Merriam-Webster's VISUAL Dictionary®

Jean-Claude **Corbeil**
Ariane **Archambault**

Merriam-Webster, Incorporated
Springfield, Massachusetts
USA

Merriam-Webster

Merriam-Webster Inc.

Published by Merriam-Webster Inc. 2007

First printing 2006

ISBN 13: 978-0-87779-051-8
ISBN 10: 0-87779-051-5

The original French Edition was first published in Canada by Québec Amérique, Montréal (Québec), under the title ***Le Visuel Définitions***

Printed and bound in Singapore
10 9 8 7 6 5 4 3 2 07 06 05 04 03
www.qa-international.com

ACKNOWLEDGEMENTS

We would like to extend our deepest thanks to the individuals, organizations and companies who generously agreed to review the definitions and, when needed, suggested changes that helped to clarify them.

Arcand, Denys (motion picture director); Audet, Nathalie (Radio Canada); Beaudouin, Yves (University of Quebec at Montreal); Beaudry, Jean (Longeuil Police Department); Beaulieu, Jacques (Sainte-Thérèse Automotive Vocational Training Center); Bordeleau, André (astronomer); Bugnet-Buchwalter, Marie-Odile (Music Librarian, University of Montreal); Butler, Philip (Stewart Museum); Christian, Ève (meteorology consultant); Delorme, Michel (Montreal Biodôme); Deschamps, Laurent; Desjardins, Jean-Pierre (UQAM); Doray, Francine (Hydro-Québec); Doyon, Philippe (Ministry of Natural Resources, Wildlife, and Parks); Dupré, Céline (terminologist); Dupuis, Laval (Montreal Trade School of Motorized Equipment); Faucher, Claude (Communications Transcript); Fournier, Jacques (Éditions Roselin); Gagnon, Roger (astronomer); Garceau, Gaétan (Sainte-Thérèse Automotive Vocational Training Center); Harou, Jérôme (Montreal School of Construction Trades); Lachapelle, Jacques (School of Architecture, University of Montreal); Lafleur, Claude (science journalist); Lapierre, Robert (chief machinist); Le Tirant, Stéphane (Montreal Insectarium); Lemay, Lucille (Leclerc Weaving Center); Lemieux-Bérubé, Louise (Montreal Center of Contemporary Textiles); Lévesque, Georges (ER doctor); Marc, Daniel (Montreal School of Construction Trades); Marchand, Raymond G. (Laval University); Martel, Félix (information technology consultant); McEvoy, Louise (Air Canada Linguistic Services); Michotte, Pierre (Maritime Institute of Quebec); Morin, Nadia (Montreal Fire Department Training Center); Mosimann, François (Sherbrooke University); Neveu, Bernard (University of Quebec at Trois-Rivières); Normand, Denis (telecommunications consultant); Ouellet, Joseph (Montreal School of Construction Trades); Ouellet, Rosaire (Cowansville Vocational Education Training Centre); Papillon, Mélanie (aeronautical engineer); Paquette, Luc (Montreal Trade School of Motorized Equipment); Paradis, Serge (Pratt & Whitney); Parent, Serge (Montreal Biodôme); Prichonnet, Gilbert (UQAM); Rancourt, Claude (Montreal Trade School of Motorized Equipment); Revéret, Jean-Pierre (UQAM); Robitaille, Jean-François (Laurentian University, Ontario); Ruel, Jean-Pierre (Correctional Service Canada); Thériault, Joël.

Merriam-Webster's Visual Dictionary was created and produced by :
QA International
329, rue de la Commune Ouest, 3e étage
Montréal (Québec) H2Y 2E1 Canada
T 514.499.3000 F 514.499.3010

EDITORIAL STAFF

Publisher: Jacques Fortin
Authors: Jean-Claude Corbeil and Ariane Archambault
Editorial Director: François Fortin
Editor-in-Chief: Serge D'Amico
Graphic Design: Anne Tremblay

PRODUCTION

Mac Thien Nguyen Hoang
Guylaine Houle

TERMINOLOGICAL RESEARCH

Jean Beaumont
Catherine Briand
Nathalie Guillo

ENGLISH DEFINITIONS

Nancy Butchart
Rita Cloghesy
Tom Donovan
Diana Halpenny
John Woolfrey

ILLUSTRATIONS

Art Direction: Jocelyn Gardner
Jean-Yves Ahern
Rielle Lévesque
Alain Lemire
Mélanie Boivin
Yan Bohler
Claude Thivierge
Pascal Bilodeau
Michel Rouleau
Anouk Noël
Carl Pelletier

LAYOUT

Pascal Goyette
Janou-Ève LeGuerrier
Véronique Boisvert
Josée Gagnon
Karine Raymond
Geneviève Théroux Béliveau

DOCUMENTATION

Gilles Vézina
Kathleen Wynd
Stéphane Batigne
Sylvain Robichaud
Jessie Daigle

DATA MANAGEMENT

Programmer: Daniel Beaulieu
Josée Gagnon

REVISION

Marie-Nicole Cimon

PREPRESS

Sophie Pellerin
Kien Tang
Karine Lévesque
Tony O'Riley

MERRIAM-WEBSTER EDITORS

Daniel B. Brandon
Christopher C. Connor
Ilya A. Davidovich
Anne Eason
Daniel J. Hopkins
Anne P. Miller
Neil S. Serven
Peter A. Sokolowski
Paul S. Wood

Jean-Claude Corbeil is an expert in linguistic planning, with a world-wide reputation in the fields of comparative terminology and socio-linguistics. He serves as a consultant to various international organizations and governments.

Ariane Archambault, a specialist in applied linguistics, has taught foreign languages and is now a terminologist and editor of dictionaries and reference books.

CONTRIBUTIONS

QA International would like to extend a special thank you to the following people for their contribution to *Merriam-Webster's Visual Dictionary:*

Jean-Louis Martin, Marc Lalumière, Jacques Perrault, Stéphane Roy, Alice Comtois, Michel Blais, Christiane Beauregard, Mamadou Togola, Annie Maurice, Charles Campeau, Mivil Deschênes, Jonathan Jacques, Martin Lortie, Raymond Martin, Frédérick Simard, Yan Tremblay, Mathieu Blouin, Sébastien Dallaire, Hoang Khanh Le, Martin Desrosiers, Nicolas Oroc, François Escalmel, Danièle Lemay, Pierre Savoie, Benoît Bourdeau, Marie-Andrée Lemieux, Caroline Soucy, Yves Chabot, Anne-Marie Ouellette, Anne-Marie Villeneuve, Anne-Marie Brault, Nancy Lepage, Daniel Provost, François Vézina.

Introduction

A MAJOR INNOVATION

In response to public demand, QA International, in cooperation with Merriam-Webster, has created this edition of the *Visual Dictionary*. The evocative power of the illustrations (in seeing, one can identify and name) is supplemented by definitions that bring out the essential information that cannot be seen or is only suggested by the word: the inherent qualities, function and characteristics of the illustrated item.

THE DEFINITIONS

Within the hierarchical format of the *Visual Dictionary*'s presentation, the definitions fit together like a Russian doll: theme, sub-theme, title, sub-title, illustration, terminology. The definition of the theme "Animal Kingdom," for example, applies to all of the animals in the chapter, and the information within the definition for the term *insect* at the top of the page does not have to be repeated for each of the insects illustrated. Instead, the text concentrates on defining the distinguishing characteristics of each insect (the louse is a parasite, the female yellow jacket stings, and so forth).

Since the definition leaves out what is obvious from the illustration, the illustrations and definitions complement one another. Hence, the cross-section of the ear shows the exact position of each of its parts, while the definitions describe only their functions.

As the illustrations progress, the definitions become more detailed. For example, the vertebral column in the skeleton is defined as a "bony axis composed of vertebrae and containing bone marrow." The vertebral column is once again featured in the section on the nervous system, but this time it contains definitions related to bone marrow and a lumbar vertebra.

Technical words used in definitions are defined in the *Visual Dictionary*, either on the same page, elsewhere in the same chapter, or in a separate chapter. For example, the words *telson* and *uropod* are a part of the definition of the lobster's tail, but they are defined as parts of the lobster's morphology.

The vast majority of the 20,800 words in the *Visual Dictionary* are defined and can be found in the index. Terms are not defined when the illustration makes the meaning absolutely clear. In addition, the definition is not repeated when the word always has the same meaning. For example, *switch* is defined in the electricity section and the definition is repeated only when it differs significantly, as in the definition of *trigger switch*. Finally, when the illustration suggests the usual meaning of the word, the word is not defined (for example, the numerous tool handles and the various housings for objects).

STRUCTURE OF THE VISUAL

The work contains three sections: the introductory pages, including the list of themes and the table of contents; the body of the work, i.e. the detailed treatment of each theme; and the index.

The order of presentation is from the abstract to the concrete: theme, sub-theme, title, sub-title, illustration, terminology, definition.

The contents are divided into 17 THEMES, from Astronomy to Sports and Games. The most complex themes are divided into SUB-THEMES, 94 in total. For example, the theme EARTH is divided into Geography, Geology, Meteorology and Environment. In this way, the *Visual Dictionary* can present and define words in groups; most other dictionaries present them in alphabetical order in which related terms are separated from each other.

The TITLES (658 in total) have various functions. They bring together, under a single heading, illustrations of various objects that are a part of the same conceptual framework (for example, armchairs, domestic appliances); they label a complex illustration whose main parts are identified (museum, exterior of a house); or they name a single object and include the terminology that applies to its parts (glacier, castle).

The principal types within the same class of objects are sometimes gathered under the same SUB-TITLE and their names are given but no detailed terminological analysis is provided (for example, under *armchair*, one finds *examples of armchairs*).

The ILLUSTRATION is an exact and realistic likeness of an object, process or phenomenon, together with its salient details. It is an integral part of the visual definition for each of the terms it depicts.

EDITORIAL POLICY

Each word in the *Visual Dictionary* has been carefully chosen after consulting the most authoritative information sources containing the appropriate level of specialization. In some instances, the sources consulted revealed that different words are used to name the same concept. In such cases, the most authoritative sources were used in selecting the term.

Words are usually referred to in the singular, even if the illustration shows a number of individual examples. The word designates the concept, not the actual illustration.

HOW TO CONSULT THE VISUAL

The fundamental originality of the *Visual Dictionary* lies in its illustrations, which allow readers to find a word that corresponds to an idea even if they have only the vaguest idea of it. This is the great advantage of the *Visual Dictionary*; when consulting a traditional dictionary, one must first know the word.

In addition, the contents of the *Visual Dictionary* may be accessed in a number of ways:

• The list of THEMES can be referred to at the end of the introductory pages and on the back cover of the book.

• The introductory page for each THEME outlines its contents and its subdivisions into SUB-THEMES and one can see at a glance the page number where they can be found (except for Vegetable Kingdom and Clothing). Themes and sub-themes are defined on these pages.

• The INDEX may be consulted to locate a specific term and, by examining the illustration cited and reading its definition, one better understands what the term refers to and its exact meaning.

TITLE

It is featured at the top of the page and its definition is found below. If the title refers to information that continues over several pages, after the first page it is shown in a shaded tone with no definition.

COLOR REFERENCE

On the spine and back of the book this identifies and accompanies each theme to facilitate quick access to the corresponding section in the book.

TERM

Each term appears in the index with a reference to the pages on which it appears. It is given in both languages, with English as the main index entry.

SUB-THEME

The majority of themes are subdivided into sub-themes. These are shown on the introductory page of a theme along with their definitions.

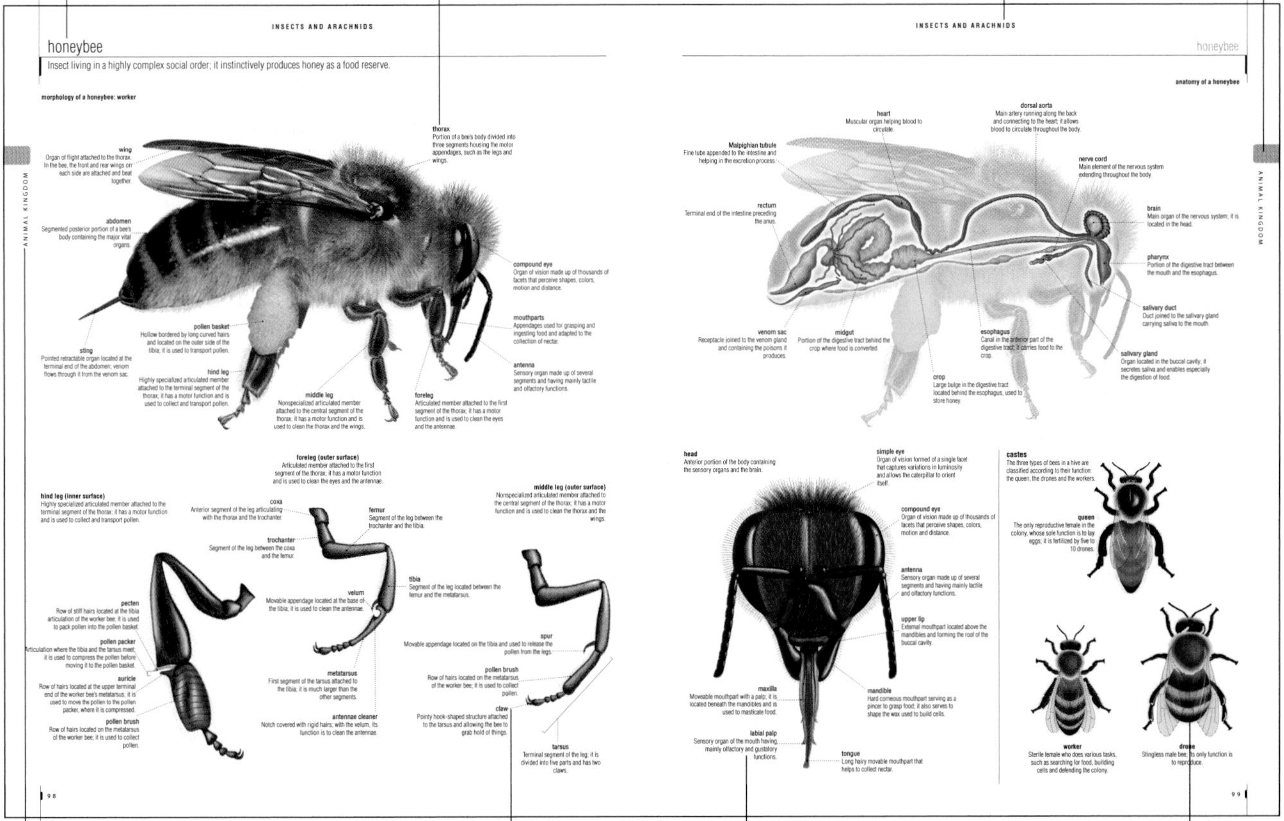

THEME

The name of the theme of each chapter, accompanied by its definition, is presented on the double-page spread at the beginning of the section. It is then repeated on each page of the section, but without the definition.

ILLUSTRATION

It is an integral part of the visual definition for each of the terms that refer to it.

NARROW LINES

These link the word to the item indicated. Where too many lines would make reading difficult, they have been replaced by color codes with captions or, in rare cases, by numbers.

DEFINITION

It explains the inherent qualities, function or characteristics of the element depicted in the illustration.

Contents

List of chapters

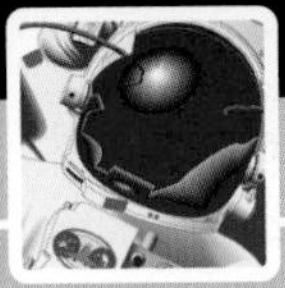
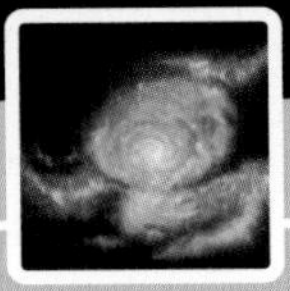

ASTRONOMY

Science whose aim is the observation and knowledge of celestial bodies: position, movement, structure, evolution and so forth.

solar system

Region of our galaxy under the influence of the Sun; includes eight planets and their natural satellites as well as dwarf planets, asteroids and comets.

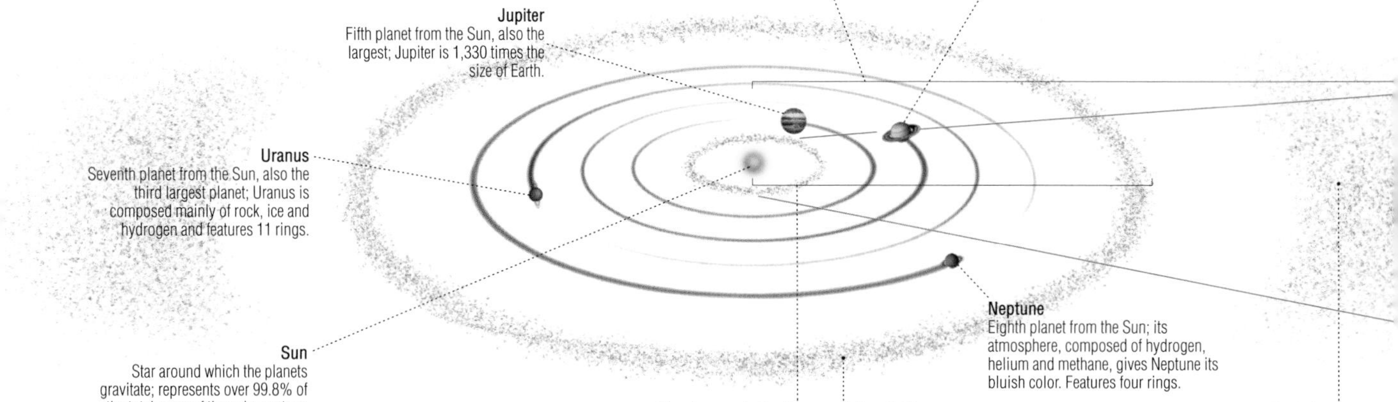

outer planets
Planets located beyond the asteroid belt; these are known as the gas giants.
50,000 astronomical units
Corresponds to about 50,000 times the Earth-Sun distance.
Saturn
Sixth planet from the Sun, also the second largest planet; Saturn is encircled by rings forming a band about 120,000 mi in diameter.
Jupiter
Fifth planet from the Sun, also the largest; Jupiter is 1,330 times the size of Earth.
Uranus
Seventh planet from the Sun, also the third largest planet; Uranus is composed mainly of rock, ice and hydrogen and features 11 rings.
Neptune
Eighth planet from the Sun; its atmosphere, composed of hydrogen, helium and methane, gives Neptune its bluish color. Features four rings.
Sun
Star around which the planets gravitate; represents over 99.8% of the total mass of the solar system.
50 astronomical units
Corresponds to about 50 times the Earth-Sun distance.
Kuiper belt
Circular region of the solar system about 50 astronomical units from the Sun; thought to be a repository of small icy bodies, the source of comets.
Oort cloud
Region of space bordering the solar system about 50,000 astronomical units from the Sun; composed of billions of comets.

planets and satellites

Planets and dwarf planets orbit the Sun, satellites orbit the planets. They are represented from left to right from the Sun, based on their relative sizes.

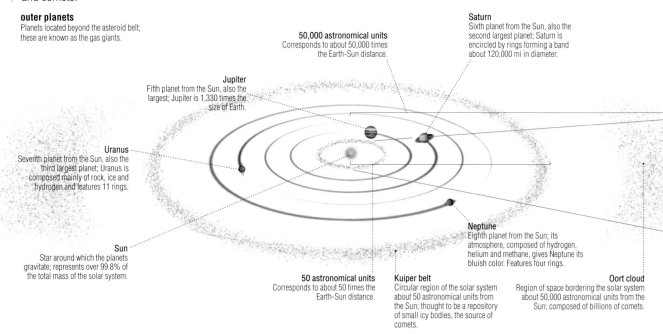

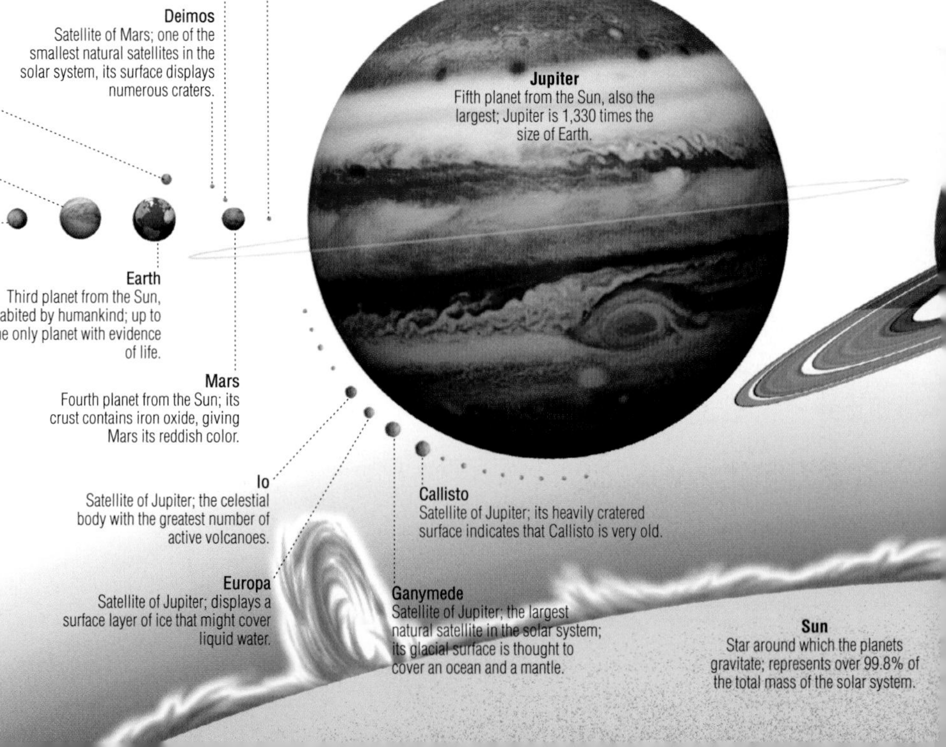

Phobos
Satellite of Mars; slightly larger than Deimos, Phobos features a large crater named Stickney.
Ceres
Discovered in 1801, it was promoted to status of dwarf planet in 2006.
Moon
Earth's only natural satellite; devoid of water and atmosphere and characterized by a highly uneven surface.
Deimos
Satellite of Mars; one of the smallest natural satellites in the solar system, its surface displays numerous craters.
Jupiter
Fifth planet from the Sun, also the largest; Jupiter is 1,330 times the size of Earth.
Venus
Second planet from the Sun; its density and chemical composition are similar to those of Earth.
Mercury
The planet closest to the Sun; devoid of atmosphere, heavily cratered and marked by extreme variations in temperature (-300°F to 800°F).
Earth
Third planet from the Sun, inhabited by humankind; up to now, the only planet with evidence of life.
Mars
Fourth planet from the Sun; its crust contains iron oxide, giving Mars its reddish color.
Io
Satellite of Jupiter; the celestial body with the greatest number of active volcanoes.
Callisto
Satellite of Jupiter; its heavily cratered surface indicates that Callisto is very old.
Europa
Satellite of Jupiter; displays a surface layer of ice that might cover liquid water.
Ganymede
Satellite of Jupiter; the largest natural satellite in the solar system; its glacial surface is thought to cover an ocean and a mantle.
Sun
Star around which the planets gravitate; represents over 99.8% of the total mass of the solar system.

solar system

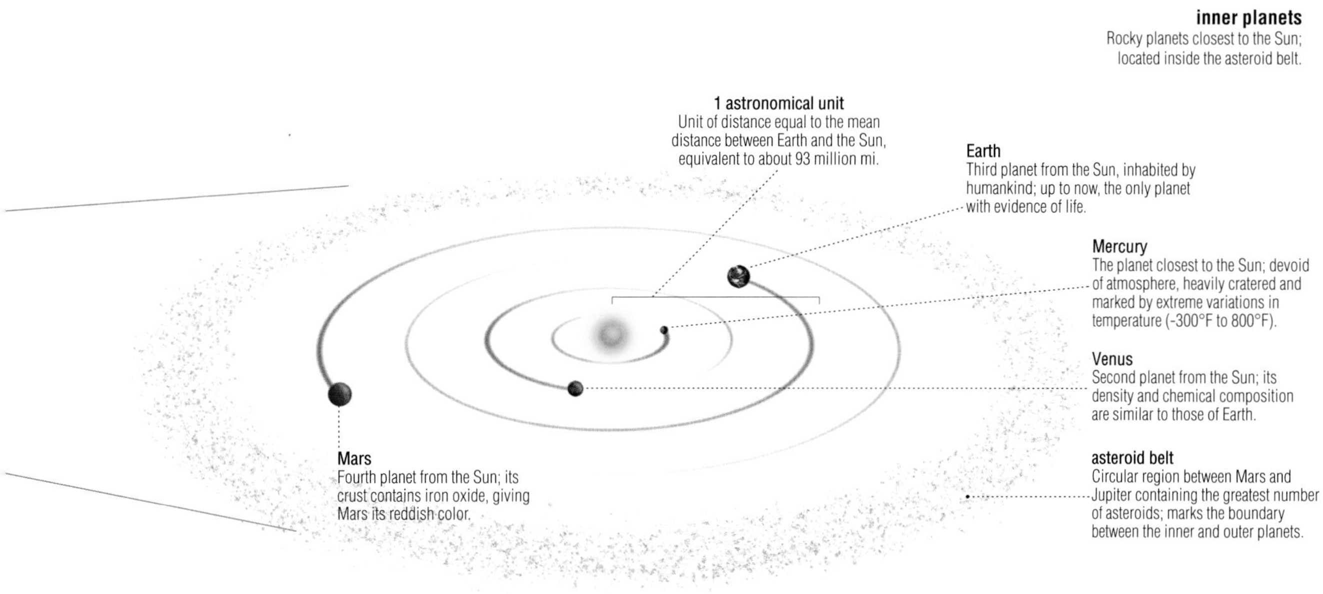
inner planets
Rocky planets closest to the Sun; located inside the asteroid belt.
1 astronomical unit
Unit of distance equal to the mean distance between Earth and the Sun, equivalent to about 93 million mi.
Earth
Third planet from the Sun, inhabited by humankind; up to now, the only planet with evidence of life.
Mercury
The planet closest to the Sun; devoid of atmosphere, heavily cratered and marked by extreme variations in temperature (-300°F to 800°F).
Venus
Second planet from the Sun; its density and chemical composition are similar to those of Earth.
Mars
Fourth planet from the Sun; its crust contains iron oxide, giving Mars its reddish color.
asteroid belt
Circular region between Mars and Jupiter containing the greatest number of asteroids; marks the boundary between the inner and outer planets.

planets and satellites

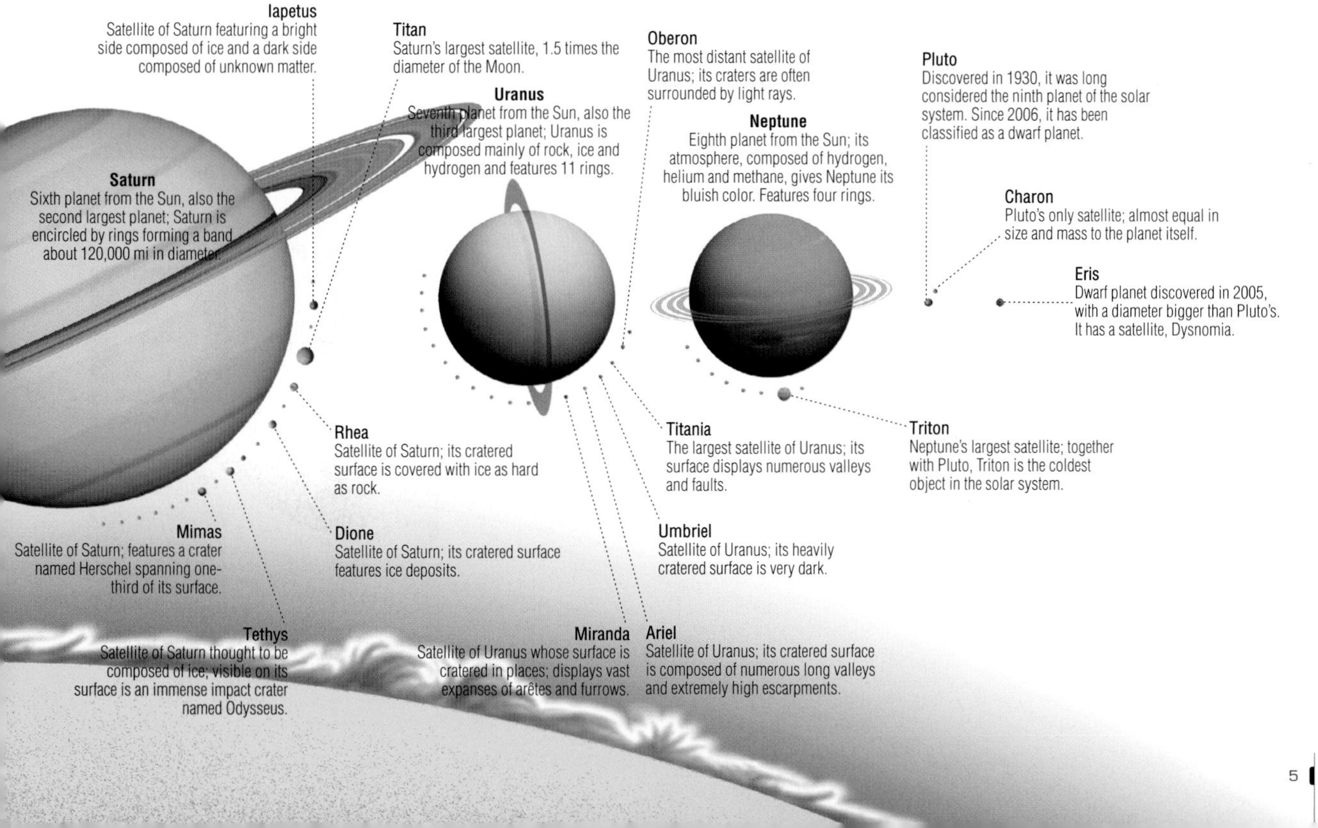
Iapetus
Satellite of Saturn featuring a bright side composed of ice and a dark side composed of unknown matter.
Titan
Saturn's largest satellite, 1.5 times the diameter of the Moon.
Oberon
The most distant satellite of Uranus; its craters are often surrounded by light rays.
Pluto
Discovered in 1930, it was long considered the ninth planet of the solar system. Since 2006, it has been classified as a dwarf planet.
Uranus
Seventh planet from the Sun, also the third largest planet; Uranus is composed mainly of rock, ice and hydrogen and features 11 rings.
Neptune
Eighth planet from the Sun; its atmosphere, composed of hydrogen, helium and methane, gives Neptune its bluish color. Features four rings.
Saturn
Sixth planet from the Sun, also the second largest planet; Saturn is encircled by rings forming a band about 120,000 mi in diameter.
Charon
Pluto's only satellite; almost equal in size and mass to the planet itself.
Eris
Dwarf planet discovered in 2005, with a diameter bigger than Pluto's. It has a satellite, Dysnomia.
Rhea
Satellite of Saturn; its cratered surface is covered with ice as hard as rock.
Titania
The largest satellite of Uranus; its surface displays numerous valleys and faults.
Triton
Neptune's largest satellite; together with Pluto, Triton is the coldest object in the solar system.
Mimas
Satellite of Saturn; features a crater named Herschel spanning one-third of its surface.
Dione
Satellite of Saturn; its cratered surface features ice deposits.
Umbriel
Satellite of Uranus; its heavily cratered surface is very dark.
Tethys
Satellite of Saturn thought to be composed of ice; visible on its surface is an immense impact crater named Odysseus.
Miranda
Satellite of Uranus whose surface is cratered in places; displays vast expanses of arêtes and furrows.
Ariel
Satellite of Uranus; its cratered surface is composed of numerous long valleys and extremely high escarpments.

Sun

Star composed of 92.1% hydrogen atoms and 7.8% helium atoms, around which the planets gravitate; represents more than 99.8% of the solar system's total mass.

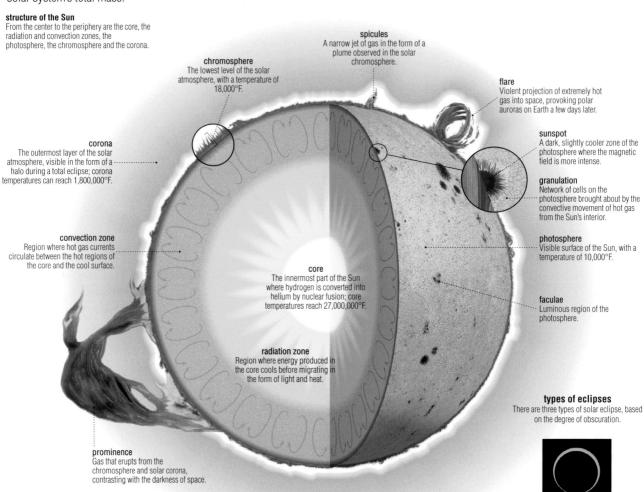

structure of the Sun
From the center to the periphery are the core, the radiation and convection zones, the photosphere, the chromosphere and the corona.

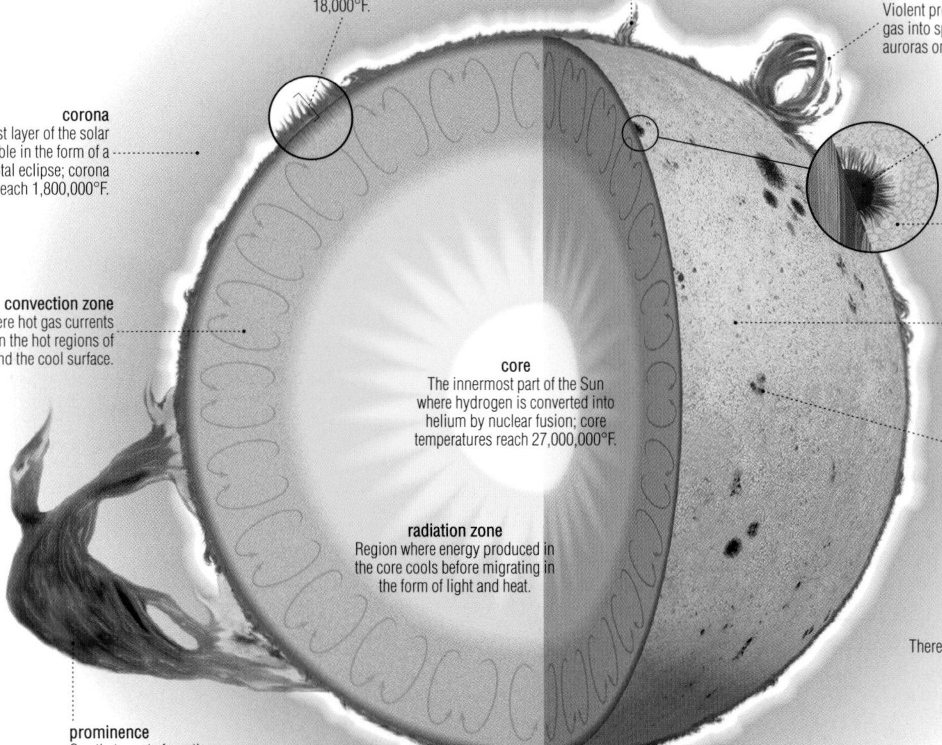

spicules
A narrow jet of gas in the form of a plume observed in the solar chromosphere.
chromosphere
The lowest level of the solar atmosphere, with a temperature of 18,000°F.
flare
Violent projection of extremely hot gas into space, provoking polar auroras on Earth a few days later.
sunspot
A dark, slightly cooler zone of the photosphere where the magnetic field is more intense.
corona
The outermost layer of the solar atmosphere, visible in the form of a halo during a total eclipse; corona temperatures can reach 1,800,000°F.
granulation
Network of cells on the photosphere brought about by the convective movement of hot gas from the Sun's interior.
convection zone
Region where hot gas currents circulate between the hot regions of the core and the cool surface.
photosphere
Visible surface of the Sun, with a temperature of 10,000°F.
core
The innermost part of the Sun where hydrogen is converted into helium by nuclear fusion; core temperatures reach 27,000,000°F.
faculae
Luminous region of the photosphere.
radiation zone
Region where energy produced in the core cools before migrating in the form of light and heat.
prominence
Gas that erupts from the chromosphere and solar corona, contrasting with the darkness of space.

types of eclipses
There are three types of solar eclipse, based on the degree of obscuration.

annular eclipse
Occurs when the Moon comes between Earth and the Sun, reducing the latter to a luminous ring.

partial eclipse
Observed by anyone within the penumbra zone during an eclipse.

total eclipse
Occurs when the lunar disk completely covers the solar disk and only the Sun's corona remains visible.

solar eclipse
Obscuration of the Sun brought about by the passage of the Moon between Earth and the Sun.

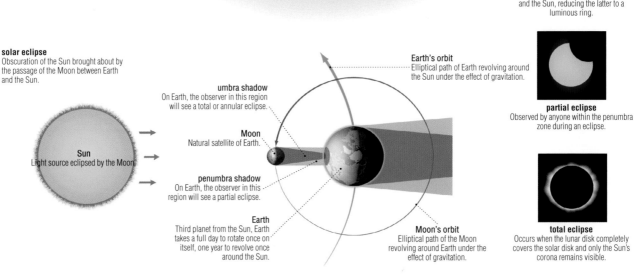

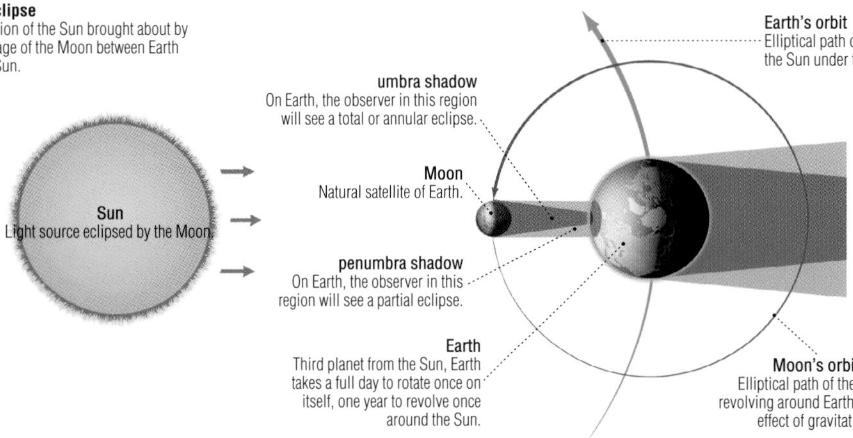

Earth's orbit
Elliptical path of Earth revolving around the Sun under the effect of gravitation.
umbra shadow
On Earth, the observer in this region will see a total or annular eclipse.
Moon
Natural satellite of Earth.
Sun
Light source eclipsed by the Moon.
penumbra shadow
On Earth, the observer in this region will see a partial eclipse.
Earth
Third planet from the Sun, Earth takes a full day to rotate once on itself, one year to revolve once around the Sun.
Moon's orbit
Elliptical path of the Moon revolving around Earth under the effect of gravitation.

Moon

Earth's only natural satellite; devoid of water and atmosphere, it displays a highly uneven surface.

types of eclipses

There are two types of eclipse based on the degree of obscuration: partial or total.

partial eclipse
When the Moon enters the umbra shadow, its bright side diminishes little by little.

total eclipse
Occurs when the Moon is completely within the umbra shadow and takes on a reddish appearance.

lunar features

Aspect of the Moon determined by past volcanic activity, meteorite impact and soil fractures.

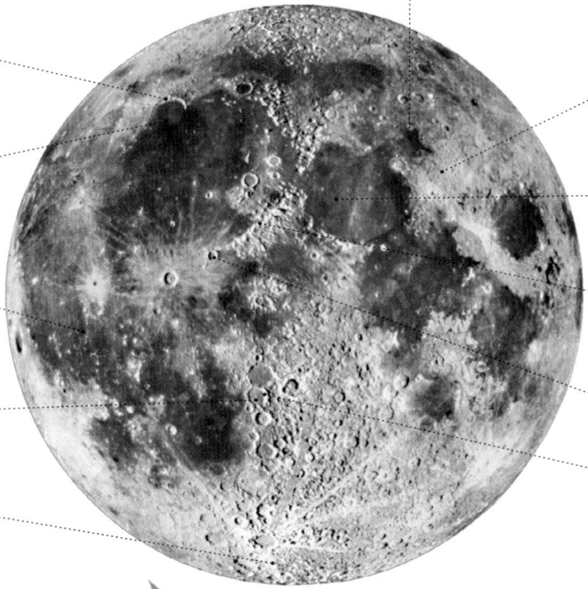
lake
Small isolated plain of hardened lava.
cliff
Steep rock face shaped by a sea.
bay
Small plain of hardened lava located along the edges of a sea.
ocean
A very large sea.
cirque
Vast crater characterized by remarkable relief; varies between 12 and 120 mi in diameter.
crater ray
Band that radiates from a young crater, the result of matter ejected during a meteorite impact.
highland
Designates bright regions riddled with craters; these oldest regions cover 85% of the surface.
sea
Designates the vast plains of hardened lava forming the dark regions; younger than the highlands, these cover 15% of the surface.
mountain range
Vestiges of the walls of a once-large crater; semicircular in shape, it can span hundreds of miles.
crater
Circular basin dug out by the impact of a meteorite.
wall
Mountain usually surrounding a cirque.

lunar eclipse

Eclipse during which the Moon enters Earth's umbra shadow in part or in full.

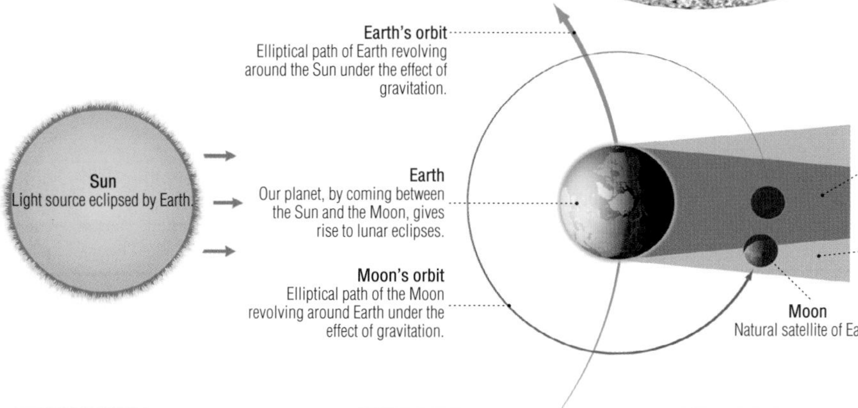
Earth's orbit
Elliptical path of Earth revolving around the Sun under the effect of gravitation.
Sun
Light source eclipsed by Earth.
Earth
Our planet, by coming between the Sun and the Moon, gives rise to lunar eclipses.
Moon's orbit
Elliptical path of the Moon revolving around Earth under the effect of gravitation.
umbra shadow
When the Moon is completely in this region, the Sun's light no longer reaches it; the eclipse is therefore total.
penumbra shadow
When the Moon enters this region, it slowly ceases to be illuminated by the Sun.
Moon
Natural satellite of Earth.

phases of the Moon

Changes in the Moon's appearance over the course of a month; result from the movement of the Moon in relation to the Sun, as seen from Earth.

new moon
The Moon lies directly between Earth and the Sun; it is not visible, as the Sun's light is too brilliant.

new crescent
The Moon is visible in the early evening in the shape of a thin crescent.

first quarter
The visible face of the Moon grows increasingly bright; the lunar crescent gradually changes until it forms a semicircle after one week.

waxing gibbous
As the Moon moves away from the Sun, its shadow gradually recedes.

full moon
The visible face of the Moon is completely illuminated by the Sun's rays.

waning gibbous
As the Moon moves closer to the Sun, its shadow begins to obscure the Sun's disk.

last quarter
The bright side gradually recedes until it becomes a half-moon.

old crescent
The Moon lies to the right of the Sun and appears in the sky at dawn in the form of a thin crescent.

meteorite

Fragment of rock, iron or another mineral that crashes into Earth instead of completely burning up as it crosses the atmosphere.

iron meteorite
Meteorite consisting mainly of iron and nickel, marked by small faults.

stony-iron meteorite
The rarest class of meteorites, characterized by the presence of almost equal quantities of rocky matter and metals.

stony meteorites
Meteorites composed mainly of rocky matter. Divided into two groups: chondrites and achondrites.

chondrite
The most common meteorite, characterized by the presence of rock or sulfurous matter in the form of minuscule spheres (chondrules).

achondrite
Meteorite whose composition is similar to that of certain terrestrial rocks; believed to come from the Moon or from Mars.

comet

Small icy body that partially evaporates as it approaches the Sun; made up of a head with a solid core and tails composed of gas and dust.

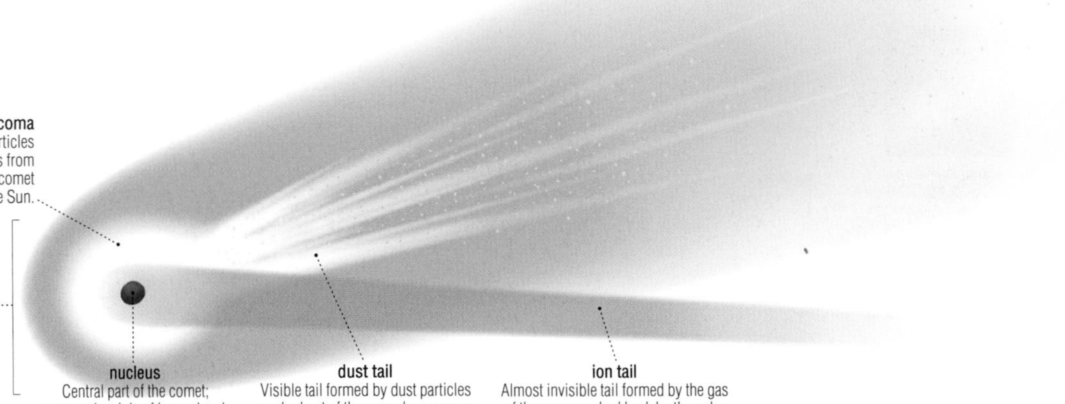
coma
Cloud of gas and dust particles emitted by the expulsion of gas from the nucleus when a comet approaches the Sun.
head
Part made up of the nucleus and the coma.
nucleus
Central part of the comet; composed mainly of ice and rocky matter.
dust tail
Visible tail formed by dust particles pushed out of the coma by pressure from the Sun's rays; can reach over 6 million mi in length.
ion tail
Almost invisible tail formed by the gas of the coma pushed back by the solar wind; can reach several hundreds of millions of miles in length.

star

A sphere of gas massive enough to generate light and heat through nuclear reactions that transform hydrogen into helium in its core.

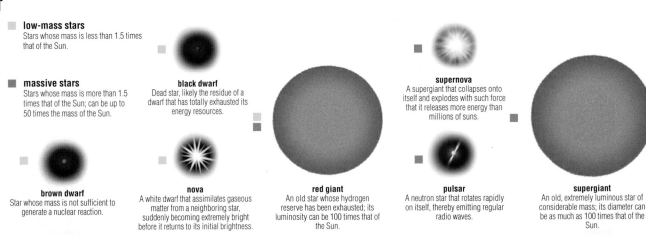

low-mass stars
Stars whose mass is less than 1.5 times that of the Sun.

massive stars
Stars whose mass is more than 1.5 times that of the Sun; can be up to 50 times the mass of the Sun.

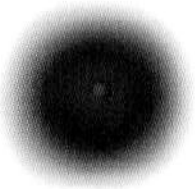

black dwarf
Dead star, likely the residue of a dwarf that has totally exhausted its energy resources.

supernova
A supergiant that collapses onto itself and explodes with such force that it releases more energy than millions of suns.

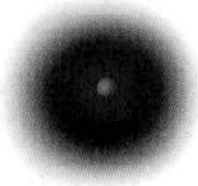

brown dwarf
Star whose mass is not sufficient to generate a nuclear reaction.

nova
A white dwarf that assimilates gaseous matter from a neighboring star, suddenly becoming extremely bright before it returns to its initial brightness.

red giant
An old star whose hydrogen reserve has been exhausted; its luminosity can be 100 times that of the Sun.

pulsar
A neutron star that rotates rapidly on itself, thereby emitting regular radio waves.

supergiant
An old, extremely luminous star of considerable mass; its diameter can be as much as 100 times that of the Sun.

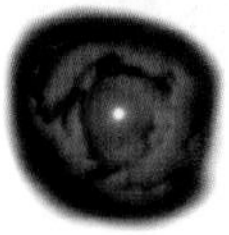

planetary nebula
Expanding gaseous envelope that corresponds to the external layer of a red giant that is gradually fading away.

white dwarf
An old, extremely dense star of faint luminosity, formed by the nucleus of a red giant contracting until it reaches the size of Earth.

main-sequence star
Star whose mass is sufficient to generate a nuclear reaction.

black hole
Results when the core of a massive star collapses; the gravitational force is so strong that not even light can escape.

neutron star
Star formed of compressed neutrons, believed to be the residue of a supernova explosion.

galaxy

Grouping of stars and interstellar matter linked together by gravitation; each galaxy comprises an average of 100 billion stars.

Hubble's classification

Classification of galaxies according to their form, devised by astronomer Edwin Hubble in the 1920s; it is still used today.

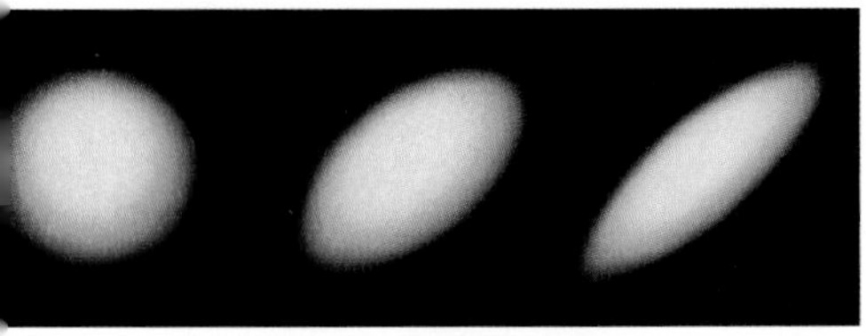

elliptical galaxy
Spherical or oval galaxy with no spiral arms.

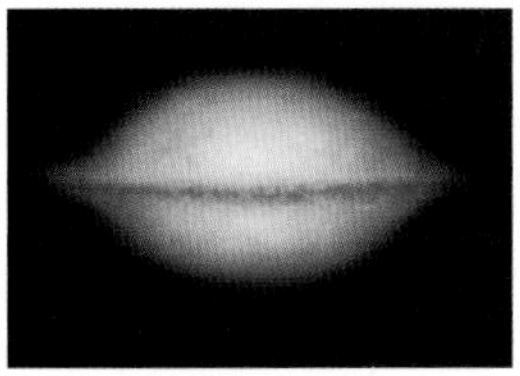

lenticular galaxy
Flat, lens-shaped galaxy with a large bulge but no arms.

normal spiral galaxy
Galaxy composed of a large nucleus from which spiral arms emerge.

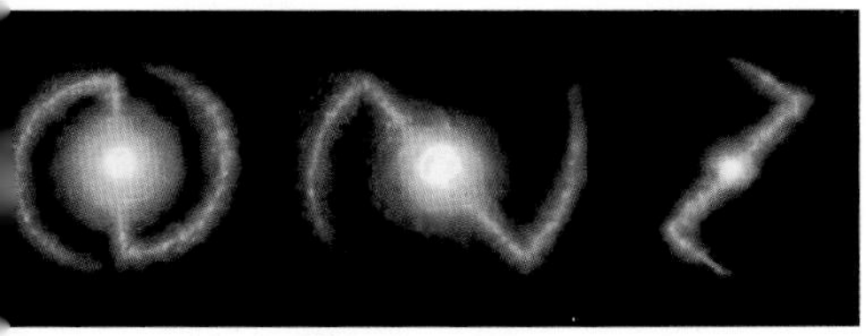

barred spiral galaxy
Galaxy crossed by a bar of stars and interstellar matter; the spiral arms emerge from the ends of the bar.

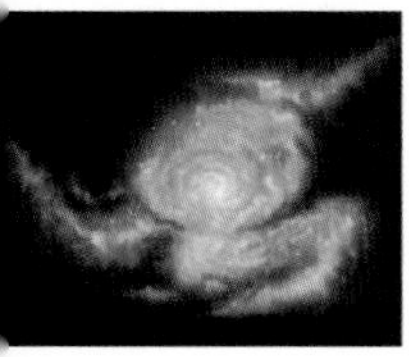

type I irregular galaxy
type of galaxy that seems to possess
al arms without displaying a specific symmetry.

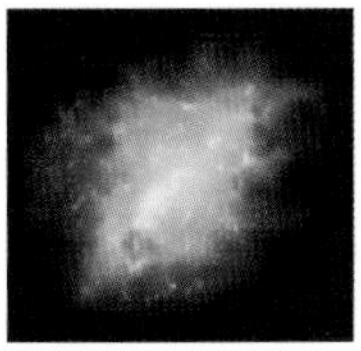

type II irregular galaxy
Rare type of galaxy whose structure obeys no specific symmetry.

Milky Way

Spiral galaxy composed of 200 to 300 billion stars, including the Sun; thought to be 10 billion years old.

Milky Way (seen from above)
From above, the Milky Way appears as a spiral that rotates on itself around a nucleus.

nucleus
Central region of the bulge; the densest and most luminous region.
spiral arm
Curved grouping of stars influenced by the rotation of the galaxy around its nucleus.

Milky Way (side view)
From the side, the Milky Way appears as a disk because its spiral arms are seen from the same angle.

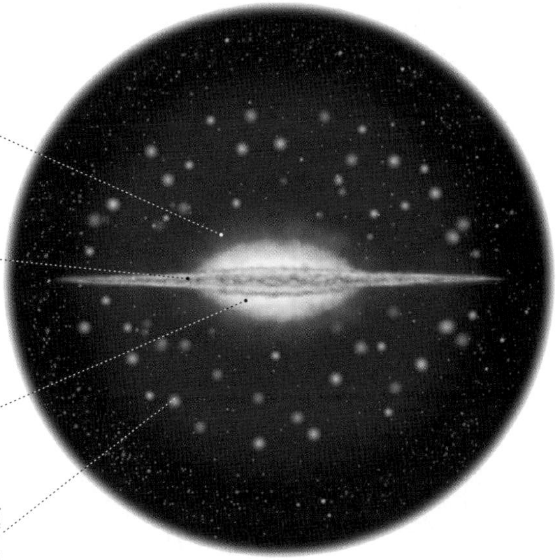
halo
Region surrounding the galaxy, inhabited by isolated stars or groupings called globular clusters; the halo has a radius of about 50,000 light-years.
disk
The main part of the galaxy, made up of a bulge and attaching arms.
bulge
The central bulge of the Milky Way's disk; the densest region of the Milky Way, with a depth of 15,000 light-years.
globular cluster
Cluster made up of hundreds of thousands of old stars.

planetarium

Structure where a projector is used to simulate the movement of the celestial bodies on a dome representing half of the celestial sphere.

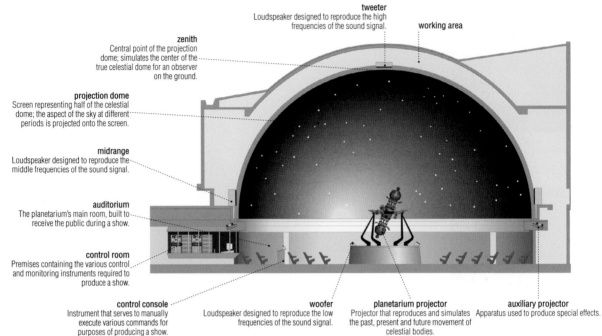

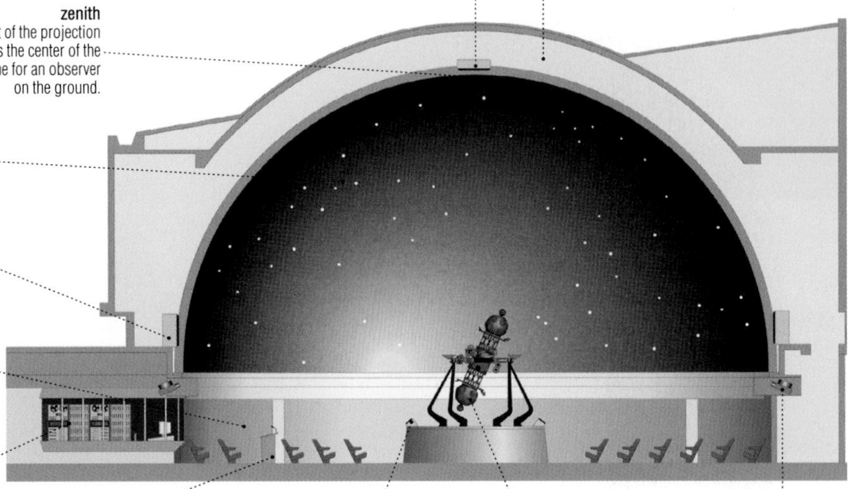
tweeter
Loudspeaker designed to reproduce the high frequencies of the sound signal.
working area
zenith
Central point of the projection dome; simulates the center of the true celestial dome for an observer on the ground.
projection dome
Screen representing half of the celestial dome; the aspect of the sky at different periods is projected onto the screen.
midrange
Loudspeaker designed to reproduce the middle frequencies of the sound signal.
auditorium
The planetarium's main room, built to receive the public during a show.
control room
Premises containing the various control and monitoring instruments required to produce a show.
control console
Instrument that serves to manually execute various commands for purposes of producing a show.
woofer
Loudspeaker designed to reproduce the low frequencies of the sound signal.
planetarium projector
Projector that reproduces and simulates the past, present and future movement of celestial bodies.
auxiliary projector
Apparatus used to produce special effects.

constellations of the Southern hemisphere

Groupings of stars whose position on the celestial dome of the Southern hemisphere, as seen from Earth, forms figures; this makes them easier to locate and has often inspired names.

1 **Cetus**
Large, mostly southern constellation containing a remarkable star, Mira Ceti; in the 16th century, Mira Ceti became the first star of varying luminosity (variable star) to be discovered.

2 **Aquarius**
Zodiac constellation between Capricorn and Pisces; contains several faint stars.

3 **Aquila**
Mostly northern constellation containing Altair, 12th brightest star in the sky.

4 **Capricornus**
Zodiac constellation marking the beginning of winter in the Gregorian calendar.

5 **Microscopium**
Small constellation recorded in the 18th century; originally formed part of the Southern Fish.

6 **Pisces Austrinus**
Constellation composed of seven stars; the brightest is named Fomalhaut, meaning "mouth of a large fish".

7 **Grus**
Constellation discovered in the 17th century whose shape recalls that of a bird in flight.

8 **Sculptor**
Constellation composed of faint stars recorded in the 18th century.

9 **Eridanus**
Large constellation containing Achernar, ninth brightest star in the sky.

10 **Fornax**
Small faint constellation discovered in the 18th century.

11 **Horologium**
Faint constellation discovered in the 18th century.

12 **Phoenix**
Faint constellation recorded in the 17th century.

13 **Tucana**
Constellation harboring the third closest galaxy to Earth, the Small Magellanic Cloud, an irregular galaxy located about 200,000 light-years away.

14 **Pavo**
Constellation recorded in the 17th century; contains only one bright star, Alpha Pavonis.

15 **Indus**
Small faint constellation discovered in the 17th century.

16 **Telescopium**
Constellation composed of faint stars discovered in the 18th century; shares stars with neighboring constellations.

17 **Corona Australis**
Small faint constellation recorded in the 2nd century.

18 **Sagittarius**
The last zodiac constellation of the fall; features, in particular, the greatest number of variable stars (stars of varying luminosity).

19 **Scutum**
Small constellation composed of five faint stars recorded in the 17th century.

20 **Scorpius**
Zodiac constellation between Libra and Sagittarius; contains Antares, 16th brightest star in the sky.

21 **Norma**
A faint constellation recorded in the 18th century.

22 **Ara**
Small faint constellation recorded in the 2nd century.

23 **Triangulum Australe**
Small constellation discovered in the 17th century whose three brightest stars form a triangle.

24 **Apus**
Constellation composed of faint stars recorded in the 17th century.

25 **Octans**
A faint constellation recorded in the 18th century; includes the South celestial pole.

26 **Hydrus**
Constellation containing only about 20 stars, most often barely visible to the naked eye; discovered in the 17th century.

27 **Mensa**
Faint constellation recorded in the 18th century; includes part of the Large Magellanic Cloud.

28 **Reticulum**
Small constellation recorded in the 18th century.

29 **Dorado**
Constellation harboring the second closest galaxy to Earth, the Large Magellanic Cloud, an irregular galaxy located about 165,000 light-years away.

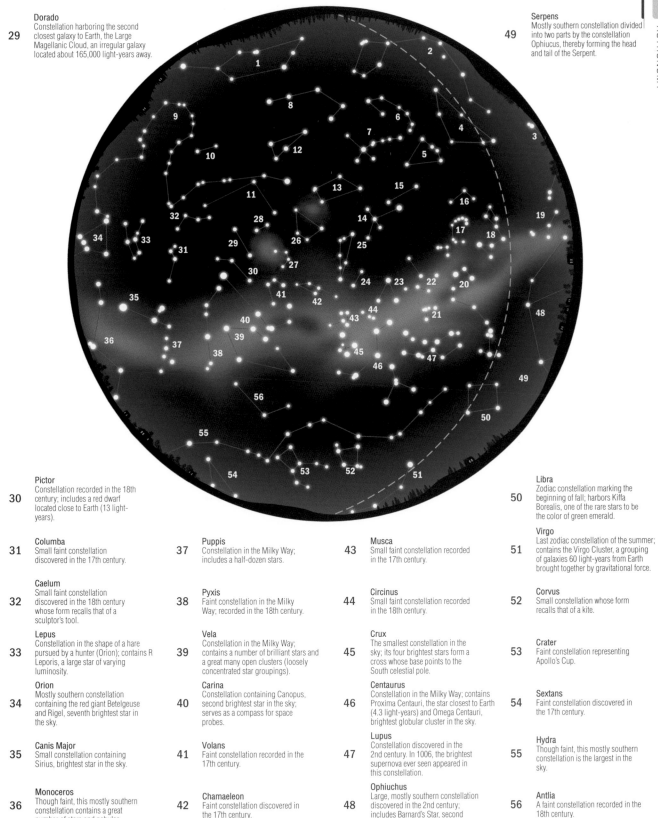

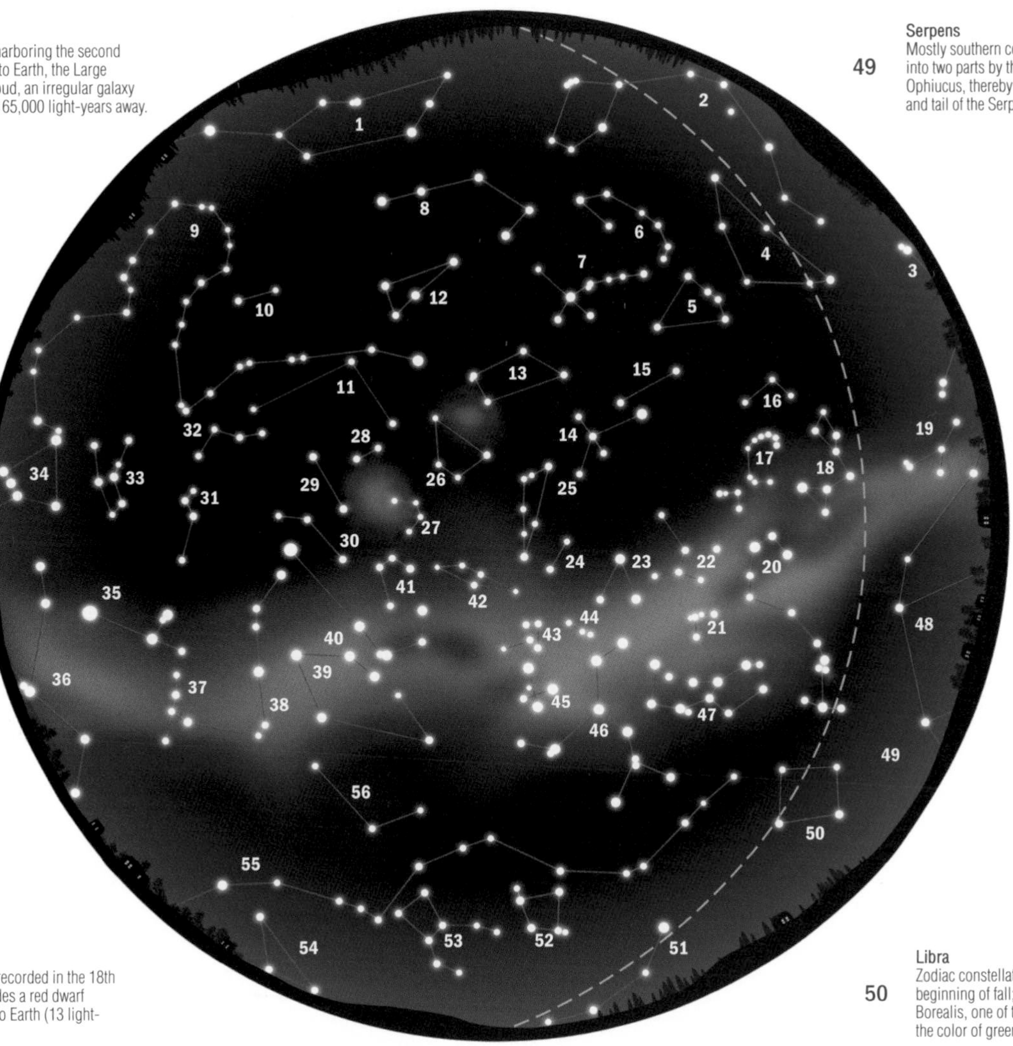

30 **Pictor**
Constellation recorded in the 18th century; includes a red dwarf located close to Earth (13 light-years).

31 **Columba**
Small faint constellation discovered in the 17th century.

32 **Caelum**
Small faint constellation discovered in the 18th century whose form recalls that of a sculptor's tool.

33 **Lepus**
Constellation in the shape of a hare pursued by a hunter (Orion); contains R Leporis, a large star of varying luminosity.

34 **Orion**
Mostly southern constellation containing the red giant Betelgeuse and Rigel, seventh brightest star in the sky.

35 **Canis Major**
Small constellation containing Sirius, brightest star in the sky.

36 **Monoceros**
Though faint, this mostly southern constellation contains a great number of stars and nebulae.

37 **Puppis**
Constellation in the Milky Way; includes a half-dozen stars.

38 **Pyxis**
Faint constellation in the Milky Way; recorded in the 18th century.

39 **Vela**
Constellation in the Milky Way; contains a number of brilliant stars and a great many open clusters (loosely concentrated star groupings).

40 **Carina**
Constellation containing Canopus, second brightest star in the sky; serves as a compass for space probes.

41 **Volans**
Faint constellation recorded in the 17th century.

42 **Chamaeleon**
Faint constellation discovered in the 17th century.

43 **Musca**
Small faint constellation recorded in the 17th century.

44 **Circinus**
Small faint constellation recorded in the 18th century.

45 **Crux**
The smallest constellation in the sky; its four brightest stars form a cross whose base points to the South celestial pole.

46 **Centaurus**
Constellation in the Milky Way; contains Proxima Centauri, the star closest to Earth (4.3 light-years) and Omega Centauri, brightest globular cluster in the sky.

47 **Lupus**
Constellation discovered in the 2nd century. In 1006, the brightest supernova ever seen appeared in this constellation.

48 **Ophiuchus**
Large, mostly southern constellation discovered in the 2nd century; includes Barnard's Star, second closest star to Earth (6 light-years).

49 **Serpens**
Mostly southern constellation divided into two parts by the constellation Ophiucus, thereby forming the head and tail of the Serpent.

50 **Libra**
Zodiac constellation marking the beginning of fall; harbors Kiffa Borealis, one of the rare stars to be the color of green emerald.

51 **Virgo**
Last zodiac constellation of the summer; contains the Virgo Cluster, a grouping of galaxies 60 light-years from Earth brought together by gravitational force.

52 **Corvus**
Small constellation whose form recalls that of a kite.

53 **Crater**
Faint constellation representing Apollo's Cup.

54 **Sextans**
Faint constellation discovered in the 17th century.

55 **Hydra**
Though faint, this mostly southern constellation is the largest in the sky.

56 **Antlia**
A faint constellation recorded in the 18th century.

constellations of the Northern hemisphere

Groupings of stars whose position on the celestial dome of the Northern hemisphere, as seen from Earth, forms figures; this makes them easier to locate and has often inspired names.

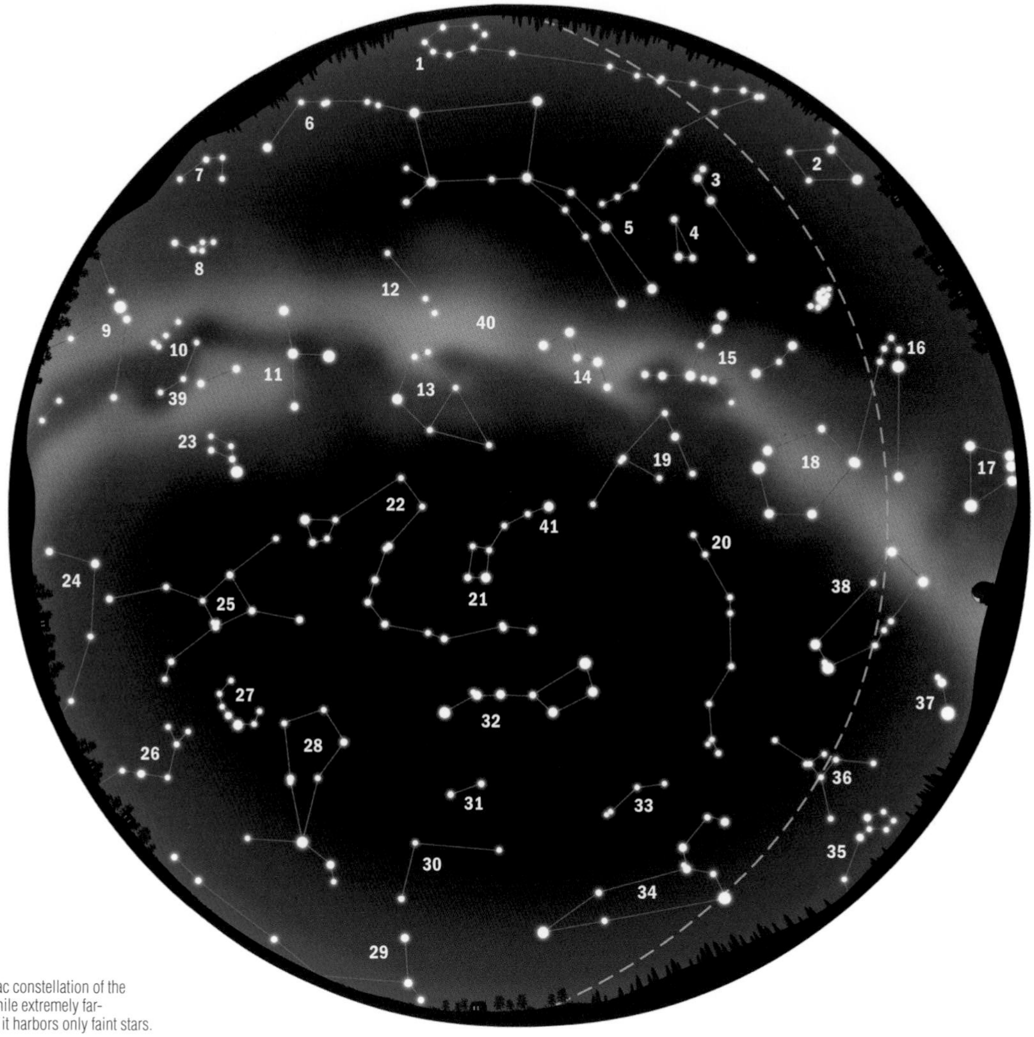

1 **Pisces**
Last zodiac constellation of the winter; while extremely far-reaching, it harbors only faint stars.

2 **Cetus**
Large, mostly southern constellation containing a remarkable star, Mira Ceti; in the 16th century, Mira Ceti became the first star of varying luminosity (variable star) to be discovered.

3 **Aries**
Zodiac constellation marking the beginning of spring in the Gregorian calendar.

4 **Triangulum**
Constellation harboring M33 (third largest galaxy close to Earth), located about 2.7 million light-years away.

5 **Andromeda**
Constellation harboring the Andromeda nebula (second largest galaxy close to Earth), located about 2.25 million light-years away.

6 **Pegasus**
Vast constellation easily located thanks to the quadrangle that three of its brilliant stars form with Sirrah (Andromeda); this asterism known as the "Great Square of Pegasus".

7 **Equuleus**
Small constellation composed of faint stars recorded in the 2nd century.

8 **Delphinus**
Small constellation harboring faint stars discovered in the 2nd century.

9 **Aquila**
Mostly northern constellation containing Altair, 12th brightest star in the sky.

10 **Sagitta**
Small constellation containing only a few stars visible to the naked eye; contains a fairly bright globular cluster.

11 **Cygnus**
Constellation whose shape recalls that of a swan in flight; contains Deneb, 20th brightest star in the sky.

12 **Lacerta**
Constellation formed of faint stars recorded in the 17th century.

13 **Cepheus**
Constellation harboring Delta Cephei, a prototype of stars of varying luminosity, named Cepheid variables for this reason.

14 **Cassiopeia**
Constellation easily identified thanks to the "W" formed by its five principal stars; contains a number of stars of varying luminosity (variable stars).

15 **Perseus**
Constellation harboring a great number of stars of varying luminosity and two large star clusters, h and Chi Persei.

16 **Taurus**
Zodiac constellation located between Aries and Gemini; contains the star Aldebaran (14th brightest star) as well as two clusters, the Hyades and Pleiades.

17 **Orion**
Mostly southern constellation containing the red giant Betelgeuse and Rigel, seventh brightest star in the sky.

18 **Auriga**
Constellation containing Capella, sixth brightest star in the sky.

19 **Camelopardalis**
Faint constellation discovered in the 17th century.

20 **Lynx**
Constellation composed of faint stars recorded in the 17th century.

21 **Ursa Minor**
Constellation containing the North Star, 47th brightest star in the sky; also called "Little Dipper" owing to its size in relation to the "Big Dipper".

22 **Draco**
Vast constellation composed of a great many faint stars.

23 **Lyra**
Constellation containing Vega, fifth brightest star in the sky.

24 **Ophiuchus**
Large, mostly southern constellation discovered in the 2nd century; includes Barnard's Star, second closest star to Earth (6 light-years).

25 **Hercules**
Large constellation containing Rasalgethi, a red giant about 830 times brighter than the Sun and more than 680 times its diameter.

26 **Serpens**
Mostly southern constellation divided into two parts by the constellation Ophiucus, thereby forming the head and tail of the Serpent.

27 **Corona Borealis**
Small constellation whose principal stars form an incomplete circle; recorded in the 2nd century.

28 **Boötes**
Constellation containing the red giant Arcturus, fourth brightest star in the sky.

29 **Virgo**
Last zodiac constellation of the summer; contains the Virgo Cluster, a grouping of galaxies 60 light-years from Earth brought together by gravitational force.

30 **Coma Berenices**
Constellation containing the Coma Cluster of galaxies, located 260 light-years from Earth.

31 **Canes Venatici**
Faint constellation harboring numerous galaxies, among them the spiral galaxy M51, located 37 million light-years from Earth.

32 **Ursa Major**
Constellation whose seven principal stars draw the outline of a giant saucepan; also called "Big Dipper". Contains several spiral galaxies.

33 **Leo Minor**
Small faint constellation discovered in the 17th century.

34 **Leo**
Zodiac constellation between Cancer and Virgo; its brightest stars form the silhouette of a lion. Harbors numerous galaxies.

35 **Hydra**
Though faint, this mostly southern constellation is the largest in the sky.

36 **Cancer**
Zodiac constellation marking the beginning of summer in the Gregorian calendar.

37 **Canis Minor**
Constellation containing Procyon, eighth brightest star in the sky.

38 **Gemini**
Last zodiac constellation of the spring; contains Castor and Pollux, 18th brightest star in the sky.

39 **Vulpecula**
Small constellation composed of faint stars recorded in the 17th century.

40 **Milky Way**
Faint milky band that is our galaxy, as seen from our spiral arm.

41 **North Star**
Star located at the end of the Little Dipper handle; nowadays serves to indicate the direction of the North celestial pole.

celestial coordinate system

Imaginary horizontal and vertical lines used to describe the position of an object on the celestial sphere.

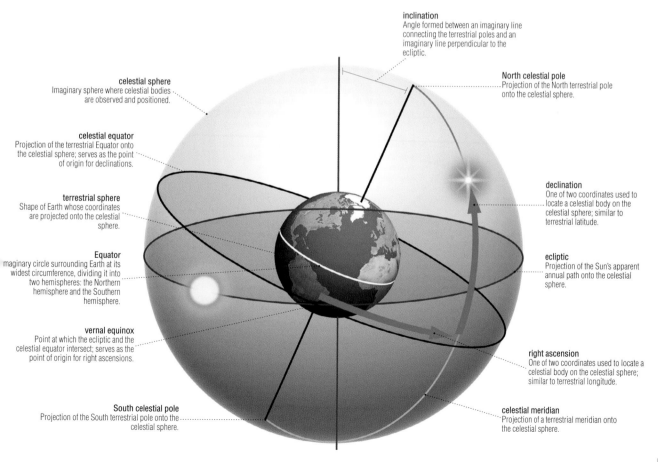

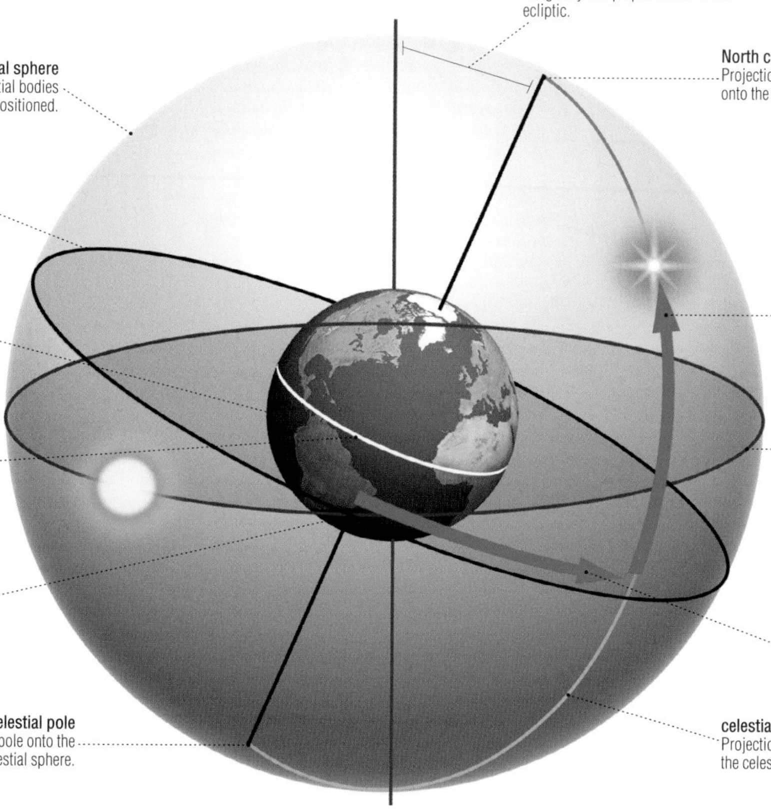
inclination
Angle formed between an imaginary line connecting the terrestrial poles and an imaginary line perpendicular to the ecliptic.
celestial sphere
Imaginary sphere where celestial bodies are observed and positioned.
North celestial pole
Projection of the North terrestrial pole onto the celestial sphere.
celestial equator
Projection of the terrestrial Equator onto the celestial sphere; serves as the point of origin for declinations.
declination
One of two coordinates used to locate a celestial body on the celestial sphere; similar to terrestrial latitude.
terrestrial sphere
Shape of Earth whose coordinates are projected onto the celestial sphere.
Equator
Imaginary circle surrounding Earth at its widest circumference, dividing it into two hemispheres: the Northern hemisphere and the Southern hemisphere.
ecliptic
Projection of the Sun's apparent annual path onto the celestial sphere.
vernal equinox
Point at which the ecliptic and the celestial equator intersect; serves as the point of origin for right ascensions.
right ascension
One of two coordinates used to locate a celestial body on the celestial sphere; similar to terrestrial longitude.
South celestial pole
Projection of the South terrestrial pole onto the celestial sphere.
celestial meridian
Projection of a terrestrial meridian onto the celestial sphere.

refracting telescope

Optical instrument that uses an objective lens to observe celestial bodies.

finderscope
Small low-magnification telescope with a wide field of view; serves to locate celestial bodies.
cradle
Part that tightens around the main tube to secure it to the base.
main tube
The barrel of a telescope housing the optical system; light rays travel through the main tube.
dew shield
Device placed in front of the objective to limit stray light and condensation.
eyepiece
Lens or system of lenses meant to magnify the image when placed before the eye.
eyepiece holder
star diagonal
Part serving to deflect the light toward the eyepiece, thereby providing a comfortable observation position.
declination setting scale
Graduated disk indicating the declination of the celestial body observed.
azimuth clamp
Clamp serving to lock the telescope along its horizontal axis.
focusing knob
Adjusting device that makes it possible to obtain a clear image of the object.
altitude clamp
Clamp serving to lock the telescope along its vertical axis.
azimuth fine adjustment
Fine-tuning device serving to position the telescope horizontally.
right ascension setting scale
Graduated disk indicating the right ascension of the observed celestial body.
altitude fine adjustment
Fine-tuning device serving to position the telescope vertically.
counterweight
Weight equal to that of the telescope; makes it possible to balance the whole.
fork
Mount with dual forks used to secure the telescope to the tripod.
tripod accessories shelf
tripod
Stable three-legged stand of variable height.

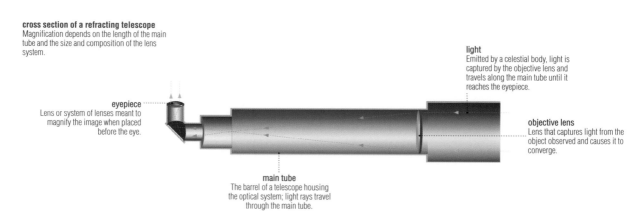

cross section of a refracting telescope
Magnification depends on the length of the main tube and the size and composition of the lens system.

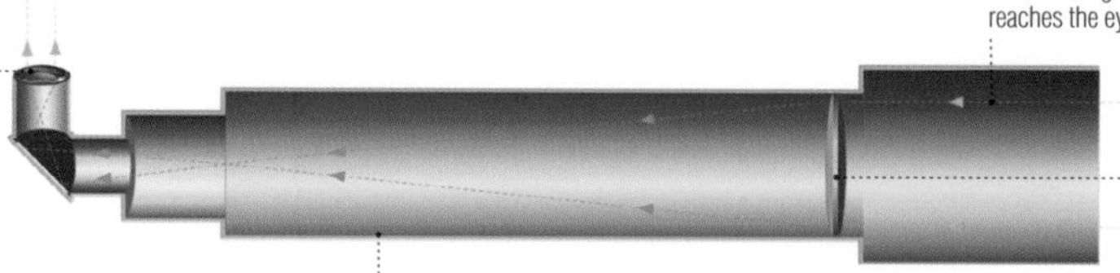
light
Emitted by a celestial body, light is captured by the objective lens and travels along the main tube until it reaches the eyepiece.
eyepiece
Lens or system of lenses meant to magnify the image when placed before the eye.
objective lens
Lens that captures light from the object observed and causes it to converge.
main tube
The barrel of a telescope housing the optical system; light rays travel through the main tube.

reflecting telescope

Optical instrument that uses an objective mirror to observe celestial bodies.

finderscope
Small low-magnification telescope with a wide field of view; serves to locate celestial bodies.
eyepiece
Lens or system of lenses meant to magnify the image when placed before the eye.
cradle
Part that tightens around the main tube to secure it to the base.
support
main tube
The barrel of the telescope through which light rays travel; houses the optical system.
focusing knob
Adjusting device that makes it possible to obtain a clear image of the object.
declination setting scale
Graduated disk indicating the declination of the celestial body observed.
right ascension setting scale
Graduated disk indicating the right ascension of the observed celestial body.
azimuth fine adjustment
Fine-tuning device that serves to position the telescope horizontally.
azimuth clamp
Clamp serving to lock the telescope along its horizontal axis.
altitude fine adjustment
Fine-tuning device that serves to position the telescope vertically.
altitude clamp
Clamp serving to lock the telescope along its vertical axis.

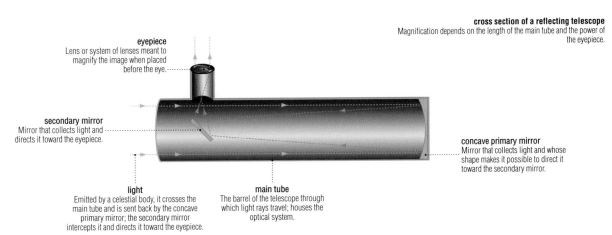

cross section of a reflecting telescope
Magnification depends on the length of the main tube and the power of the eyepiece.

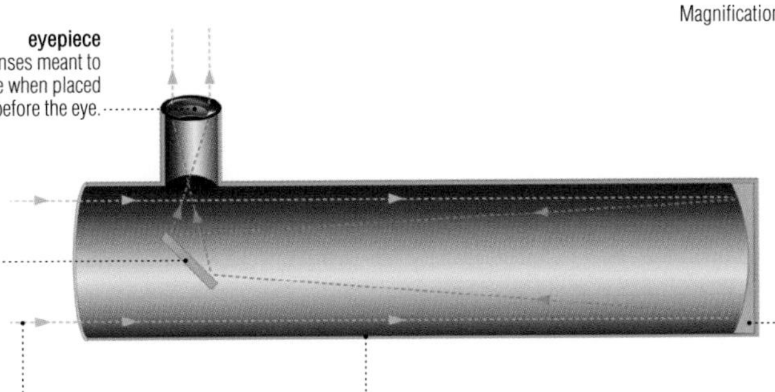
eyepiece
Lens or system of lenses meant to magnify the image when placed before the eye.
secondary mirror
Mirror that collects light and directs it toward the eyepiece.
concave primary mirror
Mirror that collects light and whose shape makes it possible to direct it toward the secondary mirror.
light
Emitted by a celestial body, it crosses the main tube and is sent back by the concave primary mirror; the secondary mirror intercepts it and directs it toward the eyepiece.
main tube
The barrel of the telescope through which light rays travel; houses the optical system.

radio telescope

Instrument used to capture, concentrate and analyze radio waves emanating from a celestial body or a region of the celestial sphere.

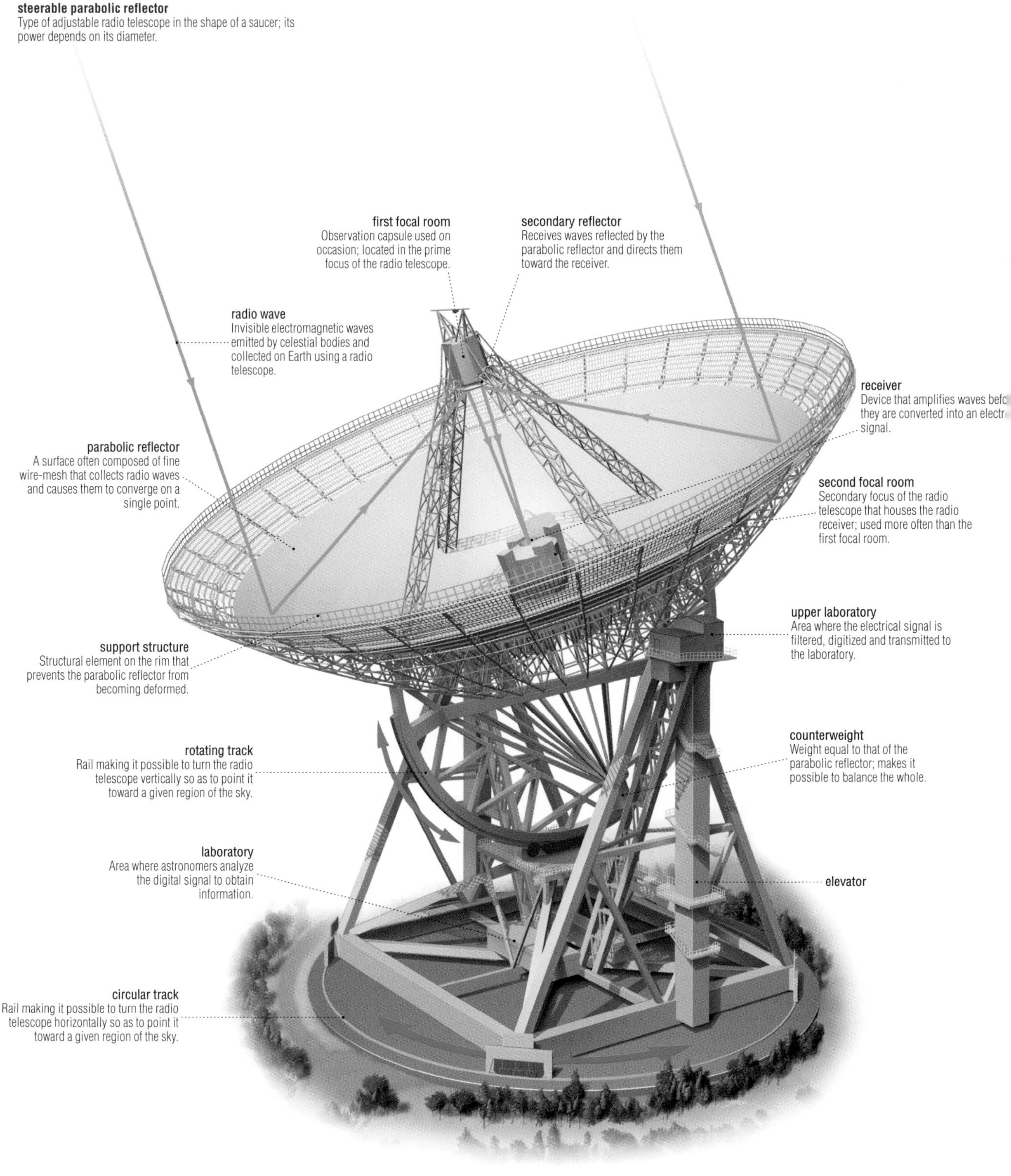

steerable parabolic reflector
Type of adjustable radio telescope in the shape of a saucer; its power depends on its diameter.
first focal room
Observation capsule used on occasion; located in the prime focus of the radio telescope.
secondary reflector
Receives waves reflected by the parabolic reflector and directs them toward the receiver.
radio wave
Invisible electromagnetic waves emitted by celestial bodies and collected on Earth using a radio telescope.
receiver
Device that amplifies waves bef
they are converted into an electr
signal.
parabolic reflector
A surface often composed of fine wire-mesh that collects radio waves and causes them to converge on a single point.
second focal room
Secondary focus of the radio telescope that houses the radio receiver; used more often than the first focal room.
upper laboratory
Area where the electrical signal is filtered, digitized and transmitted to the laboratory.
support structure
Structural element on the rim that prevents the parabolic reflector from becoming deformed.
rotating track
Rail making it possible to turn the radio telescope vertically so as to point it toward a given region of the sky.
counterweight
Weight equal to that of the parabolic reflector; makes it possible to balance the whole.
laboratory
Area where astronomers analyze the digital signal to obtain information.
elevator
circular track
Rail making it possible to turn the radio telescope horizontally so as to point it toward a given region of the sky.

Hubble space telescope

Telescope placed in orbit above Earth's atmosphere (370 mi), making it possible to observe the universe as never before.

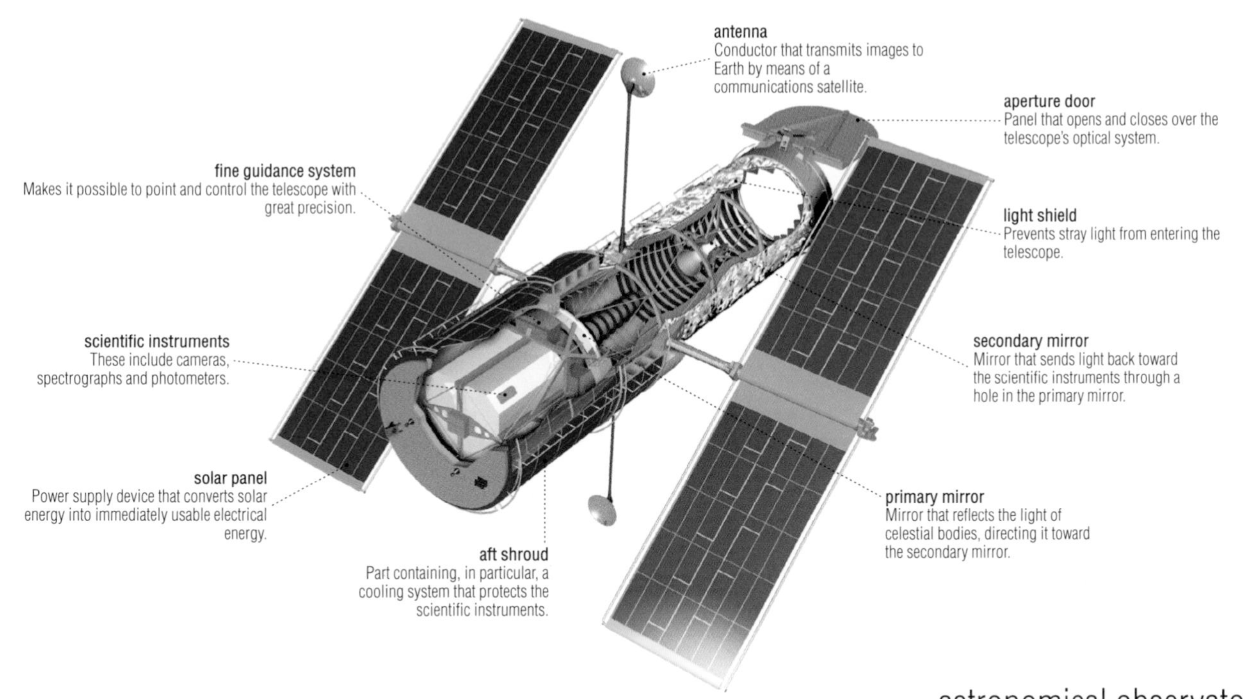

antenna
Conductor that transmits images to Earth by means of a communications satellite.
aperture door
Panel that opens and closes over the telescope's optical system.
fine guidance system
Makes it possible to point and control the telescope with great precision.
light shield
Prevents stray light from entering the telescope.
scientific instruments
These include cameras, spectrographs and photometers.
secondary mirror
Mirror that sends light back toward the scientific instruments through a hole in the primary mirror.
solar panel
Power supply device that converts solar energy into immediately usable electrical energy.
primary mirror
Mirror that reflects the light of celestial bodies, directing it toward the secondary mirror.
aft shroud
Part containing, in particular, a cooling system that protects the scientific instruments.

astronomical observatory

Building specially designed to house a large telescope.

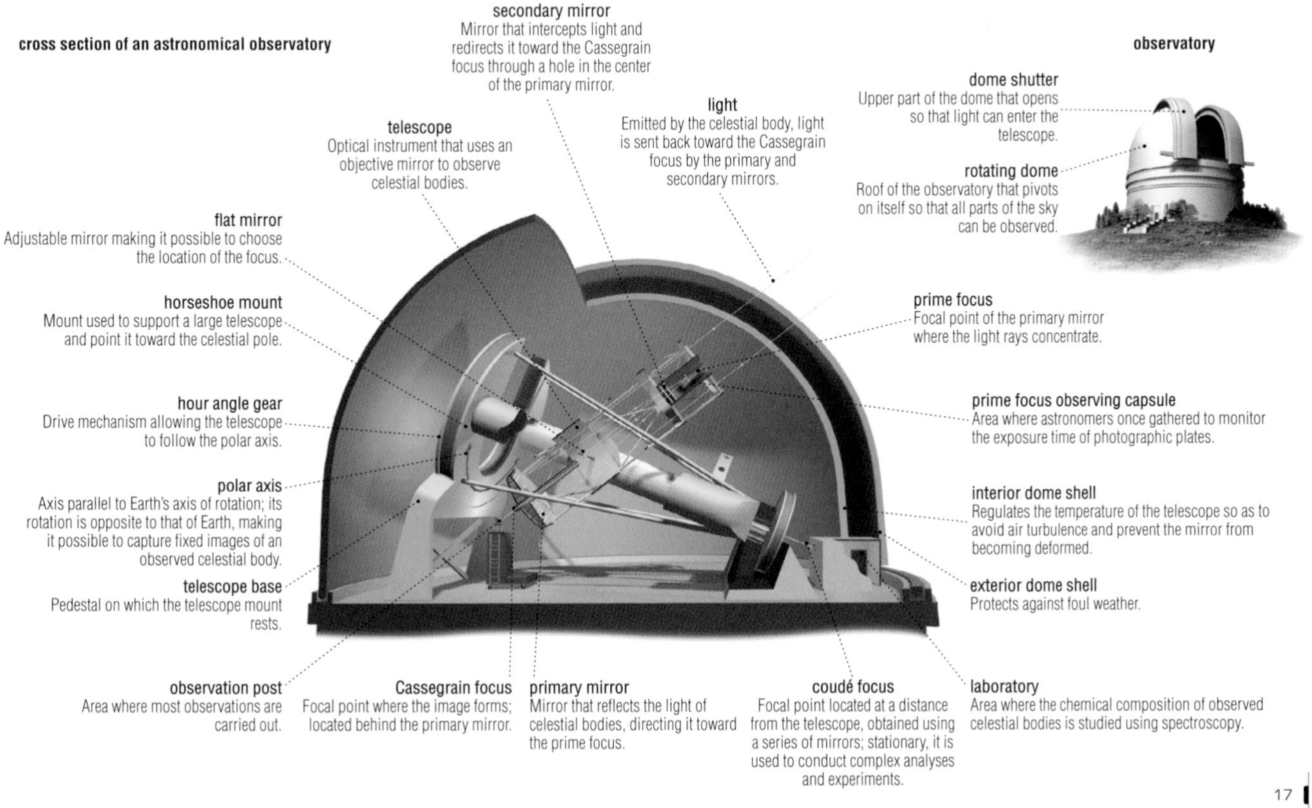

cross section of an astronomical observatory
secondary mirror
Mirror that intercepts light and redirects it toward the Cassegrain focus through a hole in the center of the primary mirror.
observatory
dome shutter
Upper part of the dome that opens so that light can enter the telescope.
light
Emitted by the celestial body, light is sent back toward the Cassegrain focus by the primary and secondary mirrors.
telescope
Optical instrument that uses an objective mirror to observe celestial bodies.
rotating dome
Roof of the observatory that pivots on itself so that all parts of the sky can be observed.
flat mirror
Adjustable mirror making it possible to choose the location of the focus.
horseshoe mount
Mount used to support a large telescope and point it toward the celestial pole.
prime focus
Focal point of the primary mirror where the light rays concentrate.
prime focus observing capsule
Area where astronomers once gathered to monitor the exposure time of photographic plates.
hour angle gear
Drive mechanism allowing the telescope to follow the polar axis.
polar axis
Axis parallel to Earth's axis of rotation; its rotation is opposite to that of Earth, making it possible to capture fixed images of an observed celestial body.
interior dome shell
Regulates the temperature of the telescope so as to avoid air turbulence and prevent the mirror from becoming deformed.
telescope base
Pedestal on which the telescope mount rests.
exterior dome shell
Protects against foul weather.
observation post
Area where most observations are carried out.
Cassegrain focus
Focal point where the image forms; located behind the primary mirror.
primary mirror
Mirror that reflects the light of celestial bodies, directing it toward the prime focus.
coudé focus
Focal point located at a distance from the telescope, obtained using a series of mirrors; stationary, it is used to conduct complex analyses and experiments.
laboratory
Area where the chemical composition of observed celestial bodies is studied using spectroscopy.

space probe

Unmanned craft launched in the direction of a celestial body in the solar system for purposes of studying it.

orbiter (Viking)
Part of the probe that flies over a celestial body before placing itself in orbit around the latter and studying it; the two Viking orbiters were launched in 1975.

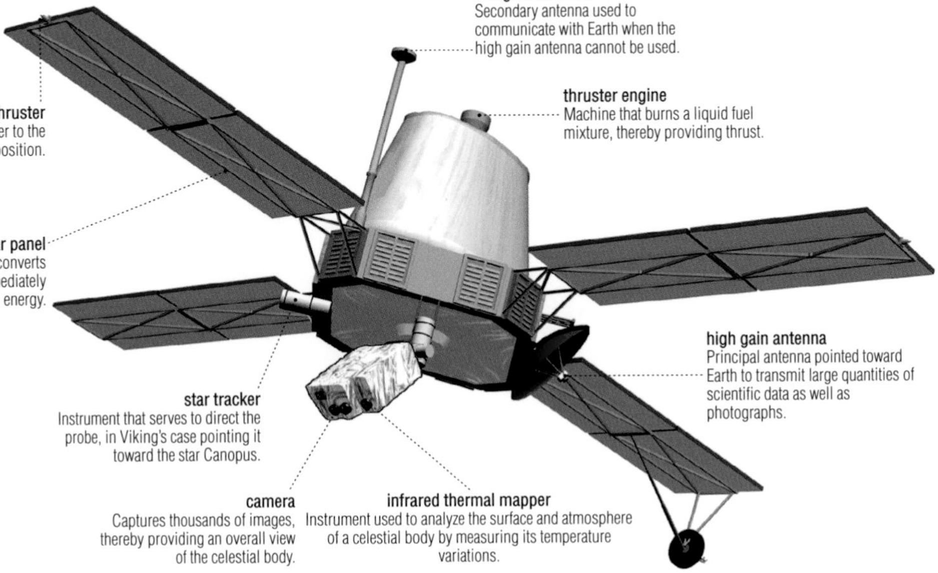

low gain antenna
Secondary antenna used to communicate with Earth when the high gain antenna cannot be used.
thruster engine
Machine that burns a liquid fuel mixture, thereby providing thrust.
attitude control thruster
Small rocket engine that directs the orbiter to the desired position.
solar panel
Power supply device that converts solar energy into immediately usable electrical energy.
high gain antenna
Principal antenna pointed toward Earth to transmit large quantities of scientific data as well as photographs.
star tracker
Instrument that serves to direct the probe, in Viking's case pointing it toward the star Canopus.
camera
Captures thousands of images, thereby providing an overall view of the celestial body.
infrared thermal mapper
Instrument used to analyze the surface and atmosphere of a celestial body by measuring its temperature variations.

lander (Viking)
Spacecraft designed to touch down on the surface of the celestial body so as to study it.

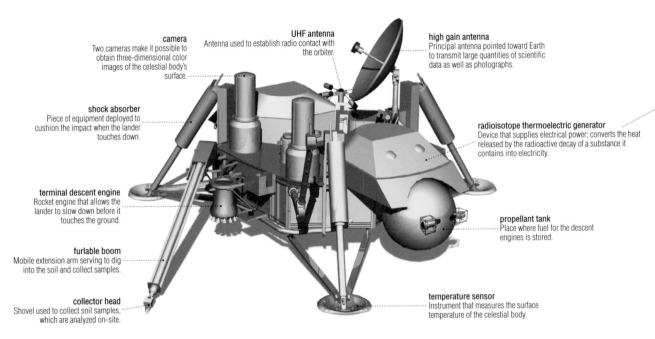

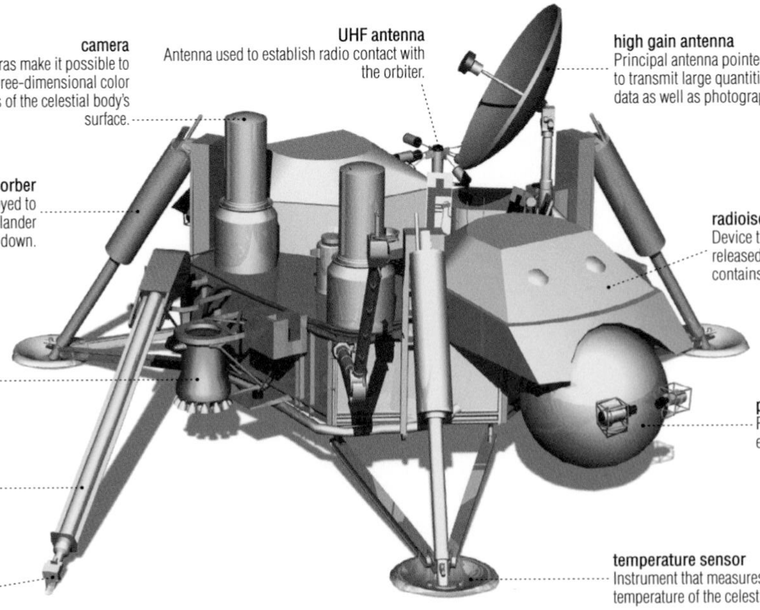

camera
Two cameras make it possible to obtain three-dimensional color images of the celestial body's surface.
UHF antenna
Antenna used to establish radio contact with the orbiter.
high gain antenna
Principal antenna pointed toward Earth to transmit large quantities of scientific data as well as photographs.
shock absorber
Piece of equipment deployed to cushion the impact when the lander touches down.
radioisotope thermoelectric generator
Device that supplies electrical power; converts the heat released by the radioactive decay of a substance it contains into electricity.
terminal descent engine
Rocket engine that allows the lander to slow down before it touches the ground.
propellant tank
Place where fuel for the descent engines is stored.
furlable boom
Mobile extension arm serving to dig into the soil and collect samples.
collector head
Shovel used to collect soil samples, which are analyzed on-site.
temperature sensor
Instrument that measures the surface temperature of the celestial body.

examples of space probes

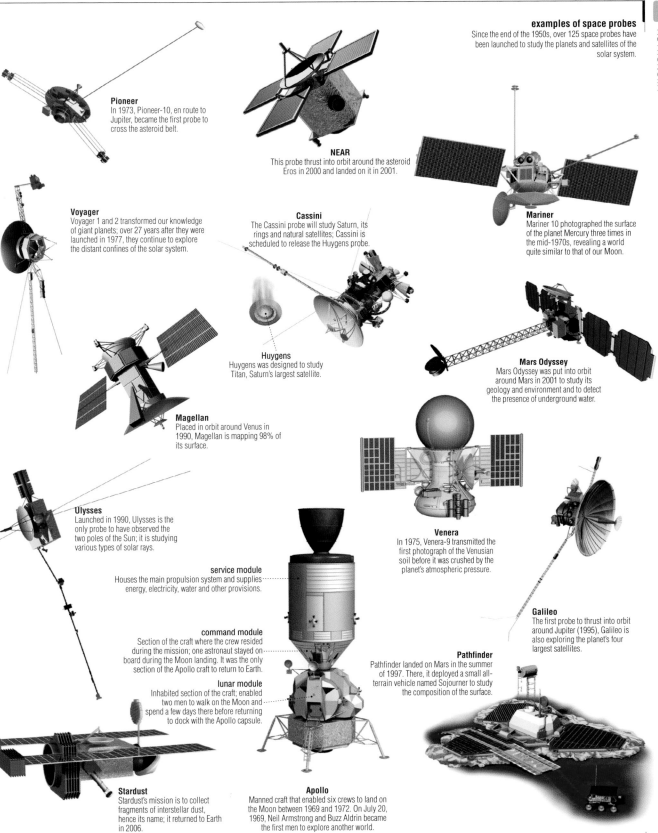

Since the end of the 1950s, over 125 space probes have been launched to study the planets and satellites of the solar system.

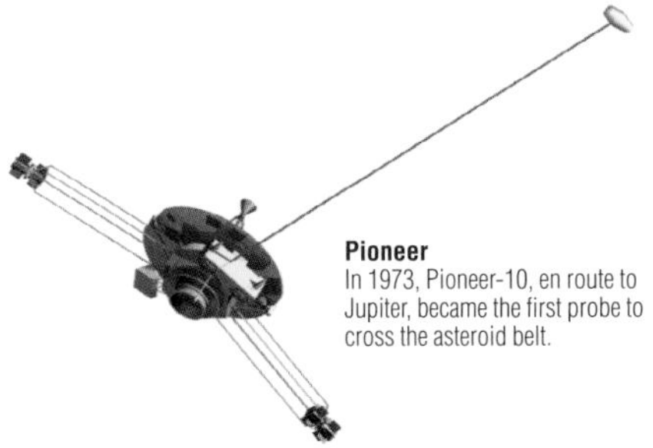

Pioneer
In 1973, Pioneer-10, en route to Jupiter, became the first probe to cross the asteroid belt.

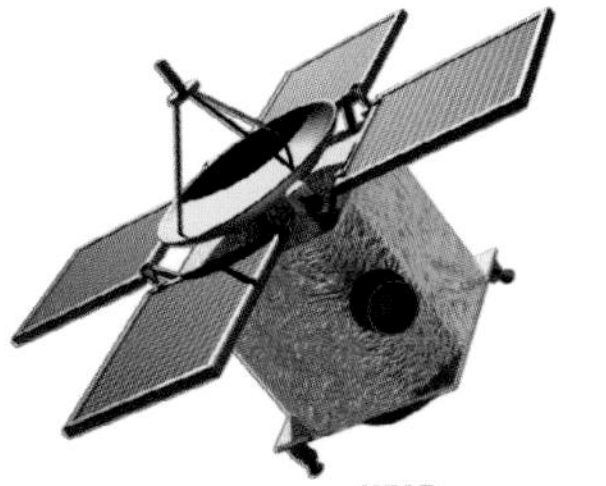

NEAR
This probe thrust into orbit around the asteroid Eros in 2000 and landed on it in 2001.

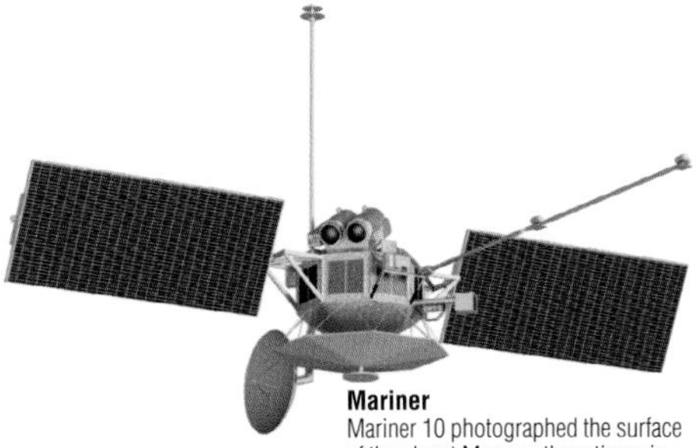

Mariner
Mariner 10 photographed the surface of the planet Mercury three times in the mid-1970s, revealing a world quite similar to that of our Moon.

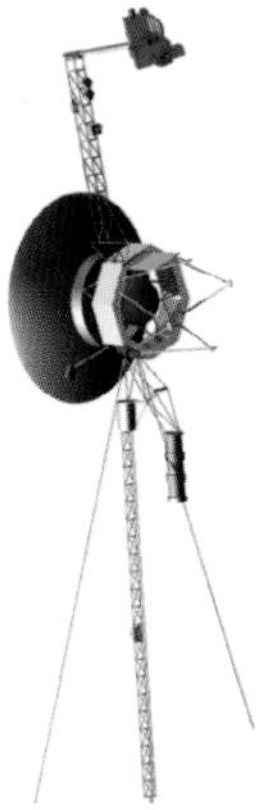

Voyager
Voyager 1 and 2 transformed our knowledge of giant planets; over 27 years after they were launched in 1977, they continue to explore the distant confines of the solar system.

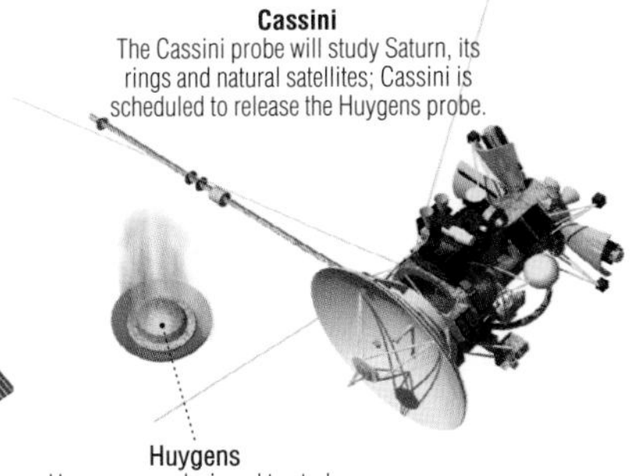

Cassini
The Cassini probe will study Saturn, its rings and natural satellites; Cassini is scheduled to release the Huygens probe.

Huygens
Huygens was designed to study Titan, Saturn's largest satellite.

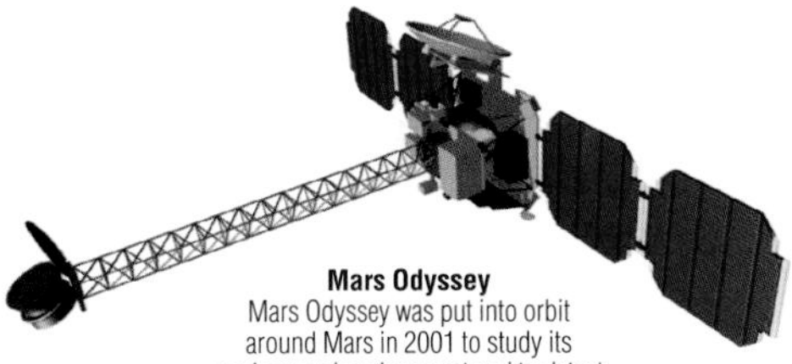

Mars Odyssey
Mars Odyssey was put into orbit around Mars in 2001 to study its geology and environment and to detect the presence of underground water.

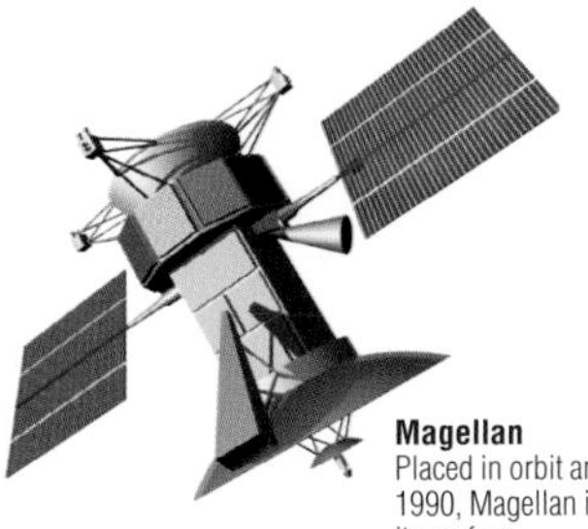

Magellan
Placed in orbit around Venus in 1990, Magellan is mapping 98% of its surface.

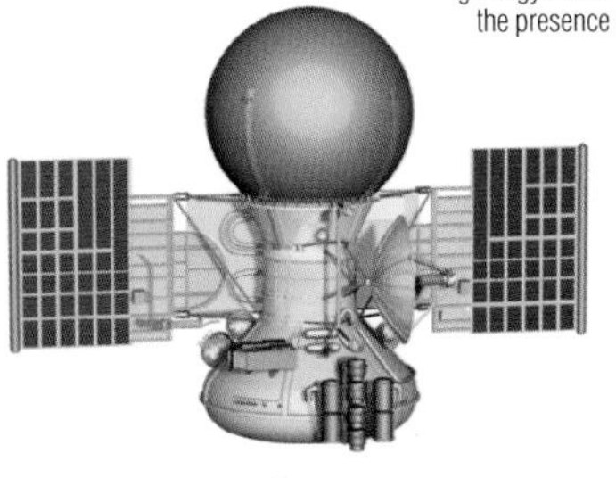

Venera
In 1975, Venera-9 transmitted the first photograph of the Venusian soil before it was crushed by the planet's atmospheric pressure.

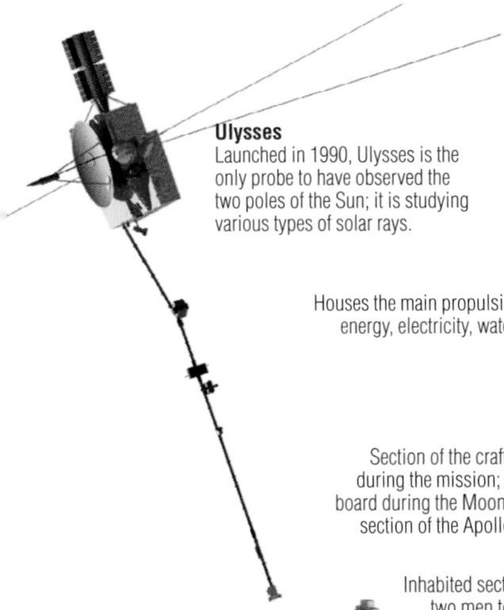

Ulysses
Launched in 1990, Ulysses is the only probe to have observed the two poles of the Sun; it is studying various types of solar rays.

Galileo
The first probe to thrust into orbit around Jupiter (1995), Galileo is also exploring the planet's four largest satellites.

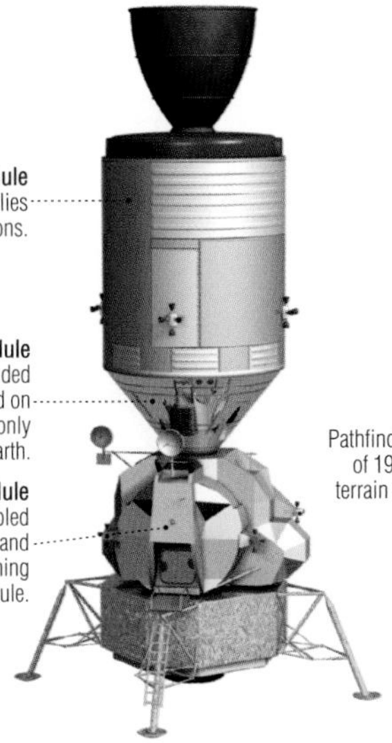

service module
Houses the main propulsion system and supplies energy, electricity, water and other provisions.

command module
Section of the craft where the crew resided during the mission; one astronaut stayed on board during the Moon landing. It was the only section of the Apollo craft to return to Earth.

lunar module
Inhabited section of the craft; enabled two men to walk on the Moon and spend a few days there before returning to dock with the Apollo capsule.

Apollo
Manned craft that enabled six crews to land on the Moon between 1969 and 1972. On July 20, 1969, Neil Armstrong and Buzz Aldrin became the first men to explore another world.

Pathfinder
Pathfinder landed on Mars in the summer of 1997. There, it deployed a small all-terrain vehicle named Sojourner to study the composition of the surface.

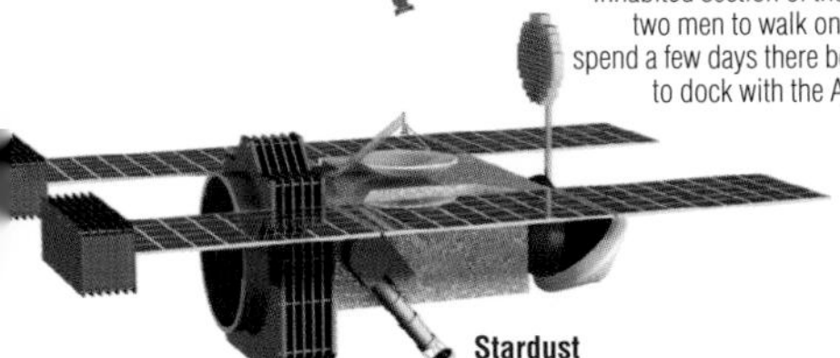

Stardust
Stardust's mission is to collect fragments of interstellar dust, hence its name; it returned to Earth in 2006.

spacesuit

A pressurized watertight suit that provides the astronaut with oxygen and protects against solar rays and meteorites during space walks.

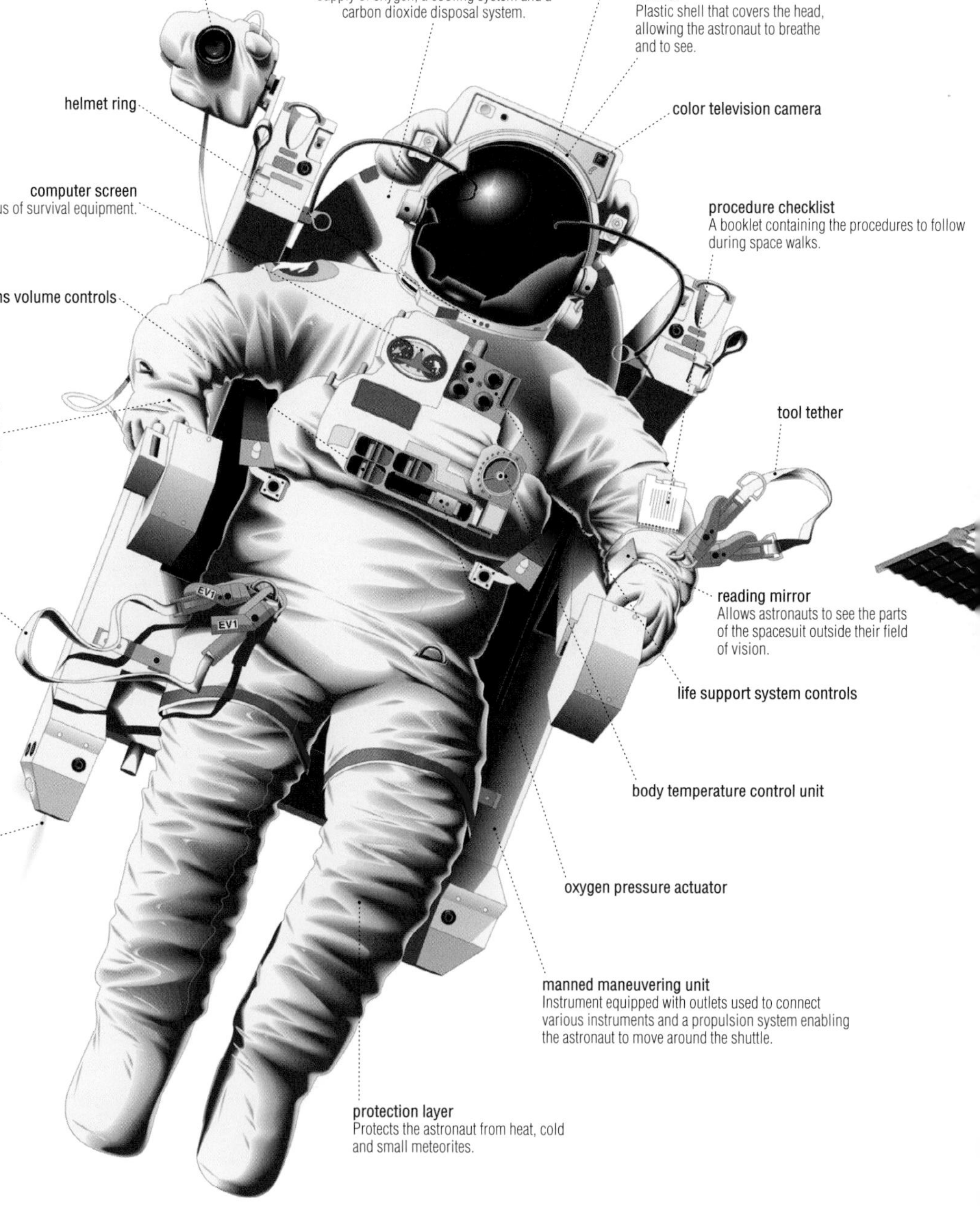

solar shield
Translucent part of the helmet that allows the astronaut to see and protects against the Sun's ultraviolet rays.
35 mm still camera
A single-objective reflex camera that uses 35 mm film to capture an image.
life support system
Module that contains, in particular, a supply of oxygen, a cooling system and a carbon dioxide disposal system.
helmet
Plastic shell that covers the head, allowing the astronaut to breathe and to see.
helmet ring
color television camera
computer screen
Makes it possible to view data on the status of survival equipment.
procedure checklist
A booklet containing the procedures to follow during space walks.
communications volume controls
glove
Covered with silicone at the fingertips to provide touch sensitivity and insulated so that objects heated by the Sun can be picked up.
tool tether
safety tether
Connects the astronaut to the shuttle, also providing a certain mobility.
EV1
EV1
reading mirror
Allows astronauts to see the parts of the spacesuit outside their field of vision.
life support system controls
body temperature control unit
thruster
Gives the astronaut the push needed to move away from the shuttle and to walk in space.
oxygen pressure actuator
manned maneuvering unit
Instrument equipped with outlets used to connect various instruments and a propulsion system enabling the astronaut to move around the shuttle.
protection layer
Protects the astronaut from heat, cold and small meteorites.

international space station

Complex made up of some 10 modules in orbit around Earth; built and assembled by 15 countries, it is used to conduct scientific and technological research on weightlessness.

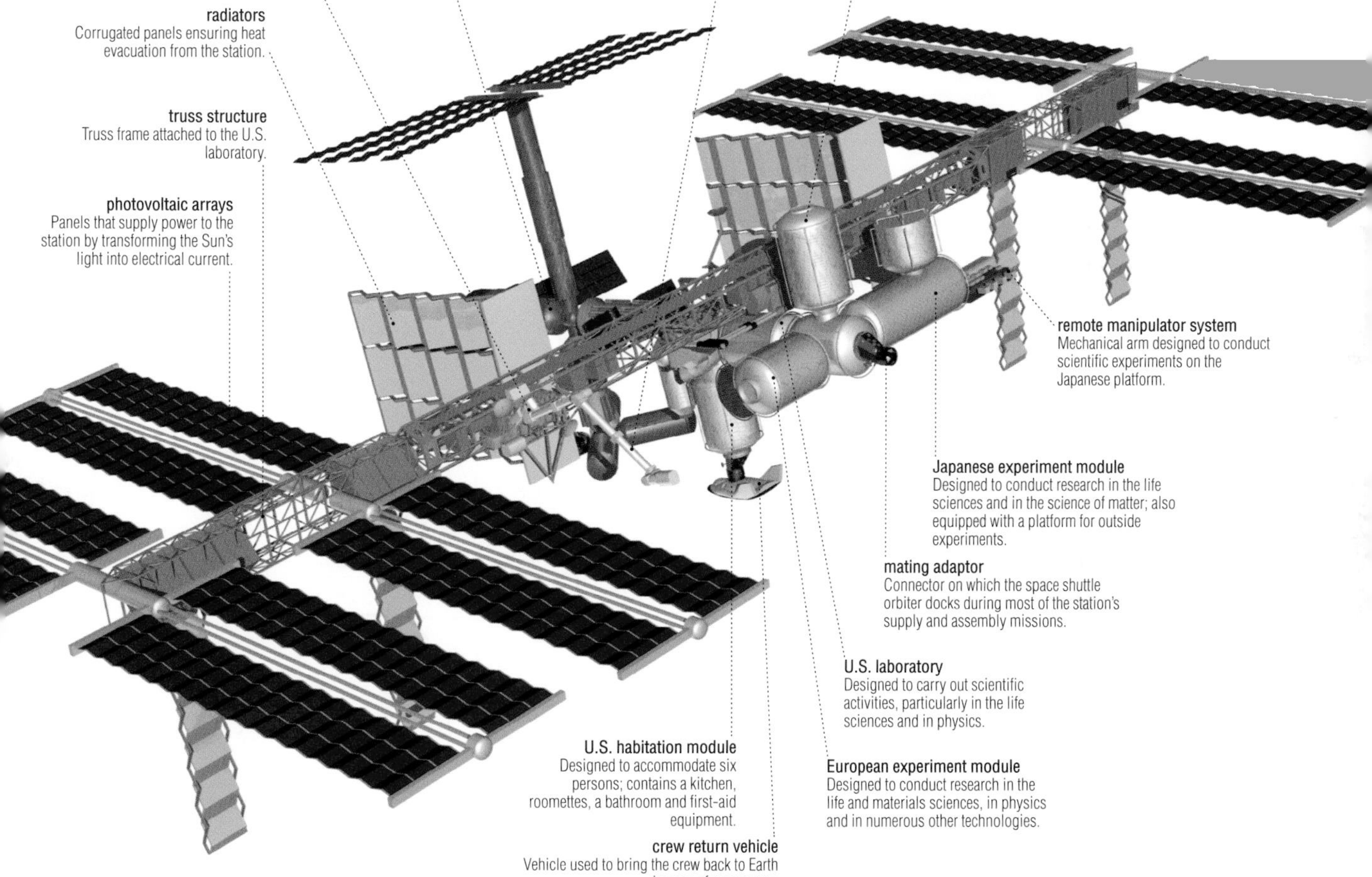

centrifuge module
Module used to create variable artificial gravity, making it possible to study the effect of gravity levels on living organisms.
remote manipulator system
This mechanical arm is used to lift heavy loads during the assembly of the station and to perform maintenance work.
mobile remote servicer
Base that supports the arm and allows it to move about the structure.
Russian module
Generates the station's electrical energy using photovoltaic cells.
radiators
Corrugated panels ensuring heat evacuation from the station.
truss structure
Truss frame attached to the U.S. laboratory.
photovoltaic arrays
Panels that supply power to the station by transforming the Sun's light into electrical current.
remote manipulator system
Mechanical arm designed to conduct scientific experiments on the Japanese platform.
Japanese experiment module
Designed to conduct research in the life sciences and in the science of matter; also equipped with a platform for outside experiments.
mating adaptor
Connector on which the space shuttle orbiter docks during most of the station's supply and assembly missions.
U.S. laboratory
Designed to carry out scientific activities, particularly in the life sciences and in physics.
U.S. habitation module
Designed to accommodate six persons; contains a kitchen, roomettes, a bathroom and first-aid equipment.
European experiment module
Designed to conduct research in the life and materials sciences, in physics and in numerous other technologies.
crew return vehicle
Vehicle used to bring the crew back to Earth in case of emergency.

space shuttle

Reusable manned space vehicle composed of an orbiter, two rockets and a fuel tank.

space shuttle at takeoff
On takeoff, the space shuttle is made up of an orbiter, two rockets and an external fuel tank.

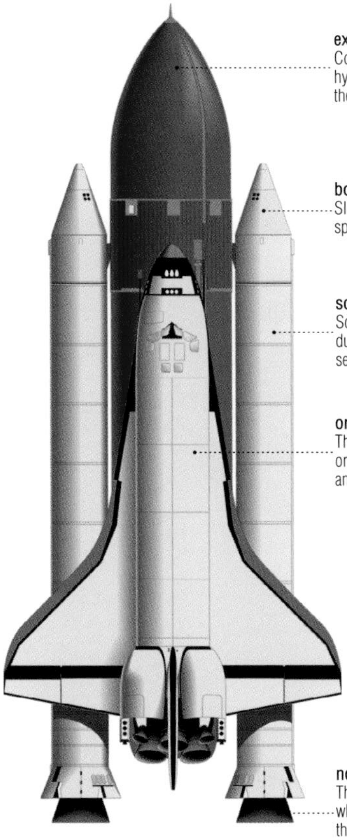
external fuel tank
Contains the liquid fuel (oxygen and hydrogen) that supplies the three engines of the orbiter tail.
booster parachute
Slows the rocket's fall after it separates from the space shuttle some two minutes after takeoff.
solid rocket booster
Solid-fuel thruster that provides most of the lift during the first few minutes of flight, after which it separates.
orbiter
The only part of the shuttle to fly in orbit; transports 13 tons of material and five to seven astronauts.
nozzle
The end portion of a rocket from which combustion gases escape, thereby creating the thrust needed to propel the craft.

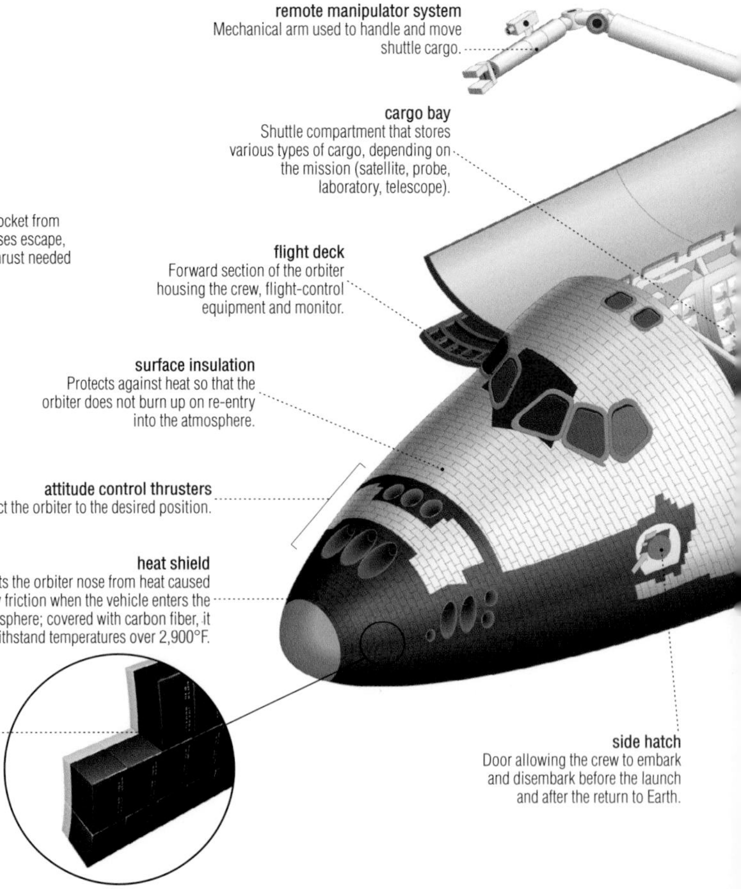
remote manipulator system
Mechanical arm used to handle and move shuttle cargo.
cargo bay
Shuttle compartment that stores various types of cargo, depending on the mission (satellite, probe, laboratory, telescope).
flight deck
Forward section of the orbiter housing the crew, flight-control equipment and monitor.
surface insulation
Protects against heat so that the orbiter does not burn up on re-entry into the atmosphere.
attitude control thrusters
Small rocket engines that direct the orbiter to the desired position.
heat shield
Protects the orbiter nose from heat caused by friction when the vehicle enters the atmosphere; covered with carbon fiber, it can withstand temperatures over 2,900°F.
tile
Covering 70% of the orbiter, the tiles protect it from heat on re-entry into the atmosphere.
side hatch
Door allowing the crew to embark and disembark before the launch and after the return to Earth.

space shuttle

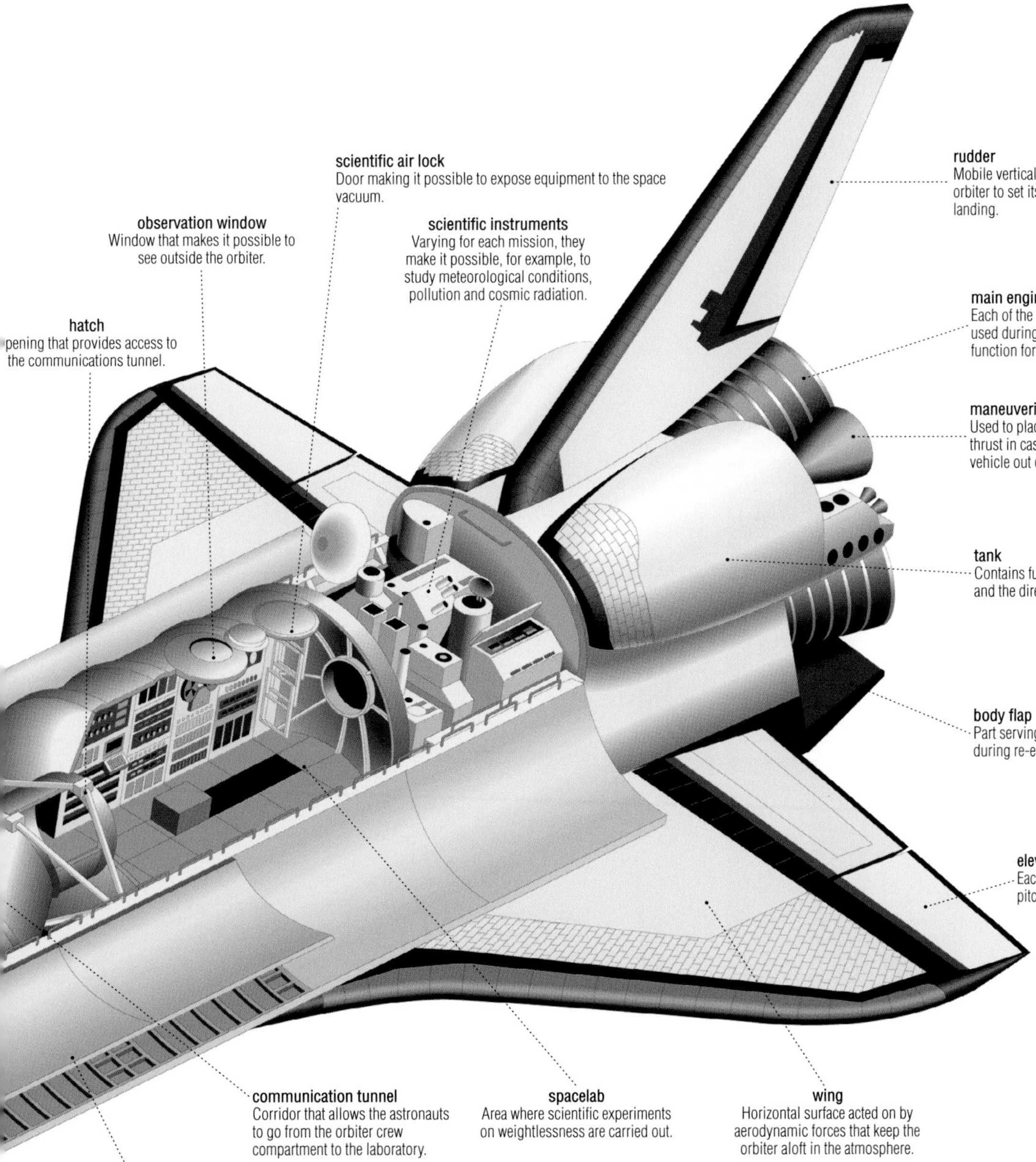
orbiter
The only part of the shuttle to fly in orbit; can transport 13 tons of material and five to seven astronauts.
rudder
Mobile vertical part that allows the orbiter to set its direction when landing.
scientific air lock
Door making it possible to expose equipment to the space vacuum.
observation window
Window that makes it possible to see outside the orbiter.
scientific instruments
Varying for each mission, they make it possible, for example, to study meteorological conditions, pollution and cosmic radiation.
hatch
pening that provides access to the communications tunnel.
main engine
Each of the orbiter's three tail engines used during takeoff; these only function for the first 8 min. of flight.
maneuvering engine
Used to place the vehicle in orbit, to provide thrust in case the orbit changes and to take the vehicle out of orbit.
tank
Contains fuel for the maneuvering engines and the directional control thrusters.
body flap
Part serving as a thermal shield for the motors during re-entry into the atmosphere.
elevon
Each of the two ailerons controls pitching during landing.
communication tunnel
Corridor that allows the astronauts to go from the orbiter crew compartment to the laboratory.
spacelab
Area where scientific experiments on weightlessness are carried out.
wing
Horizontal surface acted on by aerodynamic forces that keep the orbiter aloft in the atmosphere.
radiator panel
Discharges into space the heat produced by the functioning of onboard equipment.
cargo bay door
Remains open in orbit so as to expose the content of the cargo bay to space.

space launcher

Rocket that serves to place satellites in Earth's orbit or to send probes into the solar system.

cross section of a space launcher (Ariane V)
In service since 1996, this European launcher transports heavy payloads, including the most powerful communications satellites.

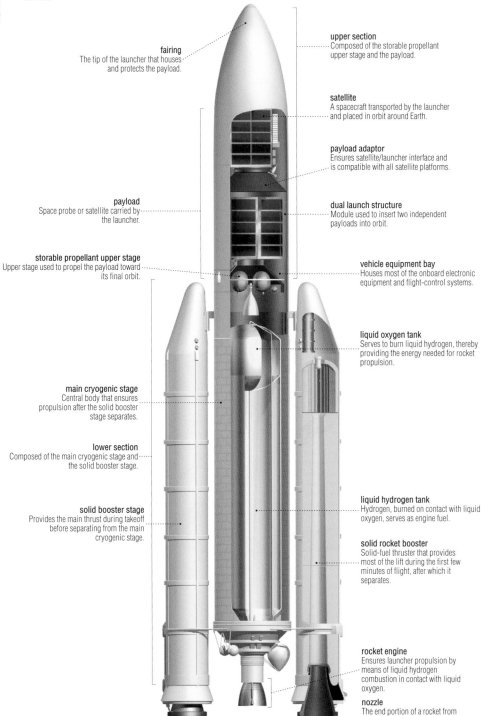

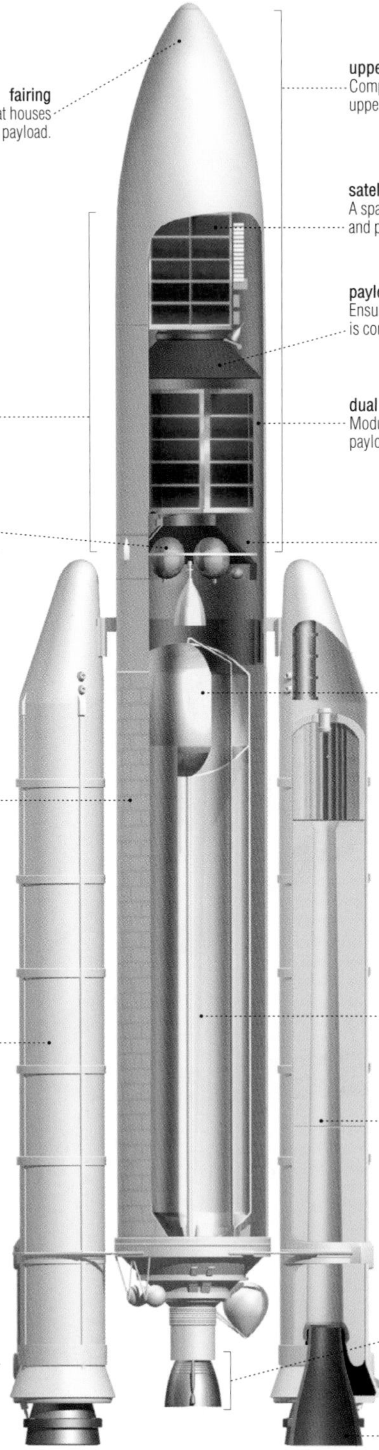
fairing
The tip of the launcher that houses and protects the payload.
upper section
Composed of the storable propellant upper stage and the payload.
satellite
A spacecraft transported by the launcher and placed in orbit around Earth.
payload adaptor
Ensures satellite/launcher interface and is compatible with all satellite platforms.
payload
Space probe or satellite carried by the launcher.
dual launch structure
Module used to insert two independent payloads into orbit.
storable propellant upper stage
Upper stage used to propel the payload toward its final orbit.
vehicle equipment bay
Houses most of the onboard electronic equipment and flight-control systems.
liquid oxygen tank
Serves to burn liquid hydrogen, thereby providing the energy needed for rocket propulsion.
main cryogenic stage
Central body that ensures propulsion after the solid booster stage separates.
lower section
Composed of the main cryogenic stage and the solid booster stage.
liquid hydrogen tank
Hydrogen, burned on contact with liquid oxygen, serves as engine fuel.
solid booster stage
Provides the main thrust during takeoff before separating from the main cryogenic stage.
solid rocket booster
Solid-fuel thruster that provides most of the lift during the first few minutes of flight, after which it separates.
rocket engine
Ensures launcher propulsion by means of liquid hydrogen combustion in contact with liquid oxygen.
nozzle
The end portion of a rocket from which combustion gases escape, thereby creating the thrust needed to propel the craft.

examples of space launchers

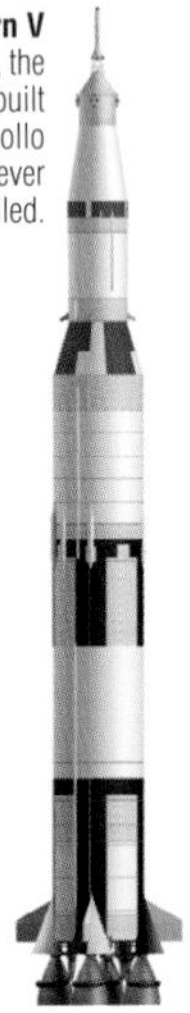

Saturn V
In service from 1967 to 1973, the most powerful rocket ever built served to launch the Apollo missions; the only launcher never to have failed.

Ariane IV
European Space Agency launcher; in service from 1989 to 1997.

Titan IV
In service since 1989, this U.S. launcher serves, in particular, to launch large military satellites.

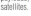

Delta II
In service since 1989, this highly versatile launcher places meteorological and communications satellites in orbit.

cross section of a space launcher (Saturn V)
Saturn V served as the launcher for the U.S. Apollo lunar exploration program.

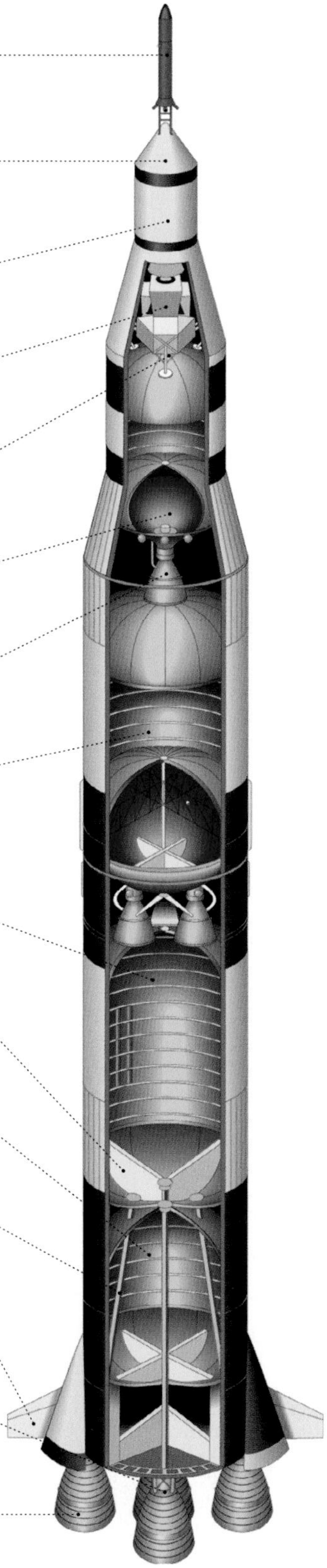

launch escape system
Makes it possible, in the event of damage, to separate the command module from the rest of the launcher and to pull it.

command module
Capsule inhabited by the crew during most of an Apollo mission; the only part of the vehicle to return to Earth.

service module
Houses the main propulsion system and supplies energy, electricity, water and other provisions.

lunar module
Inhabited section of the craft; enabled two men to walk on the Moon and spend a few days there before returning to dock with the Apollo capsule.

instrument unit
The brain of the rocket; includes the computers and all of the electronic equipment that controls the rocket during its launch.

helium sphere
Helium is used to pressurize the oxygen tank.

J-2 engine
The second and third stages are equipped with J-2 engines; these provide thrust using liquid oxygen-hydrogen combustion.

liquid hydrogen tank
Hydrogen, burned on contact with liquid oxygen, serves as engine fuel.

liquid oxygen tank
Contains liquid oxygen used to burn kerosene.

liquid oxygen tank baffle
Serves to limit the movement of liquid oxygen inside the tank.

kerosene tank
Kerosene, burned on contact with liquid oxygen, serves as fuel for F-1 engines.

fuel transfer pipe
Pipe through which liquid oxygen is sent to the rocket engines.

stabilizing fin
Fins located on either side of the launcher, serving to stabilize it.

nozzle
The end portion of a rocket from which combustion gases escape, thereby creating the thrust needed to propel the craft.

F-1 engine
The first stage is equipped with five; it provides thrust using kerosene-liquid oxygen combustion.

payload
Includes the Apollo craft, the lunar module and the third stage; the latter, after being placed in Earth's orbit, soars toward the Moon.

third stage
At an altitude of 92 mi, the third-stage engine begins to run, allowing the launcher to place itself in orbit before making its way toward the Moon.

second stage
At an altitude of 38.8 mi, the five second-stage engines ignite, burning for 6 min. 30 sec. before they are jettisoned.

first stage
Equipped with five F-1 engines that give the launcher the thrust it needs to leave the launchpad; jettisoned after 2 min. 30 sec. of flight.

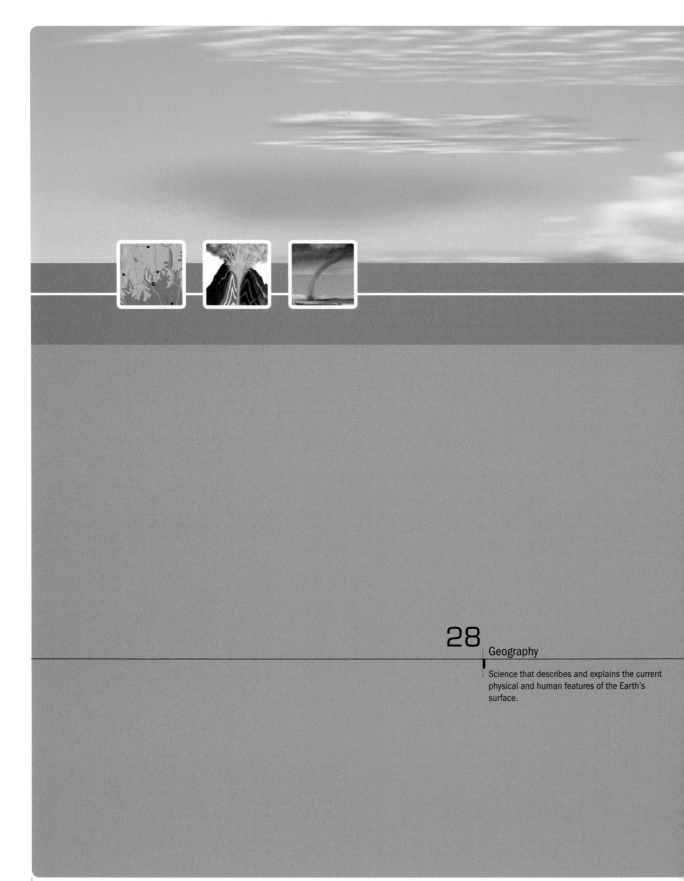

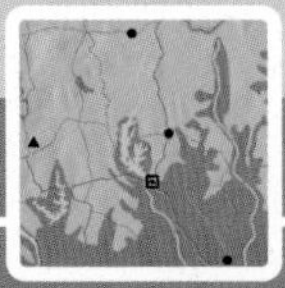

28 Geography

Science that describes and explains the current physical and human features of the Earth's surface.

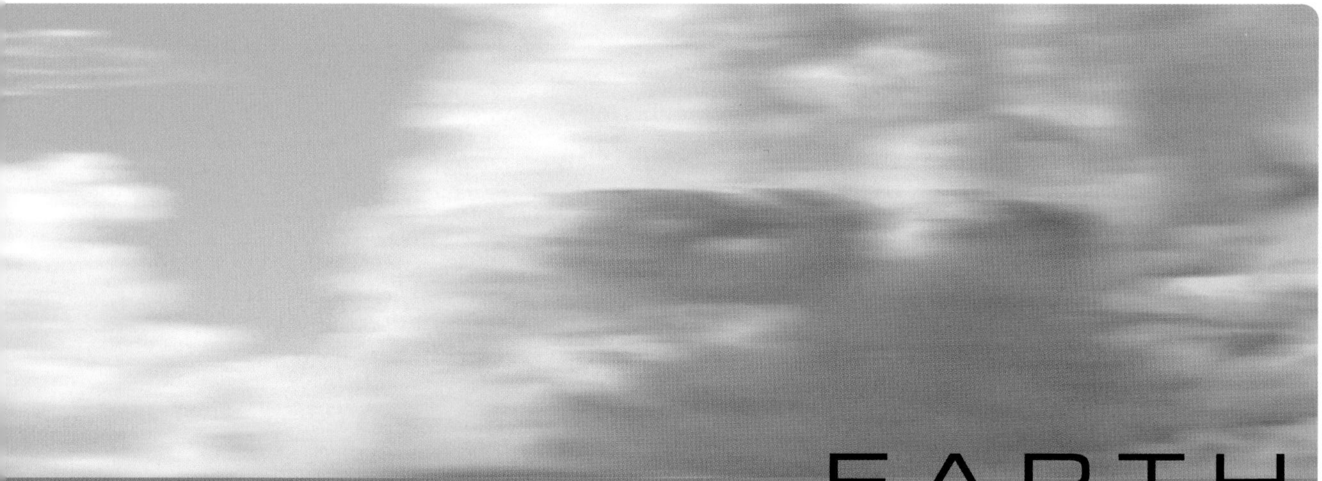

EARTH

Various sciences that study the Earth, either as a physical entity, or as a living environment for plants, animals and human beings.

42 Geology

Science whose subject is the history, structure and evolution of the terrestrial globe.

53 Meteorology

The science that studies atmospheric phenomena, with a particular focus on forecasting variations in weather.

66 Environment

Collective term for the elements that surround a living organism, some of which contribute directly to meeting its needs.

configuration of the continents

The continents are vast tracts of land surrounded by water; they cover about 30% of the Earth's surface.

planisphere
Map depicting the Earth's two hemispheres.

North Sea
Relatively shallow sea (220,000 mi²) in the North Atlantic and bordered by the coasts of Europe; some major European ports are located along its estuaries.

Mediterranean Sea
One of the largest inland seas in the world (965,000 mi²); it lies between Europe, Africa and Asia and connects to the Atlantic Ocean through the Strait of Gibraltar.

Bering Sea
Northern part of the Pacific between Kamchatka (in Asia) and Alaska; it is deepest in its southern portion.

Greenland Sea
Sea (465,000 mi²) in the North Atlantic; it is bordered by the coast of Greenland.

Black Sea
Inland sea (162,000 mi²) between Eastern Europe and Asia; it opens into the Mediterranean through two straits, the Dardanelles and the Bosporus.

South China Sea
Southern part of the China Sea bordering the entire southeast coast of Asia as well as Borneo, the Philippines and Taiwan.

Arctic
Vast region inside the north polar circle; it includes the Arctic Ocean and the lands bordering it.

Caspian Sea
The world's largest lake (140,000 mi²), located between Europe and Asia; it has no link to an ocean and is diminishing in size.

Arctic Ocean
The smallest of the oceans (5.8 million mi²), bordered by the northern coasts of Asia, America and Europe; it is largely covered with pack ice.

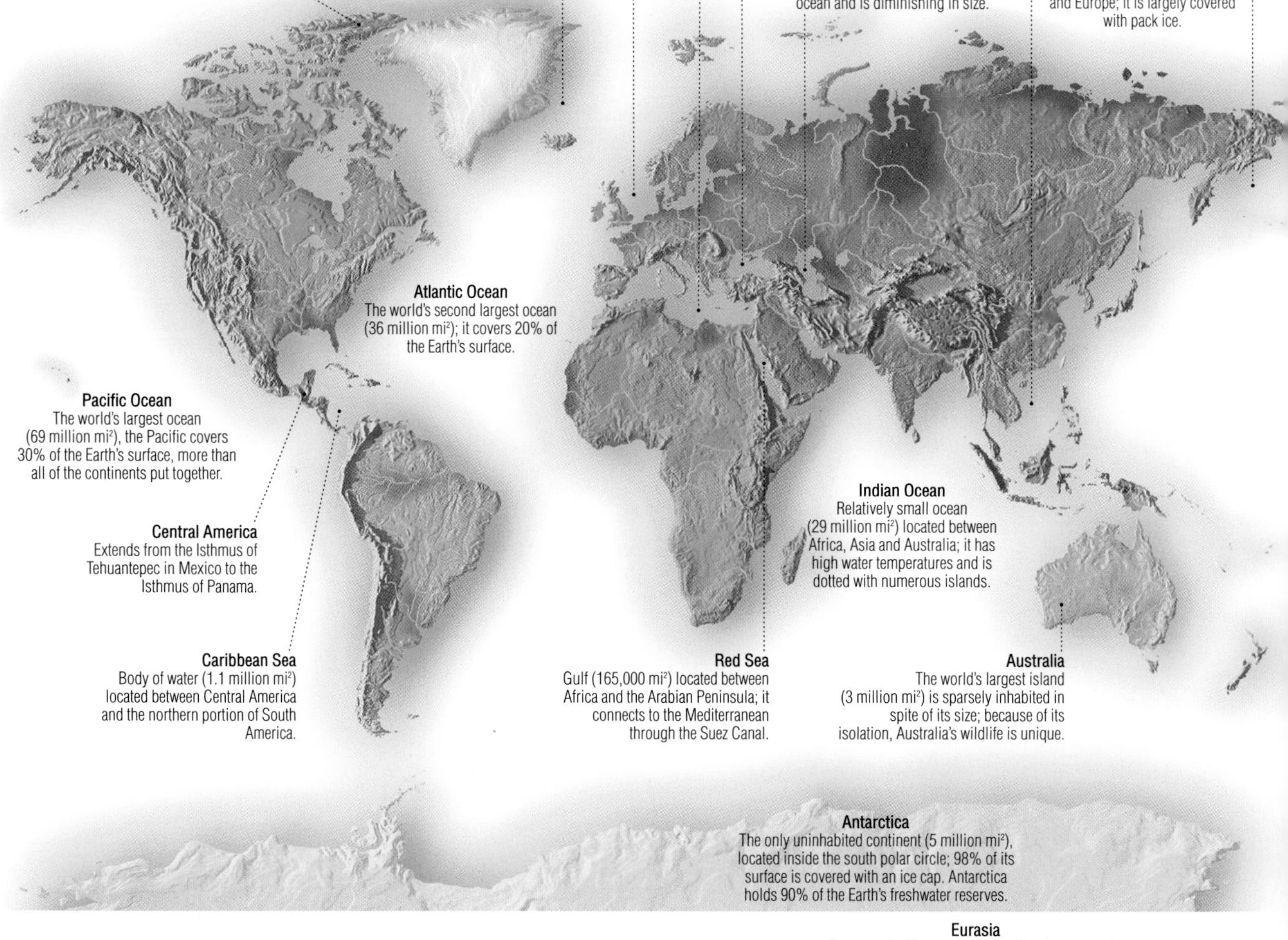

Atlantic Ocean
The world's second largest ocean (36 million mi²); it covers 20% of the Earth's surface.

Pacific Ocean
The world's largest ocean (69 million mi²), the Pacific covers 30% of the Earth's surface, more than all of the continents put together.

Indian Ocean
Relatively small ocean (29 million mi²) located between Africa, Asia and Australia; it has high water temperatures and is dotted with numerous islands.

Central America
Extends from the Isthmus of Tehuantepec in Mexico to the Isthmus of Panama.

Caribbean Sea
Body of water (1.1 million mi²) located between Central America and the northern portion of South America.

Red Sea
Gulf (165,000 mi²) located between Africa and the Arabian Peninsula; it connects to the Mediterranean through the Suez Canal.

Australia
The world's largest island (3 million mi²) is sparsely inhabited in spite of its size; because of its isolation, Australia's wildlife is unique.

Antarctica
The only uninhabited continent (5 million mi²), located inside the south polar circle; 98% of its surface is covered with an ice cap. Antarctica holds 90% of the Earth's freshwater reserves.

North America
Its area (9.3 million mi²) represents about 16% of the world's land; the Central American isthmus is an extension of North America.

South America
Represents 12% of the world's land; linked to North America by Central America; it includes the Andes in the west and plains and plateaus in east and central regions.

Oceania
Continent that represents 6% of the world's land and features a great many islands in the Pacific and Indian oceans; Australia is its true continent.

Europe
Western extremity of the vast Eurasian continent that, by convention, is separated from Asia by the Ural Mountains; it covers a relatively small area.

Asia
The largest and most populous continent, Asia represents 32% of the world's land; it is dominated by imposing mountain ranges.

Africa
Continent that represents about 20% of the world's land; two-thirds of its surface lies north of the Equator. Characterized by very hot climates, Mediterranean in the north and south, tropical and arid elsewhere.

Eurasia
Composed of Europe and Asia, Eurasia represents about 39% of the world's land; it forms a true continent that geographers have distinguished for historical and ethnographic reasons.

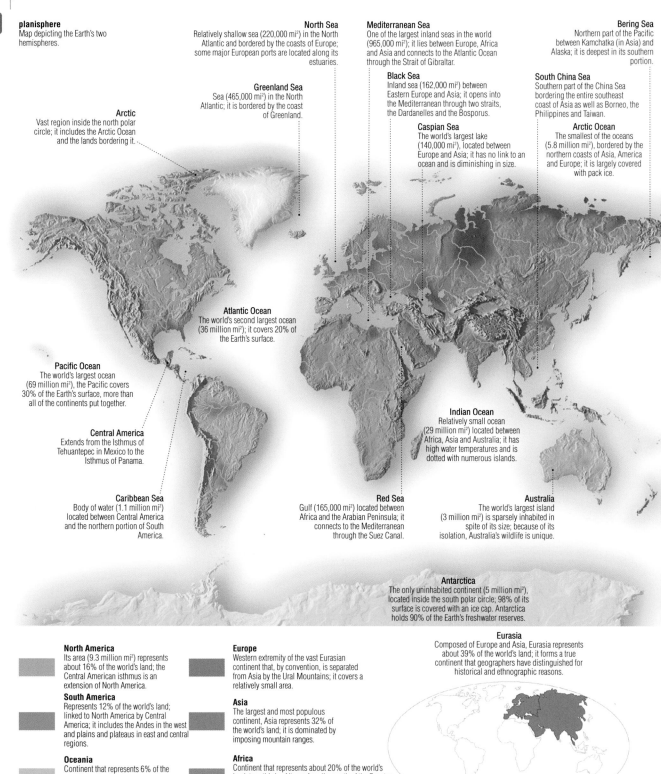

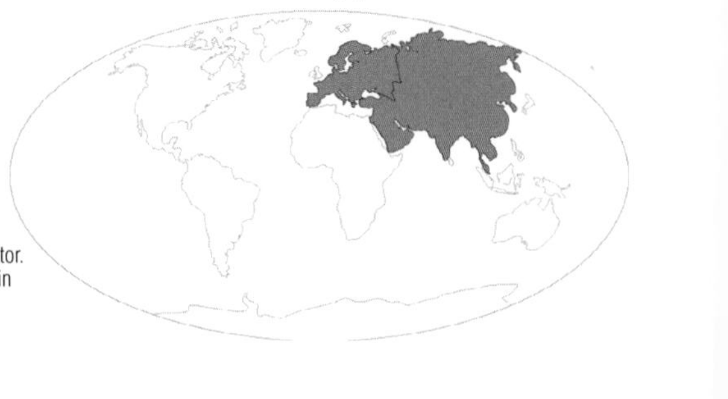

configuration of the continents

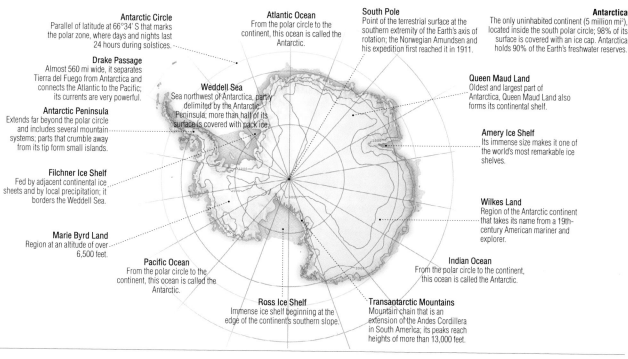

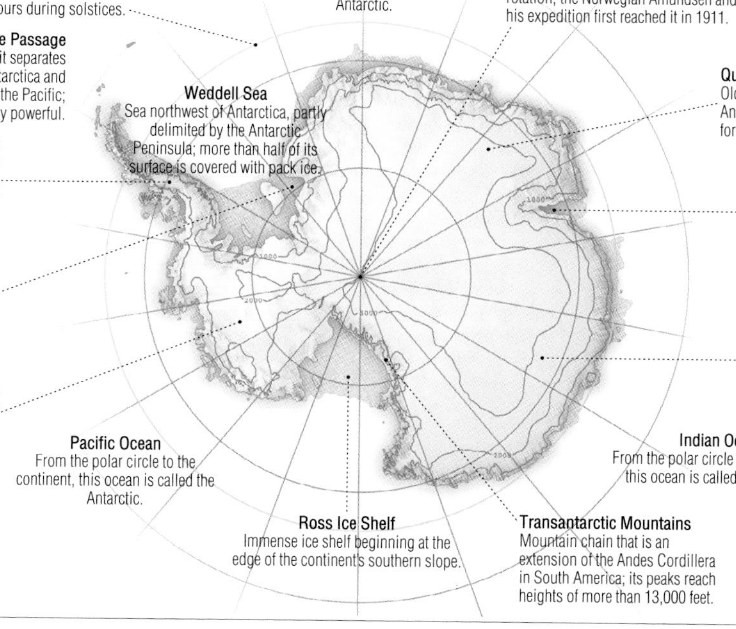
Antarctic Circle
Parallel of latitude at 66°34' S that marks the polar zone, where days and nights last 24 hours during solstices.
Atlantic Ocean
From the polar circle to the continent, this ocean is called the Antarctic.
South Pole
Point of the terrestrial surface at the southern extremity of the Earth's axis of rotation; the Norwegian Amundsen and his expedition first reached it in 1911.
Antarctica
The only uninhabited continent (5 million mi²), located inside the south polar circle; 98% of its surface is covered with an ice cap. Antarctica holds 90% of the Earth's freshwater reserves.
Drake Passage
Almost 560 mi wide, it separates Tierra del Fuego from Antarctica and connects the Atlantic to the Pacific; its currents are very powerful.
Weddell Sea
Sea northwest of Antarctica, partly delimited by the Antarctic Peninsula; more than half of its surface is covered with pack ice.
Queen Maud Land
Oldest and largest part of Antarctica, Queen Maud Land also forms its continental shelf.
Antarctic Peninsula
Extends far beyond the polar circle and includes several mountain systems; parts that crumble away from its tip form small islands.
Amery Ice Shelf
Its immense size makes it one of the world's most remarkable ice shelves.
Filchner Ice Shelf
Fed by adjacent continental ice sheets and by local precipitation; it borders the Weddell Sea.
Wilkes Land
Region of the Antarctic continent that takes its name from a 19th-century American mariner and explorer.
Marie Byrd Land
Region at an altitude of over 6,500 feet.
Pacific Ocean
From the polar circle to the continent, this ocean is called the Antarctic.
Indian Ocean
From the polar circle to the continent, this ocean is called the Antarctic.
Ross Ice Shelf
Immense ice shelf beginning at the edge of the continent's southern slope.
Transantarctic Mountains
Mountain chain that is an extension of the Andes Cordillera in South America; its peaks reach heights of more than 13,000 feet.

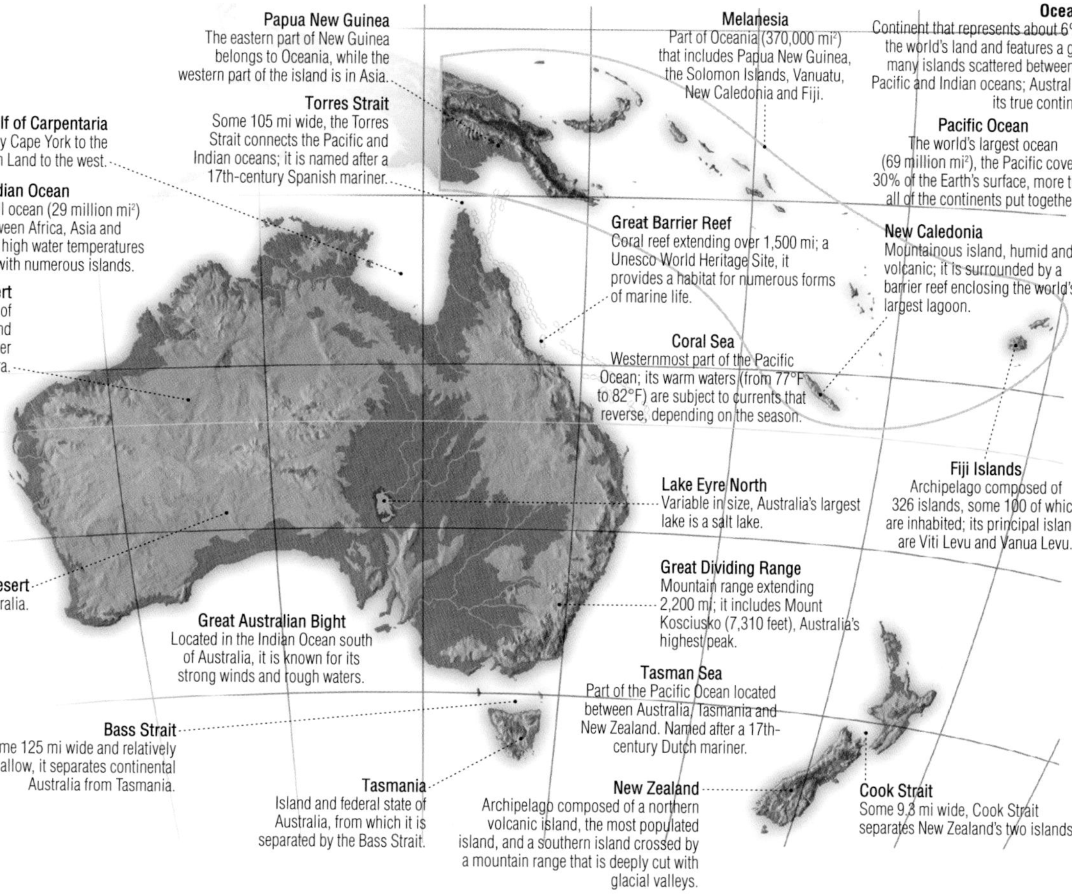
Papua New Guinea
The eastern part of New Guinea belongs to Oceania, while the western part of the island is in Asia.
Melanesia
Part of Oceania (370,000 mi²) that includes Papua New Guinea, the Solomon Islands, Vanuatu, New Caledonia and Fiji.
Oceania
Continent that represents about 6% of the world's land and features a great many islands scattered between the Pacific and Indian oceans; Australia is its true continent.
Torres Strait
Some 105 mi wide, the Torres Strait connects the Pacific and Indian oceans; it is named after a 17th-century Spanish mariner.
Gulf of Carpentaria
Gulf bounded by Cape York to the east and Arnhem Land to the west.
Pacific Ocean
The world's largest ocean (69 million mi²), the Pacific covers 30% of the Earth's surface, more than all of the continents put together.
Indian Ocean
Relatively small ocean (29 million mi²) located between Africa, Asia and Australia; it has high water temperatures and is dotted with numerous islands.
Great Barrier Reef
Coral reef extending over 1,500 mi; a Unesco World Heritage Site, it provides a habitat for numerous forms of marine life.
New Caledonia
Mountainous island, humid and volcanic; it is surrounded by a barrier reef enclosing the world's largest lagoon.
Great Sandy Desert
The northernmost desert of Australia is also the world's second largest desert (730,000 mi²) after the Sahara.
Coral Sea
Westernmost part of the Pacific Ocean; its warm waters (from 77°F to 82°F) are subject to currents that reverse, depending on the season.
Lake Eyre North
Variable in size, Australia's largest lake is a salt lake.
Fiji Islands
Archipelago composed of 326 islands, some 100 of which are inhabited; its principal islands are Viti Levu and Vanua Levu.
Great Victoria Desert
Southernmost desert of Australia.
Great Dividing Range
Mountain range extending 2,200 mi; it includes Mount Kosciusko (7,310 feet), Australia's highest peak.
Great Australian Bight
Located in the Indian Ocean south of Australia, it is known for its strong winds and rough waters.
Tasman Sea
Part of the Pacific Ocean located between Australia, Tasmania and New Zealand. Named after a 17th-century Dutch mariner.
Bass Strait
Some 125 mi wide and relatively shallow, it separates continental Australia from Tasmania.
Tasmania
Island and federal state of Australia, from which it is separated by the Bass Strait.
New Zealand
Archipelago composed of a northern volcanic island, the most populated island, and a southern island crossed by a mountain range that is deeply cut with glacial valleys.
Cook Strait
Some 9.3 mi wide, Cook Strait separates New Zealand's two islands.

configuration of the continents

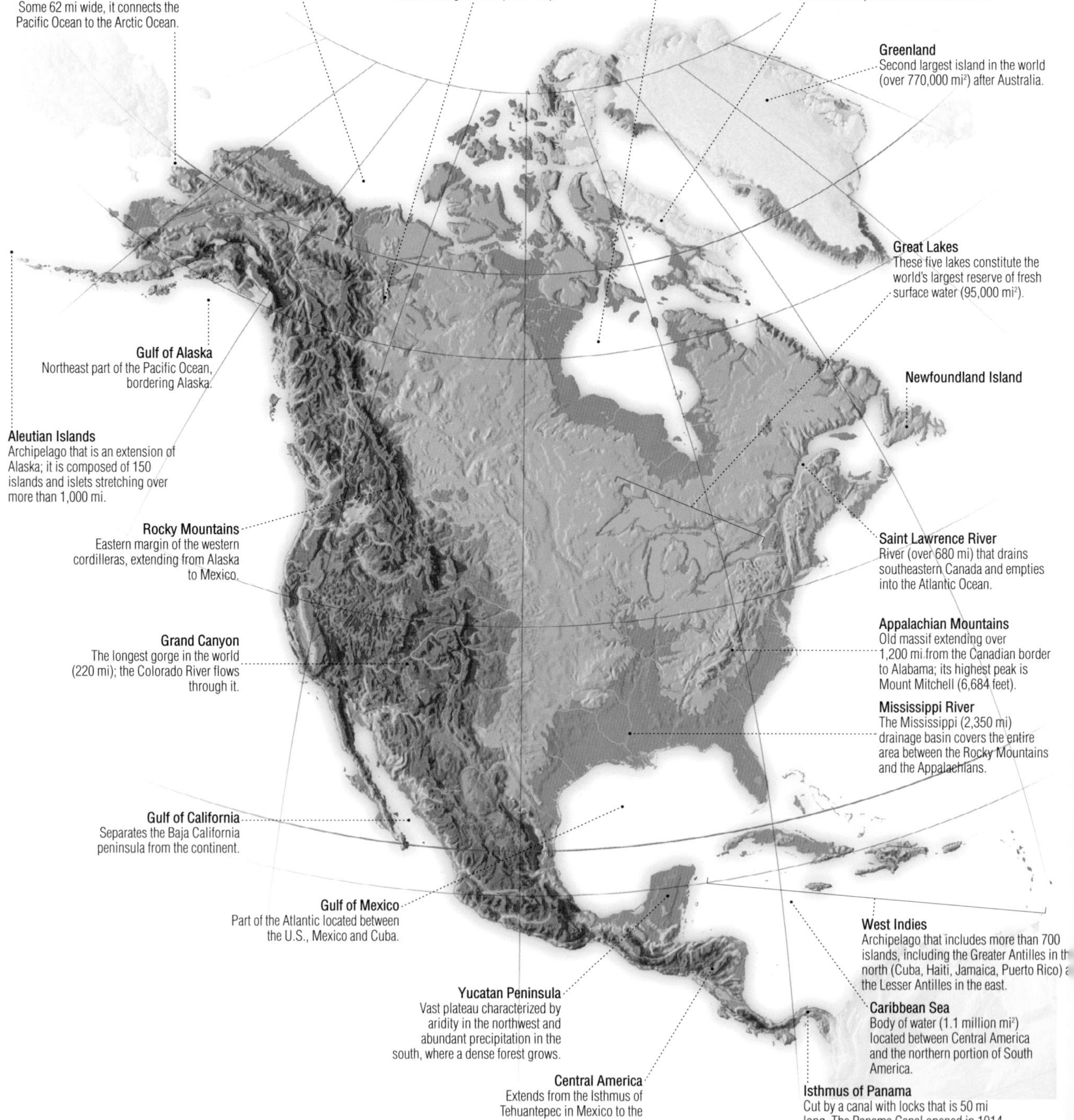
North America
The Appalachians constitute the principal relief on the eastern part of the continent, while in the west, high mountain chains (the Rocky Mountains and the Sierra Madre) follow the coast from Alaska to Mexico.
Beaufort Sea
Part of the Arctic Ocean between Alaska and the Arctic Archipelago.
Hudson Bay
Vast gulf that opens onto the Atlantic Ocean through the Hudson Strait; the bay is frozen seven months a year.
Mackenzie River
Canada's longest river (2,635 mi).
Baffin Island
Island in the Arctic Archipelago; the Baffin Sea separates it from Greenland.
Bering Strait
Some 62 mi wide, it connects the Pacific Ocean to the Arctic Ocean.
Greenland
Second largest island in the world (over 770,000 mi^2) after Australia.
Great Lakes
These five lakes constitute the world's largest reserve of fresh surface water (95,000 mi^2).
Gulf of Alaska
Northeast part of the Pacific Ocean, bordering Alaska.
Newfoundland Island
Aleutian Islands
Archipelago that is an extension of Alaska; it is composed of 150 islands and islets stretching over more than 1,000 mi.
Rocky Mountains
Eastern margin of the western cordilleras, extending from Alaska to Mexico.
Saint Lawrence River
River (over 680 mi) that drains southeastern Canada and empties into the Atlantic Ocean.
Grand Canyon
The longest gorge in the world (220 mi); the Colorado River flows through it.
Appalachian Mountains
Old massif extending over 1,200 mi from the Canadian border to Alabama; its highest peak is Mount Mitchell (6,684 feet).
Mississippi River
The Mississippi (2,350 mi) drainage basin covers the entire area between the Rocky Mountains and the Appalachians.
Gulf of California
Separates the Baja California peninsula from the continent.
Gulf of Mexico
Part of the Atlantic located between the U.S., Mexico and Cuba.
West Indies
Archipelago that includes more than 700 islands, including the Greater Antilles in th north (Cuba, Haiti, Jamaica, Puerto Rico) a the Lesser Antilles in the east.
Yucatan Peninsula
Vast plateau characterized by aridity in the northwest and abundant precipitation in the south, where a dense forest grows.
Caribbean Sea
Body of water (1.1 million mi^2) located between Central America and the northern portion of South America.
Central America
Extends from the Isthmus of Tehuantepec in Mexico to the Isthmus of Panama.
Isthmus of Panama
Cut by a canal with locks that is 50 mi long. The Panama Canal opened in 1914 allowing maritime traffic to travel between the Caribbean Sea and the Pacific Ocean.

configuration of the continents

South America
Linked to North America by Central America, its main features are the Andes Cordillera in the west and the plains and plateaus of the central and eastern regions.
Orinoco River
River in Venezuela (1,340 mi) that empties into the Atlantic through a vast delta; the volume of its flow is considerable.
Amazon River
The largest river in the world in volume of flow; it rises in the Andes and flows for 4,090 mi through more than 80% of Brazil's territory.
Gulf of Panama
Bounded in the north by the Isthmus of Panama, its coast is uneven and dotted with islands.
Equator
Imaginary circle surrounding Earth at its widest circumference, dividing it into two hemispheres: the Northern hemisphere and the Southern hemisphere.
Andes Cordillera
Longest mountain chain in the world (5,000 mi) and the second highest, it follows the western coast of South America; its highest peak is Aconcagua (22,834 feet).
Lake Titicaca
Located in the Andes Cordillera between Peru and Bolivia; at an elevation of 12,500 feet, it is the highest navigable lake in the world.
Atacama Desert
Among the driest deserts on the planet, receiving only a few inches of rain per year.
Paraná River
River (1,860 mi) with most of its course in Brazil; it marks the boundary between Brazil and Paraguay, and between Paraguay and Argentina.
Patagonia
Plateau in Chile and Argentina; it is divided into Andean Patagonia with a humid climate and abundant vegetation, and the Patagonian plateau, which is dry and sparse.
Falkland Islands
Archipelago composed of two main islands separated by the Falkland Strait, as well as some 100 islets.
Tierra del Fuego
Archipelago separated from the continent by the Magellan Strait; its cold damp climate results in perpetual snows from as low as 2,300 feet.
Cape Horn
Southernmost point of South America, only 620 mi from Antarctica; famous for its storms and dangerous reefs and shoals.
Drake Passage
Almost 560 mi wide, it separates Tierra del Fuego from Antarctica and connects the Atlantic to the Pacific; its currents are very powerful.

configuration of the continents

Europe
Western extremity of the vast Eurasian continent that, by convention, is separated from Asia by the Ural Mountains; it covers a relatively small area.

Lake Ladoga
Europe's largest lake (6,800 mi²) is located in Russia; it empties into the Baltic Sea.

Barents Sea
Area of the Arctic Ocean lying north of the Scandinavian Peninsula and Russia; it is partially ice-covered.

Ural Mountains
Mountain range extending 1,500 mi from the Caspian Sea to the Arctic; it is traditionally considered the boundary between Europe and Asia.

Kola Peninsula
Mostly mountainous peninsula located in Russia, above the Arctic polar circle.

Volga River
The longest river in Europe (2,300 mi) is ice-covered three to four months per year; its spring flood is substantial.

Gulf of Bothnia
Relatively shallow Gulf between Sweden and Finland; it is often icebound.

Norwegian Sea
Open sea west of Norway and east of Iceland.

Dnieper River
River in Russia (1,350 mi) whose flow is slow but abundant; it is a major communications artery.

Iceland
Volcanic island subject to regular earthquakes; it has over 3,100 mi of coastline.

North Sea
Relatively shallow sea (220,000 mi²) in the North Atlantic and bordered by the coasts of Europe; some major European ports are located along its estuaries.

Scandinavian Peninsula
Vast Nordic peninsula that includes Norway, Sweden and part of Finland.

Baltic Sea
Generally shallow inland sea that is low in salt content and devoid of major tides; it freezes along its coasts.

Irish Sea
Section of the Atlantic that separates Great Britain from Ireland.

Atlantic Ocean
The world's second largest ocean; it covers 20% of the Earth's surface.

English Channel
Relatively shallow sea between France and England; its extreme tides cause strong currents, making navigation difficult.

Vistula River
Poland's principal river (680 mi) has its source in the Carpathians and joins the Baltic Sea at the Gulf of Gdansk; it is ice-covered two to three months per year.

Alps
Largest mountain mass in Europe, extending 750 mi; Mont Blanc (15,771 feet) is its highest peak.

Black Sea
Inland sea (162,000 mi²) between Eastern Europe and Asia; it opens into the Mediterranean through two straits, the Dardanelles and the Bosporus.

Iberian Peninsula
Peninsula comprising Spain and Portugal; it extends from the Pyrenees to the Strait of Gibraltar.

Strait of Gibraltar
Channel (9 mi wide) between Spain and Morocco; it connects the Mediterranean to the Atlantic and is an important shipping route.

Pyrenees
Mountain range whose northern slope is in France and whose southern slope is in Spain; Pico de Aneto (11,169 feet) is its highest peak.

Danube River
Second longest river in Europe (1,770 mi); it flows into the Black Sea through a vast delta with three branches.

Balkan Peninsula
Mountainous, easternmost peninsula of Europe whose crumbling coastline features peninsulas and scattered islands.

Carpathian Mountains
Mountain range in central Europe, lower than the Alps; its highest point is at an elevation of 8,711 feet.

Mediterranean Sea
One of the world's largest inland seas, bordered by Europe, Africa and Asia; it connects to the Atlantic Ocean through the Strait of Gibraltar.

Adriatic Sea
Gulf of the Mediterranean, 520 mi long and 110 mi wide, located between Italy and the Balkan Peninsula.

Aegean Sea
Area of the Mediterranean Sea between Turkey and Greece; it contains numerous islands, the largest of which is Crete.

configuration of the continents

Asia
The largest and most populous continent, Asia represents 32% of the world's land; it is dominated by imposing mountain ranges.

Lake Baikal
The world's oldest (25 million years) and deepest (5,315 feet) lake; Lake Baikal is 370 mi long and 40 to 50 mi wide and is frozen six months of the year.

Aral Sea
Sea once connected to the Caspian Sea; it is now an immense salt lake.

Gobi Desert
One of the largest deserts in the world (400,000 mi²), shared by China and Mongolia; the Gobi is a plateau situated at an elevation of about 3,300 feet.

Caspian Sea
The world's largest lake (140,000 mi²), located between Europe and Asia; it has no link to an ocean and is diminishing in size.

Black Sea
Inland sea (162,000 mi²) between Eastern Europe and Asia; it opens into the Mediterranean through two straits, the Dardanelles and the Bosporus.

Red Sea
Gulf (165,000 mi²) located between Africa and the Arabian Peninsula; it connects to the Mediterranean through the Suez Canal.

Kamchatka Peninsula
Peninsula (12,000 mi²) on the Bering Sea; it is characterized by intense volcanic activity.

Sea of Japan (East Sea)
Area of the Pacific Ocean that separates Japan from the Asian mainland; it is divided into a warm region and a cold region.

Pacific Ocean
The world's largest ocean (69 million mi²), the Pacific covers 30% of the Earth's surface, more than all of the continents put together.

Japan
Archipelago made up of 1,000 islands, including four main islands that represent 95% of its territory; it is characterized by intense volcanic activity and frequent earthquakes.

Korean Peninsula
Peninsula that delimits the Sea of Japan; its climate is marked by monsoons in summer and typhoons in the fall.

East China Sea
Area of the China Sea between Korea, the Ryukyu Islands (south of Japan) and Taiwan.

Philippines
Archipelago with more than 7,000 islands and islets; two principal islands (Luzon and Mindanao) make up 70% of its territory.

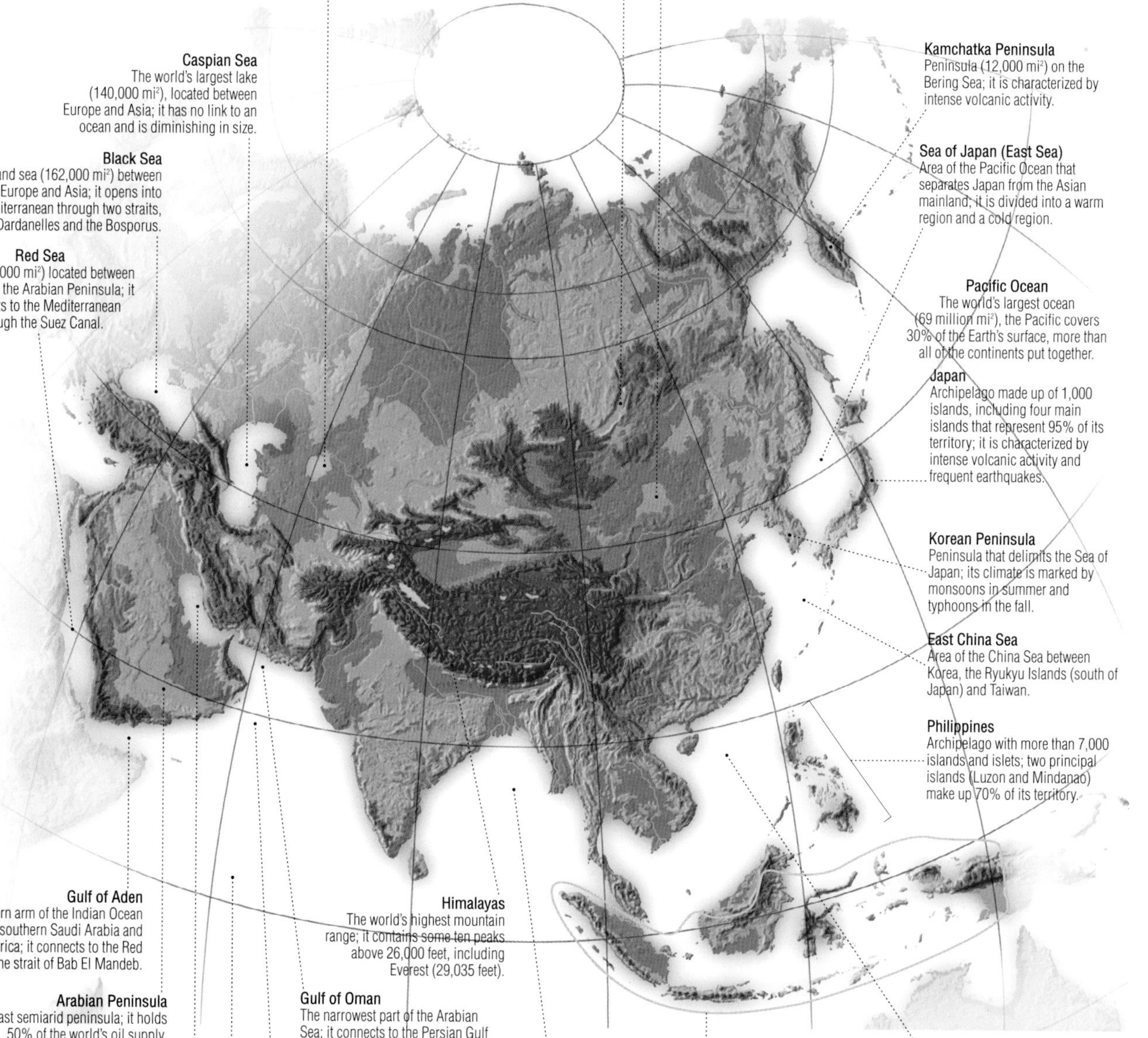

Gulf of Aden
Northwestern arm of the Indian Ocean between southern Saudi Arabia and theastern Africa; it connects to the Red ea through the strait of Bab El Mandeb.

Himalayas
The world's highest mountain range; it contains some ten peaks above 26,000 feet, including Everest (29,035 feet).

Arabian Peninsula
Vast semiarid peninsula; it holds 50% of the world's oil supply.

Gulf of Oman
The narrowest part of the Arabian Sea; it connects to the Persian Gulf through the Strait of Hormuz.

South China Sea
Southern part of the China Sea bordering the entire southeast coast of Asia as well as Borneo, the Philippines and Taiwan.

Persian Gulf
Gulf (500 mi long) bordered by Saudi Arabia, Iran and Iraq; it is also called the Arabian Gulf and is an important maritime trade route.

Arabian Sea
Area of the Indian Ocean between India and the Arabian Peninsula; the Gulf of Oman is an arm of the Arabian Sea.

Indonesia
Archipelago with almost 14,000 islands extending 3,100 mi from west to east; it is the world's most active volcanic zone.

Indian Ocean
Relatively small ocean (29 million mi²) located between Africa, Asia and Australia; it has high water temperatures and is dotted with numerous islands.

Bay of Bengal
Area of the Indian Ocean between India and the Indochinese Peninsula; the Ganges River empties into this bay through the world's largest delta.

configuration of the continents

Africa
Continent that represents about 20% of the world's land; two-thirds of its surface lies north of the Equator. Characterized by very hot climates, Mediterranean in the north and south, tropical and arid elsewhere.

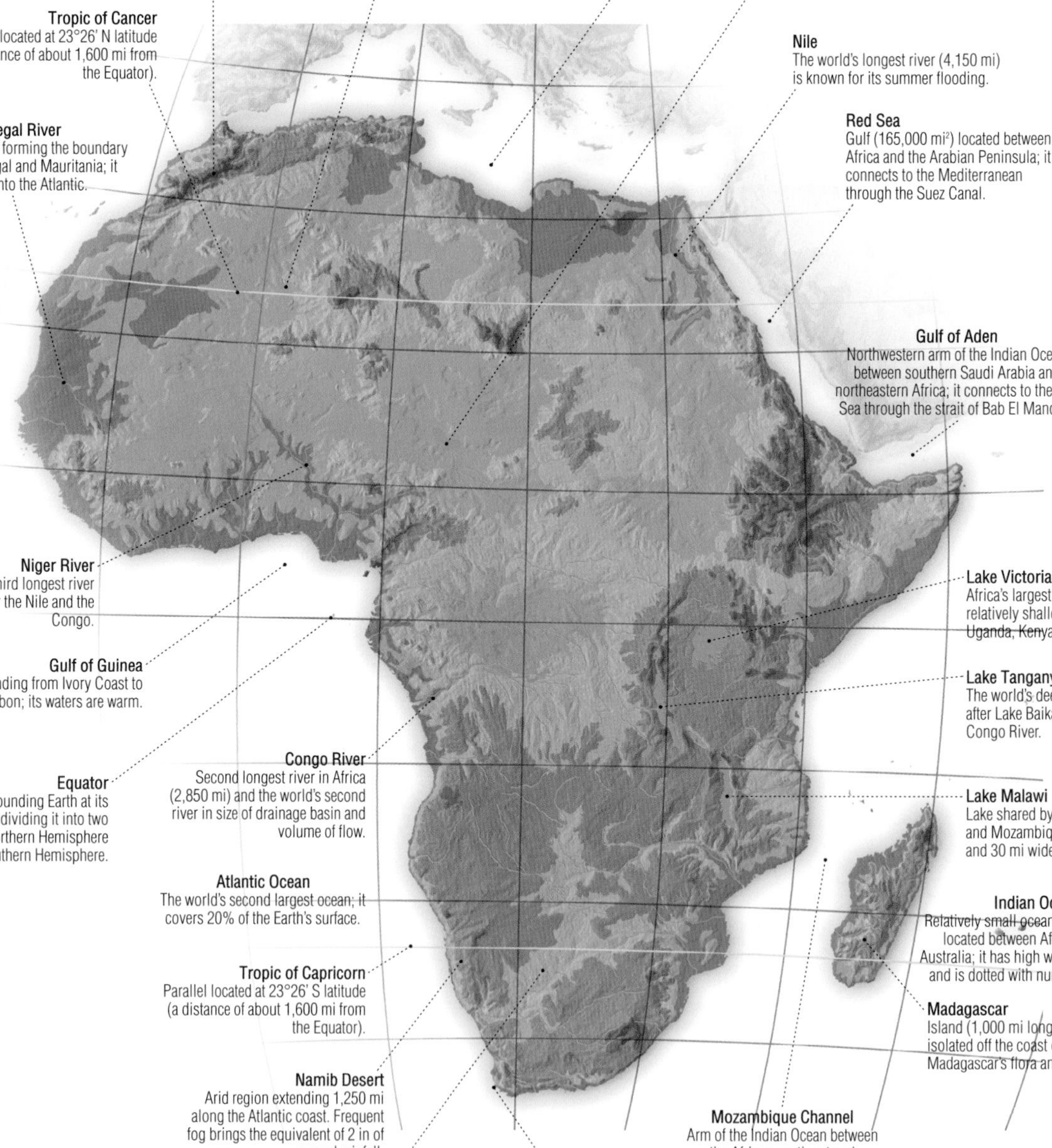
Atlas Mountains
Mountain chain composed of several ranges; it extends from Tunisia to Morocco, where Jebel Toubkal is its highest peak (13,665 feet).
Sahara Desert
Largest desert in the world (3 million mi²); it covers one-quarter of Africa.
Mediterranean Sea
One of the largest inland seas in the world (965,000 mi²); it lies between Europe, Africa and Asia and connects to the Atlantic Ocean through the Strait of Gibraltar.
Lake Chad
Large lake, shallow and marshy, the vestige of what was once a sea; it continues to diminish in size and could one day dry up.
Tropic of Cancer
Parallel located at 23°26′ N latitude (a distance of about 1,600 mi from the Equator).
Nile
The world's longest river (4,150 mi) is known for its summer flooding.
Senegal River
River (1,050 mi) forming the boundary between Senegal and Mauritania; it empties into the Atlantic.
Red Sea
Gulf (165,000 mi²) located between Africa and the Arabian Peninsula; it connects to the Mediterranean through the Suez Canal.
Gulf of Aden
Northwestern arm of the Indian Ocean between southern Saudi Arabia and northeastern Africa; it connects to the Red Sea through the strait of Bab El Mandeb.
Niger River
Africa's third longest river (2,600 mi) after the Nile and the Congo.
Lake Victoria
Africa's largest lake (26,000 mi²) is relatively shallow; it is bordered by Uganda, Kenya and Tanzania.
Gulf of Guinea
Gulf extending from Ivory Coast to Gabon; its waters are warm.
Lake Tanganyika
The world's deepest lake (4,710 fee after Lake Baikal; it empties into the Congo River.
Equator
Imaginary circle surrounding Earth at its widest circumference, dividing it into two hemispheres: the Northern Hemisphere and the Southern Hemisphere.
Congo River
Second longest river in Africa (2,850 mi) and the world's second river in size of drainage basin and volume of flow.
Lake Malawi
Lake shared by Malawi, Tanzania and Mozambique; it is 310 mi long and 30 mi wide.
Atlantic Ocean
The world's second largest ocean; it covers 20% of the Earth's surface.
Indian Ocean
Relatively small ocean (29 million mi²) located between Africa, Asia and Australia; it has high water temperatures and is dotted with numerous islands.
Tropic of Capricorn
Parallel located at 23°26′ S latitude (a distance of about 1,600 mi from the Equator).
Madagascar
Island (1,000 mi long); because it is isolated off the coast of Africa, Madagascar's flora and fauna are unique.
Namib Desert
Arid region extending 1,250 mi along the Atlantic coast. Frequent fog brings the equivalent of 2 in of annual rainfall.
Mozambique Channel
Arm of the Indian Ocean between the African continent and Madagascar.
Kalahari Desert
Semiarid region bordering the Namib Desert; the north is marshy while the south is characterized by very sparse vegetation.
Cape of Good Hope
Former island now connected to the continent by a ridge of sand; located only 90 mi to the west of Africa's southernmost point.

cartography

A collective term for the techniques and graphic arts used to develop and produce maps based on direct observation or documentation.

Earth coordinate system
The intersection of two imaginary lines, longitude and latitude, makes it possible to locate a precise point on the Earth's surface.

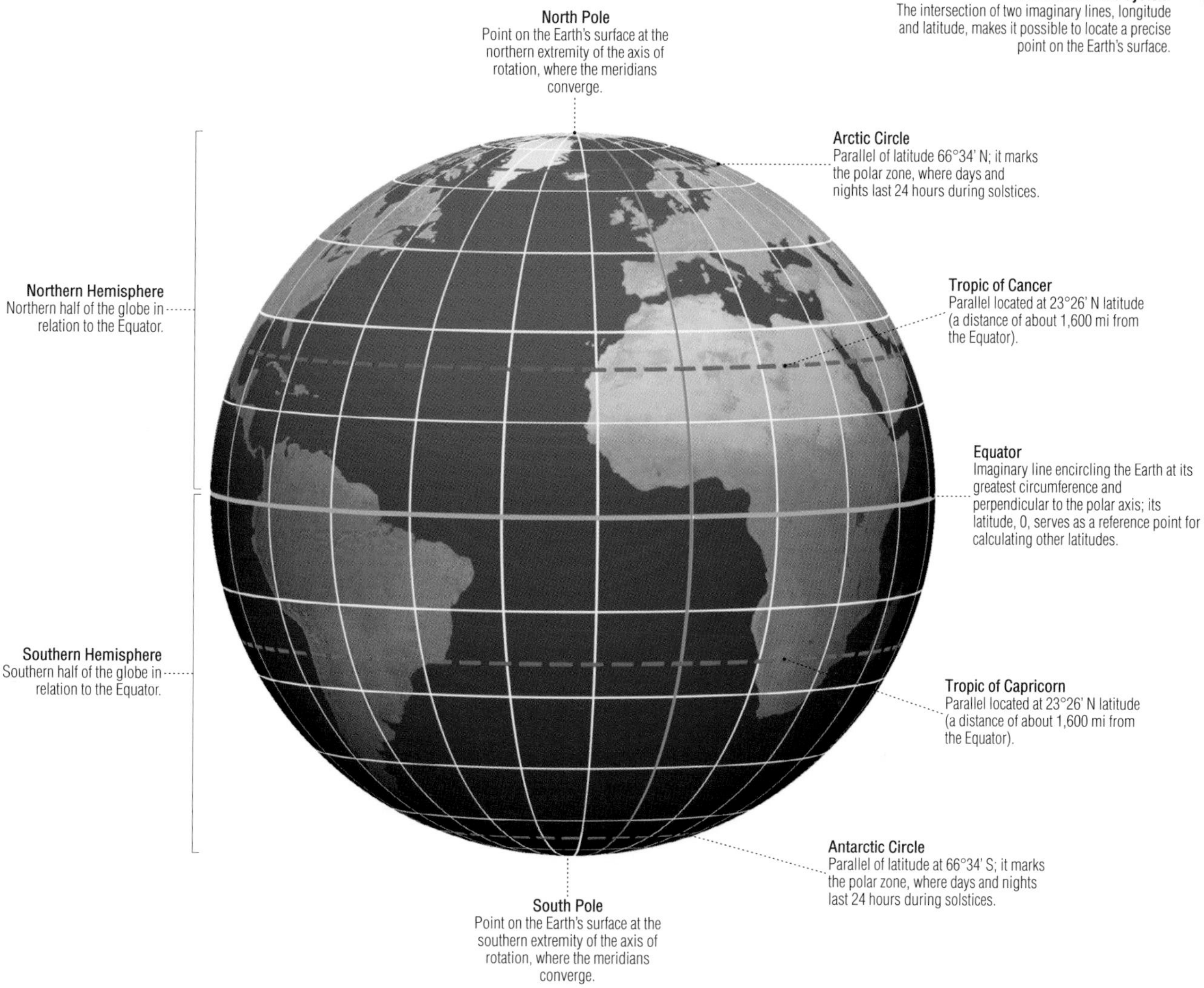

North Pole
Point on the Earth's surface at the northern extremity of the axis of rotation, where the meridians converge.
Arctic Circle
Parallel of latitude 66°34' N; it marks the polar zone, where days and nights last 24 hours during solstices.
Northern Hemisphere
Northern half of the globe in relation to the Equator.
Tropic of Cancer
Parallel located at 23°26' N latitude (a distance of about 1,600 mi from the Equator).
Equator
Imaginary line encircling the Earth at its greatest circumference and perpendicular to the polar axis; its latitude, 0, serves as a reference point for calculating other latitudes.
Southern Hemisphere
Southern half of the globe in relation to the Equator.
Tropic of Capricorn
Parallel located at 23°26' N latitude (a distance of about 1,600 mi from the Equator).
Antarctic Circle
Parallel of latitude at 66°34' S; it marks the polar zone, where days and nights last 24 hours during solstices.
South Pole
Point on the Earth's surface at the southern extremity of the axis of rotation, where the meridians converge.

hemispheres
The globe is divided by convention into four half spheres, using the Greenwich meridian or the Equator as a reference point.

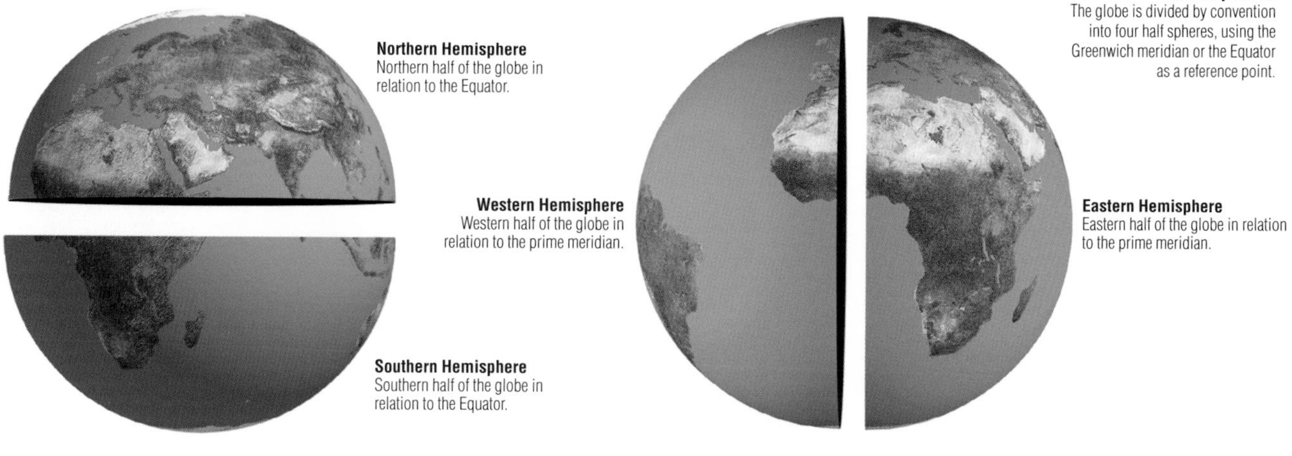

Northern Hemisphere
Northern half of the globe in relation to the Equator.
Western Hemisphere
Western half of the globe in relation to the prime meridian.
Eastern Hemisphere
Eastern half of the globe in relation to the prime meridian.
Southern Hemisphere
Southern half of the globe in relation to the Equator.

cartography

grid system
Collective term for the parallels and meridians that form an imaginary grid over the Earth's surface, making it possible to locate a specific point.

line of latitude
Coordinate of a point on the Earth's surface indicating, in degrees, its distance from the Equator.

Arctic Circle
Parallel of latitude 66°34' N; it marks the polar zone, where days and nights last 24 hours during solstices.

line of longitude
Coordinate of a point on the Earth's surface indicating, in degrees, its distance from the prime meridian.

Tropic of Cancer
Parallel located at 23°26' N latitude (a distance of about 1,600 mi from the Equator).

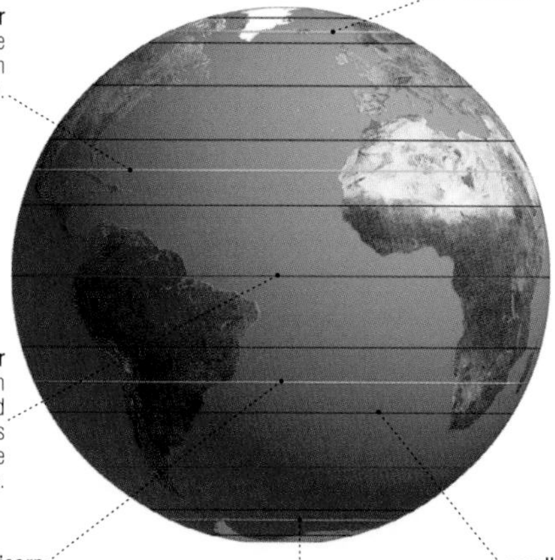

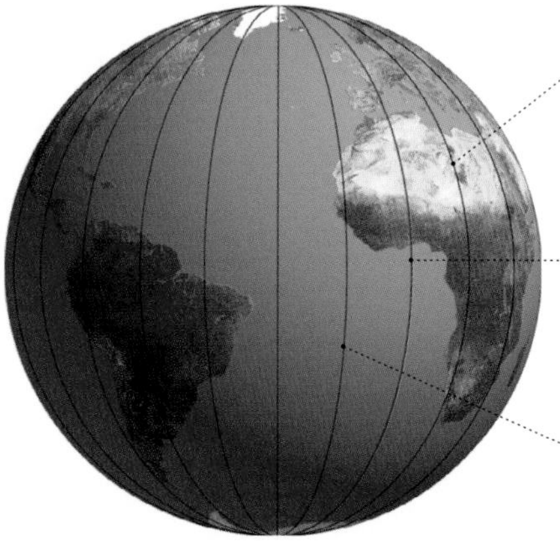

Eastern meridian
Imaginary line connecting the poles and perpendicular to the Equator; located east of the Greenwich meridian.

prime meridian
Chosen by convention as the meridian of origin; its longitude, 0 divides the Eastern and Western hemispheres.

Equator
Imaginary line encircling the Earth at its greatest circumference and perpendicular to the polar axis; its latitude, 0, serves as a reference point for calculating other latitudes.

Western meridian
Imaginary line connecting the poles and perpendicular to the Equator; located west of the Greenwich meridian.

Tropic of Capricorn
Parallel located at 23°26' N latitude (a distance of about 1,600 mi from the Equator).

Antarctic Circle
Parallel of latitude at 66°34' S; it marks the polar zone, where days and nights last 24 hours during solstices.

parallel
Imaginary circle whose plane is parallel to the Equator.

map projections
Representations of the Earth's surface on a plane.

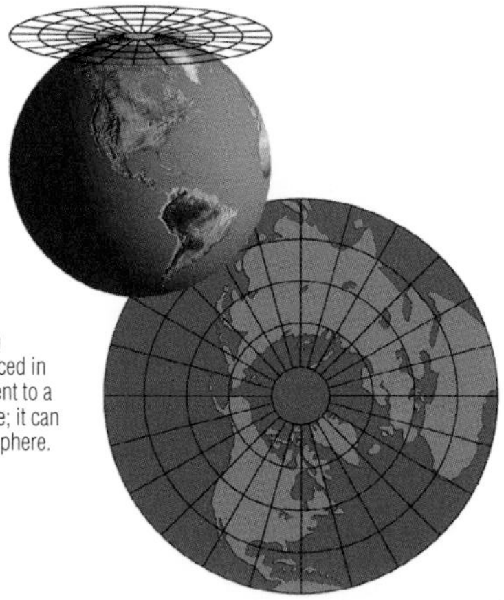

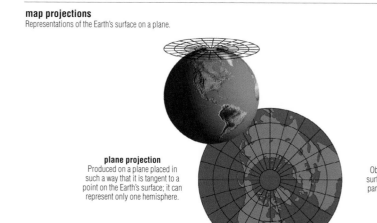

plane projection
Produced on a plane placed in such a way that it is tangent to a point on the Earth's surface; it can represent only one hemisphere.

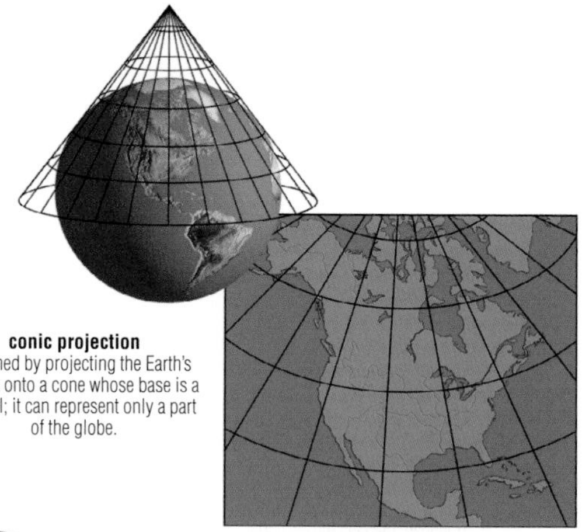

conic projection
Obtained by projecting the Earth's surface onto a cone whose base is a parallel; it can represent only a part of the globe.

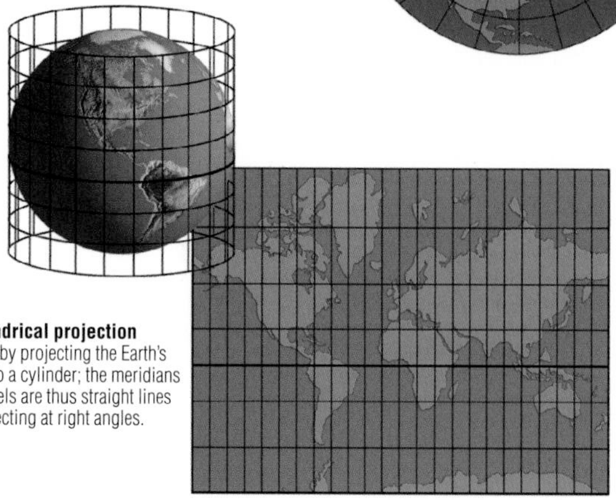

cylindrical projection
Obtained by projecting the Earth's surface onto a cylinder; the meridians and parallels are thus straight lines intersecting at right angles.

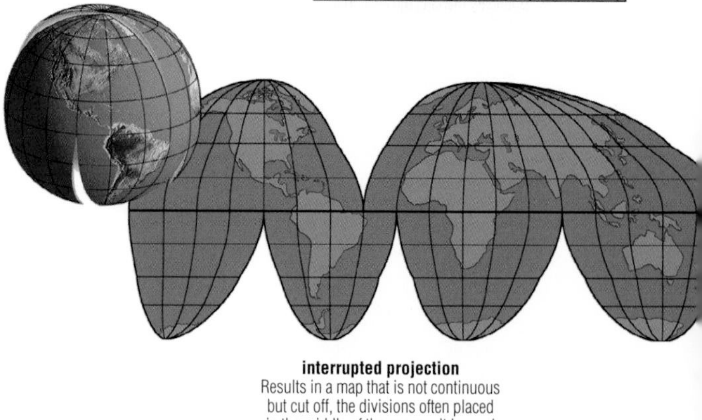

interrupted projection
Results in a map that is not continuous but cut off, the divisions often placed in the middle of the oceans; it is used to represent the continents.

compass card
Star indicating the cardinal points and the intermediary directions; it is reproduced on compass dials, marine charts and so forth.

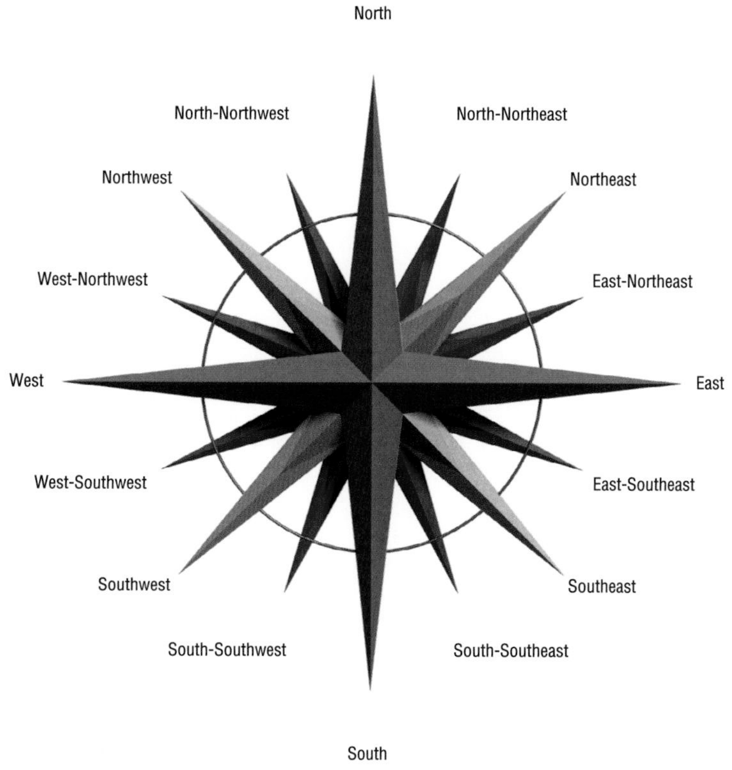
North
North-Northwest
North-Northeast
Northwest
Northeast
West-Northwest
East-Northeast
West
East
West-Southwest
East-Southeast
Southwest
Southeast
South-Southwest
South-Southeast
South

political map
Type of map representing various countries and their territorial or administrative units.

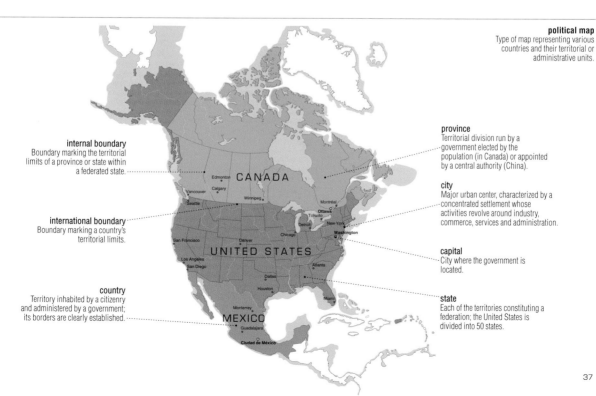

CANADA
UNITED STATES
MEXICO
Edmonton
Calgary
Vancouver
Seattle
Winnipeg
Montréal
Ottawa
Toronto
Detroit
New York
Washington
Chicago
Denver
San Francisco
Los Angeles
San Diego
Atlanta
Dallas
Houston
Miami
Monterrey
Guadalajara
Ciudad de México

internal boundary
Boundary marking the territorial limits of a province or state within a federated state.

international boundary
Boundary marking a country's territorial limits.

country
Territory inhabited by a citizenry and administered by a government; its borders are clearly established.

province
Territorial division run by a government elected by the population (in Canada) or appointed by a central authority (China).

city
Major urban center, characterized by a concentrated settlement whose activities revolve around industry, commerce, services and administration.

capital
City where the government is located.

state
Each of the territories constituting a federation; the United States is divided into 50 states.

cartography

physical map
Type of map representing the Earth's surface (topography, watercourses, aquatic areas) using various techniques (contour lines, colors).

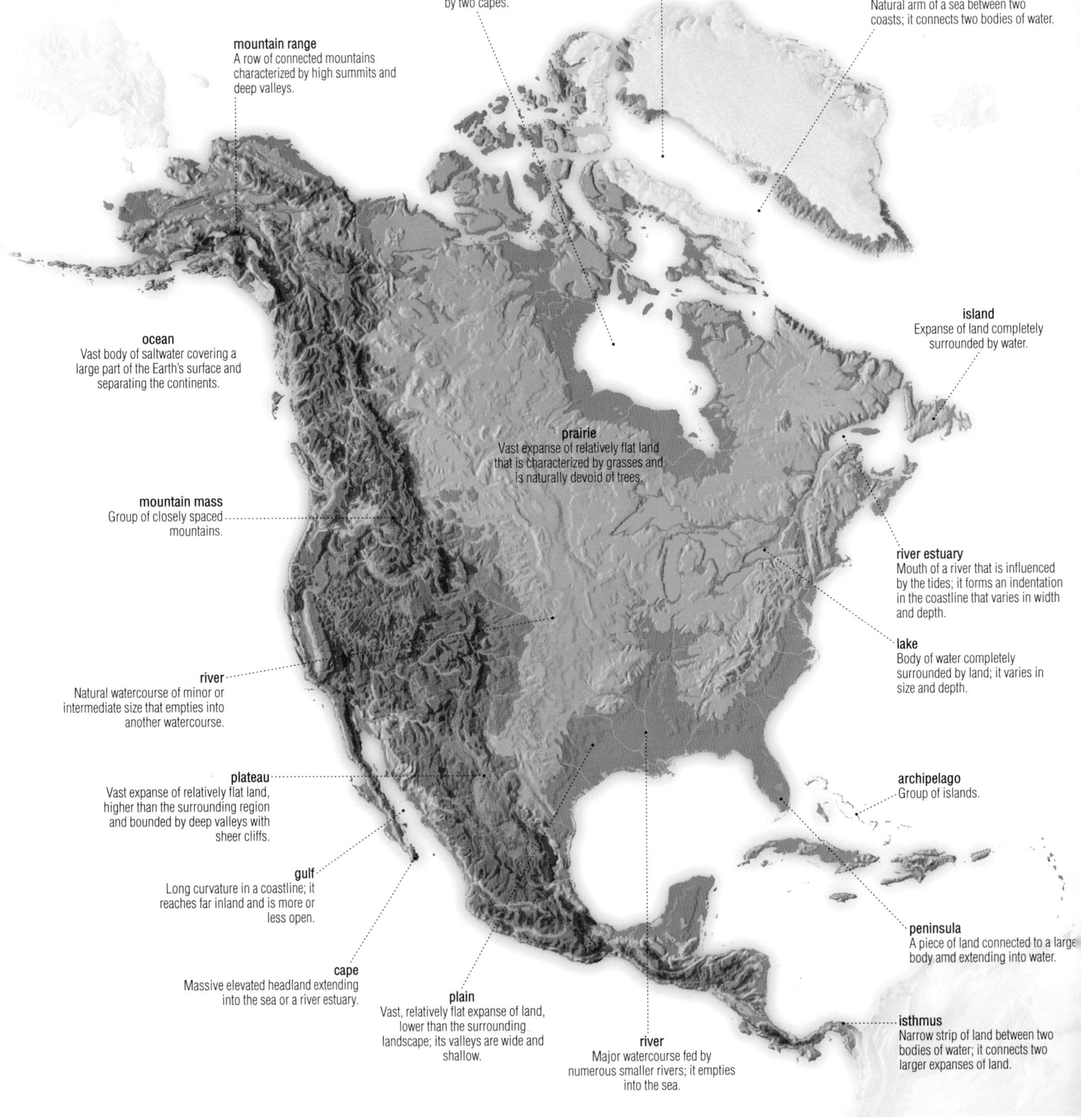
sea
Vast body of saltwater at some distance inland; it is not as deep as an ocean.
bay
Indentation in a shoreline that reaches far inland and is delimited by two capes.
strait
Natural arm of a sea between two coasts; it connects two bodies of water.
mountain range
A row of connected mountains characterized by high summits and deep valleys.
island
Expanse of land completely surrounded by water.
ocean
Vast body of saltwater covering a large part of the Earth's surface and separating the continents.
prairie
Vast expanse of relatively flat land that is characterized by grasses and is naturally devoid of trees.
mountain mass
Group of closely spaced mountains.
river estuary
Mouth of a river that is influenced by the tides; it forms an indentation in the coastline that varies in width and depth.
lake
Body of water completely surrounded by land; it varies in size and depth.
river
Natural watercourse of minor or intermediate size that empties into another watercourse.
plateau
Vast expanse of relatively flat land, higher than the surrounding region and bounded by deep valleys with sheer cliffs.
archipelago
Group of islands.
gulf
Long curvature in a coastline; it reaches far inland and is more or less open.
peninsula
A piece of land connected to a large body amd extending into water.
cape
Massive elevated headland extending into the sea or a river estuary.
plain
Vast, relatively flat expanse of land, lower than the surrounding landscape; its valleys are wide and shallow.
isthmus
Narrow strip of land between two bodies of water; it connects two larger expanses of land.
river
Major watercourse fed by numerous smaller rivers; it empties into the sea.

urban map
Precise and detailed representation of an area of a city, usually on a large scale.

railroad line
Communications route composed of two parallel rails along which trains travel.

railroad
Collective term for the network of rails and the structures needed to transport travelers and goods by train.

bridge
Structure allowing a communications route to span a natural obstacle or another communications route.

suburbs
All the cities surrounding a big city on which they depend economically.

river
Major watercourse fed by numerous smaller rivers; it empties into the sea.

woods
Small tract of land covered with trees.

circular route
High-speed road that circles the downtown area, making it possible to divert traffic away from downtown or connect two outlying communities.

traffic circle
Junction where several roads converge on a roadway that circles a round, central island; traffic moves in one direction only.

street
Thoroughfare built inside a city and usually lined with buildings.

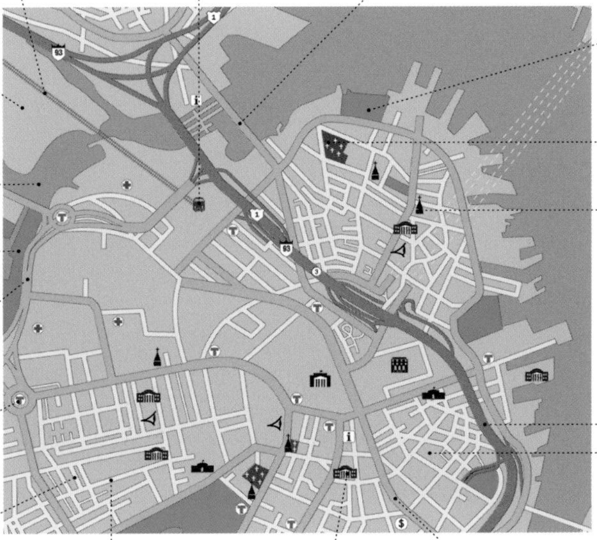

park
Area of a city set aside for leisure or recreational use.

cemetery
Place where the dead are buried.

monument
Structure that commemorates a historic event or holds aesthetic, religious or symbolic value.

highway
Large thoroughfare with separate one-way lanes and no crossing streets; reserved for high-speed traffic.

district
Area of a city having a distinguishing character.

avenue
Thoroughfare larger than a street; it services a district or an area of a city.

public building
Large building that houses public services.

boulevard
Very large, high-volume thoroughfare connecting various parts of a city.

road map
Map that uses lines to indicate a network of roads; it often features information for tourists.

road
Communications route connecting two distant geographic points, usually urban centers.

route number

highway
Large thoroughfare with separate one-way lanes and no crossing streets; reserved for high-speed traffic.

rest area
An area along a highway providing a place to rest and usually having restrooms.

service area
Area built alongside a highway providing services such as a gas station, restaurant, lodging and tourist information.

belt highway
Branch of a highway built around an urban center to facilitate inbound and outbound access and to absorb through traffic.

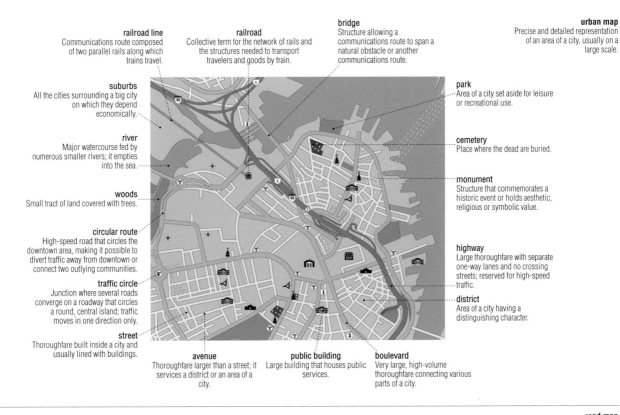

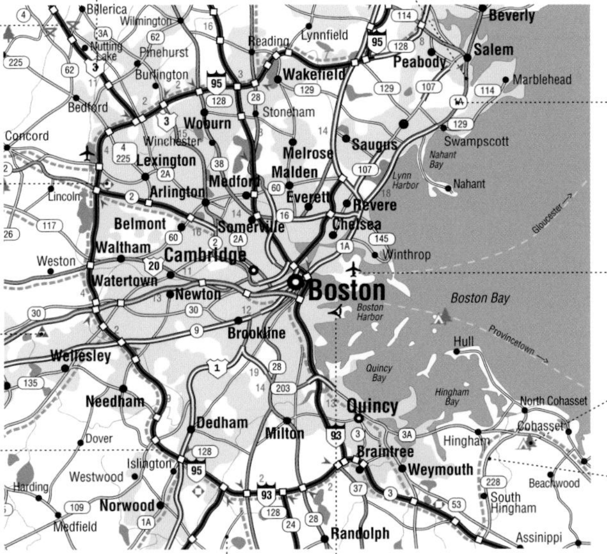

route number

airport
Location that contains all the technical and commercial facilities needed to support air traffic.

national park
Zone that the government designates with a view to protecting its natural resources; access is granted under certain conditions.

scenic route
Road offering particularly scenic landscapes for travelers.

secondary road
Road connecting two regional urban centers of lesser importance or providing access to a highway.

point of interest
A unique or attractive feature.

remote sensing

Technique that uses electromagnetic waves to obtain information about the Earth's surface and atmosphere from a distance.

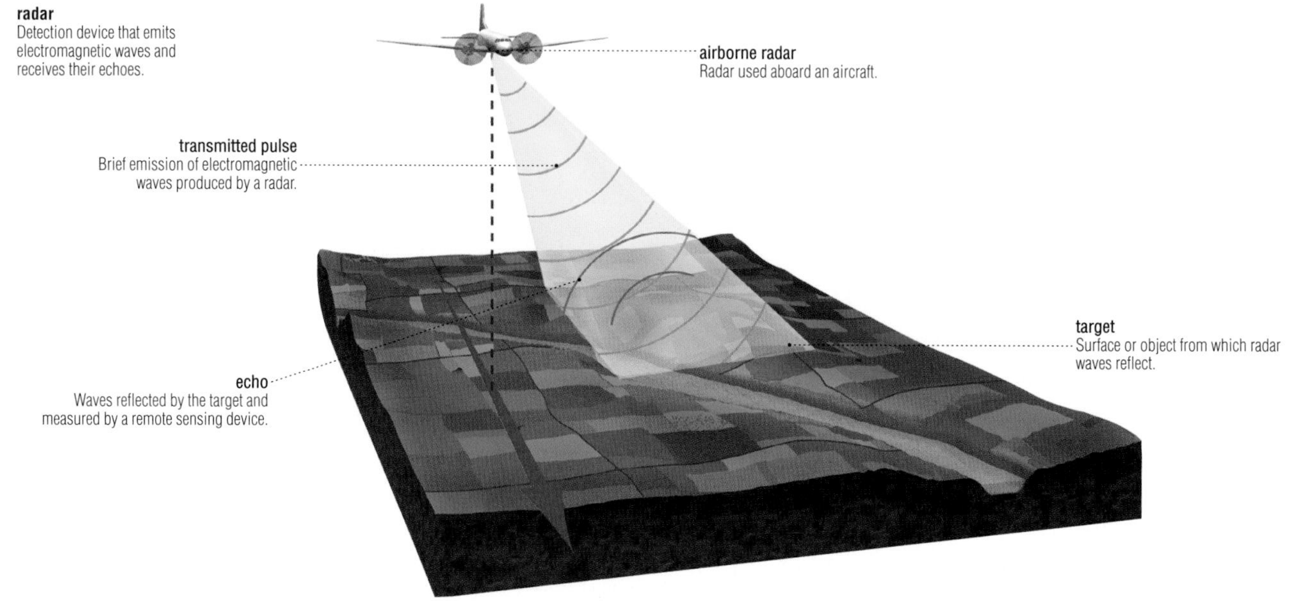

radar
Detection device that emits electromagnetic waves and receives their echoes.
airborne radar
Radar used aboard an aircraft.
transmitted pulse
Brief emission of electromagnetic waves produced by a radar.
target
Surface or object from which radar waves reflect.
echo
Waves reflected by the target and measured by a remote sensing device.

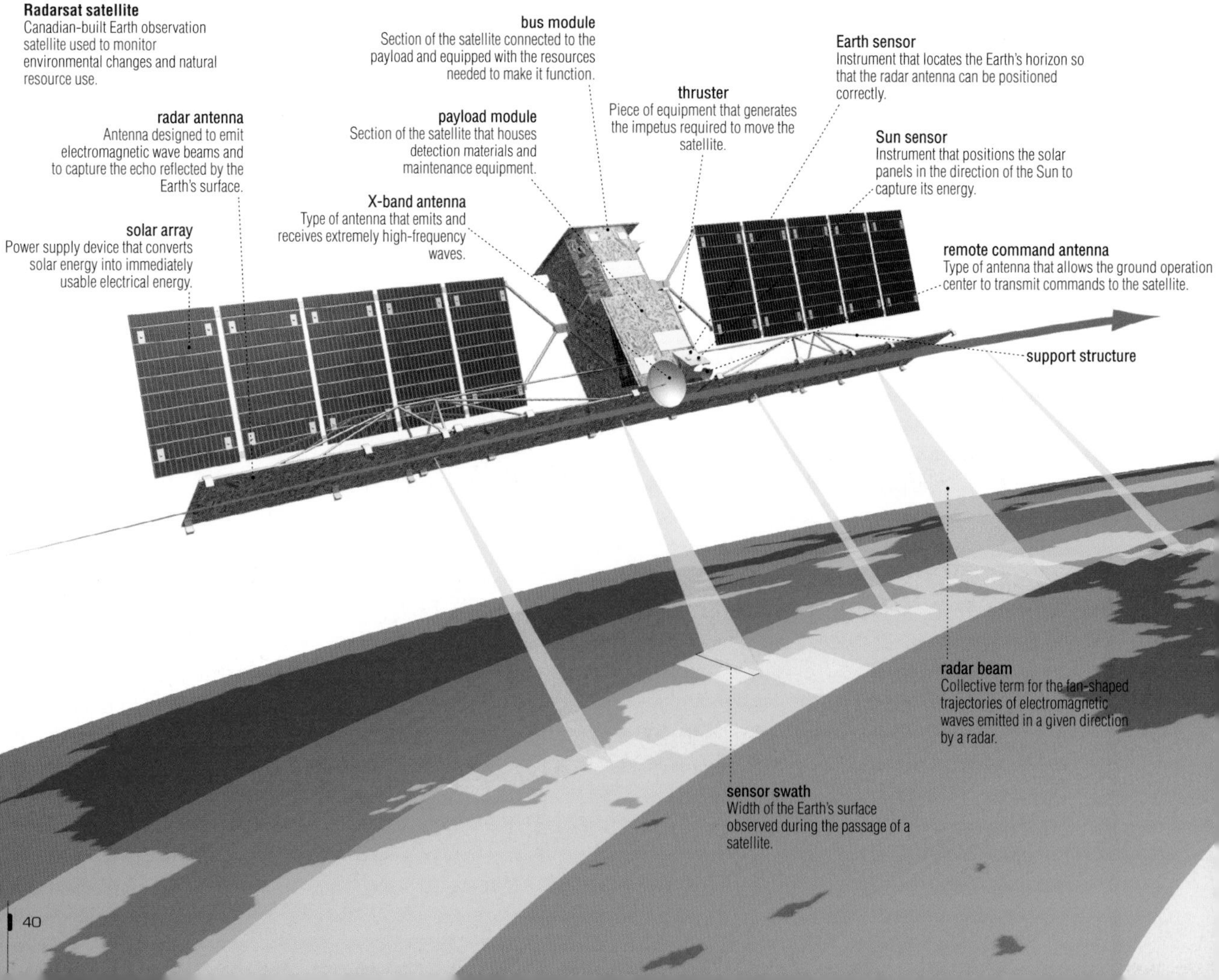

Radarsat satellite
Canadian-built Earth observation satellite used to monitor environmental changes and natural resource use.
bus module
Section of the satellite connected to the payload and equipped with the resources needed to make it function.
Earth sensor
Instrument that locates the Earth's horizon so that the radar antenna can be positioned correctly.
thruster
Piece of equipment that generates the impetus required to move the satellite.
radar antenna
Antenna designed to emit electromagnetic wave beams and to capture the echo reflected by the Earth's surface.
payload module
Section of the satellite that houses detection materials and maintenance equipment.
Sun sensor
Instrument that positions the solar panels in the direction of the Sun to capture its energy.
X-band antenna
Type of antenna that emits and receives extremely high-frequency waves.
solar array
Power supply device that converts solar energy into immediately usable electrical energy.
remote command antenna
Type of antenna that allows the ground operation center to transmit commands to the satellite.
support structure
radar beam
Collective term for the fan-shaped trajectories of electromagnetic waves emitted in a given direction by a radar.
sensor swath
Width of the Earth's surface observed during the passage of a satellite.

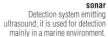

sonar
Detection system emitting ultrasound; it is used for detection mainly in a marine environment.

ship
ultrasound waves emission
Production of very high-frequency sound vibrations whose echo is captured and analyzed.
target
Surface or object from which sonar waves reflect.
echo
Waves reflected by the target and measured by a remote sensing device.

satellite remote sensing
Observation of the Earth's surface and atmosphere by a satellite equipped with a sensor.

energy source
At the origin of the remote sensing process is an energy source, for example the Sun, used to illuminate the target.

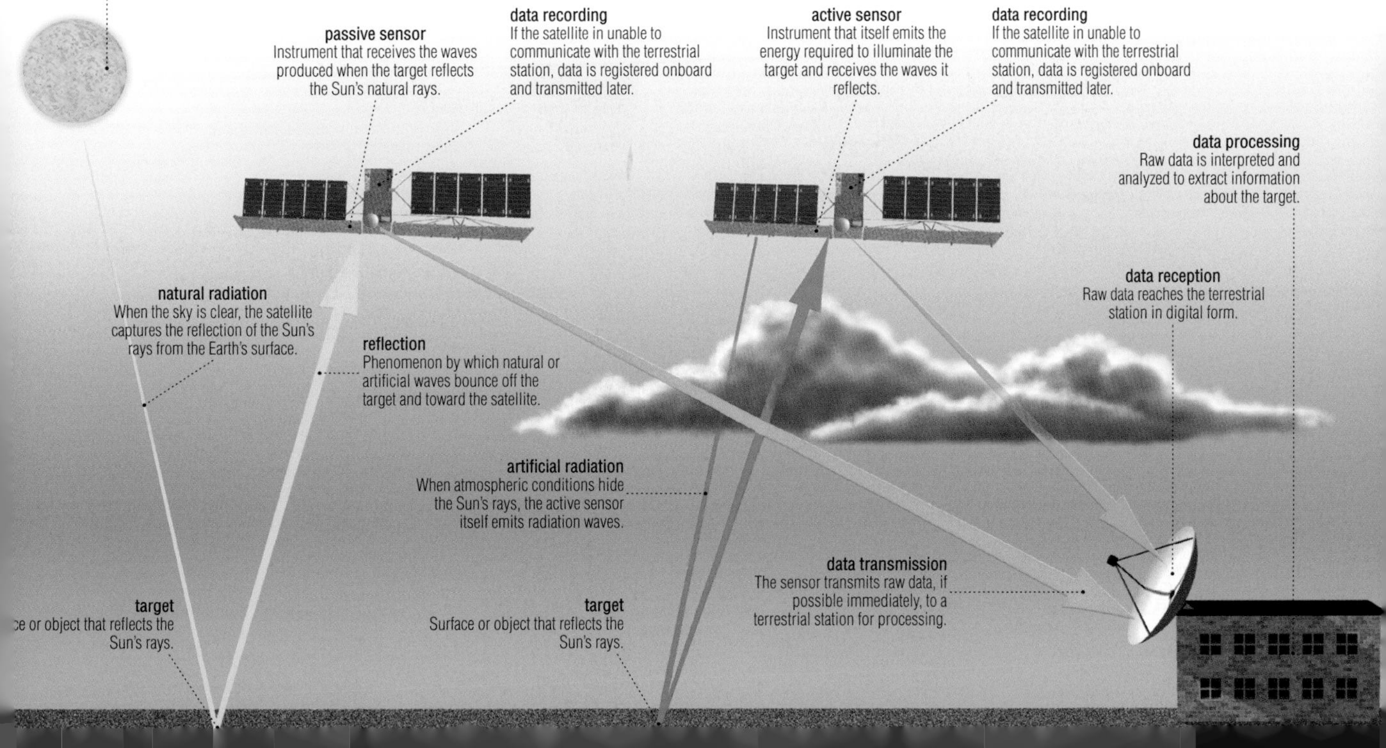
passive sensor
Instrument that receives the waves produced when the target reflects the Sun's natural rays.
data recording
If the satellite in unable to communicate with the terrestrial station, data is registered onboard and transmitted later.
active sensor
Instrument that itself emits the energy required to illuminate the target and receives the waves it reflects.
data recording
If the satellite in unable to communicate with the terrestrial station, data is registered onboard and transmitted later.
data processing
Raw data is interpreted and analyzed to extract information about the target.
data reception
Raw data reaches the terrestrial station in digital form.
natural radiation
When the sky is clear, the satellite captures the reflection of the Sun's rays from the Earth's surface.
reflection
Phenomenon by which natural or artificial waves bounce off the target and toward the satellite.
artificial radiation
When atmospheric conditions hide the Sun's rays, the active sensor itself emits radiation waves.
data transmission
The sensor transmits raw data, if possible immediately, to a terrestrial station for processing.
target
ce or object that reflects the Sun's rays.
target
Surface or object that reflects the Sun's rays.

section of the Earth's crust

The Earth's crust, continental and oceanic, is composed mainly of sedimentary, metamorphic and igneous rock.

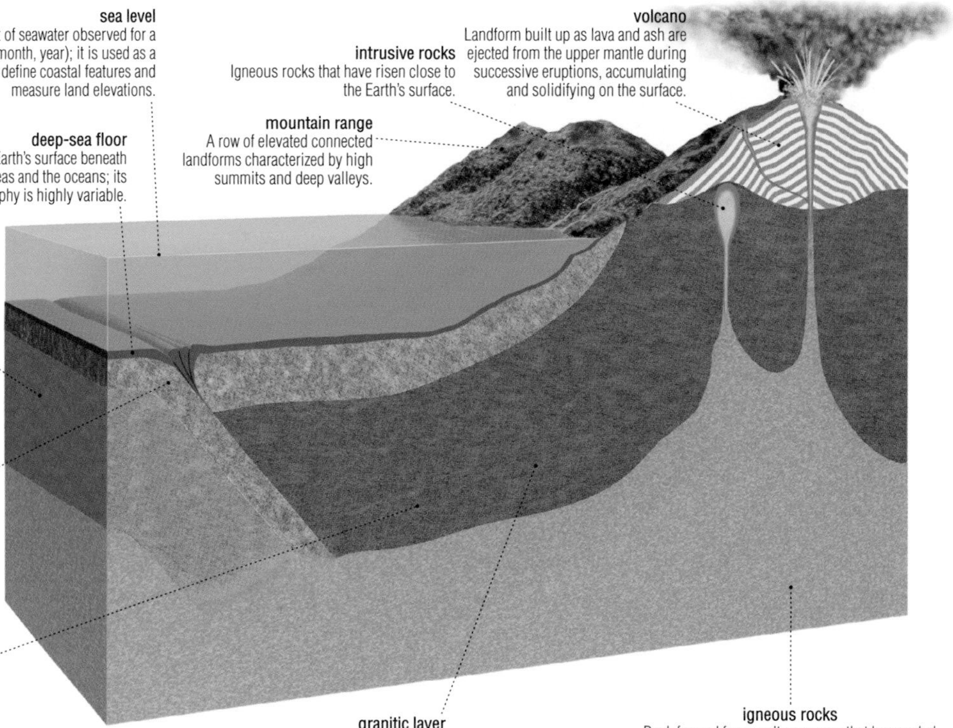

sea level
Average height of seawater observed for a given time (day, month, year); it is used as a reference point to define coastal features and measure land elevations.
intrusive rocks
Igneous rocks that have risen close to the Earth's surface.
volcano
Landform built up as lava and ash are ejected from the upper mantle during successive eruptions, accumulating and solidifying on the surface.
deep-sea floor
Part of the Earth's surface beneath the seas and the oceans; its topography is highly variable.
mountain range
A row of elevated connected landforms characterized by high summits and deep valleys.
basaltic layer
Layer of basalt, a rock denser than granite, that forms the deep-sea floor and is covered with various types of debris.
sedimentary rocks
Rocks formed by the accumulation, compaction and cementation of fragments of eroded rock and debris left by living organisms.
metamorphic rocks
Rocks made from igneous or sedimentary rocks that have been subjected to high pressure and very high temperatures.
granitic layer
Layer of granite that gives the continents their essential form.
igneous rocks
Rock formed from molten magma that has cooled and solidified inside the Earth; also called magmatic rock.

structure of the Earth

The Earth is formed of three concentric layers: the core, the mantle and the crust; these are separated by transition zones called discontinuities.

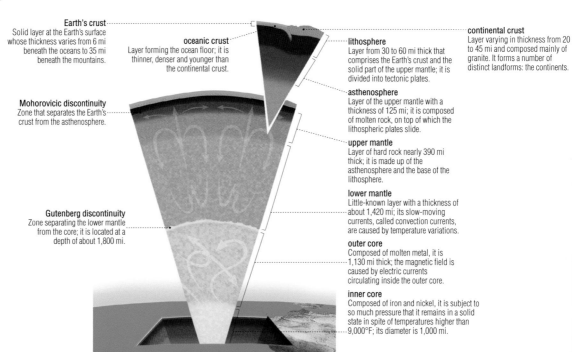

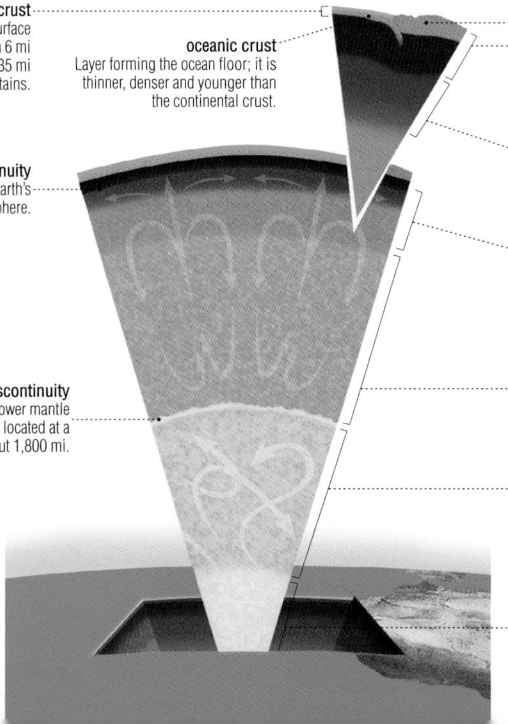

Earth's crust
Solid layer at the Earth's surface whose thickness varies from 6 mi beneath the oceans to 35 mi beneath the mountains.
oceanic crust
Layer forming the ocean floor; it is thinner, denser and younger than the continental crust.
lithosphere
Layer from 30 to 60 mi thick that comprises the Earth's crust and the solid part of the upper mantle; it is divided into tectonic plates.
continental crust
Layer varying in thickness from 20 to 45 mi and composed mainly of granite. It forms a number of distinct landforms: the continents.
Mohorovicic discontinuity
Zone that separates the Earth's crust from the asthenosphere.
asthenosphere
Layer of the upper mantle with a thickness of 125 mi; it is composed of molten rock, on top of which the lithospheric plates slide.
upper mantle
Layer of hard rock nearly 390 mi thick; it is made up of the asthenosphere and the base of the lithosphere.
lower mantle
Little-known layer with a thickness of about 1,420 mi; its slow-moving currents, called convection currents, are caused by temperature variations.
Gutenberg discontinuity
Zone separating the lower mantle from the core; it is located at a depth of about 1,800 mi.
outer core
Composed of molten metal, it is 1,130 mi thick; the magnetic field is caused by electric currents circulating inside the outer core.
inner core
Composed of iron and nickel, it is subject to so much pressure that it remains in a solid state in spite of temperatures higher than 9,000°F; its diameter is 1,000 mi.

tectonic plates

Immense portions of the lithosphere that slide over the asthenosphere; this shifting movement shapes the Earth's topography.

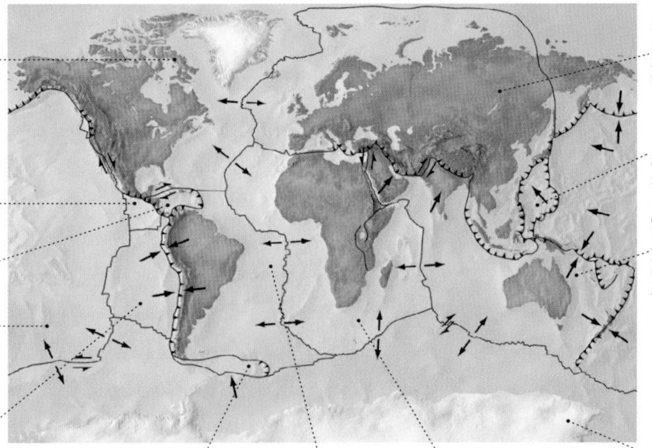

North American Plate
ether with the Pacific Plate, this
e creates the San Andreas Fault
50 mi), which extends from the
of California to San Francisco.

Cocos Plate
Plate along the coast of Mexico
d Central America; it is sinking
neath the North American Plate
and the Caribbean Plate.

Caribbean Plate
Plate subducting under the
American plates; the Caribbean
Plate created the islands of the
Lesser Antilles.

Pacific Plate
only entirely oceanic plate, it is
also among the most rapidly
shifting plates (4 in per year).

Nazca Plate
One of the most rapidly shifting
plates, moving 3 in per year.

Scotia Plate
Small plate under which the Antarctic Plate and part of the South American Plate are sliding.

South American Plate
Plate that forms the Andes cordillera by means of subduction with the Nazca Plate.

African Plate
Plate that, diverging from the South American Plate, forms an underwater mountain chain.

Antarctic Plate
The largest plate; it is stationary.

Eurasian Plate
Plate converging with the Australian-Indian Plate; it created the Himalayas.

Philippine Plate
Plate that forms the Philippines archipelago by means of subduction with the Eurasian Plate.

Australian-Indian Plate
Plate that is moving north 3 in per year; it forms the Red Sea by means of divergence from the African Plate.

subduction
Phenomenon by which an oceanic plate slides under a continental plate or under another oceanic plate, resulting in a trench.

transform plate boundaries
Plates that slide against each other, triggering earthquakes along faults of the same name.

convergent plate boundaries
Plates that collide, triggering either subduction or folding, which results in the creation of mountains.

divergent plate boundaries
Plates that are moving apart, causing magma to appear, which solidifies to generate a new crust.

earthquake

Sudden tremor in a region of the Earth's crust caused by one rock mass sliding against another.

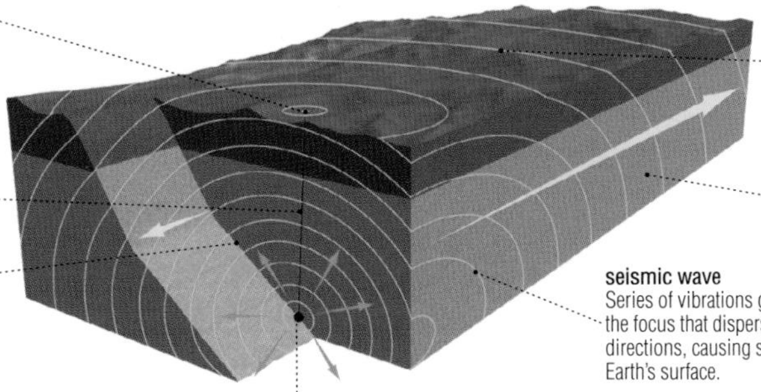

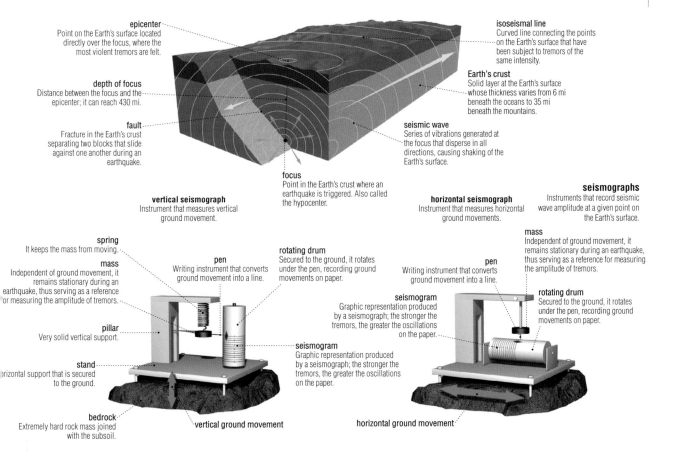

epicenter
Point on the Earth's surface located directly over the focus, where the most violent tremors are felt.

depth of focus
Distance between the focus and the epicenter; it can reach 430 mi.

fault
Fracture in the Earth's crust separating two blocks that slide against one another during an earthquake.

focus
Point in the Earth's crust where an earthquake is triggered. Also called the hypocenter.

isoseismal line
Curved line connecting the points on the Earth's surface that have been subject to tremors of the same intensity.

Earth's crust
Solid layer at the Earth's surface whose thickness varies from 6 mi beneath the oceans to 35 mi beneath the mountains.

seismic wave
Series of vibrations generated at the focus that disperse in all directions, causing shaking of the Earth's surface.

seismographs

Instruments that record seismic wave amplitude at a given point on the Earth's surface.

vertical seismograph
Instrument that measures vertical ground movement.

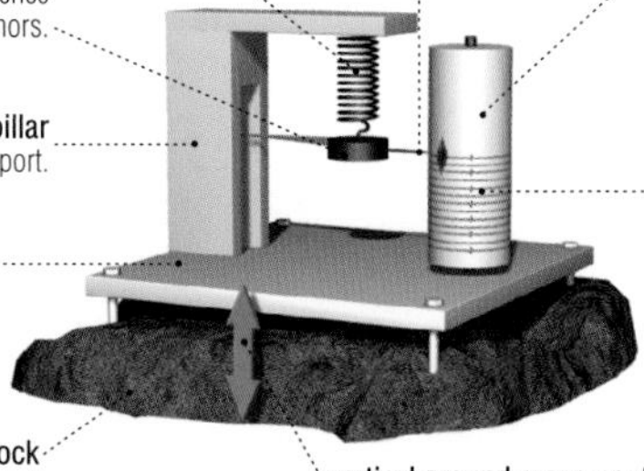

spring
It keeps the mass from moving.

mass
Independent of ground movement, it remains stationary during an earthquake, thus serving as a reference for measuring the amplitude of tremors.

pillar
Very solid vertical support.

stand
Horizontal support that is secured to the ground.

bedrock
Extremely hard rock mass joined with the subsoil.

pen
Writing instrument that converts ground movement into a line.

rotating drum
Secured to the ground, it rotates under the pen, recording ground movements on paper.

seismogram
Graphic representation produced by a seismograph; the stronger the tremors, the greater the oscillations on the paper.

vertical ground movement

horizontal seismograph
Instrument that measures horizontal ground movements.

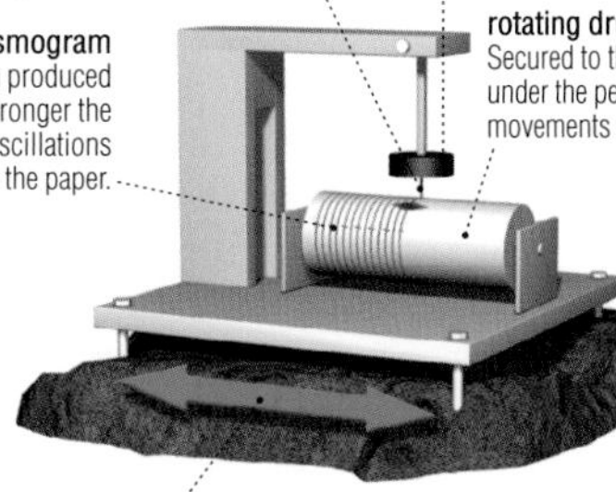

mass
Independent of ground movement, it remains stationary during an earthquake, thus serving as a reference for measuring the amplitude of tremors.

pen
Writing instrument that converts ground movement into a line.

seismogram
Graphic representation produced by a seismograph; the stronger the tremors, the greater the oscillations on the paper.

rotating drum
Secured to the ground, it rotates under the pen, recording ground movements on paper.

horizontal ground movement

volcano

Landform built up as lava and ash are ejected from the upper mantle during successive eruptions, accumulating and solidifying on the surface.

volcano during eruption
Eruption of magmatic matter (molten rock, ash, gas) from the upper mantle; it can last several years.

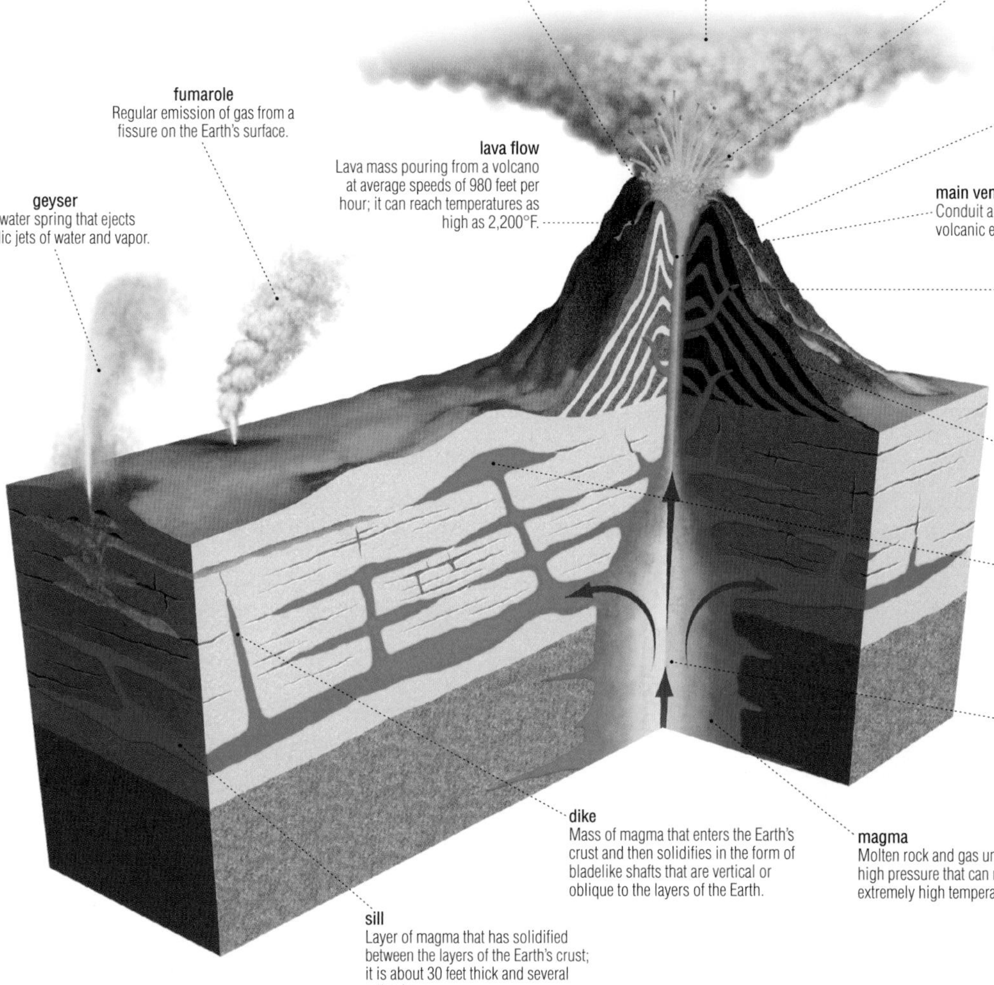

crater
Depression whose center features a chimney through which lava, gas and volcanic ejecta escape.

cloud of volcanic ash
Ash is formed of particles less than 0.08 in in diameter; it is composed of pulverized magma and ground rock.

volcanic bomb
Mass of magma ejected high into the air where it solidifies; it can be very large.

fumarole
Regular emission of gas from a fissure on the Earth's surface.

lava flow
Lava mass pouring from a volcano at average speeds of 980 feet per hour; it can reach temperatures as high as 2,200°F.

lava layer
Layer of volcanic rock formed by cooled lava.

geyser
Hot water spring that ejects sporadic jets of water and vapor.

main vent
Conduit along which lava and other volcanic ejecta rise.

side vent
Small rise that appears on the side of the volcano and is fed by the main vent.

ash layer
Ash and lava form the layers that shape the volcano over time.

laccolith
Mass of magma that enters the Earth's crust and then solidifies, causing a deformation on the Earth's surface.

magma chamber
Pocket where magma accumulates before rising to the surface.

dike
Mass of magma that enters the Earth's crust and then solidifies in the form of bladelike shafts that are vertical or oblique to the layers of the Earth.

magma
Molten rock and gas under very high pressure that can reach extremely high temperatures.

sill
Layer of magma that has solidified between the layers of the Earth's crust; it is about 30 feet thick and several miles long.

examples of volcanoes

Various types of volcanoes are characterized by the viscosity of their lava and the violence of their eruptions.

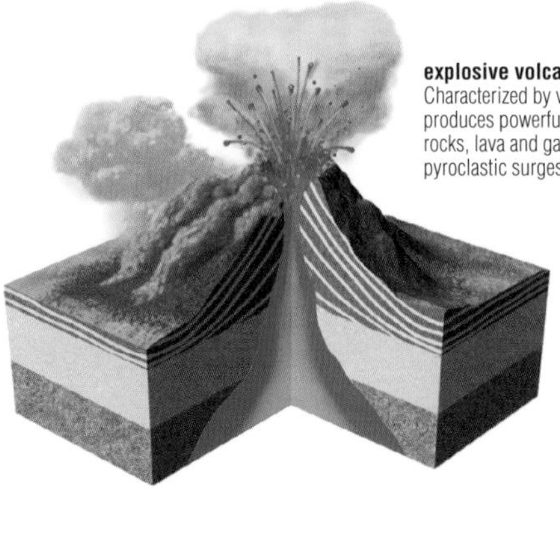

explosive volcano
Characterized by viscous lava, it produces powerful eruptions of rocks, lava and gas; it also releases pyroclastic surges.

effusive volcano
Characterized by streams of fluid lava flowing over large areas.

mountain

Elevated landform characterized by steep slopes; it is usually part of a chain.

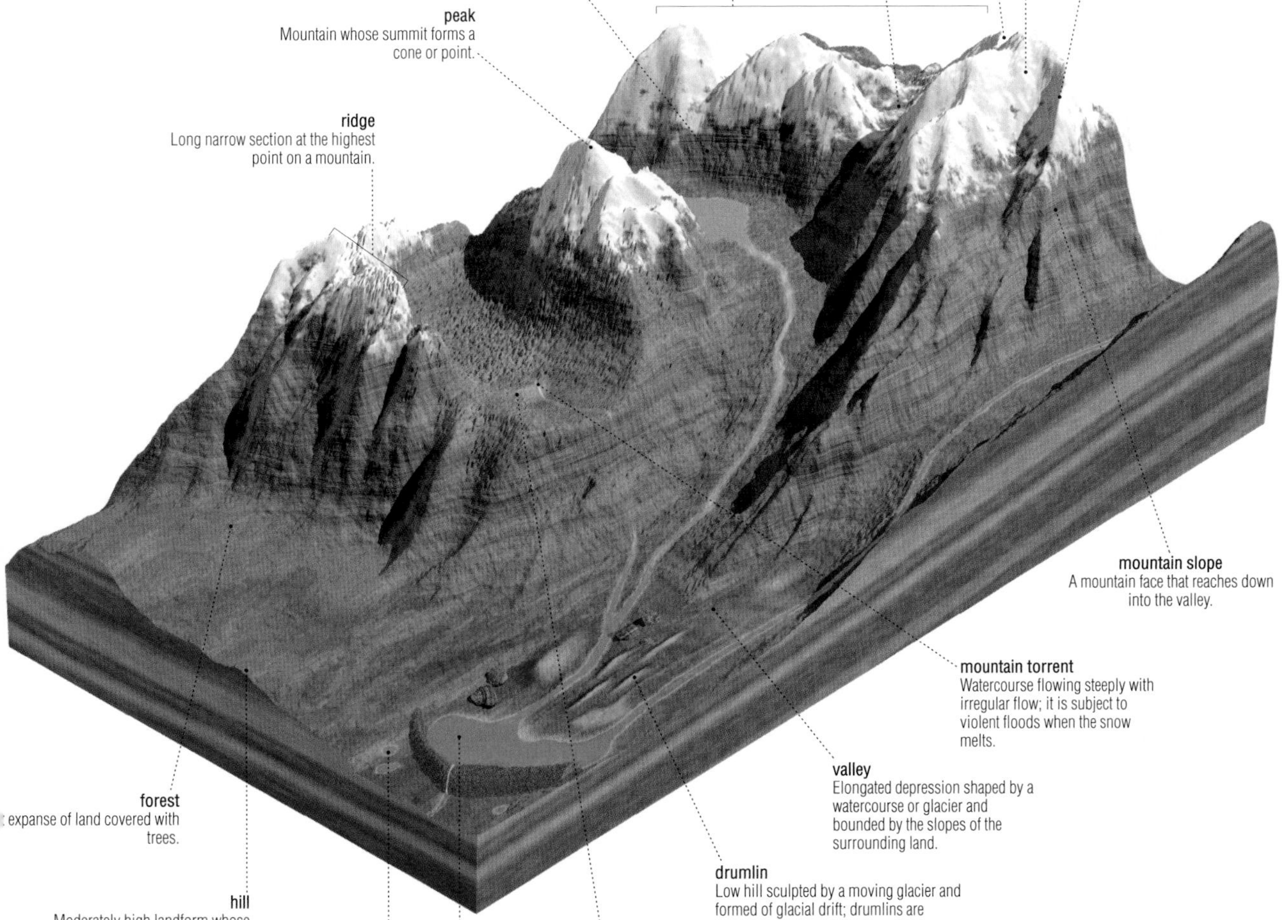
summit
The highest point on the mountain.
pass
Depression in a mountain landscape that creates a passage.
perpetual snows
Accumulations of snow on the highest reaches of a mountain that never melt.
crest
Line intersecting two mountain slopes; a crest can run all the way into the valley.
spur
A lower mountain chain bordering a principal chain.
cliff
A steep and fairly smooth slope.
peak
Mountain whose summit forms a cone or point.
ridge
Long narrow section at the highest point on a mountain.
mountain slope
A mountain face that reaches down into the valley.
mountain torrent
Watercourse flowing steeply with irregular flow; it is subject to violent floods when the snow melts.
valley
Elongated depression shaped by a watercourse or glacier and bounded by the slopes of the surrounding land.
forest
expanse of land covered with trees.
drumlin
Low hill sculpted by a moving glacier and formed of glacial drift; drumlins are usually found in parallel groupings.
hill
Moderately high landform whose slopes follow a gentle incline.
plateau
Vast expanse of relatively flat land, higher than the surrounding region and bounded by deep valleys with sheer cliffs.
kettle
Cavity formed as a mass of melting ice detaches from the tongue of a receding glacier; some kettles fill with water to form a lake.
lake
Body of water completely surrounded by land; it varies in size and depth.

glacier

Mass of ice resulting from the accumulation and compression of snow; it moves under its own weight.

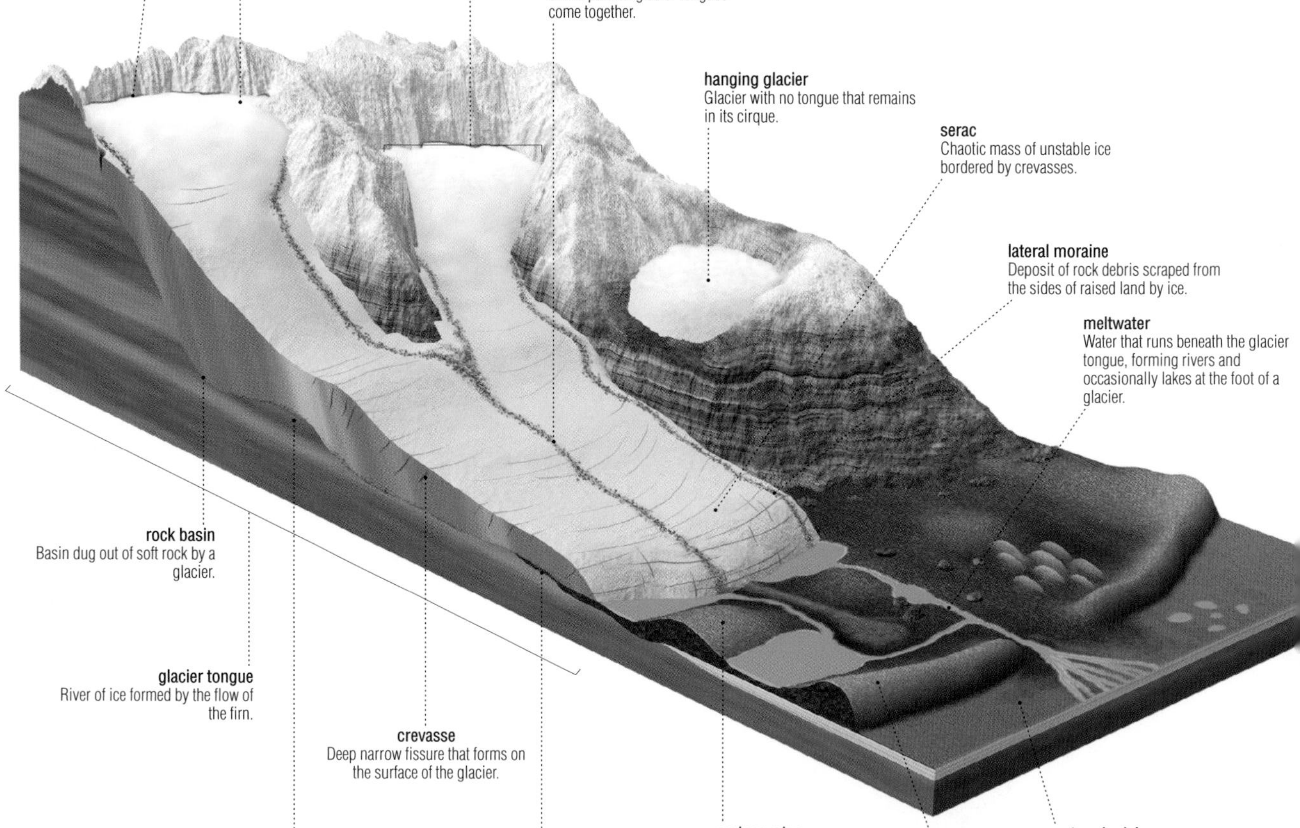
bergschrund
Crevasse between the firn and the rock face; it appears when the glacier breaks away from the rock face.
firn
Accumulation of snow inside a cirque; compressed by its own weight, it is converted into ice and feeds the glacier.
glacial cirque
Semicircular cavity with steep sides, carved out by ice.
medial moraine
Forms where the lateral moraines of two parallel glacier tongues come together.
hanging glacier
Glacier with no tongue that remains in its cirque.
serac
Chaotic mass of unstable ice bordered by crevasses.
lateral moraine
Deposit of rock debris scraped from the sides of raised land by ice.
meltwater
Water that runs beneath the glacier tongue, forming rivers and occasionally lakes at the foot of a glacier.
rock basin
Basin dug out of soft rock by a glacier.
glacier tongue
River of ice formed by the flow of the firn.
crevasse
Deep narrow fissure that forms on the surface of the glacier.
end moraine
Deposit of rock debris scraped from the ground and pushed to the front of the glacier.
outwash plain
Relatively even, gently sloping tract of land, formed by the action of a glacier's meltwater.
riegel
A rocky ridge set crosswise to the glacier tongue.
ground moraine
Deposit of rock debris (till) that is dragged along and deposited under the advancing glacier.
terminal moraine
Frontal moraine marking the glacier's most advanced position before it recedes.

cave

Natural underground cavity that results from the slow dissolution and erosion of rock by water.

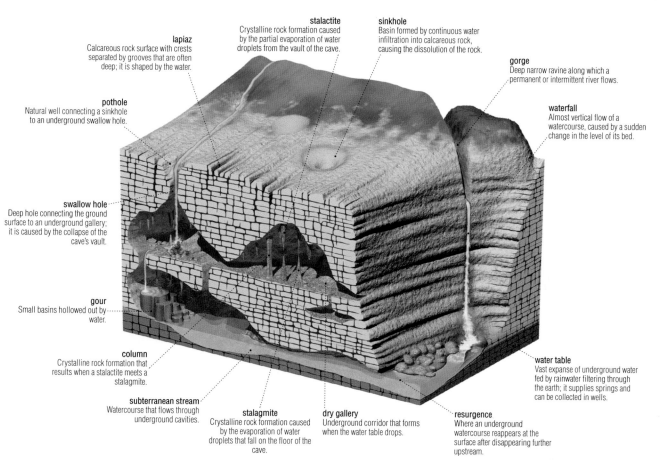

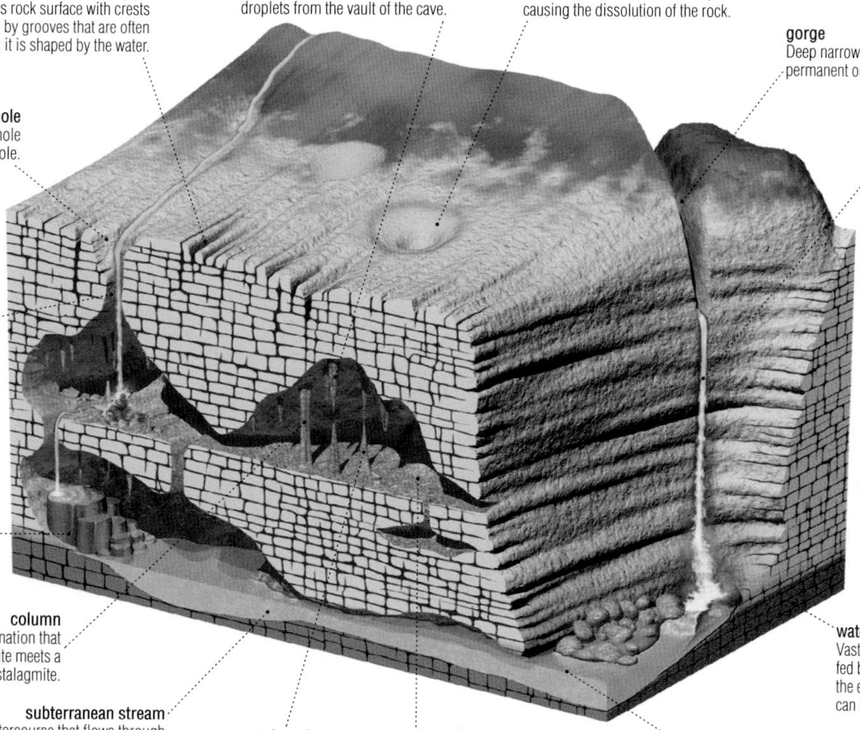

stalactite
Crystalline rock formation caused by the partial evaporation of water droplets from the vault of the cave.
sinkhole
Basin formed by continuous water infiltration into calcareous rock, causing the dissolution of the rock.
lapiaz
Calcareous rock surface with crests separated by grooves that are often deep; it is shaped by the water.
gorge
Deep narrow ravine along which a permanent or intermittent river flows.
pothole
Natural well connecting a sinkhole to an underground swallow hole.
waterfall
Almost vertical flow of a watercourse, caused by a sudden change in the level of its bed.
swallow hole
Deep hole connecting the ground surface to an underground gallery; it is caused by the collapse of the cave's vault.
gour
Small basins hollowed out by water.
column
Crystalline rock formation that results when a stalactite meets a stalagmite.
water table
Vast expanse of underground water fed by rainwater filtering through the earth; it supplies springs and can be collected in wells.
subterranean stream
Watercourse that flows through underground cavities.
stalagmite
Crystalline rock formation caused by the evaporation of water droplets that fall on the floor of the cave.
dry gallery
Underground corridor that forms when the water table drops.
resurgence
Where an underground watercourse reappears at the surface after disappearing further upstream.

landslides

Ground movements that vary in speed, depending on the slope's gradient, the nature of the soil and what triggers it.

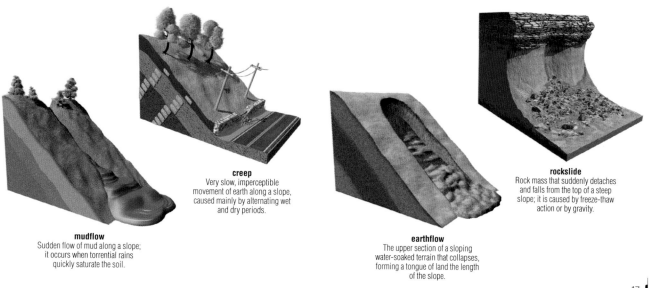

creep
Very slow, imperceptible movement of earth along a slope, caused mainly by alternating wet and dry periods.

rockslide
Rock mass that suddenly detaches and falls from the top of a steep slope; it is caused by freeze-thaw action or by gravity.

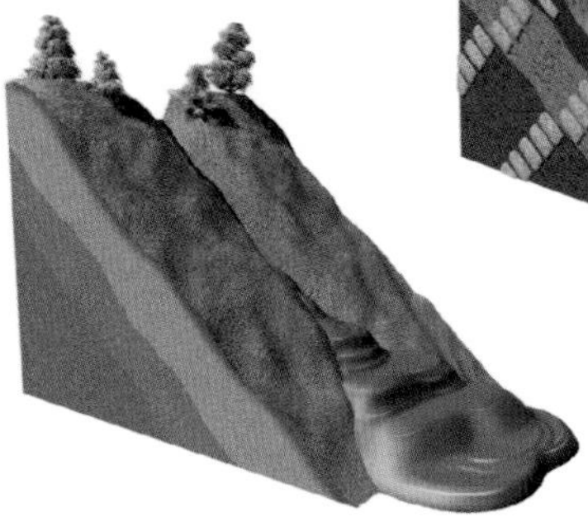

mudflow
Sudden flow of mud along a slope; it occurs when torrential rains quickly saturate the soil.

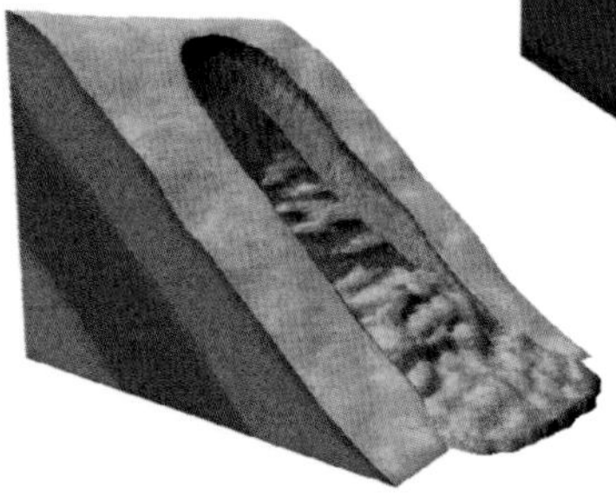

earthflow
The upper section of a sloping water-soaked terrain that collapses, forming a tongue of land the length of the slope.

watercourse

Natural flow of water that varies in size, depending on the ground slope and the number of tributaries.

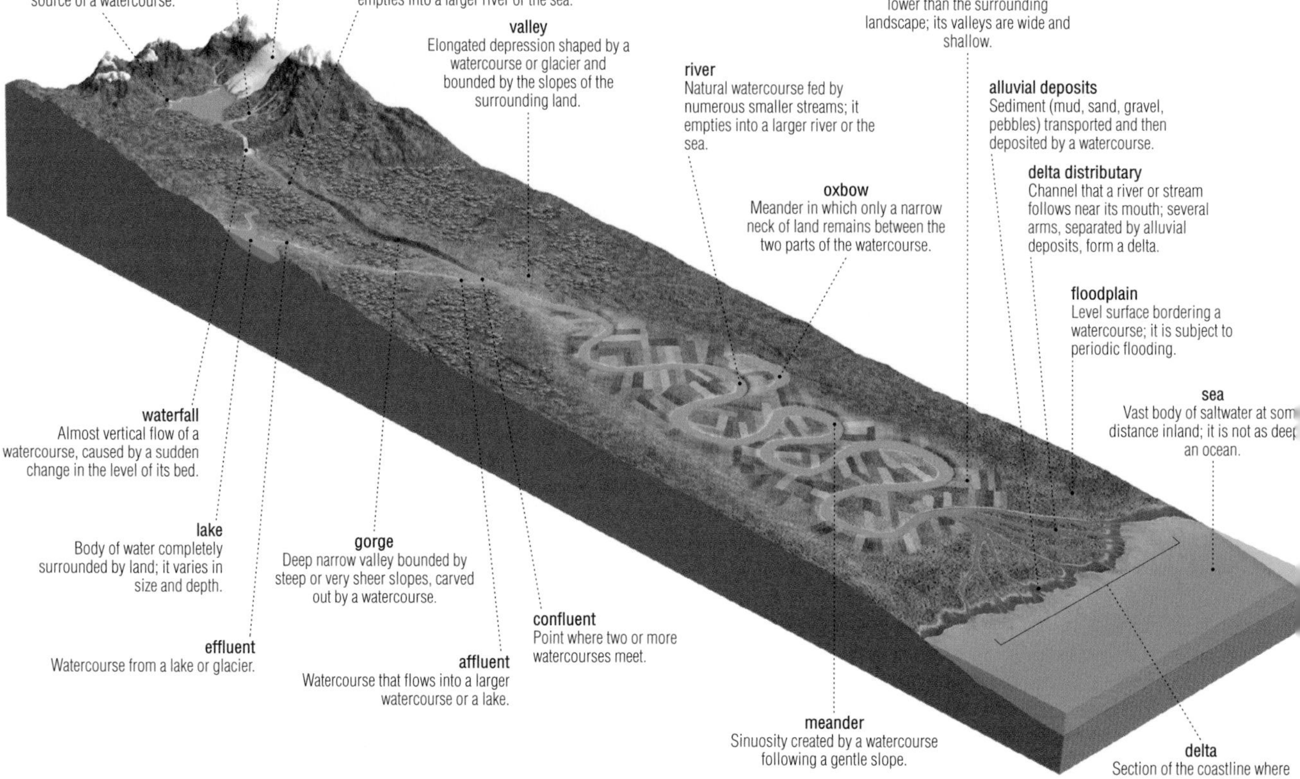
brook
Small watercourse that is a tributary of a river or a lake.
glacier
Mass of ice resulting from the accumulation and compression of snow; it moves under its own weight.
spring
Point where underground water rises to the surface; it may be the source of a watercourse.
river
Natural watercourse fed by numerous smaller streams; it empties into a larger river or the sea.
valley
Elongated depression shaped by a watercourse or glacier and bounded by the slopes of the surrounding land.
plain
Vast, relatively flat expanse of land, lower than the surrounding landscape; its valleys are wide and shallow.
river
Natural watercourse fed by numerous smaller streams; it empties into a larger river or the sea.
alluvial deposits
Sediment (mud, sand, gravel, pebbles) transported and then deposited by a watercourse.
oxbow
Meander in which only a narrow neck of land remains between the two parts of the watercourse.
delta distributary
Channel that a river or stream follows near its mouth; several arms, separated by alluvial deposits, form a delta.
floodplain
Level surface bordering a watercourse; it is subject to periodic flooding.
sea
Vast body of saltwater at som
distance inland; it is not as dee
an ocean.
waterfall
Almost vertical flow of a watercourse, caused by a sudden change in the level of its bed.
lake
Body of water completely surrounded by land; it varies in size and depth.
gorge
Deep narrow valley bounded by steep or very sheer slopes, carved out by a watercourse.
confluent
Point where two or more watercourses meet.
effluent
Watercourse from a lake or glacier.
affluent
Watercourse that flows into a larger watercourse or a lake.
meander
Sinuosity created by a watercourse following a gentle slope.
delta
Section of the coastline where sediment builds up at the mouth
a river, divided into several arms

lake

Body of water varying in size and completely surrounded by land.

glacial lake
Lake that fills a basin dug out by a glacier, whose meltwater then forms the lake.

volcanic lake
Lake that fills the crater of an extinct volcano.

tectonic lake
Lake that occupies a natural basin resulting from a collapse of the Earth's crust.

oxbow lake
Crescent-shaped lake formed when a river changes course by flowing across the neck of the oxbow.

oasis
Desert zone made fertile by the presence of underground or surface water.

artificial lake
Lake created when a dam is built on a watercourse.

wave

Undulation caused by the wind on the surface of a sea or lake.

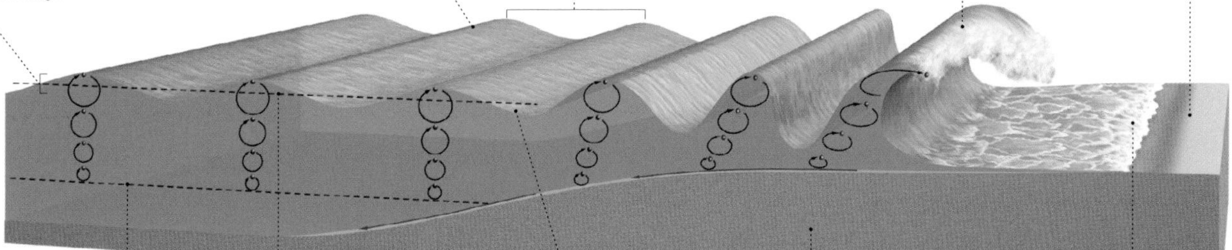

wave height
Vertical distance between the crest and the trough.

crest
The highest point of a wave.

wave length
Horizontal distance between two successive crests or troughs.

breaker
High wave that breaks on the coast.

shore
Strip of land where the sea meets the land.

wave base
Maximum depth beneath which wave action is no longer perceptible.

still water level
Level of the water surface in the absence of waves.

trough
Lowest point of the wave.

sand bar
Accumulation of sediment at the bottom of the sea, close to the shoreline; it is sometimes exposed at low tide.

foam
Whitish froth that forms on the water surface when a wave breaks.

ocean floor

Part of the Earth's surface beneath the seas and the oceans; its topography is highly variable.

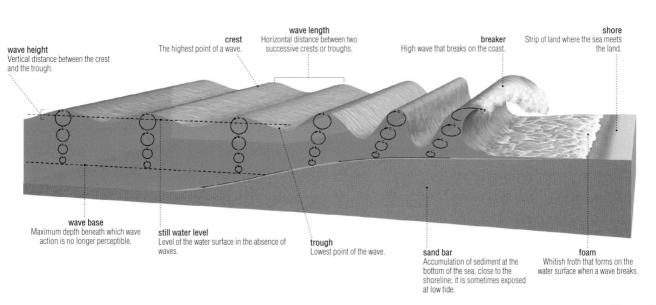

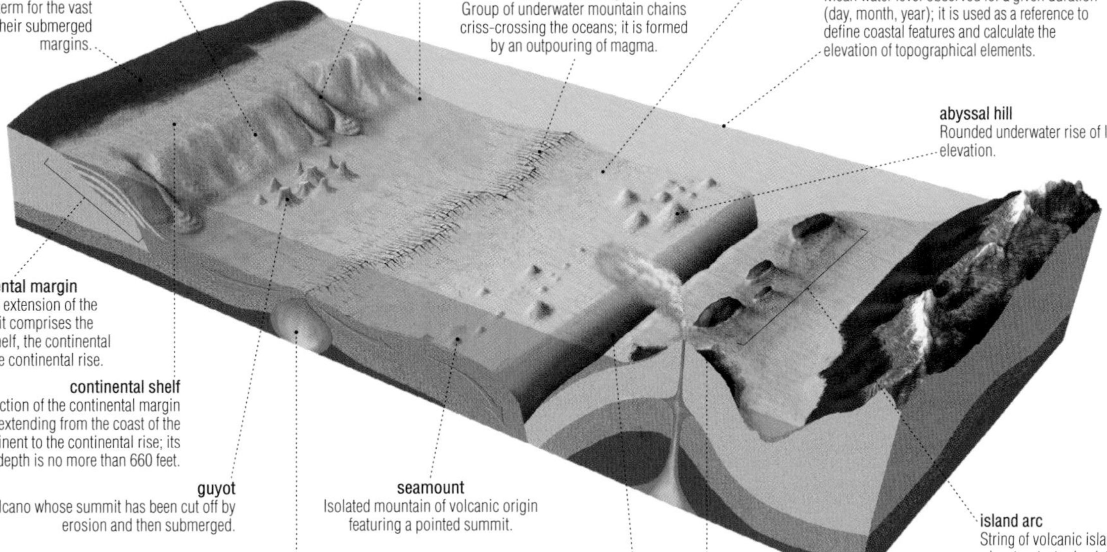

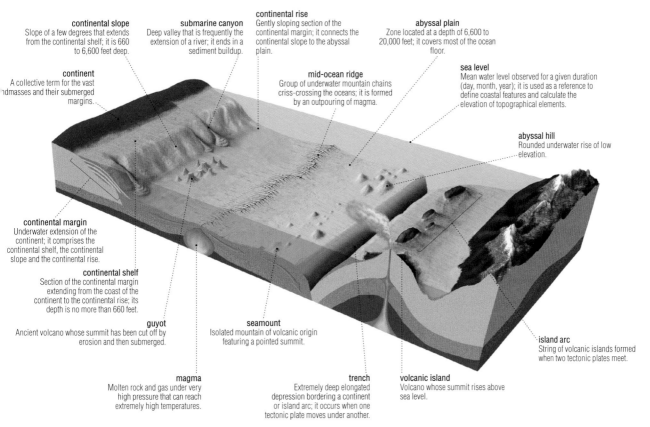

continental slope
Slope of a few degrees that extends from the continental shelf; it is 660 to 6,600 feet deep.

submarine canyon
Deep valley that is frequently the extension of a river; it ends in a sediment buildup.

continental rise
Gently sloping section of the continental margin; it connects the continental slope to the abyssal plain.

abyssal plain
Zone located at a depth of 6,600 to 20,000 feet; it covers most of the ocean floor.

continent
A collective term for the vast ıdmasses and their submerged margins.

mid-ocean ridge
Group of underwater mountain chains criss-crossing the oceans; it is formed by an outpouring of magma.

sea level
Mean water level observed for a given duration (day, month, year); it is used as a reference to define coastal features and calculate the elevation of topographical elements.

abyssal hill
Rounded underwater rise of low elevation.

continental margin
Underwater extension of the continent; it comprises the continental shelf, the continental slope and the continental rise.

continental shelf
Section of the continental margin extending from the coast of the continent to the continental rise; its depth is no more than 660 feet.

guyot
Ancient volcano whose summit has been cut off by erosion and then submerged.

seamount
Isolated mountain of volcanic origin featuring a pointed summit.

island arc
String of volcanic islands formed when two tectonic plates meet.

magma
Molten rock and gas under very high pressure that can reach extremely high temperatures.

trench
Extremely deep elongated depression bordering a continent or island arc; it occurs when one tectonic plate moves under another.

volcanic island
Volcano whose summit rises above sea level.

ocean trenches and ridges

Trench: very deep, elongated cavity bordering a continent or an island arc; it forms when one tectonic plate slides beneath another. Ridge: underwater mountain range that criss-crosses the oceans and is formed by rising magma in a zone where two plates are moving apart.

Aleutian Trench
Trench (25,600 feet) extending from Alaska to the Kamchatka Peninsula; it results from the Pacific Plate sliding beneath the North American Plate.

Europe
Western extremity of the vast Eurasian continent that, by convention, is separated from Asia by the Ural Mountains; it covers a relatively small area.

Africa
Continent that represents about 20% of the world's land; two-thirds of its surface lies north of the Equator. Characterized by very hot climates, Mediterranean in the north and south, tropical and arid elsewhere.

Ryukyu Trench
Trench (24,629 feet) located near the Ryukyu Islands; it marks the boundary between the Philippine Plate and the Eurasian Plate.

North America
Its area (9.3 million mi²) represents about 16% of the world's land; the Central American isthmus is an extension of North America.

Mid-Atlantic Ridge
Ridge about 7,000 mi long, located in the middle of the Atlantic Ocean; some of its mountains reach the surface, forming islands such as Iceland.

Asia
The largest and most populous continent, Asia represents 32% of the world's land; it is dominated by imposing mountain ranges.

Japan Trench
Trench (27,929 feet) located east of Japan, on the boundary between the Pacific Plate and the Eurasian Plate; this zone is marked by intense seismic activity.

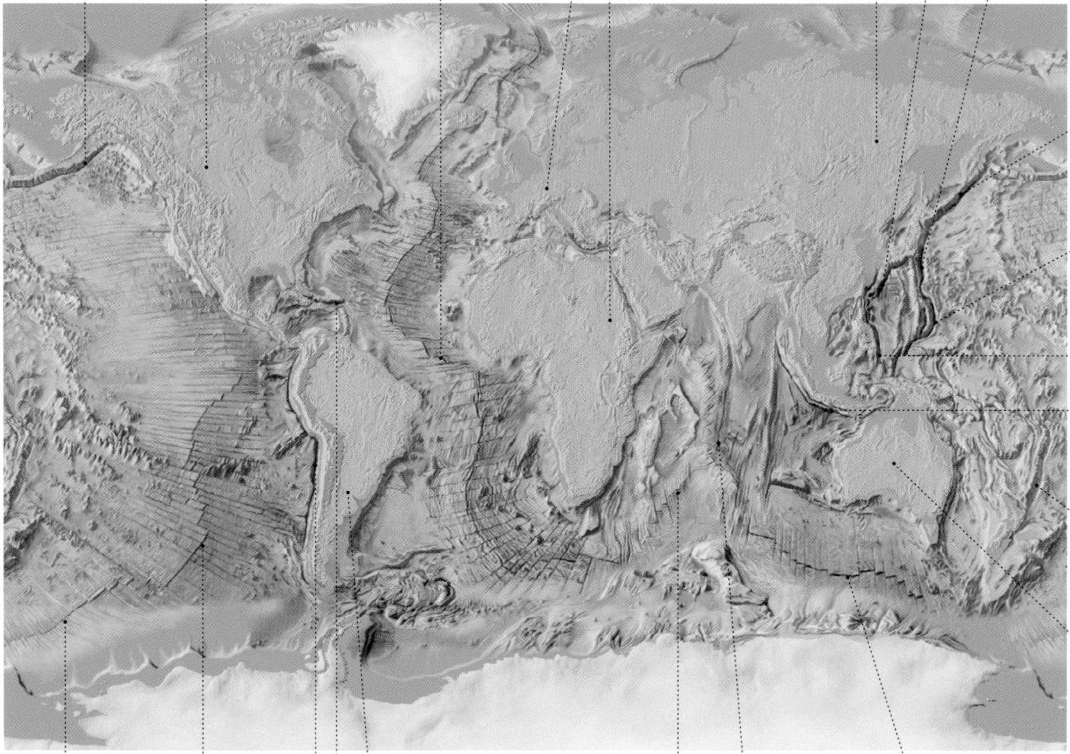

Kuril Trench
Trench (34,587 feet) located northeast of Japan; it results from Pacific Plate sliding beneath the Eurasian Plate.

Mariana Trench
Cavity located near the Mariana Isl where the Pacific Plate and the Phi Plate converge; it is the world's de trench (about 36,000 feet).

Philippine Trench
Trench bordering the eastern Philippines, reaching depths of 34,578 feet; it results from the Phil Plate sinking beneath the Eurasian

Java Trench
Trench located south of Indonesia, between the Australian-Indian and Eurasian Plates; it is the deepest p the Indian Ocean (24,440 ft).

Kermadec-Tonga Trench
Cavity located north of New Zealan where the Pacific Plate meets the Australian-Indian Plate; it reaches depths of 35,702 feet.

Australia
The world's largest island (3 million mi²) is sparsely inhabite spite of its size; because of its isolation, Australia's wildlife is uni

East Pacific Ridge
Ridge that marks the boundary between the Pacific and Cocos Islands plates to the north, and the Pacific and Nazca plates to the south.

South America
Represents about 12% of the world's land and is linked to North America by Central America; its features include the Andes in the west and plains and plateaus in east and central regions.

Southeast Indian Ridge
Ridge separating the Antarctic Plate from the Australian-Indian Plate; its topography is more regular than the topography of the Southwest Indian and Mid-Indian ridges.

Pacific-Antarctic Ridge
Mountain range separating the Pacific and Antarctic plates; it joins the eastern Pacific Ridge off the coast of South America.

Southwest Indian Ridge
Ridge separating the African and Antarctic plates; it joins the Mid-Indian and Southeast Indian ridges off the coast of Madagascar.

Mid-Indian Ridge
Mountain range in the middle of the Indian Ocean that separates the African and Australian-Indian plates.

Peru-Chile Trench
Trench (26,460 feet) bordering South America; the world's longest trench (3,700 mi), it is located on the boundary between the Nazca Plate and the South American Plate.

Puerto Rico Trench
Trench located off the coast of Puerto Rico, on the boundary between the South American and Caribbean plates; it features the deepest point in the Atlantic Ocean (27,493 feet).

common coastal features

Area where the land meets the sea; its features vary depending on climate, wind, sea and the type of rocks of which it is composed.

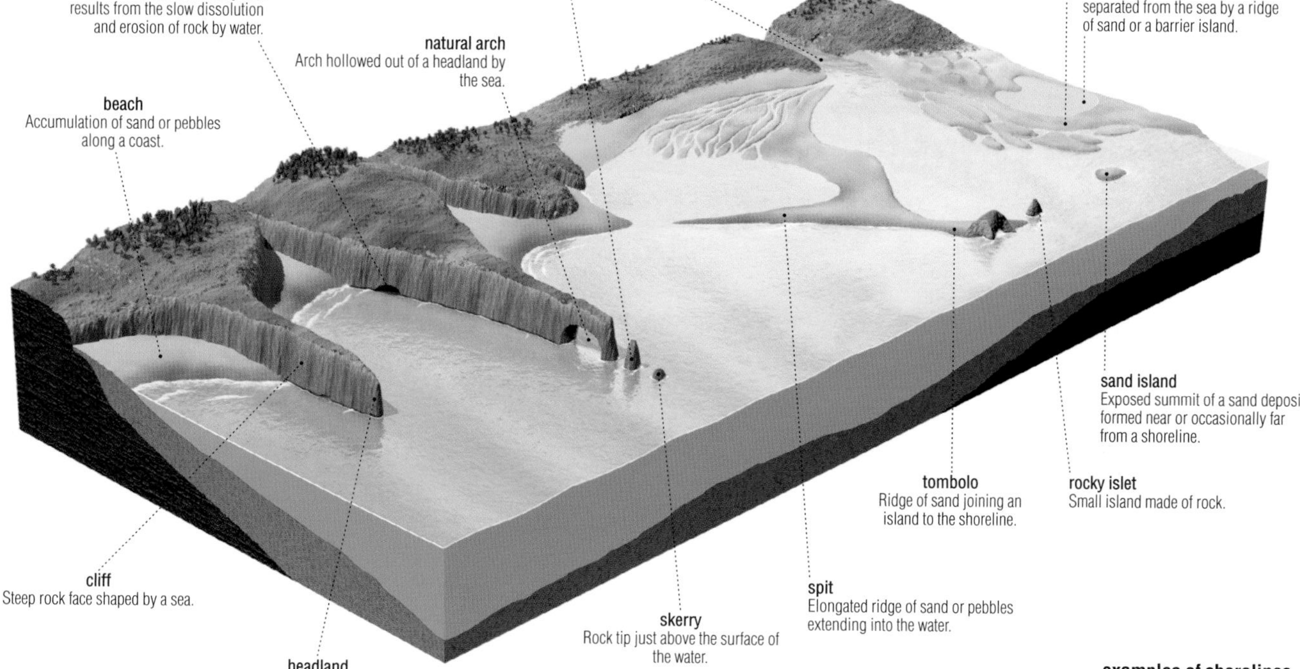
river estuary
Mouth of a river that is influenced by the tides; it forms an indentation in the coastline that varies in width and depth.
stack
Needle-shaped column resulting from the collapse of an arch.
cave
Natural underground cavity that results from the slow dissolution and erosion of rock by water.
natural arch
Arch hollowed out of a headland by the sea.
dune
Accumulation of sand shaped by the wind.
lagoon
Shallow expanse of seawater separated from the sea by a ridge of sand or a barrier island.
beach
Accumulation of sand or pebbles along a coast.
sand island
Exposed summit of a sand deposit formed near or occasionally far from a shoreline.
tombolo
Ridge of sand joining an island to the shoreline.
rocky islet
Small island made of rock.
cliff
Steep rock face shaped by a sea.
spit
Elongated ridge of sand or pebbles extending into the water.
skerry
Rock tip just above the surface of the water.
headland
Tapering strip of land jutting into the sea.

examples of shorelines

Shoreline: strip of land where the sea meets the land.

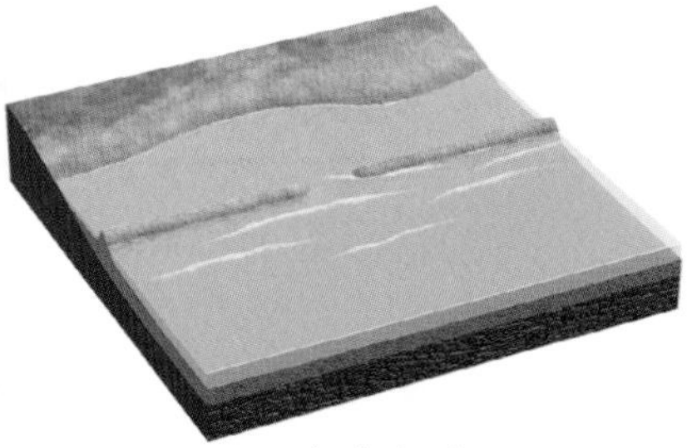

barrier beach
Usually narrow ridge of sand or pebbles bordering the shoreline.

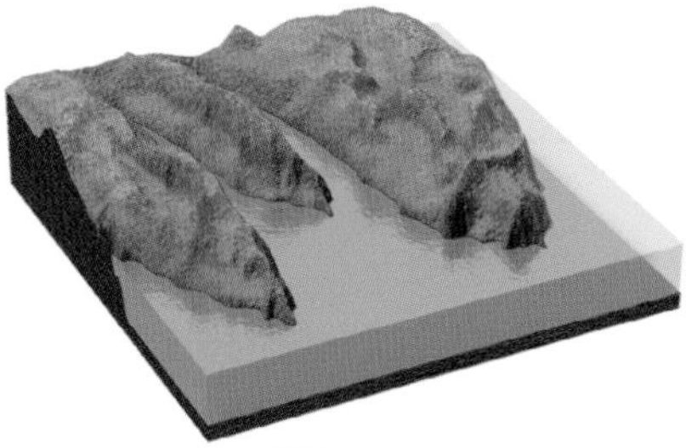

fjords
Deep glacial valleys filled with seawater and cutting into the shoreline.

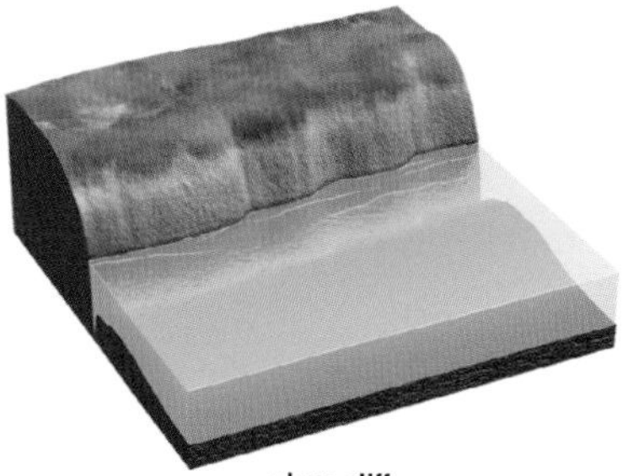

shore cliff
Steep rock-faced shoreline shaped by the sea.

delta
Section of the coastline where sediment builds up at the mouth of a river, divided into several arms.

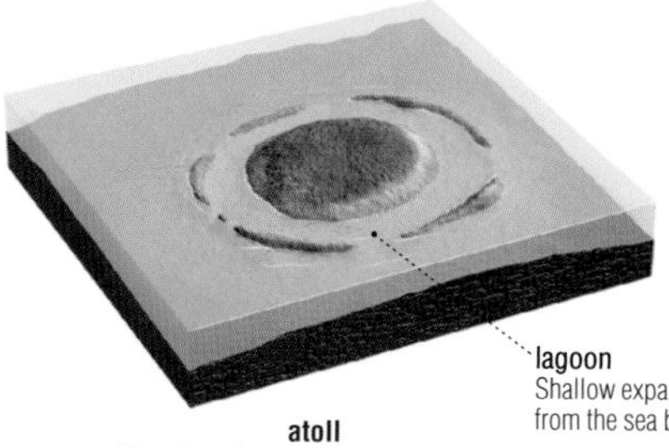
lagoon
Shallow expanse of water separated from the sea by a coral reef.

atoll
Ring-shaped coral-reef island enclosing a lagoon and often a central island.

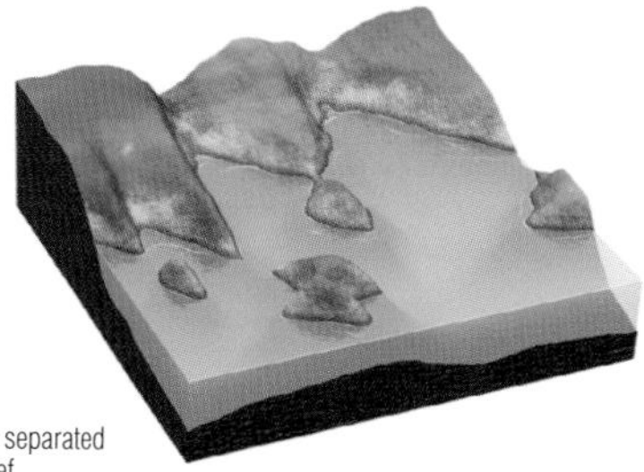

rias
Coastal valleys that are filled by the sea and get shallower inland.

desert

Hot region where aridity (less than 4 in of annual rainfall) is such that plant and animal life is almost nonexistent.

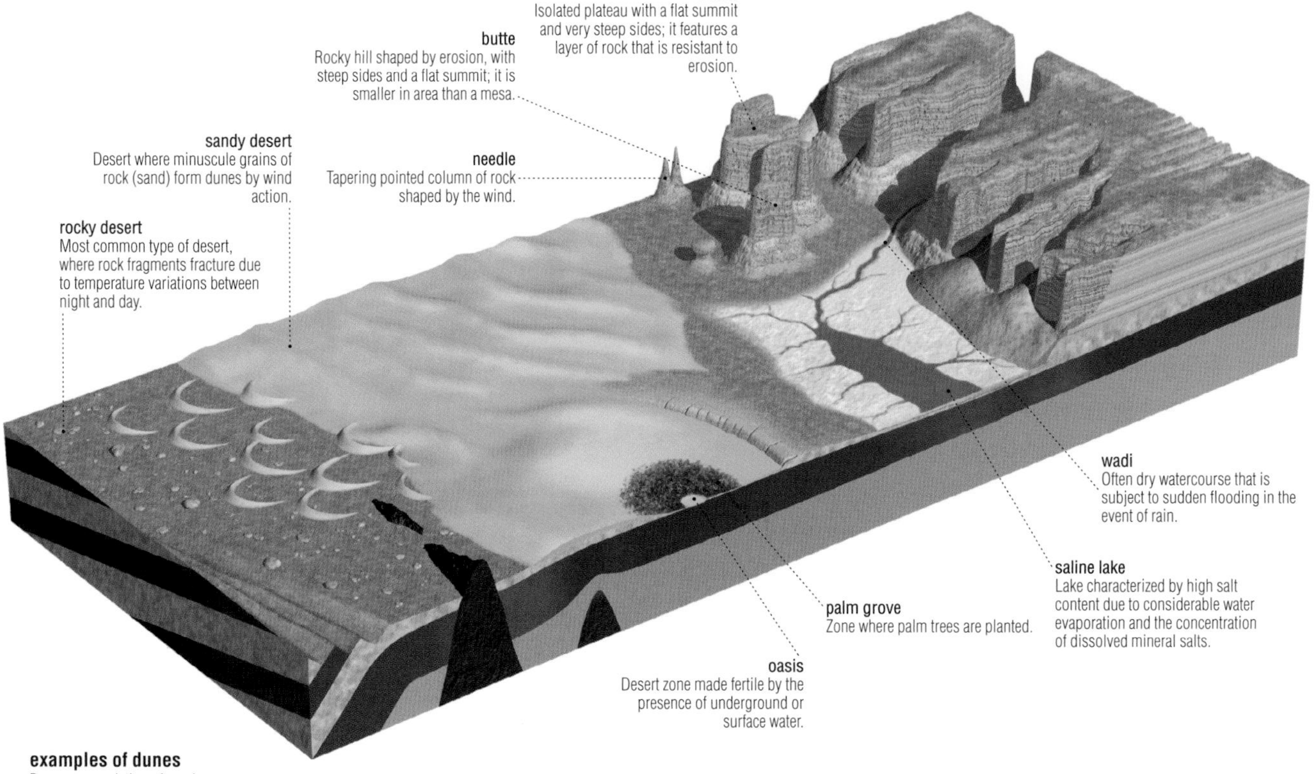
mesa
Isolated plateau with a flat summit and very steep sides; it features a layer of rock that is resistant to erosion.
butte
Rocky hill shaped by erosion, with steep sides and a flat summit; it is smaller in area than a mesa.
sandy desert
Desert where minuscule grains of rock (sand) form dunes by wind action.
needle
Tapering pointed column of rock shaped by the wind.
rocky desert
Most common type of desert, where rock fragments fracture due to temperature variations between night and day.
wadi
Often dry watercourse that is subject to sudden flooding in the event of rain.
saline lake
Lake characterized by high salt content due to considerable water evaporation and the concentration of dissolved mineral salts.
palm grove
Zone where palm trees are planted.
oasis
Desert zone made fertile by the presence of underground or surface water.

examples of dunes

Dune: accumulation of sand transported by the wind, found in deserts and along coasts.

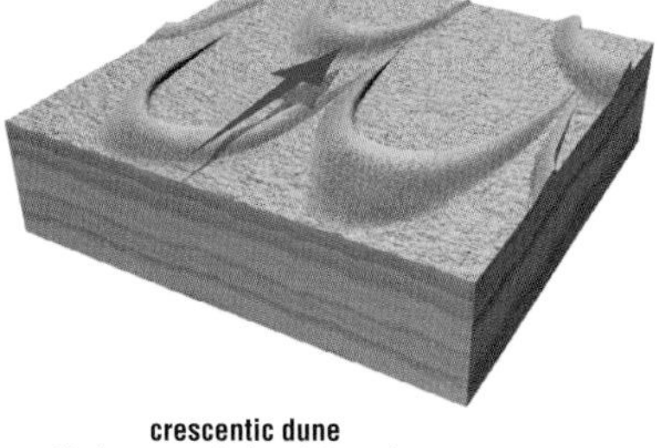

crescentic dune
Moving crescent-shaped dune whose arms extend in the same direction as the wind.

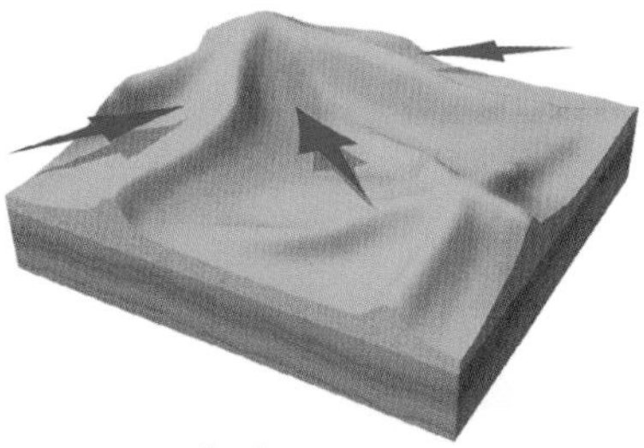

complex dune
Star-shaped dune that forms where winds blowing in various directions meet.

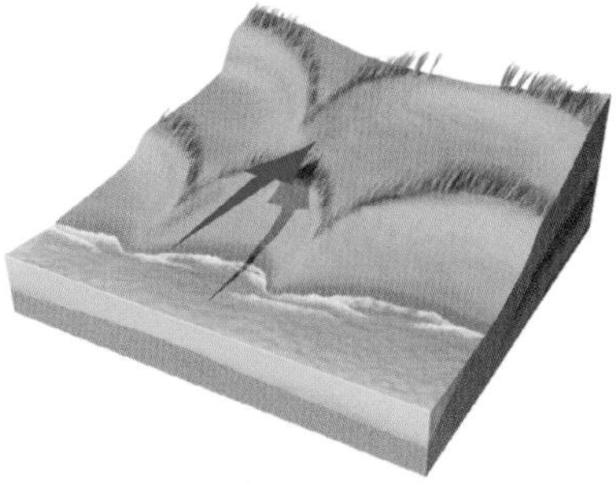

parabolic dune
Crescent-shaped coastal dune whose arms point into the wind; vegetation often keeps it in place.

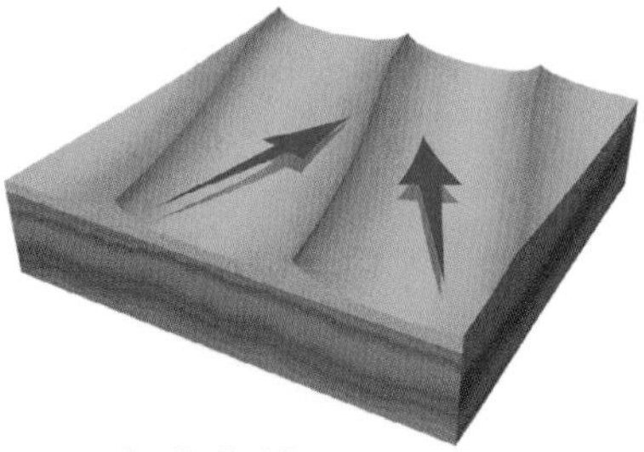

longitudinal dunes
Narrow elongated dunes that form when the wind blows in two convergent directions.

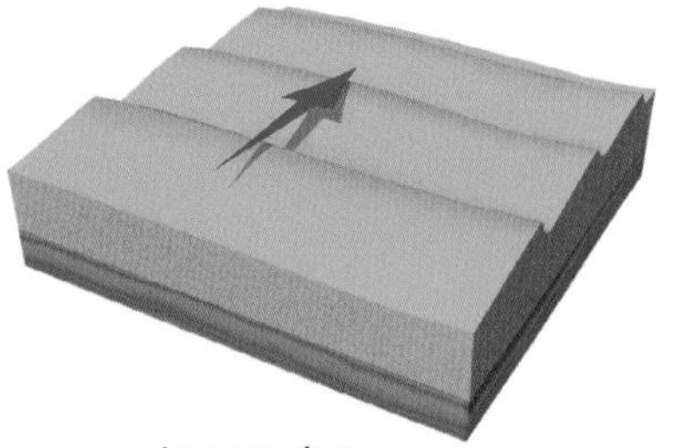

transverse dunes
Dunes that form perpendicular to the direction of the wind.

chain of dunes
Dunes aligned in the same direction, parallel to the wind.

profile of the Earth's atmosphere

Atmosphere: layer of air that surrounds the Earth and is composed mainly of nitrogen (78%) and oxygen (21%); its density decreases with altitude.

temperature scale altitude scale

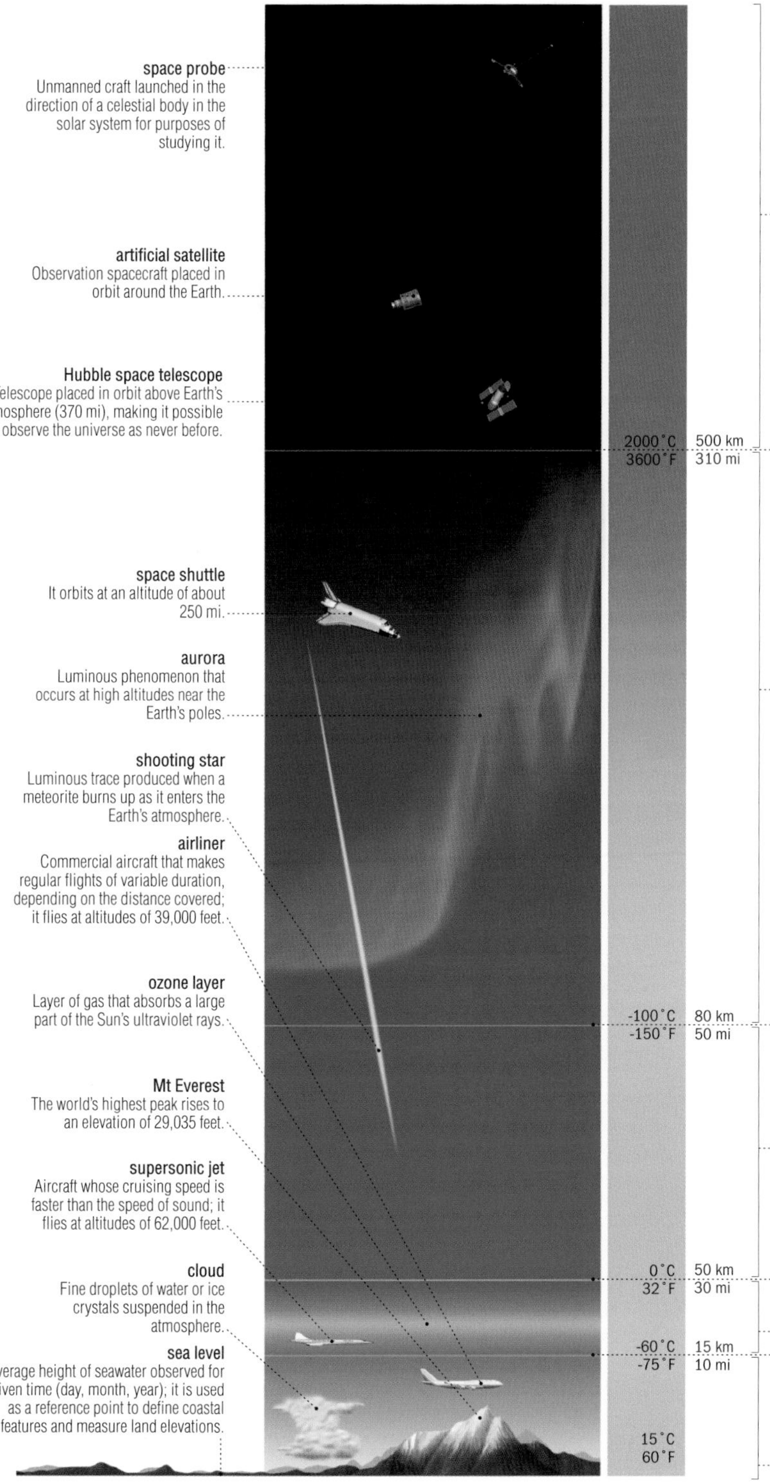

space probe
Unmanned craft launched in the direction of a celestial body in the solar system for purposes of studying it.

artificial satellite
Observation spacecraft placed in orbit around the Earth.

Hubble space telescope
Telescope placed in orbit above Earth's atmosphere (370 mi), making it possible to observe the universe as never before.

space shuttle
It orbits at an altitude of about 250 mi.

aurora
Luminous phenomenon that occurs at high altitudes near the Earth's poles.

shooting star
Luminous trace produced when a meteorite burns up as it enters the Earth's atmosphere.

airliner
Commercial aircraft that makes regular flights of variable duration, depending on the distance covered; it flies at altitudes of 39,000 feet.

ozone layer
Layer of gas that absorbs a large part of the Sun's ultraviolet rays.

Mt Everest
The world's highest peak rises to an elevation of 29,035 feet.

supersonic jet
Aircraft whose cruising speed is faster than the speed of sound; it flies at altitudes of 62,000 feet.

cloud
Fine droplets of water or ice crystals suspended in the atmosphere.

sea level
Average height of seawater observed for a given time (day, month, year); it is used as a reference point to define coastal features and measure land elevations.

exosphere
The outermost region of the atmosphere, where low-density gases disperse into space.

thermopause
Thin transition layer between the thermosphere and the exosphere.

thermosphere
Layer that absorbs a large portion of solar radiation, leading to a steady increase in its temperature.

mesopause
Thin transition layer between the mesosphere and the thermosphere.

mesosphere
The atmosphere's coldest layer, where temperatures decrease with altitude.

stratopause
Thin transition layer between the stratosphere and the mesosphere.

stratosphere
Highly stable layer of air where temperatures increase with altitude due to the absorption of solar radiation by the ozone layer.

tropopause
The boundary between the troposphere and the stratosphere; its altitude varies depending on the season, ground temperature, latitude and atmospheric pressure.

troposphere
The most dense layer, which produces most of the meteorological phenomena and where temperatures decrease with altitude.

seasons of the year

Periodic climate changes over the course of a year; they are a function of the Earth's inclination toward the Sun and its rotation around it.

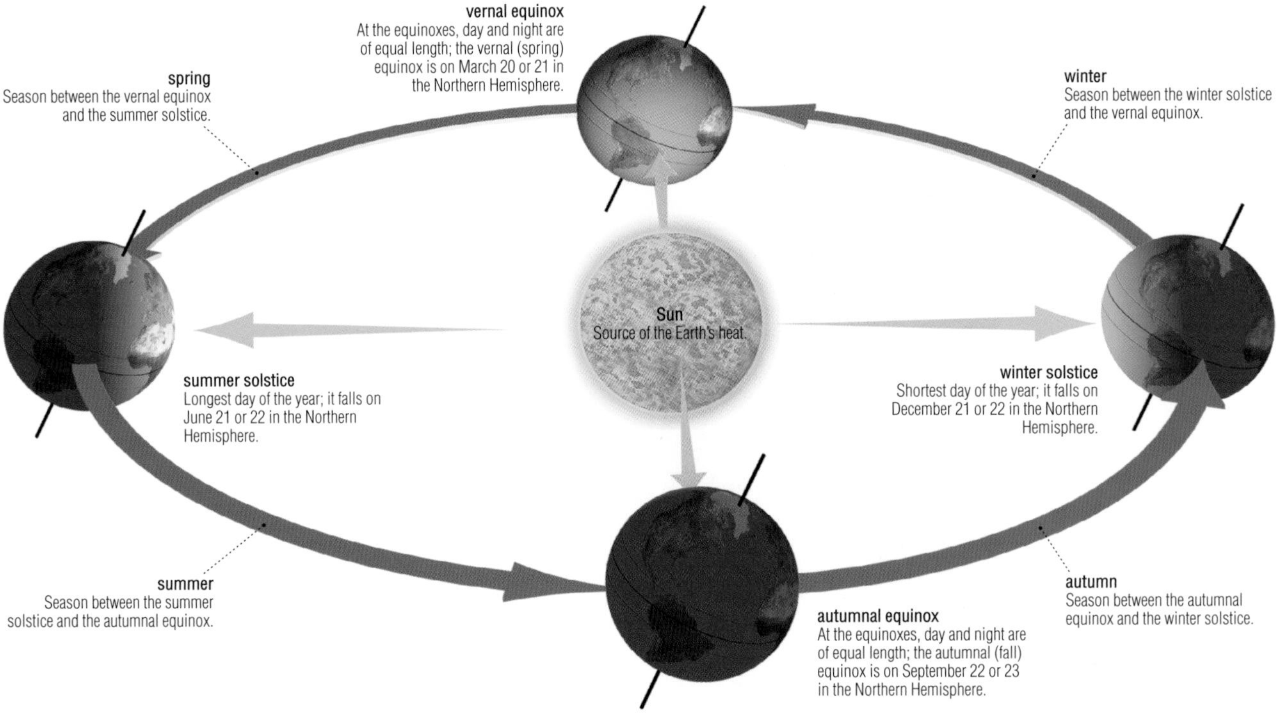
vernal equinox
At the equinoxes, day and night are of equal length; the vernal (spring) equinox is on March 20 or 21 in the Northern Hemisphere.
spring
Season between the vernal equinox and the summer solstice.
winter
Season between the winter solstice and the vernal equinox.
Sun
Source of the Earth's heat.
summer solstice
Longest day of the year; it falls on June 21 or 22 in the Northern Hemisphere.
winter solstice
Shortest day of the year; it falls on December 21 or 22 in the Northern Hemisphere.
summer
Season between the summer solstice and the autumnal equinox.
autumnal equinox
At the equinoxes, day and night are of equal length; the autumnal (fall) equinox is on September 22 or 23 in the Northern Hemisphere.
autumn
Season between the autumnal equinox and the winter solstice.

meteorological forecast

Scientific method that makes it possible to forecast atmospheric conditions in a particular region for a given period.

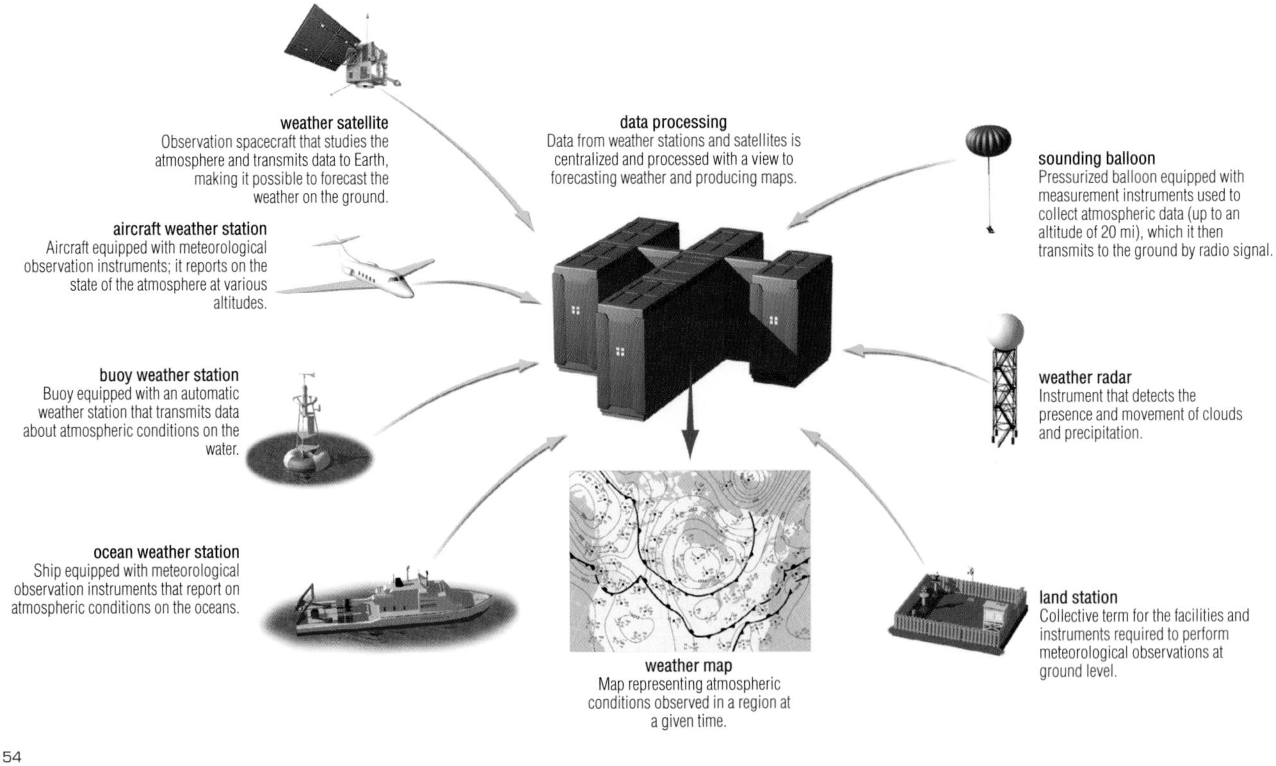
weather satellite
Observation spacecraft that studies the atmosphere and transmits data to Earth, making it possible to forecast the weather on the ground.
data processing
Data from weather stations and satellites is centralized and processed with a view to forecasting weather and producing maps.
sounding balloon
Pressurized balloon equipped with measurement instruments used to collect atmospheric data (up to an altitude of 20 mi), which it then transmits to the ground by radio signal.
aircraft weather station
Aircraft equipped with meteorological observation instruments; it reports on the state of the atmosphere at various altitudes.
weather radar
Instrument that detects the presence and movement of clouds and precipitation.
buoy weather station
Buoy equipped with an automatic weather station that transmits data about atmospheric conditions on the water.
ocean weather station
Ship equipped with meteorological observation instruments that report on atmospheric conditions on the oceans.
land station
Collective term for the facilities and instruments required to perform meteorological observations at ground level.
weather map
Map representing atmospheric conditions observed in a region at a given time.

weather map

Map representing atmospheric conditions observed in a region at a given time.

barometric pressure
Measurement of the force that air exerts at a given point on the Earth's surface; it is expressed in millibars.

isobar
Curve connecting the points on the Earth's surface that have the same atmospheric pressure.

wind direction and speed

low-pressure center
Zone characterized by relatively low pressure that increases as a function of distance from its center.

precipitation area
Zone in which atmospheric water content condenses and falls from the clouds in liquid or solid form.

trough
Elongated zone in which atmospheric pressure is relatively low.

type of the air mass
Air mass: a vast moving body of air; it takes on the climatic characteristics of the region lying below it.

high-pressure center
Zone characterized by relatively high pressure that decreases as a function of the distance from its center.

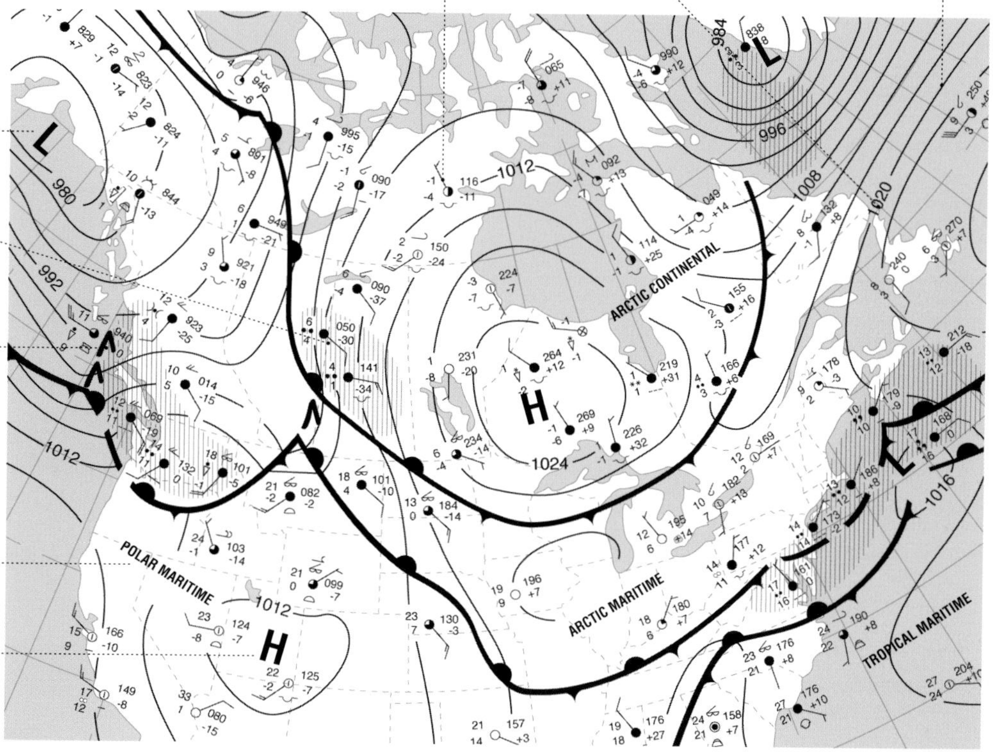

station model

Method of representing information collected by an observation station on a weather map using symbols and numbers.

type of high cloud
Type of cloud observed at altitudes higher than 20,000 feet.

type of middle cloud
Type of cloud observed at altitudes between 6,500 and 20,000 feet.

station circle
Circle on a weather map that represents an observation station; displayed around the circle is the information collected by the station.

wind speed
Wind speed is indicated by barbs and pennants whose values must be added.

air temperature
Sensation of heat or cold (°F) measured using an open-air thermometer shielded from direct sunlight.

sea-level pressure
Reference pressure that corresponds to the pressure observed at sea level; it is expressed in inches of mercury.

sky coverage
Proportion of the sky covered with cloud.

wind direction
Wind direction is indicated by the position of the wind shaft.

barometric tendency
Variation in atmospheric pressure during the three hours preceding observation.

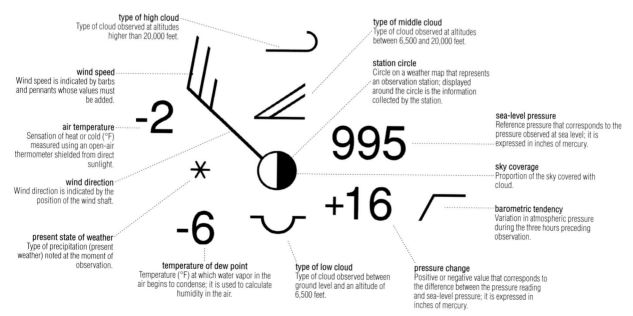

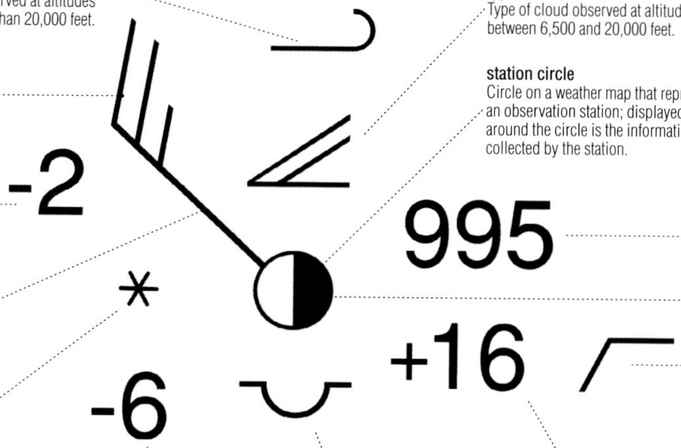

present state of weather
Type of precipitation (present weather) noted at the moment of observation.

temperature of dew point
Temperature (°F) at which water vapor in the air begins to condense; it is used to calculate humidity in the air.

type of low cloud
Type of cloud observed between ground level and an altitude of 6,500 feet.

pressure change
Positive or negative value that corresponds to the difference between the pressure reading and sea-level pressure; it is expressed in inches of mercury.

international weather symbols

Standardized map symbols used to record observations from meteorological stations all over the world.

wind

Displacement of air caused by variations in pressure between two regions of the atmosphere.

calm
Symbol indicating the absence of wind.

wind arrow
Symbol that uses the position of the shaft to indicate wind direction and the number of barbs and pennants to indicate wind speed.

shaft
Symbol of a wind blowing at a speed lower than 3 mph.

half barb
Symbol of a wind blowing between 3 and 8 mph.

barb
Symbol of a wind blowing between 9 and 14 mph.

pennant
Symbol of a wind blowing between 55 and 60 mph.

fronts

Contact surface between two air masses with different temperatures and pressure.

surface cold front
Front consisting of a cold air mass that touches the ground and displaces a warm air mass.

upper cold front
Front of a cold air mass that does not touch the Earth's surface and slides over a colder air mass.

surface warm front
Front consisting of a warm air mass that touches the ground and displaces a cold air mass.

upper warm front
Front consisting of a warm air mass that does not touch the ground and slides over a colder air mass.

occluded front
A composite front that forms when a cold front overtakes a warm front, which it pushes to a higher altitude before joining another cold front.

stationary front
Front that moves very slowly owing to the parallel movement of hot and cold air masses.

sky coverage

Proportion of the sky covered with cloud.

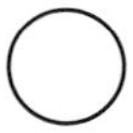

cloudless sky

clear sky

slightly covered sky

cloudy sky

very cloudy sky

overcast sky

obscured sky

clouds

Fine droplets of water or ice crystal suspended in the atmosphere; the World Meteorological Organization classifies them according to 10 types.

altostratus
Gray sheet that can completely cover the sky but allows the Sun to be seen without a halo phenomenon; it can trigger heavy precipitation.

nimbostratus
Cloud in the form of a dark layer sufficiently thick to block out the Sun; it triggers continuous precipitation.

altocumulus
Cloud composed of large white or gray flecks that sometimes form parallel layers; it foreshadows the arrival of a depression.

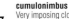

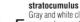

cirrus
Cloud in the form of wisps or separate strips; it usually appears in advance of a depression.

cirrostratus
Whitish layer that can completely cover the sky and that creates a halo around the Sun.

cirrocumulus
Cloud formed of white or gray flecks or strips, often arranged in rows.

stratus
Gray cloud forming a continuous veil that is similar to fog, though it never touches the ground; it can trigger light precipitation.

cumulonimbus
Very imposing cloud that can reach a thickness of 6 mi and whose base is very dark; it can trigger violent precipitation.

cumulus
Fair-weather cloud with very clear contours; it has a gray, flat base and a white top with rounded protuberances.

stratocumulus
Gray and white cloud arranged in more or less continuous rolled layers; it does not usually trigger precipitation.

international weather symbols

present weather
All atmospheric phenomena observed, with the exception of clouds; this includes forms of precipitation as well as optical and electrical phenomena.

sandstorm or dust storm

thunderstorm
Meteorological phenomenon manifested by lightning, thunder and gusts of wind, usually accompanied by rain showers or hail.

tropical storm
Low-pressure zone accompanied by precipitation and winds between 37 and 74 mph.

light intermittent rain
Rain: precipitation of water droplets produced when the air temperature is higher than 32°F.

moderate intermittent rain

heavy intermittent rain

light continuous rain

moderate continuous rain

heavy continuous rain

sleet
Precipitation in the form of water droplets or wet snow that freezes before it touches the ground.

drifting snow low
Snow that the wind blows into drifts no higher than 6 feet.

drifting snow high
Snow that the wind blows into drifts higher than 6 feet.

freezing rain
Precipitation in the form of raindrops that freeze on impact with the ground or with objects, forming a layer of ice.

heavy thunderstorm
Storm with winds higher than 57 mph, hail or heavy rain.

hurricane
Tropical cyclone comprised of a low-pressure zone accompanied by violent precipitation and winds between 74 and 185 mph.

light intermittent drizzle
Drizzle: uniform continuous precipitation of water droplets that fall very slowly and are between 0.008 and 0.02 in in diameter.

moderate intermittent drizzle

thick intermittent drizzle

light continuous drizzle

moderate continuous drizzle

thick continuous drizzle

mist
Light fog that does not limit visibility to 0.6 mi.

fog
Condensation of water vapor resulting in the suspension of microscopic droplets that reduce visibility to less than 0.6 mi.

haze
Mist composed of minuscule particles of dust, smoke, sand and other impurities; it gives the air a murky quality.

smoke
Solid or liquid particles suspended in the air; they are produced by various forms of combustion.

lightning
Brief but intense luminous phenomenon caused by an electrical discharge between two clouds or between a cloud and the ground.

tornado
Swirling column of air that extends from the ground to the base of a cumulonimbus; it produces violent winds that can reach 300 mph.

light intermittent snow
Snow: precipitation of ice crystals produced when the air temperature is lower than 32°F.

moderate intermittent snow

heavy intermittent snow

light continuous snow

moderate continuous snow

heavy continuous snow

snow shower
Sudden abundant and short-lived precipitation of ice crystals produced when the air temperature is lower than 32°F.

rain shower
Sudden abundant and short-lived precipitation of water droplets produced when the air temperature is higher than 32°F.

hail shower
Sudden abundant and short-lived precipitation of solid ice, usually in the form of pellets that vary from 0.2 to 2 in in diameter.

squall
Sudden and short-lived increase in wind speed often accompanied by showers and thunderstorms.

meteorological station

The installations and instruments required to conduct meteorological observations on the ground.

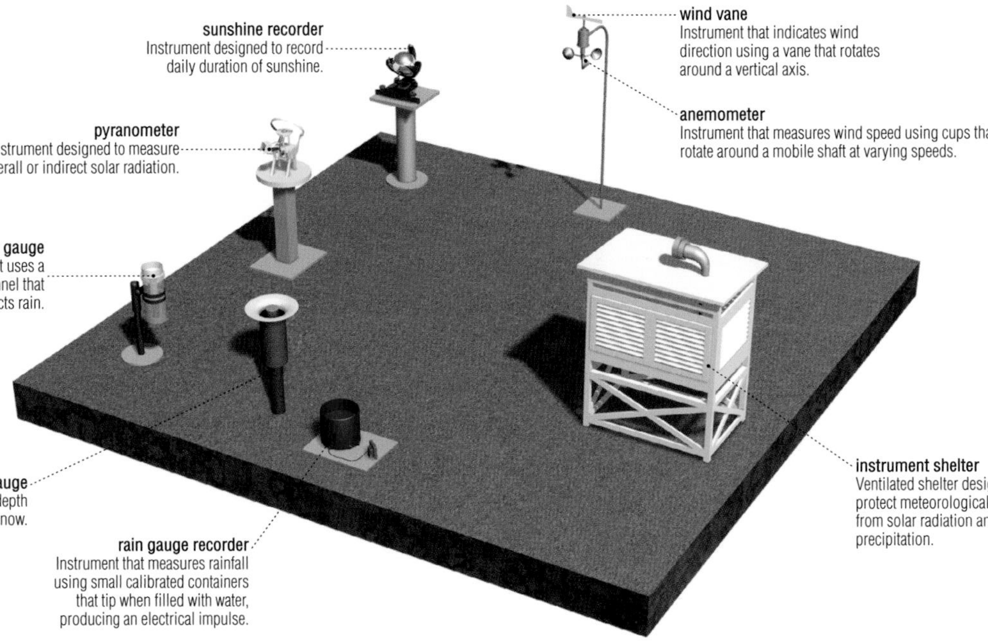

sunshine recorder
Instrument designed to record daily duration of sunshine.
wind vane
Instrument that indicates wind direction using a vane that rotates around a vertical axis.
anemometer
Instrument that measures wind speed using cups that rotate around a mobile shaft at varying speeds.
pyranometer
Instrument designed to measure overall or indirect solar radiation.
direct-reading rain gauge
Instrument that measures rainfall; it uses a measuring tube connected to a funnel that collects rain.
instrument shelter
Ventilated shelter designed to protect meteorological instruments from solar radiation and precipitation.
snow gauge
Instrument that measures the depth of water that originally fell as snow.
rain gauge recorder
Instrument that measures rainfall using small calibrated containers that tip when filled with water, producing an electrical impulse.

meteorological measuring instruments

Instruments designed to measure air temperature and humidity, sunshine, atmospheric pressure, precipitation and wind.

measure of sunshine

Sunshine: direct sunlight to which a given area is exposed.

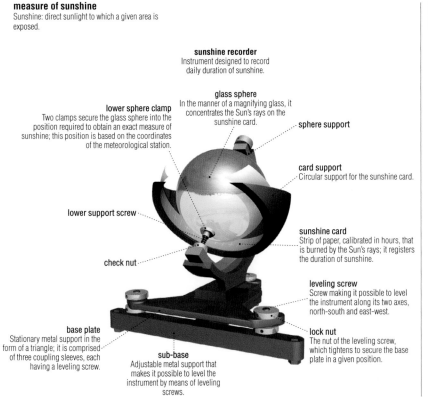

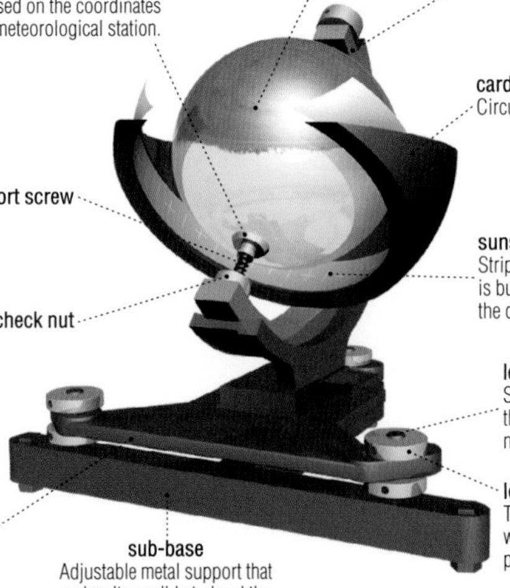

sunshine recorder
Instrument designed to record daily duration of sunshine.
glass sphere
In the manner of a magnifying glass, it concentrates the Sun's rays on the sunshine card.
lower sphere clamp
Two clamps secure the glass sphere into the position required to obtain an exact measure of sunshine; this position is based on the coordinates of the meteorological station.
sphere support
card support
Circular support for the sunshine card.
lower support screw
sunshine card
Strip of paper, calibrated in hours, that is burned by the Sun's rays; it registers the duration of sunshine.
check nut
leveling screw
Screw making it possible to level the instrument along its two axes, north-south and east-west.
base plate
Stationary metal support in the form of a triangle; it is comprised of three coupling sleeves, each having a leveling screw.
lock nut
The nut of the leveling screw, which tightens to secure the base plate in a given position.
sub-base
Adjustable metal support that makes it possible to level the instrument by means of leveling screws.

measure of sky radiation

Sky radiation: indirect solar radiation that passes through cloud and diffuses on the Earth's surface.

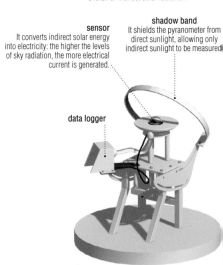

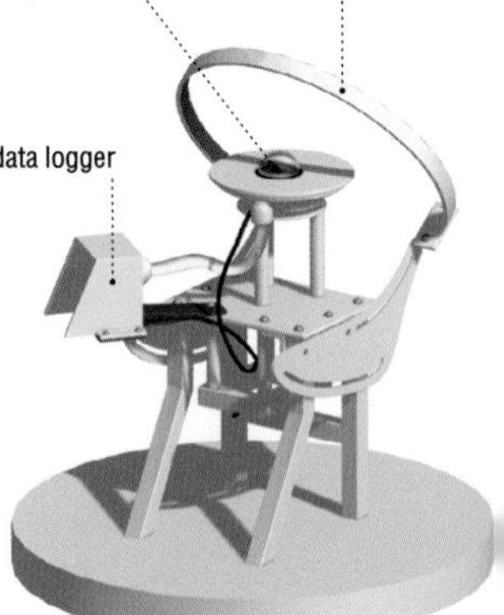

pyranometer
Instrument designed to measure overall or indirect solar radiation.
shadow band
It shields the pyranometer from direct sunlight, allowing only indirect sunlight to be measured.
sensor
It converts indirect solar energy into electricity: the higher the levels of sky radiation, the more electrical current is generated.
data logger

meteorological measuring instruments

measure of rainfall
Rainfall: quantity of water that falls to the ground during a given period.

direct-reading rain gauge
Instrument that measures rainfall; it uses a measuring tube connected to a funnel that collects rain.

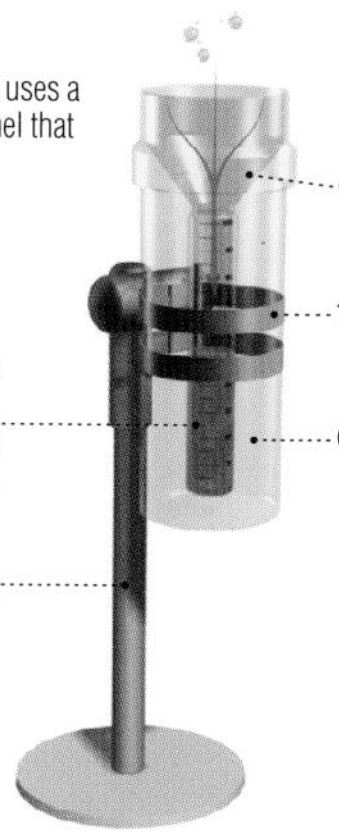

measuring tube
Calibrated in inches or millimeters, it provides a direct reading of the quantity of water in precipitation.

rain gauge recorder
Instrument that measures rainfall using small calibrated containers that tip when filled with water, producing an electrical impulse.

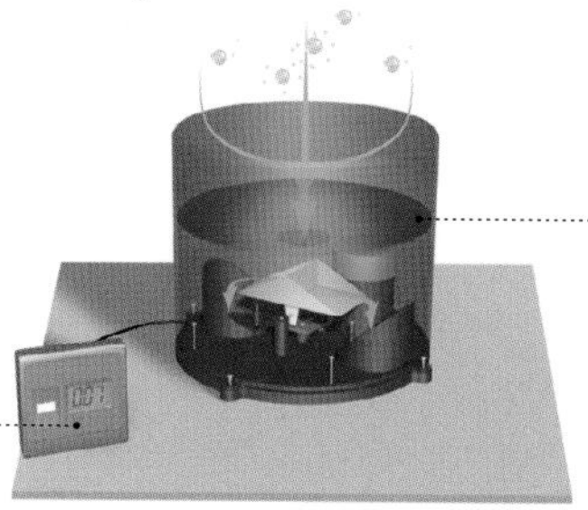

recording unit
Device connected to the collecting vessel; it records electrical impulses, whose total indicates the amount of water that fell.

upper-air sounding
Technique used to measure the pressure, temperature and humidity of air as well as wind speed and wind direction at various altitudes.

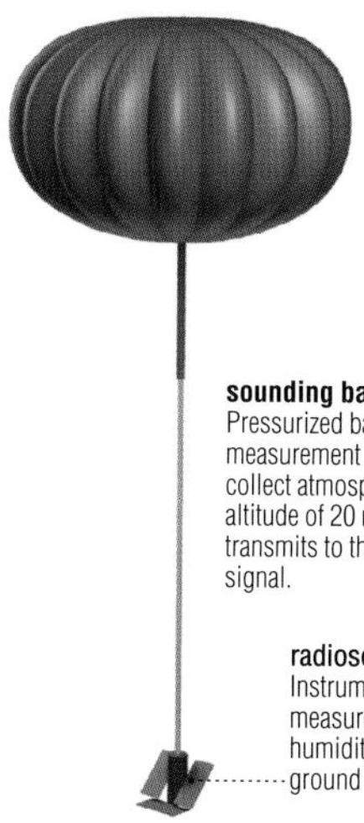

sounding balloon
Pressurized balloon equipped with measurement instruments used to collect atmospheric data (up to an altitude of 20 mi), which it then transmits to the ground by radio signal.

radiosonde
Instrument composed of sensors that measure the pressure, temperature and humidity of air; it then relays the data to ground level using a radio transmitter.

measure of air pressure
Air pressure: force exerted by an atmospheric air column on a given surface; it is expressed in inches of mercury.

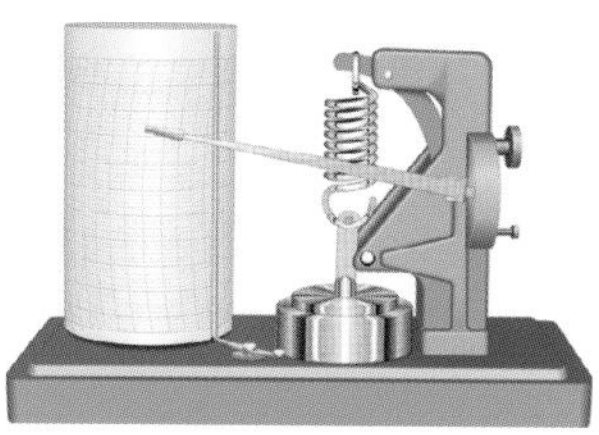

barograph
Instrument that measures variations in air pressure for a given interval.

mercury barometer
Instrument that measures atmospheric pressure using a mercury column that rises and falls with variations in air pressure.

measure of snowfall
Measurement of the depth of snow accumulation.

snow gauge
Instrument that measures the depth of water that originally fell as snow.

measure of humidity
Humidity refers to the amount of water vapor in the air.

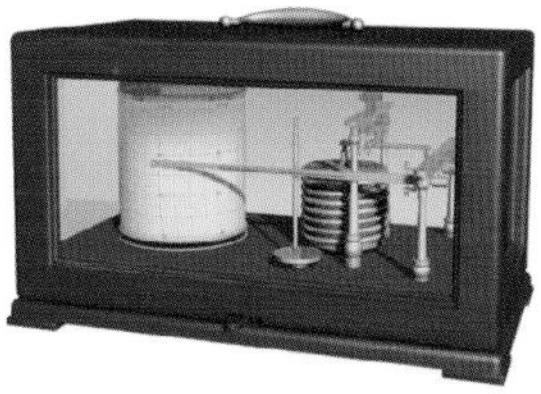

hygrograph
Instrument that registers variations in the moisture content of the air by measuring the deformation of an object that is affected by humidity.

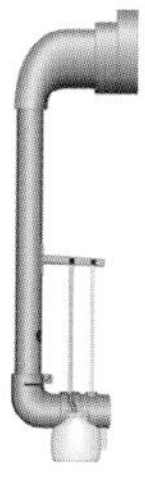

psychrometer
Instrument comprised of wet and dry thermometers that register air humidity.

measure of temperature
Measurement of heat or cold, carried out with a thermometer exposed to the air and shielded from direct sunlight.

minimum thermometer
Mercury thermometer that records the lowest temperature for a given period.

maximum thermometer
Mercury thermometer that records the highest temperature for a given period.

measure of wind direction
Wind direction: the point on the horizon from which the wind is blowing.

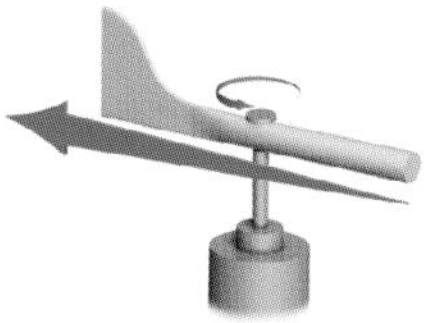

wind vane
Instrument that indicates wind direction using a vane that rotates around a vertical axis.

measure of wind strength
Wind speed: it is usually expressed in miles per hour.

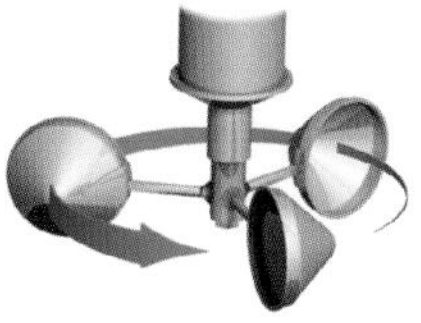

anemometer
Instrument that measures wind speed using cups that rotate around a mobile shaft at varying speeds.

measure of cloud ceiling
Cloud ceiling: altitude of the base of the clouds, expressed in feet.

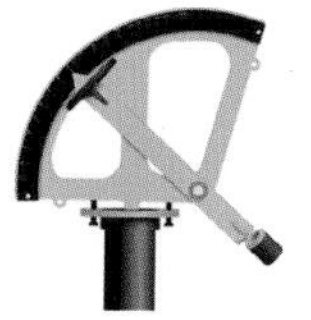

alidade
Instrument whose sighting axis, by moving along a calibrated circle, measures a cloud's angle in relation to the horizon, and thus its height.

theodolite
Instrument used to measure angles whose intervals indicate the height of a given point in relation to another.

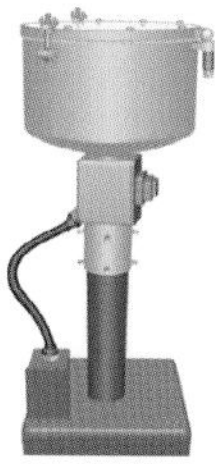

ceiling projector
Spotlight whose point of luminous impact on a cloud serves as a reference for an alidade or theodolite sighting.

weather satellites

Observation spacecraft that study the atmosphere and transmit data to Earth, making it possible to forecast the weather on the ground.

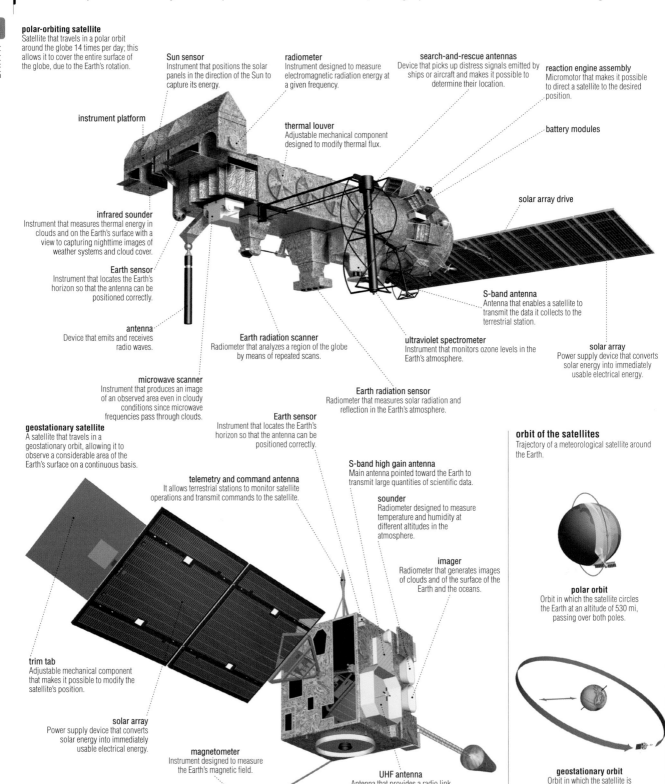

polar-orbiting satellite
Satellite that travels in a polar orbit around the globe 14 times per day; this allows it to cover the entire surface of the globe, due to the Earth's rotation.

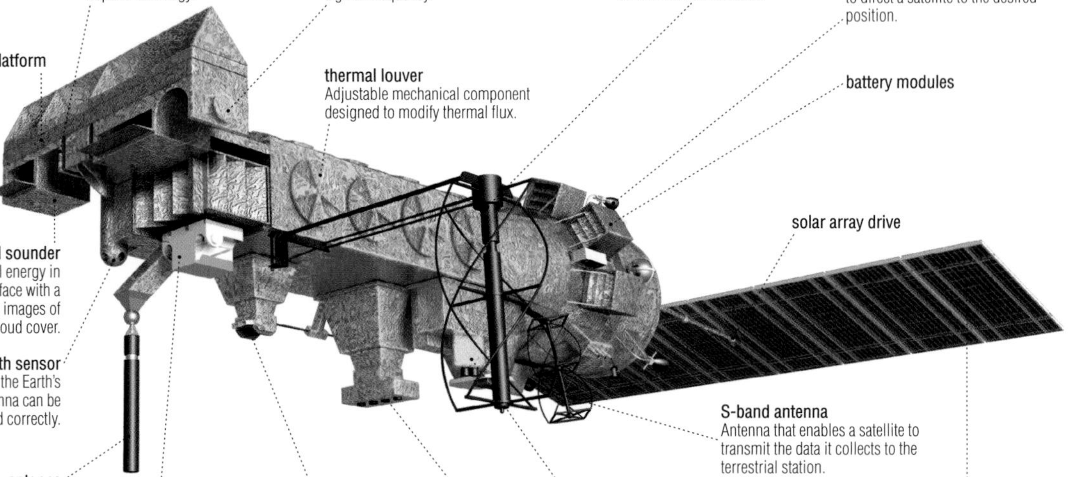

Sun sensor
Instrument that positions the solar panels in the direction of the Sun to capture its energy.

radiometer
Instrument designed to measure electromagnetic radiation energy at a given frequency.

search-and-rescue antennas
Device that picks up distress signals emitted by ships or aircraft and makes it possible to determine their location.

reaction engine assembly
Micromotor that makes it possible to direct a satellite to the desired position.

instrument platform

thermal louver
Adjustable mechanical component designed to modify thermal flux.

battery modules

solar array drive

infrared sounder
Instrument that measures thermal energy in clouds and on the Earth's surface with a view to capturing nighttime images of weather systems and cloud cover.

Earth sensor
Instrument that locates the Earth's horizon so that the antenna can be positioned correctly.

S-band antenna
Antenna that enables a satellite to transmit the data it collects to the terrestrial station.

antenna
Device that emits and receives radio waves.

Earth radiation scanner
Radiometer that analyzes a region of the globe by means of repeated scans.

ultraviolet spectrometer
Instrument that monitors ozone levels in the Earth's atmosphere.

solar array
Power supply device that converts solar energy into immediately usable electrical energy.

microwave scanner
Instrument that produces an image of an observed area even in cloudy conditions since microwave frequencies pass through clouds.

Earth radiation sensor
Radiometer that measures solar radiation and reflection in the Earth's atmosphere.

geostationary satellite
A satellite that travels in a geostationary orbit, allowing it to observe a considerable area of the Earth's surface on a continuous basis.

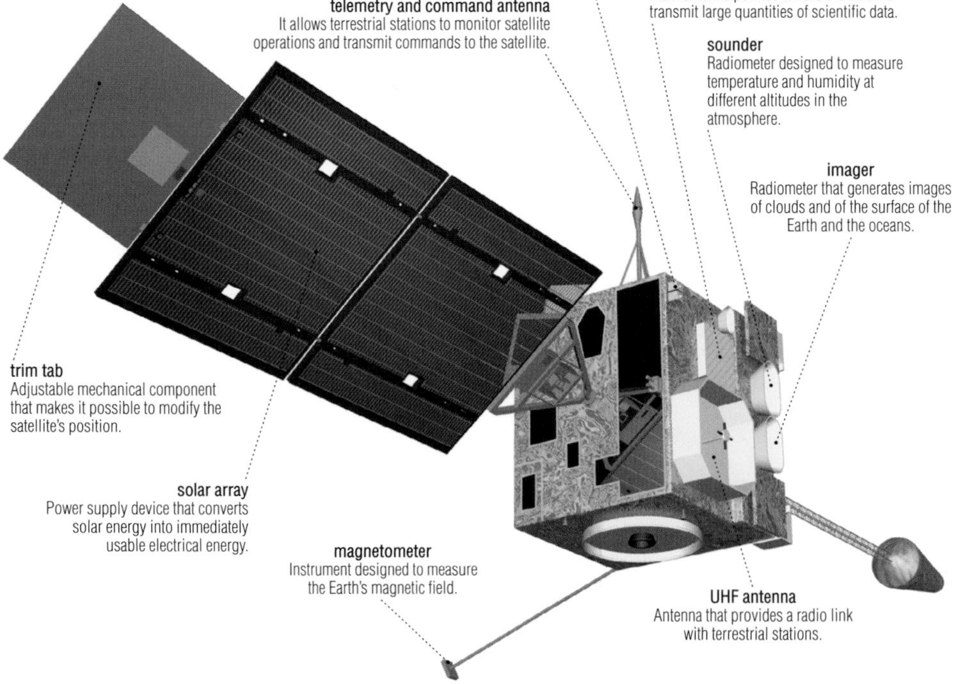

Earth sensor
Instrument that locates the Earth's horizon so that the antenna can be positioned correctly.

S-band high gain antenna
Main antenna pointed toward the Earth to transmit large quantities of scientific data.

telemetry and command antenna
It allows terrestrial stations to monitor satellite operations and transmit commands to the satellite.

sounder
Radiometer designed to measure temperature and humidity at different altitudes in the atmosphere.

imager
Radiometer that generates images of clouds and of the surface of the Earth and the oceans.

trim tab
Adjustable mechanical component that makes it possible to modify the satellite's position.

solar array
Power supply device that converts solar energy into immediately usable electrical energy.

magnetometer
Instrument designed to measure the Earth's magnetic field.

UHF antenna
Antenna that provides a radio link with terrestrial stations.

orbit of the satellites

Trajectory of a meteorological satellite around the Earth.

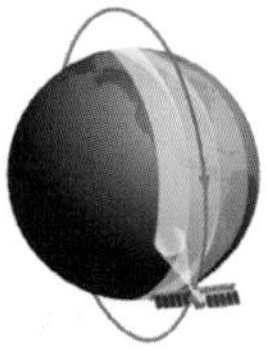

polar orbit
Orbit in which the satellite circles the Earth at an altitude of 530 mi, passing over both poles.

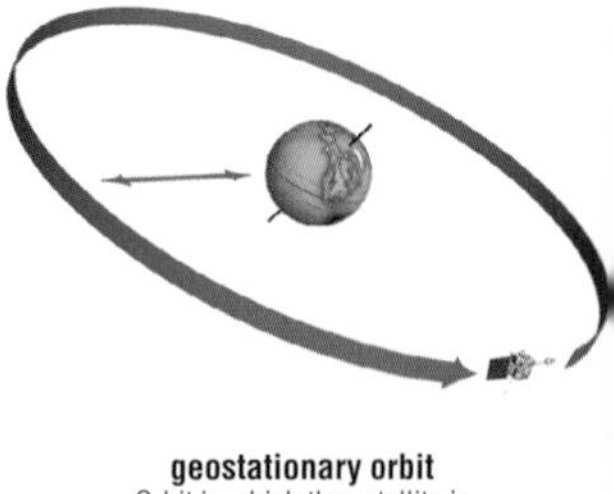

geostationary orbit
Orbit in which the satellite is synchronized with the Earth's rotation, making it appear stationary at an altitude of 22,300 mi above the Equator.

climates of the world

Climate is a collective term for the atmospheric conditions (temperature, humidity, air pressure, wind, precipitation) that characterize a given region.

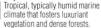

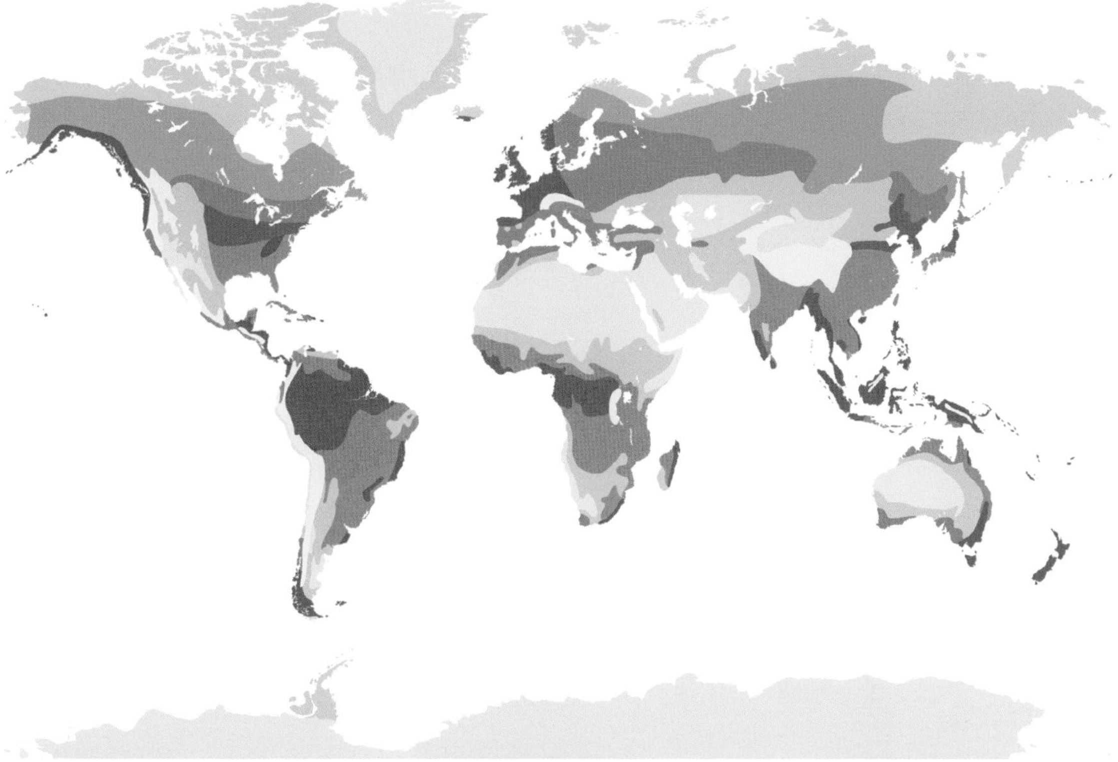

tropical climates

Climates that are hot year-round and are characterized by alternating dry and rainy seasons.

tropical rain forest
Tropical, typically humid marine climate that fosters luxuriant vegetation and dense forests.

tropical wet-and-dry (savanna)
Tropical continental climate, with an extended dry season and vegetation composed of tall grasses and scattered trees.

dry climates

Climates characterized by very low precipitation.

steppe
Region with hot summers and very cold winters; it is devoid of trees and covered with herbaceous plants adapted to arid climates.

desert
Hot region where aridity (less than 4 in of annual rainfall) is such that plant and animal life is almost nonexistent.

cold temperate climates

Climates with four clearly defined seasons, with cold winters and cool summers.

humid continental-hot summer
Climate characterized by a large annual range of temperature and relatively low rainfall. Summers are quite hot in these regions.

humid continental-warm summer
Climate characterized by a large annual range of temperature and relatively low annual rainfall. Summers are quite cool in these regions.

subarctic
Climate characterized by long, very cold winters and short cool summers; precipitation falls mainly in the summer.

warm temperate climates

Climates with four clearly defined seasons, including a mild winter and a hot or cool summer.

humid subtropical
Climate characterized by hot summers and mild winters, with precipitation distributed evenly throughout the year.

Mediterranean subtropical
Climate characterized by hot dry summers, intermediary seasons and mild rainy winters.

marine
Climate characterized by a limited annual range of temperature and by precipitation distributed throughout the year.

polar climates

Extremely cold dry climates.

polar tundra
Region where the thaw lasts only four or five months and where only mosses, lichen and a few shrubs survive the cold.

polar ice cap
The Earth's coldest region (as cold as -130°F), where the temperature, always below 32°F, creates a permanent ice cover.

highland climates

Climates where temperatures decrease and precipitation increases with altitude.

highland

clouds

Fine droplets of water or ice crystal suspended in the atmosphere; the World Meteorological Organization classifies them according to 10 types.

high clouds

Clouds at an altitude higher than 20,000 feet and composed of ice crystals; these clouds do not generate precipitation.

cirrostratus
Whitish layer that can completely cover the sky and that creates a halo around the Sun.

cirrocumulus
Cloud formed of white or gray flecks or strips, often arranged in rows.

cirrus
Cloud in the form of wisps or separate strips; it usually appears in advance of a depression.

middle clouds

Clouds at an altitude of 6,500 to 20,000 feet and composed of water droplets and ice crystals.

altostratus
Gray sheet that can completely cover the sky but allows the Sun to be seen without a halo phenomenon; it can trigger heavy precipitation.

altocumulus
Cloud composed of large white or gray flecks that sometimes form parallel layers; it foreshadows the arrival of a depression.

low clouds

Clouds that do not exceed 6,500 feet in altitude and are composed of water droplets occasionally mixed with ice crystals; they sometimes generate continuous precipitation.

stratocumulus
Gray and white cloud arranged in more or less continuous rolled layers; it does not usually trigger precipitation.

nimbostratus
Cloud in the form of a dark layer sufficiently thick to block out the Sun; it triggers continuous precipitation.

cumulus
Fair-weather cloud with very clear contours; it has a gray, flat base and a white top with rounded protuberances.

stratus
Gray cloud forming a continuous veil that is similar to fog, though it never touches the ground; it can trigger light precipitation.

clouds of vertical development

Clouds whose base is at low altitude but extend very high; the two types are cumulus and cumulonimbus.

cumulonimbus
Very imposing cloud that can reach a thickness of 6 mi and whose base is very dark; it can trigger violent precipitation.

tornado and waterspout

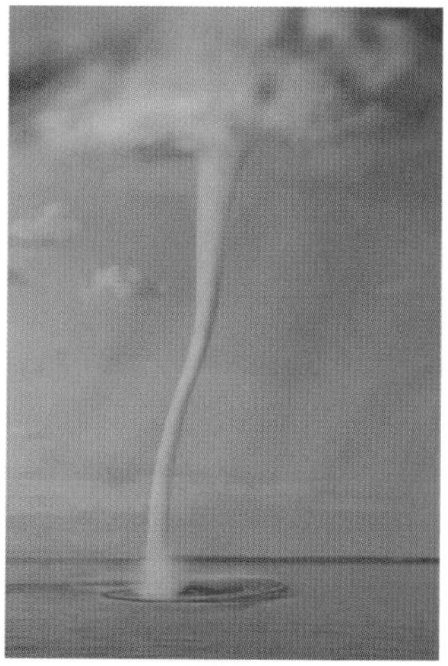

waterspout
Tornado that occurs over the sea and is not as violent as a tornado on land.

wall cloud
Ring-shaped cloud mass, usually the first sign that a tornado is imminent.

funnel cloud
Cloud that extends from another cloud's base and reaches the ground; extremely high winds whirl around it.

debris
Cloud of dust and debris swept up from the ground.

tornado
Swirling column of air that extends from the ground to the base of a cumulonimbus; it produces violent winds that can reach 300 mph.

tropical cyclone

Low-pressure zone that forms in the intertropical region and is marked by violent precipitation and swirling winds of 74 to 185 mph.

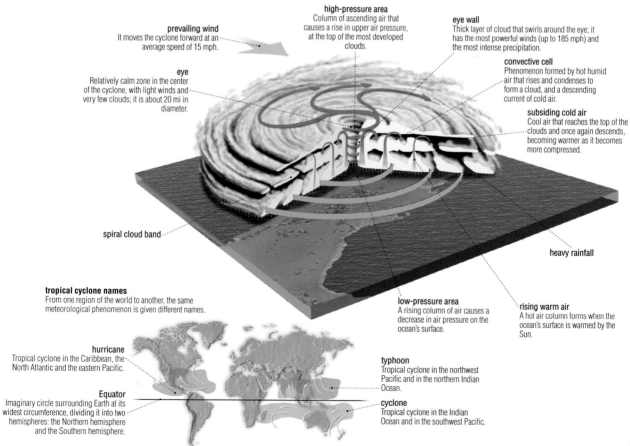

high-pressure area
Column of ascending air that causes a rise in upper air pressure, at the top of the most developed clouds.

prevailing wind
It moves the cyclone forward at an average speed of 15 mph.

eye wall
Thick layer of cloud that swirls around the eye; it has the most powerful winds (up to 185 mph) and the most intense precipitation.

convective cell
Phenomenon formed by hot humid air that rises and condenses to form a cloud, and a descending current of cold air.

eye
Relatively calm zone in the center of the cyclone, with light winds and very few clouds; it is about 20 mi in diameter.

subsiding cold air
Cool air that reaches the top of the clouds and once again descends, becoming warmer as it becomes more compressed.

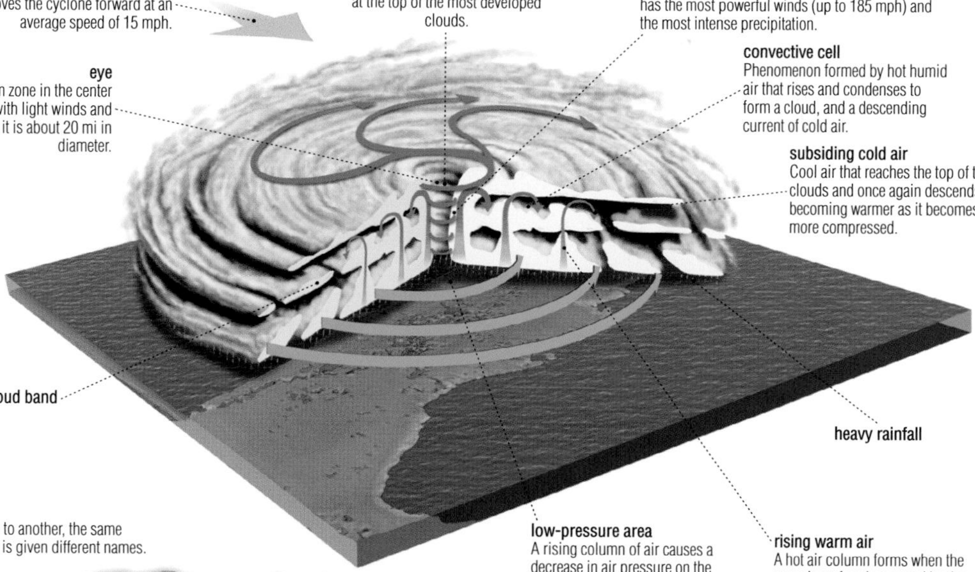

spiral cloud band

heavy rainfall

low-pressure area
A rising column of air causes a decrease in air pressure on the ocean's surface.

rising warm air
A hot air column forms when the ocean's surface is warmed by the Sun.

tropical cyclone names
From one region of the world to another, the same meteorological phenomenon is given different names.

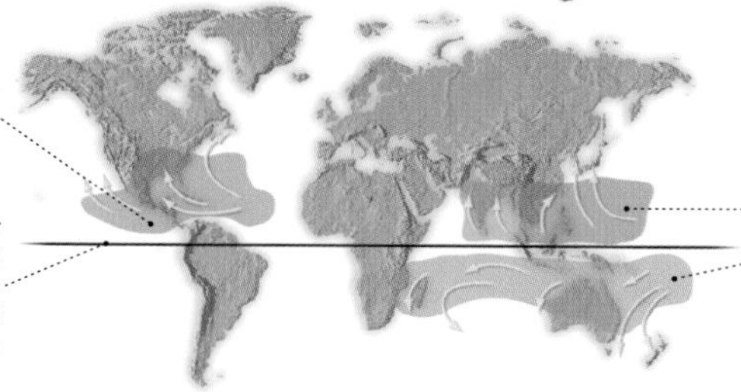

hurricane
Tropical cyclone in the Caribbean, the North Atlantic and the eastern Pacific.

Equator
Imaginary circle surrounding Earth at its widest circumference, dividing it into two hemispheres: the Northern hemisphere and the Southern hemisphere.

typhoon
Tropical cyclone in the northwest Pacific and in the northern Indian Ocean.

cyclone
Tropical cyclone in the Indian Ocean and in the southwest Pacific.

precipitation

Collective term for water particles in the atmosphere that fall or are deposited on the ground in solid or liquid form.

rain forms

By international convention, precipitation in the form of rain is classified according to the quantity that falls.

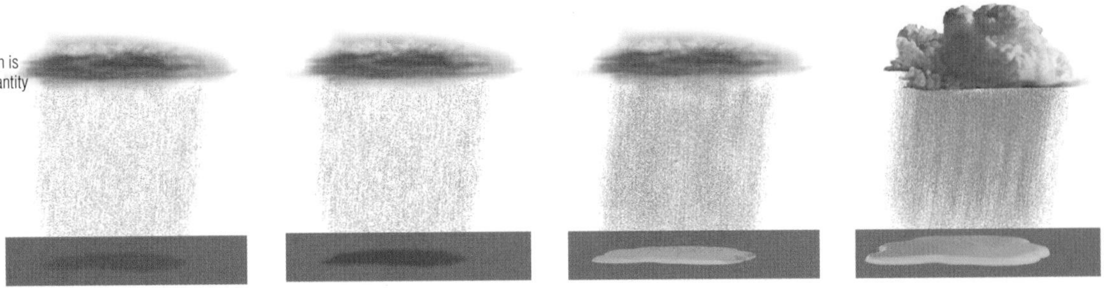

drizzle
Uniform continuous precipitation of slow-falling water droplets between 0.008 and 0.02 in in diameter.

light rain
Precipitation of water drops over 0.02 in in diameter; it results in accumulations of 0.1 in per hour.

moderate rain
Precipitation that results in 0.1 to 0.3 in accumulation per hour.

heavy rain
Precipitation that results in over 0.3 in accumulation per hour.

winter precipitations

During the winter, water can fall in various forms, depending on the air temperature.

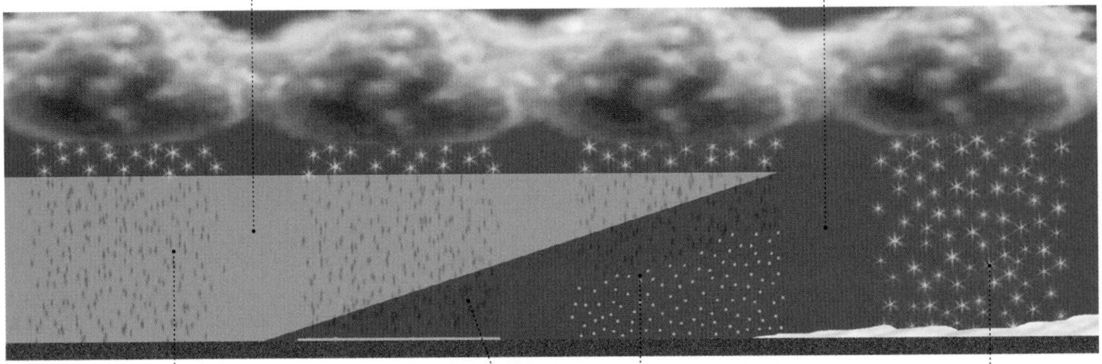

rain
Precipitation of water droplets produced when the air temperature is higher than 32°F.

freezing rain
Precipitation in the form of raindrops that freeze on impact with the ground or with objects, forming a layer of ice.

sleet
Precipitation in the form of water droplets or wet snow that freezes before it touches the ground.

snow
Precipitation of ice crystals produced when the air temperature is below 32°F.

snow crystals

Ice crystals whose form depends on temperature and humidity; they fall separately or in agglomerations of flakes.

needle
Translucent prism-shaped ice crystal; it is long and narrow and has pointed ends.

capped column
Ice crystal that is identical to the column, except for the thin hexagon-shaped cap at each extremity.

hail
Hard, usually spherical ice crystal that varies between 0.2 and 2 in in diameter; it is formed of concentric layers of clear opaque ice.

sleet
Ice crystal less than 0.2 in in diameter that results from rain drops or snow flakes freezing before they touch the ground.

snow pellet
Opaque ice crystal less than 0.2 in in diameter that froze inside a cloud.

column
Short translucent ice crystal with flat extremities; it is prism-shaped and occasionally hollow.

plate crystal
Ice crystal in the form of a thin hexagonal plate that is occasionally hollow.

spatial dendrite
Ice crystal characterized by complex branches similar to those of a tree.

irregular crystal
Ice crystal with no defined shape resulting from the agglomeration of several crystals.

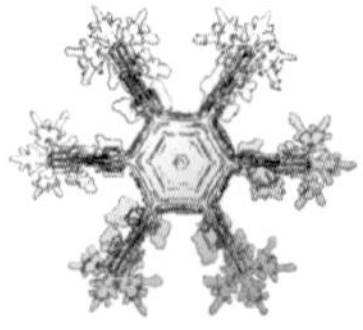

stellar crystal
Star-shaped crystal with six branches.

precipitation

stormy sky
A thunderstorm is characterized by lightning, thunder and gusts of wind, usually accompanied by rain showers or hail.

cloud
The very imposing cloud that generates thunderstorms is the cumulonimbus; it can reach a thickness of 6 mi and its base is very dark.

lightning
Brief but intense luminous phenomenon caused by an electrical discharge between two clouds or between a cloud and the ground.

rainbow
Luminous arc formed of bands of color; during a shower, it is visible in the opposite direction to the Sun.

rain
Precipitation of water droplets produced when the air temperature is higher than 32°F.

dew
Condensation of water vapor in the air that settles on cold surfaces in droplet form.

rime
Deposit of ice crystals on surfaces whose temperature is close to 32°F; it is caused by the condensation of water vapor in the air.

mist
Light fog that does not limit visibility to 0.6 mi.

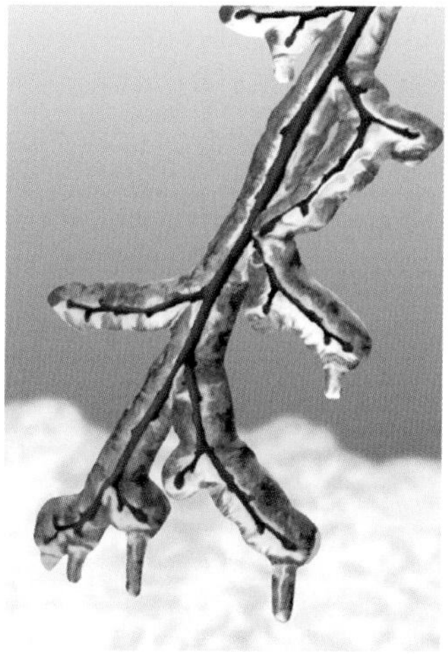

frost
Layer of ice on the ground or on an object; it is caused by the condensation of fine rain when the temperature is hovering around 32°F.

fog
Condensation of water vapor resulting in the suspension of microscopic droplets that reduce visibility to less than 0.6 mi.

vegetation and biosphere

vegetation regions

Vegetation plays an essential role in maintaining biospheric equilibrium; it varies depending on climate and soil characteristics.

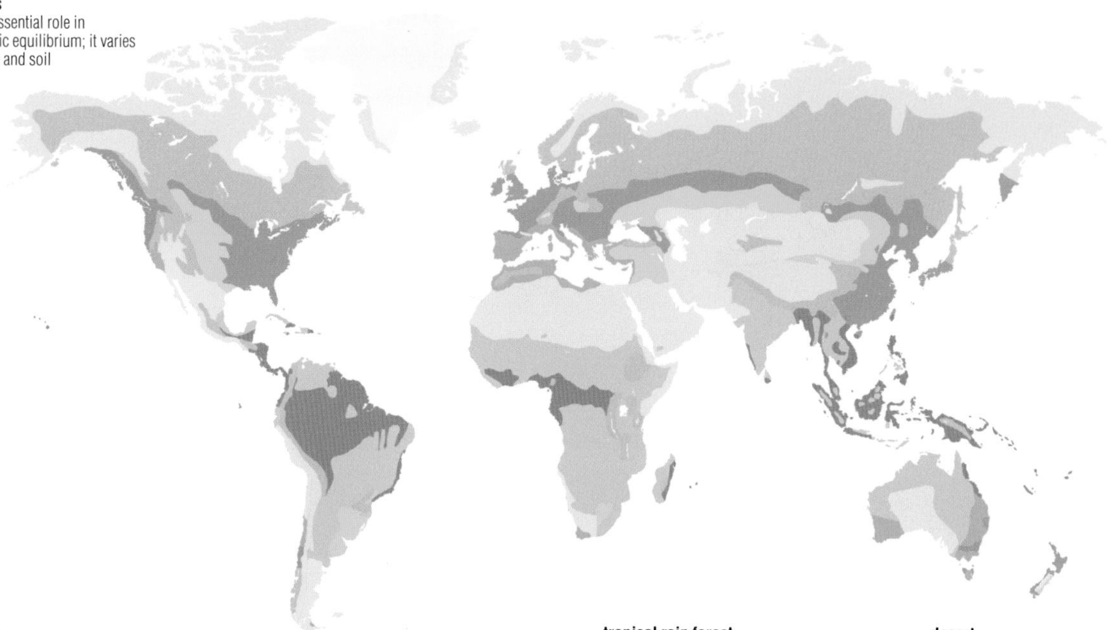

tundra
Plant formation that grows in relatively arid regions; it includes mosses, lichens, grasses, bushes and dwarf trees.

temperate forest
Forest composed mainly of deciduous trees, including oak, ash and beech.

tropical rain forest
Dense forest whose biodiversity is among the richest; its growth is fostered by abundant and regular precipitation.

desert
Hot region where aridity (less than 4 in of annual rainfall) is such that plant and animal life is almost nonexistent.

boreal forest
Vast expanse of forest composed mainly of conifers, although certain deciduous trees also grow here.

grassland
Vast expanse of herbaceous plants, mostly grasses; virtually devoid of trees, these regions are characterized by relatively cold, dry winters.

savanna
Vast expanse of herbaceous plants, dominated by tall grasses and shrubs; it is typical of hot regions that have a rainy season.

maquis
Vast expanse of degenerated vegetation composed of shrubs with evergreen leaves; it is adapted to summer drought.

elevation zones and vegetation

Types of vegetation vary depending on temperature and rainfall, which in turn depend on altitude.

glacier
Mass of ice resulting from the accumulation and compression of snow; it moves under its own weight.

tundra
Plant formation that grows in relatively arid regions; it includes mosses, lichens, grasses, bushes and dwarf trees.

coniferous forest
Forest composed mainly of softwood trees with evergreen leaves in the form of needles or scales.

mixed forest
Forest composed of conifers and deciduous trees.

deciduous forest
Forest composed mainly of trees with broad leaves that grow back every year.

tropical forest
Dense, highly varied forest in the intertropical zone, where precipitation is abundant and regular.

structure of the biosphere

Biosphere: the part of the Earth's covering where life is possible; it extends from the floor of the oceans to the summit of the highest mountains (about 12 mi).

atmosphere
Layer of air that surrounds the Earth and is composed mainly of nitrogen (78%) and oxygen (21%); only its lower portion is part of the biosphere.

lithosphere
Outer layer of the Earth's crust; only its upper portion, to a depth of 1 mi, is part of the biosphere.

hydrosphere
A collective term for the planet's waters, including the oceans, seas, lakes, watercourses and underground water systems.

food chain

Order of the relationships of predation and dependence among living organisms.

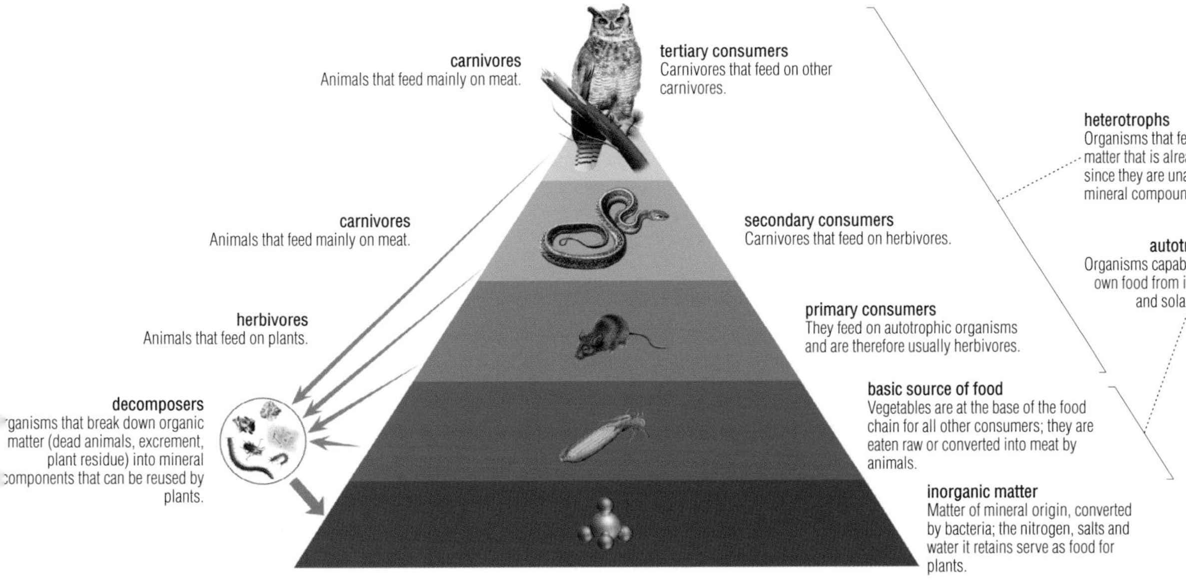
carnivores
Animals that feed mainly on meat.
tertiary consumers
Carnivores that feed on other carnivores.
heterotrophs
Organisms that feed on organic matter that is already broken down, since they are unable to feed on mineral compounds.
carnivores
Animals that feed mainly on meat.
secondary consumers
Carnivores that feed on herbivores.
autotrophs
Organisms capable of making their own food from inorganic matter and solar energy.
herbivores
Animals that feed on plants.
primary consumers
They feed on autotrophic organisms and are therefore usually herbivores.
decomposers
ganisms that break down organic matter (dead animals, excrement, plant residue) into mineral omponents that can be reused by plants.
basic source of food
Vegetables are at the base of the food chain for all other consumers; they are eaten raw or converted into meat by animals.
inorganic matter
Matter of mineral origin, converted by bacteria; the nitrogen, salts and water it retains serve as food for plants.

hydrologic cycle

Continuous circulation of water in its different states (liquid, solid and gaseous) between the oceans, the atmosphere and the Earth's surface.

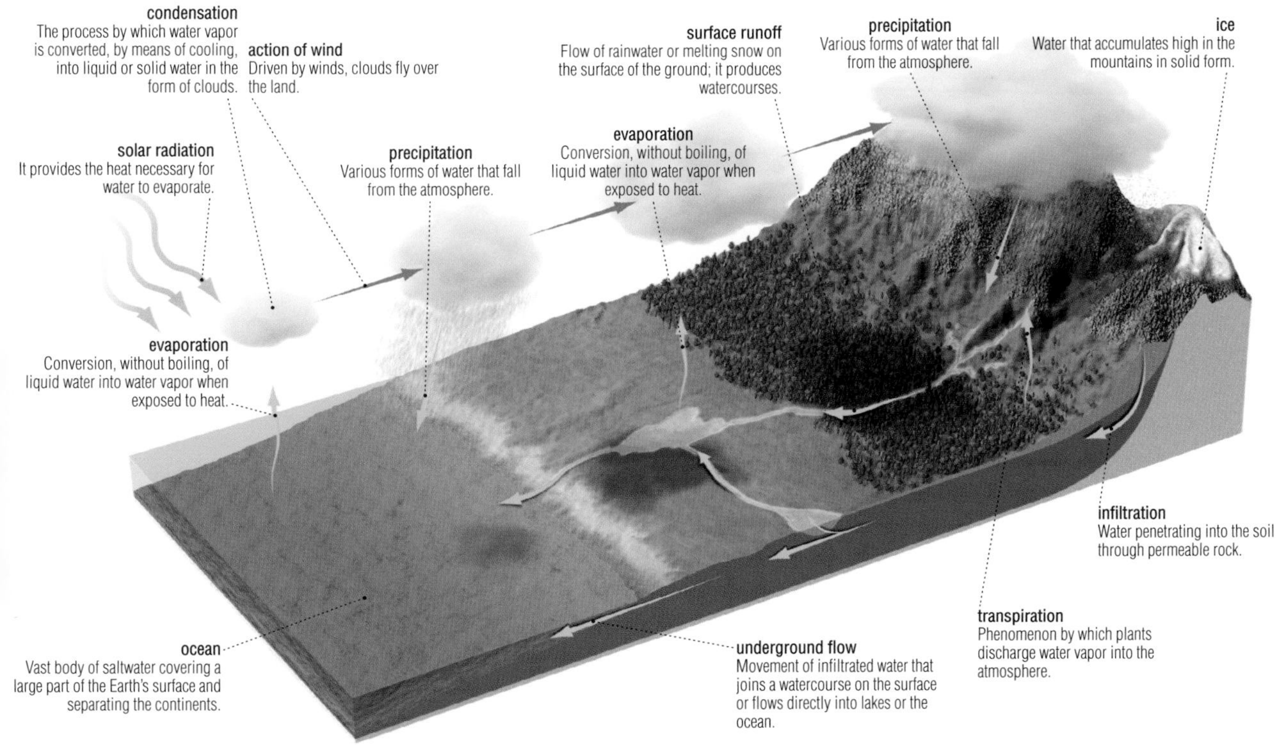
condensation
The process by which water vapor is converted, by means of cooling, into liquid or solid water in the form of clouds.
action of wind
Driven by winds, clouds fly over the land.
surface runoff
Flow of rainwater or melting snow on the surface of the ground; it produces watercourses.
precipitation
Various forms of water that fall from the atmosphere.
ice
Water that accumulates high in the mountains in solid form.
solar radiation
It provides the heat necessary for water to evaporate.
precipitation
Various forms of water that fall from the atmosphere.
evaporation
Conversion, without boiling, of liquid water into water vapor when exposed to heat.
evaporation
Conversion, without boiling, of liquid water into water vapor when exposed to heat.
infiltration
Water penetrating into the soil through permeable rock.
transpiration
Phenomenon by which plants discharge water vapor into the atmosphere.
ocean
Vast body of saltwater covering a large part of the Earth's surface and separating the continents.
underground flow
Movement of infiltrated water that joins a watercourse on the surface or flows directly into lakes or the ocean.

greenhouse effect

Warming of the atmosphere that occurs when certain gases absorb part of the solar radiation reflected by the Earth.

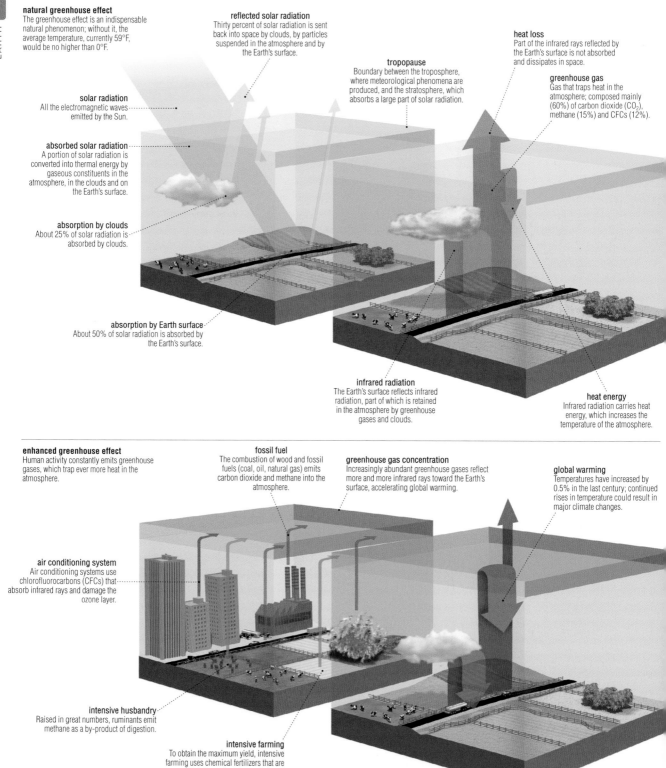

natural greenhouse effect
The greenhouse effect is an indispensable natural phenomenon; without it, the average temperature, currently 59°F, would be no higher than 0°F.

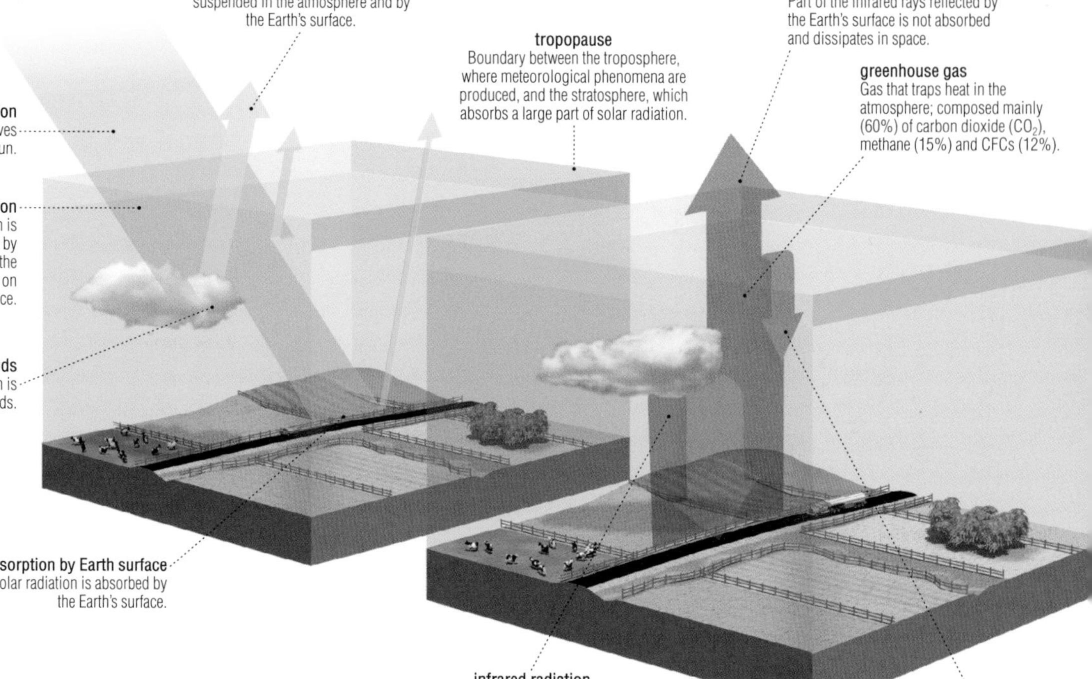

reflected solar radiation
Thirty percent of solar radiation is sent back into space by clouds, by particles suspended in the atmosphere and by the Earth's surface.

solar radiation
All the electromagnetic waves emitted by the Sun.

absorbed solar radiation
A portion of solar radiation is converted into thermal energy by gaseous constituents in the atmosphere, in the clouds and on the Earth's surface.

absorption by clouds
About 25% of solar radiation is absorbed by clouds.

absorption by Earth surface
About 50% of solar radiation is absorbed by the Earth's surface.

tropopause
Boundary between the troposphere, where meteorological phenomena are produced, and the stratosphere, which absorbs a large part of solar radiation.

heat loss
Part of the infrared rays reflected by the Earth's surface is not absorbed and dissipates in space.

greenhouse gas
Gas that traps heat in the atmosphere; composed mainly (60%) of carbon dioxide (CO_2), methane (15%) and CFCs (12%).

infrared radiation
The Earth's surface reflects infrared radiation, part of which is retained in the atmosphere by greenhouse gases and clouds.

heat energy
Infrared radiation carries heat energy, which increases the temperature of the atmosphere.

enhanced greenhouse effect
Human activity constantly emits greenhouse gases, which trap ever more heat in the atmosphere.

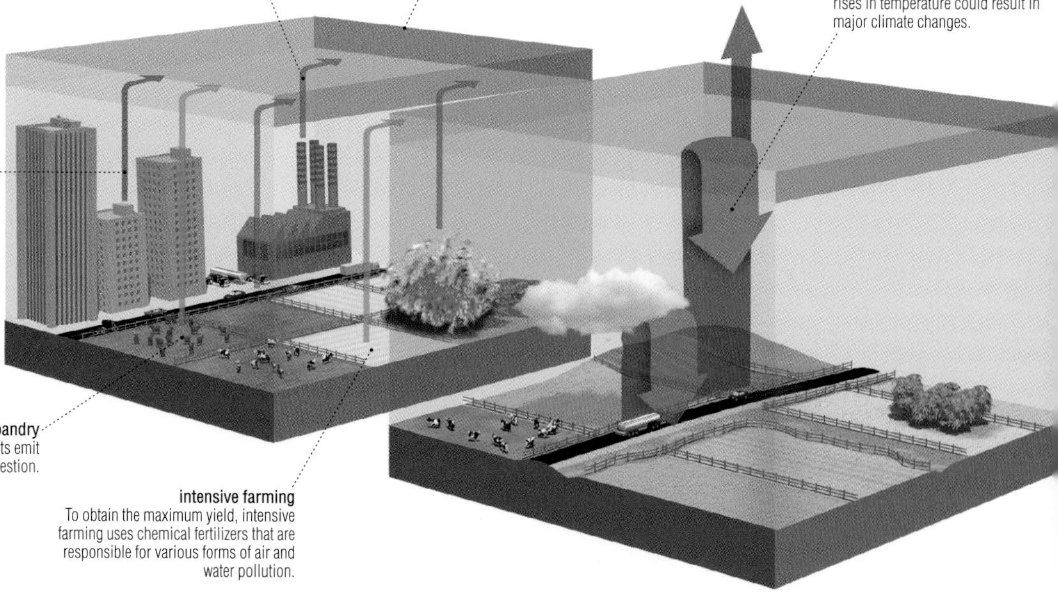

fossil fuel
The combustion of wood and fossil fuels (coal, oil, natural gas) emits carbon dioxide and methane into the atmosphere.

greenhouse gas concentration
Increasingly abundant greenhouse gases reflect more and more infrared rays toward the Earth's surface, accelerating global warming.

global warming
Temperatures have increased by 0.5% in the last century; continued rises in temperature could result in major climate changes.

air conditioning system
Air conditioning systems use chlorofluorocarbons (CFCs) that absorb infrared rays and damage the ozone layer.

intensive husbandry
Raised in great numbers, ruminants emit methane as a by-product of digestion.

intensive farming
To obtain the maximum yield, intensive farming uses chemical fertilizers that are responsible for various forms of air and water pollution.

air pollution

The presence in the atmosphere of large quantities of particles or gases produced by human activity; these are harmful to both animal and plant life.

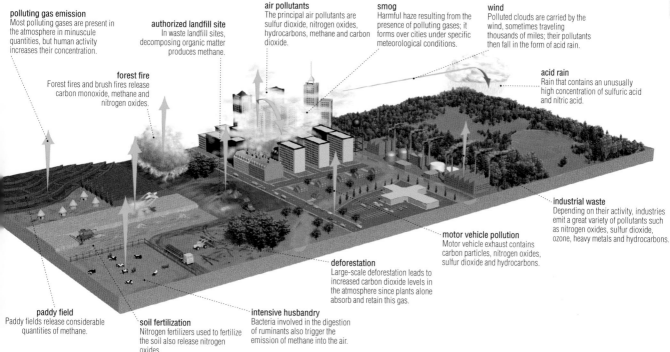

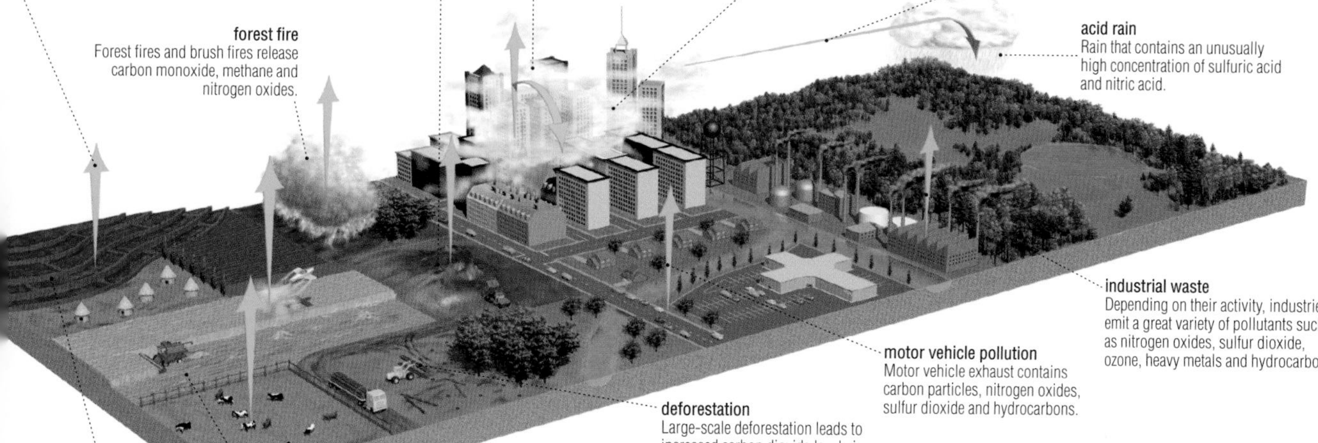
polluting gas emission
Most polluting gases are present in the atmosphere in minuscule quantities, but human activity increases their concentration.
authorized landfill site
In waste landfill sites, decomposing organic matter produces methane.
air pollutants
The principal air pollutants are sulfur dioxide, nitrogen oxides, hydrocarbons, methane and carbon dioxide.
smog
Harmful haze resulting from the presence of polluting gases; it forms over cities under specific meteorological conditions.
wind
Polluted clouds are carried by the wind, sometimes traveling thousands of miles; their pollutants then fall in the form of acid rain.
forest fire
Forest fires and brush fires release carbon monoxide, methane and nitrogen oxides.
acid rain
Rain that contains an unusually high concentration of sulfuric acid and nitric acid.
industrial waste
Depending on their activity, industries emit a great variety of pollutants such as nitrogen oxides, sulfur dioxide, ozone, heavy metals and hydrocarbons.
motor vehicle pollution
Motor vehicle exhaust contains carbon particles, nitrogen oxides, sulfur dioxide and hydrocarbons.
deforestation
Large-scale deforestation leads to increased carbon dioxide levels in the atmosphere since plants alone absorb and retain this gas.
paddy field
Paddy fields release considerable quantities of methane.
soil fertilization
Nitrogen fertilizers used to fertilize the soil also release nitrogen oxides.
intensive husbandry
Bacteria involved in the digestion of ruminants also trigger the emission of methane into the air.

land pollution

Numerous factors contribute to soil pollution (e.g., household and industrial waste, fertilizers, pesticides).

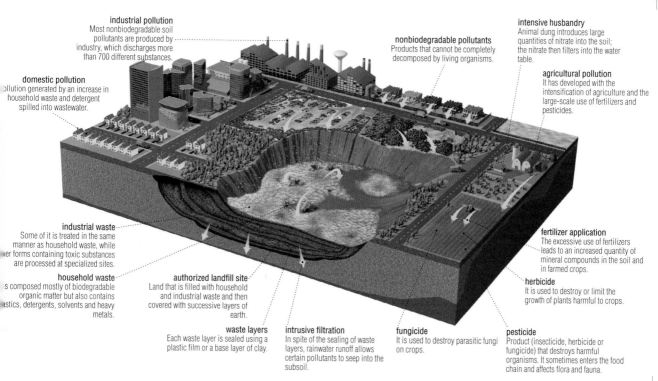

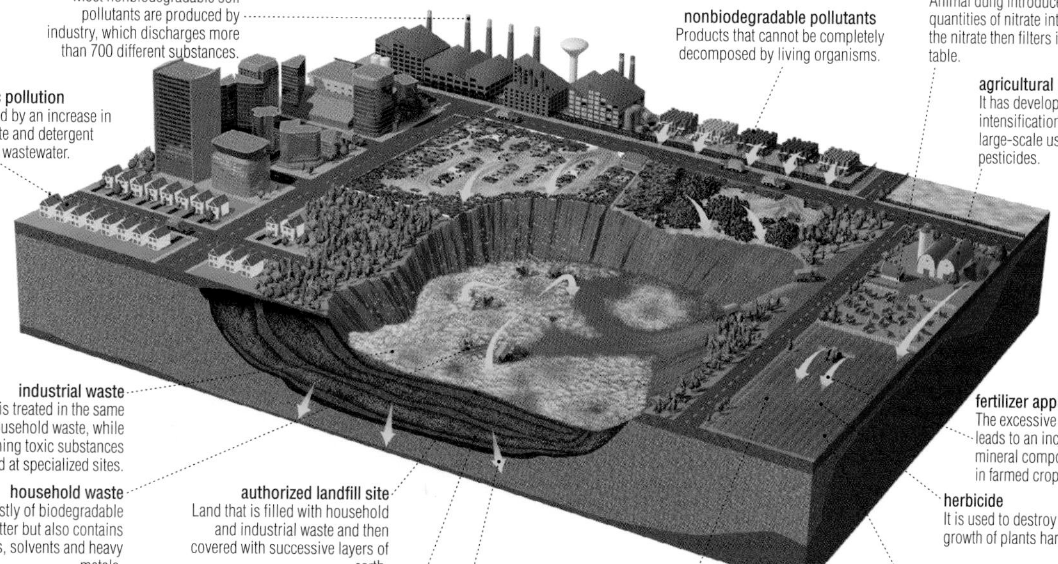
industrial pollution
Most nonbiodegradable soil pollutants are produced by industry, which discharges more than 700 different substances.
nonbiodegradable pollutants
Products that cannot be completely decomposed by living organisms.
intensive husbandry
Animal dung introduces large quantities of nitrate into the soil; the nitrate then filters into the water table.
domestic pollution
ollution generated by an increase in household waste and detergent spilled into wastewater.
agricultural pollution
It has developed with the intensification of agriculture and the large-scale use of fertilizers and pesticides.
industrial waste
Some of it is treated in the same manner as household waste, while er forms containing toxic substances are processed at specialized sites.
fertilizer application
The excessive use of fertilizers leads to an increased quantity of mineral compounds in the soil and in farmed crops.
household waste
s composed mostly of biodegradable organic matter but also contains stics, detergents, solvents and heavy metals.
authorized landfill site
Land that is filled with household and industrial waste and then covered with successive layers of earth.
herbicide
It is used to destroy or limit the growth of plants harmful to crops.
waste layers
Each waste layer is sealed using a plastic film or a base layer of clay.
intrusive filtration
In spite of the sealing of waste layers, rainwater runoff allows certain pollutants to seep into the subsoil.
fungicide
It is used to destroy parasitic fungi on crops.
pesticide
Product (insecticide, herbicide or fungicide) that destroys harmful organisms. It sometimes enters the food chain and affects flora and fauna.

water pollution

The cycle of the Earth's waters is continuous, carrying and spreading pollutants introduced by human activity all around the planet.

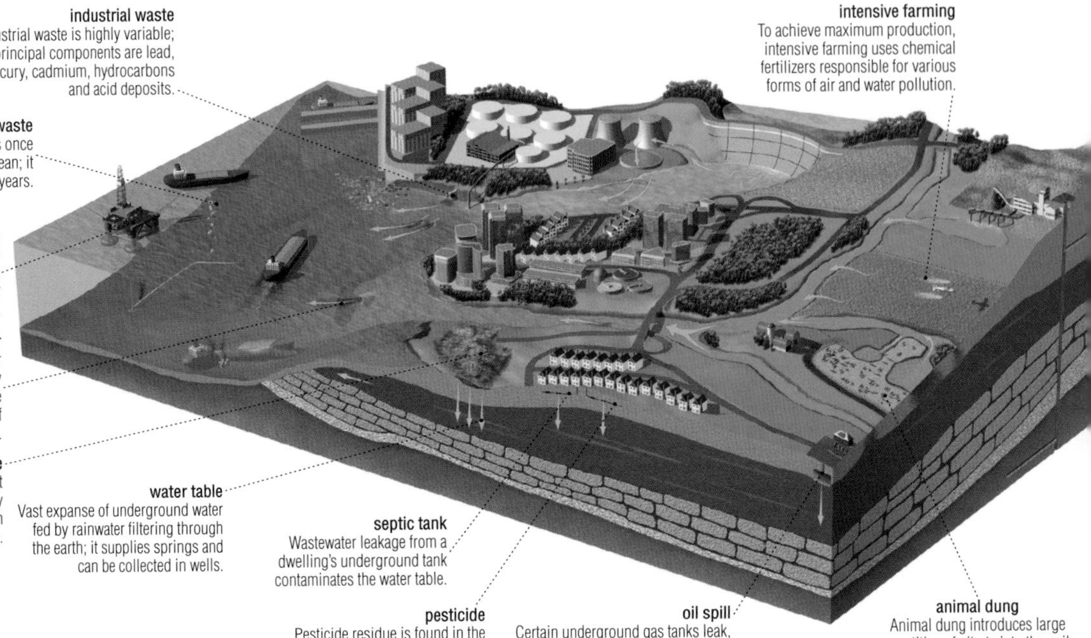

industrial waste
Industrial waste is highly variable; its principal components are lead, mercury, cadmium, hydrocarbons and acid deposits.
intensive farming
To achieve maximum production, intensive farming uses chemical fertilizers responsible for various forms of air and water pollution.
nuclear waste
Radioactive nuclear waste was once immersed at the bottom of the ocean; it has a life span of up to 1,000 years.
oil pollution
Pollution caused by leaks from refineries and offshore drilling platforms, by ships emptying their fuel tanks at sea and by oil spills.
waste water
Untreated, it contains organic matter (e.g., bacteria, viruses) and potentially pathogenic substances that cause infection and promote the growth of algae.
household waste
Burying household waste without taking any particular precautionary measures leads to contamination of the water table.
water table
Vast expanse of underground water fed by rainwater filtering through the earth; it supplies springs and can be collected in wells.
septic tank
Wastewater leakage from a dwelling's underground tank contaminates the water table.
pesticide
Pesticide residue is found in the water table and in watercourses; it makes water unfit for consumption.
oil spill
Certain underground gas tanks leak, discharging hydrocarbons into the water table.
animal dung
Animal dung introduces large quantities of nitrate into the soil; the nitrate then filters into the water table.

acid rain

Rain that contains abnormally high concentrations of sulfuric acid and nitric acid.

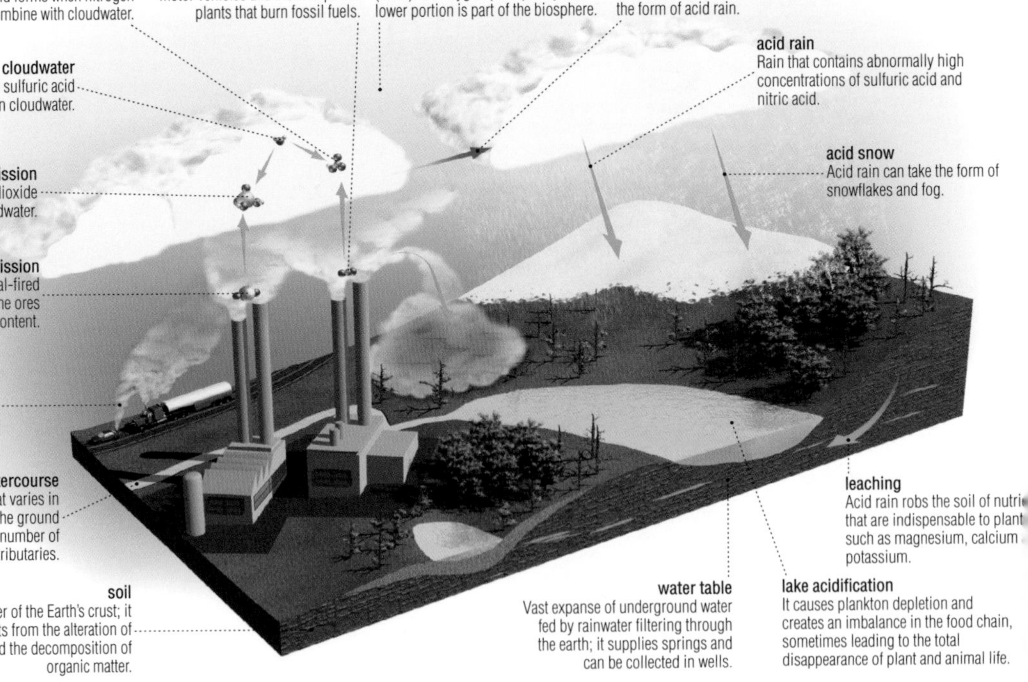

nitric acid emission
Nitric acid forms when nitrogen oxides combine with cloudwater.
nitrogen oxide emission
Nitrogen oxide is discharged by motor vehicles and thermal power plants that burn fossil fuels.
atmosphere
Layer of air that surrounds the Earth and is composed mainly of nitrogen (78%) and oxygen (21%); only its lower portion is part of the biosphere.
wind
Polluted clouds are carried by the wind, sometimes traveling thousands of miles; their pollutants then fall in the form of acid rain.
acid rain
Rain that contains abnormally high concentrations of sulfuric acid and nitric acid.
cloudwater
Nitric acid and sulfuric acid dissolve in cloudwater.
acid snow
Acid rain can take the form of snowflakes and fog.
sulfuric acid emission
Sulfuric acid forms when sulfur dioxide combines with cloudwater.
sulfur dioxide emission
Sulfur dioxide is produced mainly by coal-fired thermal power plants and smelters that refine ores with high sulfur content.
fossil fuel
The use of fossil fuels by motor vehicles and industry triggers emissions of sulfur dioxide and nitrogen oxides.
watercourse
Natural flow of water that varies in volume, depending on the ground slope and the number of tributaries.
leaching
Acid rain robs the soil of nutri
that are indispensable to plant
such as magnesium, calcium
potassium.
soil
Surface layer of the Earth's crust; it results from the alteration of bedrock and the decomposition of organic matter.
water table
Vast expanse of underground water fed by rainwater filtering through the earth; it supplies springs and can be collected in wells.
lake acidification
It causes plankton depletion and creates an imbalance in the food chain, sometimes leading to the total disappearance of plant and animal life.

selective sorting of waste

Its goal is to extract recyclable material from trash.

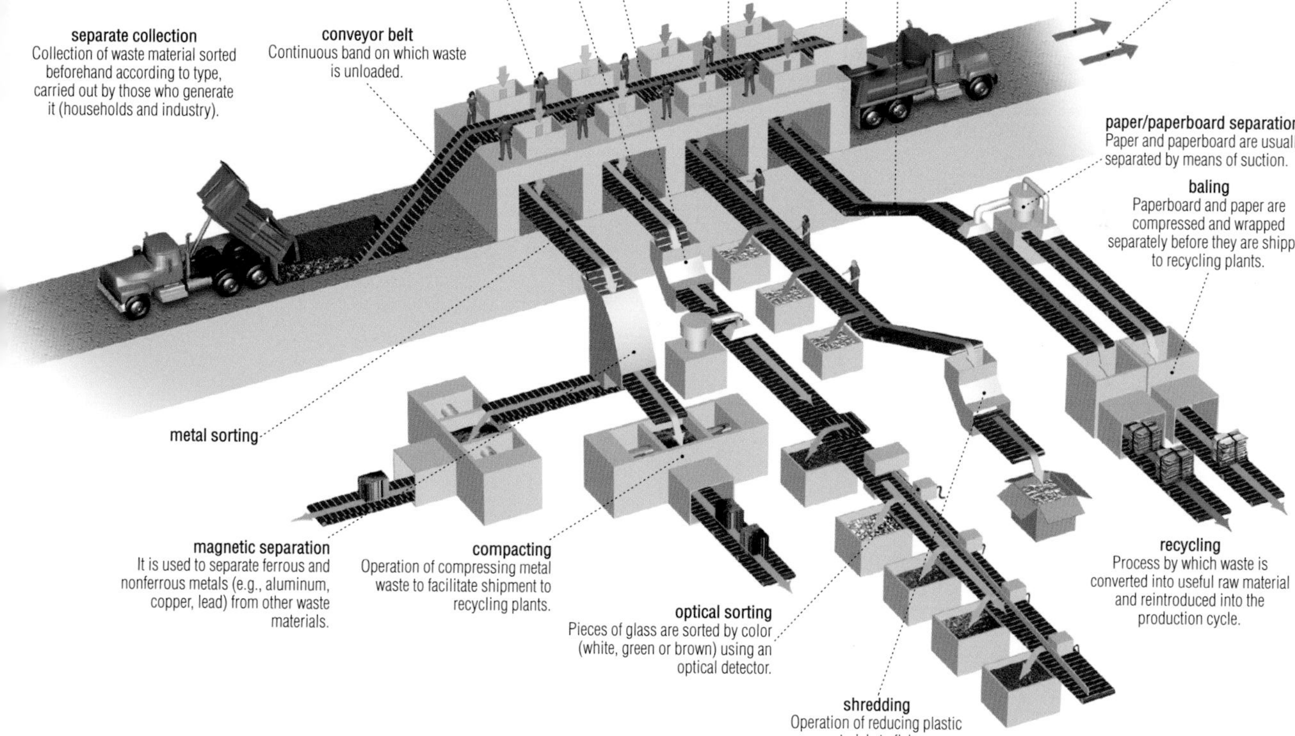
sorting plant
Facility that receives and sorts recyclable material and then delivers it to a recycling center.
crusher
paper/paperboard sorting
glass sorting
nonreusable residue waste
Waste that cannot be converted into useful matter for reintroduction into the production cycle.
burial
Operation of compressing waste into layers 7 to 10 feet thick, and then covering them with at least 6 in of earth.
incineration
Technique used to dispose of waste consisting of burning waste material until it is sterile; the gases released do not cause pollution.
manual sorting
plastics sorting
separate collection
Collection of waste material sorted beforehand according to type, carried out by those who generate it (households and industry).
conveyor belt
Continuous band on which waste is unloaded.
paper/paperboard separation
Paper and paperboard are usually separated by means of suction.
baling
Paperboard and paper are compressed and wrapped separately before they are shipped to recycling plants.
metal sorting
magnetic separation
It is used to separate ferrous and nonferrous metals (e.g., aluminum, copper, lead) from other waste materials.
compacting
Operation of compressing metal waste to facilitate shipment to recycling plants.
optical sorting
Pieces of glass are sorted by color (white, green or brown) using an optical detector.
recycling
Process by which waste is converted into useful raw material and reintroduced into the production cycle.
shredding
Operation of reducing plastic materials to flakes.

recycling containers
Containers used to collect specific types of recyclable waste material such as glass, plastic, metal and waste oil.

paper recycling container
High-volume container used by the tenants of a building to dispose of paper (e.g., newspapers, packaging).

glass recycling container
High-volume container used by the tenants of a building to dispose of glass.

aluminum recycling container
High-volume container used by the tenants of a building to dispose of metal containers.

paper collection unit
High-volume public container used by the citizens of a community to dispose of paper (e.g., newspapers, packaging).

glass collection unit
High-volume public container used by the citizens of a community to dispose of glass containers.

recycling bin
Small-volume household container used to collect recyclable household waste.

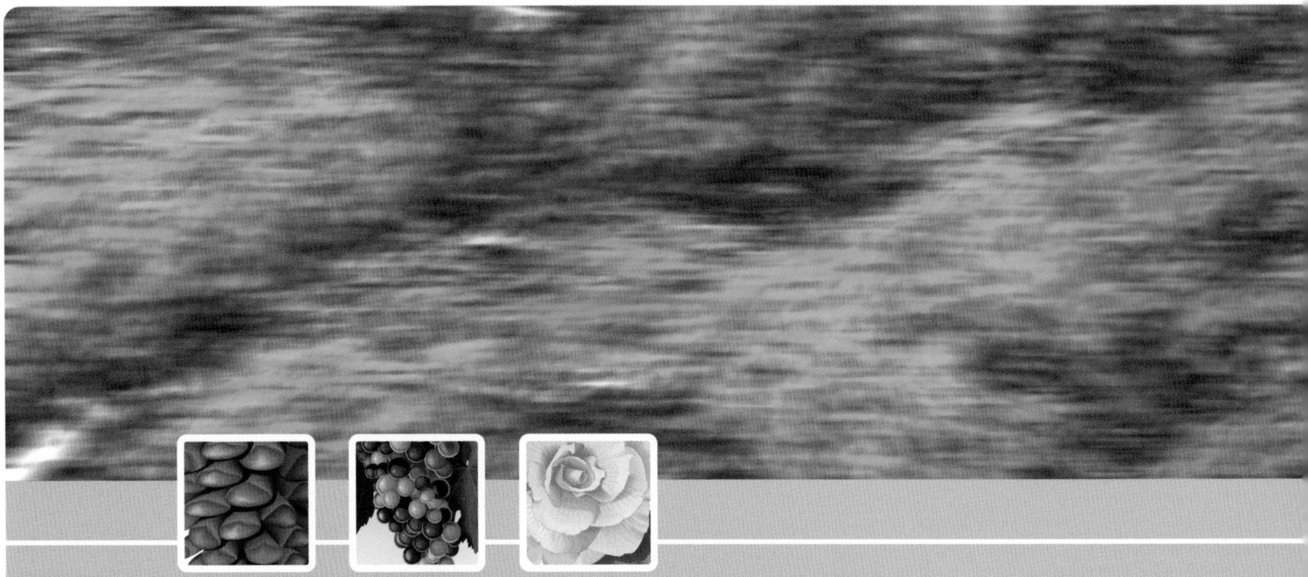

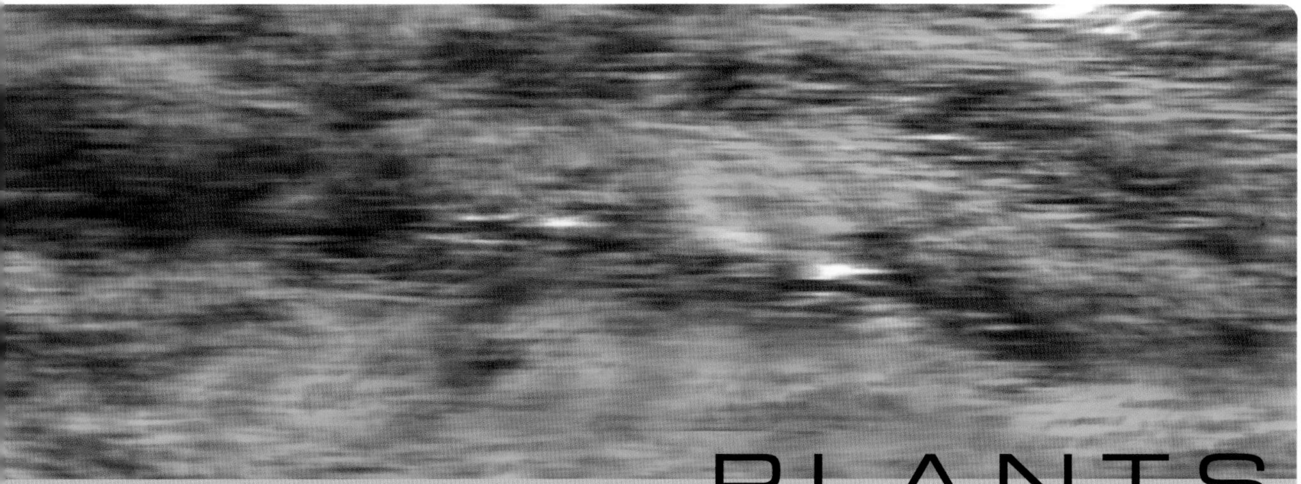

PLANTS

Classification of all living things deriving their nourishment from photosynthesis and lacking locomotive movement; the branch of knowledge associated with them.

plant cell

Smallest living structure and the constituent element of all vegetables; it varies in size and shape depending on its function.

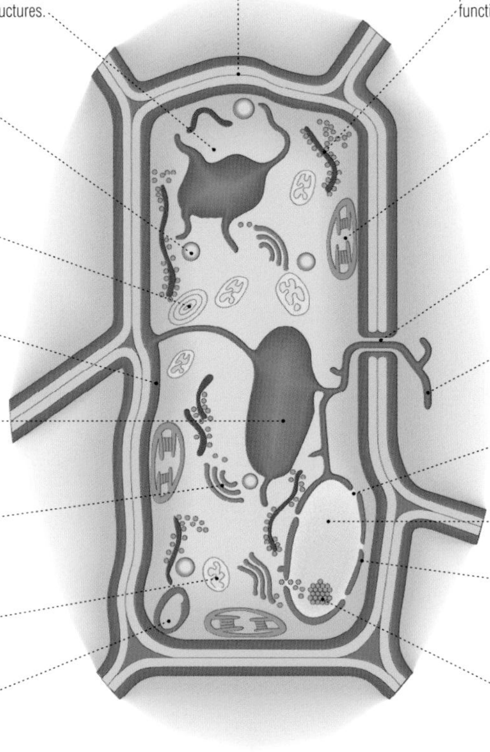
cell wall
Stiff exterior surface of the cytoplasmic membrane that gives the cell its shape.
cytoplasm
Clear gelatinous substance surrounding the various cellular structures.
ribosome
Small structure, occasionally attached to the endoplasmic reticulum; it generates proteins essential to the formation and functioning of living things.
lipid droplet
Small sac filled with essential fatty acids that are produced by the cell and stored for food.
chloroplast
Small structure, containing a green pigment called chlorophyll, which absorbs solar energy and uses it to produce glucose, the vegetable's food.
starch granule
Concentric layers of starch produced by the cell and stored for food.
plasmodesma
Perforations in the membranes allowing two adjacent cells to exchange cytoplasm.
cell membrane
Casing that covers the cell's cytoplasm; it acts as a filter, controlling the passage of certain substances in and out of the cell.
endoplasmic reticulum
Interconnecting tubes allowing substances to be transported within the cell or between the cell and its exterior environment.
vacuole
Spherical cavity containing water, waste and various substances required by the cell.
pore
Perforations in the nuclear envelope allowing for exchanges between the cytoplasm and the nucleus.
Golgi apparatus
Organelle composed of a series of pockets that receive proteins produced by the ribosomes and either transport them outside the cell or to other organelles.
nucleus
Organelle containing a cell's genes and controlling its activities.
mitochondrion
Ovoid organelle that produces the energy necessary for cell activity.
nuclear envelope
A double-layered membrane enveloping the nucleus.
leucoplast
Small colorless structure that produces and stores starch, the vegetable's food.
nucleolus
Small spherical body located inside the nucleus, within which the ribosomes, or protein-synthesizing structures, are produced.

lichen

Vegetable formed from the symbiotic association of an alga and a fungus.

structure of a lichen

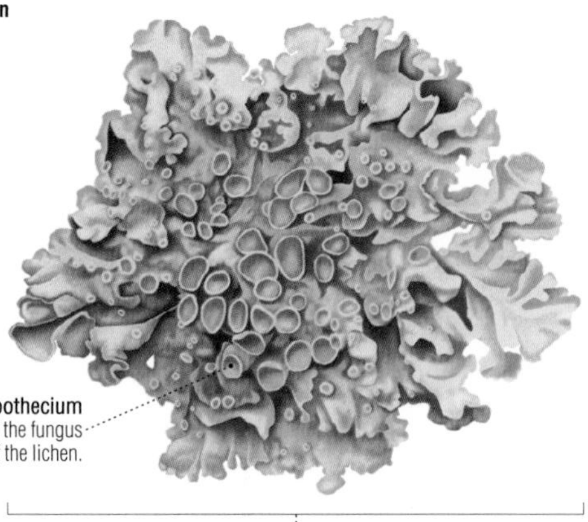
apothecium
Reproductive organ of the fungus that is a part of the lichen.
thallus
Lichen's main structure formed by the imbrication of fungal filaments and alga cells.

examples of lichens

There are more than 20,000 species of lichen, found growing out of the soil, on tree trunks or on rocks; they grow in all climatic zones.

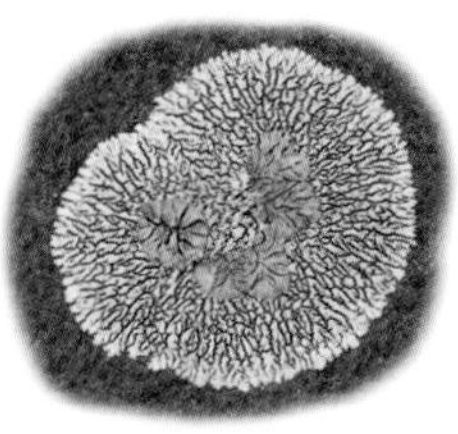

crustose lichen
Lichen whose thallus forms a crust that is firmly attached to its substrate.

fruticose lichen
Lichen whose thallus resembles a small tree; it is attached to its substrate at a single point.

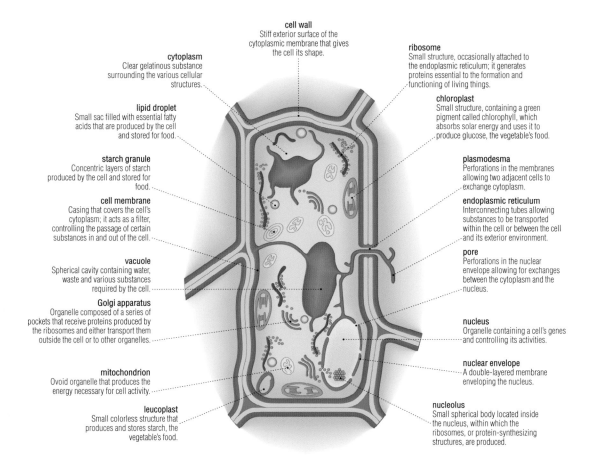

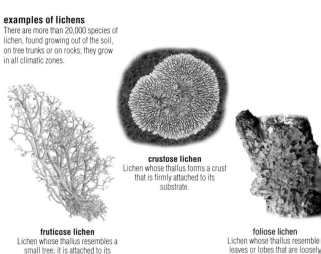

foliose lichen
Lichen whose thallus resemble leaves or lobes that are loosely attached to their substrate and c be easily removed.

moss

Flowerless vegetable, usually small in size, that grows in large tightly packed tufts to create a veritable soft carpet.

structure of a moss

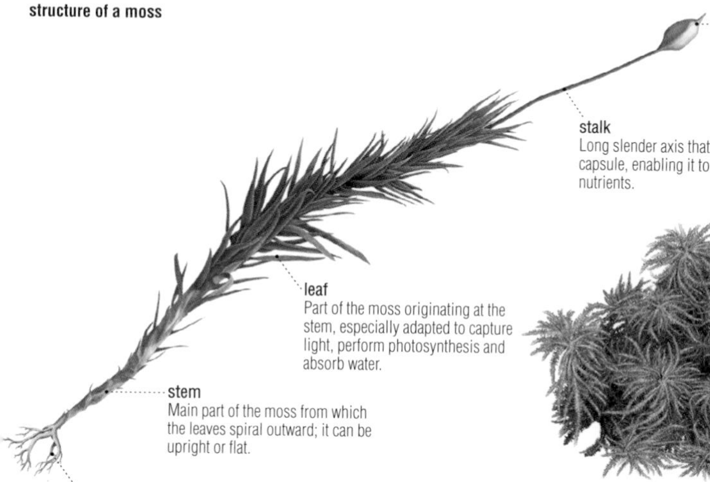

capsule
Hollow structure that manufactures spores, small seeds used in reproduction; it has a cover that opens to release the mature spores.

stalk
Long slender axis that supports the capsule, enabling it to absorb nutrients.

leaf
Part of the moss originating at the stem, especially adapted to capture light, perform photosynthesis and absorb water.

stem
Main part of the moss from which the leaves spiral outward; it can be upright or flat.

rhizoid
Rootlike filament enabling the moss to anchor itself to its substrate and absorb water and mineral salts.

examples of mosses
There are more than 13,000 species of moss; they generally grow in damp soil, on rocks or tree trunks and occasionally in fresh water.

prickly sphagnum
Bog moss that has no rhizoid and rarely bears a capsule; it has a high water content and its decomposition helps to form peat.

common hair cap moss
Ground moss with an erect stem and stiff leaves that grows in tufts, mostly in wooded areas; the capsule emerges from the end of a very long stalk.

alga

Flowerless vegetable that usually lives in aquatic environments; it produces oxygen and is at the base of the food chain.

structure of an alga

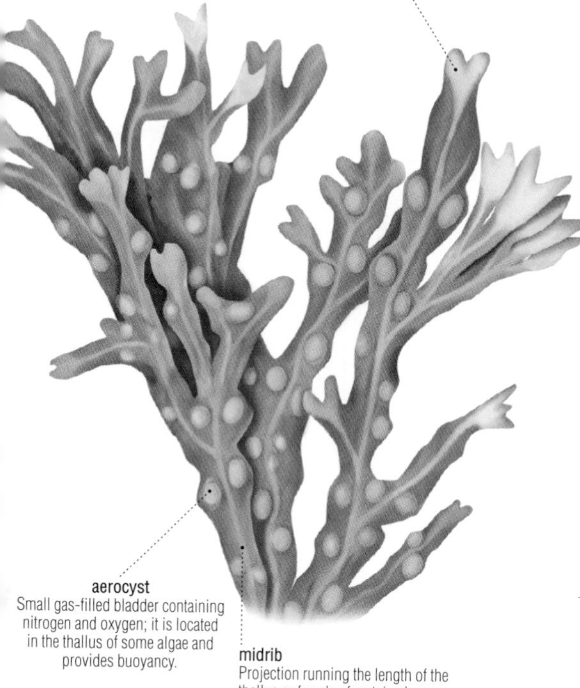

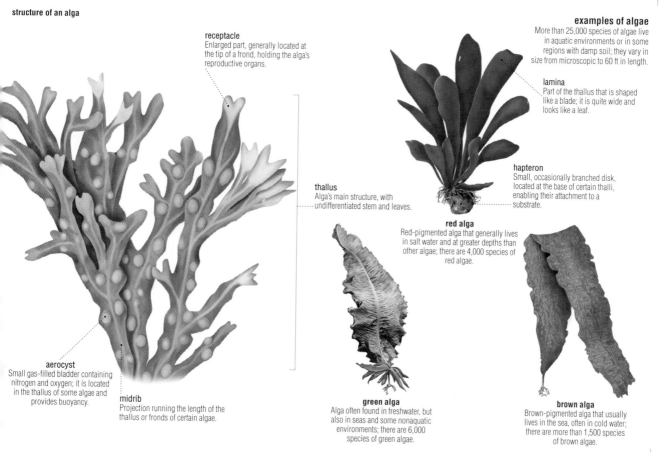

receptacle
Enlarged part, generally located at the tip of a frond, holding the alga's reproductive organs.

thallus
Alga's main structure, with undifferentiated stem and leaves.

aerocyst
Small gas-filled bladder containing nitrogen and oxygen; it is located in the thallus of some algae and provides buoyancy.

midrib
Projection running the length of the thallus or fronds of certain algae.

examples of algae
More than 25,000 species of algae live in aquatic environments or in some regions with damp soil; they vary in size from microscopic to 60 ft in length.

lamina
Part of the thallus that is shaped like a blade; it is quite wide and looks like a leaf.

hapteron
Small, occasionally branched disk, located at the base of certain thalli, enabling their attachment to a substrate.

red alga
Red-pigmented alga that generally lives in salt water and at greater depths than other algae; there are 4,000 species of red algae.

green alga
Alga often found in freshwater, but also in seas and some nonaquatic environments; there are 6,000 species of green algae.

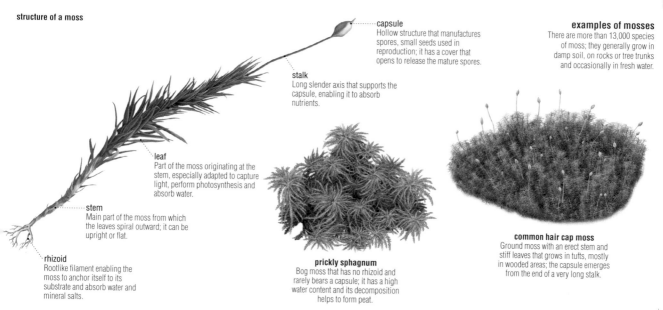

brown alga
Brown-pigmented alga that usually lives in the sea, often in cold water; there are more than 1,500 species of brown algae.

mushroom

Organism that exists parasitically or symbiotically with other living things or grows on dead organic matter.

structure of a mushroom
The mushroom is composed of an underground part (mycelium) and an aboveground, often edible part that is also the reproductive organ.

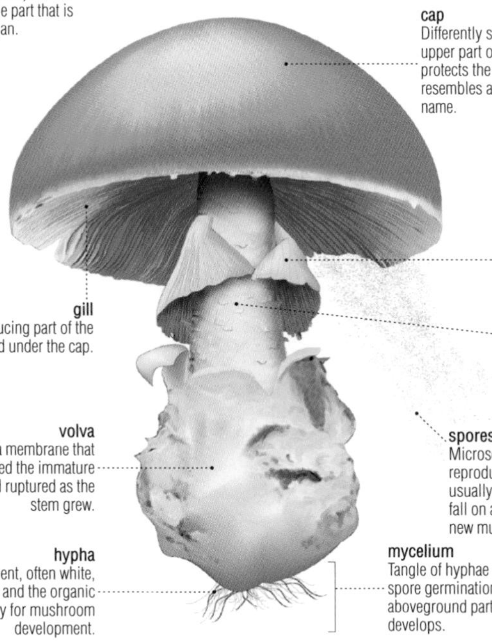

cap
Differently shaped and colored upper part of the mushroom that protects the gills; it usually resembles a headdress, hence its name.

ring
Membrane located under the cap and circling the stem; remnant of a membrane that covered the gills of the immature mushroom and ruptured as the cap grew.

gill
Fertile spore-producing part of the mushroom, located under the cap.

stem
Axis supporting the mushroom's cap.

volva
Remnant of a membrane that completely covered the immature mushroom and ruptured as the stem grew.

spores
Microscopic seeds acting as reproductive agents; they are usually released into the air and fall on a substrate to produce a new mushroom.

hypha
Microscopic filament, often white, that draws water and the organic matter necessary for mushroom development.

mycelium
Tangle of hyphae created through spore germination, from which the aboveground part of the mushroom develops.

deadly poisonous mushroom
Mushroom containing a toxin that, following contact or ingestion, produces serious effects on humans, generally resulting in death.

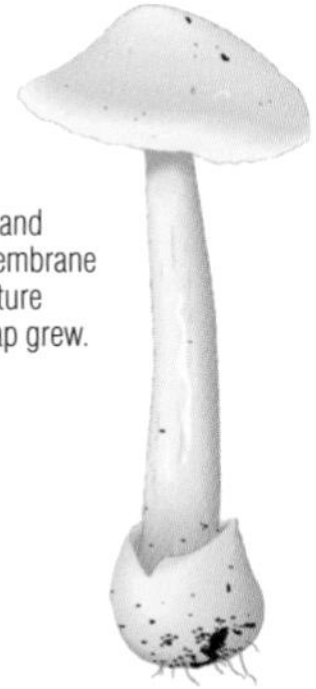

destroying angel
White ground mushroom with an unpleasant smell, growing in wooded areas; the effects of its often-deadly toxin act in a delayed manner, mainly attacking the liver.

poisonous mushroom
Mushroom containing a toxin that, following contact or ingestion, produces a range of usually nonfatal effects on humans.

fly agaric
The cap of this woodland mushroom i covered with white warts; its toxin primarily attacks the nervous system, causing hallucinations, among other symptoms.

fern

Flowerless vegetable that grows mainly in the tropics; it also grows in temperate climates in rich damp soil.

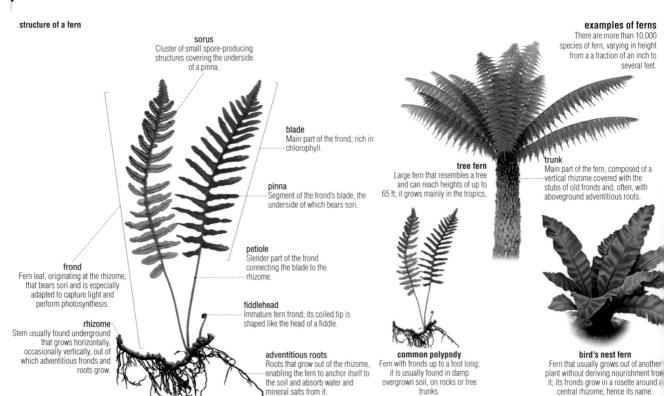

structure of a fern

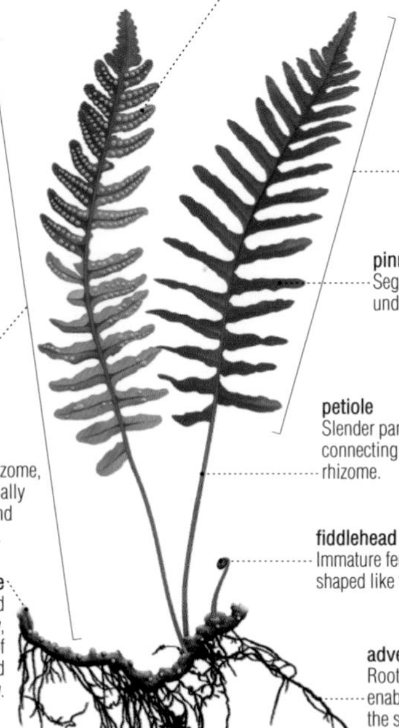

sorus
Cluster of small spore-producing structures covering the underside of a pinna.

blade
Main part of the frond, rich in chlorophyll.

pinna
Segment of the frond's blade, the underside of which bears sori.

petiole
Slender part of the frond connecting the blade to the rhizome.

frond
Fern leaf, originating at the rhizome, that bears sori and is especially adapted to capture light and perform photosynthesis.

fiddlehead
Immature fern frond; its coiled tip is shaped like the head of a fiddle.

rhizome
Stem usually found underground that grows horizontally, occasionally vertically, out of which adventitious fronds and roots grow.

adventitious roots
Roots that grow out of the rhizome, enabling the fern to anchor itself to the soil and absorb water and mineral salts from it.

examples of ferns
There are more than 10,000 species of fern, varying in height from a a fraction of an inch to several feet.

tree fern
Large fern that resembles a tree and can reach heights of up to 65 ft; it grows mainly in the tropics.

trunk
Main part of the fern, composed of a vertical rhizome covered with the stubs of old fronds and, often, with aboveground adventitious roots.

common polypody
Fern with fronds up to a foot long; it is usually found in damp overgrown soil, on rocks or tree trunks.

bird's nest fern
Fern that usually grows out of another plant without deriving nourishment fro it; its fronds grow in a rosette around a central rhizome, hence its name.

plant

Vegetable rooted in the soil, the upper part of which grows aboveground or in freshwater; it produces oxygen and is at the bottom of the food chain.

structure of a plant

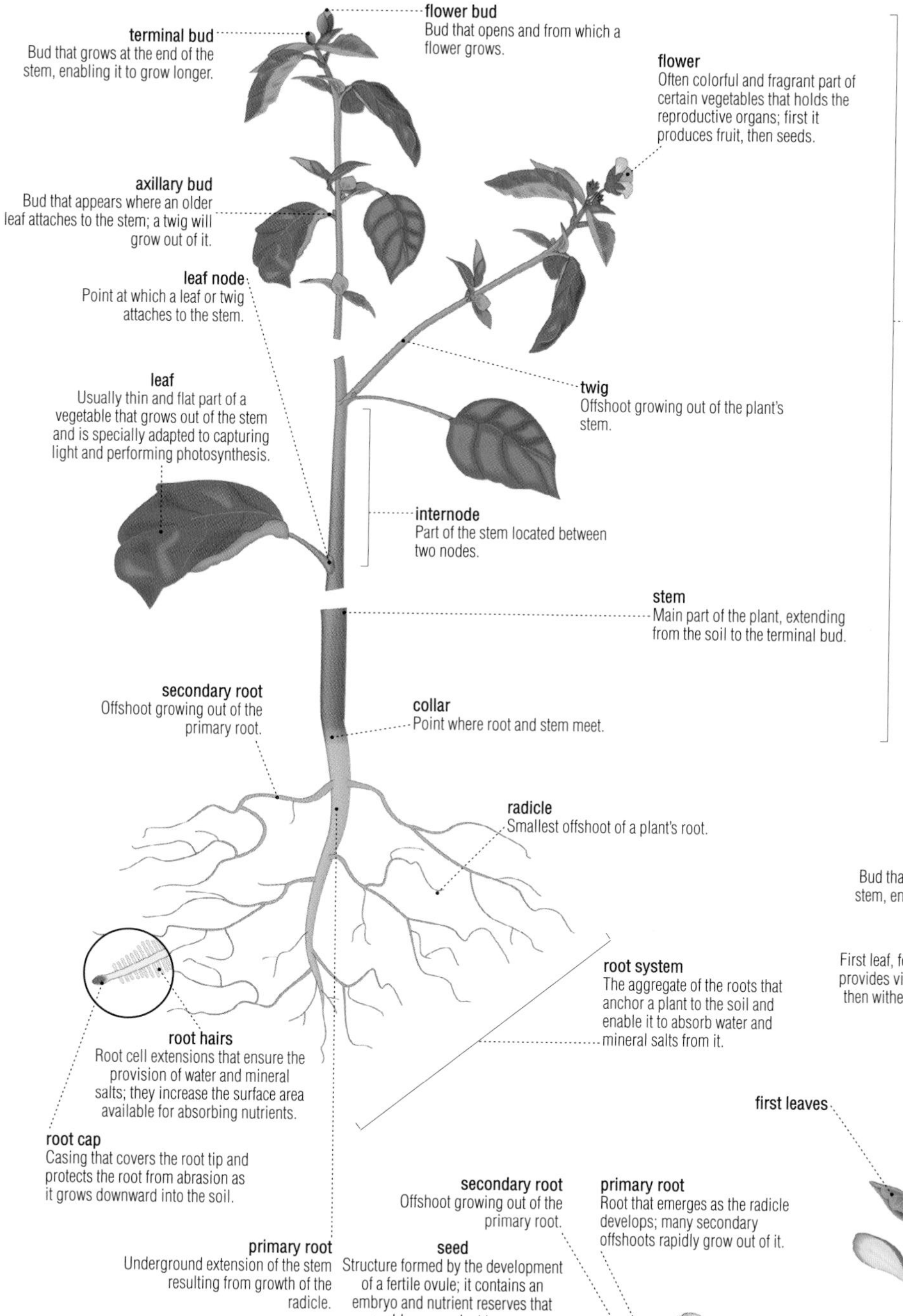
terminal bud
Bud that grows at the end of the stem, enabling it to grow longer.
flower bud
Bud that opens and from which a flower grows.
flower
Often colorful and fragrant part of certain vegetables that holds the reproductive organs; first it produces fruit, then seeds.
axillary bud
Bud that appears where an older leaf attaches to the stem; a twig will grow out of it.
leaf node
Point at which a leaf or twig attaches to the stem.
shoot
Seedling originating from a seed within the current year.
leaf
Usually thin and flat part of a vegetable that grows out of the stem and is specially adapted to capturing light and performing photosynthesis.
twig
Offshoot growing out of the plant's stem.
internode
Part of the stem located between two nodes.
stem
Main part of the plant, extending from the soil to the terminal bud.
secondary root
Offshoot growing out of the primary root.
collar
Point where root and stem meet.
radicle
Smallest offshoot of a plant's root.
root system
The aggregate of the roots that anchor a plant to the soil and enable it to absorb water and mineral salts from it.
root hairs
Root cell extensions that ensure the provision of water and mineral salts; they increase the surface area available for absorbing nutrients.
root cap
Casing that covers the root tip and protects the root from abrasion as it grows downward into the soil.
primary root
Underground extension of the stem resulting from growth of the radicle.

germination
Phenomenon by which, given favorable conditions, a seed will develop and grow into a plant.

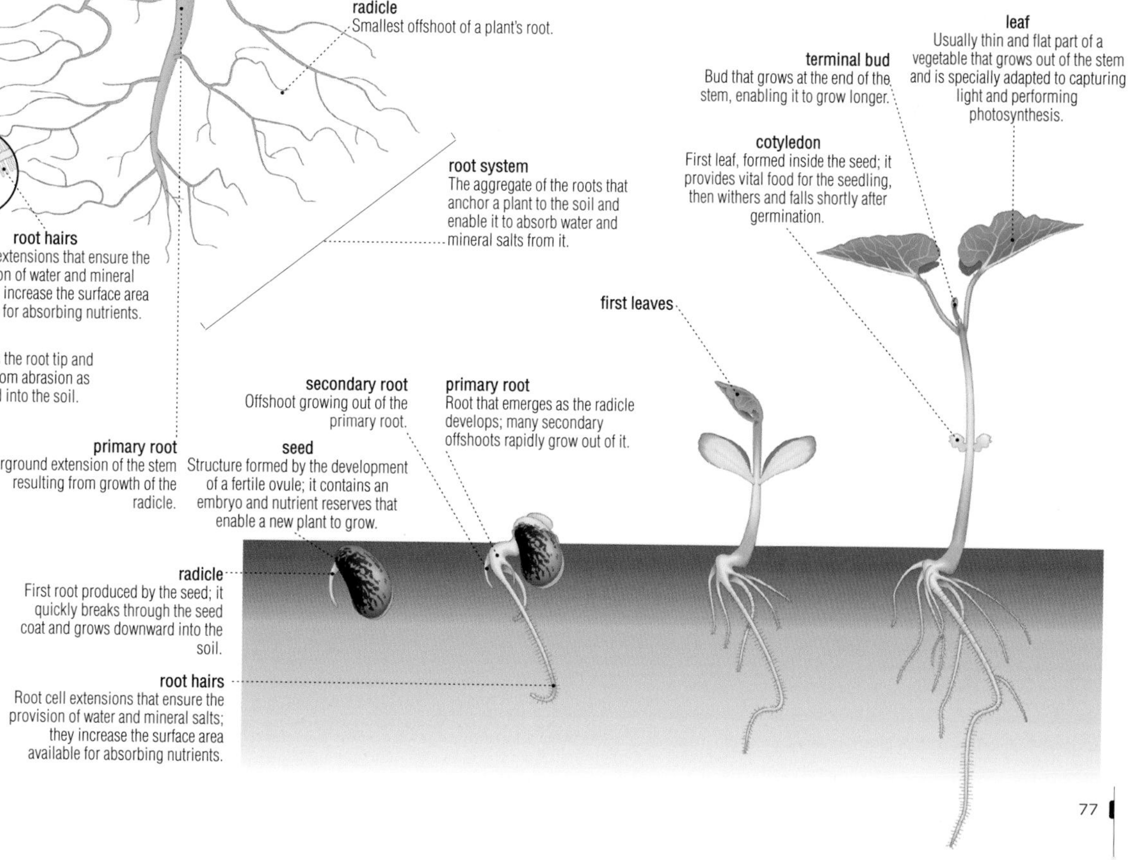
leaf
Usually thin and flat part of a vegetable that grows out of the stem and is specially adapted to capturing light and performing photosynthesis.
terminal bud
Bud that grows at the end of the stem, enabling it to grow longer.
cotyledon
First leaf, formed inside the seed; it provides vital food for the seedling, then withers and falls shortly after germination.
first leaves
secondary root
Offshoot growing out of the primary root.
primary root
Root that emerges as the radicle develops; many secondary offshoots rapidly grow out of it.
seed
Structure formed by the development of a fertile ovule; it contains an embryo and nutrient reserves that enable a new plant to grow.
radicle
First root produced by the seed; it quickly breaks through the seed coat and grows downward into the soil.
root hairs
Root cell extensions that ensure the provision of water and mineral salts; they increase the surface area available for absorbing nutrients.

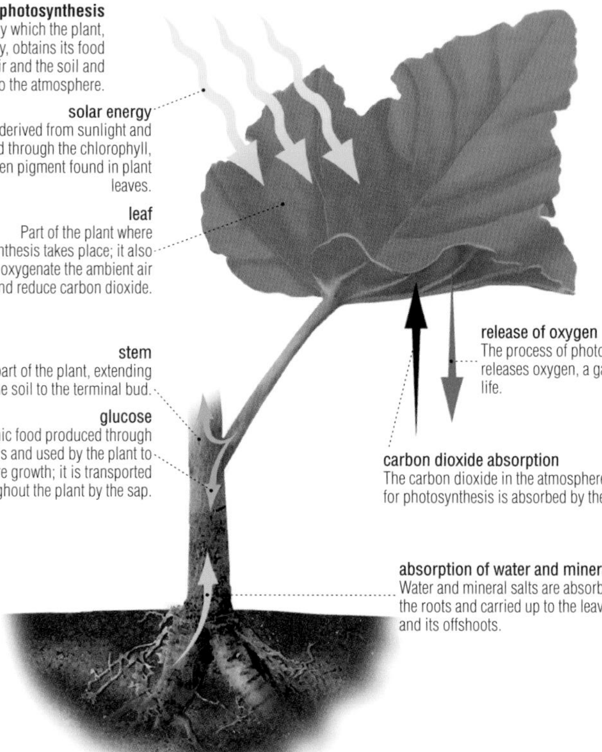

photosynthesis
Phenomenon by which the plant, helped by solar energy, obtains its food (glucose) from the air and the soil and releases oxygen into the atmosphere.

solar energy
Energy derived from sunlight and absorbed through the chlorophyll, the green pigment found in plant leaves.

leaf
Part of the plant where photosynthesis takes place; it also helps oxygenate the ambient air and reduce carbon dioxide.

release of oxygen
The process of photosynthesis releases oxygen, a gas essentia life.

stem
Main part of the plant, extending from the soil to the terminal bud.

glucose
Organic food produced through photosynthesis and used by the plant to ensure growth; it is transported throughout the plant by the sap.

carbon dioxide absorption
The carbon dioxide in the atmosphere required for photosynthesis is absorbed by the leaf.

absorption of water and mineral salts
Water and mineral salts are absorbed througl the roots and carried up to the leaves by the s and its offshoots.

soil profile
Soil usually has four main layers; it varies in total thickness from several inches to several feet, depending on the area.

plant litter
Upper layer of soil, composed of recently fallen animal and vegetable scraps or those in the early stages of decomposition.

topsoil
Second layer of soil, dark in color and rich in organic matter; it contains almost all of the soil's animal and vegetable life.

subsoil
Third layer of soil to which the roots extend; contains little organic matter but many nutrients leached from the topsoil.

bedrock
Rock that forms the bottom layer of soil; its physical and chemical breakdown enables the upper layers to develop.

section of a bulb
Bulb: underground structure of certain plants where nutrients are stored; it ensures seasonal regrowth of the aboveground part of the plant.

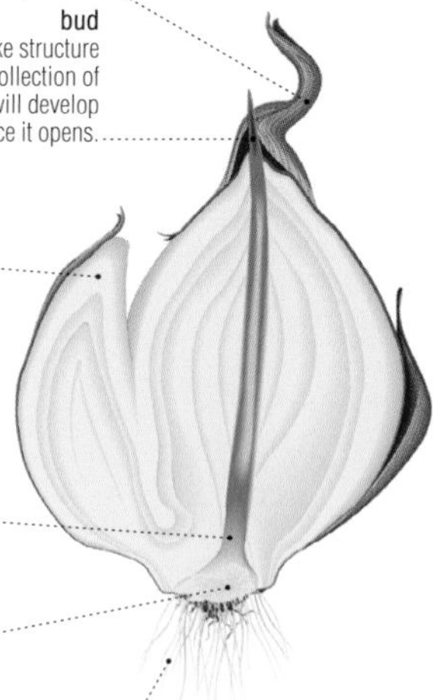

scale leaf
Bulb's external casing; it is made of layered papery leaves.

bud
Small plantlike structure constituting a collection of immature organs that will develop once it opens.

fleshy leaf
Nutrient-rich leaf underneath the scale leaf.

bulbet
A secondary bulb that develops from a bud growing out of the side of the main bulb; it can break away and grow into a new plant.

underground stem
Main part of the bulb extending from the base to the bud and protected by fleshy leaves.

base
Round part located at the bulb's base from which the stem, roots and fleshy leaves grow.

root
Underground structure that anchors the plant to the soil and enables the plant to absorb water and mineral salts.

Usually thin and flat part of a vegetable that grows out of the stem and is specially adapted to capturing light and performing photosynthesis.

simple leaves

Leaves with an undivided blade; there are many types, grouped according to shape.

cordate
Simple leaf with a heart-shaped blade.

reniform
Simple leaf with a kidney-shaped blade.

orbiculate
Simple leaf with a somewhat rounded blade.

spatulate
Simple leaf in which the blade widens, taking the shape of a spatula.

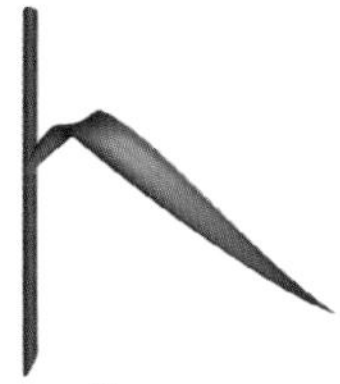

linear
Simple leaf with a long and very narrow blade and almost parallel margins.

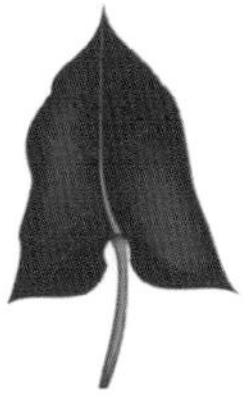

hastate
Simple leaf with a spear-shaped blade.

ovate
Simple leaf with an egg-shaped blade.

lanceolate
Simple leaf with a narrow blade that is longer than it is wide, ending in a point.

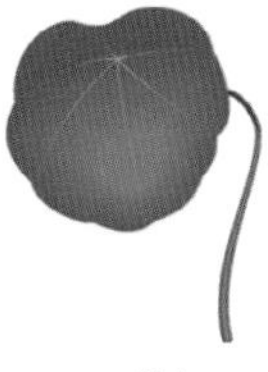

peltate
Simple leaf with a petiole attached perpendicularly to the center of the blade's underside.

structure of a leaf

tip
Apex of the leaf blade, at the opposite end from the part attached to the petiole; this part can vary markedly in shape.

vein
Branching of the midrib that carries sap to the various parts of the blade; it also functions as the leaf's skeleton.

blade
Main part of the leaf, rich in chlorophyll; it can vary markedly in shape, depending on the type of rib and size of indentation.

margin
Part that forms the outline of the leaf blade.

midrib
Hollow projection that extends the petiole into the blade and carries sap; it forms the basis of the leaf's skeleton.

petiole
Narrow part of the leaf connecting the blade to the stem.

stipule
Small outgrowth at the base of the petiole in certain leaves.

sheath
Distension of the petiole, partly or completely surrounding the stem.

leaf axil
Point at which the petiole attaches to the stem node.

leaf margin

Leaf edges vary markedly, depending on the shape and depth of their indentations.

dentate
Leaf edged with pointy teeth of similar size.

doubly dentate
Leaf edged with teeth of different sizes, the main tooth often having smaller teeth.

crenate
Leaf edge with rounded teeth.

ciliate
Leaf edge surrounded by short thin hairs called cilia.

entire
Leaf edge with no indentations.

lobate
Leaf edge indented with deep notches.

compound leaves

Leaves with blades divided into several distinct sections, called folioles, the arrangement of which determines the leaf type.

trifoliolate
Leaf having three distinct folioles.

pinnatifid
Compound leaf with folioles on both sides of a common petiole.

palmate
Compound leaf with all its folioles attached at the same point, at the apex of the petiole.

abruptly pinnate
Compound feathered leaf ending in two folioles on each side of the main petiole.

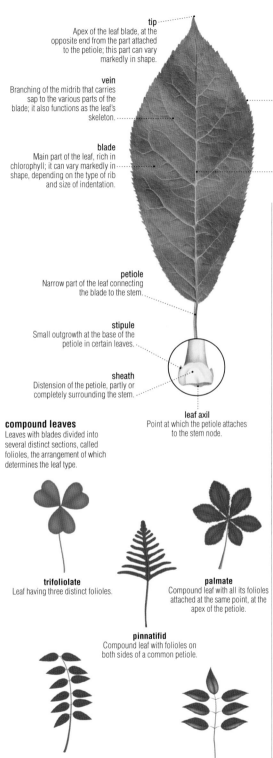

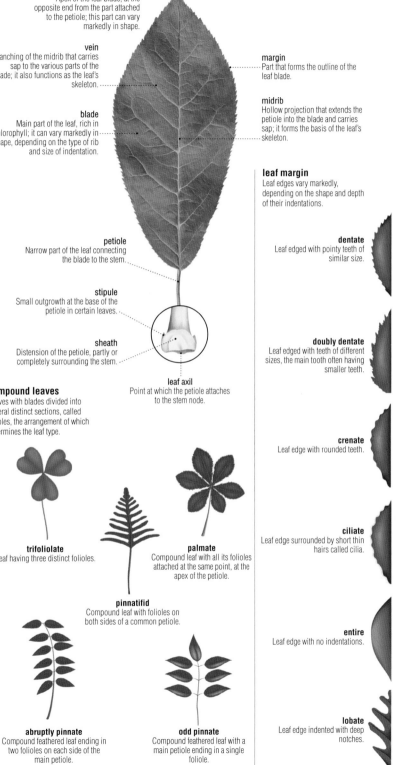

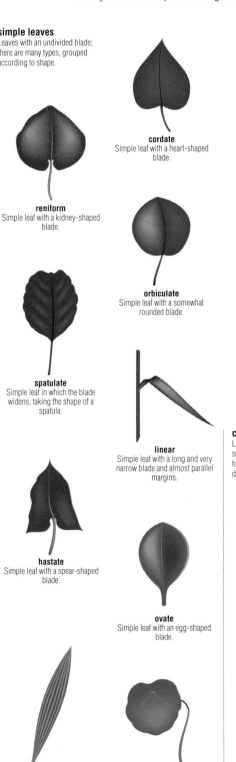

odd pinnate
Compound feathered leaf with a main petiole ending in a single foliole.

flower

Often colorful and fragrant part of certain vegetables that holds the reproductive organs; first it produces fruit, then seeds.

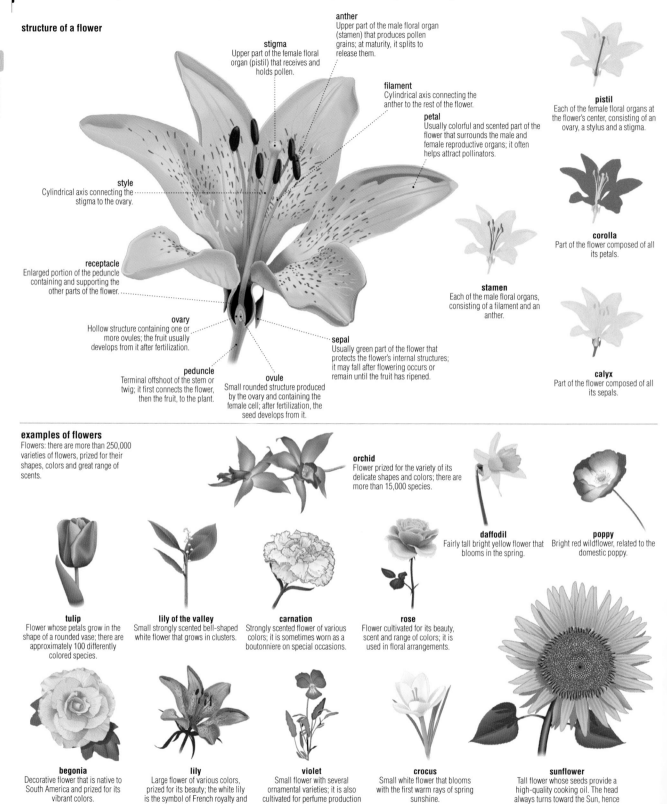

structure of a flower

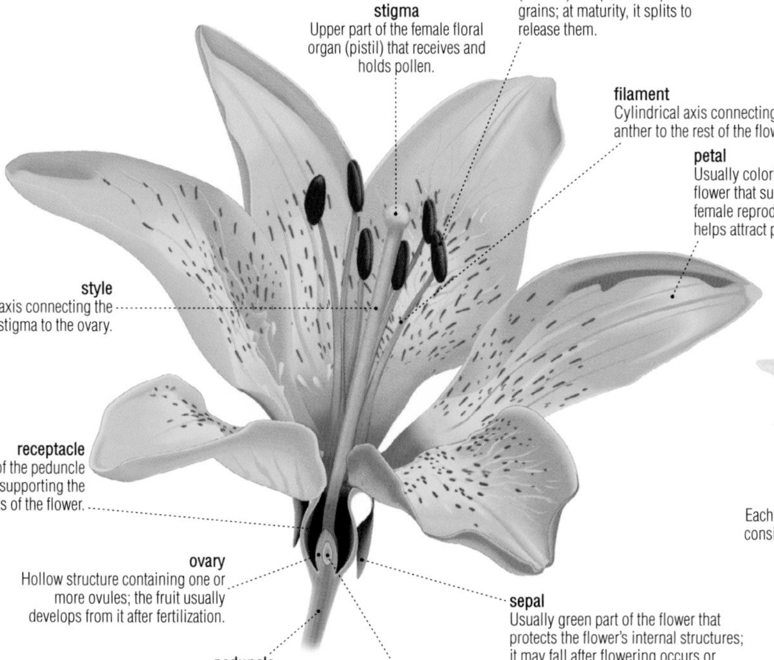

anther
Upper part of the male floral organ (stamen) that produces pollen grains; at maturity, it splits to release them.

stigma
Upper part of the female floral organ (pistil) that receives and holds pollen.

filament
Cylindrical axis connecting the anther to the rest of the flower.

petal
Usually colorful and scented part of the flower that surrounds the male and female reproductive organs; it often helps attract pollinators.

style
Cylindrical axis connecting the stigma to the ovary.

receptacle
Enlarged portion of the peduncle containing and supporting the other parts of the flower.

ovary
Hollow structure containing one or more ovules; the fruit usually develops from it after fertilization.

sepal
Usually green part of the flower that protects the flower's internal structures; it may fall after flowering occurs or remain until the fruit has ripened.

peduncle
Terminal offshoot of the stem or twig; it first connects the flower, then the fruit, to the plant.

ovule
Small rounded structure produced by the ovary and containing the female cell; after fertilization, the seed develops from it.

pistil
Each of the female floral organs at the flower's center, consisting of an ovary, a stylus and a stigma.

corolla
Part of the flower composed of all its petals.

stamen
Each of the male floral organs, consisting of a filament and an anther.

calyx
Part of the flower composed of all its sepals.

examples of flowers

Flowers: there are more than 250,000 varieties of flowers, prized for their shapes, colors and great range of scents.

orchid
Flower prized for the variety of its delicate shapes and colors; there are more than 15,000 species.

daffodil
Fairly tall bright yellow flower that blooms in the spring.

poppy
Bright red wildflower, related to the domestic poppy.

tulip
Flower whose petals grow in the shape of a rounded vase; there are approximately 100 differently colored species.

lily of the valley
Small strongly scented bell-shaped white flower that grows in clusters.

carnation
Strongly scented flower of various colors; it is sometimes worn as a boutonniere on special occasions.

rose
Flower cultivated for its beauty, scent and range of colors; it is used in floral arrangements.

begonia
Decorative flower that is native to South America and prized for its vibrant colors.

lily
Large flower of various colors, prized for its beauty; the white lily is the symbol of French royalty and the emblem of Quebec.

violet
Small flower with several ornamental varieties; it is also cultivated for perfume production and cooking.

crocus
Small white flower that blooms with the first warm rays of spring sunshine.

sunflower
Tall flower whose seeds provide a high-quality cooking oil. The head always turns toward the Sun, hence its name.

types of inflorescences

Inflorescence: the arrangement of flowers on the stem or twig of a plant.

raceme
Inflorescence composed of a main axis and laterally borne flowers with pedicels of equal length.

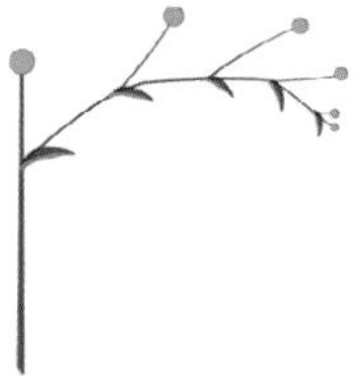

uniparous cyme
Inflorescence whose main axis ends in a flower under which a single lateral twig develops; the process is repeated under each terminal flower.

umbel
Inflorescence composed of a main axis and laterally borne flowers with pedicels of equal length, all originating from the same point.

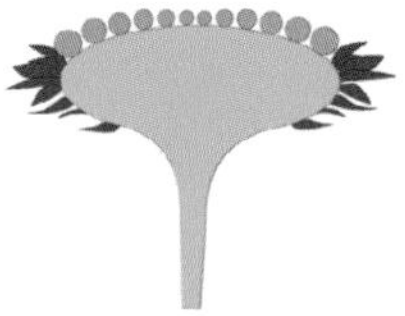

capitulum
Inflorescence composed of flowers with no pedicel, all embedded in a flat receptacle.

spike
Inflorescence composed of a main axis and laterally borne flowers with no pedicel.

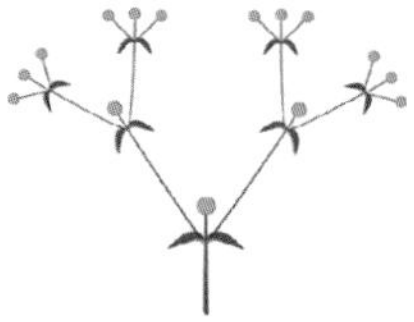

biparous cyme
Inflorescence whose main axis ends in a flower under which two lateral twigs develop; the process is repeated under each terminal flower.

corymb
Inflorescence composed of a main axis and laterally borne flowers with pedicels of unequal length, all ending at the same height.

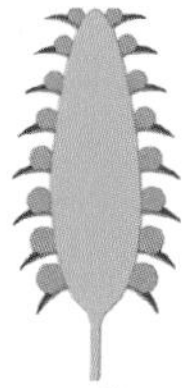

spadix
Inflorescence composed of flowers with no pedicel, all embedded in an elongated ovoid receptacle.

fruits

Vegetable structures usually resulting from the development of one or several floral ovaries that, once mature, contain seeds; they are often edible.

stone fleshy fruit

Fruit whose seed is surrounded by three distinct layers: an exocarp, a fleshy mesocarp and an extremely hard stone, or endocarp.

section of a peach

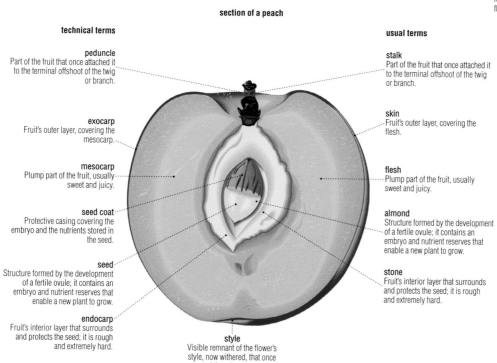

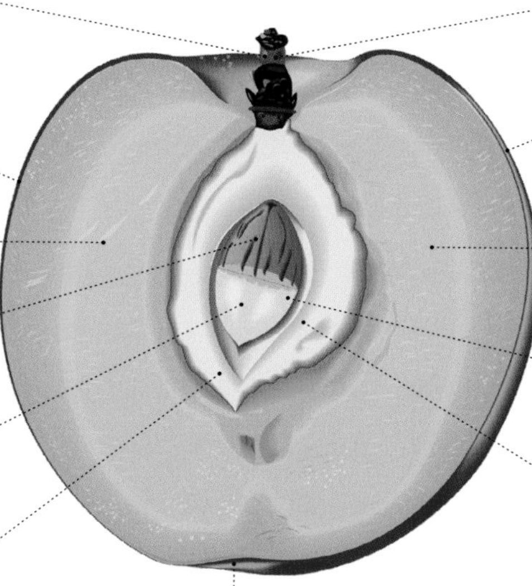

technical terms

peduncle
Part of the fruit that once attached it to the terminal offshoot of the twig or branch.

exocarp
Fruit's outer layer, covering the mesocarp.

mesocarp
Plump part of the fruit, usually sweet and juicy.

seed coat
Protective casing covering the embryo and the nutrients stored in the seed.

seed
Structure formed by the development of a fertile ovule; it contains an embryo and nutrient reserves that enable a new plant to grow.

endocarp
Fruit's interior layer that surrounds and protects the seed; it is rough and extremely hard.

style
Visible remnant of the flower's style, now withered, that once connected the stigma to the ovary.

usual terms

stalk
Part of the fruit that once attached it to the terminal offshoot of the twig or branch.

skin
Fruit's outer layer, covering the flesh.

flesh
Plump part of the fruit, usually sweet and juicy.

almond
Structure formed by the development of a fertile ovule; it contains an embryo and nutrient reserves that enable a new plant to grow.

stone
Fruit's interior layer that surrounds and protects the seed; it is rough and extremely hard.

pome fleshy fruit
Fruit with a seed, or pip, surrounded by three distinct layers: an exocarp, a fleshy mesocarp and a stiff endocarp containing loculi.

section of an apple

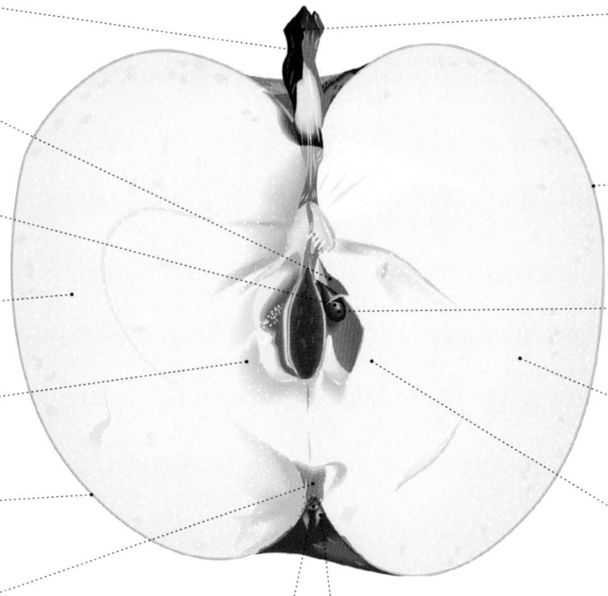
technical terms
peduncle
Part of the fruit that once attached it to the terminal offshoot of the twig or branch.
loculus
Small cavity located under the endocarp, usually containing two seeds.
seed
Structure formed by the development of a fertile ovule; it contains an embryo and nutrient reserves that enable a new plant to grow.
mesocarp
Plump part of the fruit, usually sweet and juicy.
endocarp
The stiff inner layer of the fruit, surrounding and protecting the seed and covering the loculi.
exocarp
Fruit's outer layer, covering the mesocarp.
style
Visible remnant of the flower's style, now withered, that once connected the stigma to the ovary.
stamen
Remnant of the flower's stamens, visible as small hairs in the center of the depression on the bottom of the fruit.
sepal
Remnant of the flower's sepal, visible as small flowers around a depression on the bottom of the fruit.
usual terms
stalk
Part of the fruit that once attached it to the terminal offshoot of the twig or branch.
skin
Fruit's outer layer, covering the flesh.
pip
Structure formed by the development of a fertile ovule; it contains an embryo and nutrient reserves that enable a new plant to grow.
flesh
Plump part of the fruit, usually sweet and juicy.
core
Central inedible part of the apple, comprising the endocarp, the loculi and the seeds within the loculi.

fleshy fruit: citrus fruit
Fruit composed of several segments, each one enclosing seeds that are in direct contact with the pulp.

section of an orange

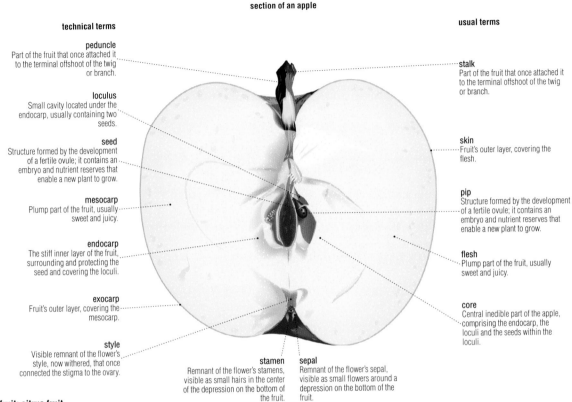

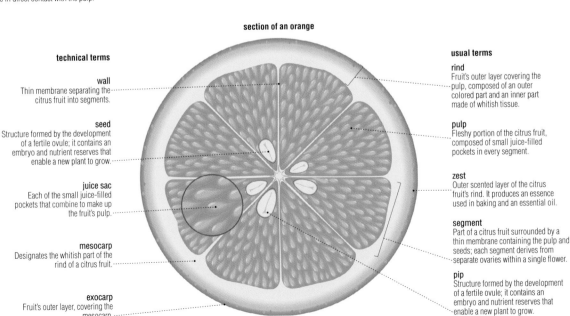

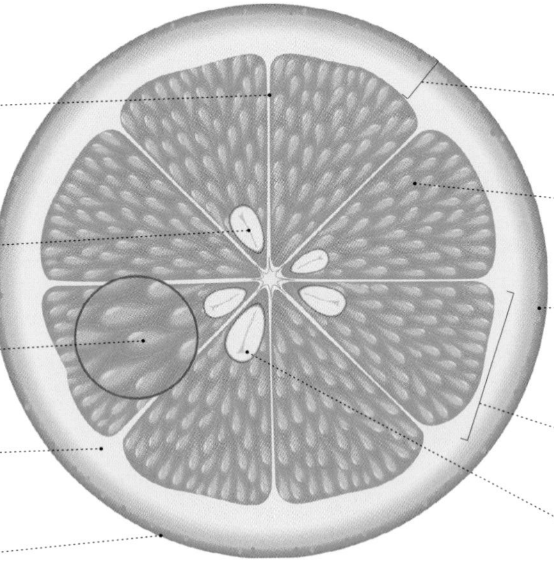
technical terms
wall
Thin membrane separating the citrus fruit into segments.
seed
Structure formed by the development of a fertile ovule; it contains an embryo and nutrient reserves that enable a new plant to grow.
juice sac
Each of the small juice-filled pockets that combine to make up the fruit's pulp.
mesocarp
Designates the whitish part of the rind of a citrus fruit.
exocarp
Fruit's outer layer, covering the mesocarp.
usual terms
rind
Fruit's outer layer covering the pulp, composed of an outer colored part and an inner part made of whitish tissue.
pulp
Fleshy portion of the citrus fruit, composed of small juice-filled pockets in every segment.
zest
Outer scented layer of the citrus fruit's rind. It produces an essence used in baking and an essential oil.
segment
Part of a citrus fruit surrounded by a thin membrane containing the pulp and seeds; each segment derives from separate ovaries within a single flower.
pip
Structure formed by the development of a fertile ovule; it contains an embryo and nutrient reserves that enable a new plant to grow.

fleshy fruit: berry fruit

Fruit in which the seed is surrounded by two distinct layers: an exocarp and a fleshy mesocarp that is in direct contact with the seed.

section of a grape

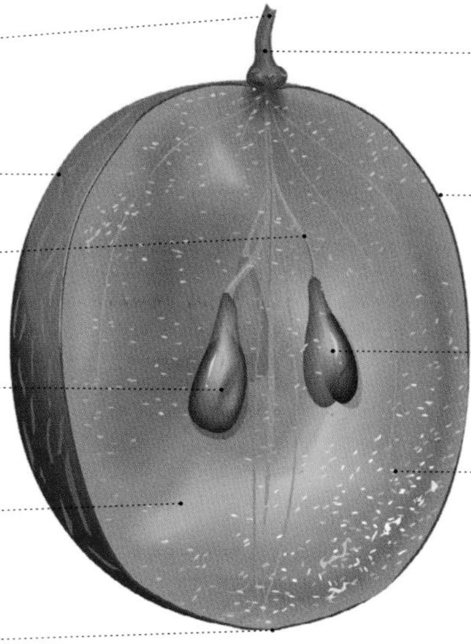

technical terms

pedicel
Part of the fruit that once connected it to the cluster's peduncle.

exocarp
Fruit's outer layer, covering the mesocarp.

funiculus
Slender strand that connects the seed to the grape's pedicel; it is used to transport food to the developing seed.

seed
Structure formed by the development of a fertile ovule; it contains an embryo and nutrient reserves that enable a new plant to grow.

mesocarp
Plump part of the fruit, usually sweet and juicy.

style
Visible remnant of the flower's style, now withered, that once connected the stigma to the ovary.

usual terms

stalk
Part of the fruit that once connected it to the cluster's peduncle.

skin
Fruit's outer layer, covering the flesh.

pip
Structure formed by the development of a fertile ovule; it contains an embryo and nutrient reserves that enable a new plant to grow.

flesh
Plump part of the fruit, usually sweet and juicy.

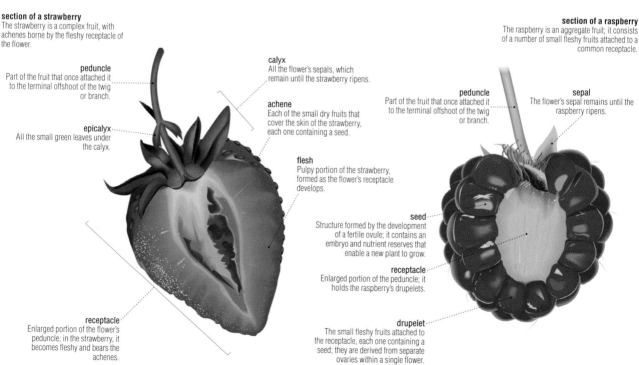

section of a strawberry

The strawberry is a complex fruit, with achenes borne by the fleshy receptacle of the flower.

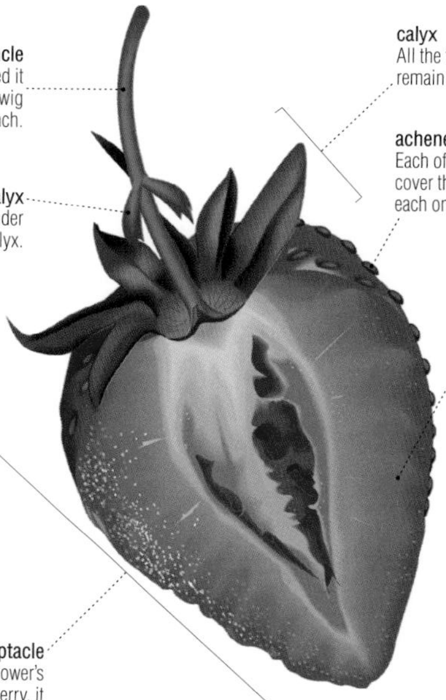

peduncle
Part of the fruit that once attached it to the terminal offshoot of the twig or branch.

epicalyx
All the small green leaves under the calyx.

calyx
All the flower's sepals, which remain until the strawberry ripens.

achene
Each of the small dry fruits that cover the skin of the strawberry, each one containing a seed.

flesh
Pulpy portion of the strawberry, formed as the flower's receptacle develops.

receptacle
Enlarged portion of the flower's peduncle; in the strawberry, it becomes fleshy and bears the achenes.

section of a raspberry

The raspberry is an aggregate fruit; it consists of a number of small fleshy fruits attached to a common receptacle.

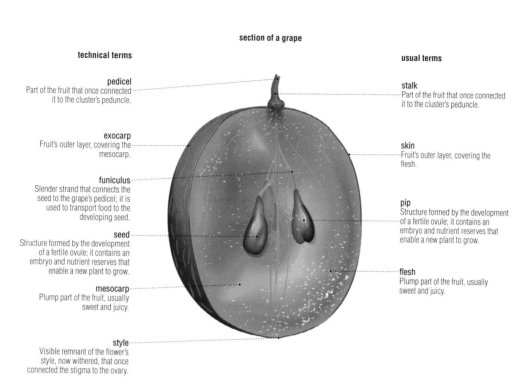

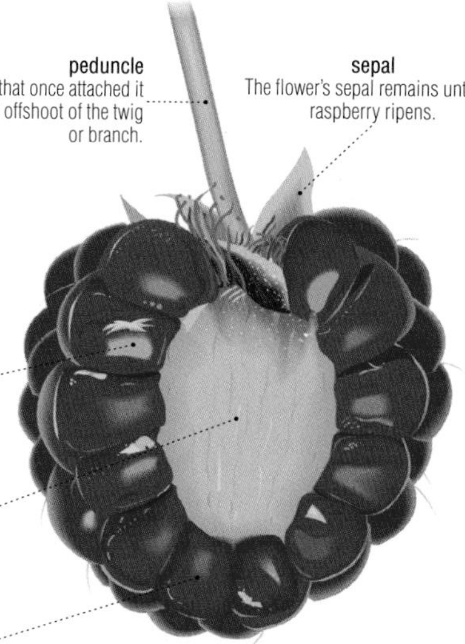

peduncle
Part of the fruit that once attached it to the terminal offshoot of the twig or branch.

sepal
The flower's sepal remains until the raspberry ripens.

seed
Structure formed by the development of a fertile ovule; it contains an embryo and nutrient reserves that enable a new plant to grow.

receptacle
Enlarged portion of the peduncle; it holds the raspberry's drupelets.

drupelet
The small fleshy fruits attached to the receptacle, each one containing a seed; they are derived from separate ovaries within a single flower.

dry fruits
Fruits with usually edible seeds, surrounded by a single dry, somewhat rigid layer.

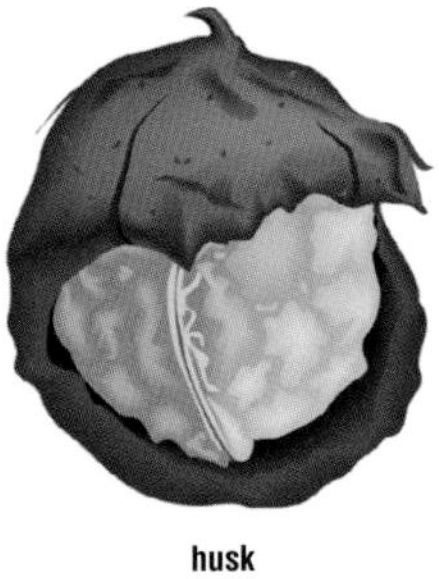

husk
Fleshy covering, first green then changing to brown, that protects the walnut shell. The husk is used to produce a stain that makes white wood look like walnut.

section of a follicle: star anise
Follicle: dry single-chambered fruit that, when ripe, splits along the suture of its casing.

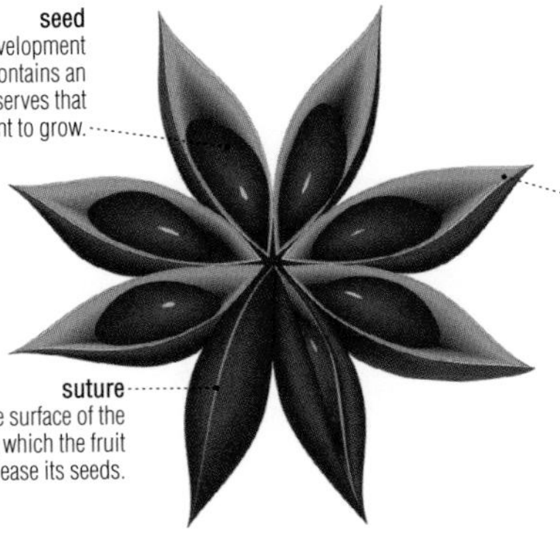

seed
Structure formed by the development of a fertile ovule; it contains an embryo and nutrient reserves that enable a new plant to grow.

follicle
Each of the eight dry fruits that make up the star anise.

suture
Visible seam on the surface of the fruit's casing, along which the fruit splits to release its seeds.

section of a silique: mustard
Silique: dry fruit with two valves that, when the fruit is ripe, split to release seeds.

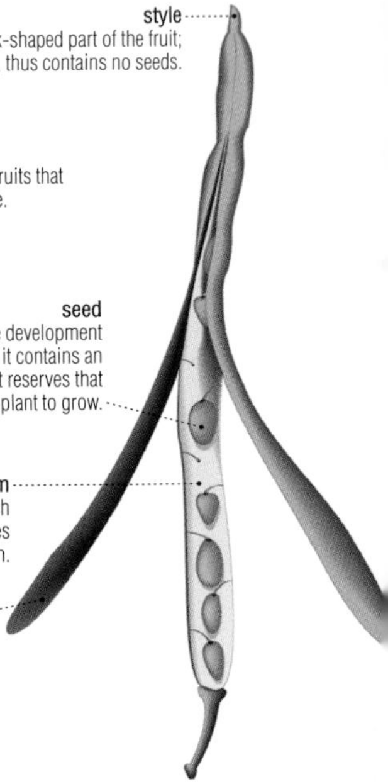

style
Upper beak-shaped part of the fruit; it is sterile, thus contains no seeds.

seed
Structure formed by the development of a fertile ovule; it contains an embryo and nutrient reserves that enable a new plant to grow.

septum
Thin barrier, bearing seeds on each side that drop when the valves open.

valve
The two parts of the fruit's casing that, when it is ripe, separate to release the seeds.

section of a hazelnut
The fruit of the hazelnut tree, the hazelnut is an achene; its pericarp is covered by a cupule.

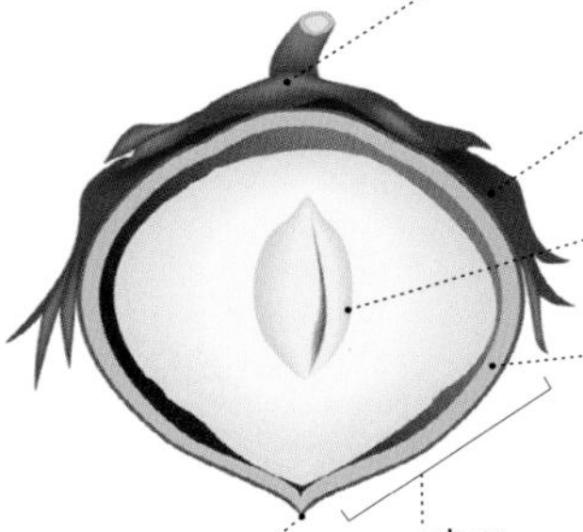

cupule
Thin scaly or prickly casing made of fused bracts; it partially or completely covers the hazelnut.

bract
Little leaf, smaller than the plant's other leaves, attached to the peduncle of the flower or fruit.

seed
Structure formed by the development of a fertile ovule; it contains an embryo and nutrient reserves that enable a new plant to grow.

pericarp

achene
Small dry fruit containing a single seed not fused to the pericarp; when ripe, the achene cannot split unaided to release its seed.

stigma
Visible remnant of the flower's stigma, now withered, forming a point at the fruit's base.

section of a walnut
The fruit of the walnut tree is the nut, which has an edible seed; its stone, or shell, is surrounded by a fleshy husk.

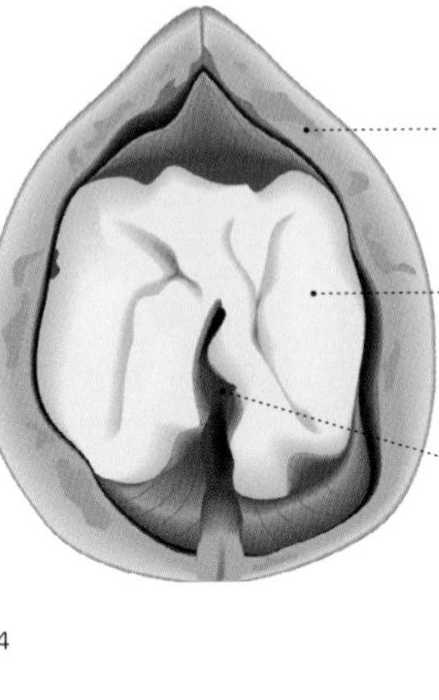

shell
Hard fibrous ovoid casing that covers and protects the green walnut.

green walnut
Kernel of the walnut, divided into two main sections by the partition.

partition
Membranous barrier that divides the walnut kernel into sections.

section of a legume: pea
Legume: dry single-chambered fruit that splits in two places when ripe: along the suture and along the midrib of its casing.

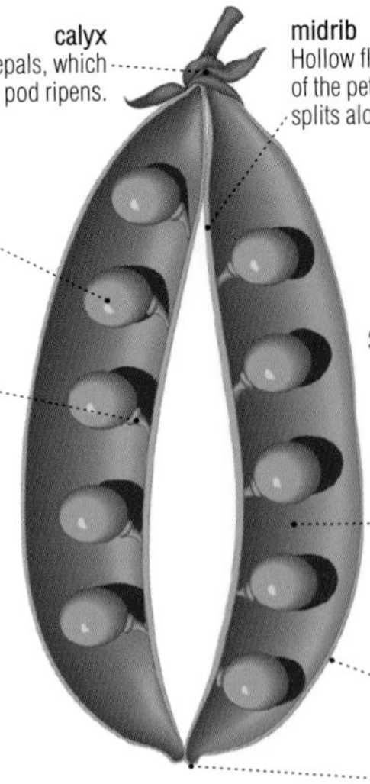

calyx
Coil of the flower's sepals, which remain until the pod ripens.

midrib
Hollow flange that is an extension of the petiole; when ripe, the fruit splits along it to release its seeds.

pea
Round green fruit seed of varying size; it is edible.

funiculus
Slender strand that connects the seed to the midrib and provides food from the plant to the developing seed.

hull
Usual term for the pod's pericarp, which bears the seeds; when the fruit is ripe, it splits in two distinct places to release the seeds.

suture
Visible seam on the surface of the fruit's casing, along which the fruit splits to release its seeds.

style
Visible remnant of the flower's style, now withered, that once connected the stigma to the ovary.

section of a capsule: poppy
Capsule: dry many-chambered fruit that opens laterally or at the apex when ripe; it contains a great many seeds.

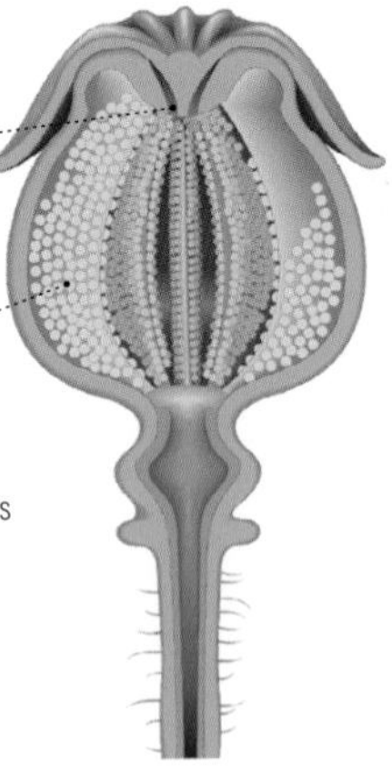

pore
Small orifice that enables the poppy casing to split open and the seeds to disperse.

seed
Structure formed by the development of a fertile ovule; it contains an embryo and nutrient reserves that enable a new plant to grow.

cereals

Plants that are often cultivated on a large scale; their grains have been a major food staple for humans and certain domestic animals for centuries.

buckwheat
Cereal cultivated for its grain, ainly ground into flour; it is also used to feed cattle and some domesticated birds.

buckwheat: raceme
The raceme is composed of a main axis and grains that have a pedicel, clustered at the stem's apex.

wheat
Cereal cultivated for its grain, important in producing food, especially foodstuffs such as flour, bread and semolina.

wheat: spike
The spike is composed of a main axis bearing seeds without a pedicel; the seeds are clustered at the stem's apex.

section of a grain of wheat
A grain of wheat is a small dry fruit whose single grain is fused to its casing; the varieties differ in size, shape and color.

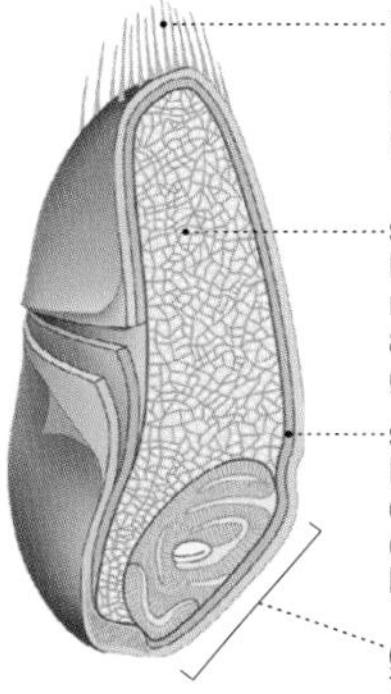

brush
Remnant of the flower's stigmas; they resemble a tuft of hair atop the grain.

starch
Part of the grain where the nutrients required for germ growth are stored; the starch can be ground into flour.

seed coat
Protective many-layered casing covering the starch and the germ; once separated from the grain, it is known as bran.

germ
The plant's embryo, located in the lower part of the grain; after germination, it enables a new plant to grow.

rice
Cereal whose grain is a major food staple in many parts of the world; rice is generally grown in flooded fields.

rice: panicle
The panicle is composed of a main axis with offshoots, each stem bearing grains that have a pedicel.

barley
Cereal cultivated for its grain; it is used mainly to produce malt for brewing beer and as cattle fodder.

barley: spike
The spike is composed of a main axis bearing seeds without a pedicel; the seeds are clustered at the stem's apex.

oats
Cereal cultivated for its grain; although it is mainly used to feed horses, humans also eat it, mostly in the form of flakes (rolled oats).

oats: panicle
The panicle is composed of a main axis with offshoots, each stem bearing grains that have a pedicel.

rye
Highly resistant cereal whose grain is used mainly to feed cattle; it is used to produce flour that can be mixed with wheat flour to make bread.

rye: spike
The spike is composed of a main axis bearing seeds without a pedicel; the seeds are clustered at the stem's apex.

sorghum
Cereal cultivated for the sugar in its sap and for its grain; it is also used as fodder, to make unleavened bread and certain kinds of beer.

sorghum: panicle
The panicle is composed of a main axis with offshoots; at its apex, each stem bears a cluster of grains that have a pedicel.

millet
Cereal cultivated as fodder or for its grain; it is used mainly to make unleavened bread and to feed domesticated birds.

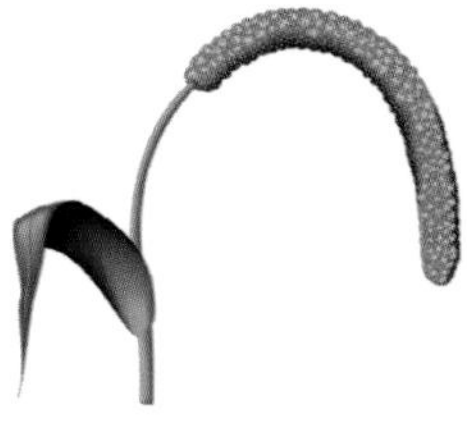

millet: spike
The spike is composed of a main axis bearing seeds without a pedicel; the seeds are clustered at the stem's apex.

corn
Native American cereal cultivated for its grains and used for human and animal food; it is also used to produce a sweet syrup and a cooking oil.

silk
Tuft of long filaments emerging from the end of the spike casing; the filaments were once attached to ovaries that have now become kernels.

cob
The cob is composed of a wide main axis with rows of tightly packed kernels; each cob grows in the axil of a leaf along the stem.

husk
Cob casing that protects the kernels and keeps them moist.

kernel
Each of the small dry fruits whose single seed is fused to its casing; a cob of corn holds several hundred kernels.

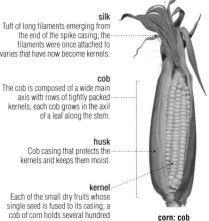

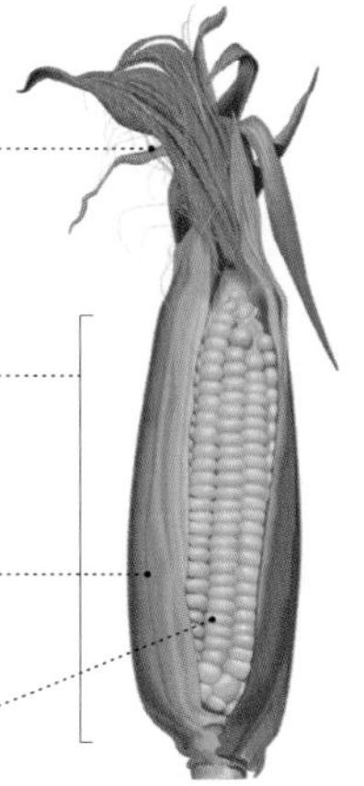

corn: cob

grape

Climbing plant usually cultivated for wine making or for the table.

bunch of grapes

branch
Secondary offshoot of a branch or a vine shoot.
pedicel
Terminal offshoot of the stem or twig; it first connects the flower, then the fruit, to the peduncle.
tendril
Spiral strand enabling the vine branch to attach itself to a natural or artificial support.
peduncle
Offshoot that connects the cluster to the branch.
grape
Differently colored fruit cultivated for the table or for wine making.

vine stock
Base of the vine on which branches grow.

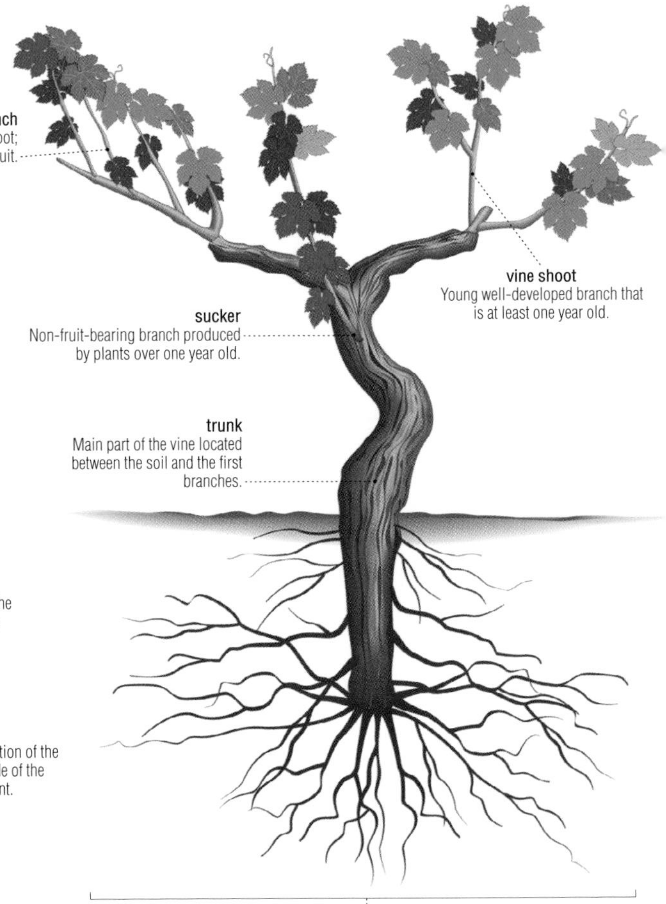
fruit branch
Secondary offshoot of a vine shoot; it first bears flowers, then fruit.
vine shoot
Young well-developed branch that is at least one year old.
sucker
Non-fruit-bearing branch produced by plants over one year old.
trunk
Main part of the vine located between the soil and the first branches.
root system
The aggregate of the roots that anchor a plant to the soil and enable it to absorb water and mineral salts from it.

grape leaf

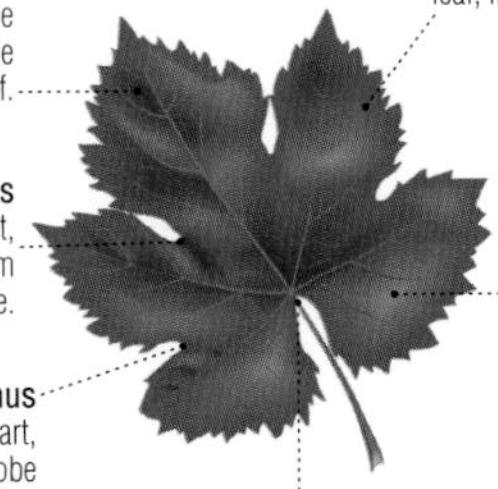
terminal lobe
Somewhat rounded section of the blade comprising the apex of the leaf.
upper lateral lobe
Somewhat rounded section of the blade located on the side of the leaf, in its upper quadrant.
upper lateral sinus
Indentation of the leaf's main part, separating the terminal lobe from the upper lateral lobe.
lower lateral lobe
Somewhat rounded section of the blade located on the side of the leaf, in its lower quadrant.
lower lateral sinus
Indentation of the leaf's main part, separating the upper lateral lobe from the lower lateral lobe.
petiolar sinus
Indentation of the leaf's main part, where it attaches to the petiole.

maturing steps

The harvest occurs about 100 days after flowering, after the grape has gone through four successive maturing steps.

flowering
First step in the maturing process, when flowers appear.

fruition
Second step in the maturing process, when the grape berries are formed.

ripening
Third step in the maturing process, when the grapes darken and become translucent.

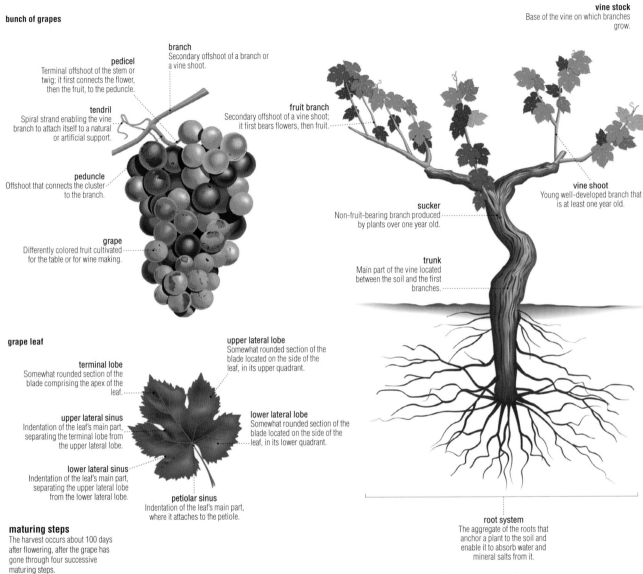

ripeness
Last step in the maturing process, when the grapes are ripe and ready to be picked.

Large vegetable whose root system and aboveground part are well developed; it produces oxygen and provides wood.

structure of a tree
The tree is composed of an underground part, the roots, and two aboveground parts, the trunk and the crown.

foliage
The aggregate of the leaves on a tree; it is especially adapted to capture light and perform photosynthesis.

branches
The aggregate of larger and smaller branches that provide support for the tree's leaves, flowers and fruit.

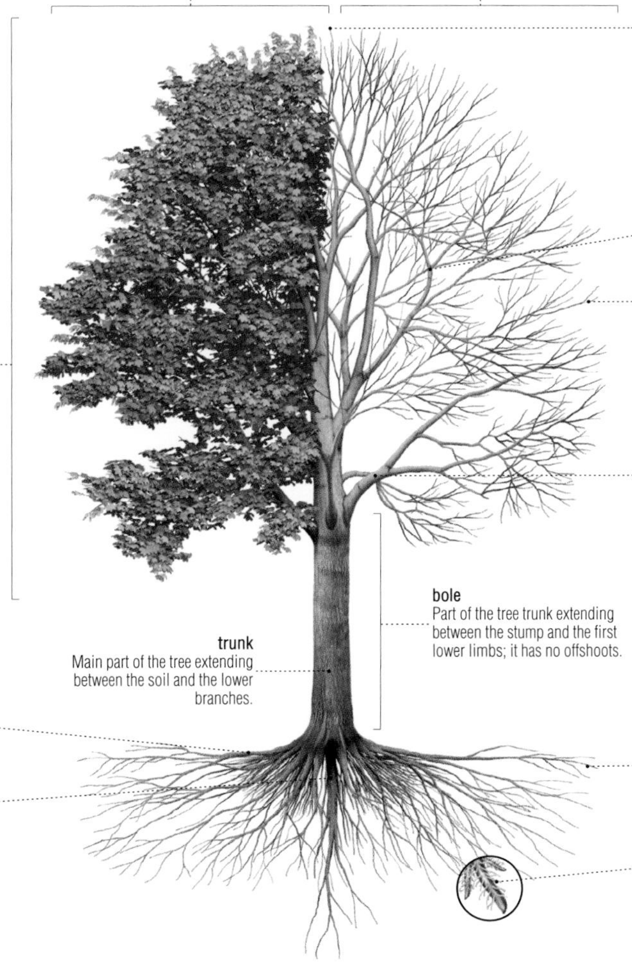

top
Apex of the tree's crown.

branch
Offshoot of one of the tree's limbs.

twig
The most slender offshoot of a tree branch.

crown
Part of the tree above the trunk, including the branches and the foliage.

limb
Offshoot growing directly out of a tree trunk, subsequently dividing into branches and twigs.

bole
Part of the tree trunk extending between the stump and the first lower limbs; it has no offshoots.

trunk
Main part of the tree extending between the soil and the lower branches.

shallow root
Root, often having many offshoots, growing somewhat horizontally into the rich moist topsoil.

taproot
First root growing out of the seed that grows vertically into the soil; it usually has few offshoots, its main function being to anchor the tree in the ground.

radicle
The most slender offshoot of a tree root.

root-hair zone
Part of the radicle covered in small absorbent hairs that ensure the tree is supplied with mineral salts and water.

cross section of a trunk
Moving from the center to the periphery there are six parts: the pith, the heartwood, the sapwood, the cambium, the phloem and the bark.

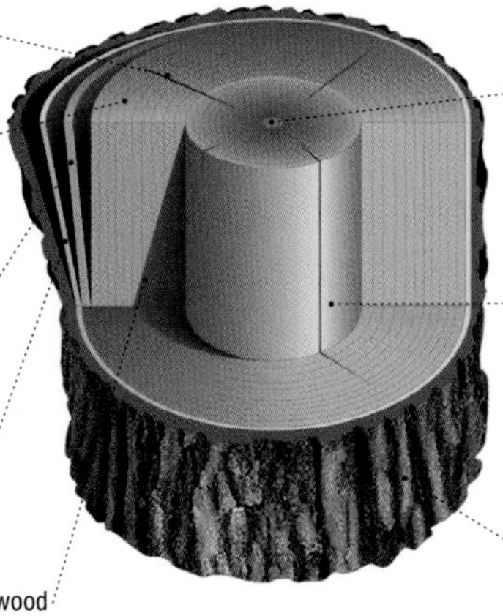

wood ray
Conduit connecting the pith to the core and circulating nutrients horizontally within the trunk.

annual ring
Each of the concentric circles resenting the layer of wood produced in one year; the age of the tree can be determined by the number of rings.

cambium
Growth tissue that simultaneously produces the external phloem and the internal sapwood, thereby enabling the tree to increase in diameter.

phloem
Tissue located immediately below the k, whose main function is to transport) transformed by photosynthesis from leaves throughout the rest of the tree.

sapwood
Relatively new layer of wood that is generally ale in color; it transports raw sap, composed f water and nutrient minerals, from the roots to the leaves.

pith
Central part of the trunk, composed of soft tissue that contains nutrients essential for sapling growth.

heartwood
Hard dark-colored wood layer made of dead sapwood; it encircles the pith and supports the trunk and branches.

bark
Tree's external protective layer; its texture and color vary depending on the species.

stump
Lower part of the trunk that remains in place, with its roots, when the tree is cut down.

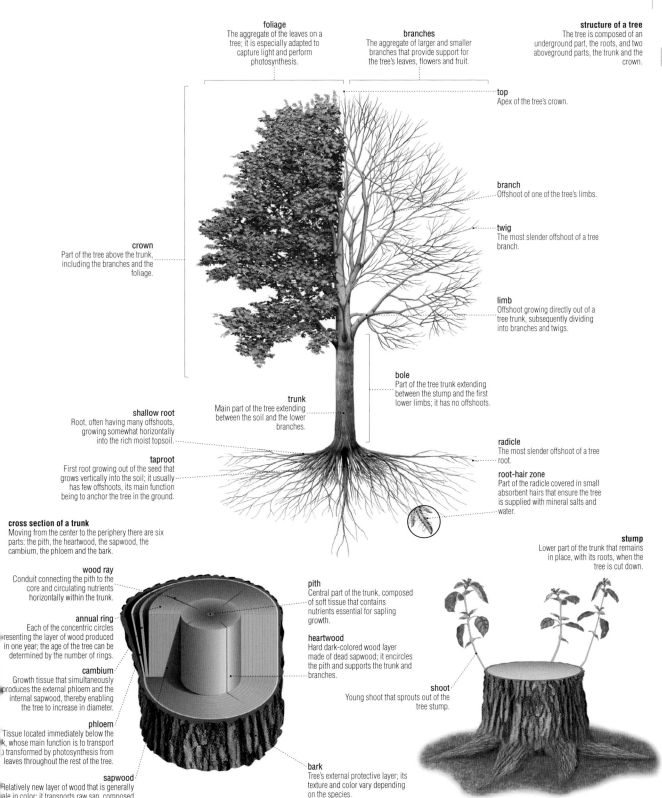

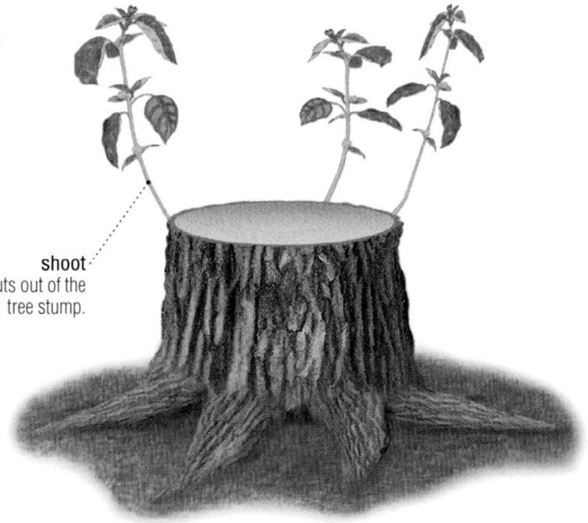

shoot
Young shoot that sprouts out of the tree stump.

examples of broadleaved trees

Broadleaved trees have mainly large flat leaves; in temperate zones, these usually fall as winter approaches.

oak
Large tree with deeply indented leaves, bearing acorns as fruit; it is prized for its hard and extremely resistant wood.

birch
Tree whose most common species has smooth white bark covered in black markings; the bark readily peels off the trunk in large sections.

weeping willow
Tree with long flexible hanging branches; it is often used for ornamental purposes and generally grows near water.

poplar
Tall slender fast-growing tree; its soft wood is used especially in woodworking and to make pulp for papermaking.

palm tree
Tree native to tropical regions; among its various species are date- and coconut-bearing kinds.

maple
Tree producing the samara, a small dry winged fruit; its wood is prized by cabinetmakers. The sugar maple tree's sap can be made into a syrup.

beech
Smooth-barked tree, prized for its ornamental value and its wood; it is used especially in woodworking and for heating.

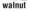

walnut
Large tree that produces an edible fruit, the walnut; its hard compact wood is prized especially by carpenters for its use in making furniture.

conifer

Tree that usually retains its needle- or scalelike leaves all winter long; it bears cones, hence its name, and produces a sticky sap known as resin.

cone
Fruit borne by conifers, consisting of scales arranged in a conical shape; when the cone is ripe, seeds develop under it.

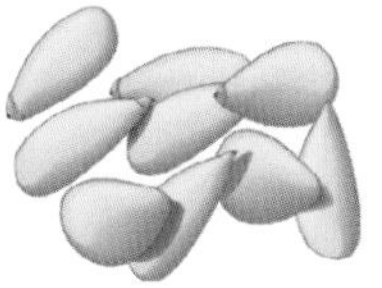

pine seed
Edible seed inside the cone of certain species of pine that is often used in cooking and baking.

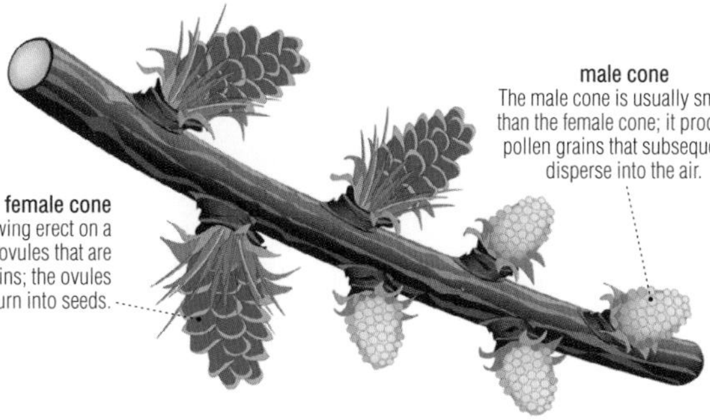

branch
Offshoot of a tree branch along which cones develop.

male cone
The male cone is usually smaller than the female cone; it produces pollen grains that subsequently disperse into the air.

female cone
Each female cone, growing erect on a branch, contains ovules that are fertilized by pollen grains; the ovules subsequently turn into seeds.

examples of leaves

Conifer leaves consist of scales or needles, varying in length and width.

fir needles
Fir leaves consist of short hard flattened needles; each needle grows directly out of the branch.

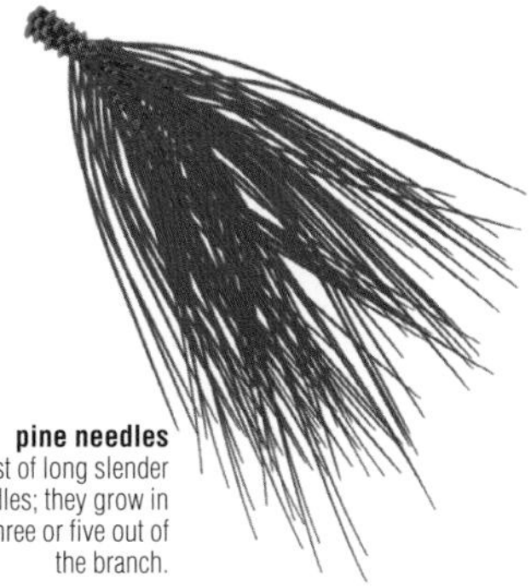

pine needles
Pine leaves consist of long slender pointed needles; they grow in groups of two, three or five out of the branch.

cypress scalelike leaves
The cypress has scales or small short stiff leaves whose blades grow directly out of the twig.

examples of conifers

There are 550 conifer species; because they are well adapted to harsh climates, they often form the tree line on mountains and in subpolar regions.

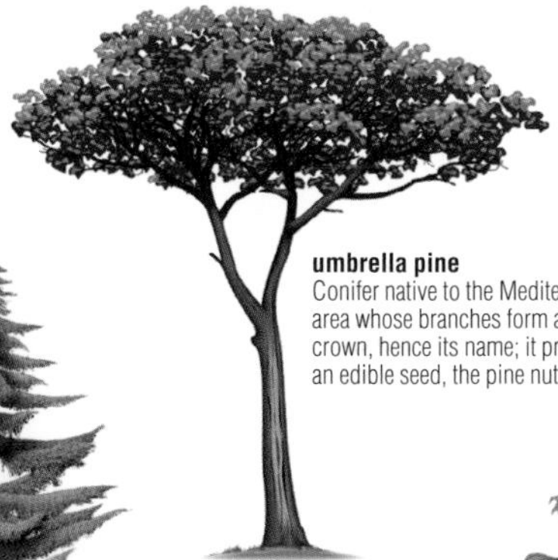

umbrella pine
Conifer native to the Mediterranean area whose branches form a flattened crown, hence its name; it produces an edible seed, the pine nut.

cedar of Lebanon
Conifer of Middle Eastern origin with a large, flattened top; now rare, former civilizations made abundant use of its wood.

spruce
Conifer with small cylindrical needles encircling the branch; it has reddish-brown bark and can grow to 180 ft.

larch
One of the few conifers that sheds its needles in the fall; its scented, resistant wood is used in construction and carpentry.

fir
Scented conifer with flat needles arranged on each side of the branch; it has grayish bark, flecked with resin. Fir is commonly used as a Christmas tree.

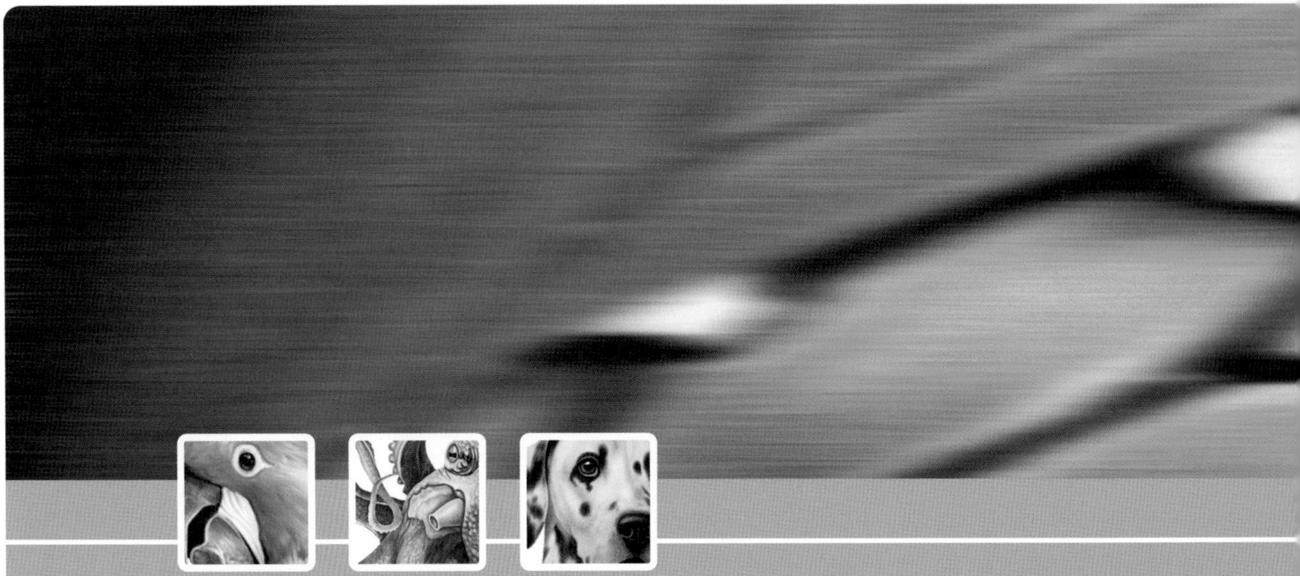

ANIMALS

Grouping of all living beings with more or less complex organs, with which they move about and feed themselves; the body of knowledge about them.

origin and evolution of species

Since its formation some 4.6 billion years ago, the Earth has witnessed the genesis of continents and oceans and the appearance of animals and vegetation.

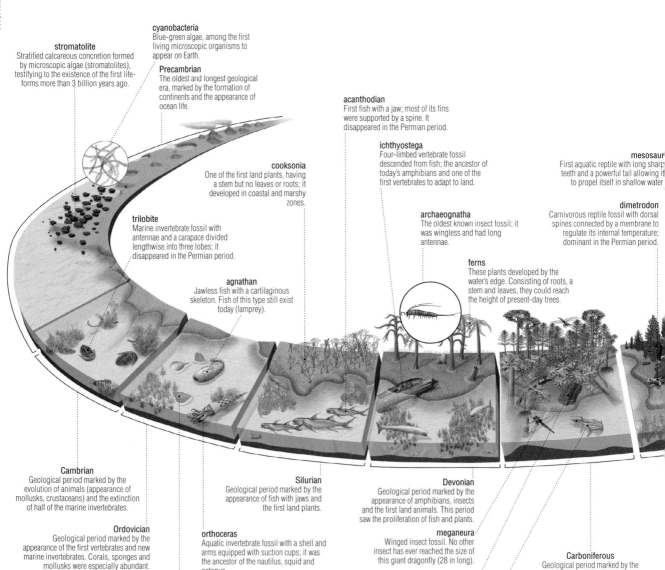

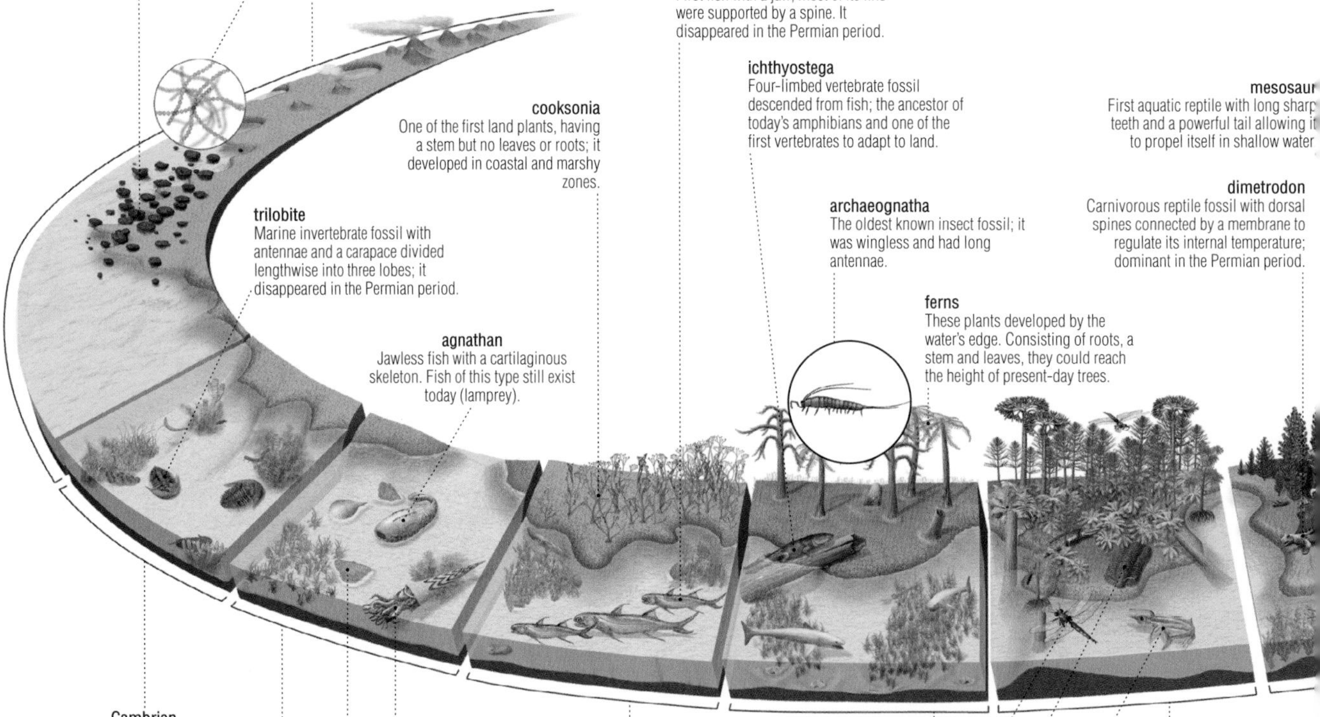

cyanobacteria
Blue-green algae, among the first living microscopic organisms to appear on Earth.
stromatolite
Stratified calcareous concretion formed by microscopic algae (stromatolites), testifying to the existence of the first life-forms more than 3 billion years ago.
Precambrian
The oldest and longest geological era, marked by the formation of continents and the appearance of ocean life.
acanthodian
First fish with a jaw; most of its fins were supported by a spine. It disappeared in the Permian period.
ichthyostega
Four-limbed vertebrate fossil descended from fish; the ancestor of today's amphibians and one of the first vertebrates to adapt to land.
mesosaur
First aquatic reptile with long sharp teeth and a powerful tail allowing it to propel itself in shallow water
cooksonia
One of the first land plants, having a stem but no leaves or roots; it developed in coastal and marshy zones.
dimetrodon
Carnivorous reptile fossil with dorsal spines connected by a membrane to regulate its internal temperature; dominant in the Permian period.
trilobite
Marine invertebrate fossil with antennae and a carapace divided lengthwise into three lobes; it disappeared in the Permian period.
archaeognatha
The oldest known insect fossil; it was wingless and had long antennae.
ferns
These plants developed by the water's edge. Consisting of roots, a stem and leaves, they could reach the height of present-day trees.
agnathan
Jawless fish with a cartilaginous skeleton. Fish of this type still exist today (lamprey).
Cambrian
Geological period marked by the evolution of animals (appearance of mollusks, crustaceans) and the extinction of half of the marine invertebrates.
Silurian
Geological period marked by the appearance of fish with jaws and the first land plants.
Devonian
Geological period marked by the appearance of amphibians, insects and the first land animals. This period saw the proliferation of fish and plants.
Ordovician
Geological period marked by the appearance of the first vertebrates and new marine invertebrates. Corals, sponges and mollusks were especially abundant.
orthoceras
Aquatic invertebrate fossil with a shell and arms equipped with suction cups; it was the ancestor of the nautilus, squid and octopus.
meganeura
Winged insect fossil. No other insect has ever reached the size of this giant dragonfly (28 in long).
Carboniferous
Geological period marked by the appearance of reptiles and winged insects. Plants (ferns, cereals) continued evolving.
brachiopod
Marine invertebrate fossil with a body protected by a bivalve shell.
arthropleura
Invertebrate fossil with a multi-segmented body. Found in damp forests, it measured almost 7 ft in length.
falcatus
Shark fossil with sharp teeth. The male had a dentate dorsal fin pointing forward.
Permian
Geological period marked by the predominance of reptiles and amphibians. The continental mass now formed into a great protocontinent: Pangea.

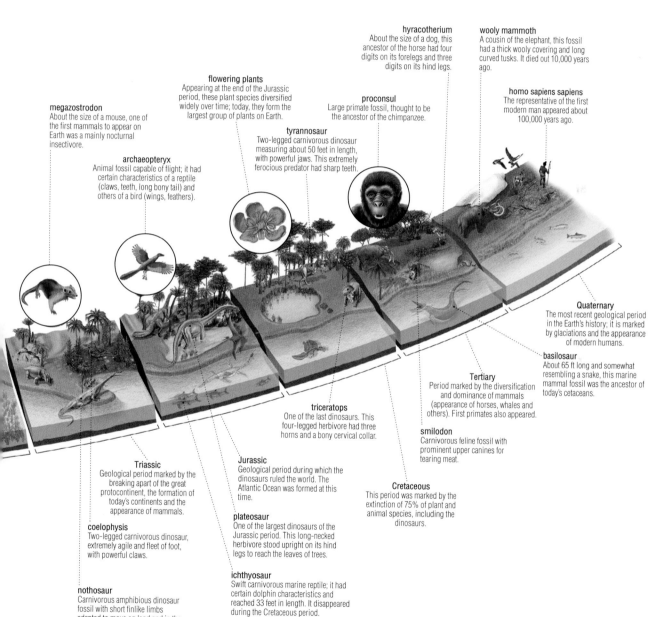

hyracotherium
About the size of a dog, this ancestor of the horse had four digits on its forelegs and three digits on its hind legs.

wooly mammoth
A cousin of the elephant, this fossil had a thick wooly covering and long curved tusks. It died out 10,000 years ago.

flowering plants
Appearing at the end of the Jurassic period, these plant species diversified widely over time; today, they form the largest group of plants on Earth.

proconsul
Large primate fossil, thought to be the ancestor of the chimpanzee.

homo sapiens sapiens
The representative of the first modern man appeared about 100,000 years ago.

megazostrodon
About the size of a mouse, one of the first mammals to appear on Earth was a mainly nocturnal insectivore.

tyrannosaur
Two-legged carnivorous dinosaur measuring about 50 feet in length, with powerful jaws. This extremely ferocious predator had sharp teeth.

archaeopteryx
Animal fossil capable of flight; it had certain characteristics of a reptile (claws, teeth, long bony tail) and others of a bird (wings, feathers).

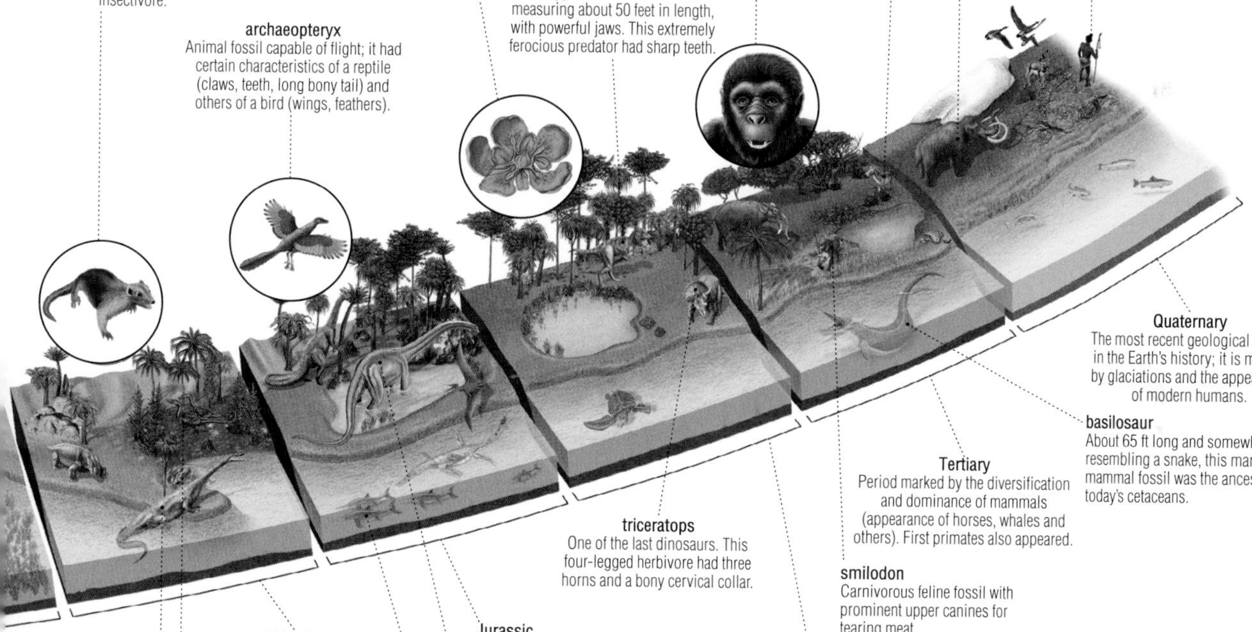

Quaternary
The most recent geological period in the Earth's history; it is marked by glaciations and the appearance of modern humans.

basilosaur
About 65 ft long and somewhat resembling a snake, this marine mammal fossil was the ancestor of today's cetaceans.

Tertiary
Period marked by the diversification and dominance of mammals (appearance of horses, whales and others). First primates also appeared.

triceratops
One of the last dinosaurs. This four-legged herbivore had three horns and a bony cervical collar.

smilodon
Carnivorous feline fossil with prominent upper canines for tearing meat.

Triassic
Geological period marked by the breaking apart of the great protocontinent, the formation of today's continents and the appearance of mammals.

Jurassic
Geological period during which the dinosaurs ruled the world. The Atlantic Ocean was formed at this time.

Cretaceous
This period was marked by the extinction of 75% of plant and animal species, including the dinosaurs.

plateosaur
One of the largest dinosaurs of the Jurassic period. This long-necked herbivore stood upright on its hind legs to reach the leaves of trees.

coelophysis
Two-legged carnivorous dinosaur, extremely agile and fleet of foot, with powerful claws.

ichthyosaur
Swift carnivorous marine reptile; it had certain dolphin characteristics and reached 33 feet in length. It disappeared during the Cretaceous period.

nothosaur
Carnivorous amphibious dinosaur fossil with short finlike limbs adapted to move on land and in the water.

animal cell

Smallest living structure and constituent unit of all animals, including human beings; its size and shape vary according to function.

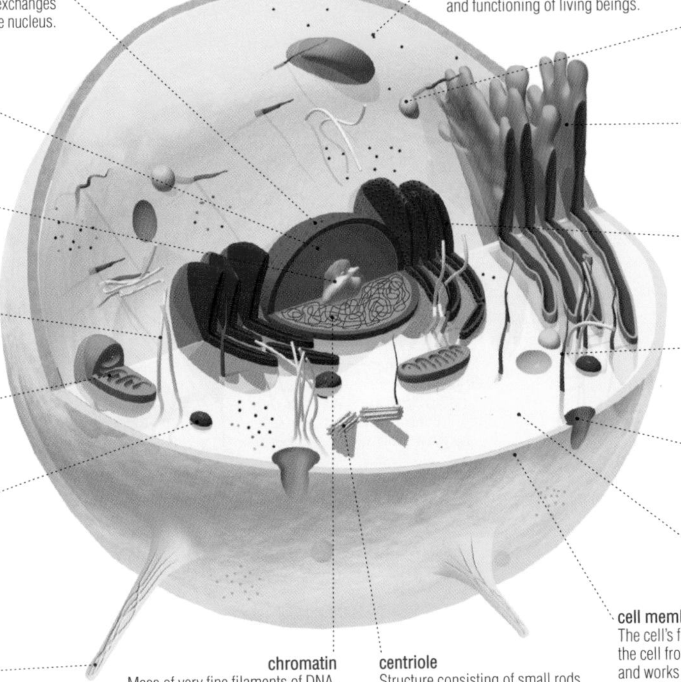

nuclear envelope
Envelope formed of two layers surrounding the nucleus and pierced with small holes, which allow exchanges between the cytoplasm and the nucleus.

nucleus
Organelle containing a cell's genes and controlling its activities.

nucleolus
Small spherical body located inside the nucleus, within which the ribosomes, or protein-synthesizing structures, are produced.

microtubule
Cylindrical structure supporting the cell and allowing organelles and substances inside the cell to move about.

mitochondrion
Ovoid organelle that produces the energy necessary for cell activity.

peroxisome
Organelle containing enzymes that neutralize the cell's toxic substances.

cilium
Filament-like extension of the cytoplasmic membrane allowing the cell and certain substances on its surface to move about.

chromatin
Mass of very fine filaments of DNA, the genetic material of the cell; it is compressed into chromosomes during cell division.

centriole
Structure consisting of small rods that play a major role in cell division. Each cell usually contains two.

ribosome
Organelle, free or attached to the endoplasmic reticulum, producing proteins essential to the constitution and functioning of living beings.

lysosome
Small spheroid organ containing enzymes that break down food, spent cell components and other harmful substances that have been absorbed.

Golgi apparatus
Organelle composed of a series of pockets that receive proteins produced by the ribosomes and either transport them outside the cell or to other organelles.

endoplasmic reticulum
Organelle formed of walls to which the ribosomes are attached.

microfilament
Rod-shaped structure supporting the cell and giving it its shape.

vacuole
Spherical cavity containing water, waste and various substances required by the cell.

cytoplasm
Clear gelatinous substance surrounding the various cellular structures.

cell membrane
The cell's flexible outer casing; it separates the cell from the surrounding environment and works as a filter to control the entry and exit of certain substances.

unicellulars

Single-cell organisms living in freshwater or salt water, in humid soil or as parasites of other organisms (plants or animals).

amoeba
Variably shaped one-cell organism, found in freshwater or salt water, in humid soil or, sometimes, as a parasite of animals. It moves about and feeds with the help of pseudopodia.

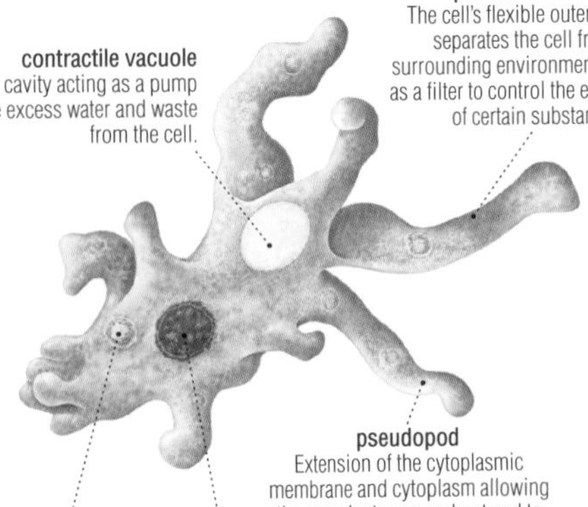

plasma membrane
The cell's flexible outer casing; it separates the cell from the surrounding environment and works as a filter to control the entry and exit of certain substances.

contractile vacuole
Spheroid cavity acting as a pump to evacuate excess water and waste from the cell.

pseudopod
Extension of the cytoplasmic membrane and cytoplasm allowing the amoeba to move about and to trap its prey.

food vacuole
Spheroid cavity in which the amoeba traps its prey to digest it.

nucleus
Organelle containing a cell's genes and controlling its activities.

paramecium
Ovoid-shaped one-cell organism generally found in freshwater and covered with cilia, which allow it to move about and to feed, mainly on bacteria.

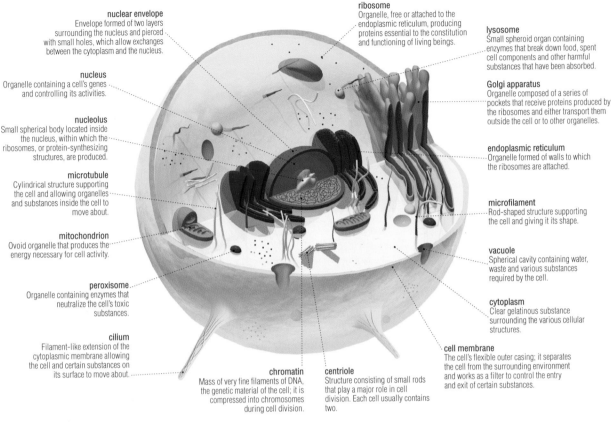

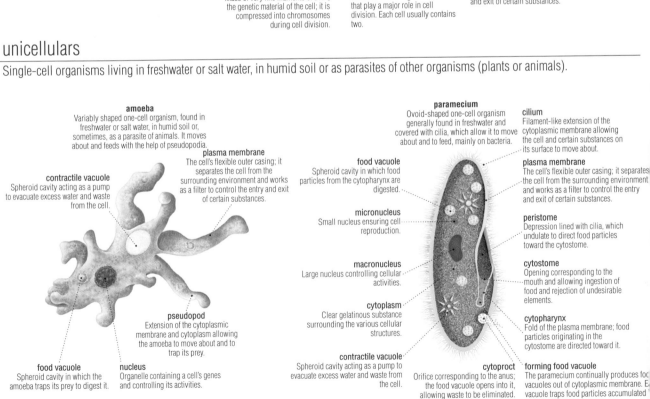

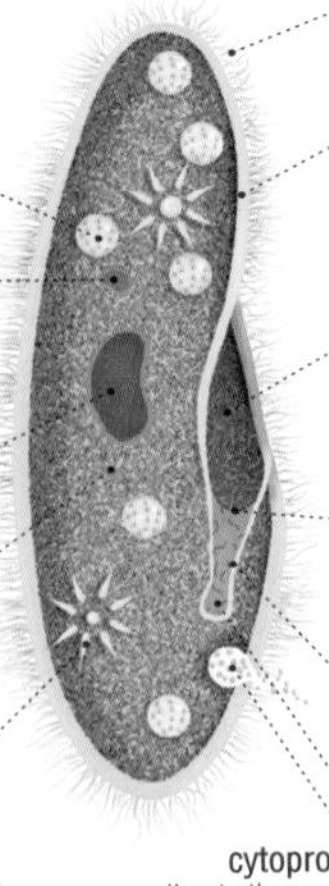

food vacuole
Spheroid cavity in which food particles from the cytopharynx are digested.

micronucleus
Small nucleus ensuring cell reproduction.

macronucleus
Large nucleus controlling cellular activities.

cytoplasm
Clear gelatinous substance surrounding the various cellular structures.

contractile vacuole
Spheroid cavity acting as a pump to evacuate excess water and waste from the cell.

cytoproct
Orifice corresponding to the anus; the food vacuole opens into it, allowing waste to be eliminated.

cilium
Filament-like extension of the cytoplasmic membrane allowing the cell and certain substances on its surface to move about.

plasma membrane
The cell's flexible outer casing; it separates the cell from the surrounding environment and works as a filter to control the entry and exit of certain substances.

peristome
Depression lined with cilia, which undulate to direct food particles toward the cytostome.

cytostome
Opening corresponding to the mouth and allowing ingestion of food and rejection of undesirable elements.

cytopharynx
Fold of the plasma membrane; food particles originating in the cytostome are directed toward it.

forming food vacuole
The paramecium continually produces foc vacuoles out of cytoplasmic membrane. E vacuole traps food particles accumulated bottom of the cytopharynx.

sponge

Porous multicell organism, mostly marine (currently about 5,000 species); it anchors itself to a support and filters water to take in food particles.

calcareous sponge
Marine sponge with a skeleton composed of small calcareous needles (spicules).

anatomy of a sponge

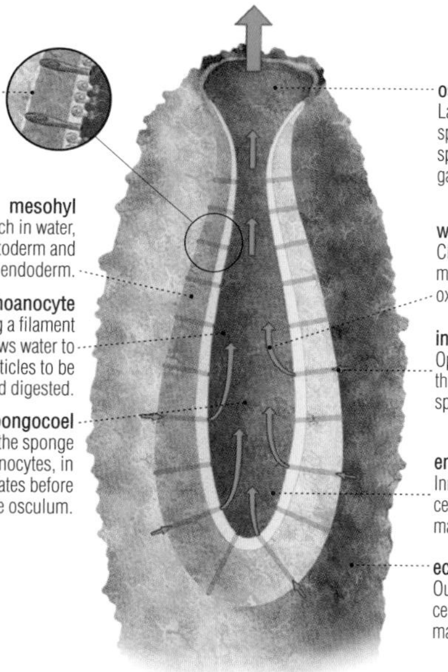

pinacocyte
Flat ectodermal cell forming the outer covering of the sponge.

mesohyl
Gelatinous substance, rich in water, located between the ectoderm and the endoderm.

choanocyte
Inner cell having a filament (flagellum), which allows water to circulate and food particles to be caught and digested.

spongocoel
Hollow portion of the sponge covered with choanocytes, in which water circulates before exiting through the osculum.

osculum
Large opening protected by spicules, through which the sponge discharges water from the gastric cavity.

water flow
Choanocyte flagella allow water to move inside the sponge, carrying oxygen and food particles to it.

incurrent pore
Opening into the gastric cavity, through which water enters the sponge.

endoderm
Inner layer of the sponge formed of cells (choanocytes) whose role is mainly to feed the organism.

ectoderm
Outer layer of the sponge formed of cells (pinacocytes) whose role is mainly to protect the organism.

echinoderms

Marine invertebrates (currently more than 6,000 species) covered with calcareous plates; an ambulacral ossicle runs along the body, helping the organism to move, anchor itself to a support and capture its prey.

anatomy of a starfish

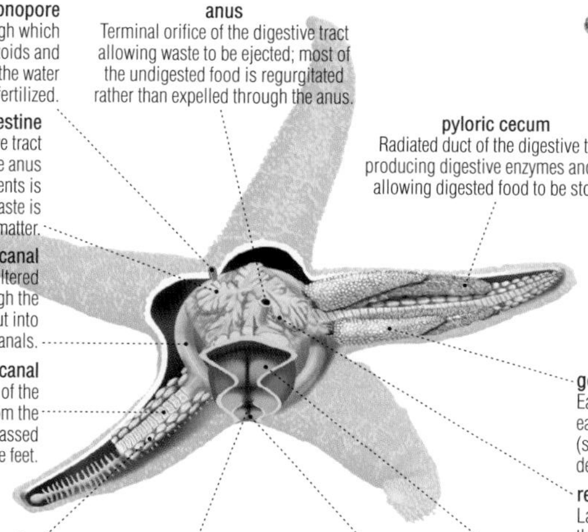

gonopore
Dorsal opening through which gametes (spermatozoids and ovules) are expelled into the water to be fertilized.

anus
Terminal orifice of the digestive tract allowing waste to be ejected; most of the undigested food is regurgitated rather than expelled through the anus.

intestine
Section of the digestive tract between the stomach and the anus where absorption of nutrients is carried out and waste is transformed into fecal matter.

pyloric cecum
Radiated duct of the digestive tract producing digestive enzymes and also allowing digested food to be stored.

ring canal
Circular canal in which filtered water enters through the nadreporite and branches out into the radiated canals.

radial canal
Canal running the length of the arm; it receives water from the annular canal, which then passed into the tube feet.

ampulla
b that contracts to let water enter e tube foot, allowing it to extend; when it dilates, the foot retracts.

gonad
Each of the two glands located in each arm, producing gametes (spermatozoids or ovules) depending on the sex of the starfish.

rectal cecum
Lateral duct of the terminal part of the digestive tract, where waste is stored before being expelled through the anus.

esophagus
Muscular membranous channel of the anterior section of the digestive tract; it allows food to reach the stomach.

mouth
Anterior cavity of the digestive tract located on the ventral surface that allows food to be ingested.

stomach
Dilated section of the digestive tract preceding the intestine; it receives food to be digested.

morphology of a starfish
Starfish: carnivorous echinoderm found in the ocean depths; it generally has five arms, which allow it to crawl slowly along surfaces.

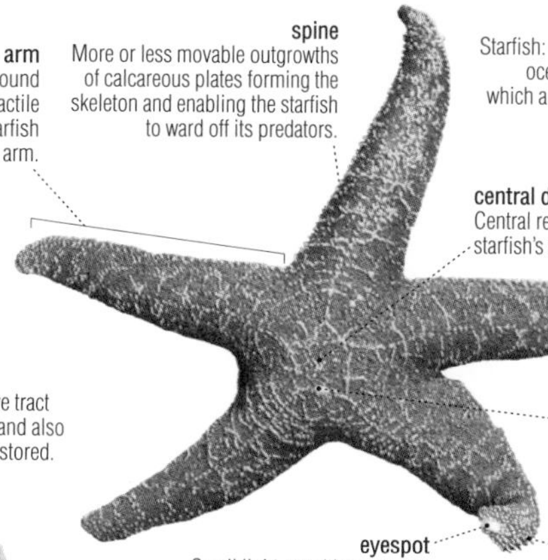

arm
Movable appendage radiating around the central disk; it has a mainly tactile and olfactory function. The starfish can regenerate an amputated arm.

spine
More or less movable outgrowths of calcareous plates forming the skeleton and enabling the starfish to ward off its predators.

central disk
Central region of the body; the starfish's arms are attached to it.

madreporite
Porous dorsal plate that allows water to enter the body; it connects the ambulacral ossicle to the outside world, and thus ensures locomotion.

eyespot
Small light-sensitive structure located at the terminal end of each arm, allowing it to locate surfaces and prey.

tube foot
Small flexible tube extending and retracting with the action of the ampulla; it mainly allows the organism to move about, anchor itself to a support and capture its prey.

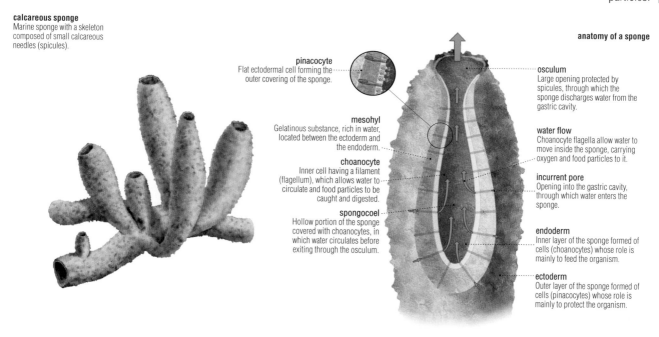

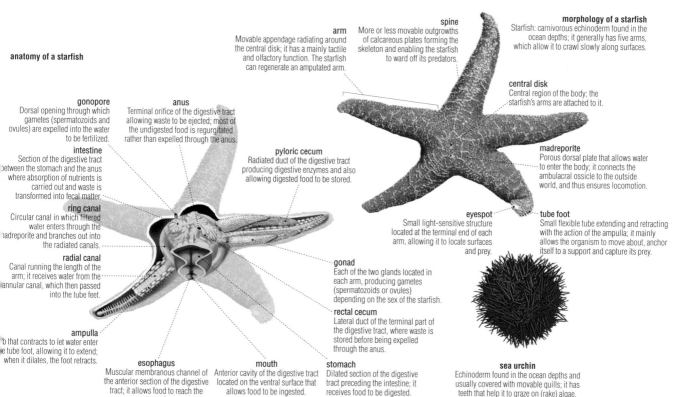

sea urchin
Echinoderm found in the ocean depths and usually covered with movable quills; it has teeth that help it to graze on (rake) algae.

butterfly

Adult insect having two pairs of wings and three pairs of legs; it emerges after the first three stages of metamorphosis: the egg, the caterpillar and the chrysalis.

morphology of a butterfly

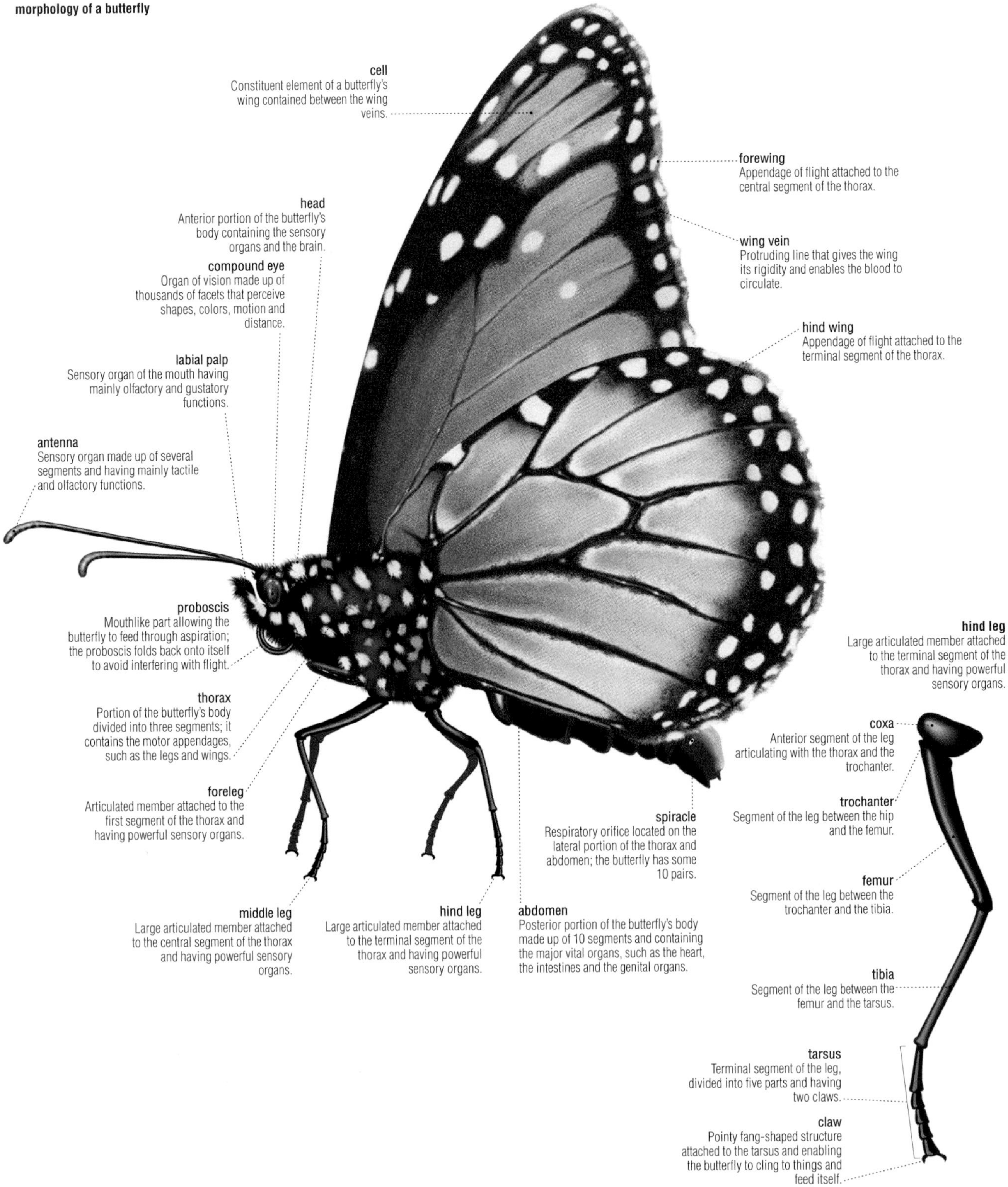
cell
Constituent element of a butterfly's wing contained between the wing veins.
forewing
Appendage of flight attached to the central segment of the thorax.
head
Anterior portion of the butterfly's body containing the sensory organs and the brain.
wing vein
Protruding line that gives the wing its rigidity and enables the blood to circulate.
compound eye
Organ of vision made up of thousands of facets that perceive shapes, colors, motion and distance.
hind wing
Appendage of flight attached to the terminal segment of the thorax.
labial palp
Sensory organ of the mouth having mainly olfactory and gustatory functions.
antenna
Sensory organ made up of several segments and having mainly tactile and olfactory functions.
hind leg
Large articulated member attached to the terminal segment of the thorax and having powerful sensory organs.
proboscis
Mouthlike part allowing the butterfly to feed through aspiration; the proboscis folds back onto itself to avoid interfering with flight.
thorax
Portion of the butterfly's body divided into three segments; it contains the motor appendages, such as the legs and wings.
coxa
Anterior segment of the leg articulating with the thorax and the trochanter.
foreleg
Articulated member attached to the first segment of the thorax and having powerful sensory organs.
trochanter
Segment of the leg between the hip and the femur.
spiracle
Respiratory orifice located on the lateral portion of the thorax and abdomen; the butterfly has some 10 pairs.
femur
Segment of the leg between the trochanter and the tibia.
middle leg
Large articulated member attached to the central segment of the thorax and having powerful sensory organs.
hind leg
Large articulated member attached to the terminal segment of the thorax and having powerful sensory organs.
abdomen
Posterior portion of the butterfly's body made up of 10 segments and containing the major vital organs, such as the heart, the intestines and the genital organs.
tibia
Segment of the leg between the femur and the tarsus.
tarsus
Terminal segment of the leg, divided into five parts and having two claws.
claw
Pointy fang-shaped structure attached to the tarsus and enabling the butterfly to cling to things and feed itself.

anatomy of a female butterfly

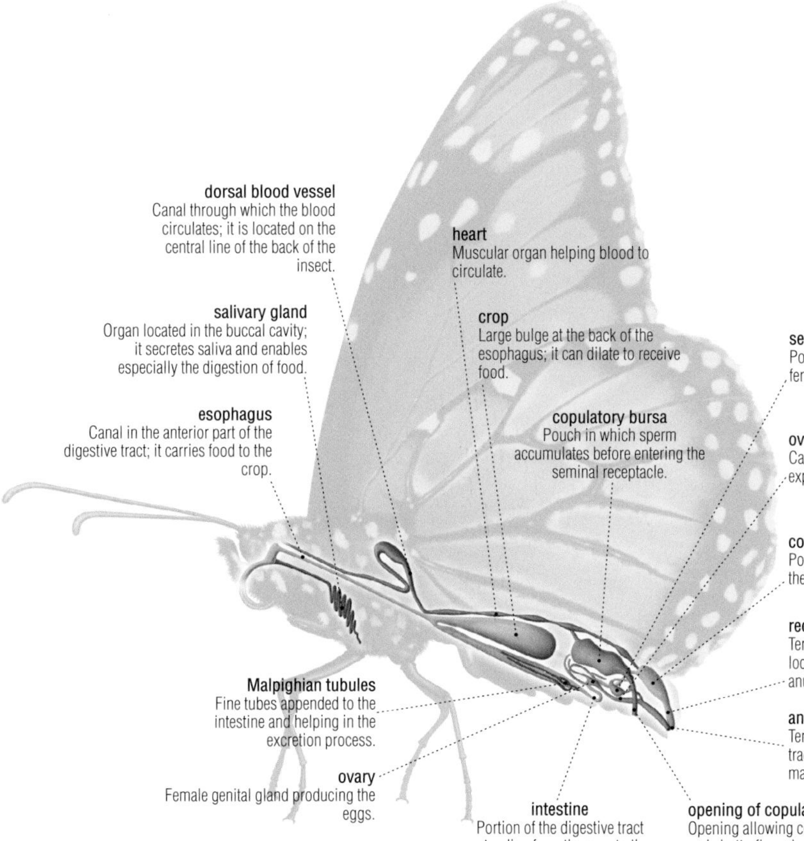
dorsal blood vessel
Canal through which the blood circulates; it is located on the central line of the back of the insect.
salivary gland
Organ located in the buccal cavity; it secretes saliva and enables especially the digestion of food.
esophagus
Canal in the anterior part of the digestive tract; it carries food to the crop.
heart
Muscular organ helping blood to circulate.
crop
Large bulge at the back of the esophagus; it can dilate to receive food.
copulatory bursa
Pouch in which sperm accumulates before entering the seminal receptacle.
seminal receptacle
Pouch where sperm is stored for fertilizing the eggs.
oviduct
Canal through which the eggs are expelled from the ovaries.
colon
Portion of the intestine in front of the rectum.
rectum
Terminal part of the intestine located between the colon and the anus.
anus
Terminal orifice of the digestive tract enabling ejection of fecal matter.
Malpighian tubules
Fine tubes appended to the intestine and helping in the excretion process.
ovary
Female genital gland producing the eggs.
intestine
Portion of the digestive tract extending from the crop to the anus.
opening of copulatory bursa
Opening allowing copulation by the male butterfly and entry of sperm into the copulatory bursa.

chrysalis

Intermediary stage between the caterpillar and the butterfly; the limbs and internal organs develop during this stage.

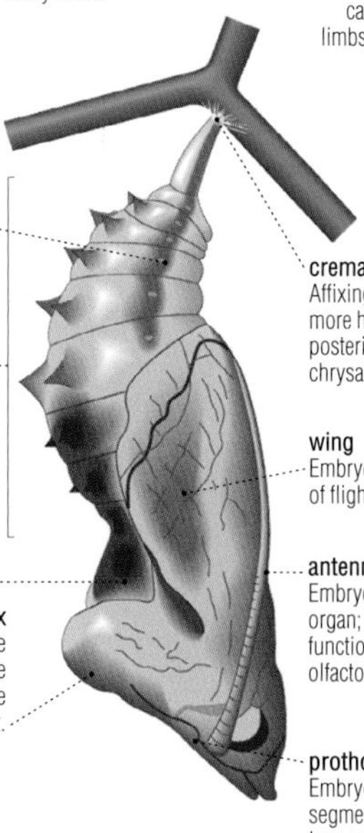
spiracle
Respiratory orifice located on the lateral portion of the thorax and the abdomen.
abdomen
Posterior portion of the chrysalis's body.
metathorax
Embryo that will become the terminal segment of the thorax; the legs and rear wings are attached to it.
mesothorax
Embryo that will become the central segment of the thorax; the middle legs and front wings are attached to it.
cremaster
Affixing element having one or more hooks; it is located at the posterior terminal end of the chrysalis's body.
wing
Embryo that will become the organ of flight; it is attached to the thorax.
antenna
Embryo that will become the sensory organ; it has several segments and its functions are mainly tactile and olfactory.
prothorax
Embryo that will become the first segment of the thorax; the front legs are attached to it, but not the wings.

caterpillar

Butterfly larva having a long body and 10 feet; the intermediary stage between the egg and the chrysalis.

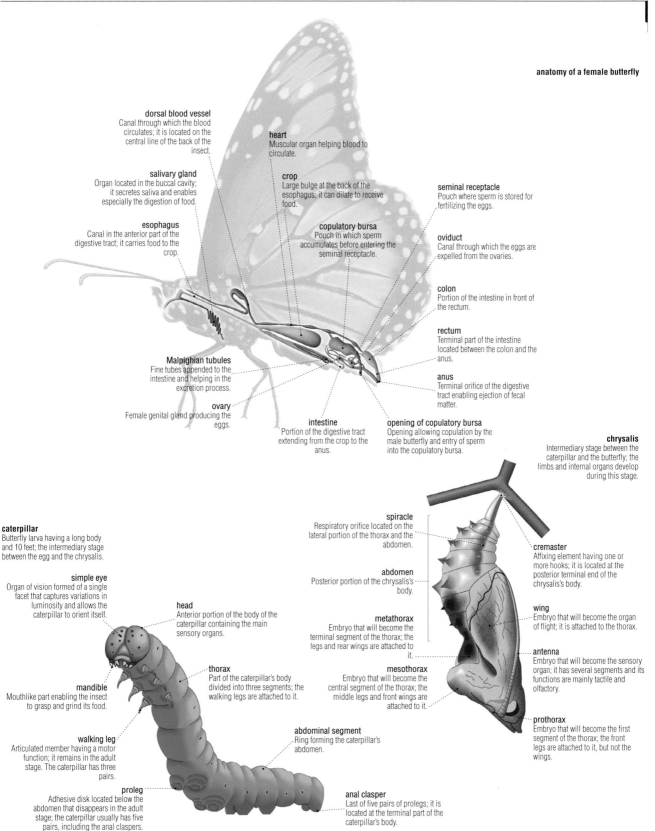

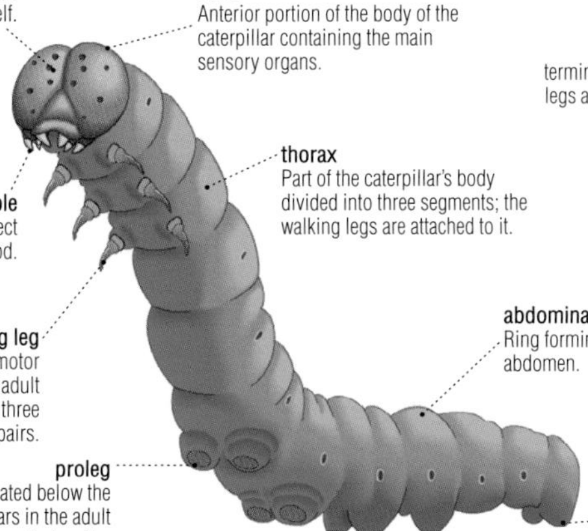
simple eye
Organ of vision formed of a single facet that captures variations in luminosity and allows the caterpillar to orient itself.
head
Anterior portion of the body of the caterpillar containing the main sensory organs.
mandible
Mouthlike part enabling the insect to grasp and grind its food.
thorax
Part of the caterpillar's body divided into three segments; the walking legs are attached to it.
walking leg
Articulated member having a motor function; it remains in the adult stage. The caterpillar has three pairs.
abdominal segment
Ring forming the caterpillar's abdomen.
proleg
Adhesive disk located below the abdomen that disappears in the adult stage; the caterpillar usually has five pairs, including the anal claspers.
anal clasper
Last of five pairs of prolegs; it is located at the terminal part of the caterpillar's body.

honeybee

Insect living in a highly complex social order; it instinctively produces honey as a food reserve.

morphology of a honeybee: worker

wing
Organ of flight attached to the thorax. In the bee, the front and rear wings on each side are attached and beat together.
abdomen
Segmented posterior portion of a bee's body containing the major vital organs.
sting
Pointed retractable organ located at the terminal end of the abdomen; venom flows through it from the venom sac.
pollen basket
Hollow bordered by long curved hairs and located on the outer side of the tibia; it is used to transport pollen.
hind leg
Highly specialized articulated member attached to the terminal segment of the thorax; it has a motor function and is used to collect and transport pollen.
middle leg
Nonspecialized articulated member attached to the central segment of the thorax; it has a motor function and is used to clean the thorax and the wings.
foreleg
Articulated member attached to the first segment of the thorax; it has a motor function and is used to clean the eyes and the antennae.
thorax
Portion of a bee's body divided into three segments housing the motor appendages, such as the legs and wings.
compound eye
Organ of vision made up of thousands of facets that perceive shapes, colors, motion and distance.
mouthparts
Appendages used for grasping and ingesting food and adapted to the collection of nectar.
antenna
Sensory organ made up of several segments and having mainly tactile and olfactory functions.

hind leg (inner surface)
Highly specialized articulated member attached to the terminal segment of the thorax; it has a motor function and is used to collect and transport pollen.

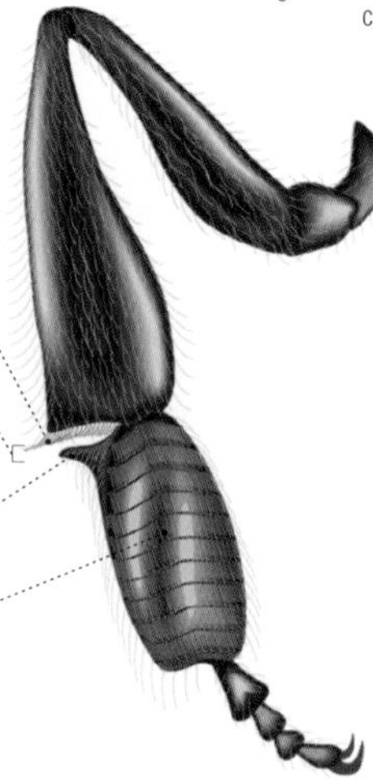

pecten
Row of stiff hairs located at the tibia articulation of the worker bee; it is used to pack pollen into the pollen basket.
pollen packer
Articulation where the tibia and the tarsus meet; it is used to compress the pollen before moving it to the pollen basket.
auricle
Row of hairs located at the upper terminal end of the worker bee's metatarsus; it is used to move the pollen to the pollen packer, where it is compressed.
pollen brush
Row of hairs located on the metatarsus of the worker bee; it is used to collect pollen.

foreleg (outer surface)
Articulated member attached to the first segment of the thorax; it has a motor function and is used to clean the eyes and the antennae.

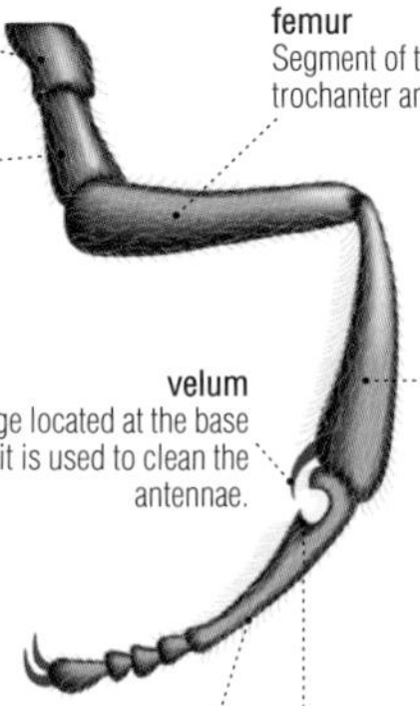

coxa
Anterior segment of the leg articulating with the thorax and the trochanter.
trochanter
Segment of the leg between the coxa and the femur.
femur
Segment of the leg between the trochanter and the tibia.
tibia
Segment of the leg located between the femur and the metatarsus.
velum
Movable appendage located at the base of the tibia; it is used to clean the antennae.
metatarsus
First segment of the tarsus attached to the tibia; it is much larger than the other segments.
antennae cleaner
Notch covered with rigid hairs; with the velum, its function is to clean the antennae.

middle leg (outer surface)
Nonspecialized articulated member attached to the central segment of the thorax; it has a motor function and is used to clean the thorax and the wings.

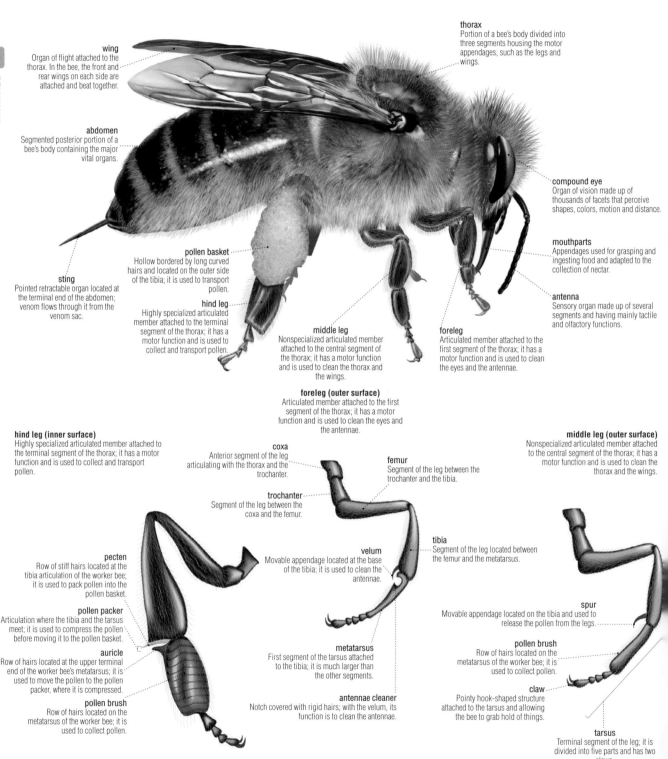

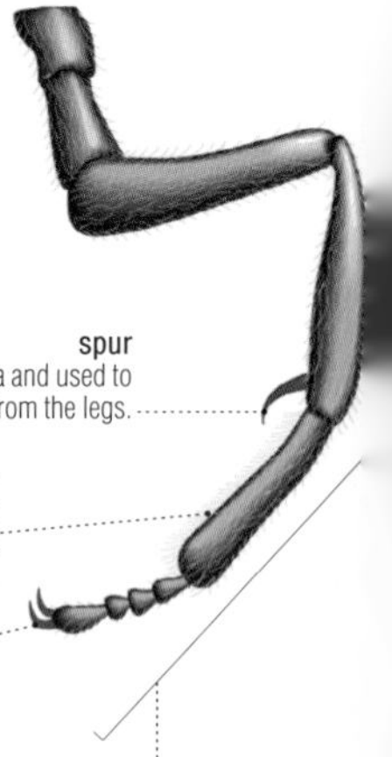

spur
Movable appendage located on the tibia and used to release the pollen from the legs.
pollen brush
Row of hairs located on the metatarsus of the worker bee; it is used to collect pollen.
claw
Pointy hook-shaped structure attached to the tarsus and allowing the bee to grab hold of things.
tarsus
Terminal segment of the leg; it is divided into five parts and has two claws.

honeybee

anatomy of a honeybee

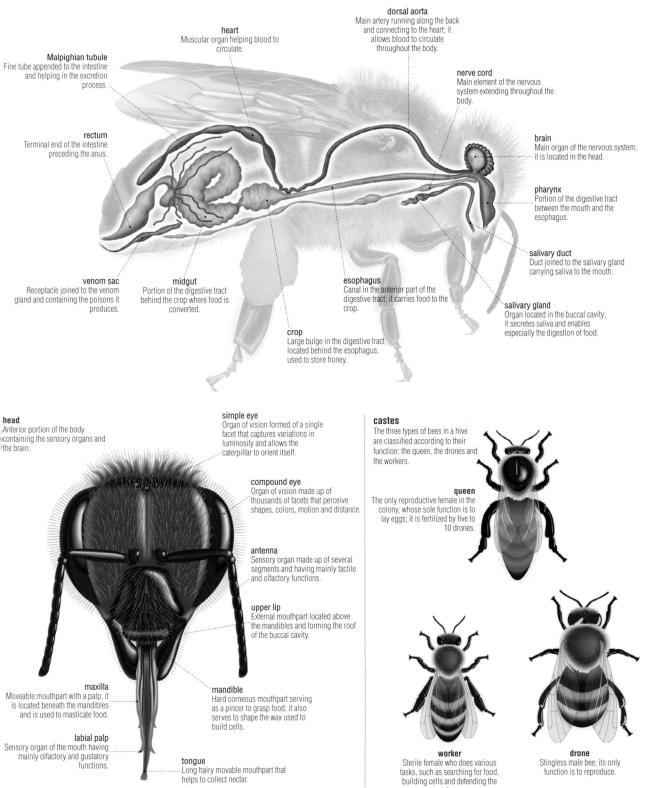

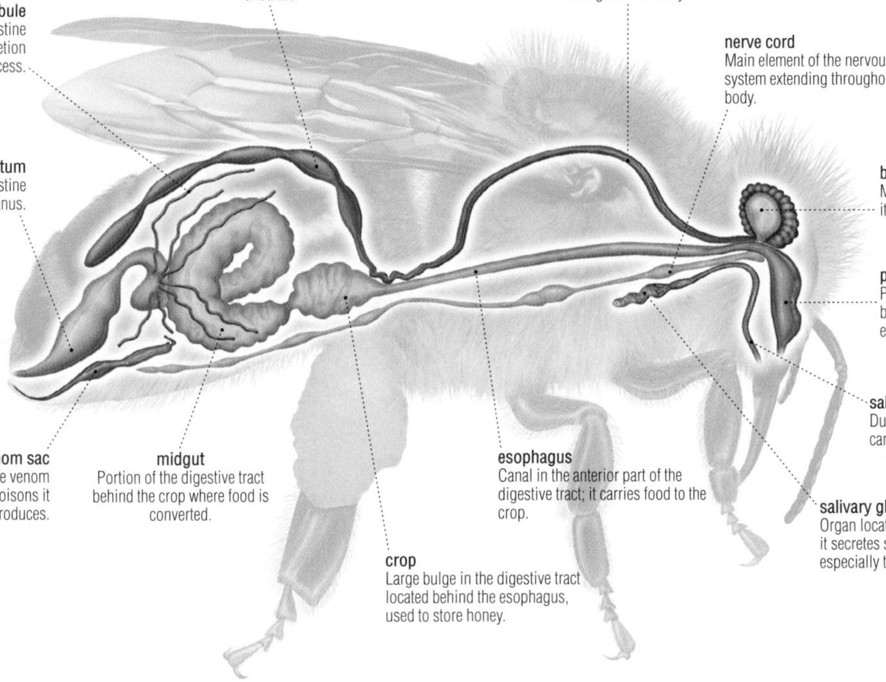
Malpighian tubule
Fine tube appended to the intestine and helping in the excretion process.
heart
Muscular organ helping blood to circulate.
dorsal aorta
Main artery running along the back and connecting to the heart; it allows blood to circulate throughout the body.
nerve cord
Main element of the nervous system extending throughout the body.
rectum
Terminal end of the intestine preceding the anus.
brain
Main organ of the nervous system; it is located in the head.
pharynx
Portion of the digestive tract between the mouth and the esophagus.
salivary duct
Duct joined to the salivary gland carrying saliva to the mouth.
venom sac
Receptacle joined to the venom gland and containing the poisons it produces.
midgut
Portion of the digestive tract behind the crop where food is converted.
esophagus
Canal in the anterior part of the digestive tract; it carries food to the crop.
salivary gland
Organ located in the buccal cavity; it secretes saliva and enables especially the digestion of food.
crop
Large bulge in the digestive tract located behind the esophagus, used to store honey.

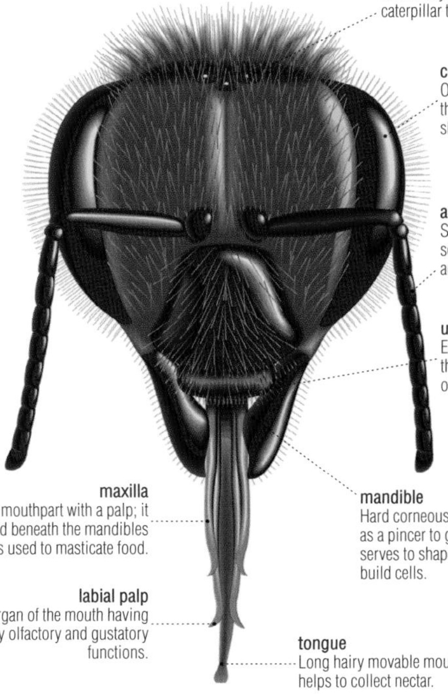
head
Anterior portion of the body containing the sensory organs and the brain.
simple eye
Organ of vision formed of a single facet that captures variations in luminosity and allows the caterpillar to orient itself.
compound eye
Organ of vision made up of thousands of facets that perceive shapes, colors, motion and distance.
antenna
Sensory organ made up of several segments and having mainly tactile and olfactory functions.
upper lip
External mouthpart located above the mandibles and forming the roof of the buccal cavity.
maxilla
Moveable mouthpart with a palp; it is located beneath the mandibles and is used to masticate food.
mandible
Hard corneous mouthpart serving as a pincer to grasp food; it also serves to shape the wax used to build cells.
labial palp
Sensory organ of the mouth having mainly olfactory and gustatory functions.
tongue
Long hairy movable mouthpart that helps to collect nectar.

castes

The three types of bees in a hive are classified according to their function: the queen, the drones and the workers.

queen
The only reproductive female in the colony, whose sole function is to lay eggs; it is fertilized by five to 10 drones.

worker
Sterile female who does various tasks, such as searching for food, building cells and defending the colony.

drone
Stingless male bee; its only function is to reproduce.

honeybee

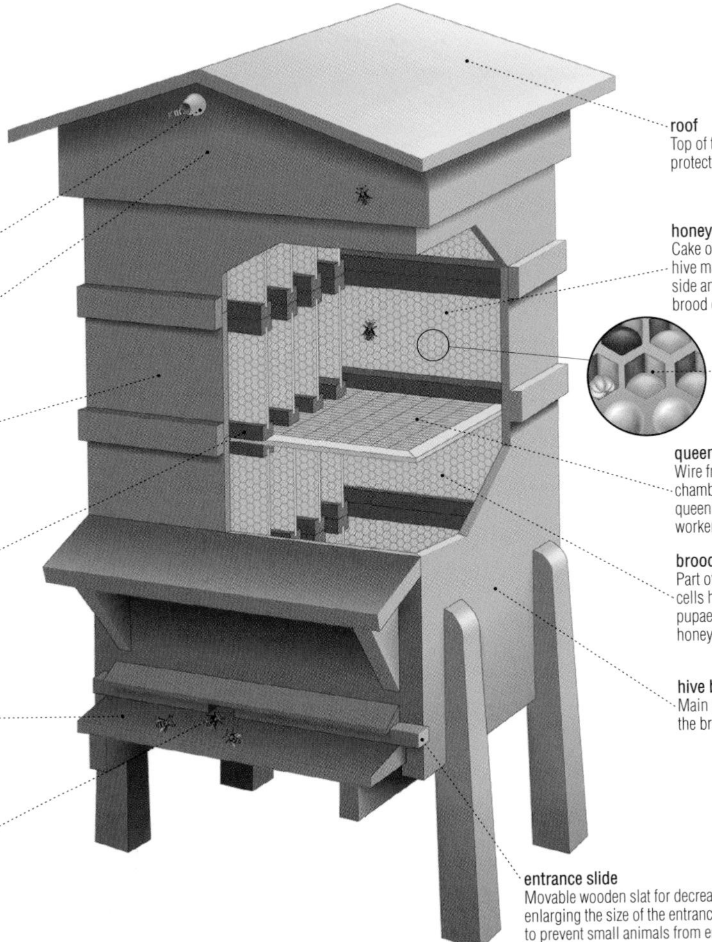
hive
Shelter constructed to house a bee colony that produces honey and pollinates fruit trees.
exit cone
Opening through which bees exit the hive, but never enter it.
outer cover
Movable outer covering of the hive, forming its roof and frame.
super
Removable container used to collect the surplus honey reserves.
frame
Wax-coated removable wooden frame; it is used as a foundation for building combs.
alighting board
Edge of the hive allowing the bees to land and take off.
entrance
Opening of the hive allowing the bees to enter and exit.
roof
Top of the hive providing protection.
honeycomb
Cake of wax made by bees in the hive made up of cells placed side by side and filled with honey or used as brood chambers for embryos.
cell
Hexagonal cavity contained within walls of wax, the constituent unit of honeycombs.
queen excluder
Wire frame separating the brood chamber from the super; it prevents the queen from entering while allowing the worker bees to pass through.
brood chamber
Part of the hive formed of combs; its cells house the queen, eggs, larvae, pupae and reserves of pollen and honey.
hive body
Main portion of the hive enclosing the brood chamber.
entrance slide
Movable wooden slat for decreasing or enlarging the size of the entrance, mainly to prevent small animals from entering the hive.

honeycomb section

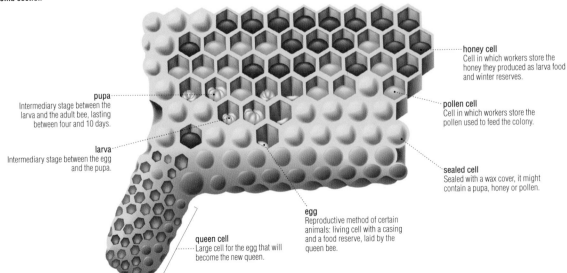

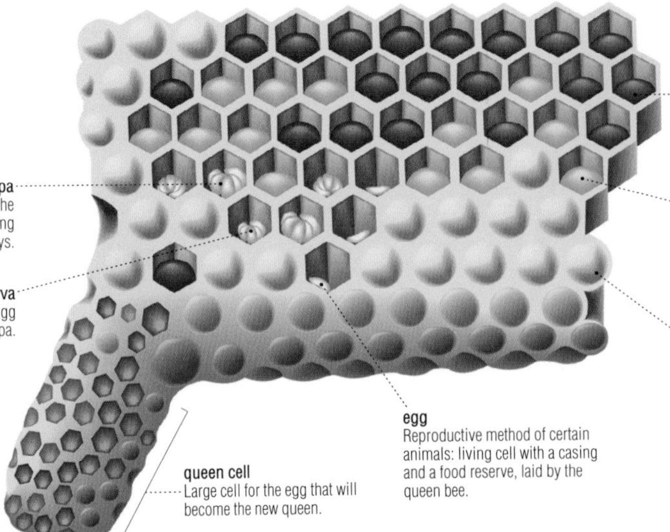
pupa
Intermediary stage between the larva and the adult bee, lasting between four and 10 days.
larva
Intermediary stage between the egg and the pupa.
honey cell
Cell in which workers store the honey they produced as larva food and winter reserves.
pollen cell
Cell in which workers store the pollen used to feed the colony.
sealed cell
Sealed with a wax cover, it might contain a pupa, honey or pollen.
egg
Reproductive method of certain animals: living cell with a casing and a food reserve, laid by the queen bee.
queen cell
Large cell for the egg that will become the new queen.

examples of insects

Insects: invertebrates with bodies divided into three parts; they usually have three pairs of legs, two pairs of wings and antennae.

flea
Extremely small, wingless leaping nsect, a parasite of certain mammals, birds and humans; it stings them to feed off their blood.

louse
Small wingless insect, a parasite of humans, mammals, birds and certain plants.

mosquito
Insect with two wings and long antennae; the female stings humans and animals to feed off their blood.

tsetse fly
Stinging African insect, a parasite of mammals, birds and humans; it is best known for transmitting sleeping sickness.

termite
Social insect that lives in hill colonies; it eats away at wood with its crushing mouthparts.

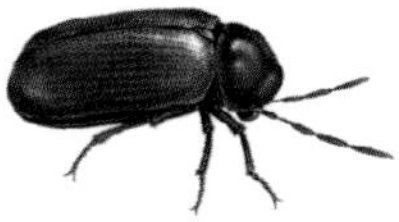

furniture beetle
Small insect, common throughout Europe; its larva feeds on lumber and dead wood.

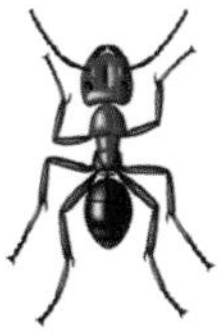

ant
Small social insect living in a highly complex colony; it has developed jaws and might or might not have wings. It consumes mainly insect pests.

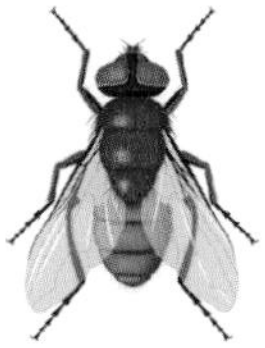

fly
Stocky insect of drab or metallic coloring and having a proboscis, two wings and short antennae; there are numerous species.

ladybug
Brightly colored round-bodied insect that preys on aphids and mealybugs.

shield bug
Small flat-bodied land insect that stings and sucks, a parasite of humans, animals and plants; it releases an unpleasant odor as a defense.

burying beetle
Insect that lays its eggs on dead animals or decomposing matter, which it buries; the egg cache gives off a strong musky smell.

yellowjacket
Social insect; the female has a venomous sting that is painful.

hornet
Large wasp with a painful and dangerous sting; it feeds mainly on insects and fruit.

horsefly
Large fly found in warm countries; the female stings animals and occasionally humans to feed off their blood.

bumblebee
Plump hairy insect related to the bee; it lives in colonies and produces honey.

oriental cockroach
currying flat-bodied nocturnal insect iat is widely dispersed; some species live in human dwellings, feeding on ste matter. It emits an unpleasant odor.

peppered moth
Large butterfly with delicate wings, active at night or at dawn; its caterpillar lives in birch trees, causing major damage.

water bug
Large carnivorous insect with a lean flat body; it is widely dispersed and lives in aquatic environments.

cockchafer
Common garden insect with fringed antennae; it eats leaves and tree roots. Infestations of this pest can cause serious damage.

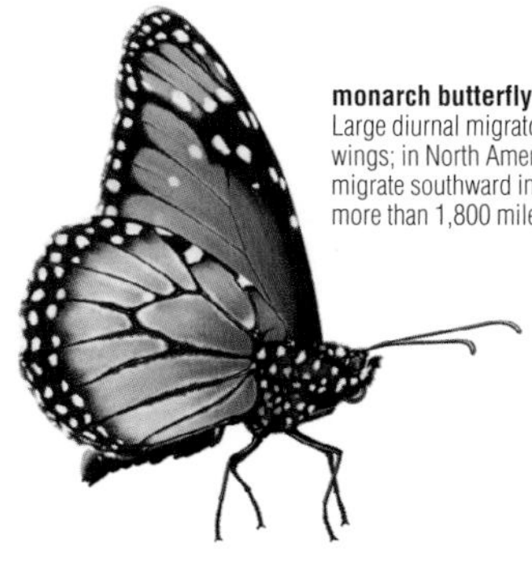

monarch butterfly
Large diurnal migratory butterfly with spotted wings; in North America, thousands of monarchs migrate southward in the autumn, sometimes more than 1,800 miles, and return north in spring.

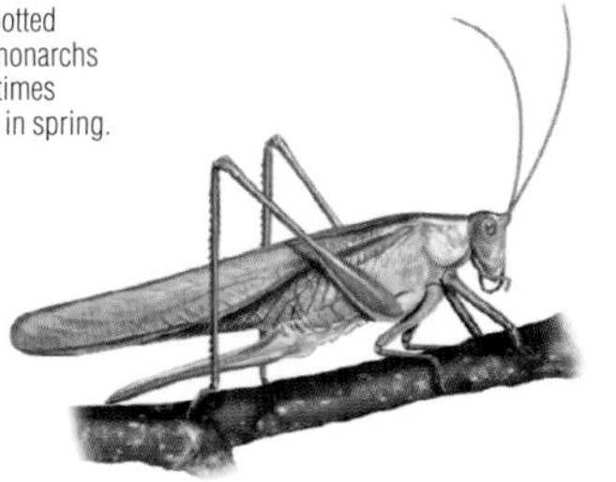

great green bush-cricket
Carnivorous leaping insect with long antennae, growing to 1 to 2 in in length; the male produces a shrill sound.

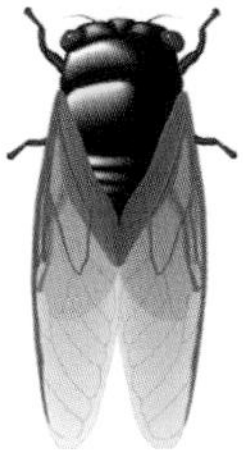

cicada
Large sap-sucking insect; the male produces a shrill monotone sound in hot weather.

examples of insects

atlas moth
Large nocturnal butterfly with colored wings and a wingspan that can reach more than 1 foot; it is found mainly in Southeast Asia.

water strider
Widespread carnivorous insect with a long thin body and six legs, of which the four longest help it to move across water.

bow-winged grasshopper
Hopping insect with short antennae and powerful hind legs; it lives especially in hot climates and emits an intense lively song.

mantid
Long-bodied carnivorous insect found in tropical regions and blending in with its surroundings; its pincer-shaped front legs have spines.

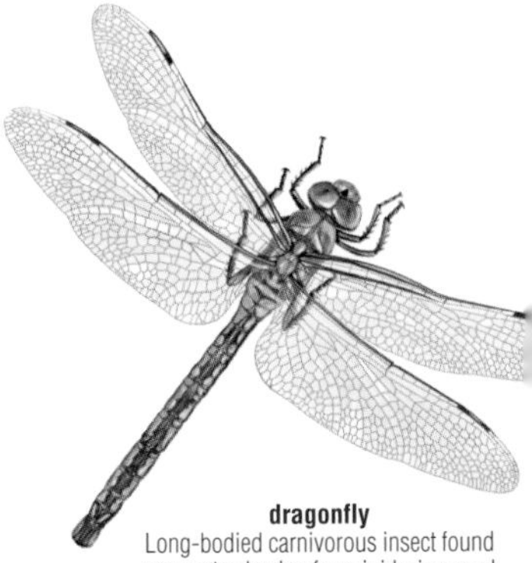

dragonfly
Long-bodied carnivorous insect found near water, having four rigid wings and the largest compound eyes of any insect.

examples of arachnids

Arachnids: invertebrates usually with four pairs of legs and two pairs of appendages attached to their heads.

crab spider
Widespread small arachnid that moves sideways and has powerful front legs; it changes color to catch its prey.

garden spider
Arachnid with a bulging stomach that weaves large webs and is commonly found in fields and gardens; its various species can be found around the world.

scorpion
Relatively large carnivorous arachnid with spines, usually found on land; it has pincers and its abdomen ends in a tail with a poisonous sting.

tick
Extremely small arachnid, parasite of animals and occasionally humans; it can transmit infectious diseases.

water spider
Aquatic arachnid found in Eurasia; to live in the water, it weaves a kind of bell that it fills with air and carries along on the hairs of its abdomen.

red-kneed tarantula
Large hairy arachnid found in Mexico, having a painful but usually innocuous bite; it lives underground in a closed compartment or cocoon.

spider

Articulated arachnid with fangs and silk-producing glands; its body ranges in size from less than an inch to 3.5 in.

spider web
Network of silk threads woven by a spider; it solidifies in the air.

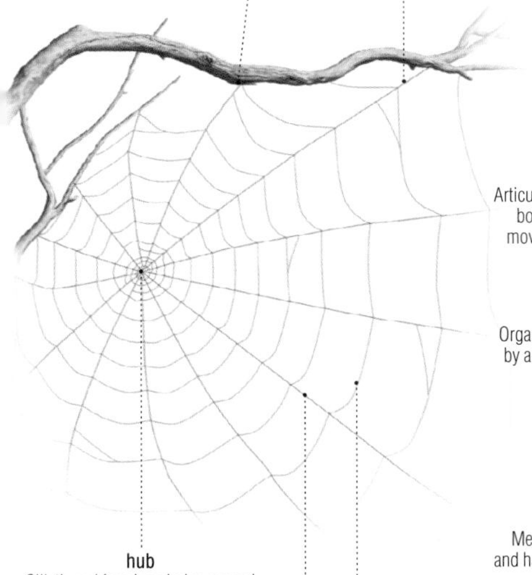

anchor point
Place where the spider affixes the web's support threads.

support thread
Terminal end of a radial thread between the last spiral and the anchor point.

hub
Silk thread forming circles around the center and acting as the juncture point of the radii to strengthen the web.

radial thread
Each of the threads that join one anchor point to the center of the web.

spiral thread
Silk thread forming circles and joining the radial threads to strengthen them.

morphology of a spider

spinneret
Appendage located near the anus, where the silk glands end; the spider generally has three pairs.

abdomen
Posterior portion of the body of a spider containing the main vital organs, including the heart, the intestines and the genital organs.

cephalothorax
Meeting point of the head and the thorax forming the anterior portion of the spider's body.

walking leg
Articulated member supporting the body and allowing the spider to move; a spider usually has eight.

eye
Organ of vision joined to the brain by a nerve; the spider usually has four pairs of simple eyes.

pedipalp
Member similar to a walking leg and having a tactile and prehensile function; a spider has two.

fang
Curved part below the eyes and attached to the venom gland; it allows the spider to catch its prey to inject it with venom.

anatomy of a female spider

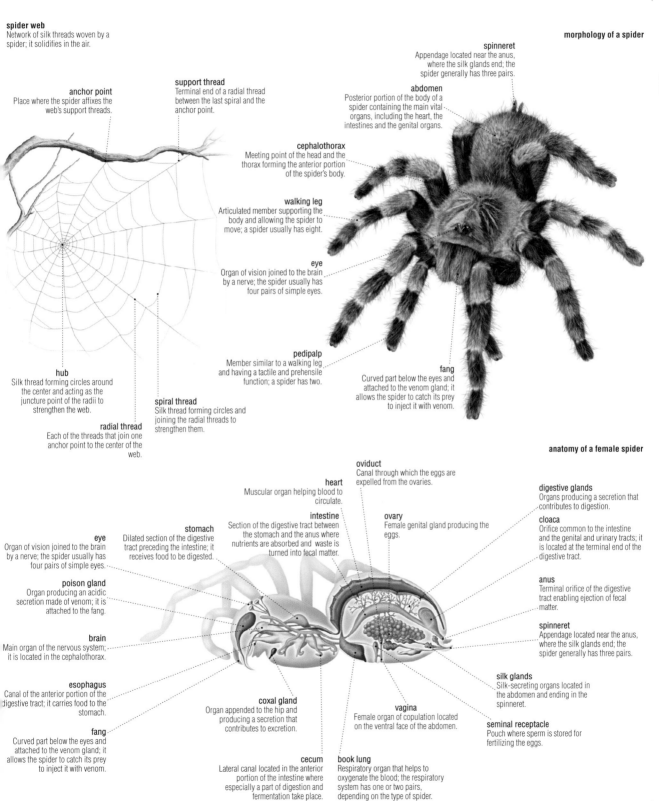

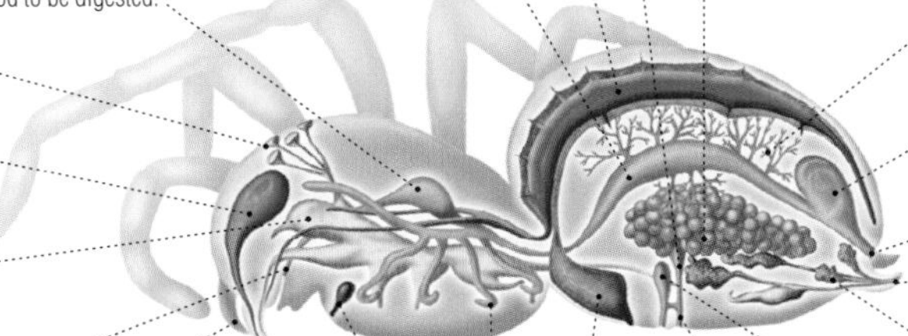

oviduct
Canal through which the eggs are expelled from the ovaries.

heart
Muscular organ helping blood to circulate.

intestine
Section of the digestive tract between the stomach and the anus where nutrients are absorbed and waste is turned into fecal matter.

stomach
Dilated section of the digestive tract preceding the intestine; it receives food to be digested.

eye
Organ of vision joined to the brain by a nerve; the spider usually has four pairs of simple eyes.

poison gland
Organ producing an acidic secretion made of venom; it is attached to the fang.

brain
Main organ of the nervous system; it is located in the cephalothorax.

esophagus
Canal of the anterior portion of the digestive tract; it carries food to the stomach.

fang
Curved part below the eyes and attached to the venom gland; it allows the spider to catch its prey to inject it with venom.

coxal gland
Organ appended to the hip and producing a secretion that contributes to excretion.

cecum
Lateral canal located in the anterior portion of the intestine where especially a part of digestion and fermentation take place.

book lung
Respiratory organ that helps to oxygenate the blood; the respiratory system has one or two pairs, depending on the type of spider.

vagina
Female organ of copulation located on the ventral face of the abdomen.

ovary
Female genital gland producing the eggs.

digestive glands
Organs producing a secretion that contributes to digestion.

cloaca
Orifice common to the intestine and the genital and urinary tracts; it is located at the terminal end of the digestive tract.

anus
Terminal orifice of the digestive tract enabling ejection of fecal matter.

spinneret
Appendage located near the anus, where the silk glands end; the spider generally has three pairs.

silk glands
Silk-secreting organs located in the abdomen and ending in the spinneret.

seminal receptacle
Pouch where sperm is stored for fertilizing the eggs.

snail

Hermaphrodite herbivore land mollusk having a spiral shell; some species of snails are edible.

morphology of a snail

whorl
Each of the swirls around the apex; they increase in diameter and form the shell.
shell
Calcareous spiral casing formed of three successive layers that protect the organs; the snail can withdraw into its shell.
growth line
Thin irregular protuberance of the whorl of the shell, corresponding to its successive growths.
apex
Crown from which the shell grows.
head
Anterior portion of the foot of the snail containing the main sensory organs.
foot
Large elongated muscular organ forming the lower portion of the snail and containing the head; it allows the snail to crawl.
eye
Organ of vision located at the terminal end of the eyestalk; the snail has poor eyesight.
eyestalk
Large muscular appendage, elongated and retractable, bearing an eye at its terminal end.
mouth
Anterior cavity of the digestive tract having a jaw and a rough tongue (radula) to graze on plants.
tentacle
Small muscular appendage, long and retractable, having a tactile role.

anatomy of a snail

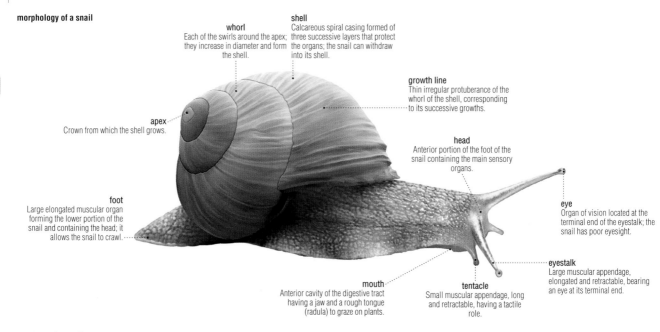

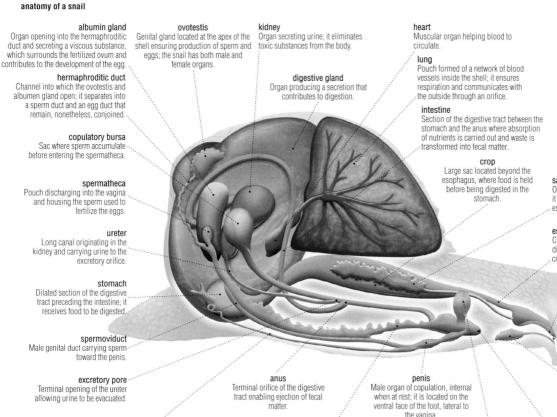

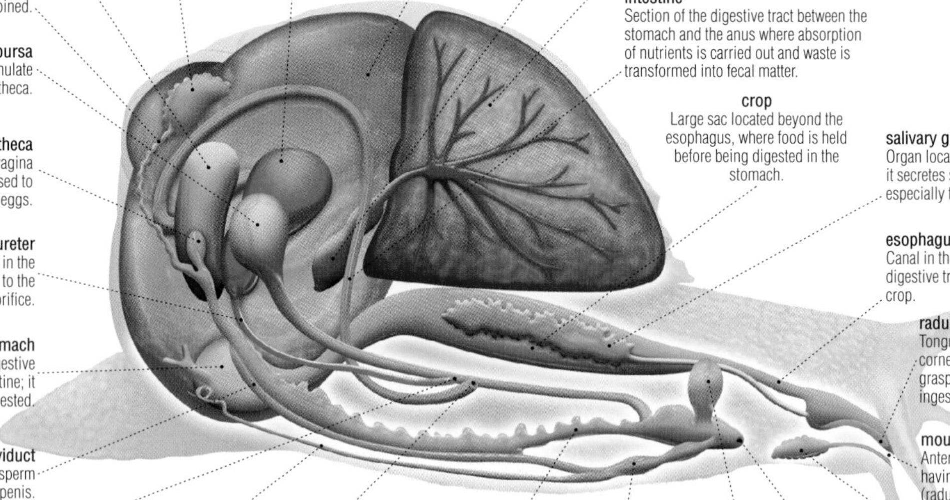
albumin gland
Organ opening into the hermaphroditic duct and secreting a viscous substance, which surrounds the fertilized ovum and contributes to the development of the egg.
ovotestis
Genital gland located at the apex of the shell ensuring production of sperm and eggs; the snail has both male and female organs.
kidney
Organ secreting urine; it eliminates toxic substances from the body.
heart
Muscular organ helping blood to circulate.
hermaphroditic duct
Channel into which the ovotestis and albumen gland open; it separates into a sperm duct and an egg duct that remain, nonetheless, conjoined.
digestive gland
Organ producing a secretion that contributes to digestion.
lung
Pouch formed of a network of blood vessels inside the shell; it ensures respiration and communicates with the outside through an orifice.
intestine
Section of the digestive tract between the stomach and the anus where absorption of nutrients is carried out and waste is transformed into fecal matter.
copulatory bursa
Sac where sperm accumulate before entering the spermatheca.
crop
Large sac located beyond the esophagus, where food is held before being digested in the stomach.
spermatheca
Pouch discharging into the vagina and housing the sperm used to fertilize the eggs.
salivary gland
Organ located in the buccal cavity; it secretes saliva and enables especially the digestion of food.
ureter
Long canal originating in the kidney and carrying urine to the excretory orifice.
esophagus
Canal in the anterior part of the digestive tract; it carries food to the crop.
radula
Tongue bearing numerous sma corneous teeth allowing the sn grasp and tear up food before ingesting it.
stomach
Dilated section of the digestive tract preceding the intestine; it receives food to be digested.
mouth
Anterior cavity of the digestive having a jaw and a rough tong (radula) to graze on plants.
spermoviduct
Male genital duct carrying sperm toward the penis.
excretory pore
Terminal opening of the ureter allowing urine to be evacuated.
anus
Terminal orifice of the digestive tract enabling ejection of fecal matter.
penis
Male organ of copulation, internal when at rest; it is located on the ventral face of the foot, lateral to the vagina.
pedal gland
Organ of the foot located near mouth; it secretes an adhesive substance that allows the snai crawl.
flagellum
Movable filament appended to the penis allowing sperm to move about during copulation.
vagina
Female organ of copulation located on the ventral surface of the foot, lateral to the penis.
dart sac
Calcareous part located inside the vagina containing the dart with which snails sting one another to achieve arousal before copulation.
gonopore
Opening common to the penis and the vagina and located at the side of the head; it allows copulation and entry of the sperm into the copulatory bursa.

univalve shell

Land or aquatic mollusk having a foot and head, which retract into a spiral shell made of a single piece.

morphology of a univalve shell

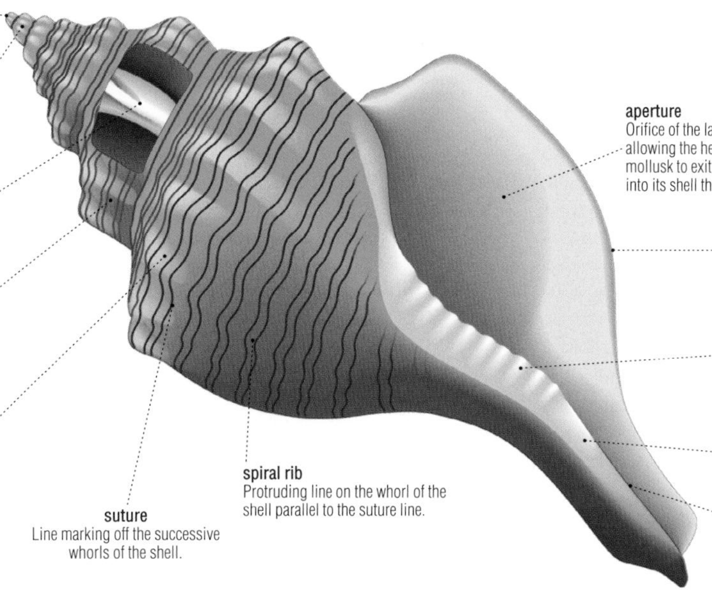

apex
Crown from which the shell grows.

nuclear whorl
First complete turn of the shell formed at the larval stage.

columella
Solid axis of the shell that can be solid or hollow; the whorls turn around it.

whorl
Each of the turns around the apex, except the last; its diameter grows.

axial rib
Protruding line on the whorl of the shell parallel to the columella.

suture
Line marking off the successive whorls of the shell.

spiral rib
Protruding line on the whorl of the shell parallel to the suture line.

aperture
Orifice of the last complete turn allowing the head and foot of the mollusk to exit; it also withdraws into its shell through this opening.

outer lip
Outer wall of the opening made by the last complete turn of the shell, opposite the inner lip.

columella fold
Small protuberance located along the columella.

inner lip
Inner wall of the opening made by the last complete turn of the shell, opposite the outer lip.

siphonal canal
Tubular extension of the opening of the last complete turn allowing water to circulate.

bivalve shell

Aquatic mollusk without a defined head but having a foot, which retracts into a shell formed of two interarticulated parts.

anatomy of a bivalve shell

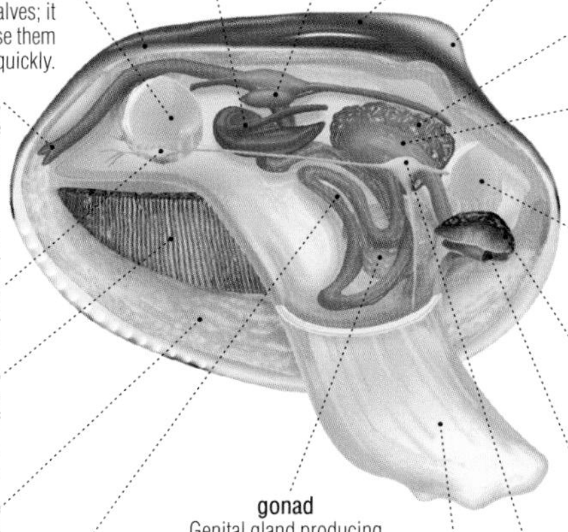

kidney
Organ secreting urine; it eliminates toxic substances from the body.

shell
Calcareous casing produced by the mantle; it has three layers and protects the main organs of the mollusk.

ligament
Corneous structure located behind the umbones and joining both valves of the shell; its elasticity allows them to pull apart.

heart
Muscular organ helping blood to circulate.

umbo
Protuberance at the terminal end of the valve, from which the shell grows.

posterior adductor muscle
Powerful muscle attached to both inside surfaces of the valves; it contracts to open or close them quickly.

digestive gland
Organ producing a secretion that contributes to digestion.

anus
erminal orifice of the digestive tract enabling ejection of fecal matter.

stomach
Dilated section of the digestive tract preceding the intestine; it receives food to be digested.

visceral ganglion
sac located near the posterior or muscle; the nervous system ade up of three pairs of ganglia ropleural, visceral and pedal).

anterior adductor muscle
Muscle attached to both inside surfaces of the valves that contracts to open or close them quickly; it is less powerful than the posterior abductor muscle.

gills
ratory organs located between foot and the mantle, formed of ers of ciliated filaments, which water and retain food particles.

labial palp
Mouthpart that grasps food particles deposited on the gills and carries them to the mouth.

mantle
hick fold of tissue forming two lateral lobes; it envelops the ganic mass of the mollusk and secretes its shell.

gonad
Genital gland producing spermatozoa (sperm) or ova (eggs), depending on the sex of the mollusk.

mouth
Anterior cavity of the digestive tract surrounded by four labial palps, which enable food particles to enter.

intestine
of the digestive tract between the h and the anus where absorption trients is carried out and waste is transformed into fecal matter.

foot
Short flat movable muscular organ located on the ventral surface; it allows the snail to move or to attach itself to a support using elastic filaments.

cerebropleural ganglion
Small sac located near the anterior abductor muscle; the nervous system is made up of three pairs of ganglia (cerebropleural, visceral and pedal).

morphology of a bivalve shell

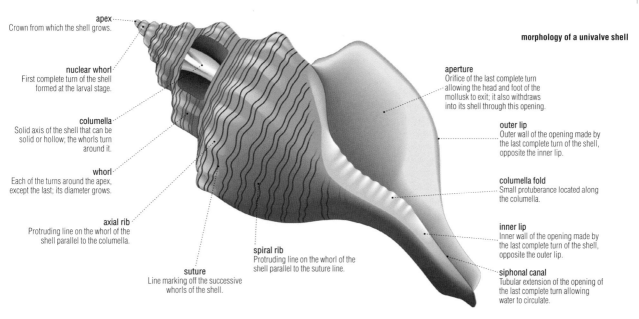

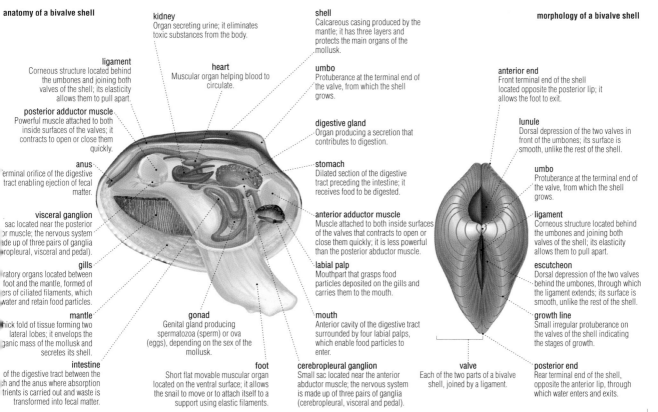

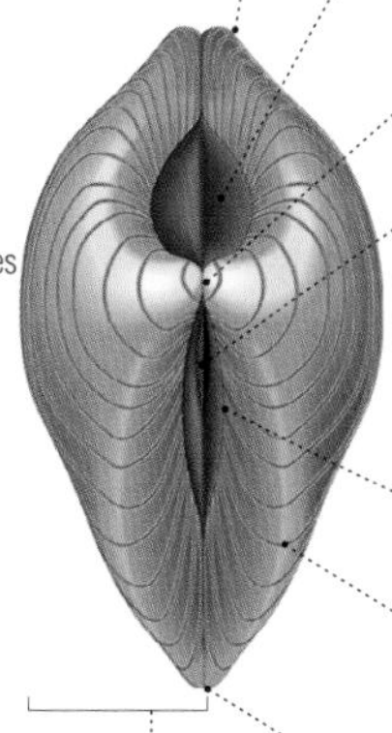

anterior end
Front terminal end of the shell located opposite the posterior lip; it allows the foot to exit.

lunule
Dorsal depression of the two valves in front of the umbones; its surface is smooth, unlike the rest of the shell.

umbo
Protuberance at the terminal end of the valve, from which the shell grows.

ligament
Corneous structure located behind the umbones and joining both valves of the shell; its elasticity allows them to pull apart.

escutcheon
Dorsal depression of the two valves behind the umbones, through which the ligament extends; its surface is smooth, unlike the rest of the shell.

growth line
Small irregular protuberance on the valves of the shell indicating the stages of growth.

valve
Each of the two parts of a bivalve shell, joined by a ligament.

posterior end
Rear terminal end of the shell, opposite the anterior lip, through which water enters and exits.

octopus

Carnivorous marine mollusk with a head bearing eight powerful arms covered with suckers; the octopus can change color to camouflage itself. Certain species are edible.

morphology of an octopus

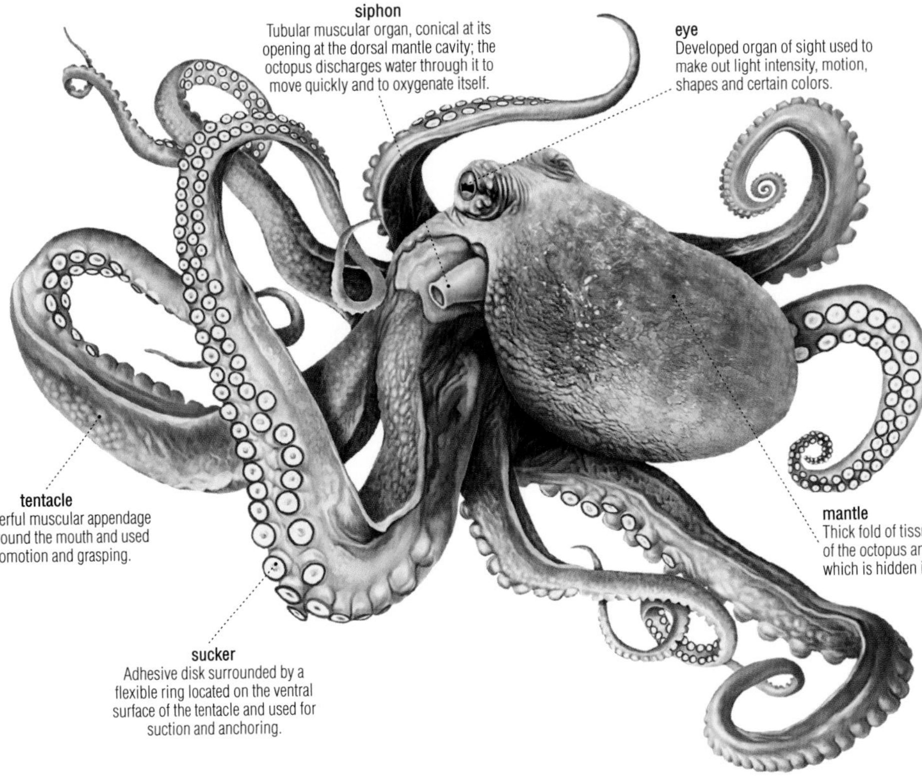

siphon
Tubular muscular organ, conical at its opening at the dorsal mantle cavity; the octopus discharges water through it to move quickly and to oxygenate itself.
eye
Developed organ of sight used to make out light intensity, motion, shapes and certain colors.
tentacle
Long powerful muscular appendage located around the mouth and used for locomotion and grasping.
mantle
Thick fold of tissue enveloping the body of the octopus and secreting the shell, which is hidden inside.
sucker
Adhesive disk surrounded by a flexible ring located on the ventral surface of the tentacle and used for suction and anchoring.

anatomy of an octopus

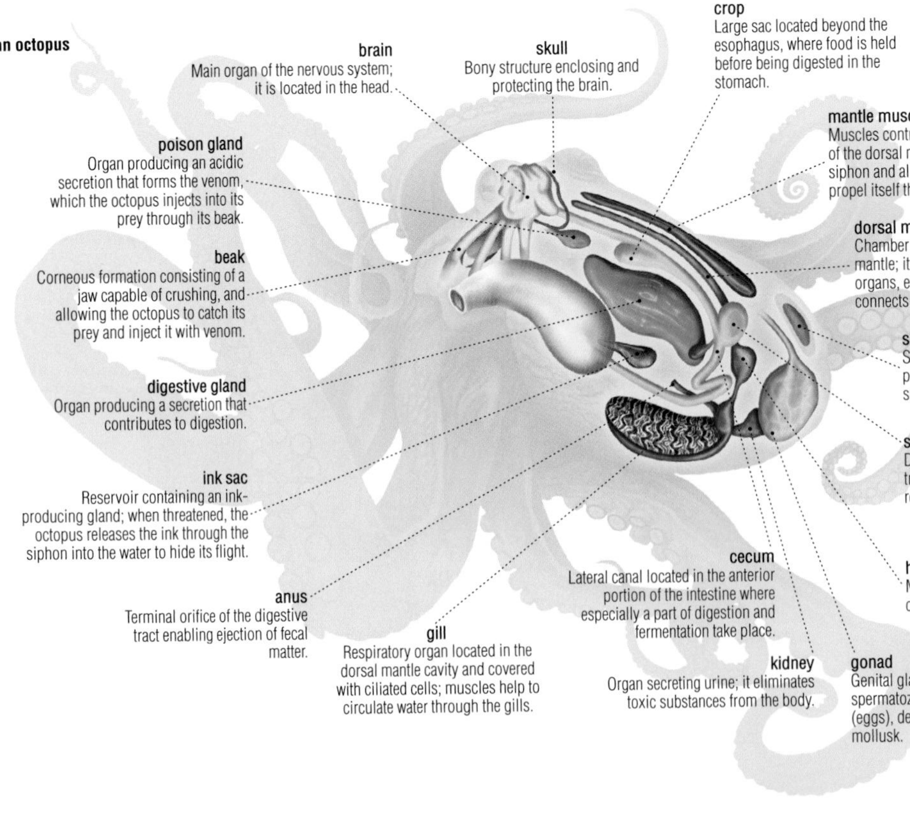

brain
Main organ of the nervous system; it is located in the head.
skull
Bony structure enclosing and protecting the brain.
crop
Large sac located beyond the esophagus, where food is held before being digested in the stomach.
poison gland
Organ producing an acidic secretion that forms the venom, which the octopus injects into its prey through its beak.
mantle muscles
Muscles contracting to force water out of the dorsal mantle cavity through the siphon and allowing the octopus to propel itself through the water.
beak
Corneous formation consisting of a jaw capable of crushing, and allowing the octopus to catch its prey and inject it with venom.
dorsal mantle cavity
Chamber formed of folds of the mantle; it contains the main organs, especially the gills, and connects to the outside.
shell
Small internal calcareous structure produced by the mantle; certain species do not have shells.
digestive gland
Organ producing a secretion that contributes to digestion.
stomach
Dilated section of the digestive tract preceding the intestine; it receives food to be digested.
ink sac
Reservoir containing an ink-producing gland; when threatened, the octopus releases the ink through the siphon into the water to hide its flight.
heart
Muscular organ helping blood to circulate.
cecum
Lateral canal located in the anterior portion of the intestine where especially a part of digestion and fermentation take place.
anus
Terminal orifice of the digestive tract enabling ejection of fecal matter.
gill
Respiratory organ located in the dorsal mantle cavity and covered with ciliated cells; muscles help to circulate water through the gills.
kidney
Organ secreting urine; it eliminates toxic substances from the body.
gonad
Genital gland producing spermatozoa (sperm) or ova (eggs), depending on the sex of the mollusk.

lobster

Large marine crustacean having a carapace and five large pairs of legs, the first of which bears powerful claws; its meat is highly prized.

morphology of a lobster

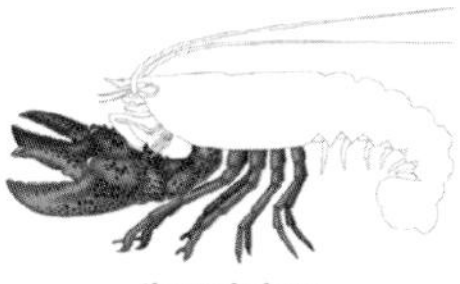

thoracic legs
Articulated limbs attached to the cephalothorax and having a prehensile and motor function; the first three legs bear pincer claws while the last two bear claws.

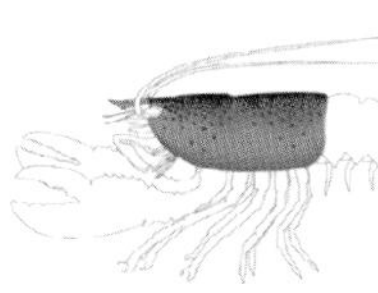

cephalothorax
Meeting of the head and the thorax that forms the anterior portion of the body of the lobster.

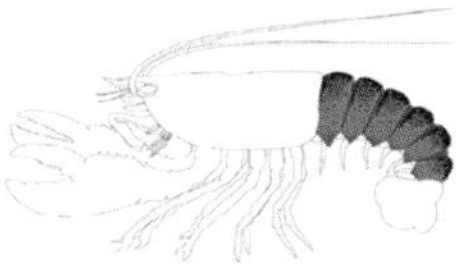

abdomen
Posterior portion of the body formed of six segments and bearing the pleopods, articulated appendages used for swimming, circulating water over the gills and holding the eggs.

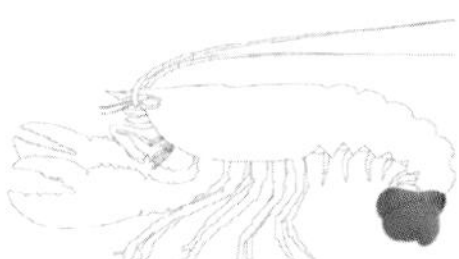

tail
Swimming organ formed of the telson and the two uropods.

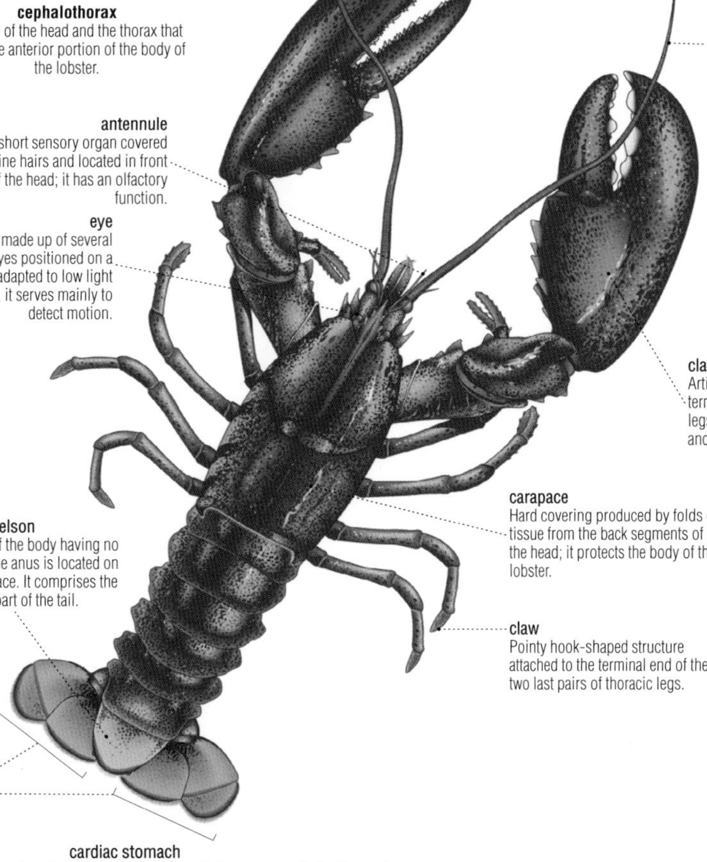

antennule
Very short sensory organ covered with fine hairs and located in front of the head; it has an olfactory function.

eye
Organ of sight made up of several individual eyes positioned on a movable axis; adapted to low light conditions, it serves mainly to detect motion.

telson
Terminal end of the body having no appendages; the anus is located on its ventral surface. It comprises the central part of the tail.

uropod
Articulated appendage attached to the last abdominal segment before the telson; it is formed of two lobes and helps the lobster to swim.

antenna
Long sensory organ having a tactile function.

claw
Articulate appendage located at the terminal end of the first three pairs of legs; it has a prehensile, defensive and, more rarely, motor function.

carapace
Hard covering produced by folds of tissue from the back segments of the head; it protects the body of the lobster.

claw
Pointy hook-shaped structure attached to the terminal end of the two last pairs of thoracic legs.

anatomy of a lobster

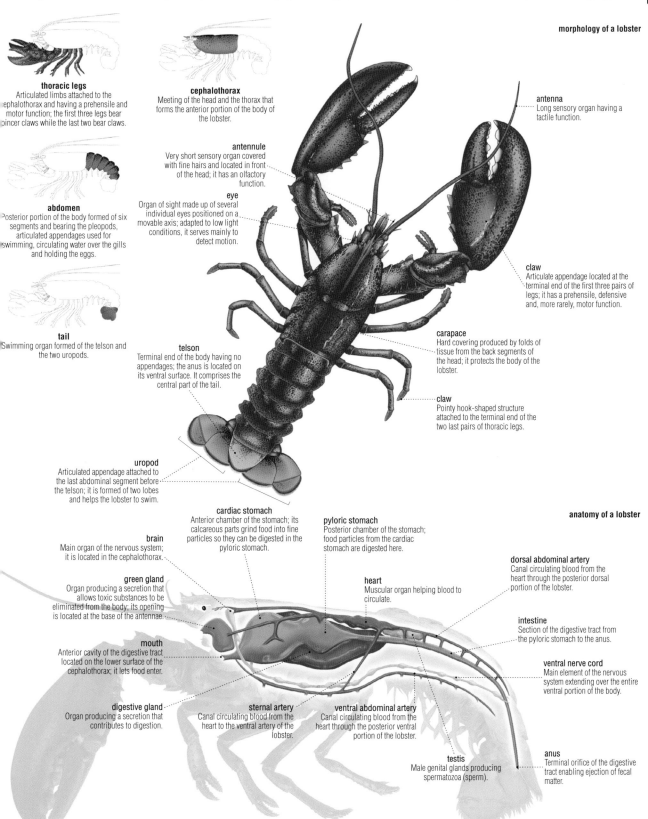

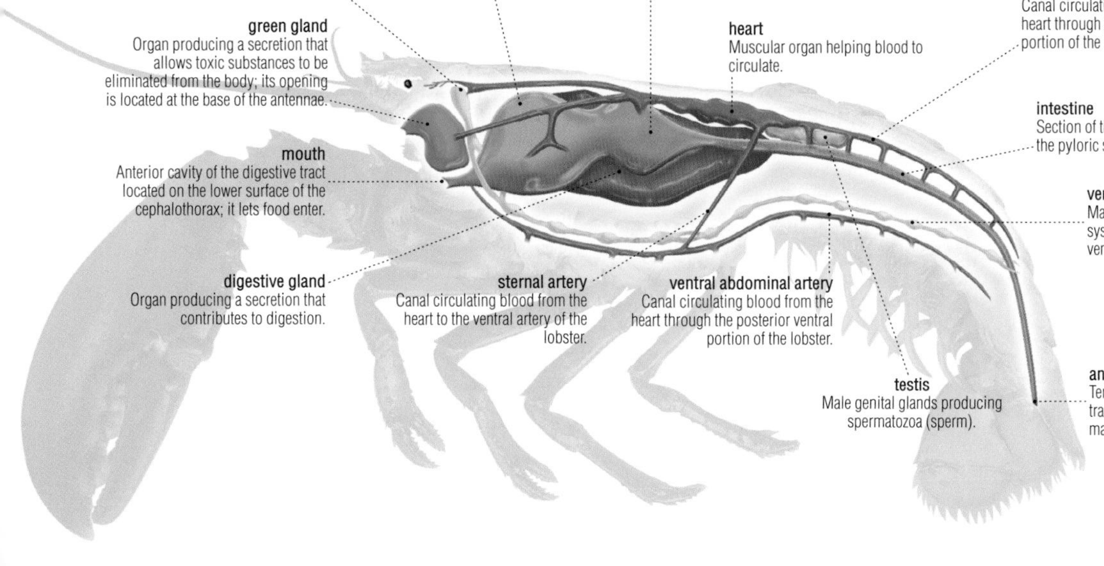

cardiac stomach
Anterior chamber of the stomach; its calcareous parts grind food into fine particles so they can be digested in the pyloric stomach.

pyloric stomach
Posterior chamber of the stomach; food particles from the cardiac stomach are digested here.

brain
Main organ of the nervous system; it is located in the cephalothorax.

green gland
Organ producing a secretion that allows toxic substances to be eliminated from the body; its opening is located at the base of the antennae.

mouth
Anterior cavity of the digestive tract located on the lower surface of the cephalothorax; it lets food enter.

digestive gland
Organ producing a secretion that contributes to digestion.

sternal artery
Canal circulating blood from the heart to the ventral artery of the lobster.

ventral abdominal artery
Canal circulating blood from the heart through the posterior ventral portion of the lobster.

heart
Muscular organ helping blood to circulate.

dorsal abdominal artery
Canal circulating blood from the heart through the posterior dorsal portion of the lobster.

intestine
Section of the digestive tract from the pyloric stomach to the anus.

ventral nerve cord
Main element of the nervous system extending over the entire ventral portion of the body.

testis
Male genital glands producing spermatozoa (sperm).

anus
Terminal orifice of the digestive tract enabling ejection of fecal matter.

cartilaginous fish

Fish whose skeleton is made of cartilage rather than bone; its skin is covered in hard scales called denticles. There are currently 700 species.

morphology of a shark
Shark: large cartilaginous carnivorous fish with a tapered body and extremely powerful toothed jaws; it rarely attacks humans.

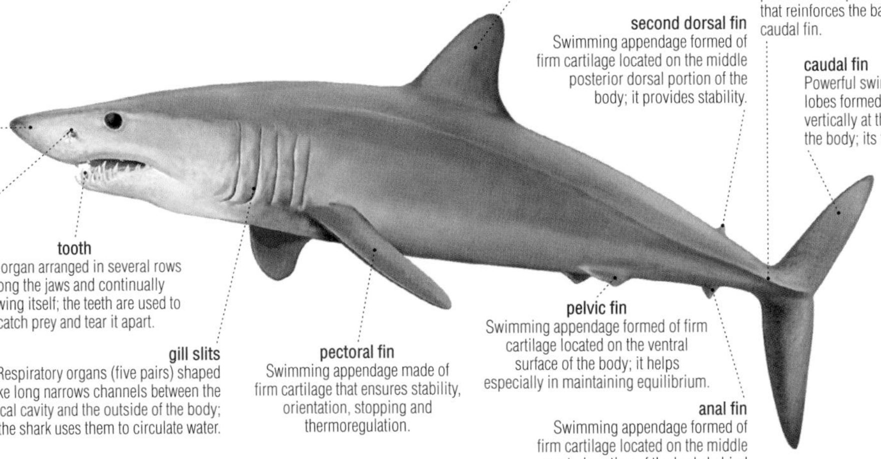
first dorsal fin
Swimming appendage, also called a flipper, made of firm cartilage located midway between the head and the tail; it provides stability.
carina
Protruding median line of the posterior side portion of the body that reinforces the base of the caudal fin.
second dorsal fin
Swimming appendage formed of firm cartilage located on the middle posterior dorsal portion of the body; it provides stability.
caudal fin
Powerful swimming appendage with t
lobes formed of firm cartilage located vertically at the posterior terminal part
the body; its function is propulsion.
snout
Pointy anterior protruding portion of the head located above the mouth and bearing the nostrils on each side.
nostril
External orifice of the nasal cavity located above the mouth with a highly developed olfactory function.
tooth
Hard organ arranged in several rows along the jaws and continually renewing itself; the teeth are used to catch prey and tear it apart.
gill slits
Respiratory organs (five pairs) shaped like long narrows channels between the buccal cavity and the outside of the body; the shark uses them to circulate water.
pectoral fin
Swimming appendage made of firm cartilage that ensures stability, orientation, stopping and thermoregulation.
pelvic fin
Swimming appendage formed of firm cartilage located on the ventral surface of the body; it helps especially in maintaining equilibrium.
anal fin
Swimming appendage formed of firm cartilage located on the middle ventral portion of the body behind the anus; it provides stability.

bony fish

Fish with a rigid skeleton and smooth flat scales; the 20,000 present-day species make up the largest group of fish.

morphology of a perch
Perch: bony carnivorous freshwater fish with an oval body and a spiny dorsal fin; its flesh is highly prized.

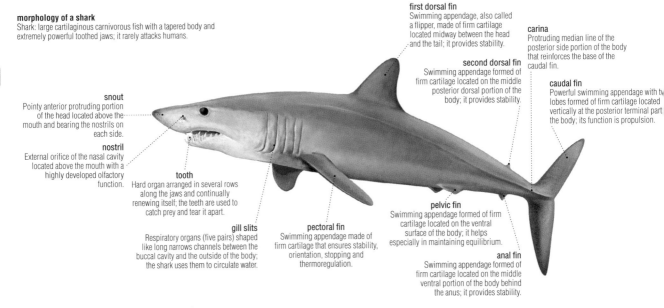

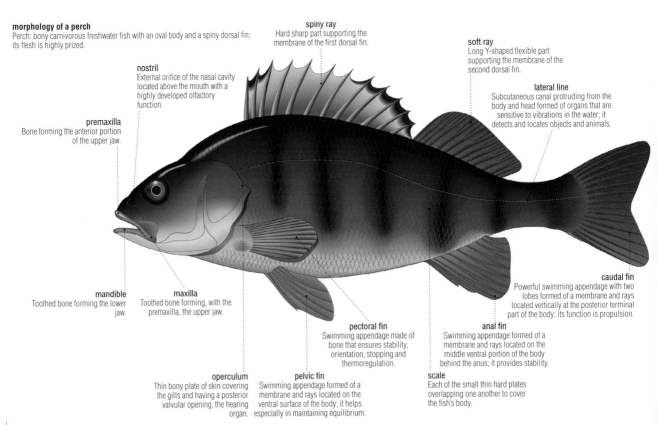

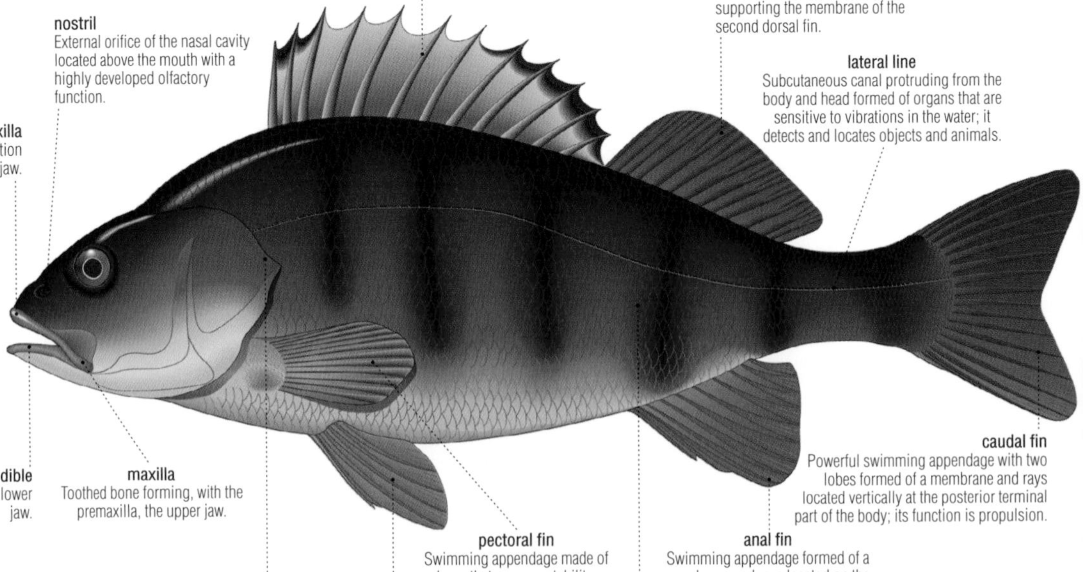
spiny ray
Hard sharp part supporting the membrane of the first dorsal fin.
soft ray
Long Y-shaped flexible part supporting the membrane of the second dorsal fin.
nostril
External orifice of the nasal cavity located above the mouth with a highly developed olfactory function.
lateral line
Subcutaneous canal protruding from the body and head formed of organs that are sensitive to vibrations in the water; it detects and locates objects and animals.
premaxilla
Bone forming the anterior portion of the upper jaw.
caudal fin
Powerful swimming appendage with two lobes formed of a membrane and rays located vertically at the posterior terminal part of the body; its function is propulsion.
mandible
Toothed bone forming the lower jaw.
maxilla
Toothed bone forming, with the premaxilla, the upper jaw.
pectoral fin
Swimming appendage made of bone that ensures stability, orientation, stopping and thermoregulation.
anal fin
Swimming appendage formed of a membrane and rays located on the middle ventral portion of the body behind the anus; it provides stability.
operculum
Thin bony plate of skin covering the gills and having a posterior valvular opening, the hearing organ.
pelvic fin
Swimming appendage formed of a membrane and rays located on the ventral surface of the body; it helps especially in maintaining equilibrium.
scale
Each of the small thin hard plates overlapping one another to cover the fish's body.

anatomy of a perch

Perch: snub-nosed bony freshwater fish with an oval body and a spiny dorsal fin; the flesh of this fish is highly valued.

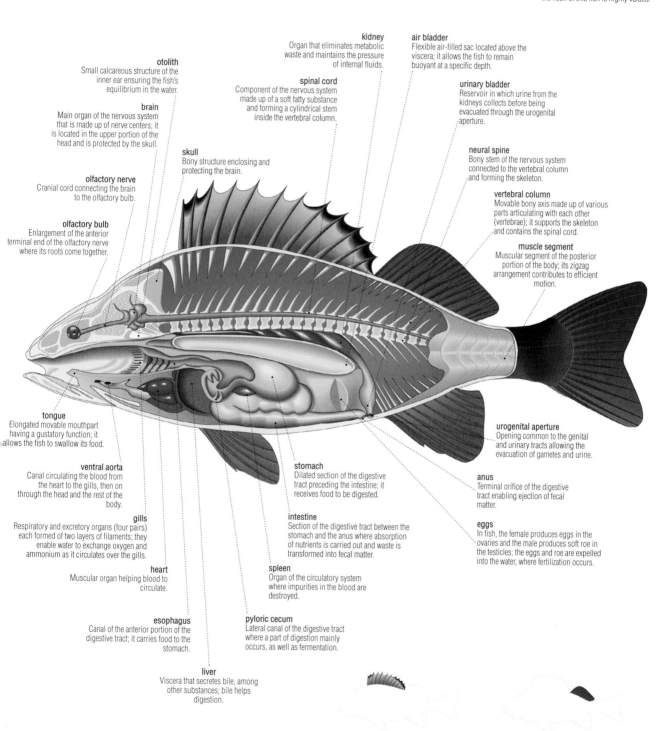

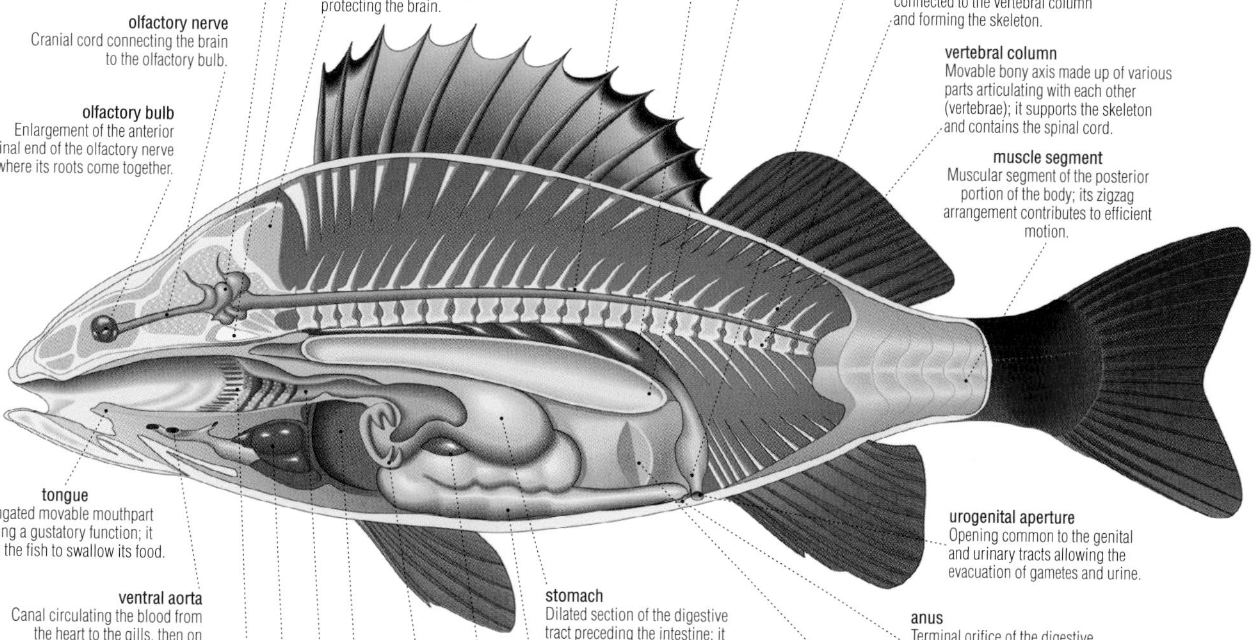
kidney
Organ that eliminates metabolic waste and maintains the pressure of internal fluids.
air bladder
Flexible air-filled sac located above the viscera; it allows the fish to remain buoyant at a specific depth.
otolith
Small calcareous structure of the inner ear ensuring the fish's equilibrium in the water.
spinal cord
Component of the nervous system made up of a soft fatty substance and forming a cylindrical stem inside the vertebral column.
urinary bladder
Reservoir in which urine from the kidneys collects before being evacuated through the urogenital aperture.
brain
Main organ of the nervous system that is made up of nerve centers; it is located in the upper portion of the head and is protected by the skull.
skull
Bony structure enclosing and protecting the brain.
neural spine
Bony stem of the nervous system connected to the vertebral column and forming the skeleton.
olfactory nerve
Cranial cord connecting the brain to the olfactory bulb.
vertebral column
Movable bony axis made up of various parts articulating with each other (vertebrae); it supports the skeleton and contains the spinal cord.
olfactory bulb
Enlargement of the anterior terminal end of the olfactory nerve where its roots come together.
muscle segment
Muscular segment of the posterior portion of the body; its zigzag arrangement contributes to efficient motion.
tongue
Elongated movable mouthpart having a gustatory function; it allows the fish to swallow its food.
urogenital aperture
Opening common to the genital and urinary tracts allowing the evacuation of gametes and urine.
ventral aorta
Canal circulating the blood from the heart to the gills, then on through the head and the rest of the body.
stomach
Dilated section of the digestive tract preceding the intestine; it receives food to be digested.
anus
Terminal orifice of the digestive tract enabling ejection of fecal matter.
gills
Respiratory and excretory organs (four pairs) each formed of two layers of filaments; they enable water to exchange oxygen and ammonium as it circulates over the gills.
intestine
Section of the digestive tract between the stomach and the anus where absorption of nutrients is carried out and waste is transformed into fecal matter.
eggs
In fish, the female produces eggs in the ovaries and the male produces soft roe in the testicles; the eggs and roe are expelled into the water, where fertilization occurs.
heart
Muscular organ helping blood to circulate.
spleen
Organ of the circulatory system where impurities in the blood are destroyed.
esophagus
Canal of the anterior portion of the digestive tract; it carries food to the stomach.
pyloric cecum
Lateral canal of the digestive tract where a part of digestion mainly occurs, as well as fermentation.
liver
Viscera that secretes bile, among other substances; bile helps digestion.

first dorsal fin
Swimming appendage formed of a membrane and usually prickly rays located on the middle anterior dorsal portion of the body; it provides stability.

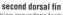

second dorsal fin
Swimming appendage formed of a membrane and rays located on the middle posterior dorsal portion of the body; it provides stability.

frog

Cold-blooded freshwater amphibian with smooth moist skin and powerful back legs for hopping and swimming.

morphology of a frog

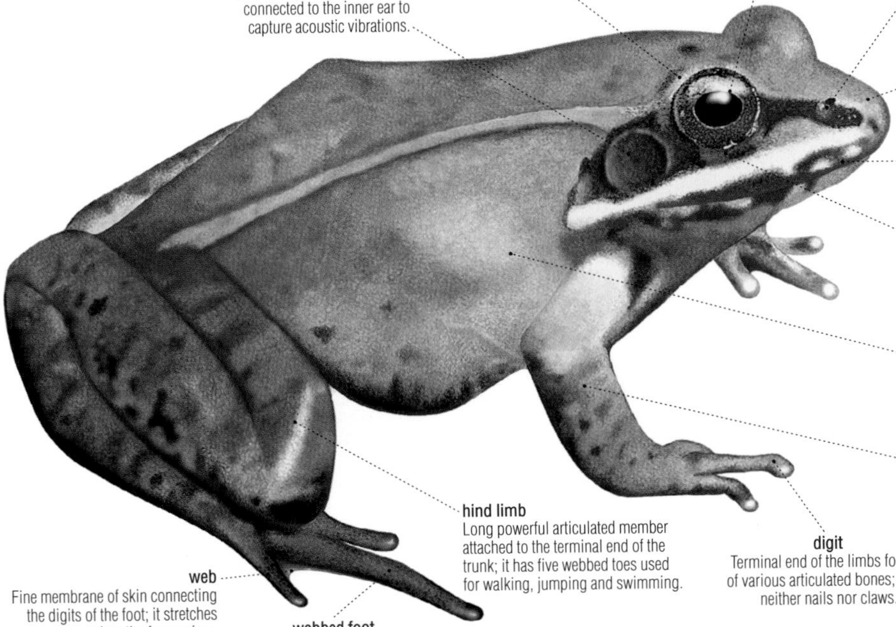
eyeball
Protruding organ of sight contained in the bony cavity at the top of the head used to perceive light intensity, motion and shapes.
upper eyelid
Thick fixed membrane.
nostril
External orifice of the nasal cavity located above the mouth and having olfactory and respiratory functions.
tympanum
Thin strong elastic membrane connected to the inner ear to capture acoustic vibrations.
snout
Anterior round protruding portion of the head that forms the mouth and the nostrils.
mouth
Anterior cavity of the digestive tract located on the ventral surface that allows food to be ingested.
lower eyelid
Thin muscular membrane that is translucent and movable; it rises from the lower edge of the eye to protect and cleanse it.
trunk
Bony portion of the body to which the head and limbs are attached.
forelimb
Short articulated member located behind the head; it has four digits and is used for walking.
hind limb
Long powerful articulated member attached to the terminal end of the trunk; it has five webbed toes used for walking, jumping and swimming.
digit
Terminal end of the limbs formed of various articulated bones; it has neither nails nor claws.
web
Fine membrane of skin connecting the digits of the foot; it stretches when the frog swims.
webbed foot
Each of the digits of the foot, connected by membranes; when spread, they make swimming easier.

anatomy of a male frog

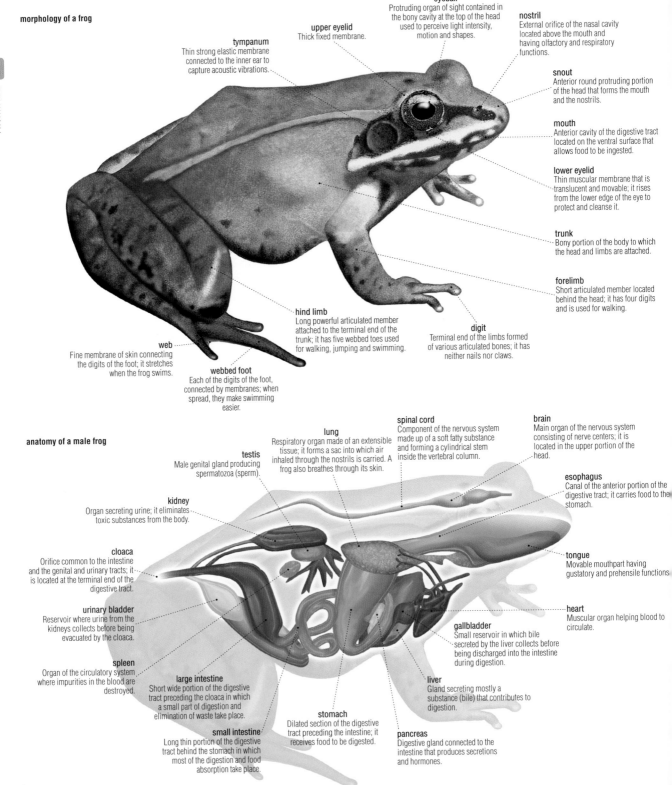

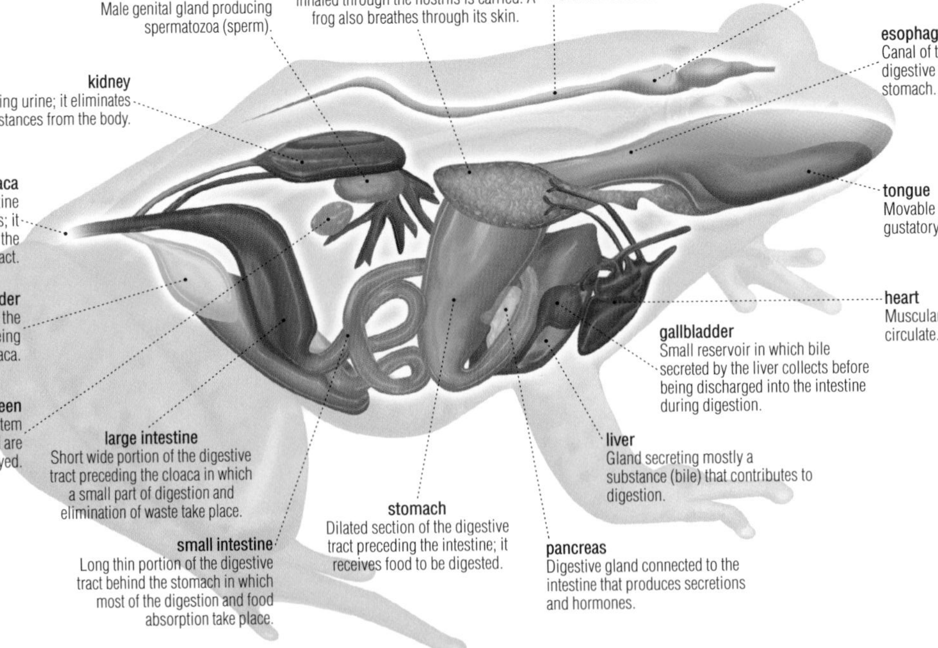
spinal cord
Component of the nervous system made up of a soft fatty substance and forming a cylindrical stem inside the vertebral column.
brain
Main organ of the nervous system consisting of nerve centers; it is located in the upper portion of the head.
lung
Respiratory organ made of an extensible tissue; it forms a sac into which air inhaled through the nostrils is carried. A frog also breathes through its skin.
testis
Male genital gland producing spermatozoa (sperm).
esophagus
Canal of the anterior portion of the digestive tract; it carries food to the stomach.
kidney
Organ secreting urine; it eliminates toxic substances from the body.
cloaca
Orifice common to the intestine and the genital and urinary tracts; it is located at the terminal end of the digestive tract.
tongue
Movable mouthpart having gustatory and prehensile functions.
urinary bladder
Reservoir where urine from the kidneys collects before being evacuated by the cloaca.
heart
Muscular organ helping blood to circulate.
gallbladder
Small reservoir in which bile secreted by the liver collects before being discharged into the intestine during digestion.
spleen
Organ of the circulatory system where impurities in the blood are destroyed.
large intestine
Short wide portion of the digestive tract preceding the cloaca in which a small part of digestion and elimination of waste take place.
liver
Gland secreting mostly a substance (bile) that contributes to digestion.
stomach
Dilated section of the digestive tract preceding the intestine; it receives food to be digested.
small intestine
Long thin portion of the digestive tract behind the stomach in which most of the digestion and food absorption take place.
pancreas
Digestive gland connected to the intestine that produces secretions and hormones.

frog

skeleton of a frog

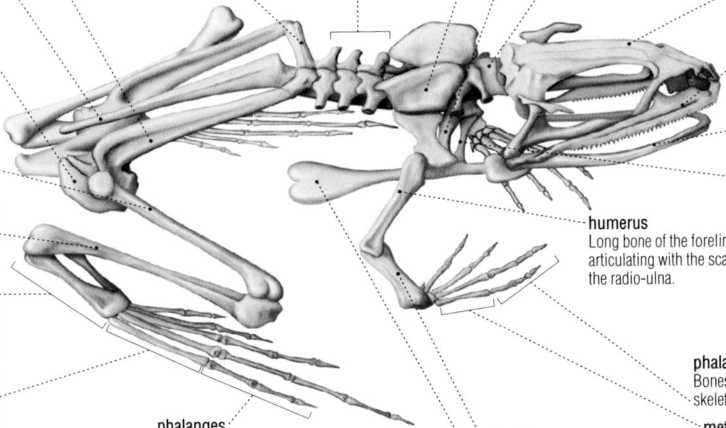

ilium
Large flat bone articulating backward with the sacral vertebra; the juncture of the ilium and the ischium is where the hind limb is attached.

sacral vertebra
Short vertebra located in the posterior portion of the central bony axis and articulating with the ilium.

scapula
Large flat back bone.

coracoid
Ventral bone articulating with the sternum; the juncture of the scapula, clavicle and coracoid is the point where the hind limb is attached.

urostyle
Long bone of the posterior portion of the central bony axis; it is formed by several fused vertebrae.

vertebrae
Short bony parts of the dorsal area of the body forming the central bony axis.

atlas
First cervical vertebra supporting the head and supported by the axis.

frontoparietal
Large flat bone of the upper anterior portion of the cranial box.

maxilla
Toothed bone comprising the upper jaw.

ischium
Bone situated behind the ilium.

mandible
Smooth curved movable bone comprising the lower jaw.

femur
Long bone of the hind limb articulating with the ilium and the tibiofibula.

clavicle
Long bone located between the sternum and the scapula.

tibiofibula
Located between the femur and the tarsus, the tibia and the fibula fuse to form one long bone.

humerus
Long bone of the forelimb articulating with the scapula and the radio-ulna.

tarsus
Part of the hind limb formed of several short bones; it is located between the tibiofibula and the metatarsus.

phalanges
Bones articulating to form the skeleton of the digits.

metatarsus
Part of the hind limb formed of five long parallel bones; it connects the tarsus with the first phalanges of the digits.

phalanges
Bones articulating to form the skeleton of the digits.

sternum
Long flat bone located in the mid-ventral portion of the body; the clavicle and the coracoid, in particular, are attached to it.

radio-ulna
Located between the humerus and the metacarpus, the radius and the ulna fuse to form one long bone.

metacarpus
Part of the forelimb formed of four long bones; it connects the radio-ulna to the first phalanges of the digits.

life cycle of the frog

The stages of development are the egg, the tadpole and the adult; each stage usually lasts several weeks, but can last up to two years in some species.

eggs
Embryonic stage of the frog resulting when the egg is fertilized by the sperm.

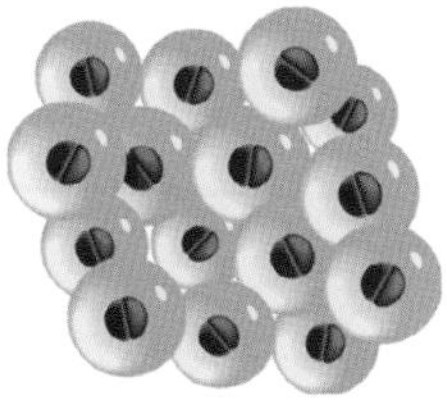

tadpole
Aquatic larva of the frog having a large head and a slender body ending in a tail; it breathes through gills.

external gills
Respiratory organs that filter water and take in food particles; they are later replaced by internal gills.

hind limb
The hind limbs appear after the gills.

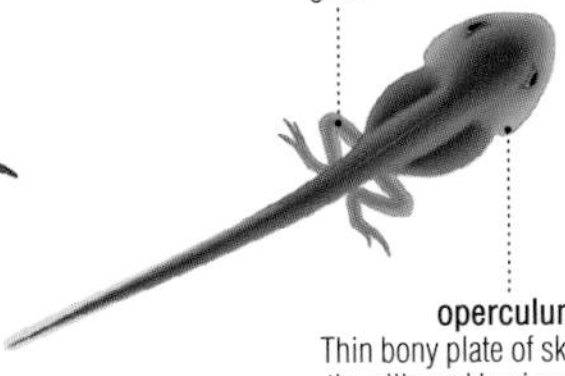

operculum
Thin bony plate of skin covering the gills and having a posterior valvular opening, the hearing organ.

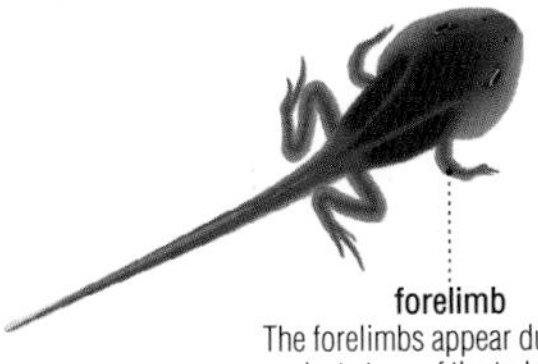

forelimb
The forelimbs appear during the last stage of the tadpole's metamorphosis.

examples of amphibians

There are about 4,000 species of amphibians divided into three main groups, depending on whether or not they have a tail and limbs.

salamander
Nocturnal amphibian, mainly insectivorous, with a tail; there are land and aquatic species.

wood frog
Tailless amphibian found mostly in the woods of North America; it feeds on various small animals.

common frog
Squat tailless amphibian usually found on land, mostly in Europe; it feeds on various small animals.

tree frog
Small tailless, usually insectivorous amphibian found mostly in trees near water; its digits are fitted with suction cups.

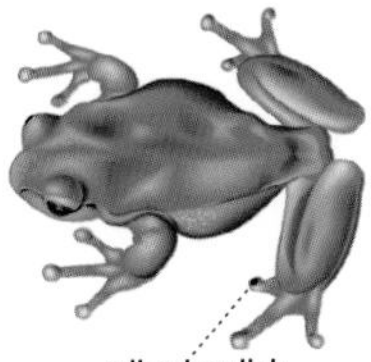

adhesive disk
Adhesive disk surrounded by a ring; it is located at the terminal end of the limbs and used for anchoring.

newt
Amphibian with a flat tail found mainly in freshwater and usually feeding on insects.

common toad
Tailless nocturnal insectivorous amphibian usually found on land and not very adept at jumping; its body is covered with small outgrowths.

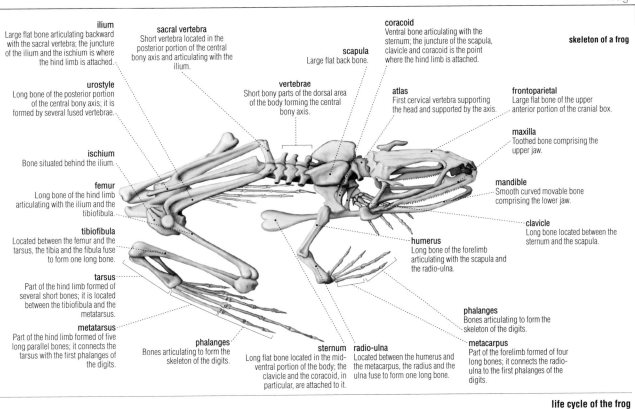

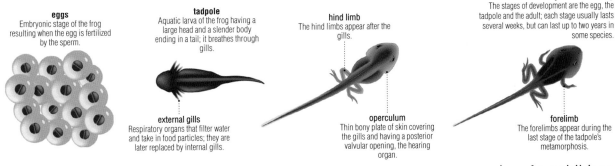

Northern leopard frog
Tailless, mostly nocturnal amphibian with a spotted body that is covered with ridges; it lives mainly in North America.

snake

Legless reptile with a very long cylindrical body and tail, moving by undulation; there are about 2,700 species.

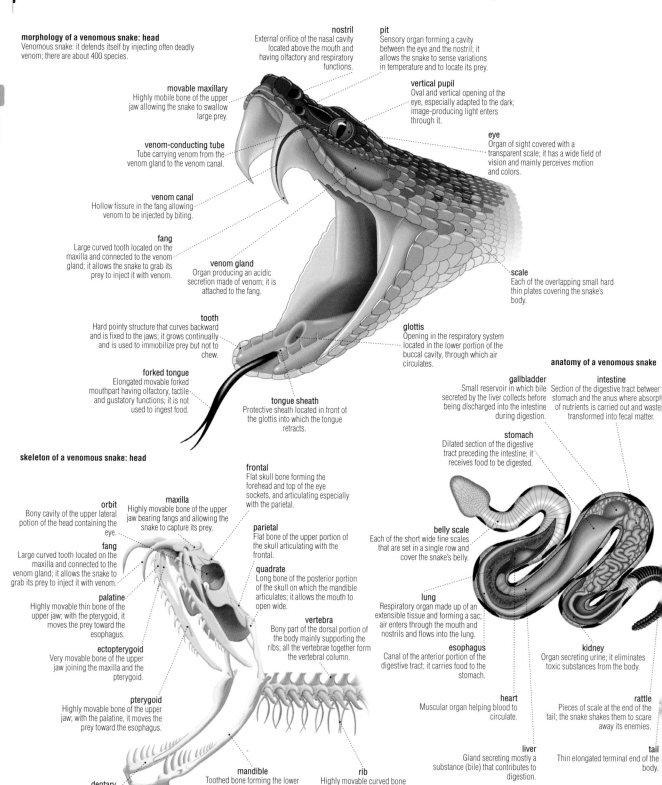

morphology of a venomous snake: head
Venomous snake: it defends itself by injecting often deadly venom; there are about 400 species.

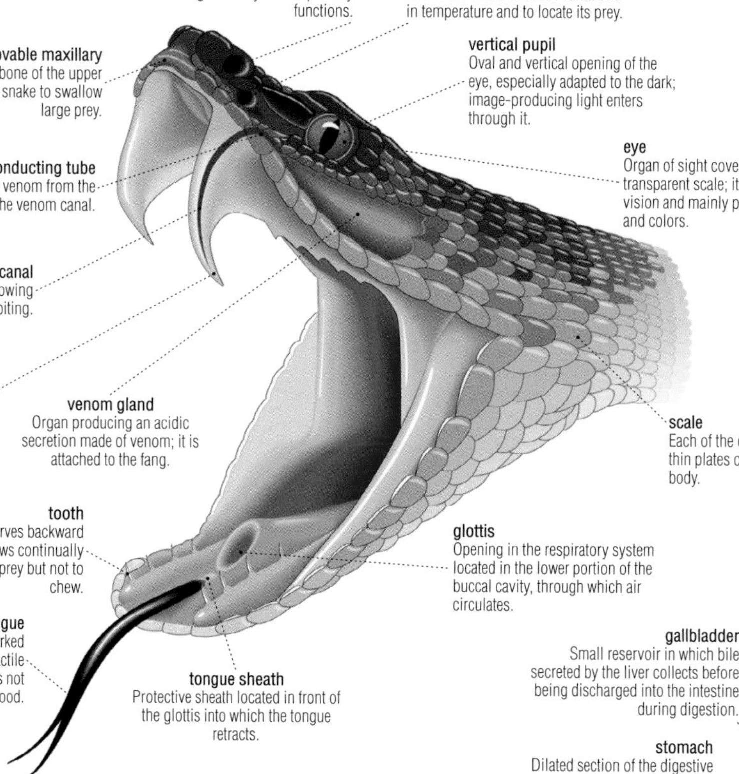
nostril
External orifice of the nasal cavity located above the mouth and having olfactory and respiratory functions.
pit
Sensory organ forming a cavity between the eye and the nostril; it allows the snake to sense variations in temperature and to locate its prey.
movable maxillary
Highly mobile bone of the upper jaw allowing the snake to swallow large prey.
vertical pupil
Oval and vertical opening of the eye, especially adapted to the dark; image-producing light enters through it.
eye
Organ of sight covered with a transparent scale; it has a wide field of vision and mainly perceives motion and colors.
venom-conducting tube
Tube carrying venom from the venom gland to the venom canal.
venom canal
Hollow fissure in the fang allowing venom to be injected by biting.
fang
Large curved tooth located on the maxilla and connected to the venom gland; it allows the snake to grab its prey to inject it with venom.
venom gland
Organ producing an acidic secretion made of venom; it is attached to the fang.
scale
Each of the overlapping small hard thin plates covering the snake's body.
tooth
Hard pointy structure that curves backward and is fixed to the jaws; it grows continually and is used to immobilize prey but not to chew.
glottis
Opening in the respiratory system located in the lower portion of the buccal cavity, through which air circulates.
forked tongue
Elongated movable forked mouthpart having olfactory, tactile and gustatory functions; it is not used to ingest food.
tongue sheath
Protective sheath located in front of the glottis into which the tongue retracts.

anatomy of a venomous snake

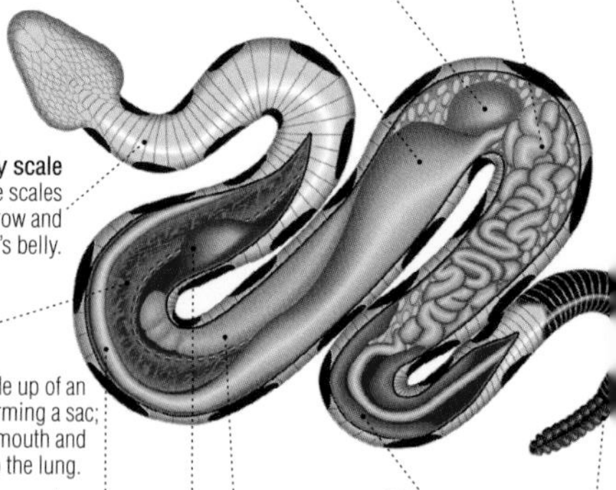
gallbladder
Small reservoir in which bile secreted by the liver collects before being discharged into the intestine during digestion.
intestine
Section of the digestive tract between stomach and the anus where absorp
of nutrients is carried out and waste transformed into fecal matter.
stomach
Dilated section of the digestive tract preceding the intestine; it receives food to be digested.
belly scale
Each of the short wide fine scales that are set in a single row and cover the snake's belly.
lung
Respiratory organ made up of an extensible tissue and forming a sac; air enters through the mouth and nostrils and flows into the lung.
esophagus
Canal of the anterior portion of the digestive tract; it carries food to the stomach.
kidney
Organ secreting urine; it eliminates toxic substances from the body.
heart
Muscular organ helping blood to circulate.
rattle
Pieces of scale at the end of the tail; the snake shakes them to scare away its enemies.
liver
Gland secreting mostly a substance (bile) that contributes to digestion.
tail
Thin elongated terminal end of the body.

skeleton of a venomous snake: head

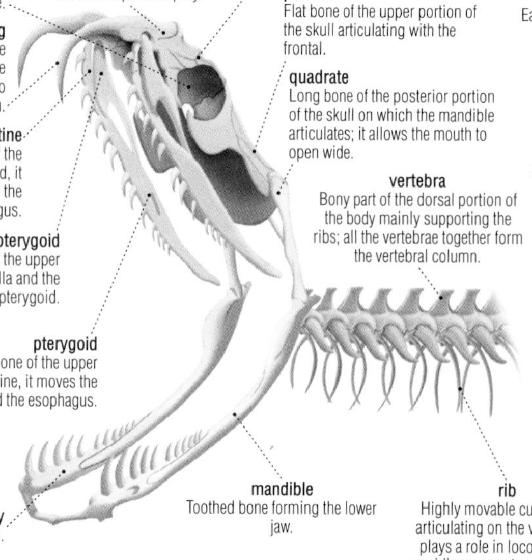
frontal
Flat skull bone forming the forehead and top of the eye sockets, and articulating especially with the parietal.
orbit
Bony cavity of the upper lateral potion of the head containing the eye.
maxilla
Highly movable bone of the upper jaw bearing fangs and allowing the snake to capture its prey.
parietal
Flat bone of the upper portion of the skull articulating with the frontal.
fang
Large curved tooth located on the maxilla and connected to the venom gland; it allows the snake to grab its prey to inject it with venom.
quadrate
Long bone of the posterior portion of the skull on which the mandible articulates; it allows the mouth to open wide.
palatine
Highly movable thin bone of the upper jaw; with the pterygoid, it moves the prey toward the esophagus.
vertebra
Bony part of the dorsal portion of the body mainly supporting the ribs; all the vertebrae together form the vertebral column.
ectopterygoid
Very movable bone of the upper jaw joining the maxilla and the pterygoid.
pterygoid
Highly movable bone of the upper jaw; with the palatine, it moves the prey toward the esophagus.
mandible
Toothed bone forming the lower jaw.
rib
Highly movable curved bone articulating on the vertebrae; it plays a role in locomotion by providing support on the ground.
dentary
Bone of the mandible bearing teeth.

turtle

Squat land or aquatic reptile with short legs and bearing a carapace into which it retracts; there are about 250 species.

morphology of a turtle

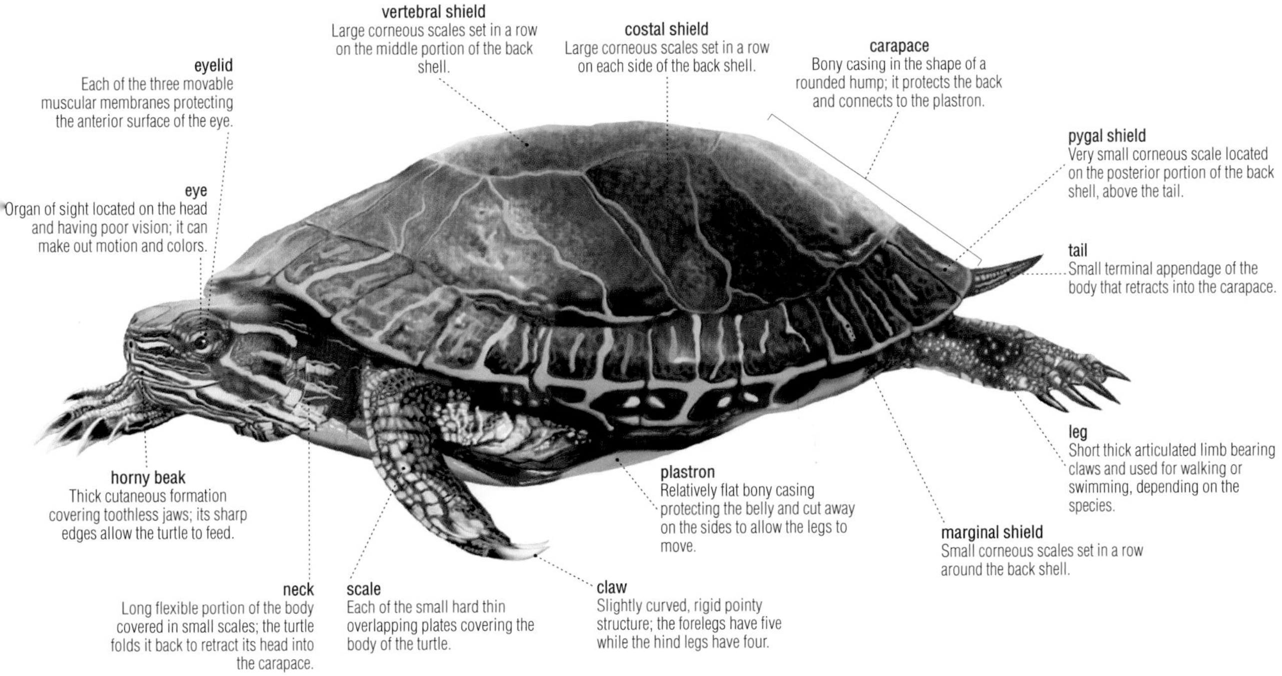
vertebral shield
Large corneous scales set in a row on the middle portion of the back shell.
costal shield
Large corneous scales set in a row on each side of the back shell.
carapace
Bony casing in the shape of a rounded hump; it protects the back and connects to the plastron.
eyelid
Each of the three movable muscular membranes protecting the anterior surface of the eye.
pygal shield
Very small corneous scale located on the posterior portion of the back shell, above the tail.
eye
Organ of sight located on the head and having poor vision; it can make out motion and colors.
tail
Small terminal appendage of the body that retracts into the carapace.
leg
Short thick articulated limb bearing claws and used for walking or swimming, depending on the species.
horny beak
Thick cutaneous formation covering toothless jaws; its sharp edges allow the turtle to feed.
plastron
Relatively flat bony casing protecting the belly and cut away on the sides to allow the legs to move.
marginal shield
Small corneous scales set in a row around the back shell.
neck
Long flexible portion of the body covered in small scales; the turtle folds it back to retract its head into the carapace.
scale
Each of the small hard thin overlapping plates covering the body of the turtle.
claw
Slightly curved, rigid pointy structure; the forelegs have five while the hind legs have four.

anatomy of a turtle

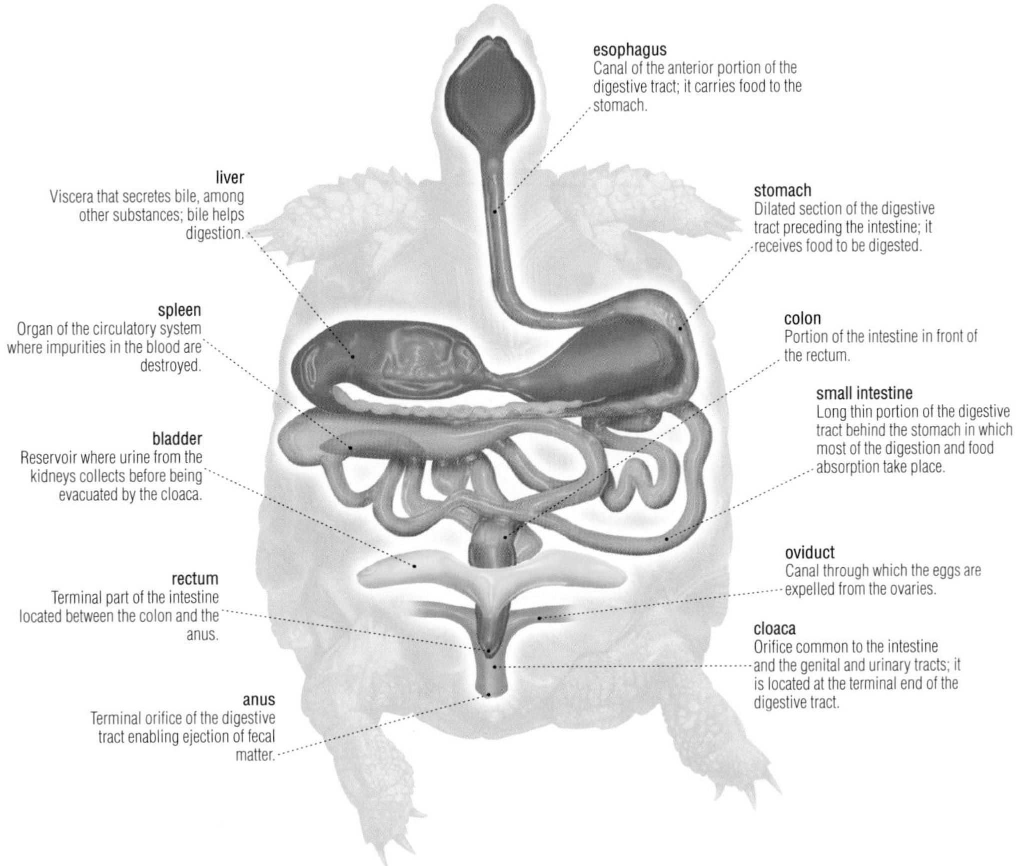
esophagus
Canal of the anterior portion of the digestive tract; it carries food to the stomach.
liver
Viscera that secretes bile, among other substances; bile helps digestion.
stomach
Dilated section of the digestive tract preceding the intestine; it receives food to be digested.
spleen
Organ of the circulatory system where impurities in the blood are destroyed.
colon
Portion of the intestine in front of the rectum.
small intestine
Long thin portion of the digestive tract behind the stomach in which most of the digestion and food absorption take place.
bladder
Reservoir where urine from the kidneys collects before being evacuated by the cloaca.
oviduct
Canal through which the eggs are expelled from the ovaries.
rectum
Terminal part of the intestine located between the colon and the anus.
cloaca
Orifice common to the intestine and the genital and urinary tracts; it is located at the terminal end of the digestive tract.
anus
Terminal orifice of the digestive tract enabling ejection of fecal matter.

examples of reptiles

Reptiles: cold-blooded vertebrates covered in scales (about 6,000 species) having limbs that are sometimes atrophied or absent.

viper
Venomous snake found in hot arid regions of Eurasia and Africa with a flat triangular head and short tail; its bite can be fatal.

garter snake
Widespread nonvenomous snake with a slightly flat oval head; its tail is longer than that of the viper.

chameleon
Insectivorous lizard of Africa and India with a prehensile tail; it lives in trees and can change color to hide itself.

lizard
Widespread diurnal and mainly insectivorous land reptile with a long brittle tail.

rattlesnake
Venomous land snake of the Americas; it rattles its scaly tail to warn off enemies.

cobra
Venomous snake found in tropical regions of Asia and Africa; it inflates its neck when threatened.

coral snake
Slender venomous snake of the Americas living under rocks or hidden in the ground; its bite can be fatal.

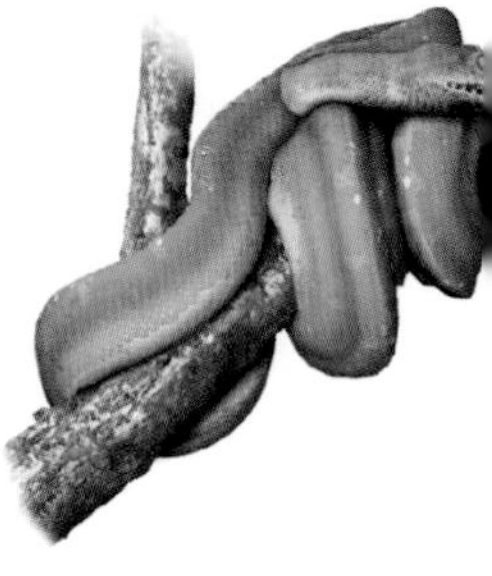

python
Large nocturnal nonvenomous snake found in hot regions of Asia, Africa and Australia; it lives mainly in trees and kills its prey by strangulation.

monitor lizard
Large diurnal carnivorous lizard with an elongated head found in hot regions of Africa, Asia and Australia; there are land and aquatic species.

iguana
Giant lizard found in tropical regions of the Americas and the Pacific islands and having a spiny dorsal crest; it lives mainly in trees.

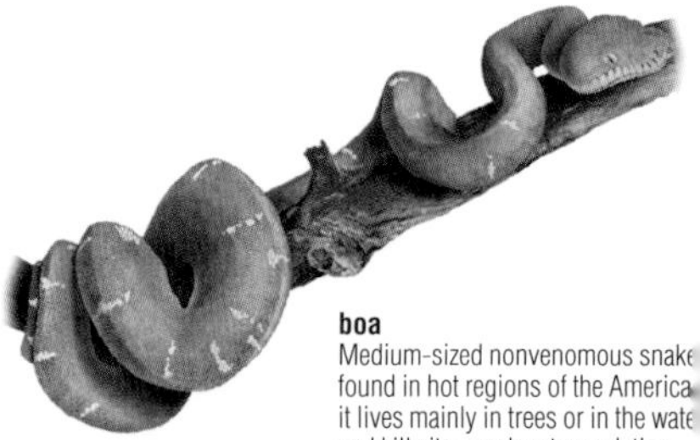

boa
Medium-sized nonvenomous snake found in hot regions of the Americas; it lives mainly in trees or in the water and kills its prey by strangulation.

alligator
Short-legged aquatic reptile found in North America and China; its head is shorter and wider than that of the crocodile.

crocodile
Aquatic and land reptile found in hot regions; it has an elongated head, strong jaws, short legs and a powerful tail.

caiman
Medium-sized aquatic reptile found in Central and South America; it is less aggressive than the crocodile and the alligator.

bird

Vertebrate with a feather-covered body and a toothless bill; its forelimbs (wings) are usually adapted for flight.

morphology of a bird

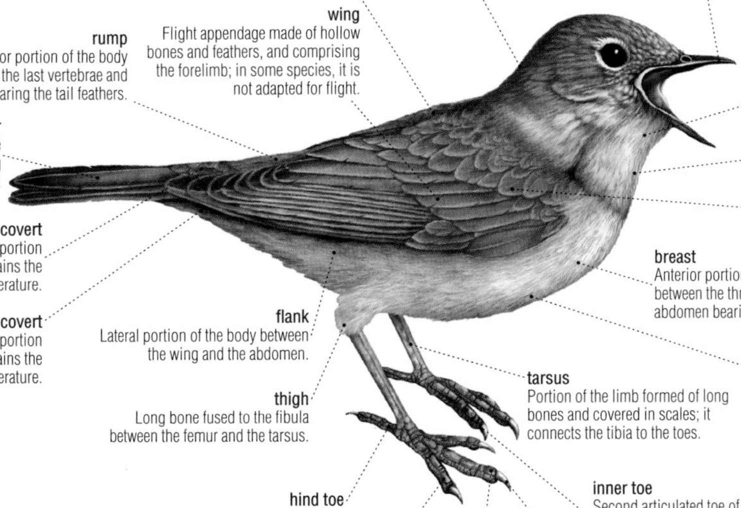

back
Upper posterior portion of the body between the head and the tail.

nape
Posterior portion of the neck below the head.

bill
Corneous formation covering toothless jaws; the bird uses it to feed.

wing
Flight appendage made of hollow bones and feathers, and comprising the forelimb; in some species, it is not adapted for flight.

rump
Posterior portion of the body formed by the last vertebrae and bearing the tail feathers.

chin
Portion of the head below the mandible.

tail feather
g stiff tail feather carried on the mp; it controls direction during flight.

throat
Anterior lateral portion of the neck between the chin and the breast.

wing covert
Short feather covering the upper portion of the base of the wing; it maintains internal body temperature.

upper tail covert
hort feather covering the upper portion of the base of the tail; it maintains the body's internal temperature.

breast
Anterior portion of the body between the throat and the abdomen bearing the wings.

under tail covert
hort feather covering the lower portion of the base of the tail; it maintains the body's internal temperature.

flank
Lateral portion of the body between the wing and the abdomen.

abdomen
Ventral portion of the body between the breast and the tail.

tarsus
Portion of the limb formed of long bones and covered in scales; it connects the tibia to the toes.

thigh
Long bone fused to the fibula between the femur and the tarsus.

hind toe
First articulated toe of the foot, usually made of a single phalange and pointing toward the back; it is also called the thumb.

inner toe
Second articulated toe of the foot, usually consisting of two phalanges.

claw
Pointy hook-shaped structure attached to the terminal end of the toes; it allows the bird to anchor itself.

outer toe
Fourth articulated bone of the foot, usually consisting of four phalanges.

middle toe
Third articulated toe of the foot; it is long and usually consists of three phalanges.

contour feather

Large rigid feather of the wings and tail enabling flight.

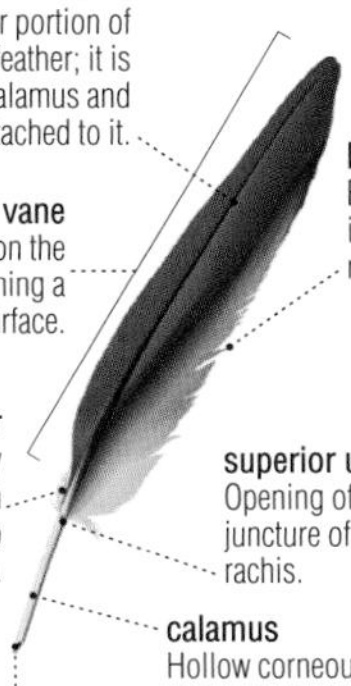

rachis
Solid corneous upper portion of the shaft of the contour feather; it is an extension of the calamus and the barbs are attached to it.

barb
Each of the self-adhering filaments implanted on each side of the rachis.

vane
All the interconnected barbs on the same side of the rachis forming a waterproof surface.

afterfeather
Small soft light feathers usually located at the base of the main athers on the abdomen; they help to insulate the body.

superior umbilicus
Opening of the shaft located at the juncture of the calamus and the rachis.

calamus
Hollow corneous anterior portion of the shaft of the contour feather extending through the rachis.

inferior umbilicus
Opening of the shaft located at the lower portion of the calamus; it is implanted in the skin.

head

Anterior portion of the body containing the main sensory organs and the brain.

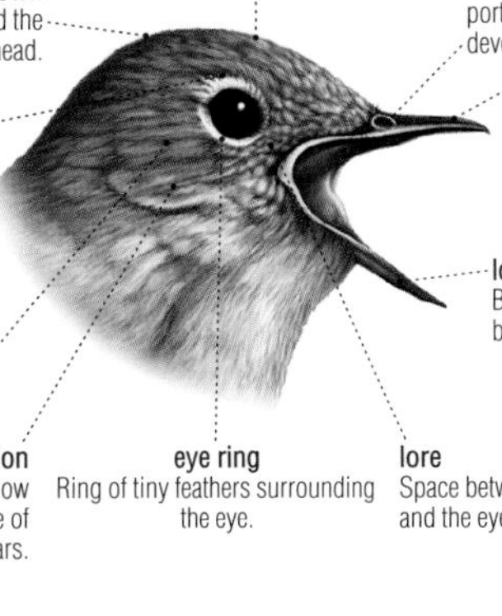

forehead
Upper front part of the head, between the bill and the crown.

nostril
External orifice of the nasal cavity located at the base of the upper portion of the bill having a poorly developed olfactory function.

crown
Top part of the skull, behind the forehead.

upper mandible
Bone forming the upper portion of the bill.

eyebrow stripe
Band of small feathers above the eye.

lower mandible
Bone forming the lower portion of the bill.

auriculars
Lateral portion of the head in back of the malar region at the level of the eye.

malar region
Lateral portion of the head below the eye extending from the base of the bill to the auriculars.

eye ring
Ring of tiny feathers surrounding the eye.

lore
Space between the base of the beak and the eye.

wing

Appendage of flight formed of hollow bones and feathers, and comprising the forelimb; in certain species, the wing is not adapted for flight.

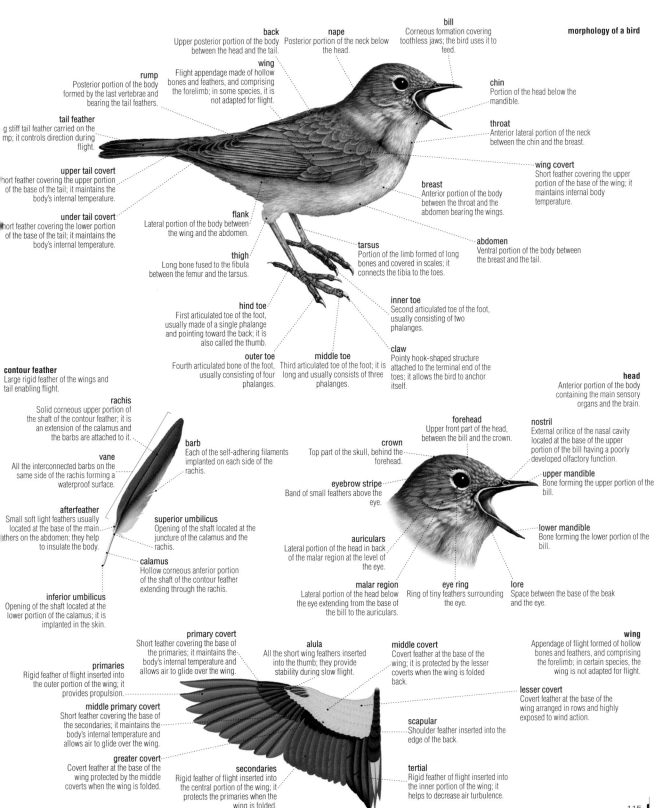

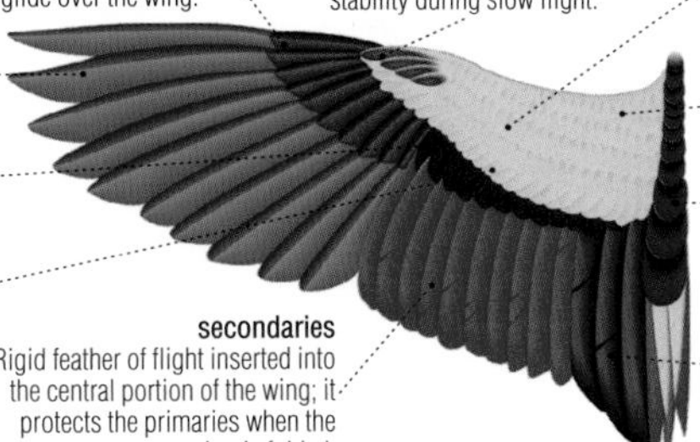

primary covert
Short feather covering the base of the primaries; it maintains the body's internal temperature and allows air to glide over the wing.

alula
All the short wing feathers inserted into the thumb; they provide stability during slow flight.

middle covert
Covert feather at the base of the wing; it is protected by the lesser coverts when the wing is folded back.

primaries
Rigid feather of flight inserted into the outer portion of the wing; it provides propulsion.

lesser covert
Covert feather at the base of the wing arranged in rows and highly exposed to wind action.

middle primary covert
Short feather covering the base of the secondaries; it maintains the body's internal temperature and allows air to glide over the wing.

scapular
Shoulder feather inserted into the edge of the back.

greater covert
Covert feather at the base of the wing protected by the middle coverts when the wing is folded.

secondaries
Rigid feather of flight inserted into the central portion of the wing; it protects the primaries when the wing is folded.

tertial
Rigid feather of flight inserted into the inner portion of the wing; it helps to decrease air turbulence.

bird

skeleton of a bird

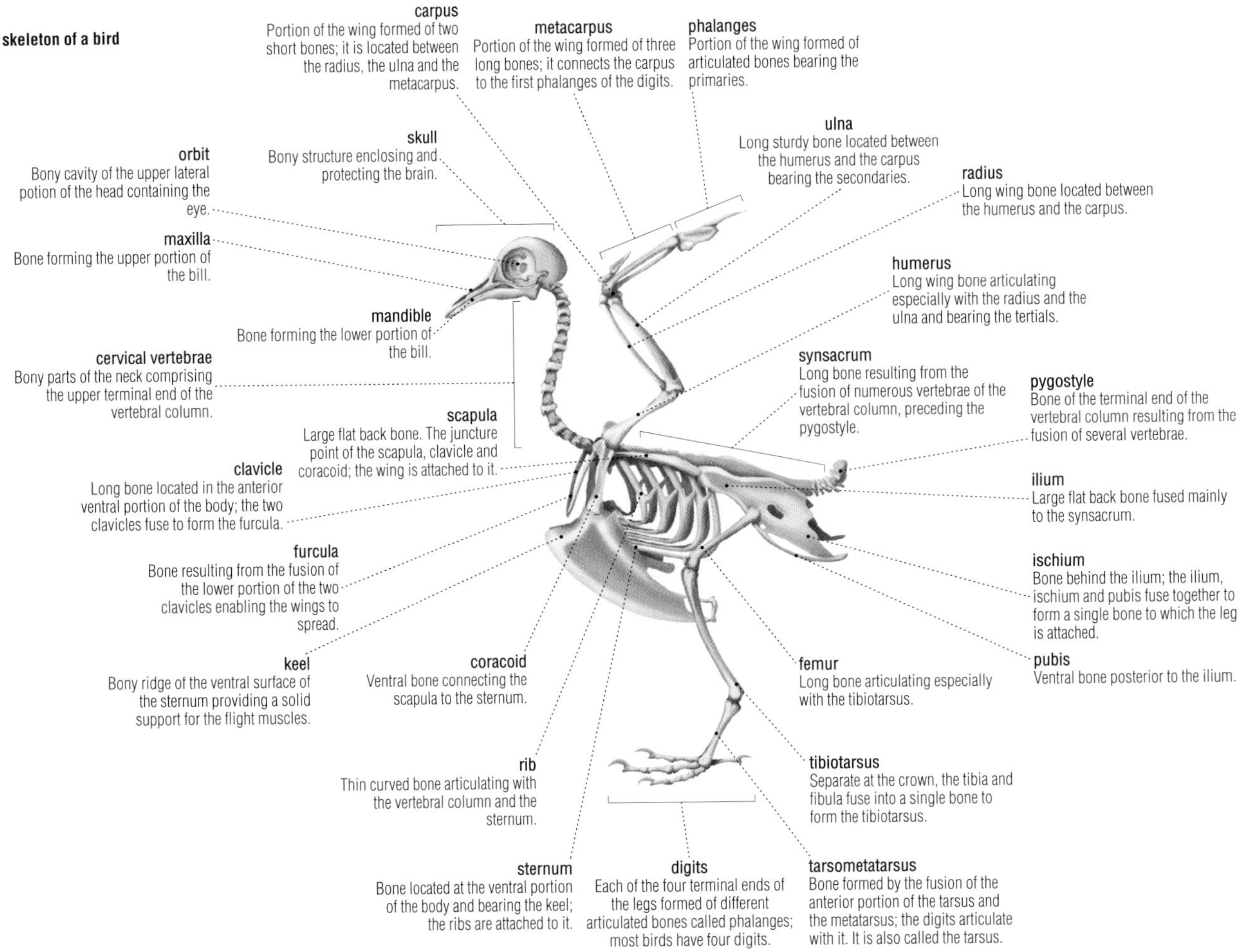
carpus
Portion of the wing formed of two short bones; it is located between the radius, the ulna and the metacarpus.
metacarpus
Portion of the wing formed of three long bones; it connects the carpus to the first phalanges of the digits.
phalanges
Portion of the wing formed of articulated bones bearing the primaries.
skull
Bony structure enclosing and protecting the brain.
orbit
Bony cavity of the upper lateral potion of the head containing the eye.
ulna
Long sturdy bone located between the humerus and the carpus bearing the secondaries.
radius
Long wing bone located between the humerus and the carpus.
maxilla
Bone forming the upper portion of the bill.
humerus
Long wing bone articulating especially with the radius and the ulna and bearing the tertials.
mandible
Bone forming the lower portion of the bill.
cervical vertebrae
Bony parts of the neck comprising the upper terminal end of the vertebral column.
synsacrum
Long bone resulting from the fusion of numerous vertebrae of the vertebral column, preceding the pygostyle.
pygostyle
Bone of the terminal end of the vertebral column resulting from the fusion of several vertebrae.
scapula
Large flat back bone. The juncture point of the scapula, clavicle and coracoid; the wing is attached to it.
clavicle
Long bone located in the anterior ventral portion of the body; the two clavicles fuse to form the furcula.
ilium
Large flat back bone fused mainly to the synsacrum.
furcula
Bone resulting from the fusion of the lower portion of the two clavicles enabling the wings to spread.
ischium
Bone behind the ilium; the ilium, ischium and pubis fuse together to form a single bone to which the leg is attached.
keel
Bony ridge of the ventral surface of the sternum providing a solid support for the flight muscles.
coracoid
Ventral bone connecting the scapula to the sternum.
femur
Long bone articulating especially with the tibiotarsus.
pubis
Ventral bone posterior to the ilium.
rib
Thin curved bone articulating with the vertebral column and the sternum.
tibiotarsus
Separate at the crown, the tibia and fibula fuse into a single bone to form the tibiotarsus.
sternum
Bone located at the ventral portion of the body and bearing the keel; the ribs are attached to it.
digits
Each of the four terminal ends of the legs formed of different articulated bones called phalanges; most birds have four digits.
tarsometatarsus
Bone formed by the fusion of the anterior portion of the tarsus and the metatarsus; the digits articulate with it. It is also called the tarsus.

anatomy of a bird

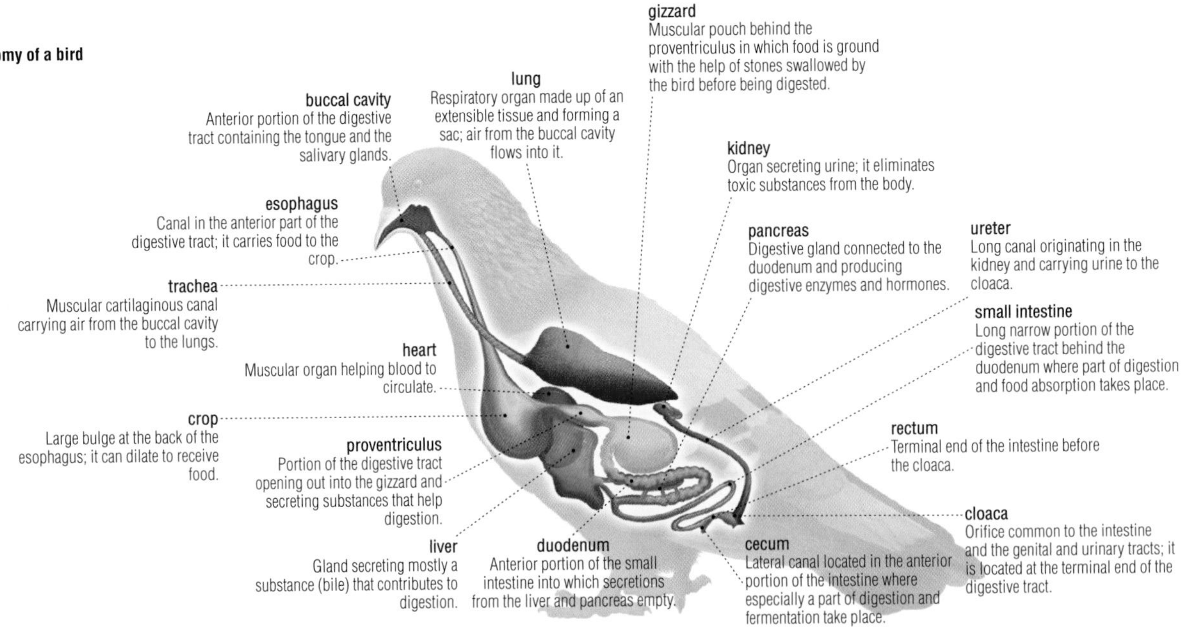
gizzard
Muscular pouch behind the proventriculus in which food is ground with the help of stones swallowed by the bird before being digested.
lung
Respiratory organ made up of an extensible tissue and forming a sac; air from the buccal cavity flows into it.
buccal cavity
Anterior portion of the digestive tract containing the tongue and the salivary glands.
kidney
Organ secreting urine; it eliminates toxic substances from the body.
esophagus
Canal in the anterior part of the digestive tract; it carries food to the crop.
pancreas
Digestive gland connected to the duodenum and producing digestive enzymes and hormones.
ureter
Long canal originating in the kidney and carrying urine to the cloaca.
trachea
Muscular cartilaginous canal carrying air from the buccal cavity to the lungs.
small intestine
Long narrow portion of the digestive tract behind the duodenum where part of digestion and food absorption takes place.
heart
Muscular organ helping blood to circulate.
crop
Large bulge at the back of the esophagus; it can dilate to receive food.
rectum
Terminal end of the intestine before the cloaca.
proventriculus
Portion of the digestive tract opening out into the gizzard and secreting substances that help digestion.
cloaca
Orifice common to the intestine and the genital and urinary tracts; it is located at the terminal end of the digestive tract.
liver
Gland secreting mostly a substance (bile) that contributes to digestion.
duodenum
Anterior portion of the small intestine into which secretions from the liver and pancreas empty.
cecum
Lateral canal located in the anterior portion of the intestine where especially a part of digestion and fermentation take place.

bird

egg
Reproductive method of certain animal species: a living cell with a casing and a food reserve, produced by the female.

blastodisc
Evidence of fertilization of the egg on the surface of the vitelline membrane; the embryo grows from it.

shell
Hard porous calcareous casing of the egg; it provides protection, fights bacteria and helps respiration.

vitelline membrane
Thin flexible transparent tissue enveloping the yolk.

shell membrane
Flexible porous tissue made of two superimposed layers covering the inside of the shell; it contributes to respiration and fights bacteria.

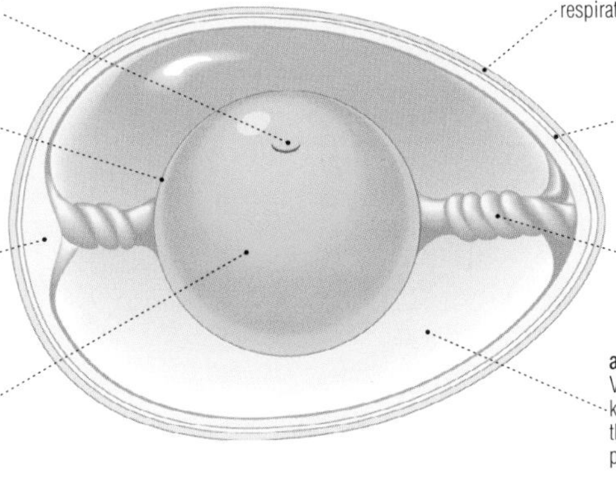

air space
Pocket of air contained between the two layers of the shell membrane at the base of the egg; it forms once the egg has cooled after being laid.

chalaza
Spiral filament of albumen maintaining the yolk in the center of the egg.

yolk
The embryo's food reserve located in the center of the egg.

albumen
Viscous liquid substance, popularly known as white of egg, surrounding the yolk and containing water and the proteins the embryo requires.

examples of bills
A bill's shape is characteristic of the lifestyle of the bird species. Its main function is to allow the bird to feed, to construct its nest and to defend itself.

aquatic bird
The large flat bill, with corneous lateral plates, filters water and mud to extract food.

granivorous bird
The short sturdy conical bill is used to hull seeds: the sharp lower mandible cracks the seed, which the tongue holds in place on the upper maxilla.

bird of prey
The short sturdy hooked bill tears apart large prey.

insectivorous bird
The long thin pointed bill allows the bird to catch insects in flight.

wading bird
The long curved bill allows the bird to extract small animals and plants buried deep in the ground, in mud and in marshes.

examples of feet
The feet of birds are adapted to their lifestyle. They usually have four toes: one posterior (the hind toe) and three anterior.

perching bird
The four toes end in a nail, which wraps around a support when the bird is resting; the hind toe provides equilibrium.

toe
The terminal end of the legs formed of articulated bones allowing the bird to perch or walk.

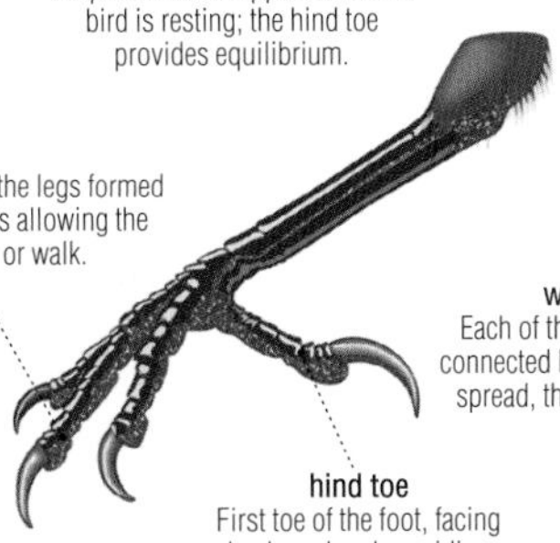

hind toe
First toe of the foot, facing backward and providing equilibrium.

bird of prey
Poorly adapted to locomotion, these sturdy powerful legs have talons to grip prey, immobilizing and killing it.

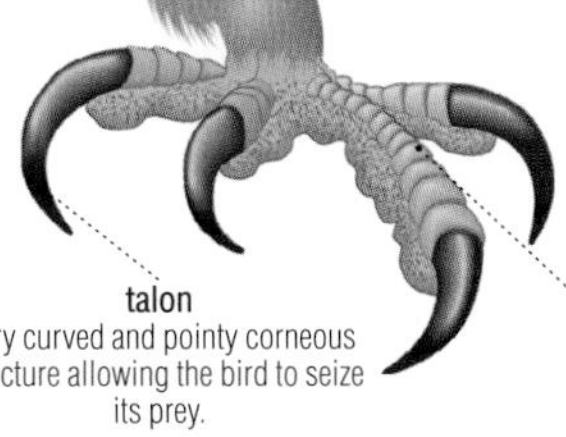

talon
ery curved and pointy corneous ructure allowing the bird to seize its prey.

scale
Each of the small hard thin scales covering the toes in layers.

aquatic bird
Bird with webbed feet for ease of swimming.

webbed toe
Each of the digits of the foot, connected by membranes; when spread, they make swimming easier.

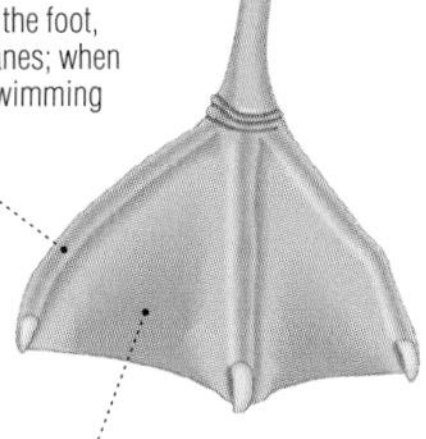

web
Fine membrane of skin connecting the digits of the foot; it stretches when the bird swims.

aquatic bird
Bird with lobed toes for ease of swimming.

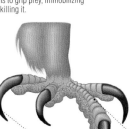

lobe
Each of the round cutaneous divisions encircling the toes that allow the bird to swim.

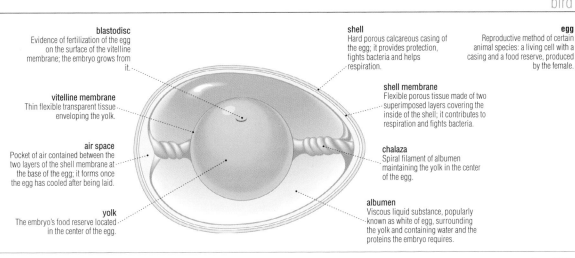

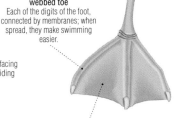

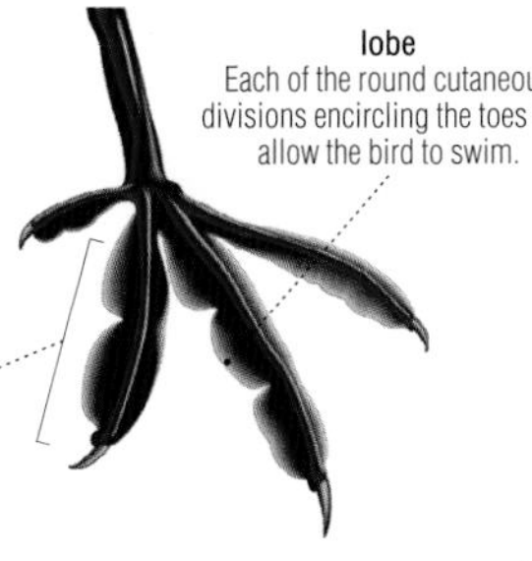

lobate toe
Each of the flat toes surrounding the lobes; they provide propulsion in the water and prevent slipping out of the water.

examples of birds

There are more than 9,000 species of birds scattered around the world.

hummingbird
Tiny brightly colored bird with a long thin bill found on the North American continent; it can hover and fly backward.

European robin
European perching bird found in woods and gardens characterized by a bright red throat and chest and emitting a fairly loud, lively melodious song.

finch
Widespread bird with a melodious song.

goldfinch
Brightly plumed songbird feeding mainly on the seeds of the thistle.

bullfinch
Red-breasted bird found in the woods and parks of Eurasia and the Americas; it feeds mainly on seeds and insects.

sparrow
Bird that feeds mainly on seeds and insects; it is widespread in cities and in the countryside.

nightingale
Bird with a melodious song that feeds on insects and fruit; it is found in the bushes of forests and parks.

swallow
Widespread in the Northern hemisphere and found in highly diverse habitats; it usually feeds on insects caught in flight.

kingfisher
Colorful fish-eating bird that spends most of its time perched by the water's edge.

magpie
Noisy omnivore found in trees and bushes in temperate regions of the Northern hemisphere.

cardinal
Brightly colored bird with a tuft of upright feathers on its head; it is found mostly in North American woods and gardens.

jay
Usually noisy, brightly colored bird found in forests; it feeds mainly on fruit and insects.

starling
Straight-billed omnivorous bird with dark plumage; it lives in trees.

swift
Widespread and very swift insectivore; it is usually airborne since its toes make it difficult to perch.

northern saw-whet owl
Nocturnal bird of prey found in the forests of North America.

lapwing
Mainly insectivorous bird found in the wetlands and marshes of Eurasia and Africa; it has a tuft of upright feathers on its head.

oystercatcher
Swift long-billed bird found in Eurasia; it feeds mainly on shellfish.

partridge
Land-based bird that flies with difficulty.

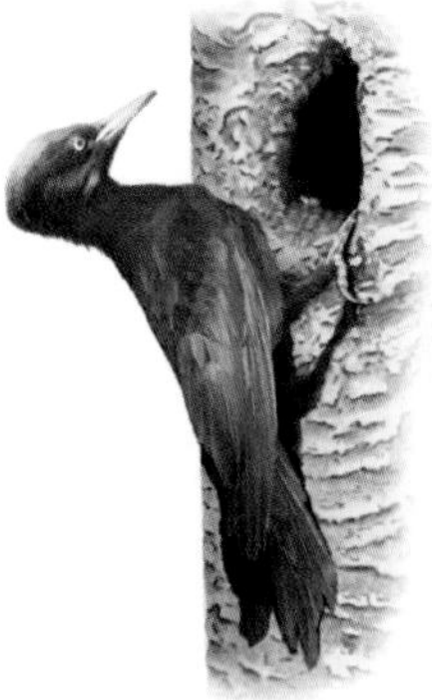

woodpecker
Widespread insectivore that pecks at the bark of trees to find food and to nest.

raven
Strong-billed scavenger with usually black plumage; it sometimes damages crops.

macaw
Noisy brightly colored perching bird found in the tropical forests of the Americas; it feeds mainly on seeds and fruit.

cockatoo
Noisy perching bird with drab plumage and a tuft of upright feathers on its head, found mainly in Australia; it can mimic human speech.

tern
Widespread web-footed aquatic bird with long wings and a forked tail; it dives for the fish it feeds on.

examples of birds

albatross
Web-footed aquatic bird of the south seas; its wingspan can reach 10 ft, allowing it to glide for hours.

toucan
Large yet gentle bird found in the forests of the Americas; its dentate bill allows it to feed especially on fruits and insects.

falcon
Diurnal bird of prey with piercing eyes and powerful talons and beak; it captures its prey in flight and is sometimes trained to hunt.

great horned owl
Nocturnal raptor found in the forests of North America, with a protruding tuft of feathers on each side of its head.

heron
Widespread wading bird found in shallow waters and marshes, mostly piscivorous, with a neck that folds into an S when it is at rest.

condor
Diurnal scavenger of the Americas, with a bald head and neck; one California species is facing extinction.

eagle
Widely prevalent raptor with piercing eyes, a hooked beak and sharp talons allowing it to catch live prey.

penguin
Piscivorous marine bird living in colonies in the Southern hemisphere; it has webbed feet and wings that have evolved into fins.

pelican
Web-footed bird with a lower jaw featuring an extensible pouch for catching fish.

stork
Wading bird found in marshes and fields; two species are threatened with extinction.

vulture
Diurnal raptor of the Americas and Eurasia, mainly a scavenger, with a bald head and neck, powerful beak and weak talons.

ostrich
Flightless bird of Africa reaching over 7 ft in height, with powerful two-toed legs; it is raised for its feathers and meat.

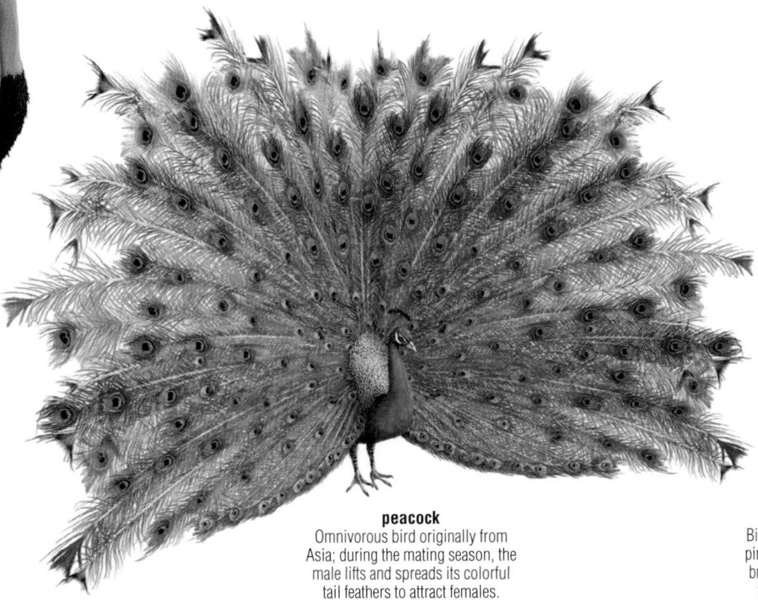

peacock
Omnivorous bird originally from Asia; during the mating season, the male lifts and spreads its colorful tail feathers to attract females.

flamingo
Bird with webbed feet and usually pink plumage living in colonies in brackish or salt water; it feeds by filtering water through its bill.

examples of birds

chick
Newly hatched bird covered in down.

quail
Bird found in fields and meadows and much prized as game; certain species are domesticated.

pigeon
Generally grain-eating bird prized for its meat and its keen sense of direction (carrier pigeon).

duck
Web-footed aquatic bird spending most of its time on water; the domestic duck is raised for its meat and for the production of foie gras.

hen
Domestic fowl (female of the rooster) with a small serrated comb raised in captivity for its eggs and meat.

rooster
Domestic bird (male of the hen) with a large serrated comb and a long-plumed tail.

pheasant
Bird originally from Asia and characterized by its long tail; its meat is highly prized. Certain pheasants are raised solely for hunting.

guinea fowl
Wild terrestrial bird with a bald head and horned comb originally from Africa and domesticated in Europe for its meat.

goose
Web-footed bird of the Northern hemisphere better adapted to land than water; certain species are raised mainly for the production of foie gras.

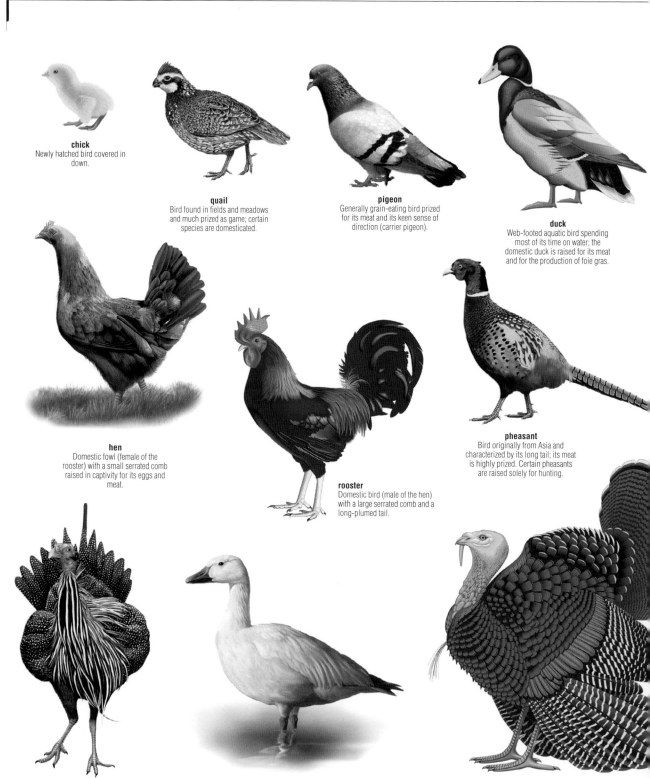

turkey
Bird originating in the Americas with a bald head and neck covered with outgrowths; it is raised in captivity for its meat.

mole

Insectivorous mammal (about 20 species) found in Eurasia and the Americas; it digs underground tunnels with its front limbs to reach its food.

morphology of a mole

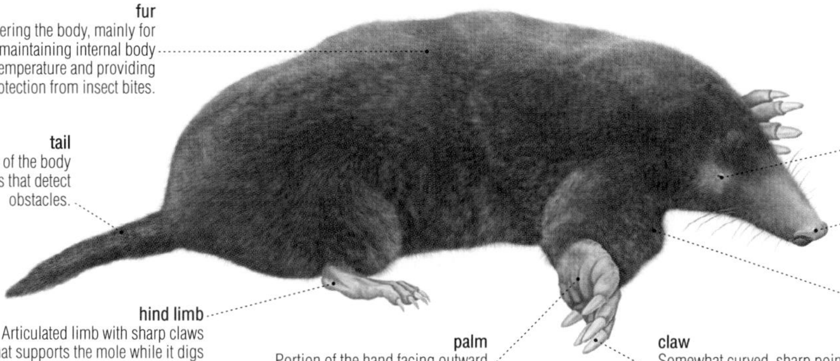

fur
Hair covering the body, mainly for maintaining internal body temperature and providing protection from insect bites.

tail
Terminal appendage of the body having tactile hairs that detect obstacles.

hind limb
Articulated limb with sharp claws that supports the mole while it digs in the earth.

palm
Portion of the hand facing outward to make digging easier and to push the earth aside more efficiently.

claw
Somewhat curved, sharp pointy structure at the terminal end of the digits for digging in the earth.

eye
Organ of sight covered with hairs that can perceive variations in light intensity; some moles are almost blind.

snout
Elongated front portion of the head covered with many sensory hairs, which have a highly developed tactile and olfactory function.

forelimb
Wide powerful articulated limb ending in a scoop-shaped paw allowing the mole to dig in the earth.

skeleton of a mole

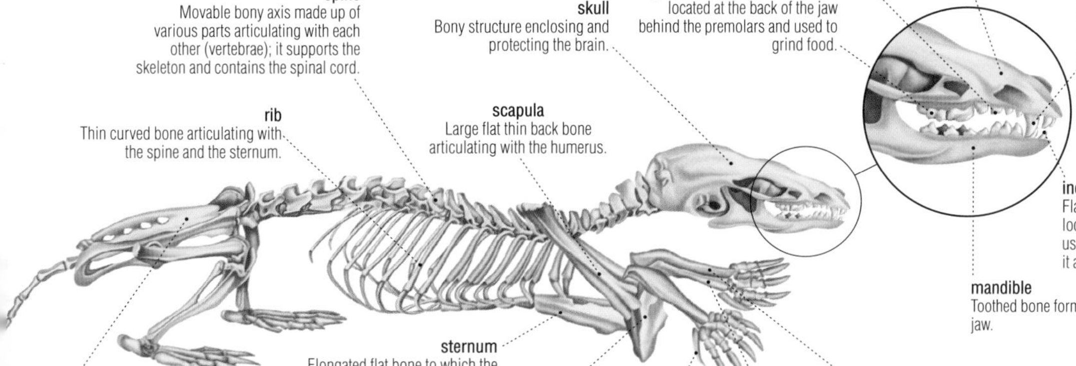

premolar
Tooth with usually a single root; it is located between the canines and the molars, and used to grind food.

maxilla
Toothed bone comprising the upper jaw.

molar
Large tooth with several roots; it is located at the back of the jaw behind the premolars and used to grind food.

canine
Pointed tooth with a single root; it is located between the incisors and the premolars, and used for gripping food and tearing it apart.

spine
Movable bony axis made up of various parts articulating with each other (vertebrae); it supports the skeleton and contains the spinal cord.

skull
Bony structure enclosing and protecting the brain.

rib
Thin curved bone articulating with the spine and the sternum.

scapula
Large flat thin back bone articulating with the humerus.

incisor
Flat tooth with a single root; it is located at the front of the jaw, and used for gripping food and tearing it apart.

mandible
Toothed bone forming the lower jaw.

sternum
Elongated flat bone to which the ribs in particular are attached and bearing a crest on its ventral surface.

pelvis
Bony girdle to which the hind limbs are attached.

ulna
Long bone forming the inner limb between the humerus and the paw.

humerus
Bone of the forelimb articulating with the scapula, as well as with the radius and the ulna; it provides a large base for the muscles.

falciform sesamoid bone
Small curved bone located near the thumb reinforcing the paw and forming a cutting inner edge.

radius
Long bone forming the outer part of the limb between the humerus and the paw.

examples of insectivorous mammals

mole
Insectivorous mammal (about 20 species) found in Eurasia and the Americas; it digs underground tunnels with its front limbs to reach its food.

hedgehog
Insectivorous mammal of Eurasia (about 10 species) with a body usually covered with stiff hairs or barbs, which stand on end when it rolls itself into a ball for protection.

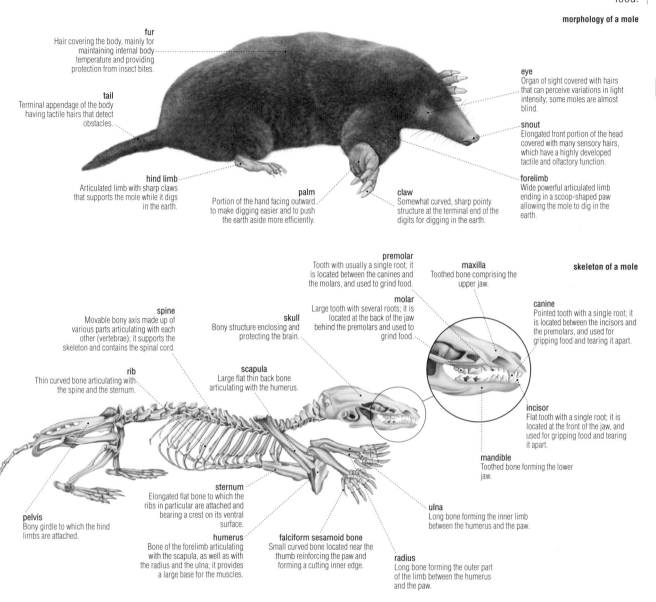

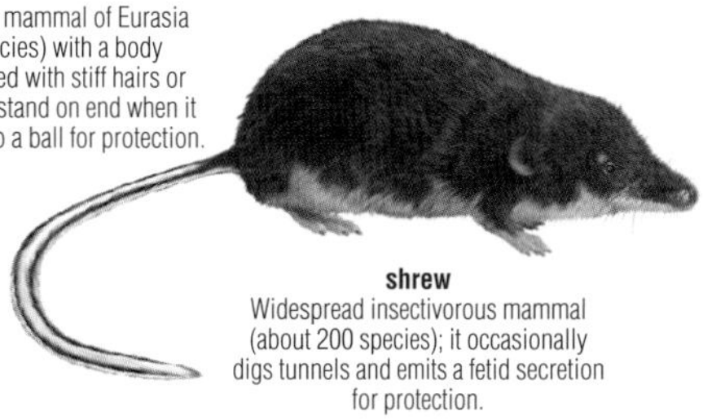

shrew
Widespread insectivorous mammal (about 200 species); it occasionally digs tunnels and emits a fetid secretion for protection.

rodent

Herbivorous or omnivorous vertebrate (over 2,000 species) with four limbs, a body covered in hair and sharp incisors that grow constantly.

morphology of a rat
Rat: omnivorous gnawing mammal with a long tail; it is extremely voracious and prolific.

pinna
External part of the ear made of cartilaginous lobes that capture sounds.

vibrissa
Long tactile hair located around the nose and mouth used to detect obstacles during nocturnal forays.

nose
Middle protuberance of the head with two orifices located above the mouth and having an olfactory and respiratory function.

digit
Terminal end of the limbs formed of various articulated bones bearing a claw and used mainly to feed and move about.

fur
Hair covering the entire body, except the nose; its main function is to maintain body temperature.

tail
Terminal appendage of the body covered with scales and containing blood vessels; it is used mainly for equilibrium.

claw
Somewhat curved, sharp pointy structure used especially for digging and defense.

skeleton of a rat

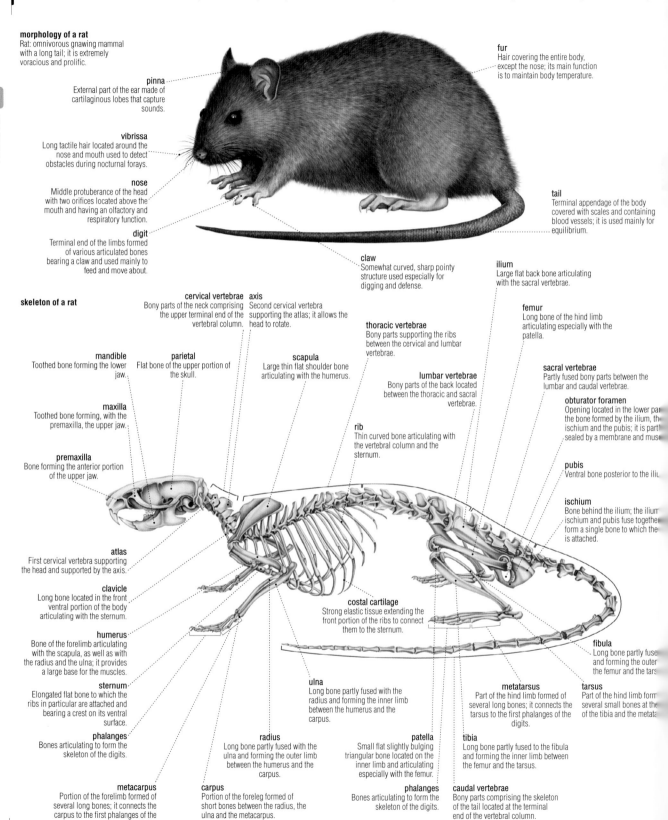

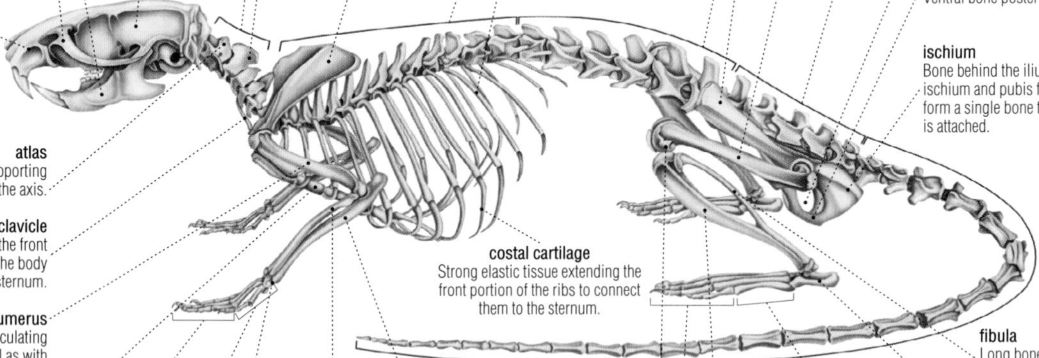

cervical vertebrae
Bony parts of the neck comprising the upper terminal end of the vertebral column.

axis
Second cervical vertebra supporting the atlas; it allows the head to rotate.

mandible
Toothed bone forming the lower jaw.

parietal
Flat bone of the upper portion of the skull.

scapula
Large thin flat shoulder bone articulating with the humerus.

thoracic vertebrae
Bony parts supporting the ribs between the cervical and lumbar vertebrae.

lumbar vertebrae
Bony parts of the back located between the thoracic and sacral vertebrae.

ilium
Large flat back bone articulating with the sacral vertebrae.

femur
Long bone of the hind limb articulating especially with the patella.

sacral vertebrae
Partly fused bony parts between the lumbar and caudal vertebrae.

obturator foramen
Opening located in the lower pa
the bone formed by the ilium, th
ischium and the pubis; it is part
sealed by a membrane and mus

maxilla
Toothed bone forming, with the premaxilla, the upper jaw.

rib
Thin curved bone articulating with the vertebral column and the sternum.

premaxilla
Bone forming the anterior portion of the upper jaw.

pubis
Ventral bone posterior to the iliu

ischium
Bone behind the ilium; the ilium
ischium and pubis fuse togethe
form a single bone to which the
is attached.

atlas
First cervical vertebra supporting the head and supported by the axis.

clavicle
Long bone located in the front ventral portion of the body articulating with the sternum.

costal cartilage
Strong elastic tissue extending the front portion of the ribs to connect them to the sternum.

humerus
Bone of the forelimb articulating with the scapula, as well as with the radius and the ulna; it provides a large base for the muscles.

fibula
Long bone partly fuse
and forming the outer
the femur and the tars

ulna
Long bone partly fused with the radius and forming the inner limb between the humerus and the carpus.

metatarsus
Part of the hind limb formed of several long bones; it connects the tarsus to the first phalanges of the digits.

tarsus
Part of the hind limb form
several small bones at th
of the tibia and the metata

sternum
Elongated flat bone to which the ribs in particular are attached and bearing a crest on its ventral surface.

phalanges
Bones articulating to form the skeleton of the digits.

radius
Long bone partly fused with the ulna and forming the outer limb between the humerus and the carpus.

patella
Small flat slightly bulging triangular bone located on the inner limb and articulating especially with the femur.

tibia
Long bone partly fused to the fibula and forming the inner limb between the femur and the tarsus.

metacarpus
Portion of the forelimb formed of several long bones; it connects the carpus to the first phalanges of the digits.

carpus
Portion of the foreleg formed of short bones between the radius, the ulna and the metacarpus.

phalanges
Bones articulating to form the skeleton of the digits.

caudal vertebrae
Bony parts comprising the skeleton of the tail located at the terminal end of the vertebral column.

examples of rodents

field mouse
Rodent found in woods and fields; it moves about by hopping and can cause serious crop damage.

chipmunk
Small, mainly vegetarian North American rodent found in hardwood forests and bushes.

jerboa
Rodent found in the deserts of Asia and Africa adapted for hopping and able to survive without drinking water.

hamster
Rodent of the Eurasian steppes sometimes domesticated and used for laboratory experiments; it stores its food in its cheek pouches.

squirrel
Mostly vegetarian rodent found in woods and forests around the world, except in Australia; some squirrels move about by gliding from tree to tree.

rat
mnivorous rodent characterized by s intelligence; it can transmit certain viruses and bacteria to humans. Some species are domesticated.

guinea pig
Rodent originating in South America, sometimes domesticated but mainly used in laboratory experiments.

groundhog
Rodent of the Northern hemisphere prized for its fur; it hibernates six months a year and emits a high-pitched whistle when in danger.

porcupine
Rodent found on land and in trees in warm and temperate regions; its body is covered with long sharp quills, which it raises to defend itself.

beaver
Amphibious rodent found in Eurasia and North America prized for its fur; it uses branches to build lodges and dams in streams.

rodent's and lagomorph's jaws

Unlike a rodent's jaws, those of a lagomorph have a second pair of (nonfunctional) incisors on the maxilla.

rodent's jaw: rat

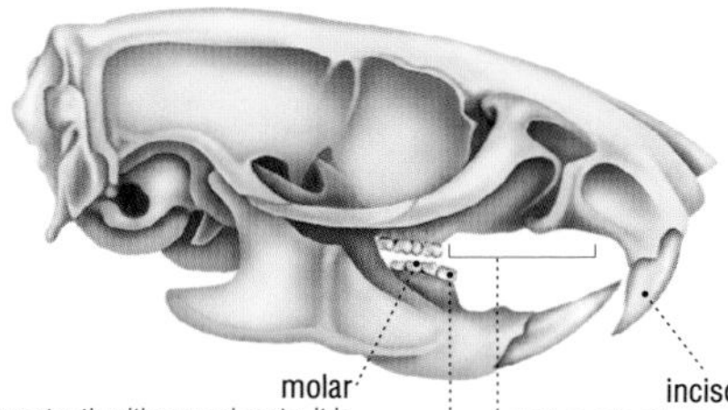

molar
_arge tooth with several roots; it is located at the back of the jaw behind the premolars and used to grind food.

premolar
Tooth usually with a single root; it is located behind the diastema and used for grinding.

incisor
Flat, constantly growing tooth with a single root; it is located in the front of the jaw and used for cutting up plants.

diastema
Large space between the incisors and the premolars due to the absence of canines.

lagomorph's jaw: rabbit

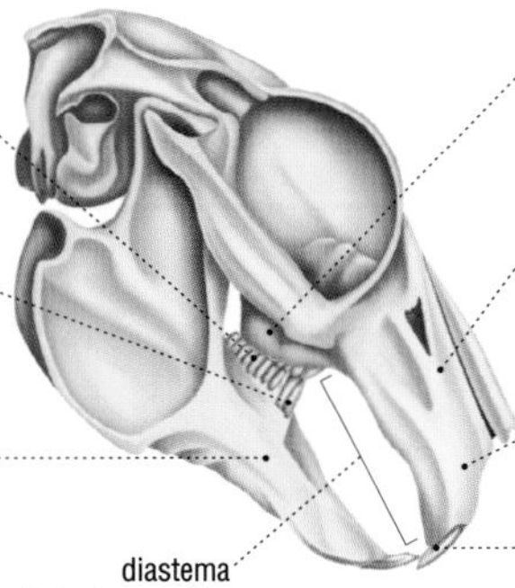

molar
Large tooth with several roots; it is located at the back of the jaw behind the premolars and used to grind food.

premolar
Tooth usually with a single root; it is located behind the diastema and used for grinding.

mandible
Toothed bone forming the lower jaw.

diastema
Space between the incisors and the premolars due to the absence of canines.

palatine
Fine bone of the maxilla; the horizontal portion forms the roof of the mouth.

maxilla
Toothed bone forming, with the premaxilla, the upper jaw.

premaxilla
Bone forming the anterior portion of the upper jaw.

incisor
Flat, constantly growing tooth with a single root; it is located in the front of the jaw and used for cutting up plants.

examples of lagomorphs

Lagomorphs: small four-legged herbivorous vertebrates (about 60 species) with dense fur, a short or absent tail and three pairs of incisors.

pika
Tailless lagomorph living in the wild in the mountains of Central Asia and North America.

rabbit
Widespread and extremely prolific lagomorph living in the wild in burrows; it is also raised for its meat and fur.

hare
Widespread lagomorph with strong hind limbs adapted for swift running; it lives in the wild and is valued especially for its meat.

horse

Maned ungulate mammal domesticated for riding and for use as a draft animal.

morphology of a horse

mane
Long stiff hairs (horsehair) covering the neck used mainly to chase away insects.
forelock
Tuft of long stiff hairs (horsehair) on the upper terminal end of the mane and falling onto the forehead between the ears.
nose
Front portion of the head extending from the base of the eyes to the nostrils.
flank
Lateral portion of the body that ripples with the action of the muscles, which allows the horse to chase away insects and warm itself.
withers
Portion of the body extending the neck and forming a protuberance above the shoulder.
lip
Each of two movable muscular fo[...] forming the contour of the mouth having a tactile function.
loin
Upper portion of the body between the back and the croup; it transmits forward the propulsion from the hind limbs.
croup
Rear portion of the body between the loin and the base of the tail; it provides propulsion.
back
Upper portion of the trunk opposite the belly between the withers and the loin.
tail
Terminal appendage of the body with long hairs; the horse whips its tail to chase away insects.
thigh
Upper portion of the hind limb having large powerful muscles.
cheek
Protruding side of the head behind the upper jaw.
muzzle
Terminal end of the upper lip having a tactile and prehens[...] function.
stifle
Articulation of the hind limb between the thigh and the leg formed of the patella and the skin that covers it.
neck
Portion of the body supporting the head and attached to the withers, the shoulders and the chest.
nostril
Each of the orifices of the nose having a respiratory and olfacto[...] function.
gaskin
Portion of the hind limb between the stifle and hock.
belly
Lower portion of the trunk opposite the back.
chest
Front portion of the body located between the neck and the limbs.
hock
Articulation of the hind limb; it contributes to movement and absorbs shocks.
elbow
Articulation of the forelimb between the upper arm and the forearm above the knee.
shoulder
Upper portion of the forelimb attached to the trunk.
cannon
Portion of the hind limb between the hock and the fetlock joint supporting the horse's weight.
fetlock joint
Articulation of the limbs between the cannon and the pastern forming a protuberance and acting as a shock absorber.
forearm
Part of the forelimb located between the shoulder and the elbow corresponding to the humerus.
pastern
Portion of the limbs between the fetlock joint and the coronet, corresponding to the first phalange of the finger.
coronet
Part of the limbs covering the upper edge of the hoof and corresponding to the second phalange of the finger.
knee
Articulation of the forelimb located below the elbow between the forearm and the cannon; it contributes to movement and acts as a shock absorber.
hoof
Thick corneous casing covering and protecting the terminal end of the limb; it rests on the ground while the horse is walking and absorbs shocks.
fetlock
Tuft of hair located behind the fetlock joint.

gaits

Natural or acquired means of locomotion used by a horse, based on limb movements. There are four principal gaits.

walk
Natural walking gait in four equal movements: each leg lifts and touches down diagonally in succession. This is a horse's slowest gait.

trot
Natural jumping gait between a walk and a gallop in two movements: both pairs of diagonal legs alternate in touching down, with a pause in between.

anatomy of a horse

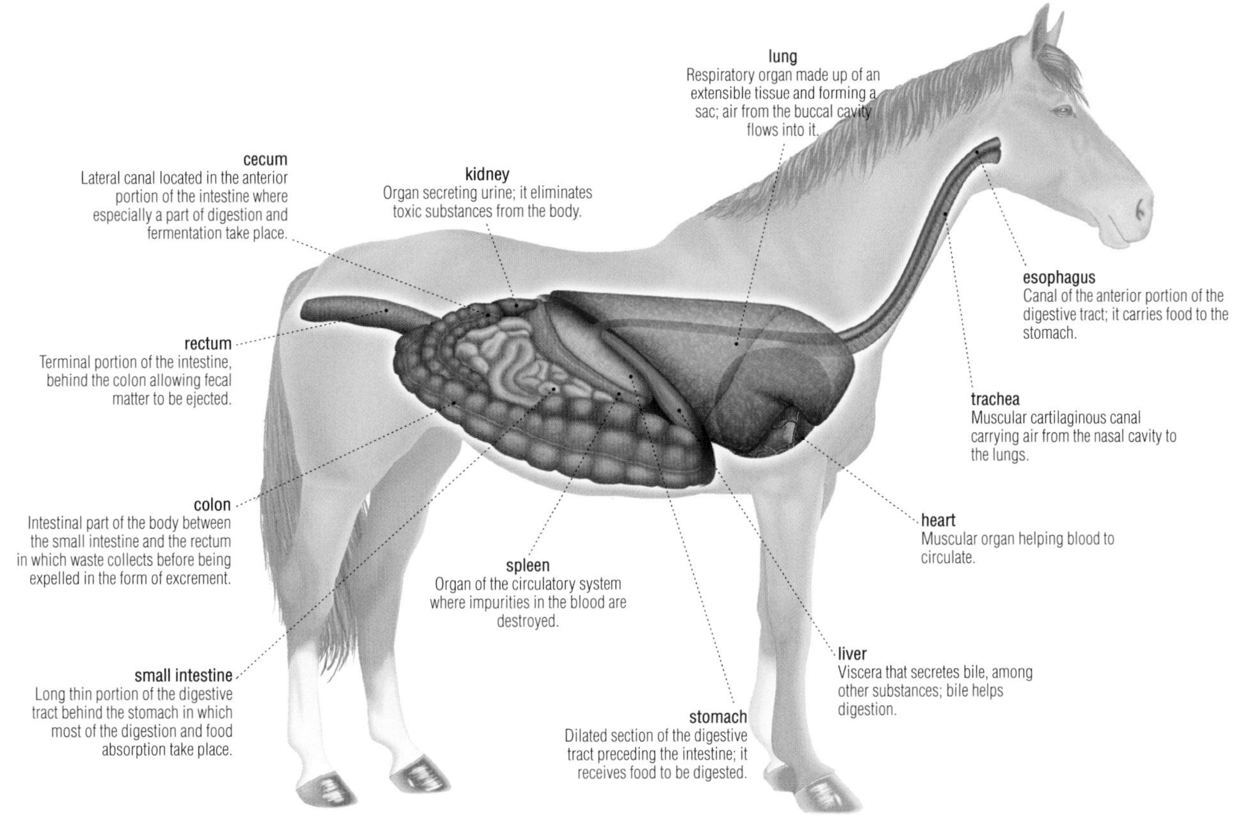
lung
Respiratory organ made up of an extensible tissue and forming a sac; air from the buccal cavity flows into it.
cecum
Lateral canal located in the anterior portion of the intestine where especially a part of digestion and fermentation take place.
kidney
Organ secreting urine; it eliminates toxic substances from the body.
esophagus
Canal of the anterior portion of the digestive tract; it carries food to the stomach.
rectum
Terminal portion of the intestine, behind the colon allowing fecal matter to be ejected.
trachea
Muscular cartilaginous canal carrying air from the nasal cavity to the lungs.
colon
Intestinal part of the body between the small intestine and the rectum in which waste collects before being expelled in the form of excrement.
heart
Muscular organ helping blood to circulate.
spleen
Organ of the circulatory system where impurities in the blood are destroyed.
liver
Viscera that secretes bile, among other substances; bile helps digestion.
small intestine
Long thin portion of the digestive tract behind the stomach in which most of the digestion and food absorption take place.
stomach
Dilated section of the digestive tract preceding the intestine; it receives food to be digested.

pace
Acquired jumping gait in two movements, extremely comfortable and faster than the trot; both pairs of lateral legs alternate in lifting.

canter
Natural gait performed in three unequal movements: both diagonal legs work together, while the other two work separately, with a pause in between.

horse

skeleton of a horse

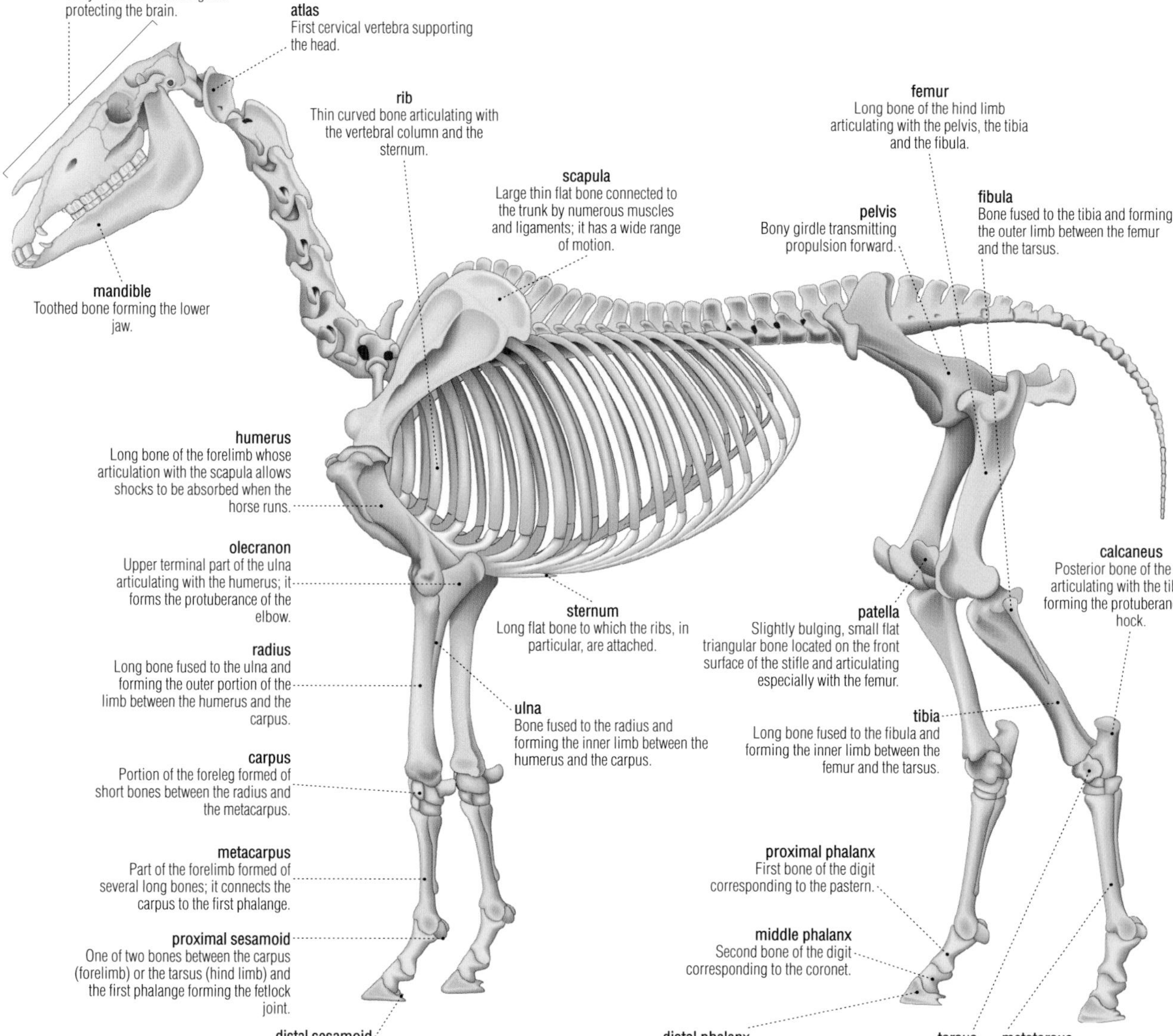
skull
Bony structure enclosing and protecting the brain.
atlas
First cervical vertebra supporting the head.
rib
Thin curved bone articulating with the vertebral column and the sternum.
scapula
Large thin flat bone connected to the trunk by numerous muscles and ligaments; it has a wide range of motion.
pelvis
Bony girdle transmitting propulsion forward.
femur
Long bone of the hind limb articulating with the pelvis, the tibia and the fibula.
fibula
Bone fused to the tibia and forming the outer limb between the femur and the tarsus.
mandible
Toothed bone forming the lower jaw.
humerus
Long bone of the forelimb whose articulation with the scapula allows shocks to be absorbed when the horse runs.
olecranon
Upper terminal part of the ulna articulating with the humerus; it forms the protuberance of the elbow.
calcaneus
Posterior bone of the tarsus articulating with the tibia an forming the protuberance of t hock.
sternum
Long flat bone to which the ribs, in particular, are attached.
patella
Slightly bulging, small flat triangular bone located on the front surface of the stifle and articulating especially with the femur.
radius
Long bone fused to the ulna and forming the outer portion of the limb between the humerus and the carpus.
ulna
Bone fused to the radius and forming the inner limb between the humerus and the carpus.
tibia
Long bone fused to the fibula and forming the inner limb between the femur and the tarsus.
carpus
Portion of the foreleg formed of short bones between the radius and the metacarpus.
metacarpus
Part of the forelimb formed of several long bones; it connects the carpus to the first phalange.
proximal phalanx
First bone of the digit corresponding to the pastern.
proximal sesamoid
One of two bones between the carpus (forelimb) or the tarsus (hind limb) and the first phalange forming the fetlock joint.
middle phalanx
Second bone of the digit corresponding to the coronet.
distal sesamoid
Small elongated bone of the third phalange of the digit allowing the lower part of the limb to move.
distal phalanx
Last phalange of the digit having a thick corneous covering upon which the horse rests.
tarsus
Part of the hind limb formed of short bones located between the tibia, the fibula and the metatarsus; it acts as a shock absorber.
metatarsus
Part of the hind limb formed of several long bones; it connects the tarsus to the first phalange of the digit.

cervical vertebrae
Bony parts of the neck comprising the upper terminal end of the vertebral column.

thoracic vertebrae
Bony parts supporting the ribs between the cervical and lumbar vertebrae.

lumbar vertebrae
Bony parts of the back located between the thoracic and sacral vertebrae.

sacral vertebrae
Bony parts that are fused together between the lumbar and caudal vertebrae; the pelvis articulates with them.

caudal vertebrae
Bony parts comprising the skeleton of the tail located at the terminal end of the vertebral column.

horse

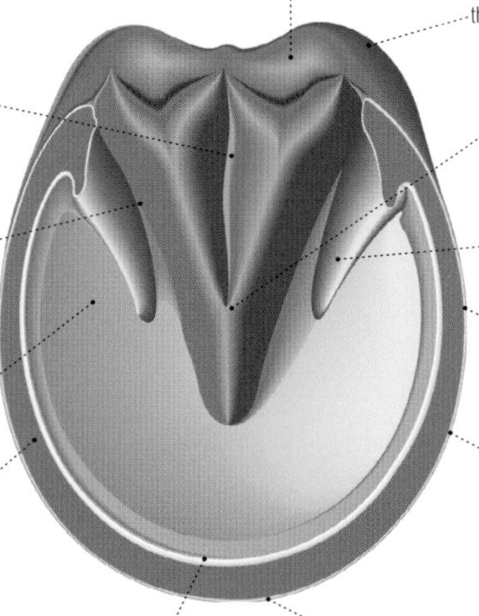

plantar surface of the hoof
Corneous lower surface of the hoof in contact with the ground.
bulb
Corneous eminence ending at the frog and joining with the heel.
heel
Rear portion of the wall of the hoof between the quarters and opposite the toe.
median groove
Deep natural groove through the center of the frog.
frog
Part of the hoof made of soft but strong corneous material located in the notch of the sole; it is used to absorb shocks and sense the terrain.
lateral groove
Natural groove separating the frog from the bars and the sole.
bar
Terminal part of the wall of the hoof running along the edge of the frog.
quarter
Side part of the wall of the hoof between the heel and the side wall.
sole
Strong thin corneous plate comprising the lower portion of the hoof and resting on the ground.
side wall
Side part of the wall of the hoof between the toe and the quarter.
wall
Corneous material making up the perimeter of the hoof; it is produced by the coronet and grows from 0.3 to 1 in a month.
white line
Line of dense compact corneous material bringing together the sole and the inner edge of the wall of the hoof.
toe
Front part of the wall of the hoof between the side walls and opposite the heel.

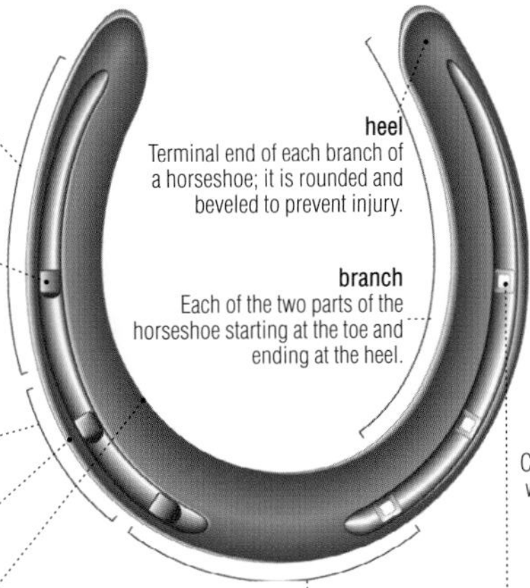

horseshoe
Curved metal band nailed under the wall of the hoof to protect it against wear, to absorb shocks and to provide better traction on the ground.
quarter
Part of the horseshoe under the quarter of the hoof.
heel
Terminal end of each branch of a horseshoe; it is rounded and beveled to prevent injury.
nail
Pointy metal pin; its head lodges in the nail hole to attach the horseshoe to the hoof.
branch
Each of the two parts of the horseshoe starting at the toe and ending at the heel.
side wall
Part of the horseshoe under the side wall of the hoof.
outer edge
Outer contour of the horseshoe.
inner edge
Inner contour of the horseshoe.
toe
Part of the horseshoe under the toe of the hoof.
nail hole
Rectangular opening made in the iron to hold the head of a nail; there are usually six to eight nail holes.

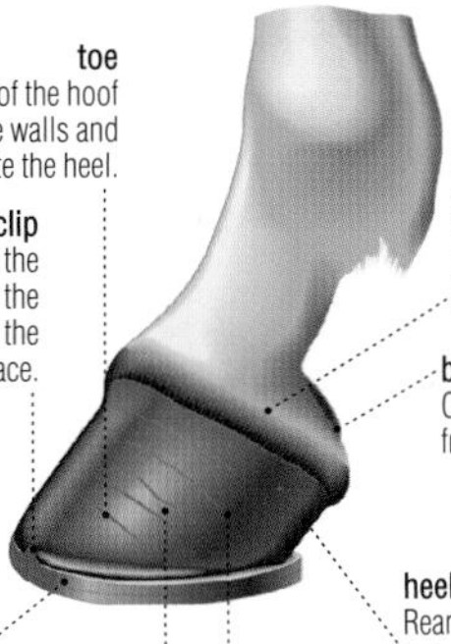

hoof
Thick corneous casing covering and protecting the terminal end of the limb; it rests on the ground while the horse is walking and absorbs shocks.
toe
Front part of the wall of the hoof between the side walls and opposite the heel.
coronet
Bulge from which the wall of the hoof grows; it secretes a varnish to protect the hoof from humidity and dryness.
toe clip
Triangular iron clip mounted on the toe of the hoof to protect the corneous material and to hold the horseshoe in place.
bulb
Corneous eminence ending at the frog and joining with the heel.
horseshoe
Curved metal band nailed under the wall of the hoof to protect it against wear, to absorb shocks and to provide better traction on the ground.
heel
Rear portion of the wall of the hoof between the quarters and opposite the toe.
side wall
Side part of the wall of the hoof between the toe and the quarter.
quarter
Side part of the wall of the hoof between the heel and the side wall.

examples of hooves

Ungulate mammals can have an odd or even number of toes (from one to five); the number can vary for the forelimbs and the hind limbs.

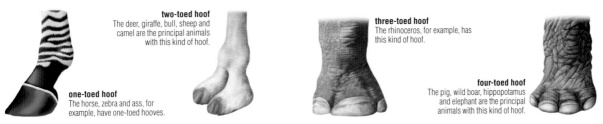

one-toed hoof
The horse, zebra and ass, for example, have one-toed hooves.

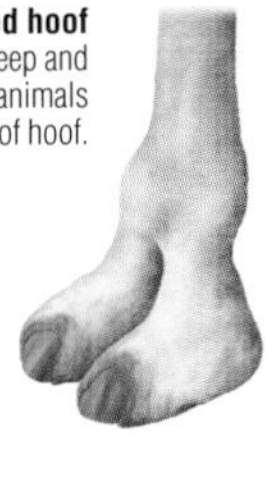

two-toed hoof
The deer, giraffe, bull, sheep and camel are the principal animals with this kind of hoof.

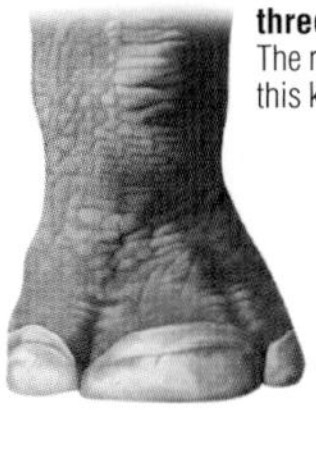

three-toed hoof
The rhinoceros, for example, has this kind of hoof.

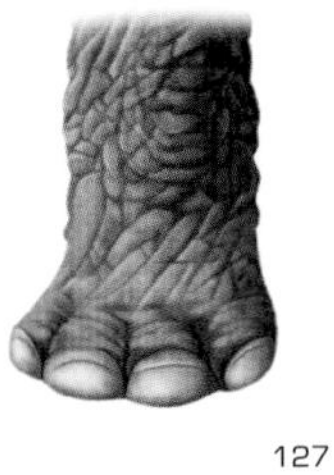

four-toed hoof
The pig, wild boar, hippopotamus and elephant are the principal animals with this kind of hoof.

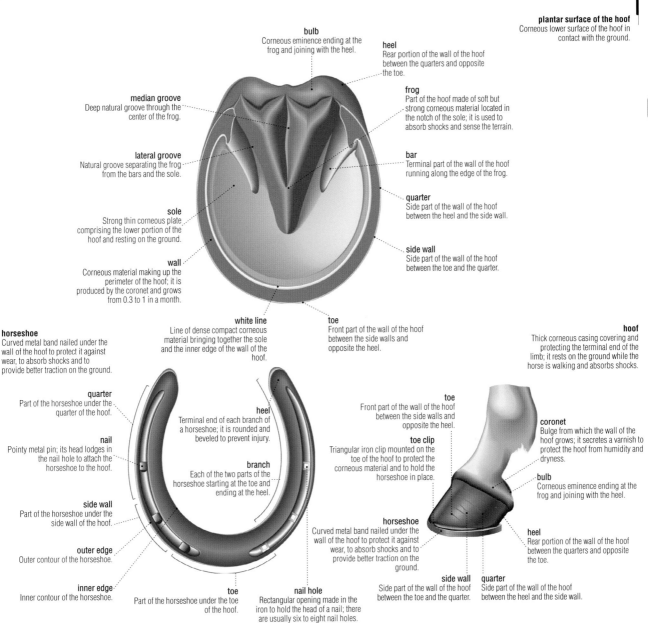

examples of ungulate mammals

There are many species of ungulate mammals; some are wild, some are domesticated and some are both.

peccary
Wild ungulate found in the forests of the Americas having a dorsal gland that emits a nauseous secretion; it is prized for its hide.

wild boar
Wild ungulate found in forests and marshes with sharp canines that it uses to defend itself; it is hunted for its hide.

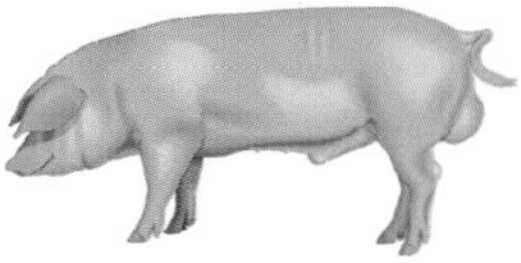

pig
Domestic omnivororous ungulate raised mainly for its meat and its hide.

goat
Ungulate ruminant with hollow horns able to jump and climb; it is domesticated for its milk and meat.

antelope
Ungulate ruminant with hollow horns found throughout Africa and Asia; it runs very fast and is prized for its meat and hide.

sheep
Ungulate ruminant covered with a thick wooly coat domesticated for its milk, meat and wool.

calf
Baby cow, male or female, up to the age of one year raised for its meat.

white-tailed deer
Wild ungulate ruminant of North America; it runs very fast and is highly prized as game.

mouflon
Extremely agile ungulate ruminant found in the wild in mountainous regions.

caribou
Ungulate ruminant found in cold regio of the Northern hemisphere; it is raise in captivity by some peoples for its me hide and milk, and as a draft animal.

elk
Wild ungulate ruminant of Canada; a good swimmer and runner, it is prized for its meat and antlers and is sometimes raised in captivity.

okapi
Ungulate ruminant of Africa with an extensible and prehensile tongue; only the male has small horns.

ass
Wild maned ungulate originally from Africa domesticated as a pack animal.

mule
Sterile male, a cross between an ass and a mare (female of the horse); it is very hardy and can carry heavy loads.

cow
Ungulate ruminant with horns (female of the bull); it is raised for its milk and meat, and for reproduction.

zebra
Maned ungulate that runs very fast; it is found in herds in the forests and steppes of Africa.

llama
Ungulate ruminant found in the mountains of South America; it can be wild or domesticated and is highly prized for its wool.

bison
Ungulate ruminant of North America and Europe, usually wild, sometimes raised for its meat.

buffalo
Ungulate ruminant found in the tropical regions of Africa and Asia; it is wild or raised in captivity for its meat and milk, and as a draft animal.

examples of ungulate mammals

ox
Castrated bovine (male of the cow) domesticated for its meat and sometimes used as a draft animal.

yak
Ruminant ungulate of Central Asia domesticated in Tibet for its milk and its hide, and as a pack animal.

horse
Maned ungulate mammal domesticated for riding and for use as a draft animal.

moose
Ruminant ungulate found in the cold regions of the Northern hemisphere with wide hooves that allow it to wade through marshes and ponds.

bactrian camel
Two-humped ruminant ungulate of Asia adapted to arid climates; it is domesticated especially for its meat, milk and hide, and as a pack animal.

dromedary camel
Single-humped ruminant ungulate of Africa adapted to arid climates; it is used especially as a pack animal and for riding.

rhinoceros
Ungulate found in the savannas and marshy areas of Africa and Asia with a one-horned or two-horned muzzle; it is threatened with extinction.

hippopotamus
Amphibious ungulate of Africa that can weigh up to 6 tons; it defends itself with its canine teeth, which grow constantly.

giraffe
Ruminant ungulate found in African savannas that can reach 23 feet in height; it has a prehensile tongue and small horns.

elephant
The largest land mammal today, found in the forests and savannas of Africa and Asia; it is hunted for its ivory tusks.

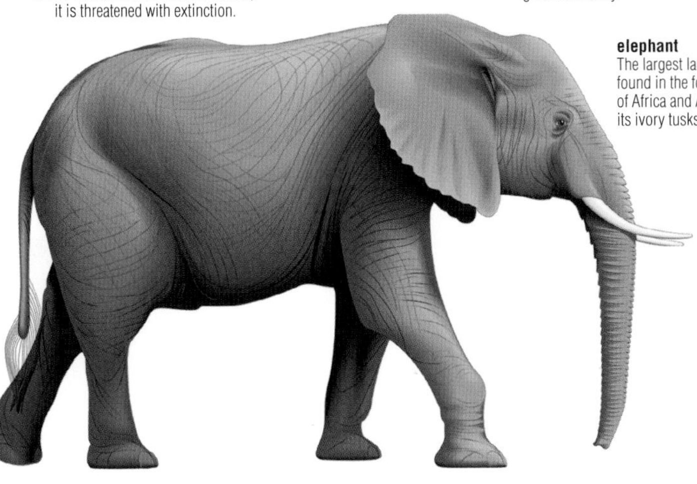

dog

Carnivorous mammal with an excellent sense of smell; it has been domesticated since prehistoric times and trained to perform a number of tasks: guarding and protecting, detecting, carrying and hunting.

morphology of a dog

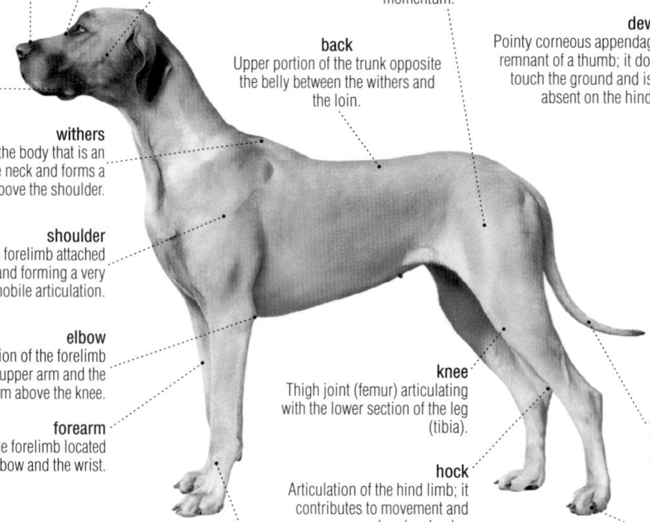
stop
Part between the top of the head and the muzzle.
cheek
Side part of the head between the muzzle and the ear, below the eye.
muzzle
Elongated front part of the head usually covered with sensory hairs (mustaches) that has a highly developed tactile and olfactory function.
thigh
Upper part of the hind limb; its muscles provide strong momentum.
flews
Movable muscular folds forming the contour of the mouth and having a tactile function.
back
Upper portion of the trunk opposite the belly between the withers and the loin.
withers
Part of the body that is an extension of the neck and forms a protuberance above the shoulder.
shoulder
Upper part of the forelimb attached to the trunk and forming a very mobile articulation.
elbow
Articulation of the forelimb between the upper arm and the forearm above the knee.
knee
Thigh joint (femur) articulating with the lower section of the leg (tibia).
forearm
Portion of the forelimb located between the elbow and the wrist.
tail
Terminal appendage of the body; the dog uses it mainly to show its reactions.
hock
Articulation of the hind limb; it contributes to movement and absorbs shocks.
wrist
Articulation of the forelimb to which the toes are attached.
toe
Terminal end of the limb supporting the body; it is formed of various articulated bones and ends in a claw.

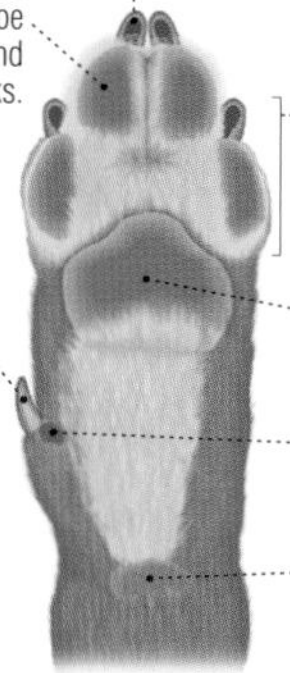
claw
Nonretractable corneous structure that is not very sharp; the dog digs with it and it provides stability and grip.
dog's forepaw
Articulated limb ending in four toes allowing the dog to move about, dig and scratch.
digital pad
Thick cutaneous bulge, elastic and resistant to wear upon which the toe rests; it contributes to locomotion and absorbs shocks.
toe
Terminal end of the limb supporting the body; it is formed of various articulated bones and ends in a claw.
dewclaw
Pointy corneous appendage, the remnant of a thumb; it does not touch the ground and is often absent on the hind limb.
palmar pad
Thick cutaneous bulge, elastic and resistant to wear supporting the metacarpus; the dog uses it to move about and it absorbs shocks.
dew pad
Thick elastic cutaneous bulge locate base of the dewclaw; it does not touc ground.
carpal pad
Thick cutaneous bulge, elastic and resistant to wear; it does not touch the ground but prevents the dog fror sliding as it lands after a jump.

dog breeds

There are about 350 breeds of dog, classified into 10 groups according to their morphology and use.

bulldog
Extremely affectionate and playful pet with a muscular body; it becomes aggressive when its owner is attacked.

schnauzer
Strong energetic dog originally from Germany, used as a guard dog and also as a pet.

poodle
Widely regarded as the most intelligent of domestic dog breeds; the poodle is bred in three varieties: standard, miniature, and toy.

chow chow
Pet originally from China, independent and reserved, it is also used as a guard dog.

collie
Scottish sheep dog and an affectionate and highly valued pet; the long-haired variety is more common than the short-haired variety.

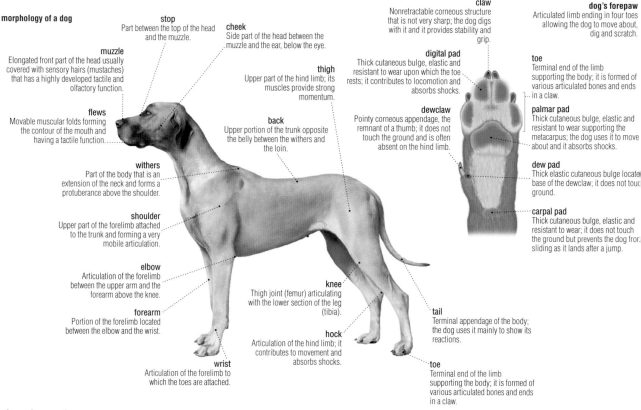

German shepherd
The most common multipurpose in the world: sheep dog, guard do police dog (detection and search), guide dog for the blind and pet.

dog

skeleton of a dog

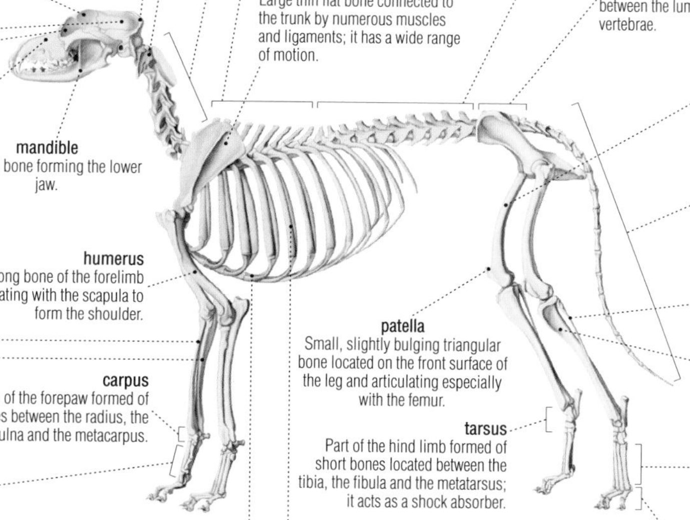

frontal bone
Flat skull bone forming the forehead and top of the eye sockets, and articulating especially with the parietal.
parietal bone
Flat bone of the upper side of the skull articulating with the frontal and occipital bones.
orbit
Bony cavity of the upper lateral potion of the head containing the eye.
maxilla
Toothed bone comprising the upper jaw.
atlas
First cervical vertebra supporting the head and supported by the axis.
occipital bone
Flat bone of the lower back part of the skull articulating with the parietal bone and the atlas.
mandible
Toothed bone forming the lower jaw.
cervical vertebrae
Bony parts of the neck comprising the upper terminal end of the vertebral column.
thoracic vertebrae
Bony parts supporting the ribs between the cervical and lumbar vertebrae.
scapula
Large thin flat bone connected to the trunk by numerous muscles and ligaments; it has a wide range of motion.
lumbar vertebrae
Bony parts of the back located between the thoracic and sacral vertebrae.
sacral vertebrae
Bony parts fused together located between the lumbar and caudal vertebrae.
femur
Long bone of the hind limb articulating with the pelvis, the tibia and the fibula.
caudal vertebrae
Bony parts comprising the skeleton of the tail located at the terminal end of the vertebral column.
radius
Long bone forming the outer limb between the humerus and the carpus.
ulna
Long bone forming the inner limb between the humerus and the carpus.
metacarpus
Portion of the forelimb formed of several long bones; it connects the carpus to the first phalange of the toe.
humerus
Long bone of the forelimb articulating with the scapula to form the shoulder.
carpus
Portion of the forepaw formed of short bones between the radius, the ulna and the metacarpus.
patella
Small, slightly bulging triangular bone located on the front surface of the leg and articulating especially with the femur.
tarsus
Part of the hind limb formed of short bones located between the tibia, the fibula and the metatarsus; it acts as a shock absorber.
fibula
Long bone forming the outer limb between the femur and the tarsus.
tibia
Long bone forming the inner limb between the femur and the tarsus.
metatarsus
Part of the hind limb formed of several long bones; it connects the tarsus to the first phalange of the toe.
phalanges
Articulated bones forming the skeleton of the toes.
sternum
Flat elongated and sometimes segmented bone to which the ribs are attached.
rib
Thin curved bone articulating with the vertebral column and the sternum.

dog breeds

dalmatian
Energetic and quite independent pet valued for its elegance; it also makes a good guard dog.

greyhound
Muscular streamlined dog; it is very swift and is used mainly for hunting and sports competitions.

Saint Bernard
Large, very muscular dog used as a rescue dog in the Alps.

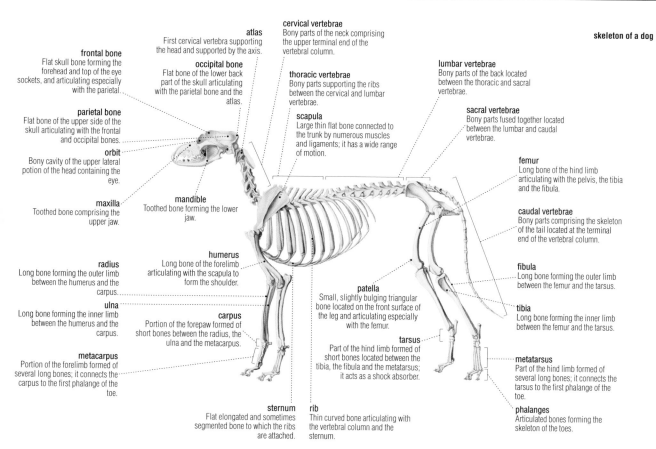

Great Dane
Very tall pet and guard dog, originally from Germany; it is affectionate and well behaved.

cat

Carnivorous mammal with a supple muscular body and paws ending in retractable claws; it is a very common pet.

cat's head
Anterior portion of the body containing the main sensory organs and the brain.

whiskers
Highly sensitive long stiff hairs located above the eyes and having a tactile function.

upper eyelid
Thin muscular membrane lowering from the upper edge of the eye to protect and clean it.

lower eyelid
Thin muscular membrane that is translucent and movable; it rises from the lower edge of the eye to protect and cleanse it.

nictitating membrane
Thin muscular membrane extending sideways from the inside corner of the eye to protect and moisten it.

whiskers
Extremely sensitive long stiff hairs (vibrissae) located on the muzzle having a tactile function.

lip
Movable muscular part forming the contour of the mouth; a cat has two upper lips lined with whiskers.

eyelashes
Hairs implanted on the free edge of the eyelid preventing dust and other particles from landing on the eye.

pupil
Central opening of the eye where light enters; it is particularly well adapted to the dark.

nose leather
Terminal end of the muzzle bearing the nostrils made of strong damp tissue; it has an olfactory and respiratory function.

muzzle
Short round front part of the head with whiskers; it has a highly developed tactile and olfactory function.

cat breeds

There are more than 30 officially recognized breeds of domestic cat, classified into three groups according to the length of their hair (short, medium-long or long).

American shorthair
Energetic and resilient cat that is in great demand in the U.S. and Japan.

Persian
Highly prized cat with silky fur, calm and affectionate; there are many varieties differentiated by the color of the fur and the eyes.

Maine coon
Sturdy cat, calm and affectionate, with a melodious meow; very popular in the U.S. but less common in Europe.

cat

morphology of a cat

ear
Highly mobile organ of hearing, also contributing to equilibrium; cats have a highly developed sense of hearing.
eye
Organ of sight especially adapted to darkness; it mainly perceives light intensity, motion and certain colors.
fur
Hair covering the body, mainly for maintaining internal body temperature and providing protection from insect bites.
tail
Terminal appendage of the body providing equilibrium when the cat jumps.

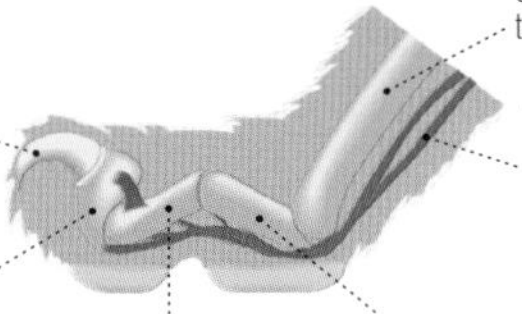
retracted claw
When a cat walks, its claws retract into a cutaneous fold (sheath) and it moves on its pads.
claw
Curved pointy retractable corneous structure allowing the cat to climb, catch its prey and defend itself.
distal phalanx
Bone of the lower terminal end of the toe bearing the claw.
middle phalanx
Bone of the central part of the toe between the proximal and distal phalanges.
proximal phalanx
Bone of the upper terminal end of the toe connected to the metacarpus.
metacarpus
Portion of the forelimb formed of several long bones; it connects the carpus to the first phalange of the toe.
tendon
Fibrous tissue connecting the muscle to the bone; relaxing the tendon causes the claw to retract.

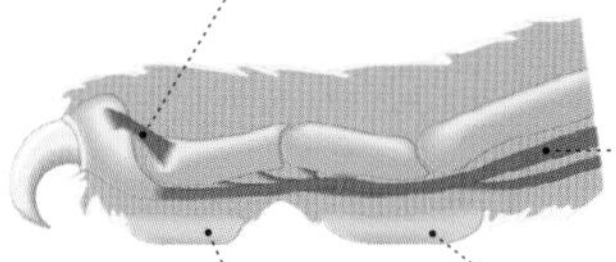
elastic ligament
Strong and elastic fibrous tissue located on the back of the distal and median phalanges allowing the claw to retract into the sheath.
extended claw
A cat uses its claws only when necessary, mainly for climbing or killing its prey.
tendon
Fibrous tissue connecting the muscle to the bone; the tendon's traction causes the claws to extend.
digital pad
Thick cutaneous bulge, elastic and resistant to wear upon which the toe rests; it contributes to locomotion and absorbs shocks.
plantar pad
Thick cutaneous bulge, elastic and resistant to wear, supporting the metacarpus; the cat uses it to move about and it absorbs shocks.

cat breeds

Siamese
Slender cat originally from Thailand, playful and affectionate; it has a loud raucous meow.

Abyssinian
Svelte cat originally from Egypt or Ethiopia, docile and energetic; it has a melodious meow.

Manx
Tailless cat with hind limbs longer than its forelimbs.

examples of carnivorous mammals

Carnivorous mammals (about 270 species) that have strong canines (fangs) and sharp molars (carnassials) adapted for eating flesh.

weasel
Very agile carnivorous mammal common in Eurasia; it is capable of attacking large prey (rats, voles, rabbits) in spite of its size.

mink
Carnivorous amphibious and mostly nocturnal mammal with webbed feet found in Eurasia and the Americas; it is hunted and raised in captivity for its highly prized fur.

stone marten
Mostly nocturnal carnivorous mammal of Eurasia; it is a good swimmer and climber and often catches fowl, domestic rabbits and rats.

marten
Mostly nocturnal agile carnivorous mammal of Eurasia and North America prized for its silky fur; it is a good climber.

fox
Very common carnivorous mammal living in a den and hunting at night (mostly rodents); its fur is highly prized.

raccoon
Mostly nocturnal carnivorous mammal of the Americas.

mongoose
Very agile carnivorous mammal of Africa and Asia; it is easily tamed and is used to destroy harmful pests (snakes, rats).

fennec
Nocturnal carnivorous mammal found in the deserts of Arabia and North Africa; it is easily tamed and capable of going without water for long periods.

river otter
Widespread carnivorous amphibious and usually nocturnal mammal with webbed feet feeding mainly on fish and prized for its fur.

skunk
Carnivorous mammal of the Americas, whose fur is prized; when threatened, it releases a nauseous and irritating secretion from its anal glands.

badger
Mostly nocturnal carnivorous mammal of the Northern hemisphere digging complex tunnels; its hairs are used to make hairbrushes and paintbrushes.

hyena
Carnivorous scavenger of Africa and Asia; hyenas live alone or in packs and will attack live prey.

lynx
Very agile and powerful carnivorous mammal found in the forests of the Northern hemisphere; it is a night hunter with piercing eyes and its fur is highly prized.

wolf
Nocturnal carnivorous mammal of Eurasia and North America; it lives in packs and hunts large mammals (deer).

cougar
Carnivorous mammal of the Americas living in various habitats (mountains, forests); it hunts only at night and is famed for its ability to leap.

examples of carnivorous mammals

cheetah
Carnivorous mammal of Africa and the Middle East with nonretractable claws; it is the fastest of the land mammals, reaching speeds of 62 mph.

leopard
Carnivorous mammal of Africa and Asia with yellow fur and black spots; it mostly lives in trees and usually hunts at night.

lion
Large carnivorous mammal common mainly in Africa that lives in groups called prides; only the male has a mane.

jaguar
Carnivorous mammal of Central and South America with spotted fur; it is an excellent swimmer and hunts at night.

tiger
Large and very powerful carnivorous mammal of Asia; it hunts at night.

black bear
Mostly nocturnal carnivorous mammal of North America; it is a good swimmer, is an excellent climber and feeds mainly on fruit and nuts.

polar bear
Carnivorous mammal of arctic regions; a good swimmer, it feeds mainly on seals and fish, and is the largest carnivorous land mammal.

dolphin

Marine mammal without hind limbs; it uses echoes of the sounds it emits (sonar) to orient itself and detect its prey.

morphology of a dolphin

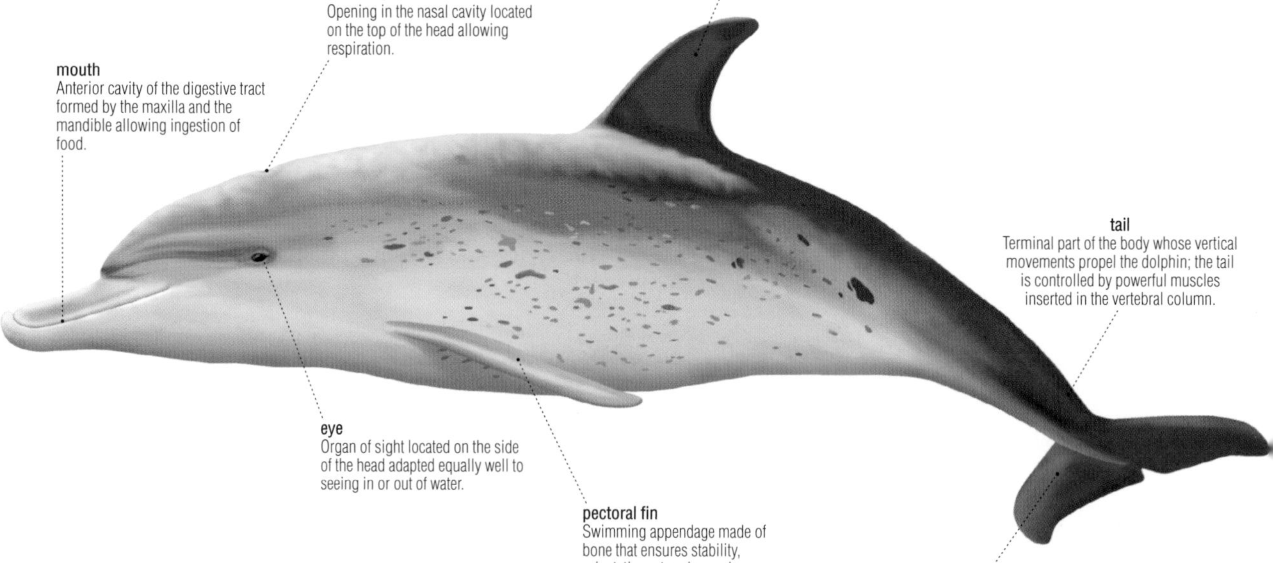
dorsal fin
Swimming appendage made of dense fibrous tissue located in the middle of the back and providing stability and thermoregulation; some marine mammals do not have a dorsal fin.
blowhole
Opening in the nasal cavity located on the top of the head allowing respiration.
mouth
Anterior cavity of the digestive tract formed by the maxilla and the mandible allowing ingestion of food.
tail
Terminal part of the body whose vertical movements propel the dolphin; the tail is controlled by powerful muscles inserted in the vertebral column.
eye
Organ of sight located on the side of the head adapted equally well to seeing in or out of water.
pectoral fin
Swimming appendage made of bone that ensures stability, orientation, stopping and thermoregulation.
caudal fin
Powerful swimming appendage with two lobes formed of dense fibrous tissue located vertically at the posterior terminal part of the body; its function is propulsion.

skeleton of a dolphin

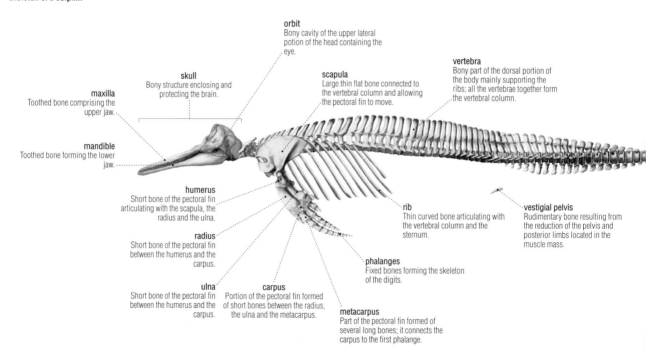

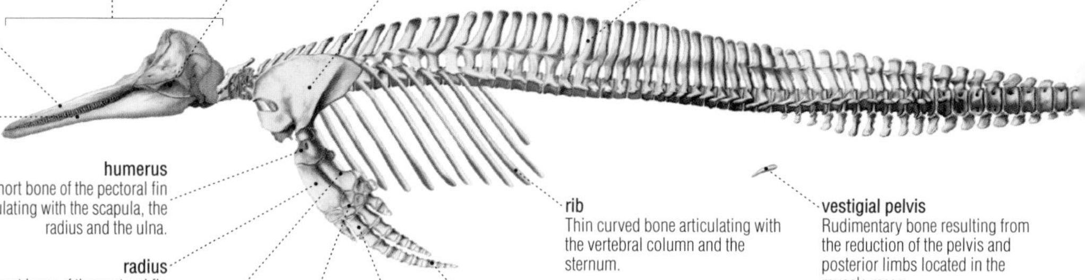
orbit
Bony cavity of the upper lateral potion of the head containing the eye.
skull
Bony structure enclosing and protecting the brain.
scapula
Large thin flat bone connected to the vertebral column and allowing the pectoral fin to move.
vertebra
Bony part of the dorsal portion of the body mainly supporting the ribs; all the vertebrae together form the vertebral column.
maxilla
Toothed bone comprising the upper jaw.
mandible
Toothed bone forming the lower jaw.
humerus
Short bone of the pectoral fin articulating with the scapula, the radius and the ulna.
rib
Thin curved bone articulating with the vertebral column and the sternum.
vestigial pelvis
Rudimentary bone resulting from the reduction of the pelvis and posterior limbs located in the muscle mass.
radius
Short bone of the pectoral fin between the humerus and the carpus.
phalanges
Fixed bones forming the skeleton of the digits.
ulna
Short bone of the pectoral fin between the humerus and the carpus.
carpus
Portion of the pectoral fin formed of short bones between the radius, the ulna and the metacarpus.
metacarpus
Part of the pectoral fin formed of several long bones; it connects the carpus to the first phalange.

examples of marine mammals

Marine mammals: many actively hunted species (more than 110 out of 116) are protected or are subject to hunting restrictions.

seal
t-haired amphibious marine mammal cking external ear flaps that moves ut on land by dragging its body; it is unted for its meat, blubber and fur.

sea lion
Amphibious marine mammal with external ear flaps that moves about on land with the help of its four limbs; it is hunted mainly for its fur.

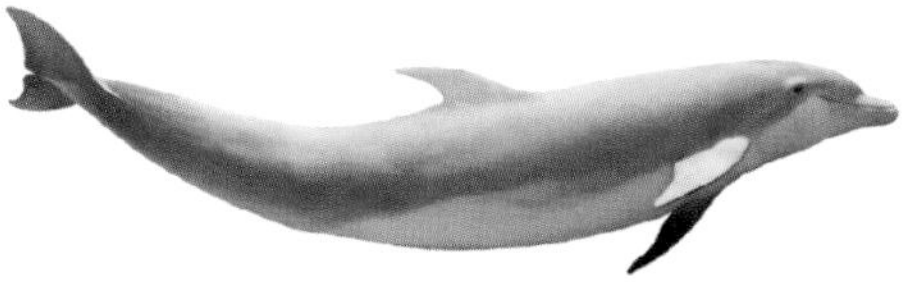

dolphin
Mammal of warm and temperate waters famed for its intelligence; it is a swift swimmer (about 28 mph).

porpoise
Mammal found in cold and temperate waters whose flesh is highly prized; it is a protected species.

narwhal
Mammal of arctic waters; the male, whose spiraled tusk can reach 10 feet in length, is hunted for its ivory.

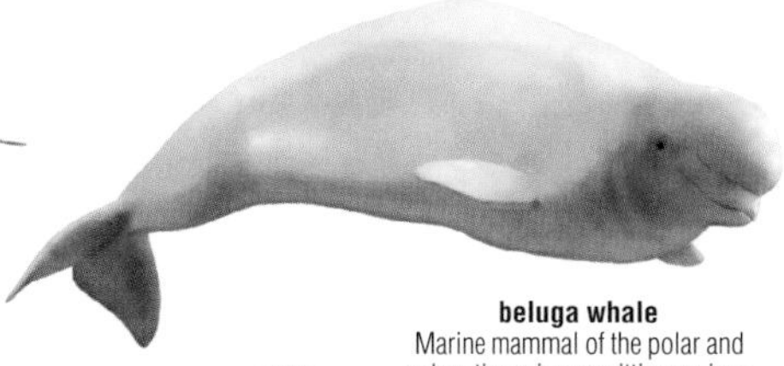

beluga whale
Marine mammal of the polar and subarctic regions emitting various whistles to communicate, hence its nickname "sea canary".

killer whale
Widespread swift aggressive marine mammal reaching up to 30 feet in length; it attacks mainly young whales and dolphins.

walrus
Amphibious marine mammal of arctic regions; it is hunted for its hide, blubber and ivory tusks.

humpback whale
Widespread marine mammal with a mouth lined with corneous plates (baleen) and numerous longitudinal grooves on its throat.

northern right whale
Marine mammal that can reach 100 feet in length and with a mouth lined with corneous plates (baleen); it was previously hunted especially for its oil and meat.

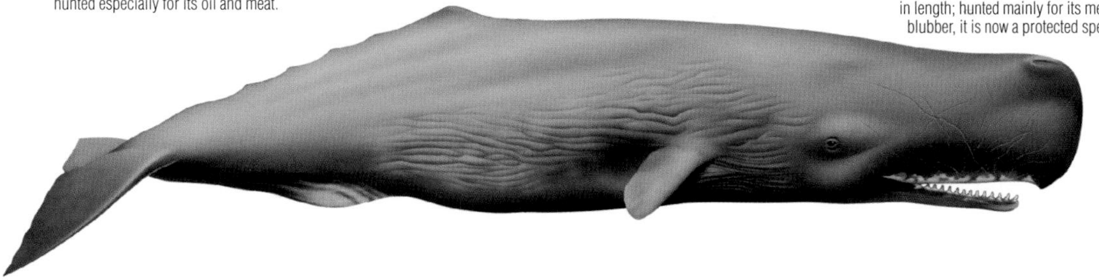

sperm whale
Mammal found in tropical and subtropical waters reaching up to 65 feet in length; hunted mainly for its meat and blubber, it is now a protected species.

gorilla

Mainly terrestrial vegetarian primate of the equatorial forests of Africa; the largest of the primates, it can reach 7 feet in height.

skeleton of a gorilla

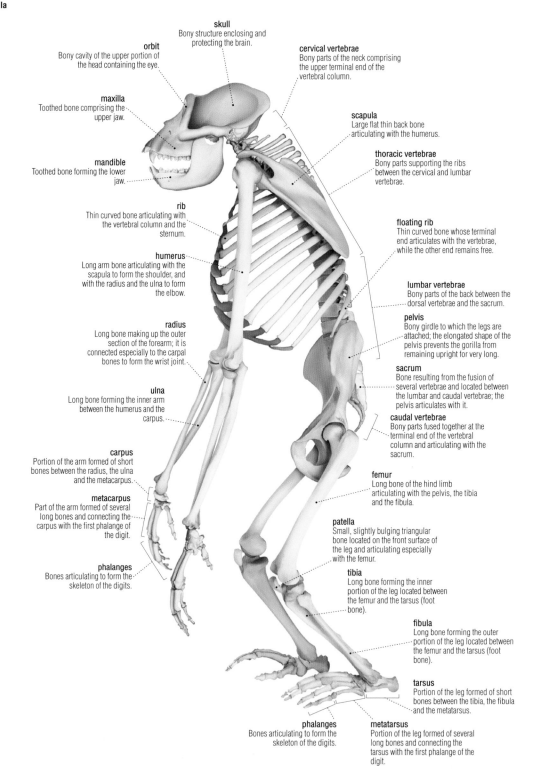

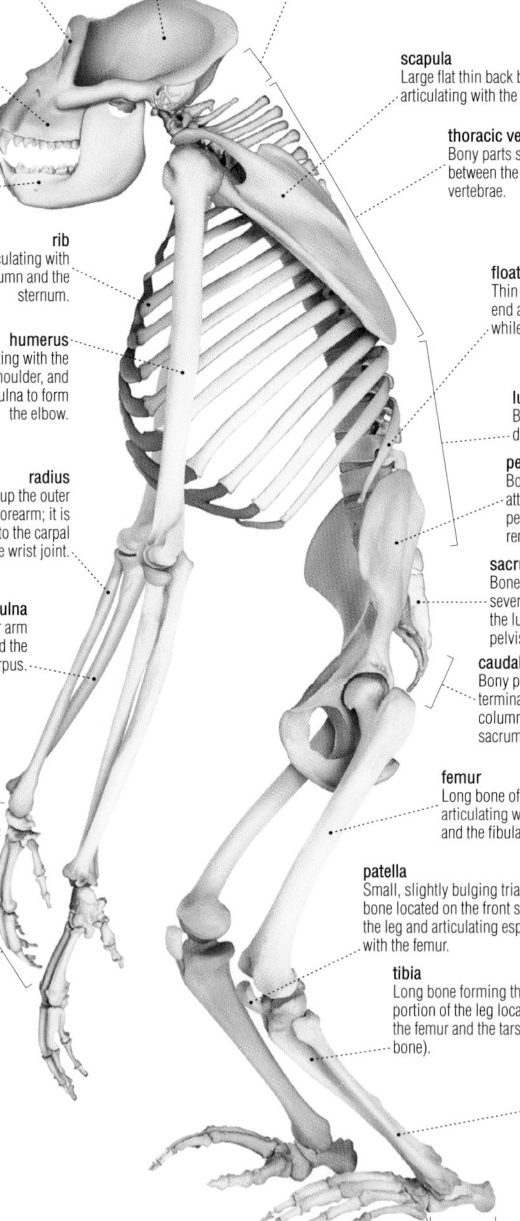

skull
Bony structure enclosing and protecting the brain.
orbit
Bony cavity of the upper portion of the head containing the eye.
cervical vertebrae
Bony parts of the neck comprising the upper terminal end of the vertebral column.
maxilla
Toothed bone comprising the upper jaw.
scapula
Large flat thin back bone articulating with the humerus.
thoracic vertebrae
Bony parts supporting the ribs between the cervical and lumbar vertebrae.
mandible
Toothed bone forming the lower jaw.
rib
Thin curved bone articulating with the vertebral column and the sternum.
floating rib
Thin curved bone whose terminal end articulates with the vertebrae, while the other end remains free.
humerus
Long arm bone articulating with the scapula to form the shoulder, and with the radius and the ulna to form the elbow.
lumbar vertebrae
Bony parts of the back between the dorsal vertebrae and the sacrum.
pelvis
Bony girdle to which the legs are attached; the elongated shape of the pelvis prevents the gorilla from remaining upright for very long.
radius
Long bone making up the outer section of the forearm; it is connected especially to the carpal bones to form the wrist joint.
sacrum
Bone resulting from the fusion of several vertebrae and located between the lumbar and caudal vertebrae; the pelvis articulates with it.
ulna
Long bone forming the inner arm between the humerus and the carpus.
caudal vertebrae
Bony parts fused together at the terminal end of the vertebral column and articulating with the sacrum.
carpus
Portion of the arm formed of short bones between the radius, the ulna and the metacarpus.
femur
Long bone of the hind limb articulating with the pelvis, the tibia and the fibula.
metacarpus
Part of the arm formed of several long bones and connecting the carpus with the first phalange of the digit.
patella
Small, slightly bulging triangular bone located on the front surface of the leg and articulating especially with the femur.
phalanges
Bones articulating to form the skeleton of the digits.
tibia
Long bone forming the inner portion of the leg located between the femur and the tarsus (foot bone).
fibula
Long bone forming the outer portion of the leg located between the femur and the tarsus (foot bone).
tarsus
Portion of the leg formed of short bones between the tibia, the fibula and the metatarsus.
phalanges
Bones articulating to form the skeleton of the digits.
metatarsus
Portion of the leg formed of several long bones and connecting the tarsus with the first phalange of the digit.

gorilla

morphology of a gorilla

face
Front portion of the head comprising especially the orifices of the sense organs.
fur
Hair covering the body, with the main exceptions of the face, palms of the hands and soles of the feet; it maintains body temperature.
prehensile digit
Articulated limb ending in a nail; along with the thumb, it is used to grasp food and to cling to objects.
opposable thumb
Short sturdy first digit of the hand facing the other digits and used for grasping and using tools; it is also used to hang from objects.
arm
Powerful muscular upper limb mainly supporting the body while walking.
hand
Terminal part of the upper limb having a tactile and prehensile function, with a thumb opposable to the other fingers.
leg
Powerful muscular lower limb supporting the body in an upright position.
foot
Terminal end of the leg bearing five digits; it rests on the ground and has a prehensile and motor function.

examples of primates

Many species are protected, especially because of deforestation (destruction of their habitat) and hunting.

tamarin
Small hopping primate of South America with elongated claws instead of nails that allow it to move about and to feed.

marmoset
Small South American primate with strong claws instead of nails that it uses to cling to the trees it lives in.

baboon
Mainly terrestrial African primate with colored ischial callosities and large cheek pouches in which it stores food.

macaque
Common primate of Asia with a nonprehensile tail living on the ground and in trees; it is often used for laboratory experiments.

orangutan
Primate found in Sumatra and Borneo with long powerful arms; it moves slowly and carefully between the trees in which it lives.

chimpanzee
Primate of equatorial Africa whose genetic makeup is very close to that of humans; it is used mainly in medical research.

lemur
Tree-dwelling agile primate of Madagascar with a long tail; it is mainly nocturnal and feeds on insects and fruit.

gibbon
Tailless tree-dwelling primate of Asia; it swings from branch to branch with agility, using its hands as hooks.

bat

Usually insectivorous nocturnal flying mammal using echoes of the sounds it produces (echolocation) to orient itself and to find its prey.

morphology of a bat

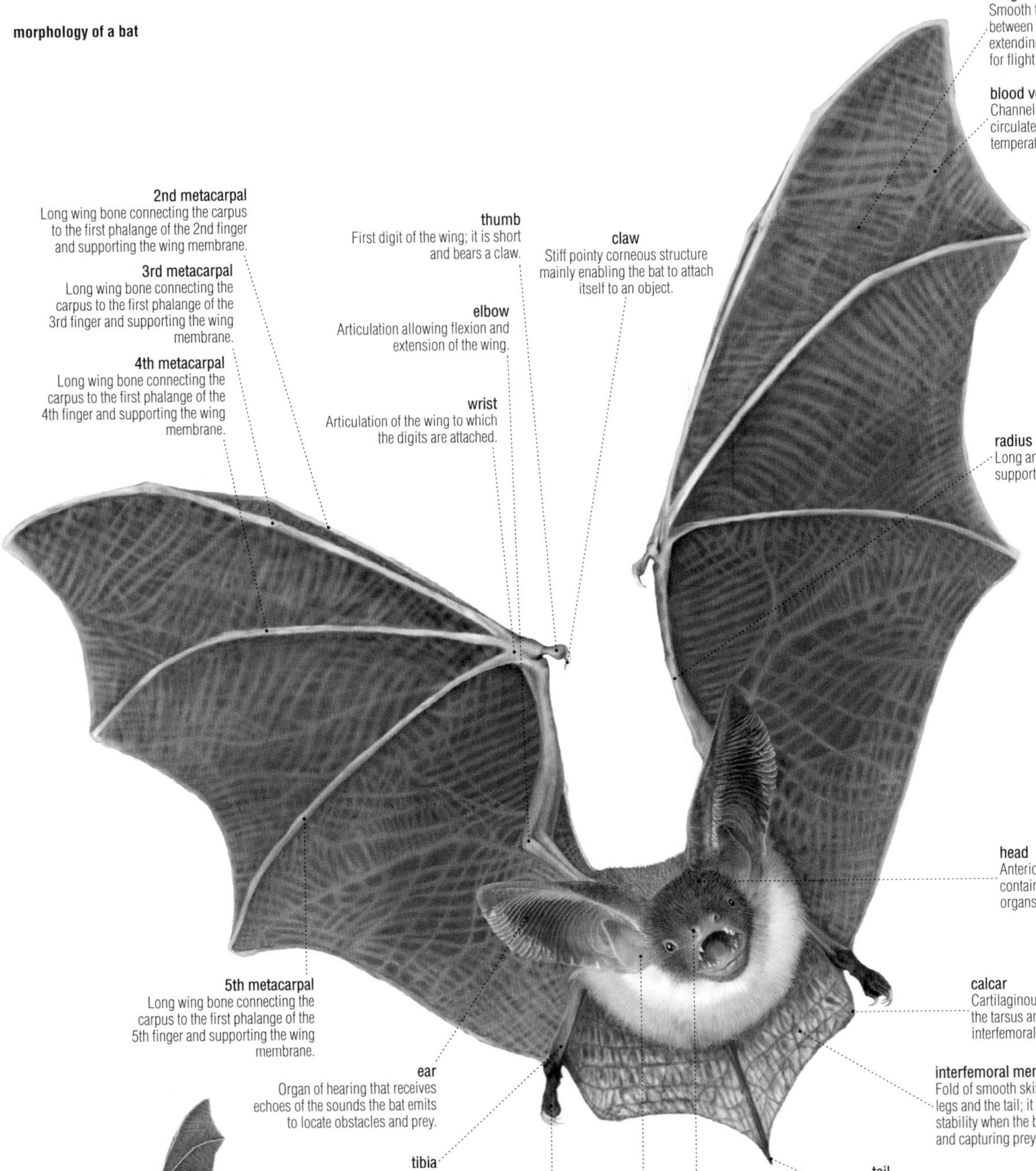

wing membrane
Smooth fold of skin stretching between the digits of the wings and extending to the feet; it is used mai for flight and thermoregulation.

blood vessels
Channels in which blood circulates; they regulate the body's temperature.

2nd metacarpal
Long wing bone connecting the carpus to the first phalange of the 2nd finger and supporting the wing membrane.

3rd metacarpal
Long wing bone connecting the carpus to the first phalange of the 3rd finger and supporting the wing membrane.

4th metacarpal
Long wing bone connecting the carpus to the first phalange of the 4th finger and supporting the wing membrane.

thumb
First digit of the wing; it is short and bears a claw.

claw
Stiff pointy corneous structure mainly enabling the bat to attach itself to an object.

elbow
Articulation allowing flexion and extension of the wing.

wrist
Articulation of the wing to which the digits are attached.

radius
Long and powerful wing bone supporting the wing membrane.

head
Anterior portion of the body containing the main sensory organs and the brain.

5th metacarpal
Long wing bone connecting the carpus to the first phalange of the 5th finger and supporting the wing membrane.

calcar
Cartilaginous structure attached to the tarsus and supporting the interfemoral membrane.

ear
Organ of hearing that receives echoes of the sounds the bat emits to locate obstacles and prey.

interfemoral membrane
Fold of smooth skin between the legs and the tail; it provides stability when the bat is in flight and capturing prey.

tibia
Long and powerful leg bone supporting especially the interfemoral membrane.

tail
Terminal appendage of the body supporting especially the interfemoral membrane.

foot
Terminal end of the foot having five toes pointing toward the back and ending in powerful claws; with it, the bat hangs upside down when at rest.

nose leaf
External opening of the nasal cavity located above the mouth and having a highly developed olfactory function in particular.

wings
Appendages of flight comprised of a cutaneous membrane supported by four very long fingers (only the thumb remains free); the bat folds its wings when resting.

tragus
Protuberance of the external opening of the ear; it improves receptivity by concentrating beams of incoming sound echoes.

skeleton of a bat

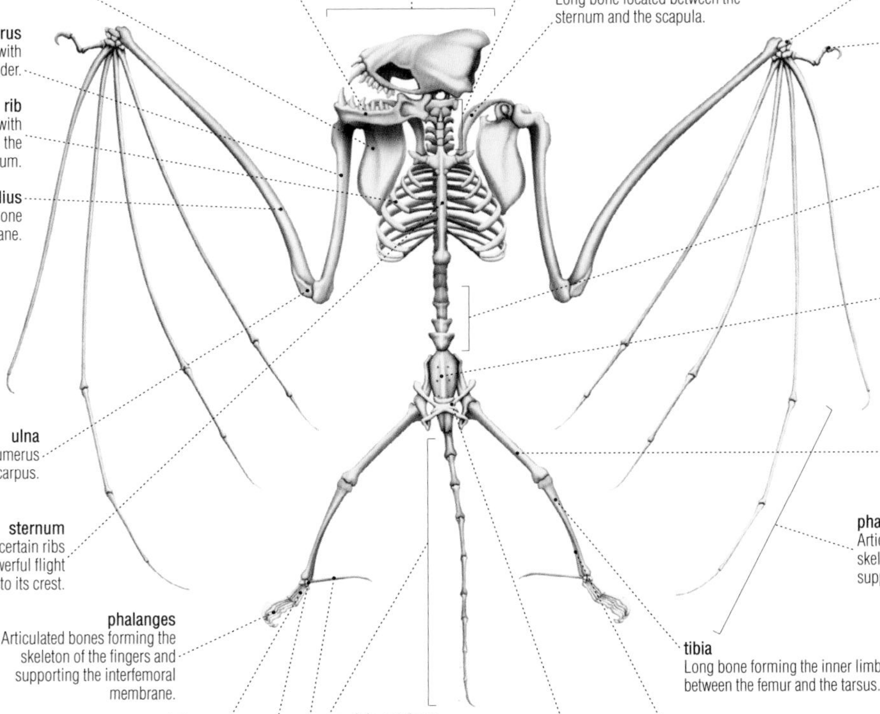
cervical vertebrae
Bony parts of the neck comprising the upper terminal end of the vertebral column.
scapula
Large thin flat bone; with the clavicle, it serves as an attachment point for the wing.
mandible
Toothed bone forming the lower jaw.
skull
Bony structure enclosing and protecting the brain.
carpus
Portion of the wing formed of two short bones; it is located between the radius, the ulna and the metacarpus.
clavicle
Long bone located between the sternum and the scapula.
humerus
Long wing bone articulating with the scapula to form the shoulder.
thumb
First digit of the wing; it is short and bears a claw.
rib
hin curved bone articulating with the vertebral column and the sternum.
radius
Long and powerful wing bone supporting the wing membrane.
lumbar vertebrae
Bony parts of the back located between the thoracic and sacral vertebrae.
sacrum
Bone resulting from the fusion of several vertebrae and located between the lumbar and caudal vertebrae; the pelvis articulates with it.
femur
Long bone of the hind limb articulating with the pelvis, the tibia and the fibula.
ulna
Wing bone between the humerus and the carpus.
sternum
Long flat bone to which certain ribs are attached; powerful flight muscles are inserted into its crest.
phalanges
Articulated bones forming the skeleton of the fingers and supporting the wing membrane.
phalanges
Articulated bones forming the skeleton of the fingers and supporting the interfemoral membrane.
tibia
Long bone forming the inner limb between the femur and the tarsus.
metatarsus
Portion of the foot formed of several long bones and connecting the tarsus to the first phalange of the digit.
caudal vertebrae
Bony parts comprising the skeleton of the tail located at the terminal end of the vertebral column.
fibula
Long bone forming the outer limb between the femur and the tarsus.
tarsus
Portion of the foot formed of short bones between the tibia, the fibula and the metatarsus.
calcar
Cartilaginous structure attached to the tarsus and supporting the interfemoral membrane.
pelvis
Bony girdle serving as an attachment point for the legs.

examples of bats

Very widespread, some 900 species of bats live mainly in colonies, in trees or in caves.

vampire bat
Tailless flying mammal of Central and South America; it feeds off the blood of animals and birds.

black flying fox
One of the largest bats in the world, it lives in Australia, feeds on fruit and has a rudimentary tail; its wingspan can reach 5 feet.

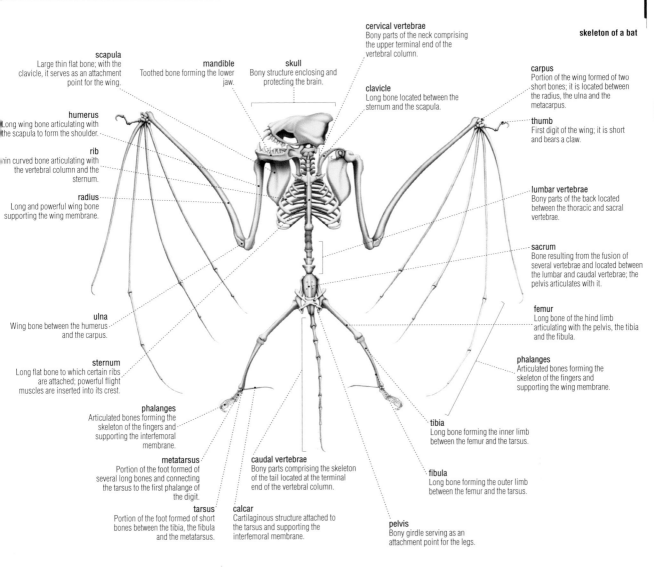

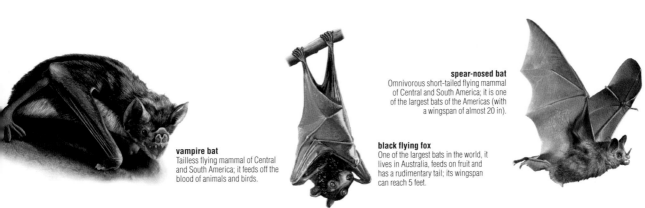

spear-nosed bat
Omnivorous short-tailed flying mammal of Central and South America; it is one of the largest bats of the Americas (with a wingspan of almost 20 in).

kangaroo

Herbivorous marsupial with a highly developed tail; it lives in groups in Australia and Tasmania and moves rapidly by leaping.

skeleton of a kangaroo

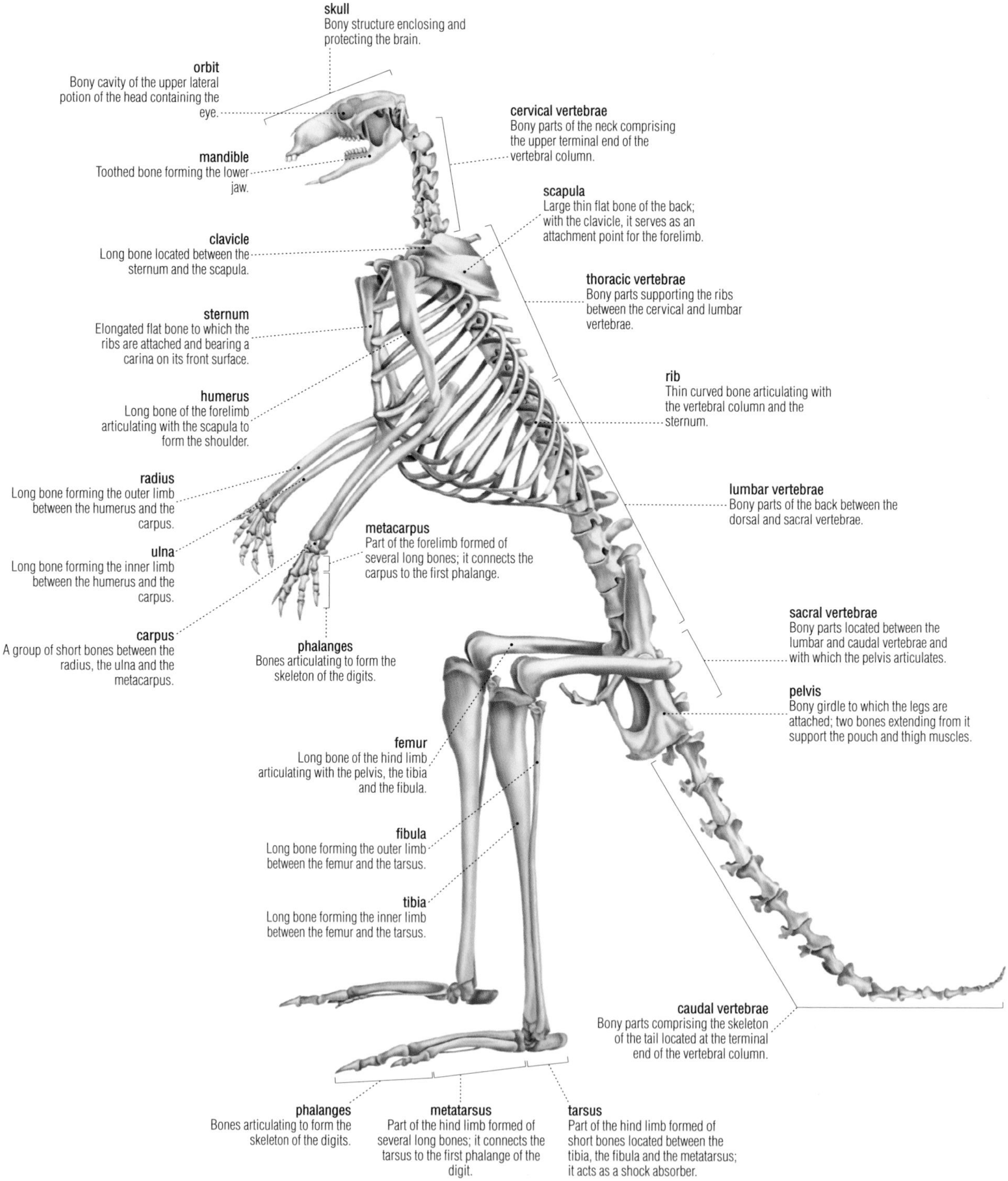
skull
Bony structure enclosing and protecting the brain.
orbit
Bony cavity of the upper lateral potion of the head containing the eye.
mandible
Toothed bone forming the lower jaw.
cervical vertebrae
Bony parts of the neck comprising the upper terminal end of the vertebral column.
scapula
Large thin flat bone of the back; with the clavicle, it serves as an attachment point for the forelimb.
clavicle
Long bone located between the sternum and the scapula.
thoracic vertebrae
Bony parts supporting the ribs between the cervical and lumbar vertebrae.
sternum
Elongated flat bone to which the ribs are attached and bearing a carina on its front surface.
rib
Thin curved bone articulating with the vertebral column and the sternum.
humerus
Long bone of the forelimb articulating with the scapula to form the shoulder.
radius
Long bone forming the outer limb between the humerus and the carpus.
lumbar vertebrae
Bony parts of the back between the dorsal and sacral vertebrae.
metacarpus
Part of the forelimb formed of several long bones; it connects the carpus to the first phalange.
ulna
Long bone forming the inner limb between the humerus and the carpus.
sacral vertebrae
Bony parts located between the lumbar and caudal vertebrae and with which the pelvis articulates.
carpus
A group of short bones between the radius, the ulna and the metacarpus.
phalanges
Bones articulating to form the skeleton of the digits.
pelvis
Bony girdle to which the legs are attached; two bones extending from it support the pouch and thigh muscles.
femur
Long bone of the hind limb articulating with the pelvis, the tibia and the fibula.
fibula
Long bone forming the outer limb between the femur and the tarsus.
tibia
Long bone forming the inner limb between the femur and the tarsus.
caudal vertebrae
Bony parts comprising the skeleton of the tail located at the terminal end of the vertebral column.
phalanges
Bones articulating to form the skeleton of the digits.
metatarsus
Part of the hind limb formed of several long bones; it connects the tarsus to the first phalange of the digit.
tarsus
Part of the hind limb formed of short bones located between the tibia, the fibula and the metatarsus; it acts as a shock absorber.

kangaroo

morphology of a kangaroo

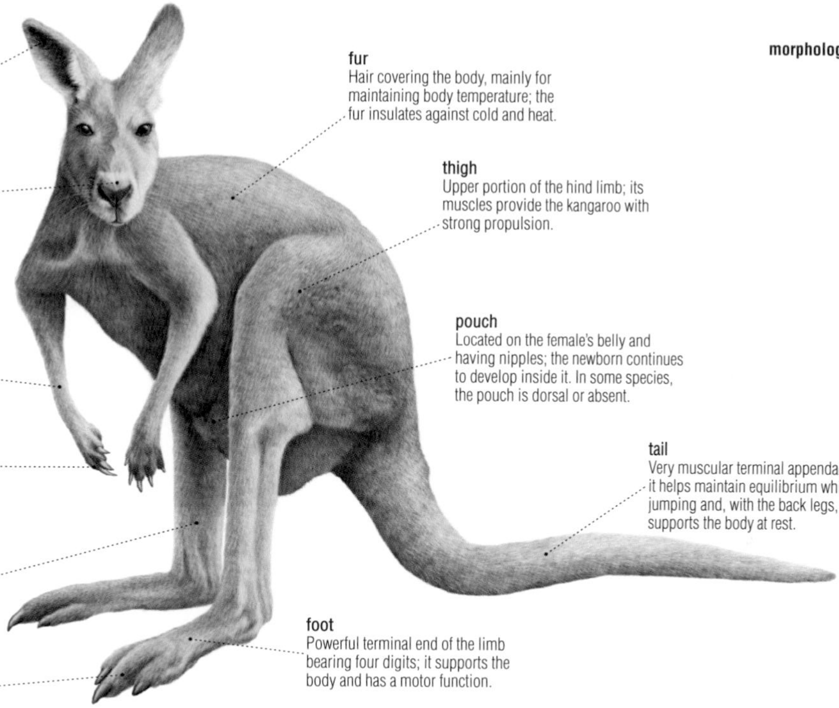
pinna
Movable outer portion of the ear made of cartilage and located on the side of the head to capture sounds.
snout
Long front portion of the head having mainly a highly developed olfactory function.
forelimb
Poorly developed articulated limb ending in five clawed digits; the kangaroo uses it to feed and to defend itself.
claw
Pointy sharp corneous structure used especially to scratch and claw adversaries during combat.
hind limb
Extremely muscular articulated limb ending in four digits allowing the kangaroo to move swiftly by powerful bounds and to strike its enemies.
digit
Articulated limb at the end of the foot. The kangaroo does not usually have a thumb. The 2nd and 3rd digits are fused, while the 4th digit ends in a strong sharp claw.
fur
Hair covering the body, mainly for maintaining body temperature; the fur insulates against cold and heat.
thigh
Upper portion of the hind limb; its muscles provide the kangaroo with strong propulsion.
pouch
Located on the female's belly and having nipples; the newborn continues to develop inside it. In some species, the pouch is dorsal or absent.
tail
Very muscular terminal appendage; it helps maintain equilibrium while jumping and, with the back legs, supports the body at rest.
foot
Powerful terminal end of the limb bearing four digits; it supports the body and has a motor function.

examples of marsupials

The 260 or so species live on land or in trees in Oceania and the Americas.

Tasmanian devil
Carnivorous scavenging nocturnal marsupial with powerful jaws that allow it to devour its prey whole (flesh, bones, fur, feathers).

koala
Tailless nocturnal marsupial of Australia; this solitary tree-dweller lives in eucalyptus forests and feeds on the tree's leaves.

wallaby
Marsupial closely related to the kangaroo and living in Australia, Tasmania and New Guinea; certain species are prized for their fur.

opossum
Omnivorous nocturnal marsupial of the Americas and Australia without a pouch; its fur is highly prized.

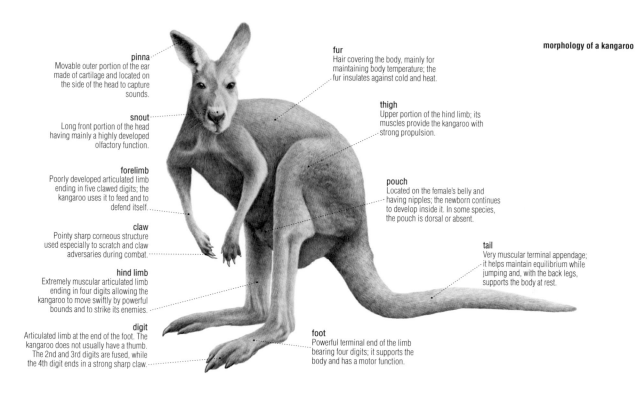

kangaroo
Herbivorous marsupial with a highly developed tail; it lives in groups in Australia and Tasmania and moves rapidly by leaping.

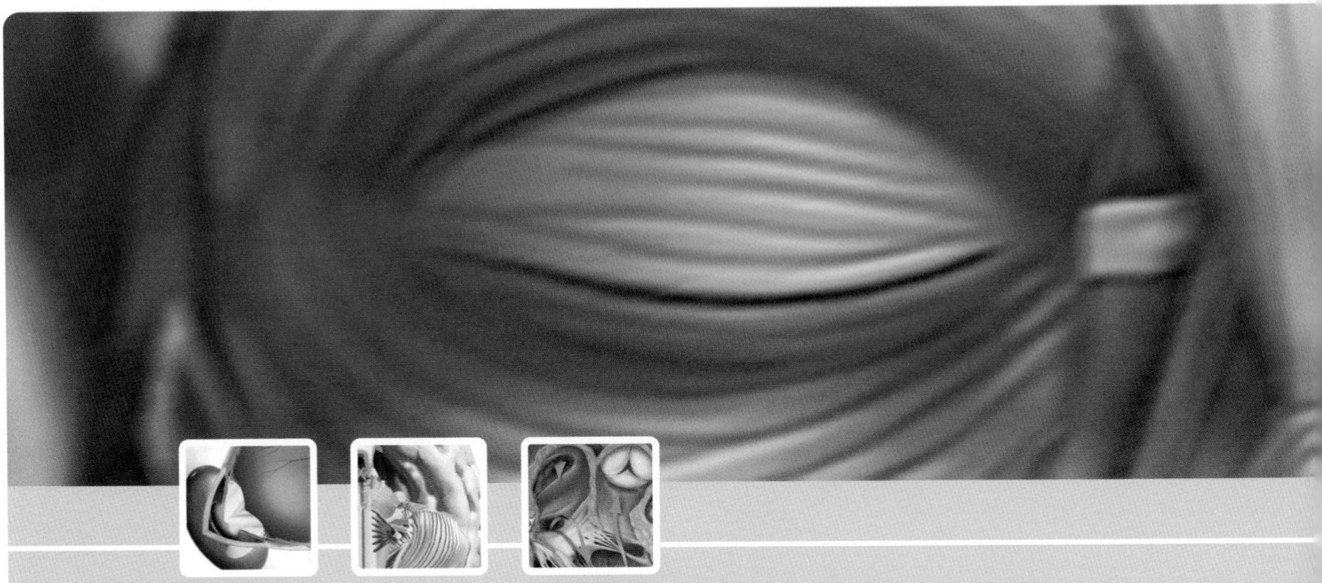

HUMAN BEING

Living being representing the most evolved species on Earth, characterized especially by upright stance, spoken language and a large brain.

man

Male human being producing cells able to fertilize the ovum (egg); the male's skeleton is generally larger and heavier than that of the female.

anterior view

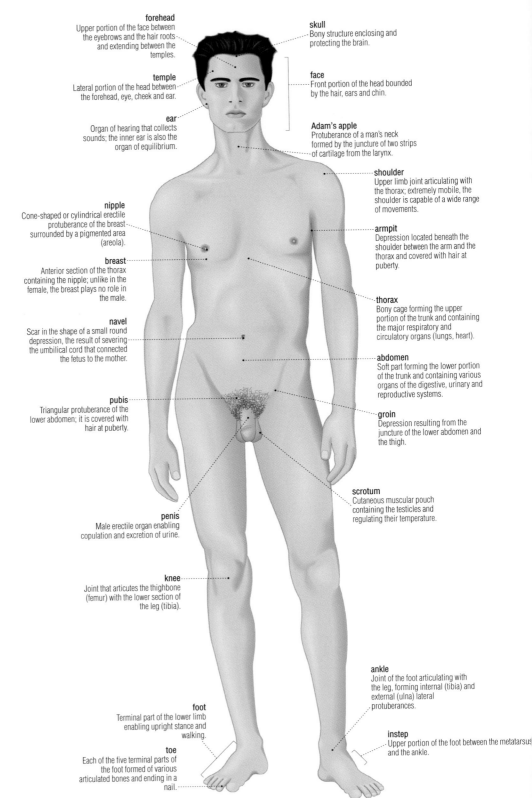

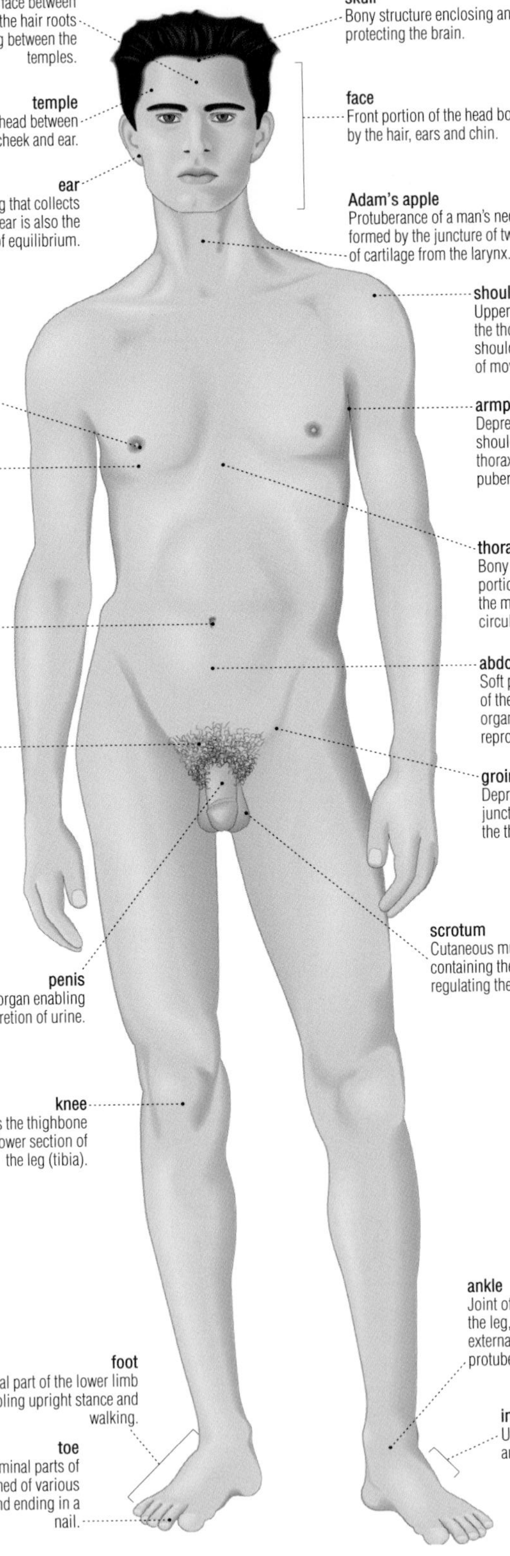

forehead
Upper portion of the face between the eyebrows and the hair roots and extending between the temples.
skull
Bony structure enclosing and protecting the brain.
temple
Lateral portion of the head between the forehead, eye, cheek and ear.
face
Front portion of the head bounded by the hair, ears and chin.
ear
Organ of hearing that collects sounds; the inner ear is also the organ of equilibrium.
Adam's apple
Protuberance of a man's neck formed by the juncture of two strips of cartilage from the larynx.
shoulder
Upper limb joint articulating with the thorax; extremely mobile, the shoulder is capable of a wide range of movements.
nipple
Cone-shaped or cylindrical erectile protuberance of the breast surrounded by a pigmented area (areola).
armpit
Depression located beneath the shoulder between the arm and the thorax and covered with hair at puberty.
breast
Anterior section of the thorax containing the nipple; unlike in the female, the breast plays no role in the male.
thorax
Bony cage forming the upper portion of the trunk and containing the major respiratory and circulatory organs (lungs, heart).
navel
Scar in the shape of a small round depression, the result of severing the umbilical cord that connected the fetus to the mother.
abdomen
Soft part forming the lower portion of the trunk and containing various organs of the digestive, urinary and reproductive systems.
pubis
Triangular protuberance of the lower abdomen; it is covered with hair at puberty.
groin
Depression resulting from the juncture of the lower abdomen and the thigh.
scrotum
Cutaneous muscular pouch containing the testicles and regulating their temperature.
penis
Male erectile organ enabling copulation and excretion of urine.
knee
Joint that articutes the thighbone (femur) with the lower section of the leg (tibia).
ankle
Joint of the foot articulating with the leg, forming internal (tibia) and external (ulna) lateral protuberances.
foot
Terminal part of the lower limb enabling upright stance and walking.
instep
Upper portion of the foot between the metatarsus and the ankle.
toe
Each of the five terminal parts of the foot formed of various articulated bones and ending in a nail.

posterior view

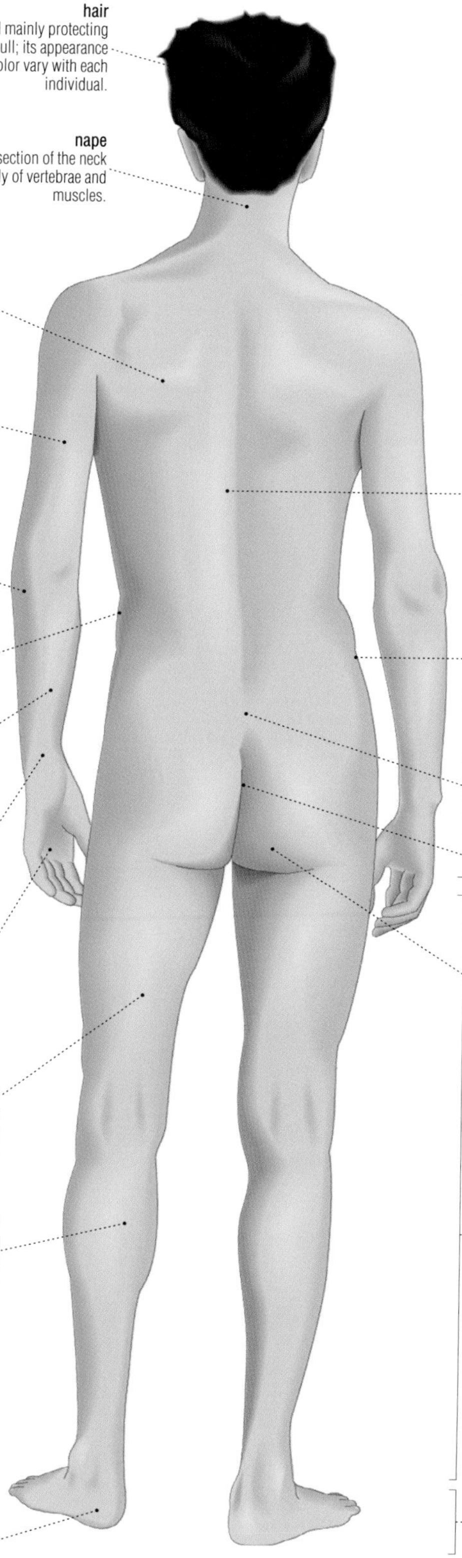

hair
Hair of the head mainly protecting the skin of the skull; its appearance and color vary with each individual.
nape
Posterior section of the neck formed mainly of vertebrae and muscles.
shoulder blade
Slender flat back bone articulating especially with the humerus (arm bone) and forming the posterior section of the shoulder.
arm
Section of the upper limb between the shoulder and the elbow and articulating especially with the scapula.
elbow
Arm joint (humerus) articulating with the forearm (radius and ulna); it protrudes when the limb is flexed.
waist
Narrowed section of the body between the base of the thorax and the hips.
forearm
Section of the upper limb between the elbow and the wrist; its muscles control the movements of the hand and fingers.
wrist
Joint of the hand (carpus) articulating with the forearm (radius).
hand
Terminal part of the upper limb having a tactile and prehensile function, with a thumb opposable to the other fingers.
thigh
Section of the leg between the hip and the knee; it contains many powerful muscles.
calf
Fleshy section formed by the muscles at the back of the leg between the knee and the ankle.
heel
Posterior section of the foot; it rests on the ground when walking.
head
Upper portion of the body supported by the neck and made up essentially of the main sensory organs and the brain.
neck
Portion of the body connecting the head to the trunk; the respiratory tract, nerve centers and blood vessels, in particular, pass through it.
back
Posterior portion of the trunk extending from the shoulders to the kidneys on each side of the vertebral column.
trunk
Portion of the body to which the head and limbs are attached; it is made up of the thorax, abdomen and pelvis.
hip
Leg joint articulating with the pelvis (base of the trunk).
loin
Lower portion of the back; it is located on each side of the vertebral column.
posterior rugae
Deep slender ridge between the two buttocks through which the anus opens.
buttock
Fleshy section made up mostly of muscles; it is located at the base of the back.
leg
Lower limb attached to the trunk; it supports the body in an upright position and during locomotion.
foot
Terminal part of the lower limb enabling upright stance and walking.

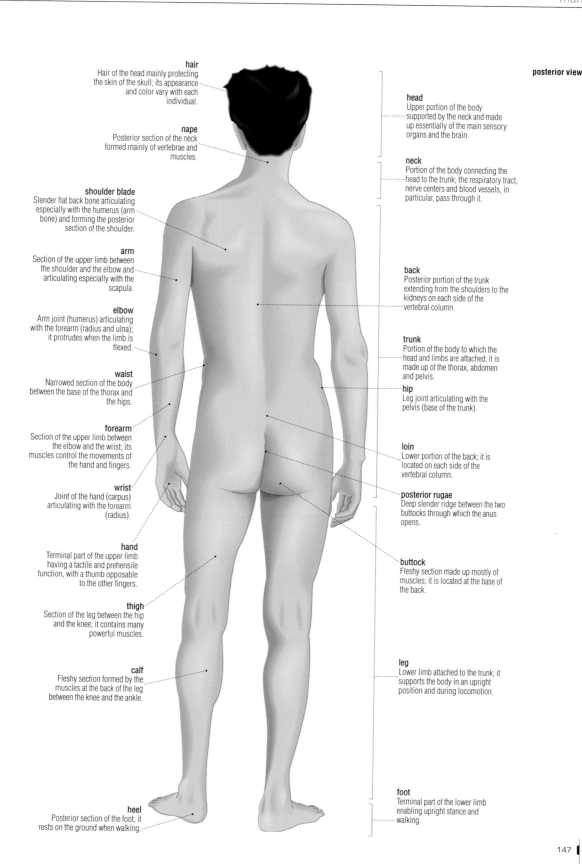

woman

Human being of the female sex capable of conceiving children from an ovum (egg) fertilized by a spermatozoon (sperm, the reproductive male cell).

anterior view

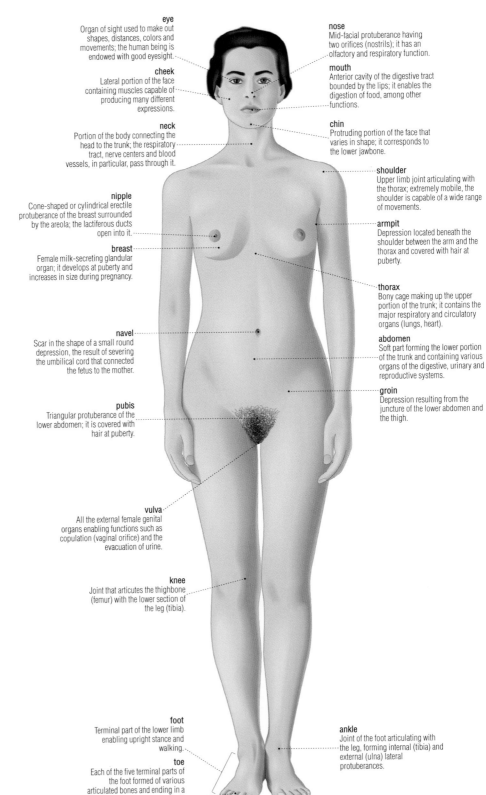

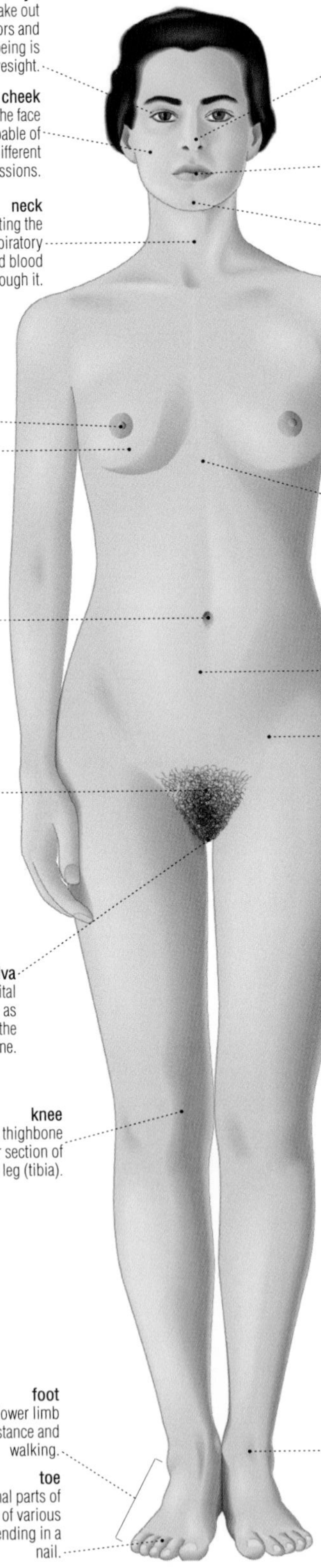

eye
Organ of sight used to make out shapes, distances, colors and movements; the human being is endowed with good eyesight.
cheek
Lateral portion of the face containing muscles capable of producing many different expressions.
neck
Portion of the body connecting the head to the trunk; the respiratory tract, nerve centers and blood vessels, in particular, pass through it.
nipple
Cone-shaped or cylindrical erectile protuberance of the breast surrounded by the areola; the lactiferous ducts open into it.
breast
Female milk-secreting glandular organ; it develops at puberty and increases in size during pregnancy.
navel
Scar in the shape of a small round depression, the result of severing the umbilical cord that connected the fetus to the mother.
pubis
Triangular protuberance of the lower abdomen; it is covered with hair at puberty.
vulva
All the external female genital organs enabling functions such as copulation (vaginal orifice) and the evacuation of urine.
knee
Joint that articutes the thighbone (femur) with the lower section of the leg (tibia).
foot
Terminal part of the lower limb enabling upright stance and walking.
toe
Each of the five terminal parts of the foot formed of various articulated bones and ending in a nail.
nose
Mid-facial protuberance having two orifices (nostrils); it has an olfactory and respiratory function.
mouth
Anterior cavity of the digestive tract bounded by the lips; it enables the digestion of food, among other functions.
chin
Protruding portion of the face that varies in shape; it corresponds to the lower jawbone.
shoulder
Upper limb joint articulating with the thorax; extremely mobile, the shoulder is capable of a wide range of movements.
armpit
Depression located beneath the shoulder between the arm and the thorax and covered with hair at puberty.
thorax
Bony cage making up the upper portion of the trunk; it contains the major respiratory and circulatory organs (lungs, heart).
abdomen
Soft part forming the lower portion of the trunk and containing various organs of the digestive, urinary and reproductive systems.
groin
Depression resulting from the juncture of the lower abdomen and the thigh.
ankle
Joint of the foot articulating with the leg, forming internal (tibia) and external (ulna) lateral protuberances.

posterior view

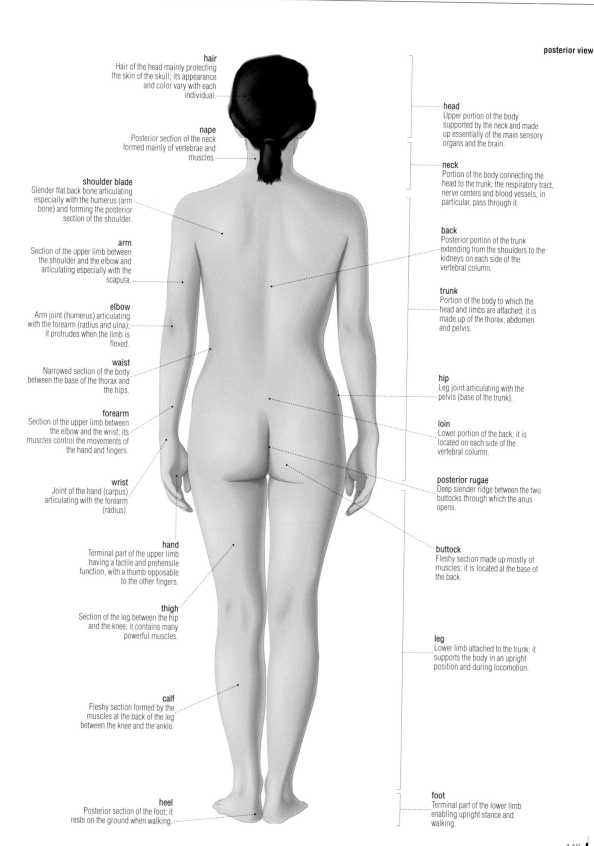

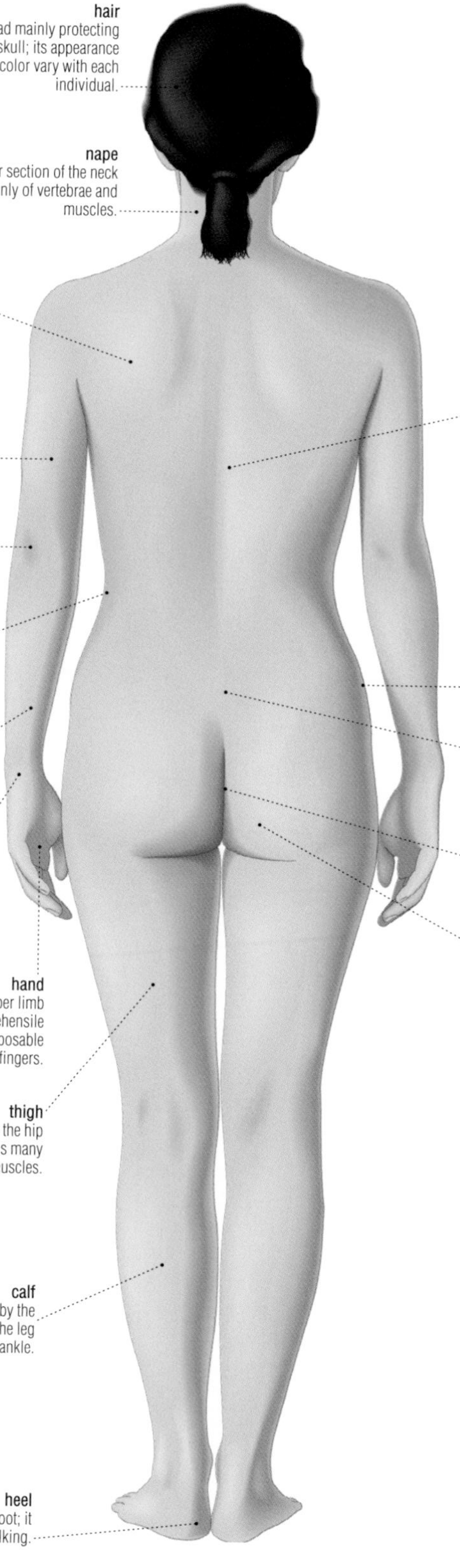

muscles

Contractile organs made of fibers allowing the body to move and maintain its posture; the human body has over 600 muscles.

anterior view

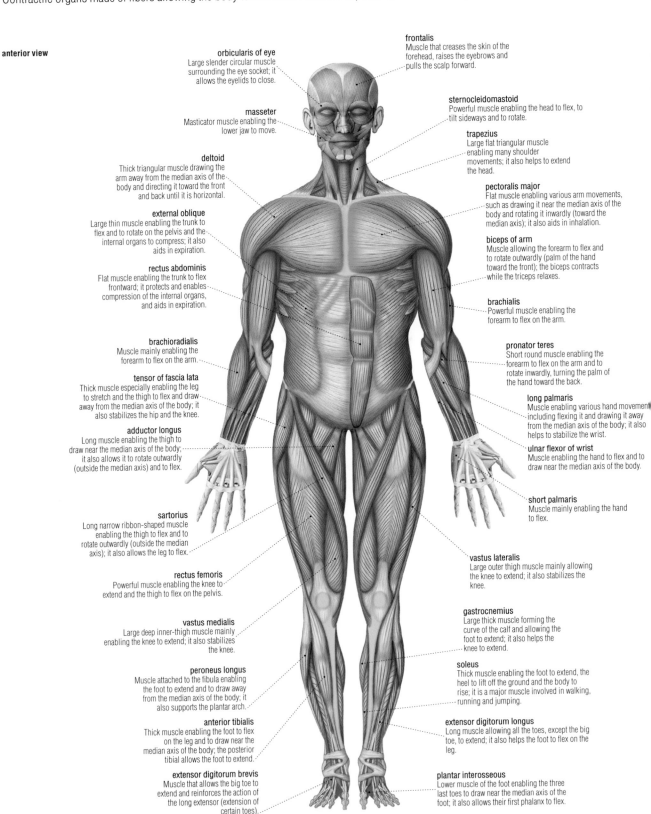

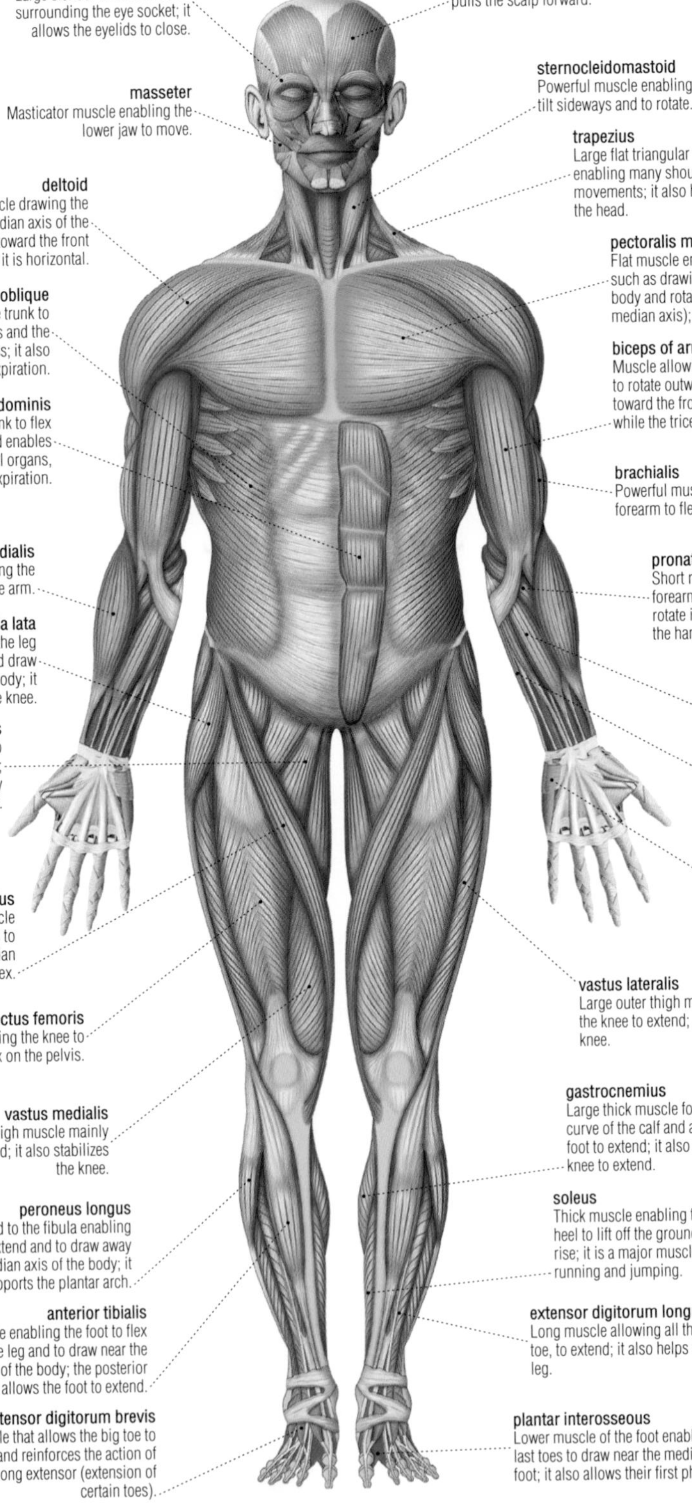
orbicularis of eye
Large slender circular muscle surrounding the eye socket; it allows the eyelids to close.
masseter
Masticator muscle enabling the lower jaw to move.
deltoid
Thick triangular muscle drawing the arm away from the median axis of the body and directing it toward the front and back until it is horizontal.
external oblique
Large thin muscle enabling the trunk to flex and to rotate on the pelvis and the internal organs to compress; it also aids in expiration.
rectus abdominis
Flat muscle enabling the trunk to flex frontward; it protects and enables compression of the internal organs, and aids in expiration.
brachioradialis
Muscle mainly enabling the forearm to flex on the arm.
tensor of fascia lata
Thick muscle especially enabling the leg to stretch and the thigh to flex and draw away from the median axis of the body; it also stabilizes the hip and the knee.
adductor longus
Long muscle enabling the thigh to draw near the median axis of the body; it also allows it to rotate outwardly (outside the median axis) and to flex.
sartorius
Long narrow ribbon-shaped muscle enabling the thigh to flex and to rotate outwardly (outside the median axis); it also allows the leg to flex.
rectus femoris
Powerful muscle enabling the knee to extend and the thigh to flex on the pelvis.
vastus medialis
Large deep inner-thigh muscle mainly enabling the knee to extend; it also stabilizes the knee.
peroneus longus
Muscle attached to the fibula enabling the foot to extend and to draw away from the median axis of the body; it also supports the plantar arch.
anterior tibialis
Thick muscle enabling the foot to flex on the leg and to draw near the median axis of the body; the posterior tibial allows the foot to extend.
extensor digitorum brevis
Muscle that allows the big toe to extend and reinforces the action of the long extensor (extension of certain toes).
frontalis
Muscle that creases the skin of the forehead, raises the eyebrows and pulls the scalp forward.
sternocleidomastoid
Powerful muscle enabling the head to flex, to tilt sideways and to rotate.
trapezius
Large flat triangular muscle enabling many shoulder movements; it also helps to extend the head.
pectoralis major
Flat muscle enabling various arm movements, such as drawing it near the median axis of the body and rotating it inwardly (toward the median axis); it also aids in inhalation.
biceps of arm
Muscle allowing the forearm to flex and to rotate outwardly (palm of the hand toward the front); the biceps contracts while the triceps relaxes.
brachialis
Powerful muscle enabling the forearm to flex on the arm.
pronator teres
Short round muscle enabling the forearm to flex on the arm and to rotate inwardly, turning the palm of the hand toward the back.
long palmaris
Muscle enabling various hand movemen including flexing it and drawing it away from the median axis of the body; it also helps to stabilize the wrist.
ulnar flexor of wrist
Muscle enabling the hand to flex and to draw near the median axis of the body.
short palmaris
Muscle mainly enabling the hand to flex.
vastus lateralis
Large outer thigh muscle mainly allowing the knee to extend; it also stabilizes the knee.
gastrocnemius
Large thick muscle forming the curve of the calf and allowing the foot to extend; it also helps the knee to extend.
soleus
Thick muscle enabling the foot to extend, the heel to lift off the ground and the body to rise; it is a major muscle involved in walking, running and jumping.
extensor digitorum longus
Long muscle allowing all the toes, except the big toe, to extend; it also helps the foot to flex on the leg.
plantar interosseous
Lower muscle of the foot enabling the three last toes to draw near the median axis of the foot; it also allows their first phalanx to flex.

posterior view

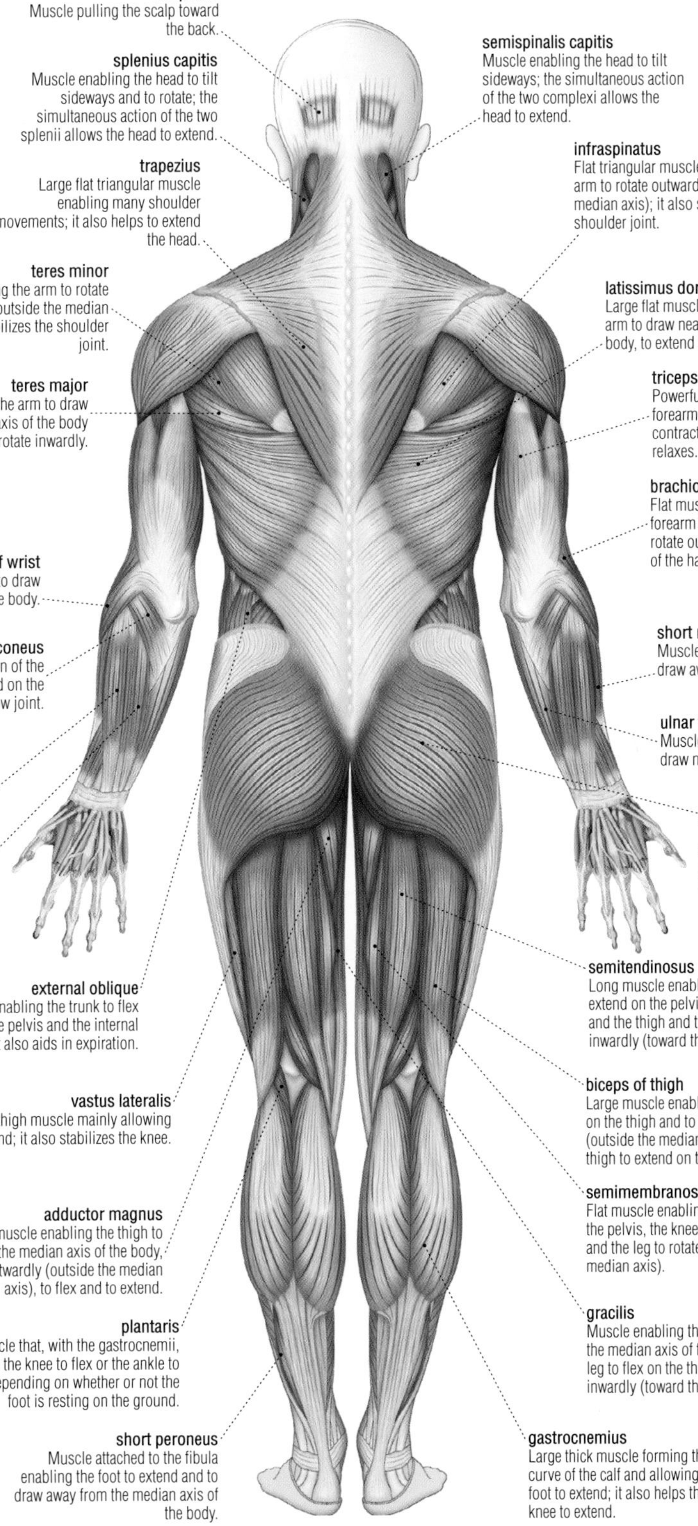
occipitalis
Muscle pulling the scalp toward the back.
splenius capitis
Muscle enabling the head to tilt sideways and to rotate; the simultaneous action of the two splenii allows the head to extend.
trapezius
Large flat triangular muscle enabling many shoulder movements; it also helps to extend the head.
teres minor
Muscle enabling the arm to rotate outwardly (outside the median axis); it also stabilizes the shoulder joint.
teres major
Muscle enabling the arm to draw near the median axis of the body and to rotate inwardly.
long radial extensor of wrist
Muscle enabling the hand to extend and to draw away from the median axis of the body.
anconeus
Short muscle reinforcing the action of the triceps; it allows the forearm to extend on the arm and also stabilizes the elbow joint.
common extensor of fingers
Muscle enabling all the fingers, except the thumb, to extend; it also helps the hand to extend on the forearm.
ulnar extensor of wrist
Muscle enabling the hand to extend and to draw near the median axis of the body.
external oblique
Large thin muscle enabling the trunk to flex and to rotate on the pelvis and the internal organs to compress; it also aids in expiration.
vastus lateralis
Large outer thigh muscle mainly allowing the knee to extend; it also stabilizes the knee.
adductor magnus
Powerful muscle enabling the thigh to draw near the median axis of the body, to rotate outwardly (outside the median axis), to flex and to extend.
plantaris
Small muscle that, with the gastrocnemii, allows the knee to flex or the ankle to extend, depending on whether or not the foot is resting on the ground.
short peroneus
Muscle attached to the fibula enabling the foot to extend and to draw away from the median axis of the body.
semispinalis capitis
Muscle enabling the head to tilt sideways; the simultaneous action of the two complexi allows the head to extend.
infraspinatus
Flat triangular muscle enabling the arm to rotate outwardly (outside the median axis); it also stabilizes the shoulder joint.
latissimus dorsi
Large flat muscle especially enabling the arm to draw near the median axis of the body, to extend and to rotate inwardly.
triceps of arm
Powerful muscle enabling the forearm to extend on the arm; it contracts whereas the biceps relaxes.
brachioradialis
Flat muscle primarily enabling the forearm to flex; it also helps it to rotate outwardly, bringing the palm of the hand toward the front.
short radial extensor of wrist
Muscle enabling the hand to extend and to draw away from the median axis of the body.
ulnar flexor of wrist
Muscle enabling the hand to flex and to draw near the median axis of the body.
gluteus maximus
Thick muscle enabling the hip to extend and to rotate outwardly (outside the median axis); it also allows the trunk to return to a vertical position.
semitendinosus
Long muscle enabling the thigh to extend on the pelvis, the knee to flex, and the thigh and the leg to rotate inwardly (toward the median axis).
biceps of thigh
Large muscle enabling the leg to flex on the thigh and to rotate outwardly (outside the median axis) and the thigh to extend on the pelvis.
semimembranosus
Flat muscle enabling the thigh to extend on the pelvis, the knee to flex, and the thigh and the leg to rotate inwardly (toward the median axis).
gracilis
Muscle enabling the thigh to draw near the median axis of the body, and the leg to flex on the thigh and to rotate inwardly (toward the median axis).
gastrocnemius
Large thick muscle forming the curve of the calf and allowing the foot to extend; it also helps the knee to extend.

skeleton

All the articulated bones (about 200), of varying sizes and shapes, forming the frame of the body, supporting the muscles and protecting the vital organs.

anterior view

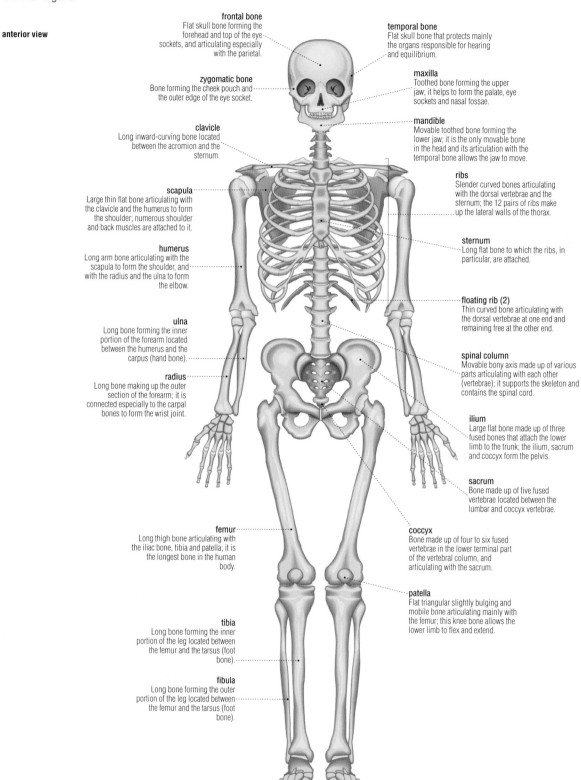

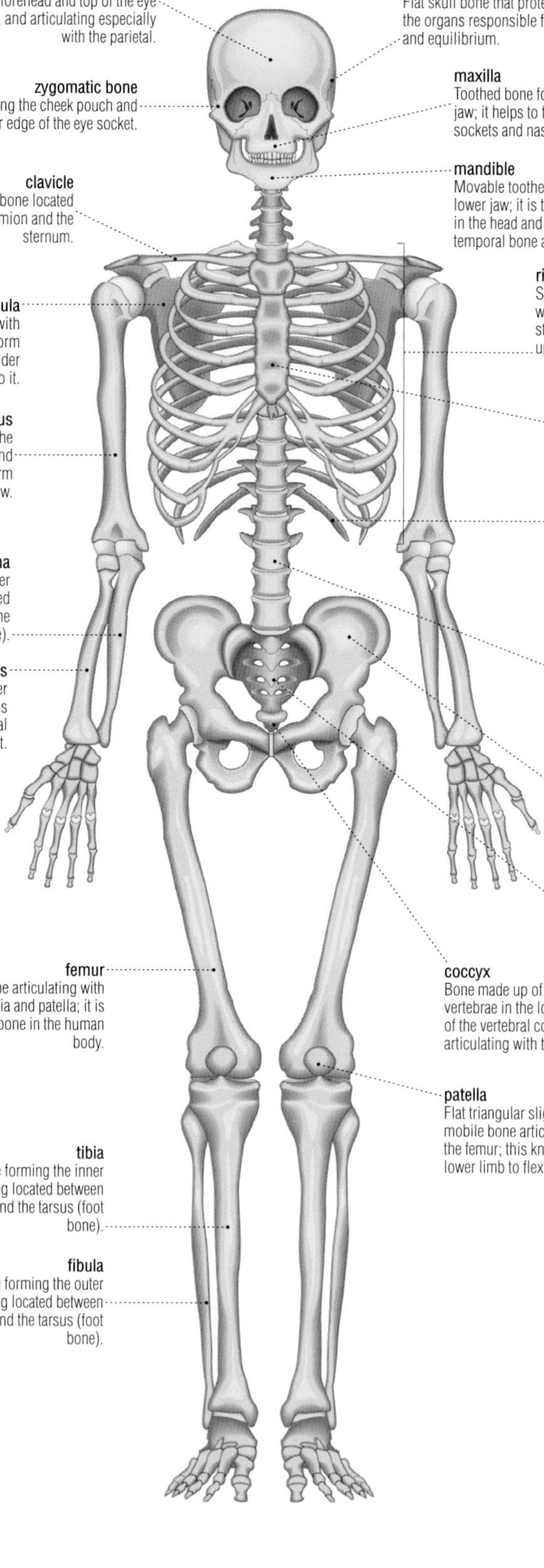

frontal bone
Flat skull bone forming the forehead and top of the eye sockets, and articulating especially with the parietal.
temporal bone
Flat skull bone that protects mainly the organs responsible for hearing and equilibrium.
zygomatic bone
Bone forming the cheek pouch and the outer edge of the eye socket.
maxilla
Toothed bone forming the upper jaw; it helps to form the palate, eye sockets and nasal fossae.
clavicle
Long inward-curving bone located between the acromion and the sternum.
mandible
Movable toothed bone forming the lower jaw; it is the only movable bone in the head and its articulation with the temporal bone allows the jaw to move.
ribs
Slender curved bones articulating with the dorsal vertebrae and the sternum; the 12 pairs of ribs make up the lateral walls of the thorax.
scapula
Large thin flat bone articulating with the clavicle and the humerus to form the shoulder; numerous shoulder and back muscles are attached to it.
sternum
Long flat bone to which the ribs, in particular, are attached.
humerus
Long arm bone articulating with the scapula to form the shoulder, and with the radius and the ulna to form the elbow.
floating rib (2)
Thin curved bone articulating with the dorsal vertebrae at one end and remaining free at the other end.
ulna
Long bone forming the inner portion of the forearm located between the humerus and the carpus (hand bone).
spinal column
Movable bony axis made up of various parts articulating with each other (vertebrae); it supports the skeleton and contains the spinal cord.
radius
Long bone making up the outer section of the forearm; it is connected especially to the carpal bones to form the wrist joint.
ilium
Large flat bone made up of three fused bones that attach the lower limb to the trunk; the ilium, sacrum and coccyx form the pelvis.
sacrum
Bone made up of five fused vertebrae located between the lumbar and coccyx vertebrae.
femur
Long thigh bone articulating with the iliac bone, tibia and patella; it is the longest bone in the human body.
coccyx
Bone made up of four to six fused vertebrae in the lower terminal part of the vertebral column, and articulating with the sacrum.
patella
Flat triangular slightly bulging and mobile bone articulating mainly with the femur; this knee bone allows the lower limb to flex and extend.
tibia
Long bone forming the inner portion of the leg located between the femur and the tarsus (foot bone).
fibula
Long bone forming the outer portion of the leg located between the femur and the tarsus (foot bone).

posterior view

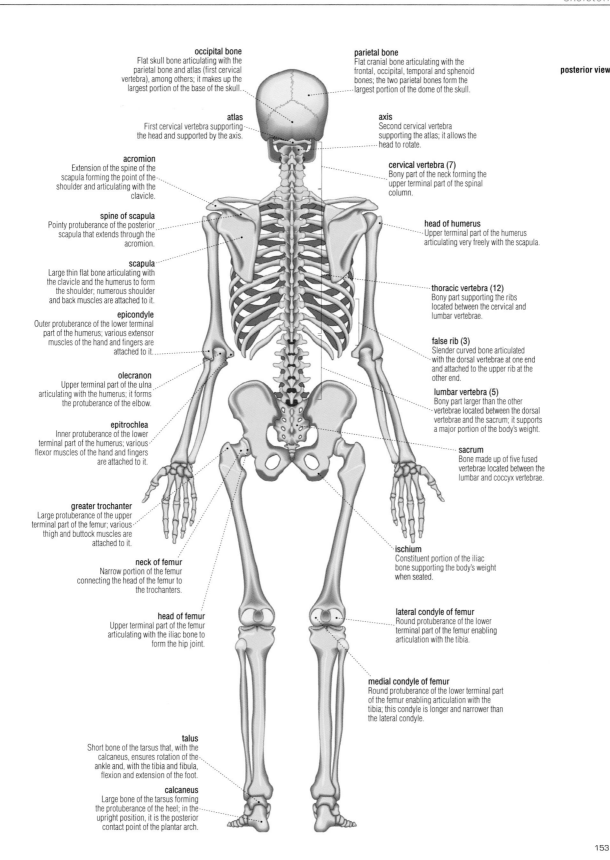

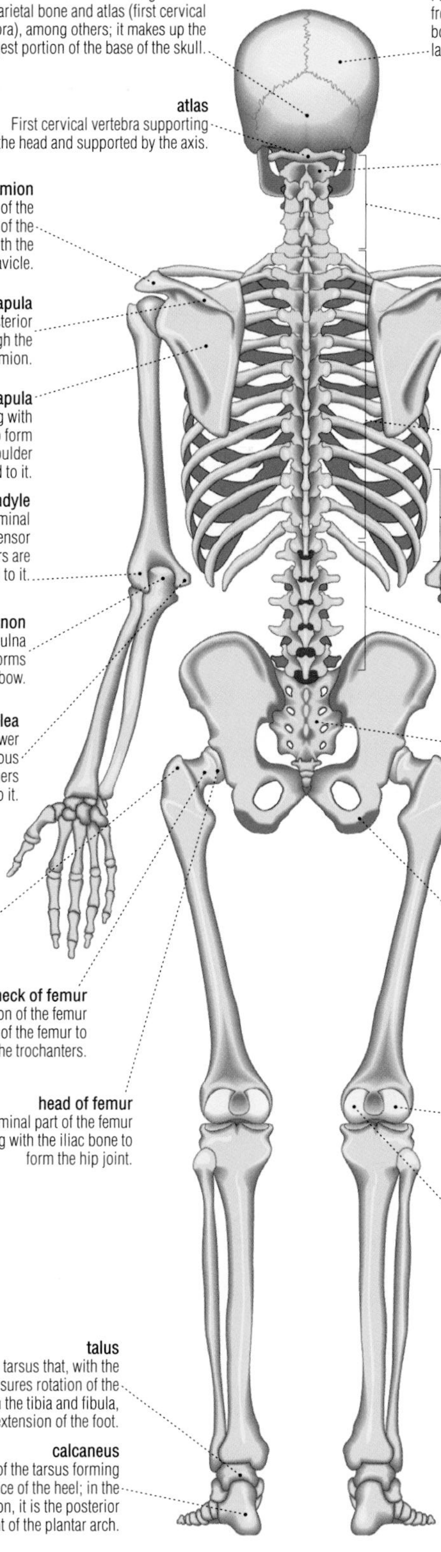

occipital bone
Flat skull bone articulating with the parietal bone and atlas (first cervical vertebra), among others; it makes up the largest portion of the base of the skull.
parietal bone
Flat cranial bone articulating with the frontal, occipital, temporal and sphenoid bones; the two parietal bones form the largest portion of the dome of the skull.
atlas
First cervical vertebra supporting the head and supported by the axis.
axis
Second cervical vertebra supporting the atlas; it allows the head to rotate.
acromion
Extension of the spine of the scapula forming the point of the shoulder and articulating with the clavicle.
cervical vertebra (7)
Bony part of the neck forming the upper terminal part of the spinal column.
spine of scapula
Pointy protuberance of the posterior scapula that extends through the acromion.
head of humerus
Upper terminal part of the humerus articulating very freely with the scapula.
scapula
Large thin flat bone articulating with the clavicle and the humerus to form the shoulder; numerous shoulder and back muscles are attached to it.
thoracic vertebra (12)
Bony part supporting the ribs located between the cervical and lumbar vertebrae.
epicondyle
Outer protuberance of the lower terminal part of the humerus; various extensor muscles of the hand and fingers are attached to it.
false rib (3)
Slender curved bone articulated with the dorsal vertebrae at one end and attached to the upper rib at the other end.
olecranon
Upper terminal part of the ulna articulating with the humerus; it forms the protuberance of the elbow.
lumbar vertebra (5)
Bony part larger than the other vertebrae located between the dorsal vertebrae and the sacrum; it supports a major portion of the body's weight.
epitrochlea
Inner protuberance of the lower terminal part of the humerus; various flexor muscles of the hand and fingers are attached to it.
sacrum
Bone made up of five fused vertebrae located between the lumbar and coccyx vertebrae.
greater trochanter
Large protuberance of the upper terminal part of the femur; various thigh and buttock muscles are attached to it.
ischium
Constituent portion of the iliac bone supporting the body's weight when seated.
neck of femur
Narrow portion of the femur connecting the head of the femur to the trochanters.
head of femur
Upper terminal part of the femur articulating with the iliac bone to form the hip joint.
lateral condyle of femur
Round protuberance of the lower terminal part of the femur enabling articulation with the tibia.
medial condyle of femur
Round protuberance of the lower terminal part of the femur enabling articulation with the tibia; this condyle is longer and narrower than the lateral condyle.
talus
Short bone of the tarsus that, with the calcaneus, ensures rotation of the ankle and, with the tibia and fibula, flexion and extension of the foot.
calcaneus
Large bone of the tarsus forming the protuberance of the heel; in the upright position, it is the posterior contact point of the plantar arch.

skeleton

hand
Terminal part of the forearm with a tactile and prehensile function and a thumb opposable to the other fingers. The skeleton of the hand has 27 bones.

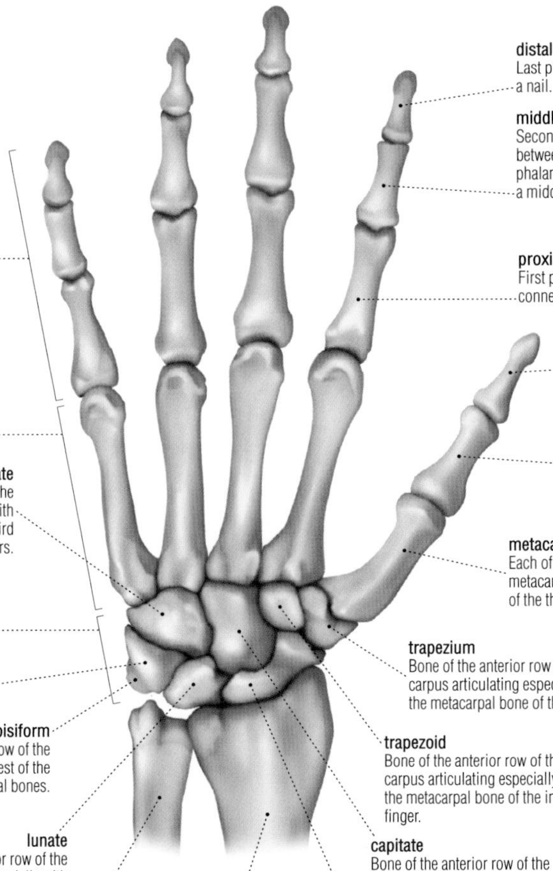

phalanges
Articulated bones forming the skeleton of the fingers; each finger has three, while the thumb has two.

metacarpus
All five long bones forming the palm of the hand; they link the anterior row of the carpus to the proximal phalanges.

hamate
Bone of the anterior row of the carpus, articulating especially with the metacarpal bones of the third and little fingers.

carpus
All eight short articulated bones, laid out in two rows, forming the wrist and giving it a wide range of motion; it connects the radius to the metacarpus.

triquetral
Last bone in the posterior row of the carpus, set opposite the thumb.

pisiform
Bone of the posterior row of the carpus; it is the smallest of the carpal bones.

lunate
Bone of the posterior row of the carpus articulating especially with the radius to form the wrist.

ulna
Long bone forming the inner portion of the forearm, and articulating especially with the radius.

radius
Long bone making up the outer section of the forearm; it is connected especially to the carpal bones to form the wrist joint.

scaphoid
The largest bone in the posterior row of the carpus articulating with the radius to form the wrist.

distal phalange
Last phalange of the finger bearing a nail.

middle phalange
Second phalange of the finger between the proximal and distal phalanges. The thumb does not have a middle phalange.

proximal phalange
First phalange of the finger; it is connected to the metacarpus.

distal phalange
Last phalange of the finger bearinc a nail.

proximal phalange
First phalange of the finger; it is connected to the metacarpus.

metacarpal
Each of the five bones forming the metacarpus. The metacarpal bone of the thumb is very mobile.

trapezium
Bone of the anterior row of the carpus articulating especially with the metacarpal bone of the thumb.

trapezoid
Bone of the anterior row of the carpus articulating especially with the metacarpal bone of the index finger.

capitate
Bone of the anterior row of the carpus articulating especially with the metacarpal bone of the middle finger.

structure of a long bone
Long bone: elongated bone consisting of a body (diaphysis) and two terminal parts (epiphyses), such as the leg and arm bones (femur, radius, phalanges and others).

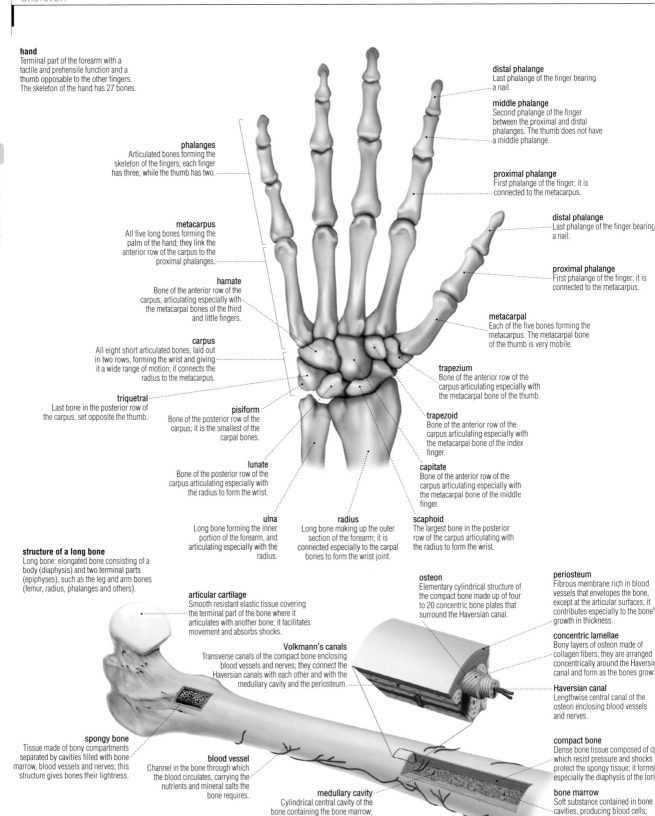

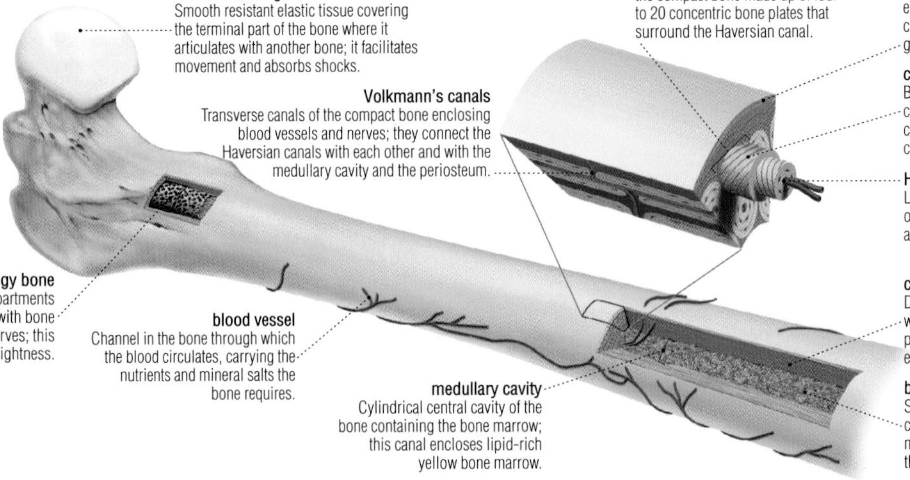

articular cartilage
Smooth resistant elastic tissue covering the terminal part of the bone where it articulates with another bone; it facilitates movement and absorbs shocks.

Volkmann's canals
Transverse canals of the compact bone enclosing blood vessels and nerves; they connect the Haversian canals with each other and with the medullary cavity and the periosteum.

osteon
Elementary cylindrical structure of the compact bone made up of four to 20 concentric bone plates that surround the Haversian canal.

periosteum
Fibrous membrane rich in blood vessels that envelopes the bone, except at the articular surfaces; it contributes especially to the bone' growth in thickness.

concentric lamellae
Bony layers of osteon made of collagen fibers; they are arranged concentrically around the Haversi canal and form as the bones grow.

Haversian canal
Lengthwise central canal of the osteon enclosing blood vessels and nerves.

spongy bone
Tissue made of bony compartments separated by cavities filled with bone marrow, blood vessels and nerves; this structure gives bones their lightness.

blood vessel
Channel in the bone through which the blood circulates, carrying the nutrients and mineral salts the bone requires.

medullary cavity
Cylindrical central cavity of the bone containing the bone marrow; this canal encloses lipid-rich yellow bone marrow.

compact bone
Dense bone tissue composed of c which resist pressure and shocks protect the spongy tissue; it forms especially the diaphysis of the lor

bone marrow
Soft substance contained in bone cavities, producing blood cells; marrow is red in children, yellow the long bones of adults.

foot
Terminal part of the leg enabling upright stance and walking. The skeleton of the foot is made up of 26 bones.

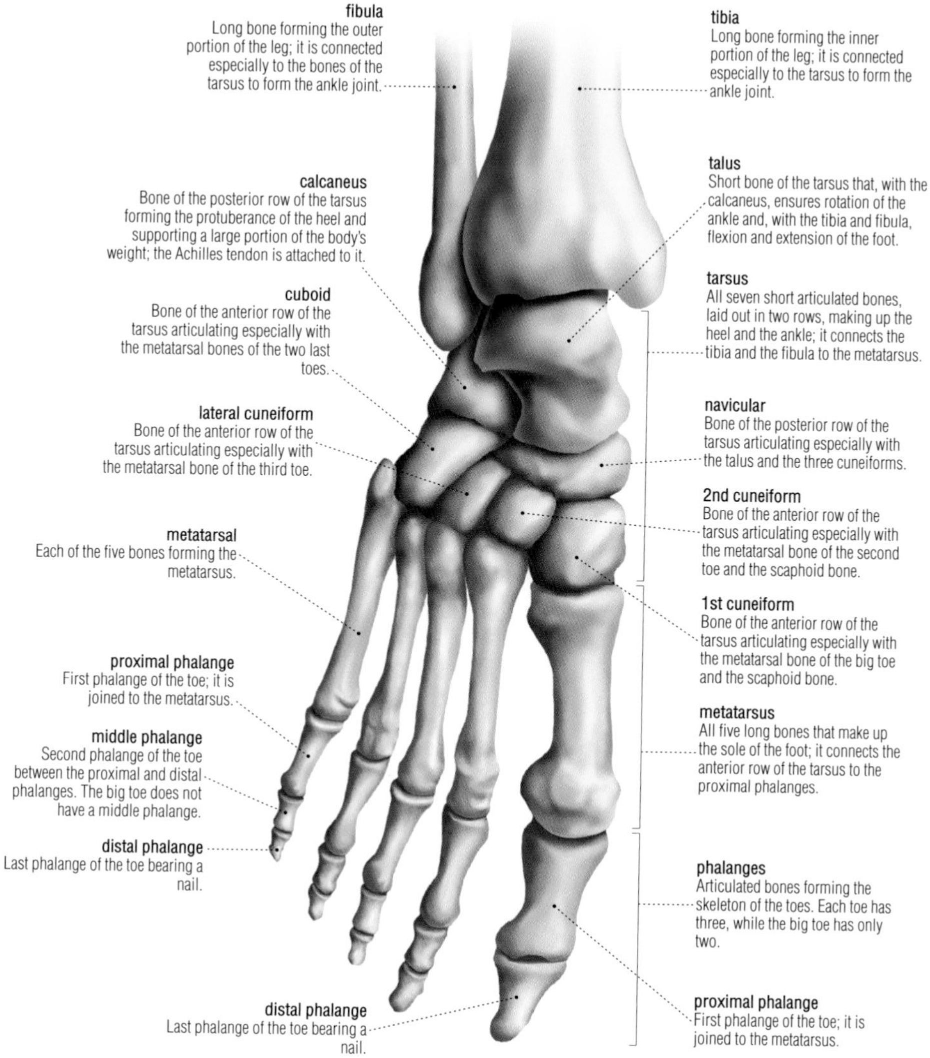
fibula
Long bone forming the outer portion of the leg; it is connected especially to the bones of the tarsus to form the ankle joint.
calcaneus
Bone of the posterior row of the tarsus forming the protuberance of the heel and supporting a large portion of the body's weight; the Achilles tendon is attached to it.
cuboid
Bone of the anterior row of the tarsus articulating especially with the metatarsal bones of the two last toes.
lateral cuneiform
Bone of the anterior row of the tarsus articulating especially with the metatarsal bone of the third toe.
metatarsal
Each of the five bones forming the metatarsus.
proximal phalange
First phalange of the toe; it is joined to the metatarsus.
middle phalange
Second phalange of the toe between the proximal and distal phalanges. The big toe does not have a middle phalange.
distal phalange
Last phalange of the toe bearing a nail.
distal phalange
Last phalange of the toe bearing a nail.
tibia
Long bone forming the inner portion of the leg; it is connected especially to the tarsus to form the ankle joint.
talus
Short bone of the tarsus that, with the calcaneus, ensures rotation of the ankle and, with the tibia and fibula, flexion and extension of the foot.
tarsus
All seven short articulated bones, laid out in two rows, making up the heel and the ankle; it connects the tibia and the fibula to the metatarsus.
navicular
Bone of the posterior row of the tarsus articulating especially with the talus and the three cuneiforms.
2nd cuneiform
Bone of the anterior row of the tarsus articulating especially with the metatarsal bone of the second toe and the scaphoid bone.
1st cuneiform
Bone of the anterior row of the tarsus articulating especially with the metatarsal bone of the big toe and the scaphoid bone.
metatarsus
All five long bones that make up the sole of the foot; it connects the anterior row of the tarsus to the proximal phalanges.
phalanges
Articulated bones forming the skeleton of the toes. Each toe has three, while the big toe has only two.
proximal phalange
First phalange of the toe; it is joined to the metatarsus.

parts of a long bone

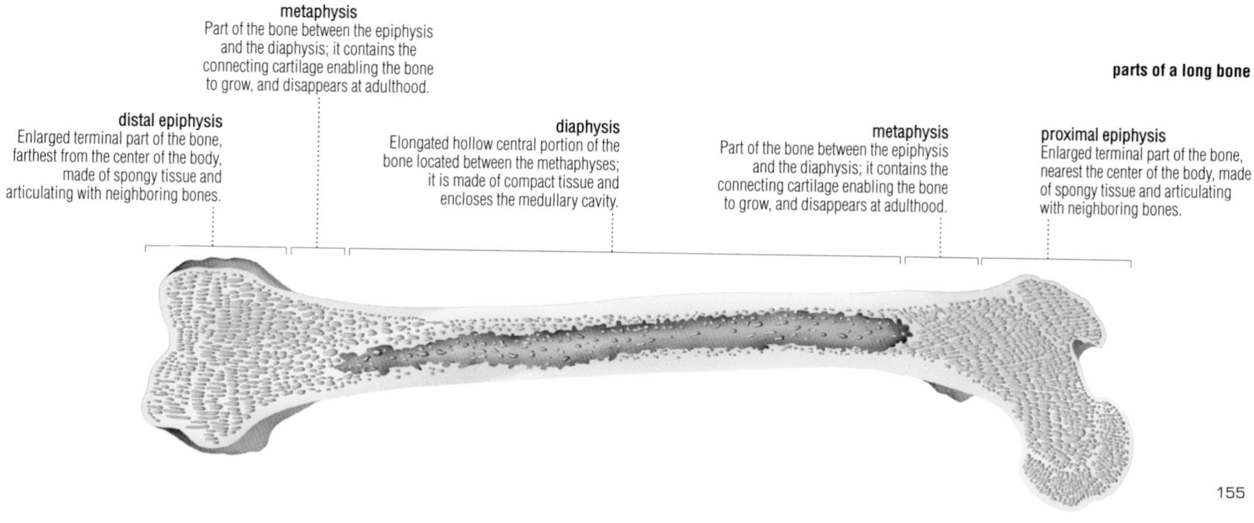
metaphysis
Part of the bone between the epiphysis and the diaphysis; it contains the connecting cartilage enabling the bone to grow, and disappears at adulthood.
distal epiphysis
Enlarged terminal part of the bone, farthest from the center of the body, made of spongy tissue and articulating with neighboring bones.
diaphysis
Elongated hollow central portion of the bone located between the methaphyses; it is made of compact tissue and encloses the medullary cavity.
metaphysis
Part of the bone between the epiphysis and the diaphysis; it contains the connecting cartilage enabling the bone to grow, and disappears at adulthood.
proximal epiphysis
Enlarged terminal part of the bone, nearest the center of the body, made of spongy tissue and articulating with neighboring bones.

skeleton

types of synovial joints

Joints bounded by a fibrous capsule whose inner membrane secretes a viscous lubricating liquid (synovia), thus allowing a wide range of motion.

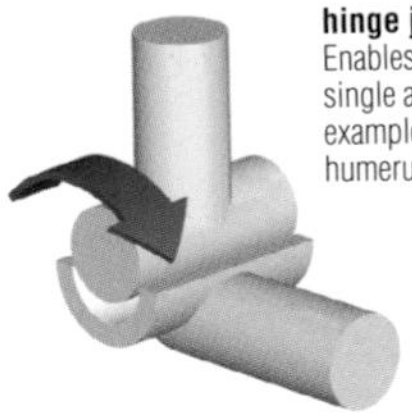

hinge joint
Enables flexion and extension along a single axis. The elbow is a particularly good example: the round terminal part of the humerus turns in the hollow of the ulna.

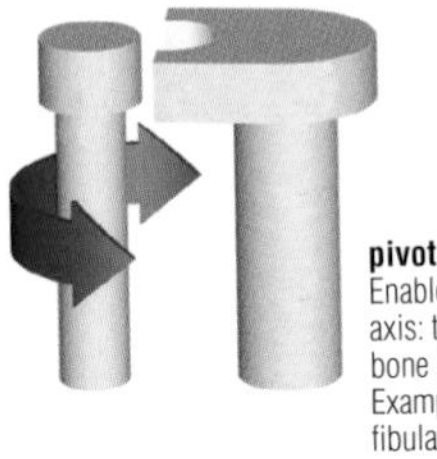

pivot joint
Enables rotation around a lengthwise axis: the cylindrical terminal part of a bone is encased in a hollow cylinder. Examples include the tibia and the fibula.

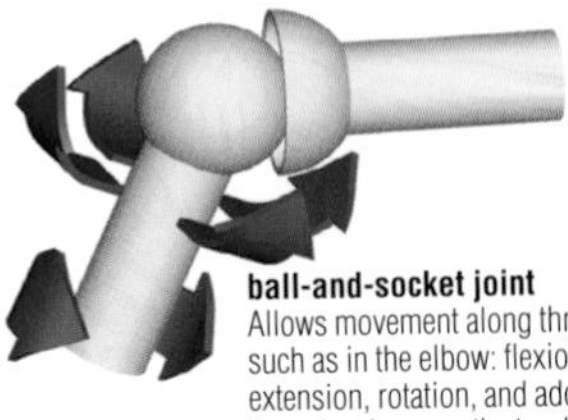

ball-and-socket joint
Allows movement along three axes, such as in the elbow: flexion and extension, rotation, and adduction (arm drawing near the trunk) and abduction (arm drawing away from the trunk).

elbow
Example of a hinged joint, between the arm and forearm.

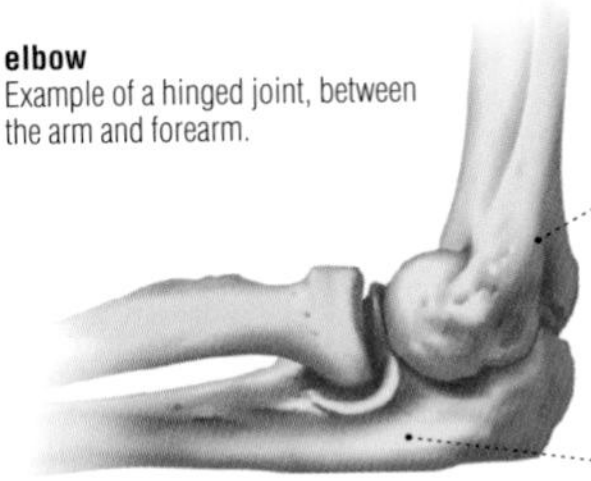

humerus
Long arm bone articulating with the scapula to form the shoulder, and with the radius and the ulna to form the elbow.

ulna
Long bone forming the inner portion of the forearm articulating especially with the humerus.

leg
Example of a pivot joint, between the fibula and the tibia.

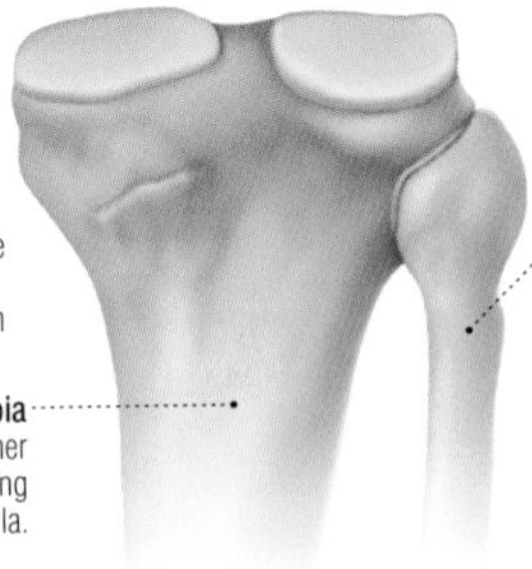

tibia
Long bone forming the inner portion of the leg articulating especially with the fibula.

fibula
Long bone forming the outer portion of the leg articulating especially with the tibia.

shoulder
Example of a ball-and-socket joint, between the humerus and the thorax.

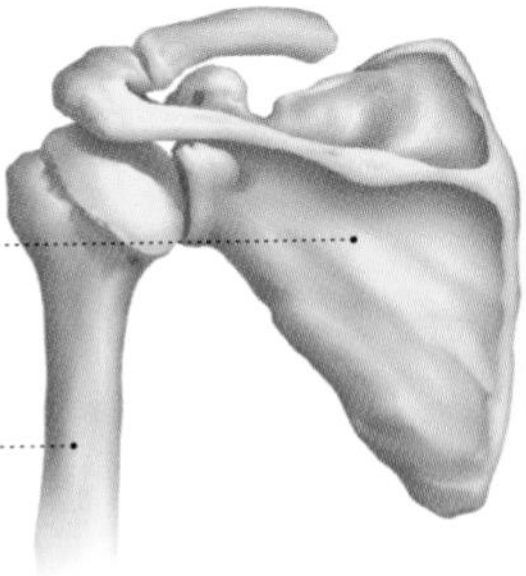

scapula
Large thin flat bone articulating with the clavicle and the humerus to form the shoulder; numerous shoulder and back muscles are attached to it.

humerus
Long arm bone articulating with the scapula to form the shoulder, and with the radius and the ulna to form the elbow.

condyloid joint
An example is the wrist, which the hand can move on two axes: flexion and extension; it can also be tilted sideways (toward the radius and ulna).

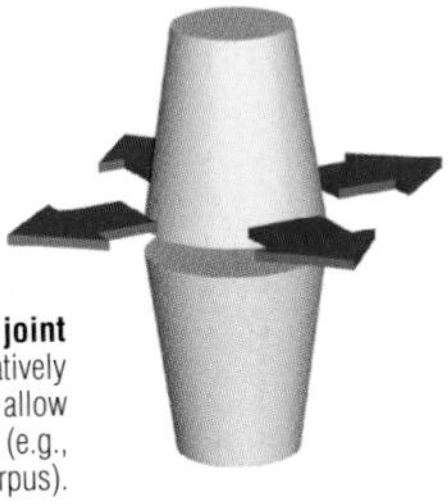

gliding joint
Surfaces of these joints are relatively flat and not very mobile; they allow only a narrow gliding range (e.g., vertebrae, certain bones of the carpus).

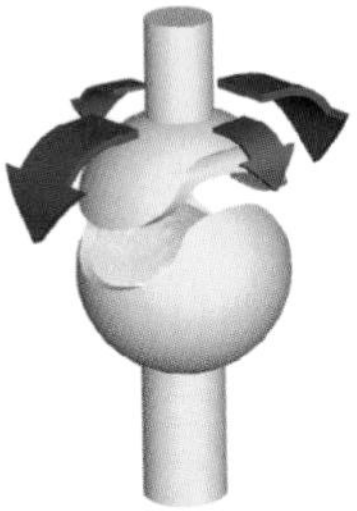

saddle joint
Resembles the condyloid joint but allows a wider range of motion; this type of joint is rare.

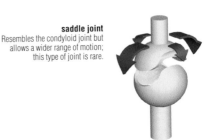

wrist
Condyloid joint of the hand (carpus) articulating with the forearm (radius); it mainly enables the hand to flex and extend.

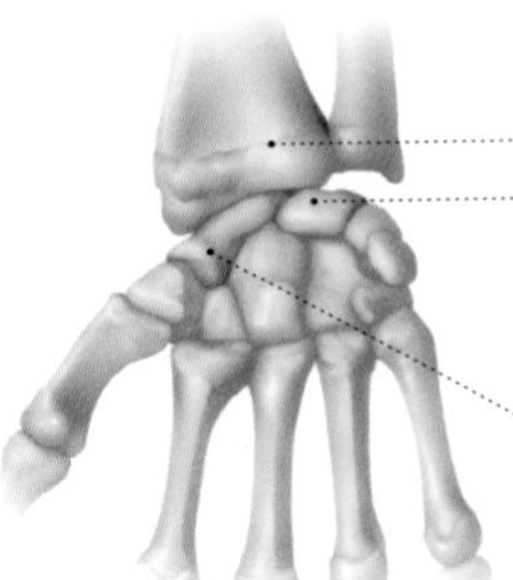

radius
Long bone making up the outer section of the forearm; it is connected especially to the carpal bones to form the wrist joint.

lunate
Bone of the posterior row of the carpus articulating especially with the radius to form the wrist.

scaphoid
Bone of the posterior row of the carpus articulating especially with the radius to form the wrist.

tarsus
Gliding joints that ensure the displacement of certain bones of the tarsus.

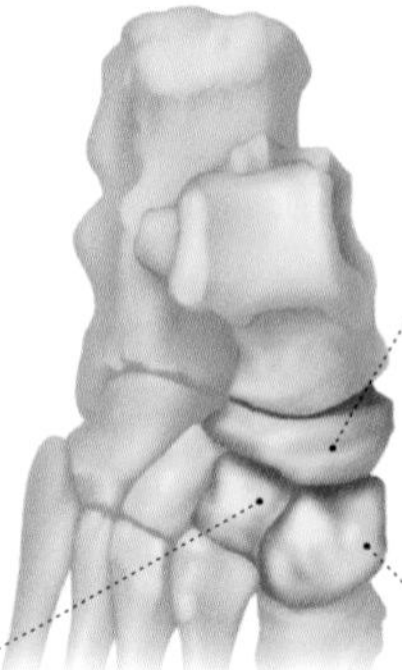

2nd cuneiform
Bone of the anterior row of the tarsus articulating especially with the metatarsal bone of the second toe and the scaphoid bone.

navicular
Bone of the posterior row of the tarsus articulating especially with the talus and the three cuneiforms.

1st cuneiform
Bone of the anterior row of the tarsus articulating especially with the metatarsal bone of the big toe and the scaphoid bone.

thumb
The thumb is an example of a saddle joint.

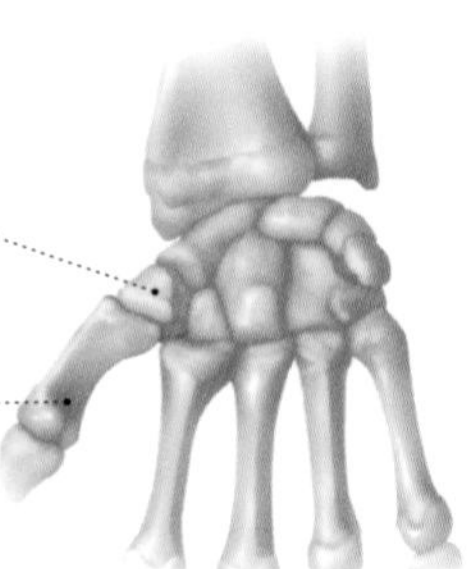

trapezium
Bone of the anterior row of the carpus articulating especially with the metacarpal bone of the thumb.

metacarpal
Each of the five bones forming the metacarpus. The metacarpal bone of the thumb is very mobile.

spinal column

The vertebral column is made up of different kinds of articulated bones (vertebrae) supporting the skeleton and protecting the spinal cord.

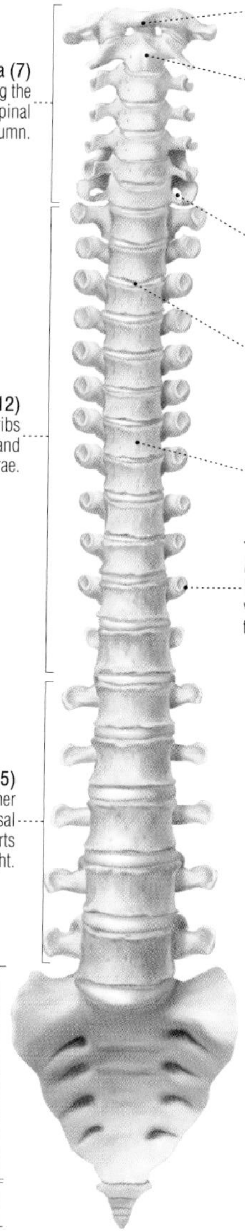
atlas
First cervical vertebra supporting the head and supported by the axis.
axis
Second cervical vertebra supporting the atlas; it allows the head to rotate.
intervertebral foramen
Orifice located between two contiguous vertebrae on each side of the column allowing nerves to pass through.
intervertebral disk
Flat rounded cartilaginous structure separating two vertebrae; its elasticity allows the vertebral column to move.
vertebral body
Anterior bony cylinder of a vertebra surrounded by two transverse processes.
transverse process
Bony protuberance extending laterally from each side of the vertebra; the muscles are attached to it.
cervical vertebra (7)
Bony part of the neck forming the upper terminal part of the spinal column.
thoracic vertebra (12)
Bony part supporting the ribs located between the cervical and lumbar vertebrae.
lumbar vertebra (5)
Bony part larger than the other vertebrae located between the dorsal vertebrae and the sacrum; it supports a major portion of the body's weight.
sacrum
Bone made up of five fused vertebrae located between the lumbar and coccyx vertebrae.
coccyx
Bone made up of four to six fused vertebrae in the lower terminal part of the spinal column, and articulating with the sacrum.

types of bones

Bones: rigid structures connected by joints to which muscles are attached. The skeleton has more than 200 bones divided into four major groups.

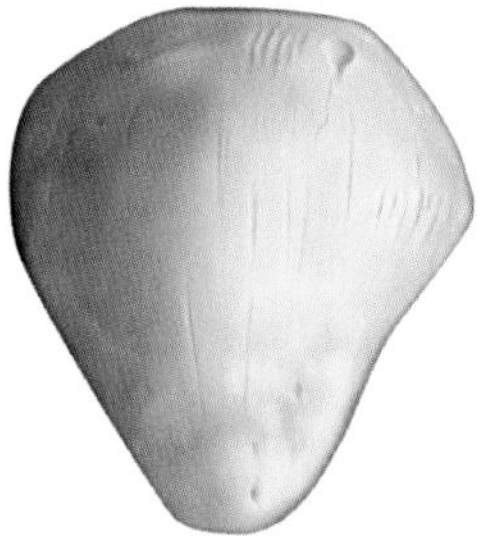

short bone
Bones shaped somewhat like cubes that facilitate flexibility of the joints; examples include the bones of the wrist and ankle.

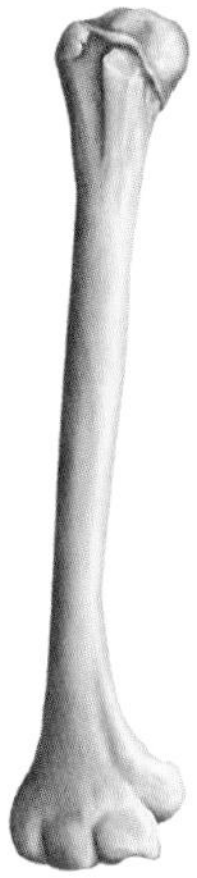

long bone
Elongated bone to which powerful muscles, such as those of the leg and arm, are attached.

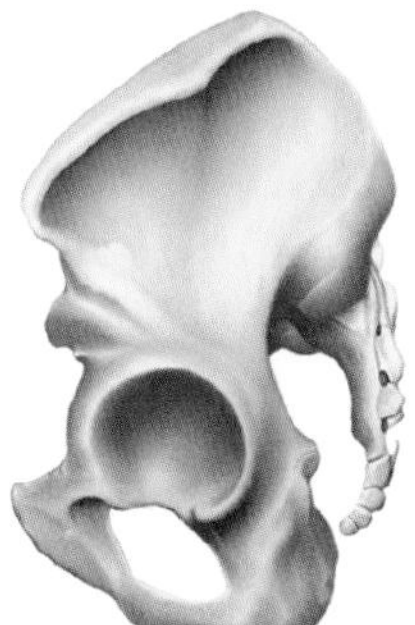

irregular bone
Bones of varying shapes and sizes, such as the vertebrae and certain bones of the skull or pelvis.

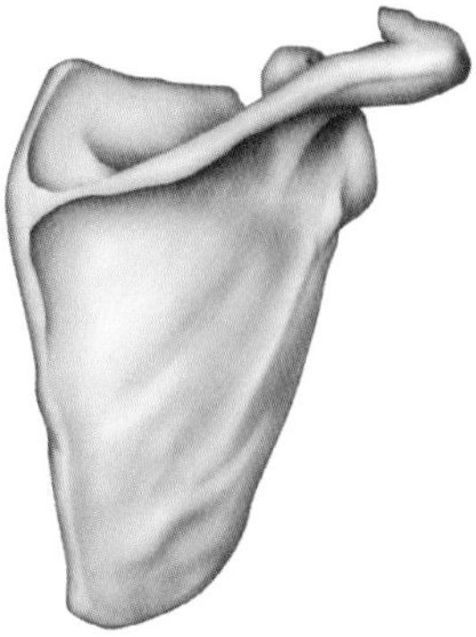

flat bone
Thin bones that protect certain organs, including most of the bones of the skull as well as the scapula.

skeleton

lateral view of skull
Skull: bony structure enclosing and protecting the brain. The eight cranial bones in an adult are fused to each other by means of sutures.

frontal bone
Flat skull bone forming the forehead and top of the eye sockets, and articulating especially with the parietal.

coronal suture
Immobile joint made of fibrous tissue connecting the frontal bone and the two parietal bones.

temporal bone
Flat skull bone that protects mainly the organs responsible for hearing and equilibrium.

squamous suture
Immobile joint made of fibrous tissue connecting the parietal and temporal bones.

sphenoid bone
Bone located behind the nasal fossae; it articulates with all the cranial bones.

parietal bone
Flat cranial bone articulating with the frontal, occipital, temporal and sphenoid bones; the two parietal bones form the largest portion of the dome of the skull.

zygomatic bone
Bone forming the cheek pouch and the outer edge of the eye socket.

lambdoid suture
Immovable joint made of fibrous tissue connecting the occipital and the two parietal bones.

nasal bone
Small flat bone making up the skeleton of the nose; the two nasal bones are joined along the bridge of the nose.

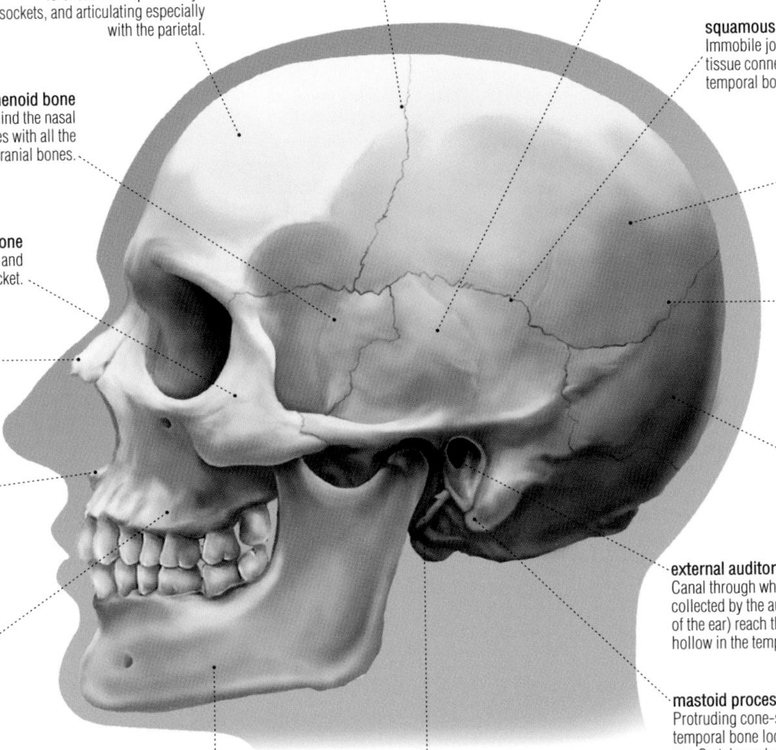

occipital bone
Flat skull bone articulating with the parietal bone and atlas (first cervical vertebra), among others; it makes up the largest portion of the base of the skull.

anterior nasal spine
Bony middle protuberance of the jawbone beneath the nasal fossae; it supports the cartilage of the dividing wall of the nose.

external auditory meatus
Canal through which sounds collected by the auricle (outer section of the ear) reach the tympanic cavity, a hollow in the temporal bone.

maxilla
Toothed bone forming the upper jaw; it helps to form the palate, eye sockets and nasal fossae.

mastoid process
Protruding cone-shaped part of the temporal bone located behind the outer ear. Certain neck muscles, such as the sternocleidomatoid, are attached to it.

mandible
Movable toothed bone forming the lower jaw; it is the only movable bone in the head and its articulation with the temporal bone allows the jaw to move.

styloid process
Elongated protuberance of the temporal bone; several tongue muscles are attached to it.

child's skull
The skull bones of the fetus and child are separated by membranous spaces (fontanelles). They disappear during the course of ossification.

anterior fontanelle
Membranous space between the frontal and two parietal bones; it closes usually at the age of two or three years. This is the largest of the fontanelles.

parietal bone
Flat cranial bone fusing especially to the frontal and occipital bones during the growth years.

coronal suture
Joint connecting the frontal and parietal bones on each side of the skull; it ossifies during the growth years (the anterior fontanelle closes up).

posterior fontanelle
Membranous space between the occipital and two parietal bones; it closes at about the age of two or three months. This fontanelle is smaller than the anterior fontanelle.

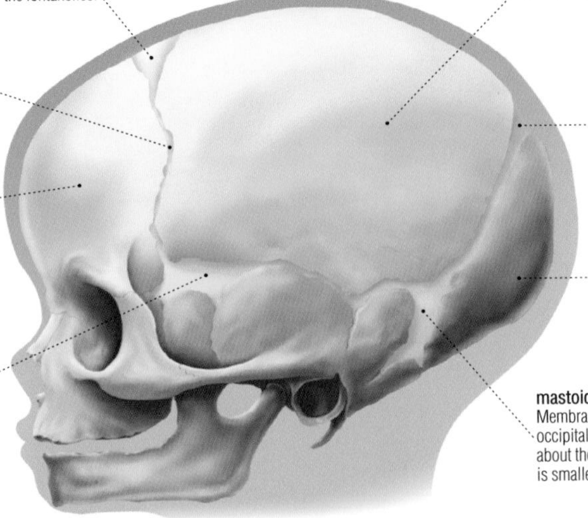

frontal bone
Flat skull bone forming the forehead and top of the eye sockets, and articulating especially with the parietal.

occipital bone
Flat cranial bone fusing especially to the parietal bone and atlas (first cervical vertebra) during the growth years.

sphenoidal fontanelle
Membranous space between the frontal, parietal, temporal and sphenoid bones; it closes at about the age of two or three months.

mastoid fontanelle
Membranous space between the parietal, occipital and temporal bones; it closes at about the age of 18 months. This fontanelle is smaller than the sphenoidal fontanelle.

teeth

Hard organs implanted in maxillae and used for masticating food; a child usually has 20 and an adult 32 (16 per jaw).

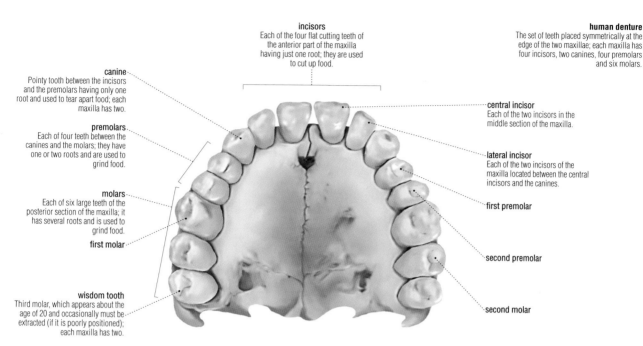

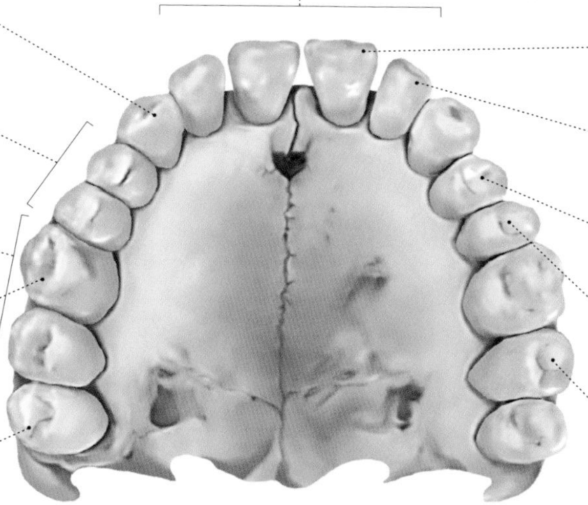
incisors
Each of the four flat cutting teeth of the anterior part of the maxilla having just one root; they are used to cut up food.
human denture
The set of teeth placed symmetrically at the edge of the two maxillae; each maxilla has four incisors, two canines, four premolars and six molars.
canine
Pointy tooth between the incisors and the premolars having only one root and used to tear apart food; each maxilla has two.
premolars
Each of four teeth between the canines and the molars; they have one or two roots and are used to grind food.
molars
Each of six large teeth of the posterior section of the maxilla; it has several roots and is used to grind food.
first molar
wisdom tooth
Third molar, which appears about the age of 20 and occasionally must be extracted (if it is poorly positioned); each maxilla has two.
central incisor
Each of the two incisors in the middle section of the maxilla.
lateral incisor
Each of the two incisors of the maxilla located between the central incisors and the canines.
first premolar
second premolar
second molar

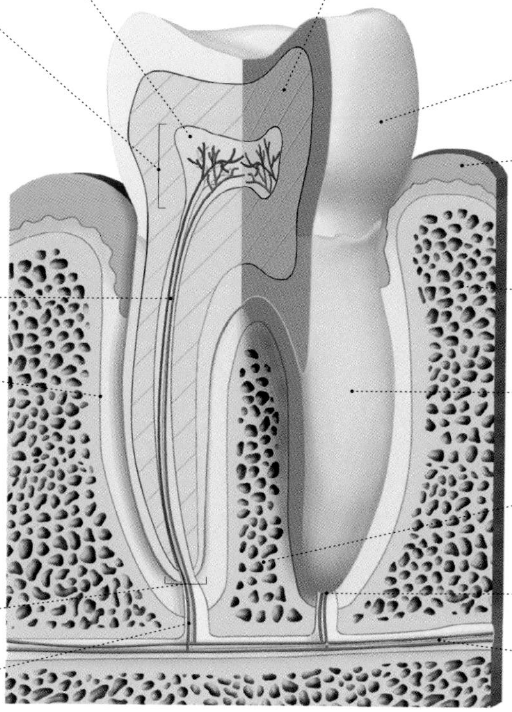
pulp chamber
Central chamber of the crown enclosing the dental pulp and extending through the root canal.
pulp
Soft conjunctive tissue that is rich in blood vessels and nerves; the pulp gives the tooth its sensitivity and plays an essential nutritional role.
dentin
Hard mineralized tissue forming the teeth; it surrounds the dental pulp and is protected by the enamel and cementum.
cross section of a molar
Teeth are formed of two main parts: the crown (the visible protruding part) and one or several roots (the part inserted into the maxilla).
crown
Part of the tooth covered with enamel and protruding outside the gum.
neck
Narrow part of the tooth surrounded by the gum separating the crown from the root.
root canal
Extension of the pulp chamber containing the dental pulp and opening at the apex of the root.
periodontal ligament
Fibrous connective tissue joining the cementum to the bone, thus fixing the tooth into its alveolus.
root
Part of the tooth covered with cementum, and implanted into the dental alveolus of the maxilla; certain teeth, such as the molars, have several roots.
dental alveolus
Bony maxillary cavity in which the root of the tooth is implanted.
apical foramen
Narrow orifice located at the terminal part of the apex allowing blood vessels and nerves to pass into the tooth.
enamel
Highly mineralized tissue covering and protecting the dentin of the crown; it is the hardest tissue in the organism.
gum
Thick section of the mucous membrane of the mouth that is rich in blood vessels and nerves; it covers the edge of the dental alveolus and adheres to the neck.
maxillary bone
Jawbone into which the teeth are inserted.
cementum
Hard mineralized tissue comparable to bone covering and protecting the dentin of the root.
alveolar bone
Section of the maxilla bone surrounding the dental alveola; its presence depends on the presence of teeth: it forms and disappears when they do.
apex
Terminal part of the dental root whose opening (apical foramen) allows blood vessels and nerves to pass through.
plexus of nerves
Grouping of blood vessels and nerves that enters the pulp through the apical foramen to nourish the tooth.

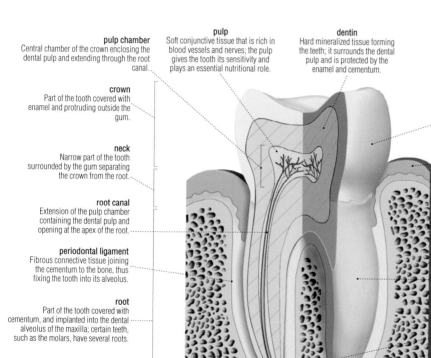

blood circulation

Propelled by the contractions of the heart, blood travels through the blood vessels of the body bringing oxygen and nutrients and removing waste.

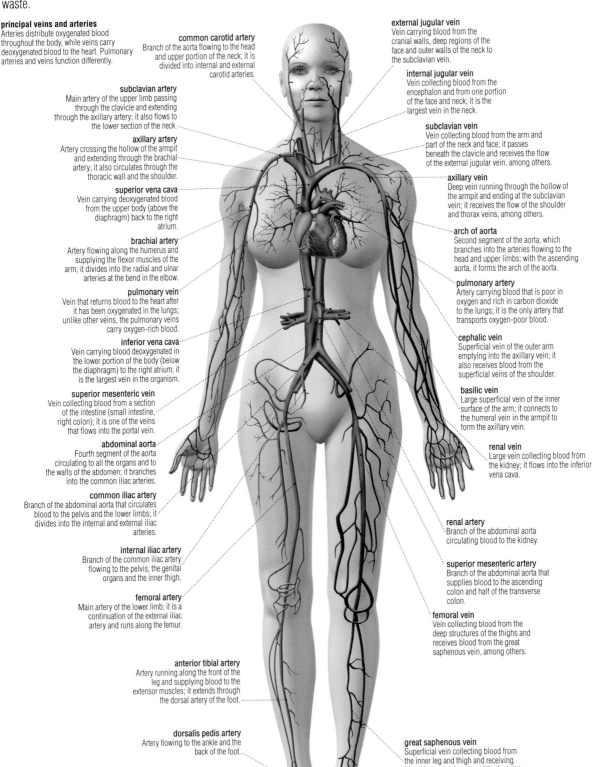

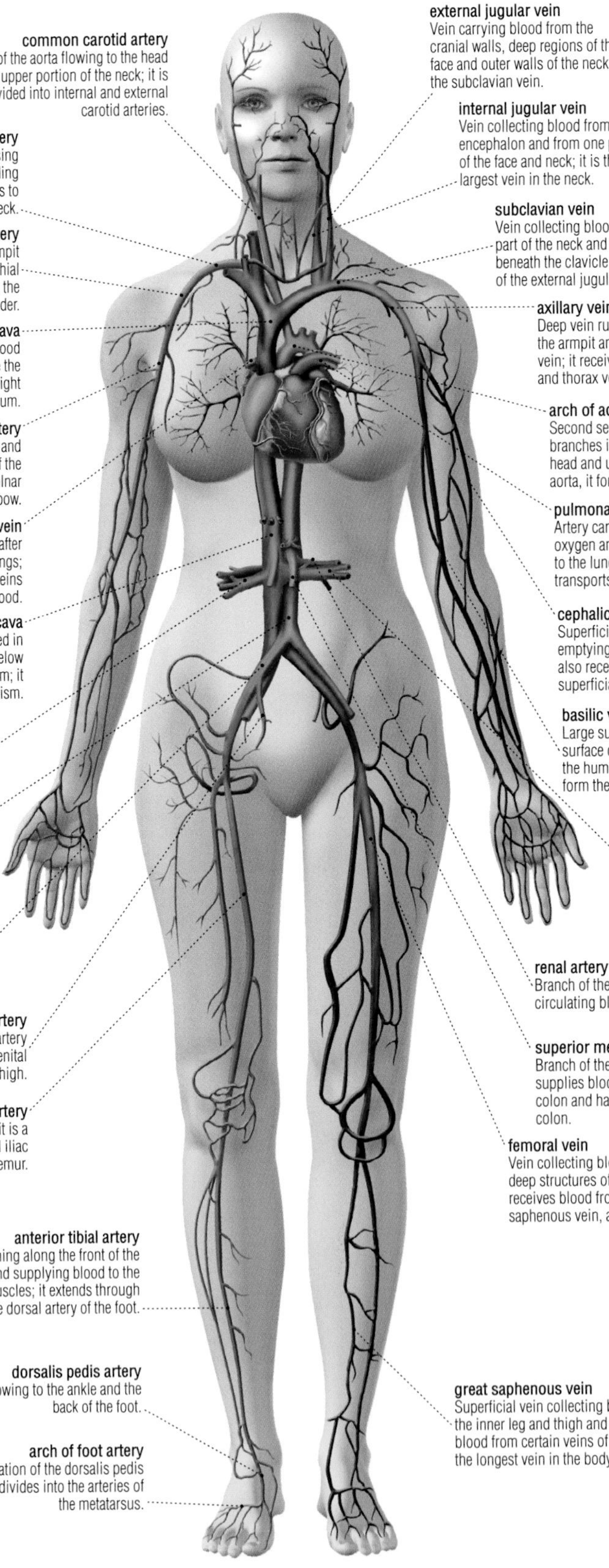

principal veins and arteries
Arteries distribute oxygenated blood throughout the body, while veins carry deoxygenated blood to the heart. Pulmonary arteries and veins function differently.

common carotid artery
Branch of the aorta flowing to the head and upper portion of the neck; it is divided into internal and external carotid arteries.

subclavian artery
Main artery of the upper limb passing through the clavicle and extending through the axillary artery; it also flows to the lower section of the neck.

axillary artery
Artery crossing the hollow of the armpit and extending through the brachial artery; it also circulates through the thoracic wall and the shoulder.

superior vena cava
Vein carrying deoxygenated blood from the upper body (above the diaphragm) back to the right atrium.

brachial artery
Artery flowing along the humerus and supplying the flexor muscles of the arm; it divides into the radial and ulnar arteries at the bend in the elbow.

pulmonary vein
Vein that returns blood to the heart after it has been oxygenated in the lungs; unlike other veins, the pulmonary veins carry oxygen-rich blood.

inferior vena cava
Vein carrying blood deoxygenated in the lower portion of the body (below the diaphragm) to the right atrium; it is the largest vein in the organism.

superior mesenteric vein
Vein collecting blood from a section of the intestine (small intestine, right colon); it is one of the veins that flows into the portal vein.

abdominal aorta
Fourth segment of the aorta circulating to all the organs and to the walls of the abdomen; it branches into the common iliac arteries.

common iliac artery
Branch of the abdominal aorta that circulates blood to the pelvis and the lower limbs; it divides into the internal and external iliac arteries.

internal iliac artery
Branch of the common iliac artery flowing to the pelvis, the genital organs and the inner thigh.

femoral artery
Main artery of the lower limb; it is a continuation of the external iliac artery and runs along the femur.

anterior tibial artery
Artery running along the front of the leg and supplying blood to the extensor muscles; it extends through the dorsal artery of the foot.

dorsalis pedis artery
Artery flowing to the ankle and the back of the foot.

arch of foot artery
Continuation of the dorsalis pedis artery; it divides into the arteries of the metatarsus.

external jugular vein
Vein carrying blood from the cranial walls, deep regions of the face and outer walls of the neck to the subclavian vein.

internal jugular vein
Vein collecting blood from the encephalon and from one portion of the face and neck; it is the largest vein in the neck.

subclavian vein
Vein collecting blood from the arm and part of the neck and face; it passes beneath the clavicle and receives the flow of the external jugular vein, among others.

axillary vein
Deep vein running through the hollow of the armpit and ending at the subclavian vein; it receives the flow of the shoulder and thorax veins, among others.

arch of aorta
Second segment of the aorta, which branches into the arteries flowing to the head and upper limbs; with the ascending aorta, it forms the arch of the aorta.

pulmonary artery
Artery carrying blood that is poor in oxygen and rich in carbon dioxide to the lungs; it is the only artery that transports oxygen-poor blood.

cephalic vein
Superficial vein of the outer arm emptying into the axillary vein; it also receives blood from the superficial veins of the shoulder.

basilic vein
Large superficial vein of the inner surface of the arm; it connects to the humeral vein in the armpit to form the axillary vein.

renal vein
Large vein collecting blood from the kidney; it flows into the inferior vena cava.

renal artery
Branch of the abdominal aorta circulating blood to the kidney.

superior mesenteric artery
Branch of the abdominal aorta that supplies blood to the ascending colon and half of the transverse colon.

femoral vein
Vein collecting blood from the deep structures of the thighs and receives blood from the great saphenous vein, among others.

great saphenous vein
Superficial vein collecting blood from the inner leg and thigh and receiving blood from certain veins of the foot; it is the longest vein in the body.

blood circulation

schema of circulation
Propelled by the heart, blood circulates through the body by two distinct routes: through the lungs (where it collects oxygen) and through the rest of the body.

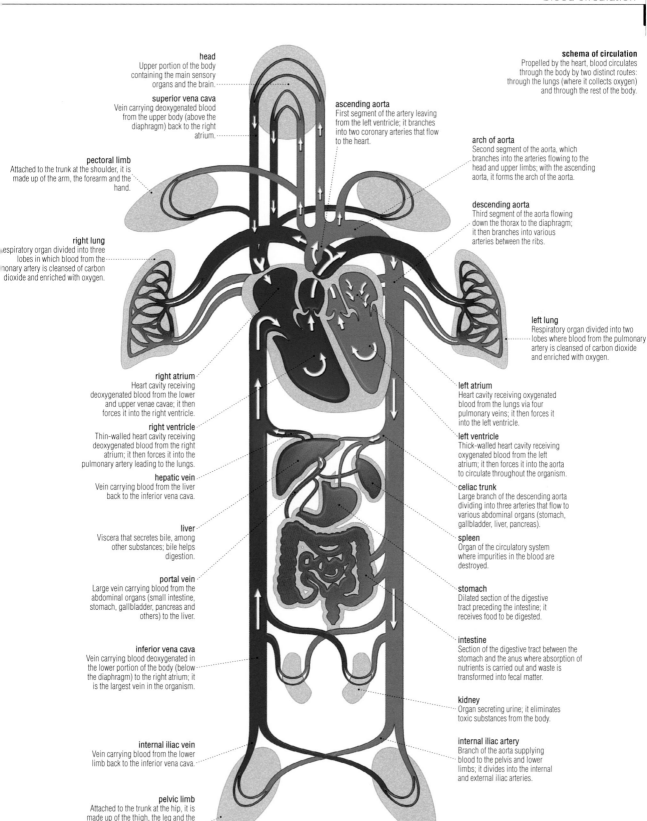

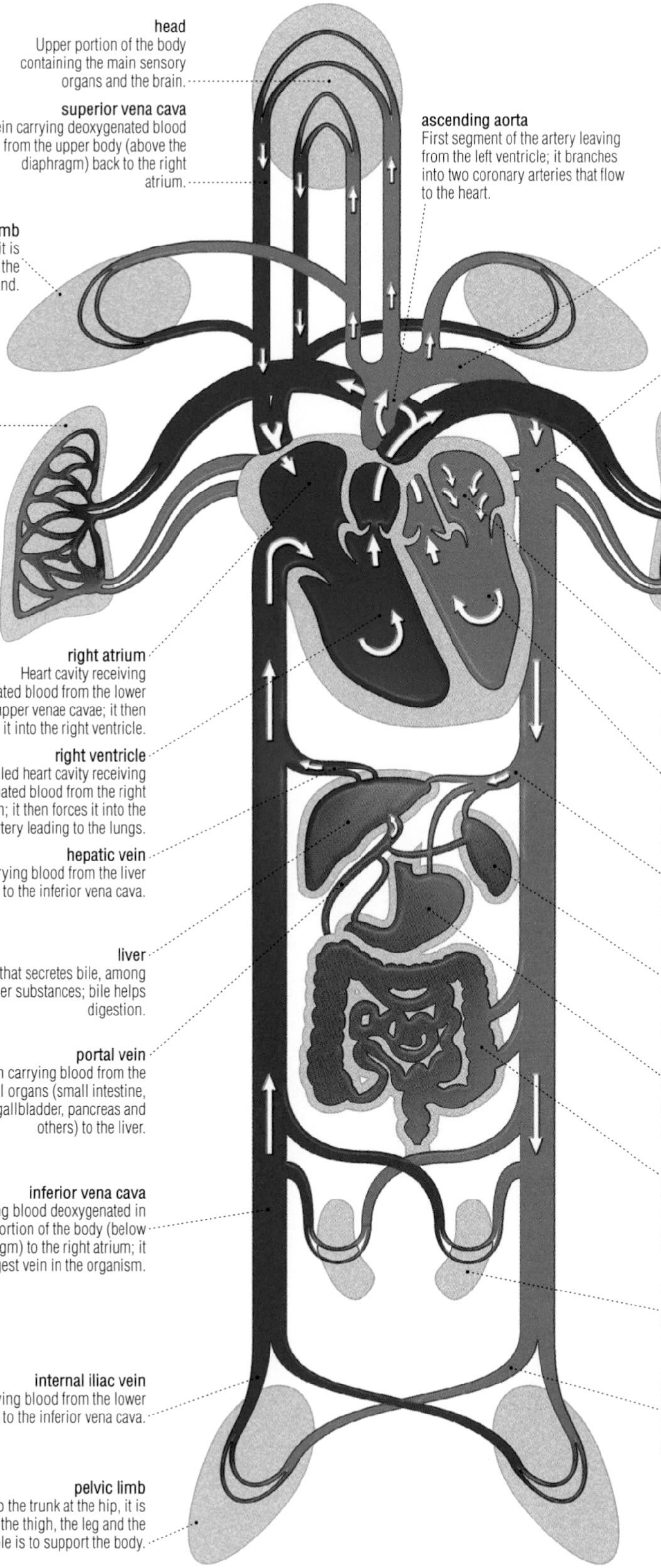

head
Upper portion of the body containing the main sensory organs and the brain.

superior vena cava
Vein carrying deoxygenated blood from the upper body (above the diaphragm) back to the right atrium.

ascending aorta
First segment of the artery leaving from the left ventricle; it branches into two coronary arteries that flow to the heart.

arch of aorta
Second segment of the aorta, which branches into the arteries flowing to the head and upper limbs; with the ascending aorta, it forms the arch of the aorta.

pectoral limb
Attached to the trunk at the shoulder, it is made up of the arm, the forearm and the hand.

descending aorta
Third segment of the aorta flowing down the thorax to the diaphragm; it then branches into various arteries between the ribs.

right lung
espiratory organ divided into three lobes in which blood from the ıonary artery is cleansed of carbon dioxide and enriched with oxygen.

left lung
Respiratory organ divided into two lobes where blood from the pulmonary artery is cleansed of carbon dioxide and enriched with oxygen.

right atrium
Heart cavity receiving deoxygenated blood from the lower and upper venae cavae; it then forces it into the right ventricle.

left atrium
Heart cavity receiving oxygenated blood from the lungs via four pulmonary veins; it then forces it into the left ventricle.

right ventricle
Thin-walled heart cavity receiving deoxygenated blood from the right atrium; it then forces it into the pulmonary artery leading to the lungs.

left ventricle
Thick-walled heart cavity receiving oxygenated blood from the left atrium; it then forces it into the aorta to circulate throughout the organism.

hepatic vein
Vein carrying blood from the liver back to the inferior vena cava.

celiac trunk
Large branch of the descending aorta dividing into three arteries that flow to various abdominal organs (stomach, gallbladder, liver, pancreas).

liver
Viscera that secretes bile, among other substances; bile helps digestion.

spleen
Organ of the circulatory system where impurities in the blood are destroyed.

portal vein
Large vein carrying blood from the abdominal organs (small intestine, stomach, gallbladder, pancreas and others) to the liver.

stomach
Dilated section of the digestive tract preceding the intestine; it receives food to be digested.

intestine
Section of the digestive tract between the stomach and the anus where absorption of nutrients is carried out and waste is transformed into fecal matter.

inferior vena cava
Vein carrying blood deoxygenated in the lower portion of the body (below the diaphragm) to the right atrium; it is the largest vein in the organism.

kidney
Organ secreting urine; it eliminates toxic substances from the body.

internal iliac vein
Vein carrying blood from the lower limb back to the inferior vena cava.

internal iliac artery
Branch of the aorta supplying blood to the pelvis and lower limbs; it divides into the internal and external iliac arteries.

pelvic limb
Attached to the trunk at the hip, it is made up of the thigh, the leg and the foot; its role is to support the body.

blood circulation

composition of the blood
Blood is made up of an aqueous liquid (plasma) in which solids (blood cells, platelets) are suspended. It accounts for 7% to 8% of the body's weight.

white blood cell
Blood cell that plays an essential role in the body's defenses (destruction of infectious agents, production of antibodies).

blood vessel
Membranous canal through which blood circulates in the organism; blood vessels form a network about 90,000 mi long.

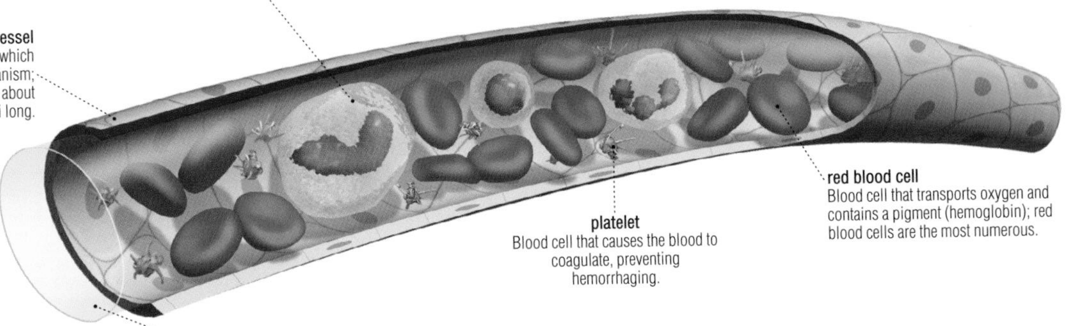

red blood cell
Blood cell that transports oxygen and contains a pigment (hemoglobin); red blood cells are the most numerous.

platelet
Blood cell that causes the blood to coagulate, preventing hemorrhaging.

plasma
Liquid part of blood consisting especially of water, mineral salts and proteins; it allows elements such as nutrients and waste to circulate in the blood.

heart
Muscular organ divided into four chambers; its regular rhythmic contractions cause blood to circulate throughout the organism.

oxygenated blood
Blood enriched with oxygen in the lungs; it leaves the left section of the heart and flows through the arteries to distribute oxygen and nutrients to the organism.

deoxygenated blood
Blood whose oxygen is depleted; the veins carry it to the right portion of the heart, after which it is re-oxygenated in the lungs.

arch of aorta
Second segment of the aorta, which branches into the arteries flowing to the head and upper limbs; with the ascending aorta, it forms the arch of the aorta.

pulmonary artery
Artery carrying blood that is poor in oxygen and rich in carbon dioxide to the lungs; this is the only artery that transports oxygen-poor blood.

pulmonary valve
Membranous fold made up of three walls; it carries blood from the right ventricle to the pulmonary artery and prevents its reflux.

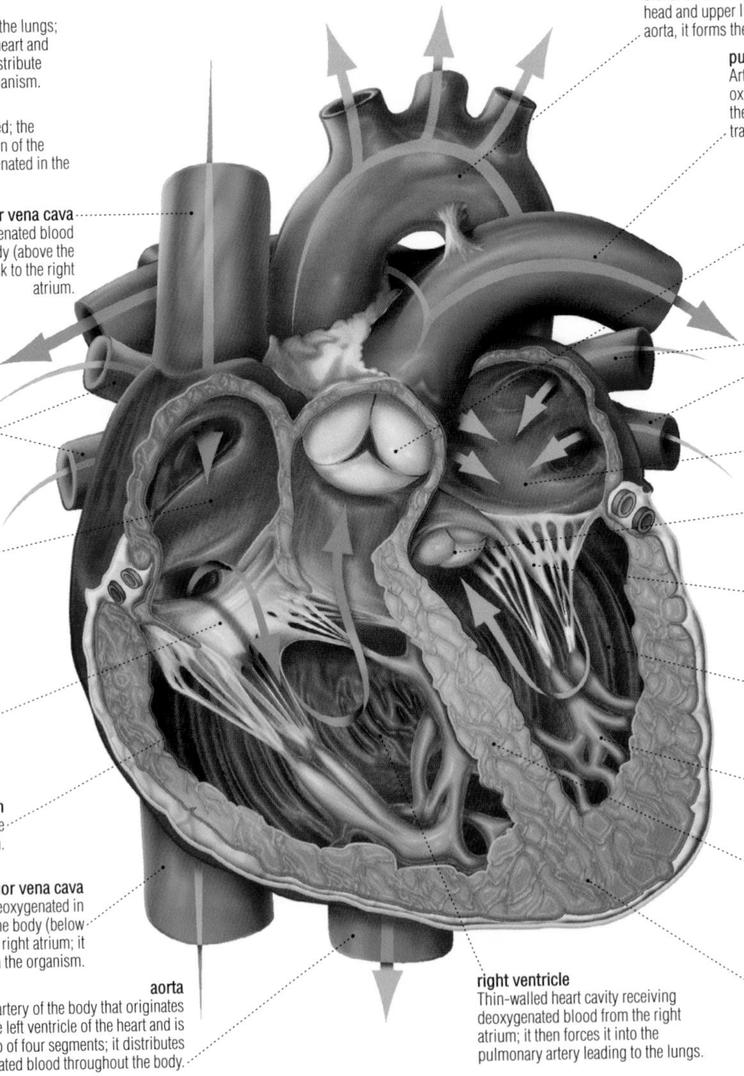

superior vena cava
Vein carrying deoxygenated blood from the upper body (above the diaphragm) back to the right atrium.

right pulmonary vein
Each of two veins returning blood oxygenated in the right lung to the left atrium of the heart.

right atrium
Heart cavity receiving deoxygenated blood from the lower and upper venae cavae; it then forces it into the right ventricle.

tricuspid valve
Membranous fold made up of three walls; it carries blood from the right atrium to the right ventricle and prevents its reflux.

endocardium
Smooth thin inner casing of the heart attached to the myocardium.

inferior vena cava
Vein carrying blood deoxygenated in the lower portion of the body (below the diaphragm) to the right atrium; it is the largest vein in the organism.

aorta
Main artery of the body that originates in the left ventricle of the heart and is made up of four segments; it distributes oxygenated blood throughout the body.

left pulmonary vein
Each of two veins returning blood, oxygenated in the left lung, to the left atrium of the heart.

left atrium
Heart cavity receiving oxygenated blood from the lungs via four pulmonary veins; it then forces it into the left ventricle.

aortic valve
Membranous fold made up of three walls; it carries blood from the left ventricle to the aorta and prevents its reflux.

mitral valve
Membranous fold made up of two w
it carries blood from the left atrium t
the left ventricle and prevents its refl

left ventricle
Thick-walled heart cavity receiving oxygenated blood from the left atriu
it then forces it into the aorta to circulate throughout the organism.

papillary muscle
Internal ventricular muscle restraini
mitral or tricuspid valve and preven
from being pushed back into the atr
during contraction of the ventricle.

interventricular septum
Mostly muscular partition separatin
the right and left ventricles of the heart.

right ventricle
Thin-walled heart cavity receiving deoxygenated blood from the right atrium; it then forces it into the pulmonary artery leading to the lungs.

myocardium
Thick muscular casing around the heart; its contraction is involuntary and depends on the autonomous nervous system.

respiratory system

It causes gaseous exchanges to take place in the lungs by ensuring that oxygen is carried to the blood through inspiration, and carbon dioxide is eliminated from the blood through expiration.

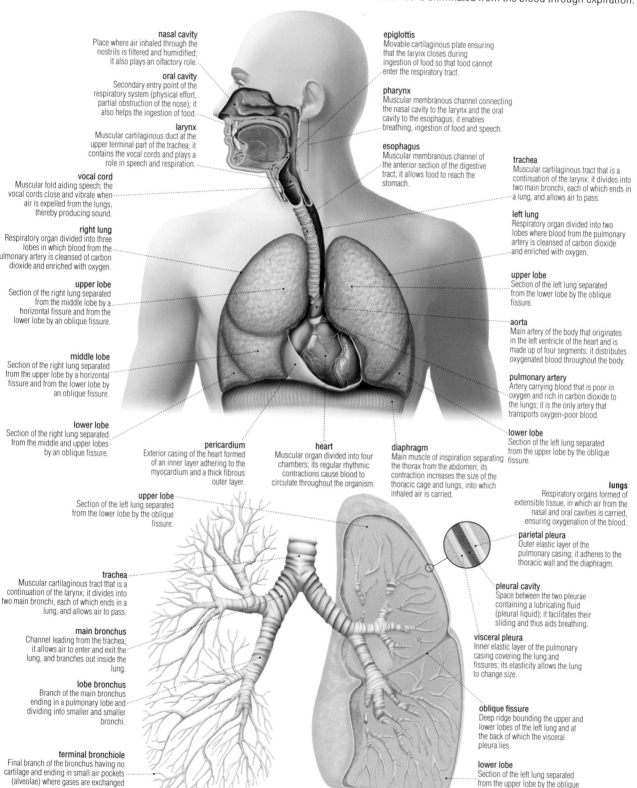

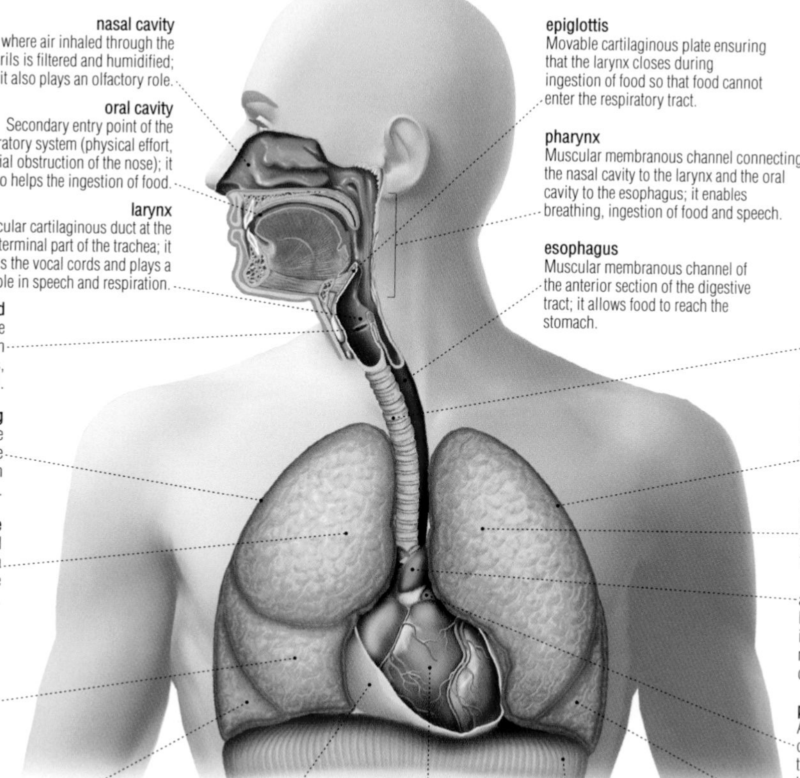

nasal cavity
Place where air inhaled through the nostrils is filtered and humidified; it also plays an olfactory role.
oral cavity
Secondary entry point of the respiratory system (physical effort, partial obstruction of the nose); it also helps the ingestion of food.
larynx
Muscular cartilaginous duct at the upper terminal part of the trachea; it contains the vocal cords and plays a role in speech and respiration.
vocal cord
Muscular fold aiding speech; the vocal cords close and vibrate when air is expelled from the lungs, thereby producing sound.
right lung
Respiratory organ divided into three lobes in which blood from the pulmonary artery is cleansed of carbon dioxide and enriched with oxygen.
upper lobe
Section of the right lung separated from the middle lobe by a horizontal fissure and from the lower lobe by an oblique fissure.
middle lobe
Section of the right lung separated from the upper lobe by a horizontal fissure and from the lower lobe by an oblique fissure.
lower lobe
Section of the right lung separated from the middle and upper lobes by an oblique fissure.
pericardium
Exterior casing of the heart formed of an inner layer adhering to the myocardium and a thick fibrous outer layer.
heart
Muscular organ divided into four chambers; its regular rhythmic contractions cause blood to circulate throughout the organism.
diaphragm
Main muscle of inspiration separating the thorax from the abdomen; its contraction increases the size of the thoracic cage and lungs, into which inhaled air is carried.
epiglottis
Movable cartilaginous plate ensuring that the larynx closes during ingestion of food so that food cannot enter the respiratory tract.
pharynx
Muscular membranous channel connecting the nasal cavity to the larynx and the oral cavity to the esophagus; it enables breathing, ingestion of food and speech.
esophagus
Muscular membranous channel of the anterior section of the digestive tract; it allows food to reach the stomach.
trachea
Muscular cartilaginous tract that is a continuation of the larynx; it divides into two main bronchi, each of which ends in a lung, and allows air to pass.
left lung
Respiratory organ divided into two lobes where blood from the pulmonary artery is cleansed of carbon dioxide and enriched with oxygen.
upper lobe
Section of the left lung separated from the lower lobe by the oblique fissure.
aorta
Main artery of the body that originates in the left ventricle of the heart and is made up of four segments; it distributes oxygenated blood throughout the body.
pulmonary artery
Artery carrying blood that is poor in oxygen and rich in carbon dioxide to the lungs; it is the only artery that transports oxygen-poor blood.
lower lobe
Section of the left lung separated from the upper lobe by the oblique fissure.

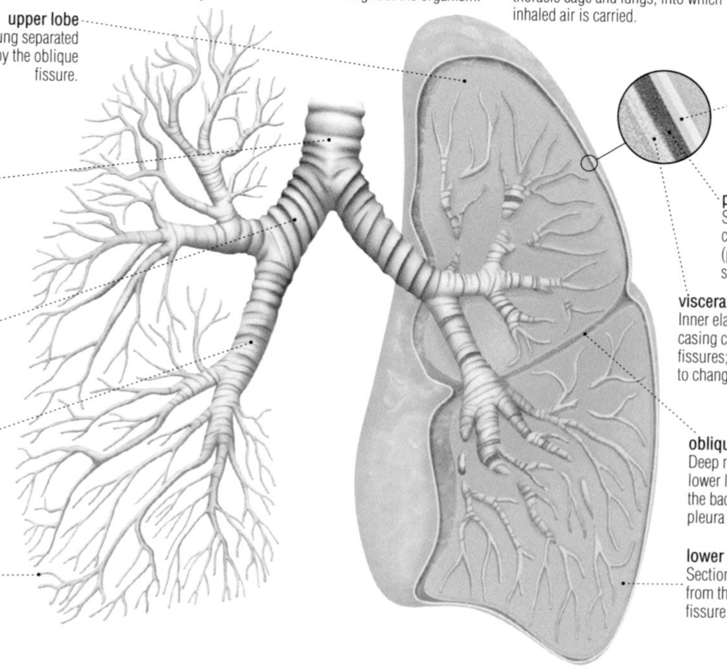

lungs
Respiratory organs formed of extensible tissue, in which air from the nasal and oral cavities is carried, ensuring oxygenation of the blood.
upper lobe
Section of the left lung separated from the lower lobe by the oblique fissure.
trachea
Muscular cartilaginous tract that is a continuation of the larynx; it divides into two main bronchi, each of which ends in a lung, and allows air to pass.
main bronchus
Channel leading from the trachea; it allows air to enter and exit the lung, and branches out inside the lung.
lobe bronchus
Branch of the main bronchus ending in a pulmonary lobe and dividing into smaller and smaller bronchi.
terminal bronchiole
Final branch of the bronchus having no cartilage and ending in small air pockets (alveolae) where gases are exchanged with the blood.
parietal pleura
Outer elastic layer of the pulmonary casing; it adheres to the thoracic wall and the diaphragm.
pleural cavity
Space between the two pleurae containing a lubricating fluid (pleural liquid); it facilitates their sliding and thus aids breathing.
visceral pleura
Inner elastic layer of the pulmonary casing covering the lung and fissures; its elasticity allows the lung to change size.
oblique fissure
Deep ridge bounding the upper and lower lobes of the left lung and at the back of which the visceral pleura lies.
lower lobe
Section of the left lung separated from the upper lobe by the oblique fissure.

digestive system

Formed of the mouth, digestive tract and appended glands, it converts ingested food so that it can be assimilated by the organism.

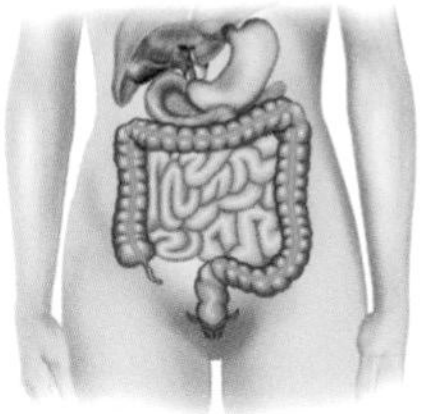

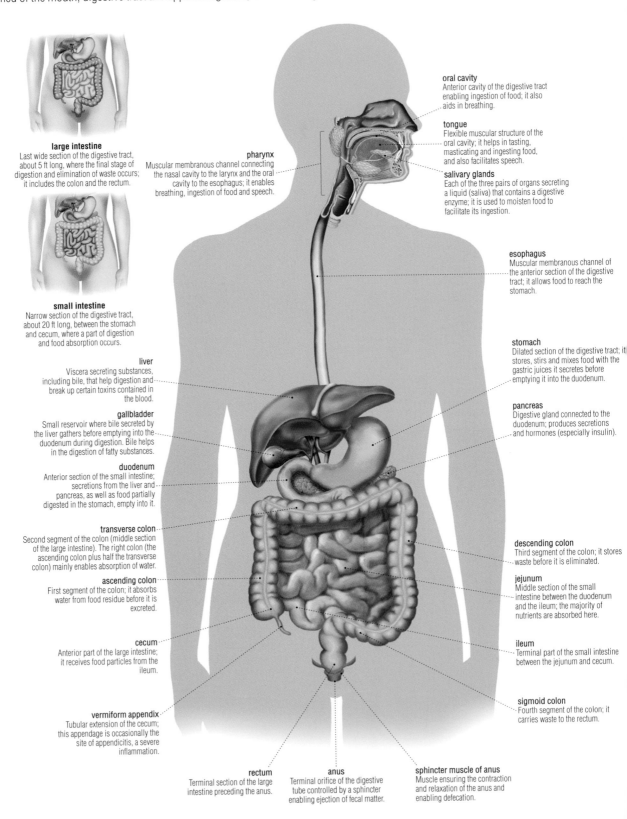

large intestine
Last wide section of the digestive tract, about 5 ft long, where the final stage of digestion and elimination of waste occurs; it includes the colon and the rectum.

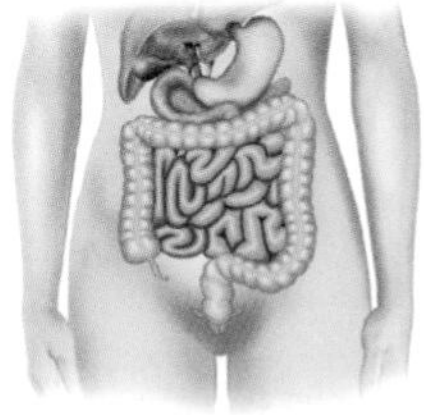

small intestine
Narrow section of the digestive tract, about 20 ft long, between the stomach and cecum, where a part of digestion and food absorption occurs.

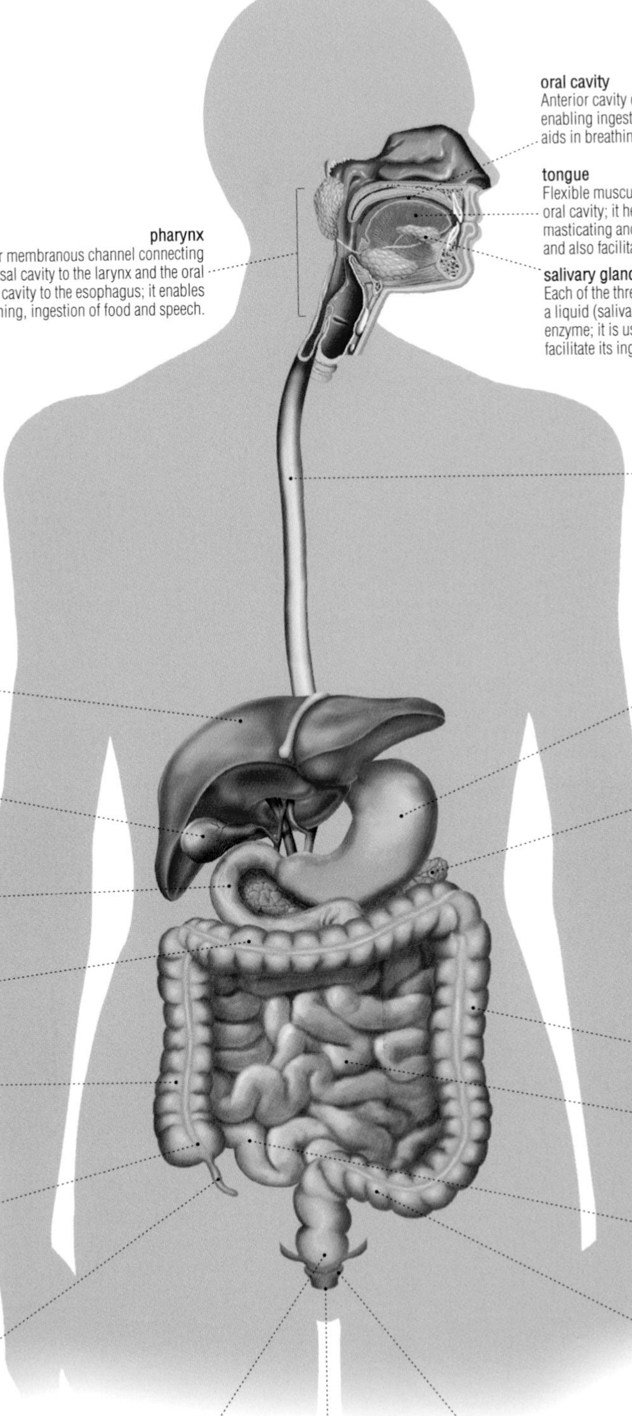

pharynx
Muscular membranous channel connecting the nasal cavity to the larynx and the oral cavity to the esophagus; it enables breathing, ingestion of food and speech.

oral cavity
Anterior cavity of the digestive tract enabling ingestion of food; it also aids in breathing.

tongue
Flexible muscular structure of the oral cavity; it helps in tasting, masticating and ingesting food, and also facilitates speech.

salivary glands
Each of the three pairs of organs secreting a liquid (saliva) that contains a digestive enzyme; it is used to moisten food to facilitate its ingestion.

esophagus
Muscular membranous channel of the anterior section of the digestive tract; it allows food to reach the stomach.

liver
Viscera secreting substances, including bile, that help digestion and break up certain toxins contained in the blood.

stomach
Dilated section of the digestive tract; it stores, stirs and mixes food with the gastric juices it secretes before emptying it into the duodenum.

gallbladder
Small reservoir where bile secreted by the liver gathers before emptying into the duodenum during digestion. Bile helps in the digestion of fatty substances.

pancreas
Digestive gland connected to the duodenum; produces secretions and hormones (especially insulin).

duodenum
Anterior section of the small intestine; secretions from the liver and pancreas, as well as food partially digested in the stomach, empty into it.

transverse colon
Second segment of the colon (middle section of the large intestine). The right colon (the ascending colon plus half the transverse colon) mainly enables absorption of water.

descending colon
Third segment of the colon; it stores waste before it is eliminated.

ascending colon
First segment of the colon; it absorbs water from food residue before it is excreted.

jejunum
Middle section of the small intestine between the duodenum and the ileum; the majority of nutrients are absorbed here.

cecum
Anterior part of the large intestine; it receives food particles from the ileum.

ileum
Terminal part of the small intestine between the jejunum and cecum.

sigmoid colon
Fourth segment of the colon; it carries waste to the rectum.

vermiform appendix
Tubular extension of the cecum; this appendage is occasionally the site of appendicitis, a severe inflammation.

rectum
Terminal section of the large intestine preceding the anus.

anus
Terminal orifice of the digestive tube controlled by a sphincter enabling ejection of fecal matter.

sphincter muscle of anus
Muscle ensuring the contraction and relaxation of the anus and enabling defecation.

urinary system

Eliminates the organism's waste through secretion and evacuation of urine; it also regulates the quantity of water and salt in the body.

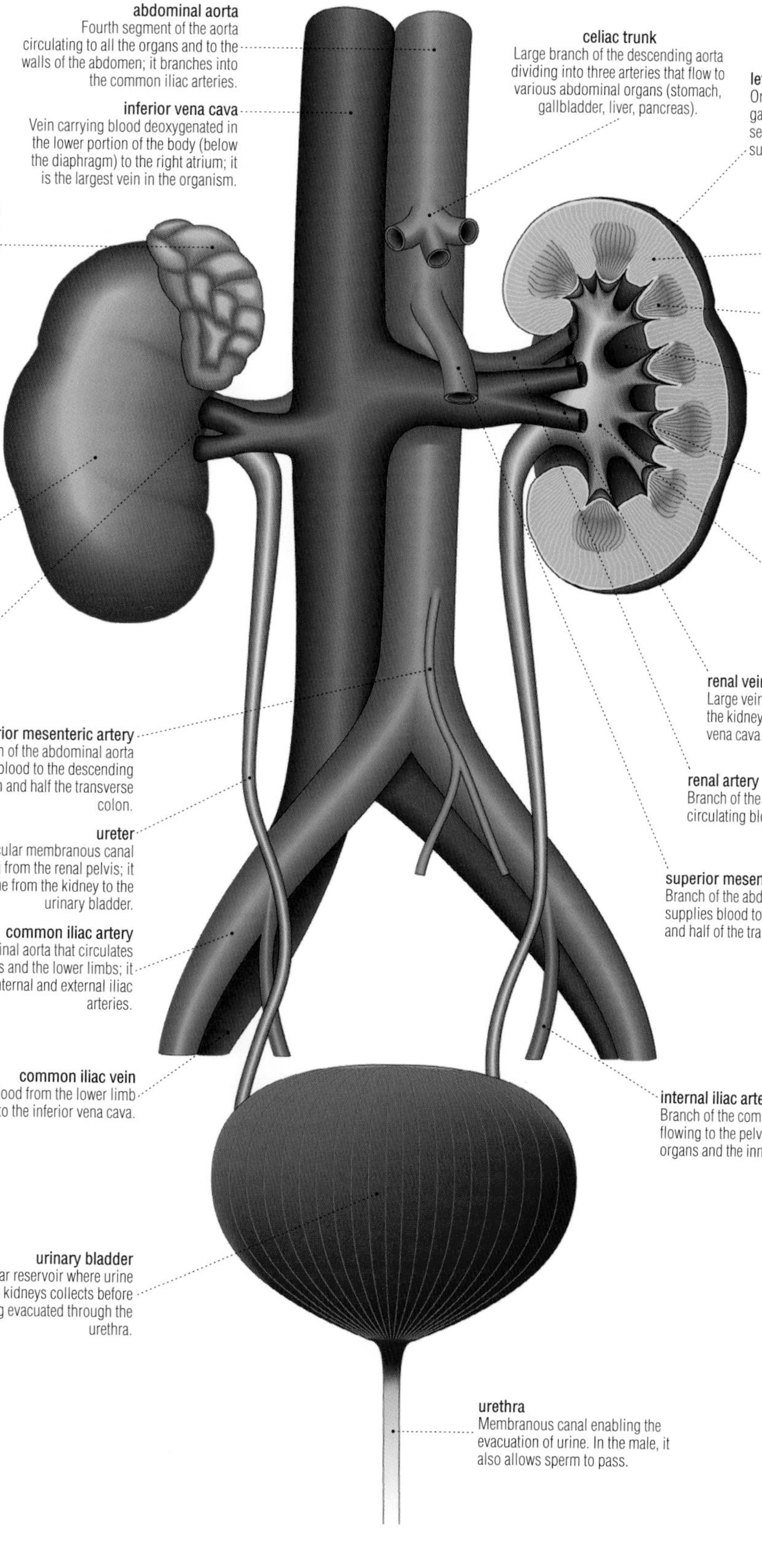

abdominal aorta
Fourth segment of the aorta circulating to all the organs and to the walls of the abdomen; it branches into the common iliac arteries.

inferior vena cava
Vein carrying blood deoxygenated in the lower portion of the body (below the diaphragm) to the right atrium; it is the largest vein in the organism.

suprarenal gland
rgan situated atop the kidney, not part of the urinary system; it secretes various hormones of the steroid and adrenal families.

right kidney
Organ located beneath the liver; it filters the blood and secretes urine to eliminate toxic substances and waste from the body.

renal hilum
Opening of the inner edge of the kidney allowing the passage of blood vessels, nerves and the ureter.

inferior mesenteric artery
Branch of the abdominal aorta circulating blood to the descending colon and half the transverse colon.

ureter
Long muscular membranous canal extending from the renal pelvis; it carries urine from the kidney to the urinary bladder.

common iliac artery
Branch of the abdominal aorta that circulates blood to the pelvis and the lower limbs; it divides into the internal and external iliac arteries.

common iliac vein
Vein carrying blood from the lower limb back to the inferior vena cava.

urinary bladder
Muscular reservoir where urine from the kidneys collects before being evacuated through the urethra.

celiac trunk
Large branch of the descending aorta dividing into three arteries that flow to various abdominal organs (stomach, gallbladder, liver, pancreas).

left kidney
Organ located beneath the gallbladder; it filters the blood and secretes urine to eliminate toxic substances and waste from the body.

cortex
Outer portion of the renal tissue inserted between the Malpighian pyramids; it is made up of small vesicles that filter the blood and produce urine.

medulla
Inner part of the renal tissue made up of Malpighian pyramids, cone-shaped structures that connect the urine collection canals.

renal papilla
Crest of the Malpighian pyramid (cone-shaped striated structure) made of urine collection canals; it opens into the calyx.

calyx
Excretory cavity of the kidney; it collects urine flowing from the papillae and opens into the renal pelvis.

renal pelvis
Broad section of the excretory renal tract resulting from the juncture of the calyxes; it extends into the ureter.

renal vein
Large vein collecting blood from the kidney; it flows into the inferior vena cava.

renal artery
Branch of the abdominal aorta circulating blood to the kidney.

superior mesenteric artery
Branch of the abdominal aorta that supplies blood to the ascending colon and half of the transverse colon.

internal iliac artery
Branch of the common iliac artery flowing to the pelvis, the genital organs and the inner thigh.

urethra
Membranous canal enabling the evacuation of urine. In the male, it also allows sperm to pass.

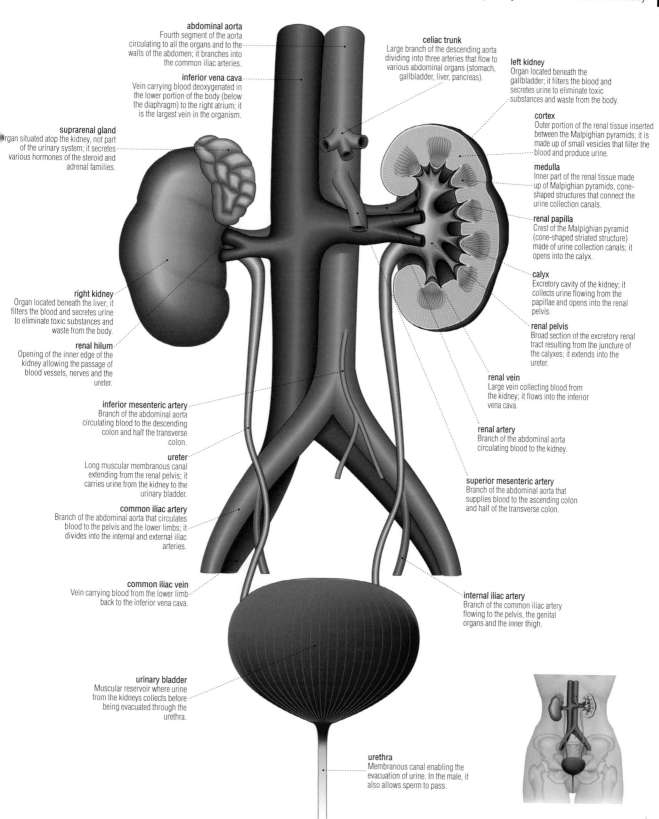

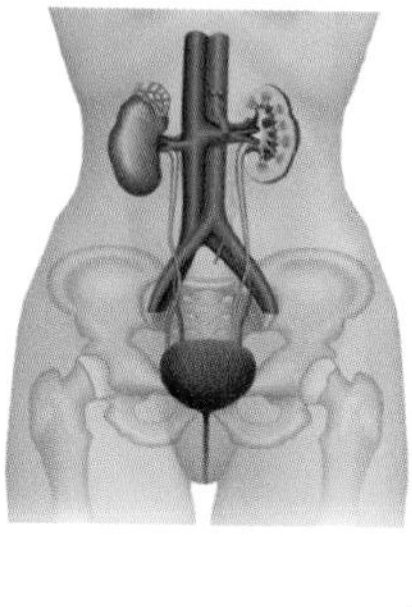

nervous system

It directs the movements of the organs and muscles and receives and interprets sensory messages coming from the body.

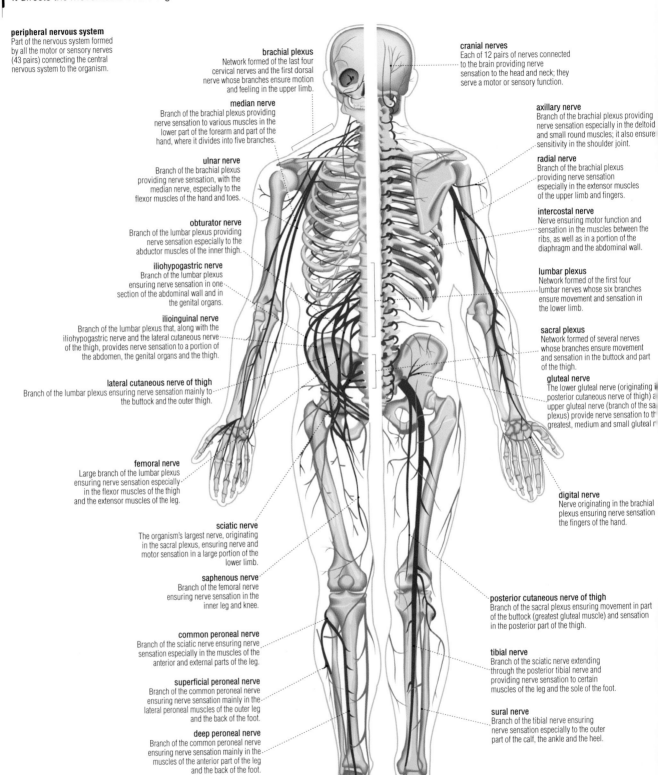

peripheral nervous system
Part of the nervous system formed by all the motor or sensory nerves (43 pairs) connecting the central nervous system to the organism.

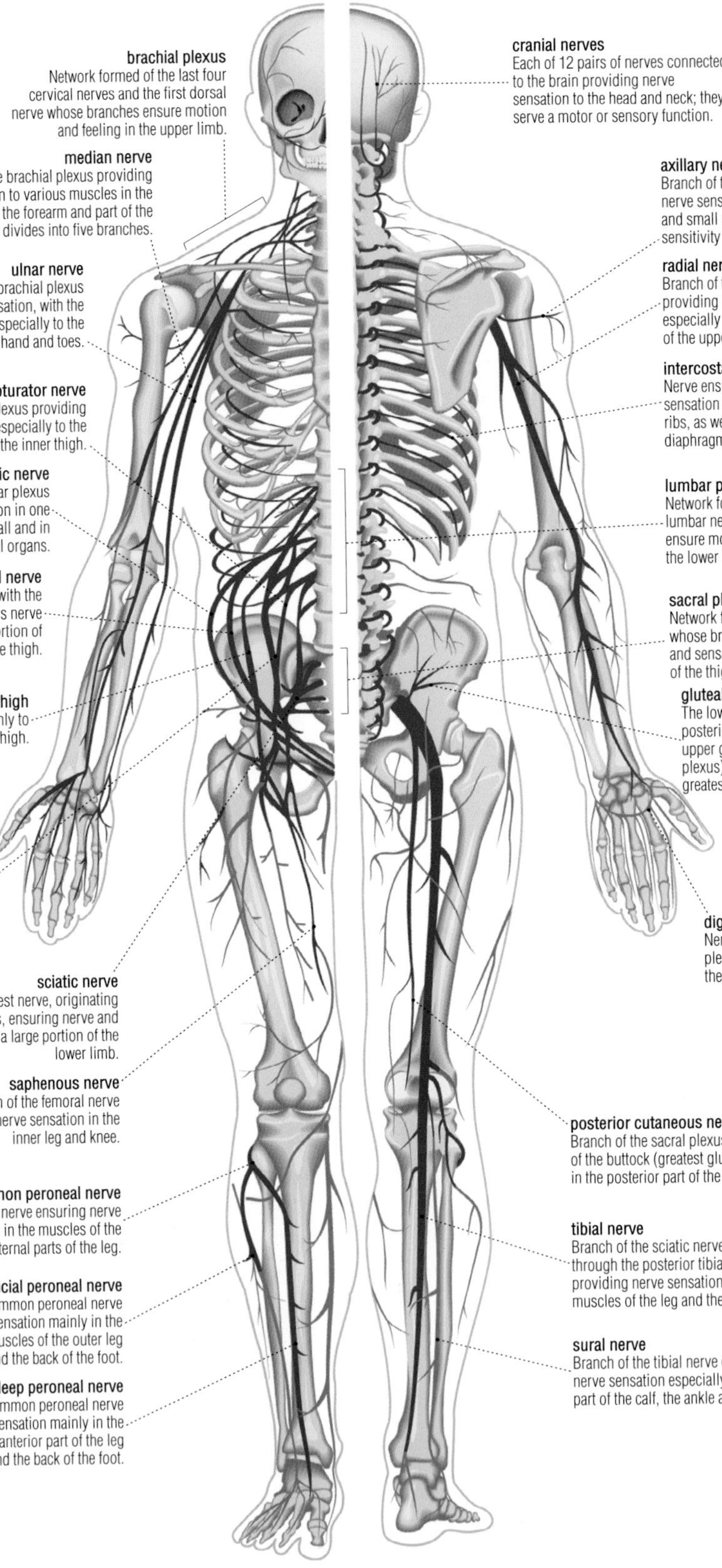

brachial plexus
Network formed of the last four cervical nerves and the first dorsal nerve whose branches ensure motion and feeling in the upper limb.

median nerve
Branch of the brachial plexus providing nerve sensation to various muscles in the lower part of the forearm and part of the hand, where it divides into five branches.

ulnar nerve
Branch of the brachial plexus providing nerve sensation, with the median nerve, especially to the flexor muscles of the hand and toes.

obturator nerve
Branch of the lumbar plexus providing nerve sensation especially to the abductor muscles of the inner thigh.

iliohypogastric nerve
Branch of the lumbar plexus ensuring nerve sensation in one section of the abdominal wall and in the genital organs.

ilioinguinal nerve
Branch of the lumbar plexus that, along with the iliohypogastric nerve and the lateral cutaneous nerve of the thigh, provides nerve sensation to a portion of the abdomen, the genital organs and the thigh.

lateral cutaneous nerve of thigh
Branch of the lumbar plexus ensuring nerve sensation mainly to the buttock and the outer thigh.

femoral nerve
Large branch of the lumbar plexus ensuring nerve sensation especially in the flexor muscles of the thigh and the extensor muscles of the leg.

sciatic nerve
The organism's largest nerve, originating in the sacral plexus, ensuring nerve and motor sensation in a large portion of the lower limb.

saphenous nerve
Branch of the femoral nerve ensuring nerve sensation in the inner leg and knee.

common peroneal nerve
Branch of the sciatic nerve ensuring nerve sensation especially in the muscles of the anterior and external parts of the leg.

superficial peroneal nerve
Branch of the common peroneal nerve ensuring nerve sensation mainly in the lateral peroneal muscles of the outer leg and the back of the foot.

deep peroneal nerve
Branch of the common peroneal nerve ensuring nerve sensation mainly in the muscles of the anterior part of the leg and the back of the foot.

cranial nerves
Each of 12 pairs of nerves connected to the brain providing nerve sensation to the head and neck; they serve a motor or sensory function.

axillary nerve
Branch of the brachial plexus providing nerve sensation especially in the deltoid and small round muscles; it also ensure sensitivity in the shoulder joint.

radial nerve
Branch of the brachial plexus providing nerve sensation especially in the extensor muscles of the upper limb and fingers.

intercostal nerve
Nerve ensuring motor function and sensation in the muscles between the ribs, as well as in a portion of the diaphragm and the abdominal wall.

lumbar plexus
Network formed of the first four lumbar nerves whose six branches ensure movement and sensation in the lower limb.

sacral plexus
Network formed of several nerves whose branches ensure movement and sensation in the buttock and part of the thigh.

gluteal nerve
The lower gluteal nerve (originating i posterior cutaneous nerve of thigh) a upper gluteal nerve (branch of the sa plexus) provide nerve sensation to th greatest, medium and small gluteal r

digital nerve
Nerve originating in the brachial plexus ensuring nerve sensation the fingers of the hand.

posterior cutaneous nerve of thigh
Branch of the sacral plexus ensuring movement in part of the buttock (greatest gluteal muscle) and sensation in the posterior part of the thigh.

tibial nerve
Branch of the sciatic nerve extending through the posterior tibial nerve and providing nerve sensation to certain muscles of the leg and the sole of the foot.

sural nerve
Branch of the tibial nerve ensuring nerve sensation especially to the outer part of the calf, the ankle and the heel.

central nervous system

Part of the nervous system connected to the peripheral nervous system formed by the brain and the spinal cord; it controls and deciphers nerve information.

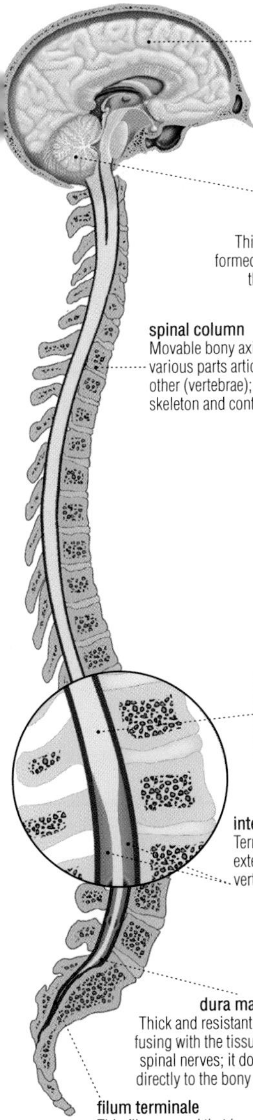
cerebrum
Large part of the brain formed of two hemispheres; it contains the control center of the higher nerve functions (motor activities, language and others).
cerebellum
Part of the brain that mainly controls motor coordination, equilibrium, muscle tone and posture.
spinal column
Movable bony axis made up of various parts articulating with each other (vertebrae); it supports the skeleton and contains the spinal cord.
spinal cord
Part of the central nervous system located in the spinal column; it receives and transmits nerve information and releases the reflexes.
internal filum terminale
Terminal part of the dura mater extending to the second sacral vertebra.
dura mater
Thick and resistant outer meninx fusing with the tissue covering the spinal nerves; it does not adhere directly to the bony vertebral wall.
filum terminale
Thin fibrous cord that is a continuation of the spinal cord between the second lumbar vertebra and the coccyx.

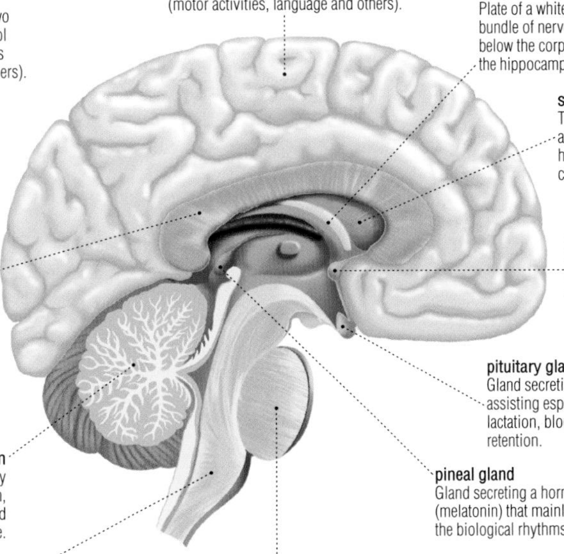
cerebrum
Large part of the brain formed of two hemispheres; it contains the control center of the higher nerve functions (motor activities, language and others).
body of fornix
Plate of a white substance formed by a bundle of nerve fibers and located below the corpus callosum; it connects the hippocampus to the hypothalamus.
septum pellucidum
Thin double membrane separating the anterior part of the two cerebral hemispheres and extending from the corpus callosum to the body of fornix.
corpus callosum
Thin plate of a white substance formed by a bundle of nerve fibers that connect the two cerebral hemispheres.
optic chiasm
Structure formed by the juncture of the optic nerves of the right and left eyes, whose fibers partially interconnect.
pituitary gland
Gland secreting a dozen hormones assisting especially in growth, lactation, blood pressure and urine retention.
cerebellum
Part of the brain that mainly controls motor coordination, equilibrium, muscle tone and posture.
pineal gland
Gland secreting a hormone (melatonin) that mainly influences the biological rhythms.
medulla oblongata
Part of the brain stem that is a continuation of the spinal cord; it mainly controls breathing, blood circulation and cardiac rhythm.
pons
Part of the cerebral trunk made up of nerve fibers; it serves as a bridge between the brain, the cerebellum and the medulla oblongata, and aids breathing.

structure of the spinal cord

The spinal cord, protected by several solid and liquid membranes, is the source of 31 pairs of spinal nerves; it connects them to the brain.

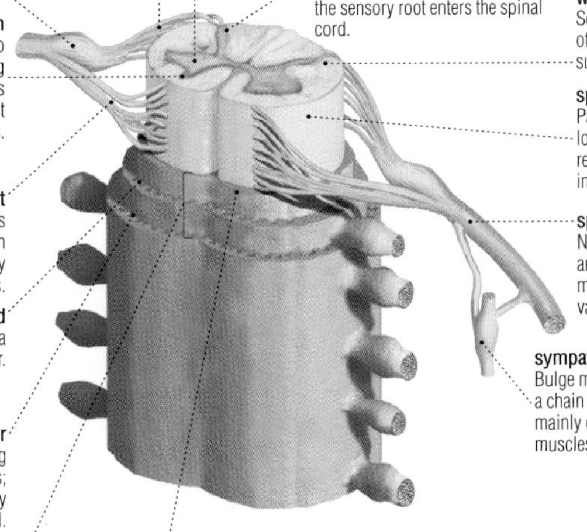
sensory root
Bundle of sensory nerve fibers (axons) communicating information from the periphery of the body to the spinal cord.
gray matter
Central part of the spinal cord primarily made of the cell bodies of neurons.
spinal ganglion
Bulge of the posterior sensory root of the spinal nerve; it encloses the cell bodies of the neuron sensors.
posterior horn
Each of the terminal parts of the two masses of gray matter enclosing the associative neurons through which the sensory root enters the spinal cord.
white matter
Section of the spinal cord made up of nerve fibers (axons) and surrounding the gray matter.
anterior horn
Each of the terminal parts of two masses of gray matter enclosing the cell bodies of motor neurons and from which the motor root originates.
spinal cord
Part of the central nervous system located in the spinal column; it receives and transmits nerve information and releases the reflexes.
motor root
Bundle of motor nerve fibers (axons) communicating information from the spinal cord to the periphery of the body, especially the muscles.
spinal nerve
Nerve formed by the union of the sensory and motor roots; it communicates nerve messages between the spinal cord and the various parts of the organism.
arachnoid
Meninx located between the dura mater and the pia mater.
sympathetic ganglion
Bulge made up of nerve cell bodies forming a chain on both sides of the spinal cord; it mainly controls contraction of the visceral muscles.
dura mater
Thick and resistant outer meninx fusing with the tissue covering the spinal nerves; it does not adhere directly to the bony vertebral wall.
meninges
Each of three fibrous membranes surrounding and protecting the central nervous system (spinal cord, brain).
pia mater
Thin and highly veined inner meninx directly covering the spinal cord and the roots of the spinal nerves.

nervous system

chain of neurons
All the interconnected complex nerve cells receiving, communicating and transmitting messages in the form of nerve impulses.

synapse
Contact zone between two neurons through which nerve impulses are transmitted.

collateral
Branch of the axon. An axon can be divided into one or several collaterals.

sheath of Schwann
Outer casing of the axon, it surrounds the myelin sheath.

cell body
Bulging part of a neuron ensuring maintenance of its structure and function.

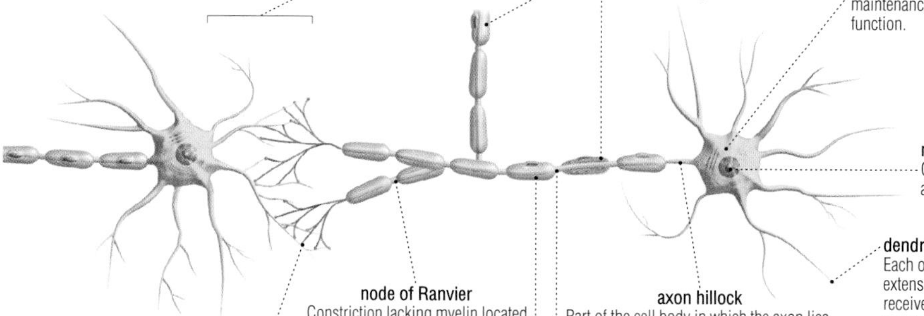

nucleus
Organelle containing a cell's genes and controlling its activities.

dendrite
Each of the short branch extensions of the cell body that receive nerve impulses from surrounding neurons.

node of Ranvier
Constriction lacking myelin located at regular intervals along the entire length of the axon; it accelerates the distribution of nerve impulses.

axon hillock
Part of the cell body in which the axon lies.

terminal arborization
Final branch of the axon storing a chemical substance (neurotransmitter) used to transfer a nerve impulse to the dendrites of the neighboring neuron.

sensory impulse
Electrical signal propagated along the nerve fibers (axons) enabling the nerve cells to communicate and to transmit messages within the organism.

myelin sheath
Casing of the axon made of a fatty substance (myelin) providing electrical insulation for the neuron and increasing the conduction speed of the nerve impulse.

axon
Neuron extension communicating nerve impulses to other cells (including nerve and muscle cells). The axons of motor neurons can be more than 3 ft long.

sensory root
Bundle of sensory nerve fibers (axons) communicating information from the periphery of the body to the spinal cord.

protoneuron
First neuron of the sensory tract; it transmits information from a sensory organ to the spinal cord.

spinal ganglion
Bulge of the posterior sensory root of the spinal nerve; it encloses the cell bodies of the neuron sensors.

motor end plate
Contact zone between the axonal end of the motor neuron and the muscle fiber that causes muscle movement.

skin
The body's outer protective casi… whose internal layer (dermis) is rich in veins and nerves.

spinal nerve
Nerve formed by the union of the sensory and motor roots; it communicates nerve messages between the spinal cord and the various parts of the organism.

white matter
Section of the spinal cord made up of nerve fibers (axons) and surrounding the gray matter.

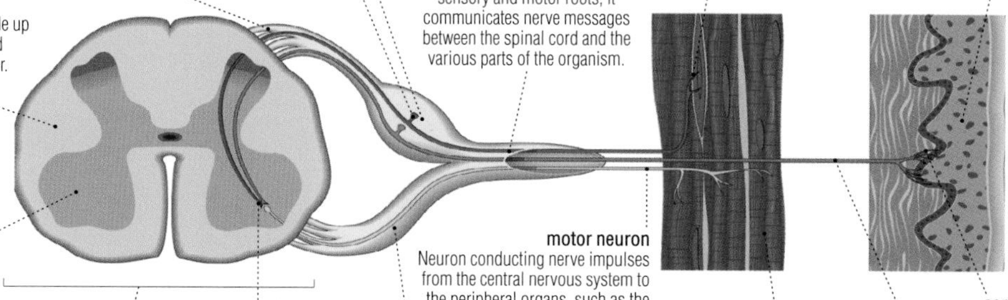

gray matter
Central part of the spinal cord primarily made of the cell bodies of neurons.

motor neuron
Neuron conducting nerve impulses from the central nervous system to the peripheral organs, such as the muscles.

sense receptor
Peripheral terminal of the senso… receiving a stimulus (touch, nois… other) and transmitting it to the s… cord in the form of nerve impuls…

spinal cord
Part of the central nervous system located in the spinal column; it receives and transmits nerve information and initiates reflex actions.

synapse
Contact zone between two neurons through which nerve impulses are transmitted.

motor root
Bundle of motor nerve fibers (axons) communicating information from the spinal cord to the periphery of the body, especially the muscles.

muscle fiber
Component tissue of the muscle; it contracts in response to a nerve impulse from the central nervous system.

sensory neuron
Neuron transmitting information gathered by sensory receptors to the central nervous system.

lumbar vertebra
Large bony part of the back located between the dorsal vertebrae and the sacrum; it supports a major portion of the body's weight.

spinous process
Posterior middle protuberance of the vertebra; the attachment point for the back muscles.

epidural space
Space filled with blood vessels and adipose tissue; separates the dura mater from the vertebra and has a protective function.

dura mater
Thick and resistant outer meninx fusing with the tissue covering the spinal nerves; it does not adhere directly to the bony vertebral wall.

cerebrospinal fluid
Fluid contained between the arachnoid and the pia mater around the spinal cord and serving mainly as a shock absorber; it protects the entire central nervous system.

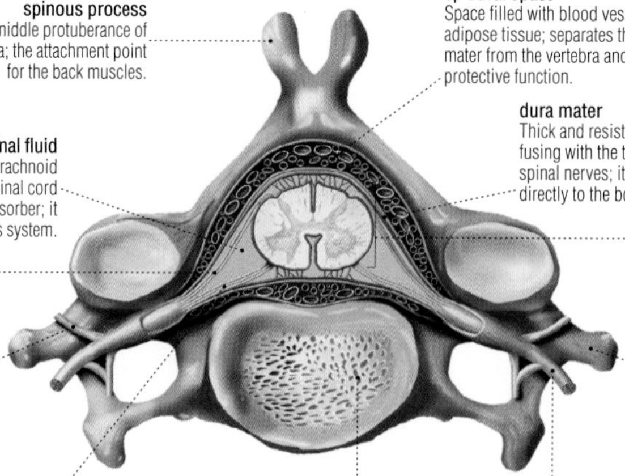

spinal cord
Part of the central nervous system located in the spinal column; it receives and transmits nerve information and initiates reflex actions.

dorsal root
Bundle of sensitive nerve fibers that carry the spinal ganglions and communicate information from the body's periphery to the spinal cord.

transverse process
Bony protuberance extending laterally from each side of the vertebra; the muscles are attached to it.

communicating ramus
Branch of the spinal nerve connecting the ganglions of the sympathetic trunk to the spinal cord.

ventral root
Bundle of motor nerve fibers (axons) communicating information from the spinal cord to the periphery of the body, especially the muscles.

vertebral body
Anterior bony cylinder of a vertebra surrounded by two transverse processes.

spinal nerve
Nerve formed by the union of the sensory and motor roots; it communicates nerve messages between the spinal cord and the various parts of the organism.

male reproductive organs

The male genitalia ensure reproduction; they produce spermatozoa and eject them into the female genital tract during copulation.

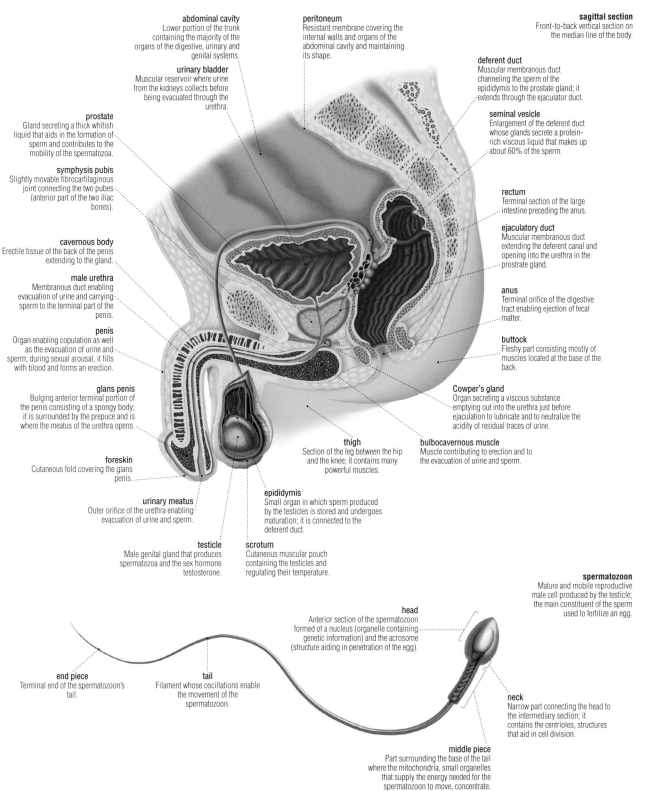

sagittal section
Front-to-back vertical section on the median line of the body.

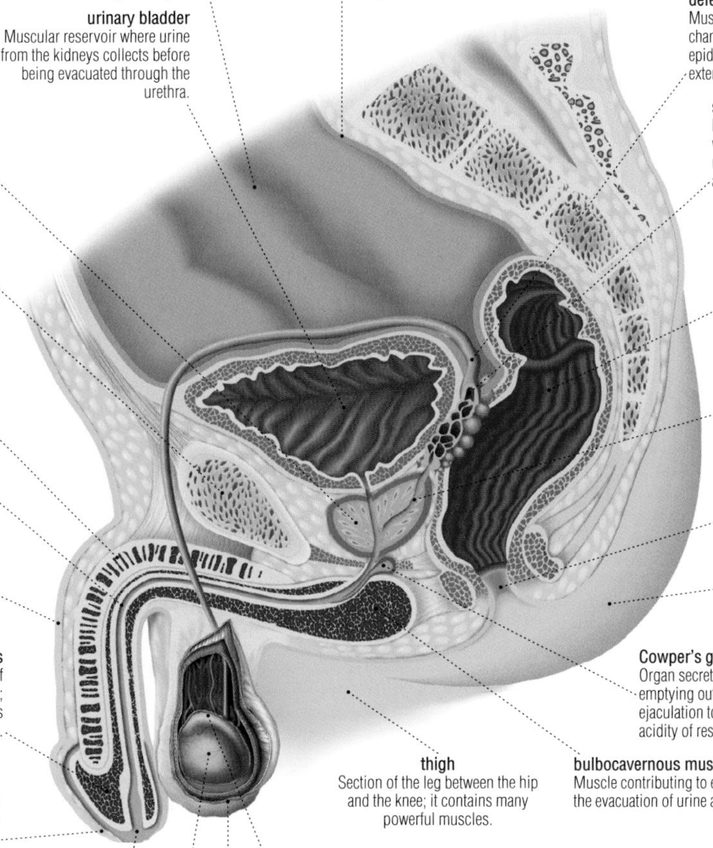

abdominal cavity
Lower portion of the trunk containing the majority of the organs of the digestive, urinary and genital systems.

peritoneum
Resistant membrane covering the internal walls and organs of the abdominal cavity and maintaining its shape.

urinary bladder
Muscular reservoir where urine from the kidneys collects before being evacuated through the urethra.

deferent duct
Muscular membranous duct channeling the sperm of the epididymis to the prostate gland; it extends through the ejaculator duct.

seminal vesicle
Enlargement of the deferent duct whose glands secrete a protein-rich viscous liquid that makes up about 60% of the sperm.

prostate
Gland secreting a thick whitish liquid that aids in the formation of sperm and contributes to the mobility of the spermatozoa.

symphysis pubis
Slightly movable fibrocartilaginous joint connecting the two pubes (anterior part of the two iliac bones).

rectum
Terminal section of the large intestine preceding the anus.

ejaculatory duct
Muscular membranous duct extending the deferent canal and opening into the urethra in the prostrate gland.

cavernous body
Erectile tissue of the back of the penis extending to the gland.

male urethra
Membranous duct enabling evacuation of urine and carrying sperm to the terminal part of the penis.

anus
Terminal orifice of the digestive tract enabling ejection of fecal matter.

penis
Organ enabling copulation as well as the evacuation of urine and sperm; during sexual arousal, it fills with blood and forms an erection.

buttock
Fleshy part consisting mostly of muscles located at the base of the back.

glans penis
Bulging anterior terminal portion of the penis consisting of a spongy body; it is surrounded by the prepuce and is where the meatus of the urethra opens.

Cowper's gland
Organ secreting a viscous substance emptying out into the urethra just before ejaculation to lubricate and to neutralize the acidity of residual traces of urine.

foreskin
Cutaneous fold covering the glans penis.

thigh
Section of the leg between the hip and the knee; it contains many powerful muscles.

bulbocavernous muscle
Muscle contributing to erection and to the evacuation of urine and sperm.

urinary meatus
Outer orifice of the urethra enabling evacuation of urine and sperm.

epididymis
Small organ in which sperm produced by the testicles is stored and undergoes maturation; it is connected to the deferent duct.

testicle
Male genital gland that produces spermatozoa and the sex hormone testosterone.

scrotum
Cutaneous muscular pouch containing the testicles and regulating their temperature.

spermatozoon
Mature and mobile reproductive male cell produced by the testicle; the main constituent of the sperm used to fertilize an egg.

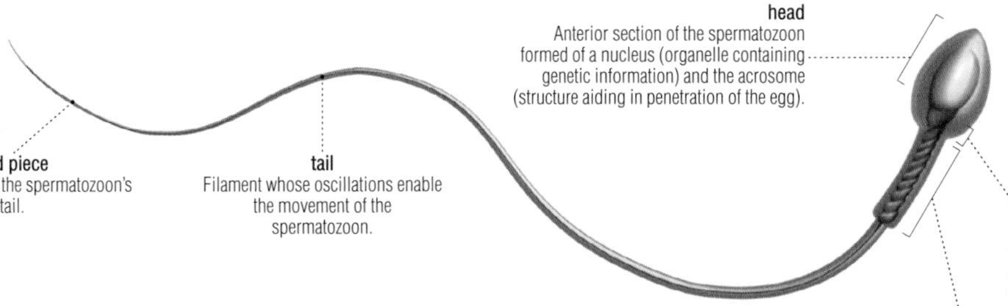

head
Anterior section of the spermatozoon formed of a nucleus (organelle containing genetic information) and the acrosome (structure aiding in penetration of the egg).

end piece
Terminal end of the spermatozoon's tail.

tail
Filament whose oscillations enable the movement of the spermatozoon.

neck
Narrow part connecting the head to the intermediary section; it contains the centrioles, structures that aid in cell division.

middle piece
Part surrounding the base of the tail where the mitochondria, small organelles that supply the energy needed for the spermatozoon to move, concentrate.

female reproductive organs

Mainly internal, they enable fertilization of the egg by the spermatozoon and the development of the embryo and fetus.

sagittal section
Front-to-back vertical section on the median line of the body.

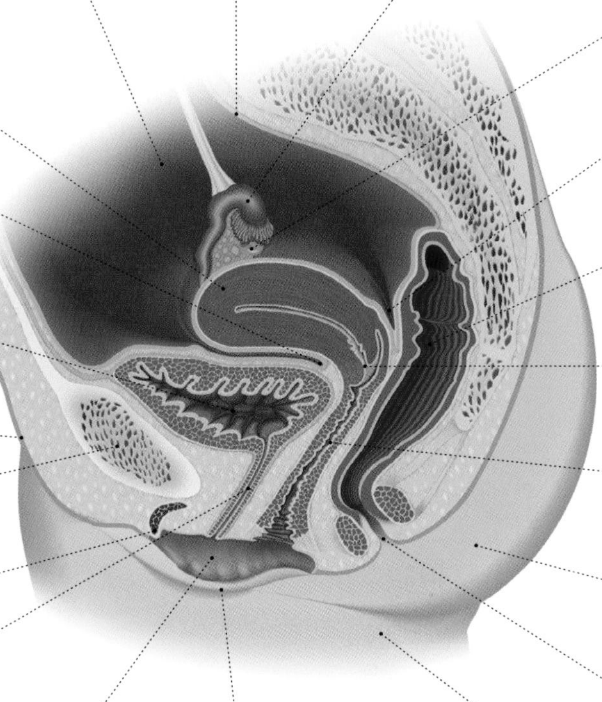
abdominal cavity
Lower portion of the trunk containing the majority of the organs of the digestive, urinary and genital systems.
peritoneum
Resistant membrane covering the internal walls and organs of the abdominal cavity and maintaining its shape.
fallopian tube
Canal through which the egg travels from the ovary to the uterus. Fertilization of the egg by the spermatozoon normally takes place in the upper section of the tube.
ovary
Female genital gland that produces eggs and the sex hormones estrogen and progesterone.
uterus
Hollow muscular organ receiving the egg and, once fertilized, enabling its development and expulsion at the end of pregnancy.
pouch of Douglas
Small pouch formed by the fold of the peritoneum between the rectum and the uterus.
uterovesical pouch
Small pouch formed by the fold of the peritoneum between the uterus and the bladder.
urinary bladder
Muscular reservoir where urine from the kidneys collects before being evacuated through the urethra.
rectum
Terminal section of the large intestine preceding the anus.
cervix of uterus
Lower narrow section of the uterus through which it connects with the vagina.
mons pubis
Middle protuberance of the pubis made of adipose tissues and covered with hair at puberty.
symphysis pubis
Slightly movable fibrocartilaginous joint connecting the two pubes (anterior part of the two iliac bones).
vagina
Muscular canal located between the neck of the uterus and the vulva enabling copulation.
clitoris
Small erectile organ at the anterior section of the vulva constituting a major erogenous zone.
buttock
Fleshy part consisting mostly of muscles located at the base of the back.
anus
Terminal orifice of the digestive tract enabling ejection of fecal matter.
urethra
Membranous canal enabling evacuation of urine from the bladder.
labia minora
Mucous folds of the vulva located between the labia majora.
labia majora
Thick cutaneous hairy folds of the vulva protecting the vaginal orifice.
thigh
Section of the leg between the hip and the knee; it contains many powerful muscles.

egg
Mature female reproductive cell produced by the ovary, which, after fertilization by a spermatozoon, enables the embryo to develop.

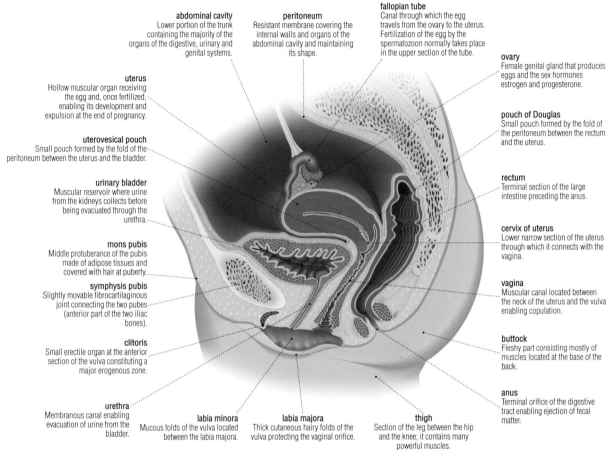

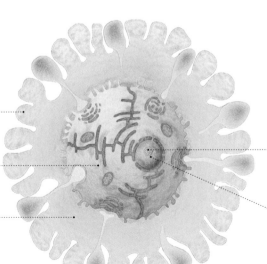

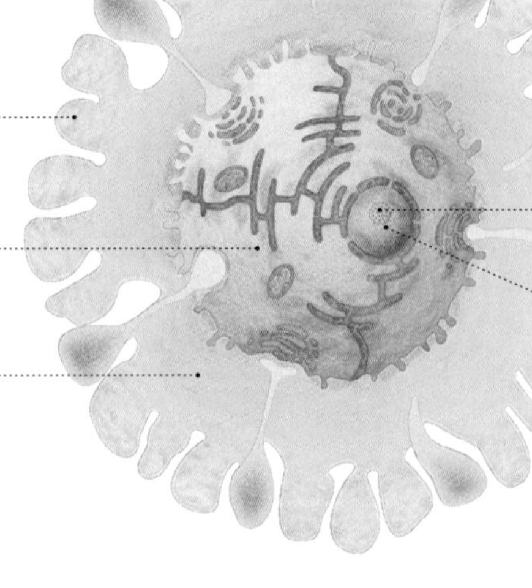
corona radiata
Collection of granular cells that forms a protective crown around the egg.
nucleolus
Small spherical body located inside the nucleus, within which the ribosomes, or protein-synthesizing structures, are produced.
cytoplasm
Clear gelatinous substance surrounding the various cellular structures.
nucleus
Organelle containing a cell's genes and controlling its activities.
zona pellucida
Fine granular coat composed of mucopolysaccharides covering the egg; it allows a single spermatozoon to penetrate the egg, which then becomes impermeable to others.

female reproductive organs

posterior view

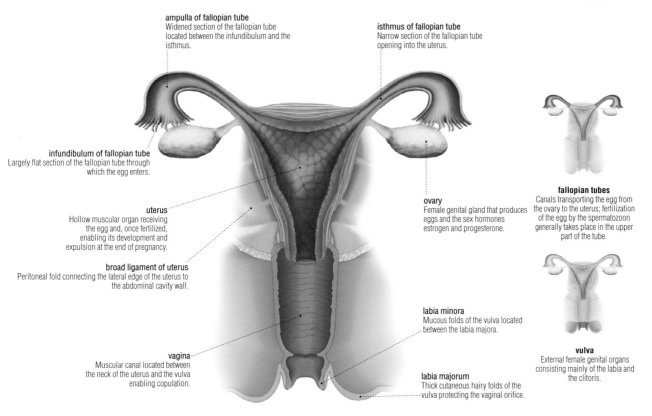

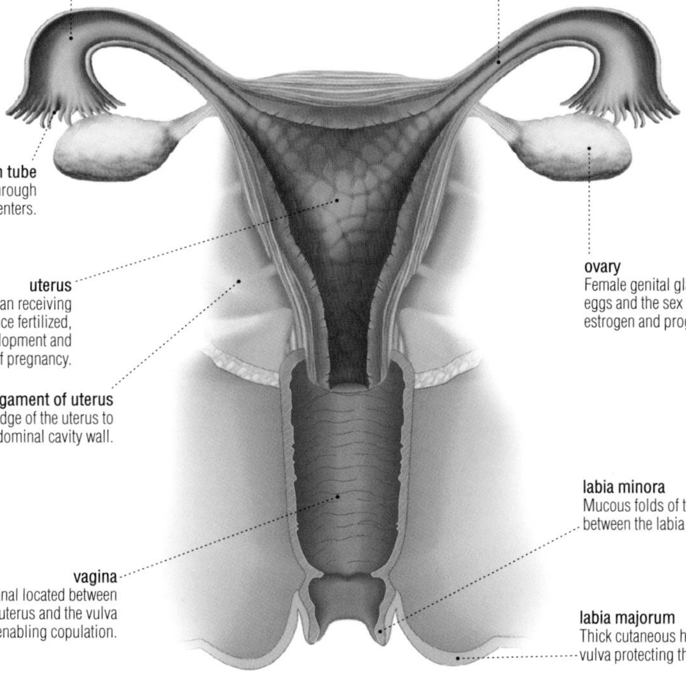
ampulla of fallopian tube
Widened section of the fallopian tube located between the infundibulum and the isthmus.
isthmus of fallopian tube
Narrow section of the fallopian tube opening into the uterus.
infundibulum of fallopian tube
Largely flat section of the fallopian tube through which the egg enters.
uterus
Hollow muscular organ receiving the egg and, once fertilized, enabling its development and expulsion at the end of pregnancy.
broad ligament of uterus
Peritoneal fold connecting the lateral edge of the uterus to the abdominal cavity wall.
vagina
Muscular canal located between the neck of the uterus and the vulva enabling copulation.
ovary
Female genital gland that produces eggs and the sex hormones estrogen and progesterone.
labia minora
Mucous folds of the vulva located between the labia majora.
labia majorum
Thick cutaneous hairy folds of the vulva protecting the vaginal orifice.

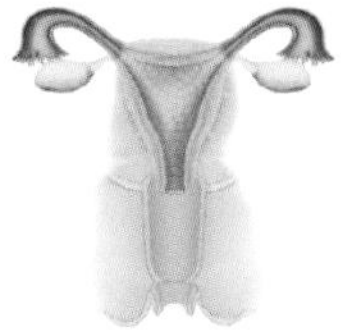

fallopian tubes
Canals transporting the egg from the ovary to the uterus; fertilization of the egg by the spermatozoon generally takes place in the upper part of the tube.

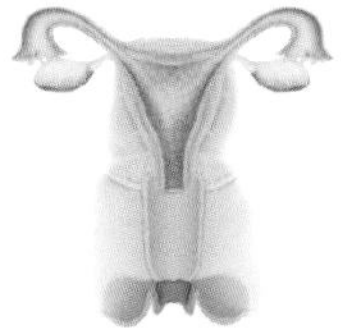

vulva
External female genital organs consisting mainly of the labia and the clitoris.

breast

Female milk-secreting glandular organ; it develops at puberty and increases in size during pregnancy.

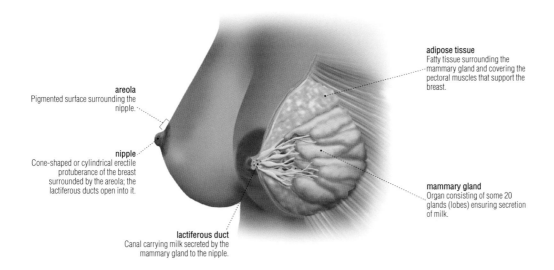

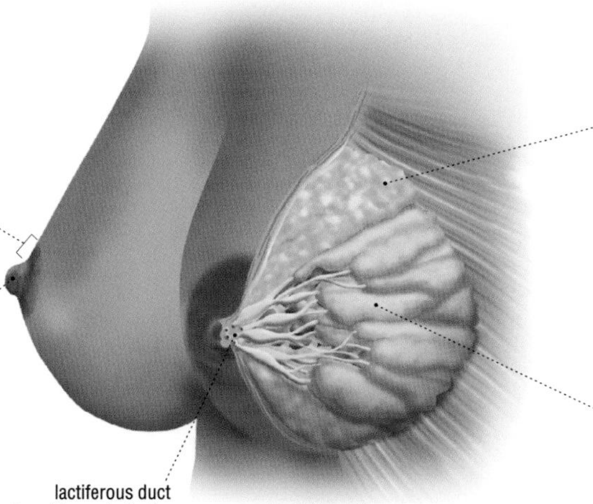
areola
Pigmented surface surrounding the nipple.
nipple
Cone-shaped or cylindrical erectile protuberance of the breast surrounded by the areola; the lactiferous ducts open into it.
lactiferous duct
Canal carrying milk secreted by the mammary gland to the nipple.
adipose tissue
Fatty tissue surrounding the mammary gland and covering the pectoral muscles that support the breast.
mammary gland
Organ consisting of some 20 glands (lobes) ensuring secretion of milk.

touch

Sense enabling the skin to detect sensations (contact, heat, pain and others) due to specialized receptors spread widely over the surface of the body.

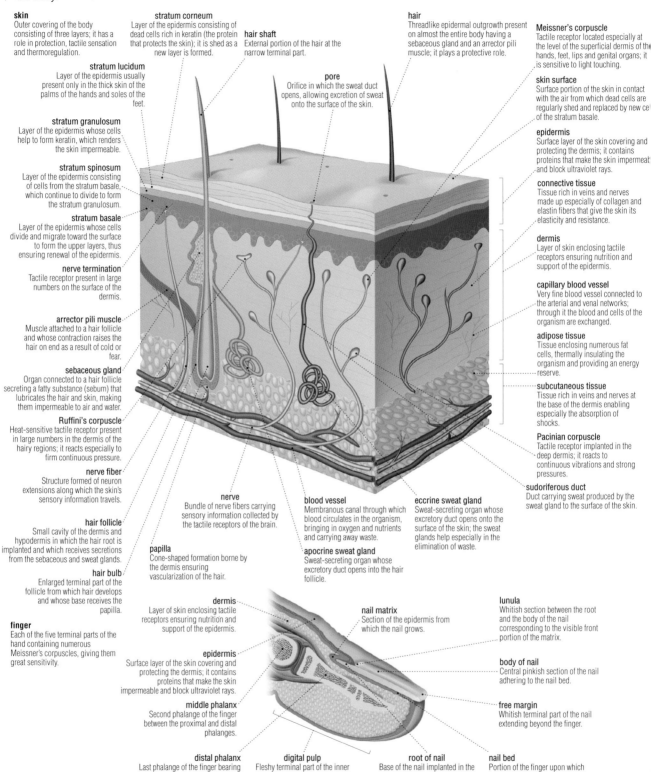

skin
Outer covering of the body consisting of three layers; it has a role in protection, tactile sensation and thermoregulation.

stratum corneum
Layer of the epidermis consisting of dead cells rich in keratin (the protein that protects the skin); it is shed as a new layer is formed.

hair shaft
External portion of the hair at the narrow terminal part.

hair
Threadlike epidermal outgrowth present on almost the entire body having a sebaceous gland and an arrector pili muscle; it plays a protective role.

Meissner's corpuscle
Tactile receptor located especially at the level of the superficial dermis of th hands, feet, lips and genital organs; it is sensitive to light touching.

stratum lucidum
Layer of the epidermis usually present only in the thick skin of the palms of the hands and soles of the feet.

pore
Orifice in which the sweat duct opens, allowing excretion of sweat onto the surface of the skin.

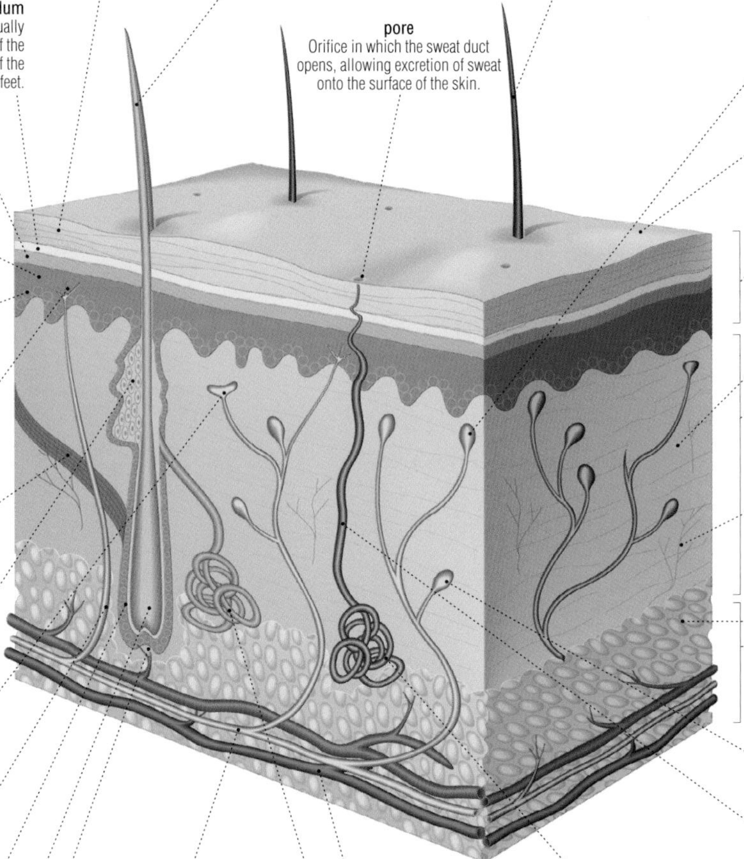

stratum granulosum
Layer of the epidermis whose cells help to form keratin, which renders the skin impermeable.

stratum spinosum
Layer of the epidermis consisting of cells from the stratum basale, which continue to divide to form the stratum granulosum.

stratum basale
Layer of the epidermis whose cells divide and migrate toward the surface to form the upper layers, thus ensuring renewal of the epidermis.

nerve termination
Tactile receptor present in large numbers on the surface of the dermis.

arrector pili muscle
Muscle attached to a hair follicle and whose contraction raises the hair on end as a result of cold or fear.

sebaceous gland
Organ connected to a hair follicle secreting a fatty substance (sebum) that lubricates the hair and skin, making them impermeable to air and water.

Ruffini's corpuscle
Heat-sensitive tactile receptor present in large numbers in the dermis of the hairy regions; it reacts especially to firm continuous pressure.

nerve fiber
Structure formed of neuron extensions along which the skin's sensory information travels.

hair follicle
Small cavity of the dermis and hypodermis in which the hair root is implanted and which receives secretions from the sebaceous and sweat glands.

hair bulb
Enlarged terminal part of the follicle from which hair develops and whose base receives the papilla.

skin surface
Surface portion of the skin in contact with the air from which dead cells are regularly shed and replaced by new ce of the stratum basale.

epidermis
Surface layer of the skin covering and protecting the dermis; it contains proteins that make the skin impermeat and block ultraviolet rays.

connective tissue
Tissue rich in veins and nerves made up especially of collagen and elastin fibers that give the skin its elasticity and resistance.

dermis
Layer of skin enclosing tactile receptors ensuring nutrition and support of the epidermis.

capillary blood vessel
Very fine blood vessel connected to the arterial and venal networks; through it the blood and cells of the organism are exchanged.

adipose tissue
Tissue enclosing numerous fat cells, thermally insulating the organism and providing an energy reserve.

subcutaneous tissue
Tissue rich in veins and nerves at the base of the dermis enabling especially the absorption of shocks.

Pacinian corpuscle
Tactile receptor implanted in the deep dermis; it reacts to continuous vibrations and strong pressures.

sudoriferous duct
Duct carrying sweat produced by the sweat gland to the surface of the skin.

nerve
Bundle of nerve fibers carrying sensory information collected by the tactile receptors of the brain.

blood vessel
Membranous canal through which blood circulates in the organism, bringing in oxygen and nutrients and carrying away waste.

eccrine sweat gland
Sweat-secreting organ whose excretory duct opens onto the surface of the skin; the sweat glands help especially in the elimination of waste.

papilla
Cone-shaped formation borne by the dermis ensuring vascularization of the hair.

apocrine sweat gland
Sweat-secreting organ whose excretory duct opens into the hair follicle.

finger
Each of the five terminal parts of the hand containing numerous Meissner's corpuscles, giving them great sensitivity.

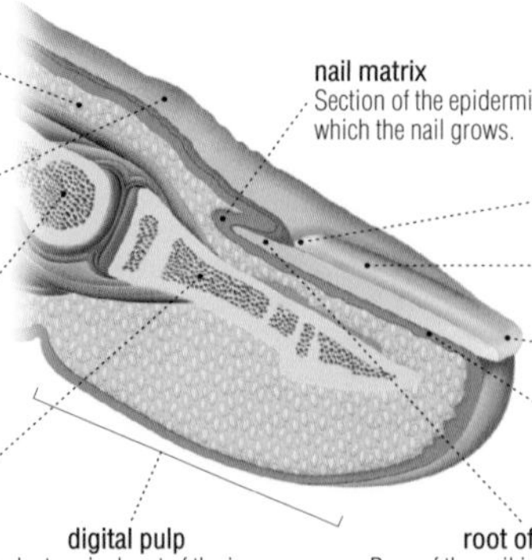

dermis
Layer of skin enclosing tactile receptors ensuring nutrition and support of the epidermis.

nail matrix
Section of the epidermis from which the nail grows.

lunula
Whitish section between the root and the body of the nail corresponding to the visible front portion of the matrix.

epidermis
Surface layer of the skin covering and protecting the dermis; it contains proteins that make the skin impermeable and block ultraviolet rays.

body of nail
Central pinkish section of the nail adhering to the nail bed.

middle phalanx
Second phalange of the finger between the proximal and distal phalanges.

free margin
Whitish terminal part of the nail extending beyond the finger.

distal phalanx
Last phalange of the finger bearing a nail.

digital pulp
Fleshy terminal part of the inner finger.

root of nail
Base of the nail implanted in the matrix and protected by a fold of skin (cuticle).

nail bed
Portion of the finger upon which the nail sits containing numerous blood vessels, thus nourishing the nail.

touch

hand

Terminal part of the upper limb having a tactile and prehensile function, with a thumb opposable to the other fingers.

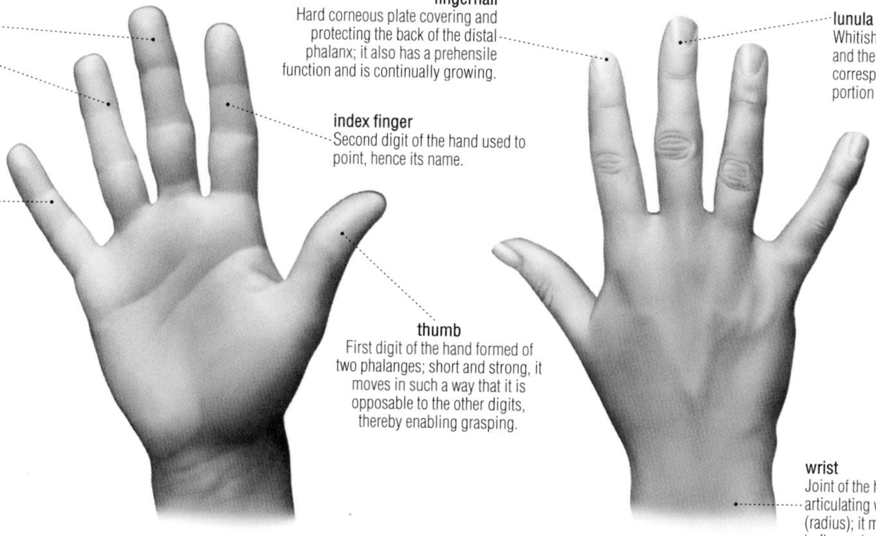

palm
Inner portion of the hand corresponding to the metacarpus and located between the wrist and the proximal phalanges of the fingers.
back
Outer part of the hand corresponding to the metacarpus and located between the wrist and the proximal phalanges of the fingers.
middle finger
Third and longest digit of the hand.
fingernail
Hard corneous plate covering and protecting the back of the distal phalanx; it also has a prehensile function and is continually growing.
lunula
Whitish section between the root and the body of the nail corresponding to the visible front portion of the matrix.
third finger
Fourth digit of the hand. Rings are worn on this finger, hence it is also called the ring finger.
index finger
Second digit of the hand used to point, hence its name.
little finger
Last and smallest of the fingers of the hand.
thumb
First digit of the hand formed of two phalanges; short and strong, it moves in such a way that it is opposable to the other digits, thereby enabling grasping.
wrist
Joint of the hand (carpus) articulating with the forearm (radius); it mainly enables the hand to flex and extend.

hearing

Sense that perceives sounds and maintains balance; the human ear is capable of distinguishing almost 400,000 sounds.

pinna

Soft cartilaginous outer portion of the ear located at the side of the head; it allows sounds to be collected.

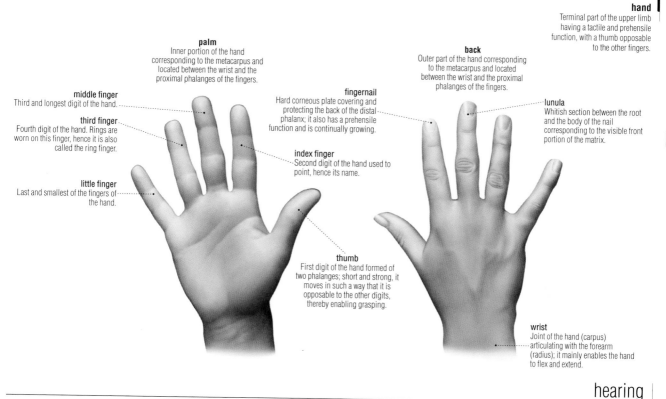

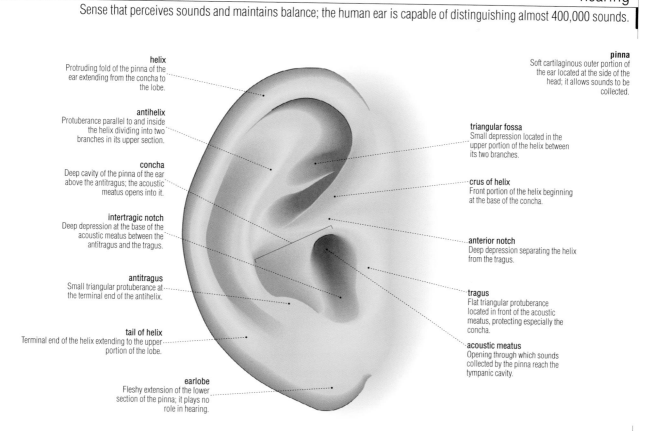

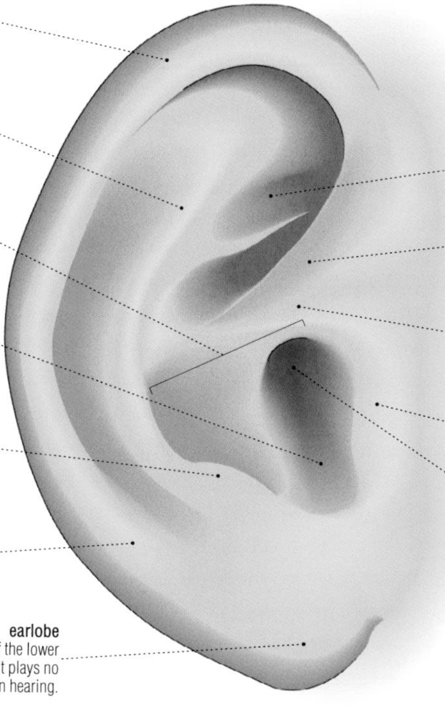

helix
Protruding fold of the pinna of the ear extending from the concha to the lobe.
antihelix
Protuberance parallel to and inside the helix dividing into two branches in its upper section.
triangular fossa
Small depression located in the upper portion of the helix between its two branches.
concha
Deep cavity of the pinna of the ear above the antitragus; the acoustic meatus opens into it.
crus of helix
Front portion of the helix beginning at the base of the concha.
intertragic notch
Deep depression at the base of the acoustic meatus between the antitragus and the tragus.
anterior notch
Deep depression separating the helix from the tragus.
antitragus
Small triangular protuberance at the terminal end of the antihelix.
tragus
Flat triangular protuberance located in front of the acoustic meatus, protecting especially the concha.
tail of helix
Terminal end of the helix extending to the upper portion of the lobe.
acoustic meatus
Opening through which sounds collected by the pinna reach the tympanic cavity.
earlobe
Fleshy extension of the lower section of the pinna; it plays no role in hearing.

hearing

structure of the ear
The ear is made up of three distinct parts; hearing is controlled by the inner ear, which contains the sensory organs.

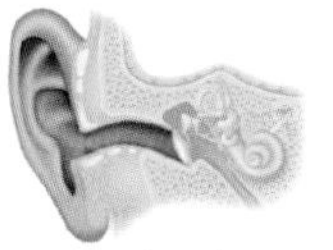

external ear
Visible portion of the ear enabling sounds to be collected and directed to the middle ear through the acoustic meatus.

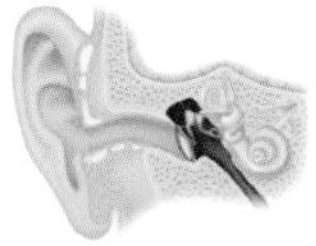

middle ear
Air-filled cavity hollowed out of the temporal bone; it receives sounds from the external ear, amplifies them through the auricles and transmits them to the internal ear.

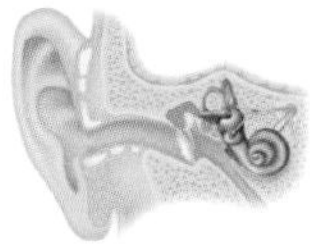

internal ear
Liquid-filled cavity hollowed out of the temporal bone that transforms sound vibrations into nerve influxes to be interpreted by the brain.

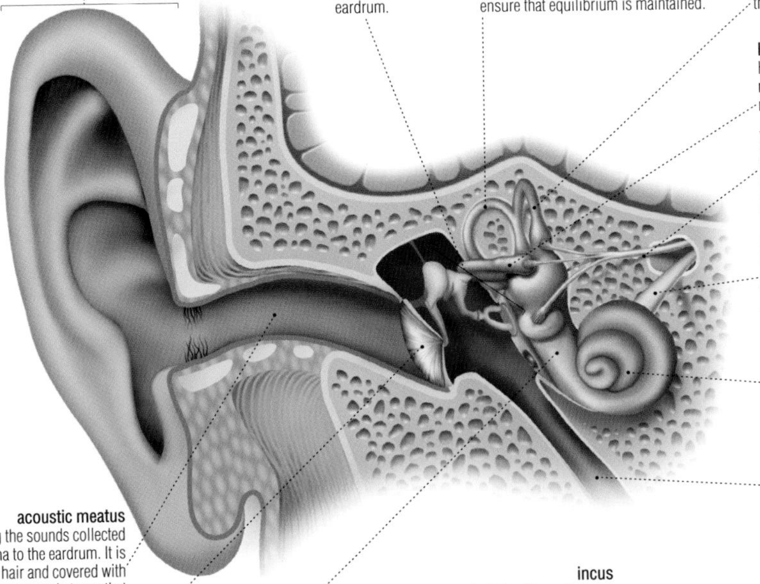

pinna
Soft cartilaginous outer portion of the ear located at the side of the head; it allows sounds to be collected.

auditory ossicles
The smallest bones in the human body, held in place by several muscles and ligaments; they amplify the vibrations of the eardrum.

posterior semicircular canal
Vertical canal parallel to the temporal bone; it monitors head movements to ensure that equilibrium is maintained.

superior semicircular canal
Vertical canal perpendicular to the temporal bone; it monitors head movements to ensure that equilibrium is maintained.

lateral semicircular canal
Horizontal canal; it monitors head movements to ensure that equilibrium is maintained.

vestibular nerve
Nerve transmitting messages related to equilibrium to the brain; it emanates from the vestibule and the semicircular canals.

cochlear nerve
Nerve transmitting auditory messages collected in the cochlea to the brain. The cochlear and vestibular nerves join to form the auditory nerve.

cochlea
Bony structure intended for hearing; it receives vibrations from the ossicles and transforms them into nervous impulses before transmitting them to the brain.

Eustachian tube
Tube connecting the middle ear to the nasopharynx; it allows outside air to pass through, thus equalizing air pressure on both sides of the eardrum.

acoustic meatus
Canal carrying the sounds collected by the pinna to the eardrum. It is lined with hair and covered with cerumen, a waxy substance that retains dust particles.

eardrum
Slender resistant elastic membrane; it vibrates when sound waves are received from the auditory canal, then transmits the waves to the ossicles.

vestibule
Bony structure into which the three semicircular canals open; with these canals, it is responsible for equilibrium.

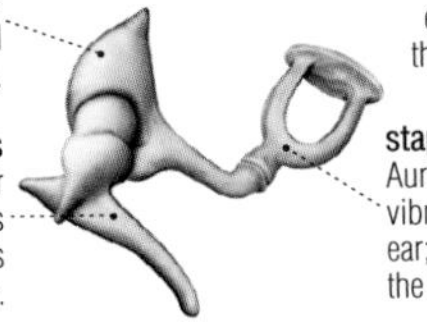

auditory ossicles
Each of the three small interarticulated bones of the middle ear that amplify the vibrations of the eardrum and transmit them to the internal ear.

incus
Auricle of the middle ear articulating with the malleus and the stapes.

malleus
Auricle of the middle ear transmitting vibrations to the incus from the ear drum (to which it is attached).

stapes
Auricle of the middle ear transmitting vibrations from the incus to the interr ear; at about .15 in long, the stapes is the smallest bone in the body.

smell and taste

Since the oral and nasal cavities are connected, the olfactory sense affects taste. The human being can distinguish four basic flavors and almost 10,000 odors.

mouth
Anterior cavity of the digestive tract; it has a role in ingesting food, tasting, breathing and speaking.

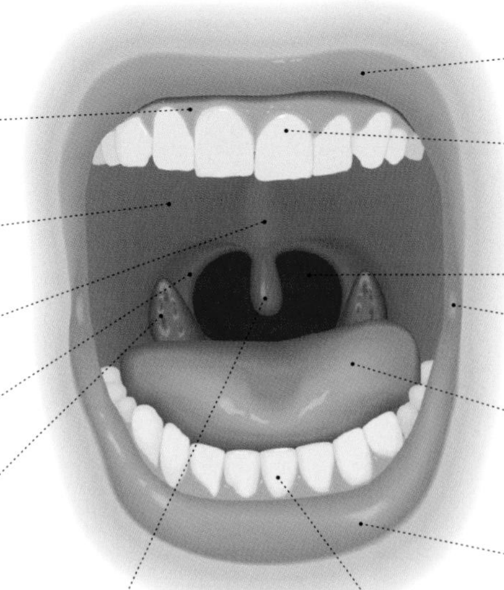

gum
Thick section of the mucous membrane of the mouth that is rich in blood vessels and nerves; it covers the edge of the dental alveolus and adheres to the neck.

hard palate
Bony section of the wall dividing the mouth from the nasal cavity; it is extended by the soft palate.

soft palate
Muscular membranous section of the wall separating the mouth from the nasal cavity; it has a role especially in ingesting food and speaking.

palatoglossal arch
Muscular lateral fold of the posterior edge of the soft palate.

tonsil
Lymphoid structure (rich in white blood cells) involved in protecting the respiratory tract by fighting bacterial infections.

uvula
Fleshy movable appendage that is an extension of the posterior edge of the soft palate; it aids in ingesting food and speaking.

inferior dental arch
Arch formed by the set of teeth of the mandible.

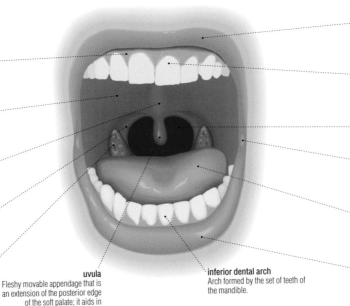

upper lip
Movable muscular fold forming the upper contour of the mouth; the main roles of the lips are protecting the teeth and helping in speech.

superior dental arch
Arch formed by the set of teeth of the maxilla.

isthmus of fauces
Orifice by which the mouth connects with the pharynx (meeting point of the respiratory and digestive tracts) enabling food to reach the esophagus.

commissure of lips of mouth
Each of the two juncture points of the upper and lower lips.

tongue
Flexible muscular structure of the oral cavity; it helps in tasting, masticating and ingesting food, and also facilitates speech.

lower lip
Movable muscular fold forming the lower contour of the mouth.

external nose

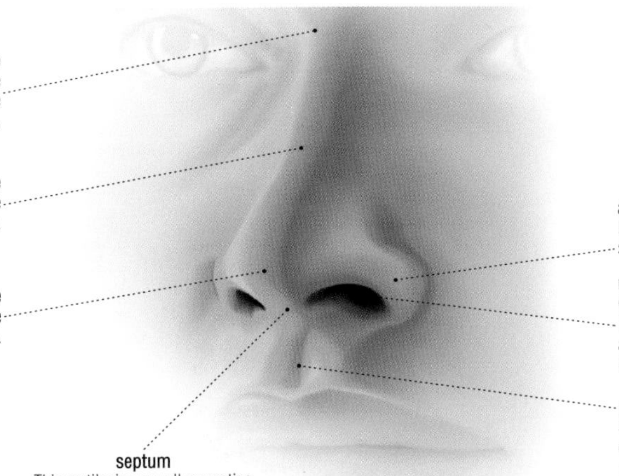

root of nose
Portion of the face between the eyes from which the nose protrudes.

dorsum of nose
Protruding median line of the nose extending from the root to the lobe.

tip of nose
Round protuberance formed by the lower terminal part of the nose.

septum
Thin cartilaginous wall separating the two nasal fossae; it is an extension of the bones of the nose.

ala
Lower cartilaginous portion of the side of the nose next to the nostril.

naris
Outer orifice of the nasal fossae lined with hairs that filter inhaled air, thus preventing the penetration of foreign bodies.

philtrum
Small cutaneous depression extending from the lower part of the nose to the upper lip.

nasal fossae

Each of two cavities separated by a middle partition; they assist in olfaction, respiration and speech.

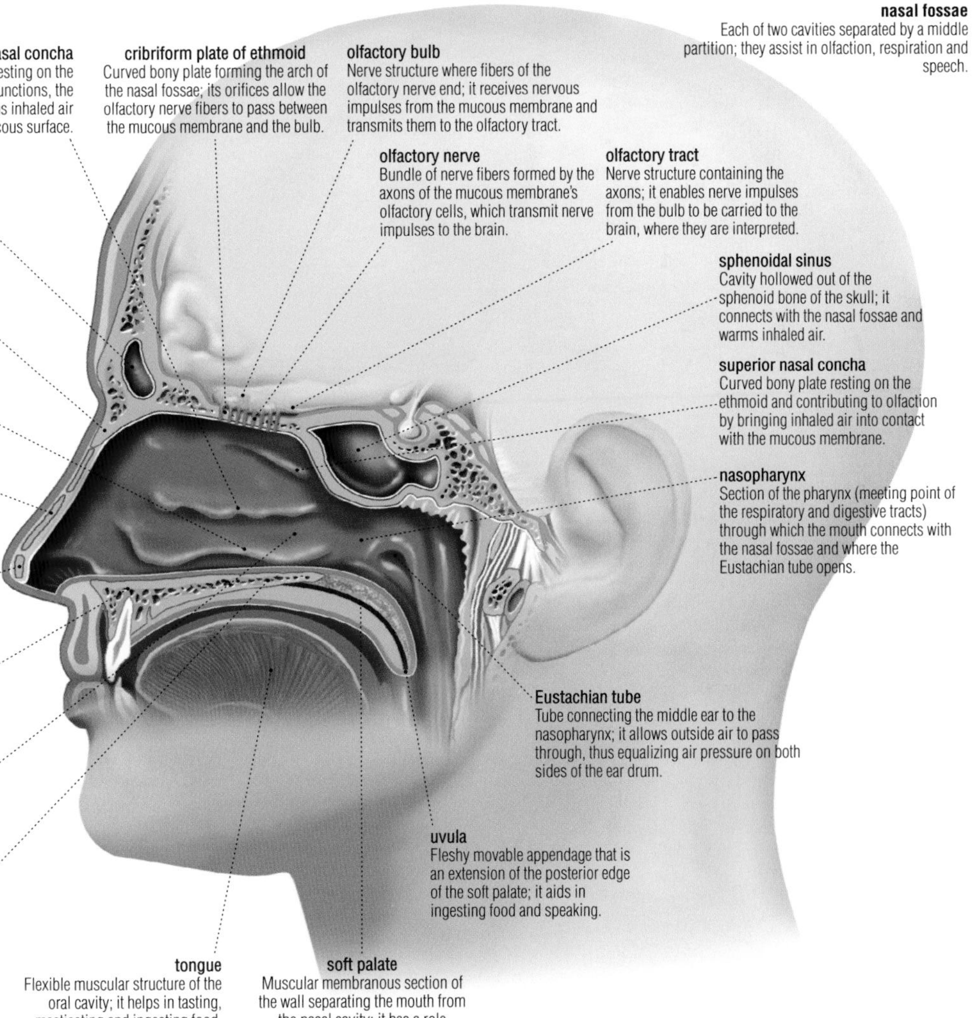

middle nasal concha
Curved bony plate resting on the ethmoid. Among its functions, the nasal chamber warms inhaled air by increasing the mucous surface.

cribriform plate of ethmoid
Curved bony plate forming the arch of the nasal fossae; its orifices allow the olfactory nerve fibers to pass between the mucous membrane and the bulb.

olfactory bulb
Nerve structure where fibers of the olfactory nerve end; it receives nervous impulses from the mucous membrane and transmits them to the olfactory tract.

frontal sinus
Cavity hollowed out of the frontal bone of the skull; it connects with the nasal fossae and warms inhaled air.

olfactory nerve
Bundle of nerve fibers formed by the axons of the mucous membrane's olfactory cells, which transmit nerve impulses to the brain.

olfactory tract
Nerve structure containing the axons; it enables nerve impulses from the bulb to be carried to the brain, where they are interpreted.

nasal bone
Small flat bone forming the skeleton of the root of the nose; the two nasal bones join along the bridge of the nose.

sphenoidal sinus
Cavity hollowed out of the sphenoid bone of the skull; it connects with the nasal fossae and warms inhaled air.

inferior nasal concha
Curved bony plate attached to the lateral wall of the nasal fossae.

superior nasal concha
Curved bony plate resting on the ethmoid and contributing to olfaction by bringing inhaled air into contact with the mucous membrane.

septal cartilage of nose
Plate of resistant elastic tissue; it extends the bones of the nose and separates the nasal fossae.

nasopharynx
Section of the pharynx (meeting point of the respiratory and digestive tracts) through which the mouth connects with the nasal fossae and where the Eustachian tube opens.

greater alar cartilage
Thin plate of resistant elastic tissue supporting the bridge of the nose and delimiting the contour of the nostril.

maxilla
Toothed bone forming the jaw. The upper jawbone forms a part of the palate. The lower jawbone is the only movable bone in the head.

Eustachian tube
Tube connecting the middle ear to the nasopharynx; it allows outside air to pass through, thus equalizing air pressure on both sides of the ear drum.

olfactory mucosa
Tissue lining a portion of the nasal fossae and containing olfactory cells, which detect odors and release nerve impulses.

uvula
Fleshy movable appendage that is an extension of the posterior edge of the soft palate; it aids in ingesting food and speaking.

hard palate
Bony section of the wall dividing the mouth from the nasal cavity; it is extended by the soft palate.

tongue
Flexible muscular structure of the oral cavity; it helps in tasting, masticating and ingesting food, and also facilitates speech.

soft palate
Muscular membranous section of the wall separating the mouth from the nasal cavity; it has a role especially in ingesting food and speaking.

smell and taste

dorsum of tongue

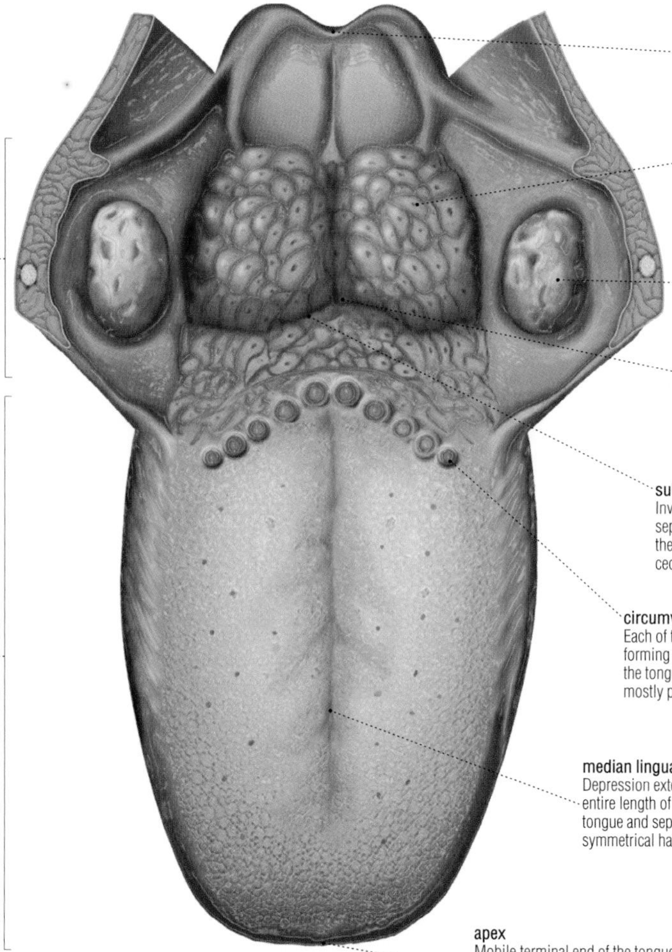
epiglottis
Movable cartilaginous plate ensuring that the larynx closes during ingestion of food so that food cannot enter the respiratory tract.
lingual tonsil
Lymphoid structure (rich in white blood cells) located at the base of the tongue; it assists in immune defense.
root
Part that fixes the tongue to the mandible and the hyoid bone of the skull; it is also joined on each side to the walls of the pharynx.
palatine tonsil
Lymphoid structure (rich in white blood cells) located on each side of the base of the tongue; it protects the respiratory tract by fighting bacteria.
foramen cecum
Small depression located at the base of the tongue, at the top of the sulcus terminalis.
sulcus terminalis
Inverted V-shaped depression separating the base of the body of the tongue, topped by the foramen cecum.
body
Free mobile portion of the tongue composed mostly of mucous-covered muscles and bearing the taste buds.
circumvallate papilla
Each of the large taste buds (about 10) forming a lingual V at the back of the body of the tongue ensuring the taste function; they mostly perceive bitter flavors.
median lingual sulcus
Depression extending over the entire length of the body of the tongue and separating it into two symmetrical halves.
apex
Mobile terminal end of the tongue; it mostly perceives sweet flavors.

taste receptors

The mucous membrane of the tongue is composed of small protuberances, lingual taste buds, distinguished by their particular sensitivity to one of the basic flavors: sweet, salty, sour, bitter.

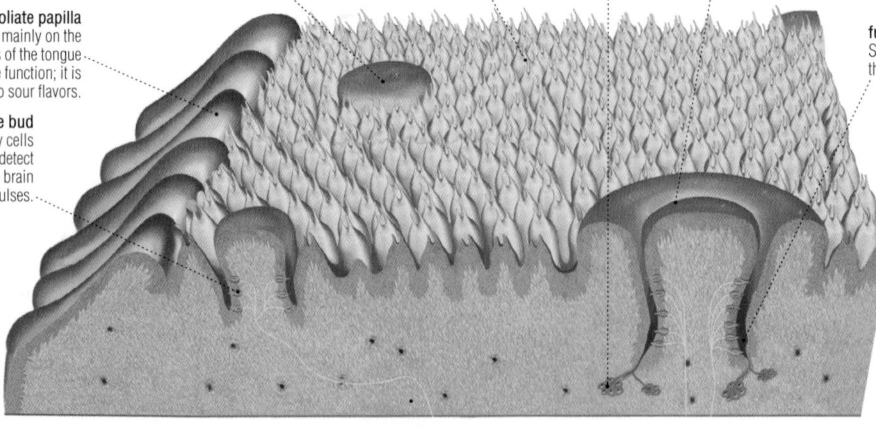
fungiform papilla
Mushroom-shaped taste bud occurring in large numbers at the apex and on the sides of the tongue and having a taste function; it reacts mainly to sweet and salty flavors.
filiform papilla
Cone-shaped taste bud covering the rear of the tongue; its function is solely tactile. These taste buds give the tongue its velvety appearance.
salivary gland
Each of the three pairs of saliva-secreting organs responsible for moistening food so that the taste buds can perceive its taste.
circumvallate papilla
Each of the large taste buds (about 10) forming a lingual V at the back of the body of the tongue ensuring the taste function; they mostly perceive bitter flavors.
foliate papilla
Taste bud located mainly on the posterior lateral edges of the tongue and having a taste function; it is most sensitive to sour flavors.
furrow
Saliva-filled depression delimiting the lingual taste buds.
taste bud
Organ of taste formed of sensory cells that, in contact with saliva, detect flavors and transmit them to the brain in the form of nerve impulses.

sight

The human being possesses a highly developed visual sensitivity, far superior to that of the other senses.

eye
Organ of vision serving to perceive shapes, distances, colors and motion.

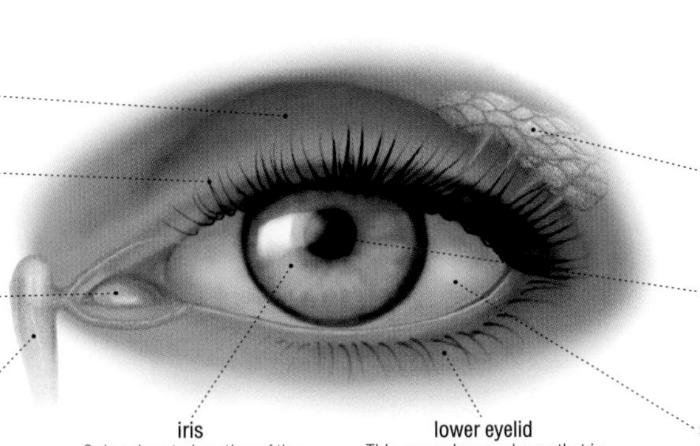

upper eyelid
Thin movable muscular membrane descending from the upper edge of the eye. The eyelids protect the eye, emit tears and discharge waste. Batting of the eyelashes is very frequent.

eyelash
Each of the hairs lining the free edge of the eyelid; they prevent dust and other particles from entering the eye.

lacrimal caruncle
Small reddish mass located at the inner corner of the eye formed by the fold of the conjunctiva.

lacrimal canal
Duct opening out into the nasal fossae through which tears produced by the tear glands are discharged.

iris
Colored central portion of the eyeball composed of muscles whose dilation or contraction controls the opening of the pupil.

lower eyelid
Thin muscular membrane that is translucent and movable; it rises from the lower edge of the eye to protect and cleanse it.

lacrimal gland
Organ secreting tears that flow over the surface of the eye to lubricate and cleanse it (eliminate dust and germs).

pupil
Central orifice of the eye whose opening varies to regulate the amount of light entering the eye; light causes the pupil to contract.

sclera
Strong fibrous opaque membrane covered by the conjunctiva; it surrounds the eyeball and protects the inner structures.

eyeball
Enclosed in a bony cavity (orbit) and moved by six muscles, this complex organ collects light signals and transmits them to the brain to form images.

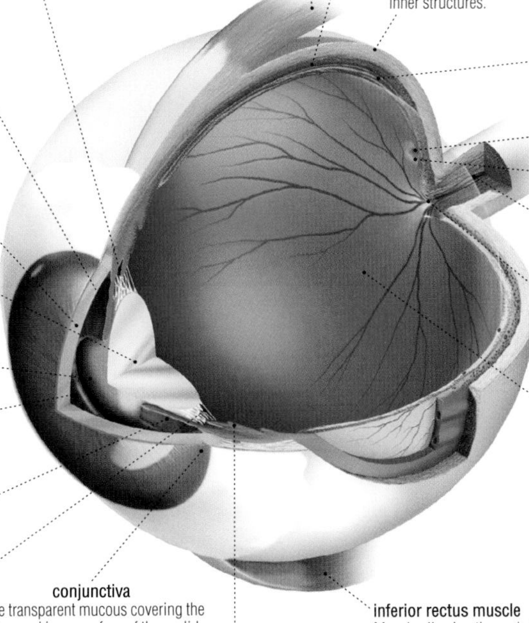

superior rectus muscle
Muscle allowing the eyeball to move upward.

choroid
Richly veined membrane located between the sclera and the retina, to which it carries nutrients and oxygen.

posterior chamber
Cavity of the eye between the iris and the lens containing the aqueous humor.

sclera
Strong fibrous opaque membrane covered by the conjunctiva; it surrounds the eyeball and protects the inner structures.

anterior chamber
Cavity of the eye between the cornea and the iris containing the aqueous humor.

cornea
Transparent fibrous membrane extending the sclera and whose curved shape makes light rays converge toward the inside of the eye.

lens
Transparent elastic area of the eye; focuses images on the retina to obtain clear vision.

pupil
Central orifice of the eye whose opening varies to regulate the amount of light entering the eye; light causes the pupil to contract.

aqueous humor
Transparent liquid contained in the anterior and posterior chambers; it nourishes the iris and maintains the pressure and shape of the eye.

iris
Colored central portion of the eyeball composed of muscles whose dilation or contraction controls the opening of the pupil.

suspensory ligament
Fibrous tissue connecting the ciliary body to the lens, holding it in place inside the eyeball.

conjunctiva
Fine transparent mucous covering the sclera and inner surface of the eyelid; it facilitates sliding thus giving the eyeball its wide range of movement.

ciliary body
Muscle tissue secreting the aqueous humor; its muscles enable the lens to change shape to adapt vision for near or far.

inferior rectus muscle
Muscle allowing the eyeball to move downward.

retina
Inner membrane at the back of the eye covered in light-sensitive nerve cells (photoreceptors); these transform light into an electrical impulse that is carried to the optic nerve.

fovea
Central depression of the yellow spot composed entirely of cones; the place where visual acuity is at its maximum.

macula
Area of the retina where the cones are concentrated; it plays an essential role in day vision and the perception of colors.

optic nerve
Nerve formed by the juncture of the nerve fibers of the retina; it carries visual information to the brain, where it is interpreted.

papilla
Protuberance formed by the anterior terminal part of the optic nerve in the retina; it has no light-sensitive cells and thus no vision. It is also called the blind spot.

vitreous body
Transparent gelatinous mass (almost 90% of the eye); it maintains constant intraocular pressure so the eye keeps its shape.

photoreceptors

Nerve cells of the retina that convert light into nerve impulses; these are transmitted to the brain, which decodes them and forms an image.

cone
Photoreceptor active in full light and responsible for perception of specific colors. There are three types: red-yellow, green and blue-violet.

rod
Photoreceptor active in dim light and responsible for night vision (in black and white).

FOOD AND KITCHEN

180 **Food**

Humans eat a wide variety of foodstuffs derived directly or indirectly from vegetable or animal sources.

222 **Kitchen**

Cooking, the main activity in a kitchen, includes anything to do with preserving, preparing or eating food.

supermarket

A large self-service store that sells food and various everyday household goods; the part accessible to shoppers is surrounded by service areas reserved for storage and for preparing and preserving merchandise.

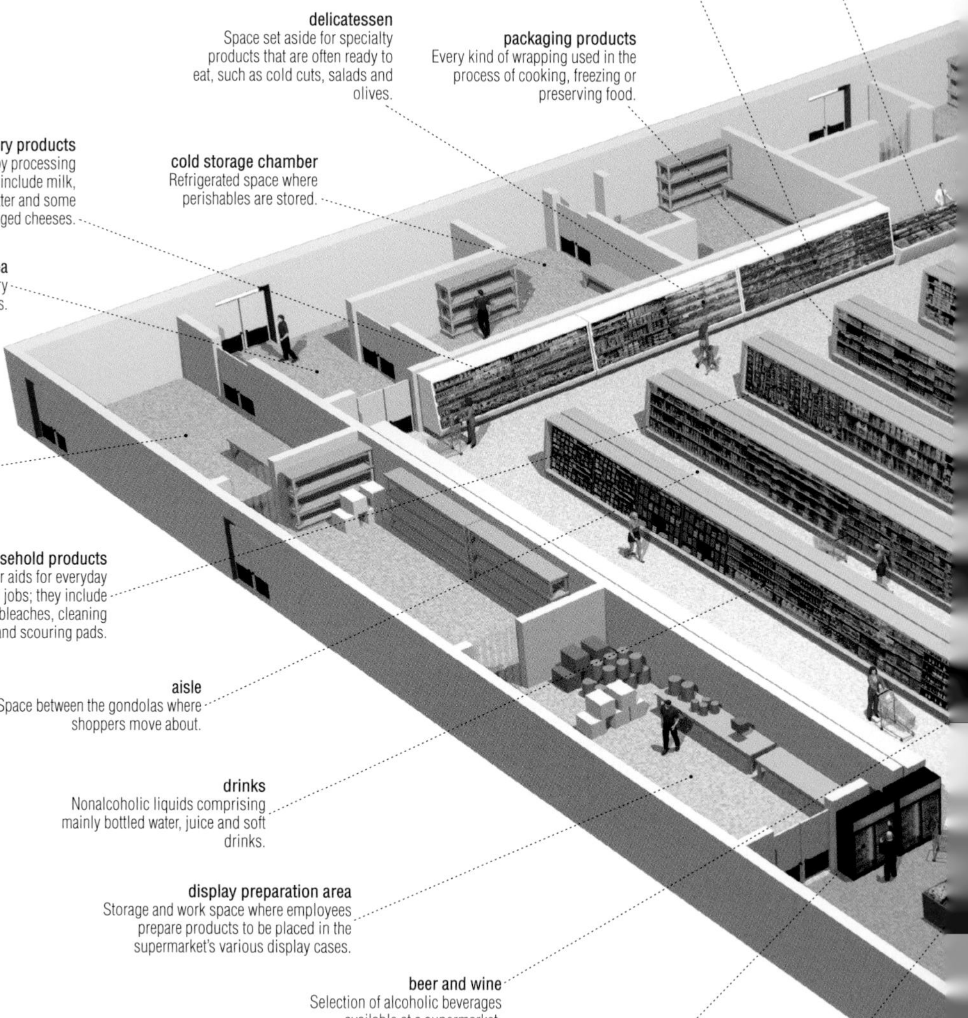

fresh meat counter
Glass display case containing pieces of meat or poultry that the butcher cuts and wraps upon request.

self-service meat counter
Display case containing pieces of meat or poultry prepared and packaged in individual or family-sized portions.

delicatessen
Space set aside for specialty products that are often ready to eat, such as cold cuts, salads and olives.

packaging products
Every kind of wrapping used in the process of cooking, freezing or preserving food.

dairy products
Foodstuffs produced by processing fresh milk; they generally include milk, cream, yogurt, butter and some prepackaged cheeses.

cold storage chamber
Refrigerated space where perishables are stored.

dairy products receiving area
Refrigerated space designed to receive dairy products.

receiving area
Space designed to receive merchandise.

household products
Products or aids for everyday household jobs; they include detergents, bleaches, cleaning products and scouring pads.

aisle
Space between the gondolas where shoppers move about.

drinks
Nonalcoholic liquids comprising mainly bottled water, juice and soft drinks.

display preparation area
Storage and work space where employees prepare products to be placed in the supermarket's various display cases.

beer and wine
Selection of alcoholic beverages available at a supermarket.

reach-in freezer
Display case used to keep drinks cool.

fruits and vegetables
Plant products sold as food, offered in bulk or prepackaged.

cold storage chamber
Refrigerated space where perishables are stored.

seafood
Section where fish and shellfish are offered for sale at a self-service counter or prepared to order.

gondola
Long unit with shelves; it is used to display self-service products.

convenience food
Food prepared and presented in such a way that it can be served quickly and easily.

frozen food storage
Refrigerated space where frozen food is stored.

frozen foods
Various foodstuffs stored at very low temperatures to preserve their quality and nutritional content for as long as possible.

cheese counter
Glass display case holding a variety of whole cheeses that the employee cuts and wraps upon request.

prepared foods
Various foodstuffs, sometimes in individual portions, prepared on-site or by a specialty supplier; they are often ready to eat.

bakery
Section where bread, pastries and other baked goods are sold, whether baked on the premises or not.

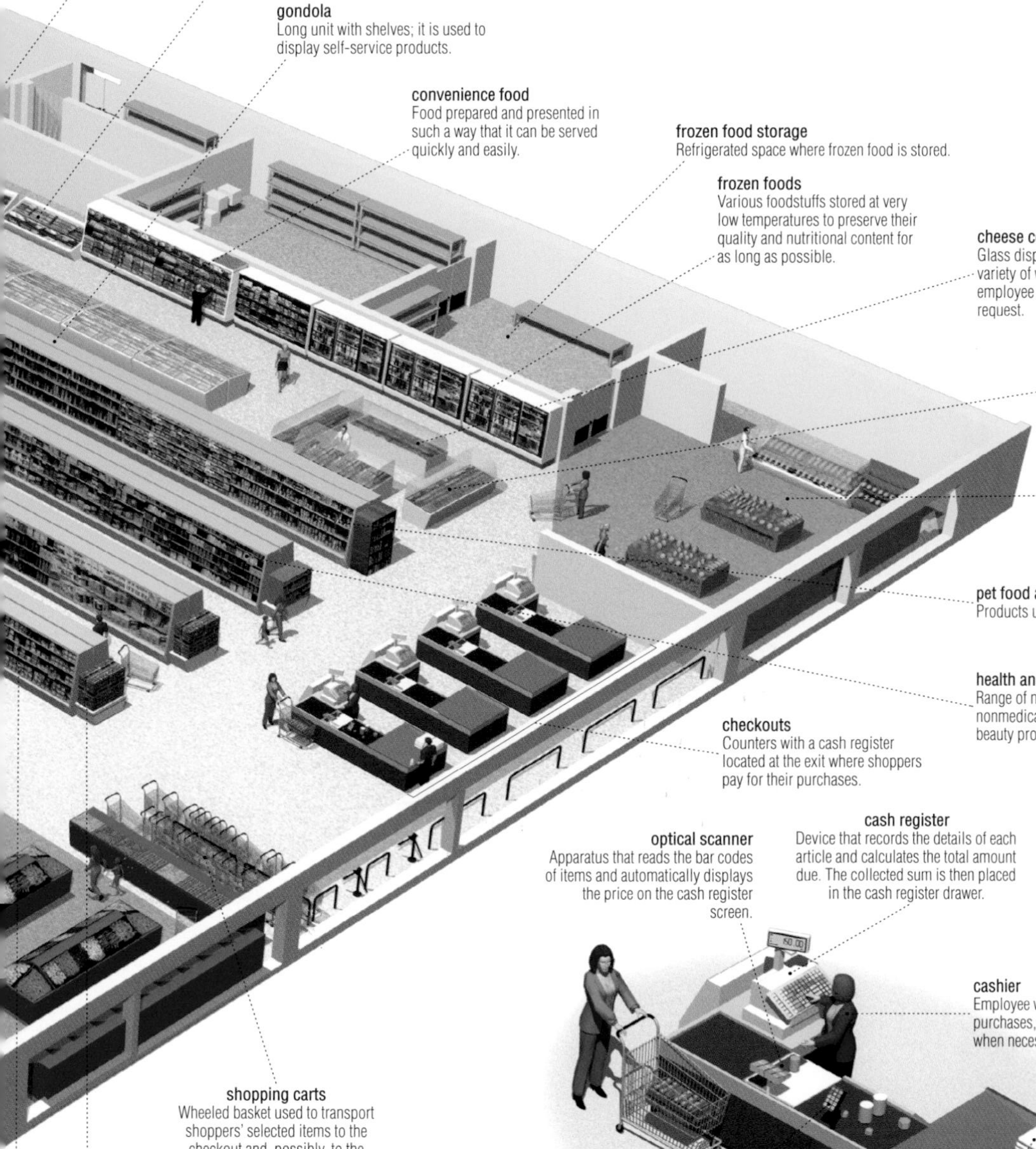

pet food and supplies
Products used to feed and care for pets.

health and beauty care
Range of nonprescription drugs, and nonmedicated personal hygiene, health and beauty products.

checkouts
Counters with a cash register located at the exit where shoppers pay for their purchases.

optical scanner
Apparatus that reads the bar codes of items and automatically displays the price on the cash register screen.

cash register
Device that records the details of each article and calculates the total amount due. The collected sum is then placed in the cash register drawer.

checkout
Counter with a cash register located at the exit where shoppers pay for their purchases.

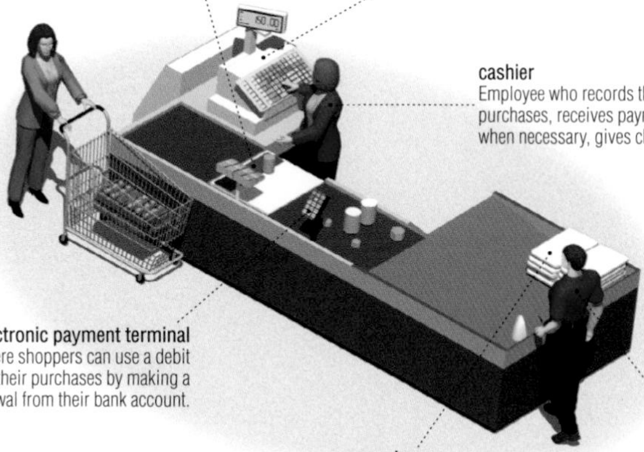

cashier
Employee who records the purchases, receives payment and, when necessary, gives change.

shopping carts
Wheeled basket used to transport shoppers' selected items to the checkout and, possibly, to the parking lot.

end aisle display
End of a gondola; it is used to highlight certain items that are on sale or whose sales need to be increased.

electronic payment terminal
Apparatus where shoppers can use a debit card to pay for their purchases by making a withdrawal from their bank account.

canned goods
Prepared foodstuffs, preserved in airtight cans or jars using a process that allows them to be kept for long periods of time.

grocery bags
Paper or flexible plastic containers in which the shoppers' purchases are packed and carried.

bagger
Employee whose main duty is to bag the shopper's purchases and, sometimes, to carry them out to the shopper's car.

farmstead

All the structures belonging to an agricultural concern and used as dwellings or in its operation.

permanent pasture
Fenced-in grassy tract of land set aside for cattle to graze on.

fallow
Arable land temporarily left unsown to allow the soil to replenish its reserves.

hayloft
Part of the barn, often the equivalent of an attic, where hay is stored to protect it from bad weather.

fodder corn
Variety of corn used as cattle feed.

dairy
Room where milk is stored and refrigerated before it is collected; it is also the place where milk is converted into butter and other by-products.

fence
Wooden or metal barrier used to delimit a section of land so it can be used for a particular purpose.

meadow
Ground covered in grass, which the farmer mows to produce fodder (hay, alfalfa, etc.) for cattle.

cowshed
Building where bovines are housed; the animals are often separated by age or type (raised for meat or for milk).

tower silo
Cylindrical structure used to store silage; it is always filled from the top, using a specially constructed apparatus.

barn
Building used mainly to store harvested crops, straw and hay.

bunker silo
Long flat structure used to store silage; filling it requires no specialized equipment.

machinery shed
Building usually meant to house farm machinery.

hen house
Building where poultry are housed; a distinction is often made between laying units and fattening units.

pigsty
Building used to house pigs usually raised to be slaughtere

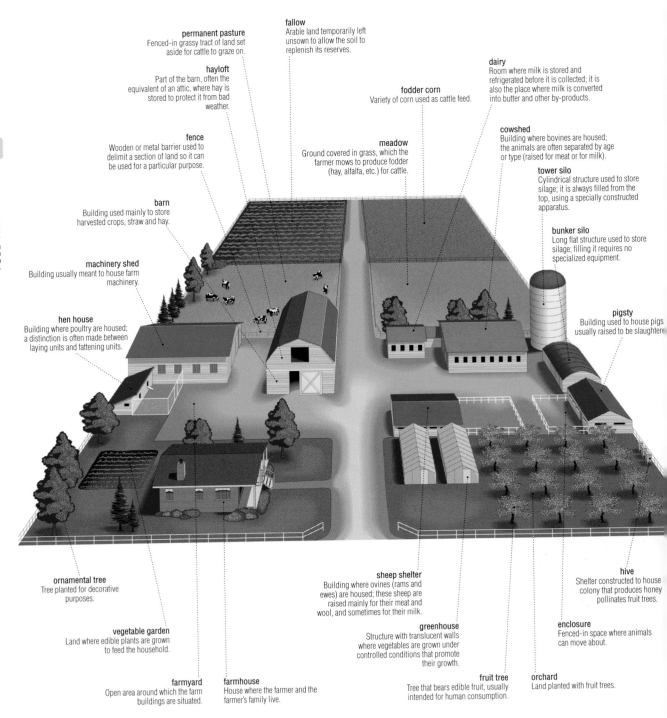

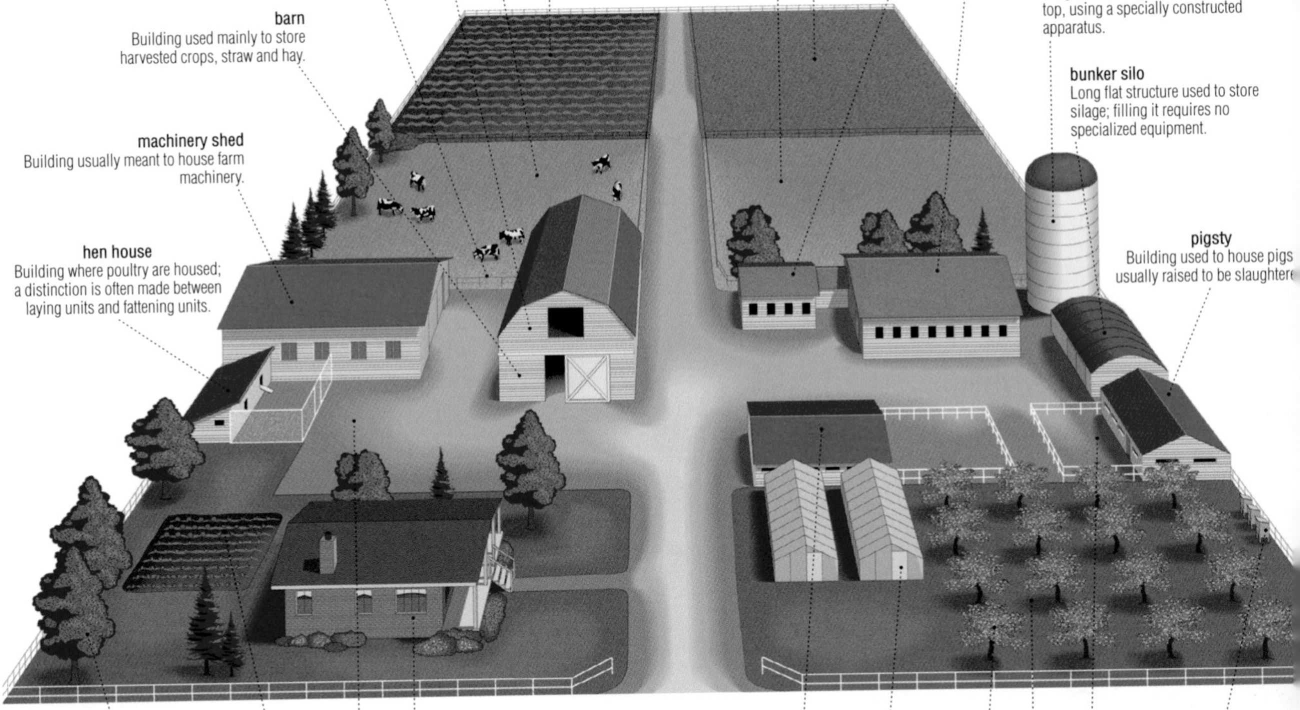

ornamental tree
Tree planted for decorative purposes.

sheep shelter
Building where ovines (rams and ewes) are housed; these sheep are raised mainly for their meat and wool, and sometimes for their milk.

hive
Shelter constructed to house colony that produces honey pollinates fruit trees.

vegetable garden
Land where edible plants are grown to feed the household.

greenhouse
Structure with translucent walls where vegetables are grown under controlled conditions that promote their growth.

enclosure
Fenced-in space where animals can move about.

farmyard
Open area around which the farm buildings are situated.

farmhouse
House where the farmer and the farmer's family live.

fruit tree
Tree that bears edible fruit, usually intended for human consumption.

orchard
Land planted with fruit trees.

mushrooms

Vegetable that grows in damp cool places; its edible varieties are served as condiments or as an ingredient in a variety of foods.

truffle
Underground mushroom hard to find and perceived as a luxury food; it is usually associated with game and poultry.

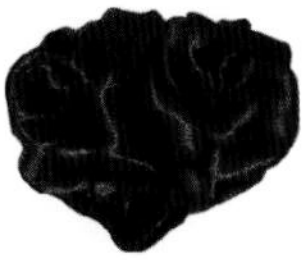

wood ear
Its tasteless gelatinous flesh is popular in Asia; it is usually eaten in soups or with vegetables.

royal agaric
Equally flavorful raw or cooked, it has been famous since ancient times; it is not to be confused with the poisonous fly agaric, which it resembles.

delicious lactarius
Secretes an orange milk when broken open; it is used primarily in spicy sauces, especially in Spain and the south of France.

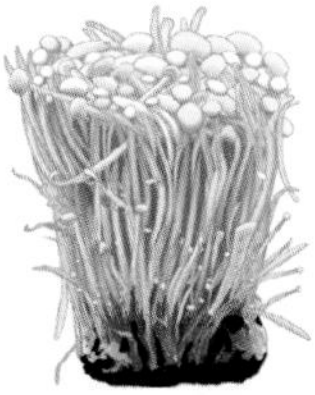

enoki mushroom
Long-stemmed, soft-fleshed resistant mushroom very popular in Asia; it is eaten raw, in salads, or cooked, in soups and Oriental dishes.

oyster mushroom
Grows on trees or on dead wood; its soft white flesh is a valued ingredient in sauces, where it can substitute for the cultivated mushroom.

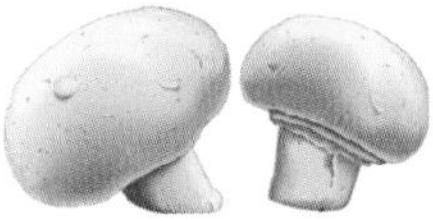

cultivated mushroom
The most widely cultivated and consumed mushroom; it is eaten raw, in salads or with dips, or cooked, primarily in sauces and on pizza.

green russula
Its white brittle flesh has an aroma of hazelnut; it can be eaten raw or cooked, preferably grilled.

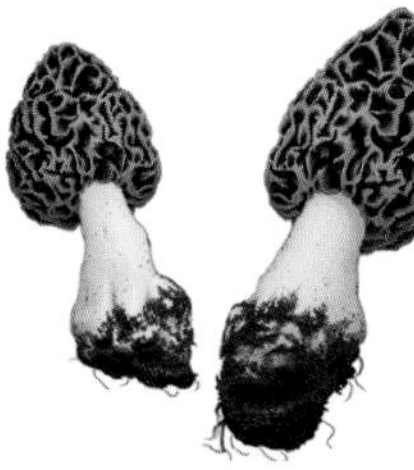

morel
The darker the specimen, the more flavorful its thin fragrant flesh; it should be thoroughly cooked to eliminate toxic substances.

edible boletus
Squat, it can grow up to 10 in in height and diameter; it is usually cooked in oil, braised or served in an omelette.

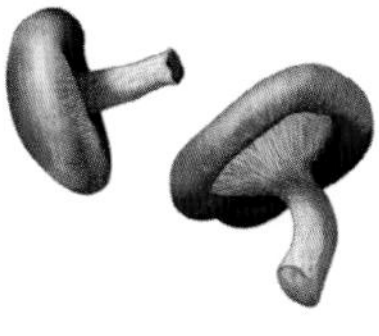

shiitake mushroom
The equivalent of the cultivated mushroom in Japan, where it is widely grown for use in Oriental dishes and sauces and for its therapeutic value.

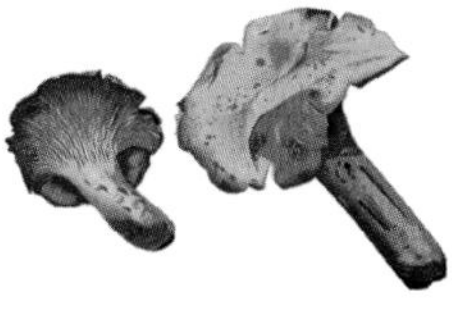

chanterelle
Pleasantly fragrant and valued by gourmets, especially those in Europe; it is served most often with meat or omelettes.

seaweed

Usually aquatic vegetables used in cooking or as dietary supplements; they are primarily produced and eaten by the Japanese.

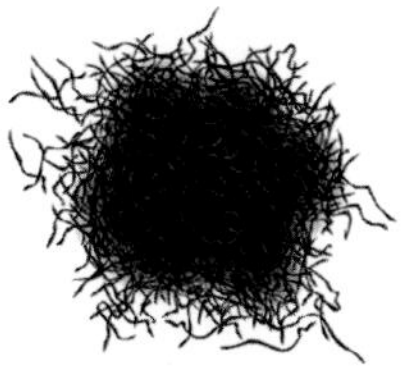

arame
Milder and less crunchy than hijiki, it is used mainly in salads and soups or served fried as a side vegetable.

wakame
Popular with the Japanese, it is rich in calcium and has a delicate texture and flavor; among its many uses, it is a often served with legume dishes.

kombu
Eaten since ancient times, it is sold in large blackish strips; it is used primarily as an ingredient in broth or to make a kind of tea.

spirulina
Microscopic freshwater alga, rich in nutrients (protein, iron, magnesium); it is used mainly as a dietary supplement.

Irish moss
Plentiful in the North Atlantic, it can only be eaten cooked; also produces carrageen, a substance used to thicken certain dishes.

hijiki
These dried twigs expand when soaked, resembling black, somewhat crunchy noodles; they are often served as a vegetable.

sea lettuce
Resembles lettuce leaves in taste and appearance; its soft leaves are eaten raw in salads or cooked in soups.

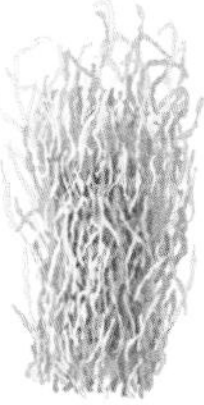

agar-agar
Translucent strips derived from red algae, which is melted to produce a jelly that can replace gelatin in numerous recipes.

nori
Purplish alga that turns black when dried; usually sold in thin dried sheets, it is used mainly to make sushi.

dulse
Iron-rich, it has long been eaten by people living along Europe's coasts; it enhances soups and salads with its soft texture and strong flavor.

vegetables

Plants used as foodstuffs; a simple way to classify vegetables is to group them according to their edible part. The sweet fruit category of plants constitutes another food category (fruits).

bulb vegetables

The main edible part of these vegetables is their bulb, the underground structure where the plant's nutrient reserves are stored.

leek
The white part is the most popular, but the green part adds flavor to puréed soups and stews; it is often combined with potatoes in a cold soup called vichyssoise.

green onion
Mild onion picked before fully ripe; it is usually sold with the stem, in bunches. It is often eaten raw in salads or cooked in sautéed dishes.

scallion
Its bulb is less developed than that of the green onion; the white part is used like the onion and the green is used to season a variety of dishes.

shallot
It has a more subtle flavor than the onion or the chive; it is eaten raw or cooked and often used as a flavoring ingredient in sauces.

water chestnut
The aquatic bulb of a Chinese plant; its white crunchy flesh is an important ingredient in many Asiar dishes.

garlic
The bulb is composed of bulblets called cloves; the germ at its center can make garlic difficult to digest.

chive
Smallest member of the onion family; its stem is used primarily tc season various hot and cold dishes.

yellow onion
The most common onion, widely used as a flavoring ingredient, either raw or cooked; it is also the essential ingredient in onion soup.

red onion
The sweetest of the onions, it is often eaten raw, in salads or sandwiches.

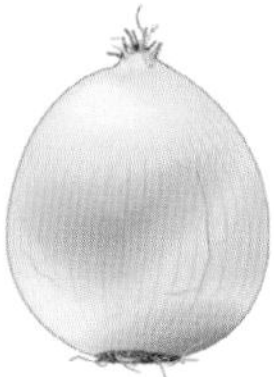

white onion
Mild and sweet, this onion is widely used as a flavoring ingredient; it is often eaten raw or deep-fried in rings.

pearl onion
Small white onion picked before fully ripe; it is primarily used to make pickles or as an ingredient i stews such as boeuf bourguignon

tuber vegetables

Tubers that are eaten like vegetables; they consist of underground growths containing the plant's nutrient reserves.

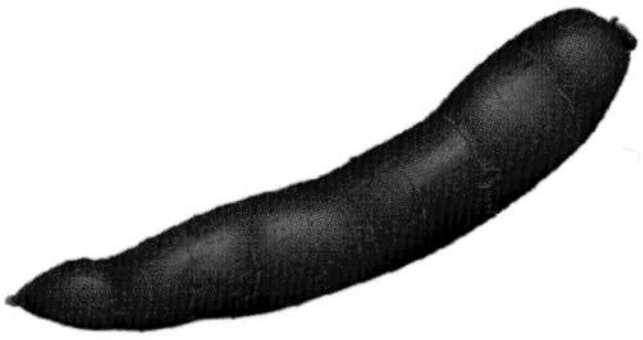

cassava
The sweet variety is eaten like the potato; the bitter one is used to make tapioca.

crosne
Native to Asia, where it is very popular although little known elsewhere; it has a slightly sweet flavor and is used and prepared like the potato.

taro
Its starchy, sweet flesh is a staple in several tropical countries; eaten raw, preferably very hot and prepared like the potato.

jicama
Its flesh is sweet, crunchy and juicy; it is eaten raw in salads, as an hors d'oeuvre or with dips; it adds a crunchy element to cooked dishes.

yam
A staple food in many countries, especially in South America and the West Indies, where it is eaten cooked, prepared like the potato.

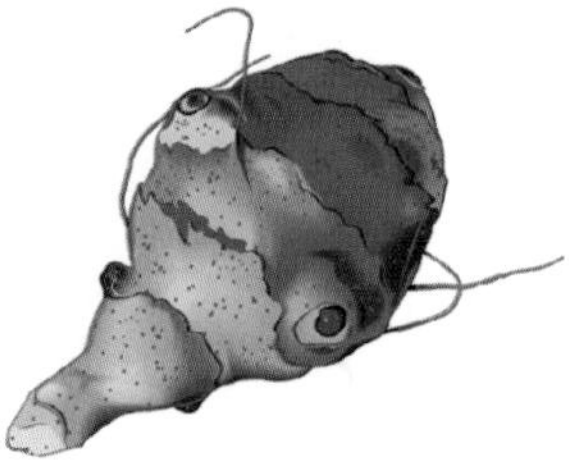

Jerusalem artichoke
Eaten raw, cooked or marinated; it has sweet, crunchy, juicy flesh.

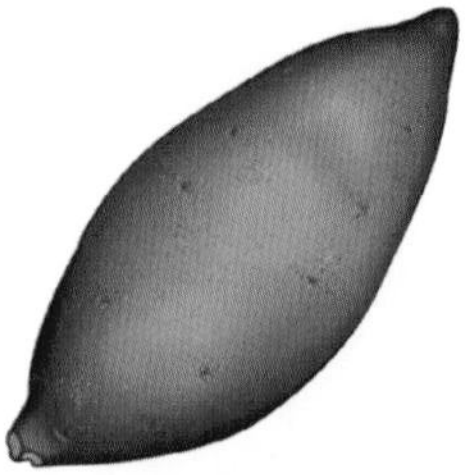

sweet potato
Sweeter than the potato and not of the same family; a staple of Creole cooking.

potato
The best-known tuber; eaten especially as a vegetable side dish, either steamed, deep-fried or mashed.

stalk vegetables

Edible plants whose stems are consumed like vegetables; the leaves of some varieties are also edible.

asparagus
Often thought of as a luxury, it is picked before fully ripe; whether served hot or cold, it is always cooked.

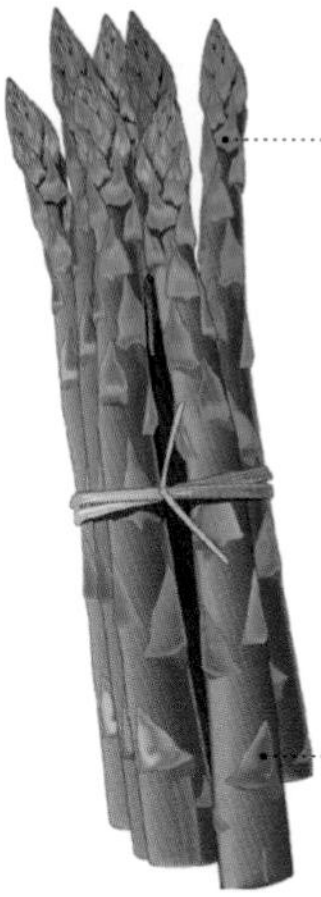

tip
Top end of the spear; the most valued part of the asparagus for cooking.

spear
Young asparagus shoot that constitutes the plant's edible part and grows out of an underground stem; its hard end is usually removed before cooking.

bundle
A number of asparagus spears tied together; asparagus is usually sold in this way.

Swiss chard
A member of the beet family, grown for its ribs, prepared like celery or asparagus, and for its leaves, often said to resemble spinach.

leaf
Thin flattened part of the chard that grows out of the rib; it is eaten cooked or raw, mainly in salads.

rib
The chard's long fleshy petiole, whitish or red depending on the variety, is both soft and crunchy.

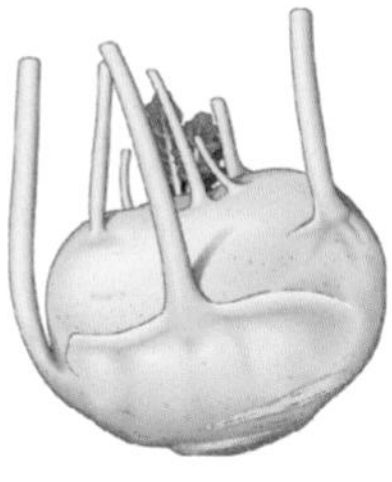

kohlrabi
Very popular in Central and Eastern Europe, where its bulbous stem is eaten raw or cooked like turnip; its cabbage-flavored leaves can also be eaten.

cardoon
A member of the artichoke family and little known in North America, its flavor is similar to that of celery; it is prepared like asparagus and served hot or cold.

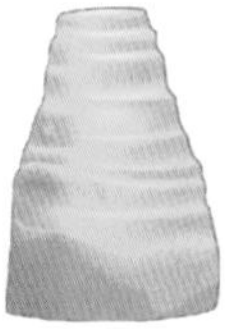

bamboo shoot
Very popular in Asia, this plant can only be eaten once cooked; it is an essential ingredient in sukiyaki, a typical Japanese dish.

fennel
Mainly associated with Italian cooking; the bulb is eaten as a vegetable while the leaves and seeds are used to season a variety of dishes.

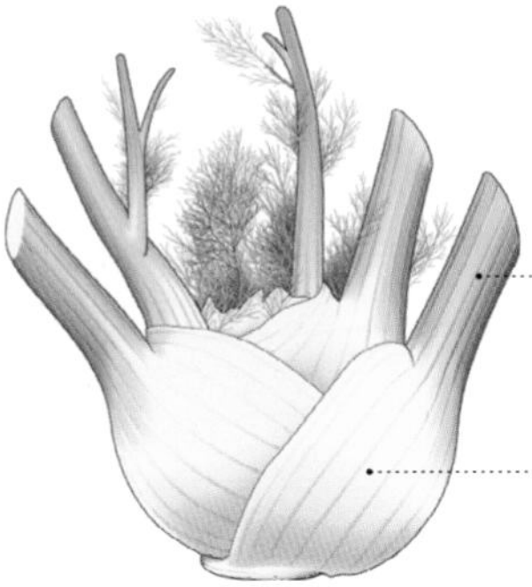

stalk
Part of the fennel growing out of the bulb and bearing small feathery dark-green leaves; it is traditionally used to flavor fish dishes.

bulb
Fleshy edible part of the fennel, composed of the overlapping enlarged parts at the base of the stems.

fiddlehead fern
When coiled, this young shoot is ready to eat; it is especially popular in salads, pasta dishes and omelettes.

rhubarb
The stems are eaten like fruit: raw, dipped in sugar or salt, or made into a compote.

celery
One of the best-known and most popular stalk vegetables, it is often served raw with dips; the leaves and seeds are used to season a variety of dishes.

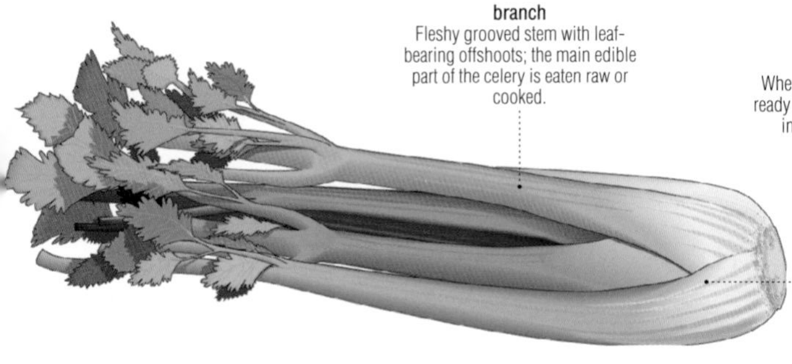

branch
Fleshy grooved stem with leaf-bearing offshoots; the main edible part of the celery is eaten raw or cooked.

head
Group of leafy branches joined at the base; the branches easily break off from the base and can then be cut to the desired length.

vegetables

leaf vegetables

Leaves of edible plants consumed as vegetables.

leaf lettuce
Lettuce having soft wavy leaves with curly edges; like most types of lettuce, it is usually eaten raw, in salads or sandwiches.

romaine lettuce
Lettuce with firm crisp leaves used especially to make Caesar salad.

celtuce
A celerylike vegetable that is derived from lettuce; it combines the flavors of celery and lettuce.

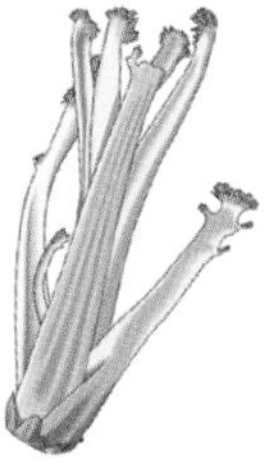

sea kale
Widely used in Europe, its leaves and wide fleshy stems are prepared like asparagus.

collards
It has thick, strongly flavored leaves and tough central ribs; it is eaten like spinach, either raw or cooked.

escarole
Its leaves are less bitter than those of the curled endive, to which it is related; it is usually eaten raw, in salads.

butterhead lettuce
Formed in a loosely compacted ball, its large soft leaves break off easily; Boston lettuce is a well-known variety of this species.

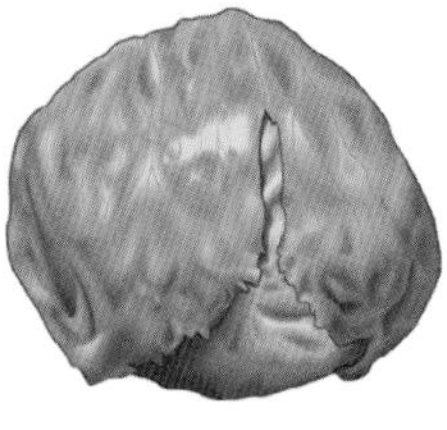

iceberg lettuce
The most widely sold lettuce in North America, it was initially covered with ice during transport, hence its name.

radicchio
Red endive native to northern Italy and having a somewhat bitter taste; it is often served with other types of lettuce.

ornamental kale
Related to the curled kale; its differently colored leaves are added to salads, soups and rice, or used to garnish serving platters.

curled kale
Its very curly, stringy tough leaves have a strong flavor; it is almost always eaten cooked.

grape leaf
Associated with Mediterranean cooking, it is used to prepare dolmades (stuffed grape leaves) and as a garnish for fruit and salad platters.

Brussels sprouts
The smallest member of the cabbage family is only eaten cooked and whole as a vegetable side dish.

red cabbage
Milder-tasting than other cabbages, it is usually eaten raw and finely chopped in salads.

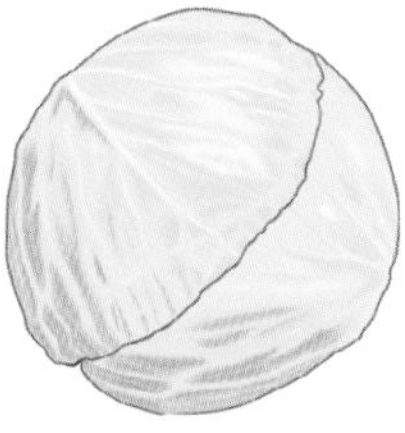

white cabbage
After fermentation, it is used to make sauerkraut; it is also used as an ingredient in stews.

savoy cabbage
Cabbage with somewhat flexible leaves, making it well suited to preparing cabbage rolls.

green cabbage
When finely chopped, it is the main ingredient in coleslaw; it is also added to soups and stews.

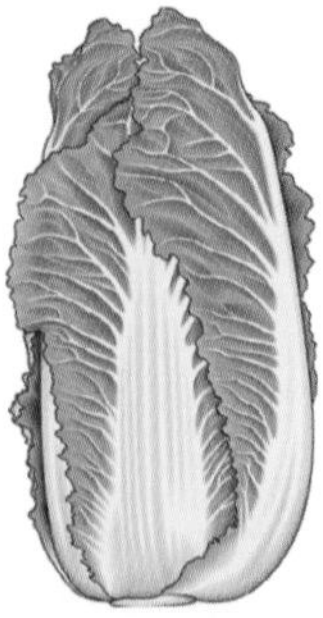

celery cabbage
A crunchy refreshing Chinese cabbage, mostly eaten cooked.

bok choy
The stems of this Chinese cabbage are juicy and crunchy; it is served in soups, with rice and in many Chinese dishes.

purslane
Both the stems and the tender fleshy leaves are eaten; it has a slightly acidic, spicy flavor.

nettle
When cooked or dried, the leaves lose their sting; it has a somewhat spicy flavor and can be prepared more or less like spinach.

watercress
Tender and juicy, it is mostly eaten raw, in salads; the delicate leaves have a slight mustardlike flavor.

dandelion
The leaves of this common plant are excellent in salads; when cooked, they can be prepared like spinach.

corn salad
Also called lamb's lettuce; its soft, mild-tasting leaves are primarily eaten raw, in salads.

arugula
Especially popular in southern France and Italy; whether raw or cooked, it should be used in moderation because of its strong flavor.

spinach
The vegetable used to make dishes à la Florentine. It is also eaten raw, in salads, and cooked, as a side dish or a stuffing ingredient.

garden cress
Picked while very young and sold in bunches; its tiny leaves add a hint of spice especially to salads, sandwiches and sauces.

garden sorrel
Its slightly lemon-flavored leaves are traditionally served with fish and veal; it is also used in a puréed soup that is a classic in a number of European countries.

curled endive
The very frilly, somewhat bitter leaves are primarily eaten raw, in salads.

Belgian endive
Its crunchy, slightly bitter leaves are much in demand for salads (used raw) or for such classic recipes as endive and ham au gratin.

inflorescent vegetables

The flowers or flower buds of edible plants eaten as vegetables.

cauliflower
The head, composed of immature buds, is either white or purple; it is eaten raw or cooked.

broccoli
Native to Italy, it is often green and occasionally white or purple; it is chosen primarily for its flower buds but the stem and leaves are also eaten.

Gai-lohn
Also called Chinese broccoli, its delicately flavored leaves and stems can be eaten raw or cooked, prepared in the same manner as broccoli.

broccoli rabe
Its slightly bitter stems, leaves and flowers can all be eaten, prepared like broccoli.

artichoke
Especially valued for its soft fleshy heart, it is often served with a dipping sauce; the leaves surrounding the heart can also be eaten.

vegetables

fruit vegetables
Fruits of edible plants consumed as vegetables.

avocado
Fruit of the avocado tree; its smooth greenish flesh is eaten raw, in salads or mashed.

tomato
Native to Central America, this fruit is essential to Italian, Provençal, Greek and Spanish cooking.

currant tomato
Very flavorful tomato characterized by its sweetness and long shelf life.

tomatillo
Picked when green, this berry is used to make sauces and is an essential ingredient in many Mexican dishes.

olive
Inedible when raw, the olive is treated to reduce its bitter taste, then cured in brine or sometimes in oil.

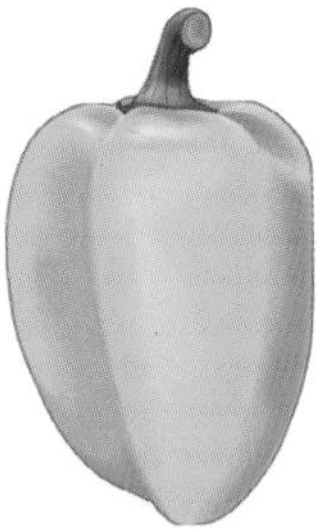

yellow sweet pepper
Mild pepper picked when ripe, it is strongly scented and has a sweet taste; it is often used in salads.

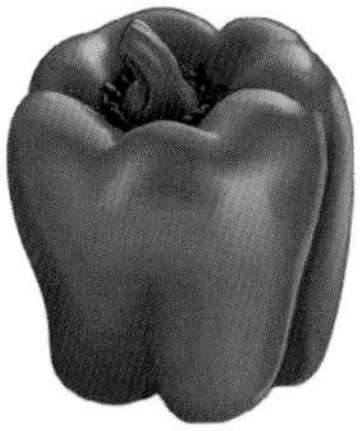

green sweet pepper
Mild pepper picked before fully ripe, it is used in many typical Mexican and Portuguese dishes.

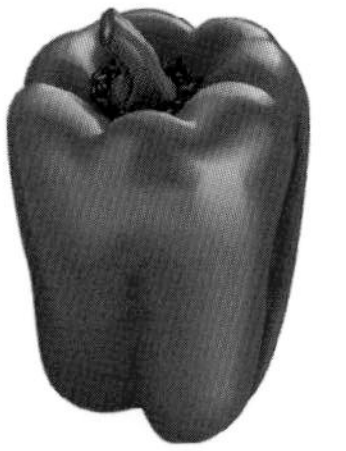

red sweet pepper
Mild pepper picked when ripe, it is very sweet and has a higher vitamin C content than the green sweet pepper.

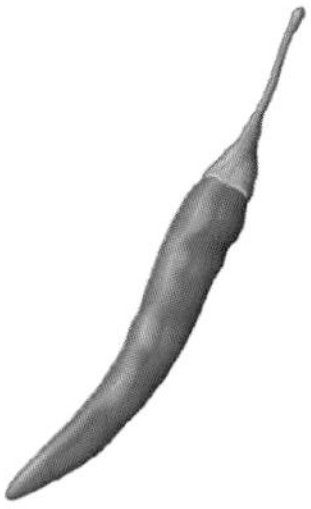

hot pepper
Cutting it or removing the seeds moderates its spicy burning taste.

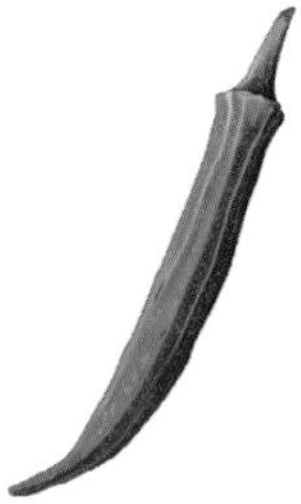

okra
Vegetable containing a substance used to thicken soups and ragouts, it is used in many Creole dishes.

gherkin
Picked when not yet ripe, it is often pickled in vinegar and eaten as a condiment; it is also served raw in salads.

cucumber
Related to squash and melons, it bears seeds and is usually eaten raw.

wax gourd
Its firm flavorful flesh is often used in puréed soups or spicy dishes.

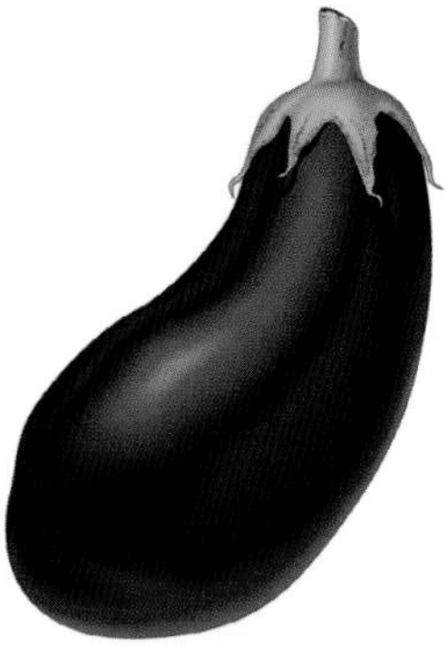

eggplant
Yellowish and spongy-fleshed vegetable that is sometimes sweated with salt to alleviate its bitter taste.

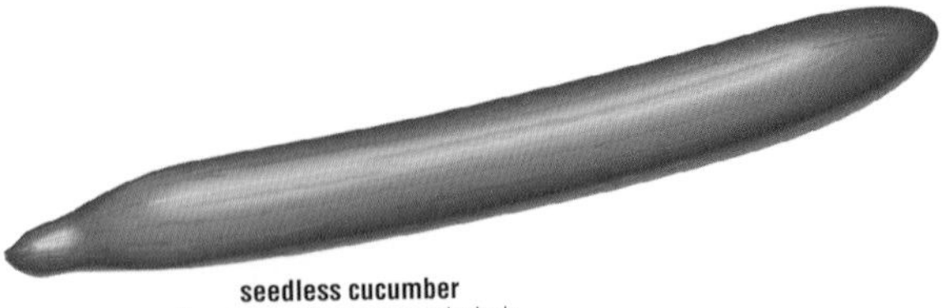

seedless cucumber
European variety grown exclusively in greenhouses without fertilization.

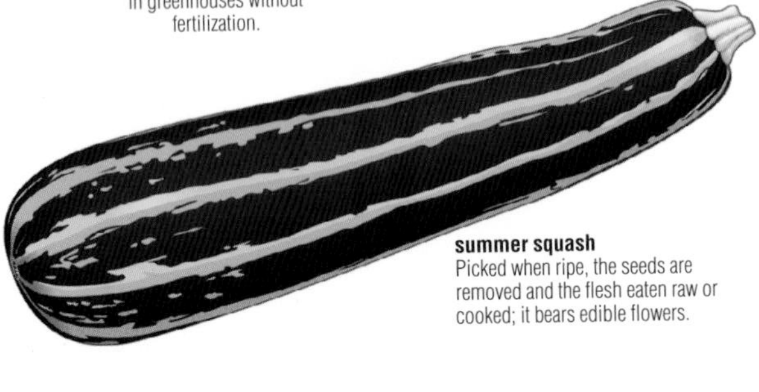

summer squash
Picked when ripe, the seeds are removed and the flesh eaten raw or cooked; it bears edible flowers.

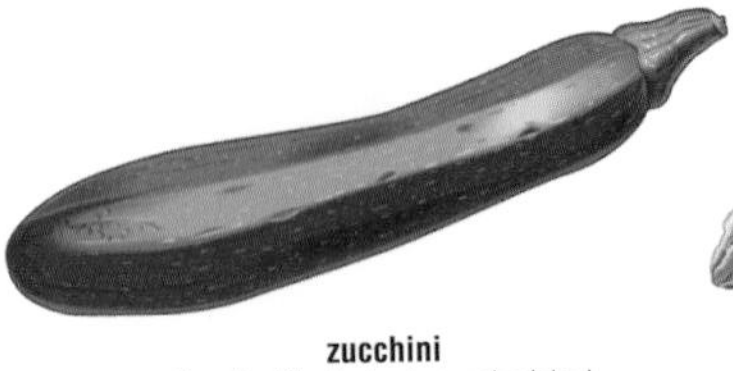

zucchini
Small white-fleshed squash picked before fully ripe; it is an essential ingredient in ratatouille.

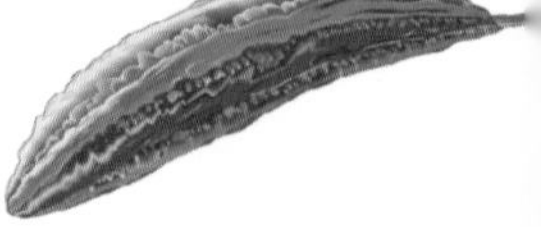

bitter melon
Too bitter to be eaten raw, it is an ingredient in various kinds of Asian cooking, such as soups or steamed dishes.

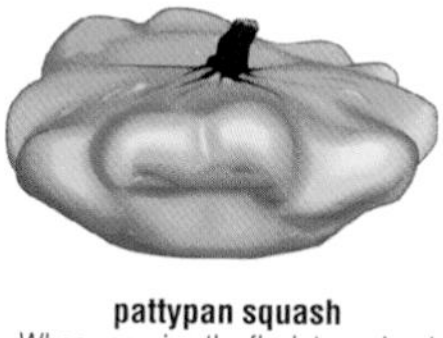

pattypan squash
When very ripe the flesh turns hard and white; its firm flesh has a flavor similar to the artichoke.

crookneck squash
The soft edible rind is covered in small ridges; best if picked very early, it can be eaten raw or cooked.

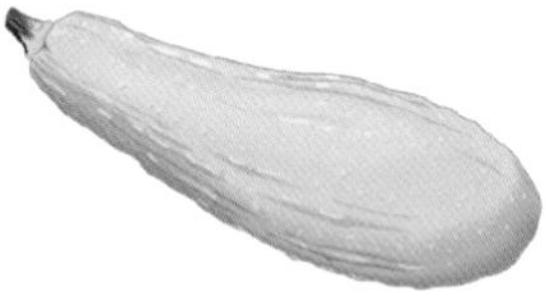

straightneck squash
The result of genetically altering the crookneck squash to eliminate the thin crooked neck; it is eaten raw or cooked.

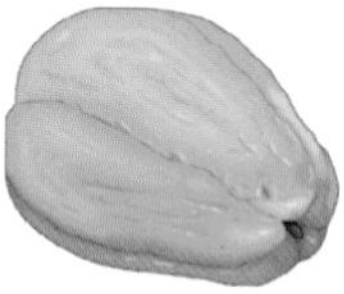

chayote
This squash, grown mainly in tropical countries, is used in Creole cooking; the central stone can be eaten once cooked.

pumpkin
Used primarily in North America, it can be recognized by its hard fibrous pedicel; its flesh is widely used in soups and desserts and its edible seeds are dried.

spaghetti squash
Derives its name from its cooked flesh, resembling spaghetti, which it can replace in most recipes.

acorn squash
Its smooth hard skin turns orange when fully ripe; the delicate, slightly fibrous flesh tastes of pepper and hazelnuts.

autumn squash
The rind can be yellow, orange or green; often confused with the pumpkin, it can be recognized by its pedicel, which is soft and enlarged where it attaches to the vegetable.

root vegetables

The fleshy roots of edible plants consumed as vegetables.

horseradish
Often used as a flavoring ingredient, especially in sauces; its strong flavor becomes milder when mixed with cream or mayonnaise.

black radish
Popular in Eastern Europe, although less juicy than the red radish; it can be cooked or sweated with salt to alleviate its bitter taste.

radish
Juicy and crunchy, it is eaten raw, as an hors d'oeuvre or in salads; it is also popular served cooked or pickled, especially in Asia.

salsify
Its sweet mild flavor is often said to resemble the oyster's; its young leaves are also edible.

carrot
Eaten in a variety of ways: plain, in salads, in deserts, as a vegetable side dish or a juice.

black salsify
Closely related to salsify, its cream-colored flesh is less stringy and more flavorful; it is an ingredient in dishes such as soups and ragouts.

parsnip
The yellowish flesh of this little-known vegetable has a slightly nutty taste and a texture similar to the turnip; it can be eaten raw or cooked.

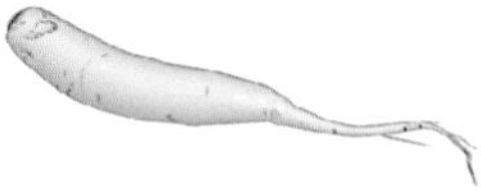

daikon
Its somewhat mild-tasting flesh, leaves and sprouted seeds are prepared in various ways; in Japan, it is served with sashimi.

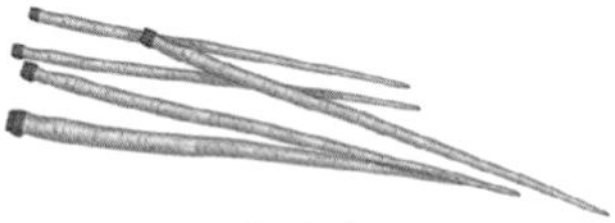

burdock
Root of a plant harvested before the floral stem develops; it is used as a vegetable or as a flavoring ingredient.

beet
Its usually red flesh contains a juice that stains readily; it is eaten raw, pickled or cooked, most famously in borscht, a hearty soup from Eastern Europe.

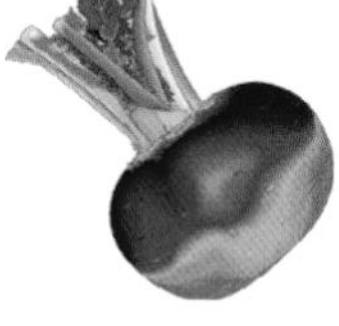

turnip
Often confused with the rutabaga, this white-fleshed vegetable is eaten raw or cooked and prepared like carrots.

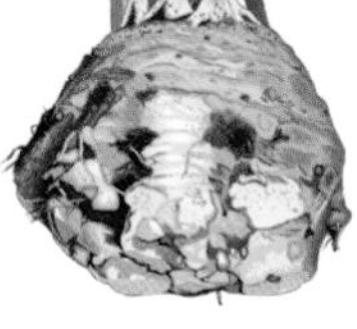

celeriac
A slightly spicy kind of celery; the raw vegetable, combined with mustard mayonnaise, becomes the classic celeriac remoulade.

rutabaga
Larger and stronger-tasting than the turnip, it can be recognized by its usually yellow flesh and by the bump on its top.

malanga
A staple in the West Indies, where it is grated and used to make fried doughnuts called acras; its strong taste hints of hazelnuts.

legumes

The main edible part of these pod-shaped fruits is their seeds, consumed fresh, dried or sprouted; if dried, they often require soaking before they can be cooked.

alfalfa
The sprouted seeds are added raw to sandwiches or used in various cooked dishes.

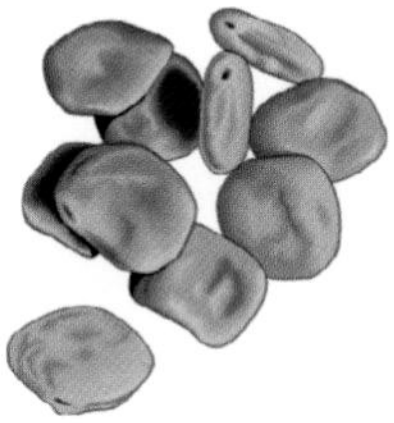

lupine
Protein-rich seed, prepared and served plain or sprinkled with lemon juice.

lentils
A main ingredient of hearty soups, they can also be puréed and made into croquettes; in India, they are often paired with rice.

peanut
Often served as a snack, it is also made into a butter and a vegetable oil and, in some countries, into a spicy sauce served with a variety of dishes.

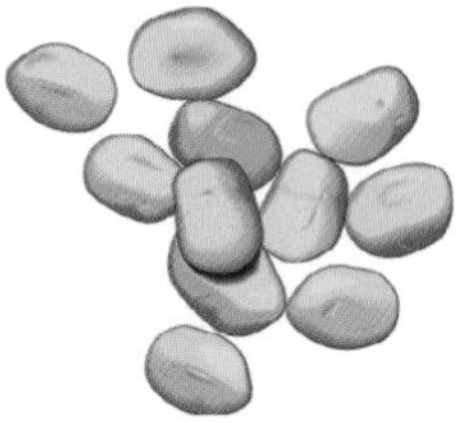

broad beans
Starchy and strong-tasting, they are typically puréed; they are also eaten whole and added to soups and stews.

peas

The rounded seeds are called "green peas" when they are fresh and "dried peas" when they are dried.

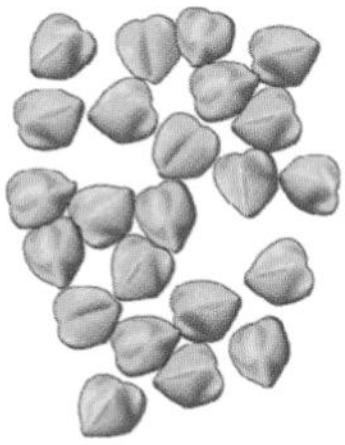

chick peas
Basic ingredient of hummus and falafel and found in couscous; they are also used to make various southern French dishes such as estouffade.

split peas
These pea seeds, dried and split in two, are generally puréed and used in various kinds of soups.

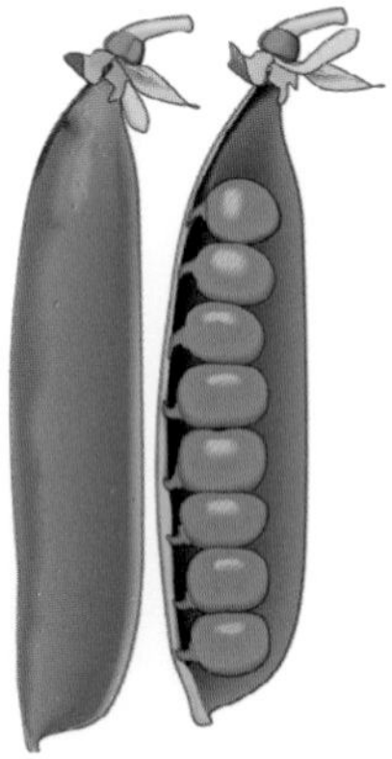

green peas
Delicious freshly picked, they are also available frozen or canned; a component of mixed vegetables and of dishes labeled "à la jardinière".

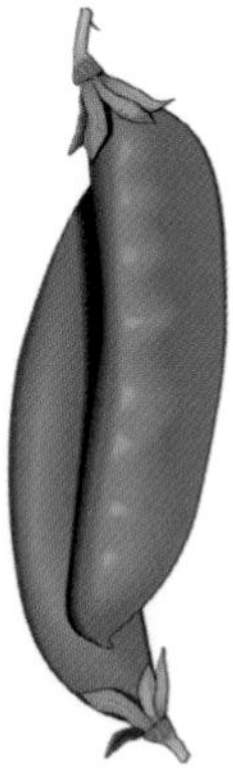

sweet peas
Eaten freshly picked with the sweet and crunchy pod, hence their name; they are especially popular in Chinese dishes.

dolichos beans

Fruit of a member of the bean family; the seeds are somewhat elongated and ovoid.

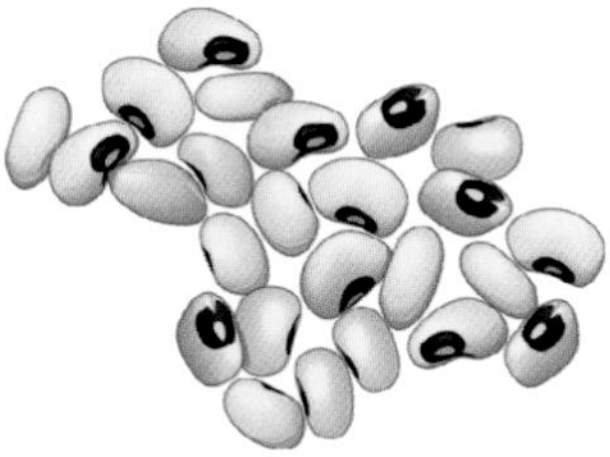

black-eyed pea
This flavorful seed has a black spot that resembles an eye, hence its name; it is typical especially of southern American cooking.

lablab bean
Characterized by a white ridge; it can be sprouted or ground into flour.

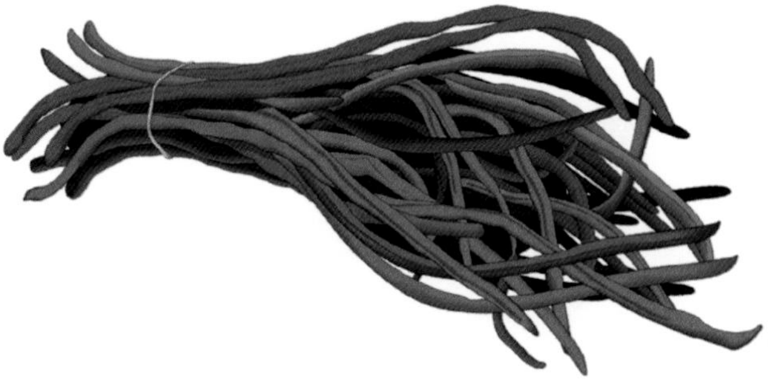

yard-long bean
Although mostly eaten fresh and whole, like the green bean, it is less juicy and sweet; its pods measure up to 3 ft in length.

beans

Fruits of plants native to Central and South America, the seeds are oval or kidney-shaped; before they are fully ripe, the pods are often edible.

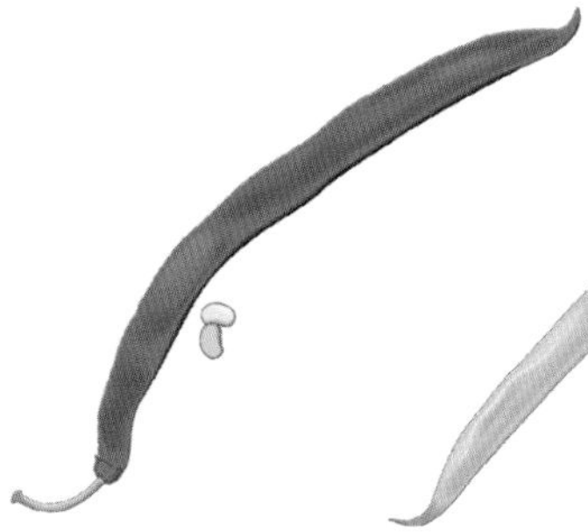

green bean
The young green pod is usually served as a vegetable side dish, sometimes with sauce or butter.

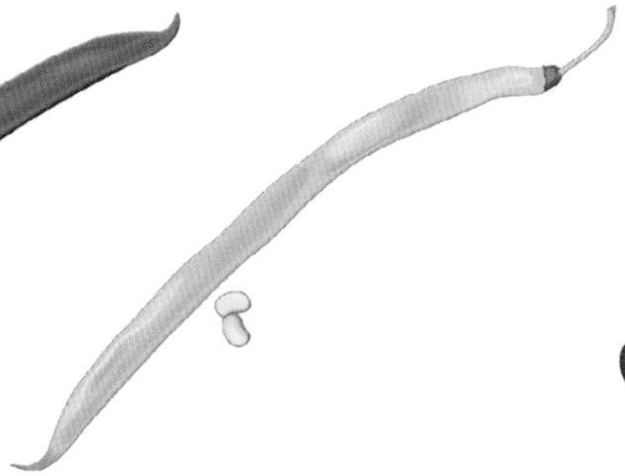

wax bean
Somewhat juicier than the green bean, it is sometimes eaten raw but mostly cooked, as a vegetable side dish.

roman bean
A staple of Italian cooking, it resembles the pinto bean, although often larger and darker; it absorbs the flavor of the foods it is cooked with.

adzuki bean
Has a delicate flavor and is often served with rice; in Asian countries, the paste made from these beans can replace tomato paste.

scarlet runner bean
The seeds are eaten fresh or dried, in which case they are prepared like the red kidney bean; a favorite accompaniment to onions, tomatoes and tuna.

mung bean
In Asia they are either puréed or ground into flour; in the West they are more commonly eaten sprouted, especially in chop suey.

Lima bean
Has a mild flavor and a starchy texture and is generally green- or cream-colored; when puréed, it can replace the potato.

pinto bean
When cooked, their spots disappear and they turn pink; because of their creamy texture, they are mostly used to make purées.

red kidney bean
One of the best-known beans, it is used to make the Mexican dish called chili con carne; it retains its shape when cooked so is often canned.

black gram
A favorite in Asia, where it is used to make a popular black sauce; in India, it is mixed with rice to make pancakes and a spicy purée.

black bean
Available mainly in Central and North America, it is a staple of Mexican cooking.

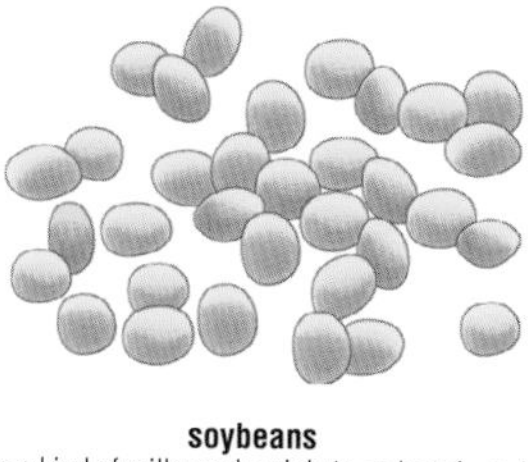

soybeans
Produces a kind of milk used mainly to make tofu and also a vegetable oil; when fermented, it is the main ingredient in soy sauce.

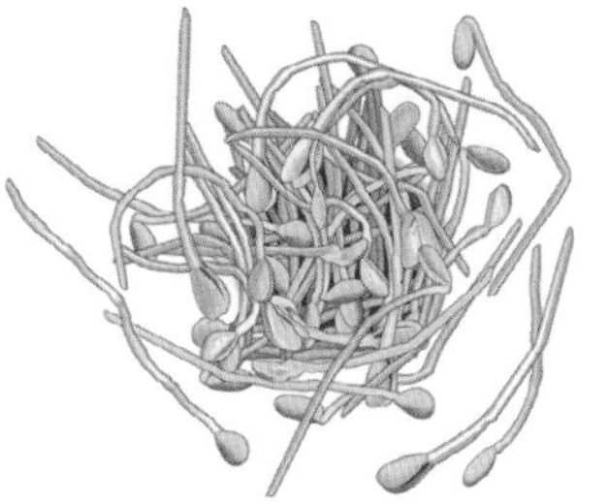

soybean sprouts
After sprouting for a few days they are ready to be eaten, either raw or lightly cooked; they are characteristic of Chinese cooking.

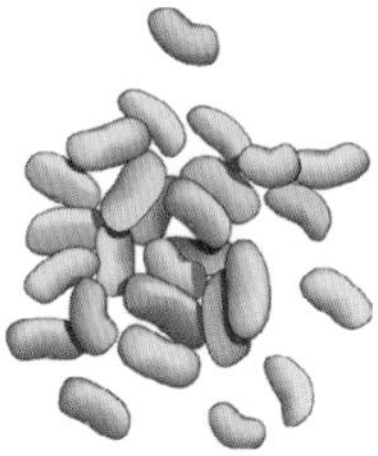

flageolet
Thin flat and less starchy than most other legumes, this bean is a favorite in France, where it is traditionally served with leg of lamb.

fruits

Usually sweet vegetables, primarily consumed at breakfast, as a snack or for dessert, and used extensively in pastry and candy making.

berries

Small fleshy fruits containing one or several usually edible seeds; when they grow together in clusters, each fruit is called a seed.

currant
Small red or white currant primarily eaten cooked due to its sour taste; its juice can replace vinegar in salad dressing.

black currant
Black berry primarily used to make coulis, jellies, wine and liqueurs such as crème de cassis, an ingredient in kir.

gooseberry
Larger than the clustered berries, it is especially popular in Europe; the British use it to make a chutney that is served with mackerel.

grape
This variously colored fruit of the vine is enjoyed worldwide, either plain, cooked, dried or in juice; it is also the main ingredient in wine.

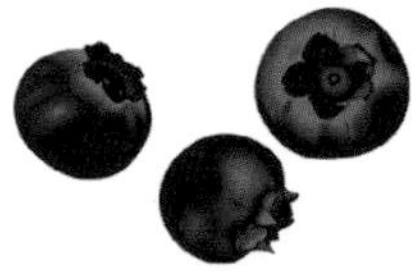

blueberry
Little known outside its native North America, it is primarily eaten plain or in desserts; the lowbush variety is the sweetest.

bilberry
Although not related to it, this berry of Europe and Asia resembles the blueberry and is used like it.

red whortleberry
Closely related to the cranberry, this small tart berry is somewhat bitter and rarely eaten raw; it is used instead to make sauces, jams and desserts.

alkekengi
Covered in a thin, inedible membrane, it is slightly tart and not very sweet; it is often used to make jams and jellies because of its high pectin content.

cranberry
Too tart to be eaten raw, it is primarily used for making desserts, sauces or juice; a traditional accompaniment to turkey in North America.

raspberry
Generally red, there are also different-colored varieties; slightly tart and very fragrant, it makes an excellent coulis that can be incorporated into desserts.

blackberry
Grows on canes as does the raspberry, and is used like that fruit; the several trailing species are comminly called dewberries.

strawberry
The cultivated strawberry was bred from the smaller and more fragrant wild strawberry; it is very flavorful and is used raw or cooked, primarily in desserts.

stone fruits

Fruits whose somewhat juicy flesh surrounds a hard, usually inedible stone.

plum
Of various colors and sizes, it is excellent either raw or cooked and is used especially to make chutney; the dried plum is called a prune.

peach
A velvety skin covers its juicy fragrant flesh; it is especially enjoyed plain, in juice and in various desserts, such as the classic peach melba.

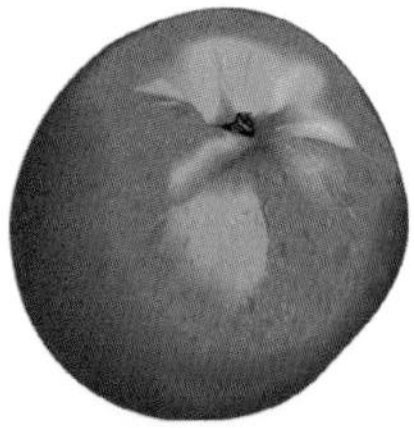

nectarine
Differentiated from the peach by its smooth, more colorful skin and by its more flavorful flesh; like the peach, it is eaten raw or used in certain desserts.

apricot
Often eaten dried or candied, its orange flesh can be mushy if picked before fully ripe; the kernel inside the stone contains a toxic substance.

cherry
An essential ingredient in Black Forest cake and, candied, in fruitcake; when artificially colored and flavored, it is used as a cocktail garnish.

date
Has a high sugar content and is often sold dried; in North America, it is primarily associated with baked goods, such as squares, muffins and cakes.

dry fruits

Often called nuts, these fruits usually have a hard dry covering called the shell that encloses an edible kernel.

macadamia nut
A popular candy ingredient, it is often sold coated in chocolate or honey; it is also a popular ingredient in mixed vegetables, curries, salads and desserts.

ginkgo nut
Extensively used in Japanese cooking but little known in the West, this nut is either eaten as is or is used in Asian dishes.

pistachio nut
Its greenish kernel is covered with a brown skin; it is extensively used in Mediterranean and Asian cooking, as well as in pastry and candy making.

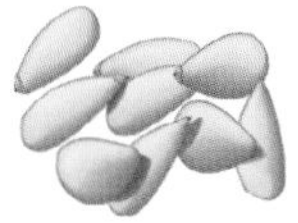

pine nut
Edible seed inside the cone of certain species of pine that is often used in cooking and baking.

cola nut
Used in drink preparations such as Coca-Cola™; it contains stimulants that are slightly less potent than those in coffee.

pecan nut
Native to North America, it is used to make certain savory dishes and numerous desserts, such as the traditional pecan pie.

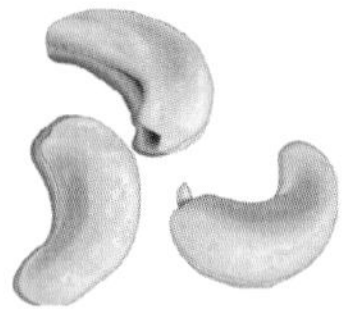

cashew
This fruit of the cashew tree is always sold shelled; its shell is covered by a juicy fleshy edible layer known as the cashew apple.

almond
Primarily used to garnish chicken and fish, and to make almond paste, candies (nougat and pralines) and an essence that flavors Amaretto and a variety of foodstuffs.

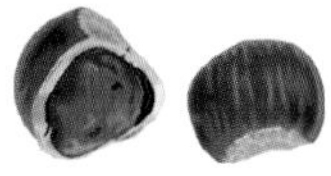

hazelnut
Primarily used to make paste, butter or a kind of flour used in cakes and cookies; in candy making, it is often combined with chocolate.

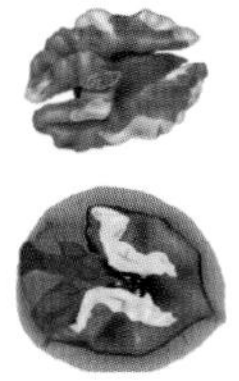

walnut
A green covering, the husk, covers the shell; the walnut is served as an appetizer, or added to a variety of desserts, salads, sauces and main dishes.

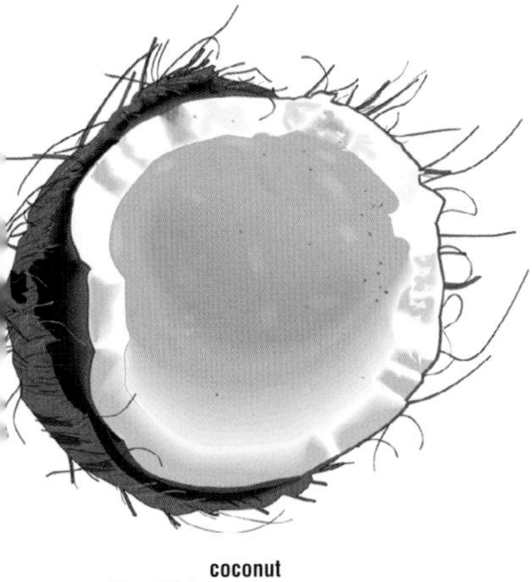

coconut
The whitish meat, known as copra, surrounds a cavity containing a refreshing liquid, not to be confused with coconut milk, which is derived from the grated flesh.

chestnut
Designates the fruit of the chestnut tree; Europeans often serve it with game and poultry. When puréed, it is the main ingredient in the dessert known as Mont Blanc.

beechnut
Fruit of the common beech tree, its flavor resembles the hazelnut's; more flavorful toasted than raw, it also yields a cooking oil.

Brazil nut
Often served as an appetizer; it is also made into candy, such as when chocolate-coated. It replaces coconut in some recipes.

pome fruits

Fruits where the flesh covers an inedible central part, the core, comprising a certain number of seeds called pips.

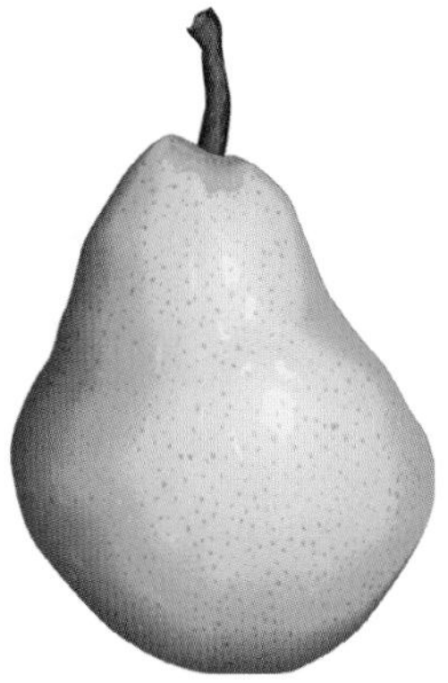

pear
Among its many and varied uses, it forms the basis for a fruit brandy; it is picked before fully ripe to prevent the flesh from acquiring a granular texture.

quince
Fruit of the quince tree, native to warm climates; inedible raw, it is traditionally made into jams and jellies.

apple
There are 7,500 known varieties; it is used to make cider and is also eaten raw or made into juice, jelly, compote or desserts, such as pie or strudel.

Japanese plum
Has thin skin, sometimes covered in fine hairs, that envelops juicy, somewhat sour flesh; whether raw or cooked, it tastes somewhat like cherries or plums.

fruits

citrus fruits

Somewhat acidic fruits with a high vitamin C content comprising numerous sections and covered with a rind that has an external layer called zest.

lemon
Highly acidic, it is especially used to flavor various recipes and enhance the flavor of certain foods; it is the main ingredient in lemonade.

kumquat
Small citrus fruit, .75 to 2 in long with a sweet tender rind that can be eaten unpeeled; its flavor is enhanced through light steeping.

lime
Intensely fragrant and used like the lemon; it is an essential ingredient in ceviche, a raw marinated fish dish.

orange
Widely available, it is often eaten plain or in juice, and it goes well with duck; it yields a flavor essence and an essential oil.

mandarin
Similar to a small, slightly flattened orange, it is less acidic than most citrus fruits and is often eaten as is; it peels easily.

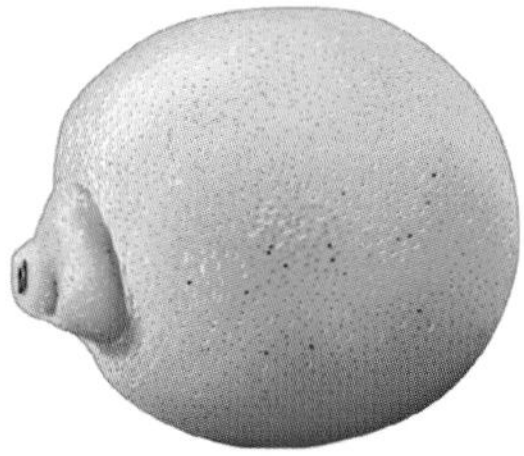

bergamot
Because its greenish flesh is inedible, it is primarily used for the zest and essential oil derived from its rind, especially in Earl Grey tea.

grapefruit
The pink grapefruit is sweeter and less bitter than the white one that has yellow flesh; it is often cut in half and eaten plain, with a spoon.

pomelo
Extremely popular in many Asian countries, it has only recently become available in the West; less juicy than the grapefruit, it is mostly cooked or candied.

citron
Extensively grown in Corsica and Israel, this somewhat dry fruit is rarely found fresh and is mostly sold candied.

melons

Related to squash and cucumbers, these tender fruits are juicy sweet and refreshing; they are primarily consumed raw.

cantaloupe
This orange-fleshed melon is characterized by its patterned textured ribs; the most widely cultivated variety is the charentais.

casaba melon
The flavor of its creamy white flesh, often less fragrant than that of other melons, can be enhanced with lemon or lime juice.

honeydew melon
Owes its name to its very sweet, green flesh; its smooth firm rind turns creamy-yellow as it ripens.

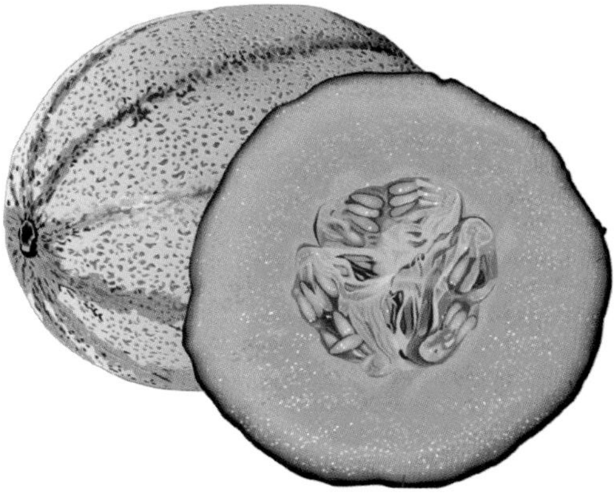

muskmelon
Named for the characteristic musky smell of its flesh; it has a textured rind and its flavorful flesh is pink or orange.

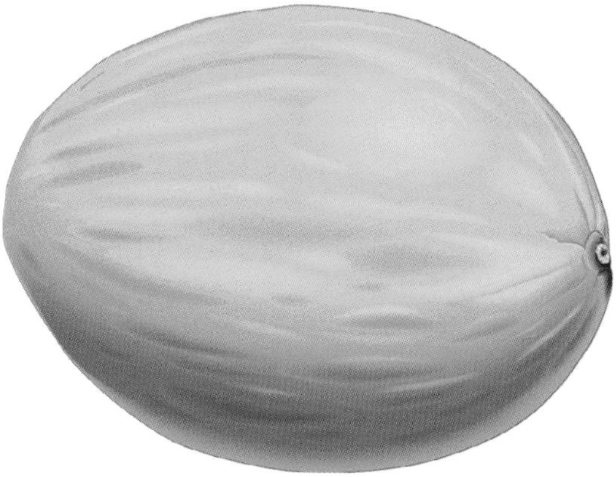

canary melon
Has sweet whitish flesh that is rose-tinted near the central cavity; it becomes very fragrant when ripe.

watermelon
This thirst-quenching fruit, named for its high water content, is primarily eaten plain, in slices.

Ogen melon
Small round melon with a hard smooth ribbed rind; its very juicy flesh is either dark pink or pale green.

fruits

tropical fruits

A variety of fruits, usually of exotic origin, more or less available in the West.

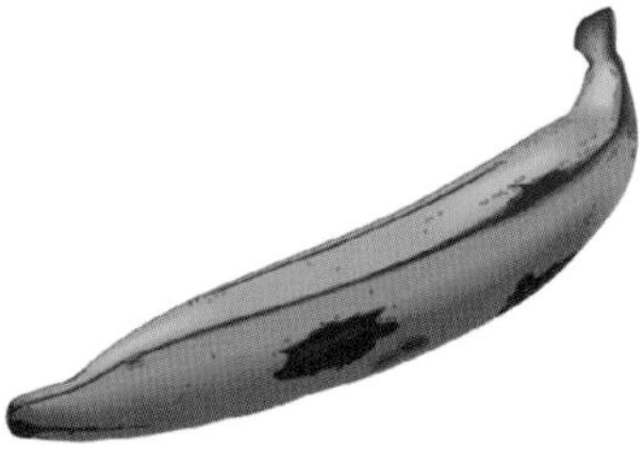

plantain
Nicknamed the "cooking banana", this staple of African and West Indian cooking is inedible when raw; it is primarily eaten as a vegetable, either steamed, roasted or fried.

banana
Eaten as is, sautéed, fried or flambéed with rum; it is a classic garnish for ice-cream dishes and is also used in muffins and cakes.

longan
Stone fruit, related to the litchi, whose whitish translucent flesh is sweet and juicy; the peeled and stoned fruit is often eaten plain.

tamarillo
Within the inedible skin there is a firm, slightly acidic flesh. If very ripe, it can be eaten raw; otherwise, it is often cooked like a vegetable.

passion fruit
Within its inedible skin that wrinkles when ripe, there is a highly aromatic gelatinous pulp; delicious plain, it is used to flavor fruit punches and cocktails.

horned melon
Its green flesh contains soft edible seeds, similar to those of the cucumber; it is often peeled and then made into juice.

mangosteen
Within the inedible skin that hardens as the fruit ages, there is a sweet juicy white flesh that is divided into sections; it is eaten as is, like an orange.

kiwi
Its juicy, slightly acidic green flesh has a high vitamin C content; delicious plain, its downy skin is generally discarded, although it can be eaten.

pomegranate
The edible part is the small, very juicy berries enclosed within the fruit's membranes; it is used to make grenadine syrup, an ingredient in drinks and desserts.

cherimoya
The skin and the seeds inside the slightly granular flesh are inedible; the flesh is sprinkled with orange juice and eaten with a spoon.

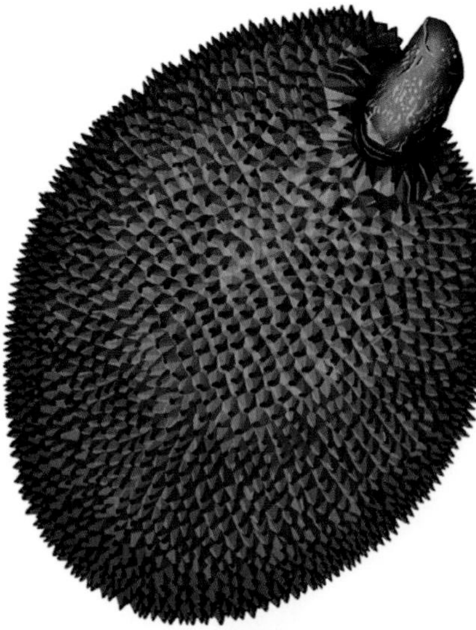

jackfruit
This very large fruit has edible seeds than can be boiled or roasted; the starchy flesh is eaten as a fruit or vegetable, either raw or cooked.

pineapple
Once the inedible rind has been removed, it is eaten raw, cooked or in juice; in North America, it is traditionally served with ham.

jaboticaba
Little known outside Brazil, it is eaten as is, like grapes, or made into jelly, jam, juice or wine; its translucent flesh is either white or pink.

litchi
Its juicy crunchy translucent flesh is more fragrant than the longan's; it is often eaten raw and the Chinese serve it with fish or meat.

fig
Among its many varieties are the black, the green and the purple fig; whether fresh or dried, it is mostly eaten raw, but can also be cooked.

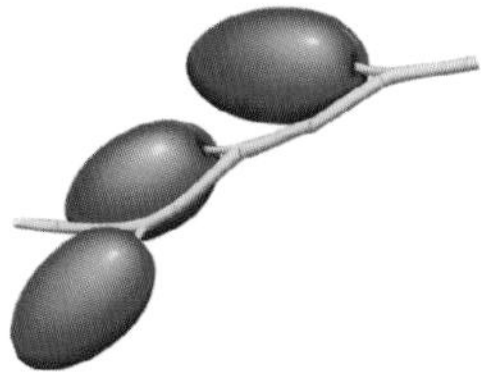

jujube
Somewhat dry stone fruit, eaten fresh or dried, raw or cooked, like the date.

sapodilla
Has juicy fragrant, slightly granular flesh that tastes like honey and apricots; it is easy to peel and is eaten raw or cooked.

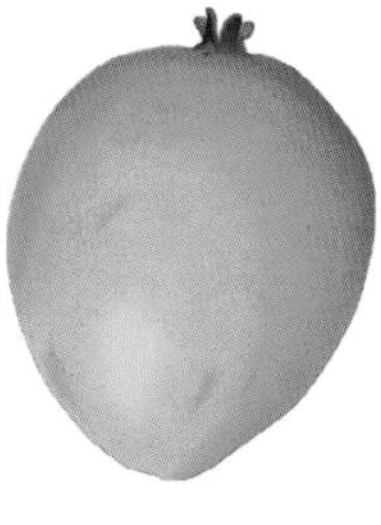

guava
Very popular in South America, its fragrant, slightly acidic flesh is eaten raw or cooked, with or without the skin and seeds.

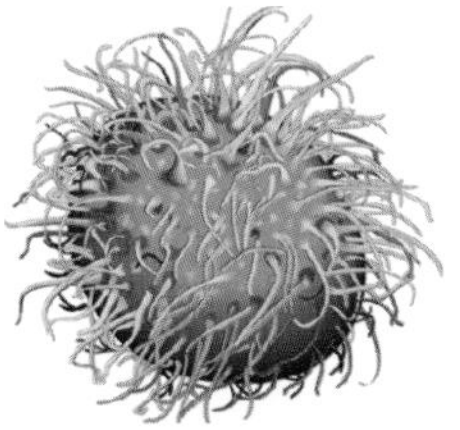

rambutan
The shell, covered in soft spikes, splits easily to reveal flesh like the litchi's but less fragrant; it is used like the litchi.

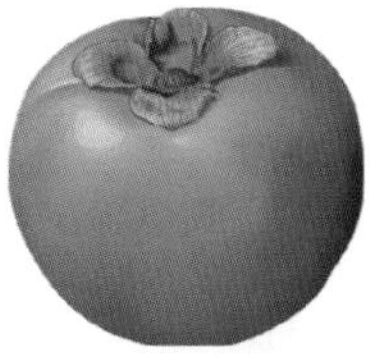

Japanese persimmon
This national fruit of Japan is often eaten plain, with a spoon; the fuyu variety is eaten like an apple.

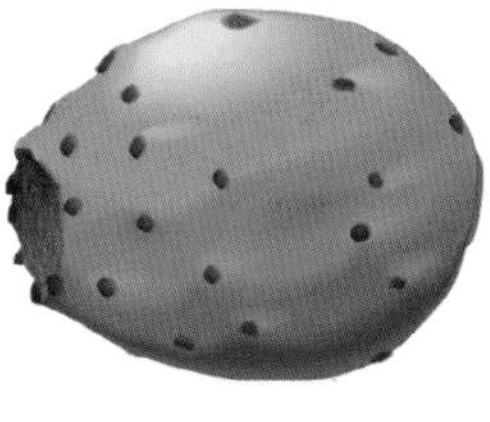

prickly pear
Fruit of a member of the cactus family; the spines and skin should be removed before eating the flesh, plain or sprinkled with lemon or lime juice.

carambola
Within the delicate edible skin is a juicy, slightly acidic flesh that can be eaten raw or cooked, as a fruit or vegetable.

Asian pear
Most popular Asian fruit, primarily eaten plain; its flesh is sweet and juicy, like the pear's, and crunchy, like the apple's.

mango
Fruit with a flattened stone and a skin that should be discarded, as it irritates the mouth; it is mostly eaten ripe, but sometimes used green, as a vegetable.

durian
Large fruit that emits a disagreeable odor when ripe; its sweet creamy flesh is often eaten plain while the seeds are used like nuts.

papaya
Its usually orange, juicy flesh is eaten like the melon and contains spicy, edible seeds; when green, it is eaten like winter squash.

pepino
The orange or yellow flesh is slightly starchy. Before fully ripe, it is often cooked and prepared like a squash; once ripe, it is eaten like a melon.

feijoa
Has sweet fragrant, slightly granular flesh; after peeling, it is eaten raw or cooked, plain or in various desserts.

spices

Plant substances, often of exotic origin, used primarily for their flavor and pungency to enhance the taste of various recipes.

juniper berry
Fruit of the juniper tree with a resinous smell and slightly bitter flavor; it is the basis for gin and also flavors marinades, sauerkraut, meat and pâtés.

clove
The dried floral bud of the clove tree. Whole, it is often used with ham or simmered onion dishes; when ground, it flavors items such as gingerbread.

allspice
Also called Jamaican spice; it is used to flavor savory or sweet dishes and certain liqueurs.

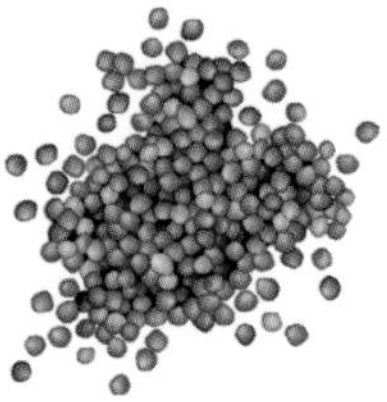

white mustard
Its seeds are larger and less pungent than the black mustard's and are used especially to make American mustard.

black mustard
The flavorful pungent seeds have a high concentration of essential oil; they are used whole, ground or as a flavoring agent.

black pepper
The most pungent and aromatic of the peppers, it comes from small berries that are picked while still green, then dried.

white pepper
Small berries picked when very ripe, then dried and skinned; this pepper is less pungent than black pepper.

pink pepper
These dried berries, with a delicate fragrant and mildly pungent flavor, do not grow on the pepper tree but on another plant; it is used like pepper.

green pepper
Small berries picked while still green and usually dried or preserved in brine or vinegar; this pepper is mild but very fragrant.

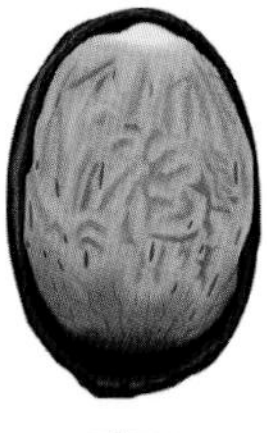

nutmeg
Its flavor complements milk products but quickly decreases once the nut is ground; its red membrane, known as mace, is also used as a spice.

caraway
Its sharp bitter flavor enhances the flavor of stewed dishes; it is used primarily in Eastern Europe, India and Arab countries.

cardamom
The pod is green, brown or white, depending on whether it was sun- or oven-dried, or bleached; its delicate peppery flavor characterizes Indian curry.

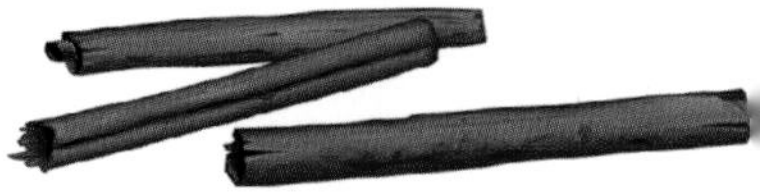

cinnamon
Dried bark of the cinnamon tree, sold in sticks, ground or as an essential oil; it is often associated with candy, sweet dishes and hot drinks.

saffron
The most expensive spice, actually derived from the handpicked and dried stigmata of the crocus flower; it is an essential ingredient in paella and bouillabaisse.

cumin
Extensively used in traditional Arab, Indian and Mexican dishes, it has a strong smell and a warm, slightly bitter flavor.

curry
A staple of Indian cooking, the pungency of this blend of spices varies, depending on how much pepper or chile is used.

turmeric
Similar to ginger, it is cooked and ground into powder; among other uses, it is added to Indian curries and chutneys and provides the color for American mustard.

fenugreek
Once roasted, the seeds have a bittersweet aftertaste; they are used in Indian cooking or, when sprouted, added to salads.

jalapeño chile
Relatively mild chile, native to Mexico and sold fresh, dried or marinated; it turns red when ripe.

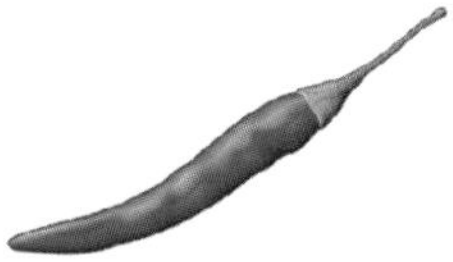

bird's eye chile
Small, intensely hot chile; removing the seeds and interior membranes alleviates the fiery taste.

crushed chiles
Dried crushed chiles that contribute flavor and spiciness to a variety of recipes; they are commonly used in pasta dishes.

dried chiles
The smaller dried chiles are generally stronger than the large ones, which can be dry-roasted before use to bring out their flavor.

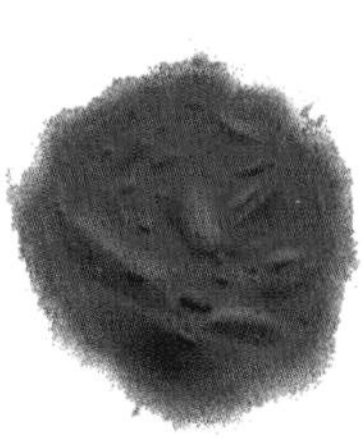

cayenne chile
Dried red chile powder used specifically to make Tabasco® sauce; it is so hot that one pinch is enough to season an entire dish.

paprika
Extensively used in Hungarian cooking, this somewhat hot powder combines dried sweet red pepper and red chiles; it is used to flavor and color numerous foods, such as eggs and potatoes.

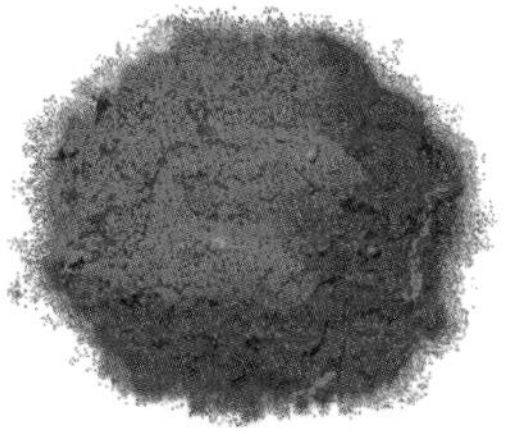

ajowan
Highly fragrant, it tastes like thyme; among other uses, it is added to starchy foods, legumes and Indian wafers.

asafetida
The dried gum derived from two species of giant fennel, its unpleasant smell dissipates with cooking; it adds flavor to vegetables, fish and Indian sauces.

garam masala
Indian spice blend of which there are countless varieties, some numbering up to 12 ingredients; it is used to season pilafs and meat dishes.

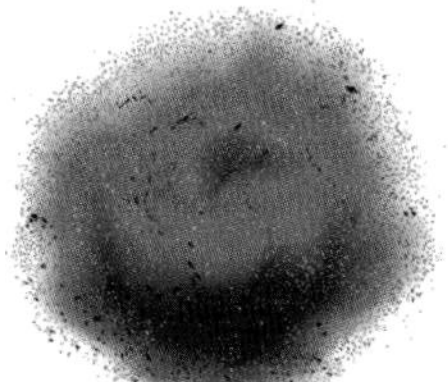

cajun spice seasoning
Its spiciness enhances the flavor of ragouts and Cajun dishes; it is also sprinkled on meat and fish before they are barbecued or roasted.

marinade spices
A mixture of spices added to fruit and vegetable preserves, chutney and vinegar; its composition varies.

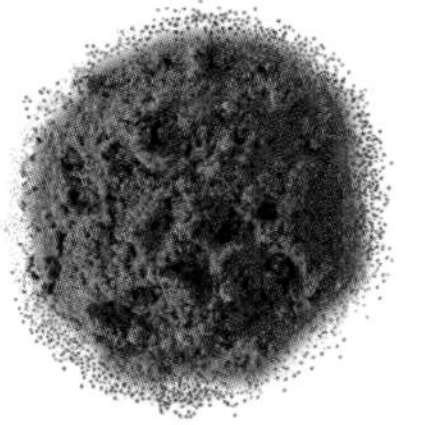

five spice powder
A blend of five ground spices used in Chinese cooking; it includes star anise, cloves, fennel seeds, cinnamon and pepper.

chili powder
Spice blend composed mainly of dried ground chiles, whose strength varies depending on the chiles used; it is widely used to flavor and color rice and pasta.

ground pepper
Although one of the most widely used cooking spices, it loses its flavor faster than peppercorns, from which it is derived.

ras el hanout
Very fragrant Moroccan spice blend with dried flowers among its up to 50 ingredients; it is used to flavor game, couscous, rice and stews called tajines.

sumac
Dried berries, sometimes ground, with a slightly acidic, lemony taste; it is very popular in the Middle East, especially in salads and fish dishes.

poppy seeds
Their nutty flavor, which intensifies with cooking, works especially well in bread, cakes and pastries; it also yields a cooking oil.

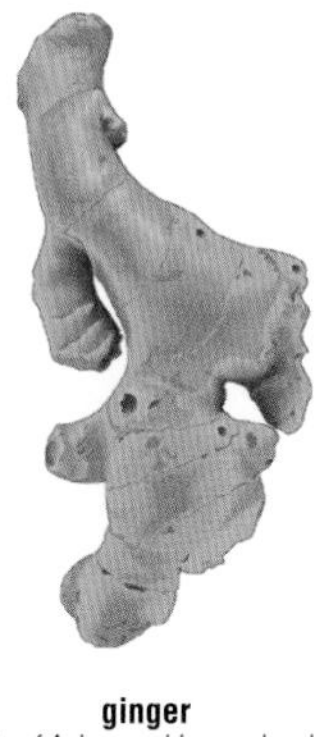

ginger
A staple of Asian cooking and a classic garnish for sushi; it is also used ground, especially in breads and cookies.

condiments

Natural or artificial substances used in cooking to bring out the flavor in a dish or to complement it.

Tabasco® sauce
Native to Louisiana, this sauce is made from crushed red chile peppers and is so pungent that a few drops are enough to season a whole dish.

Worcestershire sauce
British sauce whose exact recipe is kept secret by the manufacturer; its robust flavor goes well in cocktails, sauces, soups and many other dishes.

tamarind paste
Made from the fruit of the tamarind tree, this slightly acidic paste is used as a foodstuff and as a condiment in Asian cooking.

vanilla extract
Aromatic substance extensively used in baking; it is often made of artificial ingredients that are less tasty than real vanilla, which is more expensive.

tomato paste
Tomato coulis reduced until it turns into a paste; it is used to make ragouts and sauces.

tomato coulis
Tomato purée of medium thickness that is served either hot or cold, as a sauce.

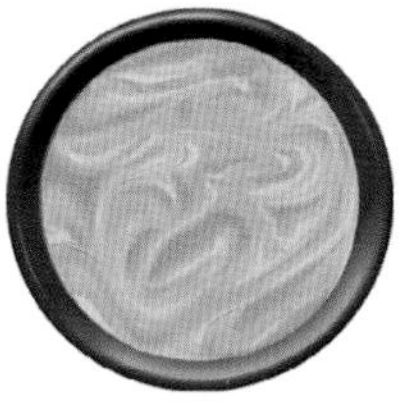

hummus
Lebanese condiment made from puréed chickpeas and sesame oil, commonly served as an hors d'oeuvre or with crudités.

tahini
Thick creamy nutty-tasting paste, made of ground sesame seeds; it is added to sauces and served with brochettes, bread, fruit and vegetables.

hoisin sauce
Thick spicy sauce made from soybeans and dried chiles; it enhances braised foods, is served with Peking duck and is used as a marinade.

soy sauce
A key condiment in Asian cooking, this extremely salty sauce is made from soybeans and is used as a flavoring ingredient, dip or marinade.

powdered mustard
Can be incorporated into shortening, used as a seasoning or mixed with water to make a paste that resembles prepared mustard.

wholegrain mustard
Native to Meaux, France, this mild spicy mustard is made from partly crushed seeds, giving it a grainy texture.

Dijon mustard
This strong mustard comes from Dijon, France; it is served with meat and is used in making sauces, salad dressings and various kinds of mayonnaise.

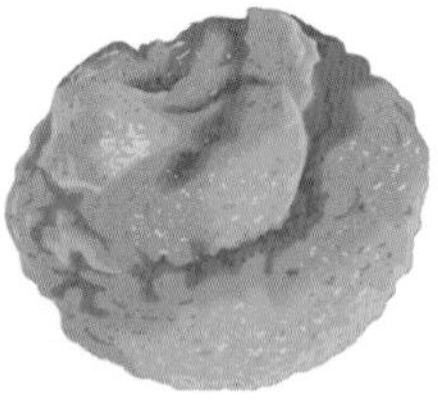

German mustard
Medium strong and slightly sweet mustard that goes well with sausages and deli meats.

English mustard
Very strong mustard, sold either prepared or powdered, traditionally served with roast beef and ham.

American mustard
Very mild, the traditional North American accompaniment to hot dogs and hamburgers; its bright yellow color comes from turmeric.

plum sauce
Sweet-and-sour Chinese sauce primarily served with deep-fried or roasted dishes, such as pork and roast duck.

mango chutney
Thick sweet-and-sour relish, originating in India and made with mangoes, sugar and vinegar; it can be served with a variety of dishes.

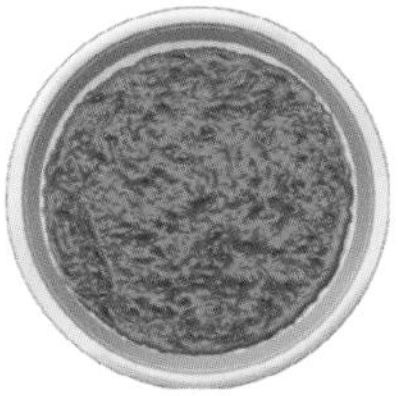

harissa
This chile-based purée is very popular in the Middle East and North Africa; it is used as is or mixed with broth and is a key ingredient in couscous.

sambal oelek
Very spicy Indonesian sauce made from chiles; it is used as a flavoring ingredient, condiment or hors d'oeuvre sauce.

ketchup
Medium spicy, traditionally English tomato purée made from numerous different recipes.

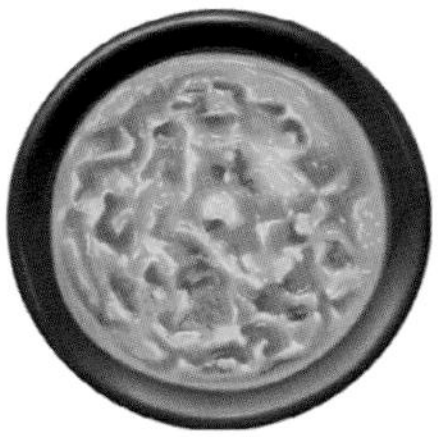

wasabi
Its very pungent taste enhances meat and fish dishes, such as Japanese sushi and sashimi.

table salt
A standard table condiment and also commonly used in cooking, it is always refined.

coarse salt
This somewhat refined version is sometimes used in cooking or to sweat vegetables and preserve foods.

sea salt
Unlike rock salt, which is whiter and comes from the subsoil, this usually grayish salt is derived from seawater through evaporation.

balsamic vinegar
Well-known condiment made from sweet white grapes and aged in wooden casks; its low acidity makes it ideal for use in salads or in hot foods.

rice vinegar
It is made from fermented rice wine and is very popular in Asian cooking; the Japanese version is sweet while the Chinese one is spicier.

apple cider vinegar
Cider-based product whose strong taste makes it unsuitable for salads; it is used primarily for deglazing or as an ingredient in fish and seafood dishes.

malt vinegar
Made from sprouted barley juice, it is much too strong for salad dressings; it is used instead to make mixed pickles and chutneys.

wine vinegar
White wine vinegar is less fragrant than the red; the former goes well with fish and seafood while the latter brings out the flavor of blander foods.

herbs

Aromatic fresh or dried plants used separately or mixed to bring out the flavor of recipes; they often make excellent infusions.

dill
Used primarily for its leaves and seeds, it imparts flavor to vinegar and pickles as well as to salmon and herring.

anise
Extensively used in making candy (licorice) and liqueurs (pastis), its edible leaves and seeds can flavor savory as well as sweet dishes.

sweet bay
The dried leaves must be used sparingly; it is an ingredient in bouquets garnis and is used to flavor soups and stews.

oregano
Wild, slightly more flavorful variety of marjoram; extensively used in Mediterranean cooking, it goes especially well with tomato dishes.

tarragon
Has a slightly bitter, peppery anise flavor that complements bland foods; it is often used with chicken and is always used in béarnaise sauce.

basil
A popular choice for seasoning tomato and pasta dishes, it is also one of the main ingredients in pistou and Italian pesto.

sage
Its pungent flavor complements a variety of dishes; it is often used with pork, duck and goose, as well as in Italian veal dishes.

thyme
Used with parsley and sweet bay to make bouquets garnis; because it withstands lengthy cooking, it is a popular choice for flavoring soups and stews.

mint
Gives a refreshing taste to numerous sweet and savory dishes, such as lamb; its aromatic essential oil is used to flavor candy, liqueurs and many other types of food.

parsley
The smooth flat-leafed parsley is less bitter and more fragrant than curly-leafed parsley; it is used to flavor numerous recipes, such as tabbouleh.

chervil
Has a subtle delicate taste and is used like parsley; it is often included with tarragon, parsley and chives in a traditional blend known as fines herbes.

coriander
Its leaves are used like parsley and it has edible musk- and lemon-scented seeds; the roots can be substituted for garlic.

rosemary
Its fairly pungent, aromatic flavor is very popular in southern France and in Italy, where it is used especially in sauces and marinades, and with roast meat.

hyssop
The highly aromatic leaves are mostly used in salads, soups, ragouts and fruit platters, as well as in some liqueurs, such as Chartreuse and Benedictine.

borage
Delicious in yogurt, cream cheese or salad dressing; the young leaves can be used in salads.

lovage
Resembles celery but with a stronger flavor; it is particularly tasty with potatoes and also goes well with ragouts, sauces and salads.

savory
Reminiscent of thyme, its flavor enhances legumes, meat and stuffing; it is also used to flavor vinegar and goat's milk cheeses.

lemon balm
Its lemon-scented leaves are used extensively in Asian cooking; it goes wel with bitter foods.

cereal

Plants that are often cultivated on a large scale; their grains have been a major food staple for humans and certain domestic animals for centuries.

rice
A universal staple, used as a side dish, in sweet and savory dishes such as risotto and paella, and for its by-products (noodles, sake).

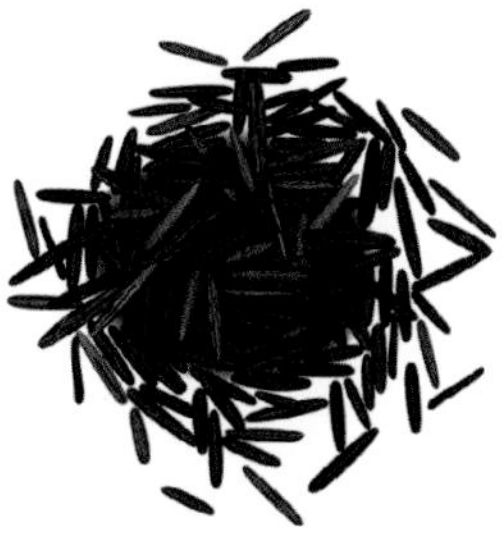

wild rice
Seeds from a North American aquatic plant; it is richer and higher in protein than rice and has a strong nutty flavor. It is sometimes mixed with other kinds of rice.

spelt wheat
Wheat variety with small brown grains that, once hulled, can be used like rice.

wheat
Cereal cultivated for its grain, of great significance in human food production; it is used to produce foodstuffs such as flour, bread and semolina.

oats
Often eaten as porridge, it is also an ingredient in date squares, fruit crisp toppings, muffins, cookies and pancakes.

rye
Yields a flour that can be combined with wheat flour to make bread; it is also used in brewing (beer) and distilling (whisky).

millet
With its strong flavor, it is mostly used for making pancakes and porridge; when sprouted and ground, millet is an ingredient in breads and muffins.

corn
Native to America, it is eaten as a vegetable, made into popcorn or ground into flour; it also yields a starch, a syrup and a cooking oil.

barley
Barley can be either hulled or pearled to remove its outer husk; it is often added to soups and ragouts and is also made into malt for brewing beer.

buckwheat
Eaten in soups and as porridge, it is also ground into a flour traditionally used to make crepes and pancakes.

quinoa
Grains should be thoroughly rinsed before cooking; it is used in South America to make an alcoholic drink called chicha.

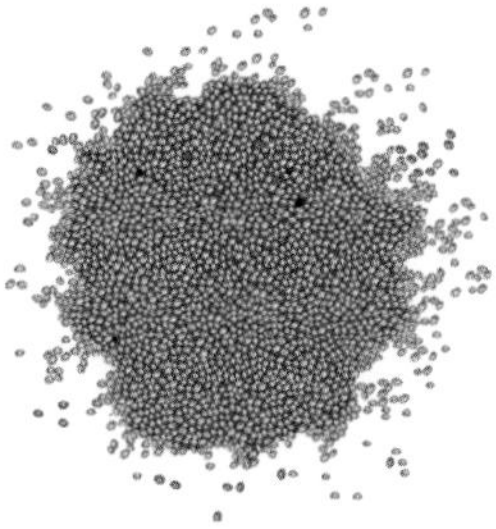

amaranth
These highly nutritious, slightly peppery grains can be eaten as is after cooking, sprouted or ground into flour.

triticale
A wheat and rye hybrid, it is mostly used to make crepes and pasta.

cereal products

Cereals that have been processed in various ways to make ground (flour, semolina), unground (rice) or manufactured products (bread, pasta, noodles).

flour and semolina

Products obtained by grinding grains and cereals; semolina is usually coarser and more granular than flour. Without a modifier, these words generally refer to wheat.

semolina
Refers to the granular flour derived from hard wheat, used to make pasta; fine semolina can also be eaten as a cereal (cream of wheat).

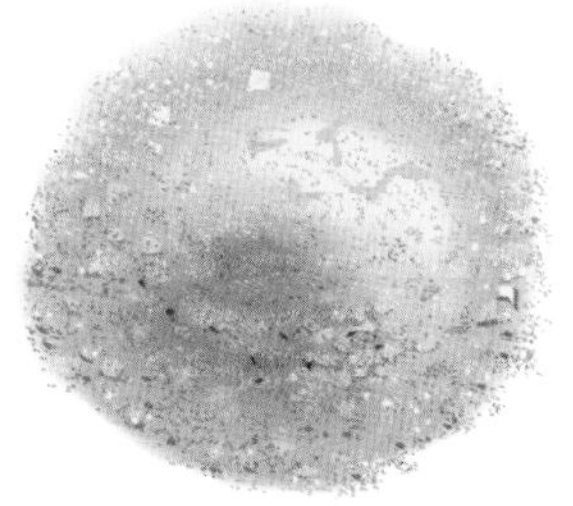

whole-wheat flour
Because it is produced by grinding the entire grain, none of the nutrients is lost; the grain's outer layer, known as bran, gives it a brownish color.

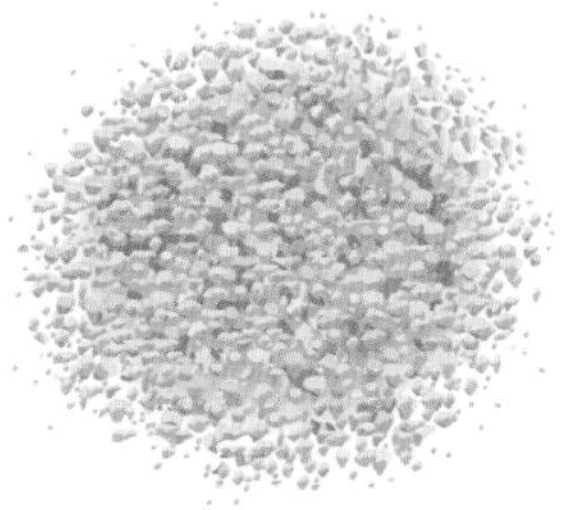

couscous
Hard wheat semolina that is formed into grains and used to prepare an eponymous dish of the Maghreb; it is traditionally steamed over broth.

all-purpose flour
This blend of ground hard and soft wheat has many uses, but is primarily used to thicken sauces or to make bread and pastry.

unbleached flour
Like white flour, it comes from grinding wheat grains from which the bran and germ have been removed, but it is not artificially whitened.

oat flour
Since it does not rise during cooking, it must be combined with wheat flour to make bread and other leavened products; it makes these products heavier.

corn flour
Primarily added to crepe, cake, muffin and bread mixes; it must be combined with wheat flour if the mixture is intended to rise.

bread

Food made from flour, water and salt, often containing an agent (leaven or yeast) that makes it rise.

croissant
A small roll of layered or puffed dough, frequently eaten as a plain or stuffed pastry; it is also used to make hors d'oeuvres and sandwiches.

black rye bread
Made from rye flour, this dense strong-tasting bread goes particularly well with seafood and smoked foods.

bagel
Jewish ring-shaped roll traditionally coated in sesame seeds; it is usually served warm, with cream cheese.

Greek bread
Round loaf with a golden crust, sometimes sprinkled with sesame seeds; olive bread is one of its many variants.

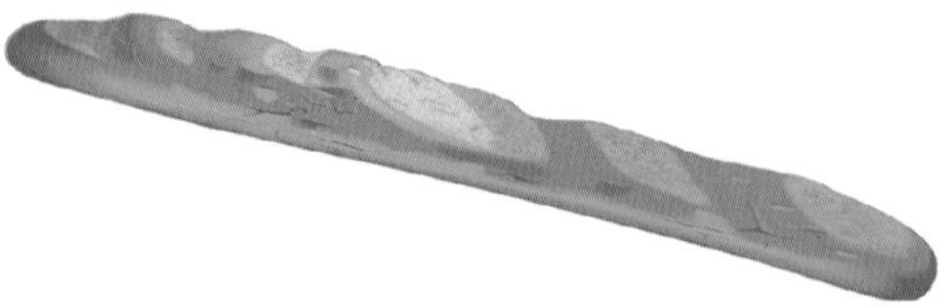

baguette
This light crusty, typically French bread is often served with a meal and also goes well with cheese and pâté; it must be eaten fresh.

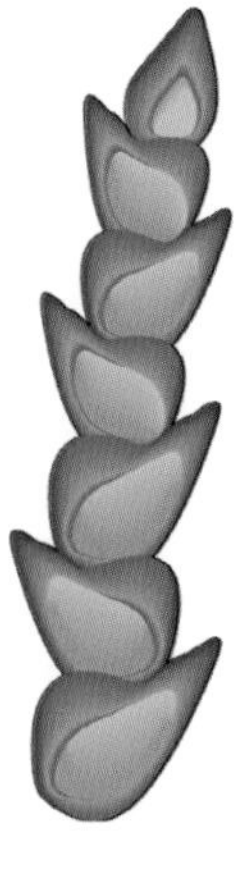

ear loaf
Baguette made so it can be easily broken into pieces by hand.

French bread
Long crusty loaf resembling an oversized baguette; it stays fresh somewhat longer than the typical baguette.

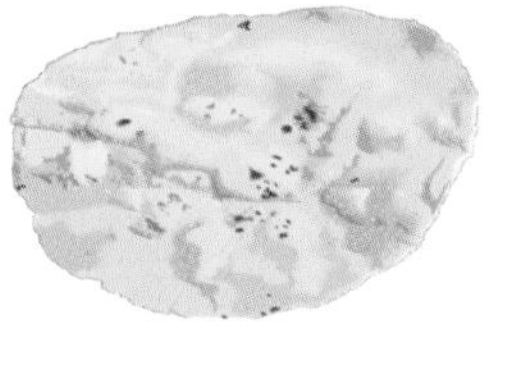

Indian chapati bread
Flat crusty, slightly puffy bread, eaten warm with vegetables and rice or used as a spoon to scoop up food.

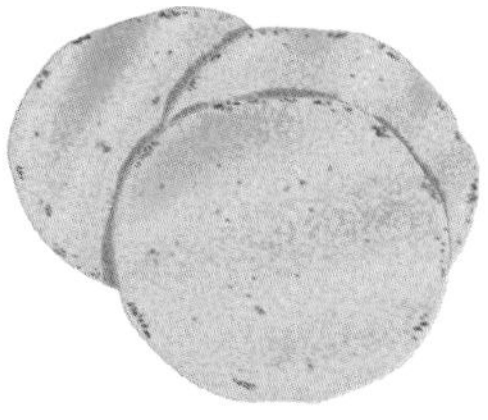

tortilla
Disk of unleavened bread made with corn flour that is the basis for many Latin-American dishes; it can be eaten plain, with a filling or cooked.

pita bread
Flat bread originally from the Middle East; its crust forms a pocket that can be filled with hot or cold kinds of stuffing.

Indian naan bread
The yogurt in the dough of this soft light sweetish bread helps it rise; it is eaten plain or stuffed.

cracked rye bread
Thin crusty flat bread made with rye flour, usually eaten with cheese.

phyllo dough
Flexible wafer-thin dough of Greek origin, used to prepare hors d'oeuvres and pastries, such as baklava.

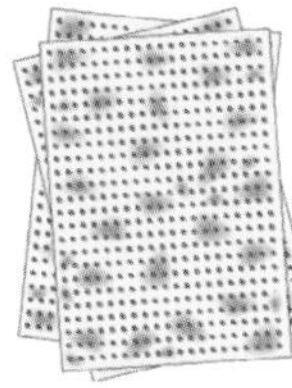

unleavened bread
Light and crusty unleavened bread, eaten mainly during Jewish Passover; it is easily digested and has a long shelf life.

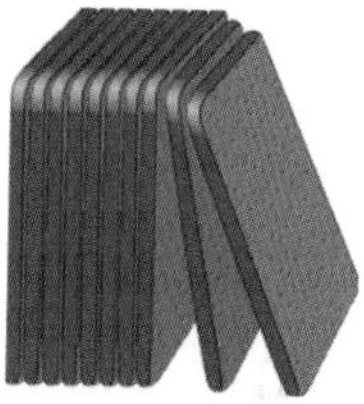

Danish rye bread
This bread is usually sweeter and lighter than German rye bread; it often contains molasses.

white bread
Bread made with white flour that comes in a variety of shapes, thickness and textures; it is less nutritious than wholemeal bread.

multigrain bread
Usually contains 80% white flour, whole wheat flour or a mixture of the two, to which other cereals (oats, rye, etc.) are added.

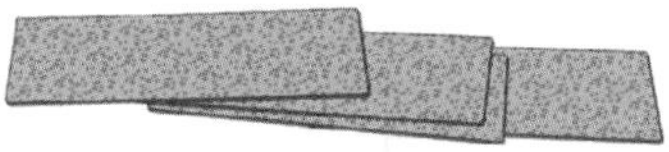

Scandinavian cracked bread
Thin crusty flat bread usually made with wheat or rye flour; it is generally served with soup, salad or cheese.

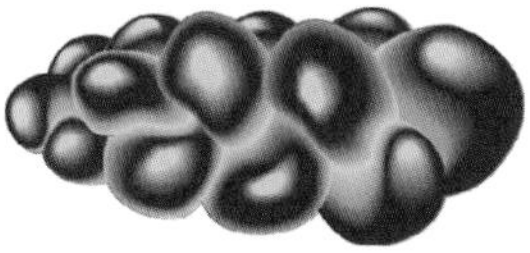

Jewish hallah
Light soft sweetish bread traditionally served on the Sabbath and other Jewish festivals; it is usually braided.

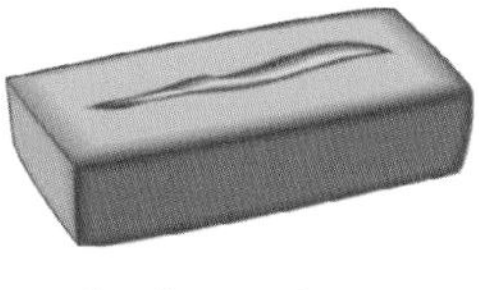

American corn bread
The crumb of this corn flour-based bread is golden in color; it is easy to make and very popular in the southern United States.

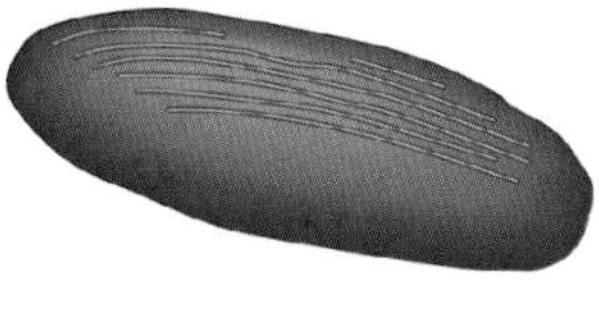

German rye bread
Dark dense bread with a strong, slightly acidic taste, made with rye and wheat flour; it has a long shelf life.

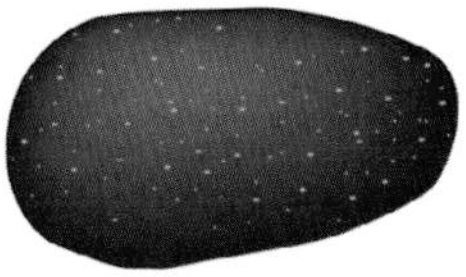

Russian pumpernickel
Made with a mixture of wheat and rye flour, it has a thin but resilient crust; it goes well with soups and ragouts.

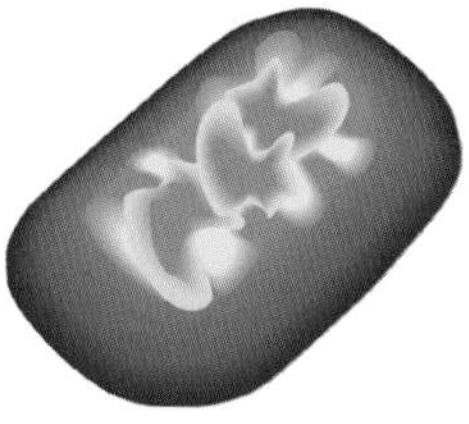

farmhouse bread
Its thick, often floury crust and slightly acidic-tasting nterior can last a long time without becoming stale; it can be used in a variety of ways.

wholemeal bread
Because it is made with whole wheat flour, it is highly nutritious and contains more minerals and protein than white bread.

Irish bread
The crust of this bread is marked with a cross; it is made with baking powder, which gives it a cakelike consistency.

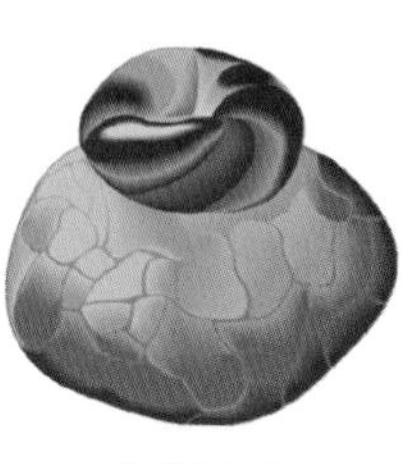

English loaf
Thin-crusted, round or rectangular bread of British origin; it is primarily used to make toast, canapés, croque-monsieurs and sandwiches.

cereal products

pasta

Made from hard wheat semolina and water, shaped into various forms and dried; it is an essential ingredient in Italian cooking that is bought ready-made.

rigatoni
This fairly large tubular pasta is suitable for serving with all kinds of sauces because they cling to it readily.

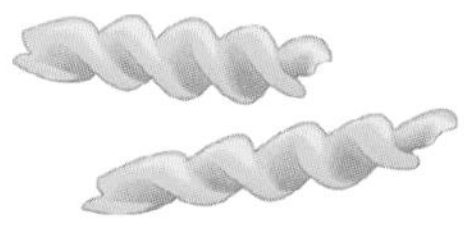

rotini
Because of its spiral grooves, it readily holds meat, cheese and vegetable sauces; it is also ideal for salads.

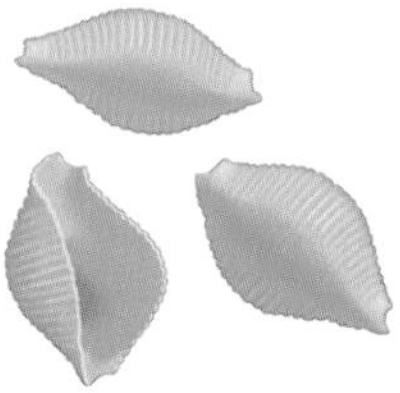

conchiglie
Small shell-shaped pasta that can be served with a sauce or added to soup or pasta salads.

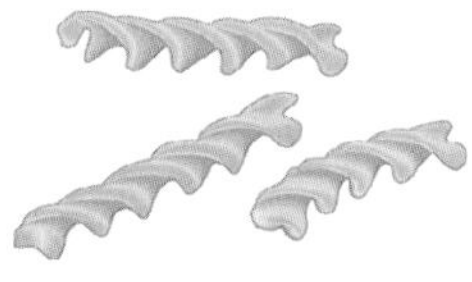

fusilli
This spiral-shaped pasta is thinner and longer than rotini, but can replace it in most recipes.

spaghetti
One of the best-known forms of pasta and the most extensively used; it is traditionally served with tomato or meat sauce.

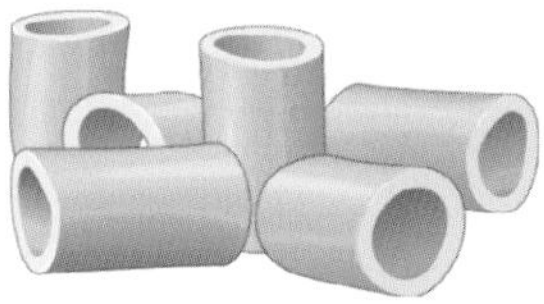

ditali
Short tube-shaped pasta that resemble fat macaroni, used especially in broth and vegetable soups.

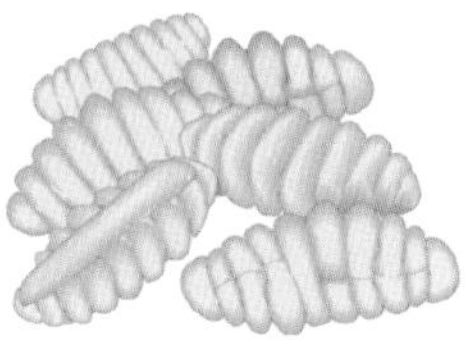

gnocchi
Often made from a potato or semolina dough with eggs and cheese; it is usually served au gratin, as an appetizer.

tortellini
Pasta stuffed with meat or cheese and sometimes colored with tomato or spinach; it is delicious with tomato or cream sauce.

spaghettini
Thinner than spaghetti but thicker than angel hair pasta or vermicelli noodles; it is particularly well suited to delicate sauces.

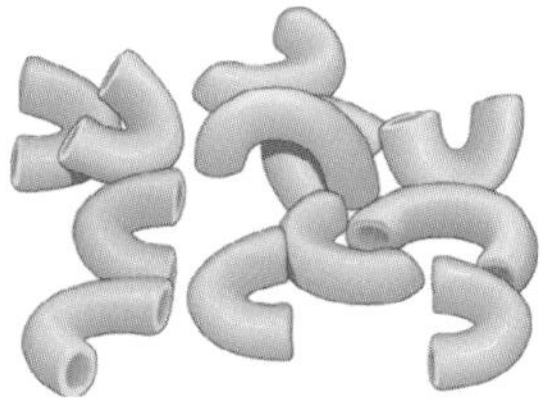

elbows
Sometimes used in a salad, this type of macaroni is also served with tomato or cheese sauce.

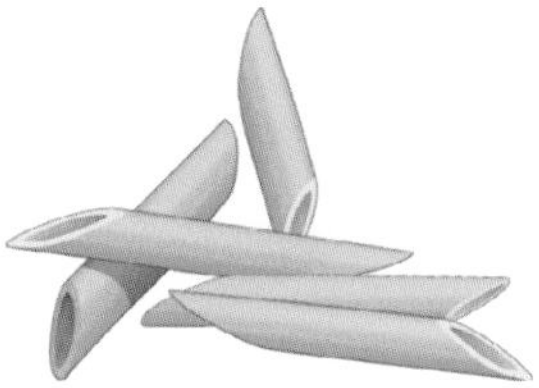

penne
Tube-shaped pasta with diagonally cut ends, often served with a spicy tomato sauce in a dish called penne all'arrabiata.

cannelloni
This fairly large tubular pasta is usually stuffed with meat or cheese, covered with tomato sauce and baked au gratin.

lasagna
These wide strips, green if spinach-flavored, are combined with a filling in alternate layers to create the eponymous dish.

ravioli
Pasta stuffed with meat, cheese or vegetables; a classic way to serve it is with tomato sauce, sprinkled with grated Parmesan.

spinach tagliatelle
Flat ribbonlike pasta made with spinach and eggs, traditionally served with meat sauce.

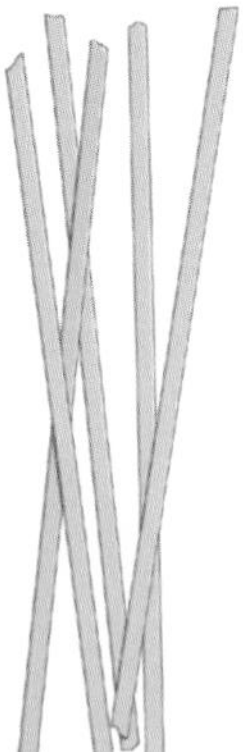

fettucine
Thicker but not as wide as tagliatelle, this pasta is often served with Alfredo sauce.

Asian noodles

This pasta is a staple of Asian cooking; generally classified according to its main ingredient: wheat, rice, buckwheat or mung beans.

soba noodles
Made with buckwheat flour, these noodles are used extensively in Japan, where they are mainly served cold, with soy sauce.

somen noodles
Fine whitish Japanese wheat noodles that go particularly well in salads and soups.

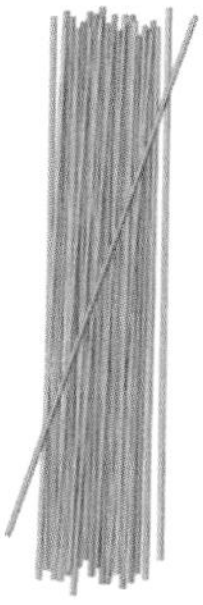

udon noodles
These Japanese wheat noodles are thicker than somen noodles; among their various uses, they can be added to soup, salads and sautéed dishes.

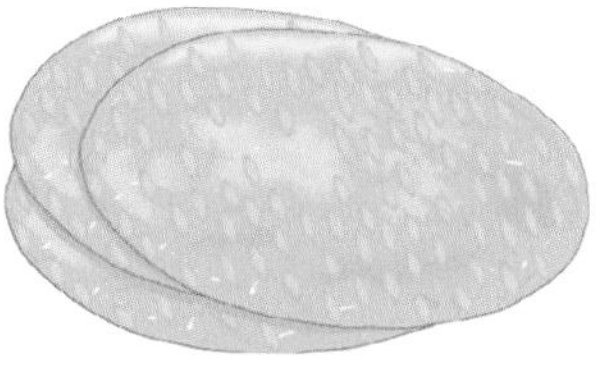

rice papers
Thin semitransparent sheets made with rice flour, used in Asia to prepare spring and imperial rolls.

rice noodles
Wide ribbons made with rice flour and water; they are often added to soup.

bean thread cellophane noodles
Transparent noodles made with mung bean flour; before adding them to a recipe, they must be soaked in hot or warm water.

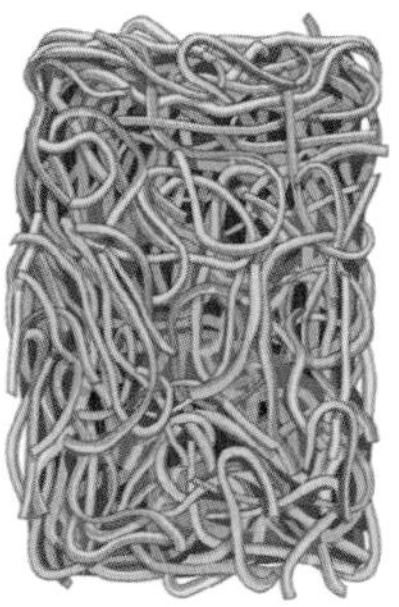

egg noodles
Wheat noodles made with eggs; they are boiled in water, then fried and used to make chow mein.

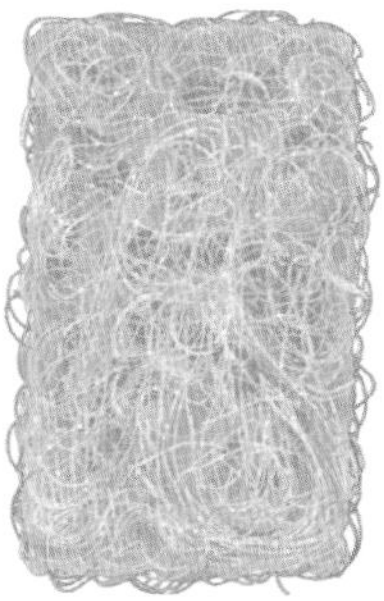

rice vermicelli
Fine rice noodles that are fried in oil and shaped into a nest that is filled with various kinds of Asian food.

won ton skins
Delicate sheets of wheat pasta that are stuffed with meat, seafood or vegetables; an essential ingredient in won ton soup.

rice

Rice is commercially classified by the shape of the grain and the processing it has undergone before being packaged.

white rice
Milled rice from which the bran and germ have been removed; it is often enriched to compensate for the loss of nutrients.

brown rice
Because it is not hulled, the grains retain the bran and germ; it is highly nutritious and has a stronger flavor than white rice.

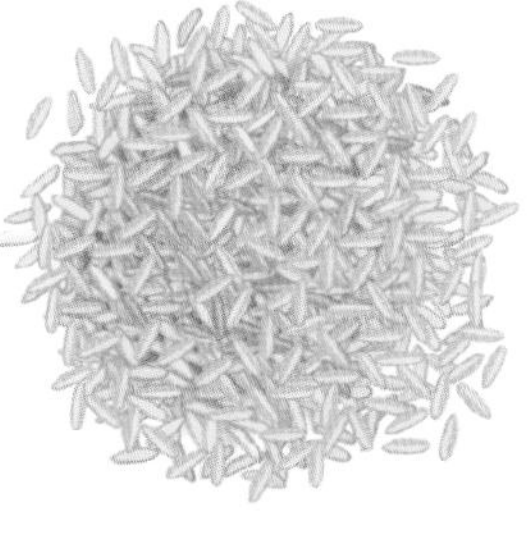

parboiled rice
More nutritious than white rice, it has undergone a steam pressure process prior to milling, to preserve the grains' vitamin and mineral content.

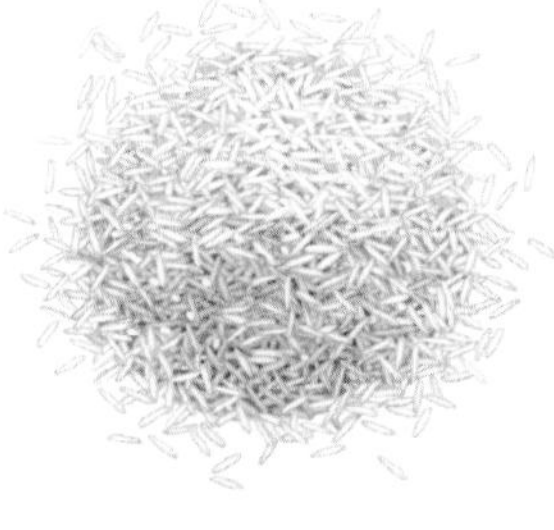

basmati rice
Variety of fine-grained rice native to India, it is known and prized for its aroma and light texture.

coffee and infusions

Aromatic beverages derived from ground beans (coffee) or dried plants (tea, herbal tea) that are combined with boiling water.

coffee

The seeds of the coffee tree can be used to prepare an extremely popular beverage, drunk hot or cold (iced coffee), and well known for its stimulant properties.

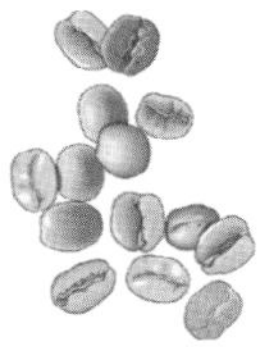

green coffee beans
The green beans remain fresh for many years but the roasted beans quickly lose their flavor.

roasted coffee beans
Roasting beans by a dry method at high temperature enhances the coffee's flavor and aroma.

herbal teas

Infusions made with aromatic dried herbs or plants, usually considered to have calming, digestive, tonic or curative properties.

linden
Tree whose dried leaves and flowers can be made into herbal teas, considered to have calming, sedative and soothing properties.

chamomile
Herbal teas made from the flowers and leaves of this plant are considered to have digestive and calming properties.

verbena
Herbal teas made from this native European plant are believed to have digestive and sedative properties.

tea

Infusion made from the dried leaves of the tea tree; drunk hot or iced, it is the world's most popular beverage after water; it is sold in bags or loose.

green tea
This unfermented product is very popular in China, Japan and Muslim countries; it has a more bitter taste than black tea.

black tea
Made from tea leaves that are fermented and then dried, it represents more than 98% of the total worldwide production of tea.

oolong tea
Semifermented tea; it has a stronger flavor than green tea but is more delicate-tasting than black tea.

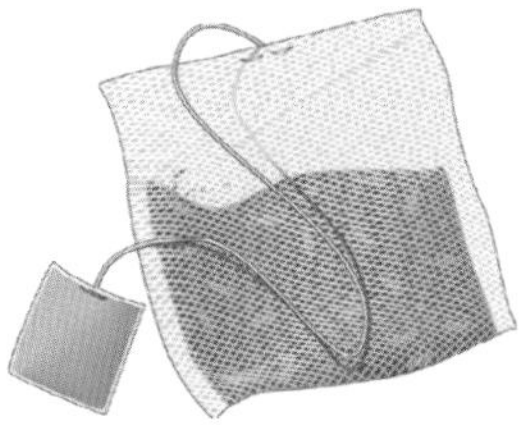

tea bag
Filled with ground leaves, it is often less flavorful than loose tea, which is composed of whole leaves.

chocolate

Smooth paste made with cocoa and sugar, extensively used in making candy and pastry and often eaten plain, as bars or squares.

dark chocolate
Includes semisweet and bitter chocolate, which contain from 35% to 70% chocolate liquor; it is often used in cooking and is also eaten plain.

milk chocolate
Made with chocolate liquor and cocoa butter mixed with powdered milk; it cannot be used in cooking because the milk solids it contains burn when heated.

cocoa
The key ingredient in chocolate; grinding the beans of the cacao tree produces chocolate liquor, which yields cocoa butter and cocoa powder.

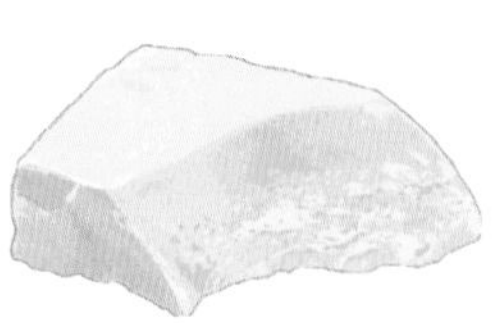

white chocolate
Sweet and creamy, it is made from cocoa butter, sugar and condensed or powdered milk.

sugar

Sweet-tasting foodstuff derived from certain plants; the most common varieties of sugar come from sugarcane and sugar beets.

granulated sugar
The most commonly used sugar in cooking and baking; it is white, fully refined and composed of small crystals.

powdered sugar
White sugar in powdered form, containing about 3% corn or wheat starch, added to prevent caking; it is used mainly for icing and decorating.

brown sugar
Fine, only slightly refined sugar crystals that still contain molasses; it has a stronger taste than white sugar.

rock candy
White or brown sugar in very large crystal form; it is used especially to sweeten fruits in brandy.

molasses
Thick liquid residue from the process of converting sugarcane into sugar; it is used to make rum, candy, soft cookies and pies.

corn syrup
Thick sweet syrup used extensively in making candy and pastry.

maple syrup
Produced by reducing sugar maple sap; it is used to make various desserts and to accompany pancakes, poach eggs and glaze ham.

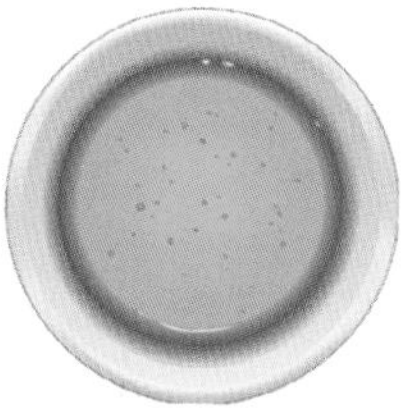

honey
Substance made by bees from flower nectar; its color and flavor vary depending on the nectar's origin.

fats and oils

Animal or vegetable fatty acids in solid or liquid form generally used to cook, flavor, thicken or preserve foods.

corn oil
Has relatively little flavor or odor; one of the most ubiquitous oils, used for cooking, frying and seasoning foods.

olive oil
This extract derived from olive pulp is essential to Mediterranean cooking, both for preparing and seasoning recipes.

sunflower-seed oil
This delicately flavored oil is the main ingredient in margarine and dressings; it is also used for frying sweet foods.

peanut oil
Heat-resistant, mild-tasting oil equally well suited to frying and to dressing salads.

sesame oil
Very popular in Asian cooking and characterized by its rich delicate toasted-nut flavor; it is not well suited to high temperatures.

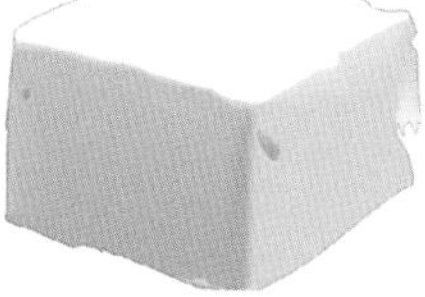

shortening
Substance produced by rendering pork fat; it is used for the lengthy cooking of certain ragouts, and for frying and for making pastry.

lard
Pork fat; fatback is rendered into shortening whereas side pork (fat streaked with lean) provides lardons and bacon.

margarine
Fatty acid used as a substitute for butter; those made with vegetable oil contain no cholesterol.

dairy products

Foods produced by processing fresh milk; they are used daily in Western countries, where they are known for their high calcium content.

yogurt
Semisolid substance produced by milk fermentation and the action of bacterial cultures; it can be eaten as is or cooked.

ghee
Clarified butter originating in Asia and traditionally made from buffalo milk; it is very popular in India and in Arab countries.

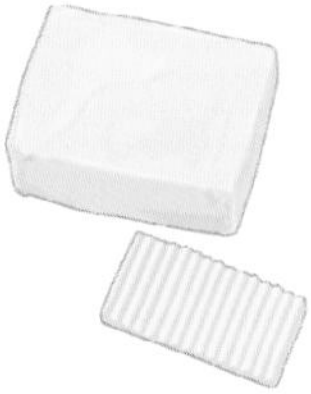

butter
Fatty rich substance produced by churning cream; it is used in cooking or is added to various recipes for sauces, pastries and creams.

milk

Highly nutritious white liquid secreted by some domesticated female mammals and consumed as food; used alone, the word refers to cow's milk.

homogenized milk
Milk processed so the fat particles remain suspended instead of rising to the surface; varieties include whole, partially skimmed or skim.

goat's milk
Whiter and stronger-tasting than cow's milk, it is also easier to digest.

evaporated milk
Milk from which a significant percentage of the water has been evaporated; it has a high milk fat content and is used primarily for making desserts.

buttermilk
Tangy liquid that separates from cream during churning; today, commercial buttermilk is made by adding bacterial culture to milk.

powdered milk
Dehydrated milk that can be stored for one year without refrigeration if the container remains unopened.

cream

This product is obtained by skimming milk and is classified according to its milk fat content; it is used extensively in cooking, as is or whipped.

whipping cream
With a minimum 30% milk fat content, this is the richest cream; it is often whipped and used to make and decorate various desserts, such as cream puffs.

sour cream
Has a thick and creamy consistency and is obtained by fermentation and bacterial action; it can be used to flavor or garnish recipes.

fresh cheeses

Nonripened cheeses that contain up to 80% water; they are smooth and mild or slightly tangy; they spoil quickly.

cottage cheese
Low in fat and grainy in texture; it works well as a spread or can be added to salads, desserts and sauces.

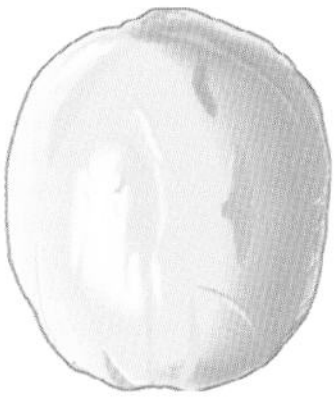

mozzarella
This native Italian cheese has a rubbery texture and is firmer than other cheeses; it is the garnish of choice for pizza.

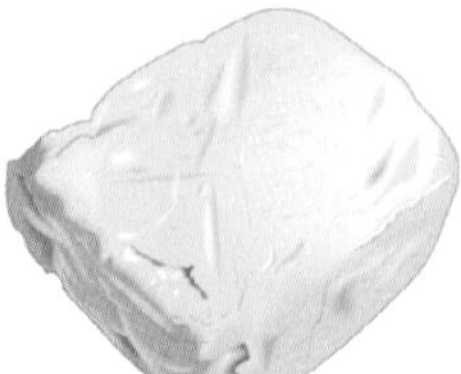

ricotta
Granular cheese with a smooth moist rind; it is used in Italian cooking, primarily for stuffed foods and desserts.

cream cheese
Made with cream, which is sometimes mixed with milk; it is smooth and spreads easily, and is used as a spread or as a dessert ingredient (e.g., in cheesecake).

goat's-milk cheeses

Cheeses made from goat's milk, which is sometimes mixed with cow's milk; these medium-strong cheeses have a smooth texture and a high water content.

Chèvre cheese
Fresh rindless cheese that has a tangy, mild taste; it is sometimes flavored with herbs.

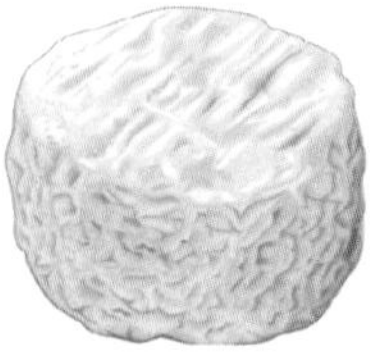

Crottin de Chavignol
Soft French cheese with a rind that is covered in mold; it is eaten fresh or dried and, as it dries, its flavor becomes more pronounced.

pressed cheeses

Ripened cheeses that are also cooked and pressed and contain less than 35% moisture; they usually have a firm compact texture and a hard rind.

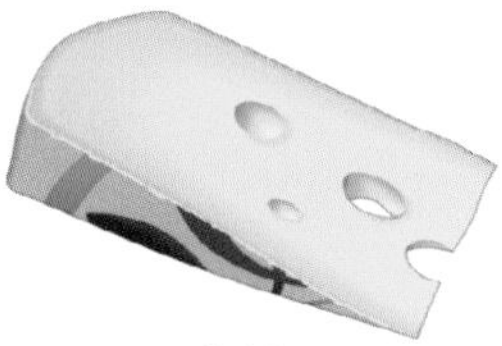

Jarlsberg
Norwegian cheese with large holes that has a characteristic nutty taste.

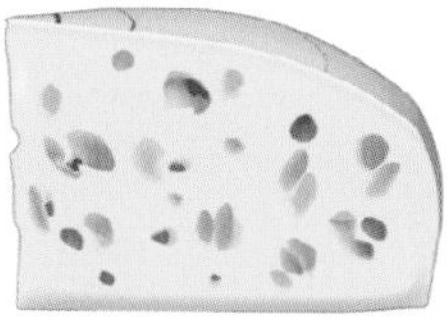

Emmenthal
Characterized by large holes, this mild Swiss cheese is very popular in fondues and au gratin dishes.

Raclette
Cheese specifically made to be used in a traditional eponymous dish that originated in the Valais region of Switzerland.

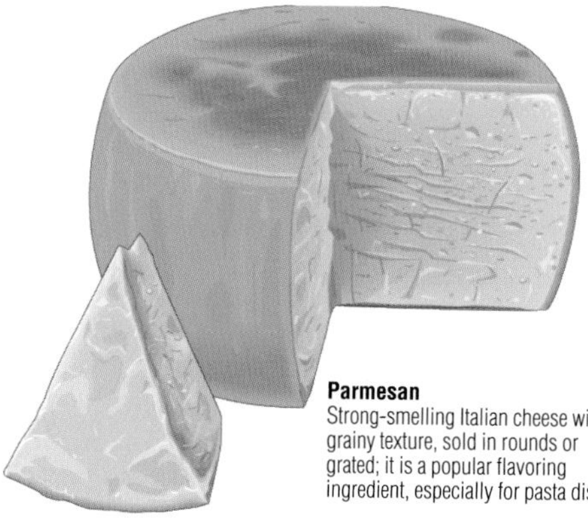

Parmesan
Strong-smelling Italian cheese with a grainy texture, sold in rounds or grated; it is a popular flavoring ingredient, especially for pasta dishes.

Gruyère
Swiss cheese with small holes called "eyes" and a medium-sweet taste; extensively used in cooking, either as is, grated or melted.

Romano
Native to Rome, this dry granular cheese is made from cow, ewe or goat's milk or a mixture of all three; it is mostly used in grated form.

blue-veined cheeses

Also called "blue cheese", it usually has a crumbly texture, is veined with mold and has a pungent peppery taste.

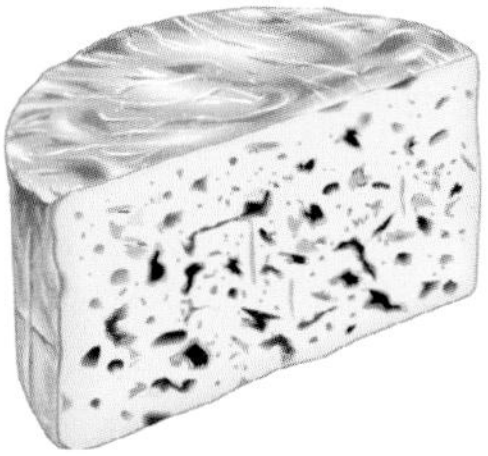

Roquefort
The best-known blue cheese, originally from Roquefort, France; it is made from ewe's milk and goes well with pears, cream and butter.

Stilton
English cheese with a firm but creamy texture; it is often served with crackers and port.

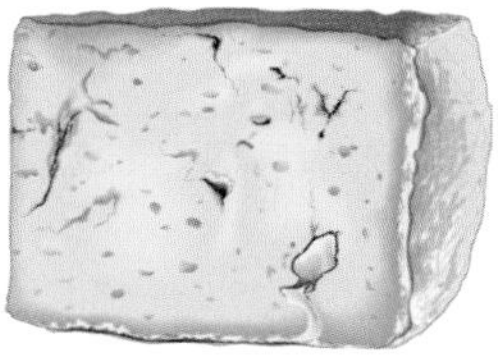

Gorgonzola
Native to Italy and recognizable by its textured gray rind, spotted with red.

Danish Blue
Native to Denmark, it has a pungent flavor, a creamy texture and a milk fat content of up to 60%.

soft cheeses

Ripened but neither pressed nor cooked, these cheeses have a soft, creamy texture and a somewhat velvety rind, which is often edible.

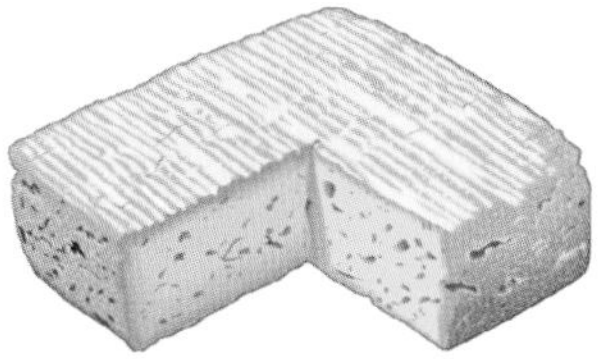

Pont-l'Évêque
Somewhat soft cheese with a pronounced odor; its name derives from the town in Normandy where it is made.

Coulommiers
Native to the area around Paris, it is similar to Brie but smaller; it contains from 45% to 50% milk fat.

Camembert
Soft and easy to spread, France's most famous cheese is smaller and slightly firmer than Brie.

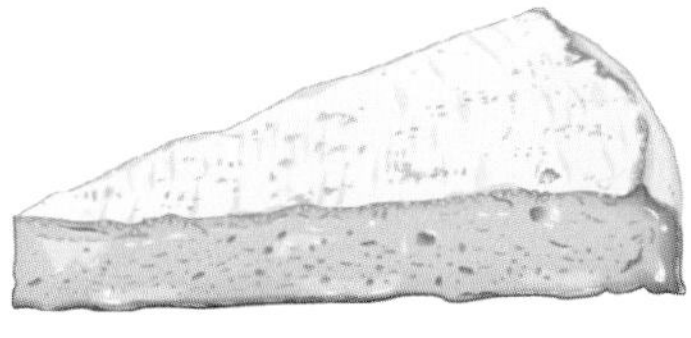

Brie
Native to Brie, near Paris, it is one of the best-known French cheeses; among its many varieties is the one from Meaux.

Munster
Cheese with a powerful penetrating odor, originally from the Alsace region; it has a creamy texture and a smooth moist rind.

variety meat

Edible parts of slaughter animals, apart from the meat.

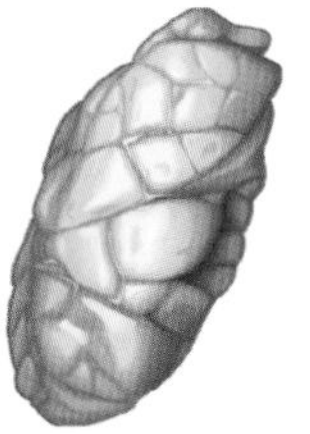

sweetbreads
Designates the tender, delicately flavored thymus gland of calves, lambs and kids; veal sweetbreads are especially prized.

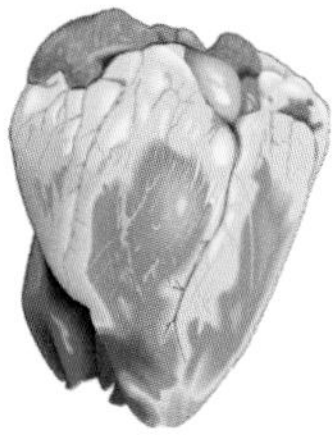

heart
Cooked in ragouts and casseroles, it can also be sautéed, roasted, braised or simmered; veal, lamb and chicken heart are the most popular.

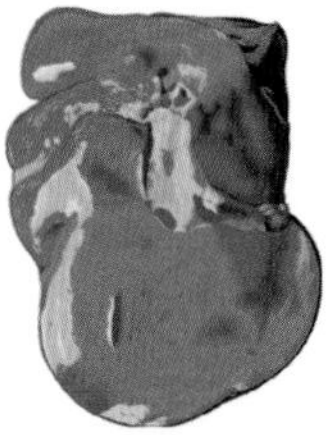

liver
People eat the liver of slaughter animals, poultry, game and some fish (cod); it has a high iron content.

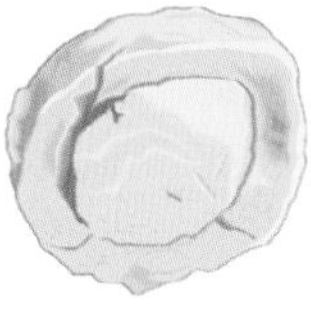

marrow
Soft fatty tissue found in the centre of bones; it is served mainly with roast beef and cardons and can also be used to add flavor to soups.

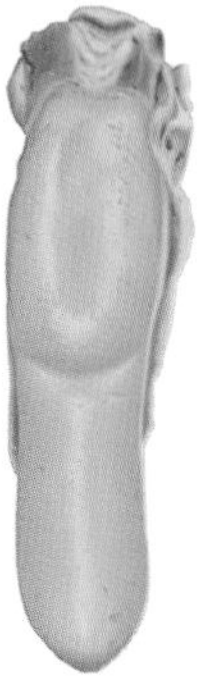

tongue
Covered with a thick skin that lift off easily once cooked; calf tongu is the most tender.

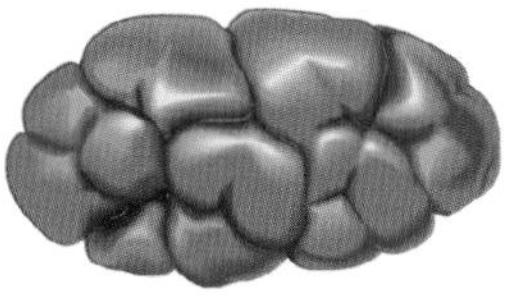

kidney
Young slaughter animals such as calves tend to have more tender kidneys; there is an unpleasant aftertaste if they are not prepared carefully.

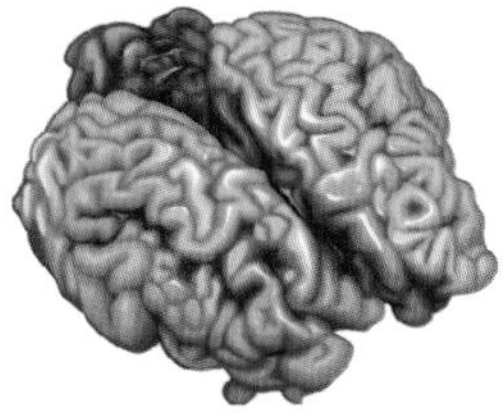

brains
Lamb, sheep and veal brains are the most prized, served in salads, au gratin, in croquettes, stuffings and sauces.

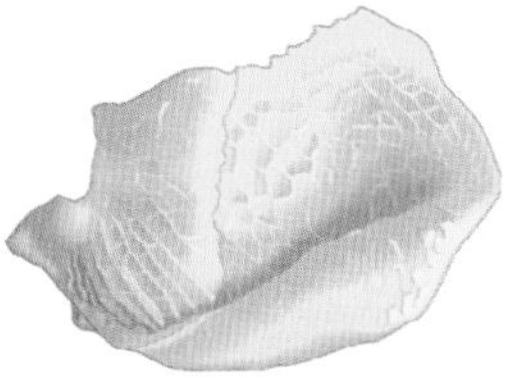

tripe
Ruminants' stomach lining, made ready for cooking; the main ingredient in many regional dishes, the best known being tripes à la mode de Caen.

game

Wild animals that can legally be hunted and eaten as food; includes large and small game animals and game birds.

quail
Roasted, braised, broiled or cooked in a casserole, this small bird is a prized delicacy; it is delicious cooked with grapes.

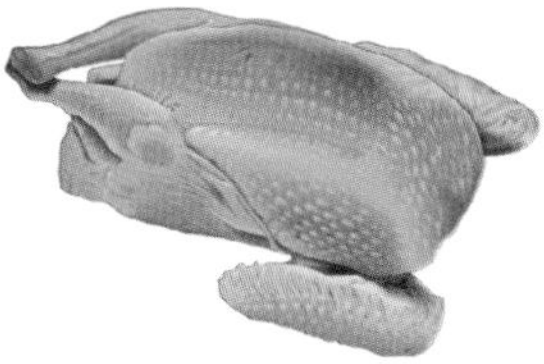

pigeon
Eaten since ancient times, pigeon is broiled, sautéed or roasted, or braised when the bird is mature; it is traditionally served with green peas.

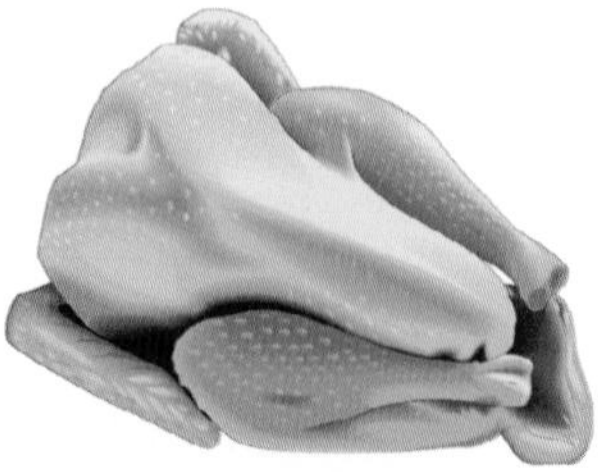

guinea fowl
The same size as a small chicken, it is more flavorful when young and weighs less than 2 lbs; its flesh is slightly gamy.

pheasant
Young pheasant are often broiled and served with a moist stuffing; as they age, they become dry and less tender and so are usually made into terrine or pâté.

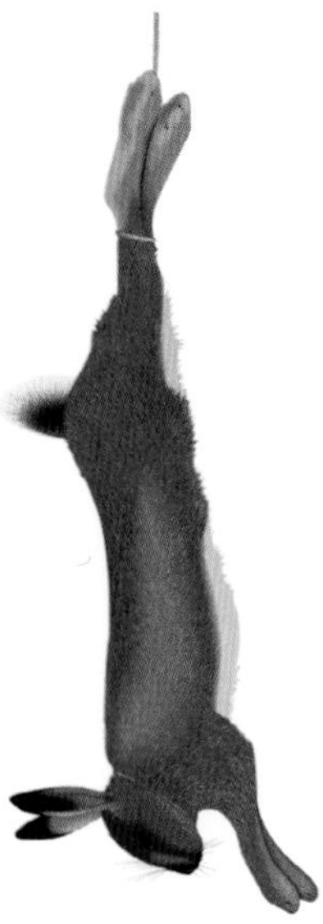

hare
The dark meat has a stronger flavor than rabbit meat. Young hares can be roasted or sautéed; older ones are marinated, then jugged or made into terrine or pâté.

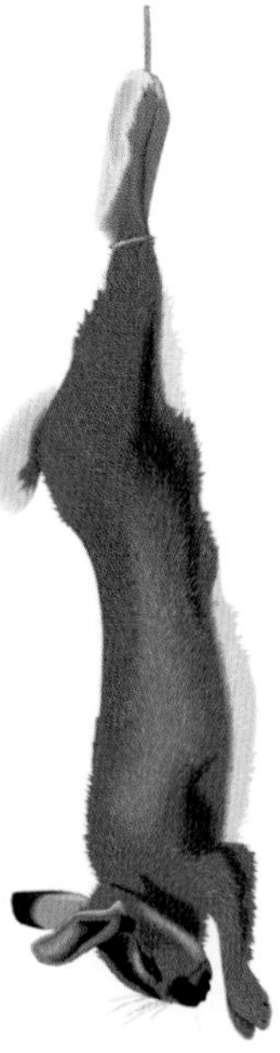

rabbit
Wild rabbit has a more pronounced flavor than domesticated rabbit, which tastes like chicken; it is often prepared with a mustard sauce.

poultry

Term that refers to barnyard fowl, most of which have been domesticated for centuries and are now mass-produced.

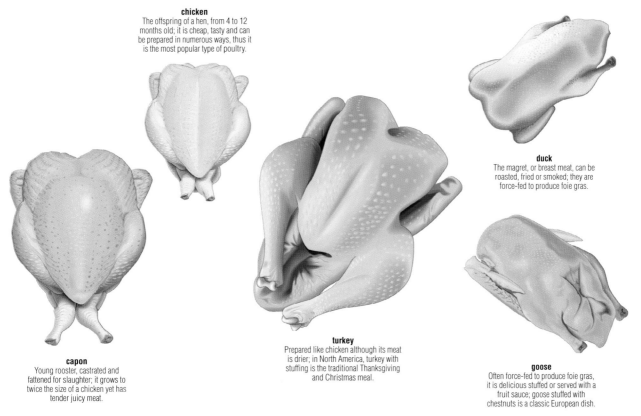

chicken
The offspring of a hen, from 4 to 12 months old; it is cheap, tasty and can be prepared in numerous ways, thus it is the most popular type of poultry.

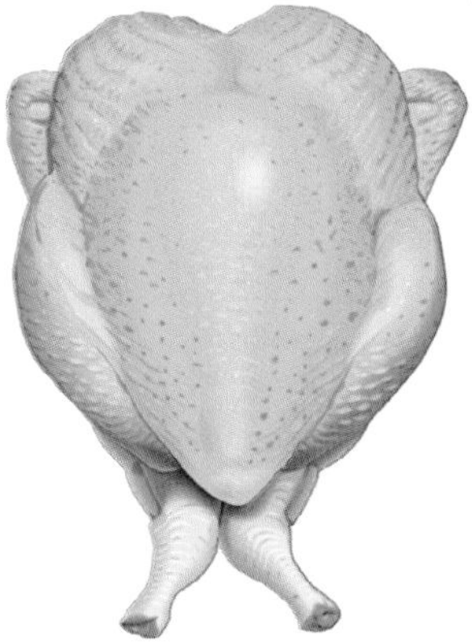

capon
Young rooster, castrated and fattened for slaughter; it grows to twice the size of a chicken yet has tender juicy meat.

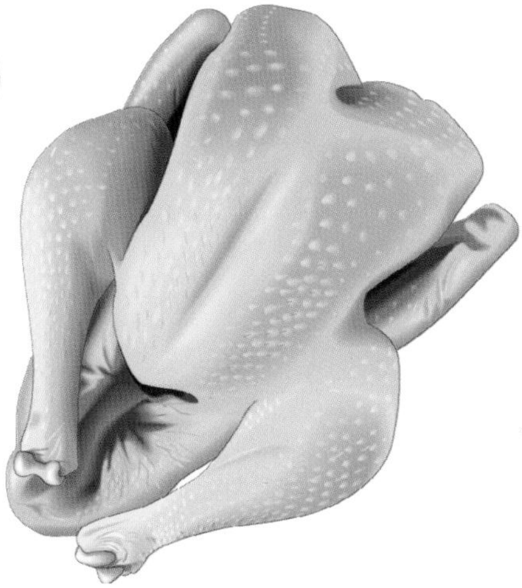

turkey
Prepared like chicken although its meat is drier; in North America, turkey with stuffing is the traditional Thanksgiving and Christmas meal.

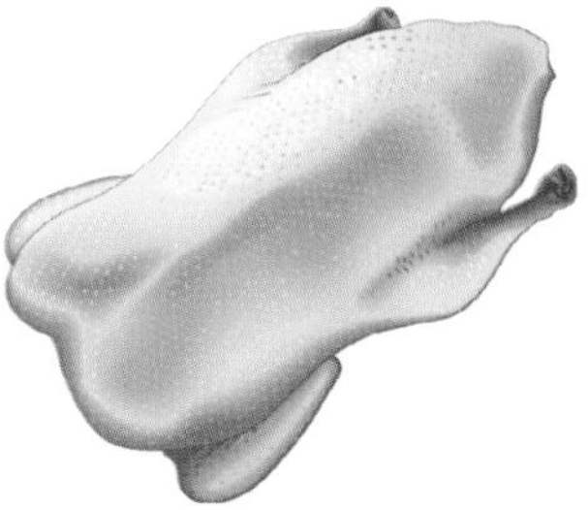

duck
The magret, or breast meat, can be roasted, fried or smoked; they are force-fed to produce foie gras.

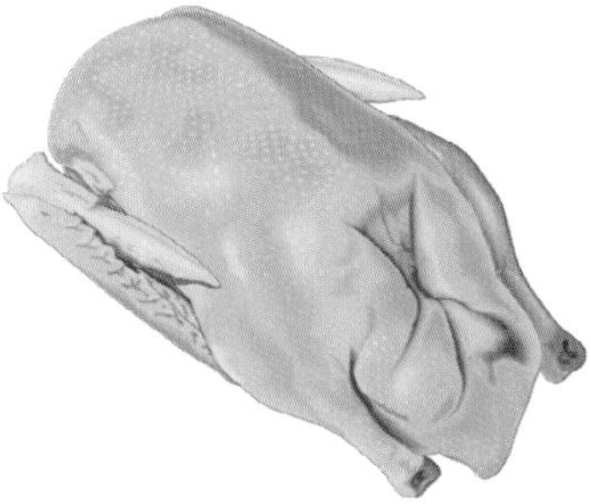

goose
Often force-fed to produce foie gras, it is delicious stuffed or served with a fruit sauce; goose stuffed with chestnuts is a classic European dish.

eggs

Foodstuff that female fowl, especially hens, produce by laying; there are many ways of preparing them: e.g., soft-boiled, scrambled and in omelettes.

ostrich egg
The largest of all eggs, it can weigh up to 5 lbs; one ostrich egg makes an omelette large enough to feed 10 people.

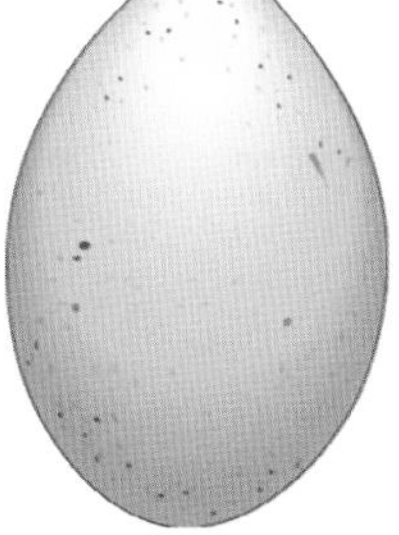

goose egg
These relatively large eggs weigh between 9 and 10.5 lbs; they are rarely found for sale.

quail egg
Very popular in China and Japan, it is usually eaten hard-boiled, often as an appetizer; it also has decorative uses.

pheasant egg
Rounder and smaller than a chicken egg, it is not readily available; it is mostly eaten hard-boiled, in salads or aspics.

duck egg
Prized in Asia for its taste, stronger than a chicken egg's; it must be boiled for at least 15 minutes to destroy harmful bacteria.

hen egg
By far the most commonly eaten, it is cooked as is or added to recipes; used alone, the word "egg" refers to a hen's egg.

meat

Flesh of slaughter animals, consumed as food; a distinction is usually made between red meat, such as beef and lamb, and white meat, such as veal and pork.

cuts of beef

Bovine carcasses are divided into quarters, then into pieces of meat that are ready to prepare.

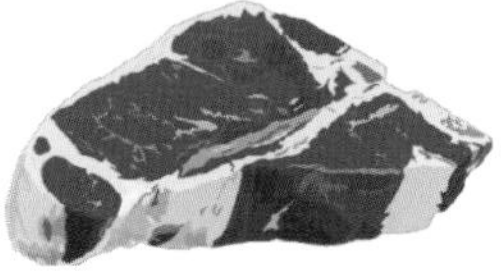

steak
Strip of meat that can be grilled or sautéed; in general, the most tender steaks, loin, sirloin and rib, come from the central section of the carcass.

beef cubes
Their tenderness varies, depending on the section from which they were cut; they are mainly used to make brochettes or ragouts, such as boeuf bourguignon.

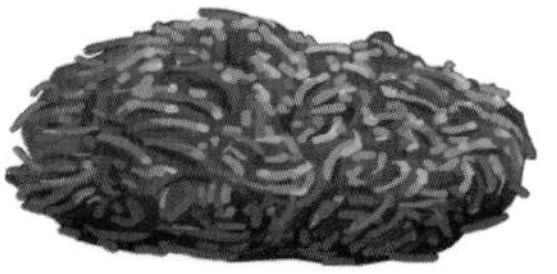

ground beef
Made from various parts of the steer; when lean and taken from the tenderloin, it is the basis for steak tartare.

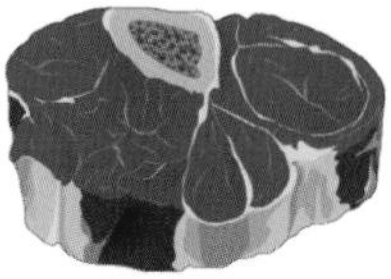

shank
Comes from a section of the front or hind leg of a steer; somewhat tough, it is primarily used in stews.

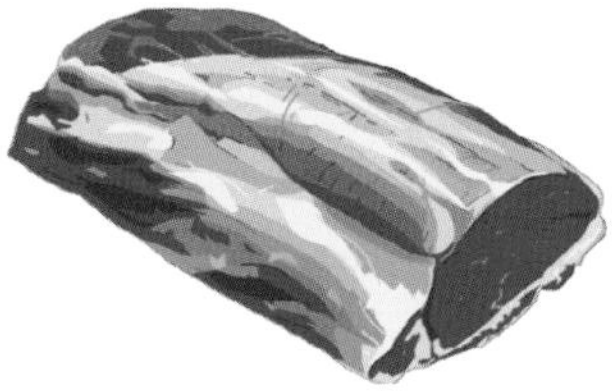

tenderloin roast
Taken from the back, along the spine, it is prized for its tenderness and is excellent when grilled; tournedos and châteaubriand come from it.

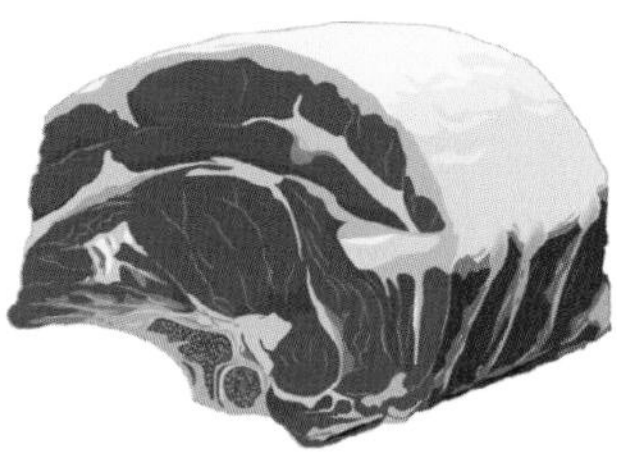

rib roast
Piece of meat intended for roasting, taken from the animal's rib section; this tender and tasty cut is one of the most popular kinds of roast beef.

back ribs
They comprise sections of rib taken from the back and the attached muscles; they are delicious with a sweet-and-sour sauce.

cuts of veal

Pieces taken from a cow's offspring, slaughtered before it reaches one year; veal is a tender delicate meat that ranges in color from whitish to pink.

veal cubes
Their tenderness varies, depending on the section of the calf they come from; they are used mainly to make brochettes or ragouts.

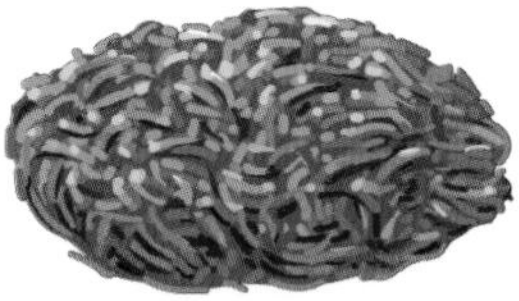

ground veal
Made from various parts of the calf, its flavor is less pronounced than that of ground beef.

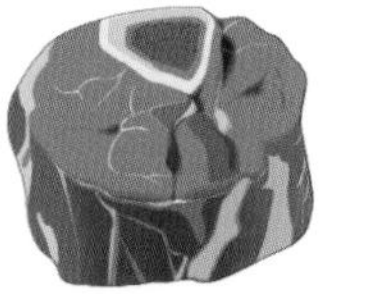

shank
Comes from a section of the front or hind leg of a calf; when sliced, it is primarily used to make the Italian dish called osso bucco.

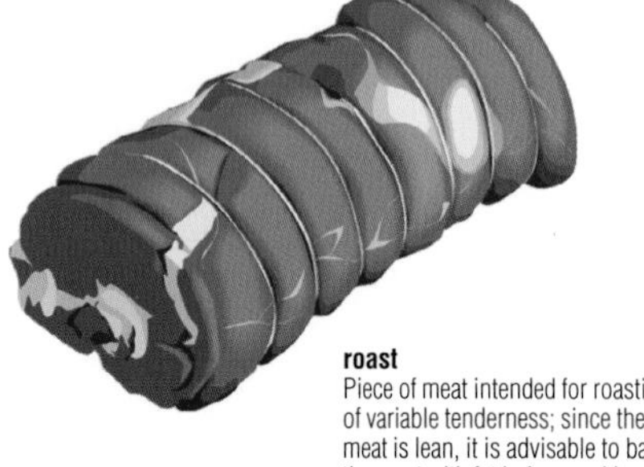

roast
Piece of meat intended for roasting, of variable tenderness; since the meat is lean, it is advisable to bard the roast with fat before cooking it.

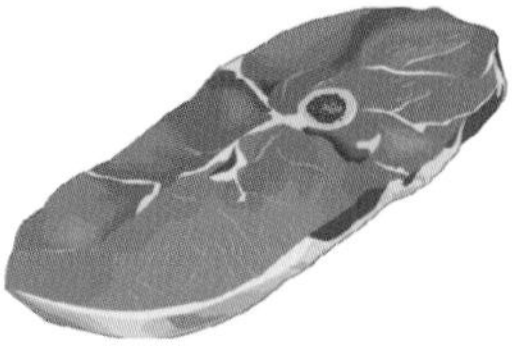

steak
Strip of meat that can be grilled or sautéed; in general, the most tender steaks, loin, sirloin and rib, come from the central section of the carcass.

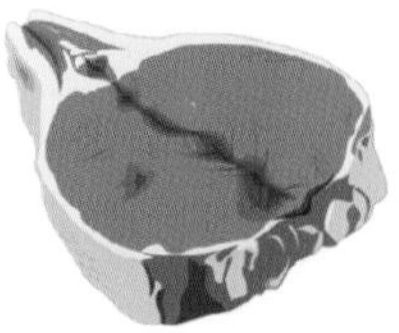

chop
Piece composed of a bone from the rib section and the attached muscles, generally eaten grilled.

cuts of lamb

Highly prized in the Middle East, lamb comes from an animal less than one year old; milk-fed lamb has a more delicate flavor than regular lamb.

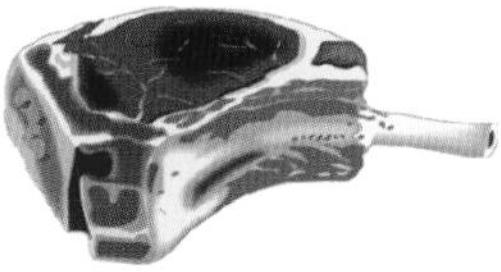

chop
Piece composed of a bone from the rib section and the attached muscles, generally eaten grilled.

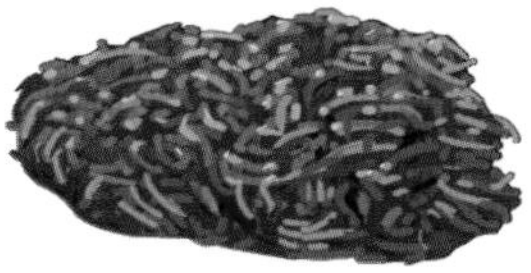

ground lamb
Made from various parts of the lamb, it is used especially to make Greek moussaka.

lamb cubes
Their tenderness varies, depending on the section of the lamb they come from; they are used mainly to make brochettes or ragouts.

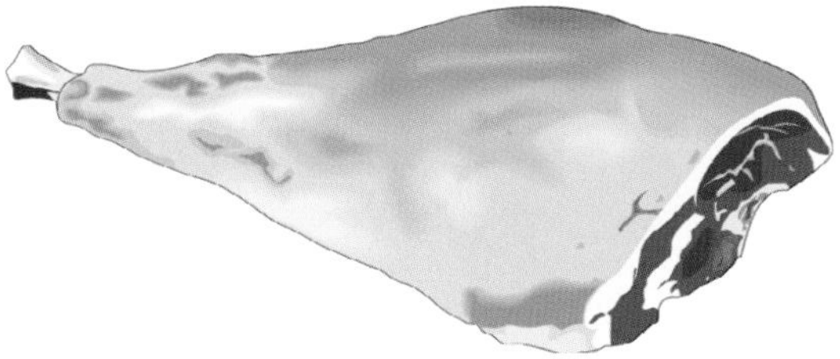

roast
Piece of meat intended for roasting; the gigot, taken from the hind section of the carcass, is the best-known cut and is a traditional Easter dish in some countries.

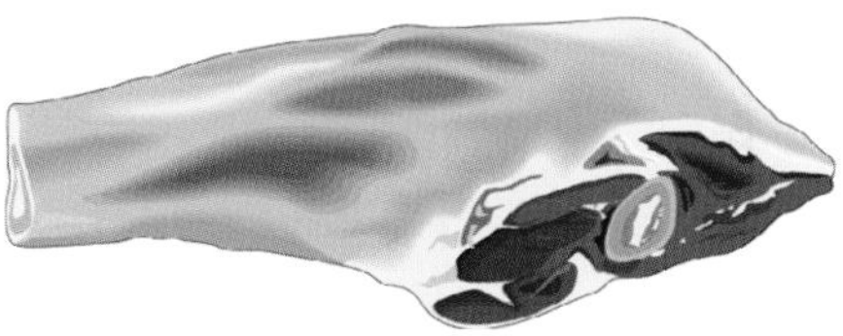

shank
Section of the front or hind leg of a lamb.

cuts of pork

Pieces taken from a pig carcass, the most tender of which come from the loin (back); the side (belly), leg (butt) and shoulder are the least tender parts.

spareribs
They comprise sections of rib taken from the back and the attached muscles; North American-style Chinese cooking usually serves them with sweet-and-sour sauce.

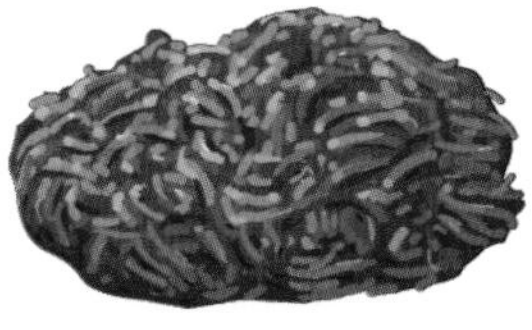

ground pork
It is made from various parts of the pig and is very tender; it is used especially to make stuffed vegetables and meat loaf.

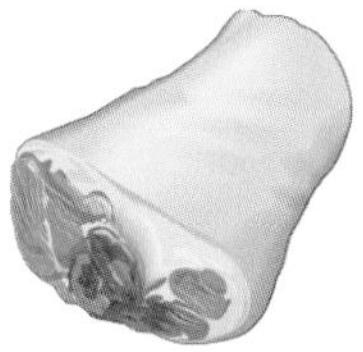

hock
Also called "shank end", it comes from the lower section of the pig's front or hind leg; it is used to make the traditional pork hock stew.

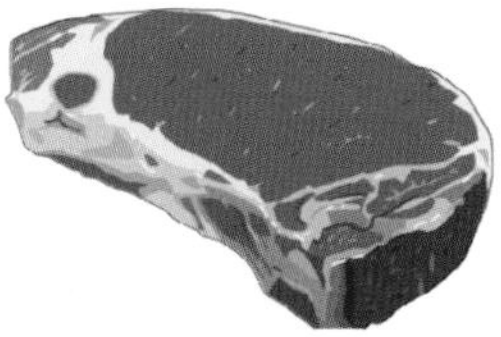

loin chop
Piece composed of a bone from the rib section and the attached muscles; some, like the butterfly chop, are sold boned.

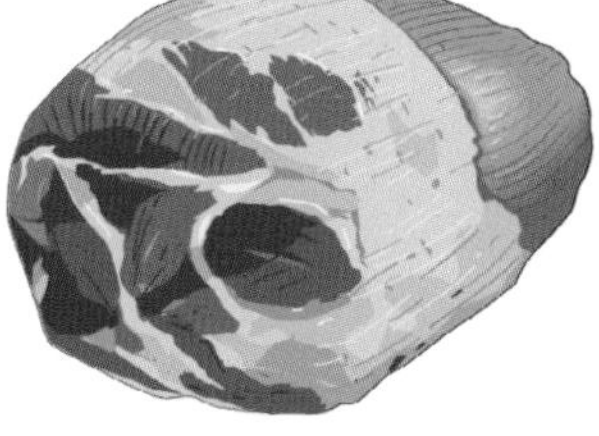

smoked ham
Taken from the pig's legs, this cut is preserved by smoking; it is sold as is, boned or sliced and can be prepared in numerous ways.

roast
Piece of meat intended for roasting, usually from the loin, leg or shoulder.

delicatessen

Foodstuff made from the meat (usually pork) or offal of various animals; among the many different varieties, some can be consumed as is, some are cooked.

rillettes
Often made with pork or goose meat and cooked in fat until the meat disintegrates; they are always served cold.

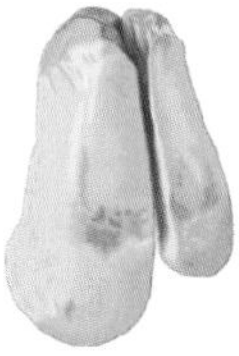

foie gras
Goose or duck liver, abnormally enlarged by force-feeding; considered a gourmet item, it is sold raw or ready to eat.

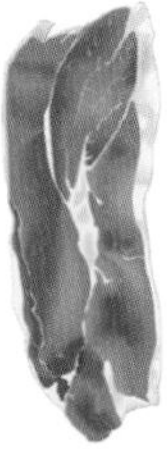

prosciutto
Raw dried ham native to the Parma region of Italy; it is mostly eaten thinly sliced and served with melon or fresh figs.

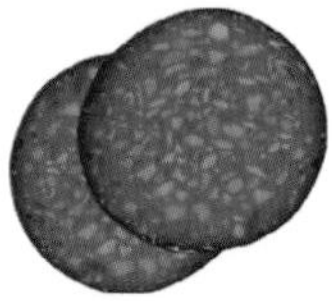

kielbasa sausage
Native to Poland, it is made with coarsely ground pork and beef, seasoned with garlic and spices.

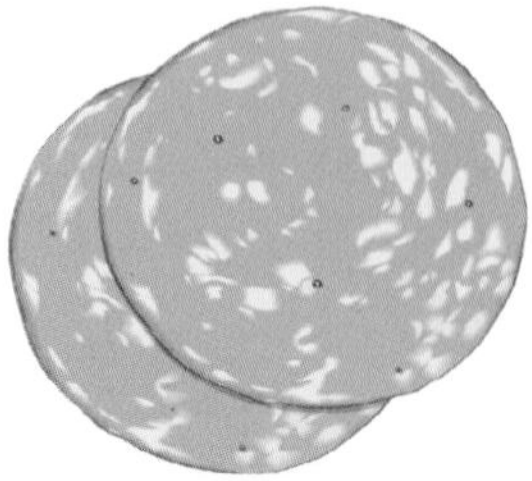

mortadella
Italian sausage made with meat and fat and flavored with peppercorns and pistachios.

blood sausage
The main ingredients in blood pudding are blood and suet (from pigs or other animals) packed into a casing; white pudding is made from white meat and milk.

chorizo
Semidry Spanish sausage seasoned with red chiles, available in several versions that vary in spiciness; it is often added to paella.

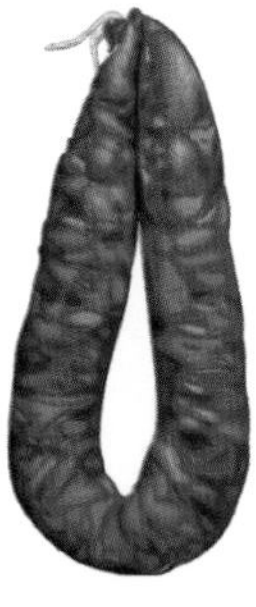

pepperoni
This dry, somewhat spicy Italian sausage is a favorite pizza topping; diced, it is added to certain dishes to give them more flavor.

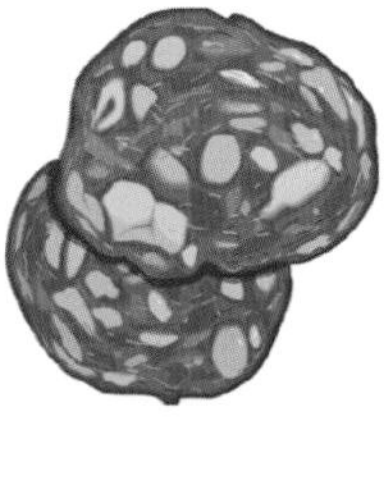

Genoa salami
Dry Italian sausage made with a mixture of pork, veal and fat; the thin slices are often served as an hors d'oeuvre.

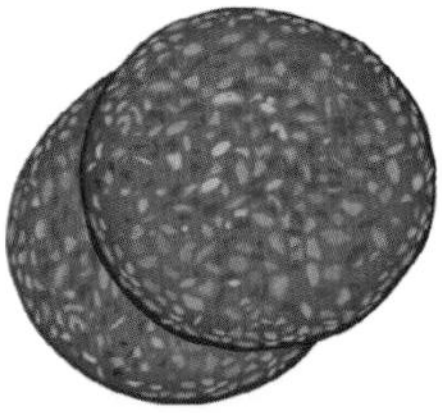

German salami
Made with finely ground beef and pork, it is usually served sliced, as an hors d'oeuvre, but also on pizza and canapés and in sandwiches.

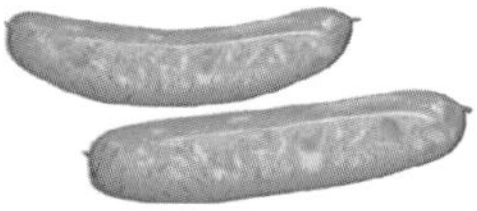

Toulouse sausage
Raw sausage, native to France, made with coarsely ground pork and pepper; often added to cassoulet.

merguez sausage
Small, highly spiced sausage made with lamb, beef or mutton; popular in North Africa and Spain, it is usually eaten fried or grilled.

andouillette
Cooked sausage made from pig or calf intestines; it can be grilled or fried and served with mustard.

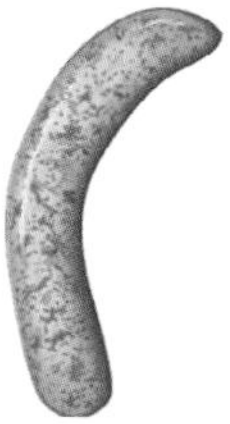

chipolata sausage
Raw pork, or pork and beef, sausage characteristically flavored with cloves; it is often grilled or fried.

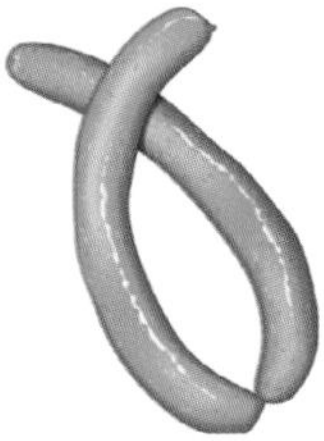

frankfurter
Smoked precooked sausage that is native to Germany and made from a pastelike pork mixture; among its many versions is the American hot dog.

pancetta
Rolled Italian bacon, sometimes spiced; it is an essential ingredient in pasta alla carbonara and also flavors sauces, soups and meat dishes.

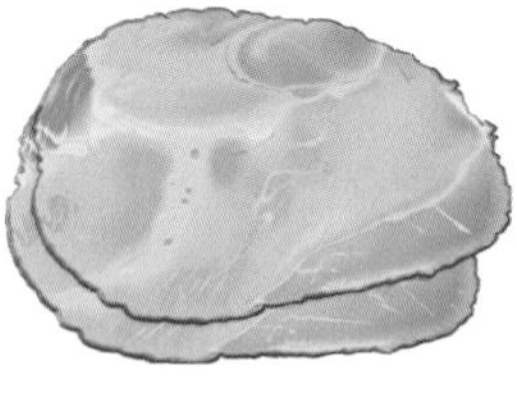

cooked ham
Salt-cured and cooked pork meat, usually served thinly sliced; it is eaten hot or cold, especially in sandwiches, and on croque-monsieurs and canapés.

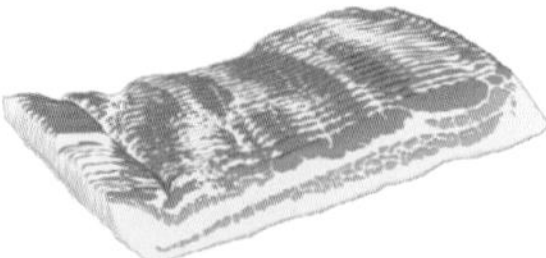

American bacon
Salted and smoked side pork, cut into thin slices; in North America, it is traditionally served with eggs, for breakfast.

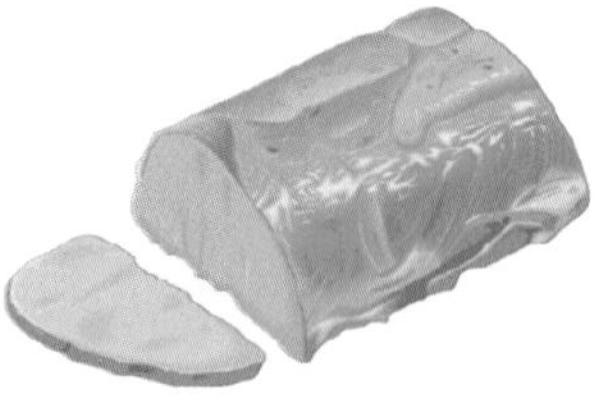

Canadian bacon
Piece of salted, usually smoked, meat from the pork loin; it goes well with eggs and in dishes such as quiches and omelets.

mollusks

Usually marine-dwelling, soft-bodied invertebrates; some have shells and are sold live.

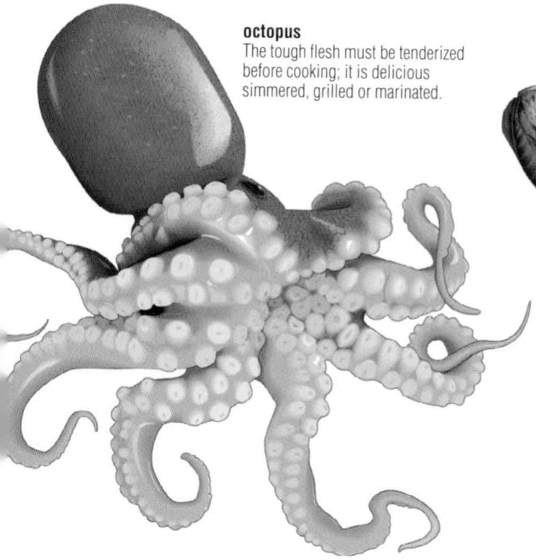

octopus
The tough flesh must be tenderized before cooking; it is delicious simmered, grilled or marinated.

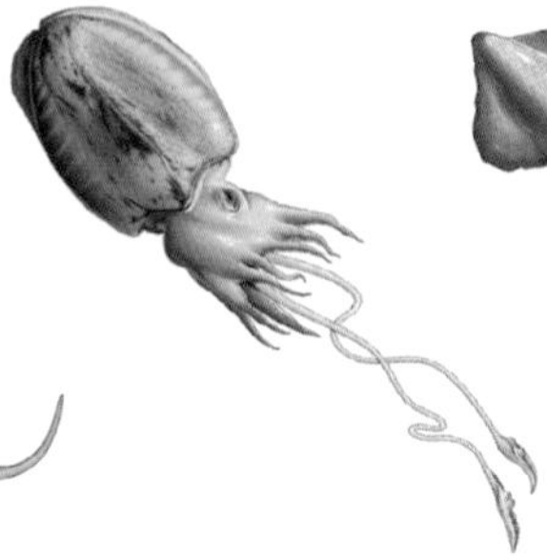

cuttlefish
The very firm flesh must be pounded before cooking and is delicious stuffed; the ink, or sepia, can also be used to color certain recipes.

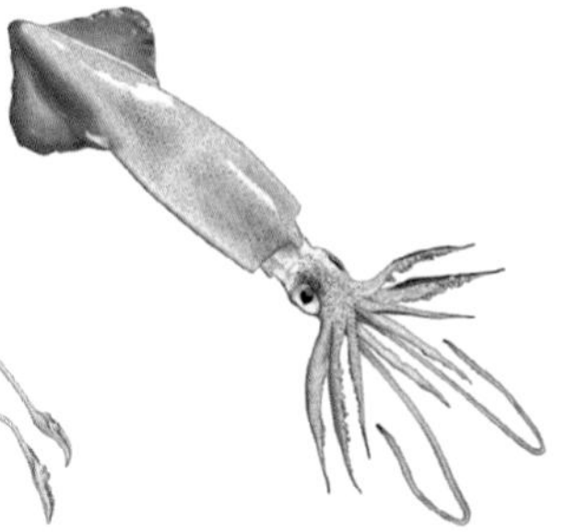

squid
The edible parts are the tentacles, the body pouch and the ink; often grilled or fried, the lean flesh can occasionally be rubbery.

scallop
The main edible part is the nut (the muscle that opens and shuts the shells) and sometimes the coral (the orange part); excellent raw or cooked, it can be prepared in numerous ways.

hard-shell clam
Mollusk with a very hard shell whose flesh can be eaten raw or cooked; they are used to make chowder, a popular New England recipe.

soft-shell clam
Primarily harvested in the Atlantic, this large soft mollusk of the clam family can replace the latter in recipes.

abalone
The muscle, also called the "foot", is delicious raw or cooked; it must be pounded before cooking.

great scallop
Related to the scallop, the delicately flavored flesh is prized by Europeans; the shells are resistant to heat and are often used as cooking and serving dishes.

snail
Snails are often sold canned, frozen or ready-cooked; served with garlic butter, they constitute a classic appetizer.

limpet
It has a single shell and is eaten raw with lemon juice or vinegar, or grilled, with butter.

common periwinkle
Its flesh resembles the snail's, which it can replace in most recipes; whether eaten hot or cold, it is always cooked first.

clam
Related to the hard-shell clam, it is as tasty raw (with or without lemon juice) as it is cooked (in soups, or stuffed, like the blue mussel).

cockle
Generally designates the European variety, although others exist; it has a firmer texture and a more pronounced flavor than oysters and mussels.

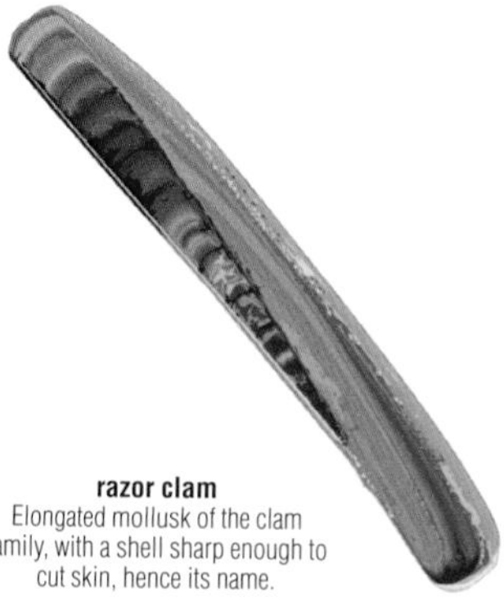

razor clam
Elongated mollusk of the clam family, with a shell sharp enough to cut skin, hence its name.

flat oyster
Less common than the cupped oyster, with a completely flat lower shell; the belon variety is particularly prized.

cupped Pacific oyster
Juicy and meaty, with a well-developed lower shell; like all oysters, it is often eaten raw, either plain or with lemon juice.

blue mussel
Fresh mussels are usually poached in broth or steamed until they open; those that fail to open should be discarded.

whelk
Resembles a large periwinkle; the flesh will toughen if it is cooked too long and it is often eaten sprinkled with lemon juice.

crustaceans

Aquatic invertebrates having a carapace over their bodies; they are sold live, frozen (raw or cooked) or canned.

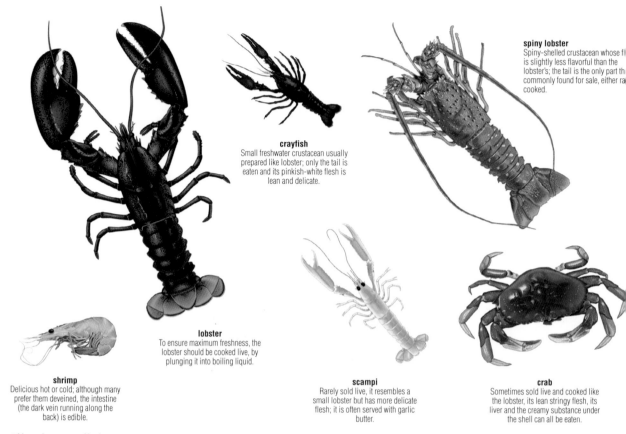

lobster
To ensure maximum freshness, the lobster should be cooked live, by plunging it into boiling liquid.

crayfish
Small freshwater crustacean usually prepared like lobster; only the tail is eaten and its pinkish-white flesh is lean and delicate.

spiny lobster
Spiny-shelled crustacean whose f is slightly less flavorful than the lobster's; the tail is the only part th commonly found for sale, either ra cooked.

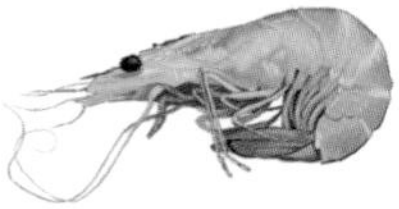

shrimp
Delicious hot or cold; although many prefer them deveined, the intestine (the dark vein running along the back) is edible.

scampi
Rarely sold live, it resembles a small lobster but has more delicate flesh; it is often served with garlic butter.

crab
Sometimes sold live and cooked like the lobster, its lean stringy flesh, its liver and the creamy substance under the shell can all be eaten.

cartilaginous fishes

Fish with skeletons made of cartilage rather than bones; their flesh usually contains no bones.

larger spotted dogfish
Shark of the Mediterranean and Atlantic; it tastes best if cooked when very fresh and served with a flavorful sauce.

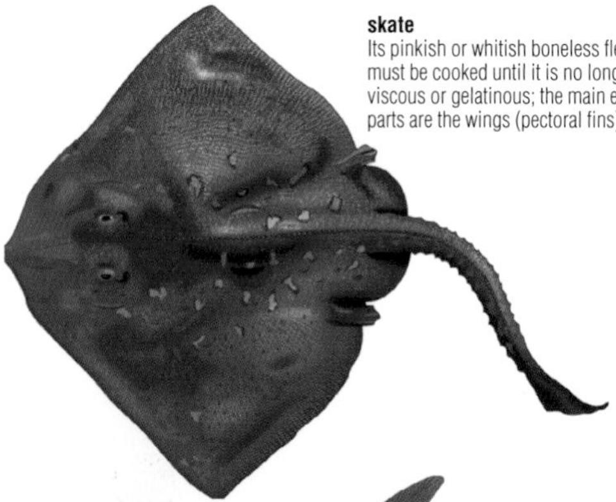

skate
Its pinkish or whitish boneless fles must be cooked until it is no longe viscous or gelatinous; the main ed parts are the wings (pectoral fins).

smooth hound
Shark of the Mediterranean, Atlantic and Pacific; its white flesh has a faint smell of ammonia that disappears with cooking.

sturgeon
This freshwater or saltwater fish of imposing size is prized for its firm flesh and its eggs, which constitute the true caviar.

bony fishes

Fish with smooth flat scales and a rigid skeleton; the various species make up the largest group of fish.

anchovy
Very popular in Mediterranean countries, this highly perishable fish is often preserved in brine, oil or salt and sold in cans or jars.

sardine
Related to the herring, it is often canned (in oil, tomato sauce or white wine) and is eaten with bread, as is or with lemon juice.

herring
One of the world's most harvested species, it is sold fresh as well as canned, marinated, salted and smoked; it can replace mackerel in most recipes.

smelt
The somewhat oily cucumber-scented flesh is the main part eaten, but the head, bones, tail and eggs are also considered edible; it is most often simply gutted and fried.

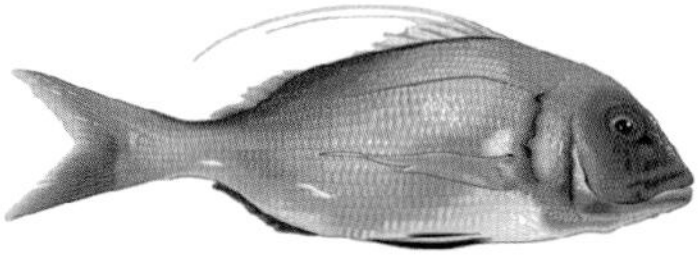

sea bream
Its delicate lean white flesh can be prepared in many ways although the simplest are the best; it is delicious smoked, in sashimi or in ceviche.

goatfish
In spite of its many bones, it is highly prized, especially in southern France, for its particularly delicate flavor.

mackerel
Traditionally served with gooseberry chutney, its somewhat oily flesh spoils rapidly if not eaten promptly.

eel
Prized in Europe and Asia for its delicate firm oily flesh; its excess fat is removed when it is skinned.

gurnard
Somewhat lean, it is often used in soups such as bouillabaisse and in fish stews; it is also excellent baked, poached, fried or smoked.

lamprey
The flavor of its oily boneless flesh is more delicate than the eel's; lamproie à la bordelaise is a famous French gourmet recipe.

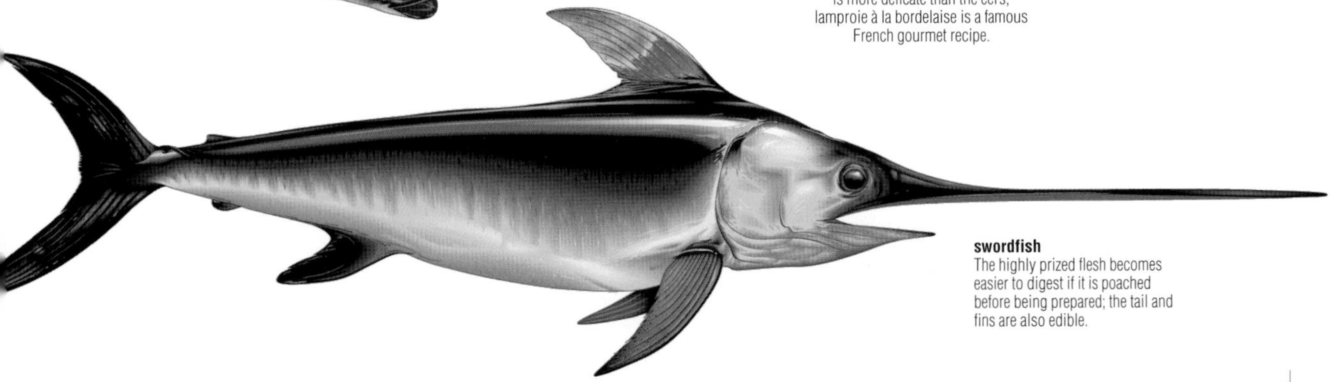

swordfish
The highly prized flesh becomes easier to digest if it is poached before being prepared; the tail and fins are also edible.

bony fishes

bass
Rarely found for sale, this sport fishing species has lean flaky flesh that is well suited to all cooking methods.

mullet
Excellent hot or cold, it is well suited to all cooking methods; its eggs are used to make boutargue provençale and the Greek taramosalata (a creamy spread).

carp
Soaking in vinegar water will make the sometimes muddy taste of the wild varieties disappear; it is especially prized for its tongue and lips.

perch
Related to the pike perch, it is often poached, steamed or floured and fried in butter; its bony flesh has a delicate flavor.

shad
Acidic ingredients such as sorrel and rhubarb are often used to prepare its somewhat oily, tender flesh; the bones of the female are more easily removed.

pike
The flesh sometimes has a slightly muddy taste that disappears with soaking; because it has many bones, it is often made into pâtés or quenelles.

pike perch
Freshwater fish with a lean firm delicate flesh that can be cooked in many ways; whole and filleted, it is prepared like perch or pike.

bluefish
Very popular in the U.S., this lean fish is often grilled, braised or poached; it is prepared like mackerel.

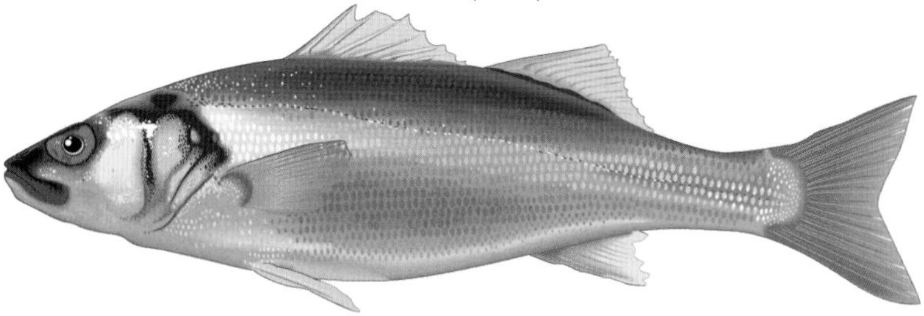

sea bass
Its firm lean flesh has few bones and withstands cooking well; it is best cooked simply, to avoid overpowering the delicate taste.

monkfish
Also called "angler fish", only its tail is eaten and the taste is said to be similar to lobster; it is delicious cold, served with a dressing.

tuna
Often canned in oil or water, it is one of the main ingredients in the Italian dish vitello tonnato; it is also used to make salads, sushi and sashimi.

redfish
Excellent raw, cooked or smoked; if cooked in broth or grilled, it is best to leave the skin on to prevent its flaky flesh from falling apart.

whiting
Its delicate flaky flesh is similar to cod's and is easy to digest; it is often wrapped in tinfoil or cooked in a flavored broth.

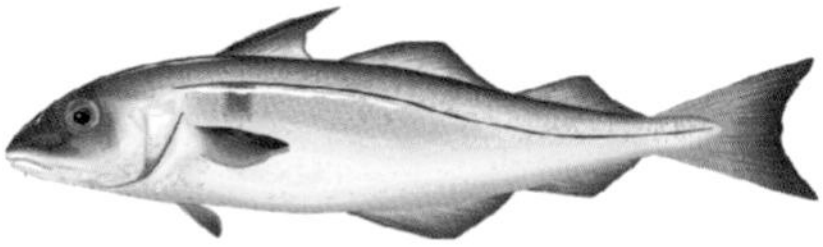

haddock
Related to cod but with flesh that is sweeter and more delicate; it is often smoked.

black pollock
Especially popular in England, it is also used in Canada to make surimi, a paste from which imitation seafood is made.

Atlantic cod
It is often dried or salted and its liver yields an oil that is rich in vitamin D; it is fished extensively off the Canadian and American coasts.

trout
Freshwater fish with medium-oily delicate and fragrant flesh that is delicious smoked; rainbow trout is the species most often raised in captivity.

Pacific salmon
King salmon (or chinook) has the oiliest flesh and is greatly prized; the leaner and less oily varieties are often canned.

Atlantic salmon
The only species of salmon inhabiting the Atlantic; it is prized for its pink, somewhat oily and fragrant flesh and is sold fresh, frozen and smoked.

brook trout
Native to Canada, it resembles the trout and is greatly prized for its delicate flesh, which is best when simply prepared.

John dory
Usually prepared like sole or turbot, its medium-firm flesh contains gelatinous bones that make an excellent fish stock.

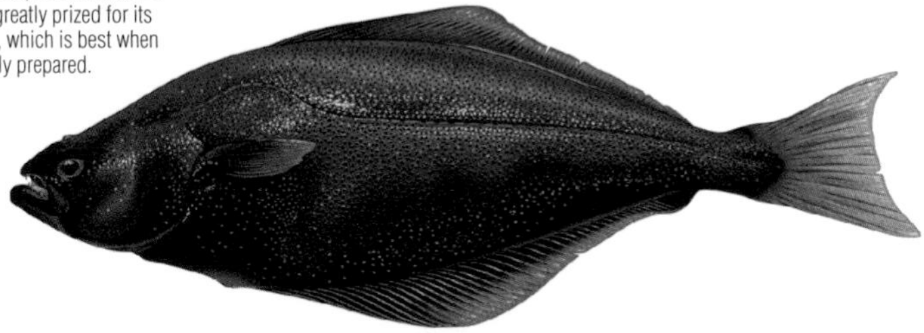

halibut
The largest of the flatfish family, it is commonly cooked in wine or served with anchovy butter; its lean flaky flesh has few bones.

turbot
One of the tenderest saltwater fish, with lean white flavorful flesh; sold whole or filleted, it is usually poached or grilled.

common plaice
Because it has so many bones, it is often sold filleted and is one of the varieties used in fish-and-chips; it is found primarily off the European coast.

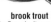

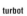

sole
Often confused with plaice, it is only found in waters off the European coast; the most highly prized variety is the common or Dover sole.

packaging

Anything to do with the packing or wrapping of food, whether to sell, cook, freeze or preserve it.

pouch
A small bag.

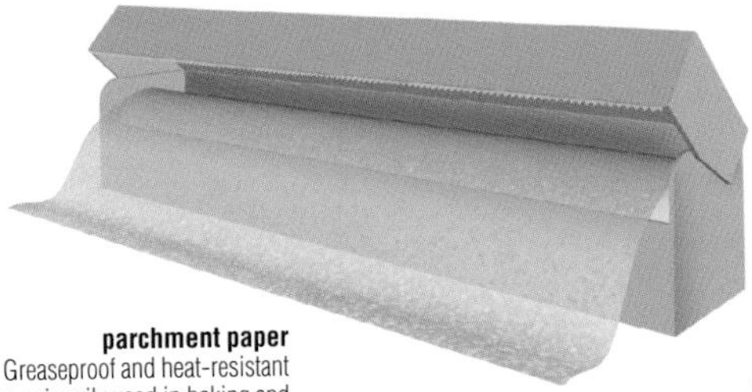

parchment paper
Greaseproof and heat-resistant paper; primarily used in baking and for cooking en papillote.

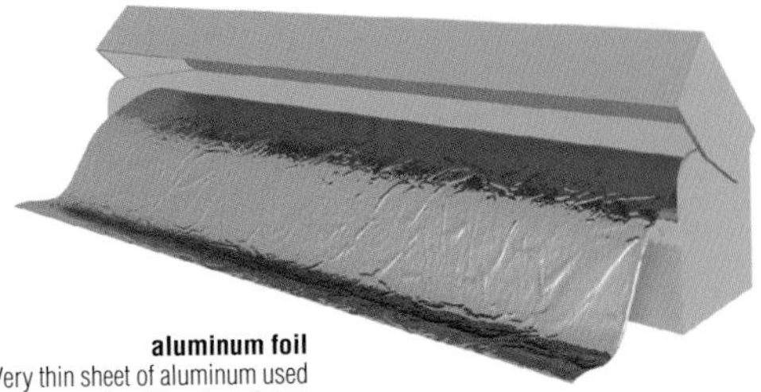

aluminum foil
Very thin sheet of aluminum used to wrap, cook, refrigerate or freeze food.

freezer bag
Airtight bag used to freeze food.

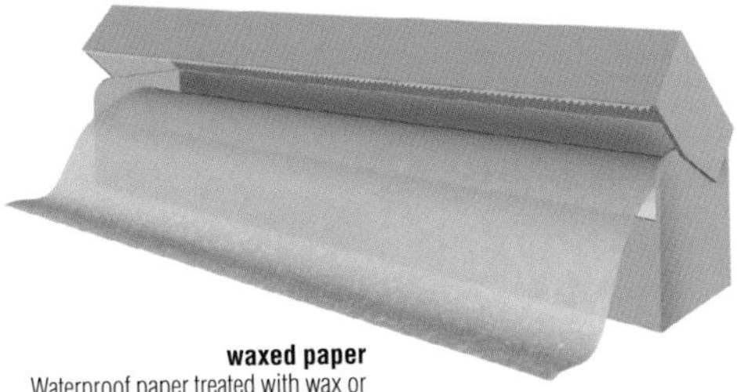

waxed paper
Waterproof paper treated with wax or paraffin that is somewhat heat resistant; it is used mainly to protect work surfaces while cooking.

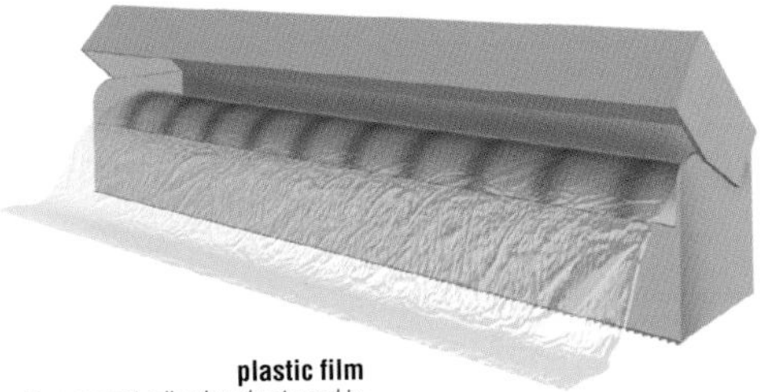

plastic film
Transparent adhesive sheet used to wrap food or cover containers.

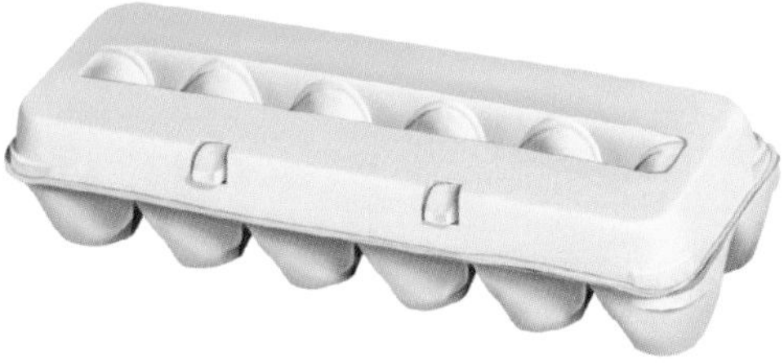

egg carton
Rigid receptacle, usually made of cardboard or plastic, composed of six or 12 cavities designed to hold eggs.

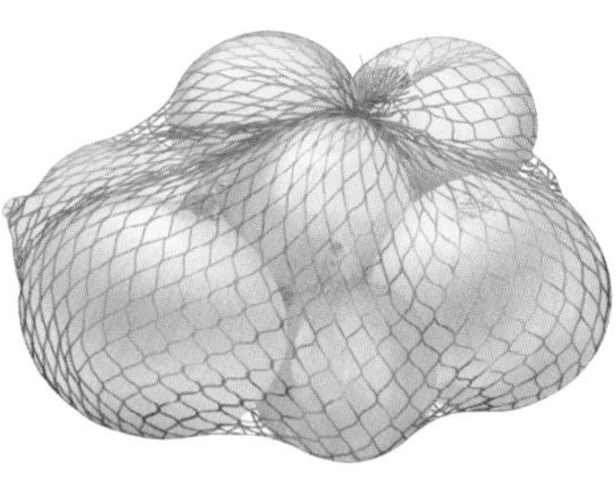

mesh bag
Bag made of netting that allows fruit and vegetables to breathe.

canisters
Airtight containers designed to contain dry goods.

food tray
Small molded receptacle, light and rigid, used to sell, freeze or reheat food.

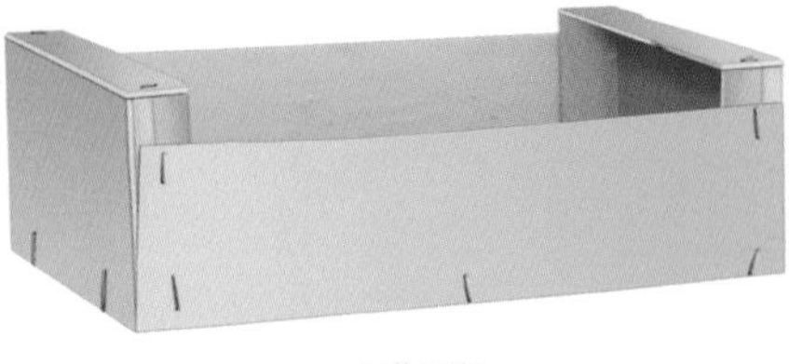

small crate
Small wooden or cardboard case usually designed for shipping and handling fruit.

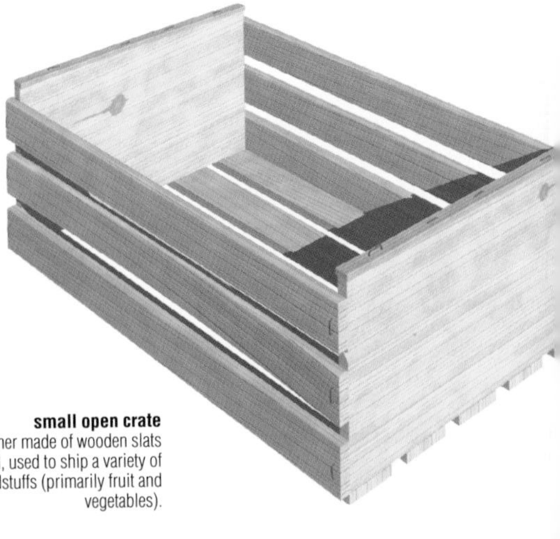

small open crate
Container made of wooden slats with no lid, used to ship a variety of foodstuffs (primarily fruit and vegetables).

packaging

screw cap
Threaded stopper that can be screwed on the top of a bottle.

glass bottle
Narrow-necked, elongated receptacle containing drinks (mineral water, wine, etc.) or liquid foodstuffs such as sauces.

food can
Airtight metal container that holds cooked food.

pull tab
Small metal strip that can be lifted with a fingernail and fingertip to open a can.

beverage can
Small cylindrical aluminum container filled with products such as beer and soft drinks.

multipack
Multiple products packaged together to facilitate shipping and handling.

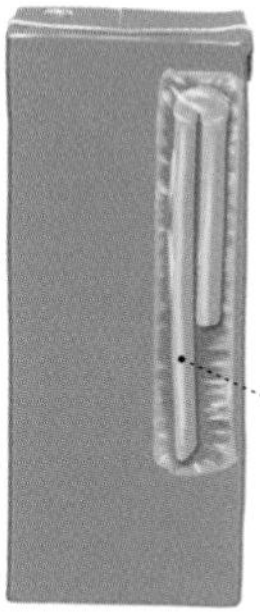

straw
A hollow tube used for sucking up a liquid.

drink box
Small single-serving box in which juice can be kept for a long time.

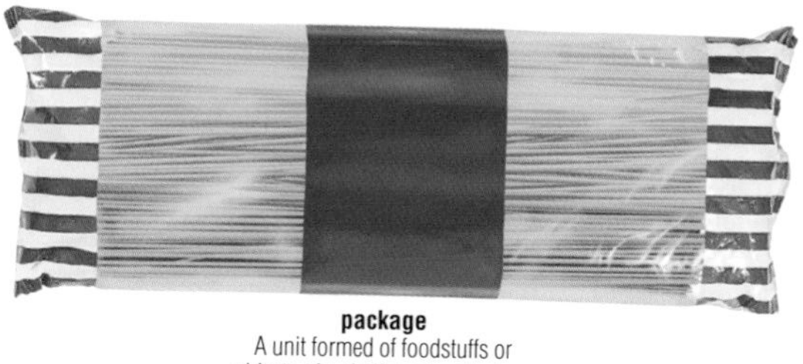

package
A unit formed of foodstuffs or objects of a similar nature that are packaged together.

heat-sealed film
Sheet that can be sealed by heat, making a container airtight.

cup
Vessel of various sizes used for selling prepared foodstuffs.

tube
Flexible cylinder-shaped packaging with a flattened base containing a paste that is squeezed out by finger pressure.

milk/cream cup
Single-serving portion served with coffee.

butter cup
Single-serving portions served with bread in restaurants.

brick carton
Container in which milk, juice and other drinks can be kept for a long time.

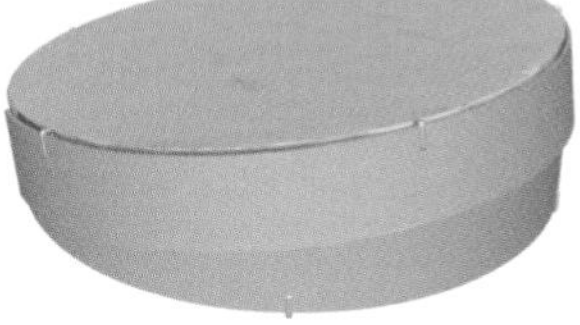

cheese box
Small cylindrical container, generally made of wood or cardboard, containing a round of cheese wrapped in paper.

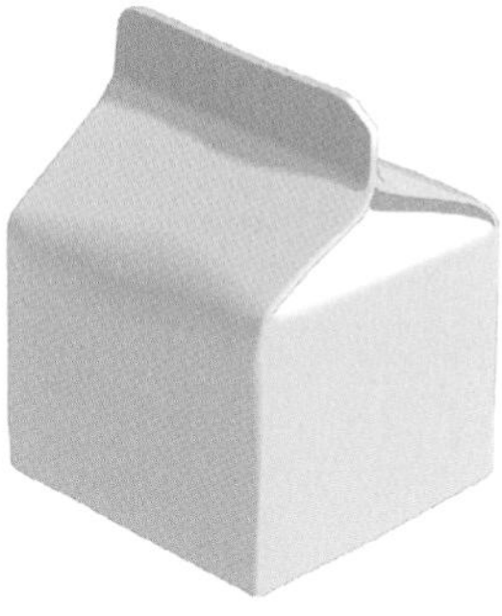

small carton
Small watertight container, usually filled with milk or cream; it comes in pint and half-pint sizes.

gabletop
Top part of a carton closed by flaps, one end of which can turn into a pouring spout.

carton
Watertight container for the sale of liquid foodstuffs such as milk and juice; it comes in one- or two-quart sizes.

kitchen

Room where meals are prepared.

range hood
Ventilation appliance expelling or recycling air that contains cooking fumes and odors.

drawer
Sliding compartment encased in a piece of furniture.

wall cabinet
Storage cupboard, usually with shelves, located above the countertop.

cooktop
Top surface of the oven on which heating elements are located.

ice cube dispenser
Appliance with a water source that makes and distributes ice cubes.

oven
Closed part of the range, equipped with an upper heating element (broiler) and a lower heating element, in which food is cooked or heated.

freezer
Appliance used to freeze and preserve food.

countertop
Flat work surface designed primarily to prepare food.

refrigerator
Appliance for storing food at low temperatures.

sink
Basin with a water source and a drain, essential for cooking tasks.

pantry
Storage place for food not needir refrigeration.

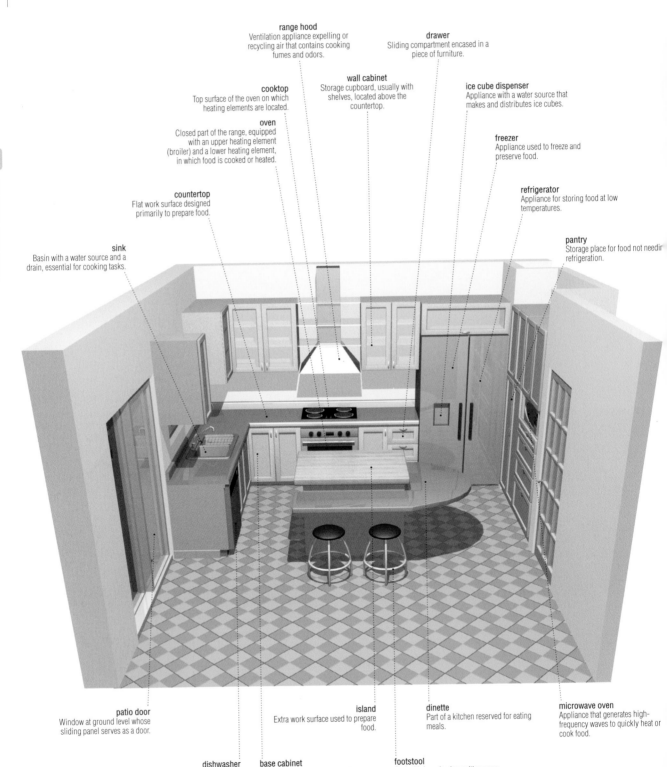

patio door
Window at ground level whose sliding panel serves as a door.

island
Extra work surface used to prepare food.

dinette
Part of a kitchen reserved for eating meals.

microwave oven
Appliance that generates high-frequency waves to quickly heat or cook food.

dishwasher
Appliance designed to automatically wash and dry dishes.

base cabinet
Storage cupboard, usually with shelves, located below the countertop.

footstool
Seat with legs, having neither arms nor back, of various heights.

glassware

Drinking receptacles; some are used to measure volume for cooking.

liqueur glass
Very small stemmed glass used for drinking liqueurs with a high alcohol content.

port glass
Small rounded stemmed glass used to serve port and dessert wines.

sparkling wine glass
Stemmed glass, wider than it is tall, used to serve champagne and sparkling wines.

brandy snifter
Short-stemmed glass whose pear shape allows the cognac to warm up, and whose narrow lip concentrates the aroma.

Alsace glass
Glass with a long stem, usually green, used to serve Alsatian white wines.

burgundy glass
Stemmed glass whose wide mouth ensures maximum oxygenation of the wine; it is used mainly for Burgundies.

bordeaux glass
Tulip-shaped stemmed glass, mainly used for Bordeaux; tapering slightly at the top, it concentrates the aroma.

white wine glass
Somewhat narrow stemmed glass usually used for white wines.

water goblet
Large stemmed glass used to serve water at the table; taller and wider than wine glasses.

cocktail glass
Conical stemmed glass used to serve certain cocktails; before serving, the rim of the glass can be frosted or decorated with fruit.

highball glass
Tall narrow straight glass used for serving liquor such as gin, often over ice or sometimes mixed with water, soda, etc.

old-fashioned glass
Wide short straight glass with a thick bottom primarily used for serving whiskey.

beer mug
Large cylindrical vessel with a handle used to serve beer; it is usually made of thick glass, ceramic or stoneware.

champagne flute
Tall and very thin stemmed glass used for champagne and sparkling wines; because the air bubbles break more slowly, the wine retains its effervescence longer.

small decanter
Small carafe used in restaurants to serve wine.

decanter
Glass or crystal carafe with a wide base and a narrow neck used to serve water or wine.

dinnerware

Receptacles of various sizes, shapes and materials used to present food and for eating it.

demitasse
Small cup for serving coffee.

cup
Cup, larger than the demitasse, used to serve tea.

coffee mug
Large cup used to serve café au lait.

creamer
Small jug used to serve cream at the table.

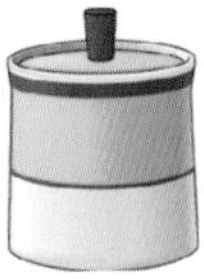

sugar bowl
Small pot used to serve sugar at the table.

salt shaker
Small receptacle used to serve salt at the table, often paired with the pepper shaker.

pepper shaker
Small receptacle used to serve pepper at the table, often paired with the salt shaker.

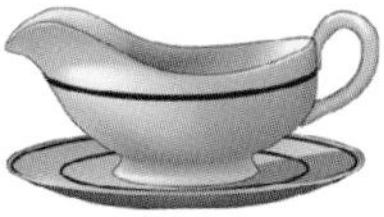

gravy boat
Receptacle used to serve sauces at the table.

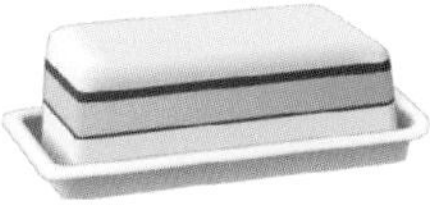

butter dish
Flat covered receptacle from which guests serve themselves butter.

ramekin
Small containers, suitable for oven and table, used to cook and serve individual portions.

soup bowl
Deep round container used to serve individual portions of soup.

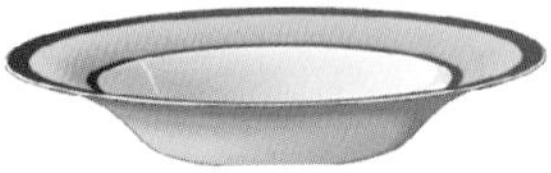

rim soup bowl
Shallower round container used to serve individual portions of soup.

dinner plate
Large piece of flat or shallow dinnerware, usually containing individual portions of solid food.

salad plate
Flat plate commonly used to serve salads or appetizers.

bread and butter plate
Small flat plate used to serve desserts.

teapot
Receptacle used for steeping and serving tea.

platter
Large oval plate used to present and serve various solid foods, such as cuts of meat, roasts, grilled meat and omelettes.

vegetable bowl
Large receptacle used to bring side vegetables to the table.

fish platter
Large oval plate used to serve a whole cooked fish.

hors d'oeuvre dish
Serving platter divided into sections used to serve several complementary foods.

water pitcher
Receptacle with a handle and a spout used mainly to serve juice and water.

salad bowl
Container of medium depth used to toss and serve salad.

salad dish
Small container used to serve individual portions of salad.

soup tureen
Large bowl with a removable lid used for bringing soup to the table and serving it.

silverware

Utensils used at the table, generally knives, forks and spoons, to which other utensils may be added, depending on the menu.

knife
Piece of silverware consisting of a handle and a sharp blade used to cut food into bite-sized pieces.

blade
Thin flat piece of metal forming the sharp part of a knife.

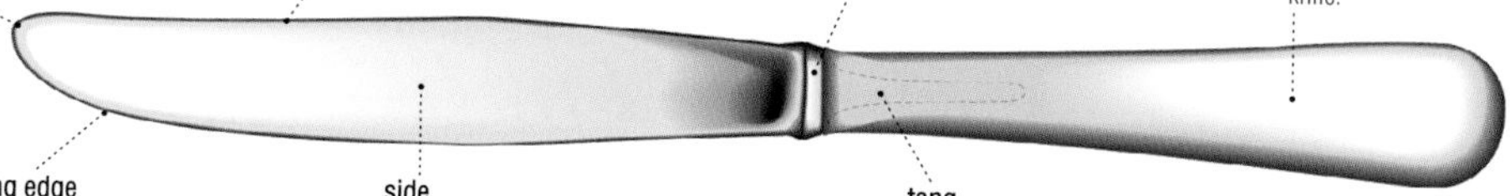
tip
Front, usually rounded, end of the blade.
back
Blunt side of the blade.
bolster
Protruding part that prevents the blade from touching the surface of the table when the knife is laid flat.
handle
Part used to pick up and handle the knife.
cutting edge
Tapered edge of the blade designed for cutting.
side
Flat surface of the blade between the back and the cutting edge.
tang
Part of the blade extending into the handle, by which it is attached.

fork
Utensil with tines used to spear food and carry it to the mouth.

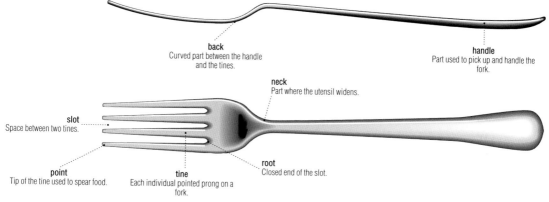

back
Curved part between the handle and the tines.
handle
Part used to pick up and handle the fork.

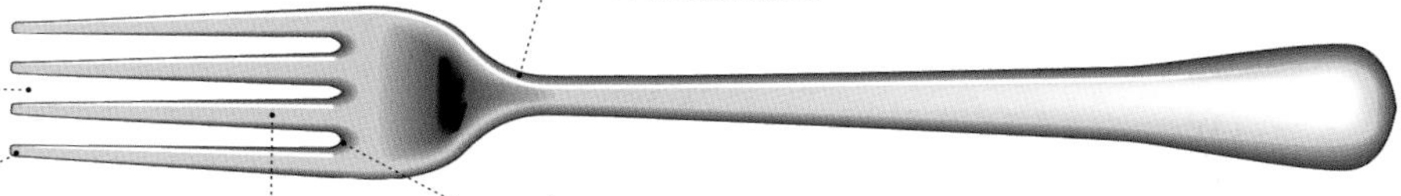
neck
Part where the utensil widens.
slot
Space between two tines.
root
Closed end of the slot.
point
Tip of the tine used to spear food.
tine
Each individual pointed prong on a fork.

spoon
Utensil consisting of a handle and a hollow part used to eat liquid or semisolid foods.

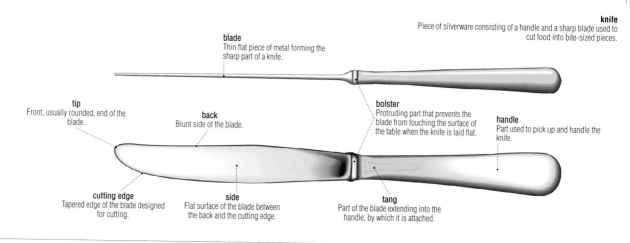

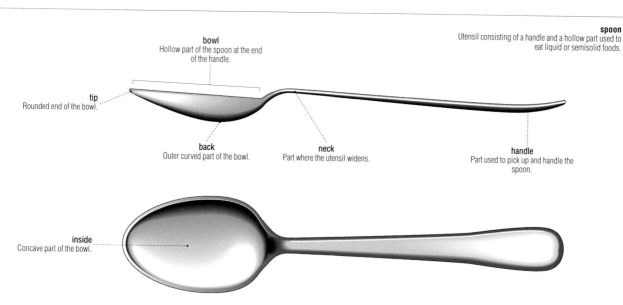

bowl
Hollow part of the spoon at the end of the handle.
tip
Rounded end of the bowl.
back
Outer curved part of the bowl.
neck
Part where the utensil widens.
handle
Part used to pick up and handle the spoon.

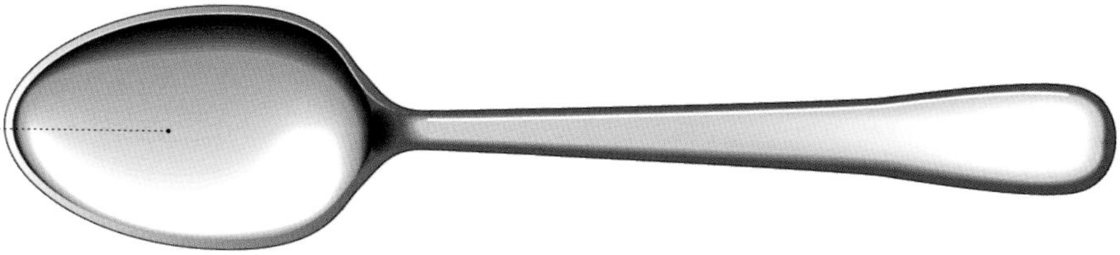
inside
Concave part of the bowl.

silverware

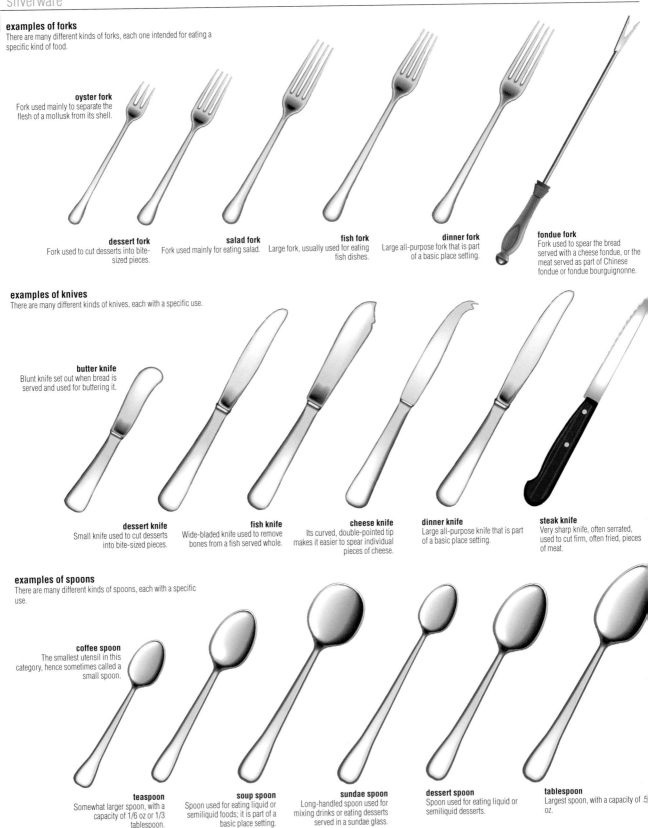

examples of forks

There are many different kinds of forks, each one intended for eating a specific kind of food.

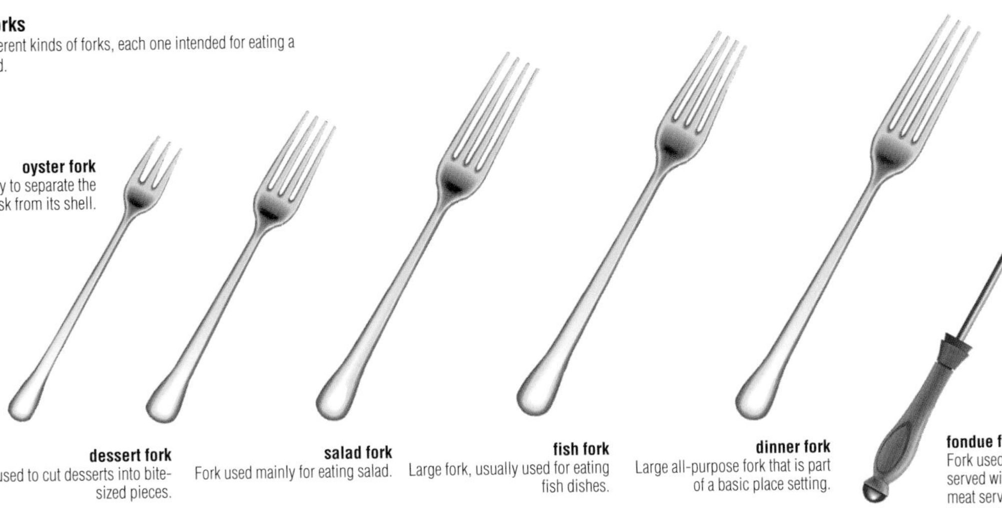

oyster fork
Fork used mainly to separate the flesh of a mollusk from its shell.

dessert fork
Fork used to cut desserts into bite-sized pieces.

salad fork
Fork used mainly for eating salad.

fish fork
Large fork, usually used for eating fish dishes.

dinner fork
Large all-purpose fork that is part of a basic place setting.

fondue fork
Fork used to spear the bread served with a cheese fondue, or the meat served as part of Chinese fondue or fondue bourguignonne.

examples of knives

There are many different kinds of knives, each with a specific use.

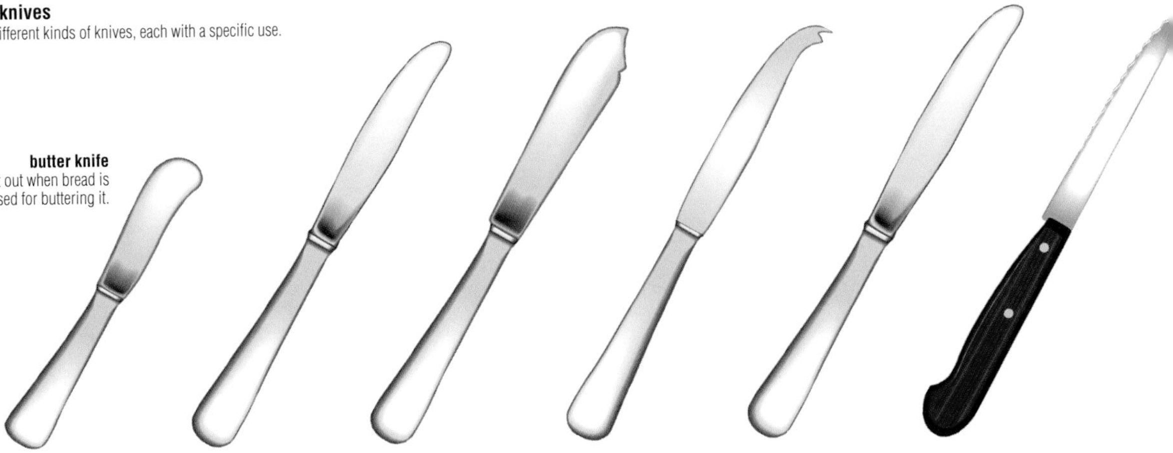

butter knife
Blunt knife set out when bread is served and used for buttering it.

dessert knife
Small knife used to cut desserts into bite-sized pieces.

fish knife
Wide-bladed knife used to remove bones from a fish served whole.

cheese knife
Its curved, double-pointed tip makes it easier to spear individual pieces of cheese.

dinner knife
Large all-purpose knife that is part of a basic place setting.

steak knife
Very sharp knife, often serrated, used to cut firm, often fried, pieces of meat.

examples of spoons

There are many different kinds of spoons, each with a specific use.

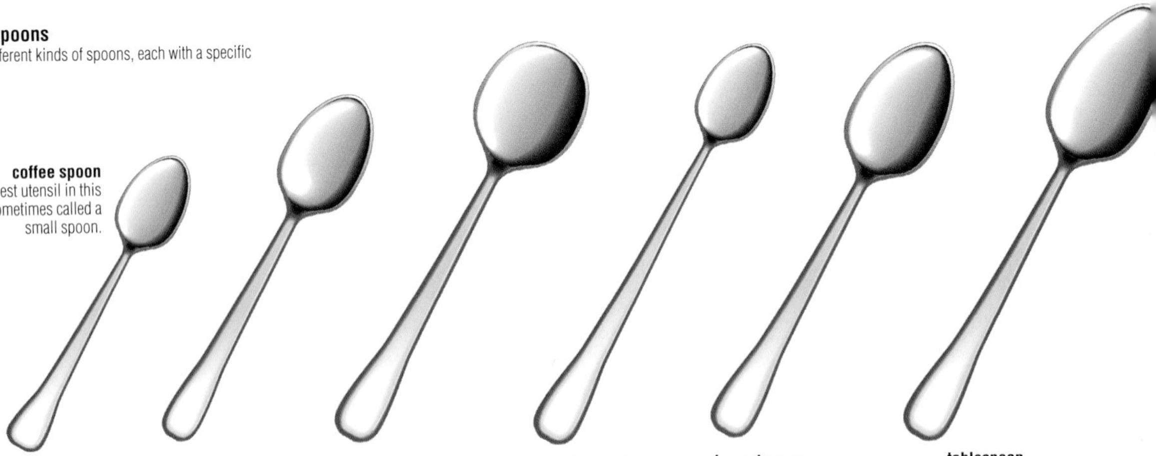

coffee spoon
The smallest utensil in this category, hence sometimes called a small spoon.

teaspoon
Somewhat larger spoon, with a capacity of 1/6 oz or 1/3 tablespoon.

soup spoon
Spoon used for eating liquid or semiliquid foods; it is part of a basic place setting.

sundae spoon
Long-handled spoon used for mixing drinks or eating desserts served in a sundae glass.

dessert spoon
Spoon used for eating liquid or semiliquid desserts.

tablespoon
Largest spoon, with a capacity of .5 oz.

kitchen utensils

Accessories or simple mechanical devices used for preparing food.

kitchen knife

Kitchen knives are used to prepare (cut, slice, bone, trim) food.

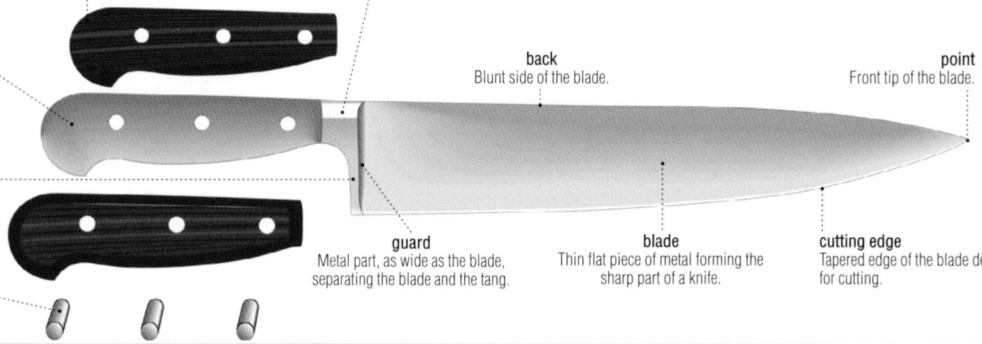

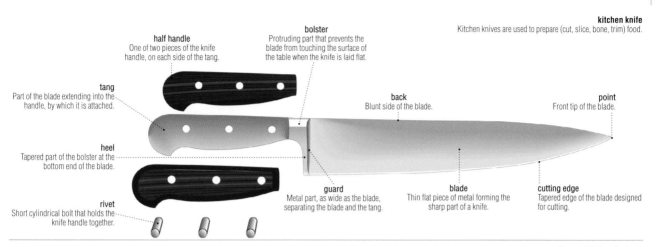

half handle
One of two pieces of the knife handle, on each side of the tang.

bolster
Protruding part that prevents the blade from touching the surface of the table when the knife is laid flat.

tang
Part of the blade extending into the handle, by which it is attached.

back
Blunt side of the blade.

point
Front tip of the blade.

heel
Tapered part of the bolster at the bottom end of the blade.

guard
Metal part, as wide as the blade, separating the blade and the tang.

blade
Thin flat piece of metal forming the sharp part of a knife.

cutting edge
Tapered edge of the blade designed for cutting.

rivet
Short cylindrical bolt that holds the knife handle together.

examples of kitchen knives

The shape and size of kitchen knives vary depending on their use and the type of food for which they are intended.

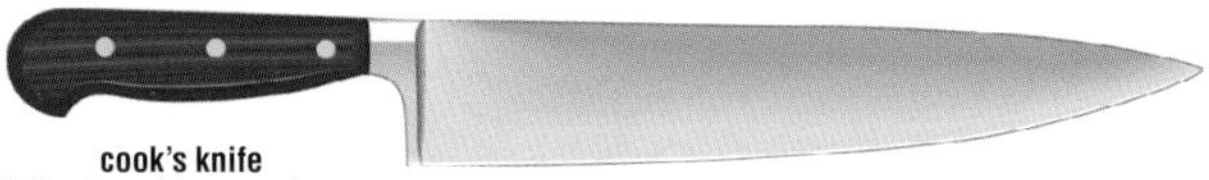

cook's knife
Knife with a wide range of uses, from cutting large pieces of meat to chopping fresh herbs.

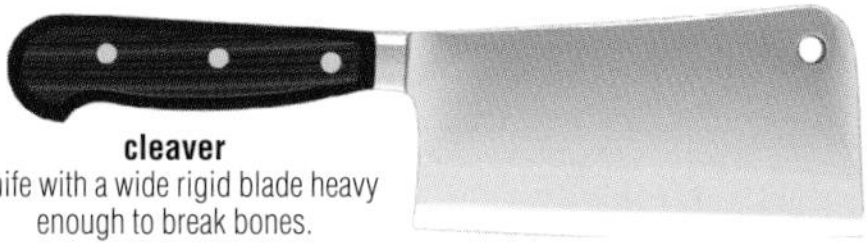

cleaver
Knife with a wide rigid blade heavy enough to break bones.

bread knife
Serrated knife used for cutting fresh bread.

carving knife
Knife with a narrow blade used to slice pieces of cooked meat into portions.

ham knife
Knife with a ridged blade used to cut whole cooked ham.

filleting knife
Knife with a long pointed blade used for separating fish into fillets.

paring knife
Miniature version of the cook's knife, it is used to clean, scrape and slice small pieces of food.

carving fork
Fork used to hold a piece of meat in place when it is being cut into portions.

sharpening steel
Cylindrical steel rod with narrow grooves used for honing a knife edge.

boning knife
Small pointed knife with a tapered blade used to separate the meat from the bones.

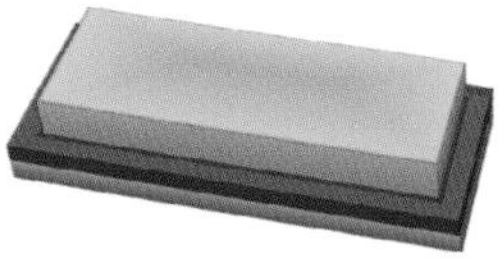

sharpening stone
Abrasive stone used to sharpen knife edges.

grapefruit knife
Knife used to detach citrus fruit pulp.

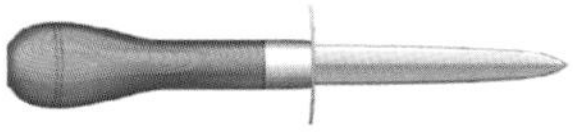

oyster knife
Double-edged knife with a guard used to open oyster shells by severing the muscle that holds them closed.

zester
Knife whose blade curves at the end and has five small cutting holes; it is used to remove thin strips of rind from citrus fruits.

peeler
Its pivoting blade follows the contours of the fruits and vegetables it is used to peel.

butter curler
Utensil with a serrated hook that creates butter curls when scraped across cold butter.

cutting board
Made of plastic or wood and used for cutting up foods.

groove
Furrow where cooking juices collect.

kitchen utensils

for opening

Instruments that remove lids, caps or corks from containers in order to provide access to their contents.

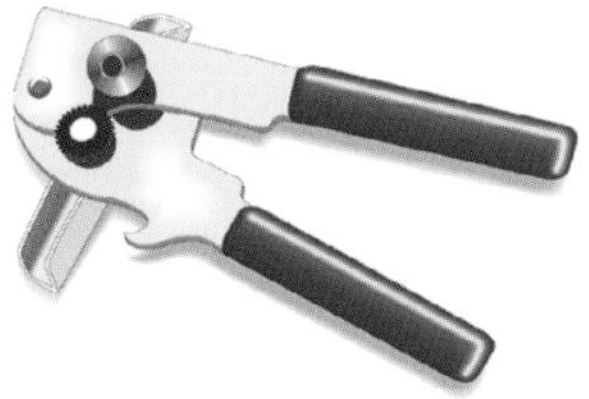

can opener
Tool used to open cans by cutting along the inside edge of the lid.

bottle opener
Instrument used to remove caps from bottles.

wine waiter corkscrew
Instrument with a screw and a lever that open wine bottles by leverage, a blade for cutting the hood around the top, and a bottle opener.

lever corkscrew
Instrument with a screw and two wings that rise as the screw penetrates the cork; they then act as levers to open the bottle.

for grinding and grating

Instruments that can reduce food to fine particles, shavings, powder, purées, etc.

mortar
Hemispheric receptacle made of marble, porcelain or hardwood in which certain foods can be ground with a pestle.

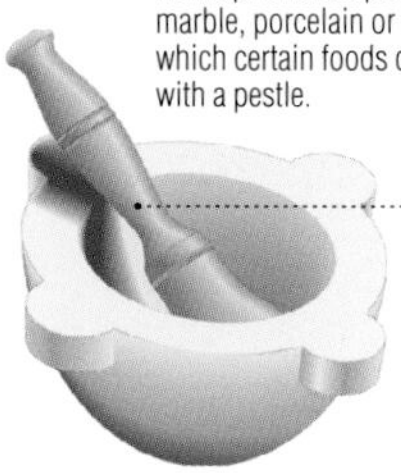

pestle
Usually heavy instrument whose short handle extends into a head; it is used mainly to grind seeds, dry ingredients and garlic.

meat grinder
Instrument with a knife and interchangeable disks used to grind meat; the perforations in the disks determine the size of the grind.

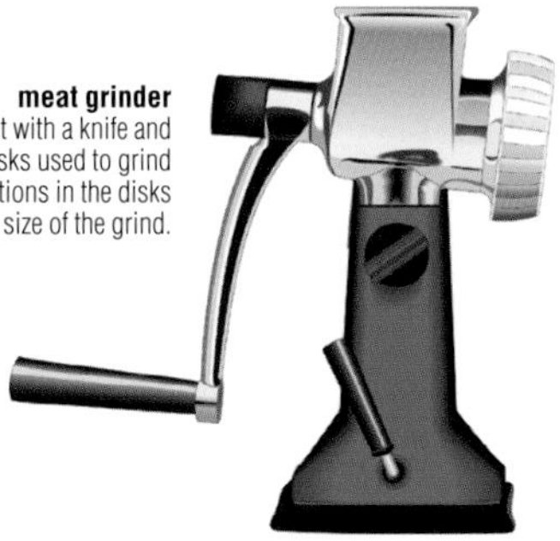

nutcracker
Tongs used to break nutshells and release the kernel inside.

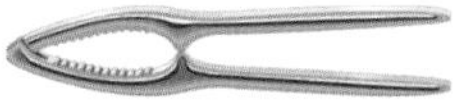

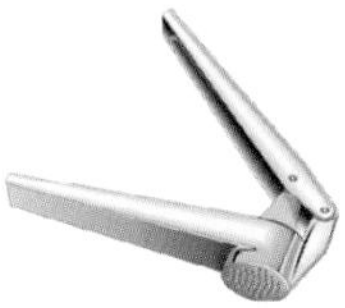

garlic press
Utensil used to finely crush garlic cloves.

citrus juicer
Instrument used to extract juice from citrus fruits, usually lemons or oranges.

nutmeg grater
Small conical grater used to reduce nutmeg seeds to a powder.

grater
Instrument used to reduce food such as vegetables, cheese and nuts into fine particles or a powder.

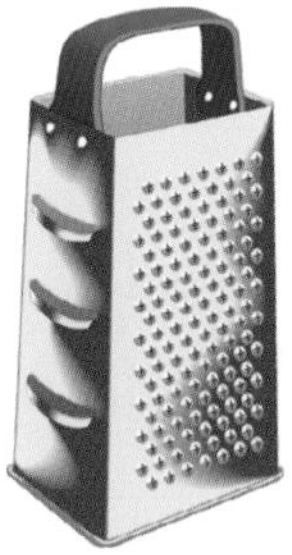

rotary cheese grater
Instrument used to grate cheese by scraping it against the teeth of a rotating drum.

pusher
Bent part of the handle that presses the piece of cheese against the drum.

crank
Angled lever that makes the drum rotate.

drum
Cylindrical part of the utensil that grates the cheese.

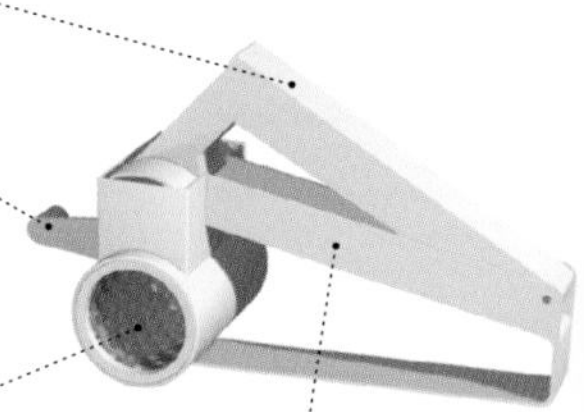

handle
Part enabling the user to hold the grater and exert pressure on the pusher.

pasta maker
Instrument that can roll out and cut pasta dough into different shapes with its removable blades.

food mill
Instrument used to reduce cooked fruit and vegetables to a purée, the consistency of which depends on the disk used.

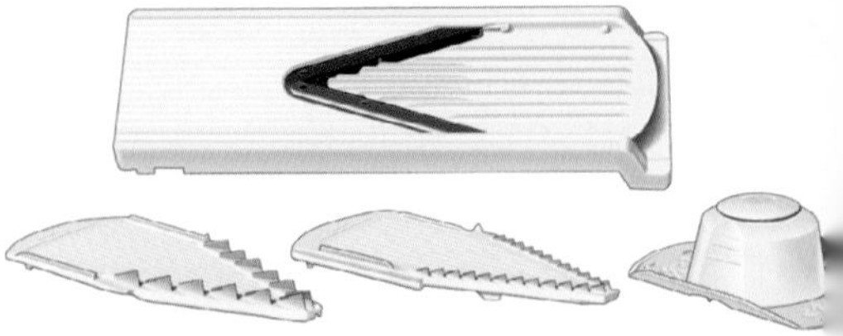

mandoline
Instrument comprising interchangeable cutting blades inserted in a frame; it slices vegetables in different ways, depending on the blade used.

kitchen utensils

for measuring

Instruments designed to measure the volume or weight of ingredients, food temperature, and cooking or preparation time.

measuring spoons
The bowls on these spoons correspond to an exact quantity of an ingredient, and are used to measure it.

measuring cups
Receptacles used to measure the exact quantity of an ingredient.

candy thermometer
Thermometer that is placed in hot liquid sugar mixtures to measure their exact temperature.

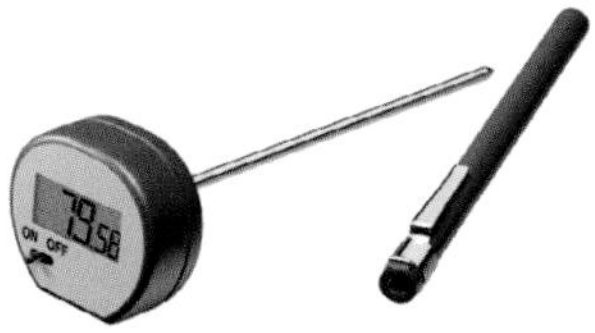

instant-read thermometer
Digital thermometer that, when inserted into a roast, instantly indicates the meat's internal temperature.

measuring cup
Graduated container with a pouring spout used for measuring liquids.

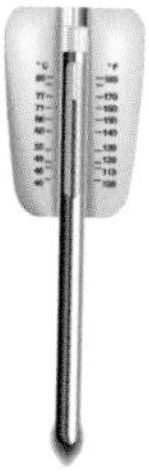

meat thermometer
Thermometer inserted into a roast to check its degree of doneness.

oven thermometer
Thermometer that is placed inside an oven to check the exact temperature.

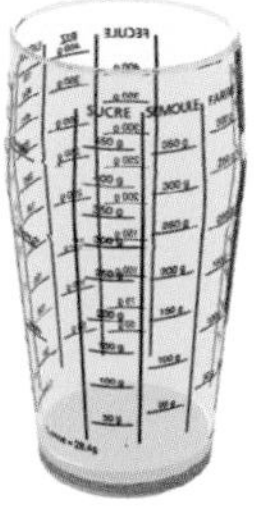

measuring beaker
Graduated container used to measure dry and liquid ingredients.

kitchen timer
Device used to measure a period of time; once that time has elapsed, the timer rings.

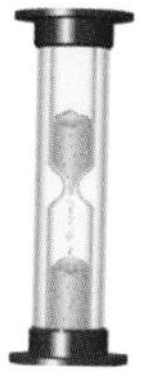

egg timer
Device with two glass vials, one of which is filled with sand; the flow of the sand between the vials measures a precise time period.

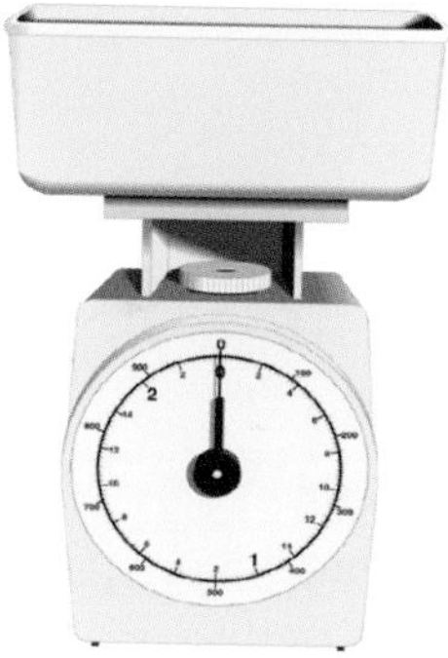

kitchen scale
Instruments used to weigh dry ingredients (e.g., flour, sugar, rice).

for straining and draining

Instruments used to filter dry or liquid foods, or to remove the liquid used to wash, blanch, cook or fry certain foods.

mesh strainer
Instrument used to sift dry ingredients or filter liquid ones.

muslin
Cloth woven into a fine loose mesh and used to strain creamed soups and sauces so they become finer and smoother.

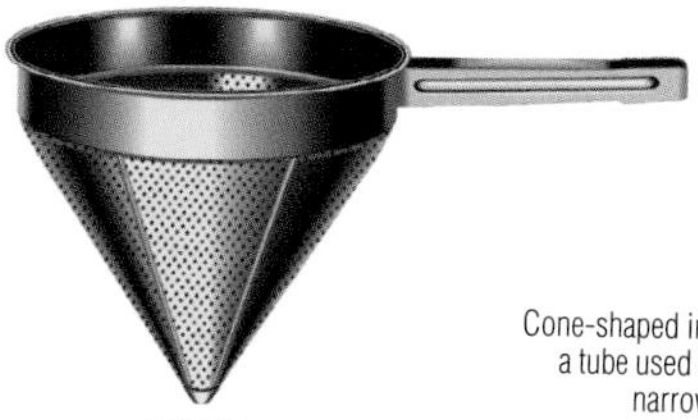

chinois
Finely meshed cone-shaped strainer used to filter broth and sauces, and to reduce food to a purée.

funnel
Cone-shaped instrument ending in a tube used to pour liquid into a narrow-necked container.

colander
Instrument used to drain food.

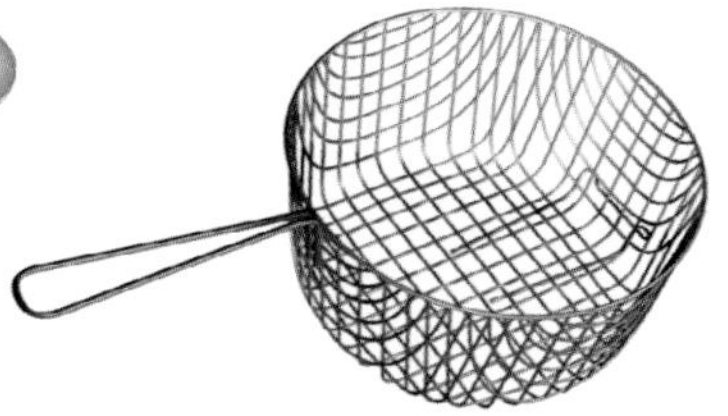

fry basket
Metal mesh receptacle designed to hold foods during frying and drain them afterward.

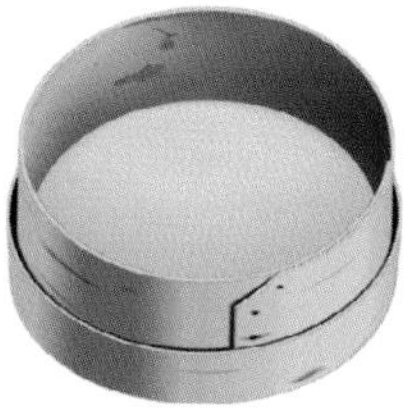

sieve
Strainer made of woven nylon, metal or silk strands and attached to a wooden frame; it is used to strain dry and liquid ingredients.

salad spinner
Apparatus that uses centrifugal force to remove water from freshly washed lettuce leaves.

kitchen utensils

baking utensils

Baking: refers to the production of cakes, cookies and other usually sweet comestibles made from cooked dough, pastry or batter.

icing syringe
Fitted with interchangeable nozzles that are filled with icing, it is used to decorate baked goods and molded desserts.

pastry cutting wheel
Device used for cutting dough; the indented wheel gives it a fluted edge.

pastry brush
Device with silk or nylon bristles at one end, used to coat, brush or glaze pastries, or to grease baking pans.

egg beater
Mechanical device with two whisks activated by a crank handle; it is used to beat liquid and semiliquid ingredients.

whisk
Utensil made of several curved and intersecting steel wires used to blend, beat or whip liquid and semiliquid ingredients.

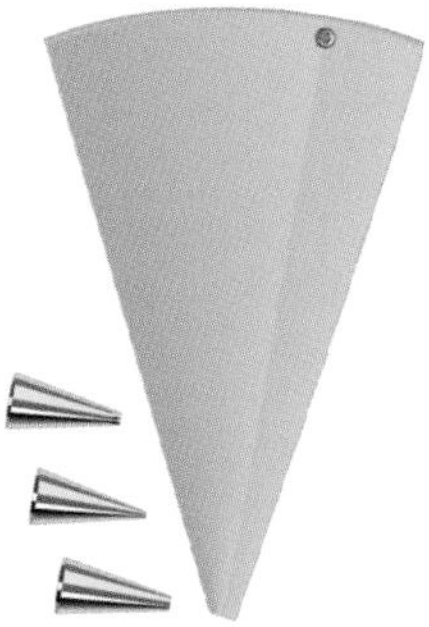

pastry bag and nozzles
Leakproof bag into which interchangeable nozzles are inserted; it is used to decorate dishes, baked goods and molded desserts, or to make pastries.

sifter
Device used to sieve flour; it has a spring-loaded handle that moves the flour about and makes it lighter.

cookie cutters
Hollow metal molds used to cut dough into soft shapes that will be retained after baking.

dredger
Container with a perforated lid used for sprinkling food with flour, sugar or grated cheese.

pastry blender
Utensil used to blend fatty ingredients with flour.

mixing bowls
Round containers of various sizes used to prepare or mix food and ingredients.

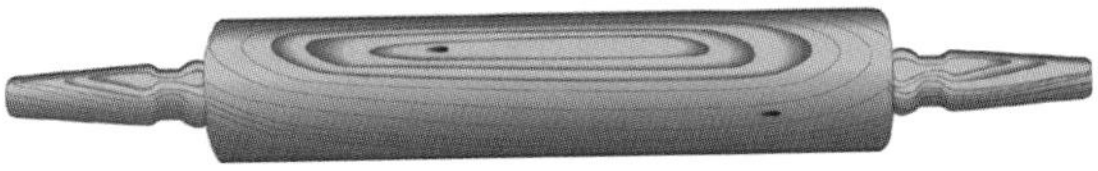

rolling pin
Wooden cylinder that rolls freely between two lateral handles; it is used to roll out pastry.

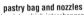

baking sheet
Rectangular pan with low sides, usually made of aluminum, used for baking cookies, cakes and other pastries that do not require molding.

muffin pan
Baking pan with indentations used to give muffins their distinctive shape.

soufflé dish
Deep porcelain dish that prevents the rising soufflé from overflowing as it cooks.

charlotte mold
Deep metal pan shaped like a pail and used to cook a cream-based sweet dessert surrounded by biscuits.

removable-bottomed pan
Metal baking pan whose bottom, and sometimes its side, come apart so the contents can be removed more easily.

pie pan
Metal pan used to make a pie crust and to bake a pie in the oven.

quiche plate
Metal baking pan with a scalloped edge that makes the crust of the quiche more attractive.

cake pan
Relatively deep metal baking pan with enough room to allow the cake to rise.

kitchen utensils

set of utensils

Main kitchen utensils, often matching, stored in a stand.

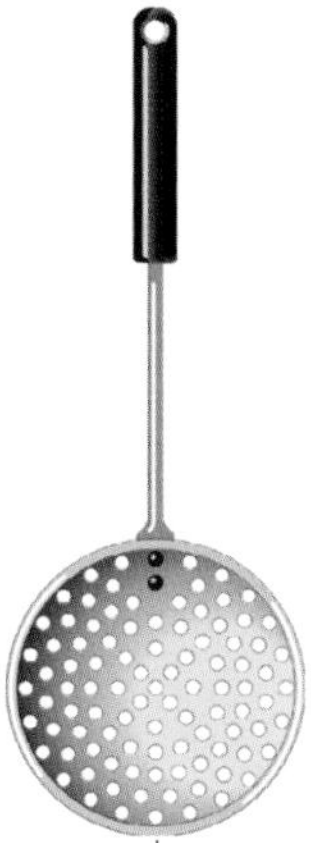

skimmer
Large round slightly concave spoon with perforations; it is used to skim broth and sauce, or to remove food from its cooking liquid.

draining spoon
Large elongated slightly concave spoon with perforations; it is used to remove small pieces of food from their cooking liquid.

spatula
Long blade of variable width used to turn food over during cooking.

turner
Utensil used to handle cooked food without breaking it.

ladle
Spoon with a deep bowl and a long handle; it is used to decant liquid or semiliquid food.

potato masher
Utensil used to manually purée cooked fruits and vegetables.

miscellaneous utensils

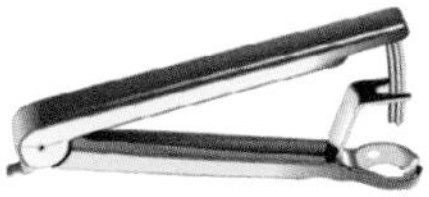

stoner
Tonglike device used to remove stones from olives and cherries without damaging the flesh.

larding needle
Tool used to insert strips of lard, ham or truffles into cuts of meat.

apple corer
Utensil used to remove the core from apples and pears.

melon baller
Spoon used to cut small round pieces from the flesh of fruits or vegetables.

trussing needle
Tool used to thread pieces of string through poultry or to tie a roast.

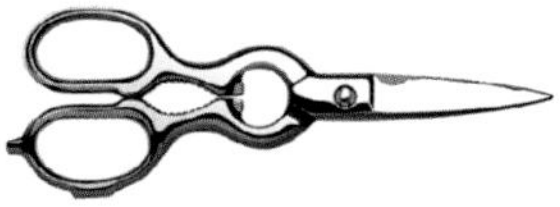

kitchen shears
Multipurpose utensil used for cutting fresh herbs, trimming meat and vegetables.

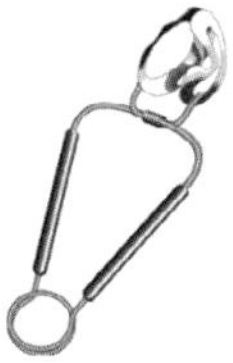

snail tongs
Utensil used to hold snail shells so the snail can be extracted.

snail dish
Has several indentations for holding snails when they are served.

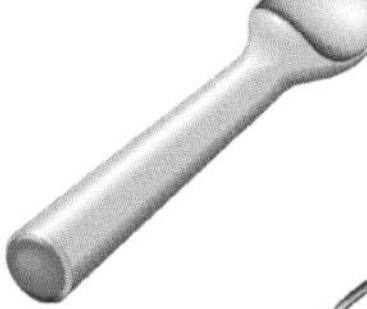

ice cream scoop
Spoon used to remove a serving of ice milk or ice cream from a container.

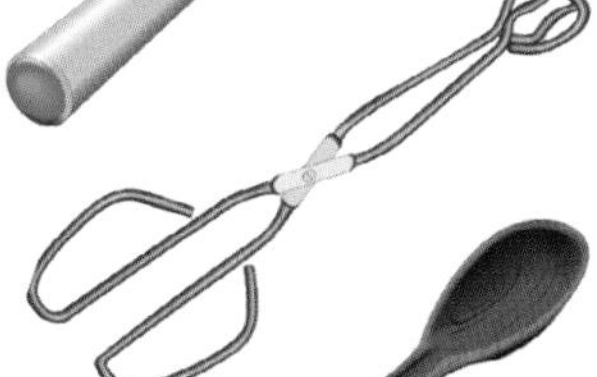

tongs
Utensil used for holding, turning and serving food.

poultry shears
Utensil used to cut poultry into pieces.

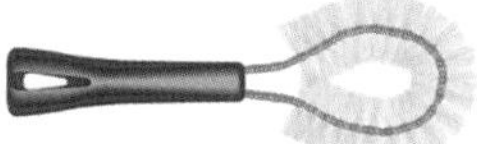

vegetable brush
Utensil used to clean certain vegetables, such as potatoes.

egg slicer
Device that uses taut steel wires to slice a hard-boiled egg.

tasting spoon
Wooden spoon consisting of two bowls joined by a shallow groove used to take and taste liquids.

tea ball
Hollow sphere that holds dried tea leaves during steeping.

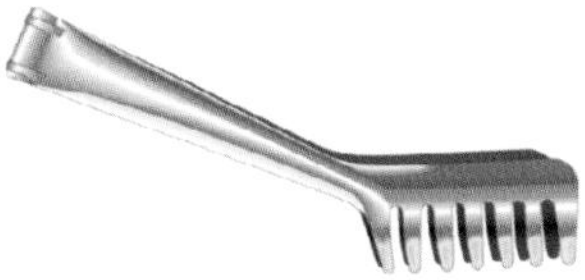

spaghetti tongs
Two-armed utensil with teeth at the end that facilitate serving long strips of pasta.

baster
Utensil with a graduated tube and a rubber bulb; it is used to suck up cooking liquid and drizzle it over the meat.

cooking utensils

Utensils used for cooking food, especially in the oven or on the stove.

wok set
Cooking utensil native to Asia used for rapidly cooking food in very little fat.

lid
Removable part that covers the wok during cooking.

rack
Half-moon-shaped grating used to drain or set aside food.

wok
Large cone-shaped frying pan; food collects at the center of the rounded bottom, where the heat is most intense.

burner ring
Metal base used to balance the wok over the burner or hot plate.

tajine
Varnished earthenware dish with a cone-shaped airtight lid used in northwestern Africa to cook an eponymous dish.

fondue set
Utensil designed to prepare and serve various kinds of fondue, such as meat, cheese or chocolate.

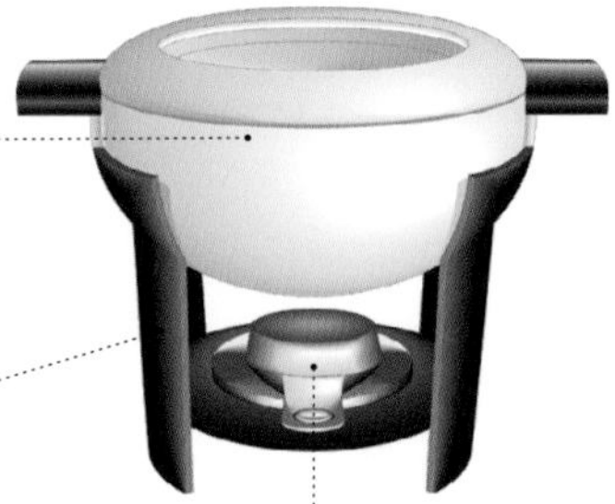

fondue pot
Container with one or two side handles used for cooking fondue.

stand
Metal base designed to hold the fondue pot and the burner.

burner
Compartment containing a flammable liquid that keeps the fondue pot warm throughout the meal.

fish poacher
Oblong receptacle that has a rack and a cover; it is used to cook whole fish.

rack
Perforated sheet; the hooks allow it to be lifted so that, once cooked, the fish can be drained and removed.

lid
Removable part that covers the fish poacher during cooking.

dripping pan
Slightly concave rectangular pan used to roast meat or to catch the meat's cooking juices.

terrine
Container with a perforated lid that allows steam to escape; it is designed for cooking recipes with or without jelly.

roasting pans
Somewhat deep large-capacity utensils used to roast meat in the oven.

pressure cooker
Stock pot with a screw-on, airtight lid designed to cook food rapidly using pressurized steam.

pressure regulator
Device maintaining the pressure at a constant level.

safety valve
Device that regulates escaping steam when the stock pot is under pressure.

Dutch oven
Somewhat deep stock pot used for cooking food in a liquid.

stock pot
Container used for cooking large quantities of food in a liquid.

couscous kettle
Double container in which steam from the broth in which the food in the bottom part is simmering cooks and flavors the semolina in the top part.

frying pan
Utensil used to fry, sauté or brown food.

steamer
Utensil comprising two saucepans; the steam from the boiling water in the bottom one cooks the food in the top one.

egg poacher
Device used to poach eggs by placing them in indentations in a tray suspended over a hot liquid.

sauté pan
Similar to a frying pan but with a straight edge, used to cook food in fat, over high heat.

small saucepan
Deeper than a frying pan, this utensil is used to simmer or braise dishes.

diable
Utensil composed of two skillets of porous clay that fit tightly together; it is used for braising food.

pancake pan
Round thick-bottomed skillet with a shallow edge that allows a spatula to loosen and flip the pancake.

steamer basket
Perforated receptacle that is placed in a saucepan above the water level and filled with food to be steam-cooked.

double boiler
Utensil comprising two saucepans; the bottom one contains boiling water, which cooks or heats the food in the top one.

saucepan
Low-sided receptacle commonly used to heat liquids or cook food in a liquid.

domestic appliances

Domestic appliances operating on electricity.

for mixing and blending

Appliances used for stirring, for blending several ingredients together or for changing the appearance of an ingredient.

blender
Electric appliance comprising a motor unit with a container on top, in which raw or cooked food is mixed, crushed or puréed.

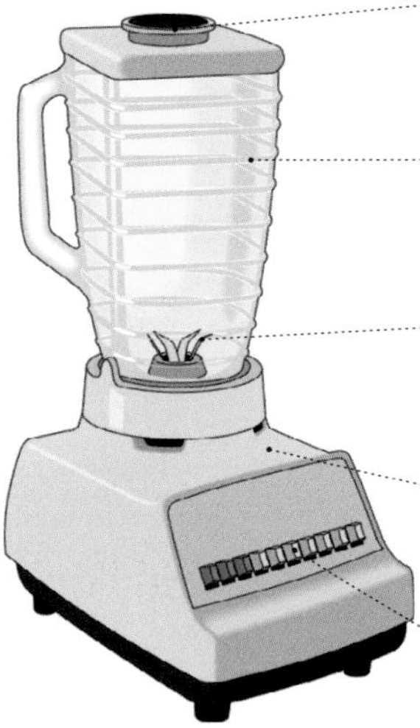

cap
Part that gives the container an airtight seal.

container
Glass jug in which food or ingredients are placed.

cutting blade
Propeller blade that mixes or grinds food as it turns.

motor unit
Part containing the motor and the various circuits making the appliance work.

push button
Buttons used to start the appliance and select blade speed.

hand mixer
Electric appliance comprising two beaters and a motor unit used to beat or mix liquid or semiliquid food.

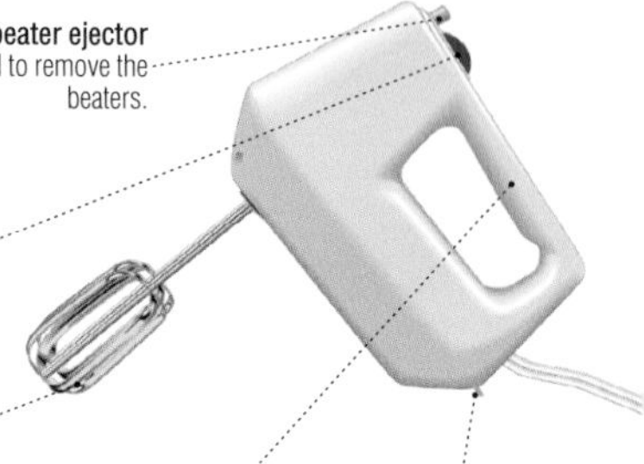

beater ejector
Button pressed to remove the beaters.

speed selector
Device for selecting the speed at which the beaters rotate.

beater
Device used to beat or mix food; the beaters are inserted into cogwheels that turn in opposite directions.

handle
Part used to pick up and handle the mixer.

heel rest
Part on which the mixer rests when it is not in use.

hand blender
Electric appliance with a handheld motor unit; less powerful than the blender, it is used for mixing liquids and grinding soft foods.

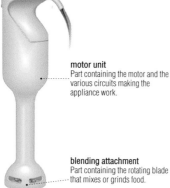

motor unit
Part containing the motor and the various circuits making the appliance work.

blending attachment
Part containing the rotating blade that mixes or grinds food.

table mixer
Electric appliance comprising a powerful motor unit, two beaters and a stand used to beat or mix liquid or semiliquid foods.

beater ejector
Button pressed to remove the beaters.

speed control
Device for selecting the speed at which the beaters rotate.

beater
Device used to beat or mix food; the beaters are inserted into cogwheels that turn in opposite directions.

tilt-back head
The motor unit rotates on an axis so the beaters can be lowered into the bowl and lifted out of it.

mixing bowl
Round container of various sizes used to mix food in.

turntable
Enables the mixing bowl to be rotated so the contents will be beaten or mixed uniformly.

stand
Base that holds the mixing bowl and the tilt-back head.

beaters

Instruments used to mix, beat or knead liquid or semiliquid foods.

four blade beater
All-purpose beater used to mix, beat or whisk various ingredients.

spiral beater
Beater used primarily to mix and knead light dough.

wire beater
Beater used to mix, emulsify or beat many different ingredients or to incorporate air into a mixture.

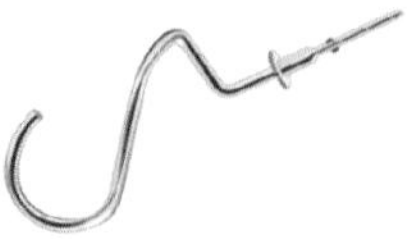

dough hook
Beater used to mix and knead dough.

domestic appliances

for cutting
Appliances used primarily for separating elements into small parts or portions.

food processor
Electric appliance comprising a motor unit, a blade and a set of disks used for cutting, chopping, slicing, grating, mixing, kneading, etc.

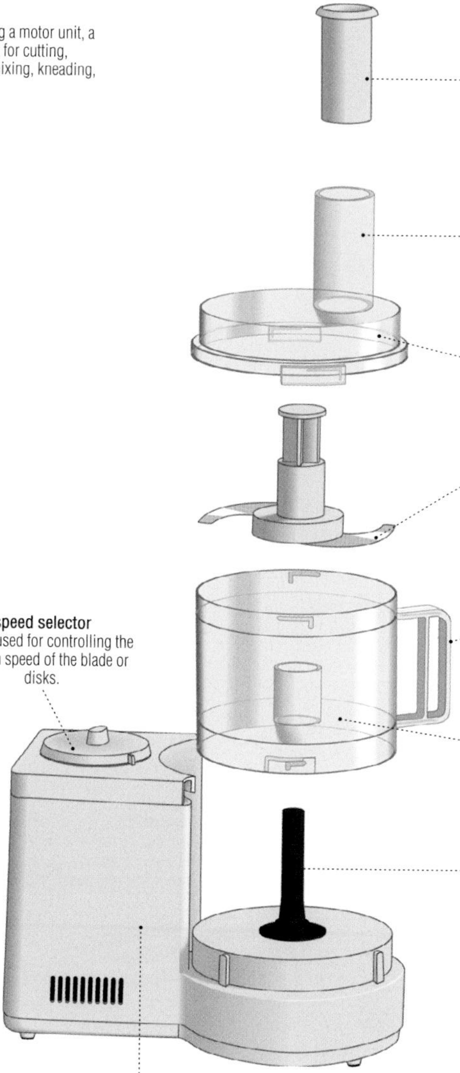

pusher
Device that pushes food into the bowl.

feed tube
Conduit in which food is placed.

lid
Removable part covering the bowl.

blade
Propeller blade that mixes or grinds food as it turns.

handle
Part used to pick up and move the bowl.

speed selector
Device used for controlling the rotation speed of the blade or disks.

bowl
Container in which food or ingredients are placed.

spindle
Shaft that transmits the motor's movement to the blade or disks.

motor unit
Part containing the motor and the various circuits making the appliance work.

disks
Blades that can replace the cutting mechanism to grate or mince food.

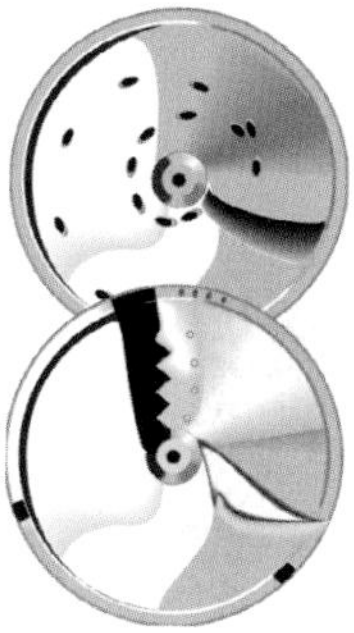

electric knife
Electric appliance with a blade that has a back-and-forth motion used to facilitate cutting a piece of meat.

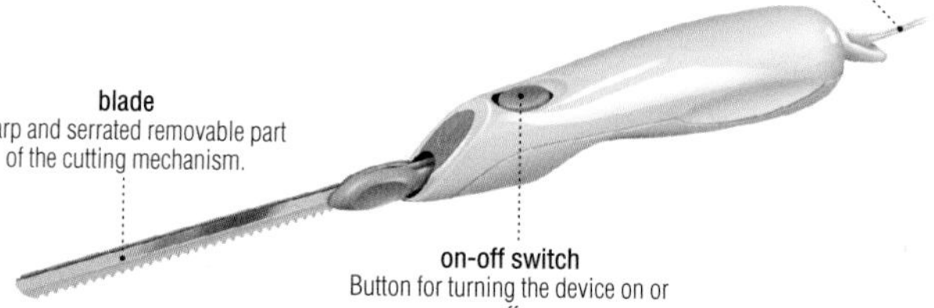

power cord
Flexible electric wire housing the leads connecting the appliance to the electric circuit.

blade
Sharp and serrated removable part of the cutting mechanism.

on-off switch
Button for turning the device on or off.

for juicing
Device designed to extract juice from fruit, especially citrus fruit, when pressure is exerted upon it.

citrus juicer
Electric appliance designed to extract the juice from citrus fruit.

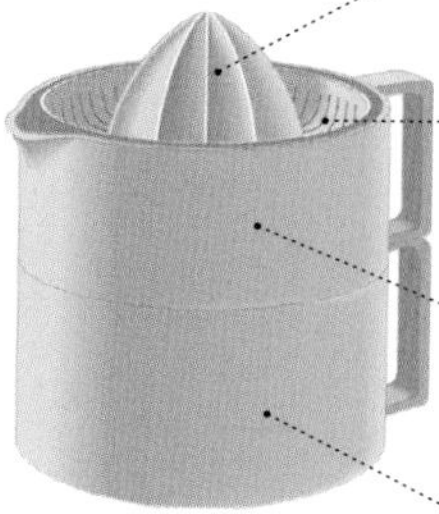

reamer
Device upon which the fruit half is placed and which reams it as it turns.

strainer
Part of the juicer that catches the seeds and the pulp.

bowl with serving spout
Container that collects the juice; it has a pouring spout.

motor unit
Part containing the motor and the various circuits making the appliance work.

FOOD AND KITCHEN

domestic appliances

for cooking
Appliances that bring raw food into contact with a heat source in order to cook them.

microwave oven
Appliance that generates high-frequency waves to quickly heat or cook food.

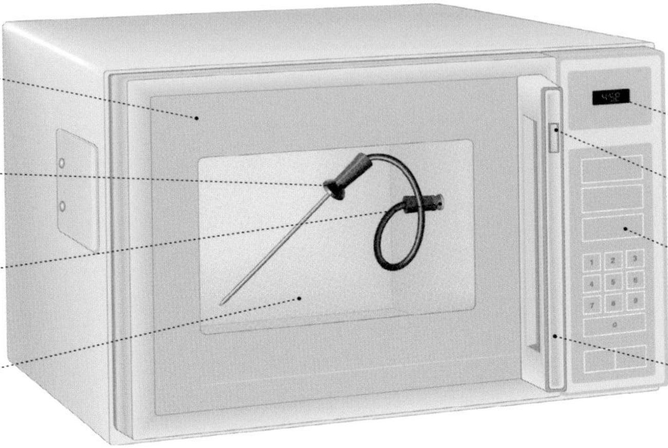

door
Movable part that closes the microwave oven.

sensor probe
Instrument that is inserted into food and used to check internal temperature and monitor cooking.

probe receptacle
Place where the sensor probe's plug is connected.

window
Thick window for looking inside the oven.

clock timer
Displays either real time or the programmed cooking time.

latch
Device that opens the door when pushed.

control panel
Panel containing the programming keys.

handle
Part used to open or close the microwave oven door.

waffle iron
Appliance comprising two indented plates, each one covering a heating element; it is used to cook waffles or grill food.

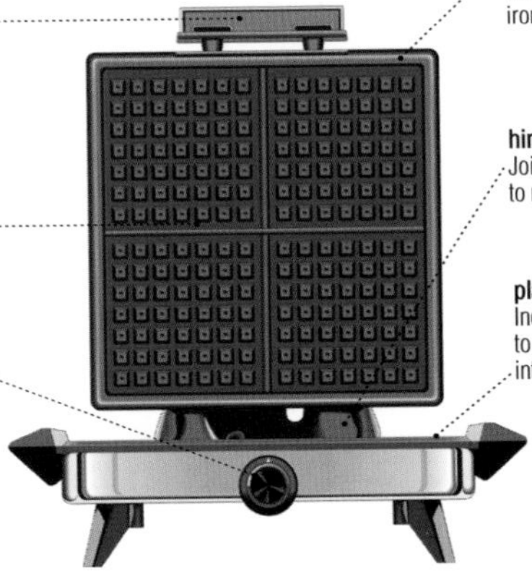

handle
Part used to raise and lower the lid.

plate
Indented cooking surface that, because it is attached to the inside of the lid, can be raised and lowered.

temperature selector
Device used to regulate plate temperature.

lid
Movable part that closes the waffle iron.

hinge
Jointed part that makes it possible to raise and lower the lid.

plate
Indented cooking surface designed to receive waffle batter or food intended for grilling.

toaster
Appliance with heating elements that toast slices of bread.

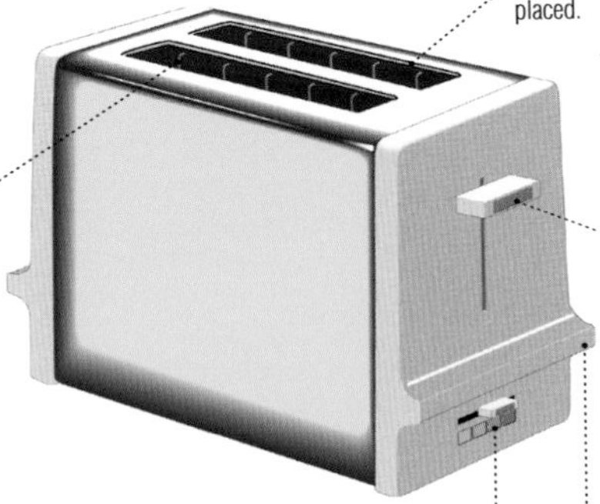

slot
Opening in which the bread slice is placed.

lever
Spring-loaded device that the carriage holding the br slices.

bread guide
Metal grating for holding bread slices in place.

temperature control
Device used to regulate cooking temperature.

handle
Part used to pick up and mov toaster.

deep fryer
Container with a heating element that raises the temperature of fat high enough to deep-fry food.

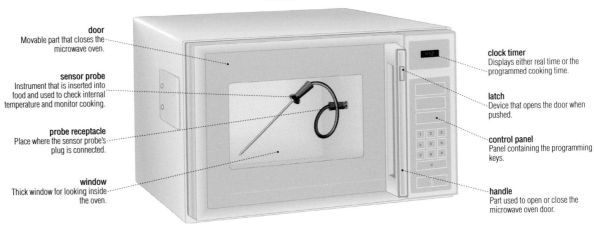

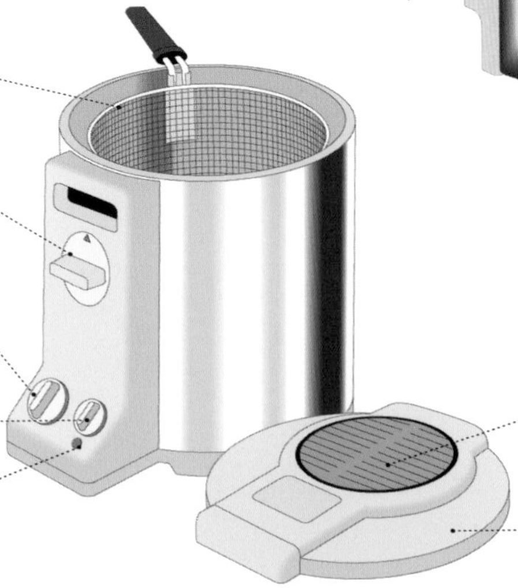

basket
Wire mesh container with a detachable handle designed to hold foods during frying and drain them once cooked.

rack
Notched device used to raise or lower the basket.

timer
Device used to monitor cooking time.

thermostat
Device used to regulate fat temperature.

signal lamp
Light indicating when the desired temperature has been reached.

filter
Device that absorbs the steam from hot fat.

lid
Removable part that covers the deep fryer during cooking.

raclette with grill
Appliance with covered heating elements used to melt cheese or grill meat and side vegetables.

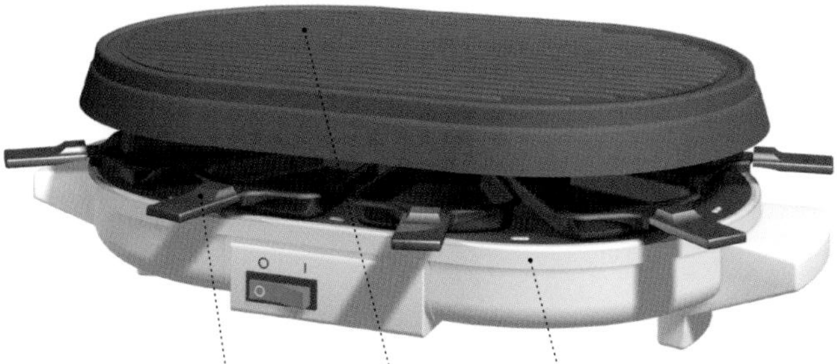

dish
Small shallow nonstick container used for cooking individual servings of food.

cooking plate
Ribbed cooking surface covering the heating elements; it is used for grilling food.

base
Stand supporting the raclette with grill; it contains the heating elements that cook the food.

electric steamer
Electric appliance comprising two dishes resting on a water-filled base; it is used to steam food separately.

cooking dishes
Containers that have a perforated base so the food they contain can be steamed.

water level indicator
Device that indicates the water level in the appliance's reservoir.

signal lamp
Light indicating that the heating element has been turned on.

timer
Device used to monitor cooking time.

indoor electric grill
Electric appliance comprising a metal grill and a heating element used to cook food.

insulated handle
art used to pick up and move the grill without burning oneself.

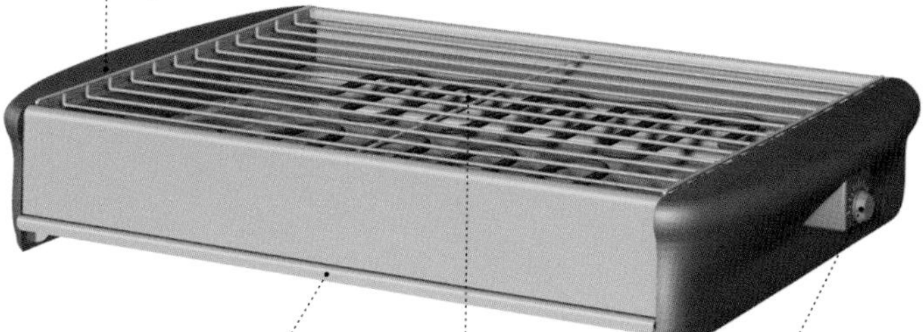

drip pan
Container into which the cooking juices drain.

cooking surface
Metal grill on which the food is cooked.

adjustable thermostat
Device used to regulate baking temperature.

bread machine
Electric appliance used to raise and bake bread dough.

lid
Movable part that closes the bread machine.

control panel
Panel containing the programming keys.

window
Thick glass through which the bread dough can be seen inside the mold.

loaf pan
Container for the bread dough, which, once baked, will become bread.

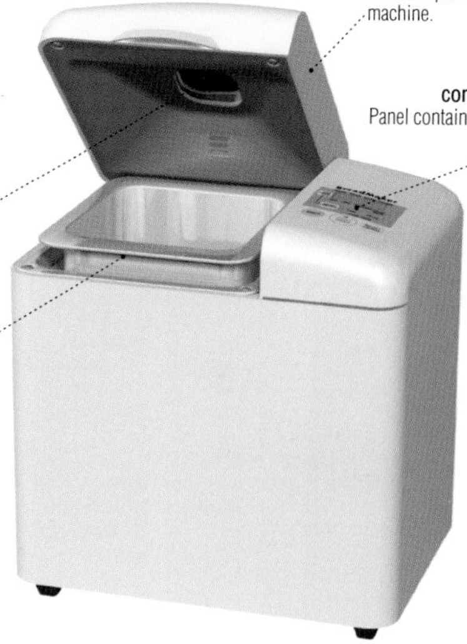

griddle
Electric appliance comprising a cooking surface and used for grilling food.

cooking surface
Often nonstick cooking plate on which food is placed.

handle
Part used to pick up and move the griddle.

detachable control
Device used to regulate grill temperature and that can be detached from the unit.

grease well
Hole through which cooking juices drain.

miscellaneous domestic appliances

can opener
Tool used to open cans by cutting along the inside edge of the lid.

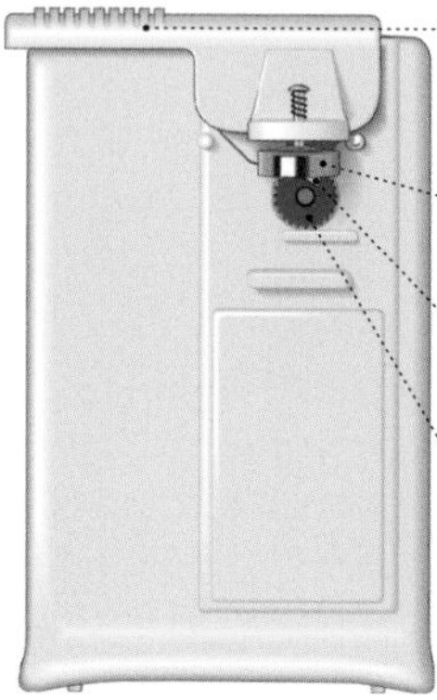

pierce lever
Device connected to the blade that the user presses down so it pierces the can lid.

magnetic lid holder
Part that holds the lid once it has been removed from the can.

cutting blade
Knife that separates the lid from the can.

drive wheel
Cogwheel that helps rotate the can so the lid can be removed.

coffee mill
Appliance that uses a rotating blade to finely grind coffee beans or other items, such as spices.

lid
Removable part that covers the coffee mill when it is in use.

blade
Instrument used to grind coffee beans or other items.

on-off button
Device that turns the appliance on or off.

motor unit
Part containing the motor and the various circuits making the appliance work.

kettle
Container with a heating element used to boil water.

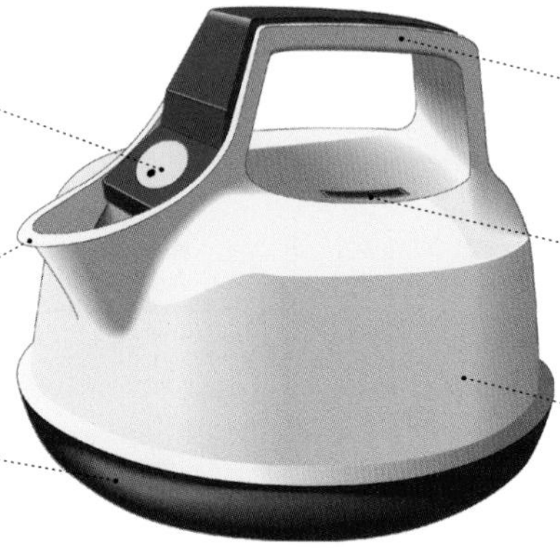

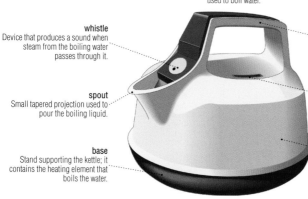

whistle
Device that produces a sound when steam from the boiling water passes through it.

spout
Small tapered projection used to pour the boiling liquid.

base
Stand supporting the kettle; it contains the heating element that boils the water.

handle
Part used to pick up and move the kettle.

signal lamp
Light showing that the appliance is on.

body
Part of the kettle that holds the water to be boiled.

ice cream freezer
Appliance comprising a freezer bucket in which revolving paddles make sherbet and ice cream.

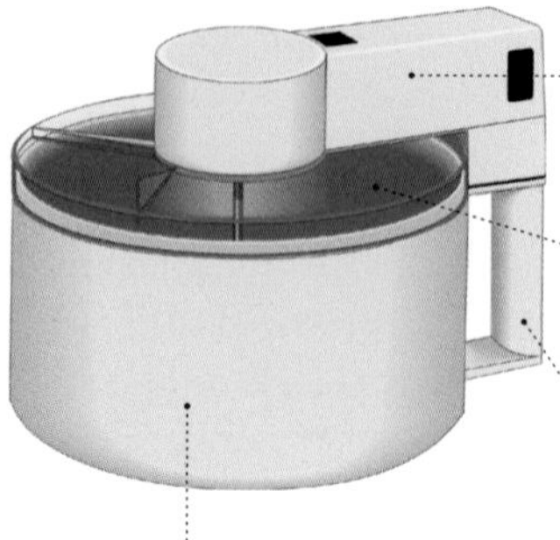

motor unit
Part containing the motor and the various circuits making the appliance work.

cover
Movable part that covers the freezer bucket during food preparation.

handle
Part used to pick up and move the ice cream freezer.

freezer bucket
Container designed to keep its contents cold.

juicer
Appliance that uses centrifugal force to extract the juice from vegetables and fruit, except citrus fruits, which must be reamed.

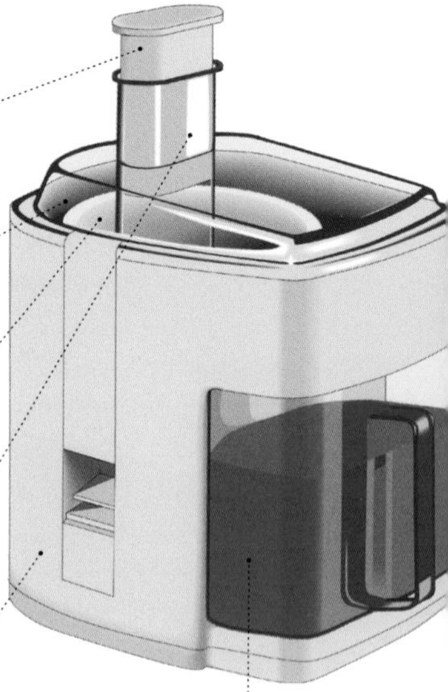

pusher
Device that pushes the fruits or vegetables into the appliance.

lid
Movable part that covers the juicer when it is in operation.

strainer
Device that allows only the fruit or vegetable juice to pass through.

feed tube
Conduit into which fruit or vegetables are placed to extract their juice.

motor unit
Part containing the motor and the various circuits making the appliance work.

bowl
Container into which the juice drains.

coffee makers

Utensils used to brew coffee; each of the various models produces coffee that has a distinctive flavor.

automatic drip coffee maker
Electric coffee maker that allows hot water to drain into a paper filter containing the ground beans, and coffee to drip into the carafe below.

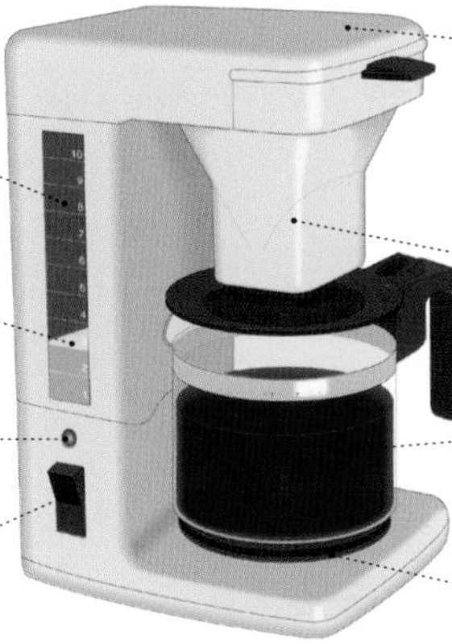

reservoir
Container holding the water to be heated.

water level
Indicates how many cups of coffee can be made.

signal lamp
Light showing that the appliance is on.

on-off switch
Button for turning the device on or off.

lid
Removable part covering the reservoir and under which the basket is located.

basket
Removable container that holds the filter with the ground beans.

carafe
Container with a spout into which the coffee drips and that is used to pour it.

warming plate
Surface used to keep the coffee warm.

Neapolitan coffee maker
Coffee maker that is placed on a heat source to boil the water; it is then turned over so the boiling water filters through the ground beans into the serving compartment.

espresso machine
Electric coffee maker that allows hot water to be forced under pressure through the ground beans.

on-off switch
Button for turning the device on or off.

tamper
Tool used to pack the ground beans into the filter.

drip tray
Compartment into which excess liquid drains.

steam nozzle
Device that emits steam used to foam milk.

steam control knob
Device used to regulate the steam coming out of the nozzle.

filter holder
Removable part with a handle into which the metal filter containing the ground beans is inserted.

water tank
Reservoir where the water is kept before it is required for heating.

vacuum coffee maker
Coffee maker that brews coffee by causing the water to pass through the ground beans twice.

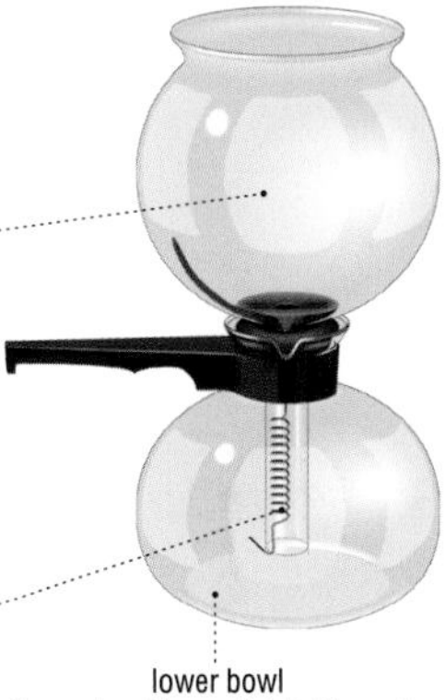

upper bowl
Compartment into which the brewed coffee rises and from which it drains into the lower bowl as the heat source cools.

stem
Conduit through which the hot water rises.

lower bowl
Compartment from which boiling water rises under pressure into the upper bowl, passing through the ground beans; the brewed coffee drains into it for serving.

plunger
Coffee maker that allows hot water to be poured over ground beans; once the grounds have steeped, the plunger is depressed to push the grounds to the bottom of the carafe.

espresso coffee maker
Coffee maker that allows boiling water from the lower compartment to be forced through the ground beans into the upper compartment.

percolator
Electric coffee maker that allows the hot water to rise several times through a tube to percolate through ground beans.

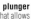

spout
Tube-shaped part through which the coffee is poured.

signal lamp
Light showing that the appliance is on.

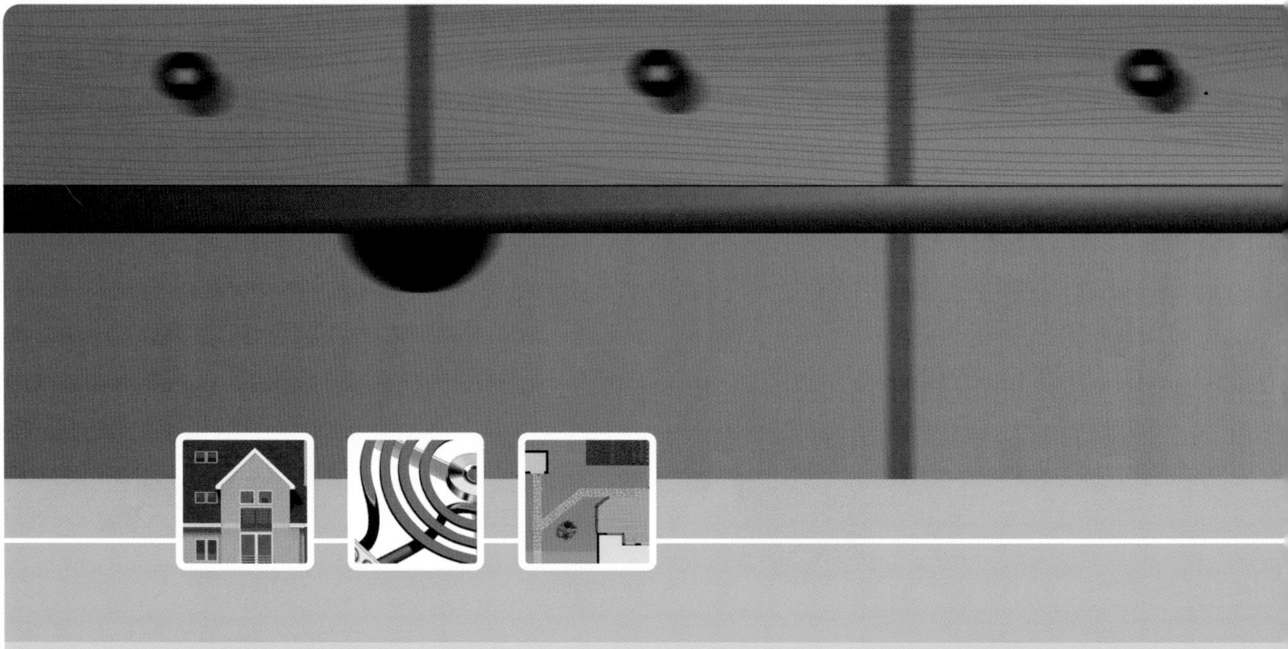

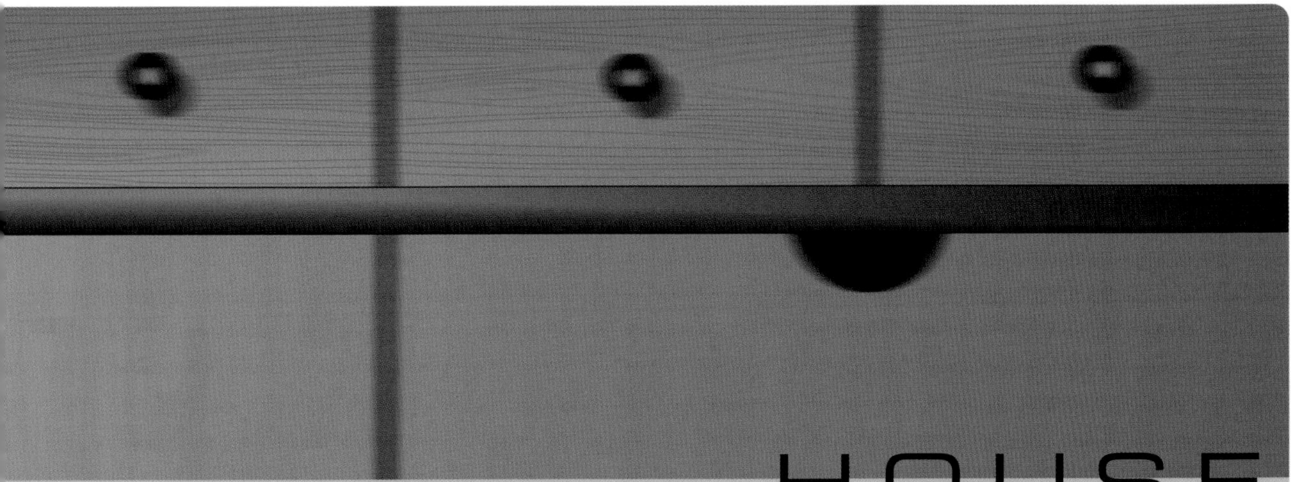

HOUSE

Structure built as a dwelling and equipped to provide a comfortable and secure life for people.

exterior of a house

View of a house on its site with the components of its exterior structure.

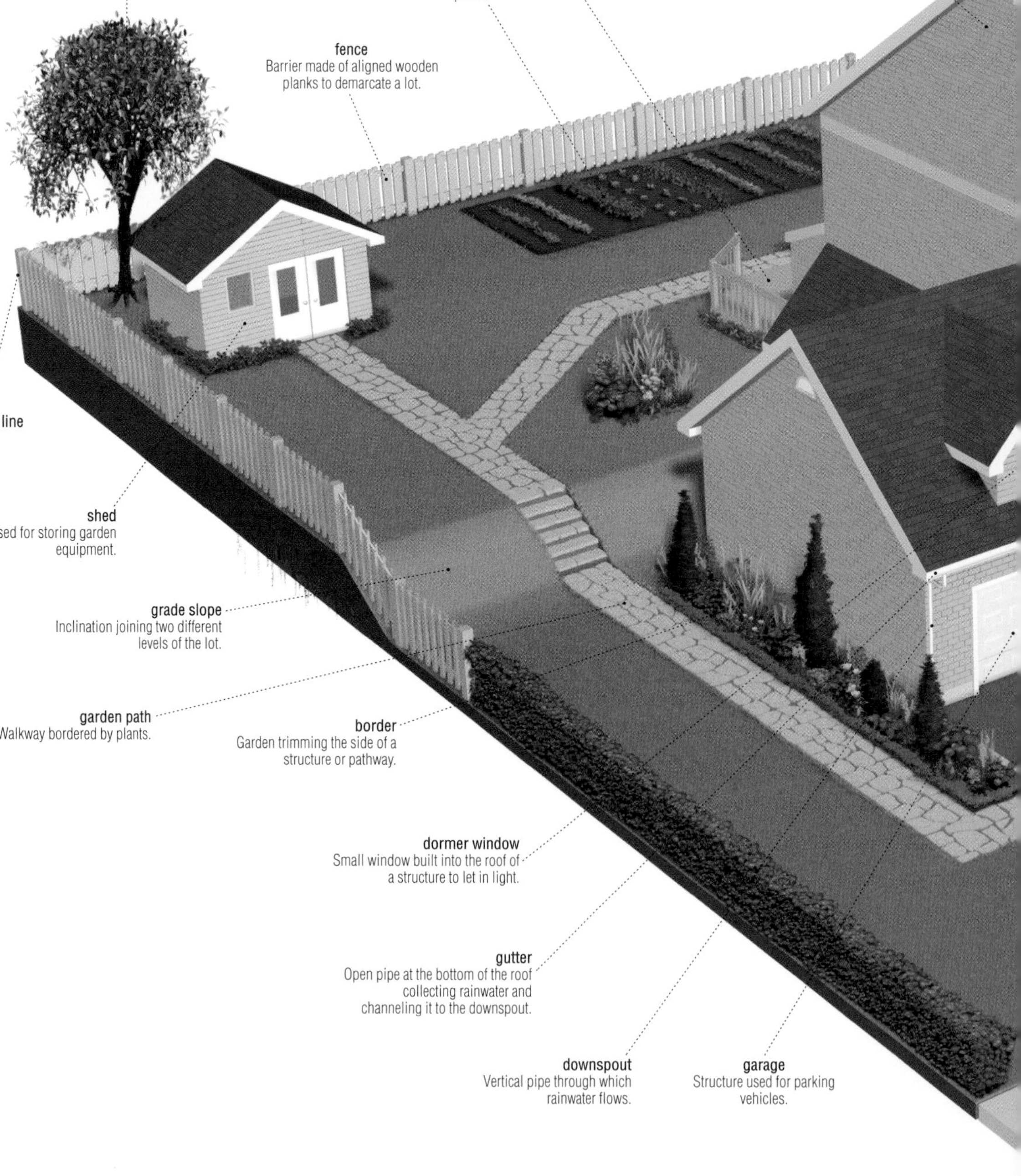
patio
Outdoor area adjacent to the house that is often paved and adapted for ourdoor dining.
gable vent
Opening in the side of a gable for ventilation.
ornamental tree
Tree planted for decorative purposes.
vegetable garden
Plot of land for growing edible plants.
gable
Upper triangular section of a wall supporting the sides of the roof.
fence
Barrier made of aligned wooden planks to demarcate a lot.
property line
shed
Structure used for storing garden equipment.
grade slope
Inclination joining two different levels of the lot.
garden path
Walkway bordered by plants.
border
Garden trimming the side of a structure or pathway.
dormer window
Small window built into the roof of a structure to let in light.
gutter
Open pipe at the bottom of the roof collecting rainwater and channeling it to the downspout.
downspout
Vertical pipe through which rainwater flows.
garage
Structure used for parking vehicles.

exterior of a house

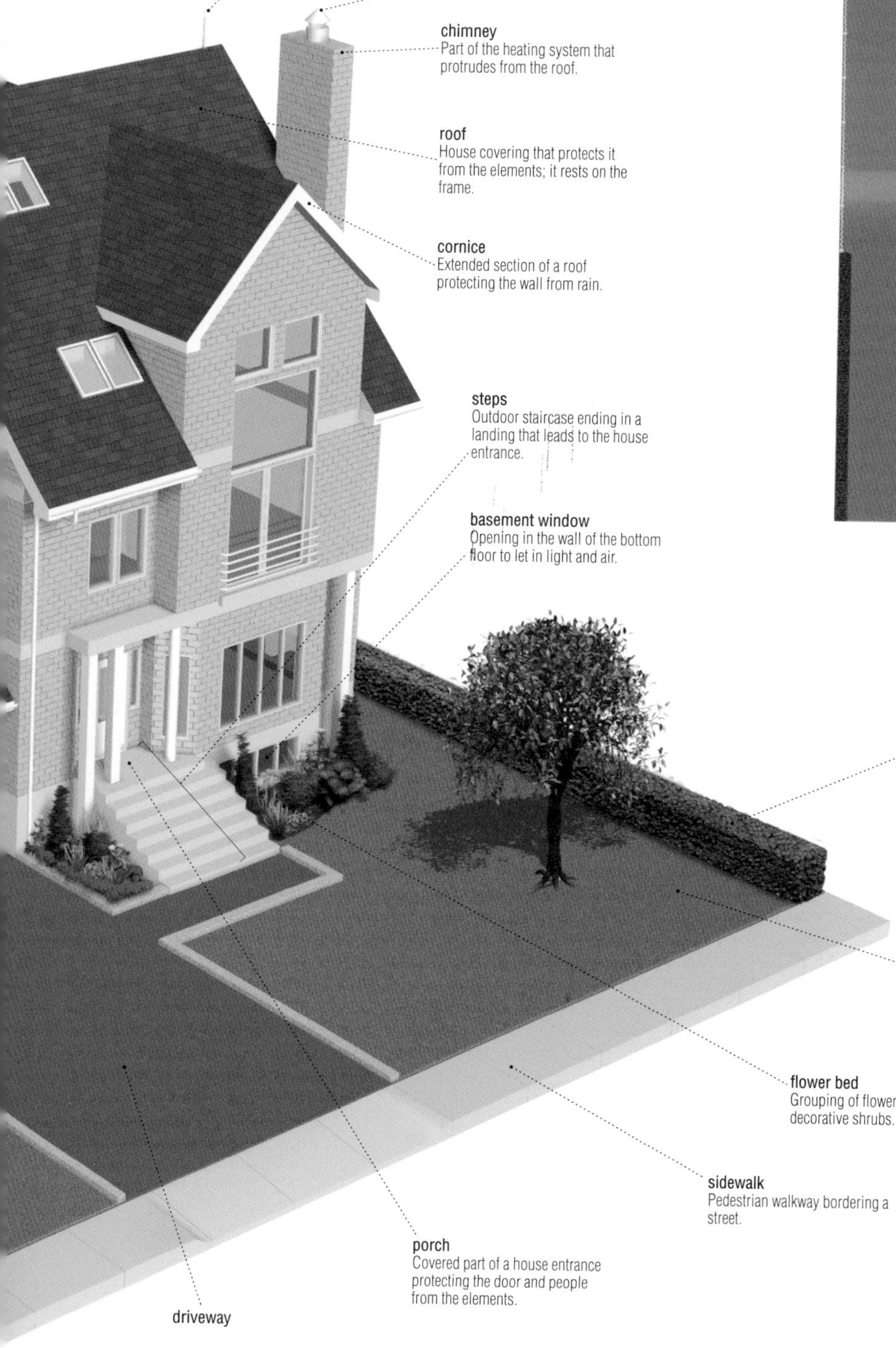
skylight
Window protruding through the roof to ventilate and illuminate the room below.
lightning rod
Metal spike attached to the roof; it protects the house by conducting lightning to the ground.
chimney pot
Topmost part of the chimney; it is covered by a piece of metal.
chimney
Part of the heating system that protrudes from the roof.
roof
House covering that protects it from the elements; it rests on the frame.
cornice
Extended section of a roof protecting the wall from rain.
steps
Outdoor staircase ending in a landing that leads to the house entrance.
basement window
Opening in the wall of the bottom floor to let in light and air.
hedge
Bushes planted in a row to demarcate a lot.
lawn
Land covered by short thick grass requiring regular mowing.
flower bed
Grouping of flowers and decorative shrubs.
sidewalk
Pedestrian walkway bordering a street.
porch
Covered part of a house entrance protecting the door and people from the elements.
driveway

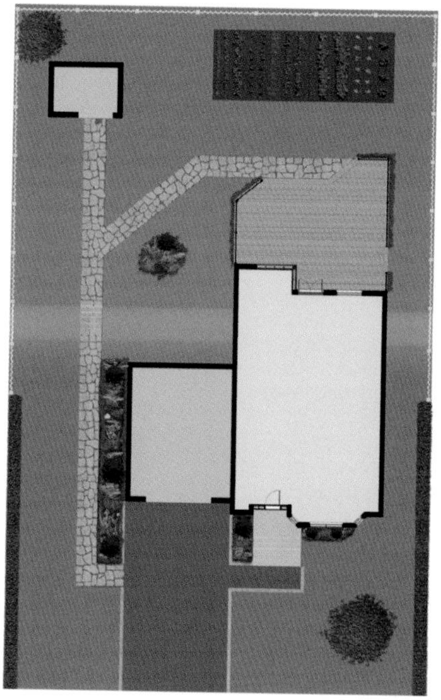

site plan
Graphical representation of the horizontal projection of a lot.

pool

Man-made basin designed for swimming.

above ground swimming pool

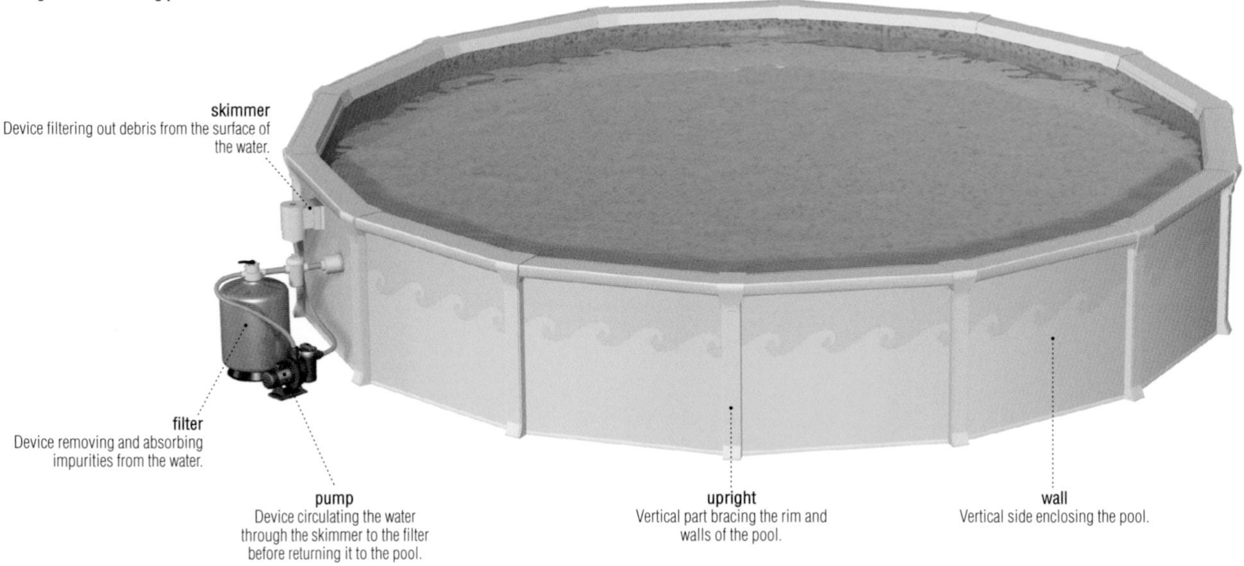
skimmer
Device filtering out debris from the surface of the water.
filter
Device removing and absorbing impurities from the water.
pump
Device circulating the water through the skimmer to the filter before returning it to the pool.
upright
Vertical part bracing the rim and walls of the pool.
wall
Vertical side enclosing the pool.

in-ground swimming pool

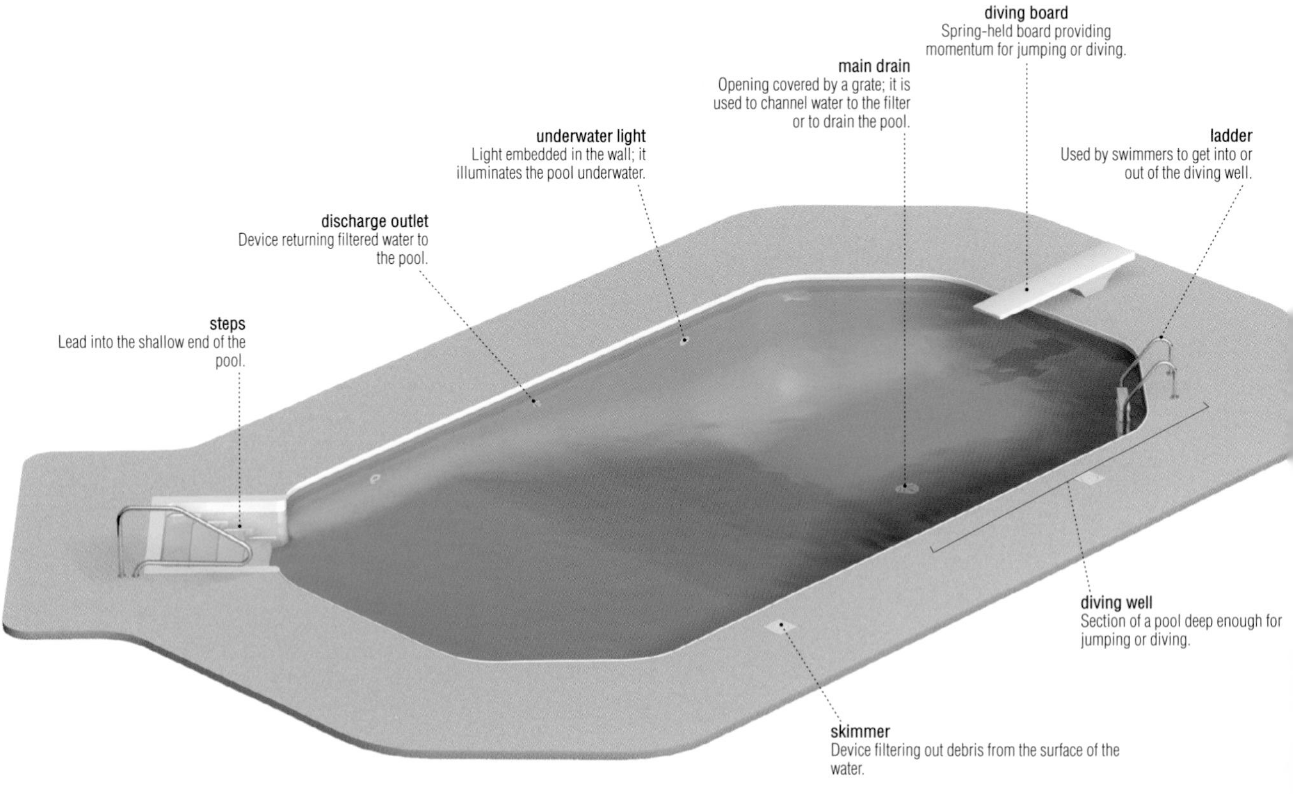
diving board
Spring-held board providing momentum for jumping or diving.
main drain
Opening covered by a grate; it is used to channel water to the filter or to drain the pool.
underwater light
Light embedded in the wall; it illuminates the pool underwater.
ladder
Used by swimmers to get into or out of the diving well.
discharge outlet
Device returning filtered water to the pool.
steps
Lead into the shallow end of the pool.
diving well
Section of a pool deep enough for jumping or diving.
skimmer
Device filtering out debris from the surface of the water.

exterior door

The exterior door comprises a moving part, the leaf, plus a frame. It provides access to and egress from the house.

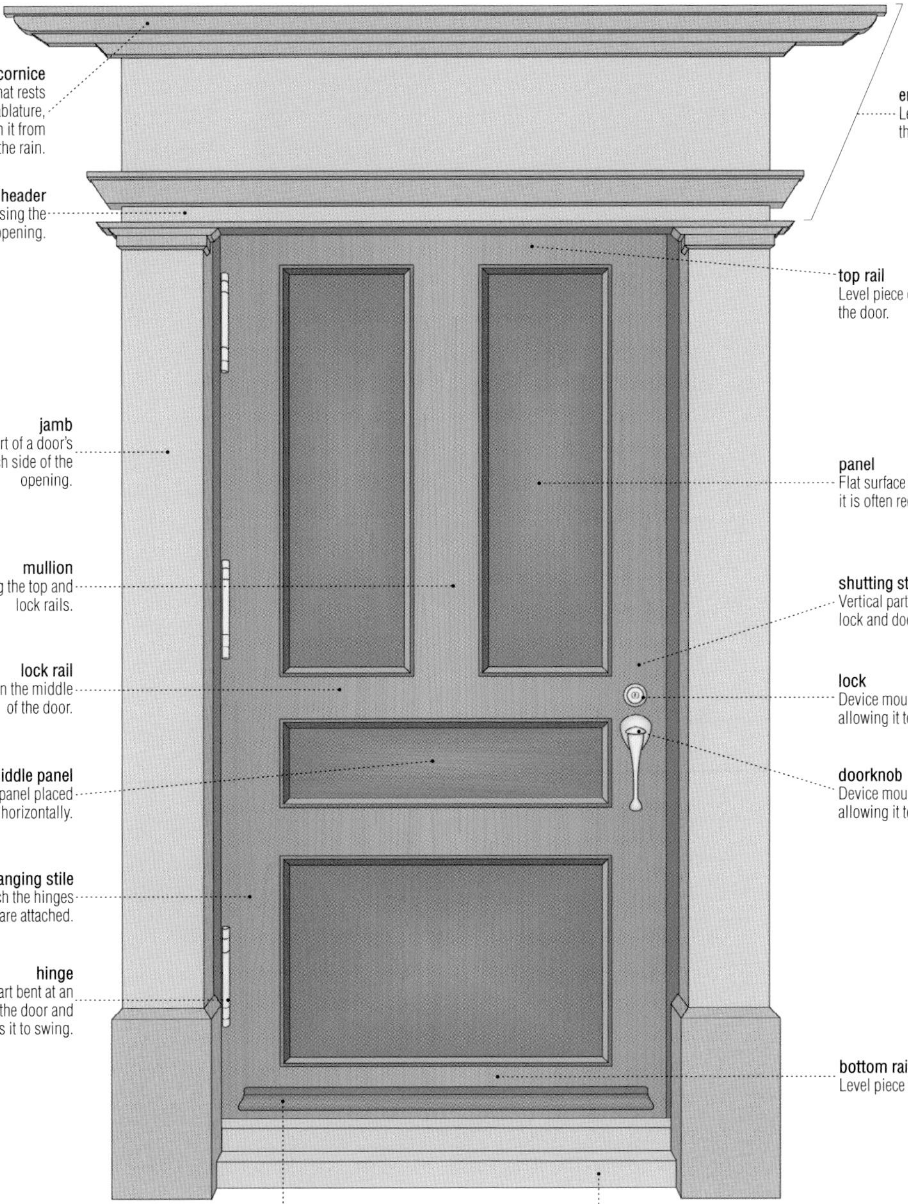
cornice
Protruding molding that rests horizontally across the entablature, protecting the parts beneath it from the rain.
entablature
Level set of woodwork covering the doorway.
header
Level frame part enclosing the upper part of a door's opening.
top rail
Level piece of wood at the top of the door.
jamb
Protruding part of a door's framework on each side of the opening.
panel
Flat surface bordered by molding; it is often recessed.
mullion
Vertical piece of wood joining the top and lock rails.
shutting stile
Vertical part of the door on which the lock and doorknob are mounted.
lock rail
Level piece of wood in the middle of the door.
lock
Device mounted on the door allowing it to lock by using a key.
middle panel
Long narrow panel placed horizontally.
doorknob
Device mounted on the door allowing it to open.
hanging stile
Vertical part of the door to which the hinges are attached.
hinge
Cylindrical metal part bent at an angle; it supports the door and allows it to swing.
bottom rail
Level piece of wood at the bottom of the door.
weather strip
Sloped strip of wood allowing water to flow away from the door.
threshold
Surface forming the bottom part of the door opening.

HOUSE

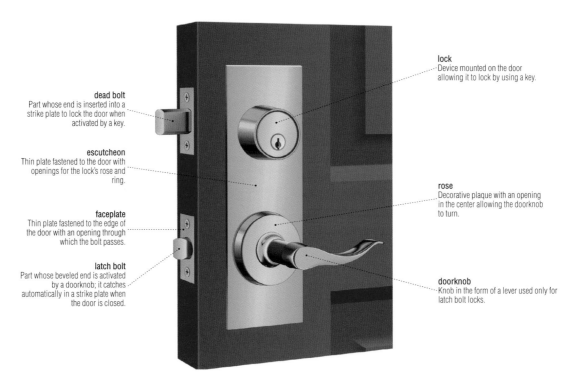

lock

Device mounted on the door allowing it to lock by using a key.

general view

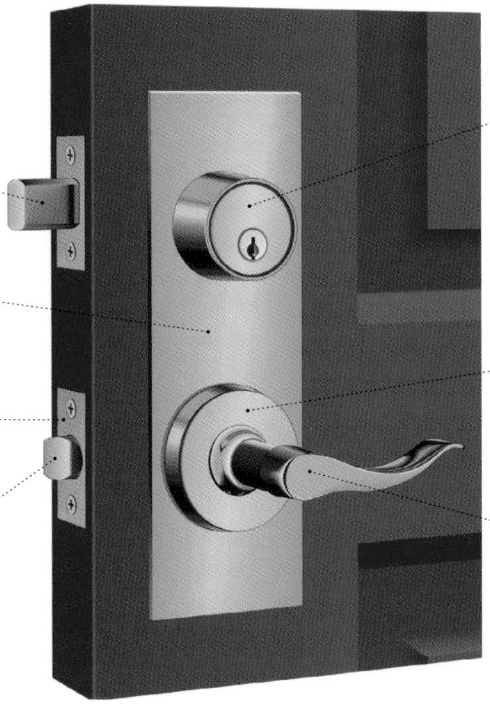
dead bolt
Part whose end is inserted into a strike plate to lock the door when activated by a key.
escutcheon
Thin plate fastened to the door with openings for the lock's rose and ring.
faceplate
Thin plate fastened to the edge of the door with an opening through which the bolt passes.
latch bolt
Part whose beveled end is activated by a doorknob; it catches automatically in a strike plate when the door is closed.
lock
Device mounted on the door allowing it to lock by using a key.
rose
Decorative plaque with an opening in the center allowing the doorknob to turn.
doorknob
Knob in the form of a lever used only for latch bolt locks.

tubular lock
Lock whose knobs activate a latch bolt and is locked by pushing a button; it is used for interior doors.

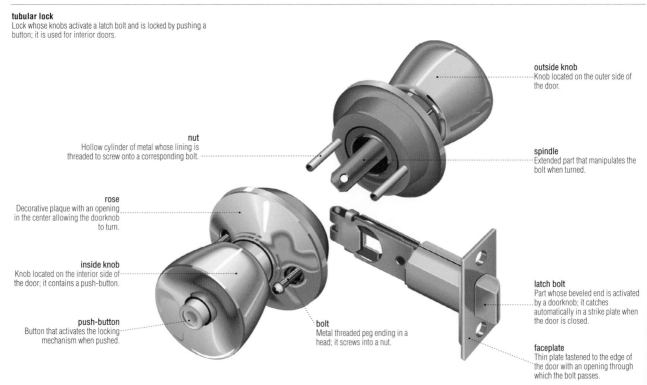

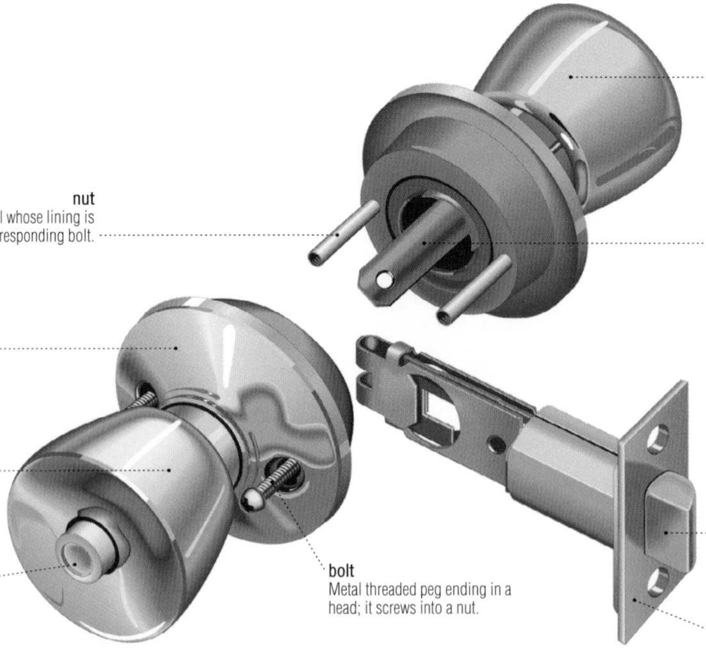
outside knob
Knob located on the outer side of the door.
nut
Hollow cylinder of metal whose lining is threaded to screw onto a corresponding bolt.
spindle
Extended part that manipulates the bolt when turned.
rose
Decorative plaque with an opening in the center allowing the doorknob to turn.
inside knob
Knob located on the interior side of the door; it contains a push-button.
latch bolt
Part whose beveled end is activated by a doorknob; it catches automatically in a strike plate when the door is closed.
push-button
Button that activates the locking mechanism when pushed.
bolt
Metal threaded peg ending in a head; it screws into a nut.
faceplate
Thin plate fastened to the edge of the door with an opening through which the bolt passes.

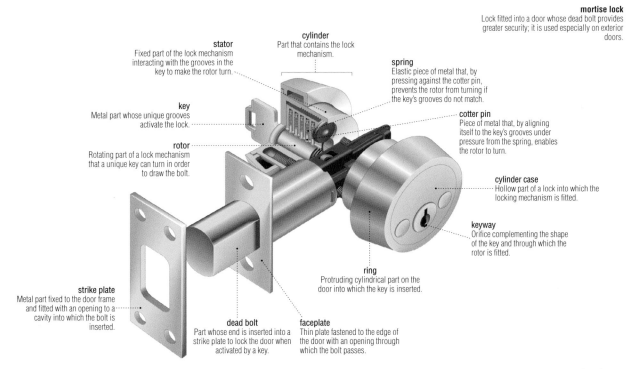

lock

mortise lock
Lock fitted into a door whose dead bolt provides greater security; it is used especially on exterior doors.

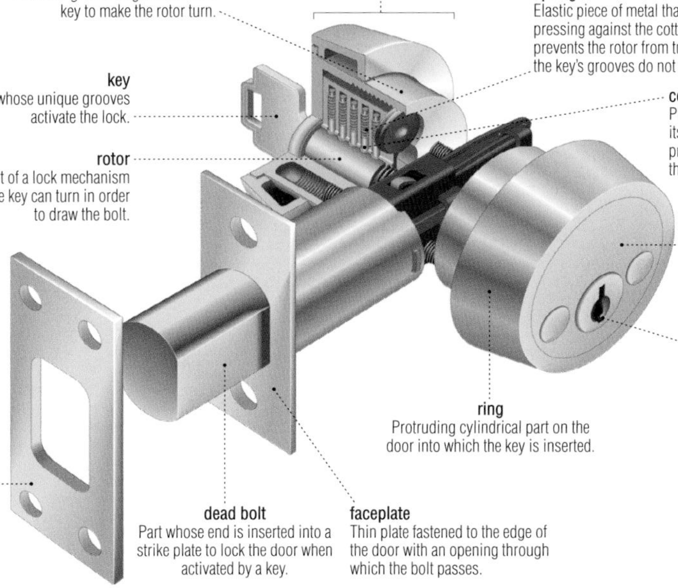
cylinder
Part that contains the lock mechanism.
stator
Fixed part of the lock mechanism interacting with the grooves in the key to make the rotor turn.
spring
Elastic piece of metal that, by pressing against the cotter pin, prevents the rotor from turning if the key's grooves do not match.
key
Metal part whose unique grooves activate the lock.
cotter pin
Piece of metal that, by aligning itself to the key's grooves under pressure from the spring, enables the rotor to turn.
rotor
Rotating part of a lock mechanism that a unique key can turn in order to draw the bolt.
cylinder case
Hollow part of a lock into which the locking mechanism is fitted.
keyway
Orifice complementing the shape of the key and through which the rotor is fitted.
ring
Protruding cylindrical part on the door into which the key is inserted.
strike plate
Metal part fixed to the door frame and fitted with an opening to a cavity into which the bolt is inserted.
dead bolt
Part whose end is inserted into a strike plate to lock the door when activated by a key.
faceplate
Thin plate fastened to the edge of the door with an opening through which the bolt passes.

window

Opening in a wall fitted with glass to let in light and air.

structure

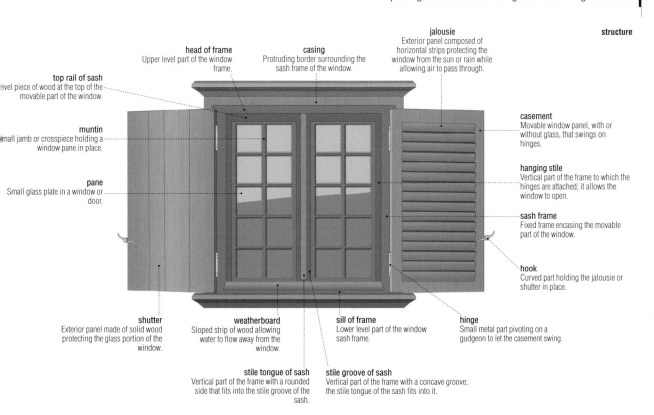

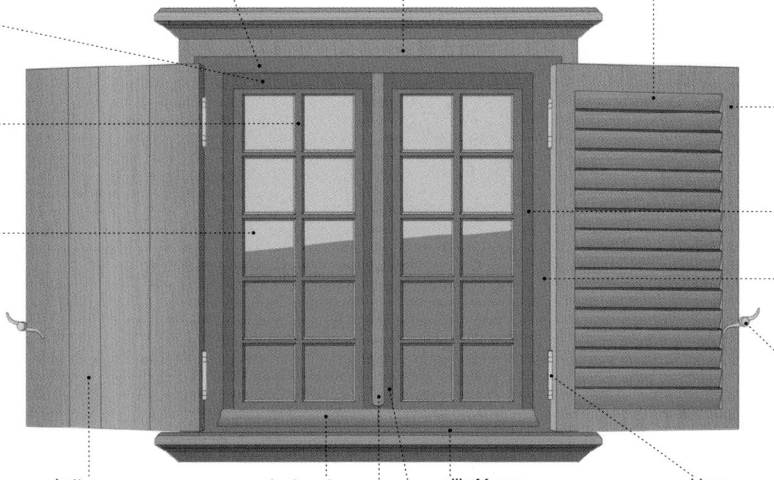
jalousie
Exterior panel composed of horizontal strips protecting the window from the sun or rain while allowing air to pass through.
head of frame
Upper level part of the window frame.
casing
Protruding border surrounding the sash frame of the window.
top rail of sash
evel piece of wood at the top of the movable part of the window.
casement
Movable window panel, with or without glass, that swings on hinges.
muntin
mall jamb or crosspiece holding a window pane in place.
hanging stile
Vertical part of the frame to which the hinges are attached; it allows the window to open.
pane
Small glass plate in a window or door.
sash frame
Fixed frame encasing the movable part of the window.
hook
Curved part holding the jalousie or shutter in place.
shutter
Exterior panel made of solid wood protecting the glass portion of the window.
weatherboard
Sloped strip of wood allowing water to flow away from the window.
sill of frame
Lower level part of the window sash frame.
hinge
Small metal part pivoting on a gudgeon to let the casement swing.
stile tongue of sash
Vertical part of the frame with a rounded side that fits into the stile groove of the sash.
stile groove of sash
Vertical part of the frame with a concave groove; the stile tongue of the sash fits into it.

main rooms

elevation
Vertical representation of the projection of the house.

third floor
Floor immediately below roof containing rooms or an unfinishe part of the house.

second floor
Part of the house defined by a floo and a ceiling; it is located above the first floor.

first floor
Part of the house closest to groun level.

basement
Part of the house that is underground or partially so; it lies under the ground floor.

first floor
Part of the house closest to ground level.

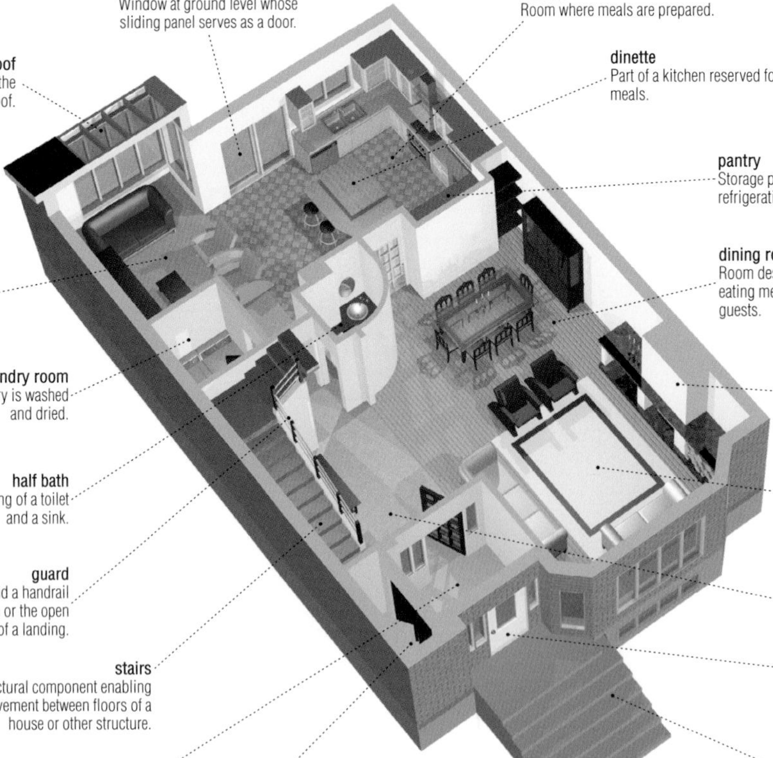

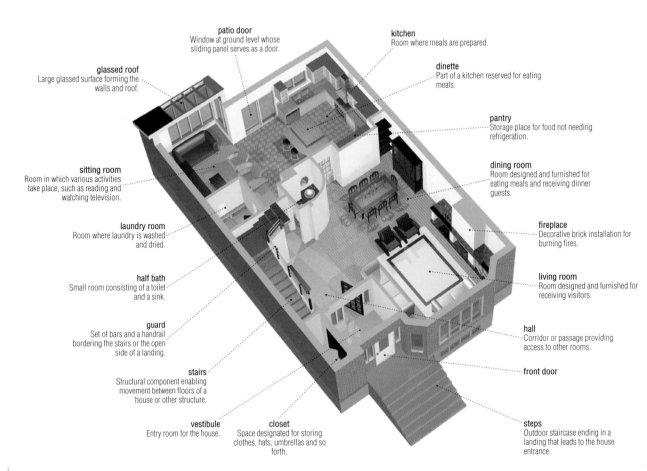

patio door
Window at ground level whose sliding panel serves as a door.

kitchen
Room where meals are prepared.

glassed roof
Large glassed surface forming the walls and roof.

dinette
Part of a kitchen reserved for eating meals.

pantry
Storage place for food not needing refrigeration.

sitting room
Room in which various activities take place, such as reading and watching television.

dining room
Room designed and furnished for eating meals and receiving dinner guests.

laundry room
Room where laundry is washed and dried.

fireplace
Decorative brick installation for burning fires.

half bath
Small room consisting of a toilet and a sink.

living room
Room designed and furnished for receiving visitors.

guard
Set of bars and a handrail bordering the stairs or the open side of a landing.

hall
Corridor or passage providing access to other rooms.

front door

stairs
Structural component enabling movement between floors of a house or other structure.

vestibule
Entry room for the house.

closet
Space designated for storing clothes, hats, umbrellas and so forth.

steps
Outdoor staircase ending in a landing that leads to the house entrance.

main rooms

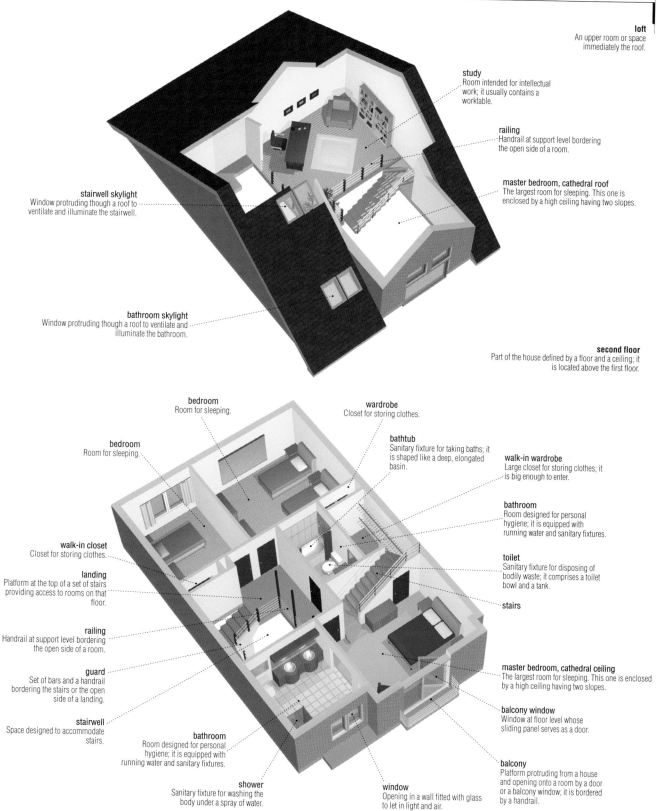

loft
An upper room or space immediately the roof.

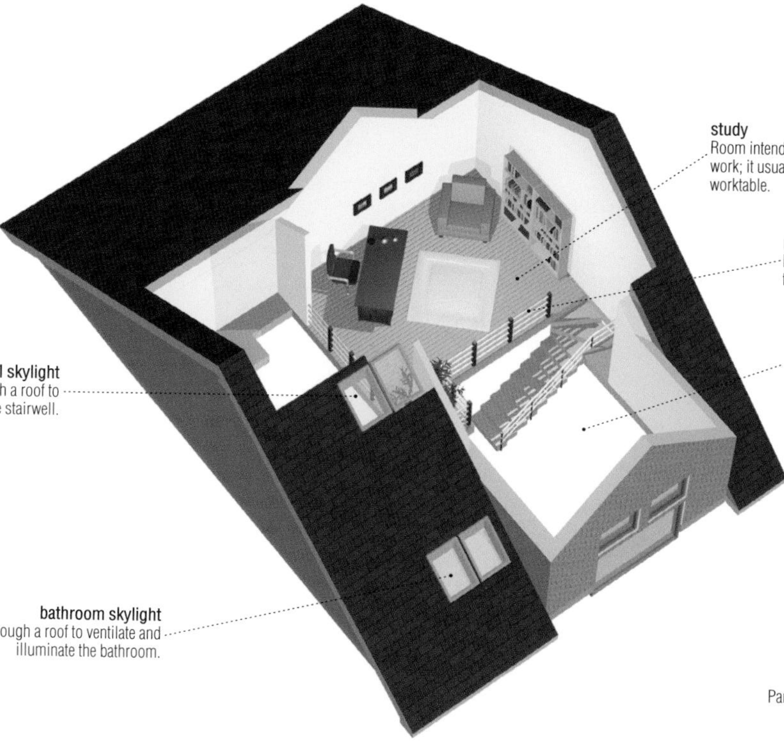

study
Room intended for intellectual work; it usually contains a worktable.
railing
Handrail at support level bordering the open side of a room.
master bedroom, cathedral roof
The largest room for sleeping. This one is enclosed by a high ceiling having two slopes.
stairwell skylight
Window protruding though a roof to ventilate and illuminate the stairwell.
bathroom skylight
Window protruding though a roof to ventilate and illuminate the bathroom.

second floor
Part of the house defined by a floor and a ceiling; it is located above the first floor.

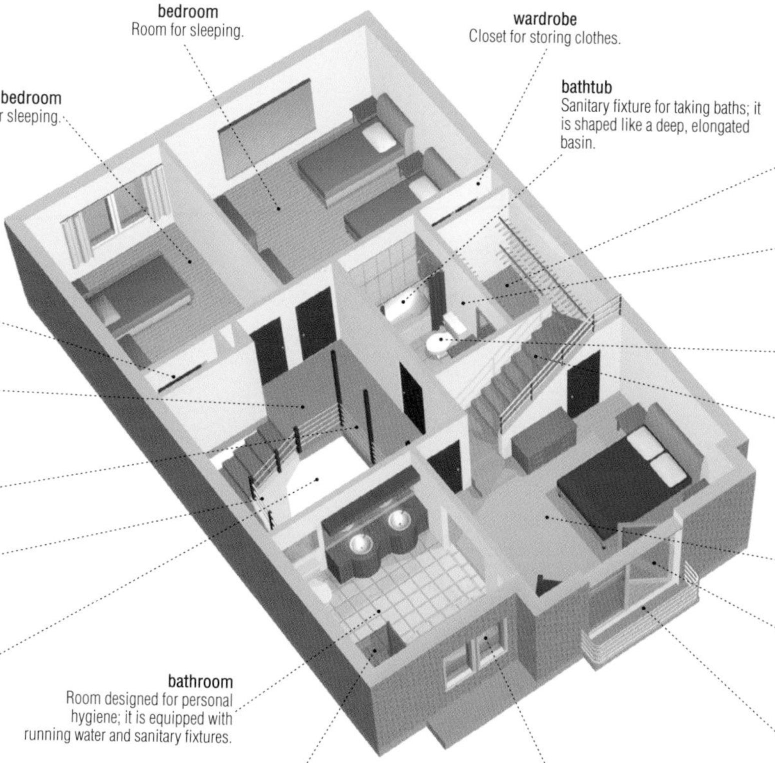

bedroom
Room for sleeping.
wardrobe
Closet for storing clothes.
bedroom
Room for sleeping.
bathtub
Sanitary fixture for taking baths; it is shaped like a deep, elongated basin.
walk-in wardrobe
Large closet for storing clothes; it is big enough to enter.
bathroom
Room designed for personal hygiene; it is equipped with running water and sanitary fixtures.
walk-in closet
Closet for storing clothes.
toilet
Sanitary fixture for disposing of bodily waste; it comprises a toilet bowl and a tank.
landing
Platform at the top of a set of stairs providing access to rooms on that floor.
stairs
railing
Handrail at support level bordering the open side of a room.
guard
Set of bars and a handrail bordering the stairs or the open side of a landing.
master bedroom, cathedral ceiling
The largest room for sleeping. This one is enclosed by a high ceiling having two slopes.
balcony window
Window at floor level whose sliding panel serves as a door.
stairwell
Space designed to accommodate stairs.
bathroom
Room designed for personal hygiene; it is equipped with running water and sanitary fixtures.
balcony
Platform protruding from a house and opening onto a room by a door or a balcony window; it is bordered by a handrail.
shower
Sanitary fixture for washing the body under a spray of water.
window
Opening in a wall fitted with glass to let in light and air.

frame

Assembly of members that consists of the load-bearing structure of a building and that provides stability to it.

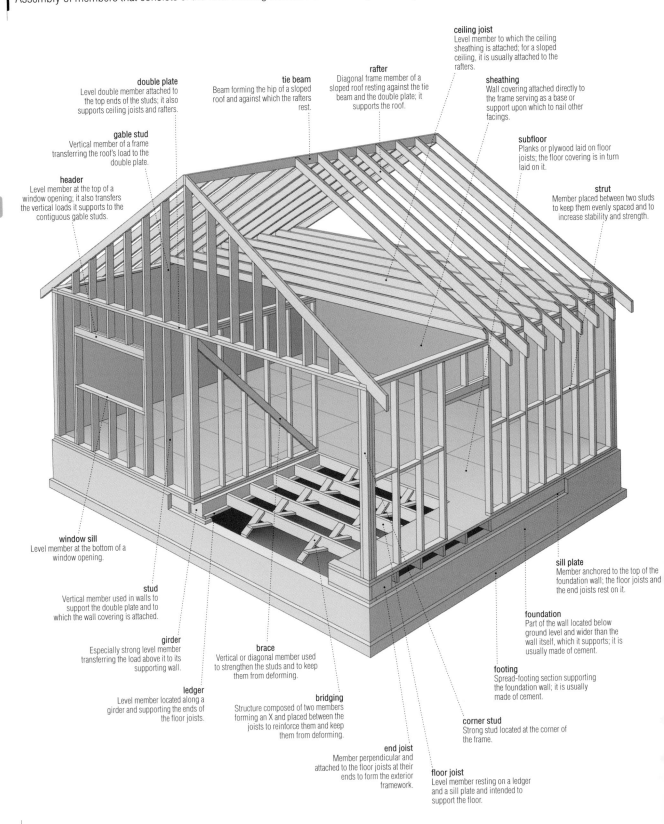

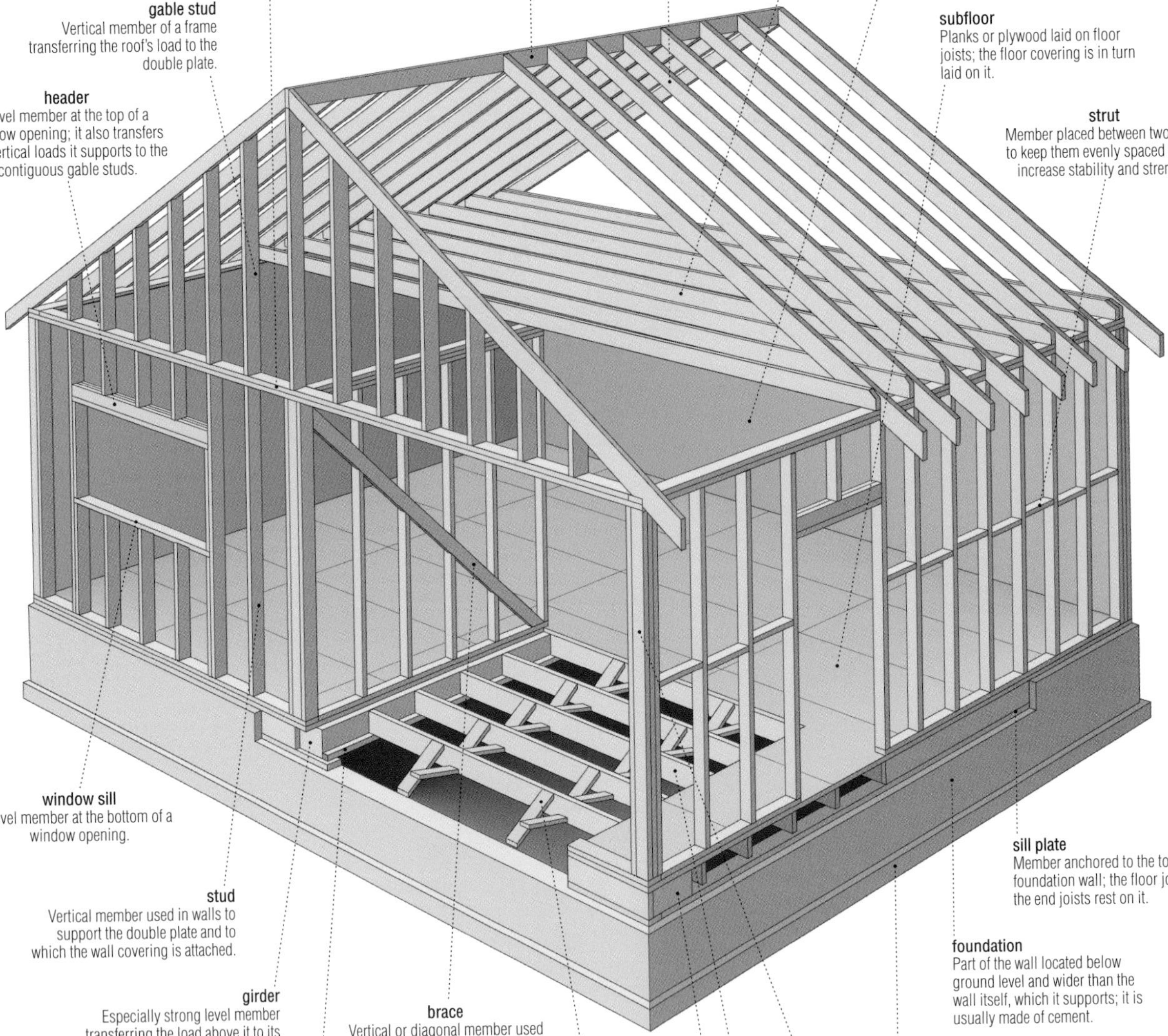

ceiling joist
Level member to which the ceiling sheathing is attached; for a sloped ceiling, it is usually attached to the rafters.

rafter
Diagonal frame member of a sloped roof resting against the tie beam and the double plate; it supports the roof.

tie beam
Beam forming the hip of a sloped roof and against which the rafters rest.

double plate
Level double member attached to the top ends of the studs; it also supports ceiling joists and rafters.

sheathing
Wall covering attached directly to the frame serving as a base or support upon which to nail other facings.

gable stud
Vertical member of a frame transferring the roof's load to the double plate.

subfloor
Planks or plywood laid on floor joists; the floor covering is in turn laid on it.

header
Level member at the top of a window opening; it also transfers the vertical loads it supports to the contiguous gable studs.

strut
Member placed between two studs to keep them evenly spaced and to increase stability and strength.

window sill
Level member at the bottom of a window opening.

sill plate
Member anchored to the top of the foundation wall; the floor joists and the end joists rest on it.

stud
Vertical member used in walls to support the double plate and to which the wall covering is attached.

foundation
Part of the wall located below ground level and wider than the wall itself, which it supports; it is usually made of cement.

girder
Especially strong level member transferring the load above it to its supporting wall.

brace
Vertical or diagonal member used to strengthen the studs and to keep them from deforming.

footing
Spread-footing section supporting the foundation wall; it is usually made of cement.

ledger
Level member located along a girder and supporting the ends of the floor joists.

bridging
Structure composed of two members forming an X and placed between the joists to reinforce them and keep them from deforming.

corner stud
Strong stud located at the corner of the frame.

end joist
Member perpendicular and attached to the floor joists at their ends to form the exterior framework.

floor joist
Level member resting on a ledger and a sill plate and intended to support the floor.

roof truss

Assembly of members composed of a triangular substructure to form the frame of a sloped roof; it supports the roof.

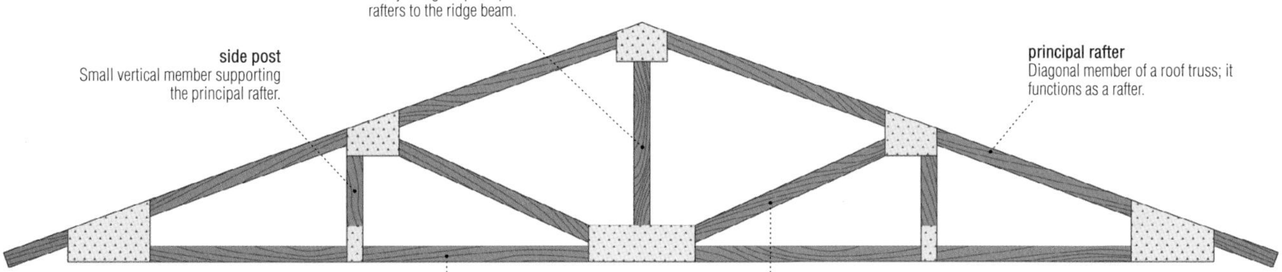

king post
Vertical member supporting the tie beam and joining the principal rafters to the ridge beam.
side post
Small vertical member supporting the principal rafter.
principal rafter
Diagonal member of a roof truss; it functions as a rafter.
ridge beam
Level member at the base of a truss upon which the side posts and the king post rest; these in turn support the principal rafters.
strut
Diagonal member supporting the principal rafter, joining it to the junction of the king post and the ridge beam.

foundation

Work done on-site in cement or masonry; it supports a structure's load and transfers it to the ground, thus providing stability.

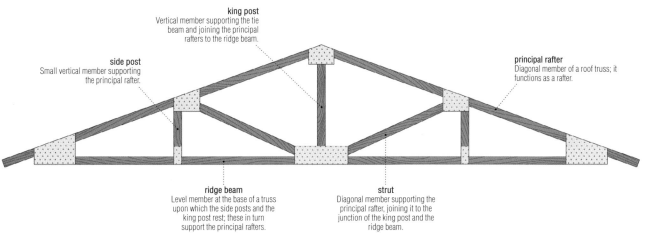

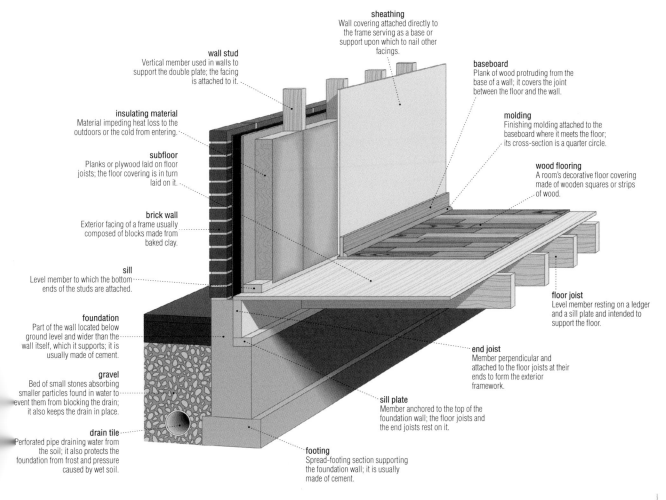

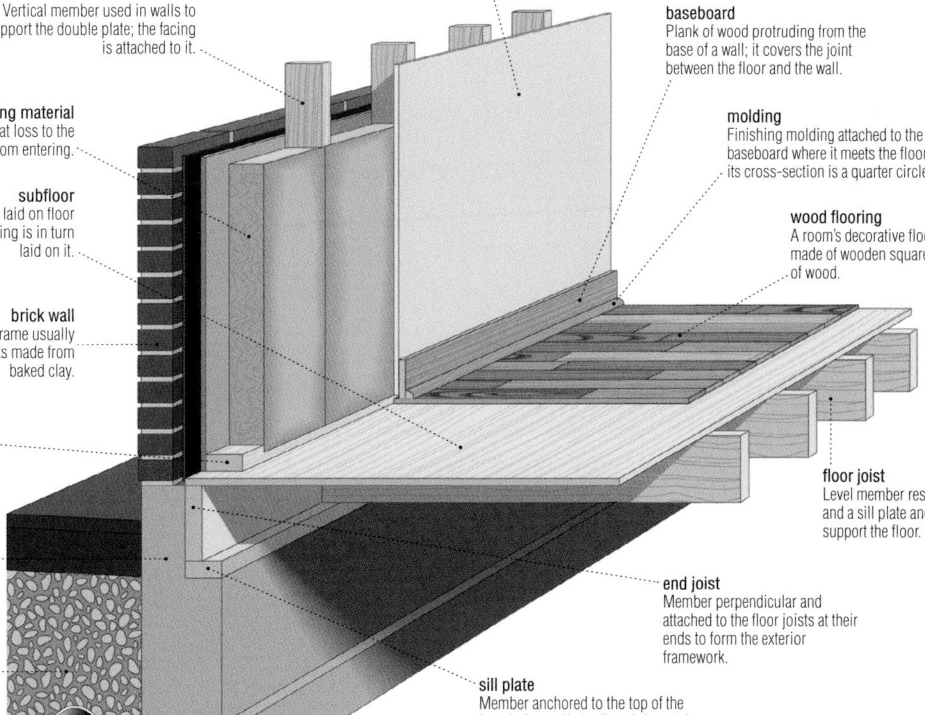

sheathing
Wall covering attached directly to the frame serving as a base or support upon which to nail other facings.
wall stud
Vertical member used in walls to support the double plate; the facing is attached to it.
baseboard
Plank of wood protruding from the base of a wall; it covers the joint between the floor and the wall.
insulating material
Material impeding heat loss to the outdoors or the cold from entering.
molding
Finishing molding attached to the baseboard where it meets the floor; its cross-section is a quarter circle.
subfloor
Planks or plywood laid on floor joists; the floor covering is in turn laid on it.
wood flooring
A room's decorative floor covering made of wooden squares or strips of wood.
brick wall
Exterior facing of a frame usually composed of blocks made from baked clay.
sill
Level member to which the bottom ends of the studs are attached.
floor joist
Level member resting on a ledger and a sill plate and intended to support the floor.
foundation
Part of the wall located below ground level and wider than the wall itself, which it supports; it is usually made of cement.
end joist
Member perpendicular and attached to the floor joists at their ends to form the exterior framework.
gravel
Bed of small stones absorbing smaller particles found in water to event them from blocking the drain; it also keeps the drain in place.
sill plate
Member anchored to the top of the foundation wall; the floor joists and the end joists rest on it.
drain tile
Perforated pipe draining water from the soil; it also protects the foundation from frost and pressure caused by wet soil.
footing
Spread-footing section supporting the foundation wall; it is usually made of cement.

wood flooring

A room's decorative floor covering made of wooden squares or strips of wood.

wood flooring on cement screed
Wood flooring that is supported by a layer of cement.

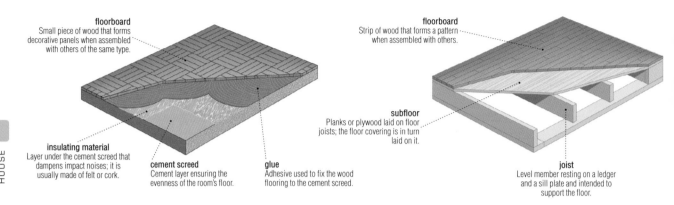

floorboard
Small piece of wood that forms decorative panels when assembled with others of the same type.

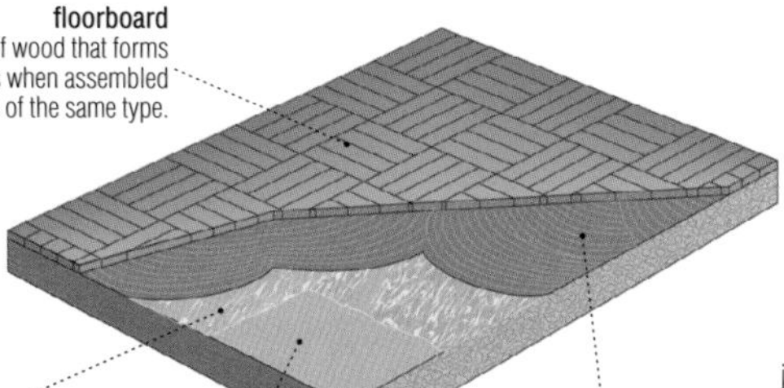

insulating material
Layer under the cement screed that dampens impact noises; it is usually made of felt or cork.

cement screed
Cement layer ensuring the evenness of the room's floor.

glue
Adhesive used to fix the wood flooring to the cement screed.

wood flooring on wooden structure
Wood flooring that is supported by a subfloor made of wood.

floorboard
Strip of wood that forms a pattern when assembled with others.

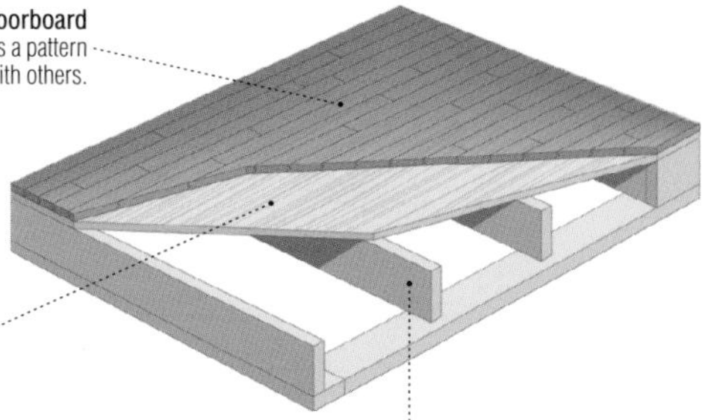

subfloor
Planks or plywood laid on floor joists; the floor covering is in turn laid on it.

joist
Level member resting on a ledger and a sill plate and intended to support the floor.

wood flooring arrangements
Strip flooring and parquetry are vehicles for creating various artistic patterns.

overlay flooring
Wood flooring with floorboards of different lengths laid parallel; its joints are distributed randomly.

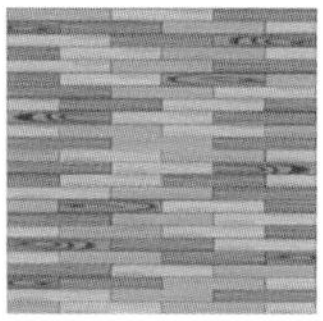

strip flooring with alternate joints
Wood flooring with floorboards of identical lengths laid parallel; its joints are offset by half a length from one row to the next.

herringbone parquet
Wood flooring of rectangular wood strips of equal lengths laid one against the other to form an angle of 45°.

herringbone pattern
Wood flooring of equal lengths whose jo meet at 45° to 60° cuts.

inlaid parquet
Wood flooring of parquetry assembled in a checkerboard pattern.

basket weave pattern
Wood flooring of parquetry creating a woven effect.

Arenberg parquet
Wood flooring composed of a border and of different geometric figures. Inspired by the Château d'Arenberg in Belgium.

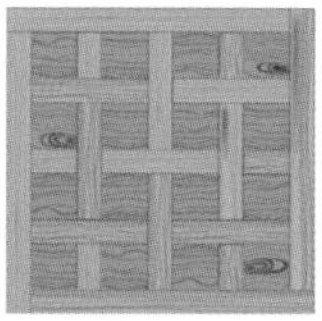

Chantilly parquet
Wood flooring composed of a border and of compartments positioned at right angles to it. Inspired by the Château de Chantilly in France.

Versailles parquet
Wood flooring composed of a borde and of compartments positioned diagonally in relation to it. Inspired b the Château de Versailles in France.

textile floor coverings

Textile floor coverings, such as rugs and pile carpets, are comfortable and attractive, and dampen impact noise.

rug
Piece of thick heavy fabric usually having a nap and covering a section of the floor; it is removable.

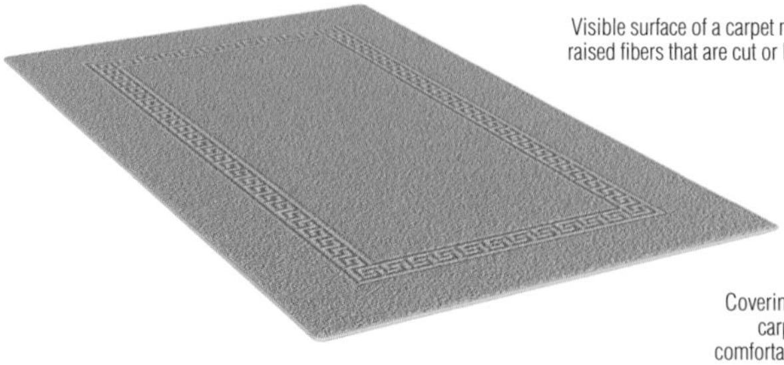

pile carpet
Piece of thick heavy fabric attached to and covering the entire floor of a room.

pile
Visible surface of a carpet made of raised fibers that are cut or looped.

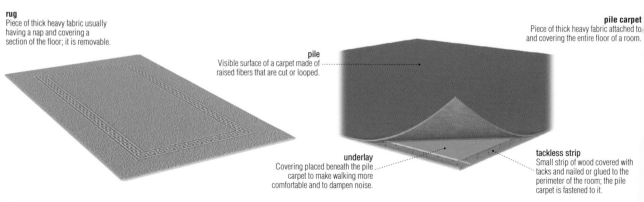

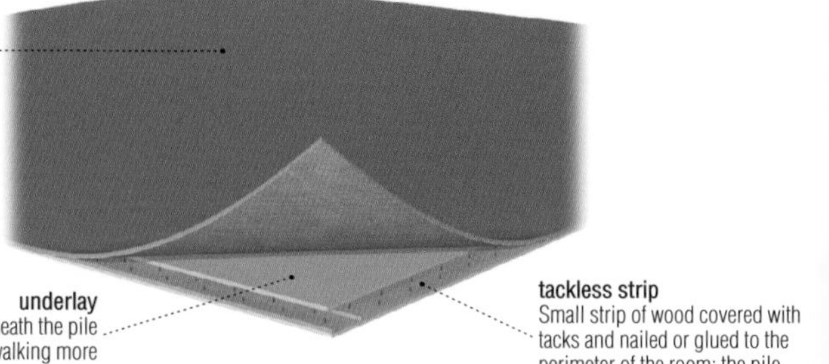

underlay
Covering placed beneath the pile carpet to make walking more comfortable and to dampen noise.

tackless strip
Small strip of wood covered with tacks and nailed or glued to the perimeter of the room; the pile carpet is fastened to it.

HOUSE

stairs

Structural component enabling movement between floors of a house or other structure.

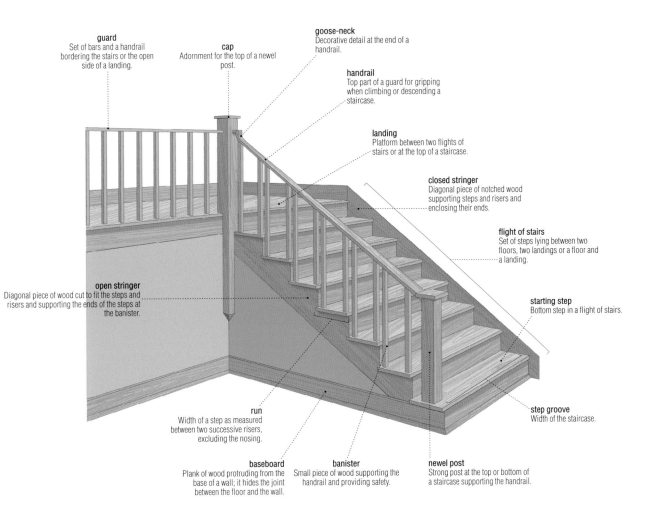

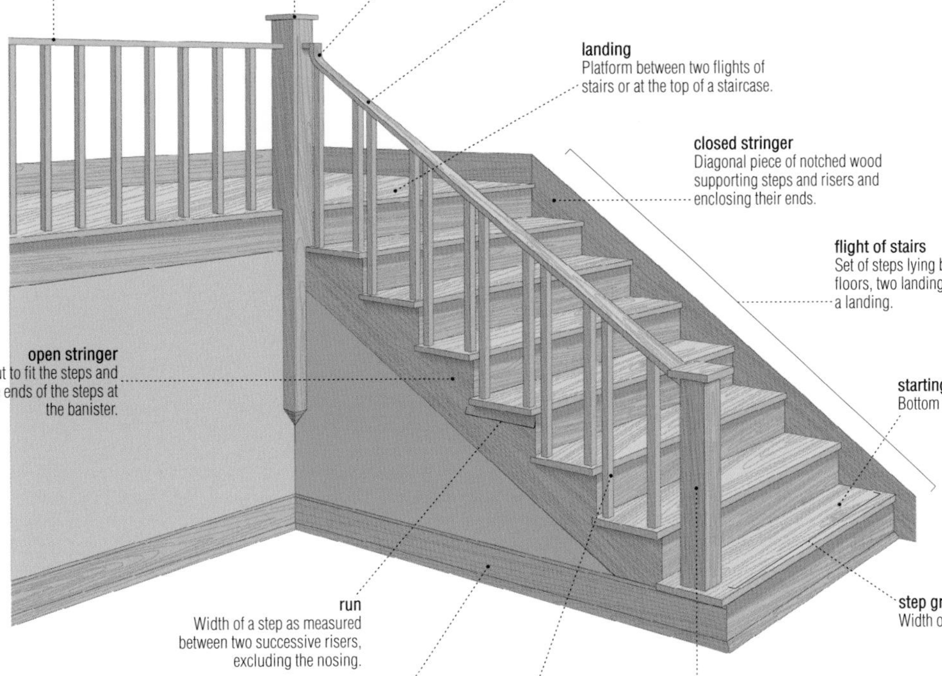
guard
Set of bars and a handrail bordering the stairs or the open side of a landing.
cap
Adornment for the top of a newel post.
goose-neck
Decorative detail at the end of a handrail.
handrail
Top part of a guard for gripping when climbing or descending a staircase.
landing
Platform between two flights of stairs or at the top of a staircase.
closed stringer
Diagonal piece of notched wood supporting steps and risers and enclosing their ends.
flight of stairs
Set of steps lying between two floors, two landings or a floor and a landing.
open stringer
Diagonal piece of wood cut to fit the steps and risers and supporting the ends of the steps at the banister.
starting step
Bottom step in a flight of stairs.
step groove
Width of the staircase.
run
Width of a step as measured between two successive risers, excluding the nosing.
baseboard
Plank of wood protruding from the base of a wall; it hides the joint between the floor and the wall.
banister
Small piece of wood supporting the handrail and providing safety.
newel post
Strong post at the top or bottom of a staircase supporting the handrail.

step

Part of a staircase composed of a tread and a riser.

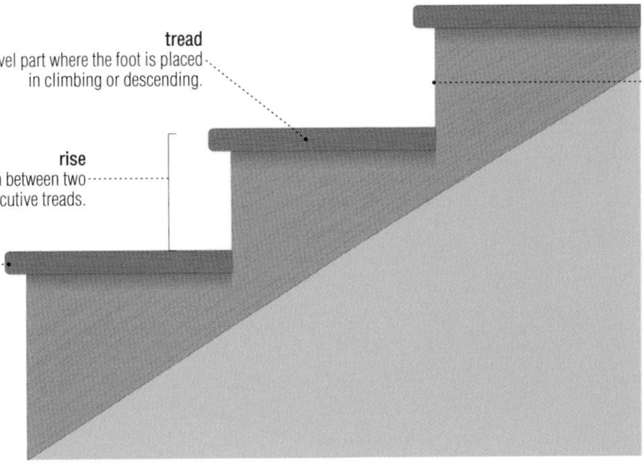
tread
Level part where the foot is placed in climbing or descending.
riser
Vertical surface beneath a tread and forming its front.
rise
Vertical length between two consecutive treads.
nosing
End of a tread that juts out over the riser below it.

wood firing

Creates heat by burning wood; nowadays, heating with wood is usually reserved as a backup.

fireplace
Masonry structure topped with a chimney and open in front; burning wood emits heat that is reflected from the inner hearth.

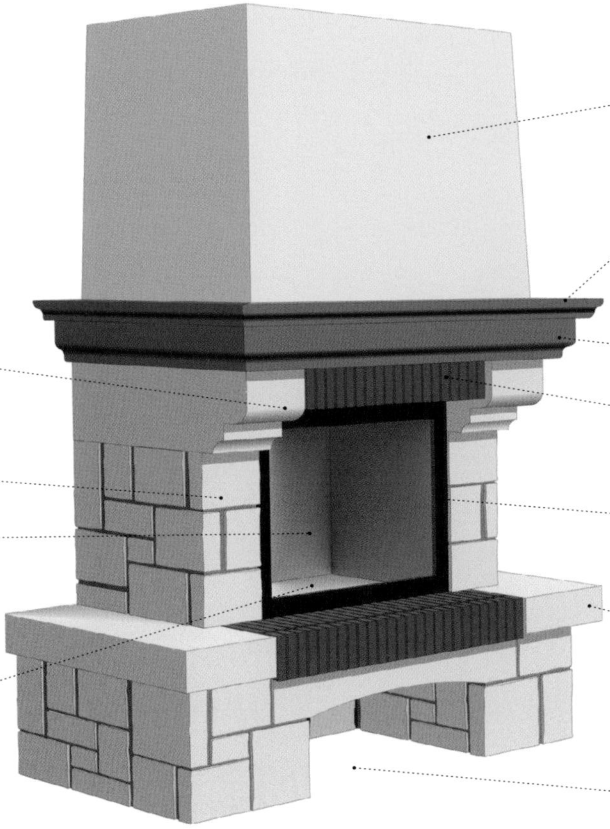

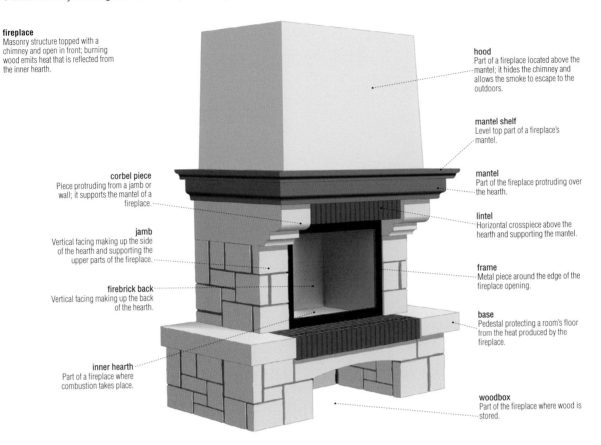

hood
Part of a fireplace located above the mantel; it hides the chimney and allows the smoke to escape to the outdoors.

mantel shelf
Level top part of a fireplace's mantel.

corbel piece
Piece protruding from a jamb or wall; it supports the mantel of a fireplace.

mantel
Part of the fireplace protruding over the hearth.

lintel
Horizontal crosspiece above the hearth and supporting the mantel.

jamb
Vertical facing making up the side of the hearth and supporting the upper parts of the fireplace.

frame
Metal piece around the edge of the fireplace opening.

firebrick back
Vertical facing making up the back of the hearth.

base
Pedestal protecting a room's floor from the heat produced by the fireplace.

inner hearth
Part of a fireplace where combustion takes place.

woodbox
Part of the fireplace where wood is stored.

slow-burning stove
Closed heating device; the amount of air entering the fire box is controlled to slow down combustion.

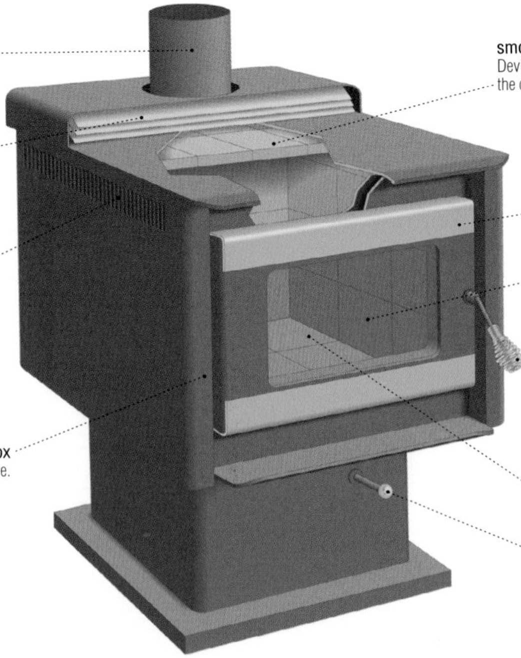

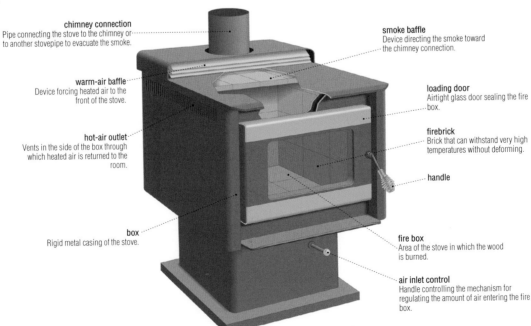

chimney connection
Pipe connecting the stove to the chimney or to another stovepipe to evacuate the smoke.

smoke baffle
Device directing the smoke toward the chimney connection.

warm-air baffle
Device forcing heated air to the front of the stove.

loading door
Airtight glass door sealing the fire box.

hot-air outlet
Vents in the side of the box through which heated air is returned to the room.

firebrick
Brick that can withstand very high temperatures without deforming.

handle

box
Rigid metal casing of the stove.

fire box
Area of the stove in which the wood is burned.

air inlet control
Handle controlling the mechanism for regulating the amount of air entering the fire box.

wood firing

chimney
Channel through which smoke and combustion gases from a heating device are evacuated while ensuring the free flow of air.

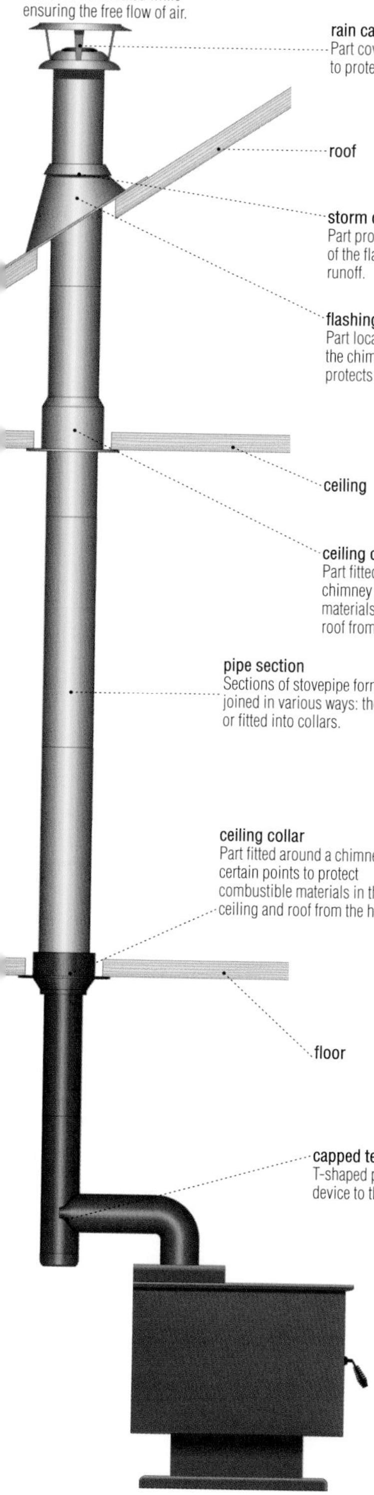

rain cap
Part covering the top of a chimney to protect it from wind and rain.

roof

storm collar
Part protecting the watertightness of the flashing by diverting water runoff.

flashing
Part located where the exterior of the chimney joins the roof; it protects against water seepage.

ceiling

ceiling collar
Part fitted around a section of the chimney to protect combustible materials in the floor, ceiling and roof from the heat.

pipe section
Sections of stovepipe forming the chimney are joined in various ways: they are screwed, welded or fitted into collars.

ceiling collar
Part fitted around a chimney at certain points to protect combustible materials in the floor, ceiling and roof from the heat.

floor

capped tee
T-shaped pipe joining a heating device to the chimney stovepipe.

fire irons
Tools used to grasp and move burning wood, revive the fire and collect the ashes.

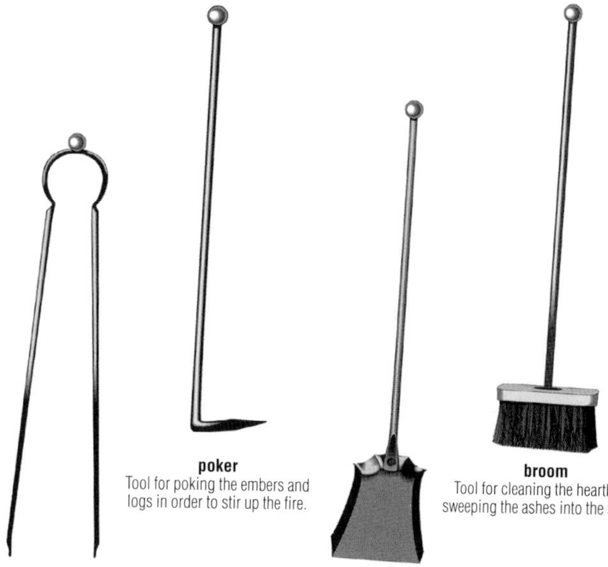

log tongs
Tool for grasping and moving logs and embers.

poker
Tool for poking the embers and logs in order to stir up the fire.

shovel
Tool for collecting the ashes.

broom
Tool for cleaning the hearth and sweeping the ashes into the shovel.

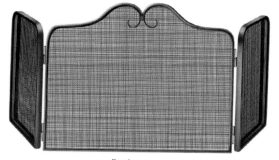

andirons
Metal supports placed in the hearth for cradling the logs; they allow air to circulate during combustion.

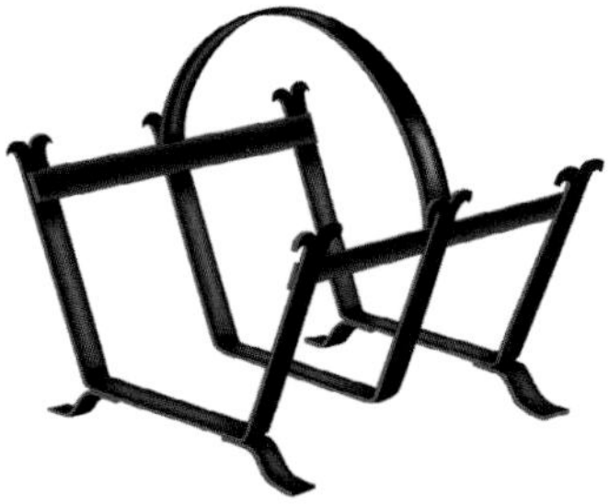

log carrier
Basket for carrying firewood and storing it near the fireplace.

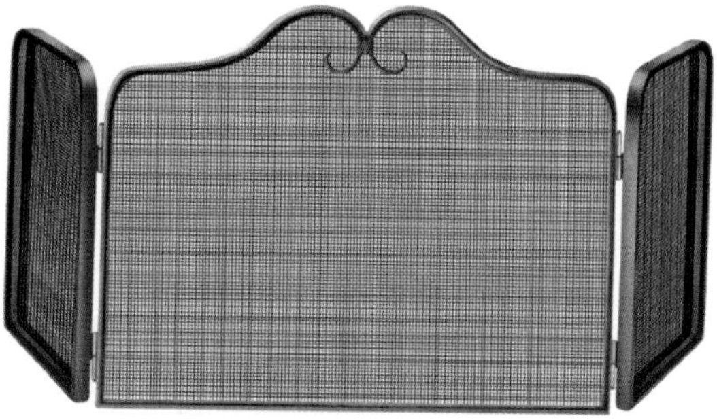

fireplace screen
Device placed in front of the fireplace opening to protect the floor from sparks.

forced warm-air system

In this type of system, air is heated in a furnace and blown by a fan through a network of ducts to the rooms of a dwelling.

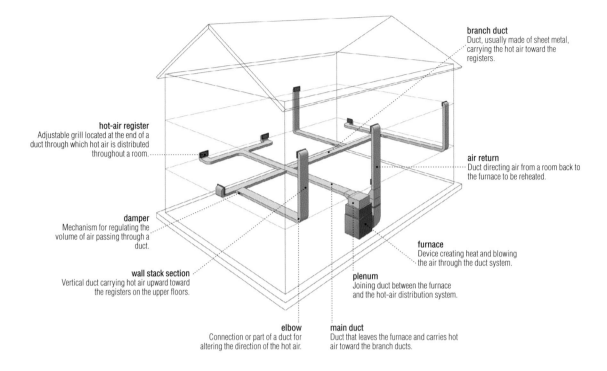

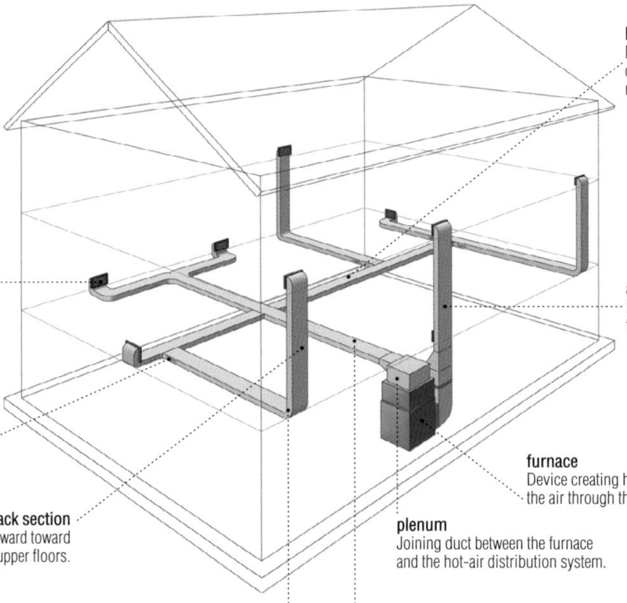
branch duct
Duct, usually made of sheet metal, carrying the hot air toward the registers.
hot-air register
Adjustable grill located at the end of a duct through which hot air is distributed throughout a room.
air return
Duct directing air from a room back to the furnace to be reheated.
damper
Mechanism for regulating the volume of air passing through a duct.
furnace
Device creating heat and blowing the air through the duct system.
wall stack section
Vertical duct carrying hot air upward toward the registers on the upper floors.
plenum
Joining duct between the furnace and the hot-air distribution system.
elbow
Connection or part of a duct for altering the direction of the hot air.
main duct
Duct that leaves the furnace and carries hot air toward the branch ducts.

electric furnace

Device using electricity for creating heat and blowing it through the duct system.

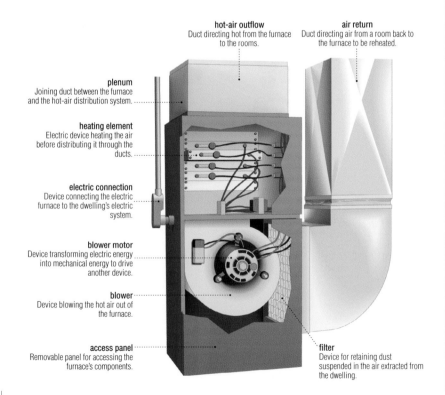

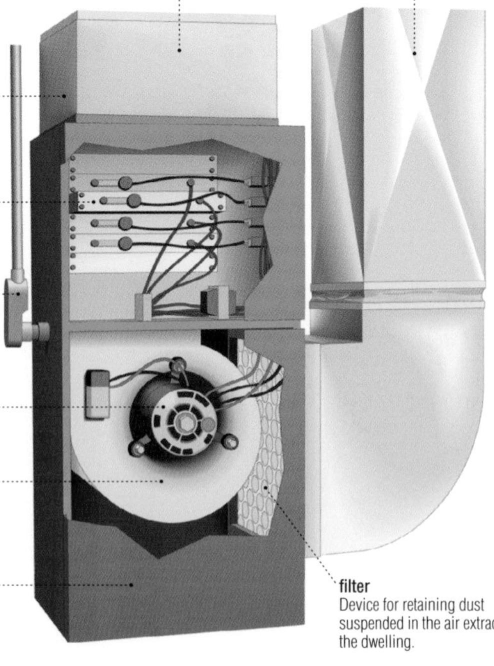
hot-air outflow
Duct directing hot from the furnace to the rooms.
air return
Duct directing air from a room back to the furnace to be reheated.
plenum
Joining duct between the furnace and the hot-air distribution system.
heating element
Electric device heating the air before distributing it through the ducts.
electric connection
Device connecting the electric furnace to the dwelling's electric system.
blower motor
Device transforming electric energy into mechanical energy to drive another device.
blower
Device blowing the hot air out of the furnace.
access panel
Removable panel for accessing the furnace's components.
filter
Device for retaining dust suspended in the air extracted from the dwelling.

types of registers

Registers are located at the ends of the ducts and are fitted at the bottom of a wall, in a floor or near the ceiling.

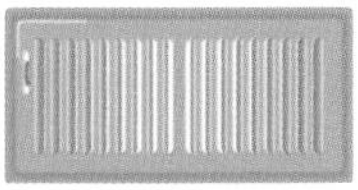

baseboard register
Adjustable grill located at the end of a duct through which hot air is distributed throughout a room.

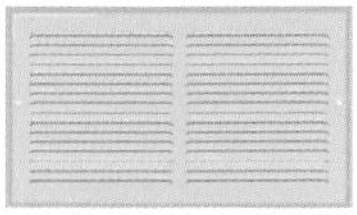

wall register
Grill at the end of an air-return duct, which returns a room's air to the furnace.

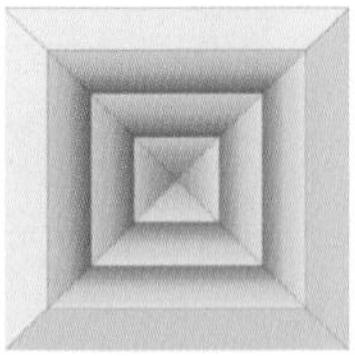

ceiling register
Grill at the end of a duct through which a room's air is drawn to mix it with the forced hot air.

forced hot-water system

Water heated in a boiler flows up to the radiators, where it releases its heat to the ambient air; the water then returns to the boiler to be reheated.

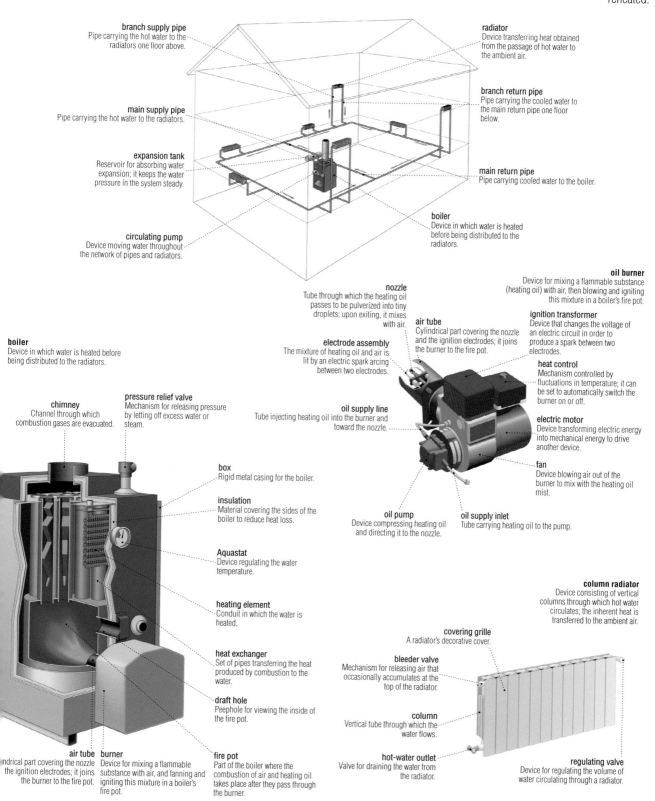

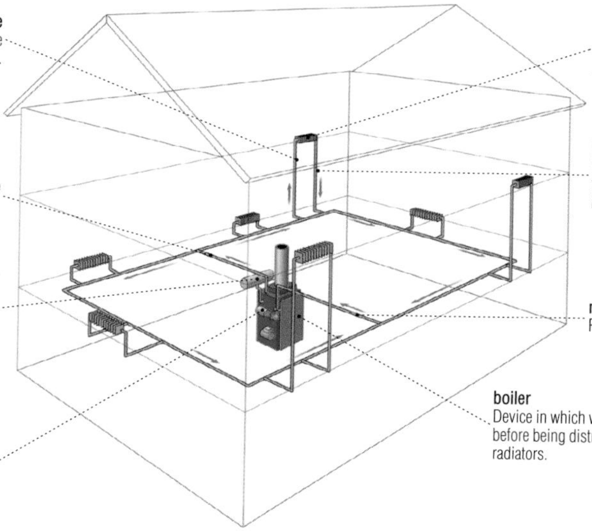

branch supply pipe
Pipe carrying the hot water to the radiators one floor above.
main supply pipe
Pipe carrying the hot water to the radiators.
expansion tank
Reservoir for absorbing water expansion; it keeps the water pressure in the system steady.
circulating pump
Device moving water throughout the network of pipes and radiators.
radiator
Device transferring heat obtained from the passage of hot water to the ambient air.
branch return pipe
Pipe carrying the cooled water to the main return pipe one floor below.
main return pipe
Pipe carrying cooled water to the boiler.
boiler
Device in which water is heated before being distributed to the radiators.

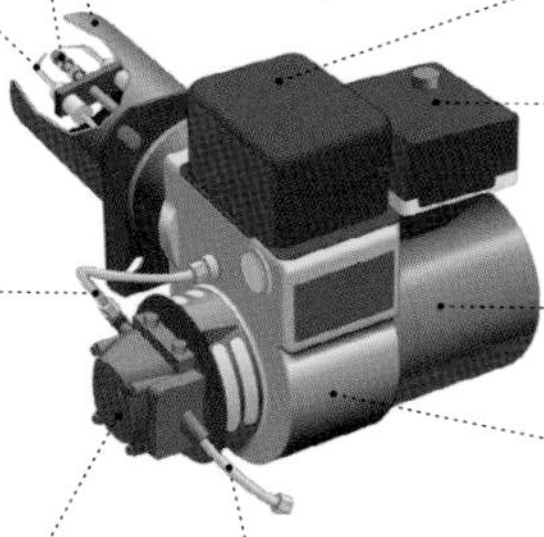

oil burner
Device for mixing a flammable substance (heating oil) with air, then blowing and igniting this mixture in a boiler's fire pot.
nozzle
Tube through which the heating oil passes to be pulverized into tiny droplets; upon exiting, it mixes with air.
air tube
Cylindrical part covering the nozzle and the ignition electrodes; it joins the burner to the fire pot.
ignition transformer
Device that changes the voltage of an electric circuit in order to produce a spark between two electrodes.
electrode assembly
The mixture of heating oil and air is lit by an electric spark arcing between two electrodes.
heat control
Mechanism controlled by fluctuations in temperature; it can be set to automatically switch the burner on or off.
oil supply line
Tube injecting heating oil into the burner and toward the nozzle.
electric motor
Device transforming electric energy into mechanical energy to drive another device.
fan
Device blowing air out of the burner to mix with the heating oil mist.
oil pump
Device compressing heating oil and directing it to the nozzle.
oil supply inlet
Tube carrying heating oil to the pump.

boiler
Device in which water is heated before being distributed to the radiators.

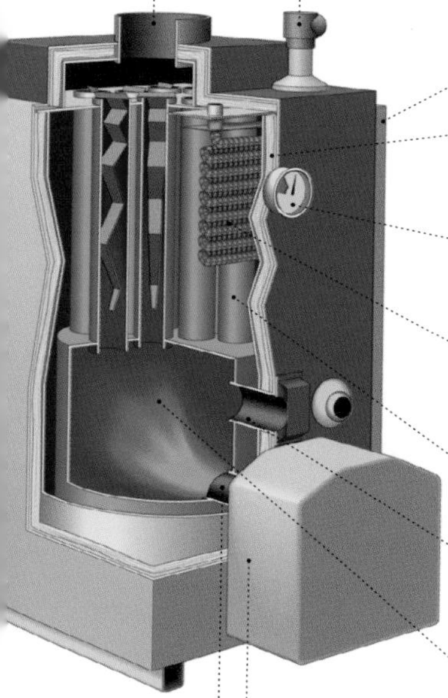

chimney
Channel through which combustion gases are evacuated.
pressure relief valve
Mechanism for releasing pressure by letting off excess water or steam.
box
Rigid metal casing for the boiler.
insulation
Material covering the sides of the boiler to reduce heat loss.
Aquastat
Device regulating the water temperature.
heating element
Conduit in which the water is heated.
heat exchanger
Set of pipes transferring the heat produced by combustion to the water.
draft hole
Peephole for viewing the inside of the fire pot.
fire pot
Part of the boiler where the combustion of air and heating oil takes place after they pass through the burner.
air tube
ndrical part covering the nozzle the ignition electrodes; it joins the burner to the fire pot.
burner
Device for mixing a flammable substance with air, and fanning and igniting this mixture in a boiler's fire pot.

column radiator
Device consisting of vertical columns through which hot water circulates; the inherent heat is transferred to the ambient air.

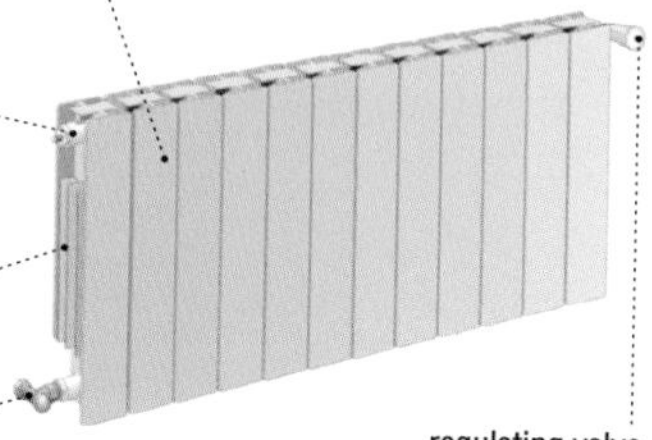

covering grille
A radiator's decorative cover.
bleeder valve
Mechanism for releasing air that occasionally accumulates at the top of the radiator.
column
Vertical tube through which the water flows.
hot-water outlet
Valve for draining the water from the radiator.
regulating valve
Device for regulating the volume of water circulating through a radiator.

HOUSE

heat pump

Device exchanging heat between two environments of different temperatures; it can either heat or cool a house, depending on how the circuit is set.

circuit breaker
Mechanism automatically cutting off the power supply in the event of overload.

fan
Propeller-shaped blades drawing in outdoor air (heating mode) or expelling indoor air (cooling mode).

outdoor unit
Part of the pump in which, depending on the setting, the outside air is tapped (heating mode) or the indoor air is cooled (cooling mode).

compressor
Device compressing the refrigerant to the desired pressure.

supply duct
Duct carrying forced hot air (heating mode) or cool air (cooling mode) into the house.

indoor unit
Part of the pump that, depending on th setting, either transfers outdoor heat into the house (heating mode) or transfers heat from the indoors to the outdoors (cooling mode).

refrigerant tubing
Conduit circulating a refrigerant, thus enabling the heat transfer.

electric connection
Conduit connecting the heat pump to the dwelling's electric system.

refrigerant tubing

auxiliary heating

electric baseboard radiator
Device using electricity to heat air by drawing it in at its base and releasing it at the top by convection.

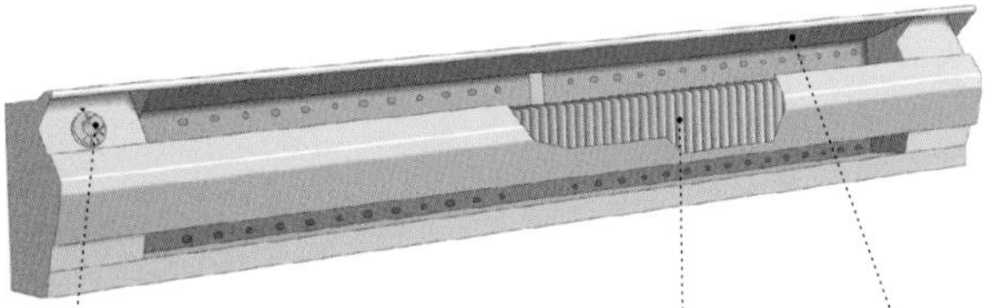

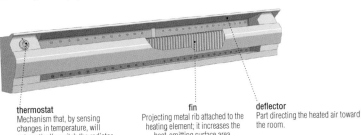

thermostat
Mechanism that, by sensing changes in temperature, will automatically switch the radiator on or off.

fin
Projecting metal rib attached to the heating element; it increases the heat-emitting surface area.

deflector
Part directing the heated air toward the room.

fan heater
Device in which the air is heated by electric elements and diffused by a fan.

convector
Device that, by convection, draws air through its base, heats it inside, then diffuses it through a grille on the top.

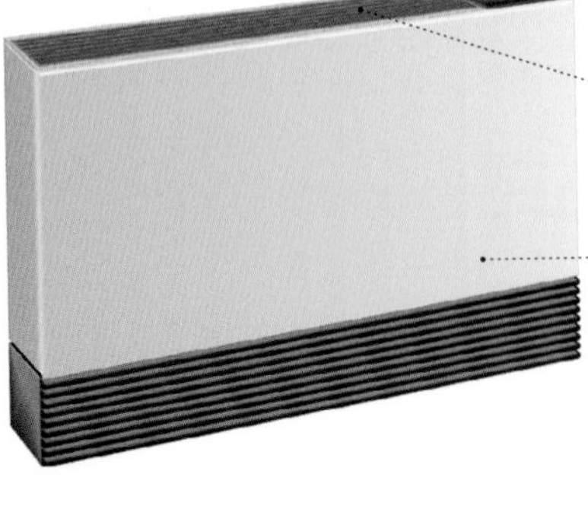

outlet grille
Grille through which the heated air is diffused in the room.

casing
Rigid metal box protecting the heater.

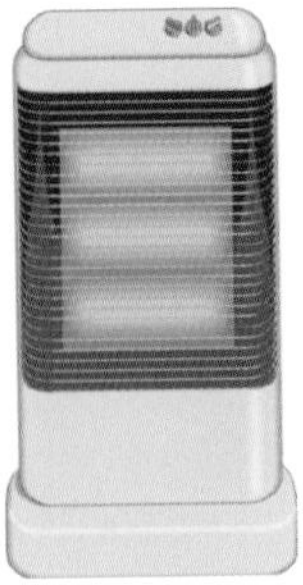

radiant heater
Device producing heat from a heating element and diffusing it in the form of light waves.

oil-filled heater
Device made of tubes that circulate oil heated by electric elements.

air-conditioning appliances

These appliances help make a house comfortable by cooling, filtering and humidifying or dehumidifying the ambient air.

ehumidifier
evice that lowers the humidity level
a room's air by cooling it.

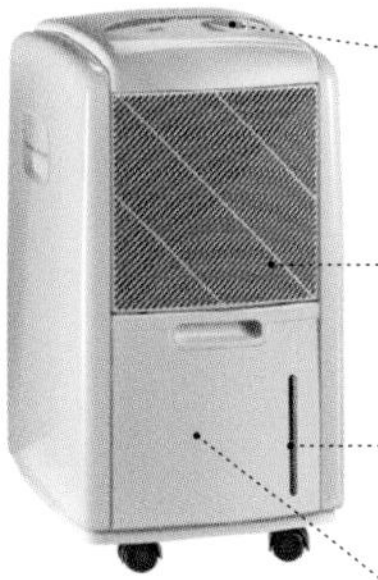
humidistat
Mechanism that, by sensing changes in humidity, can be set to automatically switch the humidifier on or off.
front grille
Perforated panel through which the air enters a room.
water level
bucket
Tank collecting the water droplets formed from the cooled air.

ceiling fan
Device whose rotating blades draw the warm air in a room upward in summer or push it downward in winter.

rod
Cylinder linking the fan to the ceiling and housing the electric wires.
motor
Device transforming electric energy into mechanical energy to drive another device.
blade
Part whose long flat surface moves the ambient air when it rotates.

rogrammable thermostat
lectronic device for keeping a
ouse or a room at a certain
mperature; it can be programmed
 follow a schedule.

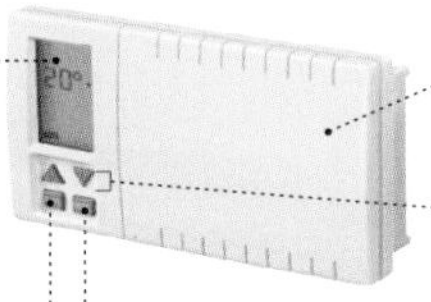
display
Screen showing digital data (time and temperature).
housing
arrow key
Button for changing the programmed time and house temperature.
choosing key
Button for confirming the selected time and temperatures programmed.
programming control
Button for regulating the thermostat according to the schedule chosen.

room thermostat
Mechanism that, by sensing changes in temperature, can be set to automatically switch the heating or air-conditioning or off in a room or house.

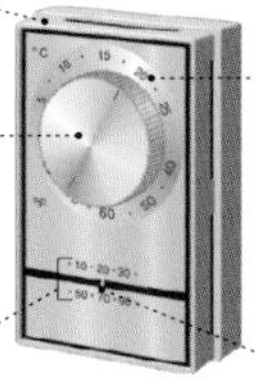
cover
desired temperature
Desired temperature of the ambient air.
temperature control
Knob for selecting the desired temperature.
pointer
Metal needle attached to the thermometer showing the ambient temperature.
actual temperature
A built-in thermometer shows the current temperature of the room in which it is located.

humidifier
Device that increases the humidity level in the air of a room.

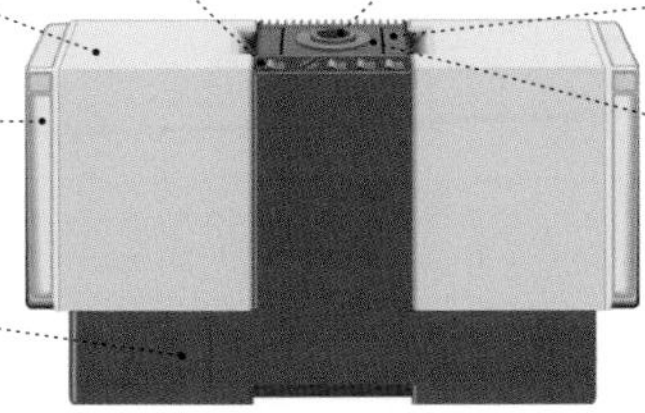
control panel
Panel containing the controls for operating the humidifier.
vaporizer
Device blending air with a fine mist of water before blowing it into the room.
water tank
Reservoir containing the water to be vaporized in the room.
air filter
Device that absorbs dust suspended in the air.
vaporizing grille
Perforated panel dispersing the humidified air.
water level
tray

ir purifier
evice drawing air in from a room
 filter it by removing its
ollutants before returning it.

room air conditioner
Device installed in a window for cooling and circulating the air in a room.

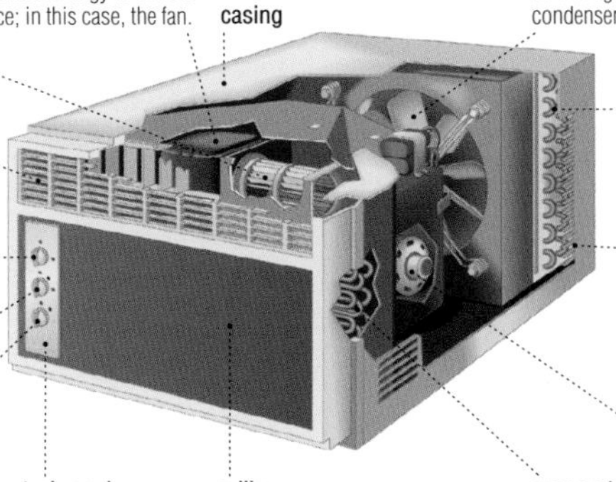
evaporator blower
Device drawing in warm air from the room, directing it over the cold evaporator coils and then returning it to the room.
fan motor
Device transforming electric energy into mechanical energy to drive a device; in this case, the fan.
casing
condenser fan
Propeller-shaped fan drawing outdoor air through the vents and over the hot condenser coils to cool them.
louver
Device directing cool air into the room.
condenser coil
Tube in which the hot refrigerant dissipates the room's heat to the outdoors.
thermostat
Mechanism that, by sensing changes in temperature, will automatically switch the air conditioner on or off.
vent
Grate through which outdoor air is drawn inward.
fan control
Knob for regulating the rate of air flow.
blower motor
Device transforming electric energy into mechanical energy to drive a device; in this case, the fan.
function selector
Knob for regulating the temperature and the fan speed.
control panel
Panel containing the controls that operate the air conditioner.
grille
Grille through which the heated air is diffused in the room.
evaporator coil
Tube carrying refrigerant that absorbs the room's heat.

ygrometer
evice measuring the amount of
umidity in a room's air.

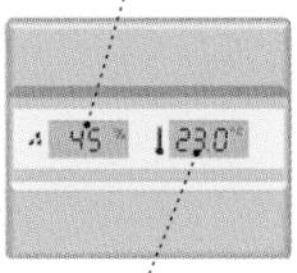
humidity
temperature

plumbing system

In a house, there are four plumbing systems enabling water to circulate: hot and cold water distribution, pipe ventilation and wastewater evacuation.

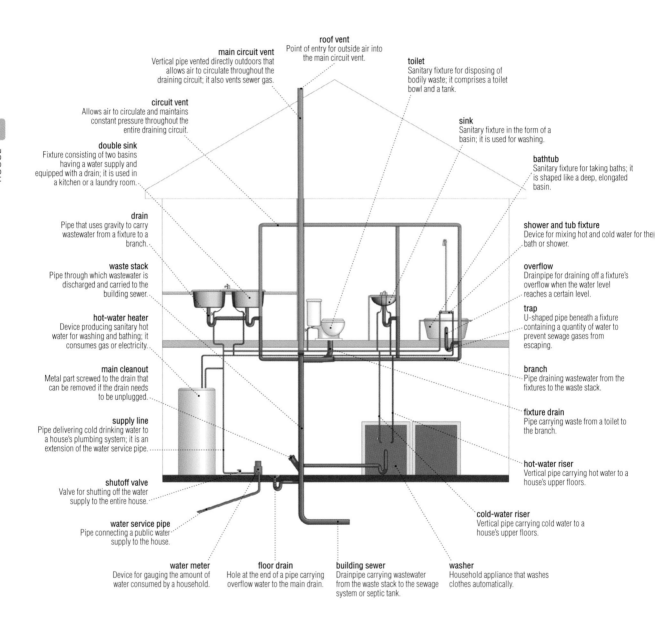

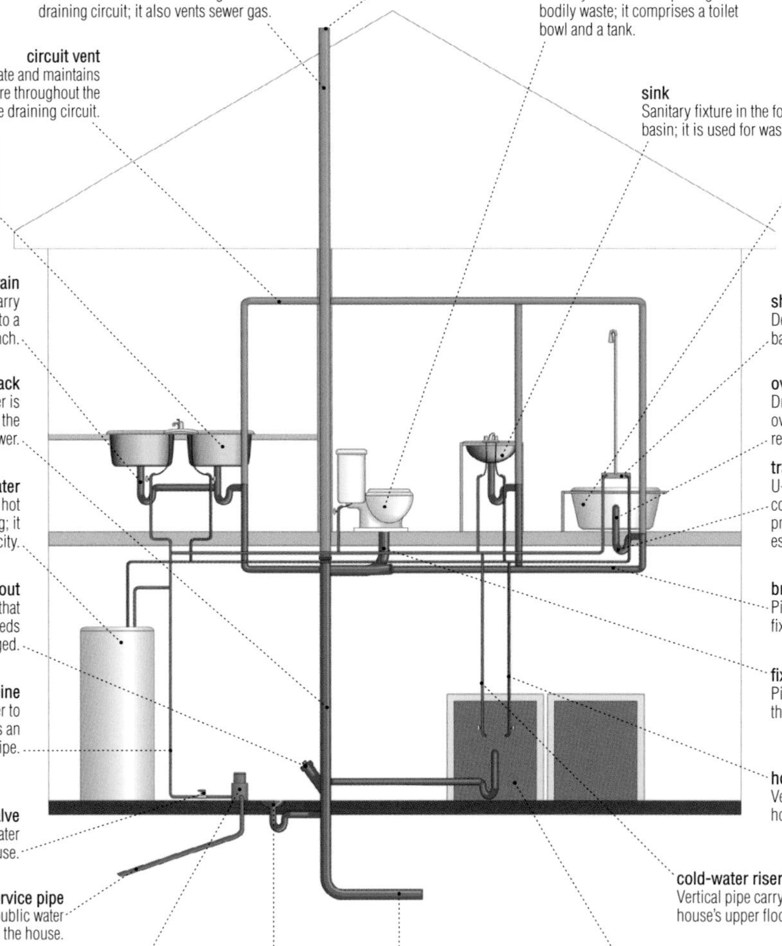
roof vent
Point of entry for outside air into the main circuit vent.
main circuit vent
Vertical pipe vented directly outdoors that allows air to circulate throughout the draining circuit; it also vents sewer gas.
toilet
Sanitary fixture for disposing of bodily waste; it comprises a toilet bowl and a tank.
circuit vent
Allows air to circulate and maintains constant pressure throughout the entire draining circuit.
sink
Sanitary fixture in the form of a basin; it is used for washing.
double sink
Fixture consisting of two basins having a water supply and equipped with a drain; it is used in a kitchen or a laundry room.
bathtub
Sanitary fixture for taking baths; it is shaped like a deep, elongated basin.
drain
Pipe that uses gravity to carry wastewater from a fixture to a branch.
shower and tub fixture
Device for mixing hot and cold water for the bath or shower.
waste stack
Pipe through which wastewater is discharged and carried to the building sewer.
overflow
Drainpipe for draining off a fixture's overflow when the water level reaches a certain level.
hot-water heater
Device producing sanitary hot water for washing and bathing; it consumes gas or electricity.
trap
U-shaped pipe beneath a fixture containing a quantity of water to prevent sewage gases from escaping.
main cleanout
Metal part screwed to the drain that can be removed if the drain needs to be unplugged.
branch
Pipe draining wastewater from the fixtures to the waste stack.
supply line
Pipe delivering cold drinking water to a house's plumbing system; it is an extension of the water service pipe.
fixture drain
Pipe carrying waste from a toilet to the branch.
hot-water riser
Vertical pipe carrying hot water to a house's upper floors.
shutoff valve
Valve for shutting off the water supply to the entire house.
cold-water riser
Vertical pipe carrying cold water to a house's upper floors.
water service pipe
Pipe connecting a public water supply to the house.
water meter
Device for gauging the amount of water consumed by a household.
floor drain
Hole at the end of a pipe carrying overflow water to the main drain.
building sewer
Drainpipe carrying wastewater from the waste stack to the sewage system or septic tank.
washer
Household appliance that washes clothes automatically.

ventilating circuit
Set of interconnected pipes allowing air to circulate in the circuit.

draining circuit
Set of interconnected pipes allowing wastewater to drain into the building sewer.

cold-water circuit
Set of interconnected pipes distributing cold drinking water throughout a house.

hot-water circuit
Set of interconnected pipes distributing ho water from a hot-water heater.

pedestal-type sump pump

Device removing water from a pit dug in the ground in order to evacuate it to a sewer or septic tank.

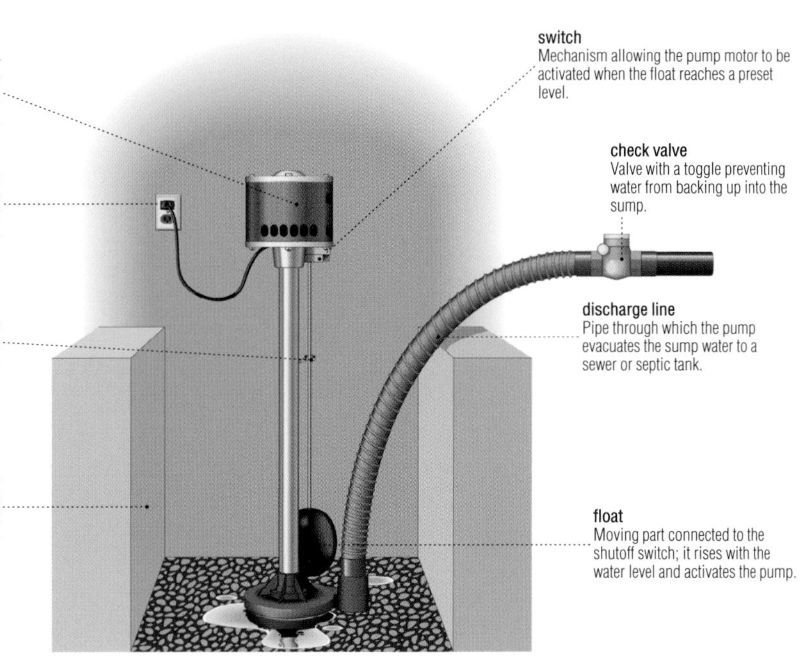

pump motor
Device transforming electric energy into mechanical energy to drive another device.
grounded receptacle
Device for supplying electricity and ensuring the transfer of the current to the ground in the event of device malfunction; it prevents electrocution.
float clamp
Metal part keeping the float line in place.
sump
Pit in which water runoff is collected in the event the basement floods.
switch
Mechanism allowing the pump motor to be activated when the float reaches a preset level.
check valve
Valve with a toggle preventing water from backing up into the sump.
discharge line
Pipe through which the pump evacuates the sump water to a sewer or septic tank.
float
Moving part connected to the shutoff switch; it rises with the water level and activates the pump.

septic tank

Underground system in which sewage is treated and dispersed.

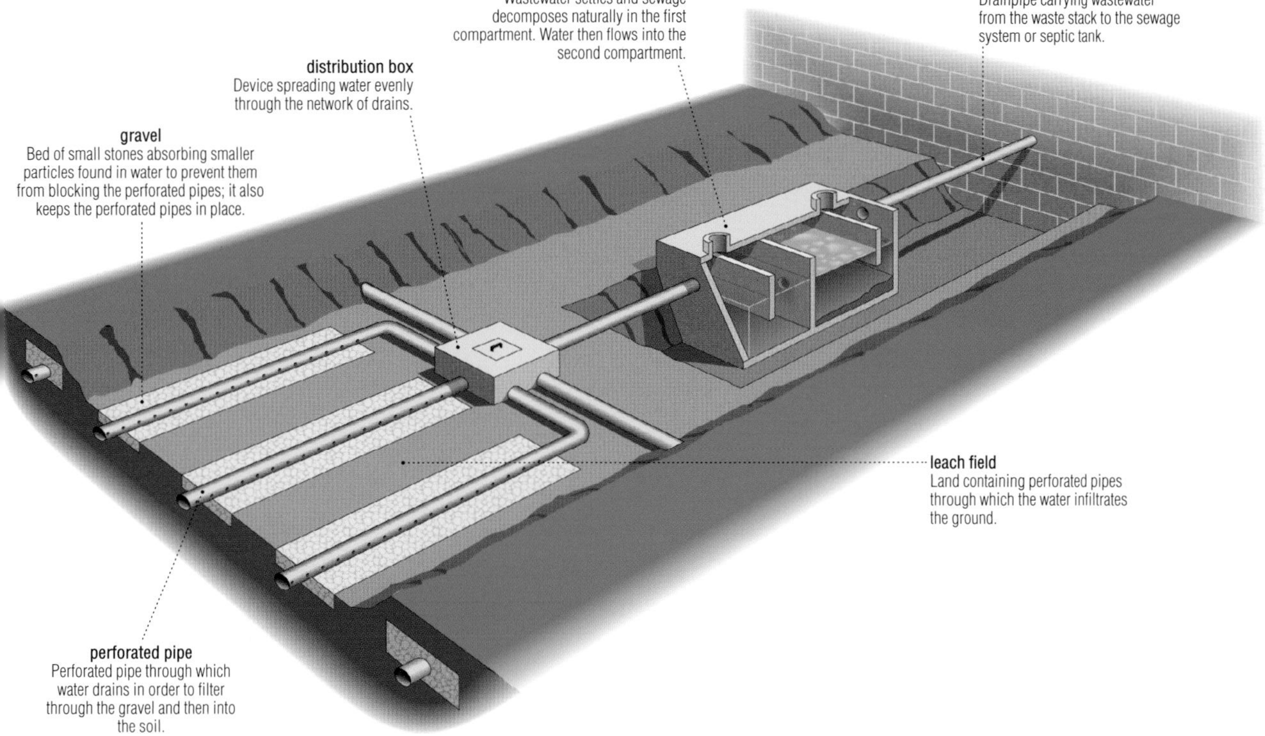

tank
Wastewater settles and sewage decomposes naturally in the first compartment. Water then flows into the second compartment.
building sewer
Drainpipe carrying wastewater from the waste stack to the sewage system or septic tank.
distribution box
Device spreading water evenly through the network of drains.
gravel
Bed of small stones absorbing smaller particles found in water to prevent them from blocking the perforated pipes; it also keeps the perforated pipes in place.
leach field
Land containing perforated pipes through which the water infiltrates the ground.
perforated pipe
Perforated pipe through which water drains in order to filter through the gravel and then into the soil.

HOUSE

bathroom

Room designed for personal hygiene; it is equipped with running water and sanitary fixtures.

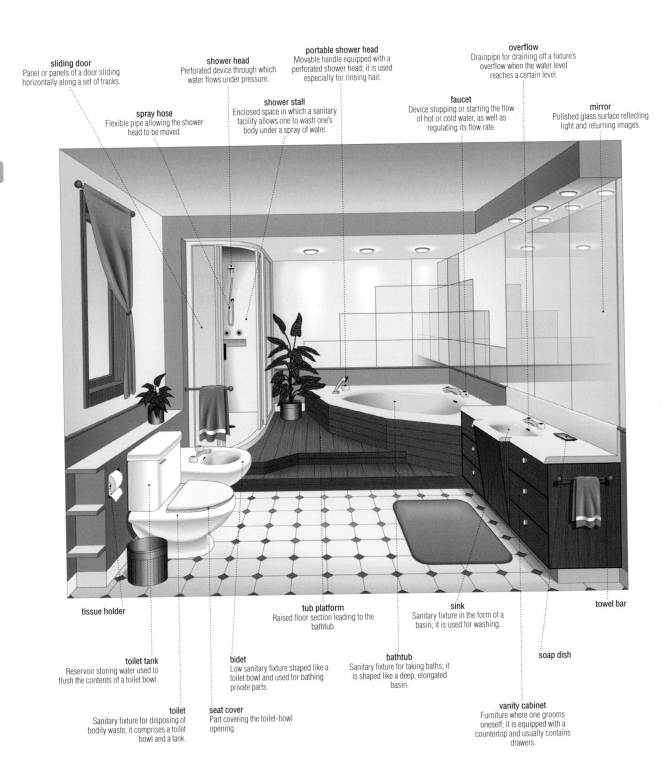

sliding door
Panel or panels of a door sliding horizontally along a set of tracks.

shower head
Perforated device through which water flows under pressure.

portable shower head
Movable handle equipped with a perforated shower head; it is used especially for rinsing hair.

overflow
Drainpipe for draining off a fixture's overflow when the water level reaches a certain level.

spray hose
Flexible pipe allowing the shower head to be moved.

shower stall
Enclosed space in which a sanitary facility allows one to wash one's body under a spray of water.

faucet
Device stopping or starting the flow of hot or cold water, as well as regulating its flow rate.

mirror
Polished glass surface reflecting light and returning images.

tissue holder

tub platform
Raised floor section leading to the bathtub.

sink
Sanitary fixture in the form of a basin; it is used for washing.

towel bar

toilet tank
Reservoir storing water used to flush the contents of a toilet bowl.

bidet
Low sanitary fixture shaped like a toilet bowl and used for bathing private parts.

bathtub
Sanitary fixture for taking baths; it is shaped like a deep, elongated basin.

soap dish

toilet
Sanitary fixture for disposing of bodily waste; it comprises a toilet bowl and a tank.

seat cover
Part covering the toilet-bowl opening.

vanity cabinet
Furniture where one grooms oneself; it is equipped with a countertop and usually contains drawers.

toilet

Sanitary fixture for disposing of bodily waste; it comprises a toilet bowl and a tank.

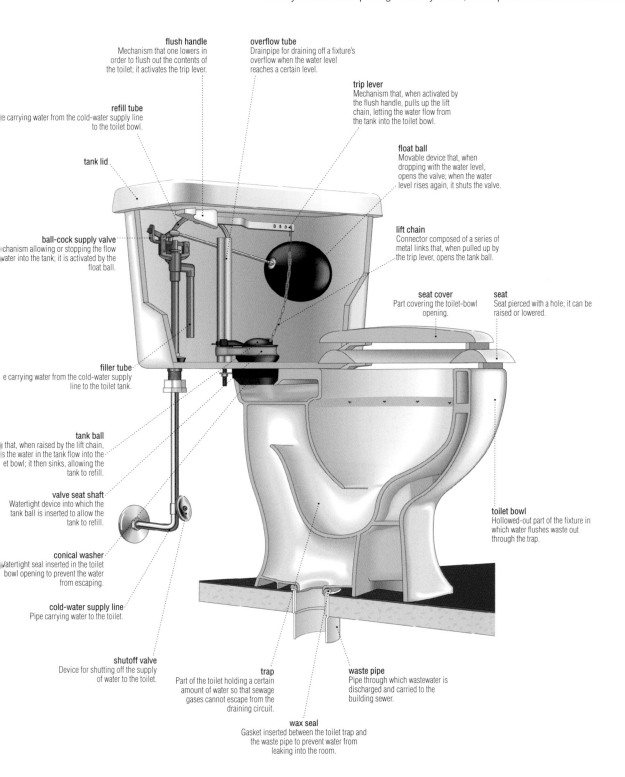

flush handle
Mechanism that one lowers in order to flush out the contents of the toilet; it activates the trip lever.

overflow tube
Drainpipe for draining off a fixture's overflow when the water level reaches a certain level.

trip lever
Mechanism that, when activated by the flush handle, pulls up the lift chain, letting the water flow from the tank into the toilet bowl.

refill tube
e carrying water from the cold-water supply line to the toilet bowl.

tank lid

float ball
Movable device that, when dropping with the water level, opens the valve; when the water level rises again, it shuts the valve.

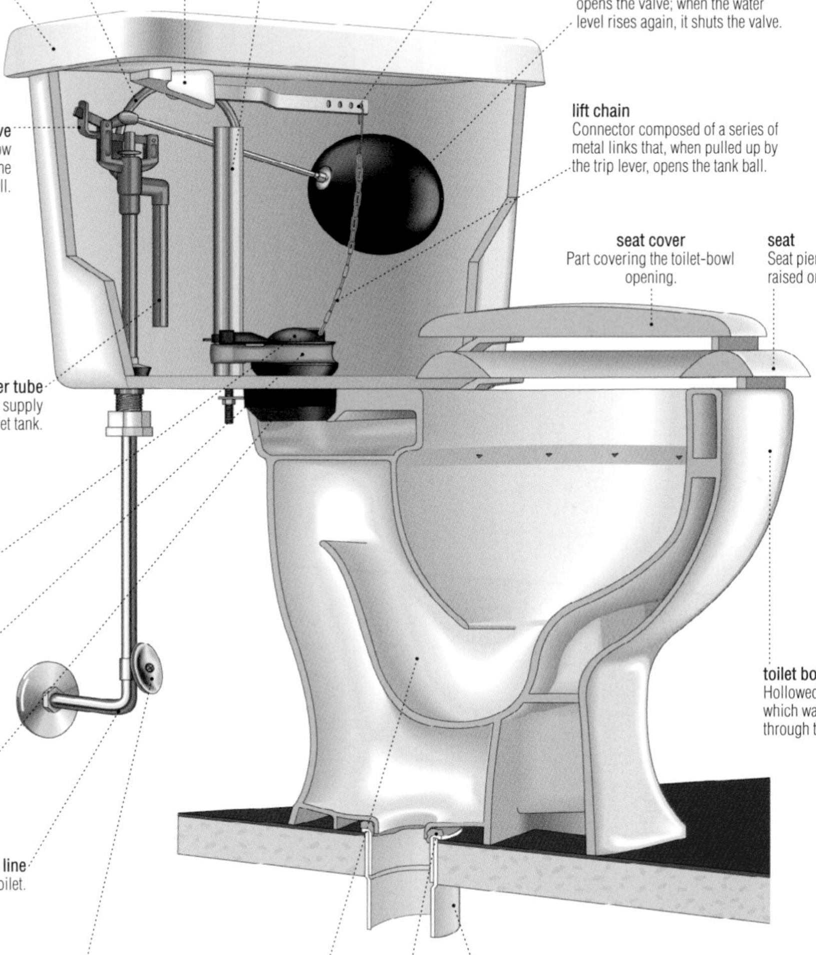

ball-cock supply valve
chanism allowing or stopping the flow vater into the tank; it is activated by the float ball.

lift chain
Connector composed of a series of metal links that, when pulled up by the trip lever, opens the tank ball.

seat cover
Part covering the toilet-bowl opening.

seat
Seat pierced with a hole; it can be raised or lowered.

filler tube
e carrying water from the cold-water supply line to the toilet tank.

tank ball
that, when raised by the lift chain, s the water in the tank flow into the et bowl; it then sinks, allowing the tank to refill.

valve seat shaft
Watertight device into which the tank ball is inserted to allow the tank to refill.

toilet bowl
Hollowed-out part of the fixture in which water flushes waste out through the trap.

conical washer
Vatertight seal inserted in the toilet bowl opening to prevent the water from escaping.

cold-water supply line
Pipe carrying water to the toilet.

shutoff valve
Device for shutting off the supply of water to the toilet.

trap
Part of the toilet holding a certain amount of water so that sewage gases cannot escape from the draining circuit.

waste pipe
Pipe through which wastewater is discharged and carried to the building sewer.

wax seal
Gasket inserted between the toilet trap and the waste pipe to prevent water from leaking into the room.

water-heater tank

Device producing sanitary hot water for washing and bathing; it consumes gas or electricity.

electric water-heater tank

cold-water supply
Inlet pipe for cold water to the tank.
hot-water outlet
Outlet pipe for hot water flowing into the hot-water circuit.
anode rod
Magnesium-coated electrode protecting the tank from the corrosive effects of the water.
pressure relief valve
Device for lowering the pressure inside the tank by releasing excess hot water.
high-temperature cutoff
Mechanism cutting off the flow of electric current when the temperature of the water exceeds a set value.
upper thermostat
Device that senses changes in temperature and automatically switches the upper heating element on or off.
upper heating element
Coated electric resistor immersed in the upper part of the tank to heat the water.
access panel
tank
Insulated reservoir in which hot water is stored; it is usually cylindrical and enameled or glazed.
insulation
Material placed between the tank and the outer walls of the hot-water tank in order to reduce heat loss.
electric supply
Point where the hot-water tank connects with the household circuit.
overflow pipe
Pipe through which water escapes when maximum pressure is exceeded.
lower thermostat
Device that senses changes in temperature and automatically switches the lower heating element on or off.
lower heating element
Coated electric resistor immersed in the lower part of the tank to heat the water.
drain valve
Device for emptying water from the tank.

gas water-heater tank

hot-water outlet
Outlet pipe for hot water flowing into the hot-water circuit.
flue hat
Device reducing the amount of air withdrawn by convection.
outer jacket
Metal casing protecting the tank.
pressure-relief valve
Device for lowering the pressure inside the tank by releasing excess hot water.
overflow pipe
Pipe through which water escapes when maximum pressure is exceeded.
insulation
Material placed between the tank and the outer walls of the hot-water tank in order to reduce heat loss.
cold-water supply line
Inlet pipe for cold water to the tank.
flue
Channel through which combustion gases are evacuated.
glass-lined tank
Insulated reservoir protected against corrosion by an enamel or glaze coating.
reset button
Mechanism allowing the burner to be manually restarted.
gas cock
Mechanism cutting off the gas supply when the water reaches the desired temperature.
control box
Box containing the set of controls that measure temperature and operate the burner.
temperature control
Device for setting the temperature.
drain valve
Device for emptying the water from the tank.
thermostat
Mechanism controlled by fluctuations in temperature; it can be set to automatically switch the burner on or off.
gas burner
Combustion device for an air-gas mixture.

faucets

The double-handle faucet controls the flow of hot and cold water; the single-lever faucet mixes the hot and cold water and controls their flow.

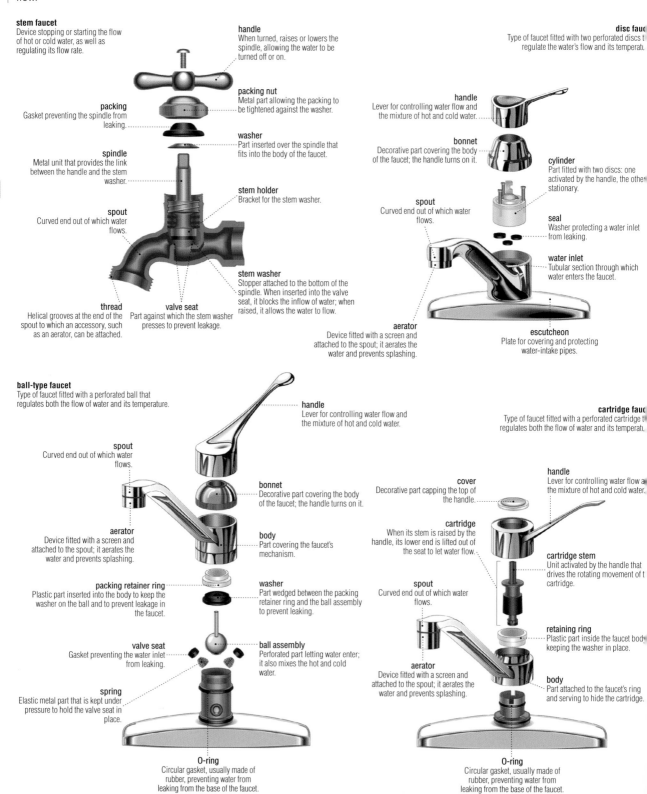

stem faucet
Device stopping or starting the flow of hot or cold water, as well as regulating its flow rate.

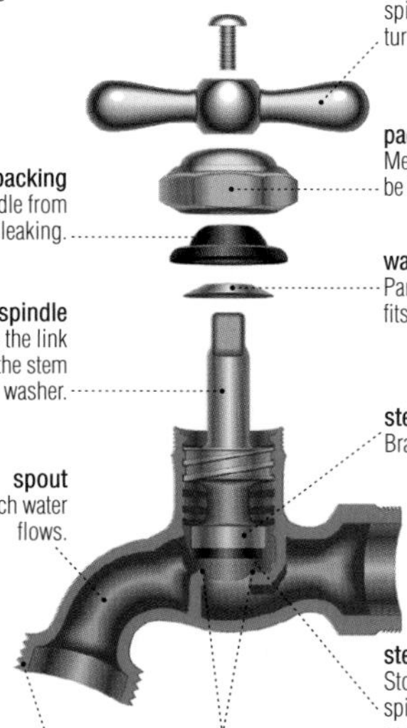
handle
When turned, raises or lowers the spindle, allowing the water to be turned off or on.
packing nut
Metal part allowing the packing to be tightened against the washer.
packing
Gasket preventing the spindle from leaking.
washer
Part inserted over the spindle that fits into the body of the faucet.
spindle
Metal unit that provides the link between the handle and the stem washer.
stem holder
Bracket for the stem washer.
spout
Curved end out of which water flows.
stem washer
Stopper attached to the bottom of the spindle. When inserted into the valve seat, it blocks the inflow of water; when raised, it allows the water to flow.
thread
Helical grooves at the end of the spout to which an accessory, such as an aerator, can be attached.
valve seat
Part against which the stem washer presses to prevent leakage.

disc fauc
Type of faucet fitted with two perforated discs t regulate the water's flow and its temperatu

handle
Lever for controlling water flow and the mixture of hot and cold water.
bonnet
Decorative part covering the body of the faucet; the handle turns on it.
cylinder
Part fitted with two discs: one activated by the handle, the othe stationary.
spout
Curved end out of which water flows.
seal
Washer protecting a water inlet from leaking.
water inlet
Tubular section through which water enters the faucet.
aerator
Device fitted with a screen and attached to the spout; it aerates the water and prevents splashing.
escutcheon
Plate for covering and protecting water-intake pipes.

ball-type faucet
Type of faucet fitted with a perforated ball that regulates both the flow of water and its temperature.

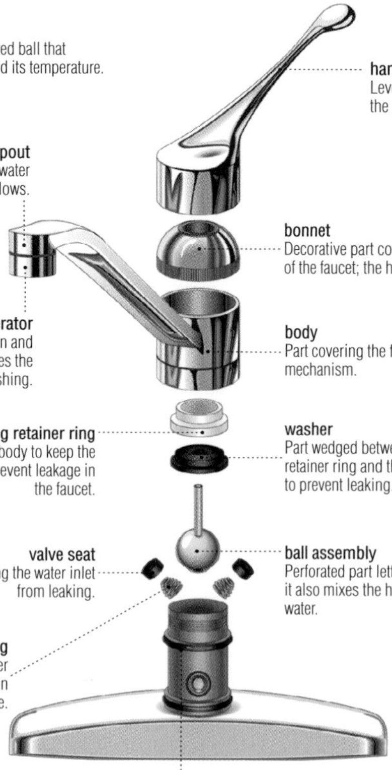
handle
Lever for controlling water flow and the mixture of hot and cold water.
spout
Curved end out of which water flows.
bonnet
Decorative part covering the body of the faucet; the handle turns on it.
aerator
Device fitted with a screen and attached to the spout; it aerates the water and prevents splashing.
body
Part covering the faucet's mechanism.
packing retainer ring
Plastic part inserted into the body to keep the washer on the ball and to prevent leakage in the faucet.
washer
Part wedged between the packing retainer ring and the ball assembly to prevent leaking.
valve seat
Gasket preventing the water inlet from leaking.
ball assembly
Perforated part letting water enter; it also mixes the hot and cold water.
spring
Elastic metal part that is kept under pressure to hold the valve seat in place.
O-ring
Circular gasket, usually made of rubber, preventing water from leaking from the base of the faucet.

cartridge fauc
Type of faucet fitted with a perforated cartridge t regulates both the flow of water and its temperatu

handle
Lever for controlling water flow a the mixture of hot and cold water.
cover
Decorative part capping the top of the handle.
cartridge
When its stem is raised by the handle, its lower end is lifted out of the seat to let water flow.
cartridge stem
Unit activated by the handle that drives the rotating movement of t cartridge.
spout
Curved end out of which water flows.
retaining ring
Plastic part inside the faucet bod keeping the washer in place.
aerator
Device fitted with a screen and attached to the spout; it aerates the water and prevents splashing.
body
Part attached to the faucet's ring and serving to hide the cartridge.
O-ring
Circular gasket, usually made of rubber, preventing water from leaking from the base of the faucet.

fittings

Transition fittings are used for joining components made of different materials, whereas fittings are used to join components of the same material.

examples of transition fittings

Transition fittings allow tubes of different materials to be joined.

steel to plastic
The tubes are joined by a threaded tube for the steel end, and by compression coupling or, for a plastic end, by gluing.

copper to plastic
The tubes are joined by union or compression coupling.

copper to steel
The tubes are joined by a threaded tube on the steel end, and by union or compression coupling on the copper end.

examples of fittings

Fittings are used to join two or more pipes, a pipe to a device, or a pipe to a cap or plug.

offset
itting joining two pipes so that the pipe can bypass an obstacle.

tee
Fitting joining three pipes, one of which is perpendicular to the other two.

Y-branch
Fitting joining three pipes, one of which is oblique to the other two.

trap
U-shaped pipe beneath a fixture containing a quantity of water to prevent sewage gases from escaping.

cap
Plug inserted into the end of a pipe to close it off.

U-bend
itting joining two pipes in order to change their direction by 180°.

threaded cap
Plug screwed onto the end of a male threaded pipe to close it off.

90° elbow
Fitting for joining two pipes in order to change their direction.

45° elbow
Fitting for joining two pipes in order to change their direction by 45°.

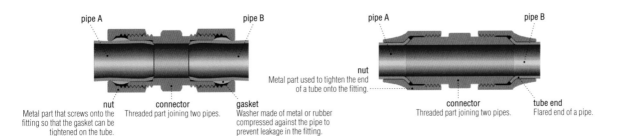

pipe coupling
Threaded fitting with two female ends; it is used to join two pipes of the same diameter.

hexagon bushing
with a hexagonal head. It joins two pipes rent diameters: one pipe is screwed onto le end, and the other into the female end.

flush bushing
Fitting joining two pipes of different diameters. The larger pipe screws onto the male end and the smaller pipe screws into the female end.

nipple
Threaded fitting having two male ends; it is used to join two pipes of the same diameter.

reducing coupling
Fitting joining two pipes of different diameters in order to reduce the diameter of a pipe run.

square head plug
Cap screwed into the end of a threaded female pipe to close it off.

mechanical connectors

Pipes joined using nuts and threaded metal parts; a gasket is inserted to tighten them, thus preventing leakage.

union
Formed by using a nut to tighten a male union nut in a female union nut; leakage is prevented by placing a gasket where the two tubes meet.

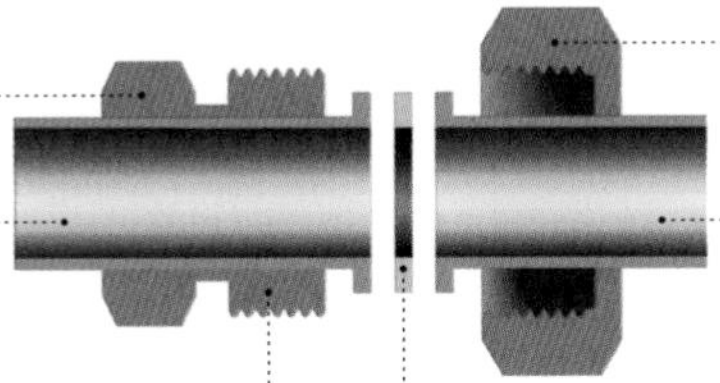

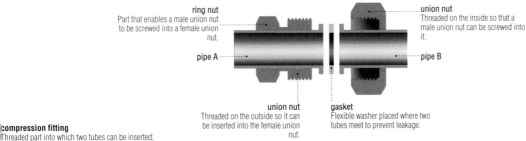

ring nut
Part that enables a male union nut to be screwed into a female union nut.

union nut
Threaded on the inside so that a male union nut can be screwed into it.

pipe A

pipe B

union nut
Threaded on the outside so it can be inserted into the female union nut.

gasket
Flexible washer placed where two tubes meet to prevent leakage.

compression fitting
Threaded part into which two tubes can be inserted; they are made watertight by a gasket tightened with a nut.

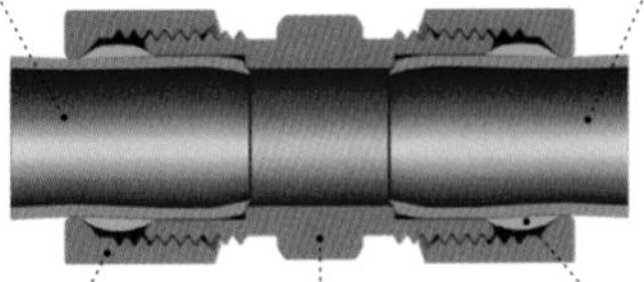

pipe A

pipe B

nut
Metal part that screws onto the fitting so that the gasket can be tightened on the tube.

connector
Threaded part joining two pipes.

gasket
Washer made of metal or rubber compressed against the pipe to prevent leakage in the fitting.

flare joint
Threaded part over which two tubes having bell-shaped ends can be tightened by a nut.

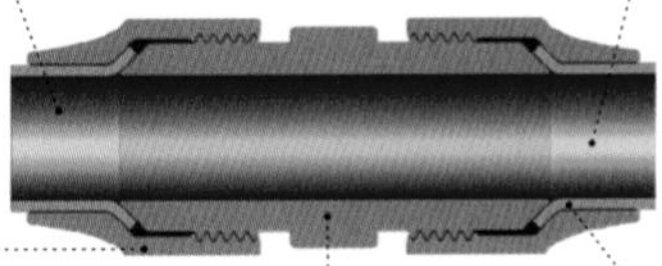

pipe A

pipe B

nut
Metal part used to tighten the end of a tube onto the fitting.

connector
Threaded part joining two pipes.

tube end
Flared end of a pipe.

HOUSE

examples of branching

Branching: the way in which an appliance is hooked up to a house's plumbing system.

garbage disposal sink
Appliance used in a kitchen, sometimes with two basins, that is fed by water and equipped with a drain and a garbage disposal unit.

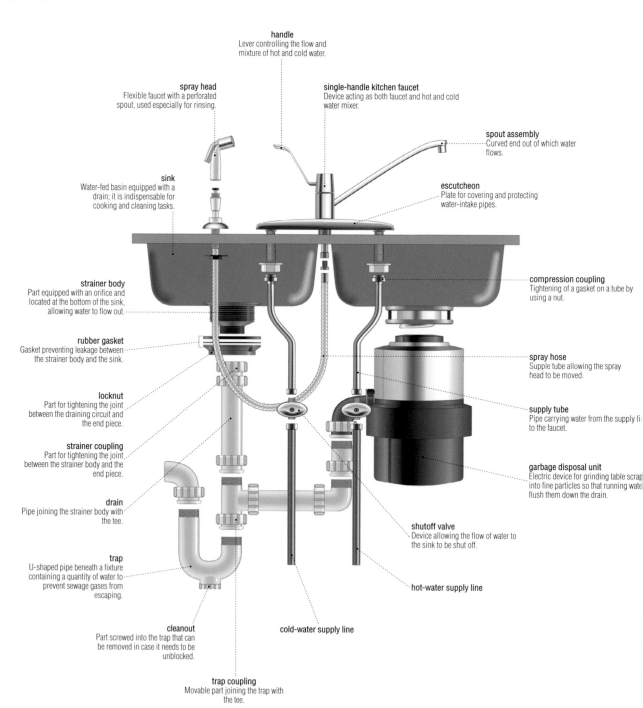

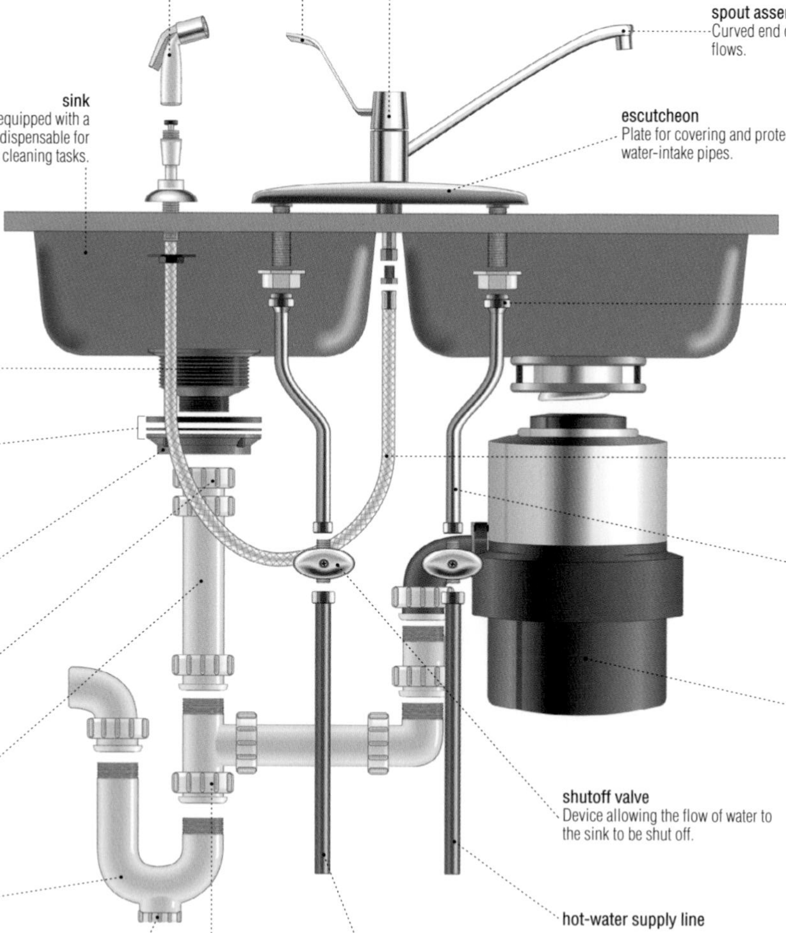

handle
Lever controlling the flow and mixture of hot and cold water.
spray head
Flexible faucet with a perforated spout, used especially for rinsing.
single-handle kitchen faucet
Device acting as both faucet and hot and cold water mixer.
spout assembly
Curved end out of which water flows.
sink
Water-fed basin equipped with a drain; it is indispensable for cooking and cleaning tasks.
escutcheon
Plate for covering and protecting water-intake pipes.
strainer body
Part equipped with an orifice and located at the bottom of the sink, allowing water to flow out.
compression coupling
Tightening of a gasket on a tube by using a nut.
rubber gasket
Gasket preventing leakage between the strainer body and the sink.
spray hose
Supple tube allowing the spray head to be moved.
locknut
Part for tightening the joint between the draining circuit and the end piece.
supply tube
Pipe carrying water from the supply li
to the faucet.
strainer coupling
Part for tightening the joint between the strainer body and the end piece.
garbage disposal unit
Electric device for grinding table scra
into fine particles so that running wat
flush them down the drain.
drain
Pipe joining the strainer body with the tee.
shutoff valve
Device allowing the flow of water to the sink to be shut off.
trap
U-shaped pipe beneath a fixture containing a quantity of water to prevent sewage gases from escaping.
hot-water supply line
cleanout
Part screwed into the trap that can be removed in case it needs to be unblocked.
cold-water supply line
trap coupling
Movable part joining the trap with the tee.

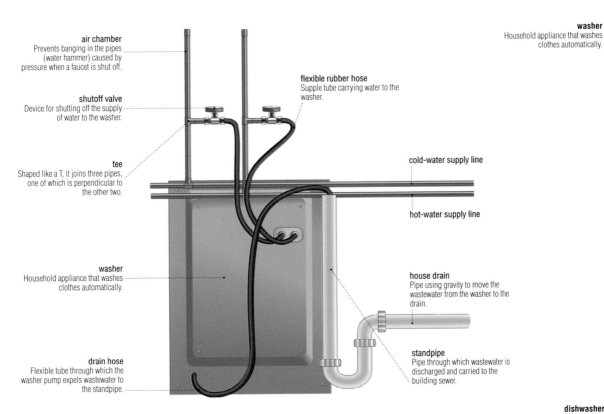

washer
Household appliance that washes clothes automatically.

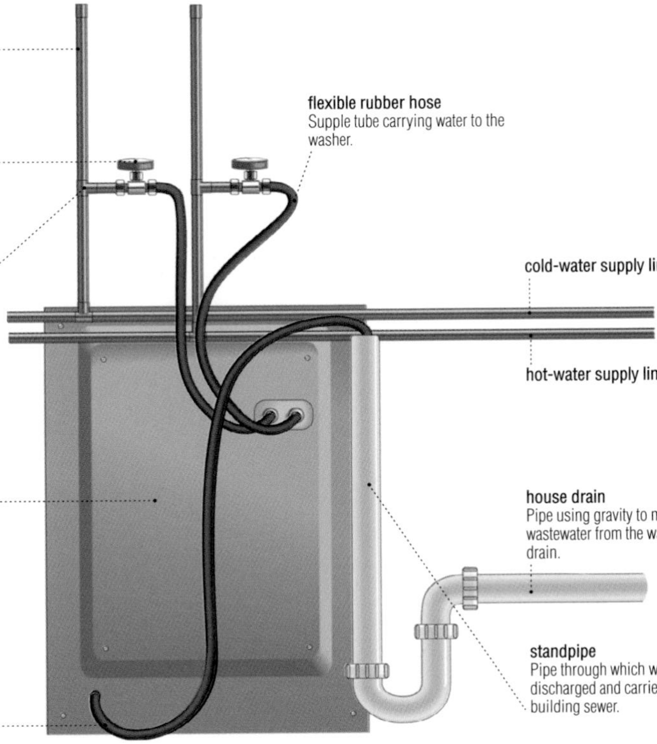
air chamber
Prevents banging in the pipes (water hammer) caused by pressure when a faucet is shut off.
shutoff valve
Device for shutting off the supply of water to the washer.
tee
Shaped like a T, it joins three pipes, one of which is perpendicular to the other two.
washer
Household appliance that washes clothes automatically.
drain hose
Flexible tube through which the washer pump expels wastewater to the standpipe.
flexible rubber hose
Supple tube carrying water to the washer.
cold-water supply line
hot-water supply line
house drain
Pipe using gravity to move the wastewater from the washer to the drain.
standpipe
Pipe through which wastewater is discharged and carried to the building sewer.

dishwasher
Appliance designed to automatically wash and dry dishes.

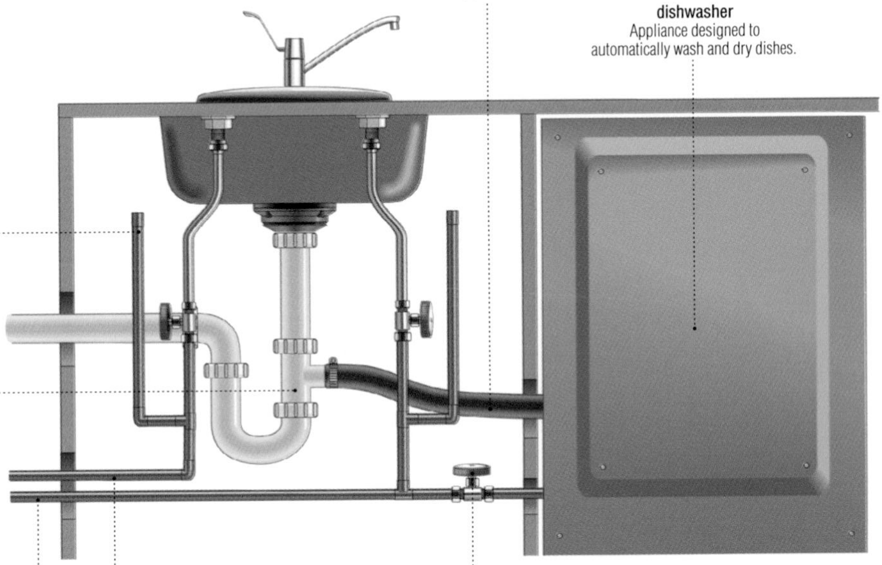
drain hose
Pipe collecting wastewater from the dishwasher and carrying it to the drain.
dishwasher
Appliance designed to automatically wash and dry dishes.
air chamber
Prevents banging in the pipes (water hammer) caused by pressure when a faucet is shut off.
waste tee
Shaped like a T, it joins three pipes, one of which is perpendicular to the other two.
hot-water supply line
cold-water supply line
shutoff valve
Device for shutting off the supply of water to the dishwasher.

distribution panel

Set of devices forming the junction of the public electricity grid and the electric circuits of a dwelling.

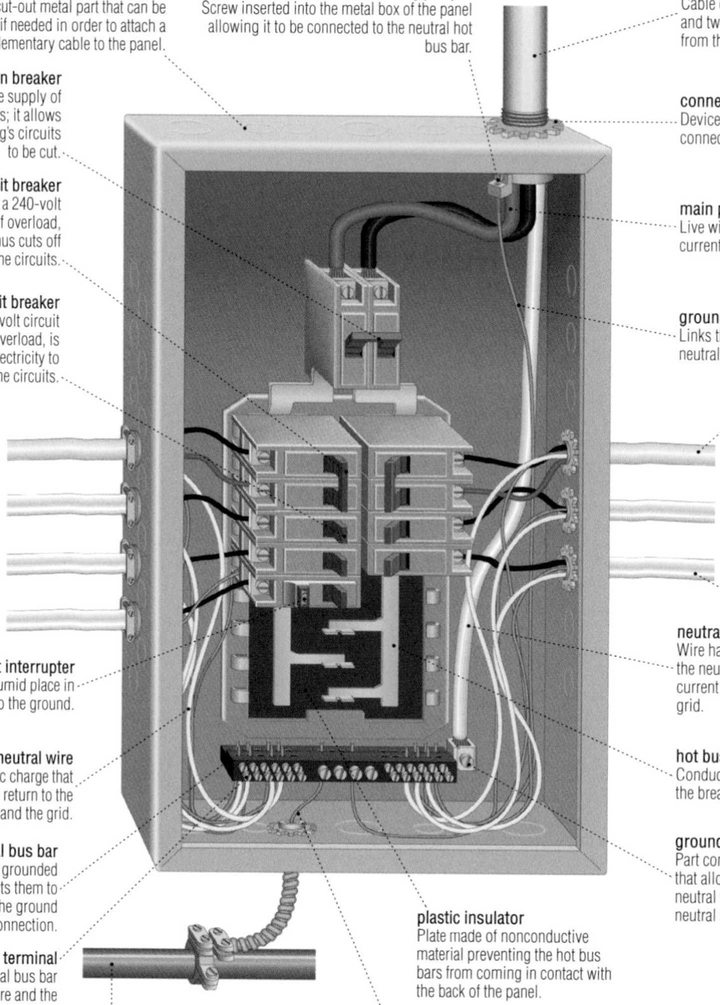

knockout
Partially cut-out metal part that can be removed if needed in order to attach a supplementary cable to the panel.

bonding jumper
Screw inserted into the metal box of the panel allowing it to be connected to the neutral hot bus bar.

240-volt feeder cable
Cable consisting of three wires, one neutral and two live, conducting an electric current from the grid to the distribution panel.

main breaker
Mechanism controlling the supply of electricity to the hot bus bars; it allows the current to all the dwelling's circuits to be cut.

connector
Device for screwing the electric-connection conduit to the panel box.

double circuit breaker
Protection device for a 240-volt circuit that, in the event of overload, is released and thus cuts off electricity to the circuits.

main power cable
Live wire conducting the electric current.

single circuit breaker
Protection device for a 120-volt circuit that, in the event of overload, is released and thus cuts off electricity to the circuits.

ground bond
Links the bonding jumper to the neutral hot bus bar.

240-volt circuit
Composed of two lives wires, one neutral wire and one grounded wire; this allows electricity to reach devices requiring a lot of power.

120-volt circuit
Composed of one live wire, one neutral wire and one grounded wire; it allows electricity to reach a small appliance or a light.

neutral service wire
Wire having no electric charge that, via the neutral hot bus bar, returns the current from domestic circuits to the grid.

ground fault circuit interrupter
Device reducing the risk of electric shock in a humid place in the event of an accidental leak of current to the ground.

hot bus bar
Conductive part of the panel into which the breakers for each circuit are plugged.

neutral wire
Wire having no electric charge that allows the current to return to the distribution panel and the grid.

ground
Part connecting the neutral hot bus bar that allows the current from the circuits' neutral wires to be transferred to the neutral service wire.

ground/neutral bus bar
Receives the current from the neutral grounded wires of the various circuits and conducts them to the neutral service wire and the ground connection.

plastic insulator
Plate made of nonconductive material preventing the hot bus bars from coming in contact with the back of the panel.

terminal
Part of the ground/neutral bus bar to which a neutral wire and the ground wire of a circuit are attached.

ground connection
Metal conductor attached to the ground wire in order to ground the entire circuit.

ground wire
Wire conducting the current from the ground/neutral bus bar to the ground connection in the event of a short circuit.

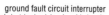

examples of fuses

Fuses: electric connection devices devised for interrupting the current in the event of electric overload by melting one of its components.

cartridge fuse
Having a maximum capacity of 60 amperes, it protects a circuit of 240 volts.

plug fuse
Having a maximum capacity of 30 amperes, it screws in like a lightbulb and protects a circuit of 120 volts.

knife-blade cartridge fuse
Having a capacity of 60 to 600 amperes, it protects the main electric circuit.

network connection

Set of equipment and conductors allowing a customer's electric installation to be connected to the public grid.

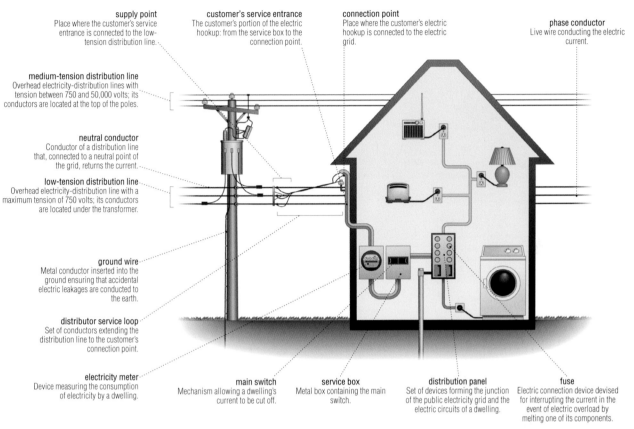

supply point
Place where the customer's service entrance is connected to the low-tension distribution line.

customer's service entrance
The customer's portion of the electric hookup: from the service box to the connection point.

connection point
Place where the customer's electric hookup is connected to the electric grid.

phase conductor
Live wire conducting the electric current.

medium-tension distribution line
Overhead electricity-distribution lines with tension between 750 and 50,000 volts; its conductors are located at the top of the poles.

neutral conductor
Conductor of a distribution line that, connected to a neutral point of the grid, returns the current.

low-tension distribution line
Overhead electricity-distribution line with a maximum tension of 750 volts; its conductors are located under the transformer.

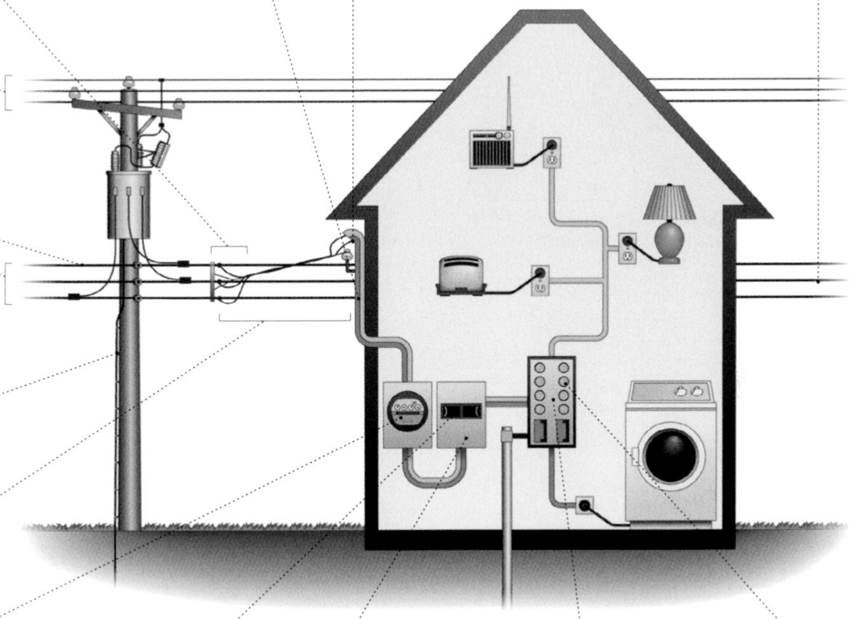

ground wire
Metal conductor inserted into the ground ensuring that accidental electric leakages are conducted to the earth.

distributor service loop
Set of conductors extending the distribution line to the customer's connection point.

electricity meter
Device measuring the consumption of electricity by a dwelling.

main switch
Mechanism allowing a dwelling's current to be cut off.

service box
Metal box containing the main switch.

distribution panel
Set of devices forming the junction of the public electricity grid and the electric circuits of a dwelling.

fuse
Electric connection device devised for interrupting the current in the event of electric overload by melting one of its components.

electricity meter

Device measuring the consumption of electricity by a dwelling.

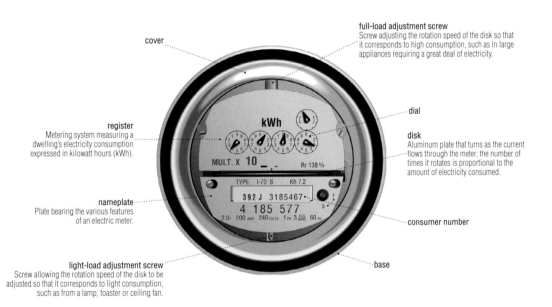

full-load adjustment screw
Screw adjusting the rotation speed of the disk so that it corresponds to high consumption, such as in large appliances requiring a great deal of electricity.

cover

dial

register
Metering system measuring a dwelling's electricity consumption expressed in kilowatt hours (kWh).

disk
Aluminum plate that turns as the current flows through the meter; the number of times it rotates is proportional to the amount of electricity consumed.

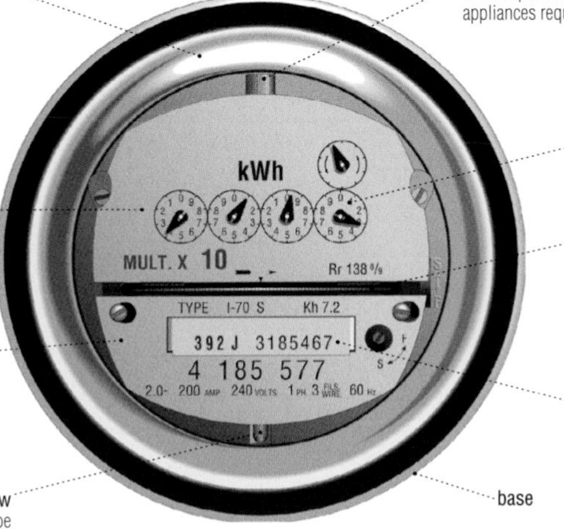

nameplate
Plate bearing the various features of an electric meter.

consumer number

light-load adjustment screw
Screw allowing the rotation speed of the disk to be adjusted so that it corresponds to light consumption, such as from a lamp, toaster or ceiling fan.

base

contact devices

Examples of components that connect a device to an electric circuit.

European plug
End part of an electric wire equipped with pins that are inserted into the socket contacts of an outlet to establish contact.

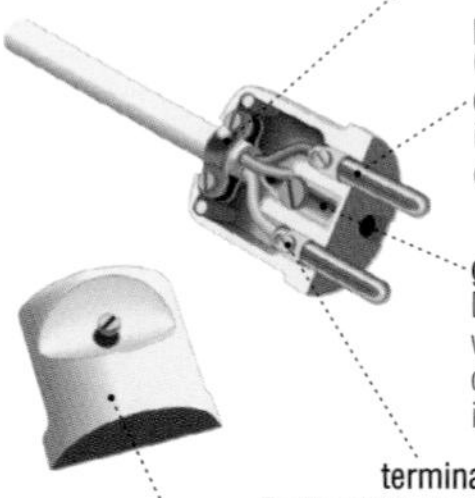

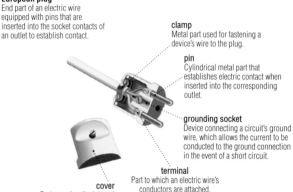

clamp
Metal part used for fastening a device's wire to the plug.

pin
Cylindrical metal part that establishes electric contact when inserted into the corresponding outlet.

grounding socket
Device connecting a circuit's ground wire, which allows the current to be conducted to the ground connection in the event of a short circuit.

terminal
Part to which an electric wire's conductors are attached.

cover
Part covering the internal components of a plug.

American plug
End part of an electric wire equipped with blades that are inserted into an outlet to establish contact.

blade
Flat metal part inserted into the slot of an outlet to establish electric contact.

grounding prong
Device connecting a circuit's ground wire, which allows the current to be conducted to the ground connection in the event of a short circuit.

switch
Mechanism allowing the current in an electric circuit to be established or interrupted.

switch plate
Protective plate covering an outl
or, in this case, a switch.

European outlet
Device fitted with sockets connecting an electric circuit to an electric device when the plug is inserted into it.

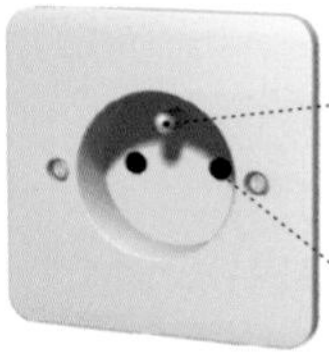

grounding prong
Device connecting a circuit's ground wire, which allows the current to be conducted to the ground connection in the event of a short circuit.

socket-contact
Hole intended to receive a plug's pin and establish electric contact.

plug adapter
Electric accessory adapting a plug to an outlet of a different configuration.

outlet
Device connecting an electric circuit that conducts the current to an electric device when a plug is inserted.

electrical box
Box housing the electric connections in order to protect the part of the dwelling's frame upon which it is mounted.

dimmer switch
Switch for varying the brightnes
of a lighting installation.

lighting

Set of devices allowing light to be diffused in a dwelling.

incandescent lamp
Lamp in which a filament heated by an electric current produces light rays.

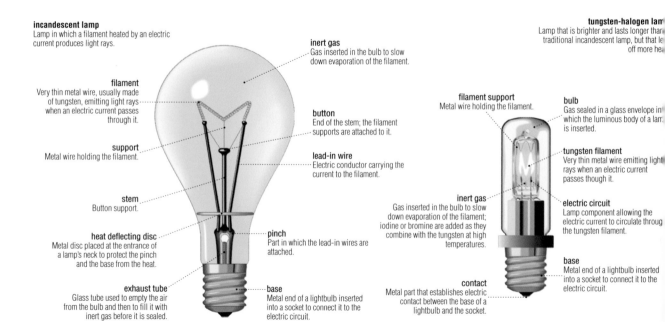

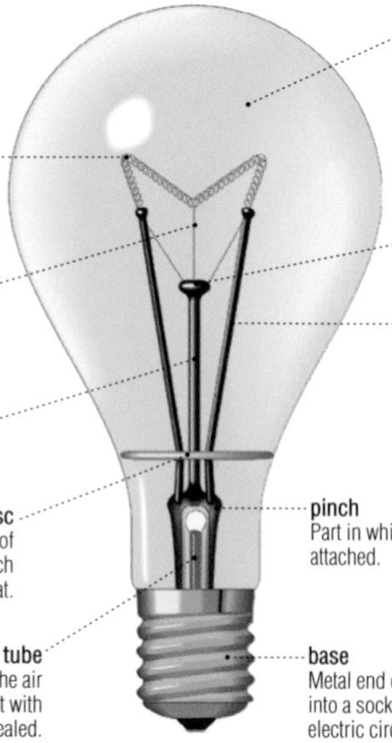

inert gas
Gas inserted in the bulb to slow down evaporation of the filament.

filament
Very thin metal wire, usually made of tungsten, emitting light rays when an electric current passes through it.

button
End of the stem; the filament supports are attached to it.

support
Metal wire holding the filament.

lead-in wire
Electric conductor carrying the current to the filament.

stem
Button support.

heat deflecting disc
Metal disc placed at the entrance of a lamp's neck to protect the pinch and the base from the heat.

pinch
Part in which the lead-in wires are attached.

exhaust tube
Glass tube used to empty the air from the bulb and then to fill it with inert gas before it is sealed.

base
Metal end of a lightbulb inserted into a socket to connect it to the electric circuit.

tungsten-halogen lam
Lamp that is brighter and lasts longer thar
traditional incandescent lamp, but that le
off more he

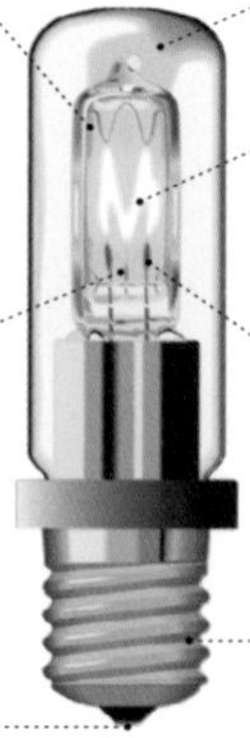

filament support
Metal wire holding the filament.

bulb
Gas sealed in a glass envelope in
which the luminous body of a lam
is inserted.

tungsten filament
Very thin metal wire emitting light
rays when an electric current
passes though it.

inert gas
Gas inserted in the bulb to slow down evaporation of the filament; iodine or bromine are added as they combine with the tungsten at high temperatures.

electric circuit
Lamp component allowing the
electric current to circulate throug
the tungsten filament.

base
Metal end of a lightbulb inserted into a socket to connect it to the electric circuit.

contact
Metal part that establishes electric contact between the base of a lightbulb and the socket.

arts of a lamp socket

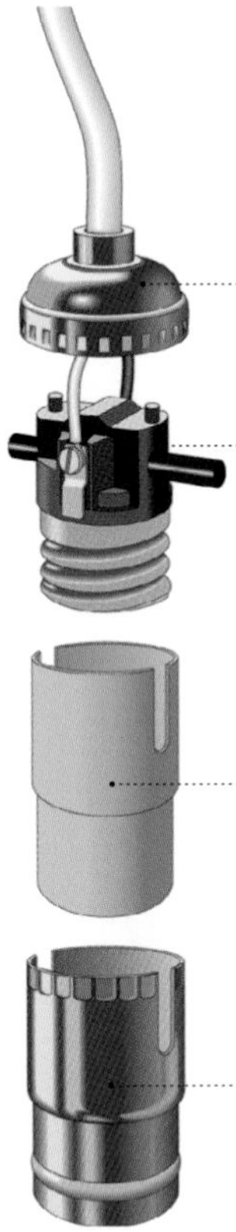
cap
Component fitting onto the outer shell and covering the upper end of a lamp's socket.
socket
Device into which a lamp's base is inserted in order to connect it to the electric-supply circuit and to keep it in place.
insulating sleeve
Component protecting the outer shell from the heat.
outer shell
Decorative component covering the socket and the insulating sleeve.

lamp socket
Device composed of a socket, its protective components and a switch.

bayonet base
Base fitted with two short metal pins so that it can be placed in the corresponding socket.

screw base
Base fitted with a screw pitch so it can be inserted into the corresponding socket.

bulb
Gas sealed in a glass envelope into which the luminous body of a lamp is inserted.

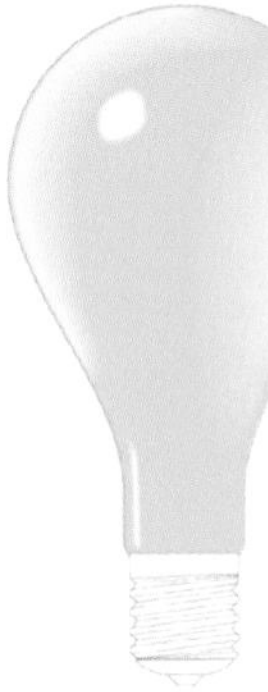

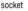

energy-saving bulb
Bulb whose electricity consumption is lower and its life longer than an incandescent bulb.

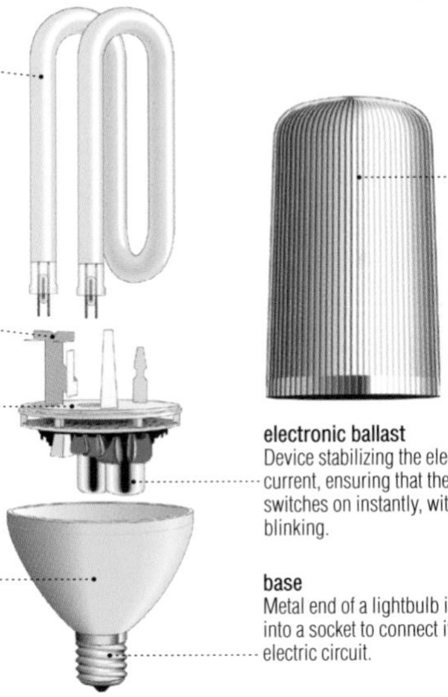
fluorescent tube
Tube in which the electric current produces ultraviolet radiation converted into visible light by a layer of a fluorescent substance.
bulb
Gas sealed in a glass envelope into which the luminous body of a lamp is inserted.
tube retention clip
Part into which the fluorescent tube is inserted to connect it.
mounting plate
Plate on which the lamp's working devices are attached.
electronic ballast
Device stabilizing the electric current, ensuring that the light switches on instantly, without blinking.
housing
base
Metal end of a lightbulb inserted into a socket to connect it to the electric circuit.

luorescent tube
ube in which the electric current roduces ultraviolet radiation onverted into visible light by a layer f a fluorescent substance.

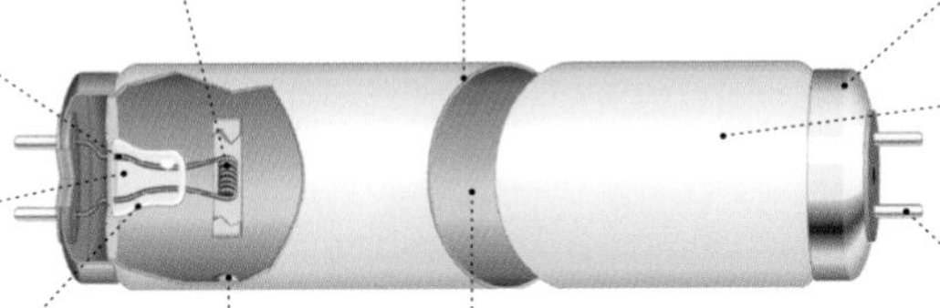
electrode
A device placed at each end of the tube; an electric discharge arcs between the two of them.
phosphorescent coating
The tube's internal coating; it is composed of phosphate particles that convert ultraviolet rays into visible light.
pin base
End of the tube equipped with two pins that, when inserted into the socket, connect the tube with the electric circuit.
lead-in wire
Electric conductor carrying the current to the filament.
bulb
Long glass cylinder enclosing the components of this type of tube and diffusing light.
exhaust tube
Glass tube used to empty the air from the bulb and then to fill it with inert gas before it is sealed.
pin
Cylindrical metal part that establishes electric contact when inserted into the corresponding outlet.
pinch
Part in which the lead-in wires are attached.
mercury
A small amount of vaporized mercury, added to the gas, emits ultraviolet radiation during the electric discharge.
gas
The tube is filled with an inert gas under low pressure, with mercury added.

tungsten-halogen lamp
Lamp that is brighter and lasts longer than a traditional incandescent lamp, but that lets off more heat.

pin
Cylindrical metal part that establishes electric contact when inserted into the corresponding outlet.

HOUSE

armchair

Chair consisting of arms, a back and legs.

parts

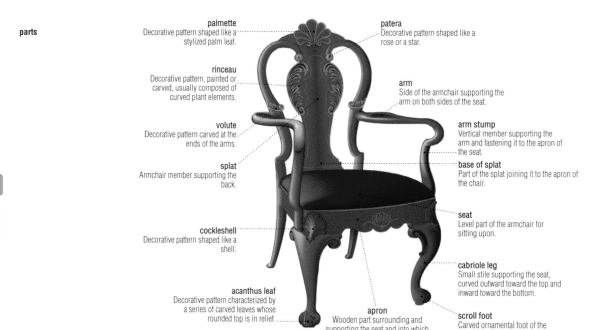

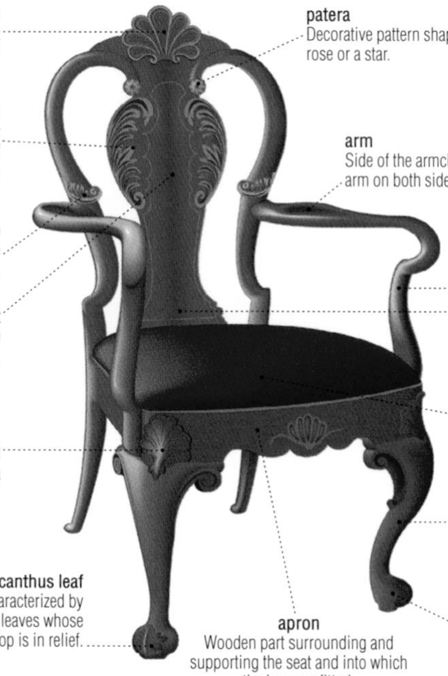
palmette
Decorative pattern shaped like a stylized palm leaf.
rinceau
Decorative pattern, painted or carved, usually composed of curved plant elements.
volute
Decorative pattern carved at the ends of the arms.
splat
Armchair member supporting the back.
cockleshell
Decorative pattern shaped like a shell.
acanthus leaf
Decorative pattern characterized by a series of carved leaves whose rounded top is in relief.
apron
Wooden part surrounding and supporting the seat and into which the legs are fitted.
patera
Decorative pattern shaped like a rose or a star.
arm
Side of the armchair supporting the arm on both sides of the seat.
arm stump
Vertical member supporting the arm and fastening it to the apron of the seat.
base of splat
Part of the splat joining it to the apron of the chair.
seat
Level part of the armchair for sitting upon.
cabriole leg
Small stile supporting the seat, curved outward toward the top and inward toward the bottom.
scroll foot
Carved ornamental foot of the armchair.

examples of armchairs

Wassily chair
Armchair with a tubular metal frame and whose back and seat are made of leather.

director's chair
Wooden armchair with a canvas back and seat that folds up in the middle.

rocking chair
Armchair with curved runners to rock on.

cabriolet
Wooden 18th-century armchair with a curved back and armrests that curve outward.

méridienne
Sofa with an irregular back joining two arms of different heights.

récamier
Long lounge chair on which one can recline, equipped with an upholstered headrest and back, the latter extending only a part of the length of the chair.

club chair
Large deep upholstered armchair, usually made of leather.

bergère
Upholstered armchair with a cushioned seat.

sofa
Long upholstered armchair that seats several people.

love seat
Sofa that seats two people.

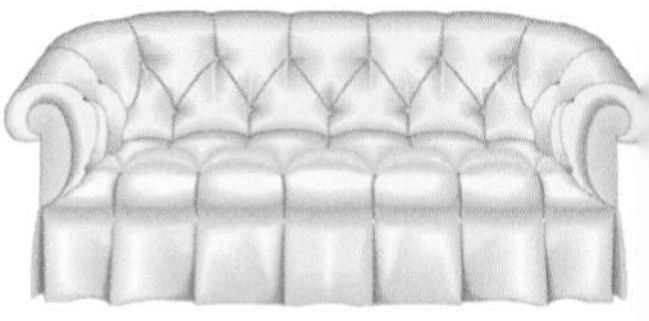

chesterfield
Upholstered quilted sofa whose arms are the same height as its back.

side chair

Seat consisting of a back and legs but no arms.

parts

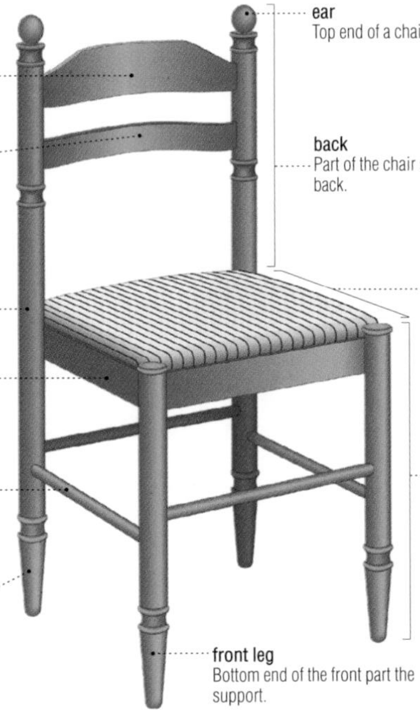

ear
Top end of a chair's stile.

top rail
Horizontal member located at the top of the back.

cross rail
Horizontal member located in the center of the back.

back
Part of the chair supporting the back.

seat
Level part of the chair for sitting upon.

stile
Part of a chair supporting both the back and the rear of the apron.

apron
Wooden part surrounding and supporting the seat and into which the legs are fitted.

support
Grouping that supports the seat, composed of the legs, spindle and apron.

spindle
Horizontal member joining two of the chair's legs.

rear leg
Bottom end of the stile completing the chair's support.

front leg
Bottom end of the front part the support.

examples of chairs

rocking chair
Chair equipped with curved runners to rock on.

stacking chairs
Chairs designed to be placed one atop the other for storing.

folding chair
Chair whose seat and legs fold up for ease of storage and carrying.

chaise longue
Folding chair upon which one can recline.

seats

Furniture designed for sitting.

ottoman
Low upholstered seat having neither arms nor back.

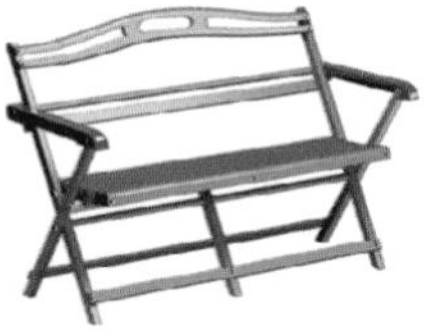

bench
Long narrow unupholstered seat with or without a back, seating several people.

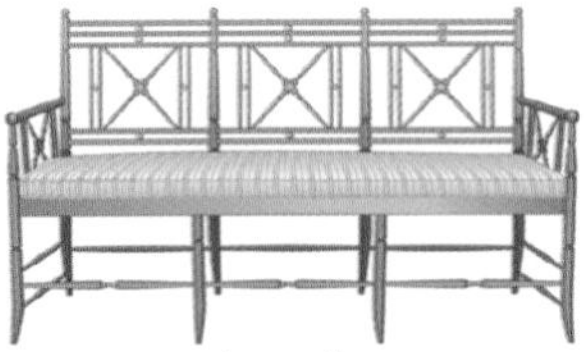

banquette
Bench with an upholstered seat.

bean bag chair
Seat composed of an upholstered bag; it assumes the form of the human body.

step chair
Chair whose foldaway lower part can be pulled out to form a step.

footstool
Seat with legs, having neither arms nor back, of various heights.

bar stool
Seat with legs, having neither arms nor back, high enough so that a person can sit at the level of a bar.

table

Piece of furniture consisting of a level top supported by one or several legs and whose uses are numerous.

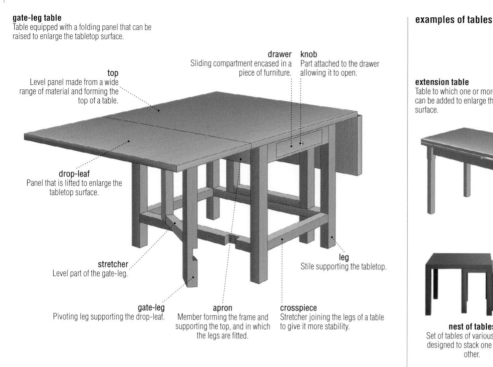

gate-leg table
Table equipped with a folding panel that can be raised to enlarge the tabletop surface.

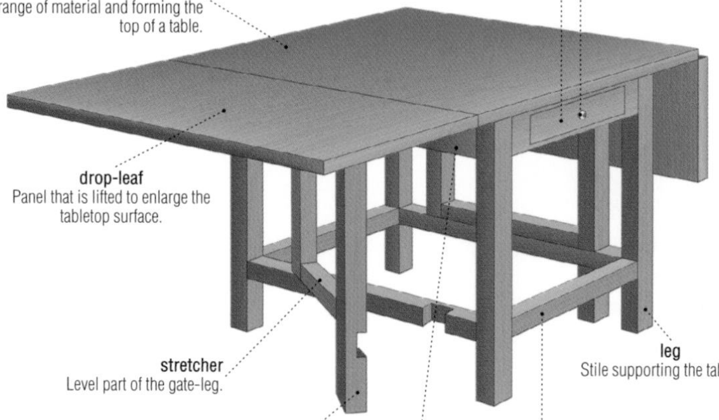
drawer
Sliding compartment encased in a piece of furniture.
knob
Part attached to the drawer allowing it to open.
top
Level panel made from a wide range of material and forming the top of a table.
drop-leaf
Panel that is lifted to enlarge the tabletop surface.
stretcher
Level part of the gate-leg.
leg
Stile supporting the tabletop.
gate-leg
Pivoting leg supporting the drop-leaf.
apron
Member forming the frame and supporting the top, and in which the legs are fitted.
crosspiece
Stretcher joining the legs of a table to give it more stability.

examples of tables

extension table
Table to which one or more extensions can be added to enlarge the tabletop surface.

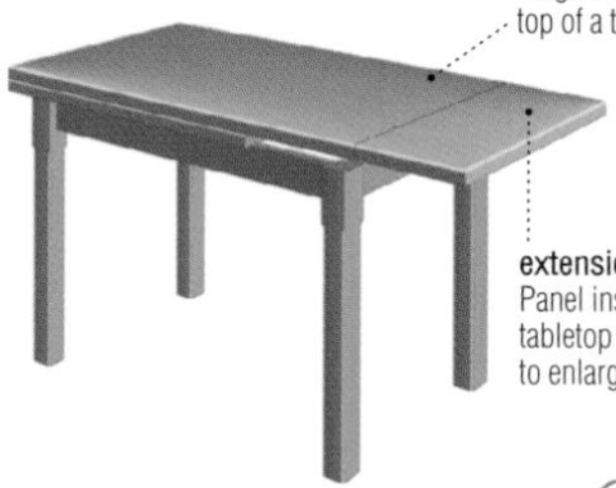
top
Level panel made from a wide range of material and forming th
top of a table.
extension
Panel inserted at the end of the tabletop or between the two halv
to enlarge the surface.

nest of tables
Set of tables of various heights designed to stack one atop the other.

serving cart
Piece of furniture on which to plac the dishes when the table is cleared.

storage furniture

Furniture serving to archive, support or protect various objects.

armoire
Tall piece of furniture enclosed by panels and equipped with shelves to store items such as linens, clothing and supplies.

frame
Set of stiles and rails comprising an armoire's structure.

door
Each of an armoire's moving parts, acting as doors.

frieze
Ornamental molding above the cornice.
top rail
Horizontal wooden member located at the top of the frame.
center post
Fixed center stile of an armoire's frame.
diamond point
Decorative pattern whose embossment resembles the facets of a diamond.
rail
Flat section of the panel between two decorative relief patterns.
bottom rail
Horizontal wooden member located at the bottom of the frame.
foot
Wooden member, usually decorative, supporting the armoire.
bracket base
Lower part of the frame.
cornice
Set of protruding moldings across the top of an armoire.
door panel
Carved or painted surface demarcated by a molding.
hanging stile
Vertical member of the frame to which the hinges are fastened.
lock
Device mounted on the door allowing it to lock by using a key.
frame stile
Wooden member making up the sides of the frame.
hinge
Cylindrical metal part bent at an angle; it supports the door and allows it to swing.
peg
Dowel made of wood or metal used for fastening various members.

storage furniture

linen chest
Low piece of furniture shaped like a chest and closed by a lid.

compartment
Compartment for storing various objects.

fall front
Panel closing the upper part of the secretary; it is lowered to form a writing table.

secretary
Piece of furniture for storing office supplies and stationery; it includes a drop panel serving as a writing table.

dresser
Piece of furniture for the bedroom equipped with drawers, used for storing clothes; it often has a mirror mounted on top.

closet
Part of an armoire equipped with a rod for hanging clothes.

shelf
Level board on which clothes are stored.

wardrobe
Piece of furniture in which one part is equipped with shelves and drawers for storing clothes and the other with a rod for hanging them.

drawer
Sliding compartment encased in a piece of furniture.

chiffonier
Tall narrow piece of furniture equipped with stacked drawers for storing accessories and clothes.

display cabinet
Glass cabinet for displaying collectibles and knickknacks.

corner cupboard
Piece of furniture designed to be placed in the angle formed by two walls.

glass-fronted display cabinet
Piece of furniture consisting of a buffet in the lower part and shelves for displaying dishes in the upper part.

buffet
Dining room or kitchen furniture for storing dishes, silverware and table linens.

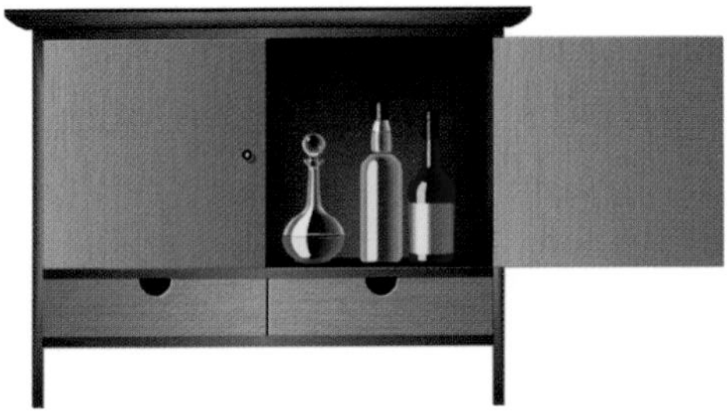

liquor cabinet
Piece of furniture for storing liquor and the accessories used for making drinks.

bed

Piece of furniture to stretch out on for resting or sleeping.

sofa bed
Sofa that can be converted into a bed.

futon
Cotton mattress of Japanese origin.
frame
Set of components forming the structure of the piece of furniture.

parts

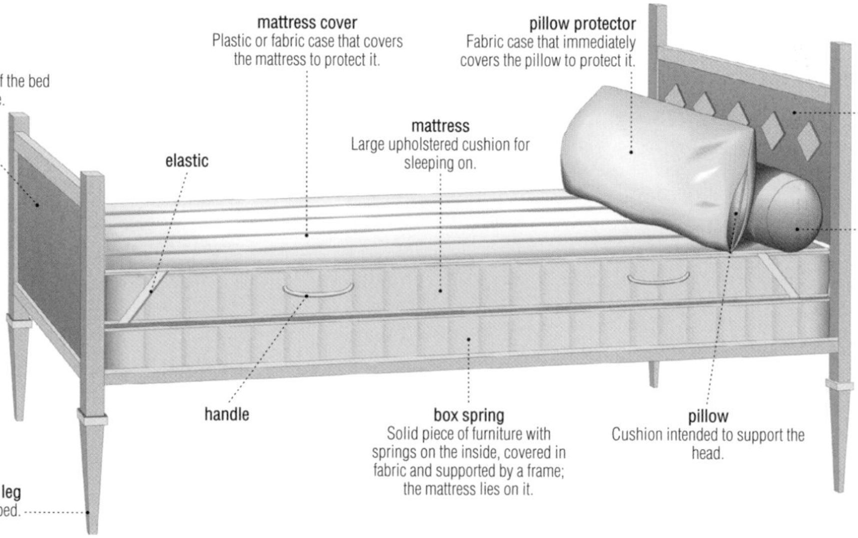
mattress cover
Plastic or fabric case that covers the mattress to protect it.
pillow protector
Fabric case that immediately covers the pillow to protect it.
footboard
Panel forming the end of the bed where the feet lie.
headboard
Panel forming the end of the be
where the head lies.
mattress
Large upholstered cushion for sleeping on.
elastic
bolster
Cylindrical cushion on which th
pillow rests; it usually extends t
entire width of the bed.
handle
box spring
Solid piece of furniture with springs on the inside, covered in fabric and supported by a frame; the mattress lies on it.
pillow
Cushion intended to support the head.
leg
Stile supporting the bed.

linen
Set of fabrics, blankets and pillows covering a bed.

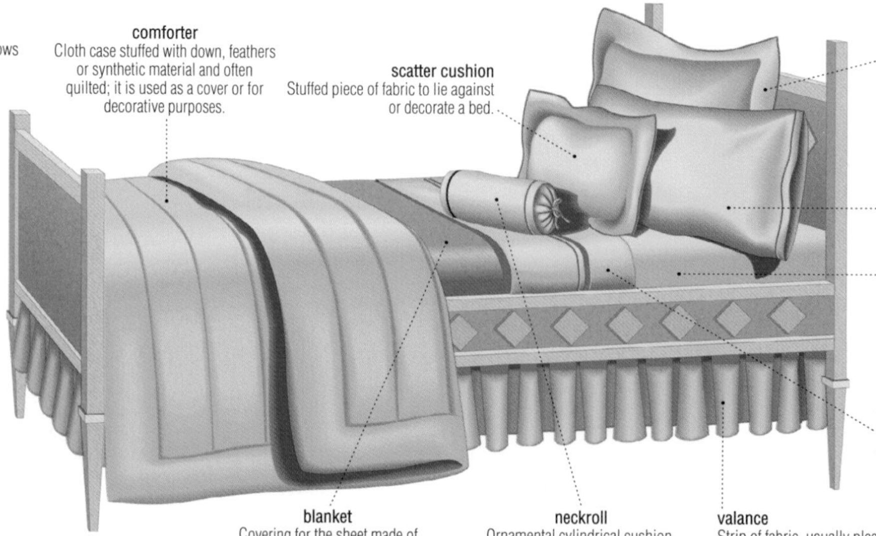
comforter
Cloth case stuffed with down, feathers or synthetic material and often quilted; it is used as a cover or for decorative purposes.
scatter cushion
Stuffed piece of fabric to lie against or decorate a bed.
sham
Decorative cloth envelope coveri
a pillow that matches the bedcov
pillowcase
Cloth envelope covering a pillow
fitted sheet
Piece of fabric whose corners an
edges are designed to tuck snugl
under the mattress.
flat sheet
Piece of fabric between the body and the blanket.
blanket
Covering for the sheet made of various warm fabrics; it protects against the cold.
neckroll
Ornamental cylindrical cushion.
valance
Strip of fabric, usually pleated, trimming the base of the bed.

children's furniture

Furniture designed and adapted for young children.

playpen
Bed that closes up, usually used when traveling.

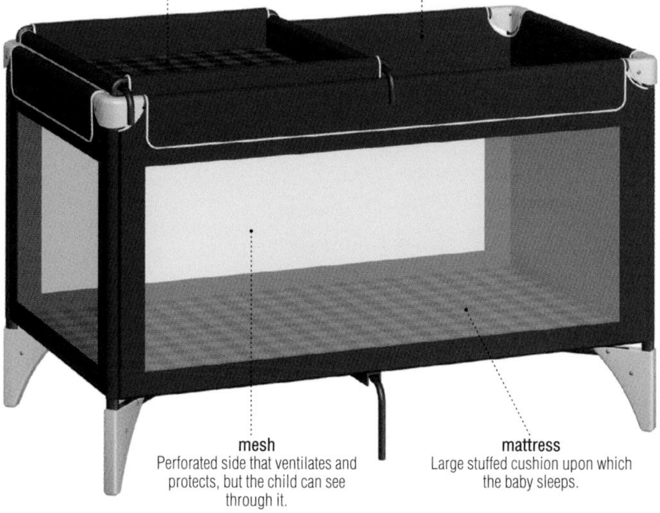

booster seat
Seat that, when set upon a chair, raises the child so that he or she can sit at table level.

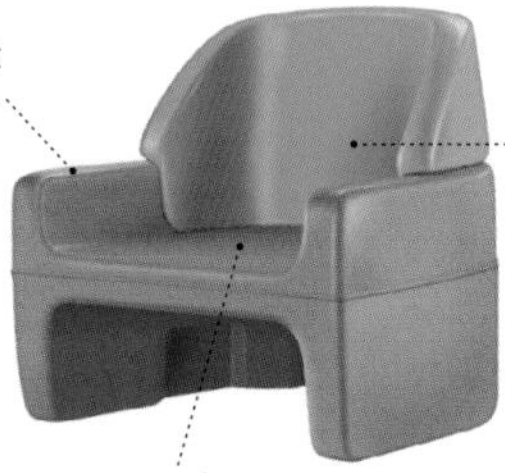

changing table
Piece of furniture equipped with storage space and a changing area.

high chair
Elevated seat, closed in front by a removable tray, in which a baby sits for feeding.

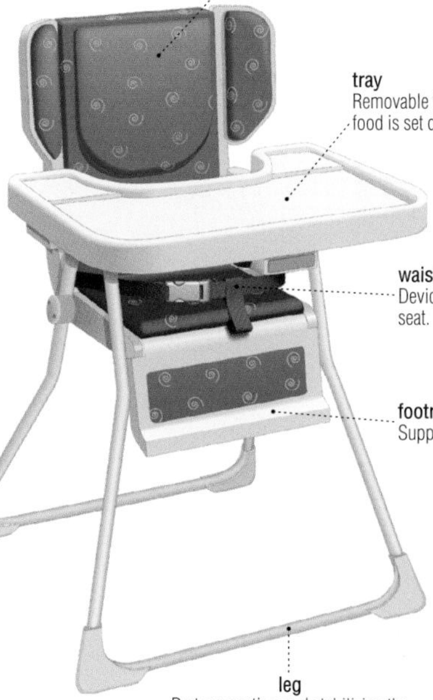

back
Part supporting the back.
tray
Removable tray on which the child's food is set down.
waist belt
Device keeping the child in the seat.
footrest
Support for the feet.
leg
Part supporting and stabilizing the chair.

crib
Deep bed for a baby surrounded by bars, one side of which can be lowered; it is equipped with a mattress whose height can be changed.

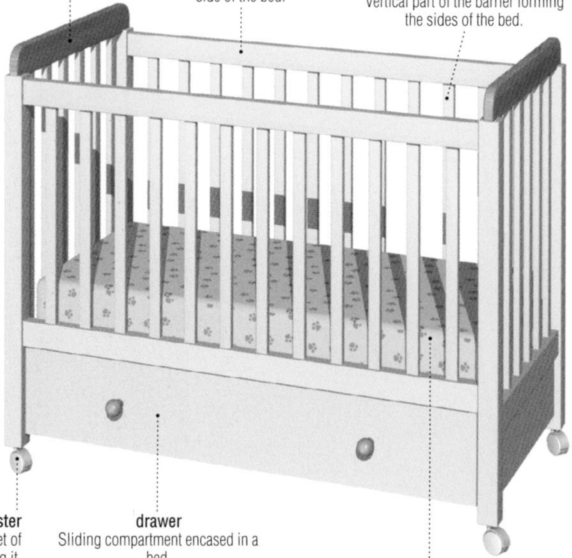

headboard
End of the bed where the head of the baby is placed.
barrier
Assembly of bars enclosing the side of the bed.
slat
Vertical part of the barrier forming the sides of the bed.
caster
Small wheels attached to the feet of the bed to facilitate moving it.
drawer
Sliding compartment encased in a bed.
mattress
Large stuffed cushion upon which the baby sleeps.

window accessories

Set of elements decorating a window.

indoor shutters
Decorative wood panels placed in front of a window composed of adjustable horizontal louvers for controlling the amount of light entering a room.

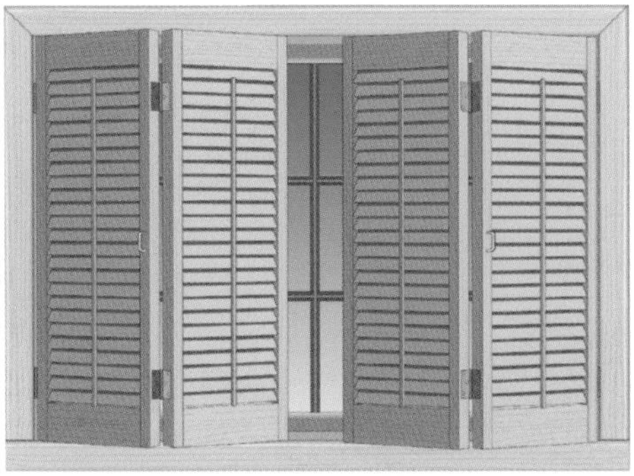

glass curtain
Curtain placed in front of a window, attached in various ways, in combination or separately.

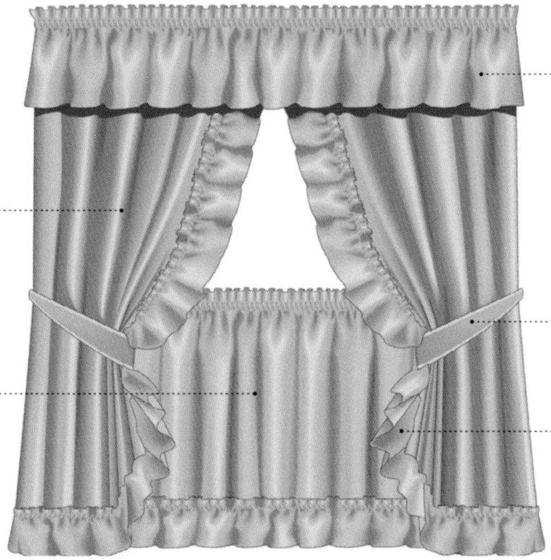

valance
Pleated or gathered strip of fabric hiding the curtain rod.

cottage curtain
Curtain held to the side by a tieback, usually trimmed with a ruffle.

tieback
Strip of fabric or rope holding back and supporting a curtain.

café curtain
Curtain whose rod is located halfway up the window; it lets in light while providing privacy.

ruffle
Pleated or gathered strip of fabric trimming the curtain border.

curtain
Formal drapery placed in front of a window, often composed of several layers of curtains.

cornice
Strip of fabric affixed to rigid canvas or cardboard; it covers and hides the curtain rod.

overdrapery
Curtain covering another curtain.

draw drapery
Piece of decorative fabric sliding in front of a window to filter or block the light and provide privacy.

holdback
Part attached to the wall for hooking the tieback.

cord tieback
Plaited rope serving as a tieback.

tassel
Decorative end of a cord tieback.

sheer curtain
Curtain made of a light fabric that filters the light entering a room.

window accessories

examples of pleats

Pleats: creases in fabric giving volume to a curtain.

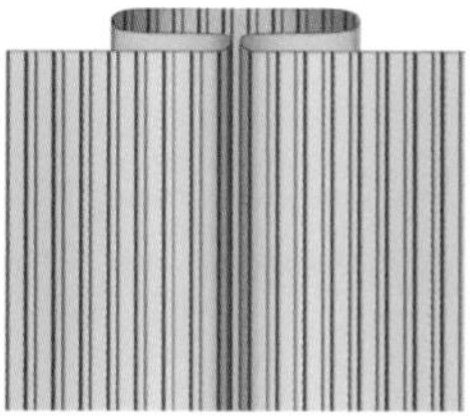

box pleat
Pleat formed by two folds that meet in front and touch on the outside of the fabric, thus forming a hollow in the fabric.

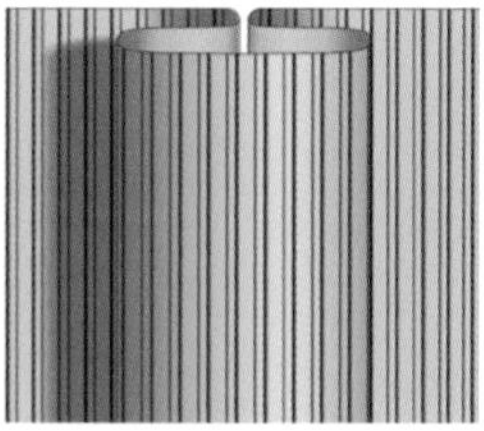

inverted pleat
Pleat formed from two pleats that meet on the reverse of the fabric.

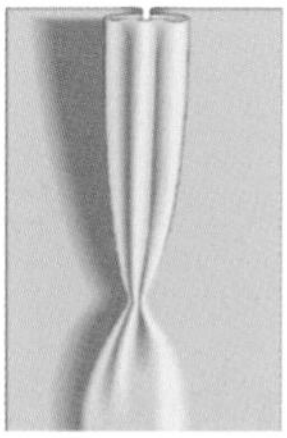

pinch pleat
Pleat formed from three pleats stitched together at the bottom to keep them together.

examples of headings

Headings: decorative pleated, shirred or draped parts at the top of the curtains.

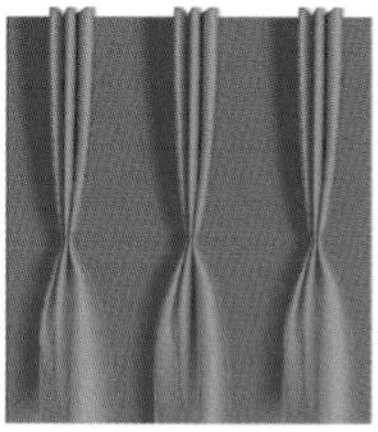

pleated heading
Heading made of pleats spaced at regular intervals.

pencil pleat heading
Heading whose small vertical pleats are shaped like tubes; they are made by pulling on two threads sewn through the fabric.

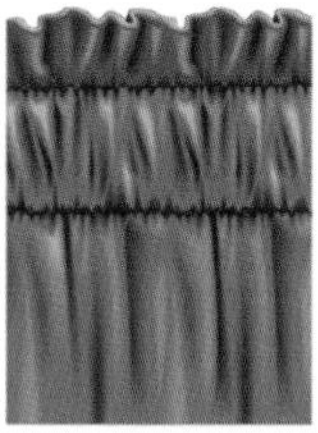

shirred heading
Heading made of pleats created by pulling on strings inserted through a ribbon.

draped swag
Strip of fabric placed in front of the curtain to hide the rod; it is arranged to form loose pleats.

examples of curtains

The various types of curtains can create a particular atmosphere in a room.

attached curtain
Curtain on two curtain rods; it has pleated sleeves at the top and bottom of the fabric.

crisscross curtains
Curtains whose held-back sides form an overlap.

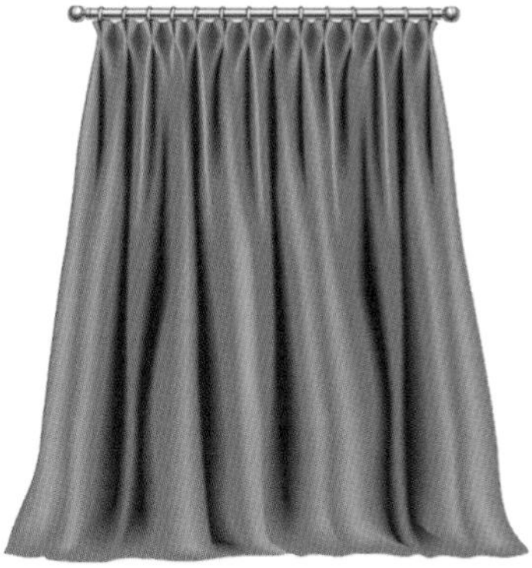

loose curtain
Curtain hung from a single curtain rod and falling in soft pleats.

balloon curtain
Curtain that is raised like a blind and whose pleats are gathered to make them puffy.

window accessories

poles
Rods of various shapes and materials from which a curtain hangs.

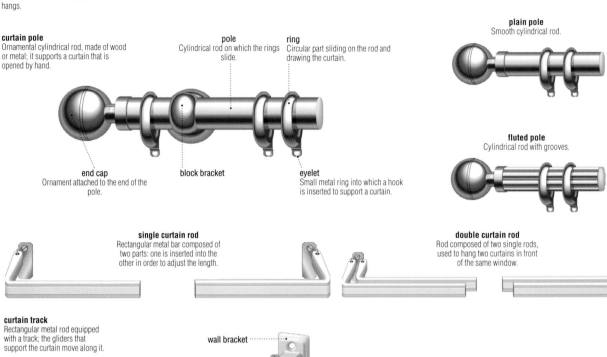

curtain pole
Ornamental cylindrical rod, made of wood or metal; it supports a curtain that is opened by hand.

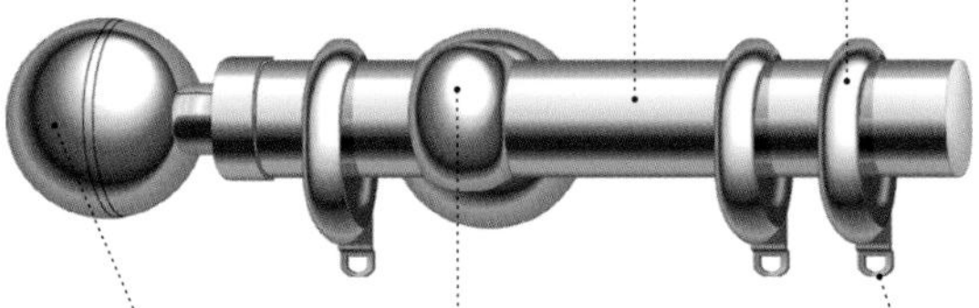

pole
Cylindrical rod on which the rings slide.

ring
Circular part sliding on the rod and drawing the curtain.

end cap
Ornament attached to the end of the pole.

block bracket

eyelet
Small metal ring into which a hook is inserted to support a curtain.

plain pole
Smooth cylindrical rod.

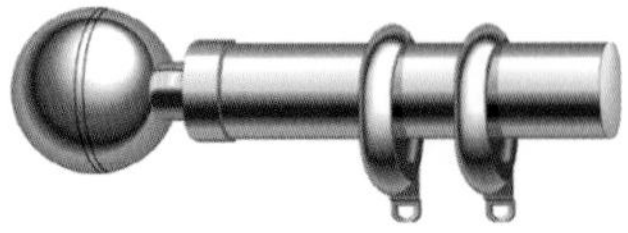

fluted pole
Cylindrical rod with grooves.

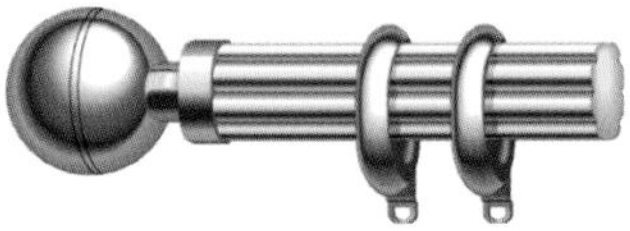

single curtain rod
Rectangular metal bar composed of two parts: one is inserted into the other in order to adjust the length.

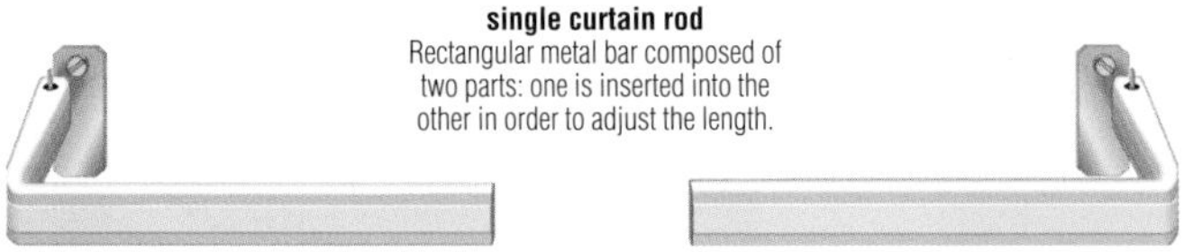

double curtain rod
Rod composed of two single rods, used to hang two curtains in front of the same window.

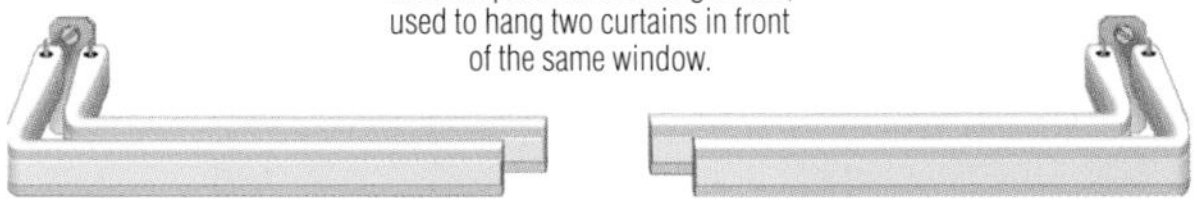

curtain track
Rectangular metal rod equipped with a track; the gliders that support the curtain move along it.

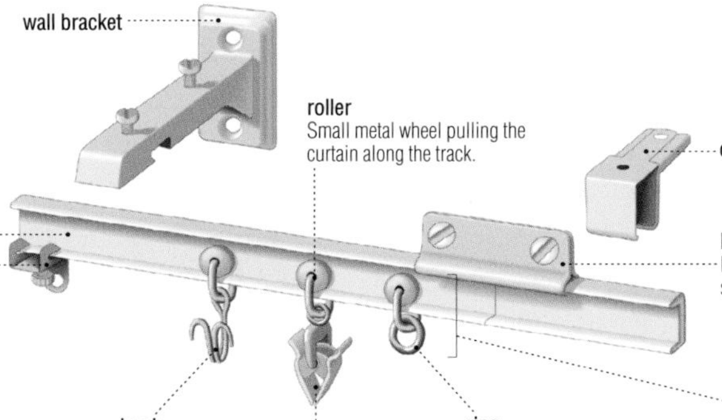

wall bracket

roller
Small metal wheel pulling the curtain along the track.

ceiling bracket

track
Grooved metal rail along which the rollers move.

end stop
Metal part serving as a stopper at the ends of the track.

bridge
Metal part joining two track sections.

carrier
Part composed of a roller for moving the curtain along the track as well as a hooking device supporting the curtain.

hook
Metal part to which the curtain heading is attached.

clip
Implement composed of two articulated prongs that grip the curtain in order to hang it.

ring
Circular piece to take the hook supporting the curtains.

traverse rod
Rectangular metal rod that adjusts to the exact width of a window and along which the carriers move, activated by an operating cord.

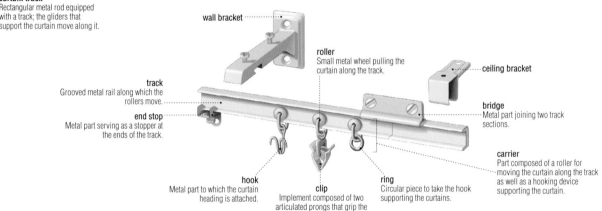

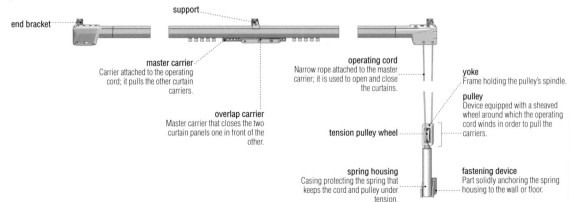

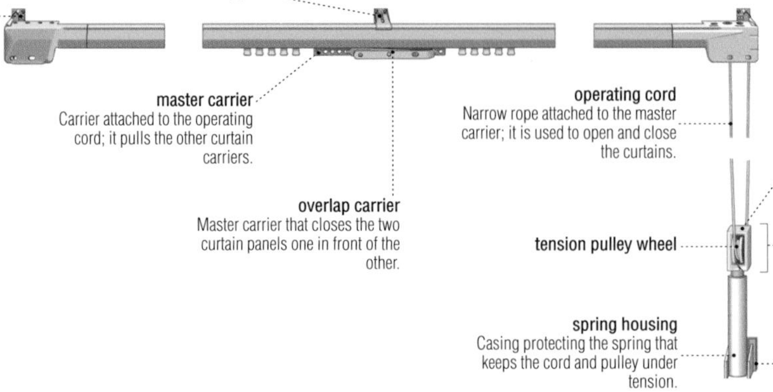

support

end bracket

master carrier
Carrier attached to the operating cord; it pulls the other curtain carriers.

operating cord
Narrow rope attached to the master carrier; it is used to open and close the curtains.

yoke
Frame holding the pulley's spindle.

pulley
Device equipped with a sheaved wheel around which the operating cord winds in order to pull the carriers.

overlap carrier
Master carrier that closes the two curtain panels one in front of the other.

tension pulley wheel

spring housing
Casing protecting the spring that keeps the cord and pulley under tension.

fastening device
Part solidly anchoring the spring housing to the wall or floor.

HOUSE

blinds

Devices that roll or fold up, serving to filter or block light and provide privacy.

roller shade

Shade with a roller containing a spring that causes the shade cloth to roll up.

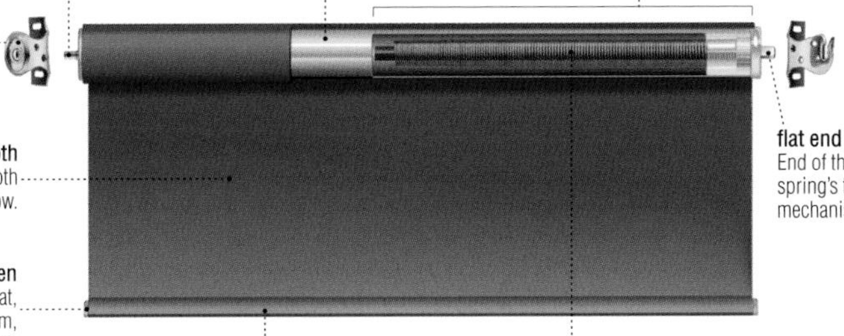

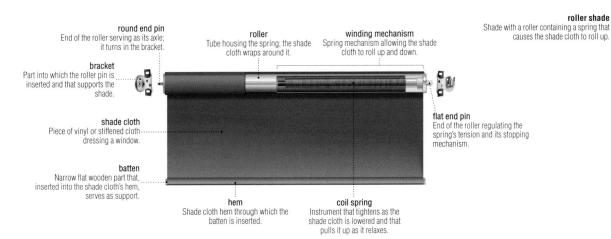

round end pin
End of the roller serving as its axle; it turns in the bracket.

roller
Tube housing the spring; the shade cloth wraps around it.

winding mechanism
Spring mechanism allowing the shade cloth to roll up and down.

bracket
Part into which the roller pin is inserted and that supports the shade.

shade cloth
Piece of vinyl or stiffened cloth dressing a window.

flat end pin
End of the roller regulating the spring's tension and its stopping mechanism.

batten
Narrow flat wooden part that, inserted into the shade cloth's hem, serves as support.

hem
Shade cloth hem through which the batten is inserted.

coil spring
Instrument that tightens as the shade cloth is lowered and that pulls it up as it relaxes.

Venetian blind

Shade made of adjustable horizontal laths containing a mechanism for controlling its height and orientation.

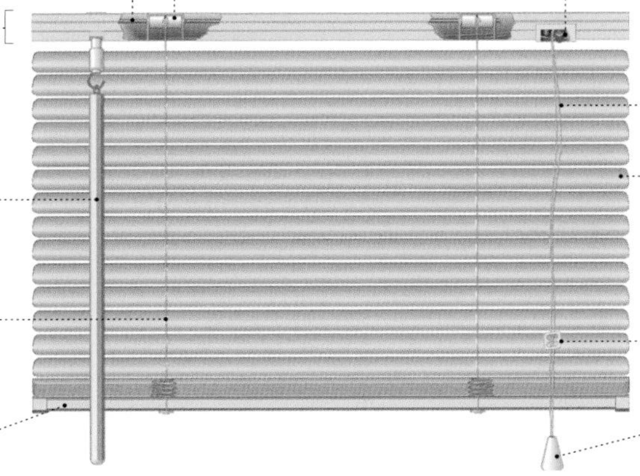

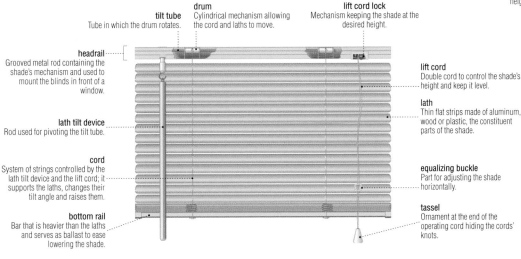

tilt tube
Tube in which the drum rotates.

drum
Cylindrical mechanism allowing the cord and laths to move.

lift cord lock
Mechanism keeping the shade at the desired height.

headrail
Grooved metal rod containing the shade's mechanism and used to mount the blinds in front of a window.

lift cord
Double cord to control the shade's height and keep it level.

lath
Thin flat strips made of aluminum, wood or plastic, the constituent parts of the shade.

lath tilt device
Rod used for pivoting the tilt tube.

cord
System of strings controlled by the lath tilt device and the lift cord; it supports the laths, changes their tilt angle and raises them.

equalizing buckle
Part for adjusting the shade horizontally.

tassel
Ornament at the end of the operating cord hiding the cords' knots.

bottom rail
Bar that is heavier than the laths and serves as ballast to ease lowering the shade.

roman shade
Shade that forms layered pleats as it is raised by means of cords sliding through rings on the back of the cloth.

roll-up blind
Shade made of nonadjustable laths rolled up by a system of cords and pulleys.

lights

Fixed or portable devices designed and used to diffuse electric light.

clamp spotlight
Small portable spotlight with a concentrated beam; it can be mounted on furniture with a clamp.

ceiling fitting
Light mounted directly on the ceiling.

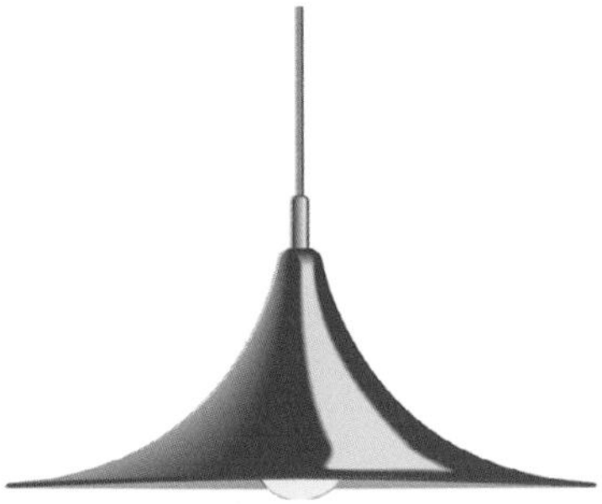

hanging pendant
Light designed to be hung from the ceiling.

halogen desk lamp
Desk lamp of greater luminous intensity and longer duration than a traditional lamp but that emits more heat.

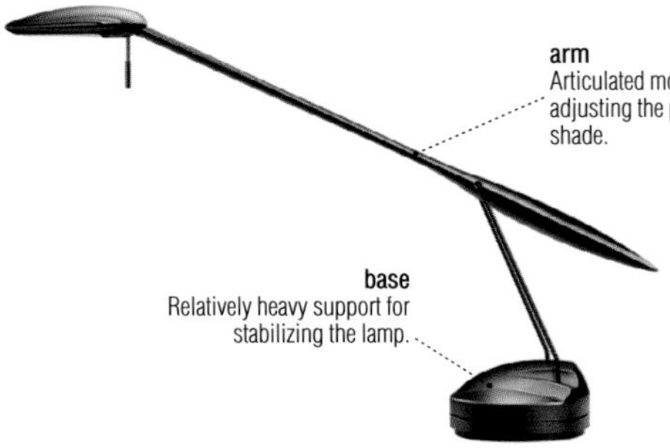
arm
Articulated moving bar for adjusting the position of the lamp shade.
base
Relatively heavy support for stabilizing the lamp.

adjustable lamp
Multidirectional light usually mounted on a worktable by an adjustable clamp.

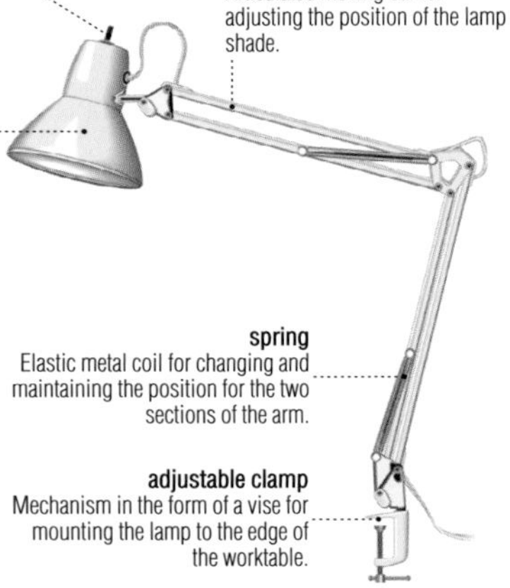
on-off switch
Button for turning the device on or off.
arm
Articulated moving bar for adjusting the position of the lamp shade.
shade
Opaque shield directing the lamp's light onto the work surface.
spring
Elastic metal coil for changing and maintaining the position for the two sections of the arm.
adjustable clamp
Mechanism in the form of a vise for mounting the lamp to the edge of the worktable.

bed lamp
Small reading light that can be mounted on the back of a book or the headboard of a bed.

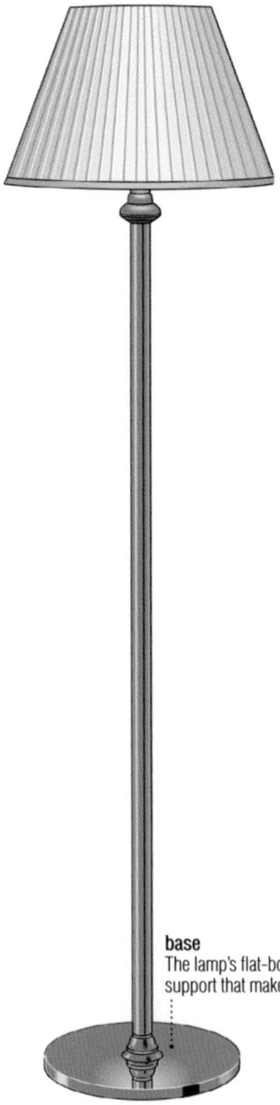
base
The lamp's flat-bottomed circular support that makes it stable.

floor lamp
Portable lamp having a high stand that is placed on the floor.

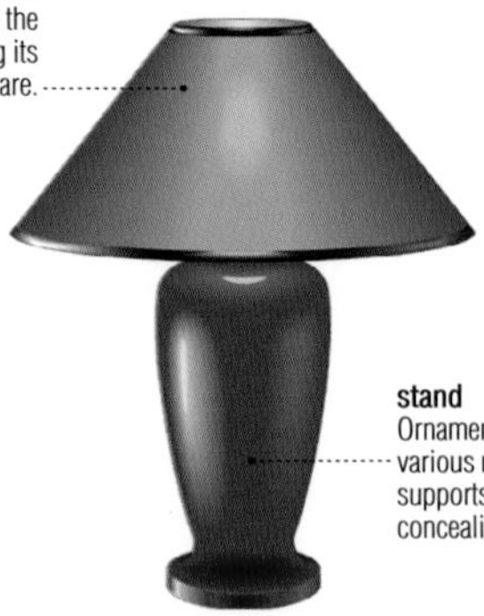
shade
Translucent screen directing the lamp's light while decreasing its glare.
stand
Ornamental base of a lamp of various materials and shapes; it supports the socket while concealing the electric wires.

table lamp
Movable light with a short stand; it is placed on furniture.

desk lamp
Portable light equipped with an opaque shield that directs and diffuses the light onto the worktable.

handelier
.ight suspended from the ceiling
nd consisting of several lamps.

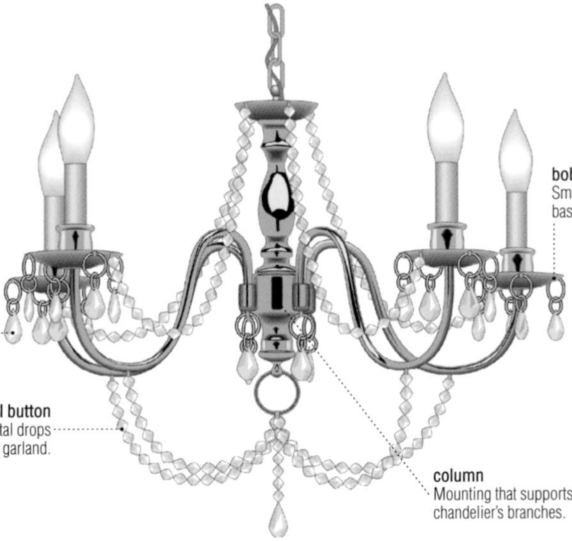

bobeche
Small ornamental cup placed at the base of the socket.

crystal drop
Crystal ornament hanging from the bobeches.

crystal button
Ornamental set of crystal drops arranged in a garland.

column
Mounting that supports the chandelier's branches.

post lantern
Exterior light having a high stand that is fixed to the ground; it consists of a translucent or transparent cage containing a light source.

track lighting
Device mounted to the ceiling to support spots and supply electricity to them.

bar frame
Part of the track fitted with two metal strips; the electric current passes through it.

transformer
)evice adapting the electric current rom the track to the spot's voltage.

contact lever
Device for attaching the transformer and plugging it into the bar frame.

spot
Small adjustable spotlight with a concentrated beam.

wall lantern
Exterior light mounted on a wall, consisting of a translucent or transparent cage containing a light source.

wall fitting
Interior light mounted on a wall.

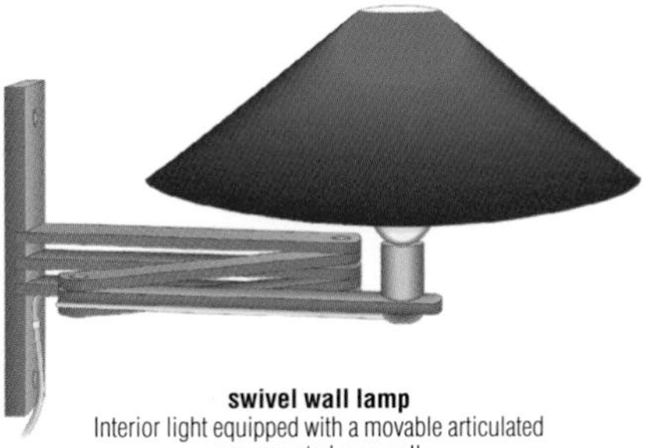

swivel wall lamp
Interior light equipped with a movable articulated arm mounted on a wall.

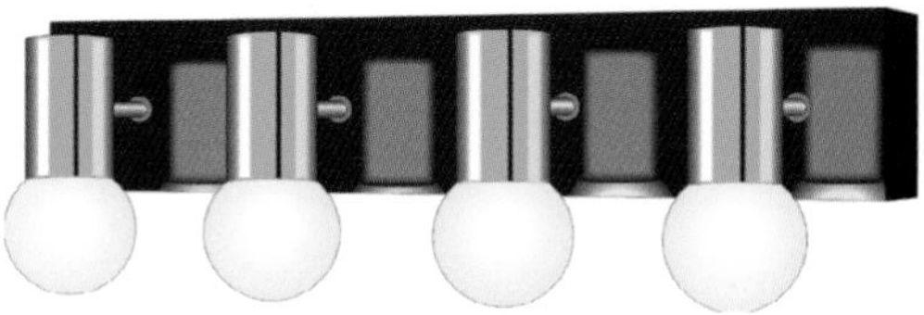

strip light
Device composed of a set of lights that are mounted on the same base.

domestic appliances

Domestic appliances operating on electricity.

steam iron
Electric appliance producing steam and used to iron fabric.

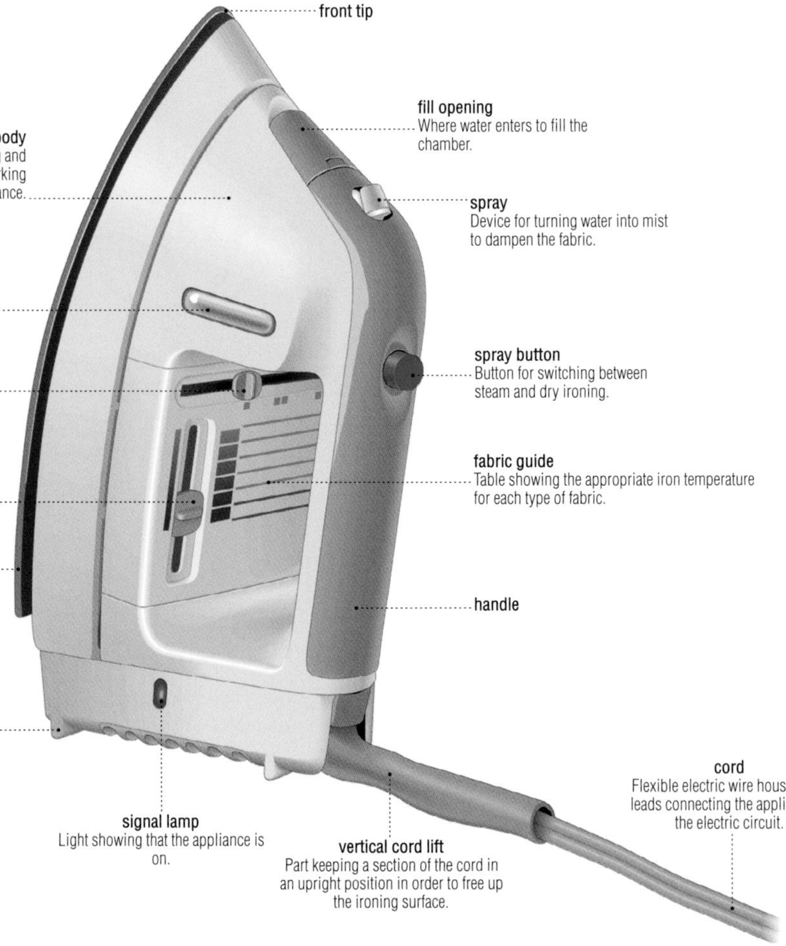

front tip
fill opening
Where water enters to fill the chamber.
body
Rigid casing covering and protecting the various working elements of the appliance.
spray
Device for turning water into mist to dampen the fabric.
water-level tube
spray button
Button for switching between steam and dry ironing.
spray control
Device regulating the flow of steam.
fabric guide
Table showing the appropriate iron temperature for each type of fabric.
temperature control
Device for regulating the iron's temperature.
soleplate
Flat metal part that presses the fabric, with orifices through which the steam escapes.
handle
heel rest
Part upon which the iron rests while not in use.
cord
Flexible electric wire housing the leads connecting the appliance to the electric circuit.
signal lamp
Light showing that the appliance is on.
vertical cord lift
Part keeping a section of the cord in an upright position in order to free up the ironing surface.

hand vacuum cleaner
Portable cordless appliance for vacuuming dust and dirt.

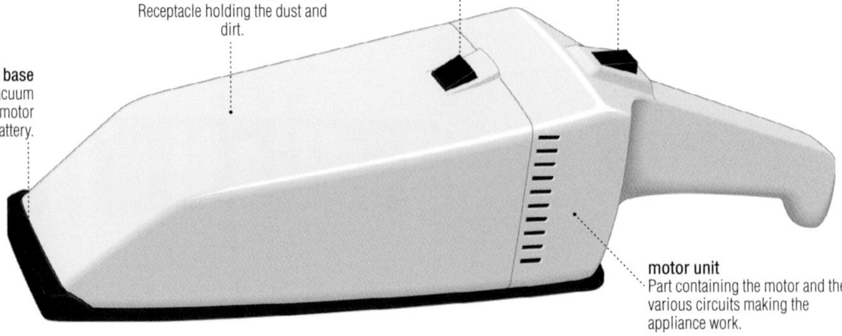

locking button
Mechanism keeping the dust receiver on the motor unit.
on-off switch
Button for turning the device on or off.
dust receiver
Receptacle holding the dust and dirt.
recharging base
Electric base on which the vacuum cleaner rests to recharge the motor unit's battery.
motor unit
Part containing the motor and the various circuits making the appliance work.

upright vacuum cleaner
Vertical one-piece vacuum cleaner that is steered by means of a handle-grip.

on-off switch
Button for turning the device on or off.

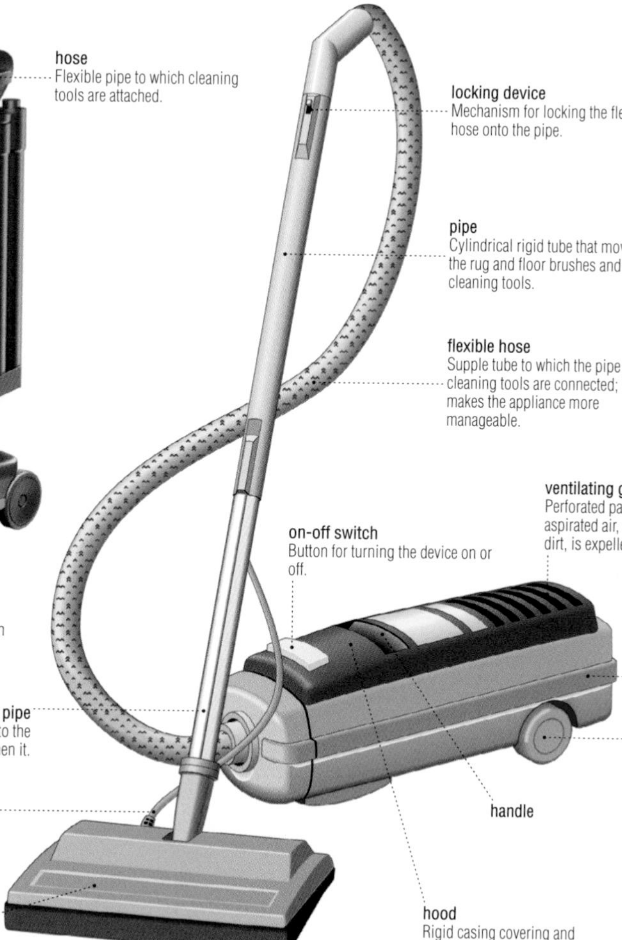

cylinder vacuum cleaner
Electric appliance for vacuuming dust and dirt; it is equipped with wheels and a flexible hose.

tool storage area
Space for storing the cleaning tools.

hose
Flexible pipe to which cleaning tools are attached.

locking device
Mechanism for locking the flexible hose onto the pipe.

pipe
Cylindrical rigid tube that moves the rug and floor brushes and other cleaning tools.

bag compartment
Space for housing the bag that collects the dust and dirt.

flexible hose
Supple tube to which the pipe and cleaning tools are connected; it makes the appliance more manageable.

cleaner height adjustment knob
Mechanism for controlling brush height depending on the thickness of the rug or pile carpet to be cleaned.

ventilating grille
Perforated panel through which aspirated air, cleansed of dust and dirt, is expelled.

on-off switch
Button for turning the device on or off.

tools
Small accessories that one attaches to the end of the hose to vacuum dust and dirt.

brush
Rotating instrument equipped with bristles for dislodging dirt encrusted in the rug or pile carpet fibers.

bumper
Trim protecting the furniture if the vacuum cleaner collides with it.

caster

extension pipe
Cylindrical tube inserted into the end of the pipe to lengthen it.

handle

cord
Flexible electric wire housing the leads connecting the appliance to the electric circuit.

hood
Rigid casing covering and protecting the various working elements of the appliance.

rug and floor brush
Accessory devised to vacuum dust and dirt from a rug, pile carpet or floor.

cleaning tools
Small accessories that one attaches to the end of the hose to vacuum dust and dirt.

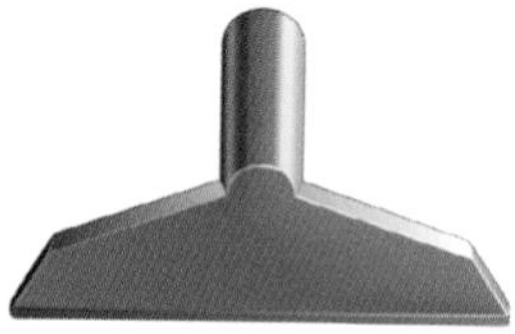

upholstery nozzle
Accessory for vacuuming dust and dirt from fabric.

dusting brush
Accessory for vacuuming dust from various surfaces.

crevice tool
Accessory for vacuuming dust and dirt from hard-to-reach places.

floor brush
Accessory equipped with bristles to avoid scratching the floor while vacuuming.

domestic appliances

range hood
Ventilation appliance expelling or recycling air that contains cooking fumes and odors.

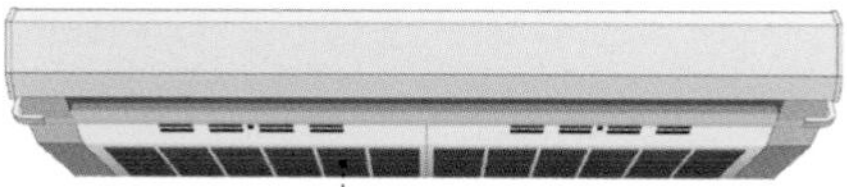

filter
Device catching the cooking grease.

surface element
Heating element on which cooking takes place.

tubular element
Spiral-shaped electric resistor that heats up as a current passes through it.

terminal
Metal part making electric contact.

drip bowl
Small container placed beneath the surface element to catch cooking spills.

trim ring
Decorative part supporting the drip bowl and surface element.

gas rang
Appliance for cooking foo equipped with gas-fed burners ar an ove

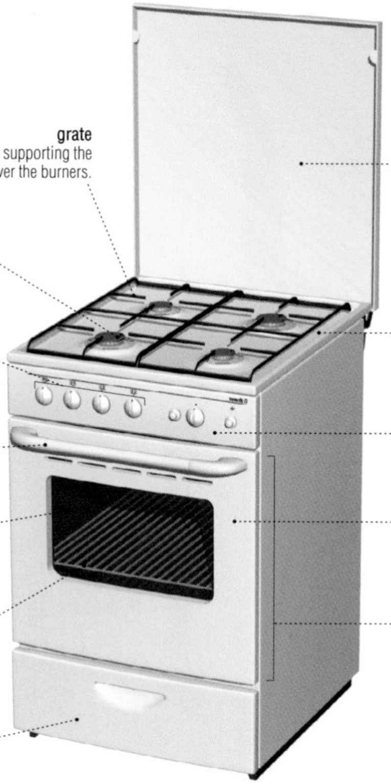

grate
Metal grille supporting the cookware over the burners.

burner
Device producing a flame in order to cook food.

burner control knobs
Instrument for starting and stopping the supply of gas and for controlling its flow.

handle
Part for opening and closing the oven door.

window
Thick window for looking inside the oven.

rack
Metal grille for supporting cookware; its height is adjustable.

drawer
Sliding drawer at the bottom of the range in which sundry cookware is stored.

lid
Flat top that is lowered to cover th appliance's cooktop when not in use.

cooktop
Surface of the range on which the burners are arranged.

control panel
Panel containing the programmin keys for the burners and the oven.

door

oven
Closed part of the range, equippec with an upper heating element (broiler) and a lower heating eleme in which food is cooked or heated.

electric rang
Electric appliance for cooking fooc equipped with surface elements c griddles and an over

oven control knob
Instruments for turning on the oven and controlling the mode of cooking and temperature.

clock timer
Multifunction timekeeping mechanism; it shows the time, times cooking duration, starts the oven at a preset time, etc.

backguard
Vertical part across the back of the range containing the appliance's various controls.

timed outlet
Electric-feed device for switching on an appliance at a preset time.

cooktop
Surface of the range on which the elements are arranged.

rack
Metal grille for supporting cookware; its height is adjustable.

oven
Closed part of the range, equipped with an upper heating element (broiler) and a lower heating element, in which food is cooked or heated.

drawer
Sliding drawer at the bottom of the range in which sundry cookware is stored.

signal lamp
Light showing that a surface element is on.

control knob
Instrument for making or cutting electric contact and for regulating the intensity of the surface elements' heat.

control panel
Panel containing the programming keys.

surface element
Heating element on which cooking takes place.

cooktop edge
Protruding edge along the sides of the cooking surface.

handle
Part for opening and closing the oven door.

window
Thick window for looking inside the oven.

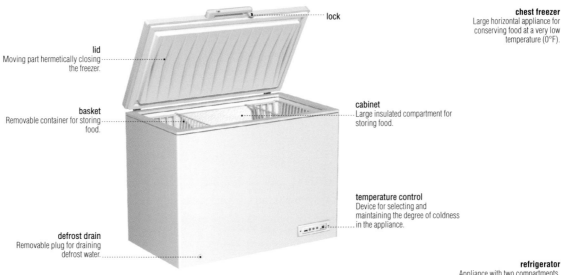

chest freezer
Large horizontal appliance for conserving food at a very low temperature (0°F).

lock
lid
Moving part hermetically closing the freezer.
basket
Removable container for storing food.
cabinet
Large insulated compartment for storing food.
temperature control
Device for selecting and maintaining the degree of coldness in the appliance.
defrost drain
Removable plug for draining defrost water.

refrigerator
Appliance with two compartments, one for keeping food cold and the other for freezing it.

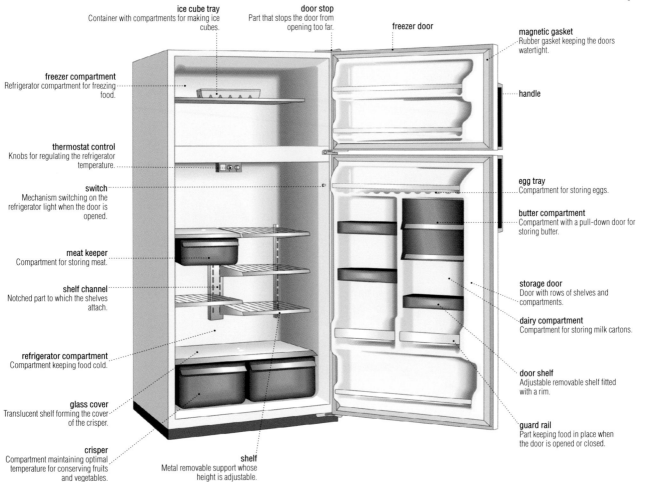

ice cube tray
Container with compartments for making ice cubes.
door stop
Part that stops the door from opening too far.
freezer door
magnetic gasket
Rubber gasket keeping the doors watertight.
freezer compartment
Refrigerator compartment for freezing food.
handle
thermostat control
Knobs for regulating the refrigerator temperature.
switch
Mechanism switching on the refrigerator light when the door is opened.
egg tray
Compartment for storing eggs.
butter compartment
Compartment with a pull-down door for storing butter.
meat keeper
Compartment for storing meat.
shelf channel
Notched part to which the shelves attach.
storage door
Door with rows of shelves and compartments.
dairy compartment
Compartment for storing milk cartons.
refrigerator compartment
Compartment keeping food cold.
door shelf
Adjustable removable shelf fitted with a rim.
glass cover
Translucent shelf forming the cover of the crisper.
guard rail
Part keeping food in place when the door is opened or closed.
crisper
Compartment maintaining optimal temperature for conserving fruits and vegetables.
shelf
Metal removable support whose height is adjustable.

domestic appliances

washer
Household appliance that washes clothes automatically.

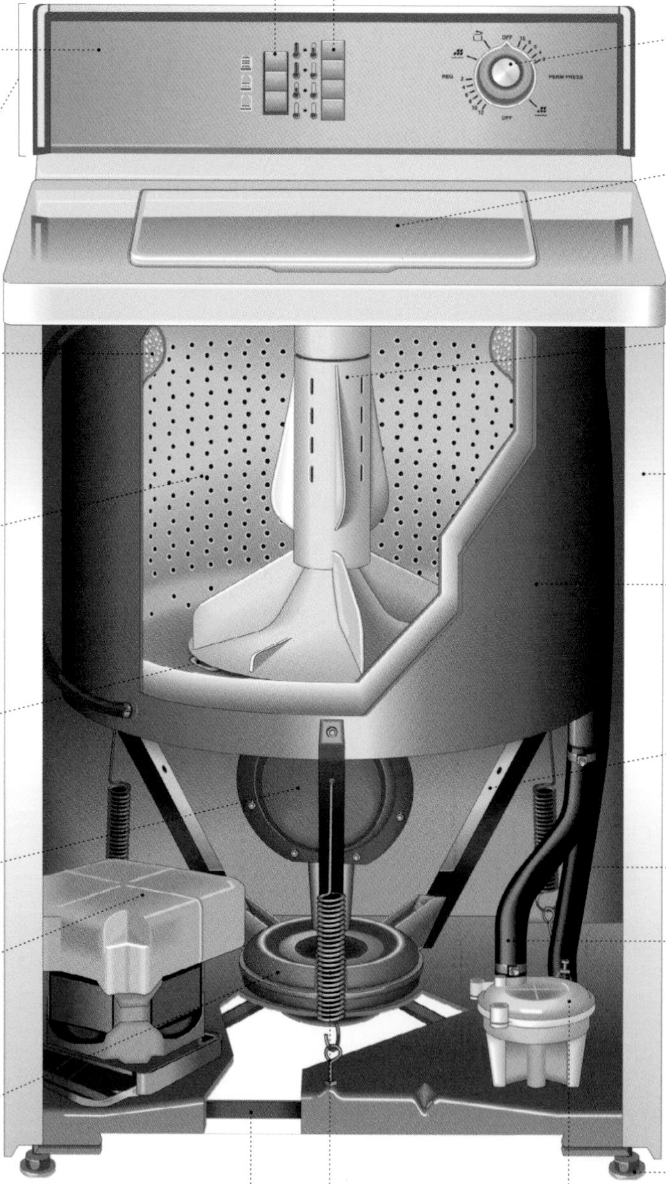

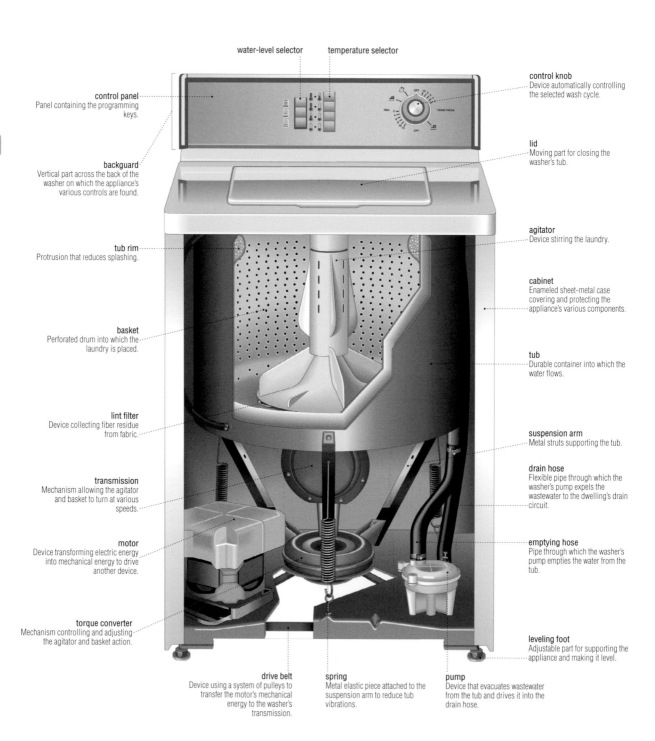

water-level selector

temperature selector

control panel
Panel containing the programming keys.

control knob
Device automatically controlling the selected wash cycle.

lid
Moving part for closing the washer's tub.

backguard
Vertical part across the back of the washer on which the appliance's various controls are found.

agitator
Device stirring the laundry.

tub rim
Protrusion that reduces splashing.

cabinet
Enameled sheet-metal case covering and protecting the appliance's various components.

basket
Perforated drum into which the laundry is placed.

tub
Durable container into which the water flows.

lint filter
Device collecting fiber residue from fabric.

suspension arm
Metal struts supporting the tub.

transmission
Mechanism allowing the agitator and basket to turn at various speeds.

drain hose
Flexible pipe through which the washer's pump expels the wastewater to the dwelling's drain circuit.

motor
Device transforming electric energy into mechanical energy to drive another device.

emptying hose
Pipe through which the washer's pump empties the water from the tub.

torque converter
Mechanism controlling and adjusting the agitator and basket action.

leveling foot
Adjustable part for supporting the appliance and making it level.

drive belt
Device using a system of pulleys to transfer the motor's mechanical energy to the washer's transmission.

spring
Metal elastic piece attached to the suspension arm to reduce tub vibrations.

pump
Device that evacuates wastewater from the tub and drives it into the drain hose.

electric dryer
Appliance for automatically drying laundry.

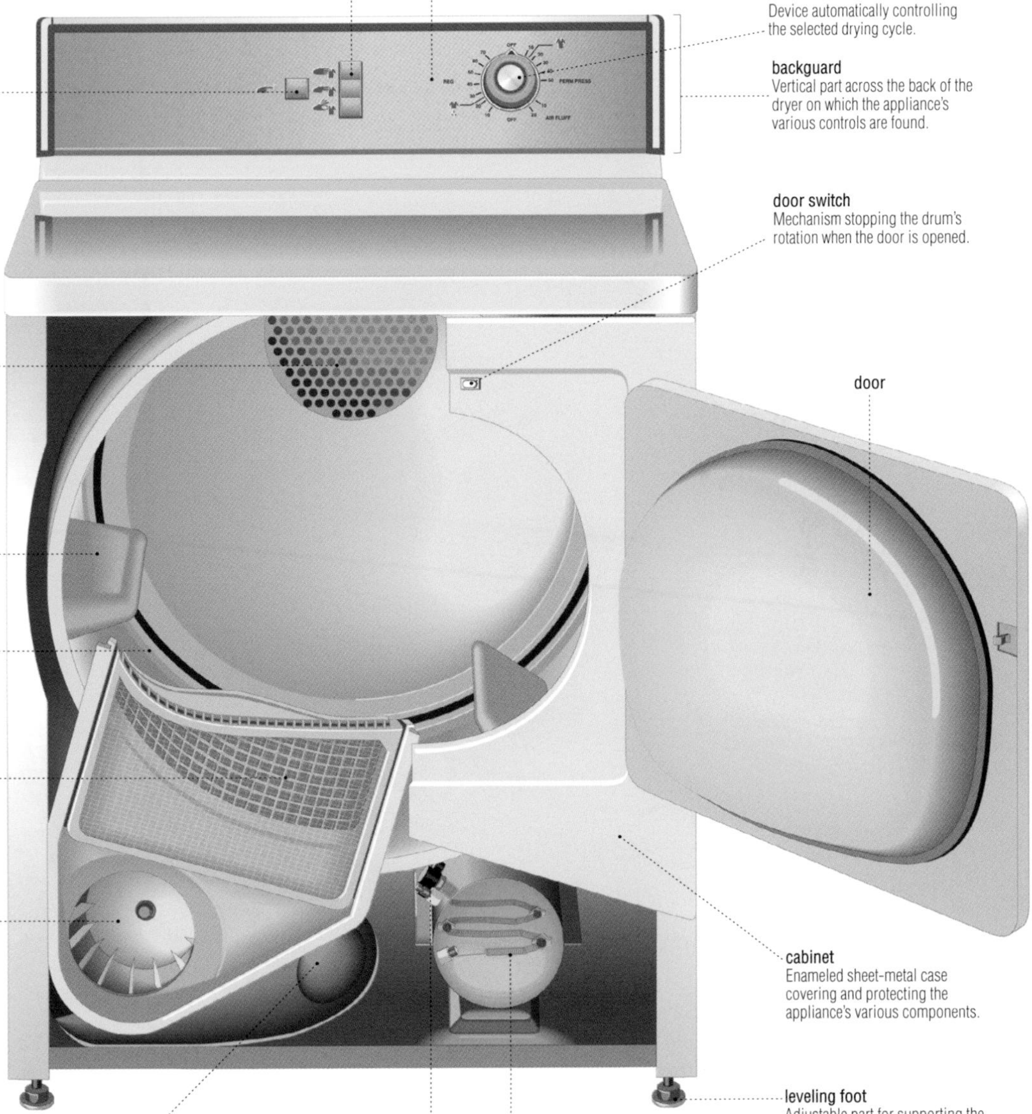
control panel
Panel containing the programming keys.
temperature selector
control knob
Device automatically controlling the selected drying cycle.
start switch
backguard
Vertical part across the back of the dryer on which the appliance's various controls are found.
door switch
Mechanism stopping the drum's rotation when the door is opened.
heating duct
Conduit in which air is heated and directed toward the drum.
door
vane
Part causing the laundry to tumble while drying.
drum
Cylinder whose rotation tumbles the laundry to dry it.
lint trap
Device collecting fiber residue from fabric.
fan
Device circulating the hot air in the drum.
cabinet
Enameled sheet-metal case covering and protecting the appliance's various components.
leveling foot
Adjustable part for supporting the appliance and making it level.
motor
Device transforming electric energy into mechanical energy to drive another device.
safety thermostat
Device interrupting the current if the heating element temperature is too high.
heating element
Electric resistor heating the air before it enters the drum.

domestic appliances

control panel
Panel containing the programming keys.

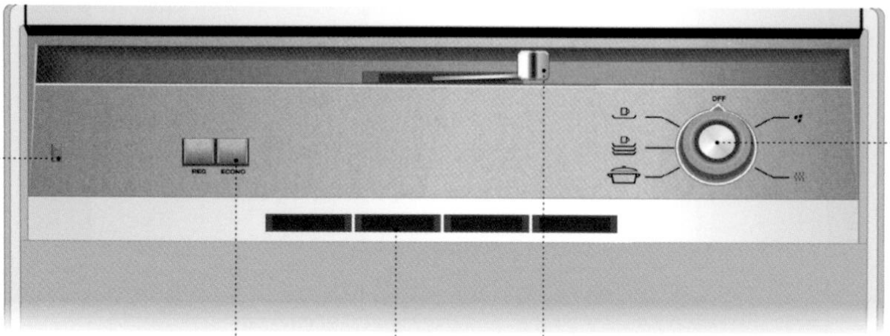

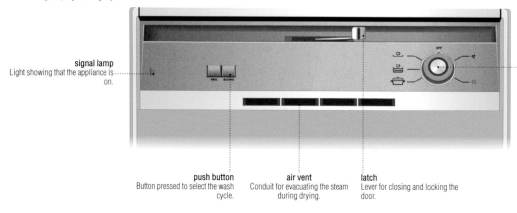

signal lamp
Light showing that the appliance is on.

control knob
Device automatically controlling the selected wash cycle.

push button
Button pressed to select the wash cycle.

air vent
Conduit for evacuating the steam during drying.

latch
Lever for closing and locking the door.

dishwasher
Appliance designed to automatically wash and dry dishes.

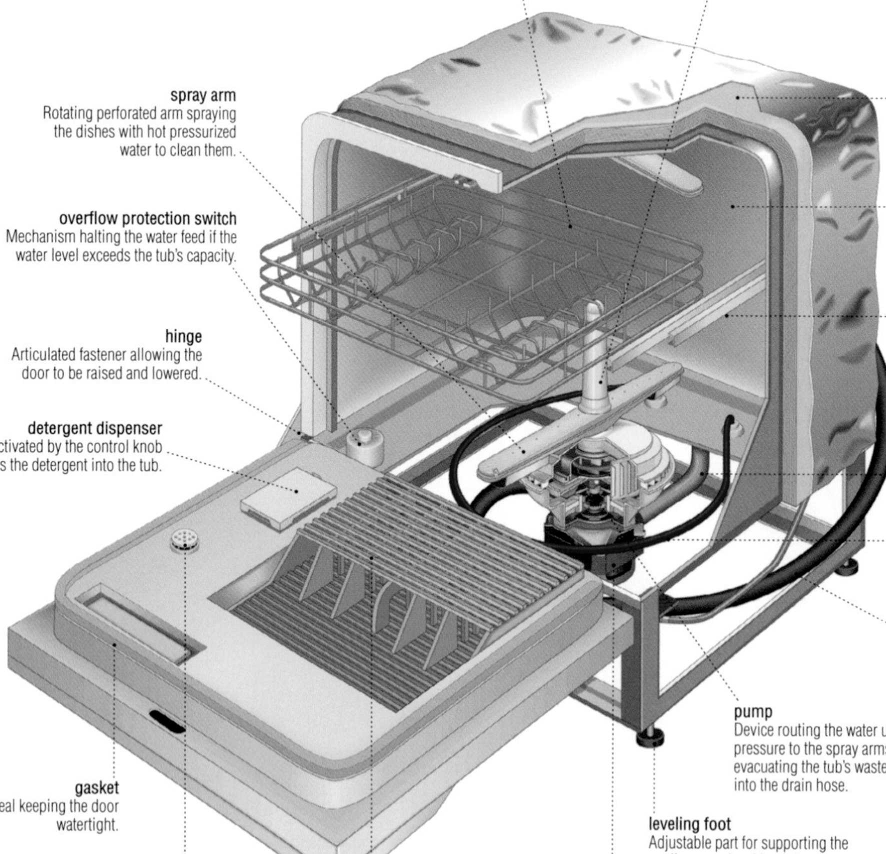

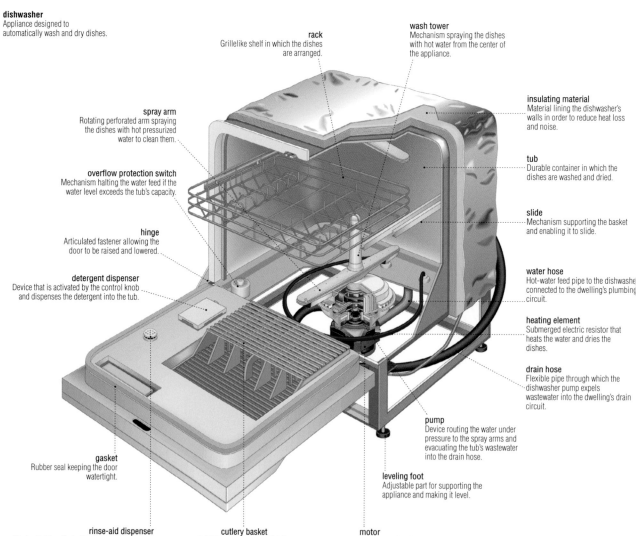

rack
Grillelike shelf in which the dishes are arranged.

wash tower
Mechanism spraying the dishes with hot water from the center of the appliance.

spray arm
Rotating perforated arm spraying the dishes with hot pressurized water to clean them.

insulating material
Material lining the dishwasher's walls in order to reduce heat loss and noise.

tub
Durable container in which the dishes are washed and dried.

overflow protection switch
Mechanism halting the water feed if the water level exceeds the tub's capacity.

slide
Mechanism supporting the basket and enabling it to slide.

hinge
Articulated fastener allowing the door to be raised and lowered.

water hose
Hot-water feed pipe to the dishwashe connected to the dwelling's plumbin circuit.

detergent dispenser
Device that is activated by the control knob and dispenses the detergent into the tub.

heating element
Submerged electric resistor that heats the water and dries the dishes.

drain hose
Flexible pipe through which the dishwasher pump expels wastewater into the dwelling's drain circuit.

pump
Device routing the water under pressure to the spray arms and evacuating the tub's wastewater into the drain hose.

gasket
Rubber seal keeping the door watertight.

leveling foot
Adjustable part for supporting the appliance and making it level.

rinse-aid dispenser
Device that is activated by the control knob and dispenses a rinsing agent into the tub.

cutlery basket
Grillelike container in which the cutlery is placed.

motor
Device transforming electric energy into mechanical energy to drive another device.

household equipment

Objects used for cleaning a dwelling.

kitchen towel
Piece of cloth used to dry dishes, furniture and so on.

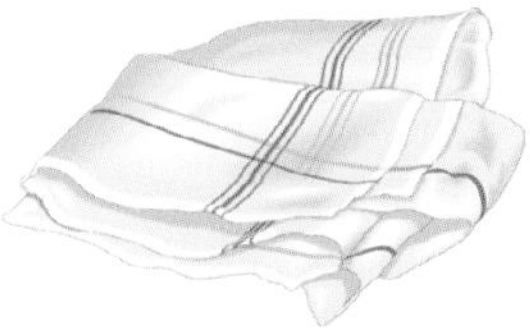

dustpan
Instrument used to collect dust and dirt.

broom
Instrument equipped with fibers attached to a handle for collecting dust and dirt.

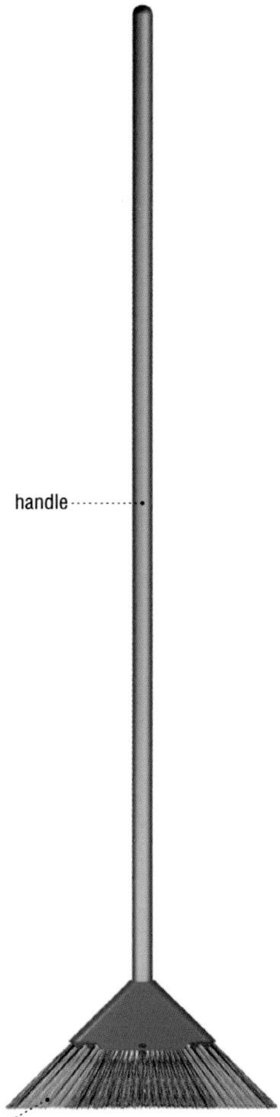

handle
fibers
Relatively rigid fabric strands for scrubbing and cleaning.

mop
Instrument equipped with fabric strips attached to a handle for washing floors.

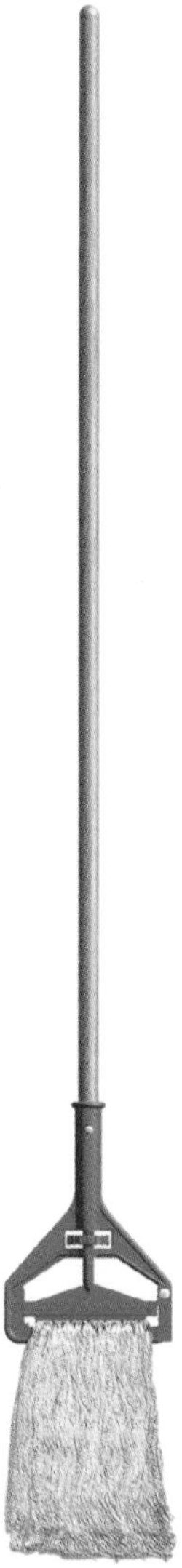

scouring pad
Object with one abrasive surface for cleaning and scouring, and a spongy surface for wiping objects and surfaces.

brush
Utensil with fibers attached to a mounting used to scrub and clean.

block
fibers
Relatively rigid fabric strands for scrubbing and cleaning.

refuse container
Container into which household trash is placed.

pail
Container for carrying water used for household chores.

pouring spout
handle
Part shaped like a semicircle for gripping the pail.

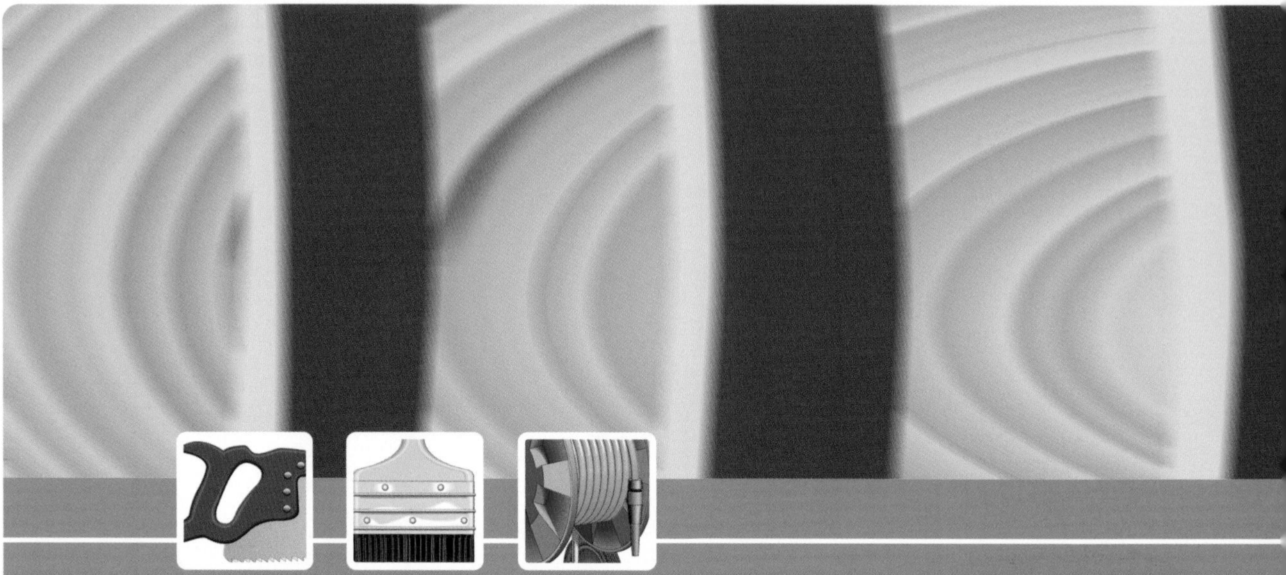

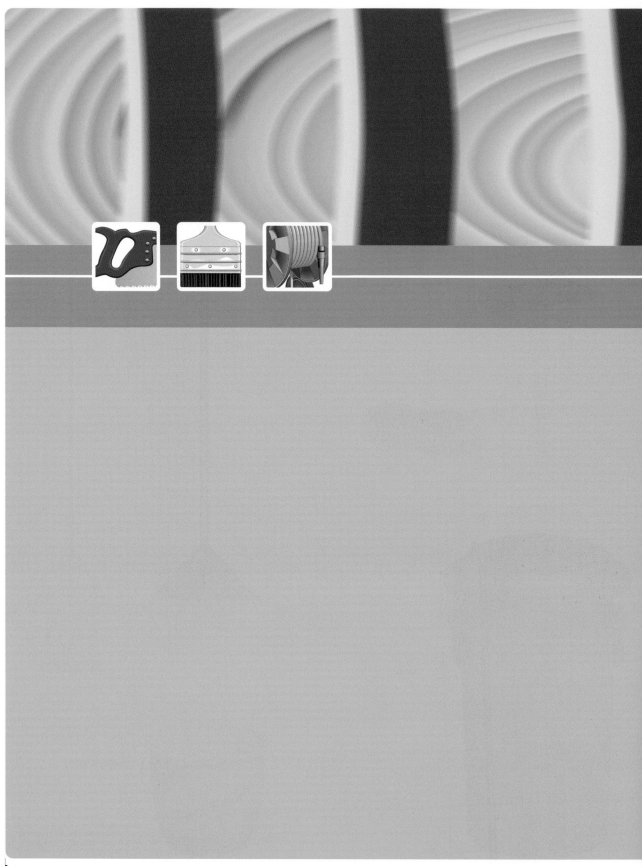

DO-IT-YOURSELF AND GARDENING

basic building materials

Components that, when assembled, form the structure of a building.

brick

Block of compressed baked clay, laid in rows with the help of mortar to form various masonry work, such as walls, partitions and chimneys.

solid brick
Small brick, not perforated, used especially in building or covering various types of walls.

perforated brick
Small brick with vertical holes, whose dimensions are usually no greater than 40% of the brick.

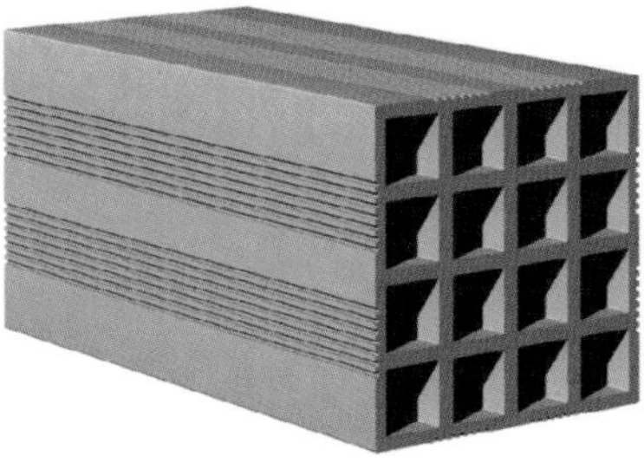

hollow brick
Large brick, over 40% of which is composed of horizontal cells.

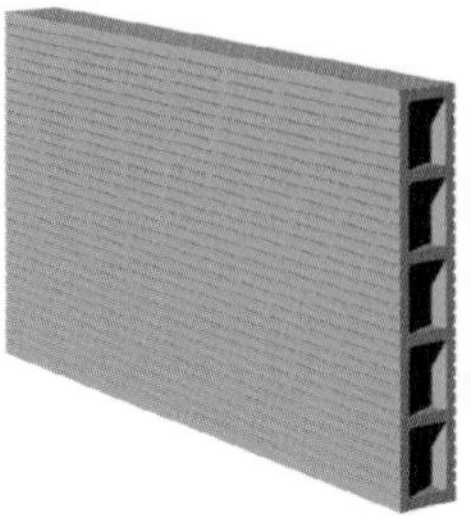

partition tile
Hollow brick, usually worked wit the help of plaster, used to build c line partitions.

brick wall

firebrick
Brick that can withstand very high temperatures without deforming.

mortar
Mixture of fine aggregates (pebbles, gravel, sand), water and a binder (cement or lime), used to join masonry components or to coat masonry after it is completed.

stone

Block of mineral matter, of irregular shape, used for masonry or as a facing.

flagstone
Flat stone of irregular shape, used to cover floors and walls.

rubble
Small block of rough or crudely carved stone, usually assembled with the help of mortar to build a wall.

cut stone
Stone cut in regular shapes so that it can be fitted without a joint or with very thin joints.

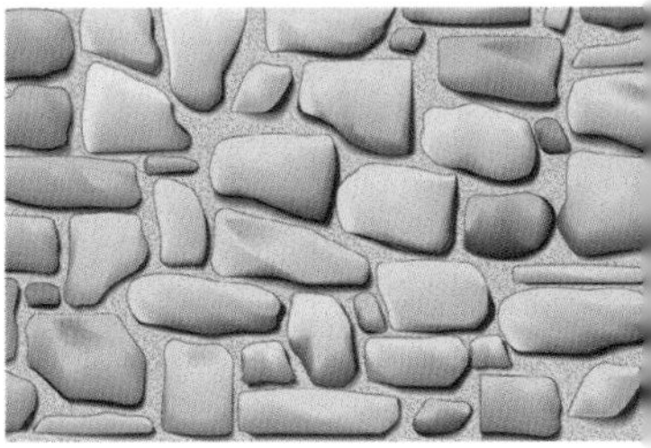

stone wall

concrete

Material composed of aggregates (pebbles, gravel, sand) and water mixed together by a binder (cement or lime) that, after hardening in a mold, forms a substance that is resistant to compression.

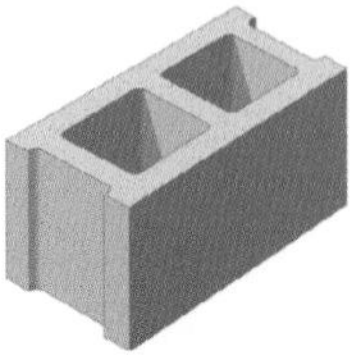

concrete block
Concrete component, solid or hollow, used mainly in the construction of masonry as a substitute for brick.

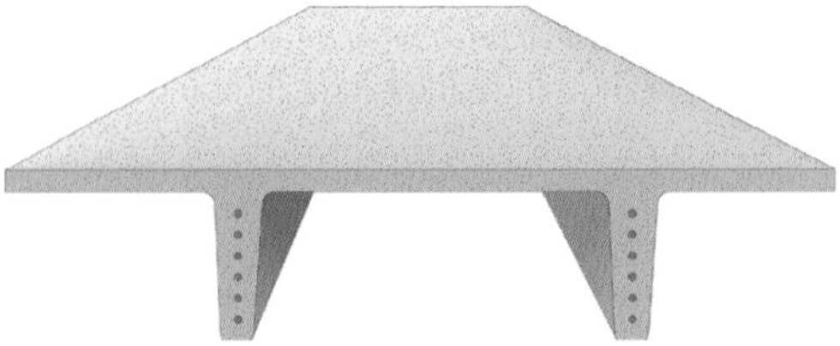

prestressed concrete
Concrete whose steel bars are stretched before cooling, creating a highly resistant and durable material; it is used to manufacture beams with long spans.

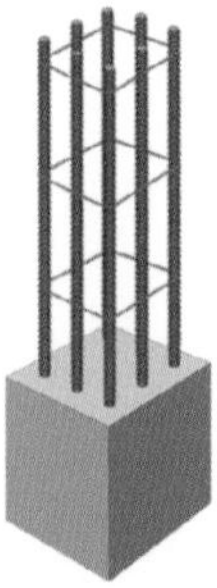

reinforced concrete
Concrete reinforced by steel bars, often used in the manufacture of load-bearing units in a building.

steel
Iron- and carbon-based metal, ve durable, frequently used in structures.

covering materials

Materials covering a surface, usually for the purpose of protecting or decorating it.

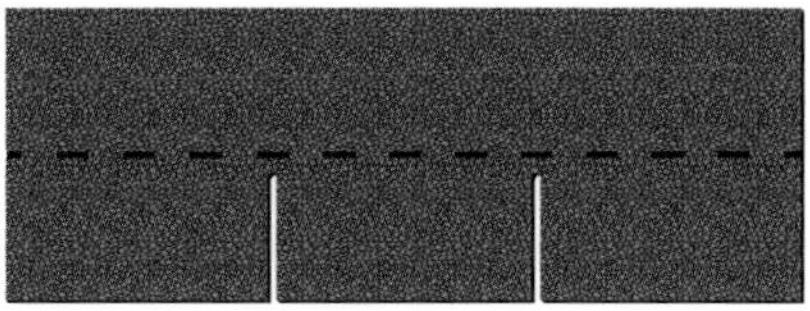

asphalt shingle
Roof-covering material, made with a framework (fiberglass, felt) coated with bitumen and covered with fine aggregate.

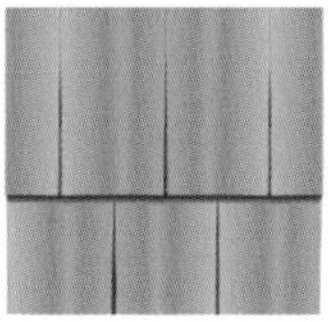

shingle
Small wooden plank used to cover roofs and walls that are especially exposed to inclement weather.

diamond mesh metal lath
Metal grid used as a framework or support for plaster and other coatings.

tar paper
Paper usually stapled directly to the roof or exterior walls, under the covering, in order to enhance impermeability.

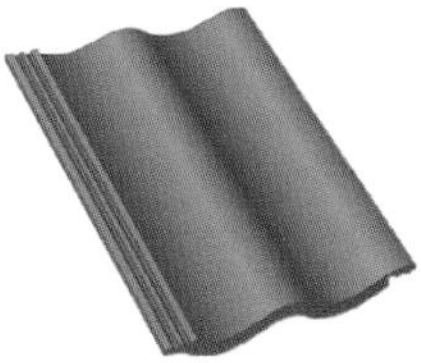

tile
Hard surface, usually made of baked molded clay, used as a covering for roofs.

gypsum tile
Small molded-plaster component, solid or hollow, with holes on the sides; it is used to construct and repair walls.

floor tile
Small flat component of regular shape, made from various materials and used for covering floors and walls.

gypsum board
Large panel made of a layer of plaster covered with paperboard, usually used as a finishing material on a dwelling's interior walls.

insulating materials

Materials impeding the transfer of heat to the outside, or cold to the inside, of a building or a duct.

loose fill insulation

spring-metal insulation

vinyl insulation

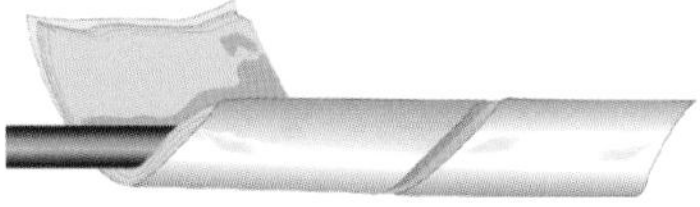

pipe-wrapping insulation

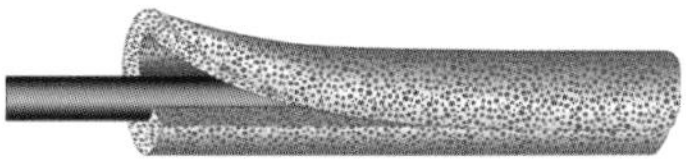

molded insulation

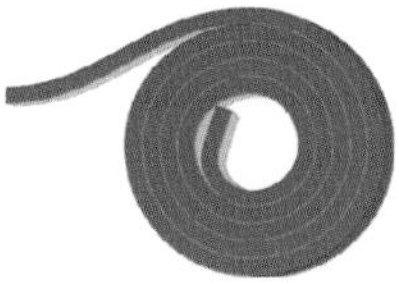

foam-rubber insulation

blanket insulation

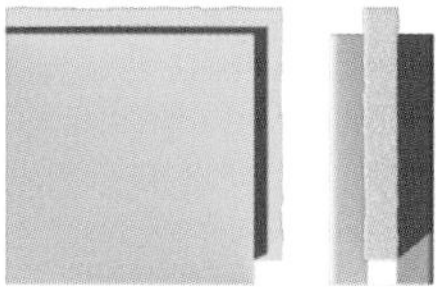

board insulation

foam insulation

wood

Relatively hard, dense substance forming the trunks, branches and roots of trees. The wood of each species has distinct characteristics.

section of a log

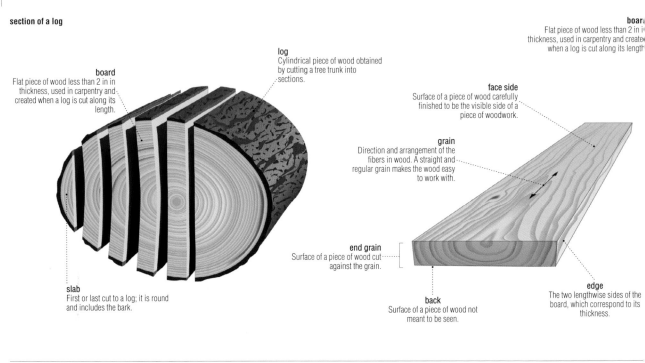

log
Cylindrical piece of wood obtained by cutting a tree trunk into sections.

board
Flat piece of wood less than 2 in in thickness, used in carpentry and created when a log is cut along its length.

slab
First or last cut to a log; it is round and includes the bark.

boar
Flat piece of wood less than 2 in i
thickness, used in carpentry and create
when a log is cut along its lengt

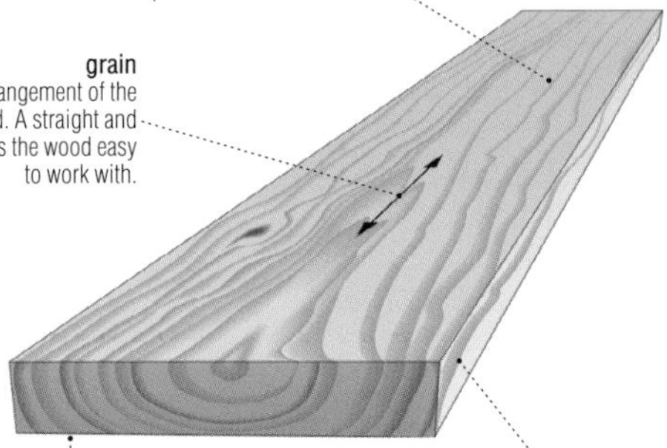

face side
Surface of a piece of wood carefully finished to be the visible side of a piece of woodwork.

grain
Direction and arrangement of the fibers in wood. A straight and regular grain makes the wood easy to work with.

end grain
Surface of a piece of wood cut against the grain.

back
Surface of a piece of wood not meant to be seen.

edge
The two lengthwise sides of the board, which correspond to its thickness.

wood-based materials

Materials obtained when a log is converted; also when various wood elements are assembled or agglomerated.

peeled veneer
Thin sheet obtained from rotating a log on a peeling machine and applying a blade (lathe) to it.

ply
Thin sheets of wood (veneer) of equal thickness, used for the manufacture of plywood.

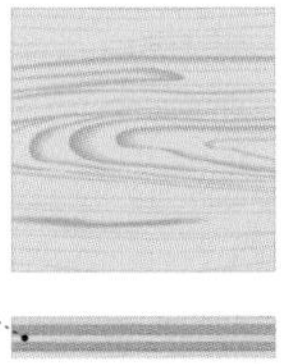

multi-ply plywood
Panel made from at least five layers, each glued to the other with their respective grains running perpendicular to the adjacent layer.

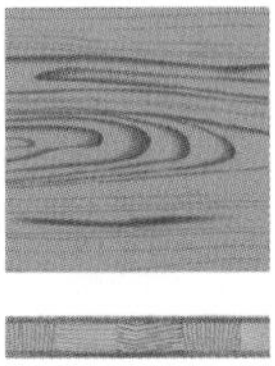

blockboard
Panel made of two layers sandwiching a central part (core), which is made up of wid
slats glued side by side.

laminboard
Panel made of two layers sandwiching a central part (core), which is made up of wide slats, or laminations, glued side by side.

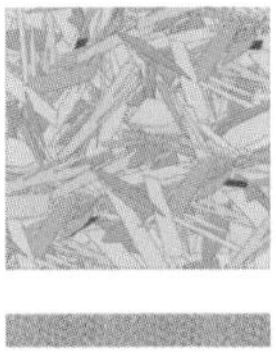

waferboard
Panel made from wood chips mixed with glu
then pressed at a high temperature to bond the

hardboard
Smooth and homogeneous board made when minuscule wood fibers are soaked in resin and pressed at a high temperature.

perforated hardboard

plastic-laminated particle board
Particle board with a melamine surface layer that is hard, smooth and easy to wash.

particle board
Board made from sawdust mixed with glue, then pressed at a high temperature to bond them.

carpentry: nailing tools

Carpentry: working with wood to build simple furniture or carry out construction and renovation projects.

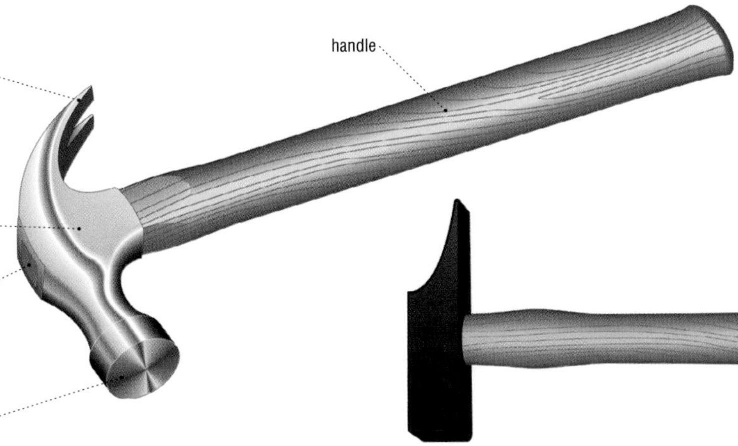

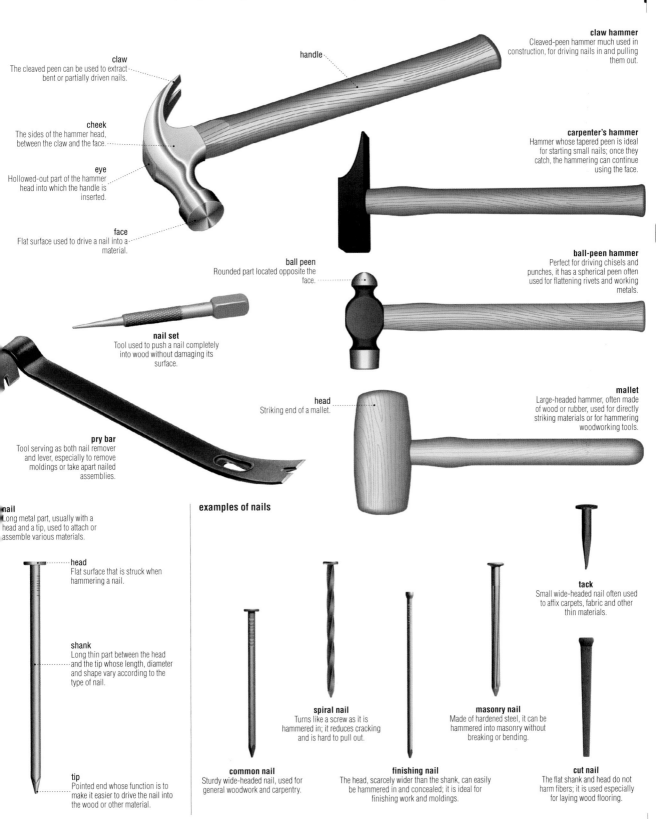

claw hammer
Cleaved-peen hammer much used in construction, for driving nails in and pulling them out.

handle

claw
The cleaved peen can be used to extract bent or partially driven nails.

cheek
The sides of the hammer head, between the claw and the face.

eye
Hollowed-out part of the hammer head into which the handle is inserted.

face
Flat surface used to drive a nail into a material.

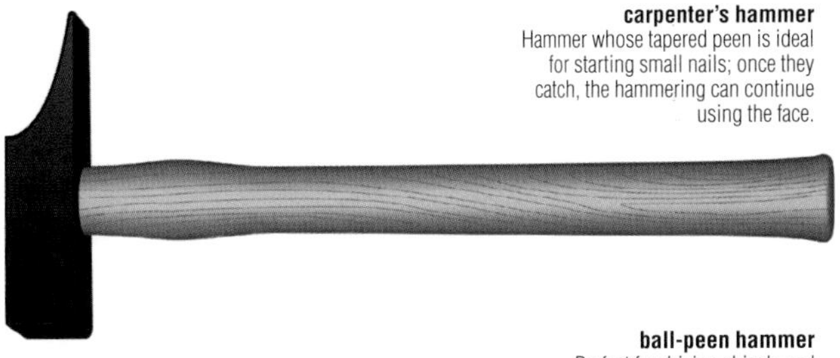

carpenter's hammer
Hammer whose tapered peen is ideal for starting small nails; once they catch, the hammering can continue using the face.

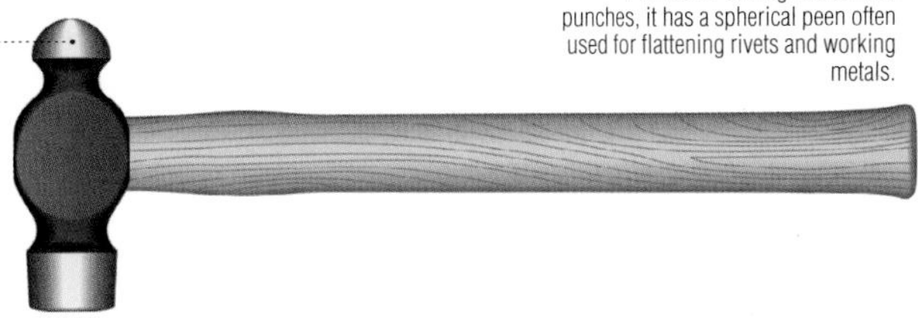

ball-peen hammer
Perfect for driving chisels and punches, it has a spherical peen often used for flattening rivets and working metals.

ball peen
Rounded part located opposite the face.

nail set
Tool used to push a nail completely into wood without damaging its surface.

pry bar
Tool serving as both nail remover and lever, especially to remove moldings or take apart nailed assemblies.

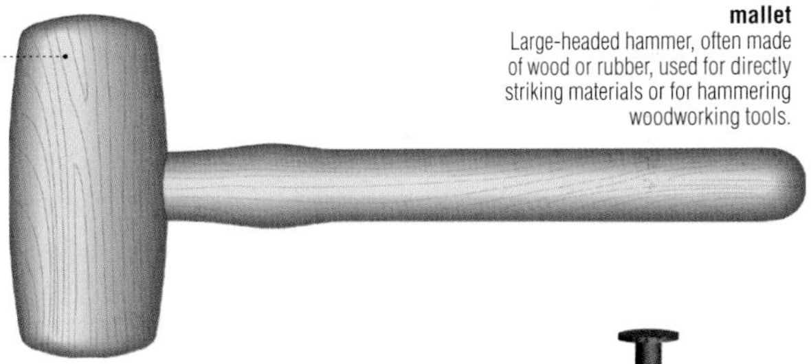

mallet
Large-headed hammer, often made of wood or rubber, used for directly striking materials or for hammering woodworking tools.

head
Striking end of a mallet.

nail
Long metal part, usually with a head and a tip, used to attach or assemble various materials.

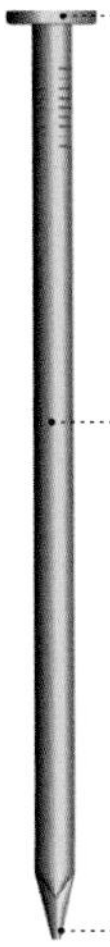

head
Flat surface that is struck when hammering a nail.

shank
Long thin part between the head and the tip whose length, diameter and shape vary according to the type of nail.

tip
Pointed end whose function is to make it easier to drive the nail into the wood or other material.

examples of nails

common nail
Sturdy wide-headed nail, used for general woodwork and carpentry.

spiral nail
Turns like a screw as it is hammered in; it reduces cracking and is hard to pull out.

finishing nail
The head, scarcely wider than the shank, can easily be hammered in and concealed; it is ideal for finishing work and moldings.

masonry nail
Made of hardened steel, it can be hammered into masonry without breaking or bending.

tack
Small wide-headed nail often used to affix carpets, fabric and other thin materials.

cut nail
The flat shank and head do not harm fibers; it is used especially for laying wood flooring.

carpentry: screwing tools

screwdriver
Hand tool used for tightening or loosening screws and bolts by applying a rotating motion.

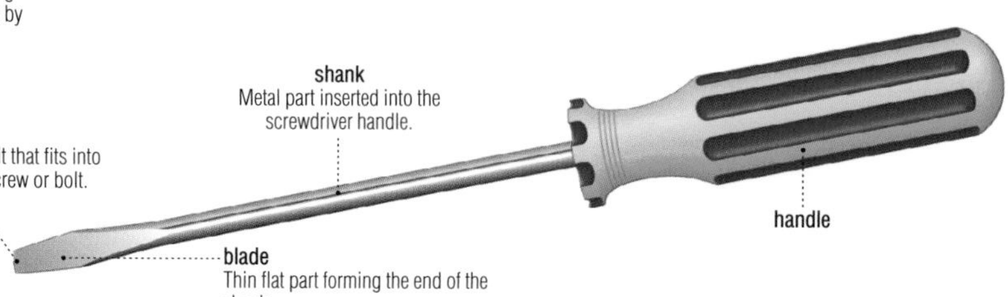
shank
Metal part inserted into the screwdriver handle.
tip
End of the blade or bit that fits into the groove of the screw or bolt.
handle
blade
Thin flat part forming the end of the shank.

spiral screwdriver
Screwdriver with interchangeable bits fitted into a mechanism for screwing or unscrewing by simply pushing the handle.

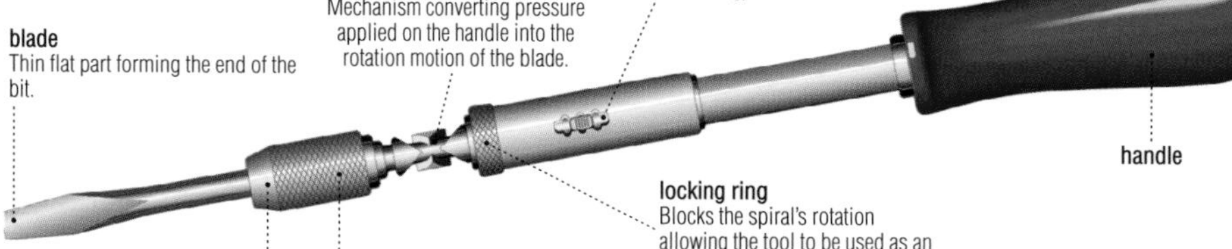
ratchet
Mechanical instrument for setting the direction of rotation of the spiral and the blade (screwing or unscrewing).
spiral
Mechanism converting pressure applied on the handle into the rotation motion of the blade.
blade
Thin flat part forming the end of the bit.
handle
locking ring
Blocks the spiral's rotation allowing the tool to be used as an ordinary screwdriver.
jaw
The parts of the chuck that grip the tool to keep it firmly in place.
chuck
Device with jaws for attaching the bit or drill to the tool.

cordless screwdriver
Battery-driven screwdriver with interchangeable bits, used for tightening and loosening screws and bolts.

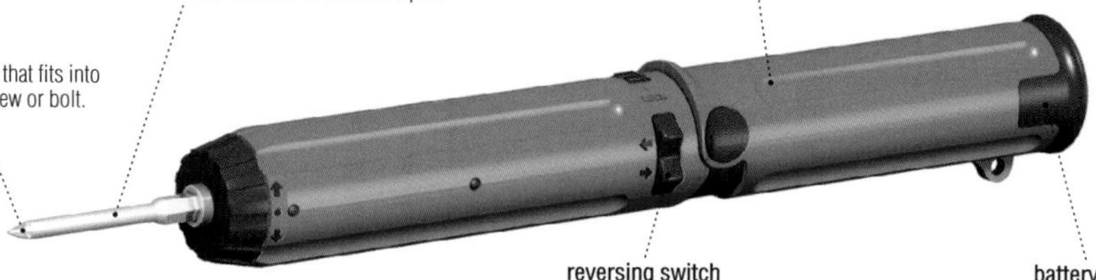
bit
Detachable shank rotated by the motor to screw or unscrew a part.
handle
tip
End of the blade or bit that fits into the groove of the screw or bolt.
reversing switch
Switch for selecting the bit's direction of rotation (screwing or unscrewing).
battery
Device that stores chemical energy while charging, then converts it to electric energy.

screw
Metal part, composed of a head and a partially or completely threaded shank, used to secure fastenings and assemblies.

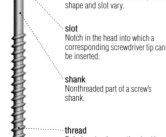

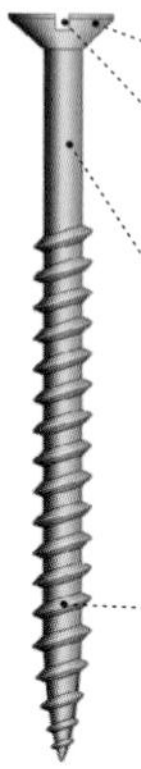
head
Broadened end of the screw, whose shape and slot vary.
slot
Notch in the head into which a corresponding screwdriver tip can be inserted.
shank
Nonthreaded part of a screw's shank.
thread
Spiral protrusion on the shank's surface, for driving the screw into a solid material by turning.

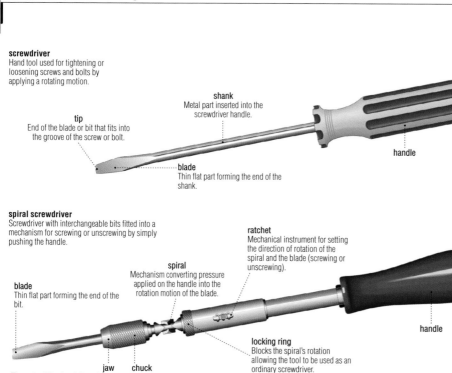

examples of tips

Tip: end part of the blade or bit; it adapts to the screw or bolt's groove.

square-headed tip
Tip whose end cut fits into a socket-head screw.

cross-headed tip
Tip whose crisscross end fits into a cross-headed screw.

flat tip
Tip that fits into a screw's slot.

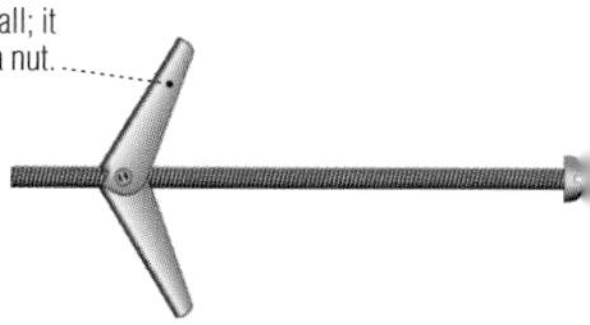
spring wing
The spring under the wing keeps it folded along the bolt as it passes through a hole made in the wall; it then opens and acts like a nut.

toggle bolt
Part composed of a bolt with wings that deploy inside the wall to ensure a solid fastening.

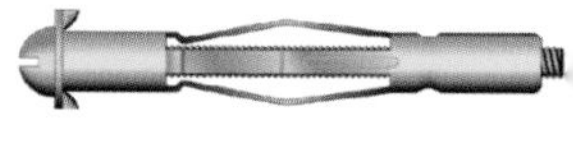

expansion bolt
Part composed of a bolt in a sheath that bends when the bolt is inserted, then flattens out against the inside of the wall.

examples of heads

Head: broadened end of the screw, whose shape and slot vary.

flat head
Slotted head becoming flush with the surface of the wood when completely embedded.

round head
Slotted rounded head whose base is flat so that it presses against the wood or metal surface.

one-way head
Slotted head having two opposing quarters removed so that the screw can be turned one way only, making it very difficult to unscrew.

Phillips
Head whose crisscross indentation keeps the screwdriver in the middle of the head, providing a very firm grip.

socket head
Head with a square socket that varies in size.

oval head
Slotted head topped with an ornamental spherical part that is not driven beneath the wood's surface.

carpentry: sawing tools

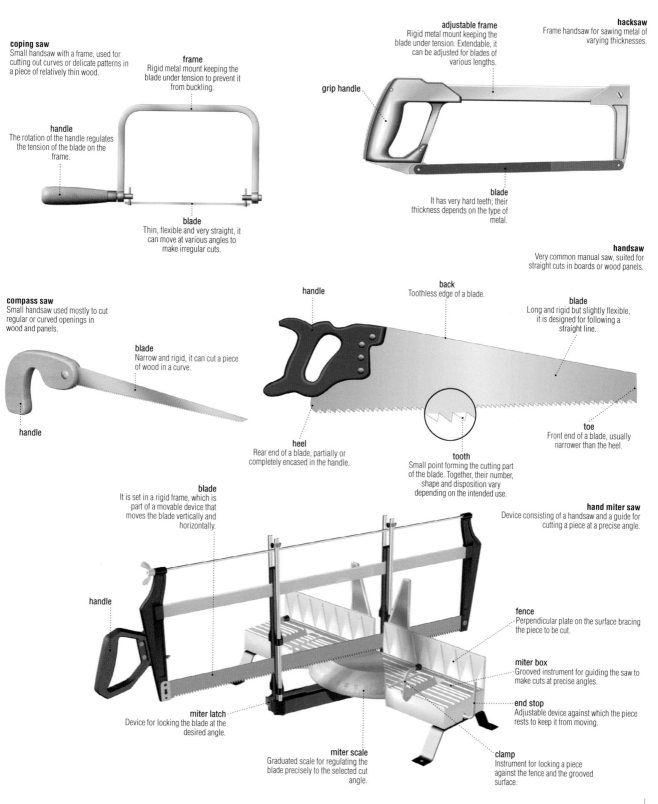

coping saw
Small handsaw with a frame, used for cutting out curves or delicate patterns in a piece of relatively thin wood.

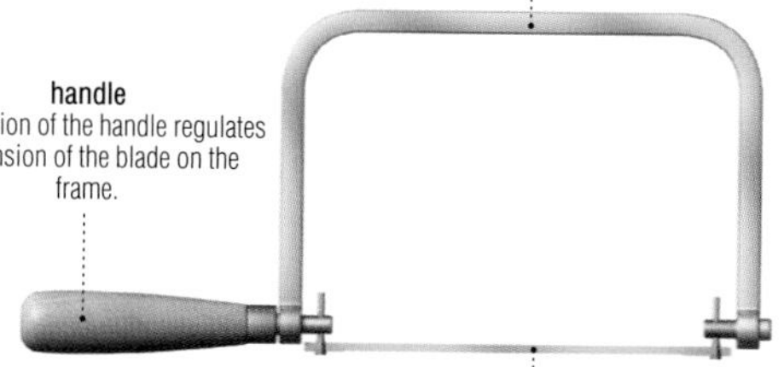
frame
Rigid metal mount keeping the blade under tension to prevent it from buckling.
handle
The rotation of the handle regulates the tension of the blade on the frame.
blade
Thin, flexible and very straight, it can move at various angles to make irregular cuts.

hacksaw
Frame handsaw for sawing metal of varying thicknesses.

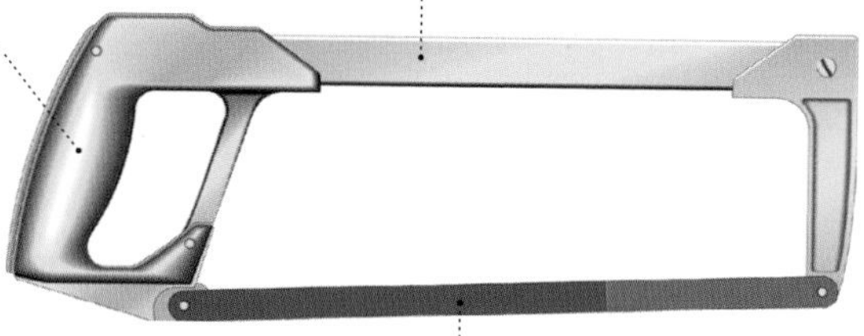
adjustable frame
Rigid metal mount keeping the blade under tension. Extendable, it can be adjusted for blades of various lengths.
grip handle
blade
It has very hard teeth; their thickness depends on the type of metal.

compass saw
Small handsaw used mostly to cut regular or curved openings in wood and panels.

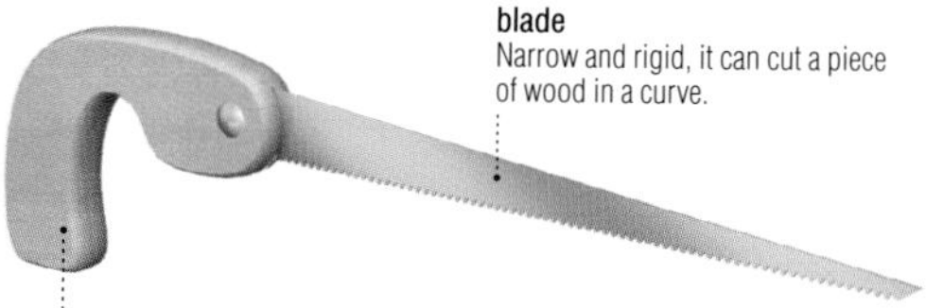
blade
Narrow and rigid, it can cut a piece of wood in a curve.
handle

handsaw
Very common manual saw, suited for straight cuts in boards or wood panels.

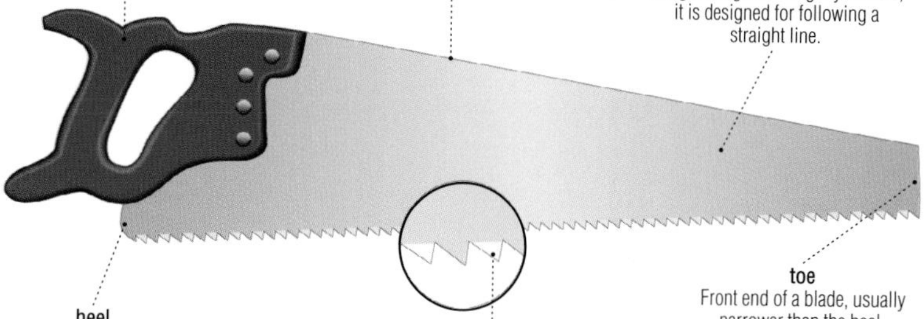
handle
back
Toothless edge of a blade.
blade
Long and rigid but slightly flexible, it is designed for following a straight line.
heel
Rear end of a blade, partially or completely encased in the handle.
tooth
Small point forming the cutting part of the blade. Together, their number, shape and disposition vary depending on the intended use.
toe
Front end of a blade, usually narrower than the heel.

hand miter saw
Device consisting of a handsaw and a guide for cutting a piece at a precise angle.

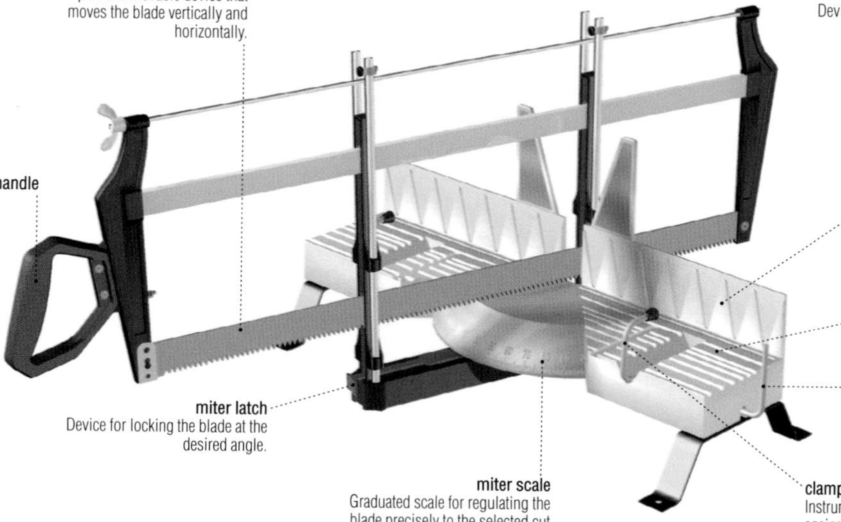
blade
It is set in a rigid frame, which is part of a movable device that moves the blade vertically and horizontally.
handle
fence
Perpendicular plate on the surface bracing the piece to be cut.
miter box
Grooved instrument for guiding the saw to make cuts at precise angles.
end stop
Adjustable device against which the piece rests to keep it from moving.
miter latch
Device for locking the blade at the desired angle.
miter scale
Graduated scale for regulating the blade precisely to the selected cut angle.
clamp
Instrument for locking a piece against the fence and the grooved surface.

carpentry: sawing tools

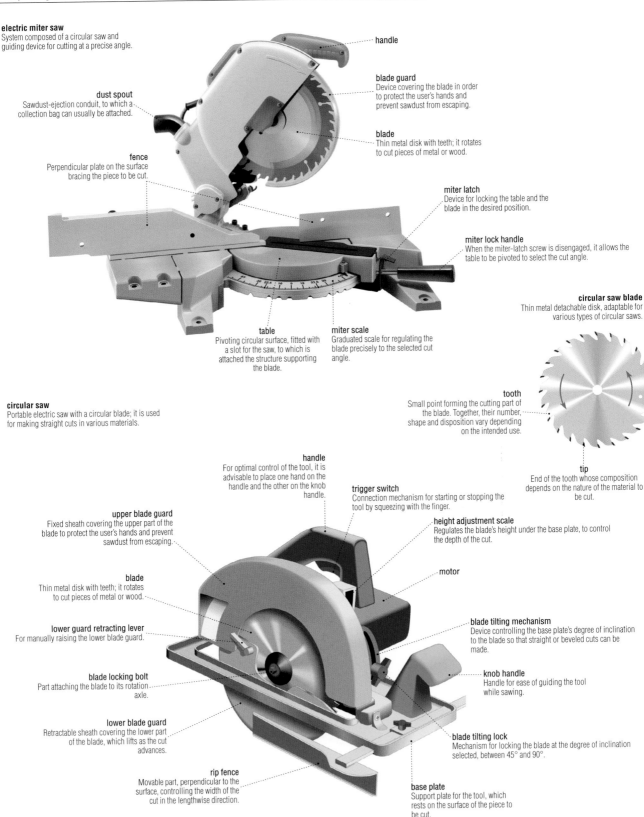

electric miter saw
System composed of a circular saw and guiding device for cutting at a precise angle.

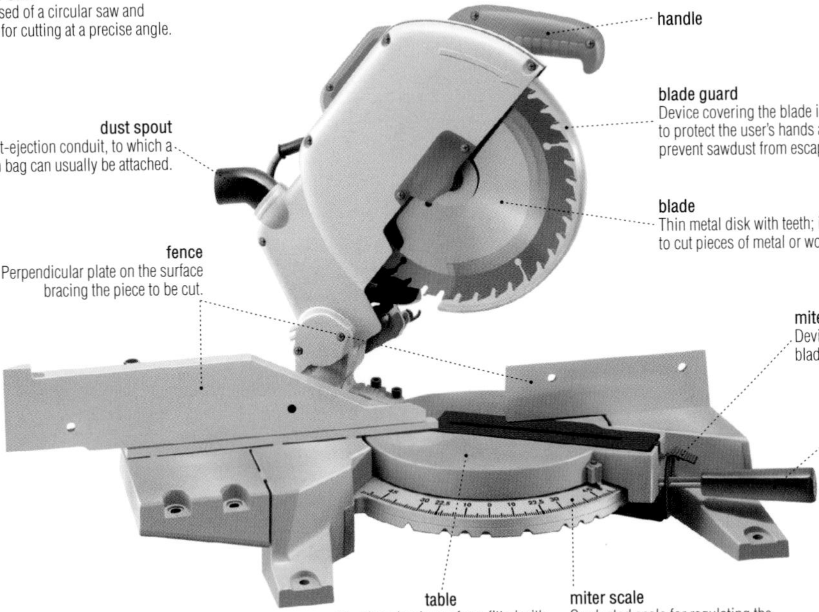
handle
blade guard
Device covering the blade in order to protect the user's hands and prevent sawdust from escaping.
dust spout
Sawdust-ejection conduit, to which a collection bag can usually be attached.
blade
Thin metal disk with teeth; it rotates to cut pieces of metal or wood.
fence
Perpendicular plate on the surface bracing the piece to be cut.
miter latch
Device for locking the table and the blade in the desired position.
miter lock handle
When the miter-latch screw is disengaged, it allows the table to be pivoted to select the cut angle.
table
Pivoting circular surface, fitted with a slot for the saw, to which is attached the structure supporting the blade.
miter scale
Graduated scale for regulating the blade precisely to the selected cut angle.

circular saw blade
Thin metal detachable disk, adaptable for various types of circular saws.

tooth
Small point forming the cutting part of the blade. Together, their number, shape and disposition vary depending on the intended use.
tip
End of the tooth whose composition depends on the nature of the material to be cut.

circular saw
Portable electric saw with a circular blade; it is used for making straight cuts in various materials.

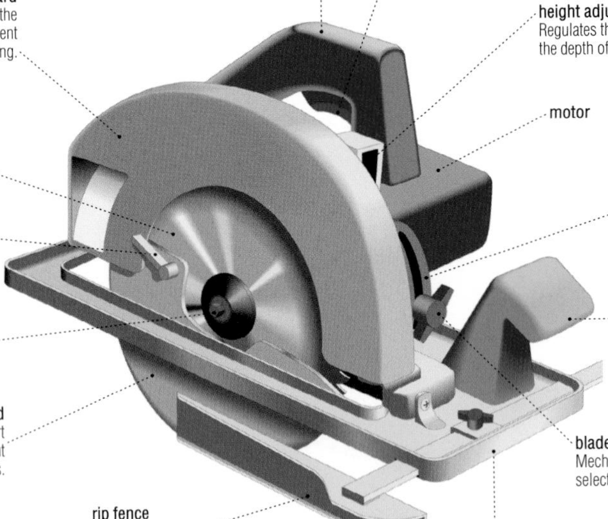
handle
For optimal control of the tool, it is advisable to place one hand on the handle and the other on the knob handle.
trigger switch
Connection mechanism for starting or stopping the tool by squeezing with the finger.
upper blade guard
Fixed sheath covering the upper part of the blade to protect the user's hands and prevent sawdust from escaping.
height adjustment scale
Regulates the blade's height under the base plate, to control the depth of the cut.
motor
blade
Thin metal disk with teeth; it rotates to cut pieces of metal or wood.
blade tilting mechanism
Device controlling the base plate's degree of inclination to the blade so that straight or beveled cuts can be made.
lower guard retracting lever
For manually raising the lower blade guard.
knob handle
Handle for ease of guiding the tool while sawing.
blade locking bolt
Part attaching the blade to its rotation axle.
lower blade guard
Retractable sheath covering the lower part of the blade, which lifts as the cut advances.
blade tilting lock
Mechanism for locking the blade at the degree of inclination selected, between 45° and 90°.
rip fence
Movable part, perpendicular to the surface, controlling the width of the cut in the lengthwise direction.
base plate
Support plate for the tool, which rests on the surface of the piece to be cut.

carpentry: sawing tools

jig saw
Electric portable saw whose blade has an up-and-down motion; it is used for making straight or curved cuts.

speed selector switch
Device for controlling the rhythm of the blade's up-and-down motion.
trigger switch
Connection mechanism for starting or stopping the tool by squeezing with the finger.
orbital-action selector
Mechanism regulating the pendular motion of the blade. A slight or no pendular motion gives a better finish but takes longer.
chip cover
Protective cover preventing sawdust and fragments from flying toward the user or toward the cutting line.
blade
It moves up and down but can also move from front to back, which increases the efficiency of the sawing.
base
The tool's support plate, which rests on the surface of the piece to be cut. It can be inclined to make beveled cuts.
lock-on button
Device locking the switch in position to keep the saw working continuously during long or complex cuts.
handle
power cord
Flexible electric wire housing the leads connecting the appliance to the electric circuit.

table saw
Set composed of a table, a circular saw and guiding accessories, for making straight or oblique cuts to large pieces.

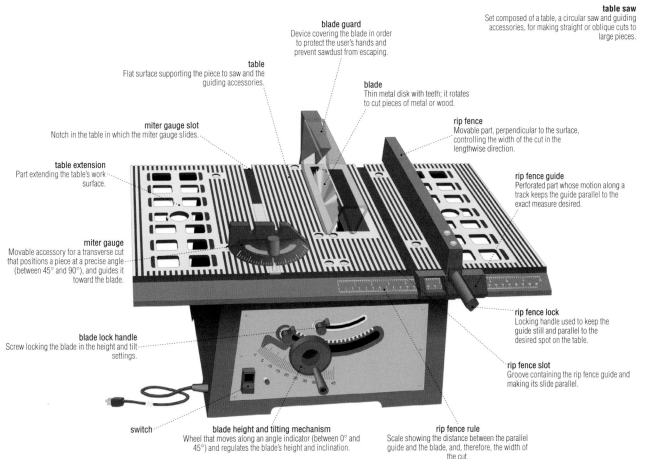

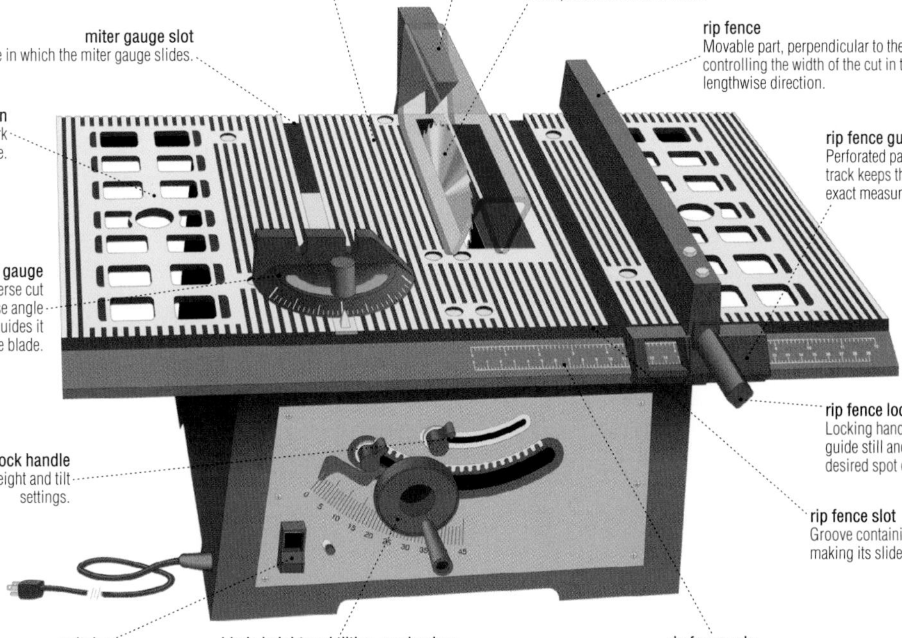
blade guard
Device covering the blade in order to protect the user's hands and prevent sawdust from escaping.
table
Flat surface supporting the piece to saw and the guiding accessories.
blade
Thin metal disk with teeth; it rotates to cut pieces of metal or wood.
miter gauge slot
Notch in the table in which the miter gauge slides.
rip fence
Movable part, perpendicular to the surface, controlling the width of the cut in the lengthwise direction.
table extension
Part extending the table's work surface.
rip fence guide
Perforated part whose motion along a track keeps the guide parallel to the exact measure desired.
miter gauge
Movable accessory for a transverse cut that positions a piece at a precise angle (between 45° and 90°), and guides it toward the blade.
rip fence lock
Locking handle used to keep the guide still and parallel to the desired spot on the table.
blade lock handle
Screw locking the blade in the height and tilt settings.
rip fence slot
Groove containing the rip fence guide and making its slide parallel.
switch
blade height and tilting mechanism
Wheel that moves along an angle indicator (between 0° and 45°) and regulates the blade's height and inclination.
rip fence rule
Scale showing the distance between the parallel guide and the blade, and, therefore, the width of the cut.

carpentry: drilling tools

cordless drill-driver
Battery-powered portable electric tool used to drill holes and to screw and unscrew.

speed selector switch
Device for regulating the chuck's rotation speed.

screwdriver bit
Detachable tool inserted into the chuck and used for screwing and unscrewing.

keyless chuck
Chuck with a regulating ring that automatically tightens the jaws on the tool's shank.

torque adjustment collar
Ringlike part controlling the tool's torsion power. Screwing needs lower torque than drilling.

battery pack
Device that stores chemical energy while charging, then converts it to electric energy.

trigger switch
Connection mechanism for starting or stopping the tool by squeezing with the finger.

reversing switch
Switch for selecting the bit's or drill's direction of rotation (screwing or unscrewing).

charger
Electrical device for recharging the tool's battery.

battery pack
Device that stores chemical energy while charging, then converts it to electric energy.

chuck key
Part for tightening and loosening the chuck's jaws.

electric drill
Portable electric tool using variable-speed rotation to pierce holes and to drive drills and bits.

nameplate
Plate showing the name of the manufacturer, the serial number of the device and certain technical characteristics (tension, power, etc.).

warning plate
Plate providing certain safety precautions to avoid injuries caused by misuse of the tool.

switch lock
Device locking the switch in position to keep the saw working for a prolonged period.

housing

chuck
Device with jaws for attaching the bit or drill to the tool.

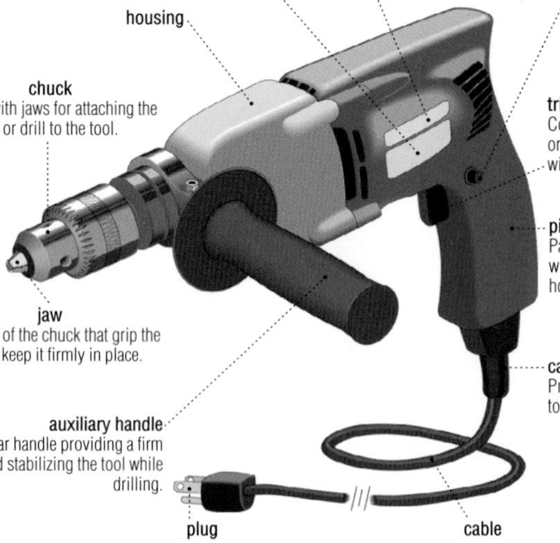

trigger switch
Connection mechanism for starting or stopping the tool by squeezing with the finger.

pistol grip handle
Part shaped like a pistol grip so the wrist remains straight while holding the tool.

jaw
The parts of the chuck that grip the tool to keep it firmly in place.

cable sleeve
Protective casing around the cable to avoid twisting and prevent wear.

auxiliary handle
Tubular handle providing a firm grip and stabilizing the tool while drilling.

plug

cable

examples of bits and drills

While both are intended for drilling holes in various materials, the bit has a center point while the drill ends in a cutting-edge cone.

twist bit
Bit with a spiral drill flu
straight uniform holes
practical for inserting c

shank
Upper part of the bit, on which pressure from the chuck's jaws is exerted.

flute
Groove in the body of the bit that removes debris from the hole while drilling.

body
Part between the shank and the lead screw.

fluted land
Cutting edge forming the edge of the land.

land
Flat surface between the flutes.

lead screw
Threaded pointed end for cent
the bit in the middle of the ho
the start of drilling.

solid center auger bit
Bit made up of a central shank encircled by a twist; it is very durable and especially designed for making deep holes.

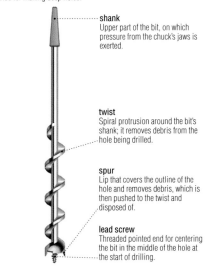

shank
Upper part of the bit, on which pressure from the chuck's jaws is exerted.

twist
Spiral protrusion around the bit's shank; it removes debris from the hole being drilled.

spur
Lip that covers the outline of the hole and removes debris, which is then pushed to the twist and disposed of.

lead screw
Threaded pointed end for centering the bit in the middle of the hole at the start of drilling.

masonry drill
The carbide and tungsten tip, hard and durable, is designed to drill through material such as brick, concrete and stone.

twist drill
Usually used to drill holes in metal or wood, it is the most common type of drill.

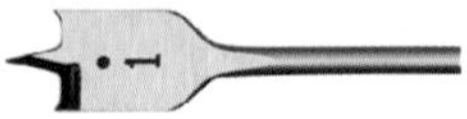

spade bit
Bit designed for shallow holes of wide diameter; it has a long lead screw for positioning on the center of the hole.

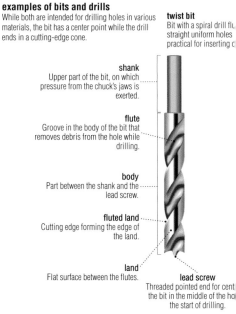

double-twist auger bit
Bit made up of two opposing twists; it re
debris quickly as the hole is drille

carpentry: drilling tools

hand drill
Gear-driven hand tool, used mainly to drill holes in wood, soft metal and plastic.

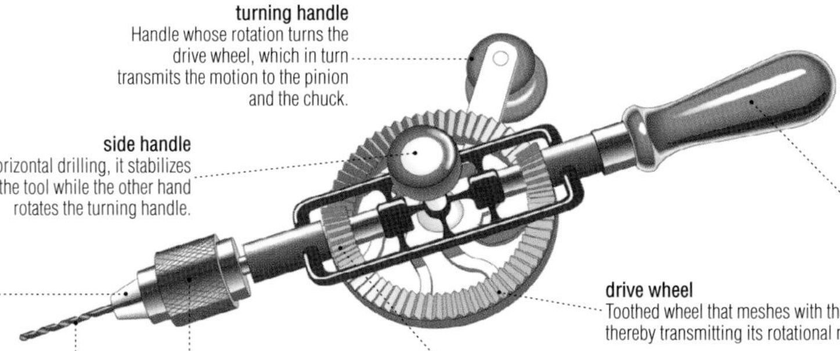

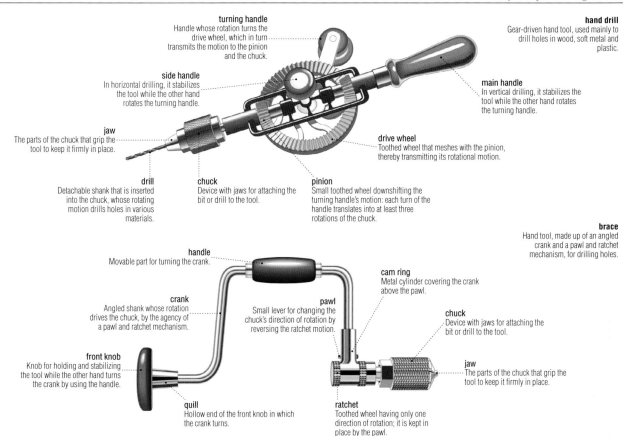

turning handle
Handle whose rotation turns the drive wheel, which in turn transmits the motion to the pinion and the chuck.

side handle
In horizontal drilling, it stabilizes the tool while the other hand rotates the turning handle.

jaw
The parts of the chuck that grip the tool to keep it firmly in place.

drill
Detachable shank that is inserted into the chuck, whose rotating motion drills holes in various materials.

chuck
Device with jaws for attaching the bit or drill to the tool.

pinion
Small toothed wheel downshifting the turning handle's motion: each turn of the handle translates into at least three rotations of the chuck.

drive wheel
Toothed wheel that meshes with the pinion, thereby transmitting its rotational motion.

main handle
In vertical drilling, it stabilizes the tool while the other hand rotates the turning handle.

brace
Hand tool, made up of an angled crank and a pawl and ratchet mechanism, for drilling holes.

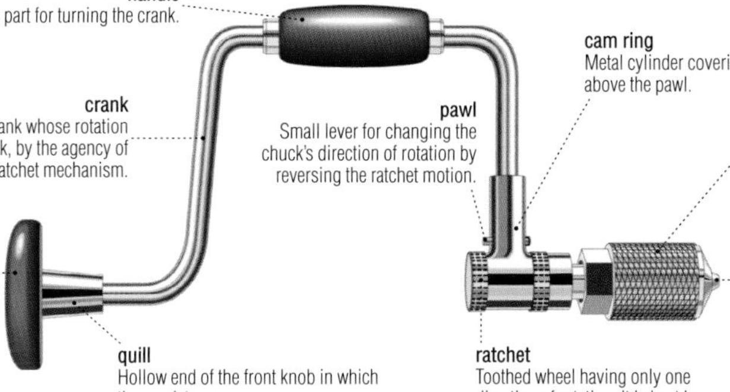

handle
Movable part for turning the crank.

crank
Angled shank whose rotation drives the chuck, by the agency of a pawl and ratchet mechanism.

front knob
Knob for holding and stabilizing the tool while the other hand turns the crank by using the handle.

quill
Hollow end of the front knob in which the crank turns.

pawl
Small lever for changing the chuck's direction of rotation by reversing the ratchet motion.

cam ring
Metal cylinder covering the crank above the pawl.

chuck
Device with jaws for attaching the bit or drill to the tool.

jaw
The parts of the chuck that grip the tool to keep it firmly in place.

ratchet
Toothed wheel having only one direction of rotation; it is kept in place by the pawl.

drill press
Set made up of an electric drill and a table mounted on a column, for drilling holes of a given depth in succession.

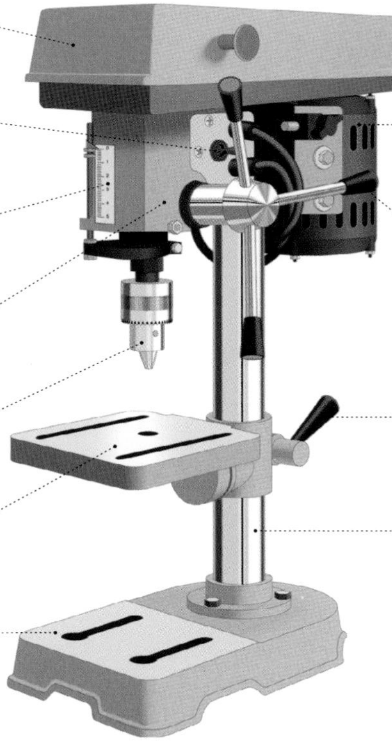

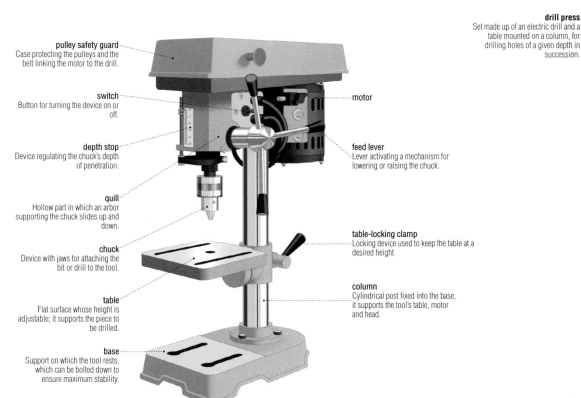

pulley safety guard
Case protecting the pulleys and the belt linking the motor to the drill.

switch
Button for turning the device on or off.

depth stop
Device regulating the chuck's depth of penetration.

quill
Hollow part in which an arbor supporting the chuck slides up and down.

chuck
Device with jaws for attaching the bit or drill to the tool.

table
Flat surface whose height is adjustable; it supports the piece to be drilled.

base
Support on which the tool rests, which can be bolted down to ensure maximum stability.

motor

feed lever
Lever activating a mechanism for lowering or raising the chuck.

table-locking clamp
Locking device used to keep the table at a desired height.

column
Cylindrical post fixed into the base; it supports the tool's table, motor and head.

carpentry: shaping tools

angle grinder
Portable electric tool used for grinding, polishing, shaping and more.

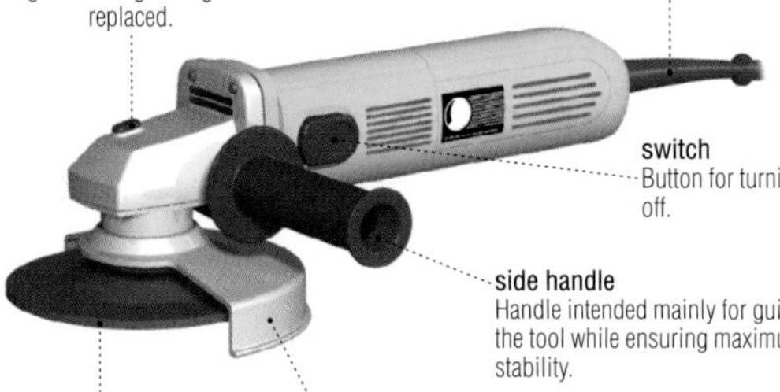

random orbit sander
Portable electric tool whose abrasive disk moves two ways (rotating and eccentric) to sand various types of surface.

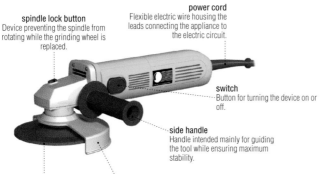

grinding wheel
Somewhat rigid abrasive disk mounted on a grinder's spindle, whose roughness varies with the task (e.g., grinding, polishing, shaping).

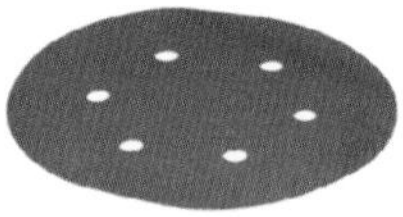

sanding disk
Paper, usually perforated and self-adhesive, that fits the sander's sanding pad.

sand paper
Paper usually coated with glass powder, used by itself or mounted on a tool for smoothing.

router
Portable electric tool using rotating bits to mill moldings, grooves and wood joints.

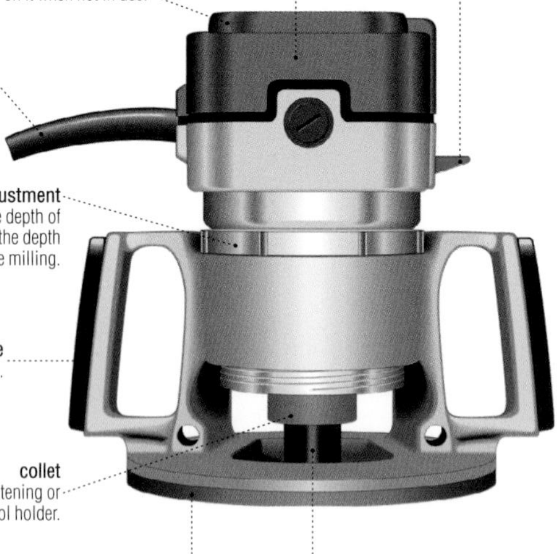

motor
head
Flat top of the router; the tool rests on it when not in use.
switch
Button for turning the device on or off.
cord sleeve
Protective casing around the cable to lessen twisting and prevent wear.
depth adjustment
Device that regulates the depth of the bit, thus controlling the depth of the milling.
guide handle
Used to hold and guide the tool.
collet
Ring-shaped part for tightening or loosening the tool holder.
base
Support plate for the tool, which rests on the surface of the piece to be worked on.
tool holder
Device fitted with jaws for attaching the bit to the router.

examples of bits

Bits: detachable tools fitted with edges or abrasive parts; a router applies a rotating motion on them to mill a piece of work.

rounding-over bit
Depending on the way it is positioned, it is a bit for rounding the edge of a piece of wood or for making a convex molding with a shoulder.

rabbet bit
Bit for cutting an edge at right angles, used especially for making frames and for various cabinetmaking joints.

core box bit
Bit usually used to mill grooves in wood in the shape of semicircles.

dovetail bit
Bit for making cuts shaped like a dove's tail, often used in joining drawers.

cove bit
Bit used especially for concave moldings or for cutting articulating joints for a gate-leg table.

chamfer bit
Bit for beveling edges at a 45° angle to create decorative edges and joints.

plane
Hand tool with a cutting blade, intended mainly for planing a wood surface or to give it a shape (e.g., beveled, chamfered).

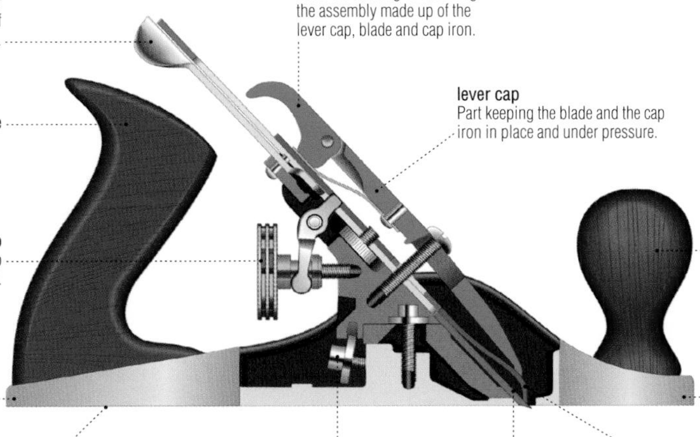

lateral-adjustment lever
Device for aligning the cutting edge of the blade with the plane of the sole.

wedge lever
Lever for holding or releasing the assembly made up of the lever cap, blade and cap iron.

lever cap
Part keeping the blade and the cap iron in place and under pressure.

handle

depth-of-cut adjustment knob
rew for controlling the motion of the blade in relation to the sole; this determines the depth of the cut.

knob
Handle for guiding and stabilizing the tool.

heel
Rear end of the tool.

toe
Front end of the tool.

sole
Support plate, which rests on the surface of the piece to be planed.

frog-adjustment screw
Screw adjusting the blade's slant and, therefore, the width of the opening (mouth) that removes the shavings.

blade
Metal plate whose beveled edge constitutes the cutting edge of the plane.

cap iron
Metal part in apposition to the blade; it breaks off the wood shavings to facilitate their removal.

jointer plane
The longest in the plane family, it is used for planing large pieces of wood and is not thrown off by bumps or indentations.

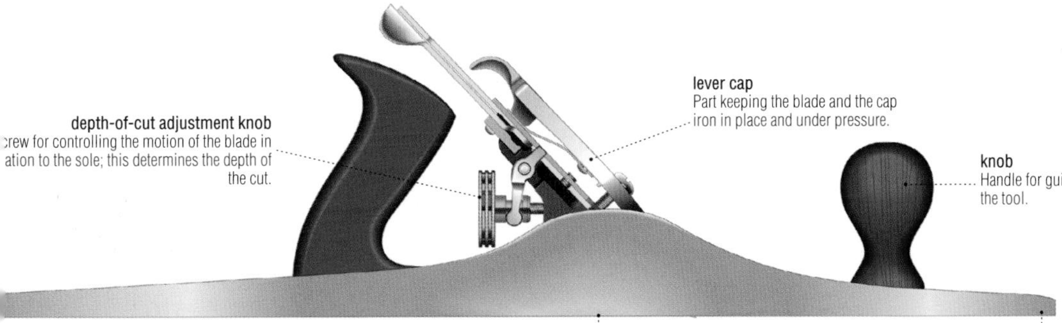

lever cap
Part keeping the blade and the cap iron in place and under pressure.

depth-of-cut adjustment knob
:rew for controlling the motion of the blade in ation to the sole; this determines the depth of the cut.

knob
Handle for guiding and stabilizing the tool.

el
ar end of the tool.

sole
Support plate, which lies on the surface of the piece to be planed.

toe
Front end of the tool.

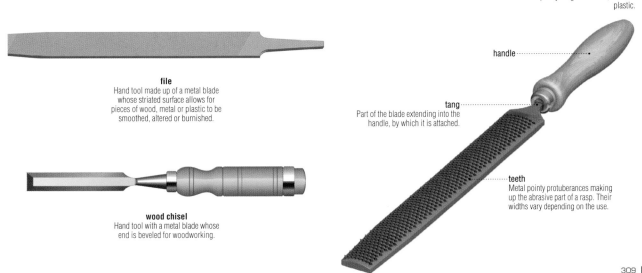

rasp
Hand tool made up of a metal blade whose tooth-covered surface can quickly rough out wood, metal or plastic.

file
Hand tool made up of a metal blade whose striated surface allows for pieces of wood, metal or plastic to be smoothed, altered or burnished.

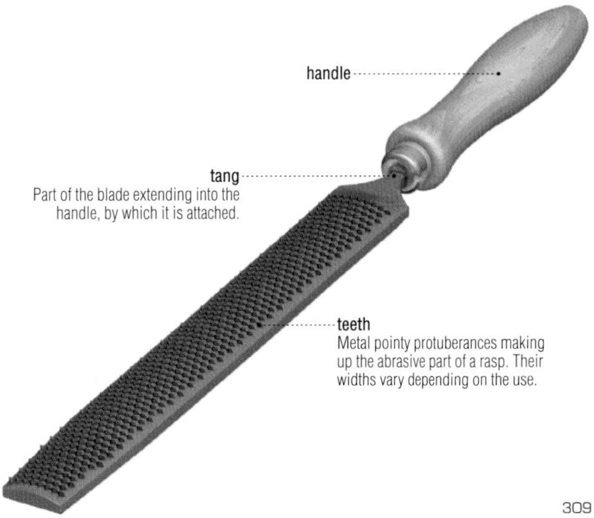

handle

tang
Part of the blade extending into the handle, by which it is attached.

teeth
Metal pointy protuberances making up the abrasive part of a rasp. Their widths vary depending on the use.

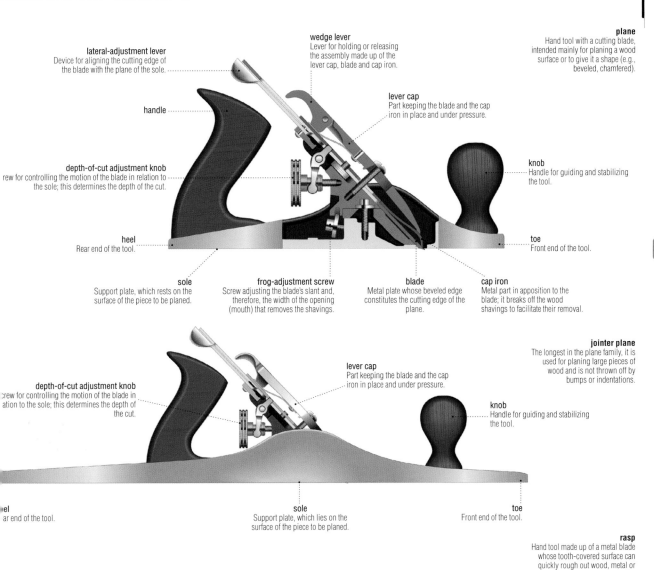

wood chisel
Hand tool with a metal blade whose end is beveled for woodworking.

carpentry: gripping and tightening tools

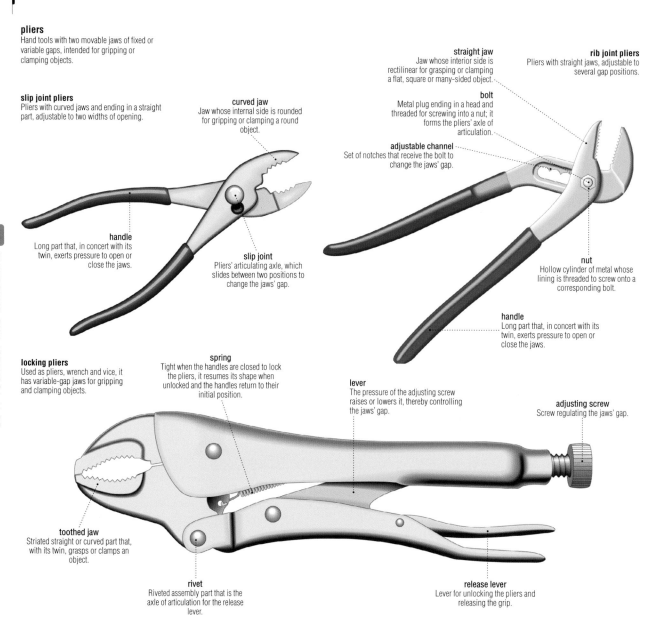

pliers

Hand tools with two movable jaws of fixed or variable gaps, intended for gripping or clamping objects.

slip joint pliers

Pliers with curved jaws and ending in a straight part, adjustable to two widths of opening.

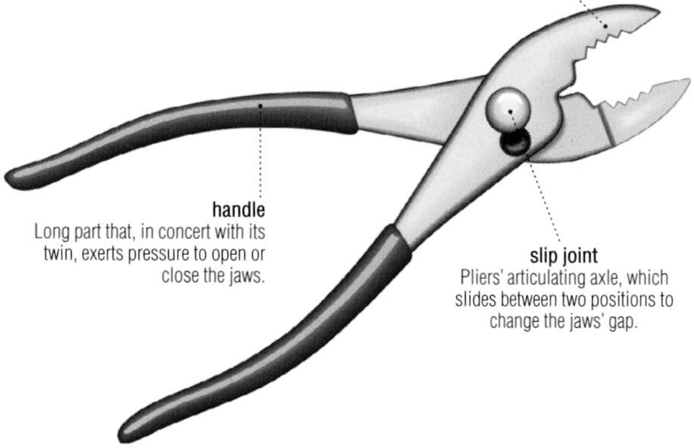

curved jaw
Jaw whose internal side is rounded for gripping or clamping a round object.

handle
Long part that, in concert with its twin, exerts pressure to open or close the jaws.

slip joint
Pliers' articulating axle, which slides between two positions to change the jaws' gap.

rib joint pliers

Pliers with straight jaws, adjustable to several gap positions.

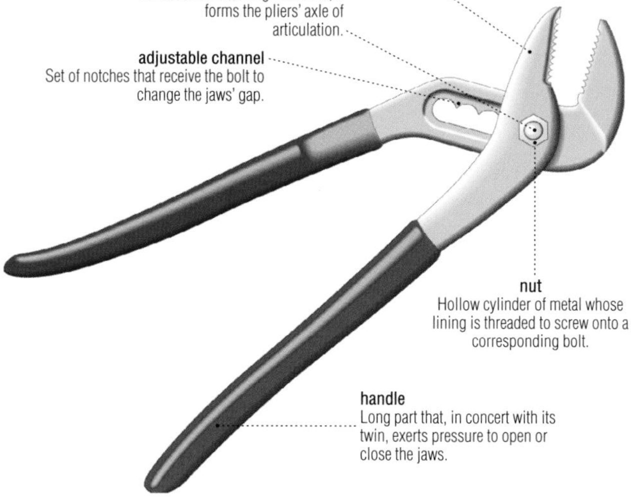

straight jaw
Jaw whose interior side is rectilinear for grasping or clamping a flat, square or many-sided object.

bolt
Metal plug ending in a head and threaded for screwing into a nut; it forms the pliers' axle of articulation.

adjustable channel
Set of notches that receive the bolt to change the jaws' gap.

nut
Hollow cylinder of metal whose lining is threaded to screw onto a corresponding bolt.

handle
Long part that, in concert with its twin, exerts pressure to open or close the jaws.

locking pliers

Used as pliers, wrench and vice, it has variable-gap jaws for gripping and clamping objects.

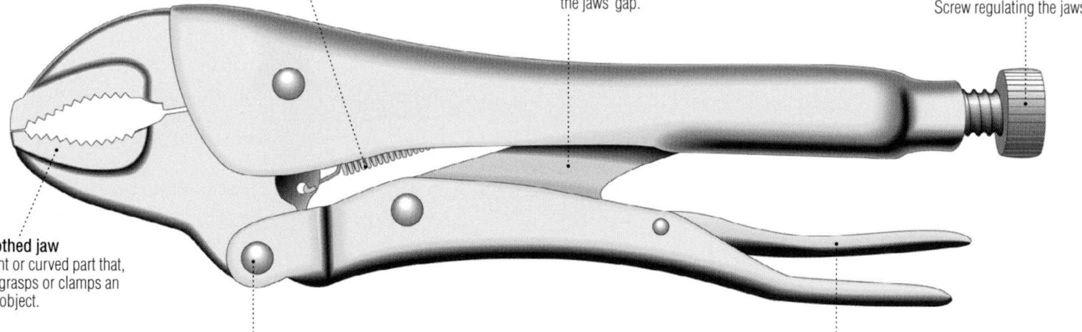

spring
Tight when the handles are closed to lock the pliers, it resumes its shape when unlocked and the handles return to their initial position.

lever
The pressure of the adjusting screw raises or lowers it, thereby controlling the jaws' gap.

adjusting screw
Screw regulating the jaws' gap.

toothed jaw
Striated straight or curved part that, with its twin, grasps or clamps an object.

rivet
Riveted assembly part that is the axle of articulation for the release lever.

release lever
Lever for unlocking the pliers and releasing the grip.

washers

Ringlike parts placed between a nut or a bolt and a part to be tightened; they distribute the stress.

flat washer
Placed underneath a screw or the head of a bolt, it distributes the pressure while protecting the work surface.

lock washer
Slightly spiral-shaped washer, which acts as a spring to prevent screws from loosening.

external tooth lock washer
Washer having protuberances on the outside so that a screw tightens securely and will not loosen.

internal tooth lock washer
Washer having protuberances on the inside so that a screw tightens securely and will not loosen.

carpentry: gripping and tightening tools

wrenches

Hand tools with fixed or variable openings, used for tightening and loosening nuts and bolts, and for assembling and disassembling objects.

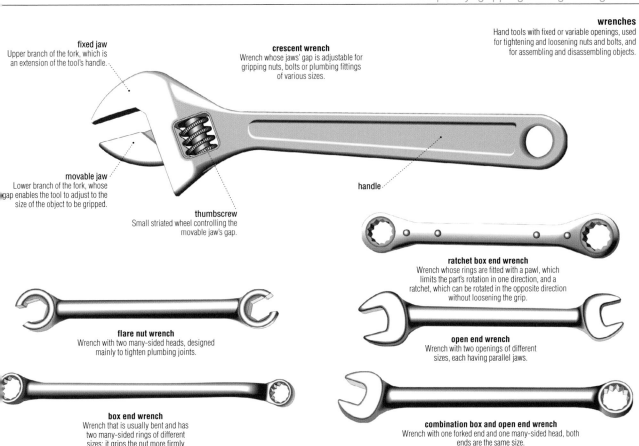

crescent wrench
Wrench whose jaws' gap is adjustable for gripping nuts, bolts or plumbing fittings of various sizes.

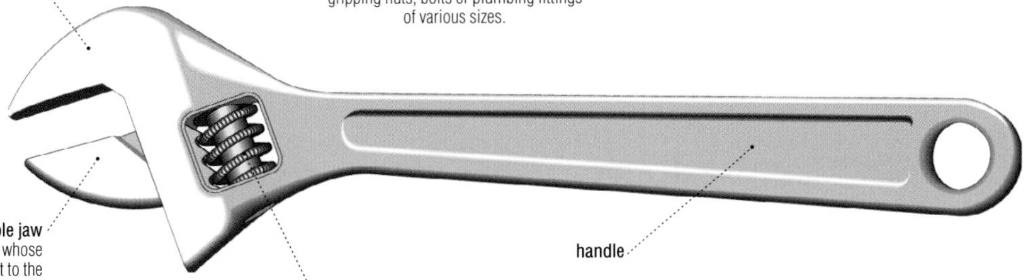

fixed jaw
Upper branch of the fork, which is an extension of the tool's handle.

movable jaw
Lower branch of the fork, whose gap enables the tool to adjust to the size of the object to be gripped.

thumbscrew
Small striated wheel controlling the movable jaw's gap.

handle

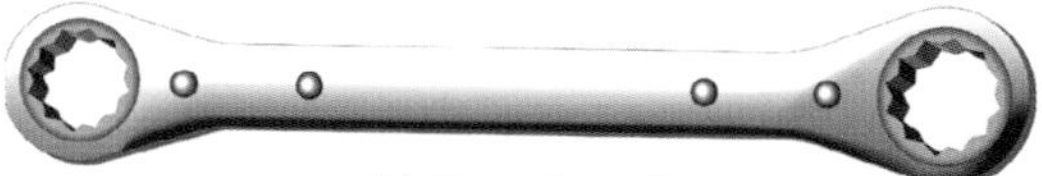

ratchet box end wrench
Wrench whose rings are fitted with a pawl, which limits the part's rotation in one direction, and a ratchet, which can be rotated in the opposite direction without loosening the grip.

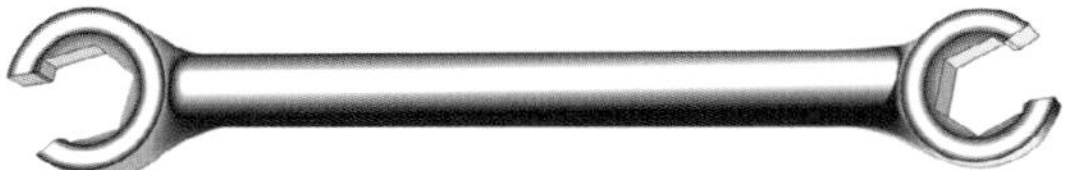

flare nut wrench
Wrench with two many-sided heads, designed mainly to tighten plumbing joints.

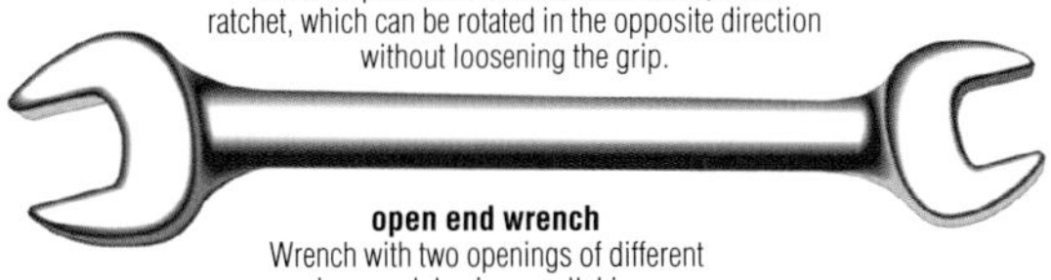

open end wrench
Wrench with two openings of different sizes, each having parallel jaws.

box end wrench
Wrench that is usually bent and has two many-sided rings of different sizes; it grips the nut more firmly than the open end wrench.

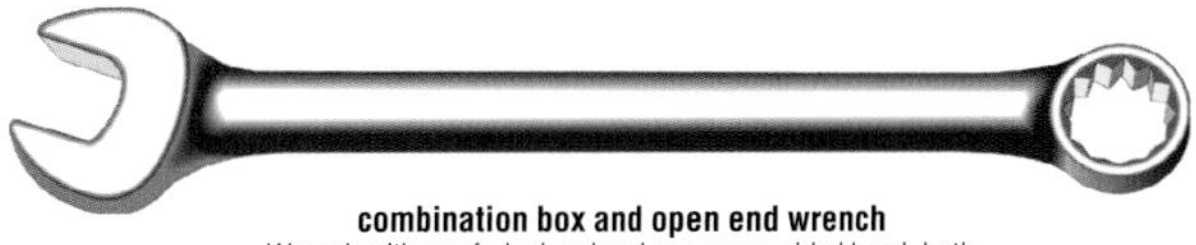

combination box and open end wrench
Wrench with one forked end and one many-sided head, both ends are the same size.

ratchet socket wrench
Wrench fitted with a pawl and a ratchet: the pawl sets the direction of rotation, while the ratchet lets the handle turn in the opposite direction over the socket.

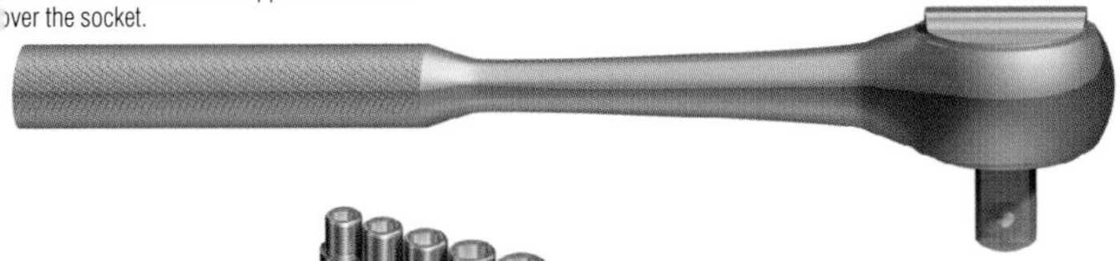

socket set
Set made up of hollow cylinders of different sizes and interior profiles that fit onto a ratchet socket wrench.

nuts

Metal parts with holes whose surfaces are threaded for screwing onto the corresponding bolts.

hexagon nut
Most common nut; it has six sides for tightening with a wrench.

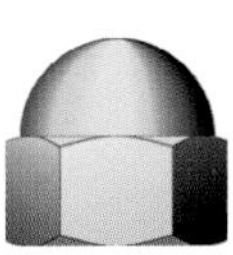

acorn nut
Nut capped with a hollow dome that covers and protects the threaded end of the bolt.

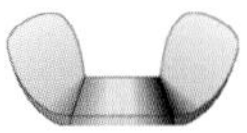

wing nut
Nut comprised of two protruding ends for tightening or loosening by hand.

bolts

Metal plugs ending in a head and threaded so they can be tightly screwed into nuts to secure fastenings and assemblies.

bolt
Metal threaded plug ending in a head; it is tightly screwed into a nut to secure fastenings and assemblies.

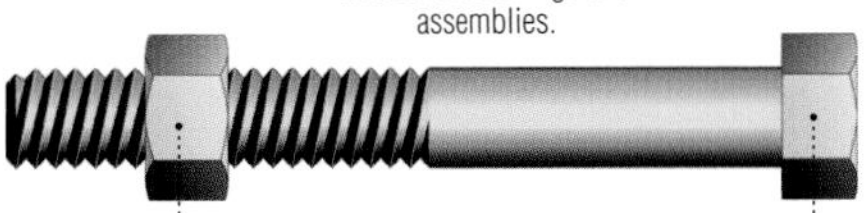

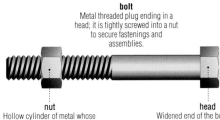

nut
Hollow cylinder of metal whose lining is threaded to screw onto a corresponding bolt.

head
Widened end of the bolt, of various shapes and sizes.

shoulder bolt
Bolt whose head comprises a section of smaller diameter for concentrating the tightening pressure.

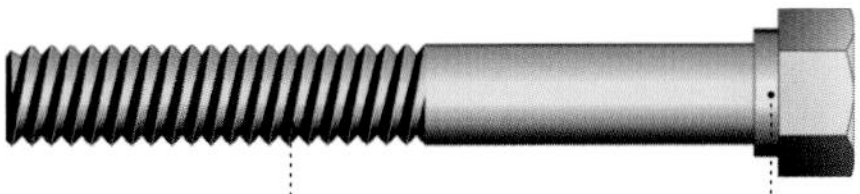

threaded rod
Elongated part whose surface has a spiral protrusion for screwing into a corresponding nut.

shoulder
Cylindrical nonthreaded protrusion used as a bracket as the bolt is being tightened.

carpentry: gripping and tightening tools

C-clamp
Portable tool with a C-shaped frame, used for keeping objects from moving while working on them.

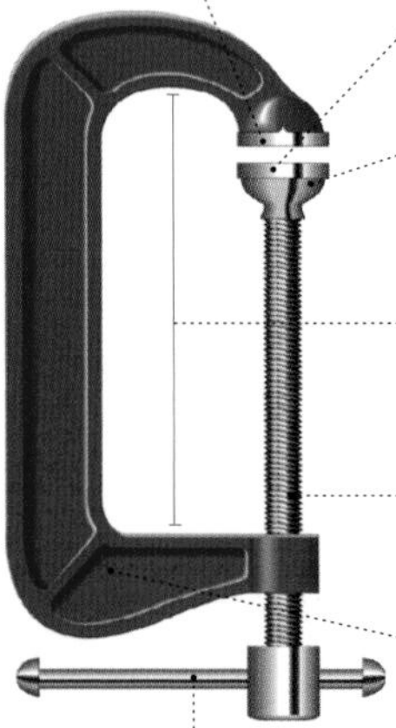

fixed jaw
Smooth or striated part against which the movable jaw presses an object.

movable jaw
Smooth or striated jaw that presses an object against the fixed jaw.

swivel head
End of the tightening screw; it pivots to adjust to irregularly shaped objects.

throat
Opening made by the frame.

adjusting screw
Threaded shank whose rotation is controlled by the handle; it moves the jaw toward or away from the piece to be clamped.

frame
Rigid metal support in the shape of a C, having the fixed jaw on one end, while the other end contains a hole for the adjusting screw.

handle
Sliding bar for tightening or loosening the adjusting screw, thereby spreading or closing the jaws.

vis
Press with two jaws; it is attache to a worktable and used fo clamping objects

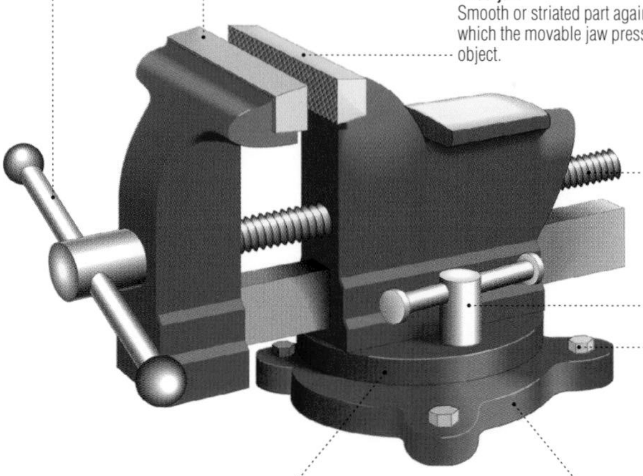

handle
Sliding bar for tightening or loosening the adjusting screw, thereby spreading or closing the jaws.

movable jaw
Smooth or striated jaw that presses an object against the fixed jaw.

fixed jaw
Smooth or striated part against which the movable jaw presses an object.

adjusting screw
Threaded shank whose rotation is controlled by the handle; it moves the jaw toward or away from the piece to be clamped.

swivel lock
Sliding bar clamping down the swivel base by locking it into the desired position.

bolt
Threaded metal plug with a head that is tightly screwed into a nut to secure the vise to a work bench.

swivel base
Rotating surface surmounting the fixed base, which allows the vise to turn 360°.

fixed base
The tool's supporting block, usually bolted onto a work bench.

pipe clamp
Large press comprising a metal pipe supporting a jaw and a tail stop.

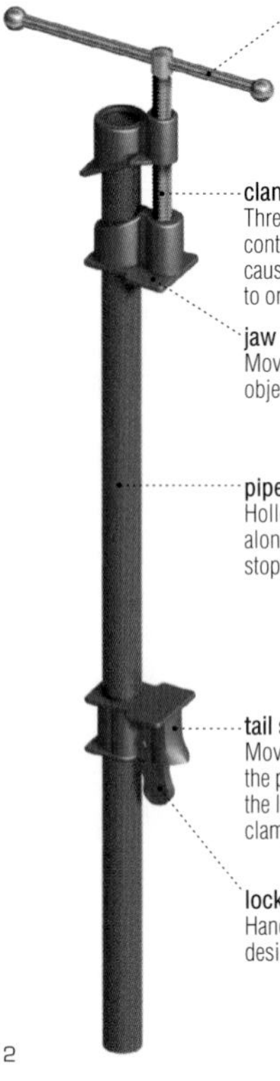

handle
Sliding bar that adjusts the screw to slide the tail stop's jaw up or down the pipe.

clamping screw
Threaded shank whose rotation, controlled by the clamping lever, causes the jaw to slide along the pipe to or from the object to be clamped.

jaw
Movable part for pressing more objects against the tail stop.

pipe
Hollow cylinder of varying length, along which the jaw and the tail stop slide.

tail stop
Movable jaw whose motion along the pipe quickly adjusts the tool to the length of the object to be clamped.

locking lever
Handle that fixes the tail stop at the desired position on the pipe.

work bench and vis
Small, usually folding, worktabl whose top surface (tray) i composed of two adjustable jaw for clamping objects

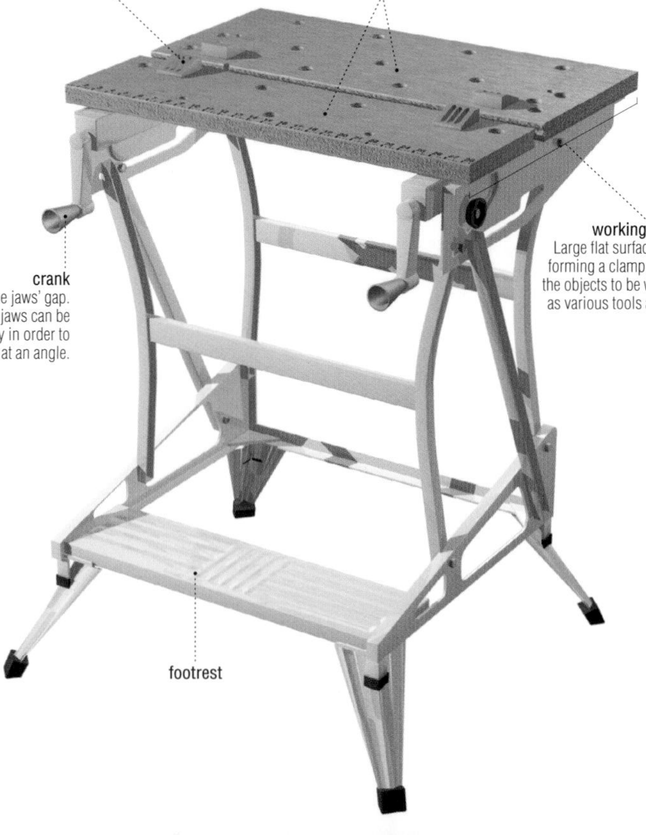

peg
Detachable part inserted into one of the openings on the work surface to clamp an object between its jaws.

jaws
The parts of the working surface that spread apart or close together to clamp one or more objects.

working surface
Large flat surface with two forming a clamp, which sup the objects to be worked on a as various tools and access

crank
Handle for regulating the jaws' gap. The two ends of the jaws can be adjusted independently in order to clamp a part at an angle.

footrest

carpentry: measuring and marking tools

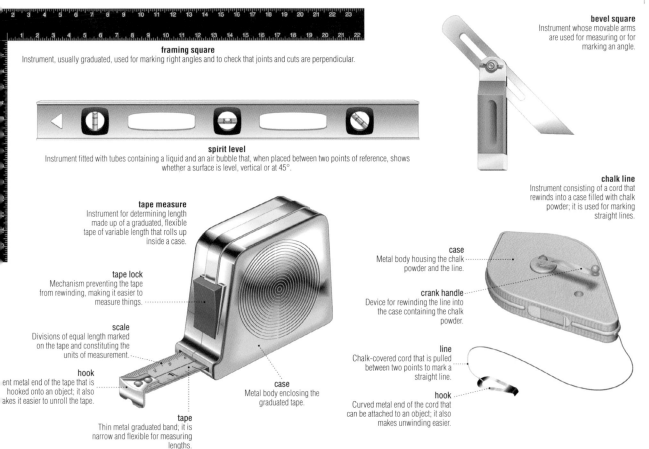

framing square
Instrument, usually graduated, used for marking right angles and to check that joints and cuts are perpendicular.

spirit level
Instrument fitted with tubes containing a liquid and an air bubble that, when placed between two points of reference, shows whether a surface is level, vertical or at 45°.

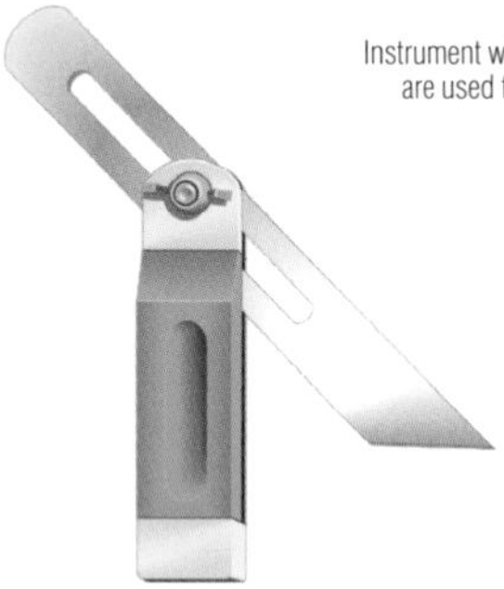

bevel square
Instrument whose movable arms are used for measuring or for marking an angle.

tape measure
Instrument for determining length made up of a graduated, flexible tape of variable length that rolls up inside a case.

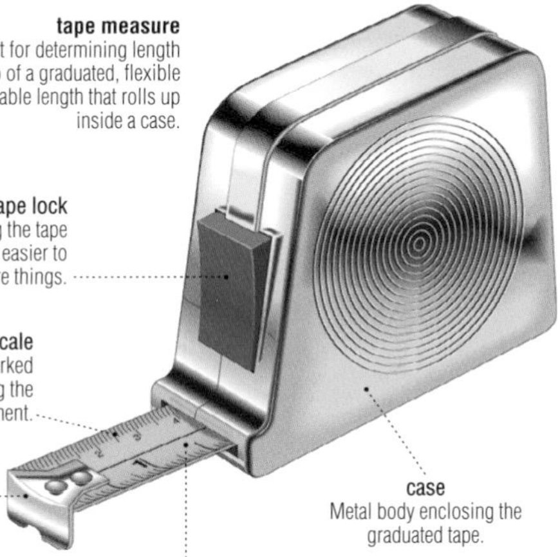

tape lock
Mechanism preventing the tape from rewinding, making it easier to measure things.

scale
Divisions of equal length marked on the tape and constituting the units of measurement.

hook
ent metal end of the tape that is hooked onto an object; it also akes it easier to unroll the tape.

case
Metal body enclosing the graduated tape.

tape
Thin metal graduated band; it is narrow and flexible for measuring lengths.

chalk line
Instrument consisting of a cord that rewinds into a case filled with chalk powder; it is used for marking straight lines.

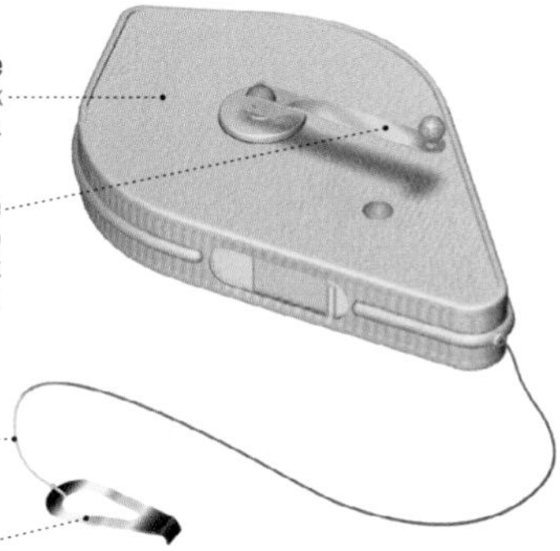

case
Metal body housing the chalk powder and the line.

crank handle
Device for rewinding the line into the case containing the chalk powder.

line
Chalk-covered cord that is pulled between two points to mark a straight line.

hook
Curved metal end of the cord that can be attached to an object; it also makes unwinding easier.

carpentry: miscellaneous material

tool box
Rigid container, fitted with a cover and a tray, for storing and carrying tools.

tray
Rigid detachable container, divided into compartments and usually used for storing hardware or small tools.

tool belt
Band worn around the waist, fitted with pockets and accessories for holding tools and instruments needed close at hand.

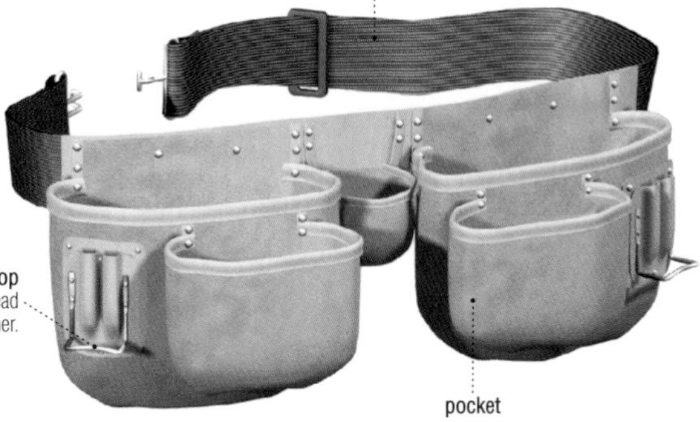

hammer loop
Metal bracket for holding the head of a hammer.

plumbing tools

The purpose of plumbing is to install, maintain and repair a dwelling's pipes and sanitary fixtures.

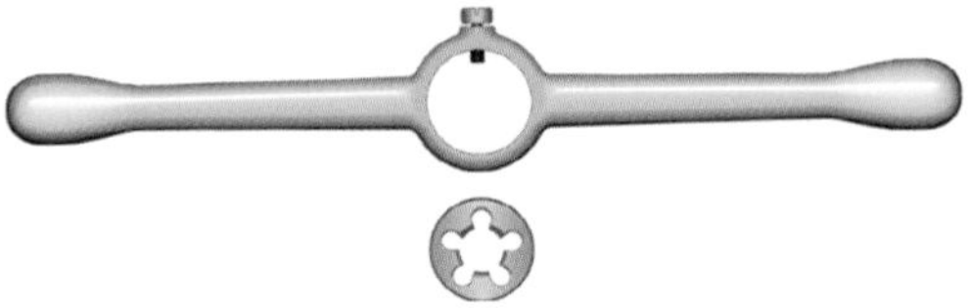

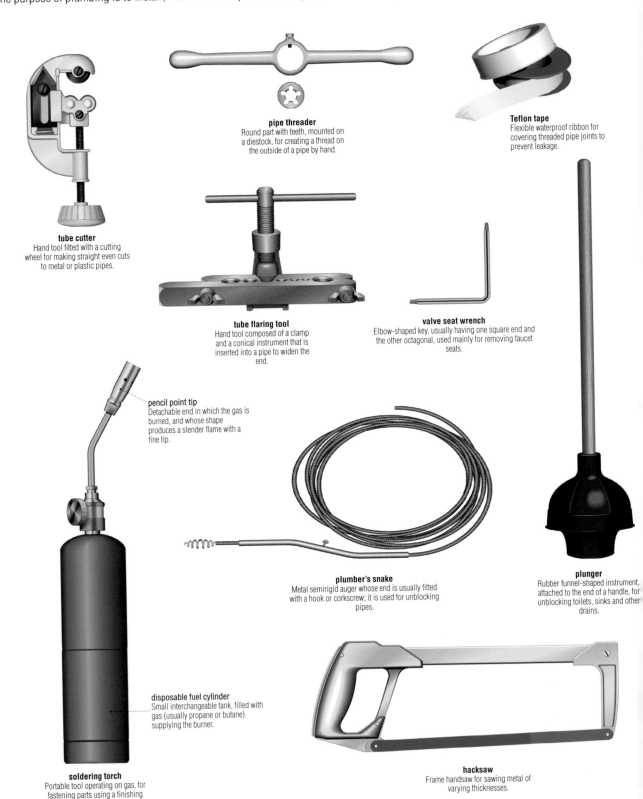

pipe threader
Round part with teeth, mounted on a diestock, for creating a thread on the outside of a pipe by hand.

Teflon tape
Flexible waterproof ribbon for covering threaded pipe joints to prevent leakage.

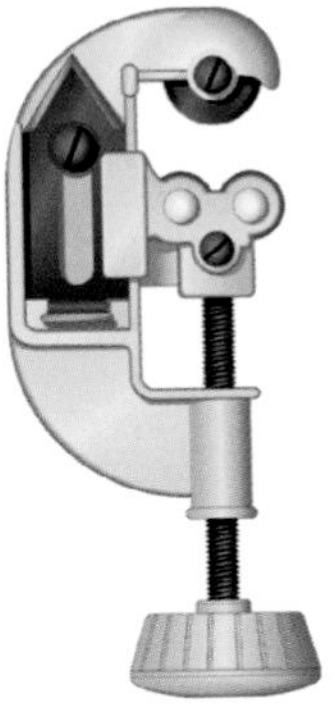

tube cutter
Hand tool fitted with a cutting wheel for making straight even cuts to metal or plastic pipes.

tube flaring tool
Hand tool composed of a clamp and a conical instrument that is inserted into a pipe to widen the end.

valve seat wrench
Elbow-shaped key, usually having one square end and the other octagonal, used mainly for removing faucet seats.

pencil point tip
Detachable end in which the gas is burned, and whose shape produces a slender flame with a fine tip.

disposable fuel cylinder
Small interchangeable tank, filled with gas (usually propane or butane) supplying the burner.

soldering torch
Portable tool operating on gas, for fastening parts using a finishing metal with a low melting point, such as lead.

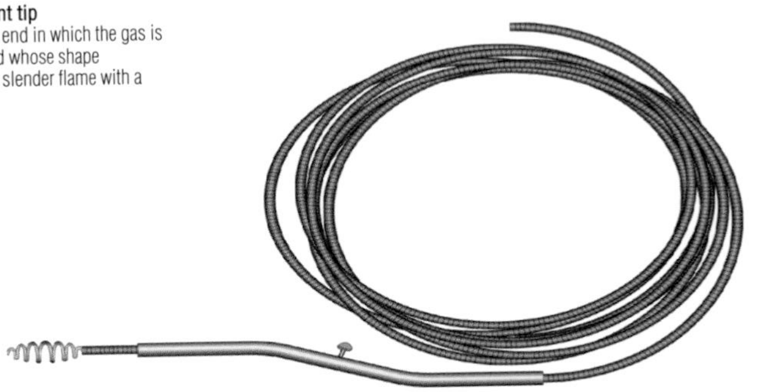

plumber's snake
Metal semirigid auger whose end is usually fitted with a hook or corkscrew; it is used for unblocking pipes.

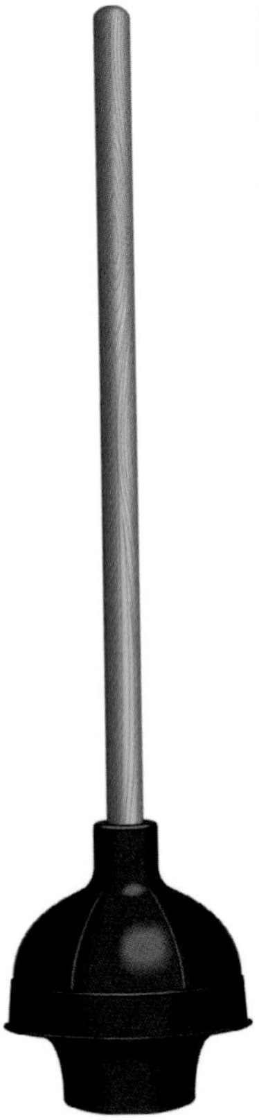

plunger
Rubber funnel-shaped instrument, attached to the end of a handle, for unblocking toilets, sinks and other drains.

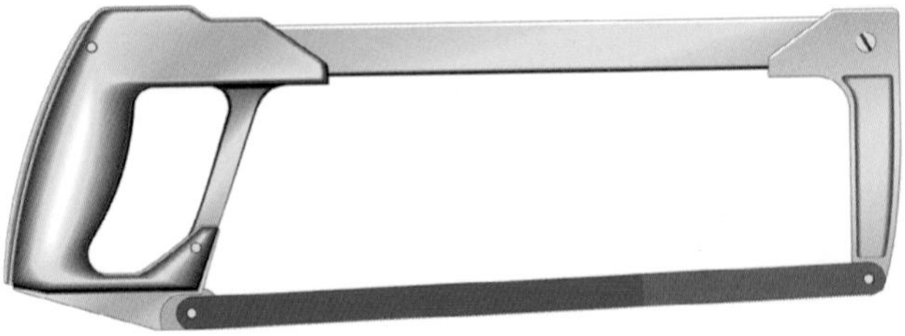

hacksaw
Frame handsaw for sawing metal of varying thicknesses.

plumbing tools

wrenches
Hand tools with fixed or variable openings, used for tightening and loosening nuts and bolts, and for assembling and disassembling objects.

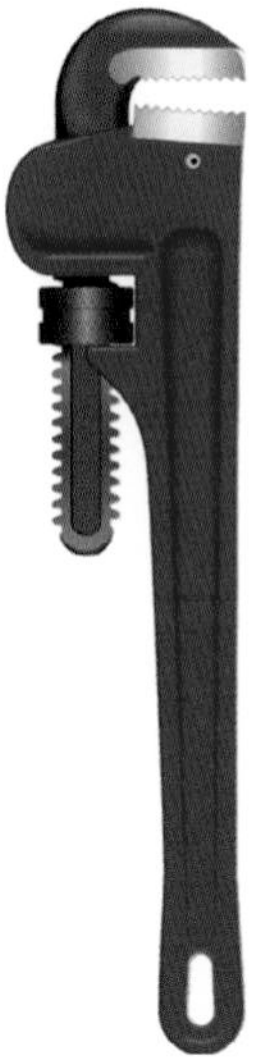

pipe wrench
Wrench with notched jaws and adjustable opening for firmly gripping nuts, couplings and thick-walled pipes.

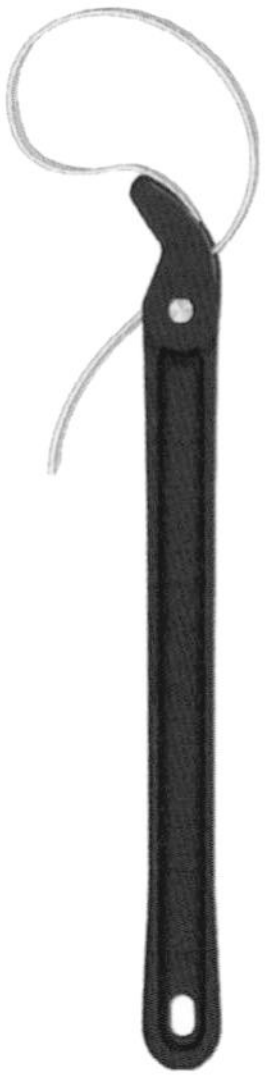

strap wrench
Wrench whose strap acts as a jaw to grip objects that are difficult to access or whose surfaces must not be damaged.

chain pipe wrench
Wrench whose chain acts as a jaw for gripping large pipes and irregularly shaped objects.

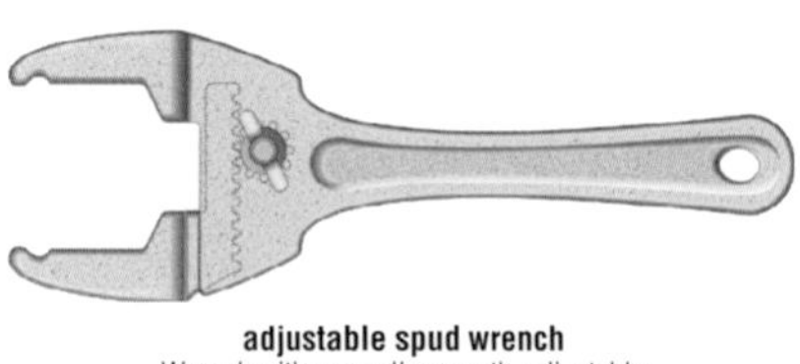

adjustable spud wrench
Wrench with a usually smooth, adjustable opening, for tightening objects that are somewhat fragile.

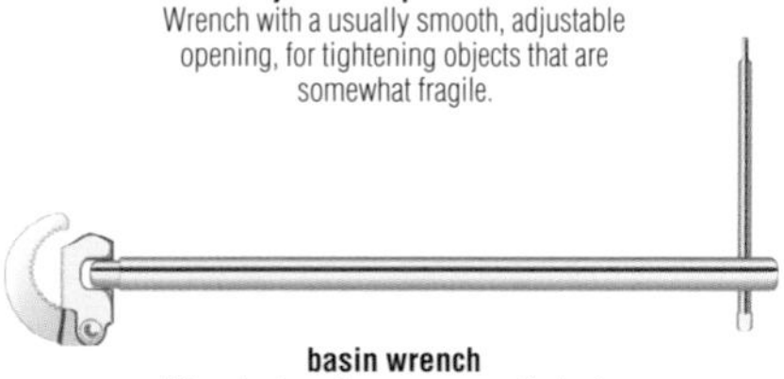

basin wrench
Wrench whose jaws are perpendicular to a telescoping handle, and pivot to open at variable positions; it is used for working in cramped spaces.

masonry tools

The purpose of masonry is to build and repair structures or to cover walls with brick, stone or concrete blocks.

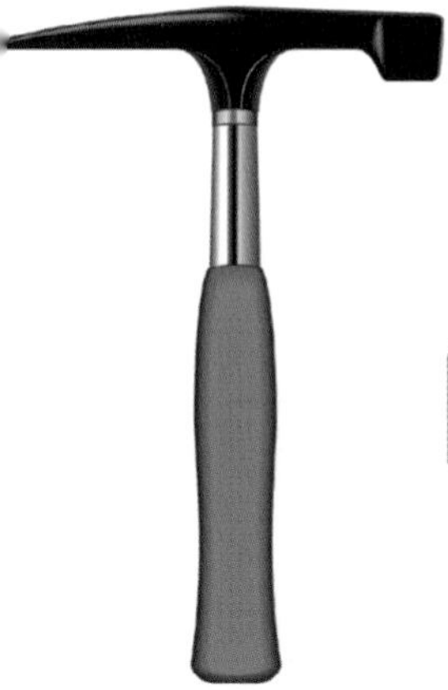

bricklayer's hammer
Hammer with a long, pointed peen, used for finishing brick and stone and for removing a damaged covering.

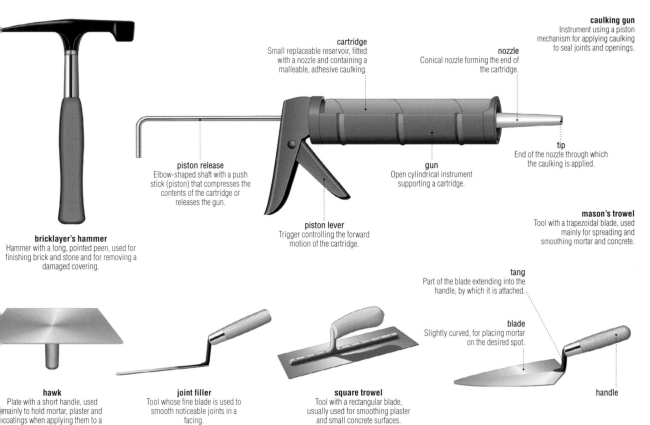

caulking gun
Instrument using a piston mechanism for applying caulking to seal joints and openings.

cartridge
Small replaceable reservoir, fitted with a nozzle and containing a malleable, adhesive caulking.

nozzle
Conical nozzle forming the end of the cartridge.

tip
End of the nozzle through which the caulking is applied.

gun
Open cylindrical instrument supporting a cartridge.

piston release
Elbow-shaped shaft with a push stick (piston) that compresses the contents of the cartridge or releases the gun.

piston lever
Trigger controlling the forward motion of the cartridge.

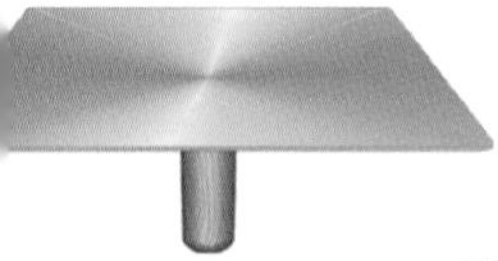

hawk
Plate with a short handle, used mainly to hold mortar, plaster and coatings when applying them to a facing.

joint filler
Tool whose fine blade is used to smooth noticeable joints in a facing.

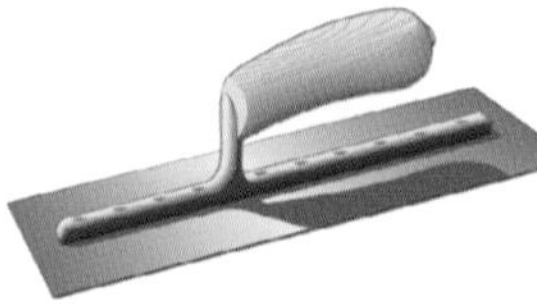

square trowel
Tool with a rectangular blade, usually used for smoothing plaster and small concrete surfaces.

mason's trowel
Tool with a trapezoidal blade, used mainly for spreading and smoothing mortar and concrete.

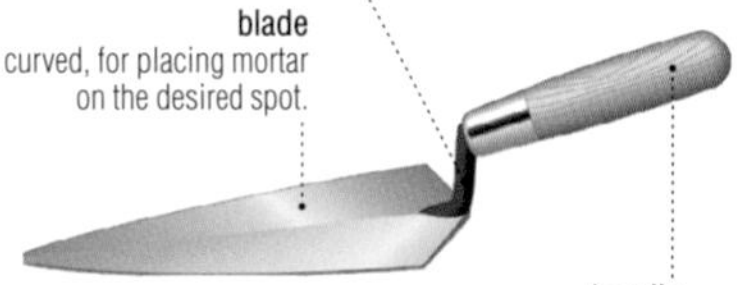

tang
Part of the blade extending into the handle, by which it is attached.

blade
Slightly curved, for placing mortar on the desired spot.

handle

electricity tools

The purpose of the electrical trade is to install, maintain and repair electrical wiring and devices in a place or building.

multimeter
Device for measuring, among other things, a conductor's resistance, the voltage between two points and the strength of the current.

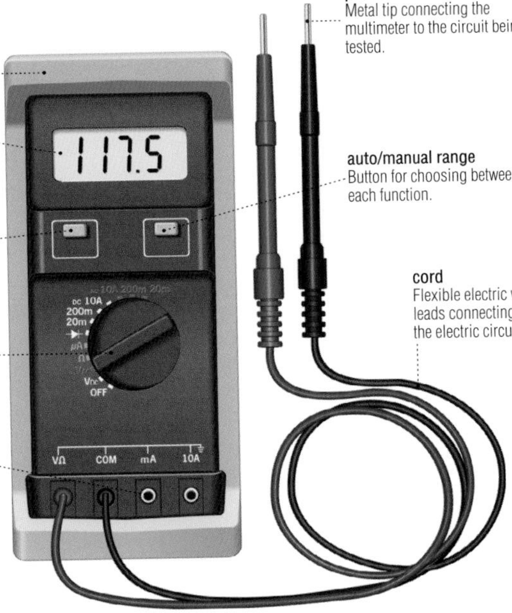

housing

digital display
Liquid-crystal screen displaying the reading taken by the device.

data hold
Function for keeping certain readings in memory.

selector switch
Device for selecting the desired function and the appropriate gauge for the measurement.

input terminal
Socket for receiving a probe's cord.

probe
Metal tip connecting the multimeter to the circuit being tested.

auto/manual range
Button for choosing between the automatic and manual gauge for each function.

cord
Flexible electric wire housing the leads connecting the appliance to the electric circuit.

voltage tester
Screwdriver used for detecting an electric current in appliances, devices and low-voltage circuits.

insulated blade

insulated handle
Part for gripping the tool, made from a material that prevents an electric current from passing through it.

neon lamp
Small tube that lights up when the blade is in contact with a live conductor.

continuity tester
Instrument for detecting short circuits and open circuits and for testing fuses.

drop light
Portable electric lamp protected by a guard and fitted with a long cord allowing it to be moved.

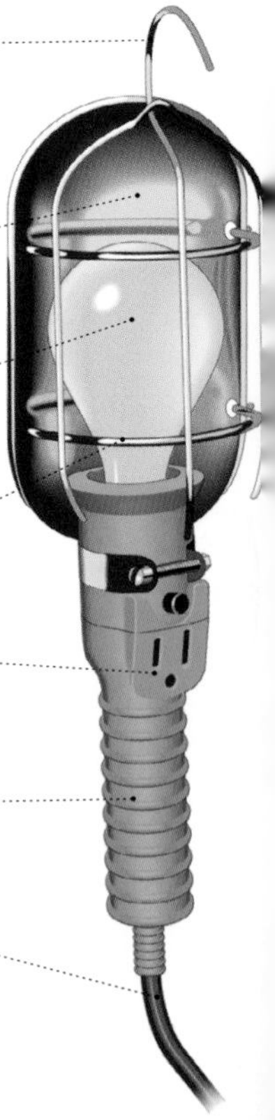

hook

reflector
Metal half sphere concentrating and directing the light from a lightbulb.

bulb
Glass envelope filled with gas, in which a luminous body is inserted.

guard
Metal mesh protecting the lightbulb while the drop light is being handled.

convenience outlet
Device connected to an electric circuit; it transmits the current to an electrical appliance when its plug is inserted into the outlet.

handle

cord
Flexible electric wire housing the leads connecting the appliance to the electric circuit.

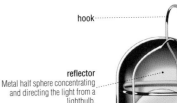

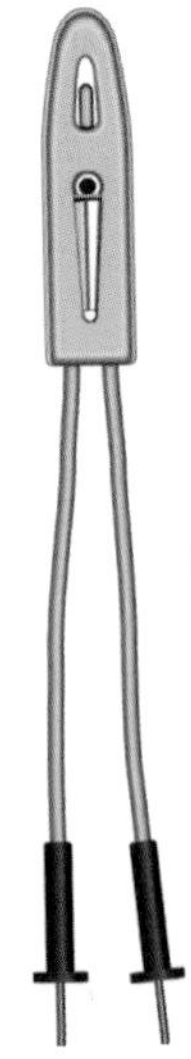

neon tester
Instrument used for detecting the presence of an electric current in low-voltage appliances, devices and circuits.

receptacle analyzer
Instrument for detecting any faults in the receptacle, such as grounding problems and crossed or unconnected wires.

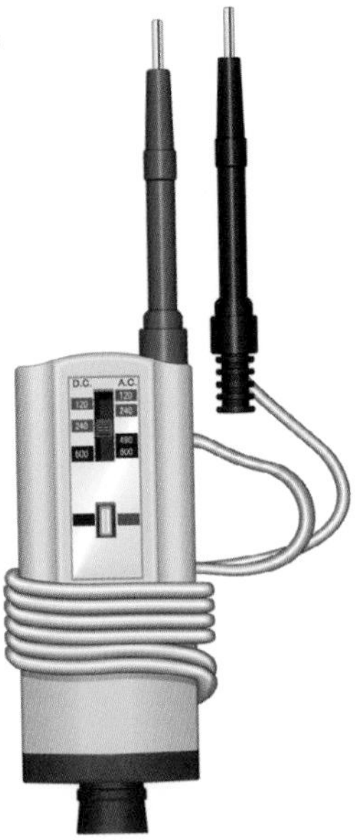

high-voltage tester
Instrument used for detecting an electric current in high-voltage appliances, devices and circuits.

electricity tools

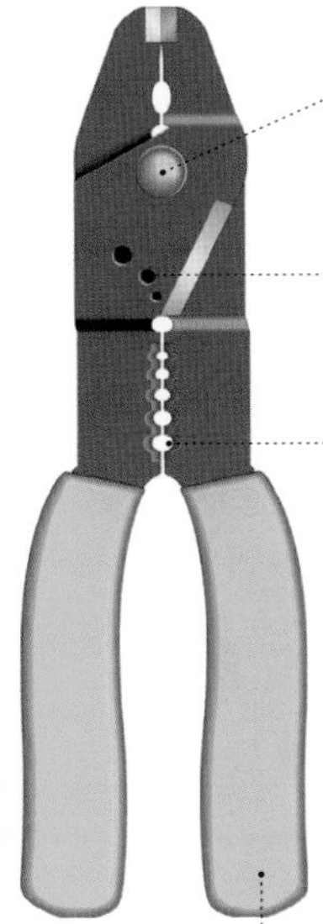

multipurpose tool
Pliers fitted with straight jaws, used especially for gripping, cutting and stripping electric wires.

pivot
Pliers' axle of articulation, which allows the jaws to open and close.

wire cutter
Cutting edge for cropping an electric wire.

wire stripper
Pliers' cutting notch, of various diameters, in which the end of an electric cable is clamped for stripping.

insulated handle
Long part of the pliers, covered with a material preventing the flow of electricity.

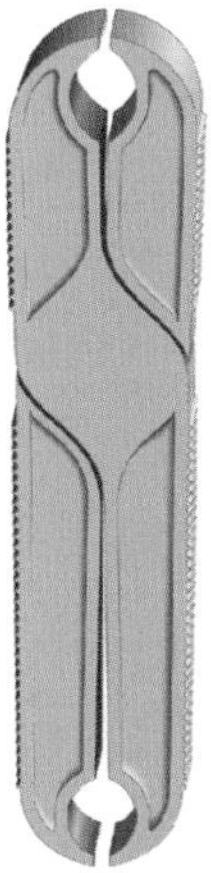

fuse puller
Insulated pliers designed for handling cartridge fuses.

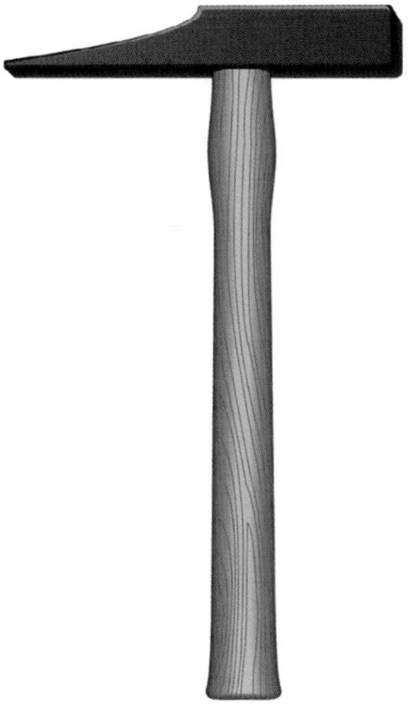

hammer
Hammer with an elongated head and a tapered peen, for attaching small parts and nailing in cramped spaces.

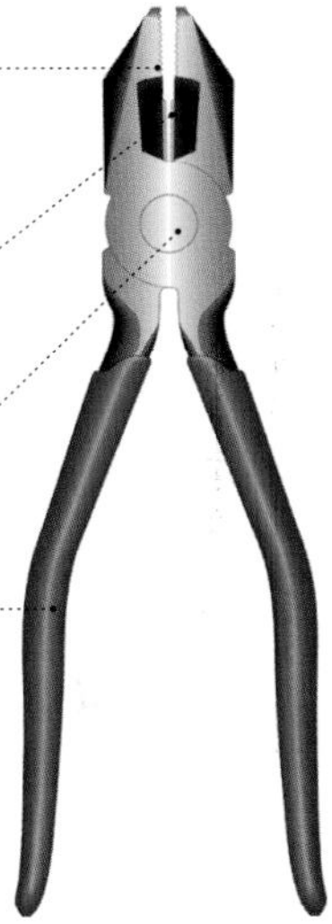

lineman's pliers
Pliers fitted with straight jaws that provide a powerful grip; they also include a wire cutter and jaws for pulling fish wire.

jaw
Straight striated part that, with its twin, opens and closes to grip, twist or cut an electric cable, wire or other object.

wire cutter
Part fitted with two cutting edges for cropping an electric wire.

pivot
Pliers' axle of articulation, which allows the jaws to open and close.

insulated handle
Long part of the pliers, covered with a material preventing the flow of electricity.

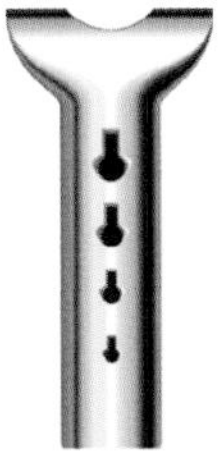

cable ripper
Tool with openings of various diameters for stripping a nonmetal electric cable or wire.

cutter
Knife with a curved blade used mainly for making incisions in the sheathing of a nonmetal electric cable or wire.

wire nut
Hollow part inside which electric wires are connected.

fish wire
Metal wire ending in a hook, used mainly for running electric cables through walls.

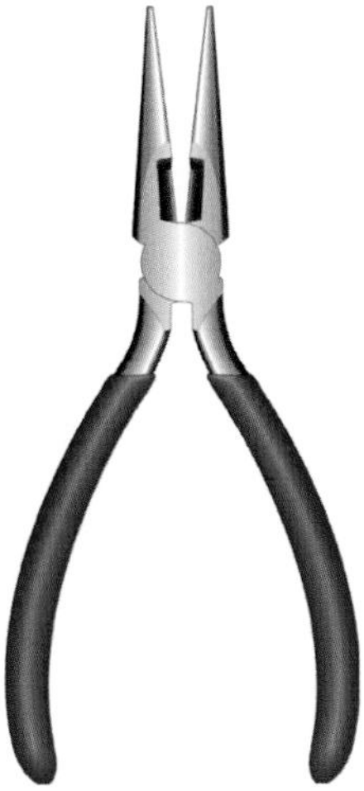

needle-nose pliers
Pliers with long narrow jaws for doing delicate work or accessing hard-to-reach parts.

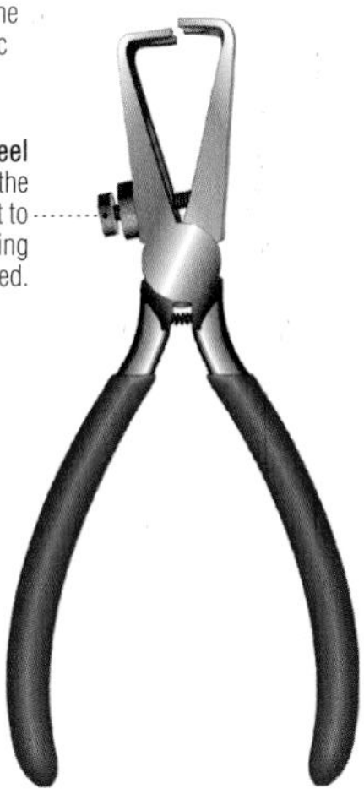

adjustment wheel
Small striated wheel controlling the movement of the jaws so they adapt to the diameter of the electric wire being stripped.

wire stripper
Pliers with adjustable cutting jaws for removing the insulating sheathing from an electric cable or wire.

soldering and welding tools

Welding joins two parts by fusing their edges, while soldering does so by fusing a finishing metal (solder) placed on the joint.

soldering gun
Electric tool that is more powerful than a soldering iron; it uses finishing metal with a low melting point, such as lead, to join parts.

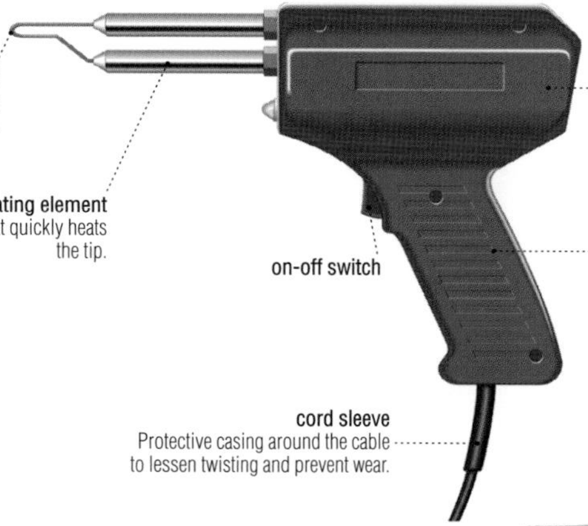

tip
Metal part forming the end of the gun, used to heat a solder.

heating element
Electrical resistor that quickly heats the tip.

on-off switch

housing
Case enclosing and protecting the device's mechanism.

pistol grip handle
Part shaped like a pistol grip so the wrist remains straight while holding the tool.

cord sleeve
Protective casing around the cable to lessen twisting and prevent wear.

soldering iron
Electric tool with a tip for heating a solder, used to join parts that can take only weak mechanical pressure.

welding curtain
Movable panel that stops the sparks and harmful light rays emitted while welding.

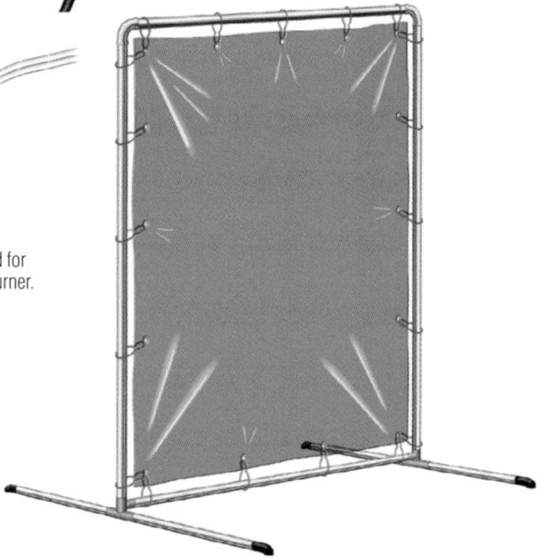

solder
Metal wire that, by fusing over a joint, joins two parts.

tip cleaners
Fine metal needles of various sizes used for clearing the inside of a nozzle, head or burner.

striker
Instrument producing a spark for lighting the gas emitted by a nozzle, head or burner.

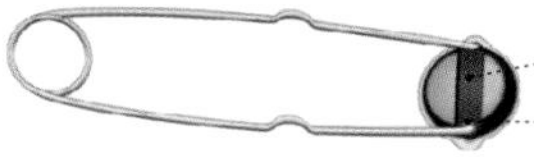

friction strip
Abrasive surface on which a flint is struck to produce a spark.

flint
Small stone that is scraped against an abrasive surface to produce a spark.

arc welding
Welding process in which the heat needed for fusing is provided by an electric arc between the electrode and the part to be welded.

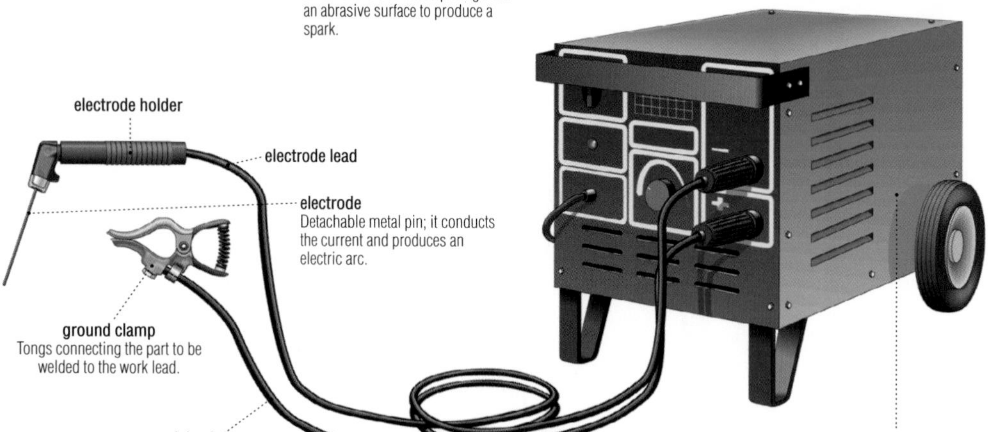

electrode holder

electrode lead

electrode
Detachable metal pin; it conducts the current and produces an electric arc.

ground clamp
Tongs connecting the part to be welded to the work lead.

work lead
Cable returning the current to the arc welding machine.

arc welding machine
Device providing a current to the electrode; the current's intensity depends on the nature of the parts to be welded and the electrode's characteristics.

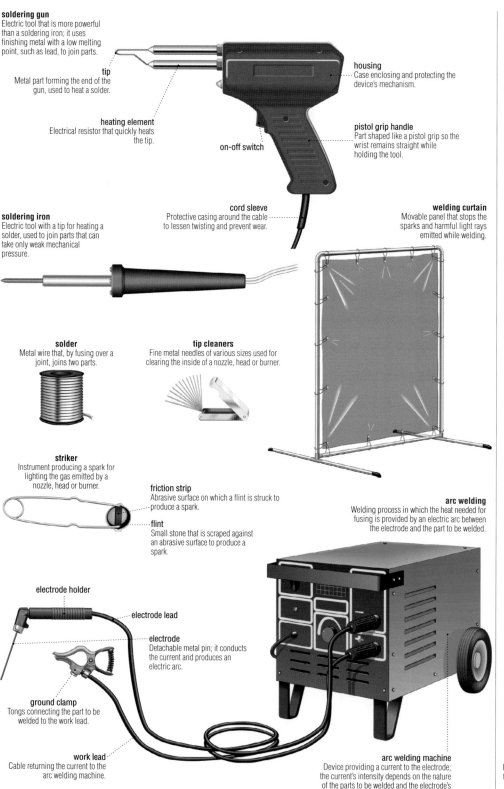

protective clothing

goggles

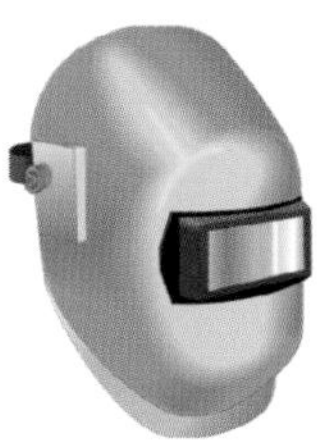

face shield

hand shield

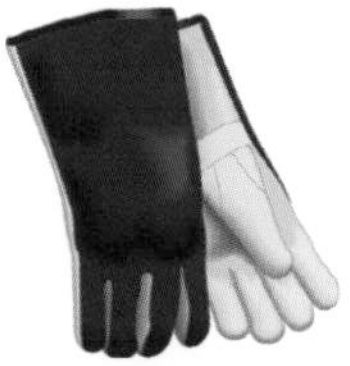

gauntlet
Fireproof article of clothing that covers the hand and wrist and takes the shape of the fingers.

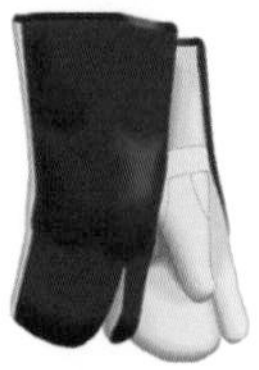

mitten
Fireproof article of clothing entirely covering the hand and the wrist but leaving the thumb free.

soldering and welding tools

cutting torch
Burning acetylene produces a very hot flame that can cut through metals such as steel.

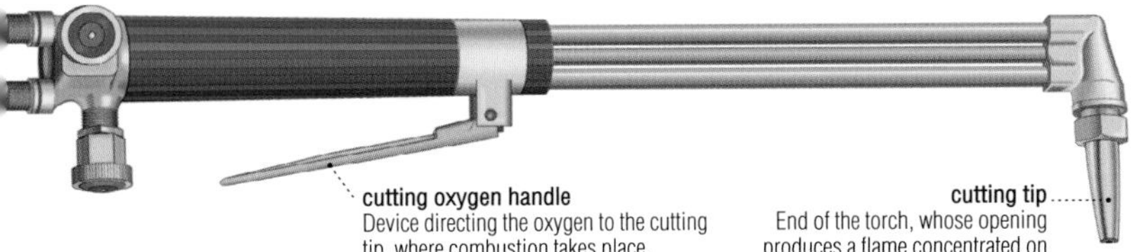

cutting oxygen handle
Device directing the oxygen to the cutting tip, where combustion takes place.

cutting tip
End of the torch, whose opening produces a flame concentrated on the surface to be cut.

pressure regulator
Device placed at the outlet port of each cylinder; it lowers and stabilizes the gas pressure reaching the torch.

cylinder pressure gauge
Dial-operated device whose needle shows the gas pressure in the cylinder.

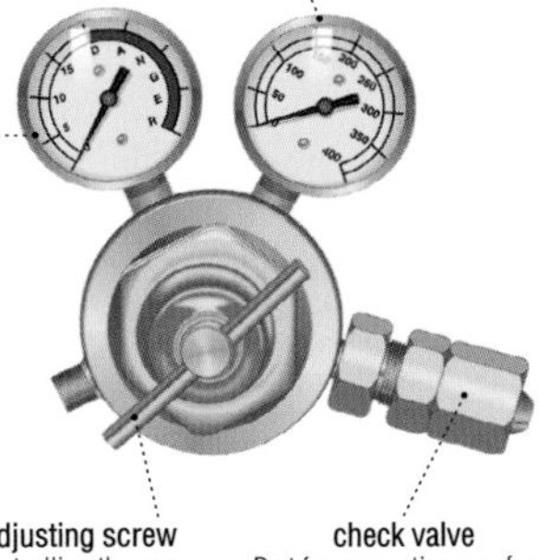

working pressure gauge
Dial-operated device whose needle shows the gas pressure at the outlet port of the pressure regulator.

adjusting screw
Screw for controlling the gas pressure at the regulator outlet port, which corresponds to the gas pressure at the inlet of the torch.

check valve
Part for preventing gas from returning to the cylinder after passing through the pressure regulator.

oxygen valve
Valve controlling the volume of oxygen introduced into the welding torch.

welding torch
Torch for joining metal parts using a flame produced by burning gas.

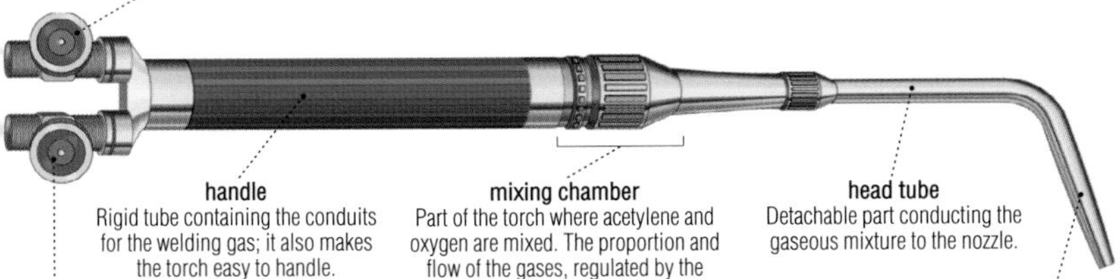

handle
Rigid tube containing the conduits for the welding gas; it also makes the torch easy to handle.

mixing chamber
Part of the torch where acetylene and oxygen are mixed. The proportion and flow of the gases, regulated by the valves, determine the flame's properties.

head tube
Detachable part conducting the gaseous mixture to the nozzle.

acetylene valve
Valve controlling the volume of acetylene entering the torch.

tip
End of the head tube; combustion takes place where it opens.

oxyacetylene welding
Welding process in which the heat required for fusion is provided by the burning of an acetylene and oxygen mixture in the end of the torch.

soldering torch
Portable tool operating on gas, for fastening parts using a finishing metal with a low melting point, such as lead.

pencil point tip
Detachable end in which the gas is burned, and whose shape produces a slender flame with a fine tip.

flame spreader tip
Detachable end producing a wide flame for covering a larger surface.

disposable fuel cylinder
Small interchangeable tank, filled with gas (usually propane or butane) supplying the burner.

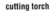

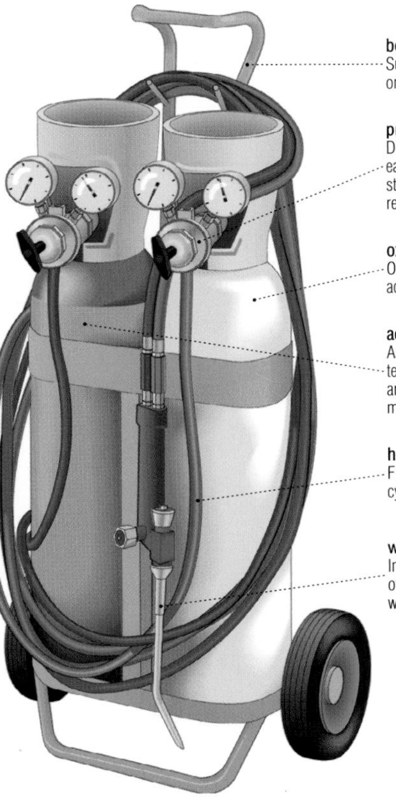

bottle cart
Support for the welding material, on wheels for easy moving.

pressure regulator
Device placed at the outlet port of each cylinder; it lowers and stabilizes the gas pressure reaching the torch.

oxygen cylinder
Oxygen is the gas used to make the acetylene burn.

acetylene cylinder
As acetylene burns at very high temperatures (6,000°F), it is used in steel and metal work, where a high temperature must be attained quickly.

hose
Flexible tube bringing gas from the cylinder to the torch.

welding torch
Instrument burning gas to produce a flame of a given shape and intensity; it is used to weld and cut metal.

painting upkeep

The main purpose of this type of work is to apply paint, stain or varnish to a surface.

spray paint gun
Pneumatic device atomizing paint onto a surface, giving it a smooth uniform finish.

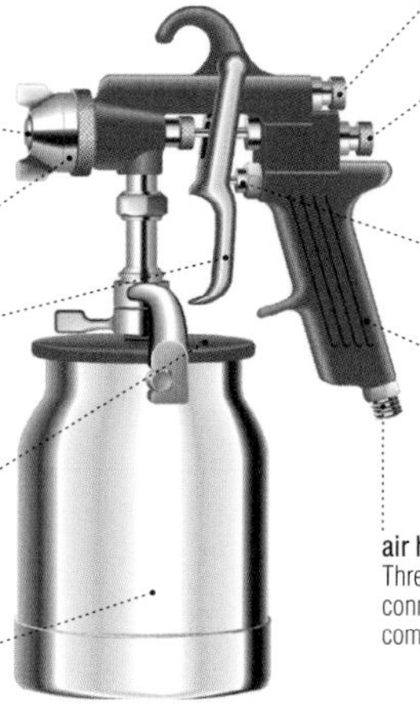

nozzle
Opening through which the paint flows; its size depends on the position of a conical part (pointer).

air cap
Part directing the compressed air toward the nozzle; here the air comes in contact with the paint jet, which is atomized.

trigger
Device that controls the supply of both air and paint.

vent hole
Opening through which the air enters the container to maintain the atmospheric pressure.

container
Reservoir for the paint, which is connected to the gun by a tube; here a low-pressure zone is created causing the liquid to be sucked in.

spreader adjustment screw
Movable part whose opening is controlled by a screw that controls the volume of air pushed into the air cap, thereby defining the size and shape of the paint jet.

fluid adjustment screw
Screw for controlling the maximum size of a pointer, thereby determining the amount of paint emitted by the nozzle.

air valve
Movable part whose opening is regulated by the trigger; it lets compressed air into the gun.

gun body

air hose connection
Threaded part receiving a flexible tube; it is connected to a compressor that allows the compressed air into the body of the gun.

brush
Natural or synthetic bristles attached to a handle, used for spreading paint, varnish or stain on a base.

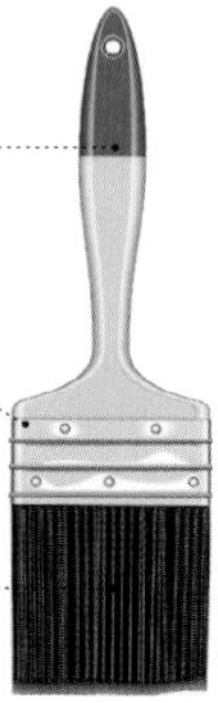

handle

ferrule
Metal part clamped around the end of the handle to keep the bristles firmly in place.

bristles
Stiff hairs made from natural or synthetic materials; they are filled with paint, varnish or stain to apply them.

scraper
Instrument with a blade used to remove paint or varnish from a surface.

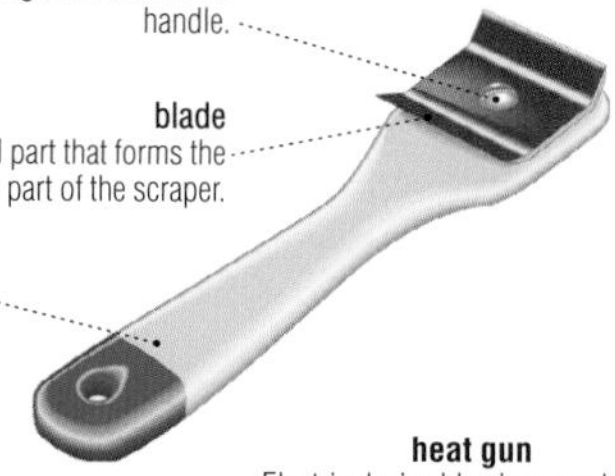

knurled bolt
Bolt fastening the blade on the handle.

blade
Thin flat metal part that forms the cutting part of the scraper.

handle

air compressor
Machine compressing and storing the air that supplies a spray paint gun or other pneumatic tool.

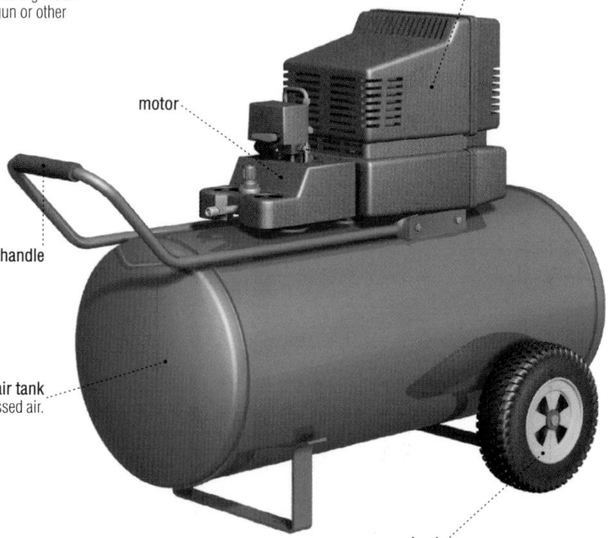

pump
Machine drawing in ambient air and forcing it under pressure into the tank.

motor

handle

air tank
Container storing compressed air.

wheel
Circular instrument rotating around an axle so that the device can be moved.

heat gun
Electric device blowing very hot air, used mainly to soften paint and varnish to ease scraping them.

nozzle
End of the tool through which a jet of hot air is forced by a fan. It is usually possible to attach various accessories to it.

switch
Device's start and stop button, regulating the intensity of the hot-air flow.

tray
Container used with a roller; it has a deep area to hold the paint and a ribbed area for coating the roller cover with the amount of paint required.

paint roller
Instrument fitted with a detachable handle for spreading the paint evenly on a large surface.

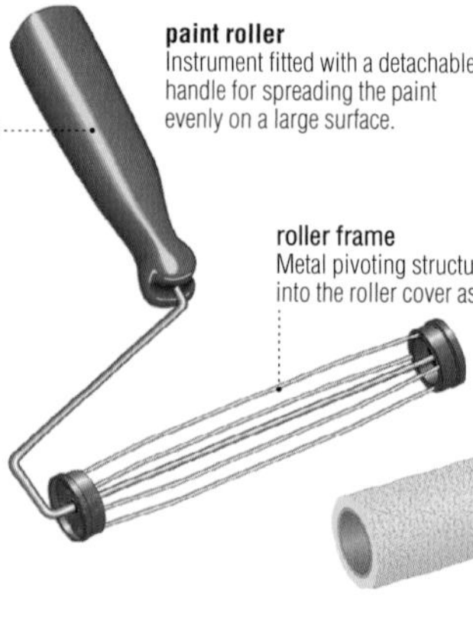

handle

roller frame
Metal pivoting structure inserted into the roller cover as support.

roller cover
Detachable cylindrical part, covered with natural or synthetic fibers adapted to the nature of the product being applied.

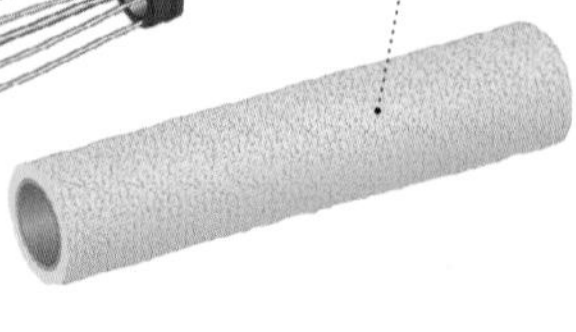

ladders and stepladders

Movable devices of wood or metal, composed of rungs or steps and used to reach relatively high areas.

foldaway ladder
Articulating ladder that can be folded up into a trap door.

straight ladder
Ladder that leans against a wall, comprised of two parallel side rails joined by rungs.

hook ladder
Straight ladder with one end having fixed or detachable hooks to keep the ladder in place on a structure.

extension ladder
Straight ladder of adjustable height, made up of two superimposed planes that slide one on the other.

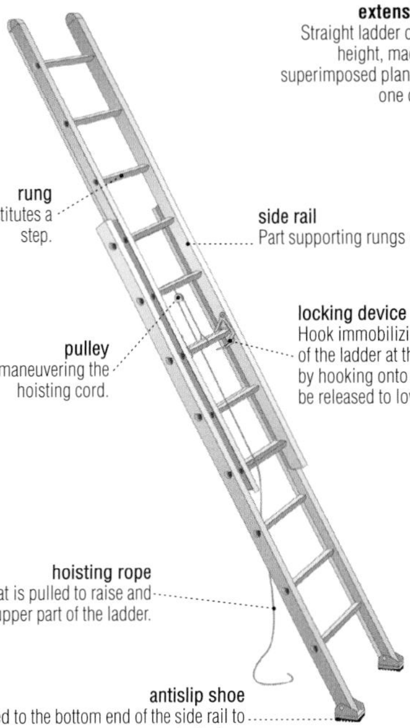

rung
Bar on a ladder that constitutes a step.

side rail
Part supporting rungs or steps.

locking device
Hook immobilizing the upper part of the ladder at the desired height by hooking onto a rung; it can also be released to lower the upper part.

pulley
Small wheel for maneuvering the hoisting cord.

hoisting rope
Rope that is pulled to raise and lower the upper part of the ladder.

antislip shoe
Part attached to the bottom end of the side rail to prevent slipping.

ladder scaffold
Movable structure made up of two vertical ladders and a work platform as well as wheels fitted with blocking devices.

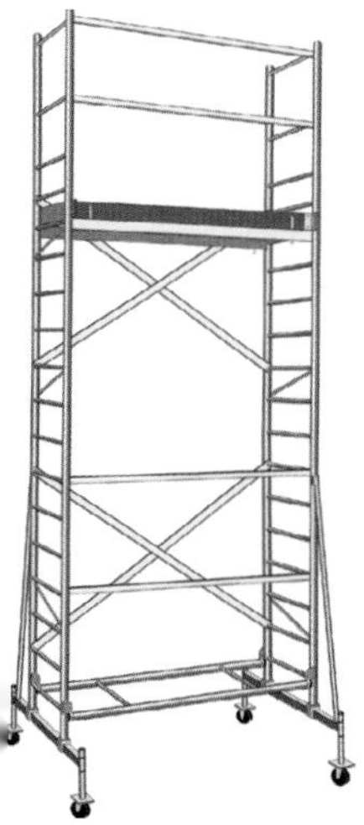

rope ladder
Suspension ladder whose side rails and rungs are made of cord.

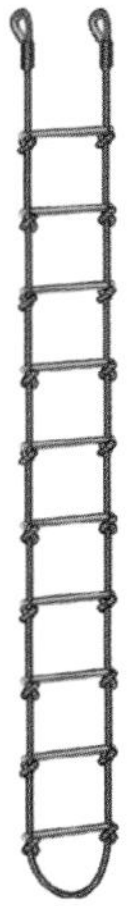

fruit-picking ladder
Double ladder specially designed for picking fruit and for pruning and maintaining trees.

multipurpose ladder
Ladder with several folds, which can be locked in a number of positions.

rolling ladder
Movable ladder fitted with a platform and a safety rail; it can be moved on wheels equipped with blocking devices.

stepladder
Small ladder, often folding, that is usually composed of three to six steps.

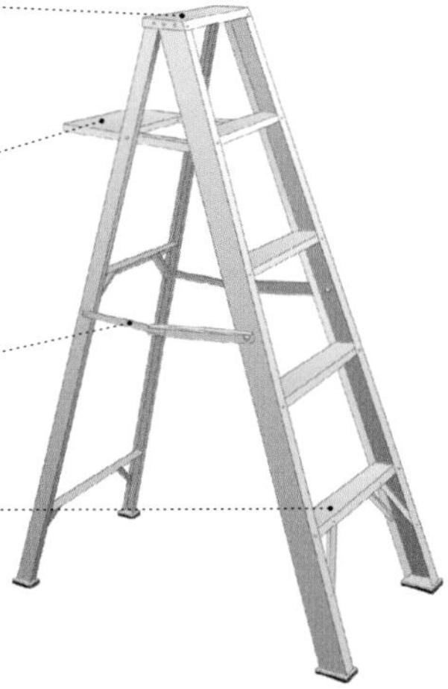

top
Flat top of a stepladder upon which objects can be placed.

tool shelf
Flat folding surface upon which tools can be placed.

brace
Folding cross piece maintaining the gap between the two opposite side rails, thereby providing stability.

step
Flat narrow surface that supports the feet when climbing, descending or standing.

step stool
Stool equipped with steps usually folding under the seat.

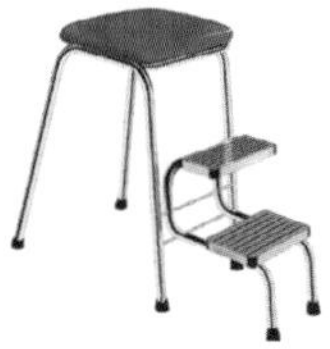

platform ladder
Small indoor ladder, usually folding, that comprises a small number of steps.

safety rail
Part serving as a support and protection barrier.

shelf
Flat folding shelf upon which objects can be placed.

platform
Wider step for standing on safely.

frame
Parts supporting the steps and the platform of a platform ladder.

rubber tip
Rubber part attached to the ends of the frame to prevent slipping.

step
Flat narrow surface that supports the feet when climbing, descending or standing.

pleasure garden

Private plot reserved for cultivating ornamental plants where one strolls and relaxes.

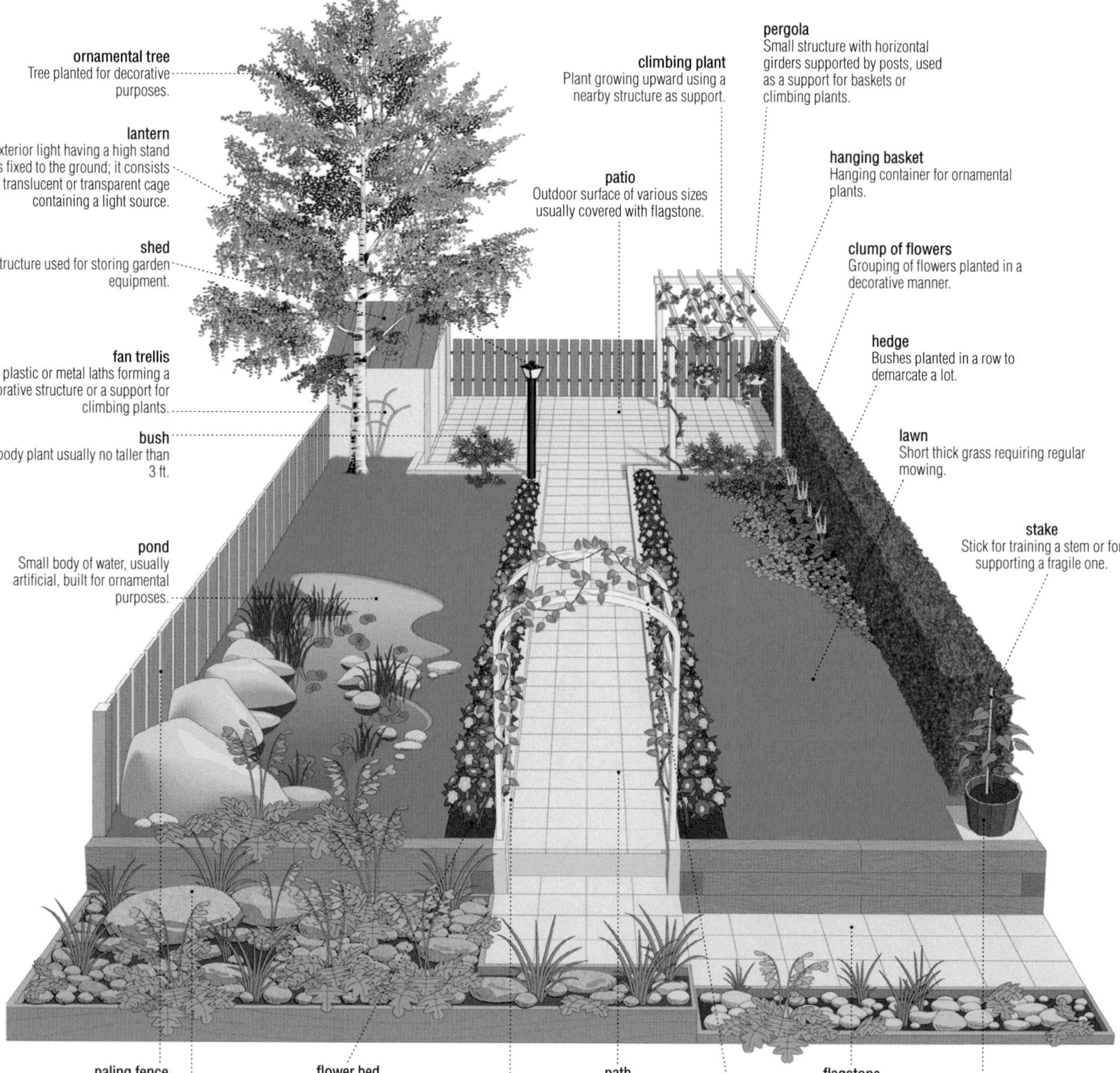
ornamental tree
Tree planted for decorative purposes.
lantern
Exterior light having a high stand that is fixed to the ground; it consists of a translucent or transparent cage containing a light source.
shed
Structure used for storing garden equipment.
fan trellis
Wood, plastic or metal laths forming a decorative structure or a support for climbing plants.
bush
Woody plant usually no taller than 3 ft.
pond
Small body of water, usually artificial, built for ornamental purposes.
climbing plant
Plant growing upward using a nearby structure as support.
pergola
Small structure with horizontal girders supported by posts, used as a support for baskets or climbing plants.
patio
Outdoor surface of various sizes usually covered with flagstone.
hanging basket
Hanging container for ornamental plants.
clump of flowers
Grouping of flowers planted in a decorative manner.
hedge
Bushes planted in a row to demarcate a lot.
lawn
Short thick grass requiring regular mowing.
stake
Stick for training a stem or for supporting a fragile one.
paling fence
Barrier made of aligned wooden planks to demarcate a lot.
flower bed
Small plot of land adorned with plants, usually flowers.
path
Walkway bordered by plants.
flagstone
Stone, marble or cement tile for covering a surface.
rock garden
Area of land strewn with ornamental rocks, among which plants grow.
edging
Row of stones or other solid material demarcating a path.
arbor
Decorative doorway with rounded apex.
tub
Container for ornamental or edible plants.

miscellaneous equipment

motorized earth auger
Machine using a rotating bit to quickly dig holes of various sizes in the ground.

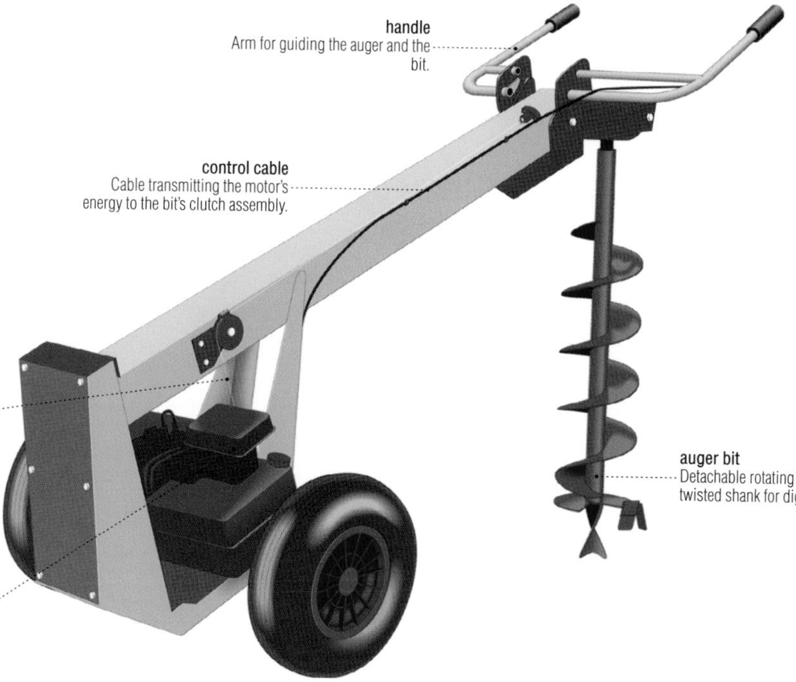
handle
Arm for guiding the auger and the bit.
control cable
Cable transmitting the motor's energy to the bit's clutch assembly.
starting cable
Electric cable controlling the starter.
motor
Device converting the combustion of fuel and air into mechanical energy.
auger bit
Detachable rotating part, with a twisted shank for digging holes.

compost bin
Container for decomposing organic waste from the garden and kitchen to produce fertilizer (compost).

wheelbarrow
Small one-wheeled handcart for transporting material such as supplies, tools, soil and debris.

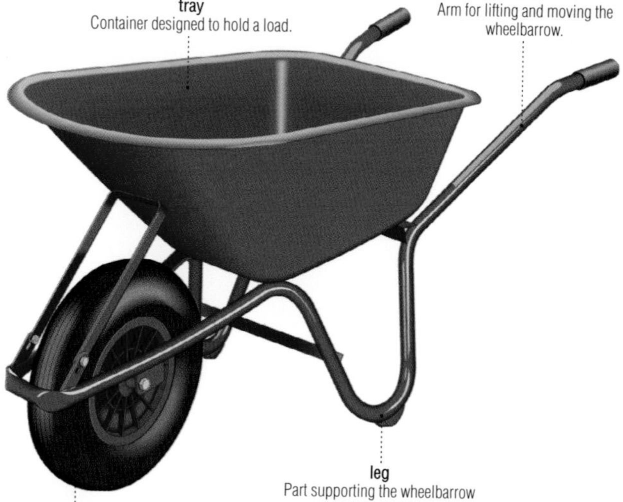
tray
Container designed to hold a load.
handle
Arm for lifting and moving the wheelbarrow.
leg
Part supporting the wheelbarrow when at rest.
wheel
Circular object rotating around an axle so that the wheelbarrow can be moved.

seeding and planting tools

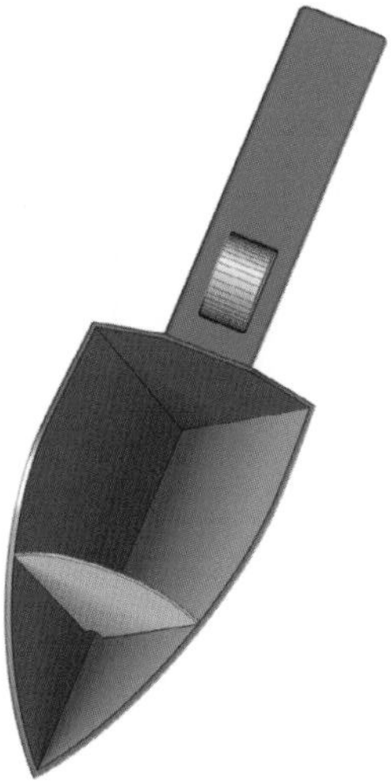

seeder
Small shovel fitted with a distribution device for sowing seeds without touching them.

dibble
Pointed tool for digging a small hole in the ground in which to plant seeds or bulbs.

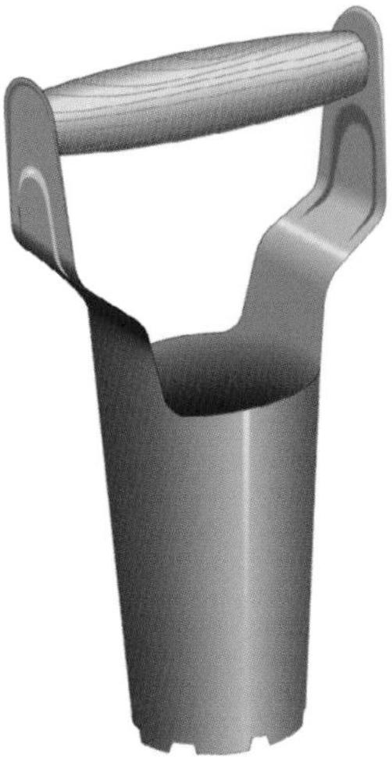

bulb dibble
Tool with a cylindrical container for removing a core of soil to create a hole in which plant bulbs or young plants are planted.

spreader
Small handcart with a reservoir and distribution mechanism for evenly spreading seeds or fertilizer on an area.

garden line
Cord stretched between two stakes and used as a guide for marking straight furrows and edges for a border or a hedge, or for demarcating sections of a vegetable garden.

stake
Stick for training a stem or for supporting a fragile one.

hand tools

Instruments used for working the soil in cramped spaces, such as a flower bed, small clumps, containers and baskets.

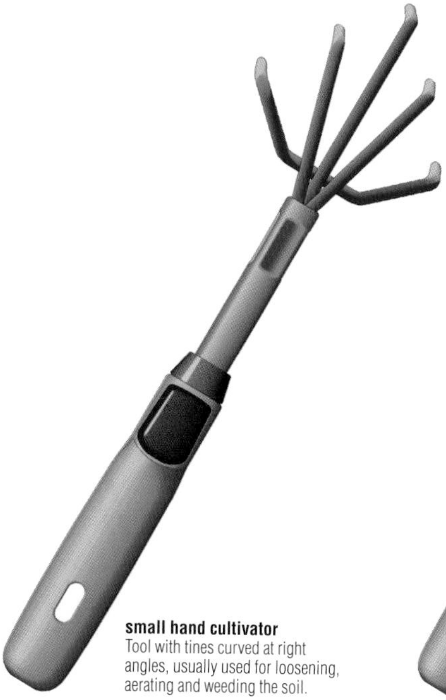

small hand cultivator
Tool with tines curved at right angles, usually used for loosening, aerating and weeding the soil.

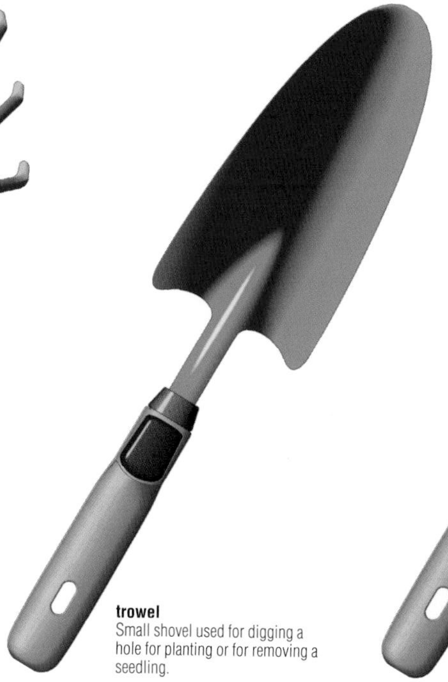

trowel
Small shovel used for digging a hole for planting or for removing a seedling.

weeder
Tool with a narrow blade for pulling up weeds with deep roots.

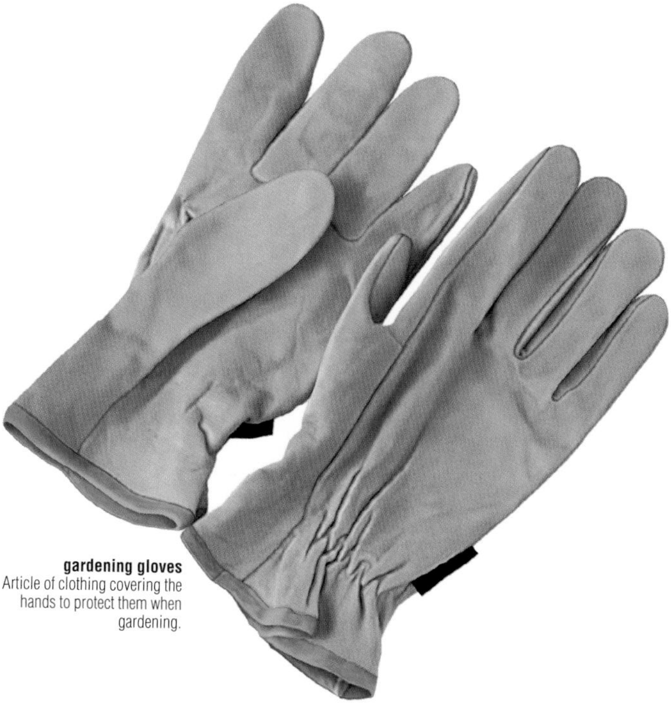

gardening gloves
Article of clothing covering the hands to protect them when gardening.

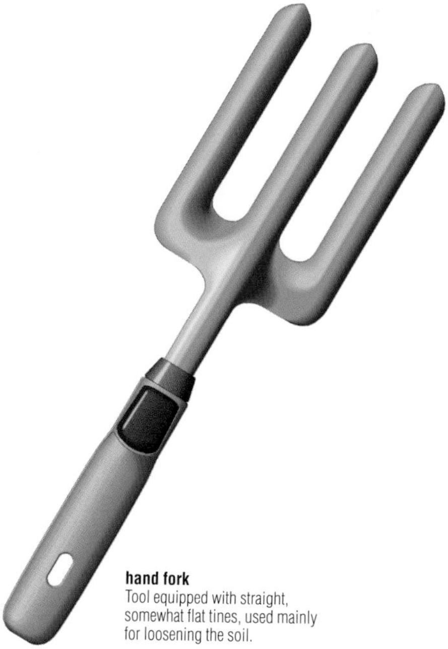

hand fork
Tool equipped with straight, somewhat flat tines, used mainly for loosening the soil.

tools for loosening the earth

shovel
Tool used for digging holes and manipulating various objects, such as soil, sand and compost.

spade
Tool with a flat or slightly concave blade, used mainly for turning over soil.

spading fork
Tool with metal tines, which make it easier to loosen soil that is hard or contains many stones or roots.

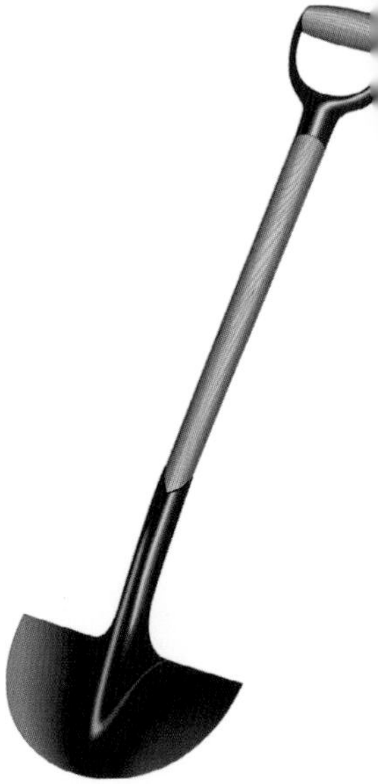

lawn edger
Tool with a semicircular blade for trimming the edge of the lawn, usually along a driveway, a patio or flower bed.

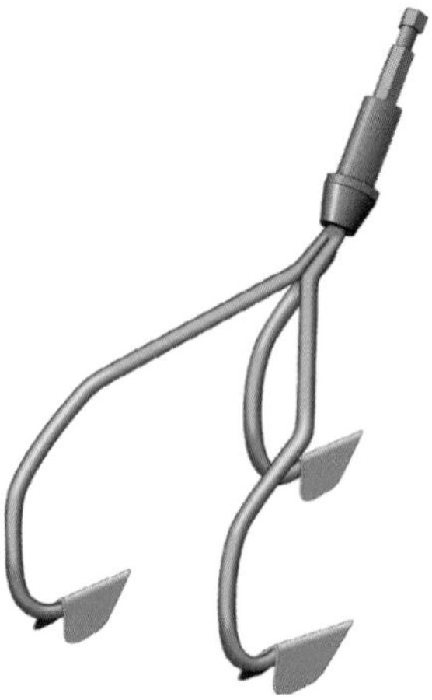

weeding hoe
Tool with claws designed mainly for loosening and weeding soil.

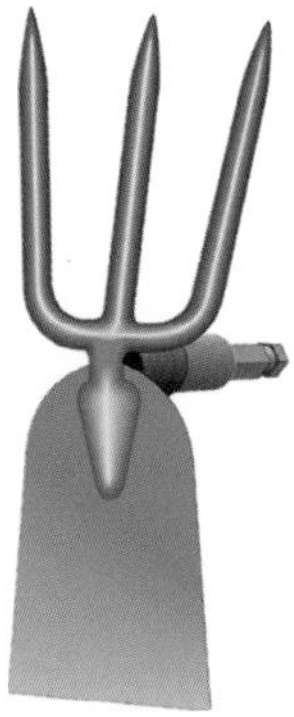

hoe-fork
Tool with a blade, which serves as a hoe, and tines; it is used especially for making furrows.

draw hoe
Tool whose blade loosens, weeds and aerates the soil; it is also used to groom the soil around a plant.

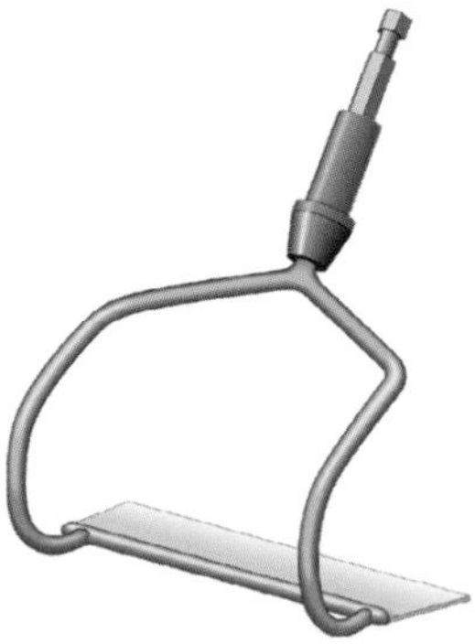

scuffle hoe
Tool whose blade, more slanted that that of the draw hoe, loosens, weeds and aerates the soil; it is also used for harvesting root vegetables.

tools for loosening the earth

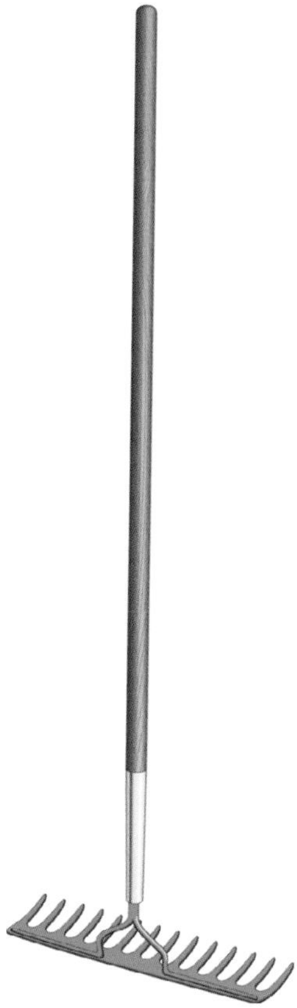

rake
Tool with tines perpendicular to the handle, for leveling the soil, removing pebbles and gathering debris.

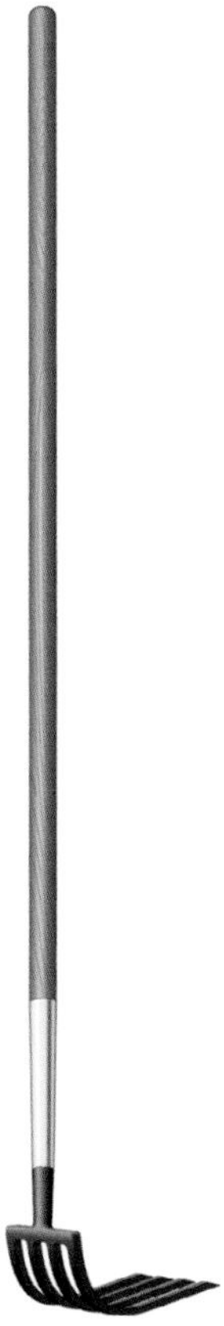

hook
Tool with curved tines, used to handle fertilizer and compost, pull up root vegetables and loosen or weed the soil.

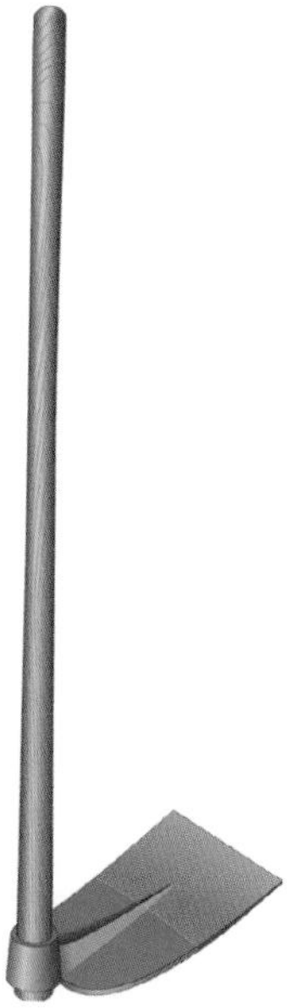

hoe
Tool with a thick sturdy blade attached directly to the handle; it is used especially for loosening and weeding dense soil.

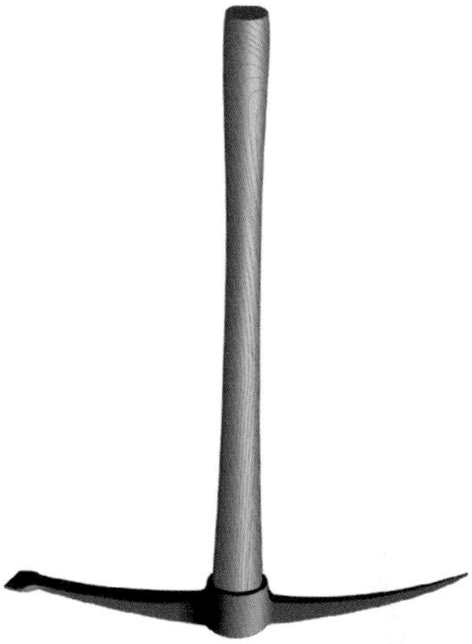

pick
Tool whose head is pointed on one end and has a cutting edge on the other; it is used to break up hard or rocky soil.

tiller
Motorized machine that uses its rotating tines to turn over and loosen the soil and mix fertilizer into it.

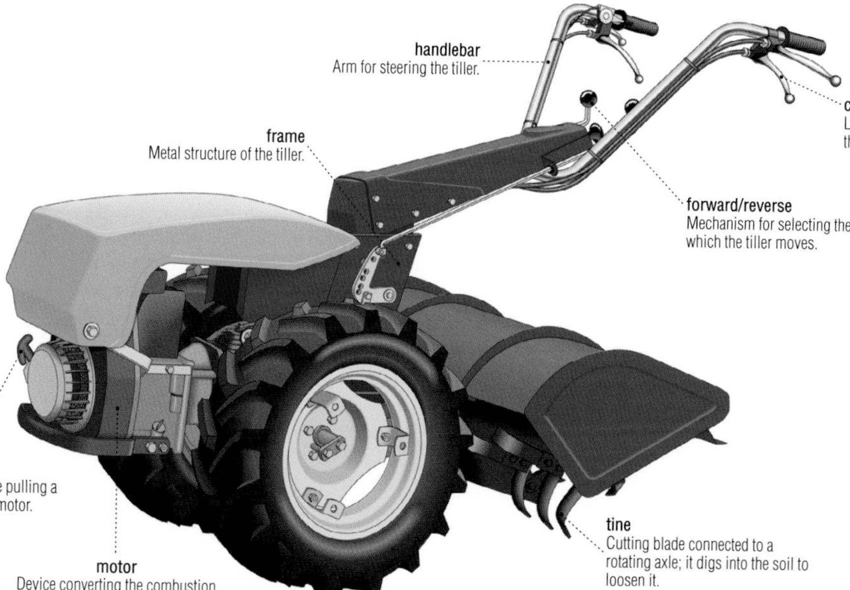

handlebar
Arm for steering the tiller.

clutch lever
Lever controlling the tiller's motion and the tines' rotation.

frame
Metal structure of the tiller.

forward/reverse
Mechanism for selecting the direction in which the tiller moves.

starter
Hand-activated device pulling a cable to start the motor.

tine
Cutting blade connected to a rotating axle; it digs into the soil to loosen it.

motor
Device converting the combustion of fuel and air into mechanical energy.

watering tools

hose trolley
Reel mounted on a cart, for transporting and storing a garden hose.

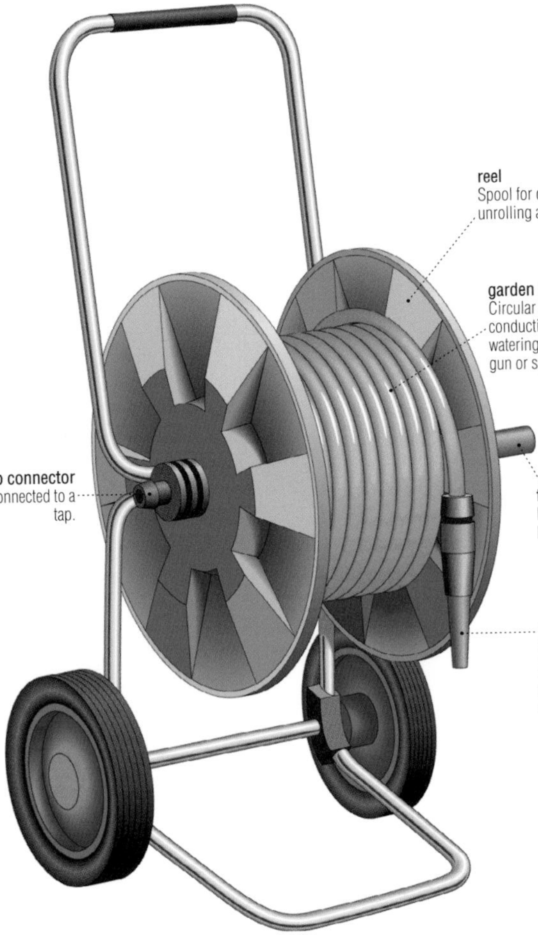

reel
Spool for quickly rolling and unrolling a garden hose.

garden hose
Circular pipe, flexible or semirigid, conducting water from a tap to a watering device such as a nozzle, gun or sprinkler.

tap connector
Threaded part receiving a hose connected to a tap.

trolley crank
Handle for rolling up the garden hose on the reel.

hose nozzle
Detachable instrument attached to the end of a garden hose, for adjusting the shape and flow of the water spray.

sprinkler hose
Hose with small openings through which water flows; placed on the ground, it deeply waters large areas.

tank sprayer
Device with a tank and a wand that sprays fine droplets of water or treatment products on plants and soil.

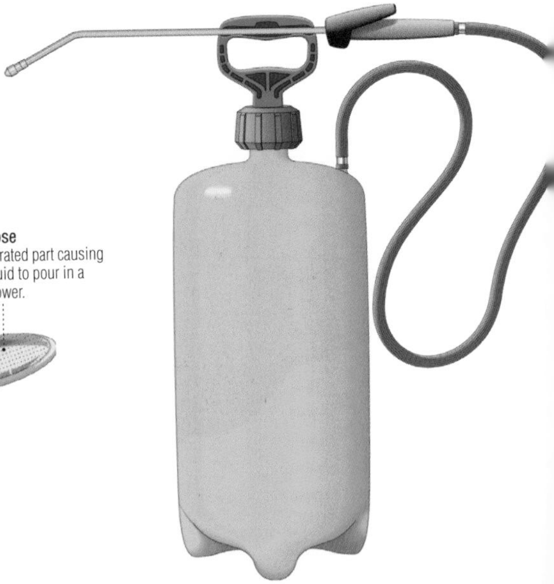

watering can
Container fitted with a long neck, usually with a rose at its end, used for sprinkling plants with water or treatment products.

handle
Part shaped like a semicircle for gripping the can.

rose
Detachable perforated part causing water or a liquid to pour in a shower.

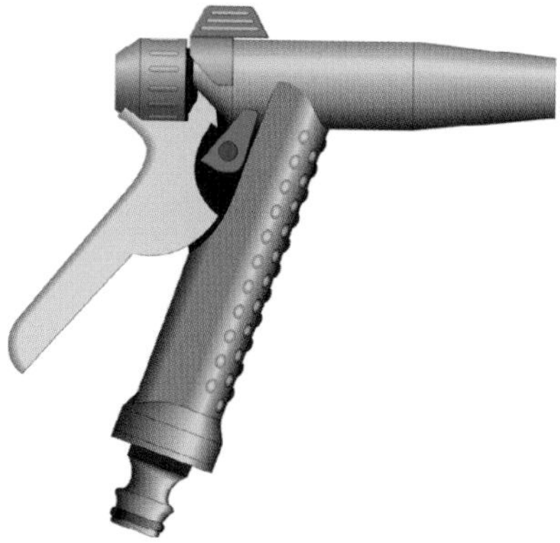

pistol nozzle
Watering nozzle activated by means of a trigger flow switch.

sprayer
Small atomizer used mainly for spraying plant foliage and seedlings.

spray nozzle
Watering gun with a wide head that contains small holes, used for watering flowers and delicate plants with a fine shower.

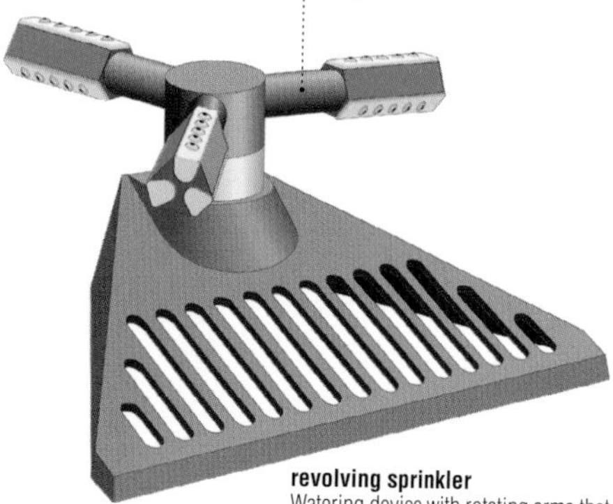

arm
Part attached to the sprinkler's pivot for distributing water.

revolving sprinkler
Watering device with rotating arms that distribute water in a full circle.

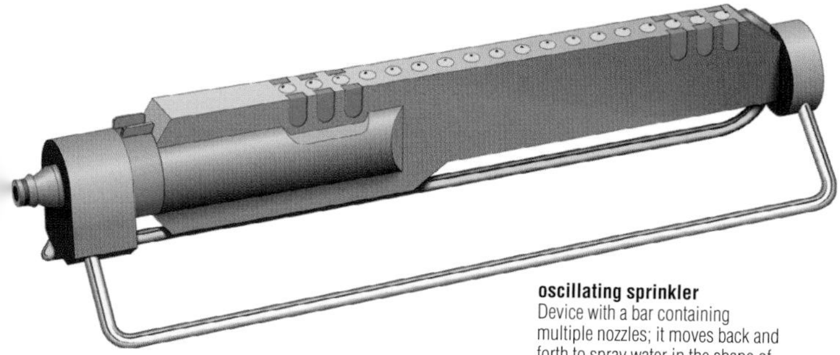

oscillating sprinkler
Device with a bar containing multiple nozzles; it moves back and forth to spray water in the shape of a fan over large areas.

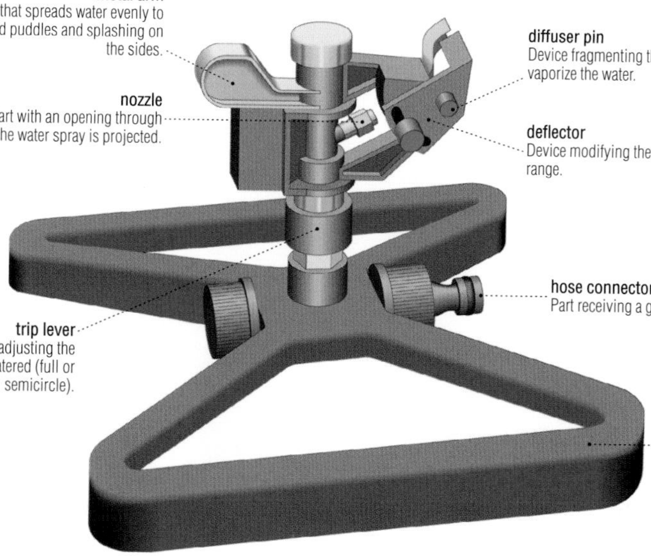

impulse sprinkler
Watering device whose single nozzle is mounted on a pivot that rotates in jerks, emitting a powerful spray to distribute water in a circle or arc.

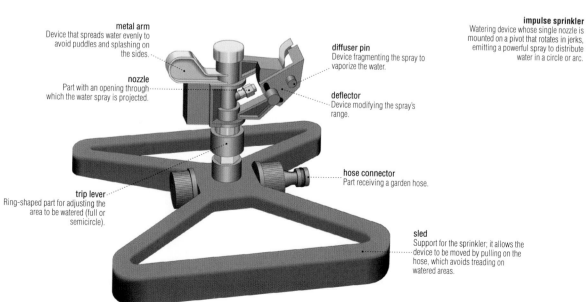

metal arm
Device that spreads water evenly to avoid puddles and splashing on the sides.

nozzle
Part with an opening through which the water spray is projected.

diffuser pin
Device fragmenting the spray to vaporize the water.

deflector
Device modifying the spray's range.

hose connector
Part receiving a garden hose.

trip lever
Ring-shaped part for adjusting the area to be watered (full or semicircle).

sled
Support for the sprinkler; it allows the device to be moved by pulling on the hose, which avoids treading on watered areas.

pruning and cutting tools

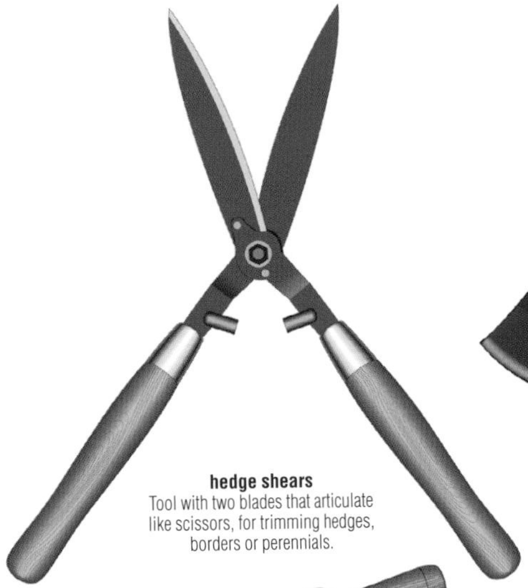

hedge shears
Tool with two blades that articulate like scissors, for trimming hedges, borders or perennials.

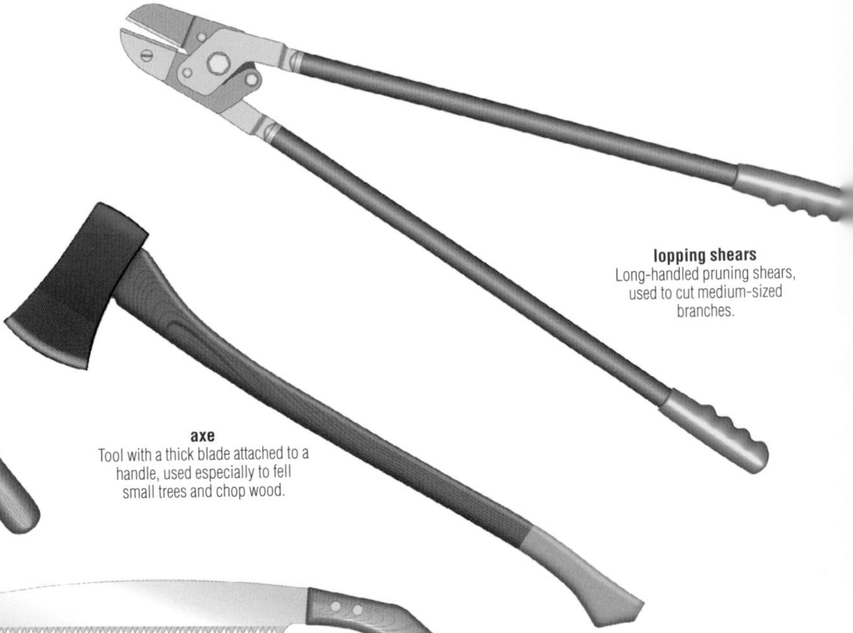

lopping shears
Long-handled pruning shears, used to cut medium-sized branches.

axe
Tool with a thick blade attached to a handle, used especially to fell small trees and chop wood.

pruning saw
Handsaw with a straight or slightly curved blade, used to cut relatively large branches.

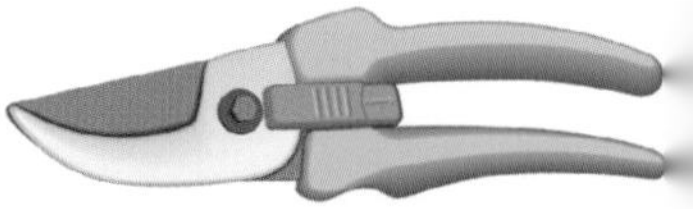

pruning shears
Tool resembling large scissors, used mainly for cutting stems and small branches.

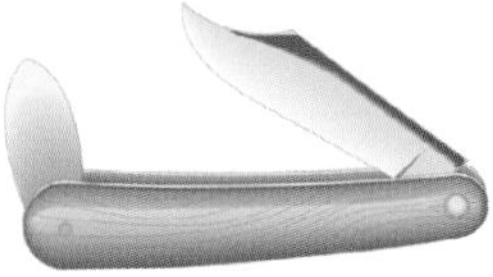

grafting knife
Small pointed knife, very sharp, designed to make grafting cuts.

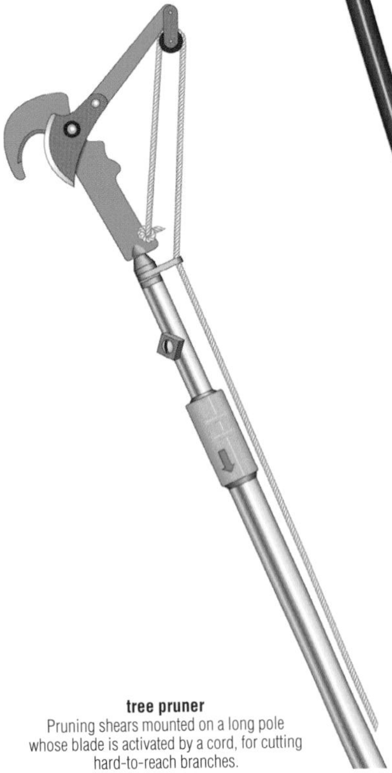

tree pruner
Pruning shears mounted on a long pole whose blade is activated by a cord, for cutting hard-to-reach branches.

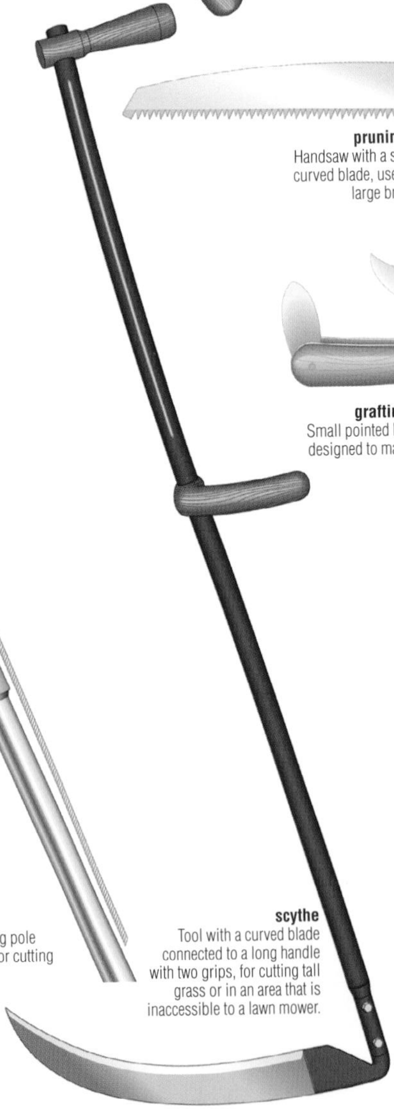

scythe
Tool with a curved blade connected to a long handle with two grips, for cutting tall grass or in an area that is inaccessible to a lawn mower.

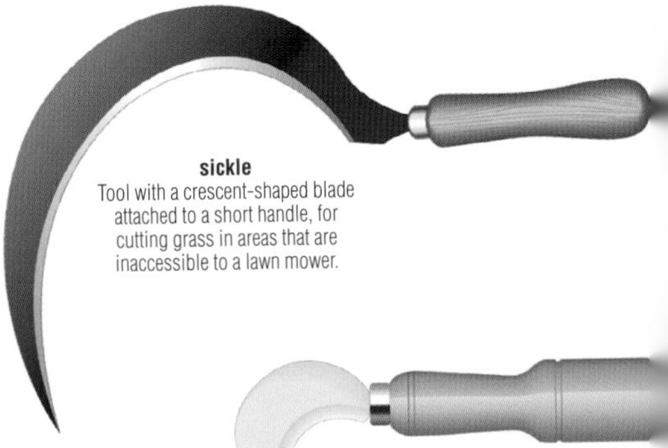

sickle
Tool with a crescent-shaped blade attached to a short handle, for cutting grass in areas that are inaccessible to a lawn mower.

pruning knife
Small billhook for cutting small branches or performing various tasks requiring a light cut.

billhook
Tool with a powerful hooked blade, used especially to cut branches and undergrowth.

pruning and cutting tools

hedge trimmer
Portable electric tool with a toothed blade, for trimming hedges and borders.

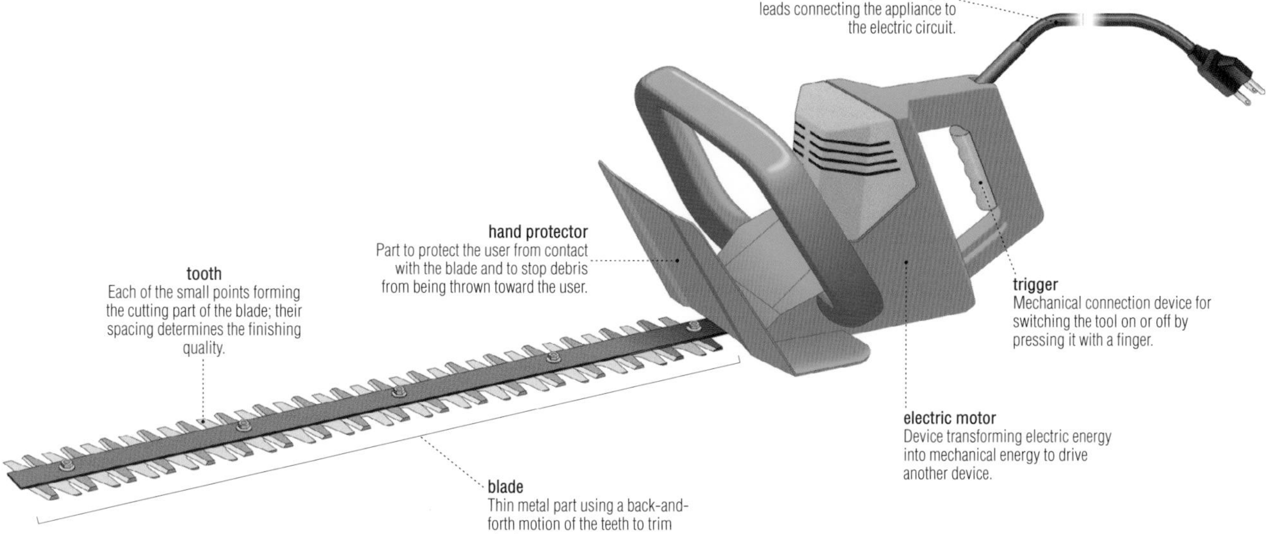
cord
Flexible electric wire housing the leads connecting the appliance to the electric circuit.
hand protector
Part to protect the user from contact with the blade and to stop debris from being thrown toward the user.
tooth
Each of the small points forming the cutting part of the blade; their spacing determines the finishing quality.
trigger
Mechanical connection device for switching the tool on or off by pressing it with a finger.
electric motor
Device transforming electric energy into mechanical energy to drive another device.
blade
Thin metal part using a back-and-forth motion of the teeth to trim plants.

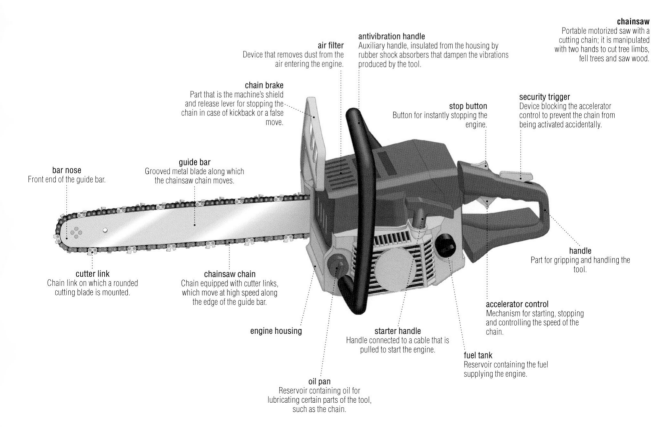

chainsaw
Portable motorized saw with a cutting chain; it is manipulated with two hands to cut tree limbs, fell trees and saw wood.

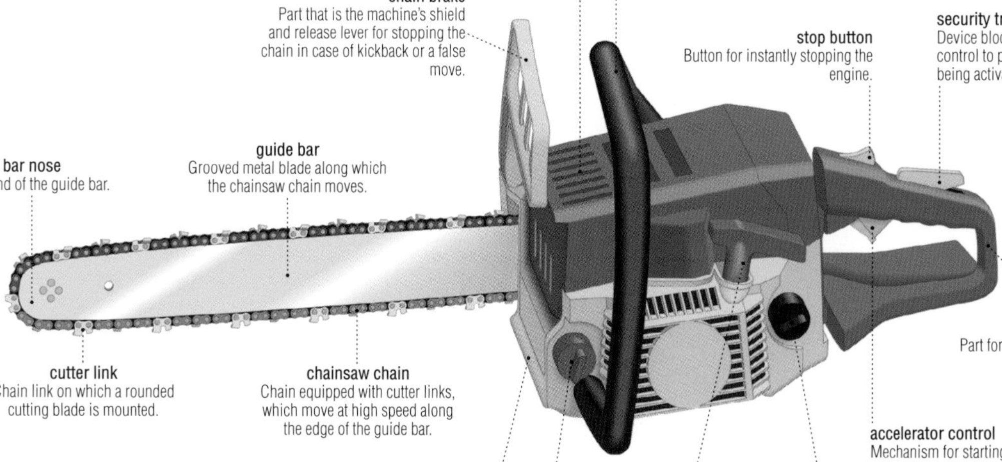
air filter
Device that removes dust from the air entering the engine.
antivibration handle
Auxiliary handle, insulated from the housing by rubber shock absorbers that dampen the vibrations produced by the tool.
chain brake
Part that is the machine's shield and release lever for stopping the chain in case of kickback or a false move.
stop button
Button for instantly stopping the engine.
security trigger
Device blocking the accelerator control to prevent the chain from being activated accidentally.
bar nose
Front end of the guide bar.
guide bar
Grooved metal blade along which the chainsaw chain moves.
handle
Part for gripping and handling the tool.
cutter link
Chain link on which a rounded cutting blade is mounted.
chainsaw chain
Chain equipped with cutter links, which move at high speed along the edge of the guide bar.
accelerator control
Mechanism for starting, stopping and controlling the speed of the chain.
engine housing
starter handle
Handle connected to a cable that is pulled to start the engine.
fuel tank
Reservoir containing the fuel supplying the engine.
oil pan
Reservoir containing oil for lubricating certain parts of the tool, such as the chain.

lawn care

lawn trimmer
Portable motorized tool, equipped with nylon yarn rotating at high speed, used for cutting grass in places inaccessible to a lawn mower.

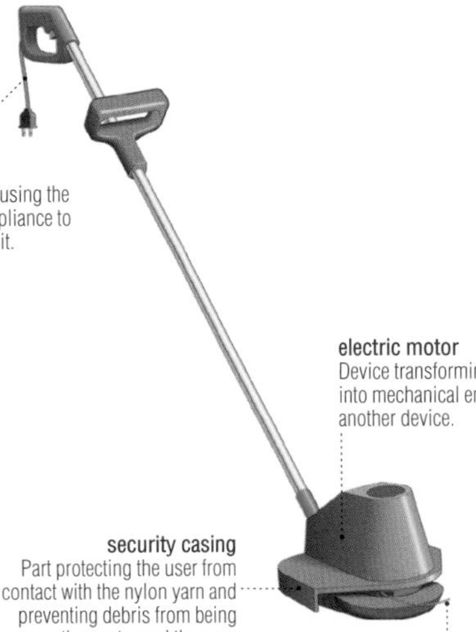

cord
Flexible electric wire housing the leads connecting the appliance to the electric circuit.

electric motor
Device transforming electric energy into mechanical energy to drive another device.

security casing
Part protecting the user from contact with the nylon yarn and preventing debris from being thrown toward the user.

nylon yarn
Nylon cord that, due to its high-speed rotation, cuts the grass.

hand mower
Hand tool equipped with a rotating cutting cylinder, used for mowing the grass over a small area.

blade
Spiral metal part that, together with the other blades, forms the cutting cylinder.

cutting cylinder
Part with several rotating blades that push the grass back against a fixed blade to cut it.

power mower
Motorized device using a rotating horizontal blade to cut grass over large areas.

ignition key
Part that is inserted into the ignition switch to start or stop the motor.

handle
Bar for moving and guiding the mower.

speed control
Mechanism for controlling the blade's rotation speed and the motion of the mower.

safety handle
Lever controlling both the blade rotation and the wheel motion.

grassbox
Detachable container collecting the cut grass.

starter
Hand-activated device pulling a cable to start the motor.

motor
Device converting the combustion of fuel and air into mechanical energy.

filler cap
Cylindrical part plugging a tank's filler opening.

accelerator cable
Cable connecting the speed control to the motor.

spark plug
Instrument with electrodes that produce sparks that ignite the gaseous mixture in the motor's combustion chamber.

deflector
Part deflecting the cut grass toward the grassbox.

casing
Part supporting and covering a rotating blade for cutting the grass.

lawn care

roller
Tool consisting of a hollow cylinder, filled with water or sand; it is rolled over the soil in order to tamp it down and even it.

lawn aerator
Roller fitted with points for puncturing the lawn in order to aerate it and facilitate the entry of substances such as water and fertilizers.

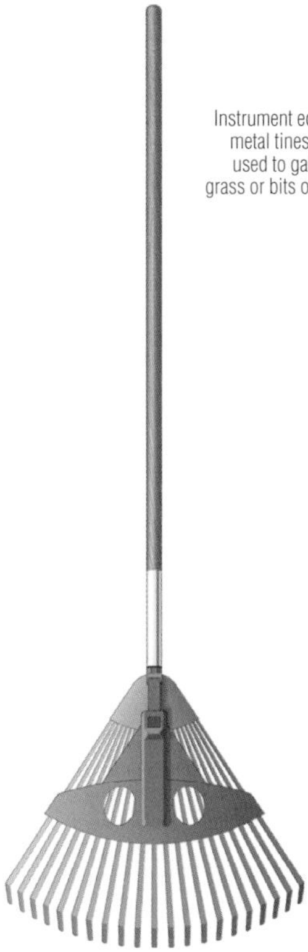

lawn rake
Instrument equipped with flexible metal tines, arranged like a fan, used to gather dead leaves, cut grass or bits of debris on the lawn.

lawn tractor
Small motorized vehicle upon which a mower deck is fixed, for cutting large expanses of grass.

seat
Part for sitting while operating the vehicle.

ignition key
Part that is inserted into the ignition switch to start or stop the motor.

steering wheel
Circular instrument used by the operator for steering the front wheels.

cruise control lever
Mechanism for selecting the vehicle's speed.

mower deck lift lever
Lever for adjusting the mower deck's height.

brake pedal
ever that the operator presses with the foot to activate the brake system.

hood
Lidlike part of the body covering and protecting the motor.

rear wheel
Circular part rotating around an axle upon which a device rests; in is case, the rear of the vehicle. Its rear wheels are the driving force.

forward travel pedal
Lever that is held down to let the vehicle go forward.

headlight
Lamp on the front of the vehicle to light up the space in front.

reverse travel pedal
Lever that is held down to let the vehicle back up.

deflector
ecting the cut grass to the side.

front wheel
Circular part rotating around an axle upon which a device rests; in this case, the front of the vehicle. Its front wheels guide the lawn tractor.

mower deck
Mobile structure supporting and covering one or more rotating blades that cut the grass.

gauge wheel
Small adjustable wheel following the contours of the terrain to give a uniform cut over uneven surfaces.

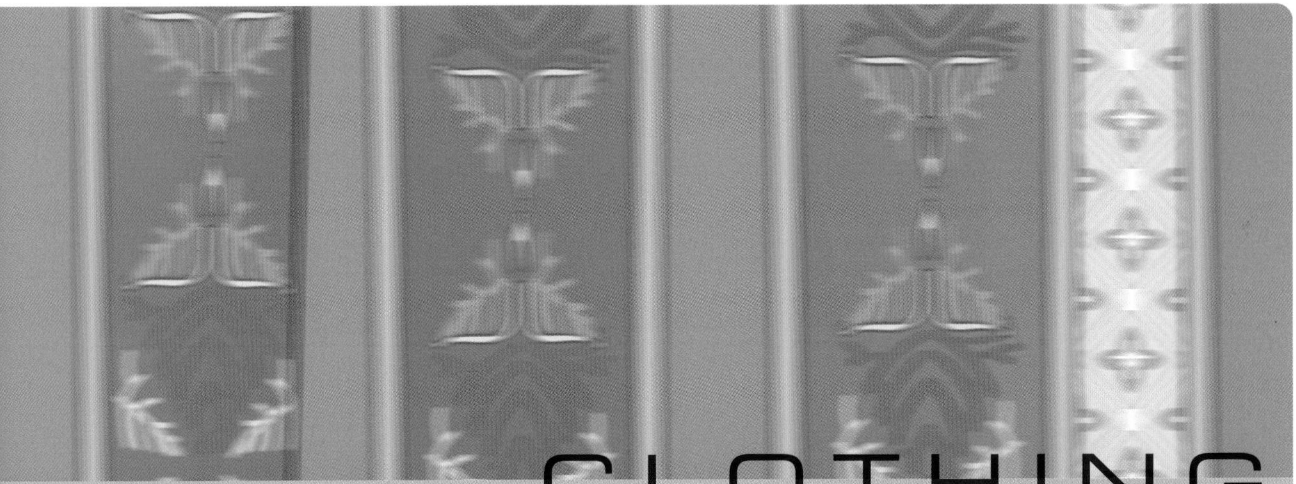

CLOTHING

Any object that covers the body to protect, conceal or adorn it.

elements of ancient costume

Examples of different articles of clothing characteristic of a period, country, condition or occasion.

peplos
In ancient times, a rectangle of woolen fabric wrapped around the torso and pinned at the shoulders, worn by Greek women.

fibula
In ancient times, a pin or metal fastener used to secure clothing.

fold
Part of the cloth folded over the belt to make it puff out.

toga
Very long length of woolen fabric that Romans wrapped around themselves, draping it over the left shoulder and arm and leaving the right arm free.

sinus
Part of the toga that draped down over the left shoulder and went under the right arm, creating carefully arranged folds.

purple border
In ancient Rome, the purple border was worn by magistrates and by boys until the age of 16.

stola
Long full robe with or without sleeves and drawn in with a belt; it was worn by Roman women.

palla
Long rectangular piece of cloth, folded in half lengthwise and used as a cloak by Roman women.

chlamys
In ancient times, a rectangle of woolen fabric pinned on one shoulder; it was worn by soldiers next to the skin or over a chiton.

chiton
Tunic worn by Greek men and women in ancient times, made of two rectangles of linen sewn together to form a tube and belted at the waist.

floating sleeve
Sleeve characterized by a long, sometimes ankle-length panel falling from the elbow.

vertical pocket
Pocket cut along the grain of the fabric.

cotehardie
In the 14th century, the cotehardie was a kind of low-cut fitted surcoat with long sleeves left open from the elbow.

short sleeve
Half sleeve covering the upper arm and extended by another half sleeve of various shapes.

sleeve
Part of the garment covering the arm; it can be of various shapes and lengths.

fringe
Strip of material with hanging threads used to decorate the border of clothing.

dress with crinoline
A 19th-century dress worn over several underskirts, including a full one made of horsehair.

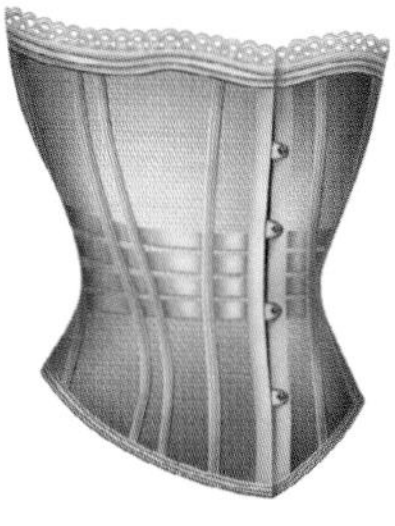

corset
Tight-fitting undergarment with stays that appeared in the 18th century; women laced it up under their dresses to shape their waists and hold in their stomachs.

underskirt
From the 16th century, the underskirt was a short skirt worn under other skirts; by the late 18th and 19th century, it had become a skirt revealed by an open-fronted dress.

shawl
In fashion since the 19th century, the shawl is a square, rectangular or triangular length of fabric used by women to cover their shoulders.

surcoat
n over a tunic by men and women from 3th to the 15th century; the women's was y long, with greatly enlarged armholes, which were often decorated with fur.

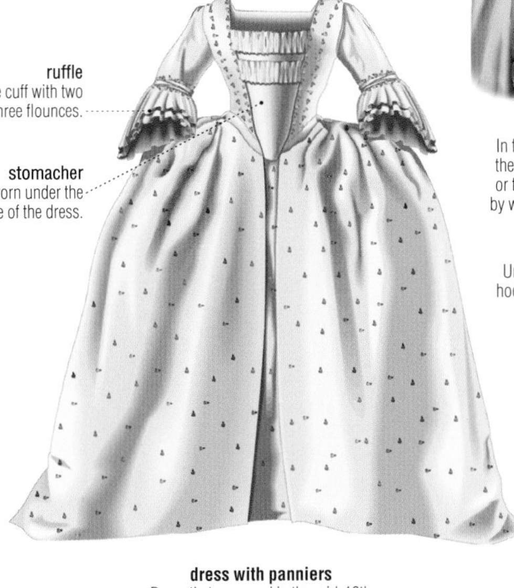

ruffle
Funnel-shaped lace cuff with two or three flounces.

stomacher
Decorative triangle worn under the bodice of the dress.

dress with panniers
Dress that appeared in the mid-18th century; it was worn over an underskirt with two hoops that made it puff out at the hips.

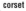

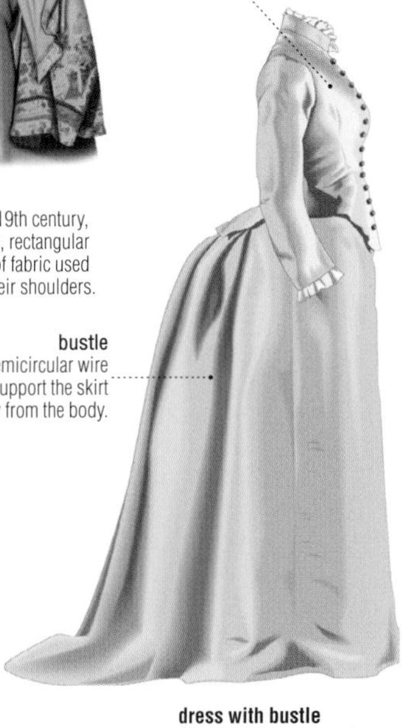

caraco jacket
Close-fitting bodice with sleeves, cut off at the hip and buttoned in front; it appeared in the second half of the 18th century.

bustle
Underskirt with a semicircular wire hoop at the back to support the skirt and draw it away from the body.

dress with bustle
Dress that appeared about 1870; it was worn over a bustle; which gave fullness to the back of the skirt.

frock coat
In the 19th century, a vest with no pockets that was extended by two long panels in the back.

waistcoat
Worn since the end of the 18th century, the waistcoat is tight and sleeveless; the front is buttoned and made of quality material while the back is made of lining.

breeches
Tight knee-length pants that appeared in the second half of the 17th century.

justaucorps
Long garment for men that was close-fitting and slightly flared at the bottom. It was initially worn as a military uniform; after 1670 it became an item of civilian clothing.

vest
In the 17th and 18th centuries, the vest was worn under the justaucorps; it hung straight and had two pockets with flaps and tight sleeves.

cuff
Reverse side of the sleeve or a strip of material added to the end of a sleeve and folded back.

breeches
Tight knee-length pants that appeared in the second half of the 17th century.

cape
Very full coat of variable length that covered the body and arms; it had no sleeves or armholes and sometimes had a hood and slits for the arms.

jacket
Padded and belted male garment worn between the 14th and the 16th century, based on the doublet; the belt created folds below the waist and the sleeves widened at the shoulders.

houppelande
Long full ceremonial garment (man's coat or woman's dress) worn at the end of the 14th century and in the early 15th century.

doublet
Tight padded garment with a belt and sleeves; it was worn by men from the 14th to the 17th century.

wing
Piece of fabric added to the armhole to accentuate the width of the shoulder.

hanging sleeve
Long sleeve, slashed at the elbow so the arm could extend out of it.

trunk hose
Shorter version of braies and a forerunner of breeches, trunk hose were worn from the 16th to the 17th century; they puffed out and were gathered above the knee.

braies
Full pants that were characteristic of Gallic attire; they were pulled in at the waist with a belt and tied at the ankle with straps.

hennin
In the 15th century, a high cylindrical women's headdress that was covered in expensive fabric; a transparent veil of medium length hung from it.

tricorne
Men's hat with a brim folded into three points and a relatively flat crown; it was worn in the 17th and 18th centuries.

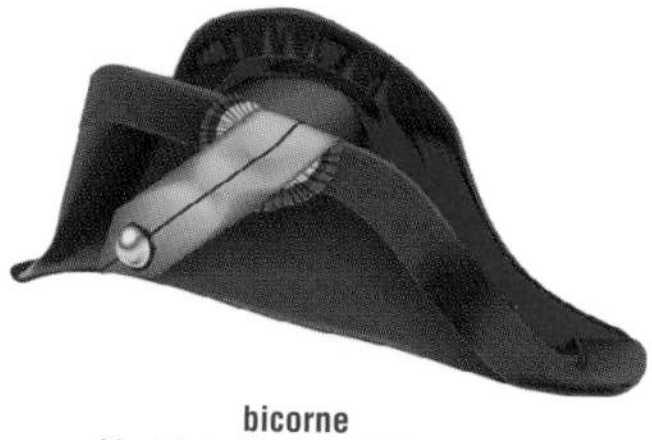

bicorne
Men's hat with a brim folded into two points; it replaced the tricorne after the French Revolution.

heeled shoe
In the 17th century, the heeled shoe had a large tongue decorated with a bow or a buckle.

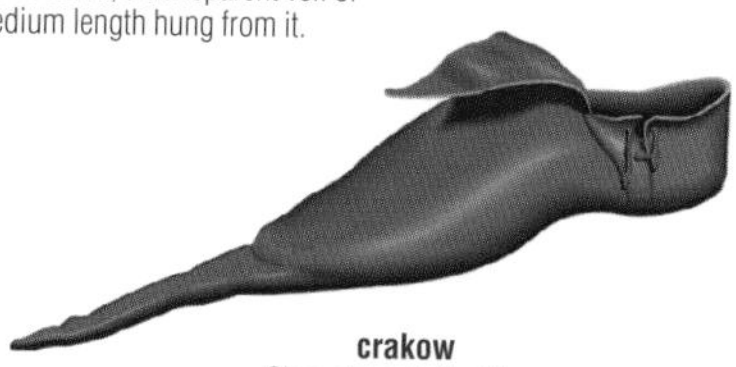

crakow
Shoe characterized by a disproportionately long toe; it was in fashion from the end of the 14th through the 15th century.

collaret
Piece of delicate, pleated or gathered fabric that adorned the neck of a dress; its shape varied greatly from one period to another.

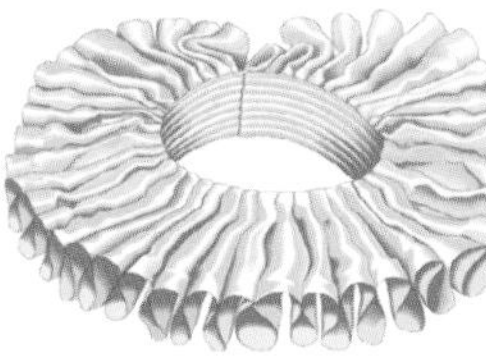

fraise
Stiff pleated collaret worn by men and women from the late 16th century to the beginning of the 17th century.

gaiter
Cover for the top of the shoe and the lower part of the leg; it was held in place by an understrap and fastened at the side with buttons or hooks.

traditional clothing

Examples of clothing that have characterized different regions for a number of generations.

boubou
Full garment made from a length of fabric folded in two; it is worn by black African men and women.

caftan
Long full garment, often richly decorated; it is worn by men as ceremonial attire in the eastern Mediterranean region.

loincloth
Piece of fabric or woven plant fibers that is worn around the waist by certain peoples of South America, Africa and Oceania.

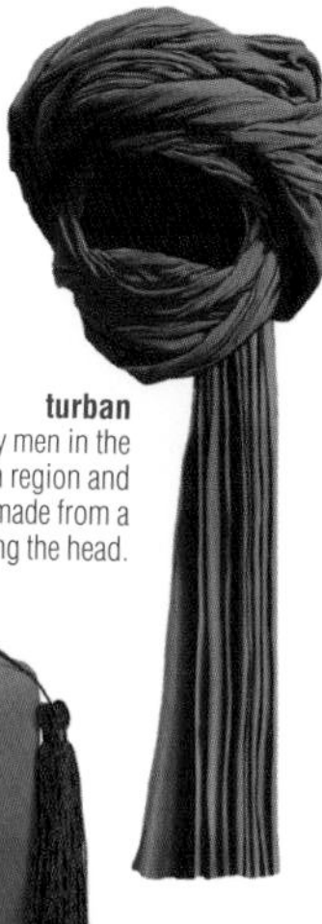

turban
Headgear worn by men in the eastern Mediterranean region and southern Asia and made from a strip of fabric encircling the head.

fez
Skullcap of white or red woolen fabric, usually bearing a tassel; it has long been the traditional Turkish headgear.

headgear

Item of attire used to cover, protect or adorn the head.

men's headgear

felt hat
Soft hat with a dented crown that is adorned with a wide ribbon; it is made from a single piece and has a brim of uniform width.

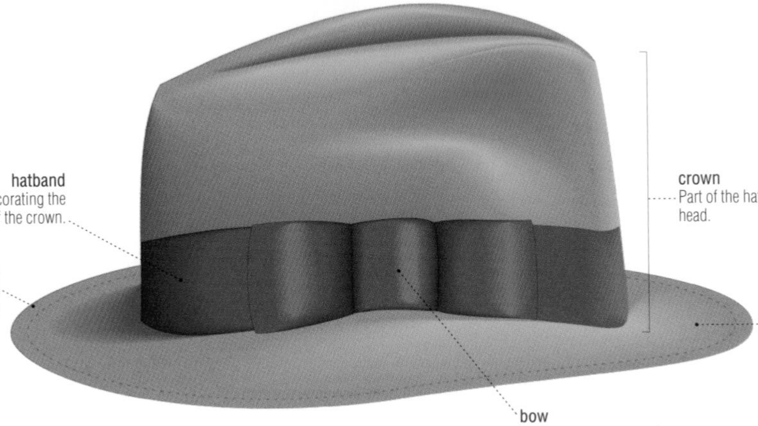

hatband
Wide silk ribbon decorating the base of the crown.

binding
Strip of fabric running along the edge of the hat.

crown
Part of the hat that fits on top of the head.

brim
Part of the hat encircling the base of the crown.

bow
Point where the ends of the hatband are tied to trim the hat.

boater
Stiff straw headgear with a flat brim of uniform width and an oval crown circled with a ribbon; it was worn at the end of the 19th century.

skullcap
Small round cap covering only the top of the head.

derby
Headgear primarily for men that appeared at the end of the 19th century; it is made of stiff felt with a circular rounded crown and an upturned narrow brim.

garrison cap
Elongated brimless headgear with a soft flexible crown; it is worn over the brow and takes the shape of the head.

top hat
Stiff silk headgear with a high cylindrical crown circled with a ribbon and a narrow brim that is turned up at the sides; it was worn toward the end of the 18th century.

shapka
Fur hat that is native to Poland; it has ear flaps that can be turned up and tied on top of the head.

hunting cap
Thick soft cap with a peak and ear flaps, which give protection against the cold.

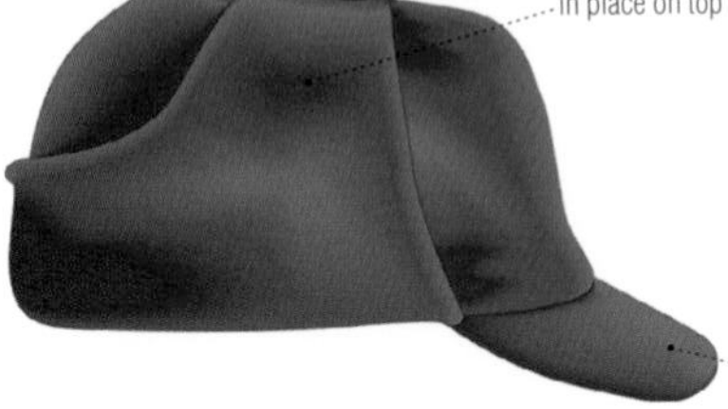

ear flap
Flap that covers the nape of the neck and the ears to keep them warm; it can be turned up and held in place on top of the head.

peak
Part that juts out over the eyes to protect them.

cap
Brimless, somewhat soft headgear that appeared at the end of the 19th century; it has a peak and a flat crown.

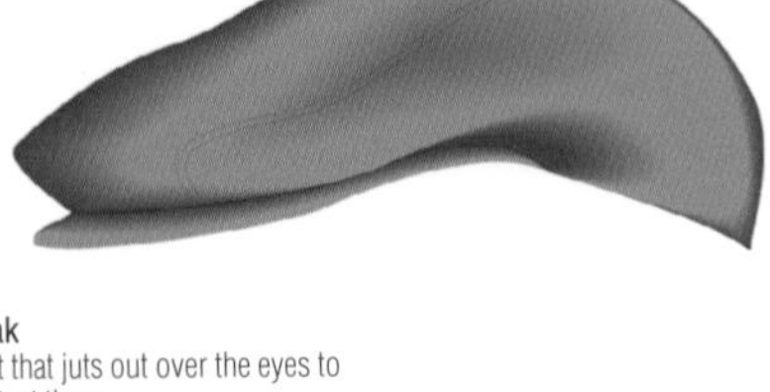

panama
Soft headgear from the end of the 19th and the early 20th century; it is made from woven jipijapa leaves and has a dented crown circled with a ribbon.

women's headgear

pillbox hat
Small low, round or oval toque worn perched on top of the head or pulled down.

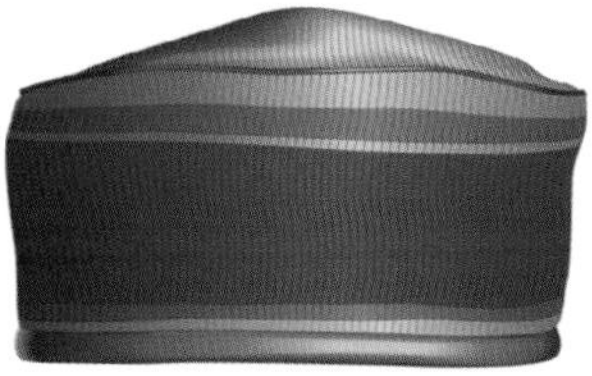

cartwheel hat
Headgear in fashion from the early 20th century, made of straw or light fibers with a large soft brim of uniform width.

cloche
Hat of the 1920s and '30s with a cylindrical crown and a narrow brim.

toque
Brimless headgear made of fabric or fur, with a cylindrical crown and a flat top that fits snugly on the head.

gob hat
Headgear made of soft light material that is worn over the brow and fits snugly on the head; the brim can be worn down to shade the face.

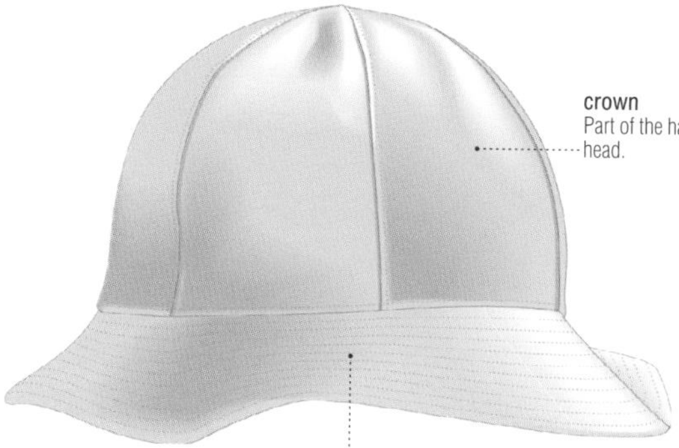

crown
Part of the hat that fits on top of the head.

brim
Part of the hat encircling the base of the crown.

turban
Headgear made of a long strip of fabric, wound around so that it covers the entire head but leaves the forehead uncovered.

southwester
Waterproof headgear with a narrow brim that widens over the nape of the neck to protect it from inclement weather.

unisex headgear
Headgear worn by members of both sexes.

balaclava
Woolen cap covering the head and neck and with an opening for the face.

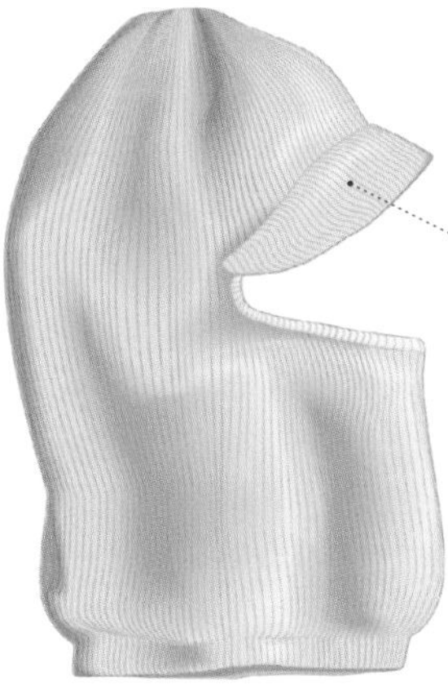

peak
Part that juts out over the eyes to protect them.

beret
Soft brimless headgear with a round flat crown that sometimes puffs out; it fits on the head by means of a simple hemmed rim or a narrow headband.

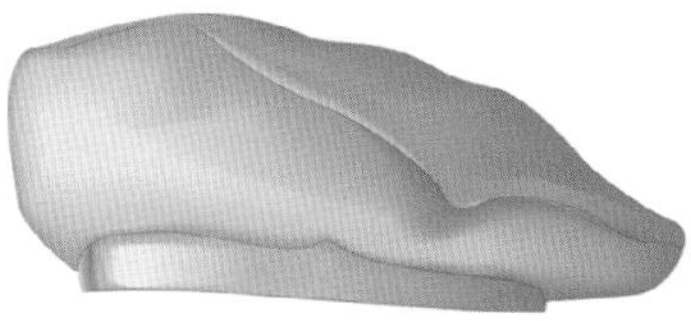

felt hat
Soft hat with a dented crown that is adorned with a wide ribbon; it is made from a single piece and has a brim of uniform width.

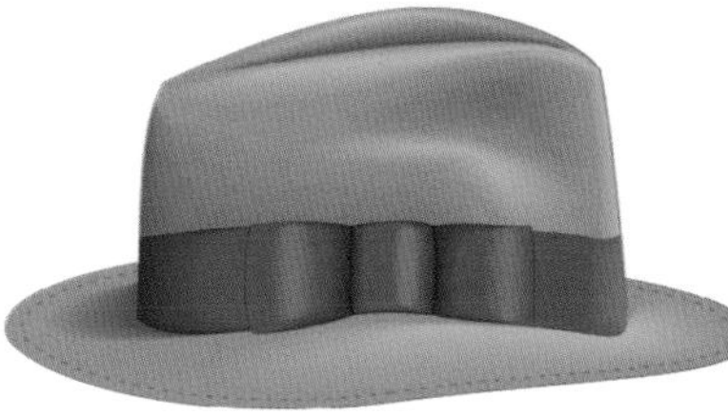

stocking cap
Woolen headgear made from a cylindrical piece that is folded over for double thickness, sewn at one end and decorated with a pompom.

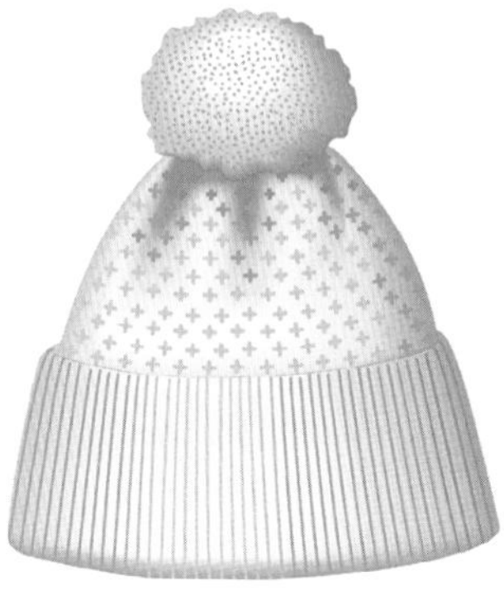

shoes

Items of attire that protect and support the foot, covering the ankle and leg to varying degrees.

men's shoes

parts of a shoe

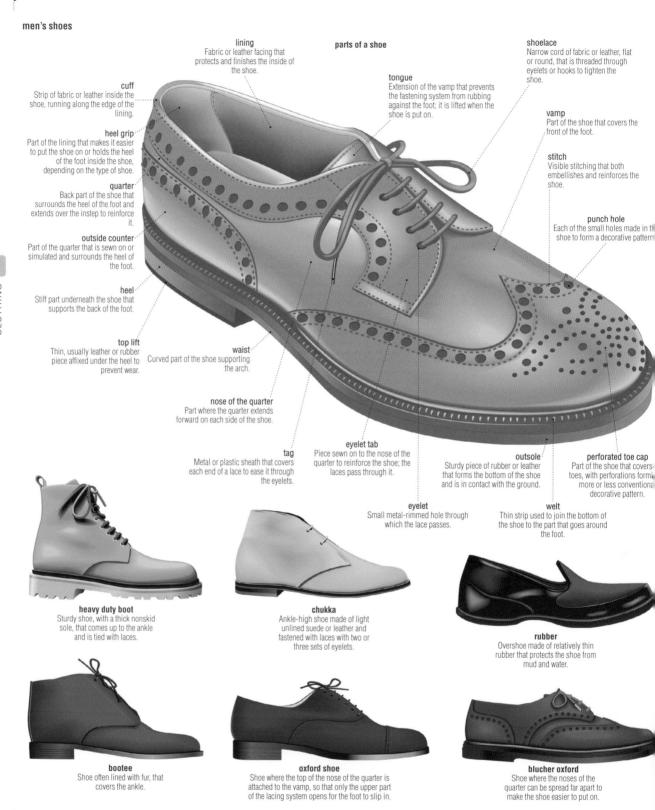

lining
Fabric or leather facing that protects and finishes the inside of the shoe.
cuff
Strip of fabric or leather inside the shoe, running along the edge of the lining.
heel grip
Part of the lining that makes it easier to put the shoe on or holds the heel of the foot inside the shoe, depending on the type of shoe.
quarter
Back part of the shoe that surrounds the heel of the foot and extends over the instep to reinforce it.
outside counter
Part of the quarter that is sewn on or simulated and surrounds the heel of the foot.
heel
Stiff part underneath the shoe that supports the back of the foot.
top lift
Thin, usually leather or rubber piece affixed under the heel to prevent wear.
waist
Curved part of the shoe supporting the arch.
nose of the quarter
Part where the quarter extends forward on each side of the shoe.
tag
Metal or plastic sheath that covers each end of a lace to ease it through the eyelets.
eyelet tab
Piece sewn on to the nose of the quarter to reinforce the shoe; the laces pass through it.
eyelet
Small metal-rimmed hole through which the lace passes.
tongue
Extension of the vamp that prevents the fastening system from rubbing against the foot; it is lifted when the shoe is put on.
shoelace
Narrow cord of fabric or leather, flat or round, that is threaded through eyelets or hooks to tighten the shoe.
vamp
Part of the shoe that covers the front of the foot.
stitch
Visible stitching that both embellishes and reinforces the shoe.
punch hole
Each of the small holes made in t
shoe to form a decorative pattern
outsole
Sturdy piece of rubber or leather that forms the bottom of the shoe and is in contact with the ground.
perforated toe cap
Part of the shoe that covers
toes, with perforations formi
more or less conventiona
decorative pattern.
welt
Thin strip used to join the bottom of the shoe to the part that goes around the foot.

heavy duty boot
Sturdy shoe, with a thick nonskid sole, that comes up to the ankle and is tied with laces.

chukka
Ankle-high shoe made of light unlined suede or leather and fastened with laces with two or three sets of eyelets.

rubber
Overshoe made of relatively thin rubber that protects the shoe from mud and water.

bootee
Shoe often lined with fur, that covers the ankle.

oxford shoe
Shoe where the top of the nose of the quarter is attached to the vamp, so that only the upper part of the lacing system opens for the foot to slip in.

blucher oxford
Shoe where the noses of the quarter can be spread far apart to make the shoe easier to put on.

women's shoes

sandal
Light shoe leaving especially the heel uncovered; it often consists only of a sole held on the foot by variously configured straps.

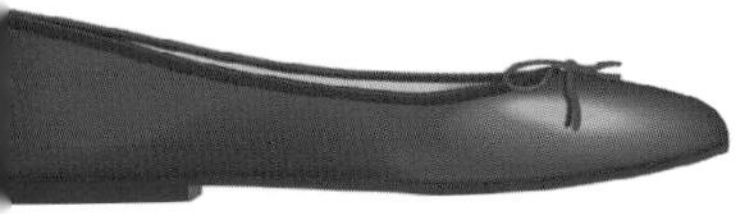

ballerina
Light supple unlined shoe that is tightened by a thin lace and sometimes has a small heel; it leaves the instep uncovered to the base of the toes.

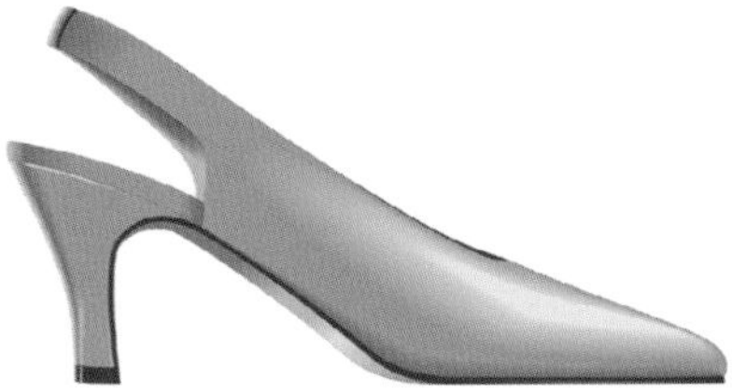

sling back shoe
Pump with a rear bar; it can be open at the toe.

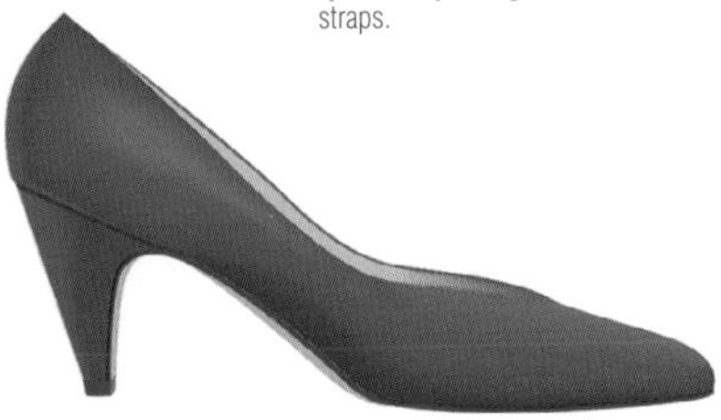

pump
Plain delicate lightweight shoe that leaves the instep uncovered; it has a heel, a thin sole and no fastening system.

T-strap shoe
Heeled shoe derived from the one-bar shoe; the vamp turns into a strap that extends over the instep and ends in a bar.

one-bar shoe
Heeled shoe characterized by a bar crossing the instep and fastened to the quarter by a buckle or button.

casual shoe
Comfortable town shoe that is suited to walking; it usually has laces and a sturdy heel.

thigh-boot
Boot that comes up to the thigh, covering most of it.

boot
Shoe that comes up to at least the calf.

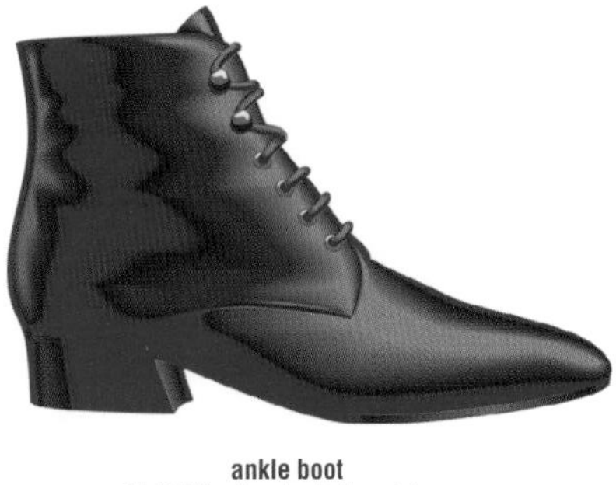

ankle boot
Tight-fitting laced or buttoned shoe that comes up over the ankle; it was worn at the turn of the 20th century.

unisex shoes

Shoes worn by members of both sexes.

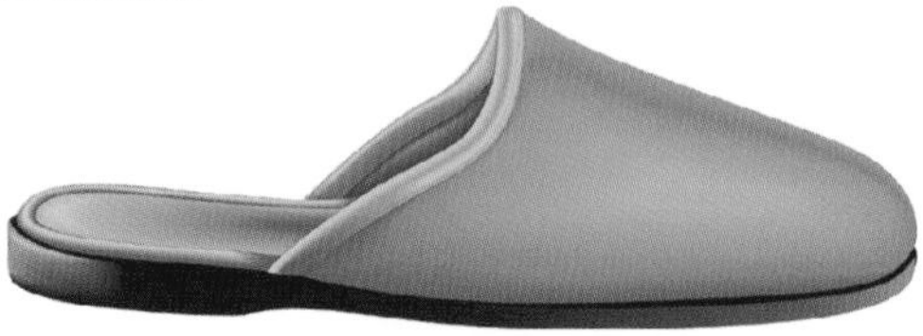

mule
Flat light, usually indoor shoe; it has a vamp only, leaving the heel bare.

tennis shoe
Flat canvas shoe with a flexible nonskid sole and a reinforced toe; the sole and toe are both made of rubber.

sandal
Shoe with a flat sole that is held on the foot by thin straps and sometimes a toe-ring.

thong
Sandal that is attached to the foot with nothing more than a Y-shaped strap, which passes between the first two toes.

sandal
Flat light sport shoe with a cutout vamp that turns into a tongue; a bar passes through the tongue and fastens at the side with a buckle.

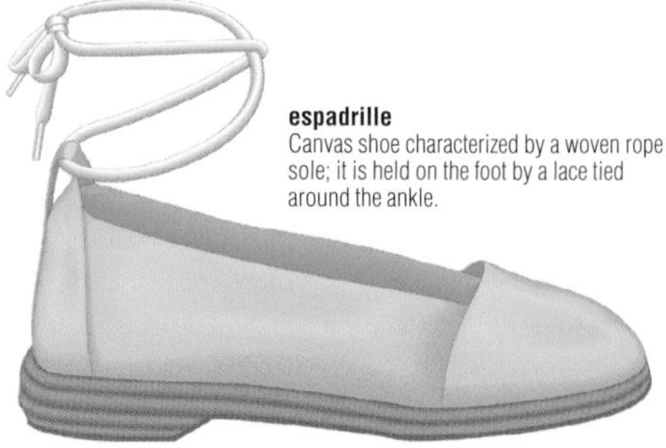

espadrille
Canvas shoe characterized by a woven rope sole; it is held on the foot by a lace tied around the ankle.

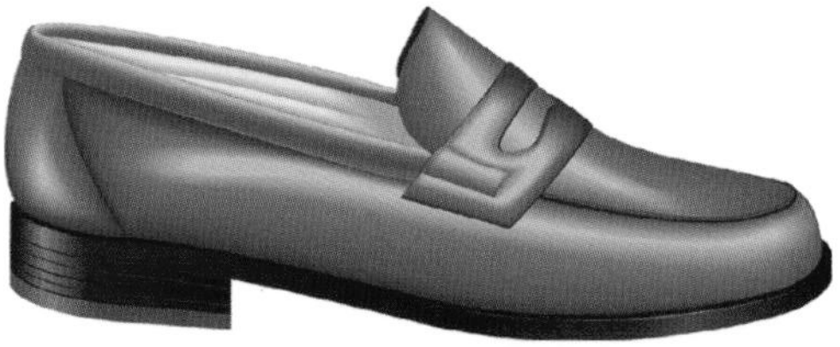

loafer
Dressy moccasin with a flat heel.

moccasin
Flat, very soft slip-on casual shoe with ridged seams; it is characterized by an apron sewn onto the vamp, which molds to the instep.

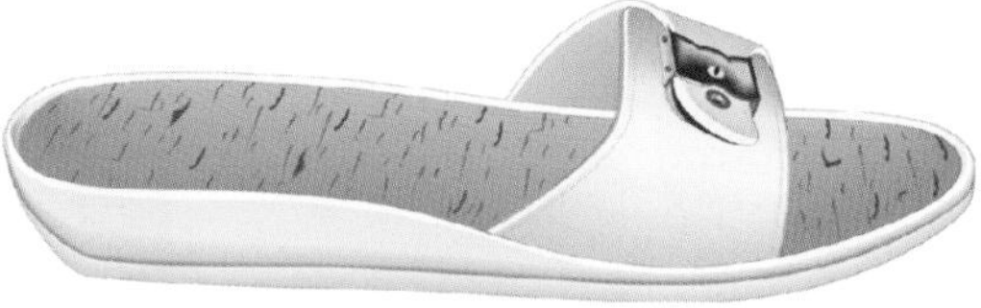

clog
Toeless mule with a thick, generally wooden sole; it is held on the foot by a thick strap.

hiking boot
Sturdy walking shoe with a thick nonskid sole; it is supported at the ankle and instep by laces threaded through hooks.

accessories

shoeshine kit
Box or case used to store various shoe care products.

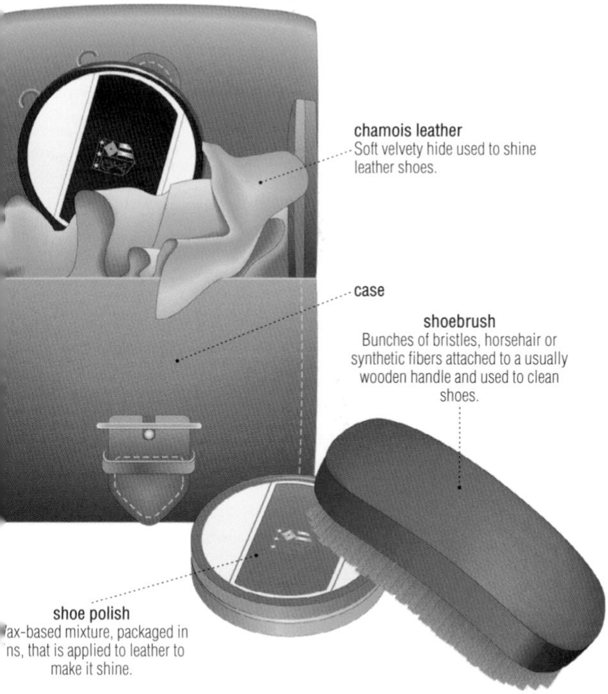

chamois leather
Soft velvety hide used to shine leather shoes.

case

shoebrush
Bunches of bristles, horsehair or synthetic fibers attached to a usually wooden handle and used to clean shoes.

shoe polish
ax-based mixture, packaged in ns, that is applied to leather to make it shine.

shoe polisher
Electric appliance with interchangeable brushes, used to polish or shine shoes.

shoehorn
Curved tongue placed at the back of the shoe to ease it onto the foot.

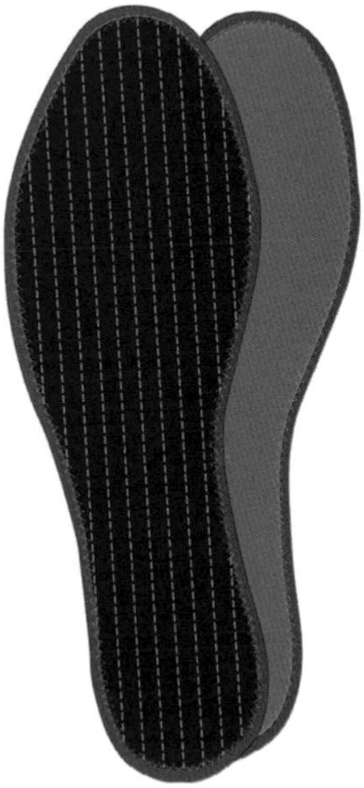

insole
Removable object placed inside the shoe to improve its fit, absorb sweat from the foot or keep it dry.

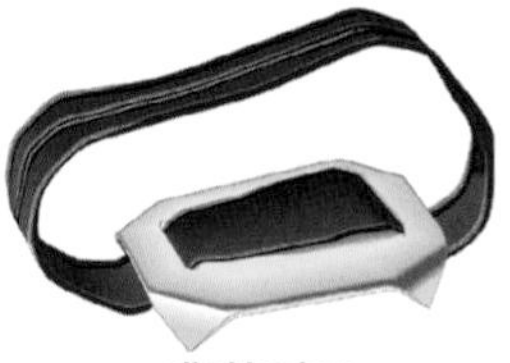

climbing iron
Object with sharp metal spikes that is attached under the shoe with a strap, making it possible to walk on hard snow or ice without slipping.

shoe rack
Device made up of one or several rows of pouches or hooks, for storing shoes.

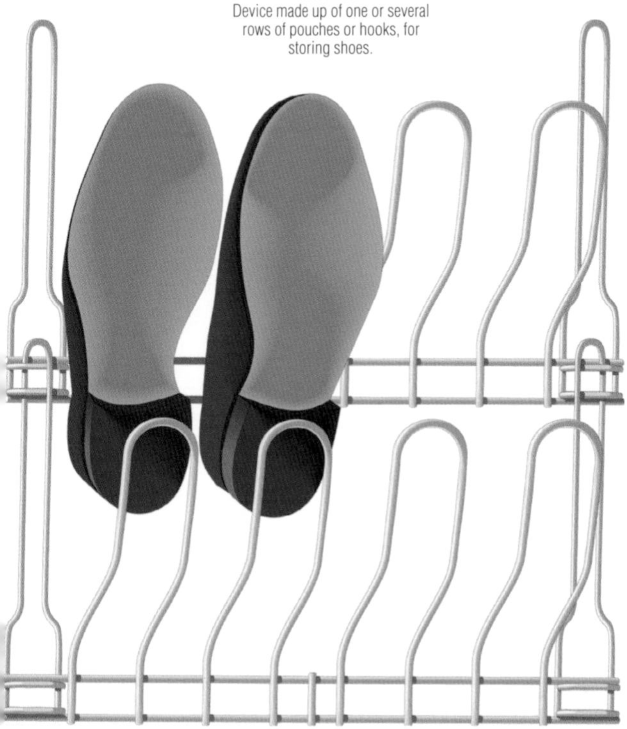

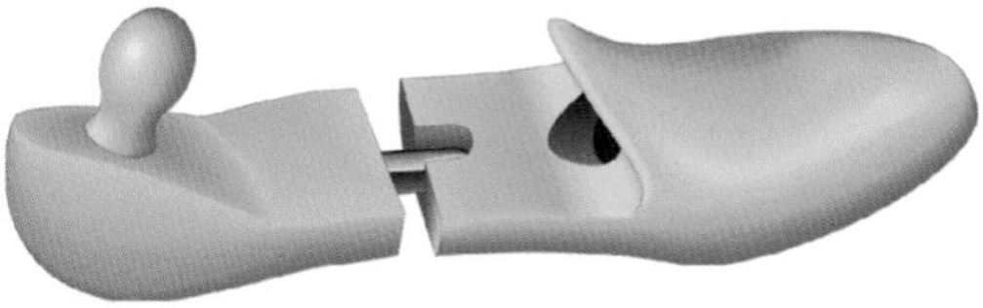

shoe tree
Wooden or plastic device that is inserted into the shoe to restore or maintain its shape.

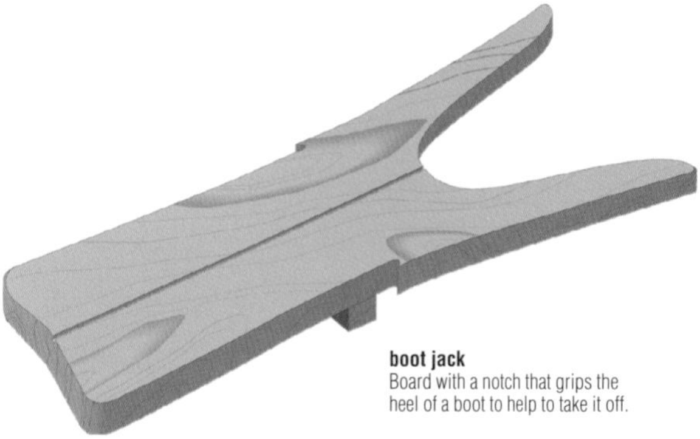

boot jack
Board with a notch that grips the heel of a boot to help to take it off.

gloves

Items of attire covering the hand to at least the wrist and having finger separations.

men's gloves

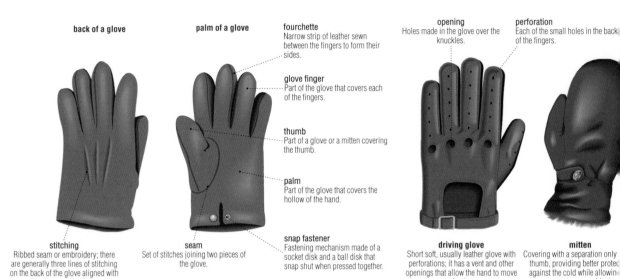

back of a glove

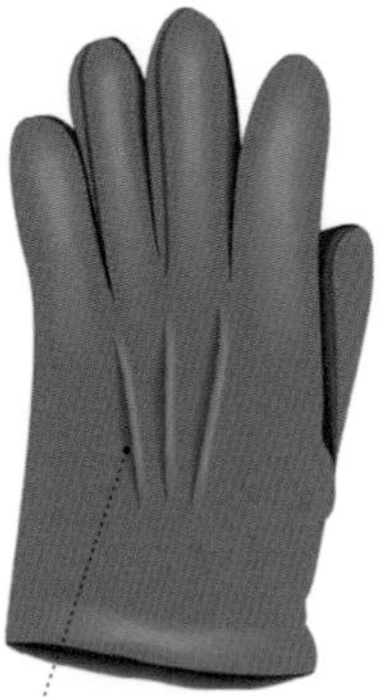

palm of a glove

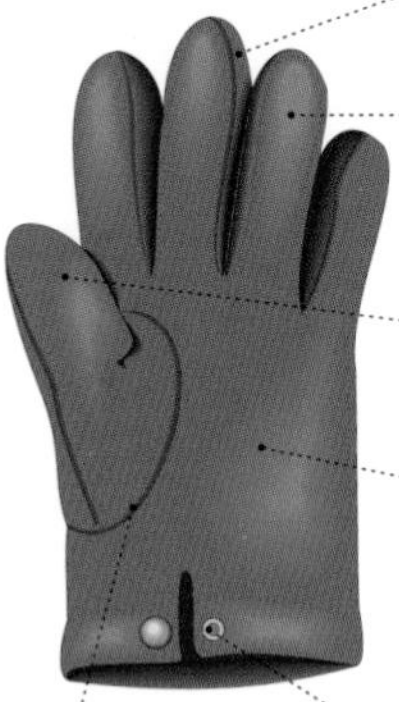

fourchette
Narrow strip of leather sewn between the fingers to form their sides.

glove finger
Part of the glove that covers each of the fingers.

thumb
Part of a glove or a mitten covering the thumb.

palm
Part of the glove that covers the hollow of the hand.

snap fastener
Fastening mechanism made of a socket disk and a ball disk that snap shut when pressed together.

stitching
Ribbed seam or embroidery; there are generally three lines of stitching on the back of the glove aligned with points between the fingers.

seam
Set of stitches joining two pieces of the glove.

opening
Holes made in the glove over the knuckles.

perforation
Each of the small holes in the back of the fingers.

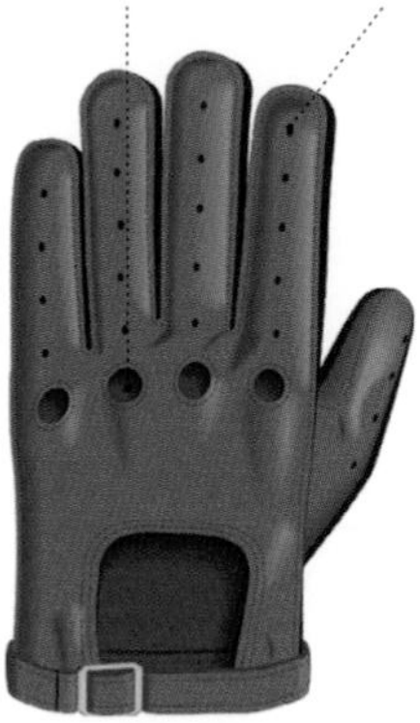

driving glove
Short soft, usually leather glove with perforations; it has a vent and other openings that allow the hand to move freely.

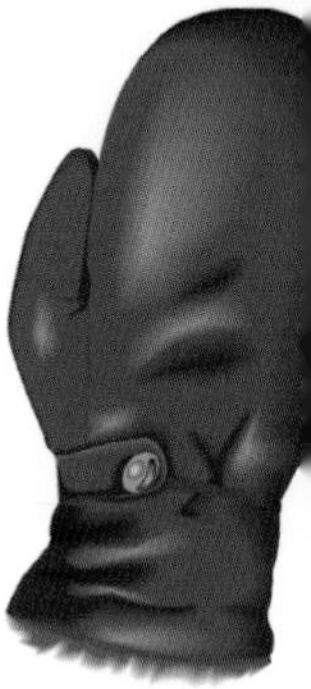

mitten
Covering with a separation only thumb, providing better protec against the cold while allowin wearer to grasp objects.

women's gloves

gauntlet
Glove to which a somewhat flared cuff is attached at the wrist; it is made of various, often decorative kinds of material.

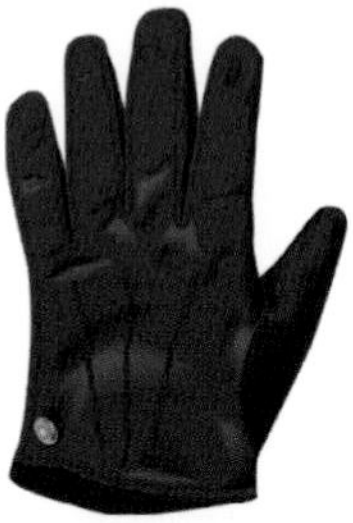

short glove
Glove covering only the hand or extending slightly over the wrist.

evening glove
Glove where the gauntlet extends over the elbow.

mitt
Often dressy glove, either long or of medium length; it fits tightly along the arm and covers only the first finger joints.

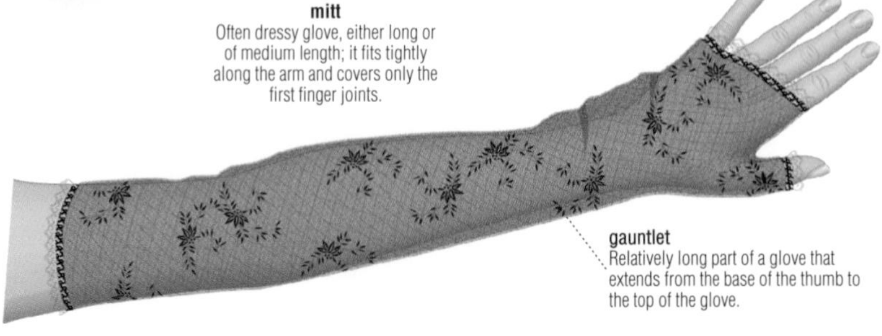

gauntlet
Relatively long part of a glove that extends from the base of the thumb to the top of the glove.

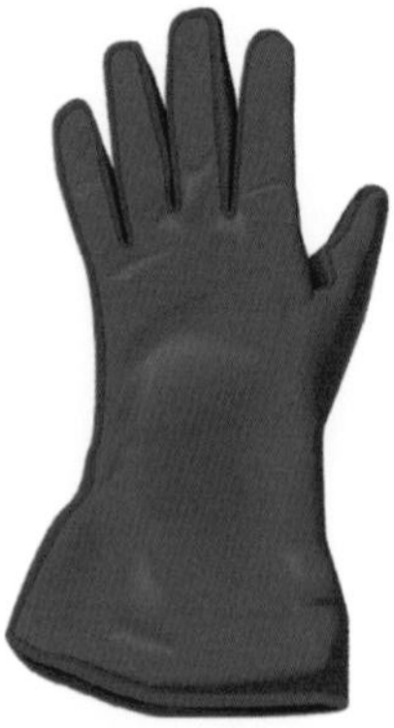

wrist-length glove
Plain unembellished glove with a flared gauntlet covering the wrist.

Most clothing has labels containing symbols showing the recommended care for the material, based on its specific characteristics.

washing

do not wash

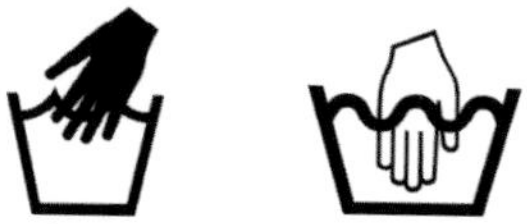
hand wash in lukewarm water

machine wash in lukewarm water at a gentle setting/reduced agitation

machine wash in warm water at a gentle setting/reduced agitation

machine wash in warm water at a normal setting

machine wash in hot water at a normal setting

do not use chlorine bleach

use chlorine bleach as directed

drying

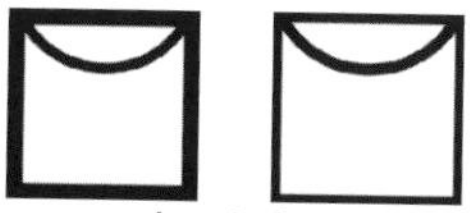
hang to dry

dry flat

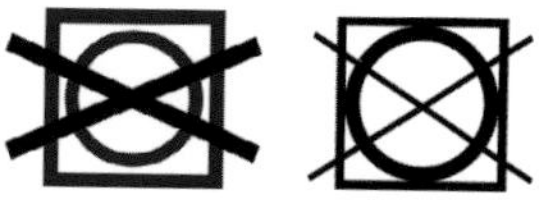
do not tumble dry

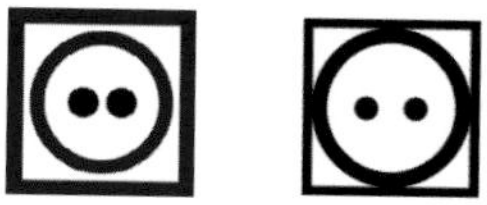
tumble dry at medium temperature

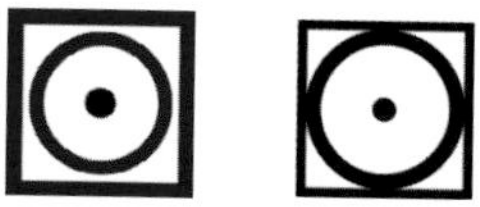
tumble dry at low temperature

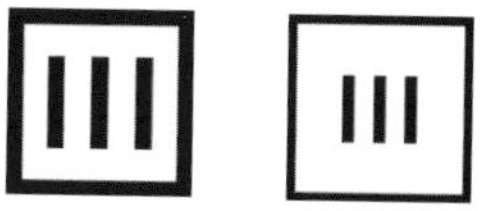
drip dry

ironing

do not iron

iron at low setting

iron at medium setting

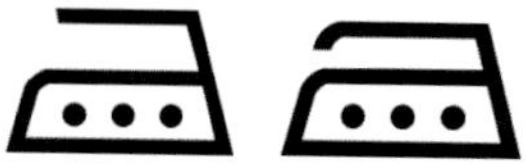
iron at high setting

eft: American symbols

right: European symbols

jackets
Sleeved garments that are open at the front and fall to the hips; they are worn over a shirt, vest, sweater, etc. The top part of a suit is called a suit jacket.

double-breasted jacket
Jacket where the front panels overlap when closed; it has a vertical double line of buttons.

collar
Piece sewn onto a garment that finishes or adorns the neck.

peaked lapel
Lapel forming a very small angle where it meets the collar.

lining
Soft fabric cut from the same pattern as the garment inside which it is sewn; it gives body to the garment, embellishes it, hides its seams and makes it warmer.

breast welt pocket
Small decorative pocket to the left of a jacket's lapel where the pocket handkerchief is placed.

sleeve
Part of the garment covering the arm; it can be of various shapes and lengths.

flap
Piece of fabric or other material that hangs from the top of a pocket opening to hide it.

outside ticket pocket
Small pocket placed at waist level above the jacket's right pocket or sometimes inside the lining on the left side.

patch pocket
Pocket of various shapes and sizes, made of a piece of material sewn onto the garment's outer surface.

side back vent
Vertical opening with overlapping edges on each side of the back of a jacket, giving it fullness.

vest
Short garment worn over a shirt and under a jacket; it is sleeveless, buttons up the front and has a deep V-neck. The back is made out of lining material.

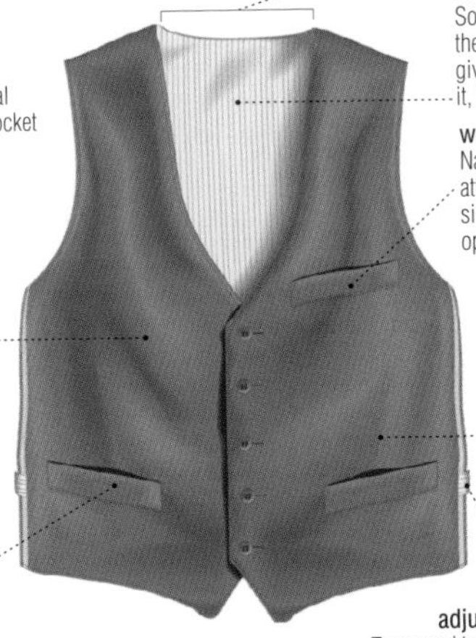

V-neck
Plunging part of the garment encircling the neck and forming a over the chest.

lining
Soft fabric cut from the same patte the garment inside which it is sew gives body to the garment, embell it, hides its seams and makes it w

welt
Narrow strip of material that is attached to the garment on three sides and decorates the pocket opening.

front
Part of the vest that covers the torso.

seam
Decorative set of stitches jc two pieces of a garment, gi distinctive line.

welt pocket
Pocket where the opening is a slit cut into the garment, edged with a welt.

adjustable waist tab
Tape used to tighten a garment around the waist by means of a buckle sewn onto the garment or onto another tab.

single-breasted jacket
Jacket that is neither close-fitting nor flared.

lapel
Part of a garment turned down over the chest, extending the collar.

notch
Angle formed where the collar and the lapel meet.

front
Part of the jacket covering the front of the torso.

lining
Soft fabric cut from the same pattern as the garment inside which it is sewn; it gives body to the garment, embellishes it, hides its seams and makes it warmer.

pocket handkerchief
Small delicate handkerchief that adorns the upper pocket of a jacket.

flap pocket
Pocket cut into the garment with a flap that can be tucked inside the pocket or worn outside.

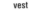

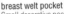

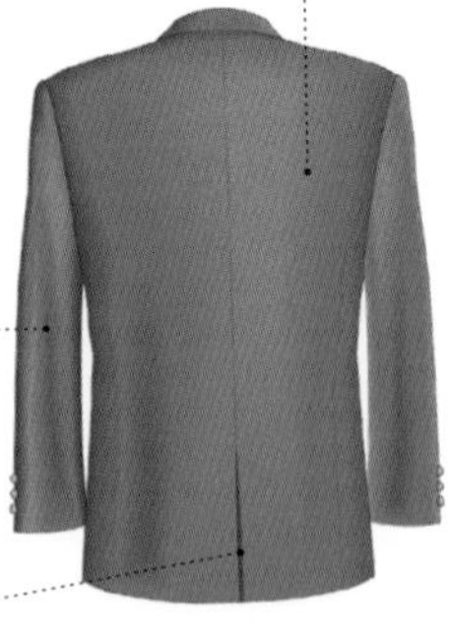

back
Part of the jacket covering the back of the torso.

sleeve
Part of the garment covering the arm; it can be of various shapes and lengths.

center back vent
Vertical opening with overlapping edges at the bottom of a jacket; it extends the center seam at the back, giving the jacket fullness.

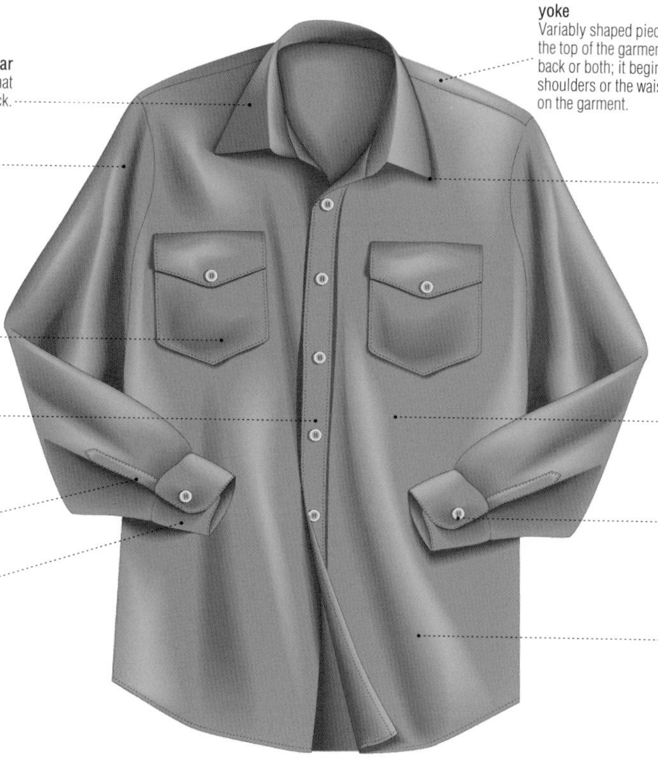
shirt
Garment covering the torso with a collar, a yoke at the back, shirttails and buttons down the front.
collar
Piece sewn onto a garment that finishes or adorns the neck.
set-in sleeve
Sleeve cut separately from the garment and sewn to the armhole.
breast pocket
Pocket of various styles usually on the side of the garment at chest height.
buttoned placket
Narrow strip of fabric along the opening of a garment containing the buttonholes.
pointed tab end
Narrow strip of fabric ending in a point and adorning the sleeve slit.
cuff
Strip of fabric sewn onto the end of the sleeve tightening it and covering the wrist.
yoke
Variably shaped piece of fabric at the top of the garment, in front, in back or both; it begins at the shoulders or the waist, depending on the garment.
collar point
Somewhat pointed tip of the collar.
front
Part of the shirt covering the front of the torso.
button
Small, often round object that is sewn onto a garment and used to fasten or adorn it.
shirttail
Extension of the bottom of the garment; it can be left hanging out or tucked into the pants.

buttondown collar
Collar whose points are buttoned to the shirtfront.

ascot tie
Wide necktie with pleats that narrow the part that goes around the neck; it is knotted loosely and worn inside the open collar of a shirt.

bow tie
Short necktie consisting of a knot at the center and a wing on each side of it.

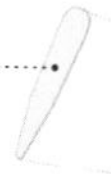
collar stay
Small plastic or metal strip inside the collar point that prevents it from curling.

spread collar
Collar whose points are spread far apart.

necktie
Long narrow strip of fabric placed under the shirt collar and knotted; the front apron, usually wider than the rear one, makes the shirt more attractive.

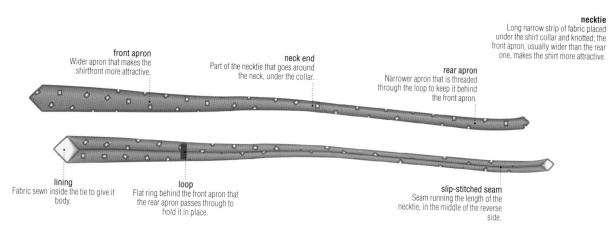

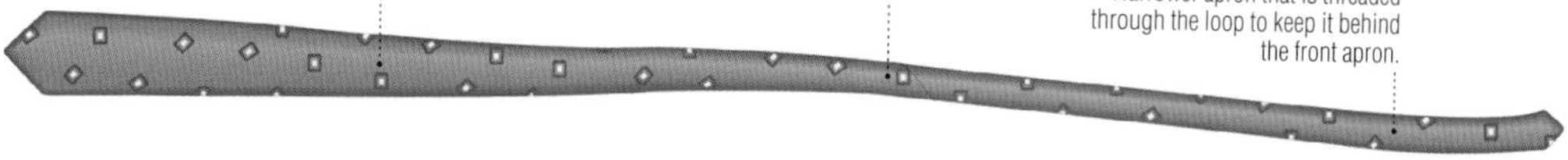
front apron
Wider apron that makes the shirtfront more attractive.
neck end
Part of the necktie that goes around the neck, under the collar.
rear apron
Narrower apron that is threaded through the loop to keep it behind the front apron.

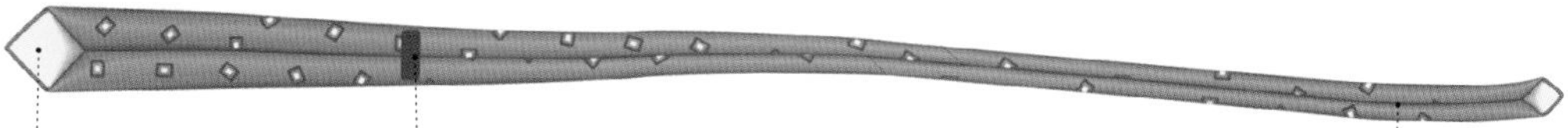
lining
Fabric sewn inside the tie to give it body.
loop
Flat ring behind the front apron that the rear apron passes through to hold it in place.
slip-stitched seam
Seam running the length of the necktie, in the middle of the reverse side.

CLOTHING

pants
Garment for the lower body; it extends from the waist or the hips to the ankles, covering each leg separately.

waistband extension
Strip of fabric that extends the waistband and is used to fasten it.

knife pleat
Pleat created by a vertical fold pointing in one direction and of constant width.

fly
Vertical opening at the middle front of the pants; it closes with buttons or a zipper and is usually covered by the folded edge of the opening.

belt loop
Thin vertical strip of material sewn at the waist of pants; a belt passes through it to hold the pants in place.

front top pocket
Front pants pocket that is often curved or diagonal; the opening is cut into the garment or is hidden inside a seam.

waistband
Strip of fabric sewn at the waist of pants forming a hem and holding them in place.

crease
Visible mark that remains where the fold has been ironed in.

cuff
Folded end of the pant leg.

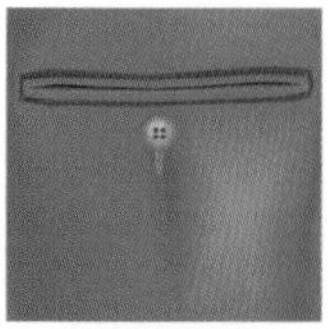

back pocket
Pocket of various kinds in the back of the pants.

suspender clip
Fastening system made up of two hinged tabs; it can replace the leather end on suspenders.

suspenders
Narrow straps of adjustable length that are often elasticized; they cross in the back, go over the shoulders and fasten to the pants to keep them in place.

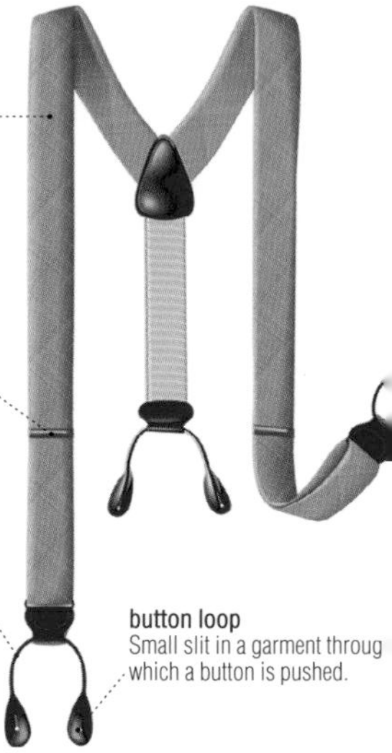

elastic webbing
Narrow strip of stretchable sturdy material.

adjustment slide
Flat ring attached to the elastic strap; it can be moved up or down to adjust the length.

leather end
Usually leather strip used to button the elastic strap to the pants.

button loop
Small slit in a garment throug which a button is pushed.

belt
Strap made of various materials often with a buckle; it is worn around the waist to adjust the fit of a garment, hold it in place or adorn it.

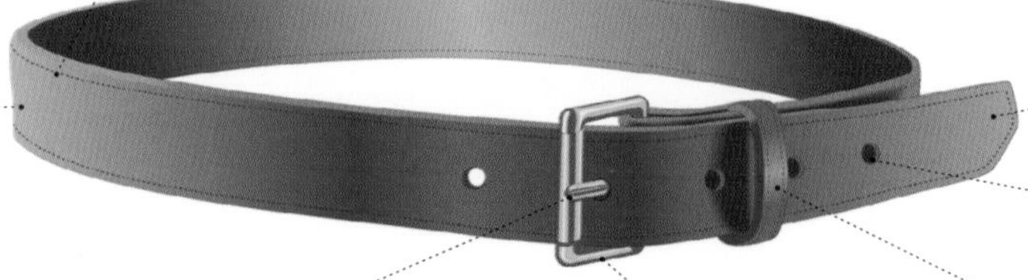

top stitching
Stitching used to embellish the belt.

panel
Smooth side of a piece of leather.

tip
End of the belt that passes through the buckle.

punch hole
Perforation in the belt through which the tongue passes.

belt loop
Flat ring next to the buckle usually made of the same material as the belt; one end of the belt passes through it.

tongue
Metal tip that pivots on the buckle's axis and fits into a hole, buckling the belt.

buckle
Fastener made up of a ring that secures the two ends of a belt.

underwear

Garments worn next to the skin and under other garments.

athletic shirt
Sleeveless tight-fitting undergarment with a very wide neck and armholes.

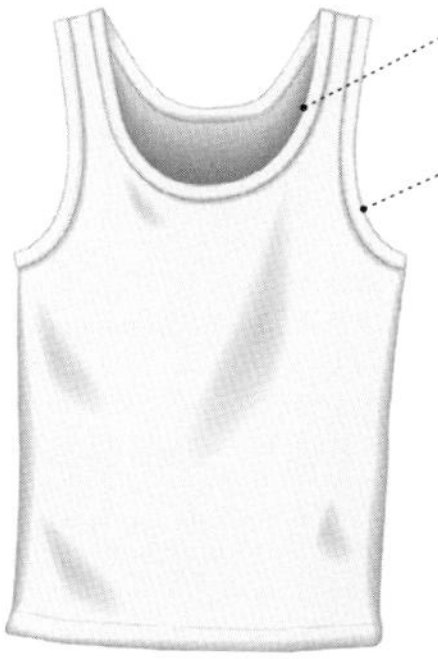

neckhole
Somewhat low part of the garment that goes around the neck.

armhole
Opening in a garment for the arm or for fitting a sleeve into.

briefs
Short legless undergarment with elastic at the waist and thighs and a fly.

waistband
Strip of elasticized material fitting snugly over the hips to hold the garment in place.

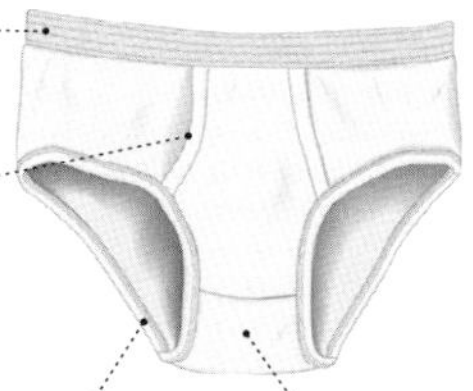

fly
Opening in the front of the briefs.

elasticized leg opening
Opening that is edged with elastic so it fits snugly around the thigh.

crotch
Part of the briefs that goes between the legs.

union suit
Warm undergarment that buttons up the front and combines a long-sleeved undershirt and long drawers.

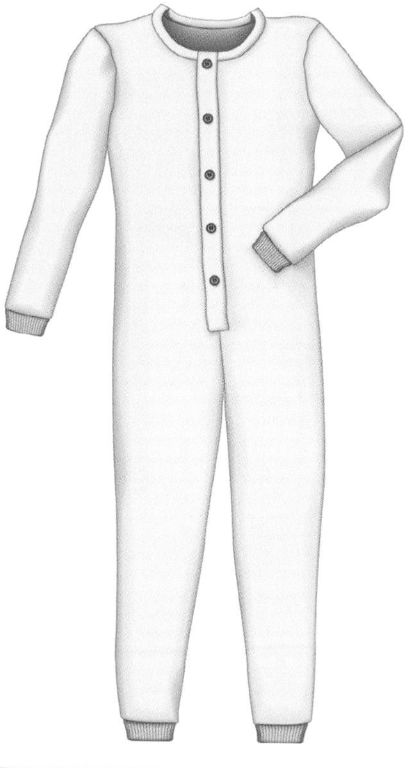

drawers
Undergarment covering the legs; it has a waistband and is gathered at the ankles with fine ribbing.

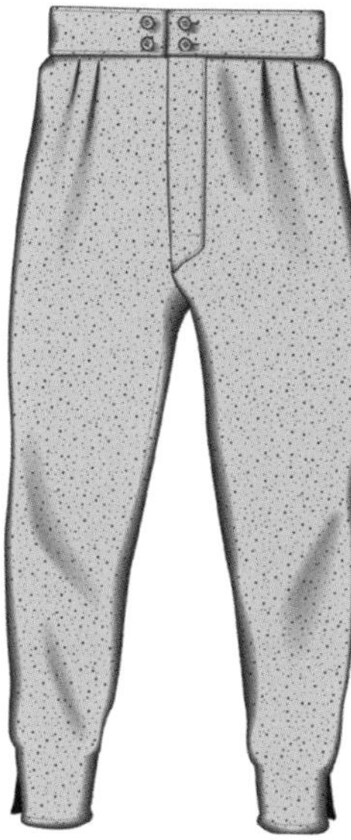

bikini briefs
Snug-fitting briefs, low-cut on the hips and high-cut on the thighs.

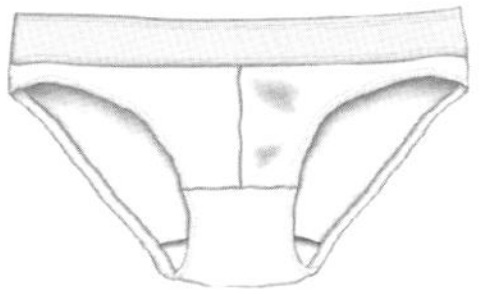

boxer shorts
Undergarment covering the tops of the thighs and held in place by an elasticized waistband.

socks

Knitted garments that cover the foot and part of the leg.

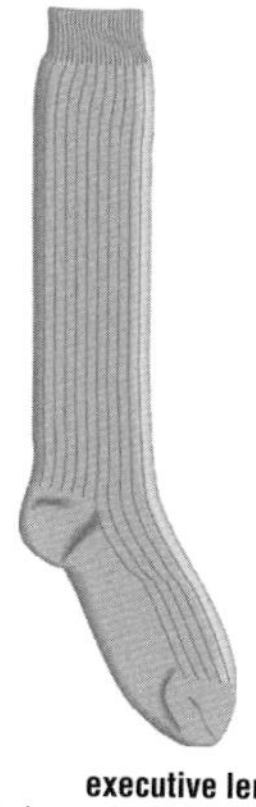

executive length
Sock covering the foot and extending to the knee.

straight-up ribbed top
Elasticized knitted strip that tightens, reinforces and adorns the sock opening.

leg
Part of the sock of varying length that extends above the foot.

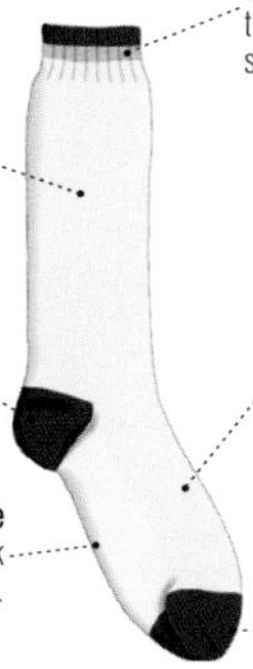

heel
Usually reinforced part of the sock that covers the heel of the foot.

instep
Part of the sock that covers the top of the foot.

sole
Usually reinforced part of the sock that covers the sole of the foot.

toe
Usually reinforced part of the sock that covers the toes of the foot.

mid-calf length
Kind of sock ending at calf level.

ankle length
Sock that covers the foot and extends slightly above the ankle.

coats
Outerwear that is fastened in front; coats are worn over other garments to protect against the cold and inclement weather.

raincoat
Coat, sometimes with a hood, that keeps the rain off because of the kind of material used to make it or because it has been waterproofed.

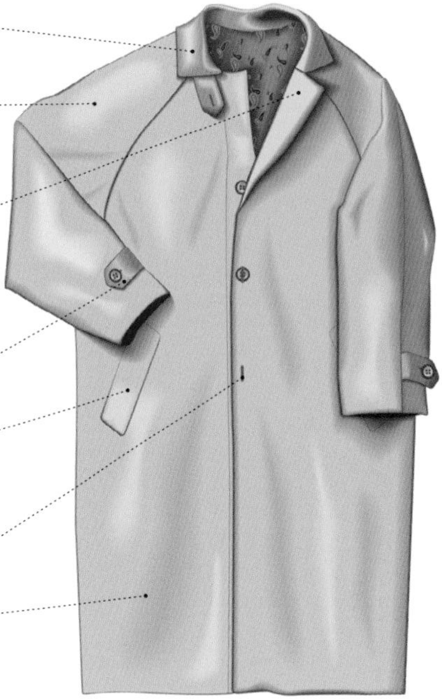

collar
Piece sewn onto a garment that finishes or adorns the neck.

raglan sleeve
Sleeve extending over the shoulder and attached front and back with a slanted seam running from under the armhole to the neck.

notched lapel
Lapel forming an angle where it meets the collar.

tab
Narrow strip of fabric attached horizontally to the sleeve end to embellish it.

broad welt side pocket
Angled pocket; the outer edge of the opening has a wide welt.

buttonhole
Small slit in a garment through which a button is pushed.

side panel
Extension of the coat that is left hanging loose.

overcoat
Coat ending below the knee and made of heavy fabric, fur or leather.

notched lapel
Lapel forming an angle where it meets the collar.

breast pocket
Pocket of various styles usually c the side of the garment at chest height.

breast dart
Pleat that is narrower at the botto than at the top; it is sewn into the reverse side of the fabric to reduc fullness around the waist.

flap pocket
Pocket whose opening is covere by a piece of fabric hanging from the top of it.

trench coat
Raincoat characterized by double-breasted buttoning, a belt, gun flaps, a collar with lapels, large pockets and tabs on the sleeves and shoulders.

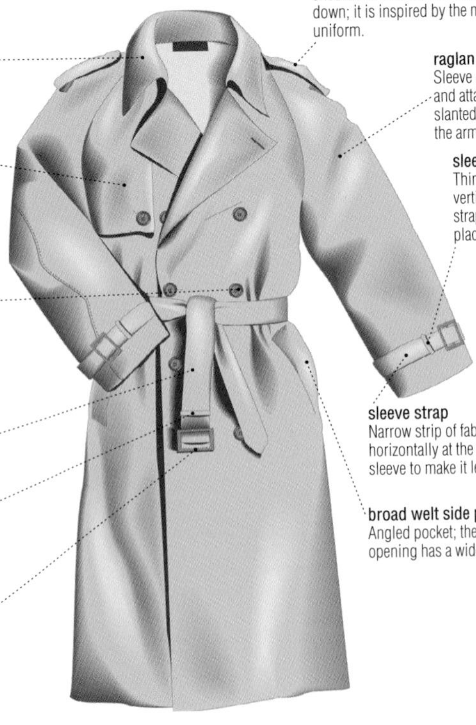

epaulet
Decorative tab attached to the shoulder and sometimes buttoned down; it is inspired by the military uniform.

two-way collar
Collar designed to be worn in various ways.

gun flap
Loose front and back yoke used as a decorative element and as protection against wind and rain.

raglan sleeve
Sleeve extending over the shoulder and attached front and back with a slanted seam running from under the armhole to the neck.

sleeve strap loop
Thin strip of material attached vertically to the sleeve; the sleeve strap threads through it to hold it in place.

double-breasted buttoning
Fastening system made up of two parallel rows of buttons.

belt
Strap made of various materials often with a frame; it is worn around the waist to adjust the fit of a garment, hold it in place or adorn it.

sleeve strap
Narrow strip of fabric that is sewn horizontally at the bottom of the sleeve to make it less full.

belt loop
Flat ring next to the frame usually made of the same material as the belt; one end of the belt passes through it.

broad welt side pocket
Angled pocket; the outer edge of the opening has a wide welt.

frame
Fastener made up of a ring that secures the two ends of a belt.

three-quarter coat
Coat ending above the knee and made of quality fabric, fur or leather, with double-breasted buttoning and outside pockets.

parka
Sporty waterproof coat that is often padded or fleece-lined; it has big pockets, a front zipper and sometimes a hood.

snap-fastening tab
Strip of material that borders the front opening of a garment, closing with a row of snap fasteners.

zipper
Closure made up of two lengths of tape edged with teeth that interlock by means of a slide.

sheepskin jacket
Three-quarter coat that crosses over in front and has a belt and patch flap pockets; it is usually made of waterproof fabric, leather or suede with a lining and a wide collar made of sheepskin.

duffle coat
Hooded casual coat ending at mid-thigh and made of heavy woolen fabric; it is characterized by a yoke and frog closures.

hood
Headgear attached at the garment's neck that can be pulled over the head as protection against cold, rain and snow.

yoke
Variably shaped piece of fabric at the top of the garment, in front, in back or both; it begins at the shoulders or the waist, depending on the garment.

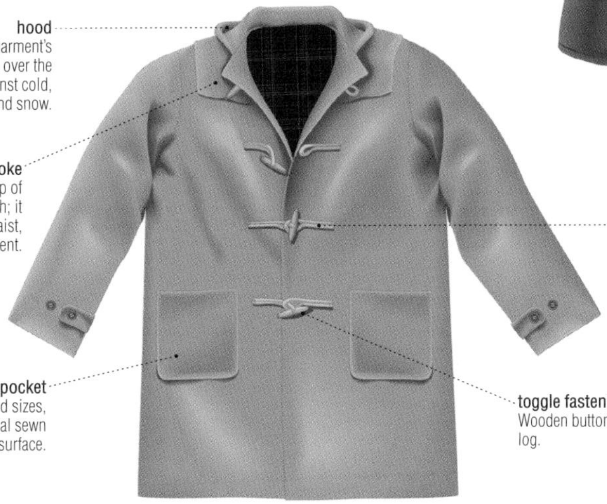

frog
Ornamental loops of braided fabric used to fasten a garment; one serves as the buttonhole and the toggle of the other one passes through it.

patch pocket
Pocket of various shapes and sizes, made of a piece of material sewn onto the garment's outer surface.

toggle fastening
Wooden button in the shape of a small log.

jacket
Full jacket ending at the waist, where it is gathered so it puffs out; it is often made of leather or waterproof material and has cuffed sleeves.

snap fastener
Fastening mechanism made of a socket disk and a ball disk that snap shut when pressed together.

hand-warmer pocket
Pocket in the front of the garment above the waist where the hand can be tucked to protect it against the cold and to rest the arm.

elastic waistband
Strip of elasticized fabric that fits snugly around the waist to hold the garment in place.

windbreaker
Jacket ending below the waist and made of leather or waterproof material.

waistband
Hem at the bottom of a garment that finishes it and encases the drawstring, which adjusts the garment around the hips.

drawstring
Thin string that is threaded inside the waistband and adjusts the windbreaker around the hips.

sweaters

Garments covering the torso and manufactured by hand or by machine from fabric with varying tightness of weave.

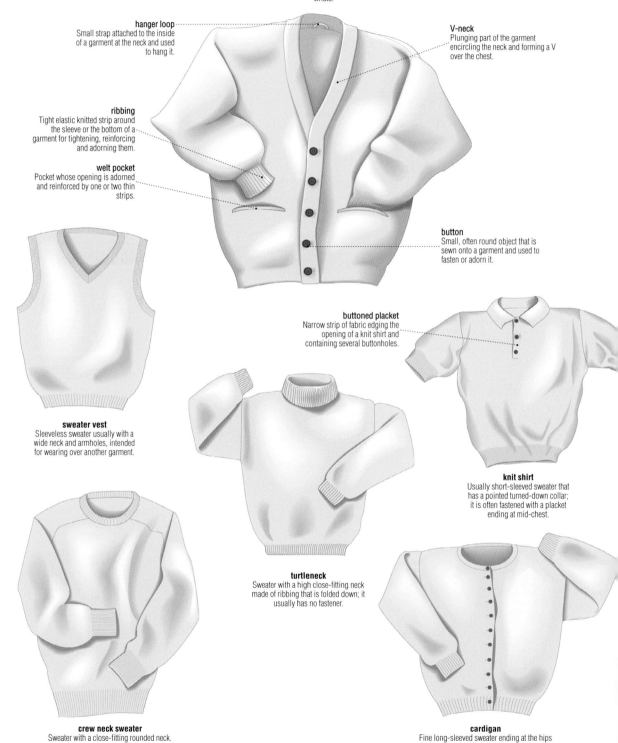

V-neck cardigan
Woolen sweater ending at the hips and characterized by front buttons, a V-neck and ribbing at the bottom and wrists.

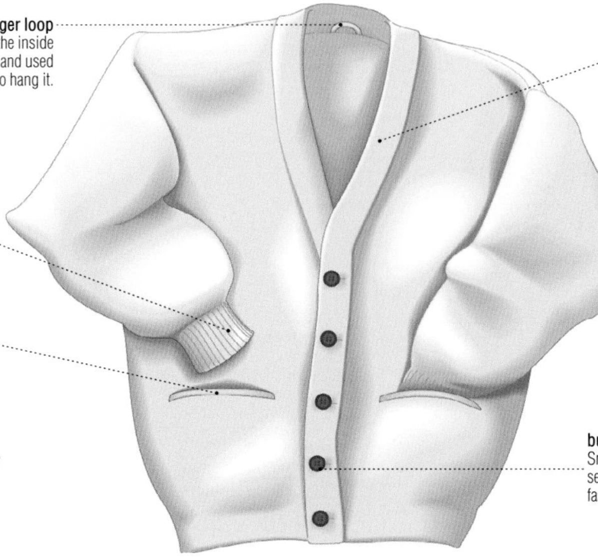

hanger loop
Small strap attached to the inside of a garment at the neck and used to hang it.

V-neck
Plunging part of the garment encircling the neck and forming a V over the chest.

ribbing
Tight elastic knitted strip around the sleeve or the bottom of a garment for tightening, reinforcing and adorning them.

welt pocket
Pocket whose opening is adorned and reinforced by one or two thin strips.

button
Small, often round object that is sewn onto a garment and used to fasten or adorn it.

sweater vest
Sleeveless sweater usually with a wide neck and armholes, intended for wearing over another garment.

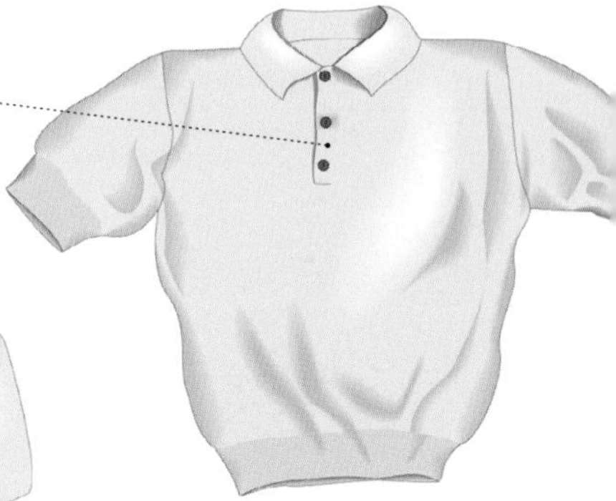

buttoned placket
Narrow strip of fabric edging the opening of a knit shirt and containing several buttonholes.

knit shirt
Usually short-sleeved sweater that has a pointed turned-down collar; it is often fastened with a placket ending at mid-chest.

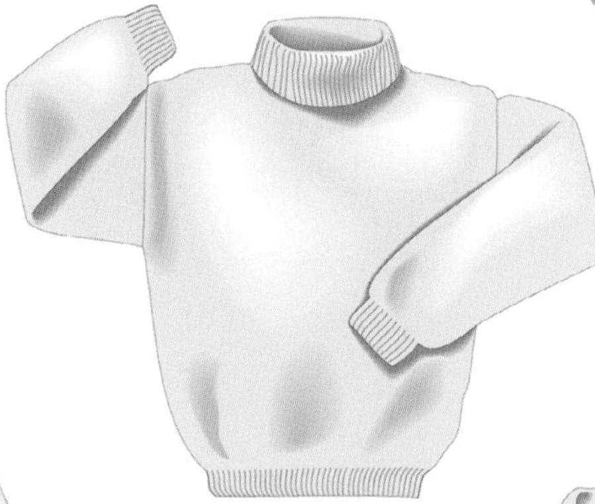

turtleneck
Sweater with a high close-fitting neck made of ribbing that is folded down; it usually has no fastener.

crew neck sweater
Sweater with a close-fitting rounded neck.

cardigan
Fine long-sleeved sweater ending at the hips and characterized by front buttoning, a round neck and a ribbed bottom and wrists.

coats

Outerwear that is fastened in front and extends at least the hips; coats are worn over other garments as protection against cold and inclement weather.

suit
Outfit made up of a skirt or pants and a long-sleeved jacket made from the same high-quality fabric.

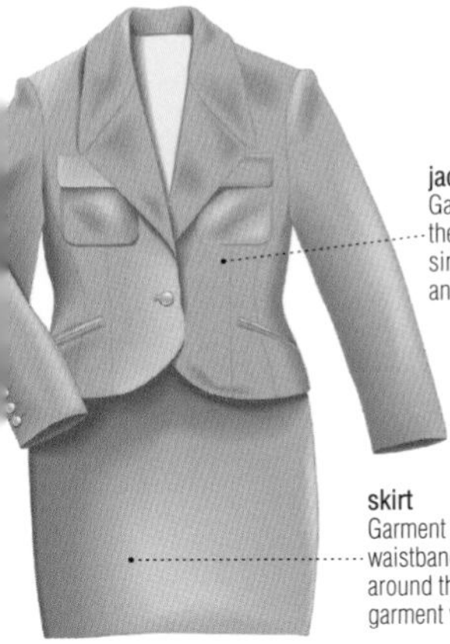

jacket
Garment with sleeves that extends to the hips; it is fastened in front with single- or double-breasted buttoning and sometimes has a belt.

skirt
Garment held in place by an inner waistband or a belt that goes around the waist; the length of the garment varies.

raglan
Somewhat full coat characterized by raglan sleeves and broad welt side pockets.

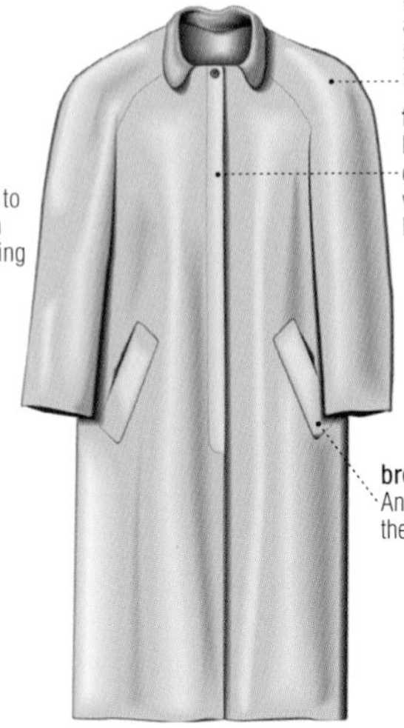

raglan sleeve
Sleeve extending over the shoulder and attached front and back with a slanted seam running from under the armhole to the neck.

fly front closing
Fastening covered by a placket and consisting of a row of buttons, which are held in place by buttonholes.

broad welt side pocket
Angled pocket; the outer edge of the opening has a wide welt.

top coat
Coat fitted at the waist and flared at the bottom.

pelerine
Coat with a short pelerine.

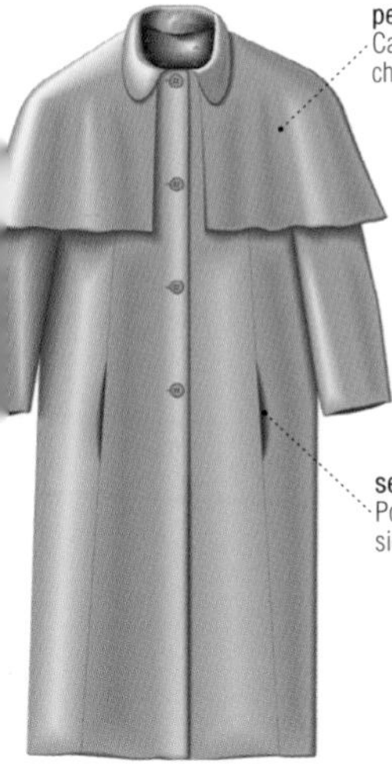

pelerine
Cape covering the shoulders and chest.

seam pocket
Pocket where the opening is in a side seam of the garment.

cape
Very full coat of variable length that covers the body and arms; it has no sleeves or armholes and sometimes has a hood and slits for the arms.

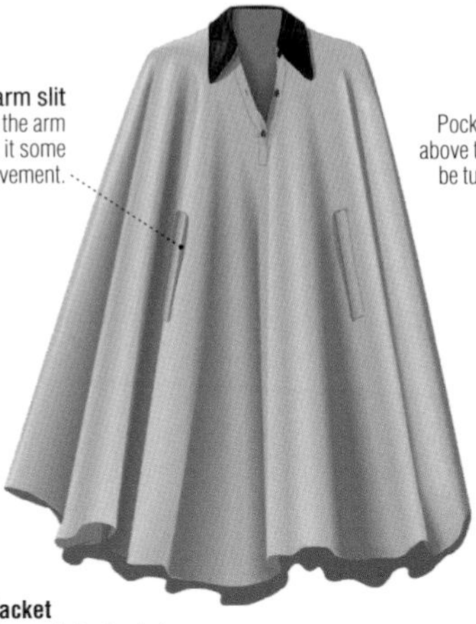

arm slit
Lateral slit through which the arm can be slipped to give it some freedom of movement.

pea jacket
Long jacket made of heavy fabric and characterized by double-breasted buttoning, a tailored collar and hand-warmer pockets.

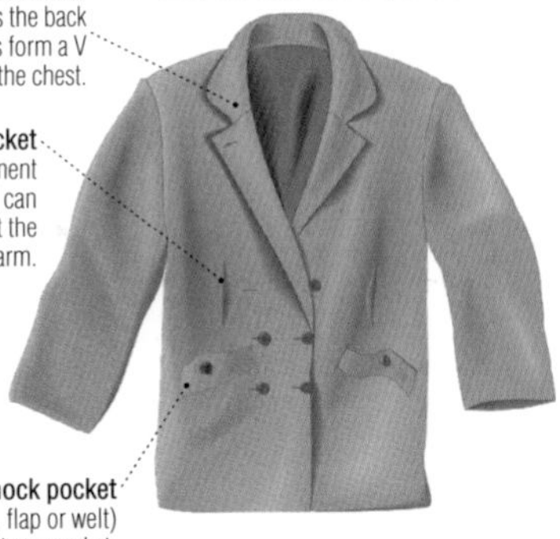

tailored collar
Collar whose fold covers the back of the neck; its lapels form a V where they cross on the chest.

hand-warmer pocket
Pocket in the front of the garment above the waist where the hand can be tucked to protect it against the cold and to rest the arm.

mock pocket
Decoration (placket, flap or welt) that simulates a pocket.

car coat
Coat loosely based on a man's three-quarter coat but changing more often to reflect the current style; it is shorter than the garment it covers and together they can make an outfit.

jacket
Garment with sleeves that extends to the hips; it is fastened in front with single- or double-breasted buttoning and sometimes has a belt.

poncho
Cape made from a rectangular piece of material with a hole in the middle for the head to go through.

overcoat
Long-sleeved article of outerwear made of heavy fabric; it extends to the calf and closes in front with various fastening systems.

examples of dresses

Dress: garment made up of a bodice with or without sleeves or a collar and extending into a skirt of variable length.

sheath dress
Unbelted, very tight form-fitting dress.

princess dress
Unbelted dress with a fitted bodice and a full or straight skirt whose cut accentuates the figure.

coat dress
Dress cut like a coat; it fastens all the way up the front and might be lined.

polo dress
Dress whose bodice imitates the knit shirt.

house dress
Simply styled dress made of light comfortable fabric; it usually has front buttons, a belt and patch pockets.

shirtwaist dress
Dress with a bodice that resembles a man's shirt; it usually has a belt and buttons all the way up the front.

drop waist dress
Dress with its waist at hip level.

trapeze dress
Unbelted dress with an increasingly flared skirt that hangs from a tight bodice.

sundress
Very low-cut dress with slim straps, which leave the back and shoulders uncovered.

wraparound dress
Dress that is open from top to bottom; it is fastened by folding one side over the other and holding them in place with a belt.

tunic dress
Two-piece dress made up of a quite long straight skirt and a straight bodice that hangs down over the skirt, sometimes to the knees.

jumper
Sleeveless dress with a very low-cut neckline and armholes; it is worn over a blouse or a sweater.

examples of skirts

Skirt: garment held in place by an inner waistband or a belt that goes around the waist; the length of the garment varies.

gored skirt
Flared skirt made up of several panels of fabric sewn vertically.

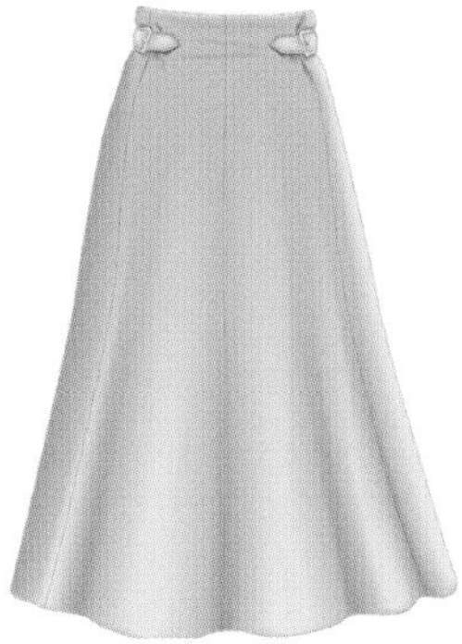

kilt
Pleated wraparound skirt made of tartan; a usually narrow panel crosses over in front and fastens with a pin or a button.

sarong
Beach skirt of variable length and made from a piece of fabric wrapped around the waist.

wraparound skirt
Skirt made up of a single panel crossing over in front or sometimes behind and buttoning on the side.

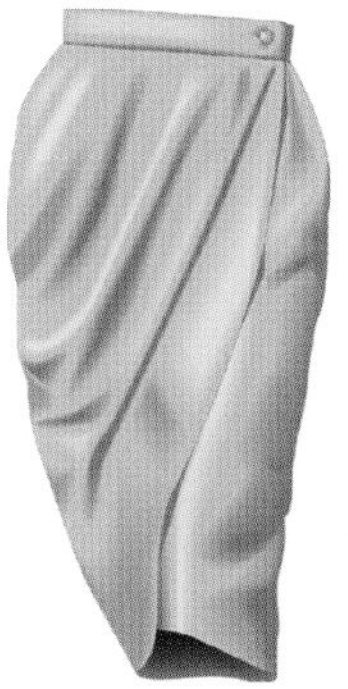

sheath skirt
Skirt that is narrow at the waist and fits tightly over the hips and legs.

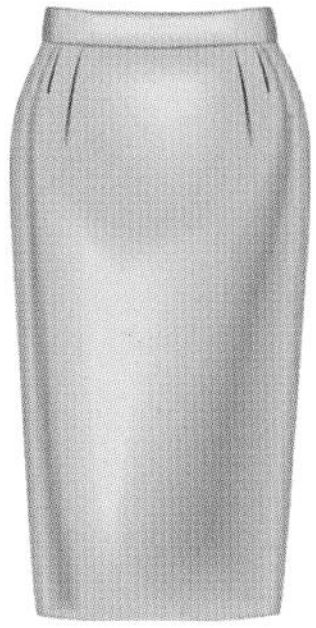

ruffled skirt
Skirt made up of several horizontal strips of material in superimposed layers; the free edge falls loose, creating folds.

straight skirt
Skirt that is narrow at the waist, tight-fitting over the hips and falls straight.

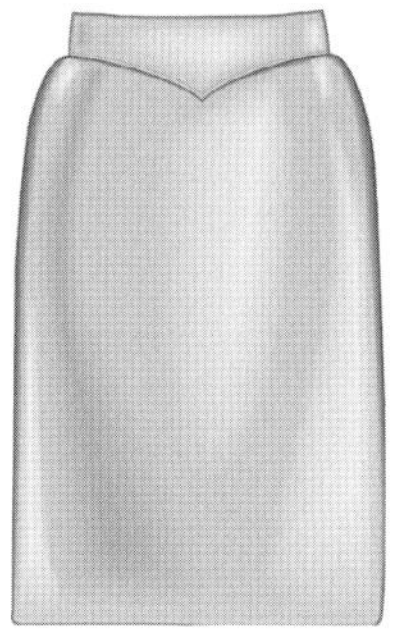

yoke skirt
Skirt with a piece added on, forming the part from the waist to the hips.

gather skirt
Skirt that is gathered at the waist and falls in wide folds.

culottes
Garment with a crotch that is hidden by its full folds thus resembling a skirt.

examples of pleats

Pleat: part of a garment folded over to form a double thickness of material.

inverted pleat
Pleat formed by two folds that meet in front and touch on the outside of the fabric, thus forming a hollow in the fabric.

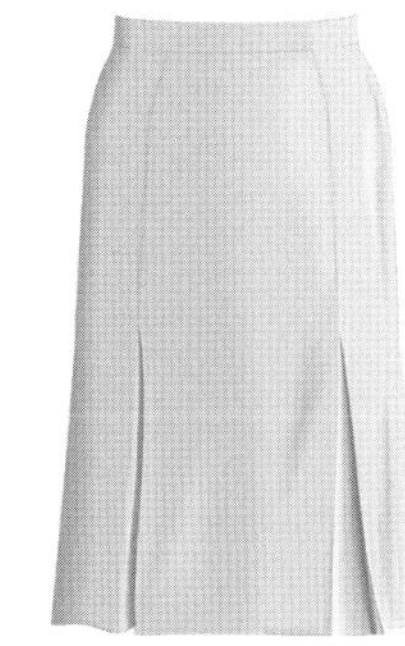

kick pleat
Inverted or flat back pleat at the bottom of a straight skirt, providing greater ease of movement.

accordion pleat
Set of thin upright pleats of uniform width along the grain of the fabric.

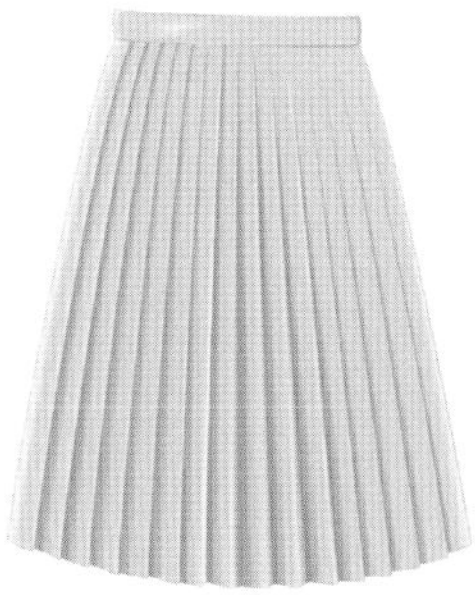

top stitched pleat
Pleat extending from a series of ornamental stitches on the outside of the fabric.

knife pleat
Pleat created by a vertical fold pointing in one direction and of constant width.

examples of pants

Pants: garment for the lower body; they extend from the waist or the hips to the ankles, covering each leg separately.

shorts
Very short pants covering only the top of the thighs.

Bermuda shorts
Long shorts ending above the knee.

knickers
Pants with full legs that are gathered below the knee or at the calf.

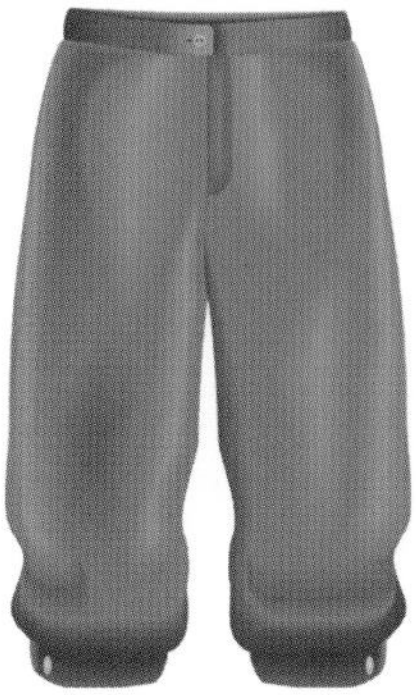

pedal pushers
Tight-fitting pants ending at mid-calf and having a slit on the outside of the leg at the knee, which can be fastened in various ways.

jeans
Pants made of durable, usually blue fabric with topstitched seams and pockets that are often reinforced by rivets.

ski pants
Generally stretchy pants with legs that narrow toward the ankle, ending in an footstrap.

footstrap
Strip of elasticized fabric that goes under the foot to keep the pants stretched tight.

jumpsuit
Garment that closes at the front and combines pants and a sometimes sleeveless bodice.

overalls
Pants with shoulder straps and a piece that covers the chest.

bell bottoms
Pants that are tight-fitting to the knee then flare out and end at the ankle.

jackets, vest and sweaters

Examples of garments covering the chest; they are worn over other garments as protection against the cold or as an accessory.

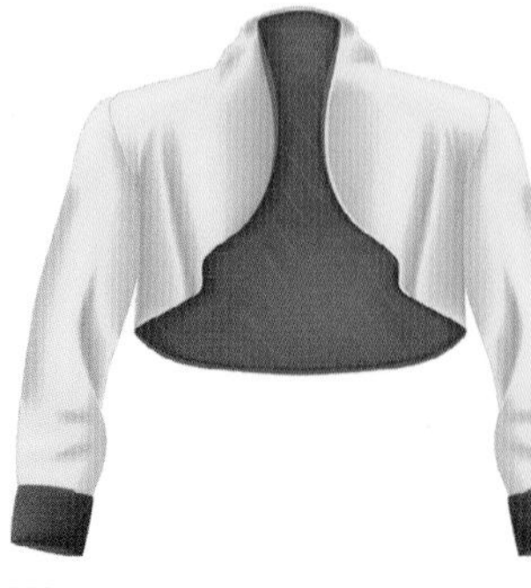

bolero
Small jacket, sometimes sleeveless and without collar or lapel, that is worn as an accessory only; it ends above the waist and does not fasten.

spencer
Tight-fitting unbelted jacket ending at the waist; it has long sleeves and often a collar with lapels.

blazer
Often navy-blue, hip-length jacket characterized by a notched collar, long wide lapels and patch pockets.

safari jacket
Lightweight long-sleeved shirt-jacket made of plain weave and having a belt and four pockets.

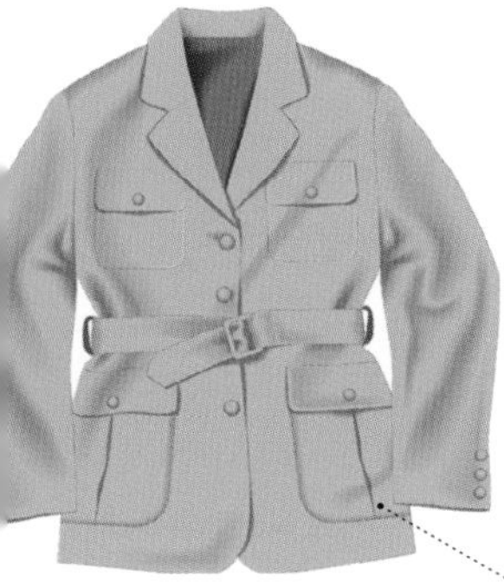

gusset pocket
Patch pocket made fuller by an expandable bottom and sides or by an inverted or round pleat in the middle of the pocket.

vest
Short garment worn over a shirt and under a jacket; it is sleeveless, buttons up the front and has a deep V-neck. The back is made out of lining material.

twin-set
Outfit made up of a sweater, often crew neck, and a matching cardigan or vest.

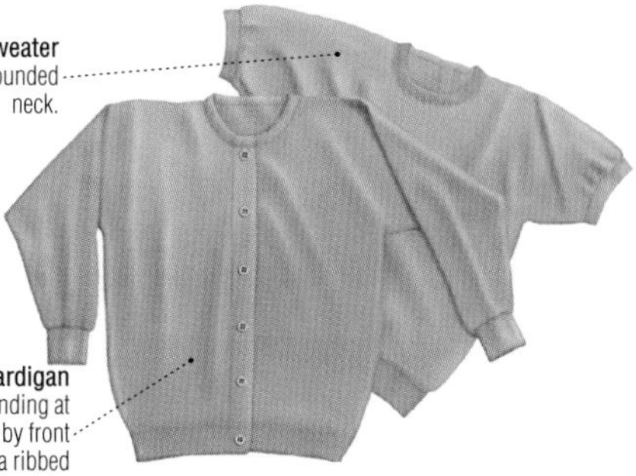

crew neck sweater
Sweater with a close-fitting rounded neck.

cardigan
Fine long-sleeved sweater ending at the hips and characterized by front buttoning, a round neck and a ribbed bottom and wrists.

examples of blouses

Blouses: women's garments covering the torso and worn directly over underwear; there are many different varieties made of all kinds of fabric.

body shirt
Tight-fitting blouse in stretchy fabric and ending in a bikini bottom.

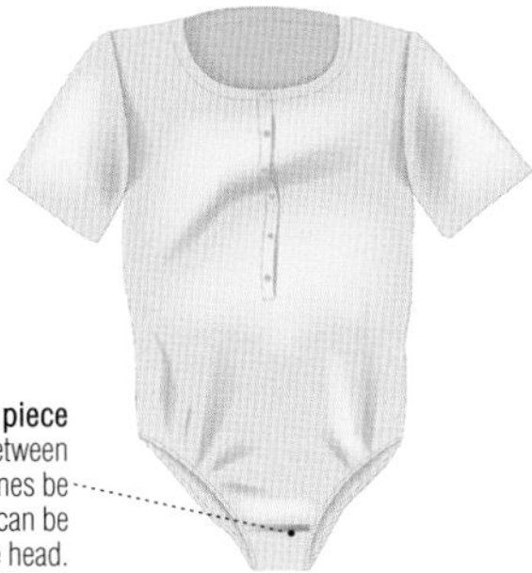

crotch piece
Part of the bikini that goes between the legs; it can sometimes be unfastened so the blouse can be put on over the head.

middy
Straight full blouse with a sailor collar and no front opening, ending at the hips.

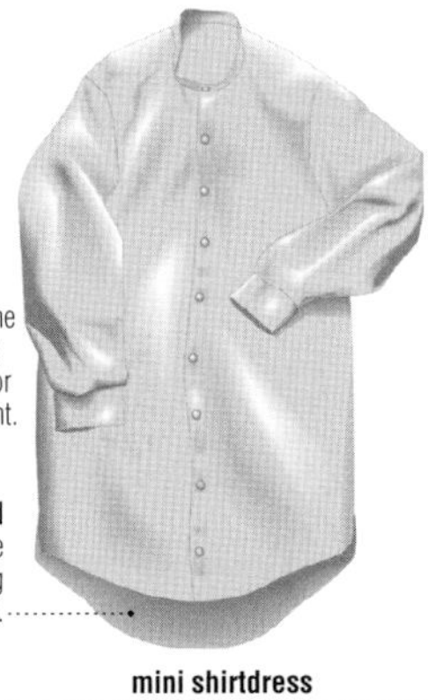

shirttail
Extension of the bottom of the garment; it can be left hanging out or tucked into the pants.

mini shirtdress
Full shirt-blouse ending at mid-thigh and usually worn over a skirt or pants; it has a side slit and rounded shirttails.

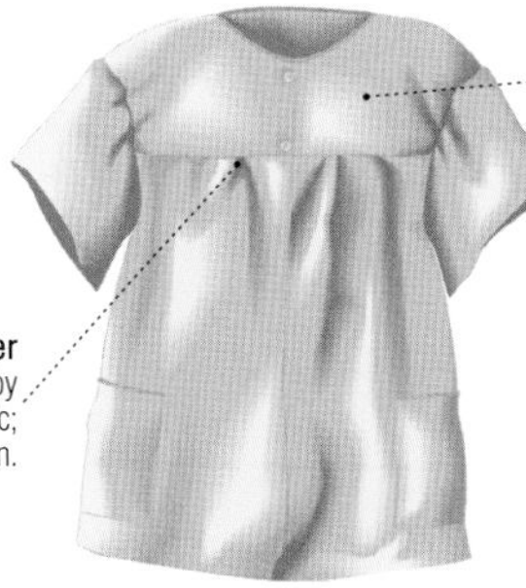

yoke
Variably shaped piece of fabric at the top of the garment, in front, in back or both; it begins at the shoulders or the waist, depending on the garment.

gather
Small narrow pleat made by drawing thread through the fabric; it is not ironed or sewn down.

smock
Long unfitted blouse made of soft lightweight material; it is often buttoned in the back and is usually worn over other garments to protect them.

classic blouse
Front-buttoning blouse with a collar and long sleeves; it is gathered at the wrists and ends at the hips.

tunic
Straight full blouse ending below the waist.

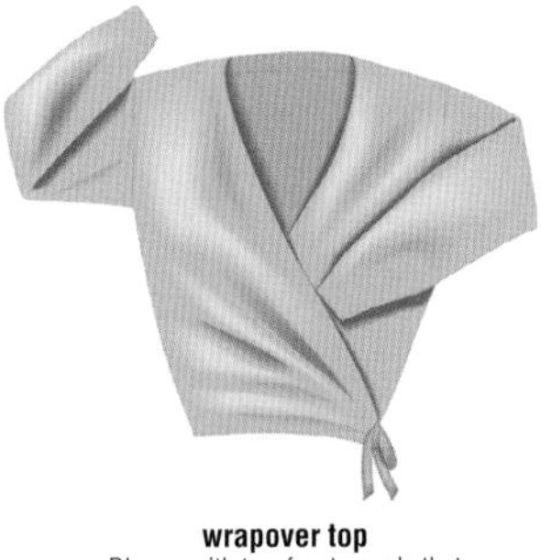

wrapover top
Blouse with two front panels that cross over one another, creating a V-neck; it has ties that fasten at the waist, back or hip.

polo shirt
Usually short-sleeved sweater that has a pointed turned-down collar; it is often fastened with a placket ending at mid-chest.

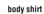

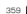

over-blouse
Straight long-sleeved tunic that is often put on over the head; it is gathered by a belt or a tie at the waist and hangs over a skirt or pants.

examples of pockets

Pocket: part of a garment used to carry things and consisting of a piece of material sewn onto or inside the garment.

gusset pocket
Patch pocket made fuller by an expandable bottom and sides or by an inverted or round pleat in the middle of the pocket.

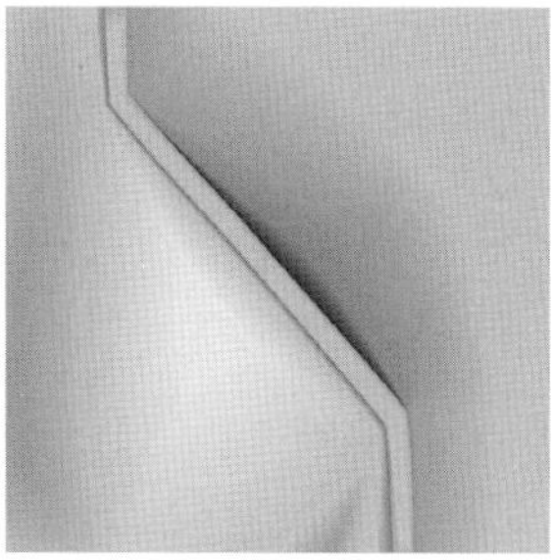

inset pocket
Pocket whose opening contains a decorative seam, giving the garment a distinctive line.

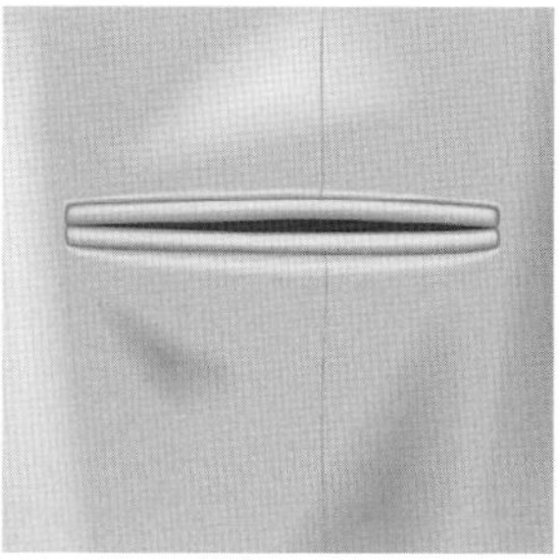

welt pocket
Pocket whose opening is adorned and reinforced by one or two thin strips.

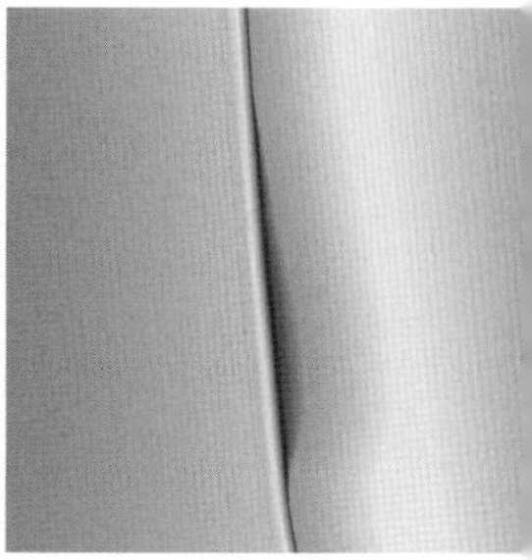

seam pocket
Pocket where the opening is in a side seam of the garment.

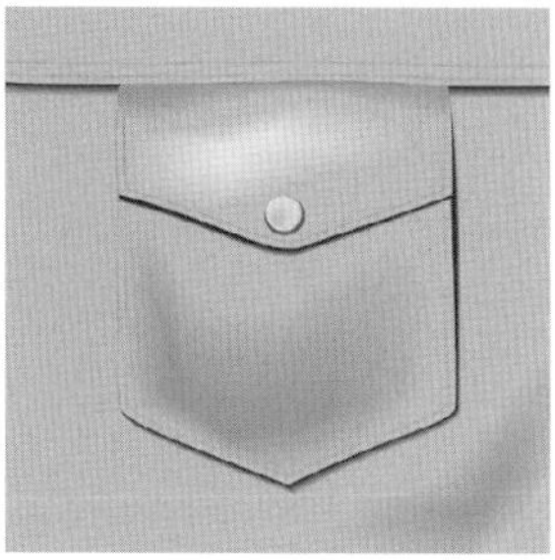

flap pocket
Pocket whose opening is covered by a piece of fabric hanging from the top of it.

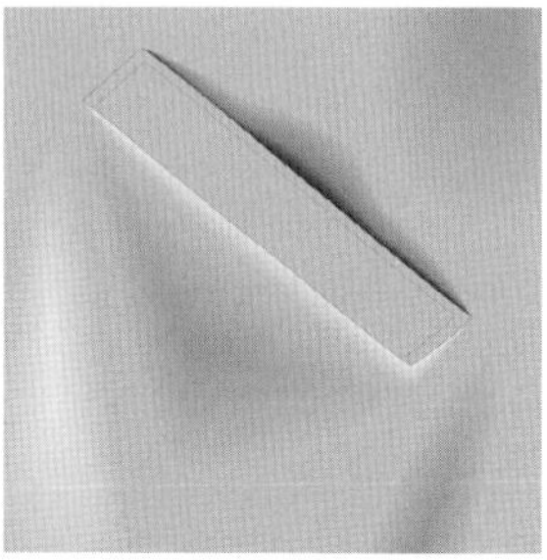

broad welt side pocket
Angled pocket; the outer edge of the opening has a wide welt.

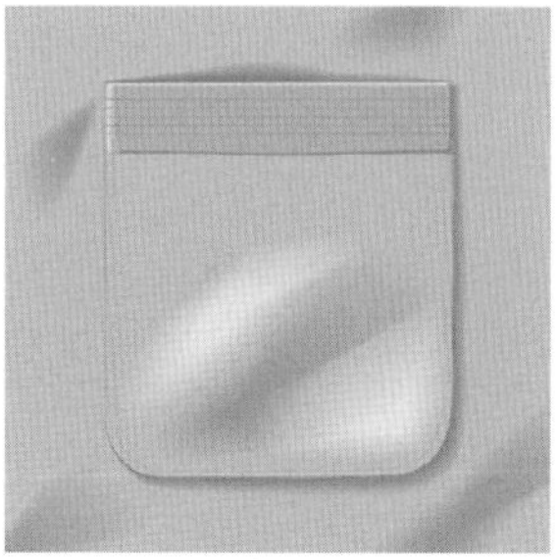

patch pocket
Pocket of various shapes and sizes, made of a piece of material sewn onto the garment's outer surface.

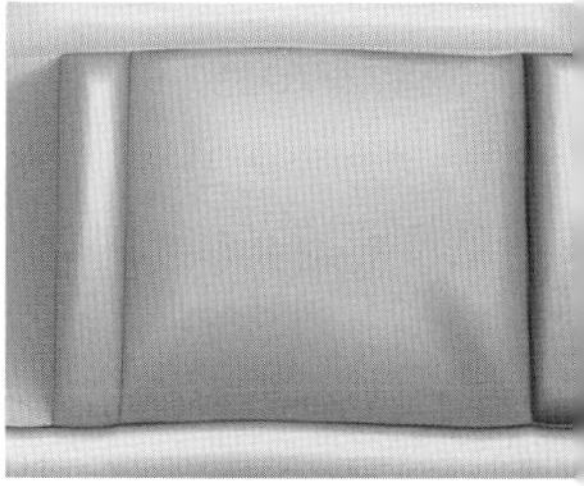

hand-warmer pouch
Patch pocket on the front of a garment; it opens vertically on one or both sides to protect the hands against the cold.

examples of sleeves

Sleeve: part of the garment that covers the arm and varies in shape and length.

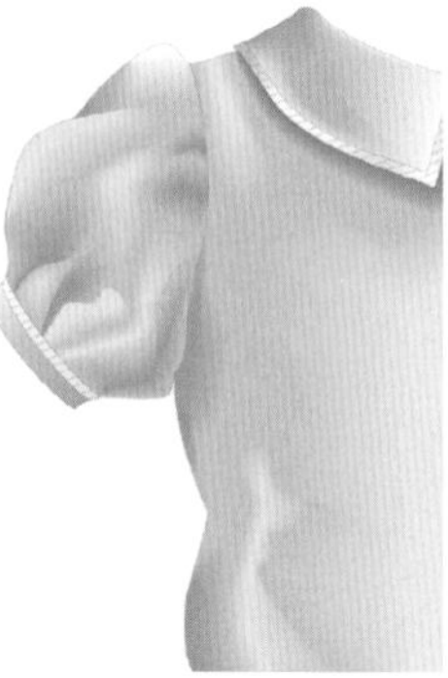

puff sleeve
Very short sleeve that puffs out because of pleats sewn at the armhole and the bottom of the sleeve; it is edged with a narrow strip of fabric or elastic.

cap sleeve
Small sleeve fitting tightly over the shoulder to fall straight or flare over the upper arm.

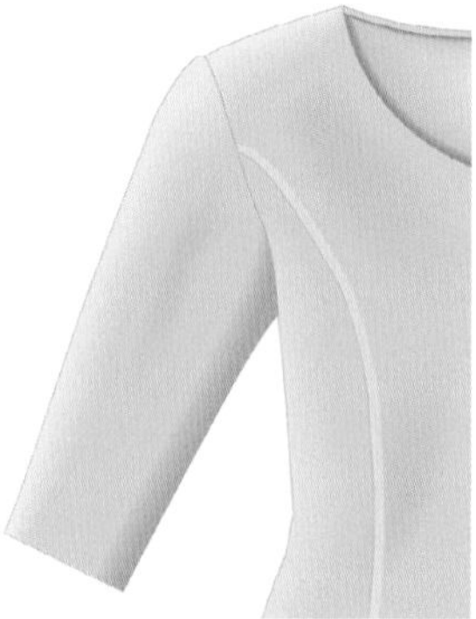

three-quarter sleeve
Sleeve that partially covers the forearm.

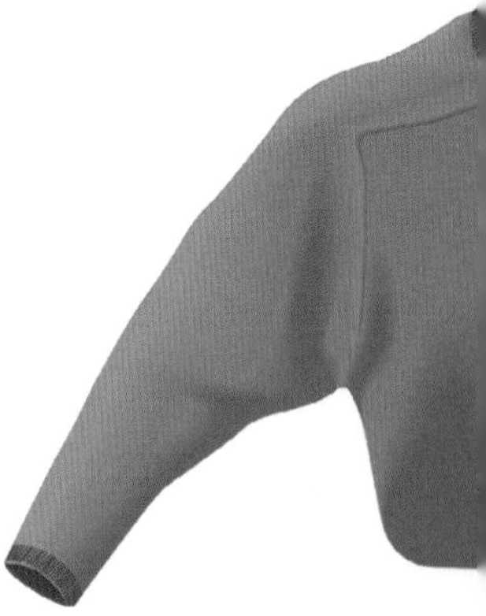

epaulet sleeve
Sleeve extending to the neck by a strip that covers the shoulder.

French cuff
Tight part of a shirt or blouse sleeve made of a wide strip of fabric, which is folded back and fastened edge to edge with cuff links.

pointed tab end
Narrow strip of fabric ending in a point and adorning the sleeve slit.

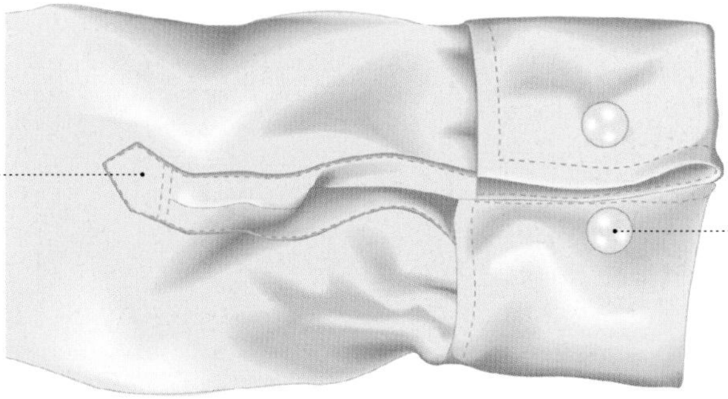

cuff link
Usually metal stud, single or paired with another, for fastening the edges of cuffs.

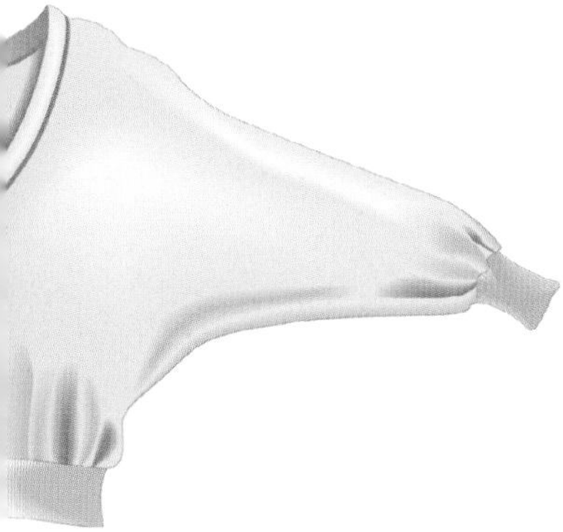

batwing sleeve
Sleeve with a large armhole that extends almost to the waist; it narrows gradually toward the wrist.

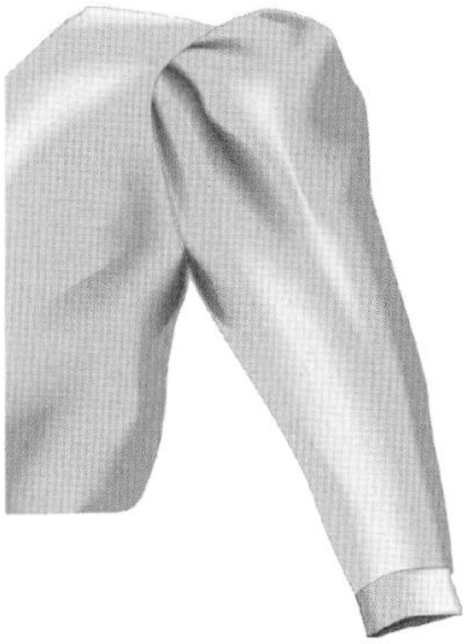

leg-of-mutton sleeve
Sleeve that is narrow from the wrist to the elbow and widens from the elbow to the shoulder, where it is gathered.

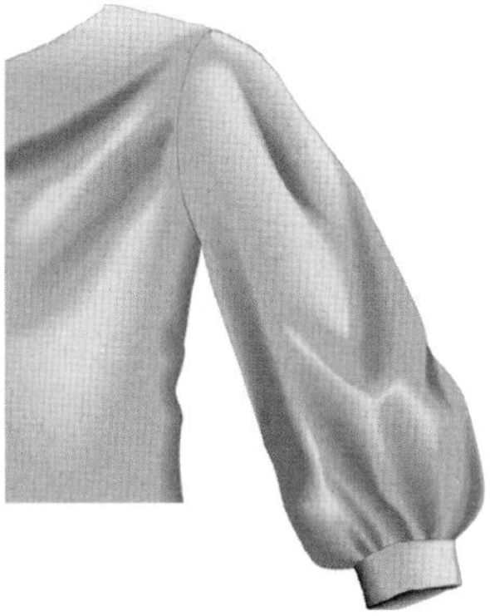

bishop sleeve
Long sleeve that puffs out because of pleats sewn at the bottom and sometimes at the armhole; it is edged with a narrow strip of fabric or elastic.

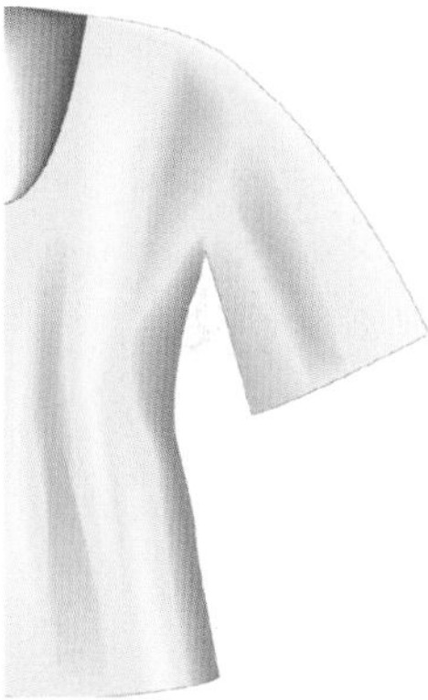

kimono sleeve
Very full sleeve with no seam at the armhole.

raglan sleeve
Sleeve extending over the shoulder and attached front and back with a slanted seam running from under the armhole to the neck.

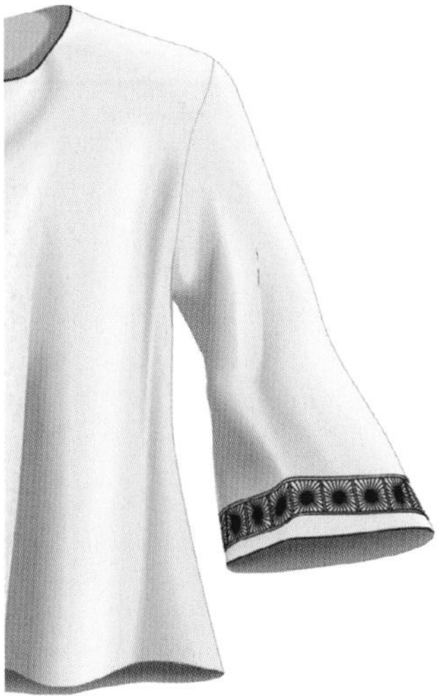

pagoda sleeve
Sleeve flaring from the elbow to the wrist.

shirt sleeve
Moderately full sleeve with a French cuff; it is slightly pleated at the bottom and is often embellished with a pointed tab end.

tailored sleeve
Long sleeve made of two pieces that are cut to follow the shape of a bent arm.

examples of collars

Collar: piece sewn onto a garment that finishes or adorns the neck.

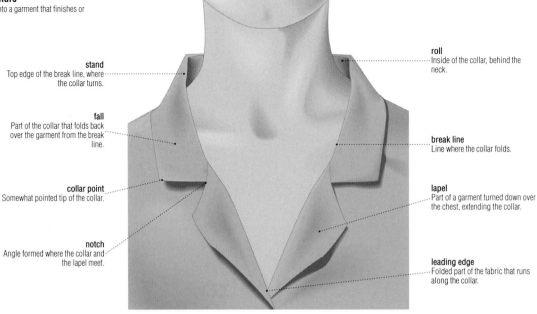

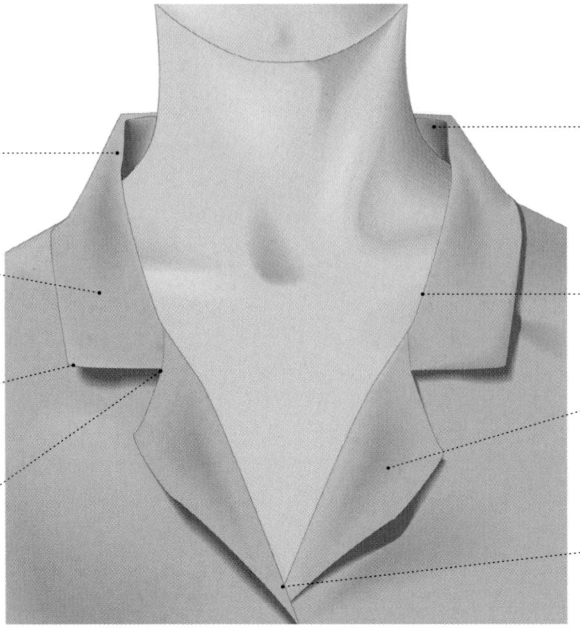
stand
Top edge of the break line, where the collar turns.
fall
Part of the collar that folds back over the garment from the break line.
collar point
Somewhat pointed tip of the collar.
notch
Angle formed where the collar and the lapel meet.
roll
Inside of the collar, behind the neck.
break line
Line where the collar folds.
lapel
Part of a garment turned down over the chest, extending the collar.
leading edge
Folded part of the fabric that runs along the collar.

collar
Piece sewn onto a garment that finishes or adorns the neck.

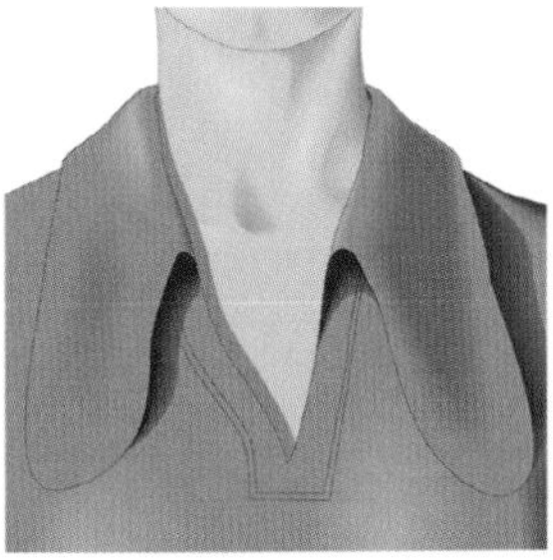

dog ear collar
Turned-down collar characterized by long, fairly wide points, which are rounded at the tips.

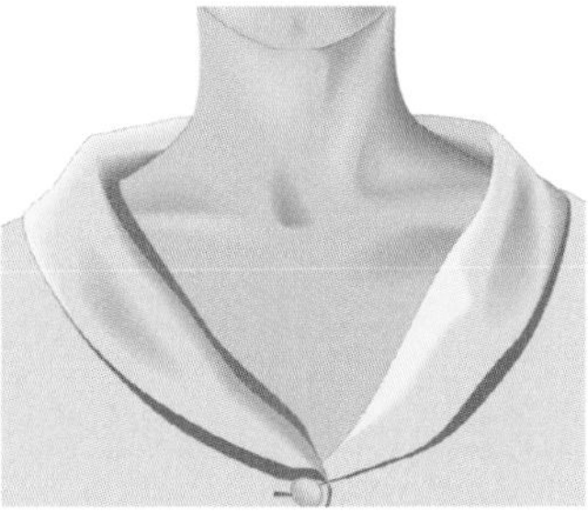

shawl collar
Wide turned-down collar with long rounded lapels that partially cross in front.

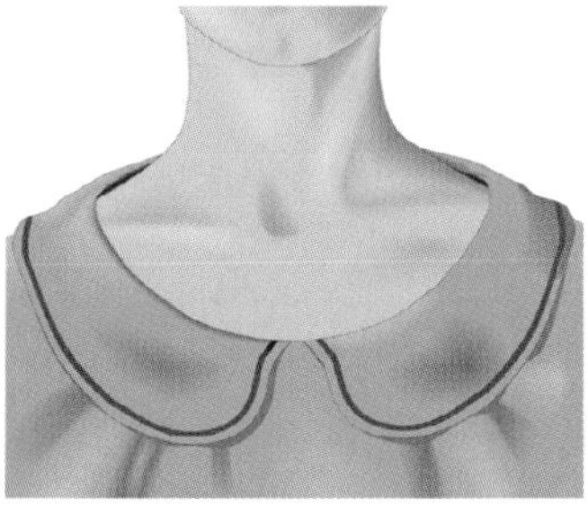

Peter Pan collar
Flat collar of uniform width with rounded tips; it is sewn onto a fairly open neck.

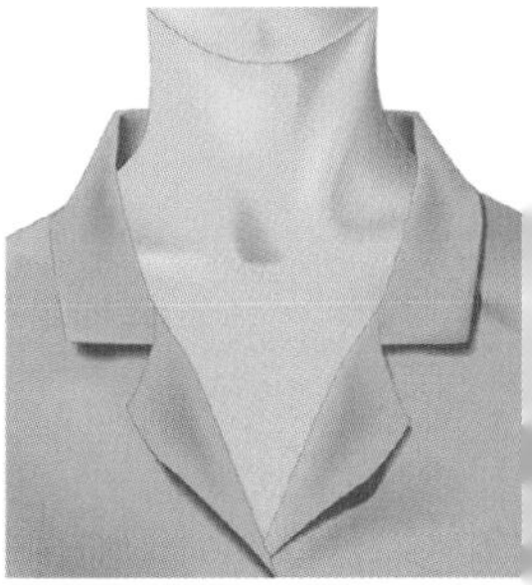

shirt collar
Collar with rounded or tapered points that is sewn onto the neck and turned down along a fold line, which is higher in back than in front.

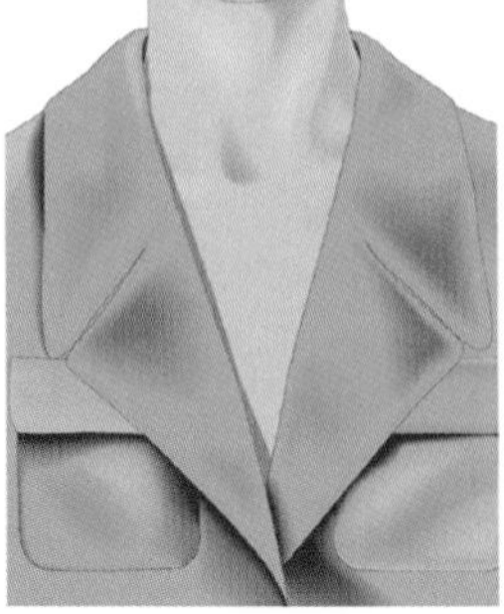

tailored collar
Collar whose fold covers the back of the neck; its lapels form a V where they cross on the chest.

bow collar
Collar made of a long strip of soft fabric sewn onto a round neck; it can be tied in front in various ways.

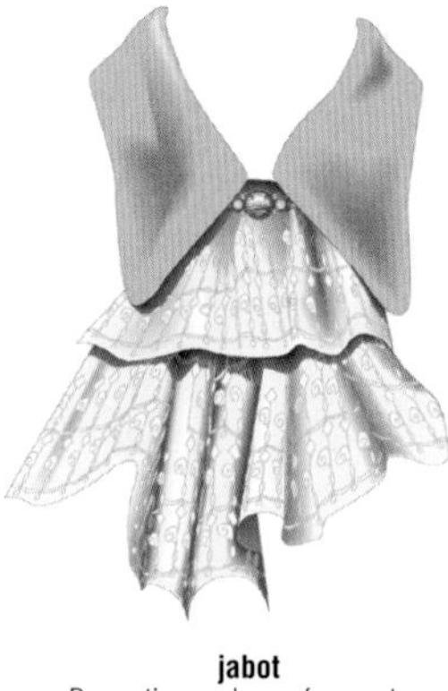

jabot
Decoration made up of one or two pieces of fine soft pleated fabric; it is attached at the base of the neck and spreads out over the chest.

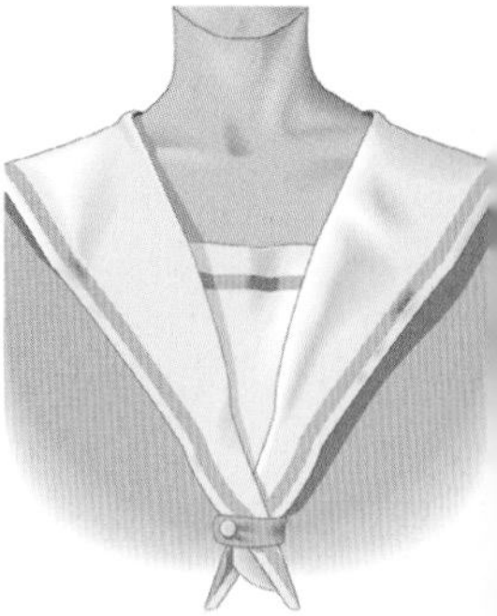

sailor collar
Collar that is square in back and has long lap extending over the chest; it is fastened to a neck and, out of modesty, the plunging neck is often concealed with a piece of fabric.

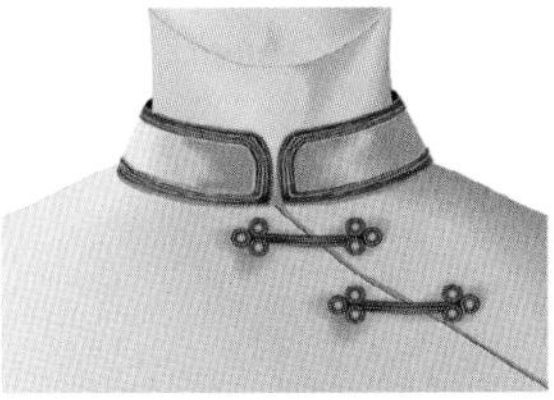

mandarin collar
Stand-up collar with rounded upper points that come together at the neck, forming a V.

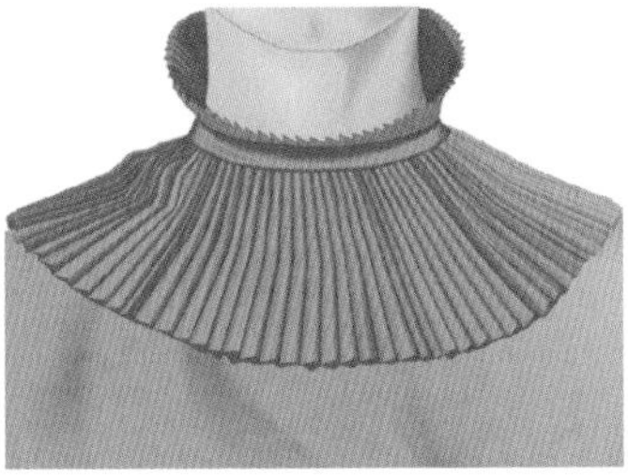

collaret
Piece of delicate, pleated or gathered fabric that adorns the neck of a dress; its shape has varied greatly from one period to another.

bertha collar
Collar made of a strip of fabric of variable width and attached to the edge of a neckline or round neck.

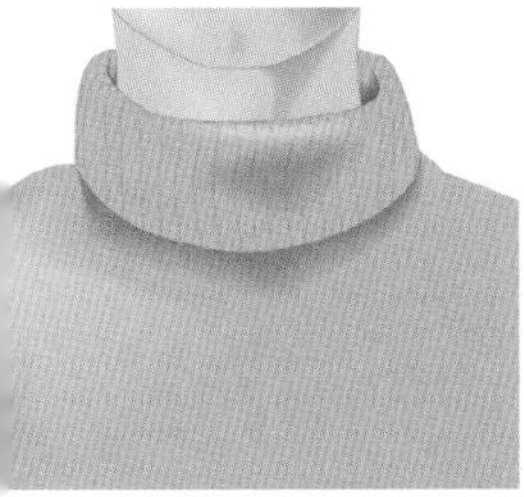

turtleneck
High-necked collar that is folded over; it is usually snug around the neck and does not fasten.

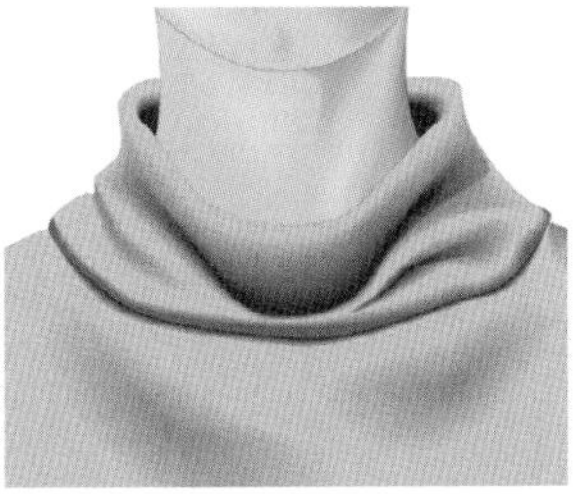

cowl neck
Turtleneck that is large enough to be draped over the head, making a kind of hood that frames the face.

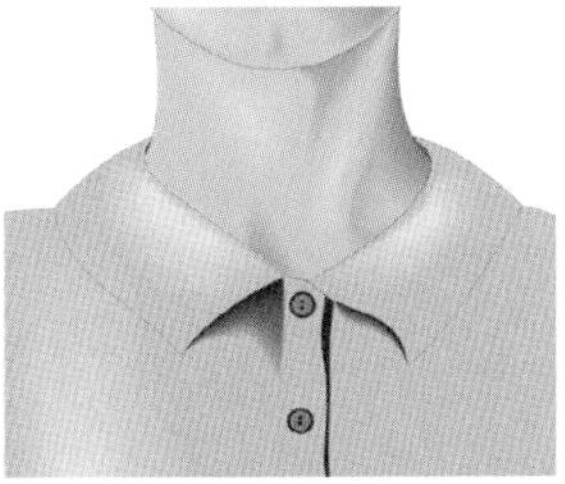

polo collar
Turned-down pointed collar fastened with a buttoned placket, which ends at mid-chest.

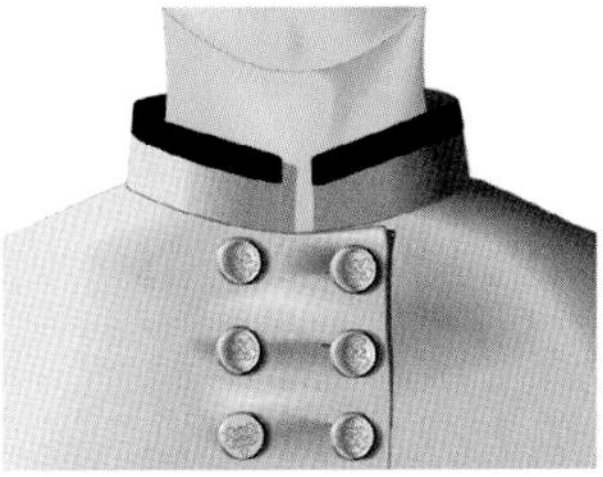

stand-up collar
Collar made of a narrow strip of fabric that sticks up from a round neck; its edges meet in front but do not fasten.

necklines and necks

The neck is that part of a garment near the wearer's neck; the neckline reveals the neck and part of the shoulders and chest.

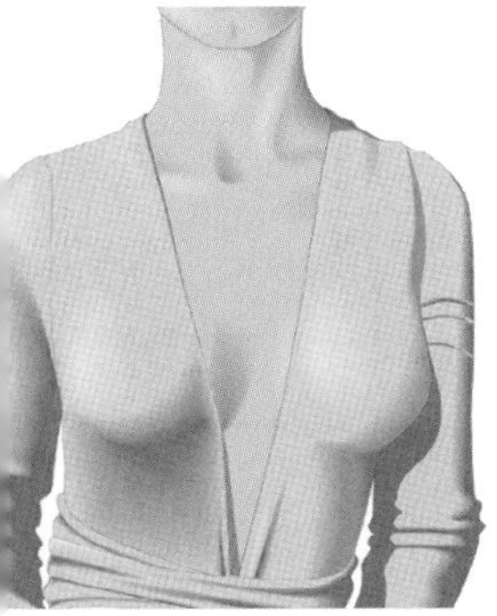

plunging neckline
Neckline that usually ends in a V and is very low in front or back.

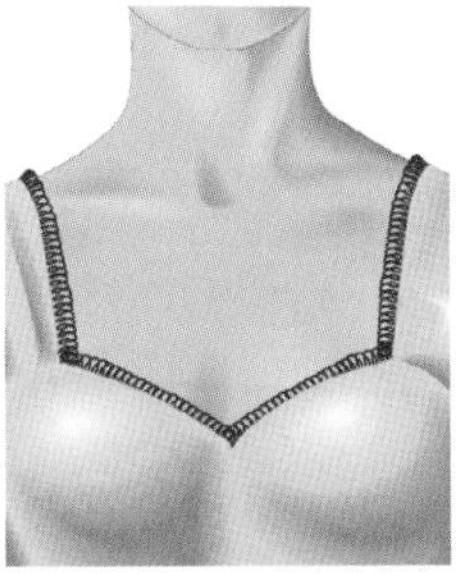

sweetheart neckline
Neckline shaped like the top of a heart.

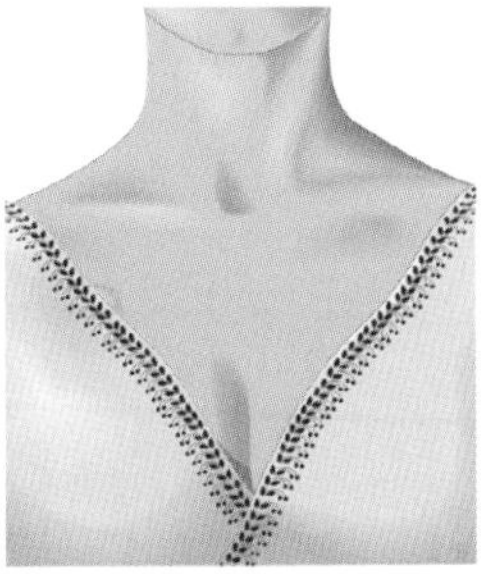

V-shaped neck
Neckline with edges coming together at mid-chest in a V shape.

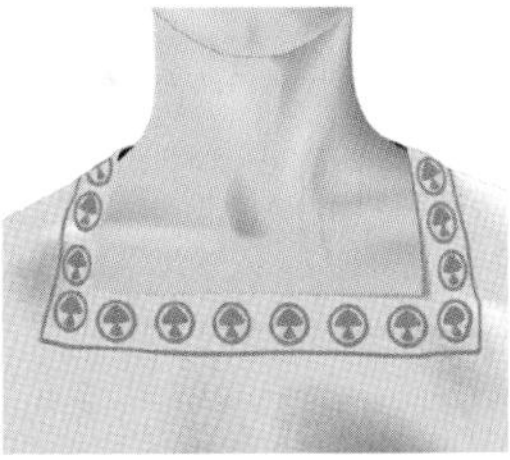

square neck
Neckline with a square neck that reveals the upper part of the chest.

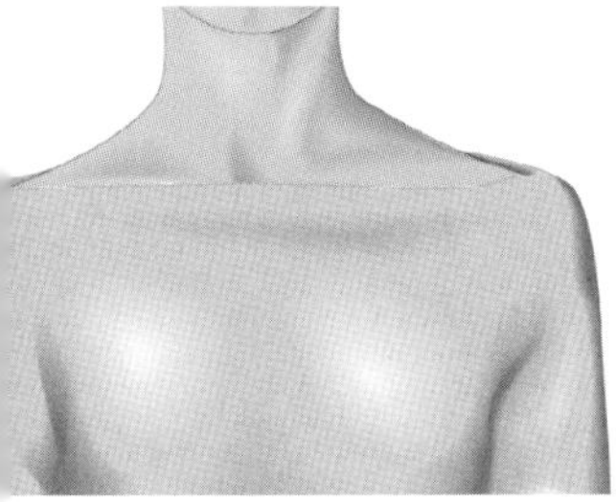

bateau neck
Neck tapering to a point on the shoulders.

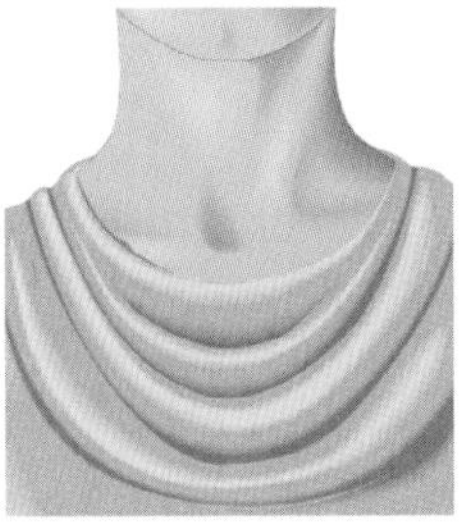

draped neck
Neck with soft pleats that can be arranged in various ways.

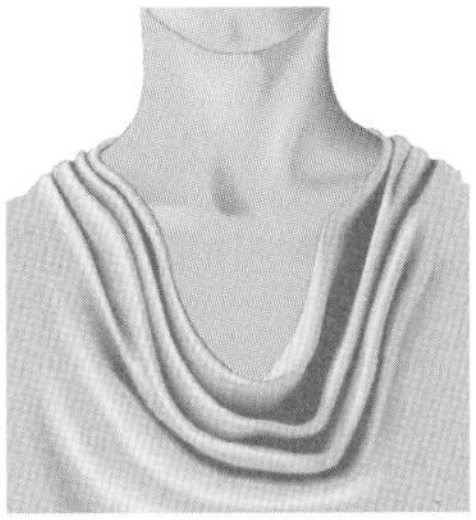

draped neckline
Neckline made up of a series of soft overlapping folds created by the fabric of the bodice.

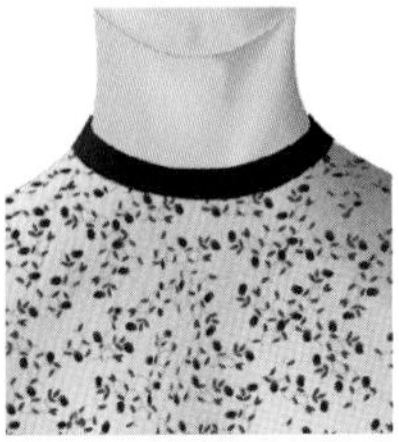

round neck
Rounded neck fitting close to the wearer's neck.

nightwear

Articles for indoor wear, some of which are worn for sleeping.

nightgown
Long wide full dress, often with shoulder straps, worn next to the skin.

baby doll
Short nightgown that ends at the top of the thighs and is worn with matching briefs.

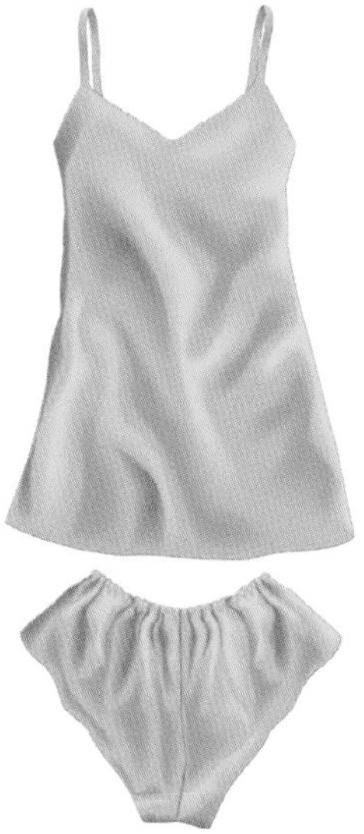

kimono
Light full dressing gown that crosses over in front; it usually has square sleeves and a belt.

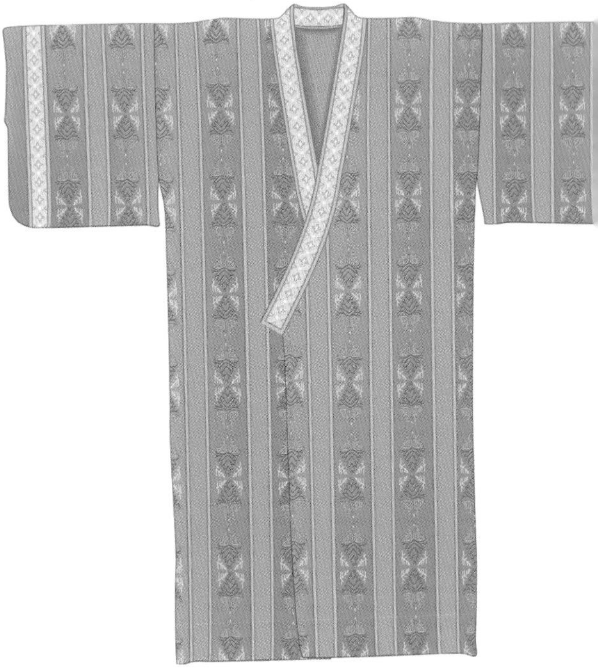

bathrobe
Full straight garment with a belt; it is usually made of terry cloth and is worn after a bath or a shower.

pajamas
Light full outfit made up of a jacket or tunic and pants with an elasticized or drawstring waist.

negligee
Light elegant women's garment, usually long and décolleté with soft lines; it often comes with a nightgown of the same fabric.

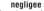

hose
Garments of various stretchy fabrics used to cover the foot and leg; each pair of hose has a different name, depending on its length.

knee-high sock
Sock covering the foot and extending to the knee.

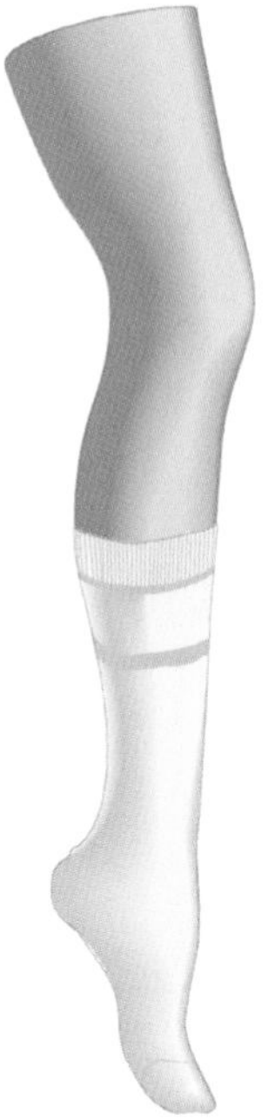

sock
Sock covering the leg to just below the knee.

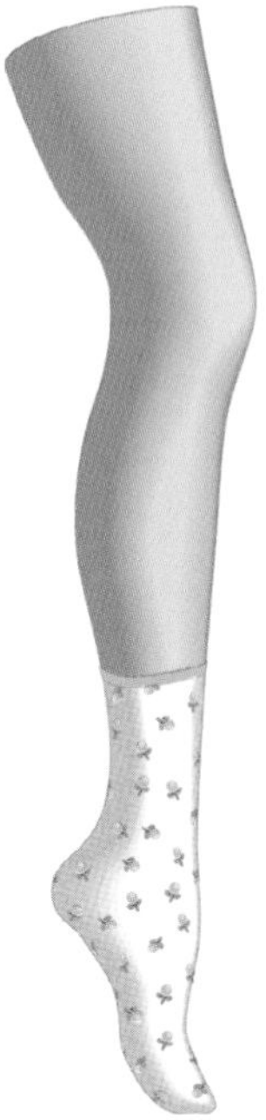

anklet
Sock that covers the foot and extends slightly above the ankle.

short sock
Light short sock covering only the foot and the ankle.

panty hose
Garment made up of two stockings joined by a pair of briefs, sometimes reinforced and held in place by an elasticized waist.

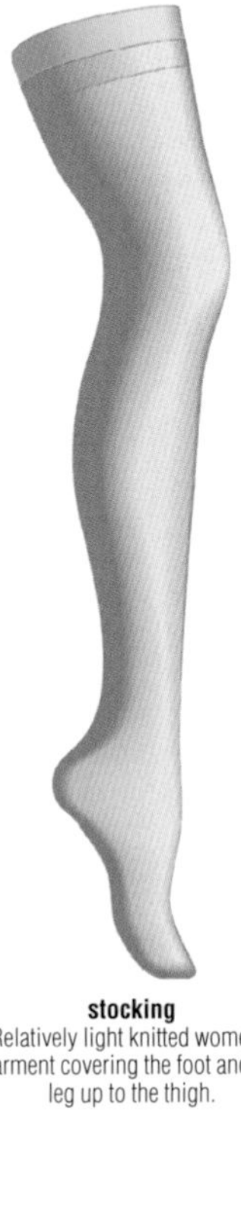

stocking
Relatively light knitted women's garment covering the foot and the leg up to the thigh.

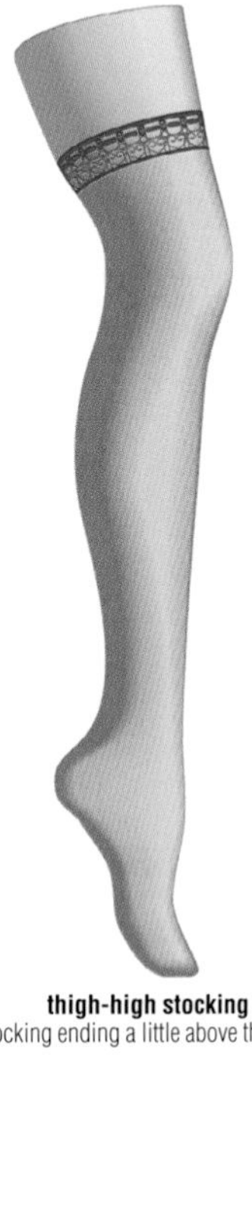

thigh-high stocking
Stocking ending a little above the knee.

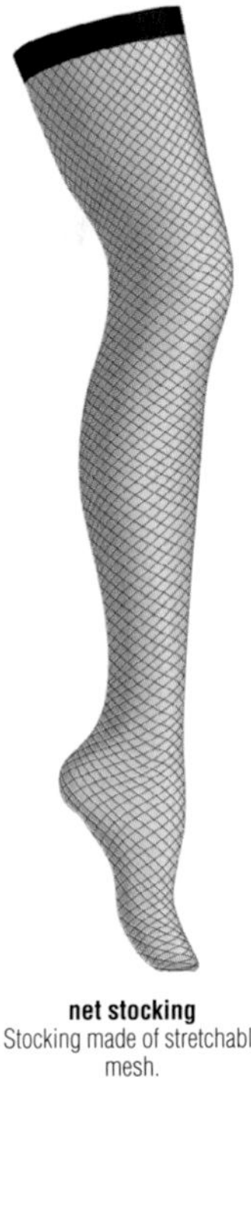

net stocking
Stocking made of stretchable mesh.

underwear

Garments worn next to the skin and under other garments.

corselette

Support undergarment combining a girdle and a bra.

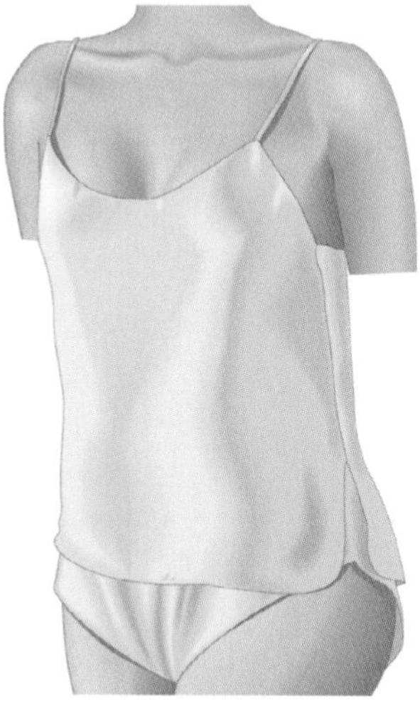

camisole

Short undergarment with an open neck and shoulder straps; the part covering the chest can be shaped like a bra.

teddy

Garment combining a camisole and briefs.

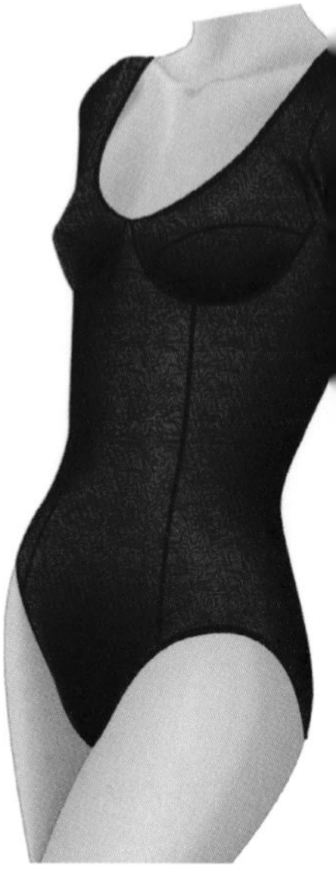

body suit

Garment combining a bodice and briefs in a single garment.

panty corselette

Undergarment combining a girdle, a bra and briefs.

half-slip

Undergarment made up of a lightweight skirt and an elasticized waist, substituting for lining.

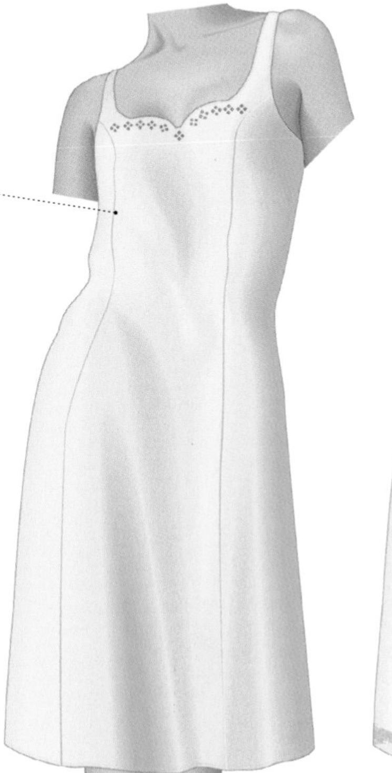

princess seaming
Decorative seam running from the shoulder or the armhole to the garment's hem, accentuating the figure.

foundation slip

Undergarment with wide nonadjustable shoulder straps, worn under a see-through dress.

slip

Undergarment with narrow adjustable shoulder straps; the part covering the chest is usually shaped like a bra.

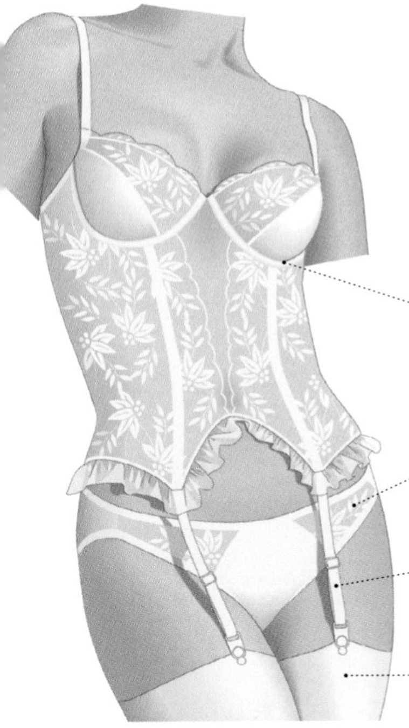

underwire
Rigid crescent that edges and reinforces the underside of the cups.

bikini
Low-waisted tight-fitting undergarment with high-cut legs.

garter
Elastic strap attached to a girdle, garter belt, etc., with a system for fastening the hose and keeping it taut.

hose
Relatively light knitted women's garment covering the foot and the leg up to the thigh.

wasp-waisted corset
Small corset made up of a bra and garter belt, slimming the figure.

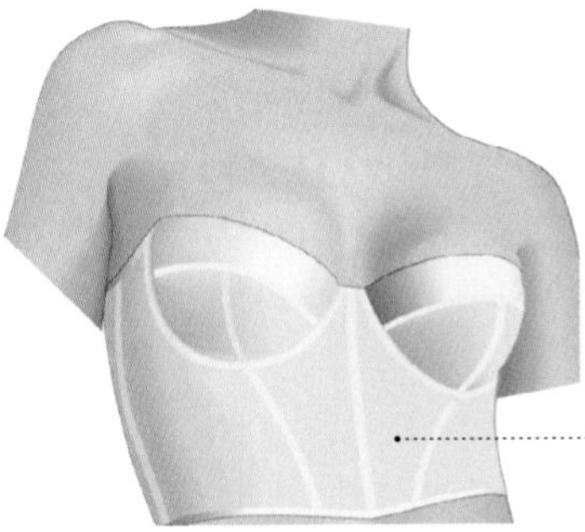

strapless bra
Bra without shoulder straps and with a midriff band that extends to the waist; the cups are preshaped and have underwires and steels.

steel
Narrow flexible strip of metal or plastic inserted into a garment to keep it stiff.

push-up bra
Bra with cups that leave the upper chest bare and with shoulder straps that sit on the outer edge of the shoulder.

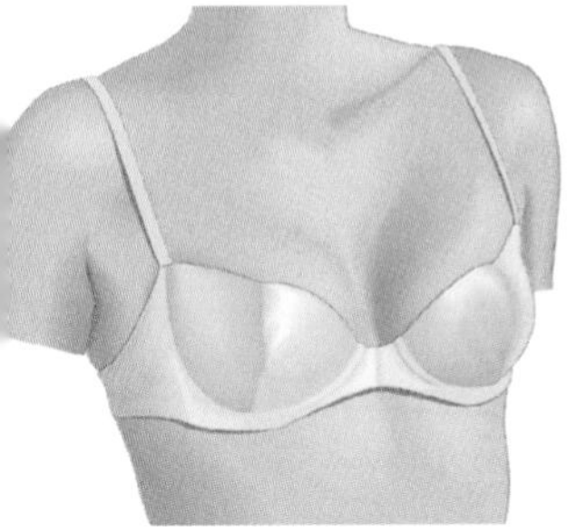

décolleté bra
Very low-cut bra with cups that extend upward toward the shoulder straps.

girdle
Elasticized undergarment with a stomach panel; it is designed to shape the waist and hips.

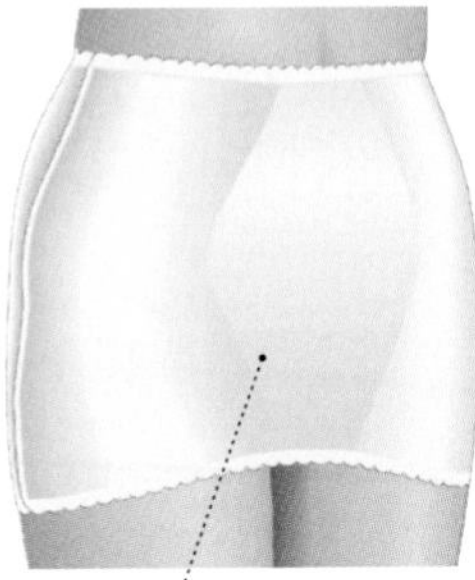

panel
Foundation piece that flattens the stomach.

shoulder strap
Narrow strip of fabric that is often adjustable; it goes over the shoulder to connect a garment's front and back.

cup
Main part of the bra that covers and supports the breasts.

midriff band
Strip of stretchable fabric connecting the cups; it varies in width and fastens with hooks.

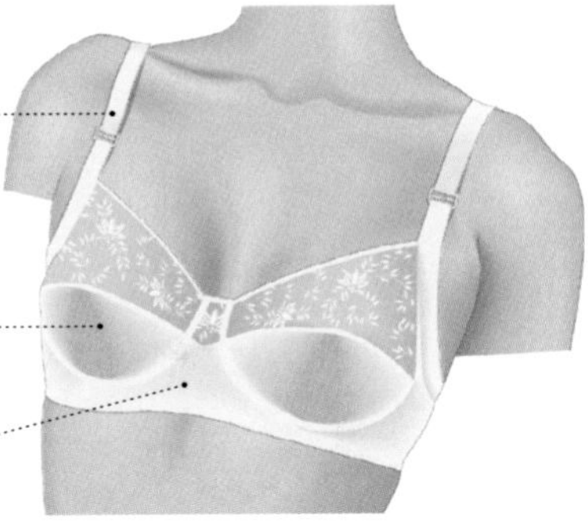

bra
Undergarment made up of cups, shoulder straps and a midriff band, designed to support the chest.

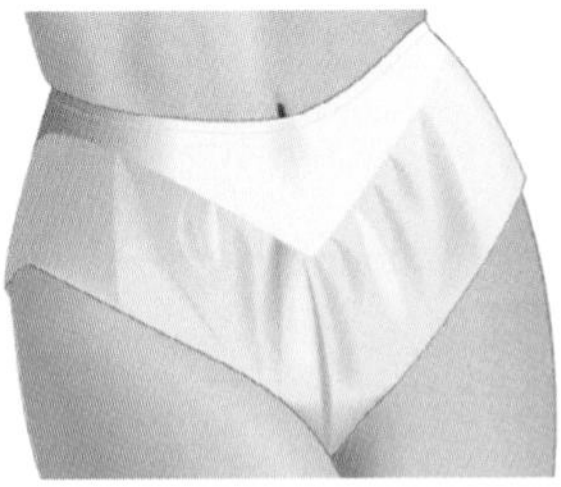

briefs
Undergarment that extends fairly low over the hips and is held in place by an elasticized waist.

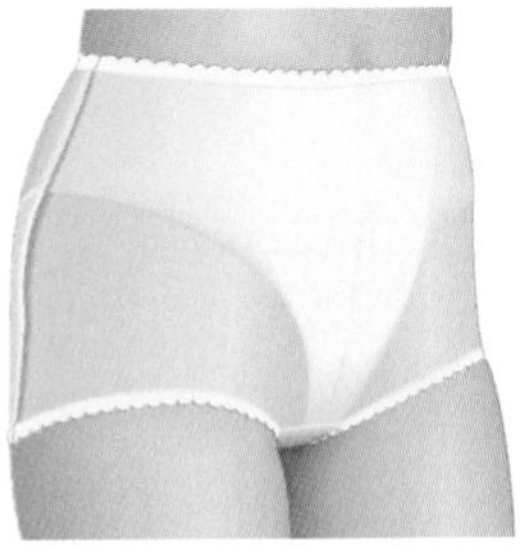

panty girdle
Girdle usually made up of briefs, with or without legs, and removable garters.

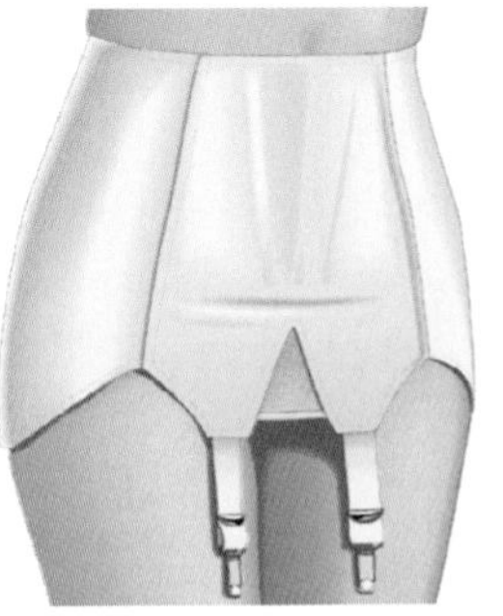

corset
Sturdy undergarment with steels and often garters; it is designed to shape the waist and hips.

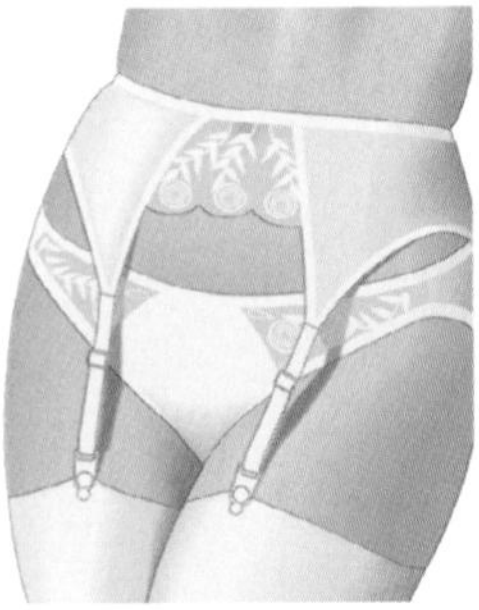

garter belt
Narrow belt with garters that fastens around the hips.

newborn children's clothing

Garments worn by children from birth to about three years of age.

jumpsuit
Low-cut one-piece sleeveless garment with legs and feet.

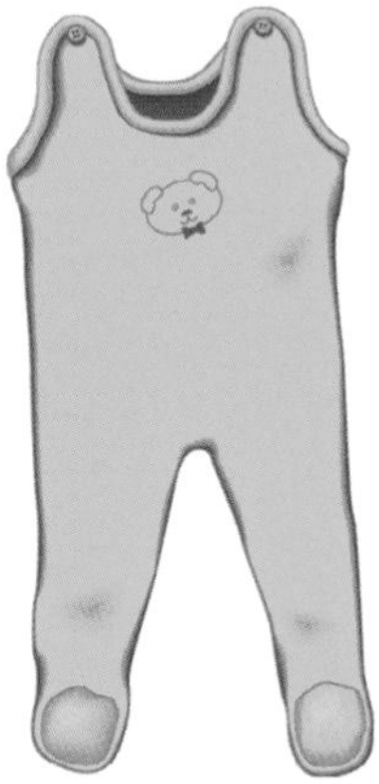

bunting bag
Hooded coat with a front zipper; it is sewn closed at the bottom and sometimes has no armholes.

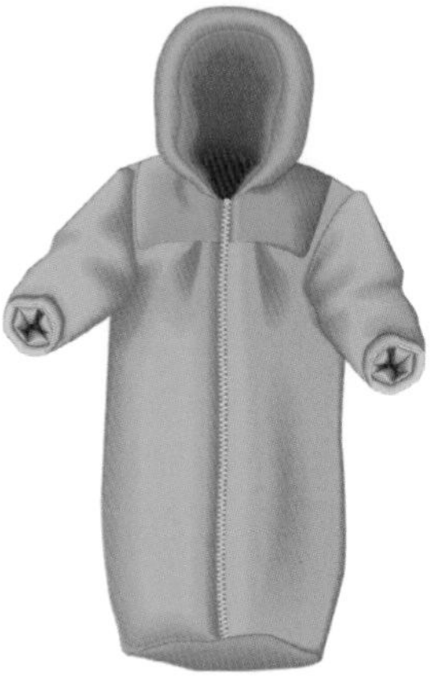

bathing wrap
Absorbent piece of fabric with a hood at one corner; it is wrapped around a baby when it comes out of the bath.

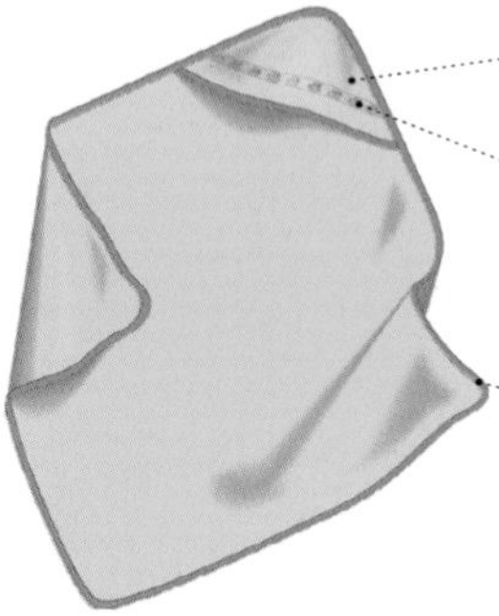

hood
Part of the garment that is pulled over the head.

decorative braid
Narrow thick closely woven piece of fabric that edges or adorns a garment.

false tuck
Strip of material designed to hide a garment's seam or decorate its edge.

nylon rumba tights
Long drawers with feet; they are made of stretchy or knitted fabric and have ruching at the back.

grow sleepers
Newborn sleepwear shaped like a bag or with feet; the garment can be lengthened in various ways: here, with snap fasteners at the waist.

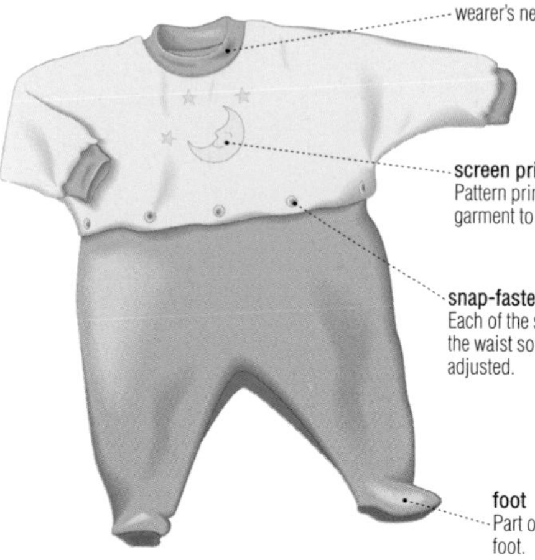

crew neck
Rounded neck fitting close to the wearer's neck.

screen print
Pattern printed or sewn on the garment to decorate it.

snap-fastening waist
Each of the snap fasteners sewn around the waist so the garment's length can be adjusted.

foot
Part of the garment covering the foot.

high-back overalls
Pants extended by a front piece covering the chest and another covering the back, connected with shoulder straps.

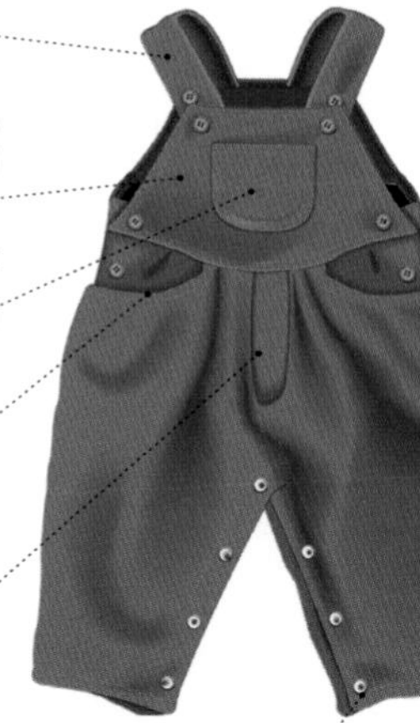

adjustable strap
Strip of adjustable fabric that goes over the shoulder to connect a garment's front and back.

bib
Upper part of the overalls, covering the chest from the waist up.

patch pocket
Pocket of various shapes and sizes, made of a piece of material sewn onto the garment's outer surface.

top stitching
Stitches on the right side of the fabric used to embellish and reinforce the garment.

fly
Vertical opening at the middle front of the pants; it closes with buttons or a zipper and is usually covered by the folded edge of the opening.

inside-leg snap-fastening
Part along the inner leg of the garment, where snap fasteners make it easier to put the pants on.

shirt
Long-sleeved baby shirt used as an under- or overgarment, depending on its weight; its characteristic lap shoulders allow the shirt's neck to expand when it is being put on.

diaper
Absorbent article of clothing used as briefs for babies.

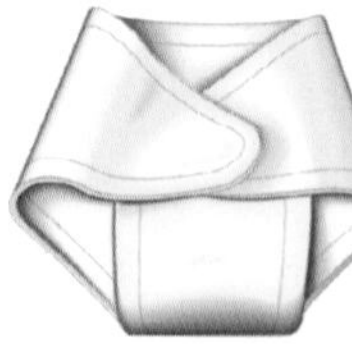

ruffled rumba pants
Undergarment with an elasticized waist that extends to the top of the thighs; it is large enough to be worn over a diaper.

ruching
One of several narrow decorative strips of light fabric, gathered and sewn onto a garment.

bib
Absorbent piece of fabric tied around a child's neck to protect its clothes from food and saliva.

disposable diaper
Throwaway piece of fabric with a waterproof outer layer and usually elasticized leg holes, which allow the child to move freely.

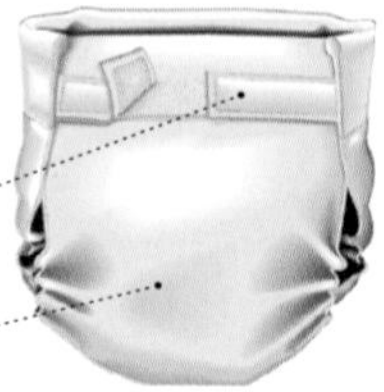

Velcro® closure
Fastening system made up of two strips with surfaces that grip on contact.

waterproof pants
Part of the diaper gathered around the top of the thighs.

blanket sleepers
ne-piece long-sleeved nightwear for bies that has legs and feet, a long front pper and a rear panel, which opens at the waist.

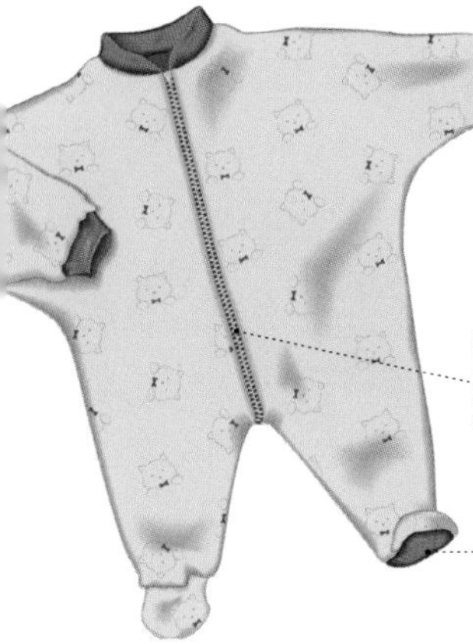

ribbing
Tight elastic knitted strip around the sleeve or the bottom of a garment for tightening, reinforcing and adorning them.

zipper
Closure made up of two lengths of tape edged with teeth that interlock by means of a slide.

vinyl grip sole
Outsole whose material or textured surface prevents the foot from slipping.

sleepers
Infant nightwear that fastens all the way up the front with snap fasteners.

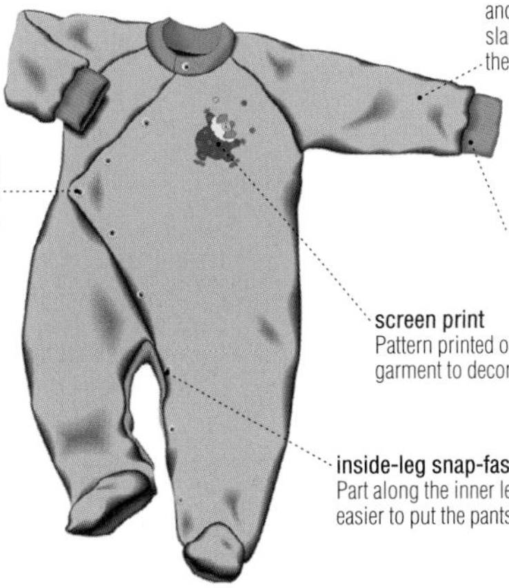

snap-fastening front
A line of snap fasteners on the front of a garment.

raglan sleeve
Sleeve extending over the shoulder and attached front and back with a slanted seam running from under the armhole to the neck.

ribbing
Tight elastic knitted strip around the sleeve or the bottom of a garment for tightening, reinforcing and adorning them.

screen print
Pattern printed or sewn on the garment to decorate it.

inside-leg snap-fastening
Part along the inner leg of the garment, where snap fasteners make it easier to put the pants on.

children's clothing

Clothing worn by children between the ages of about 3 and 12.

crossover back straps overalls
ants with a bib covering the chest and shoulder straps that cross over in the back.

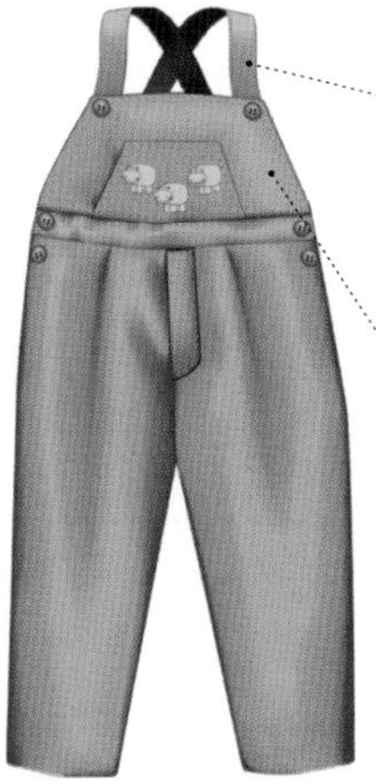

button strap
Narrow strip of fabric that is attached to the garment by buttons and connects the front and back by passing over the shoulder.

bib
Upper part of the overalls, covering the chest from the waist up.

snowsuit
Winter garment consisting of a warm one-piece suit with a hood, which is sometimes detachable and often edged with fur.

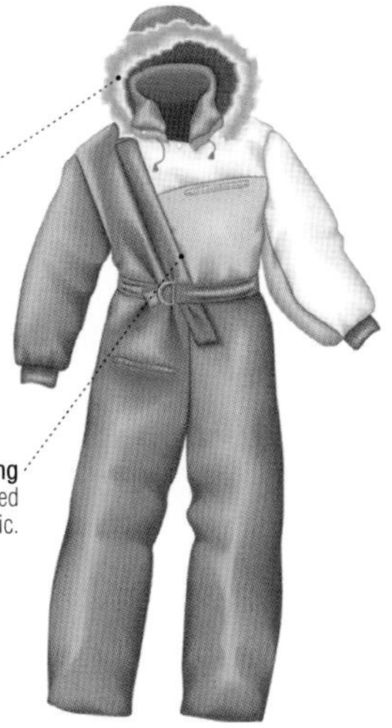

drawstring hood
Hood with a string, which draws it tight around the face.

fly front closing
Zipper or button fastening system covered by a strip of fabric.

pajamas
Nightclothes characterized by a long-sleeved, T-shirt style tunic and ribbing at the crew neck, wrists and ankles.

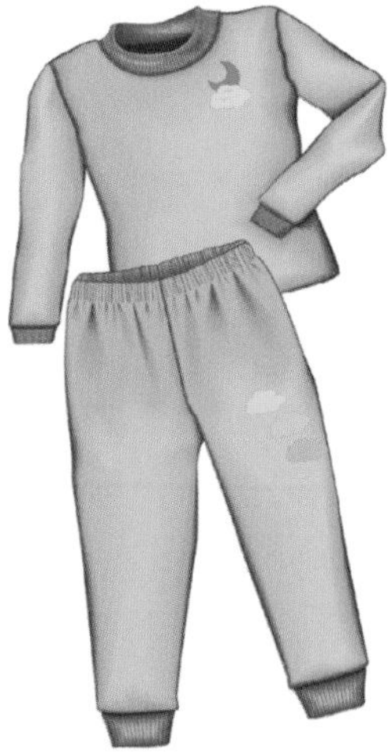

T-shirt dress
Long top in cotton jersey with a relatively high neck and usually short sleeves but with no fastening system or collar.

rompers
Infant day suit consisting of a short-sleeved blouse or a bib with shoulder straps, which are attached to puffy briefs that fasten at the crotch.

training set
Clothing designed for sports.

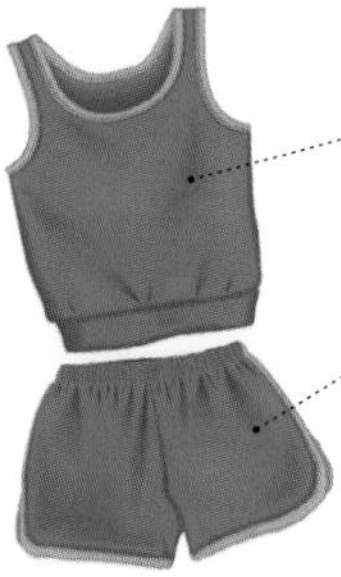

tank top
Short, fairly tight low-cut shirt without sleeves or a collar.

shorts
Very short pants covering only the top of the thighs.

jumpsuit
One-piece garment usually fastening in front with a zipper or buttons.

sportswear

Clothing and accessories designed for sports, dancing or acrobatics.

running shoe
Light but sturdy canvas and rubber or leather shoe worn for sports or leisure.

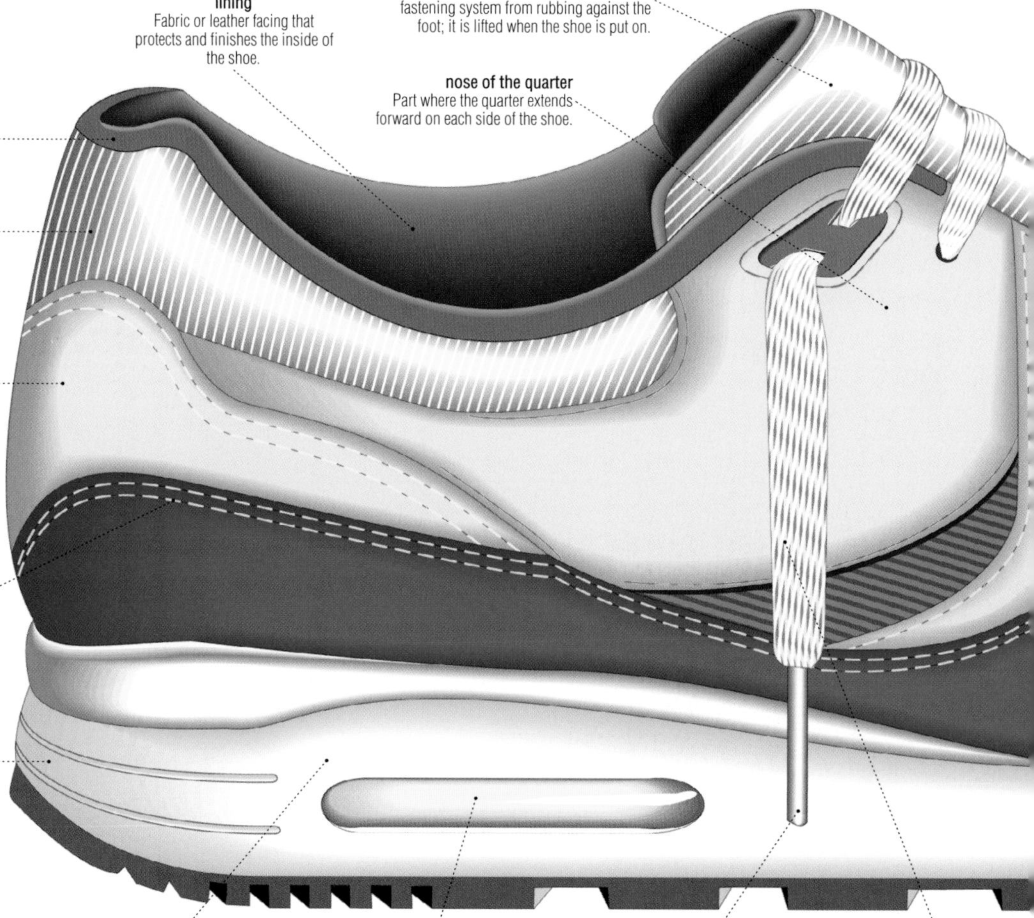

collar
Strip of fabric or leather along the edge of the lining.

counter
Piece used to reinforce the back of the shoe and keep the heel of the foot in place.

quarter
Back part of the shoe that surrounds the heel of the foot and extends over the instep to reinforce it.

stitch
Visible stitching that both embellishes and reinforces the shoe.

heel
Stiff part underneath the shoe that supports the back of the foot.

lining
Fabric or leather facing that protects and finishes the inside of the shoe.

tongue
Extension of the vamp that prevents the fastening system from rubbing against the foot; it is lifted when the shoe is put on.

nose of the quarter
Part where the quarter extends forward on each side of the shoe.

middle sole
Sole made of various materials, placed over the outsole and cushioning the entire foot.

air unit
Compartment in the middle sole that is filled with air to absorb impact.

tag
Metal or plastic sheath that covers each end of a lace to ease it through the eyelets.

shoelace
Narrow cord of fabric or leather, or round, that is threaded throu eyelets or hooks to tighten the shoe.

training suit
Outfit made up of a jacket or shirt and pants; it is usually made of jersey fleece and is worn over sports clothes or as casual wear.

hooded sweat shirt
Cotton fleece pullover that is often worn as outerwear; it has ribbing at the wrists and hips, a drawstring hood and a hand-warmer pouch.

sweat shirt
Loose fleece pullover usually with a round neck, long sleeves and ribbing at the hips and wrists.

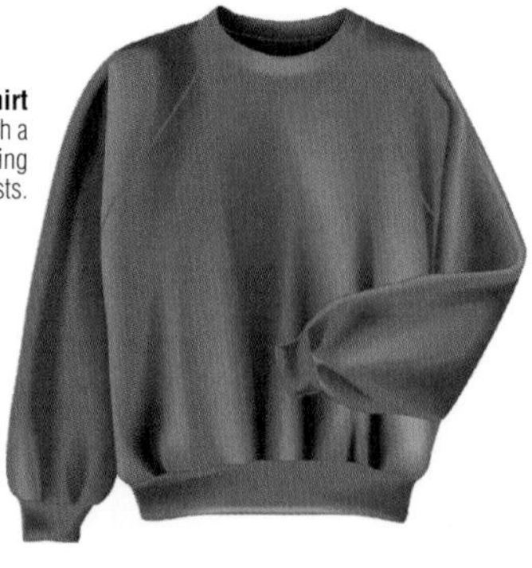

sweat pants
Training suit pants with a drawstring waist and ribbed ankles.

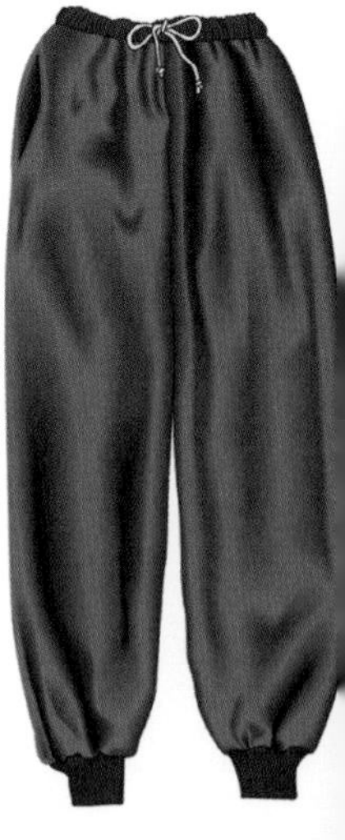

exercise wear
Clothing appropriate for sports, dancing or acrobatics.

swimming trunks
Low-waisted briefs with very high-cut legs; they are usually stretchy and tight-fitting and are worn by men for swimming.

swimsuit
Women's swimming garment that is tight-fitting and usually stretchy; it can be in one piece or consist of briefs and a bikini top.

leotard
Tight-fitting stretch knit garment combining a bodice and briefs.

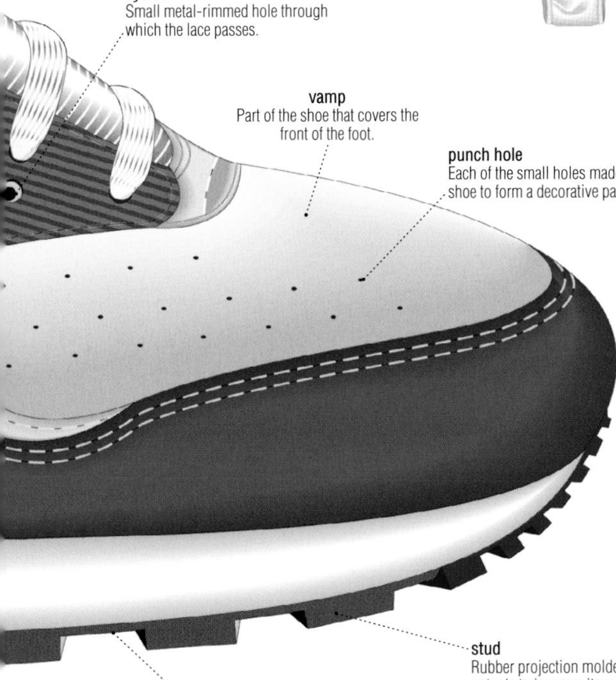

eyelet
Small metal-rimmed hole through which the lace passes.

vamp
Part of the shoe that covers the front of the foot.

punch hole
Each of the small holes made in the shoe to form a decorative pattern.

stud
Rubber projection molded into the outsole to improve its grip.

outsole
Sturdy piece of rubber or leather that forms the bottom of the shoe and is in contact with the ground.

footless tights
Tight-fitting stretch knit pants that end at the ankle and usually have an elasticized waist.

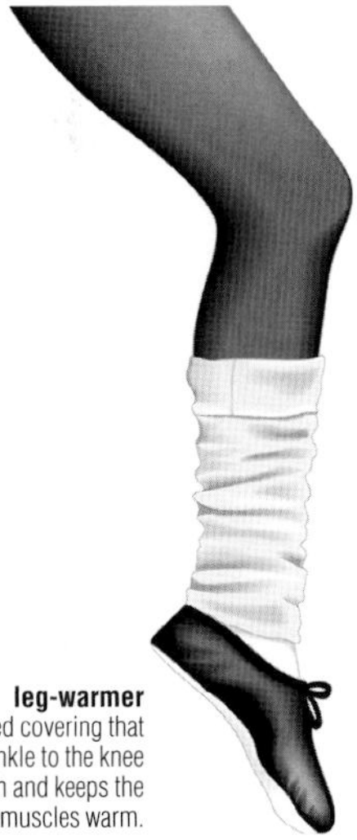

leg-warmer
Knitted tube-shaped covering that extends from the ankle to the knee or mid-thigh and keeps the muscles warm.

pants
Garment for the lower body; they extend from the waist or the hips to the ankles, covering each leg separately.

anorak
Waterproof sports jacket with long sleeves, a drawstring hood and waist and gathered wrists.

boxer shorts
Briefs covering the top of the thighs; they are gathered by an elasticized waist and have an inner bikini bottom.

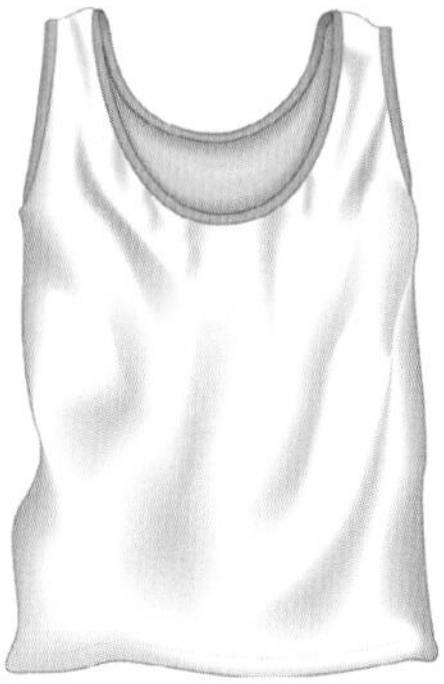

tank top
Short, fairly tight low-cut shirt without sleeves or a collar.

CLOTHING

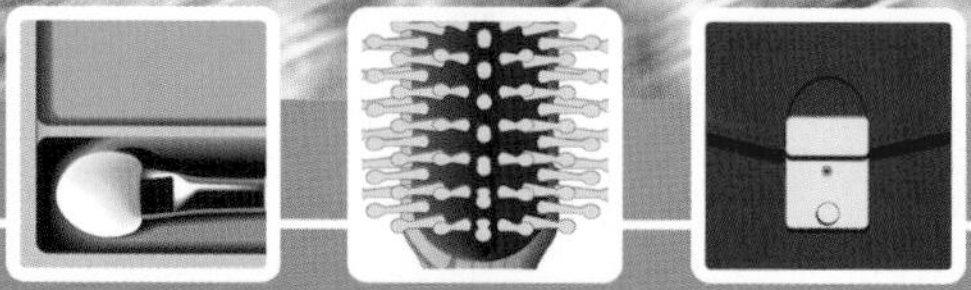

PERSONAL ACCESSORIES AND ARTICLES

374 Personal accessories

Jewelry and associated items designed to enhance a person's appearance.

383 Personal articles

Range of articles and accessories belonging to an individual who uses them every day.

jewelry

Finely crafted articles of adornment that are valued for their materials (gold, silver, gemstones) and workmanship.

earrings

Article of jewelry worn on the earlobe.

clip earrings
Earrings attached to the earlobe by a spring clip.

screw earrings
Earrings attached to the earlobe by a small screw behind the ear.

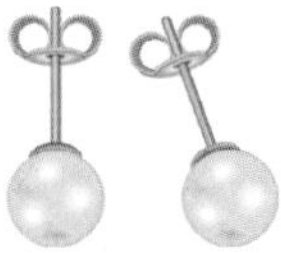

pierced earrings
Earrings with a post that passes through the pierced earlobe and is capped with a clasp.

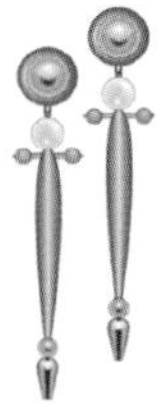

drop earrings
Earrings where the ornamental part hangs down from the ear and varies in shape and length.

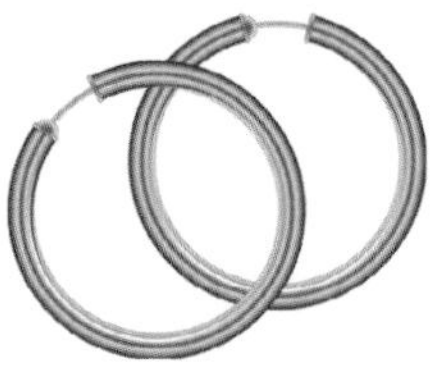

hoop earrings
Hoop-shaped earrings with a post that passes through the pierced earlobe and fits into the other end of the ring.

necklaces

Article of jewelry worn around the neck that consists of a band of gold or silver, a circle of set or unset precious stones or pearls strung together.

matinee-length necklace
Necklace that is approximately 20 in long and falls above the chest.

velvet-band choker
Choker consisting of a ribbon to which an ornament is attached.

pendant
Article of jewelry hung from a cha or a necklace.

rope
Necklace that is over 3 ft long and can be looped several times around the neck and knotted over the chest.

opera-length necklace
Necklace that is approximately 30 in long and falls over the chest.

bib necklace
Ncklace consisting of three or more rows.

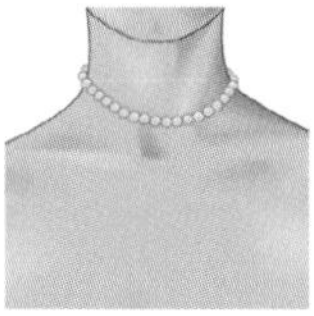

choker
Necklace that sometimes consists of many rows and is worn at the base of the neck.

locket
Usually round or oval pendant th opens to receive a memento of a loved one.

brilliant cut facets

The most common cut for a diamond is the brilliant cut; it consists of 58 facets spread over two faces, which are separated by a girdle.

side face

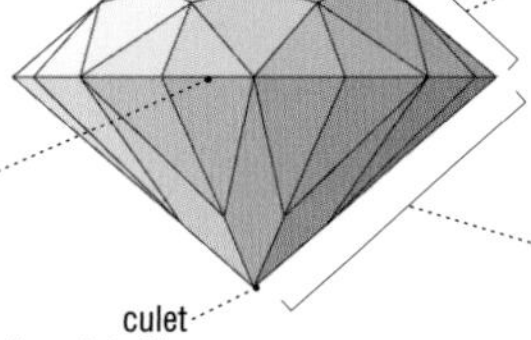

table
Upper horizontal facet of the diamond that has the shape of an octagon.

girdle
Polished or unpolished edge that separates the crown from the pavilion.

culet
Facet that is the point of the pavilion.

crown
The 32 facets situated between the girdle and the table.

pavilion
The 24 facets situated between the girdle and the culet.

top face

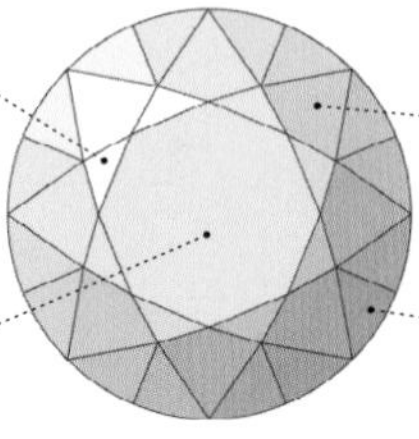

star facet (8)
Triangular facet cut on the crown face; the table is its base.

table
Upper horizontal facet of the diamond that has the shape of an octagon.

bezel facet (8)
Facet cut on the crown face; the tip touches the table, the point and the girdle.

upper girdle facet (16)
Triangular facet cut on the crown face; the base touches the girdle.

bottom face

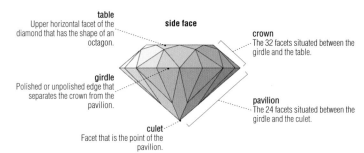

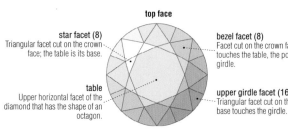

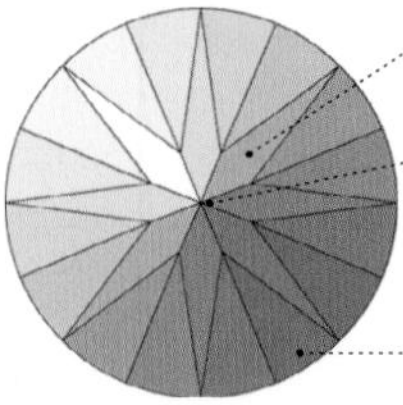

pavilion facet (8)
Facet cut on the pavilion side; one point touches the culet and the other the girdle.

culet
Facet that is the point of the pavilion.

lower girdle facet (16)
Pointed facet cut on the pavilion side; the girdle is its base.

cut for gemstones

Cutting a gemstone consists of angling the facets so that the stone's brilliance is intensified.

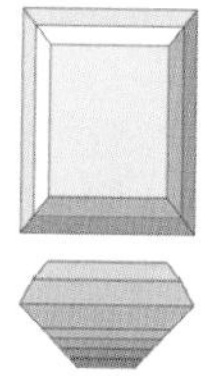

step cut
Cut where the square or rectangular girdle is surrounded by parallel rows of rectangular facets; there are more facets on the pavilion side than on the crown side.

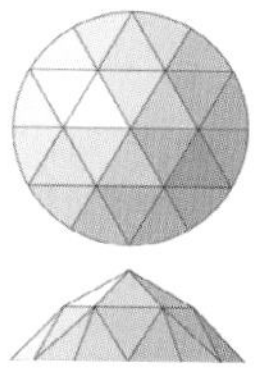

rose cut
Cut with a flat base and a dome made up of triangular facets; the total number of facets is a multiple of three.

table cut
The simplest kind of table cut; the rectangular girdle with sometimes rounded corners is surrounded on each side by a row of facets.

cabochon cut
Unfaceted cut suitable for opaque stones; it has one flat side and one or two convex sides.

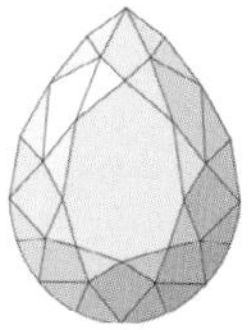

pear-shaped cut
Brilliant full cut with an elongated girdle.

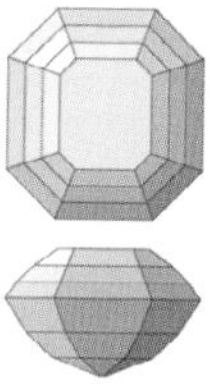

emerald cut
Classic emerald step cut that has a rectangular table with beveled corners and a girdle of the same shape with occasionally beveled corners.

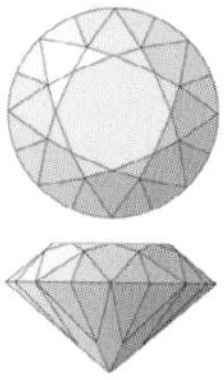

brilliant full cut
Diamond cut with 32 crown facets, 24 pavilion facets, an octagonal table and a culet.

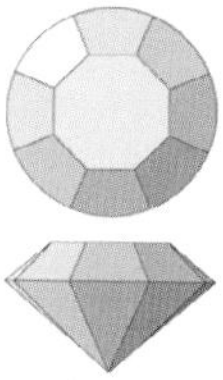

eight cut
Cut often used for smaller diamonds; it has eight crown facets, eight pavilion facets, an octagonal table and a culet.

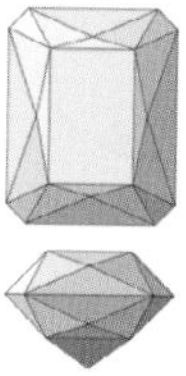

scissors cut
Step cut with triangular facets.

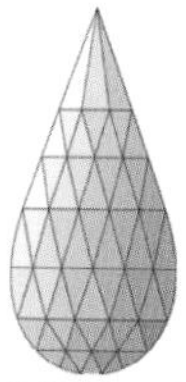

briolette cut
Elongated cut that is completely covered with triangular facets and has neither crown nor pavilion; it is used when stones are to be set in a pendant.

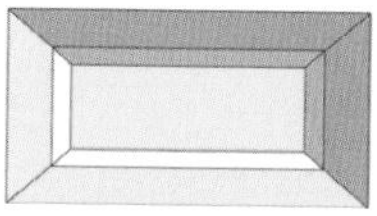

baguette cut
Step cut where the table and girdle are elongated rectangles.

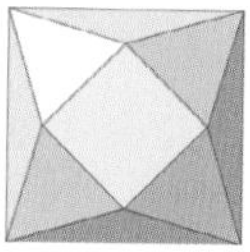

French cut
Cut where the table and the girdle are square and the facets triangular.

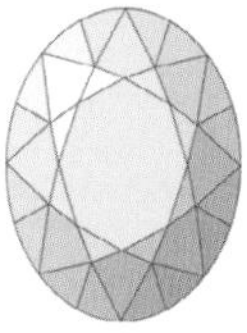

oval cut
Brilliant full cut where the girdle is oval in shape.

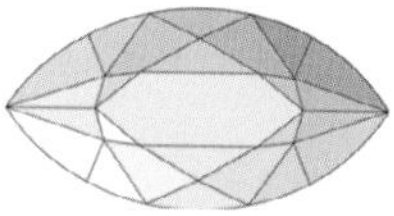

navette cut
Brilliant cut with a girdle that is shaped like a spindle with pointed ends.

semiprecious stones

Next to precious stones, these stones are the ones whose beauty and durability make them most suitable for jewelry.

amethyst
Stone whose color ranges from pale mauve to deepest purple.

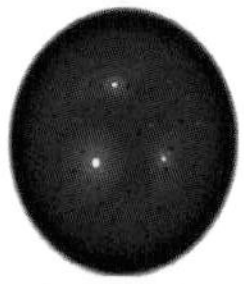

lapis lazuli
Opaque, dark blue stone that is usually speckled; the glittering flecks are proof of its authenticity.

aquamarine
Stone whose color ranges from whitish-pale blue to a deep blue-aqua color.

topaz
Stone with a wide range of colors, including yellowish-orange (the most common), green (the rarest), pink (the most sought-after), blue, brown and colorless.

tourmaline
Usually multicolored stone with a rich array of colors from red to pink and green and on to blue.

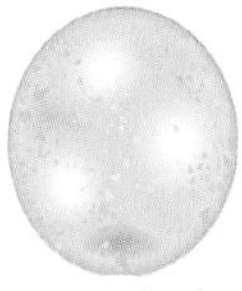

opal
Soft opaque stone that is milky-white or quite dark and gives off rainbowlike reflections.

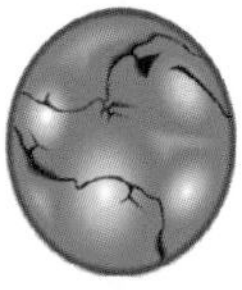

turquoise
Opaque, light blue stone with tinges of green; it often contains brown, gray or black veins.

garnet
Stone whose color ranges from green to yellow to dark red.

precious stones

The value of these four gemstones is based on their rarity, brilliance and durability.

emerald
Stone whose color varies from greenish-yellow to greenish-blue; an emerald's value is based more on its color than on its purity.

sapphire
This stone can be blue, pink, orange, yellow, green, purple or even colorless; the most sought-after color is purplish-blue.

diamond
The hardest stone is colorless although there are also blue, yellow and pink varieties; it is the most renowned precious stone.

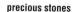

ruby
The rarest of all precious stones is extremely hard; its color varies from a bright pinkish-red to a purplish red, which is the most sought-after color.

jewelry

rings
Article of jewelry worn on the finger; it might have symbolic significance.

parts of a ring

setting
Part of the bezel surrounding and holding the stone.

claw
Small metal hook bent over the stone to hold it in place.

bezel
Single or multiple head of the ring in which the stone is held by claws.

stone
Crafted stone whose beauty, rarity and durability confer a certain value. There are three groups: precious, semiprecious and synthetic.

signet ring
Ring with a large flat top that is decorated with initials or coats of arms.

class ring
Ring worn by a graduate that is engraved with the school crest and the student's class year.

band ring
Ring of uniform width with no bezel.

engagement ring
Ring that is often decorated with a stone and is worn by an engaged woman on her left ring finger.

wedding ring
Ring that is usually a circle of precious metal or two intertwined circles; it is worn by a married person on the left ring finger.

solitaire ring
Ring decorated with a single jem that is usually brilliant cut.

bracelets
Flexible article of jewelry worn on the wrist, the arm or sometimes the ankle.

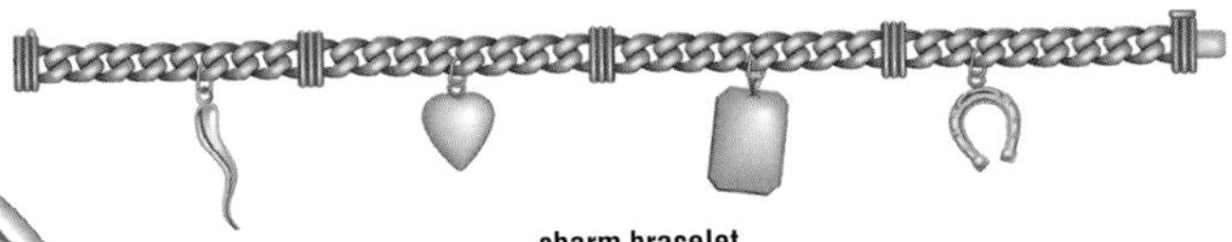

charm bracelet
Bracelet that is made of flattened links and fitted with a clasp.

bangle
Ring-shaped rigid bracelet that slips on over the hand.

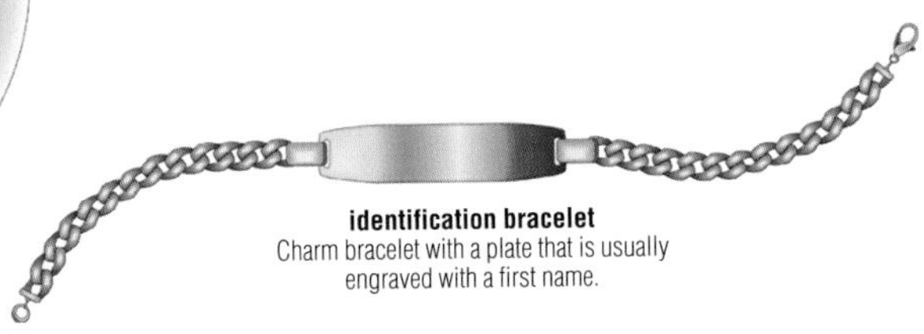

identification bracelet
Charm bracelet with a plate that is usually engraved with a first name.

charms
Small pieces of costume jewelry attached to a chain or a bracelet.

horn
Charm shaped like a horn.

horseshoe
Charm shaped like a horseshoe that is said to bring good luck.

nameplate
Charm shaped like a small plac that is usually engraved with a name.

pins
Article of jewelry used to fasten and adorn a garment.

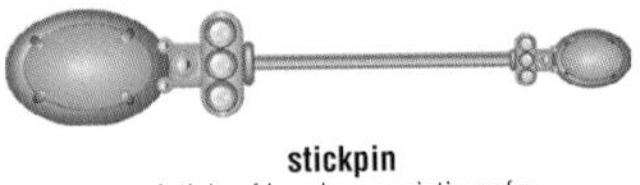

stickpin
Article of jewelry consisting of a pointed stem and a decorative head; it is usually worn on women's coat lapels.

brooch
Article of jewelry usually worn by women that consists of a pin with a decorative clasp; it is used to fasten a shawl or collar or adorn a bodice.

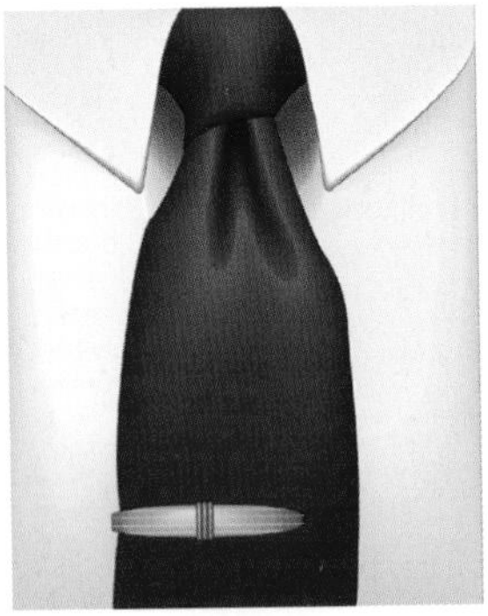

tie bar
Pincer-shaped article of jewelry clipped halfway up a tie to keep it attached to the shirt.

tiepin
Article of jewelry consisting of a short pointed stem with a head; it is used to hold the two tie aprons together.

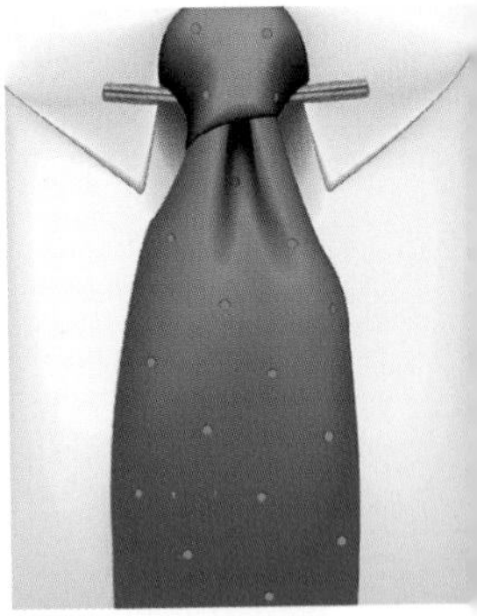

collar bar
Article of jewelry consisting of a rod with two capped pins; it is used to hold shirt collar points in place.

nail care

The means of making the hands and especially the nails more beautiful.

manicure set
Range of instruments used for nail care.

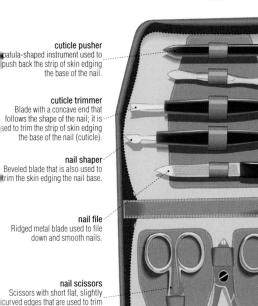

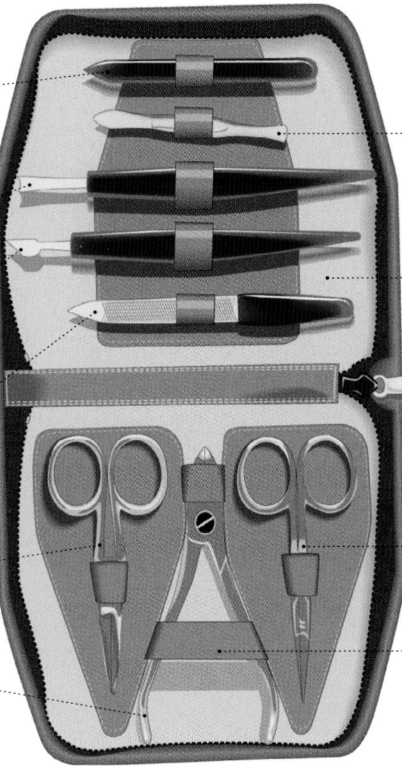

cuticle pusher
patula-shaped instrument used to push back the strip of skin edging the base of the nail.

cuticle trimmer
Blade with a concave end that follows the shape of the nail; it is sed to trim the strip of skin edging the base of the nail (cuticle).

nail shaper
Beveled blade that is also used to trim the skin edging the nail base.

nail file
Ridged metal blade used to file down and smooth nails.

nail scissors
Scissors with short flat, slightly curved edges that are used to trim fingernails and toenails.

cuticle nippers
incers with short convex jaws that are used to trim cuticles.

eyebrow tweezers
Delicate pincers used to pluck out hairs.

case
Usually rigid-sided case that is shaped to fit the articles it is designed to hold.

zipper
Closure made up of two lengths of tape edged with teeth that interlock by means of a slide.

cuticle scissors
Scissors used to trim cuticles; the thin, flat or curved blades are designed to reach the corners of the nails.

strap
Strip of leather or sometimes elasticized material keeping the instruments in place.

nail polish
Product applied to the nails that dries to become a clear or colored coating protecting and adorning the nails.

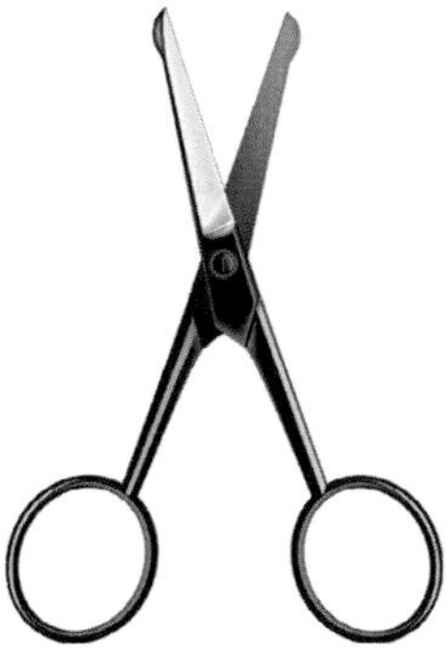

safety scissors
Scissors used to trim nails that are safer to use because of their rounded tips.

nail buffer
Curved instrument used to smooth and polish the surface of the nails.

chamois leather
Soft velvety hide used to polish nails.

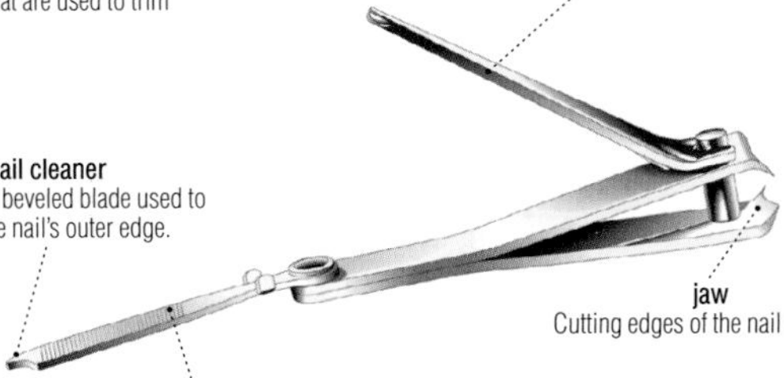

ail clippers
mall pincers with curved jaws and ten a file that are used to trim ails.

lever
Rod attached to a fulcrum that brings the jaws together when it is pressed down.

nail cleaner
ine-tipped beveled blade used to clean the nail's outer edge.

jaw
Cutting edges of the nail clippers.

folding nail file
Ridged metal blade used to file down and smooth nails.

nail whitener pencil
Pencil that is run under the outer edge of the nail to make it white.

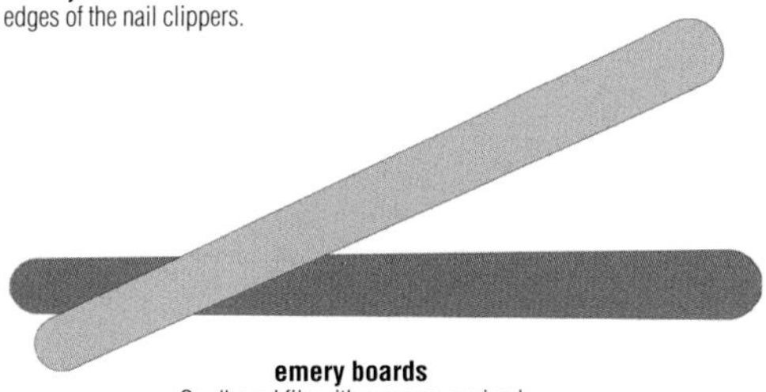

emery boards
Cardboard file with a coarse-grained side used to file down the nail and a finer-grained side to smooth it.

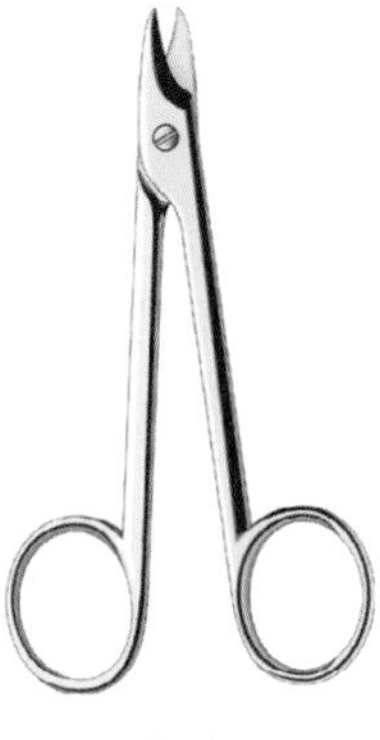

toenail scissors
Scissors with long shanks that are used to trim toenails.

makeup

Range of beauty products designed to accentuate the facial features and conceal their imperfections.

facial makeup

Range of beauty products designed to improve the appearance of facial skin.

fan brush
Very flat, very thin brush used to brush away excess loose powder.

powder puff
Small round, often cotton pad used to apply loose or pressed powder.

blusher brush
Slender round-tipped brush with soft flexible bristles; it is smaller than the loose powder brush and is used to pick up and apply powder blusher.

powder blusher
Powdered product applied to the cheekbones and cheeks to accentuate facial lines and emphasize skin tone.

compact
Small flat case housing a container with pressed powder, a powder puff and a mirror.

pressed powder
Creamy compact powder usec touch up skin tone during the c it usually comes in a compac

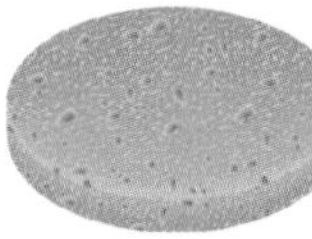

synthetic sponge
Sponge used to spread foundation evenly over the skin.

loose powder
Very fine powder that evens out skin tone, controls oily shine, sets foundation and acts as a base for blusher.

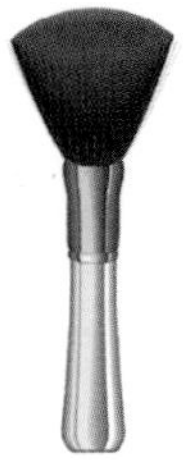

loose powder brush
Big round-tipped brush with soft flexible bristles; it is used to pick up and apply loose powder.

liquid foundation
Liquid product applied to the and neck to even out skin to

eye makeup

Range of beauty products designed to accentuate the eyes and conceal their imperfections.

eyebrow pencil
Sharp pencil used to enhance eyebrows or change their shape.

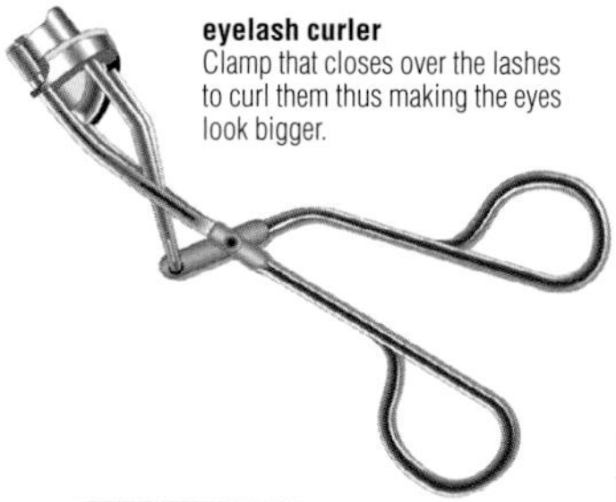

eyelash curler
Clamp that closes over the lashes to curl them thus making the eyes look bigger.

brow brush and lash comb
The brush is used to smooth the brows and the comb to separate lashes after mascara has been applied.

mascara brush
Small brush used to apply mascara to the lashes.

cake mascara
Creamy compact product applied to the lashes with a brush to lengthen or thicken them or change their color.

sponge-tipped applicator
Brush with a sponge at the tip that is used to apply and blend eyeshadow.

eyeshadow
Product that comes mainly in pressed powder form and is applied to the eyelids to give them color.

liquid eyeliner
Dark liquid product applied at the base of the lashes with a fine-tipped brush to accentuate the eyes.

liquid mascara
Liquid product applied to the lashes with a brush to lengthen or thicken them or change their color.

lip makeup

Range of beauty products designed to redraw the lipline and accentuate the lips.

lipbrush
Very delicate brush with short stiff bristles; it is used to draw the lipline and apply lipstick inside that line.

lipliner
Pencil used to redraw and enhance the lipline.

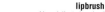

lipstick
Waxy product that comes in stick or pencil form and is applied to the lips to give them color.

body care

Range of methods promoting physical hygiene and beauty.

stopper
Device inserted into the neck of the bottle or screwed onto it to close the bottle.
bottle
Small bottle that is often made of glass.

eau de parfum
Scented concoction added to a water/alcohol mix; it is more concentrated and lingers longer than eau de toilette.

eau de toilette
Scented concoction that is more diluted with a water/alcohol mix than eau de parfum.

bubble bath
Product that is poured into the bath under the faucet water; it produces large amounts of foam and scents and colors the bathwater.

haircolor
Product applied to the hair to color it.

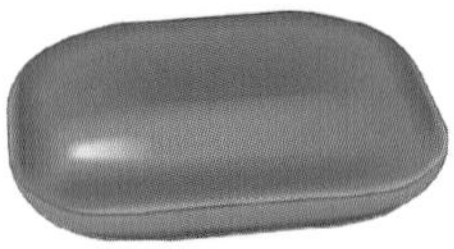

toilet soap
Fragrant fat-based product that is used for washing the body.

deodorant
Product applied to the armpits that eliminates or reduces perspiration odors.

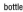

hair conditioner
Product applied to the hair after shampooing to strengthen it, improve its appearance and make styling easier.

shampoo
Product used to wash the hair and the scalp.

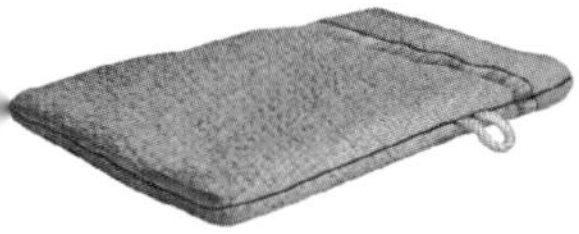

washcloth
Bath mitt usually made of terry cloth; it fits over the hand and is used for washing all or part of the body.

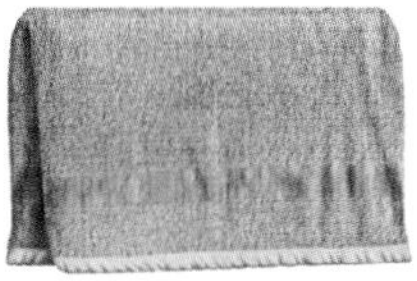

washcloth
Small square towel that is usually made of terry cloth and is used for washing the face.

massage glove
Rough glove used for rubbing the body to exfoliate the skin and stimulate the circulation.

loofah
Particularly soft, flexible absorbent material that comes from dried plant matter and is used for bathing.

bath sheet
Large bath towel used for drying the body after a shower or bath.

bath towel
Usually terry cloth article of bath linen used for drying parts of the body after bathing.

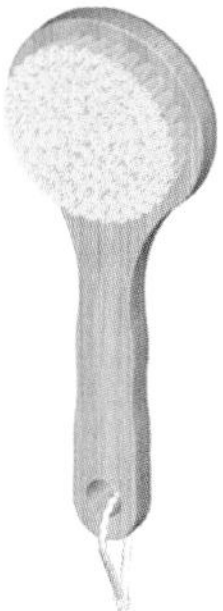

bath brush
Brush with relatively soft, flexible bristles that is used for scrubbing the body during baths or showers.

natural sponge
Particularly soft, flexible absorbent material that comes from the dried skeleton of marine animals and is used for bathing.

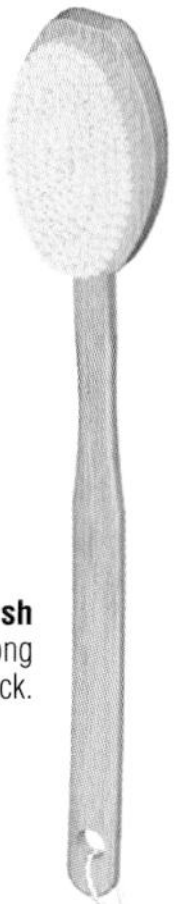

back brush
Bath brush with a handle long enough to scrub all of the back.

hairdressing

Care and styling of the hair using numerous appliances and accessories.

hairbrushes
Instruments made up of fibers of varying stiffness embedded in a backing; they are used to detangle and style hair.

flat-back brush
Brush with bristles set in a soft rubber backing that is used to detangle wet hair.

round brush
Brush with bristles that completely encircle the backing so that hair can be given a soft wave.

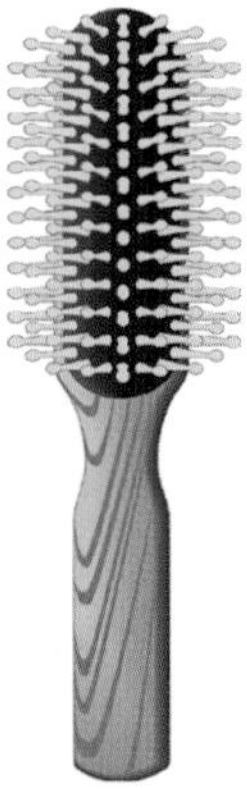

quill brush
Brush with round-tipped bristles set in a concave backing that massages the scalp; it is used for detangling and arranging hair.

vent brush
Brush with very widely spaced bristles set in a perforated backing; it is used during blow-drying to detangle hair and style it for a natural look.

combs
Devices with teeth of varying width and closeness that are used to detangle and style the hair.

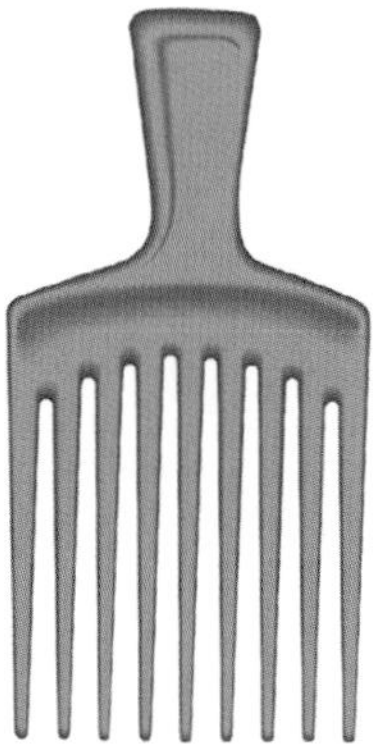

Afro pick
Comb with long, widely spaced teeth used for detangling and tidying tightly curled hair without undoing the curls.

teaser comb
Comb whose head has teeth of three different lengths; it is used to brush up the hair to give it more body.

tail comb
Comb with small, closely spaced teeth that is used to arrange the hair.

barber comb
Comb with large, widely spaced teeth for detangling the hair on one side and small, closely spaced teeth used to arrange the hair on the other side.

pitchfork comb
Comb combining a teaser comb and an Afro pick.

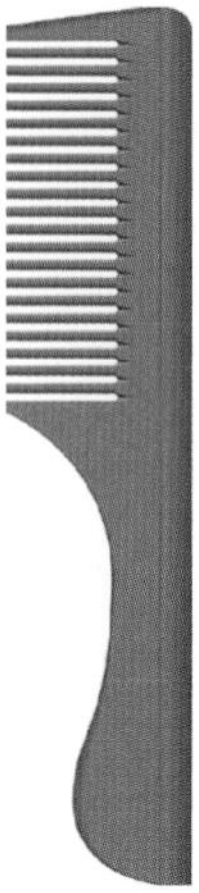

rake comb
Comb with broad, widely spac teeth for detangling hair witho damaging it.

hair roller
Instrument around which a lock of hair is wrapped to make it curl.

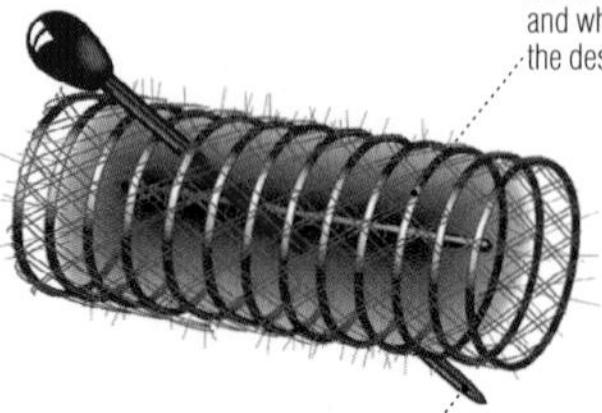

roller
Cylinder whose length depends on the length of the lock of rolled hair and whose diameter depends on the desired curl size.

hair roller pin
Pin stuck through the roller to hold the lock of wrapped hair in place.

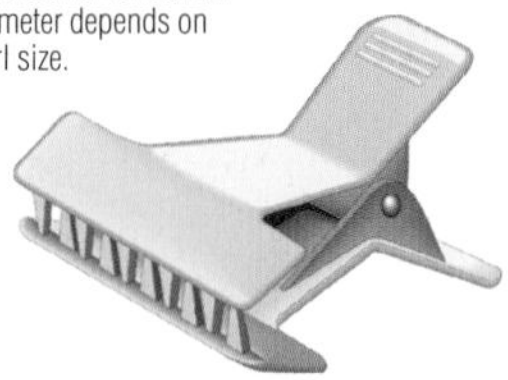

wave clip
Plastic pin with interlocking teeth used to secure a lock of hair.

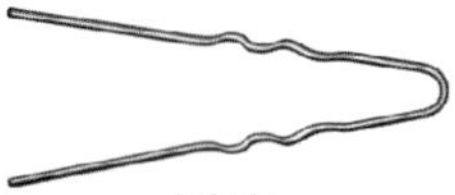

hairpin
Bent filament with spread arms that is used to loosely secure a section of hair such as a chignon.

bobby pin
Bent filament with tightly closed arms; it is used to secure a section of hair by holding it firmly in place.

hair clip
Metal pin with elongated jaws that is used during styling to separate out sections of hair not being worked on.

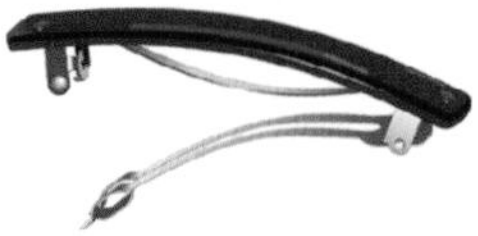

barrette
Bobby pin with a clasp; it is used as adornment or to secure a lock of hair or the whole head of hair.

hairdressing

lighted mirror
Mirror with a light fixture and swiveling panels that provide views from different angles.

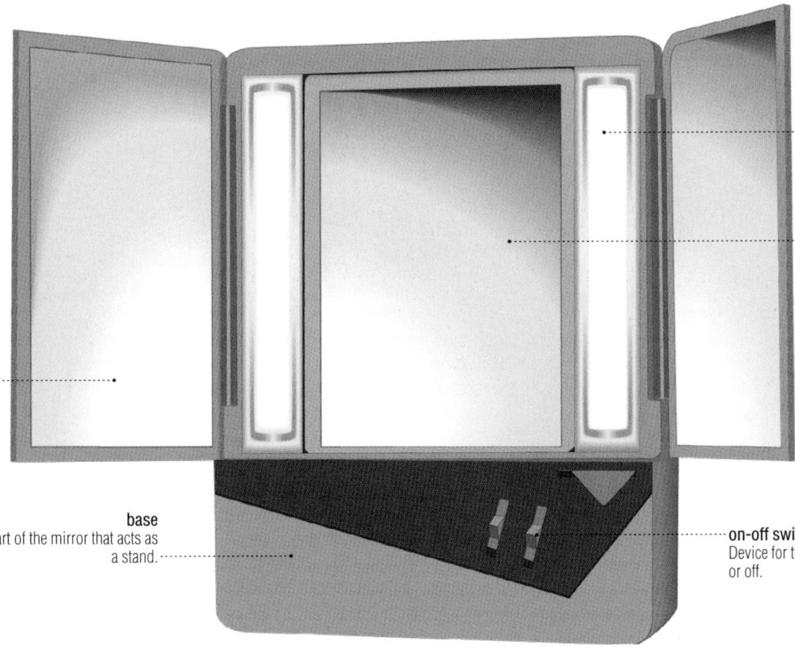

lighting
Device that emits white light that does not change the color of the hair or skin.

dual swivel mirror
Two-sided mirror, one side of which provides a magnified view.

side mirror
Mirror that can be swiveled to provide a view of the profile.

base
Lower part of the mirror that acts as a stand.

on-off switch
Device for turning the lighting on or off.

raightening iron
ectric appliance that smoothes d straightens hair.

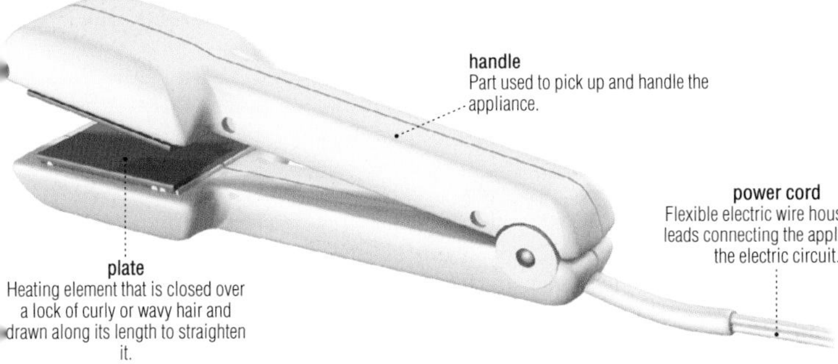

handle
Part used to pick up and handle the appliance.

power cord
Flexible electric wire housing the leads connecting the appliance to the electric circuit.

plate
Heating element that is closed over a lock of curly or wavy hair and drawn along its length to straighten it.

thinning razor
Razor whose blade has sharp teeth that can cut hair in points.

rling iron
ectric appliance used to curl hair.

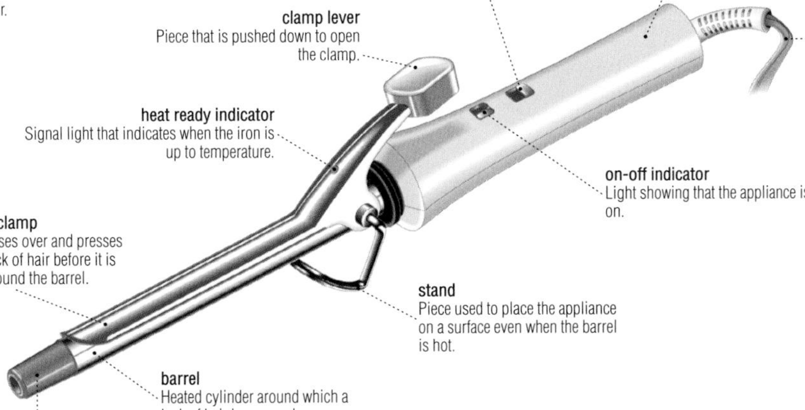

handle
Part molded to the shape of the hand; it is used to pick up and handle the appliance.

on-off switch
Button for turning the device on or off.

swivel cord
Electric cord containing insulated wires that connect the appliance to the electric circuit; the base is reinforced to reduce twisting and prevent wear.

clamp lever
Piece that is pushed down to open the clamp.

heat ready indicator
Signal light that indicates when the iron is up to temperature.

on-off indicator
Light showing that the appliance is on.

clamp
Clamp that closes over and presses down on a lock of hair before it is rolled around the barrel.

stand
Piece used to place the appliance on a surface even when the barrel is hot.

barrel
Heated cylinder around which a lock of hair is wrapped.

cool tip
End of the barrel that remains cool so that it can be touched with the fingers when handling the appliance.

clippers
Electric appliance used to trim a beard or very short hair; the adjustable head makes it possible to trim to various lengths.

hairdressing

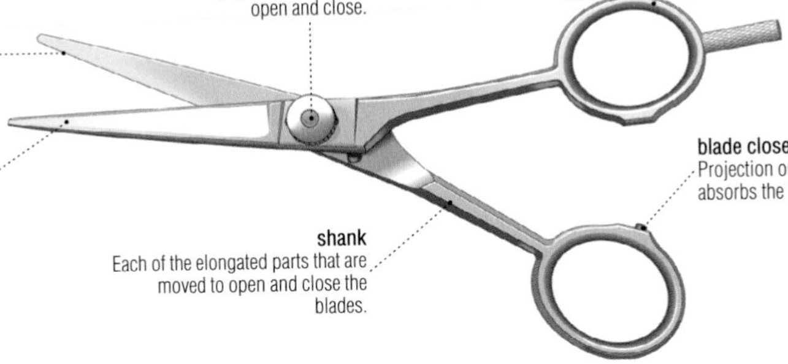
haircutting scissors
Straight-bladed scissors used to trim hair.
pivot
Hinge pin enabling the blades to open and close.
ringhandle
End of the shank of the scissors where the fingers are placed to move the blades.
cutting edge
Tapered edge of the blade designed for cutting.
blade close stop
Projection on the ring handles that absorbs the impact between them.
blade
Thin flat sharp moving part used to cut hair.
shank
Each of the elongated parts that are moved to open and close the blades.

notched single-edged thinning scissors
Scissors that can both trim and thin hair because they have a straight lower blade and a notched upper blade.
notched edge
Blade with an edge that has a row of teeth; it is used to cut hair in points.
blade
Blade with a smooth cutting edge that cuts straight across the hair.

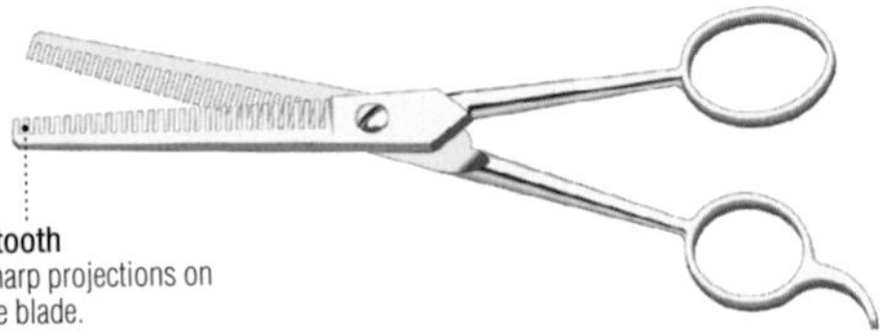
notched double-edged thinning scissors
Scissors with notched blades that thin the hair by cutting individual locks in points.
tooth
Each of the sharp projections on the blade.

hair dryer
Electric appliance that blows hot air to dry hair.
fan housing
Part of the appliance's frame that houses the motor and the fan that blows hot air.
air-inlet grille
Grating through which air is drawn in; it prevents hair and other matter from entering the appliance's housing.
barrel
Part housing the hair dryer's heating element.
air-outlet grille
Grating through which the hot air is blown; it prevents any contact with the heating element inside.
speed selector switch
Device that regulates fan speed and hence the power of the airflow.
on-off switch
Button for turning the device on or off.
heat selector switch
Device regulating air temperature.
hang-up ring
Ring for hanging the hair dryer on a hook when it is not in use.
handle
Part used to pick up and handle the appliance.
air concentrator
Piece that fits over the end of the appliance to concentrate the flow of hot air over the hair.
power supply cord
Flexible electric wire housing the leads connecting the appliance to the electric circuit.

shaving

Range of appliances and accessories used to cut the beard close to the skin.

shaving foam
roduct applied to the beard before shaving to soften the hairs and help the blade glide more smoothly.

power cord
Flexible electric wire housing the leads connecting the appliance to the electric circuit.

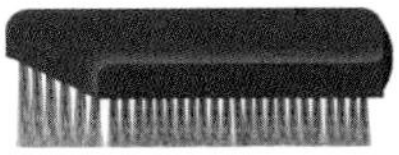

cleaning brush
Brush used for cleaning the blades and inside the heads.

electric razor
Razor with power-activated blades.

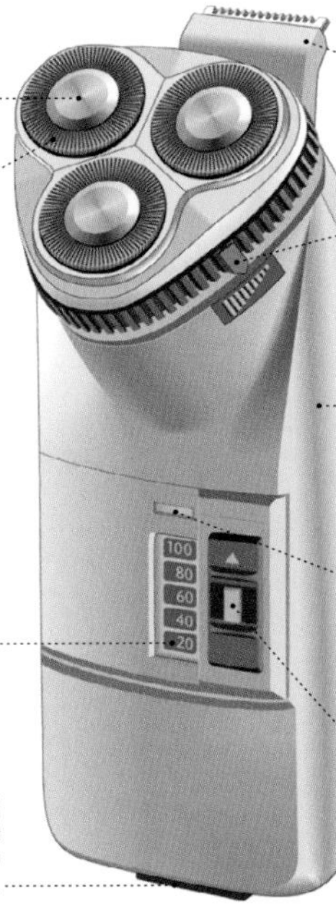

floating head
Base to which the blades are connected; it pivots as it follows the facial contours to give a close smooth shave.

screen
Grating that protects the skin from contact with the blades and positions the hair so that it can be cut more easily.

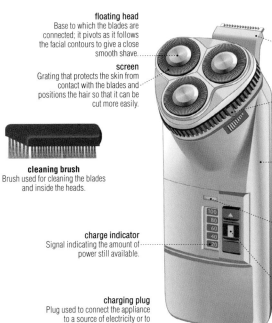

trimmer
Retractable accessory with two notched blades; it uses a back-and-forth motion to trim mustaches and sideburns.

closeness setting
Device that adjusts the height of the razor heads.

housing
Case enclosing and protecting the device's mechanism.

charge indicator
Signal indicating the amount of power still available.

charging light
Signal light that indicates when the razor is recharging or when it is finished.

on-off switch
Button for turning the device on or off.

charging plug
Plug used to connect the appliance to a source of electricity or to charge the battery.

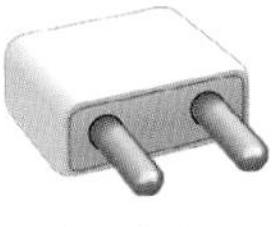

plug adapter
Electric accessory adapting a plug to an outlet of a different configuration.

shaving brush
rush with long firm bristles that is sed to apply a thin coat of shaving lather to the face.

bristle
Part of the shaving brush made of hog's hair or, more rarely, badger hair.

after shave
Lotion applied to the face after shaving to soothe and scent the skin.

straight razor
Traditional barber's razor that is made up of a very sharp blade hinged into a handle.

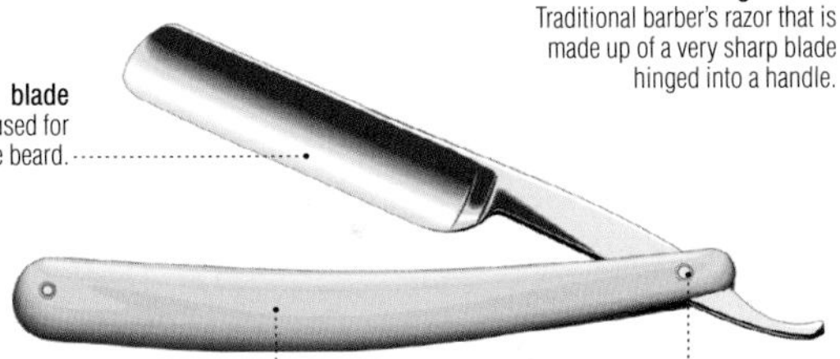

blade
Long sharp steel blade used for cutting the beard.

handle
Case made of materials such as horn, ivory and mother-of-pearl that is used to manipulate the razor during use and to store the blade when it is not in use.

pivot
Hinge pin connecting the blade and the handle.

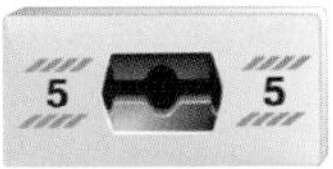

blade injector
Small metal box containing spare blades.

shaving mug
Container in which the shaving lather is made before it is applied to the beard.

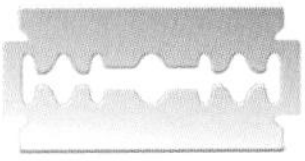

double-edged blade
Disposable blade with two cutting edges doubling the blade's useful life.

double-edged razor
Manual metal razor; it has a double-edged blade that can be replaced as needed.

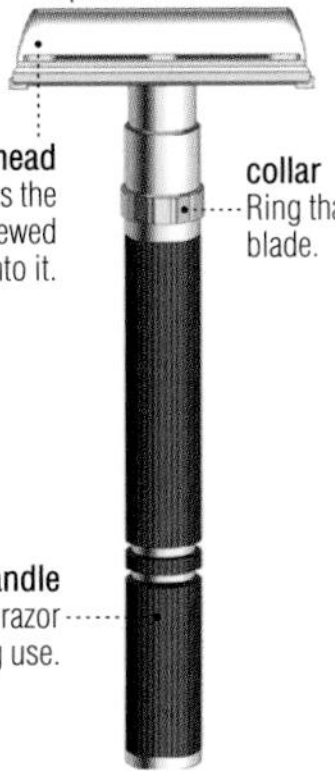

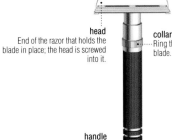

head
End of the razor that holds the blade in place; the head is screwed into it.

collar
Ring that adjusts the angle of the blade.

handle
Part used to manipulate the razor during use.

disposable razor
Plastic razor with one or more overlapping blades that can be thrown away after a few shaves.

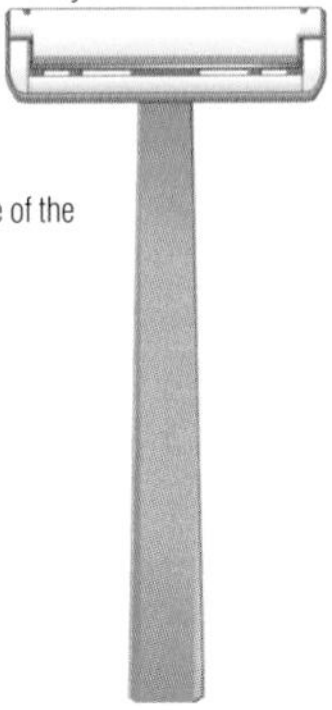

dental care

Procedures to care for the mouth and especially the teeth that include brushing, flossing and using mouthwash.

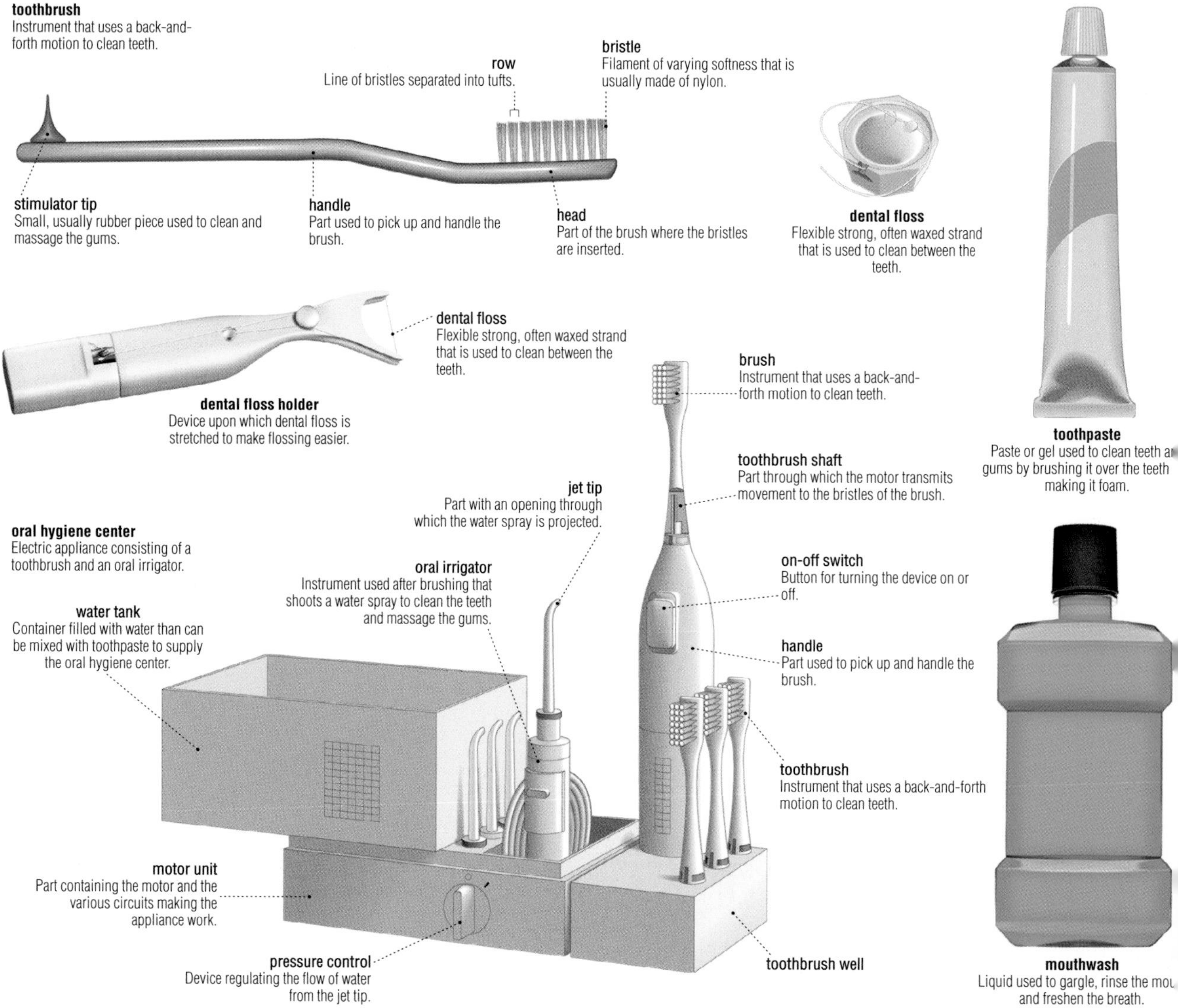
toothbrush
Instrument that uses a back-and-forth motion to clean teeth.
row
Line of bristles separated into tufts.
bristle
Filament of varying softness that is usually made of nylon.
stimulator tip
Small, usually rubber piece used to clean and massage the gums.
handle
Part used to pick up and handle the brush.
head
Part of the brush where the bristles are inserted.
dental floss
Flexible strong, often waxed strand that is used to clean between the teeth.
dental floss
Flexible strong, often waxed strand that is used to clean between the teeth.
dental floss holder
Device upon which dental floss is stretched to make flossing easier.
brush
Instrument that uses a back-and-forth motion to clean teeth.
toothpaste
Paste or gel used to clean teeth a
gums by brushing it over the teeth
making it foam.
toothbrush shaft
Part through which the motor transmits movement to the bristles of the brush.
jet tip
Part with an opening through which the water spray is projected.
oral hygiene center
Electric appliance consisting of a toothbrush and an oral irrigator.
oral irrigator
Instrument used after brushing that shoots a water spray to clean the teeth and massage the gums.
on-off switch
Button for turning the device on or off.
water tank
Container filled with water than can be mixed with toothpaste to supply the oral hygiene center.
handle
Part used to pick up and handle the brush.
toothbrush
Instrument that uses a back-and-forth motion to clean teeth.
motor unit
Part containing the motor and the various circuits making the appliance work.
toothbrush well
pressure control
Device regulating the flow of water from the jet tip.
mouthwash
Liquid used to gargle, rinse the mou
and freshen the breath.

contact lenses

Transparent visual aid placed over the cornea to correct defective vision.

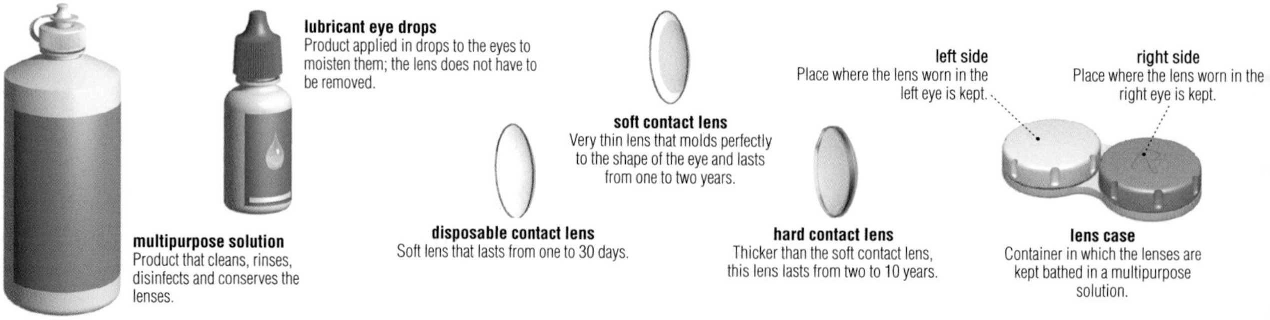
lubricant eye drops
Product applied in drops to the eyes to moisten them; the lens does not have to be removed.
left side
Place where the lens worn in the left eye is kept.
right side
Place where the lens worn in the right eye is kept.
soft contact lens
Very thin lens that molds perfectly to the shape of the eye and lasts from one to two years.
multipurpose solution
Product that cleans, rinses, disinfects and conserves the lenses.
disposable contact lens
Soft lens that lasts from one to 30 days.
hard contact lens
Thicker than the soft contact lens, this lens lasts from two to 10 years.
lens case
Container in which the lenses are kept bathed in a multipurpose solution.

eyeglasses

Lenses set in frames that are placed in front of the eyes to correct vision or to protect the eyes from the Sun's brilliant rays.

eyeglasses parts

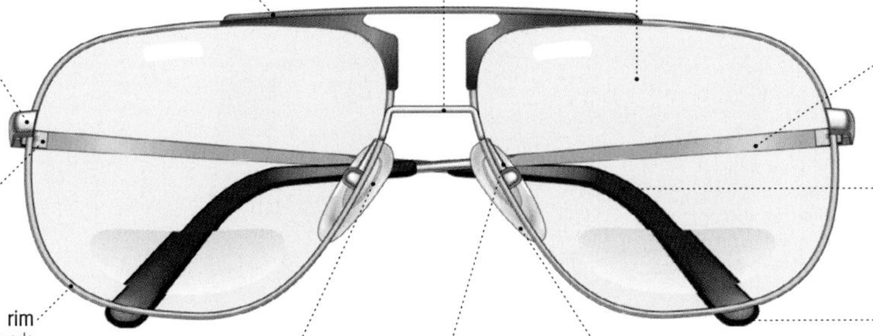

bar
Part following the line of the eyebrows and connecting the two rims.

bridge
Part of the frames that connects the two lens rims and rests on the nose.

glass lens
Transparent lens with optical characteristics designed for the needs of a specific person and shaped to fit a specific frame.

endpiece
Part attached to the side of the rim that connects the temple to the frame.

temple
Hinged stem connected to the side of the rim; the end of it bends behind the ear to hold the lenses in place in front of the eyes.

butt-strap
Part of the temple that hinges onto the endpiece so that the temple can be folded behind the frames.

bend
Part of the temple that rests on the ear and where the backward curve begins.

rim
Part of the frames that surrounds and supports the lens.

pad plate
Flat end of the pad arm to which the latter is attached.

pad arm
Metal stem connecting the nose pad to the rim.

nose pad
Small, usually plastic piece that supports the rim on the nose.

earpiece
Curved rigid round-tipped part at the far end of the temple that goes behind the ear.

frames
Mounting that supports the lenses and holds them in place in front of the eyes.

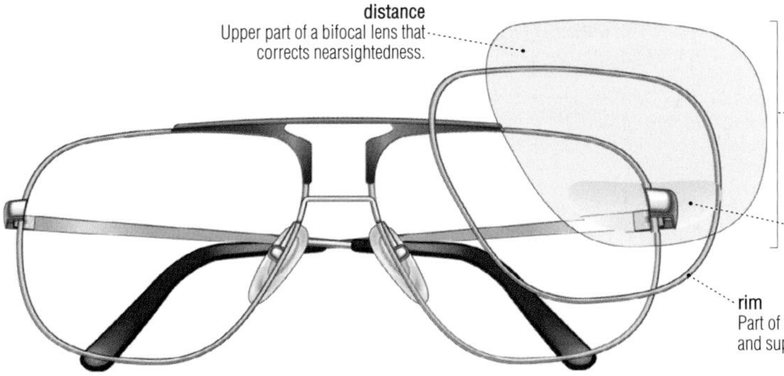

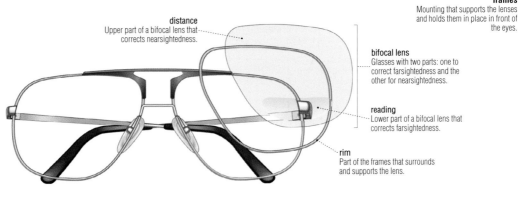

distance
Upper part of a bifocal lens that corrects nearsightedness.

bifocal lens
Glasses with two parts: one to correct farsightedness and the other for nearsightedness.

reading
Lower part of a bifocal lens that corrects farsightedness.

rim
Part of the frames that surrounds and supports the lens.

examples of eyeglasses

The shape of glasses varies depending on the period and their use (e.g., correcting far- or nearsightedness, protecting the eye, magnifying).

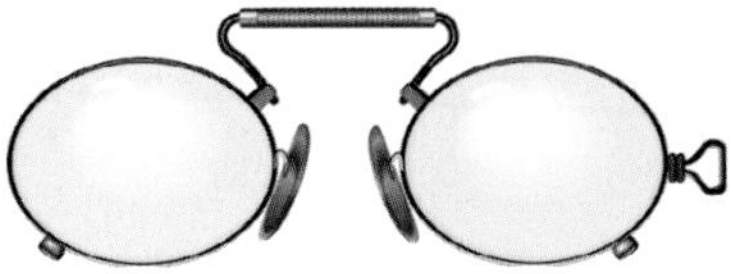

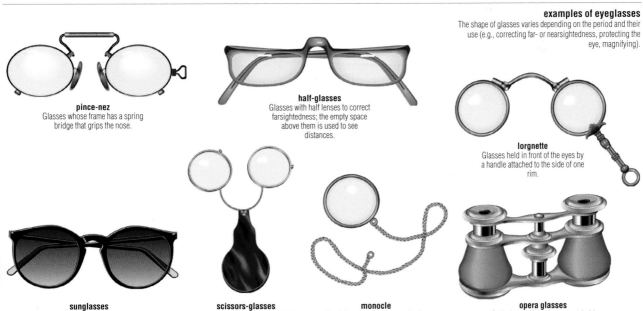

pince-nez
Glasses whose frame has a spring bridge that grips the nose.

half-glasses
Glasses with half lenses to correct farsightedness; the empty space above them is used to see distances.

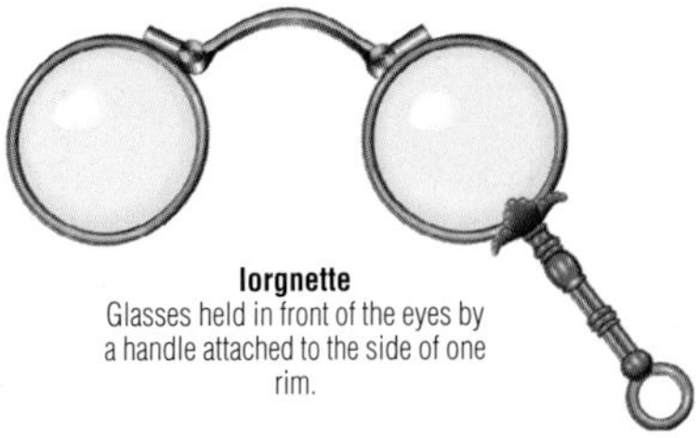

lorgnette
Glasses held in front of the eyes by a handle attached to the side of one rim.

sunglasses
Glasses with lenses that filter the sun's glare to protect the eyes.

scissors-glasses
Lorgnette whose lenses fold back over one another and can be slipped into the handle, which also acts as a case.

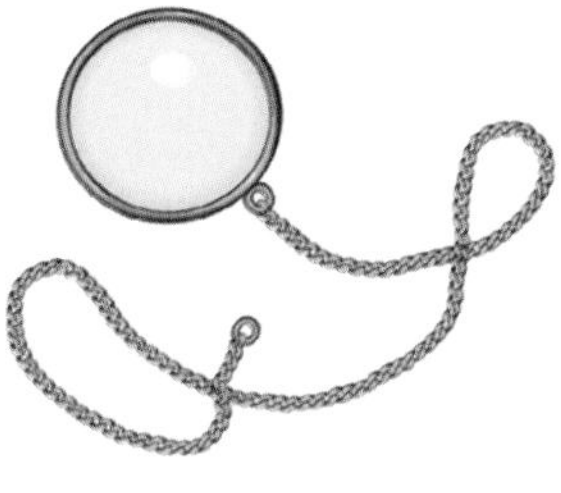

monocle
Single lens held in place under the ridge of the eyebrow.

opera glasses
Optical magnifying instrument held in front of the eyes; it is used for looking at relatively close objects such as at the theater.

leather goods

Personal articles made of leather or fake leather.

attaché case
Small plain case with rigid sides that is used to carry documents.

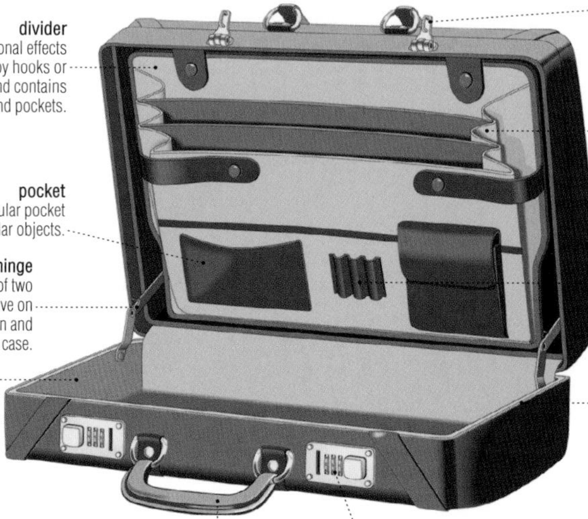

divider
Panel used to keep personal effects separate; it is held by hooks or snap fasteners and contains compartments and pockets.

pocket
Small soft flat rectangular pocket that is used to hold similar objects.

hinge
Metal structure consisting of two symmetrical pieces that move on an axis and are used to open and close the case.

lining
Fabric or leather covering that protects and embellishes the inside of the case.

clasp
Metal device such as a clip or fastener that is used to hold an object closed.

expandable file pouch
Set of overlapping pockets used to hold documents.

pen holder
Tubular piece of leather or fabric used to hold pens.

frame
Rectangular metal piece on which the shell is mounted; it supports the hinges, locks and handle.

handle
It is used to pick up and carry the case.

combination lock
Lock that is opened with a combination of numbers.

bottom-fold portfolio
Briefcase with a handle; its sides expand to accommodate more documents or books.

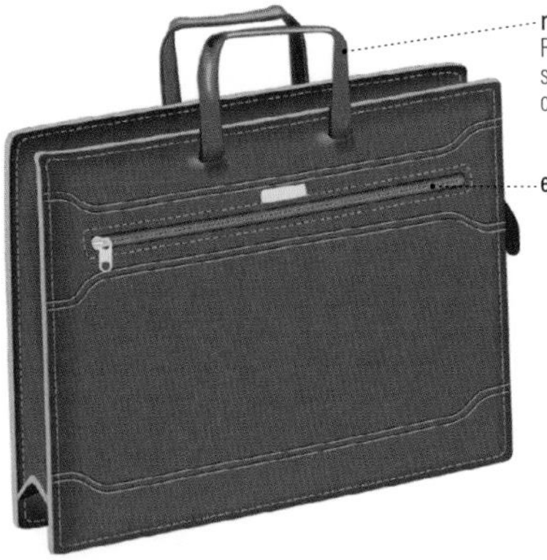

retractable handle
Rigid flat retractable handle that slides through two openings in the case.

exterior pocket

briefcase
Rectangular bag with compartments that is used to carry items such as documents, files and books.

tab
Small piece with a fastening system that extends a flap or goes over an article's opening to fasten it.

key lock
Lock that opens with a key.

gusset
Piece sewn along the bottom and up the side of a bag to increase its capacity.

checkbook/secretary clutch
Article with compartments of various sizes that is intended to hold identity papers, cards, banknotes, change, a pen and a checkbook.

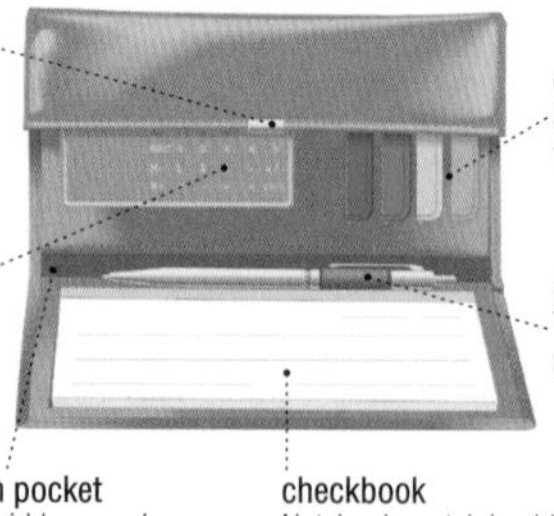

trimming
Metal piece used to reinforce the edge or the corner of certain articles.

calculator
Small self-powered electronic instrument used to automatically make numerical calculations.

hidden pocket
Pocket with a hidden opening.

checkbook
Notebook containing blank checks.

card case
Set of adjacent pockets for inserting various cards.

pen holder
Tubular piece of leather or fabric used to hold pens.

card case
Article used to hold, organize and protect identity papers and other cards while making them easily visible.

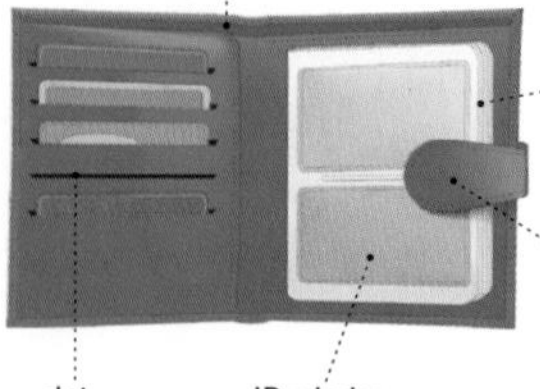

bill compartment
Flat compartment between the back and the inside of a wallet or a card case where banknotes are kept.

windows
Transparent compartments that hold photographs or identity cards.

tab
Small piece with a fastening system that extends a flap or goes over an article's opening to fasten it.

slot
Narrow elongated opening into which a card is inserted with a part of it projecting so it can be easily recognized.

ID window
A window behind which an identity cards is inserted to protect it and make its front side visible.

leather goods

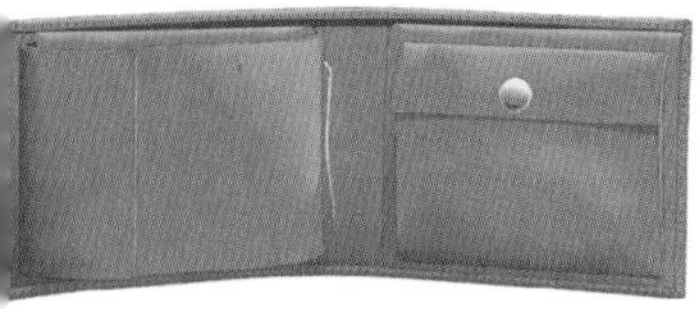

wallet
Article with compartments of various sizes that is designed to hold identity papers, cards, banknotes and change.

coin purse
Small case of various sizes that is designed to hold change and is usually carried in a pocket.

key case
Case accommodating a number of keys that is designed to protect a bag or garment from contact with them.

purse
Small soft-sided bag with a zipper or clasp that is used to store change and sometimes banknotes.

passport case
Case usually separated into several compartments; one of them is shaped to hold and protect a passport.

billfold
Case with a number of dividers that is folded in half and used only for banknotes.

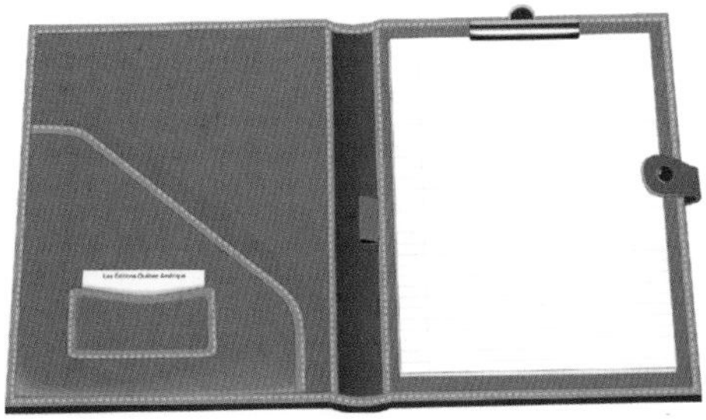

writing case
Article for holding correspondence materials such as paper and a pen; it has a rigid surface for writing.

checkbook case
Case that protects a checkbook from handling and rubbing against the inside of a pocket or bag.

eyeglasses case
Holder with relatively rigid sides that is shaped to fit glasses and used to carry and protect them.

underarm portfolio
Slim briefcase with only one compartment.

handbags

Relatively soft and light accessory that contains a pocket and is carried in the hand, under the arm or over the shoulder; it is used to carry various objects.

drawstring bag
Soft-sided cylindrical flat-bottomed bag with a single compartment that might have handles or a shoulder strap.

eyelet
Small metal-rimmed hole through which the drawstring passes.

drawstring
Narrow leather or fabric cord that is flat or round; it is threaded through the eyelets and used to close the bag.

front pocket

satchel bag
Sturdy bag with a handle and sometimes shoulder straps; it combines a handbag with a briefcase.

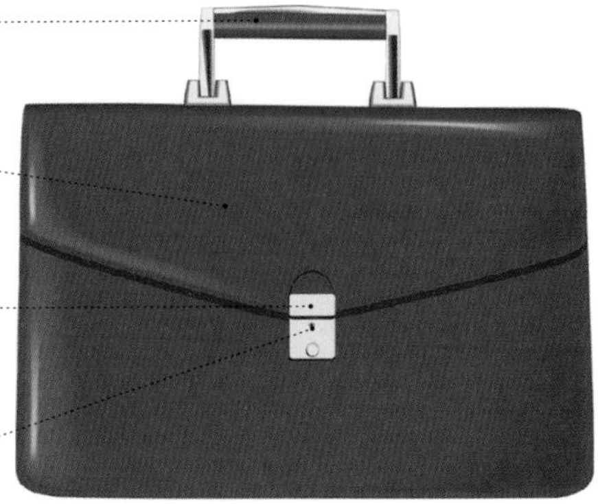

handle
It is used to pick up and carry the bag.

flap
Piece sometimes equipped with a fastening system that goes over the opening of an object to close it.

clasp
Metal device such as a clip or fastener that is used to hold an object closed.

lock
Mechanism for an owner to secure an article using a key or a combination.

handbags

box bag
Rigid-sided bag with one or two handles.

drawstring bag
Soft cylindrical bag with only one compartment that closes with a drawstring and has a shoulder strap.

shoulder bag
Bag with an adjustable shoulder strap and a flap or zipper closure.

buckle
Fastener made up of a ring that secures the two ends of a shoulder strap.

shoulder strap
Long belt often with a buckle to adjust it; it is used to carry the bag over the shoulder or diagonally across the chest.

muff
Small light flat bag with a cord that hangs from the wrist; it is used for carrying very small objects.

hobo bag
Bag whose bottom consists of a strip that comes up each side as far as the opening and then forms a point where the shoulder strap is attached.

accordion bag
Bag that has soft adjacent pockets with gussets and often zippers; the whole bag is closed with a flap.

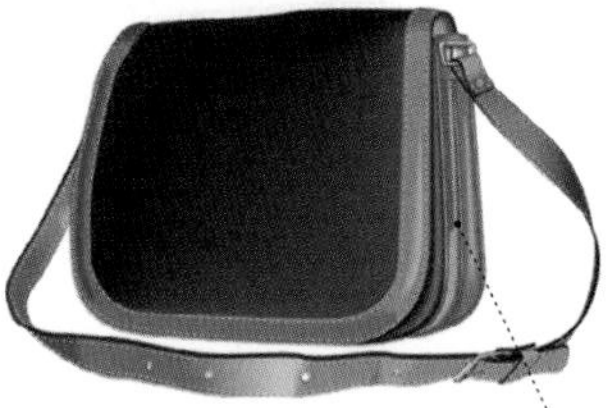

gusset
Piece sewn along the bottom and up the side of a bag to increase its capacity.

tote bag
Fairly large bag having neither divider nor pocket but with a shoulder strap; it is practical, simple and sturdy.

men's bag
Small plain, usually rectangular bag for men with a handle and sometimes a shoulder strap.

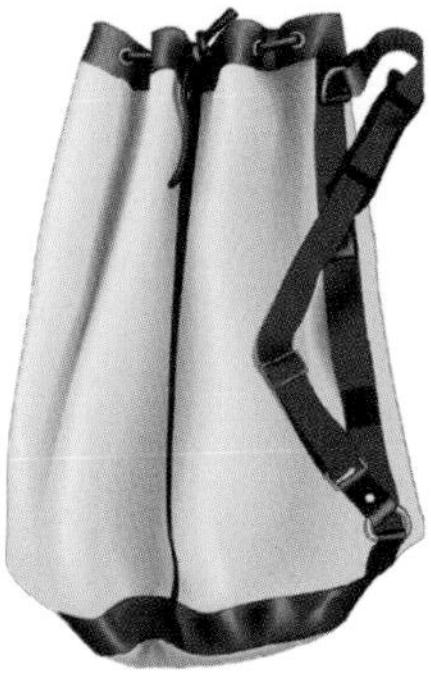

sea bag
Large, usually leather-bottomed drawstring bag with a shoulder strap attached down the side.

duffel bag
Cylindrical bag usually with a zipper along its entire length; it has two symmetrical handles or a shoulder strap.

carrier bag
Large sturdy bag with handles that is used to carry groceries.

shopping bag
Large carrier bag.

luggage

Articles such as suitcases, boxes and bags that are used to store and protect items packed for a trip.

utility case
Multicompartment case designed to hold articles such as toiletries, cosmetics and jewelry.

carry-on bag
Travel bag that can be carried into an airplane cabin because its dimensions do not exceed the limits set by carriers.

handle
It is used to pick up and carry the bag.

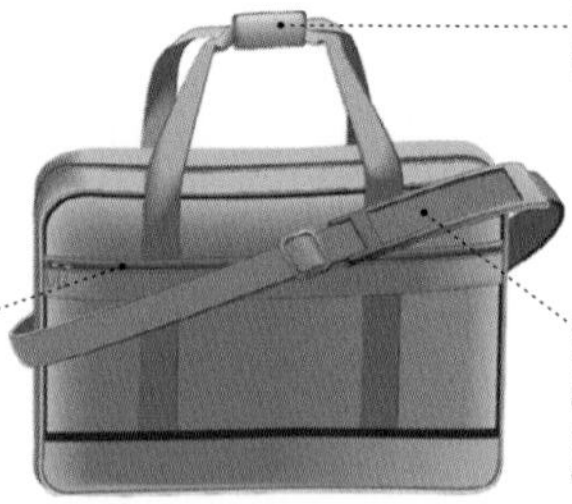

exterior pocket

shoulder strap
Long belt often with a buckle to adjust it; it is used to carry the bag over the shoulder or diagonally across the chest.

tote bag
Light travel bag with soft sides and only one compartment.

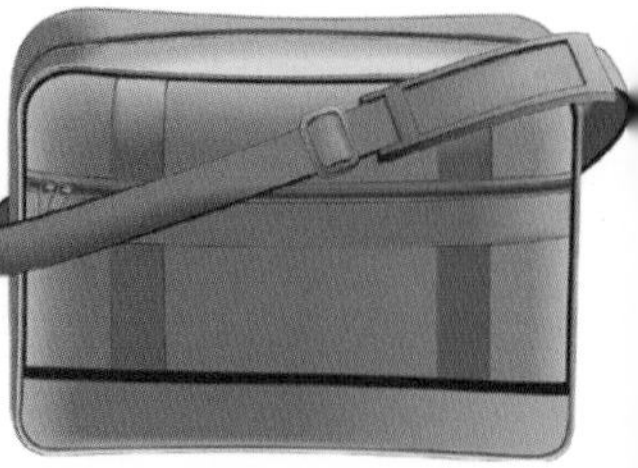

luggage

arment bag
oft-sided carrier that encases and rotects clothing; it is hung from a uilt-in hanger.

zipper
Closure made up of two lengths of tape edged with teeth that interlock by means of a slide.

Pullman case
Large rectangular piece of hand luggage that is often equipped with wheels to facilitate transport.

handle
It is used to pick up and carry the suitcase.

frame
Rectangular metal piece on which the shell is mounted; it supports the hinges, locks and handle.

pull strap
Leash attached to the suitcase that is placed over the wrist to pull the suitcase along on its wheels.

wheel
Small castor attached to a suitcase so that it can be rolled rather than carried.

identification tag
Small transparent case attached to a suitcase; a label with the owner's name and address is inserted inside it.

trim
Parts made of various materials designed to reinforce the bottom of the suitcase.

vanity case
Small, rigid-sided piece of luggage designed to hold toiletries, cosmetics and jewelry; it usually has a mirror attached to the inside of the lid.

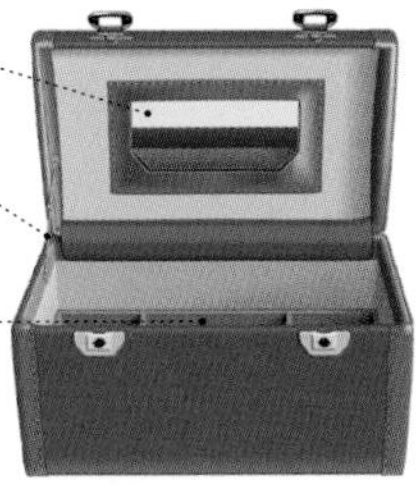

mirror
Polished glass surface reflecting light and returning images.

hinge
Metal structure consisting of two symmetrical pieces that move on an axis and are used to open and close the case.

cosmetic tray
sually removable part inside a piece of luggage; it is divided into several compartments for storing articles that are to be kept separate from others.

weekender
Small rectangular piece of hand luggage that is used for short trips.

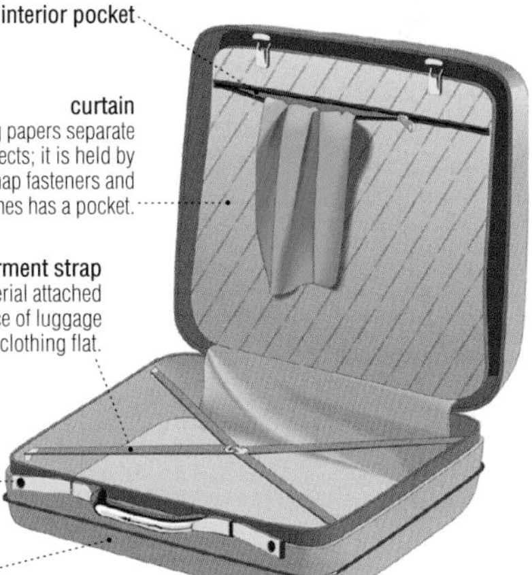

interior pocket

curtain
Panel for keeping papers separate from personal effects; it is held by hooks or snap fasteners and sometimes has a pocket.

garment strap
Strips of elastic material attached to the inside of a piece of luggage to keep clothing flat.

lock
Device attached to the piece of luggage that is used to lock it.

shell
Light metal or plastic structure that makes up the suitcase's two main pieces; they close one on top of the other.

iggage carrier
Vheeled stand that is pulled with a andle; suitcases are placed on it to ansport them.

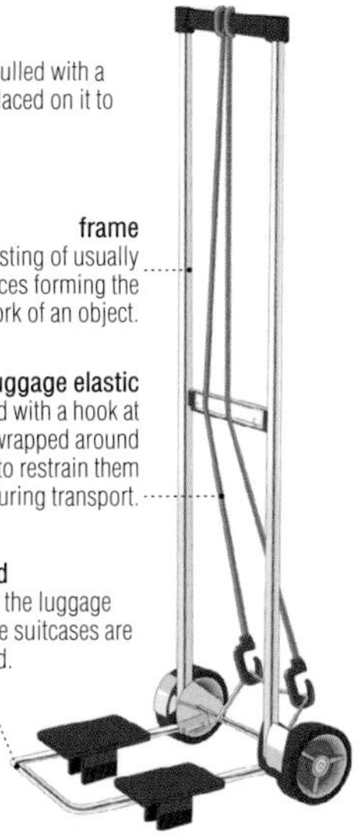

frame
Structure consisting of usually metal pieces forming the framework of an object.

luggage elastic
Sturdy elastic cord with a hook at one end that is wrapped around pieces of luggage to restrain them during transport.

stand
Foldaway part of the luggage carrier on which the suitcases are placed.

trunk
Large rigid sturdy piece of luggage that is used to transport objects.

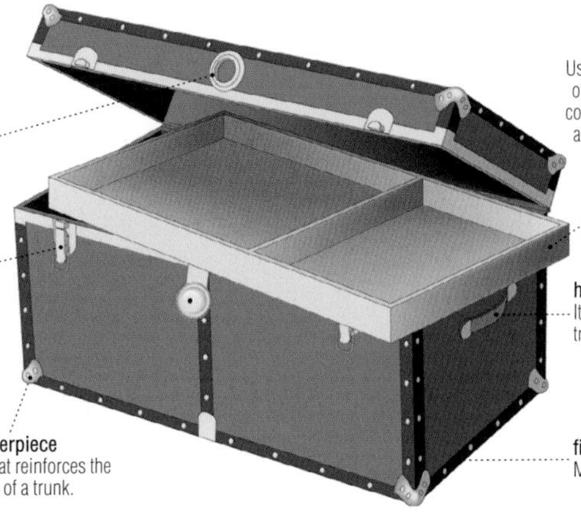

hasp
Fastener that consists of a hinged pin with a lock that is anchored to the inner wall of the trunk; it fits over a ring attached to the lid and is secured by a lock bolt.

latch
Two-part metal accessory that holds the trunk lid closed.

cornerpiece
Metal trim that reinforces the corners of a trunk.

tray
Usually removable part inside a piece of luggage; it is divided into several compartments for storing articles that are to be kept separate from others.

handle
It is used to pick up and carry the trunk.

fittings
Metal trim that reinforces the trunk.

smoking accessories

Range of objects used for smoking tobacco in pipes, cigars or cigarettes.

pipe
Instrument consisting of a tobacco hole that is filled with tobacco and a stem through which the smoke is inhaled.

bowl
Lower projecting part of the stummel that is used to hold the pipe.

shank
With the tobacco hole, it forms part of the stummel and acts as a conduit.

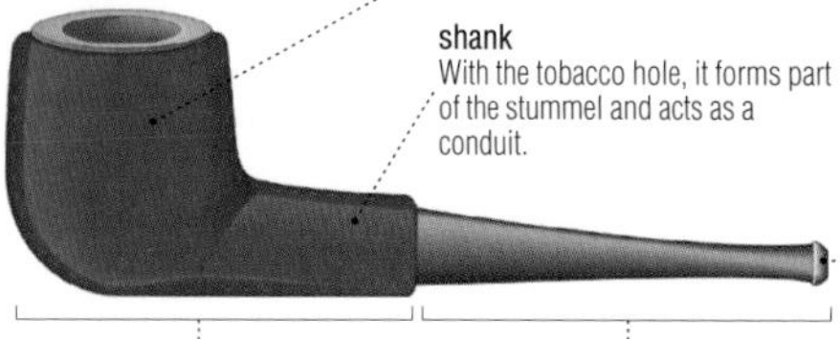

bit
Wide flat end of the stem that is held between the teeth.

stummel
Usually wooden part of a pipe that contains the tobacco hole.

stem
Part of the pipe that is usually made of hard rubber; it fits into the shank and acts as a conduit.

pipe tools
Multipurpose three-armed instrument used to tamp down tobacco in the tobacco hole and to unblock and empty it.

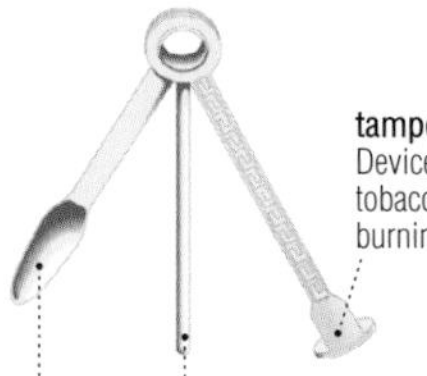

tamper
Device used to tamp down any tobacco that has expanded during burning.

scoop
Device used to remove any remaining ashes and scrape away the carbonized layer.

pick
Device used to ream the stem and empty the tobacco from the tobacco hole.

pipe cleaners
Flexible fiber-covered rods use
clean the inside of the stem

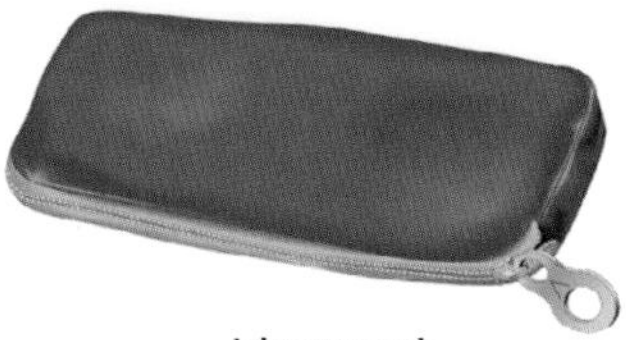

tobacco pouch
Watertight case for storing tobacco.

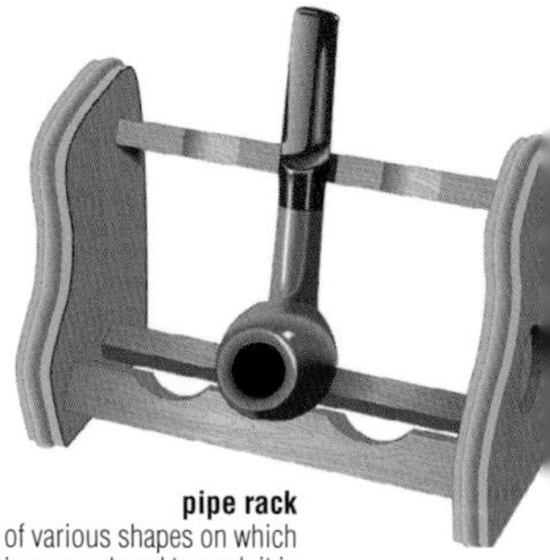

pipe rack
Object of various shapes on which pipes are placed to cool; it is designed so that the pipe stem points up for it to dry.

cross section of a pipe

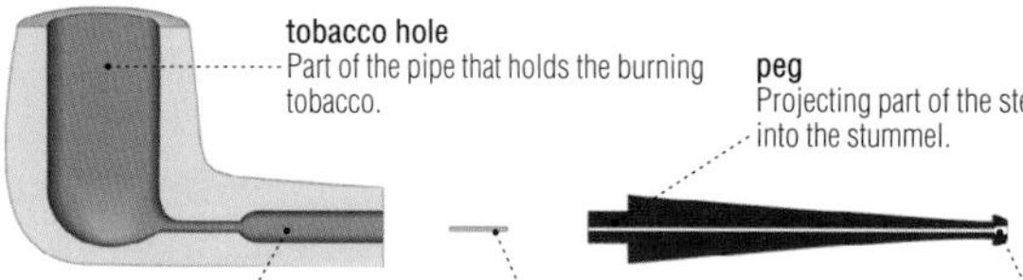

tobacco hole
Part of the pipe that holds the burning tobacco.

peg
Projecting part of the stem that fits into the stummel.

mortise
Opening made in the stummel that the peg of the stem fits into.

filter
Small aluminum tube inserted between the shank and the stem; it is intended to capture some of the smoke's toxic substances.

air hole
End of the conduit through which smoke passes into the mouth.

cigar cutter
Device made of a perforated metal plate and a blade; it is used to clip a cigar's head and tuck.

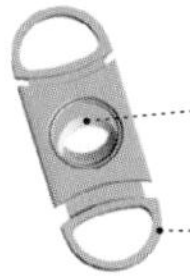

blade
Sharp object with a movable blade that cuts off the cigar's head or tuck when placed in the cigar cutter's hole.

ring handle
Rounded part through which the finger is passed to hold the cigar cutter; the movable ring activates the blade.

cigar
Roll made of pieces of tobacco leaves wrapped in a large high-grade leaf.

cigar band
Paper ring that encircles the cigar bearing the manufacturer or brand name or a company logo.

wrapper
Thin, very high-grade tobacco leaf used as a casing to wrap around a cigar.

tobacco
Product made from the dried leaves of a nicotine-rich plant; the leaves are treated and made into cigars or cigarettes for smoking.

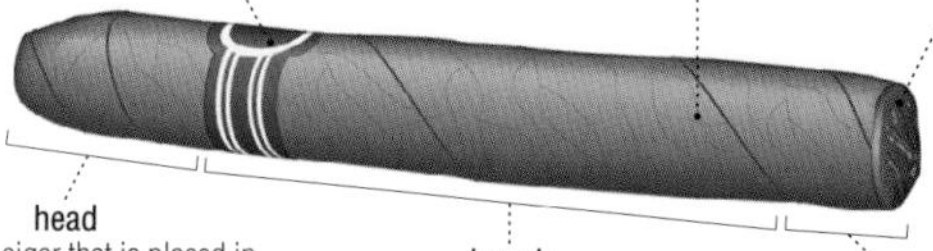

filler
Inside of a cigar made of two to four different kinds of tobacco leaves, which are cut moderately fine.

head
End of the cigar that is placed in the mouth; it must be clipped before the cigar is lit.

bunch
Body of the cigar made up of the cut tobacco leaves and the leaf that is wrapped around them.

tuck
Tip of the cigar that is to be lit; if the tuck is closed, it must be cut off before the cigar can be lit.

cigarette papers
Set of very thin sheets of paper in which tobacco is rolled so individuals can make their own cigarettes.

cigarette
Small roll of cut tobacco wrapped in thin paper; it often has a filter at one end and is made for smoking.

filter tip
Tip at the mouth end for capturing some of the smoke's toxic substances.

paper
Very thin sheet of paper that is wrapped around the tobacco.

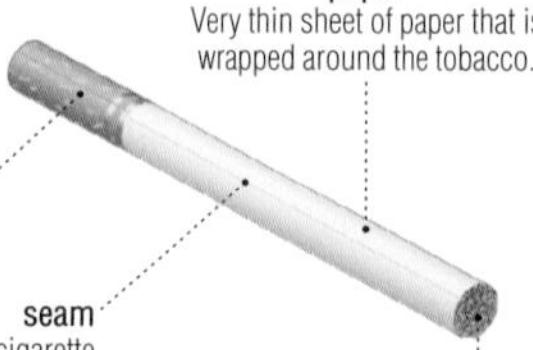

seam
Line along which the cigarette paper is sealed.

tobacco
Product made from the dried leaves of a nicotine-rich plant; the leaves are treated and made into cigars or cigarettes for smoking.

cigarette pack
Unit of sale containing 10, 20 or 25 cigarettes.

stamp
Rectangle of paper stuck on a cigarette pack to close it; it sometimes bears an excise stamp.

tear tape
Strip of plastic that is torn away to remove the plastic covering the cigarette pack.

trade name
Trademark that has been registered so that only the legal owner may use it.

carton
Unit of sale containing several cigarette packs.

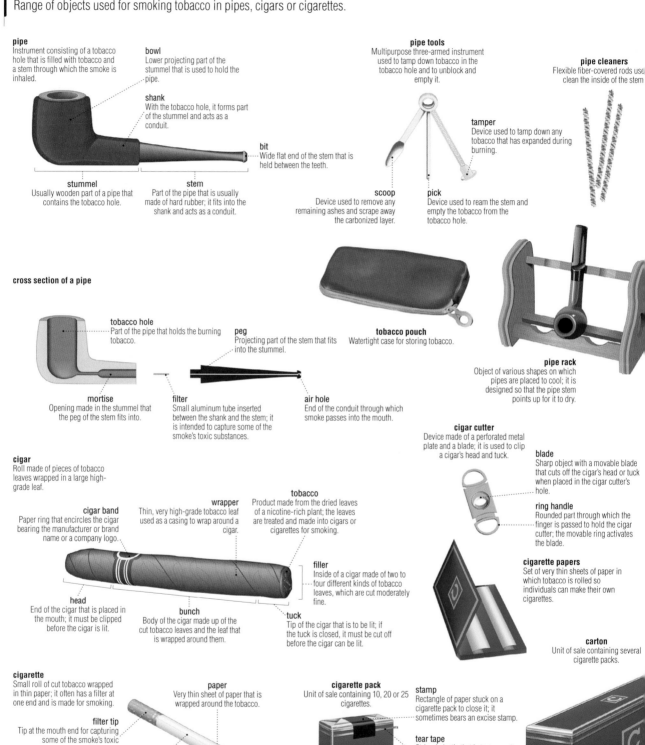

PERSONAL ACCESSORIES AND ARTICLES

smoking accessories

gas lighter
Instrument containing liquid butane sometimes mixed with propane that is ignited by a spark produced from friction.

cover
Spring-loaded hood that snaps down to extinguish the flame.

striker wheel
Small notched wheel that produces sparks when rubbed against a stone thus igniting the flow of gas.

flame adjustment wheel
Wheel that adjusts the flow of gas escaping from the tank thus increasing or decreasing the size of the flame.

butane tank
Hollow cylindrical compartment containing liquid butane.

matchbook
Case closed by a flap that contains rows of matches attached to the book.

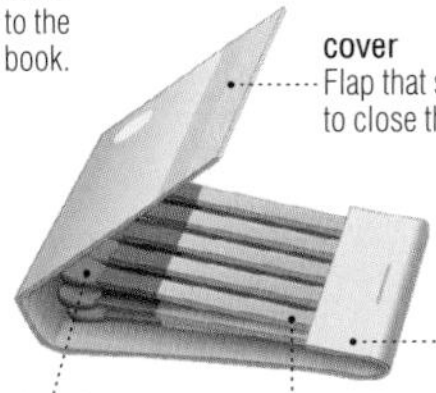

cover
Flap that slides under the front flap to close the book.

front flap
Flap under which the matches are attached.

head
End of the match with a chemical coating that lights when struck against another surface.

matchstick
Usually cardboard or wooden body of the match.

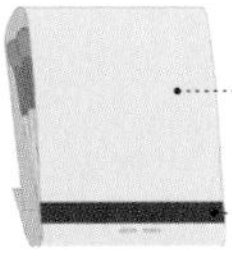

back

friction strip
Part of a book or box of matches with an abrasive coating against which the matches are struck to light them.

matchbox
Rectangular or square box with a sliding lid containing loose matches.

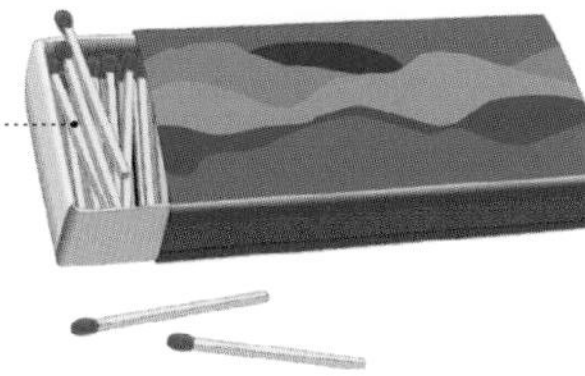

safety match
Small stem with a head that lights only when struck against a particular surface thus preventing accidental lighting.

ashtray
Receptacle into which smokers empty their pipe or leave the remains of their cigar or cigarette.

butt
Unburned portion of a cigar or cigarette.

ash
Residue left from burned tobacco.

umbrella and stick

The shape, price and materials of these personal articles vary widely according to culture, period and manufacturer.

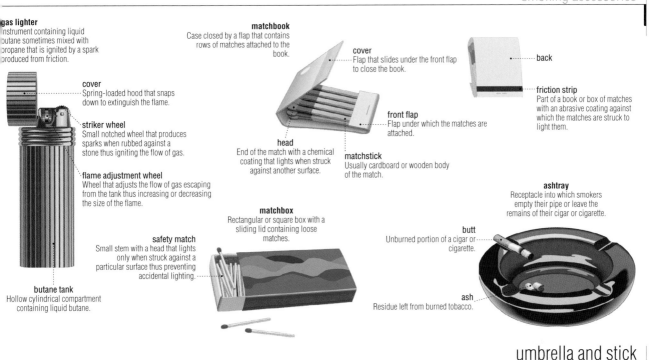

walking stick
Crafted stick used for support when walking.

umbrella stand
Variously shaped accessory or piece of furniture where umbrellas and walking sticks are kept.

telescopic umbrella
Umbrella that can become shorter when closed because it has a collapsible handle and hinged ribs that fold up.

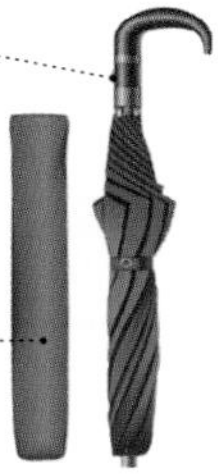

push button
Button that is pushed to activate the umbrella's opening mechanism.

cover
Elongated case that covers the umbrella when it is closed to protect its canopy.

stick umbrella
Umbrella with a handle shaped like a walking stick.

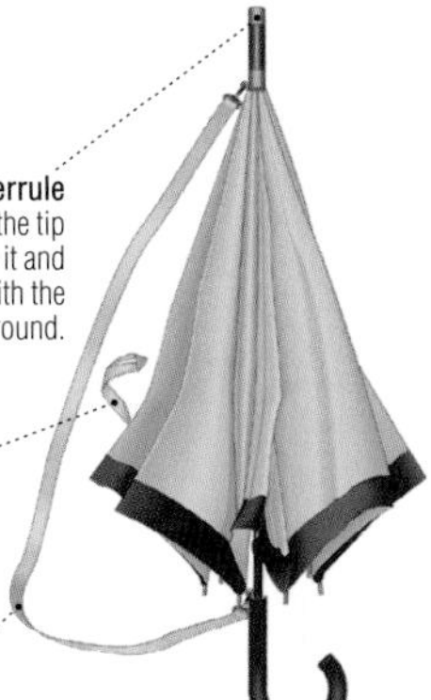

ferrule
Usually metal trim covering the tip of an umbrella to decorate it and protect if from contact with the ground.

tie closure
Strip of material with a fastener that is wrapped around the closed umbrella to hold the ribs and canopy in place.

shoulder strap
Long belt often with a buckle to adjust it; it is used to carry the umbrella over the shoulder or diagonally across the chest.

umbrella
Accessory made up of a handle and fabric stretched over a collapsible metal frame that is used as protection against the rain.

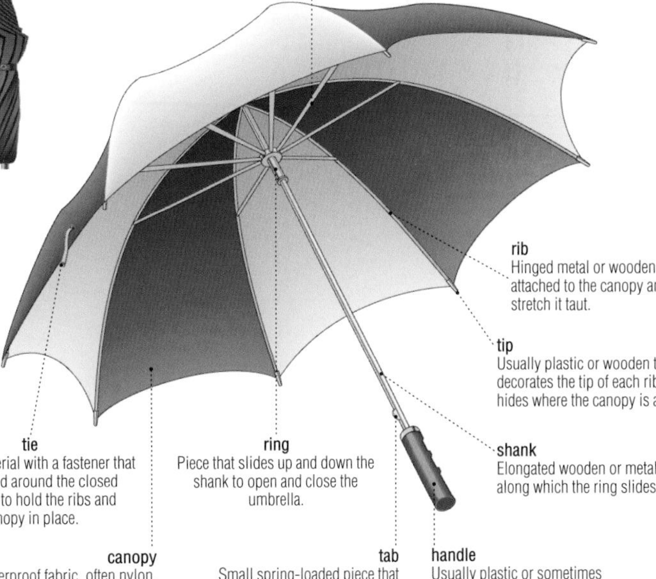

spreader
Part of the frame that is connected to both the ring and a rib.

rib
Hinged metal or wooden rod that is attached to the canopy and used to stretch it taut.

tip
Usually plastic or wooden trim that decorates the tip of each rib and hides where the canopy is attached.

shank
Elongated wooden or metal piece along which the ring slides.

tie
Strip of material with a fastener that is wrapped around the closed umbrella to hold the ribs and canopy in place.

ring
Piece that slides up and down the shank to open and close the umbrella.

canopy
Waterproof fabric, often nylon.

tab
Small spring-loaded piece that engages with the ring at the bottom and top of the shank and holds it in place to keep the umbrella open or closed.

handle
Usually plastic or sometimes wooden part that is used to hold the umbrella whether it is open or closed.

ARTS AND ARCHITECTURE

museum

Establishment where works of art are stored and exhibited.

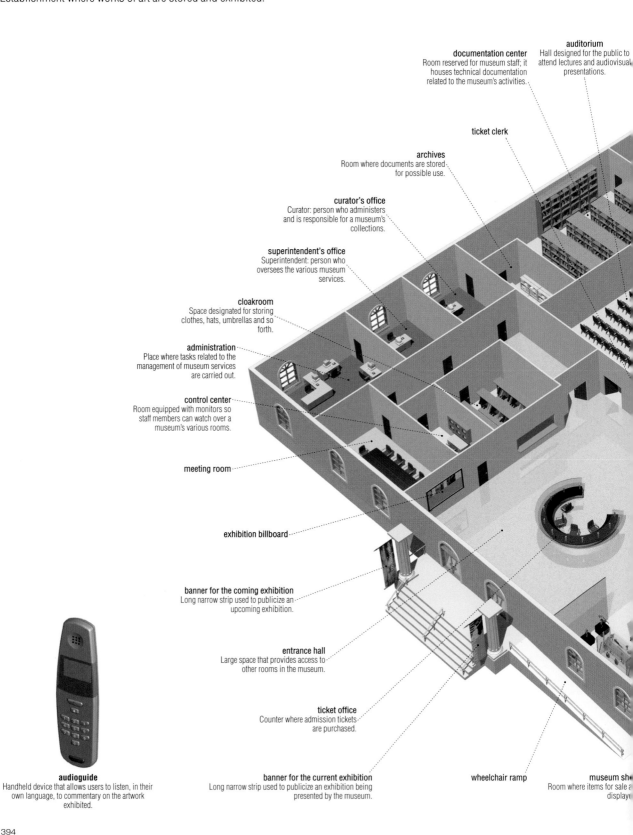

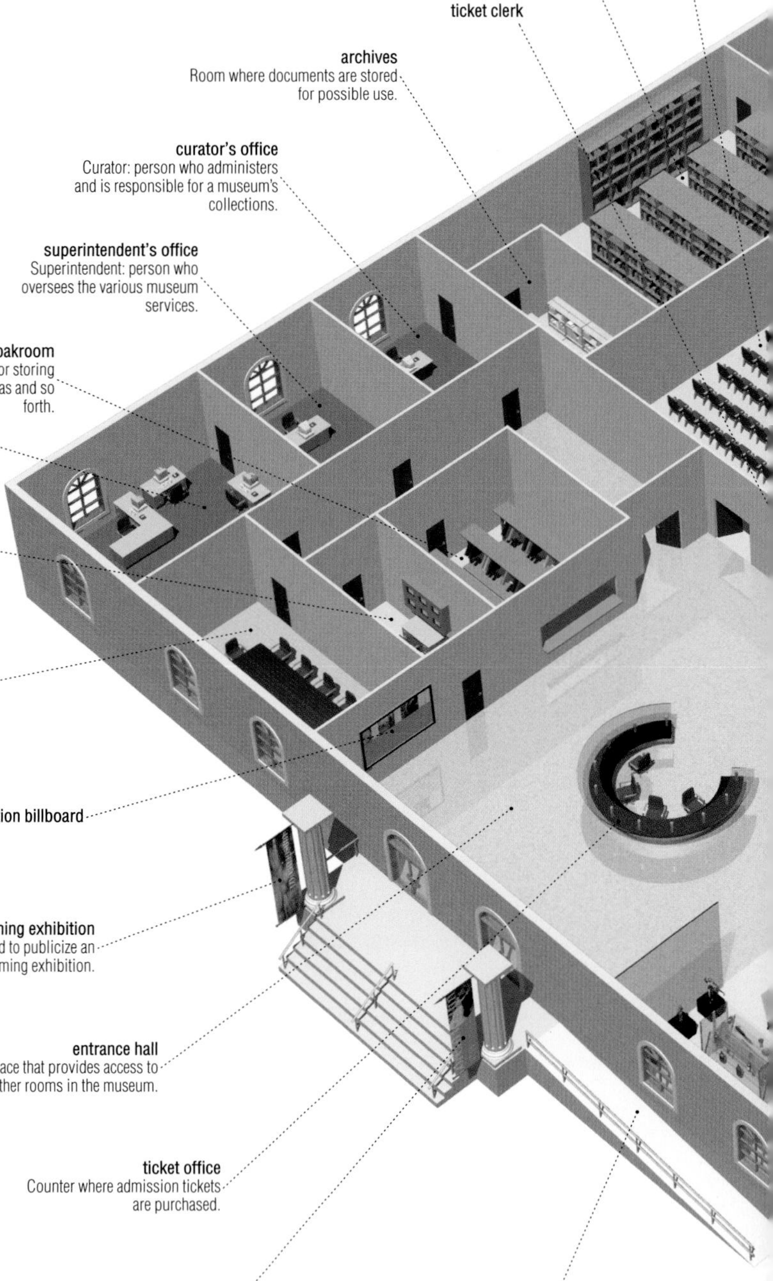

auditorium
Hall designed for the public to attend lectures and audiovisual presentations.

documentation center
Room reserved for museum staff; it houses technical documentation related to the museum's activities.

ticket clerk

archives
Room where documents are stored for possible use.

curator's office
Curator: person who administers and is responsible for a museum's collections.

superintendent's office
Superintendent: person who oversees the various museum services.

cloakroom
Space designated for storing clothes, hats, umbrellas and so forth.

administration
Place where tasks related to the management of museum services are carried out.

control center
Room equipped with monitors so staff members can watch over a museum's various rooms.

meeting room

exhibition billboard

banner for the coming exhibition
Long narrow strip used to publicize an upcoming exhibition.

entrance hall
Large space that provides access to other rooms in the museum.

ticket office
Counter where admission tickets are purchased.

banner for the current exhibition
Long narrow strip used to publicize an exhibition being presented by the museum.

wheelchair ramp

museum sh
Room where items for sale a
display

audioguide
Handheld device that allows users to listen, in their own language, to commentary on the artwork exhibited.

ARTS AND ARCHITECTURE

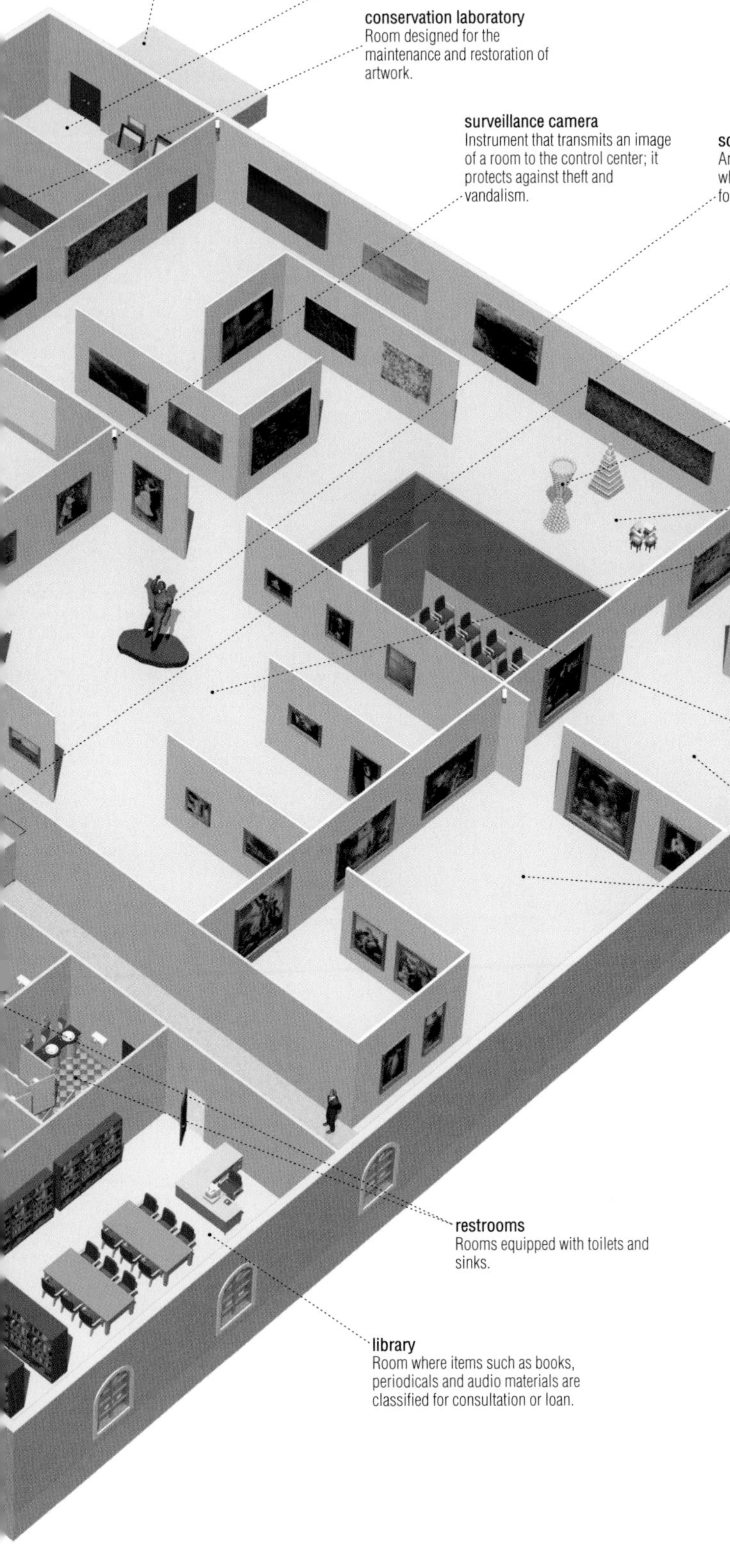
unloading dock
Facility for off-loading crates containing exhibition equipment.
receiving area
Area designed to receive artwork.
conservation laboratory
Room designed for the maintenance and restoration of artwork.
surveillance camera
Instrument that transmits an image of a room to the control center; it protects against theft and vandalism.
sculpture
Artwork created from a material, which is worked to depict a given form.
interactive terminals
Interactive computers with touch screens or keyboards that, with the visitor's participation, provide a variety of information.
installation work
Three-dimensional artwork composed of elements arranged in a precise order, in keeping with the artist's intention.
temporary exhibition rooms
Rooms designed to house short-term exhibitions of a given artist or theme.
painting
Pictorial work usually executed on a canvas, which is stretched and then framed.
projection room
Room occasionally used to present audiovisual materials related to the exhibition's artist or theme.
permanent exhibition rooms
Rooms where the museum mounts long-term showings of the works in its collection.
restrooms
Rooms equipped with toilets and sinks.
library
Room where items such as books, periodicals and audio materials are classified for consultation or loan.

frame
Rigid border around a painting or engraving that protects it and makes it possible to hang it.

painting
Pictorial work usually executed on a canvas, which is stretched and then framed.

work sheet
Stiff paper containing information about a work of art.

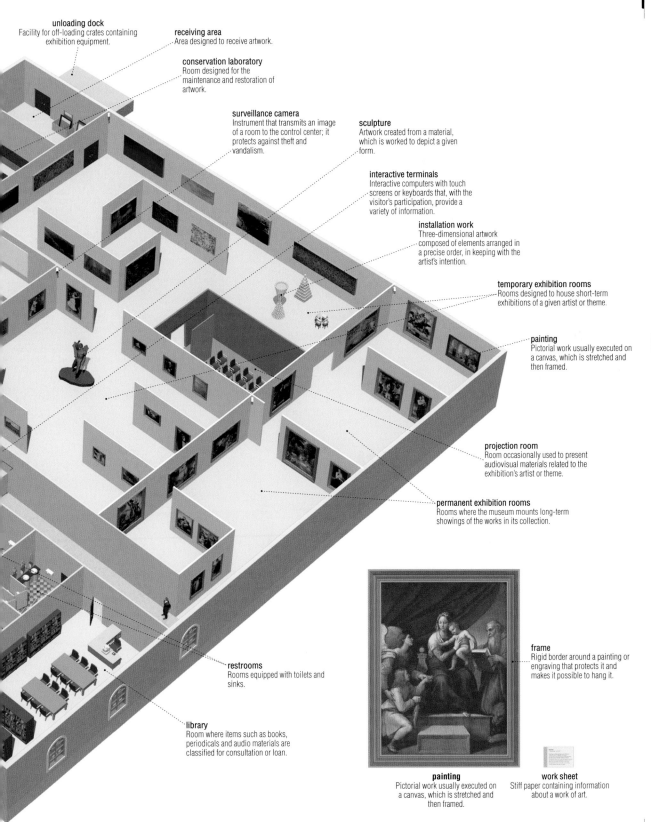

painting and drawing

Arts that use graphics and color to represent or suggest visible or imagined concepts on a surface.

major techniques

The processes used to execute drawings and paintings.

ink drawing
Technique usually involving the use of a pen to create fine and precise lines.

charcoal drawing
Sketching technique that can create tones ranging from the darkest blacks to the lightest grays.

oil painting
Technique used to achieve an opaque, transparent, matte or brilliant finish, depending on the composition of the paint.

watercolor
Mixture of pigment powder agglutinated with a water-soluble binder; when it is diluted, a transparent effect is created.

gouache
Mixture of roughly ground pigmen and chalk agglutinated with a wate soluble binder; when it is diluted, a opaque effect is created.

felt tip pen drawing
Technique for producing precise lines and gradations of color.

dry pastel drawing
Technique whose powdery line creates a velvety effect.

oil pastel drawing
Technique that provides a bold stroke similar to that of an oil painting.

colored pencil drawing
Technique for combining precise lines with color, and then applying layers of color to achieve new shades.

wax crayon drawing
Technique used mostly by children create a precise line and a brilliant c effect.

equipment

Materials, instruments and accessories used to create a drawing or painting.

oil pastel
Mixture of pigments, wax and sometimes oily substances in stick form.

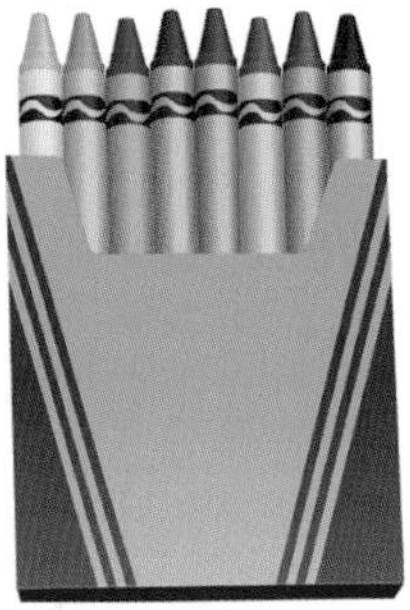

wax crayons
Sticks composed of pigment molded with wax.

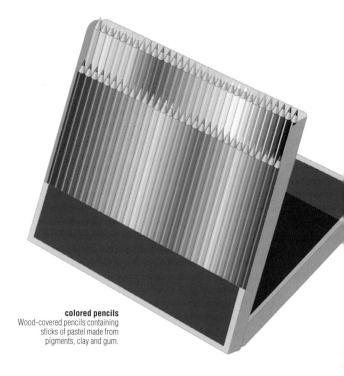

colored pencils
Wood-covered pencils containing sticks of pastel made from pigments, clay and gum.

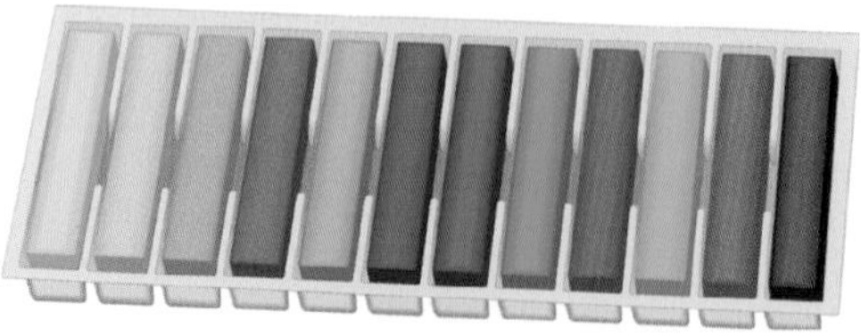

dry pastel
Mixture of pigment powder agglutinated using a gum-based binder, then shaped into sticks and dried.

marker
Bevel-tipped color felt pen of variable size.

felt tip pen
Pen whose felt tip is permeated with ink; it comes in a variety of colors.

ink
Liquid preparation, black or colored, used to write or draw.

charcoal
Stick of charcoal used for sketching; it erases easily.

oil/acrylic paint
Oil-based or acrylic pigment that comes in a tube; the artist uses oil or essences to dilute it and prepare it for application.

watercolor/gouache cakes
Small watercolor or gouache disks inserted into cells to prevent the colors from mixing.

watercolor/gouache tube
Tube containing watercolor or gouache in paste form.

spatula
Instrument with a flat flexible blade used to mix colors, spread them on a canvas or scrape down the palette.

palette knife
Instrument with a trowel-shaped blade used to mix colors and to spread them on and remove them from the canvas.

reservoir-nib pen
Drawing instrument with a curved tip containing a small amount of ink.

flat brush
Brush made from natural or synthetic bristles affixed to a handle and used mostly for oil painting on large surfaces.

sumi-e brush
Brush made from natural bristles affixed to a bamboo handle and used for drawing with India ink.

fan brush
Brush used to achieve color gradations by blending colors that have already been applied to a canvas.

brush
Natural or synthetic bristles attached to a handle, used for spreading paint, varnish or stain on a base.

painting and drawing

color chart
Sample of the different color shades provided by a manufacturer.

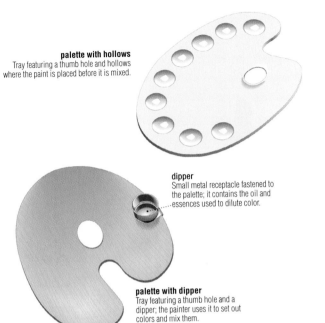

palette with hollows
Tray featuring a thumb hole and hollows where the paint is placed before it is mixed.

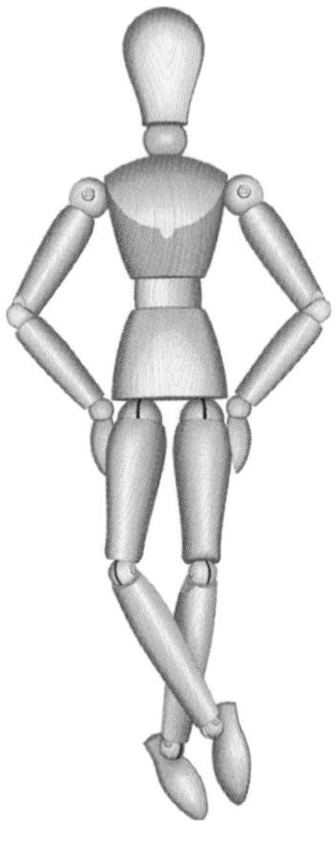

articulated mannequin
Wooden figurine used to visualize various positions assumed by the human body.

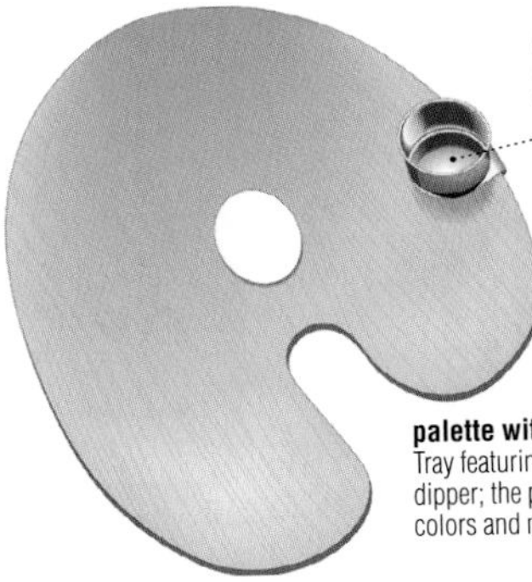

palette with dipper
Tray featuring a thumb hole and a dipper; the painter uses it to set out colors and mix them.

dipper
Small metal receptacle fastened to the palette; it contains the oil and essences used to dilute color.

airbrush

Instrument that pulverizes paint or ink by means of compressed air pressure.

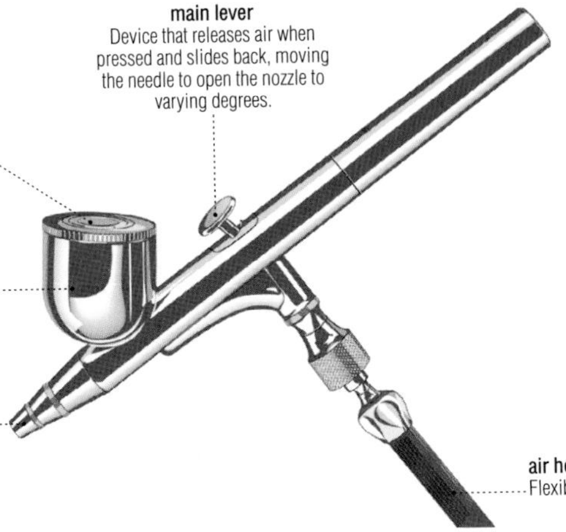

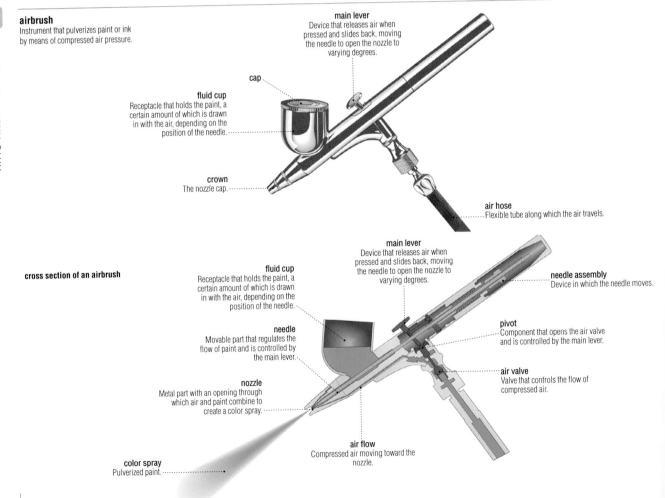

main lever
Device that releases air when pressed and slides back, moving the needle to open the nozzle to varying degrees.

cap

fluid cup
Receptacle that holds the paint, a certain amount of which is drawn in with the air, depending on the position of the needle.

crown
The nozzle cap.

air hose
Flexible tube along which the air travels.

cross section of an airbrush

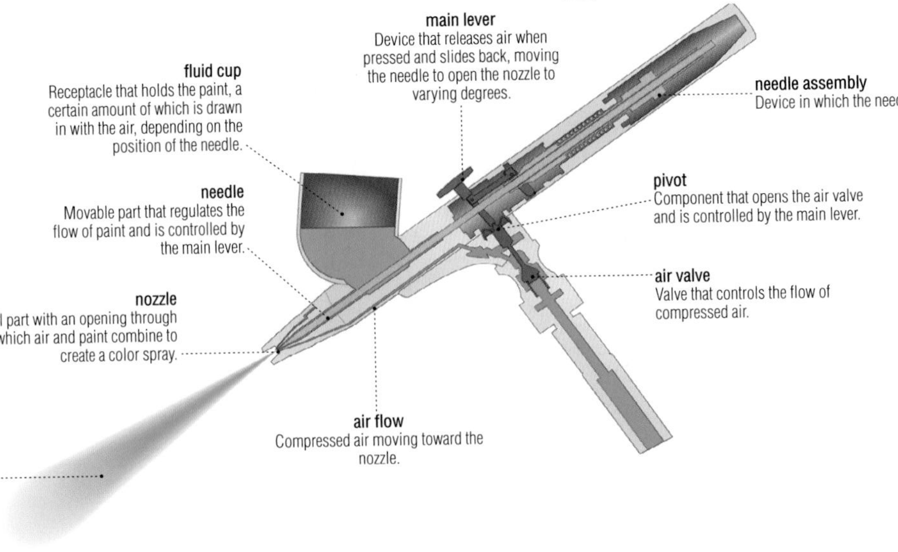

main lever
Device that releases air when pressed and slides back, moving the needle to open the nozzle to varying degrees.

fluid cup
Receptacle that holds the paint, a certain amount of which is drawn in with the air, depending on the position of the needle.

needle assembly
Device in which the needle moves.

needle
Movable part that regulates the flow of paint and is controlled by the main lever.

pivot
Component that opens the air valve and is controlled by the main lever.

air valve
Valve that controls the flow of compressed air.

nozzle
Metal part with an opening through which air and paint combine to create a color spray.

air flow
Compressed air moving toward the nozzle.

color spray
Pulverized paint.

accessories

afting table
ble whose height and incline can adjusted; it is equipped with a afting machine.

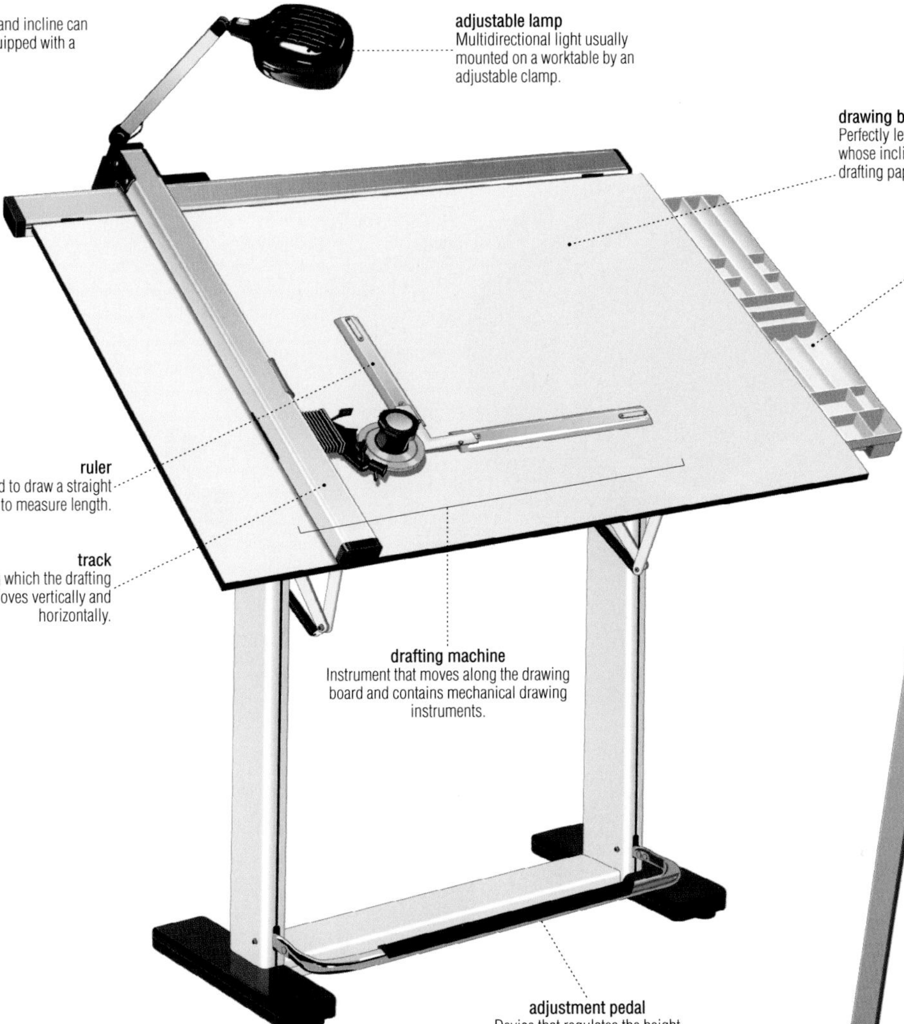

adjustable lamp
Multidirectional light usually mounted on a worktable by an adjustable clamp.

drawing board
Perfectly level wooden board whose incline can be adjusted; the drafting paper is placed on it.

storage tray

ruler
Instrument used to draw a straight line and to measure length.

track
Rail along which the drafting machine moves vertically and horizontally.

drafting machine
Instrument that moves along the drawing board and contains mechanical drawing instruments.

adjustment pedal
Device that regulates the height and angle of the drafting table.

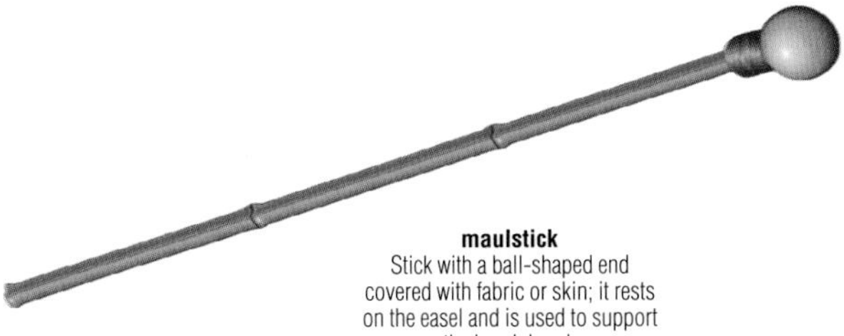

maulstick
Stick with a ball-shaped end covered with fabric or skin; it rests on the easel and is used to support the brush hand.

easel
Tripod on which a canvas is placed to execute a work or show it.

painting and drawing

color wheel
Representation of the color spectrum on a circle.

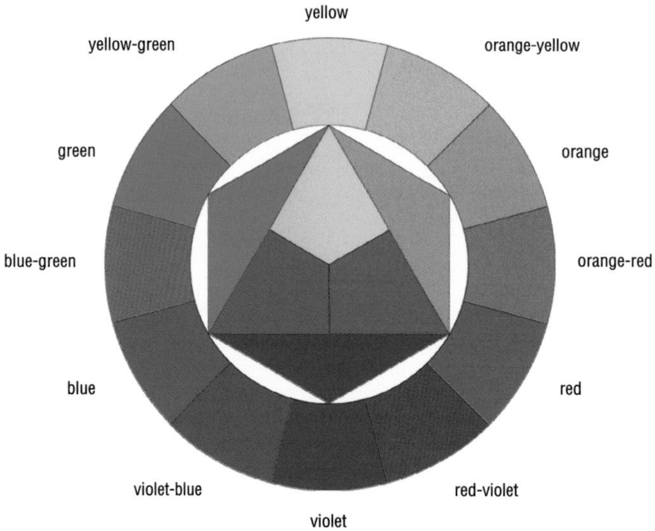

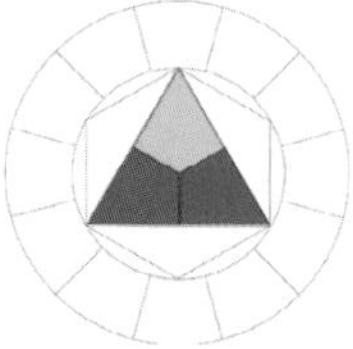

primary colors
Colors that cannot be obtained by mixing other colors.

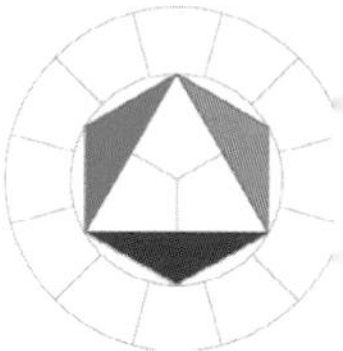

secondary colors
Colors obtained by mixing eq
proportions of two primary co

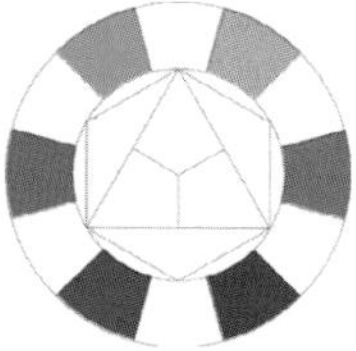

tertiary colors
Colors obtained by mixing equal proportions of a primary color and a secondary color.

utility liquids
Utility liquids are used to prepare a color or protect a work of art.

fixative
Transparent solution in liquid or aerosol form applied to protect a drawing in charcoal, chalk, pastel or pencil.

turpentine
An essential oil obtained by the distillation of natural resins and used mostly as an oil paint thinner.

linseed oil
Oil made from linseeds; it acts as a binding agent so that pigment adheres to a surface.

varnish
Preparation with no pigment; when applied to a surface, it forms a protective film.

supports
Surfaces on which paintings, drawings and engravings are created.

paper
Vegetable substance reduced to paste, rolled and then dried into thin sheets that serve as a surface for a drawing, painting or engraving.

cardboard
Somewhat rigid sheet made of several layers of paper pulp; its function is to support a drawing or painting.

canvas
Piece of fabric covered with a primer and set on a stretcher; it serves as the surface for the painting.

panel
Wooden board that serves as a rigid support for a painting.

wood carving

Art that consists of carving a piece of wood to represent or suggest an object.

steps

Phases in the development of a wood sculpture.

drawing
Step that involves drawing the piece to be carved on a wooden block.

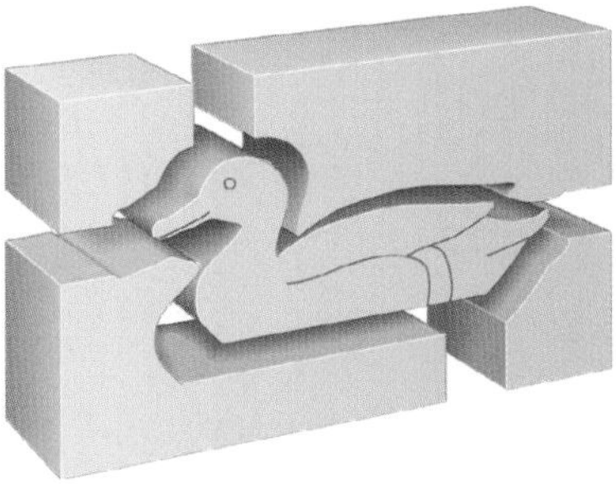

roughing out
Step that involves bringing out the basic contours of a piece.

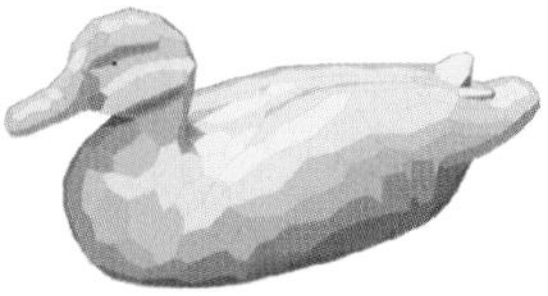

carving
Step that involves shaping and refining the piece.

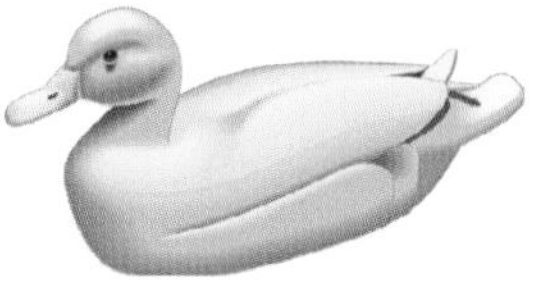

finishing
Step that involves fine-tuning the details and polishing the surface of a piece until no evidence remains of the tools used.

examples of tools

Tools: instruments used in sculpture to cut and file wood.

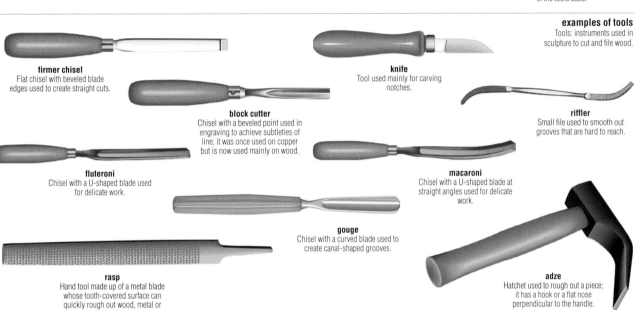

firmer chisel
Flat chisel with beveled blade edges used to create straight cuts.

knife
Tool used mainly for carving notches.

block cutter
Chisel with a beveled point used in engraving to achieve subtleties of line; it was once used on copper but is now used mainly on wood.

riffler
Small file used to smooth out grooves that are hard to reach.

fluteroni
Chisel with a U-shaped blade used for delicate work.

macaroni
Chisel with a U-shaped blade at straight angles used for delicate work.

gouge
Chisel with a curved blade used to create canal-shaped grooves.

rasp
Hand tool made up of a metal blade whose tooth-covered surface can quickly rough out wood, metal or plastic.

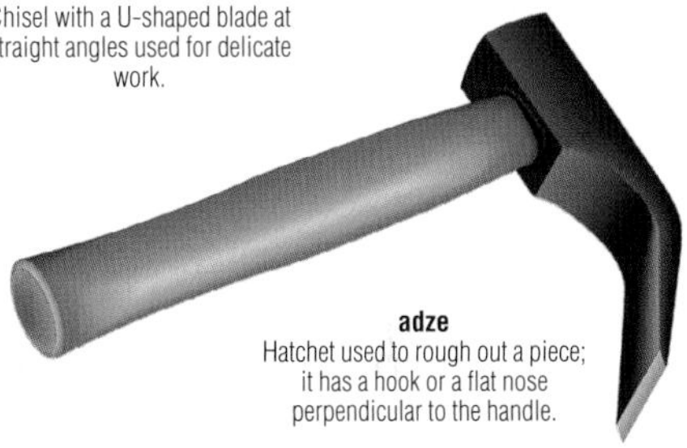

adze
Hatchet used to rough out a piece; it has a hook or a flat nose perpendicular to the handle.

major types of blades

Blade: the sharp part of a sculptor's chisel.

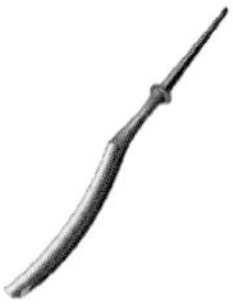

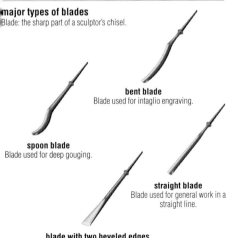

bent blade
Blade used for intaglio engraving.

spoon blade
Blade used for deep gouging.

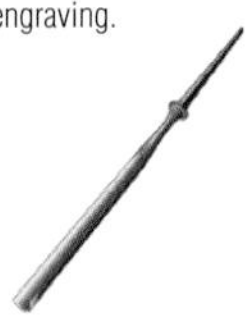

straight blade
Blade used for general work in a straight line.

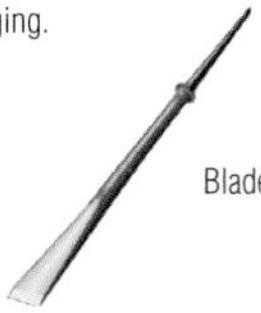

blade with two beveled edges
Blade used to execute rectilinear cuts.

accessories

stand
Small stool on which the sculptor places and secures the piece to be worked on.

carver's bench screw
Threaded instrument used to secure a piece of wood to a stand.

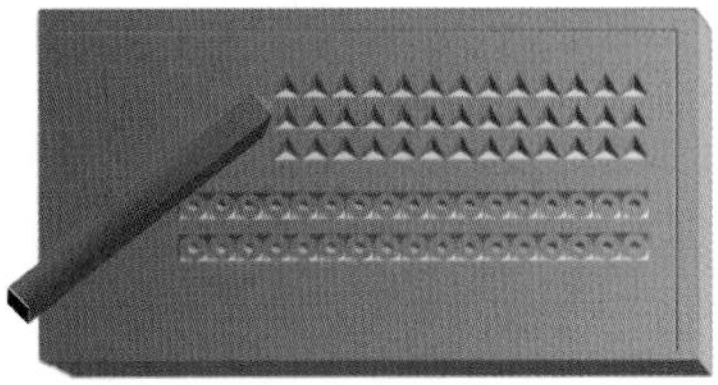

punch and pattern
The punch, a metal rod, is struck to carve motifs into a slab of wood.

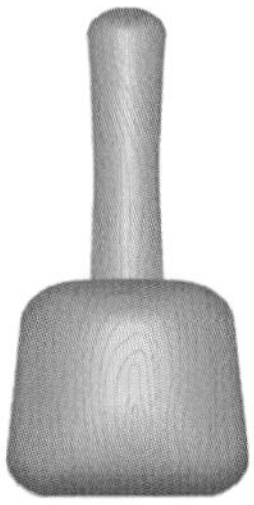

mallet
Hammer used to strike the heel of a sharp tool to force it into the wood.

pyramid

Construction with a square base and four triangular faces; it served as a tomb for the pharaohs of ancient Egypt, represented here by the pyramid of Cheops.

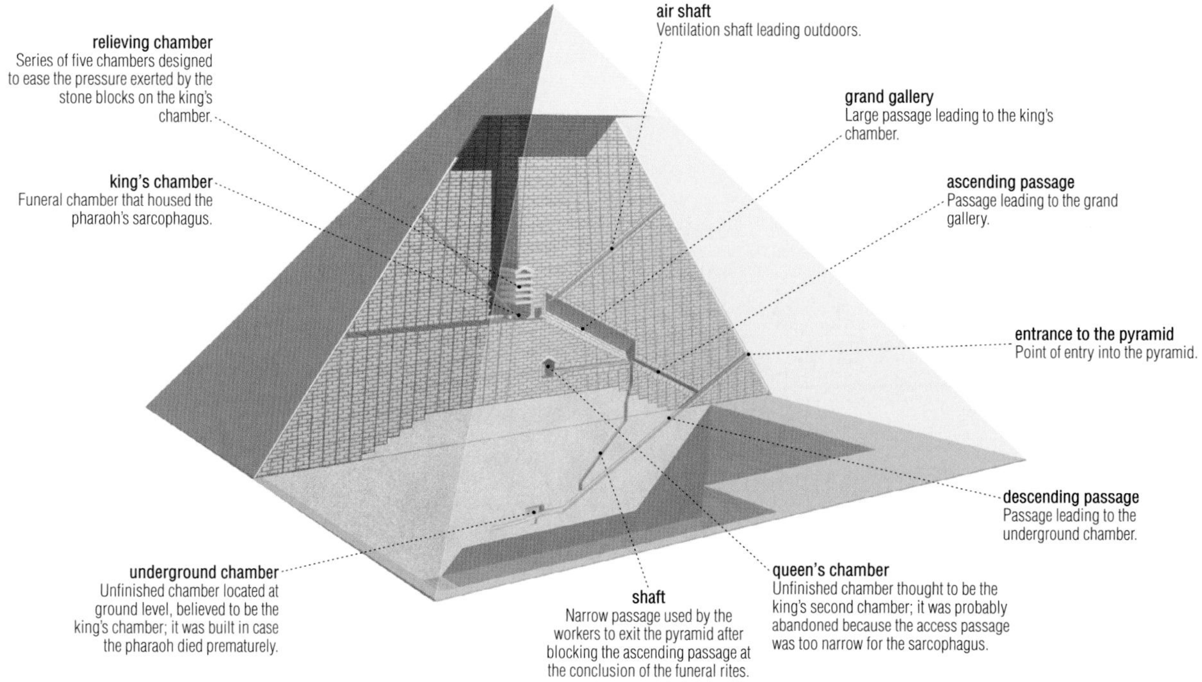
air shaft
Ventilation shaft leading outdoors.
relieving chamber
Series of five chambers designed to ease the pressure exerted by the stone blocks on the king's chamber.
grand gallery
Large passage leading to the king's chamber.
king's chamber
Funeral chamber that housed the pharaoh's sarcophagus.
ascending passage
Passage leading to the grand gallery.
entrance to the pyramid
Point of entry into the pyramid.
descending passage
Passage leading to the underground chamber.
underground chamber
Unfinished chamber located at ground level, believed to be the king's chamber; it was built in case the pharaoh died prematurely.
queen's chamber
Unfinished chamber thought to be the king's second chamber; it was probably abandoned because the access passage was too narrow for the sarcophagus.
shaft
Narrow passage used by the workers to exit the pyramid after blocking the ascending passage at the conclusion of the funeral rites.

Greek theater

Open-air structure, often built on a hillside, where theatrical performances were staged during antiquity.

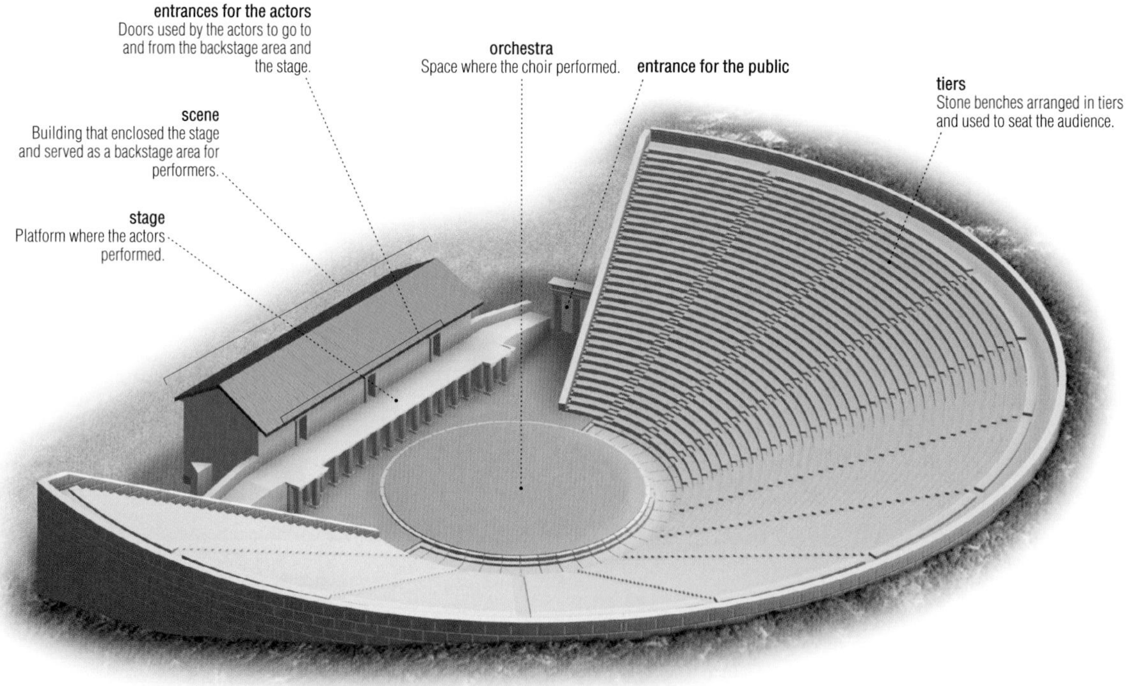
entrances for the actors
Doors used by the actors to go to and from the backstage area and the stage.
orchestra
Space where the choir performed.
entrance for the public
tiers
Stone benches arranged in tiers and used to seat the audience.
scene
Building that enclosed the stage and served as a backstage area for performers.
stage
Platform where the actors performed.

Greek temple

Building that, in antiquity, was dedicated to a divinity and featured a statue of that divinity.

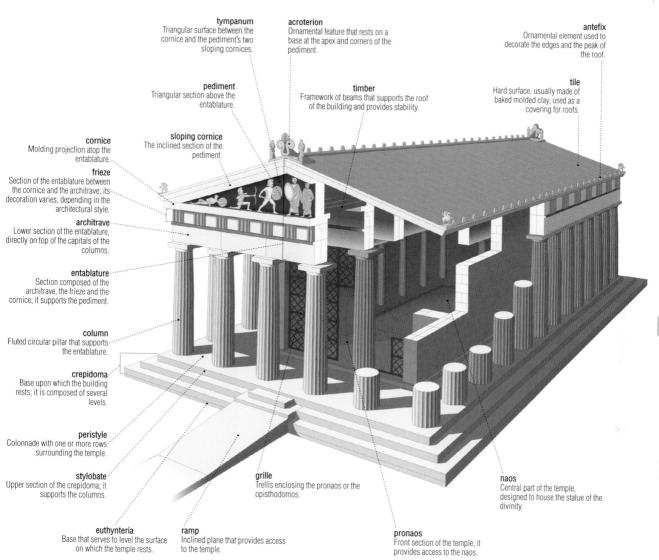

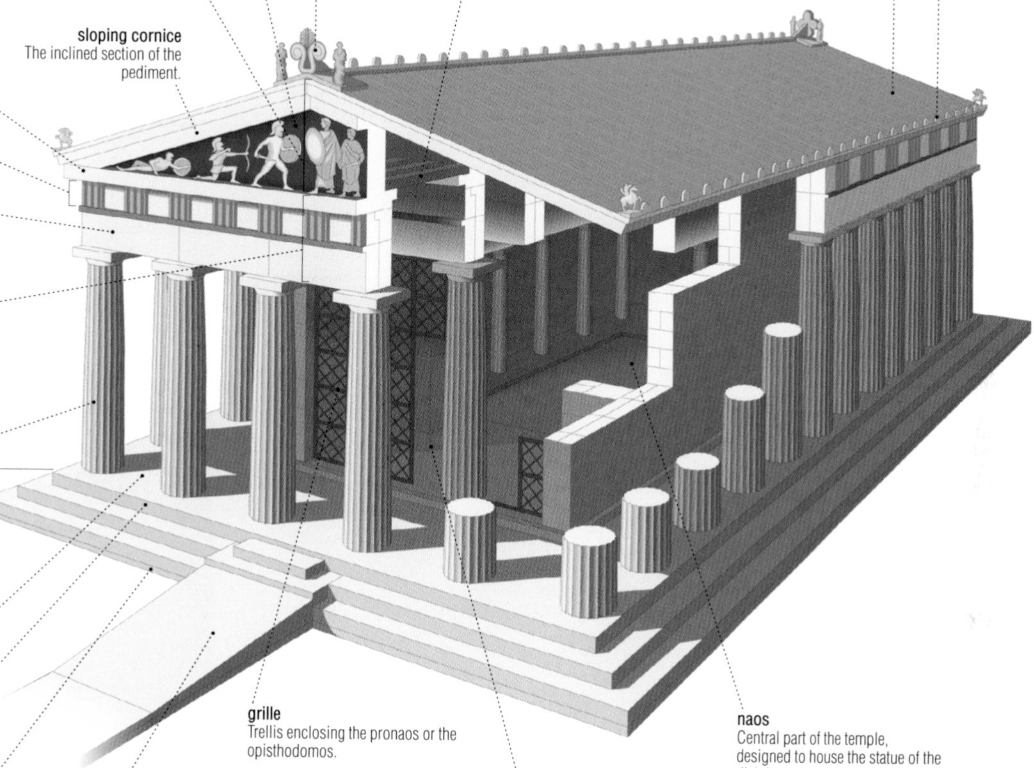
tympanum
Triangular surface between the cornice and the pediment's two sloping cornices.
acroterion
Ornamental feature that rests on a base at the apex and corners of the pediment.
antefix
Ornamental element used to decorate the edges and the peak of the roof.
pediment
Triangular section above the entablature.
timber
Framework of beams that supports the roof of the building and provides stability.
tile
Hard surface, usually made of baked molded clay, used as a covering for roofs.
cornice
Molding projection atop the entablature.
sloping cornice
The inclined section of the pediment.
frieze
Section of the entablature between the cornice and the architrave; its decoration varies, depending in the architectural style.
architrave
Lower section of the entablature, directly on top of the capitals of the columns.
entablature
Section composed of the architrave, the frieze and the cornice; it supports the pediment.
column
Fluted circular pillar that supports the entablature.
crepidoma
Base upon which the building rests; it is composed of several levels.
peristyle
Colonnade with one or more rows surrounding the temple.
stylobate
Upper section of the crepidoma; it supports the columns.
grille
Trellis enclosing the pronaos or the opisthodomos.
naos
Central part of the temple, designed to house the statue of the divinity.
euthynteria
Base that serves to level the surface on which the temple rests.
ramp
Inclined plane that provides access to the temple.
pronaos
Front section of the temple; it provides access to the naos.

plan

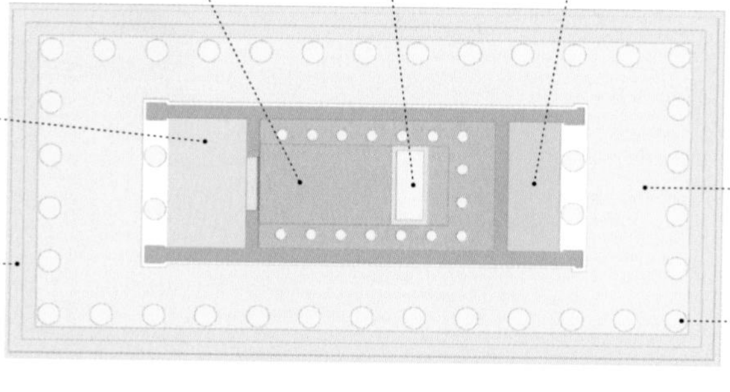
naos
Central part of the temple, designed to house the statue of the divinity.
location of the statue
Area where the statue of the divinity was placed.
opisthodomos
Rear section of the temple where offerings were left.
pronaos
Front section of the temple; it provides access to the naos.
crepidoma
Base upon which the building rests; it is composed of several levels.
peristyle
Colonnade with one or more rows surrounding the temple.
column
Circular pillar supporting the entablature; it is composed of three parts: the base, the shaft and the capital.

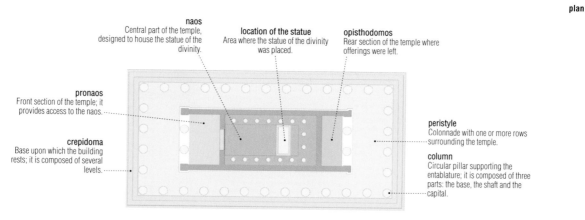

architectural styles

The architectural styles, or orders, of ancient Greece are distinguished by rules of proportion that govern a building's columns, entablature and pediment.

Doric order
Order characterized by a squat column with no base, a capital that is not sculpted and a frieze with alternating triglyphs and metopes.

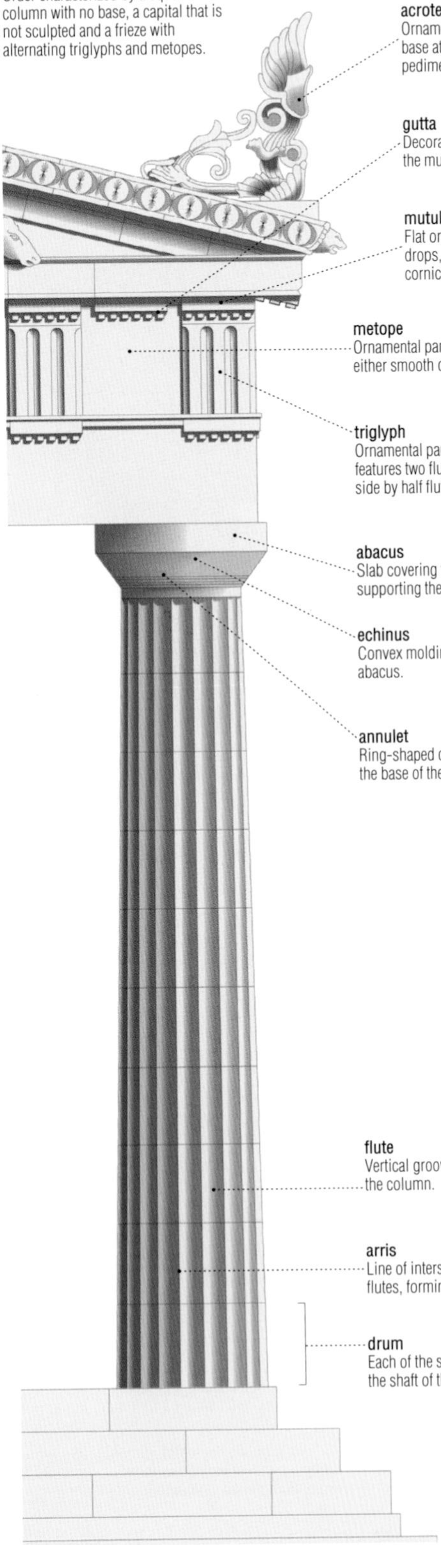

acroterion
Ornamental feature that rests on a base at the apex and corners of the pediment.

gutta
Decorative motif located beneath the mutule.

mutule
Flat ornament, often adorned with drops, attached to the base of the cornice or the frieze.

metope
Ornamental panel on the frieze; it is either smooth or sculpted.

triglyph
Ornamental panel on the frieze that features two flutes framed on each side by half flutes.

abacus
Slab covering the capital and supporting the architrave.

echinus
Convex molding supporting the abacus.

annulet
Ring-shaped ornament decorating the base of the capital.

flute
Vertical groove along the length of the column.

arris
Line of intersection between two flutes, forming a sharp angle.

drum
Each of the sections that make up the shaft of the column.

Ionic order
Order characterized by soaring columns with molded bases, capitals with volutes and a continuously sculpted frieze.

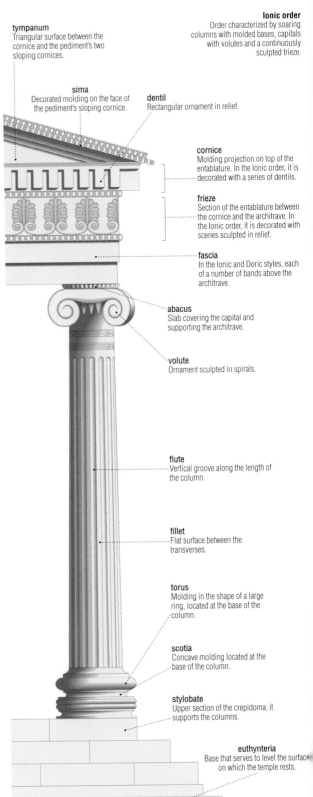

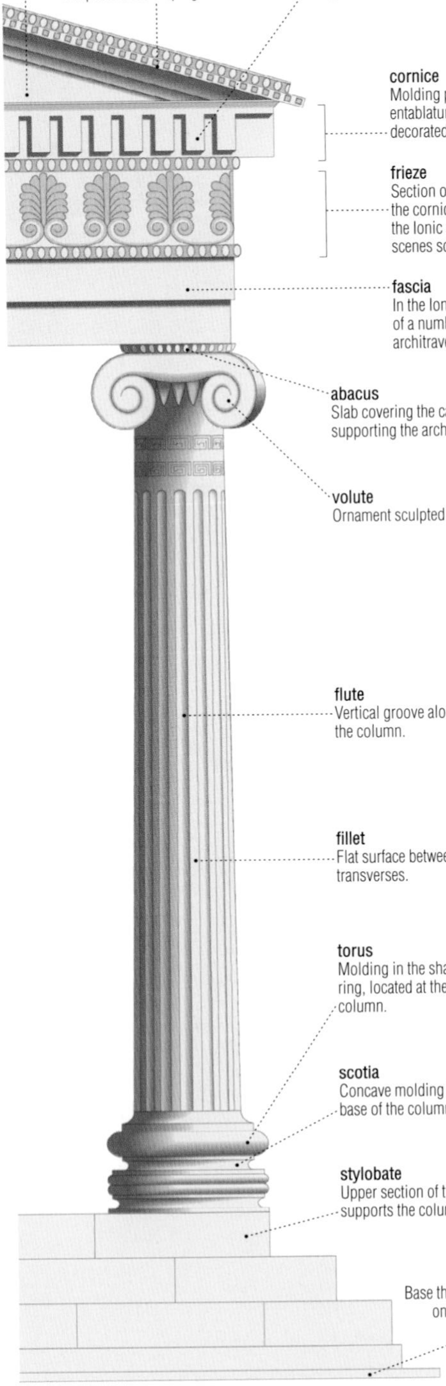

tympanum
Triangular surface between the cornice and the pediment's two sloping cornices.

sima
Decorated molding on the face of the pediment's sloping cornice.

dentil
Rectangular ornament in relief.

cornice
Molding projection on top of the entablature. In the Ionic order, it is decorated with a series of dentils.

frieze
Section of the entablature between the cornice and the architrave. In the Ionic order, it is decorated with scenes sculpted in relief.

fascia
In the Ionic and Doric styles, each of a number of bands above the architrave.

abacus
Slab covering the capital and supporting the architrave.

volute
Ornament sculpted in spirals.

flute
Vertical groove along the length of the column.

fillet
Flat surface between the transverses.

torus
Molding in the shape of a large ring, located at the base of the column.

scotia
Concave molding located at the base of the column.

stylobate
Upper section of the crepidoma; it supports the columns.

euthynteria
Base that serves to level the surface on which the temple rests.

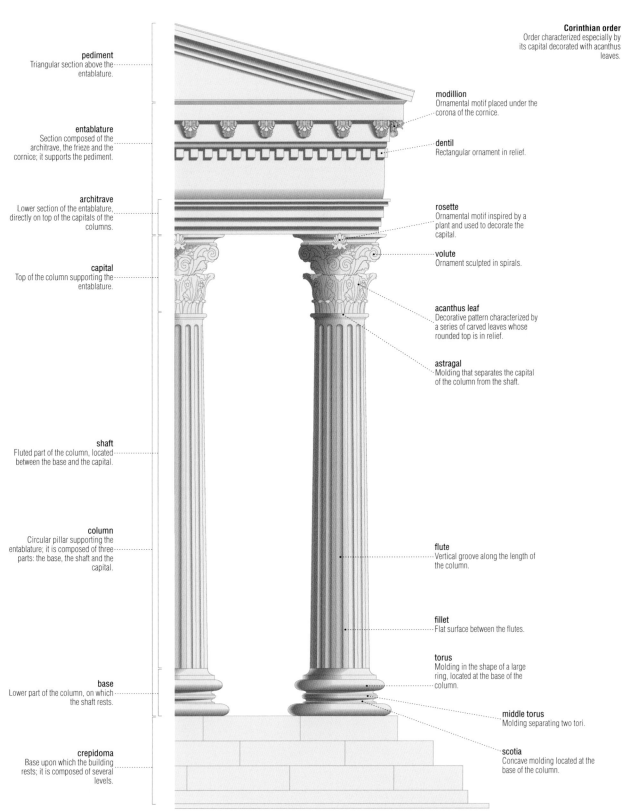

Corinthian order
Order characterized especially by its capital decorated with acanthus leaves.

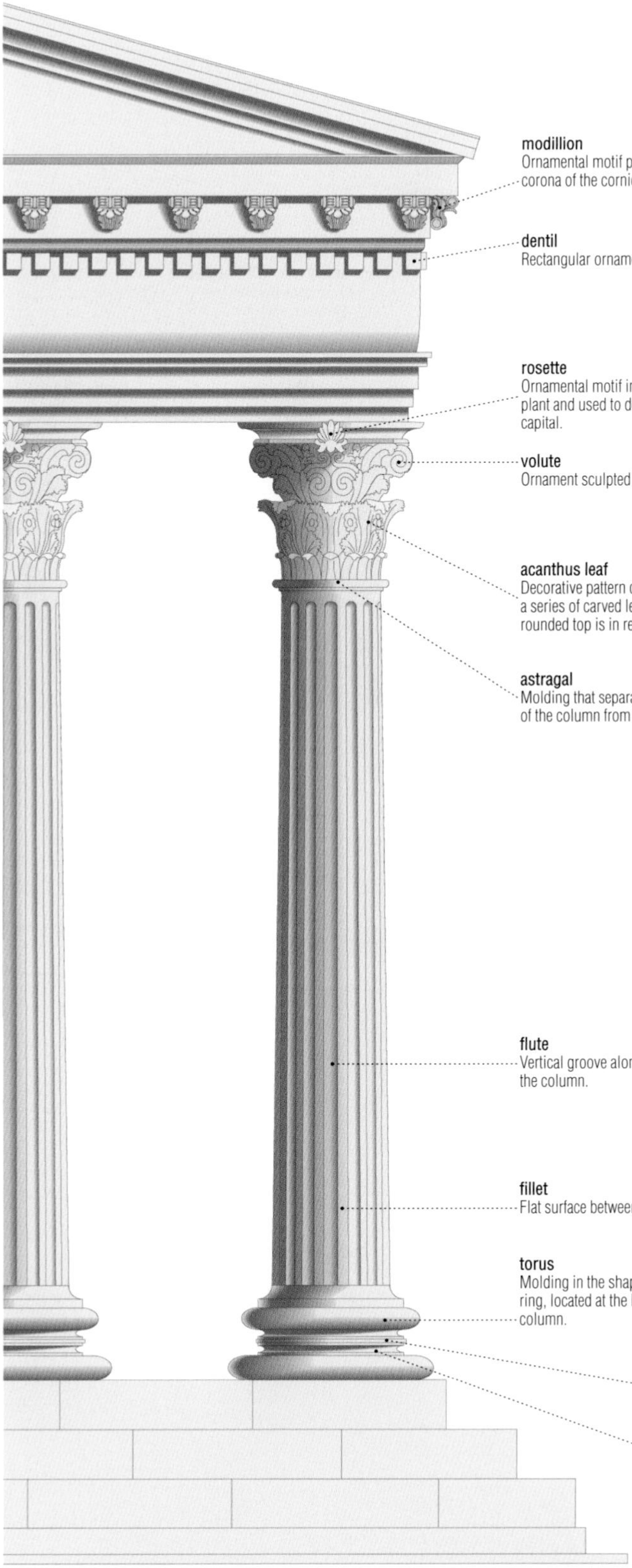

pediment
Triangular section above the entablature.

entablature
Section composed of the architrave, the frieze and the cornice; it supports the pediment.

architrave
Lower section of the entablature, directly on top of the capitals of the columns.

capital
Top of the column supporting the entablature.

shaft
Fluted part of the column, located between the base and the capital.

column
Circular pillar supporting the entablature; it is composed of three parts: the base, the shaft and the capital.

base
Lower part of the column, on which the shaft rests.

crepidoma
Base upon which the building rests; it is composed of several levels.

modillion
Ornamental motif placed under the corona of the cornice.

dentil
Rectangular ornament in relief.

rosette
Ornamental motif inspired by a plant and used to decorate the capital.

volute
Ornament sculpted in spirals.

acanthus leaf
Decorative pattern characterized by a series of carved leaves whose rounded top is in relief.

astragal
Molding that separates the capital of the column from the shaft.

flute
Vertical groove along the length of the column.

fillet
Flat surface between the flutes.

torus
Molding in the shape of a large ring, located at the base of the column.

middle torus
Molding separating two tori.

scotia
Concave molding located at the base of the column.

Roman house

For wealthy Romans, family life unfolded in spacious luxurious houses whose rooms were arranged around open-air spaces.

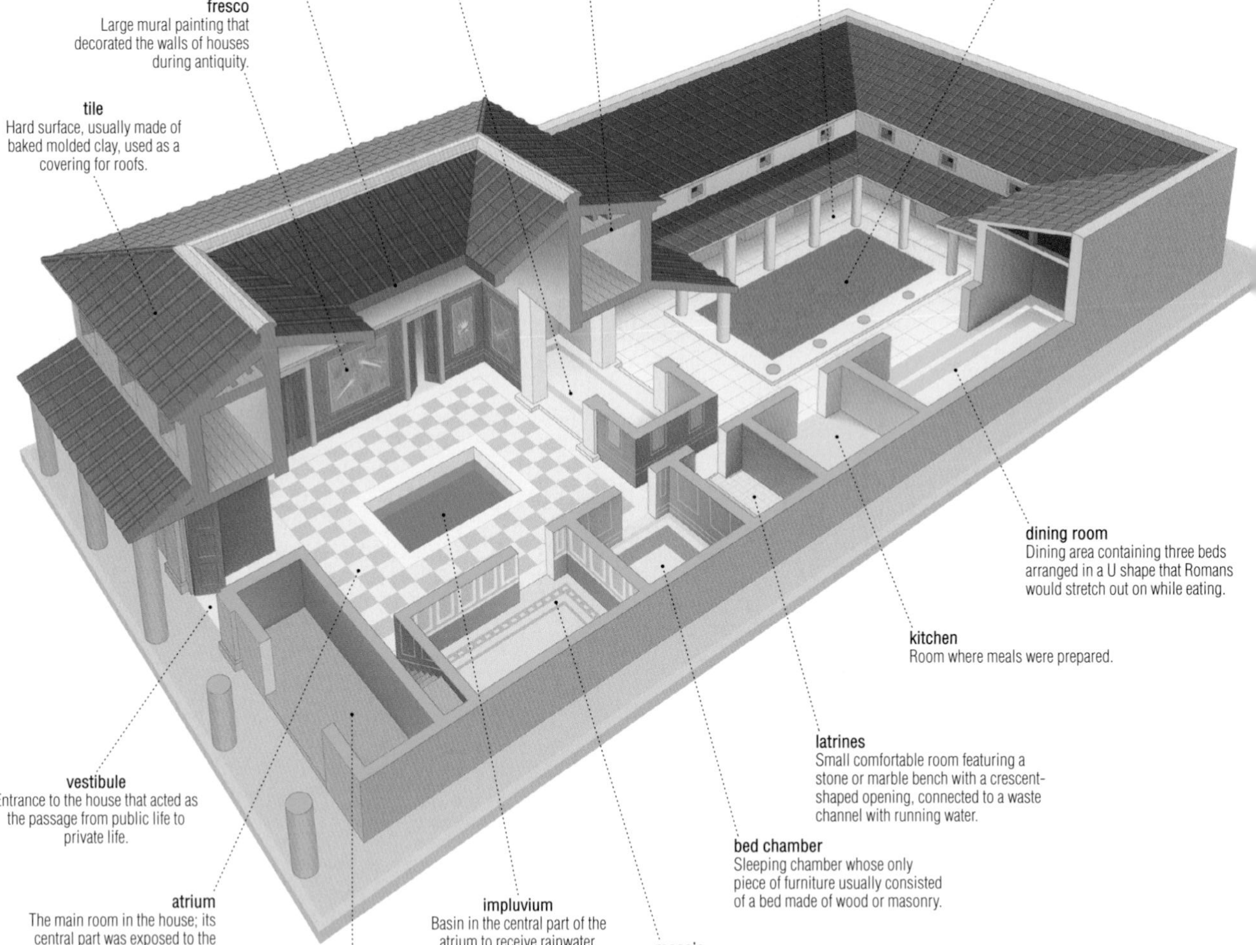

tablinum
Hall separating the peristyle from the atrium.
compluvium
Aperture built into the atrium roof to let rainwater pour into the impluvium.
timber
Framework of beams that supports the roof of the building and provides stability.
peristyle
Colonnade surrounding the inner court.
garden
Plot of land used to grow vegetables and decorated with flowers, shrubs, fountains and so forth.
fresco
Large mural painting that decorated the walls of houses during antiquity.
tile
Hard surface, usually made of baked molded clay, used as a covering for roofs.
dining room
Dining area containing three beds arranged in a U shape that Romans would stretch out on while eating.
kitchen
Room where meals were prepared.
latrines
Small comfortable room featuring a stone or marble bench with a crescent-shaped opening, connected to a waste channel with running water.
vestibule
Entrance to the house that acted as the passage from public life to private life.
bed chamber
Sleeping chamber whose only piece of furniture usually consisted of a bed made of wood or masonry.
atrium
The main room in the house; its central part was exposed to the open air to collect rainwater and let sunlight in.
impluvium
Basin in the central part of the atrium to receive rainwater.
mosaic
Collection of small fragments (e.g., stone, marble, terra-cotta) held together by mortar; it depicts a motif, and sometimes even very elaborate scenes.
shop
On the street side, the Roman house often included commercial spaces that were rented out to artisans and tradesmen.

Roman amphitheater

Oval or round building composed of an arena surrounded by tiers; it was used mainly to stage gladiator fights.

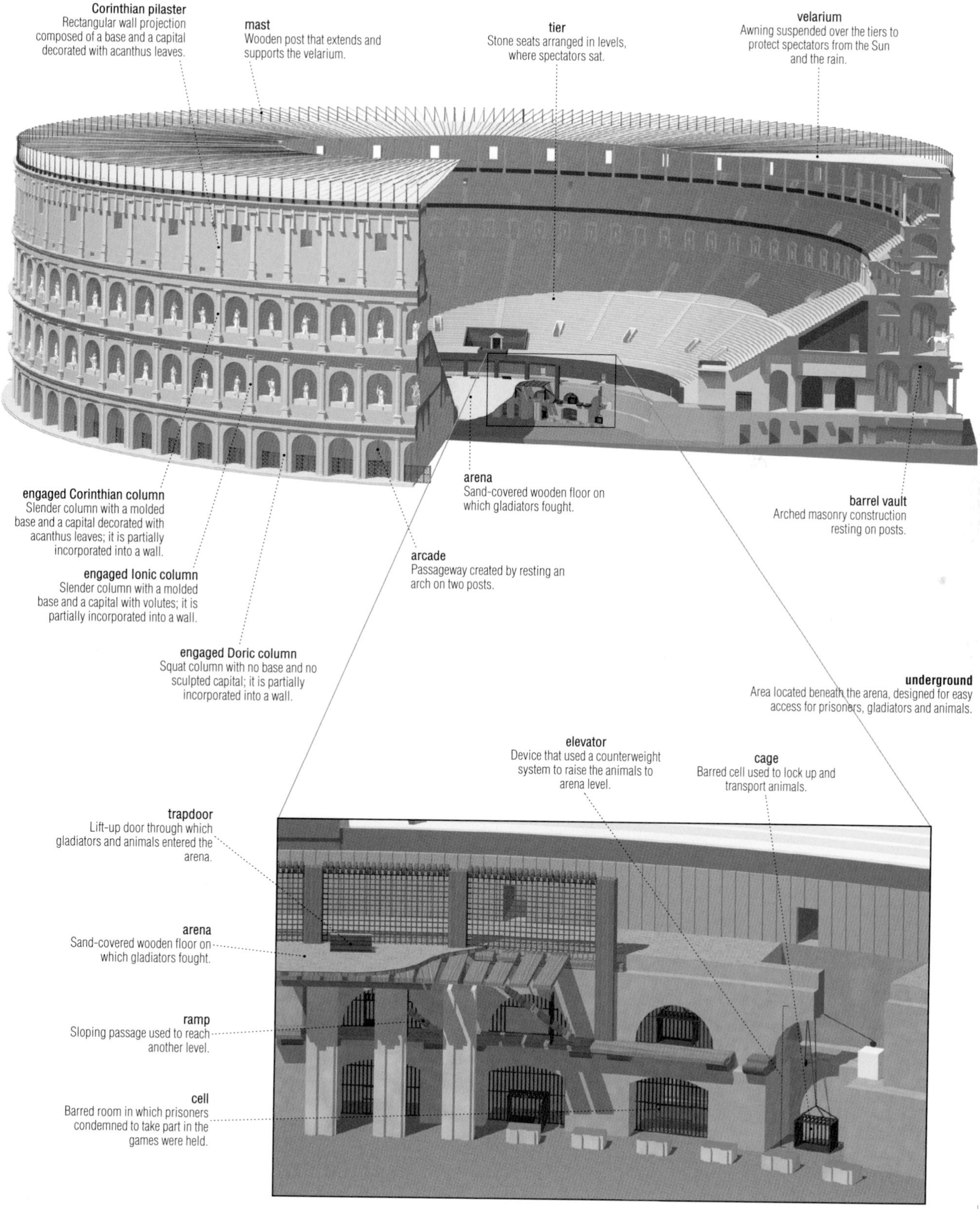
Corinthian pilaster
Rectangular wall projection composed of a base and a capital decorated with acanthus leaves.
mast
Wooden post that extends and supports the velarium.
tier
Stone seats arranged in levels, where spectators sat.
velarium
Awning suspended over the tiers to protect spectators from the Sun and the rain.
engaged Corinthian column
Slender column with a molded base and a capital decorated with acanthus leaves; it is partially incorporated into a wall.
engaged Ionic column
Slender column with a molded base and a capital with volutes; it is partially incorporated into a wall.
engaged Doric column
Squat column with no base and no sculpted capital; it is partially incorporated into a wall.
arena
Sand-covered wooden floor on which gladiators fought.
arcade
Passageway created by resting an arch on two posts.
barrel vault
Arched masonry construction resting on posts.
underground
Area located beneath the arena, designed for easy access for prisoners, gladiators and animals.
elevator
Device that used a counterweight system to raise the animals to arena level.
cage
Barred cell used to lock up and transport animals.
trapdoor
Lift-up door through which gladiators and animals entered the arena.
arena
Sand-covered wooden floor on which gladiators fought.
ramp
Sloping passage used to reach another level.
cell
Barred room in which prisoners condemned to take part in the games were held.

castle

Fortified residence of a feudal lord, designed to protect against assailants.

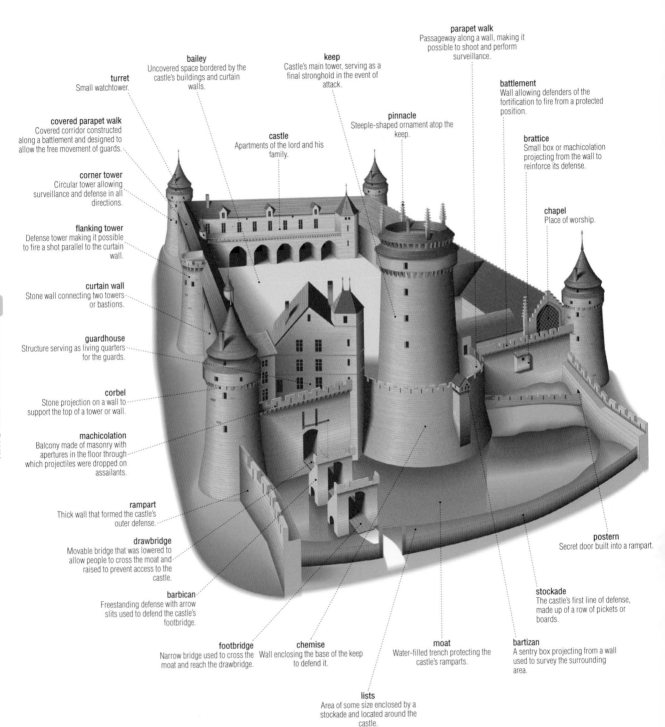

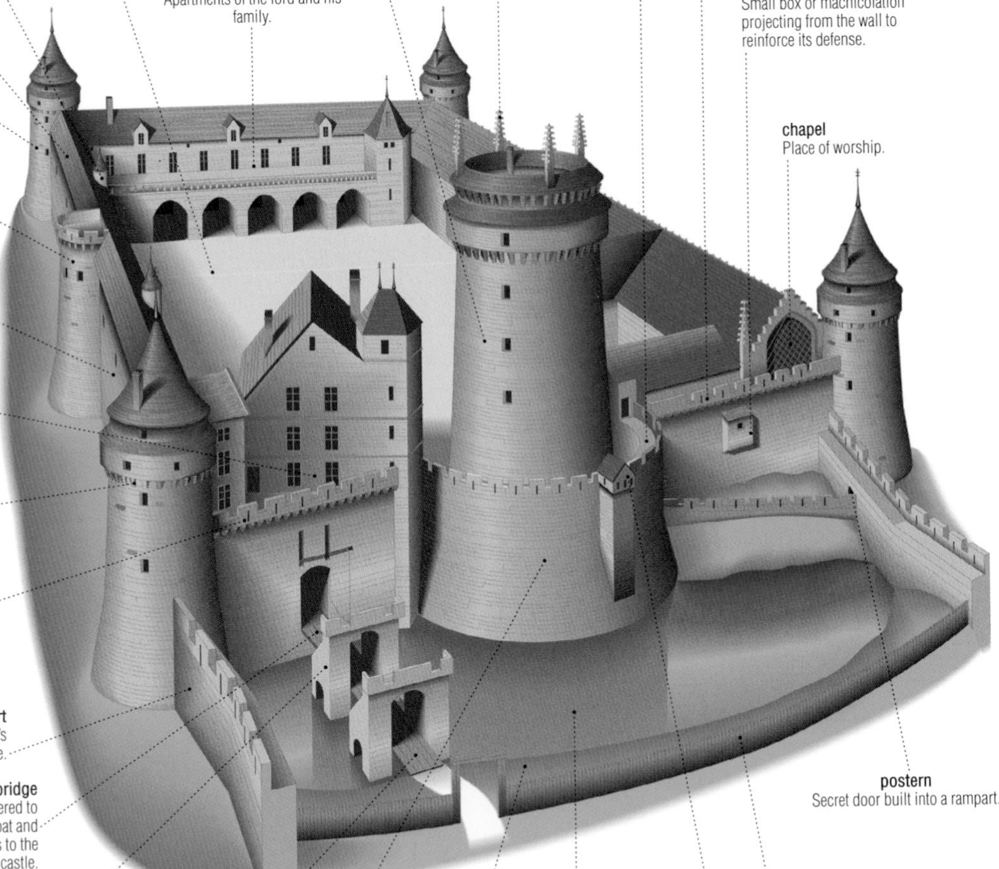

parapet walk
Passageway along a wall, making it possible to shoot and perform surveillance.
bailey
Uncovered space bordered by the castle's buildings and curtain walls.
keep
Castle's main tower, serving as a final stronghold in the event of attack.
turret
Small watchtower.
battlement
Wall allowing defenders of the fortification to fire from a protected position.
pinnacle
Steeple-shaped ornament atop the keep.
covered parapet walk
Covered corridor constructed along a battlement and designed to allow the free movement of guards.
castle
Apartments of the lord and his family.
brattice
Small box or machicolation projecting from the wall to reinforce its defense.
corner tower
Circular tower allowing surveillance and defense in all directions.
chapel
Place of worship.
flanking tower
Defense tower making it possible to fire a shot parallel to the curtain wall.
curtain wall
Stone wall connecting two towers or bastions.
guardhouse
Structure serving as living quarters for the guards.
corbel
Stone projection on a wall to support the top of a tower or wall.
machicolation
Balcony made of masonry with apertures in the floor through which projectiles were dropped on assailants.
rampart
Thick wall that formed the castle's outer defense.
drawbridge
Movable bridge that was lowered to allow people to cross the moat and raised to prevent access to the castle.
postern
Secret door built into a rampart.
barbican
Freestanding defense with arrow slits used to defend the castle's footbridge.
stockade
The castle's first line of defense, made up of a row of pickets or boards.
footbridge
Narrow bridge used to cross the moat and reach the drawbridge.
chemise
Wall enclosing the base of the keep to defend it.
moat
Water-filled trench protecting the castle's ramparts.
bartizan
A sentry box projecting from a wall used to survey the surrounding area.
lists
Area of some size enclosed by a stockade and located around the castle.

Vauban fortification

Star-shaped military fortification developed by the Frenchman Vauban in the 17th century.

parapet walk
Passageway along a wall, making it possible to shoot and perform surveillance.

retrenchment
Raised fortification of a bastion allowing the artillery to dominate the terrain.

scarp
Inner wall of a moat, closest to the fortified place.

bartizan
A sentry box projecting from a wall used to survey the surrounding area.

counterscarp
Outer wall of a moat, opposite the fortified place.

embrasure
Aperture in the battlement to allow for gun and cannon fire.

barrack buildings
Buildings used as living and instructional quarters for the garrison.

parade ground
Area serving for the assembly of troops.

battlement
Wall allowing defenders of the fortification to fire from a protected position.

flank
Part of the bastion between the curtain wall and the face, making it possible to fire parallel to the face of the neighboring bastion.

tenaille
Fortification made up of two faces forming an angle opening inward, placed in front of the curtain wall and designed to shield it.

bastion
A fortified projection consisting of two faces and two flanks, designed to reinforce a stronghold.

face
Side of the bastion exposed to the enemy.

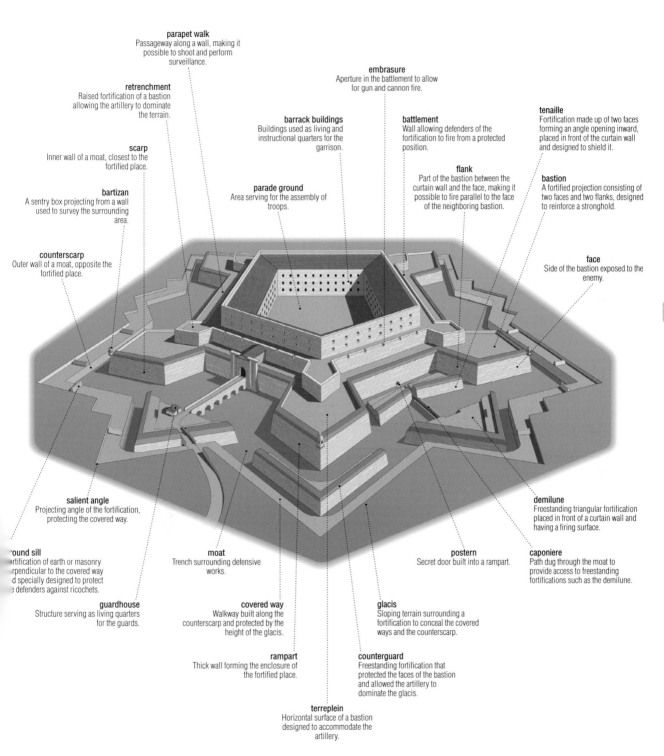

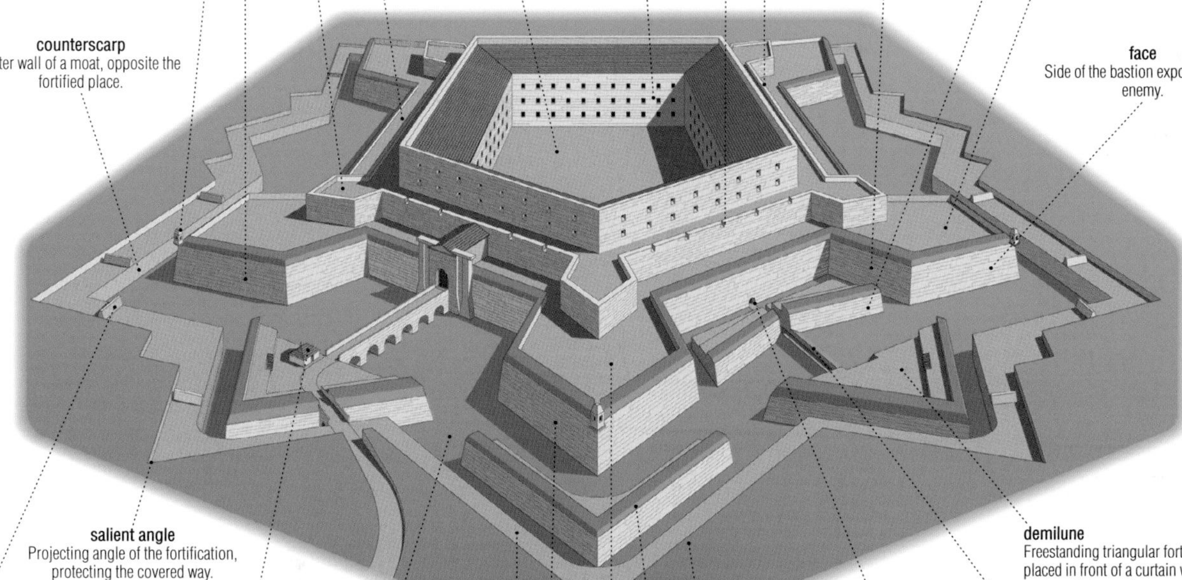

salient angle
Projecting angle of the fortification, protecting the covered way.

ound sill
rtification of earth or masonry rpendicular to the covered way d specially designed to protect e defenders against ricochets.

guardhouse
Structure serving as living quarters for the guards.

moat
Trench surrounding defensive works.

covered way
Walkway built along the counterscarp and protected by the height of the glacis.

rampart
Thick wall forming the enclosure of the fortified place.

terreplein
Horizontal surface of a bastion designed to accommodate the artillery.

glacis
Sloping terrain surrounding a fortification to conceal the covered ways and the counterscarp.

counterguard
Freestanding fortification that protected the faces of the bastion and allowed the artillery to dominate the glacis.

postern
Secret door built into a rampart.

demilune
Freestanding triangular fortification placed in front of a curtain wall and having a firing surface.

caponiere
Path dug through the moat to provide access to freestanding fortifications such as the demilune.

cathedral

The main church of a diocese, the site of the bishop's see.

Gothic cathedral
The architectural style of the medieval cathedral (12th century to the Renaissance) is characterized mainly by its ribbed, ogival vaults.

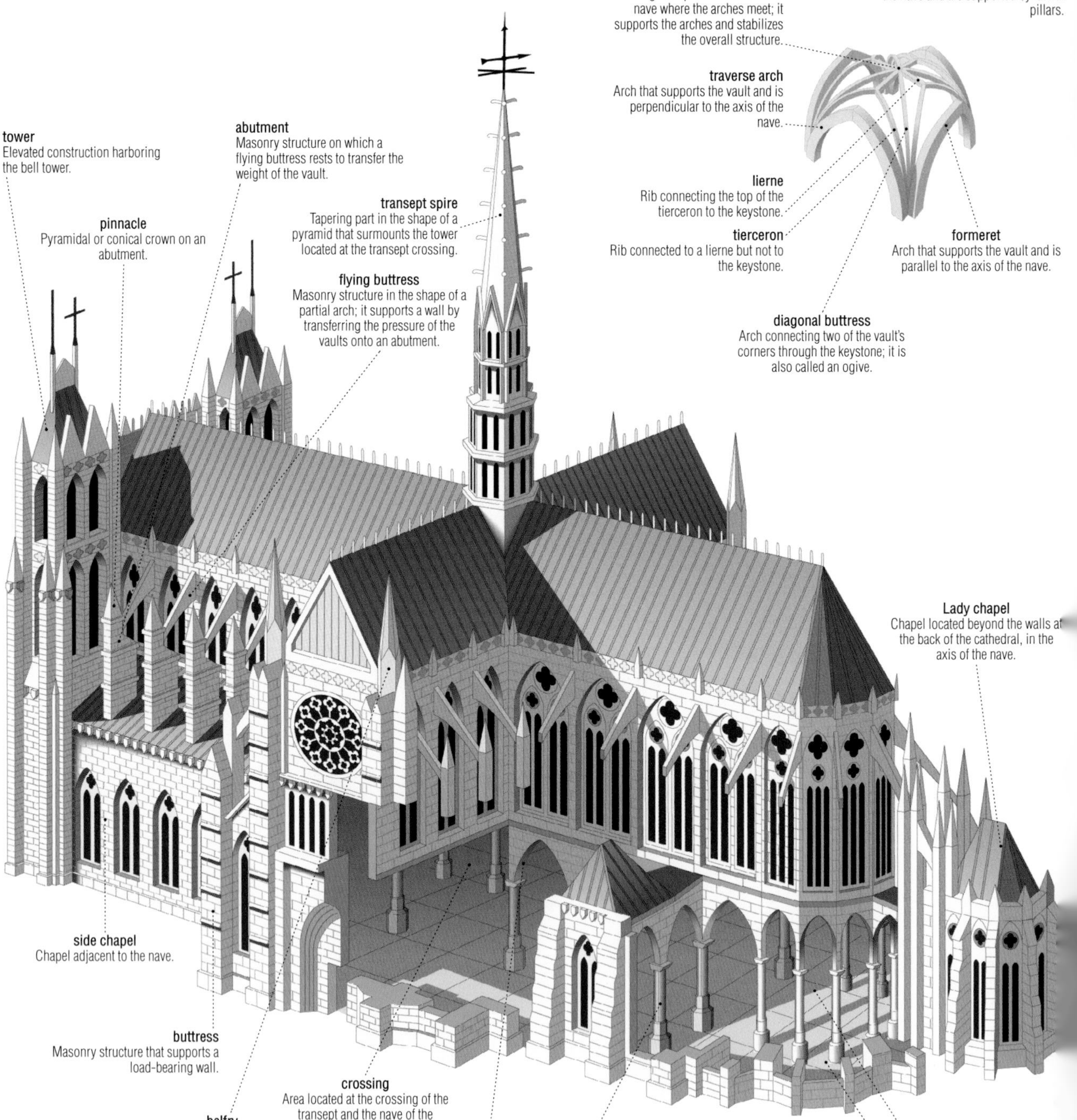
vault
The vault of a Gothic cathedral rests on a series of arches that cross at the summit of the nave and are supported by lateral pillars.
keystone
Wedge-shaped stone above the nave where the arches meet; it supports the arches and stabilizes the overall structure.
traverse arch
Arch that supports the vault and is perpendicular to the axis of the nave.
lierne
Rib connecting the top of the tierceron to the keystone.
tierceron
Rib connected to a lierne but not to the keystone.
formeret
Arch that supports the vault and is parallel to the axis of the nave.
diagonal buttress
Arch connecting two of the vault's corners through the keystone; it is also called an ogive.
tower
Elevated construction harboring the bell tower.
abutment
Masonry structure on which a flying buttress rests to transfer the weight of the vault.
pinnacle
Pyramidal or conical crown on an abutment.
transept spire
Tapering part in the shape of a pyramid that surmounts the tower located at the transept crossing.
flying buttress
Masonry structure in the shape of a partial arch; it supports a wall by transferring the pressure of the vaults onto an abutment.
Lady chapel
Chapel located beyond the walls at the back of the cathedral, in the axis of the nave.
side chapel
Chapel adjacent to the nave.
buttress
Masonry structure that supports a load-bearing wall.
crossing
Area located at the crossing of the transept and the nave of the cathedral.
belfry
Small steeplelike ornament in the shape of a pyramid; it is found on the corners of the transept or on each side of the façade.
arcade
Passageway created by resting an arch on two posts.
pillar
Column designed to support a masonry structure.
apsidiole
Small lateral chapel arranged in a semicircle behind the choir surrounding the apse.
choir
Area just beyond the transept where the clergy stand during th liturgy.

cathedral

façade

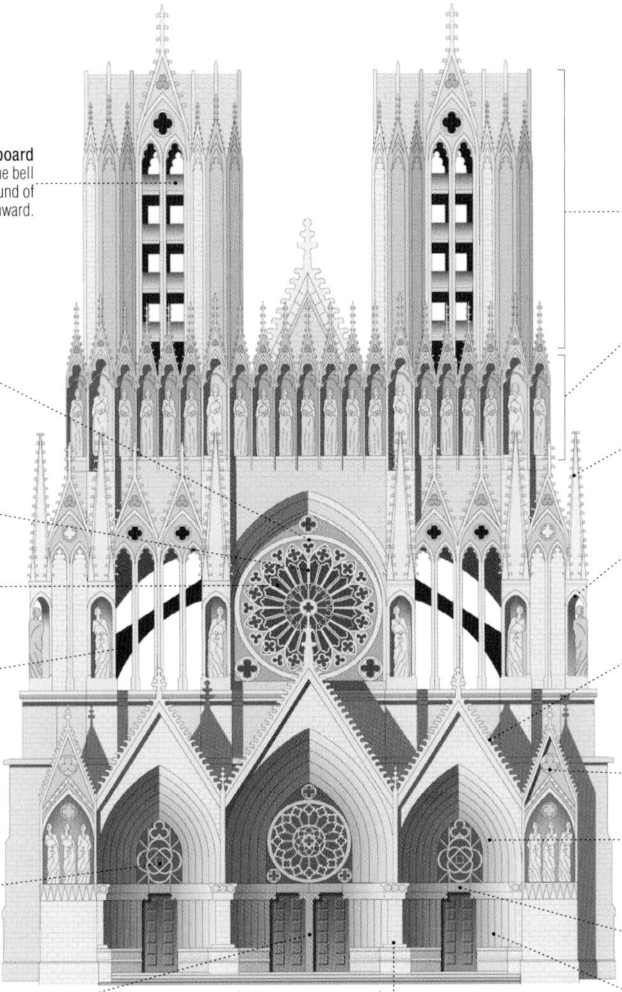
louver-board
Inclined slat located in the bell tower bay; it projects the sound of the bells downward.
rose window
Large circular bay composed of decorative tracery and stained glass; it is also called a rosette.
tracery
Stone framework adorning the inside of a bay.
stained glass
Translucent decorative work comprised of an assemblage of glass pieces, usually colored, that fills a bay.
flying buttress
Masonry structure in the shape of a partial arch; it supports a wall by transferring the pressure of the vaults onto an abutment.
tympanum
Flat portion of the portal above the door and between the orders.
pier
Pillar dividing the portal in two and supporting the lintels.
portal
Ornamental architectural feature of a façade containing one or several doors.
pier
Masonry pillar supporting the orders.
bell tower
Tower with bays in which the bells are hung.
gallery
Covered passage along the cathedral's façade, decorated with statues.
spire
Tapering part in the shape of a pyramid that surmounts the belfry.
belfry
Small steeplelike ornament in the shape of a pyramid; it is found on the corners of the transept or on each side of the façade.
gable
Triangular decorative element with molded edges, located above the portal.
trefoil
Ornamental motif comprised of three lobes.
order
Each of the receding arches that form a vault over a portal.
lintel
Horizontal section of the door frame that fills the opening above a door or portal.
splay
Recessed side of the portal that widens from its inside to its outside edge.

plan

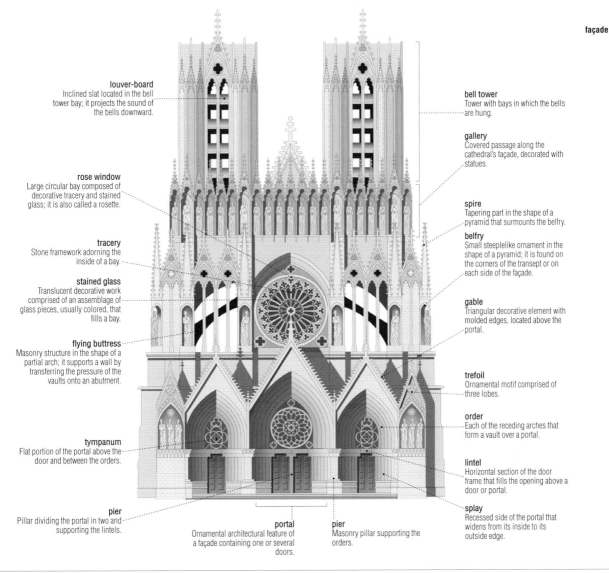

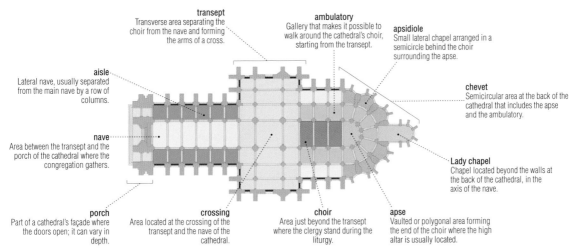

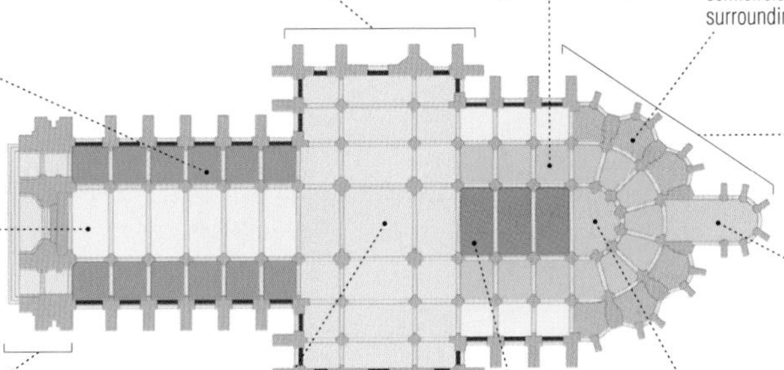
transept
Transverse area separating the choir from the nave and forming the arms of a cross.
ambulatory
Gallery that makes it possible to walk around the cathedral's choir, starting from the transept.
apsidiole
Small lateral chapel arranged in a semicircle behind the choir surrounding the apse.
aisle
Lateral nave, usually separated from the main nave by a row of columns.
chevet
Semicircular area at the back of the cathedral that includes the apse and the ambulatory.
nave
Area between the transept and the porch of the cathedral where the congregation gathers.
Lady chapel
Chapel located beyond the walls at the back of the cathedral, in the axis of the nave.
porch
Part of a cathedral's façade where the doors open; it can vary in depth.
crossing
Area located at the crossing of the transept and the nave of the cathedral.
choir
Area just beyond the transept where the clergy stand during the liturgy.
apse
Vaulted or polygonal area forming the end of the choir where the high altar is usually located.

pagoda

Place of worship for Buddhists of the Far East, usually made up of a series of stories, each with its own roof.

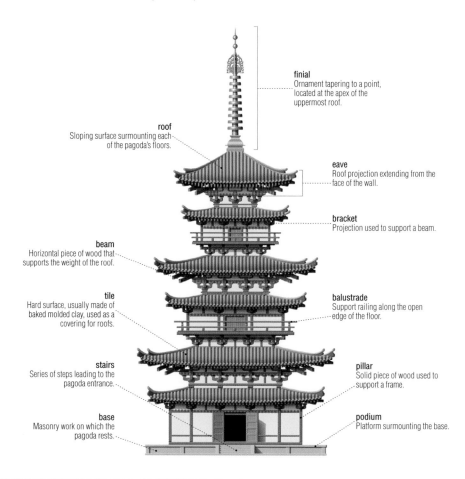

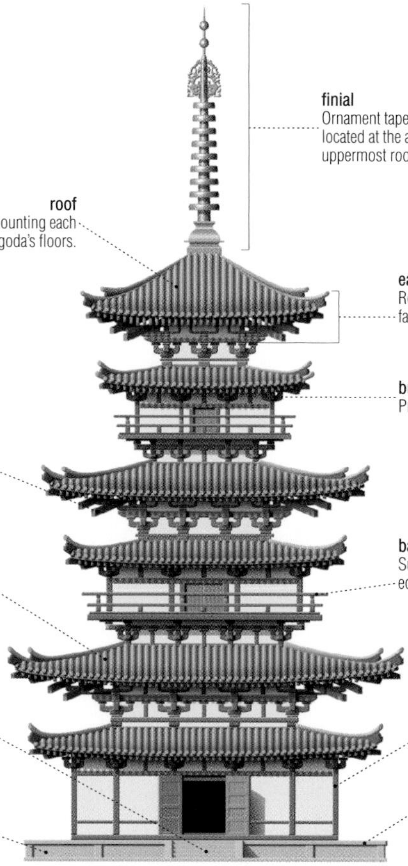
finial
Ornament tapering to a point, located at the apex of the uppermost roof.
roof
Sloping surface surmounting each of the pagoda's floors.
eave
Roof projection extending from the face of the wall.
bracket
Projection used to support a beam.
beam
Horizontal piece of wood that supports the weight of the roof.
tile
Hard surface, usually made of baked molded clay, used as a covering for roofs.
balustrade
Support railing along the open edge of the floor.
stairs
Series of steps leading to the pagoda entrance.
pillar
Solid piece of wood used to support a frame.
base
Masonry work on which the pagoda rests.
podium
Platform surmounting the base.

Aztec temple

Pyramid-shaped religious edifice of pre-Columbian Mexico featuring one or several temples.

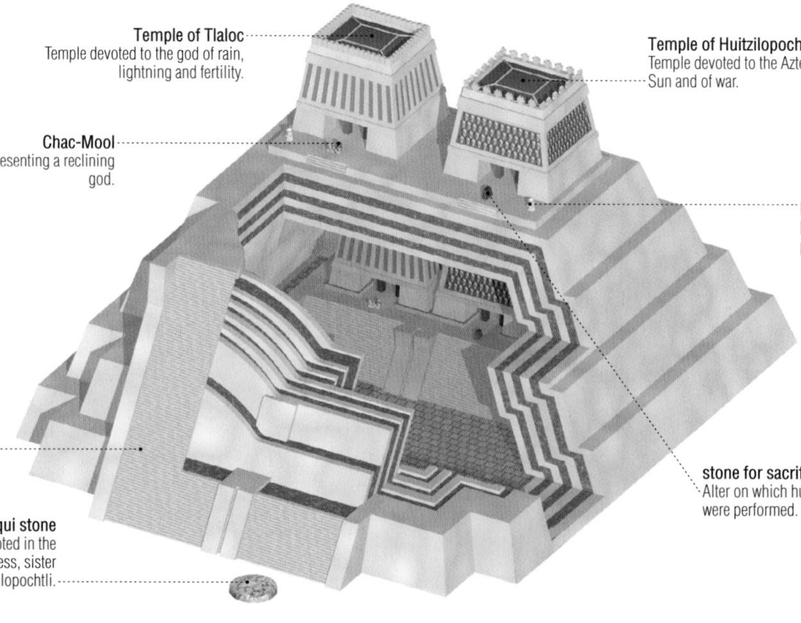
Temple of Tlaloc
Temple devoted to the god of rain, lightning and fertility.
Temple of Huitzilopochtli
Temple devoted to the Aztec god of the Sun and of war.
Chac-Mool
Sculpture representing a reclining god.
brazier
Receptacle in which the heart of the person sacrificed was burned.
stairways
Series of steps leading to the summit of the pyramid.
stone for sacrifice
Alter on which human sacrifices were performed.
Coyolxauhqui stone
Block of stone sculpted in the image of the Moon goddess, sister of Huitzilopochtli.

elements of architecture

Collective term for the components used in the construction of buildings.

semicircular arch
Arch in the form of a semicircle.

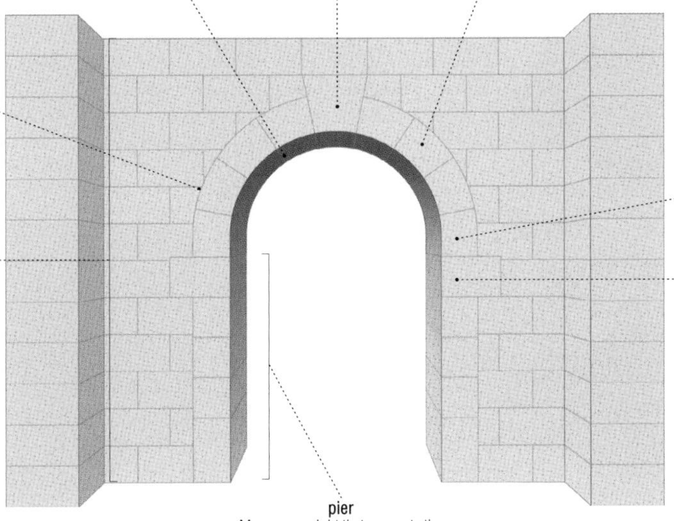
keystone
Wedge-shaped stone in the center of an arch whose function is to balance the network of voussoirs.
intrados
Interior surface of the arch.
voussoir
Each of the stone wedges that make up the arch.
extrados
Exterior surface of the arch.
springer
Stone that constitutes the arch's first voussoir and is placed on top of the pier.
spandrel
Wall surface bordered by the curve of the arch, the start of another wall and the horizontal part above it.
impost
Slightly projecting stone that surmounts the pier and supports the springer and the voussoirs.
pier
Masonry upright that supports the arch.

examples of arches

Arches: curved constructions supported on each side by piers.

equilateral
Arch forming an acute angle that is characteristic of the Gothic vault.

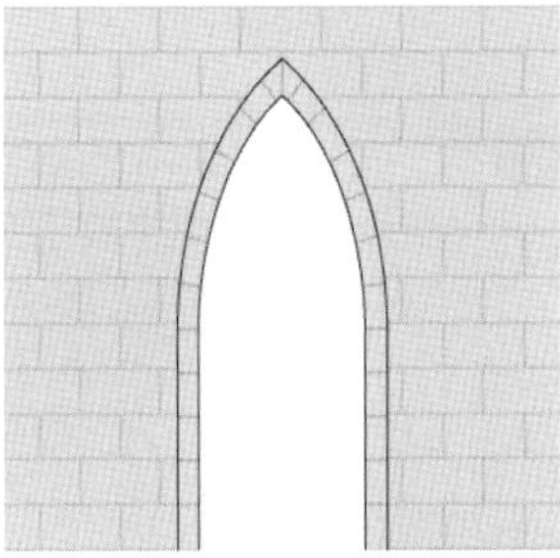

lancet
Equilateral arch whose span, or distance between the piers, is reduced.

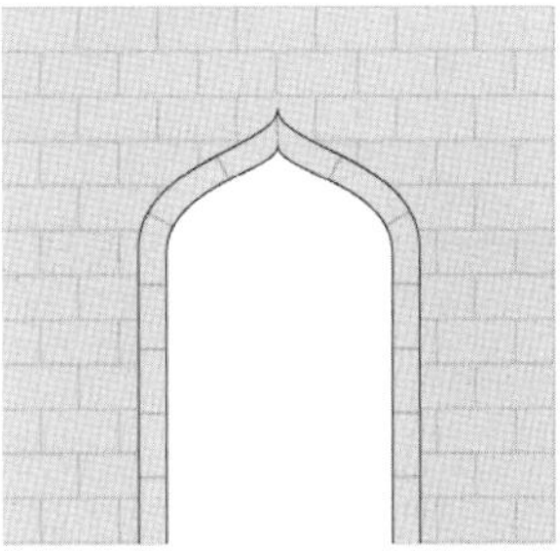

ogee
Arch comprised of two symmetrical curves that are alternately convex and concave.

horseshoe
Arch whose extremities extend beyond a semicircle; it is characteristic of Arab architecture.

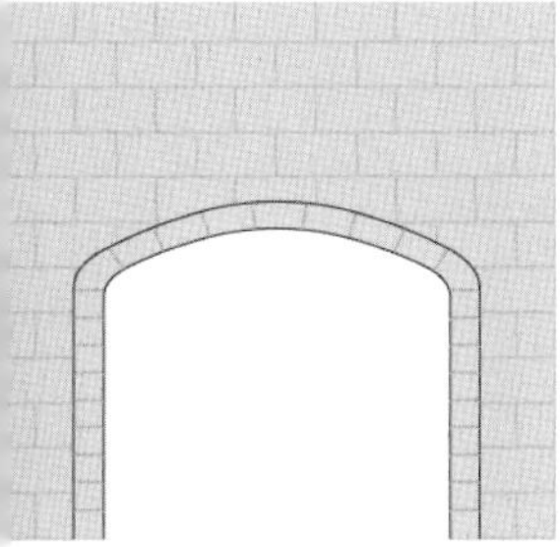

basket handle
Arch that is lower than it is wide and forms an ellipse.

stilted
Arch that takes the form of a semicircle but is higher than the semicircular arch.

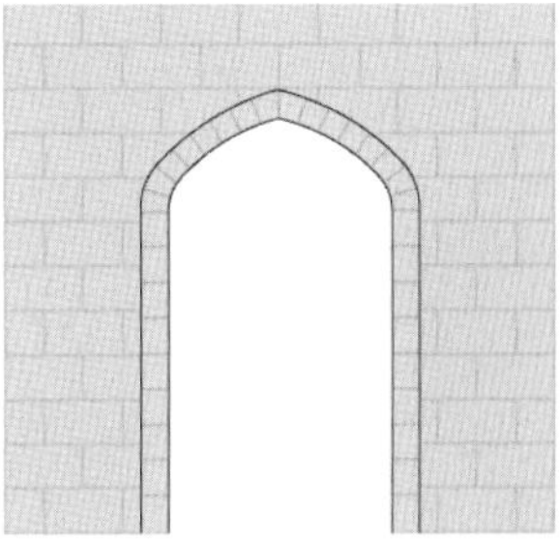

Tudor
Flattened equilateral arch that is characteristic of the style that flourished in 16th-century England.

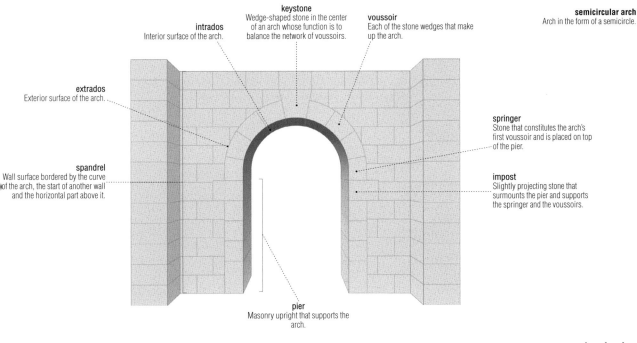

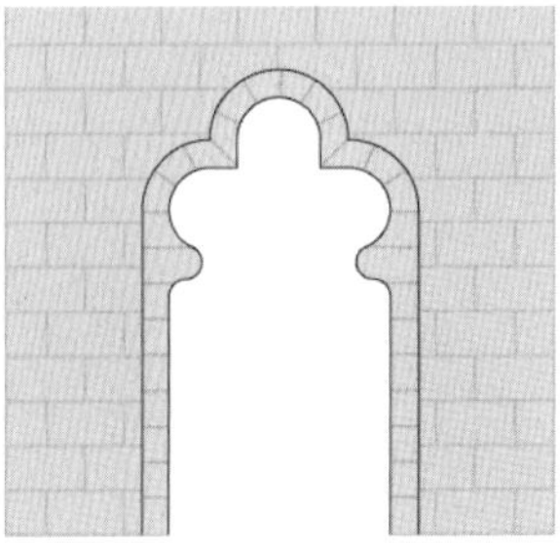

trefoil
Arch with three lobes.

elements of architecture

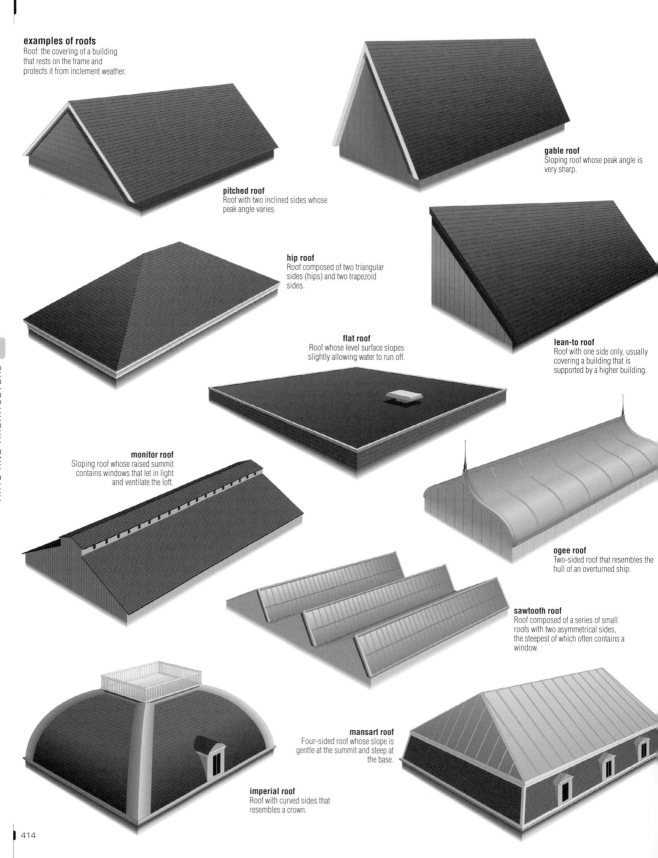

examples of roofs

Roof: the covering of a building that rests on the frame and protects it from inclement weather.

pitched roof
Roof with two inclined sides whose peak angle varies.

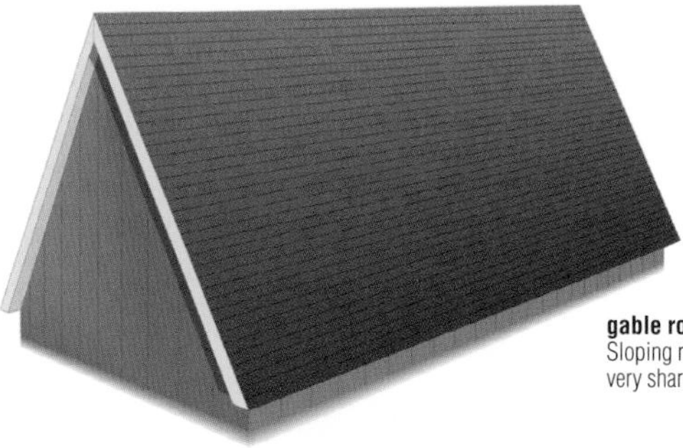

gable roof
Sloping roof whose peak angle is very sharp.

hip roof
Roof composed of two triangular sides (hips) and two trapezoid sides.

lean-to roof
Roof with one side only, usually covering a building that is supported by a higher building.

flat roof
Roof whose level surface slopes slightly allowing water to run off.

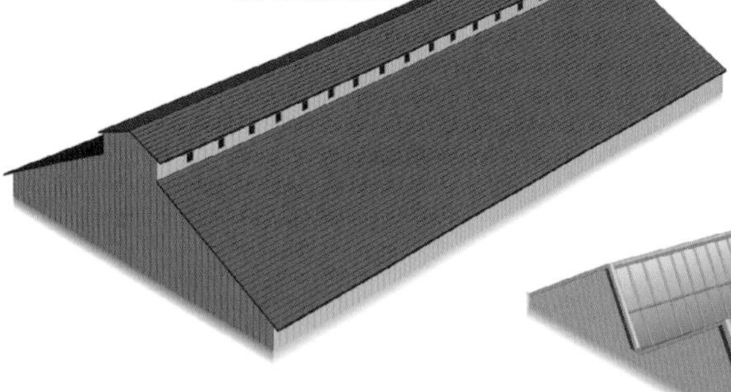

monitor roof
Sloping roof whose raised summit contains windows that let in light and ventilate the loft.

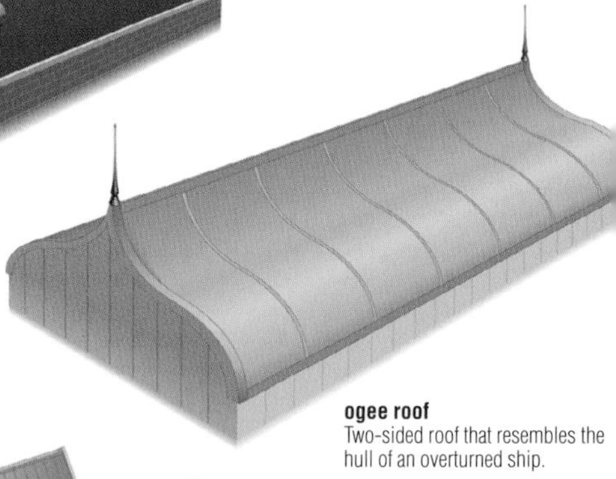

ogee roof
Two-sided roof that resembles the hull of an overturned ship.

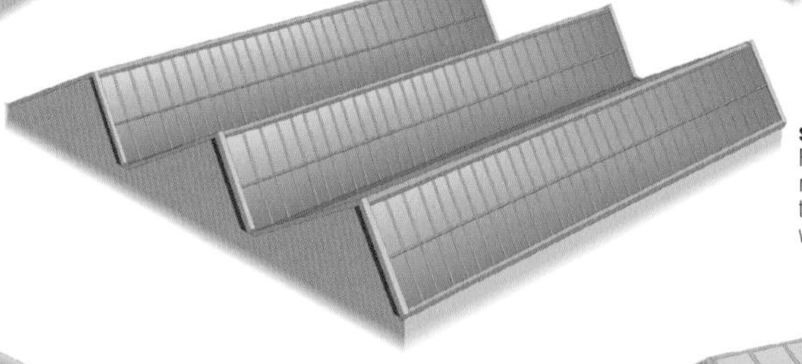

sawtooth roof
Roof composed of a series of small roofs with two asymmetrical sides, the steepest of which often contains a window.

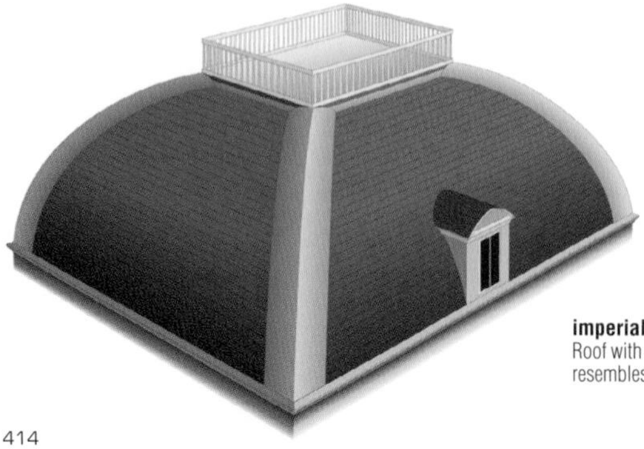

imperial roof
Roof with curved sides that resembles a crown.

mansart roof
Four-sided roof whose slope is gentle at the summit and steep at the base.

elements of architecture

pavilion roof
Roof with four triangular sides that form a pyramid.

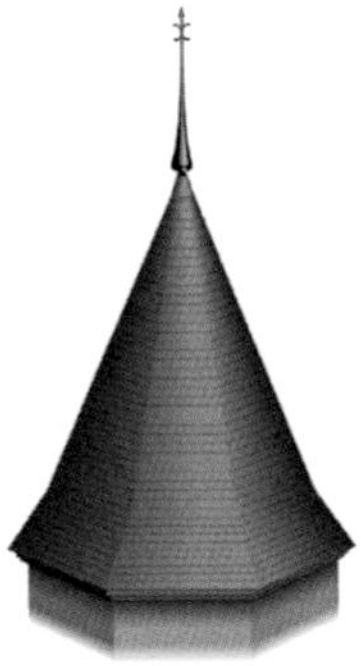

sloped turret
Many-sided roof whose slope is steep at the summit and gentle at the base.

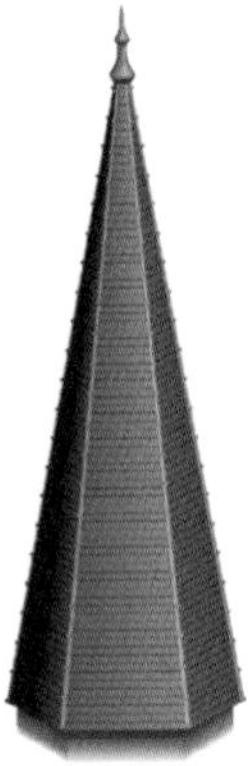

helm roof
Pyramidal or conical roof that usually surmounts a tower or bell tower.

bell roof
Roof covering the hollow semicircular vault of a building (dome).

conical broach roof
Conical roof usually surmounting a turret.

dome roof
Roof covering a large dome that sometimes rises above the rest of the roof.

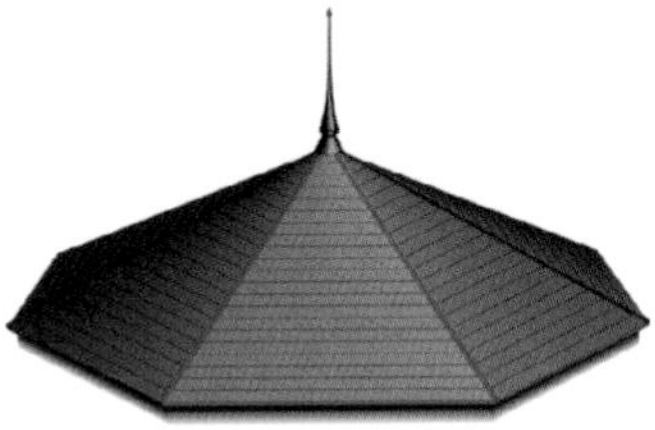

rotunda roof
Roof with several triangular sides on a polygonal base.

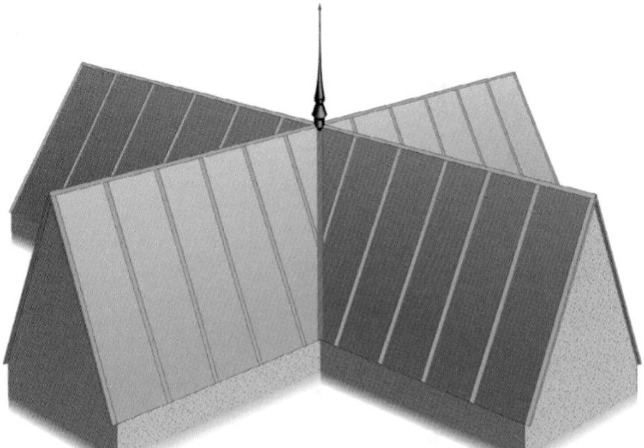

hip-and-valley roof
Roof formed where two gable roofs cross.

examples of windows

Windows: bays built into a wall and containing glass to let in light and air.

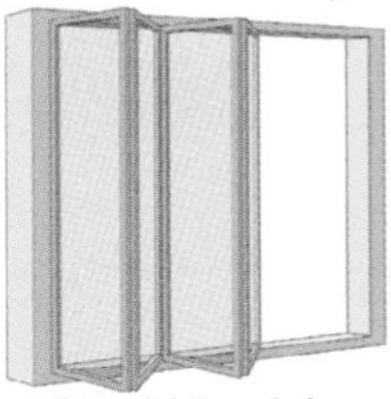

sliding folding window
Sliding window whose sash is composed of a series of articulated panels that fold together when opened.

French window
Window with two sashes that open in, pivoting vertically along a hanging stile.

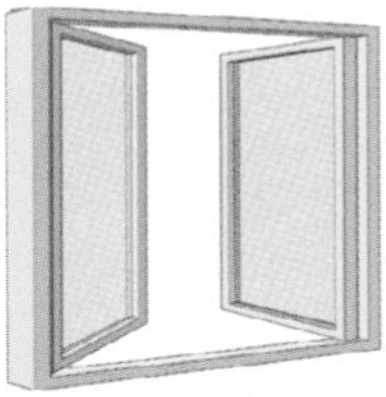

casement window
Window with one or two sashes that open out, pivoting vertically along a hanging stile.

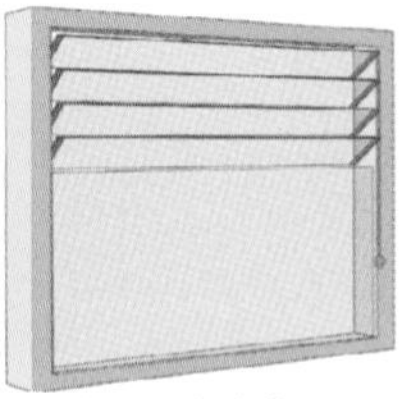

louvered window
Window whose glass louvers rotate along a horizontal axis.

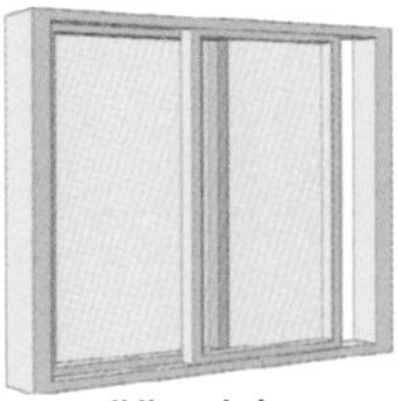

sliding window
Window with one or more sashes that move horizontally along a groove.

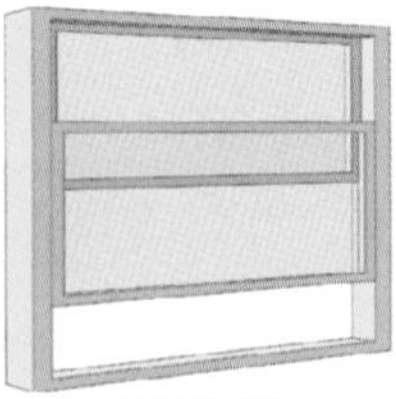

sash window
Window with one or more overlapping sashes that slide open vertically.

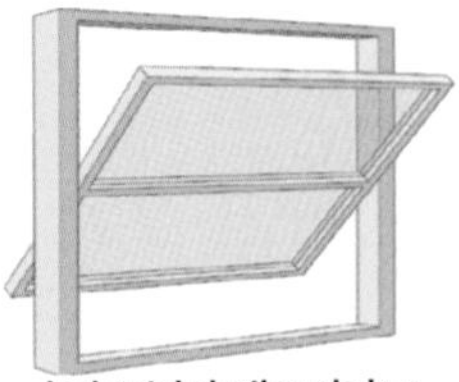

horizontal pivoting window
Window whose sash rotates along a horizontal axis located at its midpoint.

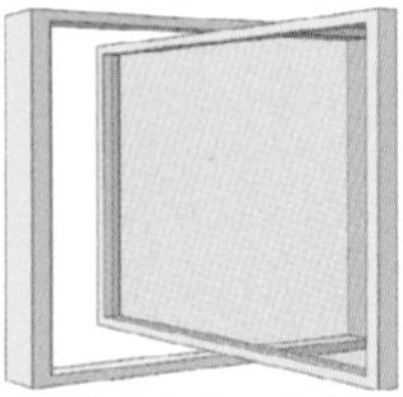

vertical pivoting window
Window whose sash rotates along a vertical axis located at its midpoint.

elements of architecture

examples of doors

Doors: composed of a movable part, the wing, and a frame; their function is to close up a bay.

manual revolving door
Rotating door comprised of three or four plateglass wings that, when pushed, pivot around a vertical axis in the manner of a turnstile.

canopy
Metal ring forming the upper part of the enclosure, where the guide rail for the wings is located.

wing
One of the vertical sections of the revolving door.

enclosure
Intermediary space between two rooms or a room and the outside, where the door is placed.

push bar
Horizontal part that is pushed to move the revolving door.

compartment
Part bordered by two wings where one or more people enter and push the door to make it rotate.

motion detector
Device that detects the presence of a person and is set to open and close the wings.

automatic sliding do
Door activated by a motion detect that causes the wings to sli along a ra

wing
The part of the door that moves.

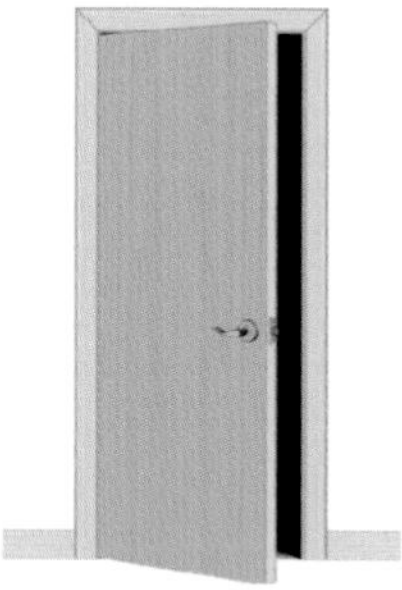

conventional door
Door made up of a wing that opens and closes by pivoting on hinges.

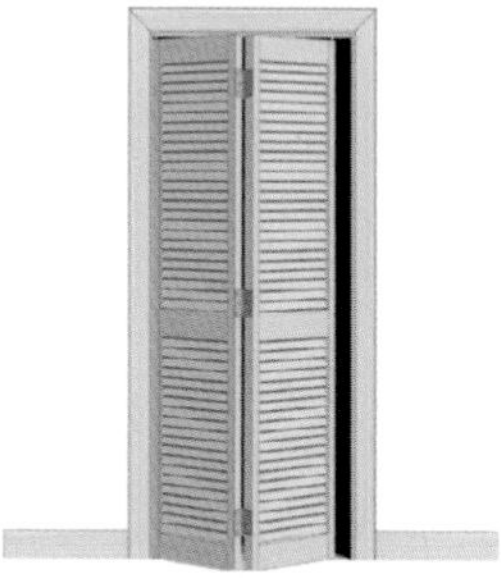

folding door
Sliding door whose wing is composed of two articulated panels that fold together when opened.

strip
Each of the flexible plastic bands that overlap to close the bay and move apart to allow a person through.

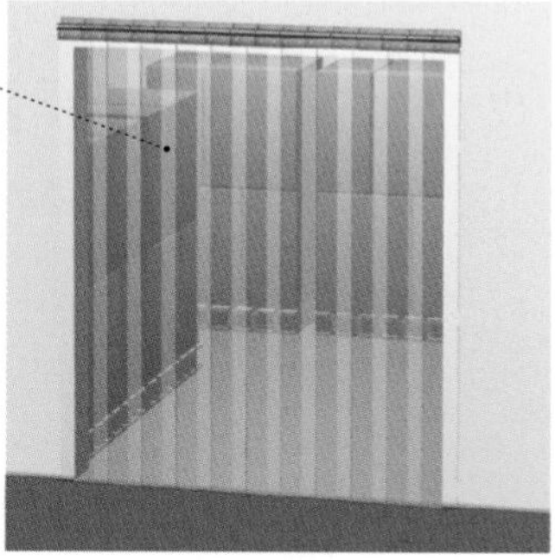

strip door
Door comprised of strips of flexible plastic; it allows easy movement between two rooms.

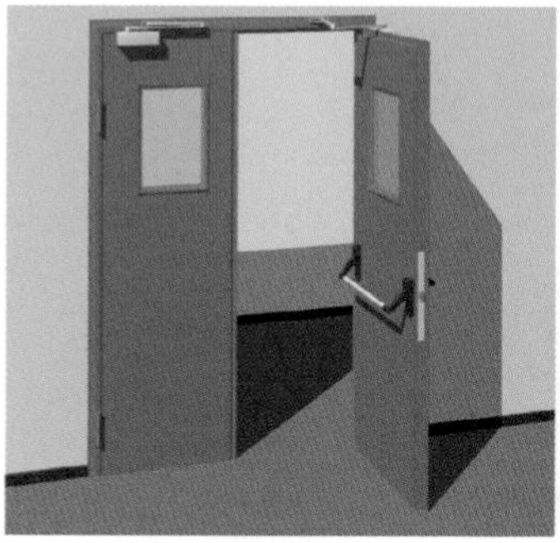

fire door
Fireproof door that delays the spread of flames and smoke during a fire.

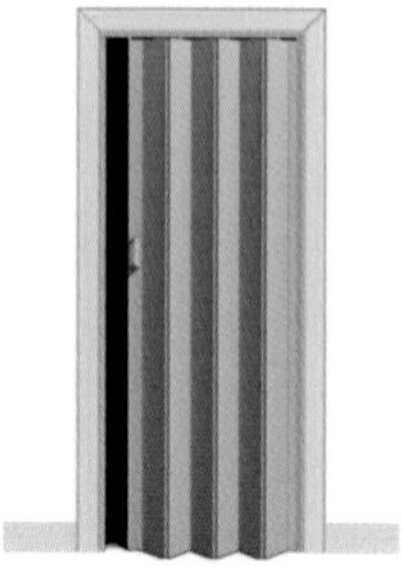

sliding folding door
Sliding door whose wing is composed of articulated panels that fold together when opened.

sliding door
Panel or panels of a door sliding horizontally along a set of tracks.

sectional garage door
Door whose wing is composed of articulated horizontal panels that slide along rails into the roof of the garage.

up and over garage door
Door made up of a wing that slides toward the ceiling of the garage.

escalator

Installation that consists of articulated steps on a continuously turning chain; it allows movement between two levels of a building.

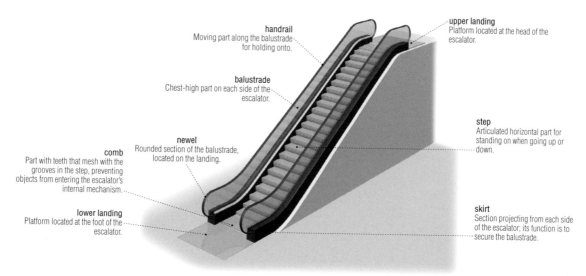

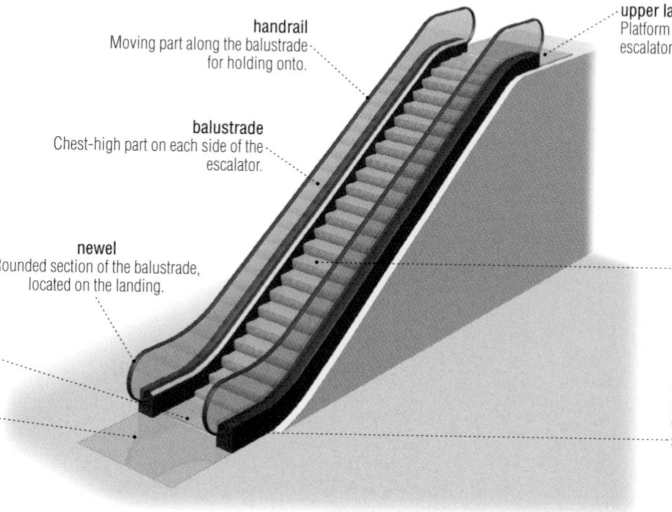
handrail
Moving part along the balustrade for holding onto.
upper landing
Platform located at the head of the escalator.
balustrade
Chest-high part on each side of the escalator.
step
Articulated horizontal part for standing on when going up or down.
newel
Rounded section of the balustrade, located on the landing.
comb
Part with teeth that mesh with the grooves in the step, preventing objects from entering the escalator's internal mechanism.
lower landing
Platform located at the foot of the escalator.
skirt
Section projecting from each side of the escalator; its function is to secure the balustrade.

elevator

Mechanical apparatus with a car that provides automated movement of people between the levels of a building.

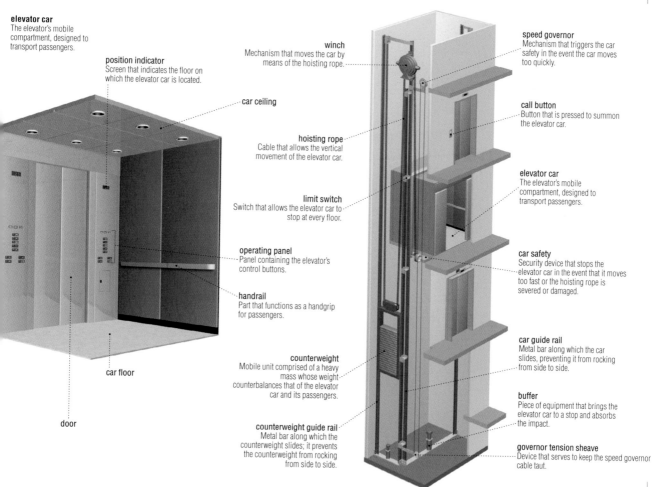

elevator car
The elevator's mobile compartment, designed to transport passengers.
position indicator
Screen that indicates the floor on which the elevator car is located.
car ceiling
operating panel
Panel containing the elevator's control buttons.
handrail
Part that functions as a handgrip for passengers.
car floor
door

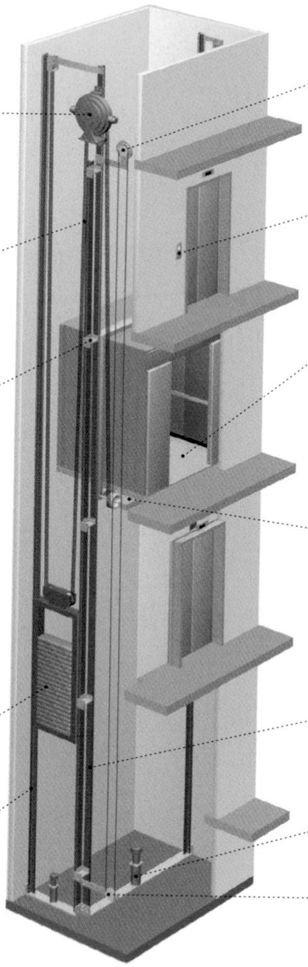
winch
Mechanism that moves the car by means of the hoisting rope.
speed governor
Mechanism that triggers the car safety in the event the car moves too quickly.
call button
Button that is pressed to summon the elevator car.
hoisting rope
Cable that allows the vertical movement of the elevator car.
elevator car
The elevator's mobile compartment, designed to transport passengers.
limit switch
Switch that allows the elevator car to stop at every floor.
car safety
Security device that stops the elevator car in the event that it moves too fast or the hoisting rope is severed or damaged.
car guide rail
Metal bar along which the car slides, preventing it from rocking from side to side.
counterweight
Mobile unit comprised of a heavy mass whose weight counterbalances that of the elevator car and its passengers.
buffer
Piece of equipment that brings the elevator car to a stop and absorbs the impact.
counterweight guide rail
Metal bar along which the counterweight slides; it prevents the counterweight from rocking from side to side.
governor tension sheave
Device that serves to keep the speed governor cable taut.

traditional houses

The dwellings, current or of former times, that characterize a given culture.

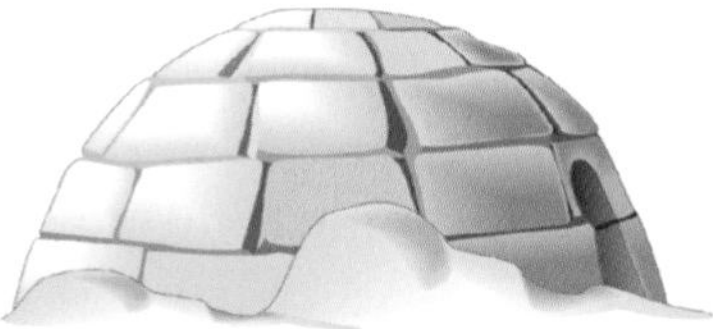

igloo
Dome-shaped Inuit dwelling made of blocks of snow or ice.

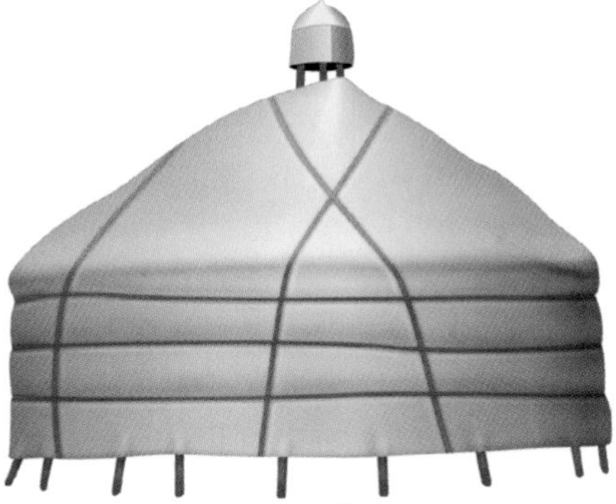

yurt
Portable dwelling of the nomadic peoples of central and northern Asia composed of a wooden frame covered with felt.

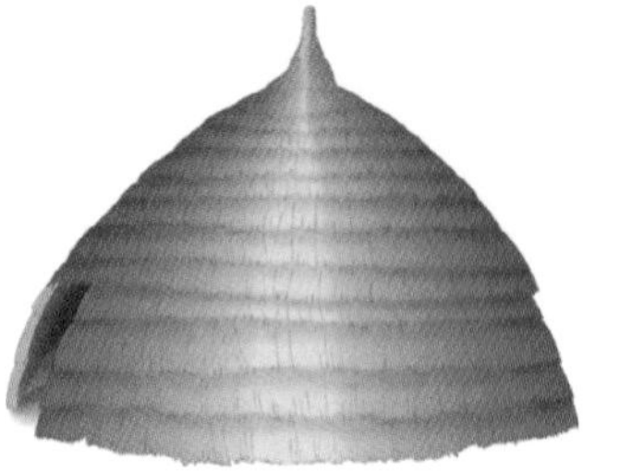

hut
Rudimentary dwelling made from tree branches and straw.

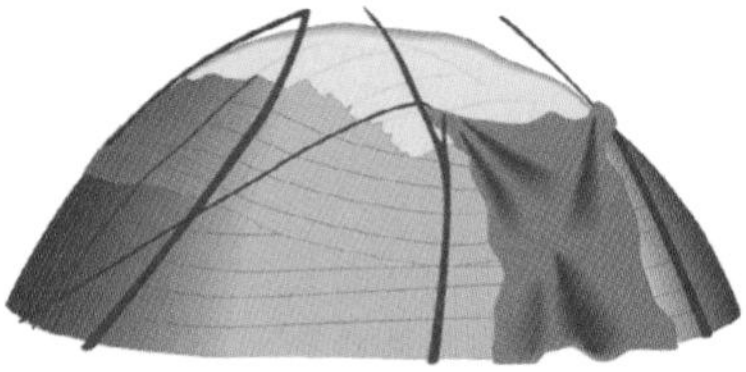

wigwam
Round or oval dwelling of North American Indians made of poles covered with bark, matting and skins.

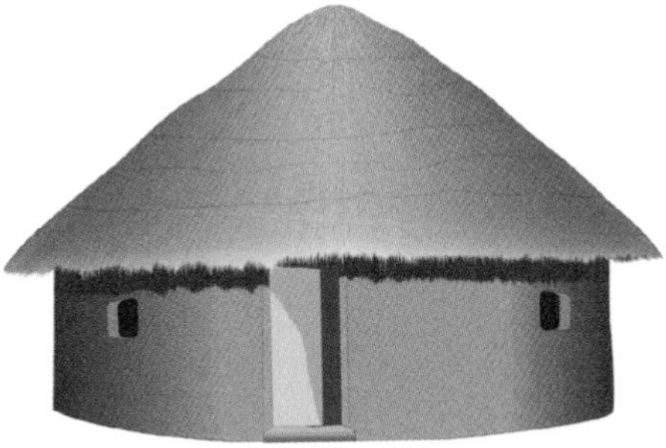

hut
Dwelling of African countries, usually made of straw and clay and covered with a straw roof.

isba
Dwelling of various countries in northern Europe, especially Russia, made of the wood of the fir tree.

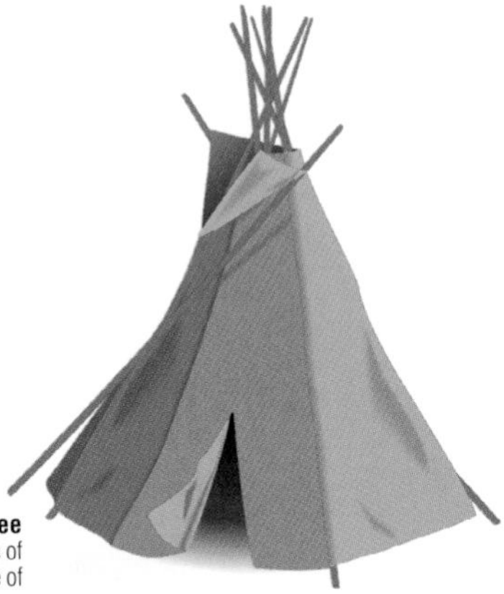

tepee
Conical dwelling of the Indians of the North American plains, made of poles covered with skins.

pile dwelling
Dwelling built over water or wet land and supported by posts.

adobe house
Dwellings found in Latin America and southwestern U.S. made of clay bricks and sun-dried straw.

beam
Heavy horizontal piece that transfers the weight of the roof onto the support structure.

ladder
Movable wooden implement with rungs, for reaching the roof.

city houses

Dwelling types found in large urban centers.

two-story house
Single-family dwelling that contains two levels, the first floor and a second floor.

one-story house
Single-family dwelling that contains only one level, the first floor.

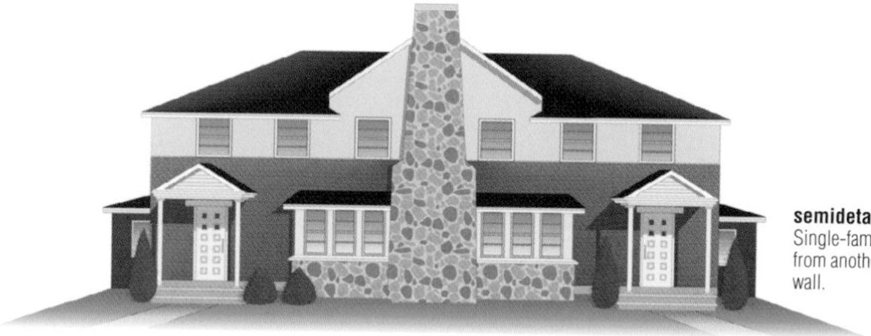

semidetached cottage
Single-family dwelling separated from another dwelling by a party wall.

town houses
Houses of the same height built in more or less the same style and separated by party walls.

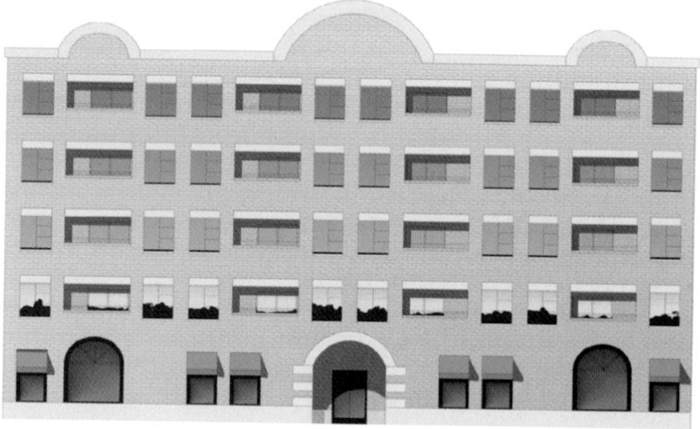

condominiums
Group of lodgings belonging to separate owners who share the building's maintenance costs.

high-rise apartment
Tall building containing multiple dwellings.

printing

Reproduction of characters or illustrations by transferring a model to a surface, usually paper, most often using ink.

relief printing
Process that consists of printing an image from a raised figure covered with a film of ink; the image is transferred to a surface by means of pressure.

intaglio printing
Process that consists of printing an image from an incised figure filled with ink; the image is transferred to a surface by means of pressure.

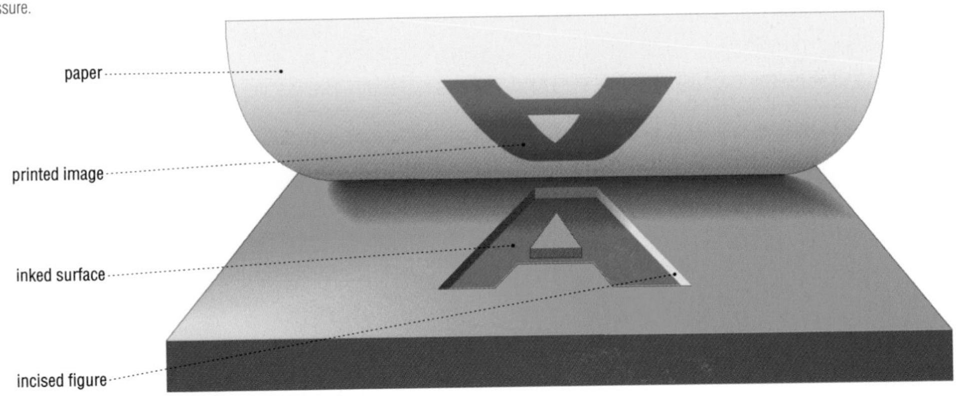

lithographic printing
Process that consists of printing an image from a figure on the same plane as the nonprinted parts, which are protected from the ink by dampening.

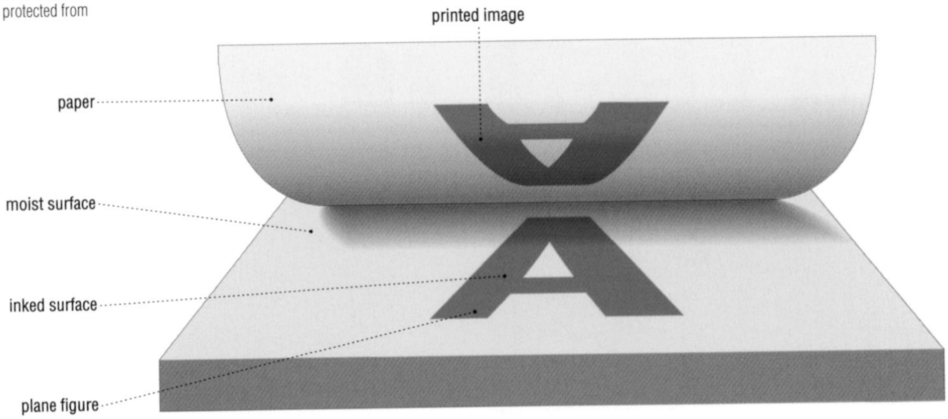

relief printing process

Technique that consists of creating a raised figure on a piece of wood.

equipment
Collective term for the materials, instruments and tools used for engraving and printing.

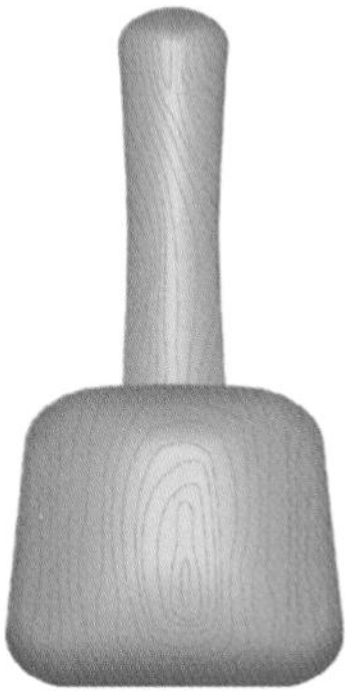

mallet
ammer used to strike the heel of a sharp tool to drive it into wood.

U-shaped gouge
Sharp U-shaped chisel used to remove areas to create large blank spaces.

V-shaped gouge
Sharp V-shaped chisel used to dig deep angular grooves and to remove areas to create smaller blank spaces.

chisel
Sharp tool with a flat beveled blade used for engraving wood in the grain direction; it removes areas to create blank space around the figure and smoothes out the background.

knife
Tool used for engraving in the grain direction of the wood; it brings out the figure by means of incisions.

block cutter
Chisel with a beveled point used in engraving to achieve subtleties of line; it was once used on copper but is now used mainly on wood.

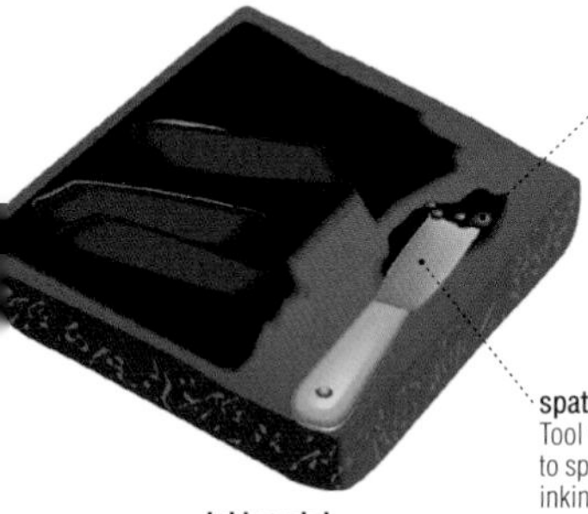

ink
Preparation in black or in color used for printing.

spatula
Tool with a flat flexible blade used to spread ink or scrape down the inking slab.

inking slab
Plate on which the ink is spread so it will be evenly distributed on the brayer.

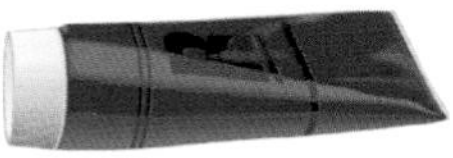

ink
Preparation in black or in color used for printing.

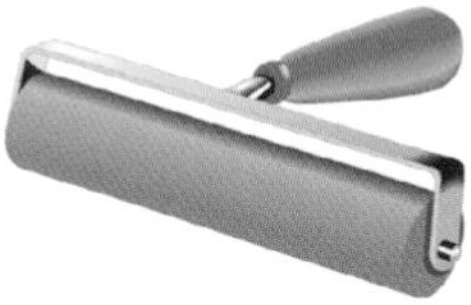

brayer
Instrument used to spread ink on a raised figure.

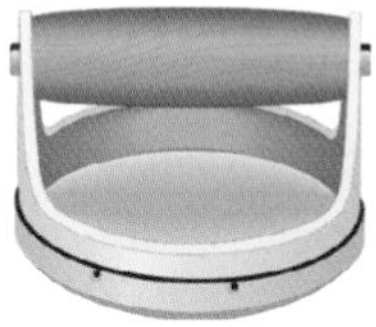

baren
Instrument that exerts pressure on the back of the paper to help the ink adhere.

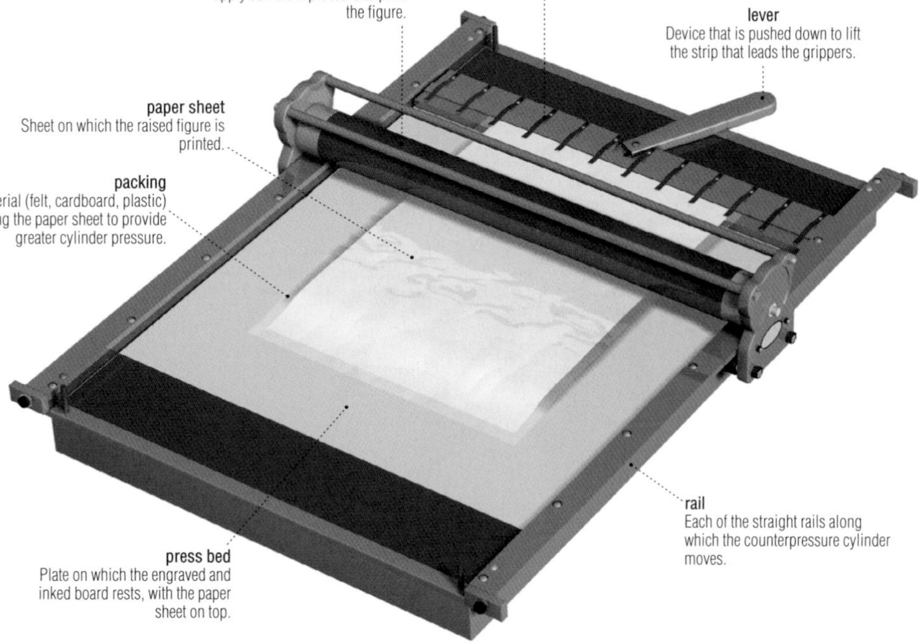

proof press
Fixed-bed printing press with a cylinder that is moved along an engraved and inked board covered with a sheet of paper.

gripper
Each of the metal pieces mounted on a strip that holds the paper in position under the cylinder.

counterpressure cylinder
Roller that is moved manually to apply sufficient pressure to print the figure.

lever
Device that is pushed down to lift the strip that leads the grippers.

paper sheet
Sheet on which the raised figure is printed.

packing
Material (felt, cardboard, plastic) covering the paper sheet to provide greater cylinder pressure.

rail
Each of the straight rails along which the counterpressure cylinder moves.

press bed
Plate on which the engraved and inked board rests, with the paper sheet on top.

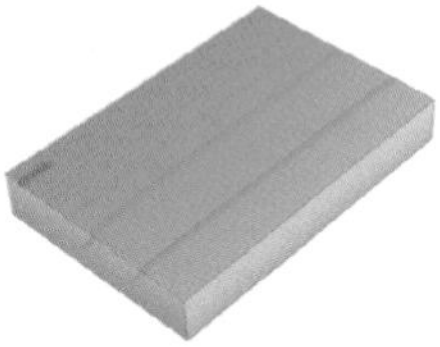

woodcut
Technique of engraving a piece of wood in the same direction as the grain.

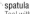

wood engraving
Technique of engraving a piece of wood against the grain.

intaglio printing process

Technique that consists of drawing a figure by engraving its lines into a surface, usually a copper plate.

equipment
Collective term for the materials, instruments and tools used for engraving and printing.

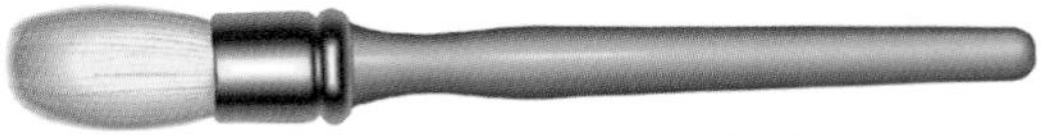

brush
Natural or synthetic bristles attached to a handle, used for spreading paint, varnish or stain on a base.

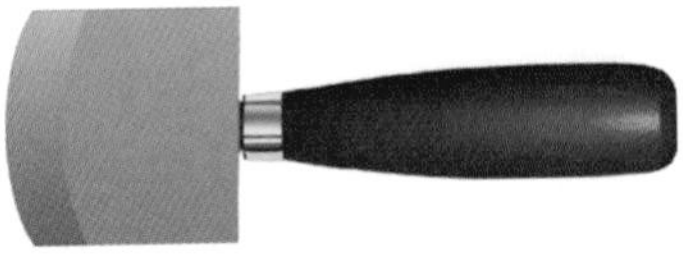

rocking tool
Tool with a thick rounded beveled steel blade; the row of vertical grooves on its sides gives the copper surface a uniform grain.

roulette
Instrument with a steel wheel containing several rows of regular asperities and used to create coarse-grained lines.

copper plate
Copper is the metal most often used in engraving because it is strong, is malleable enough for engraving and reacts to chemicals.

drypoint
Steel rod used to engrave a figure in copper by biting into the plate or the varnish covering it.

burnisher
Instrument used to refine the cuts and remove irregularities from the metal.

scraper
Tool with a pointed triangular blade used to remove burrs, thin strips of copper left on the edge of the groove made by the drypoint.

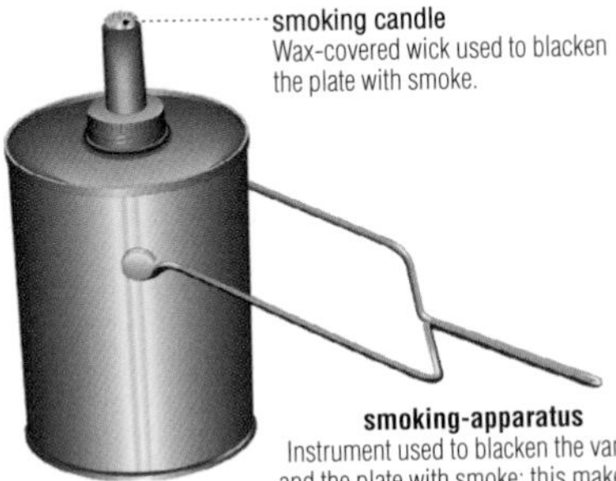

smoking candle
Wax-covered wick used to blacken the plate with smoke.

smoking-apparatus
Instrument used to blacken the varnish and the plate with smoke; this makes the figure more visible during the engraving process.

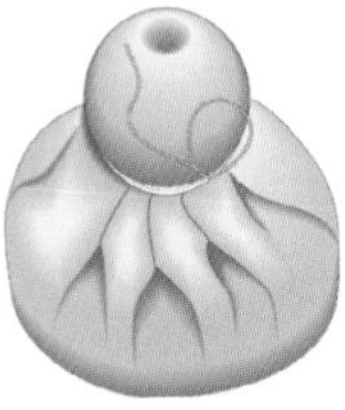

dabber
Instrument made up of a handle placed in a cotton wad and wrapped in silk; it is used to spread varnish on the plate.

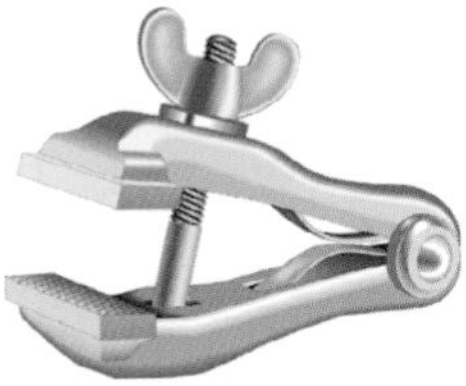

hand vise
Instrument used to hold and handle the plate while smoking it.

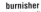

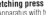

tarlatan
Muslin used to wipe excess ink from the surface of the plate.

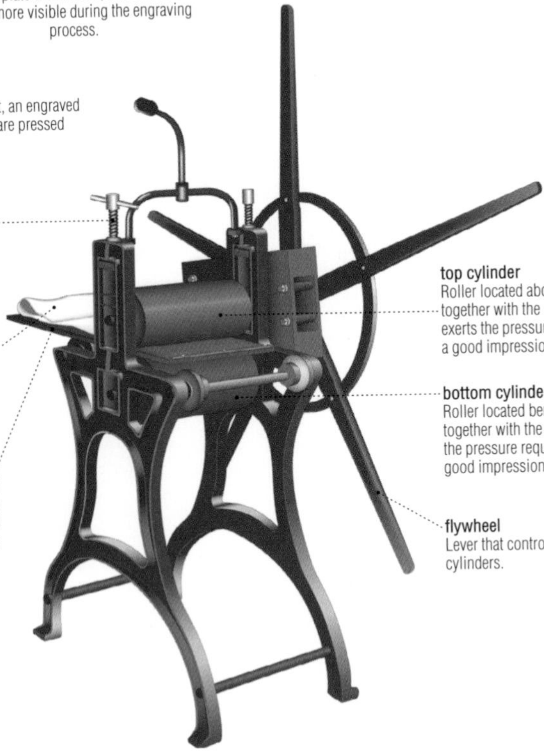

etching press
Apparatus with two cylinders; to print, an engraved and inked plate and a sheet of paper are pressed between them.

pressure screw
Part that controls cylinder pressure.

felt
Thick piece of fabric placed beneath the paper before it is put under the press; the felt cushions and distributes the pressure.

press bed
Plate that moves between the two cylinders, supporting the engraved board and the paper.

top cylinder
Roller located above the press bed; together with the bottom cylinder, it exerts the pressure required to achieve a good impression of the figure.

bottom cylinder
Roller located beneath the press bed; together with the top cylinder, it exerts the pressure required to achieve a good impression of the figure.

flywheel
Lever that controls the press cylinders.

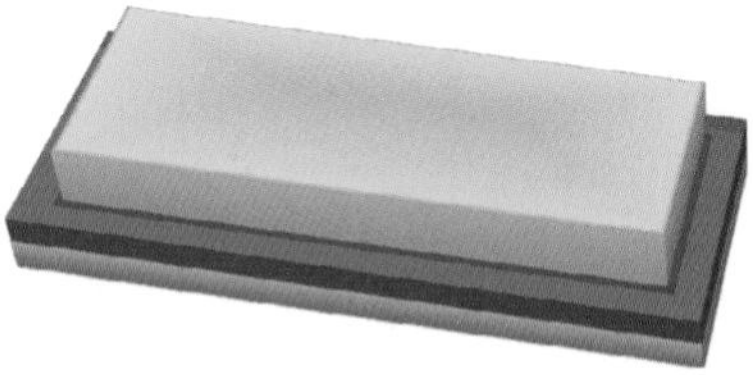

oilstone
Stone used to sharpen tools.

varnish-roller
Instrument used to spread varnish on the surface and prevent ink from adhering to it; it ensures that only the figure is inked.

lithography

Technique of printing from a plane surface using grease to draw a figure on damp limestone; the grease retains ink, the water repels it.

litho pencil
Grease pencil used to draw a figure on a lithographic stone.

drypoint
Instrument used to engrave the stone in some lithographic techniques.

pumice correcting pencil
Instrument used to polish the stone and make corrections to the figure.

litho crayon
Rectangular stick of grease chalk used to draw a figure on a lithographic stone.

red ocher pencil
Stick of hematite (iron oxide) used to produce a sketch on paper; the sketch is then transferred to the stone.

equipment
Collective term for the materials, instruments and tools used for engraving and printing.

lithographic tusche
Greasy ink in liquid or solid form used to draw a figure on a lithographic stone using a pen or a brush.

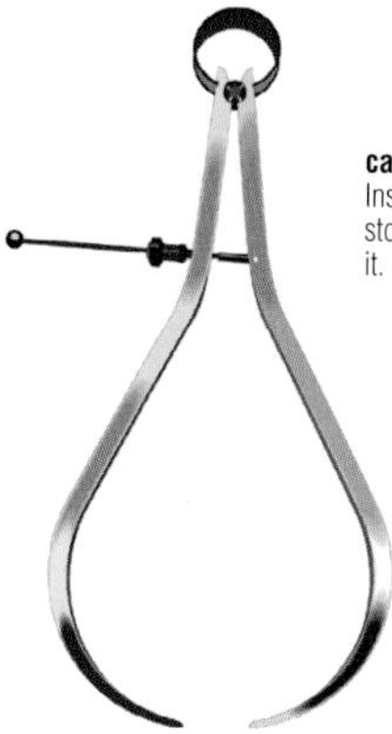

caliper
Instrument that measures the stone's thickness in order to level it.

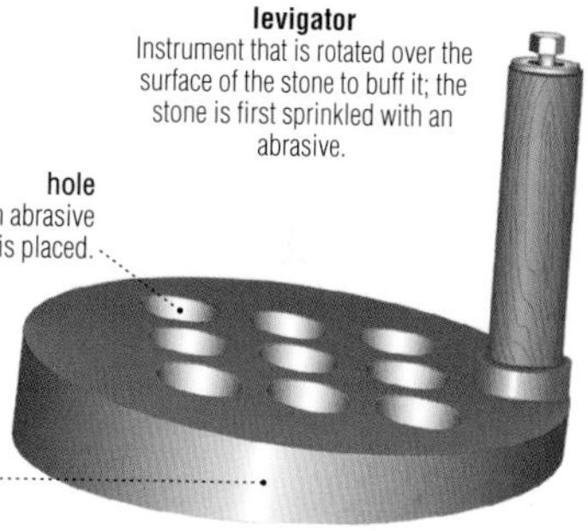

levigator
Instrument that is rotated over the surface of the stone to buff it; the stone is first sprinkled with an abrasive.

hole
Cell in which an abrasive substance is placed.

disk
Cast-iron plate with holes, used to buff the stone.

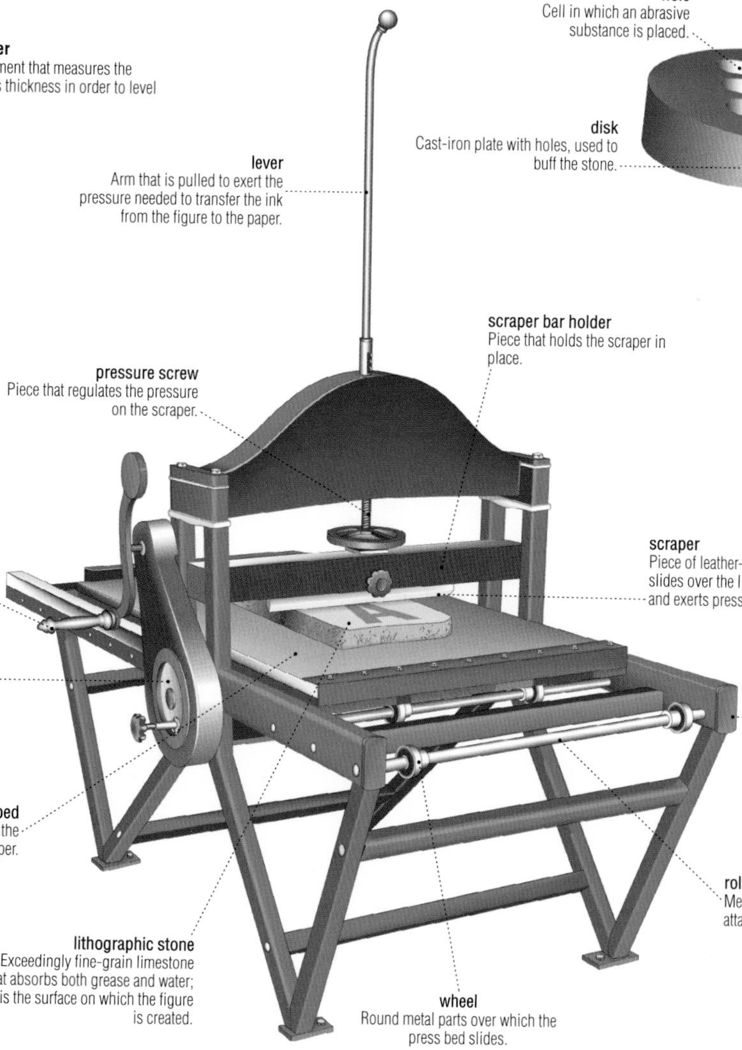

lithographic press
Manual printing press that uses pressure to print, on paper, an image created on a lithographic stone.

lever
Arm that is pulled to exert the pressure needed to transfer the ink from the figure to the paper.

scraper bar holder
Piece that holds the scraper in place.

pressure screw
Piece that regulates the pressure on the scraper.

crank handle
It manually controls the gearbox.

scraper
Piece of leather-covered wood that slides over the lithographic stone and exerts pressure.

gearbox
Device fitted with a toothed gearwheel used to move the press bed.

frame
Metal structure of the press.

press bed
Movable plate supporting the lithographic stone and the paper.

roller
Metal tube to which the wheels are attached.

lithographic stone
Exceedingly fine-grain limestone that absorbs both grease and water; it is the surface on which the figure is created.

wheel
Round metal parts over which the press bed slides.

fine bookbinding

Collective term for the manual operations required to bind the sheets of a book together and add an attractive solid cover.

sawing-in

Process for making grooves on the backs of signatures to make room for the cords.

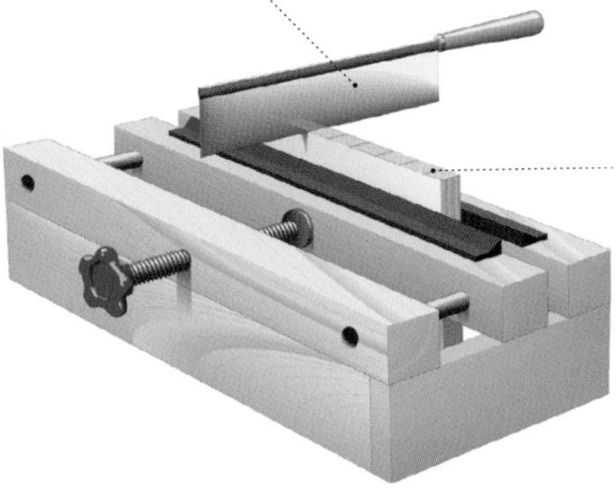

tenon saw
Small saw used to make grooves.
groove
Groove cut into the back of signatures to make room for the cords.

sewing

Process for binding the signatures of a book together using cords.

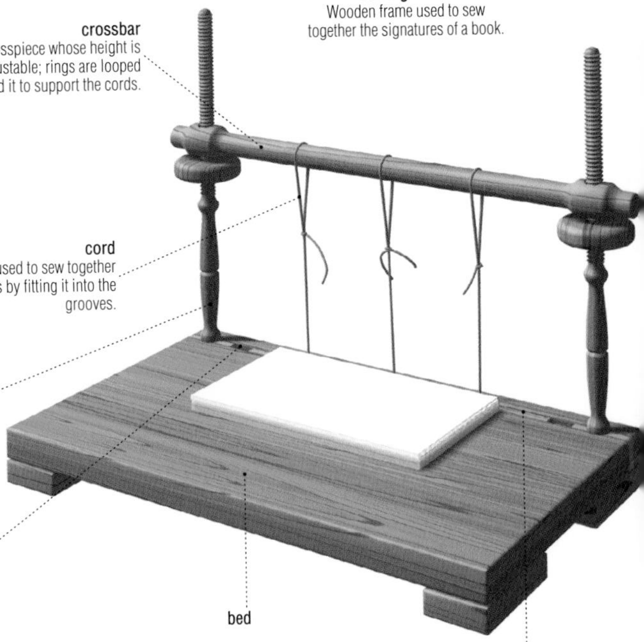

sewing frame
Wooden frame used to sew together the signatures of a book.
crossbar
Crosspiece whose height is adjustable; rings are looped around it to support the cords.
cord
Thread used to sew together signatures by fitting it into the grooves.
upright
One of two vertical pieces of threaded wood that is turned to adjust the height of the crossbar.
slot
Opening in which the cords are wedged.
bed
temple
Small movable wooden slat placed inside the slot to keep the cords in place.

trimming

The process of evening the edges of a signature using a board cutter.

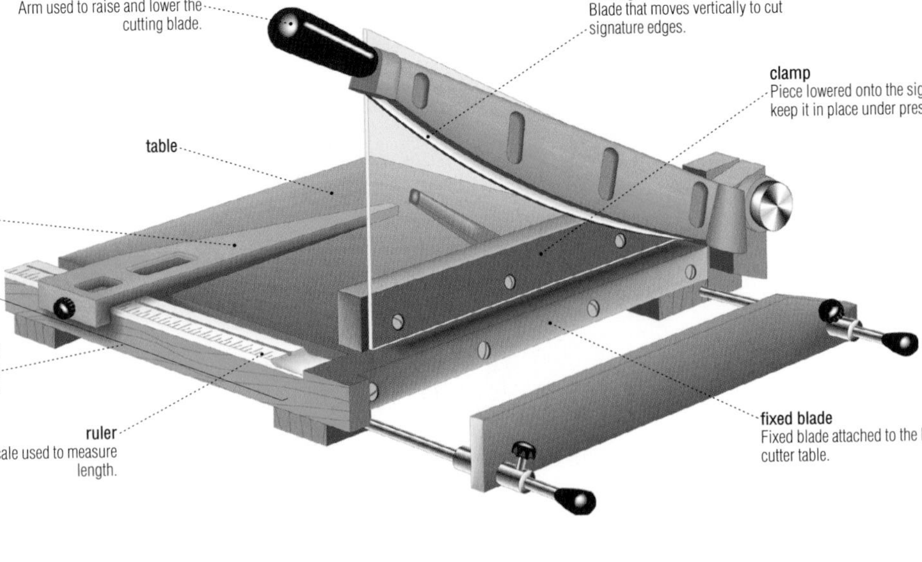

board cutter
Piece of equipment used to make square cuts in paper, cardboard, transparencies, etc.
blade lever
Arm used to raise and lower the cutting blade.
cutting blade
Blade that moves vertically to cut signature edges.
clamp
Piece lowered onto the signature to keep it in place under pressure.
table
gauge
Movable square parallel to the fixed blade for adjusting the position and dimensions of a signature.
cutting guide
Groove in which the gauge moves along the ruler.
ruler
Graduated scale used to measure length.
fixed blade
Fixed blade attached to the board cutter table.

backing
Process for creating joints, the parallel projections running the length of the book that act as hinges between the spine and the boards.

backing press
Press used to flatten a book so that the joints can be made.

spine of the book
Part that makes up the back of a book's signatures.

backing board
Metal edge of the press; the back of the signature is placed along this edge and hammered to create joints.

backing hammer
Tool used to flatten the back of signatures to give the spine a fan shape.

claw
The tapered end of the hammer, used to flatten the backs of signatures.

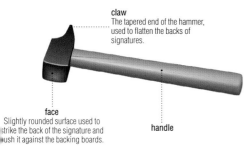

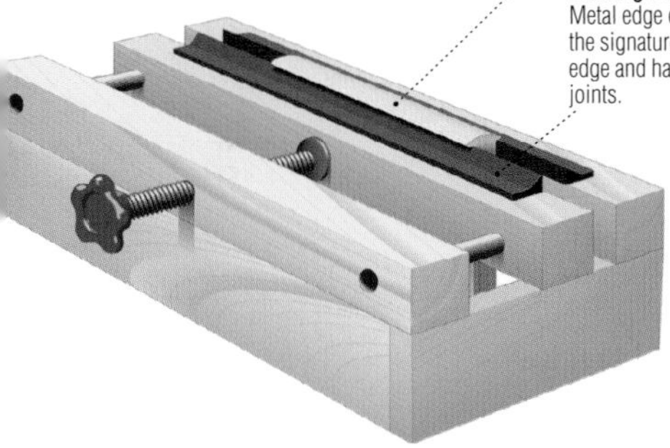

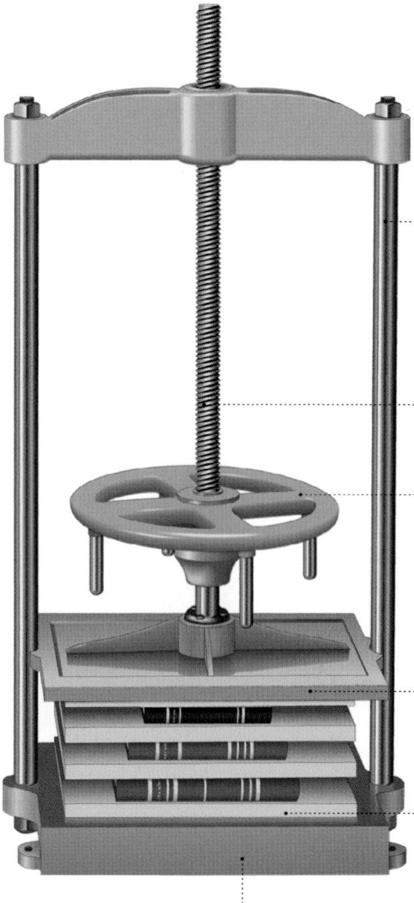

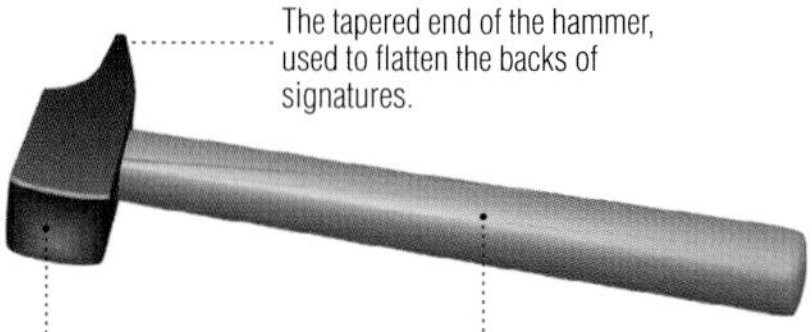

face
Slightly rounded surface used to strike the back of the signature and push it against the backing boards.

handle

standing press
Hand-operated machine for pressing books during the binding process.

pressing
Process for exerting pressure on a book being bound in order to flatten the signatures and make them more compact.

upright

central screw

handwheel
Wheel-shaped part that pivots around a central screw to move the platen.

platen
Heavy adjustable plate used to exert pressure on one or more books.

pressing board
Small board made of wood or stiff board and used to separate books, protect them and prevent warping.

base

bookbinding leather
Animal leather (e.g., goat or calf) used in bookbinding to cover a book.

covering
Process of applying a covering material (skin, fabric, paper) to the boards and spine of a book.

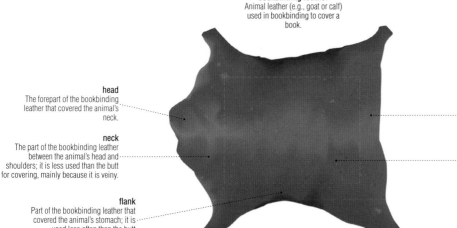

head
The forepart of the bookbinding leather that covered the animal's neck.

neck
The part of the bookbinding leather between the animal's head and shoulders; it is less used than the butt for covering, mainly because it is veiny.

flank
Part of the bookbinding leather that covered the animal's stomach; it is used less often than the butt because it warps easily.

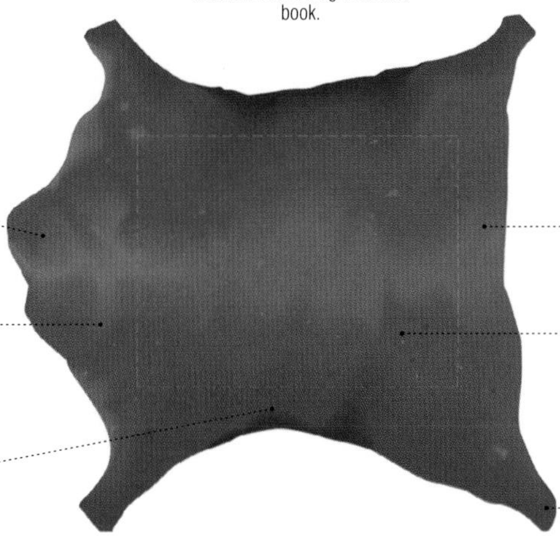

tail
Part of the skin that covered the rear portion of the animal's back and hindquarters; it is seldom used in bookbinding.

butt
Part of the skin that covered the back and hindquarters of the animal; it is the part most often used for covering because it is thick and supple.

foot
Part of the skin that covered the upper portion of the animal's legs; it is seldom used for covering.

fine bookbinding

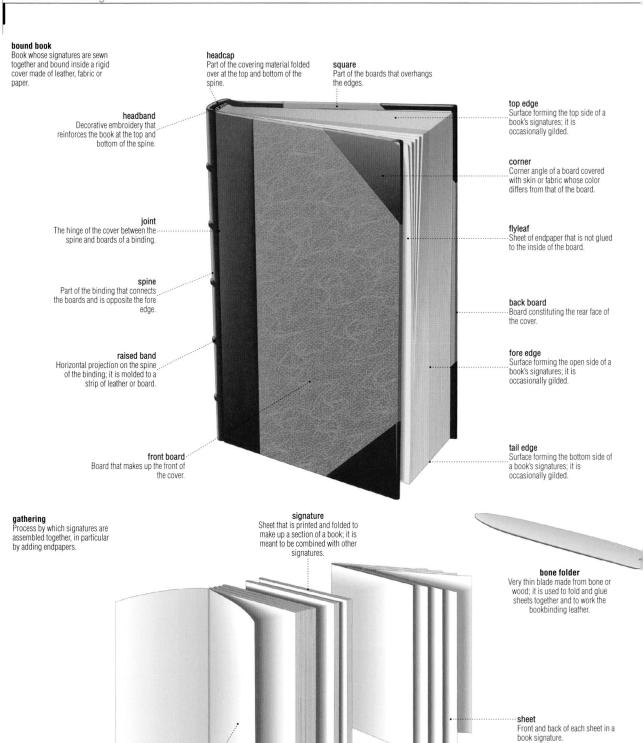

bound book
Book whose signatures are sewn together and bound inside a rigid cover made of leather, fabric or paper.

headcap
Part of the covering material folded over at the top and bottom of the spine.

square
Part of the boards that overhangs the edges.

headband
Decorative embroidery that reinforces the book at the top and bottom of the spine.

top edge
Surface forming the top side of a book's signatures; it is occasionally gilded.

corner
Corner angle of a board covered with skin or fabric whose color differs from that of the board.

joint
The hinge of the cover between the spine and boards of a binding.

flyleaf
Sheet of endpaper that is not glued to the inside of the board.

spine
Part of the binding that connects the boards and is opposite the fore edge.

back board
Board constituting the rear face of the cover.

raised band
Horizontal projection on the spine of the binding; it is molded to a strip of leather or board.

fore edge
Surface forming the open side of a book's signatures; it is occasionally gilded.

front board
Board that makes up the front of the cover.

tail edge
Surface forming the bottom side of a book's signatures; it is occasionally gilded.

gathering
Process by which signatures are assembled together, in particular by adding endpapers.

signature
Sheet that is printed and folded to make up a section of a book; it is meant to be combined with other signatures.

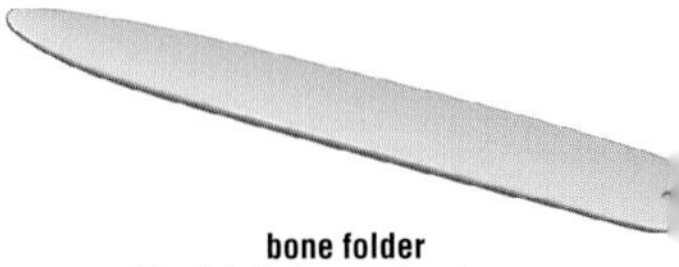

bone folder
Very thin blade made from bone or wood; it is used to fold and glue sheets together and to work the bookbinding leather.

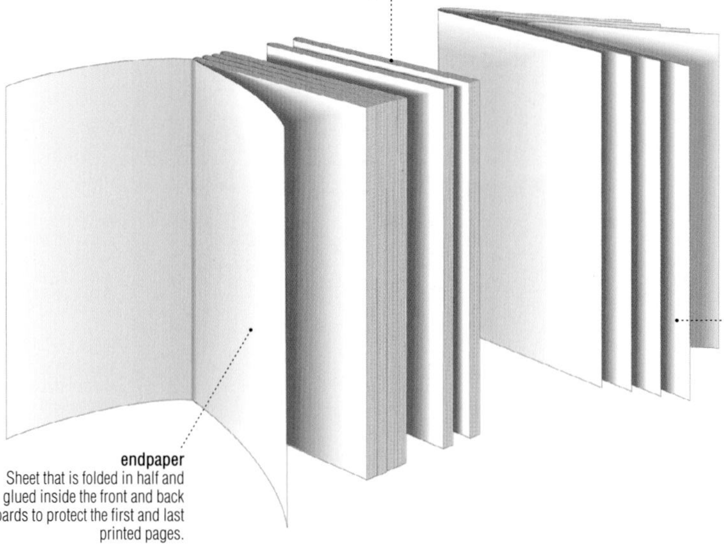

sheet
Front and back of each sheet in a book signature.

endpaper
Sheet that is folded in half and glued inside the front and back boards to protect the first and last printed pages.

movie theater

Establishment with auditoriums used for projecting films.

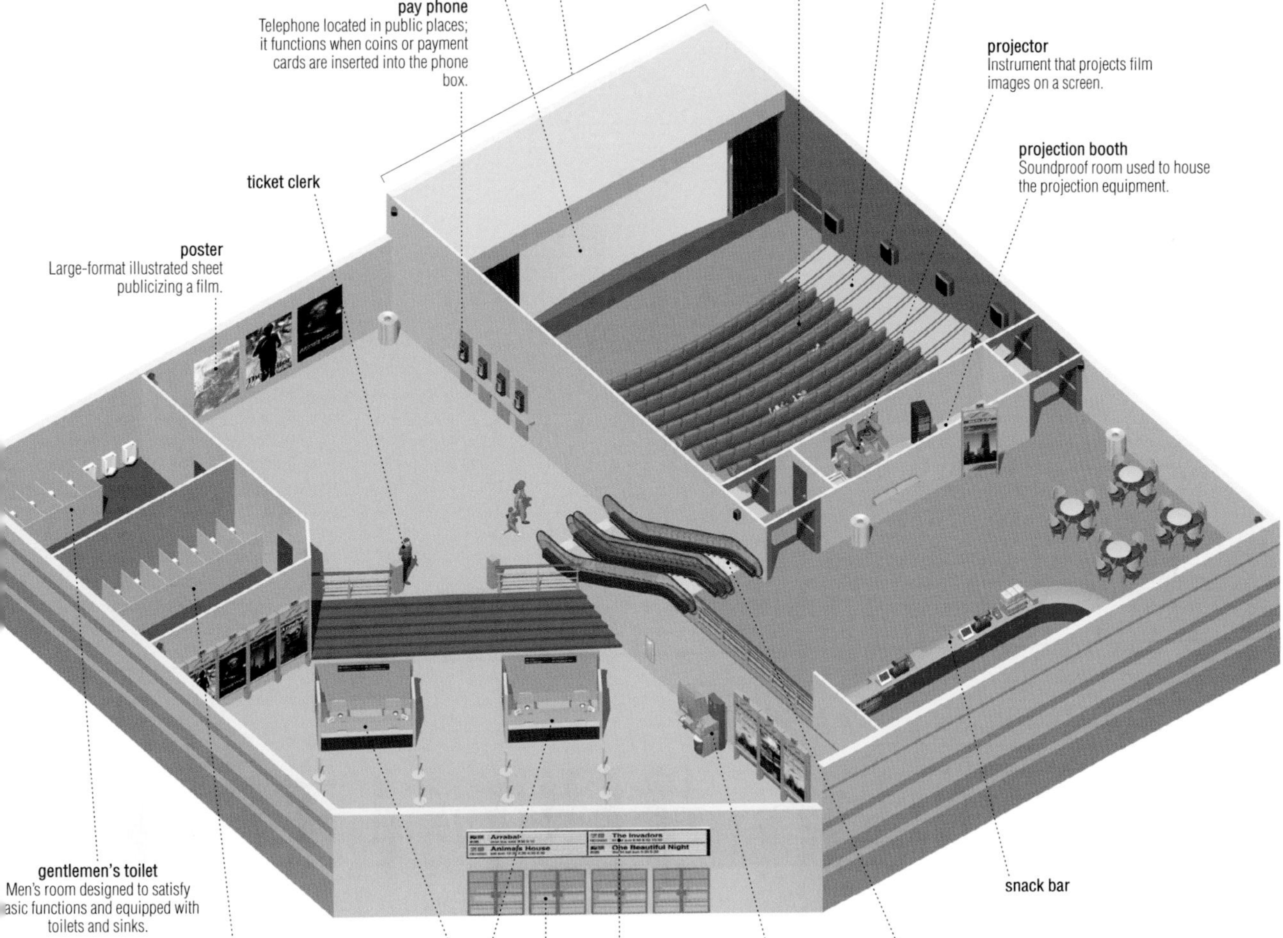
seat
Armchair used to view a movie screening.
stairs
Structural element for moving from the entrance to the auditorium and its rows of seats, arranged in tiers.
projection screen
White surface on which still or moving images are projected.
projection room
Movie theater's main room, where the public sit during a movie screening.
speaker
Device that broadcasts a film's soundtrack.
pay phone
Telephone located in public places; it functions when coins or payment cards are inserted into the phone box.
projector
Instrument that projects film images on a screen.
projection booth
Soundproof room used to house the projection equipment.
ticket clerk
poster
Large-format illustrated sheet publicizing a film.
gentlemen's toilet
Men's room designed to satisfy basic functions and equipped with toilets and sinks.
snack bar
ladies' toilet
Women's room designed to satisfy basic functions and equipped with toilets and sinks.
box office
Counter where admission tickets are purchased.
quick ticket system
Machine for using a debit card to purchase a ticket, without waiting at the box office.
escalator
Installation that consists of articulated steps on a continuously turning chain; it allows movement between two levels of a building.
entrance doors
movies' titles and schedules

movie set

Sets, materials and personnel needed to shoot a movie or a television program.

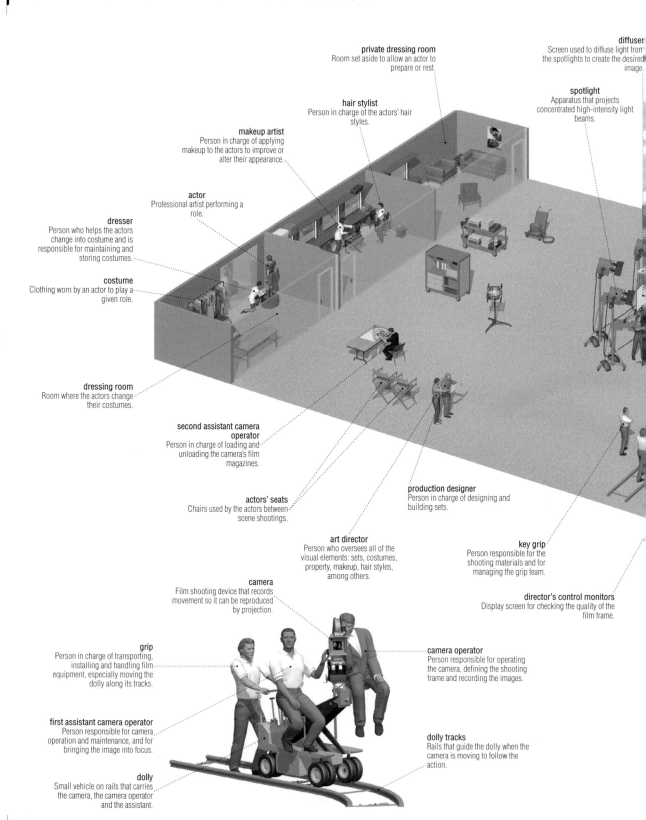

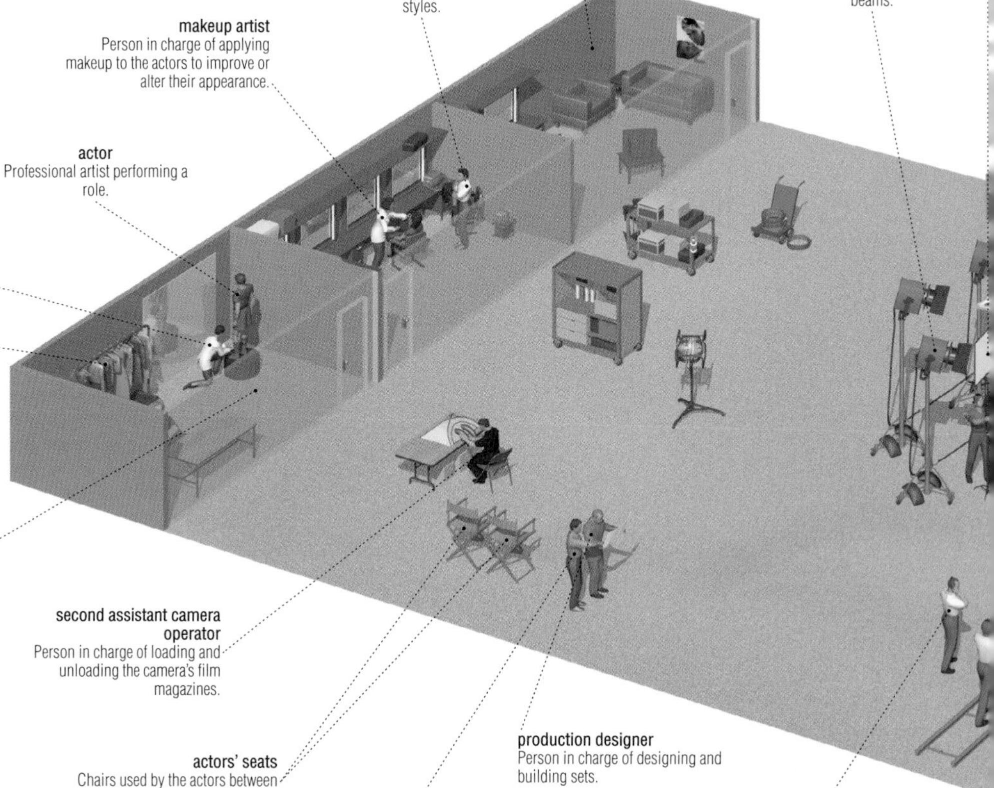
private dressing room
Room set aside to allow an actor to prepare or rest.
diffuser
Screen used to diffuse light from the spotlights to create the desired image.
hair stylist
Person in charge of the actors' hair styles.
spotlight
Apparatus that projects concentrated high-intensity light beams.
makeup artist
Person in charge of applying makeup to the actors to improve or alter their appearance.
actor
Professional artist performing a role.
dresser
Person who helps the actors change into costume and is responsible for maintaining and storing costumes.
costume
Clothing worn by an actor to play a given role.
dressing room
Room where the actors change their costumes.
second assistant camera operator
Person in charge of loading and unloading the camera's film magazines.
actors' seats
Chairs used by the actors between scene shootings.
production designer
Person in charge of designing and building sets.
art director
Person who oversees all of the visual elements: sets, costumes, property, makeup, hair styles, among others.
key grip
Person responsible for the shooting materials and for managing the grip team.
director's control monitors
Display screen for checking the quality of the film frame.

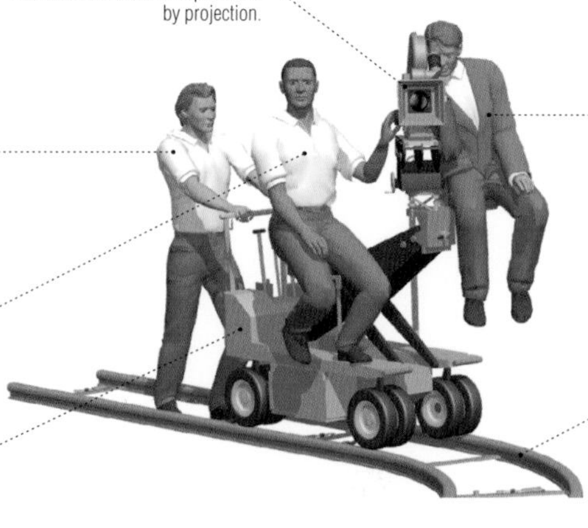
camera
Film shooting device that records movement so it can be reproduced by projection.
grip
Person in charge of transporting, installing and handling film equipment, especially moving the dolly along its tracks.
camera operator
Person responsible for operating the camera, defining the shooting frame and recording the images.
first assistant camera operator
Person responsible for camera operation and maintenance, and for bringing the image into focus.
dolly tracks
Rails that guide the dolly when the camera is moving to follow the action.
dolly
Small vehicle on rails that carries the camera, the camera operator and the assistant.

movie set

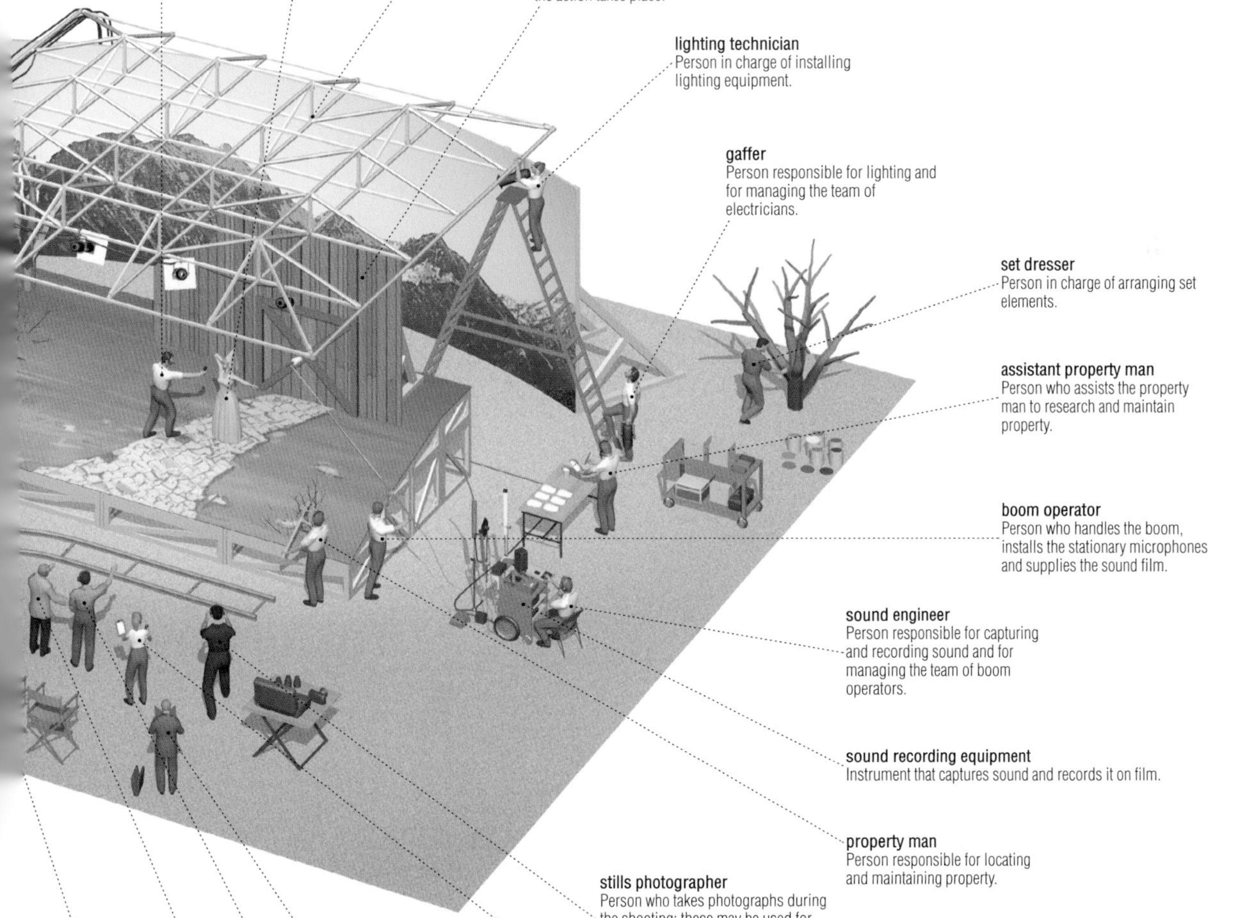
director of photography
Person responsible for the technical and artistic quality of the image.
lighting grid
Grid used to hold the spotlights.
actress
Female actor performing a role.
set
Collective term for the elements that reproduce the setting where the action takes place.
lighting technician
Person in charge of installing lighting equipment.
gaffer
Person responsible for lighting and for managing the team of electricians.
set dresser
Person in charge of arranging set elements.
assistant property man
Person who assists the property man to research and maintain property.
boom operator
Person who handles the boom, installs the stationary microphones and supplies the sound film.
sound engineer
Person responsible for capturing and recording sound and for managing the team of boom operators.
sound recording equipment
Instrument that captures sound and records it on film.
property man
Person responsible for locating and maintaining property.
stills photographer
Person who takes photographs during the shooting; these may be used for reference purposes from one shot to the next or as promotional material.
continuity person
Person who records all the technical and artistic details during shooting to ensure continuity.
producer
Person in charge of the financing and administration of a film or television program.
director's seat
Chair reserved for the director.
assistant director
Director's main assistant, in charge of preparing the shoot and ensuring that everything is done in accordance with the director's instructions.
director
Person in charge of the technical and artistic direction while a movie or a television program is being shot.

clapper/the slate
Panel consisting of two small boards that are clapped together to signal the start of shooting.
time code
Device that indicates the hour, minute, second and number of the frame; it is used to mark the sequence for editing purposes.
00.58.55.29

ARTS AND ARCHITECTURE

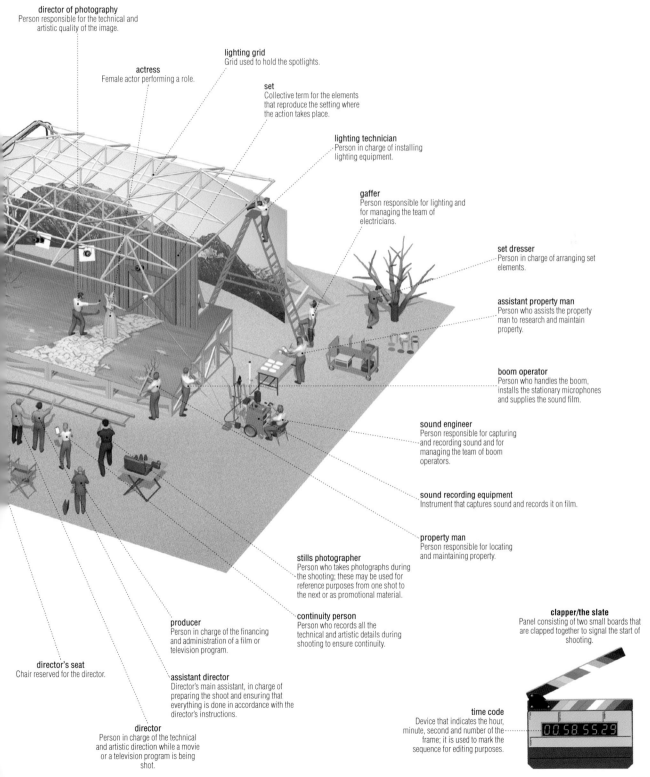

theater

Establishment built to present plays, shows, dance performances, concerts and so forth.

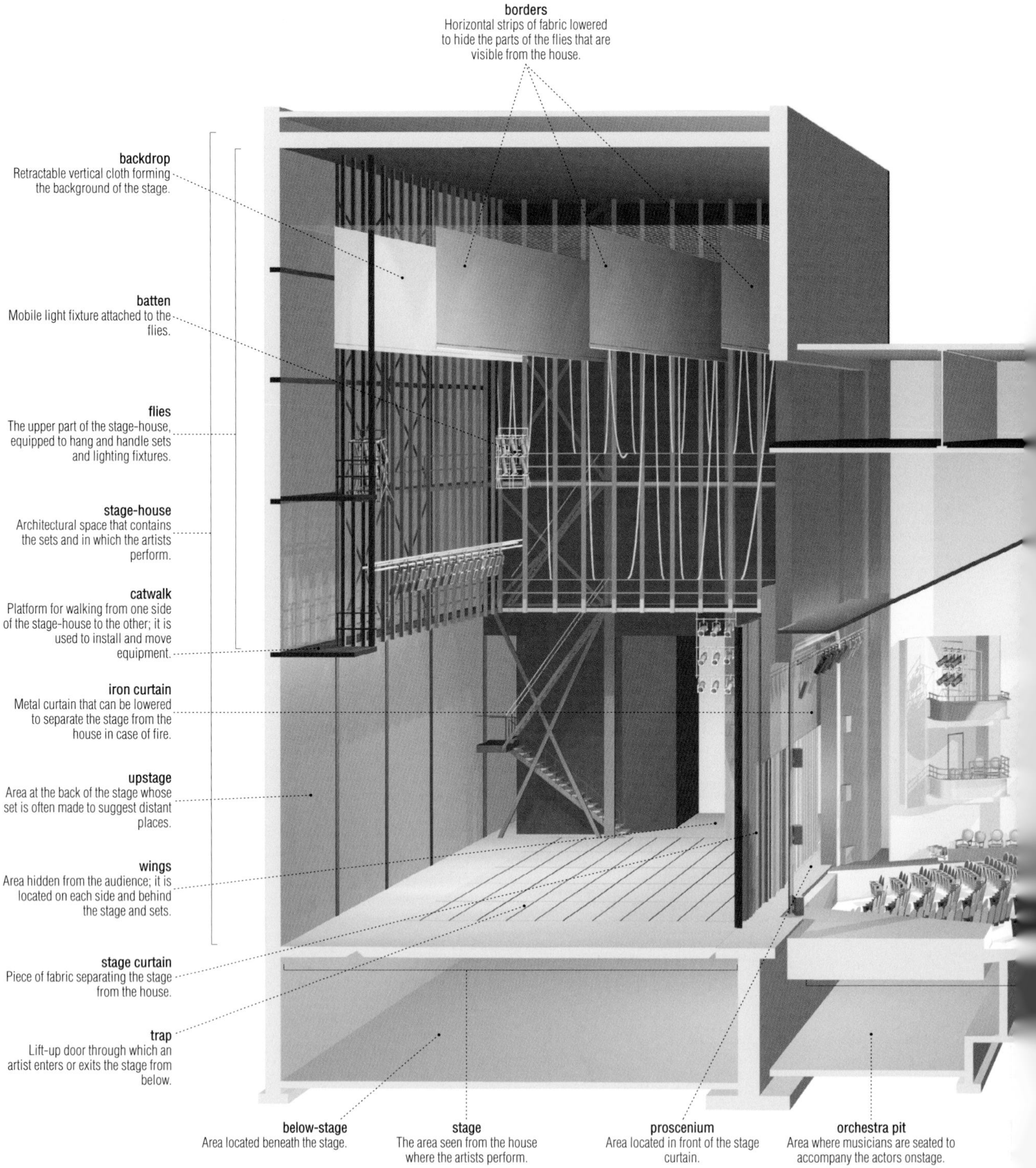
borders
Horizontal strips of fabric lowered to hide the parts of the flies that are visible from the house.
backdrop
Retractable vertical cloth forming the background of the stage.
batten
Mobile light fixture attached to the flies.
flies
The upper part of the stage-house, equipped to hang and handle sets and lighting fixtures.
stage-house
Architectural space that contains the sets and in which the artists perform.
catwalk
Platform for walking from one side of the stage-house to the other; it is used to install and move equipment.
iron curtain
Metal curtain that can be lowered to separate the stage from the house in case of fire.
upstage
Area at the back of the stage whose set is often made to suggest distant places.
wings
Area hidden from the audience; it is located on each side and behind the stage and sets.
stage curtain
Piece of fabric separating the stage from the house.
trap
Lift-up door through which an artist enters or exits the stage from below.
below-stage
Area located beneath the stage.
stage
The area seen from the house where the artists perform.
proscenium
Area located in front of the stage curtain.
orchestra pit
Area where musicians are seated to accompany the actors onstage.

stage
The area seen from the house where the artists perform.

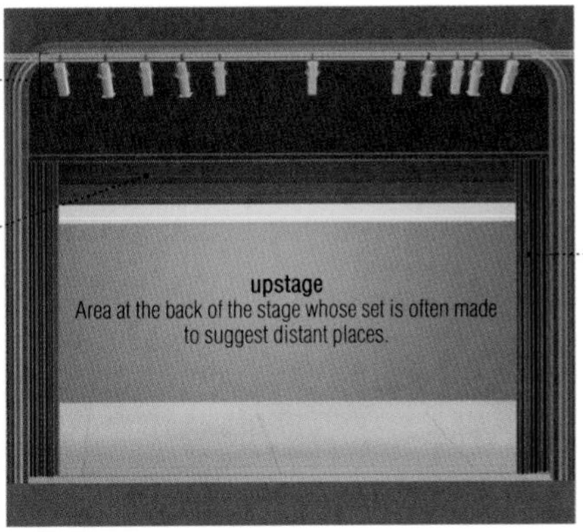

lights
Row of projectors set up above the proscenium.

border
Horizontal strip of fabric used to hide the parts of the flies that are visible from the house.

upstage
Area at the back of the stage whose set is often made to suggest distant places.

prompt side
The left side of the stage, from the audience.

stage curtain
Piece of fabric separating the stage from the house.

opposite prompt side
The right side of the stage, from the audience.

otlights
ghting device that projects a
ncentrated beam of high-
ensity light.

acoustic ceiling
Ceiling made of materials that help to project the sound into the house.

control room
Room equipped to control sound, lighting and projection.

bar
Area where alcoholic drinks are sold.

foyers
Space used by the audience before the performance and at the intermission.

stairs
Structural component enabling movement between floors of a house or other structure.

dressing room
Room that the artists use to change costumes, apply makeup and style their hair.

ıouse
Part of the theater built for seating he public during a performance.

parterre
The first floor of the house.

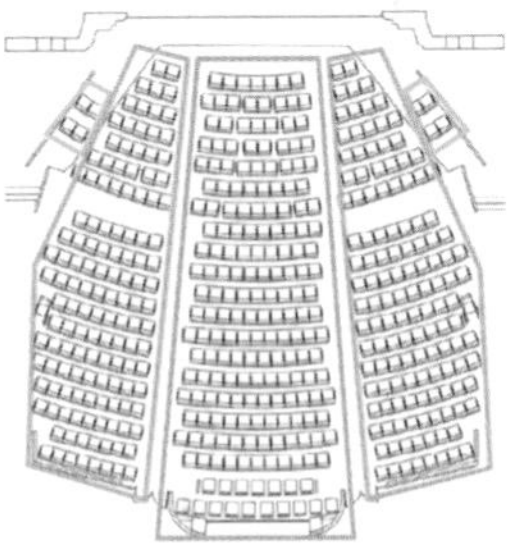

side

center

mezzanine
The floor above the parterre of the house.

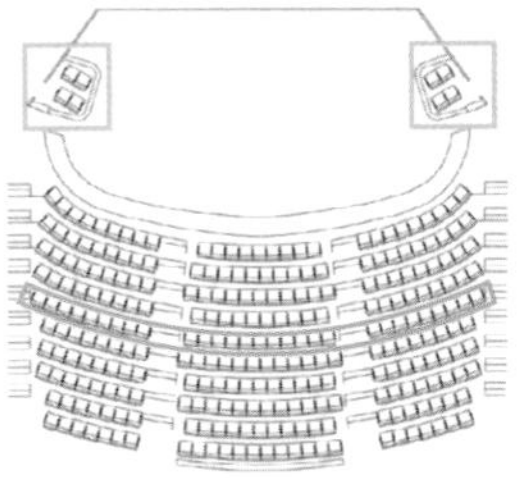

box
Small partitioned room that seats two or three people.

row
Series of seats the same distance from the stage.

balcony
Area of the house located above the mezzanine.

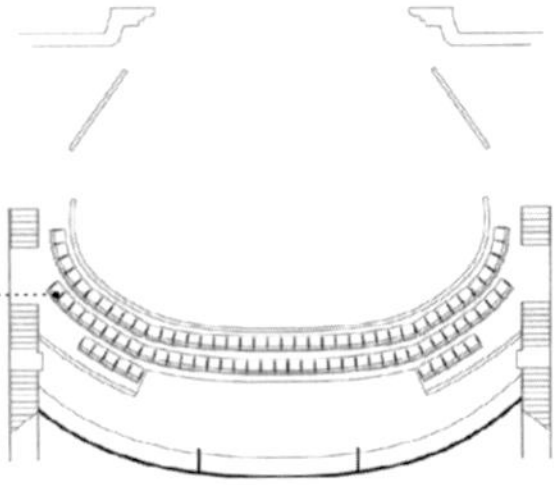

seat
Armchair used to watch a performance.

ARTS AND ARCHITECTURE

traditional musical instruments

Collective term for the instruments, current or ancient, that characterize a culture, era or style of music.

accordion
Wind instrument composed of keyboards and a manual bellows used to cause the reeds to vibrate and produce sound.

bellows strap
Piece that locks the bellows in a closed position.

treble register
Key that changes sound quality in the higher register.

treble keyboard
Keys used to play the melody.

key
White or black lever pressed to allow air from the bellows to pass, causing the reeds to vibrate and produce sound.

grille
Part through which air and sound pass.

bellows
Apparatus that contracts and expands to control air pressure and cause the reeds to vibrate.

button
Used to allow air from the bellows to enter, causing the bass keyboard reeds to vibrate.

bass keyboard
Keys that provide a harmonic complement to the treble keyboard.

bass register
Key that changes sound quality in the lower register.

harmonica
Instrument composed of small tubes with free reeds recessed in a frame, which the player causes to vibrate by exhaling and inhaling.

bagpipes
Wind instrument associated with Scottish culture; it is composed of a bellows in the shape of a windbag and several sound pipes.

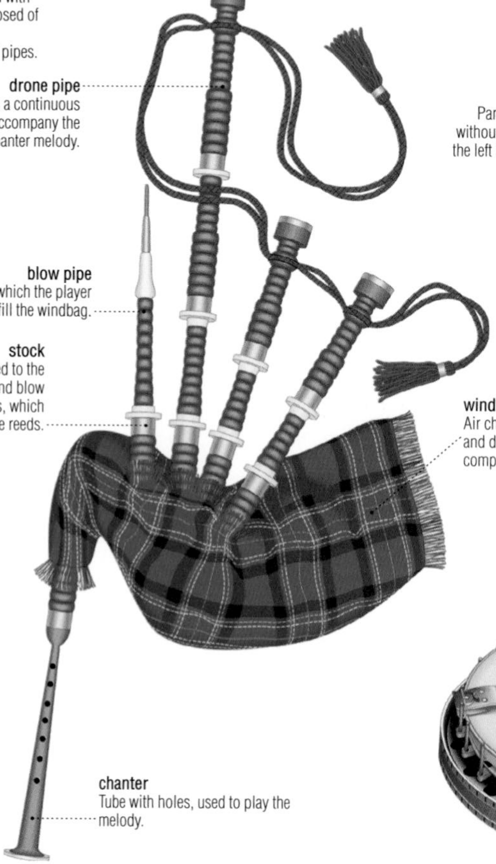

drone pipe
Tube that produces a continuous bass note to accompany the chanter melody.

blow pipe
Tube with a valve into which the player blows to fill the windbag.

stock
Each of the tubes attached to the windbag; the sound pipes and blow pipe fit inside these tubes, which also protect the reeds.

windbag
Air chamber that feeds the chanter and drone pipes by means of compression.

chanter
Tube with holes, used to play the melody.

zithe
Flat stringed instrument with r neck, associated with the music Austria and German

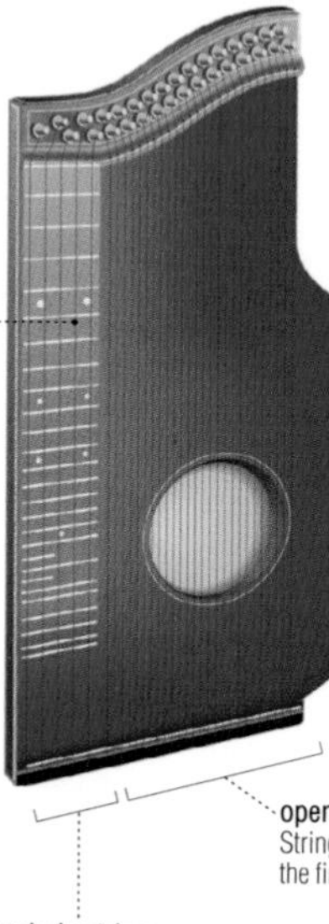

soundboard
The hollow part of the instrumen it amplifies the sound vibrations produced by the strings.

fingerboard
Part of the instrument, with or without frets, where the fingers of the left hand are placed to shorten the strings.

open strings
Strings with fixed tones, plucked with the fingers of the right hand.

melody strings
Strings of varying length that are plucked with a pick attached to the right thumb to create the melody.

banj
Afro-American stringed instrumer that was extremely popular at th dawn of the jazz era

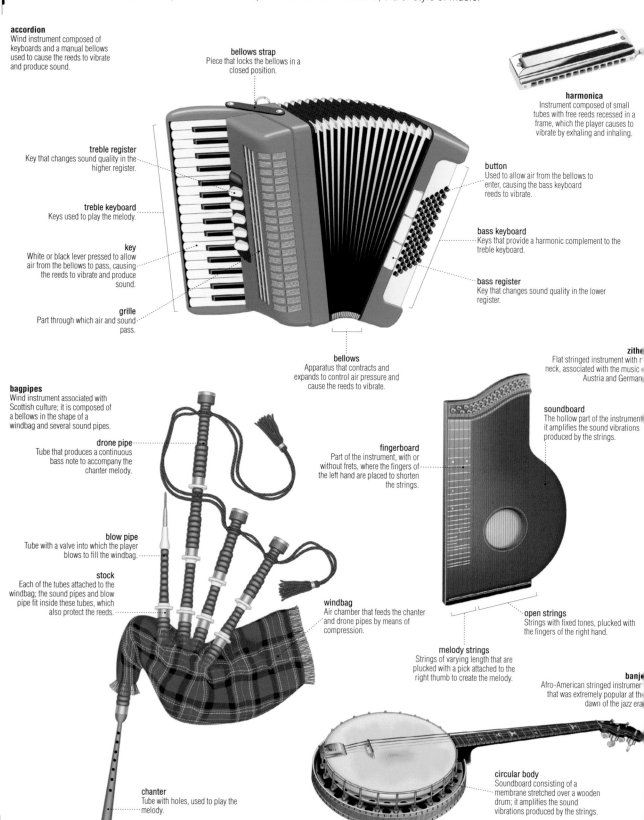

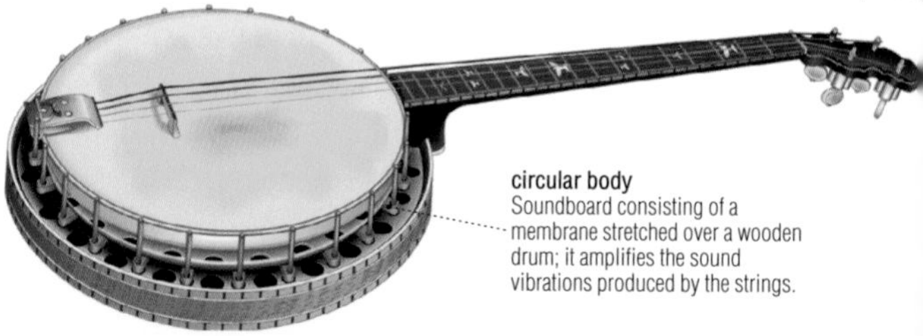

circular body
Soundboard consisting of a membrane stretched over a wooden drum; it amplifies the sound vibrations produced by the strings.

traditional musical instruments

mandolin
Plucked instrument with paired strings and a pear-shaped body, originally from Italy.

pear-shaped body
Soundboard in the shape of a half pear; it amplifies the sound vibrations produced by the strings.

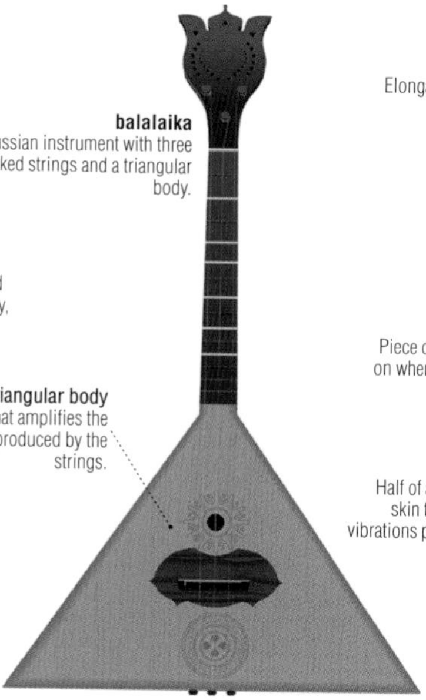

balalaika
Russian instrument with three plucked strings and a triangular body.

triangular body
Soundboard that amplifies the sound vibrations produced by the strings.

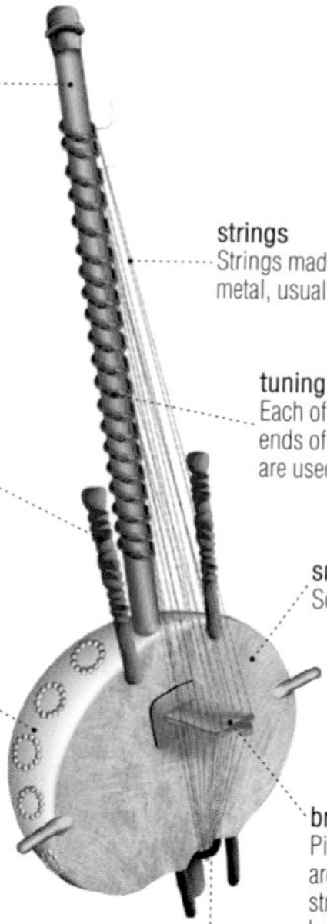

kora
Plucked string instrument used in Africa for celebrations and rituals.

neck
Elongated part of the instrument over which the strings are stretched.

strings
Strings made from gut, nylon or metal, usually numbering 21.

tuning ring
Each of the notches that the upper ends of the strings attach to; they are used to tune the instrument.

hand post
Piece of wood that the hand rests on when the instrument is played.

snare head
Soundboard made of skin.

sound box
Half of a calabash covered with skin that amplifies the sound vibrations produced by the strings.

bridge
Piece of wood on which the strings are stretched; it transmits the strings' vibrations to the snare head.

tailpiece
Piece of wood to which the bottom ends of the strings are attached.

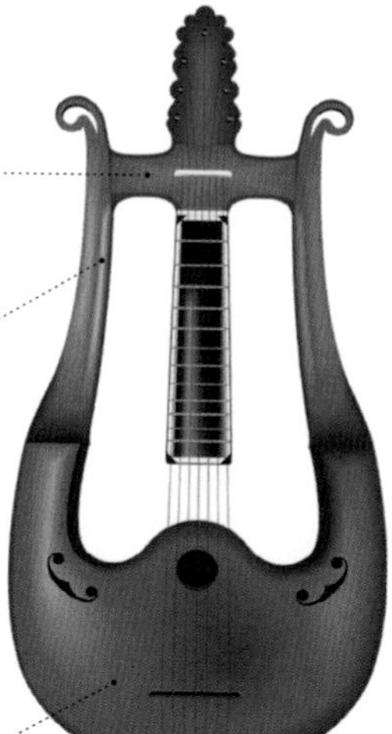

lyre
Plucked string instrument used in antiquity.

crossbar
Horizontal piece of wood supported by the arms, across which the strings are stretched.

arm
Each of the pieces of wood connecting the soundboard to the crossbar.

soundboard
The hollow part of the instrument whose shape varies; it amplifies the sound vibrations produced by the strings.

frame
Curved metal or bamboo rod held against the lips.

tongue
Flexible strip of metal attached to the frame; the player uses a finger to make it vibrate.

Jew's harp
Instrument composed of a tongue fitted to a frame; the instrument is held against the lips and the mouth is used to alter or amplify the sound vibrations.

plectrum
Accessory used to cause the strings to vibrate on certain instruments, also called a pick.

drumstick
Curved stick used to strike the skin of the talking drum.

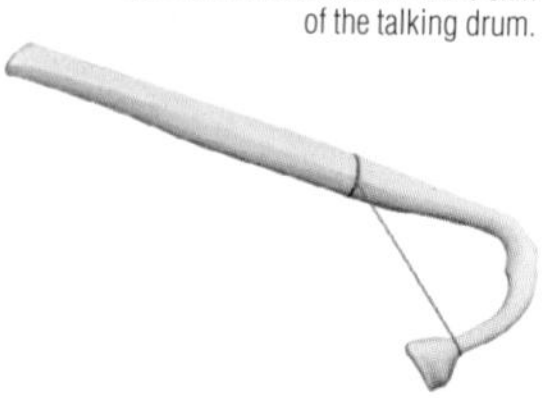

djembe
Large chalice-shaped drum used in Africa for celebrations and rituals.

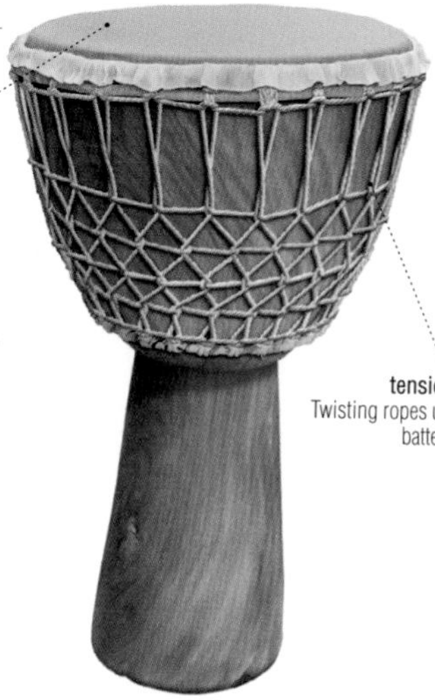

batter skin
Stretched goat or antelope skin that is struck with the hands.

sound box
Hollow cone-shaped part of the instrument that amplifies the sound vibrations produced by the hands beating on the drum.

tension rope
Twisting ropes used to tighten the batter skin.

talking drum
Drum from West Africa that is held in the armpit when played; its hourglass shape allows the tone to be adjusted by applying arm pressure to the tension ropes.

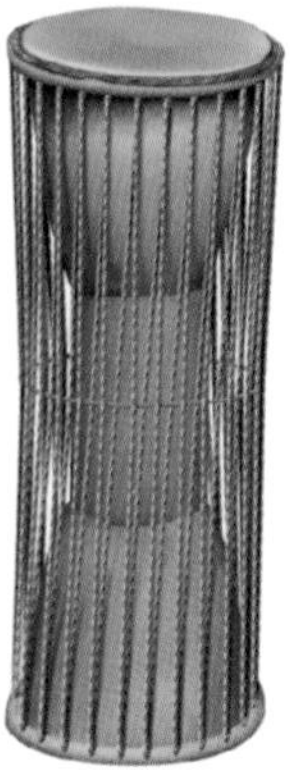

panpipe
South American instrument consisting of tubes of unequal length, each of which produces a single note.

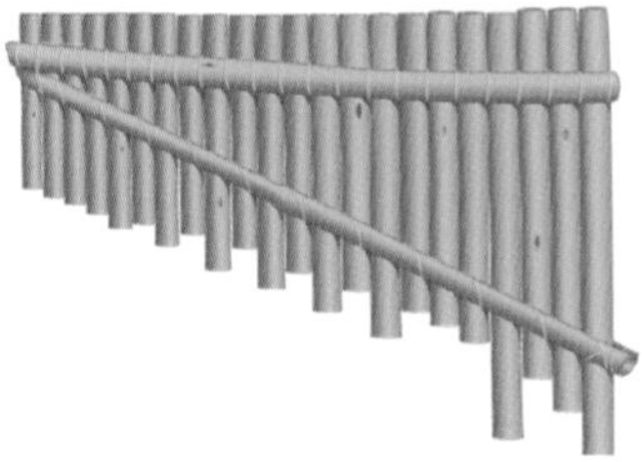

musical notation

Collective term for the signs on a staff that represent sounds and silences as well as value, pitch, measure, rhythm and so forth.

staff
A series of five lines and four spaces on which music is written and read: the lower notes are written on the bottom, the higher notes on the top; the duration of the notes is read from left to right.

space   line   ledger line

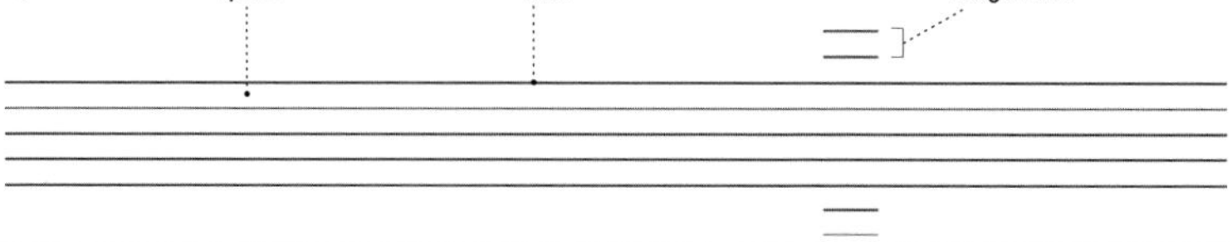

clefs
Signs placed at the beginning of the staff and named after the note they refer to.

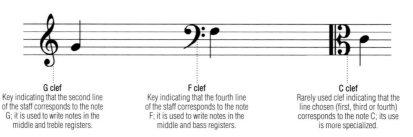

G clef
Key indicating that the second line of the staff corresponds to the note G; it is used to write notes in the middle and treble registers.

F clef
Key indicating that the fourth line of the staff corresponds to the note F; it is used to write notes in the middle and bass registers.

C clef
Rarely used clef indicating that the line chosen (first, third or fourth) corresponds to the note C; its use is more specialized.

time signatures
Section of the staff that indicates the meter of a composition, represented by a symbol in the form of a fraction or a letter, a barred C (2/2) or a C (4/4).

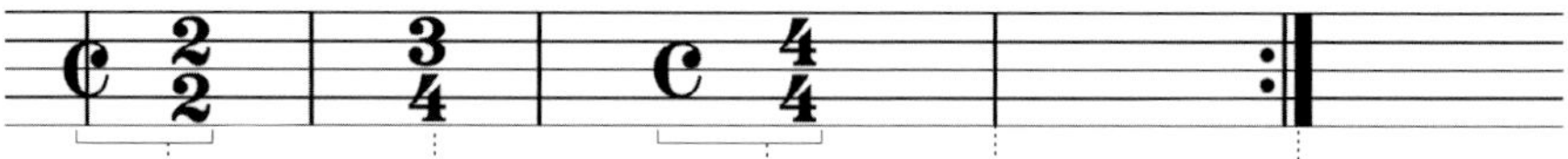

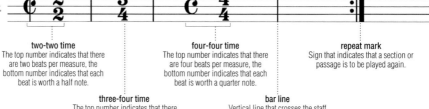

two-two time
The top number indicates that there are two beats per measure, the bottom number indicates that each beat is worth a half note.

three-four time
The top number indicates that there are three beats per measure, the bottom number indicates that each beat is worth a quarter note.

four-four time
The top number indicates that there are four beats per measure, the bottom number indicates that each beat is worth a quarter note.

bar line
Vertical line that crosses the staff lines to indicate a change in time signature.

repeat mark
Sign that indicates that a section or passage is to be played again.

intervals
Difference in pitch between two successive notes (melodic interval) or simultaneous notes (harmonic interval).

unison
Notes of the same pitch, or one or more octaves apart, produced simultaneously by several voices or instruments.

second
Interval of two tones (e.g., from C to D).

third
Interval of three tones (e.g., from C to E).

fourth
Interval of four tones (e.g., from C to F).

fifth
Interval of five tones (e.g., from C to G).

sixth
Interval of six tones (e.g., from C to A).

seventh
Interval of seven tones (e.g., from C to B).

octave
Interval of eight tones (e.g., from C to C).

scale
The diatonic scale consists of eight notes, including two semitones between E and F and between B and C. The chromatic scale is composed of 13 notes, all semitones.

C   D   E   F   G   A   B   C

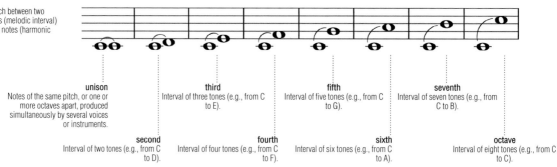

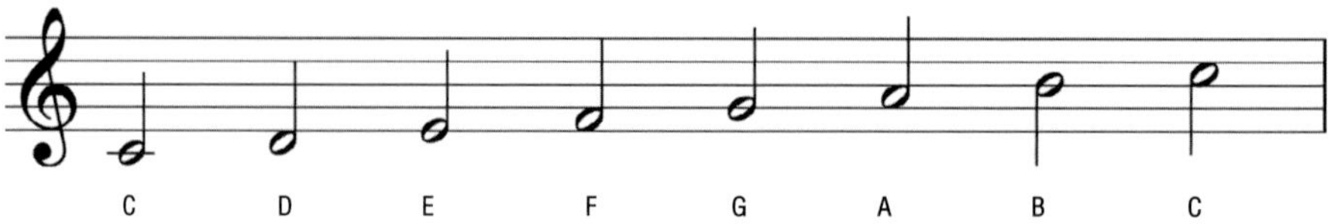

rest symbols
Symbol that marks an interruption of sound; the figure indicates duration and has the same value as the accompanying note.

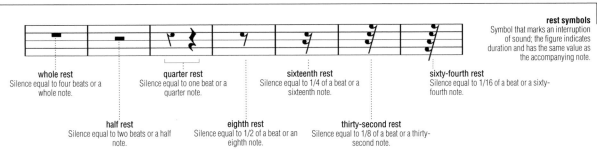

whole rest
Silence equal to four beats or a whole note.

half rest
Silence equal to two beats or a half note.

quarter rest
Silence equal to one beat or a quarter note.

eighth rest
Silence equal to 1/2 of a beat or an eighth note.

sixteenth rest
Silence equal to 1/4 of a beat or a sixteenth note.

thirty-second rest
Silence equal to 1/8 of a beat or a thirty-second note.

sixty-fourth rest
Silence equal to 1/16 of a beat or a sixty-fourth note.

ornaments
Note or series of notes used to embellish or lend variety to a melody.

appoggiatura
A short accented note played just before a principal note but immediately released.

trill
Quite rapid succession of one note with a note a semitone or a full tone above it.

turn
Series of brief notes around a principal note.

mordent
Rapid succession of two notes: the principal note and the upper mordent, or the principal note and the lower mordent, if the mordent is barred.

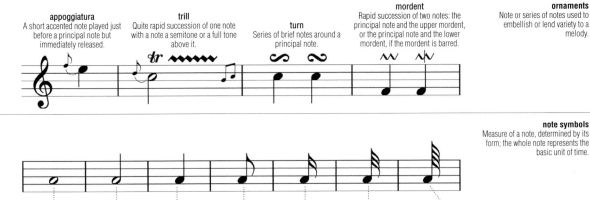

note symbols
Measure of a note, determined by its form; the whole note represents the basic unit of time.

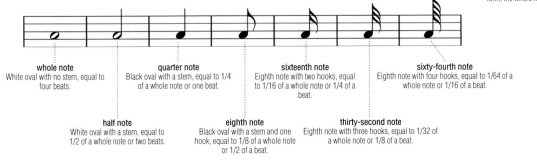

whole note
White oval with no stem, equal to four beats.

half note
White oval with a stem, equal to 1/2 of a whole note or two beats.

quarter note
Black oval with a stem, equal to 1/4 of a whole note or one beat.

eighth note
Black oval with a stem and one hook, equal to 1/8 of a whole note or 1/2 of a beat.

sixteenth note
Eighth note with two hooks, equal to 1/16 of a whole note or 1/4 of a beat.

thirty-second note
Eighth note with three hooks, equal to 1/32 of a whole note or 1/8 of a beat.

sixty-fourth note
Eighth note with four hooks, equal to 1/64 of a whole note or 1/16 of a beat.

accidentals
Signs used to change the pitch of a note.

flat
Accidental placed before a note that lowers it by a semitone.

double sharp
Accidental placed before a note that raises it by two semitones.

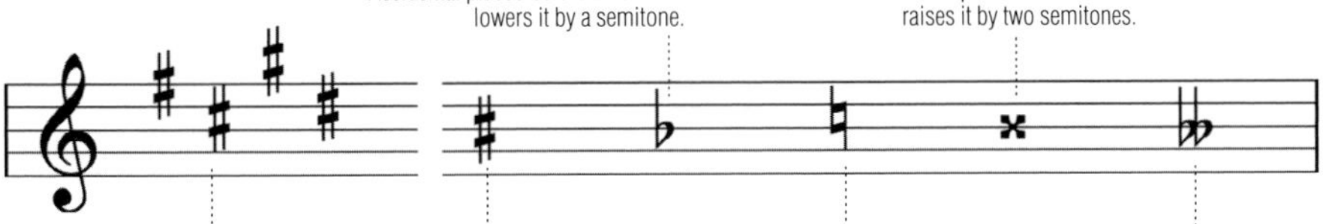

key signature
Collective term for the accidentals placed after the clef to indicate the tonality of a composition.

sharp
Accidental placed before a note that raises it by a semitone.

natural
Accidental that cancels the effect of another accidental.

double flat
Accidental placed before a note that lowers it by two semitones.

other signs
Signs that indicate how a note or series of notes should be played.

chord
Three of more notes played simultaneously.

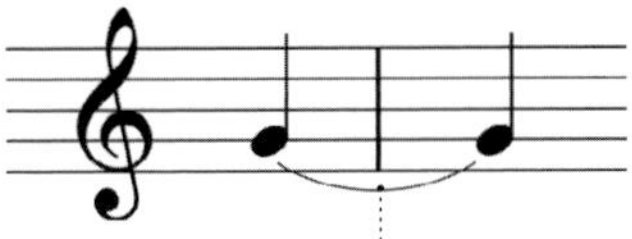

tie
Curved line indicating that the first note is prolonged by the value of the note or notes following it.

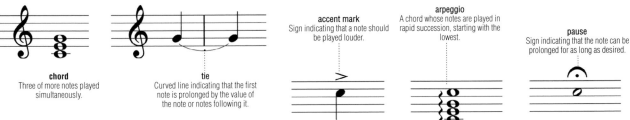

accent mark
Sign indicating that a note should be played louder.

arpeggio
A chord whose notes are played in rapid succession, starting with the lowest.

pause
Sign indicating that the note can be prolonged for as long as desired.

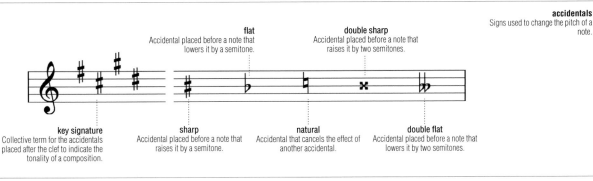

musical accessories

Instruments used by musicians to measure the tempo of a composition, tune their instruments and hold their music.

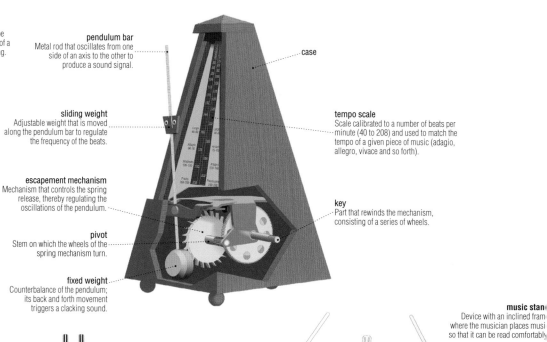

metronome
Spring-activated pendular instrument whose beats can be synchronized with the tempo of a piece of music while practicing.

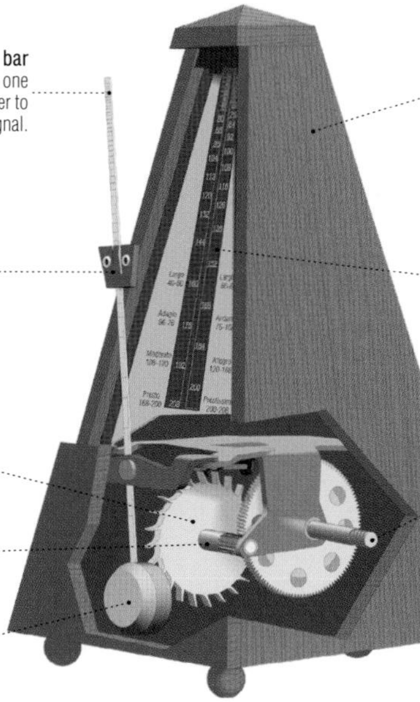

pendulum bar
Metal rod that oscillates from one side of an axis to the other to produce a sound signal.

case

sliding weight
Adjustable weight that is moved along the pendulum bar to regulate the frequency of the beats.

tempo scale
Scale calibrated to a number of beats per minute (40 to 208) and used to match the tempo of a given piece of music (adagio, allegro, vivace and so forth).

escapement mechanism
Mechanism that controls the spring release, thereby regulating the oscillations of the pendulum.

key
Part that rewinds the mechanism, consisting of a series of wheels.

pivot
Stem on which the wheels of the spring mechanism turn.

fixed weight
Counterbalance of the pendulum; its back and forth movement triggers a clacking sound.

tuning fork
Metal instrument used to tune voices and instruments; by convention, its two vibrating prongs emit an A note.

music stan
Device with an inclined fram where the musician places musi so that it can be read comfortabl

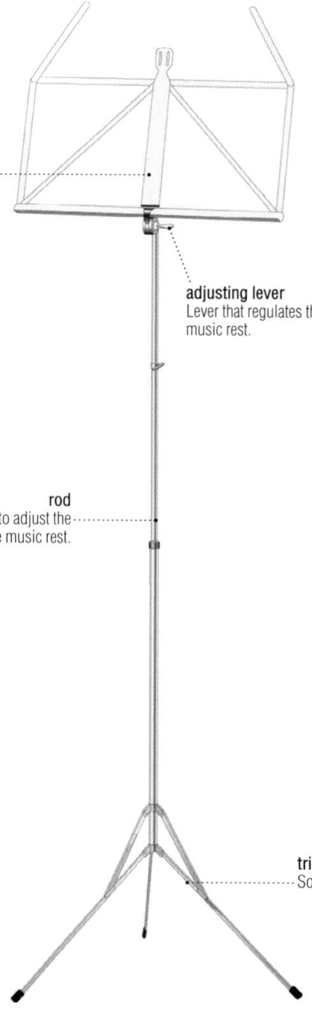

music rest
Inclined frame on which the musician places music.

adjusting lever
Lever that regulates the incline of the music rest.

rod
Telescopic piece used to adjust the height of the music rest.

tripod
Solid base with three feet.

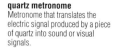

quartz metronome
Metronome that translates the electric signal produced by a piece of quartz into sound or visual signals.

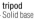

light signal
Part that translates the electronic beats of the metronome into flashing light.

standard A
Reference note established as the international standard; its frequency is 440 Hz (440 vibrations per second).

sound signal
Device that translates the metronome's electric signal into beeps; its volume can be controlled.

ARTS AND ARCHITECTURE

symphony orchestra

Group composed of numerous musicians under the direction of a conductor; it includes various categories of instruments, depending on the work to be performed.

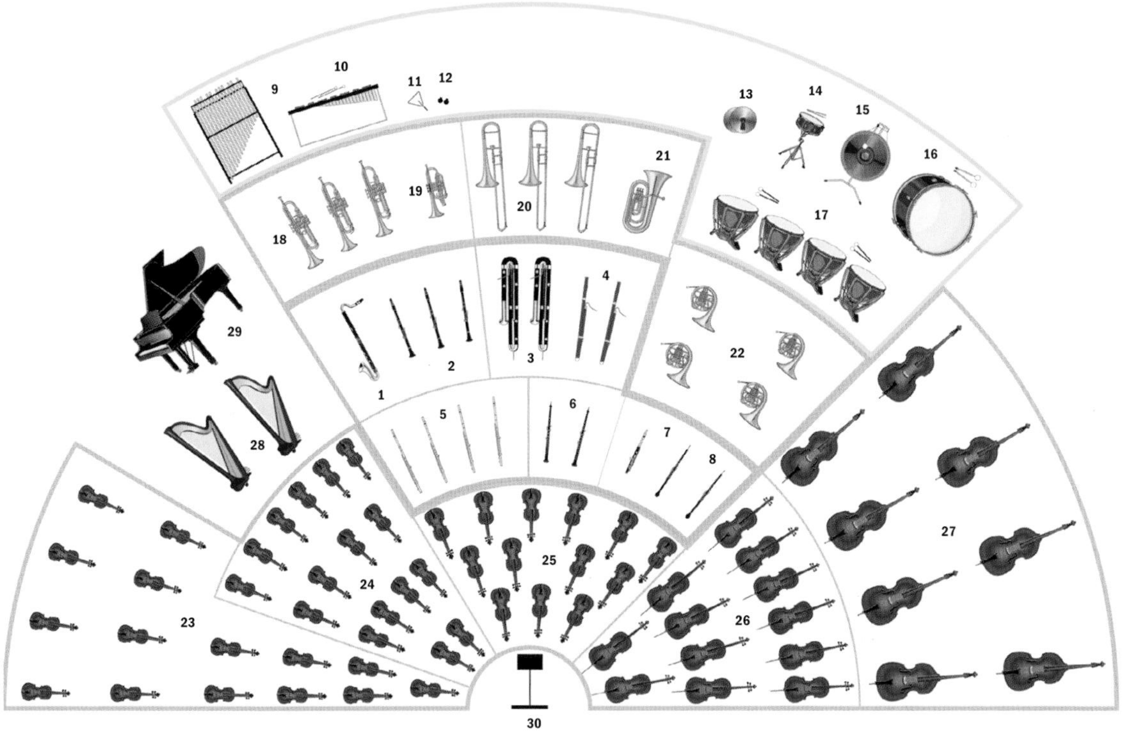

oodwind family
roup of wind instruments originally made from wood.

castanets
12 Instrument composed of two shell-shaped pieces of wood held in one hand and struck together using the fingers.

brass family
Group of wind instruments made from metal and played with cup-shaped mouthpieces.

violin family
Group of stringed instruments played with a bow.

ass clarinet
larinet with a curved tube; its nge is one octave lower than the rdinary clarinet.

piccolo
7 Small transverse flute whose range is an octave higher than the regular transverse flute.

cymbals
13 Instrument consisting of two metal disks that are struck together.

trumpets
18 Valved instruments consisting of a curved cylindrical tube and a flared bell.

first violins
23 The violins that play the melody.

arinets
ingle-reed instruments whose ylindrical tube contains holes ome closed by keys) and ends in flared bell.

English horns
8 Alto oboes with a pear-shaped bell.

snare drum
14 Flat drum consisting of two membranes; stretched across the lower head are snares that produce a rattling sound.

cornet
19 Valved instrument consisting of a curved conical tube and a flared bell.

second violins
24 The violins that support the first violins.

ontrabassoons
ouble-reed wind instruments onsisting of several tubes; their nge is one octave lower than the assoon.

percussion instruments
Group of instruments that are struck directly with the hands or with sticks, mallets, etc. to produce a sound.

gong
15 Instrument consisting of a large metal disk with a raised central portion that is struck using a mallet.

trombones
20 Instruments consisting of a curved tube with a slide that is lengthened to produce notes varying in pitch by semitones.

violas
25 Four-stringed instruments similar to a violin but played a fifth lower.

assoons
ouble-reed instruments onsisting of a curved conical ooden tube; the double-reed is serted into a curved mouthpiece.

tubular bells
9 Series of metal tubes arranged vertically in order of size; small hammers are used to strike the tops of the tubes.

bass drum
16 Large drum set on a vertical frame and struck using a pedal-controlled wooden mallet.

tuba
21 Valved instrument whose tonal range is the lowest in the brass family; it consists of a coiled conical tube and an upturned bell.

cellos
26 Four-stringed instruments placed between the legs when played; they are about twice the size of a violin and their range is one octave lower than the viola.

utes
struments with a side outhpiece and a tube containing les, some of which are closed by eys.

xylophone
10 Instrument consisting of wooden bars placed on top of resonators arranged in chromatic order in two rows; the bars are struck with mallets.

timpani
17 Instruments consisting of a parabolic copper basin covered with a stretched batter head that is struck with a mallet.

French horns
22 Valved instruments consisting of a coiled conical tube and a flared bell.

double basses
27 Four- or five-stringed instruments played upright; the largest of the violin family, they also have the lowest range.

boes
ouble-reed instruments onsisting of a conical tube with les (some closed by keys) and a lightly flared bell.

triangle
11 Instrument composed of a metal bar bent to form a triangle open at one end; the triangle is struck with a metal rod.

harps
28 Plucked stringed instruments consisting of strings of unequal length attached to a triangular frame.

piano
29 Piano whose mechanism is horizontal, allowing the pianist to better control the sound; it varies in size from 8 to 9 ft.

conductor's podium
30 Small dais that the conductor stands on to direct the musicians as they play.

examples of instrumental groups

Instrumental groups: groups of two or more instruments and musicians; a group's composition depends on the work being played.

duo
Musical work composed for two instruments.

trio
Musical work composed for three instruments.

quartet
Musical work composed for four instruments; the most common, the string quartet, features two violins, a viola and a cello.

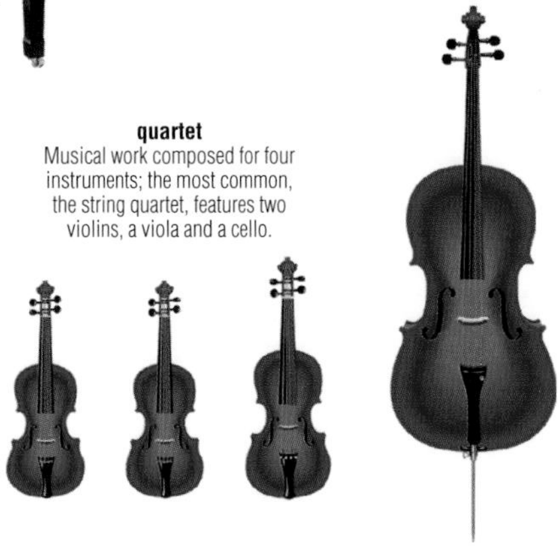

quintet
Musical work composed for five instruments.

sextet
Musical work composed for six instruments.

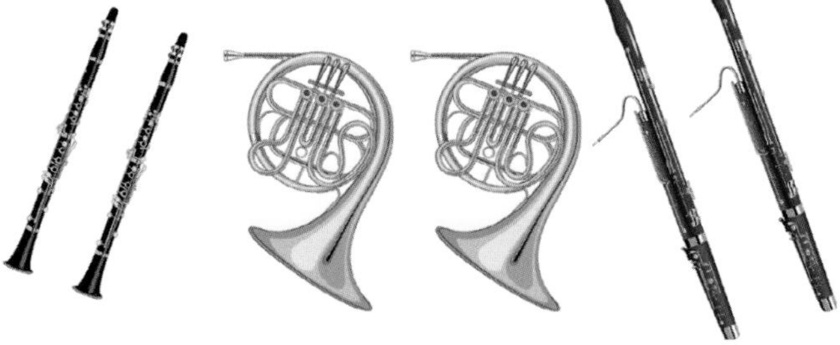

jazz band
Group composed of an indeterminate number of instruments playing an Afro-American style of music created in the early 20th century.

stringed instruments

Instruments whose sound, amplified by a sound box, is produced by the vibration of plucked or bowed strings stretched along a neck.

bow
A wooden stick with horsehair stretched from end to end; by means of friction, it makes the strings of an instrument vibrate.

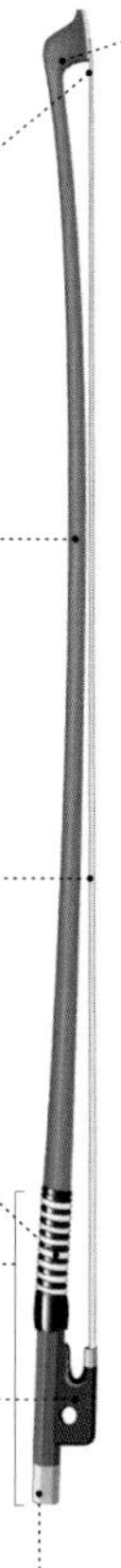

head
The upper end of the bow.

point
Part that secures the horsehair to the upper end of the bow.

stick
Thin flexible rod curved along a third of its length and along which hair is stretched.

hair
Part of the bow consisting of horsehair that is rubbed across the strings to make them vibrate.

handle
Part held when the bow is used.

heel
The lower end of the bow.

frog
Sliding part that secures the hair to the lower end of the bow; the frog is moved to adjust the tension of the hair.

screw
Threaded piece that moves the frog.

violin
Four-stringed instrument that the musician plays with a bow and holds between the shoulder and the chin.

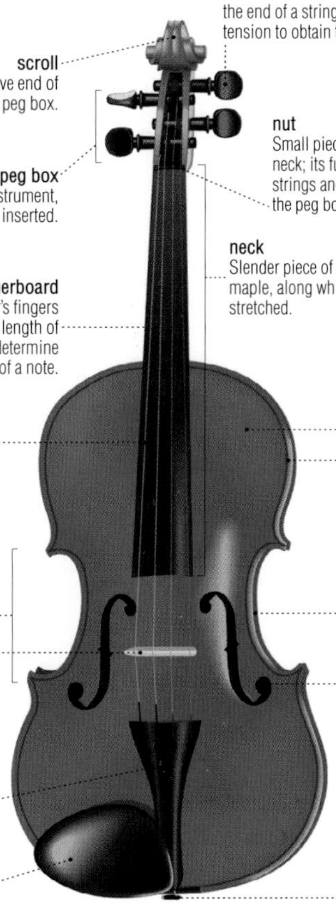

peg
Piece of wood or metal that rolls the end of a string to adjust its tension to obtain the exact note.

scroll
Spiral-shaped decorative end of the peg box.

nut
Small piece glued to the top of the neck; its function is to separate the strings and to raise them between the peg box and the bridge.

peg box
The head of a stringed instrument, where the pegs are inserted.

neck
Slender piece of wood, usually maple, along which the strings are stretched.

fingerboard
Board on which the player's fingers are placed to control the length of the vibrating string to determine the pitch of a note.

soundboard
The upper, slightly convex face of the instrument; it has two holes and receives vibrations from the bridge, which it transmits to the sound box.

string
String made of gut or metal that is rubbed with a bow; its vibrations are transmitted to the bridge.

purfling
Ornamental strip of wood around the edge of the soundboard and the bottom of the sound box.

waist
Each of the instrument's side notches in the shape of an inverted C.

rib
Each of the thin pieces of wood that form the sides of the instrument.

bridge
Piece of wood over which the strings are stretched; it transmits their vibrations to the soundboard.

sound hole
Each of the openings whose function is to release sound from the sound box.

tailpiece
Piece of wood to which the bottom ends of the strings are attached.

chin rest
Slightly concave piece of wood or plastic on which the chin rests to hold the violin against the shoulder.

end button
Ebony button used to attach the tailpiece to the sound box.

violin family
Group of stringed instruments played with a bow.

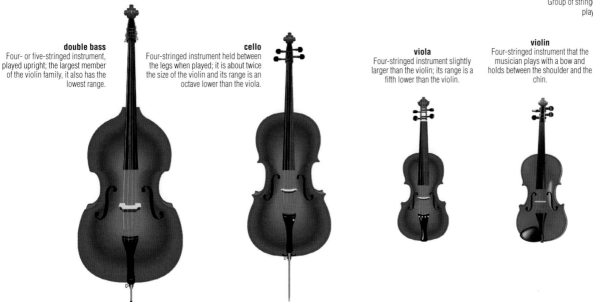

double bass
Four- or five-stringed instrument, played upright; the largest member of the violin family, it also has the lowest range.

cello
Four-stringed instrument held between the legs when played; it is about twice the size of the violin and its range is an octave lower than the viola.

viola
Four-stringed instrument slightly larger than the violin; its range is a fifth lower than the violin.

violin
Four-stringed instrument that the musician plays with a bow and holds between the shoulder and the chin.

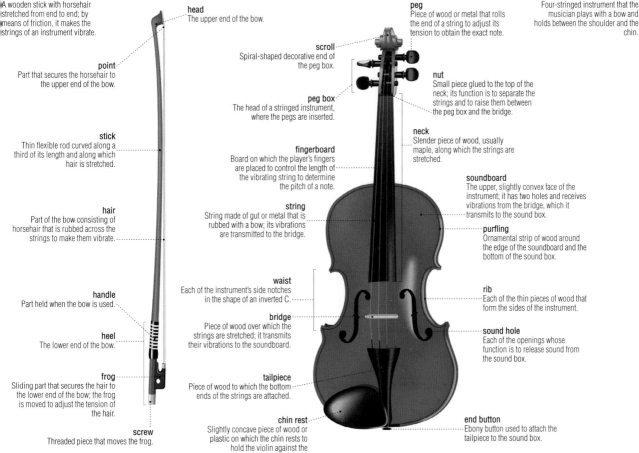

ARTS AND ARCHITECTURE

stringed instruments

harp
Plucked stringed instrument consisting of strings of various lengths attached to a triangular frame.

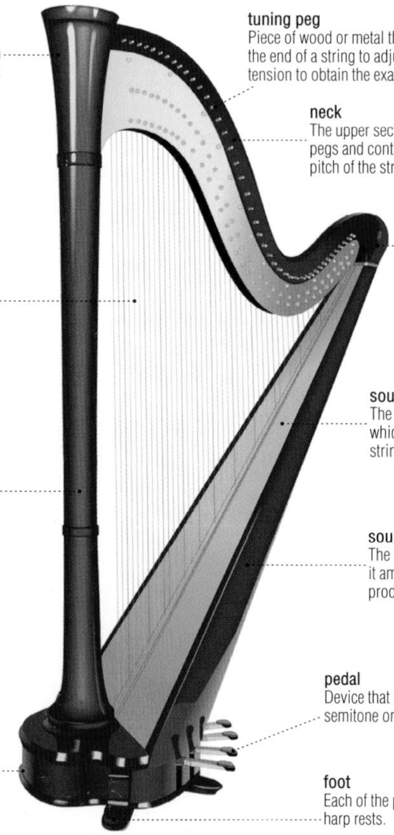

crown
The top of the pillar.

tuning peg
Piece of wood or metal that rolls the end of a string to adjust its tension to obtain the exact note.

neck
The upper section of the harp; it anchors the tuning pegs and contains a mechanism that changes the pitch of the strings by a semitone.

shoulder
Curved section of the harp's frame.

string
Made of gut, nylon or metal; its vibrations are transferred to the soundboard.

soundboard
The upper face of the sound box, which receives the vibrations of the strings.

pillar
Upright that connects the sound box to the neck; its metal rods join the pedals to the mechanism inside the neck.

sound box
The hollow part of the instrument; it amplifies the sound vibrations produced by the strings.

pedal
Device that raises the string by a semitone or a full tone.

pedestal
The base where the sound box and the pillar meet.

foot
Each of the pieces on which the harp rests.

acoustic guitar
Plucked stringed instrument whose hollow body amplifies the vibrations produced by the strings.

soundboard
The upper face of the instrument; it receives the vibrations from the bridge and transmits them to the sound box.

sound box
The hollow part of the instrument; it amplifies the sound vibrations produced by the strings.

neck
Part of the guitar separated into sections by frets and along which the strings are stretched.

head
The upper end of the neck, where the pegs are attached.

peg
Piece of wood or metal that rolls the end of a string to adjust its tension to obtain the exact note.

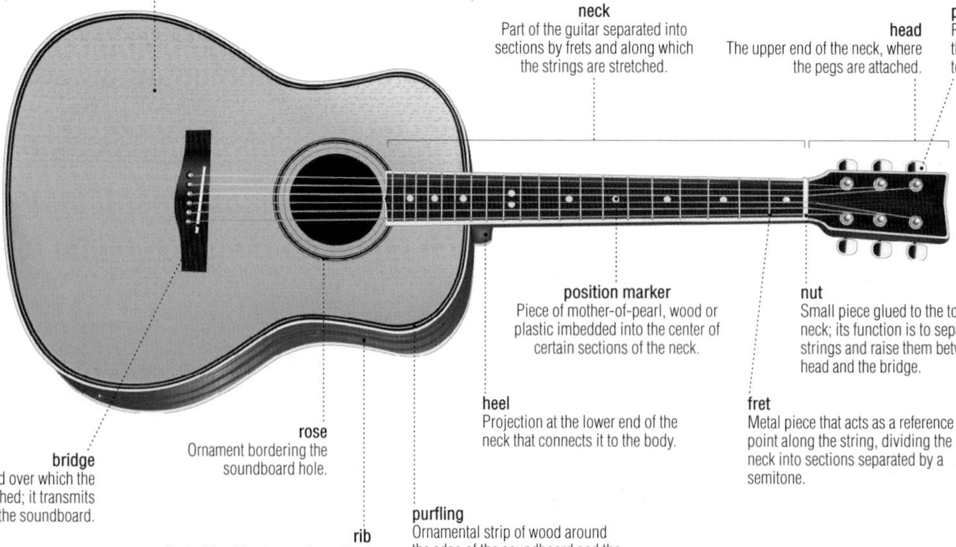

position marker
Piece of mother-of-pearl, wood or plastic imbedded into the center of certain sections of the neck.

nut
Small piece glued to the top of the neck; its function is to separate the strings and raise them between the head and the bridge.

heel
Projection at the lower end of the neck that connects it to the body.

fret
Metal piece that acts as a reference point along the string, dividing the neck into sections separated by a semitone.

rose
Ornament bordering the soundboard hole.

bridge
Piece of wood over which the strings are stretched; it transmits their vibrations to the soundboard.

purfling
Ornamental strip of wood around the edge of the soundboard and the bottom of the sound box.

rib
Each of the thin pieces of wood that form the sides of the instrument.

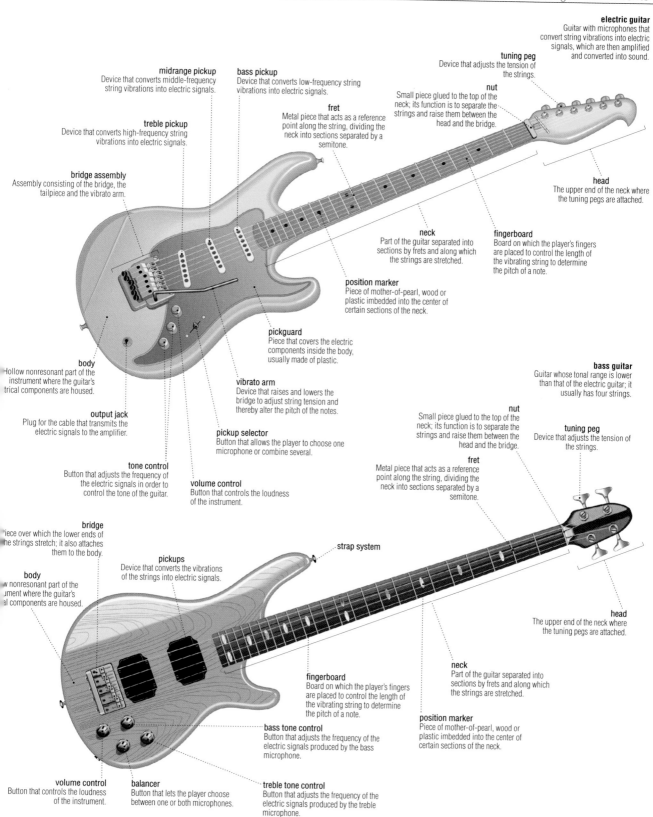

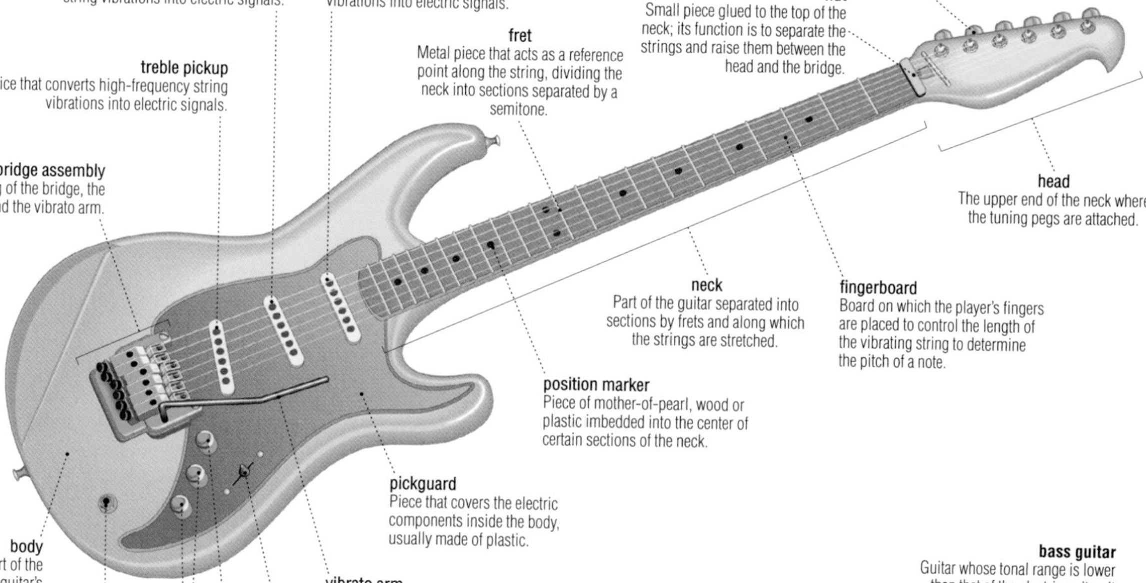
electric guitar
Guitar with microphones that convert string vibrations into electric signals, which are then amplified and converted into sound.
tuning peg
Device that adjusts the tension of the strings.
midrange pickup
Device that converts middle-frequency string vibrations into electric signals.
bass pickup
Device that converts low-frequency string vibrations into electric signals.
nut
Small piece glued to the top of the neck; its function is to separate the strings and raise them between the head and the bridge.
fret
Metal piece that acts as a reference point along the string, dividing the neck into sections separated by a semitone.
treble pickup
Device that converts high-frequency string vibrations into electric signals.
bridge assembly
Assembly consisting of the bridge, the tailpiece and the vibrato arm.
head
The upper end of the neck where the tuning pegs are attached.
neck
Part of the guitar separated into sections by frets and along which the strings are stretched.
fingerboard
Board on which the player's fingers are placed to control the length of the vibrating string to determine the pitch of a note.
position marker
Piece of mother-of-pearl, wood or plastic imbedded into the center of certain sections of the neck.
pickguard
Piece that covers the electric components inside the body, usually made of plastic.
body
Hollow nonresonant part of the instrument where the guitar's trical components are housed.
vibrato arm
Device that raises and lowers the bridge to adjust string tension and thereby alter the pitch of the notes.
output jack
Plug for the cable that transmits the electric signals to the amplifier.
pickup selector
Button that allows the player to choose one microphone or combine several.
tone control
Button that adjusts the frequency of the electric signals in order to control the tone of the guitar.
volume control
Button that controls the loudness of the instrument.

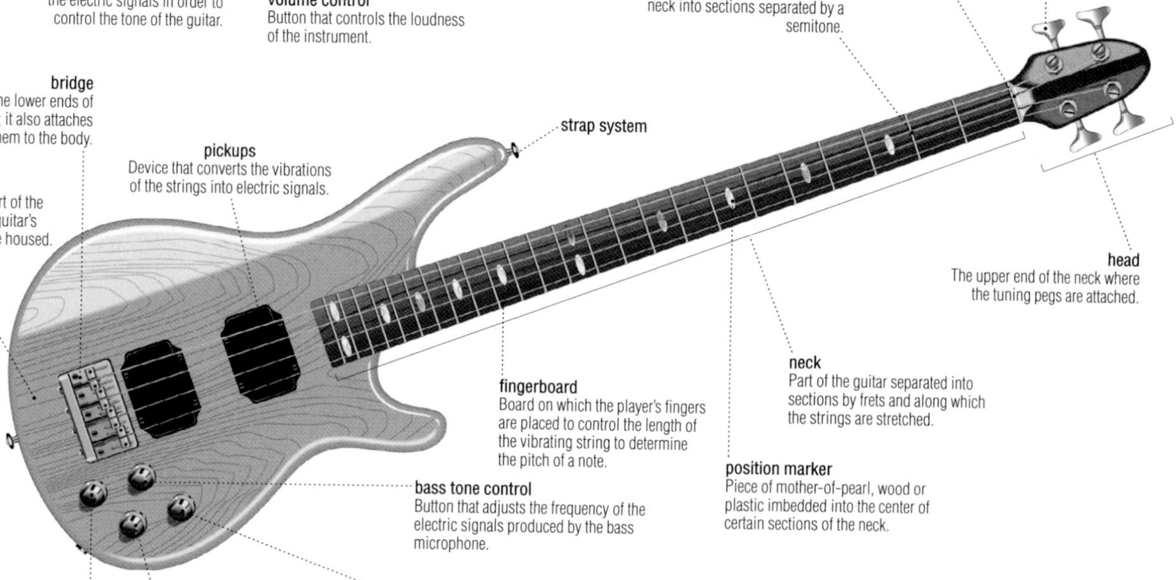
bass guitar
Guitar whose tonal range is lower than that of the electric guitar; it usually has four strings.
nut
Small piece glued to the top of the neck; its function is to separate the strings and raise them between the head and the bridge.
tuning peg
Device that adjusts the tension of the strings.
fret
Metal piece that acts as a reference point along the string, dividing the neck into sections separated by a semitone.
bridge
iece over which the lower ends of he strings stretch; it also attaches them to the body.
strap system
pickups
Device that converts the vibrations of the strings into electric signals.
body
w nonresonant part of the ument where the guitar's al components are housed.
head
The upper end of the neck where the tuning pegs are attached.
neck
Part of the guitar separated into sections by frets and along which the strings are stretched.
fingerboard
Board on which the player's fingers are placed to control the length of the vibrating string to determine the pitch of a note.
position marker
Piece of mother-of-pearl, wood or plastic imbedded into the center of certain sections of the neck.
bass tone control
Button that adjusts the frequency of the electric signals produced by the bass microphone.
volume control
Button that controls the loudness of the instrument.
balancer
Button that lets the player choose between one or both microphones.
treble tone control
Button that adjusts the frequency of the electric signals produced by the treble microphone.

keyboard instruments

Instruments with a series of keys that are pressed to strike or pluck strings and thereby produce sound.

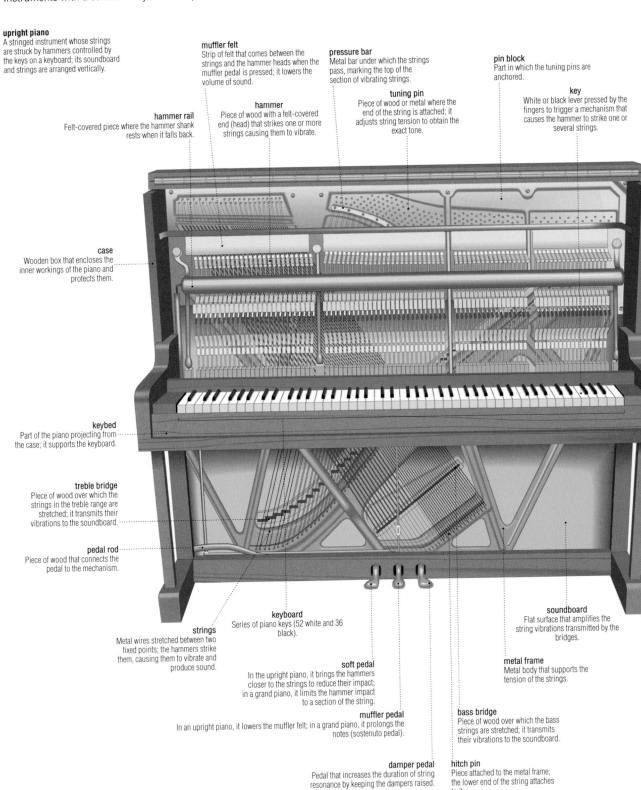

upright piano
A stringed instrument whose strings are struck by hammers controlled by the keys on a keyboard; its soundboard and strings are arranged vertically.

muffler felt
Strip of felt that comes between the strings and the hammer heads when the muffler pedal is pressed; it lowers the volume of sound.

pressure bar
Metal bar under which the strings pass, marking the top of the section of vibrating strings.

pin block
Part in which the tuning pins are anchored.

tuning pin
Piece of wood or metal where the end of the string is attached; it adjusts string tension to obtain the exact tone.

key
White or black lever pressed by the fingers to trigger a mechanism that causes the hammer to strike one or several strings.

hammer
Piece of wood with a felt-covered end (head) that strikes one or more strings causing them to vibrate.

hammer rail
Felt-covered piece where the hammer shank rests when it falls back.

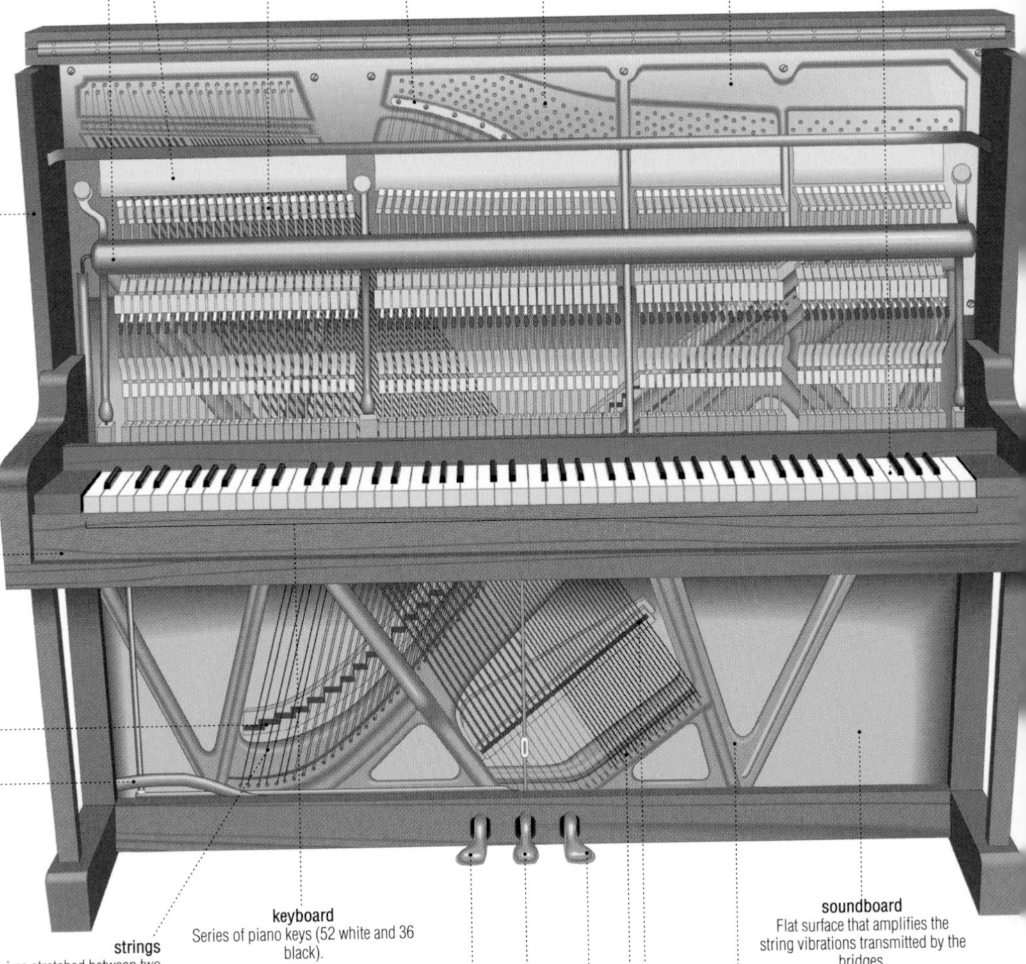

case
Wooden box that encloses the inner workings of the piano and protects them.

keybed
Part of the piano projecting from the case; it supports the keyboard.

treble bridge
Piece of wood over which the strings in the treble range are stretched; it transmits their vibrations to the soundboard.

pedal rod
Piece of wood that connects the pedal to the mechanism.

keyboard
Series of piano keys (52 white and 36 black).

strings
Metal wires stretched between two fixed points; the hammers strike them, causing them to vibrate and produce sound.

soundboard
Flat surface that amplifies the string vibrations transmitted by the bridges.

metal frame
Metal body that supports the tension of the strings.

soft pedal
In the upright piano, it brings the hammers closer to the strings to reduce their impact; in a grand piano, it limits the hammer impact to a section of the string.

muffler pedal
In an upright piano, it lowers the muffler felt; in a grand piano, it prolongs the notes (sostenuto pedal).

bass bridge
Piece of wood over which the bass strings are stretched; it transmits their vibrations to the soundboard.

damper pedal
Pedal that increases the duration of string resonance by keeping the dampers raised.

hitch pin
Piece attached to the metal frame; the lower end of the string attaches to it.

keyboard instruments

upright piano action
Combination of elements whereby energy applied to a key is transferred to the hammer, which in turn causes the strings to vibrate.

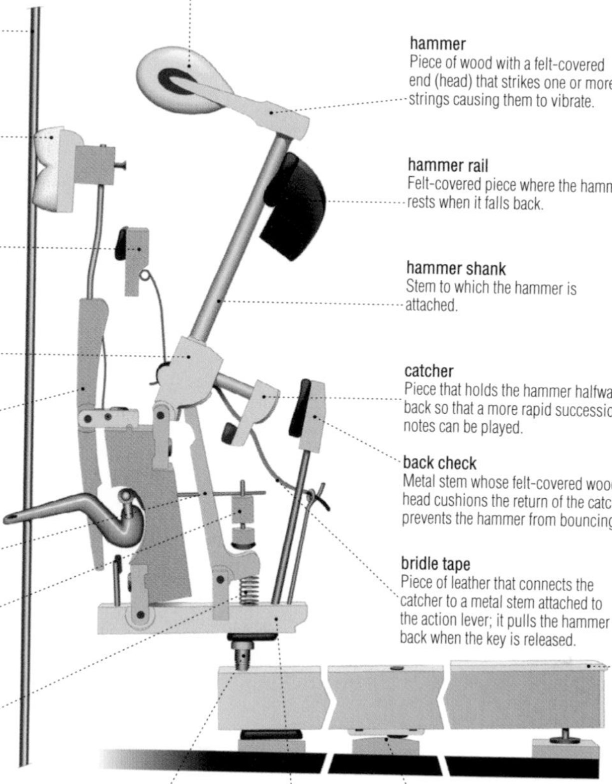

hammer felt
Felt-covered hammer head that strikes the string or strings and causes them to vibrate.

string
The strings are: single and made of copper for the bass, double and made of steel for the mid-range, and triple and made of finer steel for the treble range.

damper
Piece of felt-covered wood that rests on the string or strings to stop them from vibrating after the key is released.

damper rail
Felt-covered piece where the damper stem rests after leaving the string, allowing the string to vibrate.

hammer butt
Piece that is pushed by the jack, directing the hammer toward the string or strings.

damper lever
Stem with a spring that brings the damper back against the string when a key is released.

jack
Movable stem that transmits the movement of the action lever to the hammer butt and allows the hammer to fall back as soon as it strikes the string or strings.

regulating button
Part that pulls the jack back before the hammer strikes the string or strings.

jack spring
Spring that allows the jack to return to its position under the hammer butt once the key is released.

hammer
Piece of wood with a felt-covered end (head) that strikes one or more strings causing them to vibrate.

hammer rail
Felt-covered piece where the hammer shank rests when it falls back.

hammer shank
Stem to which the hammer is attached.

catcher
Piece that holds the hammer halfway back so that a more rapid succession of notes can be played.

back check
Metal stem whose felt-covered wooden head cushions the return of the catcher and prevents the hammer from bouncing back.

bridle tape
Piece of leather that connects the catcher to a metal stem attached to the action lever; it pulls the hammer back when the key is released.

key
White or black lever pressed by the fingers to trigger a mechanism that causes the hammer to strike one or several strings.

capstan button
Screw that controls and transmits the key movement to the action lever.

action lever
Movable piece that transmits movement to the jack.

balance rail
Piece on which the key balances.

examples of keyboard instruments

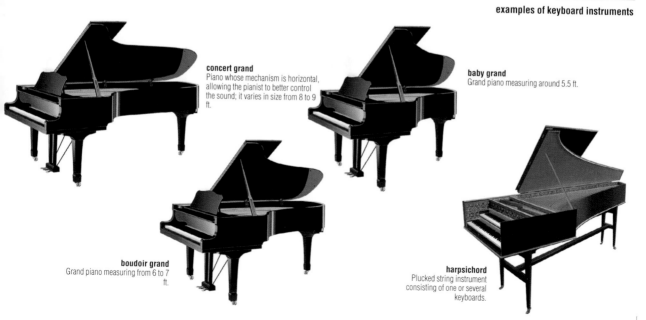

concert grand
Piano whose mechanism is horizontal, allowing the pianist to better control the sound; it varies in size from 8 to 9 ft.

baby grand
Grand piano measuring around 5.5 ft.

boudoir grand
Grand piano measuring from 6 to 7 ft.

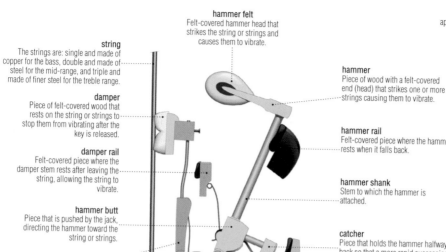

harpsichord
Plucked string instrument consisting of one or several keyboards.

keyboard instruments

organ
Wind instrument with several keyboards; it produces sound by means of pipes that are fed by a blower.

organ console
Console consisting of the mechanisms controlled by the organist (e.g., manuals, pedals, stop knobs).

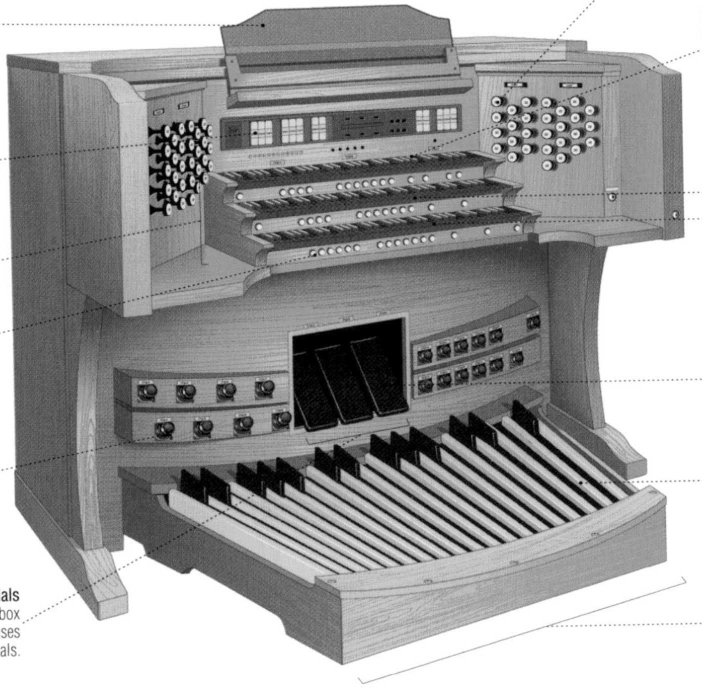

stop knob
Device attached to a stop rod that controls the slider, which allows a row of pipes to sound or remain silent.

music stand
Inclined board where the organist places music.

swell organ manual
Keyboard that controls a series of pipes enclosed in a wooden frame (swell box); its movable valves are controlled by a swell ped to obtain variations in volume.

choir organ manual
Keyboard that controls a series of pipes at the front of the organ; its timbres are softer than those of the great organ.

coupler-tilt tablet
Plate that controls the mechanism joining two or more manuals.

great organ manual
Series of keys that make up the main keyboard, which is used to play the most important parts.

manuals
Each of the series of keys that the organist plays by hand, which control one or several pipes of the same note.

thumb piston
Hand-controlled mechanism used to prepare the pipes of a manual in advance, making them sound only when the piston is pushed.

crescendo pedal
Pedal mechanism allowing certain combinations of pipes to sound and increasing their number until "tutti", when all pipes are heard.

pedal key
Lever that is lowered using the foot to allow air to enter and produce sound.

toe piston
Mechanism controlled by foot that prepares the pipes in advance, making them sound only when the pedal is pushed.

swell pedals
Mechanisms that open and close the swell box valves to control volume; the swell box houses the pipes of one or more manuals.

pedal keyboard
Series of keys that the organist operates by foot.

reed pipe
Pipe in which sound is produced by the vibration of a tongue on the open face of a pipe.

resonator
Resonant vessel that amplifies the vibrations of the shallot.

tuning wire
Metal stem that adjusts the length of the shallot's vibrating part to tune the pipe.

block
Movable part inserted into the foot of the pipe; its lower end holds the shallot.

wedge
Piece of wood that attaches the tongue to the upper end of the pipe.

shallot
Hollow pipe with one open face, on which the tongue vibrates.

tongue
Small sheet of flexible metal that vibrates on the open face of the pipe; the amplitude of the vibrations determines the pitch of the note.

foot
Lower part of the conical pipe through which air enters; it is attached to the upperboard.

foot hole
Opening through which air from the blower enters the pipe.

flue pipe
Pipe that vibrates when pressurized air passes through a narrow horizontal aperture called the mouth.

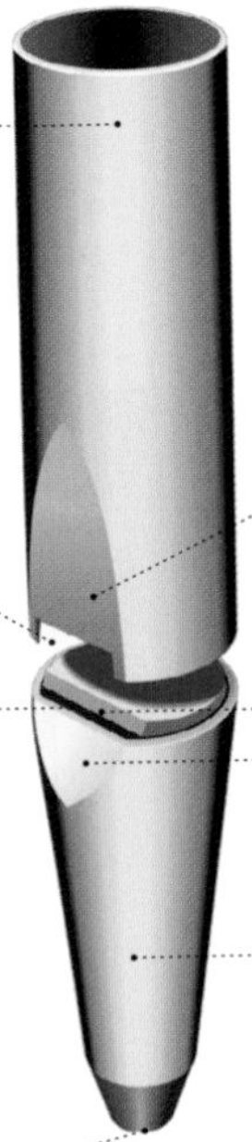

body
Upper part of the pipe; it controls the volume of vibrating air and acts as a resonator.

upper lip
Flat part of the pipe that breaks up the air exiting the flue, causing the air column in the body to vibrate.

mouth
Horizontal aperture on the front of the pipe between the body and the foot; air escapes through it to produce sound.

languid
Metal plate that the air strikes before exiting the flue.

flue
Narrow slit through which air from the foot passes after hitting the languid.

lower lip
Flat portion of the foot; it forces ai onto the languid.

foot
Lower part of the conical pipe through which air enters; it is attached to the upperboard.

foot hole
Opening through which air from the blower enters the pipe.

mechanism of the organ
All the parts between the manual keys and the pipes; in combination, they cause the organ to function.

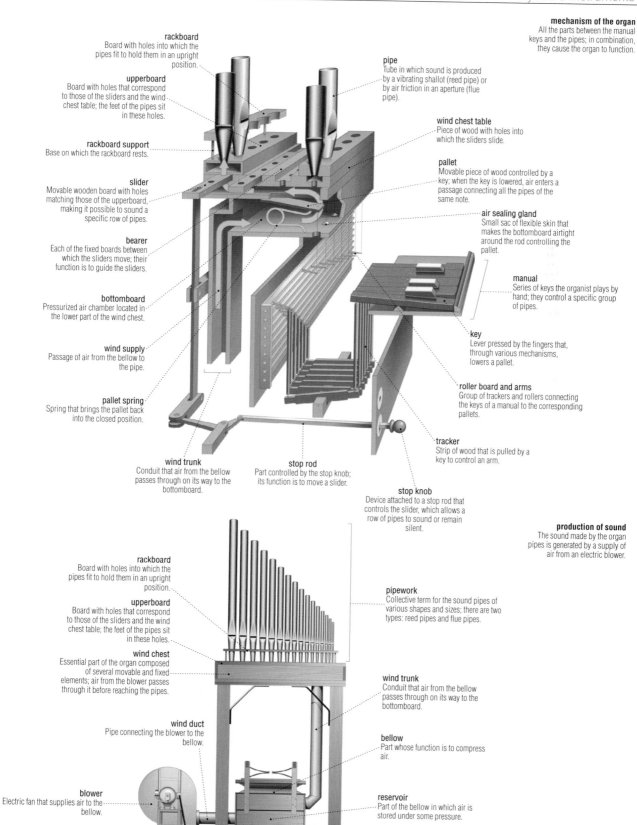

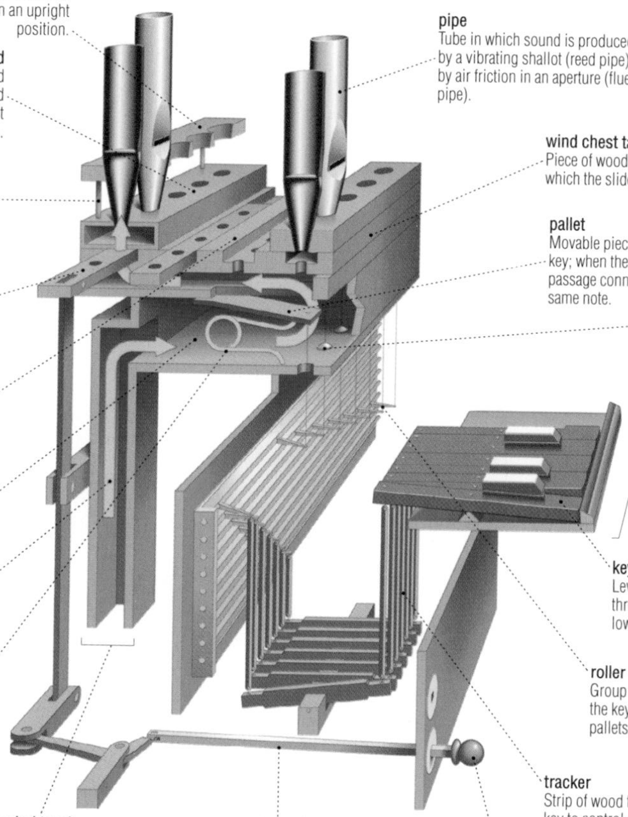
rackboard
Board with holes into which the pipes fit to hold them in an upright position.
upperboard
Board with holes that correspond to those of the sliders and the wind chest table; the feet of the pipes sit in these holes.
rackboard support
Base on which the rackboard rests.
slider
Movable wooden board with holes matching those of the upperboard, making it possible to sound a specific row of pipes.
bearer
Each of the fixed boards between which the sliders move; their function is to guide the sliders.
bottomboard
Pressurized air chamber located in the lower part of the wind chest.
wind supply
Passage of air from the bellow to the pipe.
pallet spring
Spring that brings the pallet back into the closed position.
wind trunk
Conduit that air from the bellow passes through on its way to the bottomboard.
stop rod
Part controlled by the stop knob; its function is to move a slider.
stop knob
Device attached to a stop rod that controls the slider, which allows a row of pipes to sound or remain silent.
pipe
Tube in which sound is produced by a vibrating shallot (reed pipe) or by air friction in an aperture (flue pipe).
wind chest table
Piece of wood with holes into which the sliders slide.
pallet
Movable piece of wood controlled by a key; when the key is lowered, air enters a passage connecting all the pipes of the same note.
air sealing gland
Small sac of flexible skin that makes the bottomboard airtight around the rod controlling the pallet.
manual
Series of keys the organist plays by hand; they control a specific group of pipes.
key
Lever pressed by the fingers that, through various mechanisms, lowers a pallet.
roller board and arms
Group of trackers and rollers connecting the keys of a manual to the corresponding pallets.
tracker
Strip of wood that is pulled by a key to control an arm.

production of sound
The sound made by the organ pipes is generated by a supply of air from an electric blower.

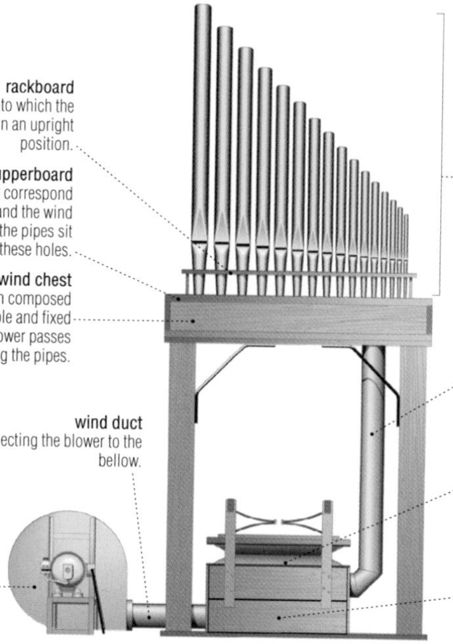
rackboard
Board with holes into which the pipes fit to hold them in an upright position.
upperboard
Board with holes that correspond to those of the sliders and the wind chest table; the feet of the pipes sit in these holes.
wind chest
Essential part of the organ composed of several movable and fixed elements; air from the blower passes through it before reaching the pipes.
wind duct
Pipe connecting the blower to the bellow.
blower
Electric fan that supplies air to the bellow.
pipework
Collective term for the sound pipes of various shapes and sizes; there are two types: reed pipes and flue pipes.
wind trunk
Conduit that air from the bellow passes through on its way to the bottomboard.
bellow
Part whose function is to compress air.
reservoir
Part of the bellow in which air is stored under some pressure.

wind instruments

Collective term for instruments that produce sound by blowing, which causes the air column inside the tube to vibrate; a reed or the lips are used to play them.

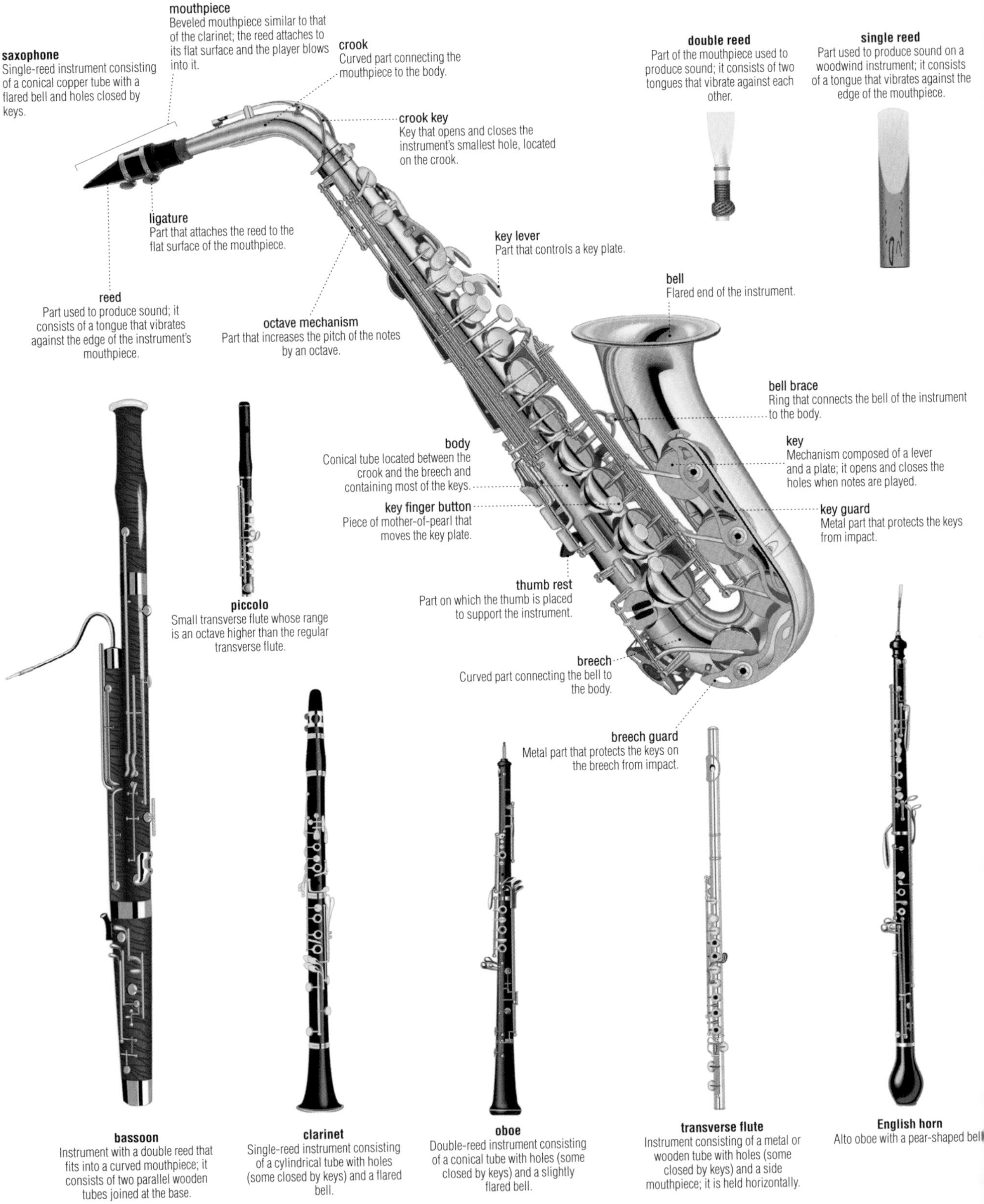
saxophone
Single-reed instrument consisting of a conical copper tube with a flared bell and holes closed by keys.
mouthpiece
Beveled mouthpiece similar to that of the clarinet; the reed attaches to its flat surface and the player blows into it.
crook
Curved part connecting the mouthpiece to the body.
crook key
Key that opens and closes the instrument's smallest hole, located on the crook.
double reed
Part of the mouthpiece used to produce sound; it consists of two tongues that vibrate against each other.
single reed
Part used to produce sound on a woodwind instrument; it consists of a tongue that vibrates against the edge of the mouthpiece.
ligature
Part that attaches the reed to the flat surface of the mouthpiece.
key lever
Part that controls a key plate.
bell
Flared end of the instrument.
reed
Part used to produce sound; it consists of a tongue that vibrates against the edge of the instrument's mouthpiece.
octave mechanism
Part that increases the pitch of the notes by an octave.
bell brace
Ring that connects the bell of the instrument to the body.
body
Conical tube located between the crook and the breech and containing most of the keys.
key
Mechanism composed of a lever and a plate; it opens and closes the holes when notes are played.
key finger button
Piece of mother-of-pearl that moves the key plate.
key guard
Metal part that protects the keys from impact.
thumb rest
Part on which the thumb is placed to support the instrument.
piccolo
Small transverse flute whose range is an octave higher than the regular transverse flute.
breech
Curved part connecting the bell to the body.
breech guard
Metal part that protects the keys on the breech from impact.
bassoon
Instrument with a double reed that fits into a curved mouthpiece; it consists of two parallel wooden tubes joined at the base.
clarinet
Single-reed instrument consisting of a cylindrical tube with holes (some closed by keys) and a flared bell.
oboe
Double-reed instrument consisting of a conical tube with holes (some closed by keys) and a slightly flared bell.
transverse flute
Instrument consisting of a metal or wooden tube with holes (some closed by keys) and a side mouthpiece; it is held horizontally.
English horn
Alto oboe with a pear-shaped bell

wind instruments

trumpet
Valved instrument consisting of a coiled cylindrical tube and a flared bell.

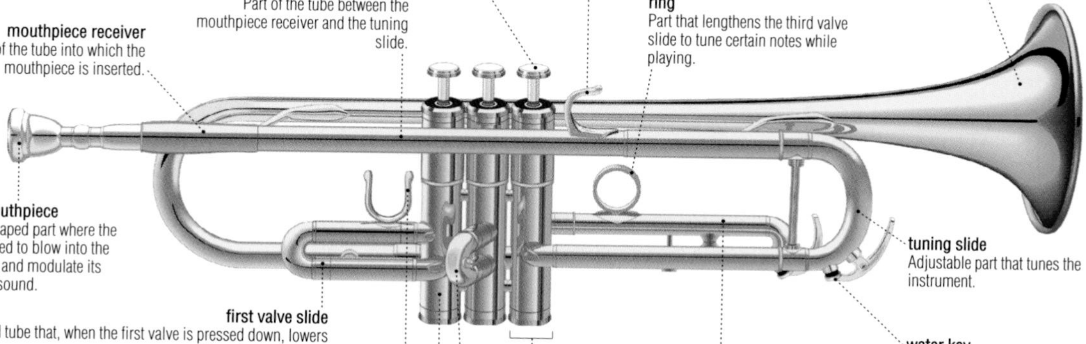

finger button
Part that is pressed to control the valves; it is often inlaid with mother-of-pearl.

little finger hook
Part used to support the little finger of the right hand.

bell
Flared end of the instrument.

mouthpipe
Part of the tube between the mouthpiece receiver and the tuning slide.

mouthpiece receiver
The end of the tube into which the mouthpiece is inserted.

ring
Part that lengthens the third valve slide to tune certain notes while playing.

mouthpiece
Small cup-shaped part where the lips are placed to blow into the instrument and modulate its sound.

tuning slide
Adjustable part that tunes the instrument.

first valve slide
Curved tube that, when the first valve is pressed down, lowers the note by one tone.

water key
Part that expels the moisture that builds up inside the instrument.

third valve slide
Curved tube that, when the third valve is pressed, lowers notes by three semitones.

thumb hook
Part in which the thumb is inserted to lengthen the first valve slide and tune certain notes while playing.

valve
Device that produces different notes by lengthening the air column inside the tube and releasing the slides.

valve casing
Cylindrical tube holding a valve.

second valve slide
Curved tube that, when the second valve is pressed down, lowers the note by a semitone.

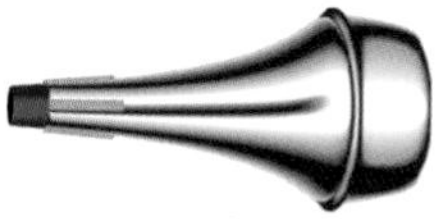

mute
Device that is inserted into the bell to muffle the sound.

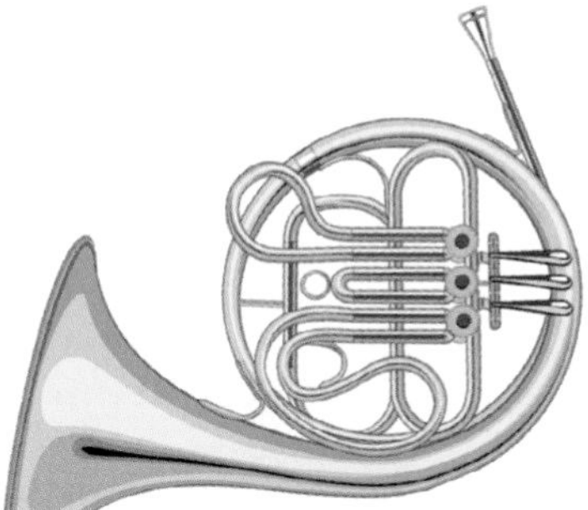

French horn
Valved instrument consisting of a coiled conical tube and a flared bell.

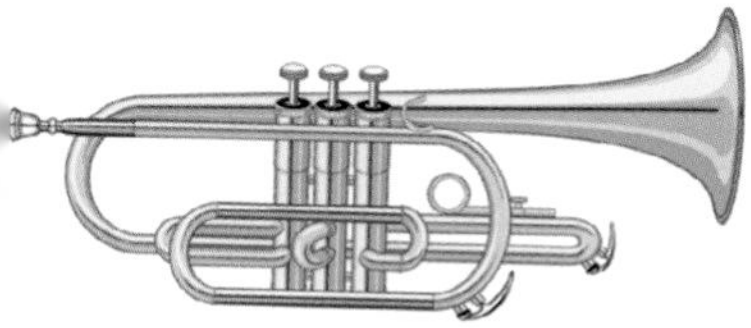

cornet
Valved instrument consisting of a curved conical tube and a flared bell.

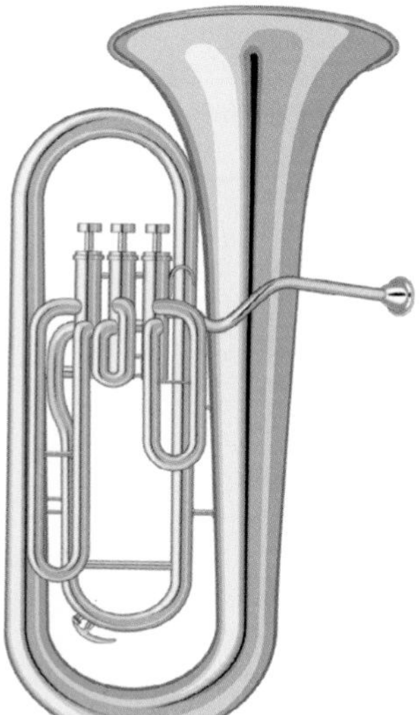

saxhorn
Valved instrument whose range is a fifth lower than the cornet; it consists of a curved conical tube and a large bell.

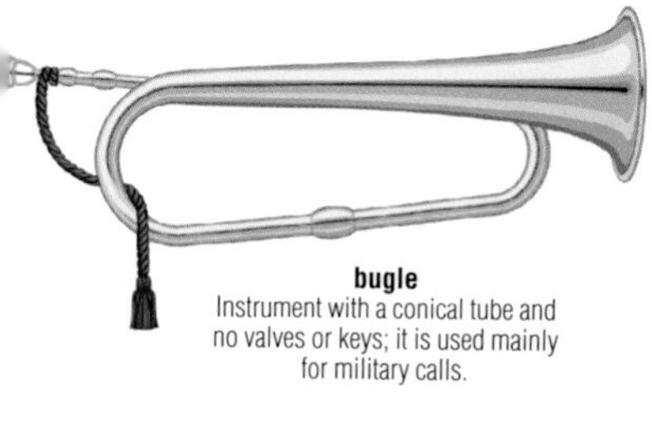

bugle
Instrument with a conical tube and no valves or keys; it is used mainly for military calls.

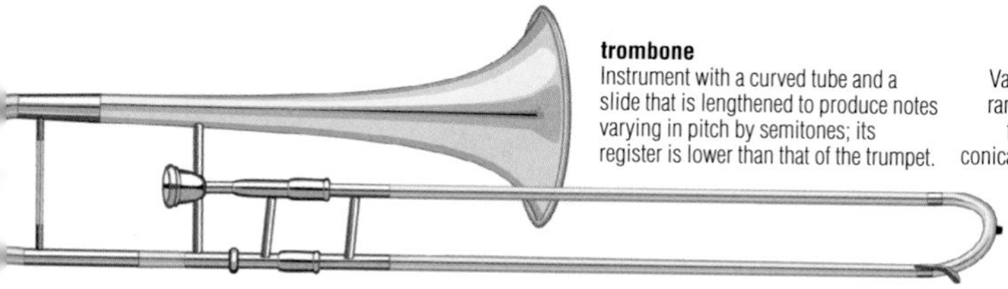

trombone
Instrument with a curved tube and a slide that is lengthened to produce notes varying in pitch by semitones; its register is lower than that of the trumpet.

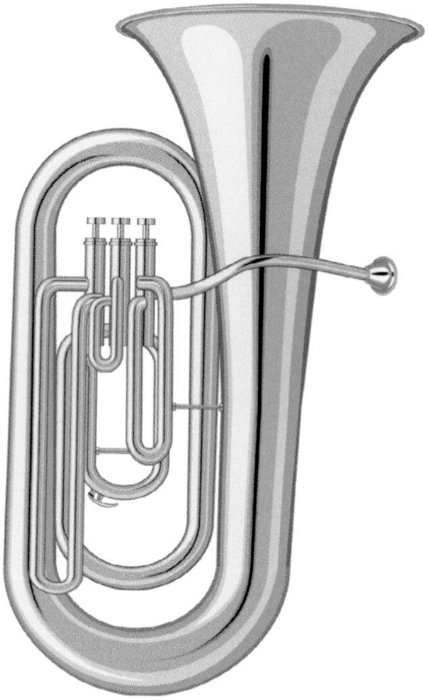

tuba
Valved instrument whose tonal range is the lowest in the brass family; it consists of a coiled conical tube and an upturned bell.

percussion instruments

Group of instruments that are struck directly with the hands or with sticks, mallets, etc. to produce a sound.

drums
All the percussion instruments played by a single musician, the drummer.
tom-tom
Instrument consisting of two single-membrane drums struck with a mallet or a drumstick.
cymbal
Instrument consisting of a metal disk mounted on a stand; it is struck with a mallet, a drumstick or a wire brush.
high-hat cymbal
Instrument consisting of two cymbals; the movable superior cymbal, controlled by a pedal, is used to strike the inferior cymbal.
superior cymbal
inferior cymbal
batter head
Stretched membrane on a snare drum that is struck with a drumstick or a wire brush.
snare drum
Flat drum consisting of two membranes; stretched across the lower membrane are snares that produce a rattling sound.
tripod stand
Solid base with three feet.
bass drum
Large drum set on a vertical frame and struck using a pedal-controlled wooden mallet.
tension screw
Part that adjusts the tension of the membrane.
stand
Part on which the bass drum and the pedal rest.
mallet
Metal rod whose end (made of felt, cork, skin, etc.) is used to strike the membrane of the bass drum.
tenor drum
Drum that makes a muted sound; it is struck with a mallet or a drumstick.
spur
Retractable metal rod attached to the bottom of a bass drum to stabilize it.
pedal
Device that controls the mallet used to strike the membrane.
leg
Part that supports the drum; its rubber end prevents the drum from sliding along the floor.

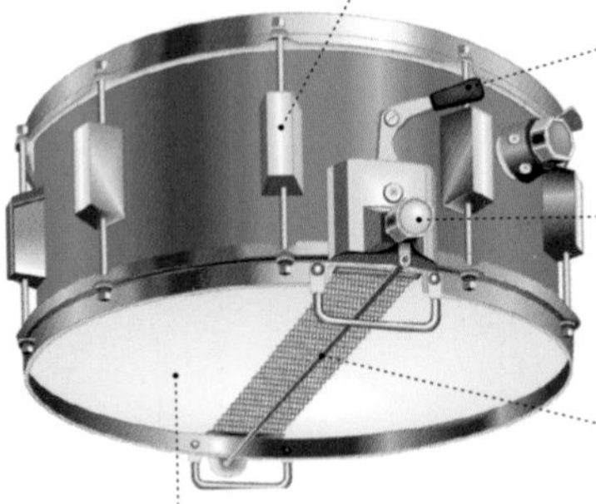
snare drum
Flat drum consisting of two membranes; stretched across the lower membrane are snares that produce a rattling sound.
lug
Part that secures the metal hoops that stretch the membranes.
tension rod
Device that brings the snare closer to or farther from the snare head.
snare strainer
Knob that adjusts snare tension and tone.
snare
Metal snares that vibrate on the snare head when the batter head is struck, producing a rattling sound.
snare head
Soundboard over which the snare is stretched.

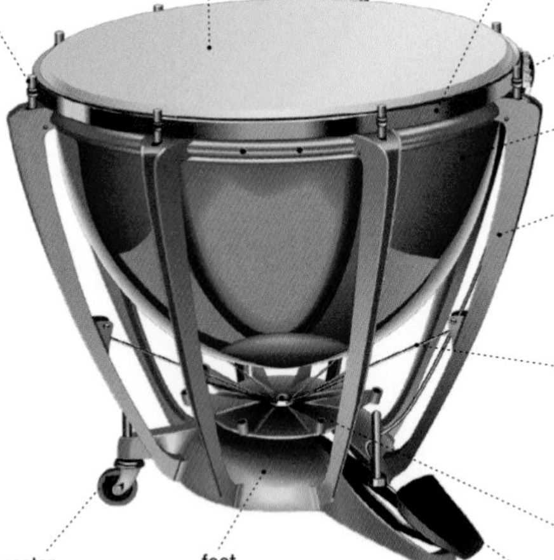
kettledrum
Instrument consisting of a parabolic copper basin covered with a stretched membrane that is struck with mallets.
metal counterhoop
Metal hoop that stretches the membrane over the shell to control the tone of the instrument.
tie rod
Metal part connected to the tension rod; by adjusting the tension of the batter head, it changes the drum's pitch.
batter head
Membrane that is struck with a mallet.
tuning gauge
Part used to adjust the pitch of a note and obtain precise tuning of the instrument.
shell
Parabolic copper basin that functions as a sound box.
strut
Metal frame with several branches; it supports the shell.
tension rod
Metal rod connecting the crown to the tie rods.
crown
Plate raised and lowered with the pedal to adjust the position of the tie rods.
pedal
Device connected to the crown tha adjusts the tension of the membrane to change the tuning of the instrument.
caster
foot
The base of the kettledrum.

sleigh bells
Set of hollow metal pieces with a free-moving steel ball inside; they are tied to a ribbon and used as accompaniment.

set of bells
Series of small bells attached to a ribbon and used as accompaniment.

sistrum
Instrument consisting of a frame with crossbars and attached metal disks that knock together when the instrument is shaken.

castanets
Instrument composed of two shell-shaped pieces of wood held in one hand and struck together using the fingers.

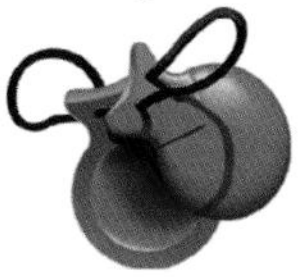

cymbals
Instrument consisting of two metal disks that are struck together.

tambourine
Instrument consisting of a wooden hoop covered with a membrane and fitted with jingles; it can be struck, brushed or shaken.

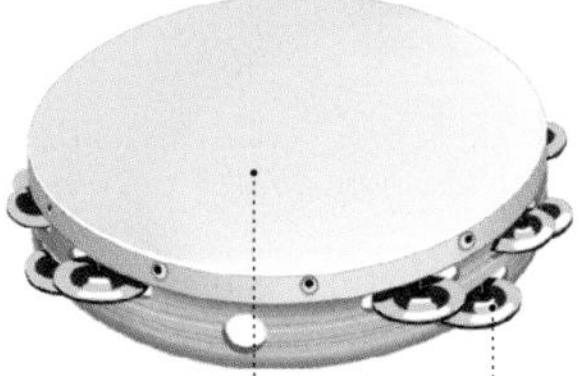

head
Membrane struck with the palm or the thumb.

jingle
Small cymbals that knock together when the tambourine is shaken.

triangle
Instrument composed of a metal bar bent to form a triangle open at one end; the triangle is struck with a metal rod.

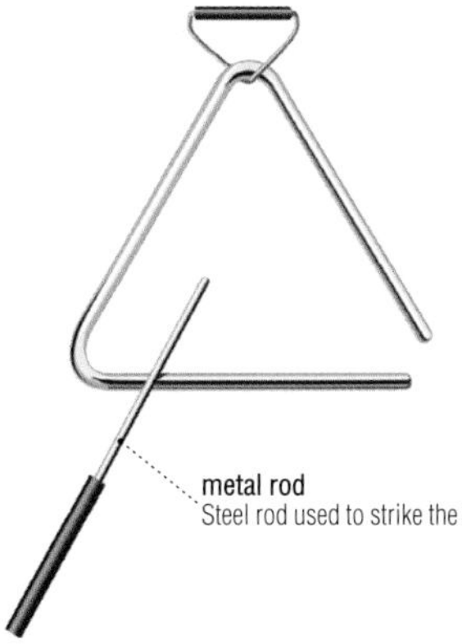

metal rod
Steel rod used to strike the triangle.

bongos
Instrument consisting of two small connected drums; they are usually struck with the hands.

gong
Instrument consisting of a large metal disk with a raised central portion that is struck using a mallet.

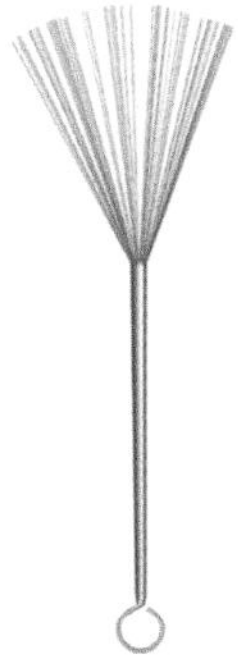

wire brush
Instrument consisting of extremely fine steel wires that are brushed across a cymbal or the batter head on a snare drum.

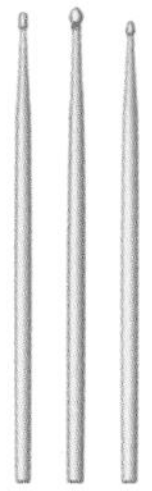

sticks
Sticks of wood with olive-shaped heads used to strike a percussion instrument.

xylophone
Instrument consisting of wooden bars placed on top of resonators arranged in chromatic order in two rows; the bars are struck with mallets.

resonator
Metal tube whose function is to amplify sound.

frame

bar
Wooden slats that the player strikes with mallets.

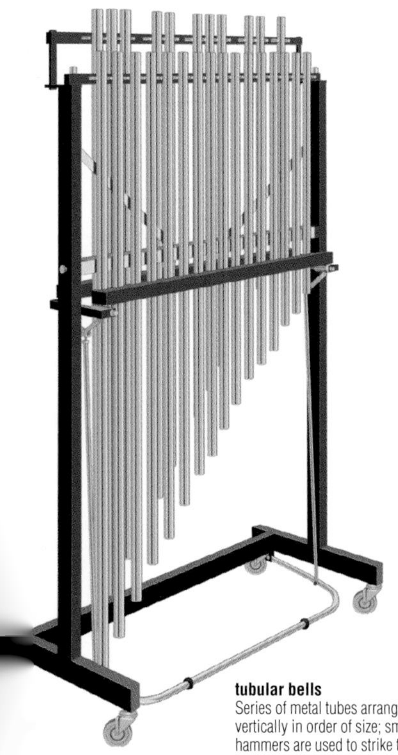

tubular bells
Series of metal tubes arranged vertically in order of size; small hammers are used to strike the tops of the tubes.

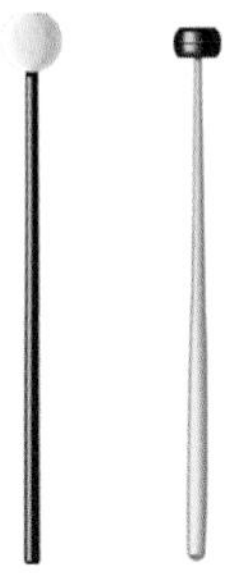

mallets
Metal or wooden rods whose end (made of felt, skin, rubber, etc.) is used to strike an instrument.

electronic instruments

Electronic instruments are designed to imitate, convert or produce sounds based on electric signals and digital data.

sequencer
Component used to record, read and change MIDI data, the digital data used to create electronic music.

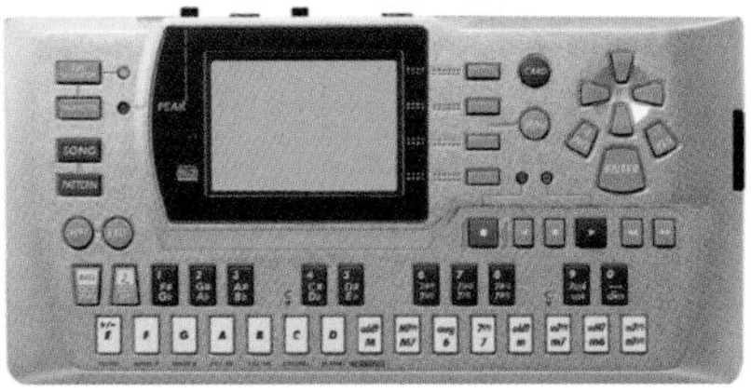

sampler
Component that digitizes and stores sounds based on recordings of various acoustic sources, and reconverts them into sound signals.

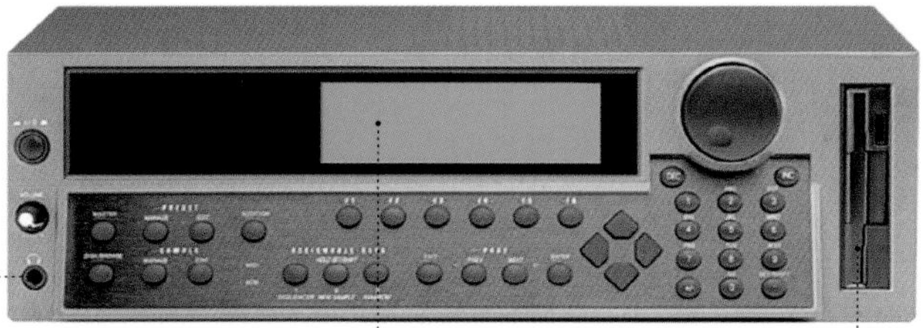

headphone jack
Slot that takes the plug from the headphones.

function display
Liquid crystal display indicating various data.

disk drive
Device used to read or record data on a diskette.

expander
Synthesizer used to produce sounds based on digital data transmitted by a keyboard, a sequencer or a computer.

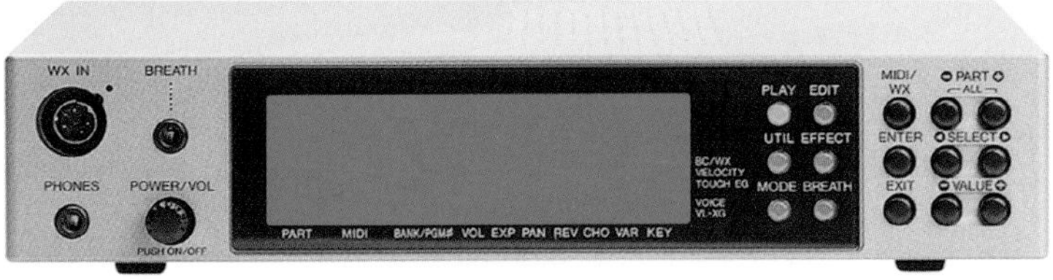

synthesizer
Instrument that imitates other instruments or creates new sounds using electric signals.

disk drive
Device used to read or record data on a diskette.

system buttons
Buttons used to select the instrument's main operations as well as musical sounds in its memory.

volume control

function display
Liquid crystal display indicating various data.

fine data entry control
Rotating device that fine-tunes a parameter.

sequencer control
Buttons that reproduce a melodic or rhythmic motif based on a prerecorded selection.

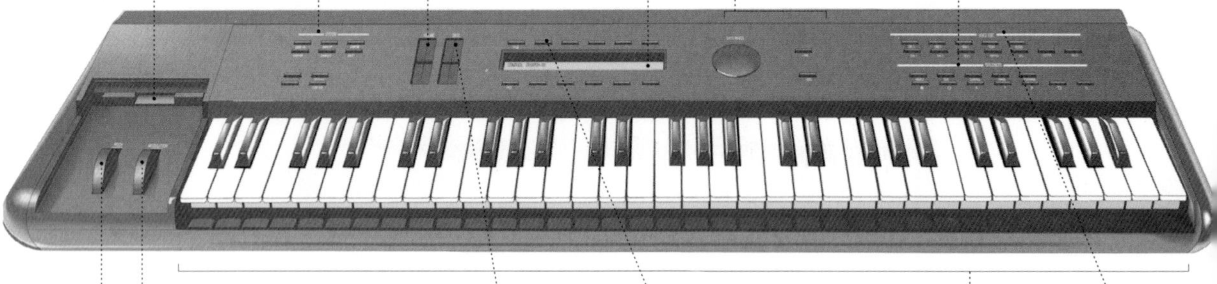

fast data entry control
Cursor used to rapidly set a parameter.

program selector
Button for selecting one of the instrument's settings (voice edit buttons, sequencer control, etc.).

keyboard
Series of keys pressed to play a melody using the timbres available on the instrument.

modulation wheel
Wheel used to adjust the quality, or timbre, of a sound, separate from its pitch or volume.

voice edit buttons
Buttons used to create or modify a sound.

pitch wheel
Wheel used to adjust the frequency of sound vibrations, or pitch.

ARTS AND ARCHITECTURE

musical instrument digital interface (MIDI) cable
Cable connecting two MIDI instruments; the MIDI interface is used to transfer digital data and electric signals.

electronic drum pad
Instrument that is struck with drumsticks to produce a percussive sound by emitting an electric signal that is converted into MIDI data.

wind synthesizer controller
Instrument connected to a synthesizer; it produces a continuous sound by emitting an electric signal that is converted into MIDI data.

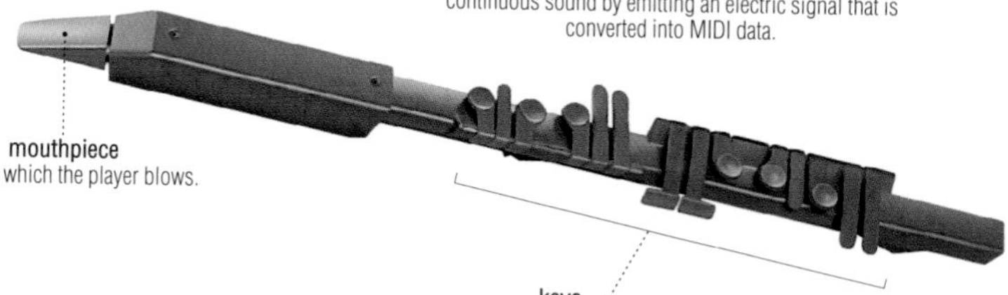

mouthpiece
Part into which the player blows.

keys
Mechanisms composed of a lever and a plate; they open and close the holes when notes are played.

electronic piano
Piano designed to reproduce the sound of an acoustic piano by converting it into digital data; it also reproduces the sound of other instruments.

rhythm selector
Buttons that allow the player to choose a rhythm (disco, rock, samba, etc.).

music stand
Inclined frame on which the musician places music.

tempo control
Buttons that allow the player to vary the tempo, or speed, of a piece of music.

volume control

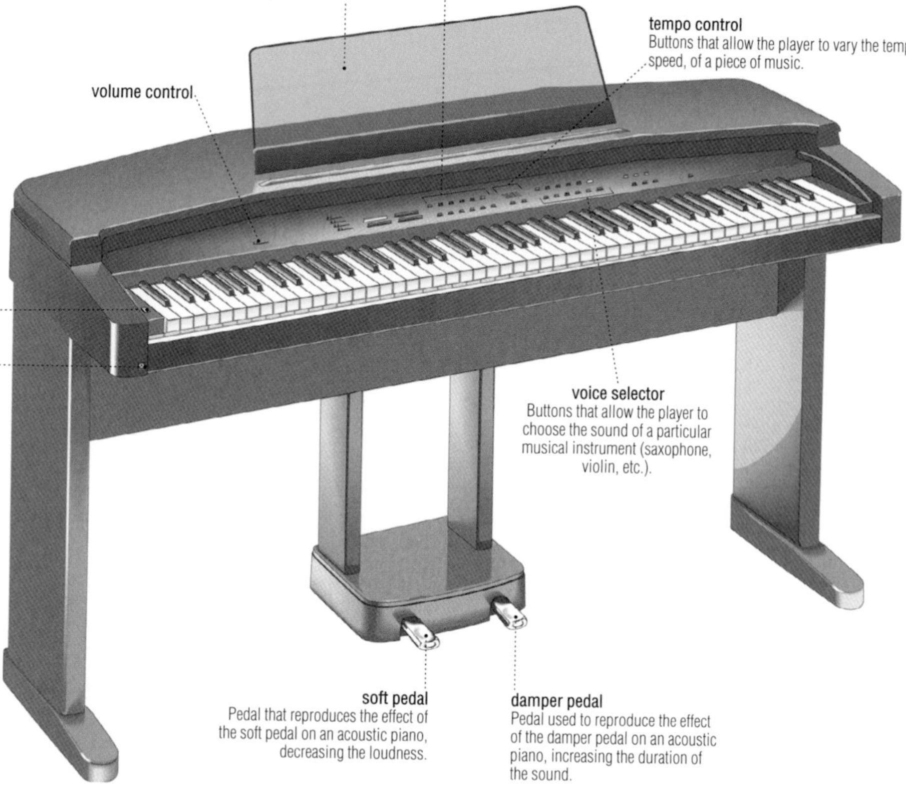

power switch
Mechanical connection that turns the instrument on or off.

headphone jack
Slot that takes the plug from the headphones.

voice selector
Buttons that allow the player to choose the sound of a particular musical instrument (saxophone, violin, etc.).

soft pedal
Pedal that reproduces the effect of the soft pedal on an acoustic piano, decreasing the loudness.

damper pedal
Pedal used to reproduce the effect of the damper pedal on an acoustic piano, increasing the duration of the sound.

sewing

Process of joining two items using a needle and a thread.

sewing machine
Machine used to assemble two pieces of fabric by means of a series of stitches made with a needle and thread.

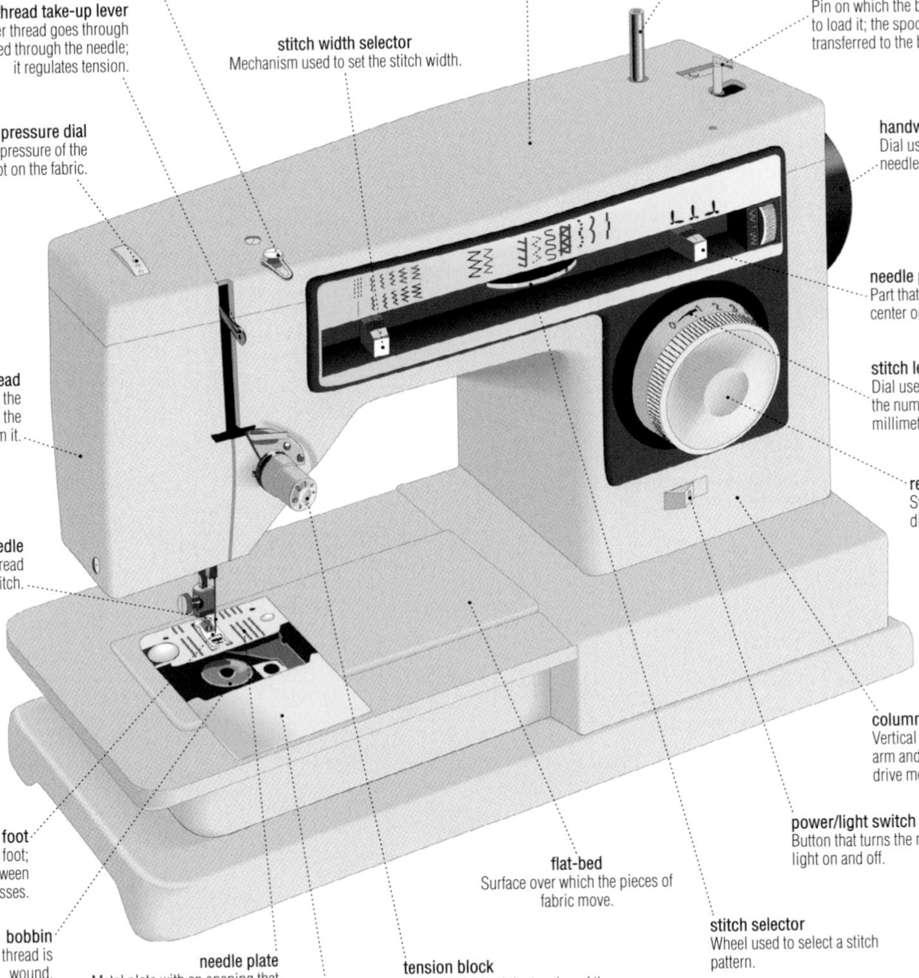

thread guide
Part used to direct the thread.

arm
Part that connects the head to the column; it houses part of the needle's drive mechanism.

spool pin
Pivot used to attach the upper spool of thread.

bobbin winder
Pin on which the bobbin is placed to load it; the spool pin thread is transferred to the bobbin winder.

thread take-up lever
Lever that the upper thread goes through before it is threaded through the needle; it regulates tension.

stitch width selector
Mechanism used to set the stitch width.

pressure dial
Mechanism used to set the pressure of the hinged presser foot on the fabric.

handwheel
Dial used to raise and lower the needle manually.

needle position selector
Part that selects the needle position (left, center or right).

head
Vertical section that completes the needle's drive mechanism; the presser foot extends from it.

stitch length regulator
Dial used to set the length of the stitch; the numbers indicate the length in millimeters.

reverse stitch button
Switch that reverses the sewing direction.

needle
Metal stem that passes the thread through the fabric to form a stitch.

column
Vertical section that supports the arm and houses part of the needle's drive mechanism.

hinged presser foot
Articulated end of the presser foot; it consists of two branches between which the needle passes.

power/light switch
Button that turns the machine and the sewing light on and off.

flat-bed
Surface over which the pieces of fabric move.

bobbin
Spool on which the lower thread is wound.

stitch selector
Wheel used to select a stitch pattern.

needle plate
Metal plate with an opening that the needle passes through and two slits from which the feed dogs for the fabric protrude.

tension block
Parts that control the tension of the upper thread.

slide plate
Plate that slides open, providing access to the lower stitching components.

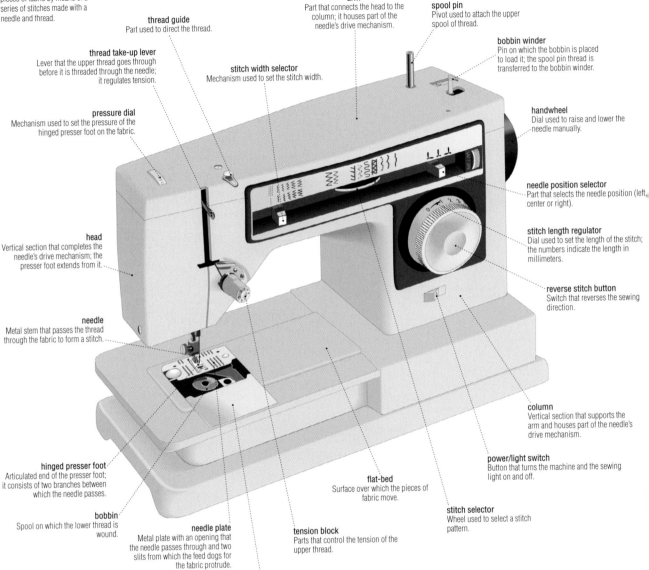

bobbin case
Case placed under the needle plate; the bobbin fits inside it.

bobbin
Spool on which the lower thread is wound.

latch lever
Mechanism that the bobbin fits into and that regulates lower thread tension.

hook
Fixed lower component containing the latch lever.

foot control
Mechanism operated by foot; it controls the sewing machine's electric motor.

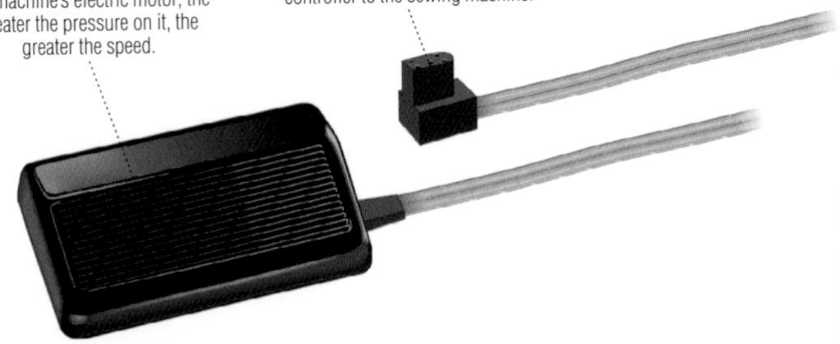

speed controller
Pedal that regulates the speed of the machine's electric motor; the greater the pressure on it, the greater the speed.

connecting terminal
Part that connects the speed controller to the sewing machine.

sewing

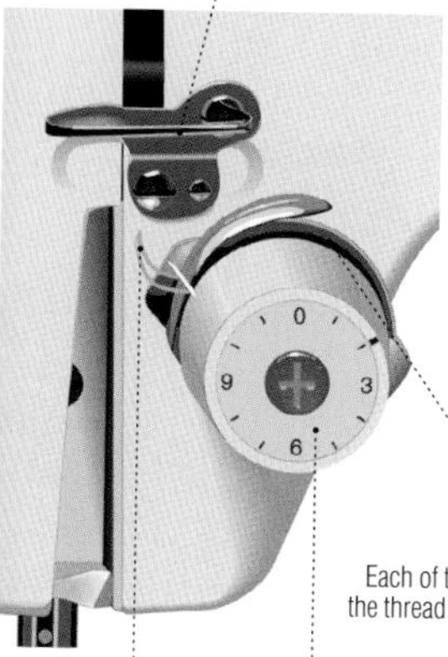

tension block
Parts that control the tension of the upper thread.

thread guide
Part that leads the thread toward the tension disk.

tension disk
Each of the parts between which the thread passes during threading.

tension dial
Graduated dial used to regulate the tension of the upper thread.

tension spring
Spring that keeps the upper thread between the tension disks.

needle
Metal stem that passes the thread through the fabric to form a stitch.

shank
Upper end of the needle that fits into the needle clamp.

groove
Narrow channel in the needle for guiding the thread.

blade
Part of the needle between the shank and the eye.

eye
Hole at the bottom of the needle that the thread passes through.

point
Lower end of the needle, used to pierce the fabric.

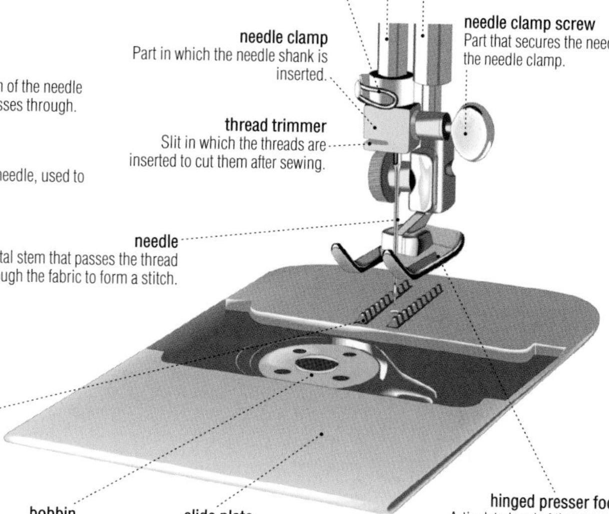

presser foot
Part of the sewing machine that keeps the fabric flat against the feed dogs during sewing.

needle bar
Cylindrical rod that supports the needle clamp at its lower end and produces the up-and-down movement of the needle.

thread guide
Part that guides the thread toward the eye of the needle.

presser bar
Cylindrical rod that ends in the presser foot.

needle clamp
Part in which the needle shank is inserted.

needle clamp screw
Part that secures the needle shank to the needle clamp.

thread trimmer
Slit in which the threads are inserted to cut them after sewing.

needle
Metal stem that passes the thread through the fabric to form a stitch.

feed dog
Each of the pointed metal pieces that move the fabric while sewing.

bobbin
Spool on which the lower thread is wound.

slide plate
Plate that slides open, providing access to the lower stitching components.

hinged presser foot
Articulated end of the presser foot; it consists of two branches between which the needle passes.

fasteners

Accessories used to open or close a garment.

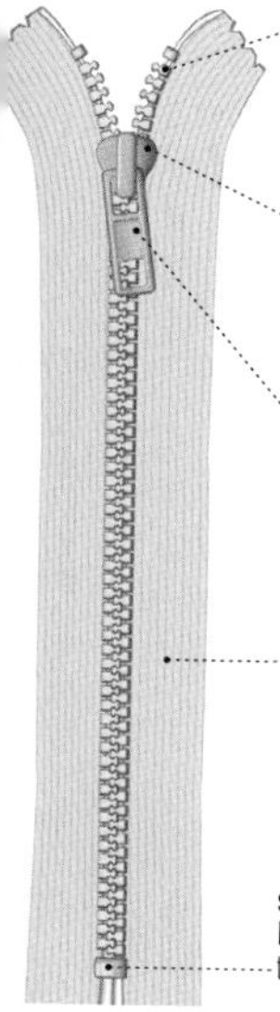

zipper
Closure made up of two lengths of tape edged with teeth that interlock by means of a slide.

tooth
Each of the metal pieces that mesh when the slide is pulled.

slide
Sliding part that joins or separates the two rows of teeth on the zipper.

tab
Metal piece used to move the slide.

tape
Strip of fabric to which the teeth are attached; it is sewed to each side of the fabric's seam.

stop
Metal piece that stops the slide at the lower end of the zipper.

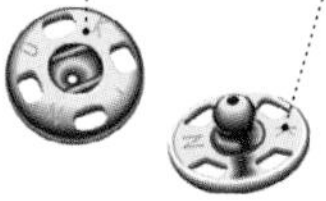

socket

ball

snap
Fastening mechanism made of a socket disk and a ball disk that snap shut when pressed together.

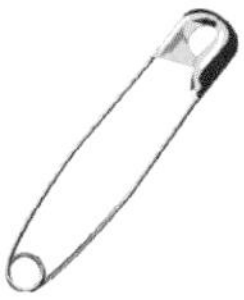

safety pin
Curved metal stem that forms a spring; the pointed extremity of its flexible arm is kept in place by a hook.

shank button
Button with a metal ring that the thread passes through to sew it to a piece of fabric.

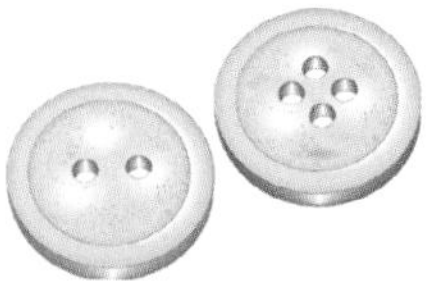

sew-through buttons
Buttons with two or four holes that the thread passes through to sew them to a piece of fabric.

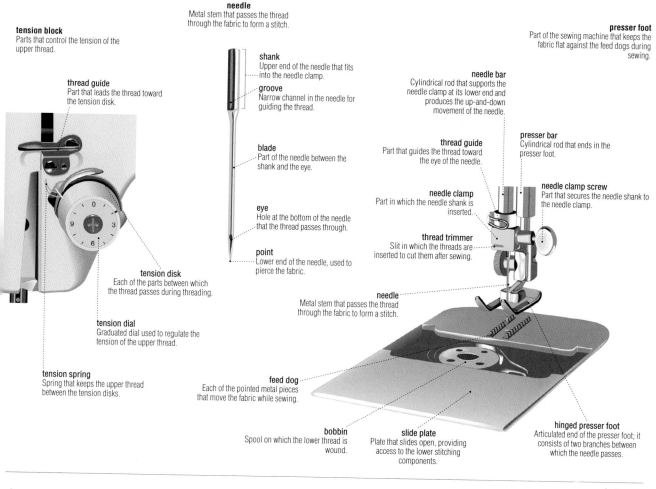

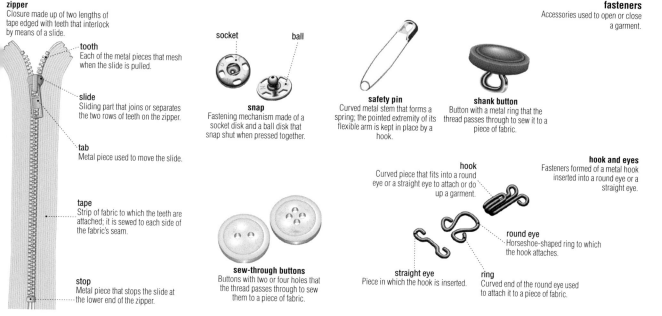

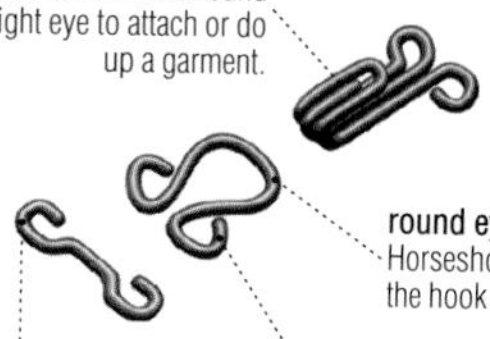

hook and eyes
Fasteners formed of a metal hook inserted into a round eye or a straight eye.

hook
Curved piece that fits into a round eye or a straight eye to attach or do up a garment.

round eye
Horseshoe-shaped ring to which the hook attaches.

straight eye
Piece in which the hook is inserted.

ring
Curved end of the round eye used to attach it to a piece of fabric.

sewing

accessories

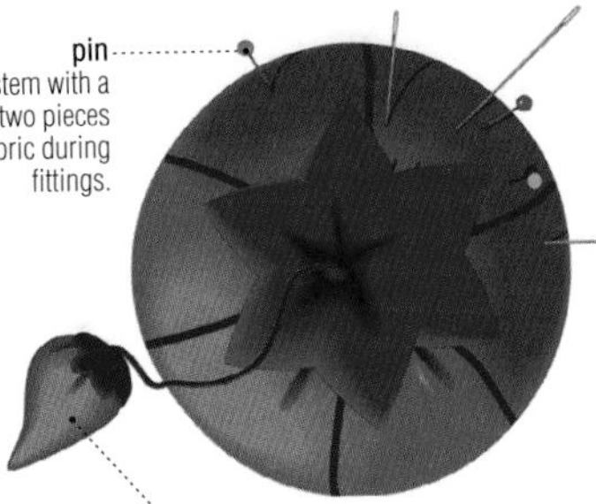

pin cushion
Small cushion used to hold pins and needles.

pin
Small pointed metal stem with a head; it is used to fasten two pieces of fabric and to mark fabric during fittings.

eye
Hole in the head of the needle through which the thread passes.

needle
Metal stem that passes the thread through the fabric to form a stitch.

emery pack
Small cushion filled with powdered emery; it is used to maintain the points of pins and needles.

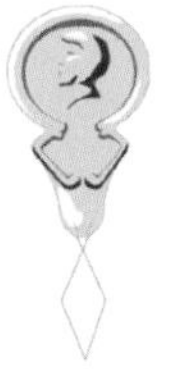

needle threader
Instrument that makes it easier to insert the thread into the eye of the needle.

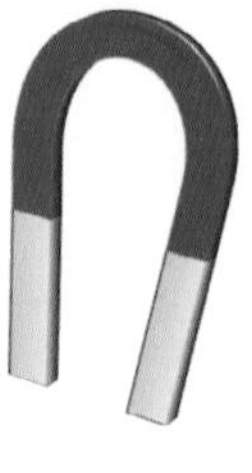

magnet
Instrument used to collect pins and needles.

thimble
Metal sleeve used to protect the middle finger, which pushes the needle when sewing by hand.

scissors
Instrument with two movable overlapping shanks having sharp inside edges; they are used for trimming and cutting.

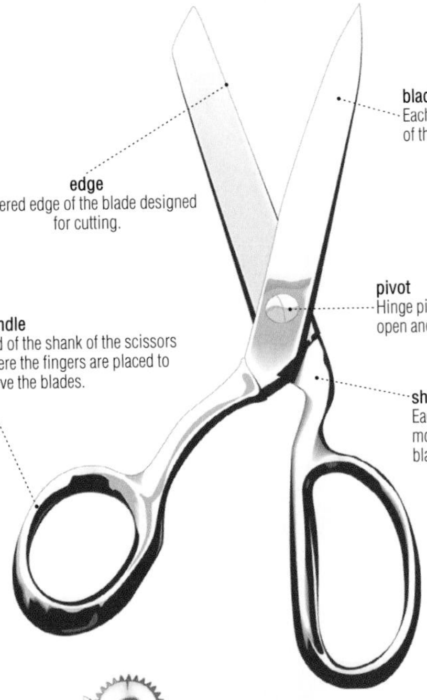

blade
Each of the sharp tapered sections of the two shanks that cut fabric.

edge
Tapered edge of the blade designed for cutting.

pivot
Hinge pin enabling the blades to open and close.

handle
End of the shank of the scissors where the fingers are placed to move the blades.

shank
Each of the elongated parts that are moved to open and close the blades.

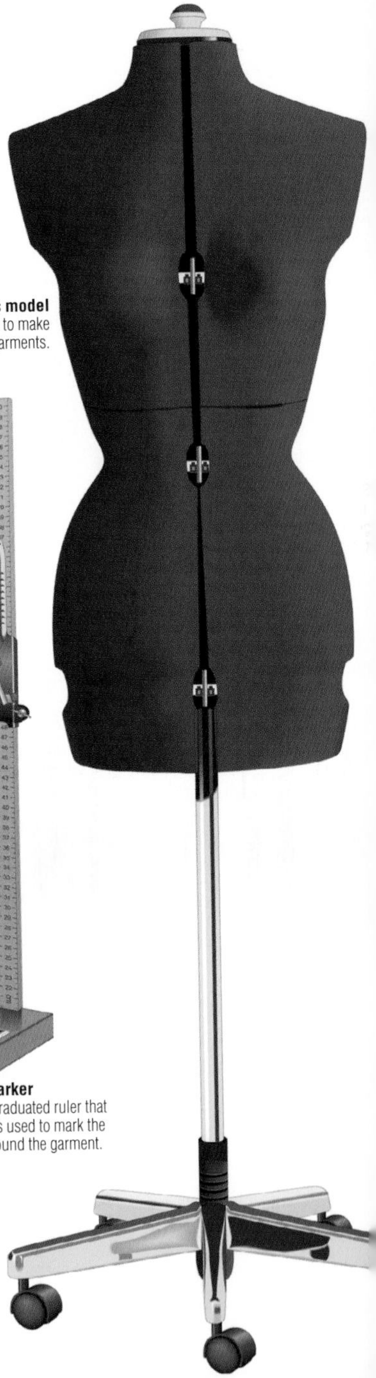

dressmaker's model
Adjustable model used to make and try on garments.

pinking shears
Scissors with a toothed blade used to give a zigzag finish.

wheel
Toothed metal wheel used to mark a piece of fabric or paper.

shank

handle

tracing wheel
Instrument that transfers the design of a pattern to a piece of fabric or another piece of paper using carbon paper.

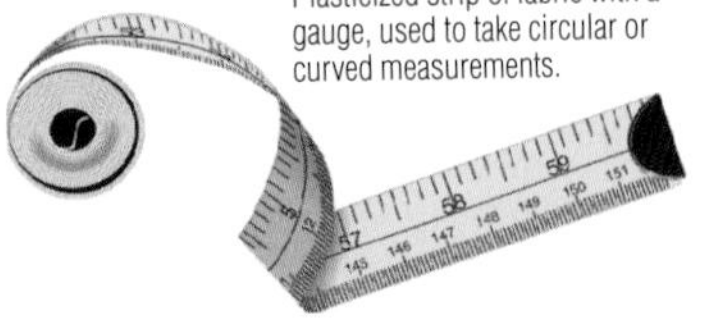

tape measure
Plasticized strip of fabric with a gauge, used to take circular or curved measurements.

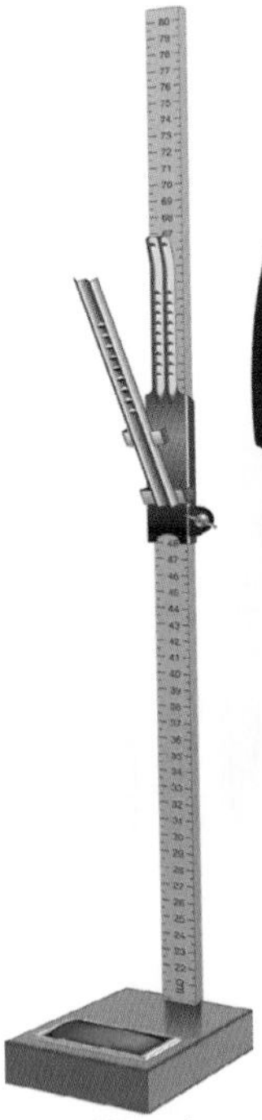

skirt marker
Device fitted with a graduated ruler that moves vertically; it is used to mark the hem of a skirt all around the garment.

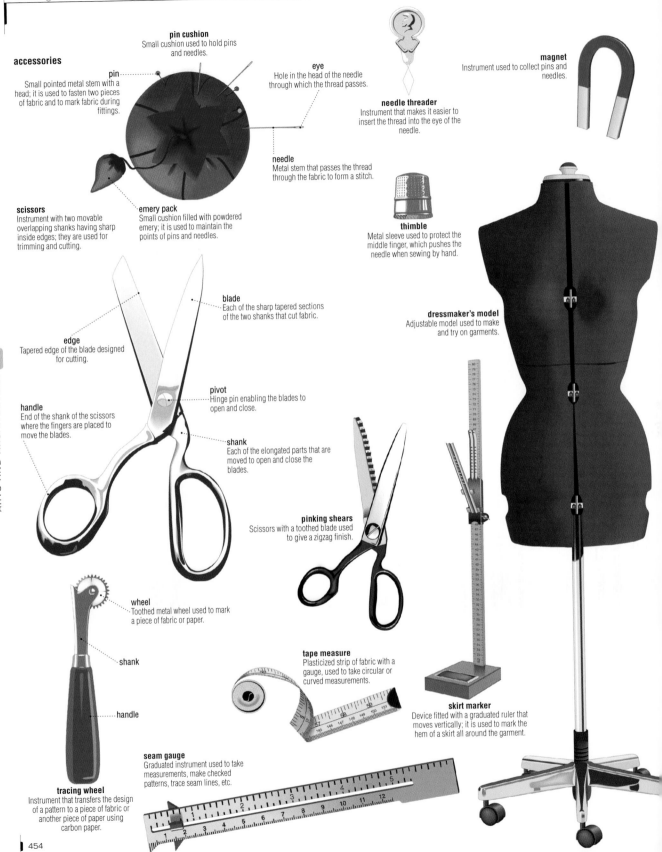

seam gauge
Graduated instrument used to take measurements, make checked patterns, trace seam lines, etc.

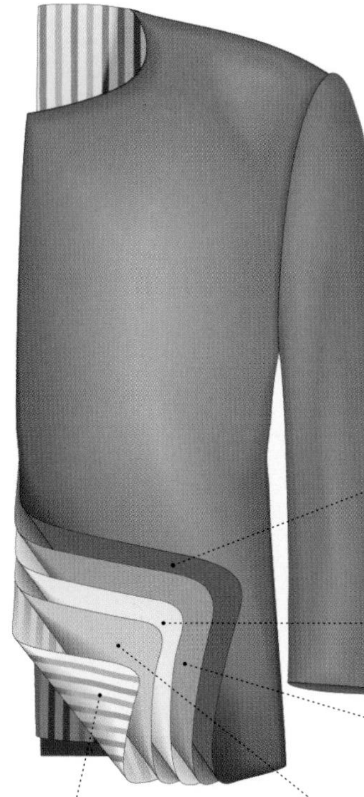

underlying fabrics
Fabrics used to hold the shape of a garment and give it a professional finish.

garment fabric
Principal material used for the garment; it covers the underlying fabrics.

interfacing
Tear-resistant fabric used to hold the shape of the garment and give it body.

underlining
Fabric used to hold the shape of the garment and make it more opaque.

lining
ft fabric cut from the same pattern as e garment inside which it is sewn; it ves body to the garment, embellishes hides its seams and makes it warmer.

interlining
Fabric used to make a garment warmer.

fabric structure
The way the threads of the material are put together during weaving.

bias
Direction of a fabric; it is diagonal to the crosswise grain and the lengthwise grain.

selvage
The finished border of a piece of fabric, woven more tightly than the piece it borders and parallel to the lengthwise grain.

crosswise grain
The threads that are passed through the lengthwise grain from one selvage to another; it is the width of the fabric.

lengthwise grain
Evenly spaced parallel threads arranged lengthwise along the fabric.

pattern
Paper template used to cut the various pieces of a garment.

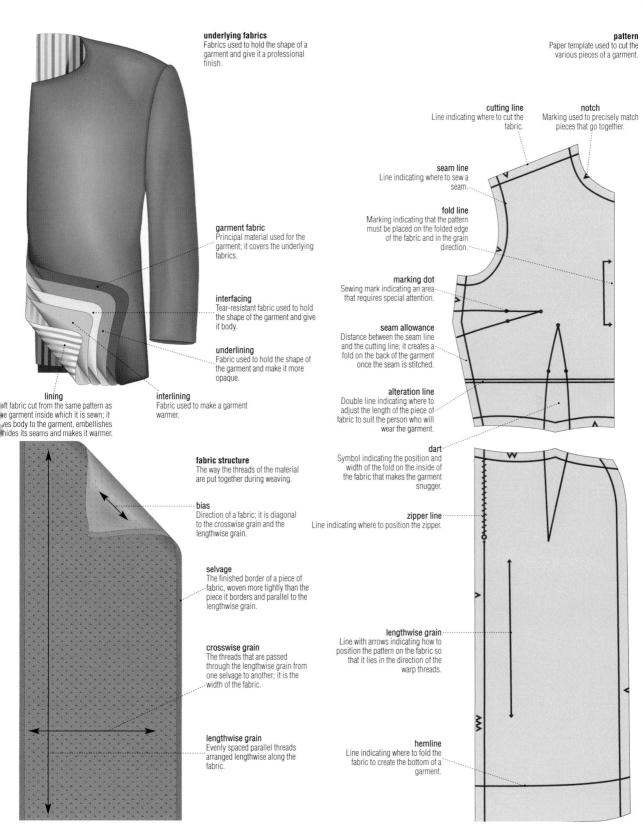

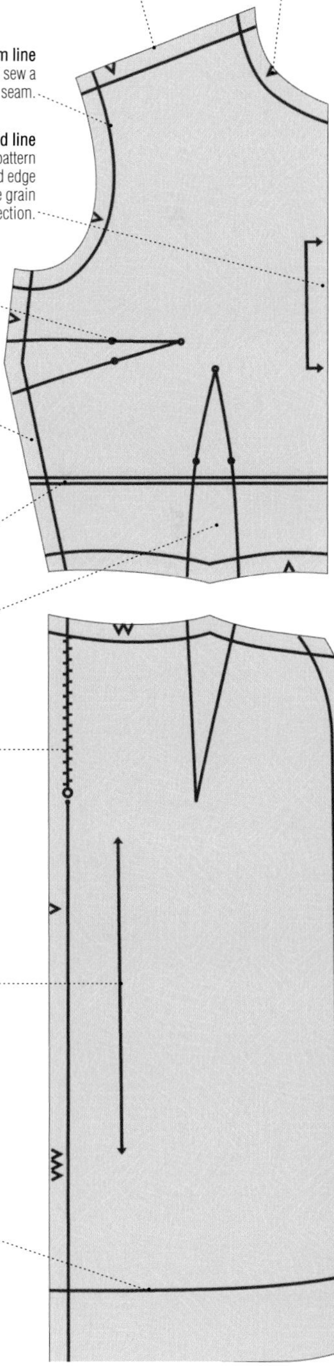

cutting line
Line indicating where to cut the fabric.

notch
Marking used to precisely match pieces that go together.

seam line
Line indicating where to sew a seam.

fold line
Marking indicating that the pattern must be placed on the folded edge of the fabric and in the grain direction.

marking dot
Sewing mark indicating an area that requires special attention.

seam allowance
Distance between the seam line and the cutting line; it creates a fold on the back of the garment once the seam is stitched.

alteration line
Double line indicating where to adjust the length of the piece of fabric to suit the person who will wear the garment.

dart
Symbol indicating the position and width of the fold on the inside of the fabric that makes the garment snugger.

zipper line
Line indicating where to position the zipper.

lengthwise grain
Line with arrows indicating how to position the pattern on the fabric so that it lies in the direction of the warp threads.

hemline
Line indicating where to fold the fabric to create the bottom of a garment.

knitting machine

Machine used to knit fabrics mechanically.

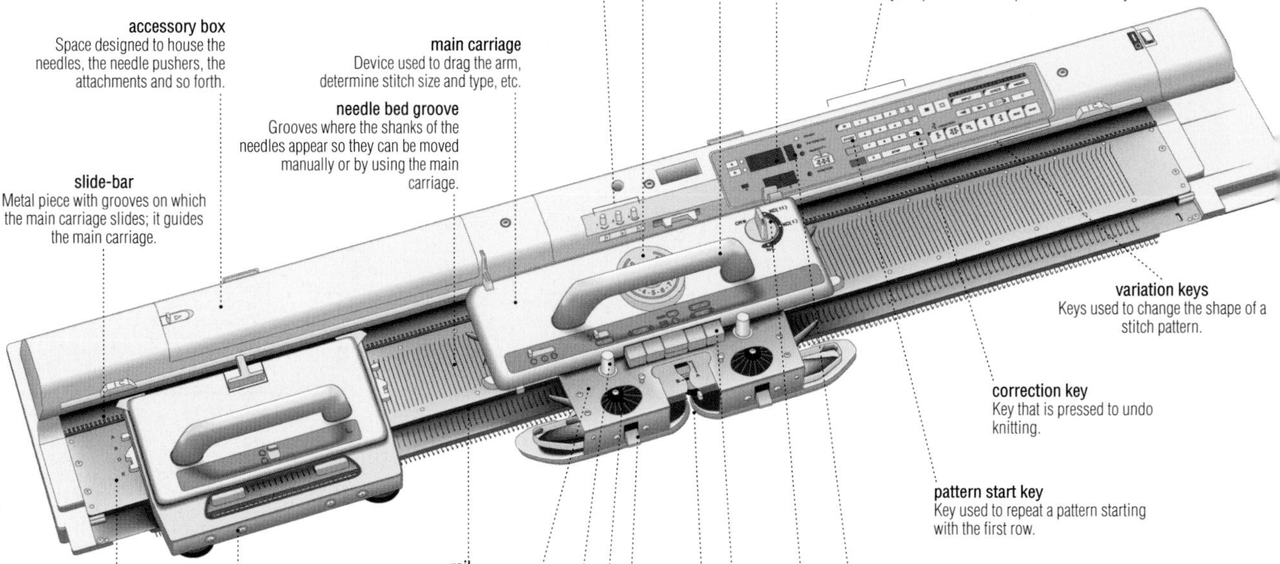

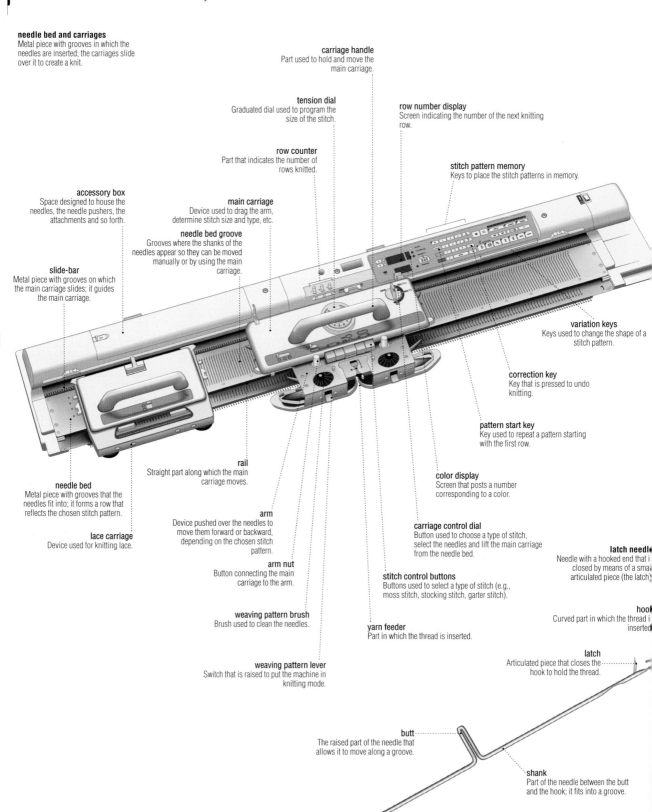

needle bed and carriages
Metal piece with grooves in which the needles are inserted; the carriages slide over it to create a knit.

carriage handle
Part used to hold and move the main carriage.

tension dial
Graduated dial used to program the size of the stitch.

row number display
Screen indicating the number of the next knitting row.

row counter
Part that indicates the number of rows knitted.

stitch pattern memory
Keys to place the stitch patterns in memory.

accessory box
Space designed to house the needles, the needle pushers, the attachments and so forth.

main carriage
Device used to drag the arm, determine stitch size and type, etc.

needle bed groove
Grooves where the shanks of the needles appear so they can be moved manually or by using the main carriage.

slide-bar
Metal piece with grooves on which the main carriage slides; it guides the main carriage.

variation keys
Keys used to change the shape of a stitch pattern.

correction key
Key that is pressed to undo knitting.

pattern start key
Key used to repeat a pattern starting with the first row.

rail
Straight part along which the main carriage moves.

color display
Screen that posts a number corresponding to a color.

needle bed
Metal piece with grooves that the needles fit into; it forms a row that reflects the chosen stitch pattern.

arm
Device pushed over the needles to move them forward or backward, depending on the chosen stitch pattern.

carriage control dial
Button used to choose a type of stitch, select the needles and lift the main carriage from the needle bed.

lace carriage
Device used for knitting lace.

arm nut
Button connecting the main carriage to the arm.

stitch control buttons
Buttons used to select a type of stitch (e.g., moss stitch, stocking stitch, garter stitch).

weaving pattern brush
Brush used to clean the needles.

yarn feeder
Part in which the thread is inserted.

weaving pattern lever
Switch that is raised to put the machine in knitting mode.

latch needl
Needle with a hooked end that i closed by means of a sma articulated piece (the latch)

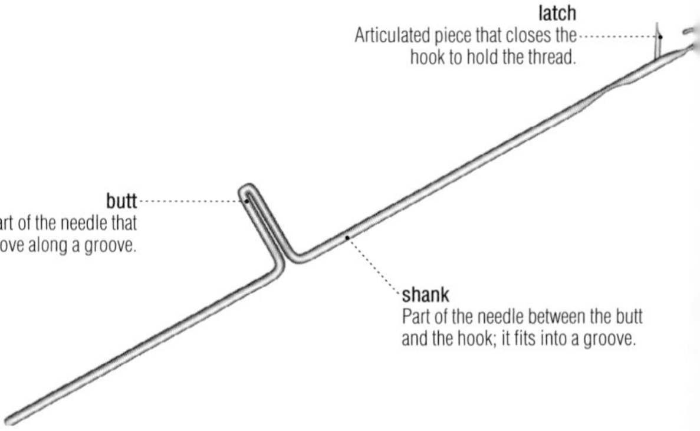

hoo
Curved part in which the thread i inserted

latch
Articulated piece that closes the hook to hold the thread.

butt
The raised part of the needle that allows it to move along a groove.

shank
Part of the needle between the butt and the hook; it fits into a groove.

knitting machine

tension block
Parts used to control thread tension.

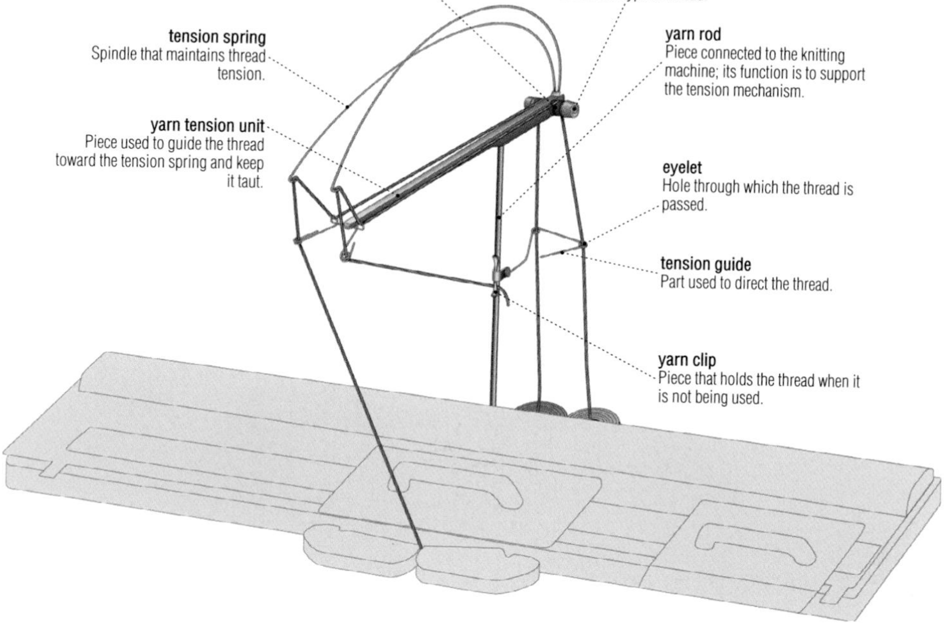
tension disk
Each of the parts between which the thread passes during threading.
tension dial
Button that adjusts the tension based on the type of thread.
tension spring
Spindle that maintains thread tension.
yarn rod
Piece connected to the knitting machine; its function is to support the tension mechanism.
yarn tension unit
Piece used to guide the thread toward the tension spring and keep it taut.
eyelet
Hole through which the thread is passed.
tension guide
Part used to direct the thread.
yarn clip
Piece that holds the thread when it is not being used.

knitting

Creating fabric by using needles to form interlacing stitches.

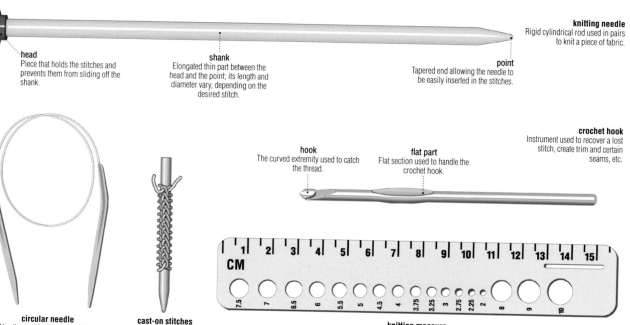

knitting needle
Rigid cylindrical rod used in pairs to knit a piece of fabric.

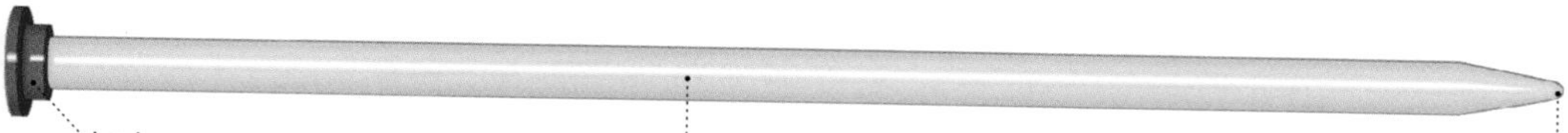
head
Piece that holds the stitches and prevents them from sliding off the shank.
shank
Elongated thin part between the head and the point; its length and diameter vary, depending on the desired stitch.
point
Tapered end allowing the needle to be easily inserted in the stitches.

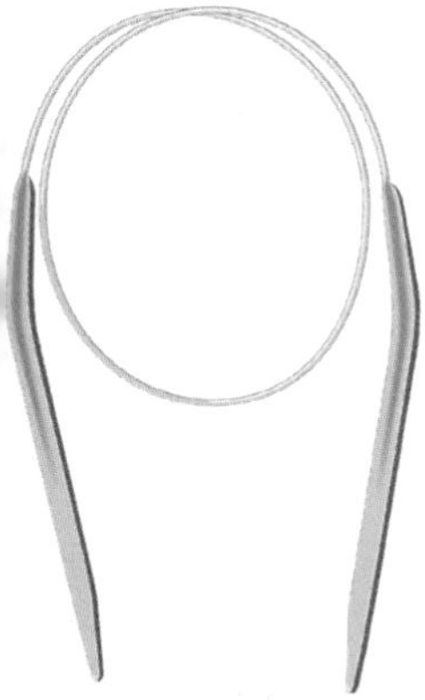

circular needle
Needle used for circular knitting, for seamless pieces or flat pieces with a great number of stitches.

cast-on stitches
Loops that form the starting point of a piece of fabric.

crochet hook
Instrument used to recover a lost stitch, create trim and certain seams, etc.

hook
The curved extremity used to catch the thread.
flat part
Flat section used to handle the crochet hook.

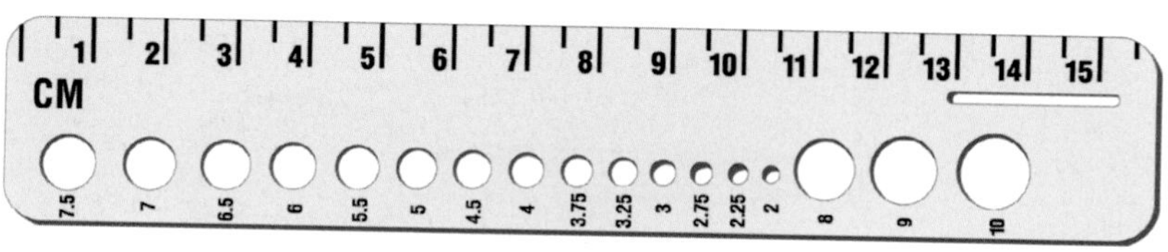
1 2 3 4 5 6 7 8 9 10 11 12 13 14 15
CM
7.5 7 6.5 6 5.5 5 4.5 4 3.75 3.25 3 2.75 2.25 2 8 9 10

knitting measure
Instrument used to measure the diameter of needles and to take measurements of a work in progress.

knitting

stitch patterns
Arrangement of groups of stitches in one or several rows; they are worked until they form a regularly repeated design or feature.

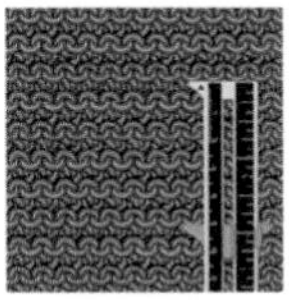

sample
Square sample used to calculate the number of stitches and rows on a 2 in² surface so that a consistent pattern can be established.

moss stitch
Stitch obtained by alternating a plain stitch with a purl stitch on one row, and then reversing the order on the next.

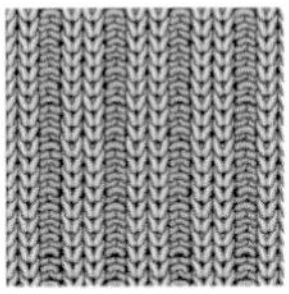

rib stitch
Stitch obtained by alternating plain and purl stitches and by repeating the same order on the following rows.

stocking stitch
Stitch obtained by alternating a plain row with a purl row.

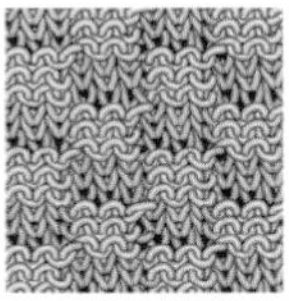

basket stitch
Stitch obtained by alternating squares composed of plain stitches with squares composed of purl stitches.

garter stitch
Stitch obtained by a succession of plain stitches on all the rows.

cable stitch
Stitch obtained by revers stitches on a row to for overlap.

bobbin lace

Openwork fabric created by interlacing thread on bobbins, using a pillow to secure the model to be reproduced.

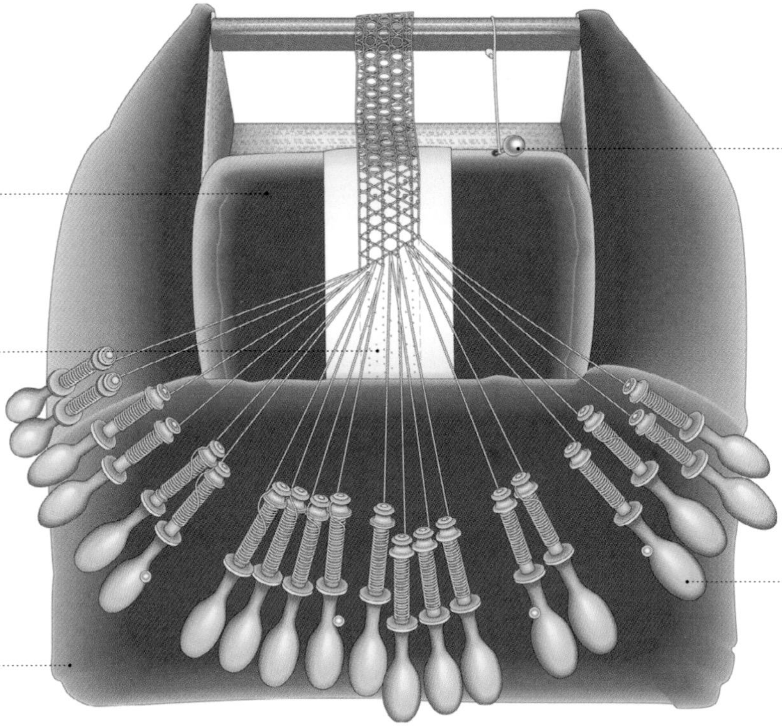

pillow
Frame used for making lace.

revolving cylinder
Movable part that secures the pattern.

pattern
Design transferred to a board by perforating it with holes; needles are inserted in the holes to create the pattern.

pillow
Stuffed piece used to spread out the bobbins.

stop
Knob that prevents the cylinder from rotating.

bobbin
Wooden tool on which thread is wound to make lace.

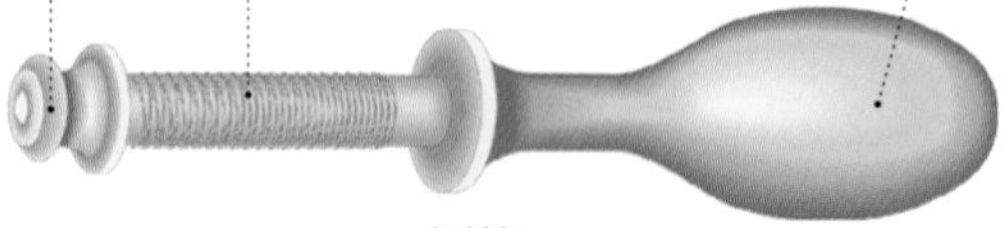

head
The end of the bobbin where the thread is tied into a stop knot.

spool
Shank on which the thread is wound.

handle
Piece of wood held between two fingers to handle the bobbin.

bobbin
Wooden tool on which thread is wound to make lace.

pricker
Needle-tipped wooden tool used to perforate the pattern so that the needle can be inserted.

embroidery

Art of stitching designs on fabric, usually using a needle and thread.

hoop
Frame consisting of two hoops; one fits inside the other and the fabric is stretched between them. The hoop is used for detail work.

frame
Device on which embroidery fabric is stretched; it is used for work on a larger scale.

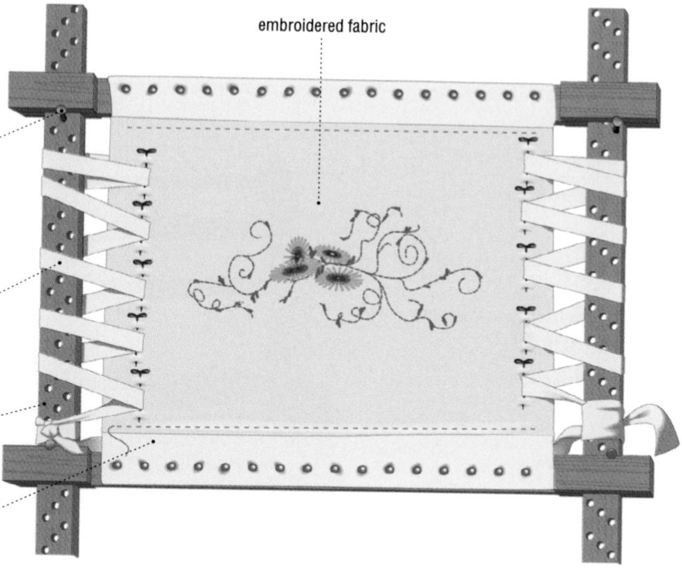

embroidered fabric

peg
Piece that immobilizes the horizontal bars to which the webbing is attached so that the fabric can be stretched vertically.

tape
Each of the strips attached to the slats and used to stretch the fabric horizontally.

slat
Horizontal bar with holes used to regulate the vertical tension of the fabric.

webbing
Strip of thick cloth attached to the horizontals bars of the frame; the embroidery fabric is attached to it.

stitches
There are more than 100 embroidery stitches, grouped into various categories.

cross stitches
Stitches made up of a succession of diagonal straight stitches that meet and then change direction.

chevron stitch
Stitch consisting of diagonal straight stitches that meet at the top and bottom of two parallel rows.

herringbone stitch
Stitch composed of intersecting diagonal straight stitches following two parallel lines.

loop stitches
Stitches forming an open or closed loop.

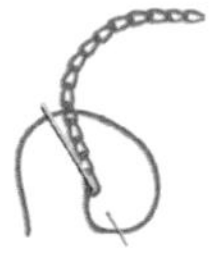

chain stitch
Stitch created by forming closed loops that are repeated like the links in a chain.

feather stitch
Stitch created by forming successive open loops, linked or unlinked.

knot stitches
Stitches created by winding the thread around the needle.

bullion stitch
Stitch created by rolling the thread several times around the needle and reinserting the needle a little farther on to create a line of thread.

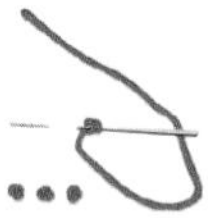

French knot stitch
Stitch created by rolling the thread two or three times around the needle and reinserting it very close to the original point of insertion to create a cluster.

flat stitches
Stitches usually used to fill in a design.

fishbone stitch
Oblique stitch alternately arranged on the left and right of an imaginary axis.

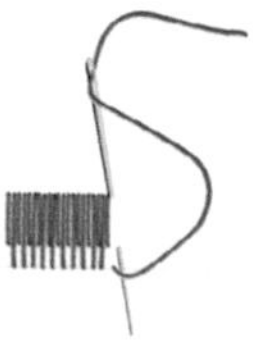

long and short stitch
Stitch consisting of overlapping rows of long and short stitches to cover a surface.

couched stitches
Stitches used to fill in and give relief to a design.

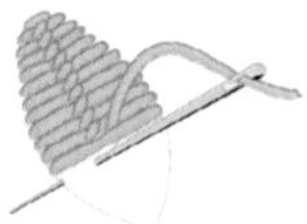

Romanian couching stitch
A stitch forms the base of the embroidery over the entire width of the line, and an angled or vertical stitch covers the center.

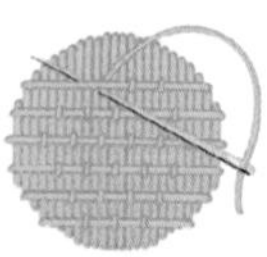

Oriental couching stitch
Vertical stitches are crossed with horizontal lines held together by isolated stitches staggered from one row to the next.

weaving

Threads (warp and weft) interlaced at right angles to form cloth.

low warp loom

Loom on which the warp threads are arranged horizontally.

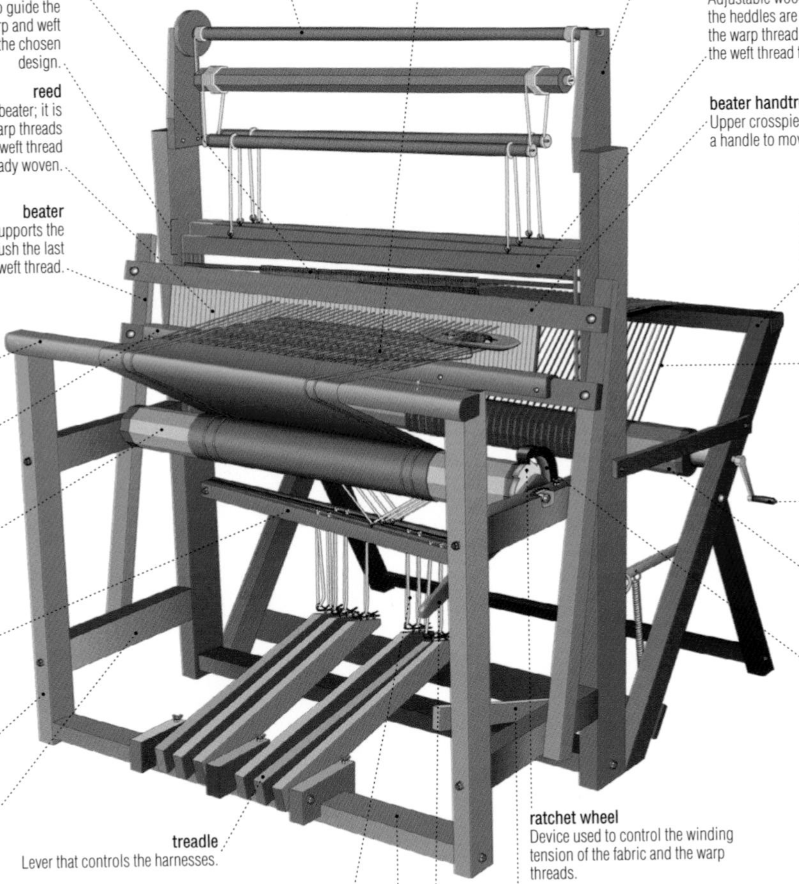

heddles
Metal wires attached to the harnesses; they contain eyes through which the warp threads pass.

head roller
Horizontal bar used to suspend the intermediate rollers supporting the harnesses, according to the setup of the loom.

weft
Threads woven across the warp thread, along the width direction of the fabric.

upright
Beam that supports the head roller.

harnesses
Series of blades used to guide the interlacing of warp and weft threads, based on the chosen design.

harness
Adjustable wooden frame to which the heddles are attached; it raises the warp thread to create a space for the weft thread to pass through.

reed
Comb imbedded in the beater; it is used to separate the warp threads and push the last weft thread against the yarn already woven.

beater handtree
Upper crosspiece of the beater; it is used as a handle to move the reed.

beater
Articulated frame that supports the reed and moves it to push the last weft thread.

back beam
Crosspiece over which the warp threads turn to keep them horizontal.

breast beam
Crosspiece over which the woven yarn passes before it is wound onto the cloth roller.

warp
Evenly spaced parallel threads arranged lengthwise along the fabric.

beater sley
The lower crosspiece of the beater.

handle
Part that controls the warp roller when the loom is set up.

cloth roller
Roller on which the fabric is wound.

warp roller
Roller on which the warp thread is wound.

lam
Lever that transfers the movement of the treadle to the harnesses.

ratchet
Movable part used to block the ratchet wheel.

post
The vertical part of the frame.

crosspiece
Wooden beam that maintains the two posts at an equal distance.

treadle
Lever that controls the harnesses.

ratchet wheel
Device used to control the winding tension of the fabric and the warp threads.

treadle cord
Cord connecting the treadle to the lam.

release treadle
Part that controls the unwinding of the warp threads so they remain taut during weaving.

crossbeam
Horizontal piece of the frame.

take-up handle
Lever that controls the cloth roller to maintain the fabric's winding tension.

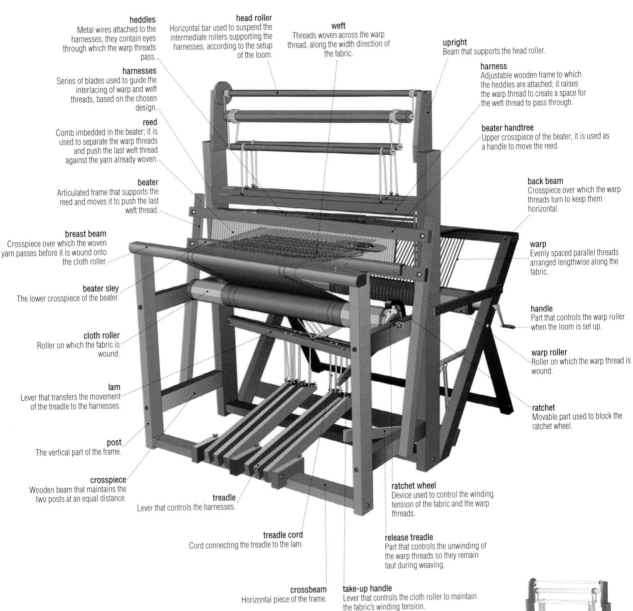

frame
Wooden structure consisting of the loom's stationary parts.

weaving

shuttle
Weaving instrument that is pushed back and forth between two sections of warp thread to insert the weft threads.

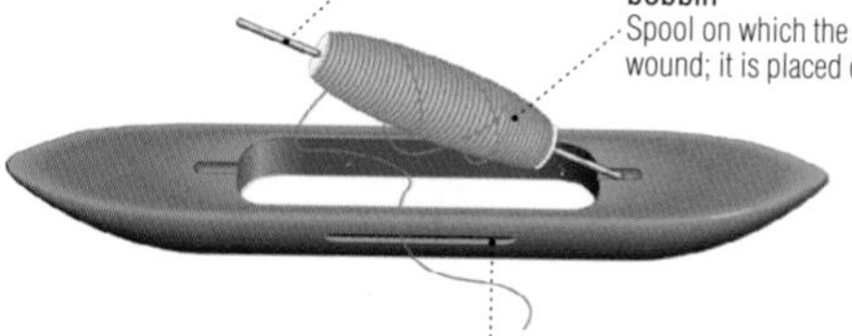

rod
Metal rod that supports the bobbin.

bobbin
Spool on which the weft thread is wound; it is placed on the shuttle.

eye
Hole through which a weft thread unrolls.

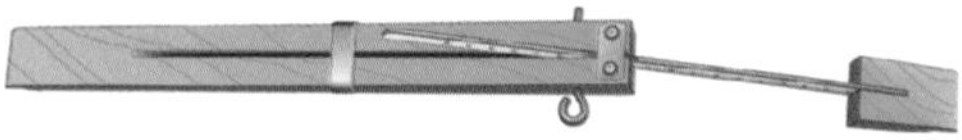

temple
Instrument that maintains a constant fabric width during weaving.

reed hooks
Hook used to pass the warp thread through the tooth of a comb or the eye of a heddle.

heddles
Metal wires that attach to the blade; they have an eye through which a warp thread passes.

eye
Hole through which a warp thread unwinds.

flat shuttle
Wooden plate on which the weft thread is wound; it replaces the shuttle when the space between the layers of warp threads is too narrow.

high warp loom
Loom on which the warp threads are arranged vertically.

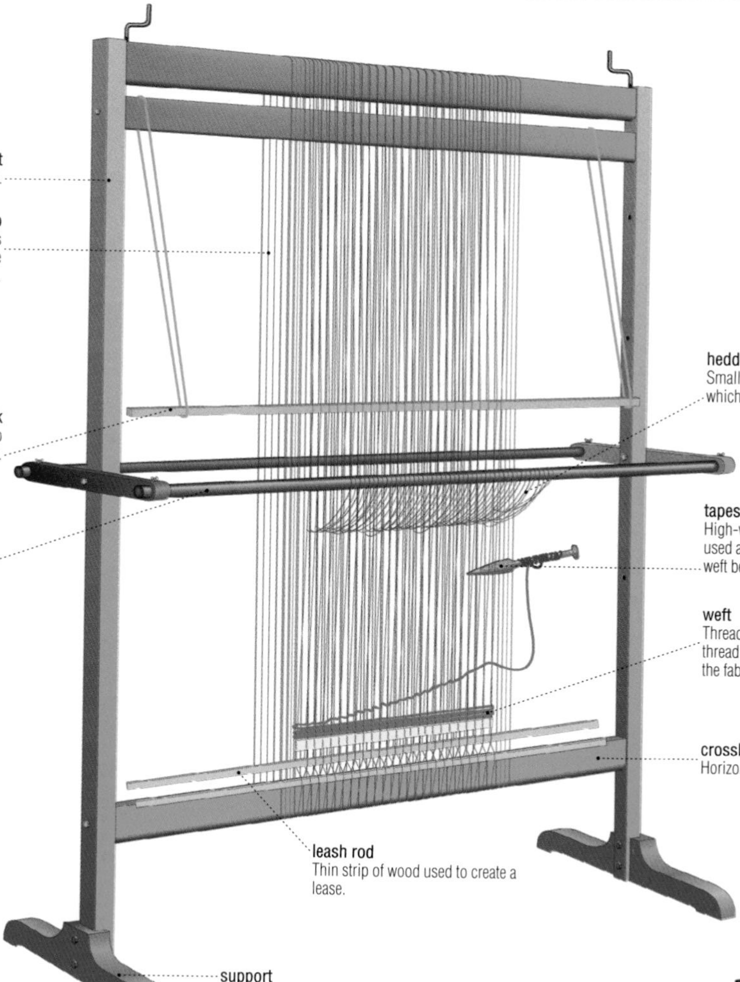

upright
Vertical section of the frame.

warp
Evenly spaced parallel threads arranged lengthwise along the fabric.

shed stick
Piece of wood that separates the warp based on the weaving pattern specified.

heddle rod
Piece of wood to which the heddles are attached.

heddles
Small wires with an eye through which the warp thread passes.

tapestry bobbin
High-warp tapestry instrument used as a shuttle to introduce the weft between the warp threads.

weft
Threads woven across the warp thread, along the width direction of the fabric.

crossbar
Horizontal section of the frame.

leash rod
Thin strip of wood used to create a lease.

support
The base on which the loom rests.

vertical frame
Wooden structure consisting of the loom's stationary parts.

tapestry bobbin
High-warp tapestry instrument used as a shuttle to introduce the weft between the warp threads.

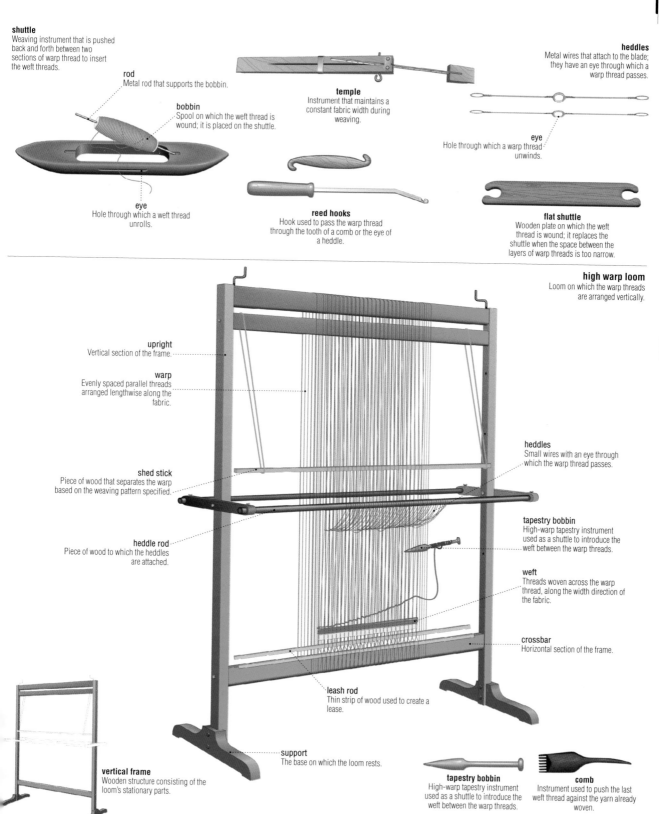

comb
Instrument used to push the last weft thread against the yarn already woven.

weaving

accessories
The tools used to facilitate various weaving processes.

bobbin winder
Device used to wind weft thread onto a bobbin.

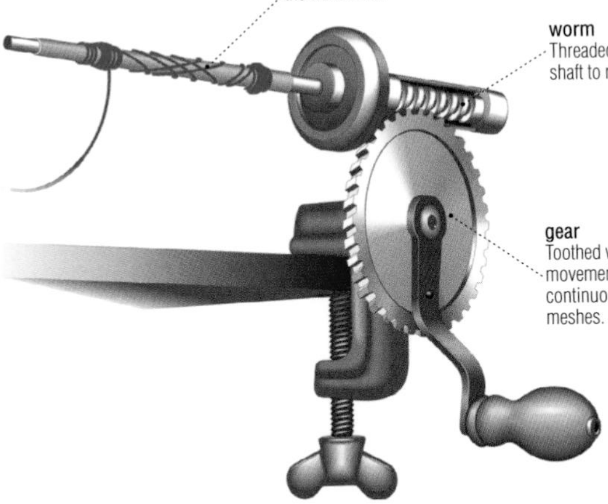

shaft
Spindle for the bobbin that holds the weft thread.

worm
Threaded device that causes the shaft to rotate.

gear
Toothed wheel whose rotating movement is transferred to the continuous worm with which it meshes.

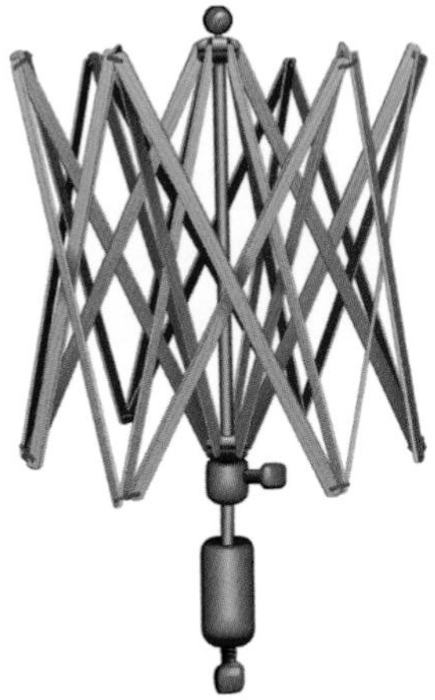

swift
Device composed of articulated slats on which warp or weft threads are disentangled, making it easier to unwind them afterward.

ball winder
Tool used to wind thread onto a ball.

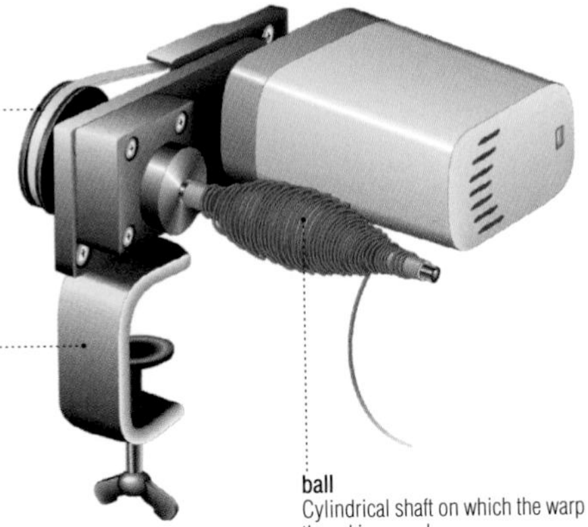

driving wheel
Wheel driven by an electric motor; it turns the shaft that winds the ball.

clamp
Tool with a C-mount used to secure the ball winder to a table.

ball
Cylindrical shaft on which the warp thread is wound.

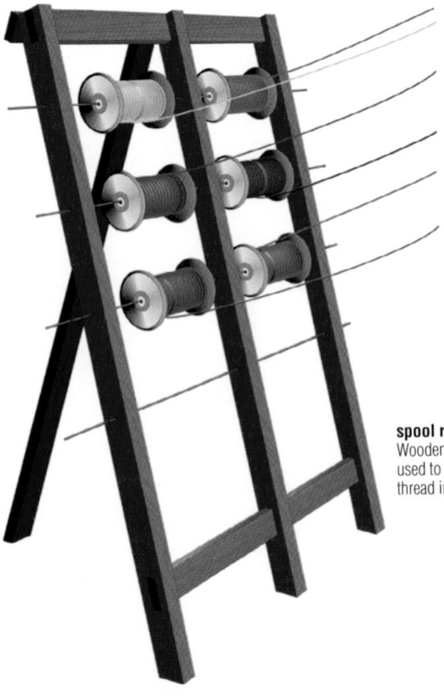

spool rack
Wooden frame with crosswise rods used to unwind spools of warp thread in various colors.

peg
Piece of wood used to create leases.

warping frame
Device on which the warp threads are arranged in parallel hanks; this makes it easier to wind them onto the warp roller.

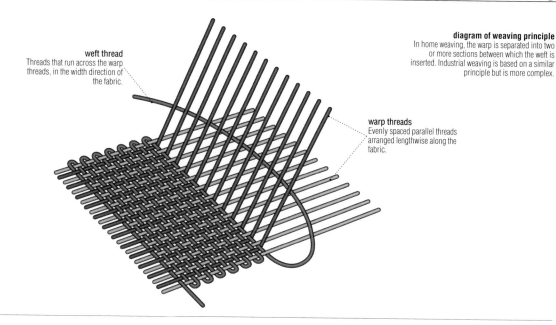

diagram of weaving principle
In home weaving, the warp is separated into two or more sections between which the weft is inserted. Industrial weaving is based on a similar principle but is more complex.

weft thread
Threads that run across the warp threads, in the width direction of the fabric.

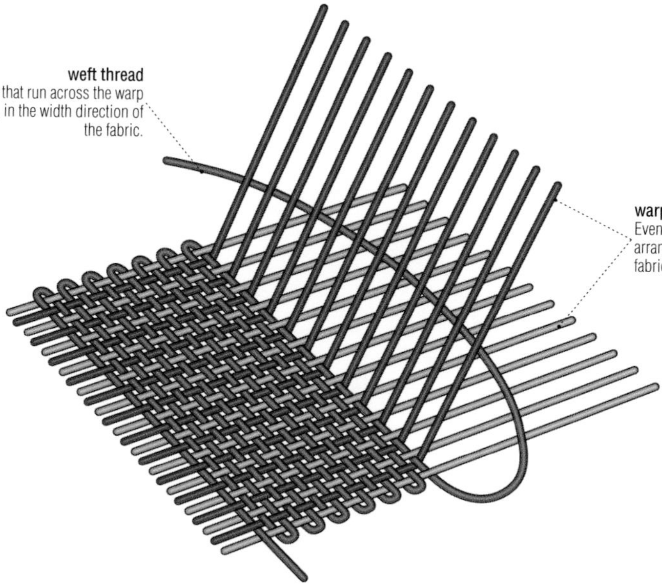

warp threads
Evenly spaced parallel threads arranged lengthwise along the fabric.

basic weaves

The principal types of weave.

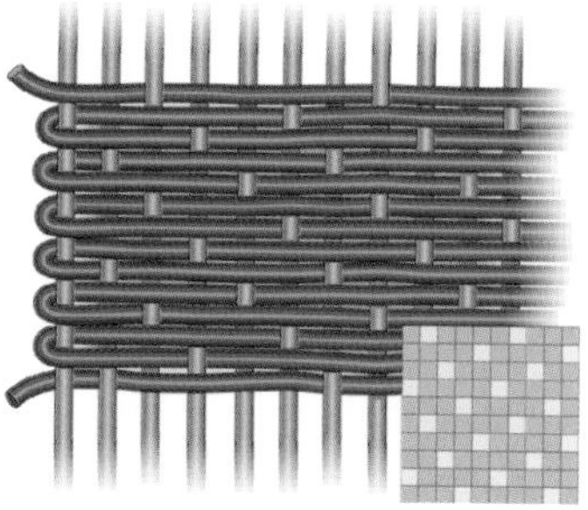

satin weave
Widely spaced weave forming a smooth surface; here, the weft thread passes over four warp threads and then under one.

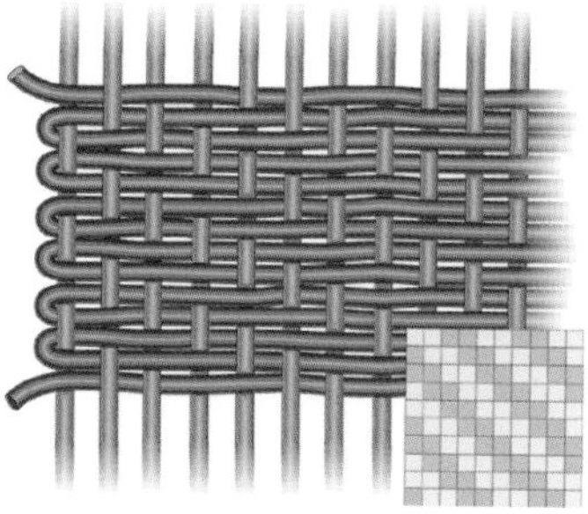

twill weave
Mesh forming oblique lines in the fabric; here, the weft thread passes over and then under two warp threads, and is staggered by one thread per row.

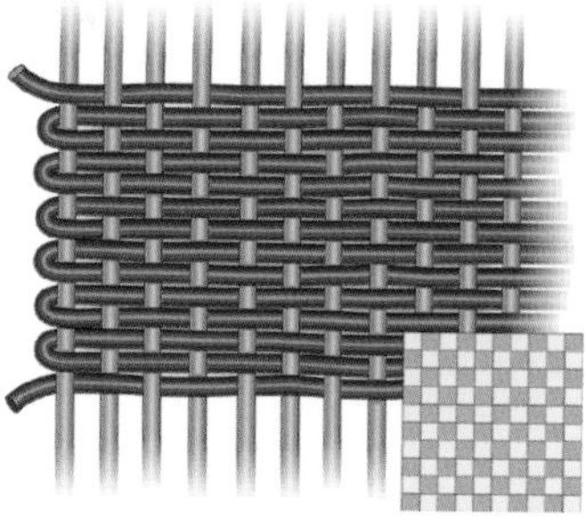

plain weave
Mesh forming a check pattern in the fabric; the weft thread passes over and under a warp thread, and is staggered by one thread per row.

other techniques

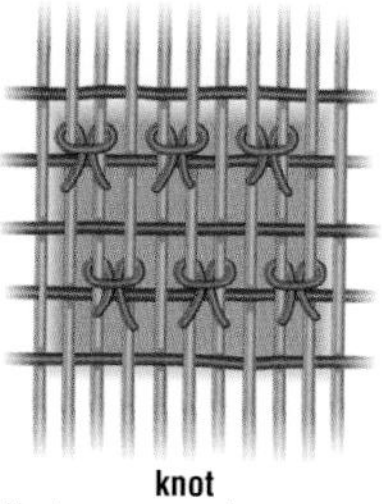

knot
Woolen yarn wound around two warp threads; its ends form the piles on a carpet.

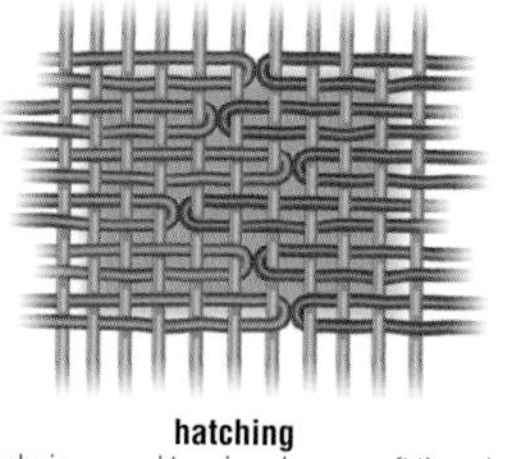

hatching
Technique used to mix colors: a weft thread enters a different color zone, interlocks with a warp thread and comes back to the original color zone.

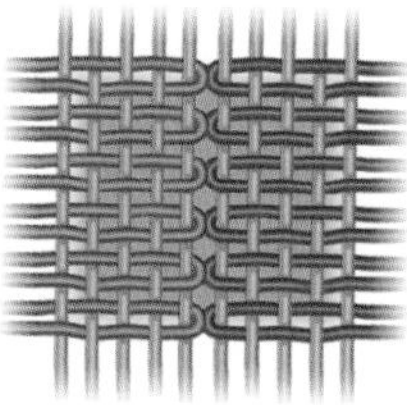

slit
The space where the thread colors change; weft threads and warp threads interlock and then return to their respective zones.

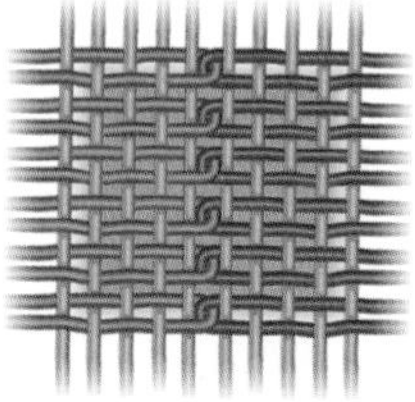

interlock
Section where the colors change; two weft threads of a different color interlock and then return to their respective zones.

pottery

Art of creating objects from a clay paste, which is shaped by hand and cooked in an oven.

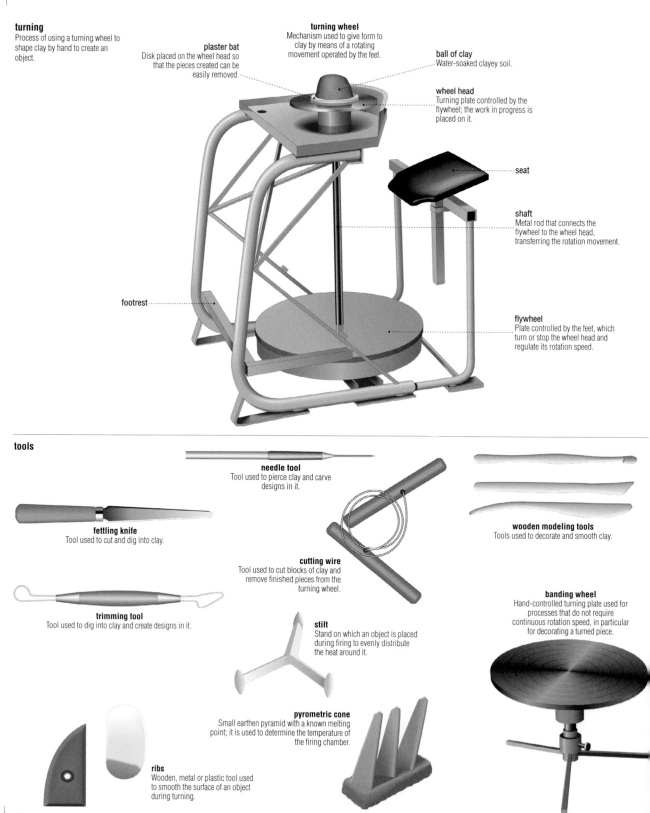

turning
Process of using a turning wheel to shape clay by hand to create an object.

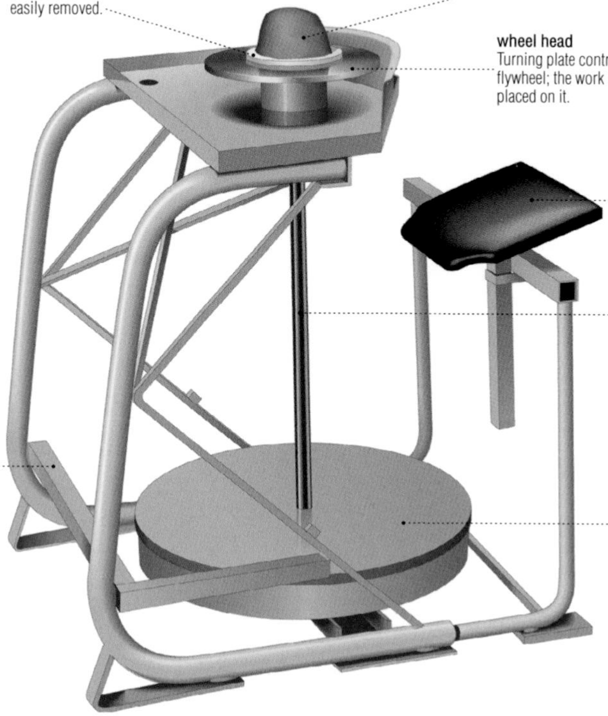

turning wheel
Mechanism used to give form to clay by means of a rotating movement operated by the feet.

plaster bat
Disk placed on the wheel head so that the pieces created can be easily removed.

ball of clay
Water-soaked clayey soil.

wheel head
Turning plate controlled by the flywheel; the work in progress is placed on it.

seat

shaft
Metal rod that connects the flywheel to the wheel head, transferring the rotation movement.

footrest

flywheel
Plate controlled by the feet, which turn or stop the wheel head and regulate its rotation speed.

tools

needle tool
Tool used to pierce clay and carve designs in it.

fettling knife
Tool used to cut and dig into clay.

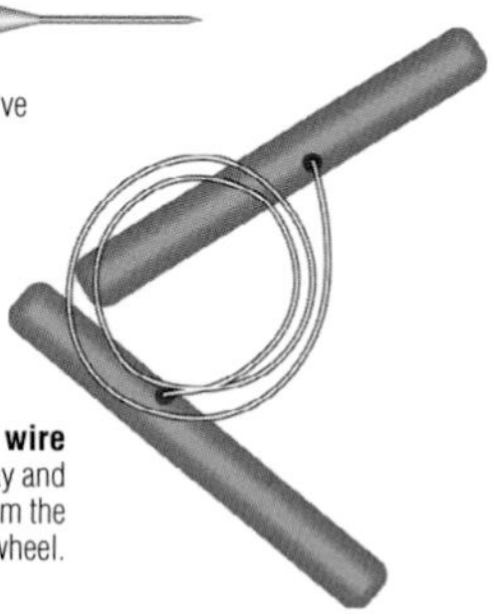

cutting wire
Tool used to cut blocks of clay and remove finished pieces from the turning wheel.

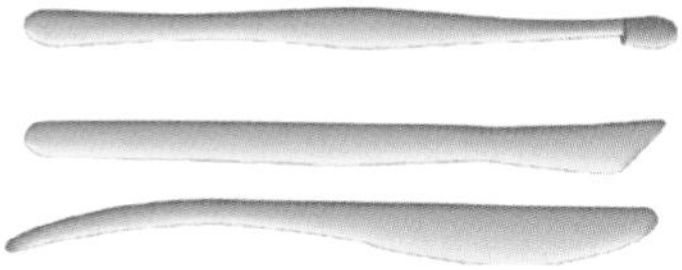

wooden modeling tools
Tools used to decorate and smooth clay.

trimming tool
Tool used to dig into clay and create designs in it.

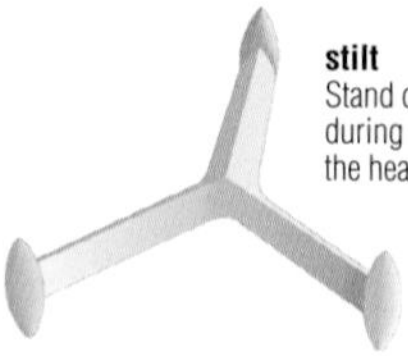

stilt
Stand on which an object is placed during firing to evenly distribute the heat around it.

banding wheel
Hand-controlled turning plate used for processes that do not require continuous rotation speed, in particular for decorating a turned piece.

pyrometric cone
Small earthen pyramid with a known melting point; it is used to determine the temperature of the firing chamber.

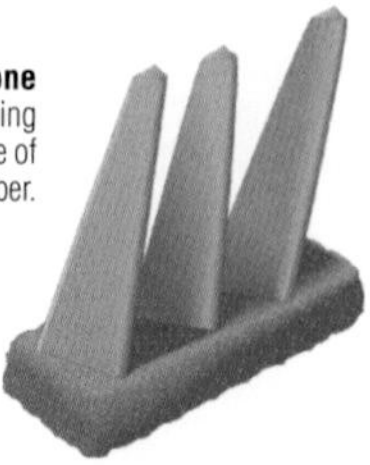

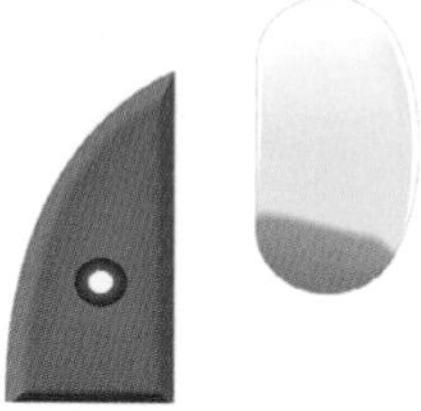

ribs
Wooden, metal or plastic tool used to smooth the surface of an object during turning.

slab building
Process by which clay is flattened with a roller, cut into slabs and then gathered together.

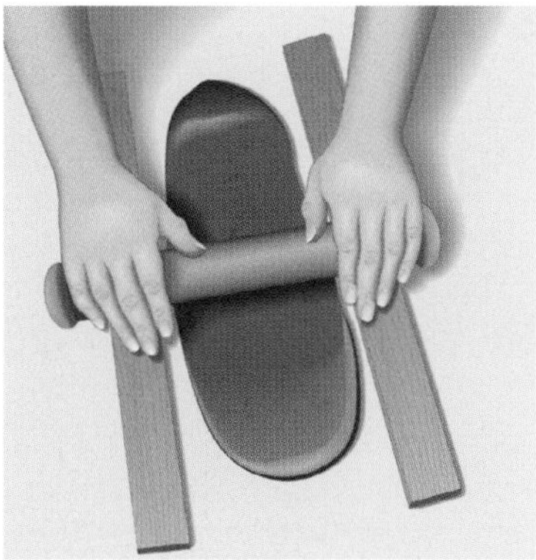

coiling
Process by which long rolls of clay are stacked and glued to create pieces without the use of a turning wheel.

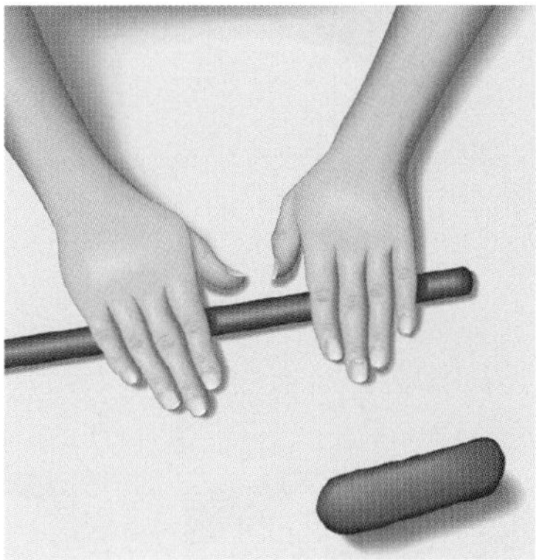

firing
Process by which clay is hardened by heating.

electric kiln
Apparatus that uses radiation to produce heat; it is used for firing clay.

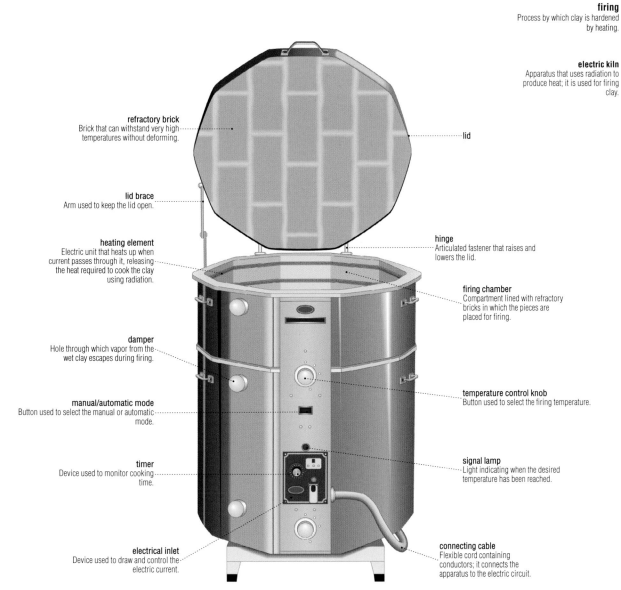

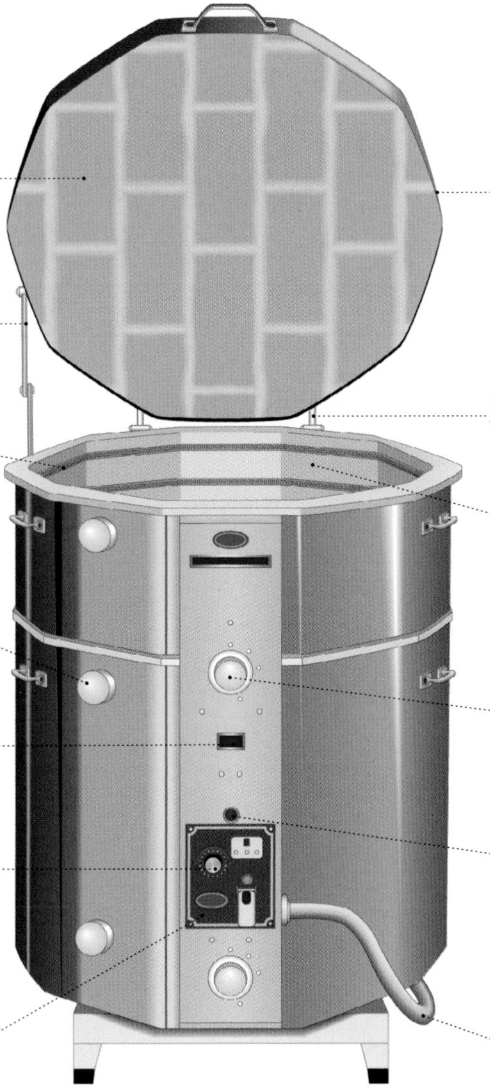

refractory brick
Brick that can withstand very high temperatures without deforming.
lid
lid brace
Arm used to keep the lid open.
heating element
Electric unit that heats up when current passes through it, releasing the heat required to cook the clay using radiation.
hinge
Articulated fastener that raises and lowers the lid.
firing chamber
Compartment lined with refractory bricks in which the pieces are placed for firing.
damper
Hole through which vapor from the wet clay escapes during firing.
temperature control knob
Button used to select the firing temperature.
manual/automatic mode
Button used to select the manual or automatic mode.
signal lamp
Light indicating when the desired temperature has been reached.
timer
Device used to monitor cooking time.
electrical inlet
Device used to draw and control the electric current.
connecting cable
Flexible cord containing conductors; it connects the apparatus to the electric circuit.

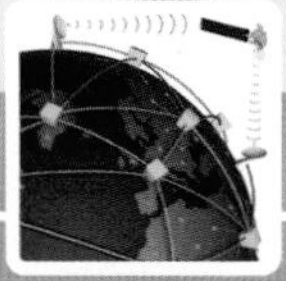

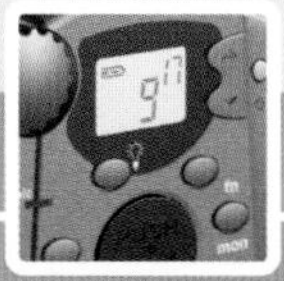

OMMUNICATIONS AND OFFICE AUTOMATION

languages of the world

There are more than 6,000 languages in the world; of these, only 250 are spoken by more than 1 million people.

major language families

Language families are grouped by their related phonetics, grammars and lexicons, or by a shared history.

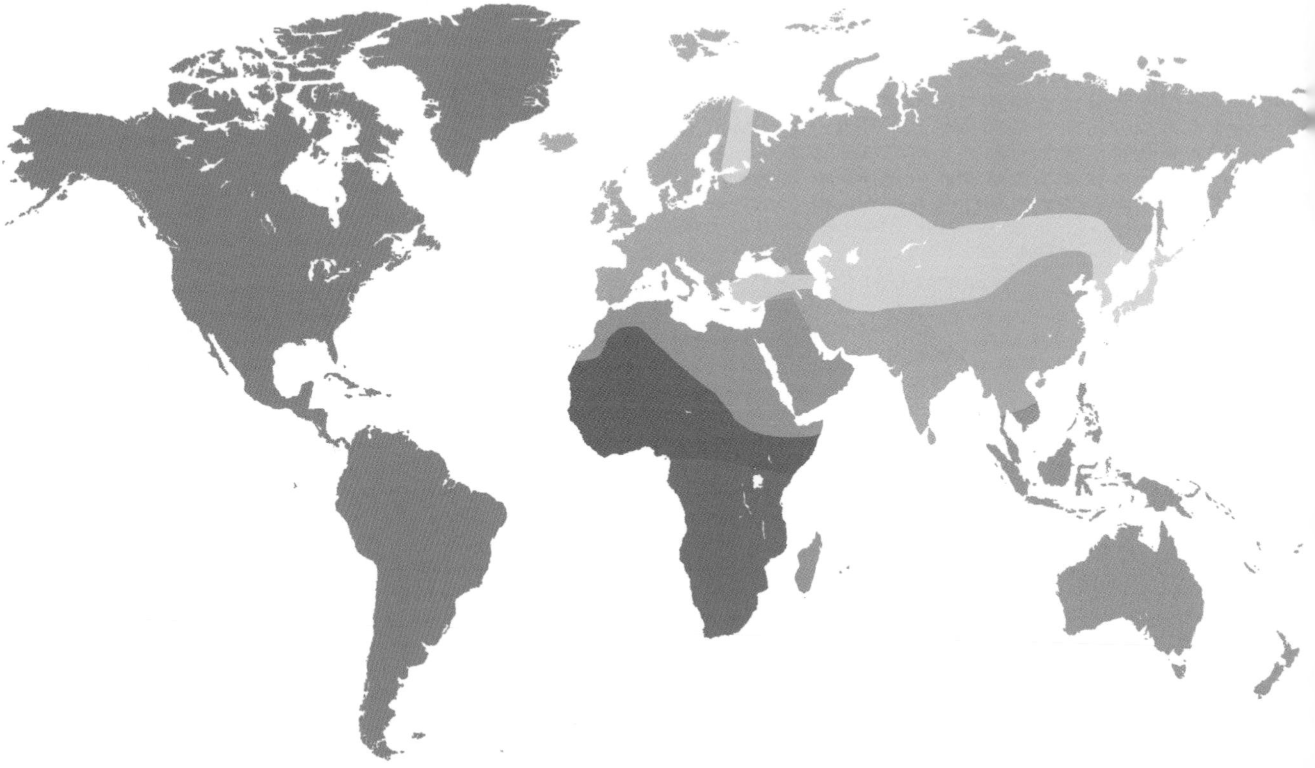

Afro-Asiatic languages

Family of some 120 living languages and several dead languages that are associated with major civilizations (Egyptian, Babylonian, Phoenician).

Arabic
Language of the Koran as well as the Afro-Asiatic language spoken by the greatest number of individuals; it is concentrated mainly in North Africa and the Middle East.

Hebrew
One of the official languages of the State of Israel; it is associated with the Jewish faith and people.

Aramaic
Spoken throughout the Middle East since antiquity; it continues to be spoken in some regions of Turkey, Syria and Iraq.

Amharic
Language spoken mainly in Ethiopia, where it has the status of official language.

Berber
Language of the Berber people of North Africa and spoken mainly in Morocco and Algeria.

Central African languages

Family grouping some 900 languages that are spoken mostly in central and western Africa.

Fulani
Language spoken along the west coast of Africa, especially in Senegal, Guinea, Nigeria and Cameroon.

Wolof
Language spoken in the western part of Africa, including in Senegal and Gambia.

Bambara
Language spoken in Mali and in some neighboring countries, including in Senegal, Guinea and Ivory Coast.

Hausa
One of the most widespread languages in western Africa; it is spoken mainly in Niger and Nigeria.

Yoruba
Language spoken mainly in Nigeria, Benin and Togo.

Bantu languages

Family of over 500 languages spoken in the southern half of the African continent.

Swahili
Bantu language spoken by the greatest number of individuals as a second language; it is concentrated mostly in eastern Africa.

Rundi
Official language of Burundi; it is very similar to Rwanda.

Rwanda
Language spoken mainly in Rwanda.

Lingala
Language spoken mainly as a second language in Congo and the Democratic Republic of the Congo.

Zulu
Language spoken by some people in South Africa and in several neighboring countries such as Swaziland and Mozambique.

Sino-Tibetan languages

Family of languages of Southeast Asia; it is spoken by about one-quarter of the world's population.

Chinese
Family of languages belonging to the same writing system using ideograms; it includes Mandarin, the most widely spoken language in the world.

Thai
Official language of Thailand; it is also spoken in certain regions of Laos and Myanmar.

Vietnamese
Language spoken mainly in Vietnam; it is usually written using a modified version of the Latin alphabet called "quoc ngu".

Burmese
Language spoken mainly in Myanmar (formerly Burma), where it enjoys the status of official language.

Tibetan
Language spoken in Tibet and certain regions of Nepal and Bhutan; the written alphabet originated in India.

Indo-European languages

Group of languages (there are more than 200) sharing a common ancestral language as deduced by a historical comparison of the grammars of the present-day languages. Latin and ancient Greek are Indo-European.

Romance languages

All the European languages derived from Latin; some have spread throughout the world.

French
Language of France and some neighboring countries that spread with the arrival of the French or Belgians to North America, Africa and Asia.

Spanish
Language of Spain that was introduced by the Spanish to most of the Americas (23 countries) and one African country (Equatorial Guinea).

Catalan
Official language of Catalonia, Valencia and Andorra; it is also spoken in the south of France.

Portuguese
Language of Portugal; it spread with the arrival of the Portuguese to Brazil, Africa and Asia.

Italian
National language of Italy and one canton of Switzerland (Tessin).

Romanian
National language of Romania.

Germanic languages

All the languages derived from an early Indo-European dialect, which has since disappeared, as deduced from similarities observed among the languages.

English
Language of England that spread with the British Empire to North America, India, Asia, Oceania and eastern and southern Africa.

German
National language of Germany, Austria and the greatest part of Switzerland.

Dutch
Language spoken mainly in the Netherlands and by the Flemish community in Belgium.

Danish
Scandinavian language spoken mainly in Denmark.

Swedish
Scandinavian language spoken mainly in Sweden and Finland.

Norwegian
Scandinavian language spoken mainly in Norway.

Icelandic
National language of Iceland; it is characterized by its great stability since the Middle Ages.

Yiddish
Language of the Ashkenazi Jews of Europe; it is a product of the fusion of Hebrew with elements of Germanic and Slavic languages.

Celtic languages

Widely spoken in western Europe throughout antiquity, these languages declined progressively and are found today in only a few regions.

Breton
Language spoken in the west of Brittany (France).

Welsh
One of the official languages of Wales (United Kingdom).

Scottish
Language closely related to Irish that is spoken mostly in Scotland (United Kingdom).

Irish
One of the official languages of the Republic of Ireland; it is also spoken in Northern Ireland (United Kingdom).

isolated languages

Some modern Indo-European languages cannot be classified into any subgroup.

Greek
The national language of Greece is directly descended from ancient Greek; its origin can be traced back several centuries before the Common Era.

Albanian
Language spoken mainly in Albania and in some neighboring regions.

Armenian
Very old language that is spoken in the Caucasus region, mainly in Armenia.

Slavic languages

Group of languages concentrated in Eastern Europe and Russia; they derive from a common extinct Slavic language.

Czech
National language of the Czech Republic that is closely related to Slovak.

Slovak
National language of Slovakia; both Slovak and Czech use the Latin alphabet.

Polish
National language of Poland; it is fairly close to Czech and Slovak.

Russian
National language of Russia that is also widely spoken in the former USSR; Russian is written with the Cyrillic alphabet.

Ukrainian
Language related to Russian that is spoken mainly in Ukraine and in several neighboring states.

Bulgarian
National language of Bulgaria that is written with the Cyrillic alphabet; it is related to Slovene and Serbo-Croatian.

Slovene
Language spoken mainly in Slovenia and written with the Latin alphabet.

Serbo-Croatian
Serbians and Montenegrins use the Cyrillic alphabet while Croatians and Bosnians use the Latin alphabet.

Indo-Iranian languages

Spoken in Asia and the Middle East, they number the largest group of speakers among all Indo-European language groups.

Persian
Language spoken mainly in Iran and Afghanistan; it is written using the Arabic alphabet.

Urdu
Language spoken mainly in Pakistan and Northern India; it is very similar to Hindi but is written using the Arabic alphabet.

Hindi
Indian language spoken by the largest number of individuals; it is written using the Devanagari alphabet, which is common to several languages derived from Sanskrit.

Ural-Altaic languages

Family made up of some 100 languages spoken in central and eastern Asia, the Middle East and northern and central Europe.

Japanese
Language spoken throughout the Japanese archipelago; it is written using ideograms or syllabic characters.

Korean
Language spoken mainly in Korea; its lexicon includes many words of Chinese origin.

Mongolian
Official language of Mongolia; it is also spoken by some communities in China and Russia.

Turkish
Official language of Turkey; it is written using the Latin alphabet.

Hungarian
Language spoken in Hungary.

Finnish
With Swedish, one of the national languages of Finland.

Malayo-Polynesian languages

Family grouping some 850 languages that are spread over a vast area, including Madagascar, parts of Southeast Asia and the Pacific.

Indonesian
National language of Indonesia; it is closely related to Malay.

Tagalog
Language spoken mainly in the Philippines, where it has the status of an official language.

Malagasy
Language spoken mainly in Madagascar, but also in Comoros and Réunion.

Samoan
Language spoken in the Samoan archipelago of Polynesia in the central Pacific.

Tahitian
Language spoken in French Polynesia.

Hawaiian
Language spoken mainly in Hawaii (United States).

Maori
One of the official languages of New Zealand.

Oceanian languages

All the languages spoken in Oceania; they usually have few ties among themselves or with other language families.

Melanesian
Language spoken in Melanesia, a group of archipelagos in the South Pacific that includes mainly New Guinea, Vanuatu, the Fiji Islands and New Caledonia.

Papuan languages
There are over 800 Papuan languages and dialects; they are spoken mainly on the island of New Guinea.

Australian aboriginal languages
There are a few hundred languages associated with the indigenous peoples of Australia; several are barely spoken today or have disappeared completely.

Amerindian languages

Several hundred languages are associated with the indigenous peoples of the Americas; several are barely spoken today or have disappeared completely.

Inuktitut
Language of the Inuit who live in Alaska, the Canadian North and Greenland.

Cree
Algonquian language associated with the Cree, the largest Amerindian community in Canada, who live in the area between Alberta and Labrador.

Montagnais
Algonquian language associated with the Montagnais, who live in Eastern Canada, mostly in Quebec (North Shore of the St. Lawrence) and in Labrador.

Navajo
Native language spoken by the Navajo people of the Southwestern United States (Arizona, New Mexico).

Nahuatl
Language of the Aztec Empire that is still widely spoken today in certain regions of southern Mexico.

Maya
Language of the Maya Empire that is spoken in certain regions of southern Mexico, especially the Yucatan Peninsula.

Quechua
Language of the Inca Empire and the language spoken today by the largest number of Amerindians in countries such as Peru, Ecuador and Bolivia.

Aymara
Language spoken mainly in Bolivia and Peru.

Guarani
Language accorded official status in Paraguay; it is also spoken in certain regions of Argentina and Bolivia.

writing instruments

The first true writing instruments were made by the Sumerians in Mesopotamia nearly 5,000 years ago.

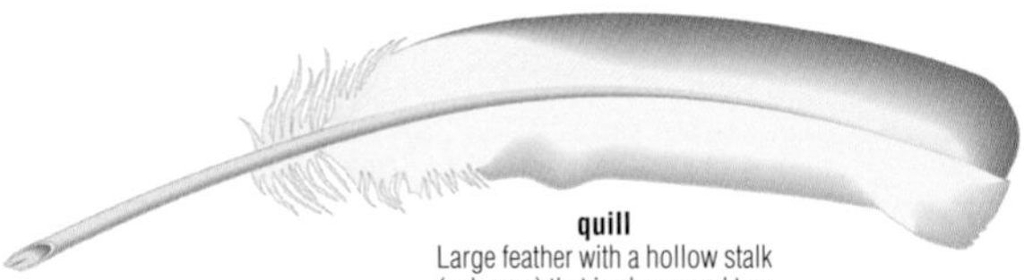

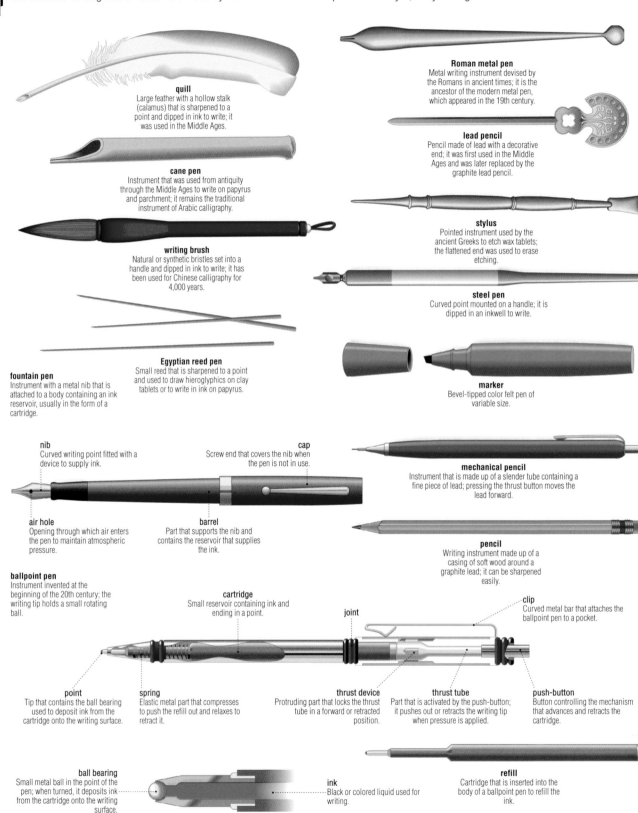

quill
Large feather with a hollow stalk (calamus) that is sharpened to a point and dipped in ink to write; it was used in the Middle Ages.

cane pen
Instrument that was used from antiquity through the Middle Ages to write on papyrus and parchment; it remains the traditional instrument of Arabic calligraphy.

writing brush
Natural or synthetic bristles set into a handle and dipped in ink to write; it has been used for Chinese calligraphy for 4,000 years.

Egyptian reed pen
Small reed that is sharpened to a point and used to draw hieroglyphics on clay tablets or to write in ink on papyrus.

Roman metal pen
Metal writing instrument devised by the Romans in ancient times; it is the ancestor of the modern metal pen, which appeared in the 19th century.

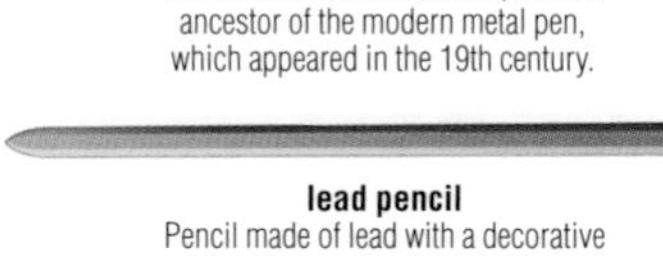

lead pencil
Pencil made of lead with a decorative end; it was first used in the Middle Ages and was later replaced by the graphite lead pencil.

stylus
Pointed instrument used by the ancient Greeks to etch wax tablets; the flattened end was used to erase etching.

steel pen
Curved point mounted on a handle; it is dipped in an inkwell to write.

marker
Bevel-tipped color felt pen of variable size.

fountain pen
Instrument with a metal nib that is attached to a body containing an ink reservoir, usually in the form of a cartridge.

nib
Curved writing point fitted with a device to supply ink.
cap
Screw end that covers the nib when the pen is not in use.
air hole
Opening through which air enters the pen to maintain atmospheric pressure.
barrel
Part that supports the nib and contains the reservoir that supplies the ink.

mechanical pencil
Instrument that is made up of a slender tube containing a fine piece of lead; pressing the thrust button moves the lead forward.

pencil
Writing instrument made up of a casing of soft wood around a graphite lead; it can be sharpened easily.

ballpoint pen
Instrument invented at the beginning of the 20th century; the writing tip holds a small rotating ball.

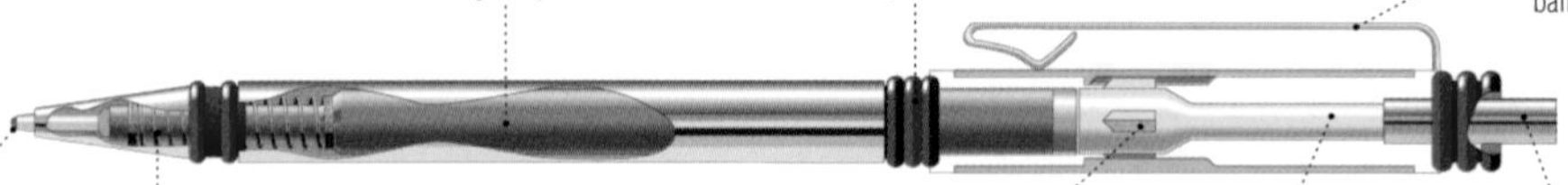

cartridge
Small reservoir containing ink and ending in a point.
joint
clip
Curved metal bar that attaches the ballpoint pen to a pocket.
point
Tip that contains the ball bearing used to deposit ink from the cartridge onto the writing surface.
spring
Elastic metal part that compresses to push the refill out and relaxes to retract it.
thrust device
Protruding part that locks the thrust tube in a forward or retracted position.
thrust tube
Part that is activated by the push-button; it pushes out or retracts the writing tip when pressure is applied.
push-button
Button controlling the mechanism that advances and retracts the cartridge.

refill
Cartridge that is inserted into the body of a ballpoint pen to refill the ink.

ball bearing
Small metal ball in the point of the pen; when turned, it deposits ink from the cartridge onto the writing surface.
ink
Black or colored liquid used for writing.

newspaper

Usually daily publication whose main purpose is to report and comment on the latest news of society, politics, the arts, sports and other areas of interest.

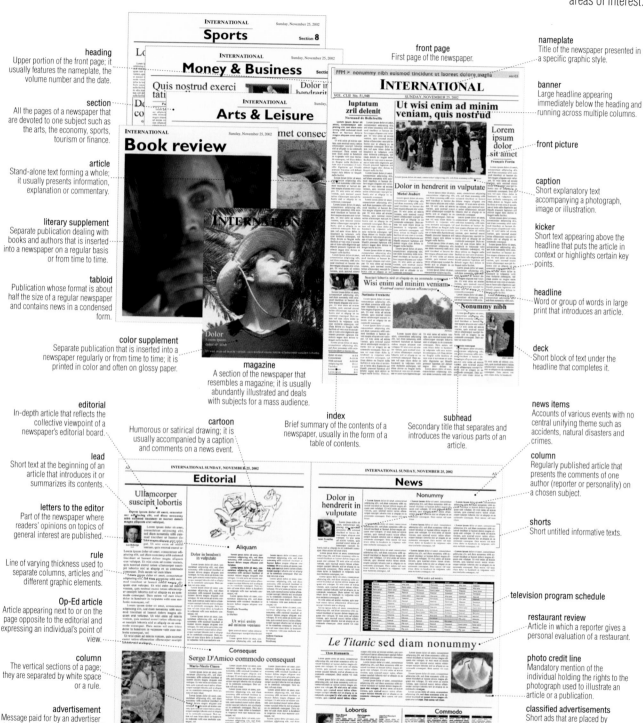

heading
Upper portion of the front page; it usually features the nameplate, the volume number and the date.

section
All the pages of a newspaper that are devoted to one subject such as the arts, the economy, sports, tourism or finance.

article
Stand-alone text forming a whole; it usually presents information, explanation or commentary.

literary supplement
Separate publication dealing with books and authors that is inserted into a newspaper on a regular basis or from time to time.

tabloid
Publication whose format is about half the size of a regular newspaper and contains news in a condensed form.

color supplement
Separate publication that is inserted into a newspaper regularly or from time to time; it is printed in color and often on glossy paper.

magazine
A section of the newspaper that resembles a magazine; it is usually abundantly illustrated and deals with subjects for a mass audience.

front page
First page of the newspaper.

nameplate
Title of the newspaper presented in a specific graphic style.

banner
Large headline appearing immediately below the heading and running across multiple columns.

front picture

caption
Short explanatory text accompanying a photograph, image or illustration.

kicker
Short text appearing above the headline that puts the article in context or highlights certain key points.

headline
Word or group of words in large print that introduces an article.

deck
Short block of text under the headline that completes it.

index
Brief summary of the contents of a newspaper, usually in the form of a table of contents.

subhead
Secondary title that separates and introduces the various parts of an article.

editorial
In-depth article that reflects the collective viewpoint of a newspaper's editorial board.

cartoon
Humorous or satirical drawing; it is usually accompanied by a caption and comments on a news event.

lead
Short text at the beginning of an article that introduces it or summarizes its contents.

letters to the editor
Part of the newspaper where readers' opinions on topics of general interest are published.

rule
Line of varying thickness used to separate columns, articles and different graphic elements.

Op-Ed article
Article appearing next to or on the page opposite to the editorial and expressing an individual's point of view.

column
The vertical sections of a page; they are separated by white space or a rule.

advertisement
Message paid for by an advertiser to inform readers about a business, product or service.

masthead
Space that usually contains information about the newspaper such its address, main contributors and subscription information.

news items
Accounts of various events with no central unifying theme such as accidents, natural disasters and crimes.

column
Regularly published article that presents the comments of one author (reporter or personality) on a chosen subject.

shorts
Short untitled informative texts.

television program schedule

restaurant review
Article in which a reporter gives a personal evaluation of a restaurant.

photo credit line
Mandatory mention of the individual holding the rights to the photograph used to illustrate an article or a publication.

classified advertisements
Short ads that are placed by individuals and grouped into categories according to the goods or services offered or sought.

obituaries
Listing of death notices and anniversaries of deaths, cards of thanks and remembrances.

typography

General term for the graphic representation of characters printed on a material or surface, with or without the use of letterpress.

characters of a font
Characters of type that make up the various fonts and are divided into two main types of characters: serif and sans serif.

sans serif type
Letter or figure without a line extension at the end of the stroke.

serif type
Letter or figure with a line extension at the end of the stroke.

abcdefghijklmnopqrstuvwxyz 0123456789

abcdefghijklmnopqrstuvwxyz 0123456789

letters   figures

shape of characters
In printing, uppercase characters, small capitals and lowercase characters can be straight (roman) or slanted (italic).

ABCDEF ABCDEF abcdef *abcdef*

uppercase
Capital letter used mostly at the beginning of a sentence and for proper names.

small capital
Capital letter that is the same height as a lowercase letter and is used mainly to write symbols.

lowercase
Smaller version of a letter that is generally used for most text wherever a capital letter is not required.

italic
Type style with characters slanting to the right; it is used mostly to identify titles, quotations and foreign words.

weight
Relative thickness of the strokes of a character; the medium and bold weights are the most commonly used.

extra-light

light

medium

semi-bold

bold

black

extra-bold

set width
Relative width of a character.

condensed   narrow   normal   wide   extended

leading
Vertical space separating two lines of characters; its precise value is proportional to the size of the characters.

Lorem ipsum dolor sit amet, consectetuer adipiscing elit, sed

Lorem ipsum dolor sit amet, consectetuer adipiscing elit, sed

Lorem ipsum dolor sit amet, consectetuer adipiscing elit, sed

simple spacing   **1.5 spacing**   **double spacing**

position of a characte[r]
With the exception of superiors an[d] inferiors, the characters of a text are usual[ly] aligned along a horizontal baselin[e].

H_2SO_4

XXe

inferior
Small character placed below the baseline and to the right of another character; it is used mostly in chemical and mathematical formulas.

superior
Small character placed above an[d] to the right of another character; [it] is sometimes used in abbreviation[s] and also to mark footnotes.

diacritic symbols

Symbols added to a letter; they usually change its pronunciation.

à
grave accent

ü
umlaut

é
acute accent

â
circumflex accent

ç
cedilla

ñ
tilde

miscellaneous symbols

Symbols are standardized marks used to refer concisely to a thing, a being or a concept.

®
registered trademark
Symbol certifying that the preceding word has been legally registered as a trademark.

©
copyright
Symbol at the beginning of a work attesting to the author's legal rights to that work; it is used to prevent plagiarism or reproduction without authorization.

&
ampersand
Symbol representing the word "and"; it is often used in company names.

's
apostrophe
Symbol used to indicate the possessive, substitute for letters and numerals that are omitted, or sometimes form a plural word.

punctuation marks

All the standardized marks used to divide a text in order to make it more legible.

.
period

;
semicolon

,
comma

...
ellipses

:
colon

*
asterisk

—
dash

( )
parentheses

[ ]
square brackets

/
virgule

!
exclamation point

?
question mark

‘ ’
single quotation marks
Marks used in pairs to indicate a concept or word of special significance or to enclose a quotation within a quotation.

“ ”
quotation marks
Marks used in pairs and shaped like inverted or regular commas.

« »
quotation marks (French)
Marks used in pairs and shaped like chevrons in French texts.

public postal network

Infrastructure with which the national postal service delivers the mail entrusted to it.

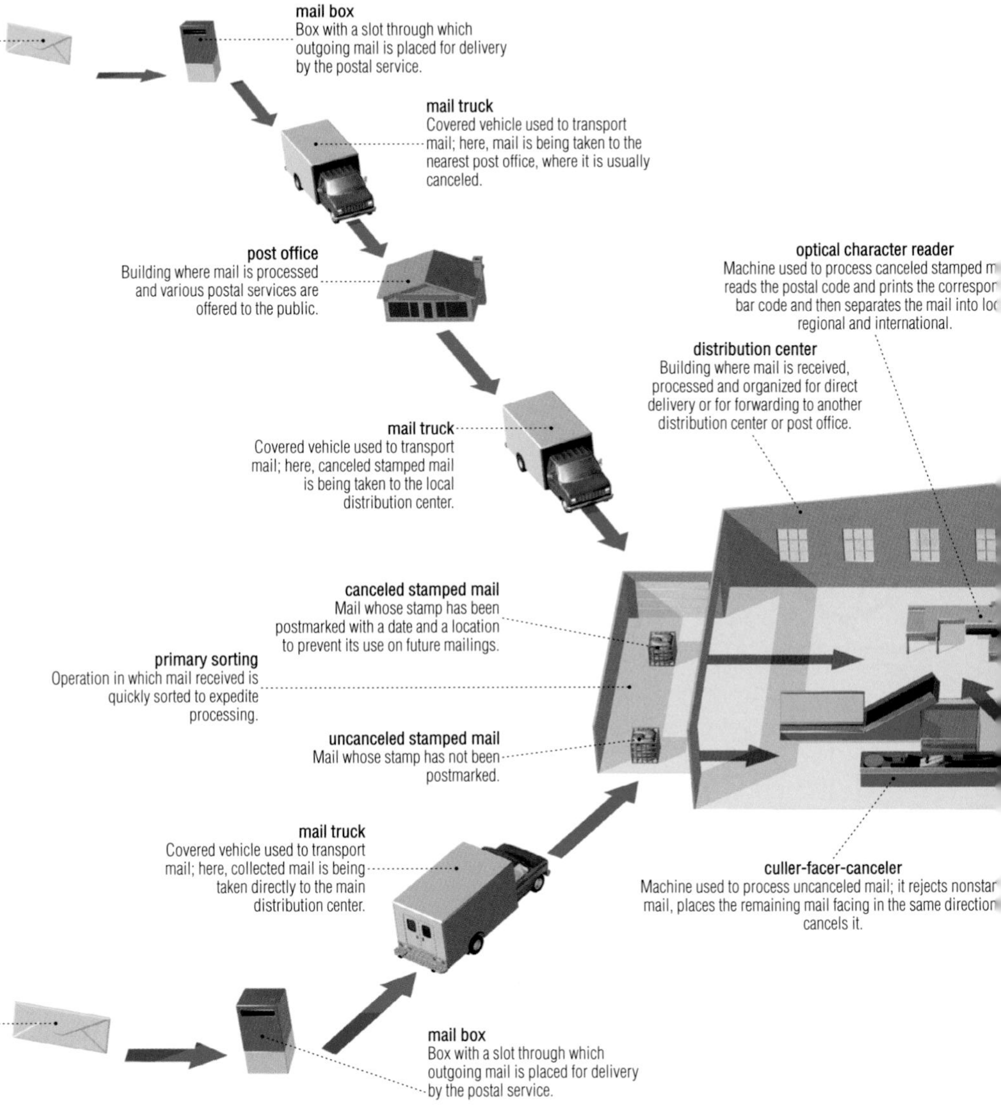
mail
Everything sent and distributed through the postal service.
mail box
Box with a slot through which outgoing mail is placed for delivery by the postal service.
mail truck
Covered vehicle used to transport mail; here, mail is being taken to the nearest post office, where it is usually canceled.
post office
Building where mail is processed and various postal services are offered to the public.
optical character reader
Machine used to process canceled stamped m
reads the postal code and prints the correspor
bar code and then separates the mail into loc
regional and international.
distribution center
Building where mail is received, processed and organized for direct delivery or for forwarding to another distribution center or post office.
mail truck
Covered vehicle used to transport mail; here, canceled stamped mail is being taken to the local distribution center.
canceled stamped mail
Mail whose stamp has been postmarked with a date and a location to prevent its use on future mailings.
primary sorting
Operation in which mail received is quickly sorted to expedite processing.
uncanceled stamped mail
Mail whose stamp has not been postmarked.
mail truck
Covered vehicle used to transport mail; here, collected mail is being taken directly to the main distribution center.
culler-facer-canceler
Machine used to process uncanceled mail; it rejects nonstar
mail, places the remaining mail facing in the same direction
cancels it.
mail
Everything sent and distributed through the postal service.
mail box
Box with a slot through which outgoing mail is placed for delivery by the postal service.

mail
Everything sent and distributed through the postal service.

postage stamp
Small adhesive label of varying denominations that is issued by a postal service and used to indicate postage paid.

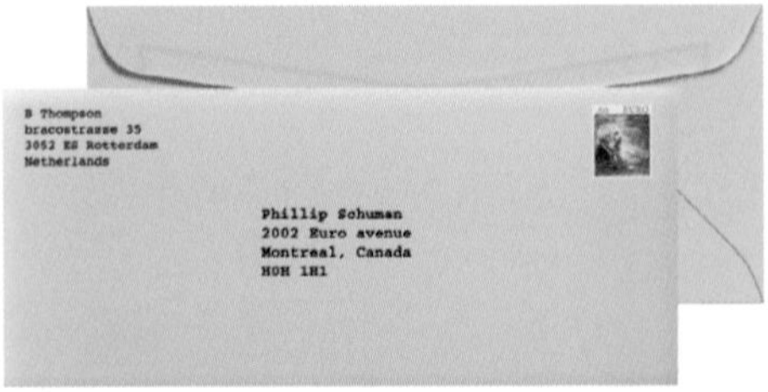

letter
Written message that is inserted into an envelope and addressed to a recipient.

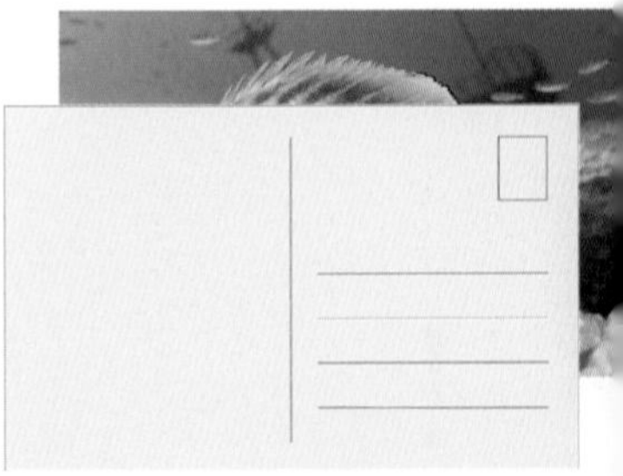

postcard
Photograph or illustration that is printed on flexible cardboard and has space on the back to write a message ar
an address.

public postal network

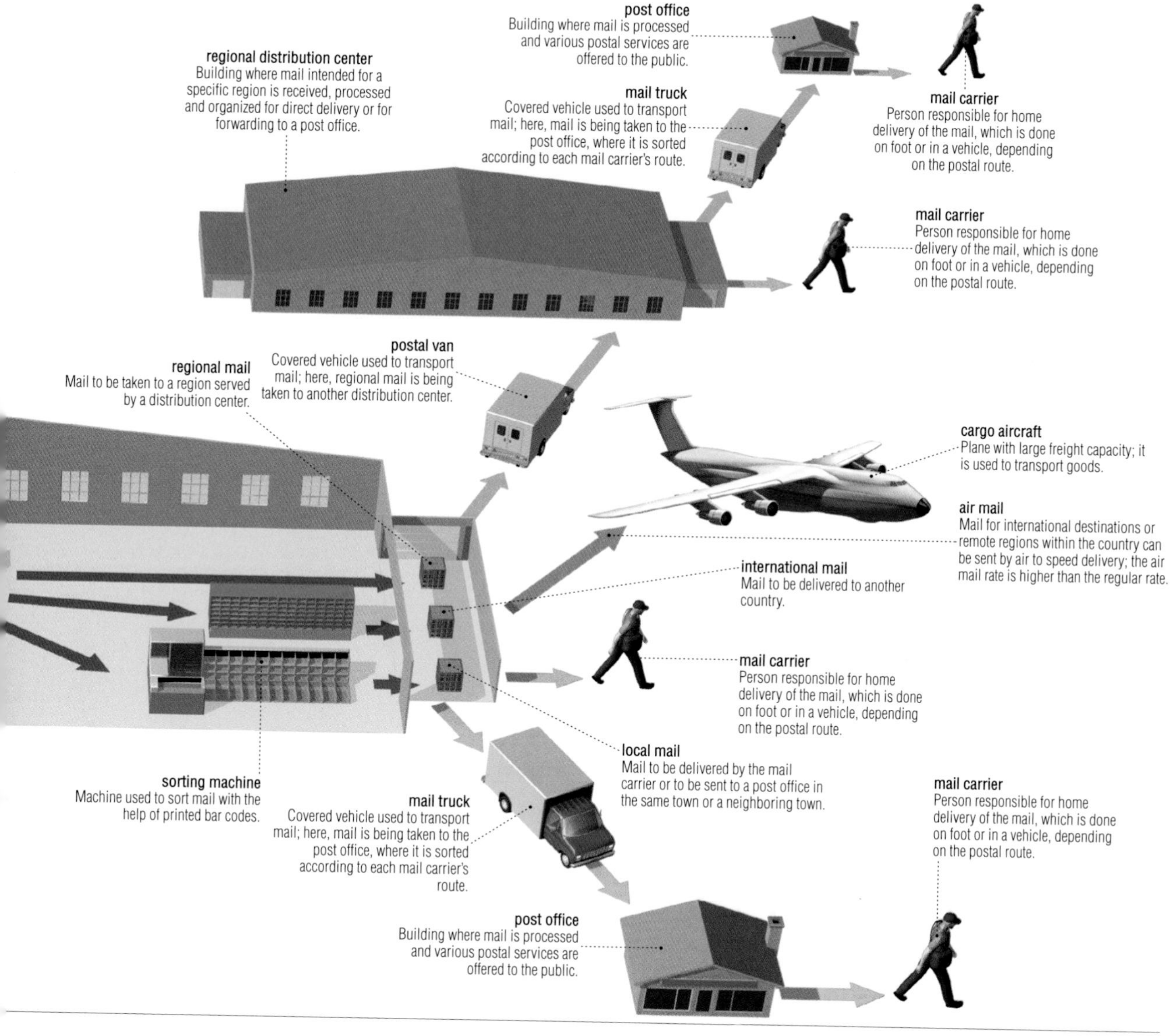
post office
Building where mail is processed and various postal services are offered to the public.
regional distribution center
Building where mail intended for a specific region is received, processed and organized for direct delivery or for forwarding to a post office.
mail truck
Covered vehicle used to transport mail; here, mail is being taken to the post office, where it is sorted according to each mail carrier's route.
mail carrier
Person responsible for home delivery of the mail, which is done on foot or in a vehicle, depending on the postal route.
mail carrier
Person responsible for home delivery of the mail, which is done on foot or in a vehicle, depending on the postal route.
postal van
Covered vehicle used to transport mail; here, regional mail is being taken to another distribution center.
regional mail
Mail to be taken to a region served by a distribution center.
cargo aircraft
Plane with large freight capacity; it is used to transport goods.
air mail
Mail for international destinations or remote regions within the country can be sent by air to speed delivery; the air mail rate is higher than the regular rate.
international mail
Mail to be delivered to another country.
mail carrier
Person responsible for home delivery of the mail, which is done on foot or in a vehicle, depending on the postal route.
local mail
Mail to be delivered by the mail carrier or to be sent to a post office in the same town or a neighboring town.
sorting machine
Machine used to sort mail with the help of printed bar codes.
mail truck
Covered vehicle used to transport mail; here, mail is being taken to the post office, where it is sorted according to each mail carrier's route.
mail carrier
Person responsible for home delivery of the mail, which is done on foot or in a vehicle, depending on the postal route.
post office
Building where mail is processed and various postal services are offered to the public.

bulk mail
Mail consisting of a large number of letters mailed at the same time by the same sender, usually at a reduced postage rate.

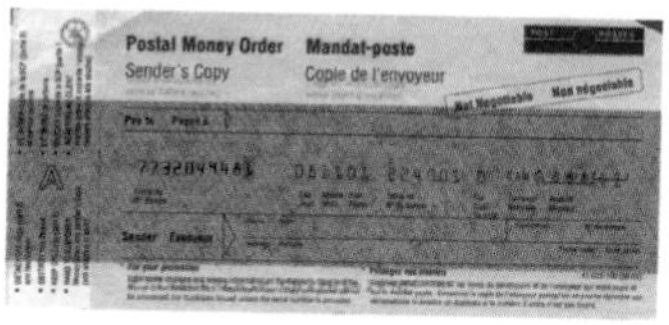

postal money order
A certificate issued by the postal service by which a sender is able to pay a specified sum to a recipient at another location.

postal parcel
Parcel sent through the mail.

photography

Process that captures an image on a light-sensitive surface by admitting light through a shutter.

single-lens reflex (SLR) camera: front view
Still camera with an interchangeable lens that can be used for both viewing and shooting, hence the term “reflex”.

exposure adjustment knob
Knob that can deliberately underexpose or overexpose a film when the camera is in automatic exposure mode.

accessory shoe
Device for attaching an accessory to the camera (usually an external flash).

hot-shoe contact
Conduction unit that links the camera’s electronic circuitry to the accessory mounted on the accessory shoe.

film advance mode
Control button used to advance the film in the camera body (frame by frame or continuously).

exposure mode
Button for choosing an automatic, semiautomatic or manual setting to control the amount of light that comes in contact with the film.

control panel
Liquid crystal display that shows the camera’s various settings.

command control dial
Dial used to adjust the various parameters of a mode.

multiple exposure mode
Control button that blocks the film from advancing to create multiple exposures (several images superimposed on the same frame).

on-off switch
Button for turning the device on or off.

film speed
Control button that sets the film’s sens to light as expressed by the ISO or AS number; the higher the number, the mo sensitive the film.

shutter release button
Button that controls the exposure through control of the focal plane shutter opening.

remote control terminal
Device that is attached to the camera by a so that it can be operated from a distance.

self-timer indicator
Light that shows the self-timer is on to delay release of the shutter; this allows the photographer to be in the photo.

focus mode selector
Button that allows the user to choose between an automatic or manual focus to ensure a clear image.

camera body
Rigid sturdy box that contains the camera’s mechanism and shields the film from light.

lens release button
Button for removing the lens from the camera body.

objective lens
Optical system made up of a set of lenses fixed on a mount; it allows a clear image to be produced on film.

depth-of-field preview button
Button that closes the diaphragm so that the relative clarity of vari depths can be seen through the viewfinder.

digital reflex camera: control panel

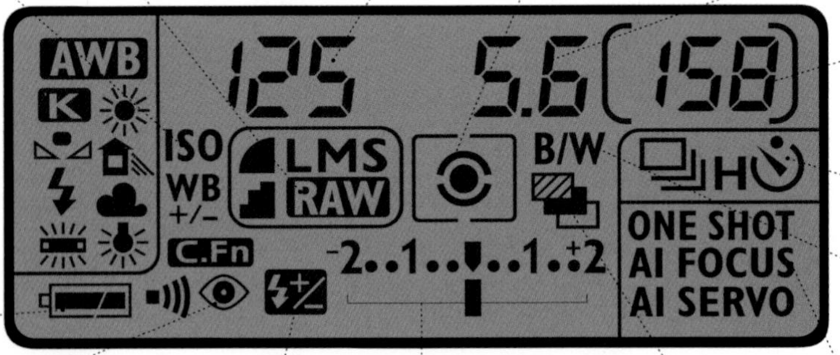

sensitivity
Value describing the sensor’s sensitivity to light, generally expressed as an ISO index.

image-recording quality
Function enabling the user to control the format and resolution of images.

shutter speed
Number indicating the interval of time during which the sensor should be exposed to light, generally measured in fractions of a second.

metering mode
Method of measuring the intensity of the light hitting and reflected by a subject in order to determine the exposure required.

aperture
Number indicating the aperture of the diaphragm, measured as an f-stop number (the higher the f-stop number, the smaller the aperture).

frames remaining/timer
Display of the number of frames remair the time before the taking of a photogra with the timer.

white balance
Correction of colors to compensate for ambient light (daylight, fluorescent or tungsten lighting, etc.)

film advance mode
Function that enables the user to choos between frame-by-frame mode (one photograph at a time) and burst mode (several consecutive photographs).

black-and-white
Function enabling an image to be recorded using only white, black, and shades of gray.

battery level
Indicator that displays the level of energy in the batteries that supply power to the camera.

red-eye reduction
Mechanism that reduces the red-eye effect by producing a small flash before the main flash goes off.

flash exposure compensation
Mechanism that deliberately reduces or increases the intensity of the flash.

exposure correction
Number representing the modification made to the exposure data when the user wishes to deliberately underexpose or overexpose the subject.

bracketing
Procedure consisting of photographing a single subject several times while varying the exposure index or the white balance.

autofocus
Automatic focusing function that ensures a sharp image.

digital reflex camera: camera back
Reflex camera that contains a sensor and a microprocessor rather than film; they record and store images in digital form on a memory card.

power switch
Button for turning the device on or off.

menu button
Button that displays menus on the picture monitor, from which the camera's settings are chosen.

liquid crystal display
Screen that uses light reflected off liquid crystals to display alphanumeric data or images.

viewfinder
Device for viewing the scene to be photographed, framing it and adjusting its clarity.

settings display button
Button for displaying the camera's settings on the screen.

compact memory card
Removable rigid card; it is a storage medium for photographs taken with a digital camera.

cover
Part covering the memory card slot.

strap eyelet
Small ring that holds a strap to help carry the camera.

multi-image jump button
utton for skipping one or several images while viewing recorded images.

video and digital terminals
Devices for attaching a camera to a television or a computer.

image review button
Button that displays recorded images.

remote control terminal
Device that is attached to the camera by a cable so that it can be operated from a distance.

index/enlarge button
Button that displays several images in index form or a specific image to be enlarged.

erase button
Button that erases a recorded image from memory.

four-way selector
Button for selecting from the various menus or scrolling through the recorded images.

eject button
Button that pushes a memory card out of the camera.

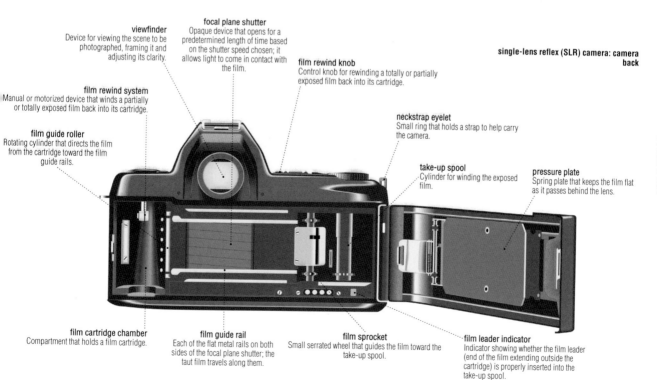

single-lens reflex (SLR) camera: camera back

viewfinder
Device for viewing the scene to be photographed, framing it and adjusting its clarity.

focal plane shutter
Opaque device that opens for a predetermined length of time based on the shutter speed chosen; it allows light to come in contact with the film.

film rewind knob
Control knob for rewinding a totally or partially exposed film back into its cartridge.

film rewind system
Manual or motorized device that winds a partially or totally exposed film back into its cartridge.

neckstrap eyelet
Small ring that holds a strap to help carry the camera.

film guide roller
Rotating cylinder that directs the film from the cartridge toward the film guide rails.

take-up spool
Cylinder for winding the exposed film.

pressure plate
Spring plate that keeps the film flat as it passes behind the lens.

film cartridge chamber
Compartment that holds a film cartridge.

film guide rail
Each of the flat metal rails on both sides of the focal plane shutter; the taut film travels along them.

film sprocket
Small serrated wheel that guides the film toward the take-up spool.

film leader indicator
Indicator showing whether the film leader (end of the film extending outside the cartridge) is properly inserted into the take-up spool.

photography

cross section of a reflex camera
A slanted mirror allows the user to view and shoot at the same time; the mirror flips up when the shutter release button is pressed.

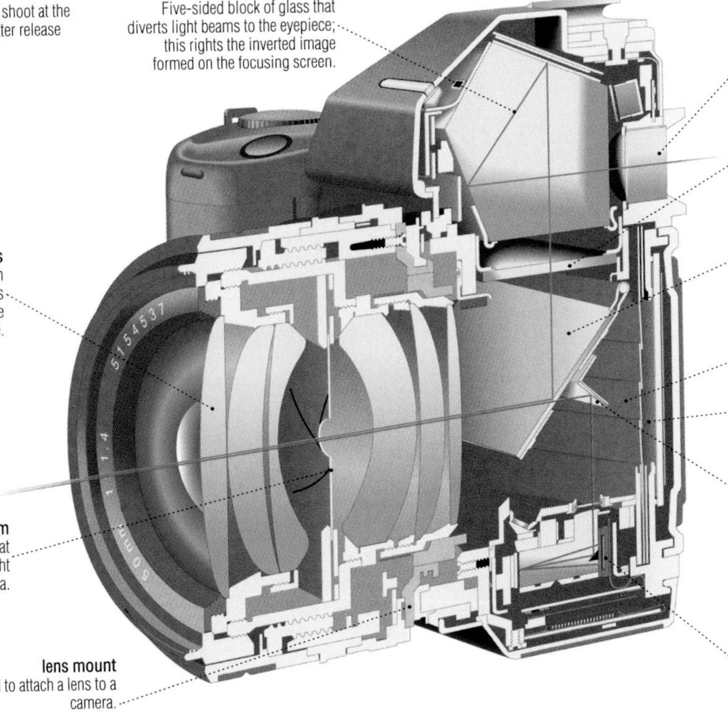

pentaprism
Five-sided block of glass that diverts light beams to the eyepiece; this rights the inverted image formed on the focusing screen.

eyepiece
Optical disk or system of disks through which the eye sees the image produced by the lens.

focusing screen
Ground glass plate on which the image caught by the lens is formed; at this point, it is inverted from right to left.

main reflex mirror
Mirror that redirects light toward the focusing screen; when the photo is taken, it retracts so that light reaches the film.

focal plane shutter
Opaque device that opens for a predetermined length of time based on the shutter speed chosen; it allows light to come in contact with the film.

film
Thin flexible transparent band that is covered with a light-sensitive emulsion, which allows images to be imprinted.

secondary mirror
Mirror that directs part of the light entering the lens through the center of the main reflex mirror and toward the light sensor.

light sensor
Sensor that measures the light intensity; it is used to determine the correct exposure (shutter speed and diaphragm opening).

lens
Transparent optical disks through which ambient light enters; the disks correct each other to improve the quality of the image.

diaphragm
Device with a variable opening that controls the amount of light entering the camera.

lens mount
Device used to attach a lens to a camera.

spotmeter
Exposure meter that uses a viewfinder to measure the brightness of precise spots on the scene to be photographed.

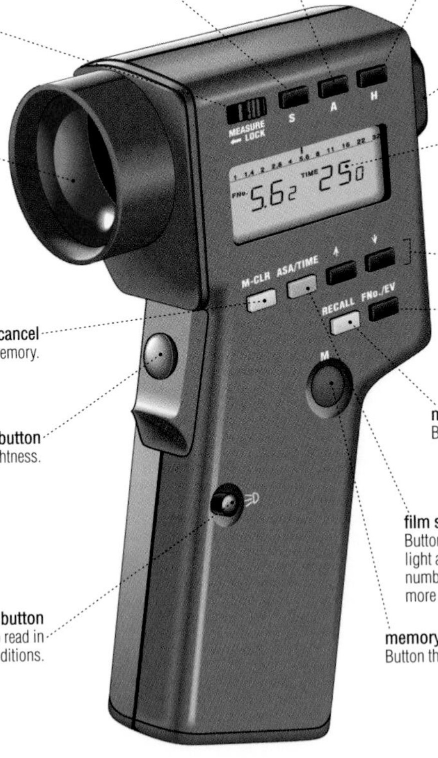

shadow key
Key that determines the correct exposure when priority is given to the darkest areas in the scene.

average key
Key that determines the correct exposure based on the average brightness of a scene.

highlight key
Key that determines the correct exposure when priority is given to the brightest areas in a scene.

lock switch
Device activating or blocking the measuring button.

eyepiece
Optical disk or system of disks through which the eye sees the image produced by the lens.

objective lens
Optical system formed of lenses attached to a mount that relay light to sensitive cells, which measure the light's intensity.

data display
Liquid crystal display showing camera readings and calculated exposure data.

shutter speed setting
Buttons that select the length of time a film is to be exposed to light (exposure time).

aperture/exposure value display
Button that displays data (diaphragm opening and exposure time) on suggested exposures based on the brightness of the scene.

memory cancel
Button that erases data stored in memory.

memory recall key
Button that displays data stored in memory.

measuring button
Control button to measure brightness.

film speed
Button that shows a film's sensitivity to light as expressed by the ISO or ASA number, where the higher the number, the more sensitive the film.

data display illumination button
Button that illuminates the display screen so it is easier to read in poor lighting conditions.

memory key
Button that stores data in memory.

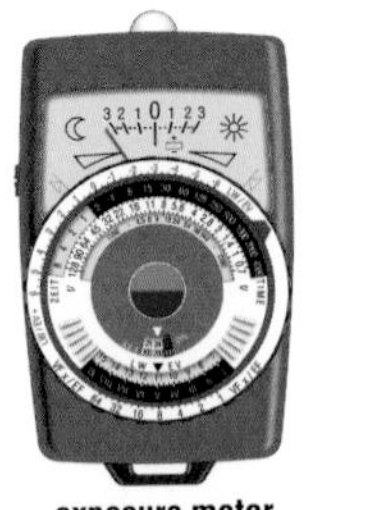

exposure meter
Device with light-sensitive cells that measures the intensity of the light strikin or reflected by the subject to determine th correct exposure for a photo.

lenses

Lenses are characterized by their focal length (between the optical center and the film), aperture (ratio between the diameter of the lens and the focal length) and angle of view (width of the captured image).

standard lens
Lens that produces an image close to that seen by the human eye.

lens
Transparent optical disks through which ambient light enters; the disks correct each other to improve the quality of the image.

distance scale
Scale that shows the distance between the lens and the subject on which it is focused.

focus setting ring
Setting ring that sharpens the image of a subject.

depth-of-field scale
Scale that shows the zone of sharpest focus around the subject; this is a function of the diaphragm's opening and the distance between the lens and the subject.

lens aperture scale
Graduated scale that controls the diaphragm's opening; it is measured in f-stops and a high f-stop indicates a small opening.

bayonet mount
Device for attaching the lens to the camera body by fitting lugs located on the lens into grooves on the camera and turning.

zoom lens
Lens with a variable focal length so that the visual field can be changed without changing the lens.

wide-angle lens
Lens with a short focal length that covers a larger visual field than a regular lens and provides significant depth of field.

macro lens
Lens designed mainly for close-up shots of small objects.

telephoto lens
Lens with a long focal length that enlarges the image of a distant subject but reduces the visual field and the depth of field.

fisheye lens
Lens with a very short focal length that covers a visual field of at least a 180°; it creates circular images.

semi-fisheye lens
Lens with a short focal length that covers a wide visual field; it emphasizes the effect of perspective.

lens accessories

All the parts that can be attached to a lens to change its focal length or alter the image projected on the film.

lens cap
Part that covers and protects the lens when it is not in use.

lens hood
Cone-shaped device that reduces the effect of intense ambient light to improve the image's contrast.

color filter
Colored glass used to alter the characteristics of the light reaching the film.

close-up lens
Optical disk that changes the focal length of the lens so that very near subjects can be photographed.

polarizing filter
Glass used to reduce reflections from nonmetallic surfaces such as water, glass and asphalt.

objective lens
Optical system made up of a set of lenses fixed on a mount; it allows a clear image to be produced on film.

tele-converter
Component inserted between the camera and the lens to increase its focal length; this enlarges the image of a distant subject.

photography

still cameras

Cameras whose principal components are a lightproof chamber and an optical system, which causes an image to be imprinted on a light-sensitive surface.

disposable camera
Small lightweight easy-to-use camera containing a film; it is designed to be used only once.

ultracompact camera
Very small camera, usually completely automatic.

single-lens reflex (SLR) camera
Camera whose interchangeable lens is used to both view and shoot through a slanted mirror that flips up (reflex).

compact camera
Small, easy-to-use camera.

medium format SLR (6 x 6)
Midsize camera with interchangeable lenses; it produces 6 cm x 6 cm images on a roll of film.

view camera
Large camera composed of two telescopic blocks connected to an expansible bellows which allows the perspective and focus to checked and adjusted as needed.

twin-lens reflex camera
Camera whose upper lens uses a mirror to view while its lower lens is used to shoot.

underwater camera
Camera composed of a watertight pressure-resistant body; it is used mainly for underwater photography.

Polaroid® camera
Camera that develops photos instantly. After a photo is taken, the exposed film is ejected from the camera and develops automatically in a few minutes.

films
Thin, flexible, transparent media covered with light-sensitive materials that enable images to be imprinted in a film camera.

sheet film
Semirigid film made to fit specific applications; it is usually loaded into a view camera.

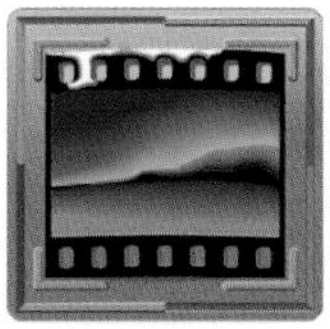

transparency slide
Positive photographic picture (with the same brightness as the original) that is mounted on a transparent backing and usually projected on a screen.

cartridge film
Small lightproof container that holds a roll of film with a number of exposures, which is loaded into a camera.

film pack
Small rigid box containing a certain number of sheet films, which are dispensed successively as the camera operates; they are used in Polaroid® cameras.

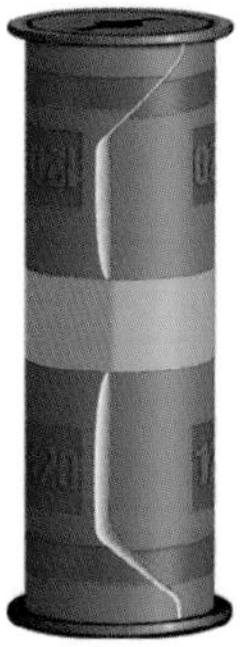

roll film
Band of film with a number of exposures; it is rolled on a spool and used in midsize cameras.

memory cards
Rigid cards used as a storage medium to record photographs taken with a digital camera.

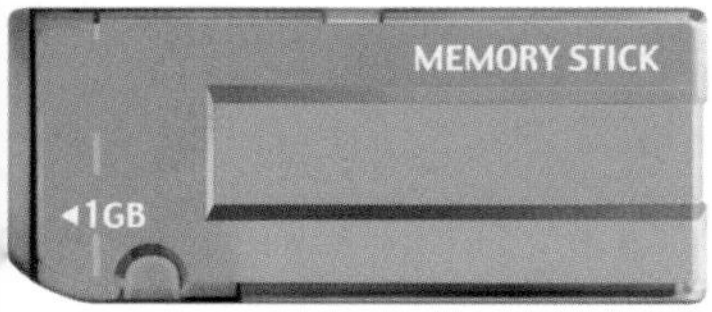

Memory Stick
Flash memory card in a rectangular-shape case. It was developed in 2000.

compact flash card
Rigid card used as a storage medium to record photos taken with digital cameras.

Secure Digital card
Small-format flash memory card that includes a copyright-protection mechanism. It was developed in 2000.

xD-Picture card
Very-small-format flash memory card, designed in 2002.

photography

photographic accessories
Add-on devices that improve or change the way a camera operates.

waterproof case
Rigid container designed to protect a camera from water or bad weather. It is used, among other things, for underwater photography.

camera bag
Bag with compartments designed to hold and protect a camera and its accessories.

cable shutter release
Flexible cable with a trigger that activates the shutter at close range thereby reducing the possibility of moving the camera.

electronic flash
Device with a lamp that produces a brief and intense flash of light; it is used to compensate for inadequate lighting.

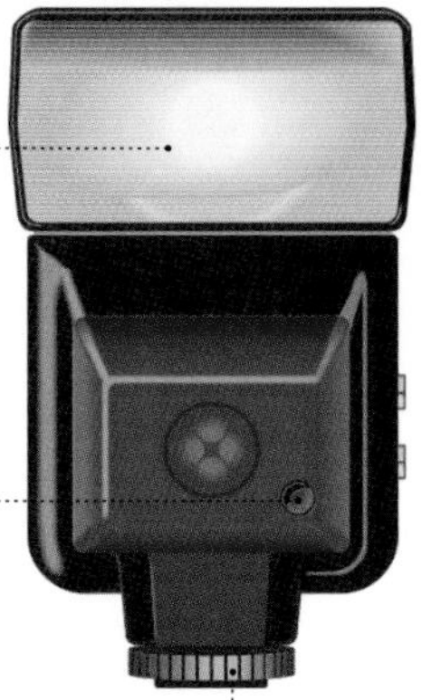

flashtube
Part that concentrates and channels light from the lamp toward the subject to be photographed.

photoelectric cell
Detector that measures the intensity of ambient light and controls the amount of light emitted by the flash.

mounting foot
Device used to mount the flash onto the accessory shoe.

tripod
Adjustable support to which a camera is attached to keep it stable, level and in focus.

camera screw
Screw used to attach the plate to the base of the camera.

camera platform
Platform that supports the plate and the camera mounted on it.

plate
Detachable plate mounted on the camera platform so that the camera can be attached and removed quickly.

quick release system
Device used to attach the plate to the camera platform and to detach it.

side-tilt lock
Grip that tilts the camera platform downward and locks it in the desired position.

horizontal motion lock
Grip that pivots the camera platform from left to right and locks it in the desired position.

column crank
Grip that adjusts the height of the column.

panoramic head
Device atop the column that allows the camera mounted on the platform to pivot horizontally and vertically.

camera platform lock
Grip used to place the camera platform in the desired position and lock it.

column lock
Device that locks the column at the desired height.

column
Upright cylinder of adjustable height that supports the panoramic head.

collet
Ring that locks the sliding components of the telescoping leg once the desired height is reached.

telescoping leg
Each of the rods used to stabilize the tripod; they are made up of sliding components, which adjust the height.

battery
Device that converts chemical energy into electrical energy to supply power to another device.

battery pack
Device that stores chemical energy during charging and converts it into electrical energy.

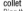

battery
Device that converts chemical energy into electrical energy to supply power to another device.

slide projector
Device with a lamp and an optical system that projects an enlarged image of a slide on a screen.

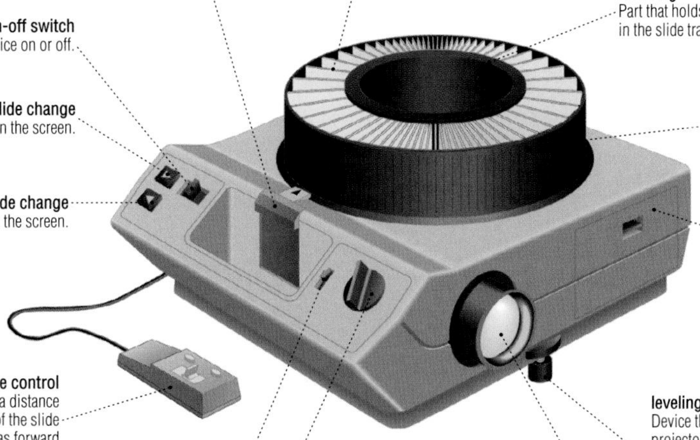

slide
Positive photographic picture (with the same brightness as the original) that is mounted on a transparent backing and usually projected on a screen.

power-off/slide-select bar
Button that causes the slide tray to advance manually so that a specific slide can be selected.

lock ring
Part that holds the slides in place in the slide tray.

on-off switch
Button for turning the device on or off.

forward slide change
Button that causes the next slide to be projected on the screen.

slide tray
Container where slides are placed in order of projection.

reverse slide change
n that causes the previous slide to be projected on the screen.

storage compartment
Compartment used for storing various items, including the power cord and the remote control.

remote control
Device manipulated from a distance that operates several of the slide projector's functions such as forward and reverse slide changes.

leveling-adjustment foot
Device that adjusts the position of the slide projector so that the image is centered on the screen.

autofocus on-off switch
Device that starts and stops the mechanism automatically controlling the sharpness of the image.

manual focusing knob
Knob for manually adjusting the sharpness of the image projected on the screen.

objective lens
System made up of a series of optical devices fixed on a mount and used to project an enlarged image of the slide on a screen.

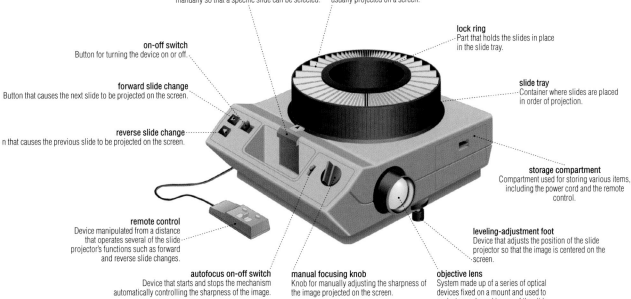

projection screen
White surface on which still or moving images are projected.

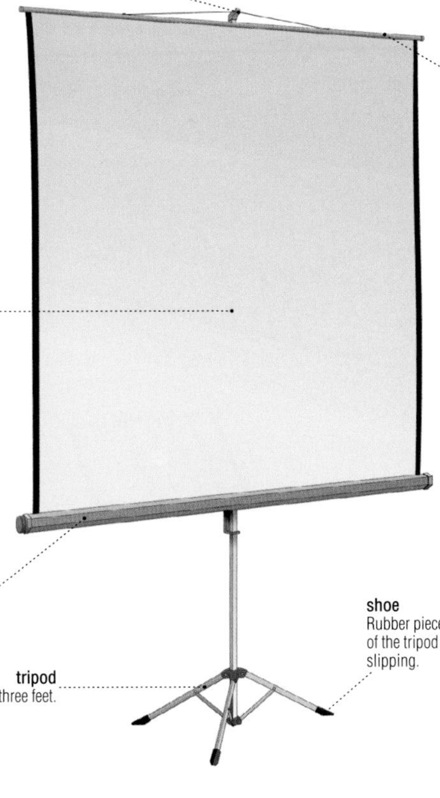

hanger

saddle

screen
Piece of rigidified fabric or vinyl that is used as a projection screen.

screen case
Cylinder into which the screen rolls up.

shoe
Rubber piece attached to the ends of the tripod to prevent it from slipping.

tripod
Solid base with three feet.

photography

darkroom equipment
Material required to process film and to print photographs in a darkened room.

developing tank
Lightproof container used during the various stages of processing an exposed film to obtain a negative.

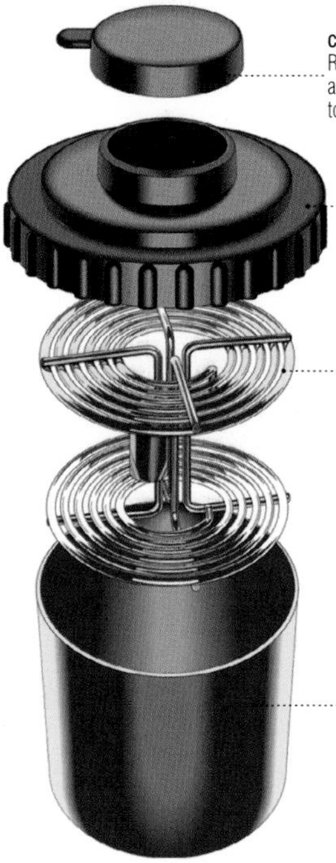

cap
Removable watertight cover allowing film processing products to be mixed in a tank.

lid
Lightproof tank cover with an opening through which film processing products are added and removed.

reel
Holder on which the film is wound; it prevents the film from sticking together and ensures uniform distribution of the processing products.

tank
Container used to hold the reel and the products required (developer, stop bath, fixer) for each of the processing steps.

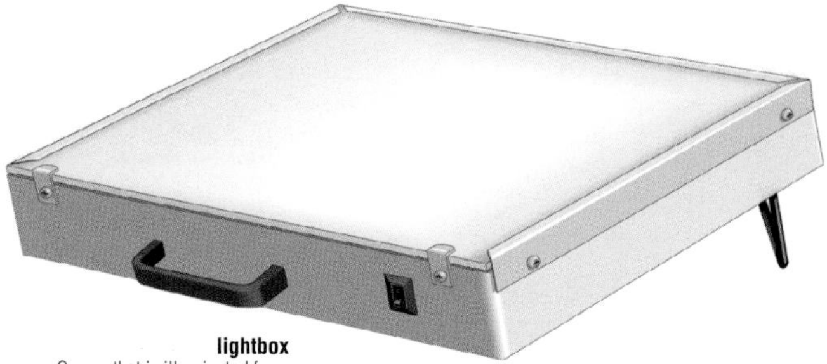

lightbox
Screen that is illuminated from behind and used to examine items such as negatives, slides, transparencies and drawings.

timer
Device with a phosphorescent dial that measures the required time for each film processing operation.

safelight
Lamp emitting light that will not affect photosensitive surfaces such as film and photographic paper.

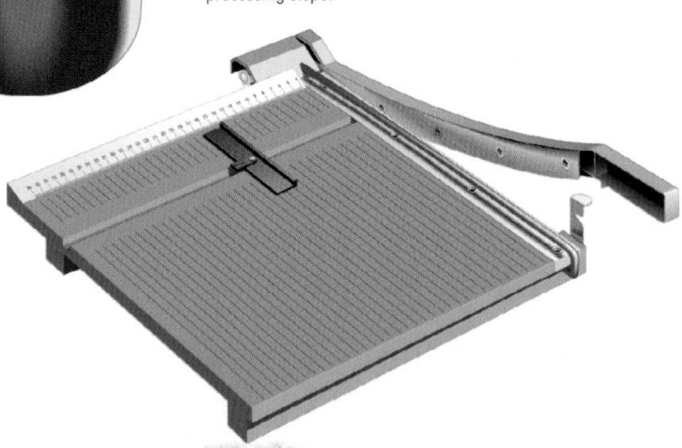

paper cutter
Piece of equipment used to make square cuts in paper, cardboard, transparencies, etc.

film drying cabinet
Enclosure with a device for circulating air where processed film and photographic paper are hung to dry.

easel
Frame used to hold paper flat under an enlarger; its movable edges make allowance for white margins on the proof.

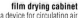

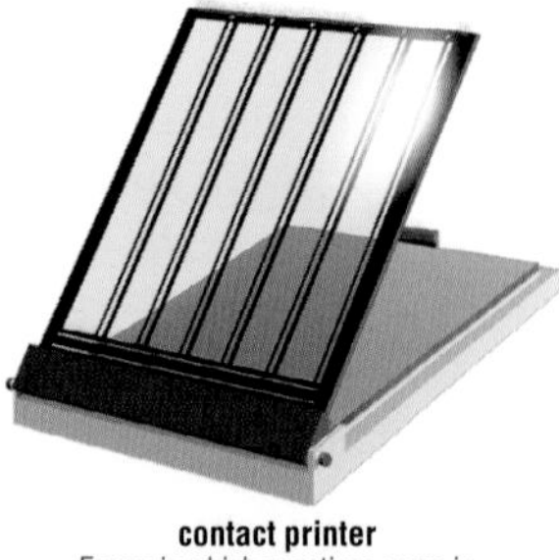

contact printer
Frame in which negatives come in contact with photographic paper and are exposed to light to print an image of the same size.

photography

enlarger
Device that projects a usually enlarged negative image in black and white onto light-sensitive photographic paper.

window
Opening that frames the image to be enlarged and stops parasitic light from reaching the baseboard.

negative
Visible still image resulting from processing an exposed film; bright areas on the original subject appear dark on the negative.

negative carrier
Device with two opaque plates that holds the negative flat between the light source and the lens of the enlarger.

enlarger timer
Device that measures the exposure time of the photographic paper on the baseboard of an enlarger.

column
Serrated bar mounted on the baseboard; it is used to support the lamphouse head and to adjust its height.

lamphouse head
Box enclosing a light source that is used to illuminate a negative.

lamphouse elevation control
Device that lifts the lamphouse head so that the negative holder can be inserted into the enlarger.

height control
Device used to adjust the height of the lamphouse head on the column.

bellows
Lightproof instrument of varying length; it is used to focus the image on photographic paper.

red safelight filter
Colored filter placed under the lens to frame or focus a black and white image directly onto photographic paper without exposing it.

height scale
Graduated scale showing the distance between the baseboard and the lens; it is used to determine the magnification ratio of the negative.

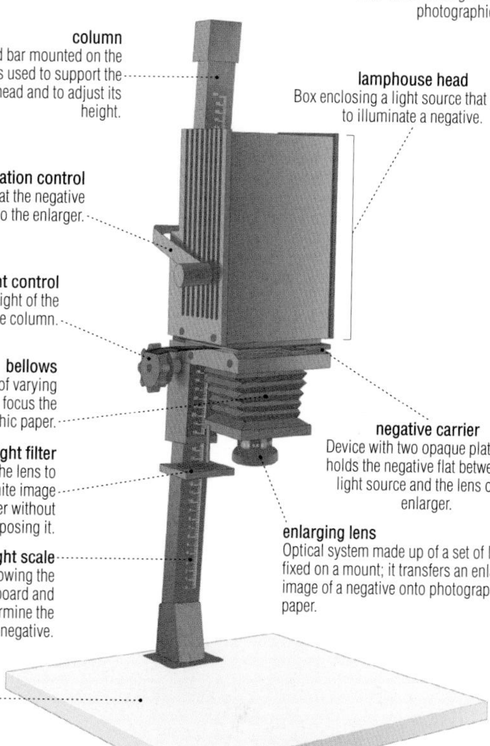

negative carrier
Device with two opaque plates that holds the negative flat between the light source and the lens of the enlarger.

enlarging lens
Optical system made up of a set of lenses fixed on a mount; it transfers an enlarged image of a negative onto photographic paper.

baseboard
Base plate on which a photographic paper is placed.

print washer
Device that uses water to eliminate residual chemicals accumulated during the processing of photographic paper.

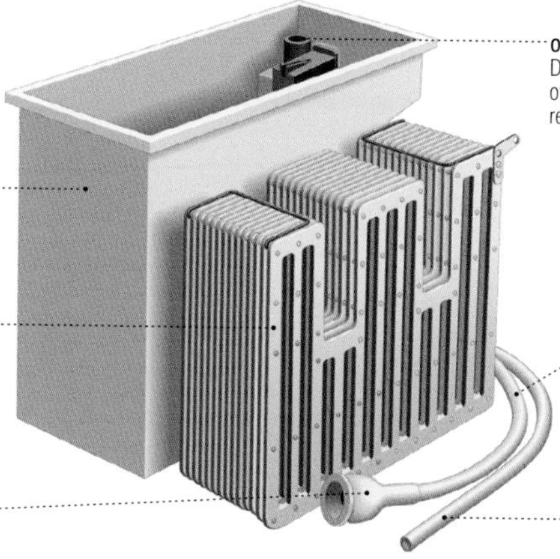

overflow tube
Drainpipe for draining off a fixture's overflow when the water level reaches a certain level.

tank

cradle
Frame where proofs are inserted to keep them from touching each other to ensure a uniform wash.

inlet hose
Flexible hose that carries water from the faucet to the tank.

adaptor
Device attached to a faucet.

outlet hose
Hose that uses gravity to drain used water from the tank to a waste collection tub or a sink.

focusing magnifier
Instrument that causes the image projected on the baseboard to be magnified and make it easier to focus.

developing baths

Trays used for the various steps in processing exposed photographic paper to obtain a proof in black and white.

developer bath
Tray containing a chemical that acts on light-exposed photographic paper to reveal an image.

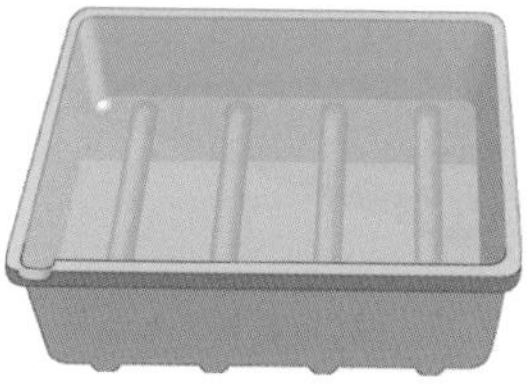

stop bath
Tray containing a chemical that stops the action of the developer.

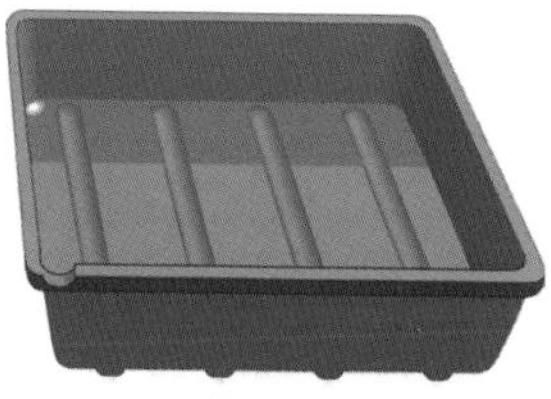

fixing bath
Tray containing a chemical that fixes the revealed image by making the photographic paper insensitive to light.

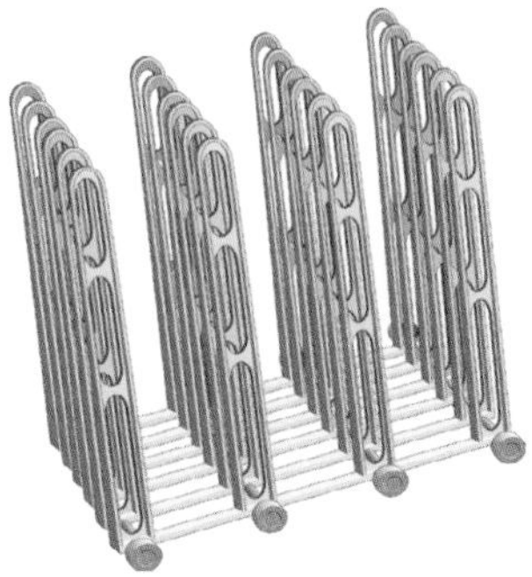

print drying rack
Frame that holds prints once they have passed through the washer so that the water evaporates.

broadcast satellite communication

Transmission of television signals (pictures and sound) to the general public by means of radio waves relayed by satellite.

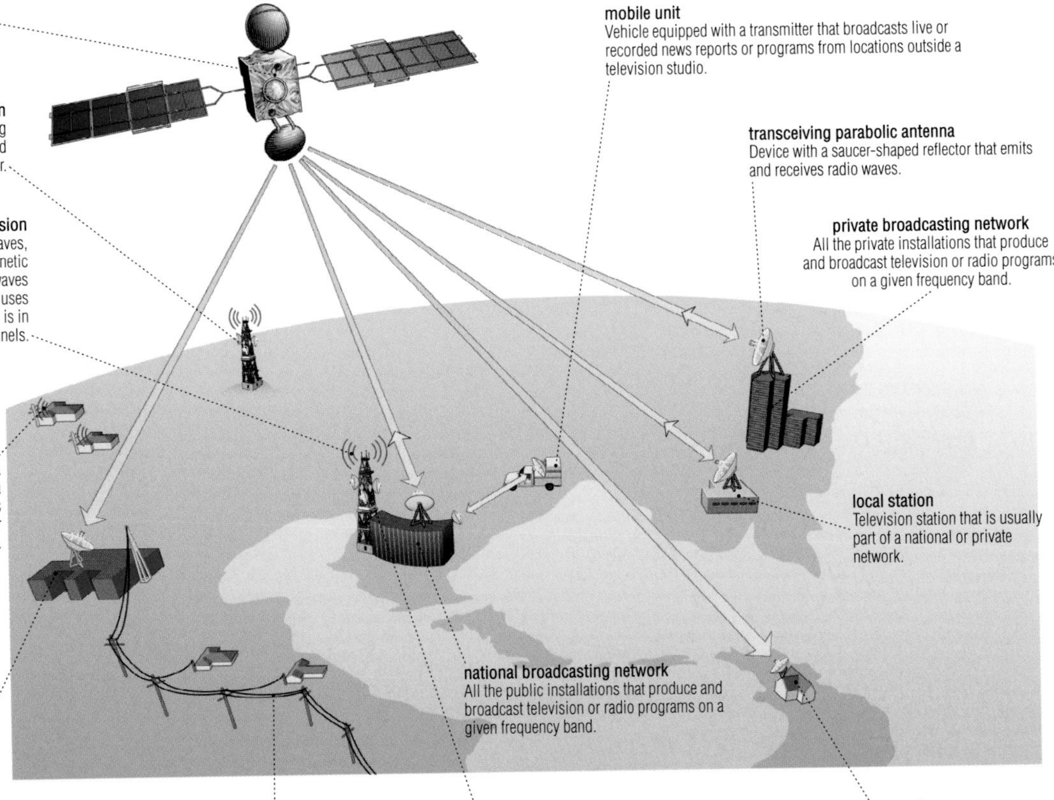

satellite
Space vehicle placed in geostationary orbit at an altitude of 22,000 mi to transmit sound and visual signals in the form of radio waves.

relay station
Facility receiving and amplifying signals from a transmitting tower and relaying them to another receiver.

Hertzian wave transmission
Hertzian waves, also called radio waves, are low-frequency electromagnetic waves; the full spectrum of radio waves is divided into bands for specific uses such as radio and TV. Each band is in turn divided into channels.

home antenna
Small receiving antenna used by a subscriber to capture radio waves emitted by a transmitting tower or relay station.

mobile unit
Vehicle equipped with a transmitter that broadcasts live or recorded news reports or programs from locations outside a television studio.

transceiving parabolic antenna
Device with a saucer-shaped reflector that emits and receives radio waves.

private broadcasting network
All the private installations that produce and broadcast television or radio programs on a given frequency band.

local station
Television station that is usually part of a national or private network.

national broadcasting network
All the public installations that produce and broadcast television or radio programs on a given frequency band.

cable distributor
Company specializing in the transmission of television signals to customers through a cable network.

distribution by aerial cable network
Signals can be relayed to the customer through a network of suspended cables.

transmitting tower
Facility used to transmit radio waves to a receiver so that television programs can be broadcast locally.

direct home reception
Radio waves are emitted by a satellite and captured directly by the subscriber's parabolic antenna.

telecommunication satellites

Space vehicles placed into geostationary orbit at an altitude of 22,000 mi to receive and broadcast long-distance signals in the form of radio waves.

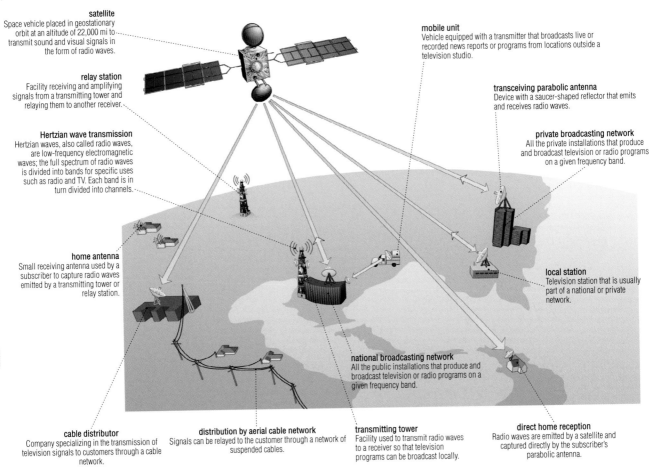

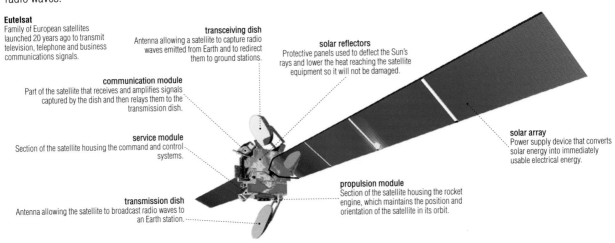

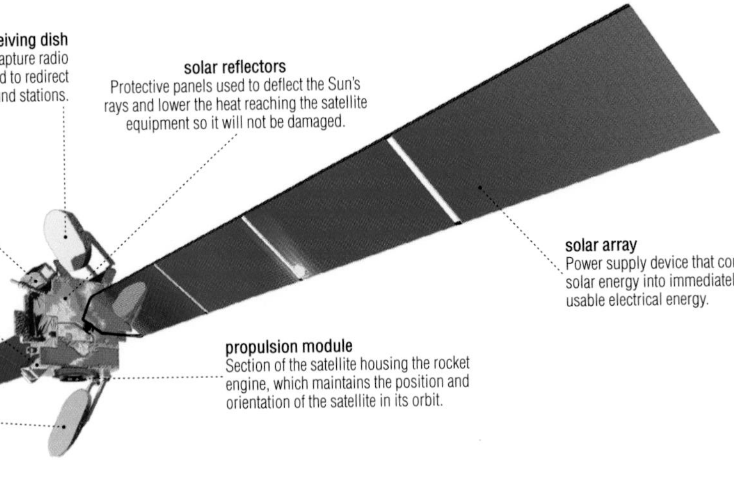

Eutelsat
Family of European satellites launched 20 years ago to transmit television, telephone and business communications signals.

transceiving dish
Antenna allowing a satellite to capture radio waves emitted from Earth and to redirect them to ground stations.

solar reflectors
Protective panels used to deflect the Sun's rays and lower the heat reaching the satellite equipment so it will not be damaged.

communication module
Part of the satellite that receives and amplifies signals captured by the dish and then relays them to the transmission dish.

service module
Section of the satellite housing the command and control systems.

solar array
Power supply device that converts solar energy into immediately usable electrical energy.

propulsion module
Section of the satellite housing the rocket engine, which maintains the position and orientation of the satellite in its orbit.

transmission dish
Antenna allowing the satellite to broadcast radio waves to an Earth station.

telecommunications by satellite

Transmission of data such as images, sound and computer data using radio waves relayed by satellites.

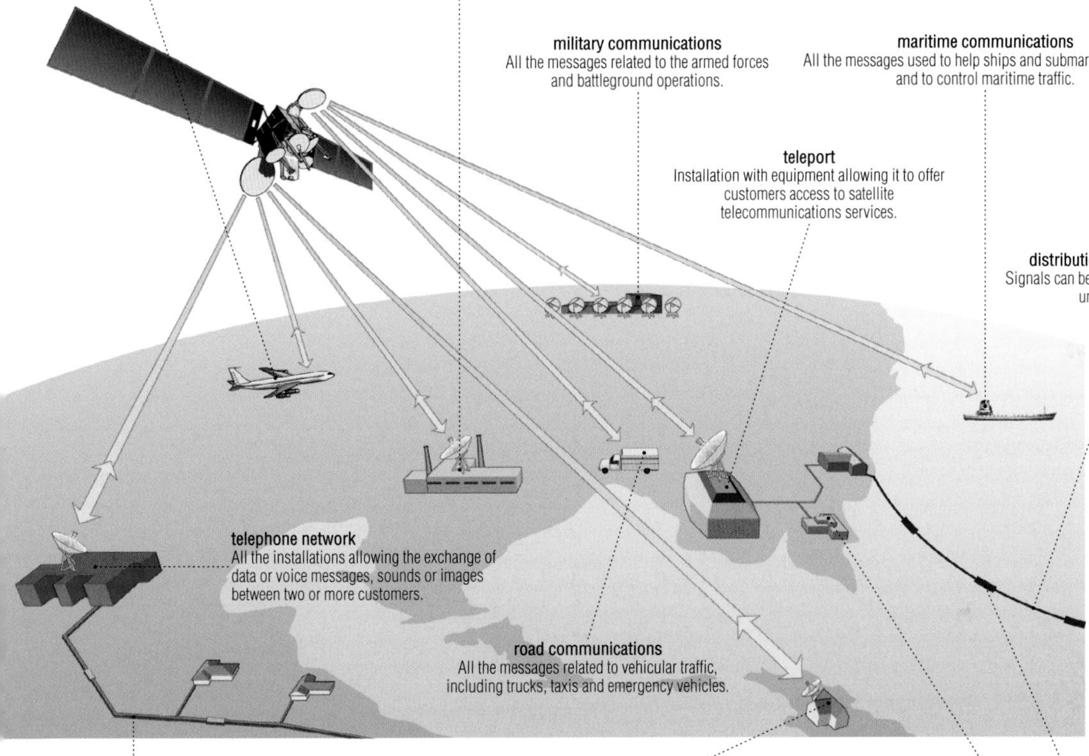
air communications
All the messages used to help aircraft navigate and to control air traffic.
industrial communications
All the messages exchanged by companies involved in the production of goods and services.
military communications
All the messages related to the armed forces and battleground operations.
maritime communications
All the messages used to help ships and submarines navigate and to control maritime traffic.
teleport
Installation with equipment allowing it to offer customers access to satellite telecommunications services.
distribution by submarine cable
Signals can be relayed through a network of underwater cables.
telephone network
All the installations allowing the exchange of data or voice messages, sounds or images between two or more customers.
road communications
All the messages related to vehicular traffic, including trucks, taxis and emergency vehicles.
distribution by underground cable network
Signals can be relayed through a network of underground cables.
personal communications
All the messages exchanged between individuals.
consumer
repeater
Device running the length of a cable that receives, amplifies and resends signals to transmit them over long distances.

telecommunication satellites

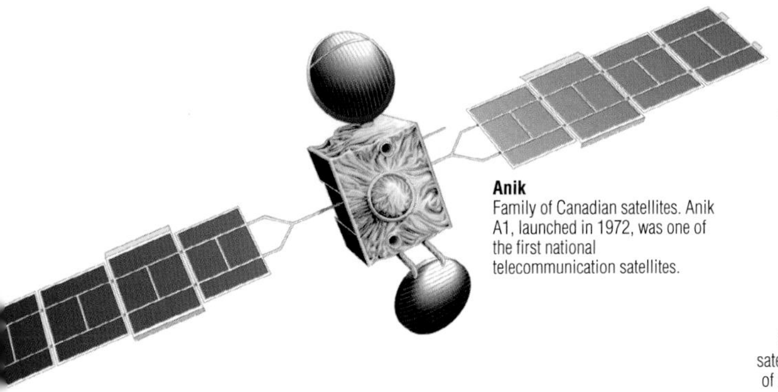
Anik
Family of Canadian satellites. Anik A1, launched in 1972, was one of the first national telecommunication satellites.

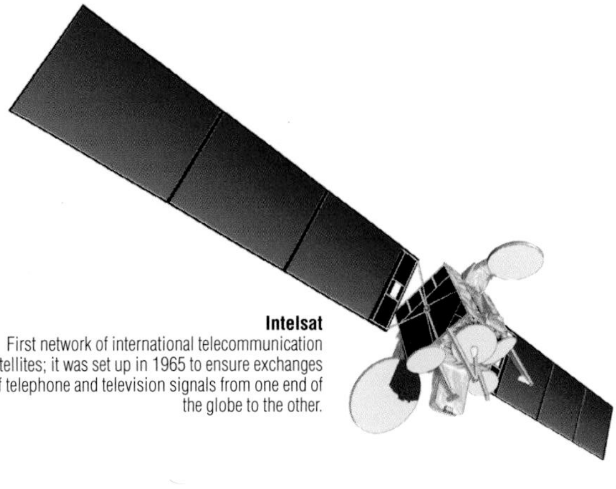
Intelsat
First network of international telecommunication satellites; it was set up in 1965 to ensure exchanges of telephone and television signals from one end of the globe to the other.

dynamic microphone

Device with a moving coil traveling in a magnetic field that converts sounds into electric pulses for broadcasting or recording.

windscreen
Screen covering and protecting a microphone; it muffles the speaker's breathing and the sound of the wind.
diaphragm
Thin sheet of metal or plastic attached to the moving coil; it vibrates from the effect of sound waves.
magnet
Material producing the magnetic field.
housing
moving coil
Metal part whose motion in a magnetic field is caused by the vibrations of the diaphragm; it creates a corresponding modulation in the electric current.
on-off switch
Power-connecting device used to turn the microphone on or off.
connector
Device used to connect the cable to the microphone.
cable
plug
Terminal end of the cable with prongs that is inserted into an electric outlet (jack).

radio: studio and control room

Area with two rooms separated by a glass window where audio programs are produced, recorded or broadcast.

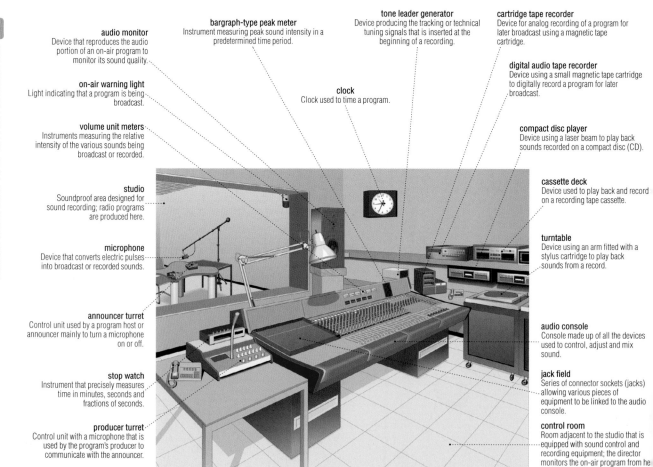

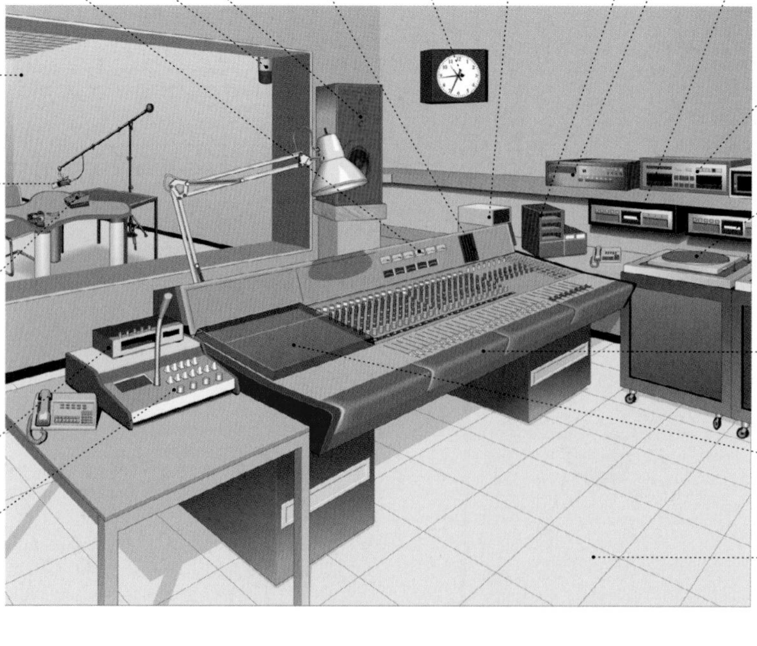
audio monitor
Device that reproduces the audio portion of an on-air program to monitor its sound quality.
bargraph-type peak meter
Instrument measuring peak sound intensity in a predetermined time period.
tone leader generator
Device producing the tracking or technical tuning signals that is inserted at the beginning of a recording.
cartridge tape recorder
Device for analog recording of a program for later broadcast using a magnetic tape cartridge.
on-air warning light
Light indicating that a program is being broadcast.
clock
Clock used to time a program.
digital audio tape recorder
Device using a small magnetic tape cartridge to digitally record a program for later broadcast.
volume unit meters
Instruments measuring the relative intensity of the various sounds being broadcast or recorded.
compact disc player
Device using a laser beam to play back sounds recorded on a compact disc (CD).
studio
Soundproof area designed for sound recording; radio programs are produced here.
cassette deck
Device used to play back and record on a recording tape cassette.
microphone
Device that converts electric pulses into broadcast or recorded sounds.
turntable
Device using an arm fitted with a stylus cartridge to play back sounds from a record.
announcer turret
Control unit used by a program host or announcer mainly to turn a microphone on or off.
audio console
Console made up of all the devices used to control, adjust and mix sound.
stop watch
Instrument that precisely measures time in minutes, seconds and fractions of seconds.
jack field
Series of connector sockets (jacks) allowing various pieces of equipment to be linked to the audio console.
producer turret
Control unit with a microphone that is used by the program's producer to communicate with the announcer.
control room
Room adjacent to the studio that is equipped with sound control and recording equipment; the director monitors the on-air program from he

television

The first long-distance transmission of black and white pictures took place in the 1920s; color television was introduced in 1951.

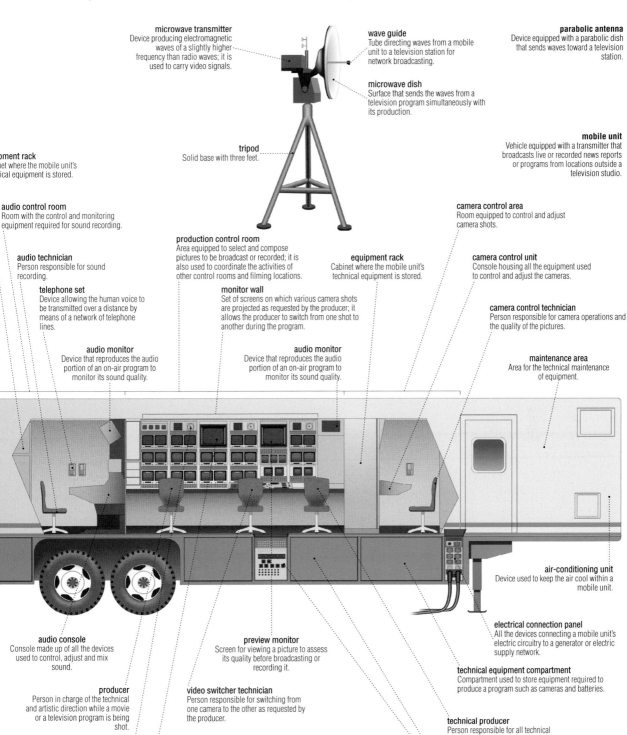

microwave transmitter
Device producing electromagnetic waves of a slightly higher frequency than radio waves; it is used to carry video signals.

wave guide
Tube directing waves from a mobile unit to a television station for network broadcasting.

parabolic antenna
Device equipped with a parabolic dish that sends waves toward a television station.

microwave dish
Surface that sends the waves from a television program simultaneously with its production.

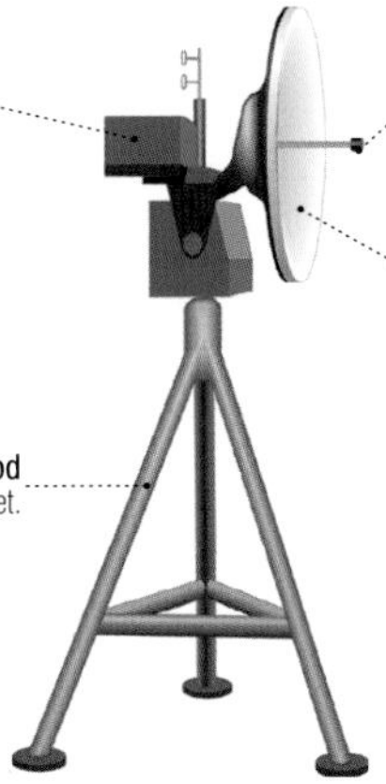

tripod
Solid base with three feet.

mobile unit
Vehicle equipped with a transmitter that broadcasts live or recorded news reports or programs from locations outside a television studio.

uipment rack
binet where the mobile unit's hnical equipment is stored.

audio control room
Room with the control and monitoring equipment required for sound recording.

camera control area
Room equipped to control and adjust camera shots.

production control room
Area equipped to select and compose pictures to be broadcast or recorded; it is also used to coordinate the activities of other control rooms and filming locations.

audio technician
Person responsible for sound recording.

equipment rack
Cabinet where the mobile unit's technical equipment is stored.

camera control unit
Console housing all the equipment used to control and adjust the cameras.

telephone set
Device allowing the human voice to be transmitted over a distance by means of a network of telephone lines.

monitor wall
Set of screens on which various camera shots are projected as requested by the producer; it allows the producer to switch from one shot to another during the program.

camera control technician
Person responsible for camera operations and the quality of the pictures.

audio monitor
Device that reproduces the audio portion of an on-air program to monitor its sound quality.

audio monitor
Device that reproduces the audio portion of an on-air program to monitor its sound quality.

maintenance area
Area for the technical maintenance of equipment.

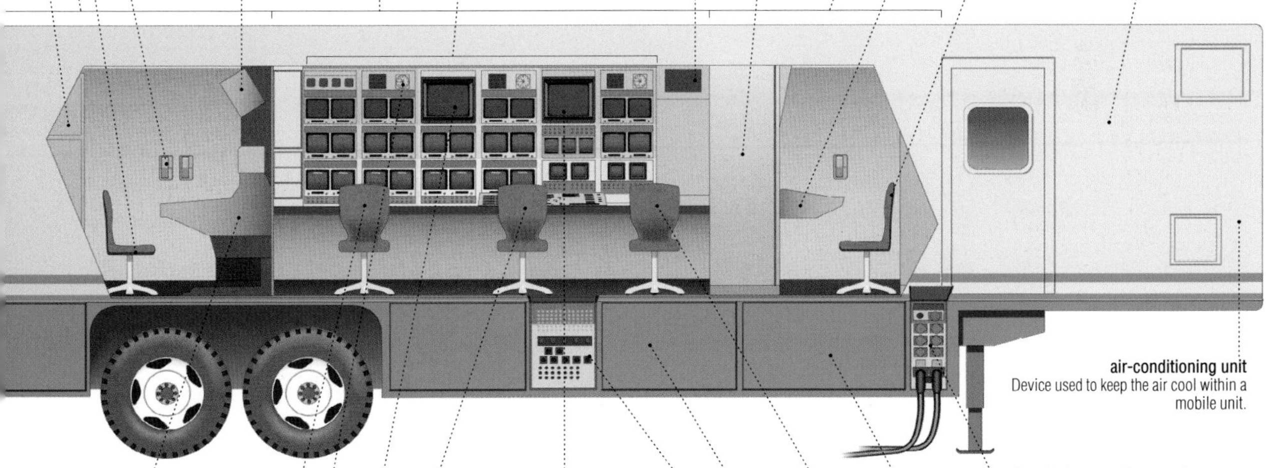

air-conditioning unit
Device used to keep the air cool within a mobile unit.

electrical connection panel
All the devices connecting a mobile unit's electric circuitry to a generator or electric supply network.

audio console
Console made up of all the devices used to control, adjust and mix sound.

preview monitor
Screen for viewing a picture to assess its quality before broadcasting or recording it.

technical equipment compartment
Compartment used to store equipment required to produce a program such as cameras and batteries.

producer
Person in charge of the technical and artistic direction while a movie or a television program is being shot.

video switcher technician
Person responsible for switching from one camera to the other as requested by the producer.

technical producer
Person responsible for all technical elements of a production, including sound and picture quality.

clock
Clock used to time a program.

output monitor
Screen for viewing a picture sent to a television station or recorded for later broadcast.

video connection panel
All the devices connecting camera cables to the control room equipment.

cable drum compartment
Compartment used to store camera and lighting cables.

television

studio and control rooms

A television studio is made up of a set and three control rooms housing a variety of facilities for controlling broadcasting and recording.

auxiliary facilities room
Room in which various technical and administrative activities are carried out.

lighting technician
Person responsible for drawing up lighting plans and supervising the installation and operation of the spotlights.

lighting control room
Room housing a set of devices used to vary the intensity of the spotlights.

lighting grid access
Area providing access to the catwalk above the lighting grid.

camera control technician
Person responsible for camera operations and the quality of the pictures.

additional production personnel
Team of assistants and consultants involved in producing a television program.

lighting board operator
Person responsible for making lighting changes during production.

lighting board
Console housing all the equipment used to control and adjust the spotlights.

camera control unit
Console housing all the equipment used to control and adjust the cameras.

technical producer
Person responsible for all technical elements of a production, including sound and picture quality.

monitor wall
Set of screens on which various camera shots are projected as requested by the producer; it allows the producer to switch from one shot to another during the program.

video switcher technician
Person responsible for switching from one camera to the other as requested by the producer.

producer
Person in charge of the technical and artistic direction while a movie or a television program is being shot.

script assistant
Assistant to the producer who is responsible mainly for the technical aspects of a program's sequences.

production adviser
Production associate who is responsible mainly for overseeing the proper flow of a program.

connection box
Panel containing all the jacks that connect control room equipment such as cameras, microphones ar intercoms.

camera
Filming device whose optical system separates light into the three primary colors and converts it into electronic signals for broadcast.

microphone boom
Arm from which a microphone is suspended and positioned above performers' heads and thus off-ca

audio console
Console made up of all the devices used to control, adjust and mix sound.

musical advisers
Production assistants for the musical portion of a program.

equipment rack
Cabinet used to store control room technical equipment.

bass trap
Device used to mute or eliminate certain low audio frequencies in a room.

audio technician
Person responsible for sound recording.

audio monitor
Device that reproduces the audio portion of an on-air program to monitor its sound quality.

studio floor
Room designed for recording television program sounds and images; it might be soundproof or not.

lighting/camera control area
Room equipped to control camera shots and lighting.

audio control room
Room with the control and monitoring equipment required for sound recording.

production control room
Area equipped to select and compos pictures to be broadcast or recorded; is also used to coordinate activities i other control rooms and the studio.

television

production control room
Area equipped to select and compose pictures to be broadcast or recorded; it is also used to coordinate activities in other control rooms and the studio.

audio/video preview unit
Module used to check sound and picture quality.

stereo phase monitor
Measuring device used to check the phase of a stereophonic signal.

preview monitors
Screens used to view a picture before broadcasting or recording it to ensure its quality.

vector/waveform monitor
Measuring device used to check the quality of a video signal (light intensity and colors).

input monitors
Screens displaying pictures taken by studio cameras or originating from various other sources such as a videocassette recorder or a telecine.

monitor wall
Set of screens on which various camera shots are projected as requested by the producer; it allows the producer to switch from one shot to another during the program.

digital video effects monitor
Screen used to view special effects generated by digital video special effects.

technical producer monitor
Screen allowing the technical producer to check a picture.

audio monitor
Device that reproduces the audio portion of an on-air program to monitor its sound quality.

output monitor
Screen for viewing a picture that was broadcast or recorded.

clock
Clock used to time a program.

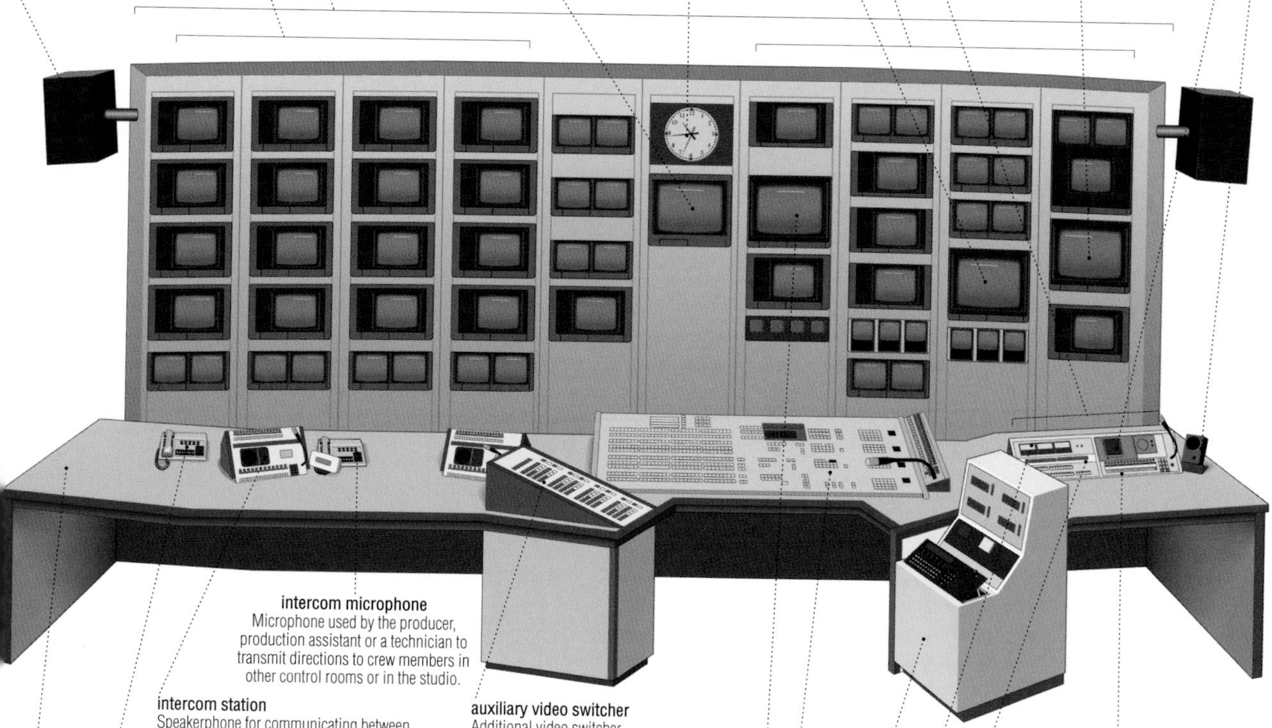

intercom microphone
Microphone used by the producer, production assistant or a technician to transmit directions to crew members in other control rooms or in the studio.

intercom station
Speakerphone for communicating between different locations in the same building.

auxiliary video switcher
Additional video switcher.

telephone
Device allowing the human voice to be transmitted over a distance by means of a network of telephone lines.

main preview monitor
Screen for viewing a program before it is broadcast or recorded.

video monitoring selector
Device for selecting a picture to be checked.

production desk
Desk housing all the technical equipment of the production control room.

production video switcher
Device used to select and transmit pictures to be broadcast or recorded; it can create various transitional effects between images.

audio monitoring selector
Device for selecting a sound source to be checked.

digital video special effects
Device used to create special effects from digital images.

audio volume unit meters
Instruments that measure the relative intensity of sounds.

television

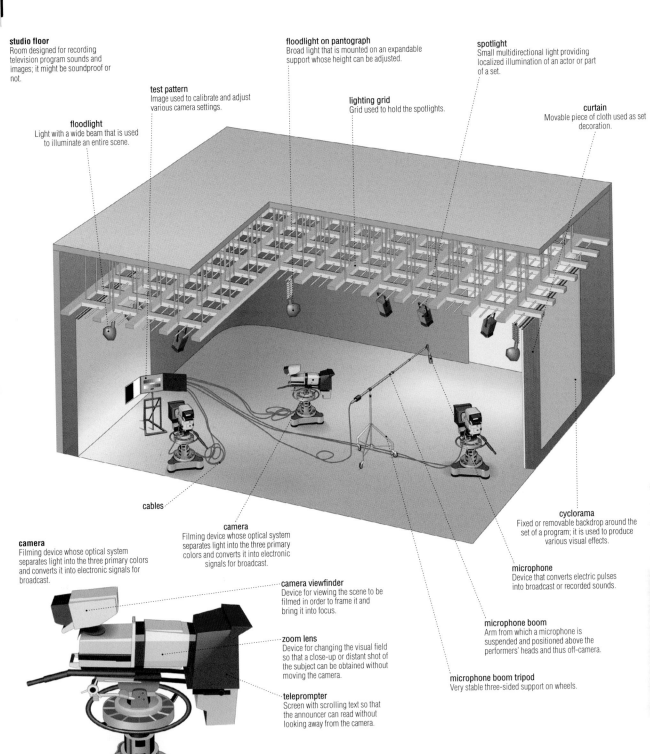

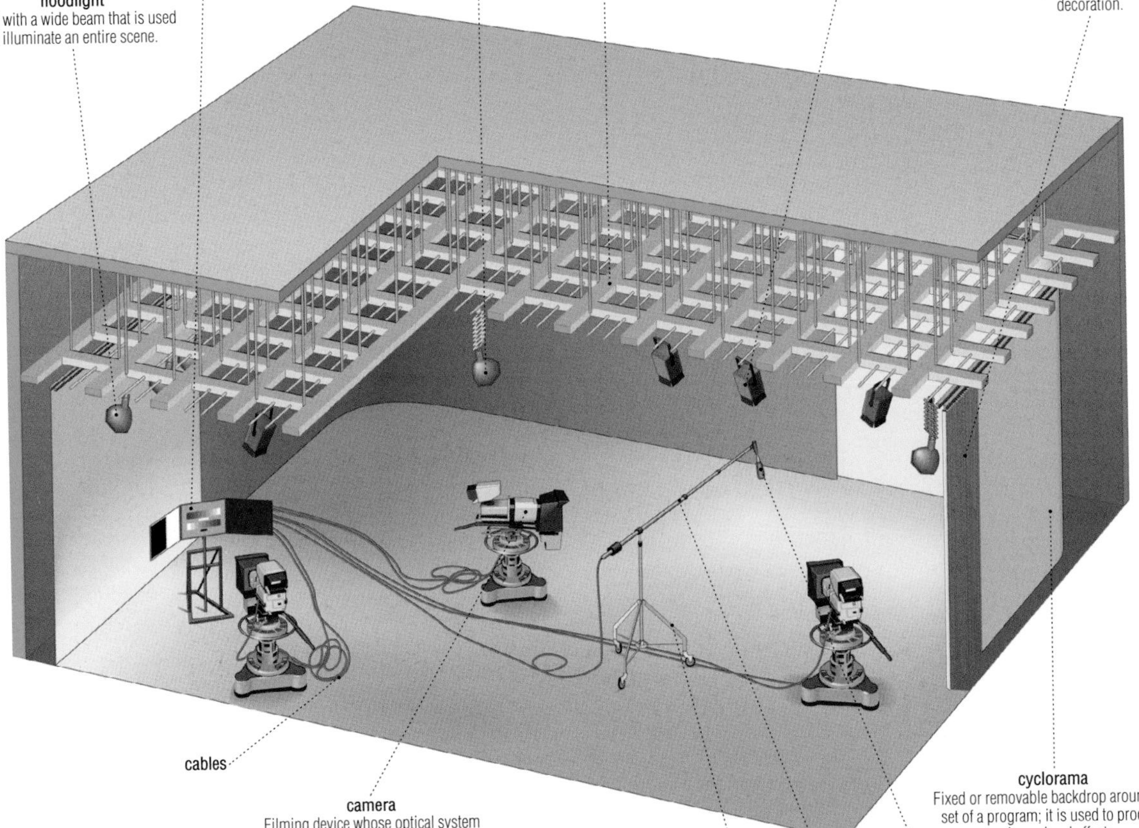
studio floor
Room designed for recording television program sounds and images; it might be soundproof or not.
test pattern
Image used to calibrate and adjust various camera settings.
floodlight
Light with a wide beam that is used to illuminate an entire scene.
floodlight on pantograph
Broad light that is mounted on an expandable support whose height can be adjusted.
lighting grid
Grid used to hold the spotlights.
spotlight
Small multidirectional light providing localized illumination of an actor or part of a set.
curtain
Movable piece of cloth used as set decoration.
cables
camera
Filming device whose optical system separates light into the three primary colors and converts it into electronic signals for broadcast.
cyclorama
Fixed or removable backdrop around the set of a program; it is used to produce various visual effects.
microphone
Device that converts electric pulses into broadcast or recorded sounds.
microphone boom
Arm from which a microphone is suspended and positioned above the performers' heads and thus off-camera.
microphone boom tripod
Very stable three-sided support on wheels.

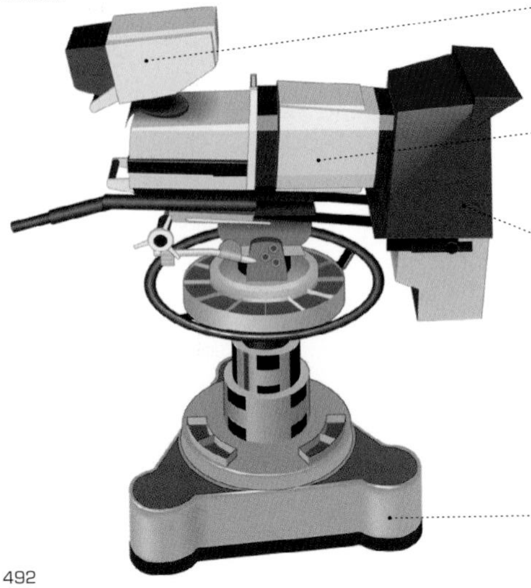
camera
Filming device whose optical system separates light into the three primary colors and converts it into electronic signals for broadcast.
camera viewfinder
Device for viewing the scene to be filmed in order to frame it and bring it into focus.
zoom lens
Device for changing the visual field so that a close-up or distant shot of the subject can be obtained without moving the camera.
teleprompter
Screen with scrolling text so that the announcer can read without looking away from the camera.
camera pedestal
Very stable three-sided support on wheels.

liquid crystal display (LCD) television
Television set with a flat, thin screen that reproduces images by reflecting light onto liquid crystals.

plasma television
Television set with a flat, thin screen that reproduces images using light emitted by a mixture of gases.

cathod ray tube (CRT) television
Receiving device that generates the sound and picture elements of programs broadcast by a television station or recorded on cassette or disc.

cabinet

screen
Surface on which TV pictures are formed.

power button
Mechanical connection that turns the television on or off.

tuning controls

remote control sensor
Device that receives infrared signals emitted by a remote control so that certain functions can be operated from a distance.

icture tube
ollow glass tube in which video ignals are converted into electron eams to produce pictures on the creen.

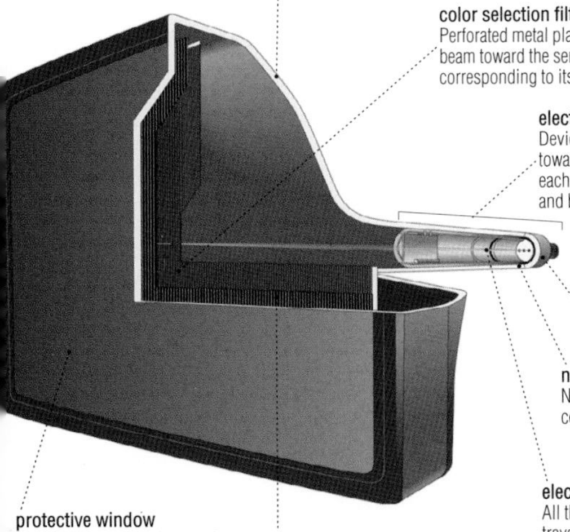

funnel
Flared rear portion of the picture tube.

color selection filter
Perforated metal plate that directs each electron beam toward the sensitive parts of the screen corresponding to its color.

electron gun
Device that emits electron beams toward the screen; there are beams for each of the primary colors, red, green and blue.

base
Terminal end of the picture tube that connects to outside circuits.

neck
Narrow part of the picture tube that contains the electron gun.

electron beam
All the negatively charged particles traveling in the same direction; their intensity varies with the video signal received.

protective window
Front portion of the picture tube that covers the screen.

screen
Surface on which pictures are formed; it is covered with sensitive dots, which emit red, green or blue light when hit by electrons.

electron gun
Device that emits electron beams toward the screen; there are beams for each of the primary colors, red, green and blue.

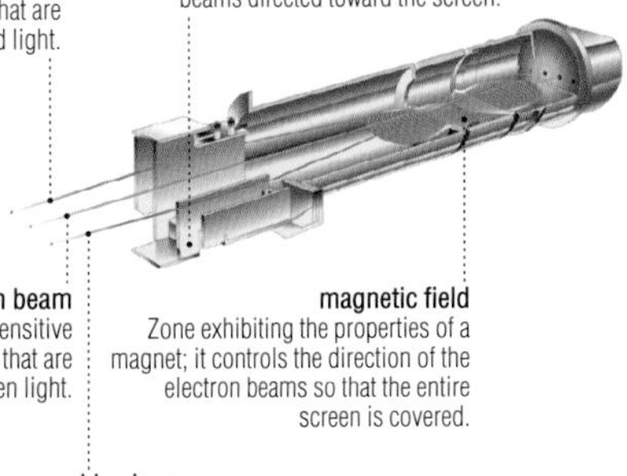

grid
Electrode with openings, which allow electrons to pass through; it helps regulate the intensity of the beams directed toward the screen.

red beam
Electron beam hitting the sensitive parts of the screen that are designed to emit red light.

green beam
Electron beam hitting the sensitive parts of the screen that are designed to emit green light.

magnetic field
Zone exhibiting the properties of a magnet; it controls the direction of the electron beams so that the entire screen is covered.

blue beam
Electron beam hitting the sensitive parts of the screen that are designed to emit blue light.

television

dish antenna
Device with a dish reflector that receives radio signals from a telecommunication satellite.

dish
Surface that collects waves and causes them to converge toward the feedhorn.

feedhorn
Device that receives, amplifies and converts waves into signals that can be used by a receiver such as a digital receiver.

pole
Tube that supports the antenna and is used to mount it.

receiv
Device that decodes digitized
signals transmitted by satellite
cable and routes them towarc
television s

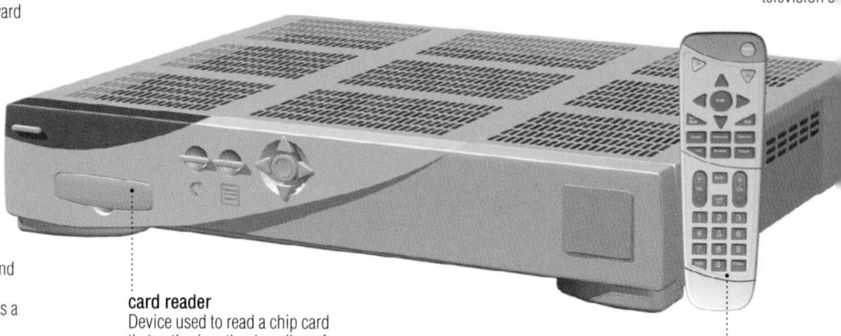

card reader
Device used to read a chip card that authorizes the decoding of signals covered by the subscription service.

remote control
Device that operates some functions of the receiver, includinc start, stop and program selection, from a distance.

home theater
Audiovisual equipment package for home use; it recreates the sound and visual effects found in movie theaters.

surround loudspeaker
Each of the small loudspeakers located about the room that generate the surround sounds.

center loudspeaker
Loudspeaker located between the two main loudspeakers that generates dialogue and certain sound effects.

large-screen television set
Television set with a screen having a length-to-height ratio greater than the norm so that it conforms to a movie theater format.

main loudspeaker
Each of the two loudspeakers located at the sides of a television set that generate most of the sounds and music.

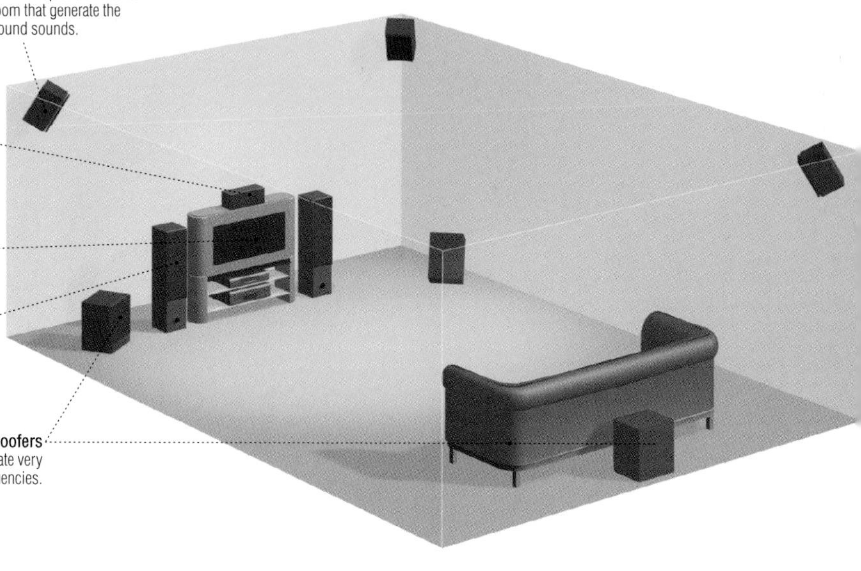

subwoofers
Large loudspeakers designed to generate very low frequencies.

videocassette recorder (VCR)
Device for playing back or recording audio and video signals on the magnetic tape of a videocassette.

cassette compartment
Space designed to receive a videocassette.

display
Liquid crystal display showing instructions for setting or operating the player.

power button
Mechanical connection that turns the VCR on or off.

remote control
Device for operating from a distance some functions of a television set, VCR or DVD player.

TV/video button
Key used to go from television mode to VCR or DVD mode.

TV mode
The keys used to operate a television set.

volume control

VCR mode
The keys used to operate a VCR.

channel selector controls
Number keys used to select a desired channel.

preset buttons
Keys used mainly to preset the recording of a television program.

VCR controls
Keys controlling the recording and playback functions of a VCR.

slow-motion button
Key used to slow the playback speed of a tape.

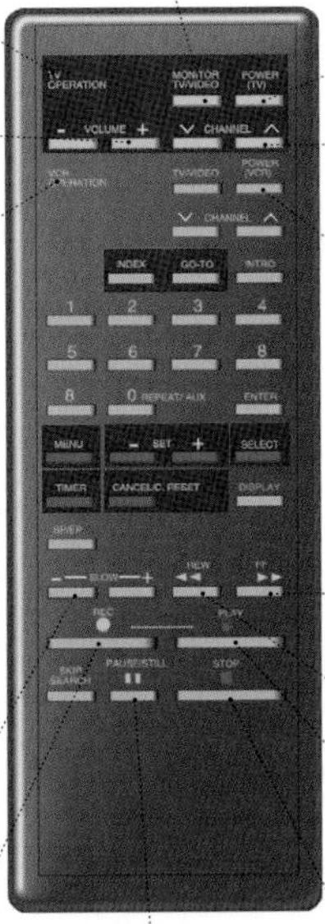

TV power button
Power connecting device used to turn a television set on or off.

channel scan button
Keys used to change channels.

VCR power button
Power connecting device used to turn a VCR on or off.

fast-forward button
Key that speeds up the forward motion of a tape; during playback, it also allows images to be scrolled forward.

rewind button
Key that controls the rewinding of a tape; during playback, it also allows images to be scrolled backward.

play button
Key used to play back a tape.

record button
Key used to begin to record a television program.

pause/still button
Key that stops a tape momentarily during playback to produce a still image on the screen.

stop button
Key used to halt playback of a tape or recording of a television program.

DVD recorder
Device that uses a laser beam to record and play back data recorded on a DVD video.

power button
Mechanical connection that turns the player on or off.

channel select
Numbered keys used to select the desired channel directly.

display
Liquid crystal display showing instructions for setting or operating the player.

record button
Button that starts recording of a program.

play button
Button that starts playback of a disc.

stop button
Button that stops playback or recording.

disc tray
Part in which a disc is inserted to be played back.

disc compartment control
Button used to open or close the disc tray.

pause/still button
Key that stops a tape momentarily during playback to produce a still image on the screen.

track search/fast operation buttons
Keys used to move to the next or previous scene, or to reverse or fast-forward the playback of a disc.

recording media
Media for recording images and sounds.

videocassette
Rigid case containing a magnetic tape on which sounds and images can be recorded.

recording tape
Flexible tape whose surface is covered with a magnetic substance; it is used as a recording medium.

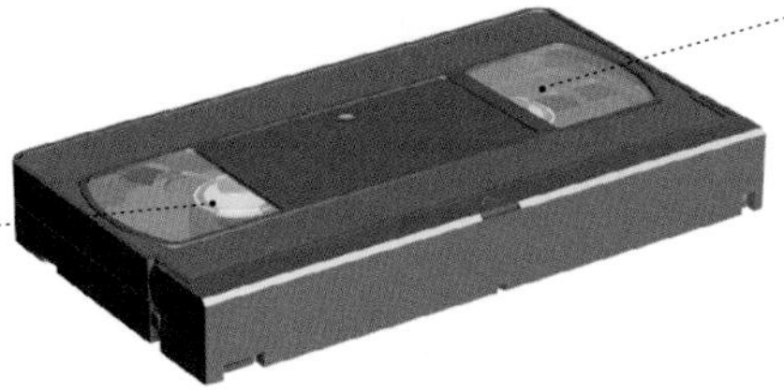

reel
Cylindrical part used to wind and unwind the magnetic tape.

digital versatile disc (DVD)
Digital recording medium available in various formats, including video, audio and multimedia; it has greater storage capacity than a compact disc.

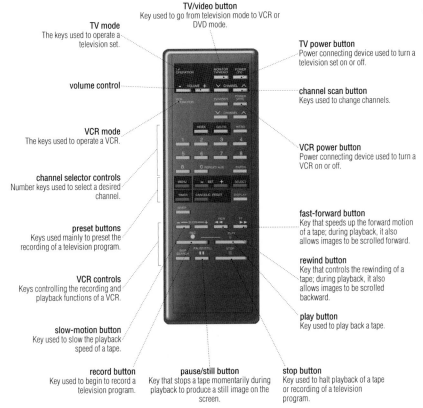

television

mini-DV camcorder: front view
Portable video camera that records sounds and images in digital format on a miniDV cassette.

zoom button
Button used to adjust the zoom to obtain a distant or close-up view of the subject being filmed.

recording mode
Button used to select a recording medium (cassette or memory card).

electronic viewfinder
Small video monitor for viewing the scene to be filmed in order to frame it and bring it into focus.

photoshot button
Button used to record a still image on a memory card.

zoom lens
Lens for changing the visual field so that a close-up or distant shot of the subject can be obtained without moving the camcorder.

power/functions switch
Button used to turn the camcorder on or off and to select the operating mode including camera, playback and battery recharge.

terminal cover
Cover that protects the camcorder's input and output jacks (microphone audio-video, DV).

lamp
Device that produces a light beam used to light the subject being filmed.

shoulder strap
Adjustable strap for carrying the camcorder over the shoulder or across the chest.

microphone
Device that converts electric pulses into broadcast or recorded sounds.

mini-DV camcorder: rear view

videotape operation controls
Buttons that control viewing of recorded images; they include playback, stop, pause, fast-forward and rewind.

focus button
Button used to focus the image automatically or manually.

nightshot button
Button for activating the mode that allows filming in the dark.

liquid crystal display
Screen that uses light reflected off liquid crystals to display alphanumeric data or images.

eyepiece
Optical disk or system of disks through which the eye sees the image produced by the lens.

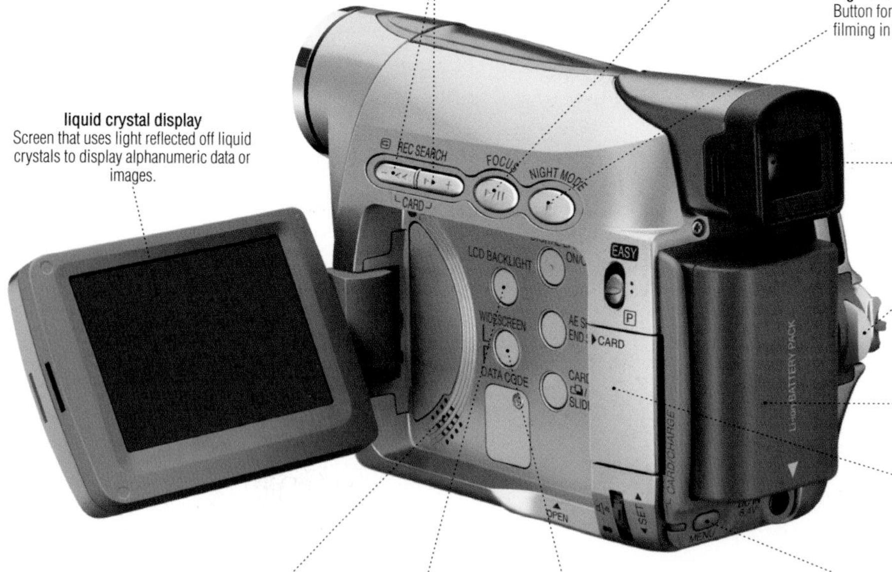

recording start/stop button
Button used to start and stop the recording of pictures and sounds.

rechargeable battery pack
Device that stores chemical energy while charging, then converts it to electric energy.

card slot
Covered slot in which a memory card is inserted to record still images taken with the camcorder.

speaker
Integrated device used to generate sound.

backlighting button
Button used to improve contrast on the LCD screen in order to improve its readability.

widescreen/data code button
Button used to start recording in widescreen format or to insert various data (date, time, etc.) onto the filmed image.

menu button
Button used to display menus for changing settings and accessing the camcorder's options.

television

hard disk drive camcorder
Portable video camera that records sounds and images in digital format on an internal hard disk.

DVD camcorder
Portable video camera that records sounds and images in digital format directly on a digital versatile disc (DVD).

cassette compartment
Space designed to receive a videocassette.

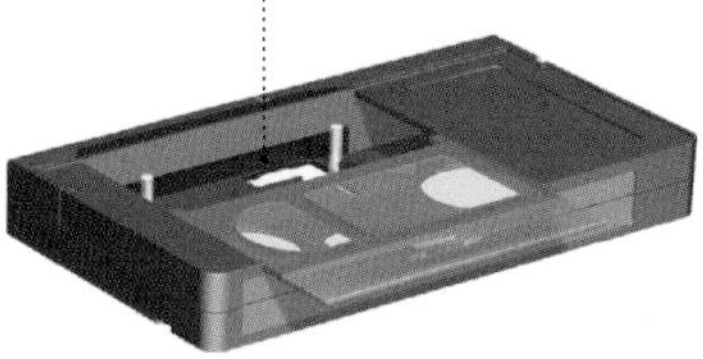

compact videocassette adapter
Case allowing a compact videocassette to be viewed using a standard VCR.

miniDV cassette
Digital videocassette onto which images and sounds are recorded.

sound reproducing system

System for reproducing sound that consists mainly of a tuner, playback equipment, an amplifier and loudspeakers.

power button
Mechanical connection that turns the tuner on or off.

memory button
Button used to hold certain stations in memory.

mode selector
Button used to select the sound reproduction mode (monophonic or stereophonic).

tuner
Device that receives signals from radio stations by selecting the appropriate frequency.

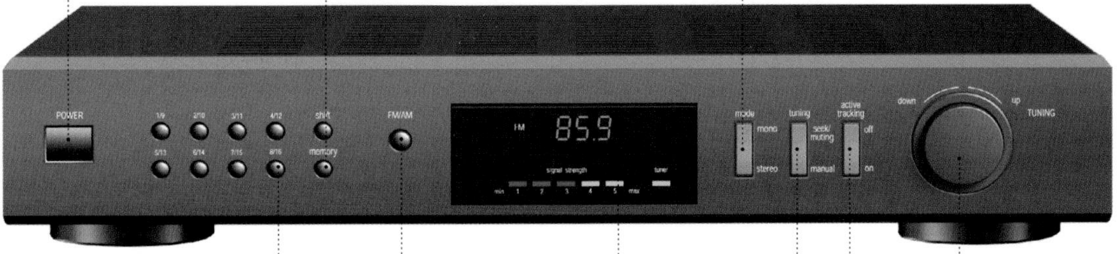

preset tuning button
Button used to tune into a station held in memory.

digital frequency display
Liquid crystal display showing the broadcast frequency of a tuned station.

tuning control
Button used to select a broadcast frequency.

band selector
Button used to select an AM or FM band.

tuning mode
Button for choosing between automatic (scanning) or manual selection of stations.

active tracking
Button used to browse the full frequency band to locate and select a station.

frequency bands
All the frequencies contained in a sound signal.

graphic equalizer
Equipment used to modulate the received signal by regulating the relative intensity of each of its frequency bands.

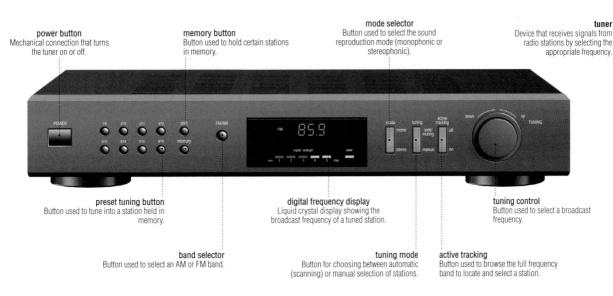

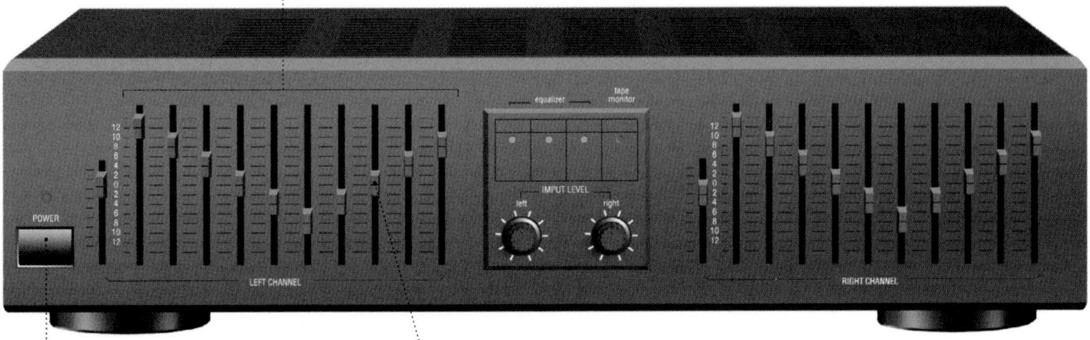

power button
Mechanical connection that turns the graphic equalizer on or off.

frequency setting slide control
Sliding part used to tone down or amplify the sound signal associated with a given frequency band.

sound reproducing system

ampli-tuner: front view
Device combining the functions of a tuner (receiving radio signals) and an amplifier (increasing the strength of a sound signal).

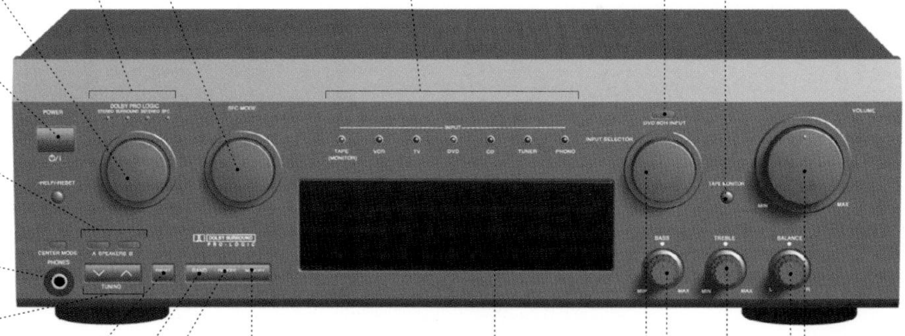

sound mode lights
Small indicator lights showing the sound mode selected.

sound field control
Dial used to select a particular listening environment, including concert hall, cabaret and live.

sound mode selector
Dial used to select the sound reproduction mode, including monophonic, stereophonic and ambiophonic.

input lights
Small indicator lights showing the selected input.

input select button
Button used to select a six-channel DVD input, which creates a three-dimensional sound environment (home theater).

tape recorder select button
Button that activates and deactivates a VCR.

power button
Mechanical connection that turns the ampli-tuner on or off.

loudspeaker system select buttons
Buttons used to activate or deactivate one or more loudspeakers.

headphone jack
Slot that takes the plug from the headphones.

tuning buttons
Buttons used to select a broadcast frequency.

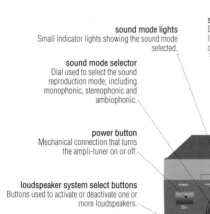

display
Liquid crystal display showing instructions for setting or operating the ampli-tuner.

volume control

preset tuning button
Button used to tune into a station held in memory.

band select button
Button used to select an AM or FM band.

memory button
Button used to hold certain stations in memory.

input selector
Button that selects the source of signals in the device including tuner, cassette deck, CD or DVD player.

balance control
Button used to adjust the relative volume of the left and right channels.

FM mode select button
Button that selects the sound reproduction mode (monophonic or stereophonic) on the FM band.

bass tone control
Button used to adjust the relative level of low-frequency sounds.

treble tone control
Button used to adjust the relative level of high-frequency sounds.

ampli-tuner: back view

ground terminal
Device that grounds the electric current to prevent electrocution due to faulty equipment.

cooling fan
Fan that circulates air to cool the internal components of the ampli-tuner.

power cord
Flexible electric wire housing the leads connecting the appliance to the electric circuit.

antenna terminals
Jacks that connect the AM and FM receiving antennas to the ampli-tuner.

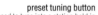

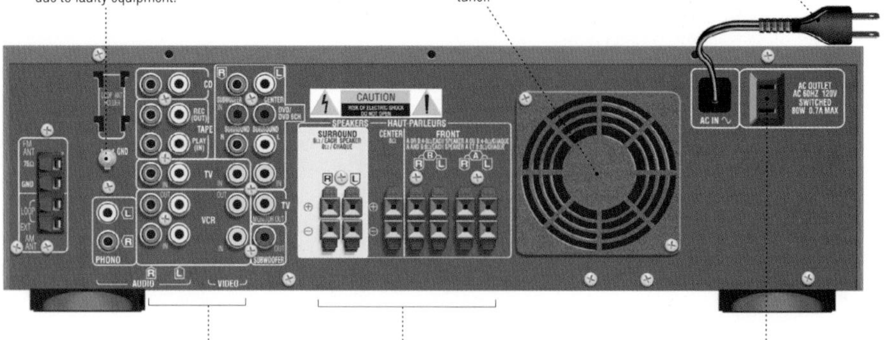

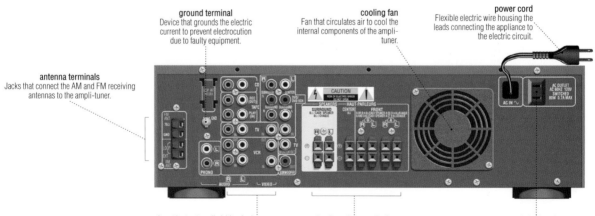

input/output audio/video jacks
Coupling jacks that transfer audio and video signals between the ampli-tuner and the various playback and recording devices.

loudspeaker terminals
Jacks that connect the loudspeakers to the ampli-tuner.

switched outlet
Device that provides electricity to the equipment connected to it when the ampli-tuner is on.

cassette
Rigid case containing a recording tape on which sounds can be recorded.

take-up reel
Cylindrical part on which the recording tape winds.

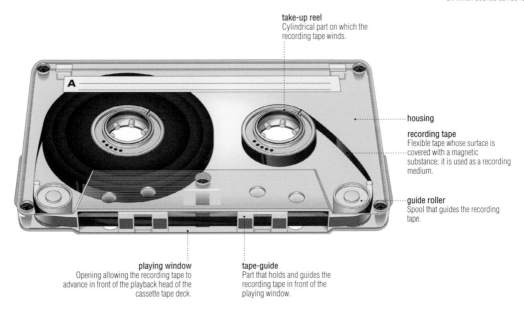

housing

recording tape
Flexible tape whose surface is covered with a magnetic substance; it is used as a recording medium.

guide roller
Spool that guides the recording tape.

playing window
Opening allowing the recording tape to advance in front of the playback head of the cassette tape deck.

tape-guide
Part that holds and guides the recording tape in front of the playing window.

cassette tape deck
Device used to play back and record sounds on a recording tape cassette.

counter reset button
Key used to reset a tape counter to zero.

play button
Key used to play back a tape.

fast-forward button
Control key used to fast-forward a tape.

eject button
Key activating the mechanism to eject a cassette from the cassette holder.

tape counter
Device showing the length of a recorded segment on a tape.

tape selector
The buttons used to indicate clearly the type of recording tape (normal, chrome or metal).

peak level meter
Device showing the intensity of the sound signals being played back or recorded.

cassette holder
Compartment receiving the cassette for playback.

stop button
Key used to interrupt the playback, recording, rewinding or fast-forwarding of a tape.

record muting button
Key used to record a blank section at the start of a track or between two tracks.

rewind button
Control key used to rewind a tape.

record button
Key used to activate the sound recording mechanism on a tape.

pause button
Key used to temporarily stop the playback or recording of a tape.

recording level control
Device used to change the intensity of the recorded sound signals.

sound reproducing system

record
Usually vinyl, circular medium on which sounds are recorded.

spiral
Blank part of the locked groove that separates two bands.

spiral-in groove
Part of the locked groove that marks the beginning of the record.

locked groove
Spiral groove etched into the surface of a record; the stylus cartridge of a record player travels along the groove from the outside in.

band
Part of the locked groove that contains a recording; the sides of the groove are marked by hills and valleys, which cause the stylus to vibrate.

tail-out groove
Part of the locked groove that marks the end of the last band.

center hole
Circular opening for inserting the record on the center of the turntable.

label
Marking affixed to the center of the record that provides information about its contents.

record player
Device using an arm fitted with a stylus cartridge to play back sounds from a record.

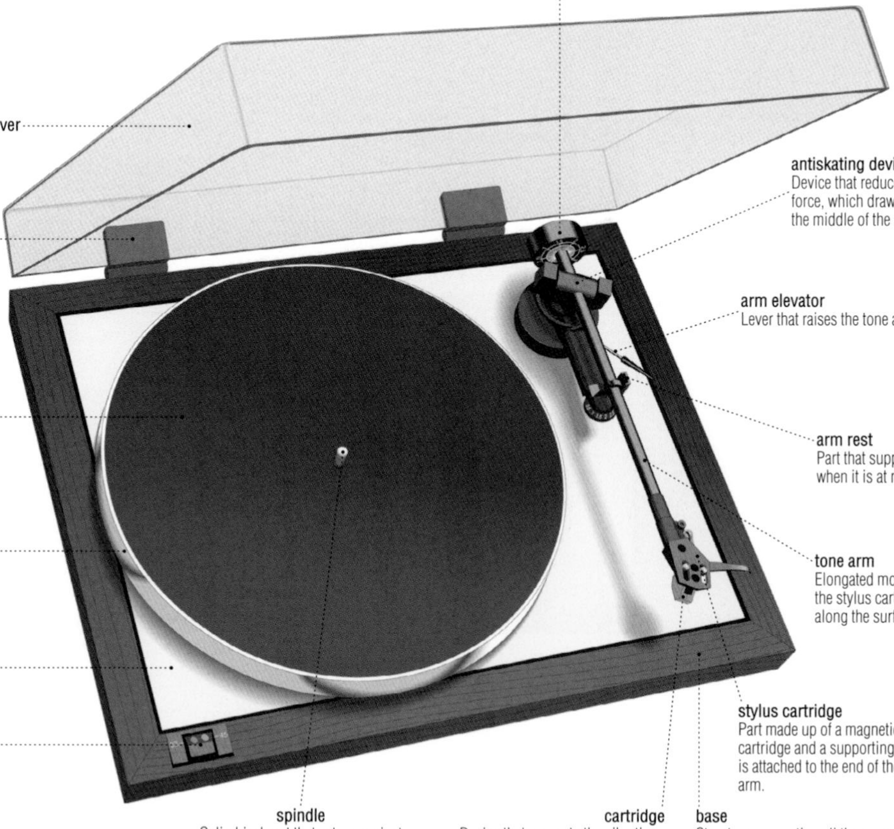

counterweight
Part that regulates the pressure of the stylus on the record groove.

dust cover

hinge

antiskating device
Device that reduces the effect of centripetal force, which draws the toner arm toward the middle of the record.

arm elevator
Lever that raises the tone arm.

rubber mat
Antiskid and antiscratch turntable cover that is usually made of felt or rubber.

arm rest
Part that supports the tone arm when it is at rest.

turntable
Rotating part on which the record rests when played.

tone arm
Elongated movable part that holds the stylus cartridge and moves it along the surface of the record.

base plate
Plate that supports the turntable; it is usually attached to the base by a springy suspension.

stylus cartridge
Part made up of a magnetic cartridge and a supporting shell; it is attached to the end of the tone arm.

speed selector
Device used to select the turntable speed (45 or 33 1/3 revolutions per minute).

spindle
Cylindrical part that acts as a pivot for the turntable and record.

cartridge
Device that converts the vibrations of the stylus into electric pulses as it travels along the locked groove.

base
Structure supporting all the record player components.

compact disc
Digital recording medium with multiple formats (including video and audio) and variable storage capacity.

technical identification band
Surface on which the disc's identification code is engraved.

pressed area
Surface that contains the recording; it is coded on a spiral groove pressed into the disc.

reading start
The track on the pressed surface is made up of a series of pits and asperities; a laser beam reads the groove from the inside out.

compact disc reading
During playback of a compact disc, a sensor analyzes laser beam variations reflected by the disc's surface to re-create the original sound signal.

objective lens
Optical system made up of a set of lenses attached to a mount; it focuses the laser beam onto the section to be played.

asperity
Each of the small protuberances of varying length that encode data on the disc's surface.

laser beam
Highly concentrated light beam that scans the surface of a disc; the pits and asperities determine how the light beam is reflected.

aluminum layer
The surface of the disc is covered with a thin layer of aluminum, which reflects the laser beam toward the sensor.

resin surface
Transparent film that covers and protects the aluminum layer.

compact disc player
Device using a laser beam to play back sounds recorded on a compact disc (CD).

shuffle play
Button used to play back tracks in random order chosen by the device.

power button
Mechanical connection that turns the player on or off.

direct disc access buttons
Buttons used to play back one of the discs inserted in the player.

repeat button
Button allowing repeated playback of one or several tracks.

track search/fast operation buttons
Buttons used to skip to the next or previous track or to accelerate playback forward or backward.

stop button
Button used to stop playback of a disc.

pause button
Button used to stop playback of a disc temporarily.

play button
Button used to start playback of a disc.

disc skip
Button used to skip to the next disc.

headphone jack
Socket for a headphone plug.

disc compartment
Compartment that contains the tray into which discs are inserted for playback.

display
LCD screen displaying device settings or operations executed.

disc compartment control
Button that opens and closes the disc tray.

sound reproducing system

headphones
Sound reproduction device made up of two earphones mounted on a headband.

headband
Flexible band that holds the earphones on the ears.

adjusting band
Device that adjusts the headband to fit the user's head.

earphone
Small speaker placed directly over the ear to listen to sounds from a stereo system or sound equipment.

resonator
Part of the headphones that is covered by a grille and houses the loudspeaker.

connecting cable
Electric cable that transmits sound to the headphones.

plug
Terminal end of the cable with prongs that is inserted into an electric outlet (jack).

loudspeakers
Case enclosing one or several speakers, which convert electric pulses into sound waves by means of an amplifier.

speaker cover
Thin grille made of fabric or metal that covers and protects the speakers.

tweeter
Loudspeaker designed to reproduce the high frequencies of the sound signal.

midrange
Loudspeaker designed to reproduce the middle frequencies of the sound signal.

woofer
Loudspeaker designed to reproduce the low frequencies of the sound signal.

diaphragm
Cone-shaped flexible part that vibrates to create sound waves in the air.

mini stereo sound system

Sound reproduction system with miniaturized components (including ampli-tuner, speakers and reader).

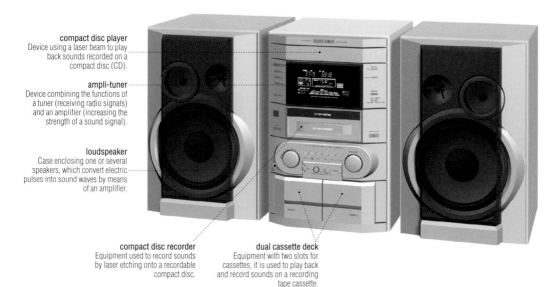

compact disc player
Device using a laser beam to play back sounds recorded on a compact disc (CD).

ampli-tuner
Device combining the functions of a tuner (receiving radio signals) and an amplifier (increasing the strength of a sound signal).

loudspeaker
Case enclosing one or several speakers, which convert electric pulses into sound waves by means of an amplifier.

compact disc recorder
Equipment used to record sounds by laser etching onto a recordable compact disc.

dual cassette deck
Equipment with two slots for cassettes; it is used to play back and record sounds on a recording tape cassette.

portable sound systems

Small self-contained sound reproduction equipment that can be carried easily from one place to another.

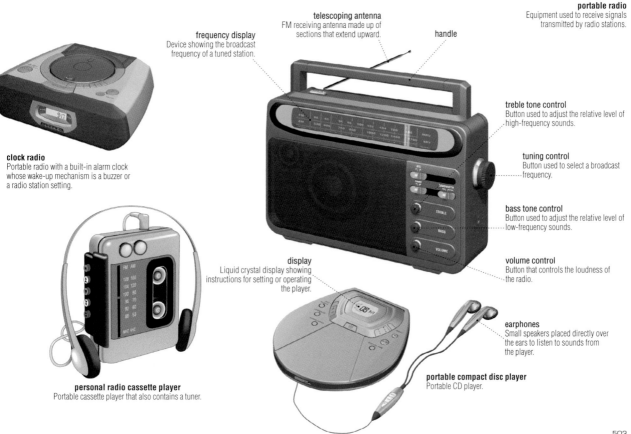

clock radio
Portable radio with a built-in alarm clock whose wake-up mechanism is a buzzer or a radio station setting.

portable radio
Equipment used to receive signals transmitted by radio stations.

telescoping antenna
FM receiving antenna made up of sections that extend upward.

frequency display
Device showing the broadcast frequency of a tuned station.

handle

treble tone control
Button used to adjust the relative level of high-frequency sounds.

tuning control
Button used to select a broadcast frequency.

bass tone control
Button used to adjust the relative level of low-frequency sounds.

volume control
Button that controls the loudness of the radio.

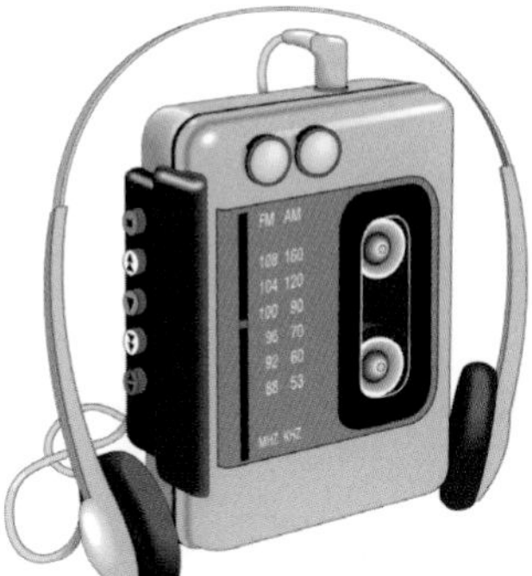

personal radio cassette player
Portable cassette player that also contains a tuner.

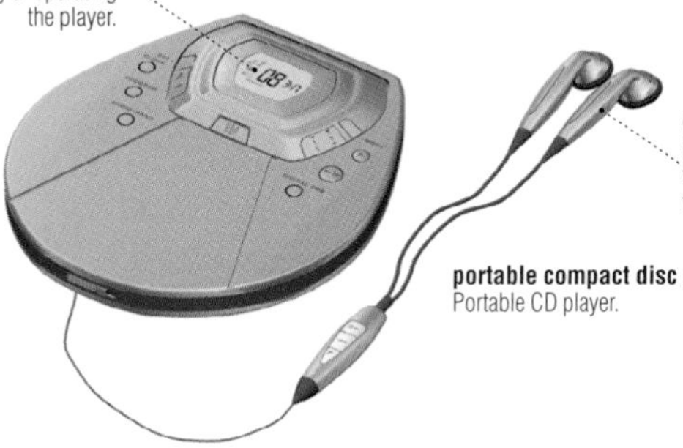

display
Liquid crystal display showing instructions for setting or operating the player.

earphones
Small speakers placed directly over the ears to listen to sounds from the player.

portable compact disc player
Portable CD player.

portable sound systems

portable digital audio player
Portable player for digital music files.

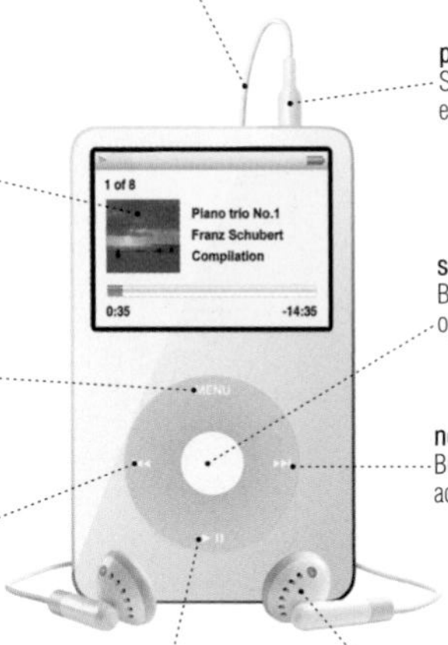

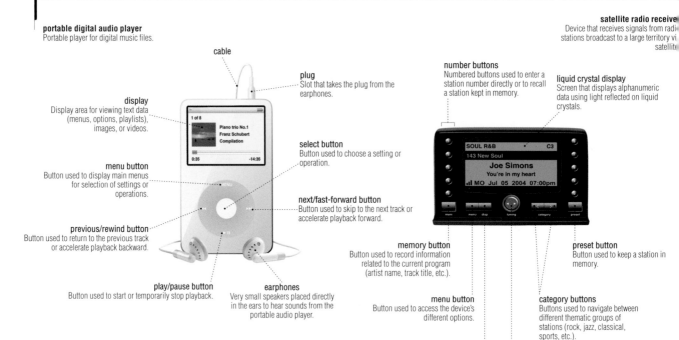

cable

plug
Slot that takes the plug from the earphones.

display
Display area for viewing text data (menus, options, playlists), images, or videos.

select button
Button used to choose a setting or operation.

menu button
Button used to display main menus for selection of settings or operations.

next/fast-forward button
Button used to skip to the next track or accelerate playback forward.

previous/rewind button
Button used to return to the previous track or accelerate playback backward.

play/pause button
Button used to start or temporarily stop playback.

earphones
Very small speakers placed directly in the ears to hear sounds from the portable audio player.

satellite radio receive
Device that receives signals from radi
stations broadcast to a large territory vi
satellit

number buttons
Numbered buttons used to enter a station number directly or to recall a station kept in memory.

liquid crystal display
Screen that displays alphanumeric data using light reflected on liquid crystals.

memory button
Button used to record information related to the current program (artist name, track title, etc.).

preset button
Button used to keep a station in memory.

menu button
Button used to access the device's different options.

category buttons
Buttons used to navigate between different thematic groups of stations (rock, jazz, classical, sports, etc.).

display button
Button used to select the items displayed on the screen (artist name, track title, duration, etc.).

tuning control
Wheel control used to choose a station or scroll through menus displayed on the screen.

portable CD radio cassette recorder
Equipment combining a radio, cassette player, CD player and speakers in the same case.

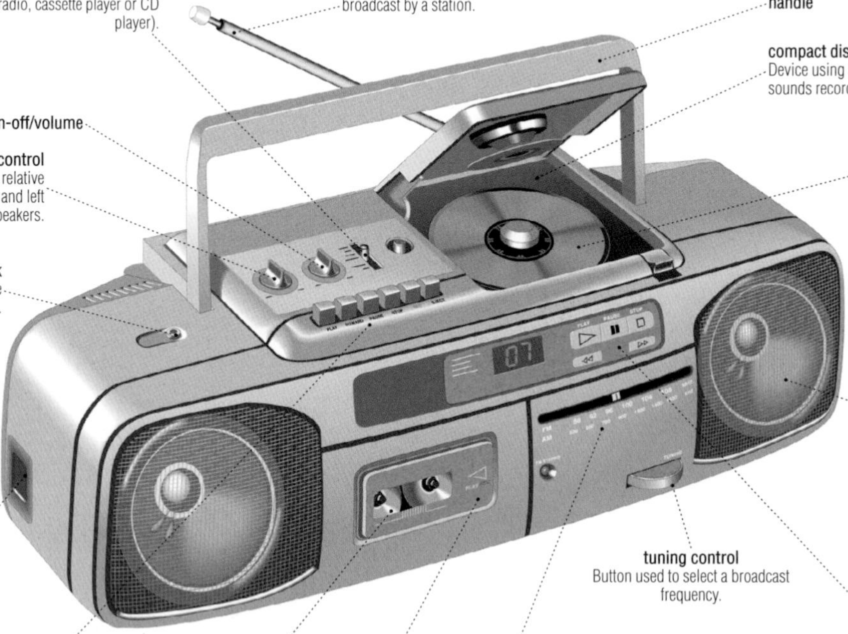

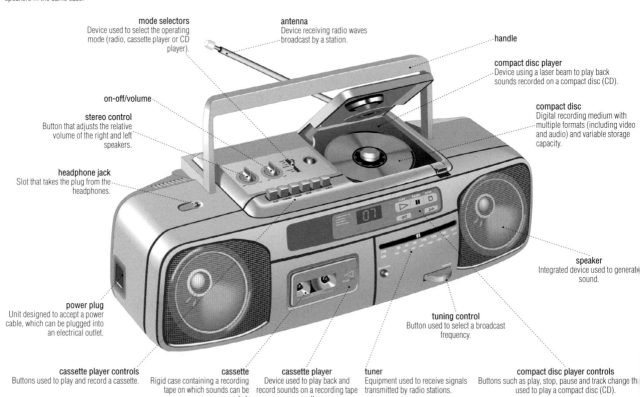

mode selectors
Device used to select the operating mode (radio, cassette player or CD player).

antenna
Device receiving radio waves broadcast by a station.

handle

compact disc player
Device using a laser beam to play back sounds recorded on a compact disc (CD).

on-off/volume

compact disc
Digital recording medium with multiple formats (including video and audio) and variable storage capacity.

stereo control
Button that adjusts the relative volume of the right and left speakers.

headphone jack
Slot that takes the plug from the headphones.

speaker
Integrated device used to generat
sound.

power plug
Unit designed to accept a power cable, which can be plugged into an electrical outlet.

tuning control
Button used to select a broadcast frequency.

cassette player controls
Buttons used to play and record a cassette.

cassette
Rigid case containing a recording tape on which sounds can be recorded.

cassette player
Device used to play back and record sounds on a recording tape cassette.

tuner
Equipment used to receive signals transmitted by radio stations.

compact disc player controls
Buttons such as play, stop, pause and track change th
used to play a compact disc (CD).

wireless communication

Transmission of voice or alphanumeric messages by radio waves; it uses small devices that are equipped with a transmitting or receiving antenna.

walkie-talkie
Portable two-way radio used to relay the human voice over short distances.

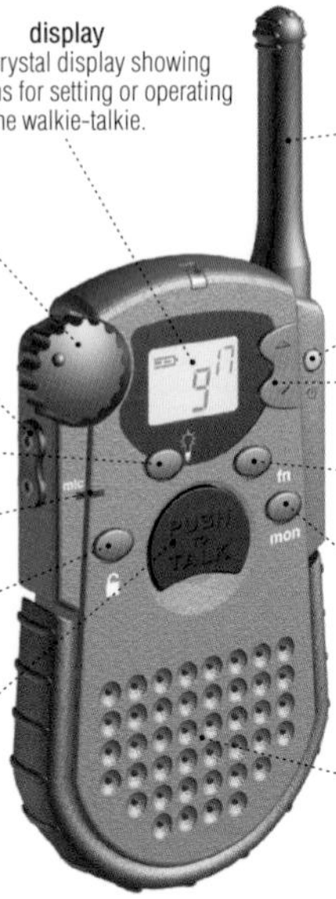

volume control
Button that controls the loudness of the walkie-talkie.

display
Liquid crystal display showing instructions for setting or operating the walkie-talkie.

antenna
Device that emits and receives radio waves.

call button
Button that signals the desire to communicate with another user.

power button
Mechanical switching device that turns the walkie-talkie on or off.

scroll button
Button that adjusts the speaker volume and changes equipment settings.

light button
Button that illuminates the display to make the data more legible in poor lighting conditions.

menu button
Button that displays the menus so that settings and operations can be selected.

microphone
Device that converts electric pulses into broadcast or recorded sounds.

monitor button
Button used to check if a broadcast or receiving channel is free before transmitting.

lock button
Button that deactivates the menu and scroll buttons to prevent equipment settings from being changed accidentally.

push-to-talk switch
When this button is pressed, voice messages can be sent from one extension to another; when it is released, messages can be received.

speaker
Integrated device used to generate sound.

numeric pager
Portable device that receives digital messages (usually the telephone number of the caller).

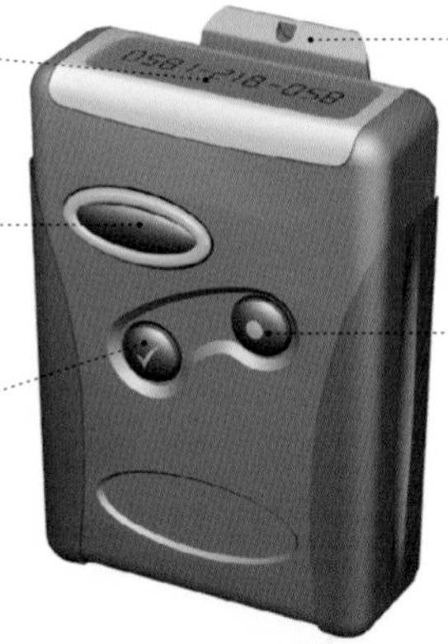

display
Liquid crystal display that shows messages received and various information about equipment settings and operations.

belt clip
Clip used to attach a pager to a belt.

read button
Button used mainly to display received messages.

menu button
Button that displays the menus so that settings and operations can be selected.

select button
Button that selects a setting or operation to be carried out.

CB radio
Two-way radio often installed in a vehicle; it transmits the human voice over reserved frequencies on a public band.

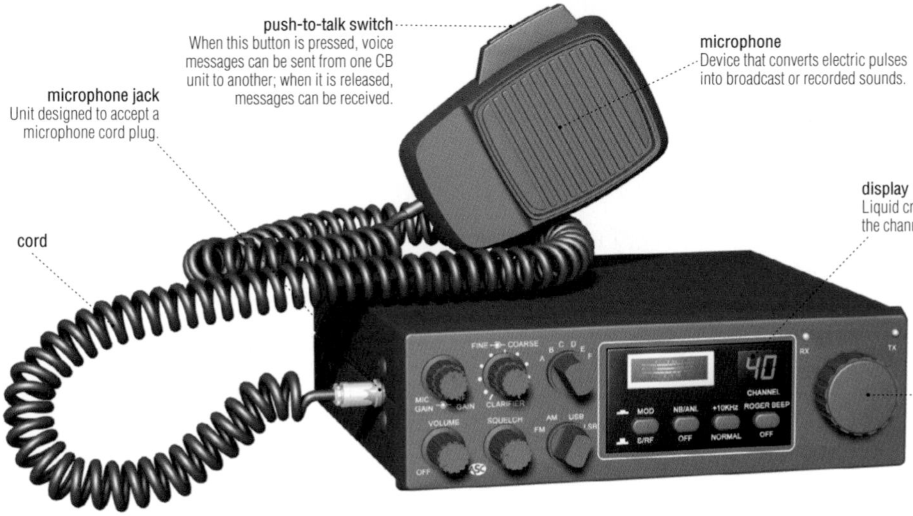

push-to-talk switch
When this button is pressed, voice messages can be sent from one CB unit to another; when it is released, messages can be received.

microphone
Device that converts electric pulses into broadcast or recorded sounds.

microphone jack
Unit designed to accept a microphone cord plug.

cord

display
Liquid crystal display that shows the channel in use.

channel selector
Button that selects a frequency channel for sending or receiving voice messages.

communication by telephone

Transmission of data, voice, audio or video messages between parties linked by a telephone network.

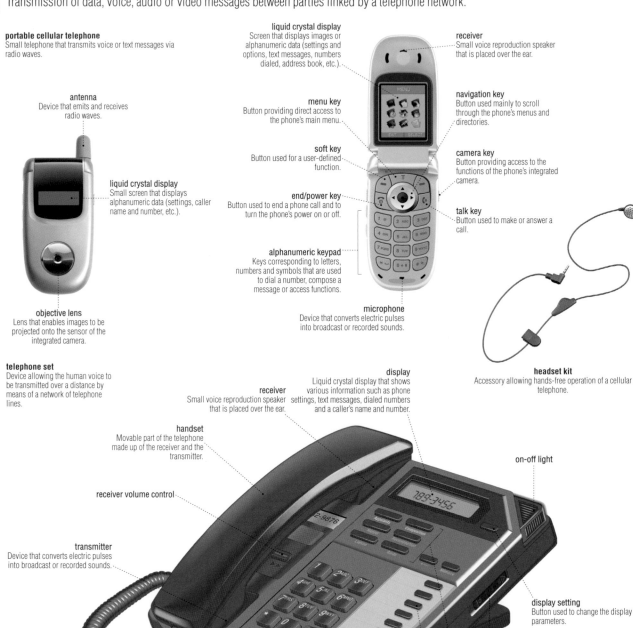

portable cellular telephone
Small telephone that transmits voice or text messages via radio waves.

antenna
Device that emits and receives radio waves.

liquid crystal display
Small screen that displays alphanumeric data (settings, caller name and number, etc.).

objective lens
Lens that enables images to be projected onto the sensor of the integrated camera.

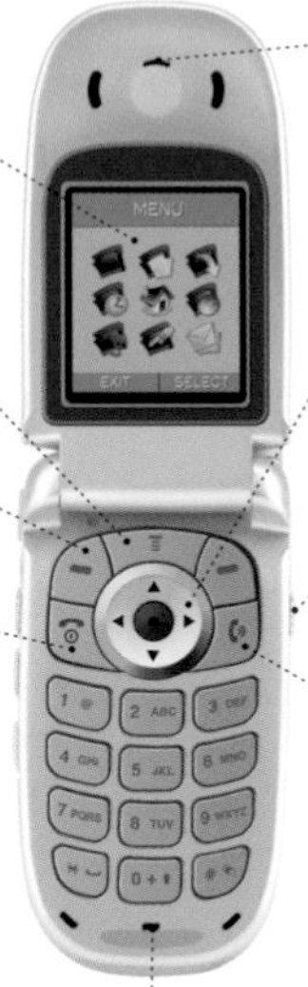

liquid crystal display
Screen that displays images or alphanumeric data (settings and options, text messages, numbers dialed, address book, etc.).

menu key
Button providing direct access to the phone's main menu.

soft key
Button used for a user-defined function.

end/power key
Button used to end a phone call and to turn the phone's power on or off.

alphanumeric keypad
Keys corresponding to letters, numbers and symbols that are used to dial a number, compose a message or access functions.

microphone
Device that converts electric pulses into broadcast or recorded sounds.

receiver
Small voice reproduction speaker that is placed over the ear.

navigation key
Button used mainly to scroll through the phone's menus and directories.

camera key
Button providing access to the functions of the phone's integrated camera.

talk key
Button used to make or answer a call.

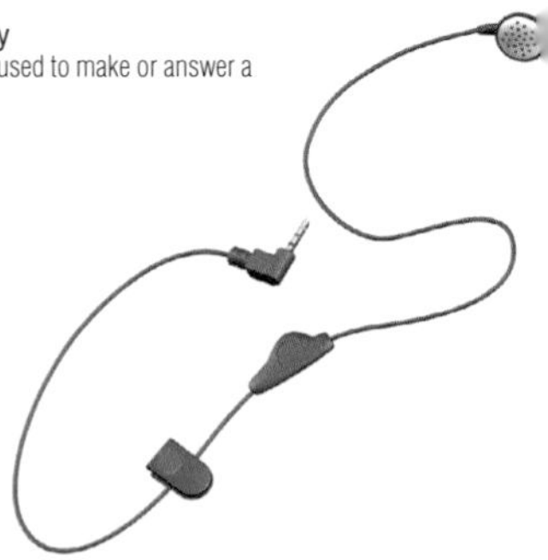

headset kit
Accessory allowing hands-free operation of a cellular telephone.

telephone set
Device allowing the human voice to be transmitted over a distance by means of a network of telephone lines.

receiver
Small voice reproduction speaker that is placed over the ear.

display
Liquid crystal display that shows various information such as phone settings, text messages, dialed numbers and a caller's name and number.

handset
Movable part of the telephone made up of the receiver and the transmitter.

on-off light

receiver volume control

transmitter
Device that converts electric pulses into broadcast or recorded sounds.

display setting
Button used to change the display parameters.

ringing volume control
Button that controls the loudness of the ringing.

handset cord

memory button
Button that automatically dials a telephone number held in memory.

function selectors
Control buttons that operate various equipment functions such as last-number redial, call hold and link.

push buttons
Keys corresponding to letters, numbers and symbols that are used to dial a number or access functions.

telephone index
List of frequently used names and telephone numbers.

automatic dialer index
List of names and telephone numbers corresponding to the memory buttons.

martphone
evice integrating the communication functions of portable cell phone and the management nctions of a personal digital assistant.

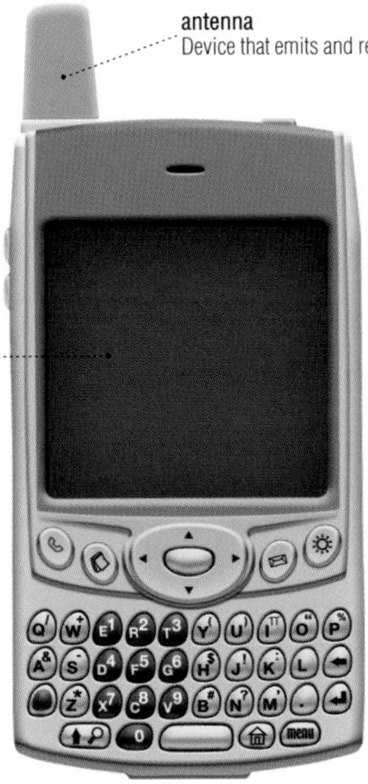

antenna
Device that emits and receives radio waves.

display
Liquid crystal display screen on which graphics or text data are displayed.

function keys
eys used to execute operations (making a phone call, sending an e-mail) or access applications (notepad, address book, agenda).

keypad
Group of keys corresponding to letters, numbers, or symbols, used to generate characters or execute functions.

ay phone
elephone located in public places; it nctions when coins or payment cards are serted into the phone box.

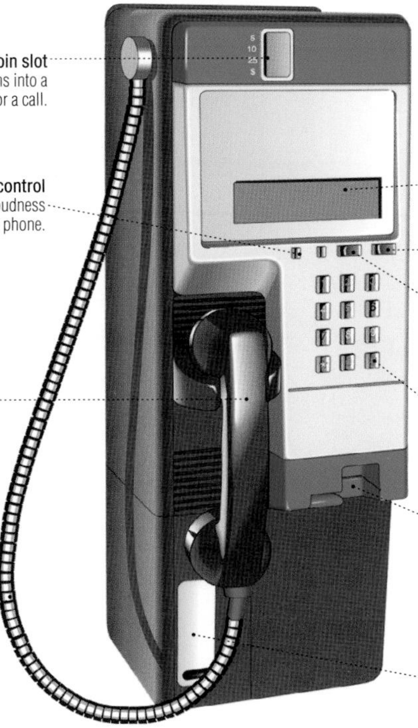

coin slot
Slot for inserting coins into a telephone to pay for a call.

volume control
Button that controls the loudness of the phone.

handset
Movable part of the telephone made up of the receiver and the transmitter.

armored cord

display
Liquid crystal display that shows a variety of information such as dialed number and prepaid card balance.

next call
Button used to make another telephone call without hanging up the handset.

language display button

push button
Key corresponding to letters, numbers and symbols that are used to dial a number or access functions.

card reader
Device used to read a payment card (credit card, calling card or prepaid card).

coin return bucket
Small chamber for retrieving coins.

examples of telephones

The shape and function of telephones is constantly evolving; today's phones relay computer data as well as voice communication.

push-button telephone
Device with alphanumeric keys to dial a number or access functions; it has gradually replaced the dial phone.

call director telephone
Device that redirects calls within an organization's internal telephone network.

cordless telephone
Device featuring a handset with an antenna that is linked by radio waves to a base.

communication by telephone

digital answering machine
Device plugged into a phone jack that answers calls with a prerecorded voice message, then records messages left by callers.

speaker
Integrated device used to generate sound.
delete
Button that erases messages recorded.
previous
Button that lets the user hear the preceding message.
setup
Button used to change different options on the device.
power button
Button that turns the device on and off.
next
Button that lets the user skip to the next message.
display
LCD screen that displays the number of messages recorded.
volume
Buttons used to adjust the speaker sound level.
play
Button that lets the user listen to a message.
stop
Button that stops message playback.
microphone
Device that converts electric pulses into broadcast or recorded sounds.

facsimile (fax) machine
Equipment used to send written documents over a telephone network.

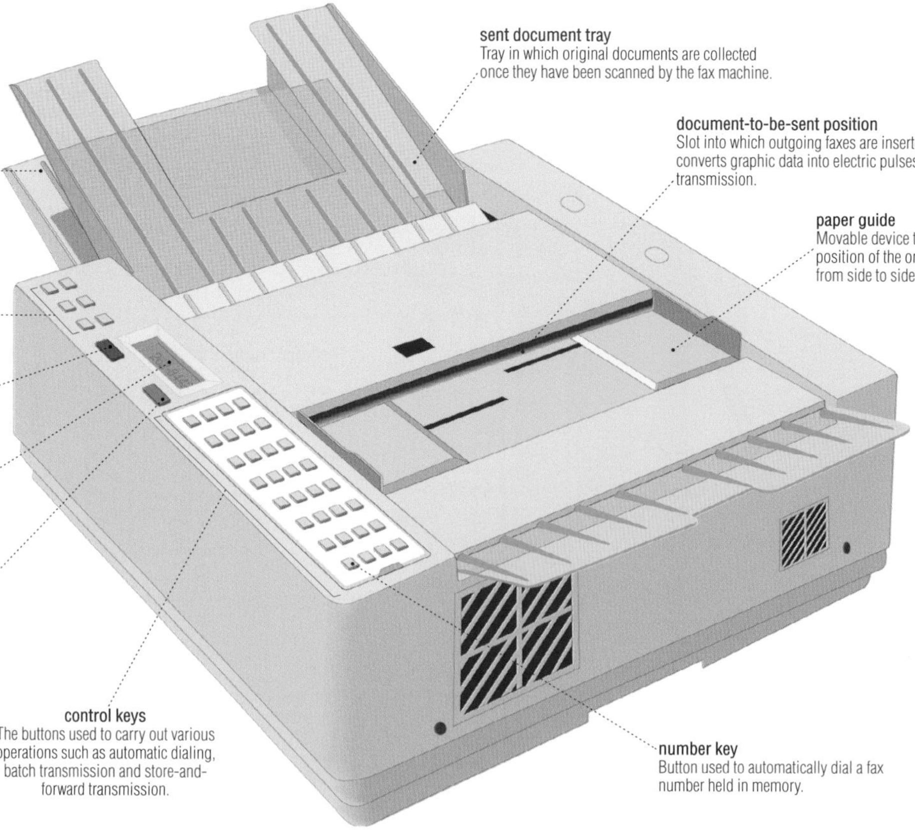
sent document tray
Tray in which original documents are collected once they have been scanned by the fax machine.
receiving tray
Tray in which incoming faxes are collected.
document-to-be-sent position
Slot into which outgoing faxes are inserted; it converts graphic data into electric pulses for transmission.
paper guide
Movable device that adjusts the position of the original document from side to side.
function keys
The buttons used to select an option or adjust parameters such as transmission mode and contrast.
reset key
Button used to cancel an operation or a setting.
data display
Liquid crystal display that shows a variety of information such as dialed number, sender's number, equipment settings and completed operations.
start key
control keys
The buttons used to carry out various operations such as automatic dialing, batch transmission and store-and-forward transmission.
number key
Button used to automatically dial a fax number held in memory.

office

Place where an organization's employees work; it can house administrative, management or production staff, depending on the company.

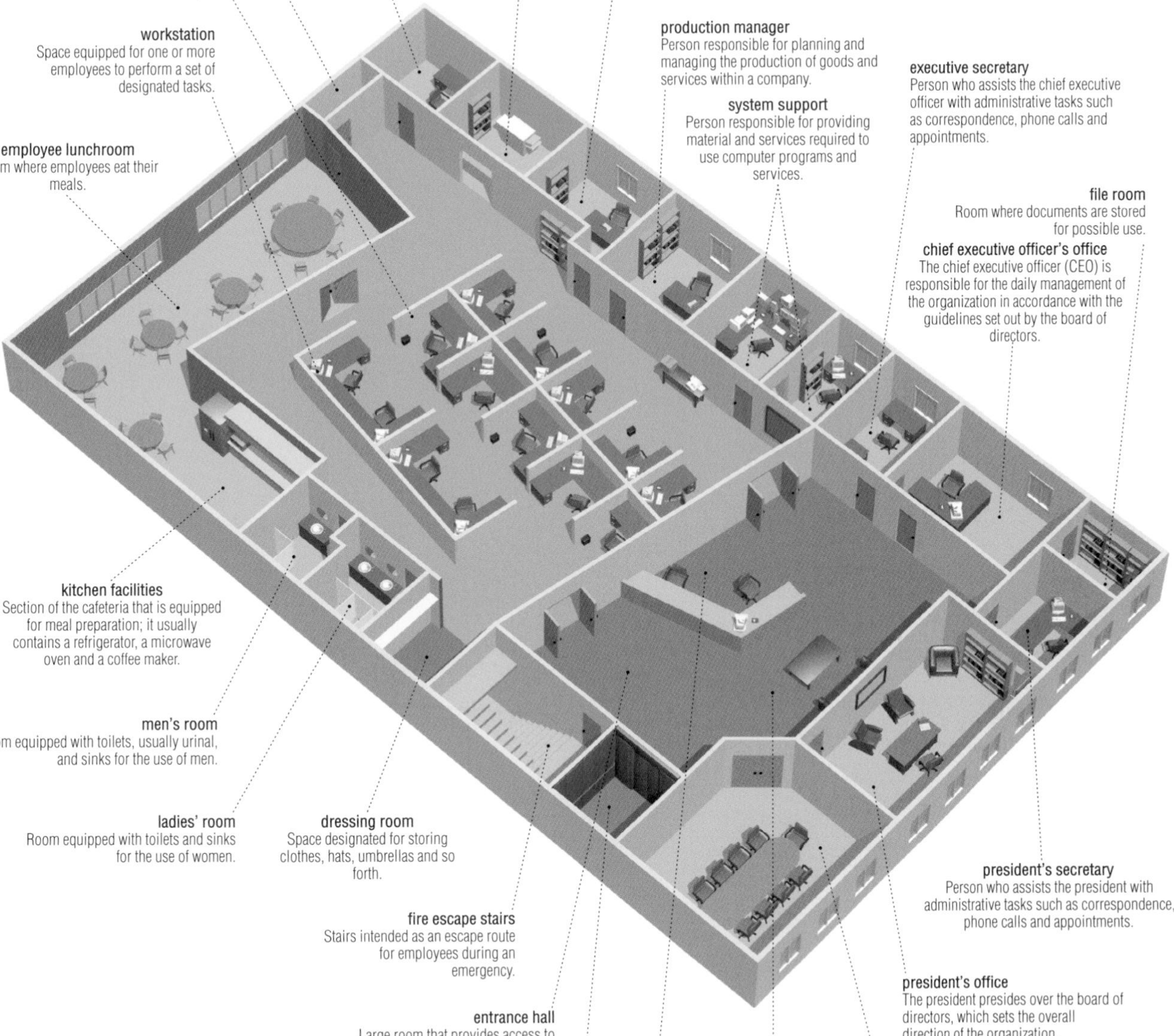
storeroom
Place where items are stored.
mail processing room
Room for sorting incoming and outgoing mail.
photocopy room
Room housing document reproduction equipment (usually photocopiers).
accountant's office
Staff responsible for keeping the account books in which an organization's financial data are recorded.
movable panel
Lightweight divider that usually has feet and is used to section off various work spaces.
workstation
Space equipped for one or more employees to perform a set of designated tasks.
production manager
Person responsible for planning and managing the production of goods and services within a company.
executive secretary
Person who assists the chief executive officer with administrative tasks such as correspondence, phone calls and appointments.
system support
Person responsible for providing material and services required to use computer programs and services.
employee lunchroom
Room where employees eat their meals.
file room
Room where documents are stored for possible use.
chief executive officer's office
The chief executive officer (CEO) is responsible for the daily management of the organization in accordance with the guidelines set out by the board of directors.
kitchen facilities
Section of the cafeteria that is equipped for meal preparation; it usually contains a refrigerator, a microwave oven and a coffee maker.
men's room
Room equipped with toilets, usually urinal, and sinks for the use of men.
ladies' room
Room equipped with toilets and sinks for the use of women.
dressing room
Space designated for storing clothes, hats, umbrellas and so forth.
president's secretary
Person who assists the president with administrative tasks such as correspondence, phone calls and appointments.
fire escape stairs
Stairs intended as an escape route for employees during an emergency.
president's office
The president presides over the board of directors, which sets the overall direction of the organization.
entrance hall
Large room that provides access to other offices.
conference room
Room used for work-related meetings between employees or with visitors.
elevator
Mechanical apparatus with a car that provides automated movement of people between the levels of a building.
waiting room
Space for visitors to wait for individuals with whom they will be meeting.
reception
Staff member assigned to welcome visitors.

office furniture

All the furniture in an office; it is intended mainly for filing, storage and carrying out work tasks.

filing furniture

Piece of furniture used to file documents by category or in a given order.

mobile filing unit
Small piece of furniture on casters; it is used to hold hanging files.

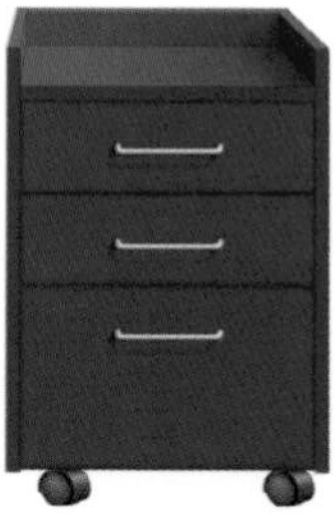

mobile drawer unit
Small piece of furniture on casters or legs; it contains drawers and is usually placed under a desk or table.

lateral filing cabinet
Compartmentalized piece of furniture with flipper doors; it is used to hold hanging files.

storage furniture

Furniture serving to archive, support or protect various objects.

display cabinet
Cabinet with usually folding, slanted shelves; it is used to display and stack books, magazines and brochures.

stationery cabinet
Large two-door cabinet with shelves; it is used to store office supplies and items used daily.

coat hook
Hook or set of hooks attached to a wall and used to hang such items as clothing, hats and umbrellas.

movable panel
Lightweight divider that usually has feet and is used to section off various work spaces.

coat tree
Small pole on legs that has to hang such items as clot hats and umbrellas.

locker
Large two-door cabinet fitted with a bar to hang clothing and a shelf to stack various items.

coat rack
Structure on legs or casters that is fitted with a rod to hang clothing.

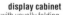

credenza
Long low office furniture with drawers or compartments to store various objects.

office furniture

work furniture
Furniture designed to facilitate office work, from writing to working at a computer or typewriter.

computer table
Table designed to hold a computer monitor and keyboard.

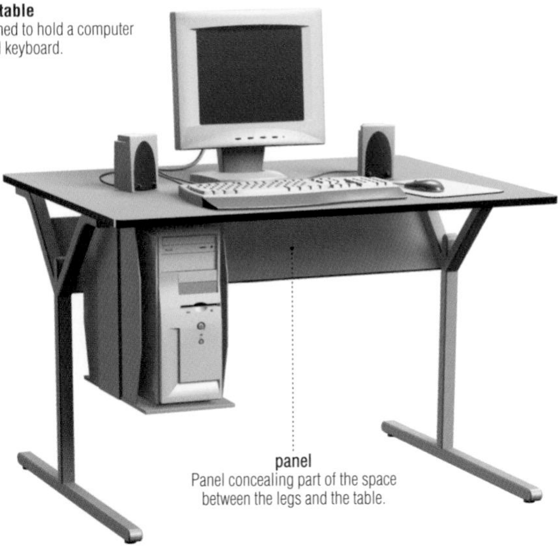

panel
Panel concealing part of the space between the legs and the table.

printer table
Table designed to hold a printer and its accessories.

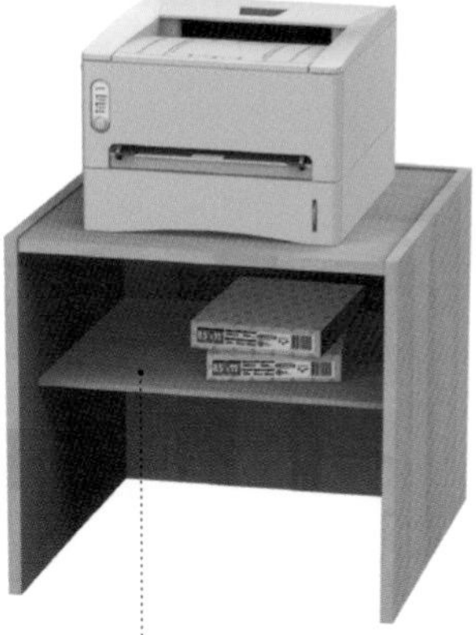

shelf
Horizontal space on which various accessories can be stored (extra paper, for example).

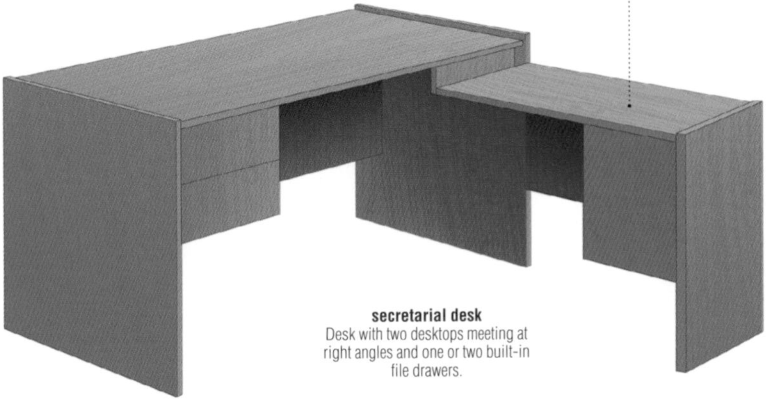

typist's chair
Padded chair on casters; the back can be tilted and adjusted for height.

executive desk
Desk with a large desktop work space and two built-in file drawers.

swivel-tilter armchair
Armchair designed to swivel horizontally around an axis and to tilt forward and back.

desk mat
Accessory on which paper is placed for writing; it protects the desktop.

return
Auxiliary desktop that is used especially to hold a typewriter or computer.

secretarial desk
Desk with two desktops meeting at right angles and one or two built-in file drawers.

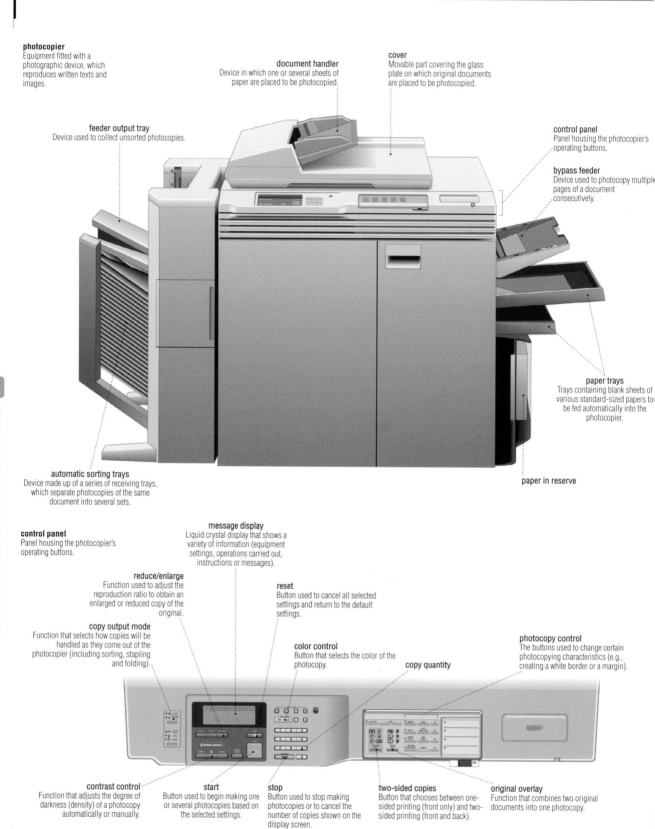

photocopier
Equipment fitted with a photographic device, which reproduces written texts and images.

document handler
Device in which one or several sheets of paper are placed to be photocopied.

cover
Movable part covering the glass plate on which original documents are placed to be photocopied.

feeder output tray
Device used to collect unsorted photocopies.

control panel
Panel housing the photocopier's operating buttons.

bypass feeder
Device used to photocopy multiple pages of a document consecutively.

paper trays
Trays containing blank sheets of various standard-sized papers to be fed automatically into the photocopier.

automatic sorting trays
Device made up of a series of receiving trays, which separate photocopies of the same document into several sets.

paper in reserve

control panel
Panel housing the photocopier's operating buttons.

message display
Liquid crystal display that shows a variety of information (equipment settings, operations carried out, instructions or messages).

reduce/enlarge
Function used to adjust the reproduction ratio to obtain an enlarged or reduced copy of the original.

reset
Button used to cancel all selected settings and return to the default settings.

copy output mode
Function that selects how copies will be handled as they come out of the photocopier (including sorting, stapling and folding).

color control
Button that selects the color of the photocopy.

copy quantity

photocopy control
The buttons used to change certain photocopying characteristics (e.g., creating a white border or a margin).

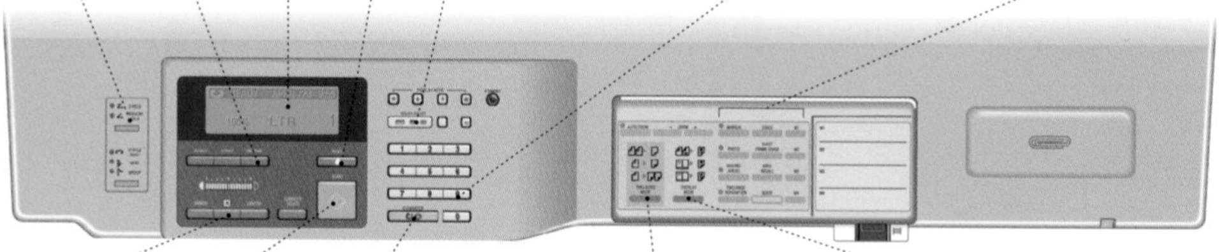

contrast control
Function that adjusts the degree of darkness (density) of a photocopy automatically or manually.

start
Button used to begin making one or several photocopies based on the selected settings.

stop
Button used to stop making photocopies or to cancel the number of copies shown on the display screen.

two-sided copies
Button that chooses between one-sided printing (front only) and two-sided printing (front and back).

original overlay
Function that combines two original documents into one photocopy.

personal computer

Compact data processor consisting of a central processing unit that is connected to a monitor, a keyboard and various other peripherals.

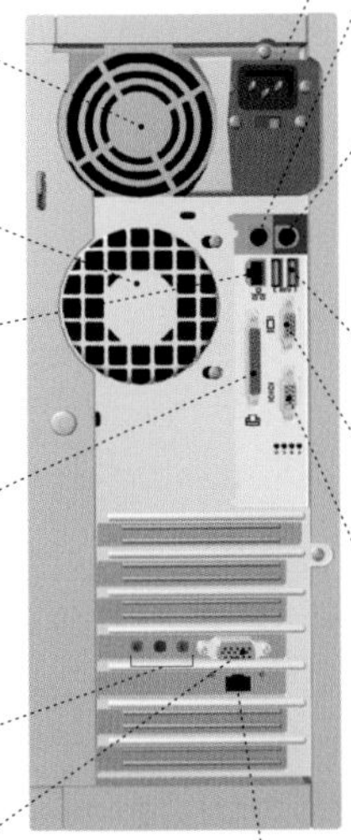

ower case: back view
power cable plug
Device with metal prongs that connects the computer by power cable to an electric circuit.
mouse port
Round connector that links the computer to the mouse.
power supply fan
Device blowing air to cool the internal components of the power supply unit.
keyboard port
Round connector that links the computer to the keyboard.
case fan
Device blowing air to cool the internal components of the tower case.
network port
Connector that attaches the computer to a network.
parallel port
Connector used mainly to attach the computer to a printer; it is faster than a serial port as it exchanges data in eight-bit groups.
audio jack
Connection device that attaches the omputer to a variety of sound recording and reproduction equipment such as a microphone and loudspeakers.
game/MIDI port
Connector that attaches the computer to a game device (e.g., a joystick) or a digital musical instrument.
internal modem port
Connector used to attach the internal modem (a two-way digital signal changing device) to a telephone line.
USB port
Connector used to link several USB standard peripherals simultaneously; it is faster than serial and parallel ports.
video port
Connector used to attach the computer monitor to the video board; the latter is inserted in the tower case and controls the display of texts and graphics.
serial port
Connector used to attach a computer to various peripherals such as an external modem; it is slower than a parallel port as it exchanges only one bit at a time.

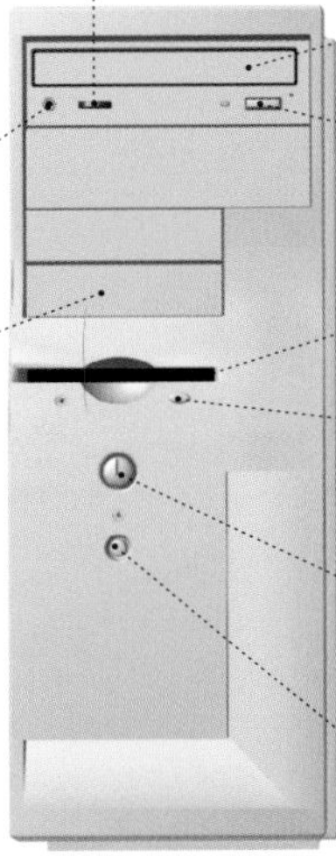

tower case: front view
Tower case: rectangular enclosure that is taller than it is wide; it houses the operating components and peripherals of a personal computer.
volume control
CD/DVD-ROM drive
Playback device using a laser beam to read the data recorded on a compact disc (CD) or digital versatile disc (DVD).
CD/DVD-ROM eject button
Button used to open the CD/DVD-ROM drive to retrieve the inserted disc.
earphone jack
Slot that takes the plug from the earphones.
bay filler panel
Standard-sized panel covering an unused compartment through which electronic hardware can be added.
floppy disk drive
Device used to read or record data on a diskette.
floppy disk eject button
Button used to retrieve a disk inserted into the floppy disk drive.
power button
Button for turning the device on or off.
reset button
Button used to reboot the computer in the event the system freezes.

tower case: interior view
battery
Electric energy reserve used to power computer functions, which are still active when the computer is turned off.
motherboard
Main circuit board that houses the components essential to the computer's operations, including the processor, chipset and connectors.
bus
The wires and circuits allowing transmission of data, in the form of electric signals, between the computer's components.
random access memory (RAM) module
Module containing RAM chips, which temporarily store programs and data while they are being used or processed.
CD/DVD-ROM drive
Playback device using a laser beam to read the data recorded on a compact disc (CD) or digital versatile disc (DVD).
power supply unit
Device that converts the power system's alternating current (AC) into direct current (DC) to supply power to the personal computer's internal components.
heat sink
Metal piece that disperses the heat generated by the processor's circuits.
random access memory (RAM) connector
Device accepting a RAM module.
processor
Central processing unit (CPU) that reads and executes programmed instructions.
floppy disk drive
Device used to read or record data on a diskette.
AGP expansion connector
Socket accepting a video board designed according to AGP standards; it is extremely fast and provides high-quality 3-D displays.
secondary hard disk drive
Device used to play and record data on a secondary hard disk that complements the primary hard disk.
filler plate
Plate covering an unused expansion connector.
speaker
Integrated device used to generate sound.
PCI expansion connector
Socket accepting a PCI expansion card; it provides a higher transmission speed than an ISA conductor.
primary hard disk drive
Device that reads and records data on the imary hard disk; it is the main storage medium for programs and data.
PCI expansion card
Circuit board designed according to PCI standards that is used to add functions to the computer; it can act as a video board, network interface board or soundboard.
chipset
The integrated circuits (chips) welded to the otherboard, which coordinates the exchange of data between the computer's various components.
ISA expansion connector
Socket accepting an expansion card designed according to ISA standards (usually a modem card or sound card).
power cable
Flexible electric cable that contains the conductors used to attach the power supply unit to the electric circuit.

input devices

Electronic devices used to transmit data and commands to a computer.

keyboard and pictograms

The keyboard contains a group of keys that correspond to characters and functions; the latter are represented by pictograms.

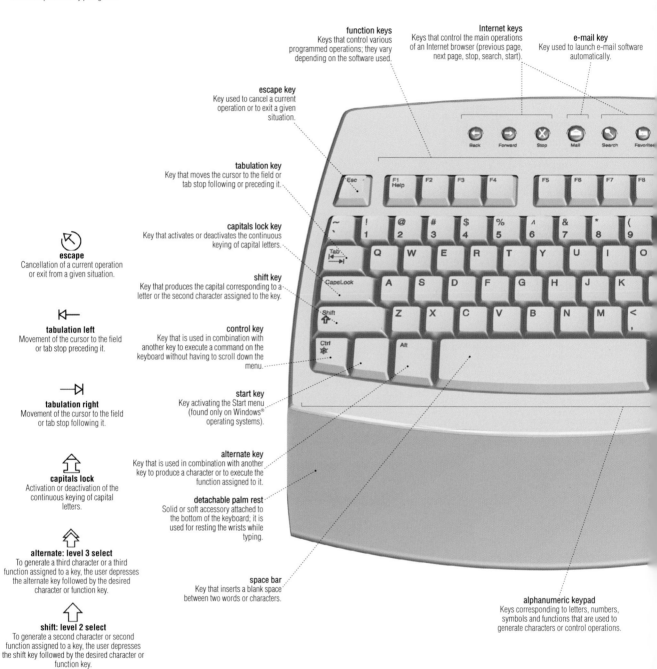

function keys
Keys that control various programmed operations; they vary depending on the software used.

Internet keys
Keys that control the main operations of an Internet browser (previous page, next page, stop, search, start).

e-mail key
Key used to launch e-mail software automatically.

escape key
Key used to cancel a current operation or to exit a given situation.

tabulation key
Key that moves the cursor to the field or tab stop following or preceding it.

capitals lock key
Key that activates or deactivates the continuous keying of capital letters.

shift key
Key that produces the capital corresponding to a letter or the second character assigned to the key.

control key
Key that is used in combination with another key to execute a command on the keyboard without having to scroll down the menu.

start key
Key activating the Start menu (found only on Windows® operating systems).

alternate key
Key that is used in combination with another key to produce a character or to execute the function assigned to it.

detachable palm rest
Solid or soft accessory attached to the bottom of the keyboard; it is used for resting the wrists while typing.

space bar
Key that inserts a blank space between two words or characters.

alphanumeric keypad
Keys corresponding to letters, numbers, symbols and functions that are used to generate characters or control operations.

escape
Cancellation of a current operation or exit from a given situation.

tabulation left
Movement of the cursor to the field or tab stop preceding it.

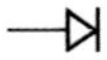

tabulation right
Movement of the cursor to the field or tab stop following it.

capitals lock
Activation or deactivation of the continuous keying of capital letters.

alternate: level 3 select
To generate a third character or a third function assigned to a key, the user depresses the alternate key followed by the desired character or function key.

shift: level 2 select
To generate a second character or second function assigned to a key, the user depresses the shift key followed by the desired character or function key.

control: group select
Symbol assigned to the control key that allows a command to be executed on the keyboard without having to scroll down the menu.

control
Other symbol assigned to the control key.

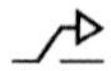

alternate
Other symbol assigned to the alternate key.

space
Insertion of a blank space between two words or characters.

nonbreaking space
Insertion of a space to keep two characters or a series of consecutive characters together on the same line.

print screen/system request key
Key used to print a copy of the data displayed on the screen or, along with other keys, to unlock the system.

backspace key
used to delete the character immediately to the left of the cursor.

indicator lights
Signal lights indicating activation of the capitals lock, numeric lock and scroll lock functions.

scrolling lock key
Key used to activate or deactivate scroll mode; this allows the contents of a window to be moved horizontally and vertically using the arrow keys.

insert key
Key that activates or deactivates the overwrite mode; this allows existing characters to be replaced by new characters during data entry.

pause/break key
Key used to pause or stop the current operation.

home key
Key that moves the cursor to the beginning of a line or a document.

numeric lock key
Key that activates or deactivates the numeric keypad.

page up key
Key used to display the preceding page screen.

page down key
Key that displays the next page screen.

enter key
Key used to confirm the execution of a command or, in the case of data entry, to move the cursor to the beginning of the next line.

end key
Key that moves the cursor to the end of a line or a document.

numeric keypad
Keys corresponding to numbers, mathematical operators and functions that are placed in a specific order to speed up numeric data entry.

cursor movement keys
Keys used to move the cursor around the screen.

delete key
Key used to delete a selected item or the character immediately to the right of the cursor.

enter key
Key used to confirm the execution of a command or, in the case of data entry, to move the cursor to the beginning of the next line.

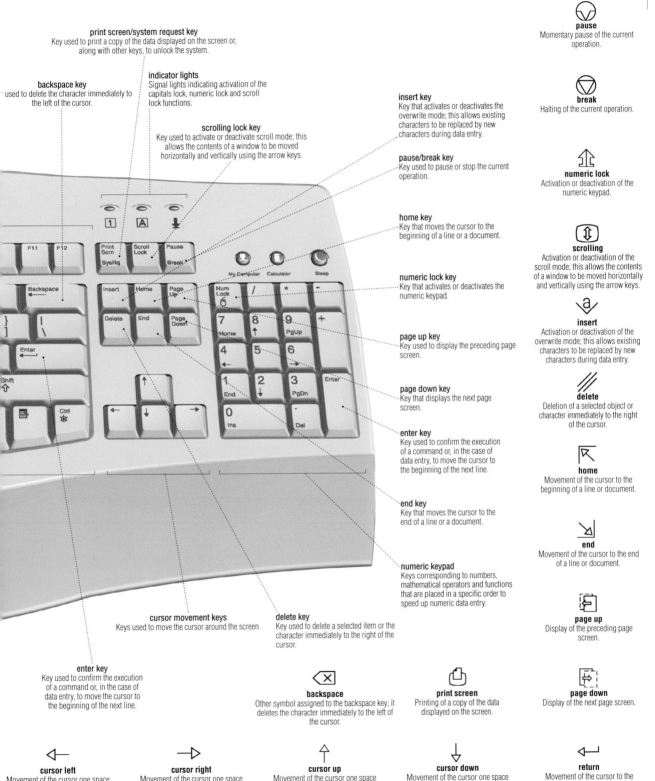

pause
Momentary pause of the current operation.

break
Halting of the current operation.

numeric lock
Activation or deactivation of the numeric keypad.

scrolling
Activation or deactivation of the scroll mode; this allows the contents of a window to be moved horizontally and vertically using the arrow keys.

insert
Activation or deactivation of the overwrite mode; this allows existing characters to be replaced by new characters during data entry.

delete
Deletion of a selected object or character immediately to the right of the cursor.

home
Movement of the cursor to the beginning of a line or document.

end
Movement of the cursor to the end of a line or document.

page up
Display of the preceding page screen.

backspace
Other symbol assigned to the backspace key; it deletes the character immediately to the left of the cursor.

print screen
Printing of a copy of the data displayed on the screen.

page down
Display of the next page screen.

cursor left
Movement of the cursor one space to the left.

cursor right
Movement of the cursor one space to the right.

cursor up
Movement of the cursor one space up.

cursor down
Movement of the cursor one space down.

return
Movement of the cursor to the beginning of the next line; the return key also has a validation function (to confirm the execution of a command).

input devices

wheel mouse
Mechanical or optical mouse that contains a scroll wheel.

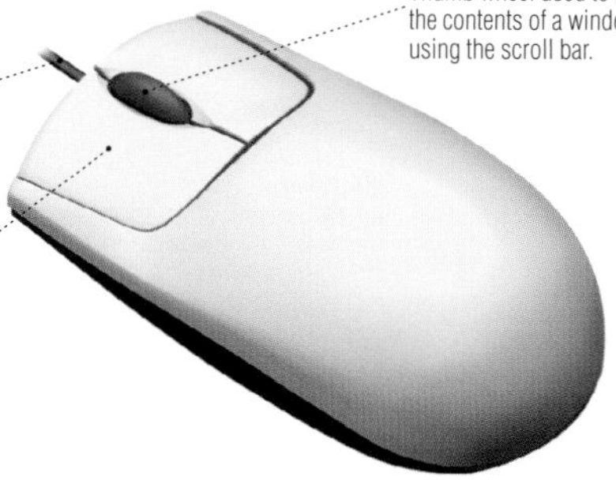

scroll wheel
Thumb wheel used to scroll down the contents of a window without using the scroll bar.

cable
Flexible cable containing the conductors by which the mouse is attached to the computer.

control button
Button that transmits various commands to the computer.

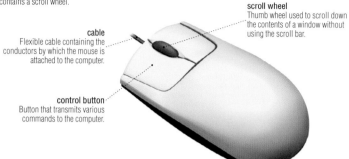

cordless mous
Mechanical or optical mous connected to the computer b infrared or radio signals

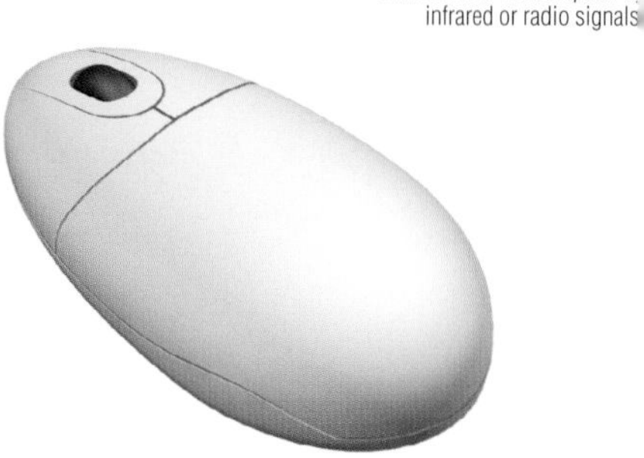

mechanical mouse
Mouse whose case contains a movable rubber ball underneath to direct the movements of the pointer on the screen.

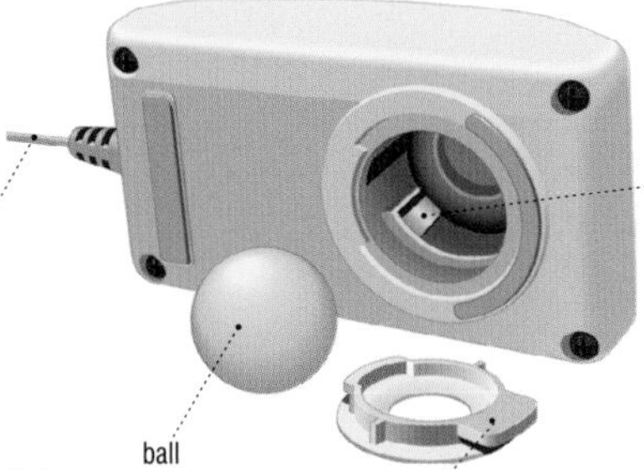

roller
Device that detects the ball's movements and transmit them to the computer.

cable
Flexible cable containing the conductors by which the mouse is attached to the computer.

ball
Movable sphere that moves over a flat surface (usually a mouse pad) to make the pointer move on the screen.

lock dial
Removable part that surrounds the ball and closes the mouse case.

optical mous
Mouse in which the ball is replace by an optical system (light emitting diode and sensor); it ha no movable parts

optical sensor
Device that measures the mouse's movements by analyzing the light rays (emitted by a diode) reflected from its support surface.

mouse pad
Smooth antiskid surface over which the mouse moves.

joystick
Device used in video games to direct the movements of an object or character and to transmit various commands.

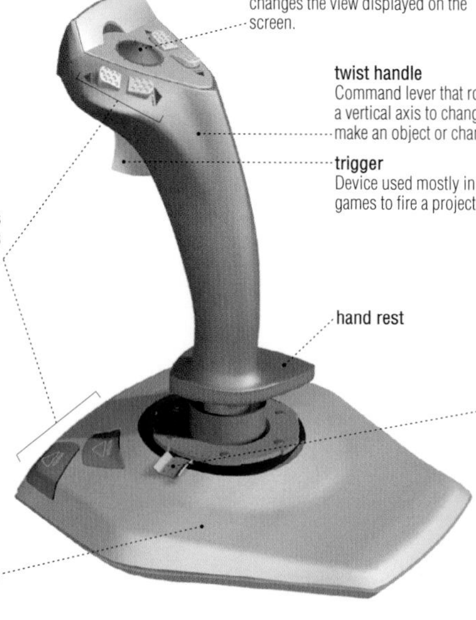

hat switch
Multidirectional button that mainly changes the view displayed on the screen.

twist handle
Command lever that rotates around a vertical axis to change the view or make an object or character turn.

trigger
Device used mostly in combat games to fire a projectile.

programmable buttons
Buttons that transmit various preset commands to the computer.

hand rest

throttle control
Device used mostly in car racing or flight simulation games to control such things as speed and thrust.

base

microphone
Device that converts electric pulses into broadcast or recorded sounds.

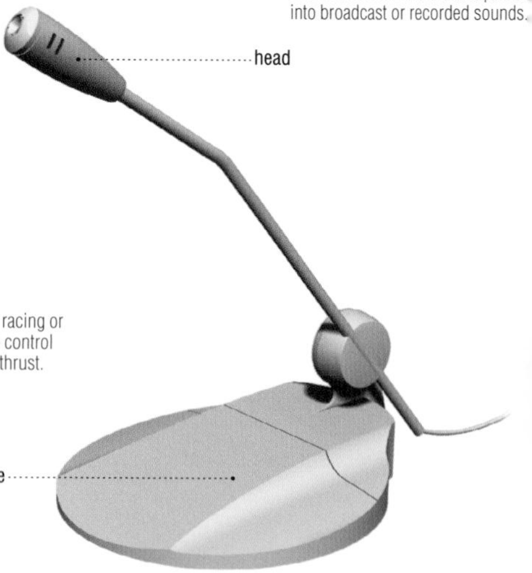

head

base

input devices

trackball
Device with a movable sphere on the upper part of its case; it directs the movements of the pointer on the screen.

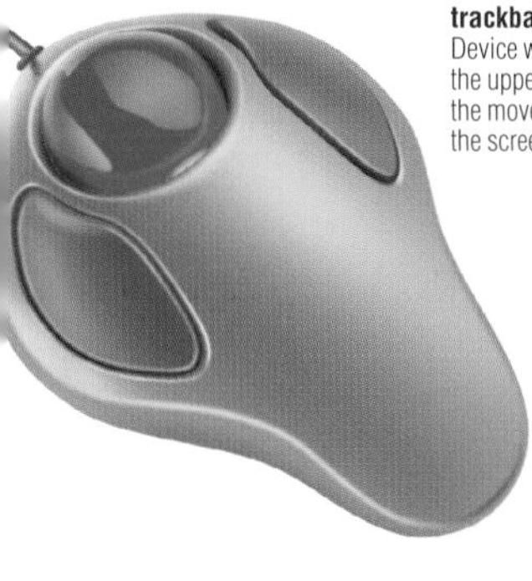

digitizing pad
Input device equipped with a touch screen on which one can write, draw or point using a stylus.

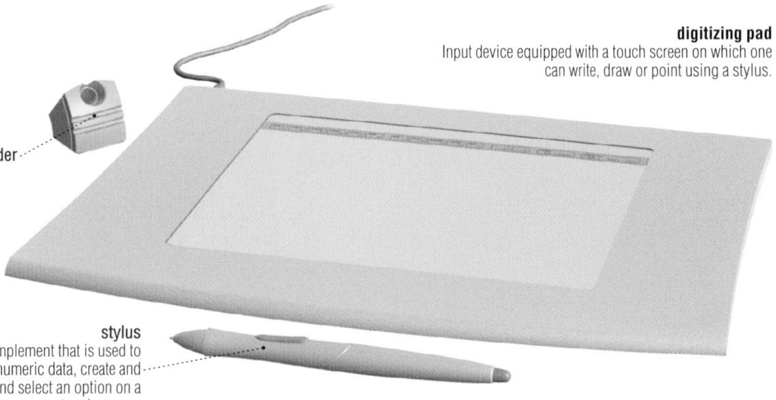

stylus
Pencillike implement that is used to enter alphanumeric data, create and retouch images and select an option on a touch screen.

CD/ROM player
Equipment that uses a laser beam to read data recorded on a compact disc.

Webcam
Miniature digital camera used to transmit video images in real time or for videoconferencing over the Internet.

cable
Flexible cable containing the conductors used to connect the Webcam to the computer.

lens
Optical system made up of a set of lenses fixed on a mount; it is used to transmit a filmed scene to a sensor.

microphone
Device that converts electric pulses into broadcast or recorded sounds.

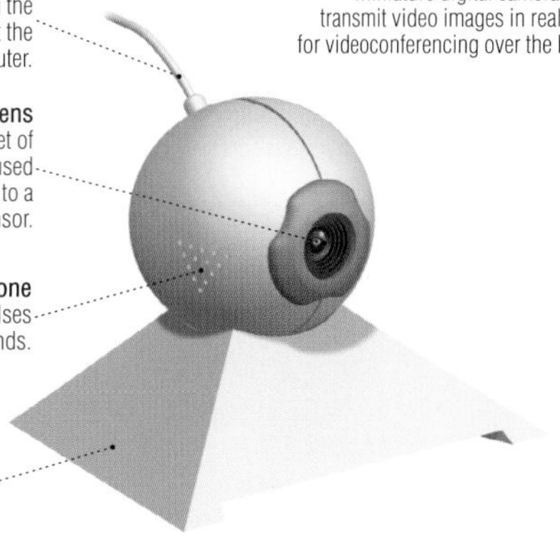

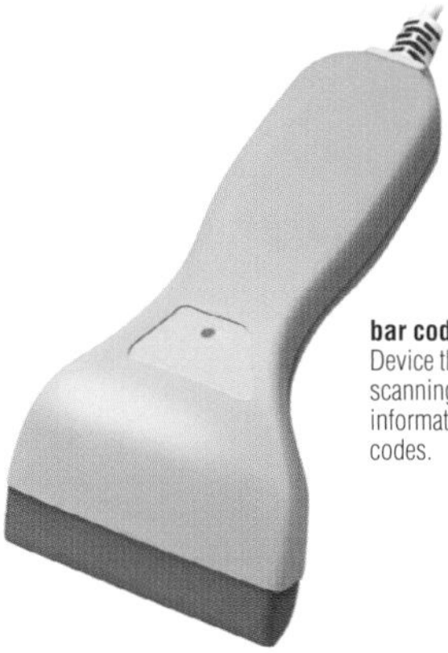

bar code reader
Device that uses an optical scanning process to decode information contained in bar codes.

digital camera
Camera that contains a sensor and a microprocessor rather than film; it records and stores images in digital form, which can then be viewed on a screen.

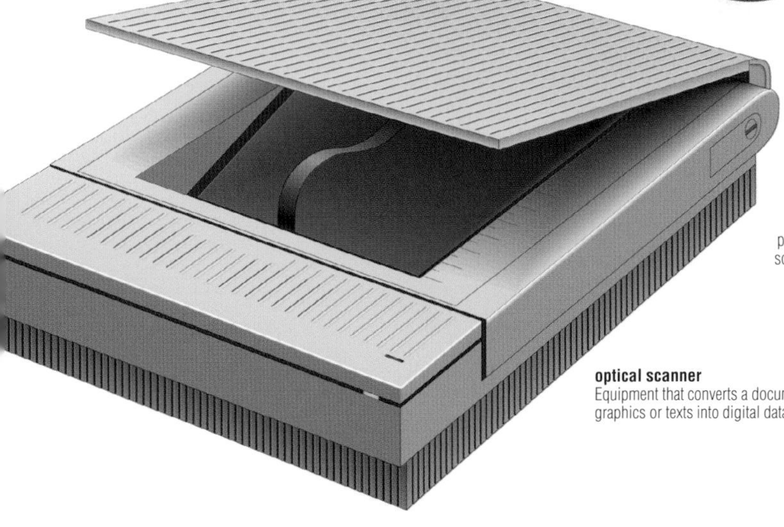

optical scanner
Equipment that converts a document's graphics or texts into digital data.

digital camcorder
Portable video camera in which the recording tape is replaced by a processor, which records and stores sounds and images in digital format.

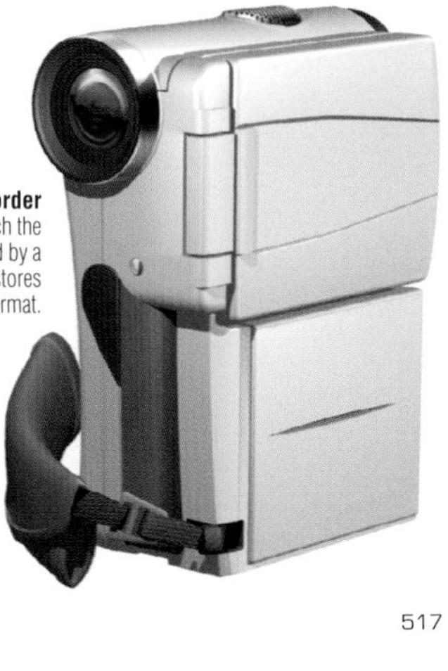

output devices

Electronic devices used to view or print the results of data processing done on a computer.

flat screen monitor
Thin screen that usually has a liquid crystal display or plasma display surface.

video monitor
Device with a cathode ray surface that displays computer-generated graphics and texts visually.

vertical control
Button that adjusts the height of the image.

horizontal control
Button that adjusts the width of the image.

centering control
Button that adjusts the position of the image on the screen.

contrast control
Button that adjusts the black and white part of an image.

power indicator
Signal light indicating that the screen is on.

power switch
Mechanical device that turns the monitor on or off.

brightness control
Button that increases or decreases the contrast between the light and dark parts of an image.

projector
Device that projects electronic images on a screen from sources such as computers, DVD players, camcorders and VCRs.

control panel
Panel housing the projector's operating buttons.

lens
Optical system made up of a set of lenses fixed on a mount; it is used to transmit enlarged video images on a projection screen.

remote sensor
Device that receives infrared signals emitted by a remote control; it activates certain projector functions from a distance.

power switch
Mechanical connection that turns the projector on or off.

connector panel
The jacks used to connect the projector to various video equipment such as DVD players, camcorders and VCRs.

computer connector
Connector that links the projector to a computer.

mouse port
Connector that links the projector to a mouse or to the mouse port of a computer.

inkjet printer
Printer with a movable printhead that sprays tiny droplets of ink onto paper to produce characters or images.

print cartridge light
Signal light that indicates a malfunction of the ink cartridge; usually it is installed incorrectly or empty.

paper feed button
Button used mainly to load or eject a sheet of paper, or to restart a suspended print job.

cancel button
Button used to interrupt the current print job.

paper feed light
Signal light that usually indicates a paper feed problem (such as a jam or empty paper tray).

front cover

power light
Signal light indicating that the printer is on.

power button
Button for turning the device on or off.

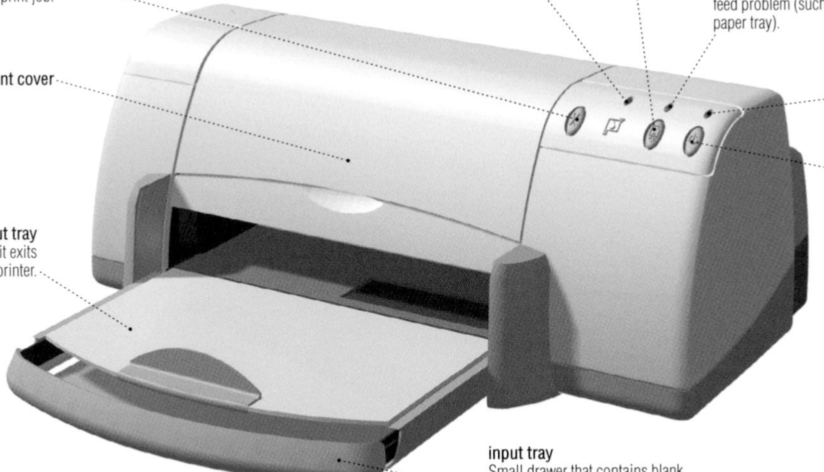

output tray
Tray that collects paper as it exits the printer.

input tray
Small drawer that contains blank sheets of standard-sized sheets of paper to be fed one at a time during printing.

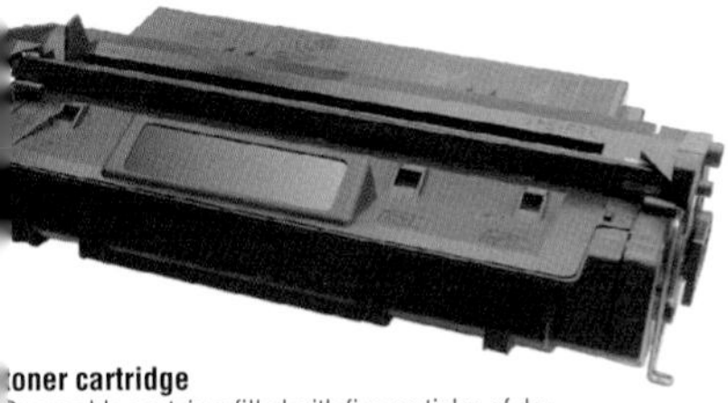

oner cartridge
emovable container filled with fine particles of dry nk; it is designed for a laser printer.

laser printer
Printer in which powdered ink in a cartridge is projected onto a rotating cylinder by laser beam and then fixed onto the paper using heated rollers.

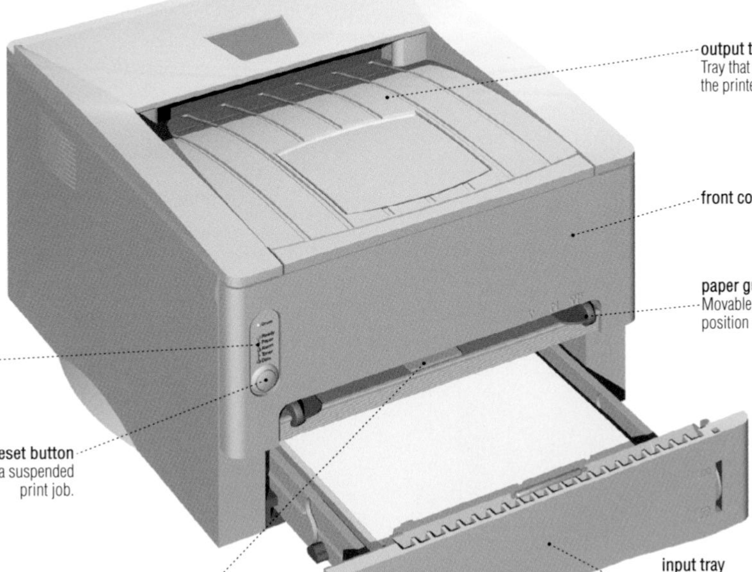

output tray
Tray that collects paper as it exits the printer.

front cover

paper guide
Movable device used to adjust the position of the paper sideways.

control lights
Signal lights indicating the operating state of the printer (standby, printing) or certain problems (paper outage, empty cartridge).

reset button
Button used to restart a suspended print job.

manual feed slot
Device used to load paper manually, one sheet at a time; it is used mainly for special or odd-sized paper.

input tray
Small drawer that contains blank sheets of standard-sized sheets of paper to be fed one at a time during printing.

output devices

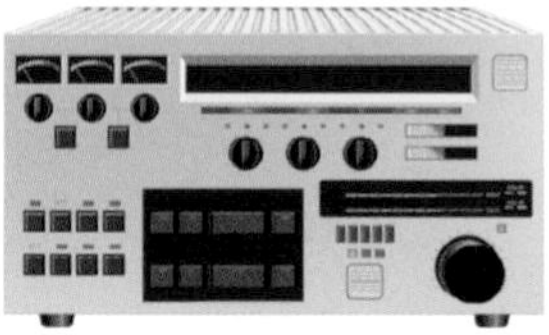

desktop video unit
Device used to produce video documents on a computer.

film recorder
Device used to transfer images displayed on a computer screen to film.

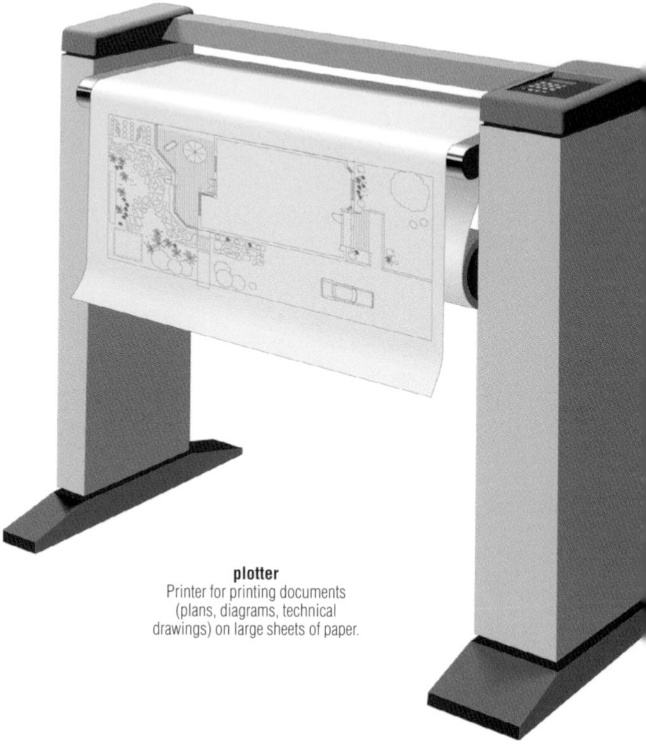

plotter
Printer for printing documents (plans, diagrams, technical drawings) on large sheets of paper.

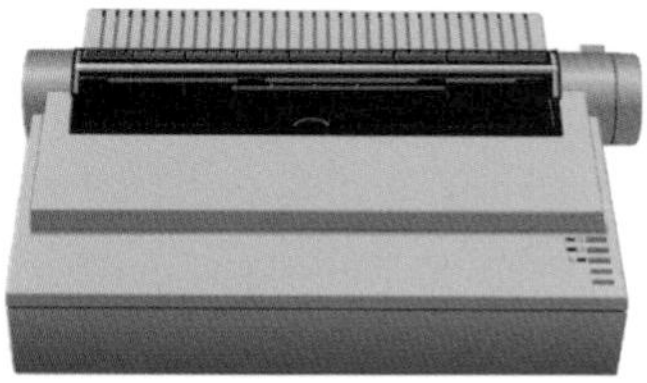

dot matrix printer
Printer with a movable printhead, which is made up of a set of small pins that strike an ink ribbon to print.

uninterruptible power supply (UPS)

Device used to regulate the power supply to the computer and its peripherals by limiting the effects of cuts, surges or dips in the electric circuit voltage.

telephone surge protection jacks
Jacks designed to protect communications equipment (such as telephones, fax machines and modems) from damage caused by too high voltage.

computer interface port
Connector attaching the UPS to the computer; software can then turn the computer off before the battery runs out completely.

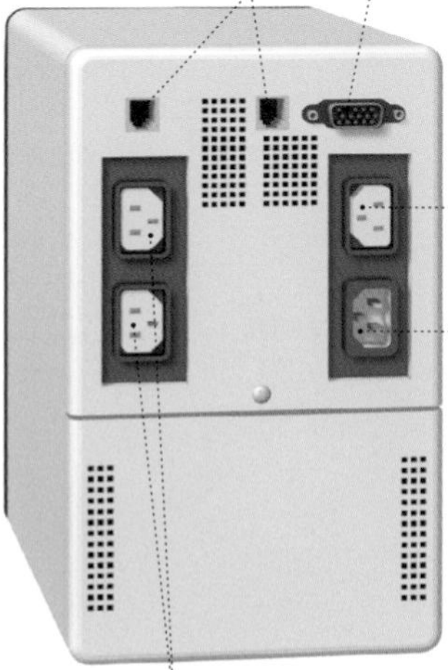

surge protection receptacle
Jack designed to protect equipment connected to it from damage caused by too high voltage.

input receptacle
Jack used to connect the UPS to the electric grid.

battery backup/surge protection receptacles
Antisurge jacks attached to a battery so that equipment connected to them have electric power in the event of a power outage.

control lights
Signal lights indicating the operating mode (main power or battery power) or certain problems (weak battery, overload).

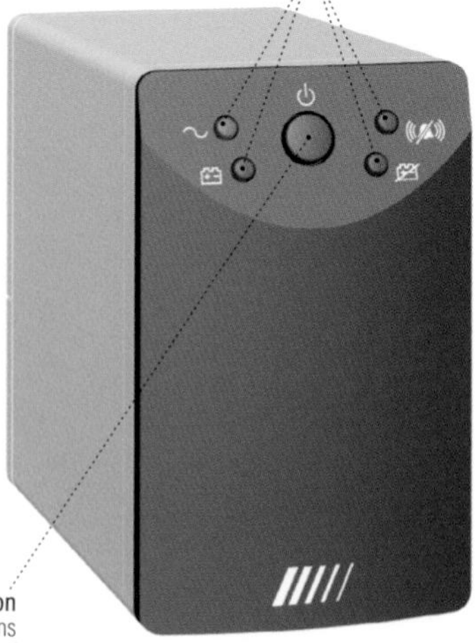

on/off/test button
Button that turns on the UPS and begins the procedure of checking the status of the battery.

data storage devices

Electronic devices used to record or save data on a magnetic or optical medium.

movable hard disk drive
and-alone device that is connected by cable to a
mputer; it is used to read and write data on a
novable hard disk.

disk eject button
Button used to retrieve a removable hard disk inserted in the drive.

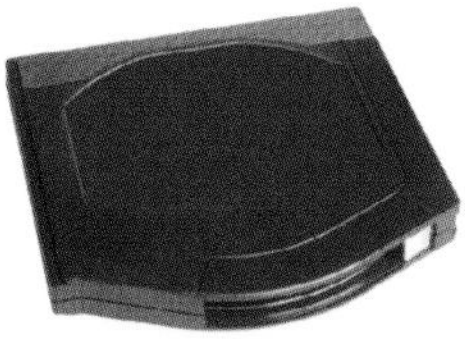

removable hard disk
Case that contains a set of hard magnetic disks for insertion into a removable hard disk drive.

hard disk drive
Device integrated into the computer that reads and writes data on the hard disk inside the case.

disk
Rigid magnetic medium that is mounted on a central axis; its surface is divided into tracks and sectors on which data are written.

disk motor
Device that converts the electric energy powering it into mechanical energy so that disks can rotate at several thousand revolutions per minute.

actuator arm
Movable arm bearing the read/write head; it moves the head across the surface of the disk.

actuator arm motor
Device that converts the electric energy powering it into mechanical energy to move the actuator arm according to the computer's instructions.

read/write head
Device used to extract stored data from a disk or to write new data on a disk.

xternal floppy disk drive
and-alone device that is linked
cable to a computer; it is used to
ad and write data on a diskette.

memory card reader
Independent device, linked to a computer via a cable or a USB connector, that reads and records data on a memory card.

USB flash drive
Small removable case containing a flash memory, which enables the user to transfer, transport, and store data.

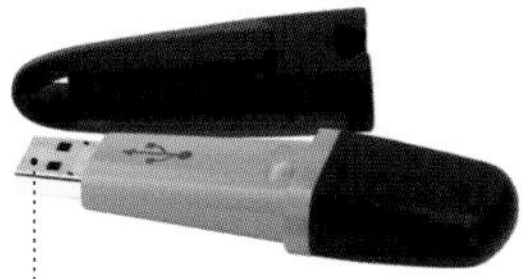

USB connector
Connector that links the flash drive to a computer's USB port.

diskette
Rigid case that contains a small flexible magnetic disk on which data can be written, erased and rewritten several times.

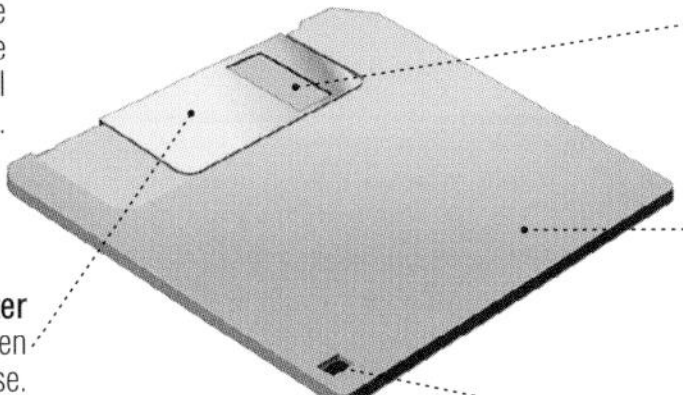

access window
Opening in the case where a disk passes in front of the read/write head of a floppy disk drive.

jacket

shutter
liding part that covers the read slot when the diskette is not in use.

protect tab
Sliding part that covers the write protection notch; it protects the diskette against any accidental changes to its contents.

assette drive
evice used to read and record data on a cassette recording
pe.

cassette
Rigid case that contains a recording tape on which data can be recorded.

DVD burner
Device used to record data on a writable or rewritable compact disc by means of laser engraving.

disc tray
Part in which a disc is inserted to be played back.

rewritable DVD disc
Digital recording medium on which data can be engraved and erased several times.

COMMUNICATIONS AND OFFICE AUTOMATION

communication devices

Electronic devices allowing computers to exchange data.

network interface card
Expansion card that connects a computer to a computer network.

network access point transceiver
Device that links a computer network linked by cable and a computer fitted with a wireless network interface card.

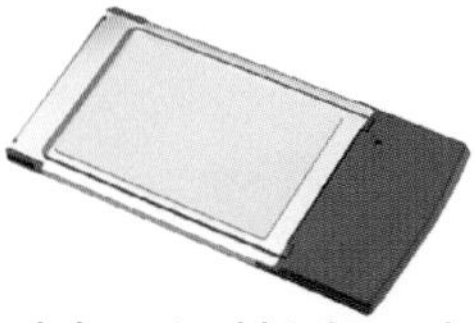

wireless network interface card
Expansion card with an integrated antenna; it links a computer to a network access point transceiver via radio waves.

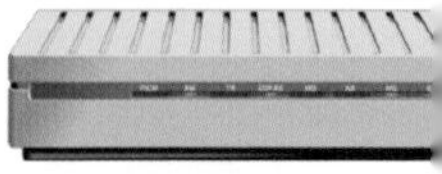

modem
Device that converts digital signals
analog signals so that computers c
communicate with each other ove
telephone lines.

examples of networks

Networks are classified mainly by size (local area or wide area network) and topography (including ring, bus and star).

ring network
Network in which all devices are connected to a ring; messages travel from one device to another in a set direction until they reach the intended receiver.

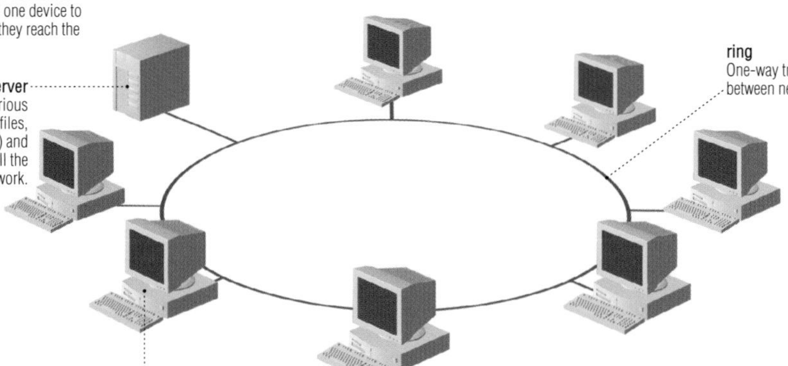

server
Computer that hosts various resources (including files, applications and databases) and places them at the disposal of all the devices connected to the network.

ring
One-way transmission of data between network components.

desktop computer
Small workstation or microcomputer designed for stationary use.

star netw
Network in which all devices
connected to a central unit (her
hub) in the shape of a s

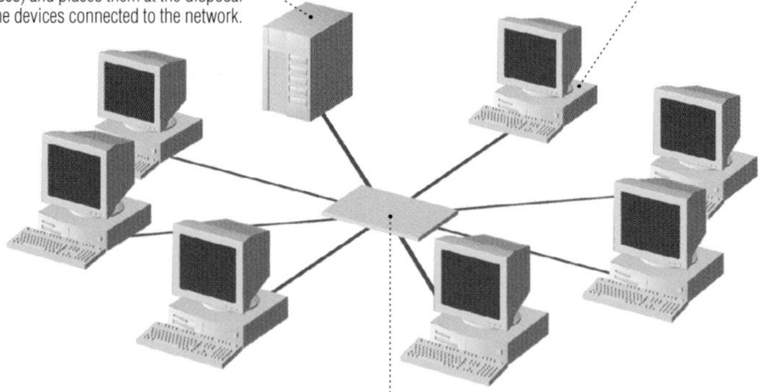

server
Computer that hosts various resources (including files, applications and databases) and places them at the disposal of all the devices connected to the network.

desktop computer
Small workstation or microcomputer designed for stationary use.

hub
Unit that receives all messages sent by the devices connected to it and redistributes them to all users.

bus network
Network in which all devices are connected to a common bus; the same message is sent to all of them but only one receives and registers it.

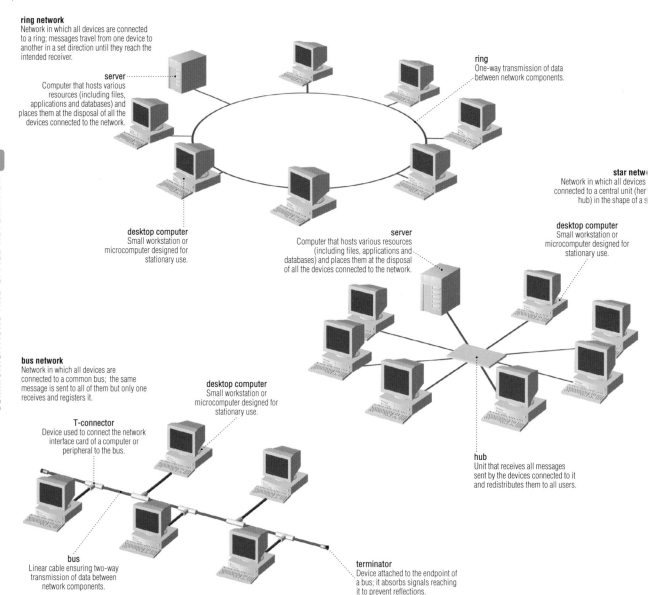

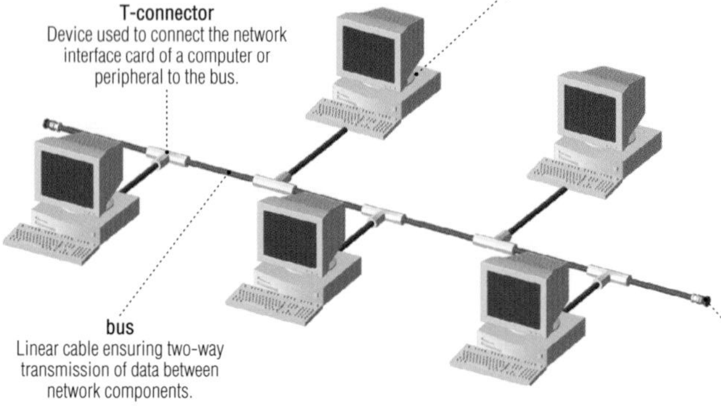

desktop computer
Small workstation or microcomputer designed for stationary use.

T-connector
Device used to connect the network interface card of a computer or peripheral to the bus.

bus
Linear cable ensuring two-way transmission of data between network components.

terminator
Device attached to the endpoint of a bus; it absorbs signals reaching it to prevent reflections.

computer network

All the computers and peripherals connected to one another, facilitating sharing of data and resources.

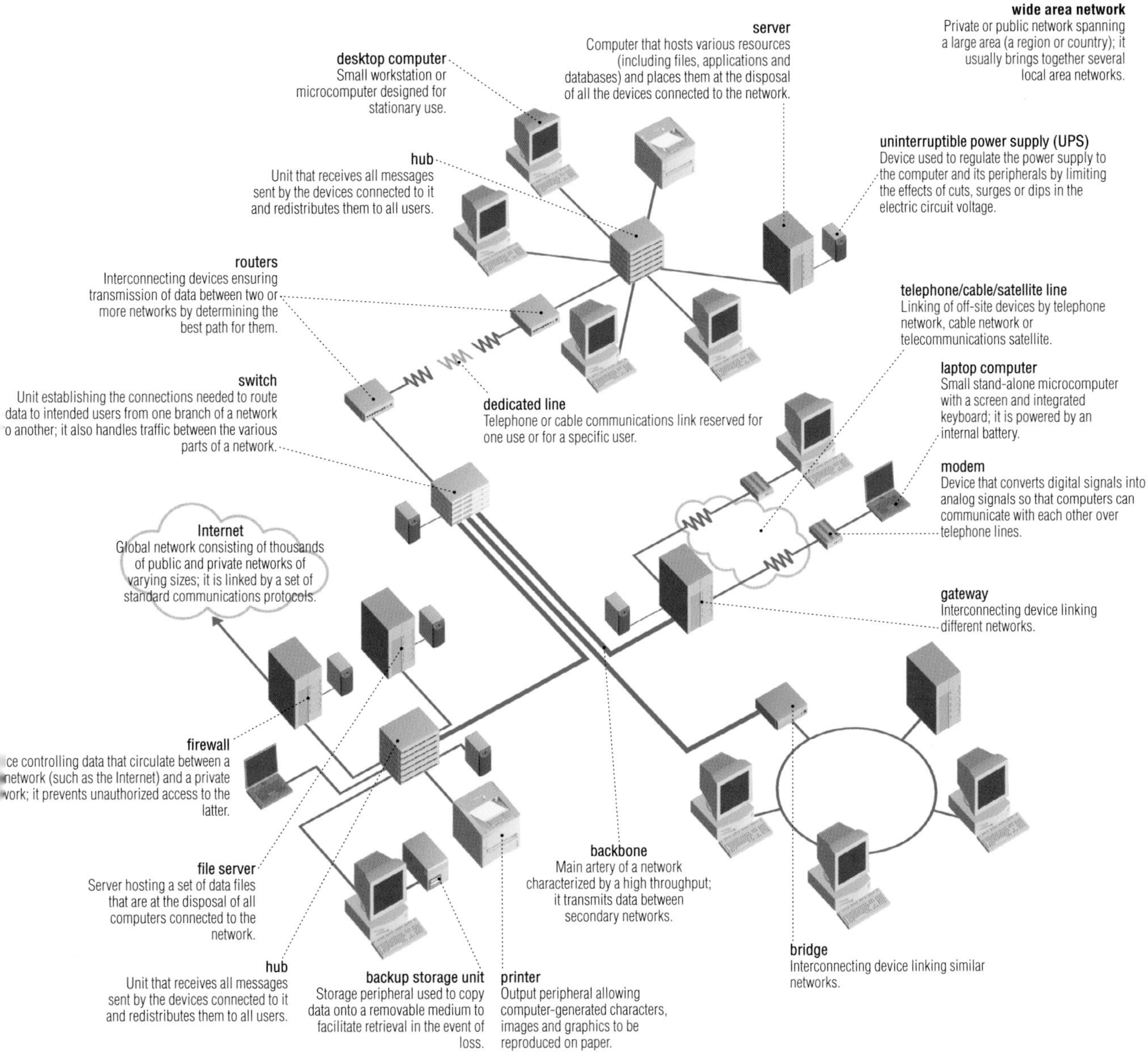
wide area network
Private or public network spanning a large area (a region or country); it usually brings together several local area networks.
server
Computer that hosts various resources (including files, applications and databases) and places them at the disposal of all the devices connected to the network.
desktop computer
Small workstation or microcomputer designed for stationary use.
hub
Unit that receives all messages sent by the devices connected to it and redistributes them to all users.
uninterruptible power supply (UPS)
Device used to regulate the power supply to the computer and its peripherals by limiting the effects of cuts, surges or dips in the electric circuit voltage.
routers
Interconnecting devices ensuring transmission of data between two or more networks by determining the best path for them.
telephone/cable/satellite line
Linking of off-site devices by telephone network, cable network or telecommunications satellite.
laptop computer
Small stand-alone microcomputer with a screen and integrated keyboard; it is powered by an internal battery.
switch
Unit establishing the connections needed to route data to intended users from one branch of a network o another; it also handles traffic between the various parts of a network.
dedicated line
Telephone or cable communications link reserved for one use or for a specific user.
modem
Device that converts digital signals into analog signals so that computers can communicate with each other over telephone lines.
Internet
Global network consisting of thousands of public and private networks of varying sizes; it is linked by a set of standard communications protocols.
gateway
Interconnecting device linking different networks.
firewall
ce controlling data that circulate between a network (such as the Internet) and a private work; it prevents unauthorized access to the latter.
file server
Server hosting a set of data files that are at the disposal of all computers connected to the network.
backbone
Main artery of a network characterized by a high throughput; it transmits data between secondary networks.
bridge
Interconnecting device linking similar networks.
hub
Unit that receives all messages sent by the devices connected to it and redistributes them to all users.
backup storage unit
Storage peripheral used to copy data onto a removable medium to facilitate retrieval in the event of loss.
printer
Output peripheral allowing computer-generated characters, images and graphics to be reproduced on paper.

cables

Protective sheaths covering one or several usually insulated wires; they transmit data between network components.

coaxial cable

Cable that holds two insulated concentric conductors; it transmits signals in the form of electric pulses without loss of quality.

twisted-pair cable

Cable that contains one or several pairs of twin wires twisted around one another; it transmits signals in the form of electric pulses.

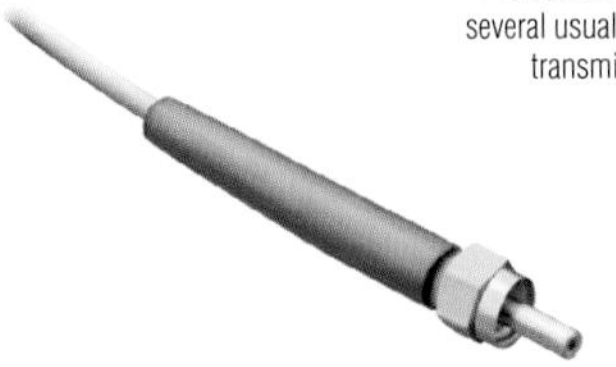

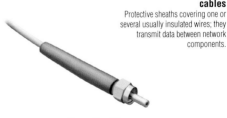

fiber optic cable

Cable that holds thin glass filaments or optical fibers that transmit signals in the form of light pulses at high speed.

Internet

Global network consisting of thousands of public and private networks of varying sizes; it is linked by a set of standard communications protocols.

uniform resource locator (URL)
All the data allowing access to a resource hosted by an Internet server (e.g., a Web page).

communication protocol
Part of the URL address specifying the language used to exchange data. The HTTP protocol, which allows the transfer of Web pages, is the best known.

domain name
Part of the URL address specifically designating the host. It must be registered with a domain name registrar.

file format
Group of letters specifying the way in which file data is encoded. For example, Web documents are generally written in HTML format.

http://www.un.org/aboutun/index.html

double virgule

second-level domain
Part of the domain name that designates the server name.

file
Part of the URL address specifying the name of the unit of data (file) corresponding to the chosen resource.

server
Part of the URL address identifying the type of server. The best known is the Web server (www), which, as its name implies, hosts Web sites.

top-level domain
Part of the domain name that designates the country of origin or the category of organization (including government agency, commercial business and educational institution).

directory
Part of the URL address showing where the resource is located on the server.

browser
Software used to search and consult Internet sites.

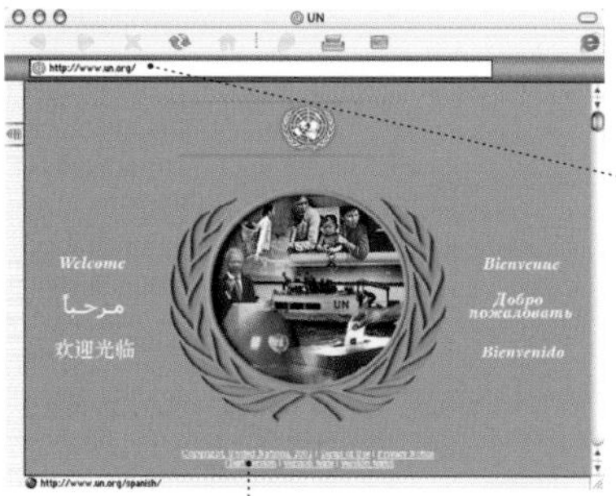

hyperlinks
Elements of a Web page (words, images or icons) that, when activated, allow direct access to another linked page.

microwave relay station
Facility that receives and amplifies signals transmitted in the form of microwaves and relays them to another receiver.

uniform resource locator (URL)
All the data allowing access to a resource hosted by an Internet server (e.g., a Web page).

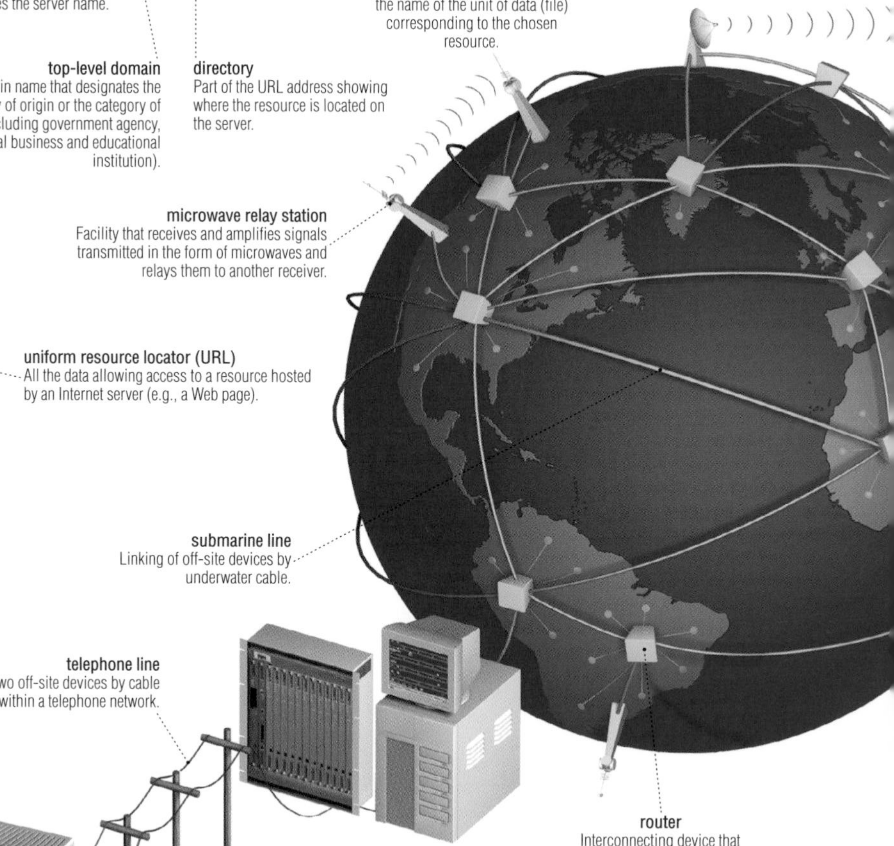

submarine line
Linking of off-site devices by underwater cable.

telephone line
Linking of two off-site devices by cable within a telephone network.

e-mail software
Software used to format, send and receive messages over the Internet.

router
Interconnecting device that transmits data between two or more networks by determining the best path for them.

dedicated line
Telephone or cable communications link reserved for one use or for a specific user.

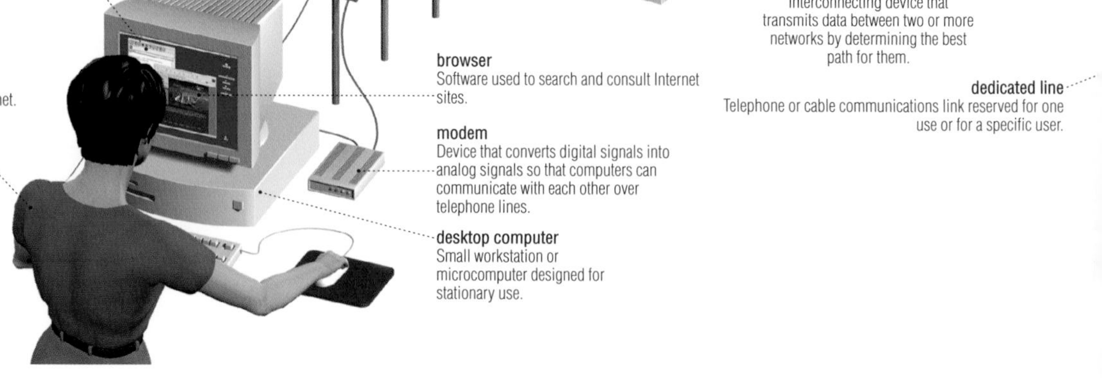

Internet user
Person using the Internet.

browser
Software used to search and consult Internet sites.

modem
Device that converts digital signals into analog signals so that computers can communicate with each other over telephone lines.

desktop computer
Small workstation or microcomputer designed for stationary use.

Internet uses

A number of user types use Internet tools and resources to communicate, find information and entertainment, make purchases and manage funds.

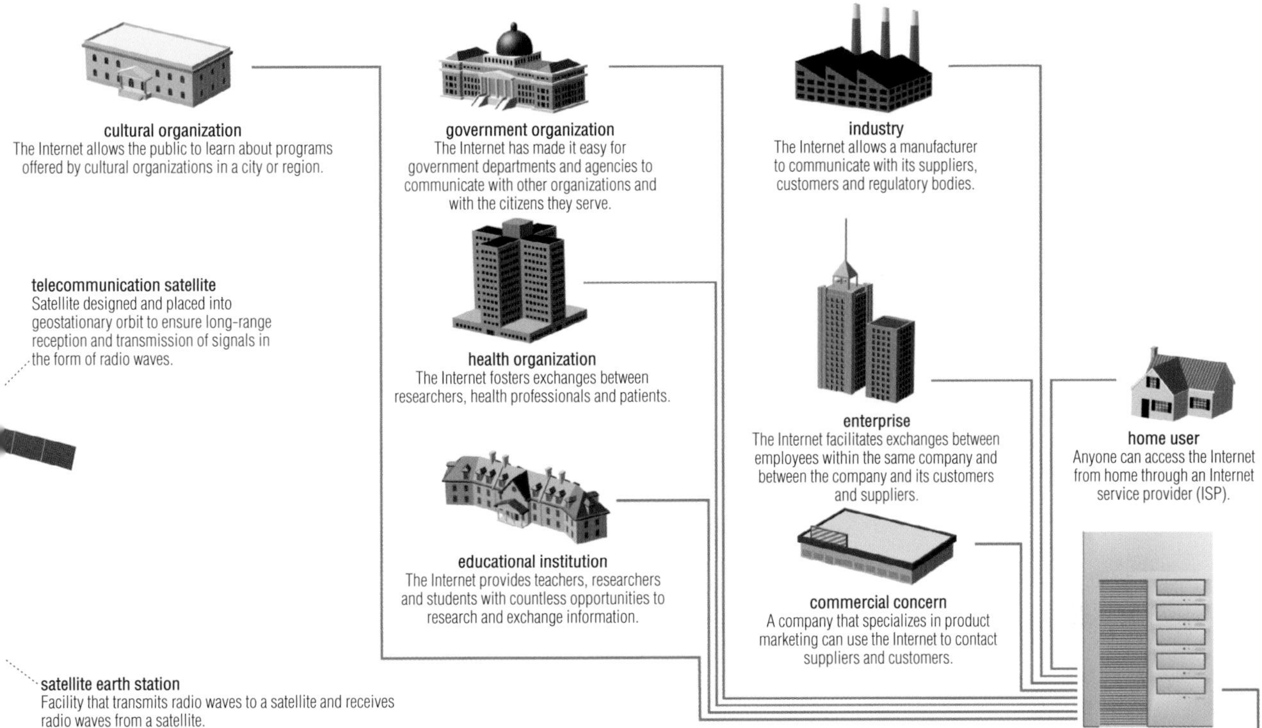

cultural organization
The Internet allows the public to learn about programs offered by cultural organizations in a city or region.

government organization
The Internet has made it easy for government departments and agencies to communicate with other organizations and with the citizens they serve.

industry
The Internet allows a manufacturer to communicate with its suppliers, customers and regulatory bodies.

telecommunication satellite
Satellite designed and placed into geostationary orbit to ensure long-range reception and transmission of signals in the form of radio waves.

health organization
The Internet fosters exchanges between researchers, health professionals and patients.

enterprise
The Internet facilitates exchanges between employees within the same company and between the company and its customers and suppliers.

home user
Anyone can access the Internet from home through an Internet service provider (ISP).

educational institution
The Internet provides teachers, researchers and students with countless opportunities to research and exchange information.

commercial concern
A company that specializes in product marketing can use the Internet to contact suppliers and customers.

satellite earth station
Facility that transmits radio waves to a satellite and receives radio waves from a satellite.

server
Computer that hosts various resources (including files, applications and databases) and places them at the disposal of all the devices connected to the network.

Internet service provider
ompany that is permanently connected to the Internet; it provides individuals and organizations with access to various Internet services.

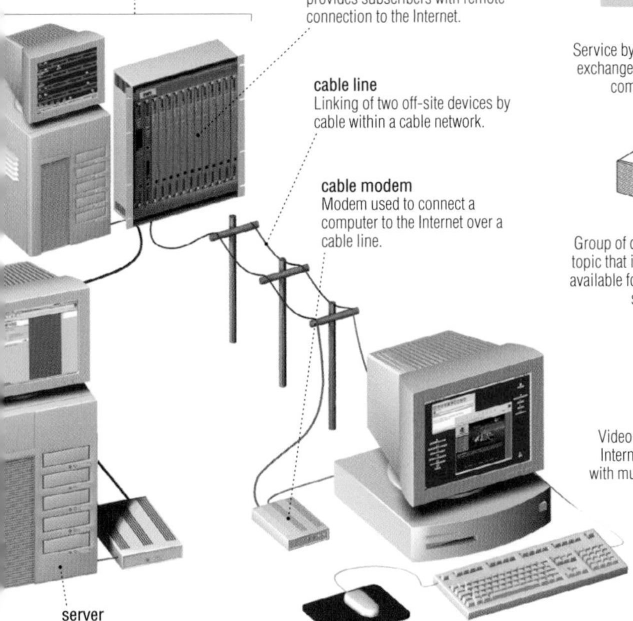

access server
Communications server that provides subscribers with remote connection to the Internet.

cable line
Linking of two off-site devices by cable within a cable network.

cable modem
Modem used to connect a computer to the Internet over a cable line.

server
Computer that hosts various resources (including files, applications and databases) and places them at the disposal of all the devices connected to the network.

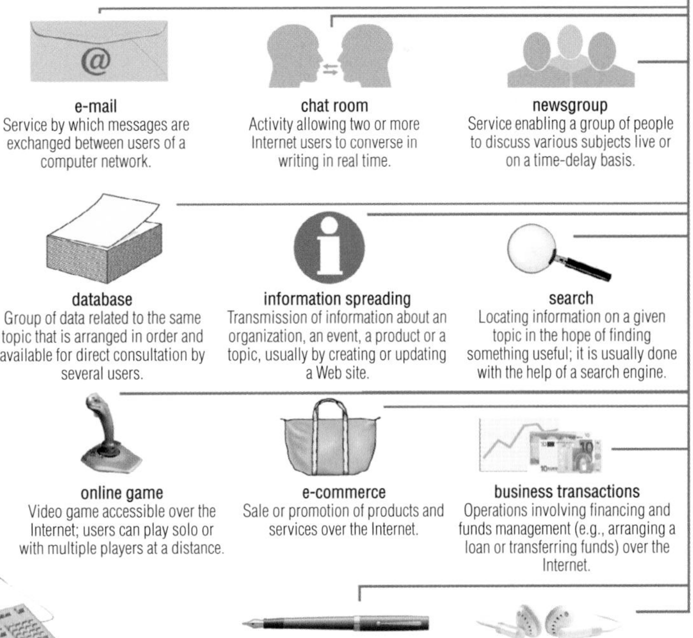

e-mail
Service by which messages are exchanged between users of a computer network.

chat room
Activity allowing two or more Internet users to converse in writing in real time.

newsgroup
Service enabling a group of people to discuss various subjects live or on a time-delay basis.

database
Group of data related to the same topic that is arranged in order and available for direct consultation by several users.

information spreading
Transmission of information about an organization, an event, a product or a topic, usually by creating or updating a Web site.

search
Locating information on a given topic in the hope of finding something useful; it is usually done with the help of a search engine.

online game
Video game accessible over the Internet; users can play solo or with multiple players at a distance.

e-commerce
Sale or promotion of products and services over the Internet.

business transactions
Operations involving financing and funds management (e.g., arranging a loan or transferring funds) over the Internet.

blog
Web site in the form of a personal journal in which a person shares opinions or impressions in notes or short articles.

podcasting
Service for automatic downloading of audio or video documents to a digital portable audio player to be listened to later.

laptop computer

Small stand-alone microcomputer with a screen and integrated keyboard; it is powered by an internal battery.

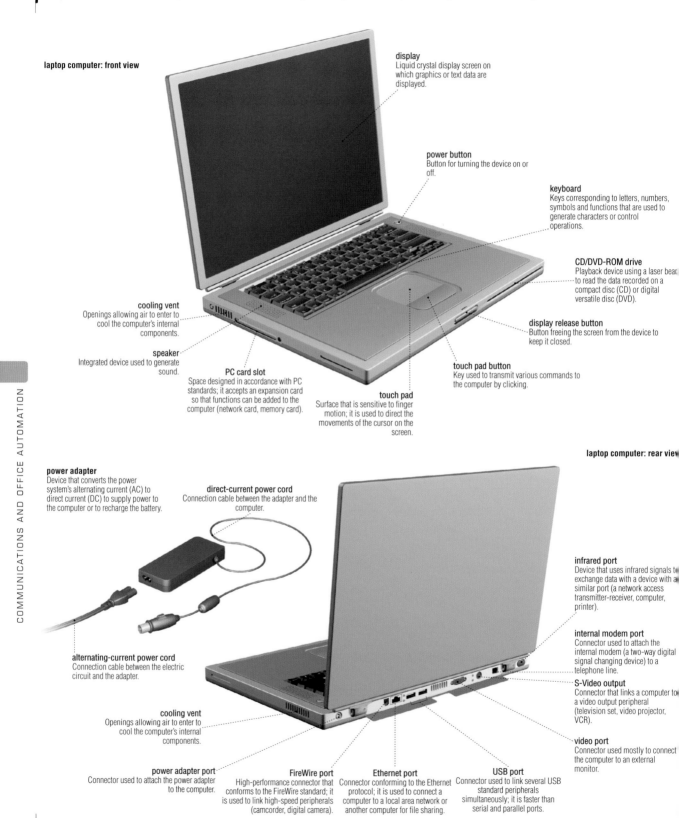

laptop computer: front view

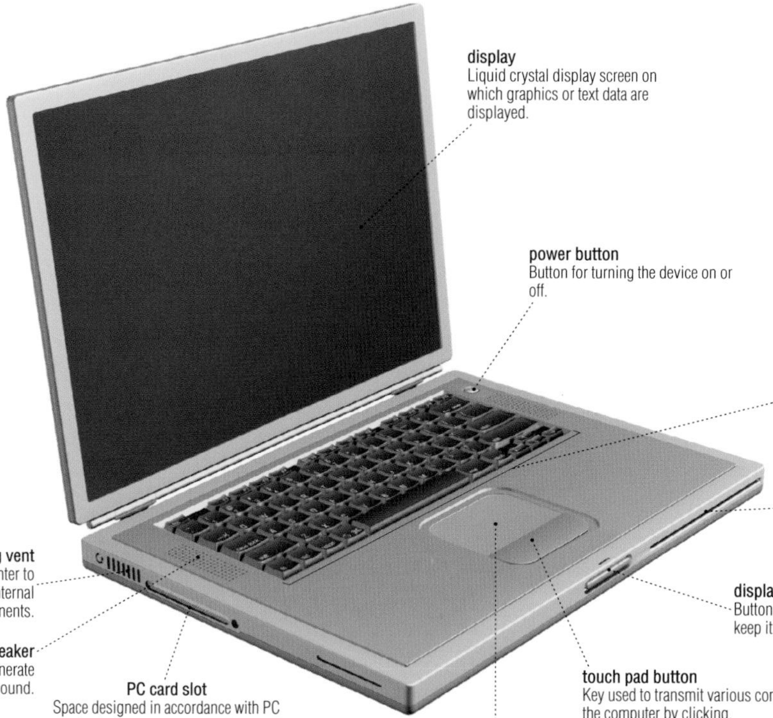

display
Liquid crystal display screen on which graphics or text data are displayed.

power button
Button for turning the device on or off.

keyboard
Keys corresponding to letters, numbers, symbols and functions that are used to generate characters or control operations.

CD/DVD-ROM drive
Playback device using a laser bear to read the data recorded on a compact disc (CD) or digital versatile disc (DVD).

display release button
Button freeing the screen from the device to keep it closed.

cooling vent
Openings allowing air to enter to cool the computer's internal components.

speaker
Integrated device used to generate sound.

PC card slot
Space designed in accordance with PC standards; it accepts an expansion card so that functions can be added to the computer (network card, memory card).

touch pad
Surface that is sensitive to finger motion; it is used to direct the movements of the cursor on the screen.

touch pad button
Key used to transmit various commands to the computer by clicking.

laptop computer: rear vie

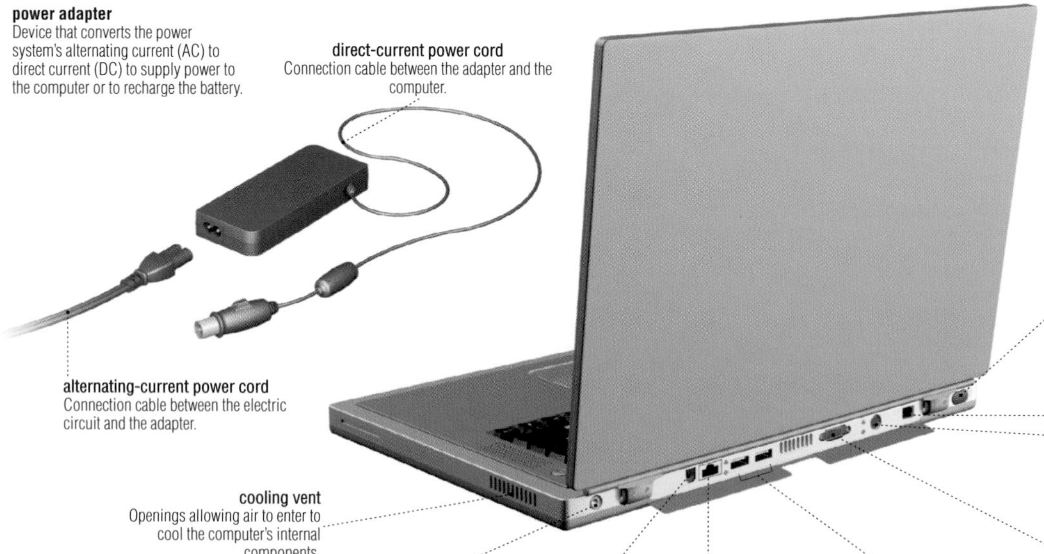

power adapter
Device that converts the power system's alternating current (AC) to direct current (DC) to supply power to the computer or to recharge the battery.

direct-current power cord
Connection cable between the adapter and the computer.

alternating-current power cord
Connection cable between the electric circuit and the adapter.

cooling vent
Openings allowing air to enter to cool the computer's internal components.

power adapter port
Connector used to attach the power adapter to the computer.

FireWire port
High-performance connector that conforms to the FireWire standard; it is used to link high-speed peripherals (camcorder, digital camera).

Ethernet port
Connector conforming to the Ethernet protocol; it is used to connect a computer to a local area network or another computer for file sharing.

USB port
Connector used to link several USB standard peripherals simultaneously; it is faster than serial and parallel ports.

infrared port
Device that uses infrared signals t exchange data with a device with a similar port (a network access transmitter-receiver, computer, printer).

internal modem port
Connector used to attach the internal modem (a two-way digital signal changing device) to a telephone line.

S-Video output
Connector that links a computer t a video output peripheral (television set, video projector, VCR).

video port
Connector used mostly to connect the computer to an external monitor.

laptop computer

laptop computer briefcase
Small briefcase with compartments; it carries a laptop computer and its accessories as well as documents.
computer compartment
document compartment
shoulder strap

electronic book

Small portable computer in the shape of a book; it is used to download, store and read electronic books.

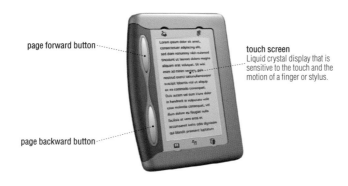

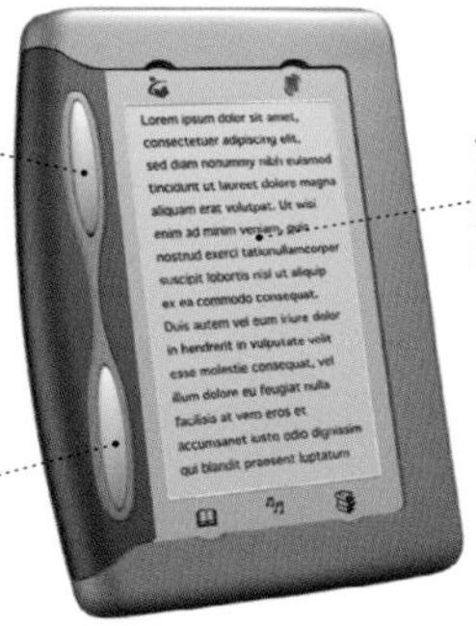
page forward button
touch screen
Liquid crystal display that is sensitive to the touch and the motion of a finger or stylus.
page backward button

handheld computer

Small portable computer with a miniature operating system; it is used mostly for personal management tasks (agenda, address book).

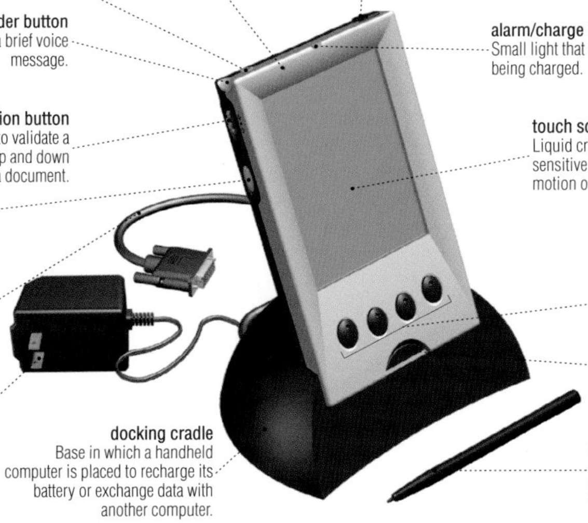
audio input/output jack
Connector used to transfer audio signals between the computer and a sound recording or reproduction device such as a microphone or headphones.
microphone
Device that converts electric pulses into broadcast or recorded sounds.
infrared port
Device that uses infrared signals to exchange data with a device with a similar port (a network access transmitter-receiver, computer, printer).
voice recorder button
Key used to record a brief voice message.
alarm/charge indicator light
Small light that signals an alarm or indicates that a battery is being charged.
dial/action button
Thumb wheel used to validate a selection or to scroll up and down through a document.
touch screen
Liquid crystal display that is sensitive to the touch and the motion of a finger or stylus.
exit button
Key used to exit an application.
application launch buttons
Keys used to directly access available applications such as word processing and Internet browsing.
sync cable
Cable that connects the docking cradle to the computer; it allows data to be exchanged between the two devices.
power and backlight button
Key used to turn a computer on or off; it also illuminates the screen in poor lighting conditions.
power plug
docking cradle
Base in which a handheld computer is placed to recharge its battery or exchange data with another computer.
stylus
Pencillike implement used to enter data or to select an option on a touch screen.

stationery

Equipment, instruments and accessories needed to carry out office tasks.

electronic typewriter
Equipment with a keyboard that is used to produce typewritten documents; it has certain word processing functions and an integrated memory.

paper support
Folding part used to keep the paper in a vertical position.

top plate

paper bail release lever
Device used to raise and lower the paper bail.

printing unit
Movable device with raised characters, which strike an inked ribbon to print on paper.

paper bail
Part that holds the paper against the platen.

pitch scale
Graduated scale that shows the different spacing available; it is measured in number of characters per unit of length.

paper release lever
Device that releases the pressure of the platen on the paper so that the paper can be cleared or moved.

platen
Rubber roller over which paper passes during printing.

variable spacer
Thumb wheel that controls the rotation of the platen so the paper can be moved up or down.

margin release
Key used to print characters outside the margin limits.

EXEGI MONUMENTUM AERE PERENIUS

tabulator
Key that moves the printing unit or cursor to the next tab stop.

indent
Key used to move the left margin temporarily to indent a line or paragraph.

character correction
Key used to erase the character next to the printing unit or cursor.

decimal tab
Key that aligns numbers columns at a preset decimal tab stop.

half indexing
Key used to automatically move the pa up and down.

margin control
Key used to set the left and right margins.

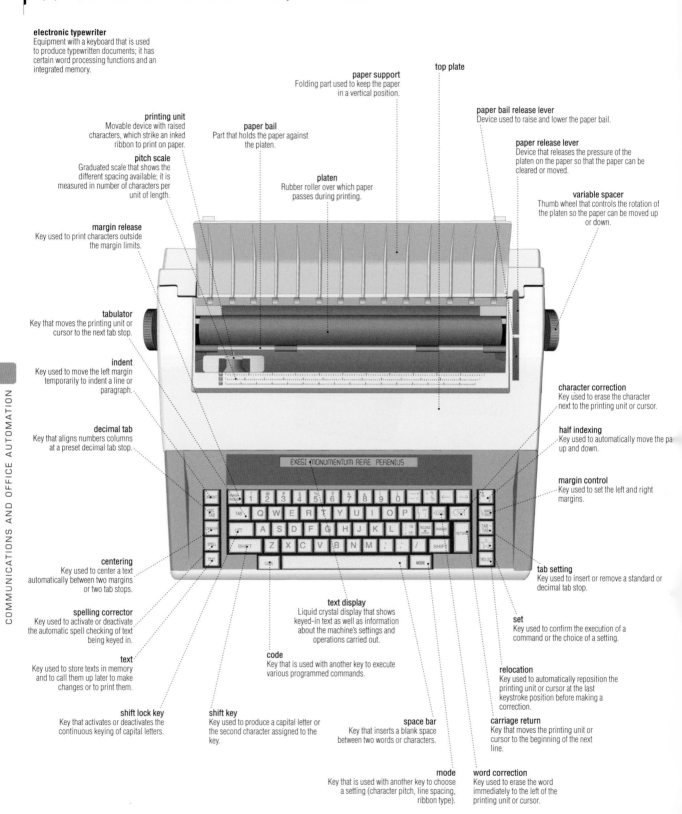

centering
Key used to center a text automatically between two margins or two tab stops.

tab setting
Key used to insert or remove a standard or decimal tab stop.

text display
Liquid crystal display that shows keyed-in text as well as information about the machine's settings and operations carried out.

spelling corrector
Key used to activate or deactivate the automatic spell checking of text being keyed in.

set
Key used to confirm the execution of a command or the choice of a setting.

text
Key used to store texts in memory and to call them up later to make changes or to print them.

code
Key that is used with another key to execute various programmed commands.

relocation
Key used to automatically reposition the printing unit or cursor at the last keystroke position before making a correction.

shift lock key
Key that activates or deactivates the continuous keying of capital letters.

shift key
Key used to produce a capital letter or the second character assigned to the key.

space bar
Key that inserts a blank space between two words or characters.

carriage return
Key that moves the printing unit or cursor to the beginning of the next line.

mode
Key that is used with another key to choose a setting (character pitch, line spacing, ribbon type).

word correction
Key used to erase the word immediately to the left of the printing unit or cursor.

pocket calculator
Small self-powered electronic instrument used to automatically make numerical calculations.

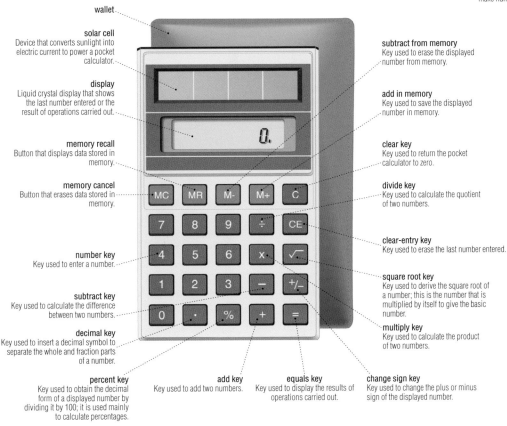

wallet

solar cell
Device that converts sunlight into electric current to power a pocket calculator.

display
Liquid crystal display that shows the last number entered or the result of operations carried out.

memory recall
Button that displays data stored in memory.

memory cancel
Button that erases data stored in memory.

number key
Key used to enter a number.

subtract key
Key used to calculate the difference between two numbers.

decimal key
Key used to insert a decimal symbol to separate the whole and fraction parts of a number.

percent key
Key used to obtain the decimal form of a displayed number by dividing it by 100; it is used mainly to calculate percentages.

add key
Key used to add two numbers.

equals key
Key used to display the results of operations carried out.

change sign key
Key used to change the plus or minus sign of the displayed number.

subtract from memory
Key used to erase the displayed number from memory.

add in memory
Key used to save the displayed number in memory.

clear key
Key used to return the pocket calculator to zero.

divide key
Key used to calculate the quotient of two numbers.

clear-entry key
Key used to erase the last number entered.

square root key
Key used to derive the square root of a number; this is the number that is multiplied by itself to give the basic number.

multiply key
Key used to calculate the product of two numbers.

scientific calculator
Calculator designed to execute mathematical operations specific to science and technology.

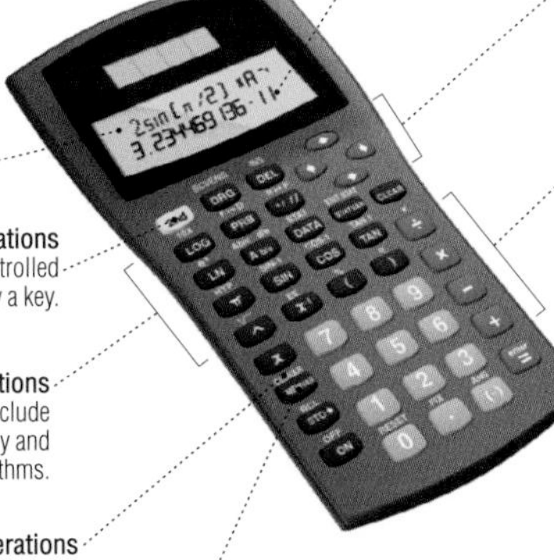

result line
Part of the screen that shows the solution to the problem.

cursor movement keys
Keys used to move the cursor around the screen.

basic operations
Basic calculations include adding, subtracting, multiplying and dividing.

entries line
Part of the screen that shows the problem to be solved.

ccess to the second level of operations
used to select a second function controlled by a key.

specific operations
Specialized calculations include square root, trigonometry and logarithms.

second level of operations
All the supplementary functions listed above the keys and accessible using the access to the second level of operations.

first level of operations
All the operations directly controlled by the scientific calculator keys.

printing calculator
Office calculator with an integrated printer; it is used mainly in business and administration.

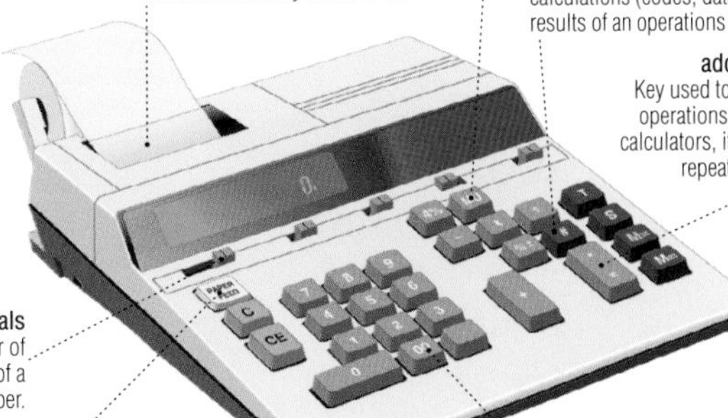

multiple use key
Key that facilitates certain financial calculations (margin, selling price, costs).

printer
Device that makes a hard copy of data transmitted by the calculator.

non-add/subtotal
Key used to print numbers other than calculations (codes, dates) or to obtain the results of an operations subset.

add/equals key
Key used to display the results of operations carried out; on some calculators, it can also be used to do repeated calculations.

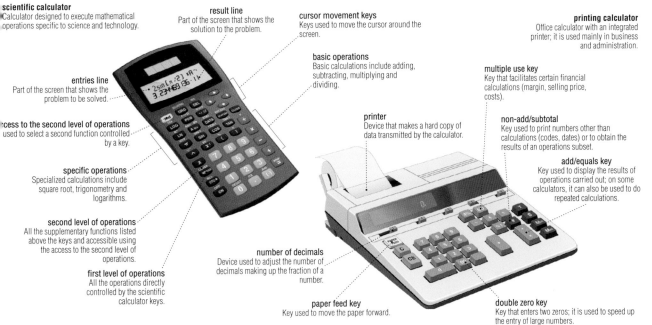

number of decimals
Device used to adjust the number of decimals making up the fraction of a number.

paper feed key
Key used to move the paper forward.

double zero key
Key that enters two zeros; it is used to speed up the entry of large numbers.

stationery

for time management

tear-off calendar
Pad of tear-off sheets printed with the day and date; it is used to jot down appointments and things to do.

calendar pad
Sheets of paper printed with the day and date and on a ring base; it is used to jot down appointments and things to do.

personal digital assistant
Small pocket computer that stores in memory and manages a variety of information such as addresses, telephone numbers and appointments.

display
Liquid crystal display screen on which graphics or text data are displayed.

alphabetical keypad
Keys corresponding to letters, symbols and functions used to generate characters or control operations.

numeric keypad
Keys corresponding to numbers, mathematical operators and functions that are placed in a specific order to speed up numeric data entry.

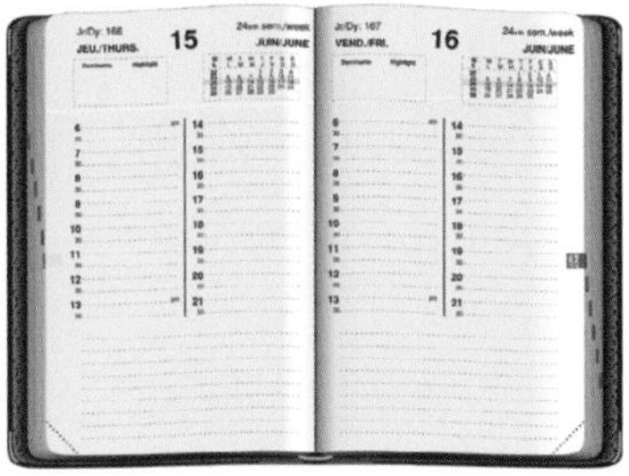

appointment book
Notebook that is printed with the day and date; it is used to jot down appointments and things to do.

self-stick note
Small piece of paper with a sticky strip on the back for temporary attachment to a surface.

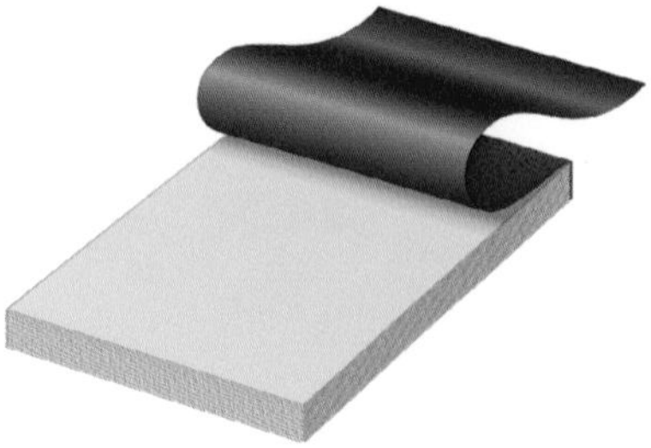

memo pad
Set of tear-off sheets of paper used mainly for taking notes.

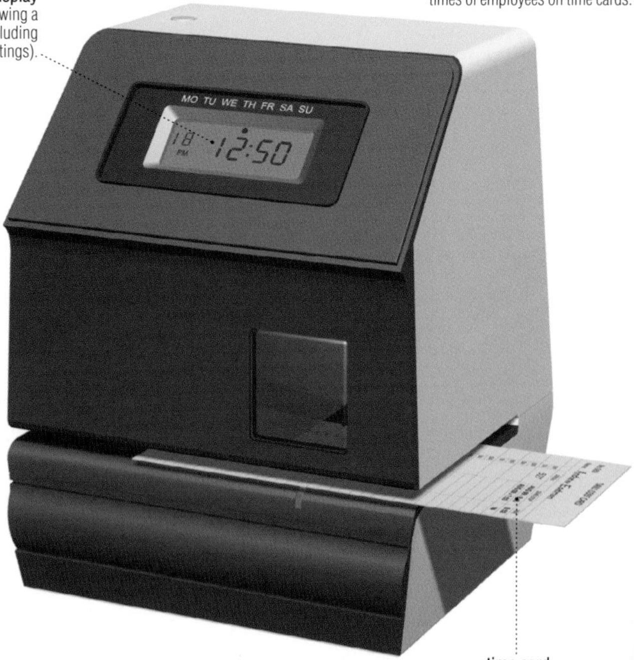

time clock
Device used to print the arrival and departure times of employees on time cards.

display
Liquid crystal display showing a variety of information (including date, hour and settings).

time card
Card on which an employee's arrival and departure times are listed so that worked time can be precisely calculated.

for correspondence

padded envelope
Envelope that is lined with bubble wrap to protect the contents from humidity and impact damage.

self-sealing flap
Flap coated with an adhesive substance; it seals an envelope on contact.

air bubbles
Small air pockets that form a protective cushion around the contents of an envelope.

letter opener
Small knife used to open envelopes and cut sheets of paper.

numbering machine
Device consisting of movable strips embossed with a series of digits; it is used to print numbers.

dater
Device consisting of movable strips embossed with a series of digits and letters; it is used to print the date.

letter scale
Scale used to weigh a letter or parcel.

steno book
Spiral-bound sheets of lined paper; these books were originally used by stenographers to take dictation.

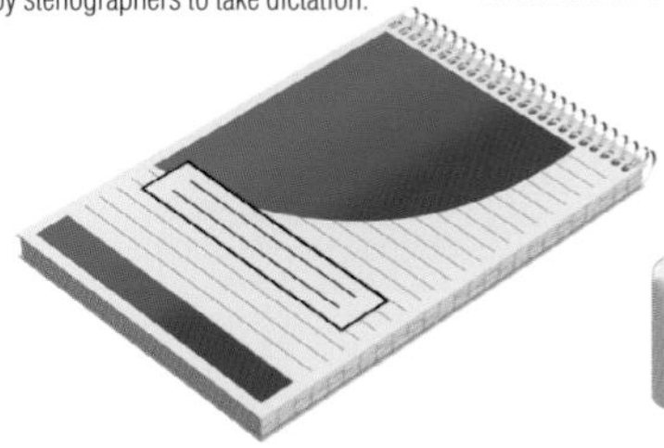

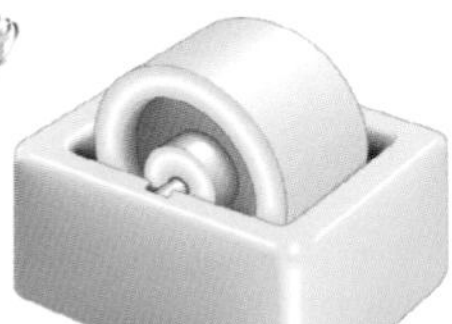

moistener
Device used to moisten postage stamps and labels.

finger tip
Rubber sheath to cover the finger; it is used mainly to turn pages more easily or to sort papers or banknotes more quickly.

stamp rack
Rack used to hold such items as rubber stamps for dating and numbering.

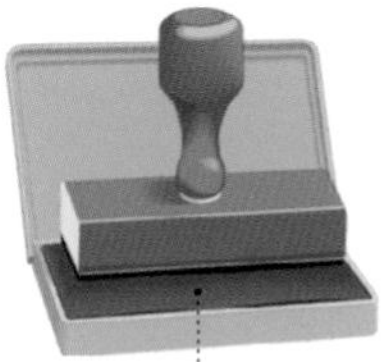

stamp pad
Ink-saturated pad on which a rubber stamp is moistened prior to stamping.

rubber stamp
Device consisting of an embossed rubber strip that is inked to print a stamp on an object or document.

signature book
Register made up of sheets of blotting paper; documents that require a manager's signature are placed in it.

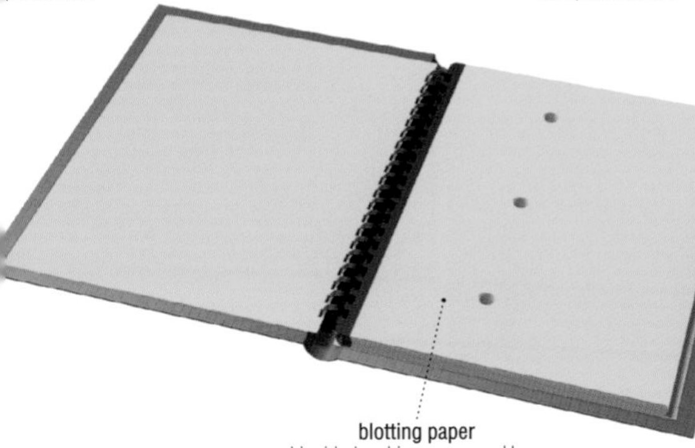

blotting paper
Liquid-absorbing paper used here to remove excess ink from newly signed documents.

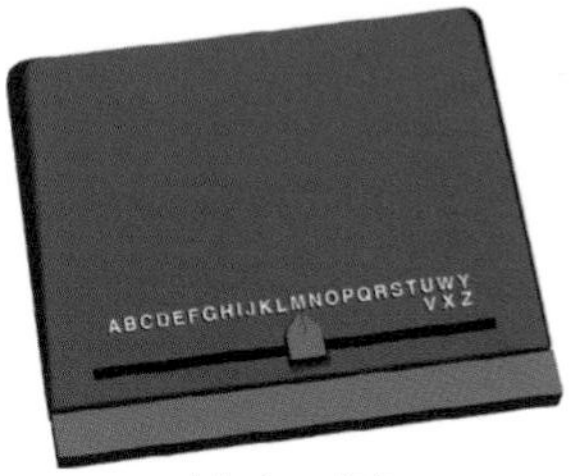

telephone index
Book in which frequently used names, addresses and telephone numbers are written and stored in alphabetical order.

rotary file
Device with a set of files that rotate on a spindle for easy consultation.

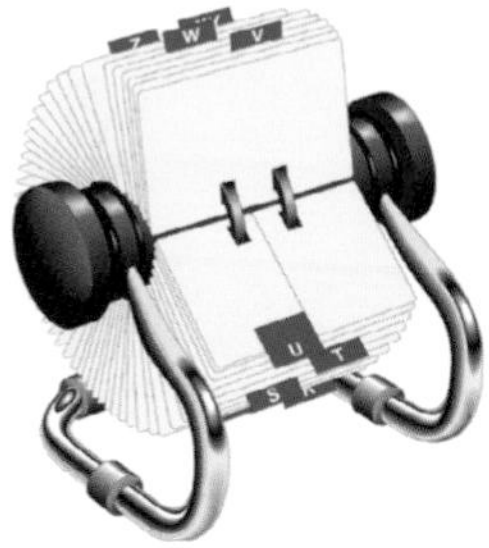

postage meter
Machine used to print a postage meter stamp on an envelope or label in lieu of using a postage stamp.

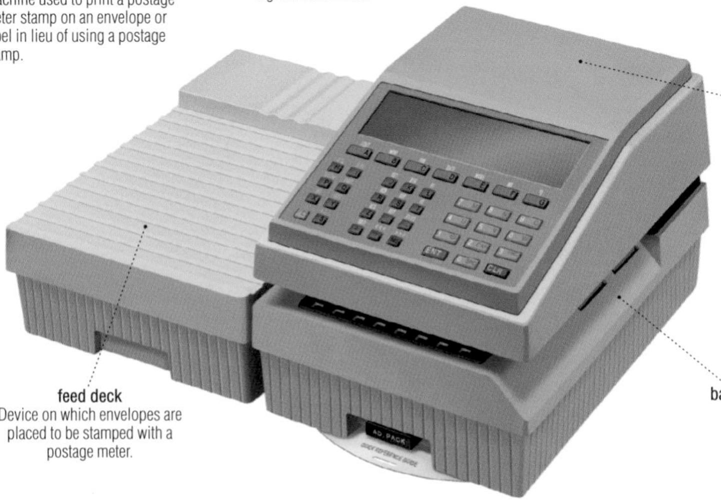

postmarking module
Unit housing the machine's control buttons; it is used to set the prepaid postage meter with the correct amount of postage.

base

feed deck
Device on which envelopes are placed to be stamped with a postage meter.

desk tray
Container that usually has several compartments; it is used to handle incoming and outgoing mail.

stationery

for filing

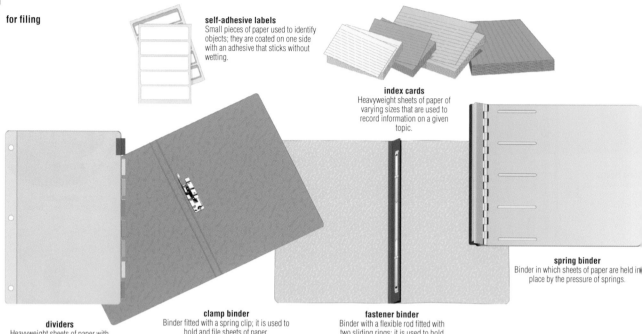

self-adhesive labels
Small pieces of paper used to identify objects; they are coated on one side with an adhesive that sticks without wetting.

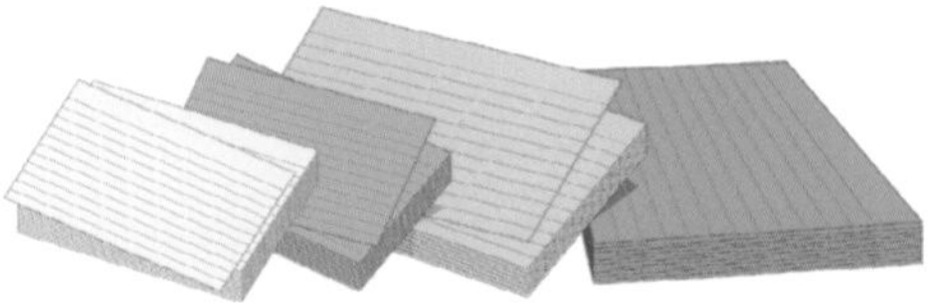

index cards
Heavyweight sheets of paper of varying sizes that are used to record information on a given topic.

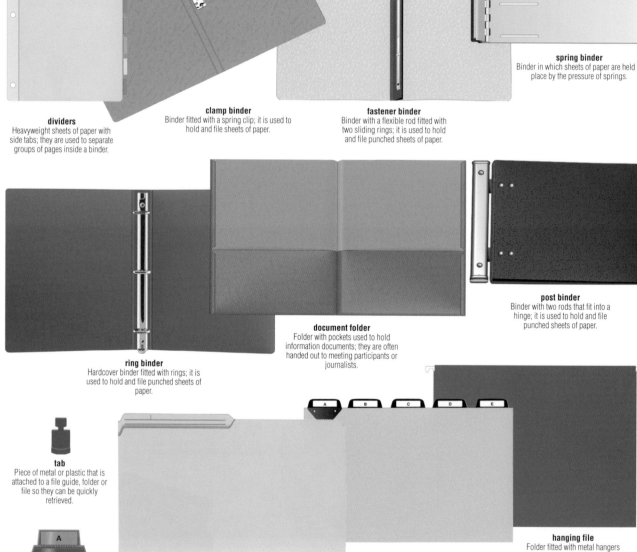

spring binder
Binder in which sheets of paper are held in place by the pressure of springs.

dividers
Heavyweight sheets of paper with side tabs; they are used to separate groups of pages inside a binder.

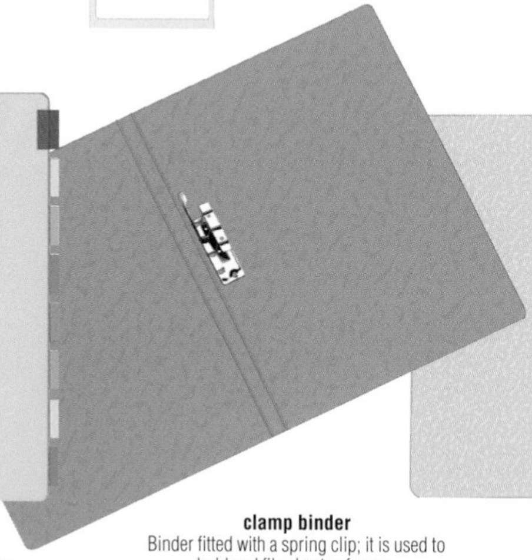

clamp binder
Binder fitted with a spring clip; it is used to hold and file sheets of paper.

fastener binder
Binder with a flexible rod fitted with two sliding rings; it is used to hold and file punched sheets of paper.

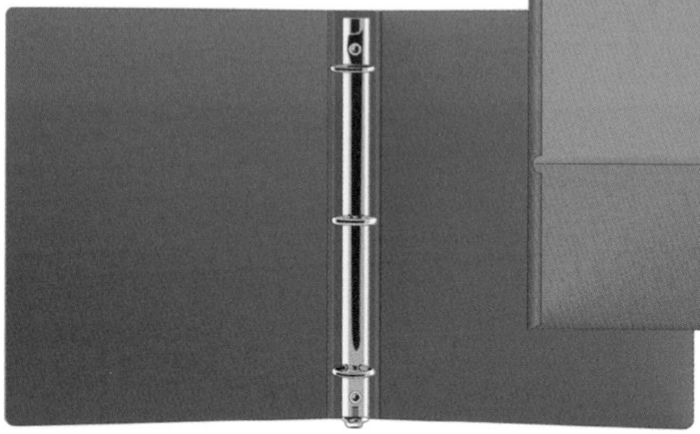

ring binder
Hardcover binder fitted with rings; it is used to hold and file punched sheets of paper.

document folder
Folder with pockets used to hold information documents; they are often handed out to meeting participants or journalists.

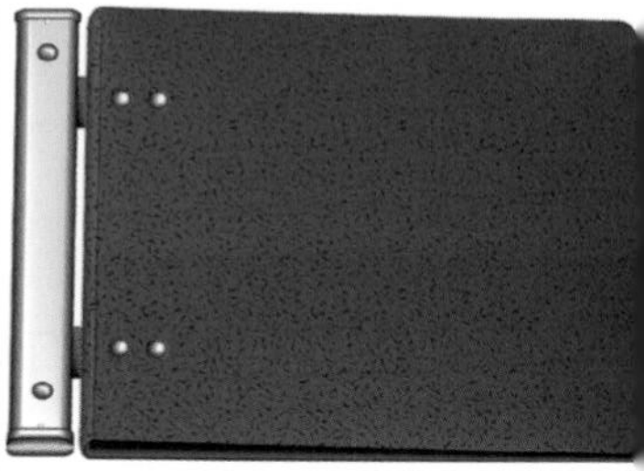

post binder
Binder with two rods that fit into a hinge; it is used to hold and file punched sheets of paper.

tab
Piece of metal or plastic that is attached to a file guide, folder or file so they can be quickly retrieved.

window tab
Tab with an opening to hold an identification label.

folder
Rigid cardboard that is folded in half; documents on the same topic are placed in it.

file guides
Heavyweight sheets of paper with a tab at the top; they are used to separate groups of documents or folders in a filing cabinet drawer.

hanging file
Folder fitted with metal hangers that is hung in a filing cabinet drawer.

stationery

spiral binder
Notebook made up of a set of punched sheets of paper bound together with a spiral wire of metal or plastic.

clipboard
Rigid board fitted with a spring clip under which sheets of paper are placed mainly to take notes.

archboard
Rigid board fitted with two arched metal clips on which punched sheets are placed.

index card drawer
Small built-in drawer designed for storage and filing of index cards.

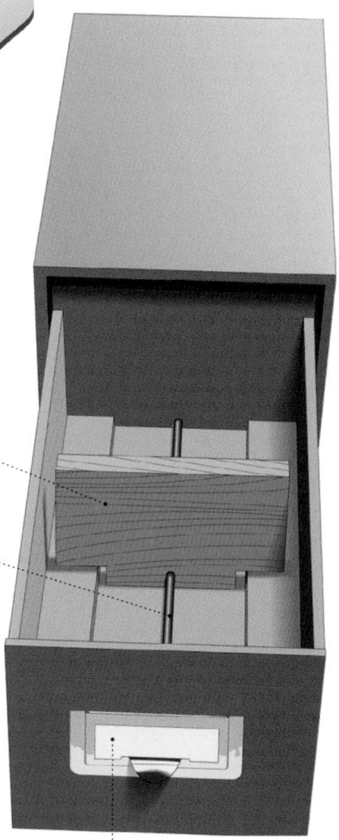

compressor
Movable panel that holds index cards in an upright position.

metal rail
Cylindrical rod along which the compressor moves.

label holder
Part with an opening to hold an identification label.

index card cabinet
Small file drawer designed to hold and store index cards in a set order.

label maker
Device used to print characters on a self-adhesive strip.

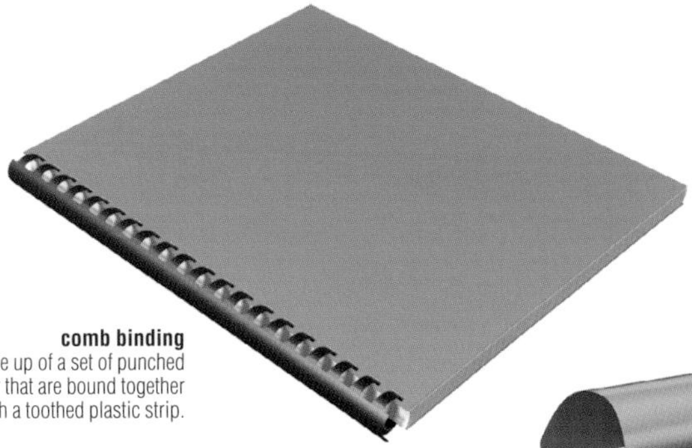

comb binding
Notebook made up of a set of punched sheets of paper that are bound together with a toothed plastic strip.

filing box
Small open cardboard box that is mainly used to hold magazines, catalogs and brochures.

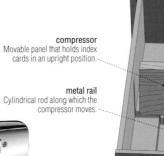

paper punch
Device used to punch holes in sheets of paper.

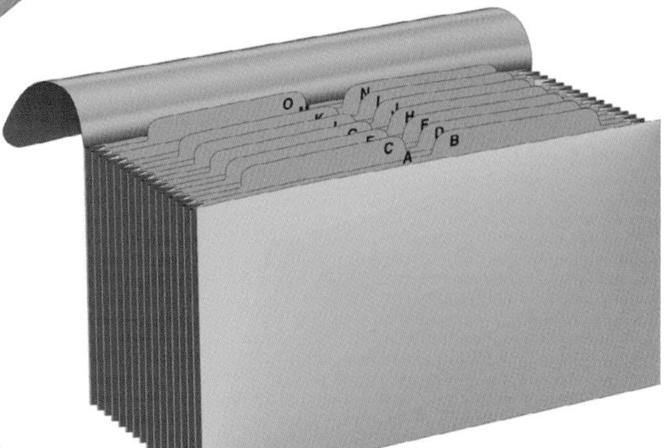

expanding file
Usually expandable file with compartments; it is used to store documents by subject.

stationery

miscellaneous articles

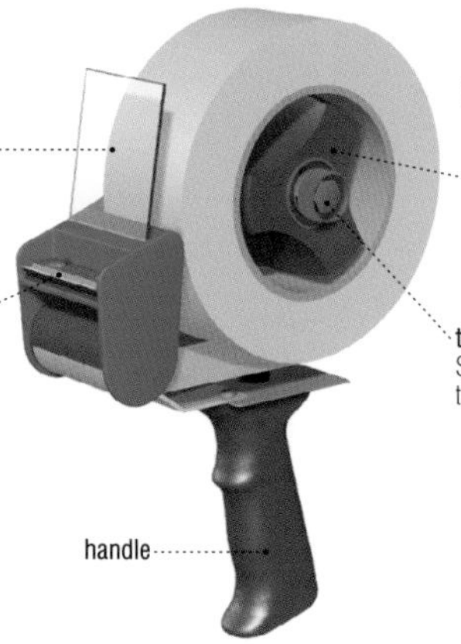

box sealing tape dispenser
Device that is used to unroll, apply and cut a roll of adhesive tape using one hand.

tape guide
Device used as a visual guide to apply the adhesive tape to a specific area.

cutting blade
Thin flat metal piece that cuts the adhesive tape to the desired length.

hub
Rotating piece on which the roll of adhesive tape is mounted.

tension adjusting screw
Screw that adjusts the speed at which the tape unrolls.

handle

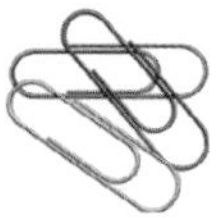

paper clips
Small clips made from a piece of bent metal wire; they are used to hold a few sheets of paper or index cards.

thumb tacks
Small tacks with short pointy ends; they are easily pushed in with the finger and are used to attach sheets of paper, cardboard or posters to a surface.

paper fasteners
Small clips made of two bars, which spread open to hold sheets of paper or cardboard.

pencil sharpener
Portable device used to sharpen pencils by rotating them in a cone-shaped chamber fitted with a blade.

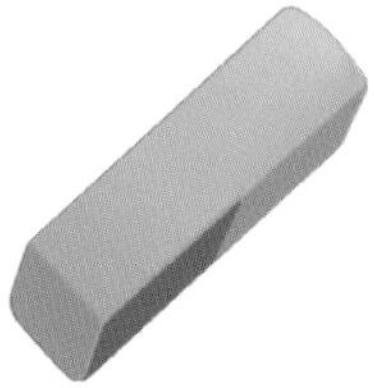

eraser
Small block of rubber used to erase pencil marks and some types of ink.

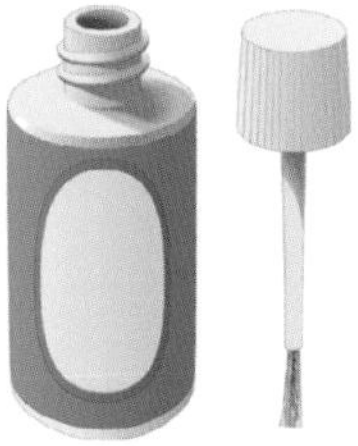

correction fluid
Liquid that covers up printed or written characters so that corrections can be made.

paper clip holder
Small box containing paper clips, which are released one by one through a magnetic opening.

magnet
Material that produces a magnetic field; it attracts paper clips to the top and holds them in place around the opening.

clip
Device with two articulated arms that are pressed together to hold such items as sheets of paper and index cards.

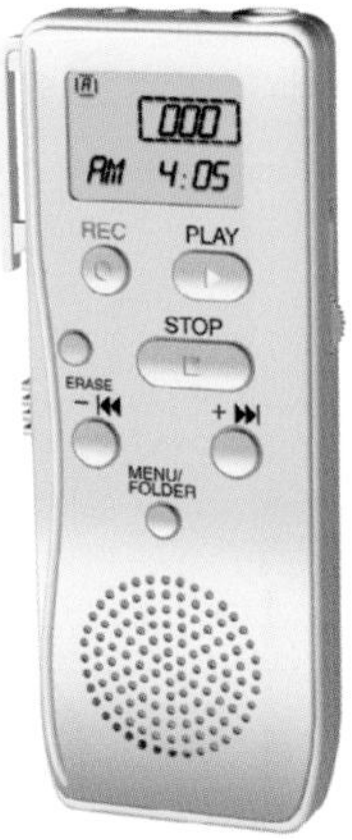

digital voice recorder
Portable device used to record voice messages in digital form.

glue stick
Tube that contains a small stick of solid adhesive matter to be applied to a surface.

pencil sharpener
Office device with a rotating blade that is controlled by a crank; it is used to sharpen pencils.

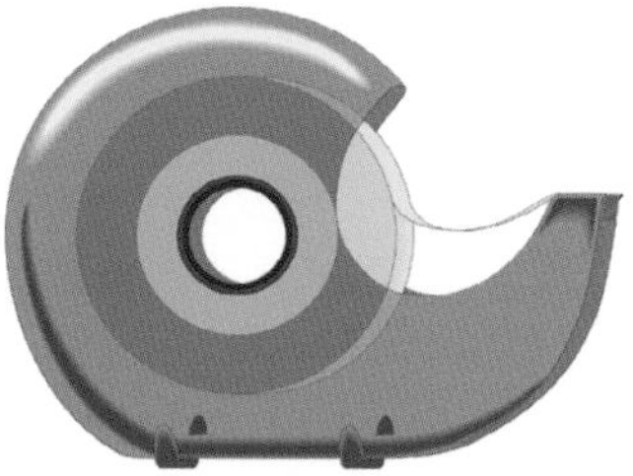

tape dispenser
Holder that eases the unrolling and cutting of a roll of adhesive tape.

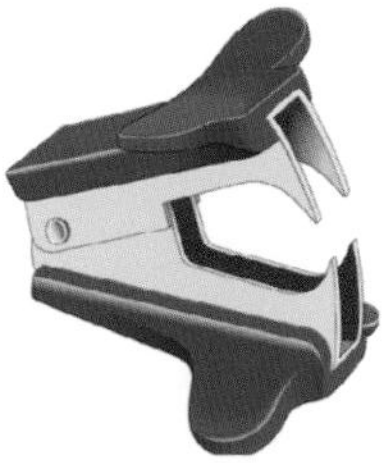

staple remover
Device used to remove staples from sheets of paper.

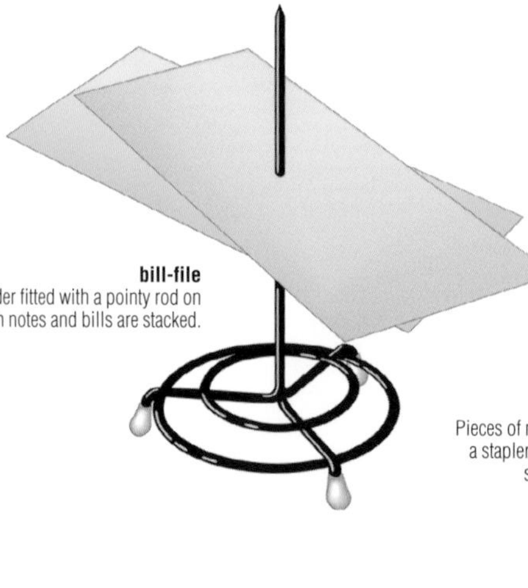

bill-file
Holder fitted with a pointy rod on which notes and bills are stacked.

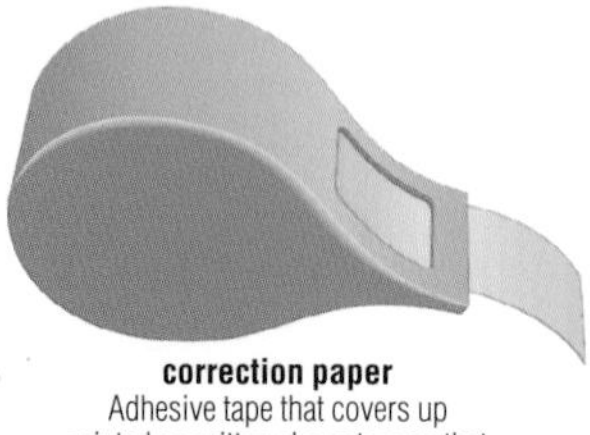

correction paper
Adhesive tape that covers up printed or written characters so that corrections can be made.

stapler
Device used to fasten two or more sheets of paper together with staples.

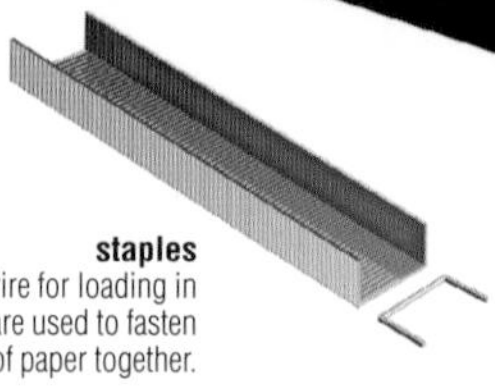

staples
Pieces of metal wire for loading in a stapler; they are used to fasten sheets of paper together.

overhead projector
Device that projects the enlarged image of a document printed on a transparency on a screen located behind the user.

projection head
Movable part that contains the lens and mirror; a focusing ring changes its position to give a clear image on the screen.

mirror
Polished glass surface that directs light from the lens toward the projection screen.

optical lens
Transparent optical disk that captures the light from the optical stage and makes it converge toward the mirror.

optical stage
Glass plate that is lit by an internal light; the document to be projected is placed on it.

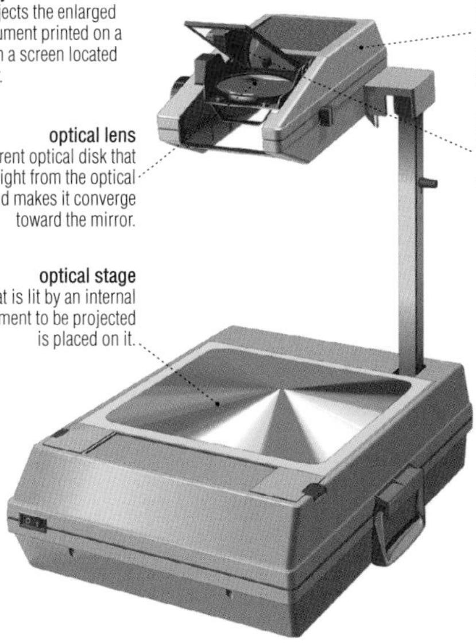

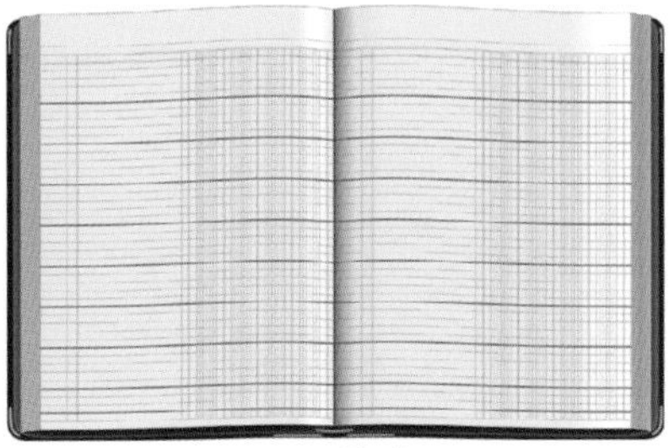

account book
Book with columns in which the financial data of an organization (such as sales, purchases, receipts and expenditures) are recorded.

cutting head
Unit with an opening where paper enters; it is fitted with a cutting device to destroy documents.

waste basket
Basket that collects shredded documents.

paper shredder
Device that reduces paper documents to illegible fragments.

waste basket
Basket in which unneeded documents are discarded.

bulletin board
Panel that hangs on a wall; messages, notices, notes and other written communications are pinned on it.

book ends
Items designed to hold binders or books tightly against one other.

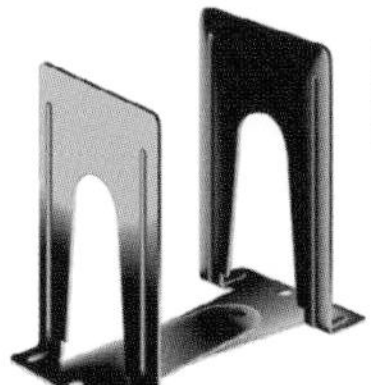

lightbox
Screen that is illuminated from behind and used to examine items such as negatives, slides, transparencies and drawings.

slotted box
Box with flaps that is formed from a single piece of sturdy cardboard; it is used to collect various items for storage or shipping.

flap
Articulated piece that folds over the opening of the box to close it.

paper cutter
Piece of equipment used to make square cuts in paper, cardboard, transparencies, etc.

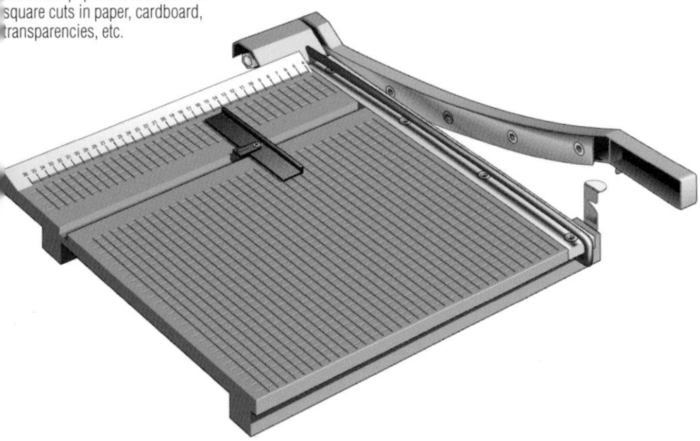

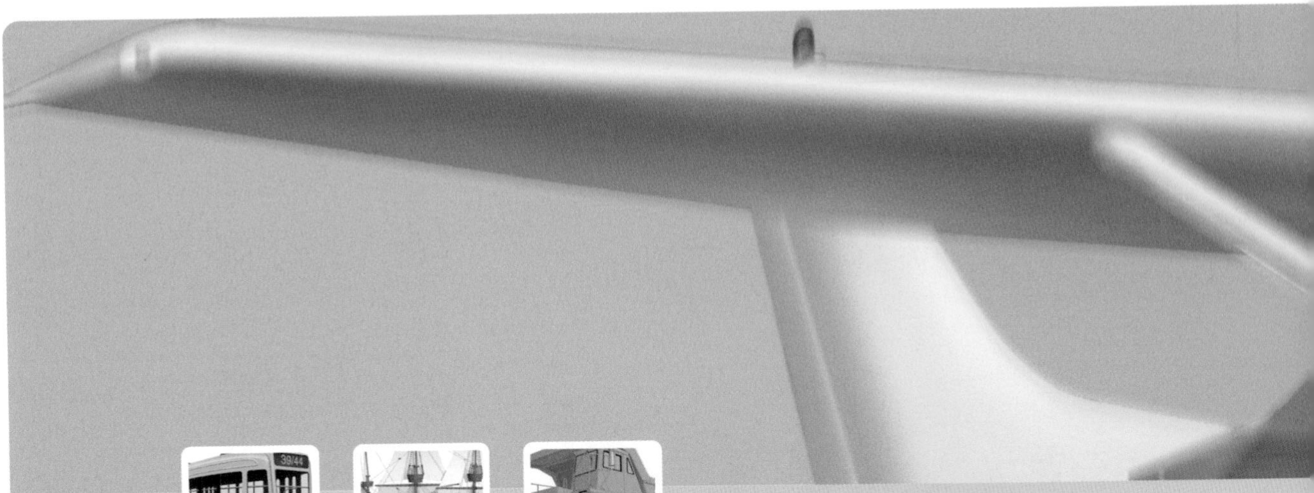

538 Road transport

The structures and equipment that together provide for the transportation of passengers and cargo by motorized vehicles.

582 Rail transport

The structures and equipment required to transport passengers and cargo by train.

596 Maritime transport

Structures and equipment required to transp
passengers and cargo by ship.

TRANSPORT AND MACHINERY

18 **Air transport**

The structures and equipment required to transport passengers and cargo by air.

632 **Handling**

Machinery and equipment used for moving and storing heavy loads.

636 **Heavy machinery**

Equipment used on large-scale projects to dig, loosen and move earth and other matter.

road system

Network of thoroughfares providing for the flow of traffic.

cross section of a road
Road: thoroughfare connecting two geographical points, usually urban centers.

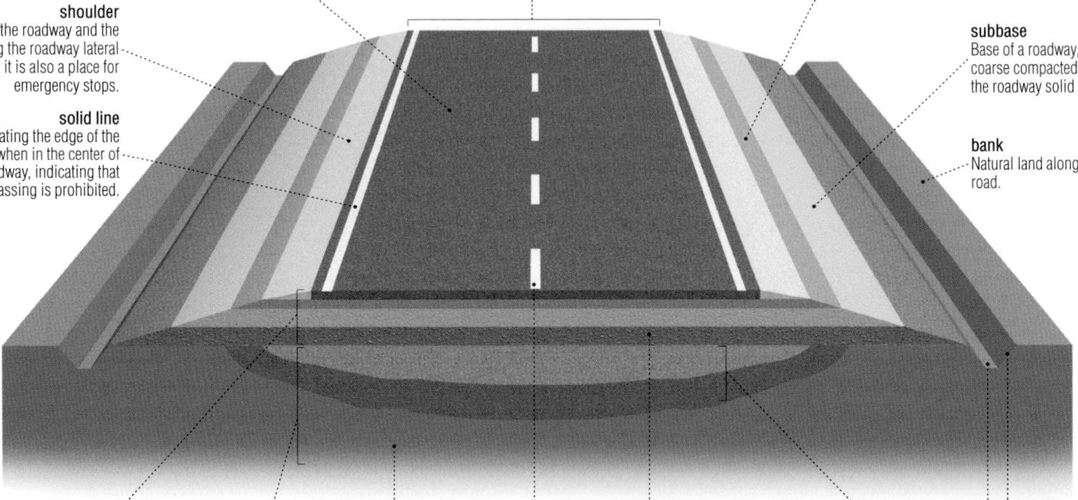

surface course
Roadway's driving surface; it is smooth, impermeable and provides a good grip for vehicles.

roadway
Surface upon which vehicles drive.

base course
Top foundation layer, made up of fine compacted material; the driving surface lies on it.

shoulder
Area between the roadway and the ditch, providing the roadway lateral support; it is also a place for emergency stops.

subbase
Base of a roadway, made up of coarse compacted gravel, making the roadway solid and stable.

solid line
Line demarcating the edge of the roadway or, when in the center of the roadway, indicating that passing is prohibited.

bank
Natural land along the edge of the road.

base
Series of layers above the embankment reducing stress exerted by the traffic and preventing the bed from deforming.

earth foundation
Part of the ground that was not excavated during the road's construction.

subgrade
Layer supporting the base course and the subbase and providing drainage.

embankment
Layers of material used to build up or level the route the road is to take.

slope
Steeply sloped ground betwe ditch and the bank and betwe ditch and the shoulder.

bed
Composed of the embankment and the earth foundation; the base rests on it.

broken line
Line demarcating the two lanes of the roadway and showing that passing is permitted.

ditch
Ditch parallel to the roadway; surface water drains into it.

examples of interchanges

Interchange: structure linking roads or freeways so they do not intersect.

cloverleaf
Interchange with four branches where the inside loops are for turning left and the direct links for turning right.

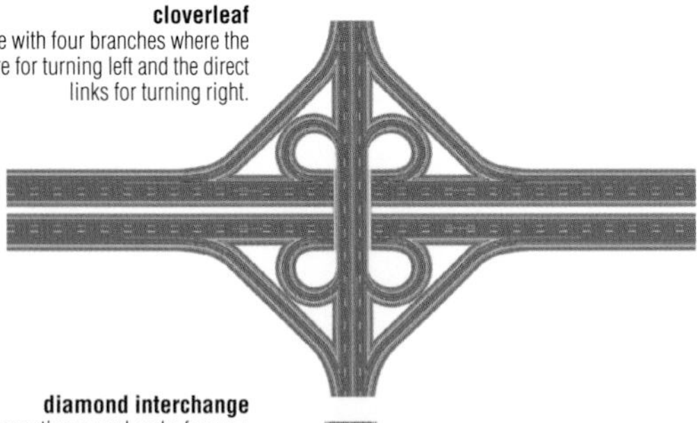

traffic circle
Interchange composed of four ramps joining each other to form a circular one-way thoroughfare.

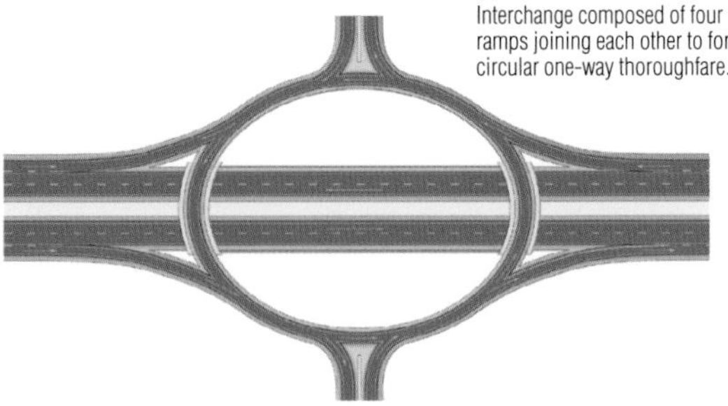

diamond interchange
Interchange connecting a road and a freeway, requiring traffic lights for left turns onto and off the road or overpass.

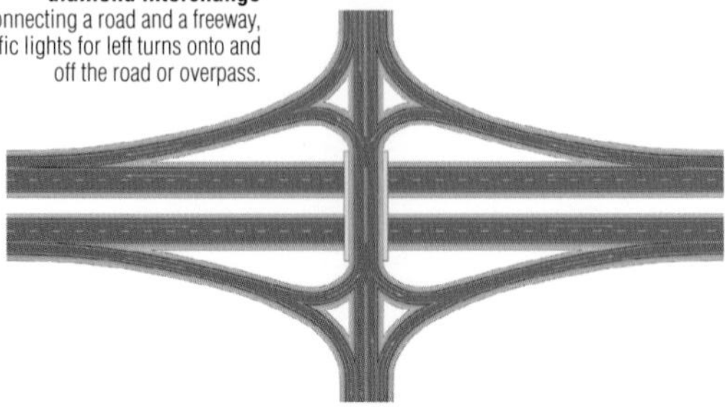

trumpet interchange
Interchange connecting a road ending at a freeway, using only one loop.

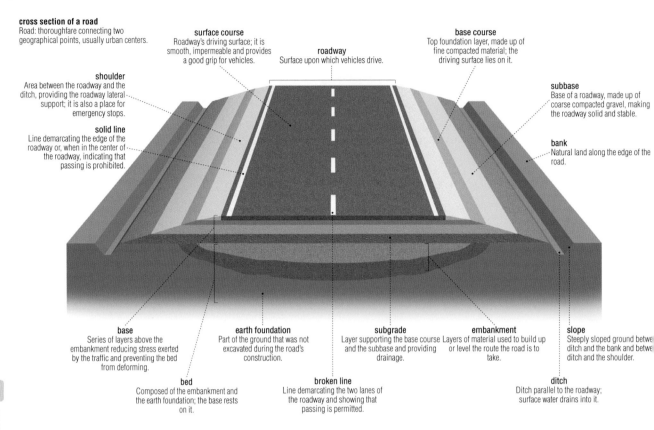

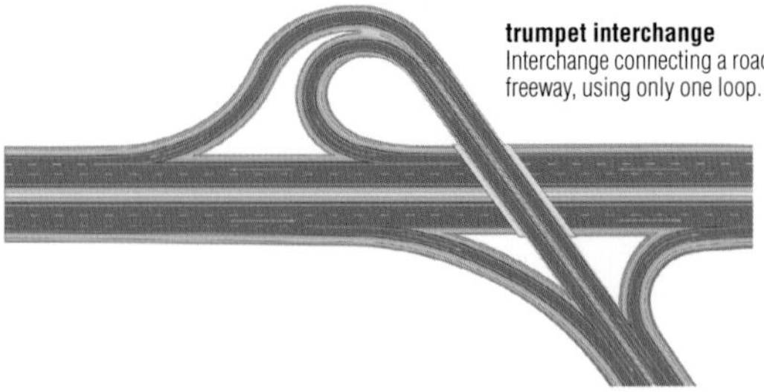

cloverleaf
Interchange with four branches where the inside loops are for turning left and the direct links for turning right.

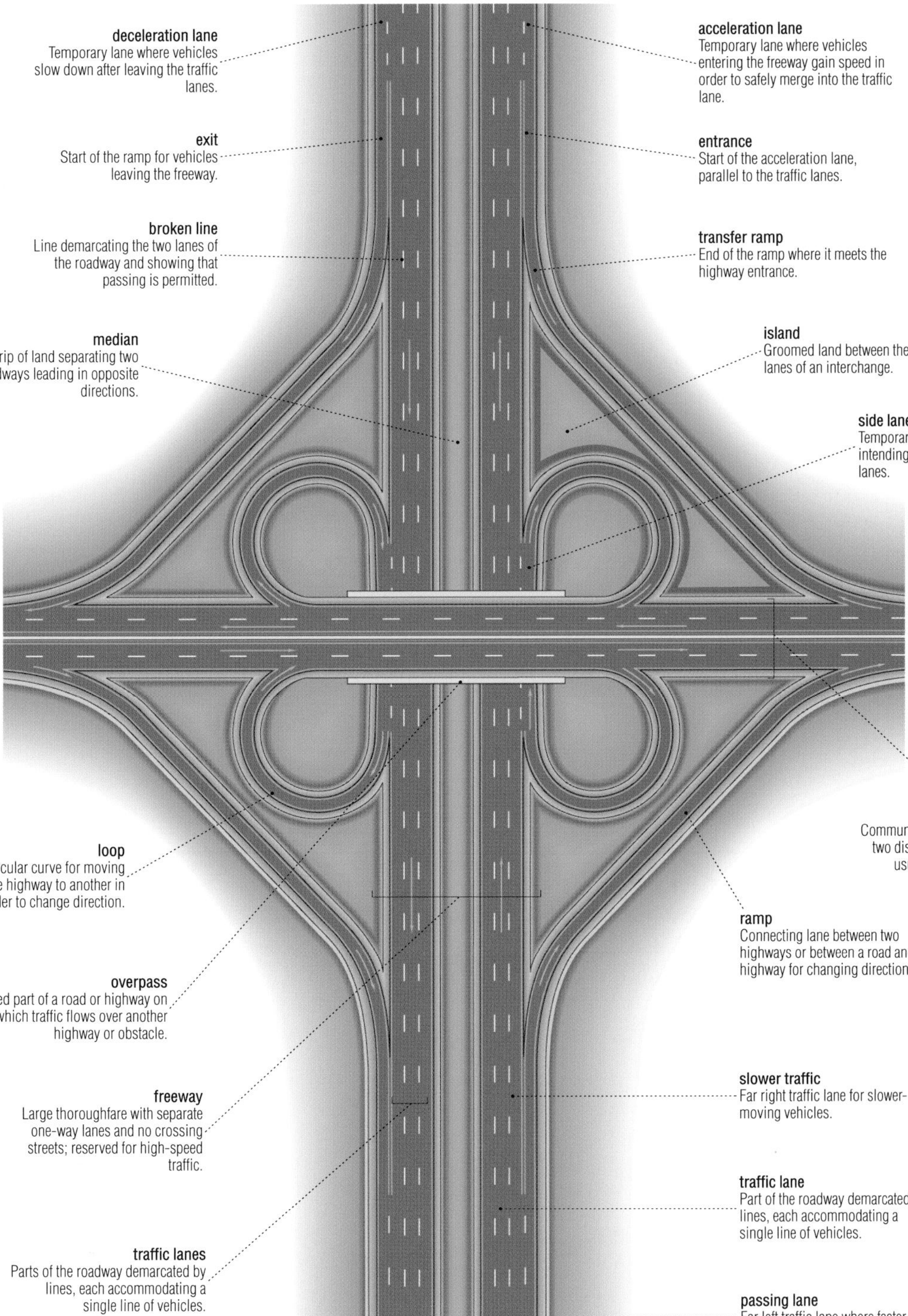

deceleration lane
Temporary lane where vehicles slow down after leaving the traffic lanes.

exit
Start of the ramp for vehicles leaving the freeway.

broken line
Line demarcating the two lanes of the roadway and showing that passing is permitted.

median
Strip of land separating two roadways leading in opposite directions.

loop
Wide circular curve for moving from one highway to another in order to change direction.

overpass
Raised part of a road or highway on which traffic flows over another highway or obstacle.

freeway
Large thoroughfare with separate one-way lanes and no crossing streets; reserved for high-speed traffic.

traffic lanes
Parts of the roadway demarcated by lines, each accommodating a single line of vehicles.

acceleration lane
Temporary lane where vehicles entering the freeway gain speed in order to safely merge into the traffic lane.

entrance
Start of the acceleration lane, parallel to the traffic lanes.

transfer ramp
End of the ramp where it meets the highway entrance.

island
Groomed land between the various lanes of an interchange.

side lane
Temporary lane for vehicles intending to enter or exit the main lanes.

highway
Communications route connecting two distant geographic points, usually urban centers.

ramp
Connecting lane between two highways or between a road and a highway for changing direction.

slower traffic
Far right traffic lane for slower-moving vehicles.

traffic lane
Part of the roadway demarcated by lines, each accommodating a single line of vehicles.

passing lane
Far left traffic lane where faster-moving vehicles pass other traffic.

fixed bridges

Structures enabling traffic to clear an obstacle, such as a river, gorge or highway.

beam bridge
Bridge whose deck is composed of one or several beams, which are supported by piers across the open space.

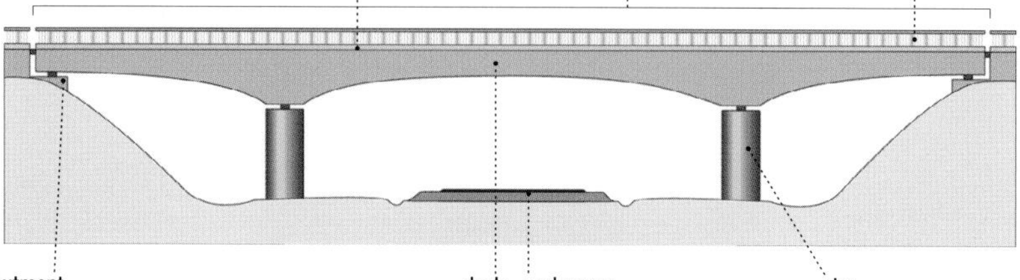

overpass
Raised part of a road or highway on which traffic flows over another highway or obstacle.

continuous beam
Extended load-bearing part supported by abutments and piers.

parapet
Chest-high barrier on each side of the deck, preventing people and vehicles from falling off.

abutment
A pier's point of support on firm ground.

deck
Set of components making up the structure that carries the bridge's traffic lanes.

underpass
Lowered part of a thoroughfare, enabling traffic to flow under another roadway or obstacle.

pier
Sturdy load-bearing component placed at intervals to support the bridge's beams.

arch bridge
Bridge whose deck is supported by suspenders attached to an arch, which exerts diagonal thrust against the lateral supports.

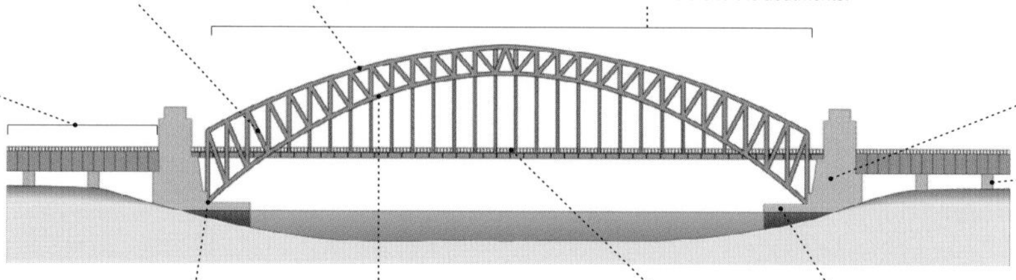

trussed arch
Arched girder consisting of two chords joined by a triangulated network of struts.

upper chord
Upper lengthwise steel girder forming the metal arch.

arch
Metal bow-shaped structure supporting the deck, whose load it transfers to the abutments.

portal frame
Part of the deck's frame over firm ground, lying on columns.

pier
Solid concrete construction actin as counterweight to the thrust of the arch against the abutment.

column
Sturdy component forming a vertical support.

thrust
Point at which the arch is supported by the abutment.

lower chord
Lower lengthwise steel girder forming the metal arch.

deck
Set of components making up the structure that carries the bridge's traffic lanes.

abutment
Base of the pier; it supports the arch's weight and thrust.

suspension bridge
Bridge whose long deck is suspended from load-bearing cables, which are supported by the towers and anchored in the ground at both ends of the bridge.

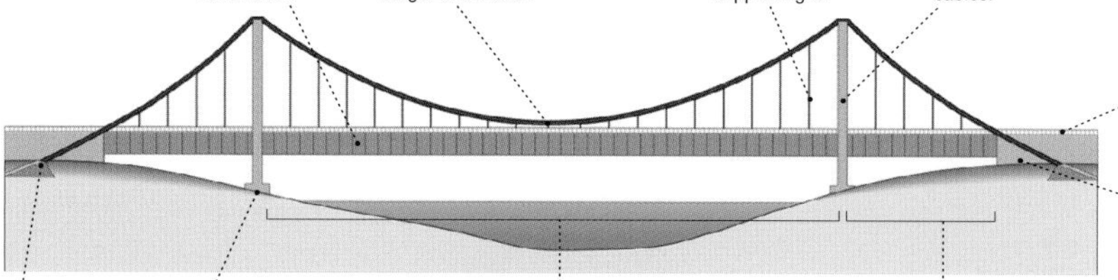

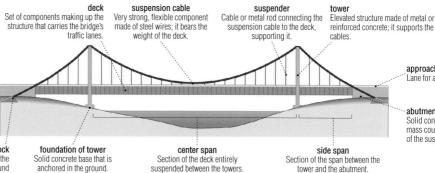

deck
Set of components making up the structure that carries the bridge's traffic lanes.

suspension cable
Very strong, flexible component made of steel wires; it bears the weight of the deck.

suspender
Cable or metal rod connecting the suspension cable to the deck, supporting it.

tower
Elevated structure made of metal or reinforced concrete; it supports the cables.

approach ramp
Lane for accessing the bridge.

abutment
Solid concrete construction whos mass counterbalances the weight of the suspended roadway.

anchorage block
Concrete structure on each side of the abutment; it is buried deep in the ground and the end of the suspension cable is attached to it.

foundation of tower
Solid concrete base that is anchored in the ground.

center span
Section of the deck entirely suspended between the towers.

side span
Section of the span between the tower and the abutment.

cantilever bridge
Bridge whose two main spans extend toward each other and support a short suspended span, which bears less load.

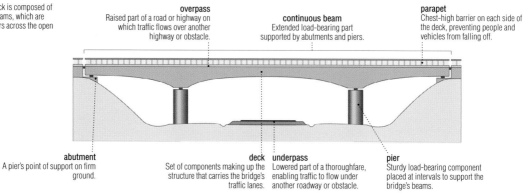

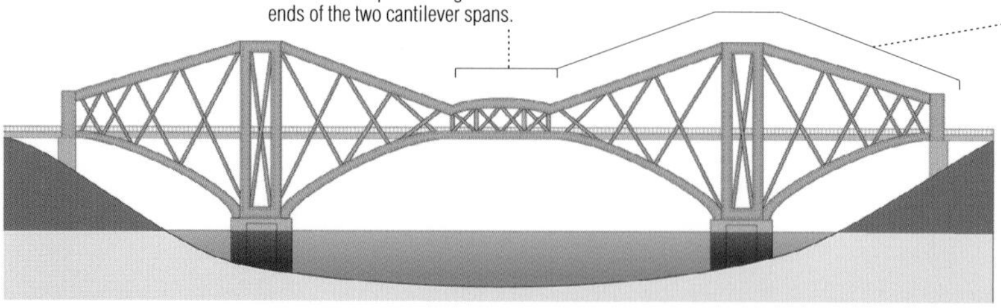

suspended span
Short center span resting on the ends of the two cantilever spans.

cantilever span
Span with a complex framework c each side of a central pillar; one end of the span rests on the grour and the other supports a suspended span.

fixed bridges

cable-stayed bridges

Bridges whose deck is supported at several points by stays and rests on one or more towers.

cable stay anchorage
Apparatus by which one end of the stay is attached to the tower and the other to the end of the deck.

stays
Usually metal cables connected at one end to the top of the tower, and supported by the deck at the other end.

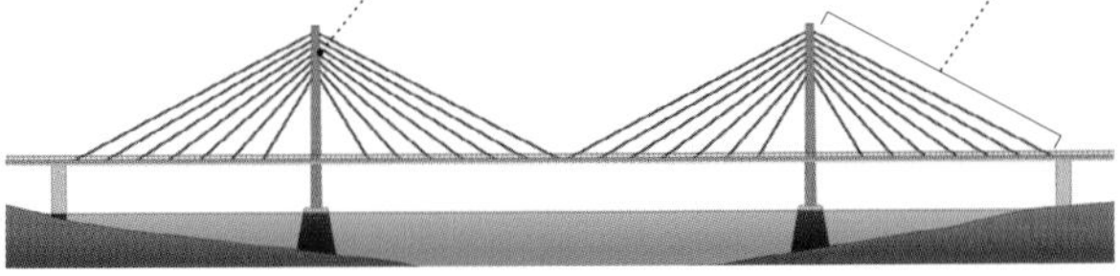

fan cable stays
Bridge for which the distance between the anchorage points of the stays on the tower is less than the distance between the anchorage points on the deck.

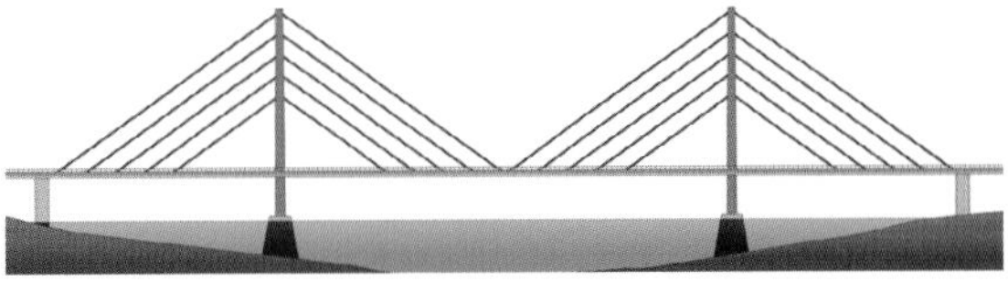

harp cable stays
Bridge whose stays are parallel.

examples of arch bridges

Among arch bridges, the position of the deck in relation to the arch varies.

deck arch bridge
Bridge whose deck is located above the arch upon which it rests.

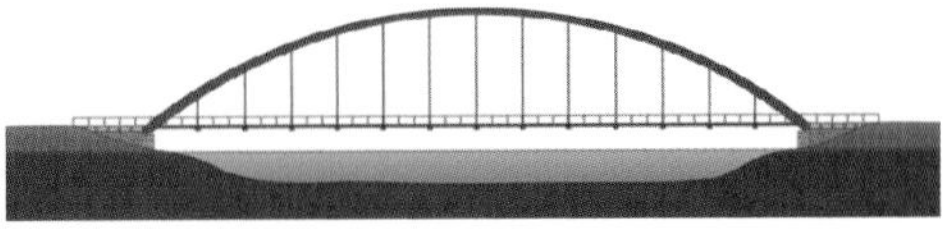

through arch bridge
Bridge whose deck is located below the arch from which it is suspended.

portal bridge
Bridge resting on diagonal beams that are embedded in the deck.

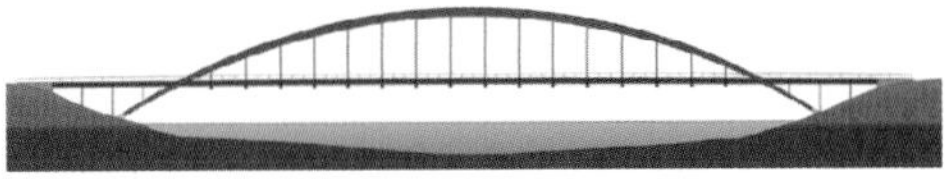

half-through arch bridge
Bridge whose deck is located within the arch from which it is suspended in the middle, and on which it rests, at each end.

examples of arches

The concept of the arch varies in relation to the way it absorbs and transfers the roadway's weight to its support points.

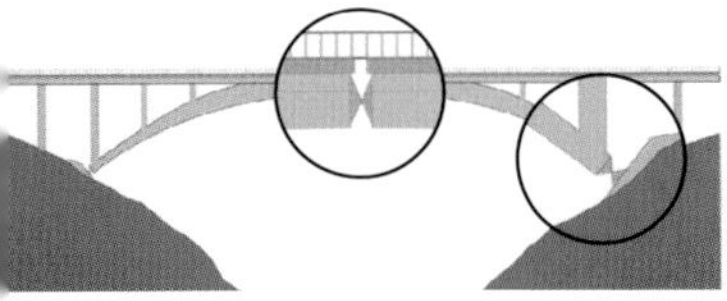

three-hinged arch
Arch with three roller joints: one at each end and one at the center.

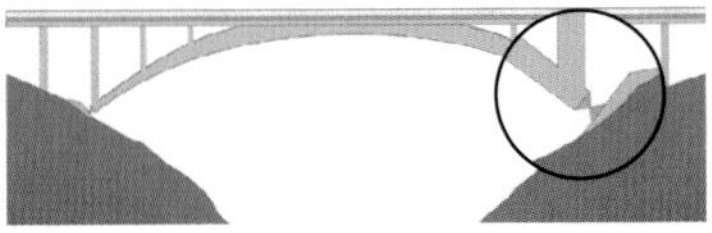

two-hinged arch
Arch whose ends rest on an abutment attached by a roller joint.

fixed arch
Nonarticulated arch, embedded in each of its supports.

examples of beam bridges

Depending on the length of the roadway above the obstacle, the bridge could comprise one or more beams.

viaduct
Bridge composed of several beams that crosses a very high valley.

multiple-span beam bridge
Bridge whose deck is composed of several juxtaposed beams, each one supported at each end.

simple-span beam bridge
Bridge whose deck is composed of only one continuous beam.

movable bridges

Bridges whose decks move to free up the transportation channel they cross, or that are built temporarily while awaiting a permanent structure.

swing bridge
Bridge whose deck pivots around a vertical axle.

turntable
Moving mechanical structure on a pier enabling the deck to pivot.

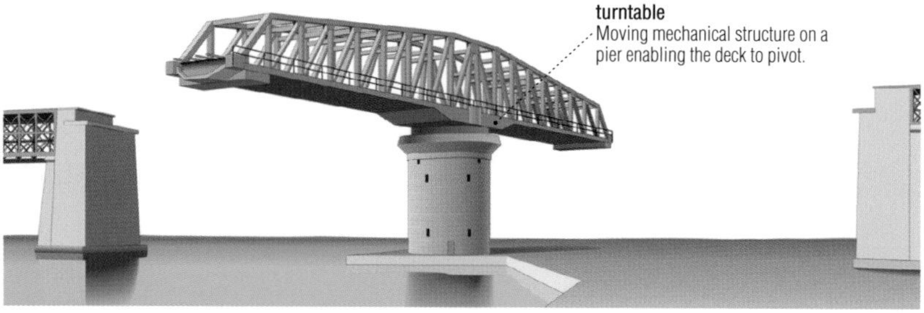

counterweight
Concrete or cast-iron mass, balancing the weight of the deck and facilitating its movement.

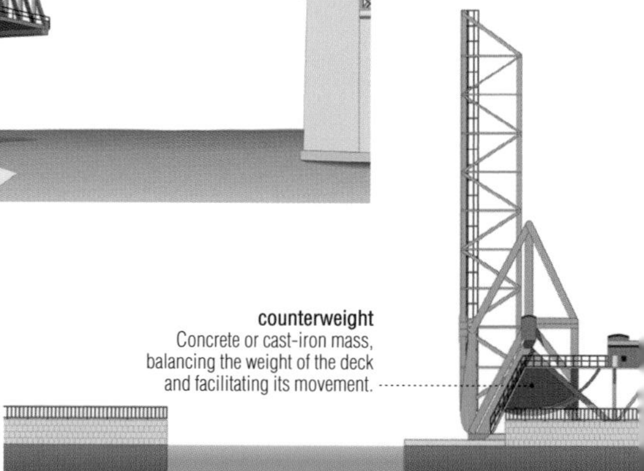

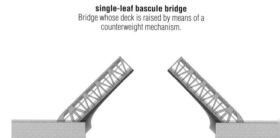

single-leaf bascule bridge
Bridge whose deck is raised by means of a counterweight mechanism.

manrope
Chest-high barrier on each side of the deck, preventing people and vehicles from falling off.

pontoon
Floating caisson filled with air and supporting the deck.

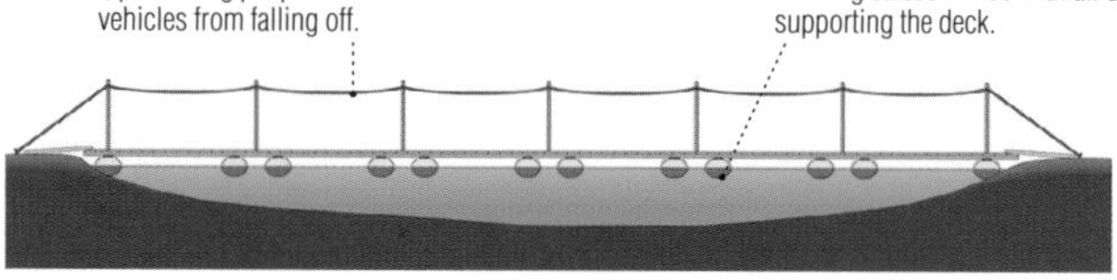

floating bridge
Bridge whose deck rests on pontoons that can be taken apart to open the bridge.

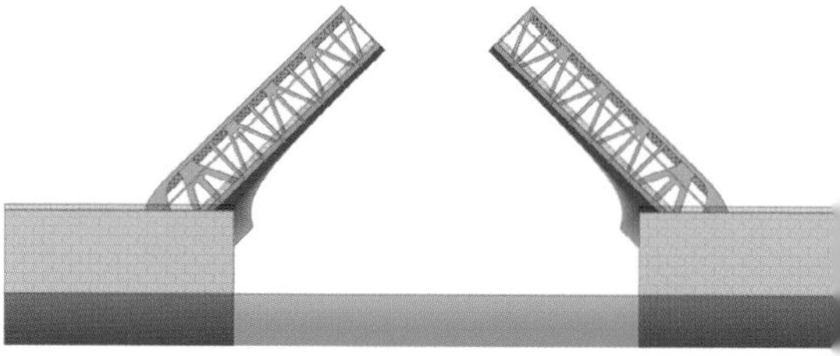

double-leaf bascule bridge
Bridge whose deck is composed of two spans joining each other at the middle of the bridge and pivoting around a vertical axle at each abutment.

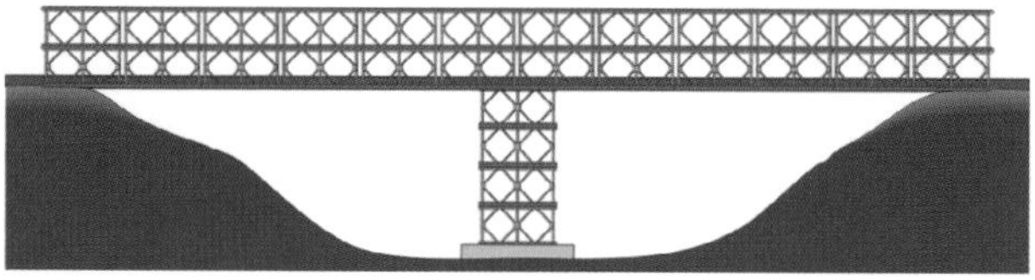

Bailey bridge
Steel bridge, often temporary, whose standardized truss components make it easy to assemble quickly.

trolley
Part of the bridge moved by a motor; it glides along rails installed under the deck.

platform
Cabin suspended from the trolley by cables; it moves from one shore to the other.

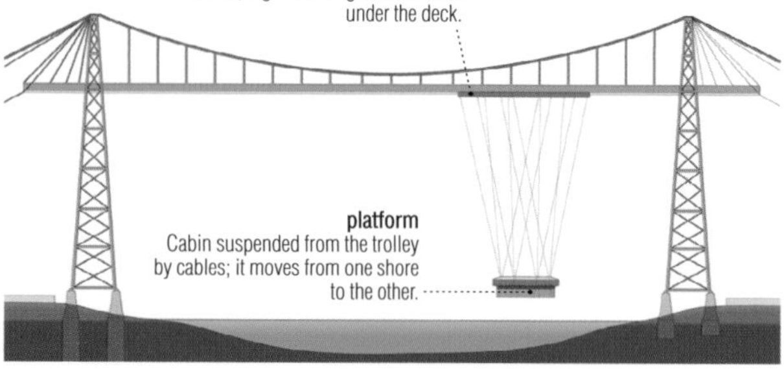

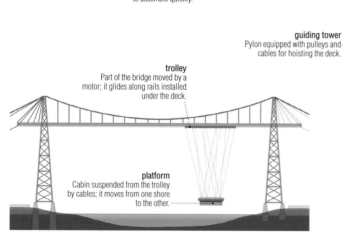

transporter bridge
Bridge with a very high deck from which a moving platform is suspended to transport pedestrians and vehicles.

guiding tower
Pylon equipped with pulleys and cables for hoisting the deck.

lift span
Deck suspended at each end by cables hoisting it up along the guiding towers.

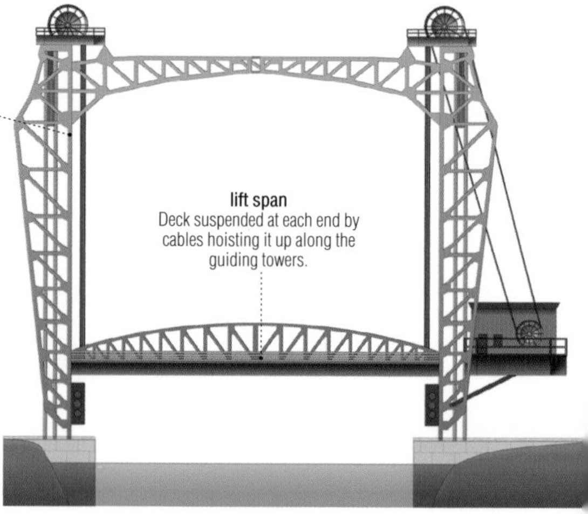

lift bridge
Bridge whose deck is raised by a system of cables.

road tunnel

Underground passage for a road under an obstacle, such as a river or a hill.

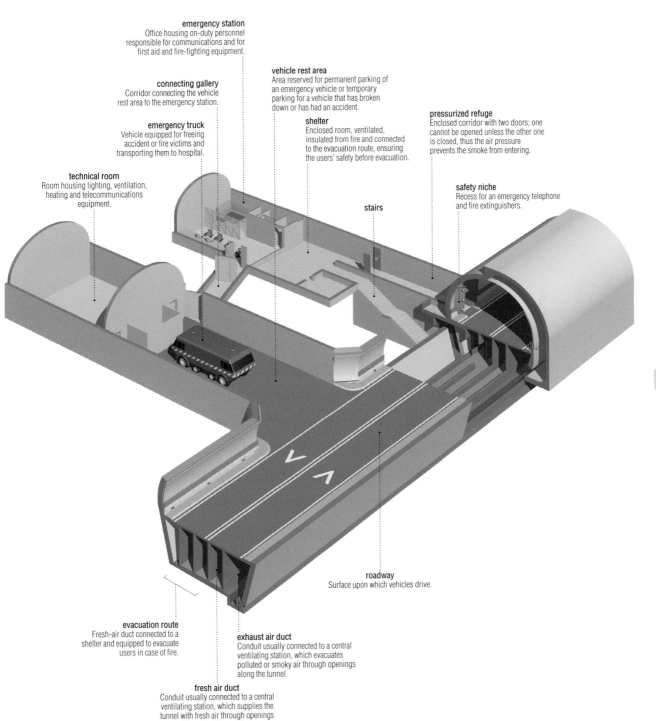

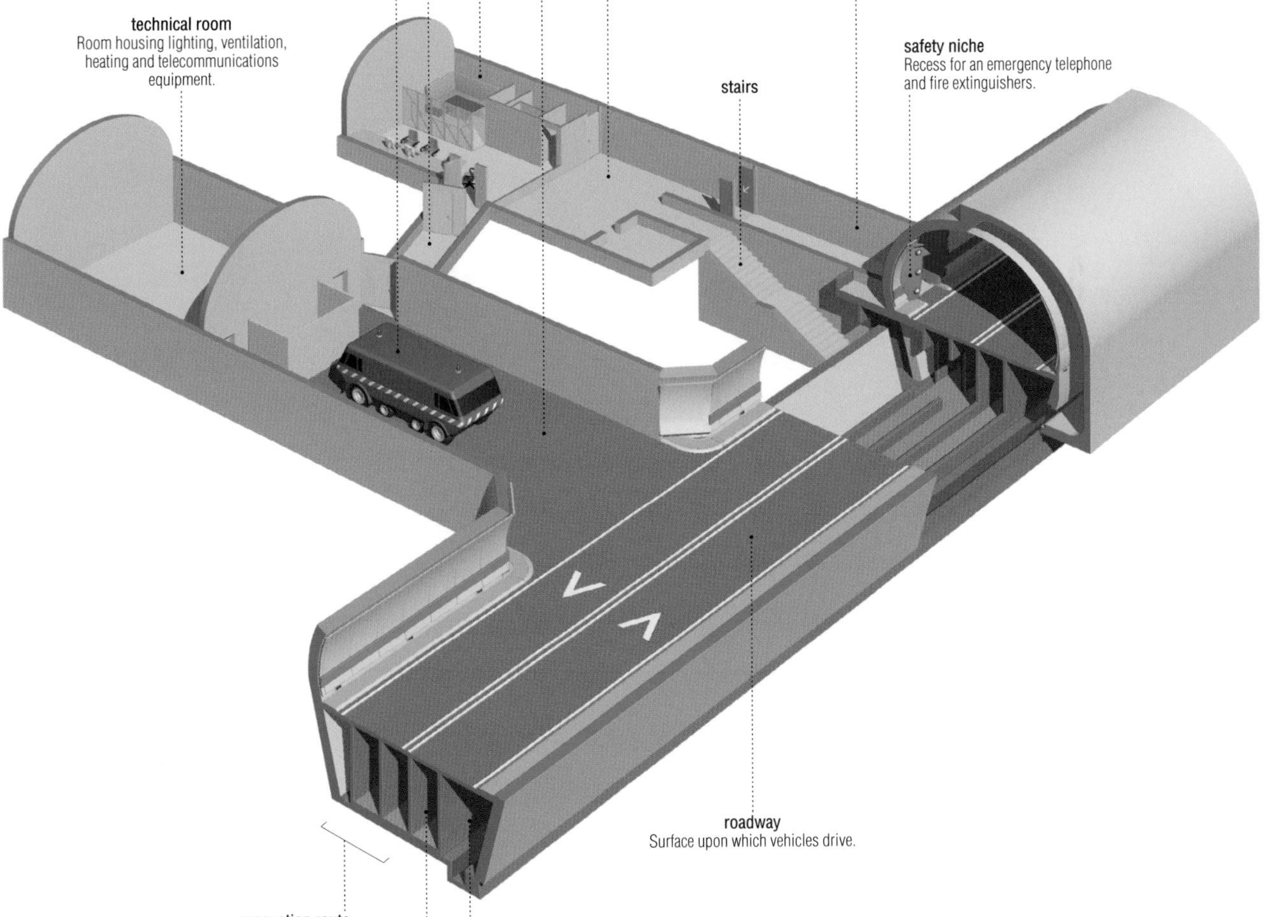

emergency station
Office housing on-duty personnel responsible for communications and for first aid and fire-fighting equipment.
connecting gallery
Corridor connecting the vehicle rest area to the emergency station.
emergency truck
Vehicle equipped for freeing accident or fire victims and transporting them to hospital.
technical room
Room housing lighting, ventilation, heating and telecommunications equipment.
vehicle rest area
Area reserved for permanent parking of an emergency vehicle or temporary parking for a vehicle that has broken down or has had an accident.
shelter
Enclosed room, ventilated, insulated from fire and connected to the evacuation route, ensuring the users' safety before evacuation.
pressurized refuge
Enclosed corridor with two doors; one cannot be opened unless the other one is closed, thus the air pressure prevents the smoke from entering.
safety niche
Recess for an emergency telephone and fire extinguishers.
stairs
roadway
Surface upon which vehicles drive.
evacuation route
Fresh-air duct connected to a shelter and equipped to evacuate users in case of fire.
exhaust air duct
Conduit usually connected to a central ventilating station, which evacuates polluted or smoky air through openings along the tunnel.
fresh air duct
Conduit usually connected to a central ventilating station, which supplies the tunnel with fresh air through openings at the side of the roadway.

road signs

Objects such as signs, traffic lights and road markings, aimed at ensuring the safety of the road's users and increasing traffic-flow efficiency.

major international road signs

Main signs used by countries complying with the Vienna International Convention, which provides some international uniformity to road signs.

right bend

double bend

roadway narrows

stop at intersection

no entry

no U-turn

passing prohibited

direction to be followed

direction to be followed

direction to be followed

direction to be followed

one-way traffic

two-way traffic

yield

priority intersection

falling rocks

overhead clearance

signal ahead

school zone

pedestrian crossing

roadwork ahead

slippery road

railroad crossing

deer crossing

steep hill

bumps

closed to bicycles

closed to motorcycles

closed to trucks

closed to pedestrians

road signs

major North American road signs

Main signs used in Canada and the United States, inspired more or less by the signs endorsed by the Vienna International Convention of 1968.

stop at intersection

no entry

yield

closed to motorcycles

closed to pedestrians

closed to bicycles

closed to trucks

direction to be followed

direction to be followed

direction to be followed

direction to be followed

no U-turn

passing prohibited

one-way traffic

two-way traffic

double bend

merging traffic

right bend

roadway narrows

slippery road

deer crossing

roadwork ahead

bumps

steep hill

falling rocks

railroad crossing

overhead clearance

signal ahead

school zone

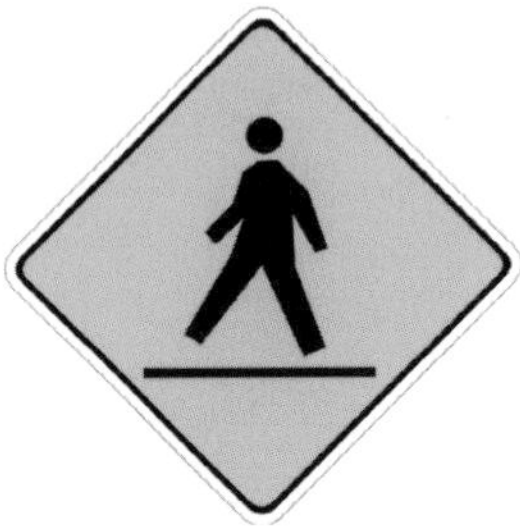
pedestrian crossing

service station

gasoline pump
Machine with a pump for refilling vehicles with fuel.

display
Surface displaying instructions for customers paying by card.

card reader slot
The card is inserted into the device, which verifies the customer's personal identification number (PIN) before the transaction can begin.

alphanumeric keyboard
Set of buttons for entering numbers, letters and other kinds of information.

slip presenter
Slot through which the user is given the payment receipt for the card payment.

type of fuel
Choice of available fuels (such as diesel and gasoline) and the price of each per volume unit (liter or gallon).

operating instructions
Set of instructions explaining the steps to follow to use the gasoline pump.

total sale display
Screen displaying the total price, corresponding to the volume of fuel pumped.

volume display
Screen displaying, in gallons or liters, the volume of fuel pumped.

price per gallon/liter
Screen displaying the price per volume unit (liter or gallon) of the fuel chosen.

pump number

pump nozzle
Gun-shaped spout at the end of the gasoline pump hose and used to pour fuel into the vehicle's tank.

gasoline pump hose
Flexible pipe connected to the pump, maintaining fuel flow.

service station
Commercial establishment comprising one or several gasoline pumps and carrying out general maintenance of vehicles.

mechanics
Workshop where engines and their related systems are maintained and repaired.

ice dispenser
Refrigerated box containing bags of ice for self-service.

car wash
Station where vehicles are automatically washed.

maintenance
Workshop where the necessary checks and adjustments are made to vehicles.

soft-drink dispenser
Automated machine serving soft drinks; it is activated by the insertion of coins into a slot.

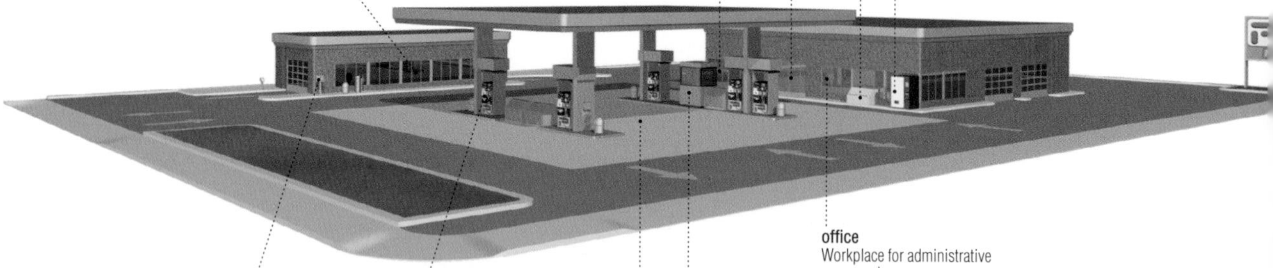

office
Workplace for administrative personnel.

air pump
Machine connected to a compressor, used for inflating tires to their required air pressure.

pump island
Space where the gasoline pumps are installed.

kiosk
Hut where customers can quickly settle their fuel bills.

gasoline pump
Machine with a pump for refilling vehicles with fuel.

automobile

Motor vehicle comprising four wheels, developed for transporting a small number of people and small loads.

examples of bodies

Styles vary from manufacturer to manufacturer and from year to year but there is little variation in the basic model.

sports car
Automobile with an aerodynamic look comprising two doors, a small trunk separate from the passenger compartment and, sometimes, narrow rear seats.

micro compact car
Very small automobile comprising two seats and integrated cargo area, designed to be driven and parked in large cities.

hatchback
Automobile comprising two doors and a lift gate, folding front seats granting access to the rear seats, and a cargo area integrated with the passenger compartment.

two-door sedan
Automobile comprising two doors, a trunk separate from the passenger compartment and four places.

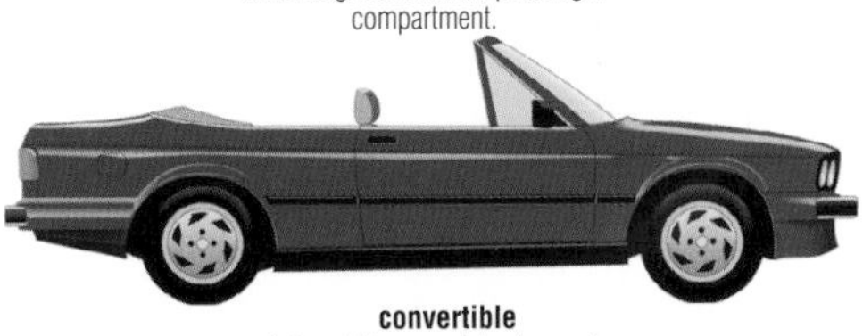

convertible
Automobile comprising two or four doors and a soft or hard retractable roof.

four-door sedan
Automobile comprising four doors and a trunk separate from the passenger compartment.

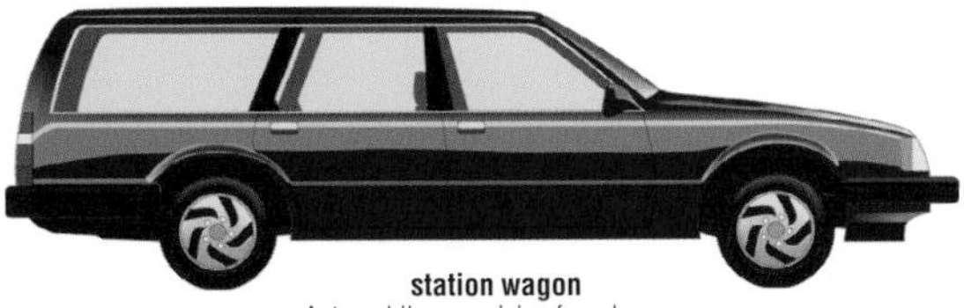

station wagon
Automobile comprising four doors, a large cargo area integrated with the passenger compartment and folding rear seats for enlarging the cargo area.

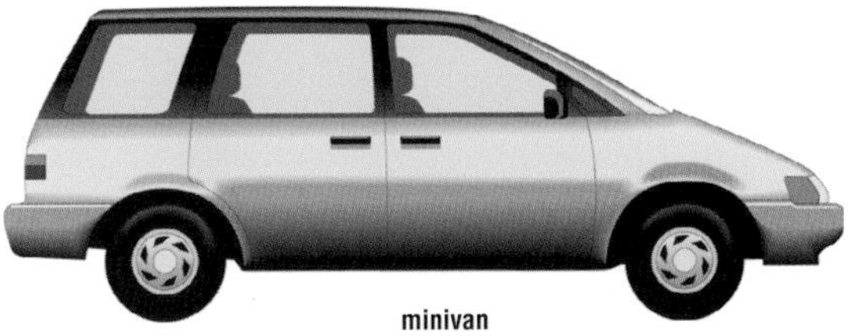

minivan
Automobile comprising three rows of seats; the last row can be folded down to enlarge the cargo area.

sport-utility vehicle
Automobile designed to be driven on any kind of roadway or on rugged terrain.

pickup truck
Automobile comprising only one row of seats and an uncovered bed closed off by a gate.

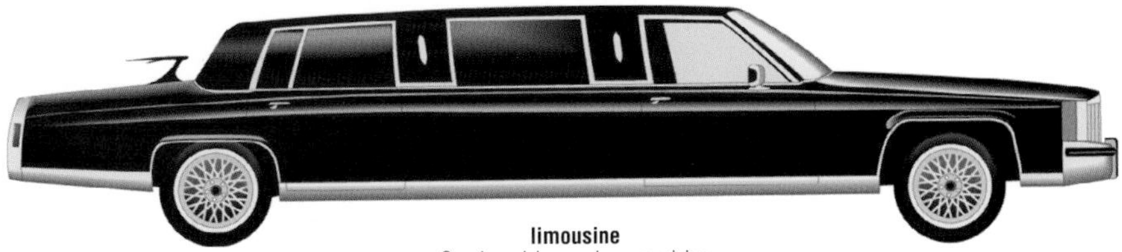

limousine
Spacious deluxe sedan comprising four or more doors; the passenger area is separated from the chauffeur's.

automobile

body
Automobile structure designed to house and protect the mechanical components, the passengers and cargo.

windshield
Glass and plastic pane protecting the occupants from inclement weather while providing good visibility.

outside mirror
Mirror fixed to the outside of the passenger compartment enabling the driver to see behind and along the sides of the vehicle without turning around.

windshield wiper
Rubber squeegee, usually mounted in a pair; it is activated by a motor and cleans the windshield.

cowl
Transverse component of the body between the hood and the windshield allowing air into the passenger compartment.

washer nozzle
Device squirting liquid on the windshield in order to clean it.

hood
Lidlike part of the body covering and protecting the engine.

grille
Plastic or metal grating in front of the vehicle protecting the radiator and serving as decoration.

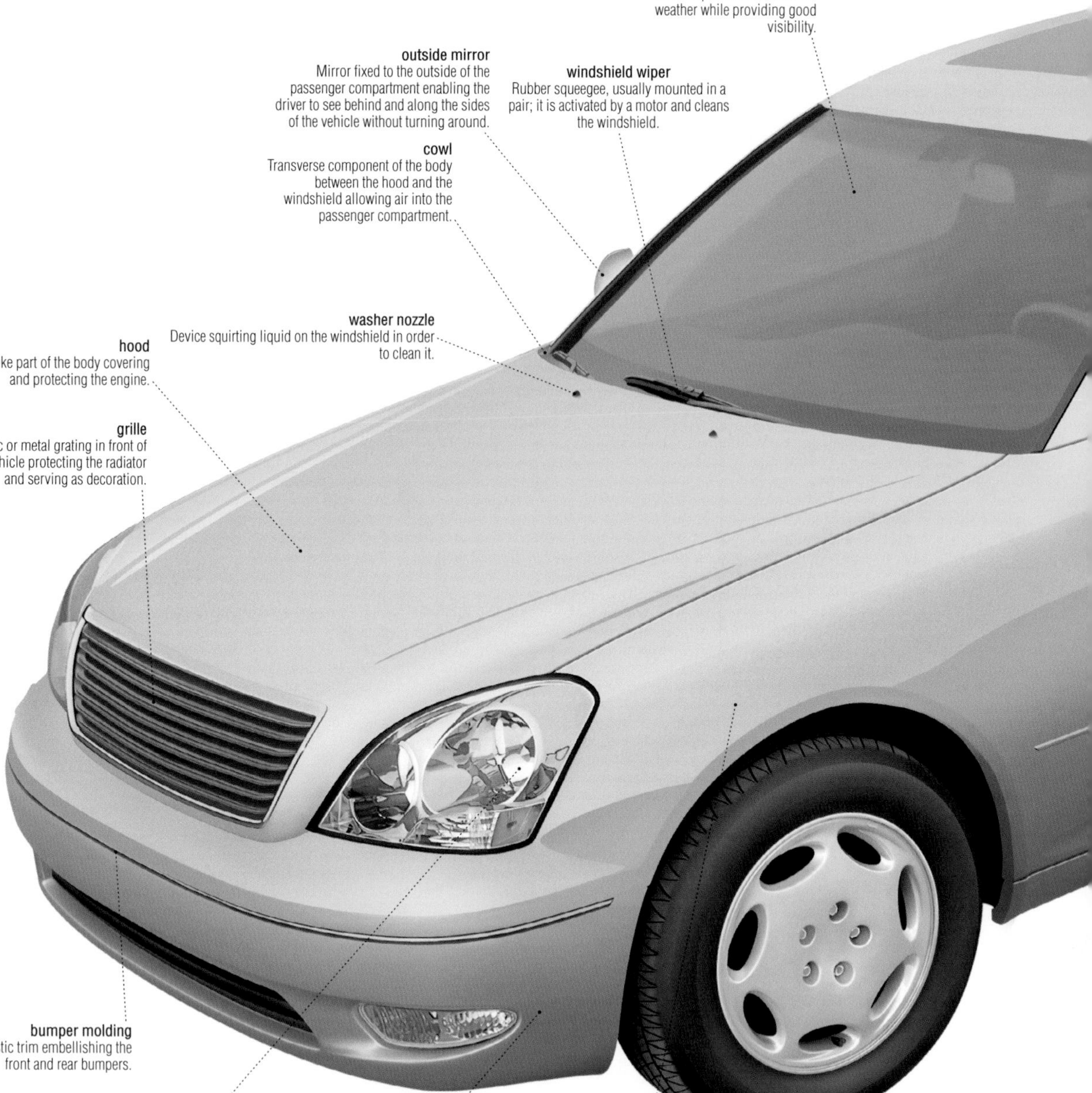

bumper molding
Metal or plastic trim embellishing the front and rear bumpers.

headlight
Lamp on the front of the vehicle to light up the space in front.

front fascia
Component on the exterior of the body below the bumpers reducing air resistance.

fender
Component of the body forming a streamlined and aerodynamic casing around the wheels.

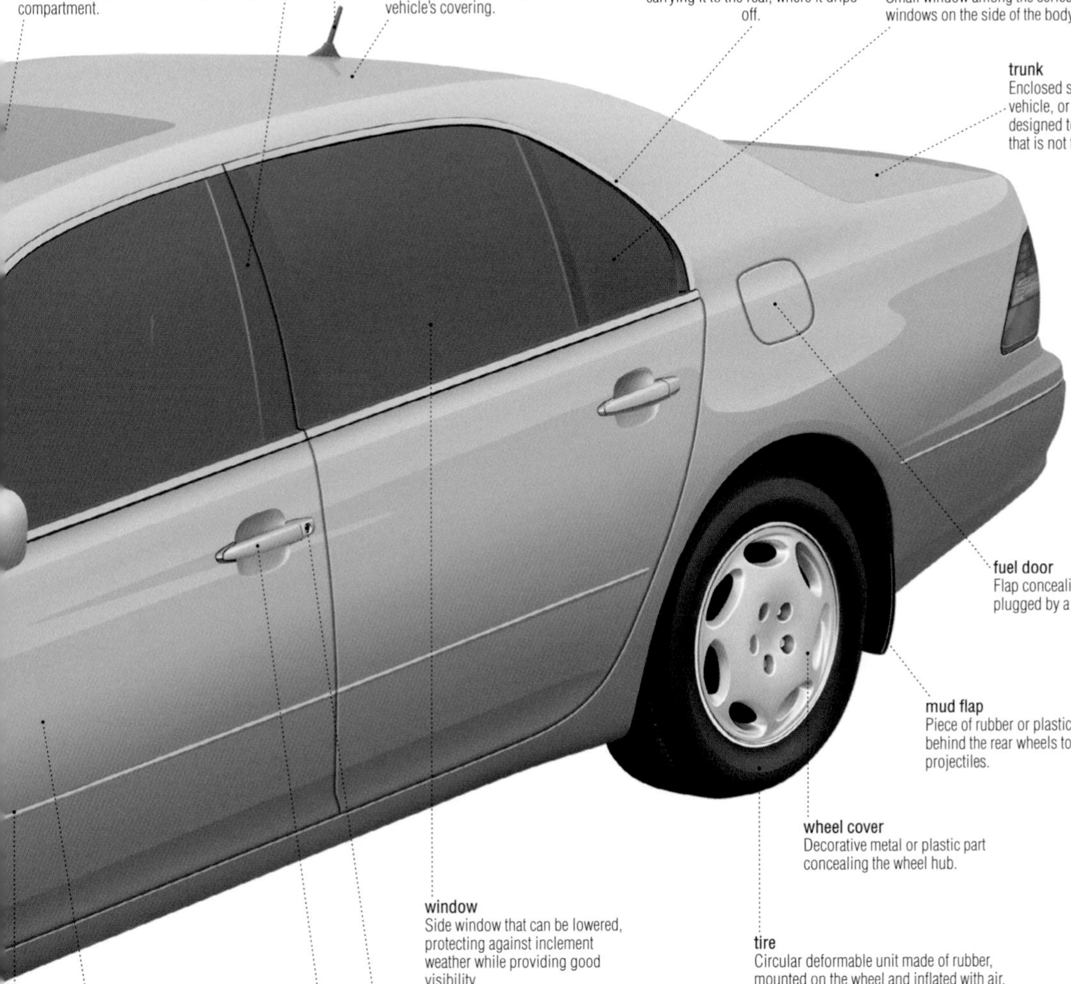

center post
Vertical safety pillar between the two doors connecting the upper part of the body to the lower part.

antenna
Device receiving radio waves broadcast by a station.

sliding sunroof
Moving part in the roof that opens up over the front seats to let air into the passenger compartment.

roof
Exterior component with a slightly curving surface forming the vehicle's covering.

drip molding
Small open canal capturing rainwater from the roof and carrying it to the rear, where it drips off.

quarter window
Small window among the series of windows on the side of the body.

trunk
Enclosed space at the rear of the vehicle, or sometimes at the front, designed to hold and transport cargo that is not too large.

fuel door
Flap concealing the fuel-tank opening, which is plugged by a cap.

mud flap
Piece of rubber or plastic attached behind the rear wheels to repel projectiles.

wheel cover
Decorative metal or plastic part concealing the wheel hub.

window
Side window that can be lowered, protecting against inclement weather while providing good visibility.

tire
Circular deformable unit made of rubber, mounted on the wheel and inflated with air, providing the connection between the car and the road, and absorbing the unevenness of the road.

door
Moving panel with a handle, attached to the body by hinges or a sliding system, providing access to the passenger compartment.

door lock
Mechanism housed in the door to lock it; it is manipulated with a key or button.

body side molding
Metal or plastic part attached along the doors to protect them against light impact.

door handle
Device for activating the door's opening mechanism.

automobile

automobile systems: main parts
A vehicle is composed of basic mechanical parts and devices making up its systems; each of them fulfills a specific function.

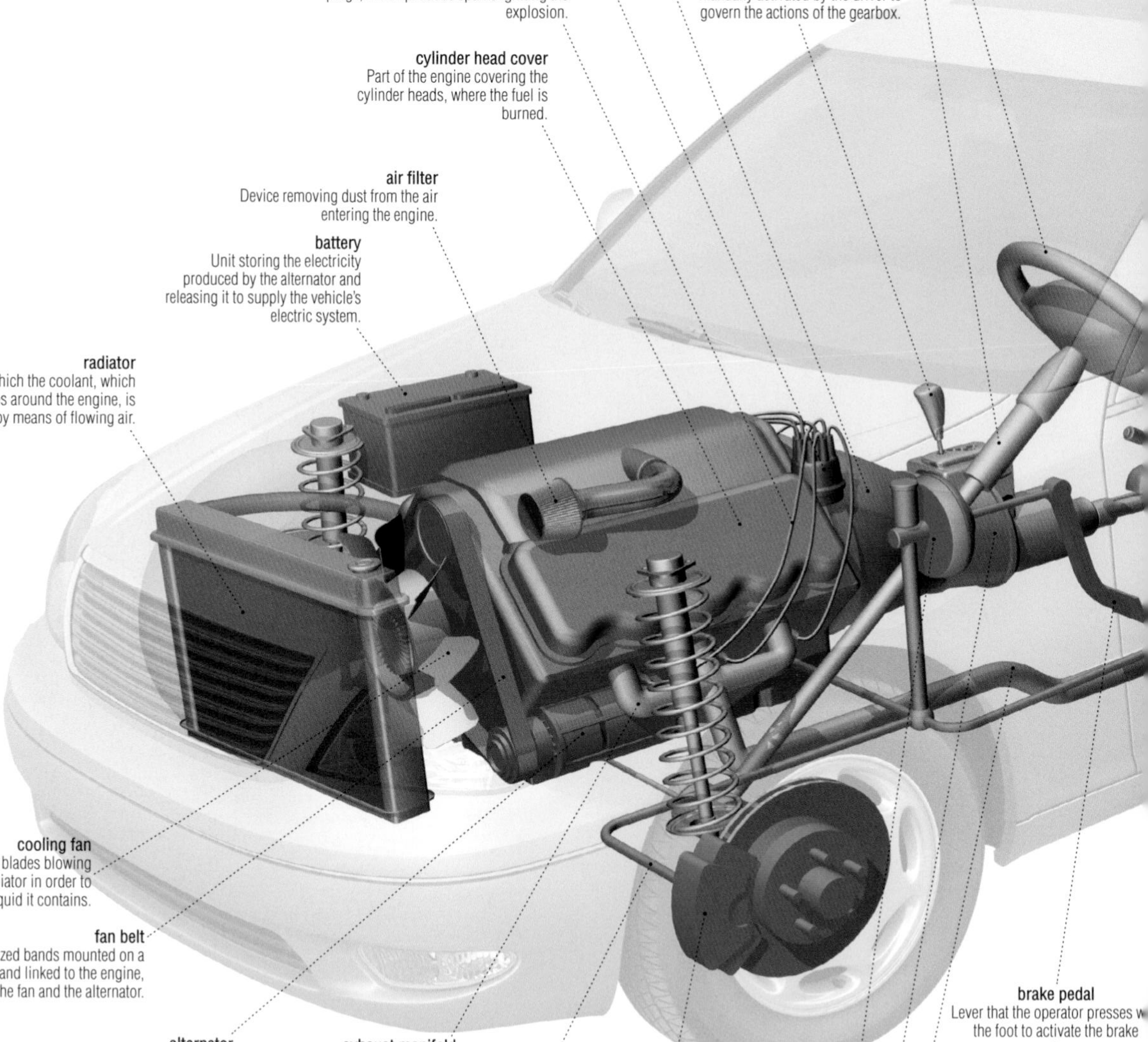
hand brak
Lever in the passenger compartmen that is connected to the rear wheels the driver manually activates it t stop the vehicle or in case c emergency
clutch
Mechanism disengaging and reengaging the engine and the gearbox in order to change gears.
steering wheel
Circular instrument used by the operator for steering the guide wheels.
distributor cap
Unit supplying the electric current necessary for producing sparks that ignite the fuel in the engine.
steering column
Mechanism transmitting the steering wheel's rotational motion to the steering gearbox.
spark plug cable
Electric wire carrying the high-voltage current from the distributor to the spark plugs, which produce sparks igniting the explosion.
gearshift lever
Control for the gearbox that is manually activated by the driver to govern the actions of the gearbox.
cylinder head cover
Part of the engine covering the cylinder heads, where the fuel is burned.
air filter
Device removing dust from the air entering the engine.
battery
Unit storing the electricity produced by the alternator and releasing it to supply the vehicle's electric system.
radiator
Vessel in which the coolant, which circulates around the engine, is cooled by means of flowing air.
cooling fan
Mechanism with blades blowing air across the radiator in order to cool the liquid it contains.
fan belt
Rubberized bands mounted on a pulley and linked to the engine, driving the fan and the alternator.
brake pedal
Lever that the operator presses w the foot to activate the brake system.
alternator
Current generator driven by the engine, which recharges the battery to supply the electric system.
exhaust manifold
Set of pipes at the exit of the cylinders, capturing the combustion gases to conduct them to the exhaust pipe.
disc brake
Braking mechanism comprising a disc attached to the wheel, whose rotation is slowed down when the brake pads exert friction on it.
exhaust pipe
Tubular conduit conducting the combustion gases from the exhaust manifold to the catalytic converter.
braking circuit
System of tubes containing a fluid that activates the brakes when they come under pressure from the pedal.
brake booster
Mechanism amplifying the force exerted by the driver on the brake pedal.
gearbox
Unit changing the ratio between the rotation speed of the engine and that of the wheels in the forward gears, or reversing the rotation in the reverse gear.

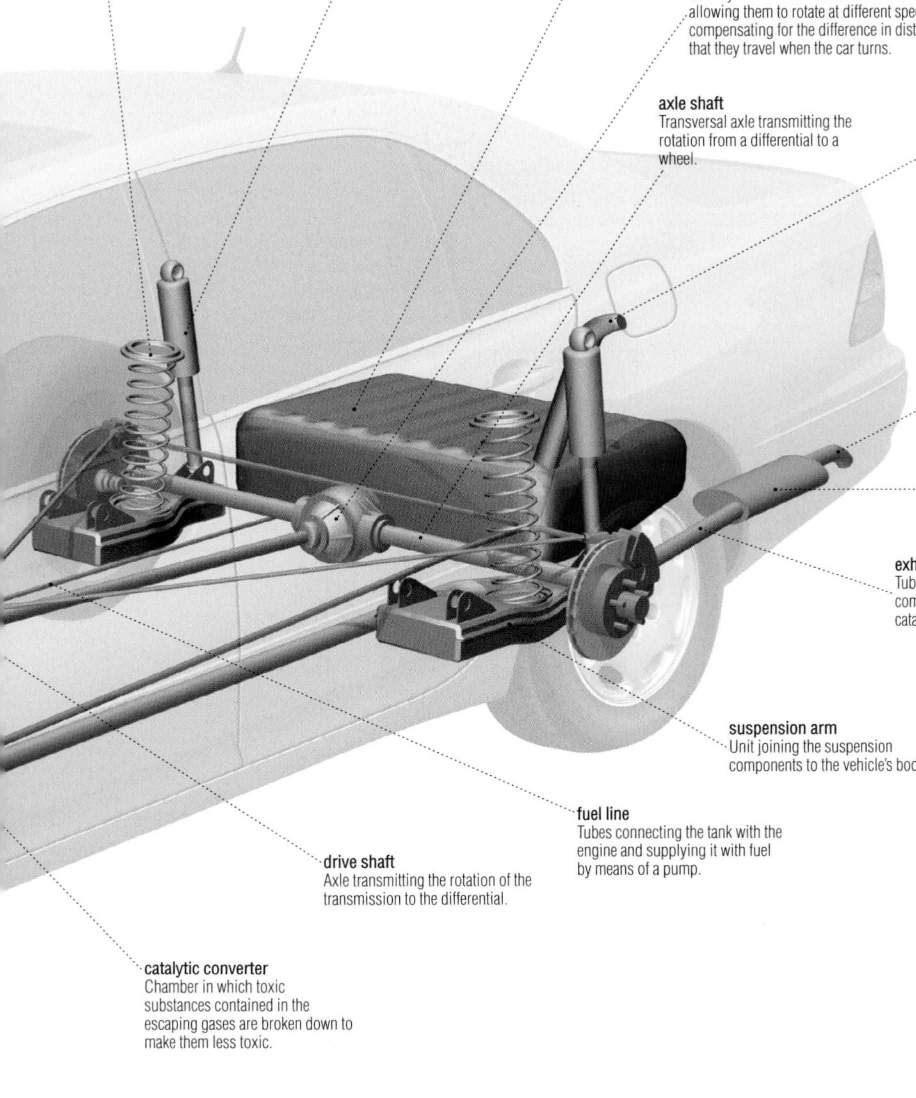
coil spring
Elastic metal shank wound up in a spiral, supporting the weight of the vehicle and absorbing the shocks used by any unevenness in the road.
shock absorber
Telescopic cylinder, pneumatic or hydraulic, reducing the spring's oscillations.
fuel tank
Reservoir containing the fuel that makes the vehicle self-sufficient.
differential
Gear system located between the two wheels, allowing them to rotate at different speeds and compensating for the difference in distance that they travel when the car turns.
axle shaft
Transversal axle transmitting the rotation from a differential to a wheel.
filler neck
Conduit connected to the tank for filling it.
tail pipe
Conduit expelling the combustion gases from the muffler to the ambient air.
muffler
Compartmentalized chamber in which the escaping gases expand, thus reducing the noise from the engine.
exhaust pipe
Tubular conduit carrying the combustion gases from the catalytic converter to the muffler.
suspension arm
Unit joining the suspension components to the vehicle's body.
fuel line
Tubes connecting the tank with the engine and supplying it with fuel by means of a pump.
drive shaft
Axle transmitting the rotation of the transmission to the differential.
catalytic converter
Chamber in which toxic substances contained in the escaping gases are broken down to make them less toxic.

automobile systems

Each system is a set of interdependent parts fulfilling a specific function and capable of functioning on its own.

suspension system
Set of components that joins the wheels to the vehicle's body while reducing shocks caused by the road's unevenness and improving the hold on the road.

transmission system
Set of components transmitting the motion produced by the motor to the wheels.

fuel supply system
Set of components supplying the fuel to the engine.

steering system
Set of components that direct the front wheels to guide the vehicle as it moves.

braking system
Set of components that reduce the vehicle's speed, eventually to a halt, and keep it in place while parked.

electrical system
Set of components supplying the necessary current for starting the vehicle and operating its electric accessories.

exhaust system
Set of components designed to expel the engine's burned gases into the ambient air.

gasoline engine
Engine in which a mixture of air and gasoline is compressed and ignited to produce an explosion whose energy is converted into mechanical energy.

cooling system
Set of components that prevents the temperature of the engine from rising excessively.

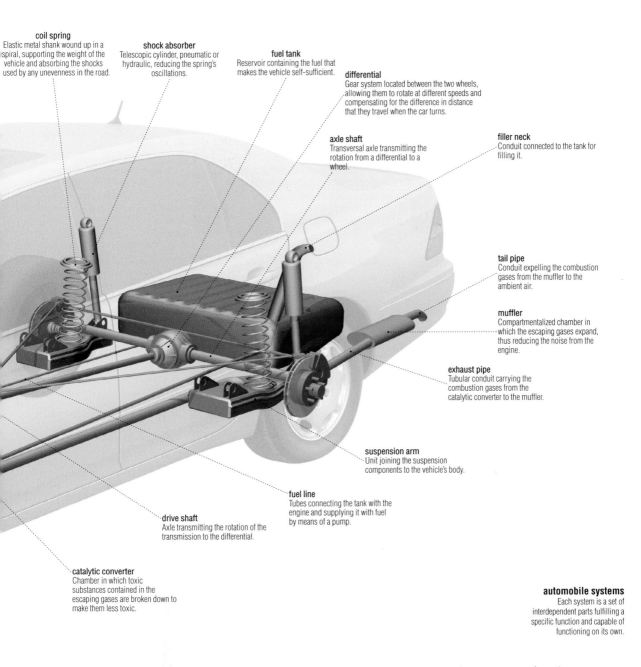

automobile

headlights
Set of regulation luminous devices placed on the front of a vehicle for illuminating and signaling.

high beam
Lamp illuminating the road over a long distance (100 yards), used outside urban areas.

low beam
Lamp illuminating the road at short distances (30 yards), used instead of high beam to avoid blinding drivers coming in the opposite direction.

fog light
Lamp whose light rays are directed toward the roadway and illuminate the road shoulder, by which the driver navigates in the event of fog.

turn signal
Device emitting an intermittent light, signaling a change of the vehicle's direction or a temporary hazard to other vehicles.

side marker light
Colored light demarcating the width of the vehicle.

taillights
Set of regulation lighting devices placed at the rear of a vehicle and used for signaling.

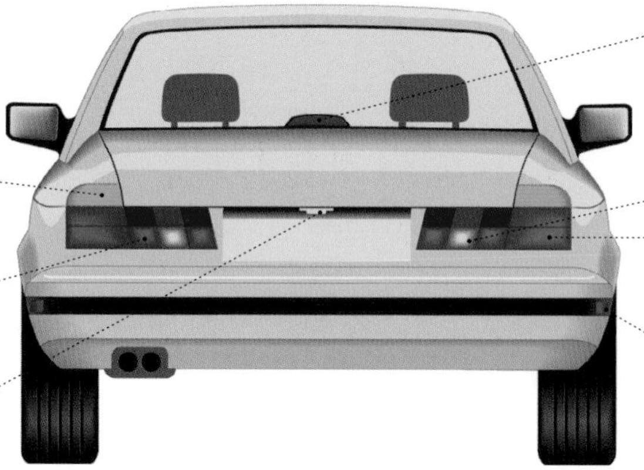

turn signal
Device emitting an intermittent light, signaling a change of the vehicle's direction or a temporary hazard to other vehicles.

brake light
Light that goes on automatically when the driver steps on the brake pedal in order to warn the vehicles following it.

license plate light
Lighting device for a vehicle's license plate, making it visible in darkness.

brake light
Light that goes on automatically when the driver steps on the brake pedal in order to warn the vehicles following it.

back-uo light
White lamp that turns on automatically to warn motorists and pedestrians when the driver puts the car in reverse.

taillight
Lamp turning on automatically when the front lights are lit, making the vehicle visible for up to 150 yards.

side marker light
Colored light demarcating the width of the vehicle.

door
Moving panel with a handle, attached to the body by hinges or a sliding system, providing access to the passenger compartment.

interior door handle
Mechanism for opening the door from the inside of the vehicle.

assist grip
Handle allowing the passenger to pull the door inward in order to close it.

outside mirror control
Lever for adjusting the position of the outside mirror from the inside.

window regulator handle
Handily placed lever that turns to activate the mechanism raising and lowering the window.

hinge
Articulating mechanism supporting the door and enabling it to pivot while it is being opened and closed.

accessory pocket
Open compartment fitted into the bottom of the door, for storing small objects.

window
Side window that can be lowered; it protects against inclement weather while ensuring good visibility.

interior door lock button
Visible end of the rod activating the lock; it is lifted or lowered to unlock and lock the door.

armrest
Support fixed to the door, for resting the arm.

lock
Mechanism housed in the door to lock it; it is manipulated with a key or button.

trim panel
Component covered with fabric, plastic or leather, upholstering the inside of the door.

inner door shell
The door's metal structure, serving to absorb impacts; it also encloses the locking mechanisms and, when it is lowered, the window.

ucket seat: front view

ucket seat: upholstered and adjustable seat that envelopes
ıe occupant's body, keeping it in place during turns and
roviding greater comfort.

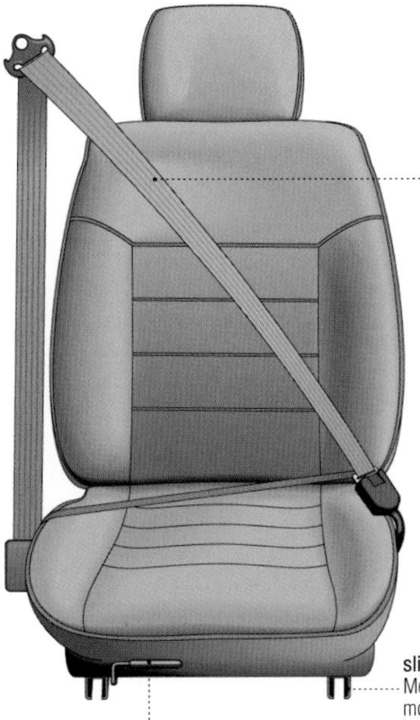
shoulder belt
Strap crossing in front of the passenger's thorax, from the shoulder to the hip.
sliding rail
Metal part along which the seat moves forward and backward.
sliding lever
Handle for moving the seat toward or away from the dashboard, in relation to the passenger's height.

bucket seat: side view

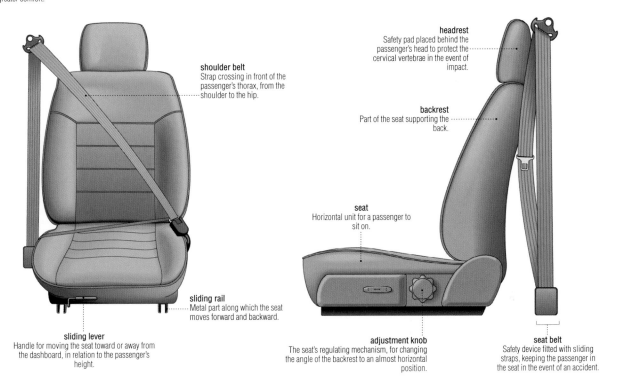

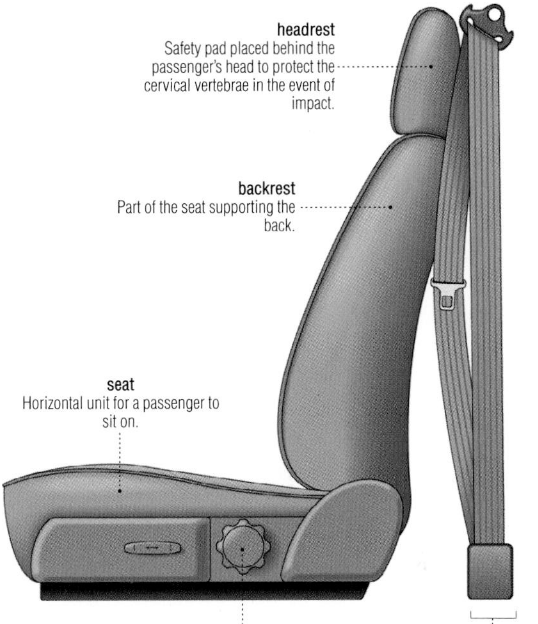
headrest
Safety pad placed behind the passenger's head to protect the cervical vertebrae in the event of impact.
backrest
Part of the seat supporting the back.
seat
Horizontal unit for a passenger to sit on.
adjustment knob
The seat's regulating mechanism, for changing the angle of the backrest to an almost horizontal position.
seat belt
Safety device fitted with sliding straps, keeping the passenger in the seat in the event of an accident.

rear seat

Bench containing several spaces installed in the rear of the passenger compartment and occupying its full width.

armrest
Folding support in the middle of the rear seat, for resting the forearm.
webbing
Center belt in the rear seat, strapping in the passenger's pelvis and restraining only the lower part of the body in the event of impact.
buckle
Clasp keeping the seat belt around the passenger and released by pressing with the finger.
bench seat
Horizontal unit for sitting on, providing up to three spaces.

automobile

dashboard
Component in the passenger compartment comprising the instrument panel, the manual controls, storage and other accessories.

rearview mirror
Mirror mounted on the windshield, positioned by the driver so that the vehicles following behind can be seen in it.

vanity mirror
Small mirror on the inside of the sun visor.

on-board computer
Computer integrated into the vehicle; it provides information about the vehicle's main components and helps the driver with tasks related to driving.

sun visor
Movable panel that the passenger can lower over the upper part of the windshield or of the side window to prevent being blinded by the Sun.

wiper switch
Electric mechanism for switching on the windshield wipers, controlling their speed and activating the windshield washer fluid.

cruise control
Mechanism enabling the driver to maintain a cruising speed for the vehicle.

glove compartment
Small storage space fitted with a locking door.

vent
Opening, usually covered by an adjustable grille, allowing warm or cold air into the passenger compartment.

ignition switch
Switch activated by a contact key allowing a current from the battery to flow to the starter.

horn
Device emitting a loud sound that the driver can use to attract the attention of a pedestrian or other user of the road.

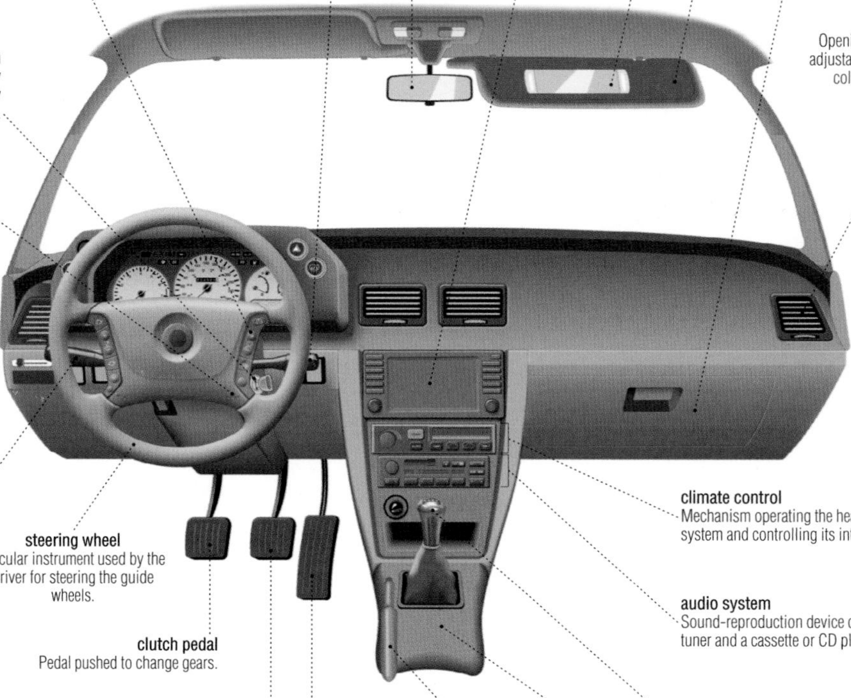

climate control
Mechanism operating the heating or air-conditioning system and controlling its intensity.

steering wheel
Circular instrument used by the driver for steering the guide wheels.

audio system
Sound-reproduction device comprising a tuner and a cassette or CD player.

clutch pedal
Pedal pushed to change gears.

gearshift lever
Control for the gearbox that is manually activated by the driver to change gears.

headlight/turn signal
Lever having several positions that control the turn signals and the low and high beams.

parking brake lever
Lever connected to the rear-wheel brakes that the driver activates manually to stop the vehicle, or in case of emergency.

center console
Component located between the front seats and containing certain accessories and control devices, especially the parking brake and gearshift levers.

brake pedal
Lever that the driver presses with the foot to activate the brake system.

gas pedal
Unit controlled by the foot to increase, maintain or decrease the vehicle's speed.

air bag restraint system
Automatic safety device containing air bags that, in the event of impact, instantly come between the occupants and the dashboard.

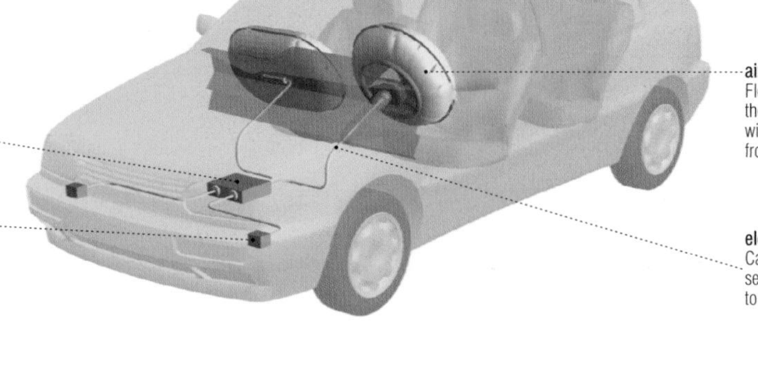

air bag
Flexible envelope encased in the dashboard, the steering wheel or the doors, which inflates with pressurized gas when it receives the sign from the safing sensor.

safing sensor
Device that receives the signal from the primary sensor and deploys the air bags. It has safeguards against deploying accidentally.

primary crash sensor
Device located at the front of the vehicle, which, in the event of collision, transmits the pulse it receives to the safing sensor.

electrical cable
Cable connecting the safing sensor, which causes the air bags to deploy.

instrument panel
Set of dials and warning lights within the driver's view that report on the vehicle's functioning.

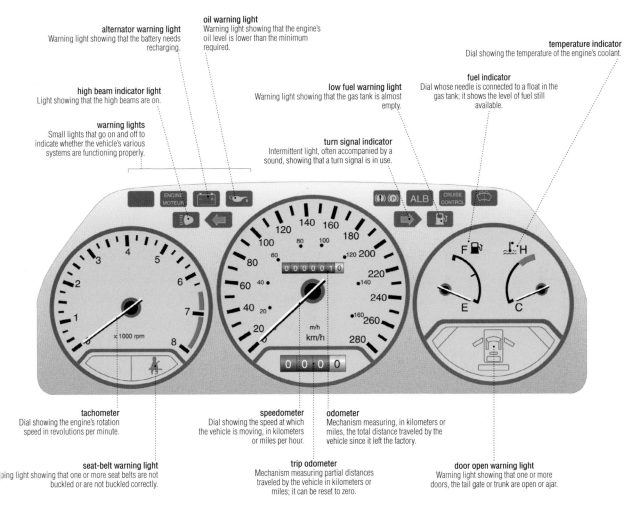

alternator warning light
Warning light showing that the battery needs recharging.

oil warning light
Warning light showing that the engine's oil level is lower than the minimum required.

temperature indicator
Dial showing the temperature of the engine's coolant.

high beam indicator light
Light showing that the high beams are on.

low fuel warning light
Warning light showing that the gas tank is almost empty.

fuel indicator
Dial whose needle is connected to a float in the gas tank; it shows the level of fuel still available.

warning lights
Small lights that go on and off to indicate whether the vehicle's various systems are functioning properly.

turn signal indicator
Intermittent light, often accompanied by a sound, showing that a turn signal is in use.

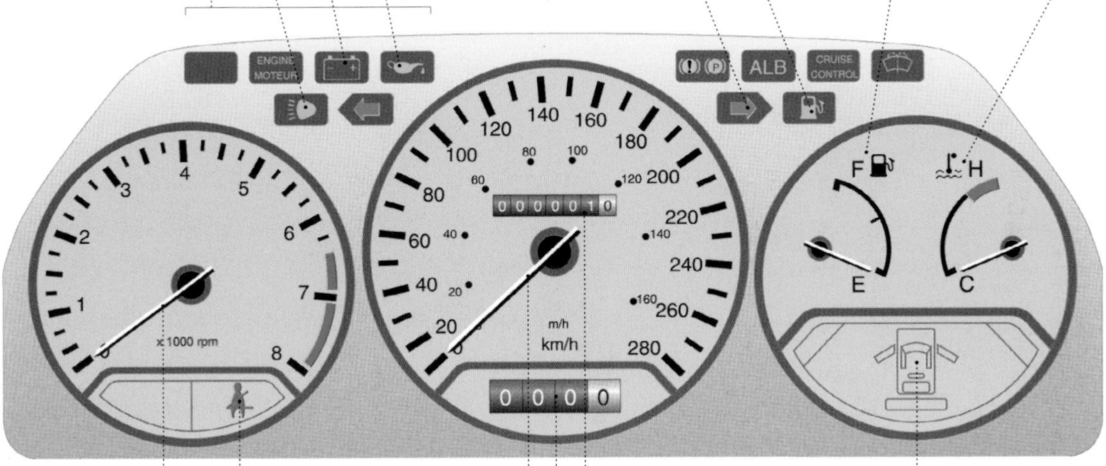

tachometer
Dial showing the engine's rotation speed in revolutions per minute.

speedometer
Dial showing the speed at which the vehicle is moving, in kilometers or miles per hour.

odometer
Mechanism measuring, in kilometers or miles, the total distance traveled by the vehicle since it left the factory.

seat-belt warning light
ning light showing that one or more seat belts are not buckled or are not buckled correctly.

trip odometer
Mechanism measuring partial distances traveled by the vehicle in kilometers or miles; it can be reset to zero.

door open warning light
Warning light showing that one or more doors, the tail gate or trunk are open or ajar.

windshield wiper
Rubber squeegee, usually mounted in a pair; it is activated by a motor and cleans the windshield.

windshield wiper blade
Metal part supporting the wiper through the actions of two small connecting rods.

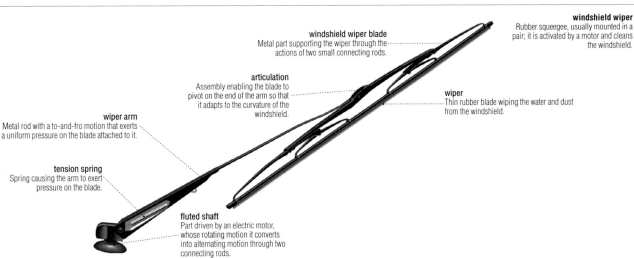

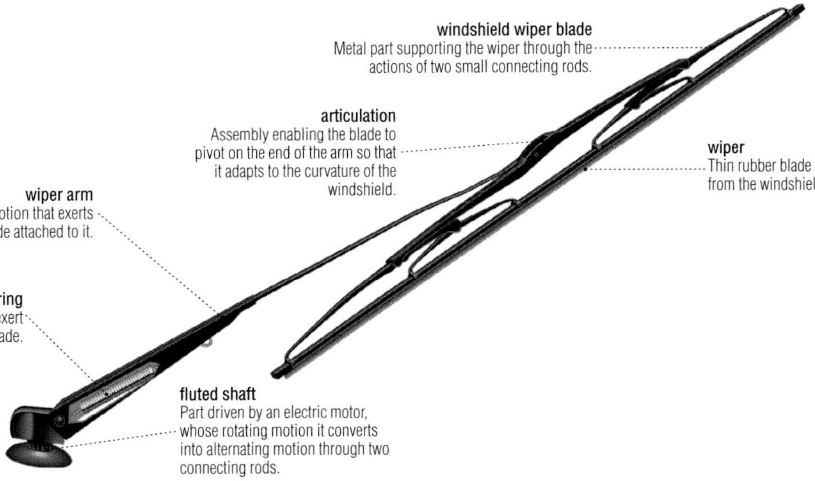

articulation
Assembly enabling the blade to pivot on the end of the arm so that it adapts to the curvature of the windshield.

wiper
Thin rubber blade wiping the water and dust from the windshield.

wiper arm
Metal rod with a to-and-fro motion that exerts a uniform pressure on the blade attached to it.

tension spring
Spring causing the arm to exert pressure on the blade.

fluted shaft
Part driven by an electric motor, whose rotating motion it converts into alternating motion through two connecting rods.

automobile

accessories

Secondary components of a vehicle, used for its maintenance, safety and such.

roller shade
Shade with a roller containing a spring that causes the shade cloth to roll up; it is usually placed on a side window.

jumper cables
Cables fitted with alligator clips for connecting an emergency battery to a discharged one.

black clamp
A black clamp is fitted on the negative terminal of the emergency battery; the other is attached to a metal part of the other car.

red clamp
A red clamp is fitted on the positive terminal of both batteries.

cable

floor mat
Fabric or rubber covering placed under the passengers' feet in order to protect the floor of the vehicle.

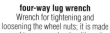

snow brush with scraper
Small broom with one end for removing snow from the vehicle and the other for scraping ice off the windows.

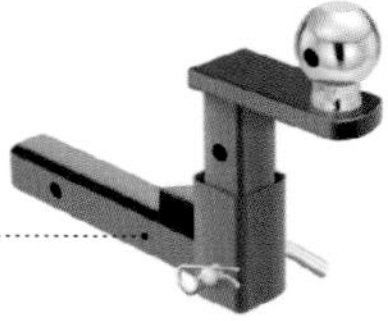

ball mount
Part attached under the rear of the vehicle, with a hitch ball on one end; the trailer's or caravan's hitch articulates with it.

hitch ball
Device for hooking up a trailer or caravan to a vehicle.

four-way lug wrench
Wrench for tightening and loosening the wheel nuts; it is made up of two crossed rods with each end having a different size.

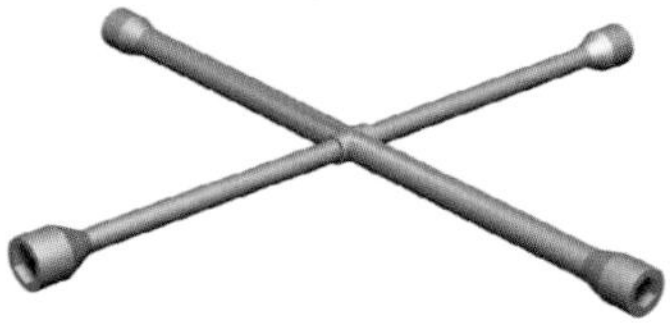

ski rack
Support placed on the vehicle's roof, for mounting and transporting skis.

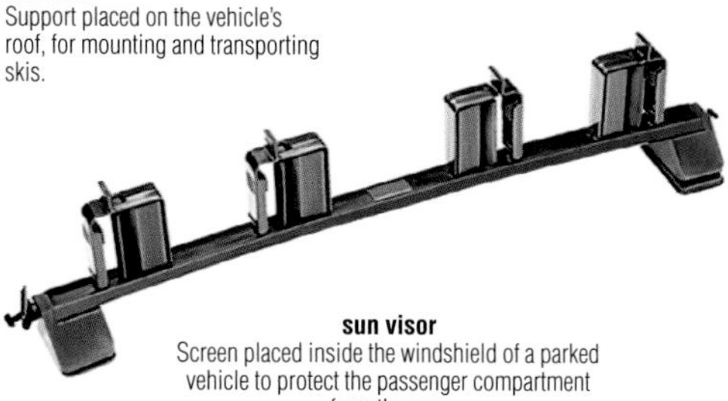

bike carrier
Support placed on the roof or the rear of the vehicle, on which one or more bicycles can be mounted and transported.

jack
Mechanism activated by a handle, for raising the vehicle.

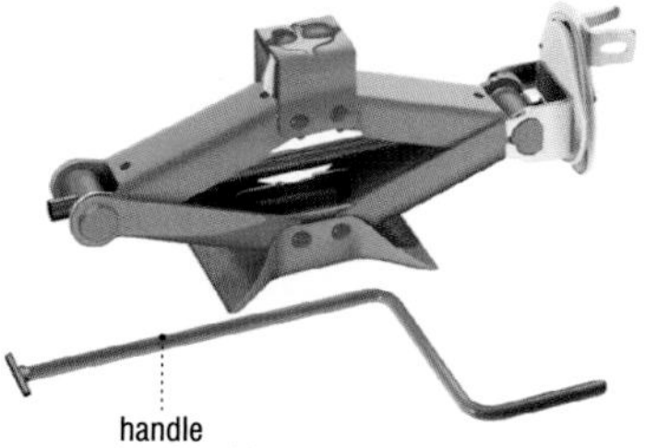

handle
Lever comprising two right-angle bends, for activating the jack mechanism to raise and lower it.

sun visor
Screen placed inside the windshield of a parked vehicle to protect the passenger compartment from the sun.

car cover
Flexible casing for covering and protecting the vehicle from the sun, dust and inclement weather.

child safety seat
Chair adapted to the size of a child; it is equipped with a safety harness for keeping the child seated and attached to the rear seat by the seat belt.

brakes

Units slowing down or stopping the rotation of the vehicle's wheels.

disc brake
Braking mechanism comprising a disc attached to the wheel, whose rotation is slowed down when the brake pads exert friction on it.

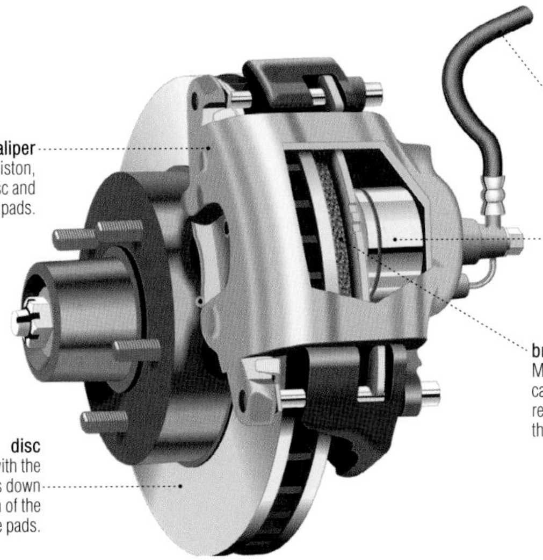

caliper
Viselike part comprising a piston, which straddles the brake disc and supports the brake pads.

disc
Round plate interlocked with the wheel whose rotation slows down as it is braked by the friction of the brake pads.

brake line
Tube carrying the brake fluid, which becomes pressurized when the driver steps on the brake pedal.

piston
Part put into motion by hydraulic pressure, which pushes the brake pads to squeeze the disc.

brake pad
Metal plate that is held by the caliper; it is covered with a heat-resistant material that rubs against the disc to slow down its rotation.

drum brake
Braking mechanism comprising a drum interlocked with the wheel; the brake shoes rub against the drum to slow down the wheel's rotation.

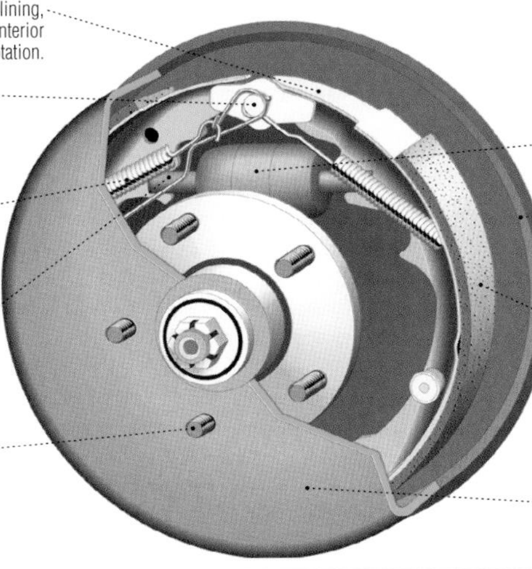

brake shoe
Crescent-shaped part interlocked with an anchor pin; it is fitted with a lining, which moves against the interior surface of the drum to slow its rotation.

anchor pin
Axle serving as an anchoring point for the brake shoe, enabling it to move when acted upon by the piston.

return spring
Spring returning the brake shoe to its initial position once the pressure on the brake pedal has ceased.

piston
Part that slides in the cylinder under hydraulic pressure and pushes the brake shoe against the drum.

lug
Part for assembling and interlocking the drum and the wheel.

wheel cylinder
Mechanism with a cylinder and two pistons that converts the hydraulic pressure in the master cylinder to mechanical force that is applied to the brake shoes.

backing plate
Fixed part serving as a mount for the brake shoes, cylinder and anchor pin.

brake lining
Band of material attached to the brake shoe; heat resistant, it increases the frictional force on the drum.

drum
Part interlocked with the wheel so that the wheel slows its rotation when the brake shoes rub against the inside of the drum.

antilock braking system (ABS)
Electronic device controlling the hydraulic pressure in the braking circuit, to prevent the wheels from locking.

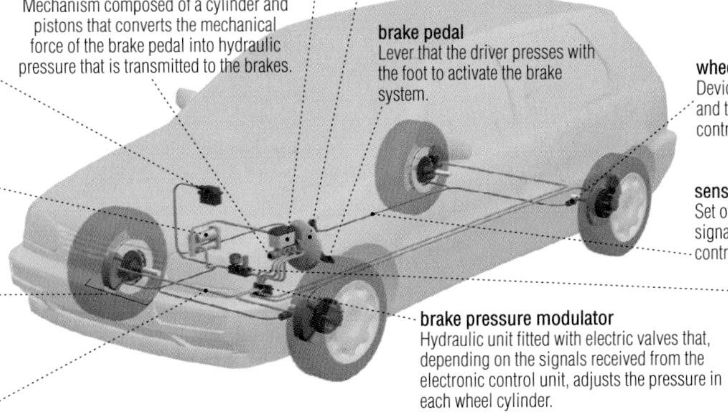

brake fluid reservoir
Reservoir supplying the master cylinder with the fluid that transmits pressure to the brakes after the driver presses the brake pedal.

brake booster
Mechanism amplifying the force exerted by the driver on the brake pedal.

electronic control unit
Device that, as a result of signals received from the wheel speed sensor, controls the brake pressure modulator to give the optimal hydraulic pressure.

master cylinder
Mechanism composed of a cylinder and pistons that converts the mechanical force of the brake pedal into hydraulic pressure that is transmitted to the brakes.

brake pedal
Lever that the driver presses with the foot to activate the brake system.

wheel speed sensor
Device sensing the rotation speed of a wheel and transmitting that information to the control unit.

pump and motor assembly
Pump driven by an electric motor, circulating the brake fluid from the accumulator to the master cylinder.

disc brake
Braking mechanism comprising a disc attached to the wheel, whose rotation is slowed down when the brake pads exert friction on it.

sensor wiring circuit
Set of electric wires transmitting the signals from the sensor to the electronic control unit.

accumulator
Device temporarily holding the hydraulic brake fluid while the modulator lowers the pressure.

braking circuit
System of tubes containing a fluid that activates the brakes when they come under pressure from the pedal.

brake pressure modulator
Hydraulic unit fitted with electric valves that, depending on the signals received from the electronic control unit, adjusts the pressure in each wheel cylinder.

tire

Circular deformable unit made of rubber, mounted on the wheel and inflated with air, providing the connection between the car and the road, and absorbing the unevenness of the road.

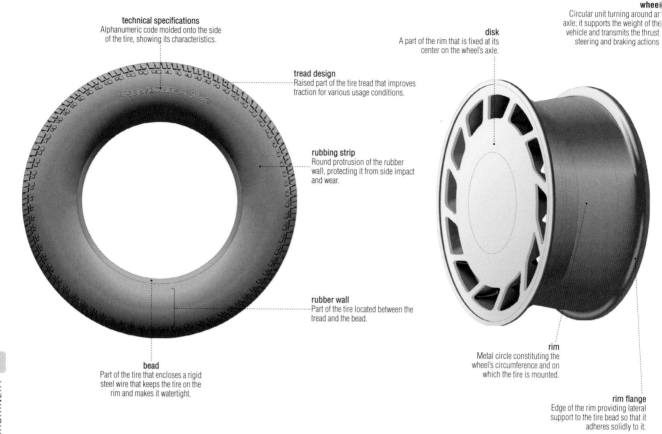

technical specifications
Alphanumeric code molded onto the side of the tire, showing its characteristics.

tread design
Raised part of the tire tread that improves traction for various usage conditions.

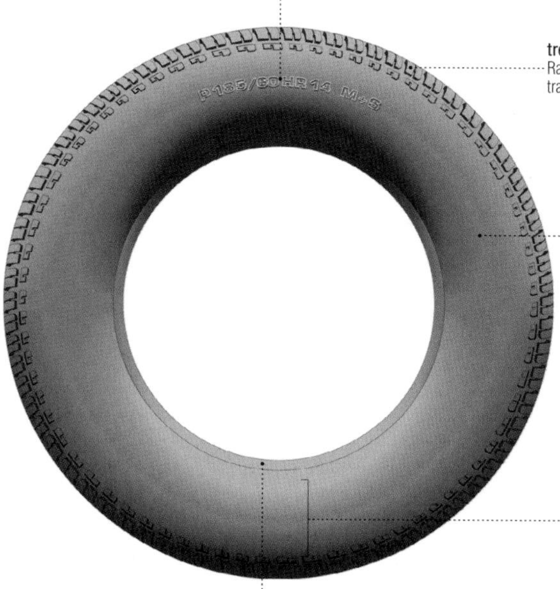

rubbing strip
Round protrusion of the rubber wall, protecting it from side impact and wear.

rubber wall
Part of the tire located between the tread and the bead.

bead
Part of the tire that encloses a rigid steel wire that keeps the tire on the rim and makes it watertight.

whee
Circular unit turning around ar axle; it supports the weight of the vehicle and transmits the thrust steering and braking actions

disk
A part of the rim that is fixed at its center on the wheel's axle.

rim
Metal circle constituting the wheel's circumference and on which the tire is mounted.

rim flange
Edge of the rim providing lateral support to the tire bead so that it adheres solidly to it.

examples of tires

Depending on the intended conditions and uses, tire construction (e.g., type of rubber, tread design, width) varies widely.

performance tire
Wide tire that withstands particularly high temperatures and offers superior performance in holding the road and handling turns.

all-season tire
Tire designed for driving on roads that are dry, wet or slightly snow-covered.

winter tire
Tire characterized by ridges providing a good grip on snow- and ice-covered roads.

touring tire
Tire designed for driving on dry or wet roads, but not recommended for snow or ice.

studded tire
Tire whose tread is fitted with metal studs, which provide a good grip on icy roads.

tire

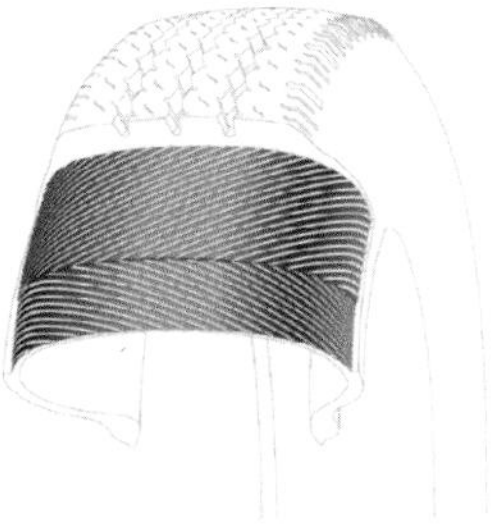

bias-ply tire
Tire with plies whose cords cross each other and are diagonal to the direction of the tread.

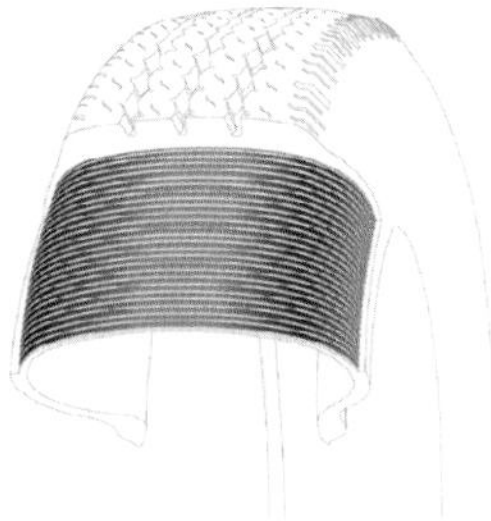

radial tire
Tire with plies whose cords are perpendicular to the direction of the tread.

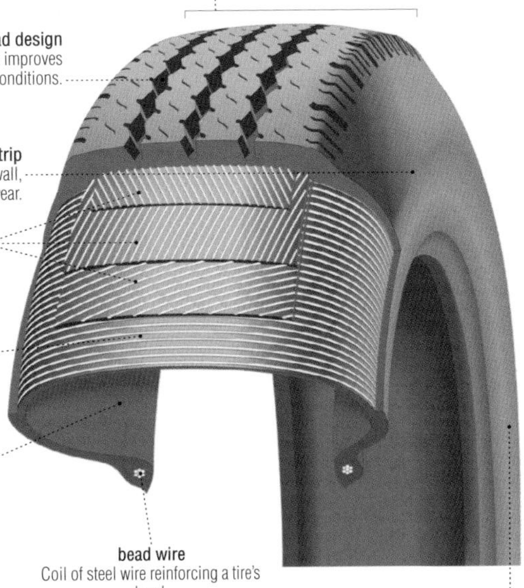

steel belted radial tire
Hybrid tire with addition belts laid on top of the plies of the radial tire; the cords of these belts crisscross each other diagonally.

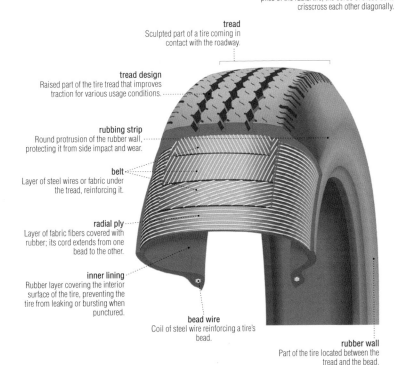

tread
Sculpted part of a tire coming in contact with the roadway.

tread design
Raised part of the tire tread that improves traction for various usage conditions.

rubbing strip
Round protrusion of the rubber wall, protecting it from side impact and wear.

belt
Layer of steel wires or fabric under the tread, reinforcing it.

radial ply
Layer of fabric fibers covered with rubber; its cord extends from one bead to the other.

inner lining
Rubber layer covering the interior surface of the tire, preventing the tire from leaking or bursting when punctured.

bead wire
Coil of steel wire reinforcing a tire's bead.

rubber wall
Part of the tire located between the tread and the bead.

radiator

Vessel in which the coolant, which circulates around the engine, is cooled by means of flowing air.

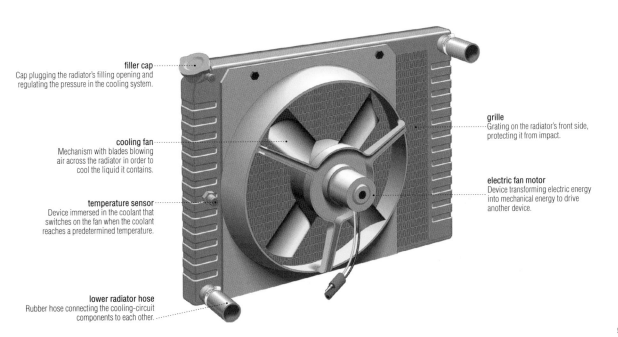

filler cap
Cap plugging the radiator's filling opening and regulating the pressure in the cooling system.

cooling fan
Mechanism with blades blowing air across the radiator in order to cool the liquid it contains.

temperature sensor
Device immersed in the coolant that switches on the fan when the coolant reaches a predetermined temperature.

lower radiator hose
Rubber hose connecting the cooling-circuit components to each other.

grille
Grating on the radiator's front side, protecting it from impact.

electric fan motor
Device transforming electric energy into mechanical energy to drive another device.

spark plug

Electric device whose two electrodes produce the spark necessary to ignite the air/gasoline mixture in the cylinder.

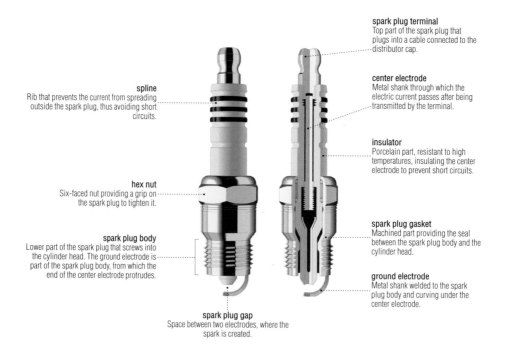

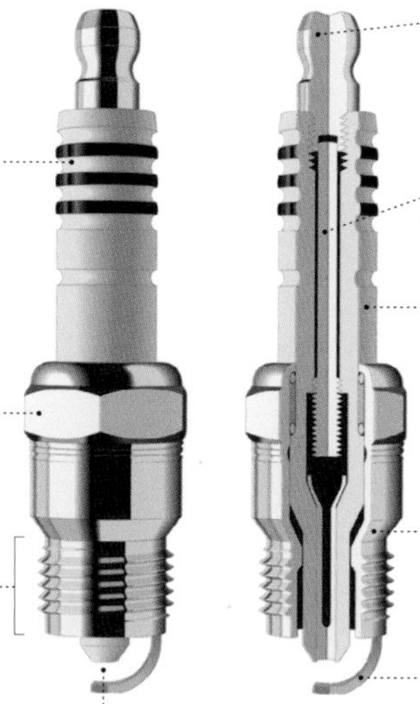
spark plug terminal
Top part of the spark plug that plugs into a cable connected to the distributor cap.
spline
Rib that prevents the current from spreading outside the spark plug, thus avoiding short circuits.
center electrode
Metal shank through which the electric current passes after being transmitted by the terminal.
insulator
Porcelain part, resistant to high temperatures, insulating the center electrode to prevent short circuits.
hex nut
Six-faced nut providing a grip on the spark plug to tighten it.
spark plug gasket
Machined part providing the seal between the spark plug body and the cylinder head.
spark plug body
Lower part of the spark plug that screws into the cylinder head. The ground electrode is part of the spark plug body, from which the end of the center electrode protrudes.
ground electrode
Metal shank welded to the spark plug body and curving under the center electrode.
spark plug gap
Space between two electrodes, where the spark is created.

battery

Unit storing the electricity produced by the alternator and releasing it to supply the vehicle's electric system.

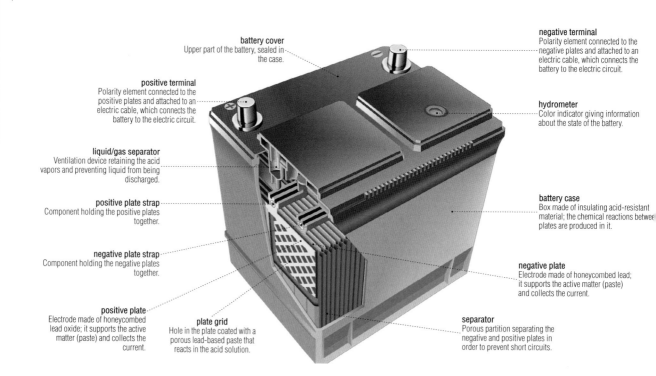

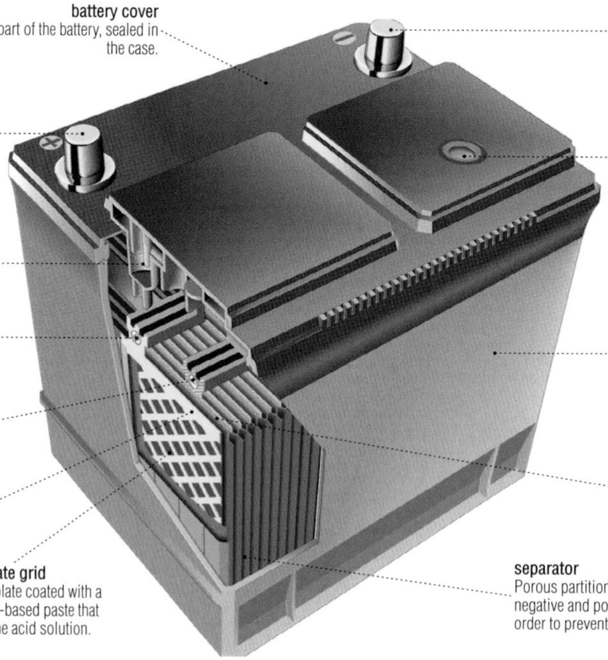
battery cover
Upper part of the battery, sealed in the case.
negative terminal
Polarity element connected to the negative plates and attached to an electric cable, which connects the battery to the electric circuit.
positive terminal
Polarity element connected to the positive plates and attached to an electric cable, which connects the battery to the electric circuit.
hydrometer
Color indicator giving information about the state of the battery.
liquid/gas separator
Ventilation device retaining the acid vapors and preventing liquid from being discharged.
positive plate strap
Component holding the positive plates together.
battery case
Box made of insulating acid-resistant material; the chemical reactions betwee plates are produced in it.
negative plate strap
Component holding the negative plates together.
negative plate
Electrode made of honeycombed lead; it supports the active matter (paste) and collects the current.
positive plate
Electrode made of honeycombed lead oxide; it supports the active matter (paste) and collects the current.
plate grid
Hole in the plate coated with a porous lead-based paste that reacts in the acid solution.
separator
Porous partition separating the negative and positive plates in order to prevent short circuits.

TRANSPORT AND MACHINERY

electric automobile

Car propelled by an electric motor whose energy is provided by a battery.

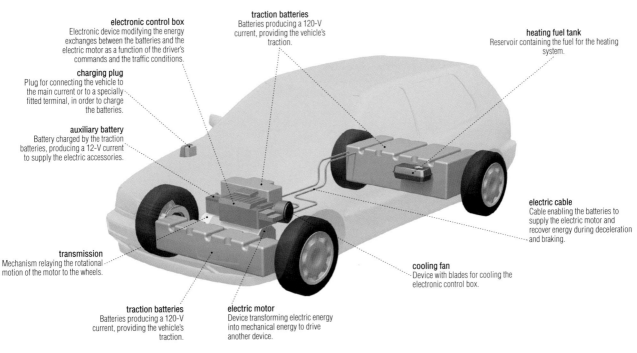

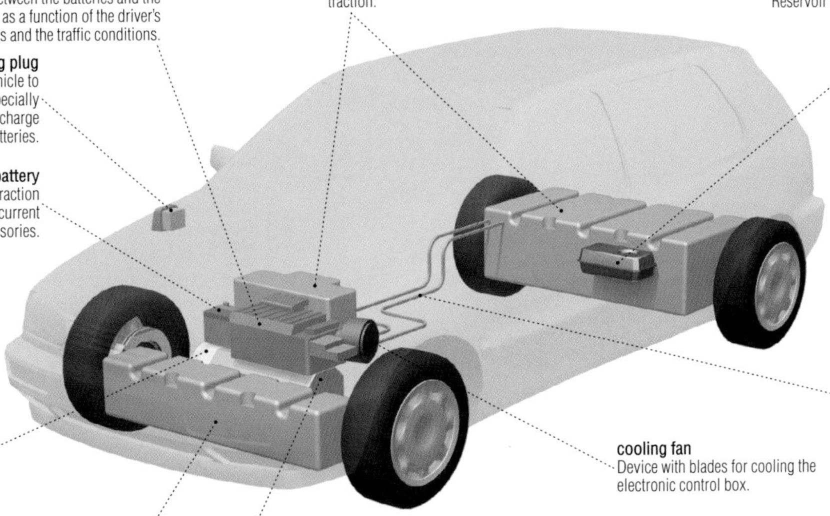
electronic control box
Electronic device modifying the energy exchanges between the batteries and the electric motor as a function of the driver's commands and the traffic conditions.
traction batteries
Batteries producing a 120-V current, providing the vehicle's traction.
heating fuel tank
Reservoir containing the fuel for the heating system.
charging plug
Plug for connecting the vehicle to the main current or to a specially fitted terminal, in order to charge the batteries.
auxiliary battery
Battery charged by the traction batteries, producing a 12-V current to supply the electric accessories.
electric cable
Cable enabling the batteries to supply the electric motor and recover energy during deceleration and braking.
transmission
Mechanism relaying the rotational motion of the motor to the wheels.
cooling fan
Device with blades for cooling the electronic control box.
traction batteries
Batteries producing a 120-V current, providing the vehicle's traction.
electric motor
Device transforming electric energy into mechanical energy to drive another device.

hybrid automobile

Car powered by an internal combustion engine and an electric motor, reducing gasoline consumption and polluting emissions.

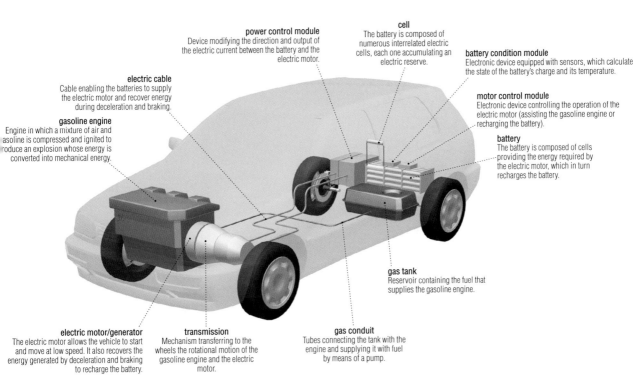

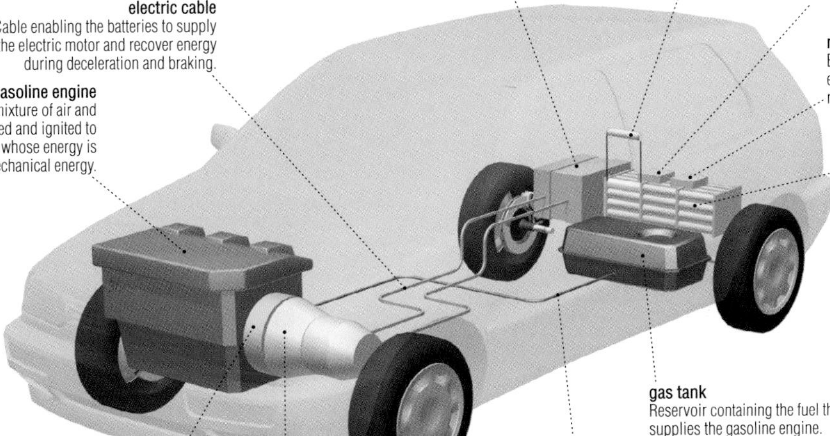
power control module
Device modifying the direction and output of the electric current between the battery and the electric motor.
cell
The battery is composed of numerous interrelated electric cells, each one accumulating an electric reserve.
battery condition module
Electronic device equipped with sensors, which calculate the state of the battery's charge and its temperature.
electric cable
Cable enabling the batteries to supply the electric motor and recover energy during deceleration and braking.
motor control module
Electronic device controlling the operation of the electric motor (assisting the gasoline engine or recharging the battery).
gasoline engine
Engine in which a mixture of air and asoline is compressed and ignited to roduce an explosion whose energy is converted into mechanical energy.
battery
The battery is composed of cells providing the energy required by the electric motor, which in turn recharges the battery.
gas tank
Reservoir containing the fuel that supplies the gasoline engine.
electric motor/generator
The electric motor allows the vehicle to start and move at low speed. It also recovers the energy generated by deceleration and braking to recharge the battery.
transmission
Mechanism transferring to the wheels the rotational motion of the gasoline engine and the electric motor.
gas conduit
Tubes connecting the tank with the engine and supplying it with fuel by means of a pump.

types of engines

Engines: machines that convert the combustion of an air/fuel mixture into mechanical energy.

turbo-compressor engine
Engine equipped with a device combining a turbine with a compressor, which increases the amount of air entering the engine to increase its efficiency.

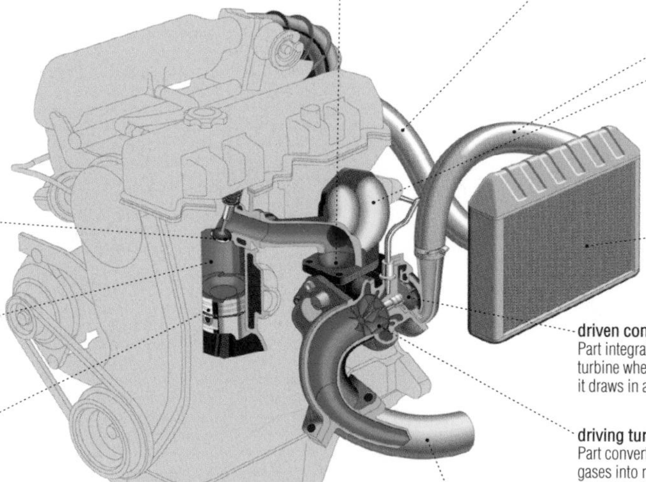

exhaust gas admission
The flow of the exhaust gas is conducted directly from the combustion chamber to the turbo compressor to drive the turbine.

intake manifold
After cooling, the air is again conducted to the combustion chamber, which takes in more air.

warm-air outlet
When compressed, the temperature of the air increases greatly, which can make it less effective.

exhaust manifold
Set of pipes at the exit of the cylinders; it captures the exhaust gases and conducts them to the turbo-compressor.

charge air cooler
The heat exchanger cools the compressed air before it enters the cylinders.

exhaust valve
Part that opens to allow the burned gases to escape.

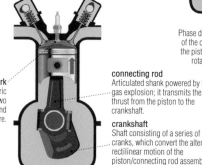

combustion chamber
Part of the cylinder in which the pressurized air/fuel mixture is ignited and burned.

piston
Metal moving part in the cylinder and attached to the connecting rod; it compresses the air/fuel mixture, then receives the thrust from the burned gases.

driven compressor wheel
Part integrated with the driving turbine wheel; it spins very quickly as it draws in air and compresses it.

driving turbine wheel
Part converting the energy from the exhaust gases into rotational energy to activate the compressor.

exhaust pipe
Tubular conduit conducting the exhaust gases from the turbo-compressor to the muffler.

four-stroke-cycle engine
Combustion engine whose cycle (intake, compression, combustion, exhaust) requires two up-and-down movements of the piston.

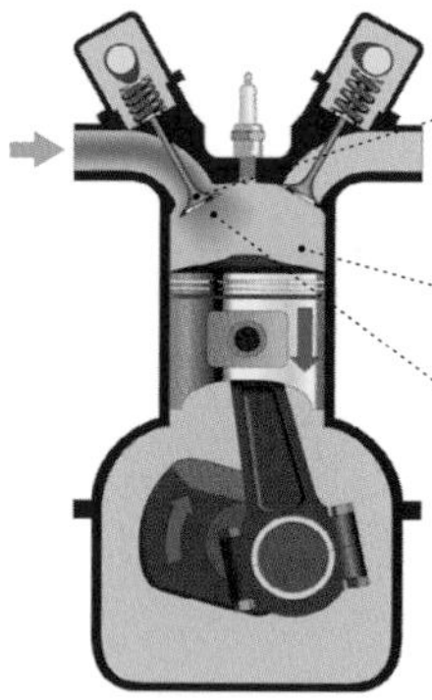

intake valve
Part that opens to let the air/fuel mixture into the cylinder.

cylinder
Chamber closed by two valves; in it, the piston moves and the air/fuel mixture is burned.

air/fuel mixture
Mixture prepared in the carburetor, containing an amount of fuel proportional to the amount of air entering.

intake
Phase during which the exhaust valve opens and the piston comes down and draws the air/fuel mixture into the combustion chamber.

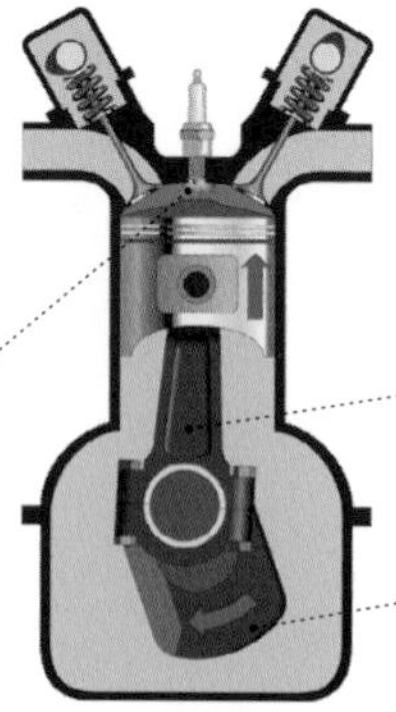

spark
Spark produced when an electric current arcs between the two electrodes of a spark plug and ignites the air/fuel mixture.

connecting rod
Articulated shank powered by the gas explosion; it transmits the thrust from the piston to the crankshaft.

crankshaft
Shaft consisting of a series of cranks, which convert the alternate rectilinear motion of the piston/connecting rod assembly into a continuous circular motion.

compression
Phase during which the piston goes up to compress the air/fuel mixture. At the height of the compression, the spark plug produces a spark.

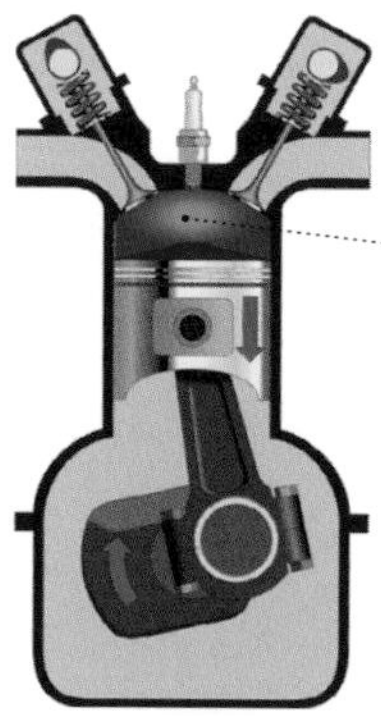

explosion
Ignition of the air/fuel mixture produces a major energy release that pushes the piston downward.

combustion
Phase during which the expansion of the combustion gases pushes the piston downward, driving the rotation of the crankshaft.

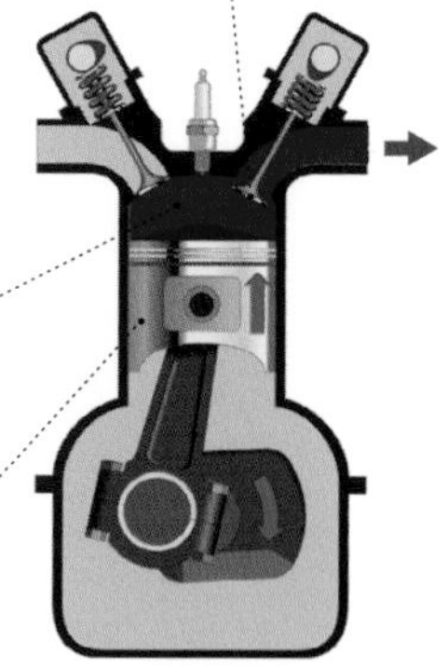

exhaust valve
Part that opens to allow the burned gases to escape.

burned gases
Mixture of gases (carbon monoxide, nitrogen oxide and unburned hydrocarbons) filling the combustion chamber after the explosion.

piston
Metal moving part in the cylinder and attached to the connecting rod; it compresses the air/fuel mixture, then receives the thrust from the burned gases.

exhaust
Phase during which the exhaust valve opens and the piston moves back up to expel the burned gases.

two-stroke-cycle engine cycle

Two-stroke engine: combustion engine whose cycle (intake, compression, combustion and exhaust) requires one up-and-down movement of the piston.

spark plug
Electric device whose two electrodes produce the spark necessary to ignite the air/fuel mixture in the cylinder.

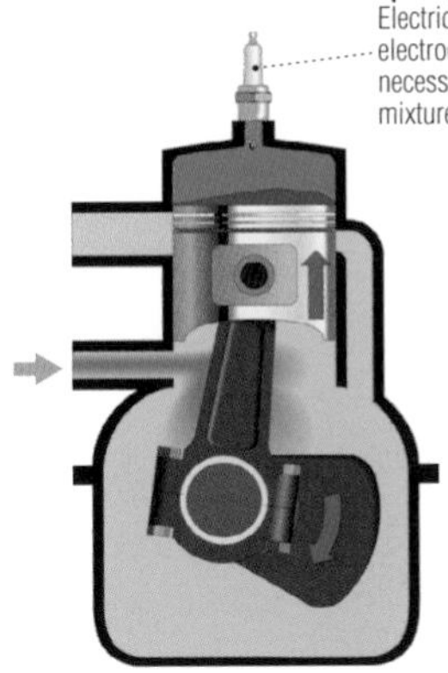

compression/intake
Beginning of the first stroke during which the piston moves up, drawing the air/fuel mixture into the crankcase and compressing the mixture in the cylinder.

exhaust port
Conduit through which the burned gases are expelled from the combustion chamber.

intake port
Conduit through which the air/fuel mixture enters the crankcase.

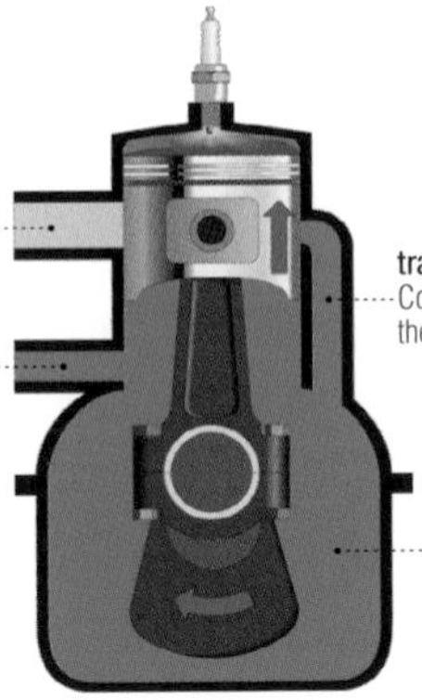

transfer port
Conduit conducting the air/fuel mixture from the crankcase to the cylinder.

crankcase
Sealed enclosure where the air/fuel mixture enters and the piston/connecting rod moves.

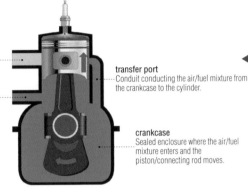

combustion
End of the first stroke during which a spark ignites the air/fuel mixture.

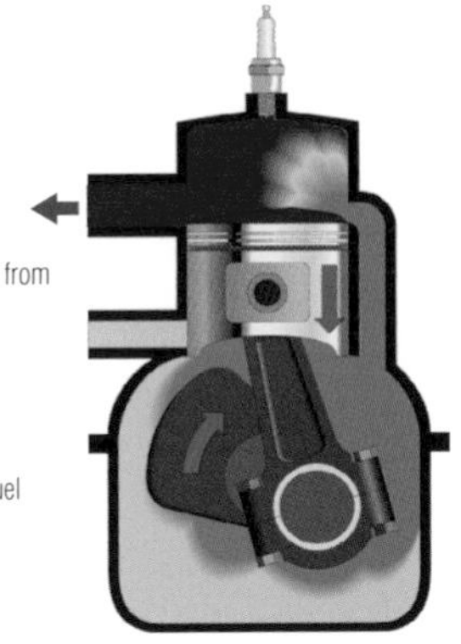

exhaust/scavaging
Second stroke during which the piston is pushed back by the expansion of the burned gases, which are then expelled and replaced by the mixture coming from the crankcase.

rotary engine cycle

Rotary engine: combustion engine in which the combustion chamber is divided by a rotor into three turning parts of unequal volume.

intake manifold
Passages through which the air/fuel mixture enters the cylinder.

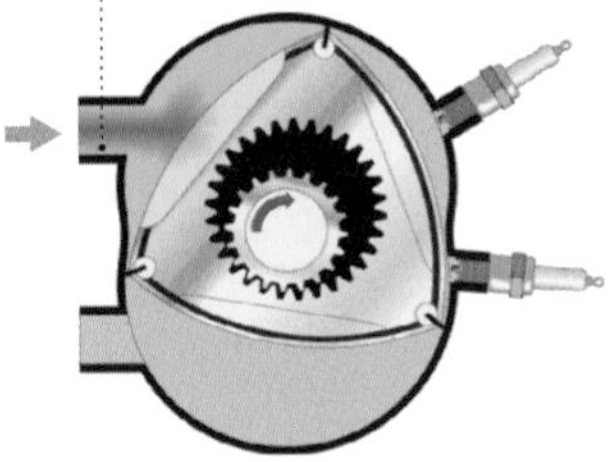

intake
The air/fuel mixture enters the cylinder through the intake manifold; the rotor's motion forces it into the next chamber.

exhaust manifold
Pipe through which the burned gases are expelled from the cylinder.

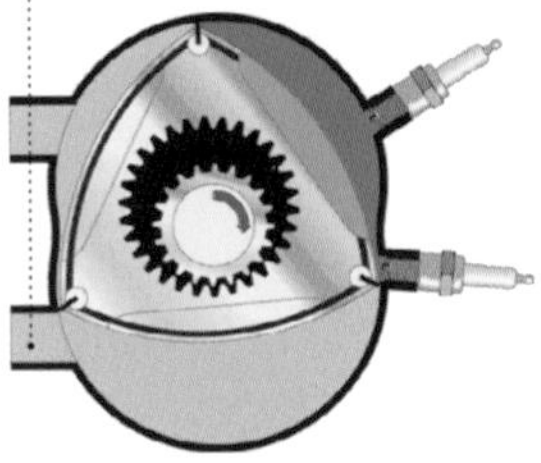

compression
The rotor's rotation reduces the volume in the chamber and compresses the mixture.

rotor
Triangular piston turning eccentrically around an axle and transmitting a rotational motion directly to the crankshaft.

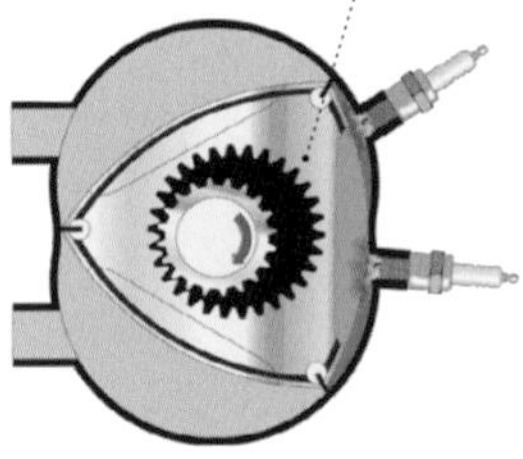

power
When the compression level is reached, the spark plugs produce sparks that ignite the air/fuel mixture.

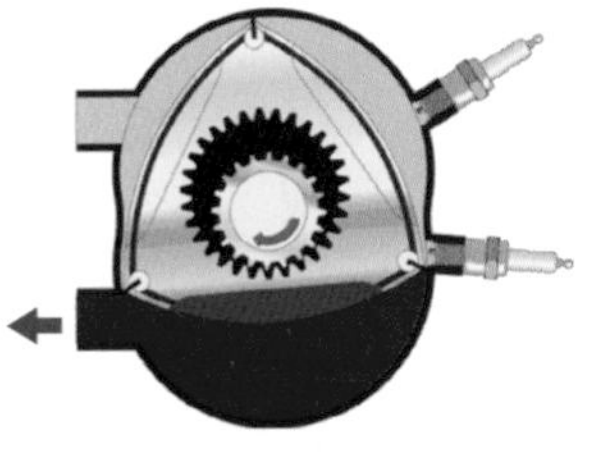

exhaust
In the passage before the exhaust manifold, the burned gases are expelled by the rotor.

diesel engine cycle

Diesel engine: combustion engine in which the compressed air becomes sufficiently hot to ignite the injected fuel.

air
Air enters the combustion chamber.

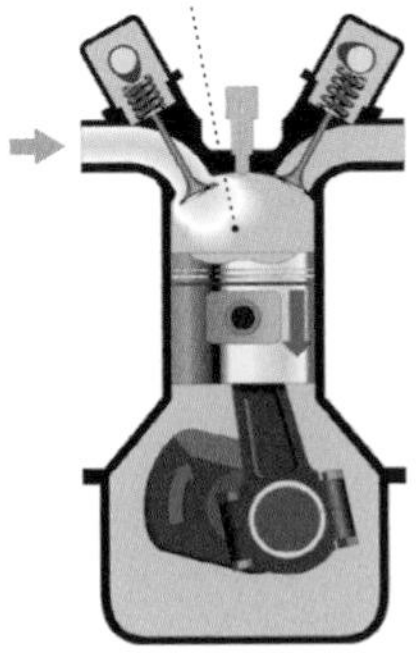

intake
Phase during which the exhaust valve opens and the piston comes down and draws the air/fuel mixture into the combustion chamber.

injection/combustion
Fuel ignites immediately when it is injected into the hot air at very high pressure.

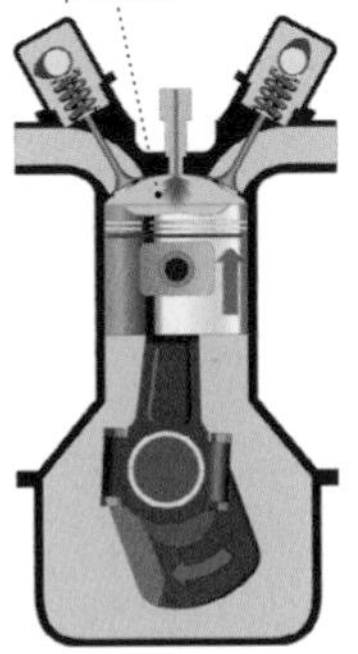

compression
Stroke during which the piston rises, compressing the air, which becomes heated under the pressure.

fuel injector
Device pulverizing the fuel in the combustion chamber.

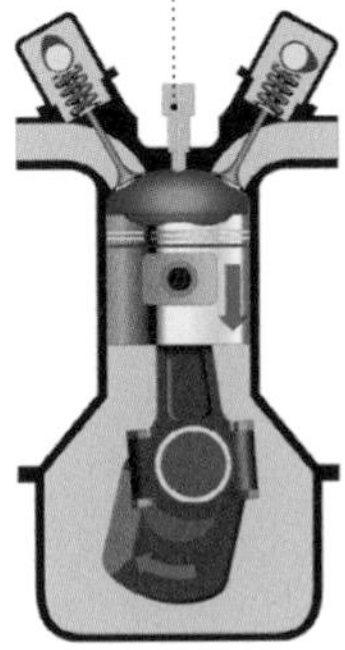

power
Stroke during which the expansion of the burning gases pushes the piston downward.

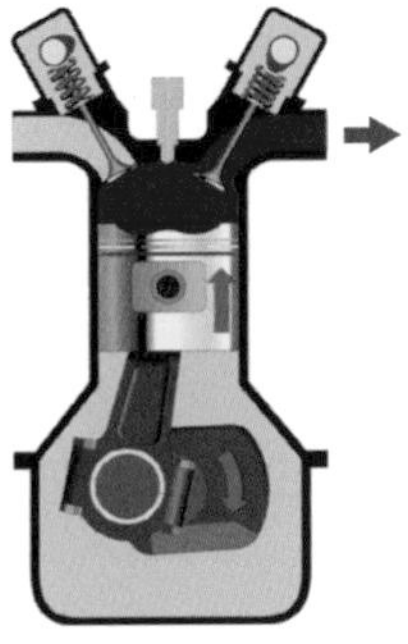

exhaust
Phase during which the piston moves up and forces the burned gases toward the exhaust valve.

types of engines

gasoline engine
Engine in which a mixture of air and gasoline is compressed and ignited to produce an explosion whose energy is converted into mechanical energy.

fuel injector
Device pulverizing the fuel in the combustion chamber.
rocker arm
Lever, activated by the camshaft, that drives the inlet and exhaust valves to open them.
camshaft
Axle driven by a belt, a chain or gears connected to the crankshaft, controlling the opening and closing of the valves.
inlet valve
Part that opens to let the air/fuel mixture into the cylinder.
intake manifold
Passages through which the air/fuel mixture enters the cylinder.
distributor cap
Unit supplying the electric current necessary for producing sparks that ignite the fuel in the engine.
timing belt
Strap connecting the crankshaft to the camshaft.
valve spring
Spring that brings the valve back into the closed position.
cylinder head cover
Part of the engine covering the cylinder heads, where the fuel is burned.
vacuum diaphragm
Device connected to the distributor cap specifying the precise moment ignition must be produced relative to the engine's rotation speed.
piston skirt
Side surface of a piston guiding it along the inside of the cylinder.
combustion chamber
Part of the cylinder in which the pressurized air/fuel mixture is ignited and burned.
piston ring
Circular ring mounted on the piston providing a seal between it and the cylinder.
spark plug cable
Electric wire carrying the high-voltage current from the distributor to the spark plugs, which produce sparks igniting the explosion.
connecting rod
Articulated shank powered by the gas explosion; it transmits the thrust from the piston to the crankshaft.
spark plug
Electric device whose two electrodes produce the spark necessary to ignite the air/fuel mixture in the cylinder.
alternator
Current generator driven by the engine, which recharges the battery to supply the electric system.
exhaust manifold
Set of pipes at the exit of the cylinders, capturing the combustion gases to conduct the to the exhaust pipe.
cooling fan
Mechanism with blades blowing air across the radiator in order to cool the liquid it contains.
flywheel
Disk connected to the crankshaft uses the kinetic energy produced combustion to regulate the crank rotation during the rest of the cyc
pulley
Part attached to a shaft, whose rotational movement it transmits by means of a belt.
exhaust valve
Part that opens to allow the burned gases to escape.
fan belt
Rubberized bands mounted on a pulley and linked to the engine, driving the fan and the alternator.
engine block
Main engine casing, which encloses the cylinders.
crankshaft
Shaft consisting of a series of cranks, which convert the alternate rectilinear motion of the piston/connecting-rod assembly into a continuous circular motion.
oil pan
Container closing the bottom of the engine block; it is the reservoir for the oil that lubricates the engine's moving parts.
air conditioner compressor
Component of the air-conditioning system circulating coolant, which cools the air in the passenger compartment when it is hot outside.
oil pan gasket
Packing providing the seal between the oil pan and the engine block.
oil drain plug
Plug closing the hole at the bottom of the oil pan through which used oil is evacuated.
piston
Metal moving part in the cylinder and attached to the connecting rod; it compresses the air/fuel mixture, then receives the thrust from the burned gases.

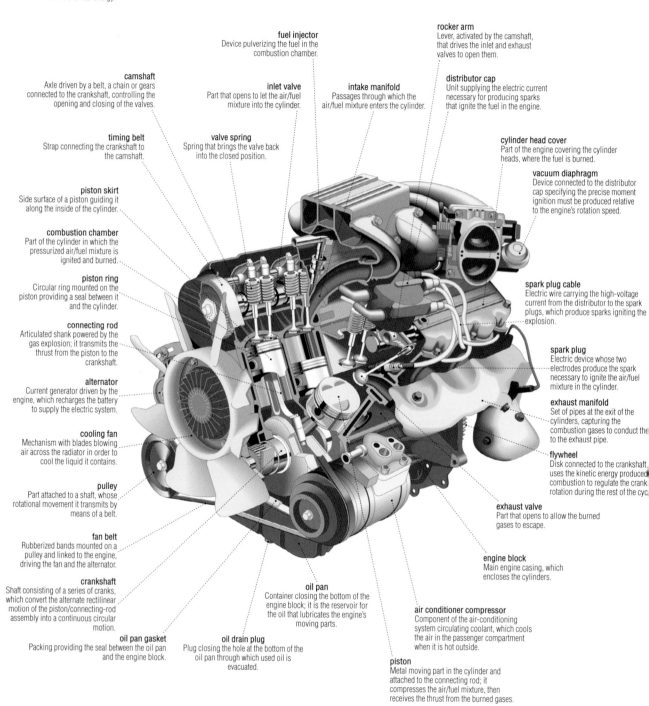

campers

Motorized or towed vehicle fitted out as a dwelling.

trailer
Caravan fitted out as a dwelling, usually pulled by an automobile.

roof vent
Opening in the roof, fitted with a cover, for letting in fresh air when parked.

side vent
Grille on the side of the body, for letting in fresh air.

body
Rigid metal frame comprising the body of the caravan.

sun visor
Device protecting against the sun.

awning channel
Track where the edge of an awning is inserted so it can be spread out in front of the caravan.

propane gas cylinder
Tank containing a gas reserve for supplying the caravan's stove and heating system.

grab handle
Vertical handle, placed at shoulder height near the door, that one holds to step up into the caravan.

hydraulic jack
Mechanism composed of a cylinder and a piston and activated by hydraulic pressure; it allows the landing gear to be deployed by turning a crank.

outlet
Device connected to the main current by an electric cord, which transmits the electric current to the appliances in the caravan.

towing hitch
Device placed at the end of the tow bar, securing the caravan to the hitch ball of the vehicle towing it.

storage compartment
mpartment for storing bulky objects, usually ssible from the inside and the outside of the caravan.

door
Opening comprising a leaf pivoting on hinge pins, for entering and exiting the caravan.

tow bar
Metal piece attached to the caravan's chassis; it comprises a towing hitch and enables the caravan to be connected to the towing vehicle.

retractable step
Folding apparatus attached to the door sill, for stepping up into or down from the caravan.

tow safety chain
Part of an antitheft device attached to the towing hitch, which stops anyone from hitching or unhitching the caravan.

landing gear
The towing hitch's telescopic support, which props up the caravan when it is parked.

lighting cable
Electric wire for connecting the caravan's lighting and signaling system to that of the vehicle towing it.

tent trailer
Caravan with a collapsible section that is opened up when at rest and folded up again before moving, to lessen wind resistance.

roof
Rigid part enclosing the top of the body and protecting the sections when they are folded up.

canopy
Canvas awning supported by a framework; it protects an outdoor space from the rain and sun.

window
Flexible canvas opening, letting in air and light, supported by a framework when it is opened out.

bunk
Area for sleeping, supported by a frame when opened out.

spare tire
Supplementary wheel for replacing a wheel whose tire is punctured.

body
Rigid metal frame comprising the body of the caravan.

stabilizer jack
Retractable support placed under the caravan to keep it steady when parked.

screen door
Door fitted with a wire cloth that lets air and light pass through while protecting against mosquitoes.

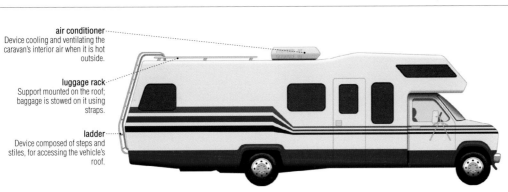

motor home
Van whose passenger compartment is fitted out as a dwelling.

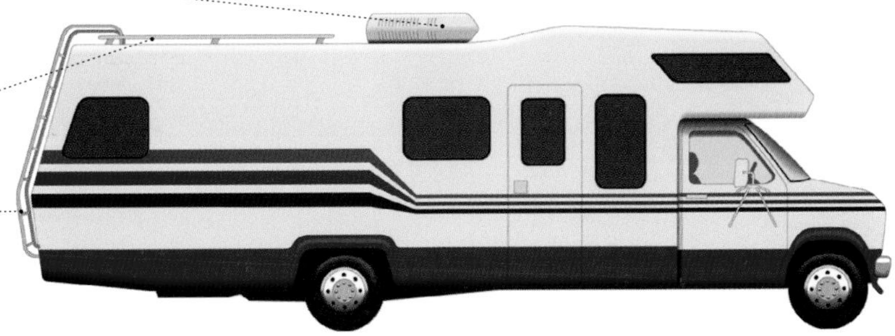

air conditioner
Device cooling and ventilating the caravan's interior air when it is hot outside.

luggage rack
Support mounted on the roof; baggage is stowed on it using straps.

ladder
Device composed of steps and stiles, for accessing the vehicle's roof.

bus

Motorized vehicle for city or intercity transportation of passengers who are standing or seated.

school bus
Motorized vehicle for transporting schoolchildren and equipped with specialized safety devices.

outside mirror
Mirror fixed to the outside of the passenger compartment enabling the driver to see behind and along the sides of the vehicle without turning around.

blind spot mirror
Exterior convex mirror providing a wider field of vision than a conventional mirror.

blinking lights
Flashing red lights at the front and rear of the bus that the driver activates at each stop to signal other vehicles to stop.

crossover mirror
Convex mirror allowing the driver to front of the bus.

city bus
Motorized vehicle for city transportation of passengers who are standing or seated.

air intake
Opening in the roof, fitted with a cover, for letting fresh air into the bus.

two-leaf door
Wide door divided into two movable parts, which double back to each side to allow several people to pass through at once.

crossing arm
Pivoting rod deployed at each stop so that the schoolchildren stay in the driver's field of vision while passing in front of the bus.

route sign
Screen usually on the front, rear and right side of the vehicle, displaying the number of the bus's route.

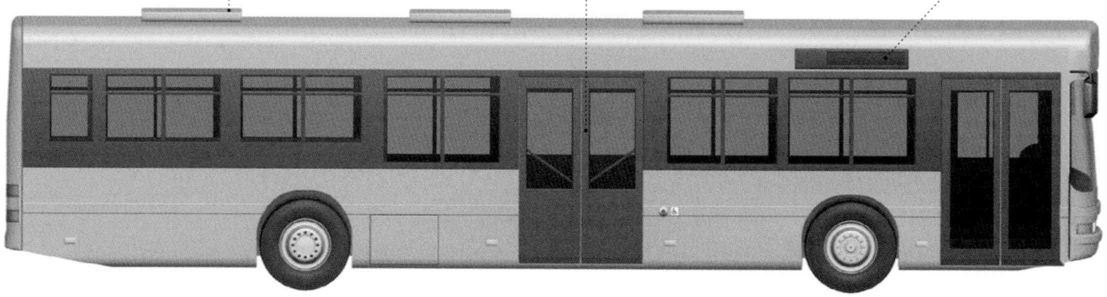

coach
Motorized vehicle for intercity transportation of seated passengers over medium and long distances.

engine air intake
Opening through which outside air enters the vehicle's engine.

entrance door

engine compartment
Housing for the engine under the vehicle's chassis, accessible by a door.

baggage compartment
Large compartment beneath the vehicle's floor, fitted with side doors, in which passengers' baggage is deposited.

double-decker bus
Bus equipped with two superimposed compartments, connected by stairs.

upper deck
Upper floor of the bus.
route sign
Screen usually on the front, rear and right side of the vehicle, displaying the number of the bus's route.

van
Motorized vehicle for transporting about 10 passengers, sometimes equipped with a lift for wheelchairs.

blind spot mirror
Exterior convex mirror providing a wider field of vision than a conventional mirror.
West Coast mirror
Mirror fixed to the outside of the passenger compartment enabling the driver to see behind and along the sides of the vehicle without turning around.
lift door
handrail
Support rail equipped with a belt restraining the wheelchair when the platform is being raised and lowered.
wheelchair lift
ifting device deployed so that a person
elchair can be raised into and lowered
from a minibus.
entrance door
platform
Horizontal part moving up and down for the wheelchair; it rests on the ground in the lower position and forms the doorsill in the upper position.

articulated bus
Bus with two aligned compartments, connected by an articulated joint.

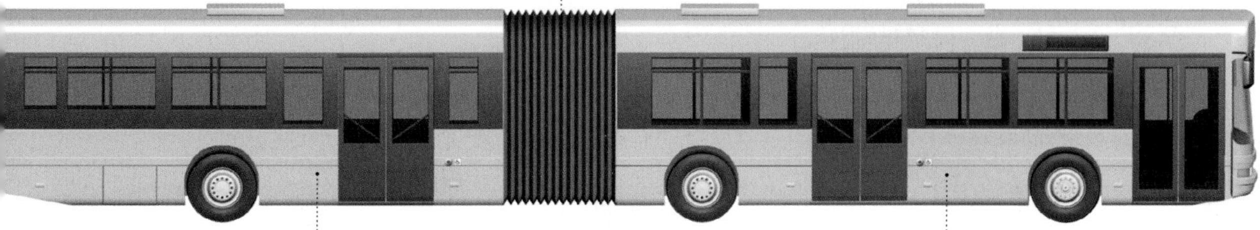

articulated joint
Part connecting the rigid sections by a waterproof bellows and a turning platform shared by the two sections.
rear rigid section
front rigid section

trucking

Transportation of cargo by truck.

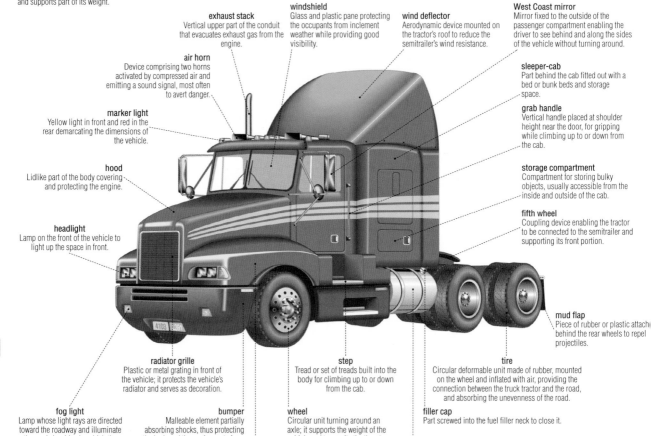

truck tractor
Motorized vehicle equipped with a fifth wheel that pulls a semitrailer and supports part of its weight.

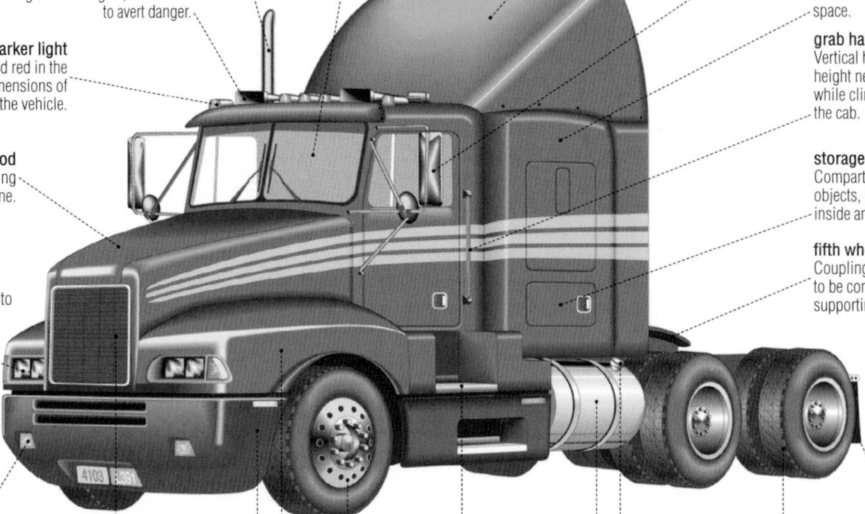

windshield
Glass and plastic pane protecting the occupants from inclement weather while providing good visibility.
exhaust stack
Vertical upper part of the conduit that evacuates exhaust gas from the engine.
wind deflector
Aerodynamic device mounted on the tractor's roof to reduce the semitrailer's wind resistance.
West Coast mirror
Mirror fixed to the outside of the passenger compartment enabling the driver to see behind and along the sides of the vehicle without turning around.
air horn
Device comprising two horns activated by compressed air and emitting a sound signal, most often to avert danger.
sleeper-cab
Part behind the cab fitted out with a bed or bunk beds and storage space.
marker light
Yellow light in front and red in the rear demarcating the dimensions of the vehicle.
grab handle
Vertical handle placed at shoulder height near the door, for gripping while climbing up to or down from the cab.
hood
Lidlike part of the body covering and protecting the engine.
storage compartment
Compartment for storing bulky objects, usually accessible from the inside and outside of the cab.
fifth wheel
Coupling device enabling the tractor to be connected to the semitrailer and supporting its front portion.
headlight
Lamp on the front of the vehicle to light up the space in front.
mud flap
Piece of rubber or plastic attach behind the rear wheels to repel projectiles.
radiator grille
Plastic or metal grating in front of the vehicle; it protects the vehicle's radiator and serves as decoration.
step
Tread or set of treads built into the body for climbing up to or down from the cab.
tire
Circular deformable unit made of rubber, mounted on the wheel and inflated with air, providing the connection between the truck tractor and the road, and absorbing the unevenness of the road.
fog light
Lamp whose light rays are directed toward the roadway and illuminate the road shoulder, by which the driver navigates in the event of fog.
bumper
Malleable element partially absorbing shocks, thus protecting the body and the engine parts from damage.
wheel
Circular unit turning around an axle; it supports the weight of the vehicle and transmits the thrust, steering and braking actions.
filler cap
Part screwed into the fuel filler neck to close it.
fender
Part of the body covering the wheel.
fuel tank
Reservoir containing the diesel fuel that makes the vehicle self-sufficient.

tandem tractor trailer
Set of vehicles comprising a tractor, a semitrailer and a trailer.

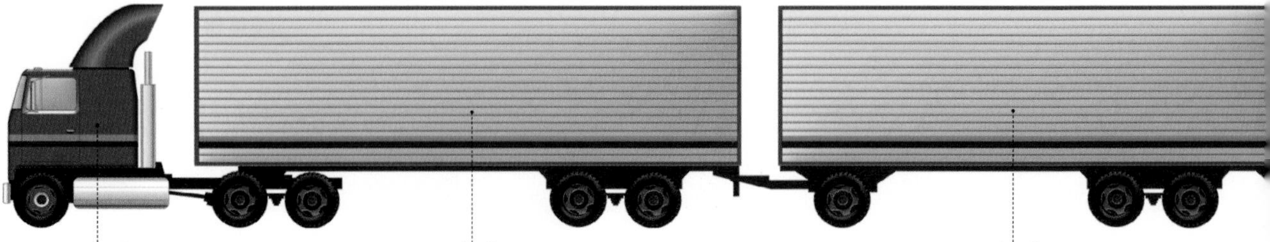

truck tractor
Motorized vehicle equipped with a fifth wheel that pulls a semitrailer and supports part of its weight.
semitrailer
Trailer whose front part is equipped with a kingpin for coupling it to the tractor.
truck trailer
Motorless vehicle for transporting cargo and connected by a coupling bar to the vehicle towing it.

refrigerated semitrailer
Semitrailer equipped with a refrigeration unit and an insulated compartment for transporting perishable goods.

marker light
Yellow light in front and red in the rear demarcating the dimensions of the vehicle.

refrigeration unit
Device using compression to lower the temperature inside the semitrailer to a predetermined level.

frontwall

sidewall

vent door
Grille through which the air cools the refrigerant.

battery box
Compartment containing the battery supplying the electric energy required to operate the refrigeration unit.

partlow chart
Device monitoring the temperature in the semitrailer.

electrical connection
Electric wire connecting the semitrailer's lighting and signaling system with that of the tractor.

reflector
Device reflecting light back toward its source so that other drivers can see the semitrailer.

landing gear
Telescopic support keeping the semitrailer level when uncoupled.

kingpin
Axle of attachment housed in the tractor's fifth wheel; it allows the semitrailer and the tractor to articulate.

nud flap
'iece of rubber or plastic attached ehind the rear wheels to repel rojectiles.

side rail
Thick piece along the length of the chassis frame, reinforcing it.

sand shoe
Part attached to the foot of the landing gear to increase stability.

auxiliary tank
Reservoir containing the fuel used to operate the refrigeration unit.

landing gear crank
Bent lever activating the elevating cylinder to deploy the landing gear.

flatbed semitrailer
Semitrailer composed of a platform around which detachable side panels can be placed.

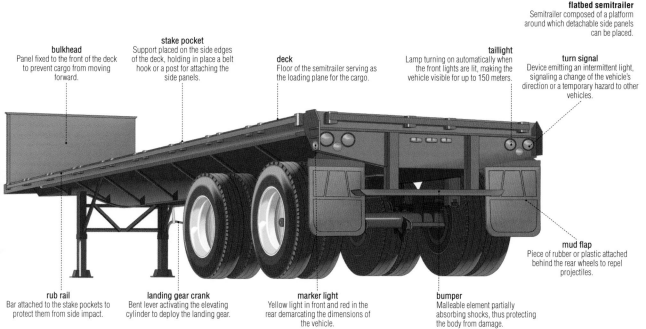

bulkhead
Panel fixed to the front of the deck to prevent cargo from moving forward.

stake pocket
Support placed on the side edges of the deck, holding in place a belt hook or a post for attaching the side panels.

deck
Floor of the semitrailer serving as the loading plane for the cargo.

taillight
Lamp turning on automatically when the front lights are lit, making the vehicle visible for up to 150 meters.

turn signal
Device emitting an intermittent light, signaling a change of the vehicle's direction or a temporary hazard to other vehicles.

mud flap
Piece of rubber or plastic attached behind the rear wheels to repel projectiles.

rub rail
Bar attached to the stake pockets to protect them from side impact.

landing gear crank
Bent lever activating the elevating cylinder to deploy the landing gear.

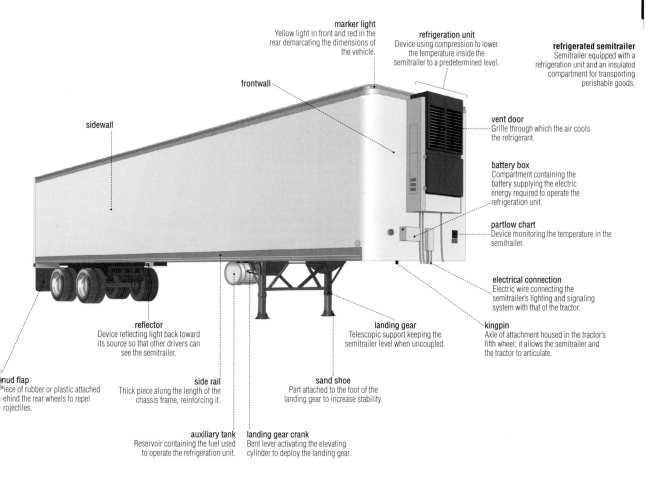

marker light
Yellow light in front and red in the rear demarcating the dimensions of the vehicle.

bumper
Malleable element partially absorbing shocks, thus protecting the body from damage.

trucking

examples of semitrailers

Semitrailers: trailers whose front portion is equipped with a kingpin for coupling them to a tractor.

tank trailer
Semitrailer for transporting bulk products in liquid, powder or gas form.

tank body
Closed tank divided into several compartments of various sizes.

automobile transport semitrailer
Semitrailer equipped with several sloped platforms for transporting vehicles.

dump body
Open or closed container; when raised by the elevation cylinder, it discharges its bulk material.

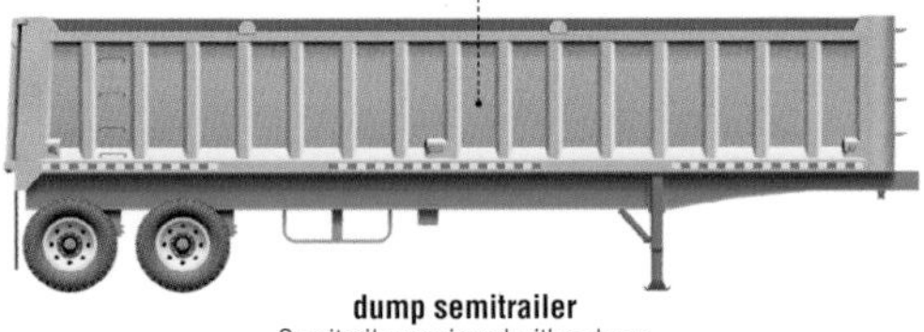

dump semitrailer
Semitrailer equipped with a dump body for transporting in bulk.

twist lock
Locking mechanism housed in each bottom corner of the container to secure it to the semitrailer.

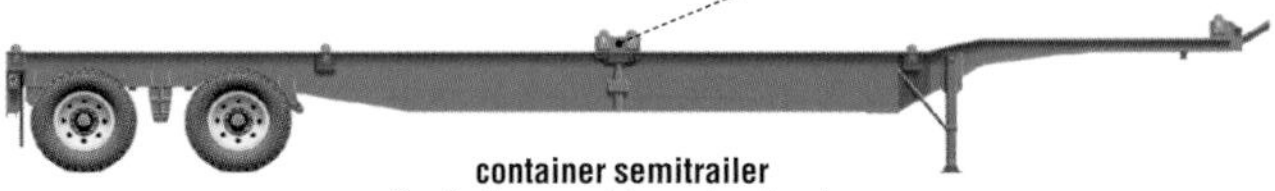

container semitrailer
Semitrailer comprising only a chassis; containers of standard sizes are loaded on it to transport cargo.

chip van
Semitrailer designed to transport wood in chip form.

double drop lowbed semitrailer
Semitrailer for transporting heavy machinery.

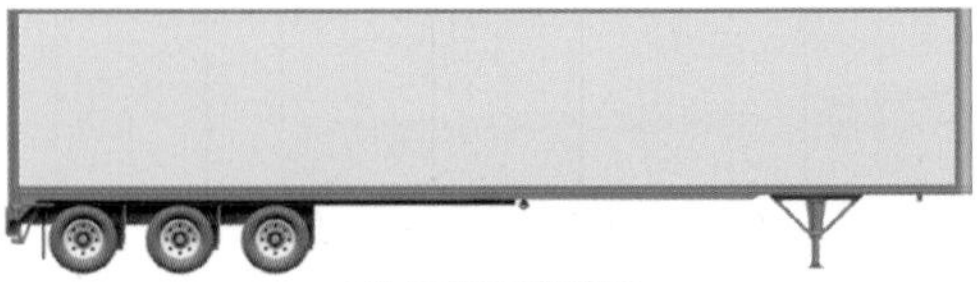

van body semitrailer
Semitrailer comprising a closed box, rigid or made of thick fabric (tarpaulin and sliding curtains).

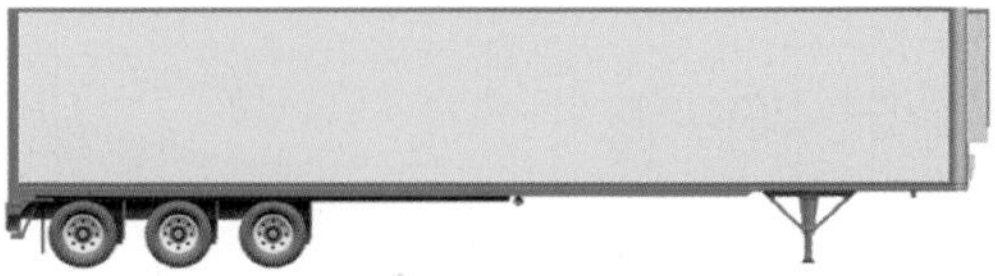

refrigerated semitrailer
Semitrailer equipped with a refrigeration unit and an insulated compartment for transporting perishable goods.

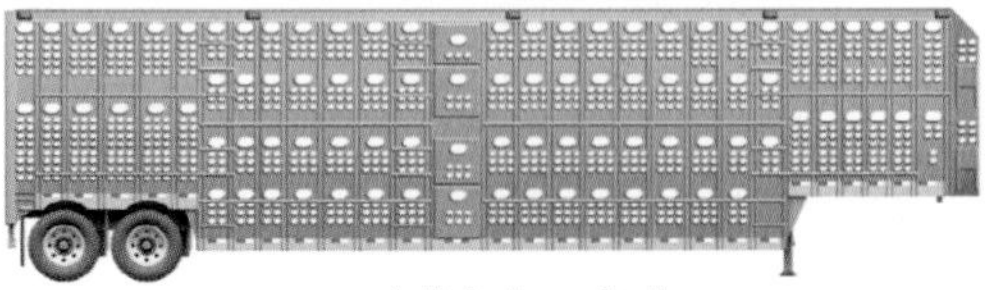

possum-belly body semitrailer
Semitrailer designed to transport livestock; it comprises several perforated compartments.

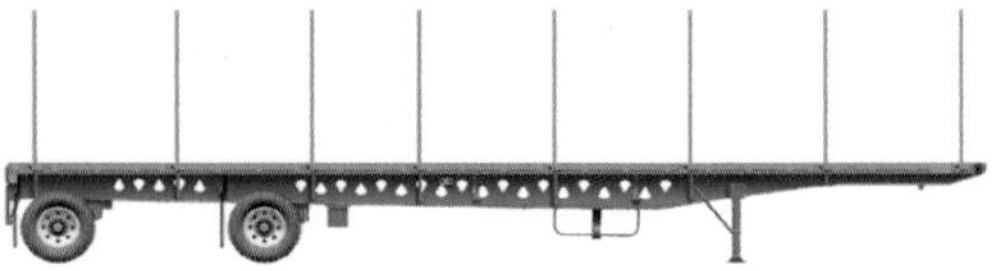

log semitrailer
Semitrailer with folding side posts for transporting tree trunks.

examples of trucks

Trucks: motorized vehicles for transporting cargo and providing maintenance and safety.

tow truck
Truck for towing vehicles that have broken down.

boom
Thick sturdy metal beam, which the elevating cylinder raises.

elevating cylinder
Hydraulic device comprising a telescopic arm, for lifting a heavy load.

cable

hook
Part that is detached from the towing device while the vehicle's front wheels placed in position, then reattached to raise it.

towing device
Lifting device where the front wheels of the towed vehicle are placed.

winch controls
Control mechanisms for the electric motor, which powers the spool's rotation.

winch
Mechanism with a steel cable rolled around a spool, for pulling and raising heavy loads, such as a vehicle that has broken down.

dump body
Open or closed container; when raised by the elevation cylinder it discharges its bulk material.

dump truck
Truck equipped with a dump body; it is used for bulk transport.

septic truck
Truck equipped with a tank, a pump and a long pipe, for emptying septic tanks and other pipes.

loading hopper
Large reservoir that takes the trash bags and then feeds them to the packer body.

packer body
Bin equipped with a hydraulic system that compresses household trash.

trash truck
Dump truck for collecting household trash.

cement mixer
Truck equipped with a rotating tub, for transporting fresh cement, which it pours out down a chute.

box van
Truck whose box is rigid and closed.

tank truck
Truck for transporting bulk products in liquid, powder or gas form.

tank body
Closed tank divided into several compartments of various sizes.

detachable body truck
Truck for transporting containers, which it loads and unloads using a mechanical arm.

street sweeper
Vehicle for cleaning city streets, equipped with a collection body, rotating brushes, a vacuum cleaner and a watering device.

collection body
Container for the trash swept up by the central brush.

central brush
Rotating brush that cleans the width of the roadway.

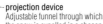

lateral brush
Rotating brush that cleans the edge of the roadway.

watering tube
Pipe supplying water to the brush as it cleans the roadway.

snowblower
Vehicle with a mechanism that draws up snow from the road and projects it some distance or into a dump truck.

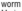

projection device
Adjustable funnel through which the snow is expelled in a chosen direction.

worm
Mechanism grinding hardened snow before a screw forces it into the projection device.

motorcycle

Two-wheeled motorized vehicle whose engine cylinder is larger than 125 cubic centimeters.

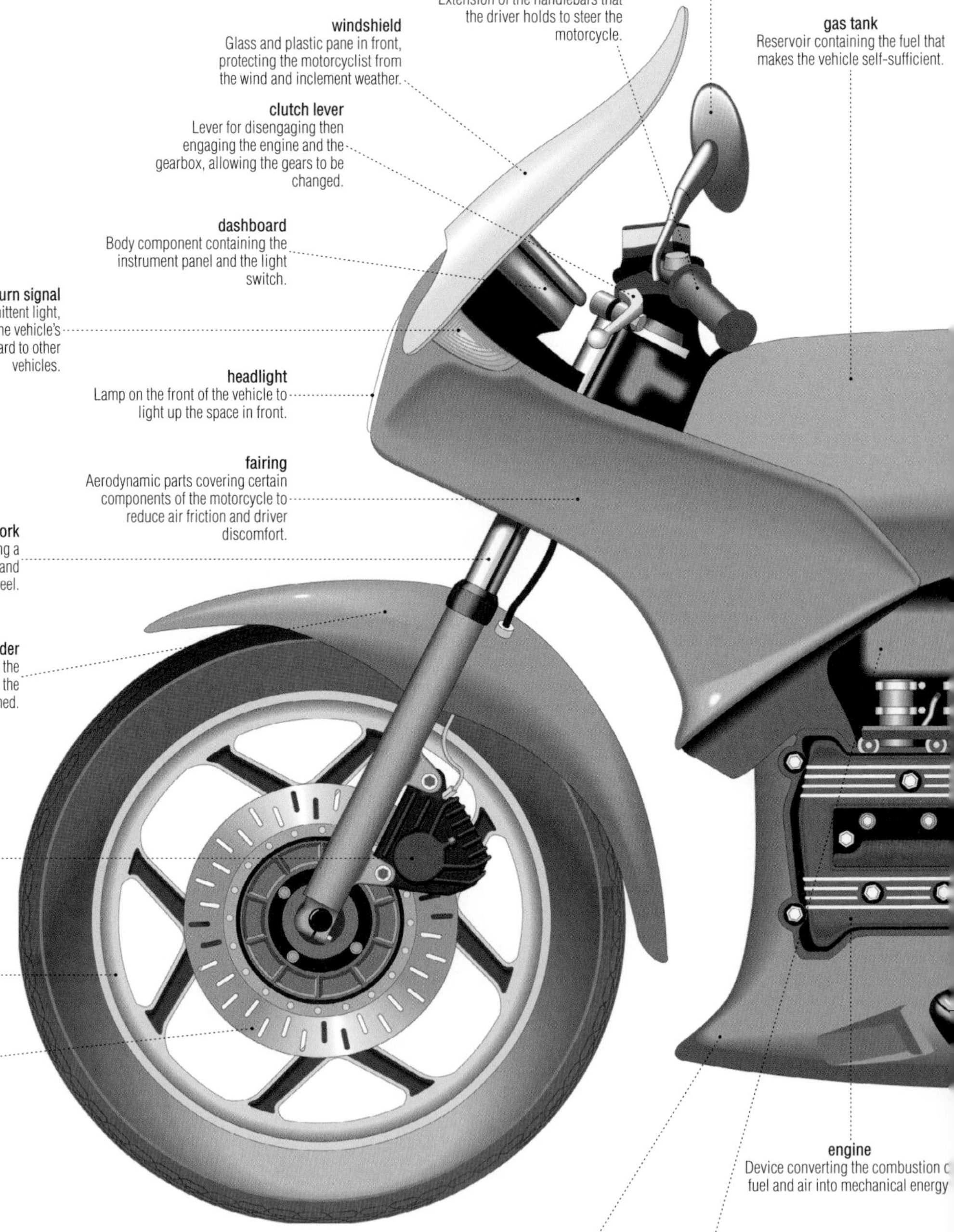
mirror
Mirror attached to the handgrip, allowing the motorcyclist to see behind and along the sides of the vehicle without turning around.
handgrip
Extension of the handlebars that the driver holds to steer the motorcycle.
gas tank
Reservoir containing the fuel that makes the vehicle self-sufficient.
windshield
Glass and plastic pane in front, protecting the motorcyclist from the wind and inclement weather.
clutch lever
Lever for disengaging then engaging the engine and the gearbox, allowing the gears to be changed.
dashboard
Body component containing the instrument panel and the light switch.
turn signal
Device emitting an intermittent light, signaling a change of the vehicle's direction or a temporary hazard to other vehicles.
headlight
Lamp on the front of the vehicle to light up the space in front.
fairing
Aerodynamic parts covering certain components of the motorcycle to reduce air friction and driver discomfort.
telescopic front fork
Pair of tubes sliding together and encasing a spring; it controls steering, suspension and shock absorption for the front wheel.
front fender
Piece of curved metal covering the front wheel, protecting the motorcyclist from being splashed.
brake caliper
Viselike part comprising a piston, which straddles the brake disc and supports the brake pads.
rim
Metal circle constituting the wheel's circumference and on which the tire is mounted.
disc brake
Braking mechanism comprising a disc attached to the wheel, whose rotation is slowed down when the brake pads exert friction on it.
engine
Device converting the combustion c
fuel and air into mechanical energy
spoiler
Partly aesthetic aerodynamic part that deflects air away from the front wheel.
carburetor
Engine mechanism that prepares the air/fuel mixture.

motorcycle

protective helmet
Rigid headgear covering the head to protect it in the event of accident.
bubble
Exterior surface made of durable materials (thermoplastic or composite materials) that absorb shocks.
visor
Transparent swing-away part, protecting the eyes while providing good visibility.
air inlet
Opening in the bubble allowing air to circulate in the helmet and preventing fog from forming on the visor.
chin protector
Part of the bubble protecting the motorcyclist's chin.
visor hinge
Articulated fastener for raising and lowering the visor.

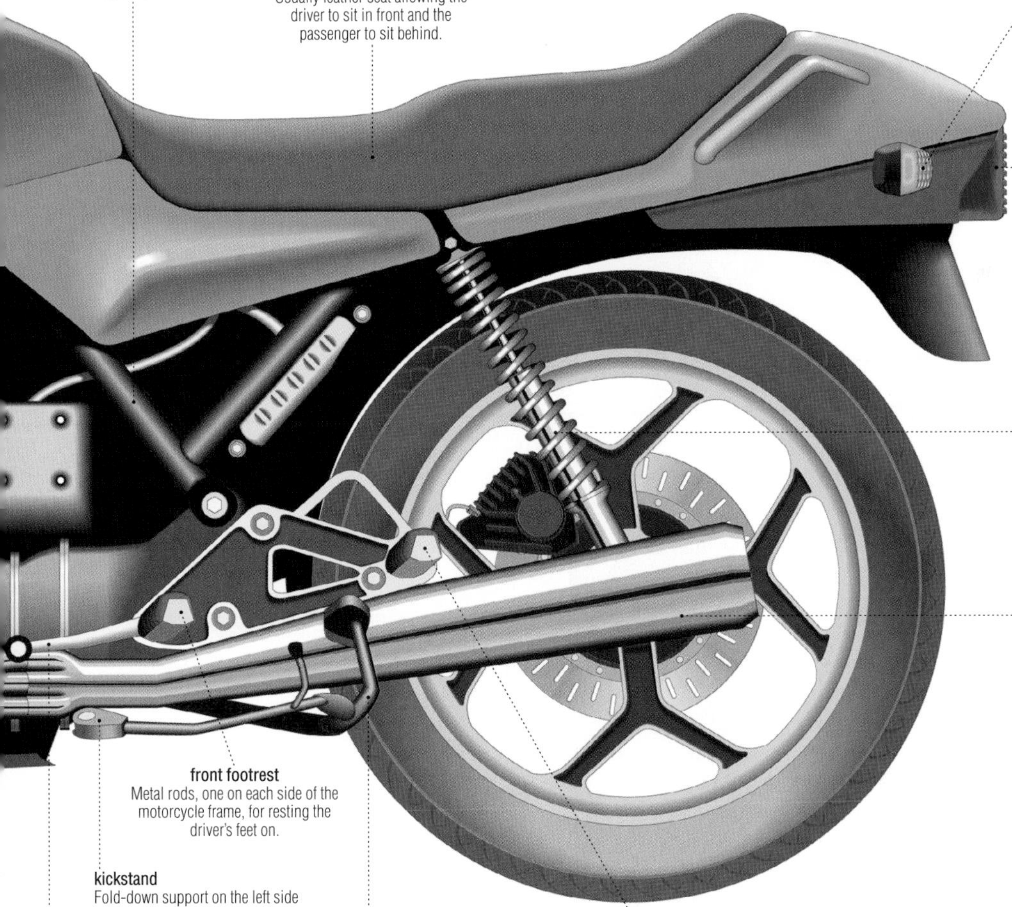
frame
Set of hollow metal tubes welded together, forming the motorcycle's framework.
dual seat
Usually leather seat allowing the driver to sit in front and the passenger to sit behind.
turn signal
Device emitting an intermittent light, signaling a change of the vehicle's direction or a temporary hazard to other vehicles.
taillight
Lamp that lights up automatically when the front lights are lit and emits a brighter light when the driver applies the brakes.
rear shock absorber
Cylindrical mechanism attached to the rear wheel and coupled with a spring; it absorbs shocks caused by unevenness in the road.
exhaust pipe
Compartmentalized chamber in which the escaping gases expand, thus reducing the noise from the engine.
front footrest
Metal rods, one on each side of the motorcycle frame, for resting the driver's feet on.
kickstand
Fold-down support on the left side of the motorcycle to keep it almost upright when at rest.
gearshift lever
Pedal located under the motorcyclist's left foot, for changing the ratio between the motor's speed of rotation and that of the wheels.
main stand
Fold-down support comprising two rods; it keeps the motorcycle upright with one of its wheels off the ground.
pillion footrest
Metal rods, one on each side of the motorcycle frame, for resting the passenger's feet on.

motorcycle

motorcycle dashboard
Body component containing the instrument panel and the ignition switch.

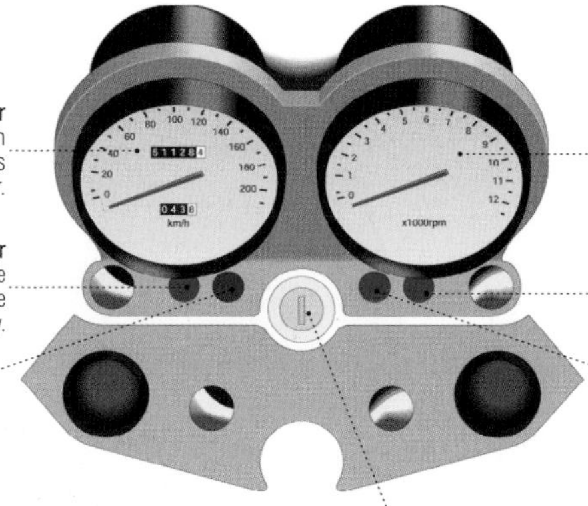

speedometer
Dial showing the speed at which the vehicle is moving, in kilometers or miles per hour.

oil pressure warning indicator
Light showing that the oil pressure in the engine's lubrication system is below the minimum necessary.

neutral indicator
Light showing that none of the gears is engaged; that is, the engine's rotation is not being transmitted to the wheels.

tachometer
Dial showing the engine's rotation speed in revolutions per minute.

high beam warning indicator
Light showing that the high beam is lit.

turn signal indicator
Intermittent light, often accompanied by a sound, showing that a turn signal is in use.

ignition switch
Switch activated by a contact key allowing a current from the battery to flow to the starter.

motorcycle: view from above

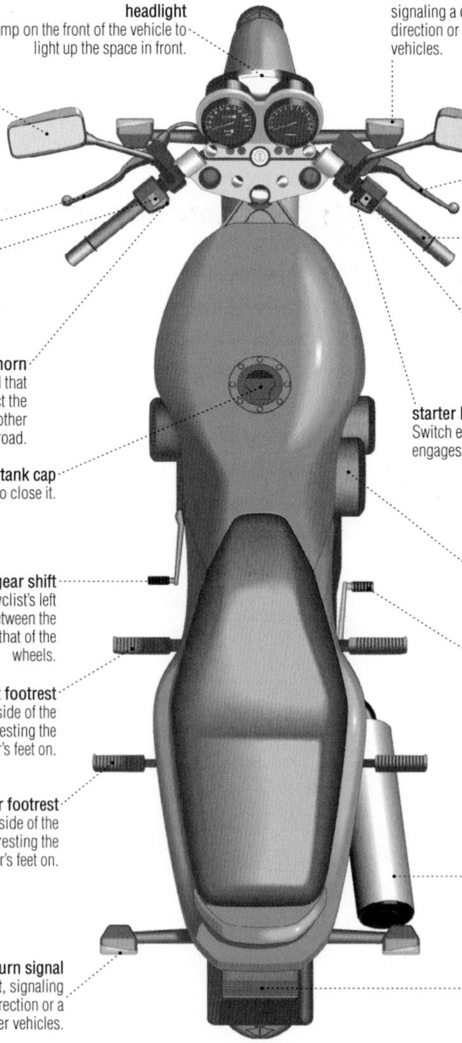

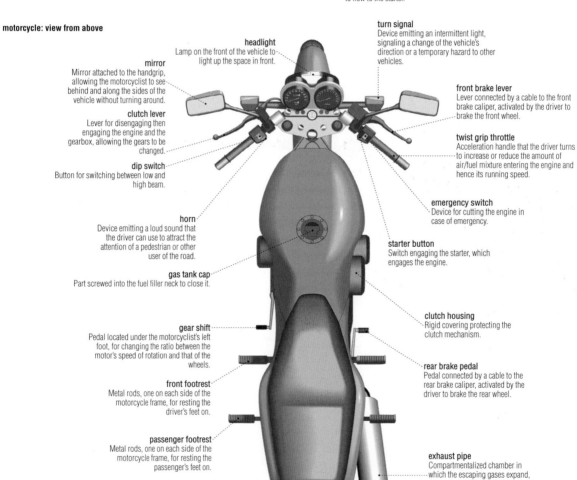

headlight
Lamp on the front of the vehicle to light up the space in front.

mirror
Mirror attached to the handgrip, allowing the motorcyclist to see behind and along the sides of the vehicle without turning around.

clutch lever
Lever for disengaging then engaging the engine and the gearbox, allowing the gears to be changed.

dip switch
Button for switching between low and high beam.

horn
Device emitting a loud sound that the driver can use to attract the attention of a pedestrian or other user of the road.

gas tank cap
Part screwed into the fuel filler neck to close it.

gear shift
Pedal located under the motorcyclist's left foot, for changing the ratio between the motor's speed of rotation and that of the wheels.

front footrest
Metal rods, one on each side of the motorcycle frame, for resting the driver's feet on.

passenger footrest
Metal rods, one on each side of the motorcycle frame, for resting the passenger's feet on.

turn signal
Device emitting an intermittent light, signaling a change of the vehicle's direction or a temporary hazard to other vehicles.

turn signal
Device emitting an intermittent light, signaling a change of the vehicle's direction or a temporary hazard to other vehicles.

front brake lever
Lever connected by a cable to the front brake caliper, activated by the driver to brake the front wheel.

twist grip throttle
Acceleration handle that the driver turns to increase or reduce the amount of air/fuel mixture entering the engine and hence its running speed.

emergency switch
Device for cutting the engine in case of emergency.

starter button
Switch engaging the starter, which engages the engine.

clutch housing
Rigid covering protecting the clutch mechanism.

rear brake pedal
Pedal connected by a cable to the rear brake caliper, activated by the driver to brake the rear wheel.

exhaust pipe
Compartmentalized chamber in which the escaping gases expand, thus reducing the noise from the engine.

taillight
Lamp that lights up automatically when the front lights are lit and emits a brighter light when the driver applies the brakes.

motorcycle

examples of motorcycles

motor scooter
Motorized vehicle with two small wheels, embellished with fairing, characterized by an open frame and a flat floor.

luggage rack
Support at the rear of the vehicle, for attaching a trunk or for lashing down luggage using straps.

seat
Usually leather seat where the driver sits.

mirror
Mirror attached to the handgrip, allowing the motorcyclist to see behind and along the sides of the vehicle without turning around.

apron
Aerodynamic component in sheet metal or plastic, trimming the steering column and protecting the driver from the wind and inclement weather.

floorboard
Wide flat surface for resting the feet on.

off-road motorcycle
Motorcycle designed for traveling over rough terrain, with features such as a raised engine, extended suspension, elevated muffler and tires with studs.

seat
Usually leather seat where the driver sits.

telescopic front fork
Pair of sliding tubes enclosing a spring; it controls steering, suspension and shock absorption on the front wheel.

knobby tread tire
Tire whose tread is fitted with blocks of rubber, providing better traction on rough terrain.

moped
Vehicle designed like a bicycle, but equipped with an engine whose cylinder is no larger than 50 cubic centimeters.

carrier
Support at the rear of the vehicle, for attaching a trunk or for lashing down luggage using straps.

kickstand
Fold-down support on the right side of the moped to keep it almost upright when at rest.

touring motorcycle
Motorcycle providing comfort for the driver and the passenger, with features such as wide fairing, extended handgrips and footrests for stretching the legs.

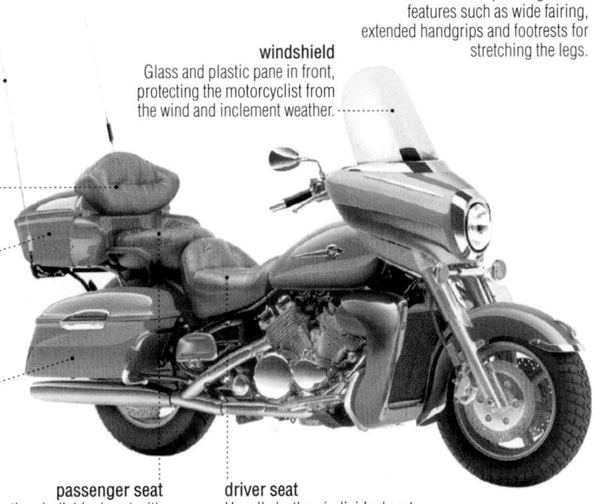

antenna
Device receiving radio waves broadcast by a station.

windshield
Glass and plastic pane in front, protecting the motorcyclist from the wind and inclement weather.

backrest
Part supporting the back.

top box
Usually rigid and waterproof compartment, behind the passenger seat, for stowing light objects.

saddlebag
Usually rigid and waterproof luggage, attached to each side of the passenger seat.

passenger seat
Usually leather, individual seat with a back; it is higher than the driver seat, for the passenger to sit.

driver seat
Usually leather, individual seat, sometimes equipped with a back, for the driver to sit.

4 X 4 all-terrain vehicle

Four-wheeled all-terrain vehicle (ATV) for traversing most kinds of terrain, equipped with a motorcycle engine.

rear cargo rack
Support at the rear of the vehicle, for attaching a trunk or for lashing down luggage using straps.

seat
Usually leather seat where the driver sits.

gas tank
Reservoir containing the fuel that makes the vehicle self-sufficient.

handgrip
Extension of the handlebars used for steering the ATV.

rear fender
Piece of curved metal covering the rear wheel, for protecting the motorcyclist from being splashed.

muffler
Compartmentalized chamber in which the escaping gases expand, thus reducing the noise from the engine.

bumper
Malleable component partly absorbing impact in the event of a front-on collision.

front shock absorber
Cylindrical mechanism attached to the front wheel and coupled with a spring; it absorbs shocks caused by unevenness in the road.

gearshift lever
Pedal located under the driver's foot, for changing the ratio between the motor's speed of rotation and that of the wheels.

bicycle

Frame vehicle steered by the front wheel and propelled by the rear wheel, which in turn is driven, via a chain, by a pedal mechanism.

parts of a bicycle

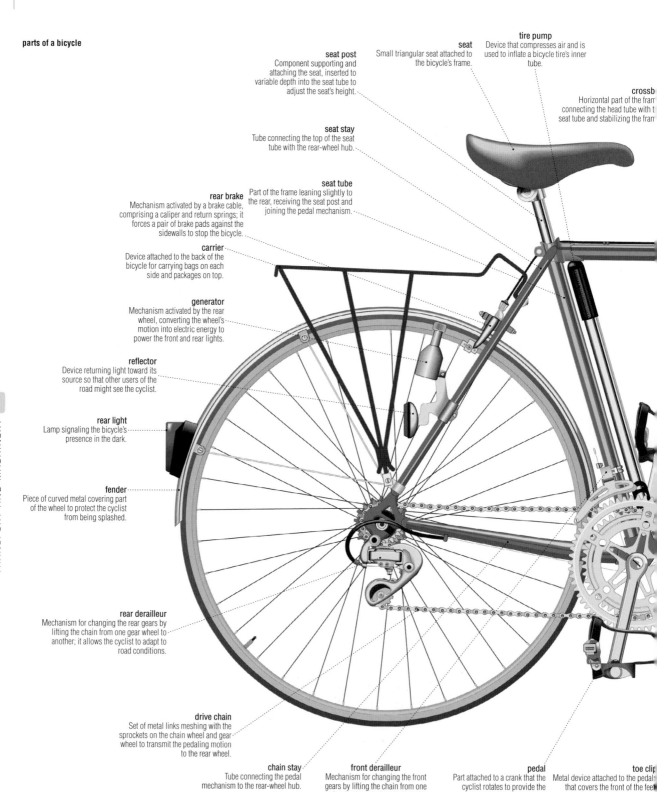

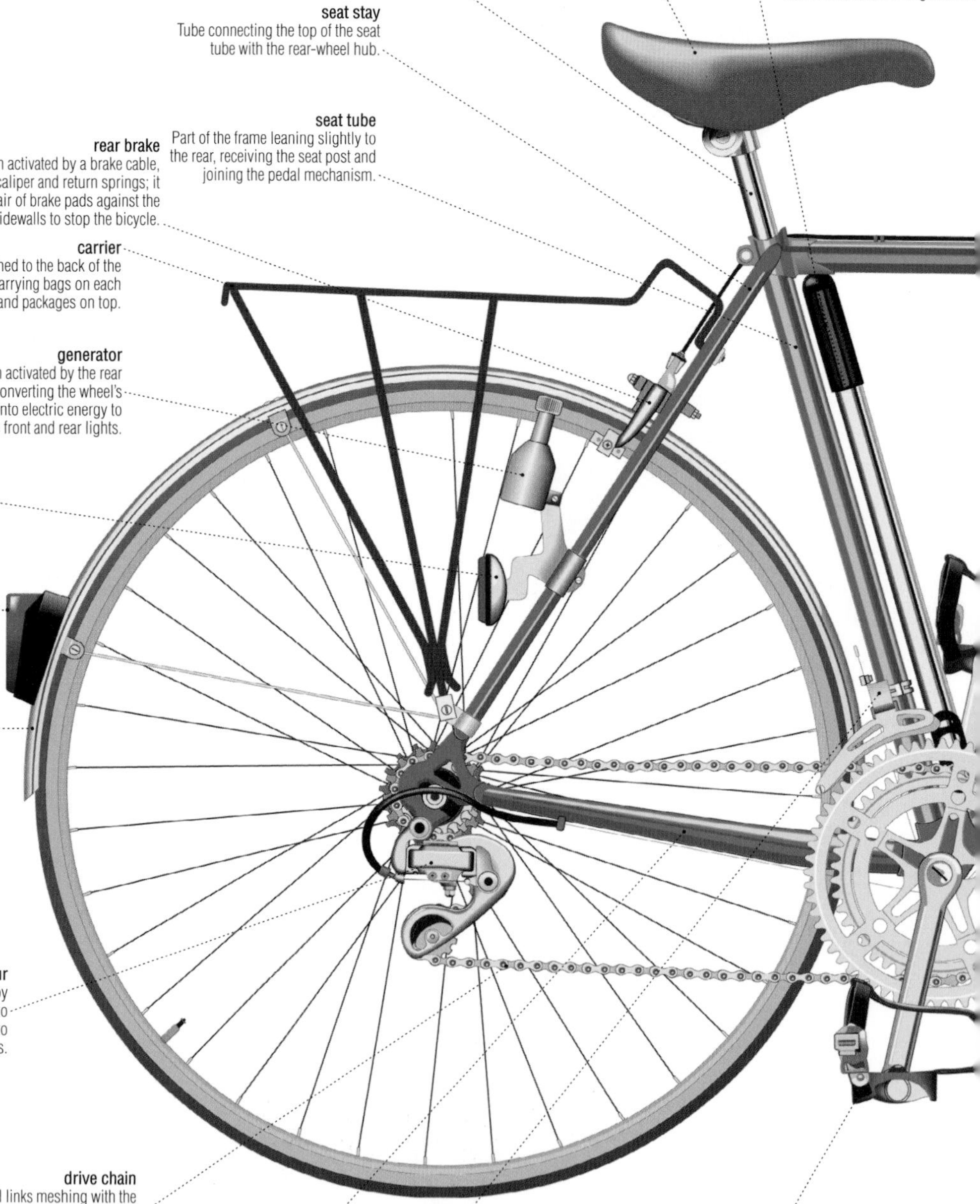

tire pump
Device that compresses air and is used to inflate a bicycle tire's inner tube.
seat
Small triangular seat attached to the bicycle's frame.
seat post
Component supporting and attaching the seat, inserted to variable depth into the seat tube to adjust the seat's height.
crossb
Horizontal part of the fram connecting the head tube with t seat tube and stabilizing the fram
seat stay
Tube connecting the top of the seat tube with the rear-wheel hub.
seat tube
Part of the frame leaning slightly to the rear, receiving the seat post and joining the pedal mechanism.
rear brake
Mechanism activated by a brake cable, comprising a caliper and return springs; it forces a pair of brake pads against the sidewalls to stop the bicycle.
carrier
Device attached to the back of the bicycle for carrying bags on each side and packages on top.
generator
Mechanism activated by the rear wheel, converting the wheel's motion into electric energy to power the front and rear lights.
reflector
Device returning light toward its source so that other users of the road might see the cyclist.
rear light
Lamp signaling the bicycle's presence in the dark.
fender
Piece of curved metal covering part of the wheel to protect the cyclist from being splashed.
rear derailleur
Mechanism for changing the rear gears by lifting the chain from one gear wheel to another; it allows the cyclist to adapt to road conditions.
drive chain
Set of metal links meshing with the sprockets on the chain wheel and gear wheel to transmit the pedaling motion to the rear wheel.
chain stay
Tube connecting the pedal mechanism to the rear-wheel hub.
front derailleur
Mechanism for changing the front gears by lifting the chain from one chain wheel to another; it allows the cyclist to adapt to road conditions.
pedal
Part attached to a crank that the cyclist rotates to provide the bicycle's power.
toe clip
Metal device attached to the pedal that covers the front of the feet keeping the feet in the prope position and increasing pedaling power

TRANSPORT AND MACHINERY

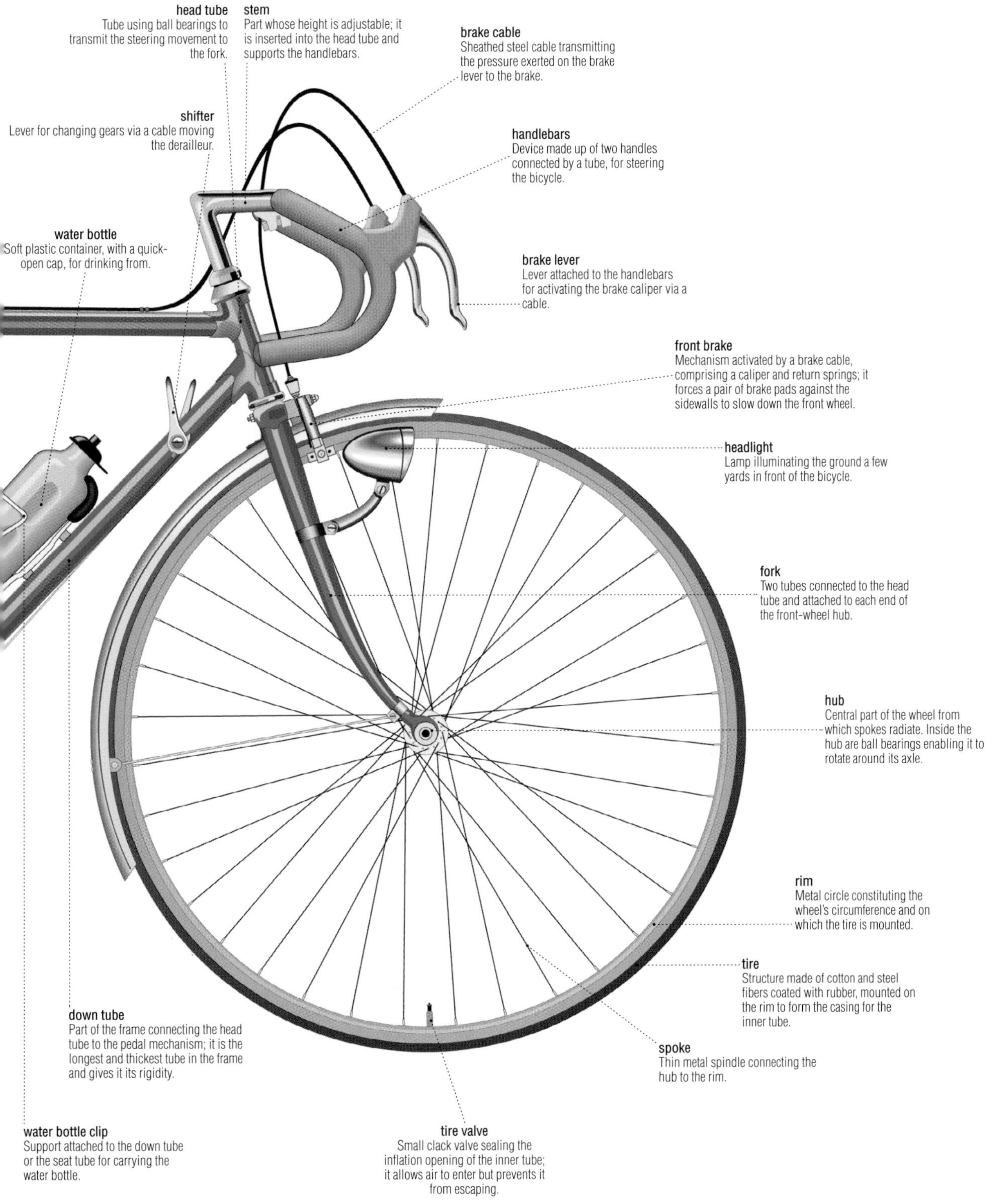
head tube
Tube using ball bearings to transmit the steering movement to the fork.
stem
Part whose height is adjustable; it is inserted into the head tube and supports the handlebars.
brake cable
Sheathed steel cable transmitting the pressure exerted on the brake lever to the brake.
shifter
Lever for changing gears via a cable moving the derailleur.
handlebars
Device made up of two handles connected by a tube, for steering the bicycle.
water bottle
Soft plastic container, with a quick-open cap, for drinking from.
brake lever
Lever attached to the handlebars for activating the brake caliper via a cable.
front brake
Mechanism activated by a brake cable, comprising a caliper and return springs; it forces a pair of brake pads against the sidewalls to slow down the front wheel.
headlight
Lamp illuminating the ground a few yards in front of the bicycle.
fork
Two tubes connected to the head tube and attached to each end of the front-wheel hub.
hub
Central part of the wheel from which spokes radiate. Inside the hub are ball bearings enabling it to rotate around its axle.
rim
Metal circle constituting the wheel's circumference and on which the tire is mounted.
tire
Structure made of cotton and steel fibers coated with rubber, mounted on the rim to form the casing for the inner tube.
down tube
Part of the frame connecting the head tube to the pedal mechanism; it is the longest and thickest tube in the frame and gives it its rigidity.
spoke
Thin metal spindle connecting the hub to the rim.
water bottle clip
Support attached to the down tube or the seat tube for carrying the water bottle.
tire valve
Small clack valve sealing the inflation opening of the inner tube; it allows air to enter but prevents it from escaping.

bicycle

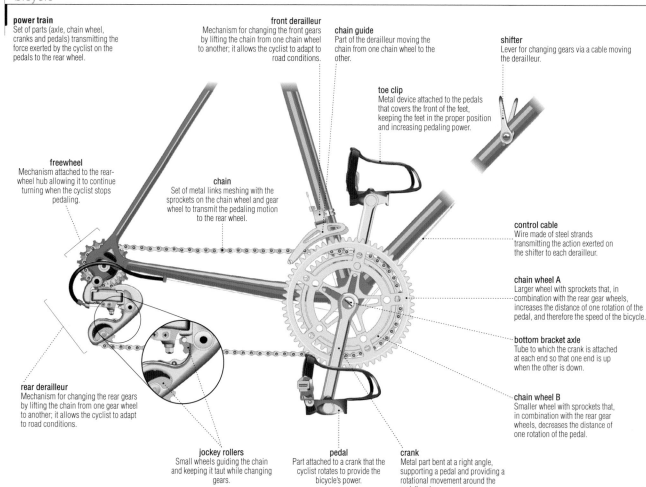

power train
Set of parts (axle, chain wheel, cranks and pedals) transmitting the force exerted by the cyclist on the pedals to the rear wheel.

front derailleur
Mechanism for changing the front gears by lifting the chain from one chain wheel to another; it allows the cyclist to adapt to road conditions.

chain guide
Part of the derailleur moving the chain from one chain wheel to the other.

shifter
Lever for changing gears via a cable moving the derailleur.

toe clip
Metal device attached to the pedals that covers the front of the feet, keeping the feet in the proper position and increasing pedaling power.

freewheel
Mechanism attached to the rear-wheel hub allowing it to continue turning when the cyclist stops pedaling.

chain
Set of metal links meshing with the sprockets on the chain wheel and gear wheel to transmit the pedaling motion to the rear wheel.

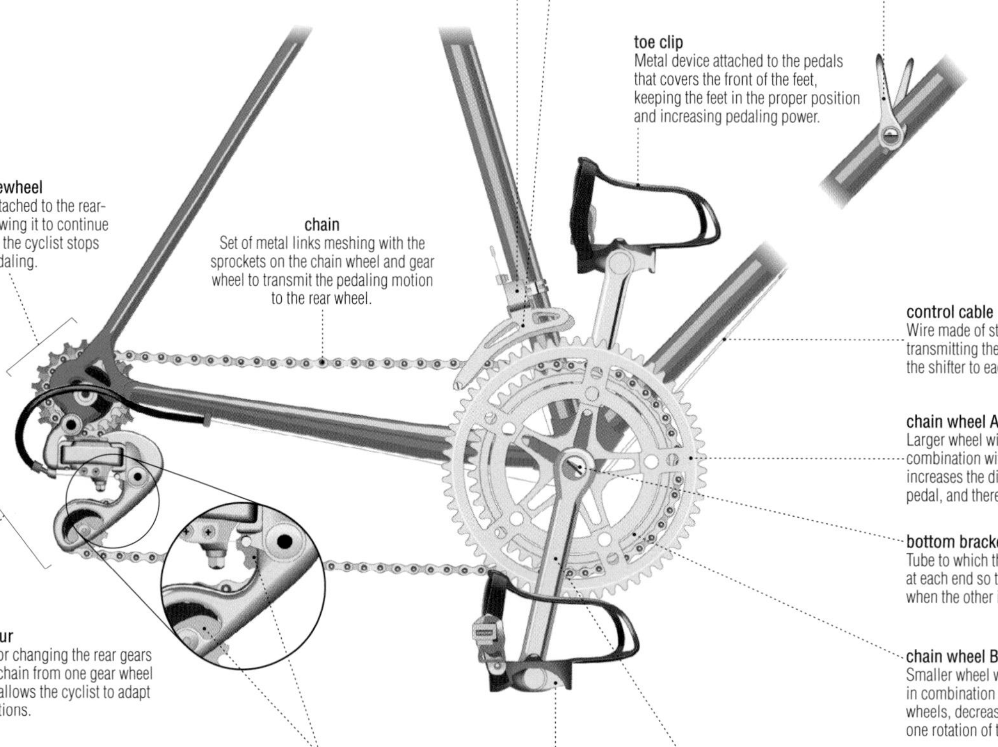

control cable
Wire made of steel strands transmitting the action exerted on the shifter to each derailleur.

chain wheel A
Larger wheel with sprockets that, in combination with the rear gear wheels, increases the distance of one rotation of the pedal, and therefore the speed of the bicycle.

bottom bracket axle
Tube to which the crank is attached at each end so that one end is up when the other is down.

rear derailleur
Mechanism for changing the rear gears by lifting the chain from one gear wheel to another; it allows the cyclist to adapt to road conditions.

chain wheel B
Smaller wheel with sprockets that, in combination with the rear gear wheels, decreases the distance of one rotation of the pedal.

jockey rollers
Small wheels guiding the chain and keeping it taut while changing gears.

pedal
Part attached to a crank that the cyclist rotates to provide the bicycle's power.

crank
Metal part bent at a right angle, supporting a pedal and providing a rotational movement around the pedal's axle.

accessories

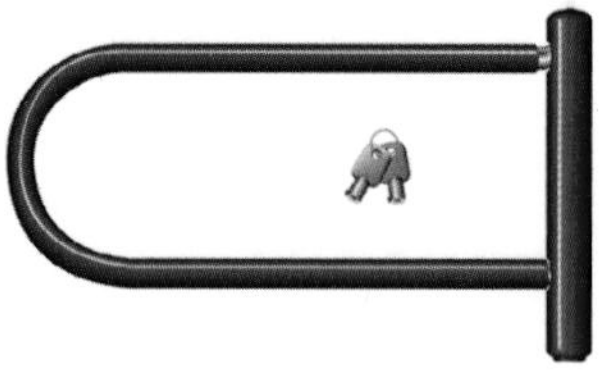

lock
Antitheft system made up of two metal shanks, one inserted into the other and fitted with a lock, for locking the bicycle to a fixed object.

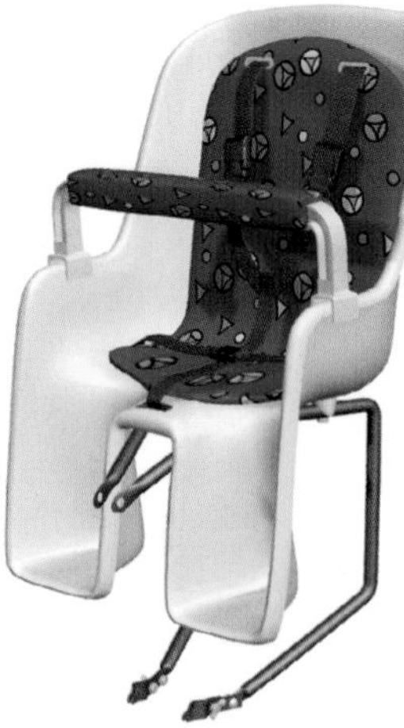

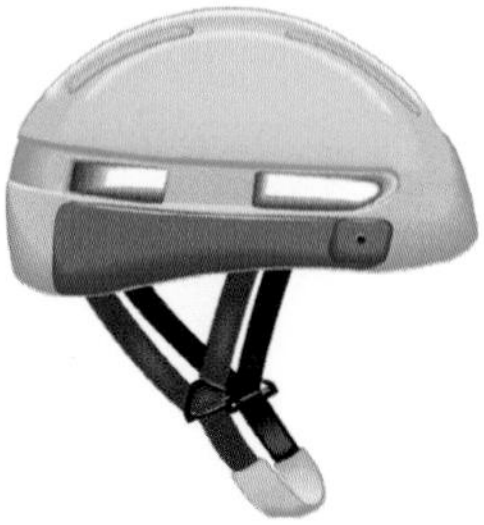

protective helmet
Rigid headgear covering the head to protect it in the event of accident.

tool kit
Set of tools for simple repairs and adjustments, such as fixing a flat tire, replacing spokes or adjusting brakes.

bicycle bag
Bag that can be attached to the handlebars or the carrier.

child carrier
Seat attached to the frame or the carrier, comprising a harness and footrests, for transporting a child.

examples of bicycles

child's tricycle
Very stable three-wheeled vehicle with pedals driving either the front wheel or the rear wheels, for the use of young children.

BMX bike
Strong small bicycle, for acrobatics and competitions on bumpy tracks.

Dutch bicycle
City bicycle designed for comfort and in such a way that the cyclist sits upright; its features include a built-in chain guard and a drop-down fender.

mountain bike
Bicycle with large wheels with treads with studs, a strong frame, numerous gears and powerful brakes, for navigating all kinds of terrain.

city bicycle
Bicycle designed for comfort and safety while taking short trips on city streets.

road bicycle
Bicycle with narrow tires, lightweight frame and handlebars that position the cyclist for optimum aerodynamics, designed for road racing.

touring bicycle
Intermediate bicycle between a road bicycle and a city bicycle, designed for traveling long distances in comfort.

tandem bicycle
Bicycle with two places; both cyclists pedal simultaneously but only the person in front steers.

passenger station

Covered building for the public where trains and passengers arrive and depart.

office
Workplace of the employees managing the station.

indicator board
Panel showing the destination and the configuration of the train, such as type and numbering of cars.

glassed roof
Large glassed surface forming the walls and roof.

baggage cart
Four-wheeled handcart available to passengers for transporting baggage inside the station.

metal structure
Set of metal components comprising the skeleton of a building and supporting its roof; here, the roof is made of glass.

baggage locker
Metal compartments for keeping luggag temporarily for a small fe

platform number

platform edge
Zone along the edge of the platform, usually demarcated by a safety line.

ticket collector
Person checking that passengers' tickets correspond to their destinations.

passenger train
Set of cars coupled together and pulled along tracks by a locomotive.

concourse
Large space for passengers and the public at large housing the various services of the station, such as ticket sales, information counter and shops.

departure time indicator

track
A pair of parallel rails laid end to end and on which trains run.

baggage room
Counter where passengers leave their baggage to be taken to the train's baggage car, if it has one.

passenger platform
Area alongside the tracks for passengers to embark and disembark trains.

schedules
Grid showing the departure and arrival times of the trains, their number and their destination or point of departure.

platform entrance
Area leading to the platforms, sometimes reserved for passengers who have valid tickets.

parcel office
Courier-service window for sending envelopes and packages to be dispatched by train.

destination
Name of the last station where the train stops at the end of its route.

railroad station

Covered building for the public where trains and passengers arrive and depart.

station platform
Area alongside the tracks, for passengers to embark and disembark the train, or for loading and unloading cargo from the cars.

passenger station
Covered building for the public where trains and passengers arrive and depart.

commuter train
Local train running frequently each day between an urban center and its suburbs or neighboring cities.

main line
Tracks for trains traveling long distances.

suburban commuter railroad
Railroad connecting an urban center to its suburbs and neighboring cities.

siding
Side track not used for railroad traffic but for shunting, marshaling or loading and unloading.

bumper
Buffer placed at the end of a track stopping the train from running off the end of the track.

grade crossing
Intersection of a railroad and a road, with or without warning lights.

parking
Area for parking vehicles.

platform shelter
Roof protecting passengers waiting on the platform from inclement weather.

footbridge
Elevated walkway for passengers to cross over a set of tracks.

semaphore
Light for relaying information such as the speed of trains and the distance between them.

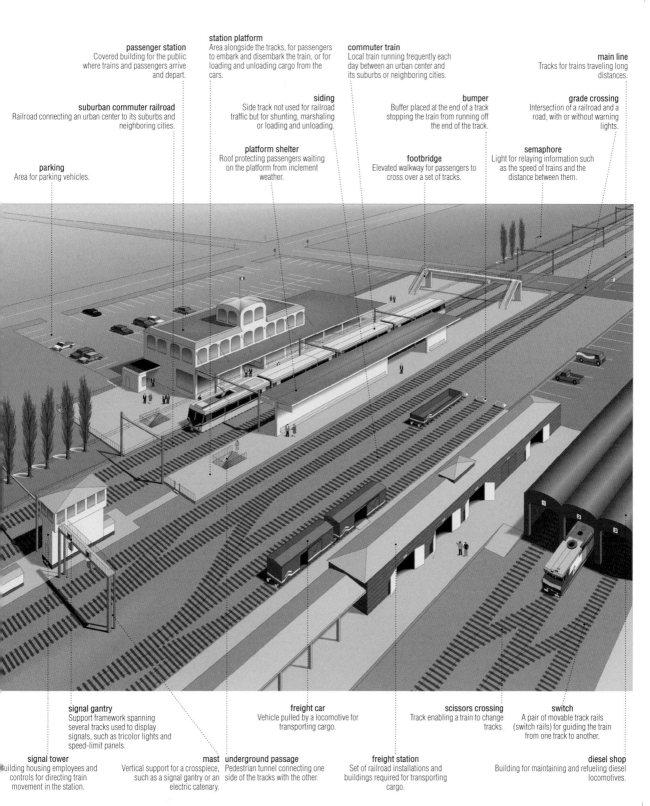

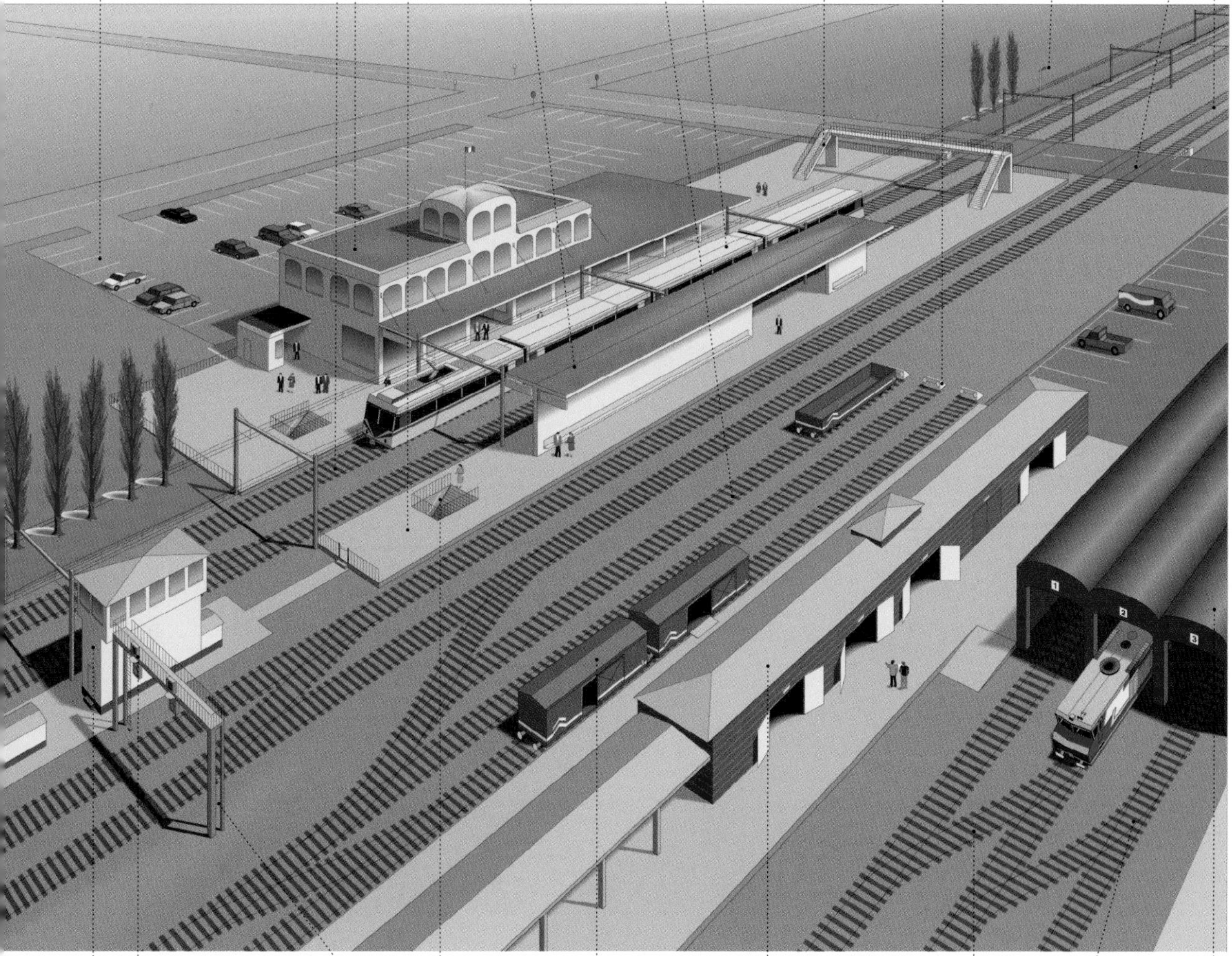

signal gantry
Support framework spanning several tracks used to display signals, such as tricolor lights and speed-limit panels.

freight car
Vehicle pulled by a locomotive for transporting cargo.

scissors crossing
Track enabling a train to change tracks.

switch
A pair of movable track rails (switch rails) for guiding the train from one track to another.

signal tower
Building housing employees and controls for directing train movement in the station.

mast
Vertical support for a crosspiece, such as a signal gantry or an electric catenary.

underground passage
Pedestrian tunnel connecting one side of the tracks with the other.

freight station
Set of railroad installations and buildings required for transporting cargo.

diesel shop
Building for maintaining and refueling diesel locomotives.

TRANSPORT AND MACHINERY

types of passenger cars

Cars: vehicles with various layouts that are pulled by locomotives, for transporting and providing services to passengers.

coach car
Car with two rows of benches or seats for transporting passengers in the seated position.

luggage rack
Space at the entrance of the car for stowing large pieces of luggage.

vestibule
Entrance compartment of the ca

adjustable seat
Seat whose back can be changed from a sitting position to a reclining position.

center aisle
Walkway between the two rows of benches or seats, for going from one end of the car to the other.

vestibule door
Sometimes sliding door on the threshold plate at the top of the steps, providing access to the car.

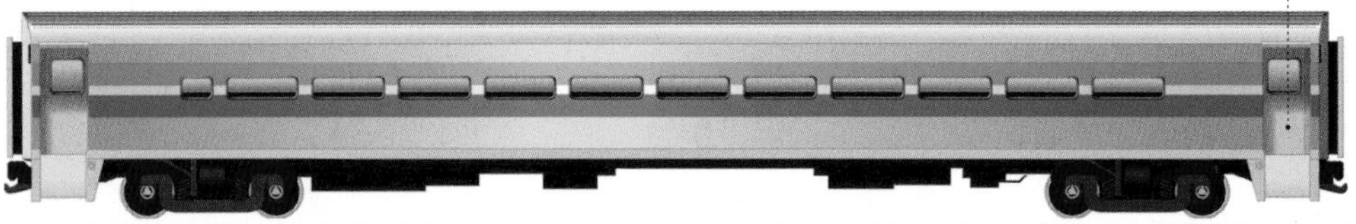

sleeping car
Car with compartments laid out as small bedrooms.

berth
Sometimes folding bench located in a compartment, for sleeping.

toilet
Compartment equipped with a toilet and a sink.

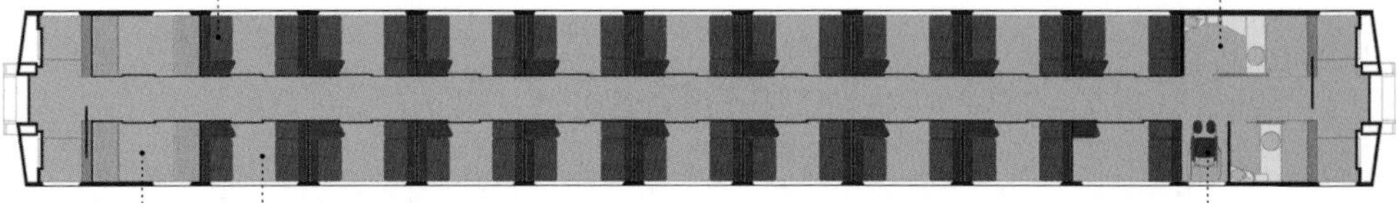

linen
Storage for linens needed for the trip, such as towels and sheets.

sleeping compartment
Compartment laid out with berths.

wheelchair
Place with special fittings designed for wheelchairs.

corridor connection
Device where two cars articulate togeth passengers and personnel can pass through to get from one car to the ne

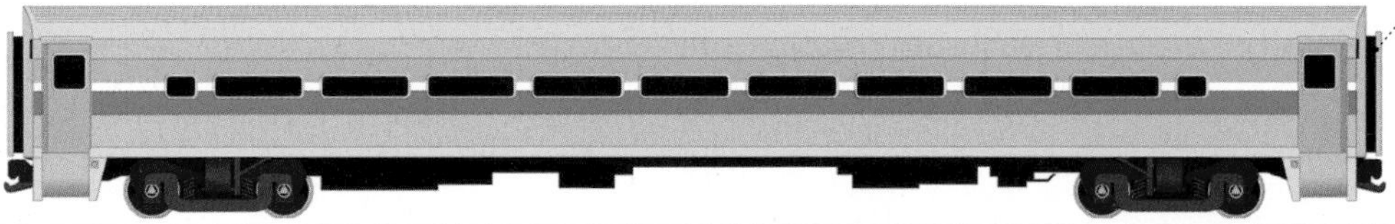

dining car
Car laid out for serving meals.

dining section
Part of the car where passengers can eat or drink.

steward's desk
Table for laying out the dishes used for the various courses and food that is ready to serve.

storage space
Place where employees keep materials for providing service during the trip.

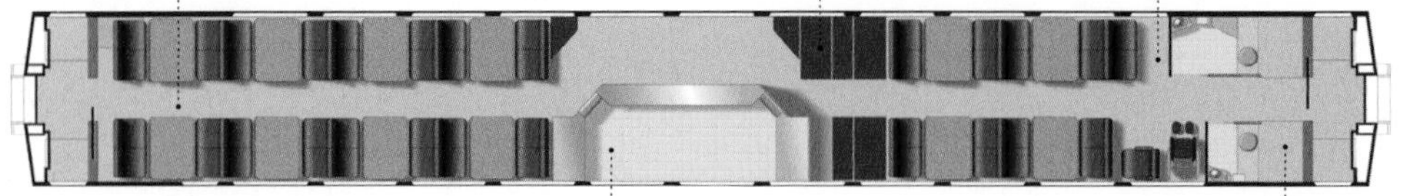

panoramic window
Large window offering an unobstructed view of the passing countryside.

kitchen
Room where meals are prepared.

crew's locker
Compartment at the entrance where personnel can stow their coats and other personal effects.

grab handle
Vertical handle at shoulder heig next to the door for gripping wh climbing up to or down from th car.

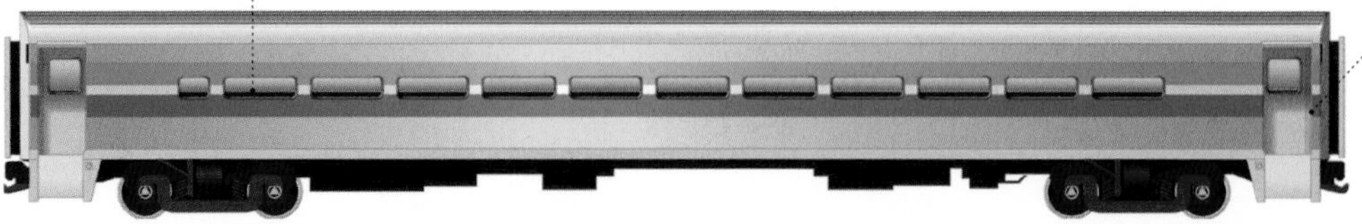

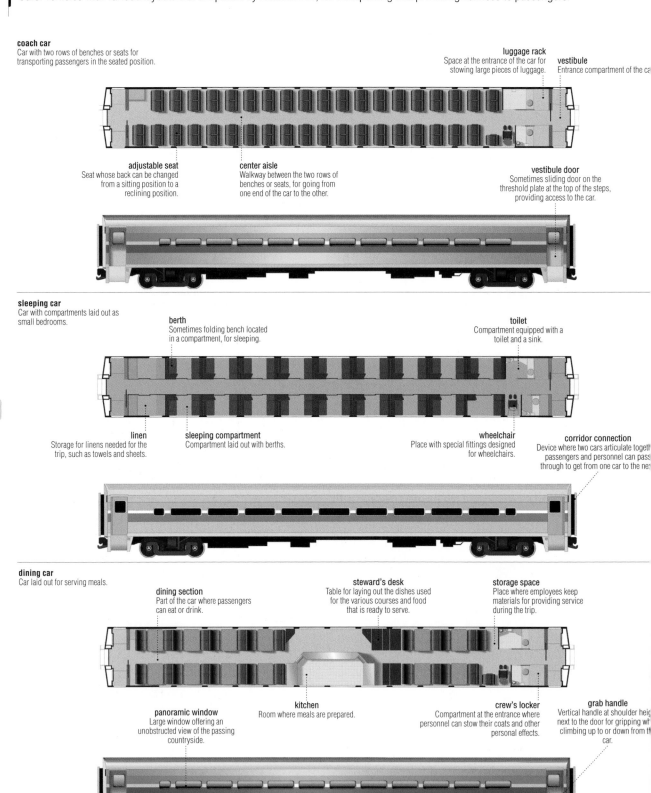

high-speed train

High-speed passenger train (between 135 and 190 mph) powered by electricity, with a power car at each end and a limited number of cars in between.

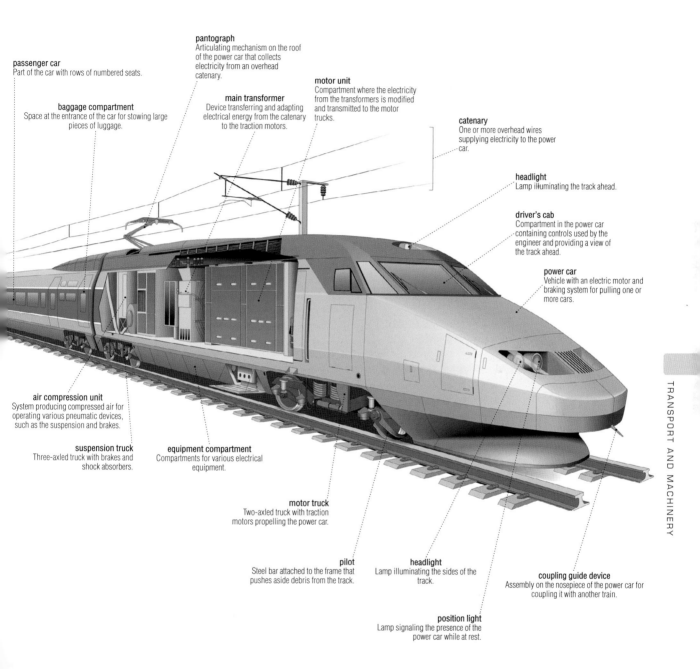

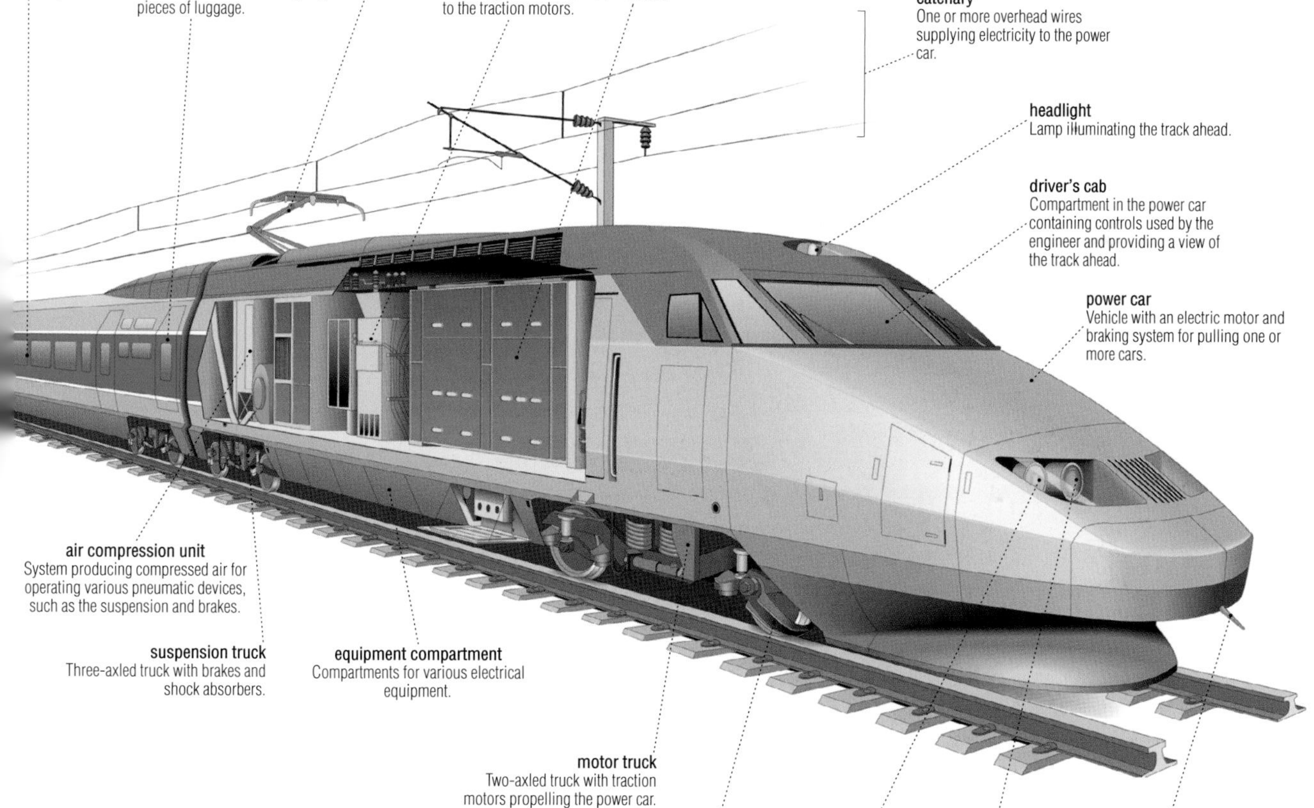
pantograph
Articulating mechanism on the roof of the power car that collects electricity from an overhead catenary.
passenger car
Part of the car with rows of numbered seats.
motor unit
Compartment where the electricity from the transformers is modified and transmitted to the motor trucks.
main transformer
Device transferring and adapting electrical energy from the catenary to the traction motors.
baggage compartment
Space at the entrance of the car for stowing large pieces of luggage.
catenary
One or more overhead wires supplying electricity to the power car.
headlight
Lamp illuminating the track ahead.
driver's cab
Compartment in the power car containing controls used by the engineer and providing a view of the track ahead.
power car
Vehicle with an electric motor and braking system for pulling one or more cars.
air compression unit
System producing compressed air for operating various pneumatic devices, such as the suspension and brakes.
suspension truck
Three-axled truck with brakes and shock absorbers.
equipment compartment
Compartments for various electrical equipment.
motor truck
Two-axled truck with traction motors propelling the power car.
pilot
Steel bar attached to the frame that pushes aside debris from the track.
headlight
Lamp illuminating the sides of the track.
coupling guide device
Assembly on the nosepiece of the power car for coupling it with another train.
position light
Lamp signaling the presence of the power car while at rest.

diesel-electric locomotive

Vehicle with a diesel engine turning a generator that in turn powers the electric traction motors.

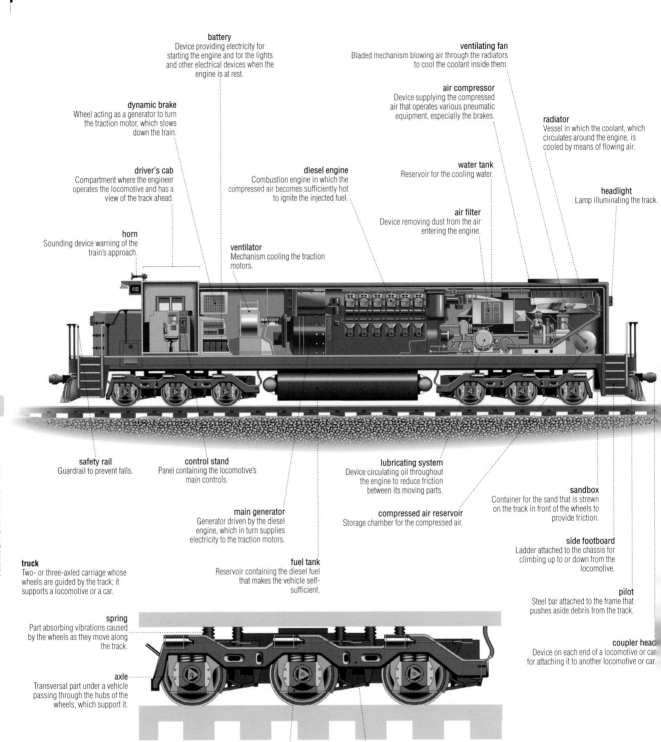

battery
Device providing electricity for starting the engine and for the lights and other electrical devices when the engine is at rest.

ventilating fan
Bladed mechanism blowing air through the radiators to cool the coolant inside them.

air compressor
Device supplying the compressed air that operates various pneumatic equipment, especially the brakes.

dynamic brake
Wheel acting as a generator to turn the traction motor, which slows down the train.

radiator
Vessel in which the coolant, which circulates around the engine, is cooled by means of flowing air.

water tank
Reservoir for the cooling water.

driver's cab
Compartment where the engineer operates the locomotive and has a view of the track ahead.

diesel engine
Combustion engine in which the compressed air becomes sufficiently hot to ignite the injected fuel.

headlight
Lamp illuminating the track.

air filter
Device removing dust from the air entering the engine.

horn
Sounding device warning of the train's approach.

ventilator
Mechanism cooling the traction motors.

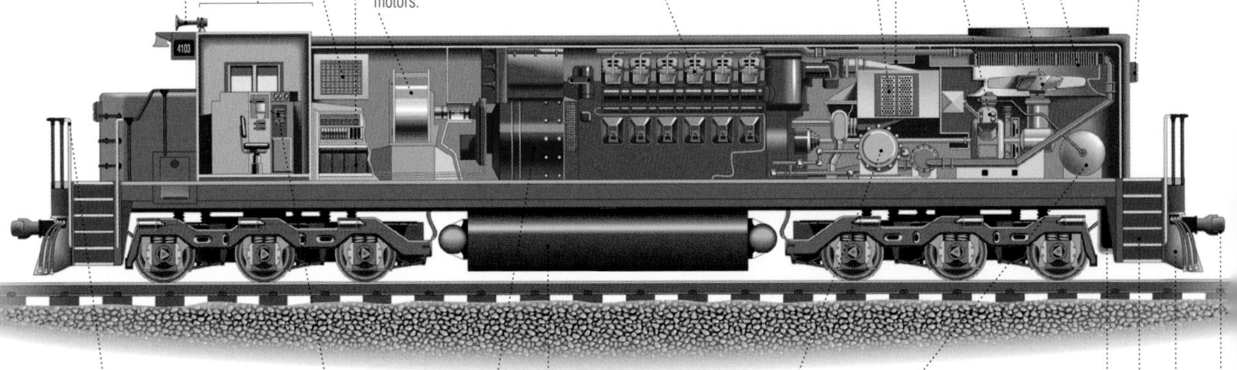

safety rail
Guardrail to prevent falls.

control stand
Panel containing the locomotive's main controls.

lubricating system
Device circulating oil throughout the engine to reduce friction between its moving parts.

sandbox
Container for the sand that is strewn on the track in front of the wheels to provide friction.

main generator
Generator driven by the diesel engine, which in turn supplies electricity to the traction motors.

compressed air reservoir
Storage chamber for the compressed air.

side footboard
Ladder attached to the chassis for climbing up to or down from the locomotive.

truck
Two- or three-axled carriage whose wheels are guided by the track; it supports a locomotive or a car.

fuel tank
Reservoir containing the diesel fuel that makes the vehicle self-sufficient.

pilot
Steel bar attached to the frame that pushes aside debris from the track.

spring
Part absorbing vibrations caused by the wheels as they move along the track.

coupler head
Device on each end of a locomotive or car for attaching it to another locomotive or car.

axle
Transversal part under a vehicle passing through the hubs of the wheels, which support it.

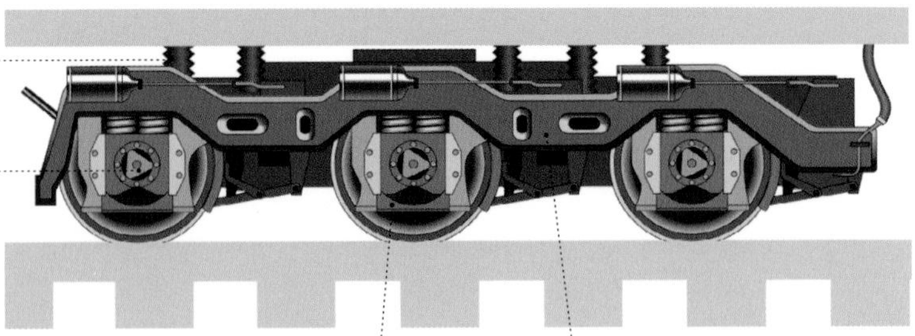

journal box
Part connecting the axle to the truck frame.

truck frame
Framework supporting the axles, suspension, brakes and traction motors.

car

Vehicle pulled by a locomotive for transporting cargo.

box car
Car covered with a waterproof casing and having sliding side doors, for transporting cargo that must be protected from the weather and theft.

hand brake wheel
Wheel for manually activating the brake.

horizontal end handhold
Crossbar for holding onto when moving from one side of the car to the other while coupling.

corner cap
Metal part reinforcing and protecting the edges of the car.

routing cardboard
Placard for a label listing the car's contents.

placard board
Placard for a label warning of dangerous material.

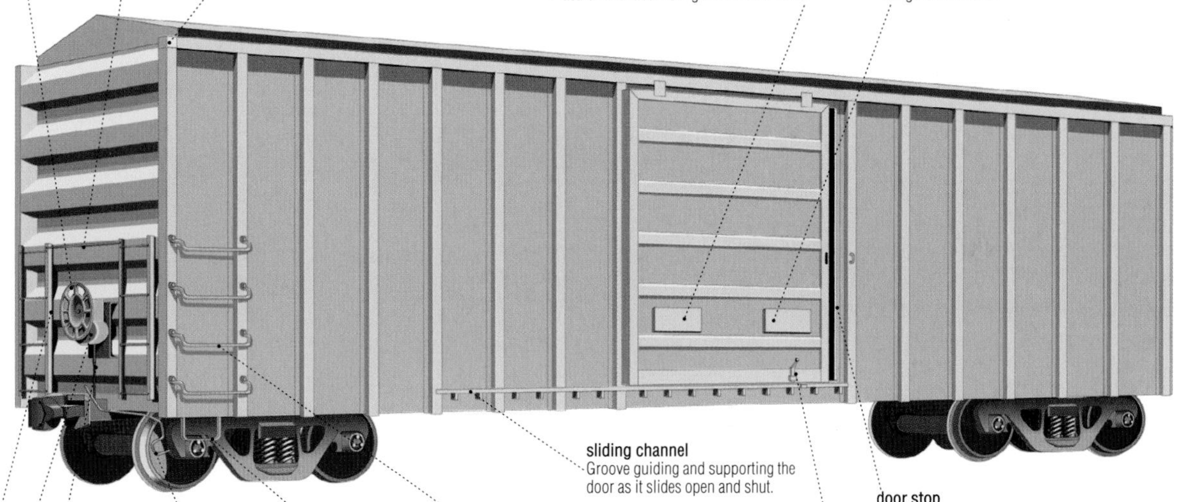

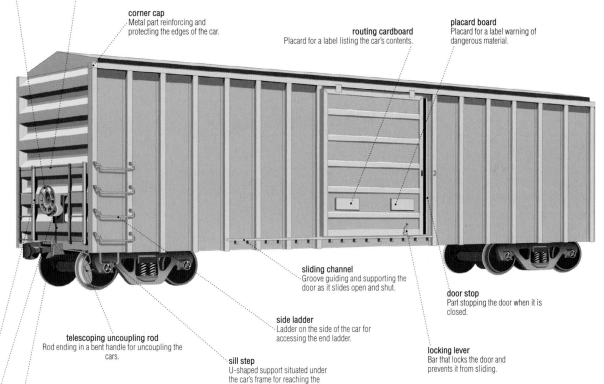

sliding channel
Groove guiding and supporting the door as it slides open and shut.

door stop
Part stopping the door when it is closed.

side ladder
Ladder on the side of the car for accessing the end ladder.

telescoping uncoupling rod
Rod ending in a bent handle for uncoupling the cars.

locking lever
Bar that locks the door and prevents it from sliding.

sill step
U-shaped support situated under the car's frame for reaching the ladder.

hand brake winding lever
Vertical metal shaft, with one end connected by a chain to the hand brake wheel and the wheel house, for setting the hand brake.

hand brake gear housing
Part covering a chain transmitting the wheel's turning movement to the hand brake winding lever.

nd ladder
adder for climbing up and down the ar to carry out certain tasks, such as ncoupling the cars and setting the and brake.

automatic coupler
Device on each end of a locomotive or car for attaching it to another locomotive or car.

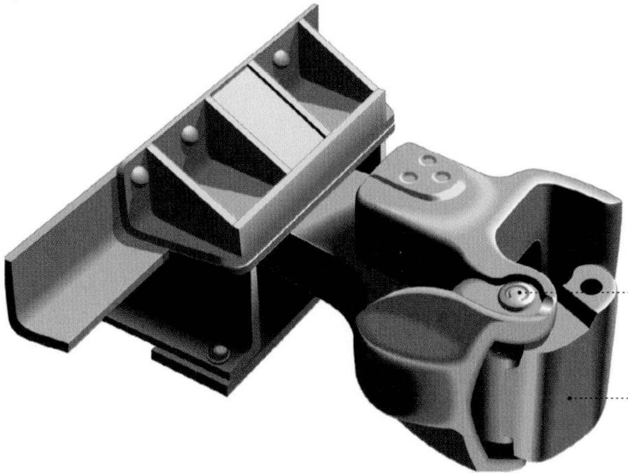

coupler knuckle pin
Part around which the coupler knuckle pivots to open and uncouple.

coupler knuckle
Articulated component that interlocks with the corresponding part on another car or locomotive.

car

examples of freight cars

The shape of the cars varies depending on the type of cargo being transported.

caboose
Car that is usually at the end of the train; it houses personnel, provisions and tools.

tank car
Car with a sealed reservoir for carrying liquids and gases.

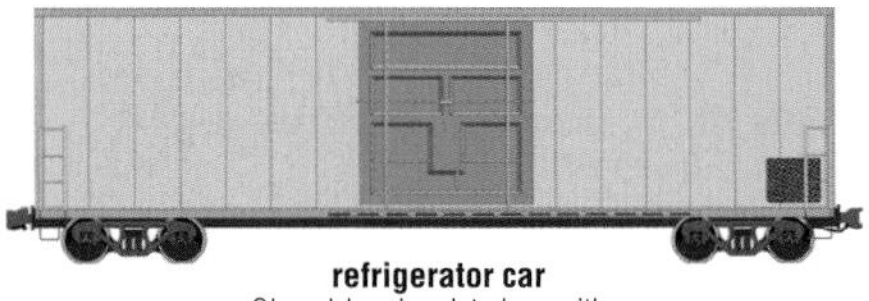

refrigerator car
Closed-box insulated car with a refrigeration unit for carrying perishable foodstuffs.

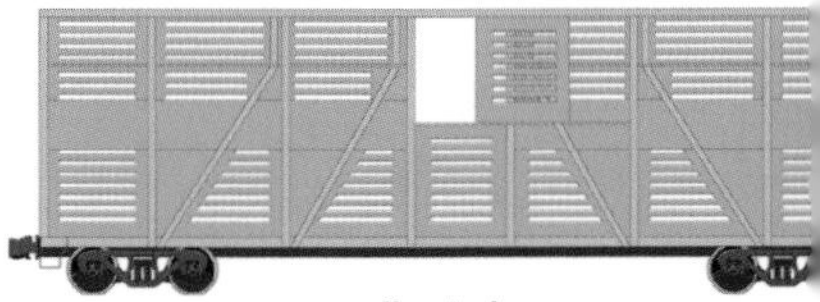

livestock car
Car with slatted sides for carrying livestock; it sometimes has two decks.

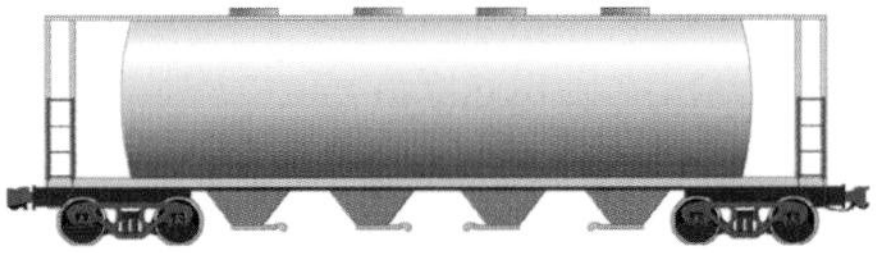

hopper car
Car for carrying bulk cargo; it has dump doors on the bottom for unloading the cargo.

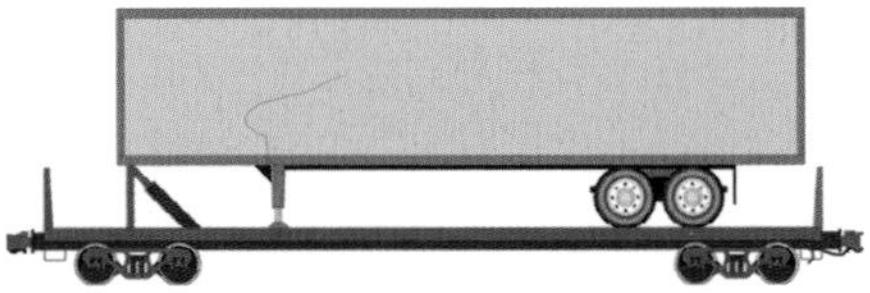

intermodal car
Flat car for carrying semitrailers.

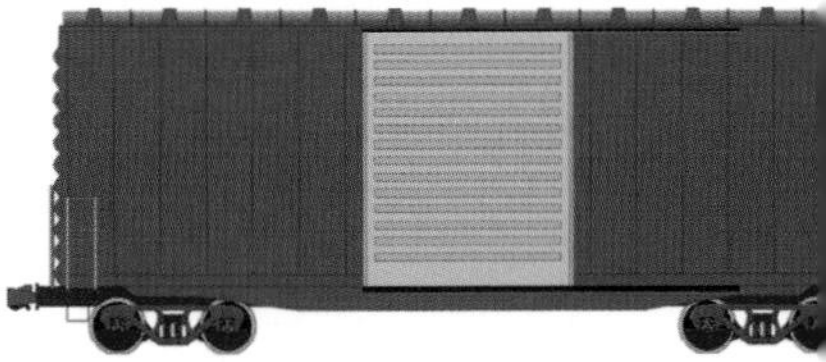

box car
Car covered with a waterproof casing and having sliding side doors, for transporting cargo that must be protected from the weather and theft.

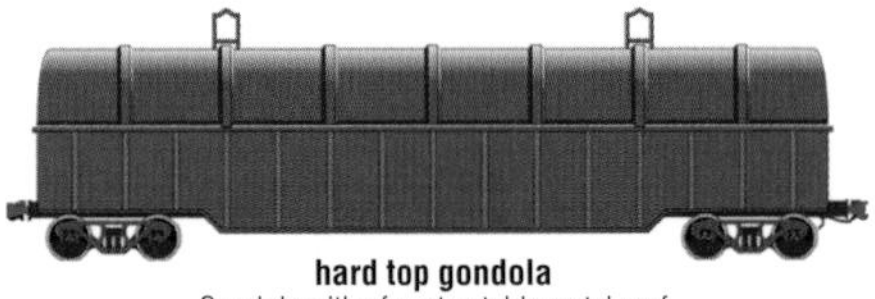

hard top gondola
Gondola with of a retractable metal roof for carrying bulk cargo.

wood chip car
Open-top gondola car with a large compartment for carrying wood chips.

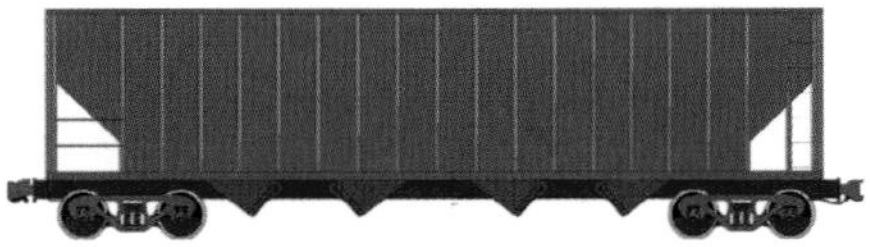

hopper ore car
Usually open-top hopper car of limited capacity for carrying minerals.

gondola car
Open-top car for carrying heavy bulk material, such as scrap metal and construction material.

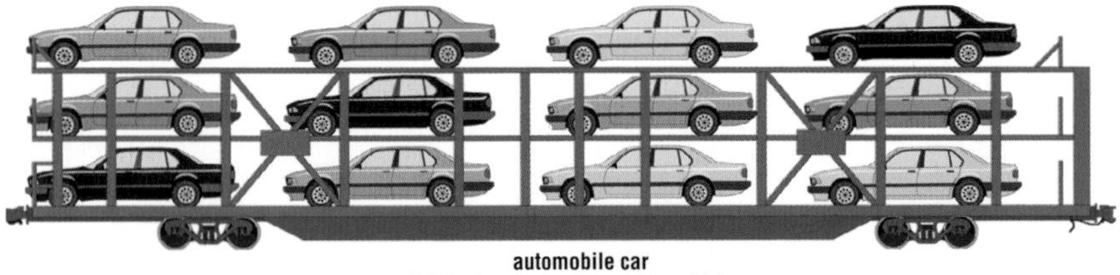

automobile car
Multilevel car for carrying vehicles, which are strapped down.

flat car
Car with a simple wooden deck for carrying large objects, such as pipes, logs and heavy machinery.

bulkhead flat car
Flat car with sturdy plates at each end for carrying loose carg (usually logs).

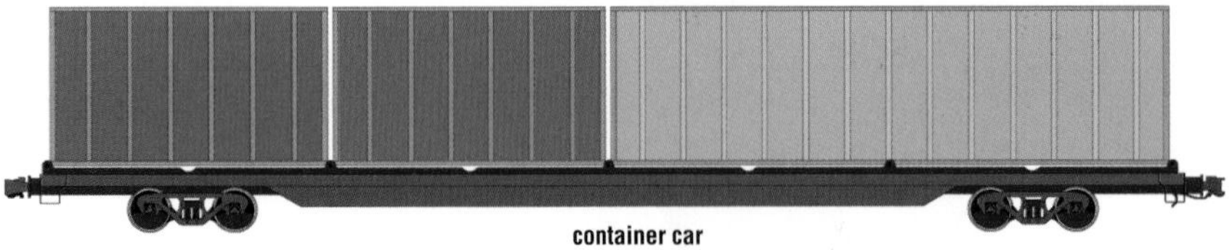

container car
Flat car for carrying standard-size shipping boxes.

depressed-center flat car
Car with two extra trucks and a lowered deck for carrying heavy equipment.

yard

Set of tracks where freight trains are reconfigured to contain cargo cars with the same destination and then dispatched.

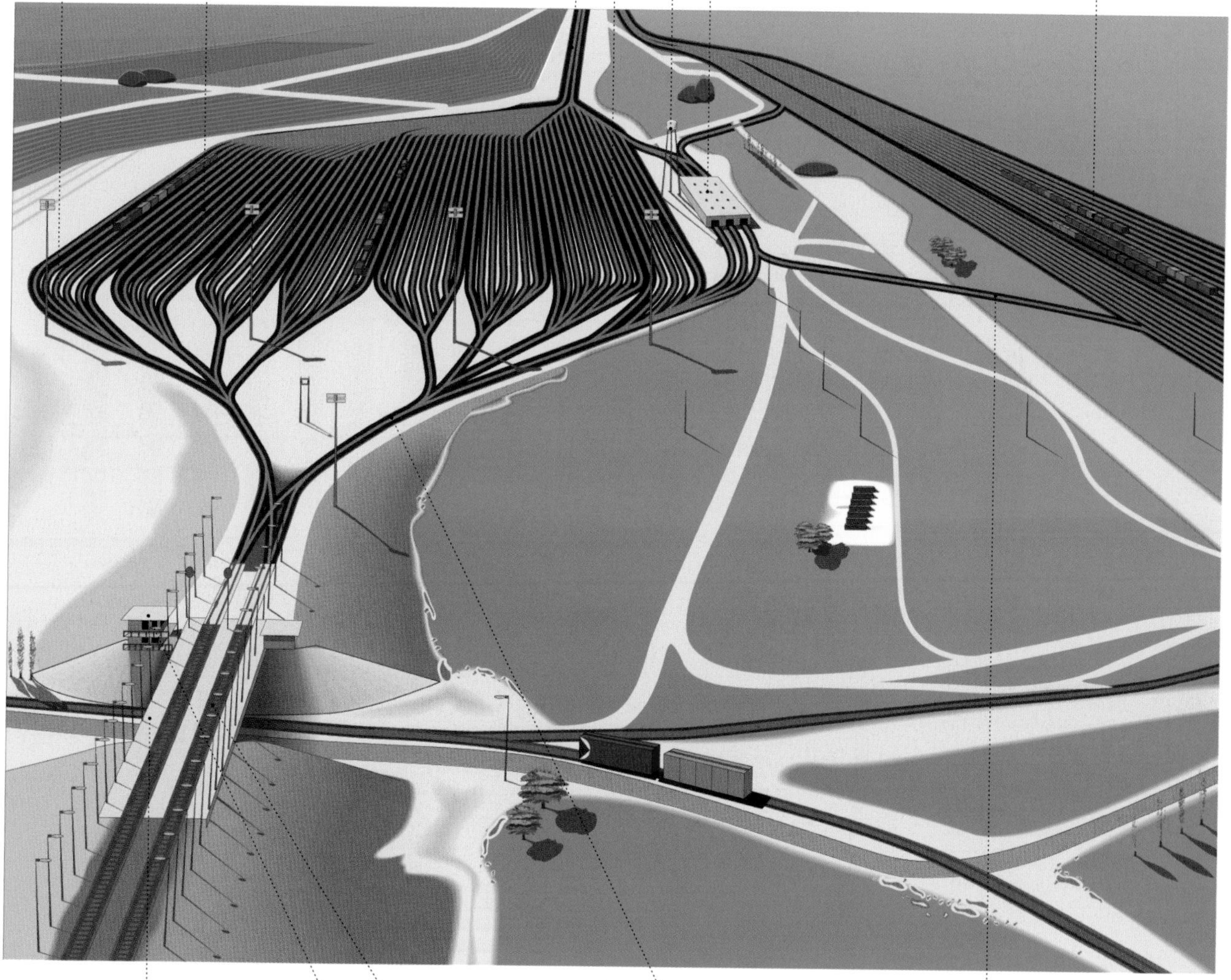
second classification track
Track where cars of known destination are assembled.
classification yard
Set of tracks where cars are hitched together to form trains with the same destination.
car cleaning yard
Set of tracks where cars are cleansed of any cargo residue before going back into circulation.
outbound track
Track that leads trains out of the yard.
water tower
Elevated reservoir containing potable water.
repair shop
Structure for repairing and maintaining locomotives and cars.
receiving yard
Set of tracks where arriving trains park and are unhitched from their locomotives.
hump
Sloped part of the track where cars are pushed up a hill (hump) by a locomotive.
first classification track
Track where cars for the second classification track are switched.
locomotive track
Track that leads locomotives to the shop for maintenance.
hump office
Office where train formations are programmed and car shunting is controlled.
hump lead
Track where cars are released to coast onto other tracks for switching onto outbound trains.

railroad track

A pair of parallel rails laid end to end and on which trains run.

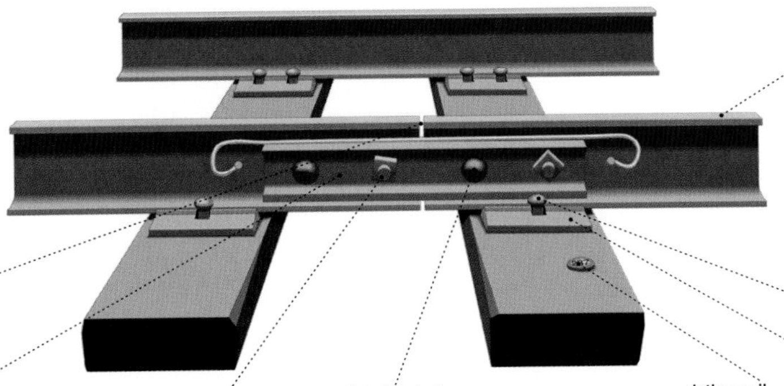
rail joint
Fasteners joining the ends of rails.
running surface
Top of the rail head on which the train wheels roll.
expansion space
Space left between two joining rails to absorb expansion due to heat.
spike
Large nail with a hooked head that fastens the base of the rail to the tie.
tie plate
Metal plate placed between the rail head and the tie that helps to distribute the weight of the train on the tie.
fishplate
Long steel plate that is fitted into the two sides of the rail webs to join them end to end.
nut
Hollow cylinder of metal whose lining is threaded to screw onto a corresponding bolt.
fishplate bolt
Bolt-and-screw assembly that fastens a fishplate to rails.
dating nail
Nail attached to a tie that bears the two last numbers of the year in which the tie was laid.

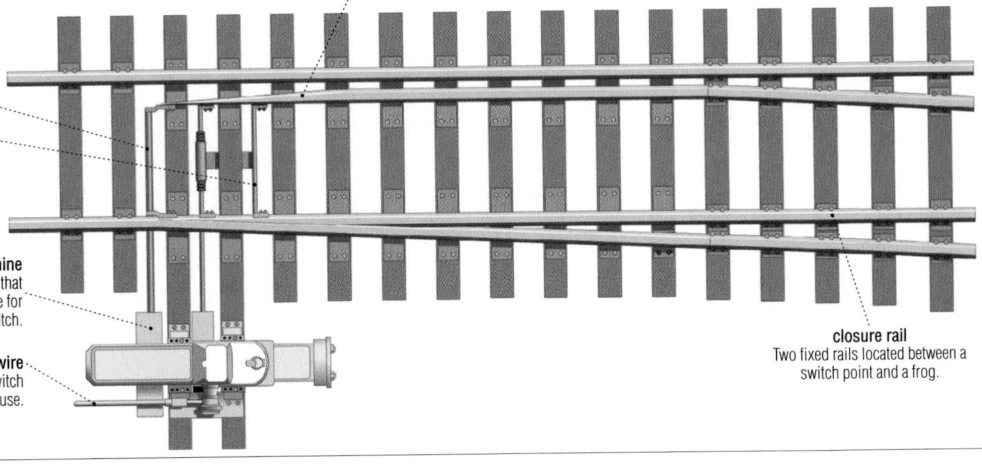
remote-controlled switch
Device operated from a distance for opening and closing a pair of movable track rails (switch points) to guide a train from one track to another.
switch point
Movable rail that is machine-tapered at the end and connected to a parallel and similarly machined switch point.
pull rod
Metal part connected to the power switch machine that opens and closes the switch points.
switch rod
Metal part located between two ties that maintains the distance between two switch points.
power switch machine
Remote-controlled motor that provides the mechanical force for opening and closing the switch.
closure rail
Two fixed rails located between a switch point and a frog.
point wire
Wire that connects the power switch machine to levers in the switch house.

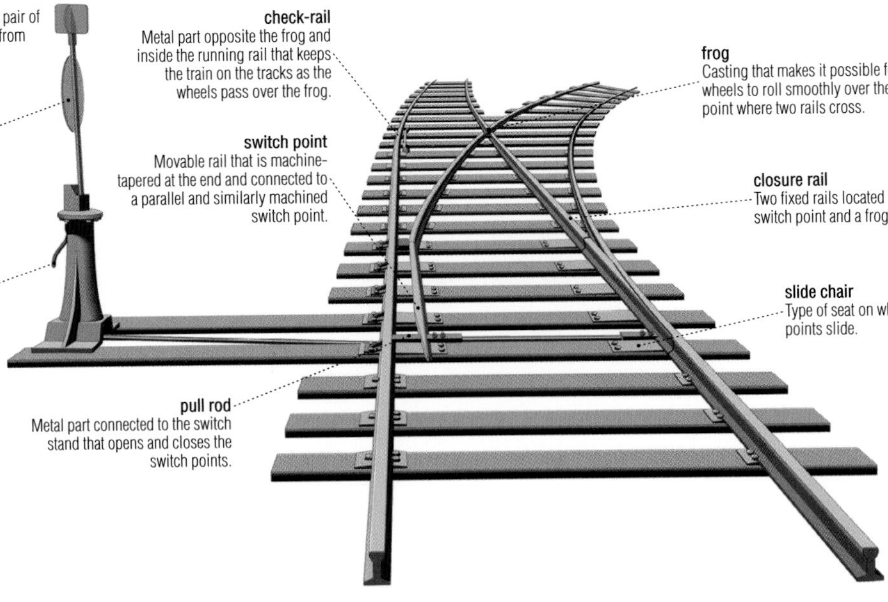
manually operated switch
Device operated by hand for opening and closing a pair of movable track rails (switch points) to guide a train from one track to another.
check-rail
Metal part opposite the frog and inside the running rail that keeps the train on the tracks as the wheels pass over the frog.
frog
Casting that makes it possible for wheels to roll smoothly over the point where two rails cross.
switch signal
Device with an arm that is controlled by the switch stand; it is raised or lowered to indicate whether the switch is open or closed.
switch point
Movable rail that is machine-tapered at the end and connected to a parallel and similarly machined switch point.
closure rail
Two fixed rails located between a switch point and a frog.
switch stand
Manually operated lever that opens and closes the switch.
slide chair
Type of seat on which the switch points slide.
pull rod
Metal part connected to the switch stand that opens and closes the switch points.

railroad track

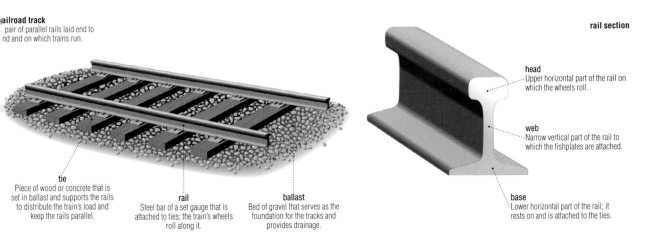

ailroad track
pair of parallel rails laid end to nd and on which trains run.

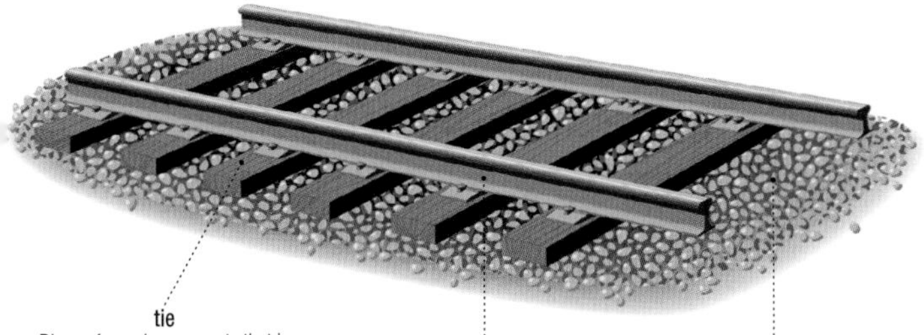

tie
Piece of wood or concrete that is set in ballast and supports the rails to distribute the train's load and keep the rails parallel.

rail
Steel bar of a set gauge that is attached to ties; the train's wheels roll along it.

ballast
Bed of gravel that serves as the foundation for the tracks and provides drainage.

rail section

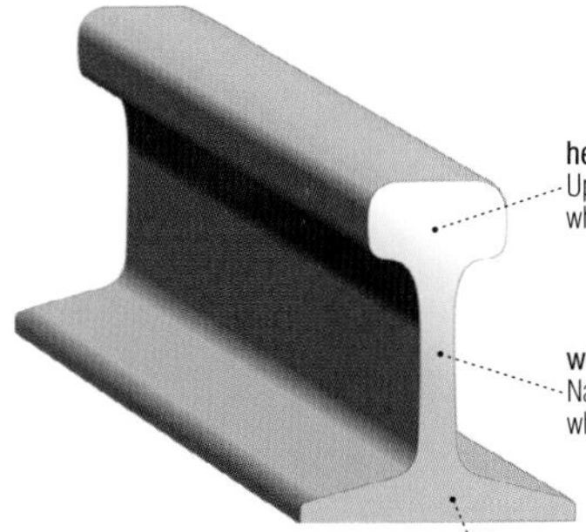

head
Upper horizontal part of the rail on which the wheels roll.

web
Narrow vertical part of the rail to which the fishplates are attached.

base
Lower horizontal part of the rail; it rests on and is attached to the ties.

highway crossing

Intersection of a railroad and a road, with or without warning lights.

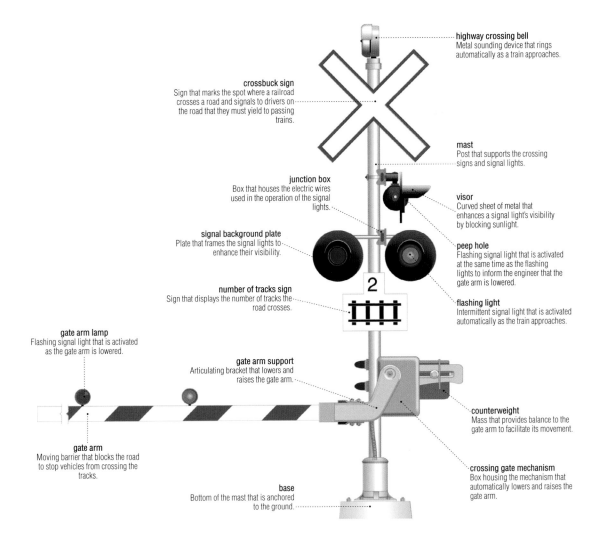

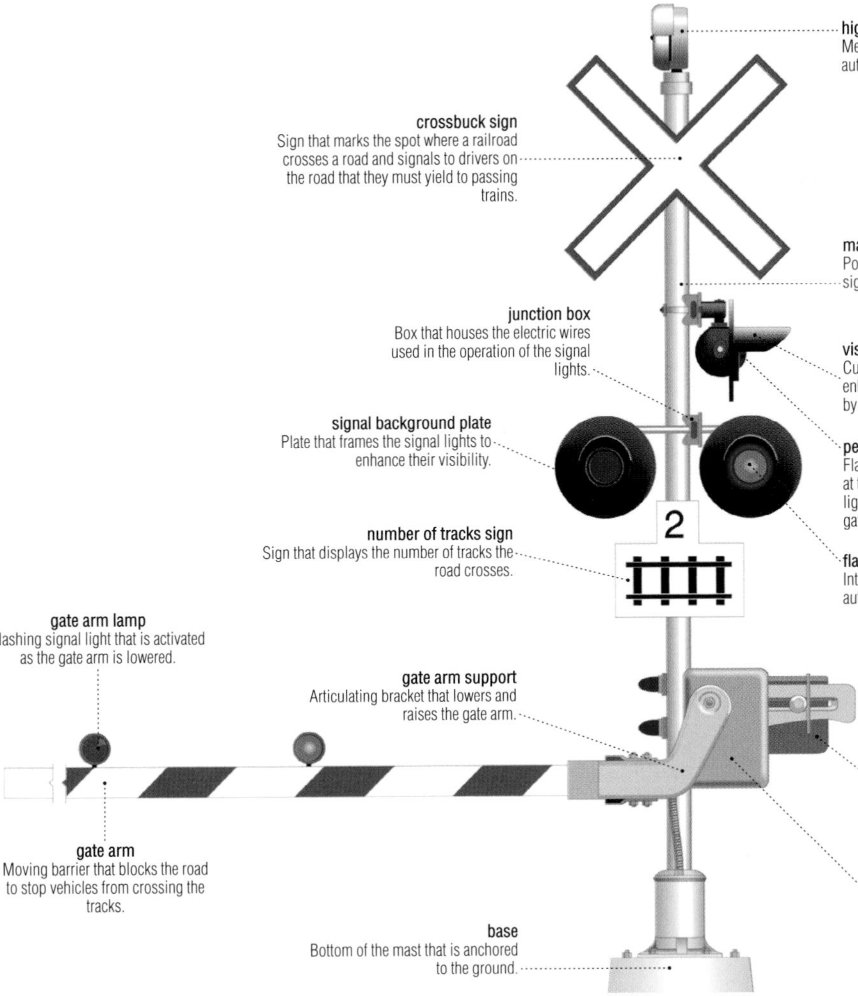

highway crossing bell
Metal sounding device that rings automatically as a train approaches.

crossbuck sign
Sign that marks the spot where a railroad crosses a road and signals to drivers on the road that they must yield to passing trains.

mast
Post that supports the crossing signs and signal lights.

junction box
Box that houses the electric wires used in the operation of the signal lights.

visor
Curved sheet of metal that enhances a signal light's visibility by blocking sunlight.

signal background plate
Plate that frames the signal lights to enhance their visibility.

peep hole
Flashing signal light that is activated at the same time as the flashing lights to inform the engineer that the gate arm is lowered.

number of tracks sign
Sign that displays the number of tracks the road crosses.

flashing light
Intermittent signal light that is activated automatically as the train approaches.

gate arm lamp
Flashing signal light that is activated as the gate arm is lowered.

gate arm support
Articulating bracket that lowers and raises the gate arm.

counterweight
Mass that provides balance to the gate arm to facilitate its movement.

gate arm
Moving barrier that blocks the road to stop vehicles from crossing the tracks.

crossing gate mechanism
Box housing the mechanism that automatically lowers and raises the gate arm.

base
Bottom of the mast that is anchored to the ground.

subway

Electrified urban railroad built mainly underground for transporting passengers at frequent intervals.

subway station
Structure and facilities that provide passengers access to the subway.

station entrance
Small structure built on a public thoroughfare that provides access to the subway station.

exterior sign
Sign placed outside the entrance to the subway that makes it visible from afar.

escalator
Installation that consists of articulated steps on a continuously turning chain; it allows movement between two levels of a building.

stairs
Structural component that enables movement between levels.

mezzanine
Intermediate level that is accessible by stairs and serves as a landing between the station entrance and the platforms.

exit turnstile
Device that allows one user at a time to exit.

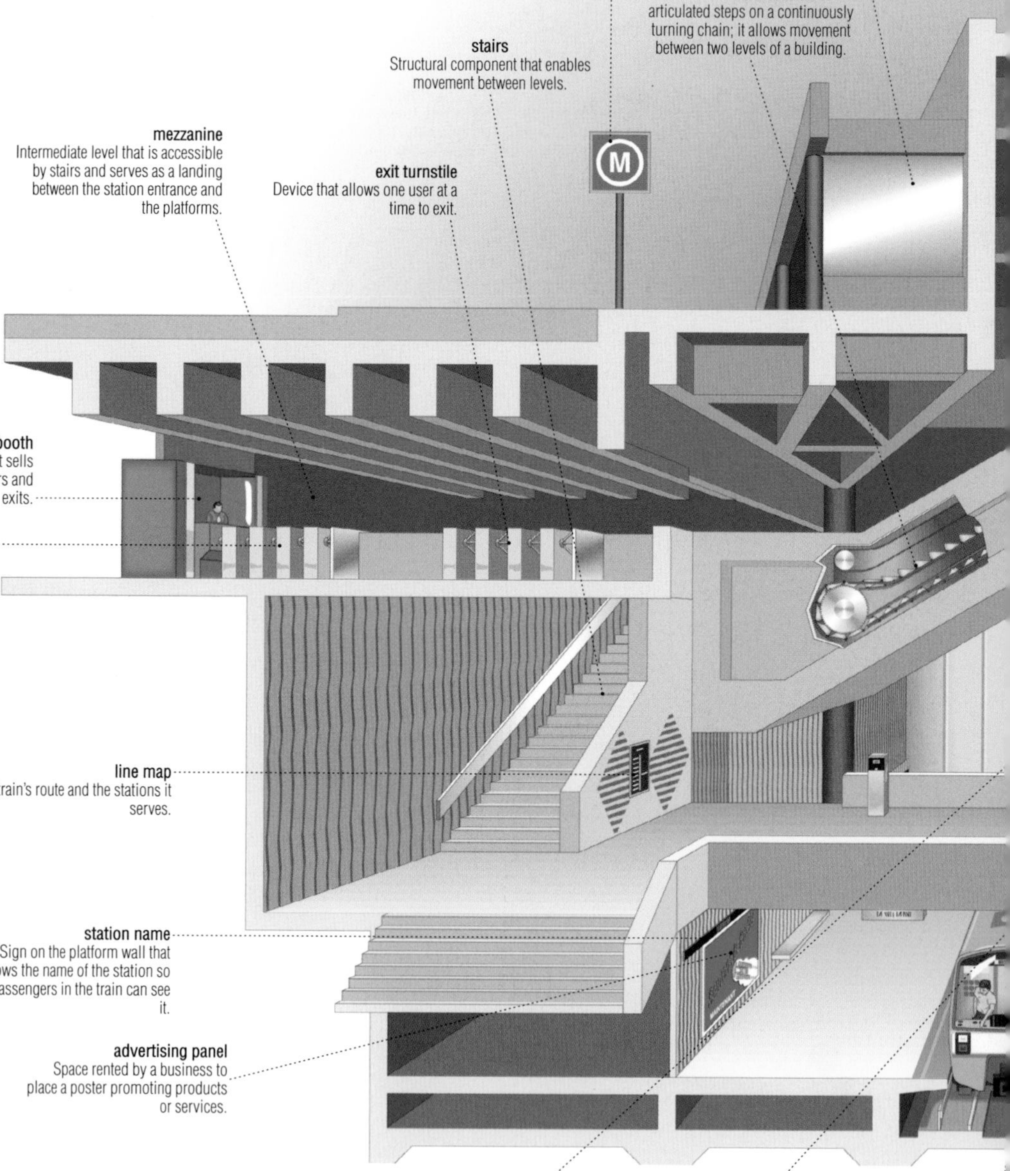

ticket collecting booth
Kiosk protected by glass where an agent sells tickets and passes, and controls who enters and exits.

entrance turnstile
Automatic device that allows a user to enter after swiping a pass or inserting a ticket or transfer.

line map
Chart that shows a train's route and the stations it serves.

station name
Sign on the platform wall that shows the name of the station so that passengers in the train can see it.

advertising panel
Space rented by a business to place a poster promoting products or services.

tunnel
Underground passageway through which the subway train travels between stations.

subway train
Set of cars that is pulled by a motor car and carries passengers.

track
Course that consists of parallel electrified rails on which trains roll.

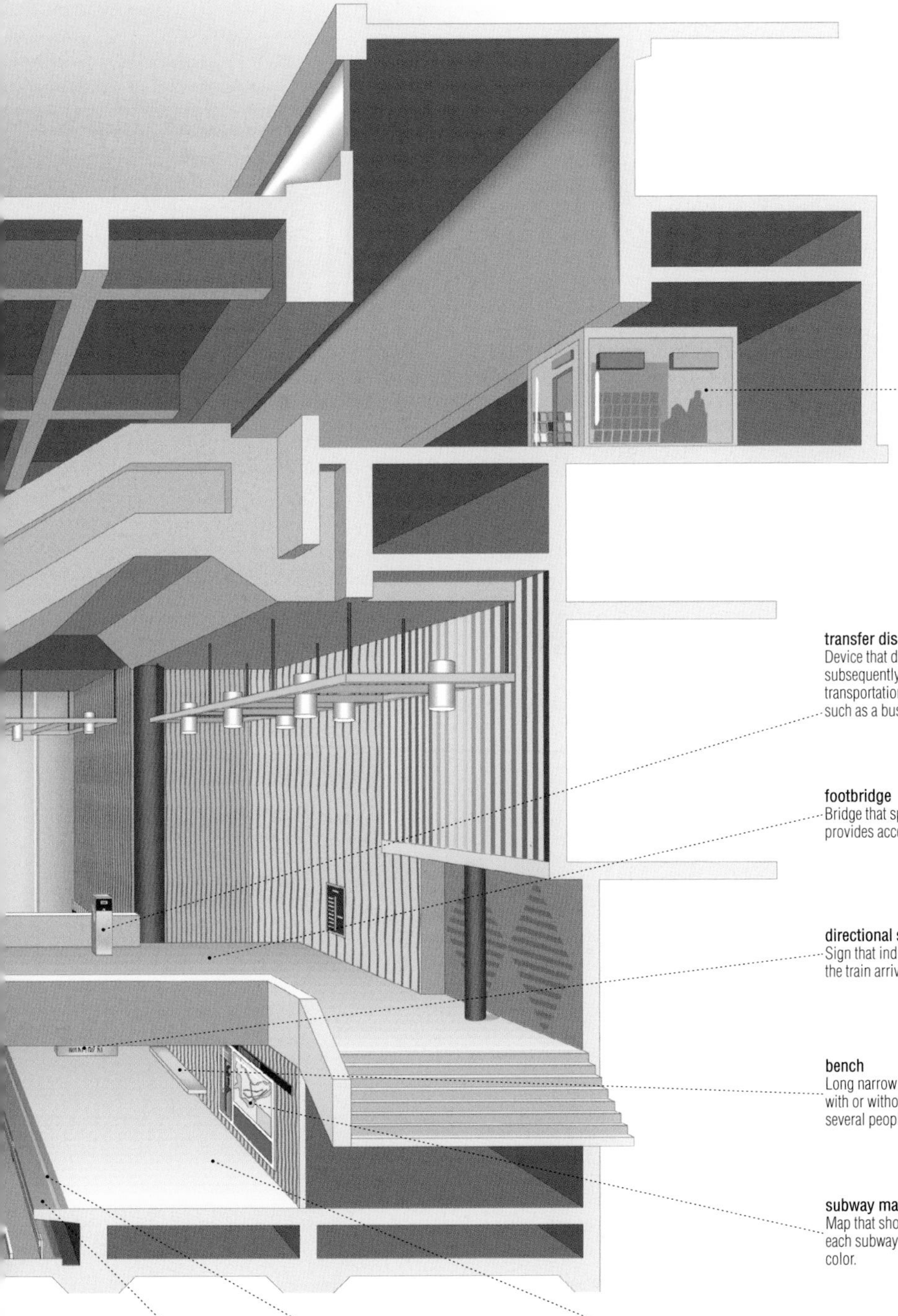
kiosk
Small store in the halls or the entrance of the station that sells newspapers and refreshments.
transfer dispensing machine
Device that dispenses tickets entitling the user to subsequently board another means of transportation linked with the subway system, such as a bus, streetcar or train.
footbridge
Bridge that spans the tracks and provides access to both platforms.
directional sign
Sign that indicates the terminus of the train arriving at that platform.
bench
Long narrow unupholstered seat with or without a back, seating several people.
subway map
Map that shows the entire subway system; each subway line is illustrated in a different color.
platform edge
Zone along the edge of the platform, usually demarcated by a safety line.
safety line
Visible or textured line warning passengers of the margin of safety.
platform
Area adjacent to the tracks where passengers board and exit trains; it is at the same level as the floor of the trains.

subway

passenger car
Vehicle that rolls along subway tracks and transports passengers.

communication set
Loudspeaker phone used for talking to the train driver.

emergency brake
Device that stops the train; it is available to users in case of emergency.

side door
Sliding door that opens onto the station platforms for passengers to enter and exit.

ventilator
Grille that circulates fresh air throughout the car.

side handrail
Handle on the wall next to the door for passengers to hold onto while the train is in motion.

light
Fixtures for illuminating the interior of the car.

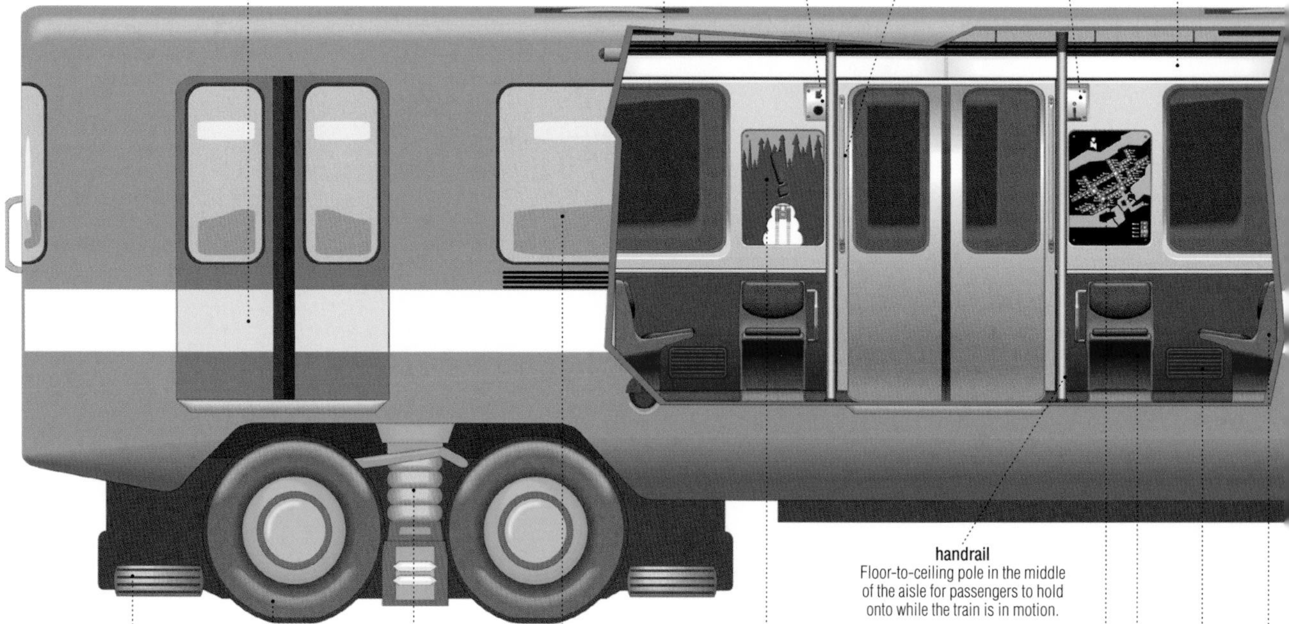

handrail
Floor-to-ceiling pole in the middle of the aisle for passengers to hold onto while the train is in motion.

inflated guiding tire
Tire mounted at right angles to the carrying tire; it rolls against the guiding bar to guide the truck.

window
Opening containing thick glass that does not open.

subway map
Map that shows the entire subway system; each subway line is illustrated in a different color.

suspension
Assembly that dissipates the vibrations occurring as the wheels roll along the tracks.

advertising sign
Poster on a space rented by a business that promotes products or services.

single seat
Seat for one passenger.

inflated carrying tire
Nitrogen-filled tire that supports and conveys the car.

heating grille
Grating through which warm air is forced to heat the car interior.

double seat
Bench with space for two passengers.

subway train
Set of cars that is pulled by a motor car and carries passengers.

motor car
Vehicle with an electric motor and braking system for pulling one or more cars.

trailer car
Freewheeling car pulled by a motor car.

motor car
Vehicle with an electric motor and braking system for pulling one or more cars.

subway

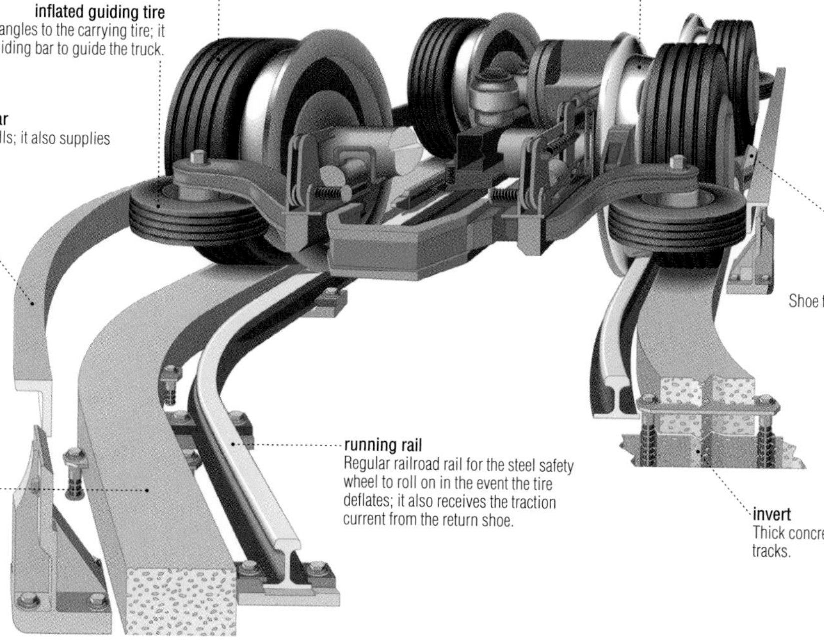
truck and track
The most up-to-date subway trucks ride on tires, which provide fast acceleration and little noise or vibration.
steel safety wheel
Auxiliary regular train wheel that comes in contact with the running rail in the event the tire deflates and during switching.
inflated carrying tire
Nitrogen-filled tire that supports and conveys the car.
inflated guiding tire
Tire mounted at right angles to the carrying tire; it rolls against the guiding bar to guide the truck.
guiding and current bar
Metal bar against which the guiding tire rolls; it also supplies the traction current.
sliding block
Shoe taking the current from the guiding and current bar.
running rail
Regular railroad rail for the steel safety wheel to roll on in the event the tire deflates; it also receives the traction current from the return shoe.
runway
Metal or concrete track that is fixed to the invert on which the tires roll.
invert
Thick concrete foundation for the tracks.

streetcar

Electrically powered vehicle for transporting people; it rolls on tracks embedded in city streets and on the edge of roadways.

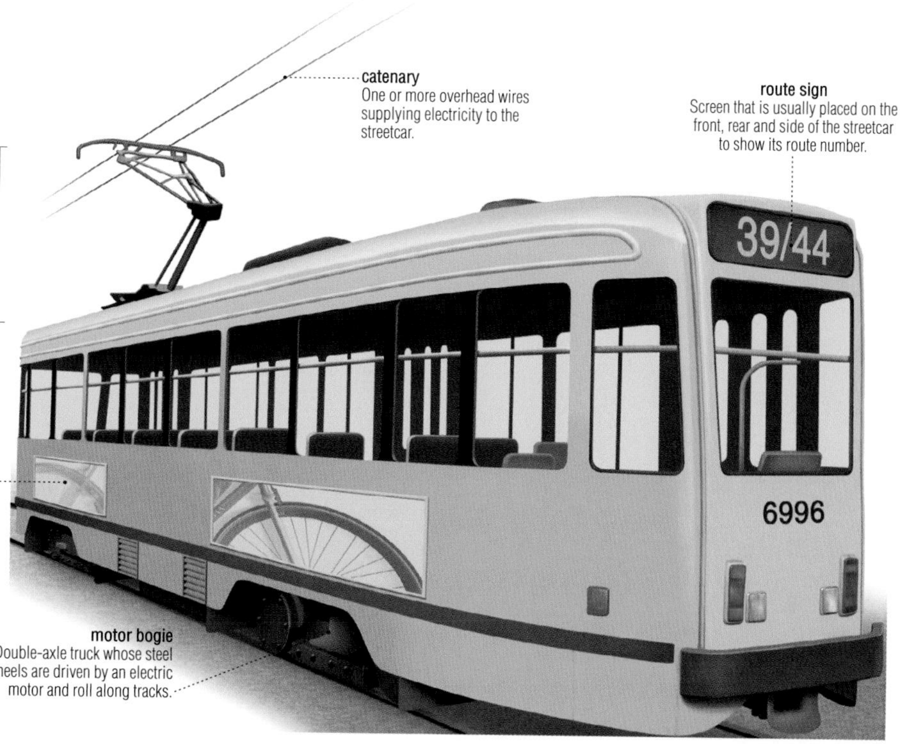
catenary
One or more overhead wires supplying electricity to the streetcar.
route sign
Screen that is usually placed on the front, rear and side of the streetcar to show its route number.
39/44
pantograph
Articulating mechanism on the roof of the streetcar that collects electricity from an overhead catenary.
advertising sign
Poster on a space rented by a business that promotes products or services.
6996
motor bogie
Double-axle truck whose steel wheels are driven by an electric motor and roll along tracks.

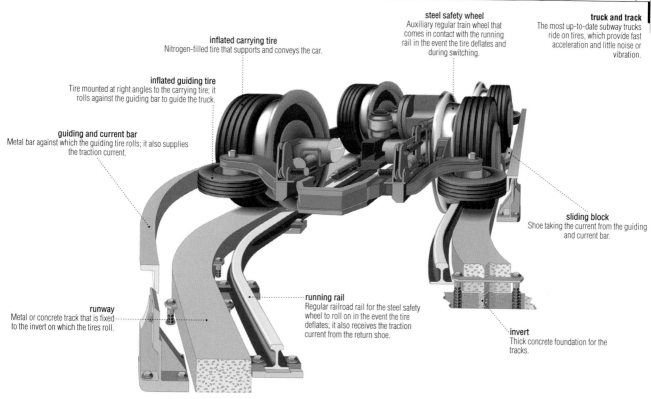

harbor

Site for refueling and repairing ships, loading and unloading cargo and embarking and disembarking passengers.

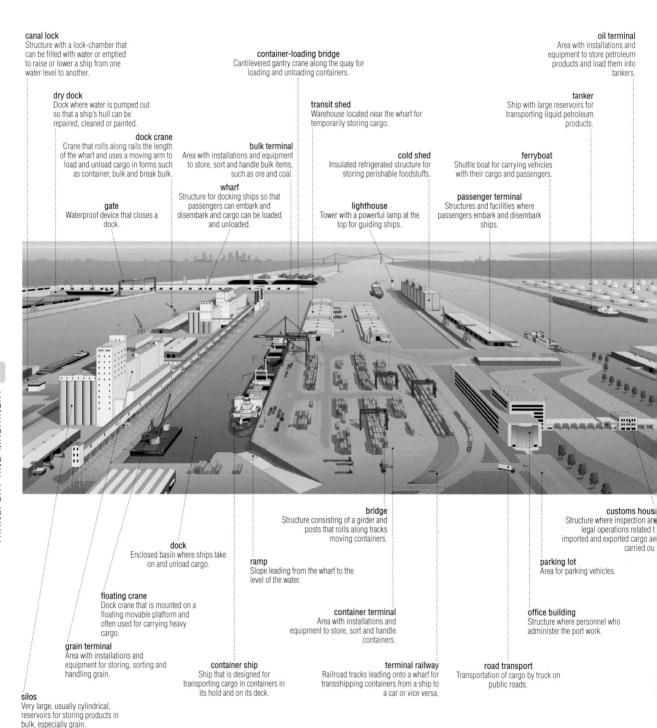

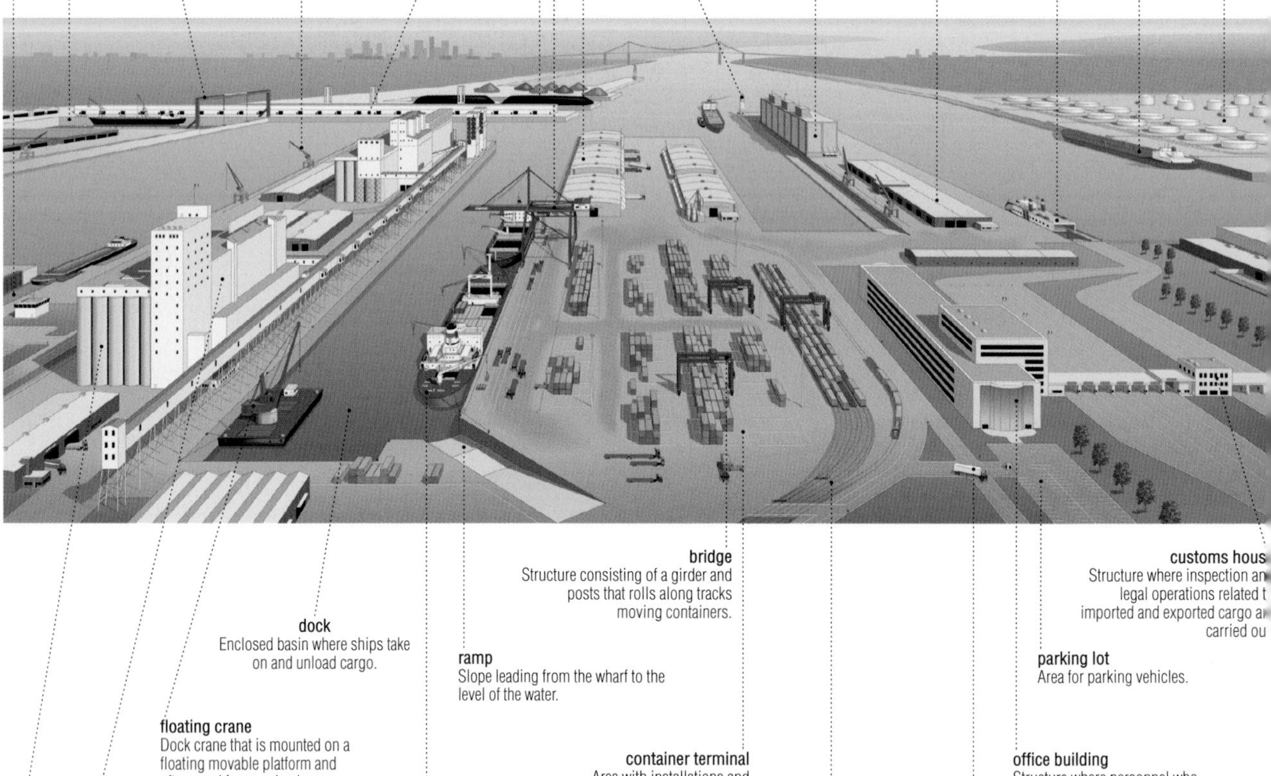

canal lock
Structure with a lock-chamber that can be filled with water or emptied to raise or lower a ship from one water level to another.

dry dock
Dock where water is pumped out so that a ship's hull can be repaired, cleaned or painted.

dock crane
Crane that rolls along rails the length of the wharf and uses a moving arm to load and unload cargo in forms such as container, bulk and break bulk.

gate
Waterproof device that closes a dock.

container-loading bridge
Cantilevered gantry crane along the quay for loading and unloading containers.

bulk terminal
Area with installations and equipment to store, sort and handle bulk items, such as ore and coal.

wharf
Structure for docking ships so that passengers can embark and disembark and cargo can be loaded and unloaded.

transit shed
Warehouse located near the wharf for temporarily storing cargo.

cold shed
Insulated refrigerated structure for storing perishable foodstuffs.

lighthouse
Tower with a powerful lamp at the top for guiding ships.

oil terminal
Area with installations and equipment to store petroleum products and load them into tankers.

tanker
Ship with large reservoirs for transporting liquid petroleum products.

ferryboat
Shuttle boat for carrying vehicles with their cargo and passengers.

passenger terminal
Structures and facilities where passengers embark and disembark ships.

bridge
Structure consisting of a girder and posts that rolls along tracks moving containers.

customs hous
Structure where inspection an legal operations related t imported and exported cargo a carried ou

dock
Enclosed basin where ships take on and unload cargo.

ramp
Slope leading from the wharf to the level of the water.

parking lot
Area for parking vehicles.

floating crane
Dock crane that is mounted on a floating movable platform and often used for carrying heavy cargo.

container terminal
Area with installations and equipment to store, sort and handle containers.

office building
Structure where personnel who administer the port work.

grain terminal
Area with installations and equipment for storing, sorting and handling grain.

container ship
Ship that is designed for transporting cargo in containers in its hold and on its deck.

terminal railway
Railroad tracks leading onto a wharf for transshipping containers from a ship to a car or vice versa.

road transport
Transportation of cargo by truck on public roads.

silos
Very large, usually cylindrical, reservoirs for storing products in bulk, especially grain.

canal lock

Structure with a lock-chamber that can be filled with water or emptied to raise or lower a ship from one water level to another.

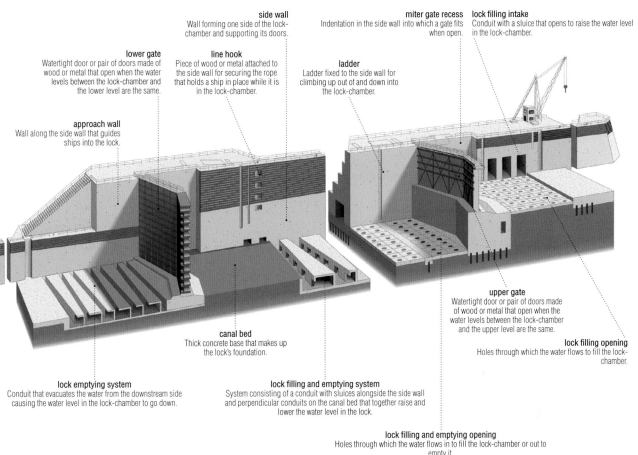

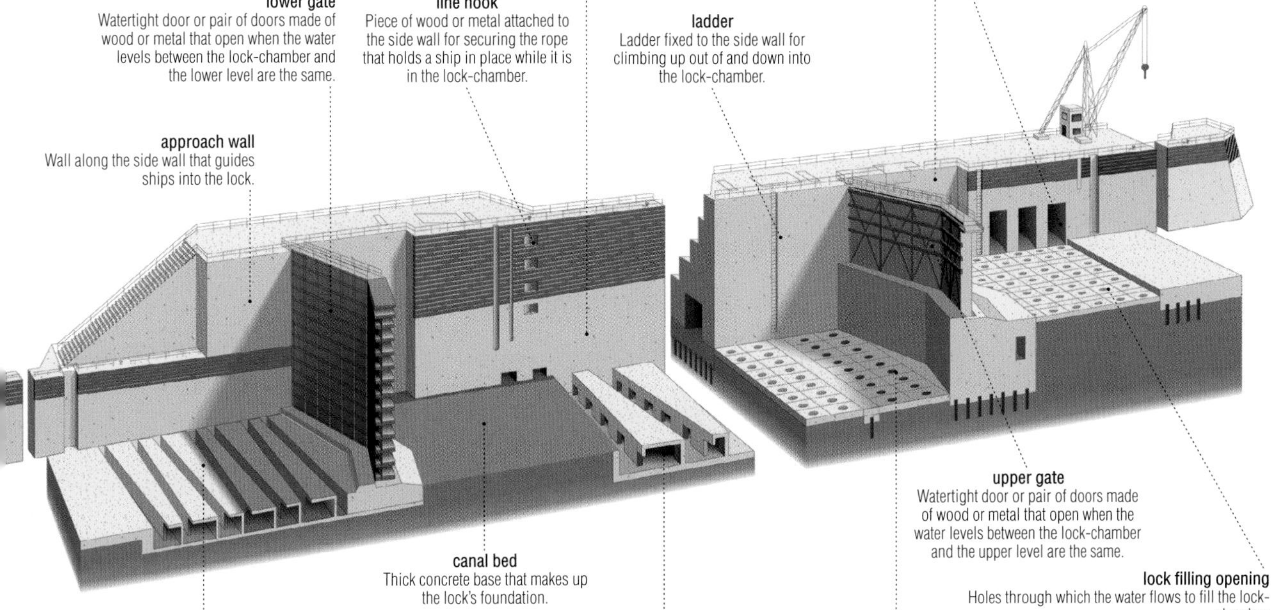

side wall
Wall forming one side of the lock-chamber and supporting its doors.
miter gate recess
Indentation in the side wall into which a gate fits when open.
lock filling intake
Conduit with a sluice that opens to raise the water level in the lock-chamber.
lower gate
Watertight door or pair of doors made of wood or metal that open when the water levels between the lock-chamber and the lower level are the same.
line hook
Piece of wood or metal attached to the side wall for securing the rope that holds a ship in place while it is in the lock-chamber.
ladder
Ladder fixed to the side wall for climbing up out of and down into the lock-chamber.
approach wall
Wall along the side wall that guides ships into the lock.
upper gate
Watertight door or pair of doors made of wood or metal that open when the water levels between the lock-chamber and the upper level are the same.
canal bed
Thick concrete base that makes up the lock's foundation.
lock filling opening
Holes through which the water flows to fill the lock-chamber.
lock emptying system
Conduit that evacuates the water from the downstream side causing the water level in the lock-chamber to go down.
lock filling and emptying system
System consisting of a conduit with sluices alongside the side wall and perpendicular conduits on the canal bed that together raise and lower the water level in the lock.
lock filling and emptying opening
Holes through which the water flows in to fill the lock-chamber or out to empty it.

canal lock: side view

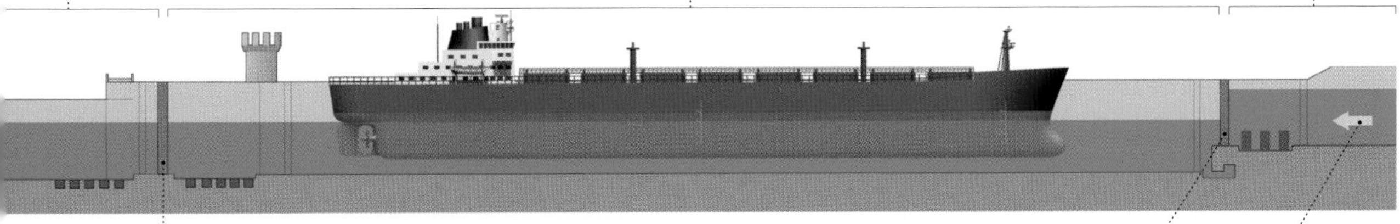

lock-chamber
Central part of the lock where the water level is raised and lowered depending on the heading of the ship.
lower level
Part of the lock at the downstream end of the lock-chamber.
upper level
Part of the lock at the upstream end of the lock-chamber.
lower gate
Watertight door or pair of doors made of wood or metal that open when the water levels between the lock-chamber and the lower level are the same.
upper gate
Watertight door or pair of doors made of wood or metal that open when the water levels between the lock-chamber and the upper level are the same.
flow
Natural current moving down the grade from upstream to downstream.

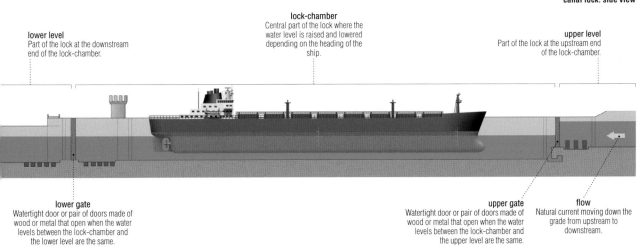

ancient ships

Over the course of history, navigation has played a key role in discovering new lands and in developing trade between peoples.

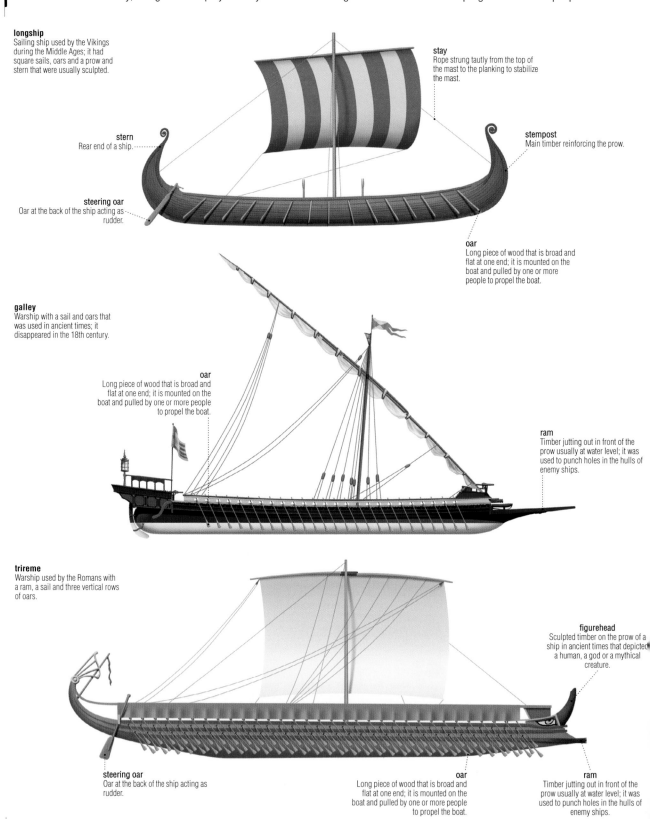

longship
Sailing ship used by the Vikings during the Middle Ages; it had square sails, oars and a prow and stern that were usually sculpted.

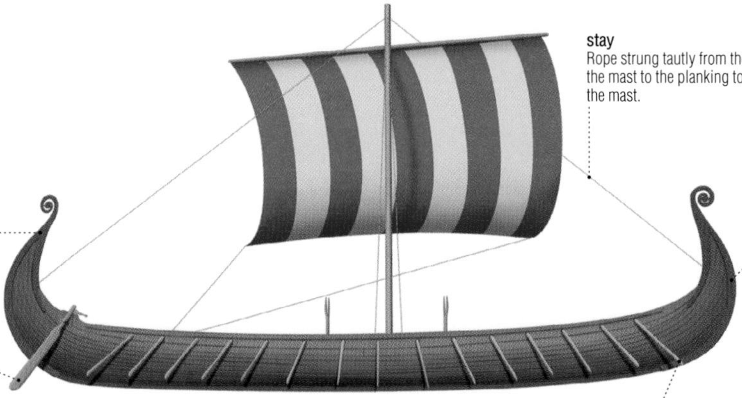
stay
Rope strung tautly from the top of the mast to the planking to stabilize the mast.
stern
Rear end of a ship.
stempost
Main timber reinforcing the prow.
steering oar
Oar at the back of the ship acting as rudder.
oar
Long piece of wood that is broad and flat at one end; it is mounted on the boat and pulled by one or more people to propel the boat.

galley
Warship with a sail and oars that was used in ancient times; it disappeared in the 18th century.

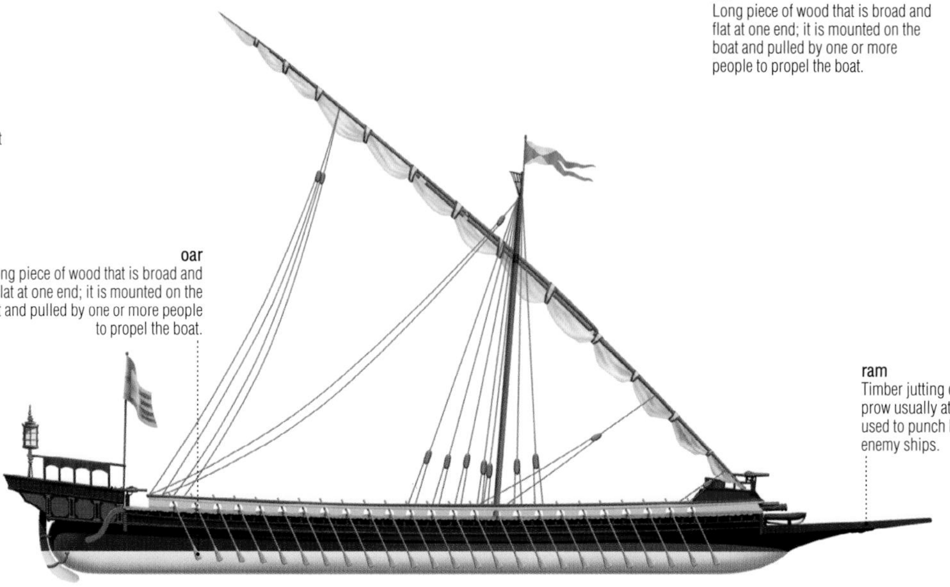
oar
Long piece of wood that is broad and flat at one end; it is mounted on the boat and pulled by one or more people to propel the boat.
ram
Timber jutting out in front of the prow usually at water level; it was used to punch holes in the hulls of enemy ships.

trireme
Warship used by the Romans with a ram, a sail and three vertical rows of oars.

figurehead
Sculpted timber on the prow of a ship in ancient times that depicted a human, a god or a mythical creature.
steering oar
Oar at the back of the ship acting as rudder.
oar
Long piece of wood that is broad and flat at one end; it is mounted on the boat and pulled by one or more people to propel the boat.
ram
Timber jutting out in front of the prow usually at water level; it was used to punch holes in the hulls of enemy ships.

ancient ships

side-wheeler
Ship used in the 19th century that was propelled by steam, which turned two paddle wheels.

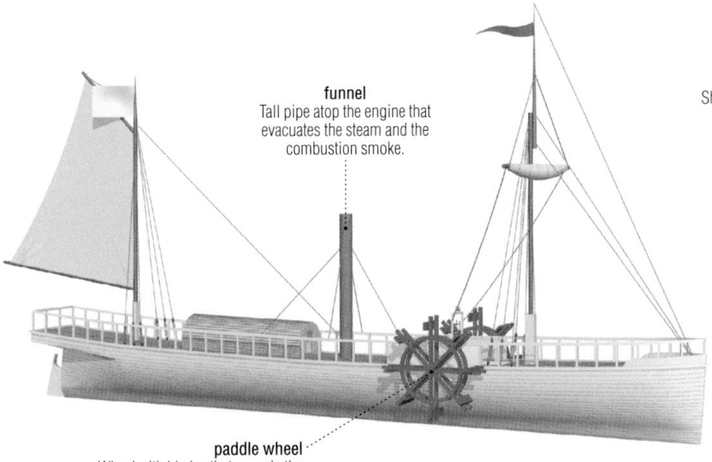

funnel
Tall pipe atop the engine that evacuates the steam and the combustion smoke.

paddle wheel
Wheel with blades that propels the boat; it is driven by a steam engine.

galleon
Large warship with sails that was used by the Spanish in the 17th and 18th centuries for trading with the colonies.

caravel
Fast ship with three or four masts; it was used especially in the 15th and 16th centuries for exploration.

traditional ships

Boats characteristic of various parts of the world for a number of generations; they are used as a means of transportation, for fishing, commerce and exploration.

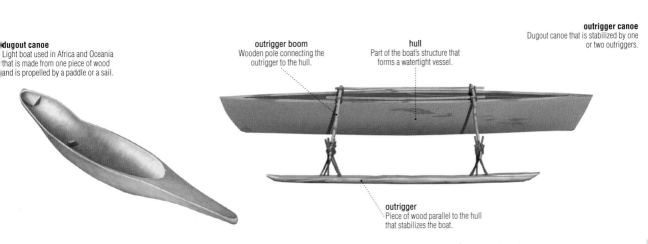

dugout canoe
Light boat used in Africa and Oceania that is made from one piece of wood and is propelled by a paddle or a sail.

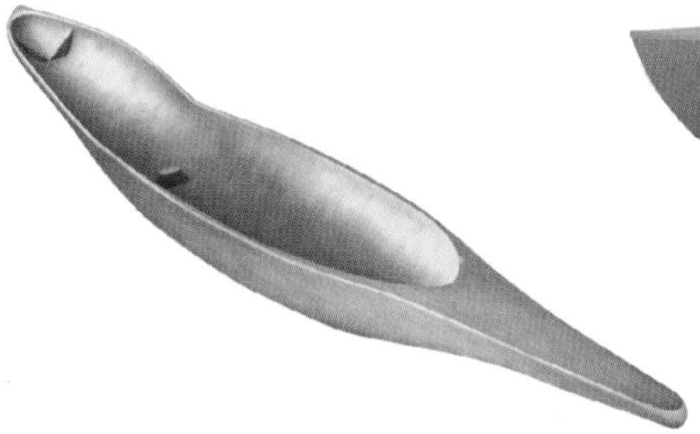

outrigger canoe
Dugout canoe that is stabilized by one or two outriggers.

outrigger boom
Wooden pole connecting the outrigger to the hull.

hull
Part of the boat's structure that forms a watertight vessel.

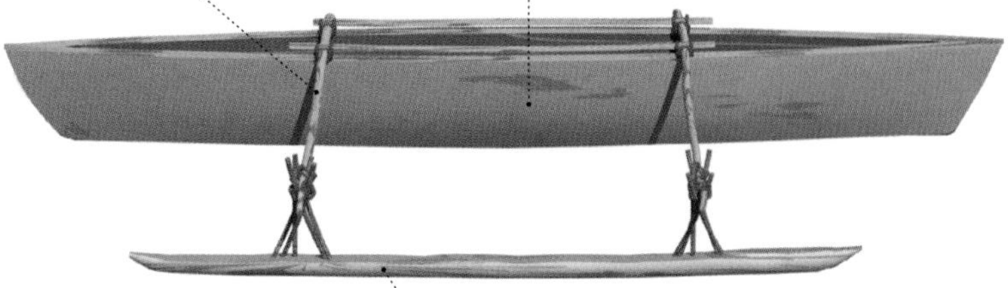

outrigger
Piece of wood parallel to the hull that stabilizes the boat.

traditional ships

junk
Boat used in the Far East for fishing and transporting cargo; its sails are made of matting or canvas and are stretched by battens.

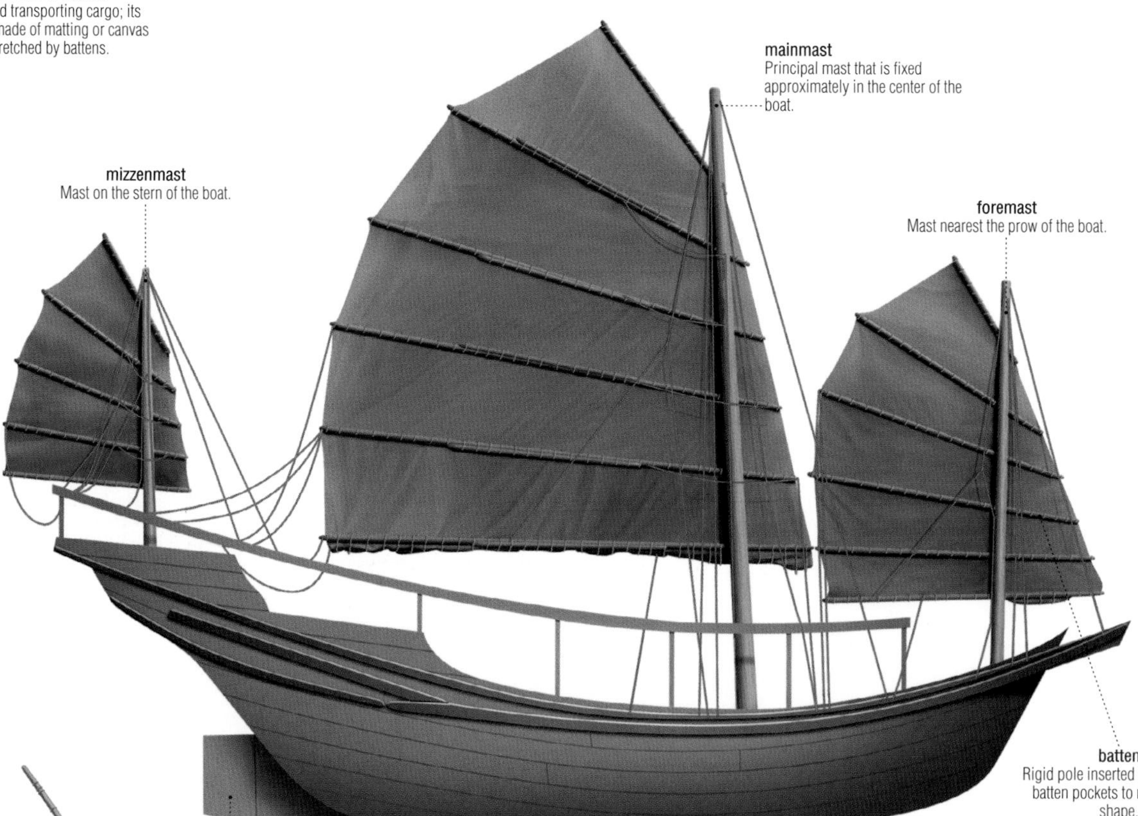
mainmast
Principal mast that is fixed approximately in the center of the boat.
mizzenmast
Mast on the stern of the boat.
foremast
Mast nearest the prow of the boat.
batten
Rigid pole inserted into the sail batten pockets to maintain its shape.
rudder
Submerged component that pivots on a vertical axle and is used to steer the boat.

oar
Long piece of wood that is broad and flat at one end; it is mounted on the boat and pulled by one or more people to propel the boat.
prow ornament
The iron prow is characteristic of gondolas; it symbolizes the pointed caps of the doges and the districts of Venice.

gondola
Venetian boat characterized by raised curved ends and steered by an oar.

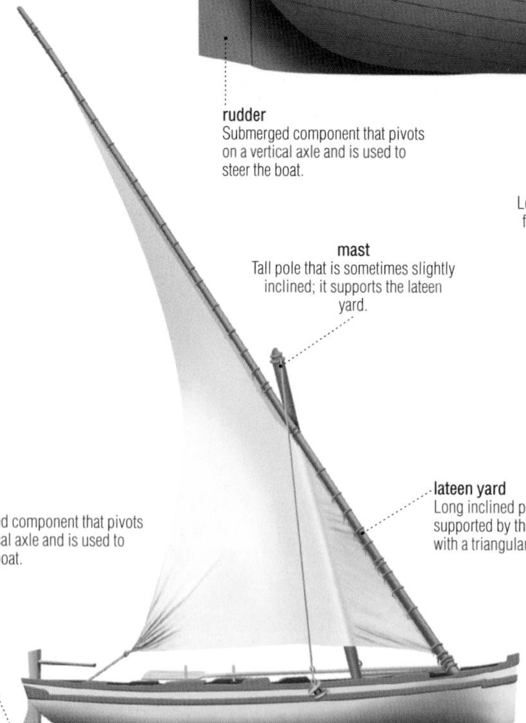
mast
Tall pole that is sometimes slightly inclined; it supports the lateen yard.
lateen yard
Long inclined pole that is supported by the mast and rigged with a triangular sail.
rudder
Submerged component that pivots on a vertical axle and is used to steer the boat.

felucca
A Mediterranean boat of ancient times that was propelled by a sail or an oar; it is still found today on the Nile.

canoe
Light boat used by Native Americans; it is propelled by a paddle and is used for transporting people and cargo.

examples of sails

Sails: sections of durable fabric that are sewn together and mounted on a mast; they create a surface that causes a boat to move when the wind blows against it.

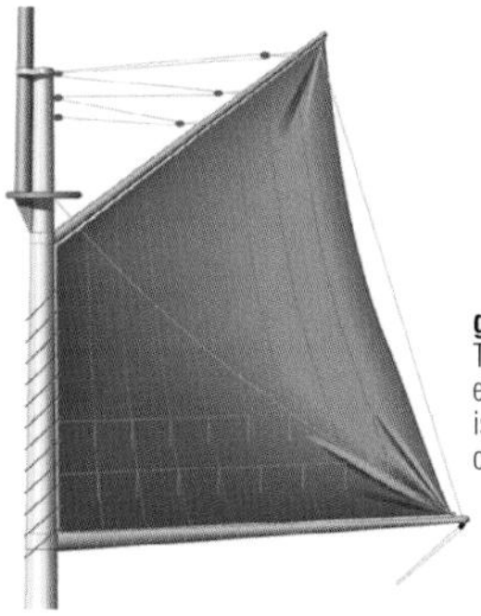

gaff sail
Trapezoidal sail that is rigged entirely aft of the mast; its top edge is supported by a diagonal yard called a gaff.

Bermuda sail
Triangular sail that is also called a Marconi sail; its longest side is attached directly to a tall mast and its base is attached to a pole called a boom.

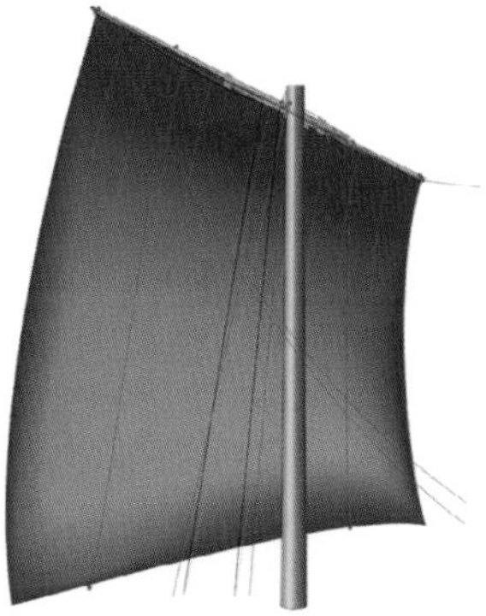

lug sail
Trapezoidal sail that hangs from a yard; it is attached to the mast one-third of the way from its end.

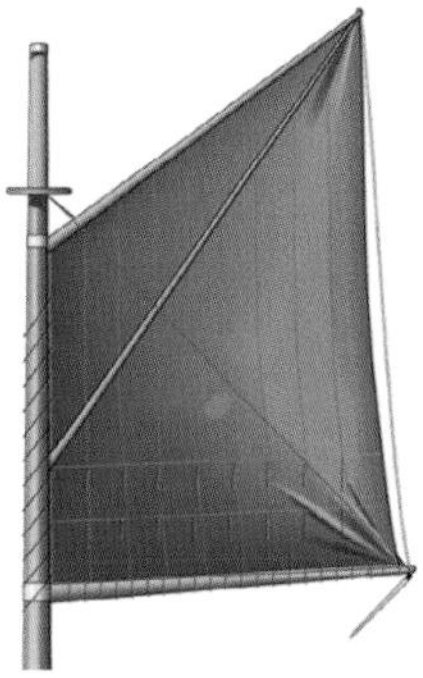

spritsail
Trapezoidal sail that is rigged entirely aft of the mast and is supported by a long, diagonal yard, called a sprit; it articulates at the bottom of the mast.

lateen sail
Triangular sail supported by a long tilted yard called a lateen yard; it is attached to the mast in its middle.

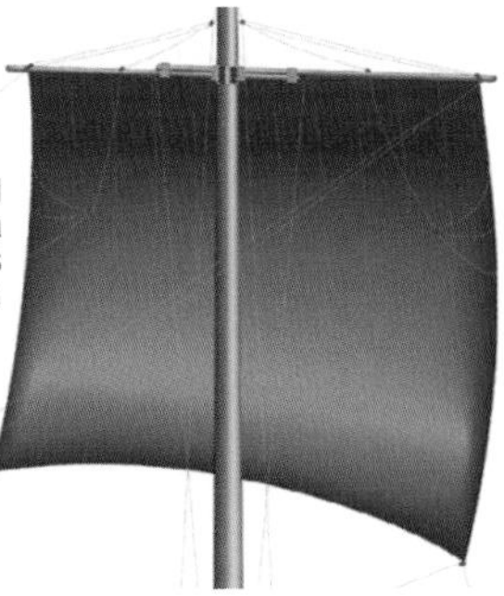

square sail
Trapezoidal sail that hangs from a yard; it is attached to the mast in its middle.

examples of rigs

Rigs: various combinations of sails that distinguish one sailboat from another.

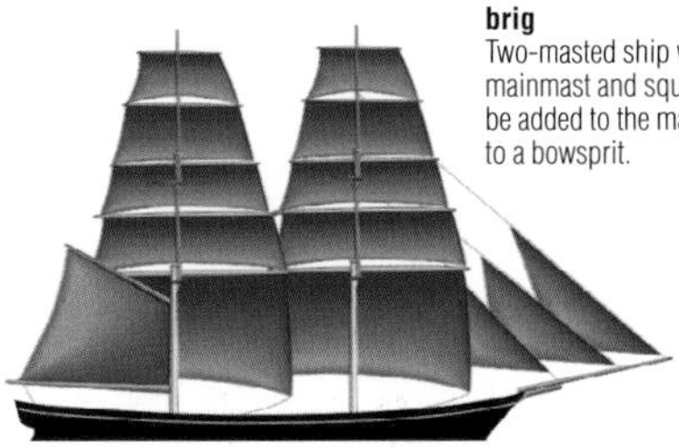

brig
Two-masted ship with a foremast and a mainmast and square sails; a spanker can be added to the mainmast and three jibs to a bowsprit.

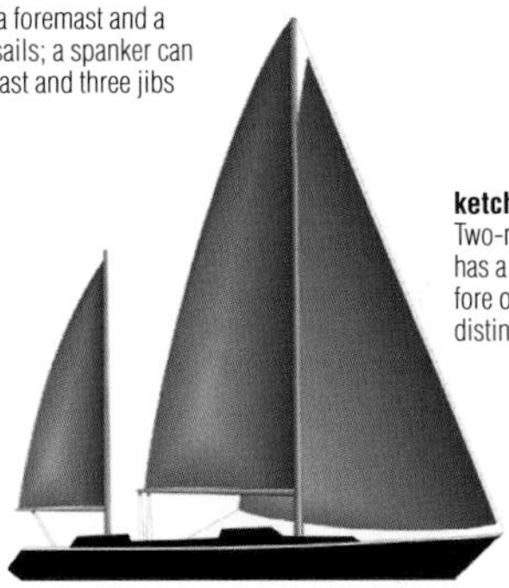

ketch
Two-masted pleasure sailboat; it has a mainmast and a mizzenmast fore of the tiller, which distinguishes it from the cutter.

brigantine
Two-masted ship that is lighter than the brig and rigged differently.

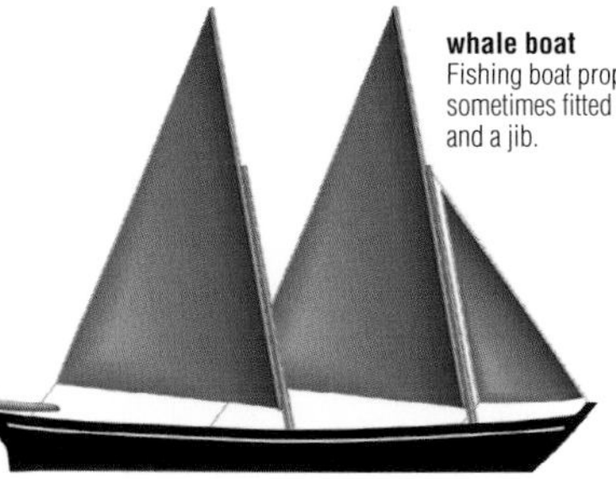

whale boat
Fishing boat propelled mainly by oars but sometimes fitted with one or two lug sails and a jib.

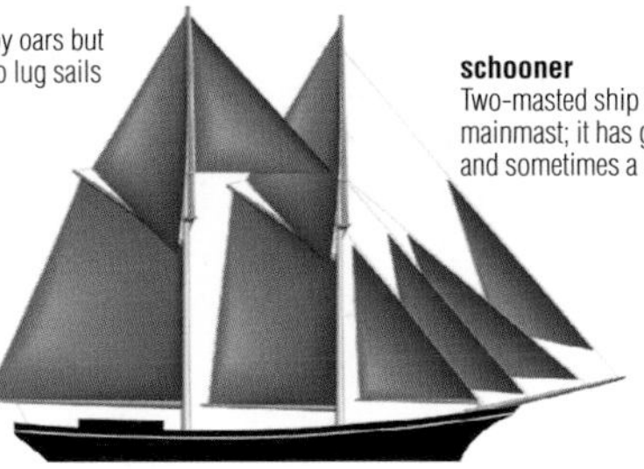

schooner
Two-masted ship with a foremast and a mainmast; it has gaff sails and topsails and sometimes a staysail.

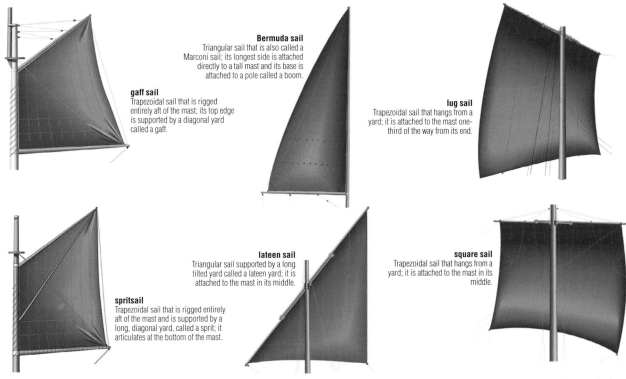

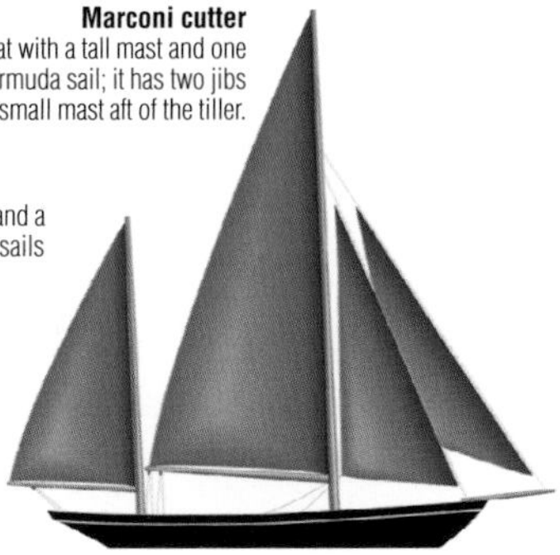

Marconi cutter
Fishing boat with a tall mast and one gaff or Bermuda sail; it has two jibs and a small mast aft of the tiller.

four-masted bark

Sailboat with four masts and square sails except for the jiggermast, which carries a gaff sail.

masting and rigging
Masting: masts, yards, ropes and other movable sailing equipment that support and manipulate the rigging.

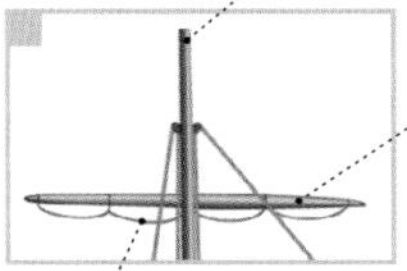

pole
Tapered top end of a mast.

yard
Long pole that is supported by the mast and holds up the edge of a sail.

footrope
Rope hanging along the entire length of a yard that is used by sailors to trim the sails.

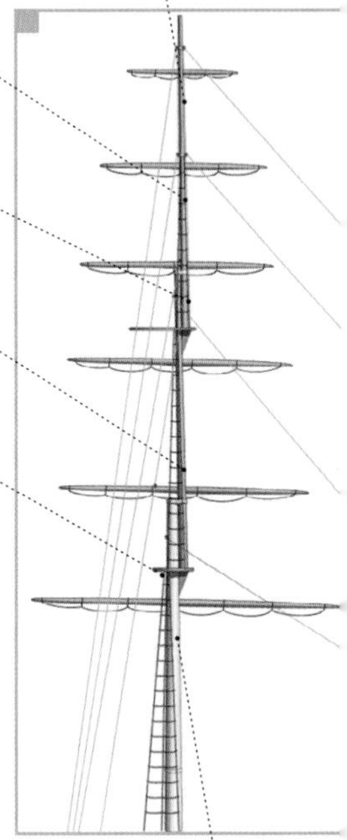

fore-royal mast
Mast above the fore-topgallant mast that carries a royal sail.

fore-topgallant mast
Mast above the fore-topmast that carries a topgallant sail.

masthead
Topmost section of a mast that is sometimes doubled with the lower section of the mast supporting it; the stays and shrouds are attached to it.

fore-topmast
Mast that is immediately above a lower mast and carries a topsail.

top
Platform at the top of the lower mast from which the upper rigging can be manipulated.

lower mast
Bottom section of a mast that is solid and thick so it can support the upper sections.

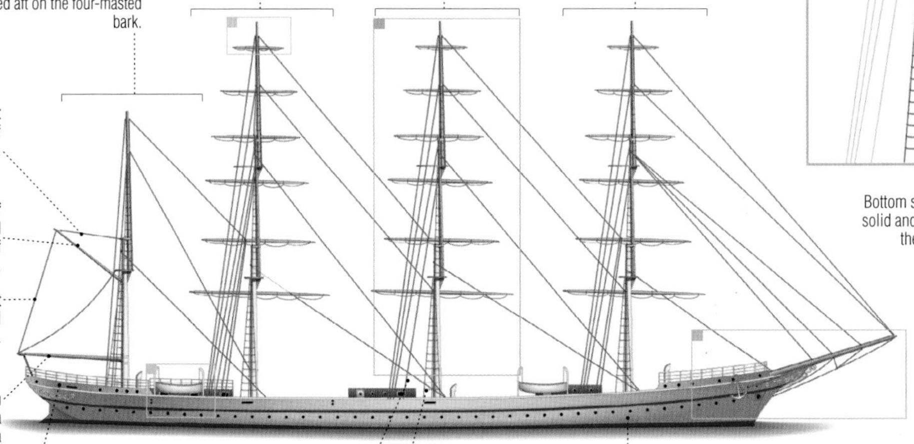

mainmast
One of the principal parts of the ship; it is located closest to the center of gravity.

mizzenmast
One of the principal masts of the ship; it is located aft of the mainmast between the ship's center of gravity and its rudder.

jiggermast
Mast located aft on the four-masted bark.

foremast
Mast nearest the prow of the boat.

topping lift
Rope that holds the sail's gaff loosely in place.

gaff
Diagonal yard aft of a mast and supporting the top part of a gaff sail.

lift
Rope connecting two yards of a sail and used to maneuver them.

gaff sail boom
Horizontal yard articulating on a mast; it keeps the bottom edge of a sail taut.

poop
Structure above the aft deck that extends athwartships; it usually serves as officers' quarters.

backstay
Long taut rope between the mast and the deck; it secures and supports the mast athwartships and aft.

shroud
Heavy taut rope between a mast and the side of the ship; it secures and supports the mast on the sides.

side
Longitudinal surface of the ship.

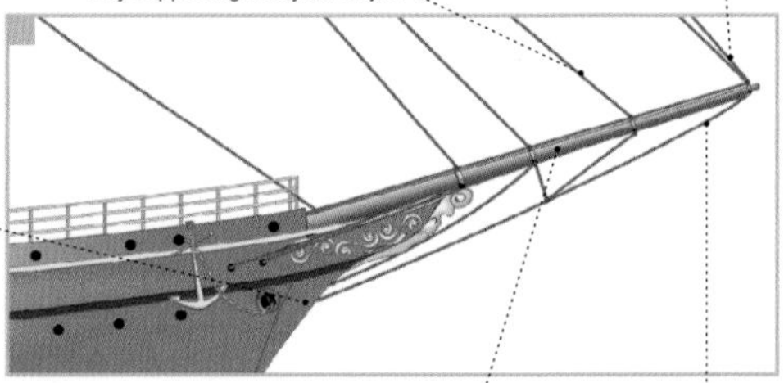

stay
Taut rope between a mast and another point on the masting; it secures and supports the mast for of it.

staysail-stay
Stay supporting a staysail or jib.

stem
Main timber reinforcing the prow.

bowsprit
Mast extending before the stem; additional jibs can be attached to it.

bobstay
Rope counterbalancing the tension caused by the stays and the staysail-stays on the bowsprit.

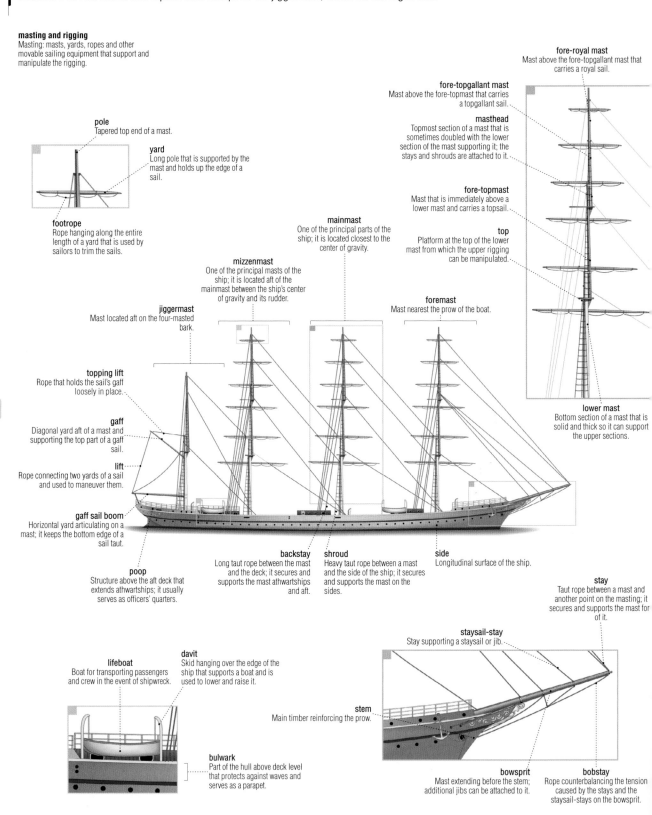

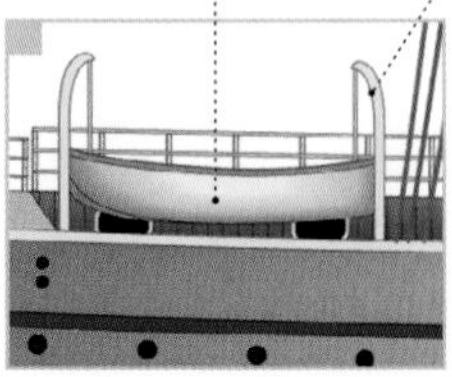

lifeboat
Boat for transporting passengers and crew in the event of shipwreck.

davit
Skid hanging over the edge of the ship that supports a boat and is used to lower and raise it.

bulwark
Part of the hull above deck level that protects against waves and serves as a parapet.

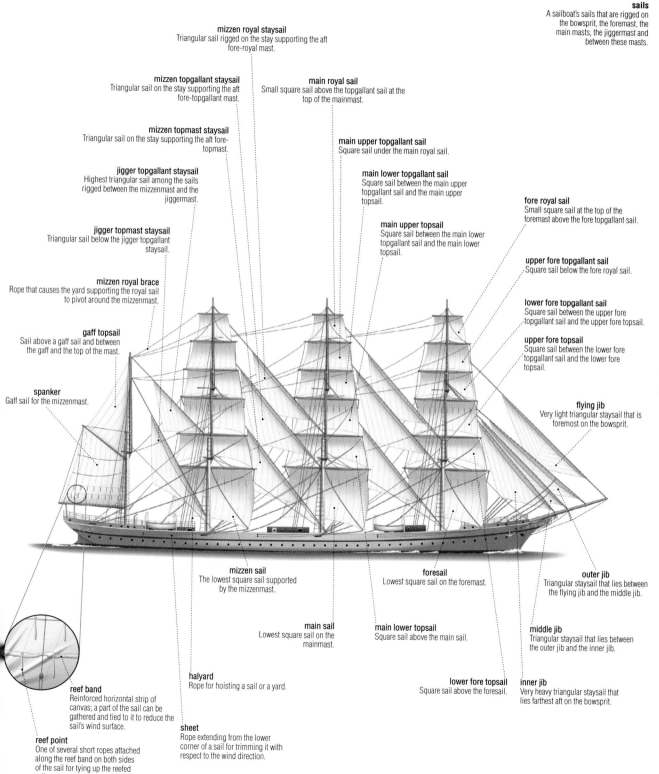

four-masted bark

sails
A sailboat's sails that are rigged on the bowsprit, the foremast, the main masts, the jiggermast and between these masts.

mizzen royal staysail
Triangular sail rigged on the stay supporting the aft fore-royal mast.

mizzen topgallant staysail
Triangular sail on the stay supporting the aft fore-topgallant mast.

main royal sail
Small square sail above the topgallant sail at the top of the mainmast.

mizzen topmast staysail
Triangular sail on the stay supporting the aft fore-topmast.

main upper topgallant sail
Square sail under the main royal sail.

jigger topgallant staysail
Highest triangular sail among the sails rigged between the mizzenmast and the jiggermast.

main lower topgallant sail
Square sail between the main upper topgallant sail and the main upper topsail.

fore royal sail
Small square sail at the top of the foremast above the fore topgallant sail.

jigger topmast staysail
Triangular sail below the jigger topgallant staysail.

main upper topsail
Square sail between the main lower topgallant sail and the main lower topsail.

upper fore topgallant sail
Square sail below the fore royal sail.

mizzen royal brace
Rope that causes the yard supporting the royal sail to pivot around the mizzenmast.

lower fore topgallant sail
Square sail between the upper fore topgallant sail and the upper fore topsail.

gaff topsail
Sail above a gaff sail and between the gaff and the top of the mast.

upper fore topsail
Square sail between the lower fore topgallant sail and the lower fore topsail.

spanker
Gaff sail for the mizzenmast.

flying jib
Very light triangular staysail that is foremost on the bowsprit.

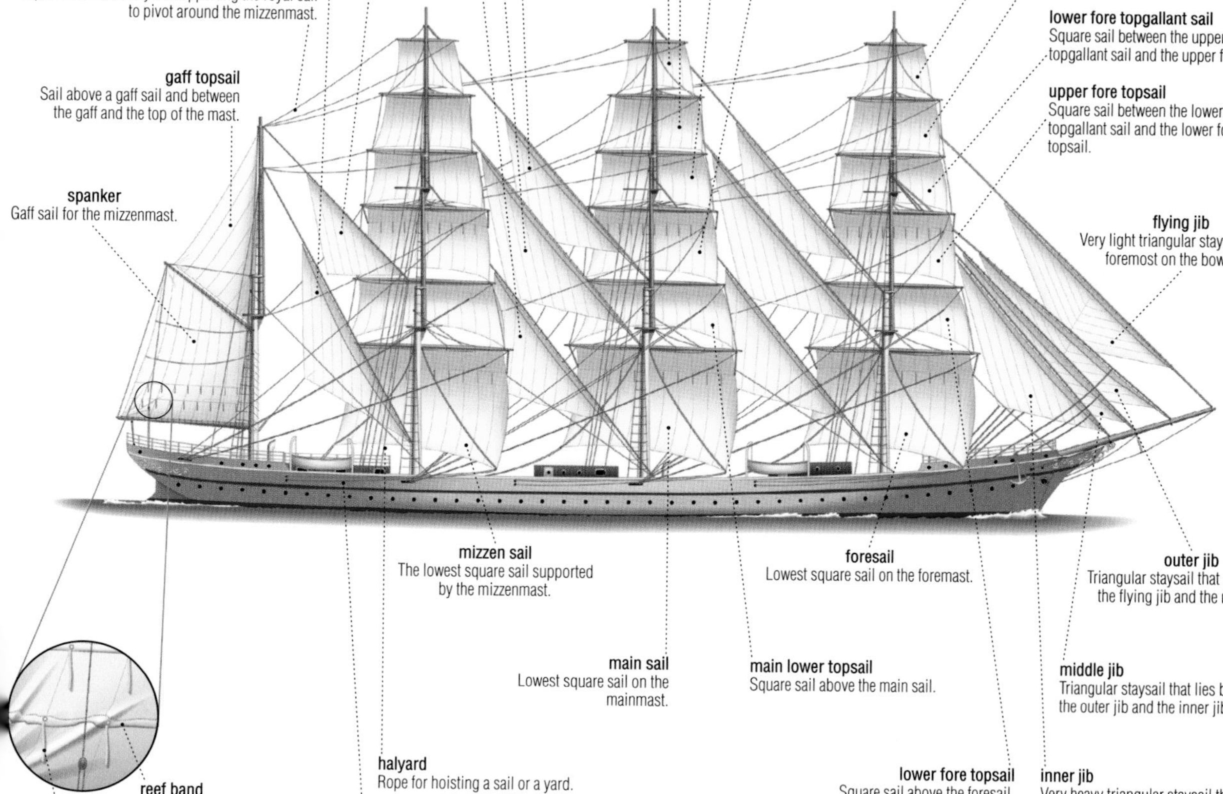

mizzen sail
The lowest square sail supported by the mizzenmast.

foresail
Lowest square sail on the foremast.

outer jib
Triangular staysail that lies between the flying jib and the middle jib.

main sail
Lowest square sail on the mainmast.

main lower topsail
Square sail above the main sail.

middle jib
Triangular staysail that lies between the outer jib and the inner jib.

halyard
Rope for hoisting a sail or a yard.

lower fore topsail
Square sail above the foresail.

inner jib
Very heavy triangular staysail that lies farthest aft on the bowsprit.

reef band
Reinforced horizontal strip of canvas; a part of the sail can be gathered and tied to it to reduce the sail's wind surface.

sheet
Rope extending from the lower corner of a sail for trimming it with respect to the wind direction.

reef point
One of several short ropes attached along the reef band on both sides of the sail for tying up the reefed sail.

examples of boats and ships

Boats and ships: floating structures for underwater exploration and transporting passengers and cargo across water.

drill ship
Ship for drilling for oil in deep water (half mile or more); it is more mobile but less stable than a drilling rig.

derrick
Metal structure erected over an oil well; tools for drilling through rock are raised and lowered through it.

bulk carrier
Ship for transporting raw dry materials, such as grain, coal and ore.

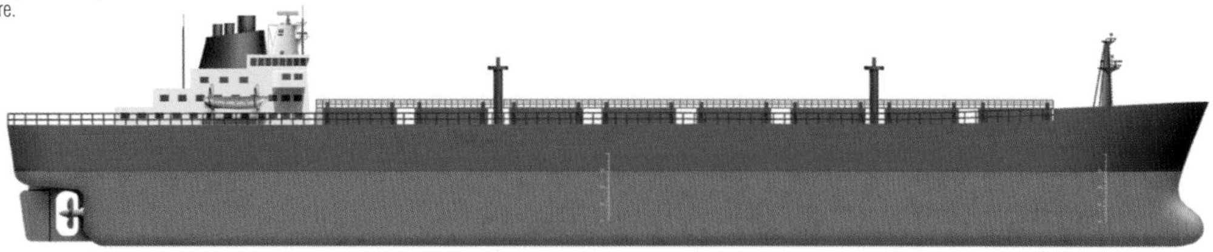

container ship
Ship that is designed for transporting cargo in containers in its hold and on its deck.

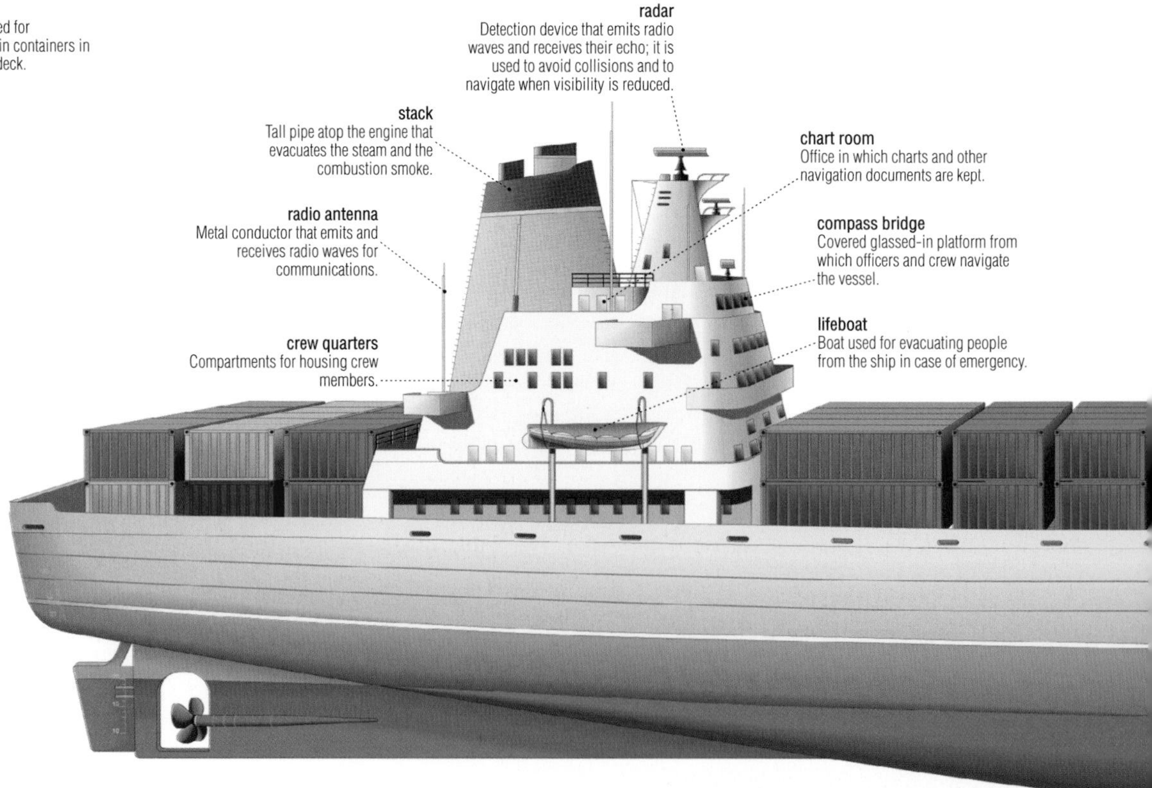
radar
Detection device that emits radio waves and receives their echo; it is used to avoid collisions and to navigate when visibility is reduced.
stack
Tall pipe atop the engine that evacuates the steam and the combustion smoke.
chart room
Office in which charts and other navigation documents are kept.
radio antenna
Metal conductor that emits and receives radio waves for communications.
compass bridge
Covered glassed-in platform from which officers and crew navigate the vessel.
lifeboat
Boat used for evacuating people from the ship in case of emergency.
crew quarters
Compartments for housing crew members.

examples of boats and ships

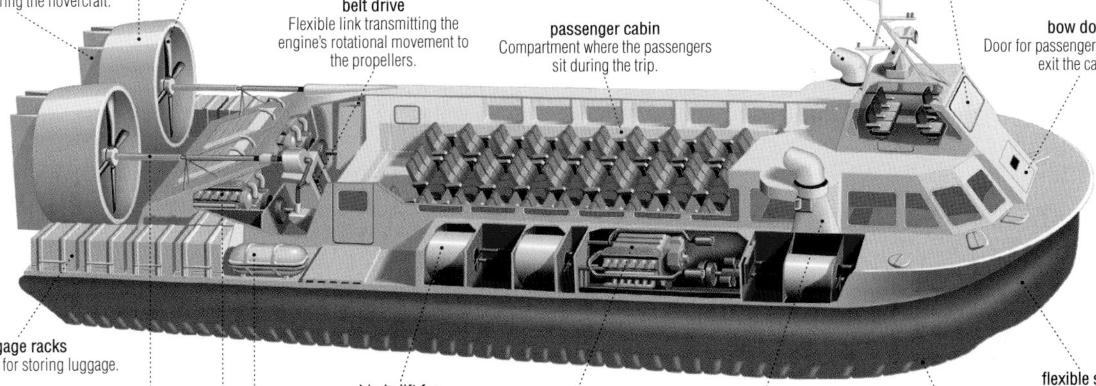
propeller duct
Metal part that surrounds the propeller and increases its power by concentrating its air intake.
dynamics propeller
Device that is made up of blades integrated with a shaft; it pushes air behind the hovercraft thus causing a forward movement.
rudder
Pivoting part behind the propeller blast for steering the hovercraft.
belt drive
Flexible link transmitting the engine's rotational movement to the propellers.
radar
Detection device that emits radio waves and receives their echo; it is used to avoid collisions and to navigate when visibility is reduced.
navigation light
Lamp that is visible from afar to signal the hovercraft's presence.
hovercraft
Propeller vehicle that moves above water (or land) by gliding on a cushion of air it creates by blowing downward.
air intake
Intake opening for the fan.
control deck
Compartment from which the pilots operate the hovercraft.
passenger cabin
Compartment where the passengers sit during the trip.
bow door
Door for passengers to enter and exit the cabin.
baggage racks
Compartment for storing luggage.
blade lift fan
Device blowing air downward under the hovercraft to keep it levitated.
lift-fan air inlet
Duct through which air enters, which is then blown downward under the hovercraft by the blade lift fan.
flexible skirt
Rubber flexible side that surrounds the edge of the hull to trap the air blown down by the lift fan; this increases pressure, which in turn causes lift.
drive shaft
Part transmitting the engine's rotational movement to the propellers.
skirt finger
Flexible and pliable extension to the skirt that adapts to the surface of the water.
life raft
Inflatable boat that transports passengers and crew in case of emergency.
diesel lift engine
Power source using the combustion of an air/fuel mixture to drive the blade lift fan.
diesel propulsion engine
Power source using the combustion of an air/fuel mixture to drive the propellers.

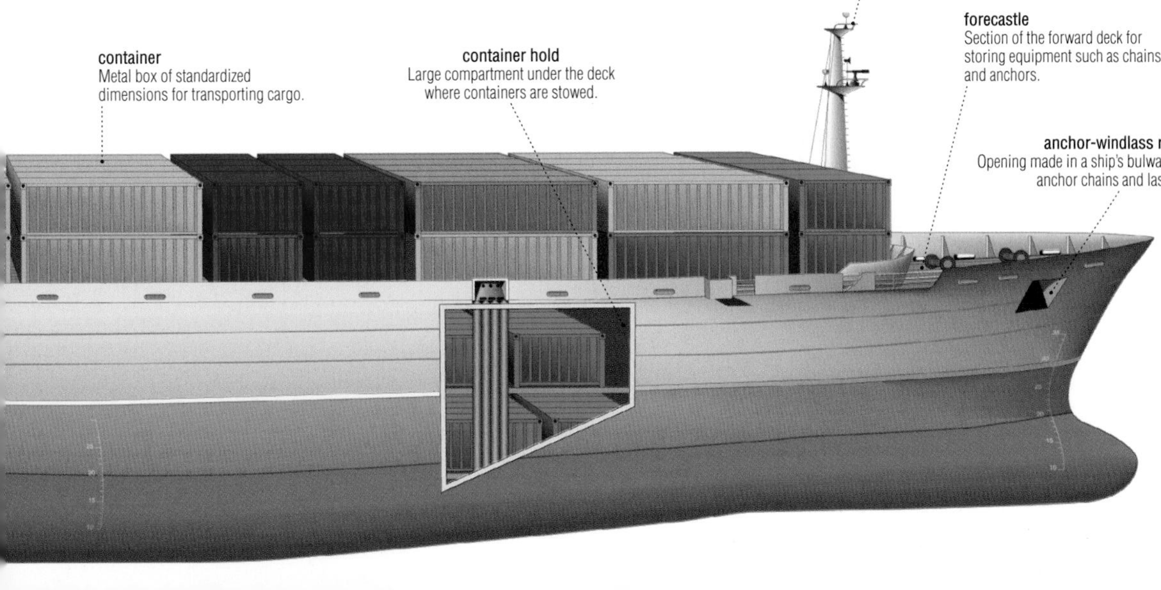
masthead light
Lamp projecting a strong light several miles ahead and to the sides of the ship.
forecastle
Section of the forward deck for storing equipment such as chains and anchors.
container
Metal box of standardized dimensions for transporting cargo.
container hold
Large compartment under the deck where containers are stowed.
anchor-windlass room
Opening made in a ship's bulwark or deck for the anchor chains and lashings.

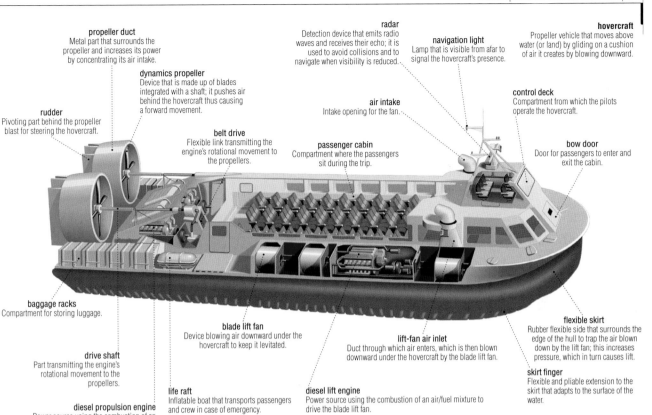

examples of boats and ships

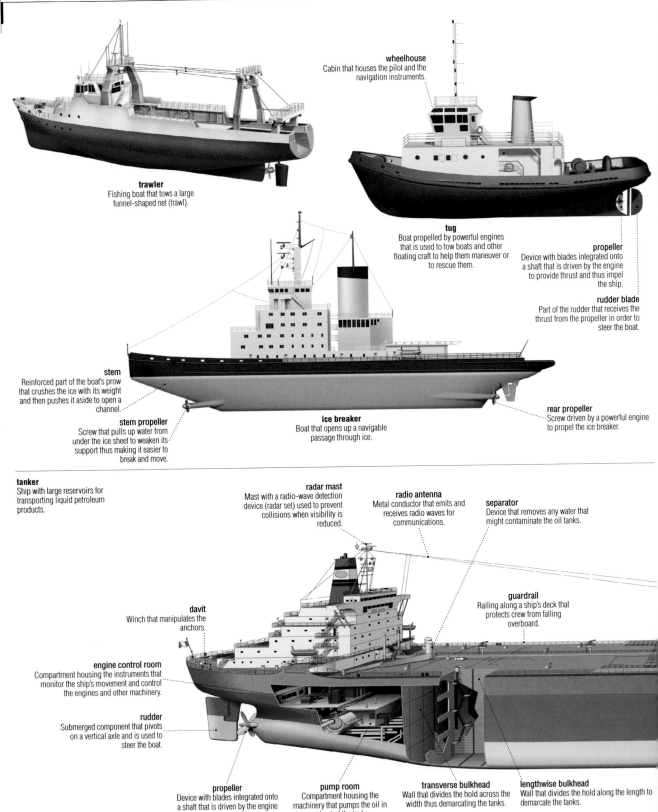

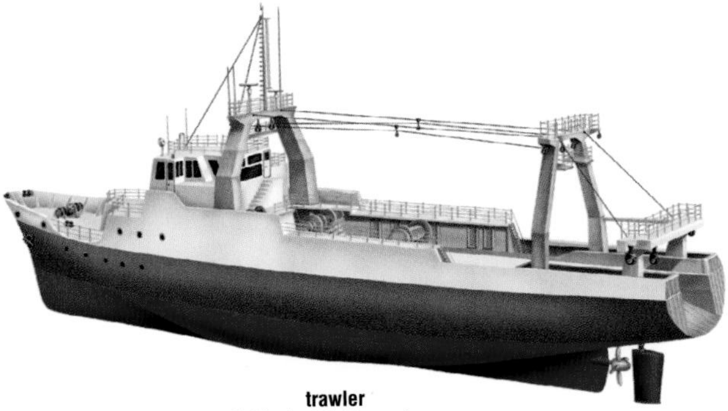
trawler
Fishing boat that tows a large funnel-shaped net (trawl).

wheelhouse
Cabin that houses the pilot and the navigation instruments.
tug
Boat propelled by powerful engines that is used to tow boats and other floating craft to help them maneuver or to rescue them.
propeller
Device with blades integrated onto a shaft that is driven by the engine to provide thrust and thus impel the ship.
rudder blade
Part of the rudder that receives the thrust from the propeller in order to steer the boat.

stem
Reinforced part of the boat's prow that crushes the ice with its weight and then pushes it aside to open a channel.
stem propeller
Screw that pulls up water from under the ice sheet to weaken its support thus making it easier to break and move.
ice breaker
Boat that opens up a navigable passage through ice.
rear propeller
Screw driven by a powerful engine to propel the ice breaker.

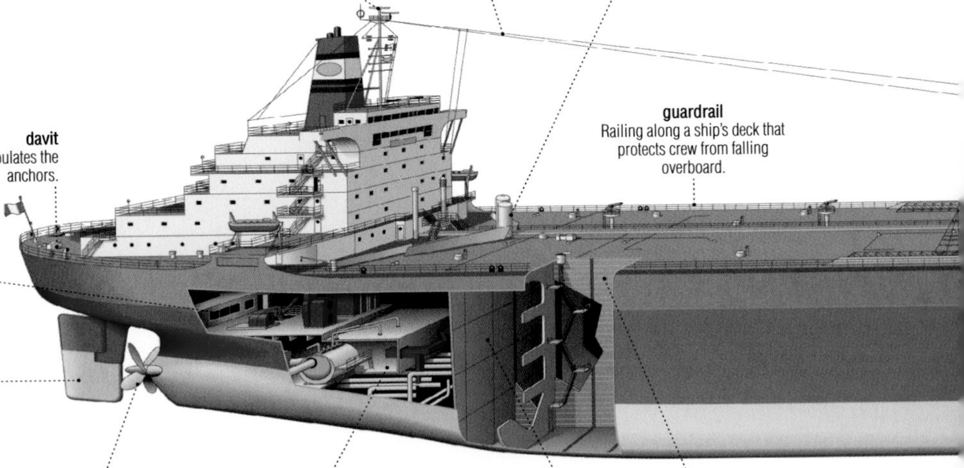
tanker
Ship with large reservoirs for transporting liquid petroleum products.
radar mast
Mast with a radio-wave detection device (radar set) used to prevent collisions when visibility is reduced.
radio antenna
Metal conductor that emits and receives radio waves for communications.
separator
Device that removes any water that might contaminate the oil tanks.
guardrail
Railing along a ship's deck that protects crew from falling overboard.
davit
Winch that manipulates the anchors.
engine control room
Compartment housing the instruments that monitor the ship's movement and control the engines and other machinery.
rudder
Submerged component that pivots on a vertical axle and is used to steer the boat.
propeller
Device with blades integrated onto a shaft that is driven by the engine to provide thrust and thus impel the ship.
pump room
Compartment housing the machinery that pumps the oil in and out of the tanks.
transverse bulkhead
Wall that divides the hold across the width thus demarcating the tanks.
lengthwise bulkhead
Wall that divides the hold along the length to demarcate the tanks.

examples of boats and ships

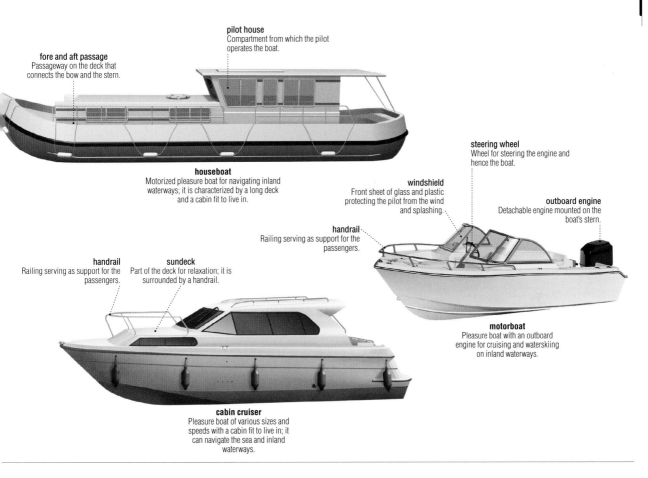

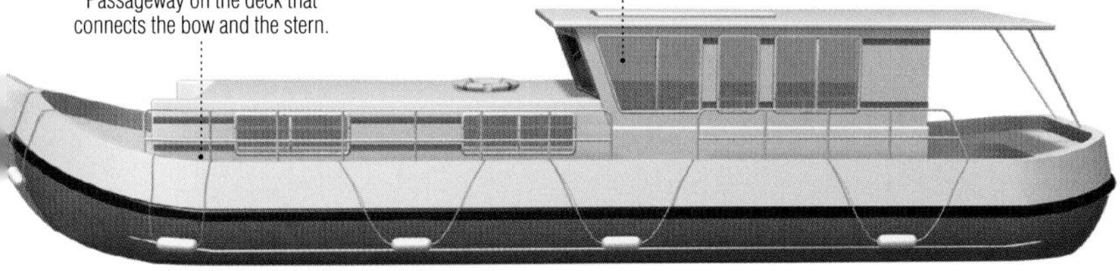
pilot house
Compartment from which the pilot operates the boat.
fore and aft passage
Passageway on the deck that connects the bow and the stern.
houseboat
Motorized pleasure boat for navigating inland waterways; it is characterized by a long deck and a cabin fit to live in.

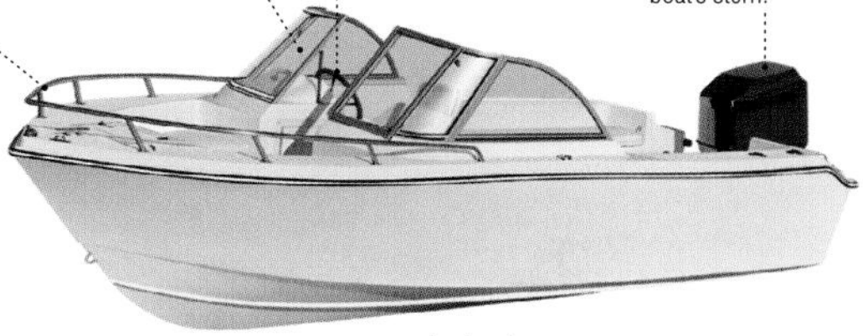
steering wheel
Wheel for steering the engine and hence the boat.
windshield
Front sheet of glass and plastic protecting the pilot from the wind and splashing.
outboard engine
Detachable engine mounted on the boat's stern.
handrail
Railing serving as support for the passengers.
motorboat
Pleasure boat with an outboard engine for cruising and waterskiing on inland waterways.

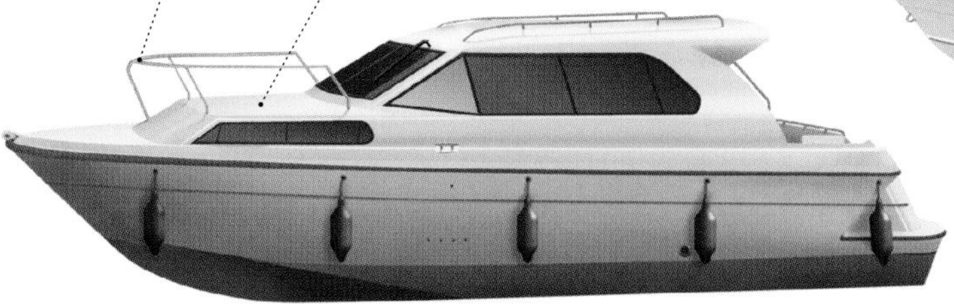
handrail
Railing serving as support for the passengers.
sundeck
Part of the deck for relaxation; it is surrounded by a handrail.
cabin cruiser
Pleasure boat of various sizes and speeds with a cabin fit to live in; it can navigate the sea and inland waterways.

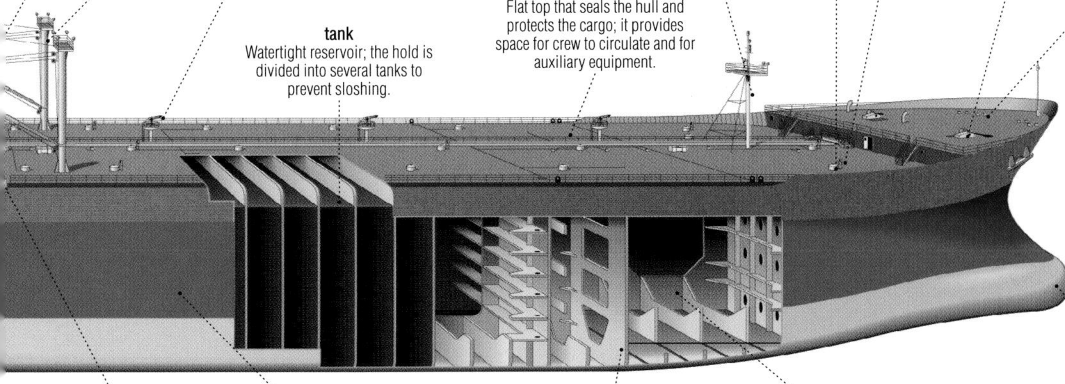
derrick
evice with pulleys that is mounted on a pivot for handling loads.
derrick mast
Short thick mast that supports the derrick.
tank hatch cover
Watertight door that provides access to a tank.
air relief valve
Device that allows air to escape as oil fills the tanks to displace it.
foremast
Mast located near the bow of the deck that supports the navigation lights.
foam monitor
Pressurized mechanism that produces foam for extinguishing fires.
mooring winch
Motorized spool around which a mooring cable is wound.
main deck
Flat top that seals the hull and protects the cargo; it provides space for crew to circulate and for auxiliary equipment.
bitt
Metal cylindrical fittings attached to the deck for fastening mooring ropes and tow lines.
tank
Watertight reservoir; the hold is divided into several tanks to prevent sloshing.
crossover cargo deck line
ick pipe that runs transversally and is used to fill and empty the tanks.
wall side
Vertical part of the hull below the water line.
web frame
Metal reinforcement that spans the hull transversally.
center keelson
Metal girder that runs along the ship's longitudinal axis to reinforce the bottom of the hull.
bulb
Bulge in the bottom part of the stem that reduces the hull's water resistance.

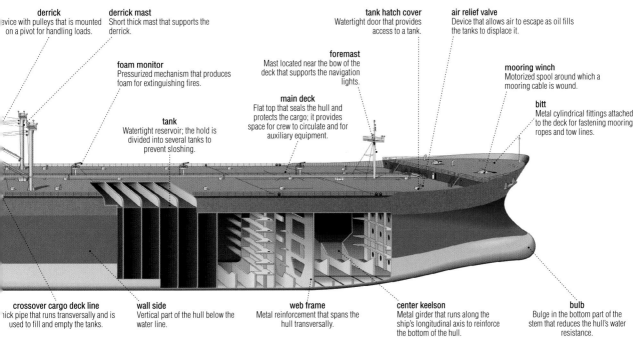

examples of boats and ships

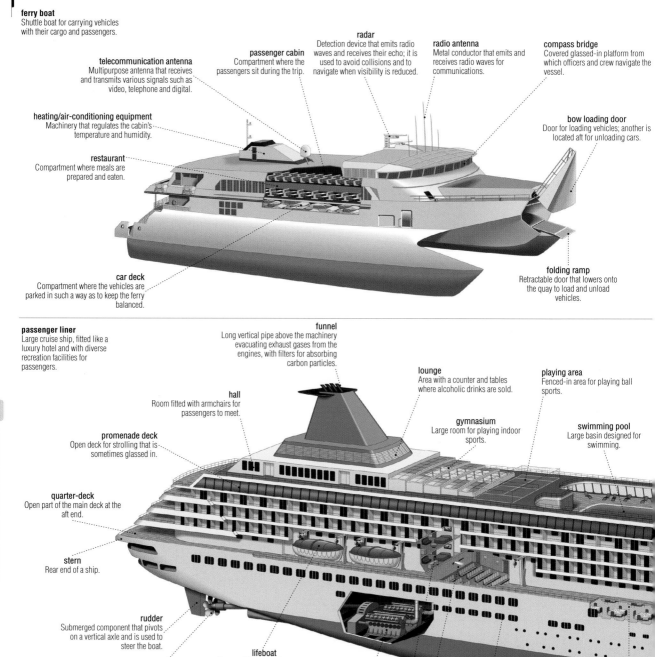

ferry boat
Shuttle boat for carrying vehicles with their cargo and passengers.

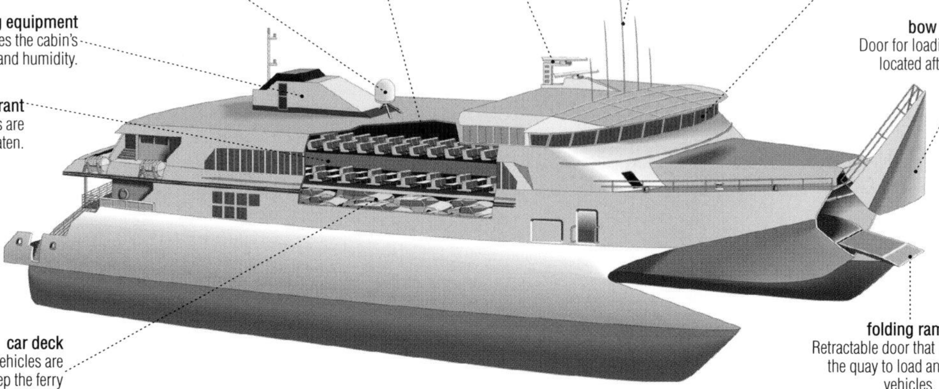

telecommunication antenna
Multipurpose antenna that receives and transmits various signals such as video, telephone and digital.

passenger cabin
Compartment where the passengers sit during the trip.

radar
Detection device that emits radio waves and receives their echo; it is used to avoid collisions and to navigate when visibility is reduced.

radio antenna
Metal conductor that emits and receives radio waves for communications.

compass bridge
Covered glassed-in platform from which officers and crew navigate the vessel.

heating/air-conditioning equipment
Machinery that regulates the cabin's temperature and humidity.

bow loading door
Door for loading vehicles; another is located aft for unloading cars.

restaurant
Compartment where meals are prepared and eaten.

car deck
Compartment where the vehicles are parked in such a way as to keep the ferry balanced.

folding ramp
Retractable door that lowers onto the quay to load and unload vehicles.

passenger liner
Large cruise ship, fitted like a luxury hotel and with diverse recreation facilities for passengers.

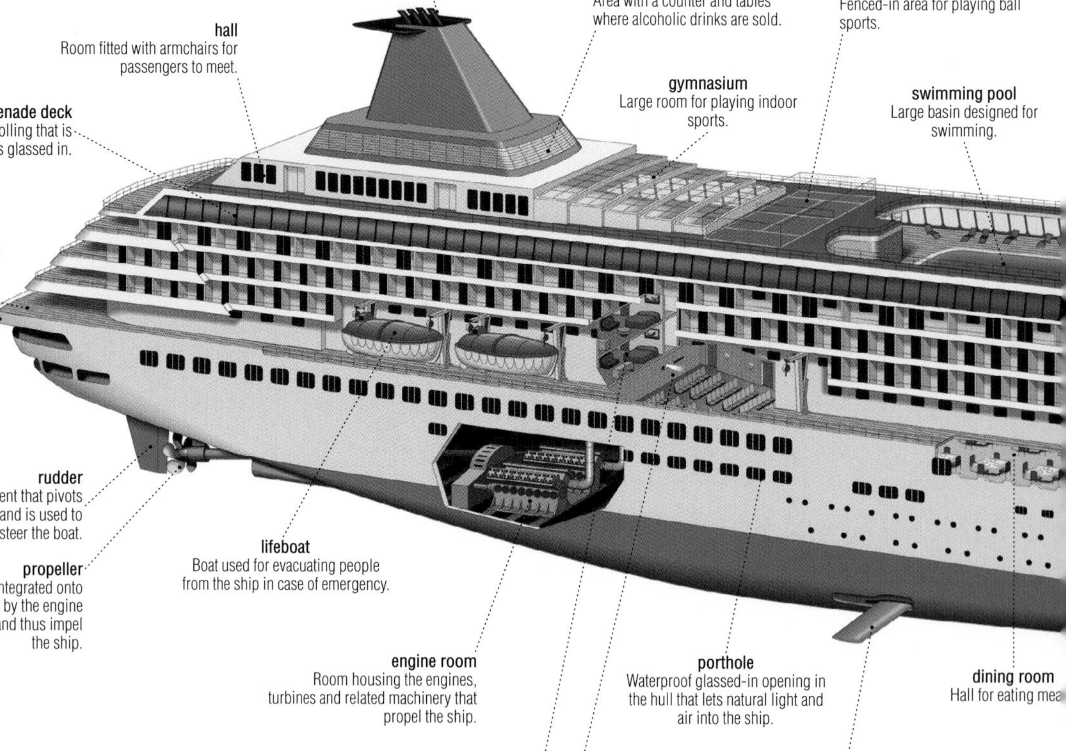

funnel
Long vertical pipe above the machinery evacuating exhaust gases from the engines, with filters for absorbing carbon particles.

lounge
Area with a counter and tables where alcoholic drinks are sold.

playing area
Fenced-in area for playing ball sports.

hall
Room fitted with armchairs for passengers to meet.

gymnasium
Large room for playing indoor sports.

swimming pool
Large basin designed for swimming.

promenade deck
Open deck for strolling that is sometimes glassed in.

quarter-deck
Open part of the main deck at the aft end.

stern
Rear end of a ship.

rudder
Submerged component that pivots on a vertical axle and is used to steer the boat.

propeller
Device with blades integrated onto a shaft that is driven by the engine to provide thrust and thus impel the ship.

lifeboat
Boat used for evacuating people from the ship in case of emergency.

engine room
Room housing the engines, turbines and related machinery that propel the ship.

porthole
Waterproof glassed-in opening in the hull that lets natural light and air into the ship.

dining room
Hall for eating mea

cabin
Room that accommodates one or several passengers.

movie theater
Room for screening films.

stabilizer fin
Small pivoting winglike flaps on each side of the hull to reduce the rolling motion.

examples of boats and ships

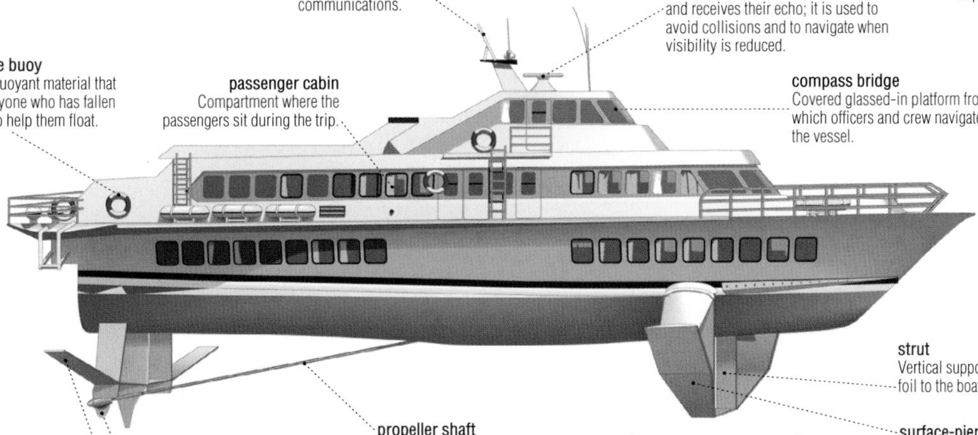
hydrofoil boat
Fast boat with foils, which lift and support the hull above water when cruising speed is reached.
radio antenna
Metal conductor that emits and receives radio waves for communications.
radar
Detection device that emits radio waves and receives their echo; it is used to avoid collisions and to navigate when visibility is reduced.
life buoy
Ring made of buoyant material that is thrown to anyone who has fallen overboard to help them float.
passenger cabin
Compartment where the passengers sit during the trip.
compass bridge
Covered glassed-in platform from which officers and crew navigate the vessel.
strut
Vertical support that connects each foil to the boat's hull.
surface-piercing foils
Parts that lift the boat when cruising speed has been reached; they also stabilize the boat.
propeller shaft
Long metal rod that transmits the motor's rotational movement to the propeller.
front foil
Wing on each side of the prow.
rear foil
Wing on each side of the stern.
propeller
Device with blades integrated onto a shaft that is driven by the engine to provide thrust and thus impel the ship.

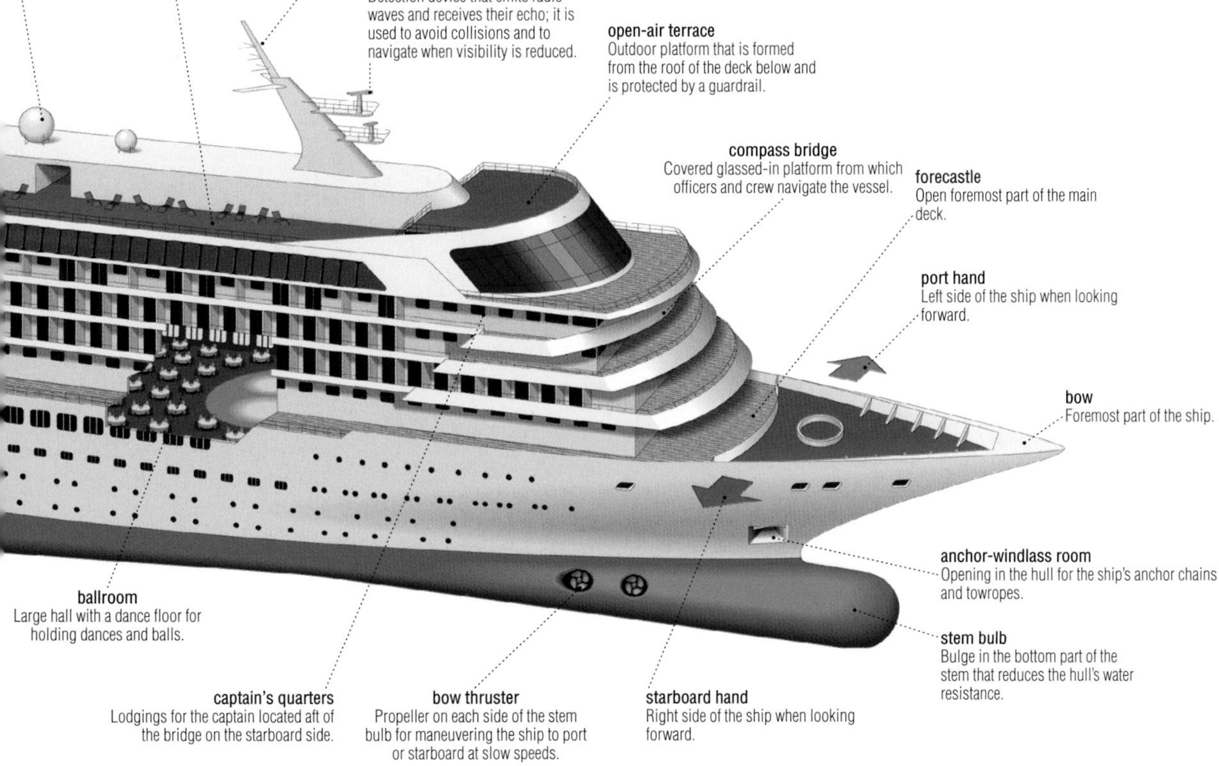
telecommunication antenna
Multipurpose antenna that receives and transmits various signals such as video, telephone and digital.
radio antenna
Metal conductor that emits and receives radio waves for communications.
sundeck
Usually the highest and sunniest deck with a pool and lounge chairs.
radar
Detection device that emits radio waves and receives their echo; it is used to avoid collisions and to navigate when visibility is reduced.
open-air terrace
Outdoor platform that is formed from the roof of the deck below and is protected by a guardrail.
compass bridge
Covered glassed-in platform from which officers and crew navigate the vessel.
forecastle
Open foremost part of the main deck.
port hand
Left side of the ship when looking forward.
bow
Foremost part of the ship.
anchor-windlass room
Opening in the hull for the ship's anchor chains and towropes.
stem bulb
Bulge in the bottom part of the stem that reduces the hull's water resistance.
ballroom
Large hall with a dance floor for holding dances and balls.
captain's quarters
Lodgings for the captain located aft of the bridge on the starboard side.
bow thruster
Propeller on each side of the stem bulb for maneuvering the ship to port or starboard at slow speeds.
starboard hand
Right side of the ship when looking forward.

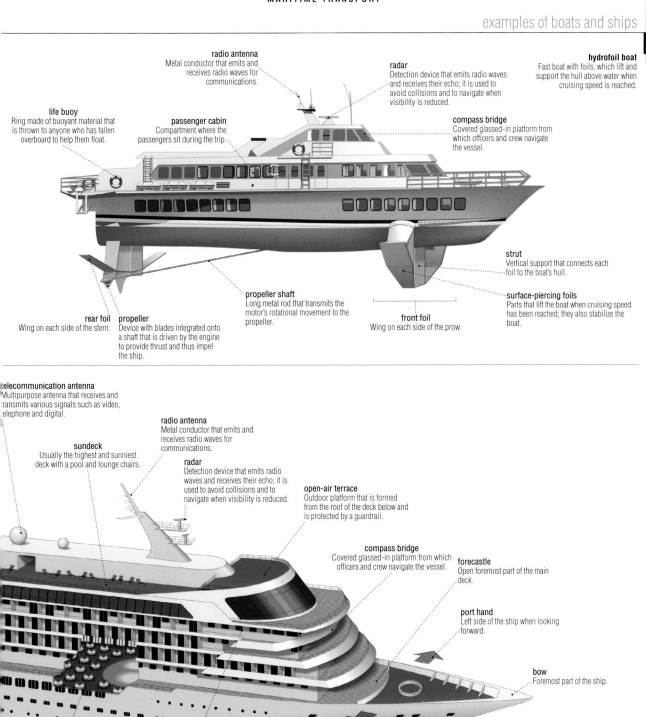

anchor

Usually steel part that is attached to a chain or cable; it hooks onto the bottom of a body of water to keep the boat from moving.

ship's anchor
The traditional anchor is made up of a shank with a stock at one end and two arms ending in palms at the other end.

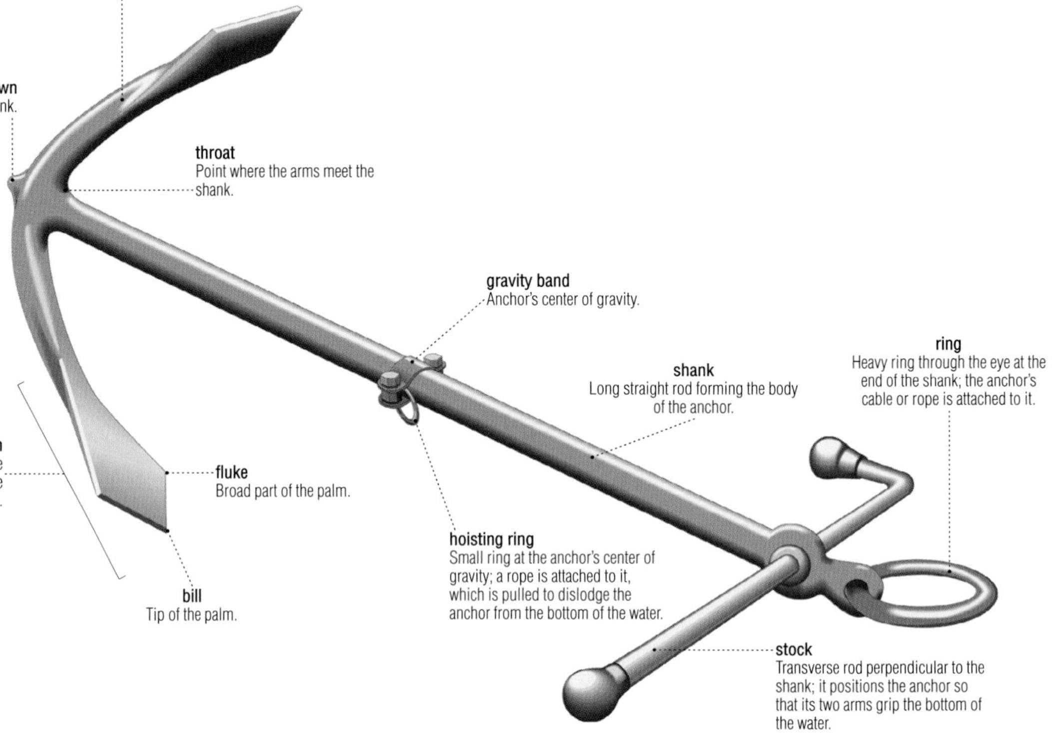

arm
Shank that curves out from the bottom end of the main shank and ends in a palm.

crown
Point at the end of the shank.

throat
Point where the arms meet the shank.

gravity band
Anchor's center of gravity.

ring
Heavy ring through the eye at the end of the shank; the anchor's cable or rope is attached to it.

shank
Long straight rod forming the body of the anchor.

palm
Flat pointed part at the end of the arm; it sinks into the bottom of the water to grip it.

fluke
Broad part of the palm.

hoisting ring
Small ring at the anchor's center of gravity; a rope is attached to it, which is pulled to dislodge the anchor from the bottom of the water.

bill
Tip of the palm.

stock
Transverse rod perpendicular to the shank; it positions the anchor so that its two arms grip the bottom of the water.

examples of anchors
The weight and the shape of the arms of anchors are designed to hook onto various bottoms (such as firm, loose or reedy).

mushroom anchor
Anchor with a large crown instead of arms.

grapnel
Small anchor with four, sometimes folding, cruciform arms.

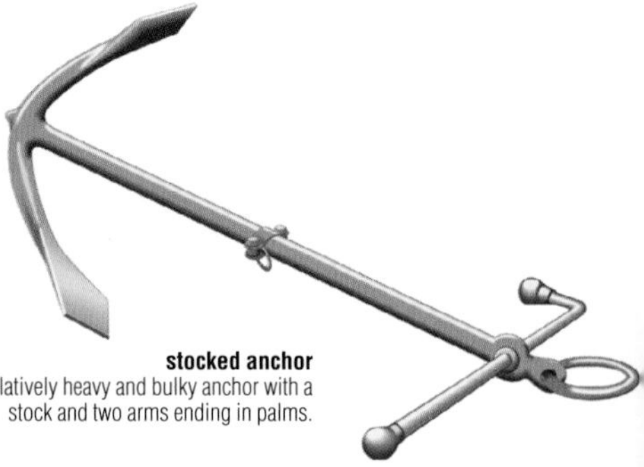

stocked anchor
Relatively heavy and bulky anchor with a stock and two arms ending in palms.

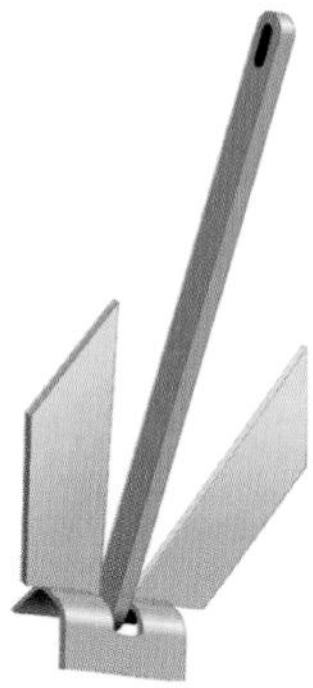

stockless anchor
Relatively light anchor with a pair of pivoting palms that fold along the shank.

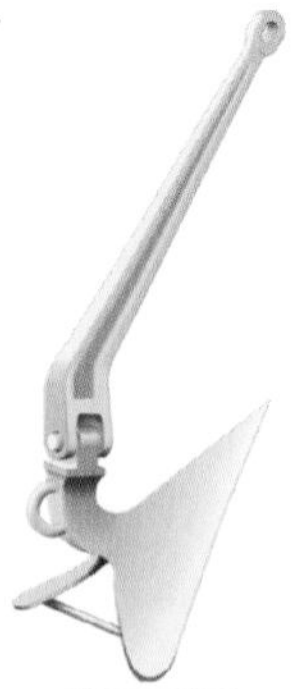

plow anchor
Anchor with a plow-shaped arm that pivots on the shank and hooks onto most bottoms.

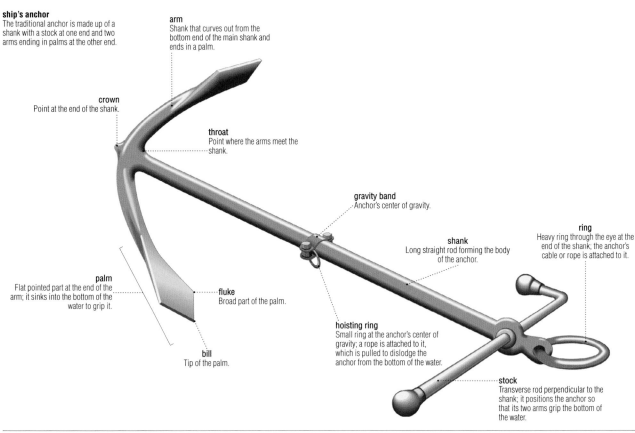

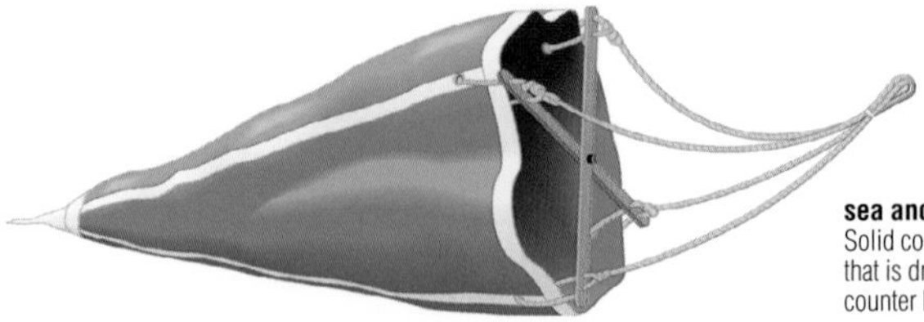

sea anchor
Solid cone-shaped canvas sack that is dragged behind a boat to counter heaving and strong winds.

life-saving equipment

Instruments and equipment for signaling a boat's presence and for saving people from drowning.

antenna
Metal rod that emits the radio signal into the atmosphere.
strobe
Lamp that produces an intense light from a gas, which glows between two electrodes.

distress beacon
Device that automatically transmits a radio distress signal giving its precise position.

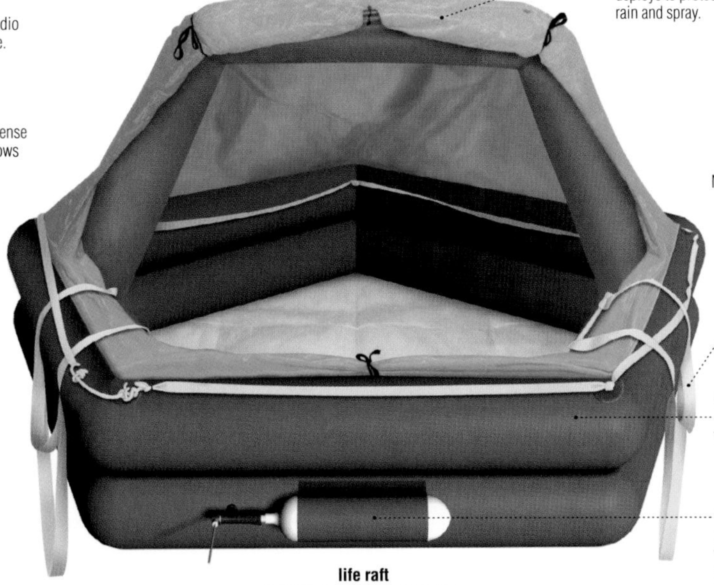
canopy
Covering that automatically deploys to protect against wind, rain and spray.
boarding ladder
Nylon straps that form steps for climbing into the life raft.
buoyancy tube
Inflatable tube that serves as a hull to make the raft float.
inflation system
Device containing pressurized air that automatically inflates the buoyancy tubes when the life raft is launched.

life raft
Inflatable boat where passengers can take refuge in case of emergency.

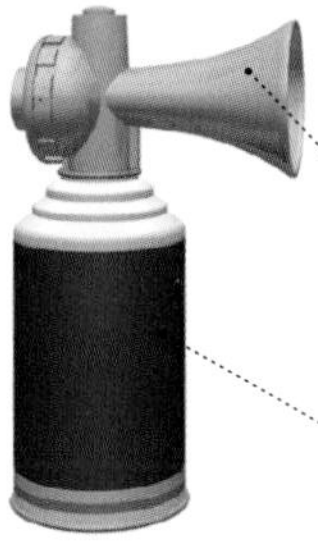
trumpet
Bell mouth that amplifies the sound emitted by a diaphragm when compressed air passes over it.
canister
Small container of compressed air.

fog horn
Instrument that makes a regulation sound when visibility is reduced to indicate the presence of a boat.

ring
Rigid buoyant circle that a person in the water slips under the arms.
rope
Nylon rope that can be caught with the boat hook to hoist a person out of the water.
retro-reflective tape
Tape that reflects light, making it easier to find a person in the water.

life buoy
Ring made of buoyant material that is thrown to anyone who has fallen overboard to help them float.

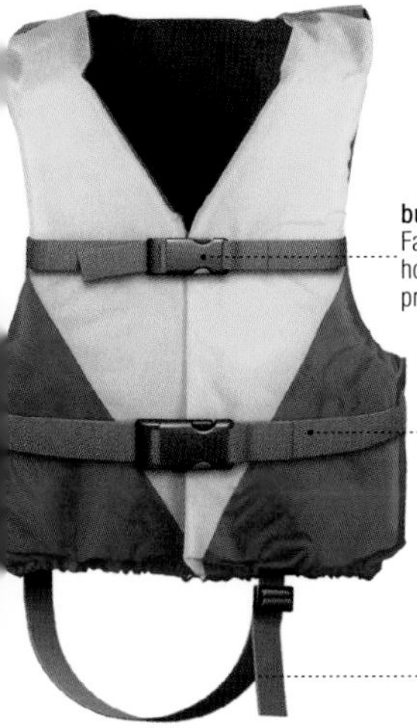
buckle
Fastener with two elements that hook together and unfasten when pressed.
belt
Nylon strap that adjusts to the wearer's size to keep the life jacket in place.
leg strap
Adjustable nylon belt that goes between the legs to prevent the life jacket from riding up.

life jacket
Buoyant vest filled with air or plastic foam that is used to keep a person afloat.

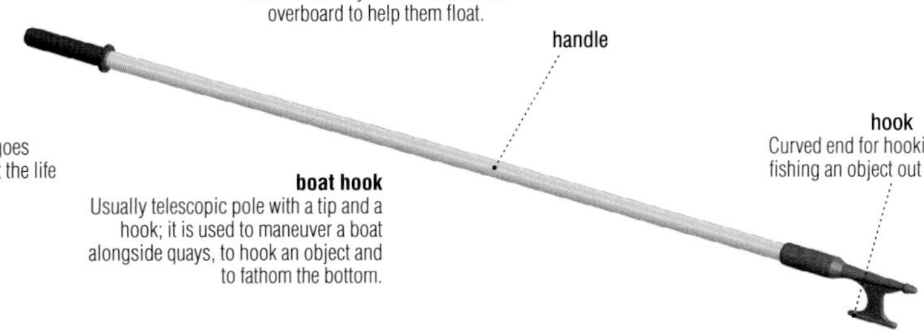
handle
hook
Curved end for hooking a rope or fishing an object out of the water.

boat hook
Usually telescopic pole with a tip and a hook; it is used to maneuver a boat alongside quays, to hook an object and to fathom the bottom.

navigation devices

Examples of instruments that are used on a ship to determine its position and to chart and stay a course.

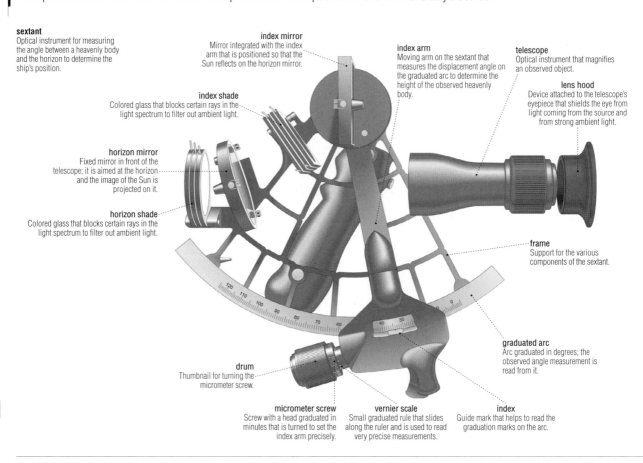

sextant
Optical instrument for measuring the angle between a heavenly body and the horizon to determine the ship's position.

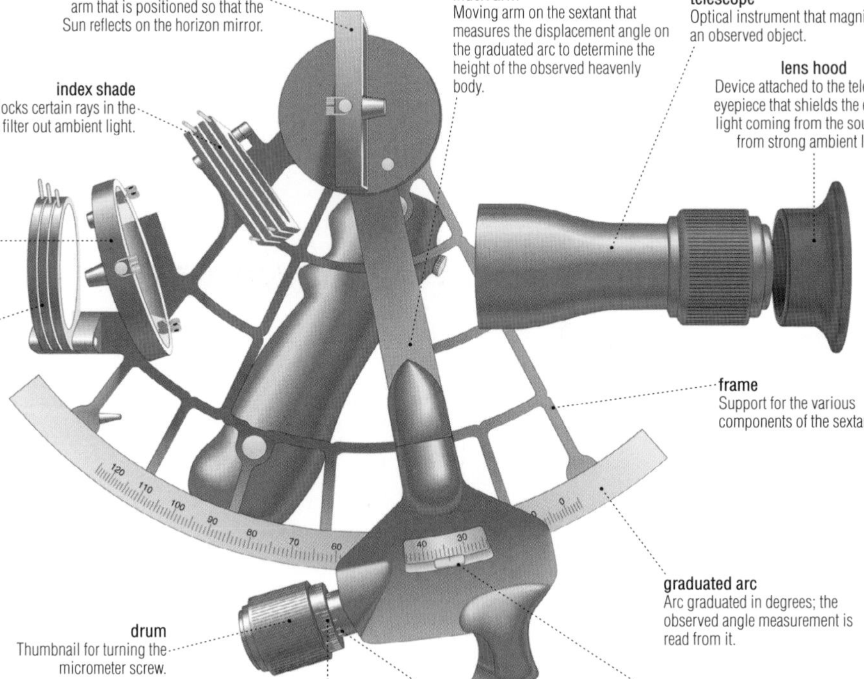

index mirror
Mirror integrated with the index arm that is positioned so that the Sun reflects on the horizon mirror.

index shade
Colored glass that blocks certain rays in the light spectrum to filter out ambient light.

horizon mirror
Fixed mirror in front of the telescope; it is aimed at the horizon and the image of the Sun is projected on it.

horizon shade
Colored glass that blocks certain rays in the light spectrum to filter out ambient light.

index arm
Moving arm on the sextant that measures the displacement angle on the graduated arc to determine the height of the observed heavenly body.

telescope
Optical instrument that magnifies an observed object.

lens hood
Device attached to the telescope's eyepiece that shields the eye from light coming from the source and from strong ambient light.

frame
Support for the various components of the sextant.

graduated arc
Arc graduated in degrees; the observed angle measurement is read from it.

drum
Thumbnail for turning the micrometer screw.

micrometer screw
Screw with a head graduated in minutes that is turned to set the index arm precisely.

vernier scale
Small graduated rule that slides along the ruler and is used to read very precise measurements.

index
Guide mark that helps to read the graduation marks on the arc.

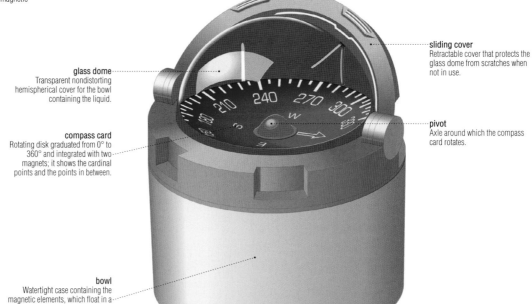

liquid compass
Instrument with magnets that floats on a liquid; it indicates magnetic north.

glass dome
Transparent nondistorting hemispherical cover for the bowl containing the liquid.

compass card
Rotating disk graduated from 0° to 360° and integrated with two magnets; it shows the cardinal points and the points in between.

bowl
Watertight case containing the magnetic elements, which float in a liquid (oil or alcohol) to reduce oscillations.

sliding cover
Retractable cover that protects the glass dome from scratches when not in use.

pivot
Axle around which the compass card rotates.

navigation devices

depth finder
Device that uses a sonic pulse to measure the depth of water below the boat.

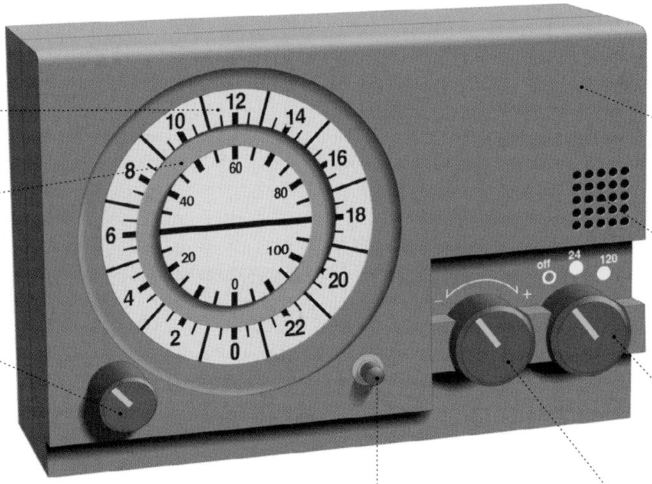

depth scale
Line graduated in feet or meters for reading the distance to the bottom.

dial-type display
Display surface where an illuminated dot appears at the point on the scale that corresponds to the depth.

housing

sound alarm
Audible signal activated when the alarm threshold is reached.

alarm threshold setting
Knob for setting the maximum depth considered to be dangerous.

on-off switch
Button for activating the sounder and for selecting the scale.

echo sounder probe
Part of the sounder that is submerged to send the ultrasound to the bottom; it receives the echo and converts it into sound.

alarm threshold display button
Button that is pushed to display the alarm threshold value.

gain control
Knob for adjusting the amplification of the signal.

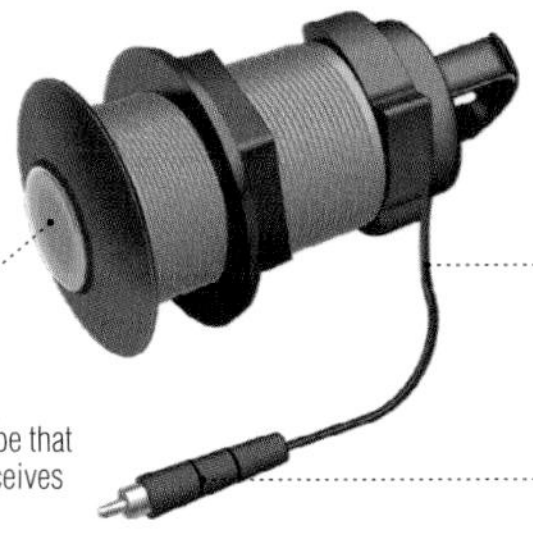

transmission cable
Electric wire that relays the electric signals between the housing and the echo sounder probe.

transducer
Part of the echo sounder probe that emits the ultrasound and receives its echoes.

plug
Metal prong that plugs into the housing.

satellite navigation system
Device that uses radio signals transmitted by a network of satellites to plot a boat's position and course on a chart.

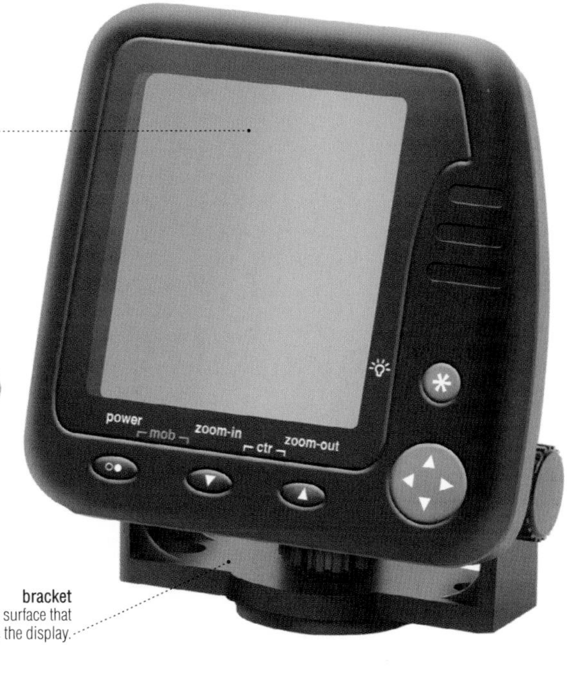

display
Liquid crystal display screen on which graphics or text data are displayed.

GPS receiver-antenna
External antenna and GPS receiver that receive radio waves from satellites to calculate the boat's position.

bracket
Support fixed onto a surface that holds the display.

maritime signals

Beacons and devices located on the sea, coasts and waterways that emit light, sound and radio waves to aid navigation.

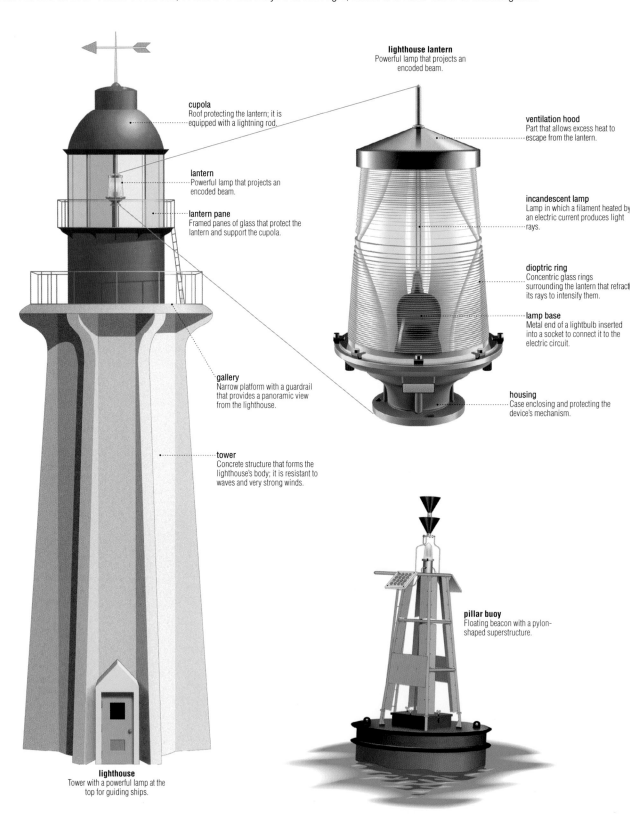

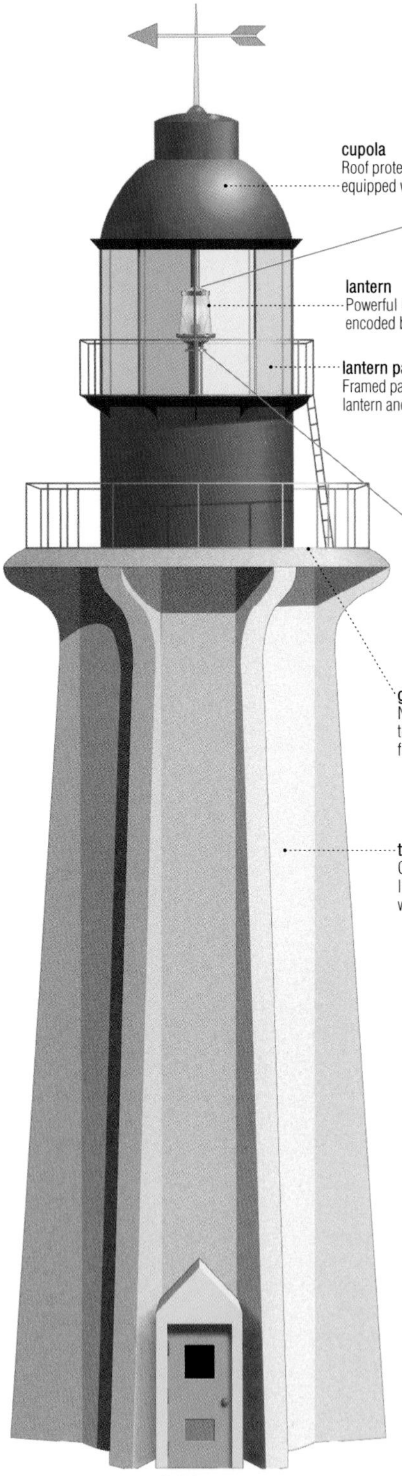
cupola
Roof protecting the lantern; it is equipped with a lightning rod.
lantern
Powerful lamp that projects an encoded beam.
lantern pane
Framed panes of glass that protect the lantern and support the cupola.
gallery
Narrow platform with a guardrail that provides a panoramic view from the lighthouse.
tower
Concrete structure that forms the lighthouse's body; it is resistant to waves and very strong winds.

lighthouse
Tower with a powerful lamp at the top for guiding ships.

lighthouse lantern
Powerful lamp that projects an encoded beam.

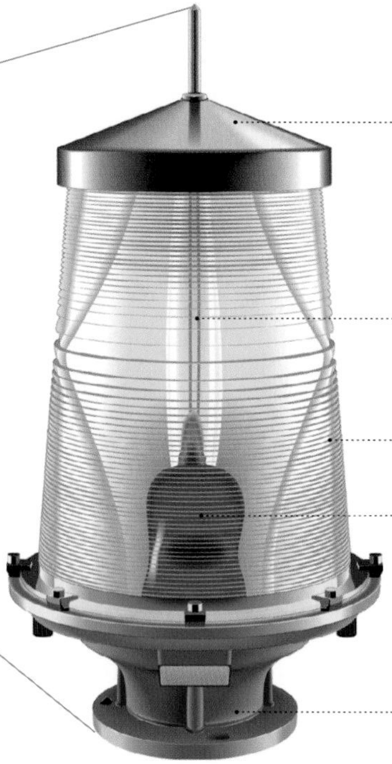
ventilation hood
Part that allows excess heat to escape from the lantern.
incandescent lamp
Lamp in which a filament heated by an electric current produces light rays.
dioptric ring
Concentric glass rings surrounding the lantern that refract its rays to intensify them.
lamp base
Metal end of a lightbulb inserted into a socket to connect it to the electric circuit.
housing
Case enclosing and protecting the device's mechanism.

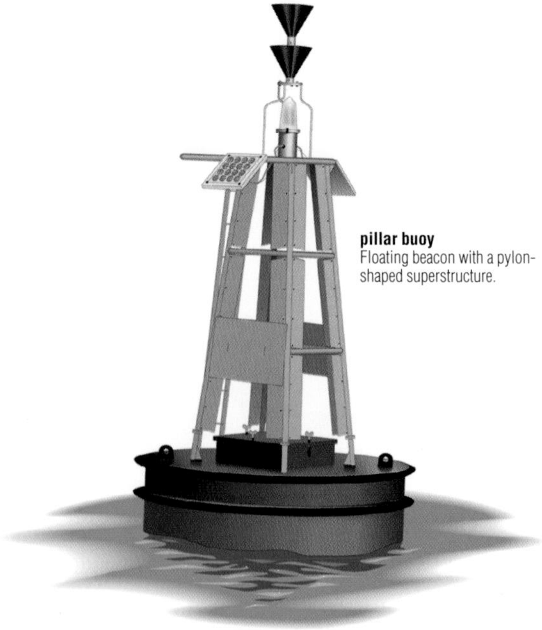

pillar buoy
Floating beacon with a pylon-shaped superstructure.

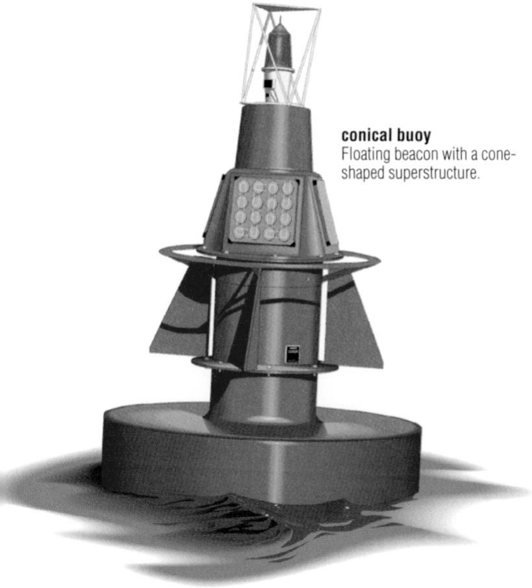

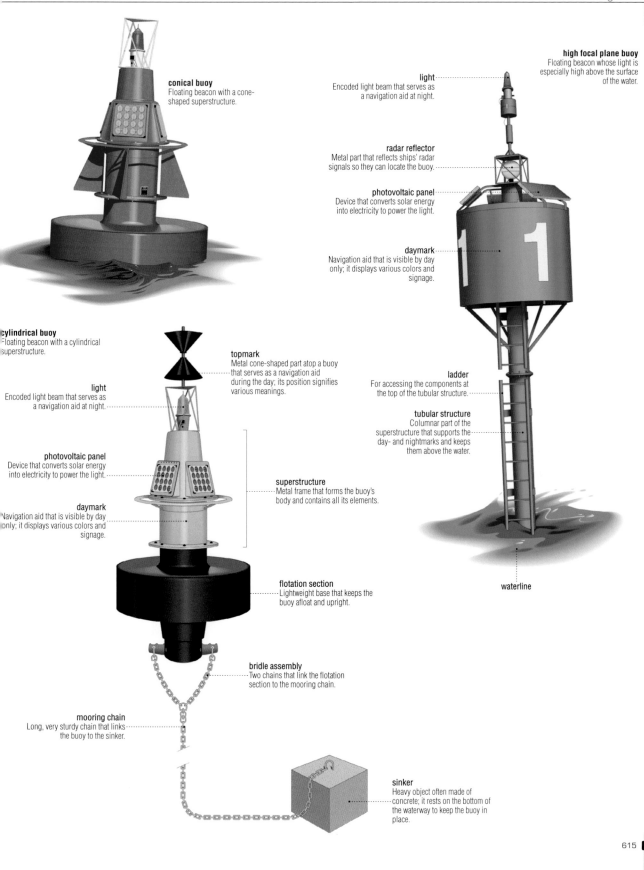

conical buoy
Floating beacon with a cone-shaped superstructure.

high focal plane buoy
Floating beacon whose light is especially high above the surface of the water.

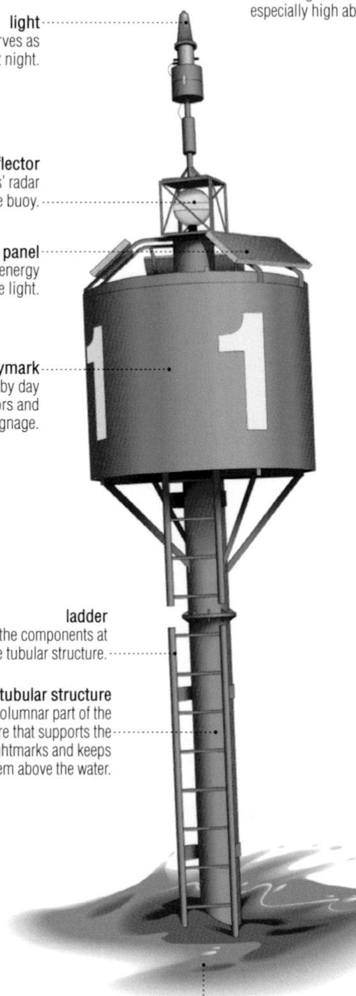

light
Encoded light beam that serves as a navigation aid at night.

radar reflector
Metal part that reflects ships' radar signals so they can locate the buoy.

photovoltaic panel
Device that converts solar energy into electricity to power the light.

daymark
Navigation aid that is visible by day only; it displays various colors and signage.

ladder
For accessing the components at the top of the tubular structure.

tubular structure
Columnar part of the superstructure that supports the day- and nightmarks and keeps them above the water.

waterline

cylindrical buoy
Floating beacon with a cylindrical superstructure.

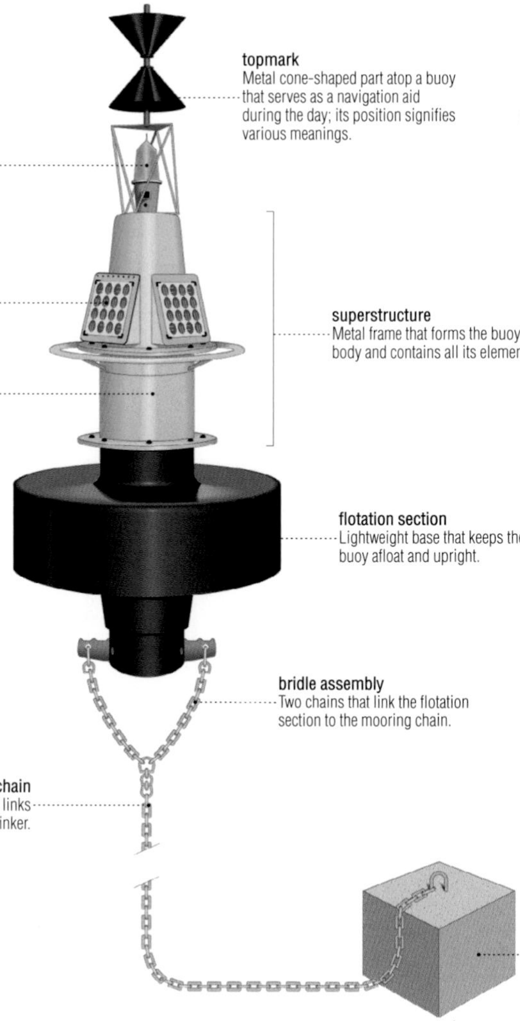

topmark
Metal cone-shaped part atop a buoy that serves as a navigation aid during the day; its position signifies various meanings.

light
Encoded light beam that serves as a navigation aid at night.

photovoltaic panel
Device that converts solar energy into electricity to power the light.

superstructure
Metal frame that forms the buoy's body and contains all its elements.

daymark
Navigation aid that is visible by day only; it displays various colors and signage.

flotation section
Lightweight base that keeps the buoy afloat and upright.

bridle assembly
Two chains that link the flotation section to the mooring chain.

mooring chain
Long, very sturdy chain that links the buoy to the sinker.

sinker
Heavy object often made of concrete; it rests on the bottom of the waterway to keep the buoy in place.

maritime buoyage system

Buoys, beacons and lights located along coasts and waterways to guide ships and boats.

cardinal marks
Buoys of standardized colors, topmarks and lights whose placement alone or in a pattern corresponds to the divisions of a compass.

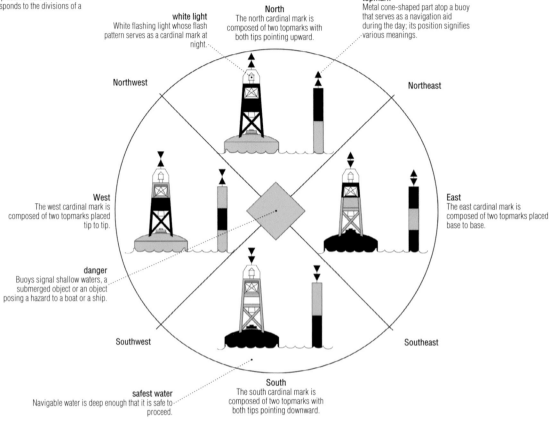

white light
White flashing light whose flash pattern serves as a cardinal mark at night.

North
The north cardinal mark is composed of two topmarks with both tips pointing upward.

topmark
Metal cone-shaped part atop a buoy that serves as a navigation aid during the day; its position signifies various meanings.

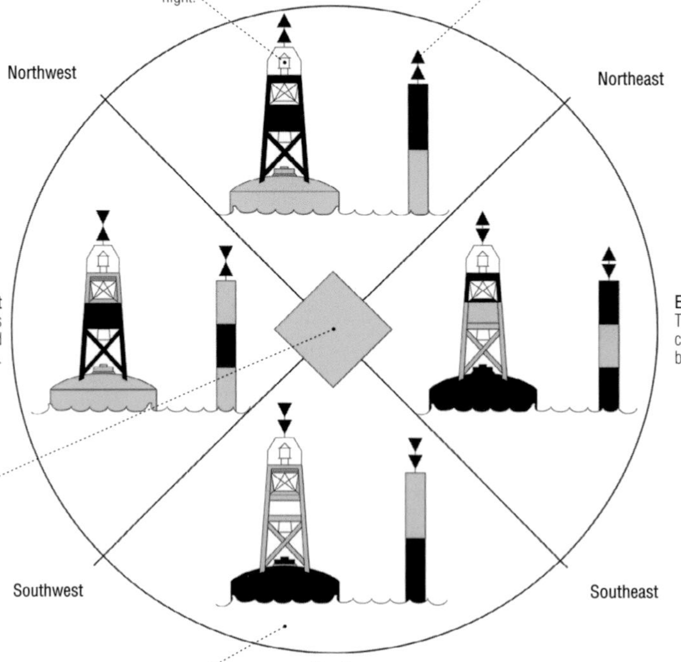

West
The west cardinal mark is composed of two topmarks placed tip to tip.

East
The east cardinal mark is composed of two topmarks placed base to base.

danger
Buoys signal shallow waters, a submerged object or an object posing a hazard to a boat or a ship.

safest water
Navigable water is deep enough that it is safe to proceed.

South
The south cardinal mark is composed of two topmarks with both tips pointing downward.

buoyage regions
The color of the buoys that indicate starboard and port is the opposite in various parts of the world.

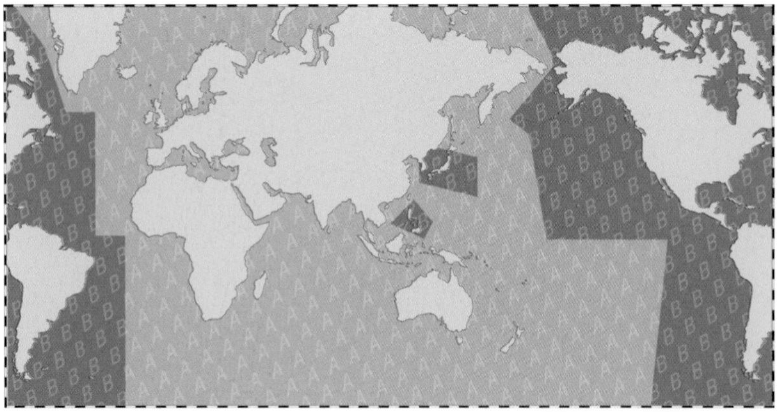

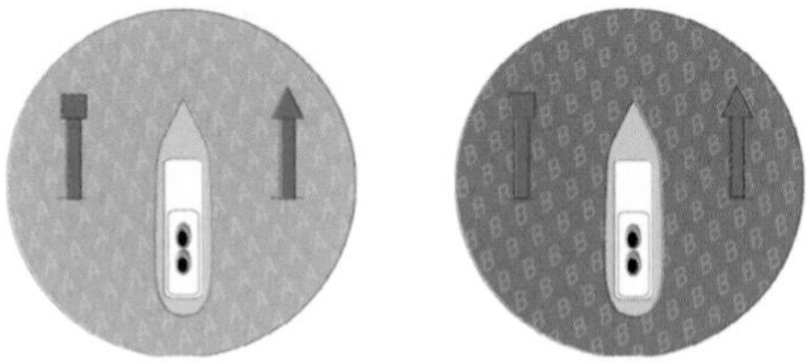

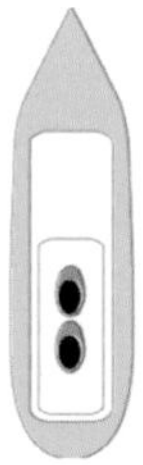

port hand
Left side of the ship when looking forward.

starboard hand
Right side of the ship when looking forward.

maritime buoyage system

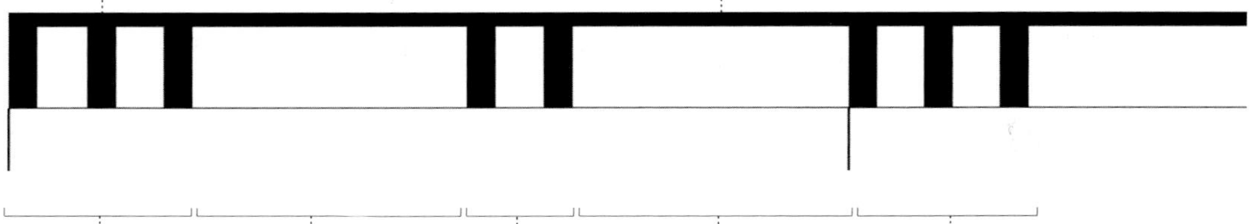
rhythm of marks by night
Lights that shine at night; their color and the frequency of their flashing signal various meanings, including the source of the light.
light
The light's color and brightness vary during the period as a function of the type of light.
darkness
No light.
period
Duration between two intervals at which time the light signals.
period
Duration between two intervals at which time the light signals.
period
Duration between two intervals at which time the light signals.
interval
Duration between two periods at which time the light remains dark.
interval
Duration between two periods at which time the light remains dark.

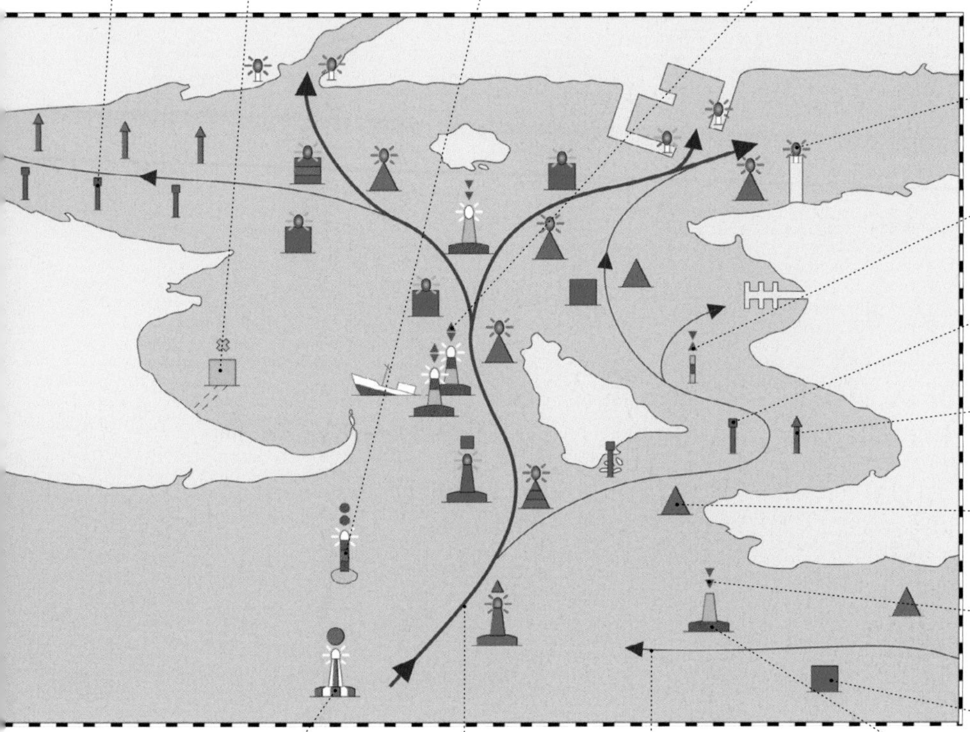
daymarks (region B)
System B combines lateral and cardinal marks. It is the opposite of system A, in which starboard marks are red and port marks are green.
spar buoy
Long tubular buoy used in harbors and in waters that have no tides.
special mark
Buoy marking an area that is regulated for a specific use (such as military exercises or fishing) or contains submerged obstacles (such as cables or pipelines).
isolated danger mark
Buoy marking an isolated danger zone beyond which the waters are navigable.
East cardinal mark
Buoy with two base-to-base topmarks that is placed to the east of a danger zone.
light
Encoded light beam that serves as a navigation aid at night.
West cardinal mark
Buoy with two point-to-point topmarks that is placed to the west of a danger zone.
port hand
Mark the ship must keep on the left side of its prow as it navigates a channel.
starboard hand
Mark the ship must keep on the right side of its prow as it navigates a channel.
conical buoy
Floating beacon with a cone-shaped superstructure.
South cardinal mark
Buoy with two topmarks pointing downward that is placed to the south of a danger zone.
lateral mark
Red or green buoy that indicates the port or starboard limits of the channel.
safe water mark
Buoy signaling that the water is navigable.
preferred channel
Navigation lane with beacons; it is the shortest and safest way to a harbor or for navigating near a coast or through a waterway.
secondary channel
Navigation lane with beacons that is longer or more difficult than the preferred channel.
pillar buoy
Floating beacon with a pylon-shaped superstructure.

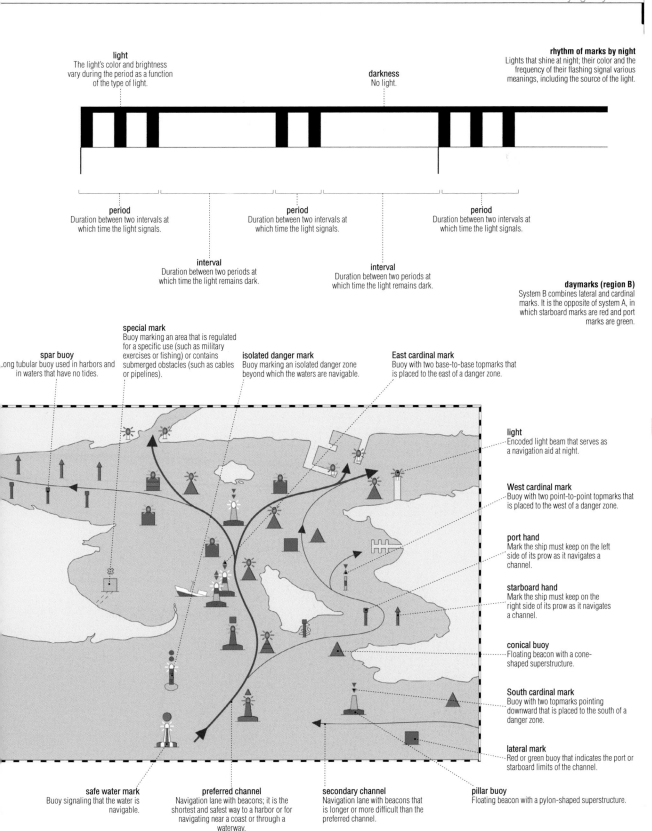

airport

Location that contains all the technical and commercial facilities needed to support air traffic.

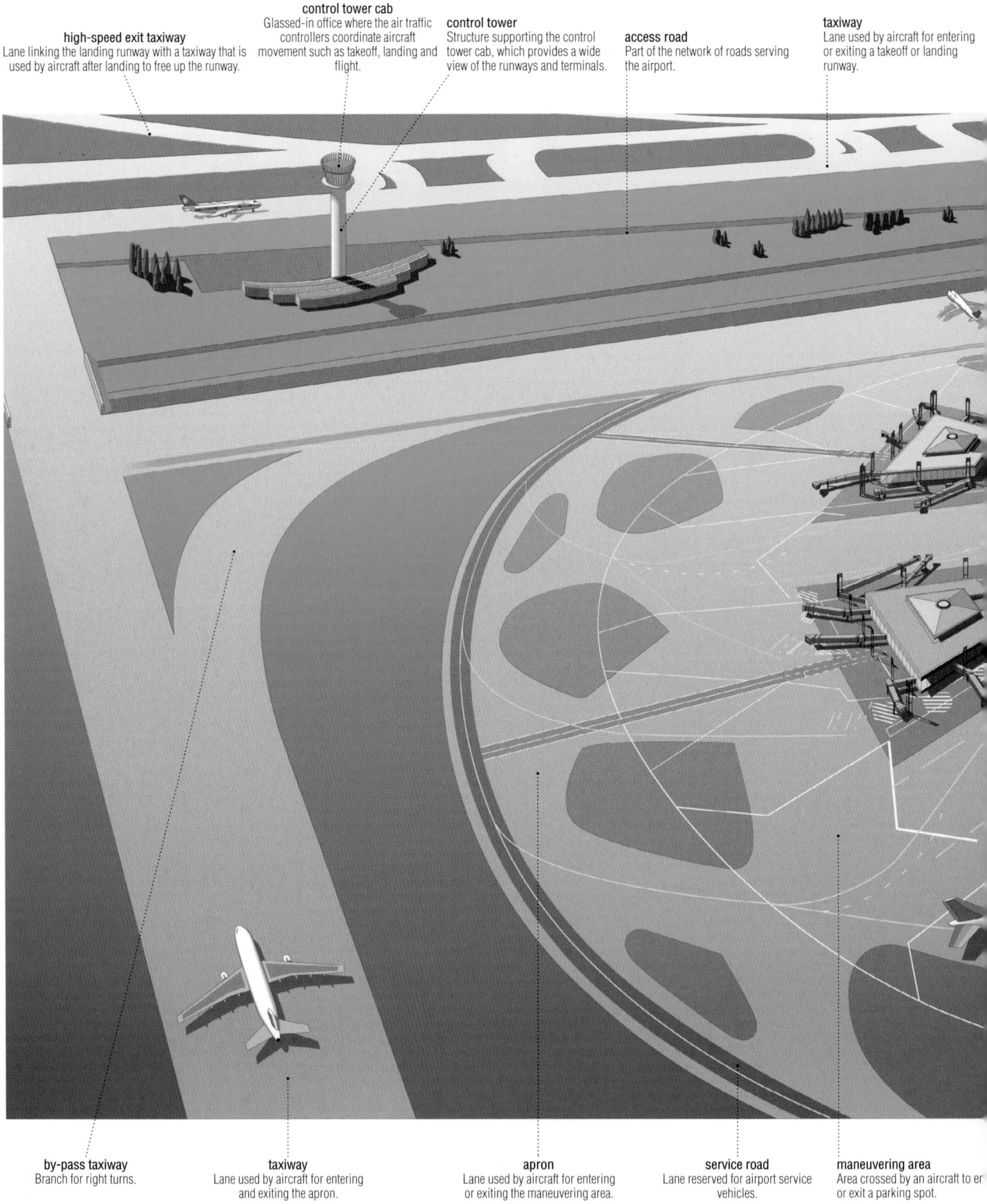
control tower cab
Glassed-in office where the air traffic controllers coordinate aircraft movement such as takeoff, landing and flight.
high-speed exit taxiway
Lane linking the landing runway with a taxiway that is used by aircraft after landing to free up the runway.
control tower
Structure supporting the control tower cab, which provides a wide view of the runways and terminals.
access road
Part of the network of roads serving the airport.
taxiway
Lane used by aircraft for entering or exiting a takeoff or landing runway.
by-pass taxiway
Branch for right turns.
taxiway
Lane used by aircraft for entering and exiting the apron.
apron
Lane used by aircraft for entering or exiting the maneuvering area.
service road
Lane reserved for airport service vehicles.
maneuvering area
Area crossed by an aircraft to er
or exit a parking spot.

passenger terminal
Structure through which passengers pass before or after their flight to pick up or leave their baggage and to go through customs.

maintenance hangar
Structure where aircraft are maintained and repaired.

parking area
Area where aircraft park between flights for maintenance or overhaul.

telescopic corridor
Mobile corridor connecting the passenger loading area with the aircraft.

service area
Area around an aircraft that is reserved for service vehicles and ground crew attending to arriving or departing aircraft.

boarding walkway
Underground corridor linking the main terminal with a radial passenger loading area.

taxiway line
Yellow line painted on the ground that shows aircraft the route to follow on the apron or the maneuvering area.

radial passenger loading area
Pavilion for passengers to reach aircraft that is linked by an underground corridor or by vehicles with the main terminal.

airport

passenger terminal
Structure through which passengers pass before or after their flight to pick up or leave their baggage and to go through customs.

information counter
Desk where information can be obtained about flights and ground transportation.

baggage claim area
Area where the baggage conveyor belt emerges for passengers to pick up their luggage.

hotel reservation desk
Counter where a hotel room can be reserved.

ticket counter
Desk where an airline or travel agent sells tickets for flights.

lobby
Large entrance hall of the terminal for passengers and the people accompanying them.

automatically controlled door
Door automatically opening and closing for people to go through.

baggage check-in counter
Desk where an employee checks and weighs passengers' baggage and issues boarding passes.

parking lot
Area for parking vehicles.

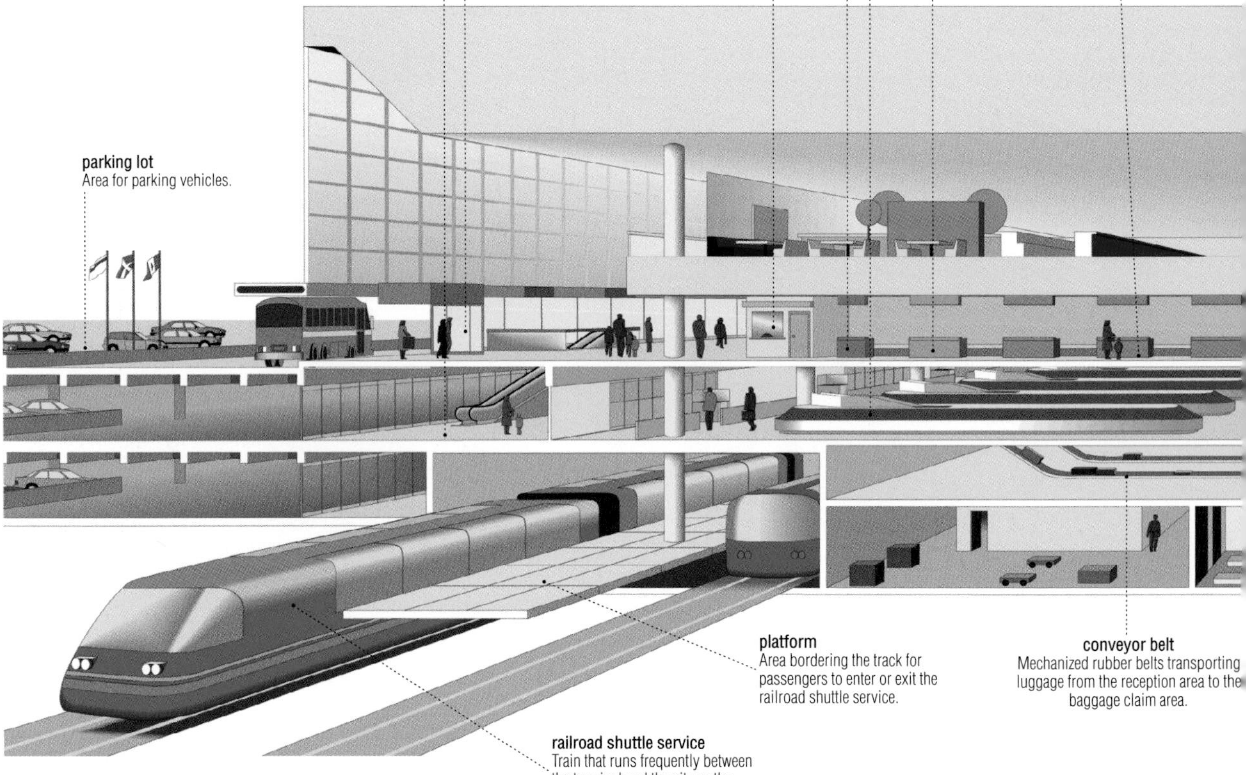

platform
Area bordering the track for passengers to enter or exit the railroad shuttle service.

conveyor belt
Mechanized rubber belts transporting luggage from the reception area to the baggage claim area.

railroad shuttle service
Train that runs frequently between the terminal and the city or the nearest station.

runway
Strip of land on which an aircraft speeds up before takeoff or brakes after landing.

holding area marking
Line that shows an aircraft where to wait for clearance from the control tower before entering the runway for takeoff.

runway designation marking
Number that, when multiplied by 10, shows the runway's position in relation to magnetic north.

runway center line markings
Wide broken white line that shows the center of the runway.

runway side stripe markings
Wide solid white line that marks the edges of the runway.

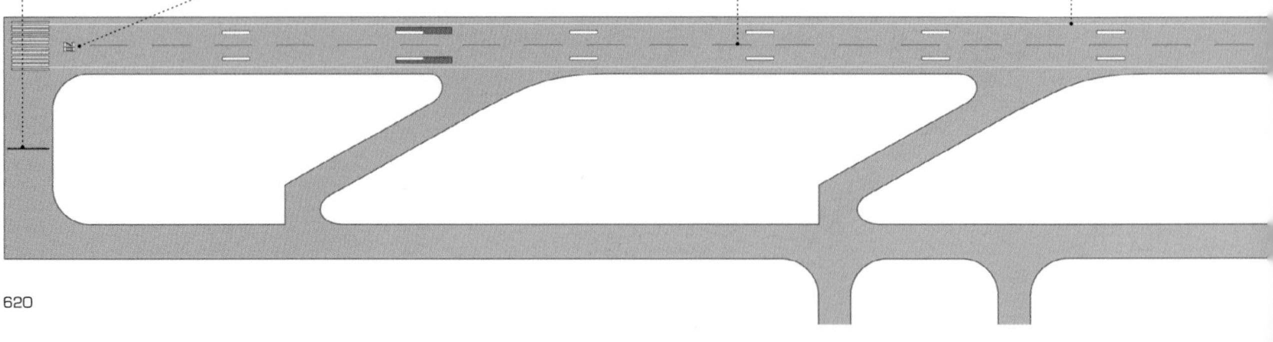

security check
Mandatory checkpoint for passengers before boarding where their identification and luggage are inspected.

duty-free shop
Store located near the boarding room where tax-free goods are sold (e.g., perfume, alcohol, leather goods).

observation deck
Mezzanine that is open to the public and overlooks the departure and arrival area and the runways.

flight information board
Panel listing and updating all the airport's arrivals and departures as well as the flight departure gate numbers.

freight dispatching
Room where luggage and cargo are inspected, sorted and loaded onto carts transporting them to the aircraft.

passport control
Booth where passengers show their passports before entering or leaving the boarding room.

waiting area
Area where passengers wait before boarding.

passenger transfer vehicle
Vertically adjustable vehicle with a cabin for transporting passengers between the aircraft and the terminal.

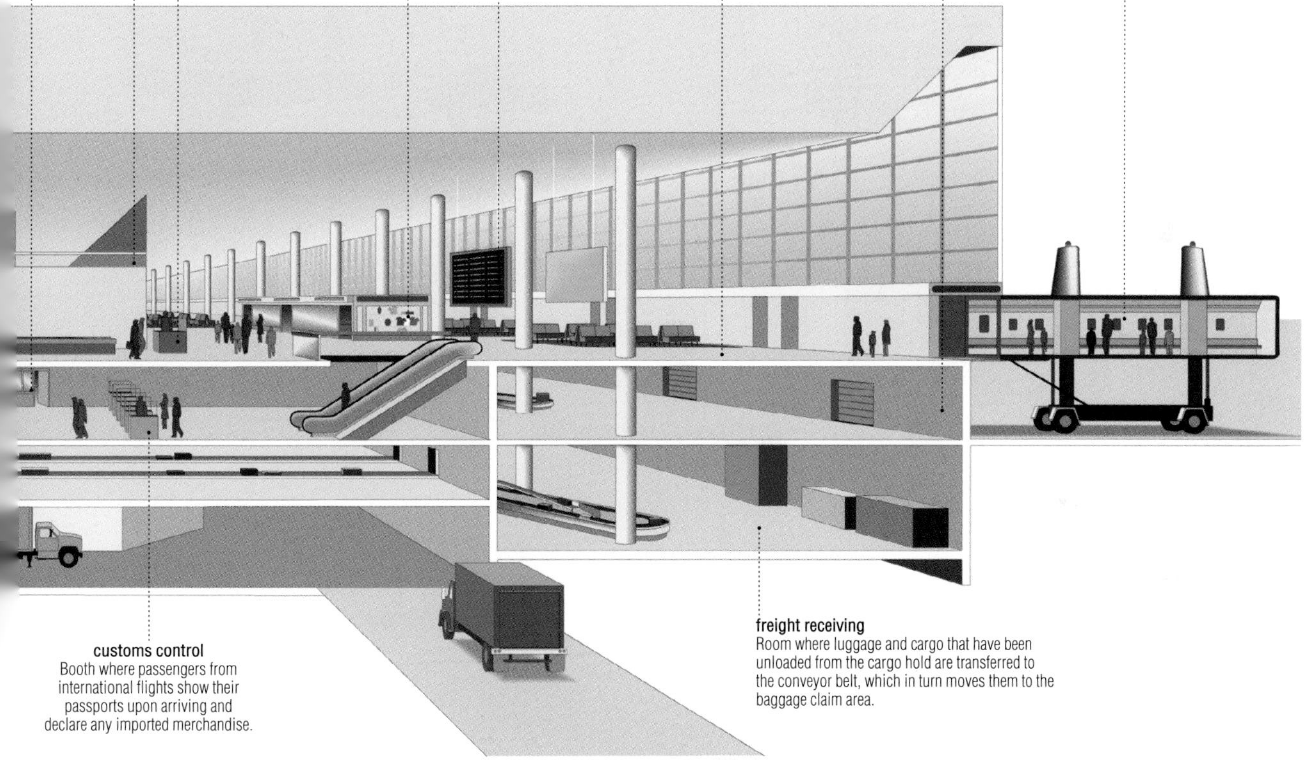

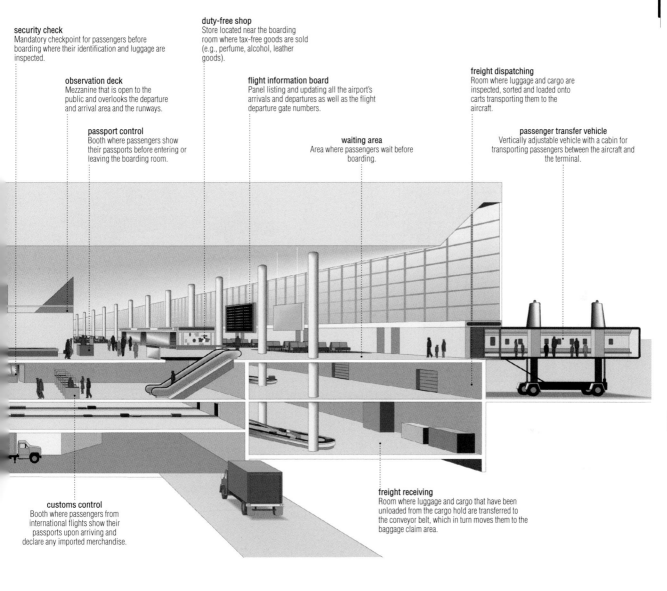

customs control
Booth where passengers from international flights show their passports upon arriving and declare any imported merchandise.

freight receiving
Room where luggage and cargo that have been unloaded from the cargo hold are transferred to the conveyor belt, which in turn moves them to the baggage claim area.

exit taxiway
Lane connecting the runway with a taxiway so that incoming aircraft can exit the runway as soon as possible after landing.

runway touchdown zone marking
Pair of lines painted at each end of the runway that shows where aircraft should touch down on the runway.

runway threshold markings
Longitudinal lines painted at each end of the runway to show its limits.

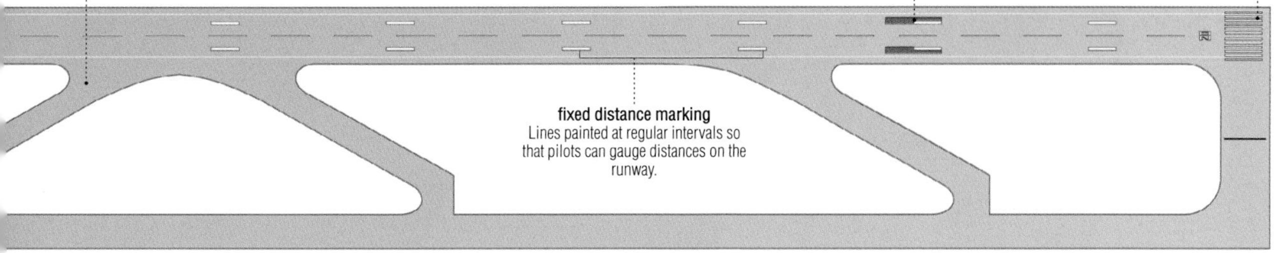

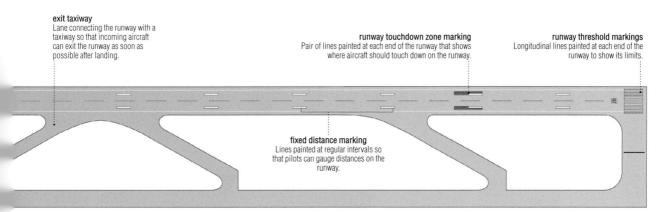

fixed distance marking
Lines painted at regular intervals so that pilots can gauge distances on the runway.

airport

ground airport equipment

Equipment and materials for preparing an aircraft for its next flight; this includes cleaning, performing checks, refueling and boarding.

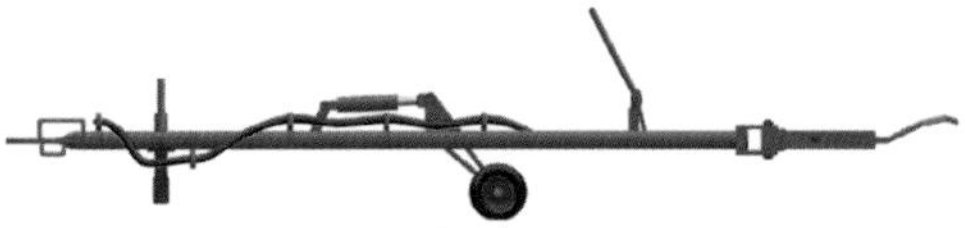

tow bar
Device that connects the tow tractor to the aircraft's front landing gear.

tow tractor
Very heavy vehicle that pulls or pushes an aircraft onto the maneuvering area or the parking area.

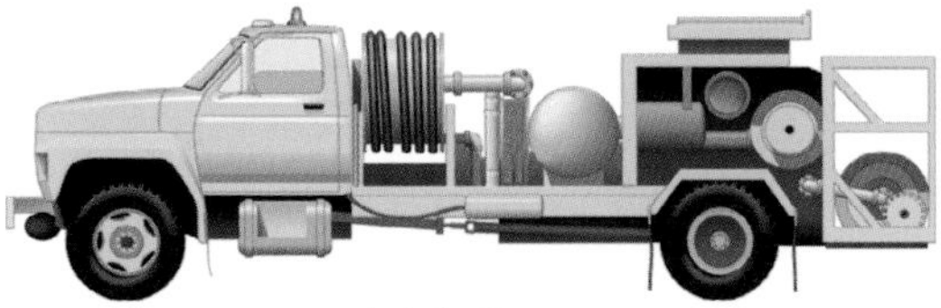

air start unit
Vehicle that is equipped with an air compressor driven by a gas turbine; it pumps air into the aircraft's jet engines to start them.

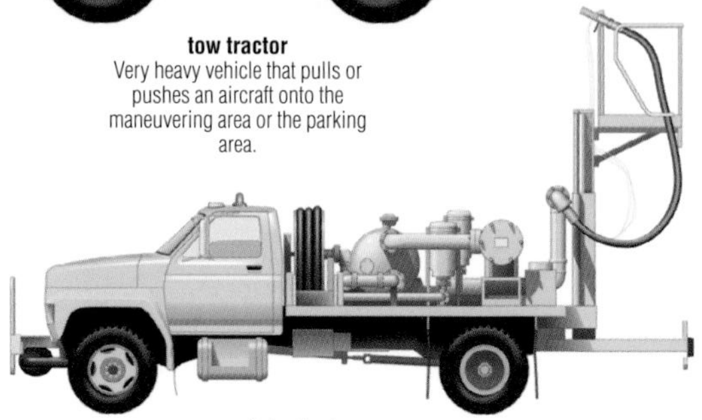

jet refueler
Truck that pumps fuel from underground tanks into the aircraft's tanks.

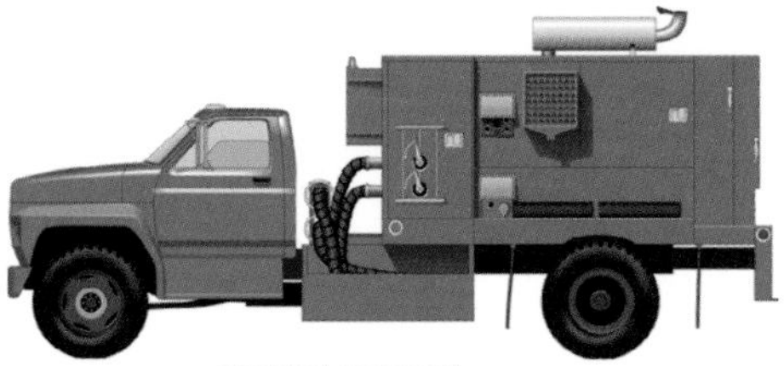

electrical power unit
Vehicle that is equipped with a transformer to provide electricity to the aircraft when its auxiliary generator set is at rest.

ground air conditioner
Truck that contains a device for treating the aircraft's interior air (ventilation and cooling or heating) when the aircraft is at rest.

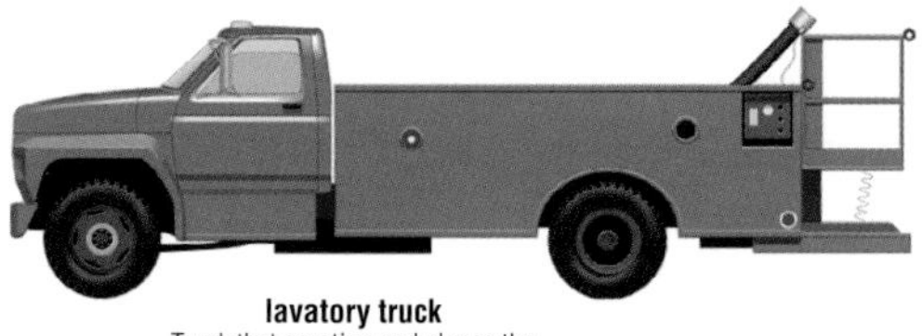

lavatory truck
Truck that empties and cleans the aircraft's toilets.

aircraft maintenance truck
Vehicle that is used by technical maintenance crew when servicing an aircraft.

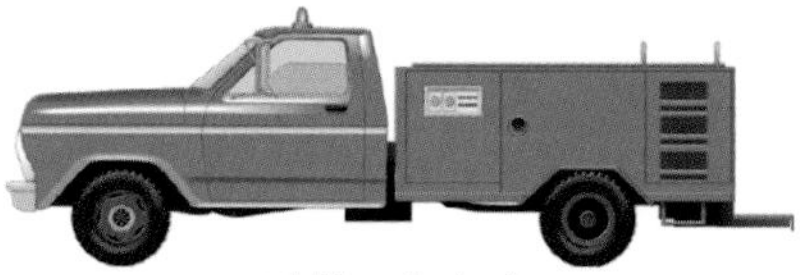

potable water truck
Truck that fills the aircraft's water tanks with drinking water.

wheel chock
Object that is placed against the landing gear's wheels to keep the aircraft stationary when on the ground.

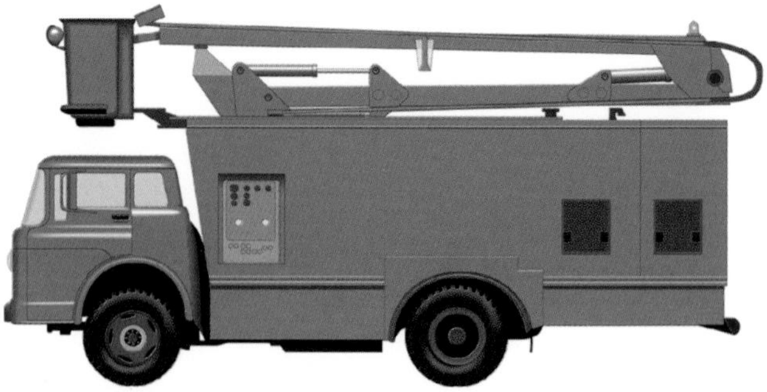

boom truck
Vehicle that is equipped with a bucket at the end of an articulating pivoting arm; technicians stand in it to work on aircraft.

tripod tail support
Adjustable tripod that supports part of the aircraft (the tail or a wing) when maintenance or repairs are carried out.

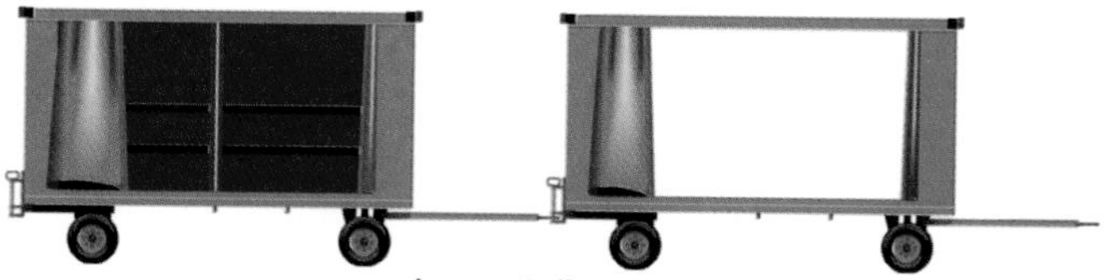

baggage trailer
Flat trailer or cart that carries containers in which baggage is transported from the terminal to the aircraft.

tow tractor
Vehicle that pulls the baggage trailer.

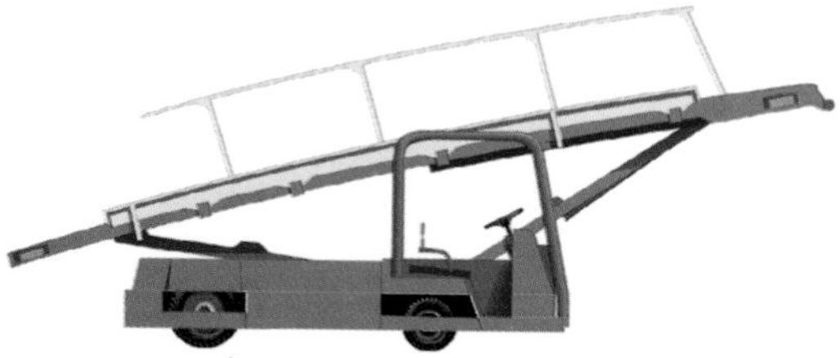

baggage conveyor
Conveyor belt of adjustable height for loading and unloading baggage and cargo.

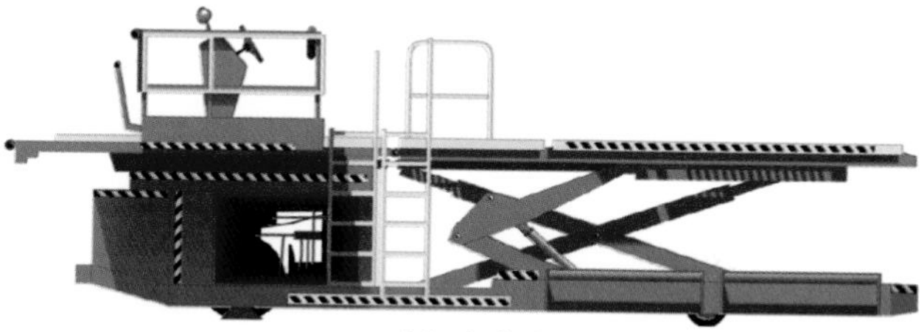

container/pallet loader
Vehicle whose articulated arms raise and lower a level platform for loading and unloading heavy cargo such as containers and cargo on pallets.

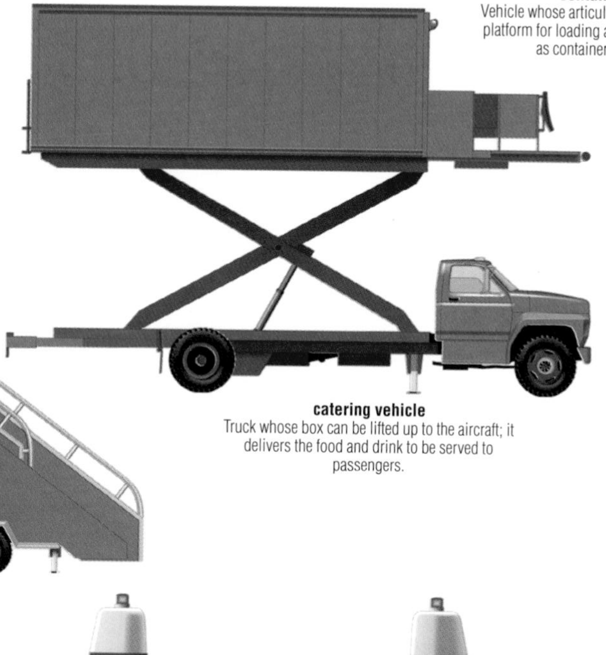

catering vehicle
Truck whose box can be lifted up to the aircraft; it delivers the food and drink to be served to passengers.

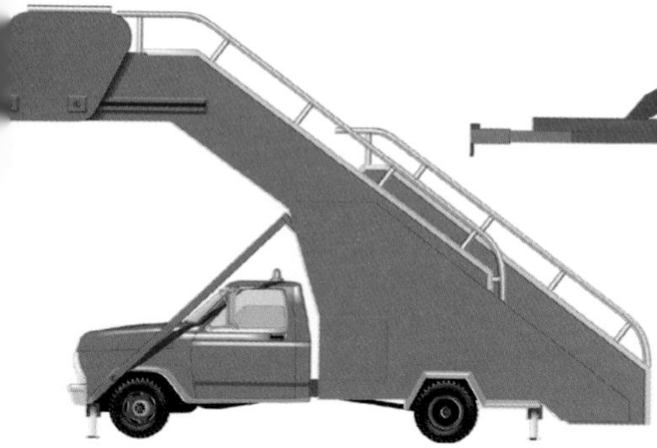

mobile passenger stairs
Truck that carries a telescopic staircase, which is positioned at an aircraft door to allow passengers to enter or exit.

universal step
Mobile staircase that is positioned manually at an aircraft door to allow passengers to enter or exit.

passenger transfer vehicle
Vertically adjustable vehicle with a cabin for transporting passengers between the aircraft and the terminal.

long-range jet

Aircraft that transports passengers and cargo traveling long distances at high altitudes (between 30,000 and 40,000 ft).

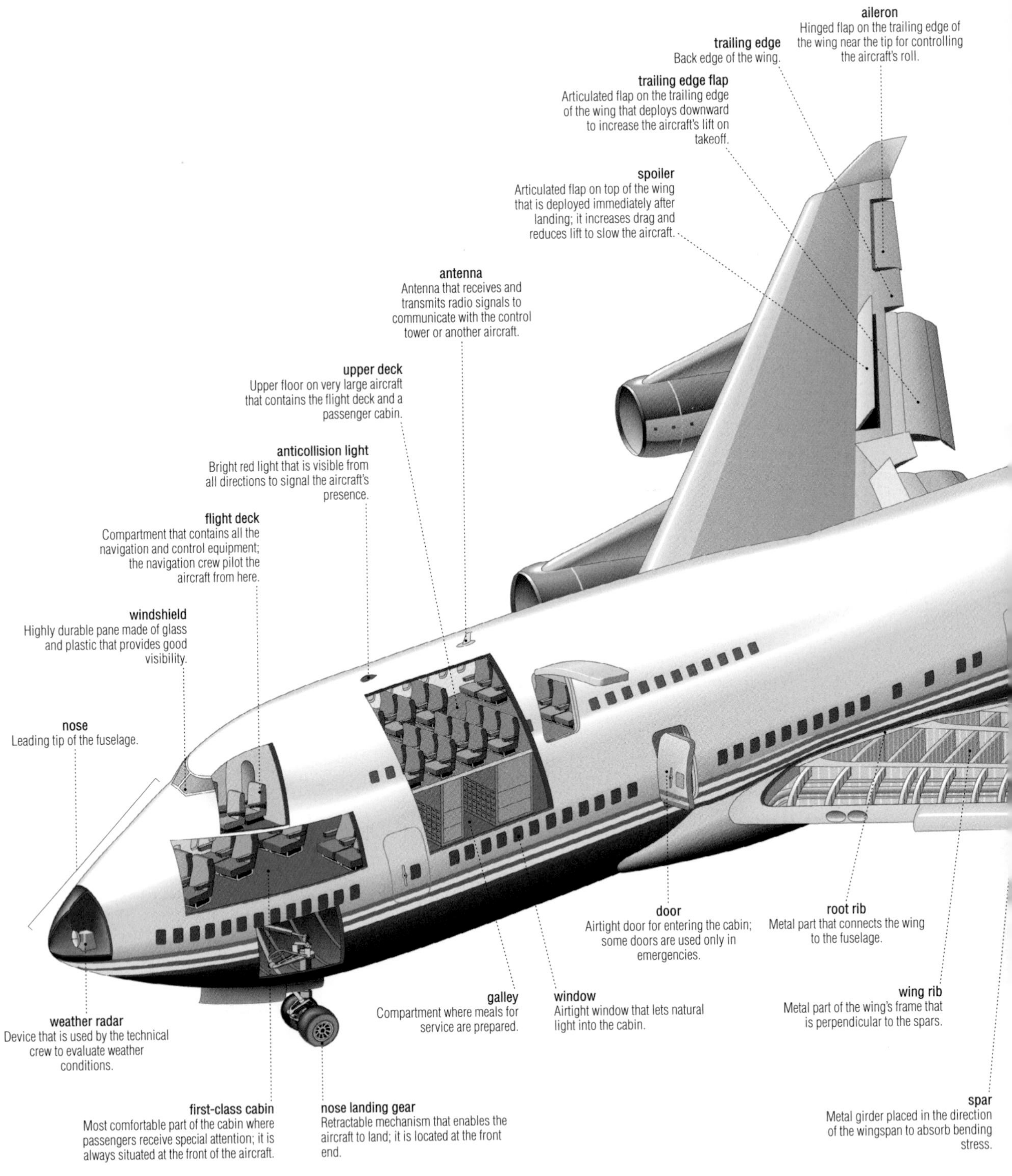
aileron
Hinged flap on the trailing edge of the wing near the tip for controlling the aircraft's roll.
trailing edge
Back edge of the wing.
trailing edge flap
Articulated flap on the trailing edge of the wing that deploys downward to increase the aircraft's lift on takeoff.
spoiler
Articulated flap on top of the wing that is deployed immediately after landing; it increases drag and reduces lift to slow the aircraft.
antenna
Antenna that receives and transmits radio signals to communicate with the control tower or another aircraft.
upper deck
Upper floor on very large aircraft that contains the flight deck and a passenger cabin.
anticollision light
Bright red light that is visible from all directions to signal the aircraft's presence.
flight deck
Compartment that contains all the navigation and control equipment; the navigation crew pilot the aircraft from here.
windshield
Highly durable pane made of glass and plastic that provides good visibility.
nose
Leading tip of the fuselage.
door
Airtight door for entering the cabin; some doors are used only in emergencies.
root rib
Metal part that connects the wing to the fuselage.
galley
Compartment where meals for service are prepared.
window
Airtight window that lets natural light into the cabin.
wing rib
Metal part of the wing's frame that is perpendicular to the spars.
weather radar
Device that is used by the technical crew to evaluate weather conditions.
first-class cabin
Most comfortable part of the cabin where passengers receive special attention; it is always situated at the front of the aircraft.
nose landing gear
Retractable mechanism that enables the aircraft to land; it is located at the front end.
spar
Metal girder placed in the direction of the wingspan to absorb bending stress.

TRANSPORT AND MACHINERY

long-range jet

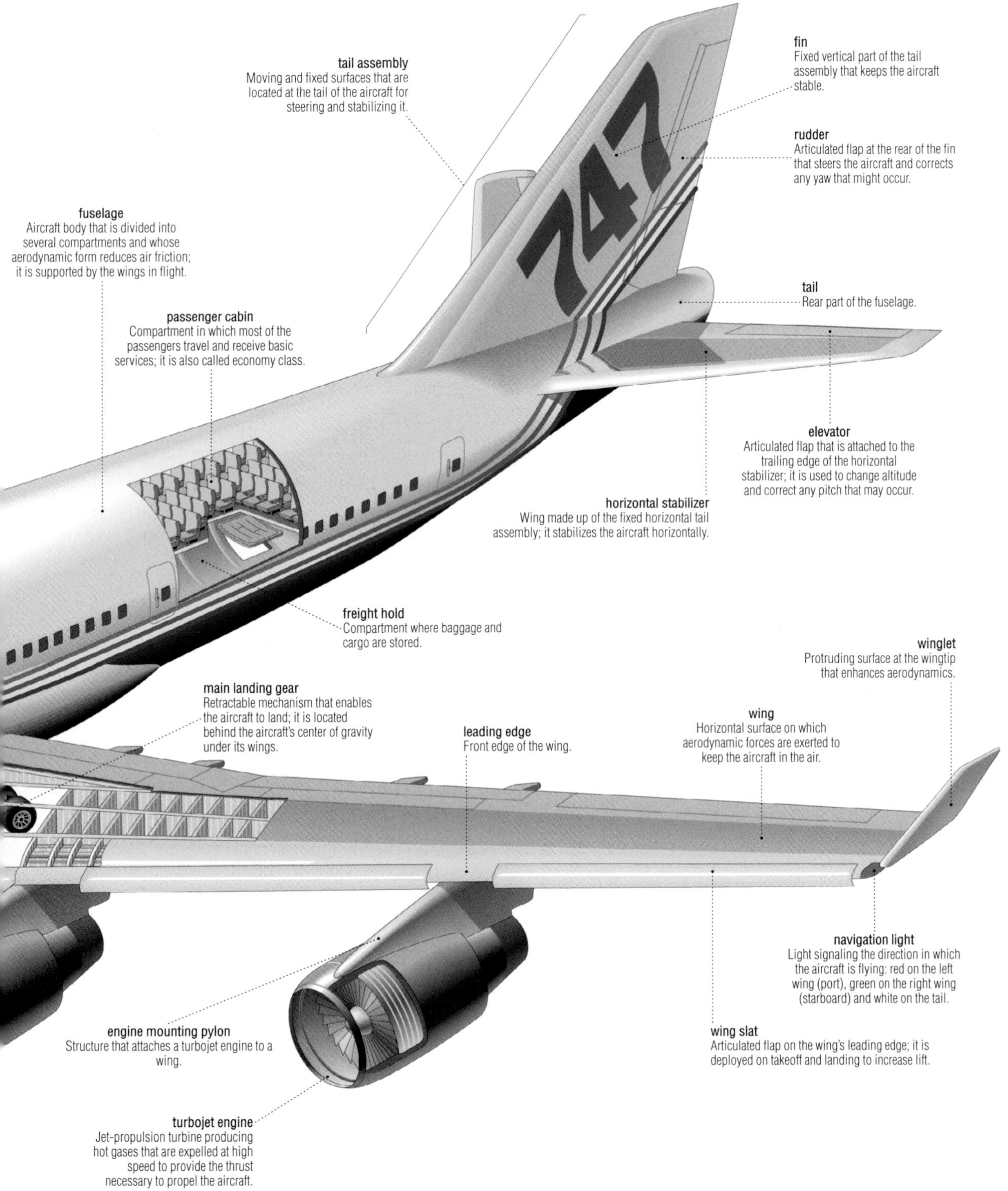
fin
Fixed vertical part of the tail assembly that keeps the aircraft stable.
tail assembly
Moving and fixed surfaces that are located at the tail of the aircraft for steering and stabilizing it.
rudder
Articulated flap at the rear of the fin that steers the aircraft and corrects any yaw that might occur.
747
fuselage
Aircraft body that is divided into several compartments and whose aerodynamic form reduces air friction; it is supported by the wings in flight.
tail
Rear part of the fuselage.
passenger cabin
Compartment in which most of the passengers travel and receive basic services; it is also called economy class.
elevator
Articulated flap that is attached to the trailing edge of the horizontal stabilizer; it is used to change altitude and correct any pitch that may occur.
horizontal stabilizer
Wing made up of the fixed horizontal tail assembly; it stabilizes the aircraft horizontally.
freight hold
Compartment where baggage and cargo are stored.
winglet
Protruding surface at the wingtip that enhances aerodynamics.
main landing gear
Retractable mechanism that enables the aircraft to land; it is located behind the aircraft's center of gravity under its wings.
wing
Horizontal surface on which aerodynamic forces are exerted to keep the aircraft in the air.
leading edge
Front edge of the wing.
navigation light
Light signaling the direction in which the aircraft is flying: red on the left wing (port), green on the right wing (starboard) and white on the tail.
engine mounting pylon
Structure that attaches a turbojet engine to a wing.
wing slat
Articulated flap on the wing's leading edge; it is deployed on takeoff and landing to increase lift.
turbojet engine
Jet-propulsion turbine producing hot gases that are expelled at high speed to provide the thrust necessary to propel the aircraft.

flight deck

Compartment that contains navigation equipment and controls and from which the crew pilots the aircraft.

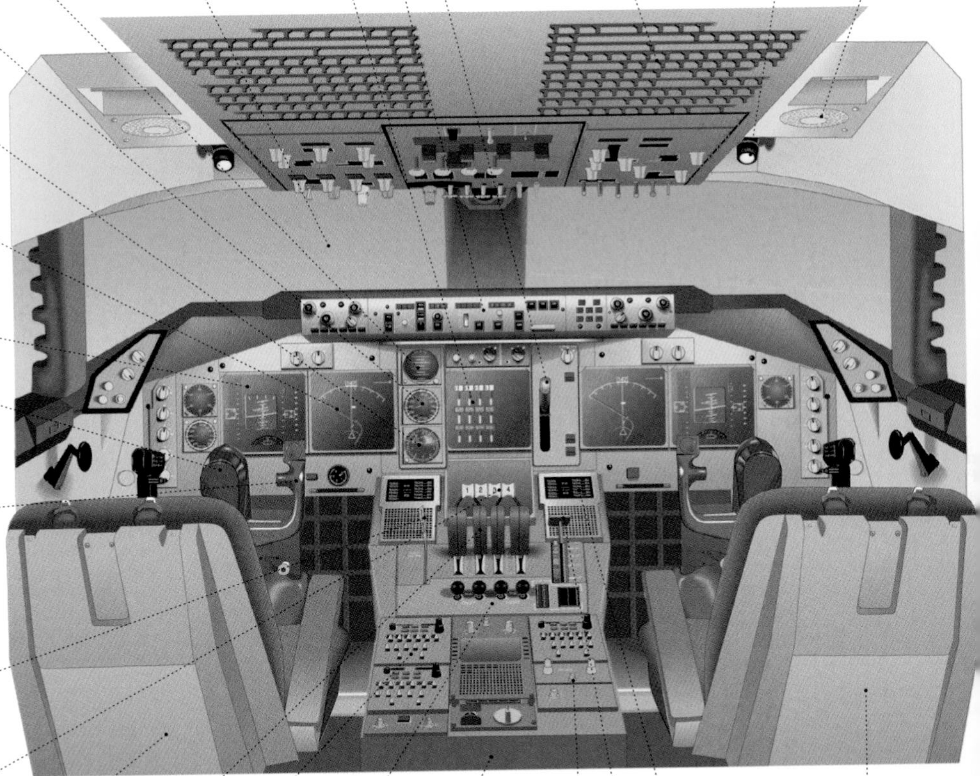

speaker
Integrated device that relays audible messages such as alarms to the pilots.

autopilot controls
Device that enables the aircraft to be piloted and kept on course automatically.

landing gear lever
Control for lowering and raising the landing gear.

lighting
Device that diffuses light over a shelf on which the pilots place navigation charts.

engine and crew alarm display
Screen that controls the engines and displays alarm signals in the event of system failure.

standby attitude indicator
Screen that shows the aircraft's position in relation to the horizon; it is used in the event the flight display fails.

windshield
Highly durable pane made of glass and plastic that provides good visibility.

overhead switch panel
Panel made up of the switches that cut the hydraulic, electric and fuel circuits.

standby airspeed indicator
Instrument that shows the aircraft's speed; it is used in the event the flight display fails.

standby altimeter
Instrument that shows the vertical distance between the aircraft and the ground; it is used in the event the flight display fails.

navigation display
Screen that shows the aircraft's position and flight plan and weather conditions.

primary flight display
Screen that shows the main parameters necessary for piloting (aircraft's position in relation to the horizon, altitude and course).

control column
Steering component that causes an aircraft to bank to the left or to the right and to ascend or descend.

control wheel
Lever that activates the control column from back to front and from side to side.

speedbrake lever
Command stick that releases the wing flaps to brake the aircraft immediately after landing.

systems display
Screen that controls various systems, such as air pressure and the electric and hydraulic circuits.

first officer's seat
Right seat occupied by the copilot, who is second in command.

captain's seat
Left seat occupied by the pilot, who is in charge of the flight and the crew.

transponder
Instruments that, with the autopilot, control the engine power and guide the aircraft on its course.

throttles
Control levers for the engines; they regulate speed and thrust.

flap lever
Control stick that activates the wing slats and the trailing edge flaps.

communication panels
Panel for selecting radio frequencies on which pilots can send or receive.

engine fuel valves
Knobs for opening and shutting the fuel supply to the engines.

control console
Component located between the two seats that contains part of the instrumentation.

air data computer
Computer that calculates the flight parameters (speed, altitude and course).

turbofan engine

Jet engine with a fan and two airflows; one airflow passes through the combustion chamber and the other bypasses it.

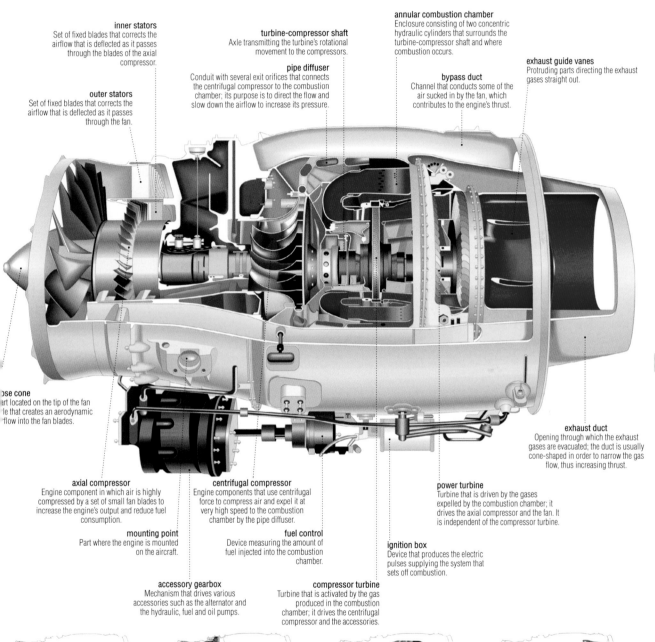

inner stators
Set of fixed blades that corrects the airflow that is deflected as it passes through the blades of the axial compressor.

outer stators
Set of fixed blades that corrects the airflow that is deflected as it passes through the fan.

turbine-compressor shaft
Axle transmitting the turbine's rotational movement to the compressors.

pipe diffuser
Conduit with several exit orifices that connects the centrifugal compressor to the combustion chamber; its purpose is to direct the flow and slow down the airflow to increase its pressure.

annular combustion chamber
Enclosure consisting of two concentric hydraulic cylinders that surrounds the turbine-compressor shaft and where combustion occurs.

bypass duct
Channel that conducts some of the air sucked in by the fan, which contributes to the engine's thrust.

exhaust guide vanes
Protruding parts directing the exhaust gases straight out.

ose cone
art located on the tip of the fan le that creates an aerodynamic flow into the fan blades.

exhaust duct
Opening through which the exhaust gases are evacuated; the duct is usually cone-shaped in order to narrow the gas flow, thus increasing thrust.

axial compressor
Engine component in which air is highly compressed by a set of small fan blades to increase the engine's output and reduce fuel consumption.

mounting point
Part where the engine is mounted on the aircraft.

centrifugal compressor
Engine components that use centrifugal force to compress air and expel it at very high speed to the combustion chamber by the pipe diffuser.

fuel control
Device measuring the amount of fuel injected into the combustion chamber.

power turbine
Turbine that is driven by the gases expelled by the combustion chamber; it drives the axial compressor and the fan. It is independent of the compressor turbine.

ignition box
Device that produces the electric pulses supplying the system that sets off combustion.

accessory gearbox
Mechanism that drives various accessories such as the alternator and the hydraulic, fuel and oil pumps.

compressor turbine
Turbine that is activated by the gas produced in the combustion chamber; it drives the centrifugal compressor and the accessories.

fan
Blower sucking air into the turbofan engine.

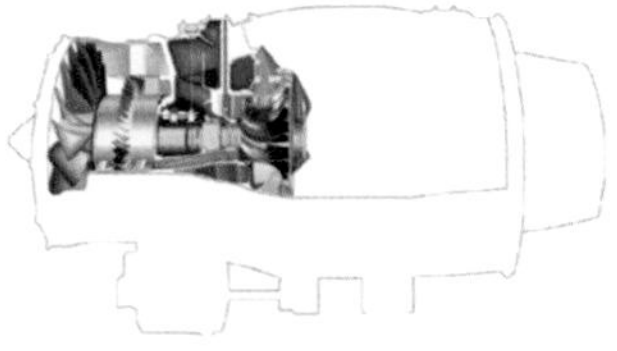

compression
Phase during which some of the air flowing through the engine is compressed before it enters the combustion chamber.

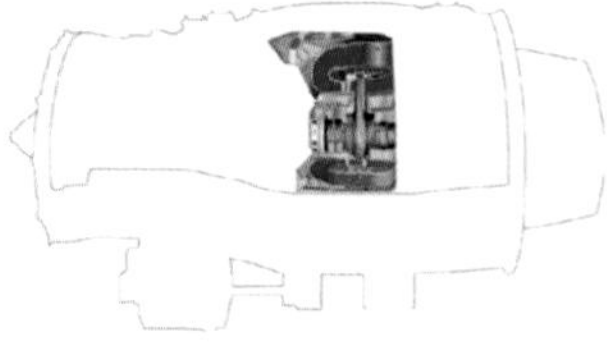

combustion
Phase during which the compressed air enters the combustion chamber, where it is mixed with fuel and ignited.

exhaust
Phase during which the air expands and produces a thrust that activates the turbines and propels the turbofan engine.

examples of airplanes

Ever since the first airplane, Éole, in 1890, the shape of aircraft has evolved constantly as new aerodynamic discoveries were made and engine power increased.

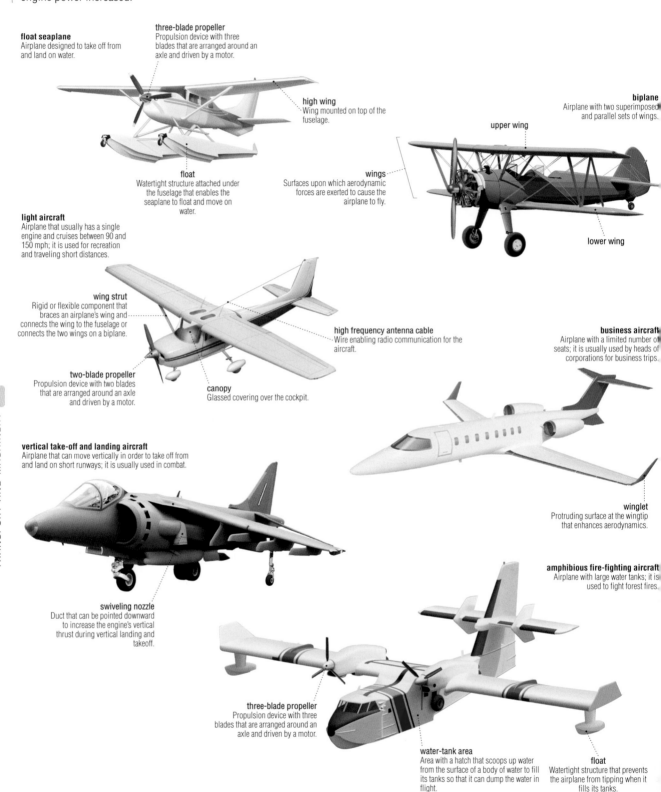

float seaplane
Airplane designed to take off from and land on water.

three-blade propeller
Propulsion device with three blades that are arranged around an axle and driven by a motor.
high wing
Wing mounted on top of the fuselage.
float
Watertight structure attached under the fuselage that enables the seaplane to float and move on water.

biplane
Airplane with two superimposed and parallel sets of wings.

upper wing
wings
Surfaces upon which aerodynamic forces are exerted to cause the airplane to fly.
lower wing

light aircraft
Airplane that usually has a single engine and cruises between 90 and 150 mph; it is used for recreation and traveling short distances.

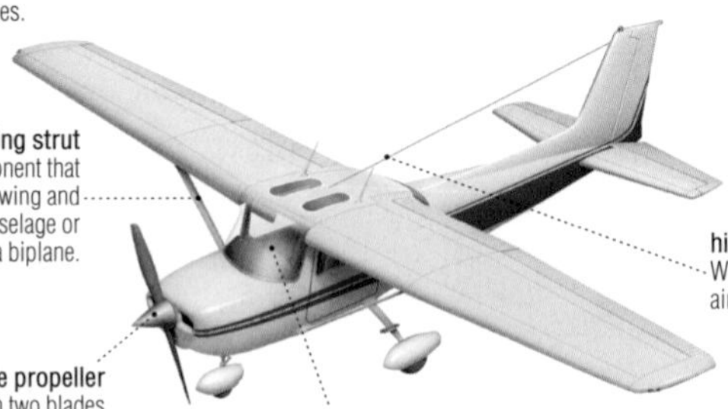
wing strut
Rigid or flexible component that braces an airplane's wing and connects the wing to the fuselage or connects the two wings on a biplane.
high frequency antenna cable
Wire enabling radio communication for the aircraft.
two-blade propeller
Propulsion device with two blades that are arranged around an axle and driven by a motor.
canopy
Glassed covering over the cockpit.

business aircraft
Airplane with a limited number of seats; it is usually used by heads of corporations for business trips.

winglet
Protruding surface at the wingtip that enhances aerodynamics.

vertical take-off and landing aircraft
Airplane that can move vertically in order to take off from and land on short runways; it is usually used in combat.

swiveling nozzle
Duct that can be pointed downward to increase the engine's vertical thrust during vertical landing and takeoff.

amphibious fire-fighting aircraft
Airplane with large water tanks; it is used to fight forest fires.

three-blade propeller
Propulsion device with three blades that are arranged around an axle and driven by a motor.
water-tank area
Area with a hatch that scoops up water from the surface of a body of water to fill its tanks so that it can dump the water in flight.
float
Watertight structure that prevents the airplane from tipping when it fills its tanks.

examples of airplanes

stealth aircraft
Aircraft that cannot be detected by radar because of the radar-absorbing facets covering its fuselage.

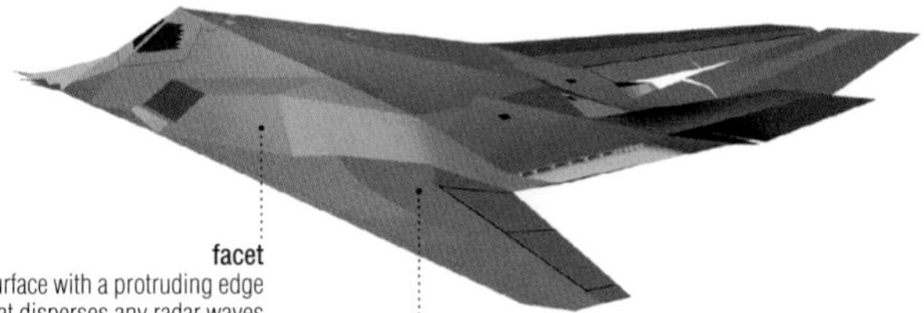

facet
Flat surface with a protruding edge that disperses any radar waves hitting it and makes them undetectable.

radar-absorbent material
Material that absorbs radar waves before they strike any metal part of the aircraft in order to muffle the sound of the echo.

radar aircraft
Surveillance aircraft for locating and identifying aircraft in flight.

rotodome
Domelike rotating structure that houses radar antennae.

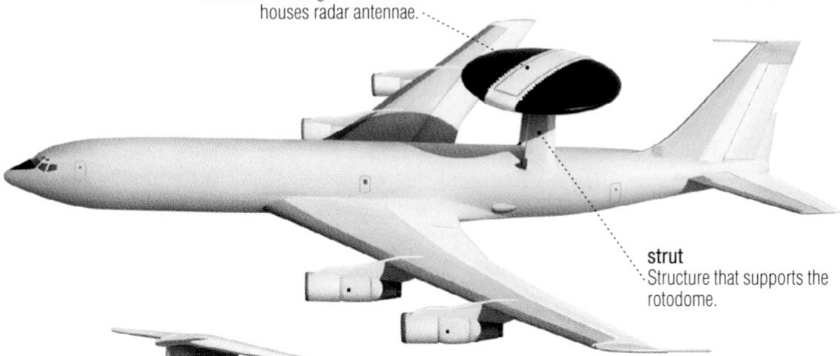

strut
Structure that supports the rotodome.

cargo aircraft
Plane with large freight capacity; it is used to transport goods.

supersonic jetliner
Passenger aircraft whose cruising speed (1500 mph) is faster than the speed of sound (761 mph). The Concorde was the best known commercial aircraft of this type.

variable ejector nozzle
Duct whose mouth widens as the plane climbs, thus enabling the engines to increase output.

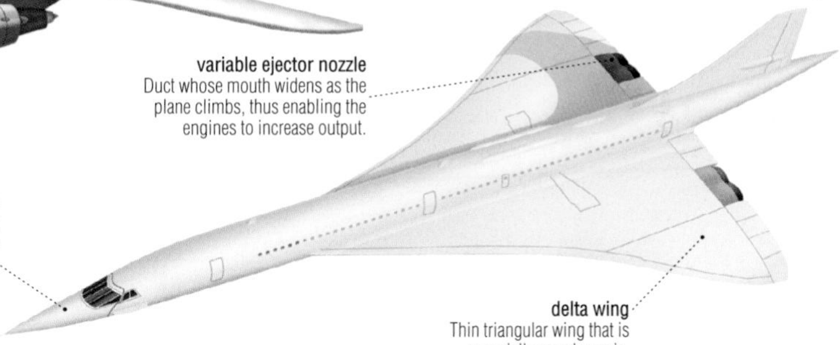

droop nose
Articulated nose that is lowered on takeoff and landing to provide the pilot with better visibility.

delta wing
Thin triangular wing that is especially aerodynamic.

examples of tail shapes

Moving and fixed surfaces that are located at the tail of the aircraft for steering and stabilizing it.

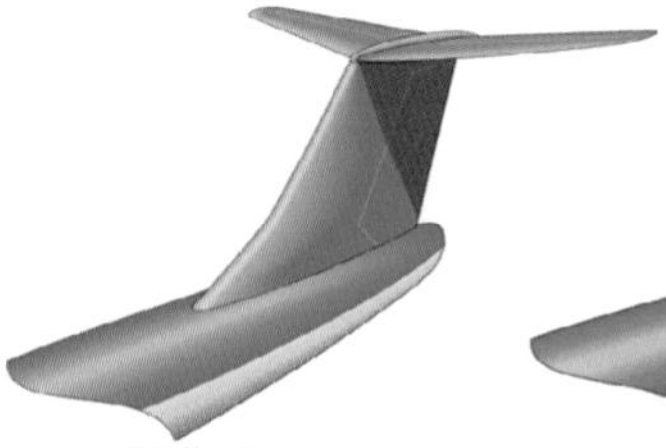

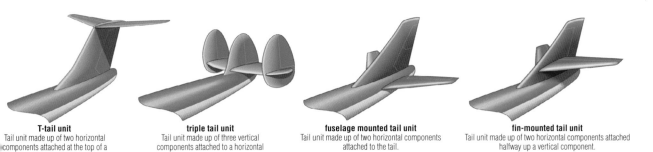

T-tail unit
Tail unit made up of two horizontal components attached at the top of a vertical component.

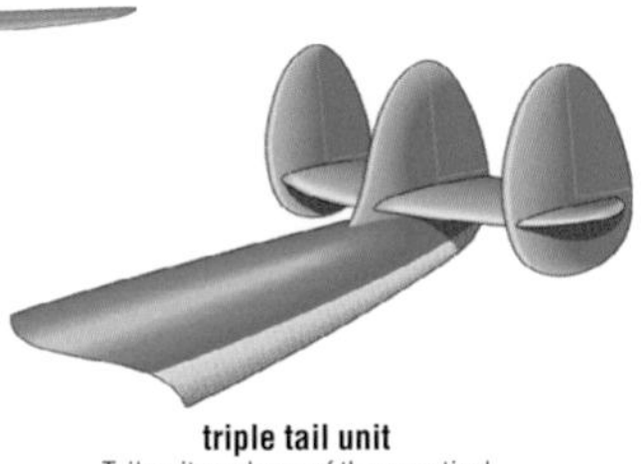

triple tail unit
Tail unit made up of three vertical components attached to a horizontal component.

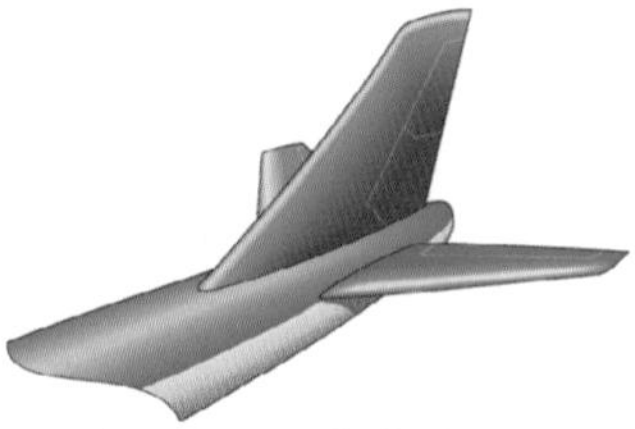

fuselage mounted tail unit
Tail unit made up of two horizontal components attached to the tail.

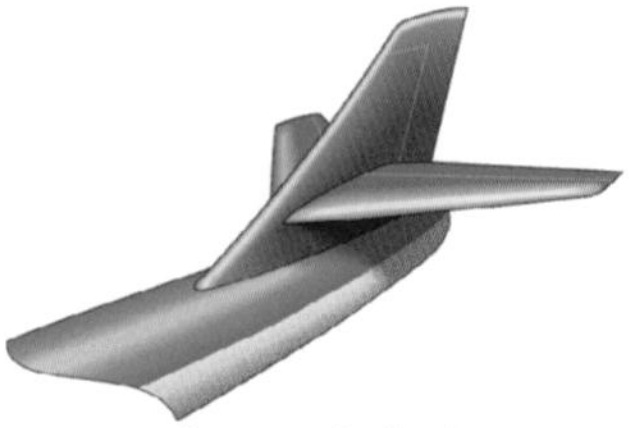

fin-mounted tail unit
Tail unit made up of two horizontal components attached halfway up a vertical component.

examples of wing shapes

From one era to the next and depending on the type of aircraft, the shape and position of the wings in relation to the fuselage has varied.

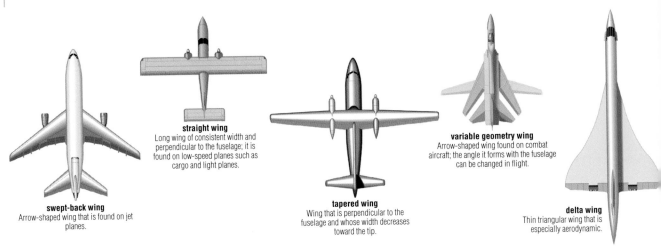

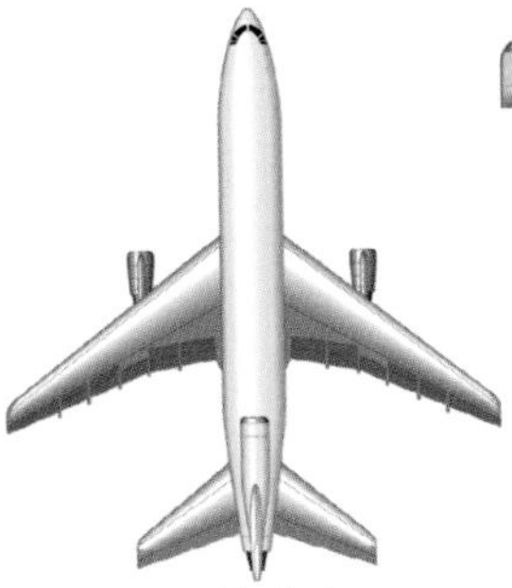

swept-back wing
Arrow-shaped wing that is found on jet planes.

straight wing
Long wing of consistent width and perpendicular to the fuselage; it is found on low-speed planes such as cargo and light planes.

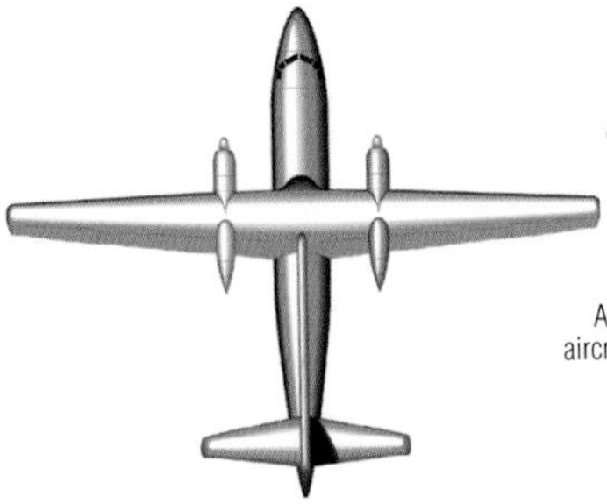

tapered wing
Wing that is perpendicular to the fuselage and whose width decreases toward the tip.

variable geometry wing
Arrow-shaped wing found on combat aircraft; the angle it forms with the fuselage can be changed in flight.

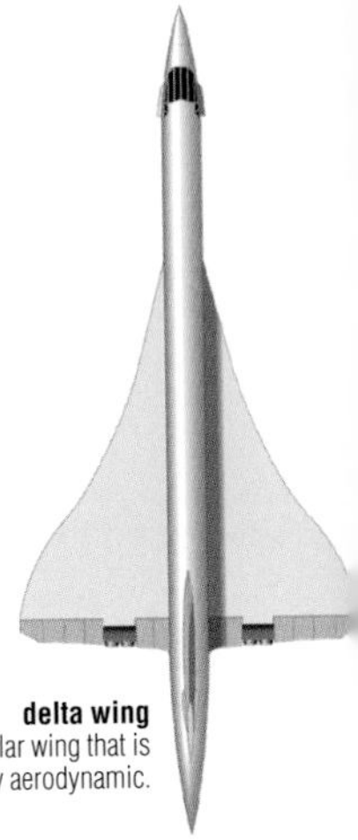

delta wing
Thin triangular wing that is especially aerodynamic.

forces acting on an airplane

Physical phenomena that affect the movement of an aircraft in flight.

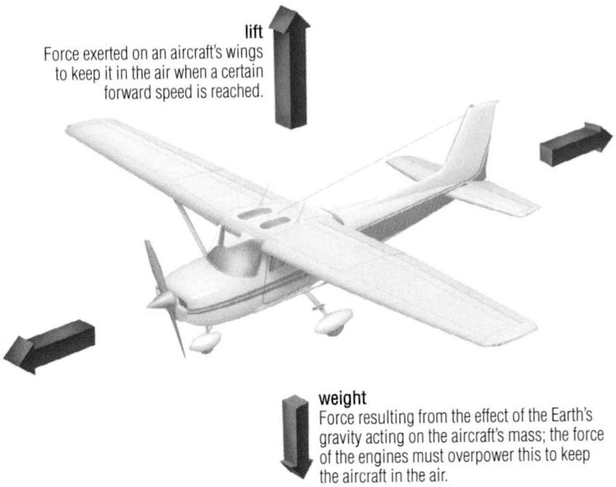

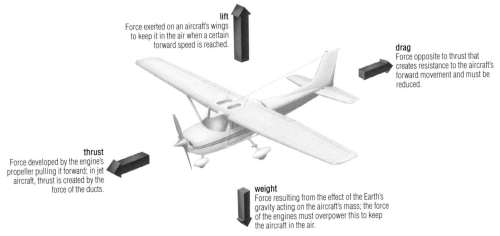

lift
Force exerted on an aircraft's wings to keep it in the air when a certain forward speed is reached.

drag
Force opposite to thrust that creates resistance to the aircraft's forward movement and must be reduced.

thrust
Force developed by the engine's propeller pulling it forward; in jet aircraft, thrust is created by the force of the ducts.

weight
Force resulting from the effect of the Earth's gravity acting on the aircraft's mass; the force of the engines must overpower this to keep the aircraft in the air.

movements of an airplane

Changes exerted on an aircraft in flight that affect its behavior; a pilot must know how to correct them.

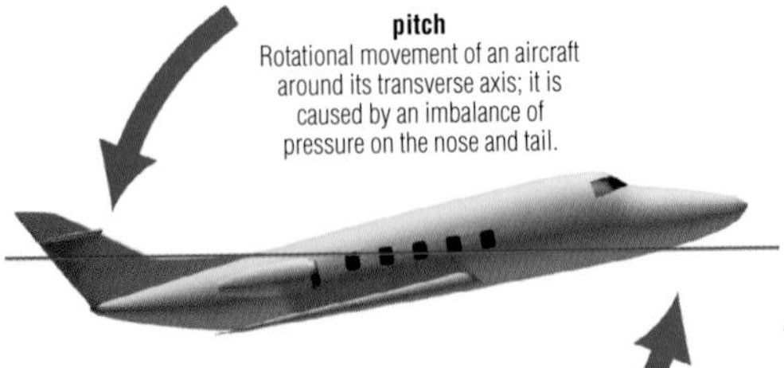

pitch
Rotational movement of an aircraft around its transverse axis; it is caused by an imbalance of pressure on the nose and tail.

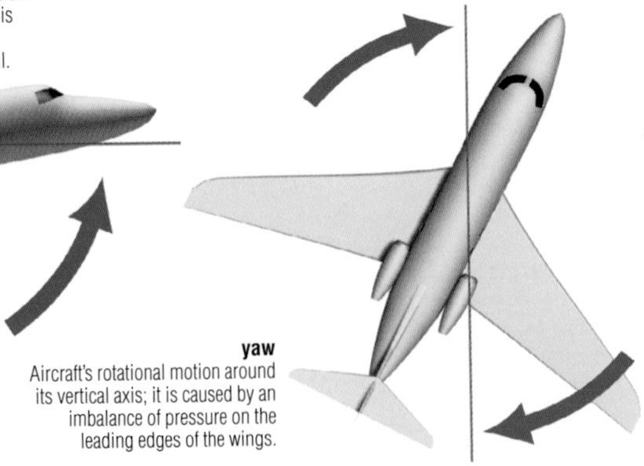

yaw
Aircraft's rotational motion around its vertical axis; it is caused by an imbalance of pressure on the leading edges of the wings.

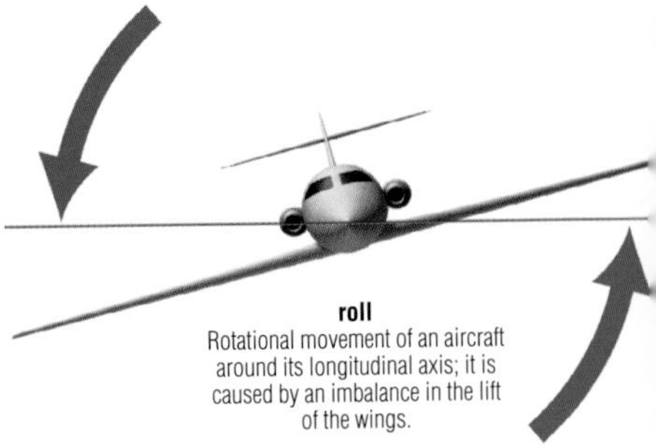

roll
Rotational movement of an aircraft around its longitudinal axis; it is caused by an imbalance in the lift of the wings.

helicopter

Aircraft whose lift agent is a rotor on a vertical axle.

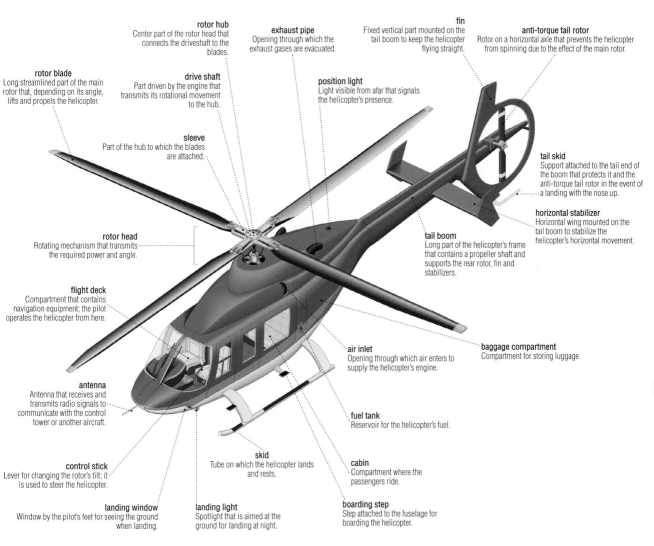

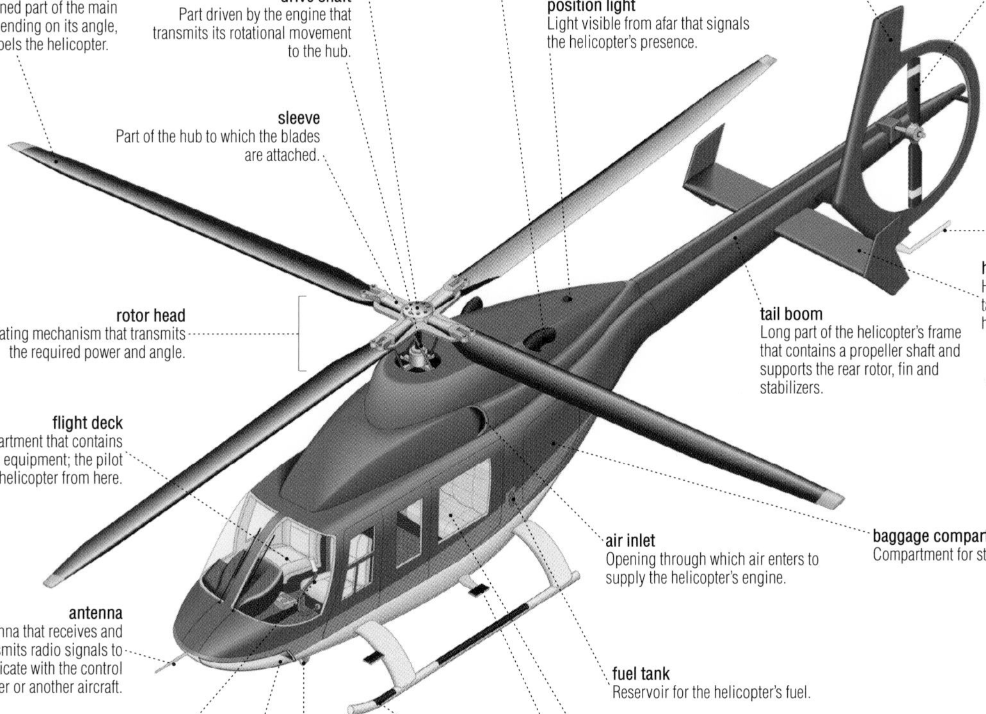
rotor hub
Center part of the rotor head that connects the driveshaft to the blades.
exhaust pipe
Opening through which the exhaust gases are evacuated.
fin
Fixed vertical part mounted on the tail boom to keep the helicopter flying straight.
anti-torque tail rotor
Rotor on a horizontal axle that prevents the helicopter from spinning due to the effect of the main rotor.
rotor blade
Long streamlined part of the main rotor that, depending on its angle, lifts and propels the helicopter.
drive shaft
Part driven by the engine that transmits its rotational movement to the hub.
position light
Light visible from afar that signals the helicopter's presence.
sleeve
Part of the hub to which the blades are attached.
tail skid
Support attached to the tail end of the boom that protects it and the anti-torque tail rotor in the event of a landing with the nose up.
horizontal stabilizer
Horizontal wing mounted on the tail boom to stabilize the helicopter's horizontal movement.
rotor head
Rotating mechanism that transmits the required power and angle.
tail boom
Long part of the helicopter's frame that contains a propeller shaft and supports the rear rotor, fin and stabilizers.
flight deck
Compartment that contains navigation equipment; the pilot operates the helicopter from here.
air inlet
Opening through which air enters to supply the helicopter's engine.
baggage compartment
Compartment for storing luggage.
antenna
Antenna that receives and transmits radio signals to communicate with the control tower or another aircraft.
fuel tank
Reservoir for the helicopter's fuel.
skid
Tube on which the helicopter lands and rests.
control stick
Lever for changing the rotor's tilt; it is used to steer the helicopter.
cabin
Compartment where the passengers ride.
landing window
Window by the pilot's feet for seeing the ground when landing.
landing light
Spotlight that is aimed at the ground for landing at night.
boarding step
Step attached to the fuselage for boarding the helicopter.

examples of helicopters

Because they can take off and land vertically, helicopters are more effective than airplanes in certain situations.

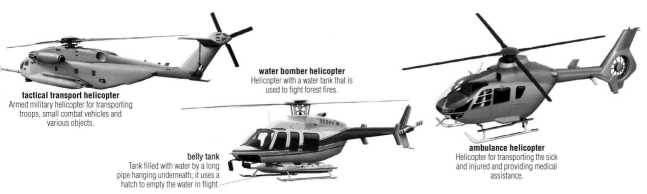

tactical transport helicopter
Armed military helicopter for transporting troops, small combat vehicles and various objects.

belly tank
Tank filled with water by a long pipe hanging underneath; it uses a hatch to empty the water in flight.

water bomber helicopter
Helicopter with a water tank that is used to fight forest fires.

ambulance helicopter
Helicopter for transporting the sick and injured and providing medical assistance.

material handling

Machines and equipment used to move and stack goods in a store or warehouse.

forklift truck
Motorized cart for lifting and moving pallets to stack them or load them onto a truck.

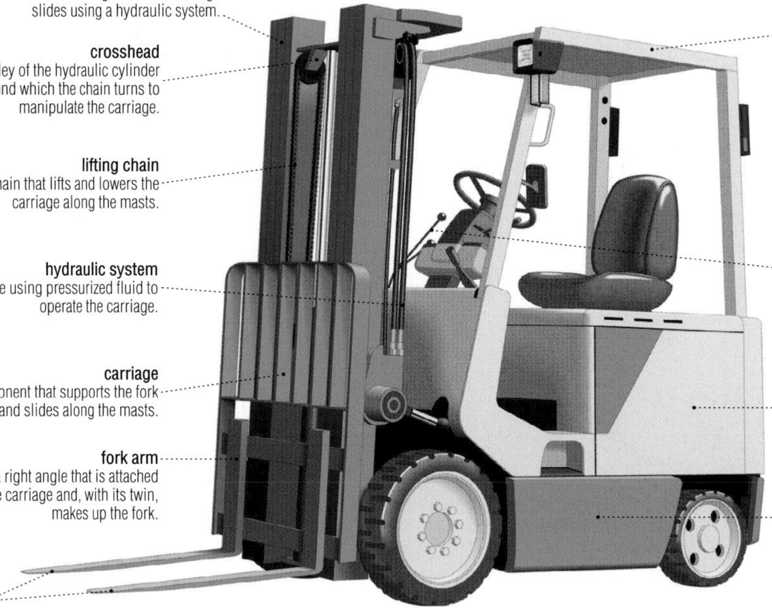
mast
Post along which the carriage slides using a hydraulic system.
crosshead
Upper pulley of the hydraulic cylinder around which the chain turns to manipulate the carriage.
lifting chain
Chain that lifts and lowers the carriage along the masts.
hydraulic system
Device using pressurized fluid to operate the carriage.
carriage
Component that supports the fork arms and slides along the masts.
fork arm
Part at a right angle that is attached to the carriage and, with its twin, makes up the fork.
fork
Instrument made up of two arms that is inserted into a pallet's entry to lift it.
overhead guard
Metal framework that protects the operator and the cab against falling goods.
mast operating lever
Lever controlled by the operator to move the carriage along the masts.
engine compartment
Electric motor or combustion engine that supplies the power to propel the truck and operate the fork.
frame
Forklift truck's metal structure.

pallets
Usually wooden platform for loads; forklift and hydraulic pallet trucks can slip their forks underneath them in order to handle goods.

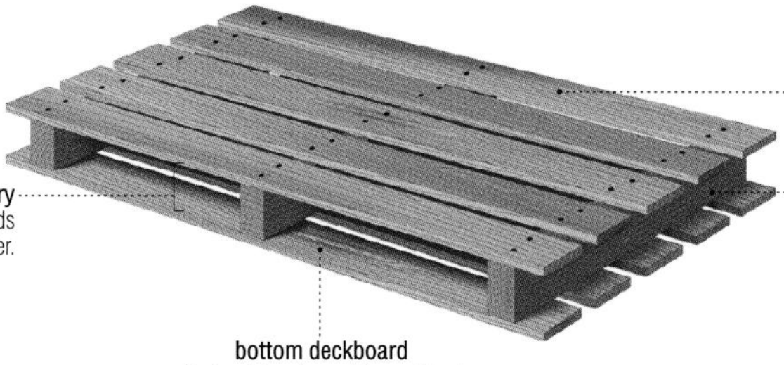
wing pallet
Pallet with overhang on one or both of its deckboards.
entry
Space between the deckboards through which the fork arms enter.
top deckboard
Flat horizontal surface with or without gaps between the planks; the goods rest on it.
stringer
Part supporting the deckboards and providing the gap for the fork arms to fit through.
bottom deckboard
Horizontal surface with or without gaps that is attached to the stringer and rests on the ground.

box pallet
Pallet with three or four sides; it is used to handle bulk merchandise.

side
Wall with or without gaps between the planks that slides back or can be removed; it keeps the goods in place and can withstand loads stacked on top.
pallet
Part of the box pallet supporting the load; it supports the box pallet on the ground and provides the place where the forks enter.
block
Supporting part underneath the deckboard that is wide enough to allow the fork arms to enter.
half-side
Half wall that is sometimes detachable; it facilitates the loading and unloading of the contents of the pallet.

double-decked palle
Pallet with an upper and lowe deckboard that is sometimes reversible

single-decked palle
Pallet with one deckboard

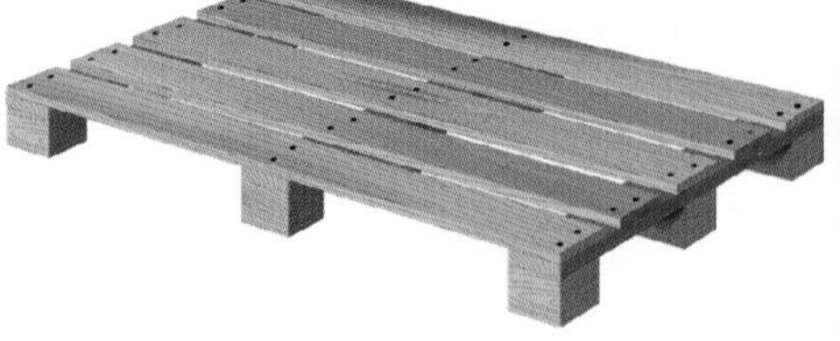

ydraulic pallet truck
art with a fork for stacking loads at various eights.

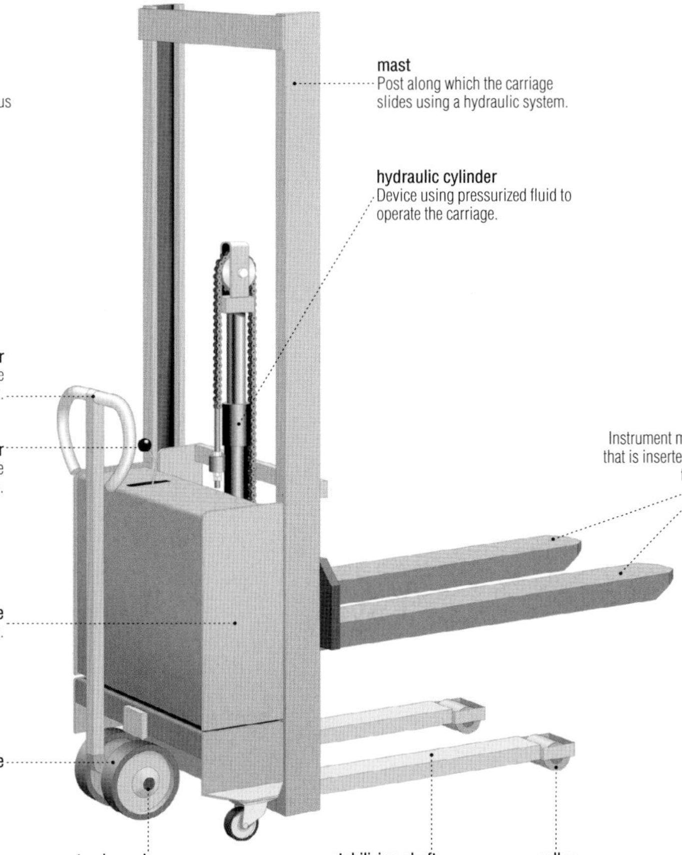

mast
Post along which the carriage slides using a hydraulic system.

hydraulic cylinder
Device using pressurized fluid to operate the carriage.

steering lever
Column linked to the steering axle for manually steering the truck.

mast control lever
Lever controlled by the operator to move the carriage along the masts.

fork
Instrument made up of two arms that is inserted into a pallet's entry to lift it.

frame
Metal structure of the truck.

solid rubber tire

steering axle
Pivoting rod connecting two wheel hubs; it rotates on a vertical assembly to change the direction of the truck when moving it.

stabilizing shaft
Long part that is placed parallel to one of the forks to balance the truck while it lifts a load, thus avoiding tipping.

roller

hand truck
Pivoting device with a nose plate that slides under a load and is then tipped up to move it.

pallet truck
Hand truck with a fork and a hydraulic system for lifting pallets slightly and moving them.

platform pallet truck
Hand truck with a metal frame that can be lowered to lift a deckboard and its load slightly and move it.

flatbed pushcart
Hand truck with a frame that supports a deckboard where the load to be moved is placed.

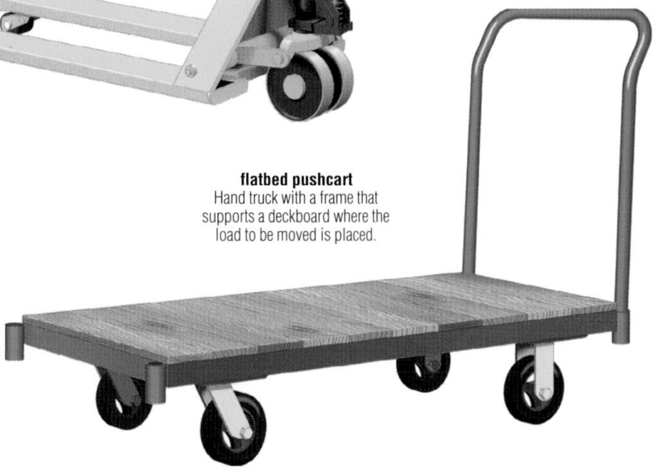

cranes

Examples of lifting devices for picking up and moving very heavy loads.

tower crane
Crane used on construction sites with a usually horizontal jib mounted on top of a tower.

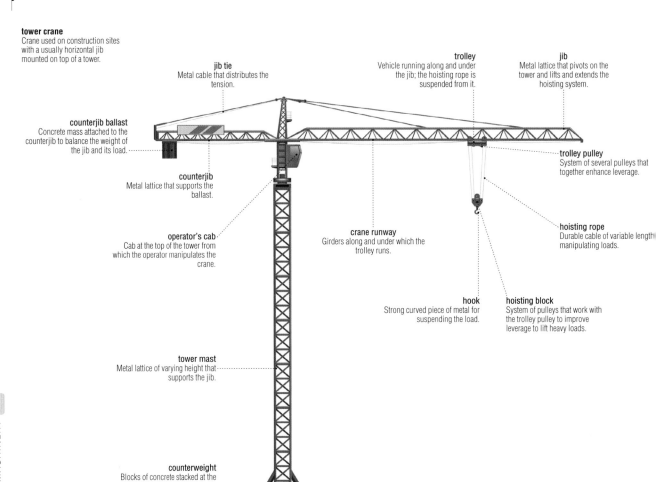

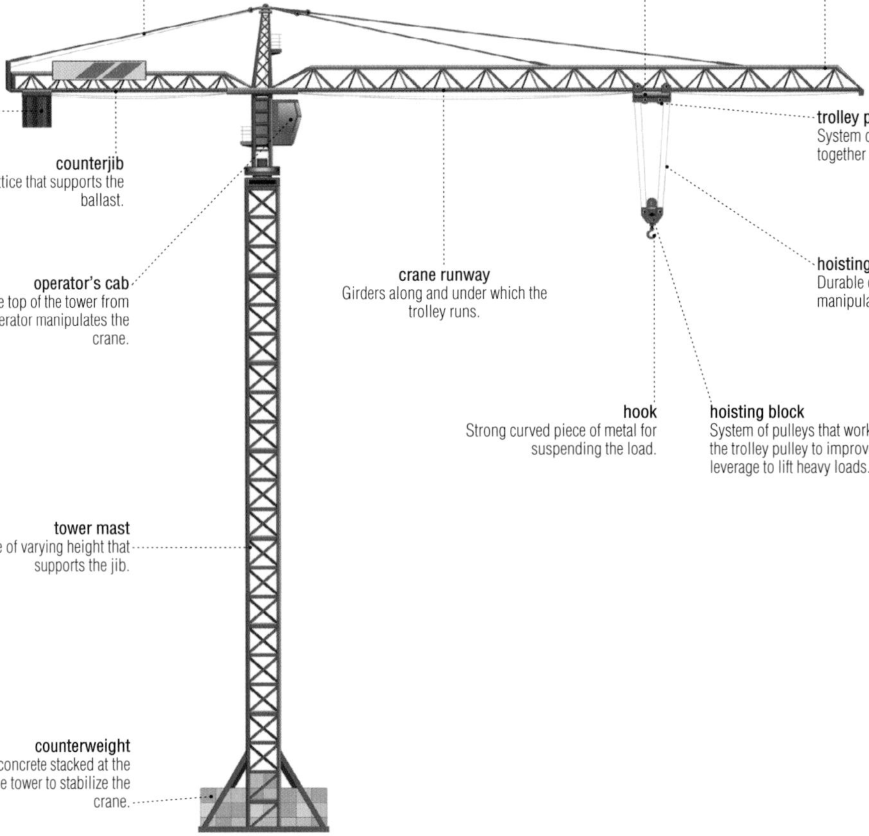
jib tie
Metal cable that distributes the tension.
trolley
Vehicle running along and under the jib; the hoisting rope is suspended from it.
jib
Metal lattice that pivots on the tower and lifts and extends the hoisting system.
counterjib ballast
Concrete mass attached to the counterjib to balance the weight of the jib and its load.
trolley pulley
System of several pulleys that together enhance leverage.
counterjib
Metal lattice that supports the ballast.
hoisting rope
Durable cable of variable length manipulating loads.
crane runway
Girders along and under which the trolley runs.
operator's cab
Cab at the top of the tower from which the operator manipulates the crane.
hook
Strong curved piece of metal for suspending the load.
hoisting block
System of pulleys that work with the trolley pulley to improve leverage to lift heavy loads.
tower mast
Metal lattice of varying height that supports the jib.
counterweight
Blocks of concrete stacked at the base of the tower to stabilize the crane.

truck crane
Mobile telescopic crane that is mounted on the chassis of a straight truck.

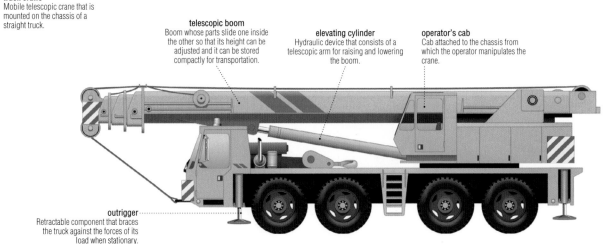

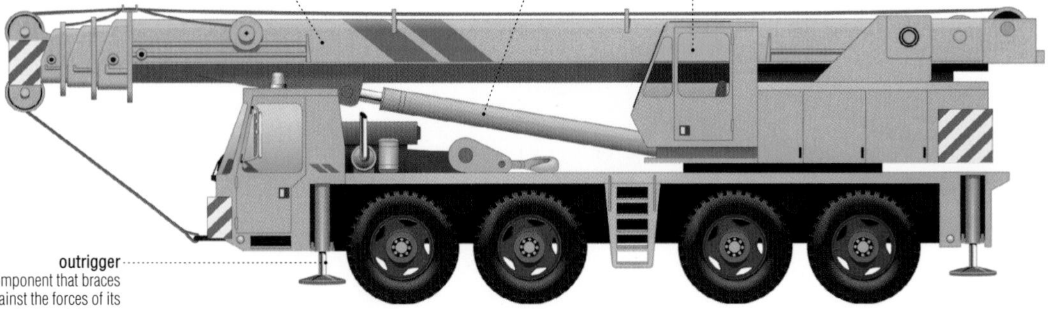
telescopic boom
Boom whose parts slide one inside the other so that its height can be adjusted and it can be stored compactly for transportation.
elevating cylinder
Hydraulic device that consists of a telescopic arm for raising and lowering the boom.
operator's cab
Cab attached to the chassis from which the operator manipulates the crane.
outrigger
Retractable component that braces the truck against the forces of its load when stationary.

cranes

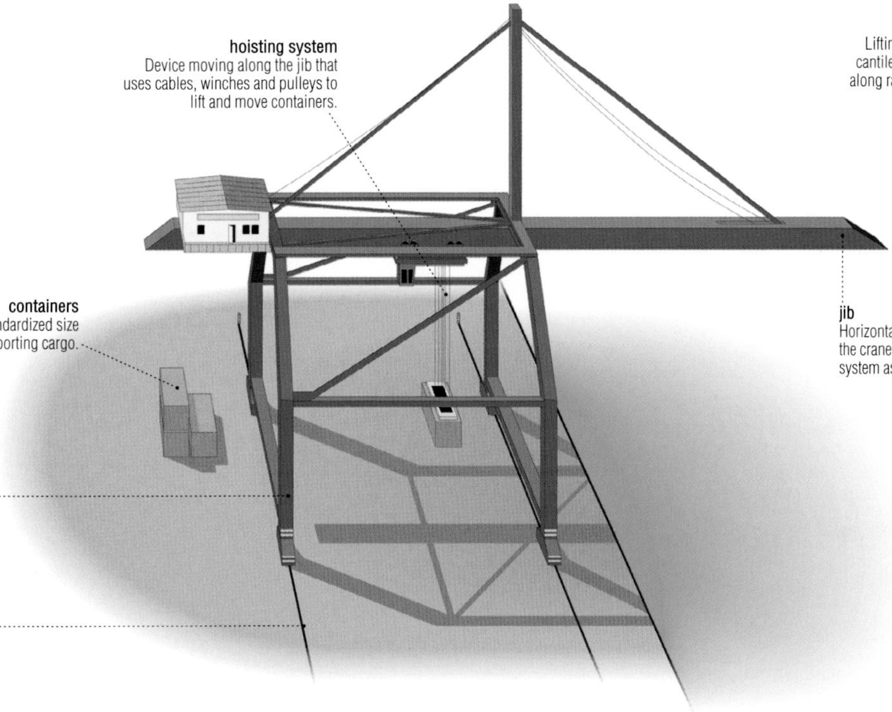

hoisting system
Device moving along the jib that uses cables, winches and pulleys to lift and move containers.
gantry crane
Lifting device with posts and cantilevered girders that move along rails or on tires to handle containers.
containers
Metal boxes of standardized size for transporting cargo.
jib
Horizontal component overhanging the crane that extends the hoisting system as far out as possible.
tower
Post that supports the crane.
running track
Rail along which the crane moves.

container

Metal box of standardized size for transporting cargo.

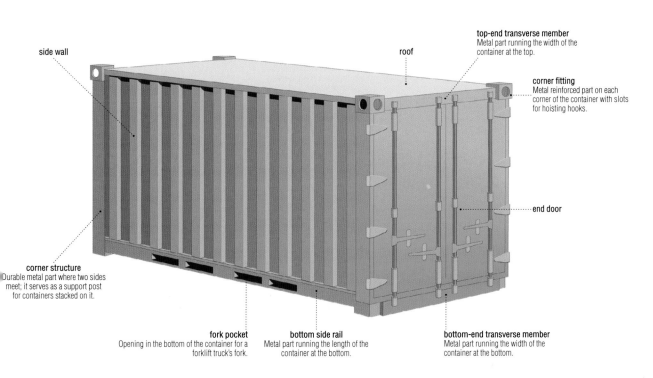

side wall
roof
top-end transverse member
Metal part running the width of the container at the top.
corner fitting
Metal reinforced part on each corner of the container with slots for hoisting hooks.
end door
corner structure
Durable metal part where two sides meet; it serves as a support post for containers stacked on it.
fork pocket
Opening in the bottom of the container for a forklift truck's fork.
bottom side rail
Metal part running the length of the container at the bottom.
bottom-end transverse member
Metal part running the width of the container at the bottom.

bulldozer

Excavation machine for pushing materials; it is made up of a crawler tractor, a blade and often a ripper.

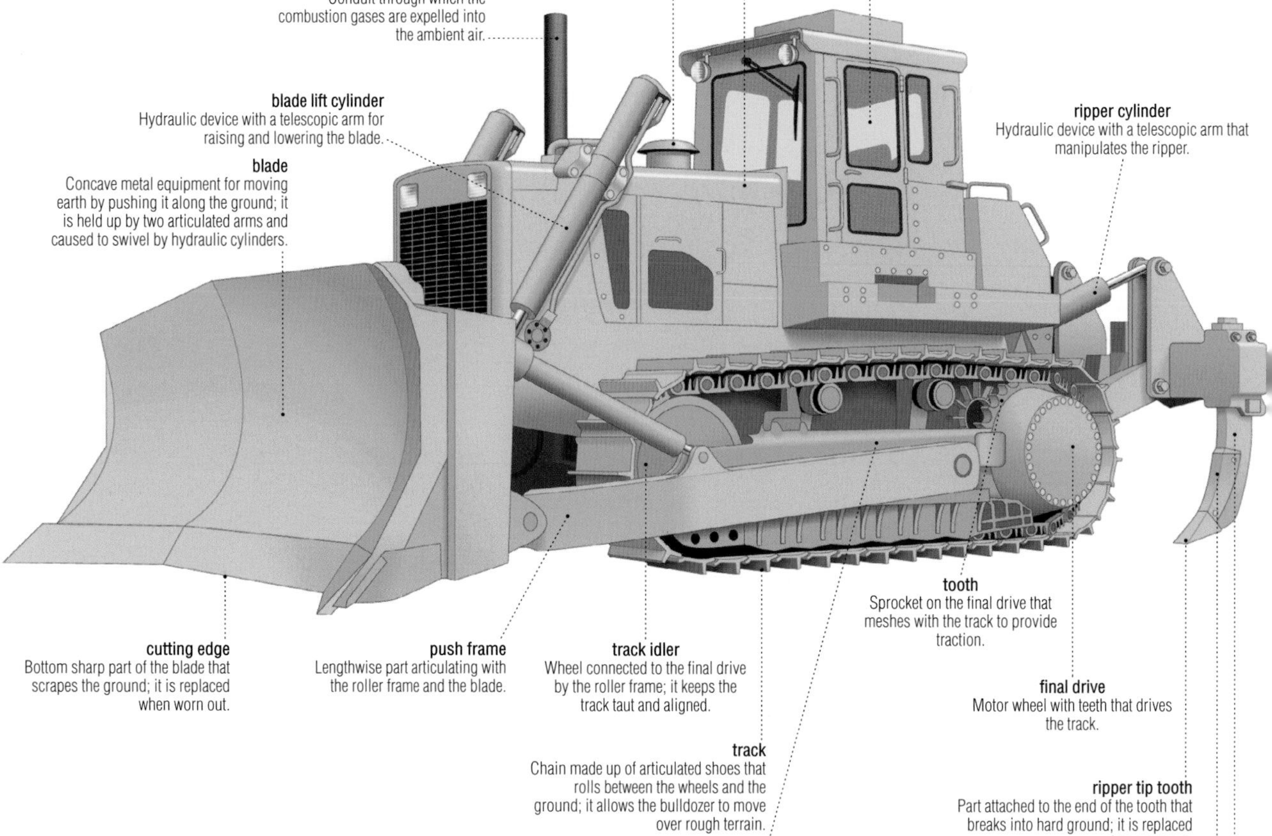

air pre-cleaner filter
Device that removes dust from the air entering the engine.
diesel motor compartment
Combustion engine in which the compressed air becomes sufficiently hot to ignite the injected fuel.
cab
Compartment from which the operator controls the bulldozer.
exhaust pipe stack
Conduit through which the combustion gases are expelled into the ambient air.
blade lift cylinder
Hydraulic device with a telescopic arm for raising and lowering the blade.
blade
Concave metal equipment for moving earth by pushing it along the ground; it is held up by two articulated arms and caused to swivel by hydraulic cylinders.
ripper cylinder
Hydraulic device with a telescopic arm that manipulates the ripper.
cutting edge
Bottom sharp part of the blade that scrapes the ground; it is replaced when worn out.
push frame
Lengthwise part articulating with the roller frame and the blade.
track idler
Wheel connected to the final drive by the roller frame; it keeps the track taut and aligned.
tooth
Sprocket on the final drive that meshes with the track to provide traction.
final drive
Motor wheel with teeth that drives the track.
track
Chain made up of articulated shoes that rolls between the wheels and the ground; it allows the bulldozer to move over rough terrain.
track roller frame
Lengthwise part forming the track's chassis; the final drive and the track idler are attached to it.
ripper tip tooth
Part attached to the end of the tooth that breaks into hard ground; it is replaced when worn out.
shank protector
Part attached on the inner side of a tooth to brace the tooth; it is replaced when worn out.
ripper shank
Part of the ripper that digs into the ground to break it up.

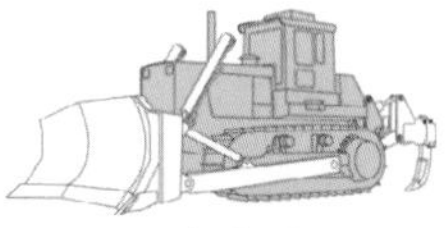

crawler tractor
Machine that can move along rough ground by means of two tracks; it is equipped with a blade and a ripper.

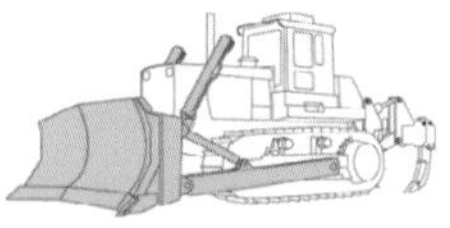

blade
Concave metal equipment for moving earth by pushing it along the ground; it is held up by two articulated arms and caused to swivel by hydraulic cylinders.

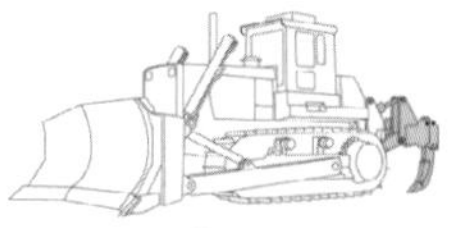

ripper
Equipment for breaking up hard earth; it is made up of a frame fitted with one to three teeth and is mounted on the back of a bulldozer.

wheel loader

Excavation machine made up of a wheel tractor, a backhoe and a front-end loader.

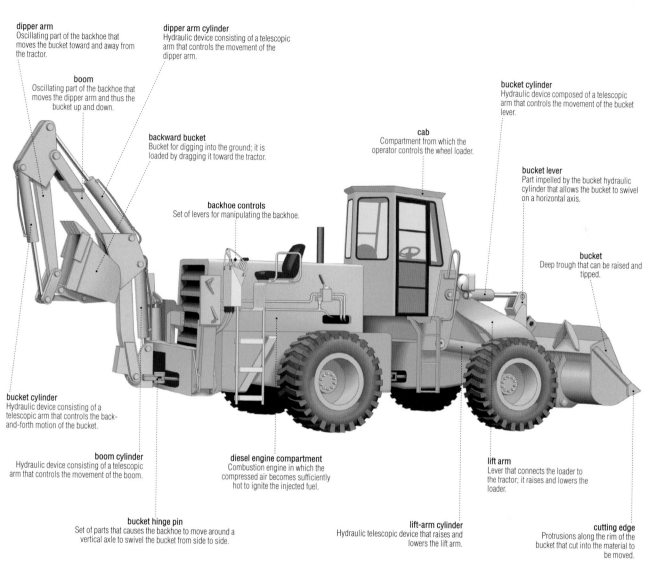

dipper arm
Oscillating part of the backhoe that moves the bucket toward and away from the tractor.

dipper arm cylinder
Hydraulic device consisting of a telescopic arm that controls the movement of the dipper arm.

boom
Oscillating part of the backhoe that moves the dipper arm and thus the bucket up and down.

bucket cylinder
Hydraulic device composed of a telescopic arm that controls the movement of the bucket lever.

backward bucket
Bucket for digging into the ground; it is loaded by dragging it toward the tractor.

cab
Compartment from which the operator controls the wheel loader.

bucket lever
Part impelled by the bucket hydraulic cylinder that allows the bucket to swivel on a horizontal axis.

backhoe controls
Set of levers for manipulating the backhoe.

bucket
Deep trough that can be raised and tipped.

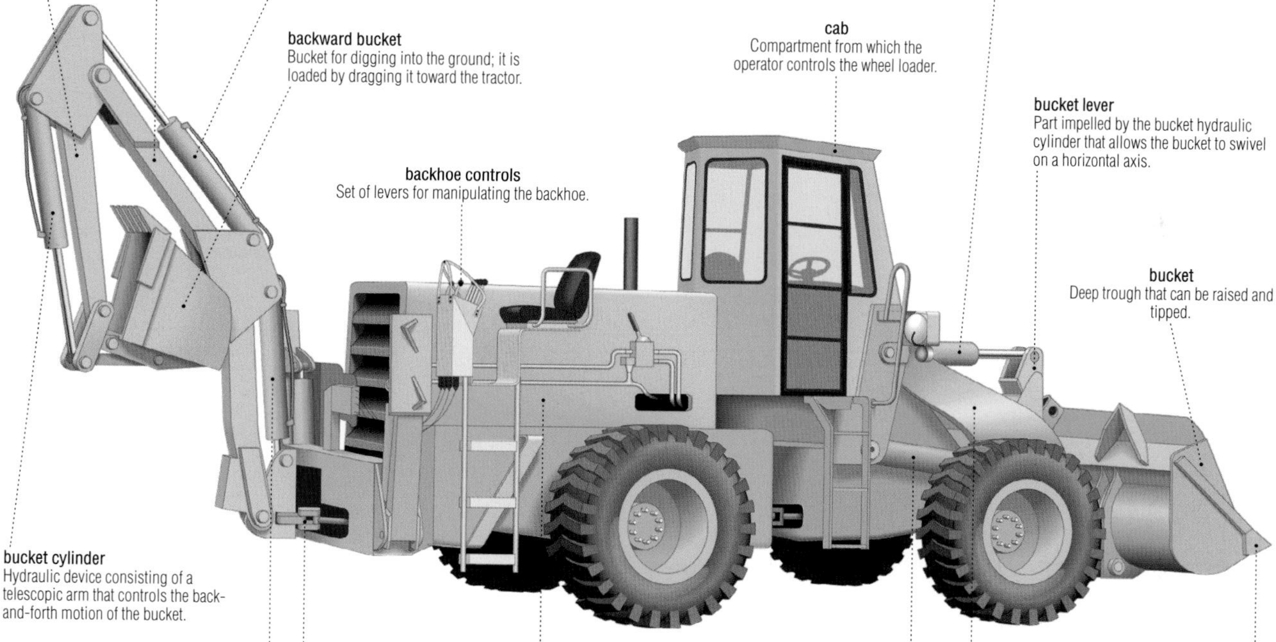

bucket cylinder
Hydraulic device consisting of a telescopic arm that controls the back-and-forth motion of the bucket.

boom cylinder
Hydraulic device consisting of a telescopic arm that controls the movement of the boom.

diesel engine compartment
Combustion engine in which the compressed air becomes sufficiently hot to ignite the injected fuel.

lift arm
Lever that connects the loader to the tractor; it raises and lowers the loader.

bucket hinge pin
Set of parts that causes the backhoe to move around a vertical axle to swivel the bucket from side to side.

lift-arm cylinder
Hydraulic telescopic device that raises and lowers the lift arm.

cutting edge
Protrusions along the rim of the bucket that cut into the material to be moved.

front-end loader
Equipment for lifting objects or material to be moved or loaded; it consists of a bucket and a lift arm impelled by hydraulic cylinders.

wheel tractor
Machine whose chassis can be articulated; it is equipped with a backhoe and a loader.

backhoe
Equipment for digging into the ground and moving rubble; it consists of a bucket, an arm and a boom impelled by hydraulic cylinders.

scraper

Machine that uses a blade to scrape the ground or roadbed and store the rubble in a bowl for disposal.

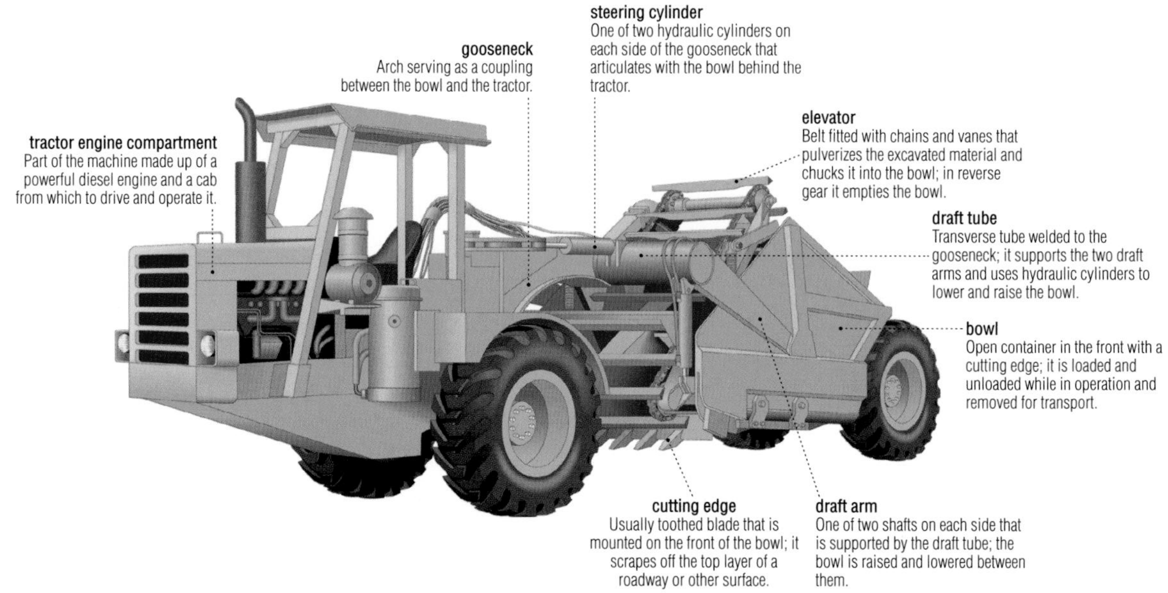
steering cylinder
One of two hydraulic cylinders on each side of the gooseneck that articulates with the bowl behind the tractor.
gooseneck
Arch serving as a coupling between the bowl and the tractor.
elevator
Belt fitted with chains and vanes that pulverizes the excavated material and chucks it into the bowl; in reverse gear it empties the bowl.
tractor engine compartment
Part of the machine made up of a powerful diesel engine and a cab from which to drive and operate it.
draft tube
Transverse tube welded to the gooseneck; it supports the two draft arms and uses hydraulic cylinders to lower and raise the bowl.
bowl
Open container in the front with a cutting edge; it is loaded and unloaded while in operation and removed for transport.
cutting edge
Usually toothed blade that is mounted on the front of the bowl; it scrapes off the top layer of a roadway or other surface.
draft arm
One of two shafts on each side that is supported by the draft tube; the bowl is raised and lowered between them.

hydraulic shovel

Machine made up of a pivot cab with a bucket attached for moving various types of material.

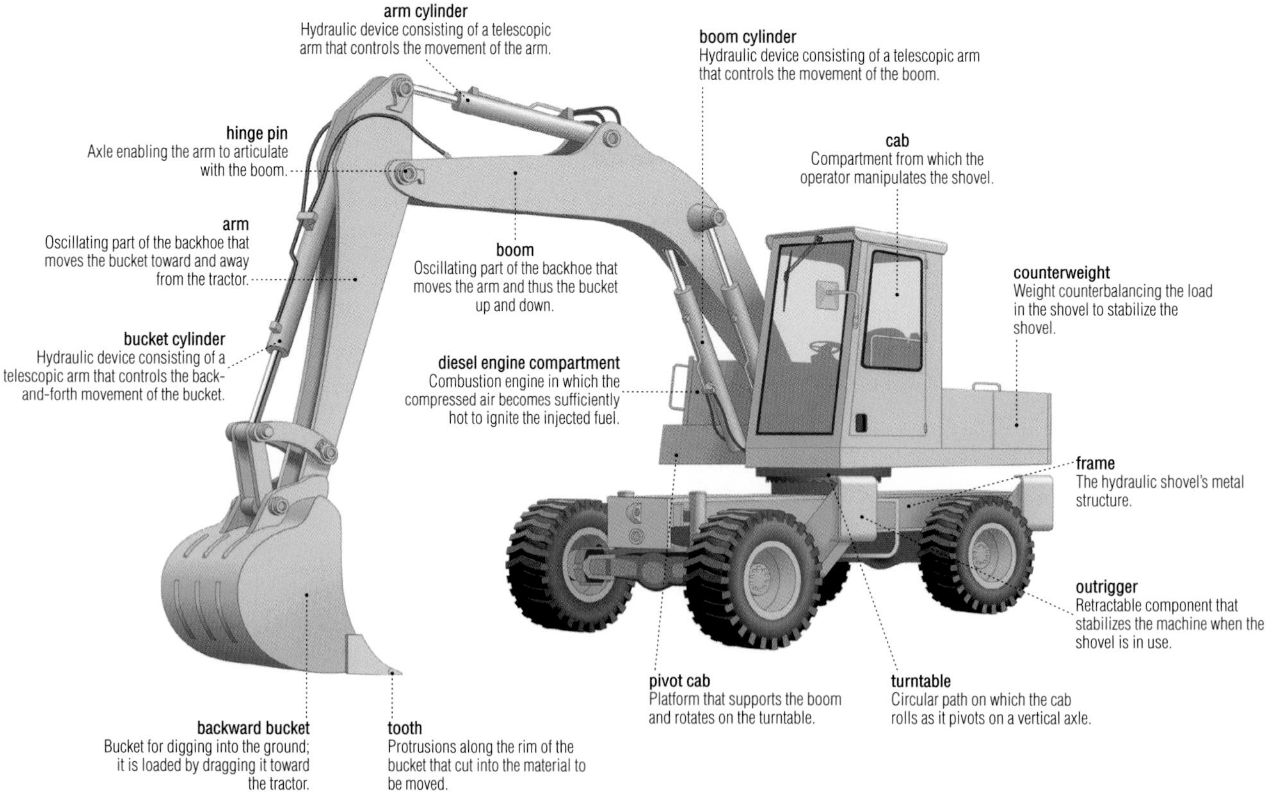
arm cylinder
Hydraulic device consisting of a telescopic arm that controls the movement of the arm.
boom cylinder
Hydraulic device consisting of a telescopic arm that controls the movement of the boom.
hinge pin
Axle enabling the arm to articulate with the boom.
cab
Compartment from which the operator manipulates the shovel.
arm
Oscillating part of the backhoe that moves the bucket toward and away from the tractor.
boom
Oscillating part of the backhoe that moves the arm and thus the bucket up and down.
counterweight
Weight counterbalancing the load in the shovel to stabilize the shovel.
bucket cylinder
Hydraulic device consisting of a telescopic arm that controls the back-and-forth movement of the bucket.
diesel engine compartment
Combustion engine in which the compressed air becomes sufficiently hot to ignite the injected fuel.
frame
The hydraulic shovel's metal structure.
outrigger
Retractable component that stabilizes the machine when the shovel is in use.
pivot cab
Platform that supports the boom and rotates on the turntable.
turntable
Circular path on which the cab rolls as it pivots on a vertical axle.
backward bucket
Bucket for digging into the ground; it is loaded by dragging it toward the tractor.
tooth
Protrusions along the rim of the bucket that cut into the material to be moved.

grader

Machine with a swiveling blade situated between two wheel shafts for leveling the ground or clearing debris off a roadway.

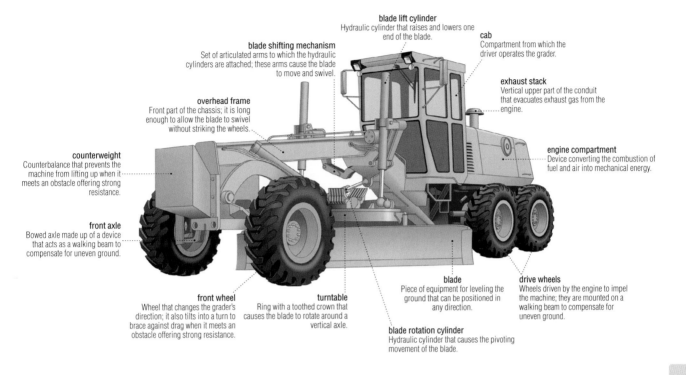

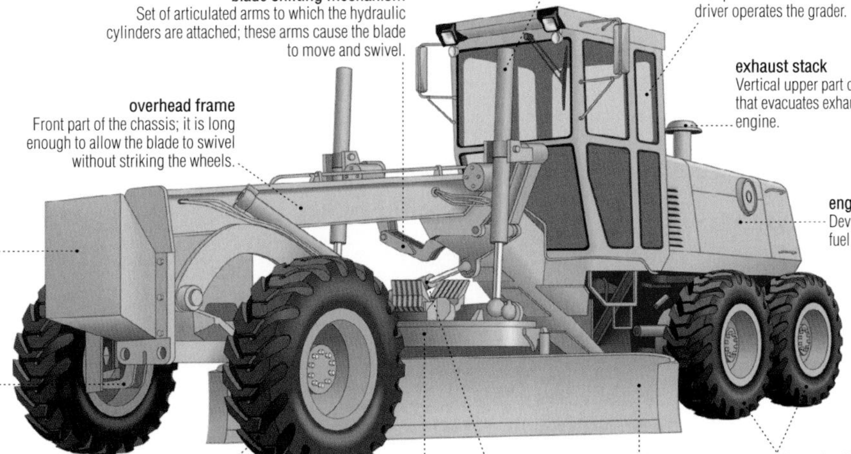

blade lift cylinder
Hydraulic cylinder that raises and lowers one end of the blade.
cab
Compartment from which the driver operates the grader.
blade shifting mechanism
Set of articulated arms to which the hydraulic cylinders are attached; these arms cause the blade to move and swivel.
exhaust stack
Vertical upper part of the conduit that evacuates exhaust gas from the engine.
overhead frame
Front part of the chassis; it is long enough to allow the blade to swivel without striking the wheels.
engine compartment
Device converting the combustion of fuel and air into mechanical energy.
counterweight
Counterbalance that prevents the machine from lifting up when it meets an obstacle offering strong resistance.
front axle
Bowed axle made up of a device that acts as a walking beam to compensate for uneven ground.
blade
Piece of equipment for leveling the ground that can be positioned in any direction.
drive wheels
Wheels driven by the engine to impel the machine; they are mounted on a walking beam to compensate for uneven ground.
front wheel
Wheel that changes the grader's direction; it also tilts into a turn to brace against drag when it meets an obstacle offering strong resistance.
turntable
Ring with a toothed crown that causes the blade to rotate around a vertical axle.
blade rotation cylinder
Hydraulic cylinder that causes the pivoting movement of the blade.

dump truck

Truck equipped with a dump body; it is used for bulk transport.

canopy
Metal surface that protects the cab from falling material during loading.
rib
Crosspiece welded to the outside walls of the dump body to reinforce it.
cab
Compartment from which the driver operates the truck.
dump body
Open or closed container; when raised by the elevation cylinder, it discharges its bulk material.
diesel engine compartment
Combustion engine in which the compressed air becomes sufficiently hot to ignite the injected fuel.
ladder
Device composed of treads and side rails that provides access to the cab.
frame
Metal structure of the dump truck.

tractor

Motorized machine used for operating farm equipment and tools.

tractor: rear view
The back end of the tractor is fitted with the equipment necessary to haul farm equipment or supply mechanical power to it.

headlight
Lamp on the rear of the vehicle that illuminates the work area.

compression link
Bar fastened to a tool that is coupled to the draft link to prevent it from tipping up or down.

taillight
Lamp that illuminates automatically when the front lights are on and shines more brightly when the operator steps on the brake pedal.

rock shaft lift arm
Part controlled by the hydraulic cylinder that raises and lowers a tool by means of the lifting link and the draft link.

hydraulic coupler
Device for attaching the hydraulic hoses so that power can be transmitted to the attached tool.

lifting link
Part adjustable to several positions that connects the draft link to the rock shaft lift arm.

hydraulic cylinder
Hydraulically powered device made up of a cylinder and a piston, which drive the draft link.

power takeoff
Mechanism consisting of a grooved shaft that uses the engine's power or the tractor's movement to drive a tool or equipment being towed.

coupler head
Linking device between the tool and the draft link.

draft link
Bar with a coupler head for towing.

towing hitch
Device for attaching the coupler-head ring of a towed piece of agricultural machinery.

tractor: front view
There are tractors with two or four driving wheels and two or four wheels that change the direction of the tractor.

steering wheel
Circular instrument used by the operator for steering the guide wheels.

exhaust stack
Vertical upper part of the conduit that evacuates exhaust gas from the engine.

fender
Part of the body that covers part of the wheel and serves as a shield from flying mud.

cab
Compartment from which the operator drives the truck and operates the tools or agricultural machinery.

rim
Metal circle constituting the wheel's circumference and upon which the tire is mounted.

headlight
Lamp on the front of the vehicle that illuminates the space in front.

step
Tread or set of treads built into the body for climbing up to or down from the cab.

tread bar
Raised part of the tire tread that improves traction for various usag conditions.

counterweight
Mass that balances and stabilizes the tool hitched to the tractor.

engine compartment
Device converting the combustion of fuel and air into mechanical energy.

front wheel
Wheel that changes the tractor's direction; it is usually smaller than the rear wheel.

driving wheel
Wheel that receives the engine's power and propels the tractor.

agricultural machinery

Mechanized devices used in farming.

ribbing plow
Plowing-tilling device for cutting up and plowing in furrow slices.

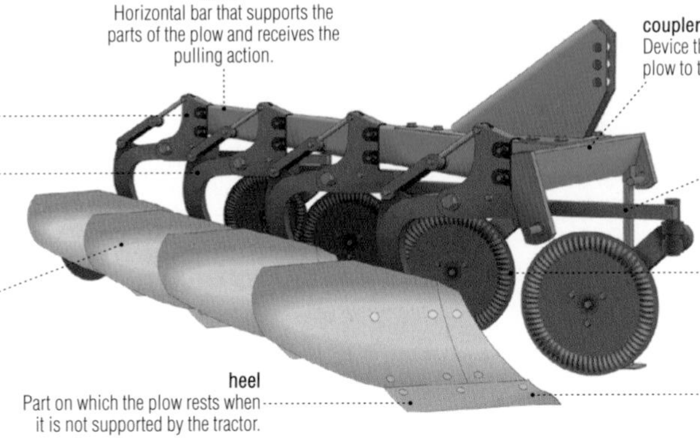

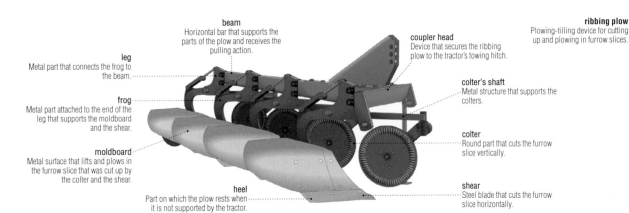

beam
Horizontal bar that supports the parts of the plow and receives the pulling action.

leg
Metal part that connects the frog to the beam.

frog
Metal part attached to the end of the leg that supports the moldboard and the shear.

moldboard
Metal surface that lifts and plows in the furrow slice that was cut up by the colter and the shear.

heel
Part on which the plow rests when it is not supported by the tractor.

coupler head
Device that secures the ribbing plow to the tractor's towing hitch.

colter's shaft
Metal structure that supports the colters.

colter
Round part that cuts the furrow slice vertically.

shear
Steel blade that cuts the furrow slice horizontally.

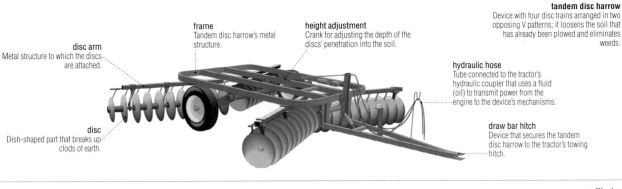

tandem disc harrow
Device with four disc trains arranged in two opposing V patterns; it loosens the soil that has already been plowed and eliminates weeds.

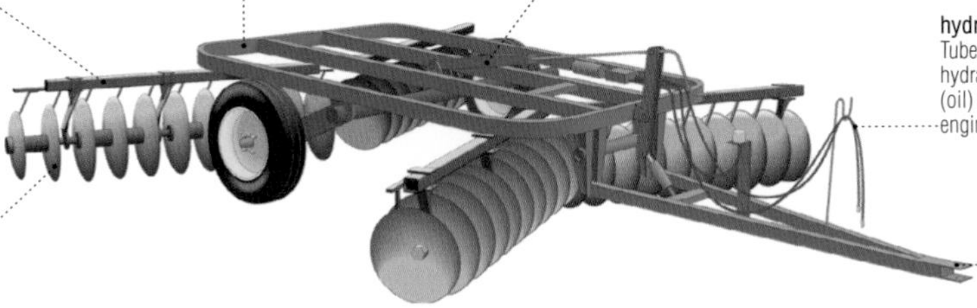

frame
Tandem disc harrow's metal structure.

height adjustment
Crank for adjusting the depth of the discs' penetration into the soil.

disc arm
Metal structure to which the discs are attached.

hydraulic hose
Tube connected to the tractor's hydraulic coupler that uses a fluid (oil) to transmit power from the engine to the device's mechanisms.

disc
Dish-shaped part that breaks up clods of earth.

draw bar hitch
Device that secures the tandem disc harrow to the tractor's towing hitch.

cultivator
Device with tines for working the top layer of the soil; it usually completes the plowing operation.

frame
Cultivator's metal structure.

rotary hoe
Device whose mechanism is powered by the towing action of the tractor; it is made up of blades that aerate and level the field.

tine
Curved prong that digs into the soil to work it by moving it sideways.

manure spreader
Device for scattering a mixture of litter and fermented animal waste over the soil to fertilize it.

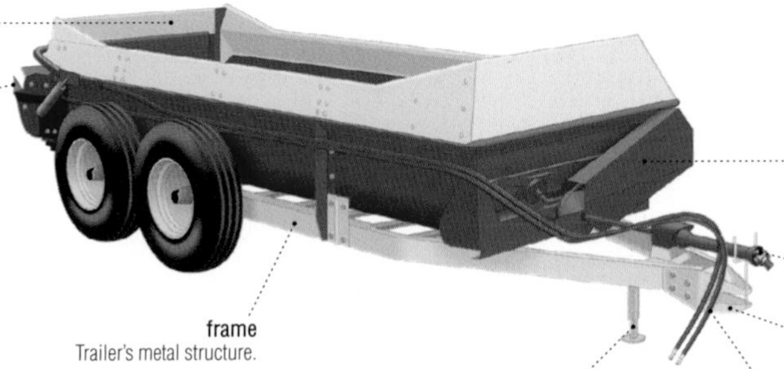

box
Container that holds the manure.

beater
Rotating device that disperses manure over the soil.

chain drive
Belt that transmits the rotational movement of the power-takeoff shaft to the moving floor of the trailer to bring the manure back to the beater.

power-takeoff shaft
Device that hitches the machine's shaft to the tractor's power train to transmit the necessary power to operate it.

frame
Trailer's metal structure.

jack stand
Telescopic support for the draw bar hitch that supports the trailer when stationary.

hydraulic hose
Tube connected to the tractor's hydraulic coupler that uses a fluid (oil) to transmit power from the engine to the device's mechanisms.

draw bar hitch
Device that secures the manure spreader to the tractor's towing hitch.

agricultural machinery

rake
Device for turning over hay.

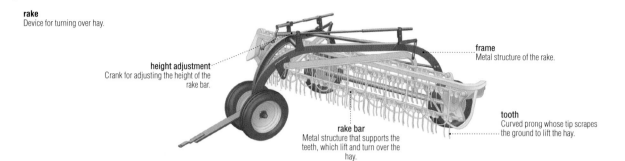

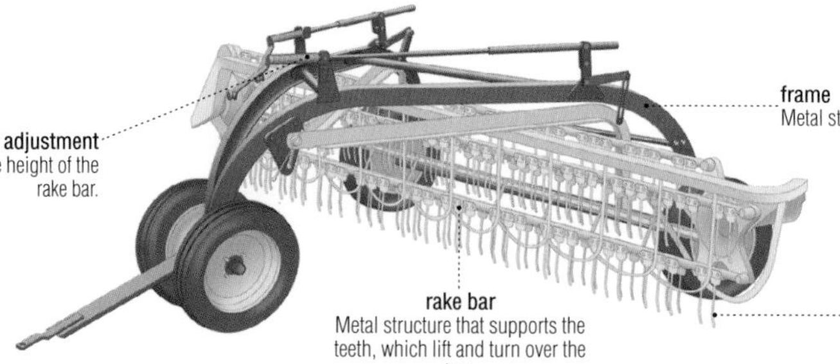
height adjustment
Crank for adjusting the height of the rake bar.
frame
Metal structure of the rake.
tooth
Curved prong whose tip scrapes the ground to lift the hay.
rake bar
Metal structure that supports the teeth, which lift and turn over the hay.

flail mower
Device that cuts the forage stalks as it moves and prepares them for the next harvesting phase (drying on the field and collection).

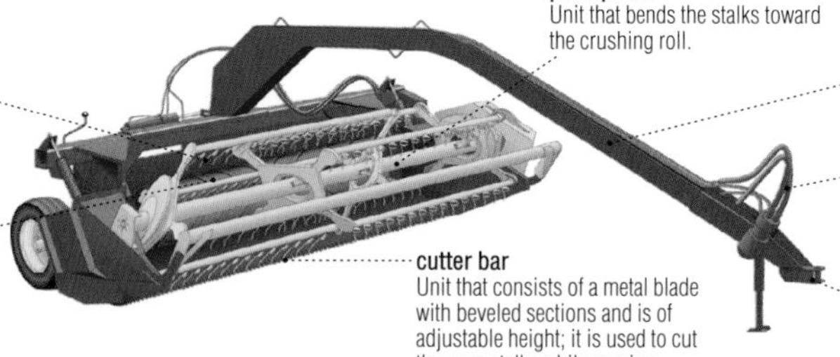
pickup reel
Unit that bends the stalks toward the crushing roll.
tow bar
Metal part with a draw bar hitch head that secures the flail mower to a tractor.
tooth
Curved tip for picking up the cut stalks.
hydraulic hose
Tube connected to the tractor's hydraulic coupler that uses a fluid (oil) to transmit power from the engine to the device's mechanisms.
crushing roll
One of two cylinders that crush and bend the stalks as they are fed between them; the crop is then deposited in a row on the ground.
cutter bar
Unit that consists of a metal blade with beveled sections and is of adjustable height; it is used to cut the crop stalks while moving.
draw bar hitch head
Device that secures the flail mower to the tractor's towing hitch.

hay baler
Device that harvests the forage and compresses it into bales.

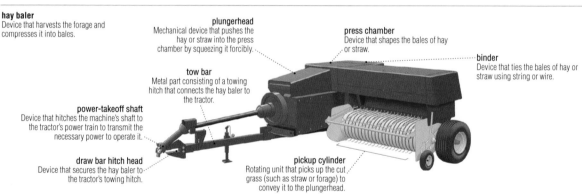

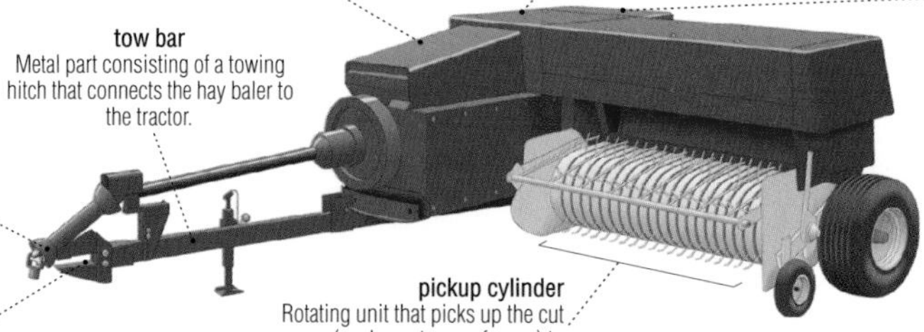
plungerhead
Mechanical device that pushes the hay or straw into the press chamber by squeezing it forcibly.
press chamber
Device that shapes the bales of hay or straw.
binder
Device that ties the bales of hay or straw using string or wire.
tow bar
Metal part consisting of a towing hitch that connects the hay baler to the tractor.
power-takeoff shaft
Device that hitches the machine's shaft to the tractor's power train to transmit the necessary power to operate it.
draw bar hitch head
Device that secures the hay baler to the tractor's towing hitch.
pickup cylinder
Rotating unit that picks up the cut grass (such as straw or forage) to convey it to the plungerhead.

forage harvester
Device that harvests herbage (such as alfalfa, clover and corn) for feeding livestock.

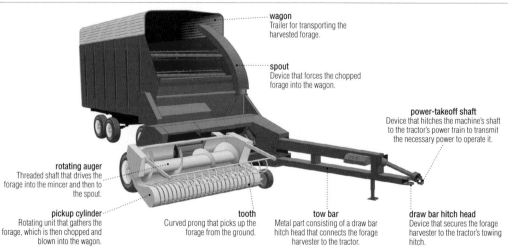

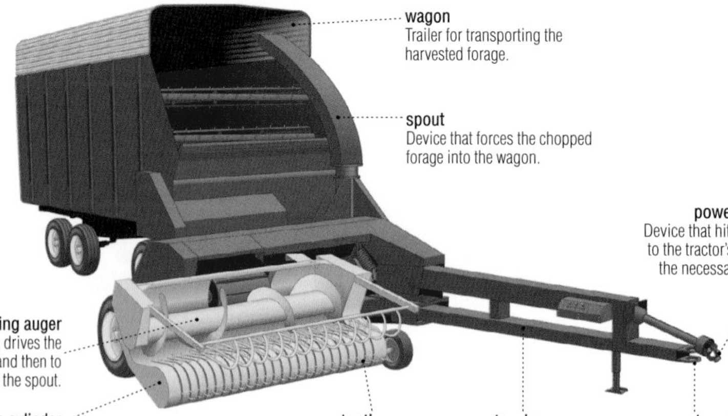
wagon
Trailer for transporting the harvested forage.
spout
Device that forces the chopped forage into the wagon.
power-takeoff shaft
Device that hitches the machine's shaft to the tractor's power train to transmit the necessary power to operate it.
rotating auger
Threaded shaft that drives the forage into the mincer and then to the spout.
pickup cylinder
Rotating unit that gathers the forage, which is then chopped and blown into the wagon.
tooth
Curved prong that picks up the forage from the ground.
tow bar
Metal part consisting of a draw bar hitch head that connects the forage harvester to the tractor.
draw bar hitch head
Device that secures the forage harvester to the tractor's towing hitch.

seed drill
Farming tool that spreads and plows seeds into the soil following straight lines (furrows).

grain tube
Tube through which the seeds flow from the bottom of the hopper to be dropped into the furrow.

hopper
Container that is usually shaped like an inverted pyramid; it holds the seeds to be sown.

chain drive
Distribution unit that regulates the flow of seeds into the grain tube.

colter
Round part that cuts the furrow slice vertically.

covering disk
One of a pair of circular parts that work together to close up the furrow.

press wheel
Wheel that tamps the earth to plow the seeds down to a certain depth.

disk spacing lever
Lever for changing the distance between the sowing lines.

forage blower
Farm machine that forces the harvested forage (e.g., grass, wheat and corn) into the silo.

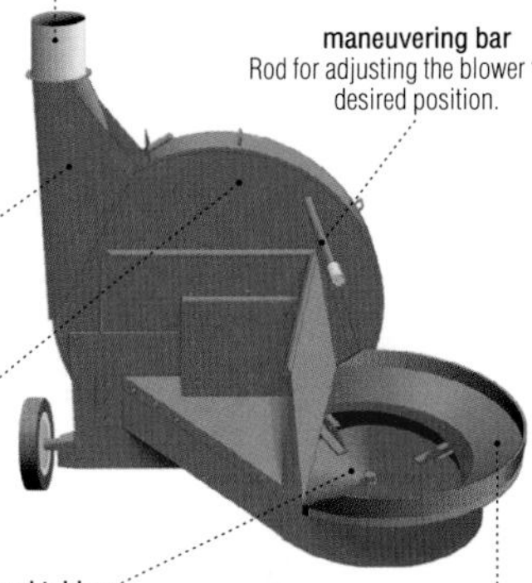

ensiling tube
Duct through which the forage is blown into the silo.

maneuvering bar
Rod for adjusting the blower to the desired position.

fan's tube
Duct through which the forage is blown toward the ensiling tube.

fan
Machine that produces airflow to force the forage through the ensiling tube and onto the silo.

feed table
Rotating plate that moves the forage into the fan.

hopper
Container that holds harvested forage coming from a trailer, truck or ensiling trailer.

combine harvester
Vehicle that harvests seed crops, usually grain; it cuts, threshes and separates the seeds from the chaff.

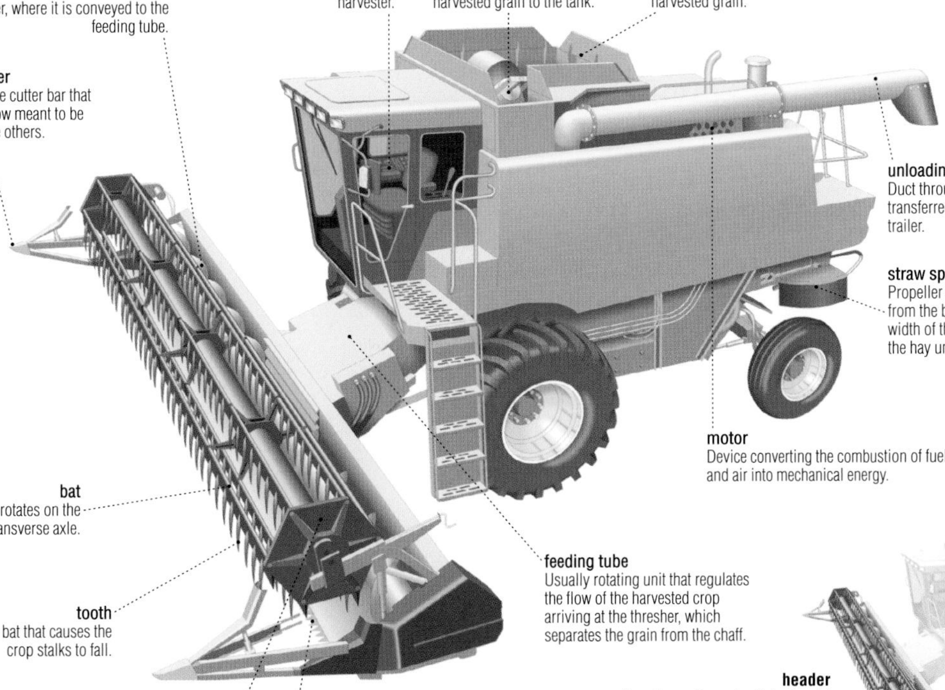

rotating auger
Double rotating worm that gathers the harvest to the center of the header, where it is conveyed to the feeding tube.

cab
Compartment from which the driver operates the combine harvester.

grain elevator
Mechanism that conveys the harvested grain to the tank.

grain tank
Container that temporarily stores harvested grain.

divider
Unit at the end of the cutter bar that separates the furrow meant to be cut from the others.

unloading tube
Duct through which the grain is transferred from the tank to a trailer.

straw spreader
Propeller device that spreads hay from the back of the harvester the width of the cut to facilitate plowing the hay under the soil.

motor
Device converting the combustion of fuel and air into mechanical energy.

bat
Toothed bar that rotates on the pickup reel's transverse axle.

tooth
Prong on the bat that causes the crop stalks to fall.

feeding tube
Usually rotating unit that regulates the flow of the harvested crop arriving at the thresher, which separates the grain from the chaff.

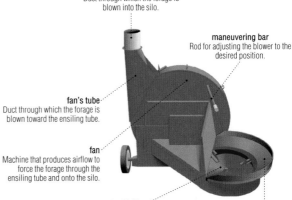

header
Trough usually made of sheet metal into which the cut crop is conveyed; from there it is sent through the feeding tube to the thresher.

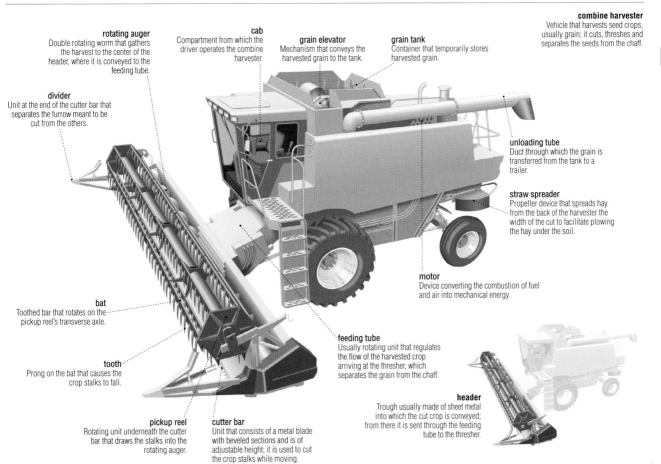

pickup reel
Rotating unit underneath the cutter bar that draws the stalks into the rotating auger.

cutter bar
Unit that consists of a metal blade with beveled sections and is of adjustable height; it is used to cut the crop stalks while moving.

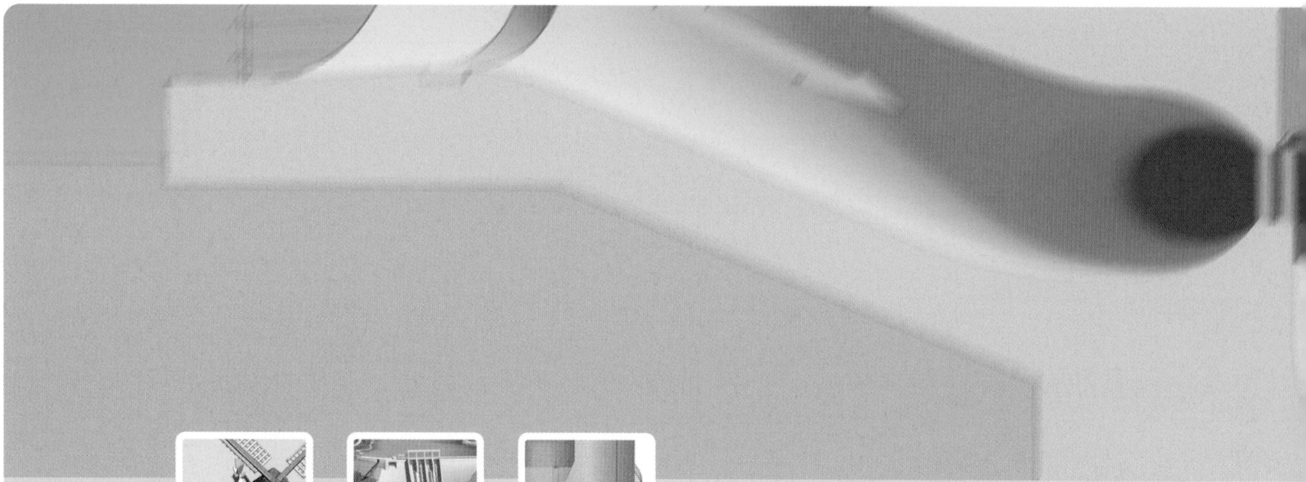

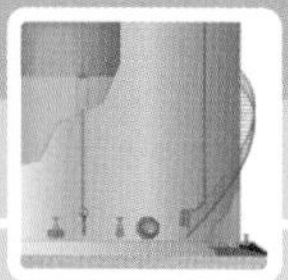

646 Geothermal and fossil energy

Geothermal energy uses the Earth's internal heat and is a renewable energy source; fossil fuels such as coal and petroleum are nonrenewable energy sources.

657 Hydroelectricity

A nonpolluting renewable energy source, hydroelectricity accounts for 20% of the electricity consumed around the world.

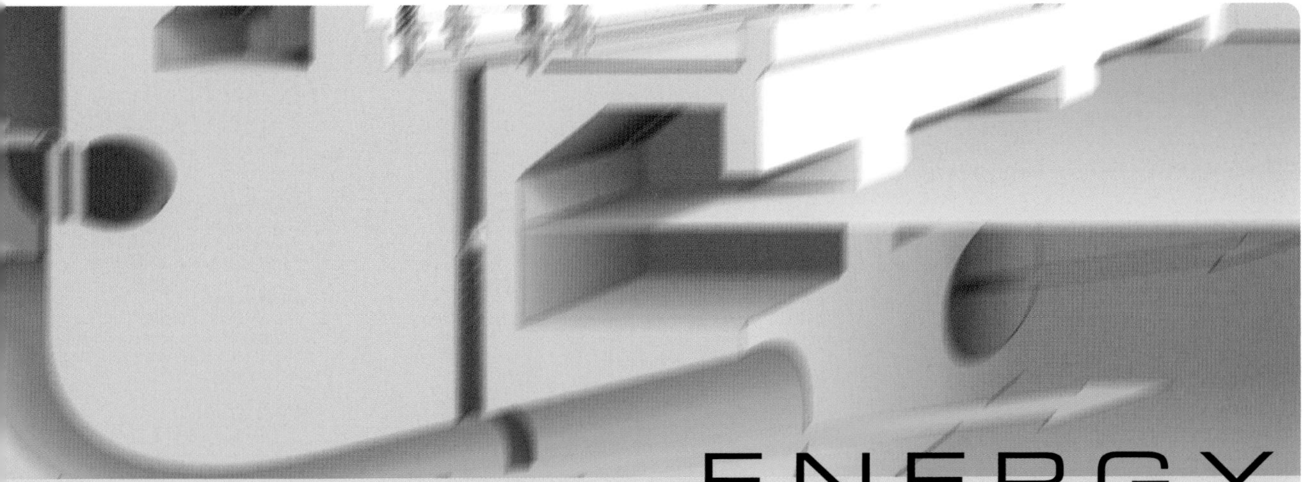

ENERGY

The power to perform work, produced from natural phenomena (e.g., the Sun and the wind) or raw materials (e.g., coal and petroleum).

665 Nuclear energy

Large quantity of energy that is released in the form of heat; this occurs during a nuclear reaction (fission of atom nuclei). The heat is used to produce electricity.

672 Solar energy

Harnessed solar radiation has many applications, including solar-panel heating and electricity produced with solar cells and solar furnaces.

676 Wind energy

A renewable energy source, wind energy harnesses the power of the wind and converts it into mechanical or electric energy.

production of electricity from geothermal energy

Hot water contained in the ground near a volcano, geyser or thermal source is piped to the surface by drilling to extract steam and produce electricity.

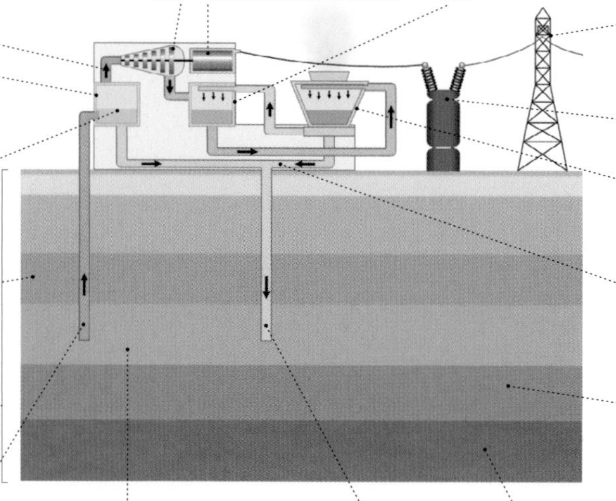
turbine
Steam-powered machine whose wheel transmits mechanical energy to the generator and causes it to rotate.
generator
Turbine-powered rotating machine that converts mechanical energy into electric energy to direct it toward a transmission network.
condenser
Circuit that cools the steam from the turbine and condenses it into water.
steam
Gaseous state of water; steam pressure operates the turbine.
high-tension electricity transmission
Using high-voltage lines to transmit electricity over long distances reduces the strength of the current and, as a result, energy losses.
separator
Device that separates water from steam, which it recovers to operate the turbine; the water is reinjected into the aquifer.
voltage increase
At the outlet end of the power plant, the transformer increases the voltage; this reduces energy losses during transmission over long distances.
water-steam mix
Hot water extracted from the aquifer; as it rises to the surface, it is partially turned into steam.
cooling tower
Device that cools the condenser's hot water on contact with the air; some of the water evaporates and the rest is reinjected into the condenser and the aquifer.
upper confining bed
Layer of impermeable rock that covers the confined aquifer.
water
Liquid made up of hydrogen and oxygen that becomes steam at 212°F; the water transfers Earth's internal heat.
geothermal field
Area of Earth's crust where a pocket of hot confined water is close enough to the surface to be exploited.
lower confining bed
Layer of impermeable rock that transmits heat from the magma chamber to the aquifer.
production well
Borehole dug into the ground to allow the hot water contained in the aquifer to be pumped to produce electricity.
confined aquifer
Layer of porous sedimentary rock between two impermeable layers where water accumulates at a temperature between 300°F and 750°F.
injection well
Borehole that is drilled into the ground to return water to the aquifer, where it is reheated after its heat has been extracted.
magma chamber
Pocket of magma (molten rock emerging from Earth's crust) that constitutes a heat source; it transmits its thermal energy to water.

thermal energy

Energy that is produced by turning water into steam through the burning of fuel (e.g., petroleum and coal) or through nuclear reaction.

production of electricity from thermal energy
The heat that is given off by burning combustible fuels in the thermal power plant converts water into steam; the steam turns a turbo-alternator unit to produce electricity.

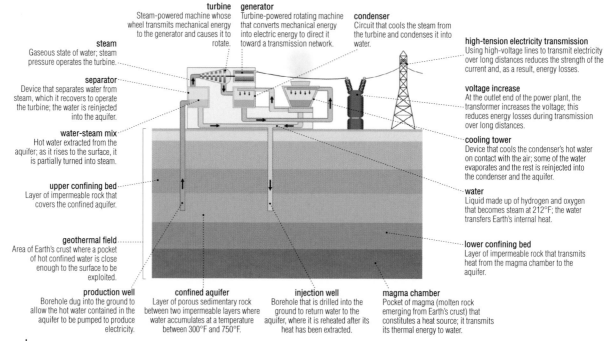

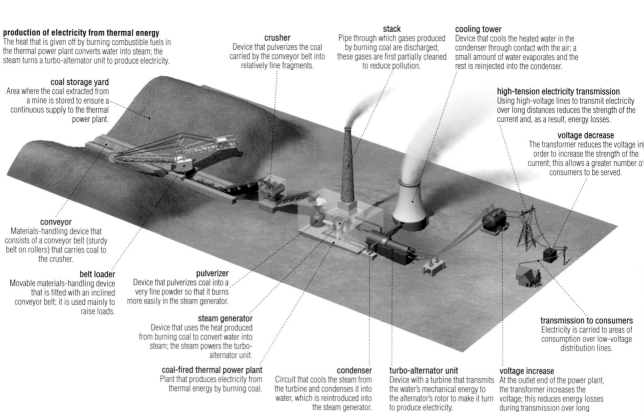

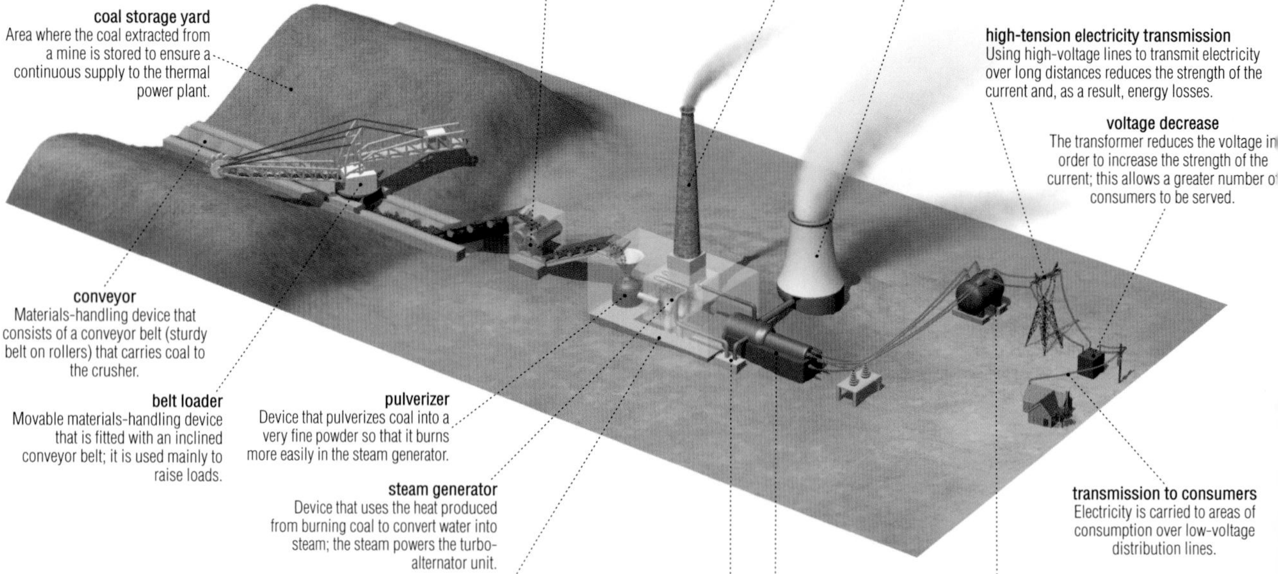
crusher
Device that pulverizes the coal carried by the conveyor belt into relatively fine fragments.
stack
Pipe through which gases produced by burning coal are discharged; these gases are first partially cleaned to reduce pollution.
cooling tower
Device that cools the heated water in the condenser through contact with the air; a small amount of water evaporates and the rest is reinjected into the condenser.
coal storage yard
Area where the coal extracted from a mine is stored to ensure a continuous supply to the thermal power plant.
high-tension electricity transmission
Using high-voltage lines to transmit electricity over long distances reduces the strength of the current and, as a result, energy losses.
voltage decrease
The transformer reduces the voltage in order to increase the strength of the current; this allows a greater number of consumers to be served.
conveyor
Materials-handling device that consists of a conveyor belt (sturdy belt on rollers) that carries coal to the crusher.
belt loader
Movable materials-handling device that is fitted with an inclined conveyor belt; it is used mainly to raise loads.
pulverizer
Device that pulverizes coal into a very fine powder so that it burns more easily in the steam generator.
steam generator
Device that uses the heat produced from burning coal to convert water into steam; the steam powers the turbo-alternator unit.
transmission to consumers
Electricity is carried to areas of consumption over low-voltage distribution lines.
coal-fired thermal power plant
Plant that produces electricity from thermal energy by burning coal.
condenser
Circuit that cools the steam from the turbine and condenses it into water, which is reintroduced into the steam generator.
turbo-alternator unit
Device with a turbine that transmits the water's mechanical energy to the alternator's rotor to make it turn to produce electricity.
voltage increase
At the outlet end of the power plant, the transformer increases the voltage; this reduces energy losses during transmission over long distances.

coal mine

The underground or open-pit facilities that are set up around a coal deposit in order to extract it.

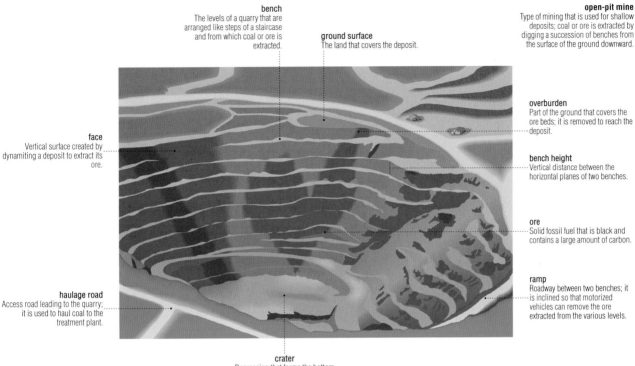

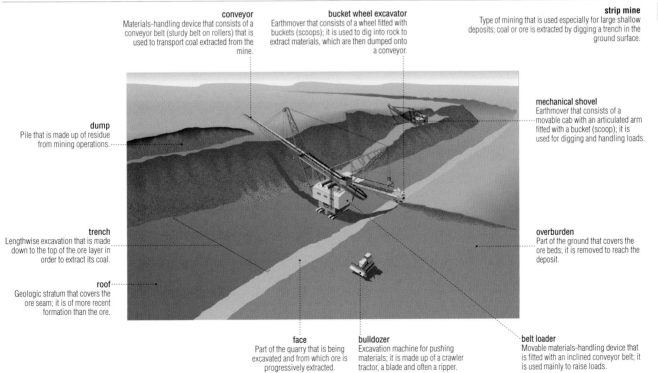

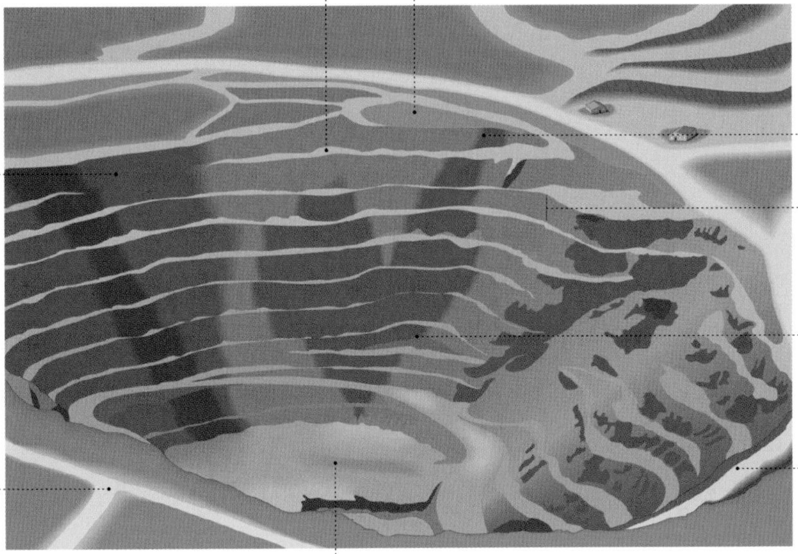
bench
The levels of a quarry that are arranged like steps of a staircase and from which coal or ore is extracted.
ground surface
The land that covers the deposit.
open-pit mine
Type of mining that is used for shallow deposits; coal or ore is extracted by digging a succession of benches from the surface of the ground downward.
overburden
Part of the ground that covers the ore beds; it is removed to reach the deposit.
face
Vertical surface created by dynamiting a deposit to extract its ore.
bench height
Vertical distance between the horizontal planes of two benches.
ore
Solid fossil fuel that is black and contains a large amount of carbon.
ramp
Roadway between two benches; it is inclined so that motorized vehicles can remove the ore extracted from the various levels.
haulage road
Access road leading to the quarry; it is used to haul coal to the treatment plant.
crater
Depression that forms the bottom of the quarry; it is a result of the extraction of deposits.

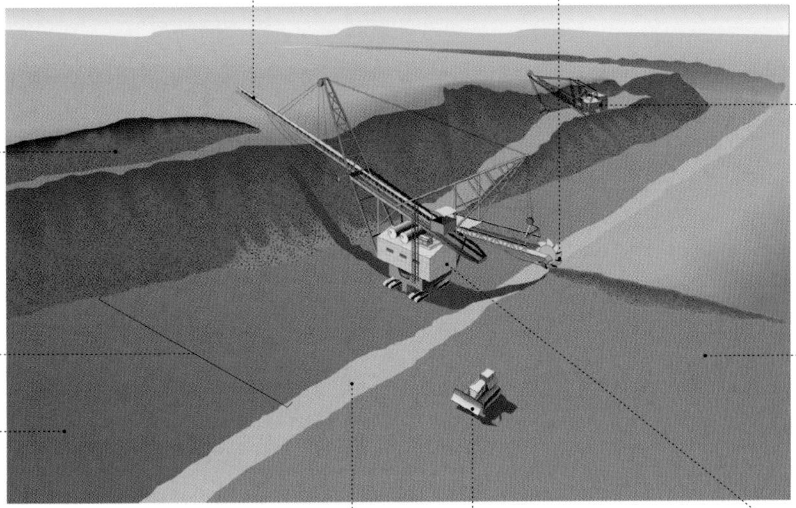
conveyor
Materials-handling device that consists of a conveyor belt (sturdy belt on rollers) that is used to transport coal extracted from the mine.
bucket wheel excavator
Earthmover that consists of a wheel fitted with buckets (scoops); it is used to dig into rock to extract materials, which are then dumped onto a conveyor.
strip mine
Type of mining that is used especially for large shallow deposits; coal or ore is extracted by digging a trench in the ground surface.
mechanical shovel
Earthmover that consists of a movable cab with an articulated arm fitted with a bucket (scoop); it is used for digging and handling loads.
dump
Pile that is made up of residue from mining operations.
trench
Lengthwise excavation that is made down to the top of the ore layer in order to extract its coal.
overburden
Part of the ground that covers the ore beds; it is removed to reach the deposit.
roof
Geologic stratum that covers the ore seam; it is of more recent formation than the ore.
face
Part of the quarry that is being excavated and from which ore is progressively extracted.
bulldozer
Excavation machine for pushing materials; it is made up of a crawler tractor, a blade and often a ripper.
belt loader
Movable materials-handling device that is fitted with an inclined conveyor belt; it is used mainly to raise loads.

ENERGY

coal mine

jackleg drill
Percussive tool that is powered by compressed air; it is used to bore holes into hard rock. The air leg makes the job easier for the drill operator.

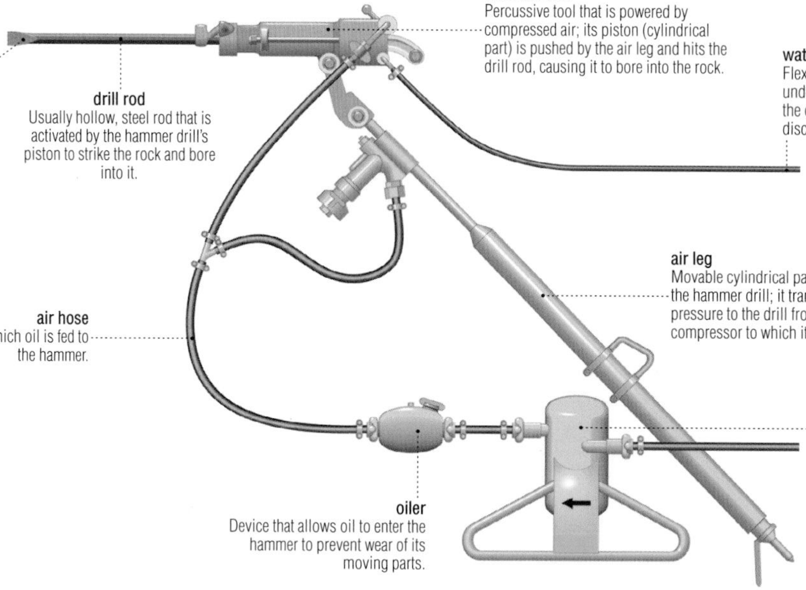

hammer drill
Percussive tool that is powered by compressed air; its piston (cylindrical part) is pushed by the air leg and hits the drill rod, causing it to bore into the rock.

water hose
Flexible hose used to inject water under pressure to prevent wear on the drill rod and the bit and to discharge waste.

bit
Cutting end of the drill rod that is used to bore into the rock.

drill rod
Usually hollow, steel rod that is activated by the hammer drill's piston to strike the rock and bore into it.

air leg
Movable cylindrical part that supports the hammer drill; it transmits air pressure to the drill from the compressor to which it is attached.

air hose
Flexible hose through which oil is fed to the hammer.

water separator
Device that removes any trace of humidity from the compressor's air to prevent damage to the hammer.

oiler
Device that allows oil to enter the hammer to prevent wear of its moving parts.

pithead
The surface facilities needed for underground mining (including extraction machinery, storage areas and offices).

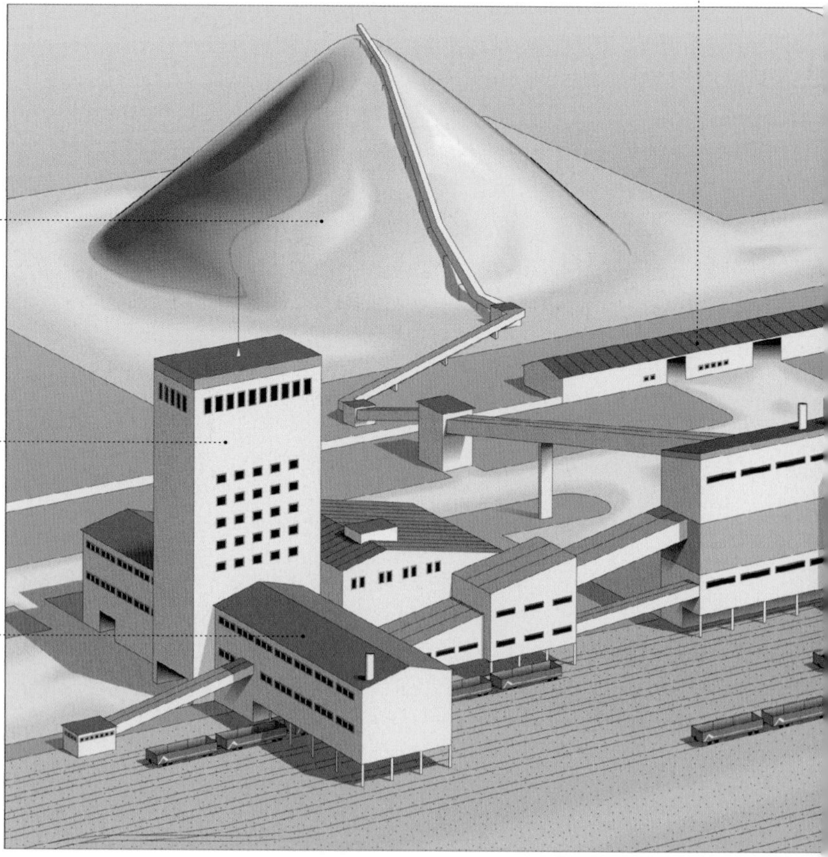

maintenance shop
Work area where machinery is maintained and repaired.

dump
Pile that is made up of residue from mining operations.

main fan
Device that ensures air exchange in the mine; air is drawn through one shaft and exits through another.

loading bunker
Reservoir where processed coal is stored before being loaded onto freight cars to be transported by rail to the power plant.

coal mine

pneumatic hammer
Percussive tool that is powered by compressed air; with the help of a piston, it activates a tool, which breaks through very hard matter such as rock and concrete.

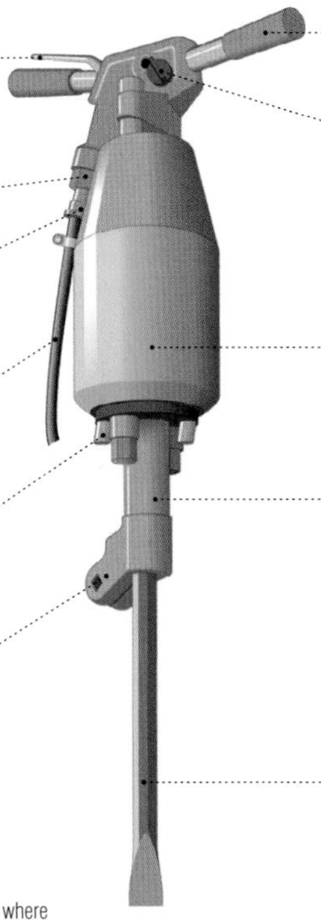

control lever
Grip used to operate the hammer; the lever opens the throttle valve so that air can enter the hammer.

throttle valve
Movable part that is opened by the control lever to let compressed air into the hammer.

flexible hose connection
Fastening device with a metal part that accepts the flexible hose so that compressed air can enter the hammer.

flexible hose
Flexible hose through which compressed air from the compressor it is attached to enters the hammer.

exhaust port
Opening through which compressed air is expelled from the pneumatic hammer.

retainer
Device that holds the tool in place in the chuck.

handle
The two elements that allow a worker to manipulate the hammer.

lubricator
Device that automatically oils the various parts of the hammer to prevent wear.

silencer
Device that lessens the noise caused when air exits the hammer.

chuck
Part of the hammer to which the tool is fastened.

tool
Cylindrical rod that is set in motion by compressed air pressure from the hammer; it is used to break hard surfaces.

headframe
Opening at the top of the shaft that connects the aboveground facilities (including ventilation fans and hoists) to the underground areas being mined.

miners' changing-room
Area with sanitary facilities (showers, toilets) where miners can go mainly to change their clothes.

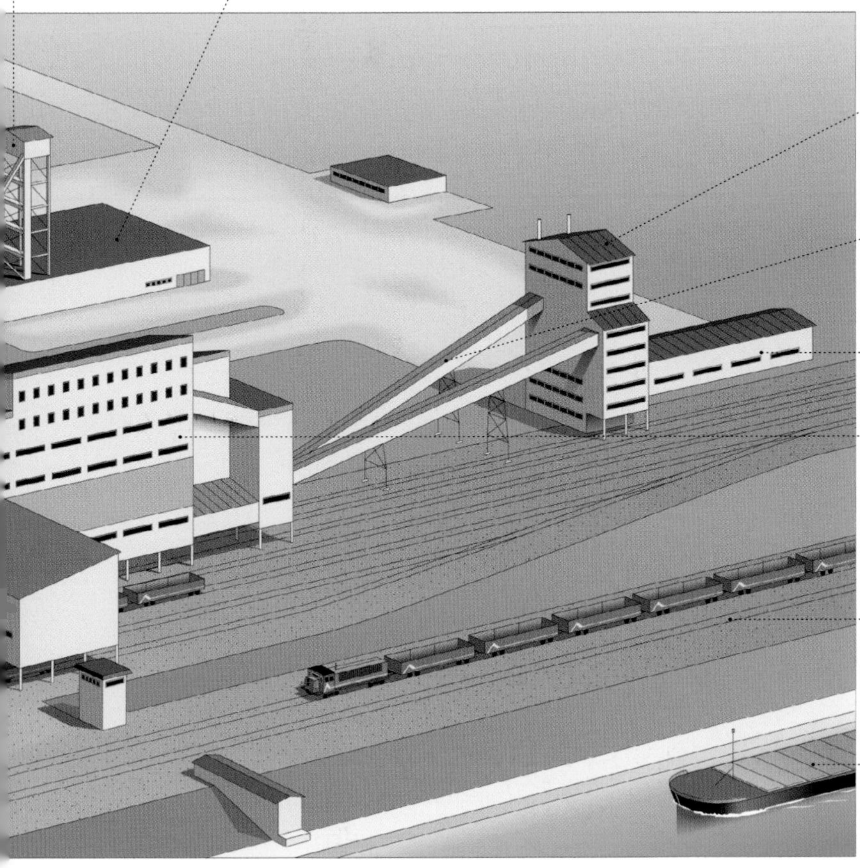

winding tower
Building that houses the shaft's hoisting equipment (including motors and hoisting cables); it provides communication between the surface and the mine galleries.

conveyor
Materials-handling device that consists of a conveyor belt (sturdy belt on rollers); it is used to carry coal to the treatment plant.

hoist room
Area that houses the hoist (cylinder) on which the hoisting cables are wound; it controls movement of the elevators and skip hoists in the shaft.

treatment plant
Place where all processing activities (including crushing and washing) are carried out to prepare the coal for market.

rail track
The tracks formed of two parallel rails on which trains travel to transport coal.

maritime transport
Means of transport that uses barges to transport coal over water.

coal mine

underground mine
Property in which excavations are carried out to extract deeply embedded (between 30 and 11,500 ft) coal for industrial mining.

headframe
Opening at the top of the shaft that connects the aboveground facilities (including ventilation fans and hoists) to the underground areas being mined.

vertical shaft
Shaft that is dug perpendicular to the surface; it serves various levels and is used mainly to transport personnel, equipment and ore.

elevator
Power lift fitted with a cab that transports coal or miners between the various levels.

chute
Vertical or inclined passageway through which ore, equipment, personnel and air move from one level of the mine to the other.

cross cut
Horizontal passageway that cuts through the ore bed perpendicularly; it provides communication between the passageways and helps to ventilate the mine.

manway
Passageway allowing workers to move around in the mine.

drift
Passageway dug horizontally along the grade line of the ore seam; it can also be dug into the ore vertically.

face
Opening that is dug laterally into the rock as coal is extracted.

winding tower
Building that houses the shaft's hoisting equipment (including motors and hoisting cables); it provides communication between the surface and the mine galleries.

winding shaft
Shaft that is dug vertically into the ground; coal is removed from the mine through it using hoisting machinery.

pillar
Mass of ore that is left unmined at regular intervals in an excavation (chamber); it provides stability for the upper layers.

room
Cavity that remains after the ore is extracted; pillars support its roof.

level
The horizontal passageways that branch off from the shaft at the same depth; they are usually at regular intervals.

top road
Horizontal passageway that serves the highest level of a panel.

deck
Extraction layer between two levels; mining is usually done in stages and in descending order.

skip
Elevator consisting of a skip bucket that is activated by a hoist; it is used to bring coal and people to the surface.

ore pass
Inclined route that takes coal to a low level; coal that falls on the mine floor is usually crushed before being brought to the surface.

panel
Unit of rock that is being mined; it is contained between vertical and horizontal planes and is demarcated by various passageways.

landing
Landing located around a shaft on each level; coal is collected here before being moved to the surface.

sump
Bottom of the shaft in which water runoff accumulates inside the mine before being pumped to the surface.

bottom road
Horizontal passageway that serves the base of a panel.

winze
Vertical or inclined passageway that connects two levels; it is dug downward from inside the mine and not from the surface.

oil

Flammable, relatively viscous oily liquid that is used as an energy source; it is made up of various hydrocarbons resulting from the decomposition of plant life over millions of year.

surface prospecting
Searching for potential oil deposits by studying the structure of the subsoil using a seismograph.

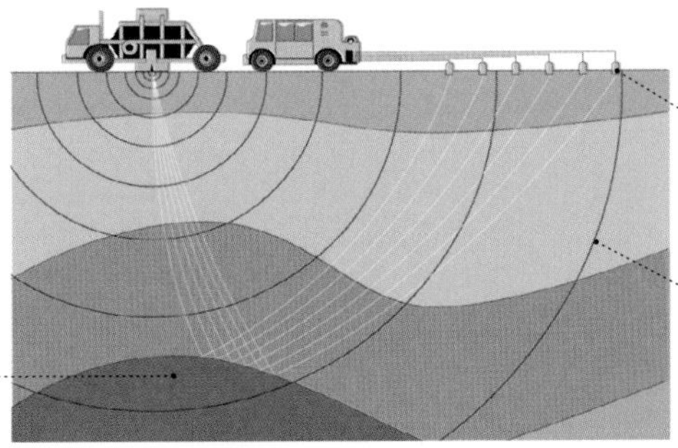

seismographic recording
A recording made using an apparatus called a seismograph; the analysis of its shock wave echoes detects the presence of rock layers that might contain pockets of petroleum or gas.

shock wave
The shock wave spreads and sends back an echo, which varies with the density and depth of the layers of subsoil; with this information, the composition of the subsoil can be determined.

petroleum trap
Assemblage of porous rocks that contain recoverable oil reserves, which are produced from marine or land deposits.

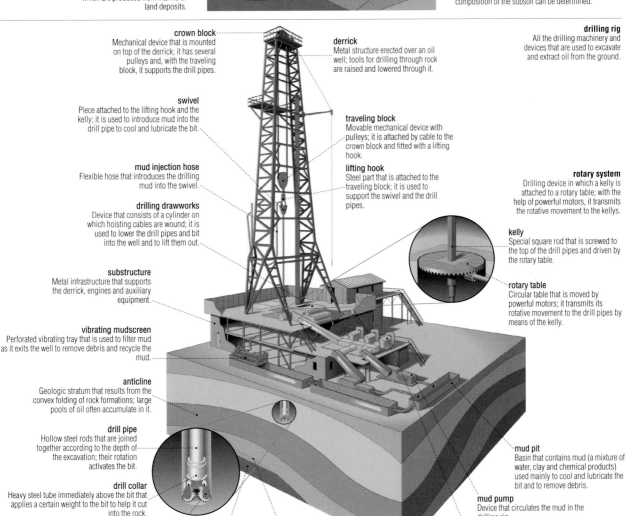

drilling rig
All the drilling machinery and devices that are used to excavate and extract oil from the ground.

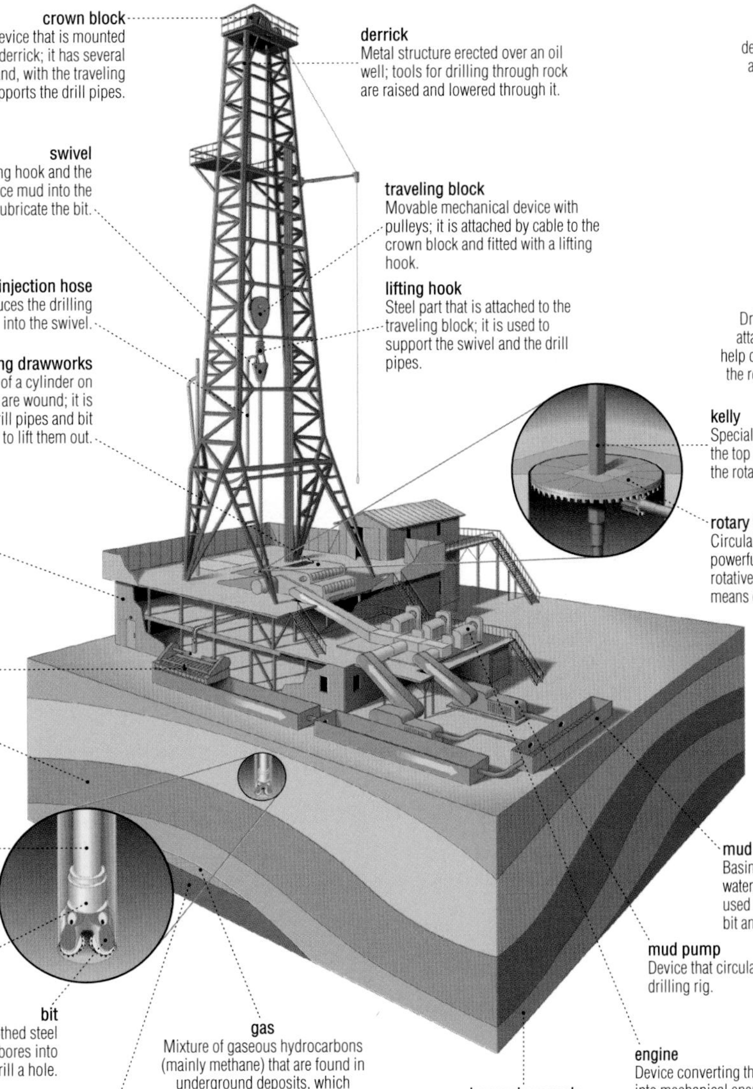

crown block
Mechanical device that is mounted on top of the derrick; it has several pulleys and, with the traveling block, it supports the drill pipes.

derrick
Metal structure erected over an oil well; tools for drilling through rock are raised and lowered through it.

swivel
Piece attached to the lifting hook and the kelly; it is used to introduce mud into the drill pipe to cool and lubricate the bit.

traveling block
Movable mechanical device with pulleys; it is attached by cable to the crown block and fitted with a lifting hook.

lifting hook
Steel part that is attached to the traveling block; it is used to support the swivel and the drill pipes.

mud injection hose
Flexible hose that introduces the drilling mud into the swivel.

rotary system
Drilling device in which a kelly is attached to a rotary table; with the help of powerful motors, it transmits the rotative movement to the kellys.

drilling drawworks
Device that consists of a cylinder on which hoisting cables are wound; it is used to lower the drill pipes and bit into the well and to lift them out.

kelly
Special square rod that is screwed to the top of the drill pipes and driven by the rotary table.

substructure
Metal infrastructure that supports the derrick, engines and auxiliary equipment.

rotary table
Circular table that is moved by powerful motors; it transmits its rotative movement to the drill pipes by means of the kelly.

vibrating mudscreen
Perforated vibrating tray that is used to filter mud as it exits the well to remove debris and recycle the mud.

anticline
Geologic stratum that results from the convex folding of rock formations; large pools of oil often accumulate in it.

drill pipe
Hollow steel rods that are joined together according to the depth of the excavation; their rotation activates the bit.

mud pit
Basin that contains mud (a mixture of water, clay and chemical products) used mainly to cool and lubricate the bit and to remove debris.

drill collar
Heavy steel tube immediately above the bit that applies a certain weight to the bit to help it cut into the rock.

mud pump
Device that circulates the mud in the drilling rig.

bit
Rotating drill bit with toothed steel or diamond wheels; it bores into rock to break it up and drill a hole.

gas
Mixture of gaseous hydrocarbons (mainly methane) that are found in underground deposits, which sometimes also contain crude oil; it is used mainly as a fuel.

engine
Device converting the combustion of fuel and air into mechanical energy.

impervious rock
Layer of impermeable rock that covers and protects the oil deposit; it prevents hydrocarbons from migrating into other rocks.

oil
Flammable, relatively viscous oily liquid that is used as an energy source; it is made up of various hydrocarbons resulting from the decomposition of plant life over millions of year.

oil

production platform
Facility used to extract underwater oil deposits; the separation and treatment of hydrocarbons are mainly done here.

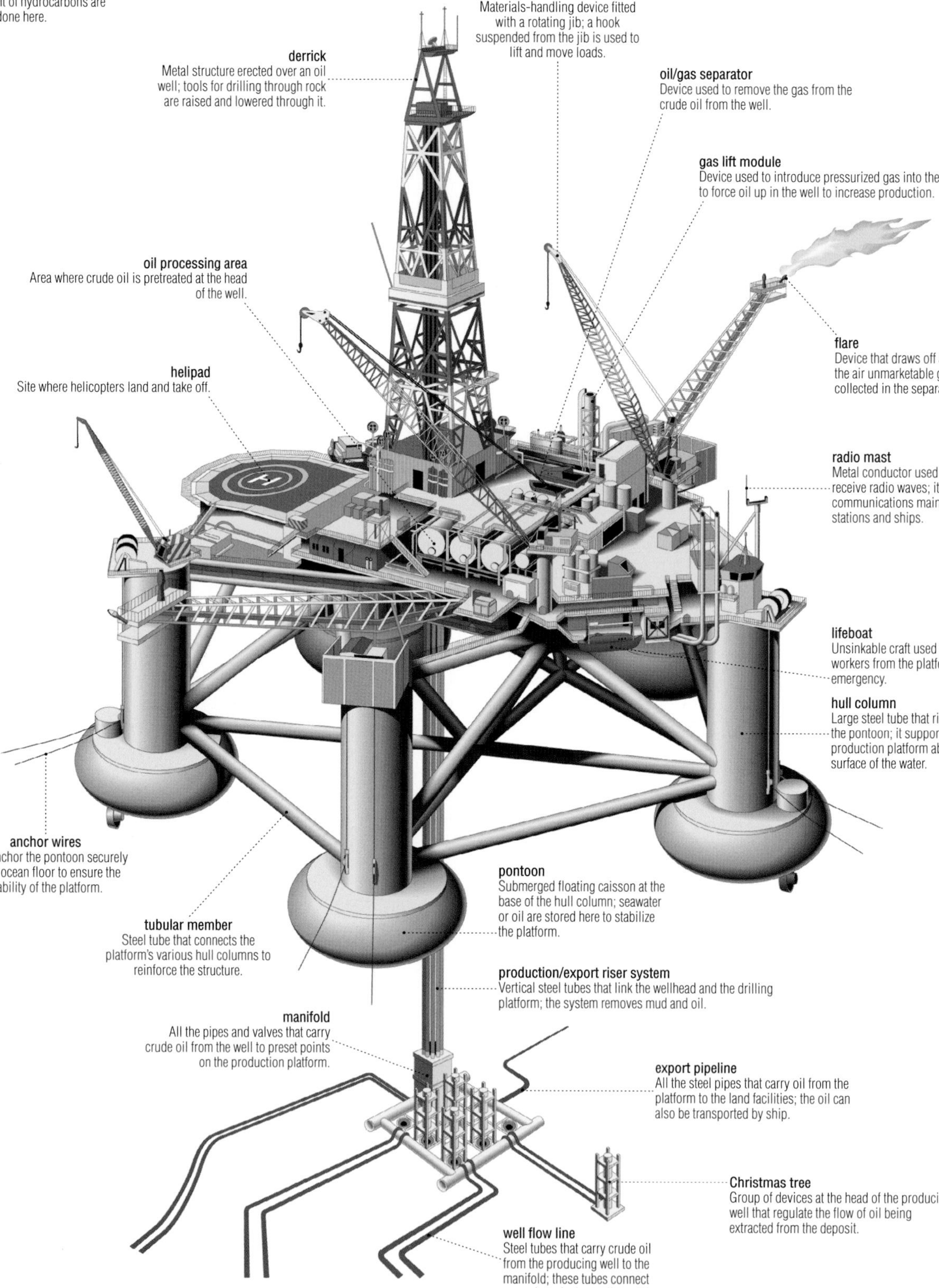
crane
Materials-handling device fitted with a rotating jib; a hook suspended from the jib is used to lift and move loads.
derrick
Metal structure erected over an oil well; tools for drilling through rock are raised and lowered through it.
oil/gas separator
Device used to remove the gas from the crude oil from the well.
gas lift module
Device used to introduce pressurized gas into the deposit to force oil up in the well to increase production.
oil processing area
Area where crude oil is pretreated at the head of the well.
flare
Device that draws off and burns in the air unmarketable gases collected in the separator.
helipad
Site where helicopters land and take off.
radio mast
Metal conductor used to send and receive radio waves; it provides communications mainly with coasta
stations and ships.
lifeboat
Unsinkable craft used to evacuate workers from the platform in an emergency.
hull column
Large steel tube that rises above the pontoon; it supports the production platform above the surface of the water.
anchor wires
They anchor the pontoon securely to the ocean floor to ensure the stability of the platform.
pontoon
Submerged floating caisson at the base of the hull column; seawater or oil are stored here to stabilize the platform.
tubular member
Steel tube that connects the platform's various hull columns to reinforce the structure.
production/export riser system
Vertical steel tubes that link the wellhead and the drilling platform; the system removes mud and oil.
manifold
All the pipes and valves that carry crude oil from the well to preset points on the production platform.
export pipeline
All the steel pipes that carry oil from the platform to the land facilities; the oil can also be transported by ship.
Christmas tree
Group of devices at the head of the producing well that regulate the flow of oil being extracted from the deposit.
well flow line
Steel tubes that carry crude oil from the producing well to the manifold; these tubes connect several producing wells together.

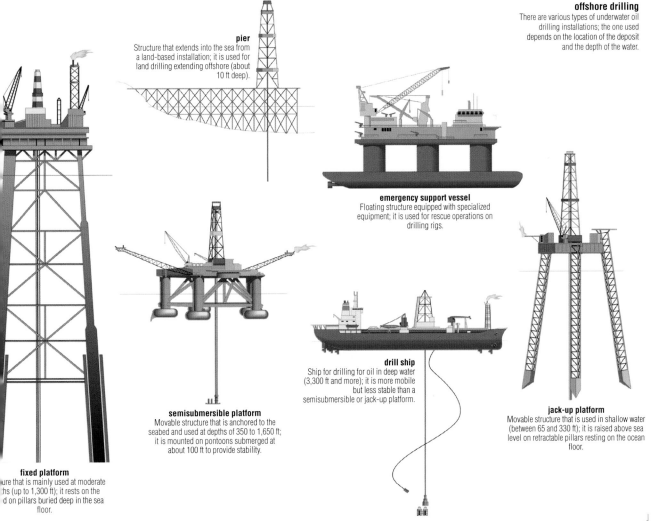

offshore prospecting
Vibrations from an exploding charge in the sea are used to locate oil deposits; prospecting offshore is more difficult than on land.

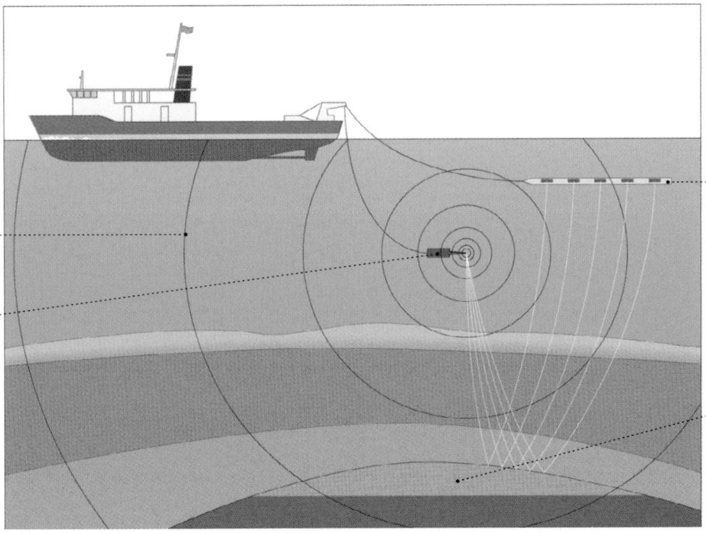

shock wave
The shock wave spreads and sends back an echo, which varies with the density and depth of the layers of subsoil; with this information, the composition of the subsoil can be determined.

blasting charge
Quantity of explosives (substances capable of discharging high-temperature gases over a very short time period) that produce shock waves when detonated.

seismographic recording
A recording made using an apparatus called a seismograph; the analysis of its shock wave echoes detects the presence of rock layers that might contain pockets of petroleum or gas.

petroleum trap
Assemblage of porous rocks that contain recoverable oil reserves, which are produced from marine or land deposits.

offshore drilling

There are various types of underwater oil drilling installations; the one used depends on the location of the deposit and the depth of the water.

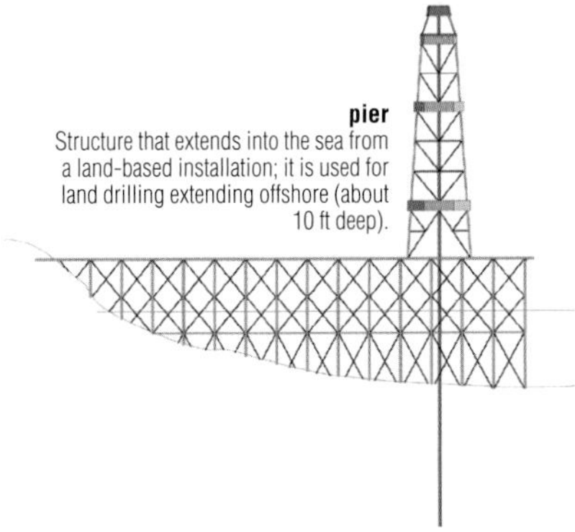

pier
Structure that extends into the sea from a land-based installation; it is used for land drilling extending offshore (about 10 ft deep).

fixed platform
...ure that is mainly used at moderate ...hs (up to 1,300 ft); it rests on the ...d on pillars buried deep in the sea floor.

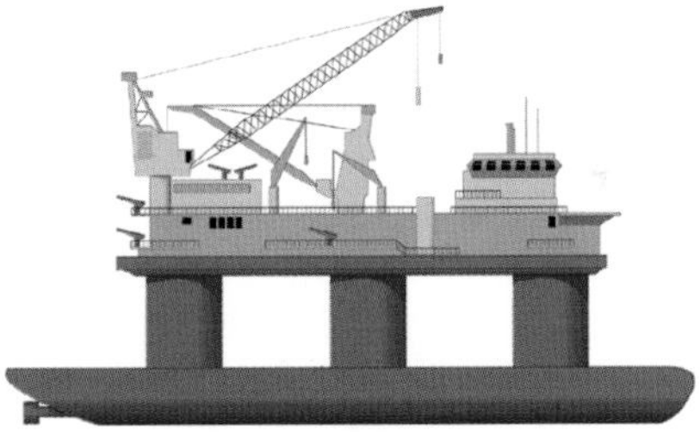

emergency support vessel
Floating structure equipped with specialized equipment; it is used for rescue operations on drilling rigs.

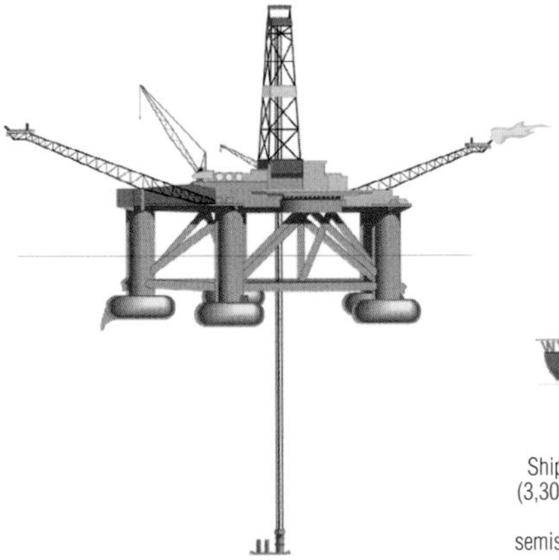

semisubmersible platform
Movable structure that is anchored to the seabed and used at depths of 350 to 1,650 ft; it is mounted on pontoons submerged at about 100 ft to provide stability.

drill ship
Ship for drilling for oil in deep water (3,300 ft and more); it is more mobile but less stable than a semisubmersible or jack-up platform.

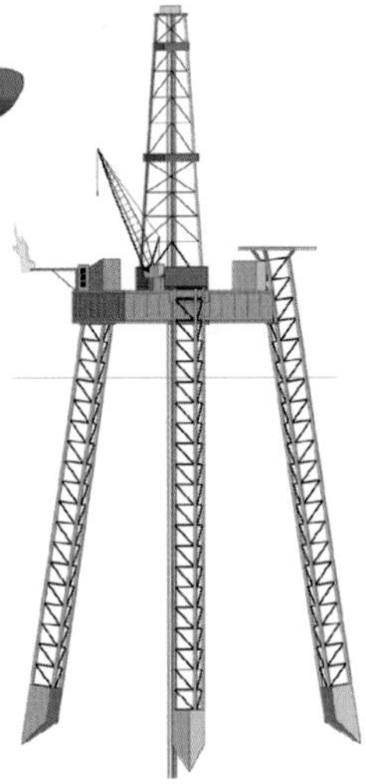

jack-up platform
Movable structure that is used in shallow water (between 65 and 330 ft); it is raised above sea level on retractable pillars resting on the ocean floor.

oil

Christmas tree
Group of devices at the head of the producing well that regulate the flow of oil being extracted from the deposit.

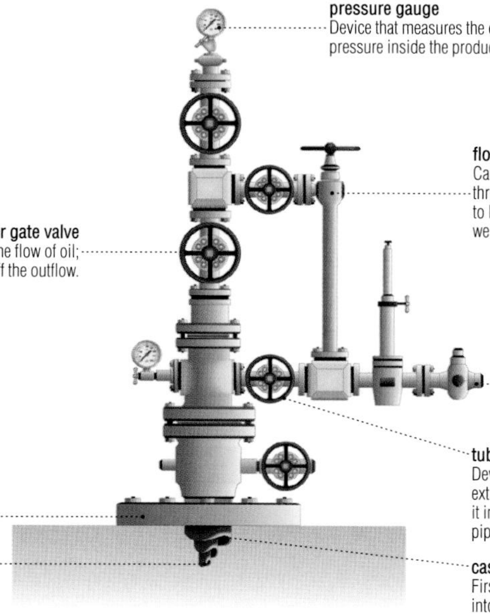

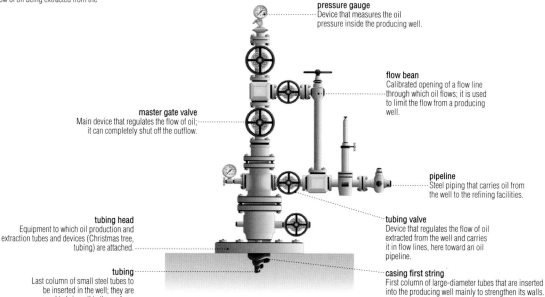

pressure gauge
Device that measures the oil pressure inside the producing well.

flow bean
Calibrated opening of a flow line through which oil flows; it is used to limit the flow from a producing well.

master gate valve
Main device that regulates the flow of oil; it can completely shut off the outflow.

pipeline
Steel piping that carries oil from the well to the refining facilities.

tubing head
Equipment to which oil production and extraction tubes and devices (Christmas tree, tubing) are attached.

tubing valve
Device that regulates the flow of oil extracted from the well and carries it in flow lines, here toward an oil pipeline.

tubing
Last column of small steel tubes to be inserted in the well; they are used to bring oil to the surface.

casing first string
First column of large-diameter tubes that are inserted into the producing well mainly to strengthen its walls.

crude-oil pipeline
Continuous underground, aboveground or underwater oil pipeline that can be thousands of miles long (the Trans-Siberian pipeline is 3,800 mi long).

offshore well
Hole dug in the sea floor to extract oil deposits; equipment such as the Christmas tree rests on the seabed.

production platform
Facility used to extract underwater oil deposits; the separation and treatment of hydrocarbons are mainly done here.

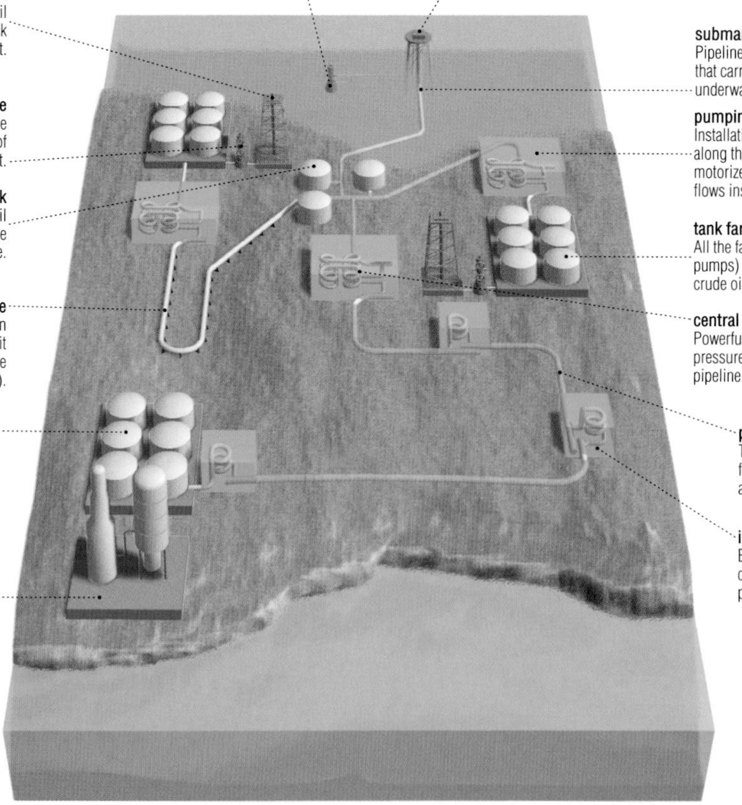

derrick
Metal structure erected over an oil well; tools for drilling through rock are raised and lowered through it.

submarine pipeline
Pipeline installed on the seabed that carries oil extracted from an underwater deposit to shore.

Christmas tree
Group of devices at the head of the producing well that regulate the flow of oil being extracted from the deposit.

pumping station
Installation located at regular intervals along the pipeline that is fitted with motorized pumps; it ensures that the oil flows inside the pipeline.

buffer tank
Large container that stores crude oil temporarily before it is pumped back into the pipeline.

tank farm
All the facilities (such as tanks and pumps) that store large quantities of crude oil to be sent later to the refinery.

aboveground pipeline
Oil pipeline that rests on aboveground supports to protect it from frozen ground (e.g., the Alaska pipeline).

central pumping station
Powerful pumping station that maintains the pressure required to move the oil along the pipeline to the next pumping station.

terminal
Facility located at the end of the pipeline that includes equipment such as tanks and pumps; it receives the crude oil before it is refined.

pipeline
The steel piping that carries oil from one treatment facility to another.

refinery
Plant in which crude oil is refined (separated and scrubbed) to obtain a broad range of finished products (including motor fuel and oils).

intermediate booster station
Booster station that reinforces the action o central station and maintains the flow of oi pipeline network.

tanks

Large covered cylindrical containers that are usually made of steel; liquid or gaseous oil products are stored here between the time they are refined and sold.

fixed-roof tank
Fixed roof that keeps the tank sealed tightly; it is used to store heavy products such as diesel fuel, kerosene and asphalt.

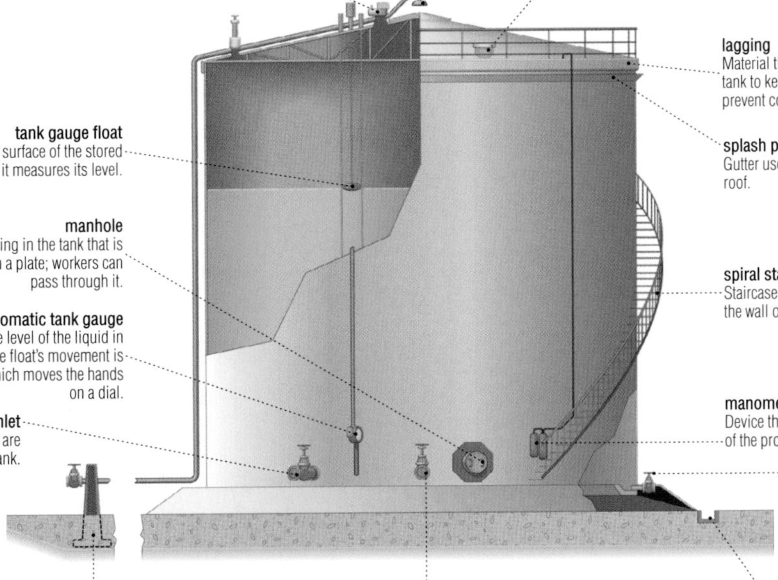
spray nozzle
Device that sprays water onto the roof of the tank to cool it when the temperature rises.
breather valve
Movable part that regulates the internal pressure of the tank; pressure fluctuates during emptying and filling and with the temperature.
manhole
Round opening in the tank that is covered with a plate; workers can pass through it.
lagging
Material that covers the wall of the tank to keep it watertight and prevent corrosion.
tank gauge float
Element that floats on the surface of the stored liquid; it measures its level.
splash plate
Gutter used to collect water draining from the roof.
manhole
Round opening in the tank that is covered with a plate; workers can pass through it.
spiral staircase
Staircase whose stairs wind around the wall of the tank to the roof.
automatic tank gauge
Device used to measure the level of the liquid in the tank; the tank gauge float's movement is transmitted to a magnet, which moves the hands on a dial.
manometer
Device that measures the pressure of the product inside the tank.
secondary inlet
Small pipe through which liquids are introduced into the tank.
drain valve
Device for emptying the liquid from the tank.
bund wall
Cement wall around the tank that protects the environment in the event of accidental leakage.
main inlet
Large pipe through which liquids are introduced into the tank.
concrete drain
Small concrete trench used to drain off the product in the event of a spill or when the tank is emptied.

floating-roof tank
Tank whose floating roof rests directly on the surface of the liquid to minimize the evaporation of hydrocarbons; it is used to store the most volatile products.

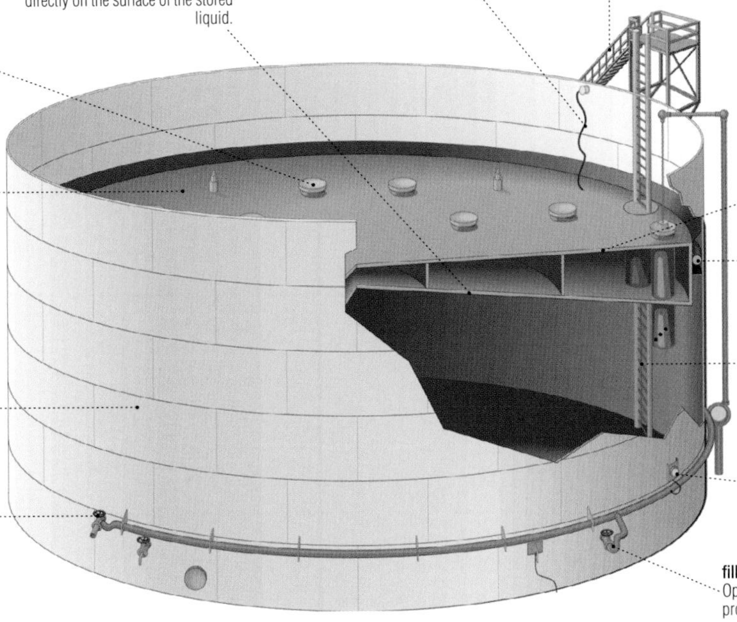
ground
Wire that connects the tank and its contents to the ground to prevent static electricity from accumulating and avoid the risk of fire.
stairs
Structural element giving access to the roof of the tank.
bottom deck
Lower part of the roof; it rests directly on the surface of the stored liquid.
manhole
Round opening in the tank that is covered with a plate; workers can pass through it.
top deck
Upper part of the roof; the space between the top and bottom decks is used to contain evaporated hydrocarbons.
floating roof
Metal cover that rests on the surface of the stored liquid; it fluctuates with the level of the fluid and slides vertically inside the shell.
sealing ring
Part that fills the space between the roof and the shell to prevent any hydrocarbons from evaporating and polluting the atmosphere.
ladder
Movable device that consists of rungs (crossbars); it is used to climb up and down.
shell
Vertical cylindrical wall of the tank.
thermometer
Device that sets and controls the temperature of the product inside the tank.
drain valve
Device for emptying the liquid from the tank.
filling inlet
Operation by which a liquid product is introduced into the tank.

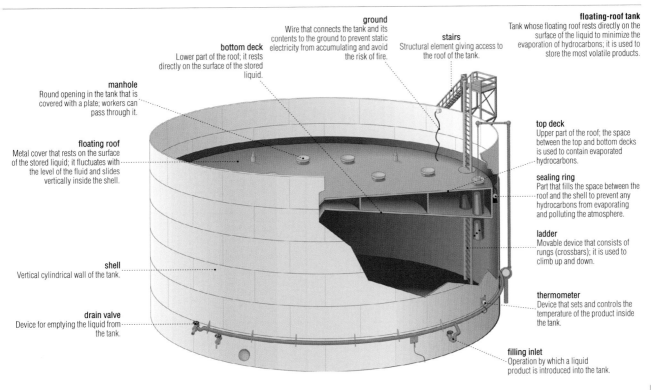

oil

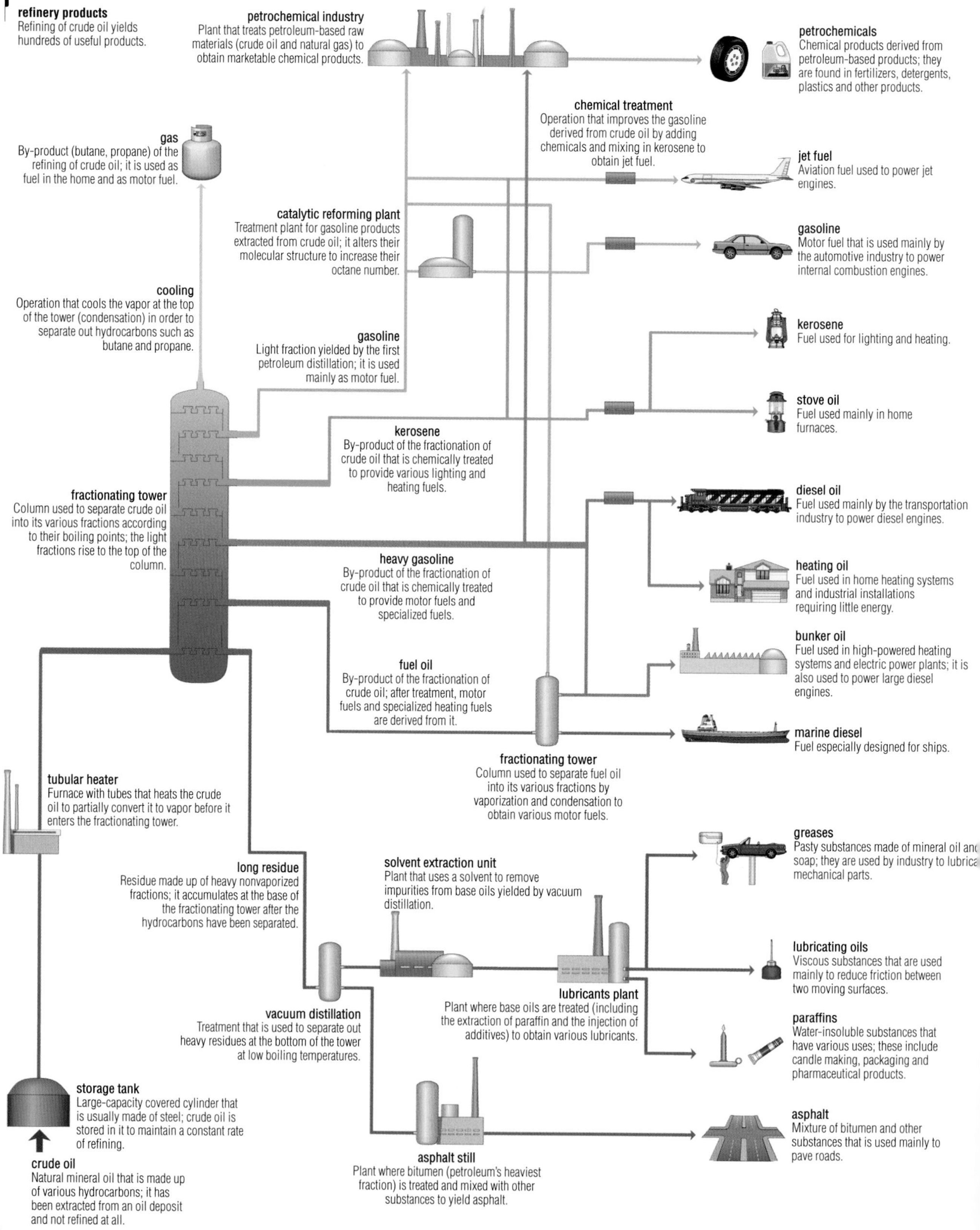
refinery products
Refining of crude oil yields hundreds of useful products.
petrochemical industry
Plant that treats petroleum-based raw materials (crude oil and natural gas) to obtain marketable chemical products.
petrochemicals
Chemical products derived from petroleum-based products; they are found in fertilizers, detergents, plastics and other products.
gas
By-product (butane, propane) of the refining of crude oil; it is used as fuel in the home and as motor fuel.
chemical treatment
Operation that improves the gasoline derived from crude oil by adding chemicals and mixing in kerosene to obtain jet fuel.
jet fuel
Aviation fuel used to power jet engines.
catalytic reforming plant
Treatment plant for gasoline products extracted from crude oil; it alters their molecular structure to increase their octane number.
gasoline
Motor fuel that is used mainly by the automotive industry to power internal combustion engines.
cooling
Operation that cools the vapor at the top of the tower (condensation) in order to separate out hydrocarbons such as butane and propane.
gasoline
Light fraction yielded by the first petroleum distillation; it is used mainly as motor fuel.
kerosene
Fuel used for lighting and heating.
stove oil
Fuel used mainly in home furnaces.
kerosene
By-product of the fractionation of crude oil that is chemically treated to provide various lighting and heating fuels.
fractionating tower
Column used to separate crude oil into its various fractions according to their boiling points; the light fractions rise to the top of the column.
diesel oil
Fuel used mainly by the transportation industry to power diesel engines.
heavy gasoline
By-product of the fractionation of crude oil that is chemically treated to provide motor fuels and specialized fuels.
heating oil
Fuel used in home heating systems and industrial installations requiring little energy.
bunker oil
Fuel used in high-powered heating systems and electric power plants; it is also used to power large diesel engines.
fuel oil
By-product of the fractionation of crude oil; after treatment, motor fuels and specialized heating fuels are derived from it.
marine diesel
Fuel especially designed for ships.
fractionating tower
Column used to separate fuel oil into its various fractions by vaporization and condensation to obtain various motor fuels.
tubular heater
Furnace with tubes that heats the crude oil to partially convert it to vapor before it enters the fractionating tower.
greases
Pasty substances made of mineral oil and soap; they are used by industry to lubricate mechanical parts.
solvent extraction unit
Plant that uses a solvent to remove impurities from base oils yielded by vacuum distillation.
long residue
Residue made up of heavy nonvaporized fractions; it accumulates at the base of the fractionating tower after the hydrocarbons have been separated.
lubricating oils
Viscous substances that are used mainly to reduce friction between two moving surfaces.
lubricants plant
Plant where base oils are treated (including the extraction of paraffin and the injection of additives) to obtain various lubricants.
vacuum distillation
Treatment that is used to separate out heavy residues at the bottom of the tower at low boiling temperatures.
paraffins
Water-insoluble substances that have various uses; these include candle making, packaging and pharmaceutical products.
storage tank
Large-capacity covered cylinder that is usually made of steel; crude oil is stored in it to maintain a constant rate of refining.
asphalt
Mixture of bitumen and other substances that is used mainly to pave roads.
crude oil
Natural mineral oil that is made up of various hydrocarbons; it has been extracted from an oil deposit and not refined at all.
asphalt still
Plant where bitumen (petroleum's heaviest fraction) is treated and mixed with other substances to yield asphalt.

hydroelectric complex

The reservoir structures and installations that use water power to produce electricity.

crest of spillway
Cement crest over which the reservoir's overflow discharges when the spillway gates are opened.
spillway gate
Movable vertical panel; it is opened to allow the reservoir's overflow to pass through.
spillway
Channel that discharges excess water from the reservoir during flooding to avoid submerging the dam.
top of dam
Upper part of the dam; it rises above the water level of the reservoir by several yards.
reservoir
Basin formed by the construction of a dam; it holds back a very large volume of water so that the flow rate can be controlled.
headbay
Part of the reservoir immediately in front of the dam where the current originates.
penstock
Channel that carries water under pressure to the power plant's turbines.
gantry crane
Hoisting device in the form of a bridge; it moves along rails.
diversion tunnel
Underground conduit that diverts water during construction.
spillway chute
Inclined surface along which discharged water flows out.
training wall
Wall that separates the spillway chutes; it is used to direct the water flow.
log chute
Structure that allows floating wood to travel from upstream to downstream of the dam.
afterbay
Area of the watercourse where water is discharged after passing through the turbines.
power plant
Plant that uses an energy source, here water, and converts it into electricity.
machine hall
Area that houses the generator units used to produce electricity.
control room
Area that contains the various control and monitoring devices required for the production of electricity.
bushing
Device that allows the conductor to pass through the wall of the transformer and separates it from the latter.
dam
Barrier built across a watercourse in order to build up a supply of water for use as an energy source.

ENERGY

hydroelectric complex

cross section of a hydroelectric power plant
Hydroelectric power plant: plant that produces electricity from energy generated by flowing water.

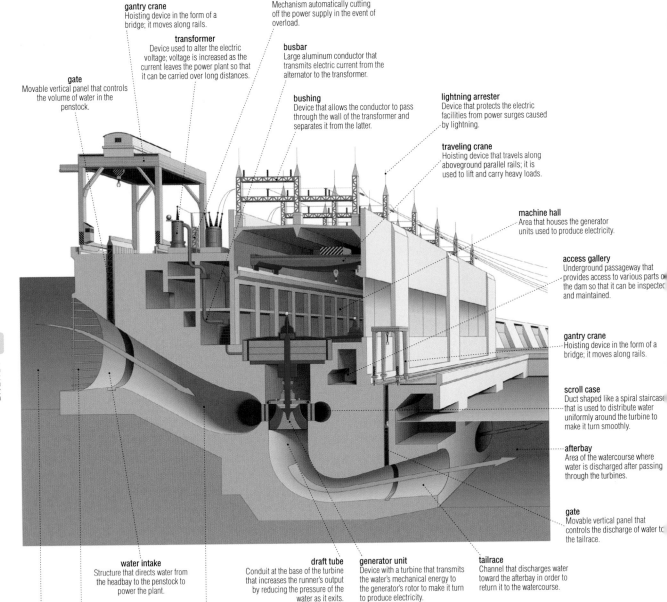

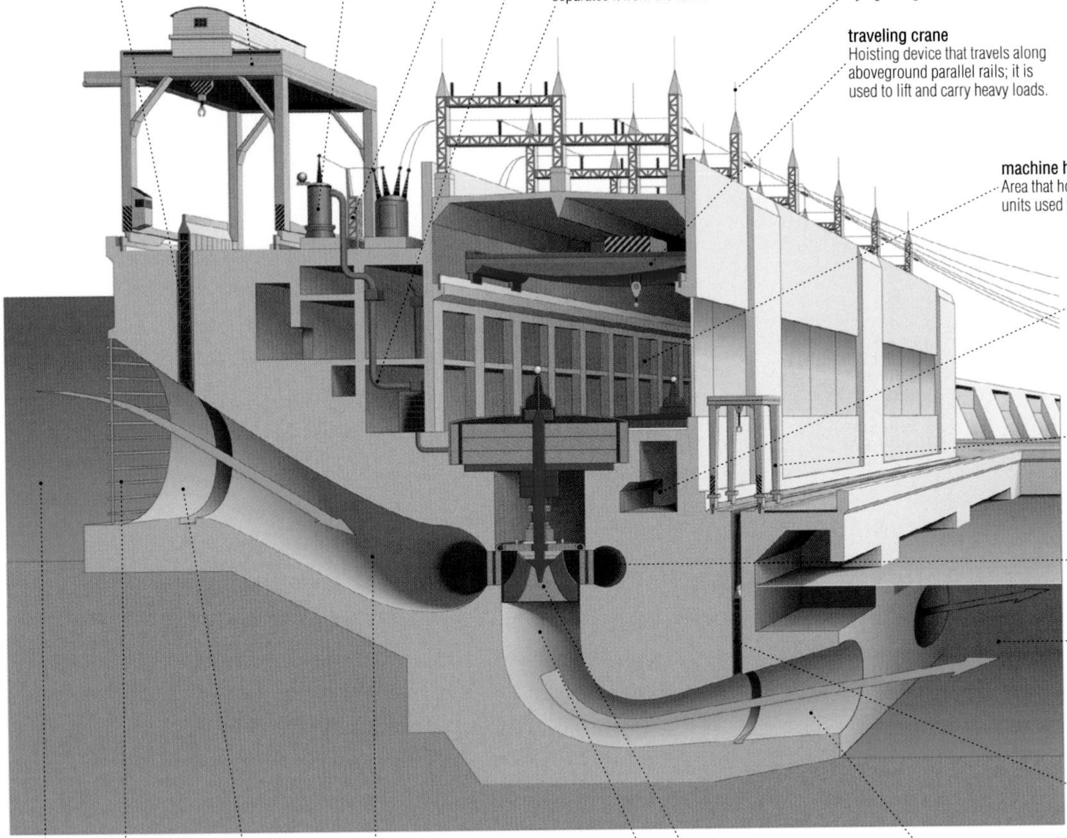

gantry crane
Hoisting device in the form of a bridge; it moves along rails.
circuit breaker
Mechanism automatically cutting off the power supply in the event of overload.
transformer
Device used to alter the electric voltage; voltage is increased as the current leaves the power plant so that it can be carried over long distances.
busbar
Large aluminum conductor that transmits electric current from the alternator to the transformer.
gate
Movable vertical panel that controls the volume of water in the penstock.
bushing
Device that allows the conductor to pass through the wall of the transformer and separates it from the latter.
lightning arrester
Device that protects the electric facilities from power surges caused by lightning.
traveling crane
Hoisting device that travels along aboveground parallel rails; it is used to lift and carry heavy loads.
machine hall
Area that houses the generator units used to produce electricity.
access gallery
Underground passageway that provides access to various parts o the dam so that it can be inspectec and maintained.
gantry crane
Hoisting device in the form of a bridge; it moves along rails.
scroll case
Duct shaped like a spiral staircase that is used to distribute water uniformly around the turbine to make it turn smoothly.
afterbay
Area of the watercourse where water is discharged after passing through the turbines.
gate
Movable vertical panel that controls the discharge of water tc the tailrace.
water intake
Structure that directs water from the headbay to the penstock to power the plant.
draft tube
Conduit at the base of the turbine that increases the runner's output by reducing the pressure of the water as it exits.
generator unit
Device with a turbine that transmits the water's mechanical energy to the generator's rotor to make it turn to produce electricity.
tailrace
Channel that discharges water toward the afterbay in order to return it to the watercourse.
screen
Assembly of bars placed in front of the water intake to hold back anything that could hinder the operation of the turbine.
penstock
Channel that carries water under pressure to the power plant's turbines.
reservoir
Basin formed by the construction of a dam; it holds back a very large volume of water so that the flow rate can be controlled.

generator unit

Device with a turbine that transmits the water's mechanical energy to the generator's rotor to make it turn to produce electricity.

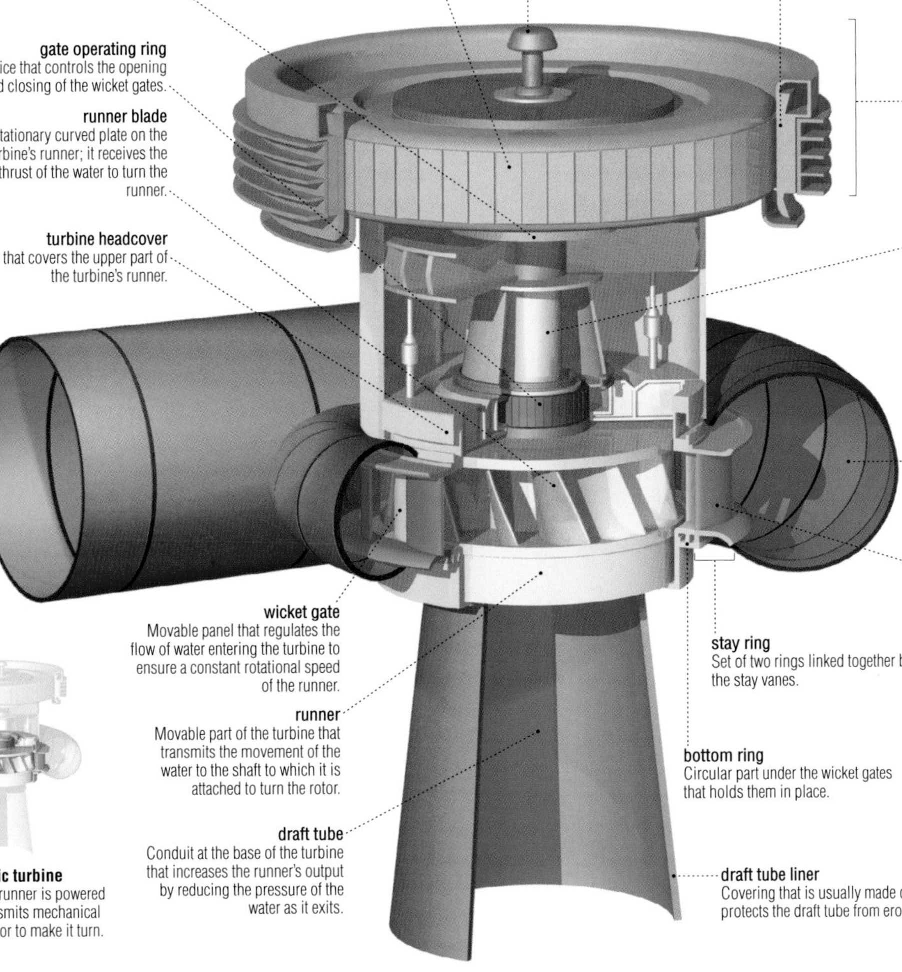

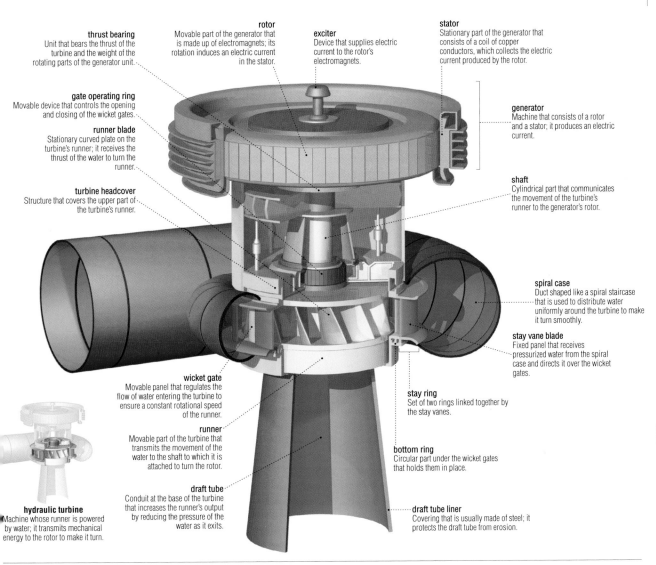

thrust bearing
Unit that bears the thrust of the turbine and the weight of the rotating parts of the generator unit.

rotor
Movable part of the generator that is made up of electromagnets; its rotation induces an electric current in the stator.

exciter
Device that supplies electric current to the rotor's electromagnets.

stator
Stationary part of the generator that consists of a coil of copper conductors, which collects the electric current produced by the rotor.

gate operating ring
Movable device that controls the opening and closing of the wicket gates.

generator
Machine that consists of a rotor and a stator; it produces an electric current.

runner blade
Stationary curved plate on the turbine's runner; it receives the thrust of the water to turn the runner.

shaft
Cylindrical part that communicates the movement of the turbine's runner to the generator's rotor.

turbine headcover
Structure that covers the upper part of the turbine's runner.

spiral case
Duct shaped like a spiral staircase that is used to distribute water uniformly around the turbine to make it turn smoothly.

stay vane blade
Fixed panel that receives pressurized water from the spiral case and directs it over the wicket gates.

wicket gate
Movable panel that regulates the flow of water entering the turbine to ensure a constant rotational speed of the runner.

stay ring
Set of two rings linked together by the stay vanes.

runner
Movable part of the turbine that transmits the movement of the water to the shaft to which it is attached to turn the rotor.

bottom ring
Circular part under the wicket gates that holds them in place.

draft tube
Conduit at the base of the turbine that increases the runner's output by reducing the pressure of the water as it exits.

draft tube liner
Covering that is usually made of steel; it protects the draft tube from erosion.

hydraulic turbine
Machine whose runner is powered by water; it transmits mechanical energy to the rotor to make it turn.

runners
Movable parts of the turbine that transmit the movement of the water to the shaft to which they are attached to turn the rotor.

Kaplan runner
Type of runner that is suited to low heights of water (usually between 30 and 200 ft) and variable flow rates.

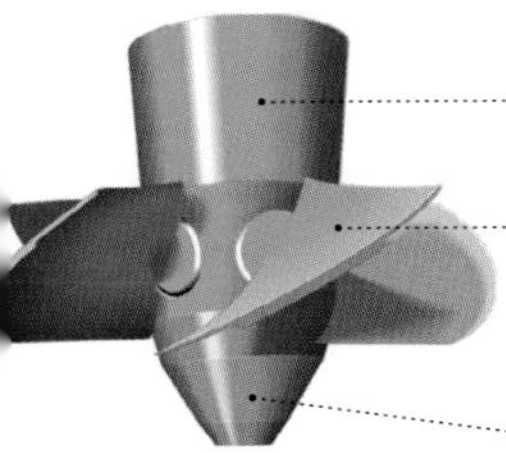

hub
Part of the runner that holds the shaft; the runner blades are attached to it.

runner blade
Movable part that is fixed to the hub of the runner; it turns through the action of water power on it.

hub cover
Cover for the lower cone-shaped part of the hub.

Pelton runner
Type of runner that is suited to high water sources (usually over 1,000 ft) and low flow rates.

bucket
Small bucket that is attached to the turbine's runner; water enters it to turn the wheel.

coupling bolt
Element made up of a nut and a bolt that attaches the runner to the shaft plate to transmit its movement to the runner.

bucket ring
Disk housing all the turbine buckets that activates the runner.

Francis runner
Most common type of runner that is suited to average heights of water (usually between 100 and 1,000 ft).

blade
Stationary curved plate on the turbine's runner; it receives the thrust of the water to turn the runner.

ring
Circular part that supports the wicket gates.

examples of dams

There are masonry dams, concrete dams and embankment dams; the choice depends on criteria such as the nature of the ground, the shape of the valley and the materials available.

buttress dam
Used mainly in wide valleys, it consists of an impermeable wall, which is shored up by a series of buttresses to transmit the thrust of the water to the foundation.

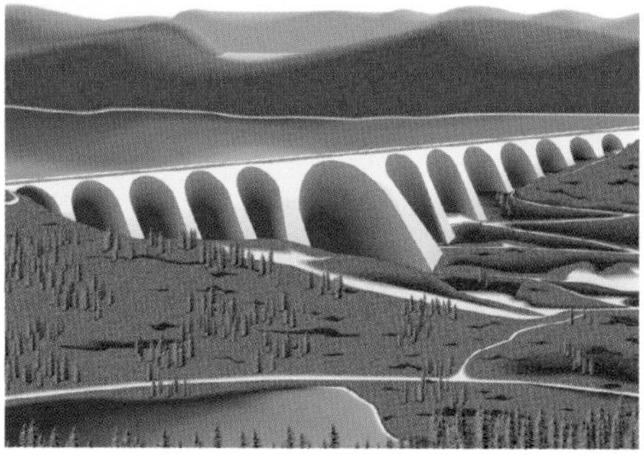

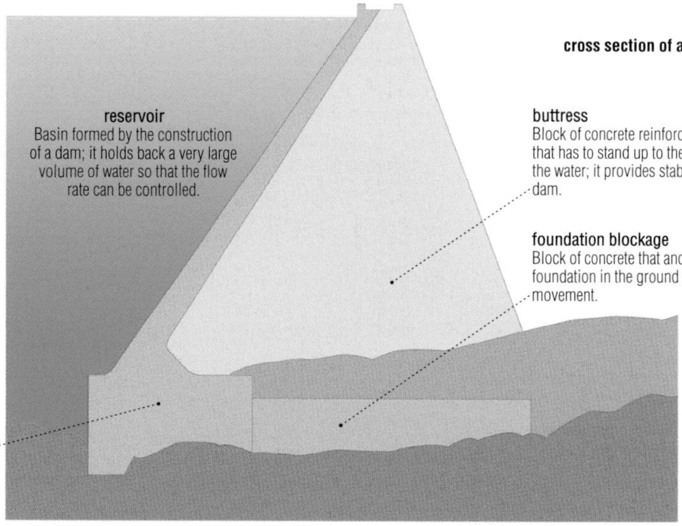

cross section of a buttress dam

reservoir
Basin formed by the construction of a dam; it holds back a very large volume of water so that the flow rate can be controlled.

buttress
Block of concrete reinforcing a wall that has to stand up to the thrust of the water; it provides stability to the dam.

foundation blockage
Block of concrete that anchors the foundation in the ground to prevent movement.

foundation
Concrete structure that supports the weight of the dam and transmits it to the ground to provide stability to the dam.

embankment dam
Formed of mounds of earth or rocks, it is used mainly when the subsoil does not allow for construction of a concrete dam.

cross section of an embankment dam

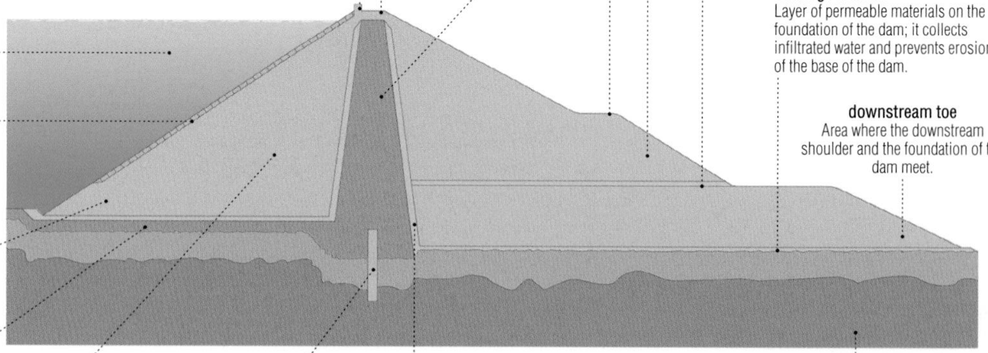

top of dam
Upper part of the dam; it rises above the water level of the reservoir by several yards.

berm
Horizontal ledge that stabilizes the upstream or downstream shoulder.

downstream shoulder
Soil embankment that, together with the upstream shoulder, provides stability to the structure.

wave wall
Small wall located at the top of the upstream shoulder that protects the dam against waves.

clay core
Central portion of the dam that is usually made of compact clay to make it watertight.

drainage layer
Layer of permeable materials that is inserted into large-scale dams to collect infiltrated water.

drainage blanket
Layer of permeable materials on the foundation of the dam; it collects infiltrated water and prevents erosion of the base of the dam.

reservoir
Basin formed by the construction of a dam; it holds back a very large volume of water so that the flow rate can be controlled.

pitching
Layer of rock or concrete blocks that covers the upstream shoulder to prevent erosion.

downstream toe
Area where the downstream shoulder and the foundation of the dam meet.

upstream toe
Area where the upstream shoulder and the foundation of the dam meet.

upstream blanket
Impermeable layer that consists of compact clay; it rests on the bottom of the dam to prevent infiltration.

upstream shoulder
Soil embankment located on the reservoir side; its mass provides stability to the dam.

cut-off trench
Area of the foundation of the dam that is connected to the core; it contains impermeable materials to limit leakage and infiltration under the dam.

sand
Granular material that is inserted between the core and the shoulder; it filters particles carried by the water flow to prevent erosion.

foundation of dam
Natural terrain (such as rock, sand or clay) on which the dam is built.

examples of dams

cross section of an arch dam

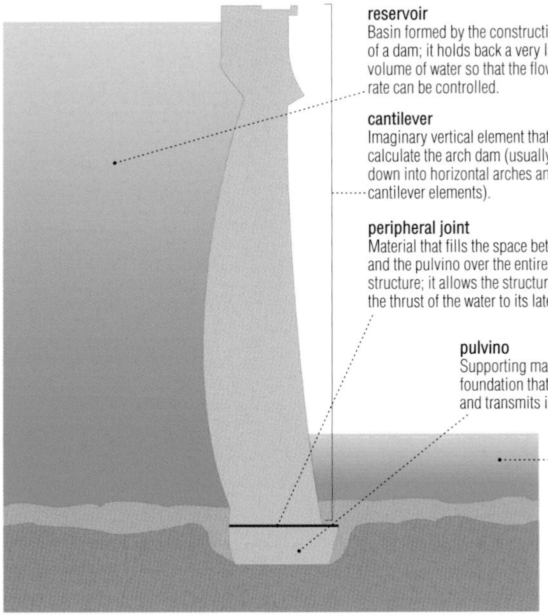
reservoir
Basin formed by the construction of a dam; it holds back a very large volume of water so that the flow rate can be controlled.
cantilever
Imaginary vertical element that is used to calculate the arch dam (usually by breaking it down into horizontal arches and vertical cantilever elements).
peripheral joint
Material that fills the space between the dam and the pulvino over the entire length of the structure; it allows the structure to transmit the thrust of the water to its lateral supports.
pulvino
Supporting mass of the dam foundation that bears its weight and transmits it to the ground.
afterbay
Area of the watercourse where water is discharged after passing through the turbines.
soil
Natural rocky ground in which the dam is anchored.

arch dam
Its curvature allows most of the water's thrust to be transmitted to the usually narrow valley slopes supporting it.

cross section of a gravity dam

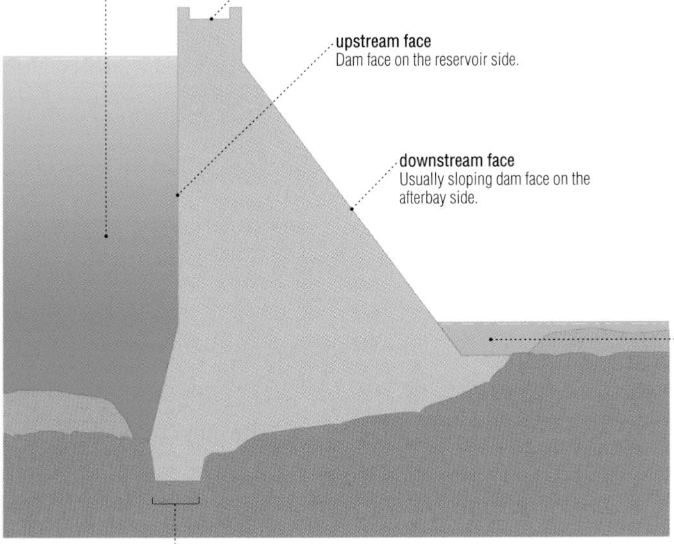
reservoir
Basin formed by the construction of a dam; it holds back a very large volume of water so that the flow rate can be controlled.
top of dam
Upper part of the dam that usually contains a roadway.
upstream face
Dam face on the reservoir side.
downstream face
Usually sloping dam face on the afterbay side.
afterbay
Area of the watercourse where water is discharged after passing through the turbines.
cut-off trench
Watertight structure that extends the foundations of the dam into the ground; it limits leakage and infiltration under the dam.

gravity dam
Its huge mass resists the thrust of the water to prevent it from overturning or sliding; this type of dam is usually used to hold back large volumes of water.

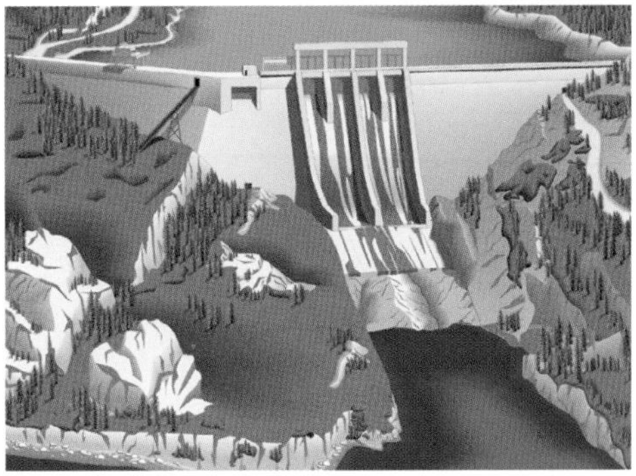

steps in production of electricity

In a hydroelectric power plant, water is turned into electricity, which is carried to consumers along a transportation and distribution network.

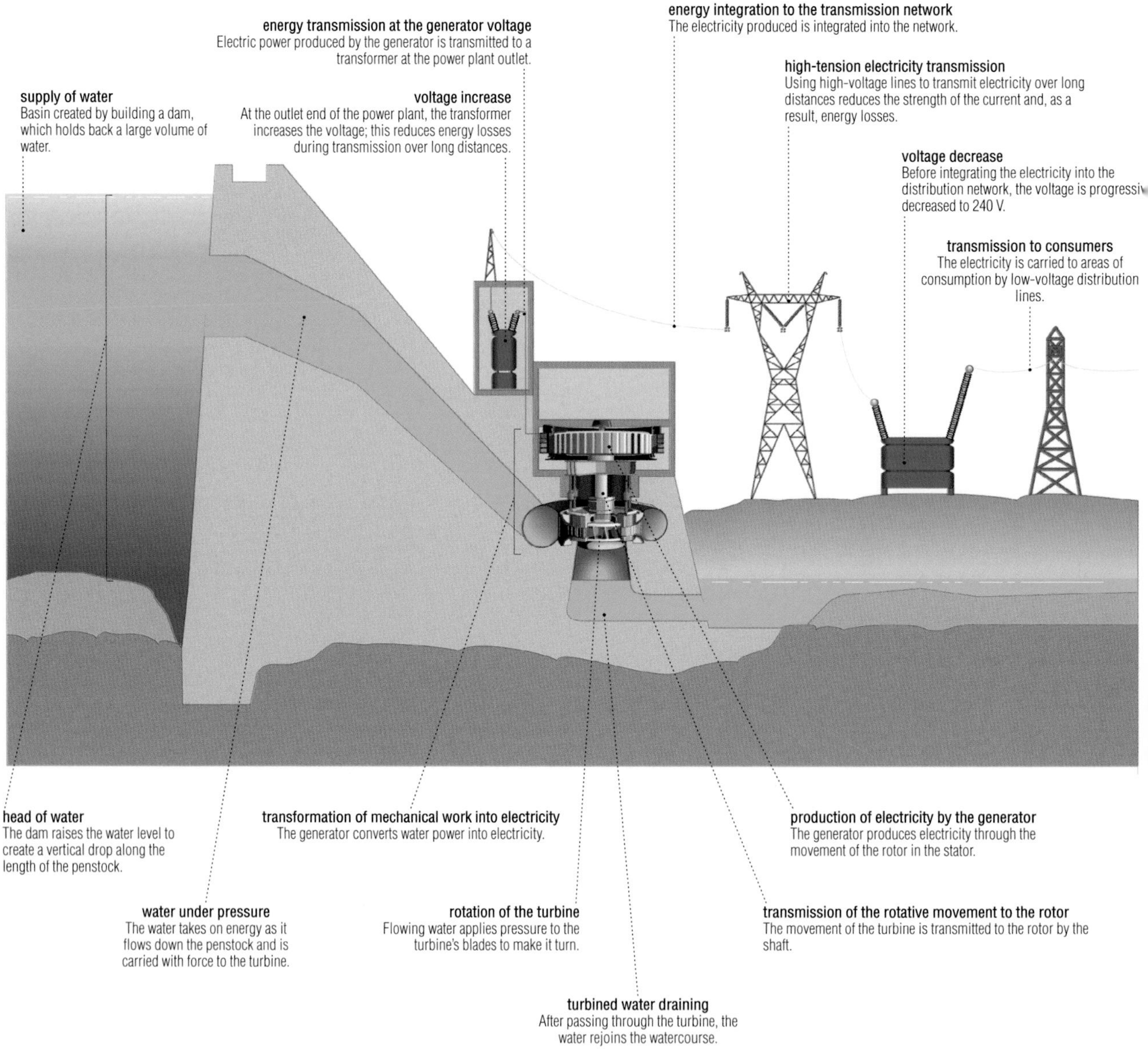

energy transmission at the generator voltage
Electric power produced by the generator is transmitted to a transformer at the power plant outlet.
energy integration to the transmission network
The electricity produced is integrated into the network.
high-tension electricity transmission
Using high-voltage lines to transmit electricity over long distances reduces the strength of the current and, as a result, energy losses.
supply of water
Basin created by building a dam, which holds back a large volume of water.
voltage increase
At the outlet end of the power plant, the transformer increases the voltage; this reduces energy losses during transmission over long distances.
voltage decrease
Before integrating the electricity into the distribution network, the voltage is progressi
decreased to 240 V.
transmission to consumers
The electricity is carried to areas of consumption by low-voltage distribution lines.
head of water
The dam raises the water level to create a vertical drop along the length of the penstock.
transformation of mechanical work into electricity
The generator converts water power into electricity.
production of electricity by the generator
The generator produces electricity through the movement of the rotor in the stator.
water under pressure
The water takes on energy as it flows down the penstock and is carried with force to the turbine.
rotation of the turbine
Flowing water applies pressure to the turbine's blades to make it turn.
transmission of the rotative movement to the rotor
The movement of the turbine is transmitted to the rotor by the shaft.
turbined water draining
After passing through the turbine, the water rejoins the watercourse.

electricity transmission

Electricity is carried by overhead and underground lines; due to high cost, underground lines are used mainly in cities.

medium-tension distribution line
Overhead line that distributes electricity at a voltage between 750 and 50,000 V; its conductors are located at the top of electricity poles.

hot line connector
Linking piece with a bolt, which is tightened to bring together two conductors to establish an electric connection between them.

insulator
Piece of nonconducting material that connects the distribution line conductors to the support.

overhead connection
The equipment and overhead conductors that connect a subscriber's electric system to the public distribution network.

crossarm
Horizontal element located at the top of an electricity pole; insulators are attached to it.

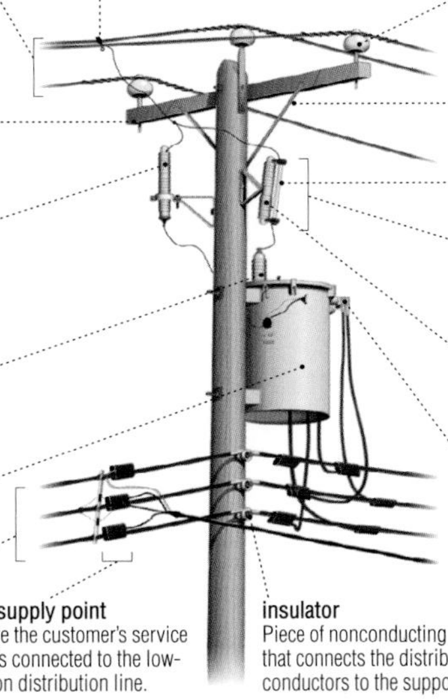

brace
Slanted part that connects the pole to the crossarm to hold it in place horizontally.

fuse
Protection device for the electric circuit; it falls from the fuse holder to cut the current in the event of a surge.

lightning arrester
Device that protects the electric facilities from power surges caused by lightning.

fuse cutout
Unit that consists of a fuse and a fuse holder.

bushing
Insulator and point where the current enters the medium-tension transformer.

fuse holder
Electric junction point where the fuse is attached and on which it articulates so the fuse can fall over.

transformer
Device that alters electric voltage; voltage is decreased before being distributed by low-tension lines to areas of consumption.

terminal
Part on which low-tension distribution line conductors are joined to the transformers.

low-tension distribution line
Overhead line that distributes electricity up to a voltage of 750 V; its conductors are located under the transformer.

supply point
Place where the customer's service entrance is connected to the low-tension distribution line.

insulator
Piece of nonconducting material that connects the distribution line conductors to the support.

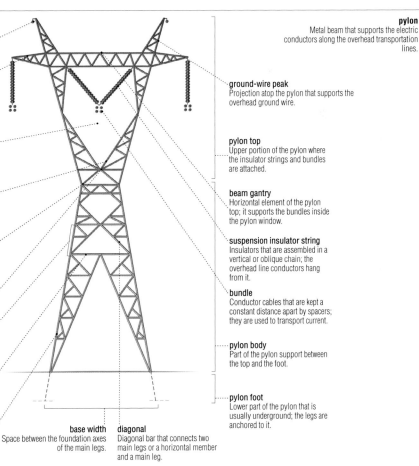

overhead ground wire
Conductor that is connected to the ground and attached above the bundles of the overhead lines to protect them from lightning.

pylon
Metal beam that supports the electric conductors along the overhead transportation lines.

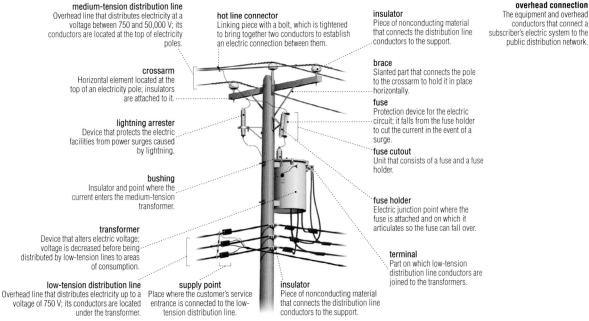

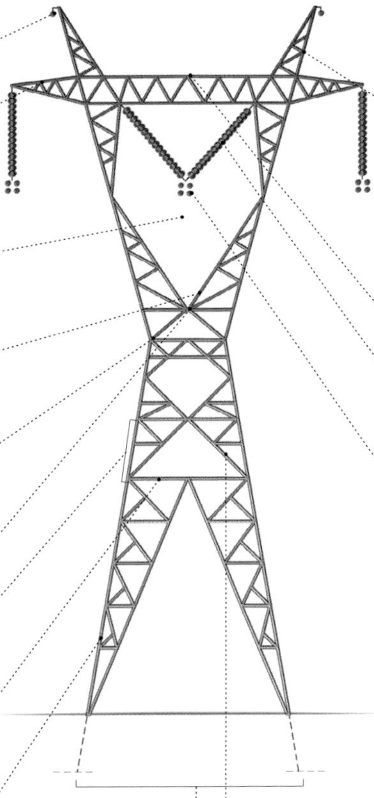

crossarm
Horizontal element that protrudes on each side of the pylon; it supports the bundles by means of suspension insulator strings.

ground-wire peak
Projection atop the pylon that supports the overhead ground wire.

pylon window
Space bounded by the inner side of the arms of the K-frame and the beam gantry.

pylon top
Upper portion of the pylon where the insulator strings and bundles are attached.

K-frame
Part of the pylon that rests on the waist; it has two branches that end at the beam gantry.

beam gantry
Horizontal element of the pylon top; it supports the bundles inside the pylon window.

waist
Demarcation bar between the pylon top and body that is held tightly between them.

suspension insulator string
Insulators that are assembled in a vertical or oblique chain; the overhead line conductors hang from it.

node
Point at which several legs and bars come together.

bundle
Conductor cables that are kept a constant distance apart by spacers; they are used to transport current.

panel
Part of the pylon between two horizontal members.

pylon body
Part of the pylon support between the top and the foot.

horizontal member
Horizontal bar that connects the main legs to strengthen them.

pylon foot
Lower part of the pylon that is usually underground; the legs are anchored to it.

main leg
The main tower legs of the pylon body; they support mainly vertical weights.

base width
Space between the foundation axes of the main legs.

diagonal
Diagonal bar that connects two main legs or a horizontal member and a main leg.

tidal power plant

Plant that harnesses tidal power (the motion of the rising and falling tides) to produce electric power.

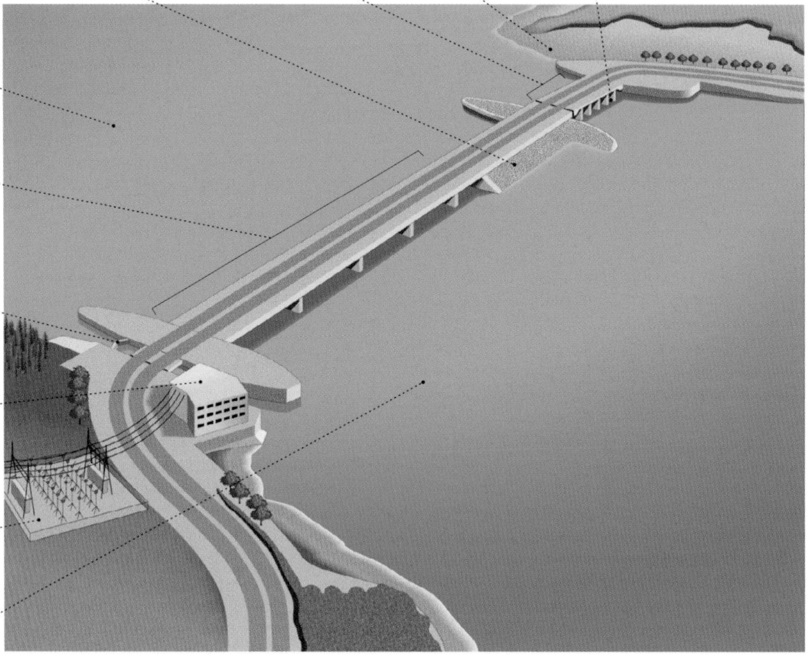
inactive dike
Part of the dam made up mainly of rocky material; it is built between the plant and the operating dam to separate the basin from the sea.
operating dam
Structure with gates that control the basin level in relation to the level of the sea.
bank
Strip of land bordering the sea.
gate
Movable vertical panel that controls the rate of flow of the water between the sea and the basin.
sea
Vast body of saltwater at some distance inland; it is not as deep as an ocean.
power plant
Part of the dam housing bulb units that are powered by the rise and fall of the sea to produce electricity.
lock
Structure with doors and gates that is built between the sea and the basin; it allows boats to pass from one level to the other.
administrative building
substation
The devices (such as transformers and changeover switches) that increase the voltage of the electricity and carry it to the network.
basin
Area in which water is stored at high tide; the basin empties out through the penstocks at low tide.

cross section of a power plant

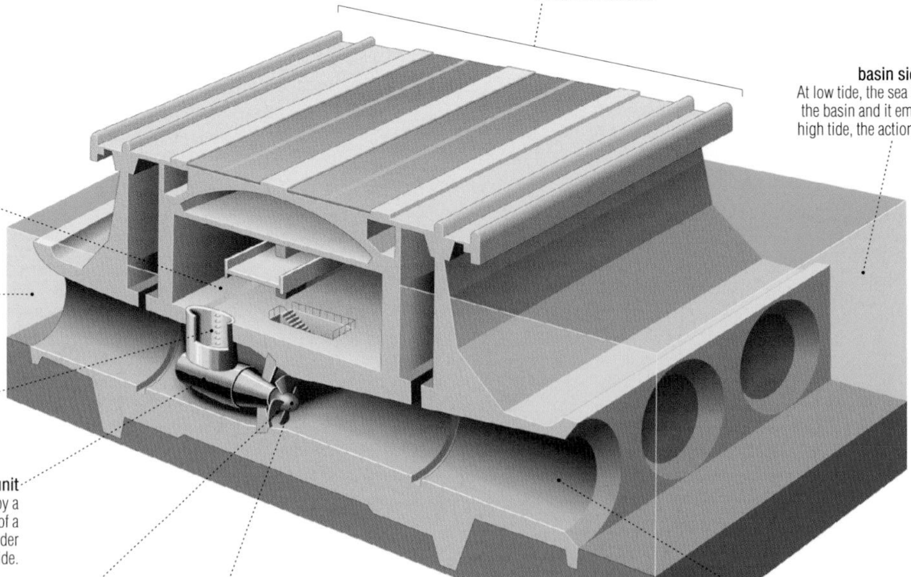
top of dam
Upper part of the plant; it usually has an access road.
basin side
At low tide, the sea is lower than the basin and it empties out; at high tide, the action is reversed.
operating floor
Part of the plant that houses the equipment needed to operate the bulb units (including maintenance and control devices).
sea side
At high tide, the sea is higher than the basin and it fills up; at low tide, the action is reversed.
access shaft
Vertical shaft connecting the operating floor to the generator so that inspection and maintenance can be carried out.
bulb unit
A turbine is connected by a horizontal axis to the rotor of a generator unit, which turns under the action of the tide.
runner blade
Movable part that is fixed to the hub of the runner; it turns through the action of water power on it.
turbine runner
Movable part of the turbine that converts energy from the water it receives into mechanical energy, which is transmitted to the generator's rotor.
penstock
Channel that carries water to the plant turbines, from the sea to the basin or from the basin to the sea.

production of electricity from nuclear energy

A nuclear fission chain reaction is started and controlled inside the reactor to produce electricity.

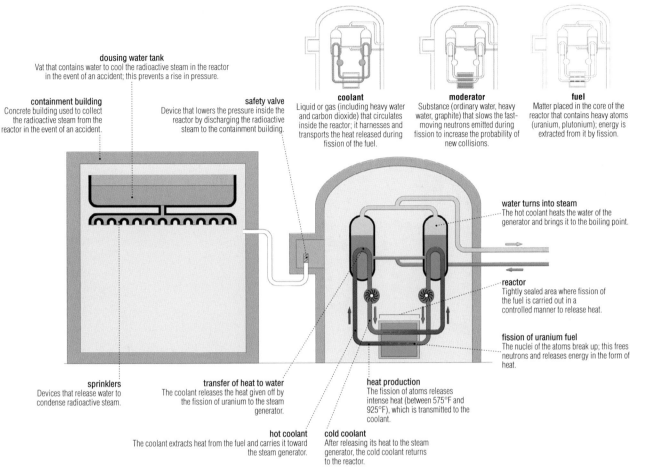

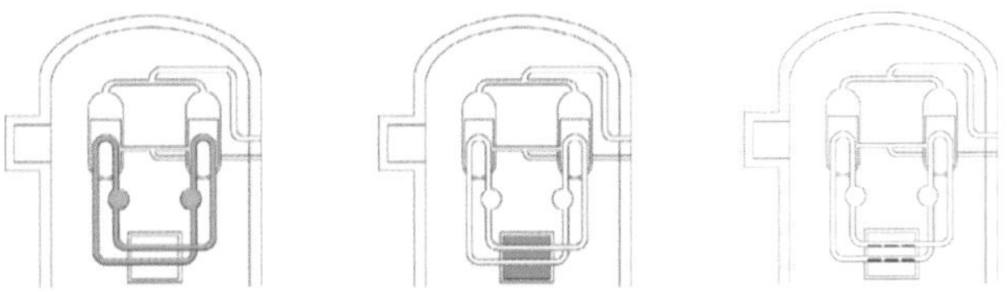

coolant
Liquid or gas (including heavy water and carbon dioxide) that circulates inside the reactor; it harnesses and transports the heat released during fission of the fuel.

moderator
Substance (ordinary water, heavy water, graphite) that slows the fast-moving neutrons emitted during fission to increase the probability of new collisions.

fuel
Matter placed in the core of the reactor that contains heavy atoms (uranium, plutonium); energy is extracted from it by fission.

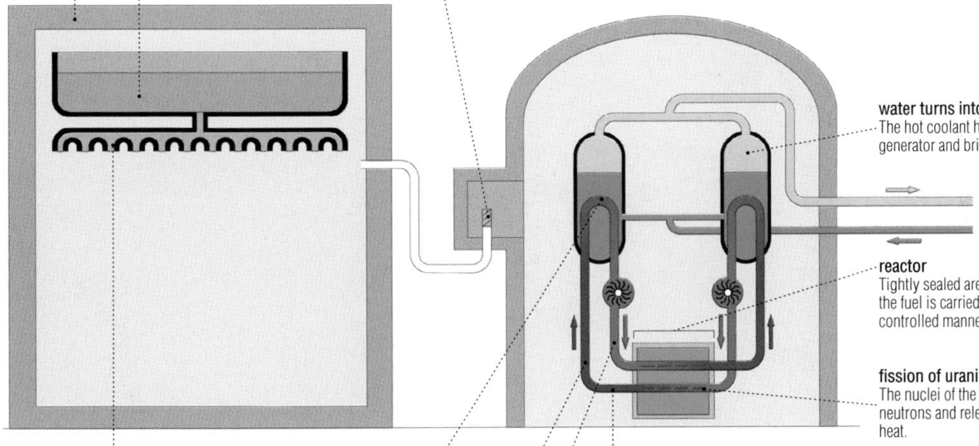
dousing water tank
Vat that contains water to cool the radioactive steam in the reactor in the event of an accident; this prevents a rise in pressure.
containment building
Concrete building used to collect the radioactive steam from the reactor in the event of an accident.
safety valve
Device that lowers the pressure inside the reactor by discharging the radioactive steam to the containment building.
water turns into steam
The hot coolant heats the water of the generator and brings it to the boiling point.
reactor
Tightly sealed area where fission of the fuel is carried out in a controlled manner to release heat.
fission of uranium fuel
The nuclei of the atoms break up; this frees neutrons and releases energy in the form of heat.
sprinklers
Devices that release water to condense radioactive steam.
transfer of heat to water
The coolant releases the heat given off by the fission of uranium to the steam generator.
heat production
The fission of atoms releases intense heat (between 575°F and 925°F), which is transmitted to the coolant.
hot coolant
The coolant extracts heat from the fuel and carries it toward the steam generator.
cold coolant
After releasing its heat to the steam generator, the cold coolant returns to the reactor.

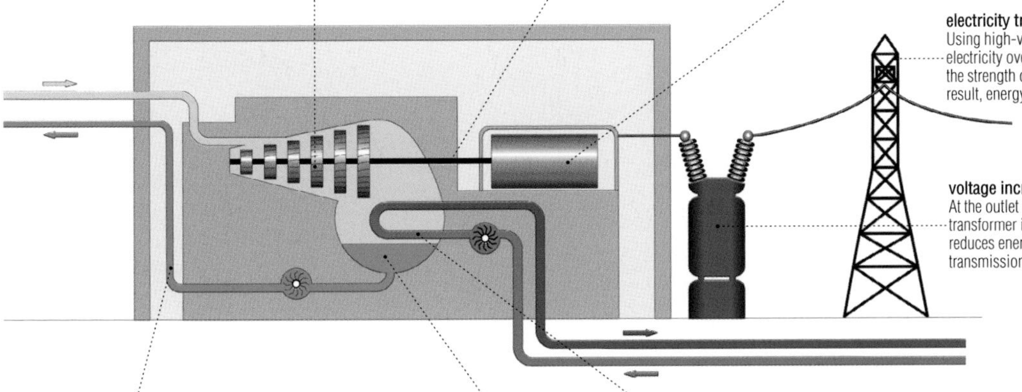
steam pressure drives turbine
Steam from the steam generator turns the turbine runner, which is connected to the generator.
turbine shaft turns generator
The rotational movement of the turbine is transmitted to the generator's rotor.
production of electricity by the generator
The generator produces electricity through the movement of the rotor in the stator.
electricity transmission
Using high-voltage lines to transmit electricity over long distances reduces the strength of the current and, as a result, energy losses.
voltage increase
At the outlet end of the power plant, the transformer increases the voltage; this reduces energy losses during transmission over long distances.
water is pumped back into the steam generator
After passing through the turbine, water produced by the condensation of the steam returns to the steam generator.
condensation of steam into water
At the turbine outlet, the steam cools and condenses into water.
water cools the used steam
Cooling of the steam from the turbine is done with river or lake water.

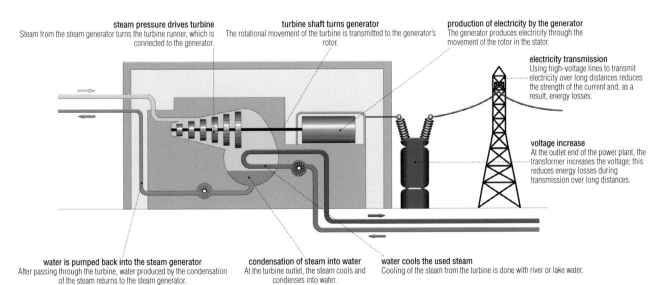

fuel handling sequence

Uranium is made into pellets, which are pressed into fuel bundles to be used in the reactor and then stored in cooling bays.

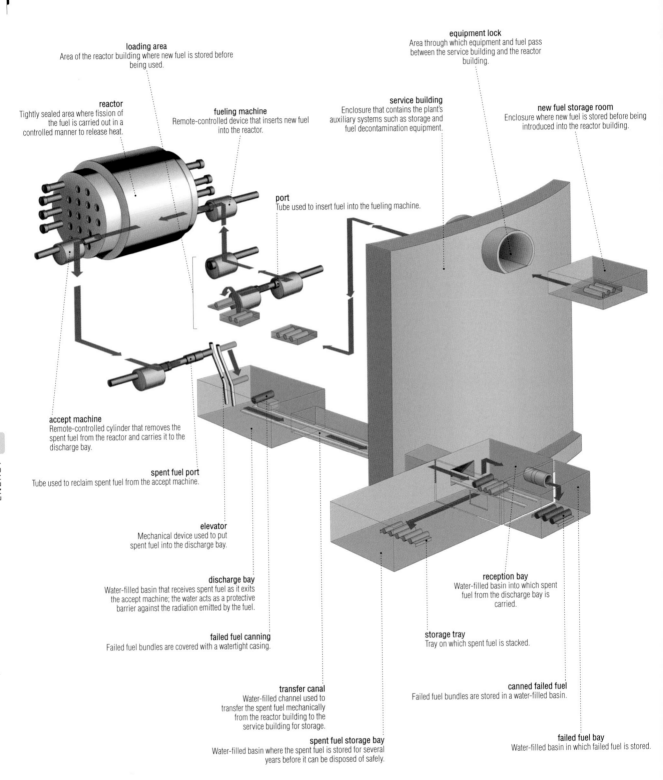

loading area
Area of the reactor building where new fuel is stored before being used.

equipment lock
Area through which equipment and fuel pass between the service building and the reactor building.

reactor
Tightly sealed area where fission of the fuel is carried out in a controlled manner to release heat.

fueling machine
Remote-controlled device that inserts new fuel into the reactor.

service building
Enclosure that contains the plant's auxiliary systems such as storage and fuel decontamination equipment.

new fuel storage room
Enclosure where new fuel is stored before being introduced into the reactor building.

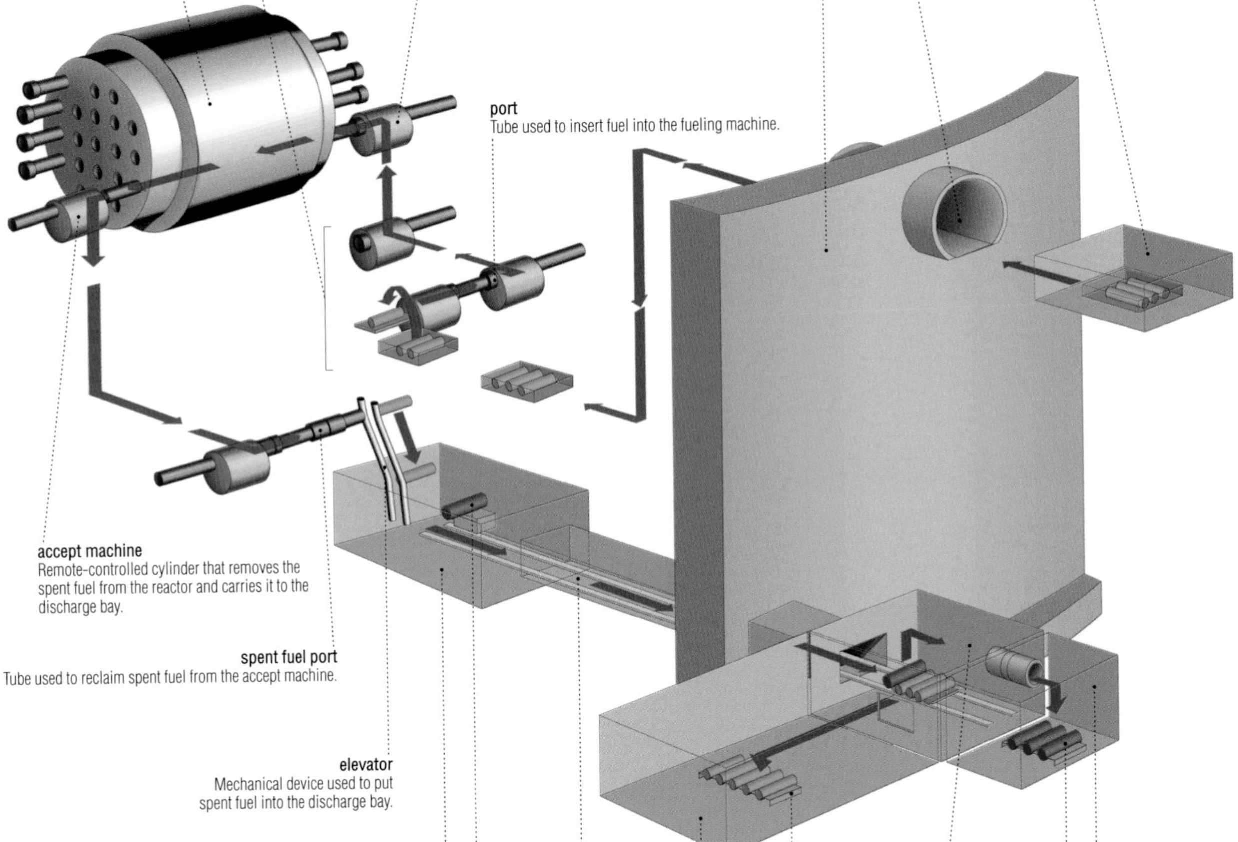

port
Tube used to insert fuel into the fueling machine.

accept machine
Remote-controlled cylinder that removes the spent fuel from the reactor and carries it to the discharge bay.

spent fuel port
Tube used to reclaim spent fuel from the accept machine.

elevator
Mechanical device used to put spent fuel into the discharge bay.

discharge bay
Water-filled basin that receives spent fuel as it exits the accept machine; the water acts as a protective barrier against the radiation emitted by the fuel.

reception bay
Water-filled basin into which spent fuel from the discharge bay is carried.

failed fuel canning
Failed fuel bundles are covered with a watertight casing.

storage tray
Tray on which spent fuel is stacked.

transfer canal
Water-filled channel used to transfer the spent fuel mechanically from the reactor building to the service building for storage.

canned failed fuel
Failed fuel bundles are stored in a water-filled basin.

spent fuel storage bay
Water-filled basin where the spent fuel is stored for several years before it can be disposed of safely.

failed fuel bay
Water-filled basin in which failed fuel is stored.

fuel bundle

Fuel pencils that are grouped in parallel for introduction into the reactor.

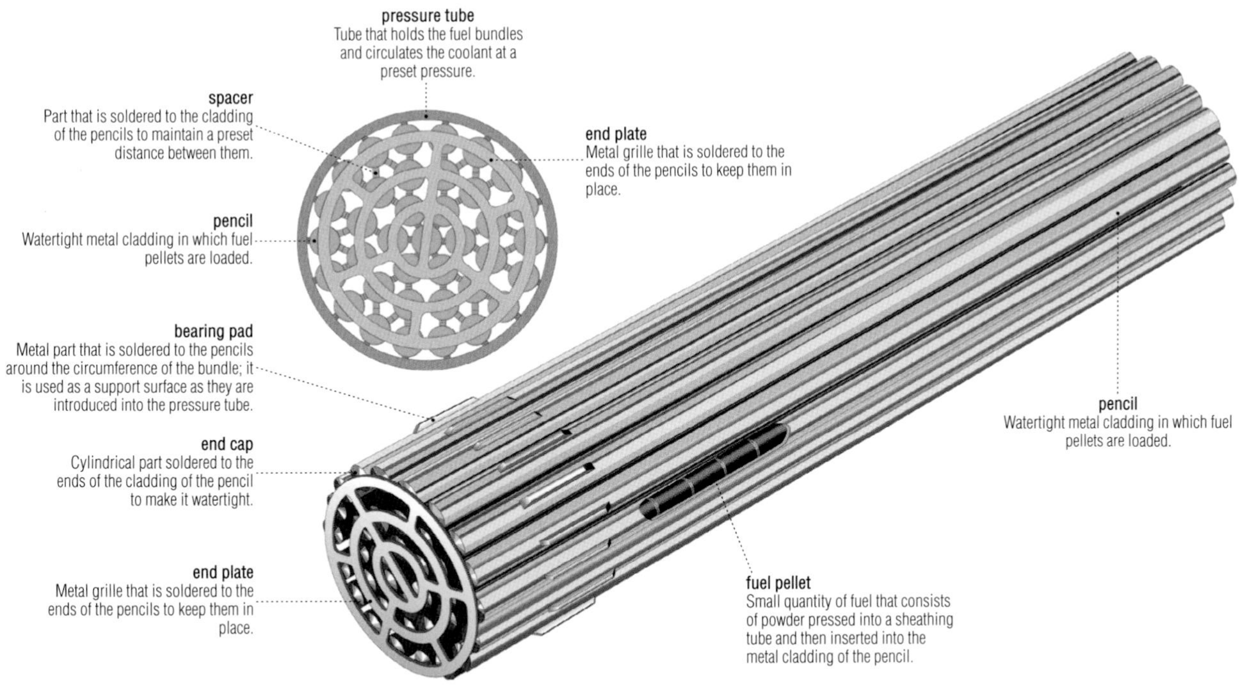
pressure tube
Tube that holds the fuel bundles and circulates the coolant at a preset pressure.
spacer
Part that is soldered to the cladding of the pencils to maintain a preset distance between them.
end plate
Metal grille that is soldered to the ends of the pencils to keep them in place.
pencil
Watertight metal cladding in which fuel pellets are loaded.
bearing pad
Metal part that is soldered to the pencils around the circumference of the bundle; it is used as a support surface as they are introduced into the pressure tube.
pencil
Watertight metal cladding in which fuel pellets are loaded.
end cap
Cylindrical part soldered to the ends of the cladding of the pencil to make it watertight.
end plate
Metal grille that is soldered to the ends of the pencils to keep them in place.
fuel pellet
Small quantity of fuel that consists of powder pressed into a sheathing tube and then inserted into the metal cladding of the pencil.

nuclear reactor

Tightly sealed area where fission of the fuel is carried out in a controlled manner to release heat.

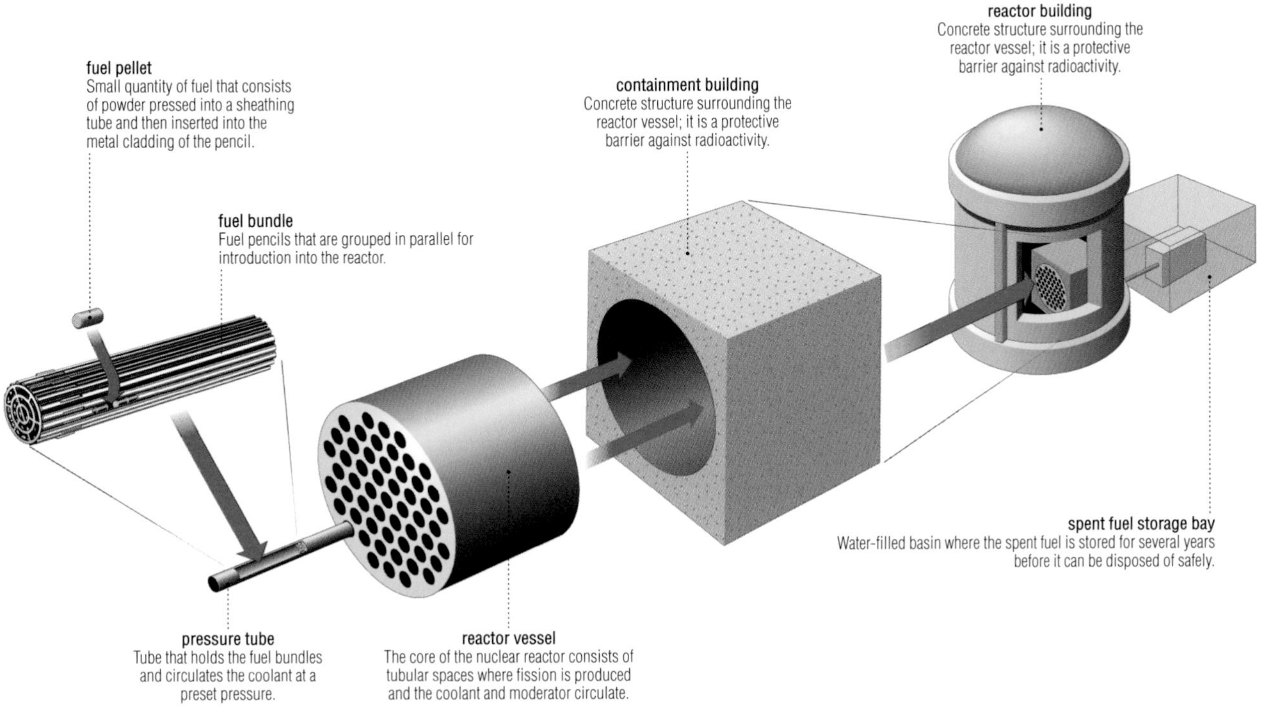
reactor building
Concrete structure surrounding the reactor vessel; it is a protective barrier against radioactivity.
fuel pellet
Small quantity of fuel that consists of powder pressed into a sheathing tube and then inserted into the metal cladding of the pencil.
containment building
Concrete structure surrounding the reactor vessel; it is a protective barrier against radioactivity.
fuel bundle
Fuel pencils that are grouped in parallel for introduction into the reactor.
spent fuel storage bay
Water-filled basin where the spent fuel is stored for several years before it can be disposed of safely.
pressure tube
Tube that holds the fuel bundles and circulates the coolant at a preset pressure.
reactor vessel
The core of the nuclear reactor consists of tubular spaces where fission is produced and the coolant and moderator circulate.

nuclear generating station

Plant that produces electricity from thermal energy generated by the fission of fuel atoms in a reactor.

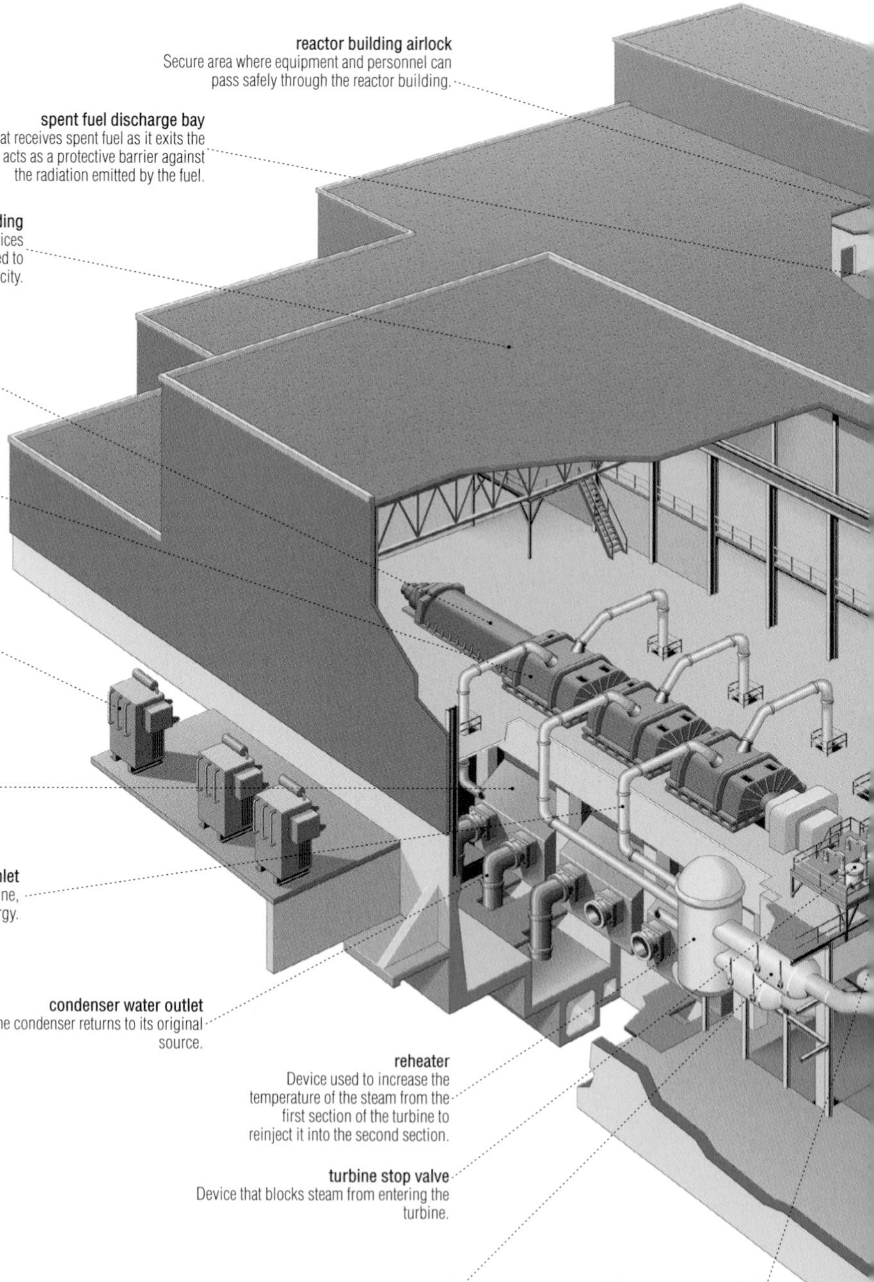

reactor building airlock
Secure area where equipment and personnel can pass safely through the reactor building.

spent fuel discharge bay
Water-filled basin that receives spent fuel as it exits the accept machine; the water acts as a protective barrier against the radiation emitted by the fuel.

turbine building
Enclosure housing the devices (turbines and generator) used to produce electricity.

generator
Turbine-powered rotating machine that converts mechanical energy into electric energy to direct it toward a transmission network.

turbine
Machine in two sections whose steam-activated runner transmits mechanical energy to the rotor shaft of the generator.

transformer
Device used to alter the electric voltage; the voltage is increased at the station outlet in order to carry the current over long distances.

condenser
Water collected from the water table flows in a circuit to cool the steam from the turbine and condense it into water.

low-pressure steam inlet
Heated steam is reinjected into the turbine, where it releases its remaining energy.

condenser water outlet
Water in the condenser returns to its original source.

reheater
Device used to increase the temperature of the steam from the first section of the turbine to reinject it into the second section.

turbine stop valve
Device that blocks steam from entering the turbine.

separator
Device that removes any water from the steam to prevent damage to the turbine's runner.

high-pressure steam inlet
Steam from the steam generators is carried to the first section of the turbine; here, it cools down and loses some of its energy.

dousing water valve
evice that releases water from the ing water tank in the reactor building) condense the radioactive steam.

steam generator
Apparatus that turns water into steam, which in turn activates the turbine.

dousing water tank
Vat that contains water to cool the radioactive steam in the reactor in the event of an accident; this prevents a rise in pressure.

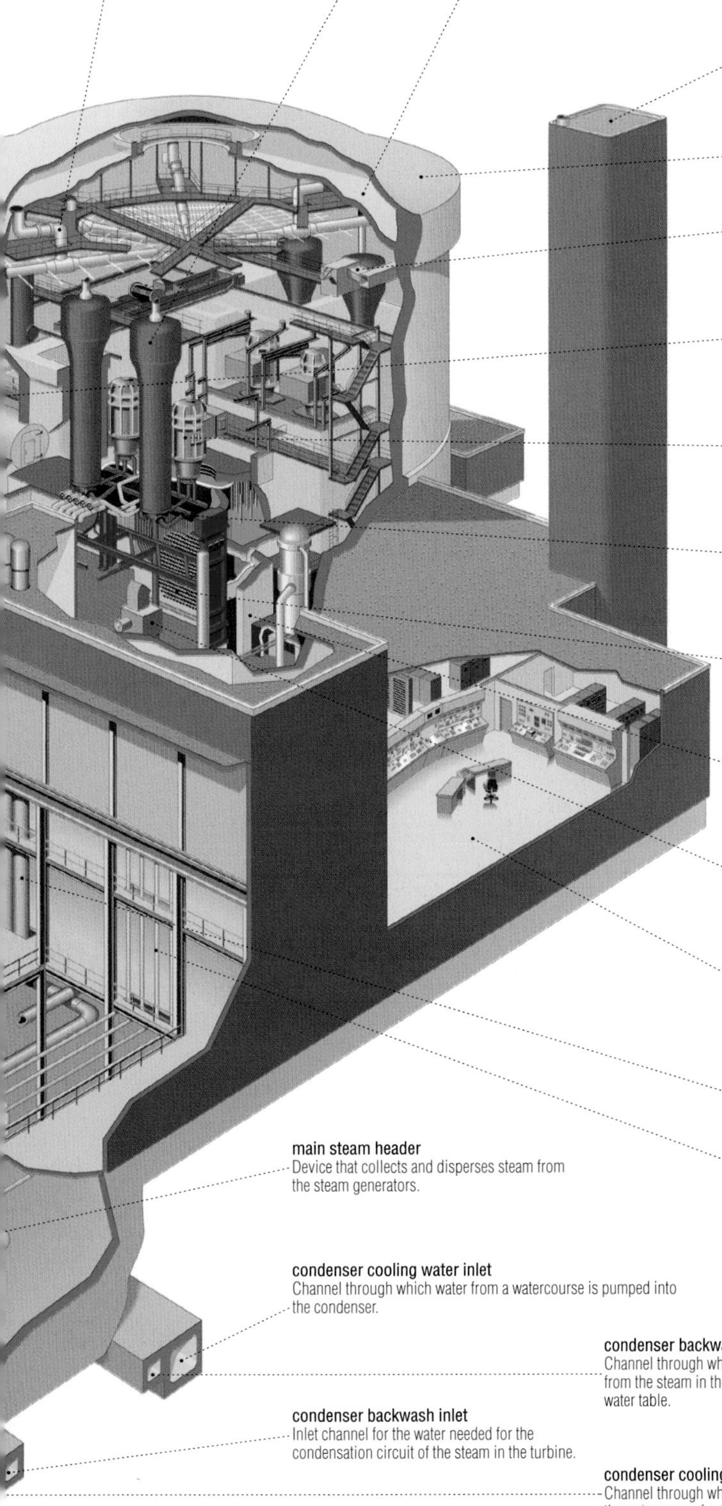

deuterium oxide upgrading
In power stations where heavy water is used as a moderator, a filter holds back steam (deuterium oxide) at the mouth of the stack.

reactor building
Concrete structure surrounding the reactor vessel; it is a protective barrier against radioactivity.

steam generator room cooler
Cooling system that controls the temperature of the room housing the generators.

spent fuel storage bay
Water-filled basin where the spent fuel is stored for several years before it can be disposed of safely.

heat transport pump
Apparatus that circulates the coolant fluid between the reactor and the steam generator.

feeder header
Large-diameter pipe that collects the coolant fluid at the reactor inlet and outlet.

reactor
Tightly sealed area where fission of the fuel is carried out in a controlled manner to release heat.

calandria
Safety containment wall that separates the reactor from the rest of the building.

fueling machine
Remote-controlled cylinder used to load and unload the reactor.

control room
Area that houses the personnel and equipment used to operate and monitor the power station.

steam release pipes
All the pipes used to carry steam to the separator outlet.

main steam header
Device that collects and disperses steam from the steam generators.

main steam pipes
All the pipes used to carry steam to the steam generator outlet.

condenser cooling water inlet
Channel through which water from a watercourse is pumped into the condenser.

condenser backwash outlet
Channel through which condensed water from the steam in the turbine returns to the water table.

condenser backwash inlet
Inlet channel for the water needed for the condensation circuit of the steam in the turbine.

condenser cooling water outlet
Channel through which the water from the condenser returns to the watercourse from which it came.

carbon dioxide reactor

Developed for the most part in Great Britain and France, it was replaced by the pressurized water reactor, which performs better and is less expensive.

fueling machine
Remote-controlled device that inserts new fuel into the reactor.

concrete shielding
Concrete structure that holds back radioactive products in the event of an accident.

carbon dioxide gas coolant
Carbon dioxide that recovers the heat from the reactor core and transfers it to the heat exchanger.

heat exchanger
Tubing system that is submerged in the hot carbon dioxide; here, water is turned into steam to power the turbine.

steam outlet
Water that has been vaporized in the carbon dioxide is carried to the turbine to produce electricity.

feedwater
Piping carries water from the condenser to the heat exchanger, where it is turned into steam.

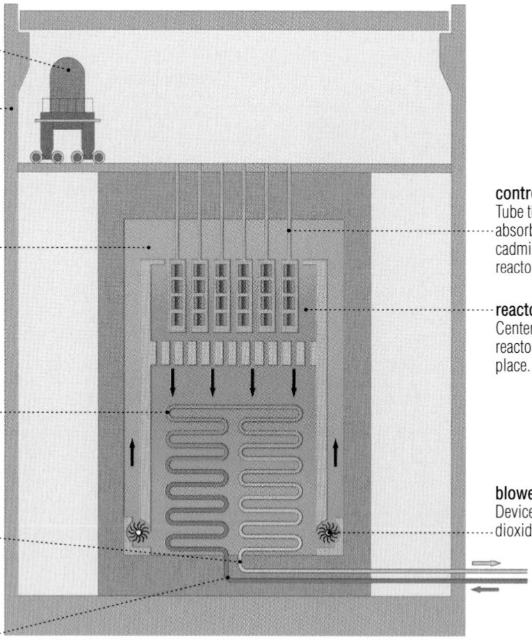

control rod
Tube that contains a neutron-absorbing material (boron, cadmium) that is introduced into the reactor core to control its power.

reactor core
Center section of the nuclear reactor where fission reactions take place.

blower
Device that circulates carbon dioxide in the reactor core.

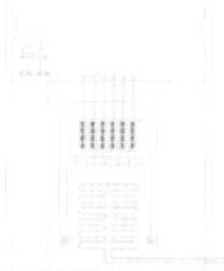

fuel: natural uranium
Natural uranium: fuel extracted from mines; consists of a mixture of three uranium isotop (uranium-234, -235 and -238).

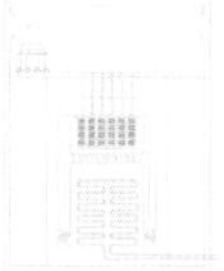

moderator: graphite
Moderator: medium that slows the speed of the neutrons to maintain a continuous chain reaction.

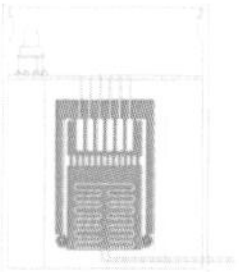

coolant: carbon dioxide
Carbon dioxide: gas that is heavier than air and is produced by burning graphite.

heavy-water reactor

The advantage of this type of reactor is that it does not require fuel enrichment; it is used mainly in Canada, Argentina and India.

pump
Apparatus that circulates the coolant fluid between the reactor and the steam generator.

control rod
Tube that contains a neutron-absorbing material (boron, cadmium) that is introduced into the reactor core to control its power.

pressurized heavy water
Heavy water that is heated in the reactor core is kept under pressure to prevent it from boiling.

fuel
Matter that is placed in the reactor core; it contains heavy atoms (uranium, plutonium) from which power is extracted by fission.

fueling machine
Remote-controlled device that inserts new fuel into the reactor.

moderator tank
Steel tank that contains cold heavy water from the moderator.

safety tank
Tank where cold heavy water from the moderator flows to stop fission reactions in the event of an emergency.

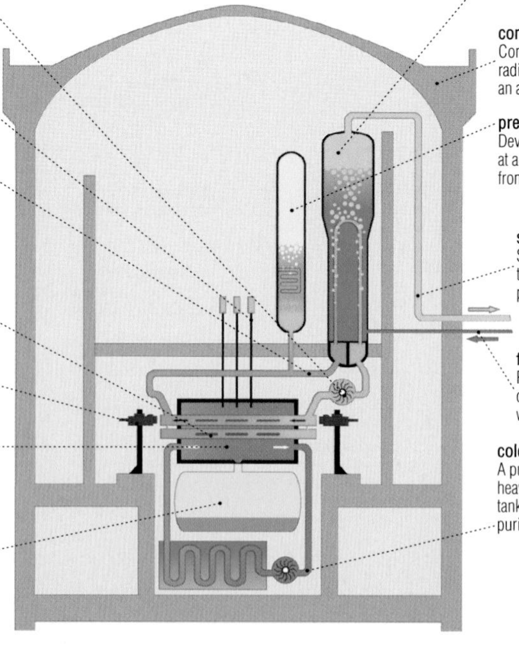

steam generator
Device that uses heat from the coolant to turn water into steam to activate the turbine.

concrete shielding
Concrete structure that holds back radioactive products in the event of an accident.

pressurizer
Device that keeps the coolant water at a preset temperature to prevent it from boiling.

steam outlet
Steam from the generator is carried to the turbine and generator to produce electricity.

feedwater
Piping carries water from the condenser to the steam generator, where it is turned into steam.

cold heavy water
A pumping system ensures that heavy water around the moderator tank circulates, cools and is purified.

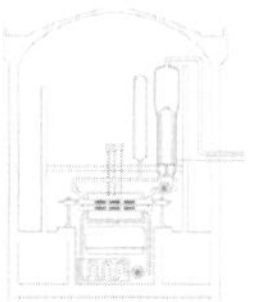

fuel: natural uranium
Natural uranium: fuel extracted from mines consists of a mixture of three uranium isoto (uranium-234, -235 and -238).

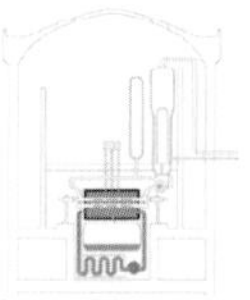

moderator: heavy water
Heavy water: water consisting of heavy hydrogen (deuterium) and oxygen; it can slow down neutrons.

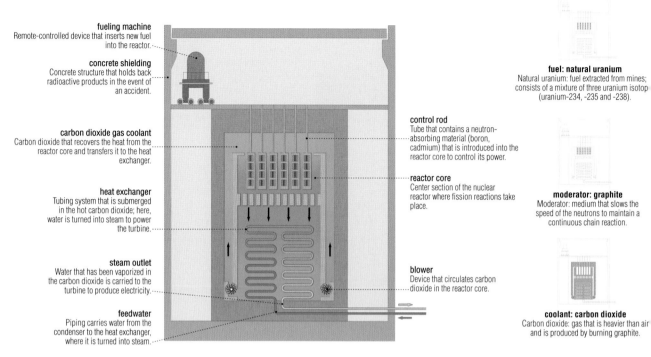

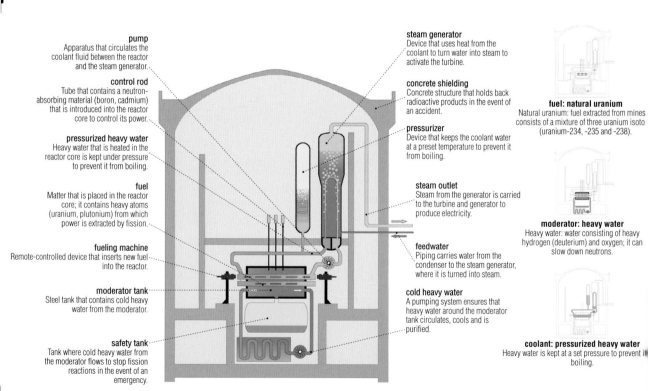

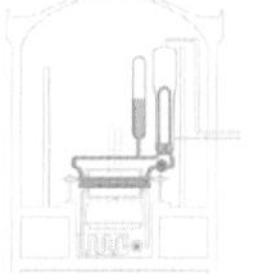

coolant: pressurized heavy water
Heavy water is kept at a set pressure to prevent i boiling.

pressurized-water reactor

The most common type of reactor in the world; water from the coolant is kept under heavy pressure to prevent it from vaporizing.

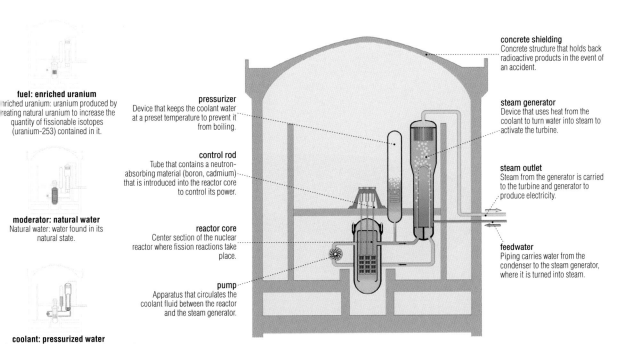

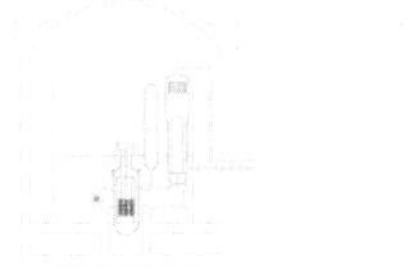

fuel: enriched uranium
nriched uranium: uranium produced by reating natural uranium to increase the quantity of fissionable isotopes (uranium-253) contained in it.

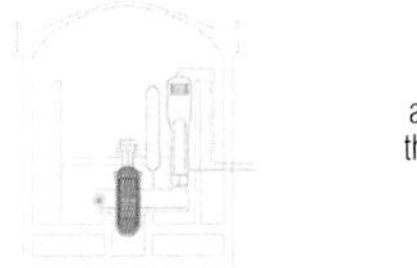

moderator: natural water
Natural water: water found in its natural state.

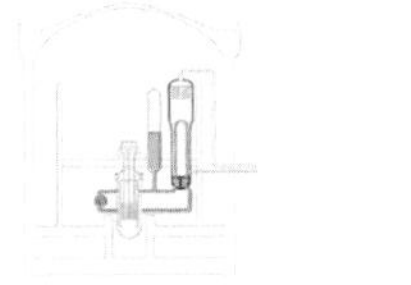

coolant: pressurized water
rized water: natural water kept under a preset pressure to prevent it from boiling.

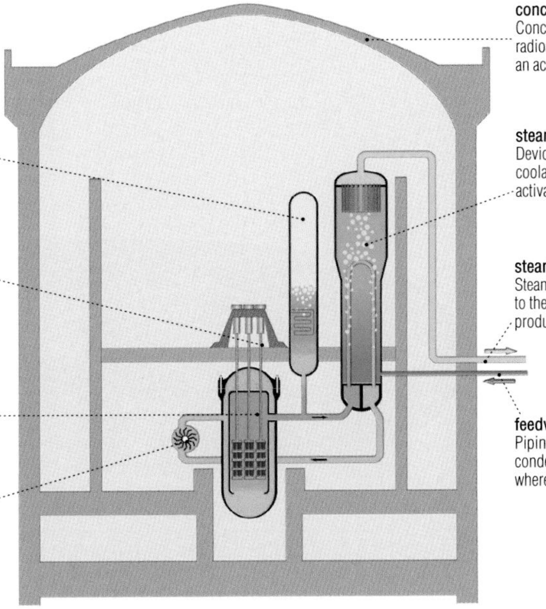

pressurizer
Device that keeps the coolant water at a preset temperature to prevent it from boiling.

control rod
Tube that contains a neutron-absorbing material (boron, cadmium) that is introduced into the reactor core to control its power.

reactor core
Center section of the nuclear reactor where fission reactions take place.

pump
Apparatus that circulates the coolant fluid between the reactor and the steam generator.

concrete shielding
Concrete structure that holds back radioactive products in the event of an accident.

steam generator
Device that uses heat from the coolant to turn water into steam to activate the turbine.

steam outlet
Steam from the generator is carried to the turbine and generator to produce electricity.

feedwater
Piping carries water from the condenser to the steam generator, where it is turned into steam.

boiling-water reactor

In this second most common reactor, boiling occurs directly in the reactor core; it is used mainly in the United States, Sweden and Japan.

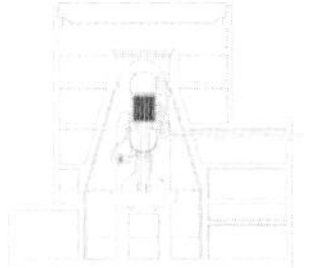

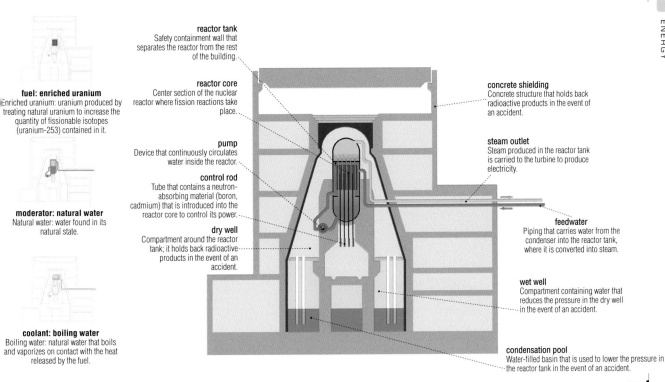

fuel: enriched uranium
Enriched uranium: uranium produced by treating natural uranium to increase the quantity of fissionable isotopes (uranium-253) contained in it.

moderator: natural water
Natural water: water found in its natural state.

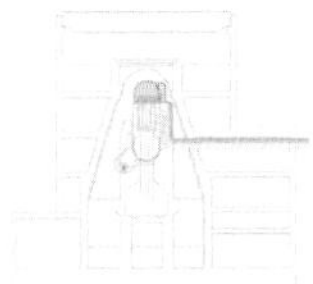

coolant: boiling water
Boiling water: natural water that boils and vaporizes on contact with the heat released by the fuel.

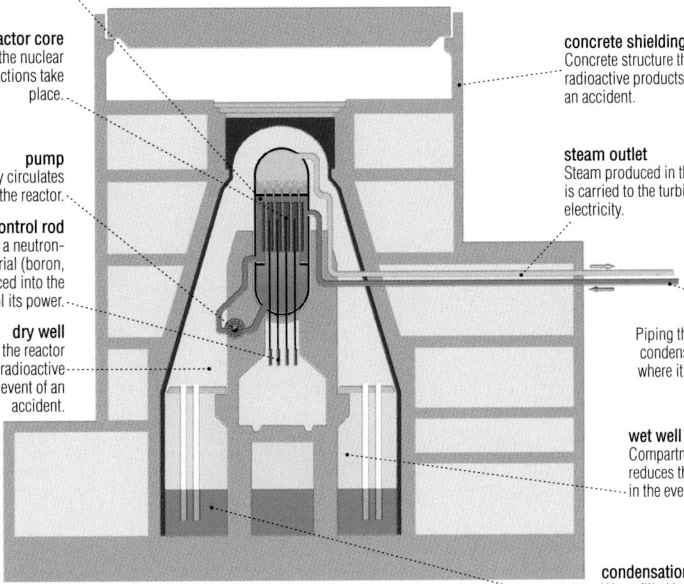

reactor tank
Safety containment wall that separates the reactor from the rest of the building.

reactor core
Center section of the nuclear reactor where fission reactions take place.

pump
Device that continuously circulates water inside the reactor.

control rod
Tube that contains a neutron-absorbing material (boron, cadmium) that is introduced into the reactor core to control its power.

dry well
Compartment around the reactor tank; it holds back radioactive products in the event of an accident.

concrete shielding
Concrete structure that holds back radioactive products in the event of an accident.

steam outlet
Steam produced in the reactor tank is carried to the turbine to produce electricity.

feedwater
Piping that carries water from the condenser into the reactor tank, where it is converted into steam.

wet well
Compartment containing water that reduces the pressure in the dry well in the event of an accident.

condensation pool
Water-filled basin that is used to lower the pressure in the reactor tank in the event of an accident.

solar cell

Device used to convert solar energy directly into electric energy (photovoltaic effect).

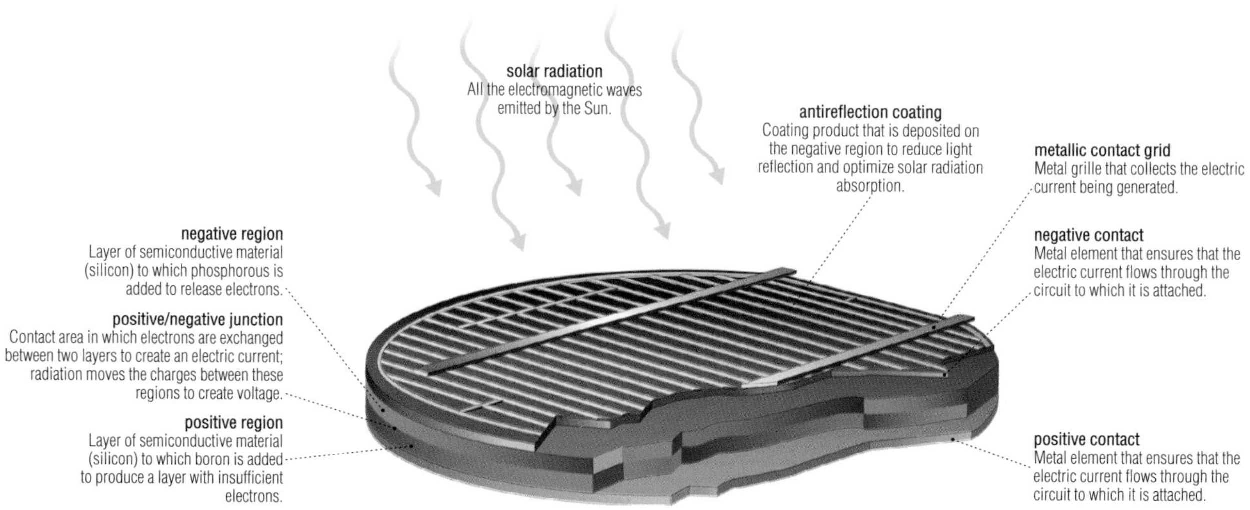
solar radiation
All the electromagnetic waves emitted by the Sun.
antireflection coating
Coating product that is deposited on the negative region to reduce light reflection and optimize solar radiation absorption.
metallic contact grid
Metal grille that collects the electric current being generated.
negative contact
Metal element that ensures that the electric current flows through the circuit to which it is attached.
negative region
Layer of semiconductive material (silicon) to which phosphorous is added to release electrons.
positive/negative junction
Contact area in which electrons are exchanged between two layers to create an electric current; radiation moves the charges between these regions to create voltage.
positive region
Layer of semiconductive material (silicon) to which boron is added to produce a layer with insufficient electrons.
positive contact
Metal element that ensures that the electric current flows through the circuit to which it is attached.

flat-plate solar collector

Device that collects solar radiation and heats a coolant, which in turn will be used in residential settings to heat water or the home.

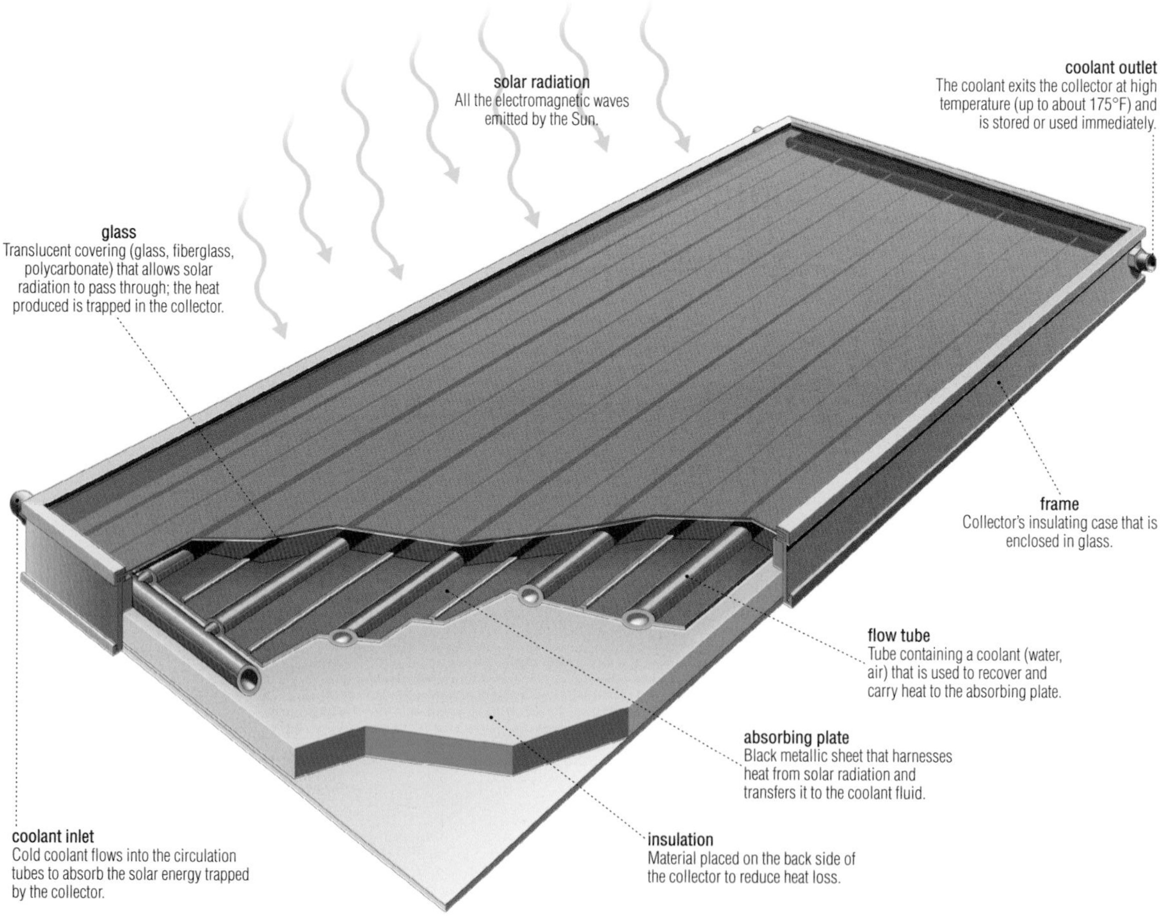
solar radiation
All the electromagnetic waves emitted by the Sun.
coolant outlet
The coolant exits the collector at high temperature (up to about 175°F) and is stored or used immediately.
glass
Translucent covering (glass, fiberglass, polycarbonate) that allows solar radiation to pass through; the heat produced is trapped in the collector.
frame
Collector's insulating case that is enclosed in glass.
flow tube
Tube containing a coolant (water, air) that is used to recover and carry heat to the absorbing plate.
absorbing plate
Black metallic sheet that harnesses heat from solar radiation and transfers it to the coolant fluid.
coolant inlet
Cold coolant flows into the circulation tubes to absorb the solar energy trapped by the collector.
insulation
Material placed on the back side of the collector to reduce heat loss.

solar-cell system

Unit that is usually made up of 36 solar cells, each of which produces a voltage of 0.5 V; it is used to power low-voltage devices.

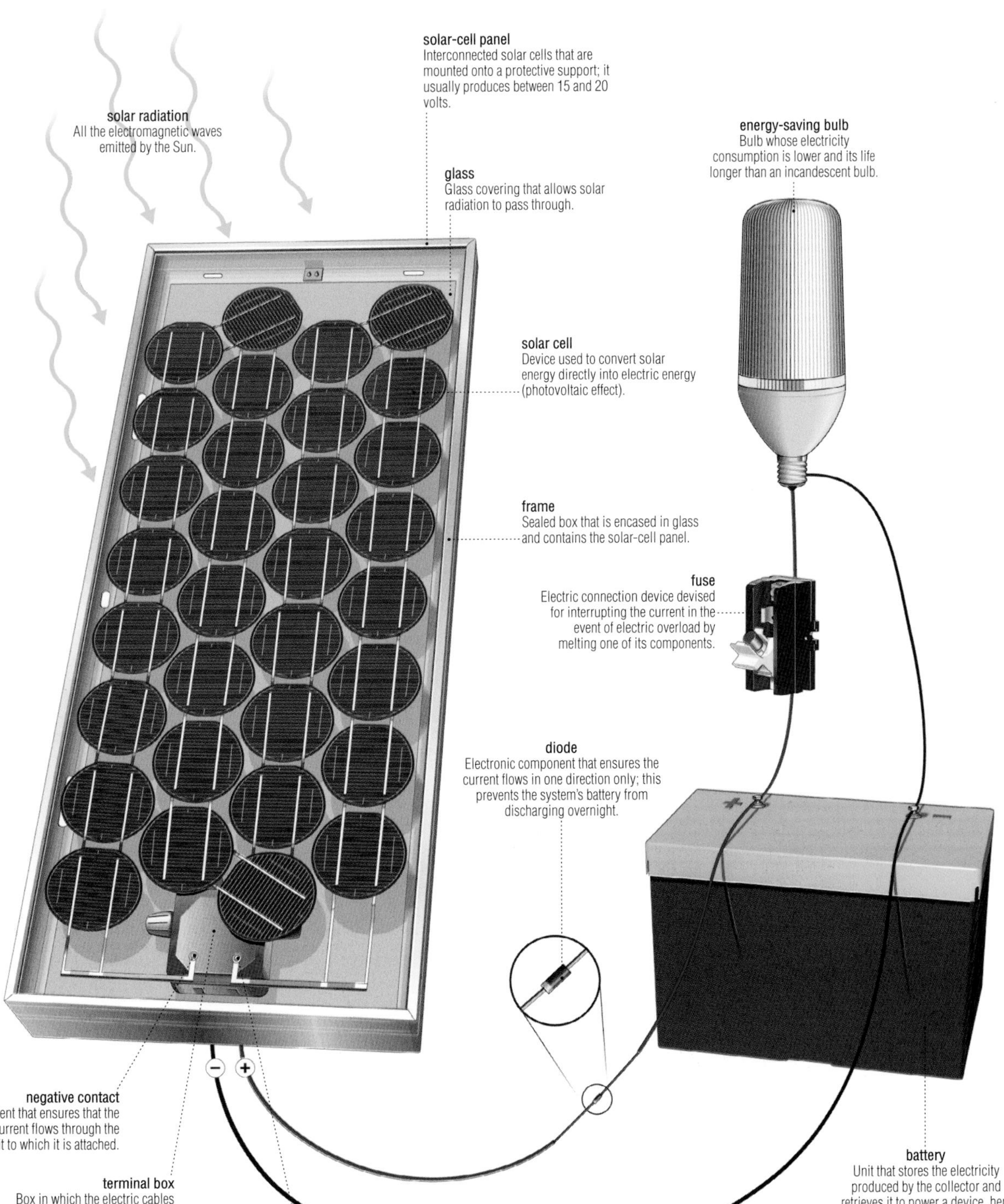
solar-cell panel
Interconnected solar cells that are mounted onto a protective support; it usually produces between 15 and 20 volts.
solar radiation
All the electromagnetic waves emitted by the Sun.
energy-saving bulb
Bulb whose electricity consumption is lower and its life longer than an incandescent bulb.
glass
Glass covering that allows solar radiation to pass through.
solar cell
Device used to convert solar energy directly into electric energy (photovoltaic effect).
frame
Sealed box that is encased in glass and contains the solar-cell panel.
fuse
Electric connection device devised for interrupting the current in the event of electric overload by melting one of its components.
diode
Electronic component that ensures the current flows in one direction only; this prevents the system's battery from discharging overnight.
negative contact
Metal element that ensures that the electric current flows through the circuit to which it is attached.
battery
Unit that stores the electricity produced by the collector and retrieves it to power a device, here an incandescent lamp.
terminal box
Box in which the electric cables powering the battery are connected to the collector's positive and negative contacts.
positive contact
Metal element that ensures that the electric current flows through the circuit to which it is attached.

solar furnace

Plant that concentrates solar radiation to reach very high temperatures (over 5,400°F) as part of a research effort to develop experimental materials (including astronautic materials and ceramics).

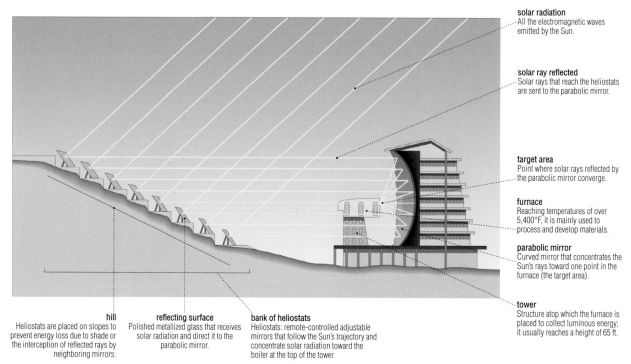

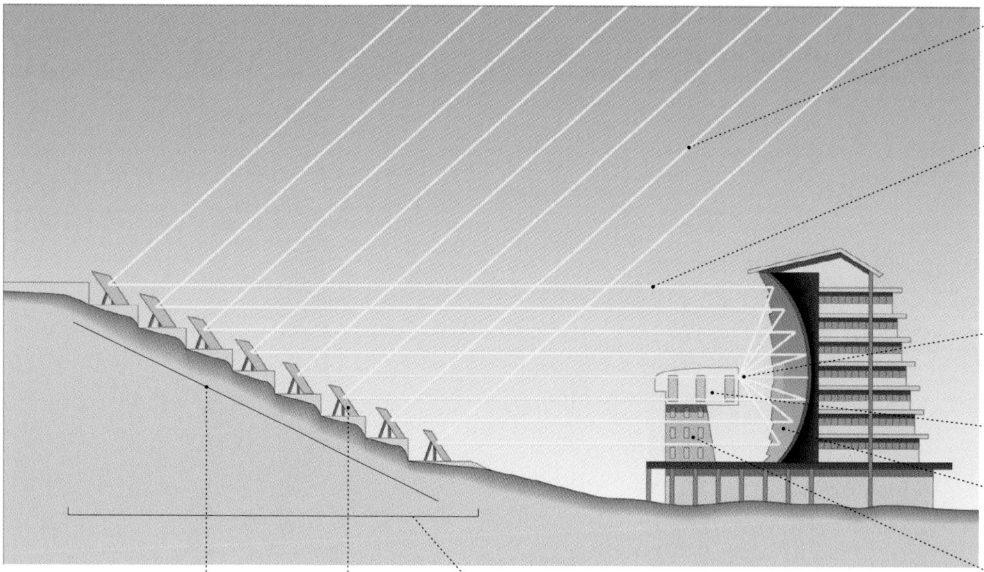
solar radiation
All the electromagnetic waves emitted by the Sun.
solar ray reflected
Solar rays that reach the heliostats are sent to the parabolic mirror.
target area
Point where solar rays reflected by the parabolic mirror converge.
furnace
Reaching temperatures of over 5,400°F, it is mainly used to process and develop materials.
parabolic mirror
Curved mirror that concentrates the Sun's rays toward one point in the furnace (the target area).
tower
Structure atop which the furnace is placed to collect luminous energy; it usually reaches a height of 65 ft.
hill
Heliostats are placed on slopes to prevent energy loss due to shade or the interception of reflected rays by neighboring mirrors.
reflecting surface
Polished metallized glass that receives solar radiation and direct it to the parabolic mirror.
bank of heliostats
Heliostats: remote-controlled adjustable mirrors that follow the Sun's trajectory and concentrate solar radiation toward the boiler at the top of the tower.

production of electricity from solar energy

Heating the coolant directly with solar rays turns water into steam, which then turns the turbo-alternator to produce electricity.

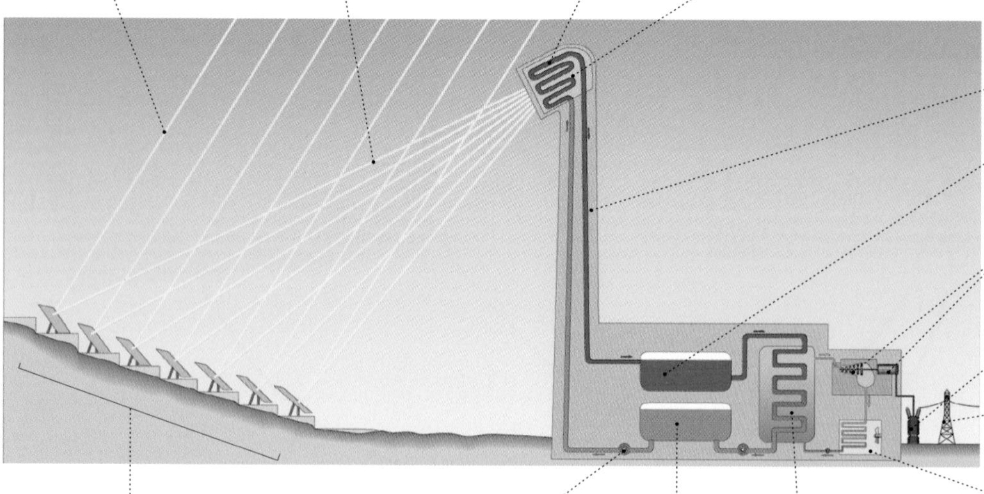
solar radiation
The Sun emits waves in the form of luminous radiation (41% visible light, 52% infrared light and 7% ultraviolet light).
solar ray reflected
Solar rays trapped by heliostats are sent to the boiler.
coolant
Fluid (e.g., a mixture of melted salts) that traps the heat from concentrated solar radiation and carries it to the turbine.
boiler
Enclosure in which the concentrated heat from the Sun's rays raises the temperature of the coolant.
tower
Structure atop which the boiler sits and colle
luminous energy; it can reach 325 ft in heigh
hot coolant
The coolant extracts heat from the boiler and carries it to the steam generator and turbine.
turbo-alternator
Device that uses steam to convert the mechanical force generated by the rotation of the turbine into electricity.
transformer
Device used to alter the electric voltage; the voltage is increased at the plant outlet in order to carry the current over long distances.
electricity transmission network
Electricity is carried over vast distances by a network of cables that extends from the power plant to consumers.
bank of heliostats
Heliostats: remote-controlled adjustable mirrors that follow the Sun's trajectory and concentrate solar radiation toward the boiler at the top of the tower.
pump
Device that ensures that the cold coolant liquid flows to the boiler.
cold coolant
After releasing its heat to the steam generator, the cold coolant returns to the boiler.
steam generator
Device that uses heat to convert water into steam to activate the turbo-alternator.
condenser
Circuit that cools the steam from the turbine and condenses it into water, which is reintroduced into the steam generator.

solar house

Solar energy can be used to heat and supply hot water to a home.

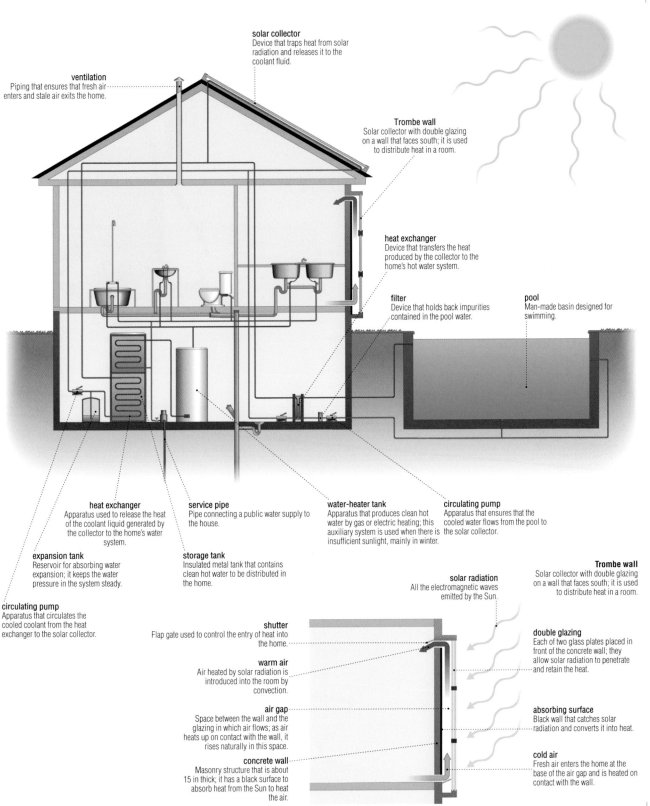

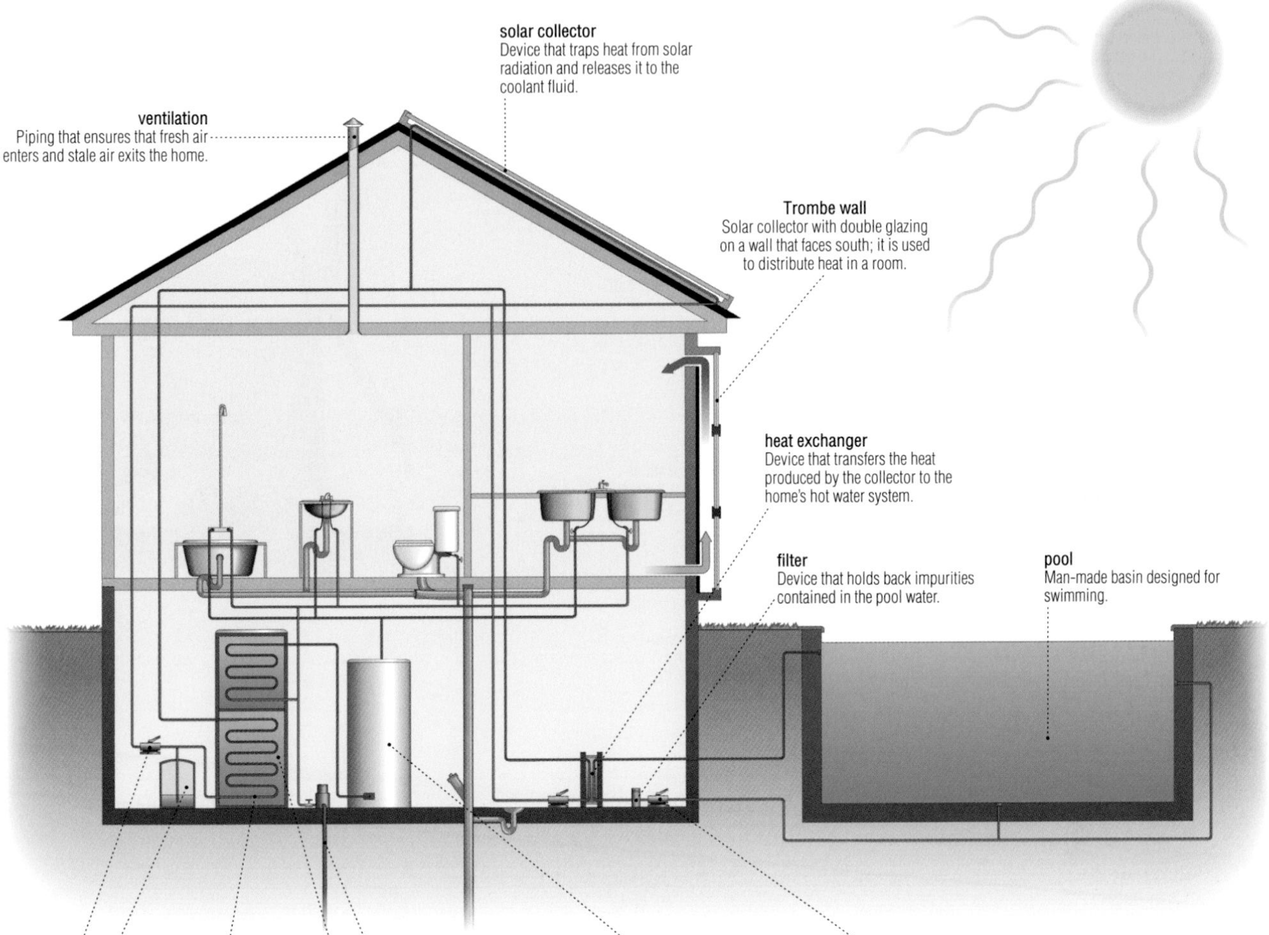
solar collector
Device that traps heat from solar radiation and releases it to the coolant fluid.
ventilation
Piping that ensures that fresh air enters and stale air exits the home.
Trombe wall
Solar collector with double glazing on a wall that faces south; it is used to distribute heat in a room.
heat exchanger
Device that transfers the heat produced by the collector to the home's hot water system.
filter
Device that holds back impurities contained in the pool water.
pool
Man-made basin designed for swimming.
heat exchanger
Apparatus used to release the heat of the coolant liquid generated by the collector to the home's water system.
service pipe
Pipe connecting a public water supply to the house.
water-heater tank
Apparatus that produces clean hot water by gas or electric heating; this auxiliary system is used when there is insufficient sunlight, mainly in winter.
circulating pump
Apparatus that ensures that the cooled water flows from the pool to the solar collector.
expansion tank
Reservoir for absorbing water expansion; it keeps the water pressure in the system steady.
storage tank
Insulated metal tank that contains clean hot water to be distributed in the home.
circulating pump
Apparatus that circulates the cooled coolant from the heat exchanger to the solar collector.

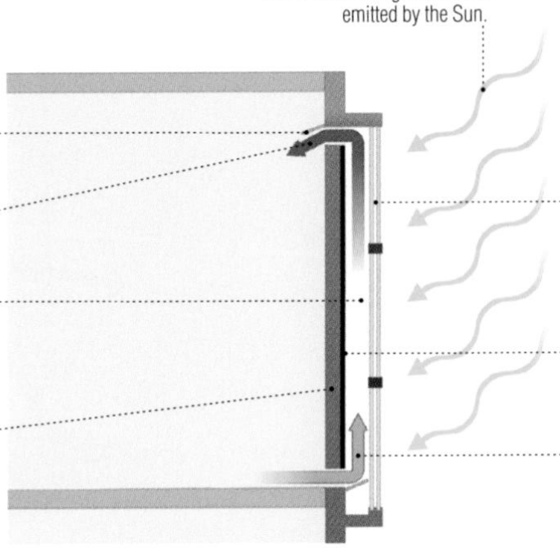
Trombe wall
Solar collector with double glazing on a wall that faces south; it is used to distribute heat in a room.
solar radiation
All the electromagnetic waves emitted by the Sun.
shutter
Flap gate used to control the entry of heat into the home.
warm air
Air heated by solar radiation is introduced into the room by convection.
air gap
Space between the wall and the glazing in which air flows; as air heats up on contact with the wall, it rises naturally in this space.
concrete wall
Masonry structure that is about 15 in thick; it has a black surface to absorb heat from the Sun to heat the air.
double glazing
Each of two glass plates placed in front of the concrete wall; they allow solar radiation to penetrate and retain the heat.
absorbing surface
Black wall that catches solar radiation and converts it into heat.
cold air
Fresh air enters the home at the base of the air gap and is heated on contact with the wall.

windmill

Machine that converts wind energy into mechanical energy; it was used in the past to mill grain and pump water.

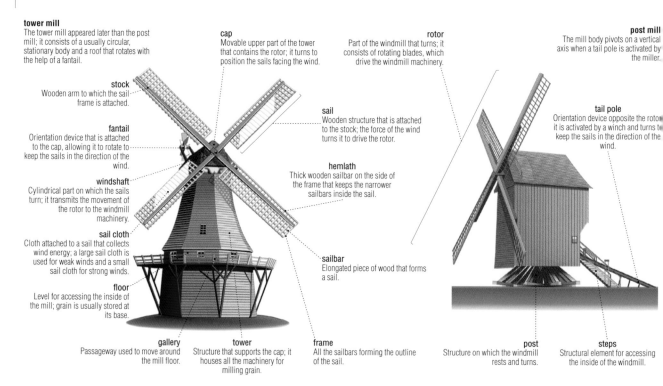

tower mill
The tower mill appeared later than the post mill; it consists of a usually circular, stationary body and a roof that rotates with the help of a fantail.

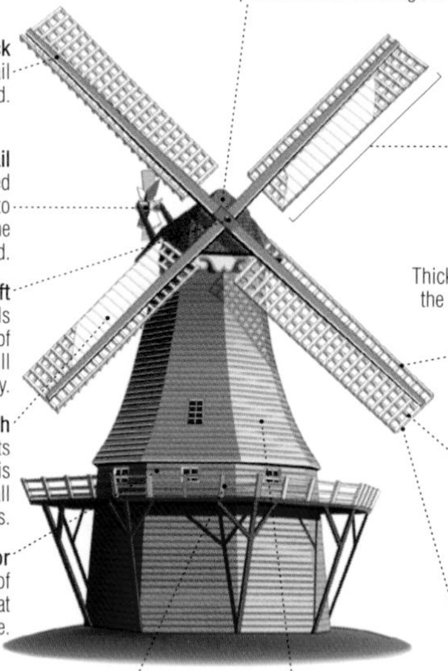

cap
Movable upper part of the tower that contains the rotor; it turns to position the sails facing the wind.

rotor
Part of the windmill that turns; it consists of rotating blades, which drive the windmill machinery.

stock
Wooden arm to which the sail frame is attached.

fantail
Orientation device that is attached to the cap, allowing it to rotate to keep the sails in the direction of the wind.

windshaft
Cylindrical part on which the sails turn; it transmits the movement of the rotor to the windmill machinery.

sail cloth
Cloth attached to a sail that collects wind energy; a large sail cloth is used for weak winds and a small sail cloth for strong winds.

floor
Level for accessing the inside of the mill; grain is usually stored at its base.

sail
Wooden structure that is attached to the stock; the force of the wind turns it to drive the rotor.

hemlath
Thick wooden sailbar on the side of the frame that keeps the narrower sailbars inside the sail.

sailbar
Elongated piece of wood that forms a sail.

gallery
Passageway used to move around the mill floor.

tower
Structure that supports the cap; it houses all the machinery for milling grain.

frame
All the sailbars forming the outline of the sail.

post mill
The mill body pivots on a vertical axis when a tail pole is activated by the miller.

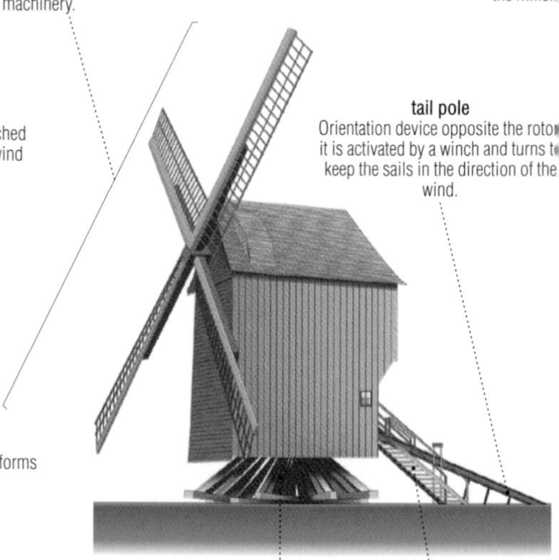

tail pole
Orientation device opposite the rotor; it is activated by a winch and turns to keep the sails in the direction of the wind.

post
Structure on which the windmill rests and turns.

steps
Structural element for accessing the inside of the windmill.

wind turbines and electricity production

Wind turbine: machine that harnesses energy from the wind and converts it into mechanical energy to activate the alternator.

vertical-axis wind turbine
Wind turbine whose axis is perpendicular to the wind.

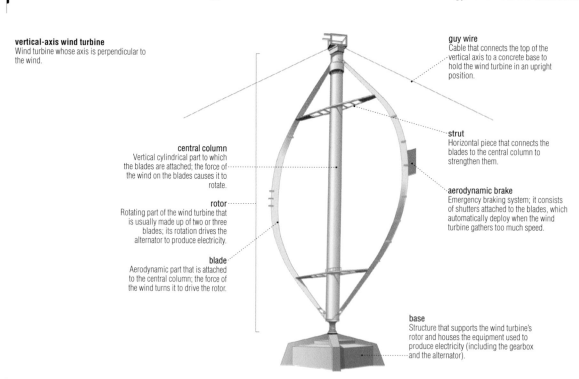

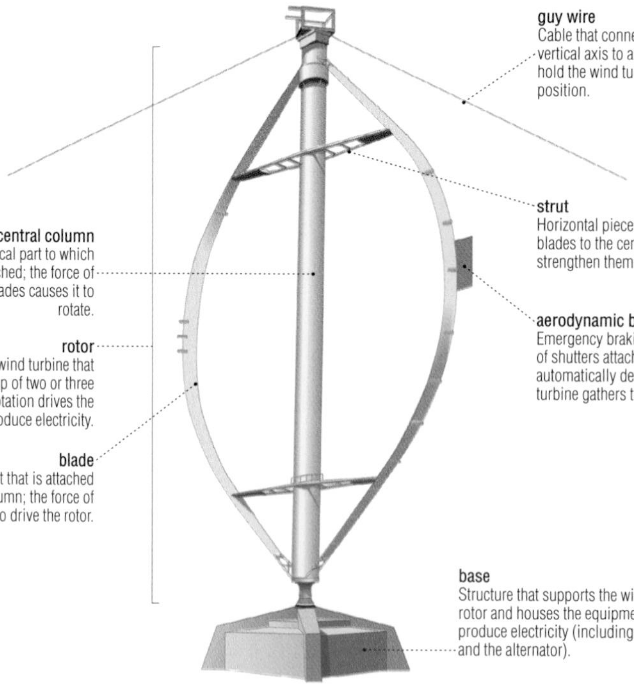

guy wire
Cable that connects the top of the vertical axis to a concrete base to hold the wind turbine in an upright position.

strut
Horizontal piece that connects the blades to the central column to strengthen them.

central column
Vertical cylindrical part to which the blades are attached; the force of the wind on the blades causes it to rotate.

aerodynamic brake
Emergency braking system; it consists of shutters attached to the blades, which automatically deploy when the wind turbine gathers too much speed.

rotor
Rotating part of the wind turbine that is usually made up of two or three blades; its rotation drives the alternator to produce electricity.

blade
Aerodynamic part that is attached to the central column; the force of the wind turns it to drive the rotor.

base
Structure that supports the wind turbine's rotor and houses the equipment used to produce electricity (including the gearbox and the alternator).

horizontal-axis wind turbine
The most common type of wind turbine; its axis positions itself in the direction of the wind.

blade
Aerodynamic part that is attached to the hub; the force of the wind causes it to rotate to drive the rotor.

hub
Part of the rotor to which the blades are attached; it turns the low-speed shaft.

nacelle
Metal structure that encloses and protects the main mechanical elements of the wind turbine (including the gearbox and the alternator).

tower
Tower that reaches 260 ft in height; it supports the nacelle and rotor and houses the electric cables.

nacelle cross-section

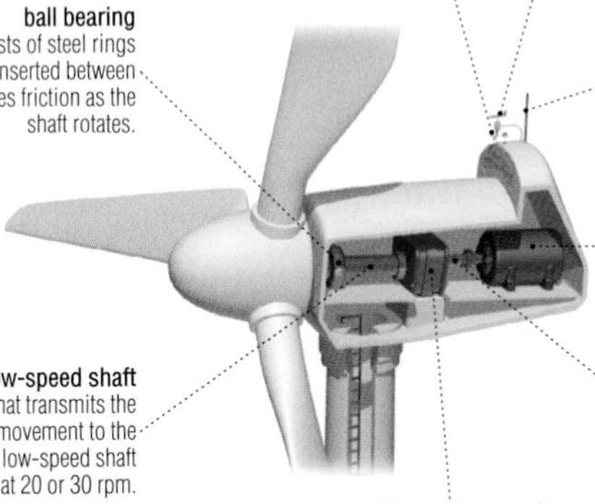

anemometer
Instrument that measures wind speed using cups that rotate around a mobile shaft at varying speeds.

wind vane
Instrument that indicates wind direction using a vane that rotates around a vertical axis.

ball bearing
Part that consists of steel rings with steel balls inserted between them; it reduces friction as the shaft rotates.

lightning rod
Metal rod that is attached to the nacelle; it protects the wind turbine from lightning, which it directs toward the ground.

alternator
Rotating machine that is driven by the high-speed shaft; it converts mechanical energy into electric energy and then directs it to the transmission network.

low-speed shaft
Cylindrical part that transmits the rotor hub's movement to the gearbox; the low-speed shaft usually turns at 20 or 30 rpm.

high-speed shaft
Cylindrical piece that transmits the high-speed movement of the rotor to the alternator; it turns at about 1,500 rpm.

speed-increasing gearbox
Part that increases the rotational speed of the rotor to drive the alternator.

production of electricity from wind energy
Wind farms contain a group of wind turbines, which are driven by the wind; they produce electricity and carry it along the transmission and distribution networks to which they are connected.

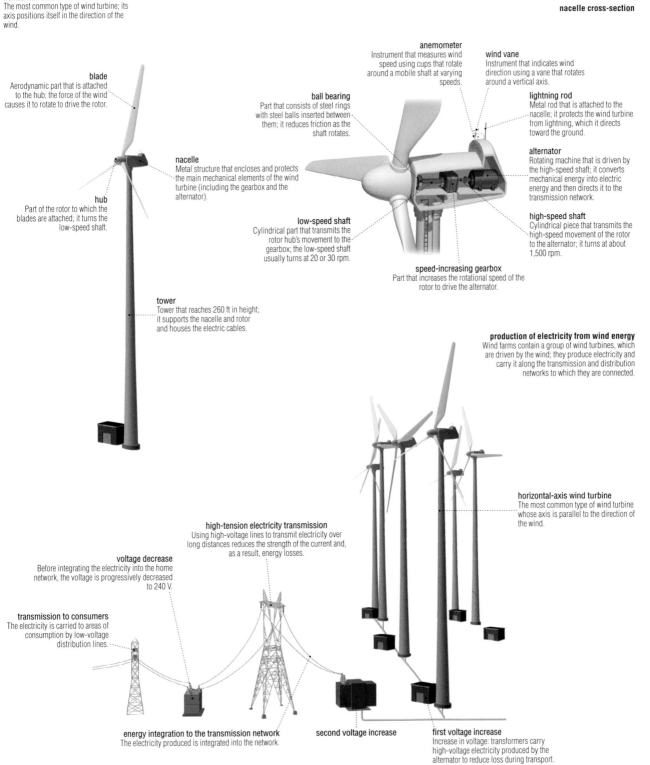

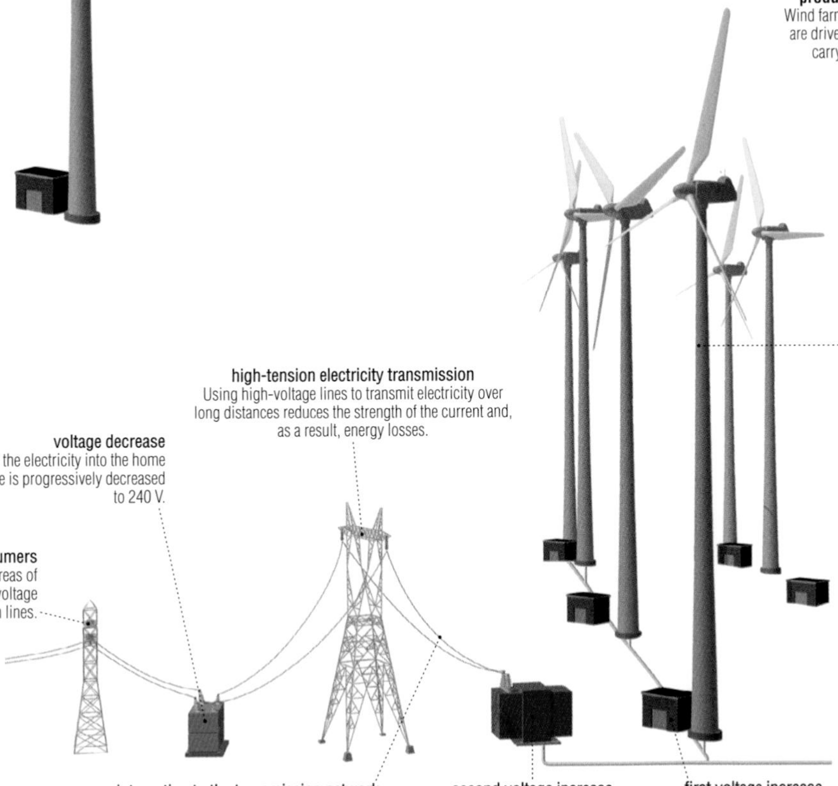

horizontal-axis wind turbine
The most common type of wind turbine whose axis is parallel to the direction of the wind.

high-tension electricity transmission
Using high-voltage lines to transmit electricity over long distances reduces the strength of the current and, as a result, energy losses.

voltage decrease
Before integrating the electricity into the home network, the voltage is progressively decreased to 240 V.

transmission to consumers
The electricity is carried to areas of consumption by low-voltage distribution lines.

energy integration to the transmission network
The electricity produced is integrated into the network.

second voltage increase

first voltage increase
Increase in voltage: transformers carry high-voltage electricity produced by the alternator to reduce loss during transport.

Chemistry is the study of the constitution of matter and its interactions; it has numerous applications, including biochemistry, electrochemistry and nuclear chemistry.

Mechanics is the study of force and motion. A mechanism is defined by two forces: the driving force (effort) and the resistant force (load).

Electromagnetism is the study of the relationship between electricity and magnetis Its many applications include motors, loudspeakers, measurement instruments and computers.

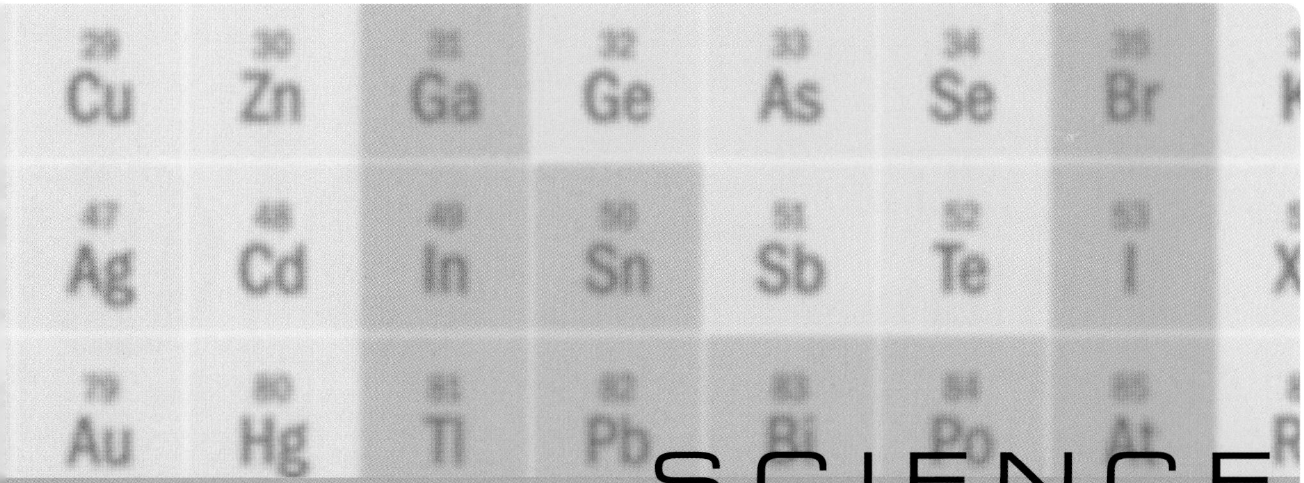
29 Cu 30 Zn 31 Ga 32 Ge 33 As 34 Se 35 Br
47 Ag 48 Cd 49 In 50 Sn 51 Sb 52 Te 53 I
79 Au 80 Hg 81 Tl 82 Pb 83 Bi 84 Po 85 At

SCIENCE

A body of knowledge, often formulated as laws and theories, based on the collection of data through observation and experiment.

matter

Any substance that has mass, is composed of atoms and occupies space.

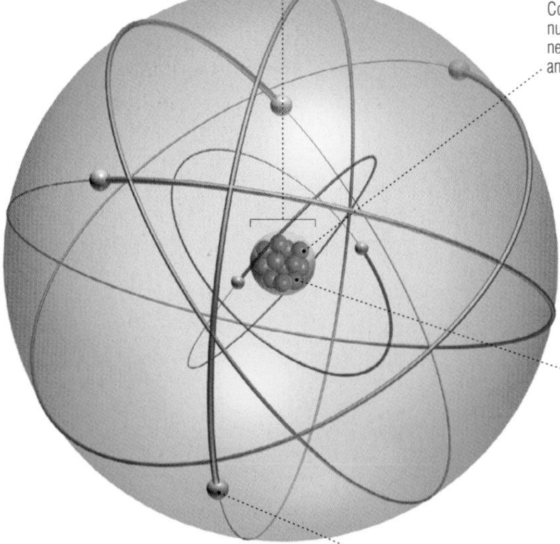
atom
Fundamental unit of matter having unique chemical properties; it is composed of a nucleus and an electron cloud. One atom is distinguished from another by the number of protons in its nucleus.
nucleus
Central part of the atom whose electric charge is positive; it is composed of protons and neutrons, around which electrons revolve.
neutron
Constituent particle of an atom's nucleus whose electric charge is neutral; it is composed of one u quark and two d quarks.
proton
Constituent particle of an atom's nucleus whose electric charge is positive; it is composed of two u quarks and one d quark.
electron
Particle having a negative electric charge that moves around the nucleus of the atom.

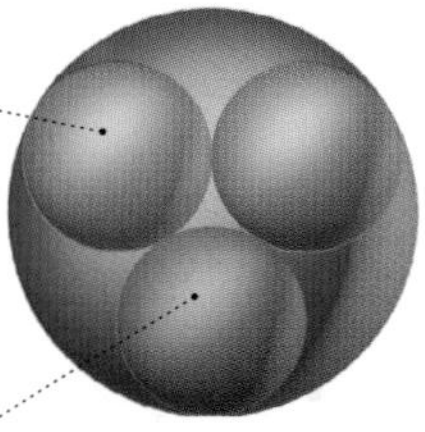
d quark
The d quark (down) is one of six types of quarks (constituent particles of protons and neutrons) having a negative electric charge.
u quark
The u quark (up) is one of six types of quarks (constituent particles of the protons and neutrons) having a positive electric charge.
neutron
Constituent particle of an atom's nucleus whose electric charge is neutral; it is composed of one u quark and two d quarks.

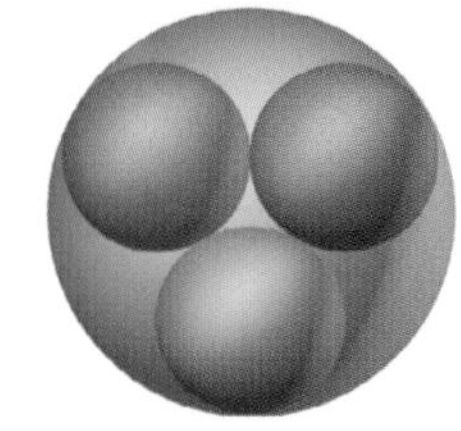
proton
Constituent particle of an atom's nucleus whose electric charge is positive; it is composed of two u quarks and one d quark.

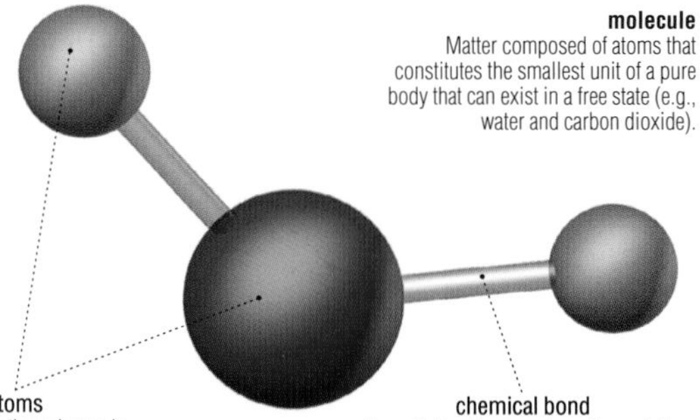
molecule
Matter composed of atoms that constitutes the smallest unit of a pure body that can exist in a free state (e.g., water and carbon dioxide).
atoms
All matter in the universe is composed of approximately 100 types of atoms.
chemical bond
Force that unites two atoms through the sharing of a common electron (covalent bond) or the transfer of electrons (ionic bond) to form a molecule.

states of matter
Matter exists in three fundamental states (solid, liquid and gaseous), which depend on the temperature and pressure to which the matter is subjected.

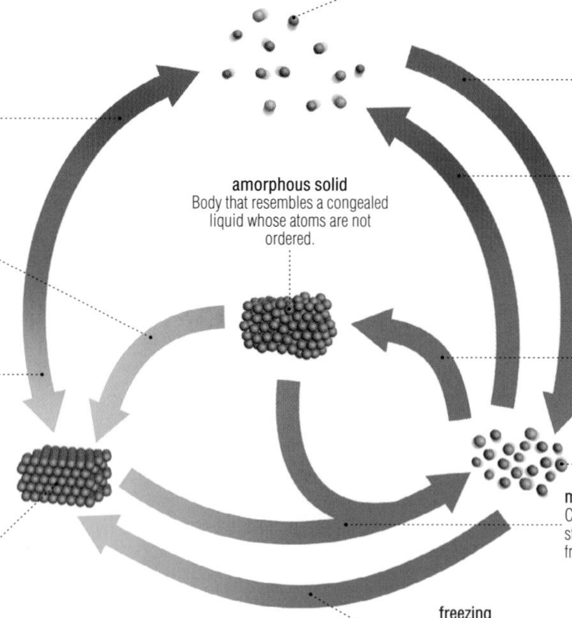
gas
Malleable and expandable matter whose only definable property is mass; its atoms are fully mobile with respect to each other.
sublimation
Change of a substance from a solid state directly to a gaseous state without passing through the liquid state; it results from heating.
condensation
Change of a substance from a gaseous state to a liquid state; it results from cooling.
amorphous solid
Body that resembles a congealed liquid whose atoms are not ordered.
evaporation
Change of a substance from a liquid state to a gaseous state; it results from heating.
crystallization
Change of a substance from an amorphous state to a crystallized state; it results from cooling, which causes the atoms to become ordered.
supercooling
The process of cooling a liquid below the point at which it normally freezes (solidifies); its atoms become unstable.
condensation
Change of a substance from a gaseous state to a liquid state; it results from cooling.
liquid
Matter having a definite mass and volume but no shape; its atoms are relatively mobile in relation to each other.
melting
Change of a substance from a solid state to a liquid state; it results from heating.
solid
Rigid body possessing mass, volume and a definite form; its atoms are linked to each other and are almost completely at rest.
freezing
Change of a substance from a liquid state to a solid state; it results from cooling.

nuclear fission
Process by which the atoms' nuclei become fragmented (e.g., in a nuclear reactor); neutrons are released and energy is produced in the form of heat.

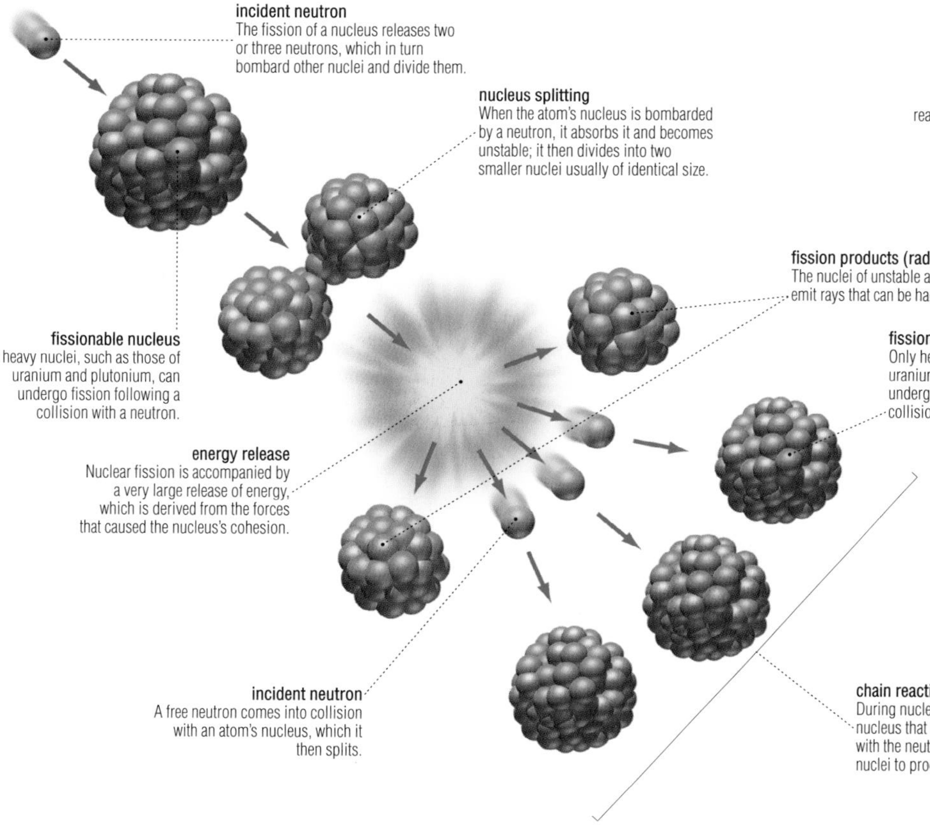
incident neutron
The fission of a nucleus releases two or three neutrons, which in turn bombard other nuclei and divide them.
nucleus splitting
When the atom's nucleus is bombarded by a neutron, it absorbs it and becomes unstable; it then divides into two smaller nuclei usually of identical size.
fission products (radioactive nuclei)
The nuclei of unstable atoms produced by fission emit rays that can be harmful to living organisms.
fissionable nucleus
Only heavy nuclei, such as those of uranium and plutonium, can undergo fission following a collision with a neutron.
fissionable nucleus
Only heavy nuclei, such as those of uranium and plutonium, can undergo fission following a collision with a neutron.
energy release
Nuclear fission is accompanied by a very large release of energy, which is derived from the forces that caused the nucleus's cohesion.
incident neutron
A free neutron comes into collision with an atom's nucleus, which it then splits.
chain reaction
During nuclear fission, parts of the atom's nucleus that have been broken off by collision with the neutron will in turn bombard other nuclei to produce more fission.

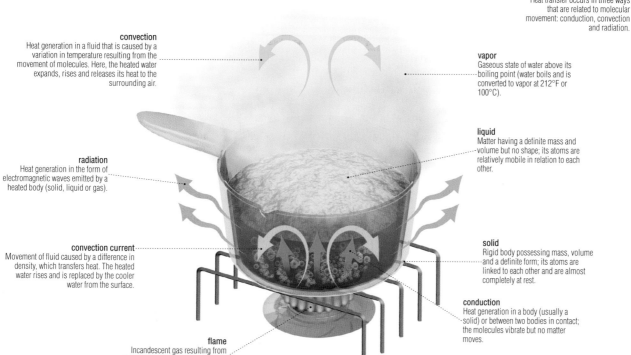

heat transfer
Heat transfer occurs in three ways that are related to molecular movement: conduction, convection and radiation.

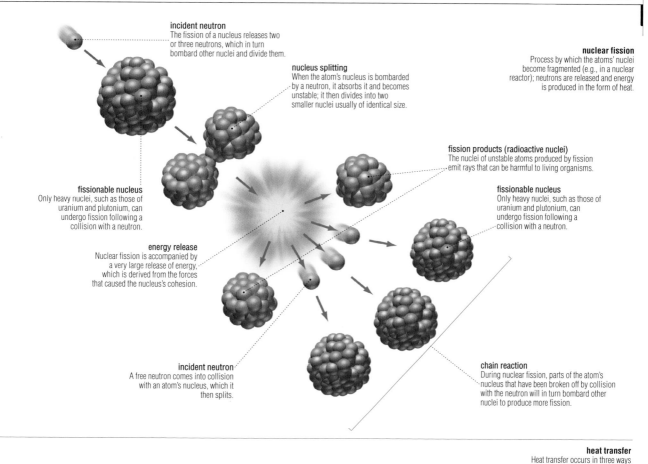

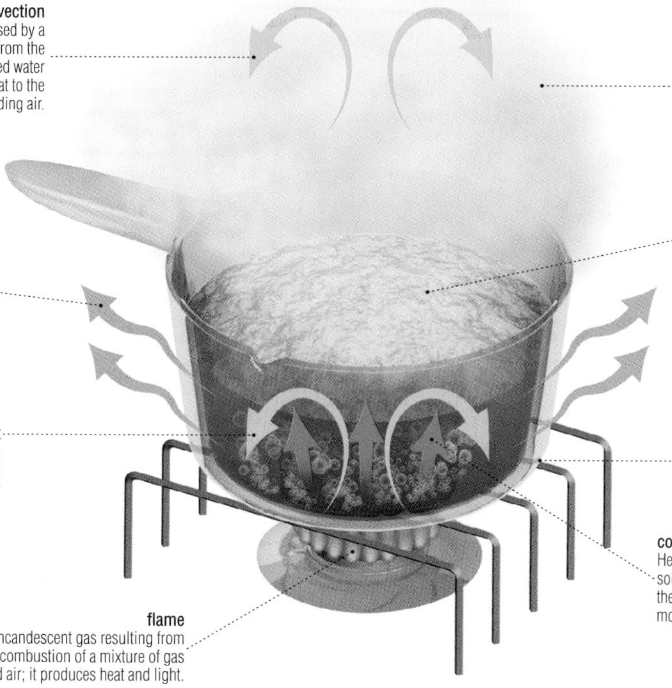
convection
Heat generation in a fluid that is caused by a variation in temperature resulting from the movement of molecules. Here, the heated water expands, rises and releases its heat to the surrounding air.
vapor
Gaseous state of water above its boiling point (water boils and is converted to vapor at 212°F or 100°C).
liquid
Matter having a definite mass and volume but no shape; its atoms are relatively mobile in relation to each other.
radiation
Heat generation in the form of electromagnetic waves emitted by a heated body (solid, liquid or gas).
convection current
Movement of fluid caused by a difference in density, which transfers heat. The heated water rises and is replaced by the cooler water from the surface.
solid
Rigid body possessing mass, volume and a definite form; its atoms are linked to each other and are almost completely at rest.
conduction
Heat generation in a body (usually a solid) or between two bodies in contact; the molecules vibrate but no matter moves.
flame
Incandescent gas resulting from the combustion of a mixture of gas and air; it produces heat and light.

chemical elements

There are more than 110 chemical elements, most of which are naturally present in the universe. The others are created artificially in the laboratory.

table of elements
Table created by Dmitry Mendeleyev in 1869 that classifies the now approximately 110 known chemical elements such as oxygen, hydrogen, iron and lead. The elements are classified in order of their atomic weight and arranged into groups having similar properties.

atomic number
Number that indicates the order of a chemical element in the table of elements and corresponds to the number of protons contained in its nucleus.

symbol
The name of each chemical element is represented by one or two letters, the first of which is in uppercase (e.g., O for oxygen, Cl for chlorine).

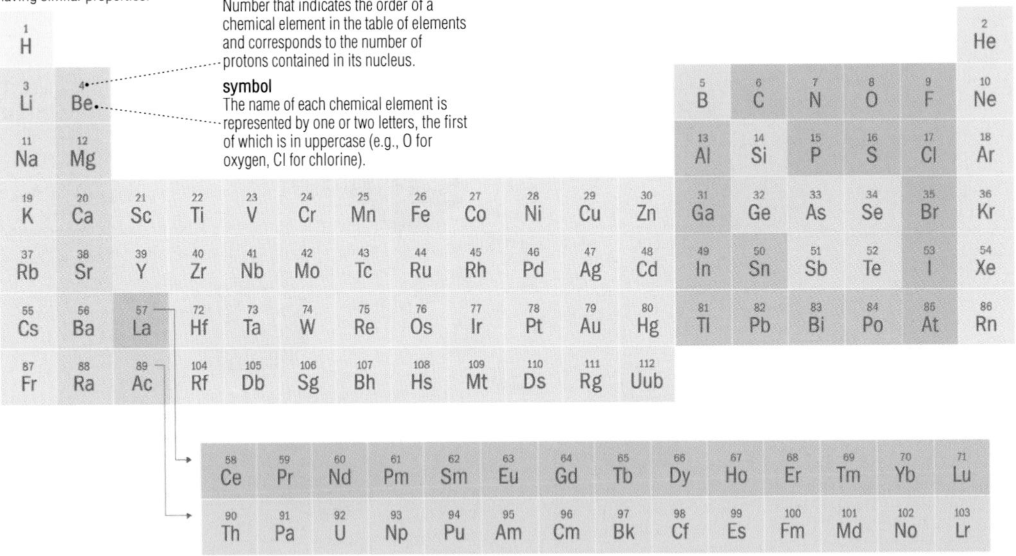

1 H
2 He
3 Li 4 Be 5 B 6 C 7 N 8 O 9 F 10 Ne
11 Na 12 Mg 13 Al 14 Si 15 P 16 S 17 Cl 18 Ar
19 K 20 Ca 21 Sc 22 Ti 23 V 24 Cr 25 Mn 26 Fe 27 Co 28 Ni 29 Cu 30 Zn 31 Ga 32 Ge 33 As 34 Se 35 Br 36 Kr
37 Rb 38 Sr 39 Y 40 Zr 41 Nb 42 Mo 43 Tc 44 Ru 45 Rh 46 Pd 47 Ag 48 Cd 49 In 50 Sn 51 Sb 52 Te 53 I 54 Xe
55 Cs 56 Ba 57 La 72 Hf 73 Ta 74 W 75 Re 76 Os 77 Ir 78 Pt 79 Au 80 Hg 81 Tl 82 Pb 83 Bi 84 Po 85 At 86 Rn
87 Fr 88 Ra 89 Ac 104 Rf 105 Db 106 Sg 107 Bh 108 Hs 109 Mt 110 Ds 111 Rg 112 Uub
58 Ce 59 Pr 60 Nd 61 Pm 62 Sm 63 Eu 64 Gd 65 Tb 66 Dy 67 Ho 68 Er 69 Tm 70 Yb 71 Lu
90 Th 91 Pa 92 U 93 Np 94 Pu 95 Am 96 Cm 97 Bk 98 Cf 99 Es 100 Fm 101 Md 102 No 103 Lr

1 H
hydrogen
This gas is the most abundant element in the universe and makes up part of the composition of water. It is used especially in petrochemistry and rocket engines.

alkali metals
Generally soft and silvery and very good conductors of heat and electricity; they are very reactant with nonmetals and break down in cold water.

3 Li
lithium
The lightest of all the metals is used especially in alloys for the aerospace industry, in household batteries and in medicine.

11 Na
sodium
Metal that is used especially in streetlights, kitchen salt (sodium chloride) and the manufacture of glass and cosmetic products.

19 K
potassium
Very reactant light metal that is used especially in fertilizer and matches; its salts are used in medicine.

37 Rb
rubidium
Metal similar to potassium but much rarer that is used in the manufacture of photoelectric cells and special kinds of glass and lasers.

55 Cs
cesium
Rare metal that is used especially in photoelectric cells, atomic clocks, infrared lamps and treating certain cancers.

87 Fr
francium
The heaviest of the alkali metals is very rare and radioactive and has a very short life span (about 22 minutes).

alkaline earth metals
Generally silvery and malleable and good conductors of heat and electricity; they react easily with nonmetals and water.

4 Be
beryllium
Uncommon metal that is used especially in alloys for the aerospace industry and as a moderator in nuclear reactors.

12 Mg
magnesium
Metal necessary for the growth and metabolism of most living organisms; it is also a component of aluminum alloys.

20 Ca
calcium
Metal that is one of the most essential elements in bones and teeth; it is also a component of cement, plaster and some alloys.

38 Sr
strontium
Relatively rare metal that is used especially in pyrotechnics (fireworks), the manufacture of magnets and medicine.

56 Ba
barium
Relatively abundant metal that is used especially in lubricants, pyrotechnics (fireworks), paint and radiology.

88 Ra
radium
Extremely radioactive metal present in very low quantities in uranium ore; it is used mainly in medicine as a cancer treatment.

semi-metals (metalloids)
Nonmetallic elements that are lusterless and solid; they possess a certain amount of electric and thermal conductivity.

5 B
boron
Semimetal that is used especially as a neutron absorber in nuclear reactors, as a rocket fuel and in detergents.

14 Si
silicon
Most common element on the planet after oxygen; it is used mostly in the manufacture of electronic devices because of its semiconductor properties.

32 Ge
germanium
Rare semimetal that is used especially in the manufacture of electronic devices and in optical equipment (camera and microscope lenses).

33 As
arsenic
Toxic semimetal that is used especially in very low doses for therapeutic uses and in the manufacture of semiconductors.

34 Se
selenium
Semimetal that is usually used in photoelectric cells and semiconductors; it is an indispensable trace element for organisms.

51 Sb
antimony
Semimetal that is used in several alloys (mostly with lead) and especially in making metal for printing type and semiconductors.

52 Te
tellurium
Rare semimetal that is used especially in the manufacture of detonators, electric resistors, rubber, ceramics and glass.

other metals
These elements are not part of any other category of metal; they are sometimes called posttransition metals.

13 Al
aluminum
Light metal that is used especially in aeronautics, cars, buildings, electric cables, kitchen utensils and packaging

31 Ga
gallium
Rare metal that is used especially in high-temperature thermometers, electroluminescent diodes and television screens (the color green).

49 In
indium
Very rare metal that is used especially in race car engines and electronic devices, and as a coating for glass.

50 Sn
tin
Metal that is used especially as an anticorrosive for copper and steel and as a component in the preparation of bronze, welding and toothpaste.

81 Tl
thallium
Metal that is used especially in infrared detectors and some kinds of glass.

82 Pb
lead
Heavy toxic metal that is used to prevent corrosion, as a protection against radiation and in accumulator batteries, paint and glass.

83 Bi
bismuth
Relatively rare metal that is used especially in alloys and cosmetics ar in medicine (treatments for gastric ulcers and diarrhea).

84 Po
polonium
Very rare radioactive metal that is us as fuel in nuclear reactors; it emits radiation that is much more powerfu than that of uranium.

SCIENCE

transition metals

Usually less reactant than alkali metals and alkaline earth metals but very good electric and thermal conductors. Many of these metals form vital alloys.

21 Sc **scandium**
Rare and very light metal that is employed in aerospace construction because of its high fusion point (about 2,700°F or 1,500°C).

22 Ti **titanium**
Metal that is used in several alloys employed in the manufacture of precision items and as a coating for light aerospace parts.

23 V **vanadium**
Metal that is used mainly in alloys, to which it provides highly anticorrosive properties.

24 Cr **chromium**
Bright metal that is used as an anticorrosive coating and in the manufacture of hard and resistant alloys; it gives emeralds and rubies their color.

25 Mn **manganese**
Hard metal that is used mainly in the manufacture of specialty steels and household batteries; it is also an indispensable trace element for humans.

26 Fe **iron**
The most used metal in the world due to its variety of alloys (steel, cast iron); it helps move oxygen through the body.

27 Co **cobalt**
Strong metal that is used in alloys (cutting tools, magnets) and in radiotherapy; it also yields a blue pigment.

28 Ni **nickel**
Hard metal that resists corrosion; it is used in the manufacture of coins and cutlery, and as a protective coating for other metals (iron, copper).

29 Cu **copper**
Reddish-brown metal that is a very good conductor of heat and electricity; it is used mainly in the manufacture of electric wire and alloys (brass, bronze).

30 Zn **zinc**
Relatively abundant metal that is resistant to corrosion; it is used especially in the manufacture of alloys, tires, paint, ointments and perfume.

39 Y **yttrium**
Rare metal used in the manufacture of alloys, electronic components, lasers, television screens and in nuclear reactors.

40 Zr **zirconium**
Metal that is used in alloys for the nuclear industry (protective sheathing, fuel rods) and in jewelry (imitation diamonds).

41 Nb **niobium**
Rare metal that is used especially in alloys for jet aircraft, missiles, nuclear reactors, ointments and cutting tools.

42 Mo **molybdenum**
Hard metal that is used in alloys (aircraft, missiles, nuclear reactors), electric lights and electronic tubes.

43 Tc **technetium**
Radioactive metal (first element to have been produced artificially) that makes steel corrosion-free and is used in medical imaging.

44 Ru **ruthenium**
Rare metal that hardens platinum and palladium; it is used in the manufacture of electric contacts, spark plugs and jewelry.

45 Rh **rhodium**
Rare metal that resists corrosion and hardens platinum and palladium; it is used especially in catalytic converters and jewelry.

46 Pd **palladium**
Rare and precious metal that is used especially in dentistry (dental prostheses), jewelry (white gold) and in catalytic converters.

47 Ag **silver**
Precious metal that is the best conductor of heat and electricity; it is used especially in the manufacture of mirrors, jewelry and coins.

48 Cd **cadmium**
Metal that is used especially as a protective covering for steel, in rechargeable batteries and in nuclear reactors (control rods).

72 Hf **hafnium**
Rare metal that is used in the control rods of nuclear reactors, filaments for incandescent lamps and jet engines.

73 Ta **tantalum**
Somewhat rare metal that is highly resistant to heat; it is used especially in nuclear reactors, missiles and capacitors.

74 W **tungsten**
Metal that is resistant to very high heat; it is used in filaments for incandescent lamps and cutting tools.

75 Re **rhenium**
Rare metal that is resistant to wear and corrosion; it is used especially in pen tips and incandescent filaments for ovens.

76 Os **osmium**
Rare metal often alloyed with iridium and platinum; it is used in pen tips, bearings, compass needles and jewelry.

77 Ir **iridium**
Rare metal that is often alloyed with platinum; it is used especially in electric contacts and jewelry.

78 Pt **platinum**
Very rare metal used especially as a catalyst in chemistry (petrochemicals, vitamins), in jewelry and in precision equipment.

79 Au **gold**
Precious metal (nuggets, flakes) that is used as currency (ingots) and in jewelry, dentistry and electronics.

80 Hg **mercury**
Rare metal that is used in measuring instruments (thermometers, barometers) and in the electricity industry.

104 Rf **rutherfordium**
Artificial radioactive element that was first produced in laboratories in the 1960s; it has applications only in scientific research.

105 Db **dubnium**
Artificial radioactive element that was first produced in laboratories in the 1960s.

106 Sg **seaborgium**
Artificial radioactive element that was first produced in laboratories in 1974; it is based on californium and oxygen.

107 Bh **bohrium**
Artificial radioactive element that was first produced in laboratories in 1976; it is based on bismuth and chromium.

108 Hs **hassium**
Artificial radioactive element that was first produced in laboratories in 1984; it is based on lead and iron.

109 Mt **meitnerium**
Artificial radioactive element that was first produced in laboratories in 1982; it is based on bismuth and iron.

110 Ds **darmstadtium**
Artificial radioactive element that was first produced in laboratories in 1994; it is based on nickel and lead.

111 Rg **roentgenium**
Artificial radioactive element that was first produced in laboratories in 1994; it is based on bismuth and nickel.

112 Uub **ununbium**
Artificial radioactive element that was first produced in laboratories in 1996; it is based on lead and zinc.

non-metals

Nonmetallic elements that are lusterless and nonmalleable; they are mostly gases and solids and are usually poor conductors of heat and electricity.

6 C **carbon**
Element common in its pure state (diamond, graphite) or found in combination (air, coal, petroleum); it is present in animal and plant tissue.

7 N **nitrogen**
Gas that constitutes about 78% of the Earth's atmosphere, present in all animal and vegetable tissue (proteins), and in fertilizer, ammonia and explosives.

8 O **oxygen**
Gas that is the most abundant element on Earth and that comprises about 20% of the atmospheric air; it is used to breathe and in the manufacture of steel.

9 F **fluorine**
Gas that is used especially for enriching uranium and manufacturing antistick coatings; it is present in bones and teeth.

15 P **phosphorus**
Solid used especially in fertilizer (phosphates), matches and pyrotechnics (fireworks); it is also necessary for human beings.

16 S **sulfur**
Solid that is quite common in nature; it is used in car batteries, fertilizer, paint, explosives, pharmaceuticals and rubber.

17 Cl **chlorine**
Abundant toxic gas that is used to whiten fabric and paper, disinfect water and manufacture various other products (solvents).

35 Br **bromine**
Very toxic liquid that is used mainly to manufacture teargas, dyes and disinfectants and in photography and medications.

53 I **iodine**
Solid that is used especially in pharmaceuticals (revulsives, antiseptics), in photography and dyes; it is also essential for the human body.

85 At **astatine**
Radioactive element that is extremely rare in nature; it is used in medicine to study the thyroid gland and to detect cancerous tumors.

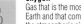

chemical elements

noble gases
Family of chemical elements also called inert, as they are weakly reactant.

2 He
helium
The lightest of the noble gases is noncombustible and abundant in the stars; it is used especially in inflating aerostats (such as balloons and dirigibles).

10 Ne
neon
Noble gas that is used mainly in lighting (billboards, television tubes and fog lamps), but also as a liquid coolant.

18 Ar
argon
Most abundant of the noble gases; it is used especially in incandescent lamps and in welding (protective gas).

36 Kr
krypton
Noble gas that is used in some incandescent lamps and in photography.

54 Xe
xenon
Rarest gas in the atmosphere; it is used mainly in discharge lamps, photoflash bulbs and lasers.

86 Rn
radon
Highly radioactive noble gas that is used mainly in medicine (destroying cancerous tumors) and in predicting earthquakes.

lanthanides (rare earth)
Very reactant elements found in the lanthanide series (monazite, xenotime); some are relatively abundant in the Earth's crust.

57 La
lanthanum
Metal that reacts with water to yield hydrogen; it is used especially in flint alloys and optical glass.

58 Ce
cerium
The most common metal of the lanthanide group and the main constituent of flint alloys (misch metal).

59 Pr
praseodymium
Metal that is used especially in protective lenses, colorants for glass, flint alloys (misch metal) and permanent magnets.

60 Nd
neodymium
One of the most reactant of rare metals; it is used mainly to manufacture lasers, eyeglasses and permanent-magnet alloys.

61 Pm
promethium
Radioactive metal that is used mainly in specialized batteries and luminescent coatings for watches, and as a source of X-rays in medicine.

62 Sm
samarium
Rare radioactive metal that is used especially in optical glass, lasers, nuclear reactors (absorbing neutrons) and permanent magnets.

63 Eu
europium
The most reactant metal of the lanthanide group; it is used especially in television screens (the color orange) and nuclear reactors (absorbing neutrons).

64 Gd
gadolinium
Metal that is often alloyed with chromed steel; it is used especially in the manufacture of permanent magnets, magnetic heads and electronic components.

65 Tb
terbium
Rare metal that is used especially in lasers and semiconductors.

66 Dy
dysprosium
Very rare metal that is used especially in permanent magnets, lasers and nuclear reactors (absorbing neutrons).

67 Ho
holmium
Very rare metal with limited applications; it is used in lasers and for coloring glass.

68 Er
erbium
Metal that is used mainly in some alloys (especially with vanadium), lasers and infrared-absorbing glass, and as a colorant for glass and enamel.

69 Tm
thulium
The rarest of the lanthanide group; it used as a source of X-rays in portab radiology equipment and in the manufacture of ferrites (magnetic ceramics).

70 Yb
ytterbium
Metal that is used in the manufactur of stainless steel, in lasers and as a source of X-rays in portable radiology equipment.

71 Lu
lutetium
Very rare metal that is difficult to separate; it has no real industrial applications but can be used as a catalyst (cracking, hydrogenation).

actinides
Radioactive elements that are abundant in nature (elements 89 to 92) or made artificially (elements 93 to 103). Most of them have no industrial applications.

89 Ac
actinium
Metal that is present in small quantities in uranium ore; it is used mainly as a source of neutrons in nuclear reactors.

90 Th
thorium
Natural metal that is used especially in alloys, photoelectric cells and uranium production.

91 Pa
protactinium
Very rare metal that is present in uranium ore; it has few applications outside of scientific research.

92 U
uranium
Naturally abundant metal that is used mainly as fuel in nuclear reactors as well as in nuclear weapons.

93 Np
neptunium
Rare metal that is produced from uranium; it is used in neutron-detection instruments.

94 Pu
plutonium
Metal that is produced from uranium; it is used especially as fuel in nuclear reactors as well as in nuclear weapons.

95 Am
americium
Metal that is produced from plutonium; it is used mainly in smoke detectors and in radiology.

96 Cm
curium
Metal that is produced in small amounts from plutonium; it is used especially in thermoelectric generators for spacecraft propulsion.

97 Bk
berkelium
Metal that is produced in small amounts from americium; it is used for scientific research only.

98 Cf
californium
Metal produced from curium that is used especially in the treatment of cancer and in some measuring instruments such as humidistats.

99 Es
einsteinium
Metal that was discovered in 1952 among the debris of the first thermonuclear explosion in the Pacific; it is used for scientific research only.

100 Fm
fermium
Metal that was discovered at the same time as einsteinium; it is used for scientific research only.

101 Md
mendelevium
Metal that is produced from einsteinium; it is named in honor of the chemist Mendeleyev (who classified the elements).

102 No
nobelium
Metal that is produced from curium; it is named in honor of Alfred Nobel (inventor of dynamite and founder of the Nobel Prize).

103 Lr
lawrencium
Metal that is produced from californium; it is used for scientific research only.

chemistry symbols
Symbols that simplify the writing of the elements, formulas and chemical reactions.

—

negative charge
Symbol that indicates a surplus of electrons in an atom, which means the atom has a negative electric charge. The chlorine atom, for example, forms a negative ion that is denoted as Cl^-.

+

positive charge
Symbol that indicates a loss of electrons in an atom, which means the atom has a positive electric charge. The sodium atom, for example, forms a positive ion that is denoted as Na+.

$\rightleftarrows$

reversible reaction
Chemical reaction that can occur in both directions; the products obtained (direct reaction) react between them to change back into the original reactants (inverse reaction).

$\longrightarrow$

reaction direction
A chemical reaction corresponds to the conversi of reactants in products and is obtained by the lo of one of the reactants. The arrow indicates the direction in which this irreversible reaction occu

laboratory equipment

These materials are highly varied: measurement instruments, various containers, heat sources, experimentation materials and mounting hardware.

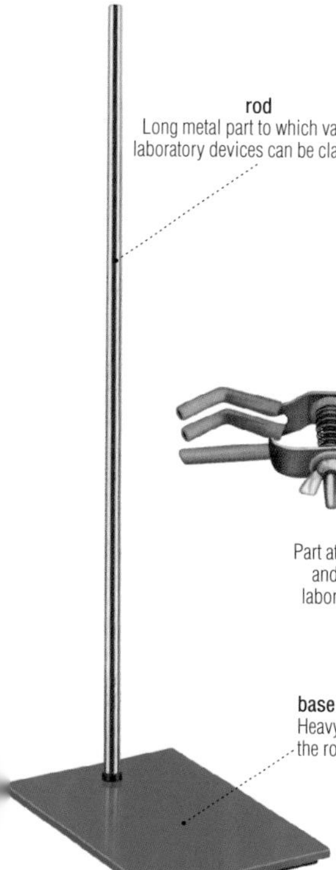

rod
Long metal part to which various laboratory devices can be clamped.

base
Heavy metal pedestal supporting the rod.

stand
Unit consisting of a base and a rod; it supports various laboratory apparatuses such as burettes and flasks.

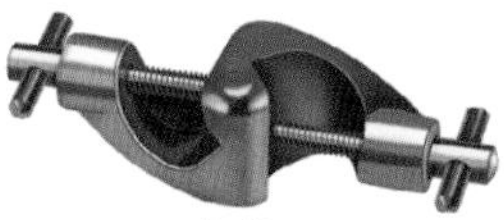

holder
Part with a screw for attaching a clamp onto the stand's rod.

clamp/holder
Part attached to the stand's rod by a holder and having tongs that clamp onto the laboratory equipment to hold it in place.

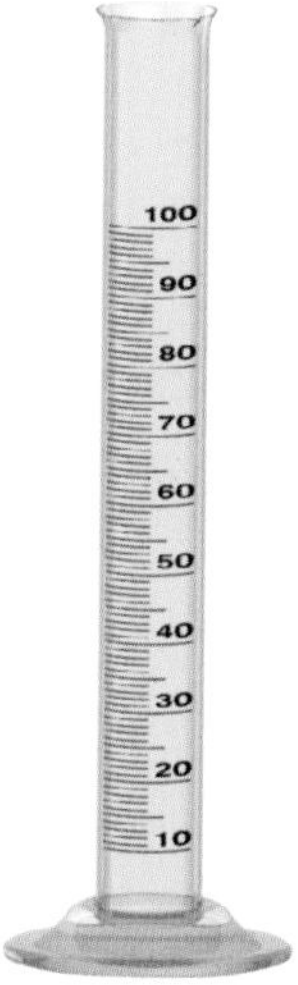

graduated cylinder
Graduated tube with a spout that is used especially for measuring small amounts of liquid with precision.

straight stopcock burette
Long graduated tube for measuring liquids with high precision; it is fitted with a valve for manually regulating the flow.

serological pipette
Fine tube that is open at both ends; it is used to transfer very precise quantities of liquids from one container to another.

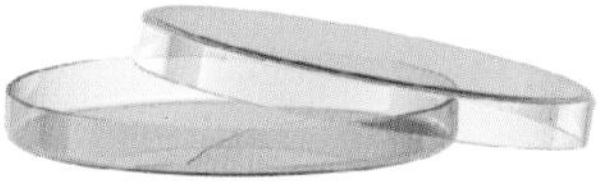

Petri dish
Flat transparent box for culturing microorganisms; it has a cover to protect them from contamination.

test tube
Cylindrical tube used to conduct various chemical experiments on small quantities (normally, it is not filled above one-third).

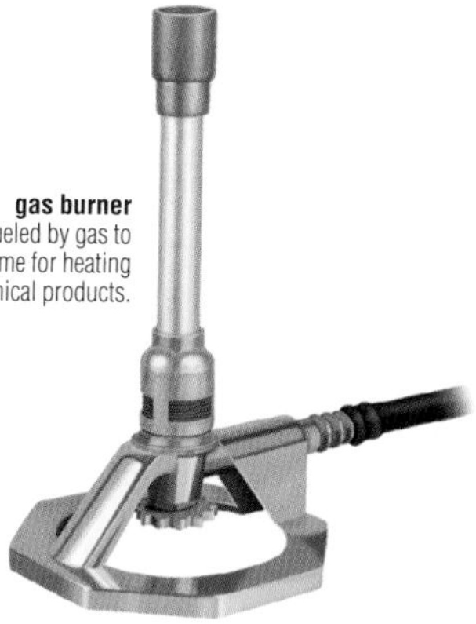

gas burner
Device that is fueled by gas to produce a flame for heating chemical products.

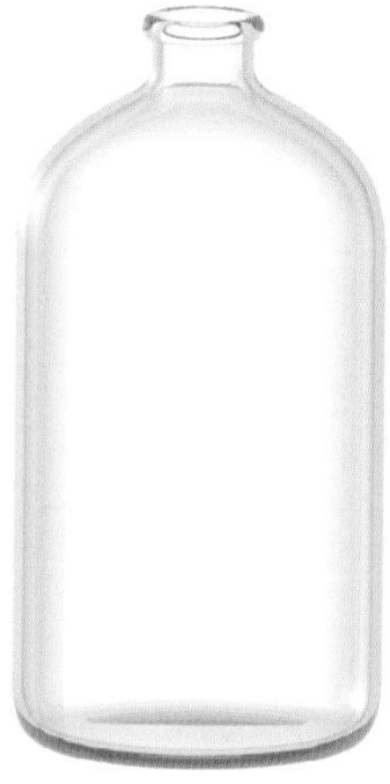

bottle
Container of various sizes and shapes and usually with a straight neck for holding liquids.

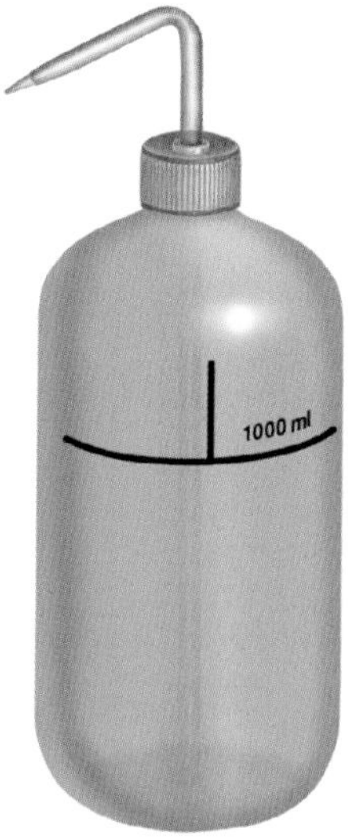

wash bottle
Flexible container that is squeezed lightly to squirt a liquid; it is used especially for cleaning equipment (test tubes, pipettes).

round-bottom flask
Spherical container used mainly for boiling liquids.

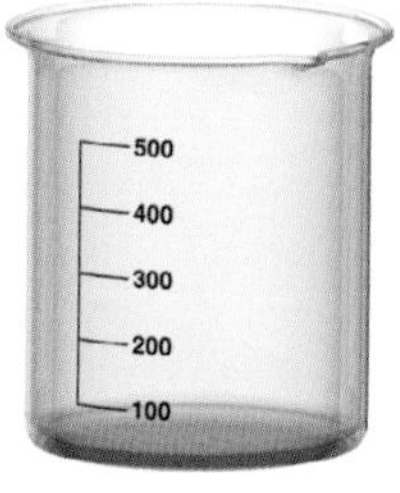

beaker
Graduated container with a spout; it is used to create reactions (precipitation, electrolysis) and to measure approximate amounts of liquid.

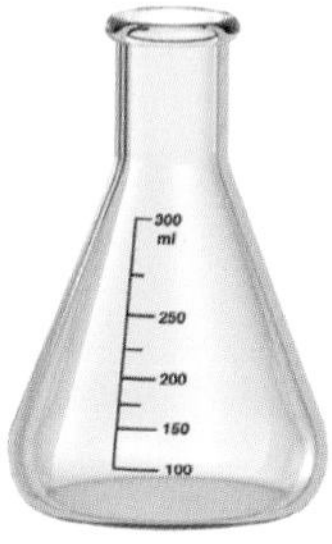

Erlenmeyer flask
Graduated cone-shaped container that is used very frequently in laboratories; it can have a stopper and is used especially for mixing and measuring liquids.

gearing systems

Mechanisms consisting of toothed parts that mesh to transmit the rotational motion of the shafts they are a part of.

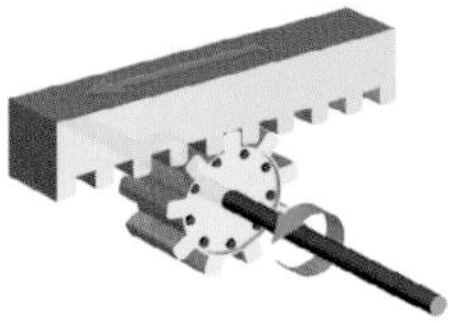

rack and pinion gear
Gearing system converting a rotational movement into a horizontal movement (and vice versa); it is often used in the steering systems of automobiles.

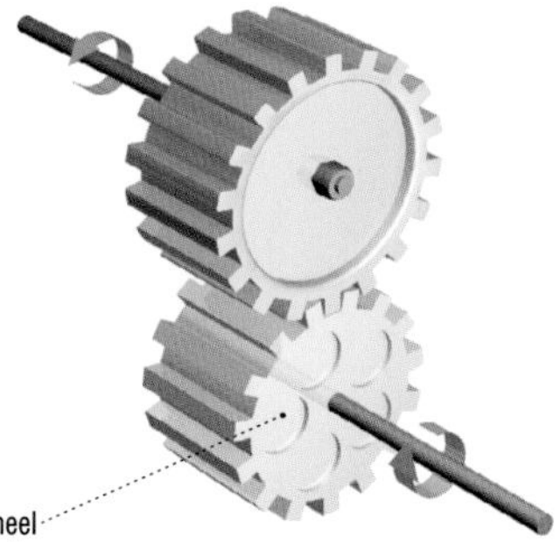

toothed wheel
Wheel with teeth that mesh with the teeth of another wheel to transmit rotational movement to it.

spur gear
Most common gearing system linking two parallel shafts that changes the speed and force of a rotation; it is used especially in automobile transmissions.

bevel gear
Gearing system linking two shafts at right angles that changes the direction of rotation; it is used especially in car jacks.

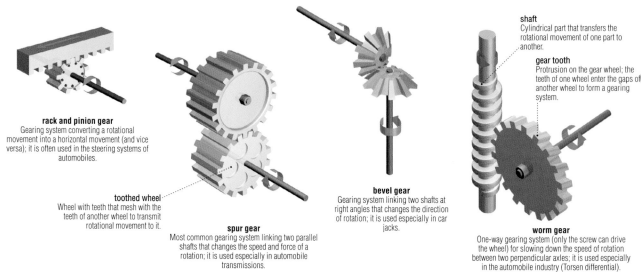

shaft
Cylindrical part that transfers the rotational movement of one part to another.

gear tooth
Protrusion on the gear wheel; the teeth of one wheel enter the gaps of another wheel to form a gearing system.

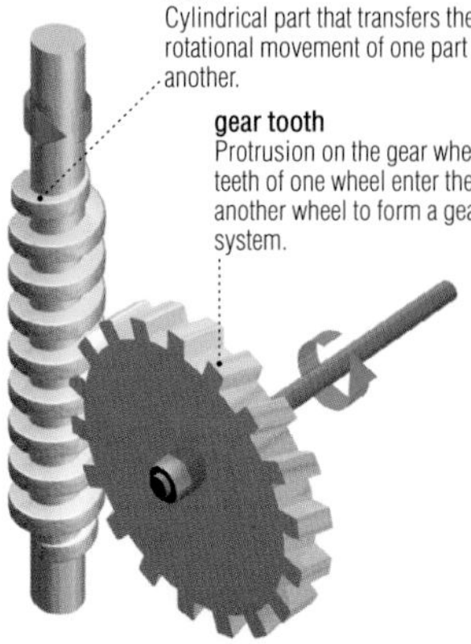

worm gear
One-way gearing system (only the screw can drive the wheel) for slowing down the speed of rotation between two perpendicular axles; it is used especially in the automobile industry (Torsen differential).

double pulley system

System consisting of two pulleys with a rope running around them to lift a load. Using two or more pulleys reduces the amount of effort needed.

pulley
Device with a grooved wheel (sheave wheel) around which a rope passes to transmit the effort exerted on the load.

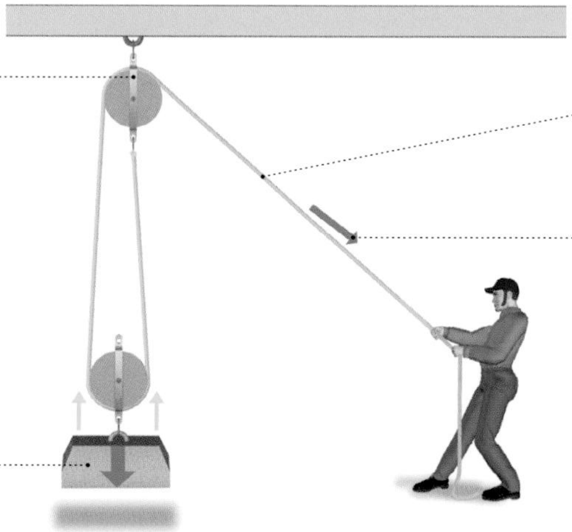

rope
Cord that slides on the pulley and is pulled to lift the load.

effort
Force exerted on the pulley's rope to lift the load.

load
Weight whose inertia exerts a force opposite to the force exerted on the rope.

lever

System consisting of a bar pivoting on a fulcrum to lift a load. The amount of effort required is related to the position of the pivot and the length of the bar.

fulcrum
Point around which the lever pivots.

load
Weight whose inertia exerts a force opposite to the effort exerted on the bar.

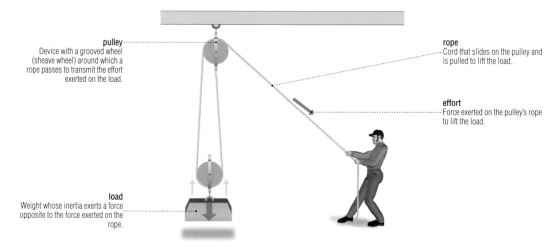

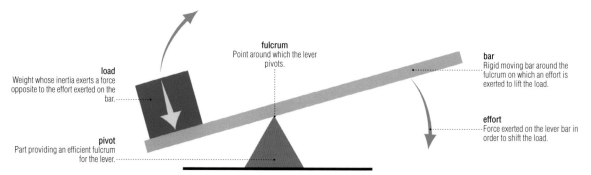

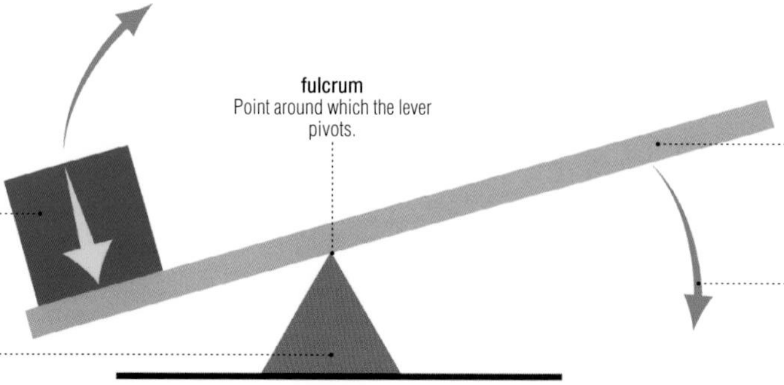

bar
Rigid moving bar around the fulcrum on which an effort is exerted to lift the load.

effort
Force exerted on the lever bar in order to shift the load.

pivot
Part providing an efficient fulcrum for the lever.

magnetism

Action exerted by magnets and magnetic fields and phenomena. Magnetism can be characterized by the forces of attraction and repulsion between two masses.

repulsion
Force by which two bodies push against each other. Two poles of the same orientation (both positive or both negative) repulse each other.

north pole
End of the magnet from which field lines originate and around which the exterior magnetic action is intense.

magnet
Body producing an exterior magnetic field; it attracts iron, nickel and cobalt as well as their alloys.

field line
Imaginary line representing the direction of the magnetic forces between the north and south poles.

south pole
End of the magnet to which the field lines are directed and around which the exterior magnetic action is intense.

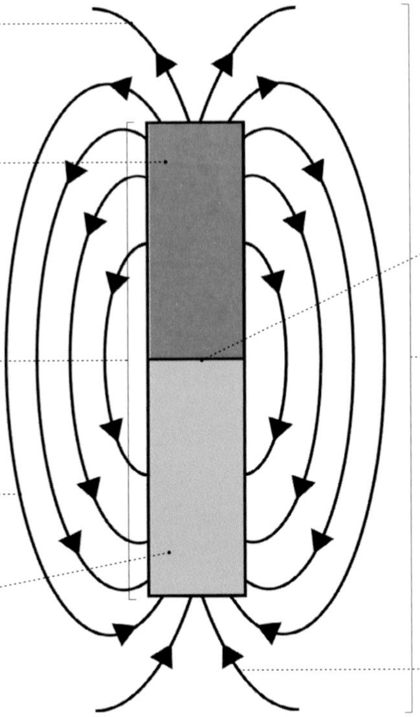

neutral line
Line separating the north and south lines of the magnet and exhibiting no magnetic phenomena.

magnetic field
Area around the magnet where magnetic forces represented by lines of force are exerted, resulting in electron movement.

attraction
Force by which two bodies are pulled toward each other; opposite poles attract each other.

parallel electrical circuit

It is divided into independent branches, through which the current flows with partial intensity (in a series circuit, all the elements receive the same intensity).

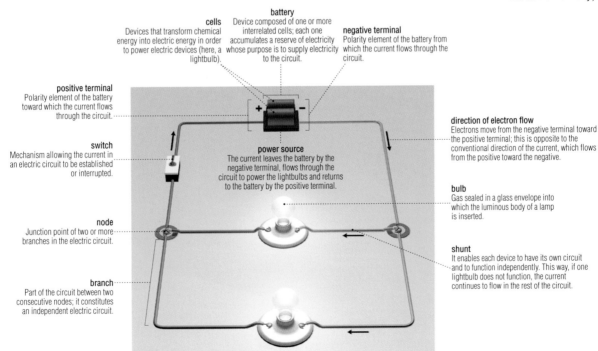

cells
Devices that transform chemical energy into electric energy in order to power electric devices (here, a lightbulb).

battery
Device composed of one or more interrelated cells; each one accumulates a reserve of electricity whose purpose is to supply electricity to the circuit.

negative terminal
Polarity element of the battery from which the current flows through the circuit.

positive terminal
Polarity element of the battery toward which the current flows through the circuit.

switch
Mechanism allowing the current in an electric circuit to be established or interrupted.

node
Junction point of two or more branches in the electric circuit.

branch
Part of the circuit between two consecutive nodes; it constitutes an independent electric circuit.

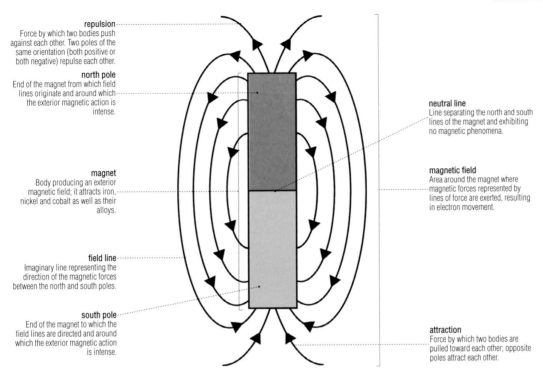

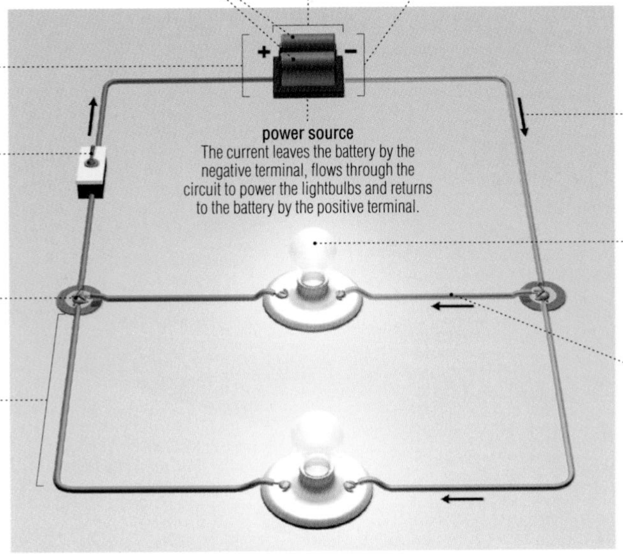

power source
The current leaves the battery by the negative terminal, flows through the circuit to power the lightbulbs and returns to the battery by the positive terminal.

direction of electron flow
Electrons move from the negative terminal toward the positive terminal; this is opposite to the conventional direction of the current, which flows from the positive toward the negative.

bulb
Gas sealed in a glass envelope into which the luminous body of a lamp is inserted.

shunt
It enables each device to have its own circuit and to function independently. This way, if one lightbulb does not function, the current continues to flow in the rest of the circuit.

generators

Devices that convert mechanical energy (here, a shaft's rotational motion) into electric energy by moving a coil inside a magnet (electromagnetic induction).

dynamo
Continuous generator of electric current; it is used, for example, on bicycles for lighting.

field electromagnet
Fixed electromagnet made up of an iron bar and coils; when exposed to an excitation current, it creates a magnetic field.

armature
Moving part of the dynamo that is made up of a coil, which produces an electric current as it rotates inside the field.

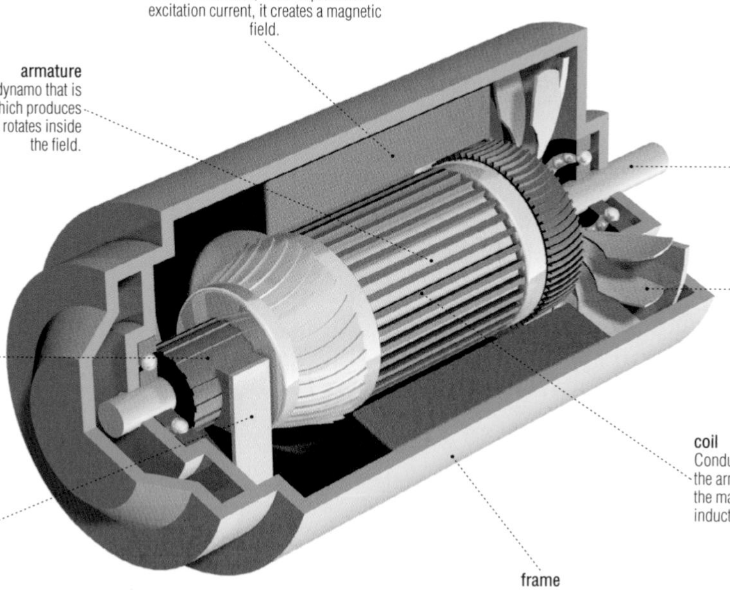

shaft
Cylindrical part that transmits a rotational motion to the dynamo's armature.

fan wheel
Device with blades that circulates air to cool the dynamo.

commutator
Conductive plates that are insulated from each other and connected to the field coil; they collect and rectify the induced alternating current.

coil
Conductive wire that is rolled around the armature cylinder, which rotates in the magnetic field produced by the inductor to create an electric current.

brush
Conductor that rubs against the commutator plates and transmits the continuous current produced by the dynamo to an exterior circuit.

frame
Metal casing that houses the magnetic field.

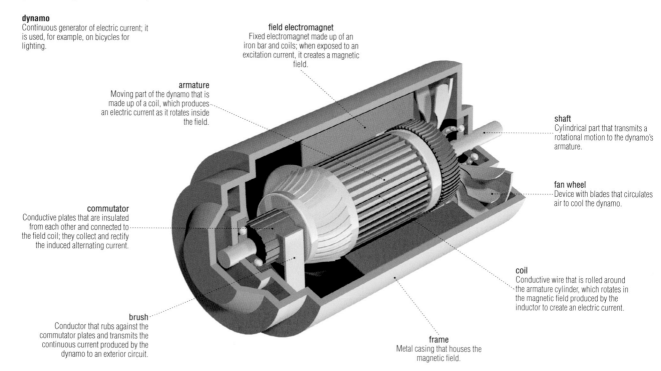

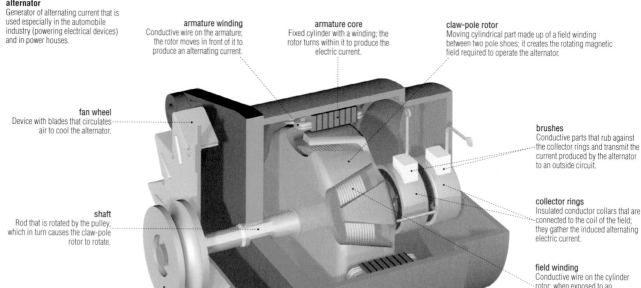

alternator
Generator of alternating current that is used especially in the automobile industry (powering electrical devices) and in power houses.

armature winding
Conductive wire on the armature; the rotor moves in front of it to produce an alternating current.

armature core
Fixed cylinder with a winding; the rotor turns within it to produce the electric current.

claw-pole rotor
Moving cylindrical part made up of a field winding between two pole shoes; it creates the rotating magnetic field required to operate the alternator.

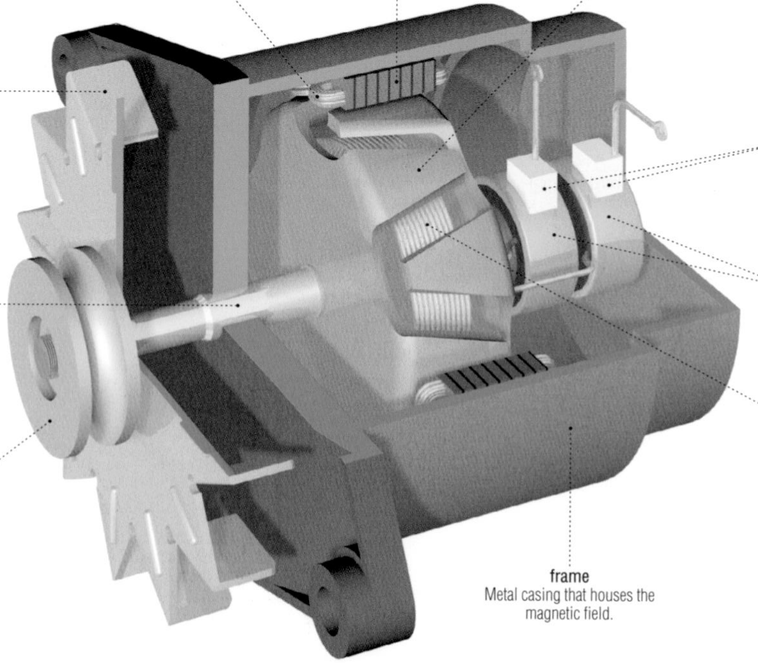

fan wheel
Device with blades that circulates air to cool the alternator.

brushes
Conductive parts that rub against the collector rings and transmit the current produced by the alternator to an outside circuit.

collector rings
Insulated conductor collars that are connected to the coil of the field; they gather the induced alternating electric current.

shaft
Rod that is rotated by the pulley, which in turn causes the claw-pole rotor to rotate.

field winding
Conductive wire on the cylinder rotor; when exposed to an excitation current, it creates a magnetic field.

drive pulley
Mechanical unit integrated with the shaft; it is rotated by a belt that is connected to an engine.

frame
Metal casing that houses the magnetic field.

dry cells

Devices that transform chemical energy into electric energy (direct current); they usually cannot be recharged and the electrolyte is fixed in place.

carbon-zinc cell
Battery that produces 1.5 V (also called Leclanché); its use is very widespread (pocket calculators, portable radios, alarm clocks).

sealing plug
Material that seals the battery.

positive terminal
Polarity element of the battery from which the current flows.

washer
Disk that compresses the depolarizing mix.

top cap
Upper metal cover; the positive terminal is located at its center.

electrolytic separator
ous paper combined with a chemical paste (ammonium chloride) that arates the two electrodes; this allows electrons to pass, thus conducting electricity.

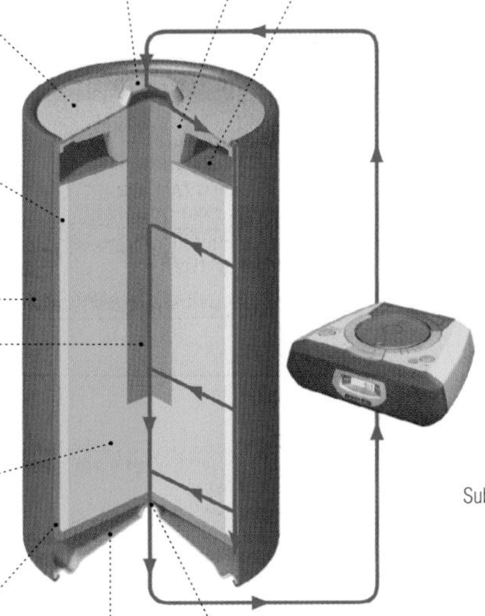

jacket
Battery's protective plastic casing.

carbon rod (cathode)
rbon rod set in the depolarizing mix; it constitutes the battery's negative electrode (cathode) collecting the electrons returning from the circuit.

depolarizing mix
Mixture of carbon and manganese ioxide that augments conductivity by acting as a barrier to polarization.

zinc can (anode)
Zinc receptacle that constitutes the battery's positive electrode (anode).

bottom cap
Lower metal cover; the negative terminal is located at its center.

negative terminal
Polarity element of the battery toward which the current flows.

alkaline manganese-zinc cell
High-performance battery that produces 1.5 V and has a longer life span than the carbon-zinc cell; it is used in devices such as flashlights, portable CD players and camera flash units.

zinc-electrolyte mix (anode)
Substance that is made up of zinc and electrolyte (potassium hydroxide); it constitutes the positive electrode (anode).

sealing material
Material (nylon) that seals the battery.

electron collector
Zinc rod that is connected to the bottom cap; it collects the electrons from the anode that are attracted to the cathode.

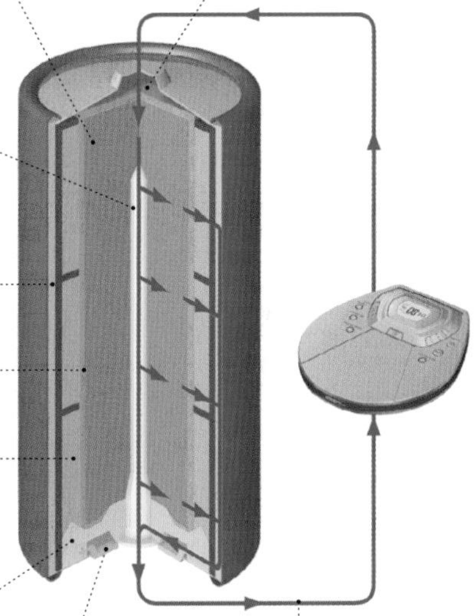

steel casing
Covering that protects the battery.

separator
Porous paper combined with a chemical paste (potassium hydroxide) that separates the two electrodes; this allows electrons to pass, thus conducting electricity.

manganese mix (cathode)
Substance made up of manganese dioxide and carbon; it constitutes the negative electrode (cathode).

sealing plug
Material that seals the battery.

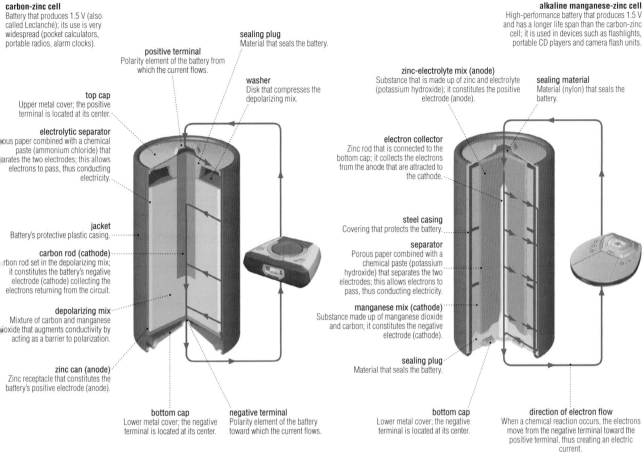

bottom cap
Lower metal cover; the negative terminal is located at its center.

direction of electron flow
When a chemical reaction occurs, the electrons move from the negative terminal toward the positive terminal, thus creating an electric current.

electronics

The scientific study of the behavior of the electron and its applications, such as computers, medicine and automation.

printed circuit board
Usually plastic insulated card with holes containing electronic components; the circuit is printed on its surface.

ceramic capacitor
Component with two conductive plates (silver, copper) separated by an insulator (ceramic); it stores weak electric charge.

electrolytic capacitors
Polarized components with two conductive components (aluminum, tantalum) separated by an insulator (electrolyte); they store strong electric charge.

plastic film capacitor
Commonly used component with two conductive plates (aluminum, tin) separated by an insulator (plastic); it stores electric charge.

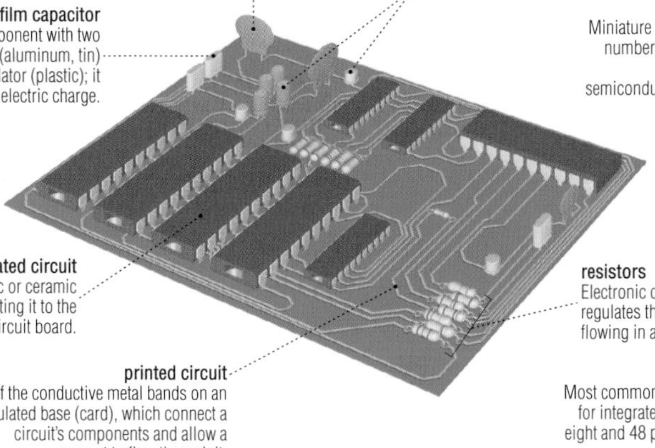

packaged integrated circuit
tric circuit under a plastic or ceramic ıg; it has pins for connecting it to the circuit board.

printed circuit
All of the conductive metal bands on an insulated base (card), which connect a circuit's components and allow a current to flow through it.

resistors
Electronic component that regulates the amount of current flowing in a circuit.

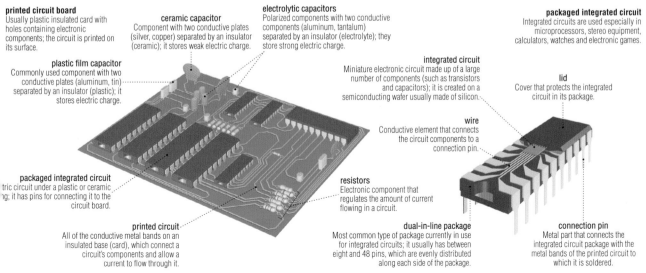

packaged integrated circuit
Integrated circuits are used especially in microprocessors, stereo equipment, calculators, watches and electronic games.

integrated circuit
Miniature electronic circuit made up of a large number of components (such as transistors and capacitors); it is created on a semiconducting wafer usually made of silicon.

lid
Cover that protects the integrated circuit in its package.

wire
Conductive element that connects the circuit components to a connection pin.

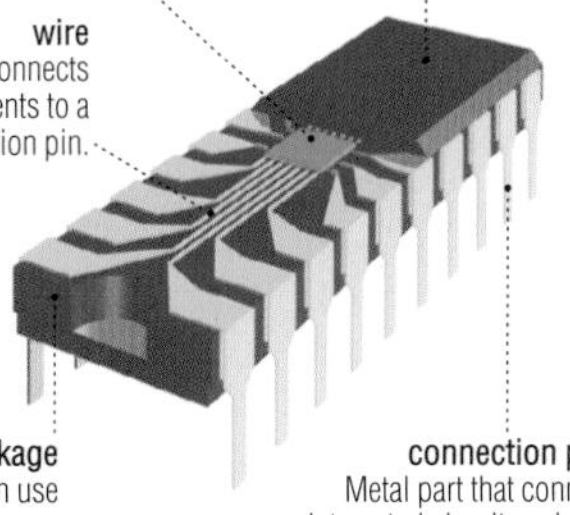

dual-in-line package
Most common type of package currently in use for integrated circuits; it usually has between eight and 48 pins, which are evenly distributed along each side of the package.

connection pin
Metal part that connects the integrated circuit package with the metal bands of the printed circuit to which it is soldered.

electromagnetic spectrum

Electromagnetic waves that are classified in ascending order of energy (frequency); they propagate at the speed of light (300,000 km/s).

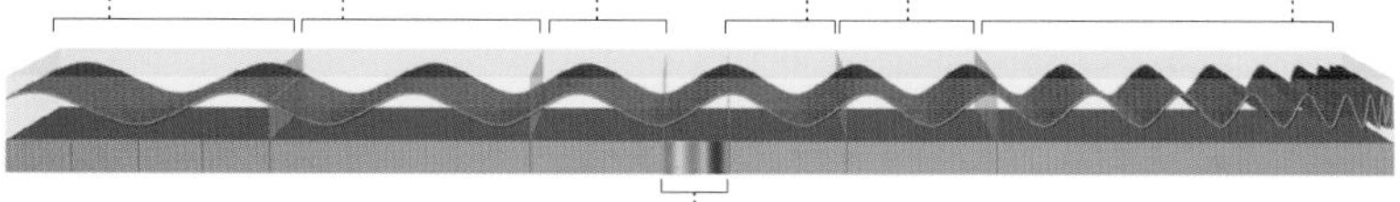

microwaves
Short electromagnetic waves; their many applications include radar detection and microwave ovens.
ultraviolet radiation
Electromagnetic waves used especially to tan skin and in microscopy, medicine and lighting (fluorescent tubes).
radio waves
Very long electromagnetic waves (about 1 meter) having low frequency; they are used to transmit information (television, radio).
infrared radiation
Electromagnetic waves emitted by warm objects; their many uses include heating, medicine, aerial photography and weaponry.
X-rays
Electromagnetic waves used especially in radiology; frequent exposure can be harmful.
gamma rays
Electromagnetic waves of very high frequency that are emitted by radioactive bodies; they are the most radiant and harmful rays and are used especially in treating cancer.
visible light
Electromagnetic radiation that is perceived by the human eye and ranges from red to violet.

wave

Oscillation caused by a disturbance; as it propagates through a medium (mechanical waves) or a vacuum (electromagnetic waves), it carries energy.

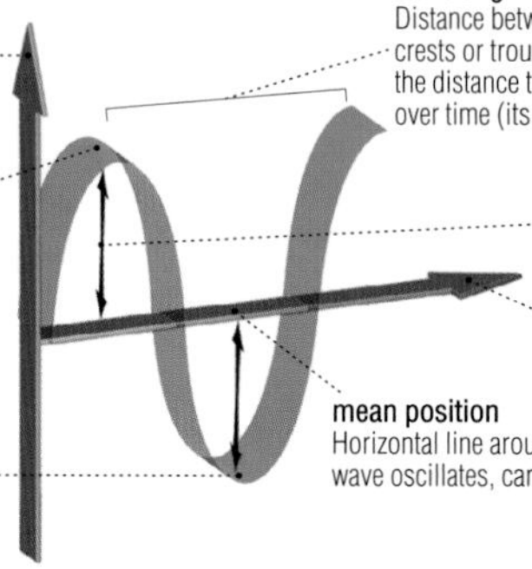

displacement
Gap in relation to the mean position.
wavelength
Distance between two consecutive crests or troughs; it corresponds to the distance traveled by the wave over time (its period).
amplitude
Maximum displacement of a wave in relation to its mean position; it corresponds to the amount of energy transmitted.
crest
Highest point of the wave.
propagation
Motion of a wave leaving its source.
mean position
Horizontal line around which the wave oscillates, carrying energy.
trough
Lowest point of the wave.

color synthesis

Technique of generating color by combining light rays or subtracting them to obtain a colored image.

additive color synthesis
The superimposition of primary colors (blue, green and red) is used especially in electronic screens (television, computer, video) to obtain intermediate tints.

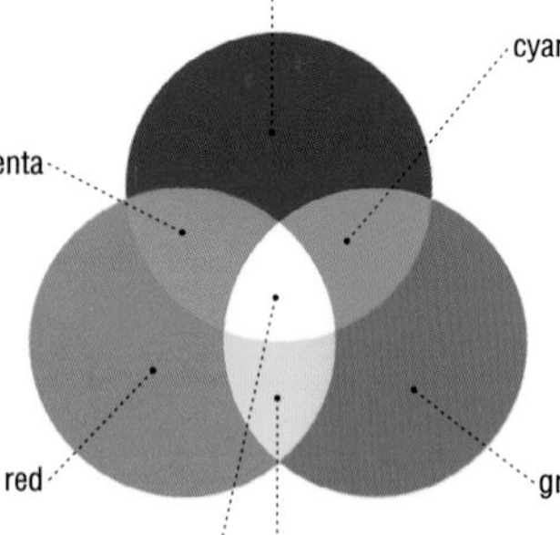

blue
cyan
magenta
red
green
white
yellow

subtractive color synthesis
The absorption of certain light rays (blue, green, red) by colored filters (yellow, magenta, cyan) is used in industries such as photography, film production and printing to obtain intermediate tints.

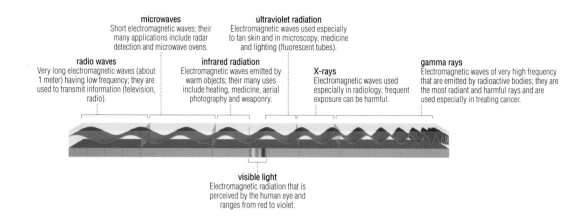

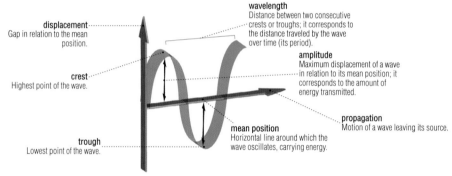

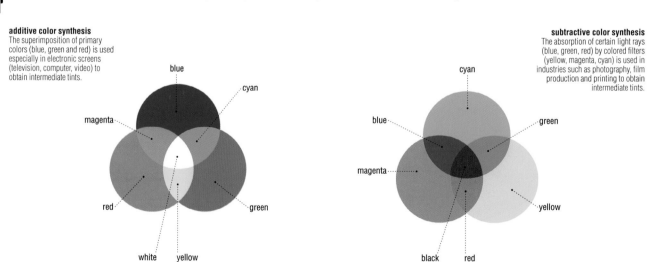

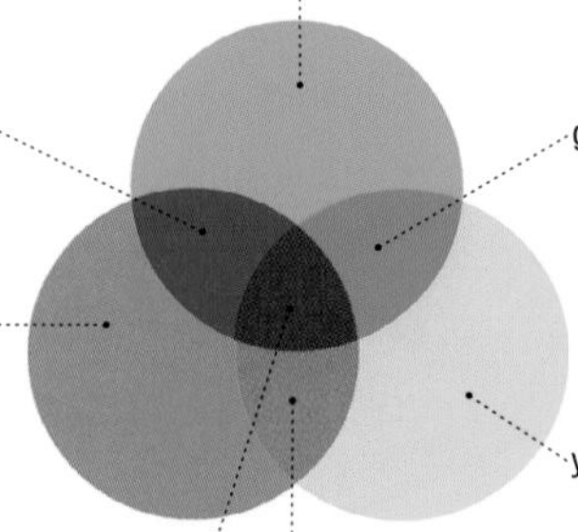

cyan
blue
green
magenta
yellow
black
red

vision

Ability to perceive shapes, distances, motion and colors; it is related to light rays and varies depending on the degree of sensitivity of the eye.

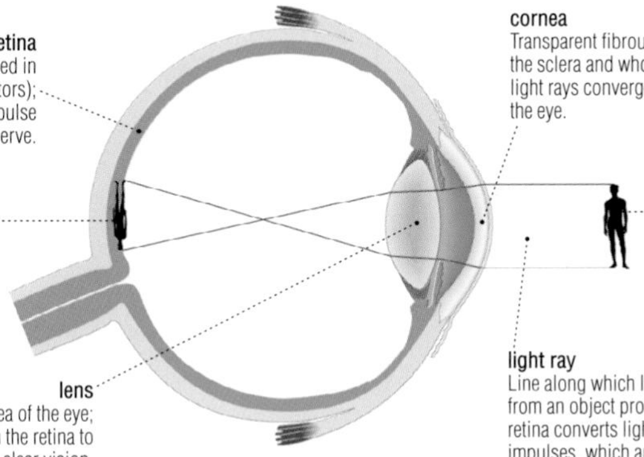

retina
Inner membrane at the back of the eye covered in light-sensitive nerve cells (photoreceptors); these transform light into an electrical impulse that is carried to the optic nerve.

focus
Point where light rays converge to form an image; the brain interprets the retina's upside-down image as right-side-up.

lens
Transparent elastic area of the eye; focuses images on the retina to obtain clear vision.

cornea
Transparent fibrous membrane extending the sclera and whose curved shape makes light rays converge toward the inside of the eye.

normal vision
The image of an object is formed on the retina after passing through the lens, which, depending on the distance of the object, expands or contracts to give a sharp image.

object
Light rays emanating from an object pass through the eye's various media to form an inverted image on the retina.

light ray
Line along which light emanating from an object propagates. The retina converts light rays into nerve impulses, which are then interpreted by the brain.

vision defects
Images do not form on the retina, thus resulting in blurry vision; such defects are corrected by eyeglasses, contact lenses or even surgery.

myopia
The image of a distant object is formed in front of the retina due to a defect in the light rays' convergence. This makes distant objects hard to see.

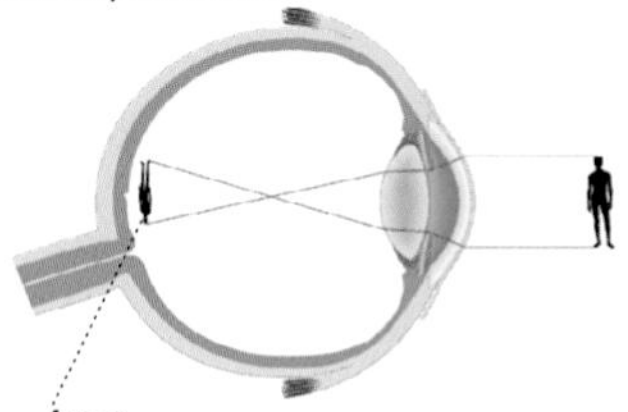

focus
Point where light rays converge to form an image; the brain interprets the retina's upside-down image as right-side-up.

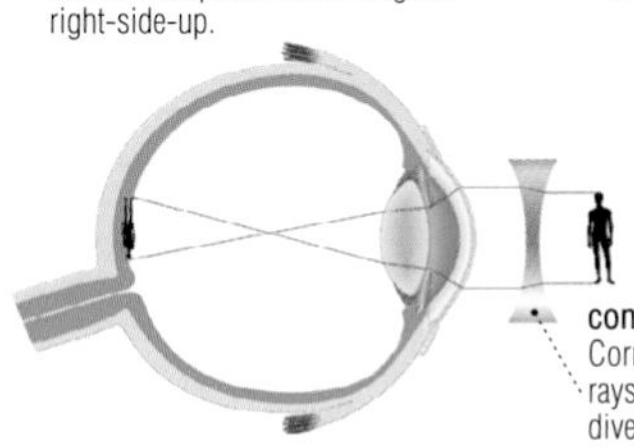

concave lens
Corrects myopia by causing light rays emanating from an object to diverge and project an image onto the focus of the retina.

hyperopia
The image of an object is formed behind the retina due to a defect in the light rays' convergence as they pass through the lens. This makes near objects hard to see.

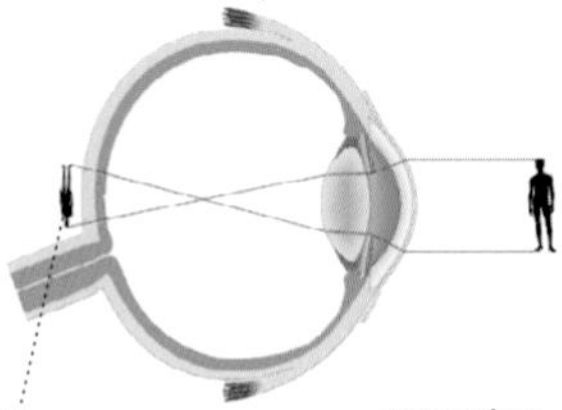

focus
Point where light rays converge to form an image; the brain interprets the retina's upside-down image as right-side-up.

convex lens
Corrects hyperopia by causing light rays emanating from an object to converge and project an image onto the focus of the retina.

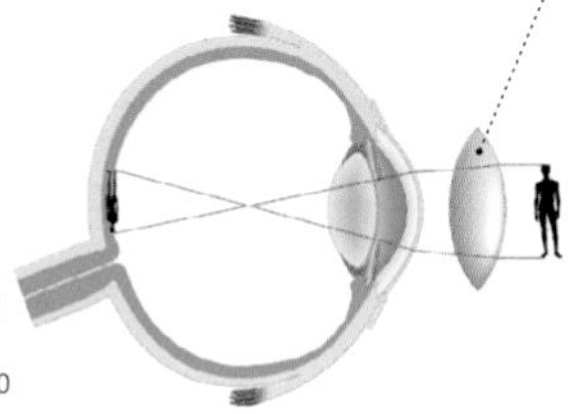

astigmatism
Usually caused by a curvature of the cornea, it is manifested by blurred vision when viewing both near and far objects, depending on various axes.

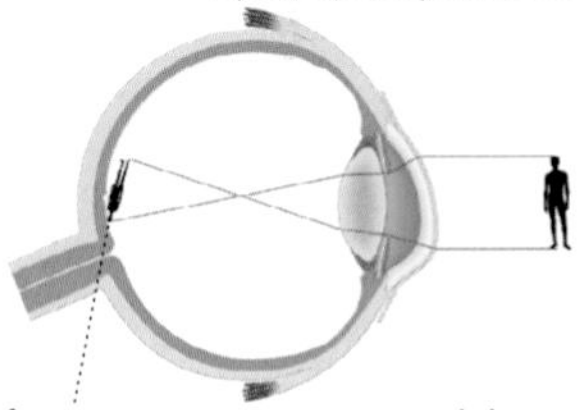

focus
Point where light rays converge to form an image; the brain interprets the retina's upside-down image as right-side-up.

toric lens
Has various powers depending on the rays' axes of convergence; it is used to offset the visual distortion caused by the cornea.

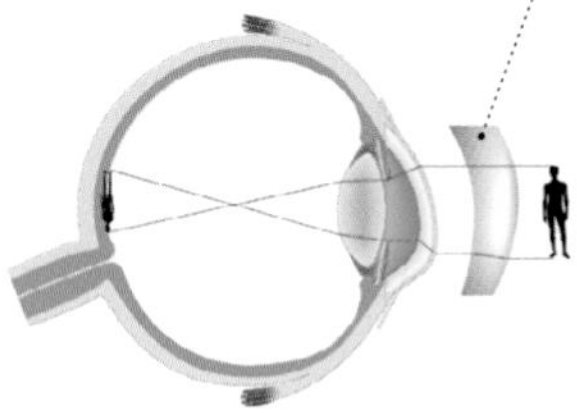

lenses

Transparent pieces of material (usually glass) that cause light rays to converge or diverge to form a sharp image (eyeglasses, microscopes, telescopes, cameras).

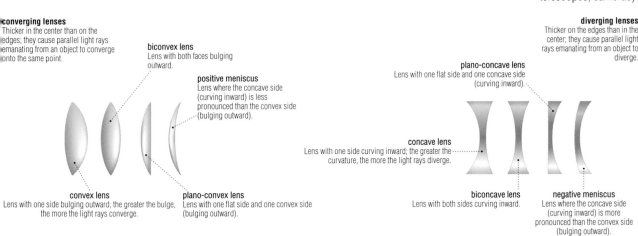

converging lenses
Thicker in the center than on the edges; they cause parallel light rays emanating from an object to converge onto the same point.

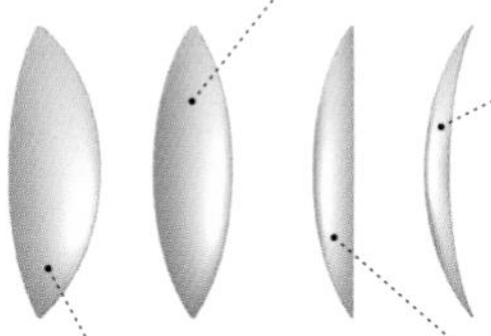

biconvex lens
Lens with both faces bulging outward.

positive meniscus
Lens where the concave side (curving inward) is less pronounced than the convex side (bulging outward).

convex lens
Lens with one side bulging outward; the greater the bulge, the more the light rays converge.

plano-convex lens
Lens with one flat side and one convex side (bulging outward).

diverging lenses
Thicker on the edges than in the center; they cause parallel light rays emanating from an object to diverge.

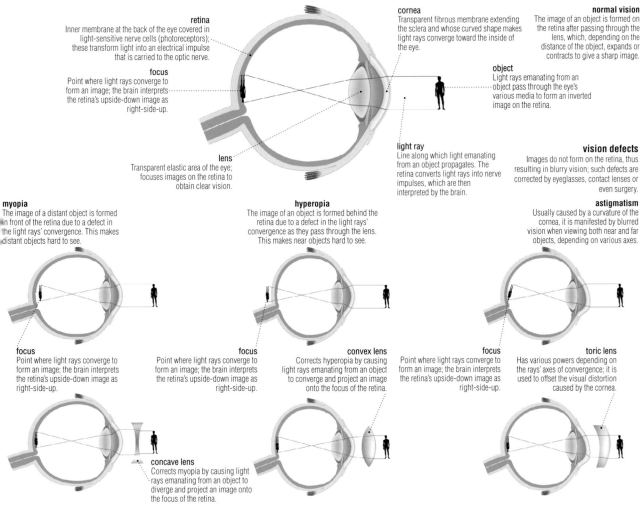

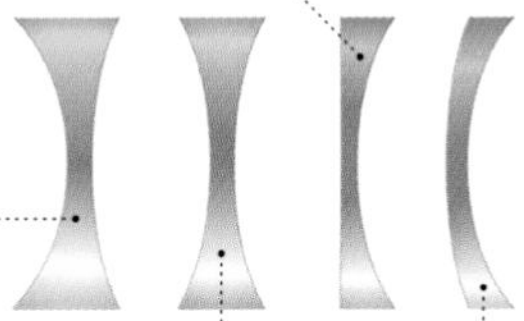

plano-concave lens
Lens with one flat side and one concave side (curving inward).

concave lens
Lens with one side curving inward; the greater the curvature, the more the light rays diverge.

biconcave lens
Lens with both sides curving inward.

negative meniscus
Lens where the concave side (curving inward) is more pronounced than the convex side (bulging outward).

SCIENCE

pulsed ruby laser

Device that produces a thin and very intense colored light beam; its various applications include fiber optics, manufacturing and surgery.

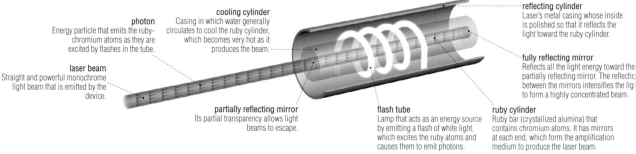

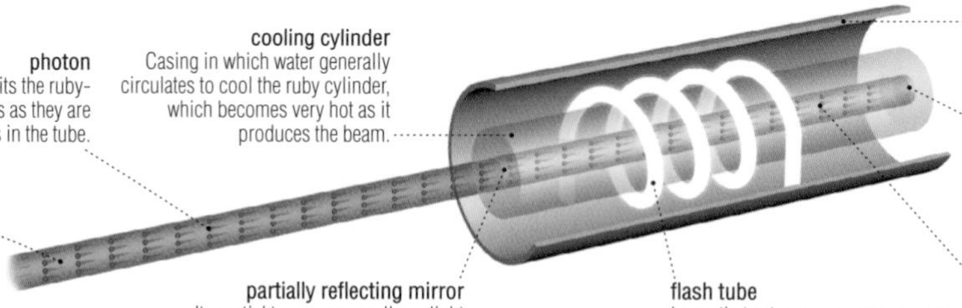
photon
Energy particle that emits the ruby-chromium atoms as they are excited by flashes in the tube.
cooling cylinder
Casing in which water generally circulates to cool the ruby cylinder, which becomes very hot as it produces the beam.
reflecting cylinder
Laser's metal casing whose inside is polished so that it reflects the light toward the ruby cylinder.
fully reflecting mirror
Reflects all the light energy toward the partially reflecting mirror. The reflectic between the mirrors intensifies the lig to form a highly concentrated beam.
laser beam
Straight and powerful monochrome light beam that is emitted by the device.
partially reflecting mirror
Its partial transparency allows light beams to escape.
flash tube
Lamp that acts as an energy source by emitting a flash of white light, which excites the ruby atoms and causes them to emit photons.
ruby cylinder
Ruby bar (crystallized alumina) that contains chromium atoms. It has mirrors at each end, which form the amplification medium to produce the laser beam.

prism binoculars

Optical instrument made up of two identical telescopes, one for each eye; it magnifies both near and distant objects.

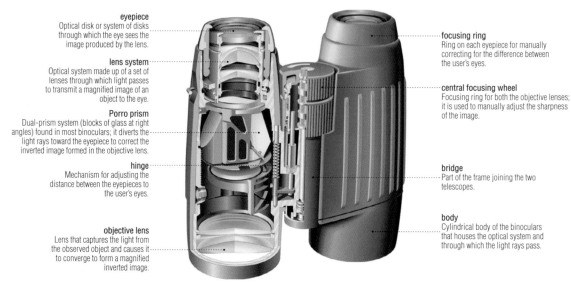

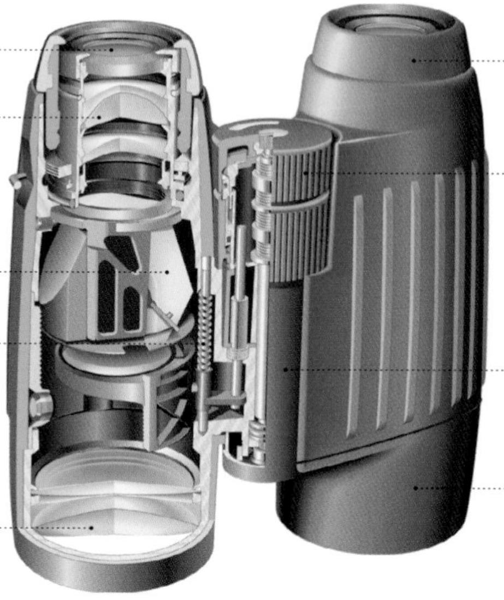
eyepiece
Optical disk or system of disks through which the eye sees the image produced by the lens.
lens system
Optical system made up of a set of lenses through which light passes to transmit a magnified image of an object to the eye.
Porro prism
Dual-prism system (blocks of glass at right angles) found in most binoculars; it diverts the light rays toward the eyepiece to correct the inverted image formed in the objective lens.
hinge
Mechanism for adjusting the distance between the eyepieces to the user's eyes.
objective lens
Lens that captures the light from the observed object and causes it to converge to form a magnified inverted image.
focusing ring
Ring on each eyepiece for manually correcting for the difference between the user's eyes.
central focusing wheel
Focusing ring for both the objective lenses; it is used to manually adjust the sharpness of the image.
bridge
Part of the frame joining the two telescopes.
body
Cylindrical body of the binoculars that houses the optical system and through which the light rays pass.

telescopic sight

Optical instrument mounted on a rifle or a measuring device to increase accuracy.

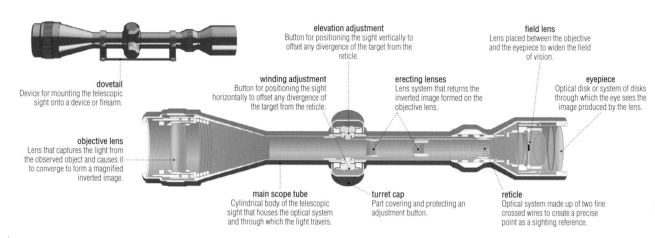

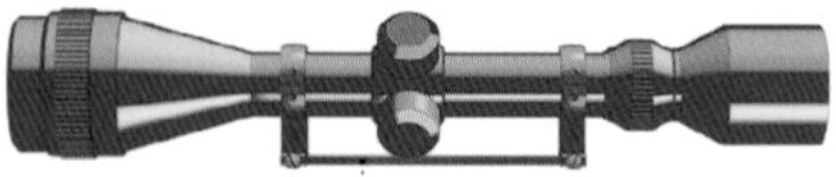
dovetail
Device for mounting the telescopic sight onto a device or firearm.

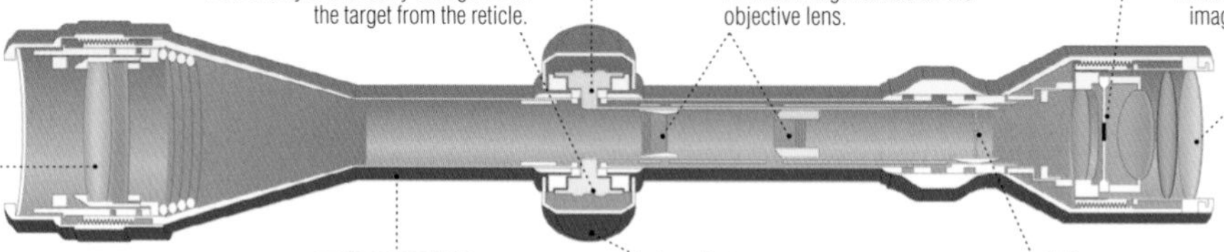
elevation adjustment
Button for positioning the sight vertically to offset any divergence of the target from the reticle.
field lens
Lens placed between the objective and the eyepiece to widen the field of vision.
winding adjustment
Button for positioning the sight horizontally to offset any divergence of the target from the reticle.
erecting lenses
Lens system that returns the inverted image formed on the objective lens.
eyepiece
Optical disk or system of disks through which the eye sees the image produced by the lens.
objective lens
Lens that captures the light from the observed object and causes it to converge to form a magnified inverted image.
main scope tube
Cylindrical body of the telescopic sight that houses the optical system and through which the light travels.
turret cap
Part covering and protecting an adjustment button.
reticle
Optical system made up of two fine crossed wires to create a precise point as a sighting reference.

magnifying glass and microscopes

Optical instruments used to magnify the image of a near object; they range in strength from low (magnifying glass) to strong (microscope).

magnifying glass
Converging lens that magnifies the image of an object.

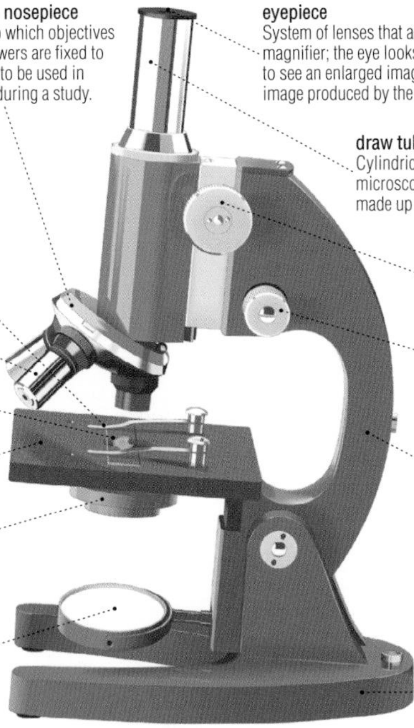

microscope
Optical instrument that consists of a system of lenses designed for observing organisms that are very small or invisible to the naked eye by magnifying their images.

revolving nosepiece
Rotating plate to which objectives of different powers are fixed to allow them to be used in succession during a study.

eyepiece
System of lenses that acts as a magnifier; the eye looks through it to see an enlarged image of the image produced by the objective.

stage clip
Springlike metal blade that keeps the glass slide on the stage.

draw tube
Cylindrical tube that houses the microscope's eyepiece; it is often made up of two converging lenses.

objective
Lens system that captures the light from an observed object and makes it converge to form an enlarged inverted image.

coarse adjustment knob
Medium-precision focusing device for adjusting the distance between the objective and the object under study.

glass slide
Fine glass plate on which the object to be studied is placed.

fine adjustment knob
High-precision focusing device for adjusting the distance between the objective and the object under study.

stage
Metal plate with an opening in the middle; the glass slide and the components keeping it in place are placed on it.

arm
Vertical part of the microscope that supports the components (draw tube, stage) and contains the focusing mechanisms.

condenser
Optical system that is usually made up of two lenses, which concentrate the light reflected by the mirror onto the object under study.

base
Support that stabilizes the microscope.

mirror
Polished glass surface that reflects the surrounding light onto the object under study to illuminate it.

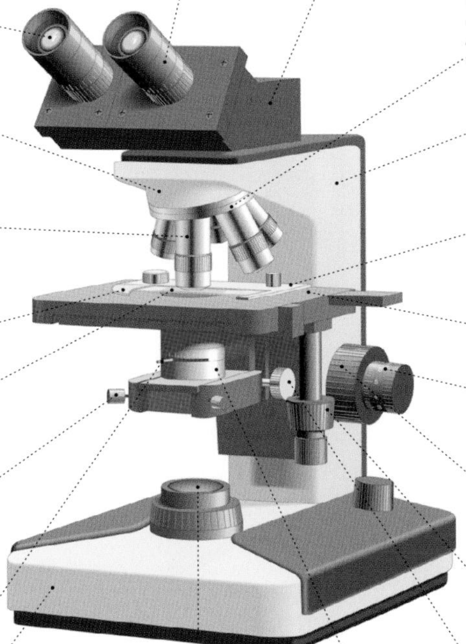

binocular microscope
Its two eyepieces allow both eyes to be fully applied; this provides a degree of depth to the image and prevents eyestrain.

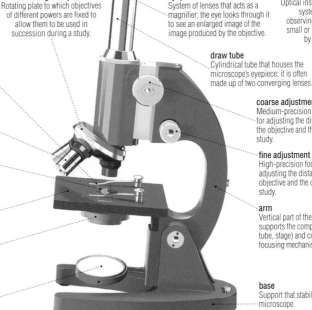

draw tube
One of two cylindrical tubes that house the eyepieces; it is often made up of two converging lenses.

body tube
Metal casing that houses the microscope's two eyepieces and through which light rays pass.

eyepiece
System of lenses that acts as a magnifier; the eye looks through it to see an enlarged image of the image produced by the objective.

revolving nosepiece
Rotating plate to which objectives of different powers are fixed to allow them to be used in succession during a study.

limb top
Upper part of the arm that supports the revolving nosepiece.

arm
Vertical part of the microscope that supports the components (draw tube, stage) and contains the focusing mechanisms.

objective
Lens system that captures the light from the observed object and makes it converge to form an enlarged inverted image.

mechanical stage
Adjustable part with two guiding screws that moves an object from right to left and from front to back on the stage.

stage clip
Springlike metal blade that keeps the glass slide on the stage.

stage
Metal plate with an opening in the middle; the glass slide and the components keeping it in place are placed on it.

glass slide
Fine glass plate on which the object to be studied is placed.

fine adjustment knob
High-precision focusing device for adjusting the distance between the objective and the object under study.

condenser adjustment knob
Screw that centers the condenser's light beam in the field of vision by moving it along a horizontal plane.

coarse adjustment knob
Medium-precision focusing device for adjusting the distance between the objective and the object under study.

field lens adjustment
Device with a variable-diameter opening that adjusts the amount of light illuminating the object.

mechanical stage control
Device for raising and lowering the mechanical stage.

base
Support that stabilizes the microscope.

lamp
Electric device that produces a light beam to illuminate the object under study.

condenser
Optical system that usually has two lenses to concentrate the light emitted from the lamp onto the object under study.

condenser height adjustment
Screw for raising and lowering the condenser.

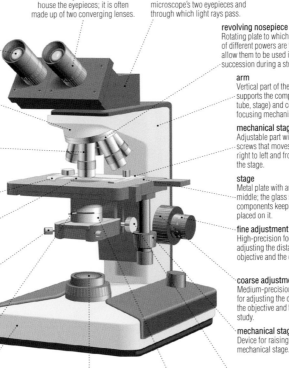

magnifying glass and microscopes

cross section of an electron microscope

Electron microscope: it uses an electron beam (as opposed to light) to provide magnification that is markedly superior to that of an optical microscope.

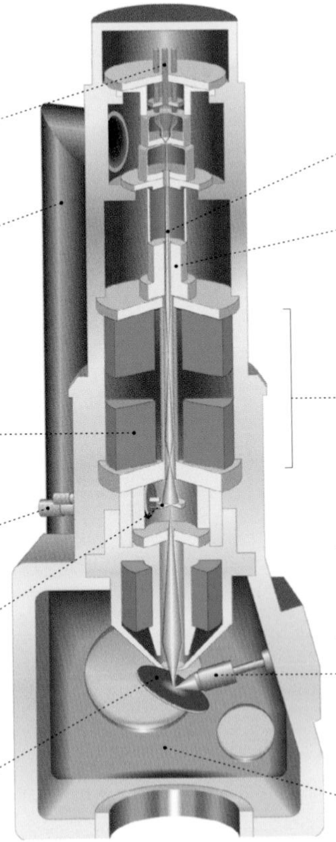

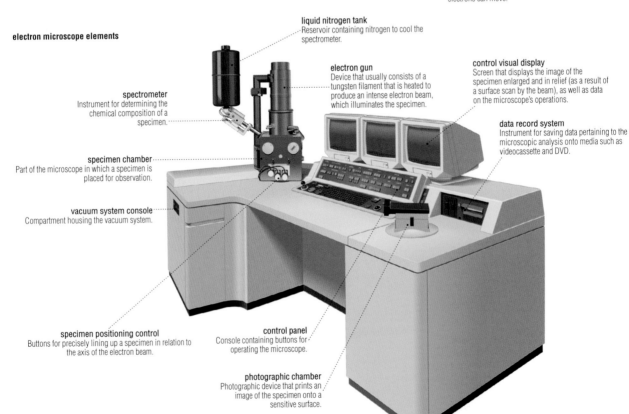

electron gun
Device that usually consists of a tungsten filament that is heated to produce an intense electron beam, which illuminates the specimen.

vacuum manifold
Conduit connected to a pump that creates enough of a vacuum in the microscope that it can function.

condenser
System of magnetic lenses (electromagnets producing a magnetic field when excited by an electric current) that concentrates the beam onto the specimen under study.

aperture changer
Device that adjusts the diaphragm opening in order to change the diameter of the beam.

aperture diaphragm
Device with an opening whose diameter can be changed to narrow or widen the diameter of the electron beam.

stage
Adjustable metal plate (stage) on which the specimen is mounted in order to study it.

electron beam
Set of negatively charged particles that propagate toward the specimen.

electron beam positioning
Control that positions the electron beam along the optical axis so that it reaches the specimen.

beam diameter reduction
The two lenses of the condenser cause the divergent electron beam emitted by the gun to converge.

focusing lenses
System of magnetic lenses (electromagnets) that concentrate the electron beam on one spot on the specimen.

visual transmission
The electron beam explores the surface of the specimen, which in turn emits electrons to form a point-by-point image on the screen.

vacuum chamber
Part of the microscope in which pressure can be reduced so that the electrons can move.

electron microscope elements

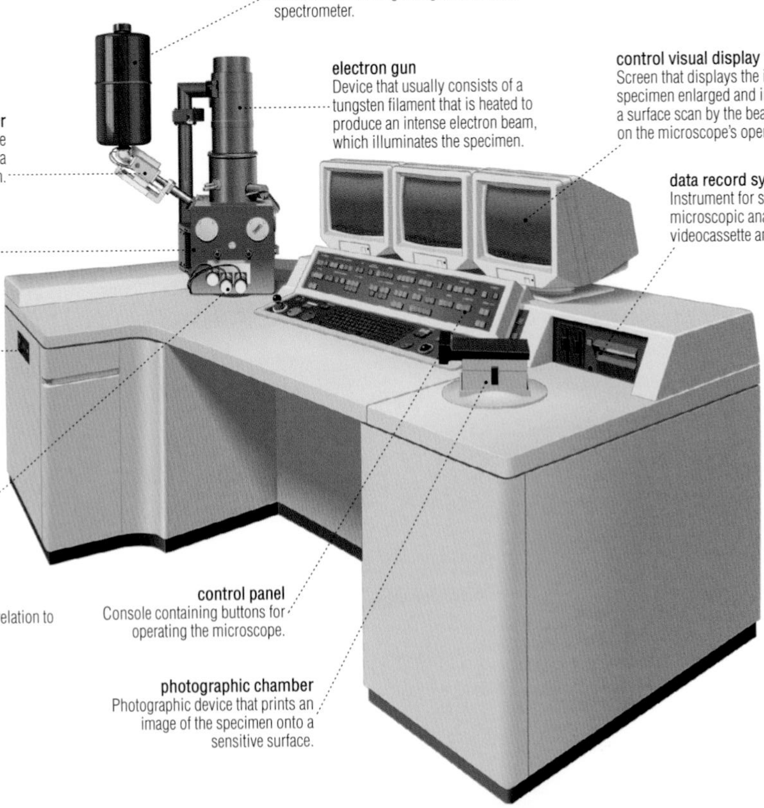

liquid nitrogen tank
Reservoir containing nitrogen to cool the spectrometer.

spectrometer
Instrument for determining the chemical composition of a specimen.

electron gun
Device that usually consists of a tungsten filament that is heated to produce an intense electron beam, which illuminates the specimen.

control visual display
Screen that displays the image of the specimen enlarged and in relief (as a result of a surface scan by the beam), as well as data on the microscope's operations.

data record system
Instrument for saving data pertaining to the microscopic analysis onto media such as videocassette and DVD.

specimen chamber
Part of the microscope in which a specimen is placed for observation.

vacuum system console
Compartment housing the vacuum system.

specimen positioning control
Buttons for precisely lining up a specimen in relation to the axis of the electron beam.

control panel
Console containing buttons for operating the microscope.

photographic chamber
Photographic device that prints an image of the specimen onto a sensitive surface.

measure of temperature

Temperature: physical quantity corresponding to the level of heat or cold, which is measured by means of a thermometer.

thermometer
Instrument for measuring temperature by means of a substance (usually a liquid or a gas) contained in a graduated tube.

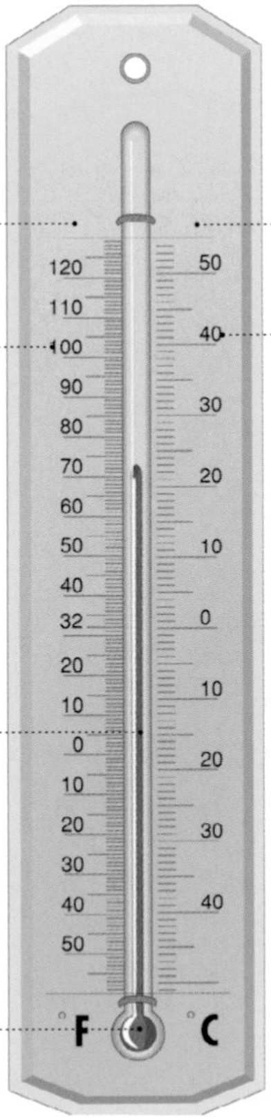

Fahrenheit scale
Temperature scale that is used in some English-speaking countries, on which the freezing point of water is at 32 and the boiling point at 212.

F degrees
Symbol representing a unit of measurement on the Fahrenheit scale (Fahrenheit degree).

alcohol column
Quantity of alcohol that is contained in the glass tube; its height varies with the temperature.

alcohol bulb
Glass reservoir containing colored alcohol (methanol, ethanol) that expands and rises in the capillary bore as the temperature rises.

Celsius scale
Temperature scale that is based on a graduation from 0 (freezing point of water) to 100 (boiling point of water); it was formerly called the centigrade scale.

C degrees
Symbol representing a unit of measurement on the Celsius scale (Celsius degree).

clinical thermometer
More precise than the alcohol thermometer, it is used to take the temperature of the human body; it is graduated from 94°F to 108°F.

expansion chamber
Space that is taken up by the gas in the capillary bore; it is pushed back as the mercury rises into it.

capillary tube
End of the glass tube in which the mercury rises or falls with the temperature; the mercury thermometer tube is filled with gas.

scale
Divisions of equal length (degrees) marked on the thermometer that constitute the units of measurement.

column of mercury
Quantity of mercury that is contained in the capillary bore; its height varies with the temperature.

stem
Glass tube containing the capillary bore.

constriction
Narrowing that prevents the mercury from spontaneously dropping into the bulb as the temperature lowers (the thermometer must be shaken to make it go down).

mercury bulb
Glass reservoir containing mercury (a liquid metal) that expands and rises in the capillary tube as the temperature rises.

bimetallic thermometer
Thermometer that uses the difference in expansion of two metals (usually iron and brass) to measure temperatures between 30°C or 86°F and 300°C or 375F°; it is used especially in industry.

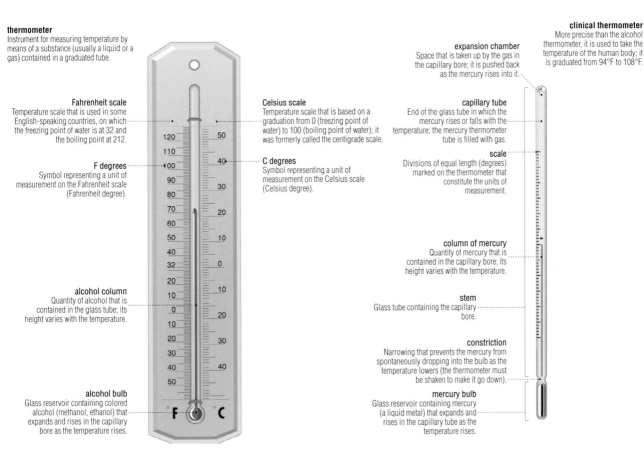

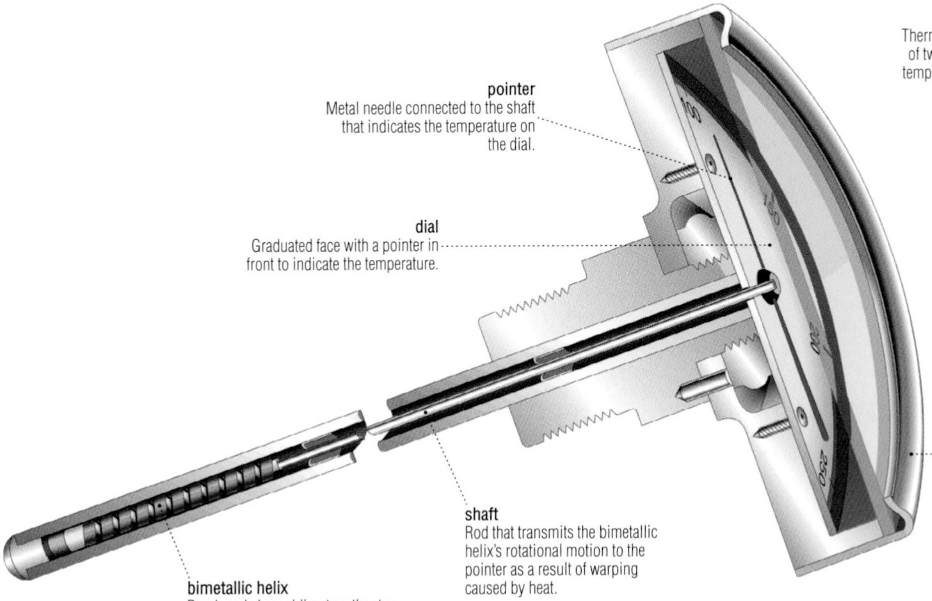

pointer
Metal needle connected to the shaft that indicates the temperature on the dial.

dial
Graduated face with a pointer in front to indicate the temperature.

case
Outer covering that encloses and protects the device's mechanism.

shaft
Rod that transmits the bimetallic helix's rotational motion to the pointer as a result of warping caused by heat.

bimetallic helix
Band made by welding together two metals with different coefficients of expansion; it curves as the temperature changes.

measure of time

Time: physical quantity corresponding to a phenomenon or an event that is measured with devices such as watches and stopwatches.

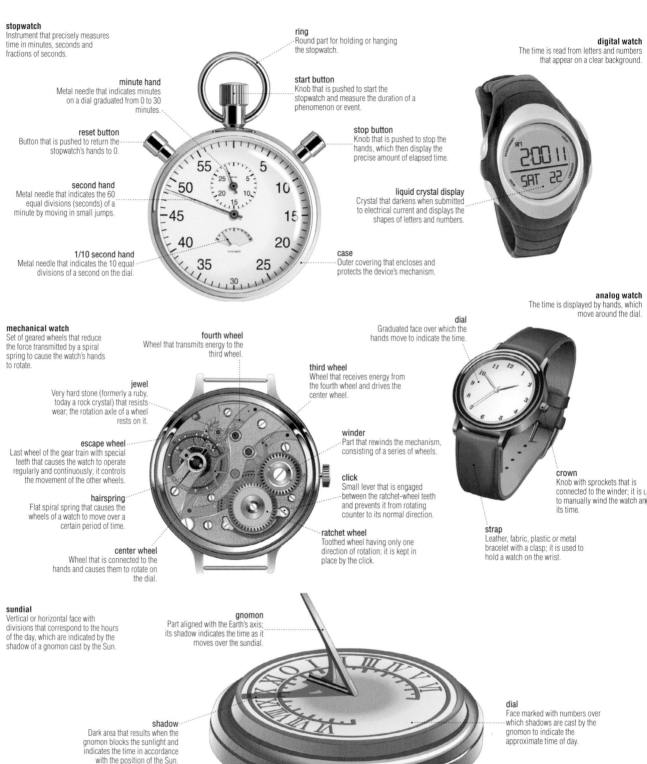

stopwatch
Instrument that precisely measures time in minutes, seconds and fractions of seconds.

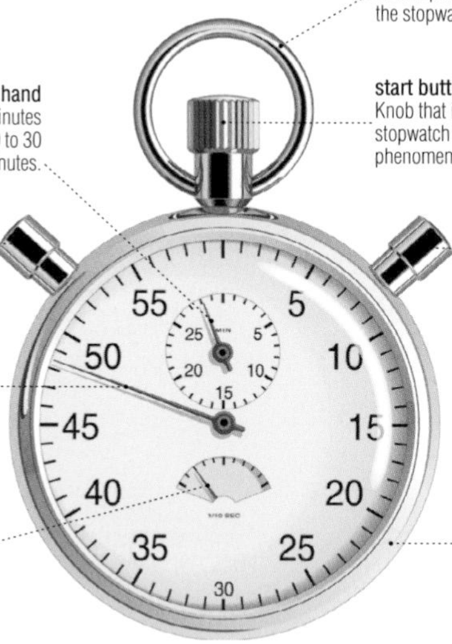

ring
Round part for holding or hanging the stopwatch.

minute hand
Metal needle that indicates minutes on a dial graduated from 0 to 30 minutes.

start button
Knob that is pushed to start the stopwatch and measure the duration of a phenomenon or event.

reset button
Button that is pushed to return the stopwatch's hands to 0.

stop button
Knob that is pushed to stop the hands, which then display the precise amount of elapsed time.

second hand
Metal needle that indicates the 60 equal divisions (seconds) of a minute by moving in small jumps.

1/10 second hand
Metal needle that indicates the 10 equal divisions of a second on the dial.

case
Outer covering that encloses and protects the device's mechanism.

digital watch
The time is read from letters and numbers that appear on a clear background.

liquid crystal display
Crystal that darkens when submitted to electrical current and displays the shapes of letters and numbers.

mechanical watch
Set of geared wheels that reduce the force transmitted by a spiral spring to cause the watch's hands to rotate.

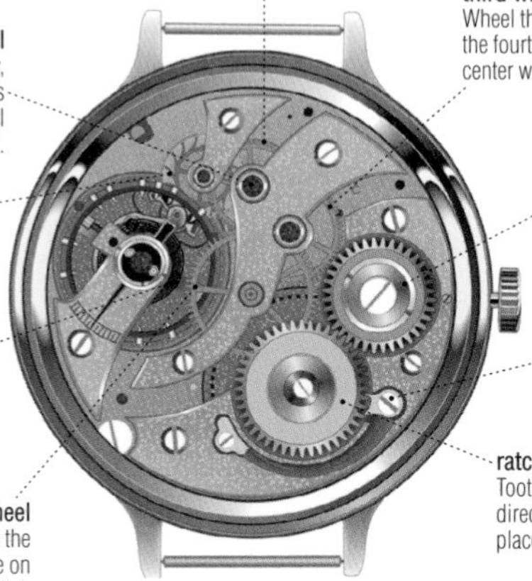

fourth wheel
Wheel that transmits energy to the third wheel.

third wheel
Wheel that receives energy from the fourth wheel and drives the center wheel.

jewel
Very hard stone (formerly a ruby, today a rock crystal) that resists wear; the rotation axle of a wheel rests on it.

escape wheel
Last wheel of the gear train with special teeth that causes the watch to operate regularly and continuously; it controls the movement of the other wheels.

winder
Part that rewinds the mechanism, consisting of a series of wheels.

hairspring
Flat spiral spring that causes the wheels of a watch to move over a certain period of time.

click
Small lever that is engaged between the ratchet-wheel teeth and prevents it from rotating counter to its normal direction.

ratchet wheel
Toothed wheel having only one direction of rotation; it is kept in place by the click.

center wheel
Wheel that is connected to the hands and causes them to rotate on the dial.

analog watch
The time is displayed by hands, which move around the dial.

dial
Graduated face over which the hands move to indicate the time.

crown
Knob with sprockets that is connected to the winder; it is u to manually wind the watch an its time.

strap
Leather, fabric, plastic or metal bracelet with a clasp; it is used to hold a watch on the wrist.

sundial
Vertical or horizontal face with divisions that correspond to the hours of the day, which are indicated by the shadow of a gnomon cast by the Sun.

gnomon
Part aligned with the Earth's axis; its shadow indicates the time as it moves over the sundial.

shadow
Dark area that results when the gnomon blocks the sunlight and indicates the time in accordance with the position of the Sun.

dial
Face marked with numbers over which shadows are cast by the gnomon to indicate the approximate time of day.

measure of time

grandfather clock
Clock with a pendulum that is operated by weights and housed in a tall (usually over 2 m high) straight body, which stands upright on the floor.

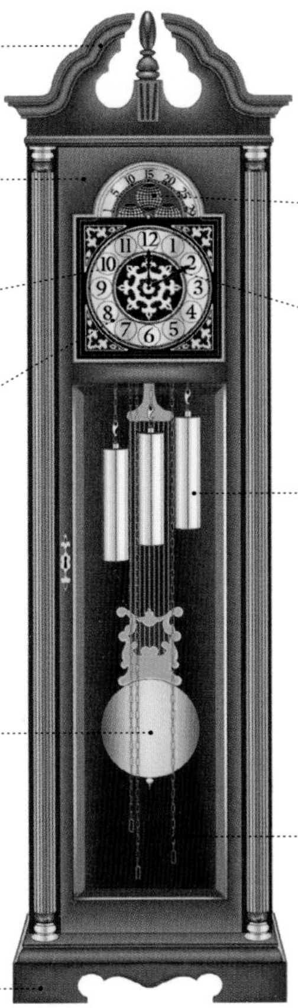

pediment
Set of decorative moldings that surmount the clock.

body
Usually wooden box that houses and protects the clock's mechanism.

hour hand
Metal needle that points at the 24 hours of a day on the dial.

dial
Graduated face over which the hands move to indicate the time.

pendulum
Unit whose regular swinging motion controls the workings of the clock's mechanism.

plinth
Base that supports the clock and makes it stable.

Moon dial
Face divided into 29 1/2 days that is represented by a moon whose movement indicates the phases of the Moon: first quarter, full moon, last quarter, new moon.

minute hand
Metal needle that points at the 60 minutes of an hour on the dial.

weight
Heavy body that hangs from the main wheel; its descent provides the necessary energy for the clock's mechanism.

chain
Series of interlaced rings to which weights are attached.

weight-driven clock mechanism
This clock is operated by weights that, under gravity, drive the hands of the clock in their rotational movement by means of a gear train.

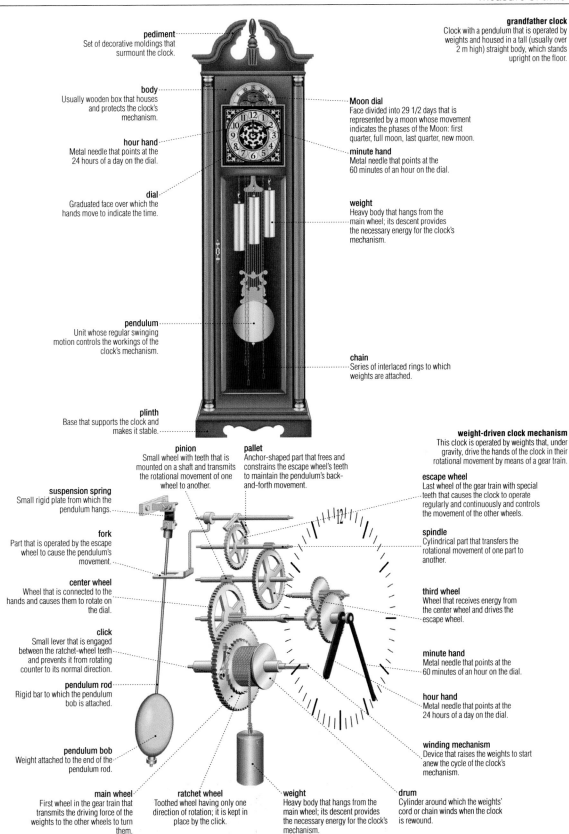

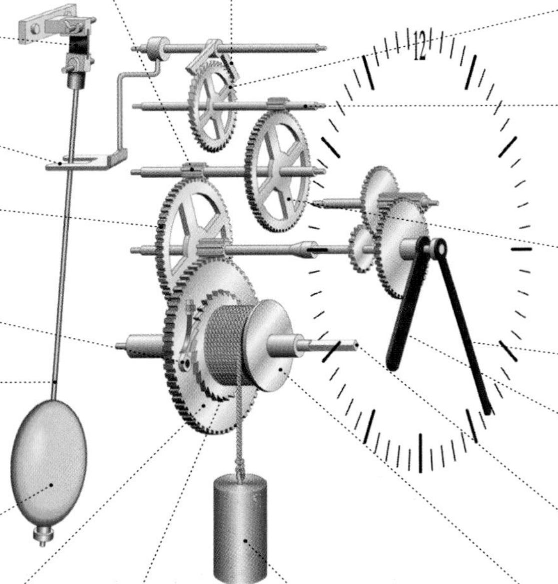

pinion
Small wheel with teeth that is mounted on a shaft and transmits the rotational movement of one wheel to another.

pallet
Anchor-shaped part that frees and constrains the escape wheel's teeth to maintain the pendulum's back-and-forth movement.

suspension spring
Small rigid plate from which the pendulum hangs.

fork
Part that is operated by the escape wheel to cause the pendulum's movement.

center wheel
Wheel that is connected to the hands and causes them to rotate on the dial.

click
Small lever that is engaged between the ratchet-wheel teeth and prevents it from rotating counter to its normal direction.

pendulum rod
Rigid bar to which the pendulum bob is attached.

pendulum bob
Weight attached to the end of the pendulum rod.

main wheel
First wheel in the gear train that transmits the driving force of the weights to the other wheels to turn them.

ratchet wheel
Toothed wheel having only one direction of rotation; it is kept in place by the click.

weight
Heavy body that hangs from the main wheel; its descent provides the necessary energy for the clock's mechanism.

drum
Cylinder around which the weights' cord or chain winds when the clock is rewound.

escape wheel
Last wheel of the gear train with special teeth that causes the clock to operate regularly and continuously and controls the movement of the other wheels.

spindle
Cylindrical part that transfers the rotational movement of one part to another.

third wheel
Wheel that receives energy from the center wheel and drives the escape wheel.

minute hand
Metal needle that points at the 60 minutes of an hour on the dial.

hour hand
Metal needle that points at the 24 hours of a day on the dial.

winding mechanism
Device that raises the weights to start anew the cycle of the clock's mechanism.

measure of weight

Mass: physical quantity that characterizes an amount of matter (mass) that is measured by means of a scale.

beam balance
Compares the mass of a body with that of another body of known mass (weight); when two pans hanging from a bar (beam) are in balance, the two weights are equal.

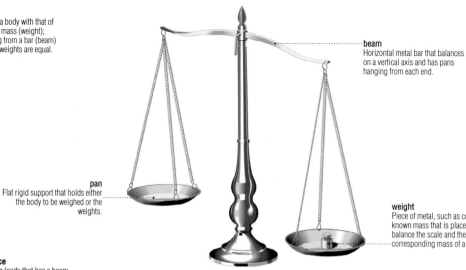

beam
Horizontal metal bar that balances on a vertical axis and has pans hanging from each end.

pan
Flat rigid support that holds either the body to be weighed or the weights.

weight
Piece of metal, such as copper or iron, of known mass that is placed on a pan to balance the scale and thereby assess the corresponding mass of a body.

unequal-arm balance
Scale used for weighing loads that has a beam with arms of different lengths; the shorter arm supports the pan and the longer arm supports the weights that slide to attain a balance.

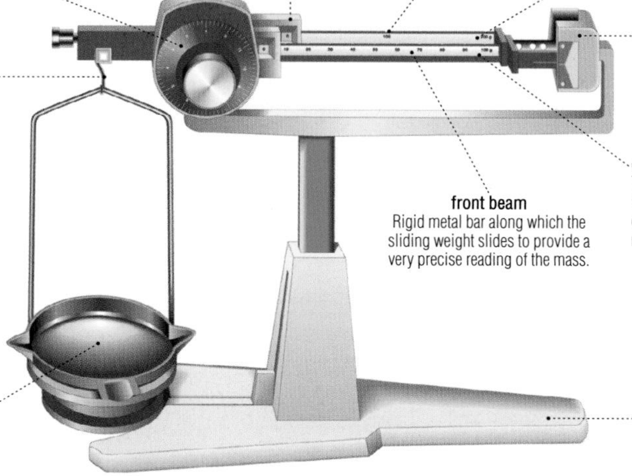

sliding weight
Sliding part that is moved along the beams until a balance between the two masses is attained.

notch
Groove in which a sliding weight catches so that a precise reading on the graduated scale can be taken.

rear beam
Rigid metal bar along which the sliding weight slides to provide a relatively precise reading of the mass.

vernier
Small graduated dial that slides along the beams and provides a very precise reading of the mass.

magnetic damping system
Device made up of magnets that reduce the beams' oscillations when the weights are moved to provide a quick reading of the mass.

pan hook
Curved part from which the pan is hung by means of rods.

graduated scale
The divisions of equal length marked on the scale's beam that constitute the units of measurement.

front beam
Rigid metal bar along which the sliding weight slides to provide a very precise reading of the mass.

pan
Flat rigid stand on which the body to be weighed is placed.

base
Support that provides stability to the scale.

Roberval's balance
Commonly used scale that operates on the same principle as the beam balance; the pans are stabilized by a shank and rest on the beam.

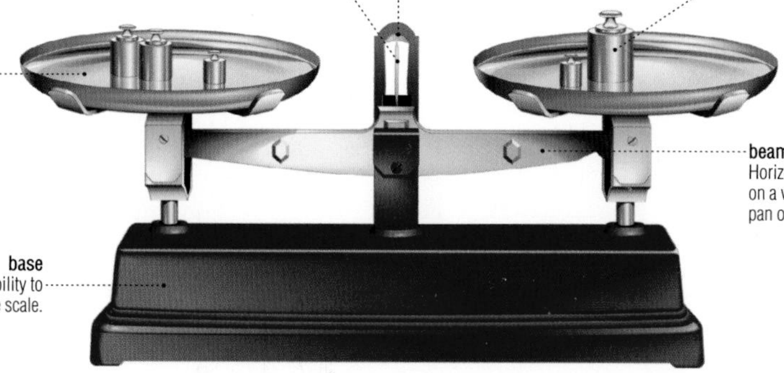

pointer
Metal needle that indicates the point of equilibrium on the dial when the beam is level.

dial
Graduated surface with a pointer in front that indicates the point of equilibrium for the two pans.

weight
Piece of metal, such as copper or iron, of known mass that is placed on a pan to balance the scale and thereby assess the corresponding mass of a body.

pan
Flat rigid support that holds either the body to be weighed or the weights.

beam
Horizontal metal bar that balances on a vertical axis and supports a pan on each end.

base
Support that provides stability to the scale.

measure of weight

spring balance
Scale made up of a hook attached to a spring that stretches in proportion to the weight of the object being weighed.

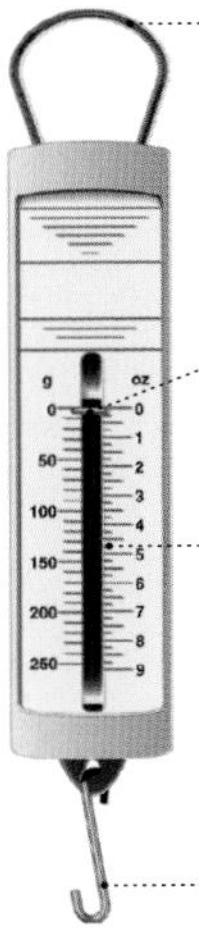

ring
Round part for holding or hanging the spring balance.

pointer
Pointer connected to the spring that moves along a graduated scale to indicate the weight of the body being weighed.

graduated scale
The divisions of equal length that are marked on the spring balance and constitute the units of measurement.

hook
Curved part on which the body to be weighed is hung.

electronic scale
Commercial scale that weighs and calculates the price of a quantity of merchandise and displays these elements.

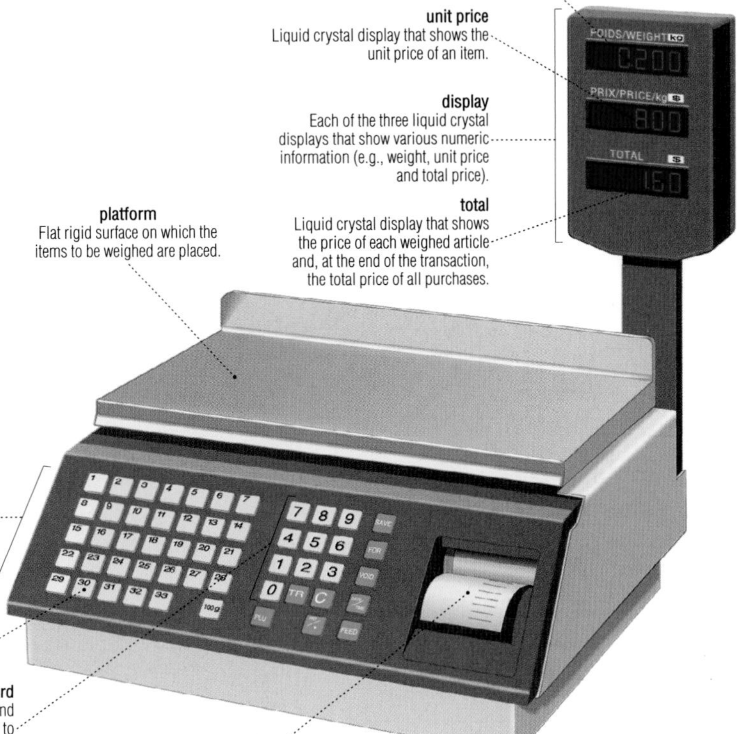

weight
Liquid crystal display that shows the weight of the item.

unit price
Liquid crystal display that shows the unit price of an item.

display
Each of the three liquid crystal displays that show various numeric information (e.g., weight, unit price and total price).

total
Liquid crystal display that shows the price of each weighed article and, at the end of the transaction, the total price of all purchases.

platform
Flat rigid surface on which the items to be weighed are placed.

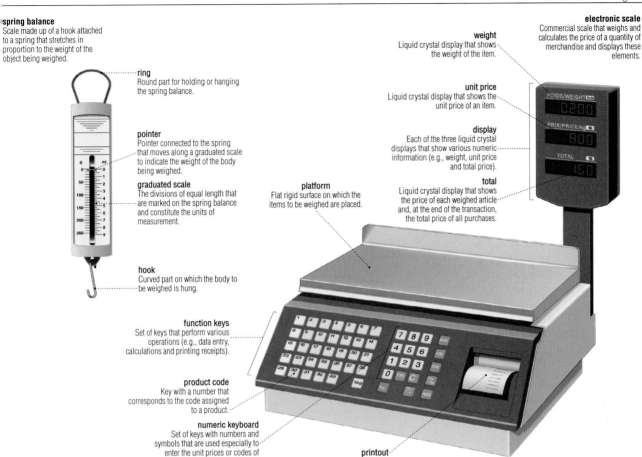

function keys
Set of keys that perform various operations (e.g., data entry, calculations and printing receipts).

product code
Key with a number that corresponds to the code assigned to a product.

numeric keyboard
Set of keys with numbers and symbols that are used especially to enter the unit prices or codes of items.

printout
Paper on which various data are printed (e.g., the weight, quantity and price of the items weighed).

bathroom scale
Scale used for weighing a person; it has a spring mechanism that compresses in proportion to the weight.

digital display
Liquid crystal display that indicates the weight in numbers.

weighing platform
Flat base that a person stands upon to be weighed.

analytical balance
Used especially in the laboratory for taking very precise weight measurements.

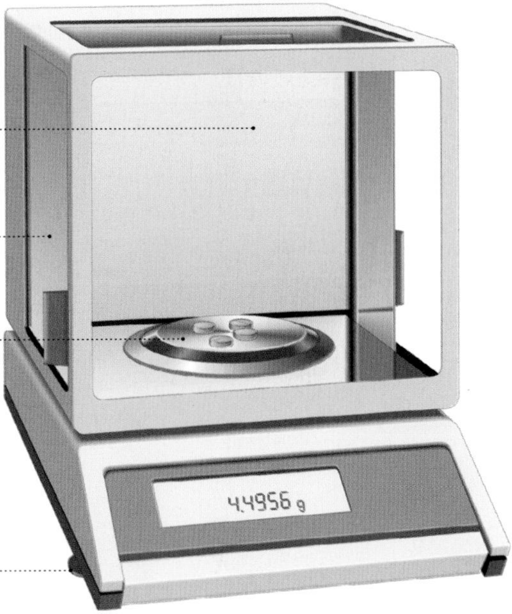

glass case
Glass box that protects the pan from air currents and dust that might cause a false reading of the weight.

door access
Sliding doors that provide easy access to the inside of the glass case.

pan
Flat rigid support on which the specimen is placed.

leveling screw
Screw for adjusting the level of the balance's base.

measure of length

Length: the longer dimension of an object as opposed to its width.

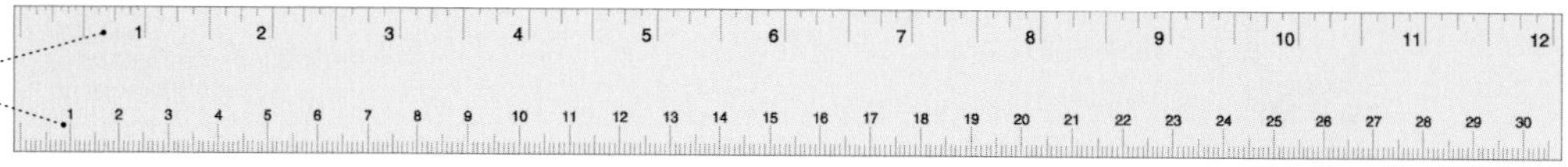

measure of distance

Distance: interval separating two points in space.

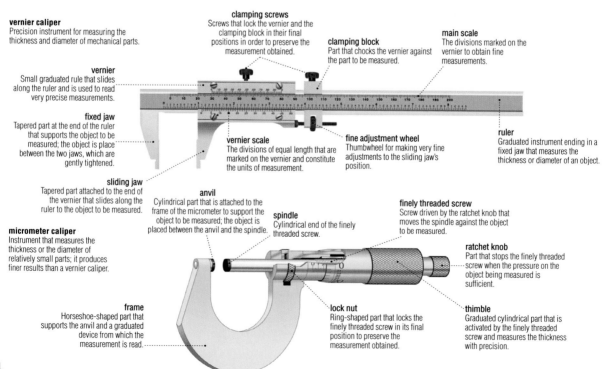

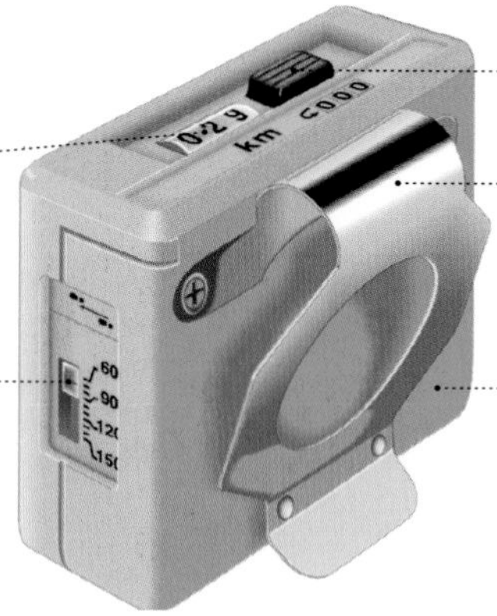
pedometer
Device that counts the number of steps taken by a walker or runner to measure the distance traveled.
distance traveled
Number of steps taken by the walker or runner converted into miles.
step setting
Button for adjusting the average length of a step in the walk or run.
reset button
Key used to reset the counter to 0.
clip
Metal fastener for attaching the pedometer to a belt or article of clothing.
case
Outer covering that encloses and protects the device's mechanism.

measure of thickness

Thickness: dimension corresponding to the distance between two surfaces of the same body.

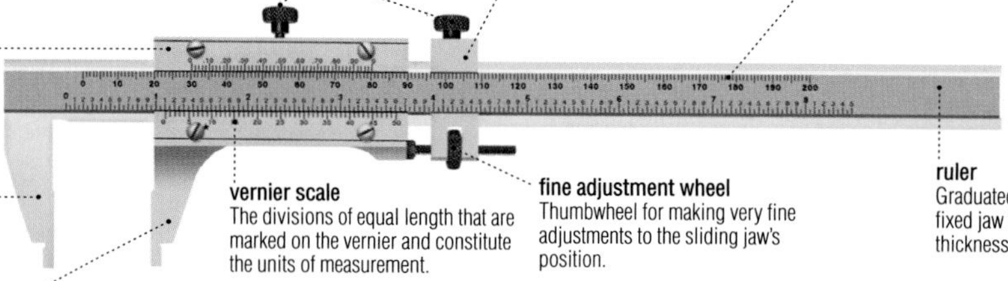
vernier caliper
Precision instrument for measuring the thickness and diameter of mechanical parts.
clamping screws
Screws that lock the vernier and the clamping block in their final positions in order to preserve the measurement obtained.
clamping block
Part that chocks the vernier against the part to be measured.
main scale
The divisions marked on the vernier to obtain fine measurements.
vernier
Small graduated rule that slides along the ruler and is used to read very precise measurements.
fixed jaw
Tapered part at the end of the ruler that supports the object to be measured; the object is place between the two jaws, which are gently tightened.
vernier scale
The divisions of equal length that are marked on the vernier and constitute the units of measurement.
fine adjustment wheel
Thumbwheel for making very fine adjustments to the sliding jaw's position.
ruler
Graduated instrument ending in a fixed jaw that measures the thickness or diameter of an object.
sliding jaw
Tapered part attached to the end of the vernier that slides along the ruler to the object to be measured.

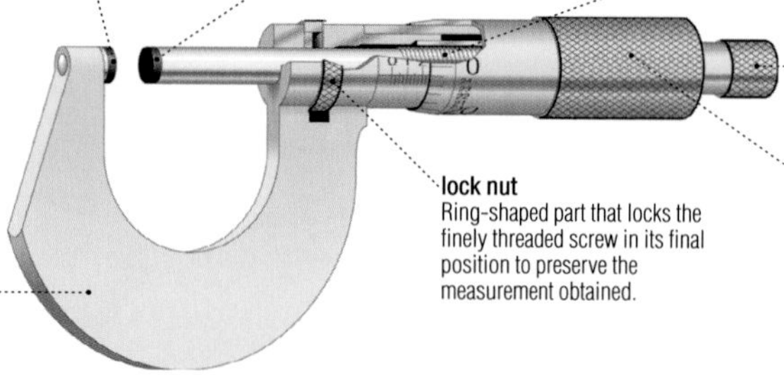
micrometer caliper
Instrument that measures the thickness or the diameter of relatively small parts; it produces finer results than a vernier caliper.
anvil
Cylindrical part that is attached to the frame of the micrometer to support the object to be measured; the object is placed between the anvil and the spindle.
spindle
Cylindrical end of the finely threaded screw.
finely threaded screw
Screw driven by the ratchet knob that moves the spindle against the object to be measured.
ratchet knob
Part that stops the finely threaded screw when the pressure on the object being measured is sufficient.
frame
Horseshoe-shaped part that supports the anvil and a graduated device from which the measurement is read.
lock nut
Ring-shaped part that locks the finely threaded screw in its final position to preserve the measurement obtained.
thimble
Graduated cylindrical part that is activated by the finely threaded screw and measures the thickness with precision.

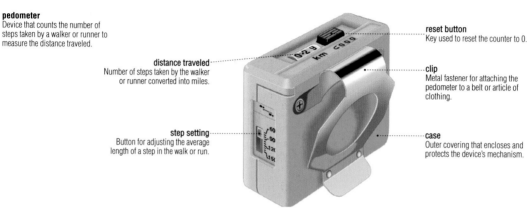

measure of angles

Angle: figure formed by two intersecting lines or planes; it is measured in degrees.

theodolite
Sighting instrument that is used especially in astronomy, geodesy and navigation for measuring horizontal and vertical angles.

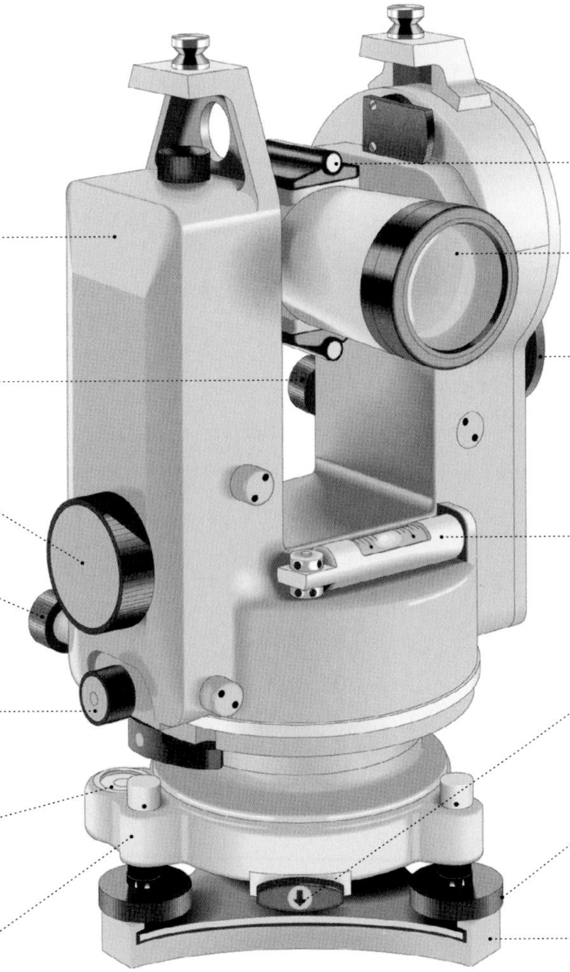

alidade
Part of the theodolite that rotates on a vertical axle to measure angles by means of the telescope.

adjustment for vertical-circle image
Knob that adjusts the sharpness of the image of the vertical circle (graduated from 0° to 360°) in order to read the angles on the vertical axis.

micrometer screw
Knob that adjusts the micrometer to give a very precise reading of the circles' measurements.

adjustment for horizontal-circle image
Knob that adjusts the sharpness of the image of the horizontal circle (graduated from 0° to 360°) in order to read the angles on the horizontal axis.

horizontal clamp
Knob that locks the alidade to prevent it from rotating.

leveling head level
Transparent tube that contains liquid and an air bubble; it serves as a guide for positioning the leveling head on the horizontal axis.

leveling head
Platform serving as a support for the theolodite.

optical sight
Device with an eyepiece that precisely aims the telescope at the target whose angles are to be measured.

telescope
Optical instrument composed of several lenses; it can be adjusted in the horizontal and vertical planes and is used to observe distant objects.

illumination mirror
Adjustable polished glass surface that reflects light onto the circles so that the angles can be read.

alidade level
Transparent tube that contains liquid and an air bubble; it serves as a guide for positioning the alidade on the vertical axis.

leveling head locking knob
Knob that locks the alidade to the leveling head.

leveling screw
Screw that adjusts the theodolite's leveling head level on the horizontal plane.

base plate
Plate to which the leveling head is attached by means of three leveling screws.

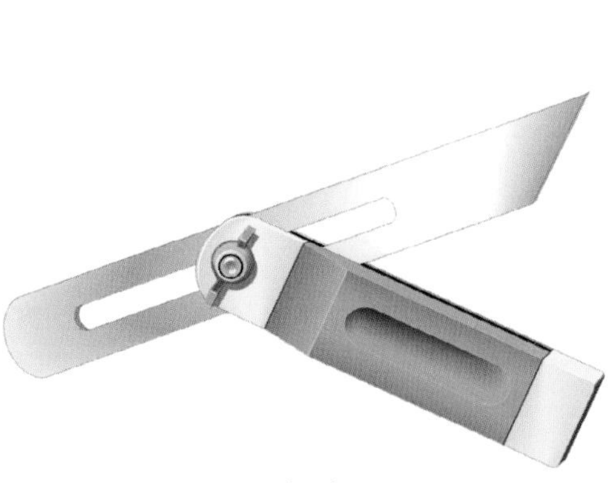

bevel square
Instrument whose movable arms are used for measuring or for marking an angle.

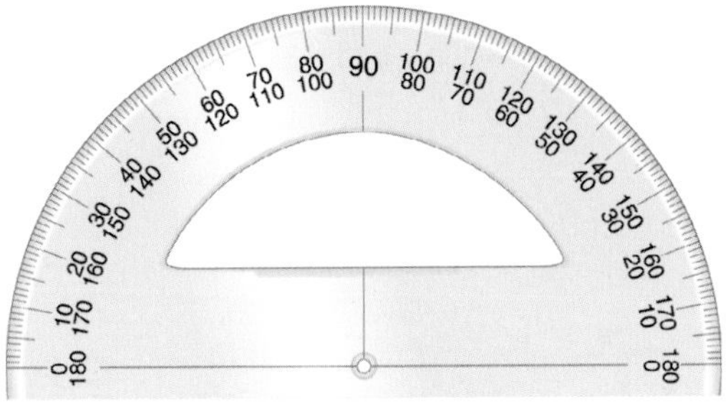

protractor
Graduated semicircular instrument for measuring and drawing angles.

SCIENCE

international system of units

Decimal system established by the 11th General Conference on Weights and Measures (GCWM) in 1960 and used by many countries.

measurement of frequency

Hz

hertz
Frequency of a periodic phenomenon whose period is 1 second.

measurement of electric potential difference

V

volt
Difference in potential between two points of a conductor carrying a constant current of 1 ampere when the power between these points is 1 watt.

measurement of electric charge

C

coulomb
Amount of electricity carried in 1 second by a current of 1 ampere.

measurement of energ

J

joule
Amount of energy released by th force of 1 newton acting through distance of 1 meter.

measurement of power

W

watt
Energy transfer of 1 joule during 1 second.

measurement of force

N

newton
Force required to impart an acceleration of 1 m/s^2 to a body having a mass of 1 kg.

measurement of electric resistance

Ω

ohm
Electrical resistance between two points of a conductor carrying a current of 1 ampere when the difference in potential between them is 1 volt.

measurement of electric curren

A

ampere
Constant current of 1 joule per second in a conductor.

measurement of length

m

meter
Distance traveled by light in a vacuum in 1/299,792,458 of a second.

measurement of mass

kg

kilogram
Mass of a platinum prototype that was accepted as the international reference in 1889; it is stored at the International Bureau of Weights and Measures.

measurement of Celsius temperature

°C

degree Celsius
Division into 100 parts of the difference between the freezing point of water (0°C) and its boiling point (100°C) at standard atmospheric pressure.

measurement of thermodynamic temperatu

K

kelvin
Zero Kelvin is equal to minus 273.16°C.

measurement of amount of substance

mol

mole
Quantity of matter equal to the number of atoms in 0.012 kg of carbon 12.

measurement of radioactivity

Bq

becquerel
Radioactivity of a substance in which one atom disintegrates per second.

measurement of pressure

Pa

pascal
Uniform pressure exerted on a flat surface of 1 m^2 with a force of 1 newton.

measurement of luminous intensity

cd

candela
Unit of light intensity equivalent to a radiant intensity of 1/683 watts per steradian (solid angle).

biology

The scientific study of living organisms (humans, animals and plants) from the point of view of their structure and how they function and reproduce.

♂

male
Symbol denoting that a being has male reproductive organs.

♀

female
Symbol denoting that a being has female reproductive organs.

Rh+

blood factor positive
Individuals are Rh positive when their red blood cells carry an Rh molecule (antigen); the Rh factor is positive in about 85% of the population.

Rh-

blood factor negative
Individuals not carrying the Rh molecule (antigen) are Rh negative; the Rh factor plays an important role in pregnancy (the parents' factors must be compatible).

†

death
Symbol placed before a date denoting a person's year of death.

*

birth
Symbol placed before a date denoting a person's year of birth.

mathematics

The science that uses deductive reasoning to study the properties of abstract entities such as numbers, space and functions and the relations between them.

$-$

minus/negative
Sign denoting that a number is to be subtracted from another; the result is a difference.

$+$

plus/positive
Sign denoting that a number is to be added to another; the result is a sum.

X

multiplied by
Sign denoting that a number is to be multiplied by another; the result is a product.

$\div$

divided by
Sign denoting a number (dividend) is to be divided by another (divisor); the result is a quotient.

$=$

equals
Sign denoting the result of an operation.

$\neq$

is not equal to
Sign denoting that the result of an operation is not close to the same value as the one on the right.

$\fallingdotseq$

is approximately equal to
Sign denoting that the result of an operation is close to the same value as the one on the right.

$\backsim$

is equivalent to
Sign denoting that the value on the left is the same magnitude as the one on the right.

$\equiv$

is identical with
Binary sign denoting that the result of the operation noted on the left has the same value as the operation noted on the right.

$\not\equiv$

is not identical with
Binary sign denoting that the result of the operation noted on the left does not have the same value as the operation noted on the right.

$\pm$

plus or minus
Sign denoting that the positive and negative values of the number that follows bracket a range of values.

$\leqslant$

is less than or equal to
Sign denoting that the result of an operation is equal to or of smaller magnitude than the number that follows.

$>$

is greater than
Sign denoting that the value on the left is of greater magnitude than the number that follows.

$\geqslant$

is greater than or equal to
Sign denoting that the result of an operation is equal to or of greater magnitude than the number that follows.

$<$

is less than
Sign denoting that the value on the left is of smaller magnitude than the number that follows.

$\emptyset$

empty set
Sign denoting that a set contains no elements.

$\cup$

union of two sets
Binary sign denoting that a set is composed of the sum of the elements of two sets.

$\cap$

intersection of two sets
Binary sign denoting that two sets M and N have elements in common.

$\subset$

is included in/is a subset of
Binary sign denoting that a set A on the left is part of the set B on the right.

%

percent
Sign denoting that the number preceding it is a fraction of 100.

$\in$

is an element of
Binary sign denoting that the element on the left is included in the set on the right.

$\notin$

is not an element of
Binary sign denoting that the element on the left is not included in the set on the right.

Σ

sum
Sign indicating that several values are to be added together (their sum).

$\sqrt{}$

square root of
Sign denoting that, when a number is multiplied by itself, the result is the number that appears below the bar.

1/2

fraction
Sign denoting that the number on the left of the slash (numerator) is one part of the number on the right of the slash (denominator).

∞

infinity
Symbol denoting that a value has no upper limit.

$\int$

integral
Result of the integral calculation used especially to determine an area and to resolve a differential equation.

!

factorial
Product of all positive whole numbers less than and equal to a given number. For example, the factorial of 4 is: 4! = 1x2x3x4 = 24.

Roman numerals

Uppercase letters that represented numbers in ancient Rome; they are still seen today in uses such as clock and watch dials and pagination.

I

one
Letter whose value is 1 unit.

V

five
Letter whose value is 5 units.

X

ten
Letter whose value is 10 units.

L

fifty
Letter whose value is 50 units.

C

one hundred
Letter whose value is 100 units.

D

five hundred
Letter whose value is 500 units.

M

one thousand
Letter whose value is 1,000 units.

geometry

Mathematical discipline that studies the relations between points, straight lines, curves, surfaces and volumes.

°
degree
Symbol placed in superscript after a number to denote the opening of an angle or the length of an arc, or in front of an uppercase letter to identify a scale of measurement.

′
minute
Symbol placed in superscript after a number that denotes degrees in sixtieths of a measure.

″
second
Symbol placed in superscript after a number that denotes degrees in sixtieths of a minute.

π
pi
Constant that represents the ratio of a circle's circumference to its diameter; its value is approximately 3.1416.

$\perp$
perpendicular
Symbol denoting that a straight line meets another at a right angle.

$\parallel$
is parallel to
Symbol denoting that two straight lines remain at a constant distance from one another.

$\nparallel$
is not parallel to
Symbol denoting that two straight lines do not remain at a constant distance from one other.

∟
right angle
Angle formed by two lines or two perpendicular planes that measures 90°.

obtuse angle
Angle between 90° and 180°.

$\angle$
acute angle
Angle that is smaller than a right angle (less than 90°).

geometrical shapes

Drawings that represent various geometric forms such as straight lines, circles and polygons.

examples of angles
Angle: figure formed by two intersecting lines or planes; it is measured in degrees.

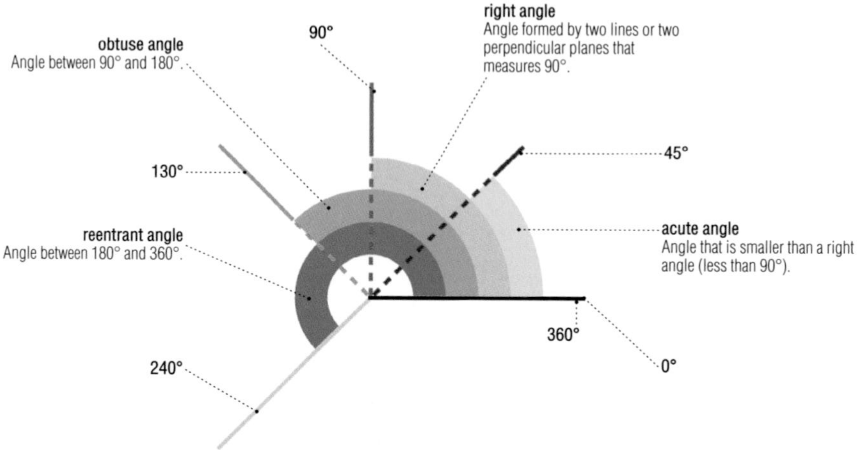

plane surfaces
Set of points on a plane that describes an area of space.

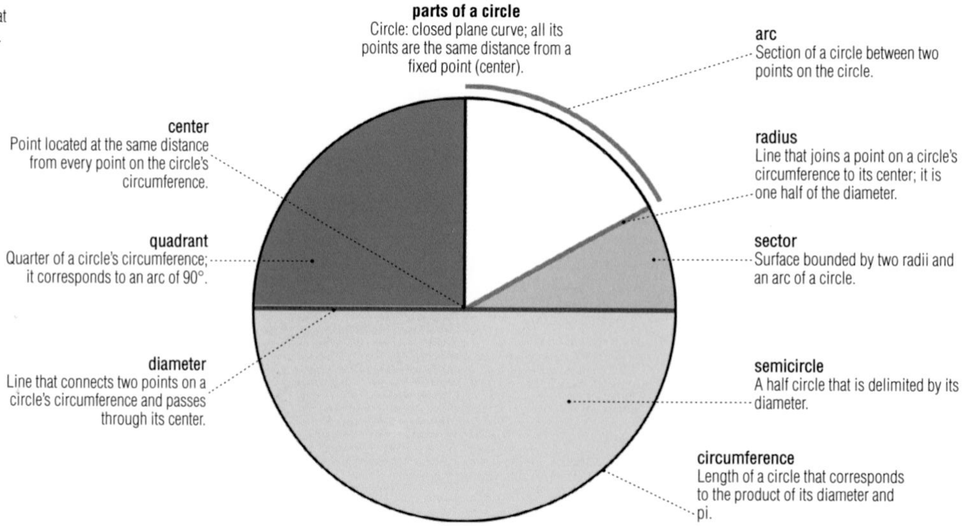

geometrical shapes

polygons

Geometric plane figures with several sides and a number of equal angles.

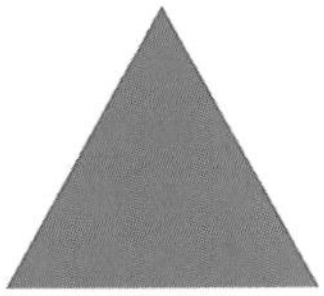

triangle
Three-sided polygon; triangles are scalene (no side is equal to any other) isosceles (two sides equal) or equilateral (all sides equal).

square
Equilateral rectangle with four right angles.

rectangle
Quadrilateral whose opposite sides are equal in length; the sides meet at right angles.

rhombus
Equilateral parallelogram.

trapezoid
Quadrilateral with two sides (bases) that are parallel. It is isosceles when it has two sides that are equal and not parallel, and rectangle when two of its sides form a right angle.

parallelogram
Trapezoid whose opposite sides are parallel and of equal length; the sides do not meet at right angles.

quadrilateral
Any plane figure with four sides and four angles.

regular pentagon
Polygon with five (penta = five) sides and equal angles.

regular hexagon
Polygon with six (hexa = six) sides and equal angles.

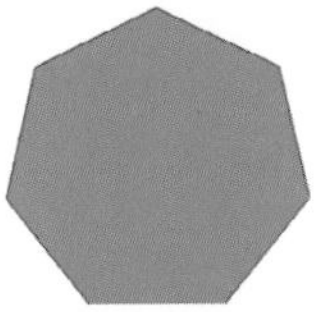

regular heptagon
Polygon with seven (hepta = seven) sides and equal angles.

regular octagon
Polygon with eight (octo = eight) sides and equal angles.

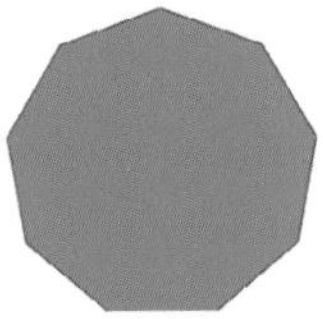

regular nonagon
Polygon with nine (nona = nine) sides and equal angles.

regular decagon
Polygon with 10 (deca = ten) sides and equal angles.

regular hendecagon
Polygon with 11 (hendeca = eleven) sides and equal angles.

regular dodecagon
Polygon with 12 (dodeca = twelve) sides and equal angles.

solids

Geometric shapes in three dimensions that are delimited by surfaces.

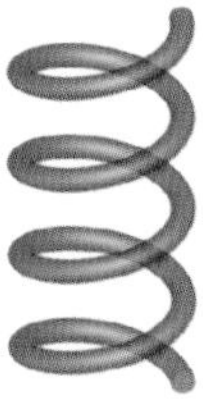

helix
Volume or solid of spiral shape that turns at a constant angle.

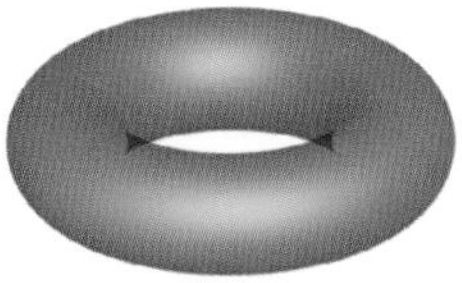

torus
Volume or solid generated by the rotation of a circle at an equal distance from its center of rotation.

hemisphere
Half sphere cut along its diameter.

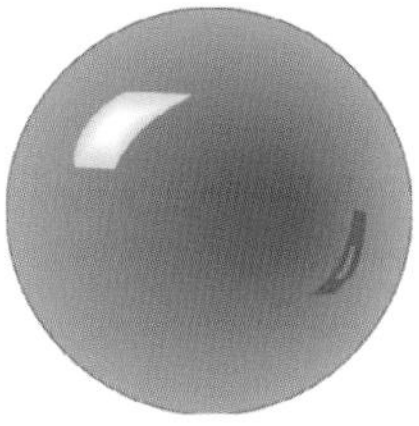

sphere
Volume with all the points on its surface the same distance from its center; the solid thus delimited is a round ball.

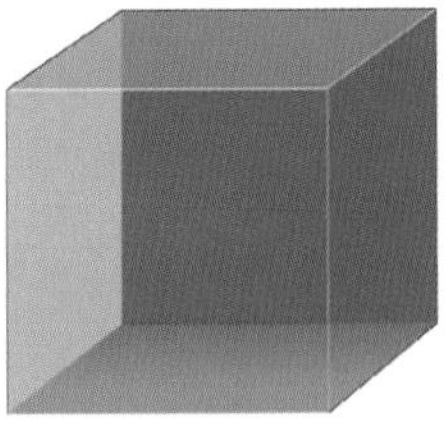

cube
Volume or solid with six square sides of equal area and six equal edges; it has eight vertices.

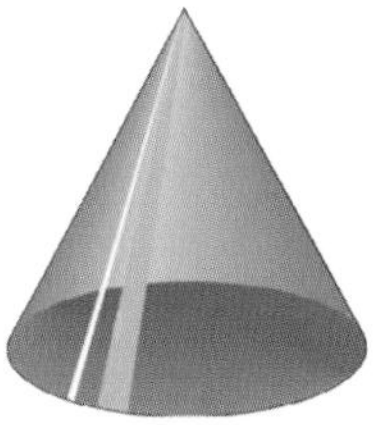

cone
Volume or solid generated by the rotation of a straight line (generatrix) along a circular line (directrix) from a fixed point (vertex).

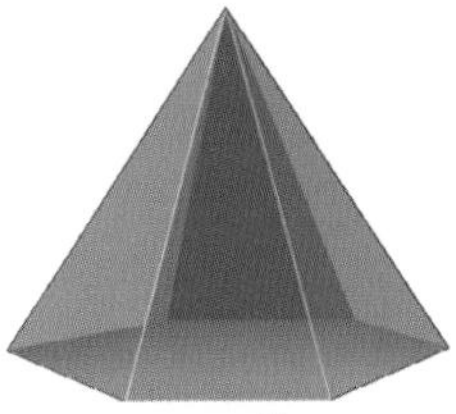

pyramid
Volume or solid generated by straight lines (edges) connecting the angles of a polygon (base) to the vertex and whose sides form triangles.

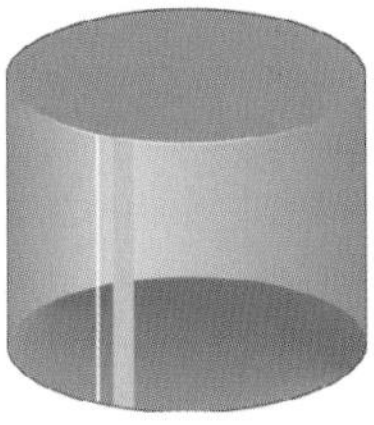

cylinder
Volume or solid generated by the rotation of a straight line (generatrix) moving along a curved line (directrix).

parallelepiped
Volume or solid with six sides (parallelograms) that are parallel in pairs.

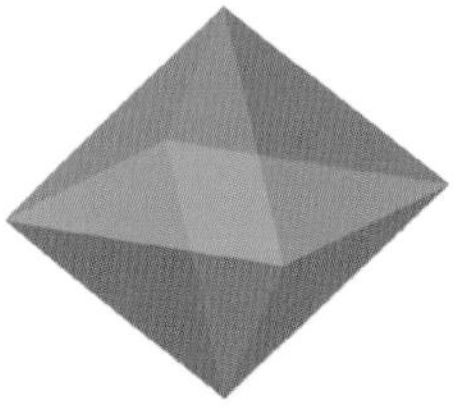

regular octahedron
Volume or solid with eight triangular sides of equal area; it has six vertices and 12 edges.

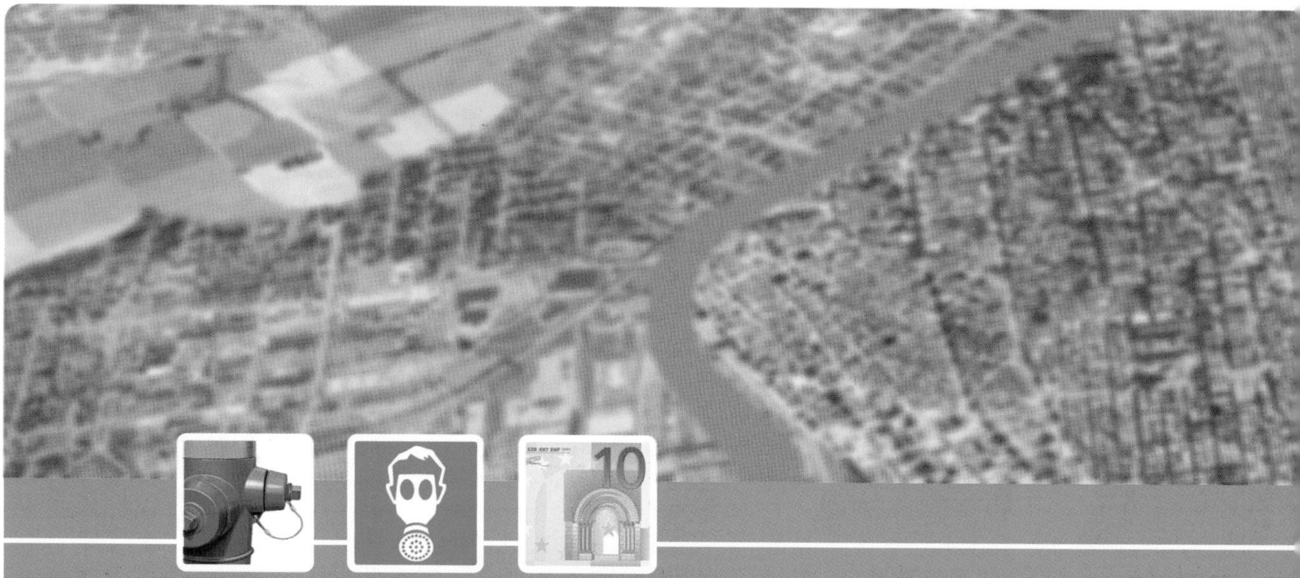

708 City
Densely populated urban area whose activities relate to commerce, industry and administration.

726 Justice
The administration of law in a society.

728 Economy and finance
All activities related to the management of assets and currencies.

732 Education
The art of educating and training an individual.

736 Religion
The belief systems, dogma and rites that characterize a human being's relationship with the sacred.

739 Politics
The art and practice of governing states and societies.

SOCIETY

Collective environment inhabited by human beings and characterized by institutions, culture, a concern for the common good and collective security.

748 Weapons

Instruments or devices used for attack or defense.

764 Safety

The measures taken and the equipment used to ensure the protection of persons and goods.

775 Health

The measures taken and the equipment used to ensure the physical and psychological well-being of the public.

784 Family

Group of persons related through common ancestry or marriage.

metropolitan area

Vast urban concentration consisting of a city and its suburbs.

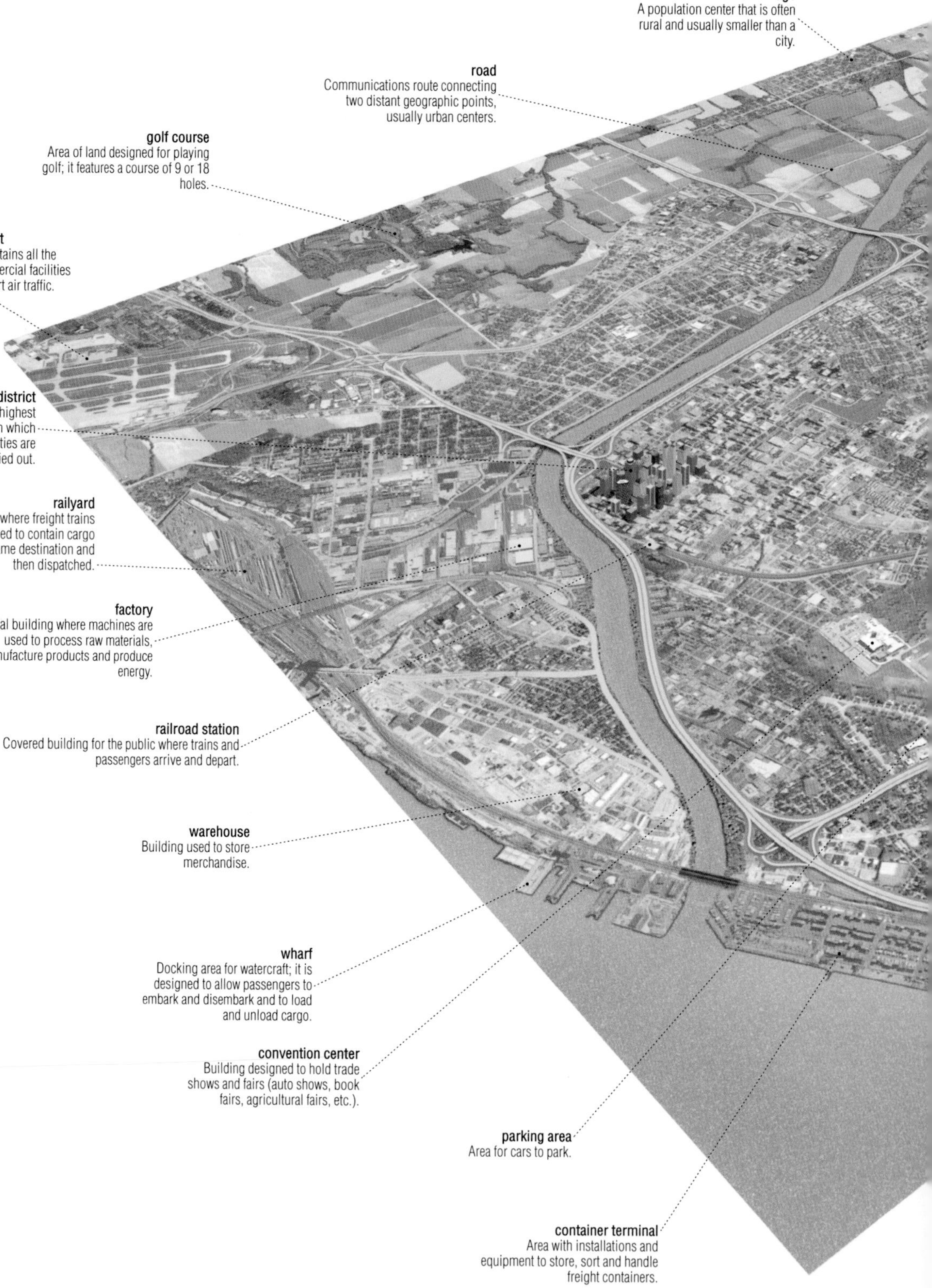

village
A population center that is often rural and usually smaller than a city.
road
Communications route connecting two distant geographic points, usually urban centers.
golf course
Area of land designed for playing golf; it features a course of 9 or 18 holes.
airport
Location that contains all the technical and commercial facilities needed to support air traffic.
central business district
Area that contains the highest concentration of uildings in which the city's economic activities are carried out.
railyard
Set of tracks where freight trains are reconfigured to contain cargo cars with the same destination and then dispatched.
factory
Industrial building where machines are used to process raw materials, manufacture products and produce energy.
railroad station
Covered building for the public where trains and passengers arrive and depart.
warehouse
Building used to store merchandise.
wharf
Docking area for watercraft; it is designed to allow passengers to embark and disembark and to load and unload cargo.
convention center
Building designed to hold trade shows and fairs (auto shows, book fairs, agricultural fairs, etc.).
parking area
Area for cars to park.
container terminal
Area with installations and equipment to store, sort and handle freight containers.

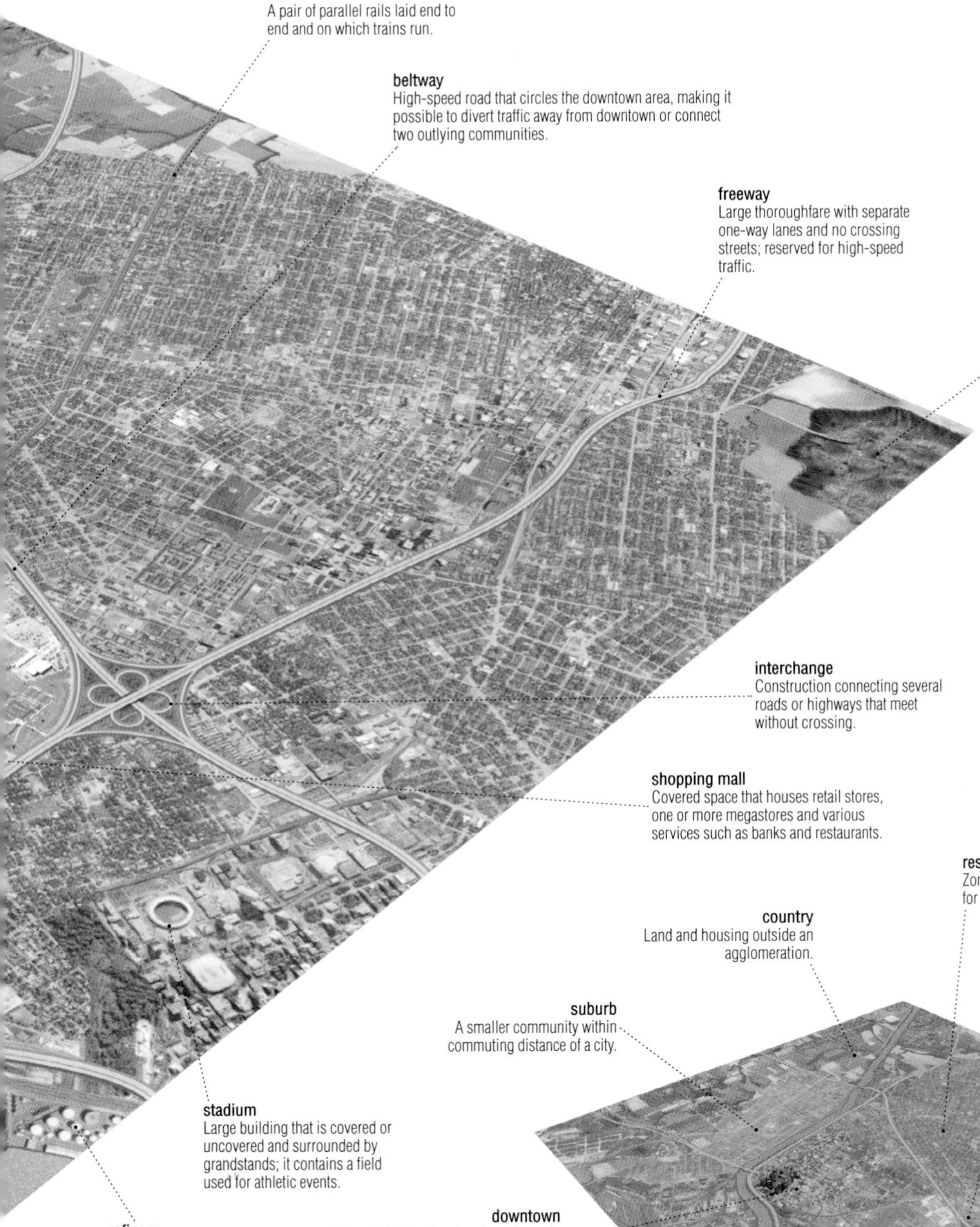
track
A pair of parallel rails laid end to end and on which trains run.
beltway
High-speed road that circles the downtown area, making it possible to divert traffic away from downtown or connect two outlying communities.
freeway
Large thoroughfare with separate one-way lanes and no crossing streets; reserved for high-speed traffic.
landfill
Site designated for waste disposal.
interchange
Construction connecting several roads or highways that meet without crossing.
shopping mall
Covered space that houses retail stores, one or more megastores and various services such as banks and restaurants.
stadium
Large building that is covered or uncovered and surrounded by grandstands; it contains a field used for athletic events.
refinery
Plant where substances such as sugar and oil are processed.

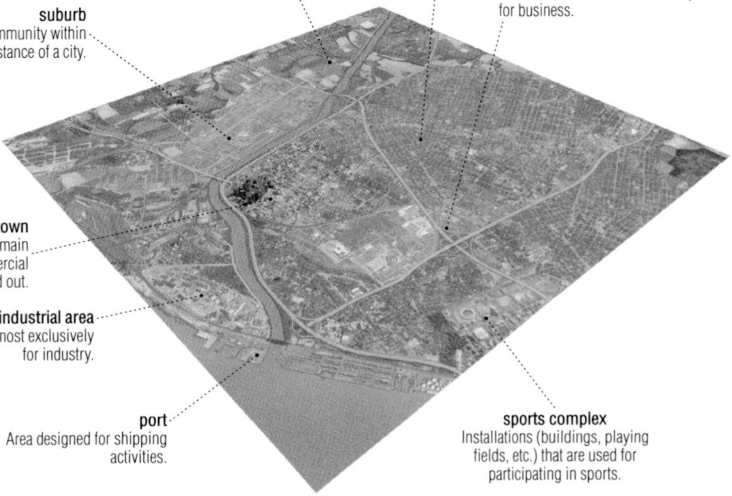
residential district
Zone reserved almost exclusively for housing.
country
Land and housing outside an agglomeration.
commercial zone
Zone reserved almost exclusively for business.
suburb
A smaller community within commuting distance of a city.
downtown
Central district of a city where the main cultural, economic and commercial activities are carried out.
industrial area
Zone reserved almost exclusively for industry.
port
Area designed for shipping activities.
sports complex
Installations (buildings, playing fields, etc.) that are used for participating in sports.

downtown

Central district of a city where the main cultural, economic and commercial activities are carried out.

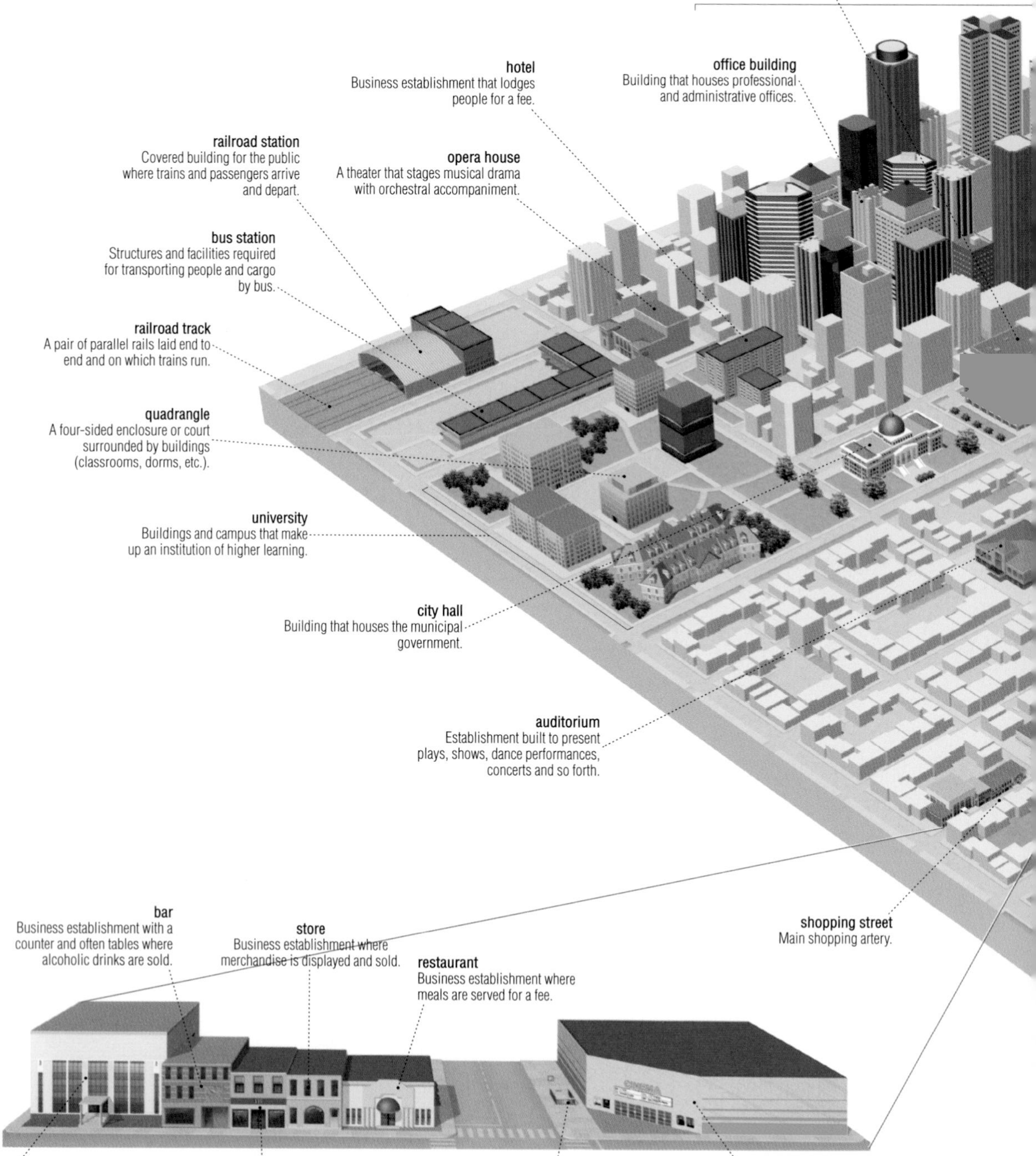
central business distric
Area that contains the highes
concentration of buildings in which th
city's economic activities are carrie
out
courthouse
Building that houses the courts.
hotel
Business establishment that lodges people for a fee.
office building
Building that houses professional and administrative offices.
railroad station
Covered building for the public where trains and passengers arrive and depart.
opera house
A theater that stages musical drama with orchestral accompaniment.
bus station
Structures and facilities required for transporting people and cargo by bus.
railroad track
A pair of parallel rails laid end to end and on which trains run.
quadrangle
A four-sided enclosure or court surrounded by buildings (classrooms, dorms, etc.).
university
Buildings and campus that make up an institution of higher learning.
city hall
Building that houses the municipal government.
auditorium
Establishment built to present plays, shows, dance performances, concerts and so forth.
shopping street
Main shopping artery.
bar
Business establishment with a counter and often tables where alcoholic drinks are sold.
store
Business establishment where merchandise is displayed and sold.
restaurant
Business establishment where meals are served for a fee.
bank
Establishment that provides a variety of financial services.
coffee shop
Business establishment where beverages such as coffee and sometimes light meals are served for a fee.
subway station
Structure and facilities that provide passengers access to the subway.
movie theater
Establishment with auditoriums used for projecting films.

SOCIETY

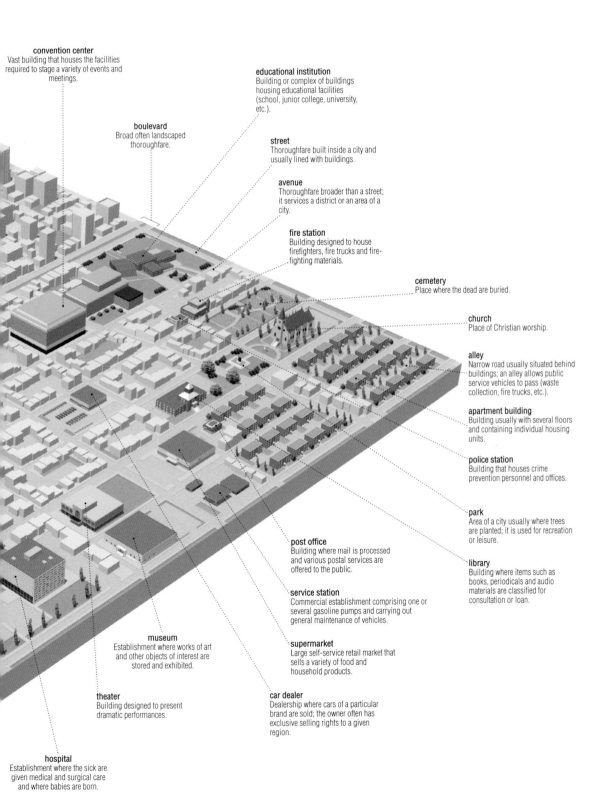

convention center
Vast building that houses the facilities required to stage a variety of events and meetings.

educational institution
Building or complex of buildings housing educational facilities (school, junior college, university, etc.).

boulevard
Broad often landscaped thoroughfare.

street
Thoroughfare built inside a city and usually lined with buildings.

avenue
Thoroughfare broader than a street; it services a district or an area of a city.

fire station
Building designed to house firefighters, fire trucks and fire-fighting materials.

cemetery
Place where the dead are buried.

church
Place of Christian worship.

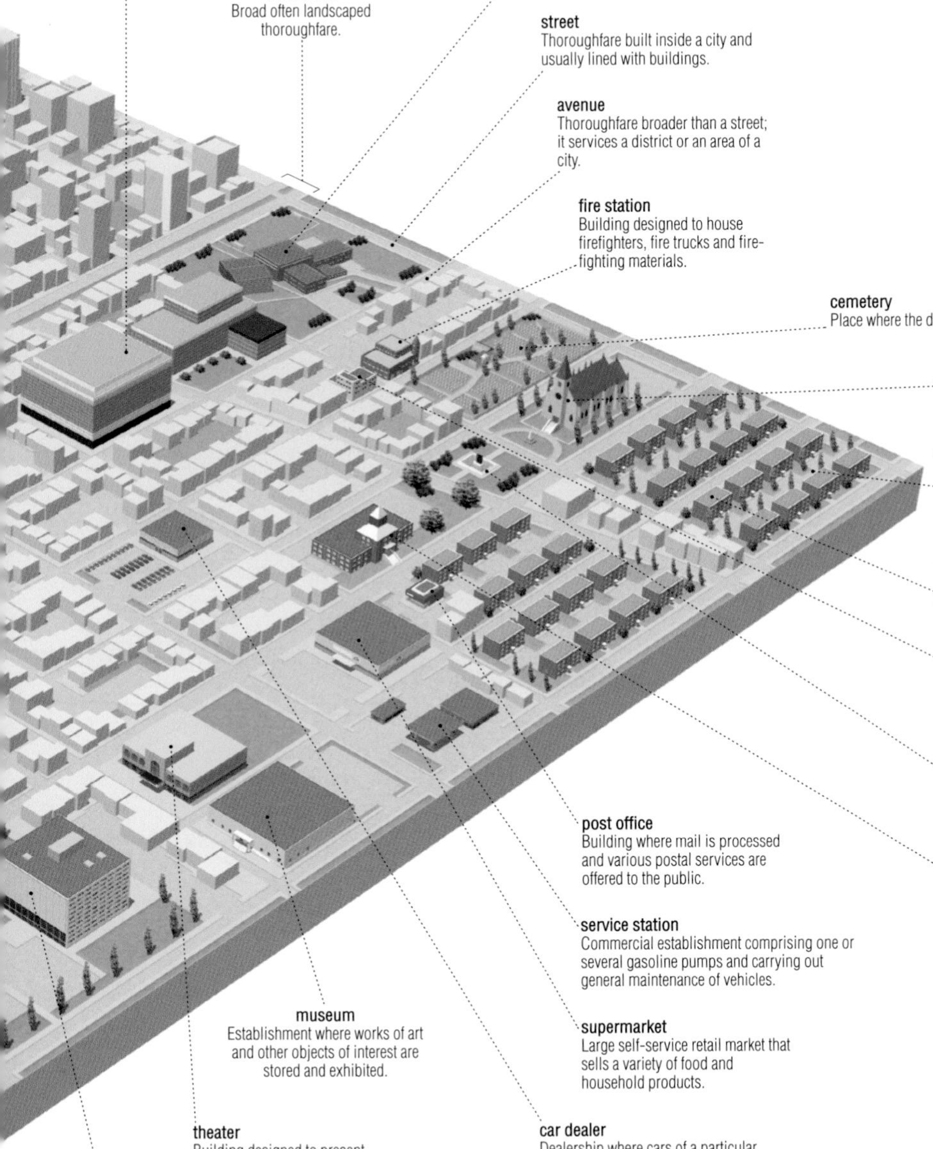

alley
Narrow road usually situated behind buildings; an alley allows public service vehicles to pass (waste collection, fire trucks, etc.).

apartment building
Building usually with several floors and containing individual housing units.

police station
Building that houses crime prevention personnel and offices.

park
Area of a city usually where trees are planted; it is used for recreation or leisure.

library
Building where items such as books, periodicals and audio materials are classified for consultation or loan.

post office
Building where mail is processed and various postal services are offered to the public.

service station
Commercial establishment comprising one or several gasoline pumps and carrying out general maintenance of vehicles.

supermarket
Large self-service retail market that sells a variety of food and household products.

museum
Establishment where works of art and other objects of interest are stored and exhibited.

theater
Building designed to present dramatic performances.

car dealer
Dealership where cars of a particular brand are sold; the owner often has exclusive selling rights to a given region.

hospital
Establishment where the sick are given medical and surgical care and where babies are born.

cross section of a street

Depiction of a network of cables and piping systems buried beneath a roadway.

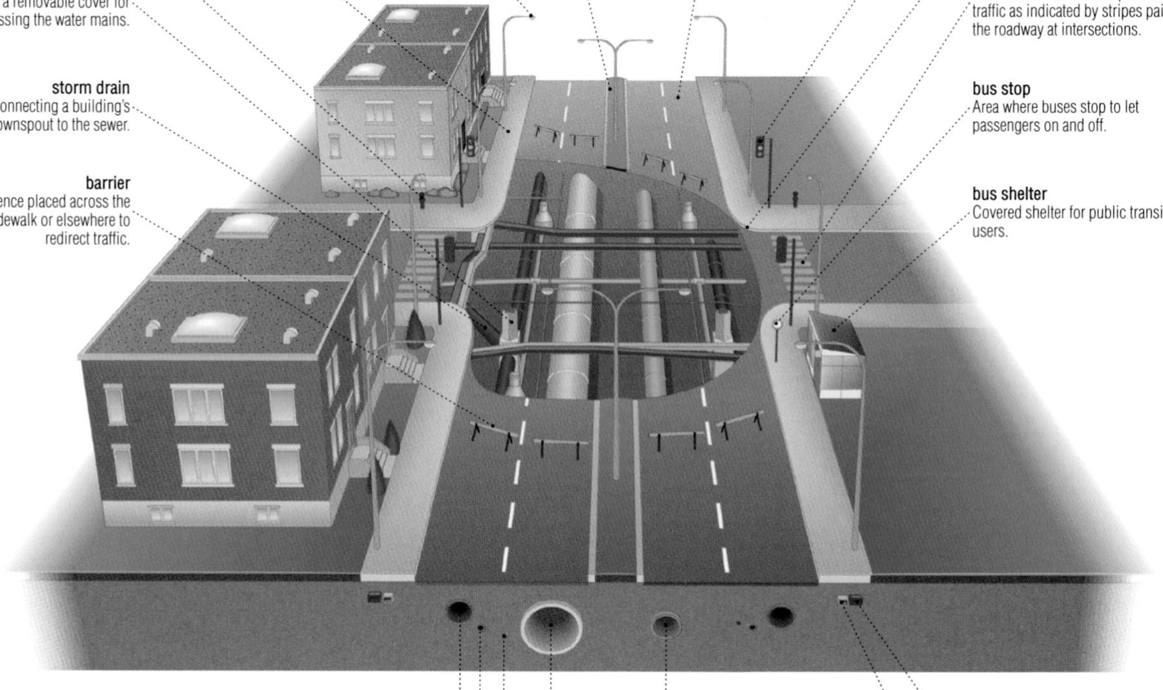

sidewalk
Pedestrian walkway bordering a street.

fire hydrant
A pipe connected to a water main; firefighters attach their hoses to it to supply their trucks.

manhole
Hole with a removable cover for accessing the water mains.

storm drain
Conduit connecting a building's downspout to the sewer.

barrier
Movable fence placed across the roadway, sidewalk or elsewhere to redirect traffic.

street light
Automated device used to illuminate a public thoroughfare.

median strip
A strip separating traffic lanes that go in opposite directions; also called a center divider.

roadway
Surface upon which vehicles drive.

traffic light
Automated lighting device that controls traffic at some intersections.

curb
Masonry construction bordering the roadway and built above it to control water flow.

pedestrian crossing
Lane that is reserved for pedestrian traffic as indicated by stripes painte the roadway at intersections.

bus stop
Area where buses stop to let passengers on and off.

bus shelter
Covered shelter for public transit users.

sewer
Pipe that collects wastewater and runoff and conveys them to the main sewer.

service main
Extremely high-flow pipe linked to smaller distribution pipes with far smaller volumes of flow.

electricity cable
Cable linking an electrical power station to its users.

main sewer
Large-diameter pipe that collects wastewater and sewer runoff and conveys them to a treatment plant.

telephone cable
Cable linking a telephone exchange to its users.

gas main
Pipe that conveys gas to buildings and houses.

water main
Pipe that conveys drinking water to buildings and residences.

traffic light
Automated lighting device that controls traffic at some intersections.

red light
The red traffic light means "stop".

yellow light
The yellow traffic light means to slow down and prepare to stop at an intersection.

green light
The green traffic light means "go".

pedestrian light
Automated lighting device that controls pedestrian traffic at some intersections.

pedestrian call button
Manual control used to obtain a green light.

office building

Building that houses professional and administrative offices.

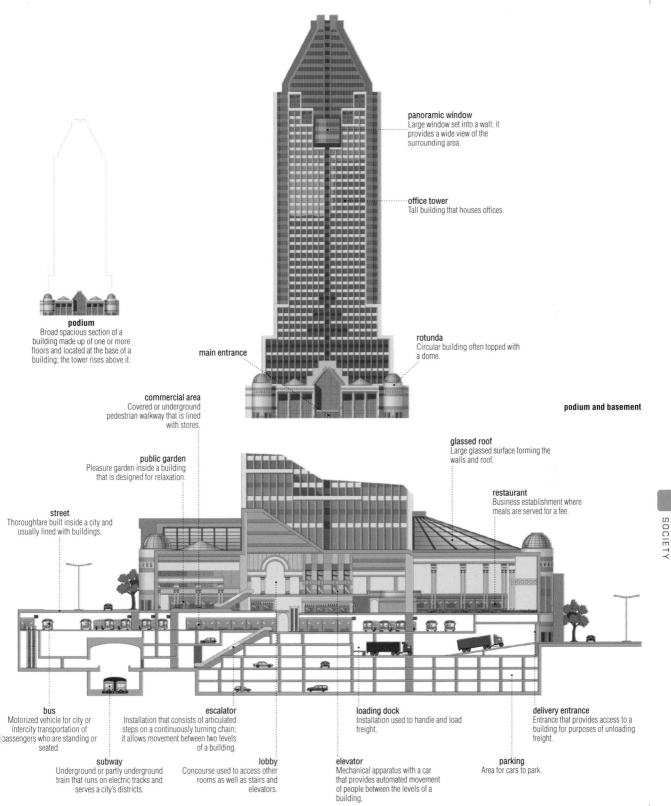

podium
Broad spacious section of a building made up of one or more floors and located at the base of a building; the tower rises above it.

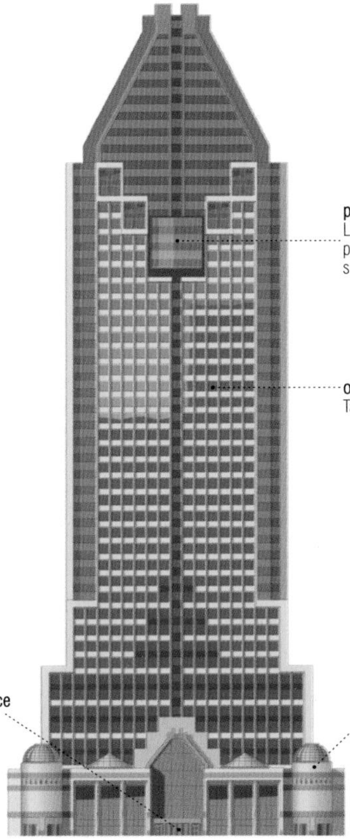

panoramic window
Large window set into a wall; it provides a wide view of the surrounding area.

office tower
Tall building that houses offices.

rotunda
Circular building often topped with a dome.

main entrance

podium and basement

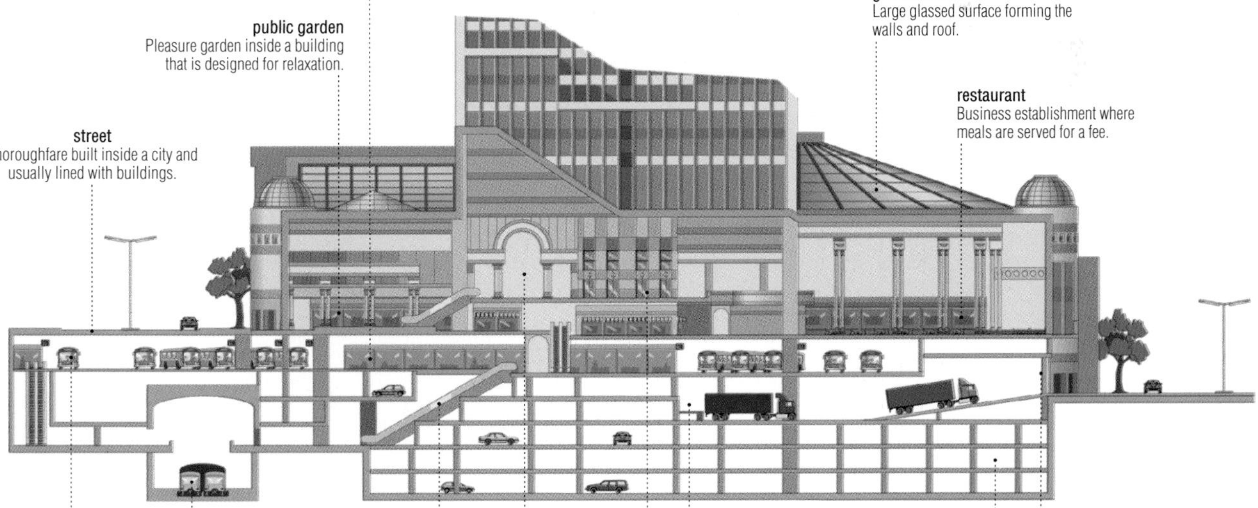

commercial area
Covered or underground pedestrian walkway that is lined with stores.

public garden
Pleasure garden inside a building that is designed for relaxation.

street
Thoroughfare built inside a city and usually lined with buildings.

glassed roof
Large glassed surface forming the walls and roof.

restaurant
Business establishment where meals are served for a fee.

bus
Motorized vehicle for city or intercity transportation of passengers who are standing or seated.

escalator
Installation that consists of articulated steps on a continuously turning chain; it allows movement between two levels of a building.

loading dock
Installation used to handle and load freight.

delivery entrance
Entrance that provides access to a building for purposes of unloading freight.

subway
Underground or partly underground train that runs on electric tracks and serves a city's districts.

lobby
Concourse used to access other rooms as well as stairs and elevators.

elevator
Mechanical apparatus with a car that provides automated movement of people between the levels of a building.

parking
Area for cars to park.

SOCIETY

shopping mall

Covered space that houses retail stores, one or more megastores and various services such as banks and restaurants.

electronics store
Retail outlet that sells electronic goods such as televisions, stereos and videocassette recorders.

restaurant
Business establishment where meals are served for a fee.

clothing store
Retail outlet that sells designer clothing that is less expensive than made-to-measure clothing.

bookstore
Retail outlet that sells books.

leather goods store
Retail outlet that sells items made of leather.

jewelry store
Retail outlet that sells articles made of precious metals and gems.

pet shop
Retail outlet that sells pets and pet supplies.

gift shop
Retail outlet that sells items for giving such as dishes, decorative objects and toys.

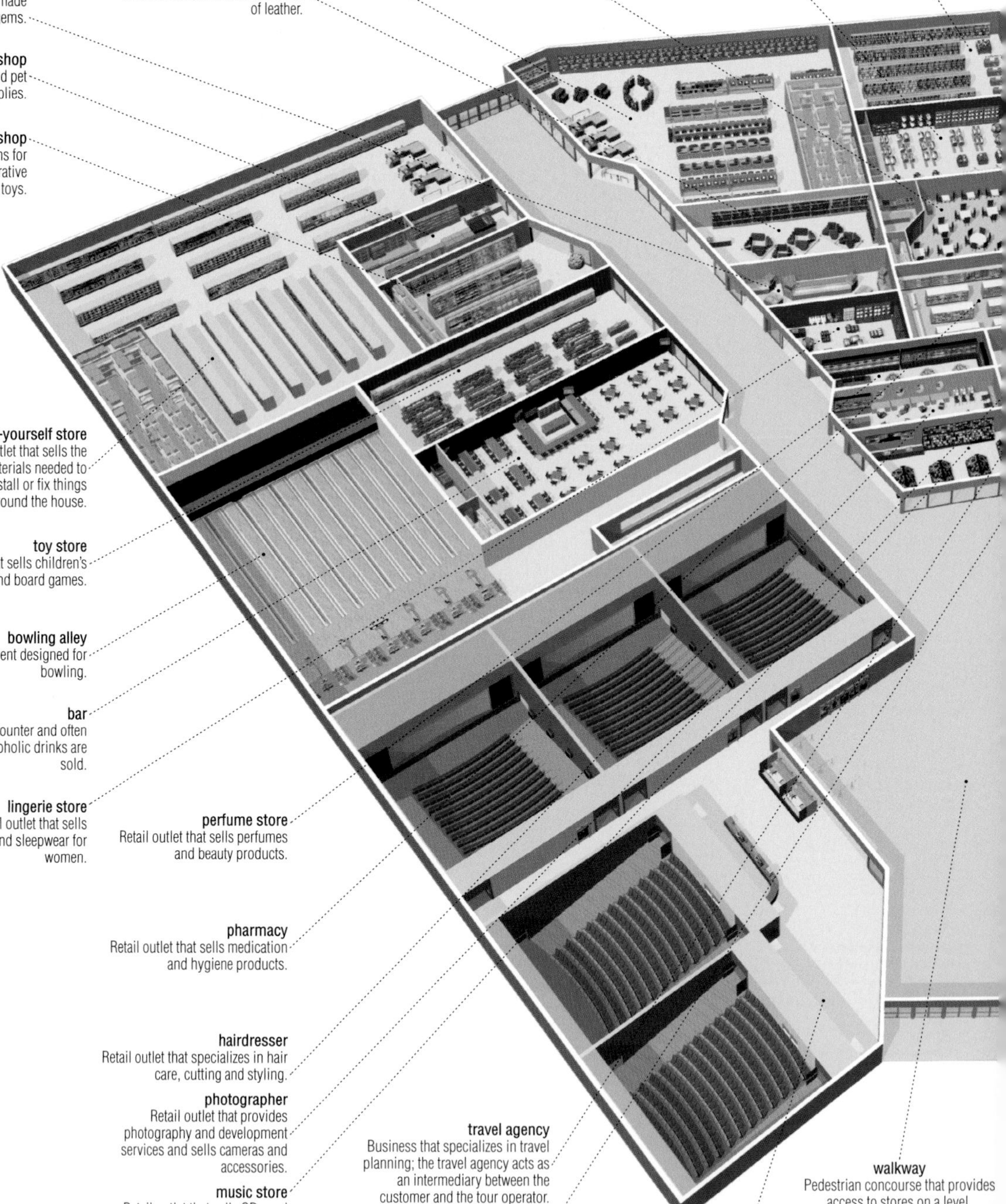

do-it-yourself store
Retail outlet that sells the equipment and materials needed to renovate, install or fix things around the house.

toy store
Retail outlet that sells children's toys and board games.

bowling alley
Establishment designed for bowling.

bar
Area with a counter and often tables where alcoholic drinks are sold.

lingerie store
Retail outlet that sells undergarments and sleepwear for women.

perfume store
Retail outlet that sells perfumes and beauty products.

pharmacy
Retail outlet that sells medication and hygiene products.

hairdresser
Retail outlet that specializes in hair care, cutting and styling.

photographer
Retail outlet that provides photography and development services and sells cameras and accessories.

music store
Retail outlet that sells CDs and cassettes.

travel agency
Business that specializes in travel planning; the travel agency acts as an intermediary between the customer and the tour operator.

smoke shop
Retail outlet that sells tobacco, cigarettes and smoking accessories.

movie theater
Establishment with auditoriums used for projecting films.

walkway
Pedestrian concourse that provides access to stores on a level.

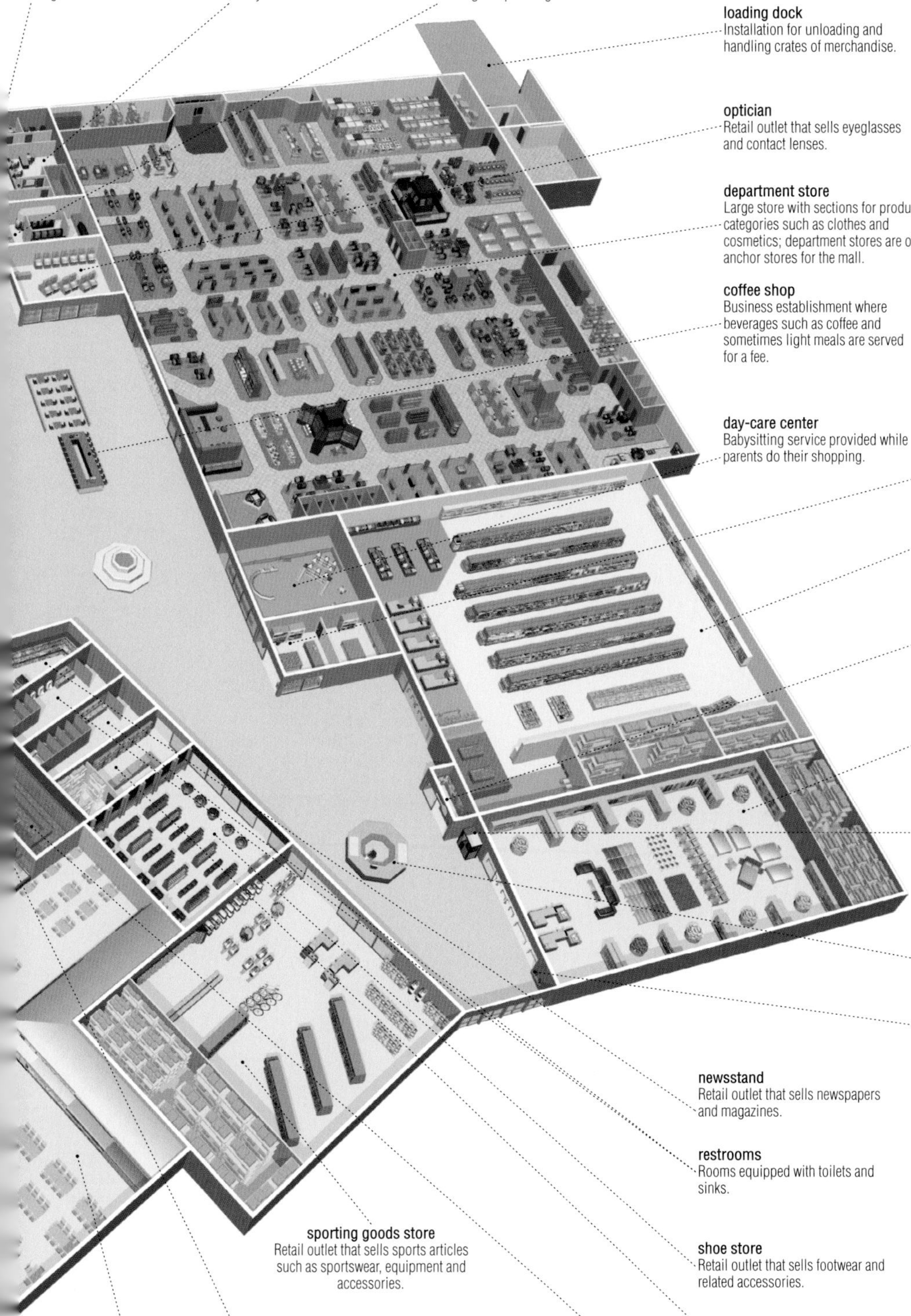

automated teller machine (ATM)
Machine used to obtain money using a debit card.

bank
Establishment that provides a variety of financial services.

dry cleaner
Retail outlet that specializes in cleaning and pressing clothes.

loading dock
Installation for unloading and handling crates of merchandise.

optician
Retail outlet that sells eyeglasses and contact lenses.

department store
Large store with sections for product categories such as clothes and cosmetics; department stores are often anchor stores for the mall.

coffee shop
Business establishment where beverages such as coffee and sometimes light meals are served for a fee.

day-care center
Babysitting service provided while parents do their shopping.

florist
Retail outlet that sells flowers and ornamental plants.

supermarket
Large self-service retail market that sells a variety of food and household products.

key cutting shop
Business that specializes in making and selling keys.

home furnishings store
Retail outlet that sells furniture and interior design accessories.

photo booth
Small booth equipped with an automated camera that takes fast-developing photographs.

information booth
Kiosk where customers can obtain information on where to find stores and services in the shopping mall.

pay phone
Telephone located in public places; it functions when coins or payment cards are inserted into the phone box.

newsstand
Retail outlet that sells newspapers and magazines.

restrooms
Rooms equipped with toilets and sinks.

shoe store
Retail outlet that sells footwear and related accessories.

sporting goods store
Retail outlet that sells sports articles such as sportswear, equipment and accessories.

fast-food restaurant
Business that serves rapidly prepared food at popular prices.

bench
Long narrow unupholstered seat with or without a back, seating several people.

pastry shop
Business that sells bread, pastries and other goods that are sometimes baked on-site.

post office
Outlet where mail is processed and various postal services are offered to the public.

department store

Large store with sections (departments) for various product categories such as clothes, stationery and cosmetics.

men's underwear
Section that sells undergarments for men.
women's casual wear
Section that sells women's clothing for everyday wear.
women's coats
Department that sells women's outerwear, which closes in front and is worn to protect against the cold and inclement weather.
checkout counter
Counter where clerks record the details of each article bought, calculate the amount due, and collect the money or the credit card information.
fitting room
Area where customers can try on articles of clothing before they decide to purchase.
swimsuits
Section that sells women's swimwear, which comes in one piece or two pieces (bikinis).
women's sweaters
Department that sells women's clothing for the upper body in a variety of fabrics and stitch patterns.
women's sportswear
lingerie
Section that sells women's undergarments and stockings.
women's suits
Section that sells women's suits, which are made up of a skirt or pants and a jacket of the same fabric.
women's nightwear
Section that sells women's clothing for indoor wear, including sleeping.
women's shoes
men's suits
Section that sells men's suits (pants, jackets, vests, etc.).
stockroom
Room used to store merchandise.
running shoes
Section where running shoes made of leather or canvas and rubber are sold; running shoes are designed to be light and flexible.
men's accessories
Department that sells men's articles such as belts, hats and scarves.
men's shoes
men's pants
mattresses and box springs
Department that sells beds in various sizes.
men's shirts
household linen
Department that sells items such as bathroom and kitchen towels, table linen and bedding.
neckties
Section that sells neckties, which are worn under the collar for decorative purposes.
audiovisual equipment
Department that sells items such as stereos, camcorders, televisions and videocassette recorders.
kitchen articles
Department that sells various utensils, articles for baking, cookware, etc.
decorative accessories
Department that sells household ornaments.
receiving area
Space designed to receive merchandise.
loading docks
Installations used to handle and unload crates and pallets of merchandise.
major domestic appliances
Section that sells kitchen and laundry appliances such as refrigerators, stoves, dishwashers, washing machines and dryers.

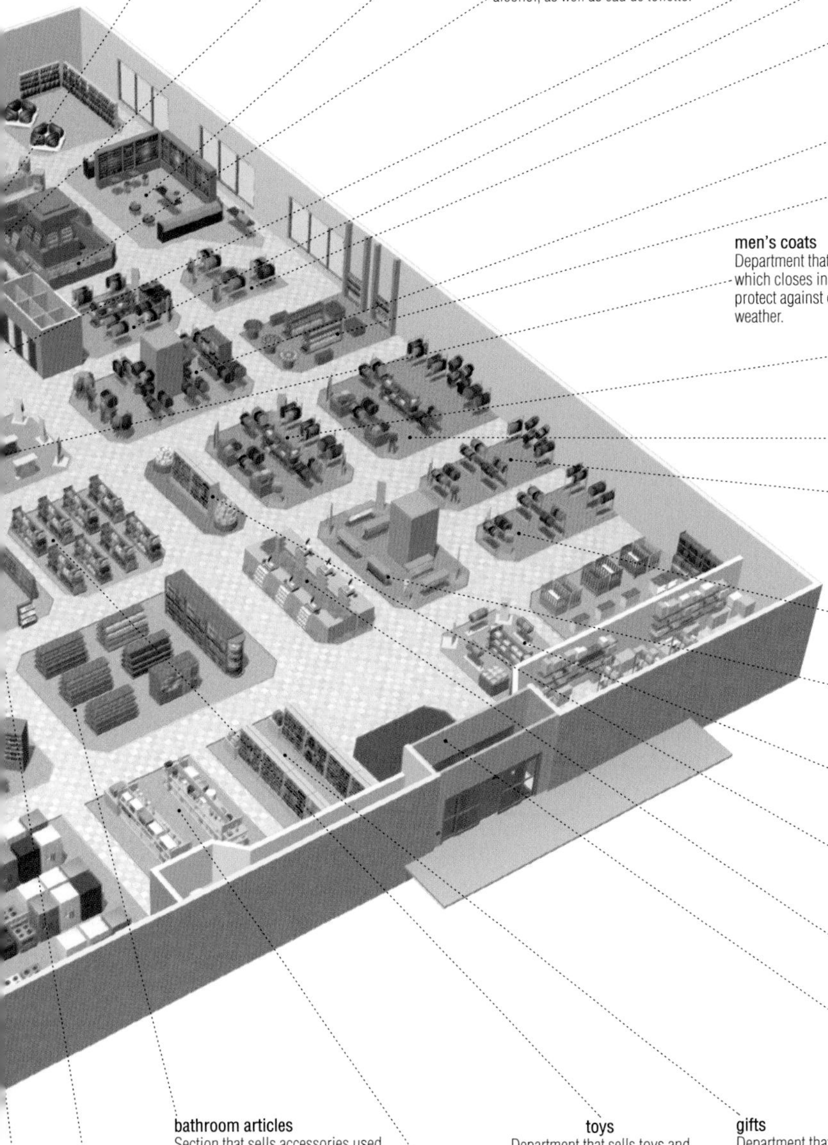

…ggage
…epartment that sells luggage used to …arry various objects and travel effects.

watches and jewelry
Department that sells watches and finely wrought ornamental objects made from precious materials (e.g., gold, silver, precious stones).

women's accessories
Department that sells women's articles such as belts, hats and scarves.

cosmetics
Department that sells facial beauty products used to bring out certain features and conceal blemishes.

perfume
Department that sells perfume, which is diluted with water and alcohol, as well as eau de toilette.

men's nightwear
Section that sells men's indoor clothing, including sleepwear.

men's sportswear
Department that sells men's clothing for participating in physical activities and informal wear.

men's sweaters
Department that sells men's clothing for the upper body that are made in a variety of fabrics and weaves.

men's casual wear
Section that sells men's clothing for everyday wear.

children's shoes

men's coats
Department that sells men's outerwear, which closes in front and is worn to protect against cold and inclement weather.

girls' wear size 7 to 17

boys' wear size 7 to 17

boys' wear size 2 to 6

girls' wear size 2 to 6

children's sportswear

baby wear

candies
Department that sells candies and chocolate.

checkout counter
Counter where clerks record the details of each article bought, calculate the amount due, and collect the money or the credit card information.

lobby
The department store's entrance area.

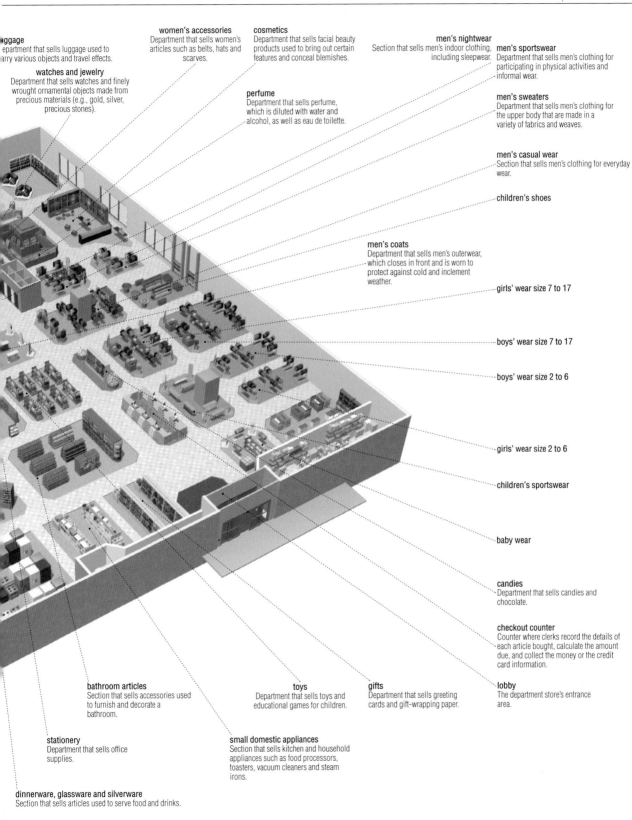

gifts
Department that sells greeting cards and gift-wrapping paper.

toys
Department that sells toys and educational games for children.

bathroom articles
Section that sells accessories used to furnish and decorate a bathroom.

small domestic appliances
Section that sells kitchen and household appliances such as food processors, toasters, vacuum cleaners and steam irons.

stationery
Department that sells office supplies.

dinnerware, glassware and silverware
Section that sells articles used to serve food and drinks.

convention center

Vast building that houses the facilities required to stage a variety of events and meetings.

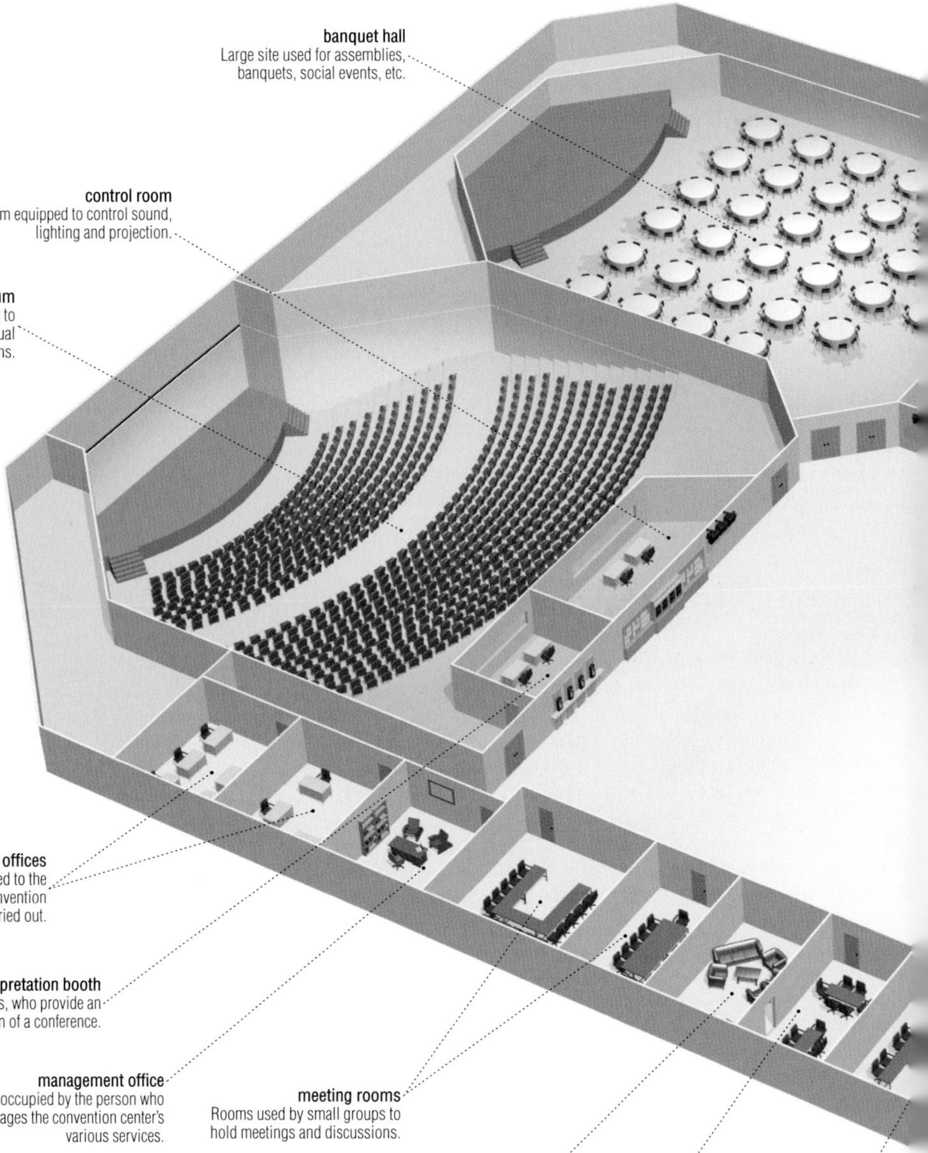

banquet hall
Large site used for assemblies, banquets, social events, etc.

control room
Room equipped to control sound, lighting and projection.

auditorium
Hall designed for the public to attend lectures and audiovisual presentations.

administrative offices
Rooms where tasks related to the management of the convention center are carried out.

simultaneous interpretation booth
Room set aside for interpreters, who provide an oral translation of a conference.

management office
Office occupied by the person who manages the convention center's various services.

meeting rooms
Rooms used by small groups to hold meetings and discussions.

VIP lounge
Room reserved for distinguished guests.

break-out room
Room designed for working sessions involving small groups.

conference room
Room that is big enough to hold a relatively large number of people.

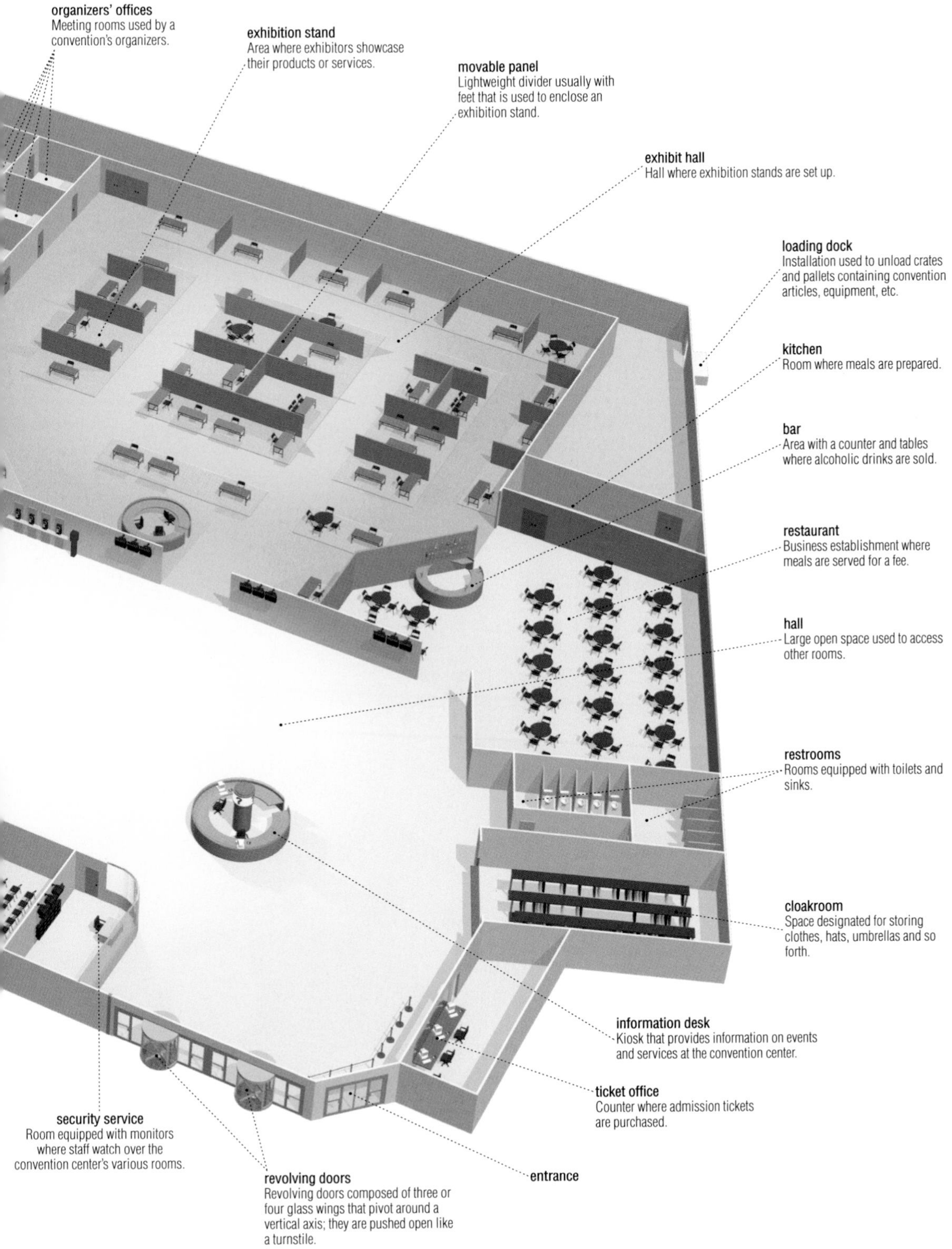
organizers' offices
Meeting rooms used by a convention's organizers.
exhibition stand
Area where exhibitors showcase their products or services.
movable panel
Lightweight divider usually with feet that is used to enclose an exhibition stand.
exhibit hall
Hall where exhibition stands are set up.
loading dock
Installation used to unload crates and pallets containing convention articles, equipment, etc.
kitchen
Room where meals are prepared.
bar
Area with a counter and tables where alcoholic drinks are sold.
restaurant
Business establishment where meals are served for a fee.
hall
Large open space used to access other rooms.
restrooms
Rooms equipped with toilets and sinks.
cloakroom
Space designated for storing clothes, hats, umbrellas and so forth.
information desk
Kiosk that provides information on events and services at the convention center.
ticket office
Counter where admission tickets are purchased.
entrance
revolving doors
Revolving doors composed of three or four glass wings that pivot around a vertical axis; they are pushed open like a turnstile.
security service
Room equipped with monitors where staff watch over the convention center's various rooms.

restaurant

Business establishment where people pay to eat a meal prepared on the premises and served at their table; a restaurant's quality and prices vary depending on the menu.

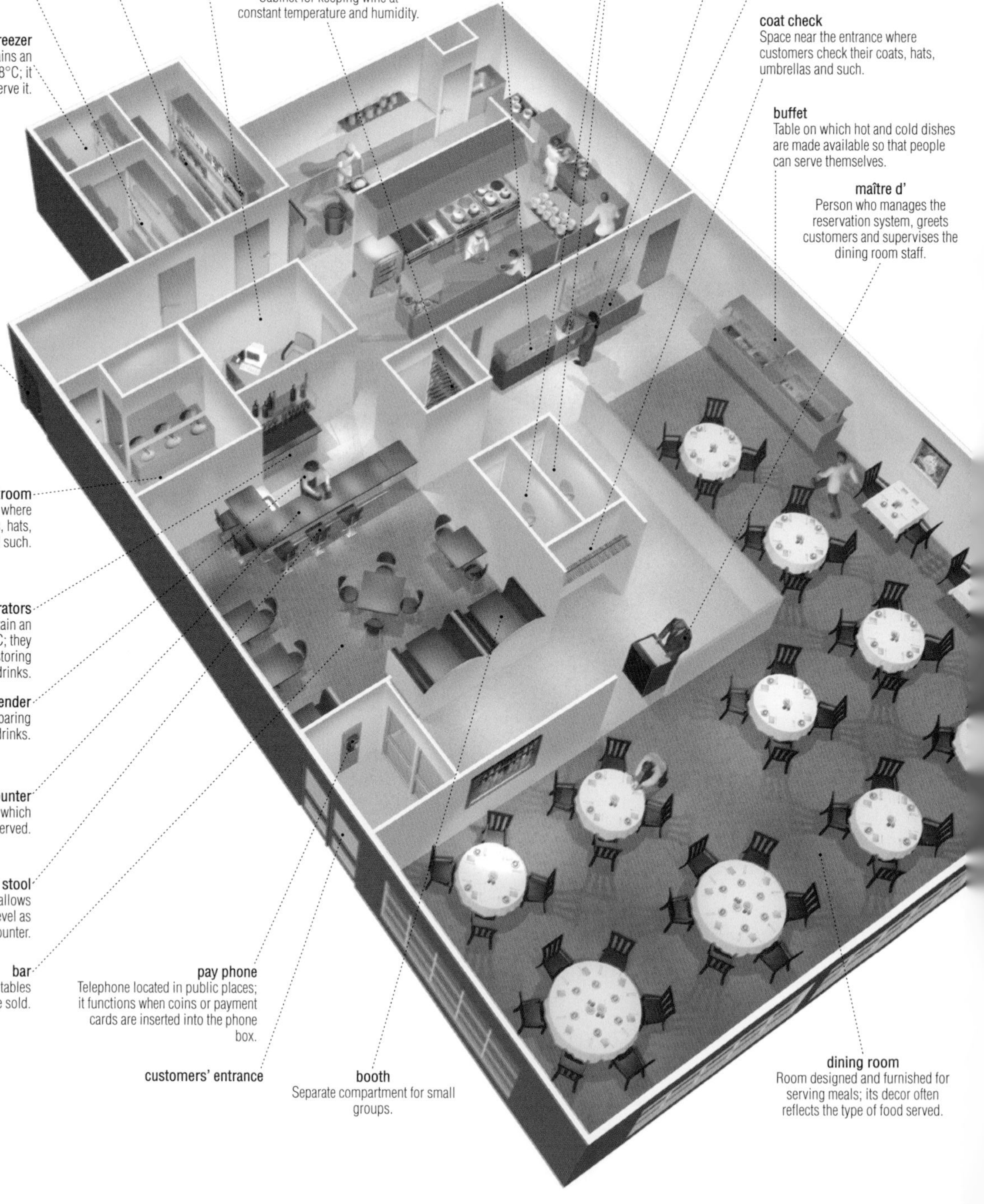

store room
Room for storing nonperishable items.
office
Workplace for administrative personnel.
refrigerated display case
Refrigerated unit for storing cold dishes that are prepared in advance.
customers' restrooms
Rooms equipped with toilets and sinks.
wine steward
Person in charge of the wine cellar; the wine steward helps customers choose a wine and sometimes serves it as well.
refrigerator
Appliance that maintains an average temperature of 4°C; it is used for storing and chilling food.
wine cellar
Cabinet for keeping wine at constant temperature and humidity.
service table
Furniture used for making extra utensils available to staff so they can provide fast service.
coat check
Space near the entrance where customers check their coats, hats, umbrellas and such.
freezer
Appliance that maintains an average temperature of -18°C; it freezes food to preserve it.
buffet
Table on which hot and cold dishes are made available so that people can serve themselves.
maître d'
Person who manages the reservation system, greets customers and supervises the dining room staff.
staff entrance
staff coatroom
Room near the entrance where employees store their clothes, hats, umbrellas and such.
refrigerators
Appliances that maintain an average temperature of 4°C; they are used for chilling and storing drinks.
bartender
Person responsible for preparing and serving drinks.
bar counter
Raised narrow counter on which drinks are served.
bar stool
Chair without arms that allows people to sit at the same level as the bar counter.
bar
Area with a counter and often tables where alcoholic drinks are sold.
pay phone
Telephone located in public places; it functions when coins or payment cards are inserted into the phone box.
customers' entrance
booth
Separate compartment for small groups.
dining room
Room designed and furnished for serving meals; its decor often reflects the type of food served.

restaurant

kitchen
Room where meals are prepared under the direction of a chef who is assisted by a kitchen staff.

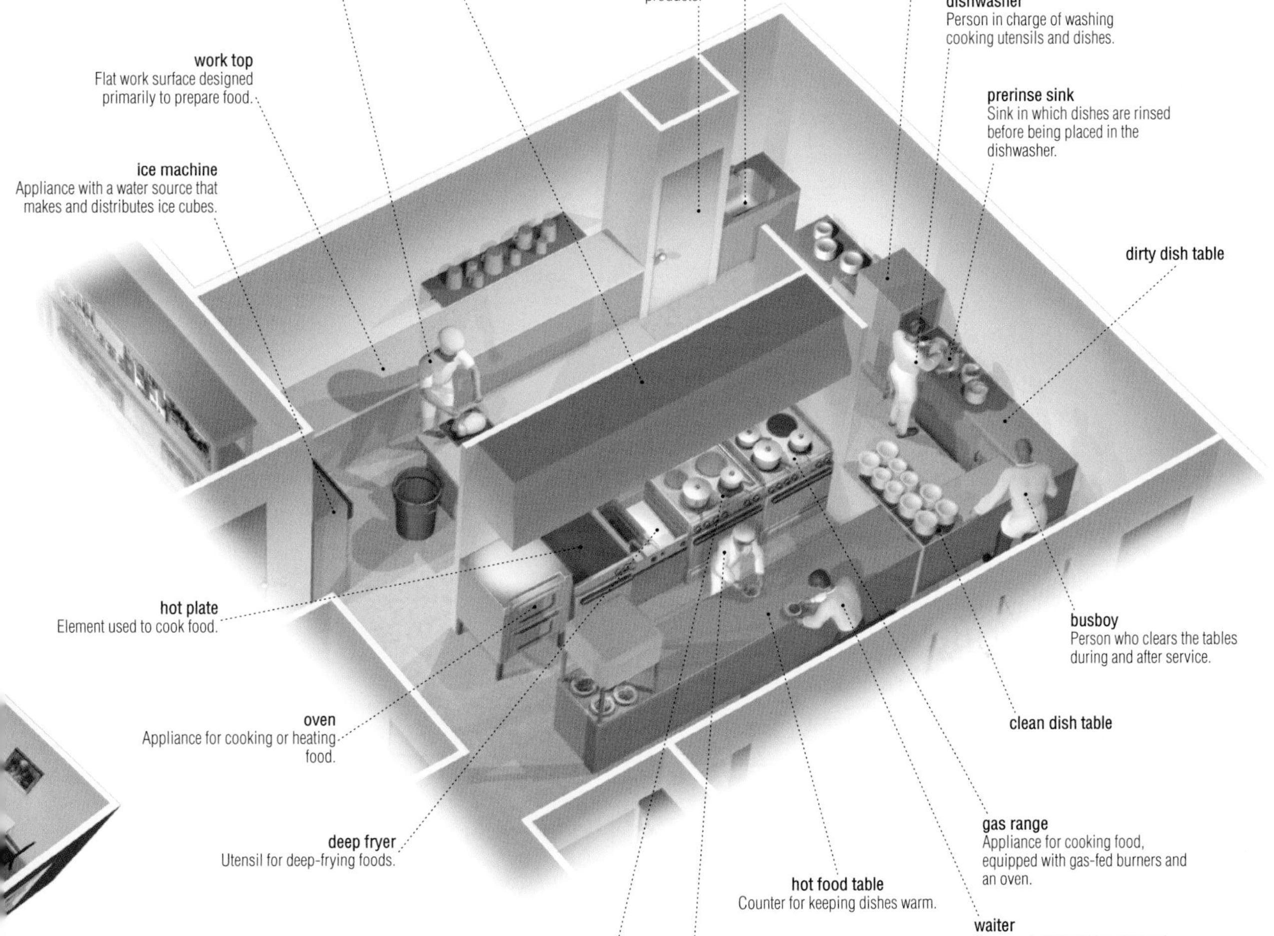

hood
Ventilation appliance expelling or recycling air that contains cooking fumes and odors.

pot-and-pan sink
Sink in which pots and pans and related cooking utensils are washed.

dishwasher
Appliance designed to automatically wash and dry dishes.

station chef
Person in charge of preparing the various dishes on the menu; specialized staff such as the sauce cook, roast cook and pastry chef answer to the station chef.

cleaning supplies
Cupboard for storing cleaning products.

dishwasher
Person in charge of washing cooking utensils and dishes.

work top
Flat work surface designed primarily to prepare food.

preringe sink
Sink in which dishes are rinsed before being placed in the dishwasher.

ice machine
Appliance with a water source that makes and distributes ice cubes.

dirty dish table

hot plate
Element used to cook food.

busboy
Person who clears the tables during and after service.

clean dish table

oven
Appliance for cooking or heating food.

gas range
Appliance for cooking food, equipped with gas-fed burners and an oven.

deep fryer
Utensil for deep-frying foods.

hot food table
Counter for keeping dishes warm.

waiter
Person who takes the customers' order, serves the meals and settles the check.

electric range
Electric appliance for cooking food, equipped with surface elements or griddles and an oven.

chef
Person whose main duties are to manage the kitchen staff, purchase supplies and plan menus.

menu
Itemized list of dishes served in a restaurant.

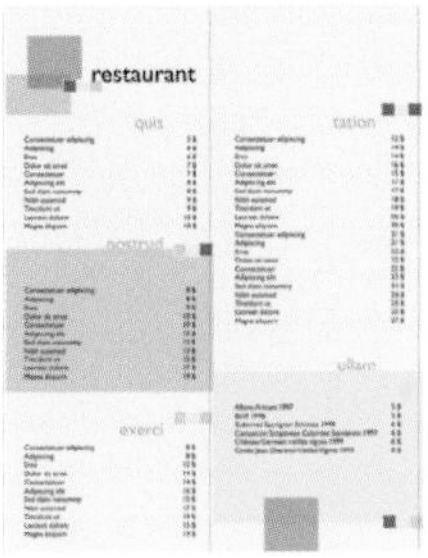

wine list
Itemized list of wines and spirits served in a restaurant.

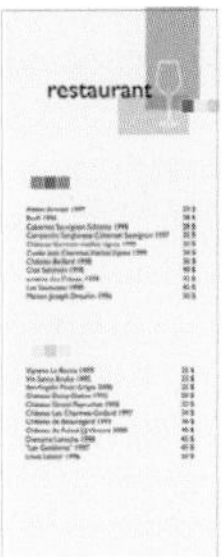

check
Bill indicating the total amount to be paid by the customer.

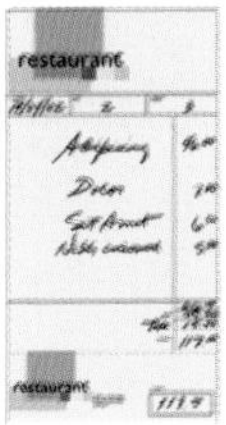

SOCIETY

self-service restaurant

Restaurant with numerous food counters where customers can put together a meal of their choosing.

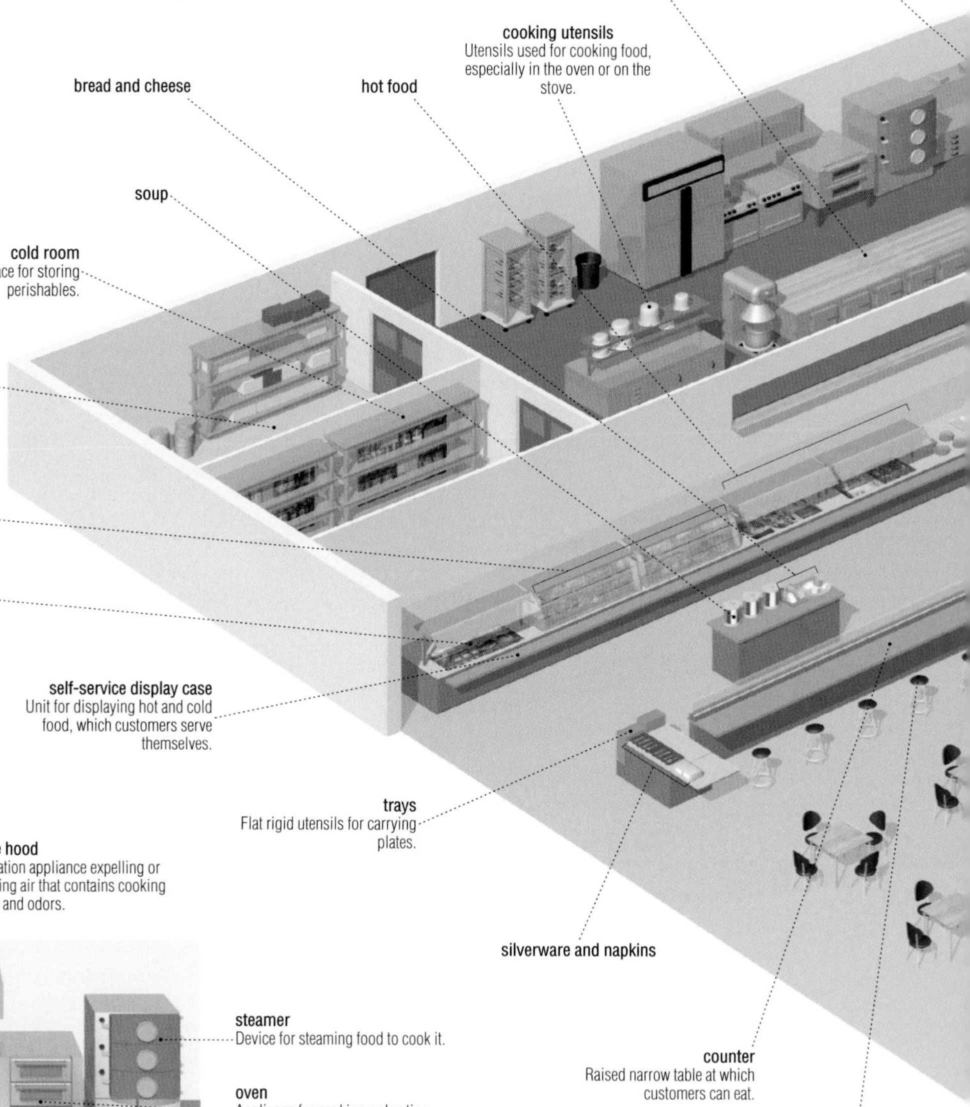
work top
Flat work surface designed primarily to prepare food.
sink
Water-fed basin equipped with a drain; it is indispensable for cooking and cleaning tasks.
cooking utensils
Utensils used for cooking food, especially in the oven or on the stove.
bread and cheese
hot food
soup
cold room
Refrigerated space for storing perishables.
store room
Room for storing nonperishable items.
hors d'oeuvres and cold food
salads
self-service display case
Unit for displaying hot and cold food, which customers serve themselves.
trays
Flat rigid utensils for carrying plates.
silverware and napkins
counter
Raised narrow table at which customers can eat.
stool
Seat without arms or back where people sit at counter level.

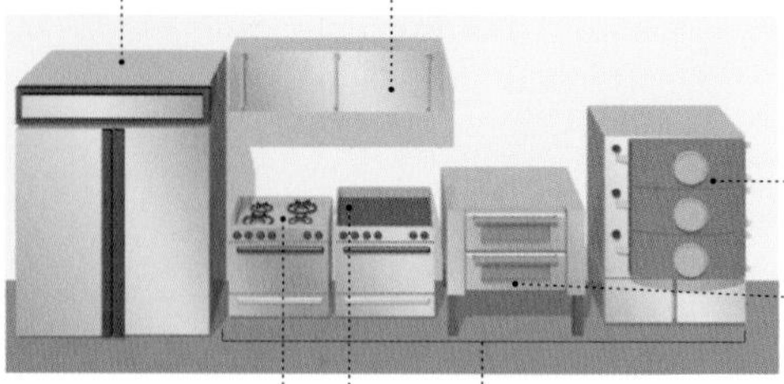
refrigerator
Appliance with two compartments, one for keeping food cold and the other for freezing it.
range hood
Ventilation appliance expelling or recycling air that contains cooking fumes and odors.
steamer
Device for steaming food to cook it.
oven
Appliance for cooking or heating food.
range
Electric appliance for cooking food.
cooking area
All the equipment needed for preparing food.
cooking plate
Element for cooking food.

self-service restaurant

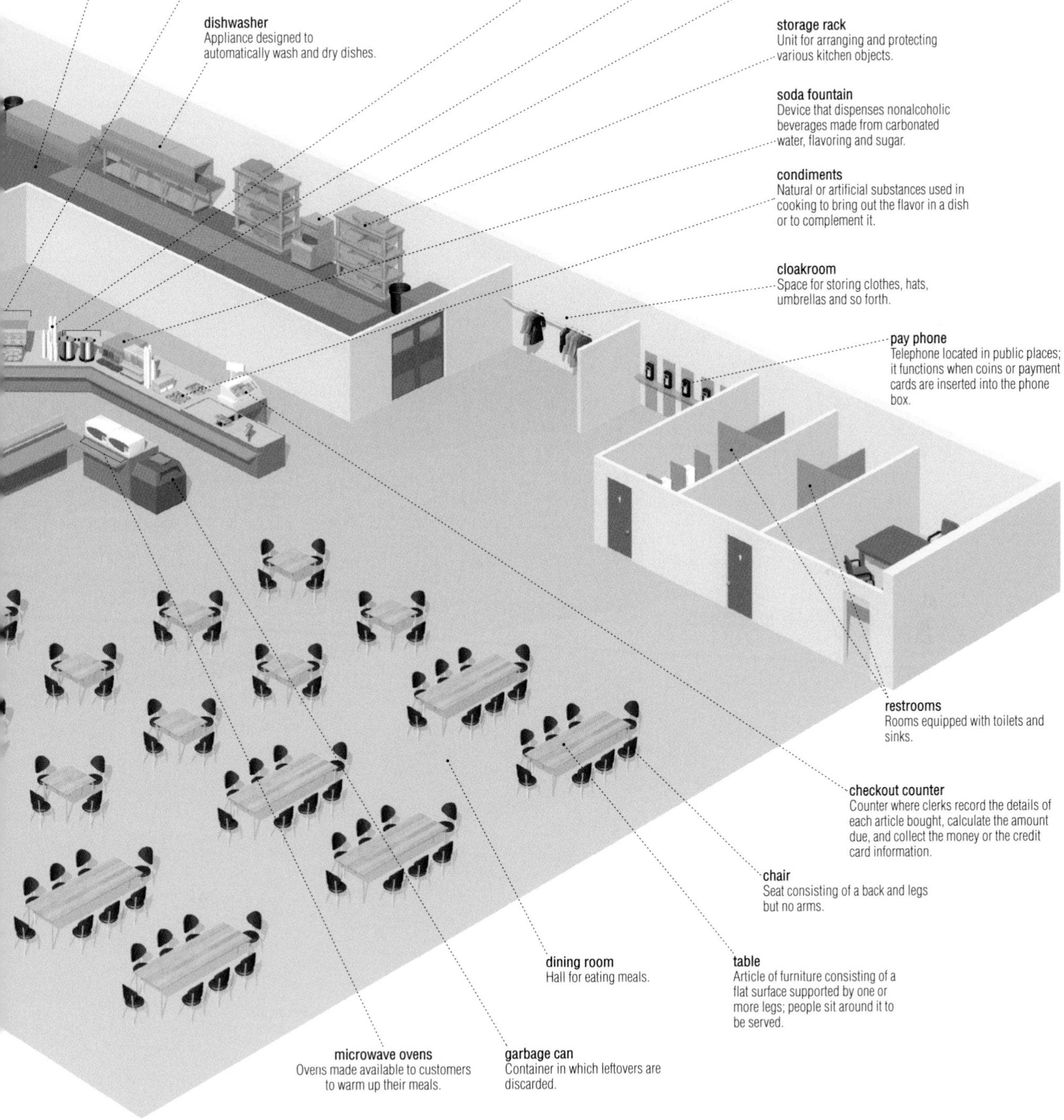
kitchen
Room where meals are prepared.
fruits and desserts
dishwasher
Appliance designed to automatically wash and dry dishes.
glasses
Receptacles for drinking.
percolators
Electric coffee makers for preparing large amounts of coffee.
glass washer
Appliance designed to automatically wash glasses.
storage rack
Unit for arranging and protecting various kitchen objects.
soda fountain
Device that dispenses nonalcoholic beverages made from carbonated water, flavoring and sugar.
condiments
Natural or artificial substances used in cooking to bring out the flavor in a dish or to complement it.
cloakroom
Space for storing clothes, hats, umbrellas and so forth.
pay phone
Telephone located in public places; it functions when coins or payment cards are inserted into the phone box.
restrooms
Rooms equipped with toilets and sinks.
checkout counter
Counter where clerks record the details of each article bought, calculate the amount due, and collect the money or the credit card information.
chair
Seat consisting of a back and legs but no arms.
table
Article of furniture consisting of a flat surface supported by one or more legs; people sit around it to be served.
dining room
Hall for eating meals.
garbage can
Container in which leftovers are discarded.
microwave ovens
Ovens made available to customers to warm up their meals.

hotel

Business establishment that lodges people for a fee.

reception level
The ground floor of the hotel.

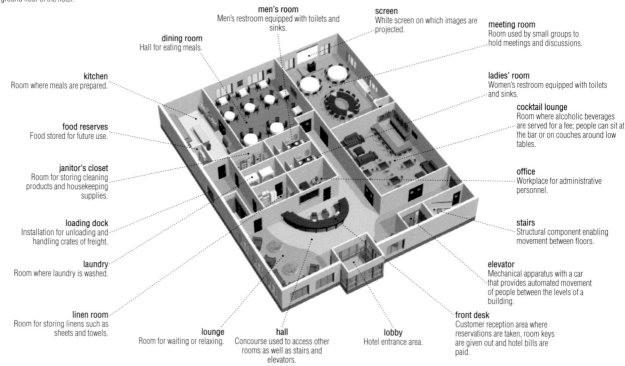

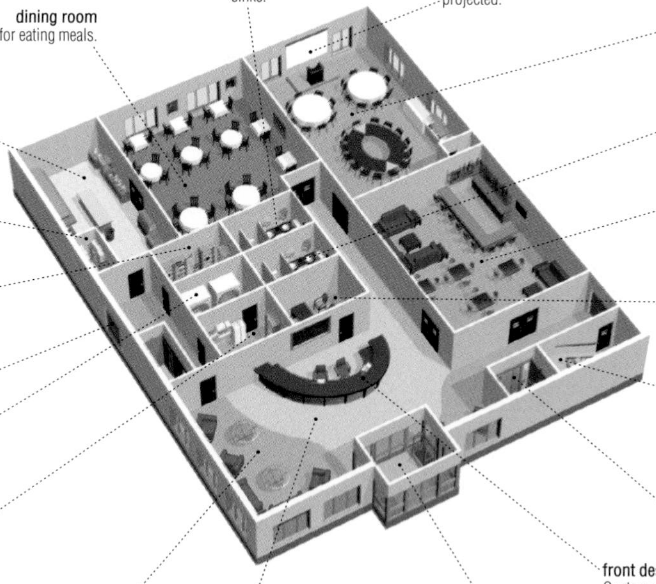
men's room
Men's restroom equipped with toilets and sinks.
screen
White screen on which images are projected.
meeting room
Room used by small groups to hold meetings and discussions.
dining room
Hall for eating meals.
kitchen
Room where meals are prepared.
ladies' room
Women's restroom equipped with toilets and sinks.
cocktail lounge
Room where alcoholic beverages are served for a fee; people can sit at the bar or on couches around low tables.
food reserves
Food stored for future use.
janitor's closet
Room for storing cleaning products and housekeeping supplies.
office
Workplace for administrative personnel.
loading dock
Installation for unloading and handling crates of freight.
stairs
Structural component enabling movement between floors.
laundry
Room where laundry is washed.
elevator
Mechanical apparatus with a car that provides automated movement of people between the levels of a building.
linen room
Room for storing linens such as sheets and towels.
front desk
Customer reception area where reservations are taken, room keys are given out and hotel bills are paid.
lounge
Room for waiting or relaxing.
hall
Concourse used to access other rooms as well as stairs and elevators.
lobby
Hotel entrance area.

hotel rooms
Rooms designed to lodge people.

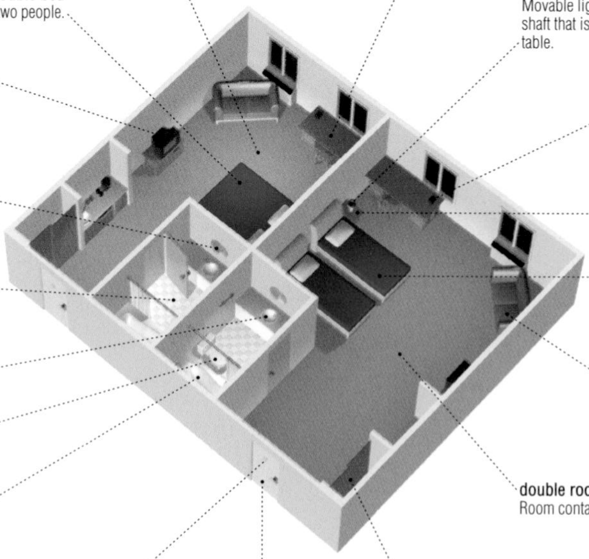
single room
Room that contains one bed and is designed for one or two people.
desk
Worktable that usually contains drawers.
double bed
Large bed designed for two people.
bedside lamp
Movable light fixture with a short shaft that is used on a bedside table.
television set
Receiving device that generates the sound and picture elements of programs broadcast by a television station or recorded on cassette or disc.
telephone
Device allowing the human voice to be transmitted over a distance by means of a network of telephone lines.
mirror
Polished glass surface that reflects light and images and used for purposes such as styling hair and applying makeup.
bedside table
Small table placed at the head of a bed; it might contain one or more drawers.
bathroom
Room designed for personal hygiene; it is equipped with running water and sanitary fixtures.
single bed
Bed designed for one person.
sink
Sanitary fixture in the form of a basin; it is used for washing.
love seat
Sofa that seats two people.
toilet
Sanitary fixture for disposing of bodily waste; it comprises a toilet bowl and a tank.
double room
Room containing two beds.
bath and shower
Sanitary facilities for washing the body; one is an elongated tub and the other, a jet of water.
room number
door
Opening connecting the hotel hallway to the room; it can be locked.
wardrobe
Closet for storing clothes.

common symbols

Pictograms used in public areas or along thoroughfares to advertise services or warn of prohibitions.

men's rest room

women's rest room

wheelchair access

no wheelchair access

camping (trailer and tent)

picnic area

picnics prohibited

camping (tent)

camping prohibited

camping (trailer)

hospital

coffee shop

telephone

restaurant

pharmacy

police

first aid

service station

fire extinguisher

information

information

lost and found articles

currency exchange

taxi transportation

prison

Place of detention designed to hold people awaiting trial and people already serving sentences.

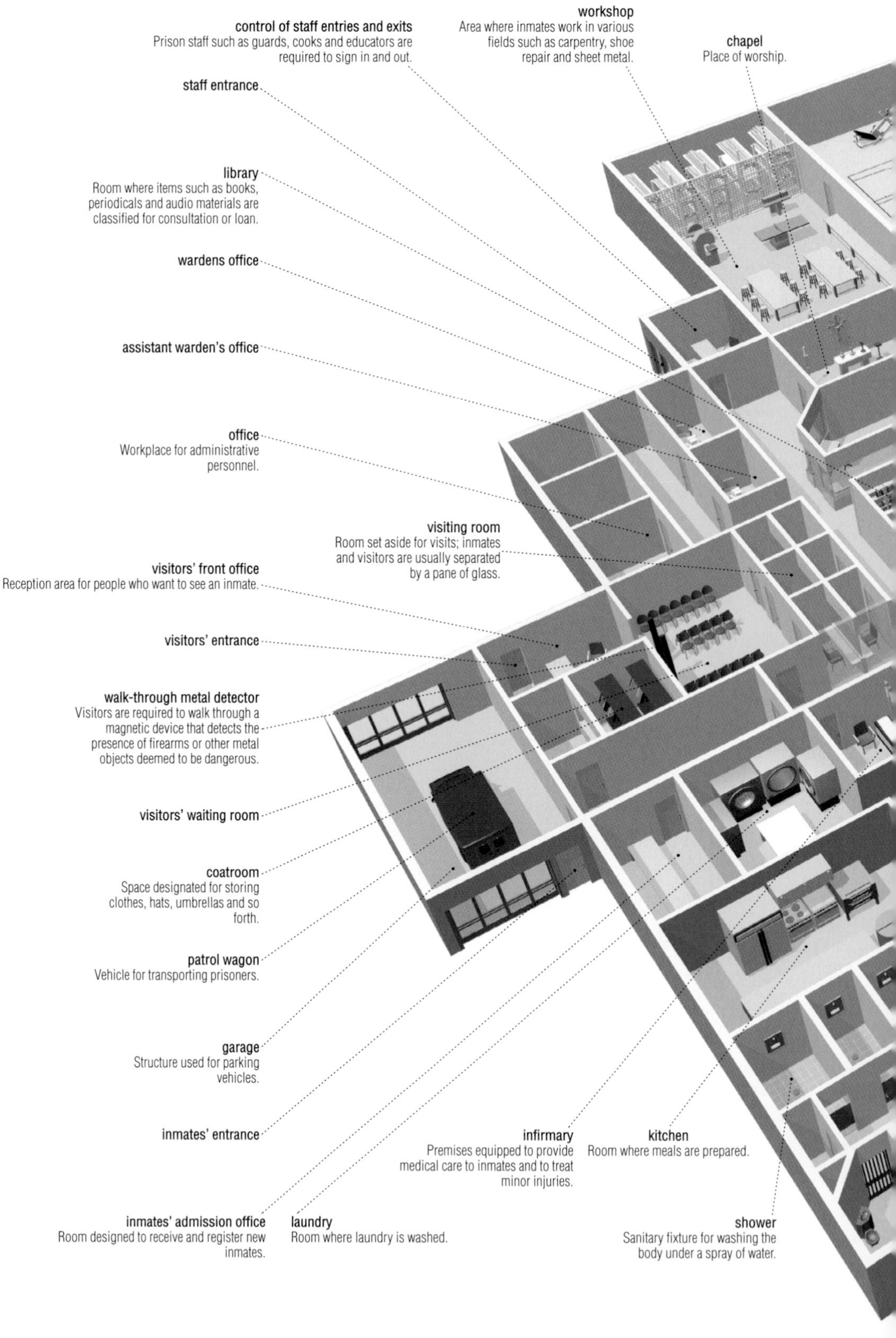
control of staff entries and exits
Prison staff such as guards, cooks and educators are required to sign in and out.
workshop
Area where inmates work in various fields such as carpentry, shoe repair and sheet metal.
chapel
Place of worship.
staff entrance
library
Room where items such as books, periodicals and audio materials are classified for consultation or loan.
wardens office
assistant warden's office
office
Workplace for administrative personnel.
visiting room
Room set aside for visits; inmates and visitors are usually separated by a pane of glass.
visitors' front office
Reception area for people who want to see an inmate.
visitors' entrance
walk-through metal detector
Visitors are required to walk through a magnetic device that detects the presence of firearms or other metal objects deemed to be dangerous.
visitors' waiting room
coatroom
Space designated for storing clothes, hats, umbrellas and so forth.
patrol wagon
Vehicle for transporting prisoners.
garage
Structure used for parking vehicles.
inmates' entrance
infirmary
Premises equipped to provide medical care to inmates and to treat minor injuries.
kitchen
Room where meals are prepared.
inmates' admission office
Room designed to receive and register new inmates.
laundry
Room where laundry is washed.
shower
Sanitary fixture for washing the body under a spray of water.

SOCIETY

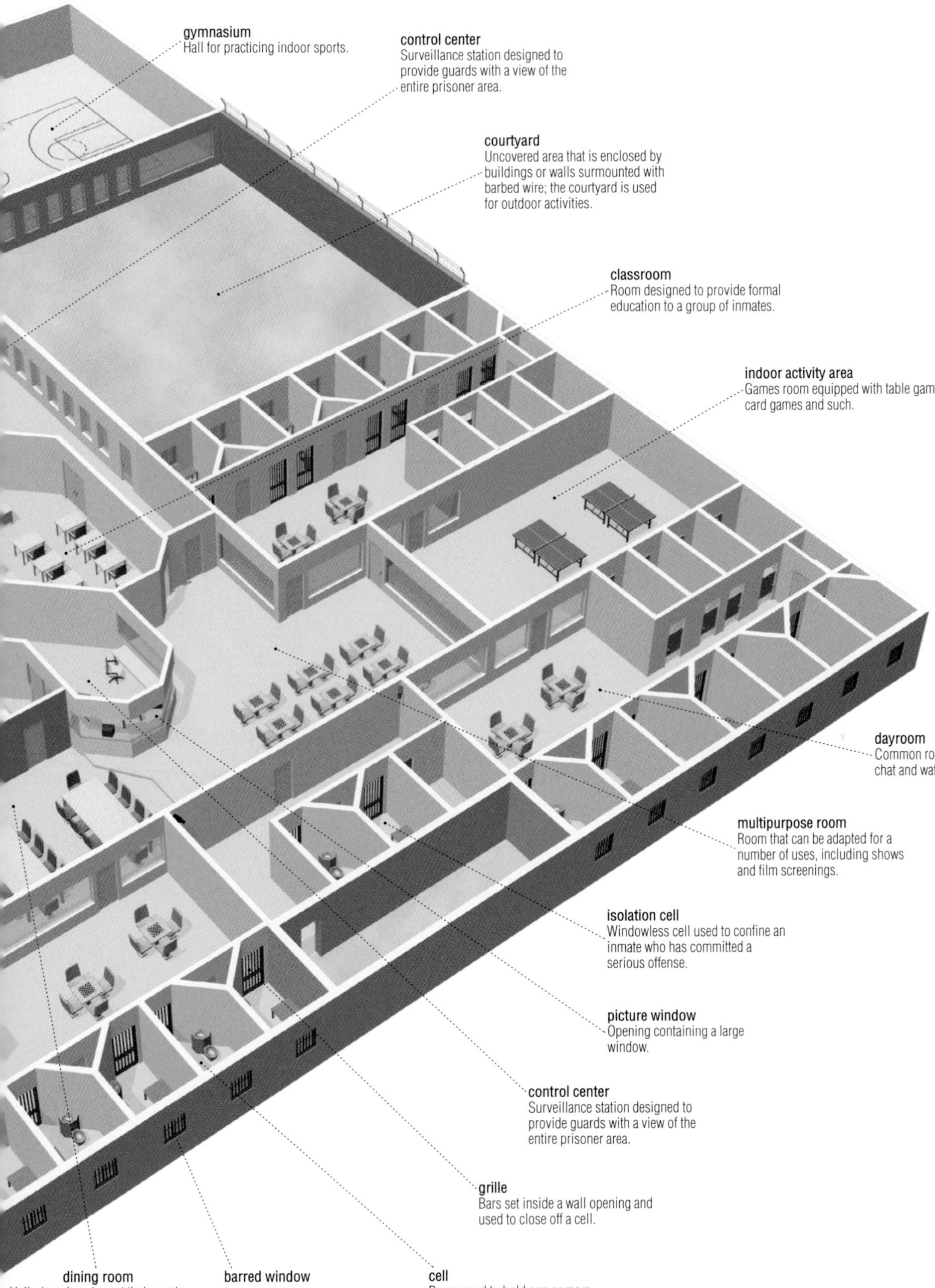
gymnasium
Hall for practicing indoor sports.
control center
Surveillance station designed to provide guards with a view of the entire prisoner area.
courtyard
Uncovered area that is enclosed by buildings or walls surmounted with barbed wire; the courtyard is used for outdoor activities.
classroom
Room designed to provide formal education to a group of inmates.
indoor activity area
Games room equipped with table games, card games and such.
dayroom
Common room used by inmates to chat and watch television.
multipurpose room
Room that can be adapted for a number of uses, including shows and film screenings.
isolation cell
Windowless cell used to confine an inmate who has committed a serious offense.
picture window
Opening containing a large window.
control center
Surveillance station designed to provide guards with a view of the entire prisoner area.
grille
Bars set inside a wall opening and used to close off a cell.
dining room
Hall where inmates eat their meals.
barred window
cell
Room used to hold one or more inmates.

court

Place where trials are held before a judge and sometimes a jury to determine if a person accused of a crime is guilty or innocent.

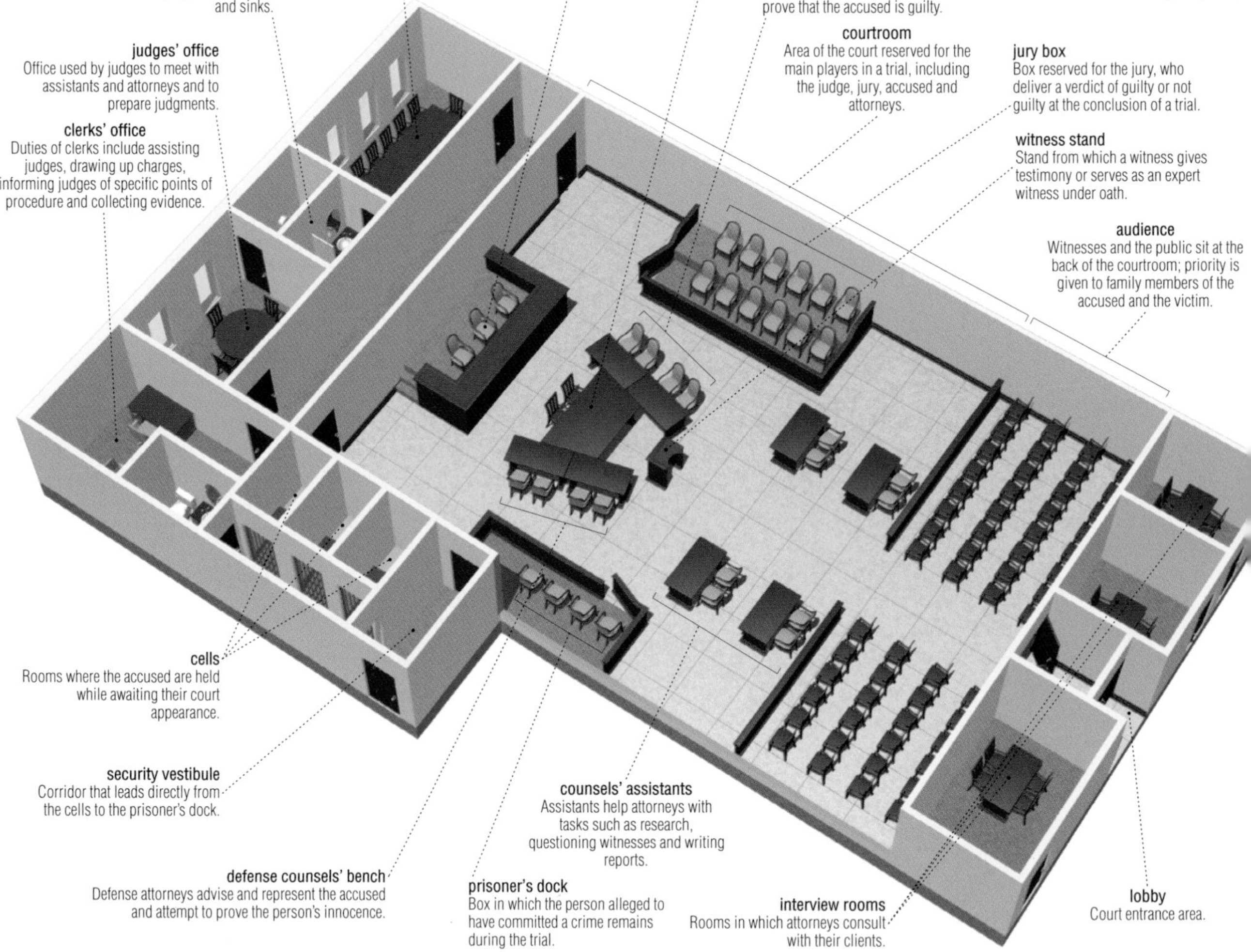
judges' bench
Judges preside over trials and ensure that proceedings are in accordance with the law; at the conclusion of a trial, the judge delivers a verdict and a sentence if the verdict is guilty.
jurors' room
Room in which jurors deliberate; jurors are citizens selected at random, usually from voters' lists.
clerks' desk
Table where clerks sit to record the proceedings.
toilet
Premises designed to satisfy basic functions and equipped with toilets and sinks.
prosecution counsels' bench
Prosecuting attorneys ensure that laws are enforced on behalf of society; they attemp prove that the accused is guilty.
judges' office
Office used by judges to meet with assistants and attorneys and to prepare judgments.
courtroom
Area of the court reserved for the main players in a trial, including the judge, jury, accused and attorneys.
jury box
Box reserved for the jury, who deliver a verdict of guilty or not guilty at the conclusion of a trial.
clerks' office
Duties of clerks include assisting judges, drawing up charges, informing judges of specific points of procedure and collecting evidence.
witness stand
Stand from which a witness gives testimony or serves as an expert witness under oath.
audience
Witnesses and the public sit at the back of the courtroom; priority is given to family members of the accused and the victim.
cells
Rooms where the accused are held while awaiting their court appearance.
security vestibule
Corridor that leads directly from the cells to the prisoner's dock.
counsels' assistants
Assistants help attorneys with tasks such as research, questioning witnesses and writing reports.
defense counsels' bench
Defense attorneys advise and represent the accused and attempt to prove the person's innocence.
prisoner's dock
Box in which the person alleged to have committed a crime remains during the trial.
interview rooms
Rooms in which attorneys consult with their clients.
lobby
Court entrance area.

examples of currency abbreviations

Currency abbreviation: abbreviation assigned to the currency of a country or group of countries; its reference value is guaranteed by a competent authority, usually a central bank.

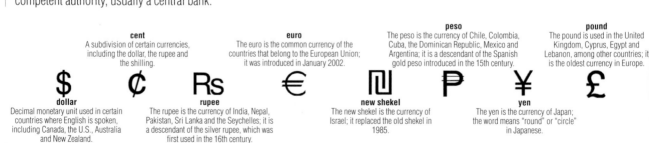

$ **dollar**
Decimal monetary unit used in certain countries where English is spoken, including Canada, the U.S., Australia and New Zealand.

¢ **cent**
A subdivision of certain currencies, including the dollar, the rupee and the shilling.

Rs **rupee**
The rupee is the currency of India, Nepal, Pakistan, Sri Lanka and the Seychelles; it is a descendant of the silver rupee, which was first used in the 16th century.

€ **euro**
The euro is the common currency of the countries that belong to the European Union; it was introduced in January 2002.

₪ **new shekel**
The new shekel is the currency of Israel; it replaced the old shekel in 1985.

₱ **peso**
The peso is the currency of Chile, Colombia, Cuba, the Dominican Republic, Mexico and Argentina; it is a descendant of the Spanish gold peso introduced in the 15th century.

¥ **yen**
The yen is the currency of Japan; the word means "round" or "circle" in Japanese.

£ **pound**
The pound is used in the United Kingdom, Cyprus, Egypt and Lebanon, among other countries; it is the oldest currency in Europe.

money and modes of payment

All the legal instruments of payment issued by a bank.

coin: obverse
The coin is currency in the form of embossed metal; specific coins are characterized by their value, appearance, weight and diameter.

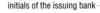

date
The year a coin was issued.

edge
Surface forming the thickness of a coin; it can be smooth, grooved or engraved.

banknote: front
A banknote is paper currency issued by a country's central bank or by an economic community.

initials of the issuing bank

security thread
A feature to prevent counterfeiting; a dark line that is visible in transmitted light is inserted into the paper.

hologram foil strip
A feature to prevent counterfeiting; the image on the strip changes when the banknote is tilted.

official signature
Banknotes are signed by people such as the central bank's governor (Canada) or president (EU) or the Secretary of the Treasury (U.S.).

watermark
A feature to prevent counterfeiting; an image that is visible in transmitted light is incorporated into the paper.

color shifting ink
A feature to prevent counterfeiting; a special ink is used that changes color when viewed from various angles.

portrait
Portrait of a famous person such as a prime minister, president, king or queen that appears on a banknote.

serial number
Each banknote is identified by a unique combination of numbers and letters.

coin: reverse

outer ring
Slightly raised ring marking the edge of a coin.

denomination
A coin's value is indicated on the reverse.

banknote: back

flag of the European Union

serial number
Each banknote is identified by a unique combination of numbers and letters.

motto
Saying or maxim that symbolizes a country or expresses an idea or a common experience.

denomination
The value of a banknote is indicated on the front and back.

name of the currency

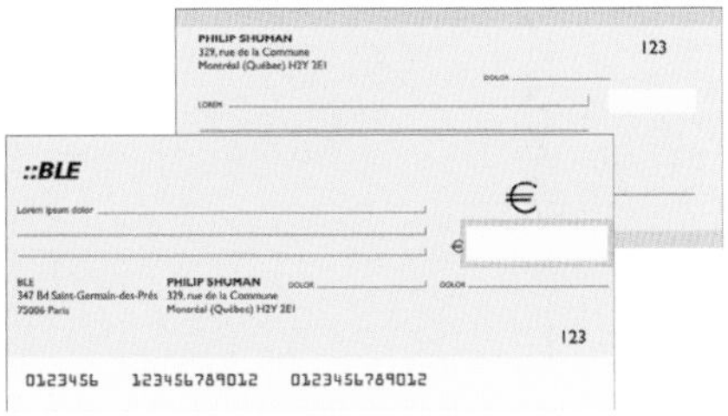

checks
Written documents by which the owner of the funds authorizes the bank to pay a third party a specific sum from the owner's account.

traveler's check
Check for a specific amount that is issued by a bank and used by travelers in lieu of cash.

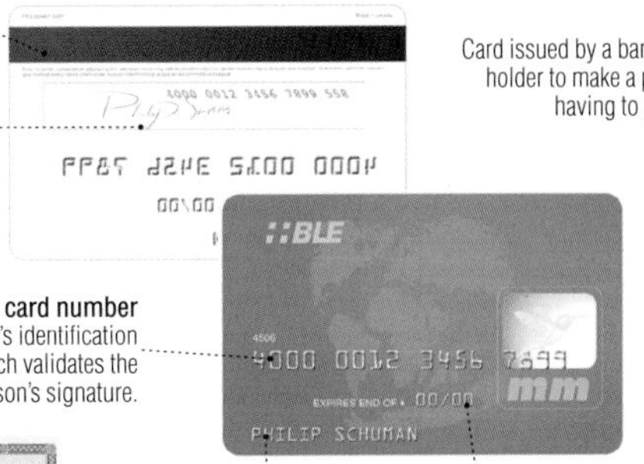

magnetic stripe
Band containing the information required to use a credit card.

cardholder's signature

credit card
Card issued by a bank that allows the holder to make a purchase without having to pay immediately.

card number
The card holder's identification number, which validates the person's signature.

cardholder's name
Name of the credit card holder.

expiration date
Date (month and year) beyond which the card is no longer valid.

bank

Establishment that provides a variety of financial services.

cash dispenser
Machine used to obtain money using a debit card.

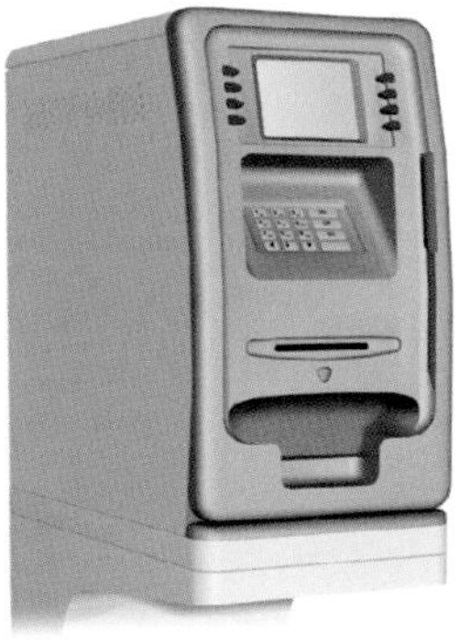

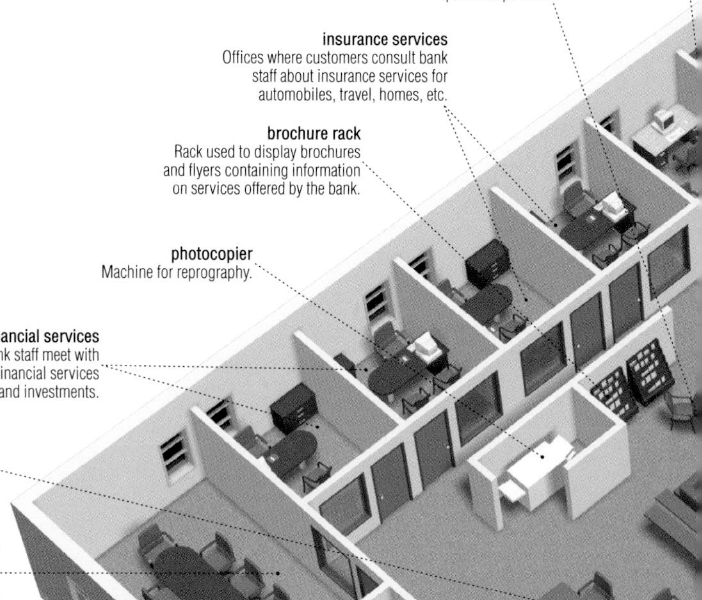

professional training office
Room reserved for providing training for bank employees.

waiting area
Space reserved for customers waiting for an appointment in a specific department.

insurance services
Offices where customers consult bank staff about insurance services for automobiles, travel, homes, etc.

brochure rack
Rack used to display brochures and flyers containing information on services offered by the bank.

photocopier
Machine for reprography.

financial services
Offices where bank staff meet with customers to discuss financial services such as mortgages and investments.

information desk
Kiosk where customers can obtain information about banking services.

conference room
Room that is big enough to hold a relatively large number of people.

reception desk
Area where customers are met.

loan services
Offices where bank staff meet with customers who are applying for a loan.

meeting room
Room used by small groups to hold meetings and discussions.

security grille
Sliding or folding bars that isolate the bank's automatic teller machines when the bank is closed.

lobby
The bank's entrance area.

automatic teller machine (ATM)
Machine where customers use a bank card or debit card to carry out banking operations such as withdrawals, deposits, transfers and bill payments.

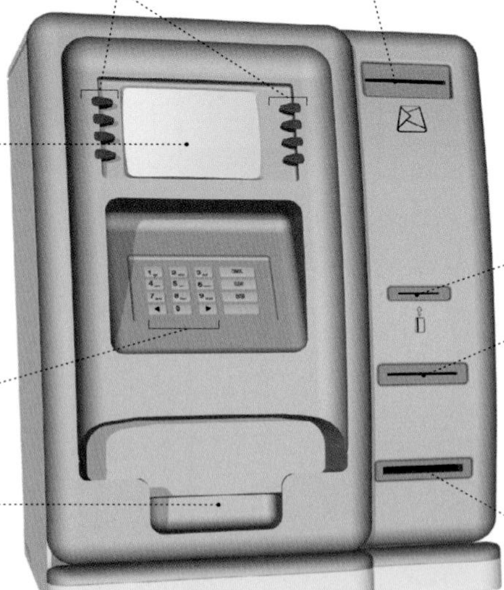

operation keys
Keys for using an on-screen menu to choose from items such as accounts, withdrawals, deposits and account balances.

deposit slot
Cash and check deposits and bill payments are enclosed in an envelope and inserted into this slot.

display
Screen featuring various menus and indicating the steps to follow to complete a transaction.

alphanumeric keyboard
Series of keys corresponding to letters and numbers that the customer uses to enter personal data such as a personal identification number and a transaction amount.

bill presenter
The machine is equipped with an optical device that calculates the number of banknotes to be issued.

card reader slot
The card is inserted into the device, which verifies the customer's personal identification number (PIN) before the transaction can begin.

transaction record slot
Receipt or record of a transaction that is printed after the transaction is complete.

passbook update slot
Customers can print out their account balances before or after a transaction.

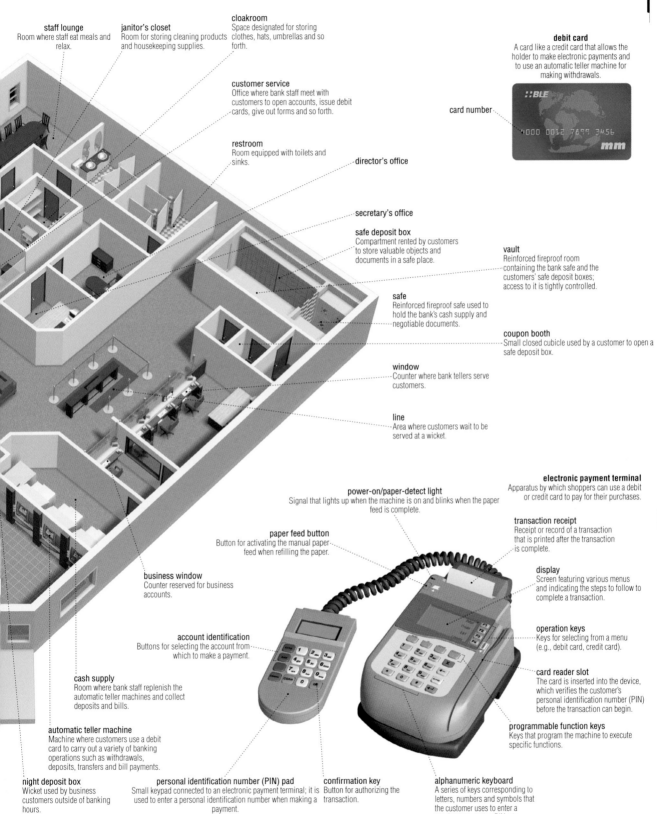

bank

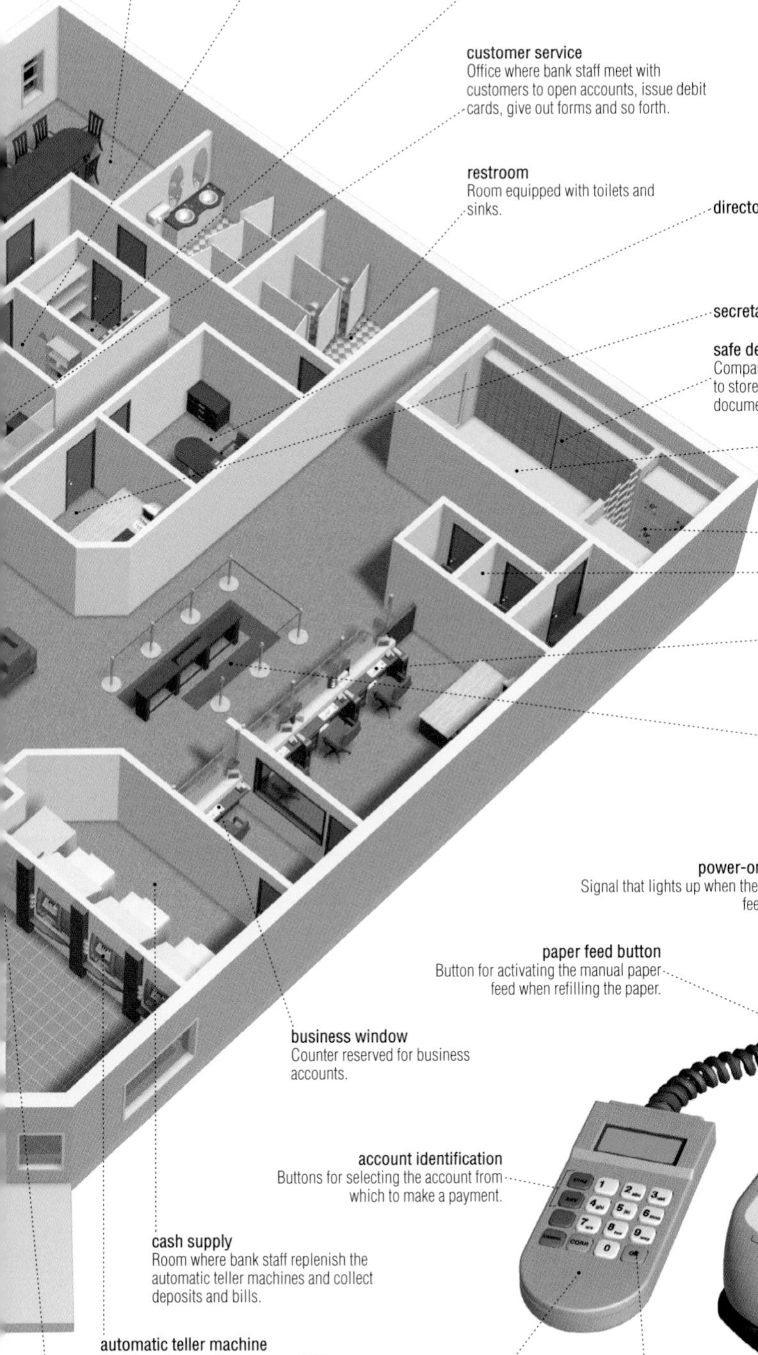

staff lounge
Room where staff eat meals and relax.

janitor's closet
Room for storing cleaning products and housekeeping supplies.

cloakroom
Space designated for storing clothes, hats, umbrellas and so forth.

customer service
Office where bank staff meet with customers to open accounts, issue debit cards, give out forms and so forth.

restroom
Room equipped with toilets and sinks.

director's office

secretary's office

safe deposit box
Compartment rented by customers to store valuable objects and documents in a safe place.

vault
Reinforced fireproof room containing the bank safe and the customers' safe deposit boxes; access to it is tightly controlled.

safe
Reinforced fireproof safe used to hold the bank's cash supply and negotiable documents.

coupon booth
Small closed cubicle used by a customer to open a safe deposit box.

window
Counter where bank tellers serve customers.

line
Area where customers wait to be served at a wicket.

business window
Counter reserved for business accounts.

cash supply
Room where bank staff replenish the automatic teller machines and collect deposits and bills.

automatic teller machine
Machine where customers use a debit card to carry out a variety of banking operations such as withdrawals, deposits, transfers and bill payments.

night deposit box
Wicket used by business customers outside of banking hours.

debit card
A card like a credit card that allows the holder to make electronic payments and to use an automatic teller machine for making withdrawals.

card number

electronic payment terminal
Apparatus by which shoppers can use a debit or credit card to pay for their purchases.

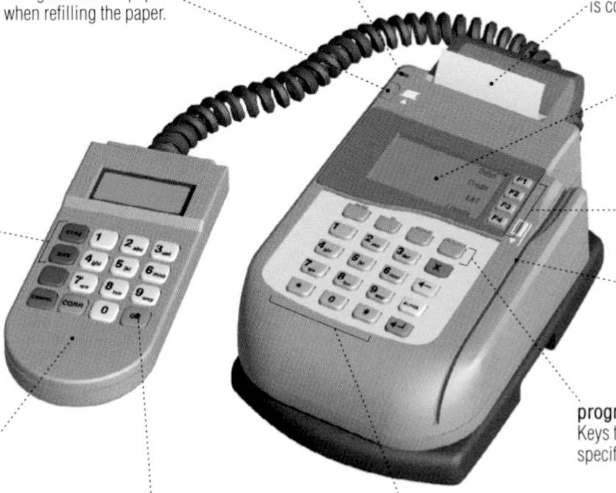

power-on/paper-detect light
Signal that lights up when the machine is on and blinks when the paper feed is complete.

paper feed button
Button for activating the manual paper feed when refilling the paper.

transaction receipt
Receipt or record of a transaction that is printed after the transaction is complete.

display
Screen featuring various menus and indicating the steps to follow to complete a transaction.

operation keys
Keys for selecting from a menu (e.g., debit card, credit card).

card reader slot
The card is inserted into the device, which verifies the customer's personal identification number (PIN) before the transaction can begin.

programmable function keys
Keys that program the machine to execute specific functions.

account identification
Buttons for selecting the account from which to make a payment.

personal identification number (PIN) pad
Small keypad connected to an electronic payment terminal; it is used to enter a personal identification number when making a payment.

confirmation key
Button for authorizing the transaction.

alphanumeric keyboard
A series of keys corresponding to letters, numbers and symbols that the customer uses to enter a purchase amount, a PIN, etc.

library

Room where items such as books, periodicals and audio materials are classified for consultation or loan.

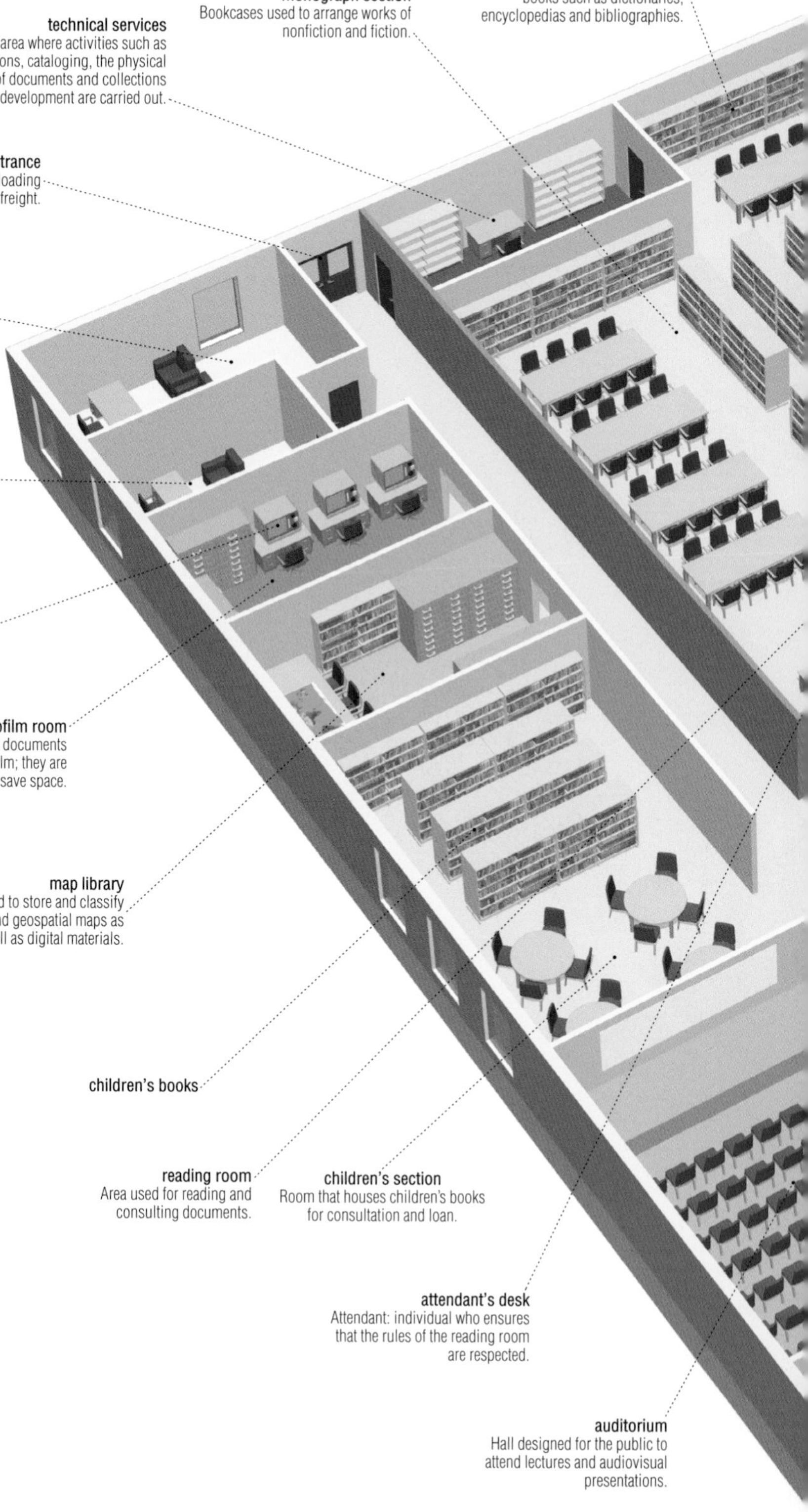
reference books
Bookcases for shelving reference books such as dictionaries, encyclopedias and bibliographies.
monograph section
Bookcases used to arrange works of nonfiction and fiction.
technical services
Staff area where activities such as acquisitions, cataloging, the physical preparation of documents and collections development are carried out.
service entrance
Entrance area used for unloading freight.
director's office
librarian's office
The librarian is responsible for the administration of the library and the development, organization and management of its collection.
microfilm reader
Device that magnifies the text reproduced on film.
microfilm room
Room used to consult documents reproduced on film; they are archived this way to save space.
map library
Room used to store and classify geographic and geospatial maps as well as digital materials.
children's books
reading room
Area used for reading and consulting documents.
children's section
Room that houses children's books for consultation and loan.
attendant's desk
Attendant: individual who ensures that the rules of the reading room are respected.
auditorium
Hall designed for the public to attend lectures and audiovisual presentations.

SOCIETY

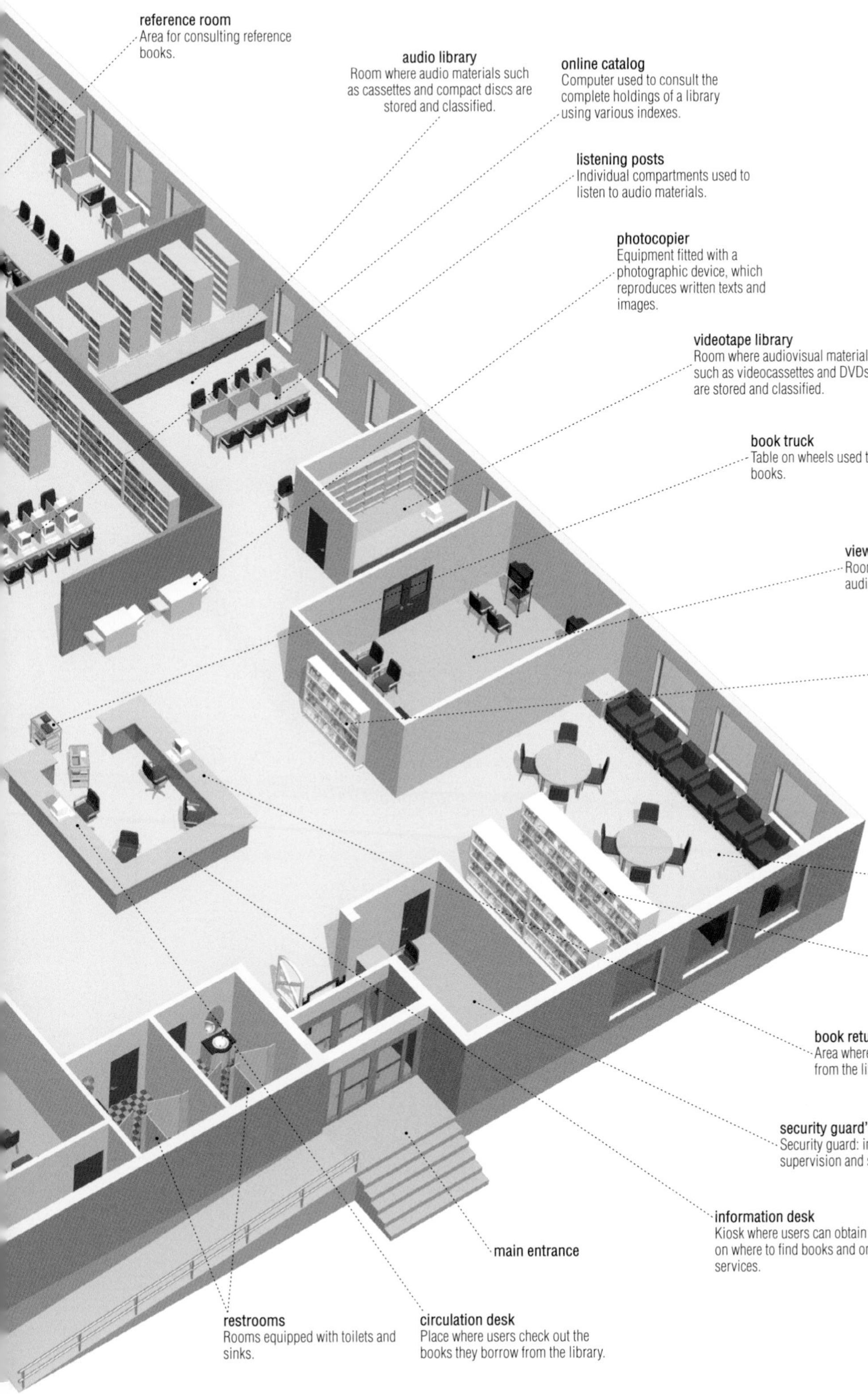
reference room
Area for consulting reference books.
audio library
Room where audio materials such as cassettes and compact discs are stored and classified.
online catalog
Computer used to consult the complete holdings of a library using various indexes.
listening posts
Individual compartments used to listen to audio materials.
photocopier
Equipment fitted with a photographic device, which reproduces written texts and images.
videotape library
Room where audiovisual materials such as videocassettes and DVDs are stored and classified.
book truck
Table on wheels used to move books.
viewing room
Room equipped for consulting audiovisual materials.
new book shelf
Shelving used to display recent acquisitions.
periodicals room
Room reserved for consulting newspapers and periodicals.
periodicals shelf
Shelving used to display recent periodicals.
book return desk
Area where users return books borrowed from the library.
security guard's office
Security guard: individual responsible for supervision and security.
information desk
Kiosk where users can obtain information on where to find books and on library services.
main entrance
restrooms
Rooms equipped with toilets and sinks.
circulation desk
Place where users check out the books they borrow from the library.

school

Teaching institution; the term "school" usually refers to an elementary or high school.

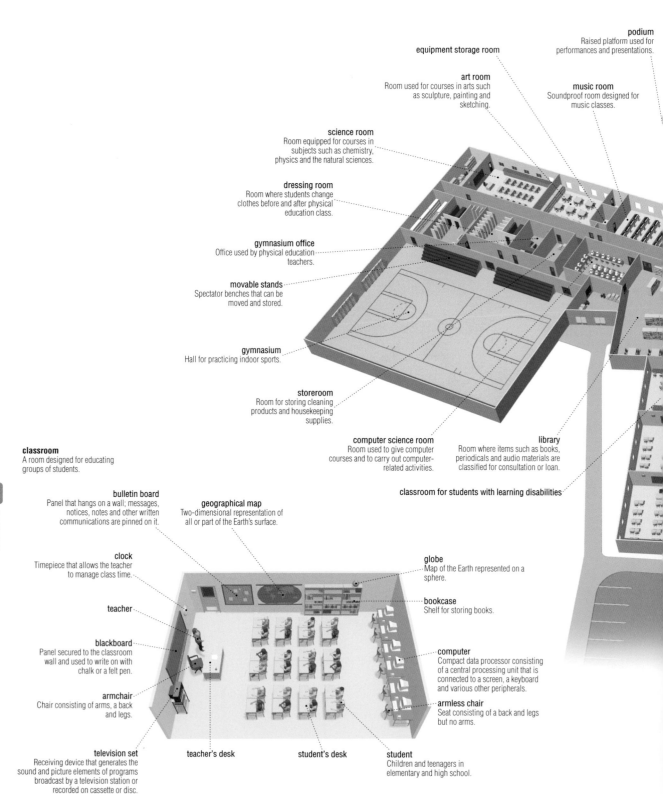

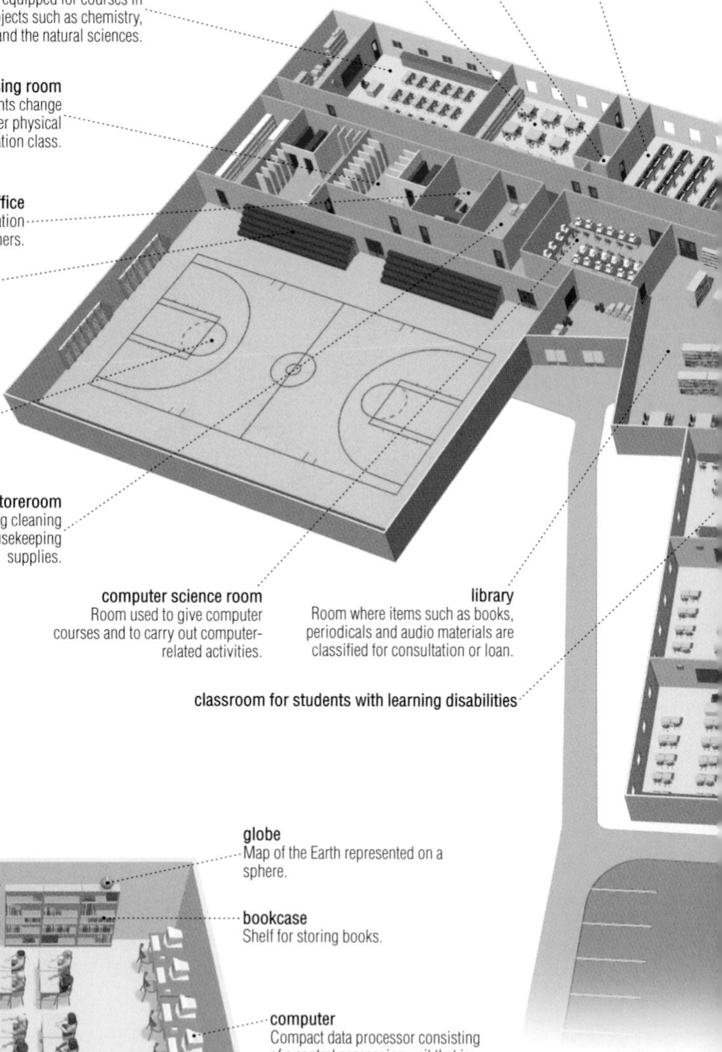
podium
Raised platform used for performances and presentations.
equipment storage room
art room
Room used for courses in arts such as sculpture, painting and sketching.
music room
Soundproof room designed for music classes.
science room
Room equipped for courses in subjects such as chemistry, physics and the natural sciences.
dressing room
Room where students change clothes before and after physical education class.
gymnasium office
Office used by physical education teachers.
movable stands
Spectator benches that can be moved and stored.
gymnasium
Hall for practicing indoor sports.
storeroom
Room for storing cleaning products and housekeeping supplies.
computer science room
Room used to give computer courses and to carry out computer-related activities.
library
Room where items such as books, periodicals and audio materials are classified for consultation or loan.
classroom for students with learning disabilities

classroom
A room designed for educating groups of students.

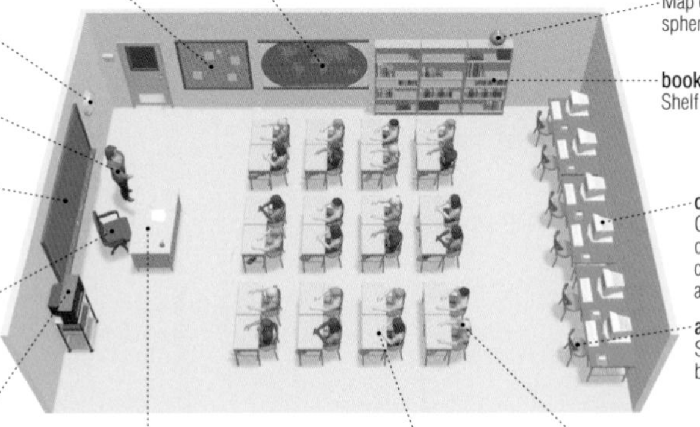
bulletin board
Panel that hangs on a wall; messages, notices, notes and other written communications are pinned on it.
geographical map
Two-dimensional representation of all or part of the Earth's surface.
clock
Timepiece that allows the teacher to manage class time.
teacher
blackboard
Panel secured to the classroom wall and used to write on with chalk or a felt pen.
armchair
Chair consisting of arms, a back and legs.
television set
Receiving device that generates the sound and picture elements of programs broadcast by a television station or recorded on cassette or disc.
teacher's desk
student's desk
student
Children and teenagers in elementary and high school.
globe
Map of the Earth represented on a sphere.
bookcase
Shelf for storing books.
computer
Compact data processor consisting of a central processing unit that is connected to a screen, a keyboard and various other peripherals.
armless chair
Seat consisting of a back and legs but no arms.

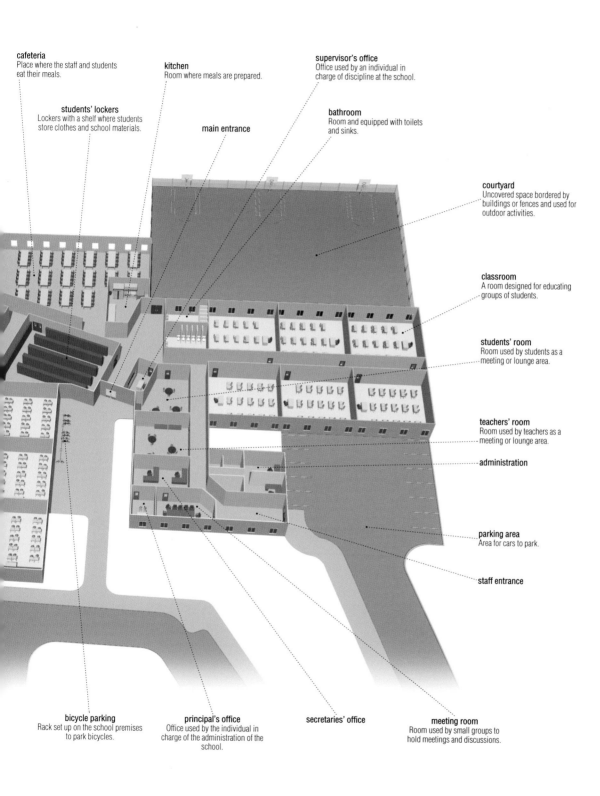

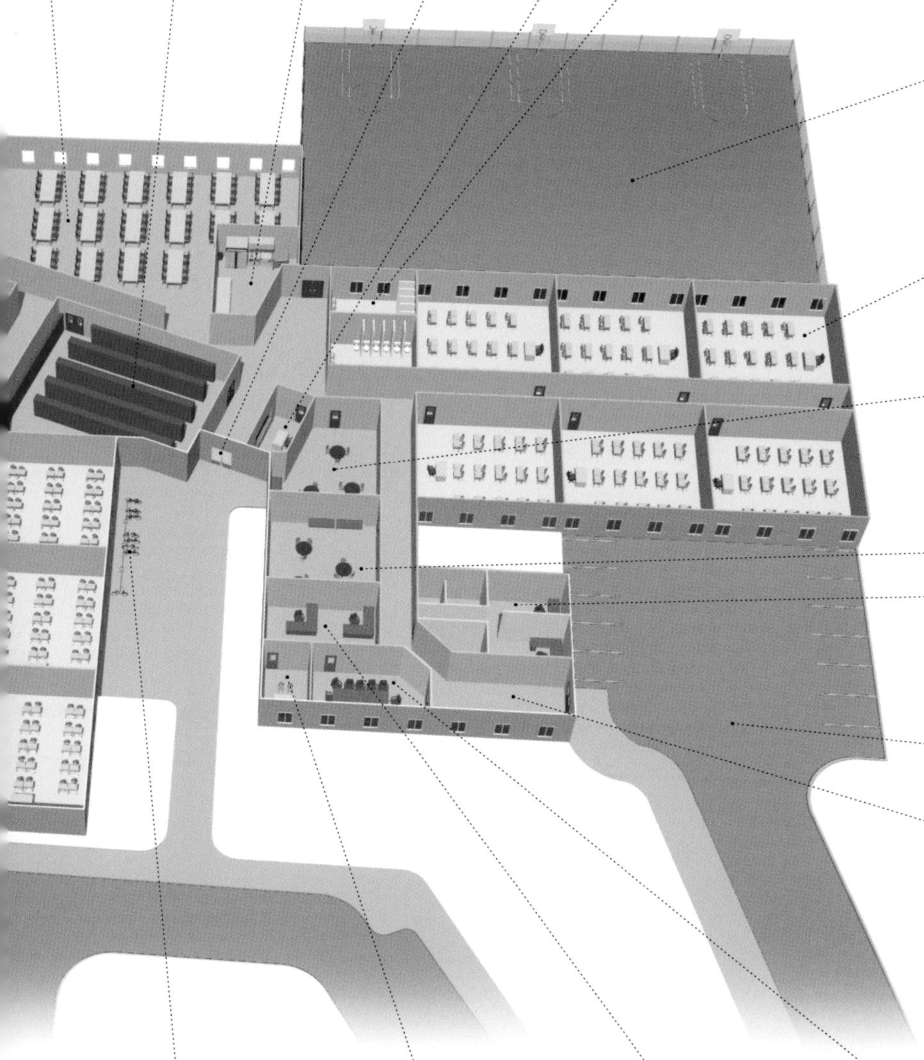
cafeteria
Place where the staff and students eat their meals.
kitchen
Room where meals are prepared.
supervisor's office
Office used by an individual in charge of discipline at the school.
students' lockers
Lockers with a shelf where students store clothes and school materials.
main entrance
bathroom
Room and equipped with toilets and sinks.
courtyard
Uncovered space bordered by buildings or fences and used for outdoor activities.
classroom
A room designed for educating groups of students.
students' room
Room used by students as a meeting or lounge area.
teachers' room
Room used by teachers as a meeting or lounge area.
administration
parking area
Area for cars to park.
staff entrance
bicycle parking
Rack set up on the school premises to park bicycles.
principal's office
Office used by the individual in charge of the administration of the school.
secretaries' office
meeting room
Room used by small groups to hold meetings and discussions.

chronology of religions

Religions have usually been signalized by a prophet or an event; they have overlapped and influenced one another throughout the course of history.

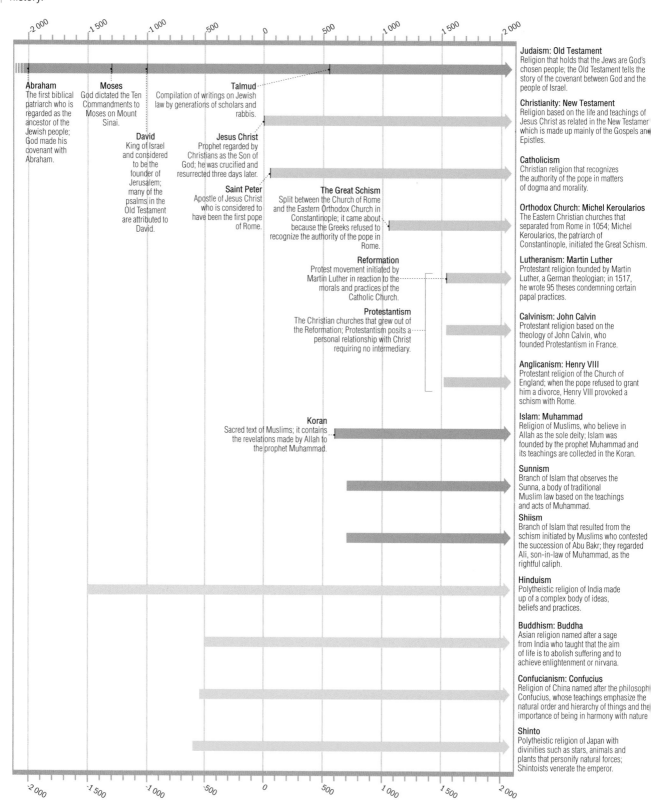

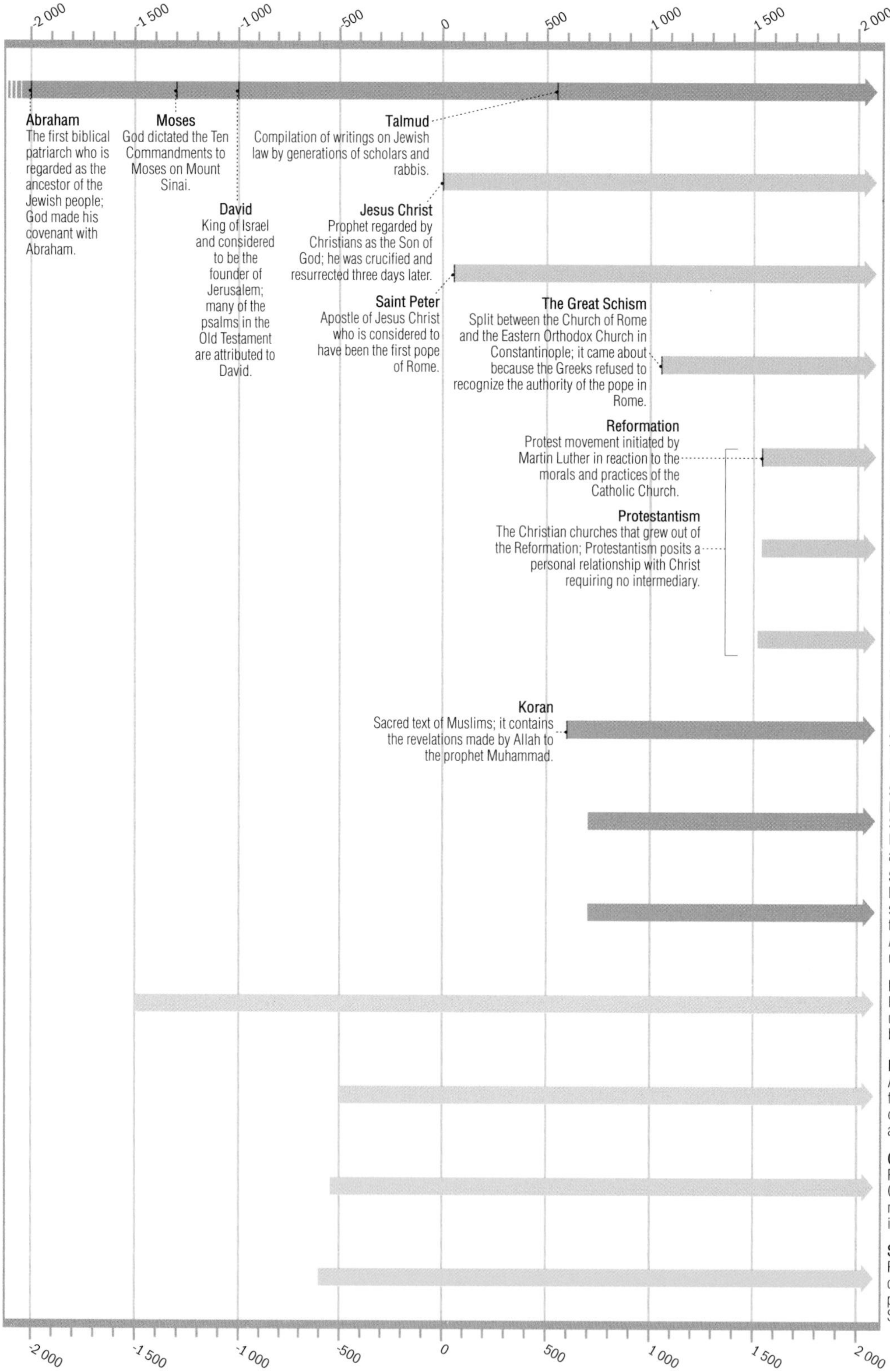
-2 000
-1 500
-1 000
-500
0
500
1 000
1 500
2 000
Abraham
The first biblical patriarch who is regarded as the ancestor of the Jewish people; God made his covenant with Abraham.
Moses
God dictated the Ten Commandments to Moses on Mount Sinai.
Talmud
Compilation of writings on Jewish law by generations of scholars and rabbis.
David
King of Israel and considered to be the founder of Jerusalem; many of the psalms in the Old Testament are attributed to David.
Jesus Christ
Prophet regarded by Christians as the Son of God; he was crucified and resurrected three days later.
Saint Peter
Apostle of Jesus Christ who is considered to have been the first pope of Rome.
The Great Schism
Split between the Church of Rome and the Eastern Orthodox Church in Constantinople; it came about because the Greeks refused to recognize the authority of the pope in Rome.
Reformation
Protest movement initiated by Martin Luther in reaction to the morals and practices of the Catholic Church.
Protestantism
The Christian churches that grew out of the Reformation; Protestantism posits a personal relationship with Christ requiring no intermediary.
Koran
Sacred text of Muslims; it contains the revelations made by Allah to the prophet Muhammad.

Judaism: Old Testament
Religion that holds that the Jews are God's chosen people; the Old Testament tells the story of the covenant between God and the people of Israel.

Christianity: New Testament
Religion based on the life and teachings of Jesus Christ as related in the New Testament which is made up mainly of the Gospels and Epistles.

Catholicism
Christian religion that recognizes the authority of the pope in matters of dogma and morality.

Orthodox Church: Michel Keroularios
The Eastern Christian churches that separated from Rome in 1054; Michel Keroularios, the patriarch of Constantinople, initiated the Great Schism.

Lutheranism: Martin Luther
Protestant religion founded by Martin Luther, a German theologian; in 1517, he wrote 95 theses condemning certain papal practices.

Calvinism: John Calvin
Protestant religion based on the theology of John Calvin, who founded Protestantism in France.

Anglicanism: Henry VIII
Protestant religion of the Church of England; when the pope refused to grant him a divorce, Henry VIII provoked a schism with Rome.

Islam: Muhammad
Religion of Muslims, who believe in Allah as the sole deity; Islam was founded by the prophet Muhammad and its teachings are collected in the Koran.

Sunnism
Branch of Islam that observes the Sunna, a body of traditional Muslim law based on the teachings and acts of Muhammad.

Shiism
Branch of Islam that resulted from the schism initiated by Muslims who contested the succession of Abu Bakr; they regarded Ali, son-in-law of Muhammad, as the rightful caliph.

Hinduism
Polytheistic religion of India made up of a complex body of ideas, beliefs and practices.

Buddhism: Buddha
Asian religion named after a sage from India who taught that the aim of life is to abolish suffering and to achieve enlightenment or nirvana.

Confucianism: Confucius
Religion of China named after the philosopher Confucius, whose teachings emphasize the natural order and hierarchy of things and the importance of being in harmony with nature.

Shinto
Polytheistic religion of Japan with divinities such as stars, animals and plants that personify natural forces; Shintoists venerate the emperor.

church

Place of Christian worship.

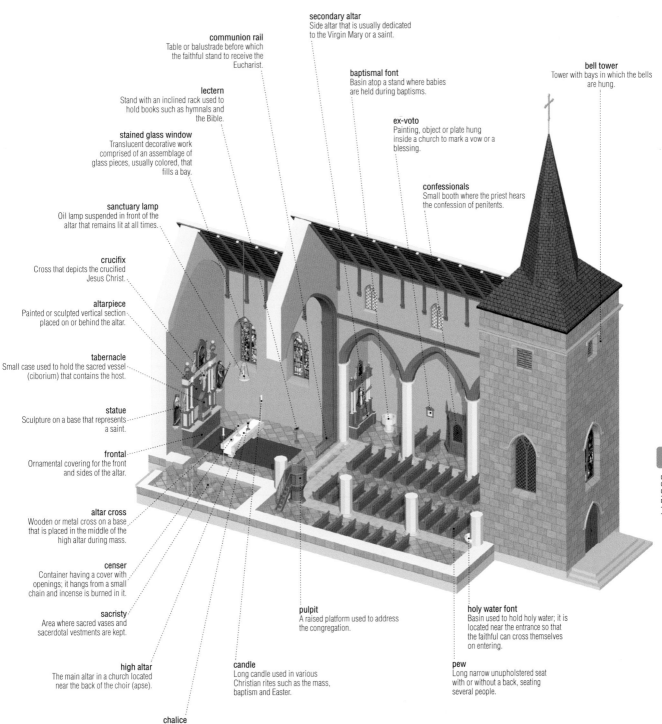

secondary altar
Side altar that is usually dedicated to the Virgin Mary or a saint.

communion rail
Table or balustrade before which the faithful stand to receive the Eucharist.

bell tower
Tower with bays in which the bells are hung.

baptismal font
Basin atop a stand where babies are held during baptisms.

lectern
Stand with an inclined rack used to hold books such as hymnals and the Bible.

ex-voto
Painting, object or plate hung inside a church to mark a vow or a blessing.

stained glass window
Translucent decorative work comprised of an assemblage of glass pieces, usually colored, that fills a bay.

confessionals
Small booth where the priest hears the confession of penitents.

sanctuary lamp
Oil lamp suspended in front of the altar that remains lit at all times.

crucifix
Cross that depicts the crucified Jesus Christ.

altarpiece
Painted or sculpted vertical section placed on or behind the altar.

tabernacle
Small case used to hold the sacred vessel (ciborium) that contains the host.

statue
Sculpture on a base that represents a saint.

frontal
Ornamental covering for the front and sides of the altar.

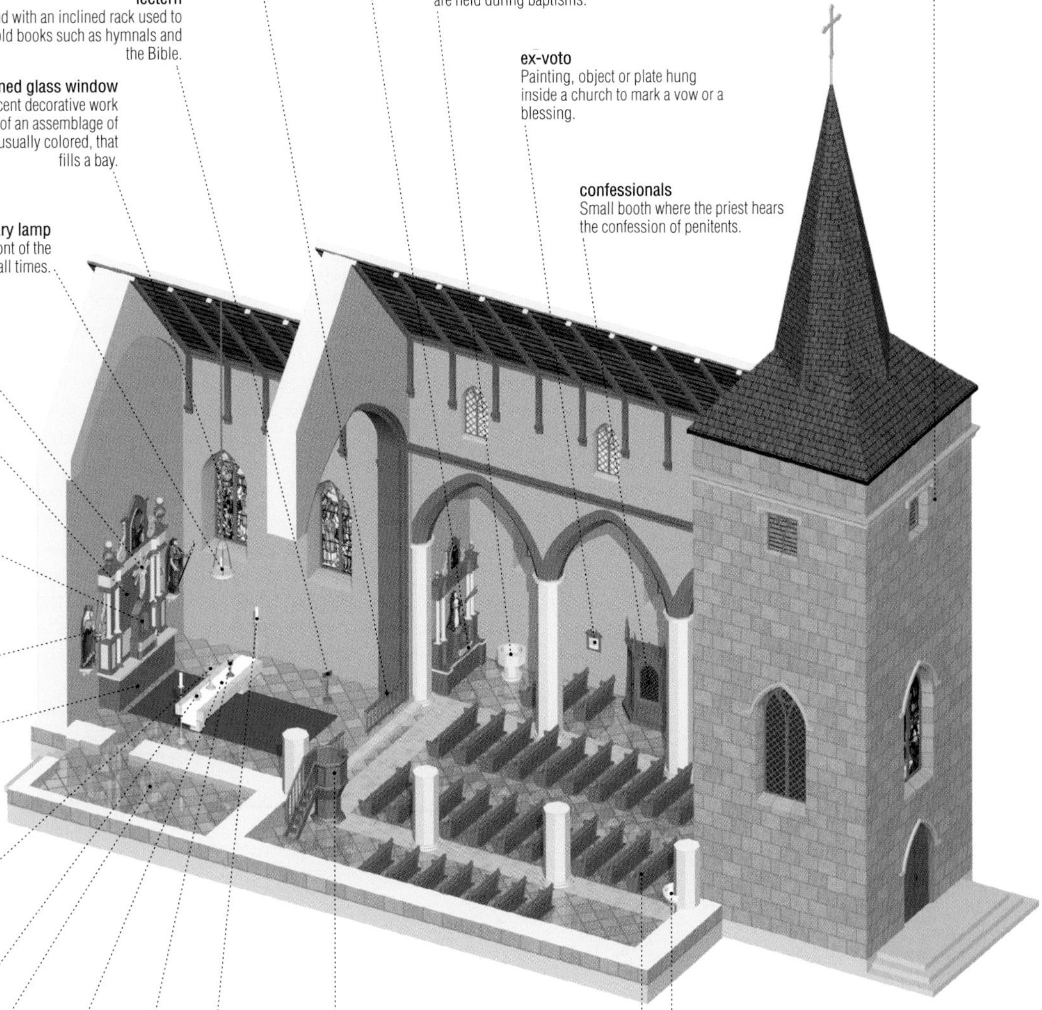

altar cross
Wooden or metal cross on a base that is placed in the middle of the high altar during mass.

censer
Container having a cover with openings; it hangs from a small chain and incense is burned in it.

sacristy
Area where sacred vases and sacerdotal vestments are kept.

pulpit
A raised platform used to address the congregation.

holy water font
Basin used to hold holy water; it is located near the entrance so that the faithful can cross themselves on entering.

high altar
The main altar in a church located near the back of the choir (apse).

candle
Long candle used in various Christian rites such as the mass, baptism and Easter.

pew
Long narrow unupholstered seat with or without a back, seating several people.

chalice
Cup in which the wine is consecrated during celebration of the mass.

synagogue

Place of worship in the Jewish religion.

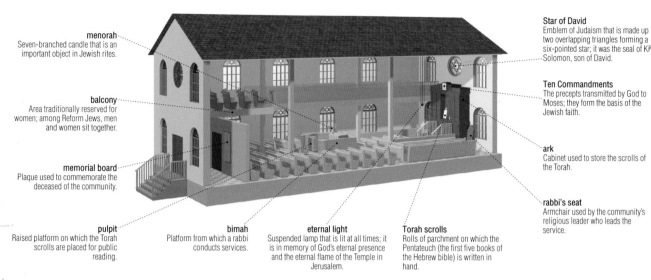

menorah
Seven-branched candle that is an important object in Jewish rites.

balcony
Area traditionally reserved for women; among Reform Jews, men and women sit together.

memorial board
Plaque used to commemorate the deceased of the community.

pulpit
Raised platform on which the Torah scrolls are placed for public reading.

bimah
Platform from which a rabbi conducts services.

eternal light
Suspended lamp that is lit at all times; it is in memory of God's eternal presence and the eternal flame of the Temple in Jerusalem.

Torah scrolls
Rolls of parchment on which the Pentateuch (the first five books of the Hebrew bible) is written in hand.

Star of David
Emblem of Judaism that is made up two overlapping triangles forming a six-pointed star; it was the seal of Ki Solomon, son of David.

Ten Commandments
The precepts transmitted by God to Moses; they form the basis of the Jewish faith.

ark
Cabinet used to store the scrolls of the Torah.

rabbi's seat
Armchair used by the community's religious leader who leads the service.

mosque

Place of worship in the Islamic religion.

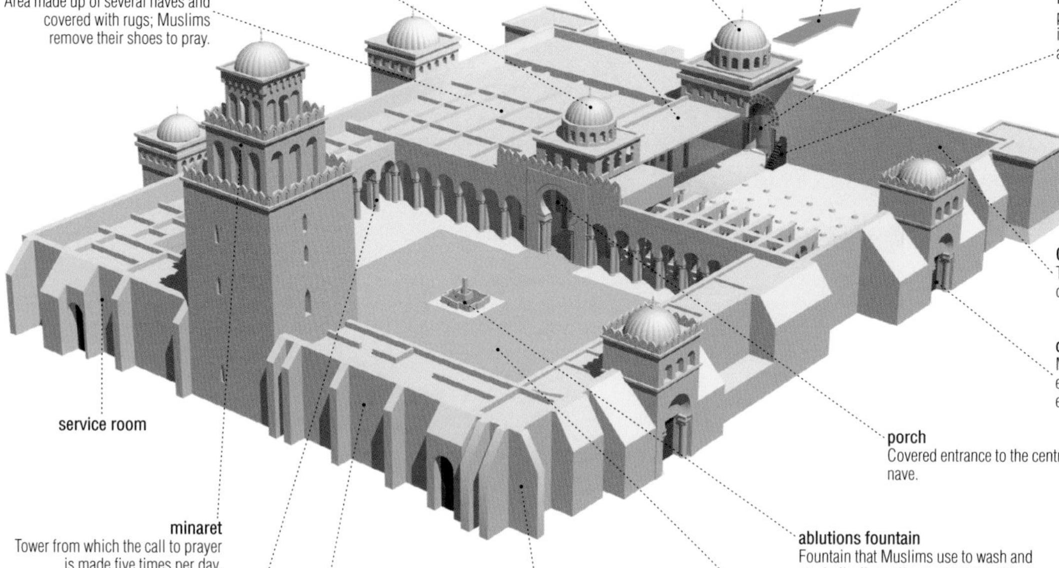

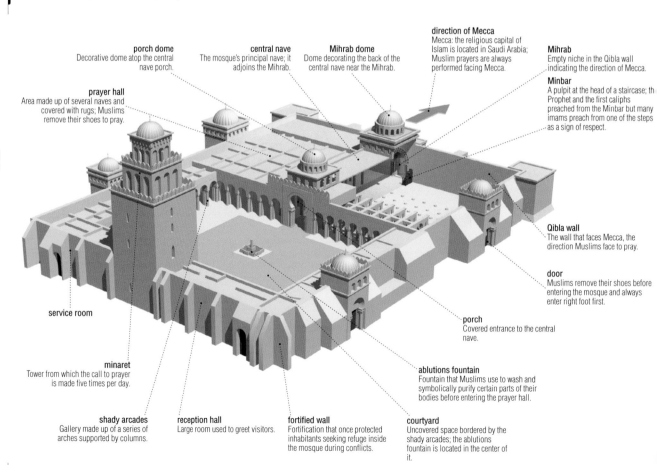

porch dome
Decorative dome atop the central nave porch.

central nave
The mosque's principal nave; it adjoins the Mihrab.

Mihrab dome
Dome decorating the back of the central nave near the Mihrab.

direction of Mecca
Mecca: the religious capital of Islam is located in Saudi Arabia; Muslim prayers are always performed facing Mecca.

Mihrab
Empty niche in the Qibla wall indicating the direction of Mecca.

Minbar
A pulpit at the head of a staircase; th Prophet and the first caliphs preached from the Minbar but many imams preach from one of the steps as a sign of respect.

prayer hall
Area made up of several naves and covered with rugs; Muslims remove their shoes to pray.

Qibla wall
The wall that faces Mecca, the direction Muslims face to pray.

door
Muslims remove their shoes before entering the mosque and always enter right foot first.

service room

porch
Covered entrance to the central nave.

minaret
Tower from which the call to prayer is made five times per day.

ablutions fountain
Fountain that Muslims use to wash and symbolically purify certain parts of their bodies before entering the prayer hall.

shady arcades
Gallery made up of a series of arches supported by columns.

reception hall
Large room used to greet visitors.

fortified wall
Fortification that once protected inhabitants seeking refuge inside the mosque during conflicts.

courtyard
Uncovered space bordered by the shady arcades; the ablutions fountain is located in the center of it.

heraldry

The study of heraldic emblems and devices used to distinguish communities and families.

parts of a flag

Flag: strip of fabric attached to a staff and bearing the emblem of a country or group.

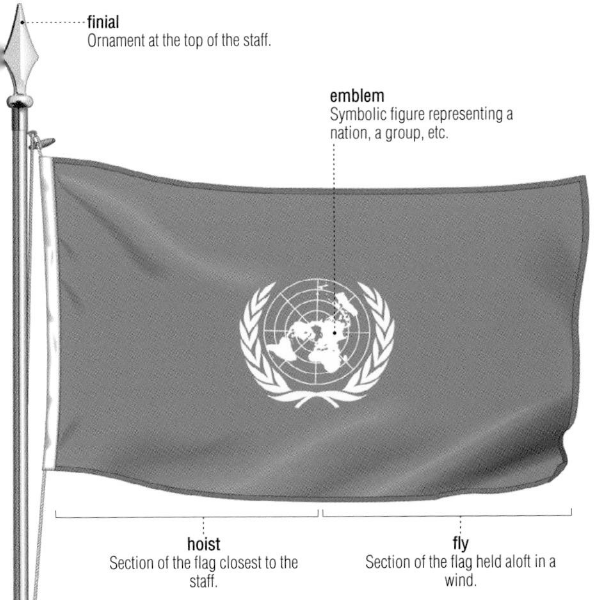
finial
Ornament at the top of the staff.
emblem
Symbolic figure representing a nation, a group, etc.
hoist
Section of the flag closest to the staff.
fly
Section of the flag held aloft in a wind.

toggle
Wooden or metal pin used to secure the flag cord to the halyard.

halyard
Cord that raises the flag.

staff
Wooden or metal arm that holds the flag.

base

flag shapes

square flag

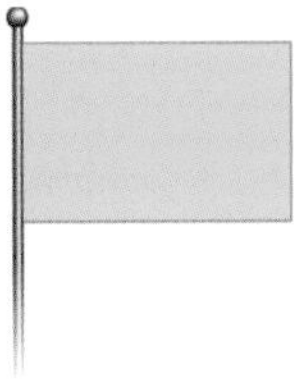

rectangular flag

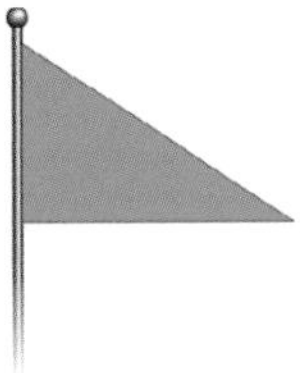

pennant
Triangular flag that the knights of the Middle Ages placed on the end of a lance when they rode off to war.

double pennant

swallowtail
Nautical flag that indicates the nationality of a vessel and the company to which it belongs; it is also used for signaling.

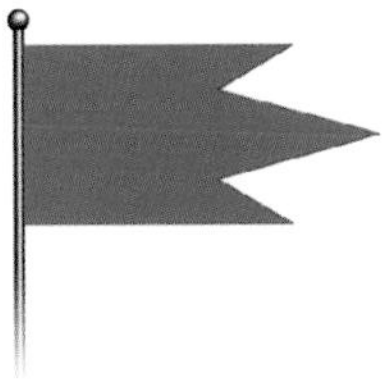

swallowtail and tongue
Flag with a long narrow piece (tongue) between two swallowtail points.

burgee
Triangular flag with two points used to indicate the affiliation of a ship.

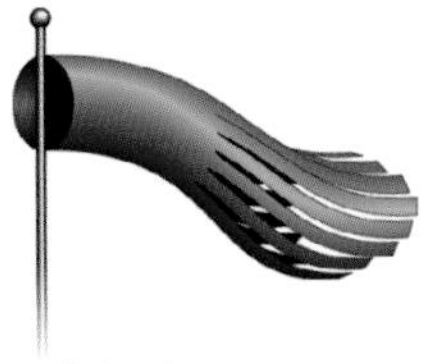

wind sock
Open-ended tube made of fabric that is used to indicate the direction and strength of the wind.

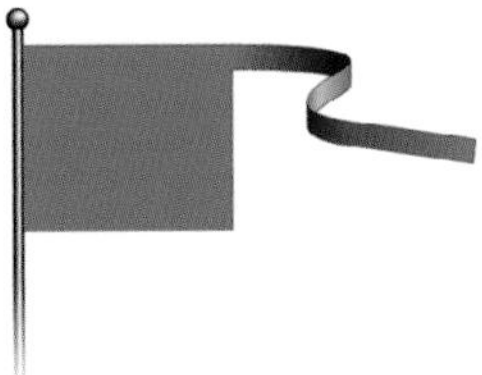

flag with Schwenkel
Square flag with a streamer extending from the top.

fanion
Small triangular flag used for a variety of purposes, such as to represent a head of state or a military unit.

gonfalon
Flag with several points parallel to the staff; in the Middle Ages, it was used as a standard to identify a lord's vassals.

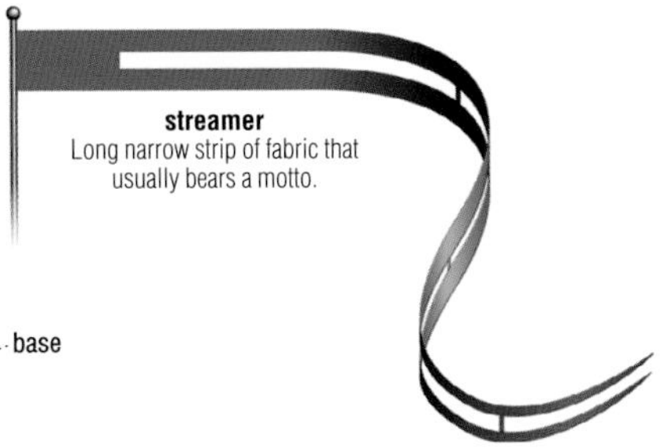

streamer
Long narrow strip of fabric that usually bears a motto.

oriflamme
Pageantry banner with several points.

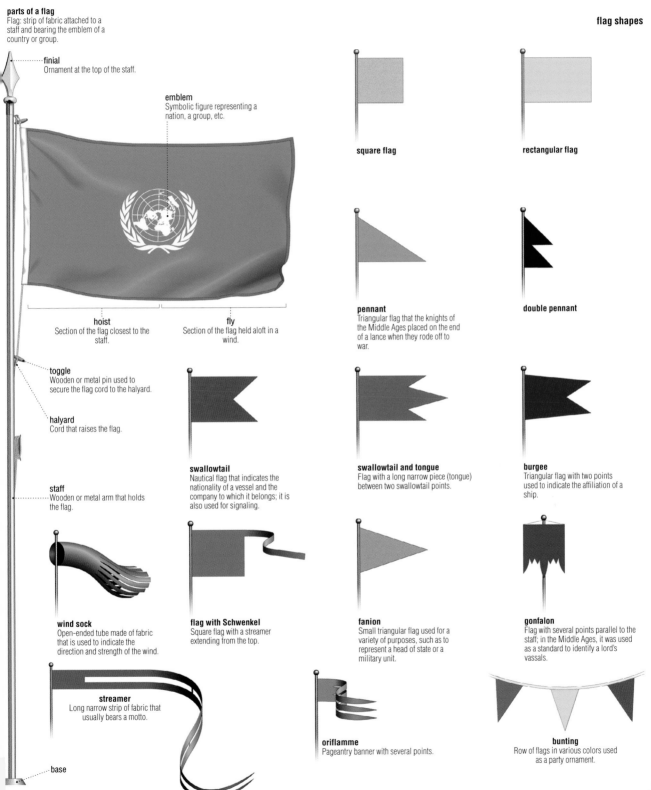

bunting
Row of flags in various colors used as a party ornament.

SOCIETY

heraldry

shield divisions

Shield: panel that is divided into nine sections and bears armorial figures.

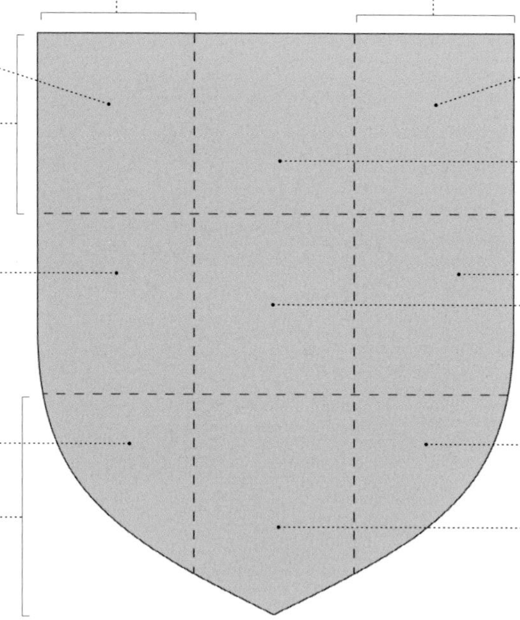
dexter
Right side of the shield (or the left side, when viewed from the front).
sinister
Left side of the shield (or the right side, when viewed from the front).
dexter chief
sinister chief
chief
The three sections that form the top of the shield.
center chief
The middle section of the chief, or the upper branch of the cross.
dexter flank
The right branch of the cross.
sinister flank
The left branch of the cross.
center point
The section located where the branches of the cross intersect.
dexter base
sinister base
base
The three sections that form the bottom of the shield.
center base
The lower branch of the cross.

examples of partitions

Partitions: divisions made by lines on the shield to form an even number of sections.

per fess
Shield divided into two sections by a horizontal line in the center.

party
Shield divided into two sections by a vertical line in the center.

per bend
Shield divided into two sections by a diagonal line from the dexter chief to the sinister base.

quarterly
Shield divided into two sections: on top, the left side of a per fess and on the bottom, the right side of a party.

examples of ordinaries

Ordinaries: divisions made by lines on the shield to form an odd number of sections.

chief
Figure covering the top third of the shield.

chevron
Figure shaped like an inverted V; its diagonal lines start in the dexter base and the sinister base and meet in the center chief.

pale
Figure covering the vertical branch of the cross.

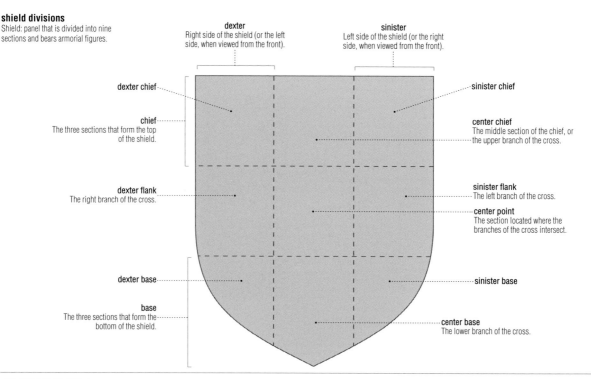

cross
Figure covering the center horizontal and vertical sections of the shield.

examples of metals
Metals: yellow represents or (gold) and white represents argent (silver).

argent
The color yellow or silver; when the shield is black and white, argent is designated by a white surface.

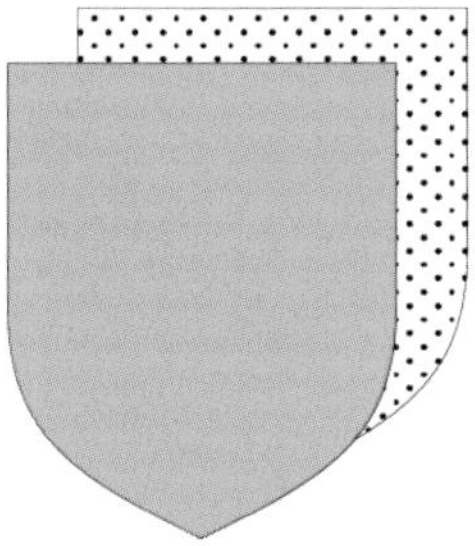

or
The color gold; when the shield is black and white, or is designated by a dotted surface.

examples of furs
Furs: combinations of colors, including metallic colors that represent fur.

ermine
Fur represented by a silver field containing sable-colored markings.

vair
Fur represented by silver and azure bells that meet where they come to a point.

examples of charges
Charge: figure represented on the shield.

fleur-de-lis
Heraldic figure often represented on old coats of arms of France and Quebec.

crescent
Crescent-shaped figure with points (horns) that usually point to the chief of the shield.

lion passant
The lion is the animal most often depicted in heraldry and symbolizes strength and courage; the lion passant is a walking lion.

eagle
The eagle is the bird most often depicted in heraldry and symbolizes power; when the tips of the wings point downward, they are said to be conjoined in lure.

mullet
Five-pointed star whose top point is directed toward the center chief.

examples of colors
Colors: colors other than metallic.

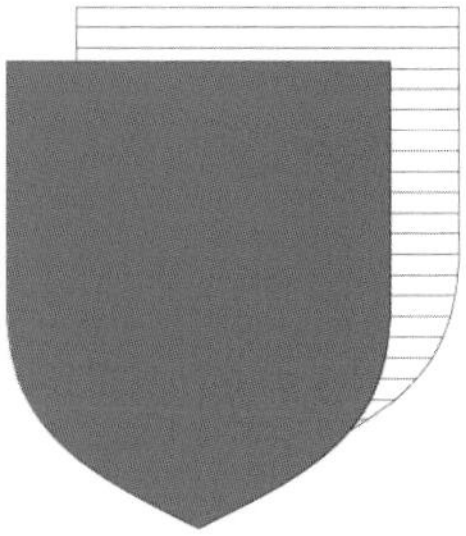

azure
A shade of blue; when the shield is black and white, azure is designated by horizontal lines.

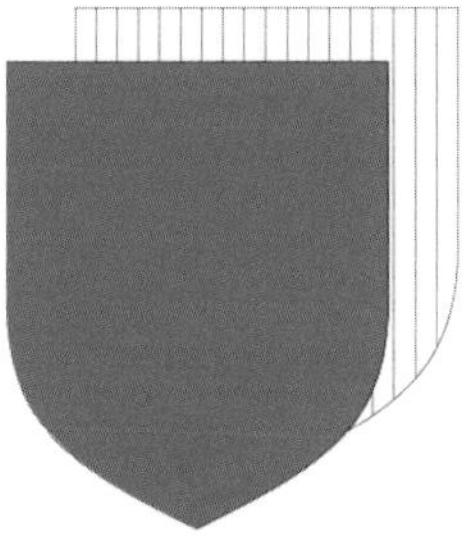

gules
The color red; when the shield is black and white, gules is designated by vertical lines.

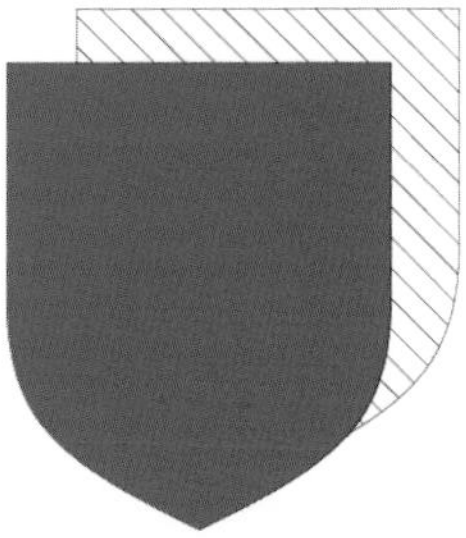

vert
The color green; when the shield is black and white, vert is designated by diagonal lines from left to right.

purpure
The color violet; when the shield is black and white, purpure is designated by diagonal lines from right to left.

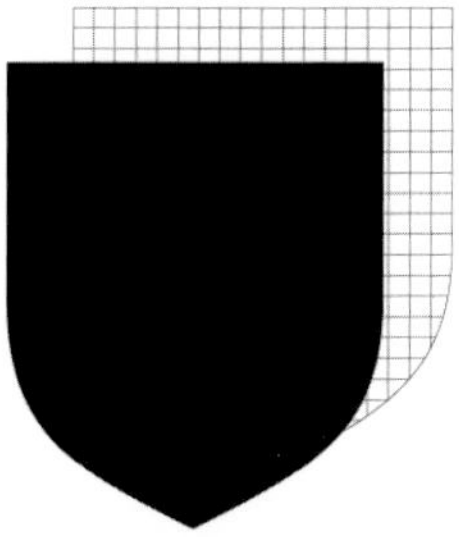

sable
The color black; when the shield is black and white, sable is designated by a cross-hatched or black surface.

flags

Emblem of a country, province or organization depicted on a piece of fabric attached to a staff or printed on a document or an escutcheon. The flags illustrated here are those of UN member countries.

Americas

1 
Canada

2 
United States of America

3 
Mexico

4 
Honduras

5 
Guatemala

6 
Belize

7 
El Salvador

8 
Nicaragua

9 
Costa Rica

10 
Panama

11 
Colombia

12 
Venezuela

13 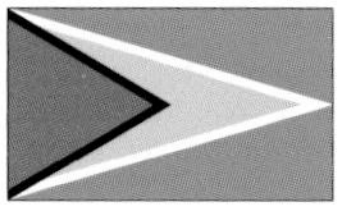
Guyana

14 
Suriname

15 
Ecuador

16 
Peru

17 
Brazil

18 
Bolivia

19 
Paraguay

20 
Chile

21 
Argentina

22 
Uruguay

Caribbean Islands

23 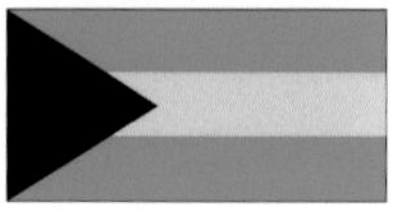
Bahamas

24 
Cuba

25 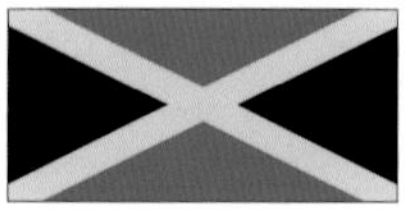
Jamaica

26 
Haiti

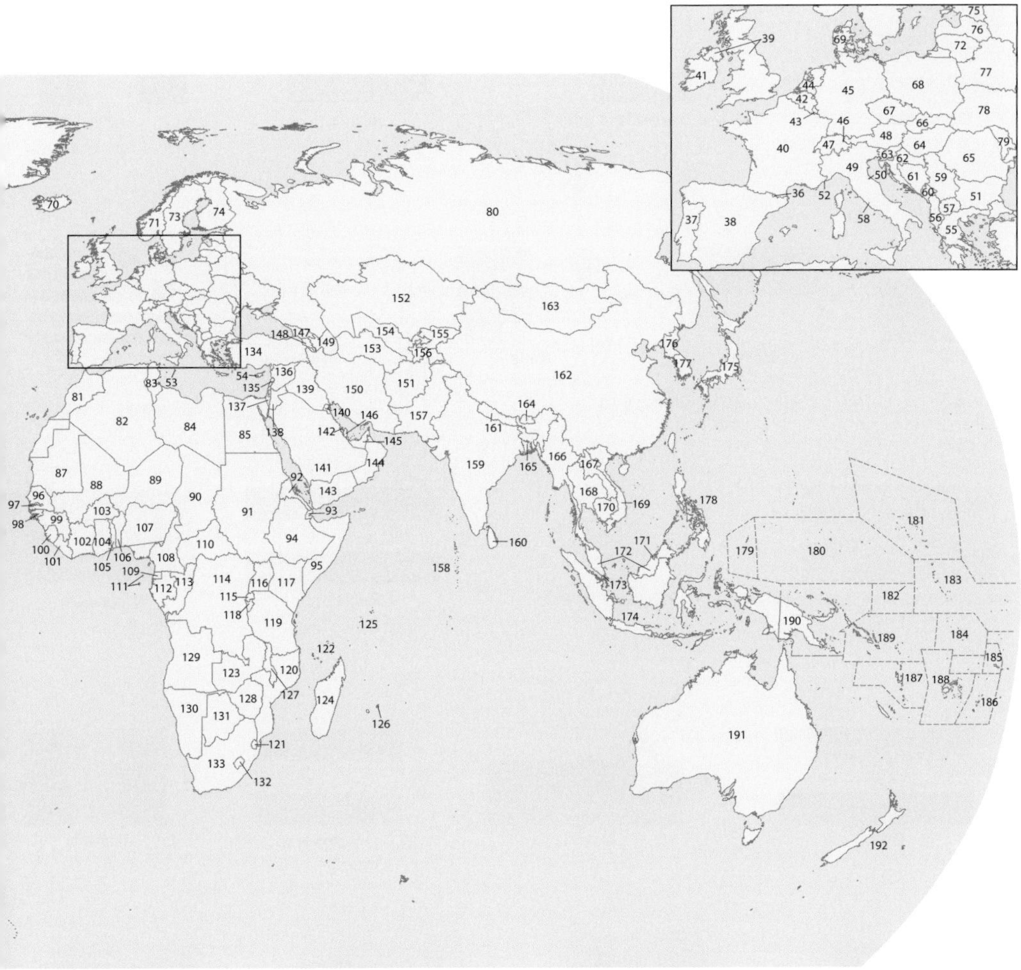

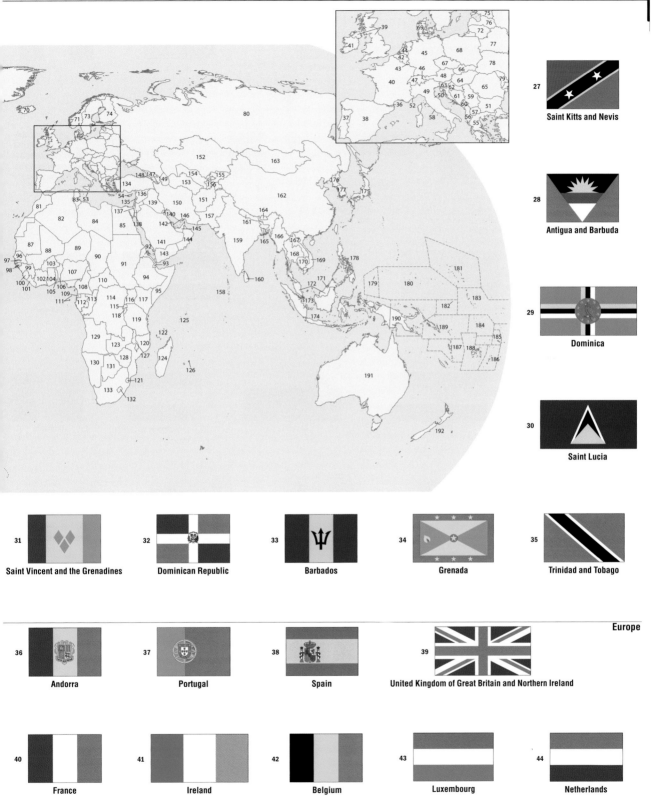

27

Saint Kitts and Nevis

28

Antigua and Barbuda

29
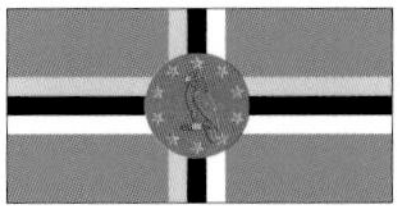
Dominica

30

Saint Lucia

31

Saint Vincent and the Grenadines

32

Dominican Republic

33

Barbados

34

Grenada

35

Trinidad and Tobago

Europe

36

Andorra

37

Portugal

38

Spain

39

United Kingdom of Great Britain and Northern Ireland

40
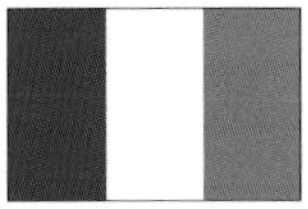
France

41

Ireland

42
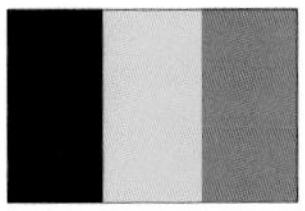
Belgium

43

Luxembourg

44

Netherlands

flags

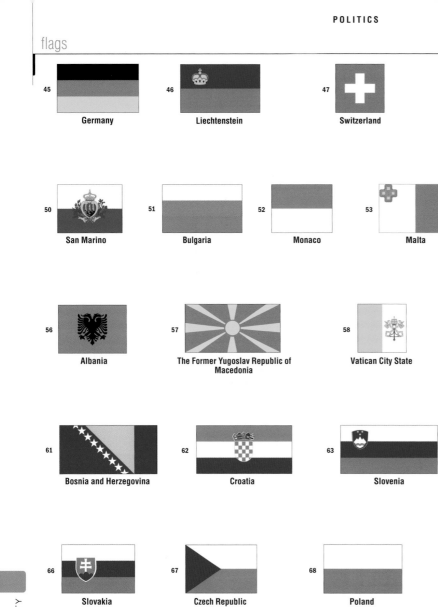

45

Germany

46

Liechtenstein

47

Switzerland

48
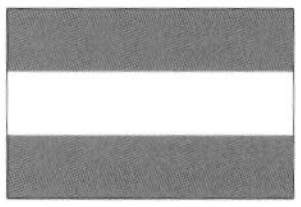
Austria

49
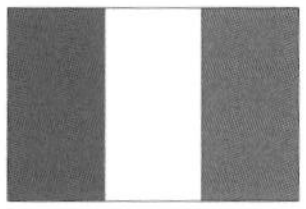
Italy

50

San Marino

51
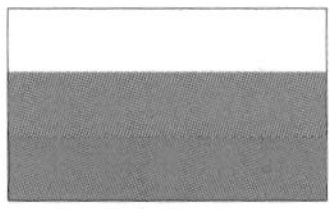
Bulgaria

52
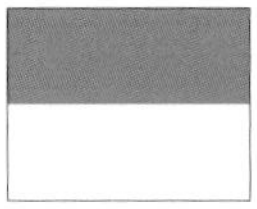
Monaco

53

Malta

54

Cyprus

55

Greece

56

Albania

57

The Former Yugoslav Republic of Macedonia

58

Vatican City State

59

Serbia

60

Montenegro

61

Bosnia and Herzegovina

62

Croatia

63

Slovenia

64

Hungary

65

Romania

66

Slovakia

67
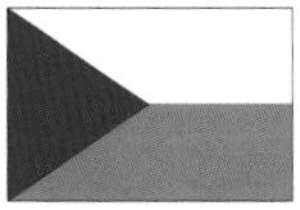
Czech Republic

68
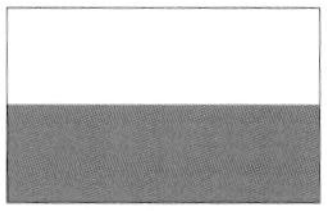
Poland

69
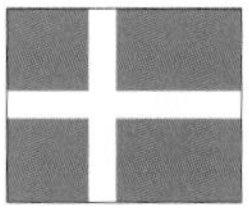
Denmark

70

Iceland

71

Norway

72
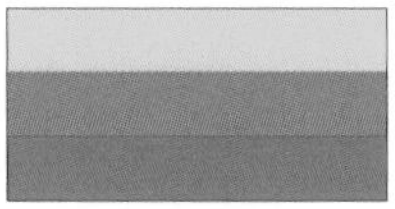
Lithuania

73

Sweden

74

Finland

75

Estonia

76

Latvia

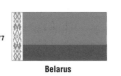

77

Belarus

78

Ukraine

79

Republic of Moldova

80

Russian Federation

Africa

81 
Morocco

82 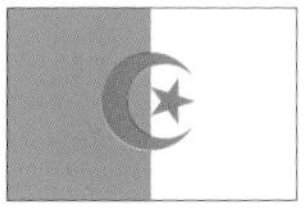
Algeria

83 
Tunisia

84 
Libyan Arab Jamahiriya

85 
Egypt

86 
Cape Verde

87 
Mauritania

88 
Mali

89 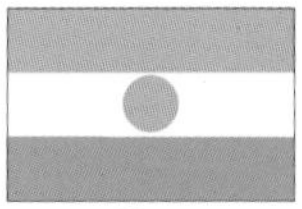
Niger

90 
Chad

91 
Sudan

92 
Eritrea

93 
Djibouti

94 
Ethiopia

95 
Somalia

96 
Senegal

97 
Gambia

98 
Guinea-Bissau

99 
Guinea

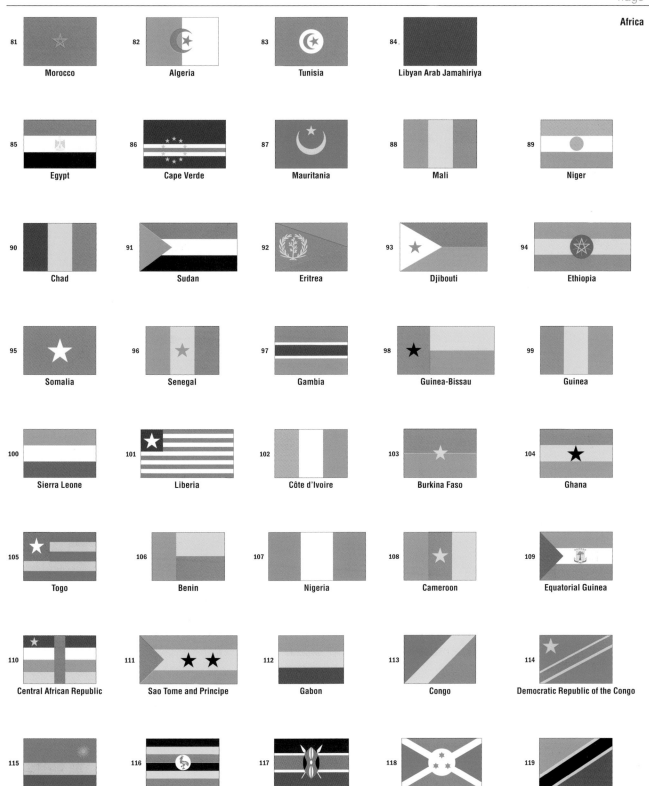

100 
Sierra Leone

101 
Liberia

102 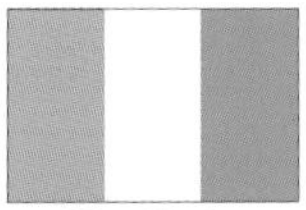
Côte d'Ivoire

103 
Burkina Faso

104 
Ghana

105 
Togo

106 
Benin

107 
Nigeria

108 
Cameroon

109 
Equatorial Guinea

110 
Central African Republic

111 
Sao Tome and Principe

112 
Gabon

113 
Congo

114 
Democratic Republic of the Congo

115 
Rwanda

116 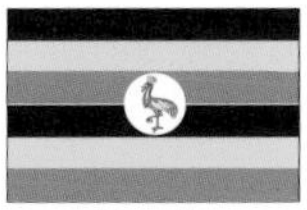
Uganda

117 
Kenya

118 
Burundi

119 
United Republic of Tanzania

flags

120 
Mozambique

121 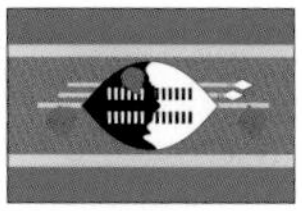
Swaziland

122 
Comoros

123 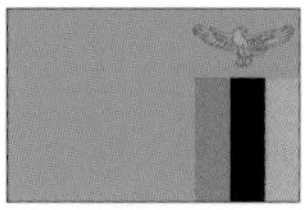
Zambia

124 
Madagascar

125 
Seychelles

126 
Mauritius

127 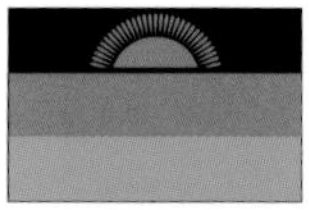
Malawi

128 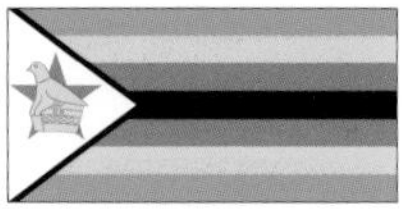
Zimbabwe

129 
Angola

130 
Namibia

131 
Botswana

132 
Lesotho

133 
South Africa

Asia

134 
Turkey

135 
Lebanon

136 
Syrian Arab Republic

137 
Israel

138 
East Timor

139 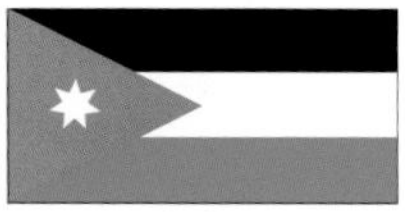
Jordan

140 
Iraq

141 
Kuwait

142 
Saudi Arabia

143 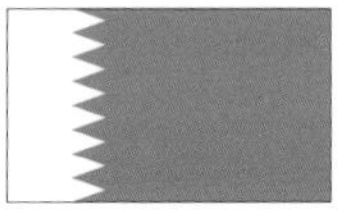
Bahrain

144 
Yemen

145 
Oman

146 
United Arab Emirates

147 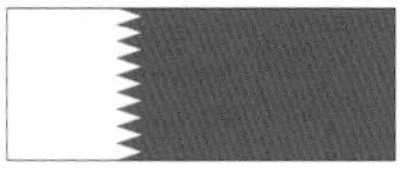
Qatar

148 
Georgia

149 
Armenia

150 
Azerbaijan

151 
Iran

152 
Afghanistan

153 
Kazakhstan

154 
Turkmenistan

155 
Uzbekistan

156 
Kyrgyzstan

157 
Tajikistan

158 
Pakistan

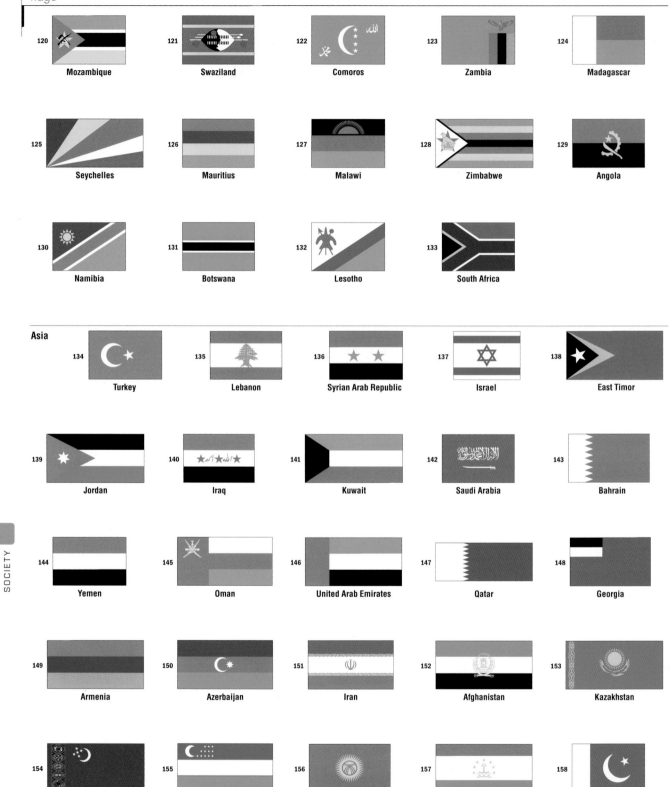

159 
Maldives

160 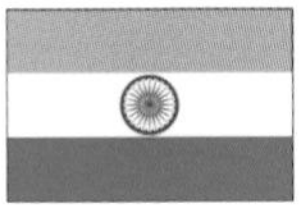
India

161 
Sri Lanka

162 
Nepal

163 
China

164 
Mongolia

165 
Bhutan

166 
Bangladesh

167 
Myanmar

168 
Lao People's Democratic Republic

169 
Thailand

170 
Viet Nam

171 
Cambodia

172 
Brunei Darussalam

173 
Malaysia

174 
Singapore

175 
Indonesia

176 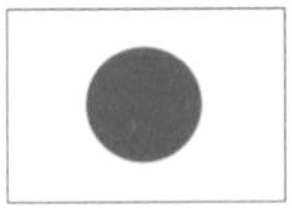
Japan

177 
Democratic People's Republic of Korea

178 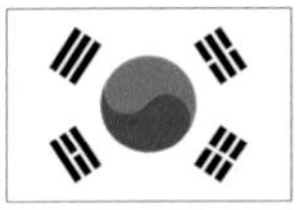
Republic of Korea

Oceania and Polynesia

179 
Philippines

180 
Palau

181 
Micronesia

182 
Marshall Islands

183 
Nauru

184 
Kiribati

185 
Tuvalu

186 
Samoa

187 
Tonga

188 
Vanuatu

189 
Fiji

190 
Solomon Islands

191 
Papua New Guinea

192 
Australia

193 
New Zealand

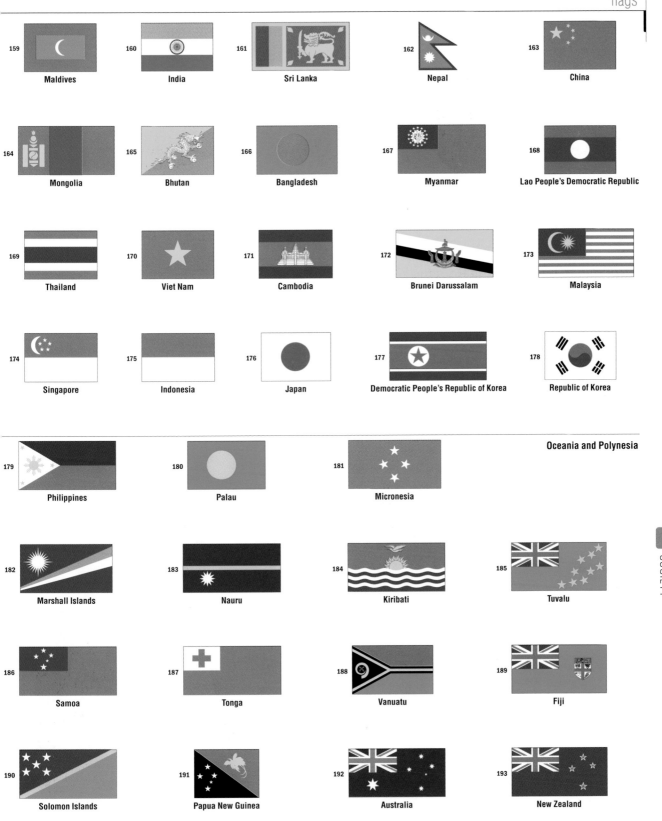

weapons in the Stone Age

Weapons used mainly for hunting in prehistory (Paleolithic and Neolithic).

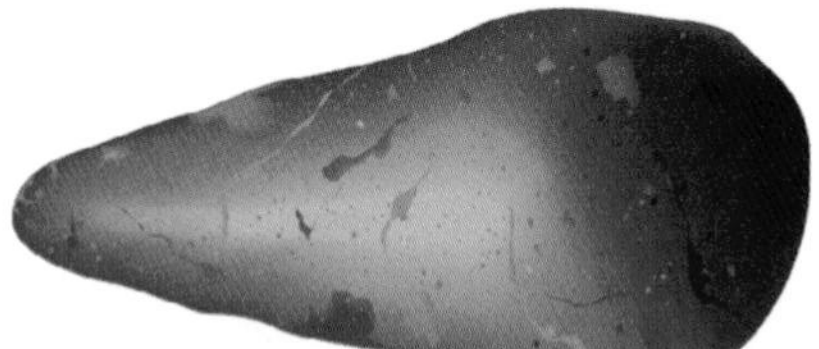

polished stone hand axe
Crudely worked stone attached to a shaft.

flint arrowhead
Flint: hard, extremely fine-grained rock (silica) used as the raw material for many weapons in prehistory.

flint knife
Piece of flint carved in the shape of a blade and mounted on a shaft.

weapons in the age of the Romans

Weapons used during the period of antiquity dominated by the Roman Empire (1st century BC to AD 476).

Roman legionary
Soldier in a Roman legion who belonged to a citizens' unit of troops, which formed the basis of the Roman army (about 6,000 men).

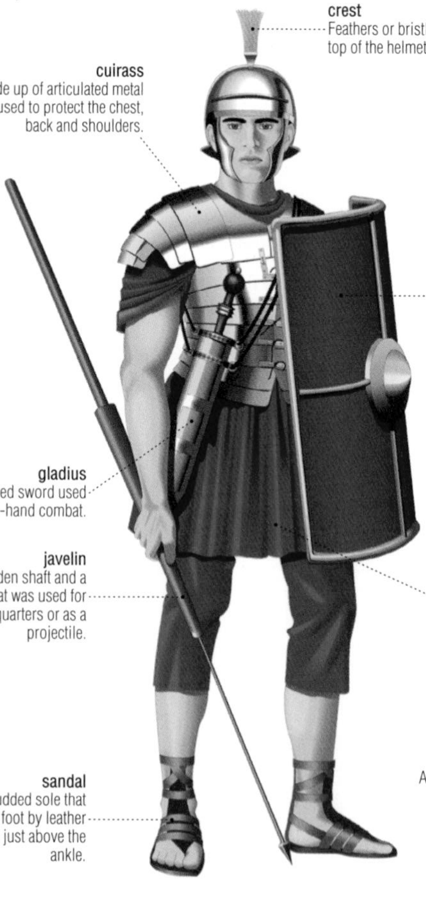
crest
Feathers or bristles decorating the top of the helmet.
cuirass
Armor made up of articulated metal strips used to protect the chest, back and shoulders.
shield
Wooden piece of armor carried on the arm to protect against enemy blows.
gladius
Short double-edged sword used for hand-to-hand combat.
javelin
Weapon with a wooden shaft and a long metal rod that was used for combat at close quarters or as a projectile.
tunic
Short-sleeved garment that legionaries wore under the cuirass.
sandal
Footwear with a studded sole that was attached to the foot by leather laces that came just above the ankle.

Gallic warric
The Gallic warrior belonged to clan governed by a chieftain; hi armor was rudimentary and h often fought bare-chested

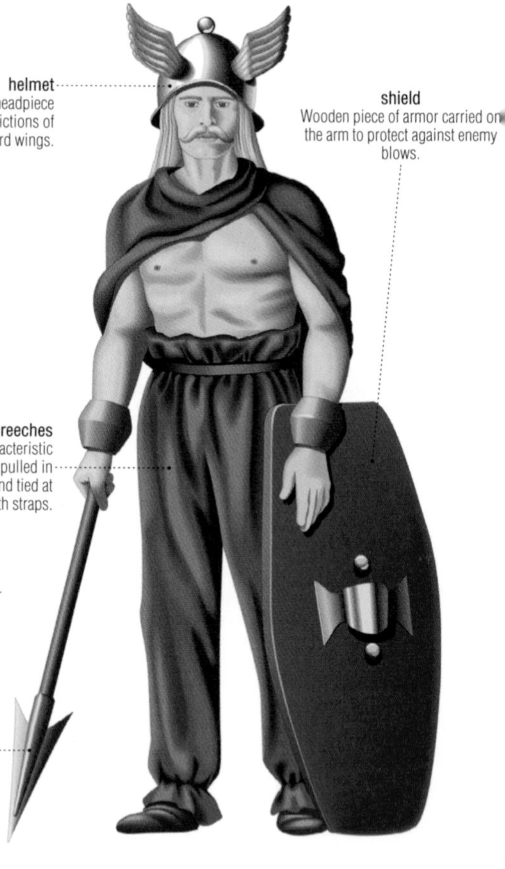
helmet
Protective metal headpiece decorated with depictions of animals, horns or bird wings.
shield
Wooden piece of armor carried on the arm to protect against enemy blows.
breeches
Full pants that were characteristic of Gallic attire; they were pulled in at the waist with a belt and tied at the ankle with straps.
spear
A long wooden pole with a pointed steel head.

SOCIETY

armor

Assemblage of molded and articulated metal pieces worn as protection during the Middle Ages.

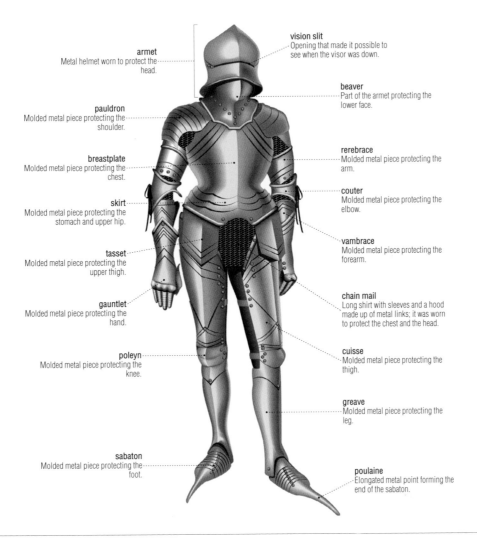

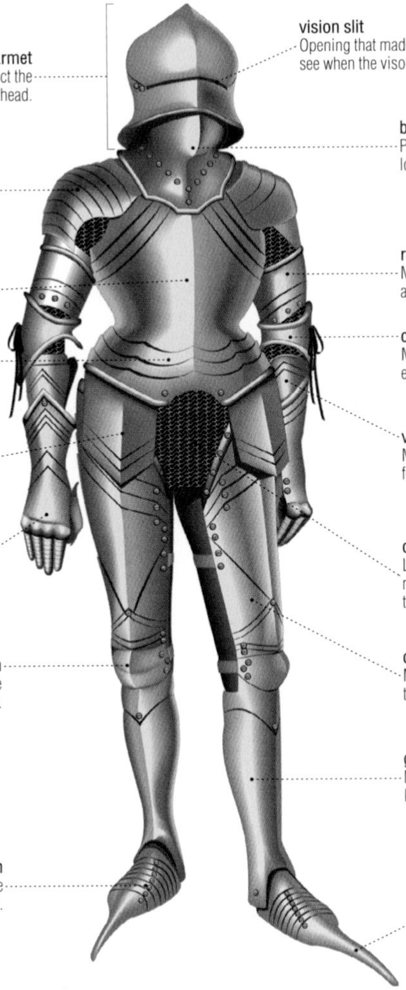
armet
Metal helmet worn to protect the head.
vision slit
Opening that made it possible to see when the visor was down.
beaver
Part of the armet protecting the lower face.
pauldron
Molded metal piece protecting the shoulder.
breastplate
Molded metal piece protecting the chest.
rerebrace
Molded metal piece protecting the arm.
couter
Molded metal piece protecting the elbow.
skirt
Molded metal piece protecting the stomach and upper hip.
vambrace
Molded metal piece protecting the forearm.
tasset
Molded metal piece protecting the upper thigh.
chain mail
Long shirt with sleeves and a hood made up of metal links; it was worn to protect the chest and the head.
gauntlet
Molded metal piece protecting the hand.
cuisse
Molded metal piece protecting the thigh.
poleyn
Molded metal piece protecting the knee.
greave
Molded metal piece protecting the leg.
sabaton
Molded metal piece protecting the foot.
poulaine
Elongated metal point forming the end of the sabaton.

armet
Metal helmet worn to protect the head.

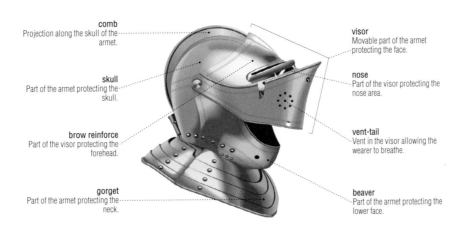

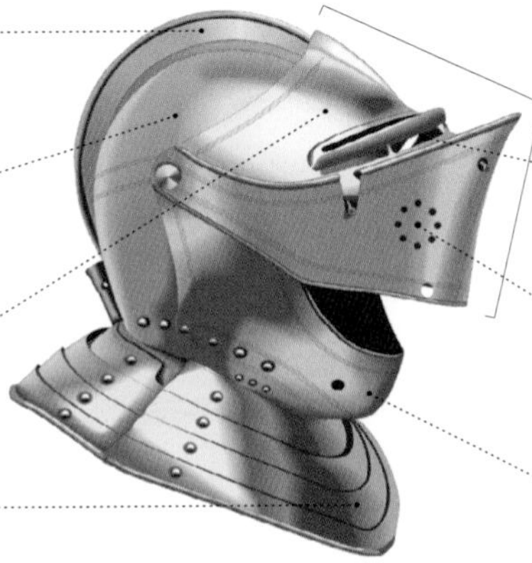
comb
Projection along the skull of the armet.
visor
Movable part of the armet protecting the face.
skull
Part of the armet protecting the skull.
nose
Part of the visor protecting the nose area.
brow reinforce
Part of the visor protecting the forehead.
vent-tail
Vent in the visor allowing the wearer to breathe.
gorget
Part of the armet protecting the neck.
beaver
Part of the armet protecting the lower face.

bows and crossbow

Weapons for hunting and war consisting of a bowstring, which is stretched to fire a projectile such as an arrow or bolt.

crossbow
Weapon consisting of a bow mounted on a tiller and fitted with tension and trigger mechanisms.

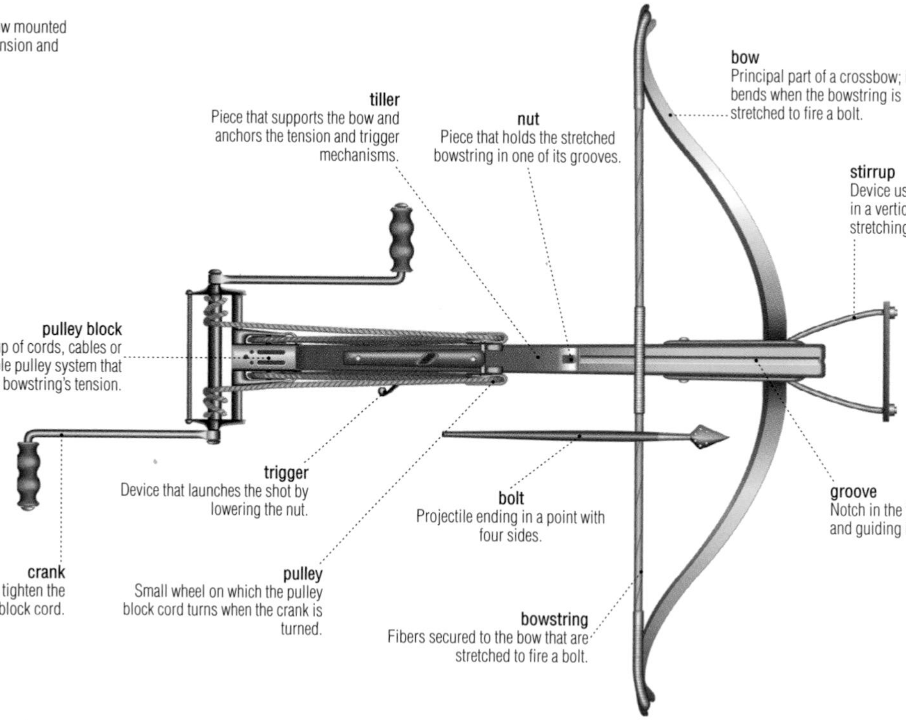

tiller
Piece that supports the bow and anchors the tension and trigger mechanisms.

nut
Piece that holds the stretched bowstring in one of its grooves.

bow
Principal part of a crossbow; it bends when the bowstring is stretched to fire a bolt.

stirrup
Device used to hold the crossbow in a vertical position when stretching the bowstring.

pulley block
Device made up of cords, cables or chains and a double pulley system that increases the bowstring's tension.

trigger
Device that launches the shot by lowering the nut.

bolt
Projectile ending in a point with four sides.

groove
Notch in the tiller holding the bolt and guiding it toward the target.

crank
Device that rotates to tighten the pulley block cord.

pulley
Small wheel on which the pulley block cord turns when the crank is turned.

bowstring
Fibers secured to the bow that are stretched to fire a bolt.

bow
Weapon with a wooden or metal shaft that bends when the bowstring is stretched to fire arrows.

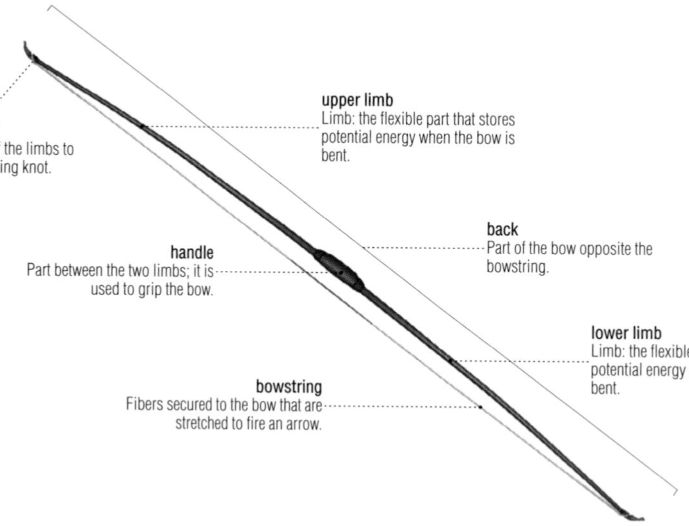

nock
Notch in the end of the limbs to take the bowstring knot.

upper limb
Limb: the flexible part that stores potential energy when the bow is bent.

back
Part of the bow opposite the bowstring.

handle
Part between the two limbs; it is used to grip the bow.

lower limb
Limb: the flexible part that stores potential energy when the bow is bent.

bowstring
Fibers secured to the bow that are stretched to fire an arrow.

arrow
Projectile fired by a bow or a crossbow; it consists of a shank, a point and a heel with a notch and fletching.

modern bow
Bow with pulleys, which increase the power of the shot.

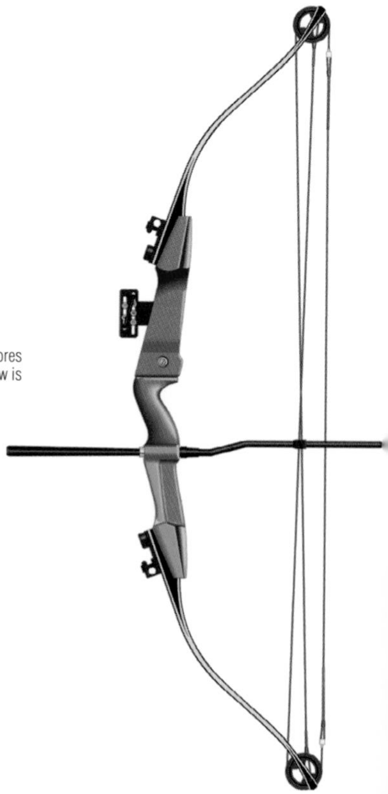

SOCIETY

thrusting and cutting weapons

Weapons with steel blades of various lengths designed to pierce or cut.

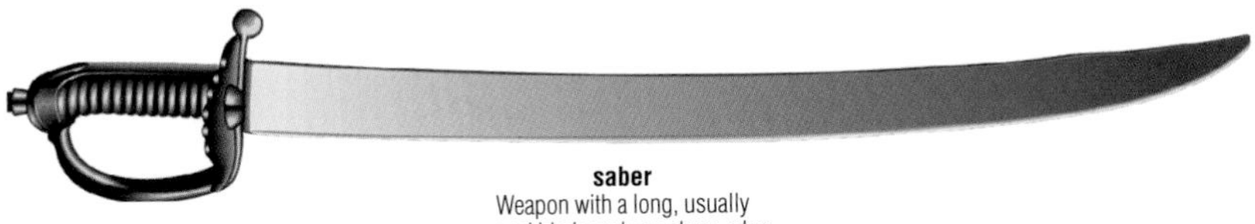

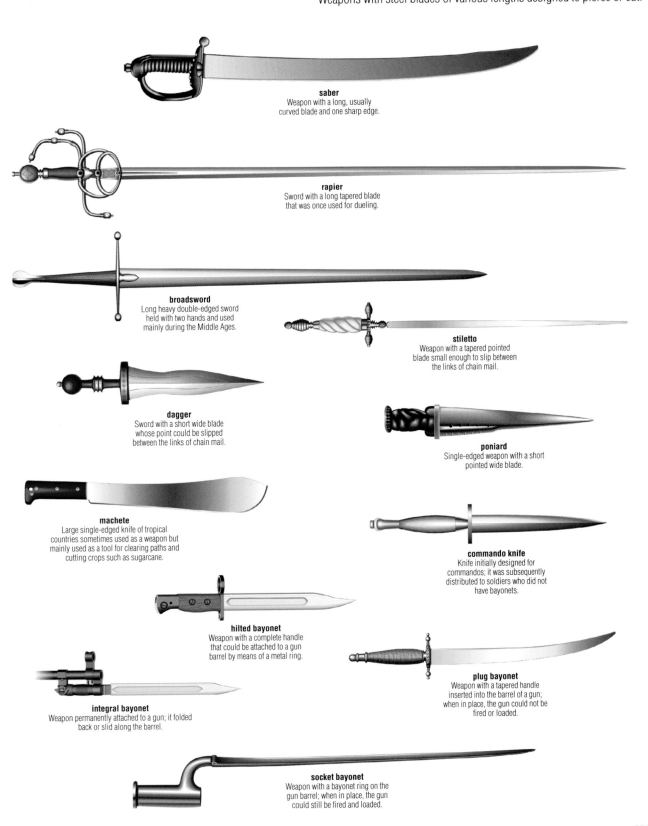

saber
Weapon with a long, usually curved blade and one sharp edge.

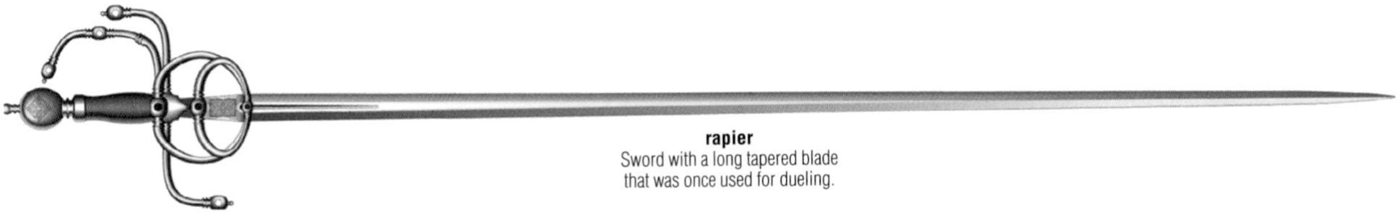

rapier
Sword with a long tapered blade that was once used for dueling.

broadsword
Long heavy double-edged sword held with two hands and used mainly during the Middle Ages.

stiletto
Weapon with a tapered pointed blade small enough to slip between the links of chain mail.

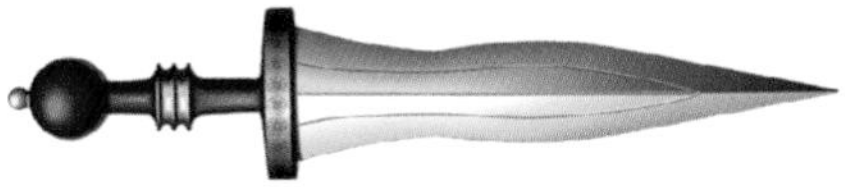

dagger
Sword with a short wide blade whose point could be slipped between the links of chain mail.

poniard
Single-edged weapon with a short pointed wide blade.

machete
Large single-edged knife of tropical countries sometimes used as a weapon but mainly used as a tool for clearing paths and cutting crops such as sugarcane.

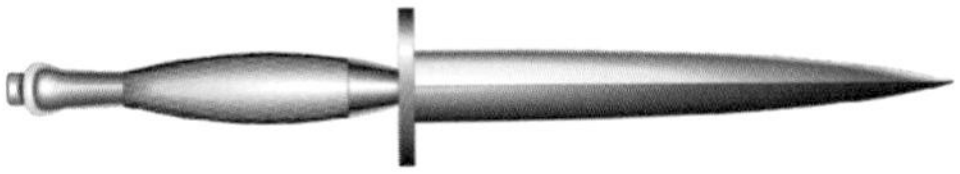

commando knife
Knife initially designed for commandos; it was subsequently distributed to soldiers who did not have bayonets.

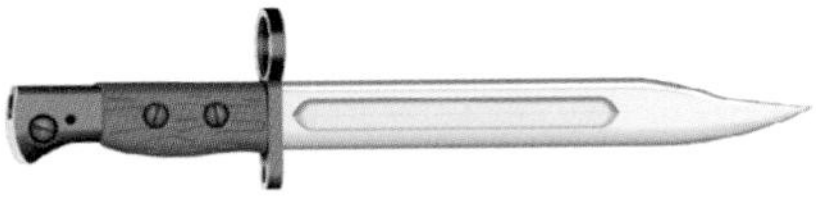

hilted bayonet
Weapon with a complete handle that could be attached to a gun barrel by means of a metal ring.

plug bayonet
Weapon with a tapered handle inserted into the barrel of a gun; when in place, the gun could not be fired or loaded.

integral bayonet
Weapon permanently attached to a gun; it folded back or slid along the barrel.

socket bayonet
Weapon with a bayonet ring on the gun barrel; when in place, the gun could still be fired and loaded.

harquebus

Firearm used until the 17th century; it was held against the shoulder and fired by means of a wick, a wheel or a flint.

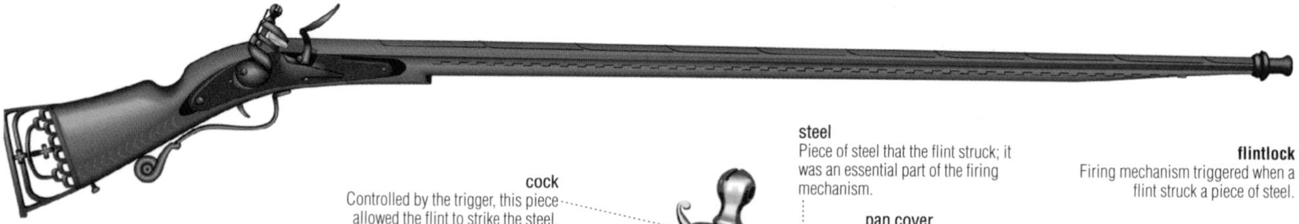

flintlock
Firing mechanism triggered when a flint struck a piece of steel.

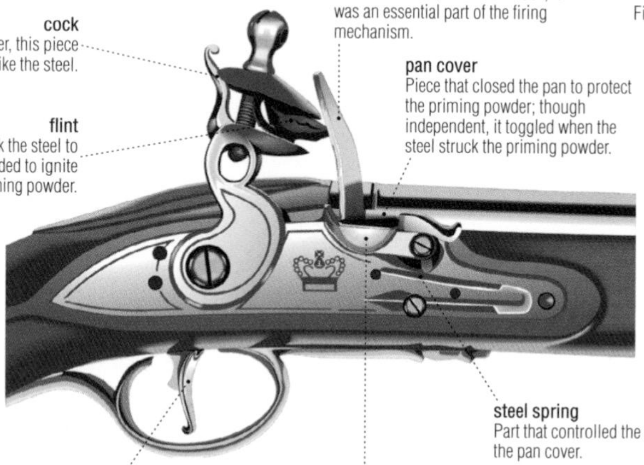

cock
Controlled by the trigger, this piece allowed the flint to strike the steel.

flint
Stone that struck the steel to produce the spark needed to ignite the priming powder.

steel
Piece of steel that the flint struck; it was an essential part of the firing mechanism.

pan cover
Piece that closed the pan to protect the priming powder; though independent, it toggled when the steel struck the priming powder.

steel spring
Part that controlled the steel and the pan cover.

trigger
Piece of the firing mechanism that was pressed to set off the shot.

pan
Container holding the priming powder.

powder flask
Container made of wood, horn or boiled leather or of brass and copper; it was used to carry the priming powder.

ball
Small lead projectile usually made by the shooter using a mold.

seventeenth century cannon and mortar

Stationary firearms designed for direct fire (cannon) or high-angle fire (mortar).

firing accessories

Instruments used to load a cannon or mortar.

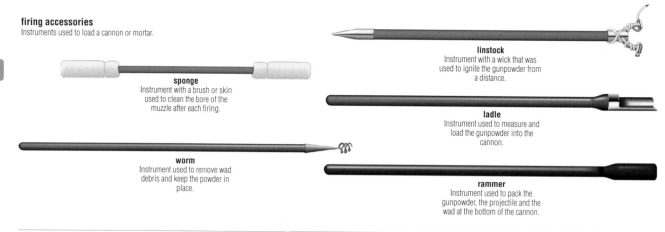

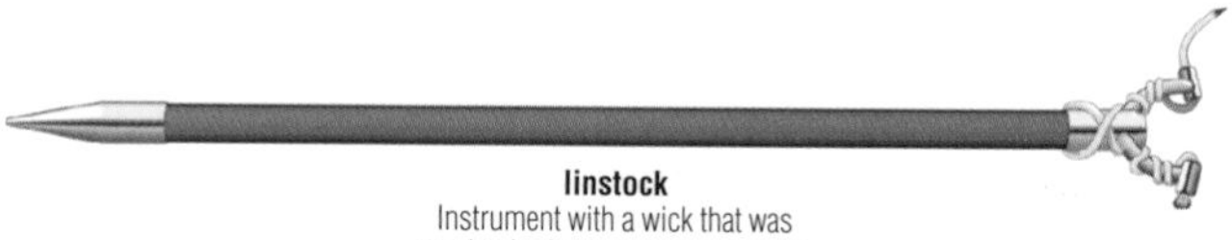

linstock
Instrument with a wick that was used to ignite the gunpowder from a distance.

sponge
Instrument with a brush or skin used to clean the bore of the muzzle after each firing.

ladle
Instrument used to measure and load the gunpowder into the cannon.

worm
Instrument used to remove wad debris and keep the powder in place.

rammer
Instrument used to pack the gunpowder, the projectile and the wad at the bottom of the cannon.

projectiles

Hard heavy objects launched by cannons and mortars.

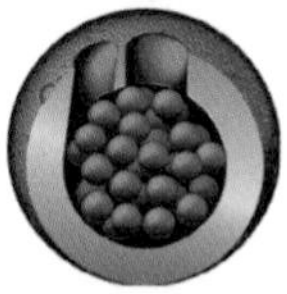

hollow shot
Spherical projectile filled with gunpowder and grapeshot that exploded on impact.

solid shot
Solid spherical projectile that was loaded into cannons; they were first made of stone, then of cast iron from the 16th century.

bar shot
Projectile made up of solid shot at opposite ends of a steel bar or a chain; it was used to destroy a ship's masting.

grapeshot
Projectile composed of lead or iron balls that dispersed on exiting the cannon.

seventeenth century cannon and mortar

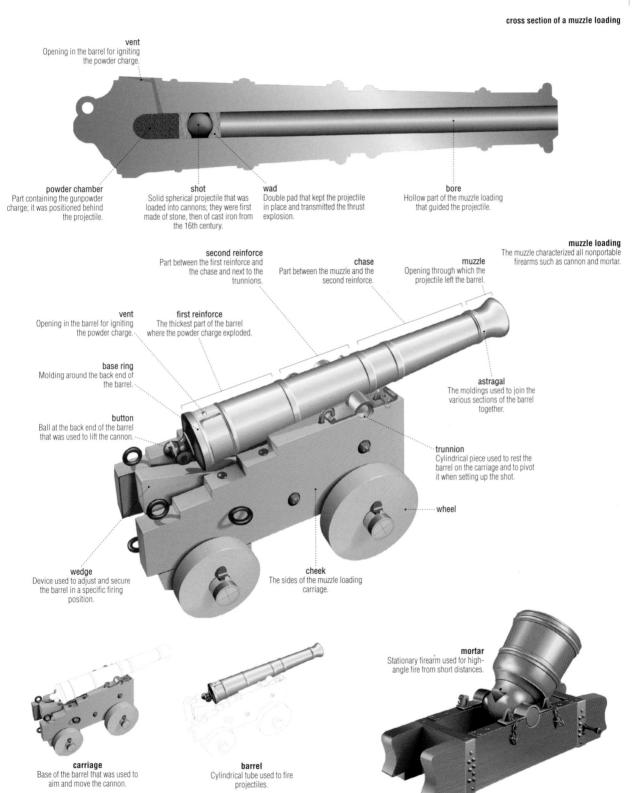

cross section of a muzzle loading

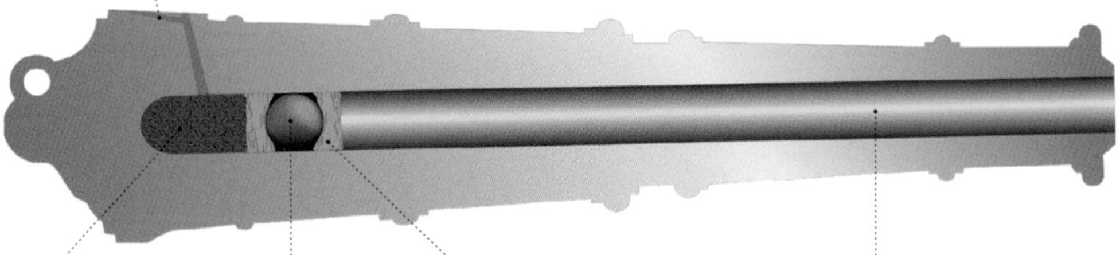

vent
Opening in the barrel for igniting the powder charge.
powder chamber
Part containing the gunpowder charge; it was positioned behind the projectile.
shot
Solid spherical projectile that was loaded into cannons; they were first made of stone, then of cast iron from the 16th century.
wad
Double pad that kept the projectile in place and transmitted the thrust explosion.
bore
Hollow part of the muzzle loading that guided the projectile.

muzzle loading
The muzzle characterized all nonportable firearms such as cannon and mortar.

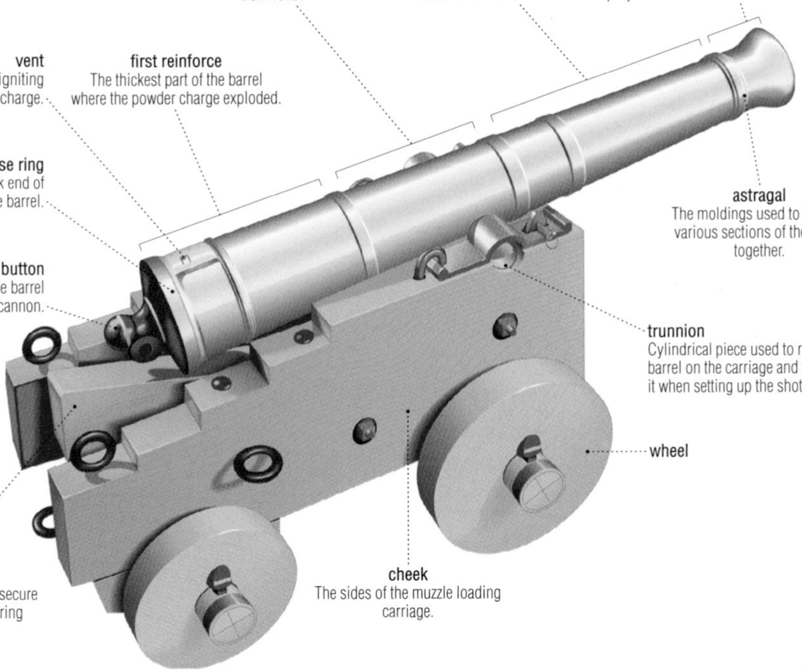

second reinforce
Part between the first reinforce and the chase and next to the trunnions.
chase
Part between the muzzle and the second reinforce.
muzzle
Opening through which the projectile left the barrel.
vent
Opening in the barrel for igniting the powder charge.
first reinforce
The thickest part of the barrel where the powder charge exploded.
base ring
Molding around the back end of the barrel.
astragal
The moldings used to join the various sections of the barrel together.
button
Ball at the back end of the barrel that was used to lift the cannon.
trunnion
Cylindrical piece used to rest the barrel on the carriage and to pivot it when setting up the shot.
wheel
wedge
Device used to adjust and secure the barrel in a specific firing position.
cheek
The sides of the muzzle loading carriage.

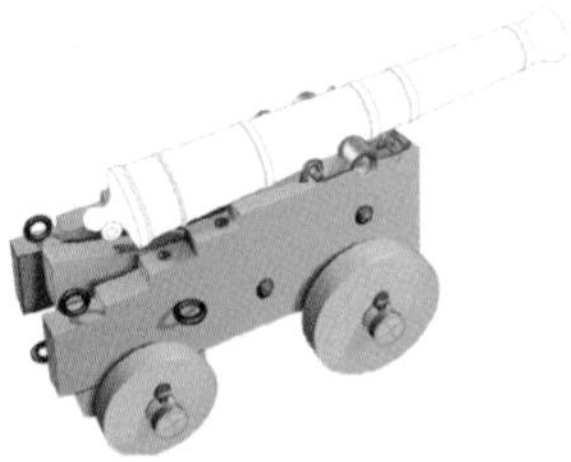

carriage
Base of the barrel that was used to aim and move the cannon.

barrel
Cylindrical tube used to fire projectiles.

mortar
Stationary firearm used for high-angle fire from short distances.

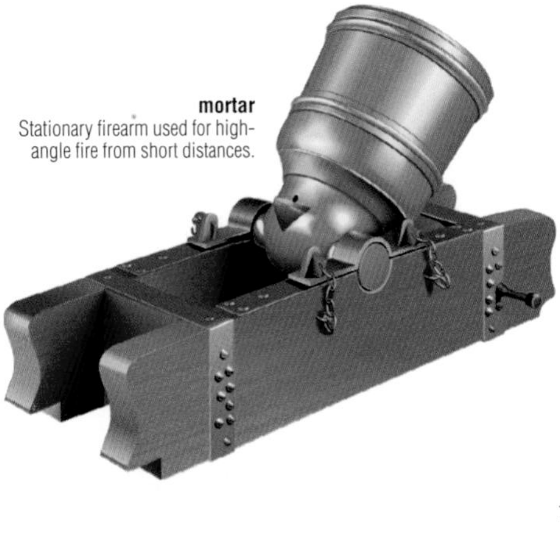

SOCIETY

submachine gun

Shoulder-held automatic assault weapon that fires handgun cartridges in bursts.

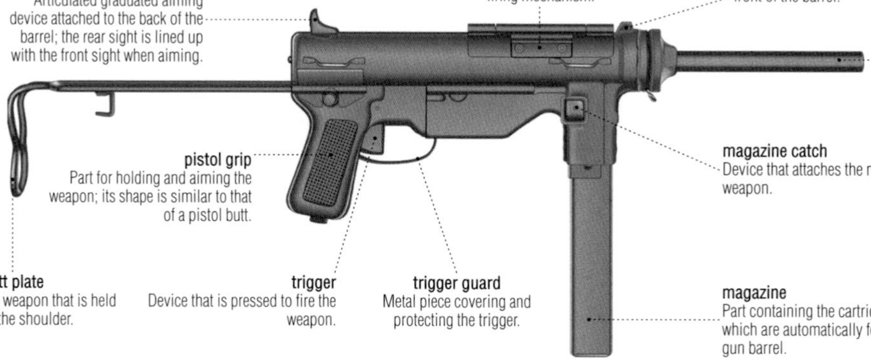
rear sight
Articulated graduated aiming device attached to the back of the barrel; the rear sight is lined up with the front sight when aiming.
receiver
Metal casing around the weapon's firing mechanism.
front sight
Metal aiming device attached to the front of the barrel.
barrel
Tubular part that guides the trajectory of the projectile.
pistol grip
Part for holding and aiming the weapon; its shape is similar to that of a pistol butt.
magazine catch
Device that attaches the magazine to the weapon.
butt plate
Back part of the weapon that is held against the shoulder.
trigger
Device that is pressed to fire the weapon.
trigger guard
Metal piece covering and protecting the trigger.
magazine
Part containing the cartridges, which are automatically fed into the gun barrel.

pistol

Short light handgun that is held in one hand; it is loaded with a magazine inside the butt.

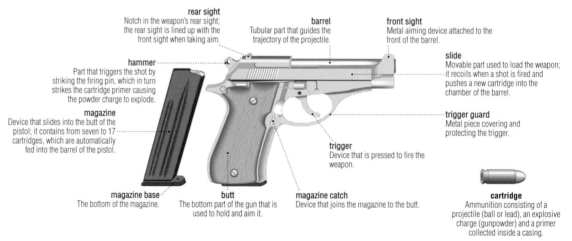

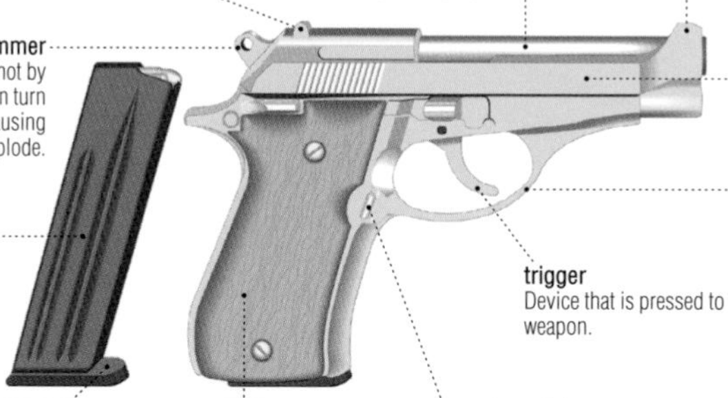
rear sight
Notch in the weapon's rear sight; the rear sight is lined up with the front sight when taking aim.
barrel
Tubular part that guides the trajectory of the projectile.
front sight
Metal aiming device attached to the front of the barrel.
hammer
Part that triggers the shot by striking the firing pin, which in turn strikes the cartridge primer causing the powder charge to explode.
slide
Movable part used to load the weapon; it recoils when a shot is fired and pushes a new cartridge into the chamber of the barrel.
magazine
Device that slides into the butt of the pistol; it contains from seven to 17 cartridges, which are automatically fed into the barrel of the pistol.
trigger guard
Metal piece covering and protecting the trigger.
trigger
Device that is pressed to fire the weapon.
magazine base
The bottom of the magazine.
butt
The bottom part of the gun that is used to hold and aim it.
magazine catch
Device that joins the magazine to the butt.

cartridge
Ammunition consisting of a projectile (ball or lead), an explosive charge (gunpowder) and a primer collected inside a casing.

revolver

Pistol with a rotary magazine, which usually contains six cartridge chambers.

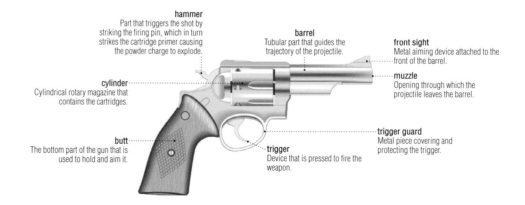

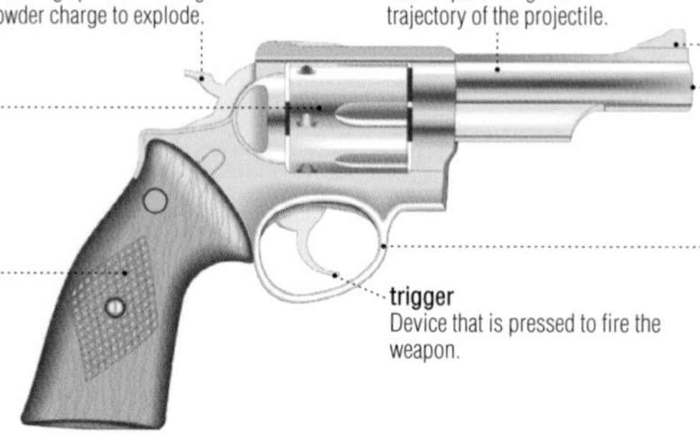
hammer
Part that triggers the shot by striking the firing pin, which in turn strikes the cartridge primer causing the powder charge to explode.
barrel
Tubular part that guides the trajectory of the projectile.
front sight
Metal aiming device attached to the front of the barrel.
cylinder
Cylindrical rotary magazine that contains the cartridges.
muzzle
Opening through which the projectile leaves the barrel.
trigger guard
Metal piece covering and protecting the trigger.
butt
The bottom part of the gun that is used to hold and aim it.
trigger
Device that is pressed to fire the weapon.

automatic rifle

Portable assault rifle that fires cartridges; in automatic weapons such as submachine guns and light machine guns, the cartridges are fed by a magazine or a belt.

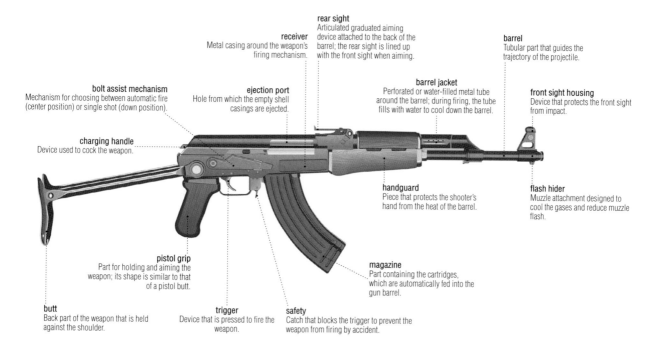

rear sight
Articulated graduated aiming device attached to the back of the barrel; the rear sight is lined up with the front sight when aiming.
receiver
Metal casing around the weapon's firing mechanism.
barrel
Tubular part that guides the trajectory of the projectile.
bolt assist mechanism
Mechanism for choosing between automatic fire (center position) or single shot (down position).
ejection port
Hole from which the empty shell casings are ejected.
barrel jacket
Perforated or water-filled metal tube around the barrel; during firing, the tube fills with water to cool down the barrel.
front sight housing
Device that protects the front sight from impact.
charging handle
Device used to cock the weapon.
handguard
Piece that protects the shooter's hand from the heat of the barrel.
flash hider
Muzzle attachment designed to cool the gases and reduce muzzle flash.
pistol grip
Part for holding and aiming the weapon; its shape is similar to that of a pistol butt.
magazine
Part containing the cartridges, which are automatically fed into the gun barrel.
butt
Back part of the weapon that is held against the shoulder.
trigger
Device that is pressed to fire the weapon.
safety
Catch that blocks the trigger to prevent the weapon from firing by accident.

light machine gun

Light automatic assault weapon that can be single-shot or automatic; its barrel is supported by a bipod.

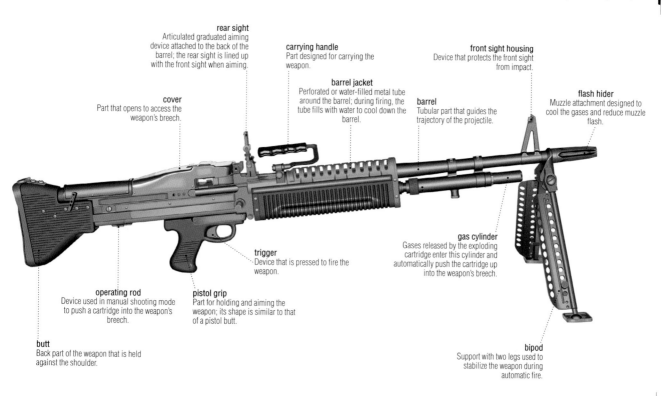

rear sight
Articulated graduated aiming device attached to the back of the barrel; the rear sight is lined up with the front sight when aiming.
carrying handle
Part designed for carrying the weapon.
front sight housing
Device that protects the front sight from impact.
barrel jacket
Perforated or water-filled metal tube around the barrel; during firing, the tube fills with water to cool down the barrel.
flash hider
Muzzle attachment designed to cool the gases and reduce muzzle flash.
cover
Part that opens to access the weapon's breech.
barrel
Tubular part that guides the trajectory of the projectile.
gas cylinder
Gases released by the exploding cartridge enter this cylinder and automatically push the cartridge up into the weapon's breech.
trigger
Device that is pressed to fire the weapon.
operating rod
Device used in manual shooting mode to push a cartridge into the weapon's breech.
pistol grip
Part for holding and aiming the weapon; its shape is similar to that of a pistol butt.
butt
Back part of the weapon that is held against the shoulder.
bipod
Support with two legs used to stabilize the weapon during automatic fire.

SOCIETY

modern howitzer

Direct-fire piece of artillery that launches a round of oval projectiles (shells); its size is between that of a cannon and a mortar.

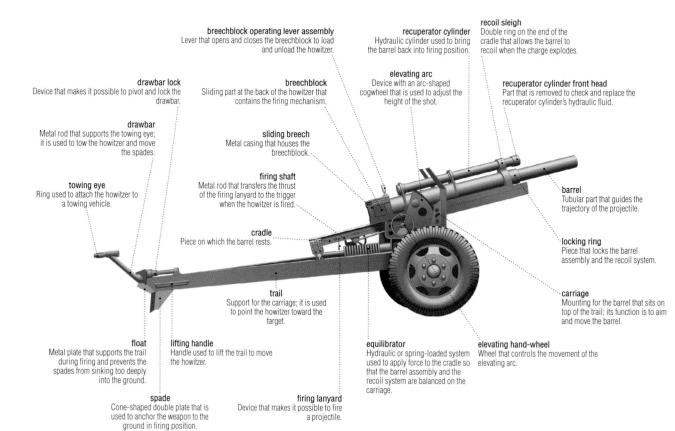

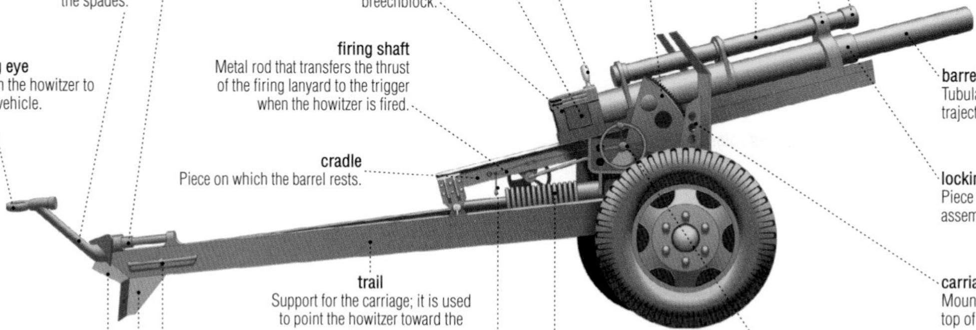
recoil sleigh
Double ring on the end of the cradle that allows the barrel to recoil when the charge explodes.
breechblock operating lever assembly
Lever that opens and closes the breechblock to load and unload the howitzer.
recuperator cylinder
Hydraulic cylinder used to bring the barrel back into firing position.
elevating arc
Device with an arc-shaped cogwheel that is used to adjust the height of the shot.
drawbar lock
Device that makes it possible to pivot and lock the drawbar.
breechblock
Sliding part at the back of the howitzer that contains the firing mechanism.
recuperator cylinder front head
Part that is removed to check and replace the recuperator cylinder's hydraulic fluid.
drawbar
Metal rod that supports the towing eye; it is used to tow the howitzer and move the spades.
sliding breech
Metal casing that houses the breechblock.
firing shaft
Metal rod that transfers the thrust of the firing lanyard to the trigger when the howitzer is fired.
towing eye
Ring used to attach the howitzer to a towing vehicle.
barrel
Tubular part that guides the trajectory of the projectile.
cradle
Piece on which the barrel rests.
locking ring
Piece that locks the barrel assembly and the recoil system.
trail
Support for the carriage; it is used to point the howitzer toward the target.
carriage
Mounting for the barrel that sits on top of the trail; its function is to aim and move the barrel.
float
Metal plate that supports the trail during firing and prevents the spades from sinking too deeply into the ground.
lifting handle
Handle used to lift the trail to move the howitzer.
equilibrator
Hydraulic or spring-loaded system used to apply force to the cradle so that the barrel assembly and the recoil system are balanced on the carriage.
elevating hand-wheel
Wheel that controls the movement of the elevating arc.
spade
Cone-shaped double plate that is used to anchor the weapon to the ground in firing position.
firing lanyard
Device that makes it possible to fire a projectile.

modern mortar

Portable muzzle-loaded infantry weapon used to discharge high-angle fire.

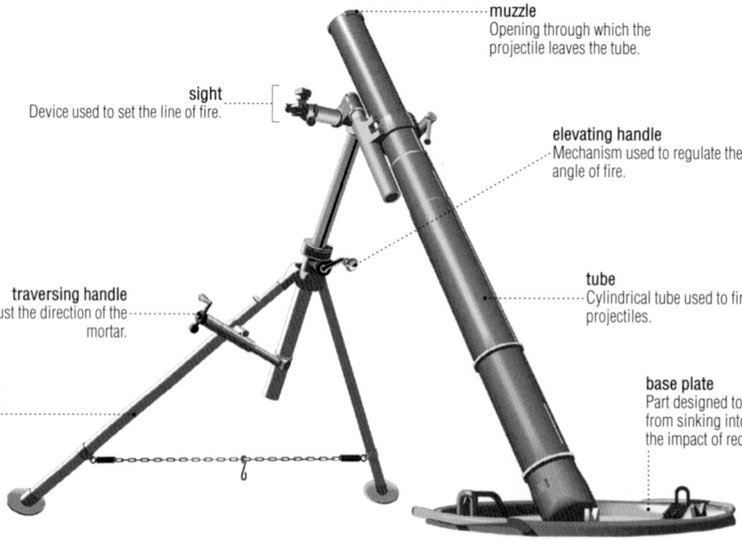
muzzle
Opening through which the projectile leaves the tube.
sight
Device used to set the line of fire.
elevating handle
Mechanism used to regulate the mortar's angle of fire.
tube
Cylindrical tube used to fire projectiles.
traversing handle
Device used to adjust the direction of the mortar.
bipod
A two-legged support whose function, with the base plate, is to stabilize the weapon during firing.
base plate
Part designed to prevent the tube from sinking into the ground from the impact of recoil.

hand grenade

Light projectile thrown by hand and made up of a metal or plastic casing loaded with an explosive charge and a firing mechanism.

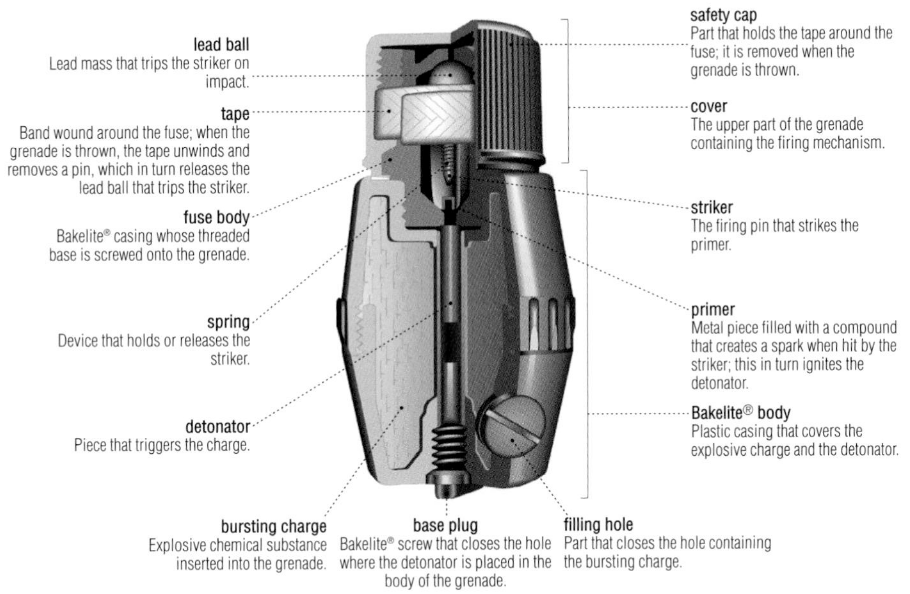

lead ball
Lead mass that trips the striker on impact.
tape
Band wound around the fuse; when the grenade is thrown, the tape unwinds and removes a pin, which in turn releases the lead ball that trips the striker.
fuse body
Bakelite® casing whose threaded base is screwed onto the grenade.
spring
Device that holds or releases the striker.
detonator
Piece that triggers the charge.
bursting charge
Explosive chemical substance inserted into the grenade.
base plug
Bakelite® screw that closes the hole where the detonator is placed in the body of the grenade.
filling hole
Part that closes the hole containing the bursting charge.
safety cap
Part that holds the tape around the fuse; it is removed when the grenade is thrown.
cover
The upper part of the grenade containing the firing mechanism.
striker
The firing pin that strikes the primer.
primer
Metal piece filled with a compound that creates a spark when hit by the striker; this in turn ignites the detonator.
Bakelite® body
Plastic casing that covers the explosive charge and the detonator.

bazooka

Portable antitank weapon that launches self-propelled projectiles (rockets).

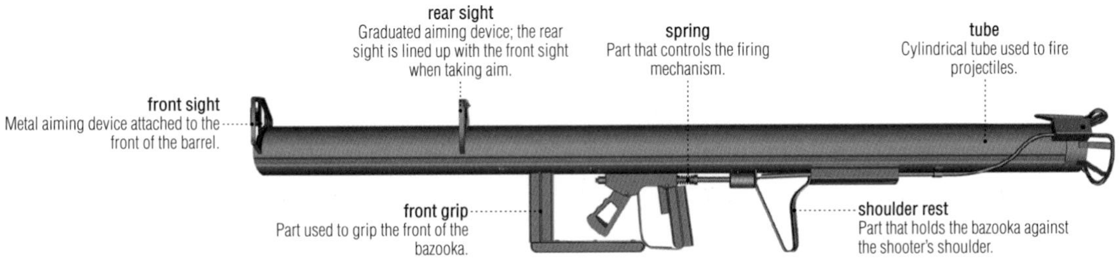

rear sight
Graduated aiming device; the rear sight is lined up with the front sight when taking aim.
spring
Part that controls the firing mechanism.
tube
Cylindrical tube used to fire projectiles.
front sight
Metal aiming device attached to the front of the barrel.
front grip
Part used to grip the front of the bazooka.
shoulder rest
Part that holds the bazooka against the shooter's shoulder.

recoilless rifle

Portable weapon that functions by balancing thrust; to prevent recoil, a projectile and a gas jet are projected in opposite directions.

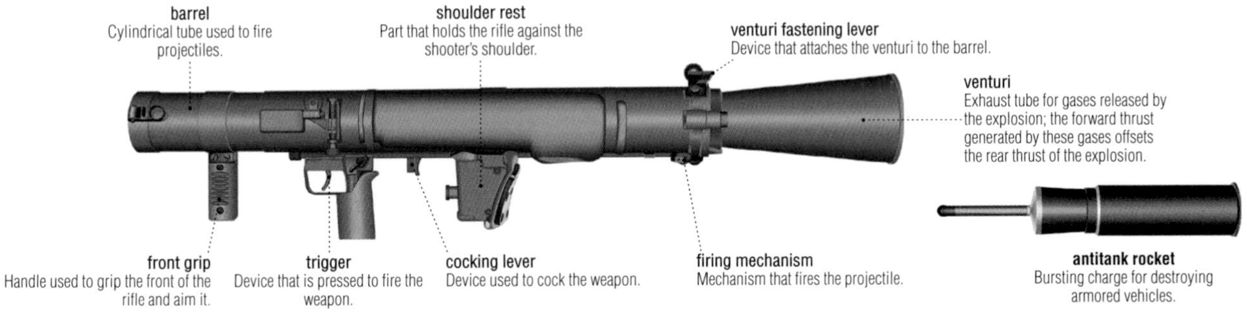

barrel
Cylindrical tube used to fire projectiles.
shoulder rest
Part that holds the rifle against the shooter's shoulder.
venturi fastening lever
Device that attaches the venturi to the barrel.
venturi
Exhaust tube for gases released by the explosion; the forward thrust generated by these gases offsets the rear thrust of the explosion.
front grip
Handle used to grip the front of the rifle and aim it.
trigger
Device that is pressed to fire the weapon.
cocking lever
Device used to cock the weapon.
firing mechanism
Mechanism that fires the projectile.
antitank rocket
Bursting charge for destroying armored vehicles.

antipersonnel mine

Explosive device designed to be triggered by a person's weight.

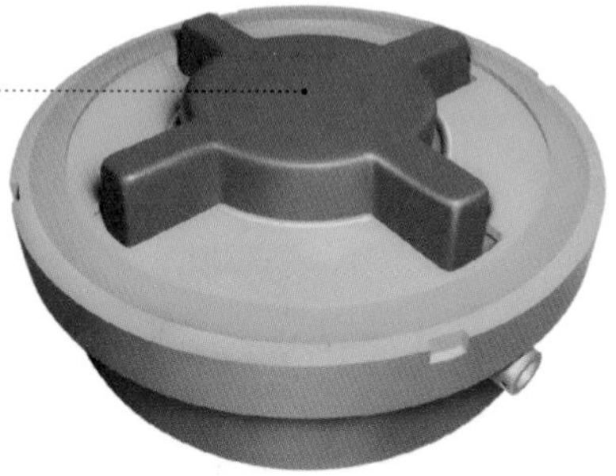
pressure plate
Device that triggers the mine's firing mechanism when pressed down.

tank

Armed and armored vehicle mounted on track shoes.

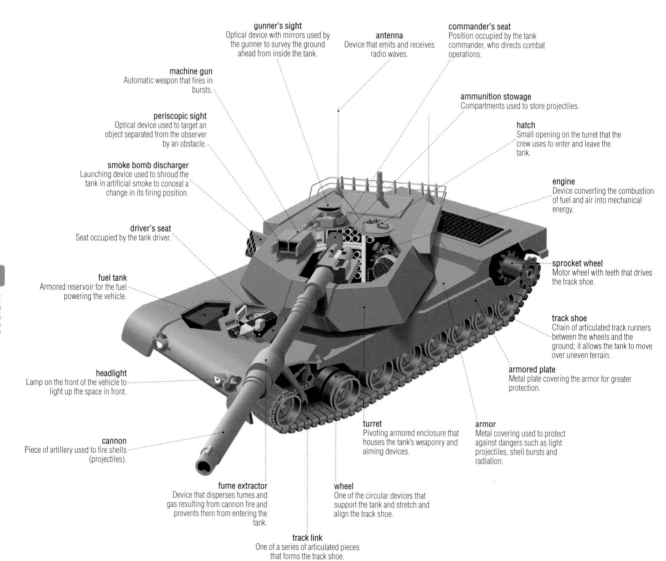

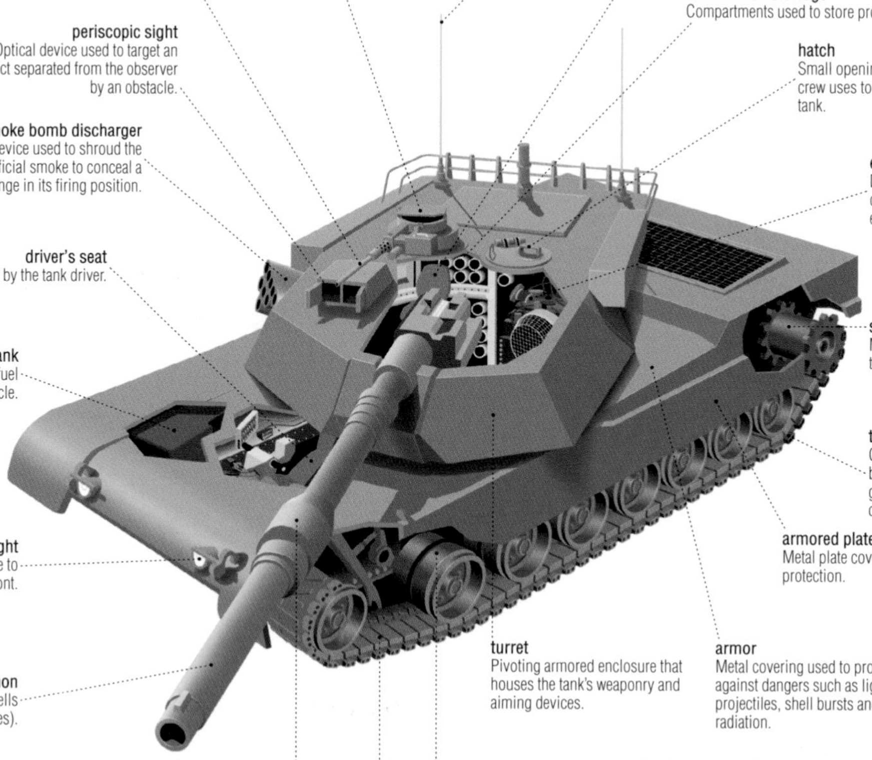
gunner's sight
Optical device with mirrors used by the gunner to survey the ground ahead from inside the tank.
antenna
Device that emits and receives radio waves.
commander's seat
Position occupied by the tank commander, who directs combat operations.
machine gun
Automatic weapon that fires in bursts.
ammunition stowage
Compartments used to store projectiles.
periscopic sight
Optical device used to target an object separated from the observer by an obstacle.
hatch
Small opening on the turret that the crew uses to enter and leave the tank.
smoke bomb discharger
Launching device used to shroud the tank in artificial smoke to conceal a change in its firing position.
engine
Device converting the combustion of fuel and air into mechanical energy.
driver's seat
Seat occupied by the tank driver.
sprocket wheel
Motor wheel with teeth that drives the track shoe.
fuel tank
Armored reservoir for the fuel powering the vehicle.
track shoe
Chain of articulated track runners between the wheels and the ground; it allows the tank to move over uneven terrain.
armored plate
Metal plate covering the armor for greater protection.
headlight
Lamp on the front of the vehicle to light up the space in front.
turret
Pivoting armored enclosure that houses the tank's weaponry and aiming devices.
armor
Metal covering used to protect against dangers such as light projectiles, shell bursts and radiation.
cannon
Piece of artillery used to fire shells (projectiles).
fume extractor
Device that disperses fumes and gas resulting from cannon fire and prevents them from entering the tank.
wheel
One of the circular devices that support the tank and stretch and align the track shoe.
track link
One of a series of articulated pieces that forms the track shoe.

missiles

Self-propelled projectiles that carry a destructive payload.

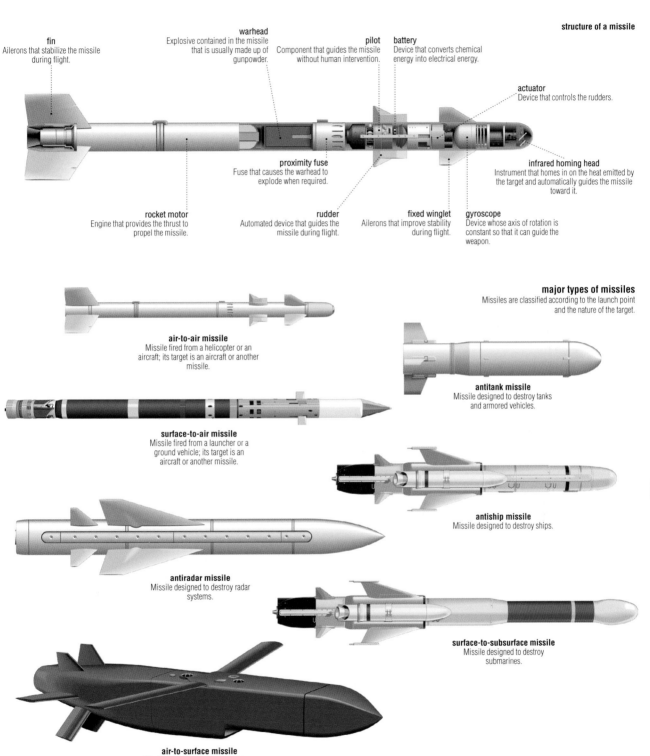

structure of a missile

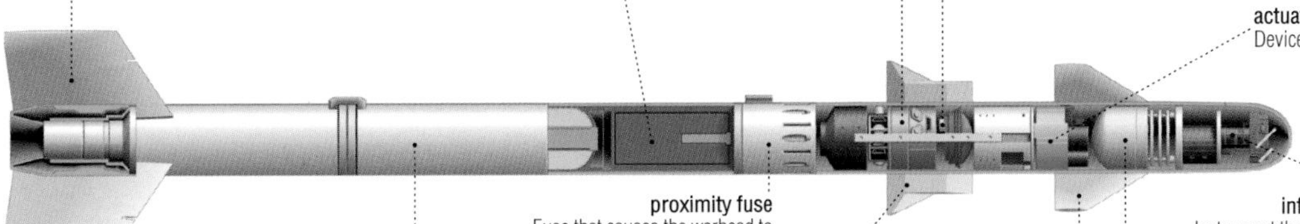
fin
Ailerons that stabilize the missile during flight.
warhead
Explosive contained in the missile that is usually made up of gunpowder.
pilot
Component that guides the missile without human intervention.
battery
Device that converts chemical energy into electrical energy.
actuator
Device that controls the rudders.
proximity fuse
Fuse that causes the warhead to explode when required.
infrared homing head
Instrument that homes in on the heat emitted by the target and automatically guides the missile toward it.
rocket motor
Engine that provides the thrust to propel the missile.
rudder
Automated device that guides the missile during flight.
fixed winglet
Ailerons that improve stability during flight.
gyroscope
Device whose axis of rotation is constant so that it can guide the weapon.

major types of missiles

Missiles are classified according to the launch point and the nature of the target.

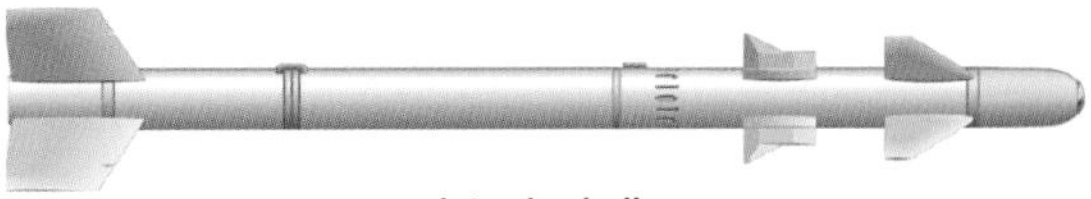

air-to-air missile
Missile fired from a helicopter or an aircraft; its target is an aircraft or another missile.

antitank missile
Missile designed to destroy tanks and armored vehicles.

surface-to-air missile
Missile fired from a launcher or a ground vehicle; its target is an aircraft or another missile.

antiship missile
Missile designed to destroy ships.

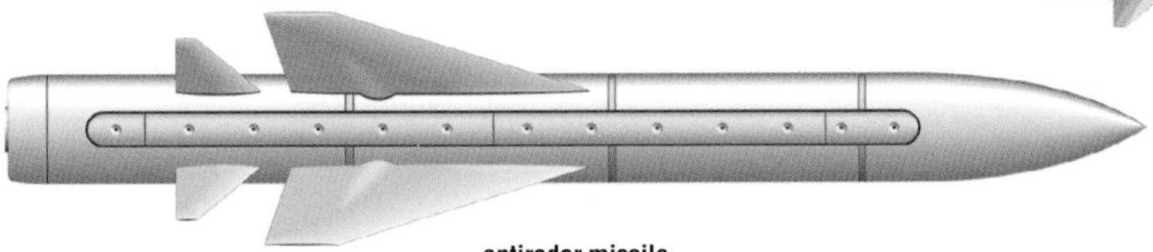

antiradar missile
Missile designed to destroy radar systems.

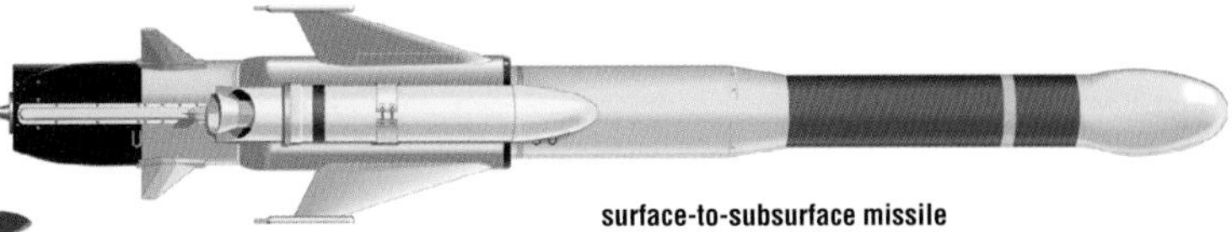

surface-to-subsurface missile
Missile designed to destroy submarines.

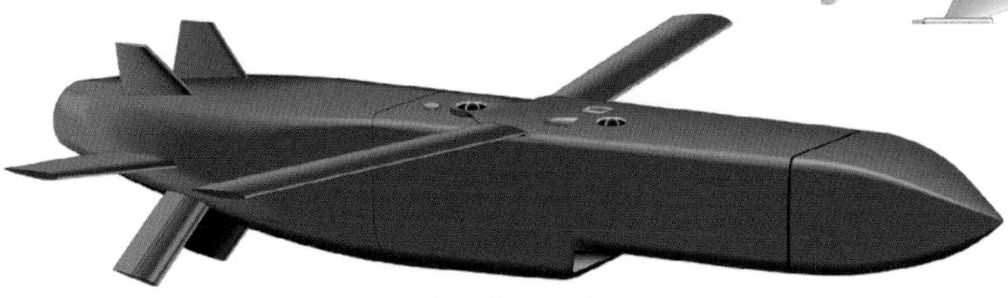

air-to-surface missile
Missile fired at a ground target from a helicopter or an aircraft.

combat aircraft

Military aircraft used for attack purposes.

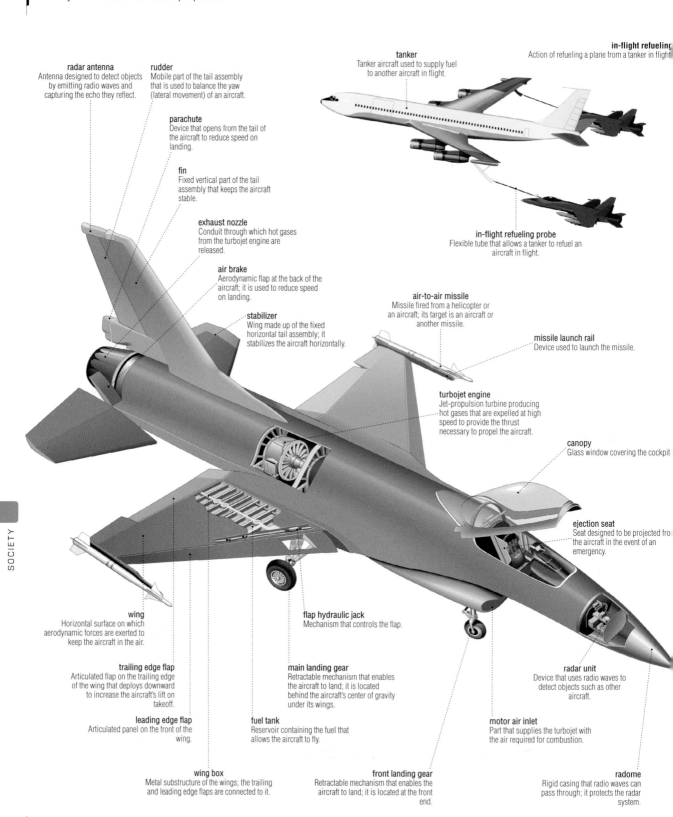

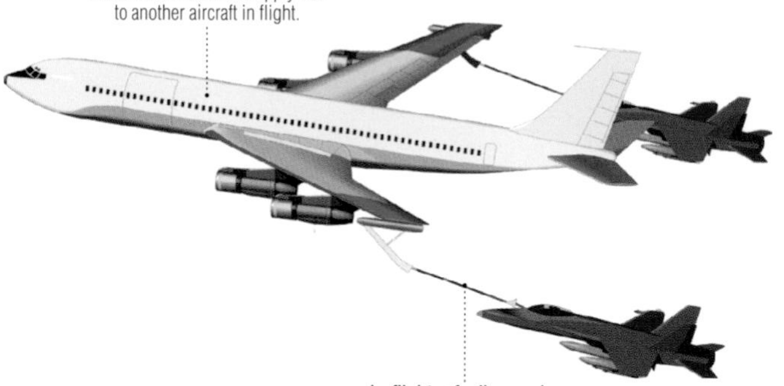
in-flight refueling
Action of refueling a plane from a tanker in flight
tanker
Tanker aircraft used to supply fuel to another aircraft in flight.
in-flight refueling probe
Flexible tube that allows a tanker to refuel an aircraft in flight.

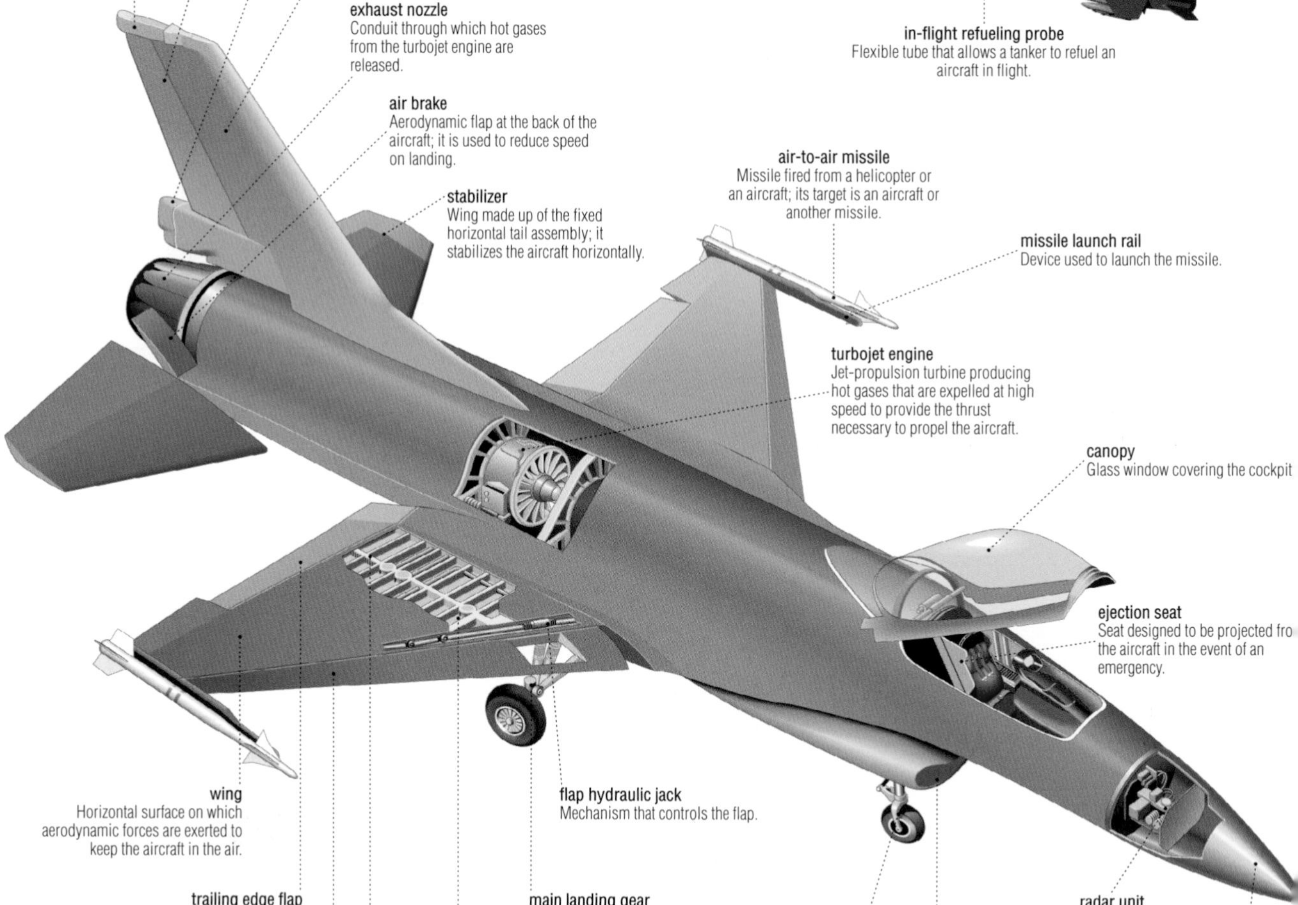
radar antenna
Antenna designed to detect objects by emitting radio waves and capturing the echo they reflect.
rudder
Mobile part of the tail assembly that is used to balance the yaw (lateral movement) of an aircraft.
parachute
Device that opens from the tail of the aircraft to reduce speed on landing.
fin
Fixed vertical part of the tail assembly that keeps the aircraft stable.
exhaust nozzle
Conduit through which hot gases from the turbojet engine are released.
air brake
Aerodynamic flap at the back of the aircraft; it is used to reduce speed on landing.
stabilizer
Wing made up of the fixed horizontal tail assembly; it stabilizes the aircraft horizontally.
air-to-air missile
Missile fired from a helicopter or an aircraft; its target is an aircraft or another missile.
missile launch rail
Device used to launch the missile.
turbojet engine
Jet-propulsion turbine producing hot gases that are expelled at high speed to provide the thrust necessary to propel the aircraft.
canopy
Glass window covering the cockpit
ejection seat
Seat designed to be projected fro the aircraft in the event of an emergency.
wing
Horizontal surface on which aerodynamic forces are exerted to keep the aircraft in the air.
flap hydraulic jack
Mechanism that controls the flap.
trailing edge flap
Articulated flap on the trailing edge of the wing that deploys downward to increase the aircraft's lift on takeoff.
main landing gear
Retractable mechanism that enables the aircraft to land; it is located behind the aircraft's center of gravity under its wings.
radar unit
Device that uses radio waves to detect objects such as other aircraft.
leading edge flap
Articulated panel on the front of the wing.
fuel tank
Reservoir containing the fuel that allows the aircraft to fly.
motor air inlet
Part that supplies the turbojet with the air required for combustion.
wing box
Metal substructure of the wings; the trailing and leading edge flaps are connected to it.
front landing gear
Retractable mechanism that enables the aircraft to land; it is located at the front end.
radome
Rigid casing that radio waves can pass through; it protects the radar system.

aircraft carrier

Warship designed to carry combat aircraft and provide a flight deck for takeoff and landing.

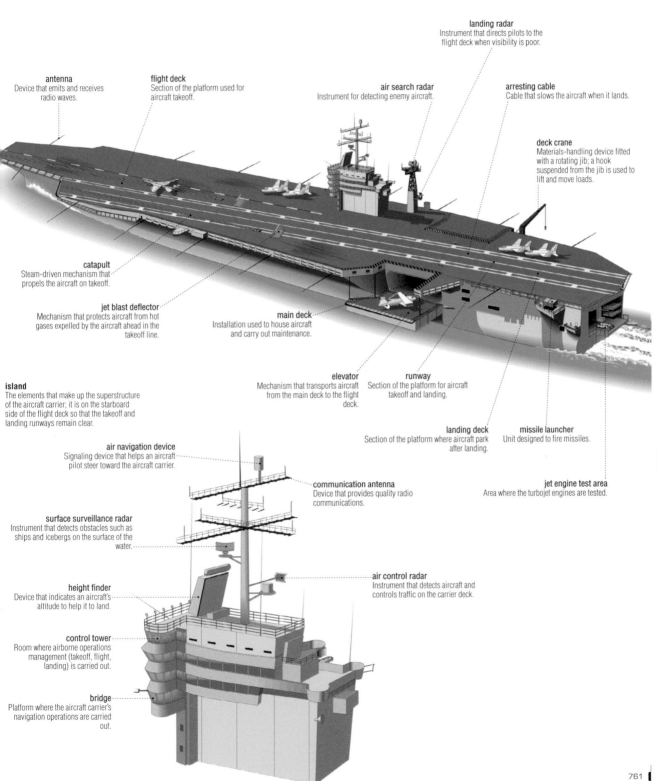

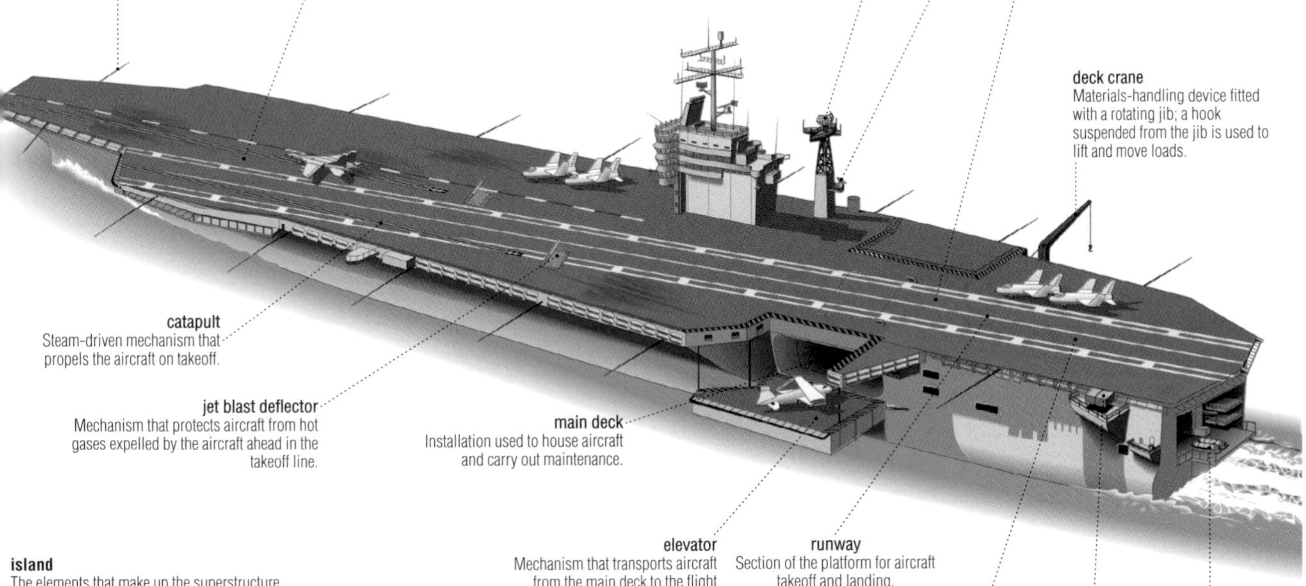
landing radar
Instrument that directs pilots to the flight deck when visibility is poor.
antenna
Device that emits and receives radio waves.
flight deck
Section of the platform used for aircraft takeoff.
air search radar
Instrument for detecting enemy aircraft.
arresting cable
Cable that slows the aircraft when it lands.
deck crane
Materials-handling device fitted with a rotating jib; a hook suspended from the jib is used to lift and move loads.
catapult
Steam-driven mechanism that propels the aircraft on takeoff.
jet blast deflector
Mechanism that protects aircraft from hot gases expelled by the aircraft ahead in the takeoff line.
main deck
Installation used to house aircraft and carry out maintenance.
elevator
Mechanism that transports aircraft from the main deck to the flight deck.
runway
Section of the platform for aircraft takeoff and landing.
landing deck
Section of the platform where aircraft park after landing.
missile launcher
Unit designed to fire missiles.
jet engine test area
Area where the turbojet engines are tested.

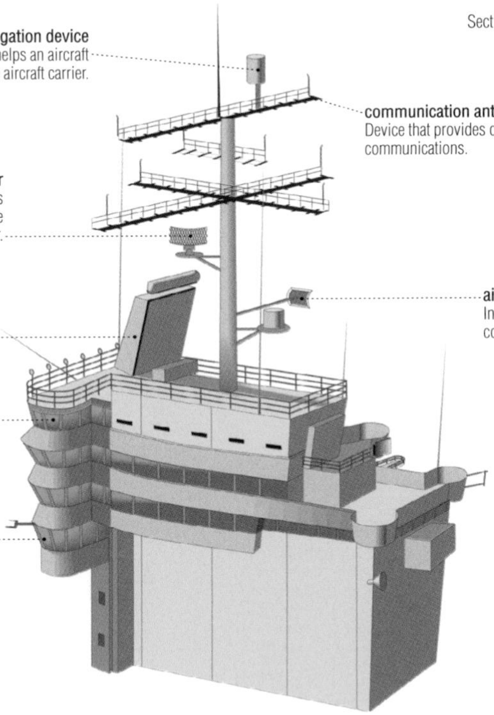
island
The elements that make up the superstructure of the aircraft carrier; it is on the starboard side of the flight deck so that the takeoff and landing runways remain clear.
air navigation device
Signaling device that helps an aircraft pilot steer toward the aircraft carrier.
communication antenna
Device that provides quality radio communications.
surface surveillance radar
Instrument that detects obstacles such as ships and icebergs on the surface of the water.
air control radar
Instrument that detects aircraft and controls traffic on the carrier deck.
height finder
Device that indicates an aircraft's altitude to help it to land.
control tower
Room where airborne operations management (takeoff, flight, landing) is carried out.
bridge
Platform where the aircraft carrier's navigation operations are carried out.

frigate

Warship used for antiaircraft, antisubmarine and antiship operations.

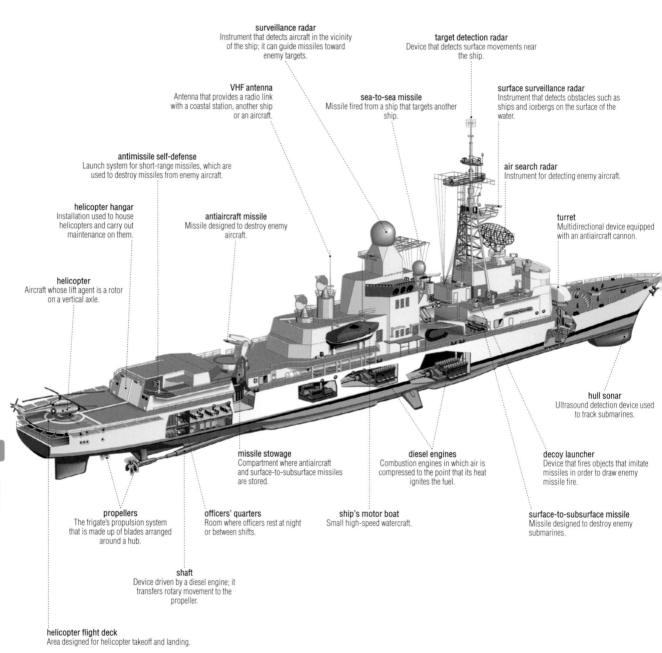

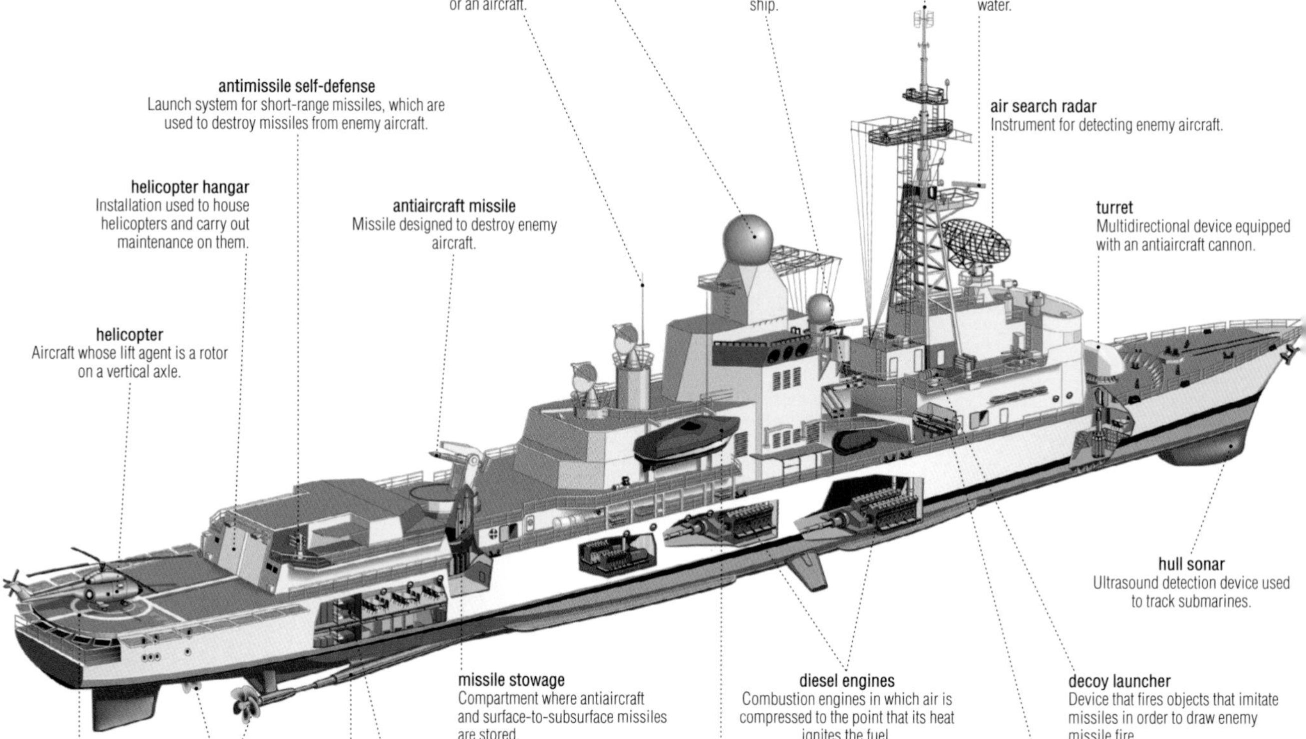

surveillance radar
Instrument that detects aircraft in the vicinity of the ship; it can guide missiles toward enemy targets.
target detection radar
Device that detects surface movements near the ship.
VHF antenna
Antenna that provides a radio link with a coastal station, another ship or an aircraft.
sea-to-sea missile
Missile fired from a ship that targets another ship.
surface surveillance radar
Instrument that detects obstacles such as ships and icebergs on the surface of the water.
antimissile self-defense
Launch system for short-range missiles, which are used to destroy missiles from enemy aircraft.
air search radar
Instrument for detecting enemy aircraft.
helicopter hangar
Installation used to house helicopters and carry out maintenance on them.
antiaircraft missile
Missile designed to destroy enemy aircraft.
turret
Multidirectional device equipped with an antiaircraft cannon.
helicopter
Aircraft whose lift agent is a rotor on a vertical axle.
hull sonar
Ultrasound detection device used to track submarines.
missile stowage
Compartment where antiaircraft and surface-to-subsurface missiles are stored.
diesel engines
Combustion engines in which air is compressed to the point that its heat ignites the fuel.
decoy launcher
Device that fires objects that imitate missiles in order to draw enemy missile fire.
propellers
The frigate's propulsion system that is made up of blades arranged around a hub.
officers' quarters
Room where officers rest at night or between shifts.
ship's motor boat
Small high-speed watercraft.
surface-to-subsurface missile
Missile designed to destroy enemy submarines.
shaft
Device driven by a diesel engine; it transfers rotary movement to the propeller.
helicopter flight deck
Area designed for helicopter takeoff and landing.

nuclear submarine

Underwater warship that operates on nuclear energy; it can remain underwater for months without surfacing.

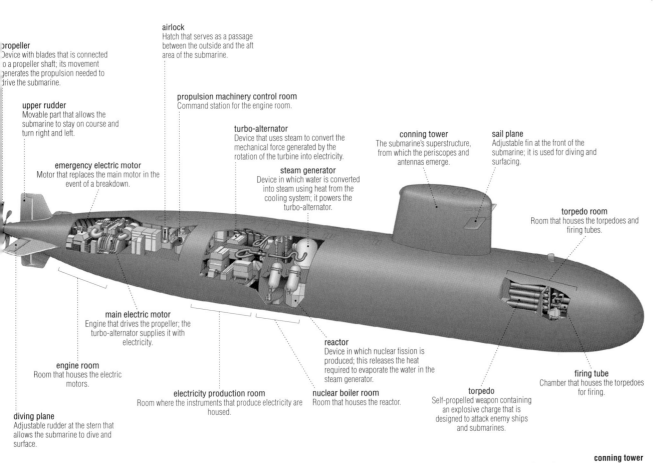

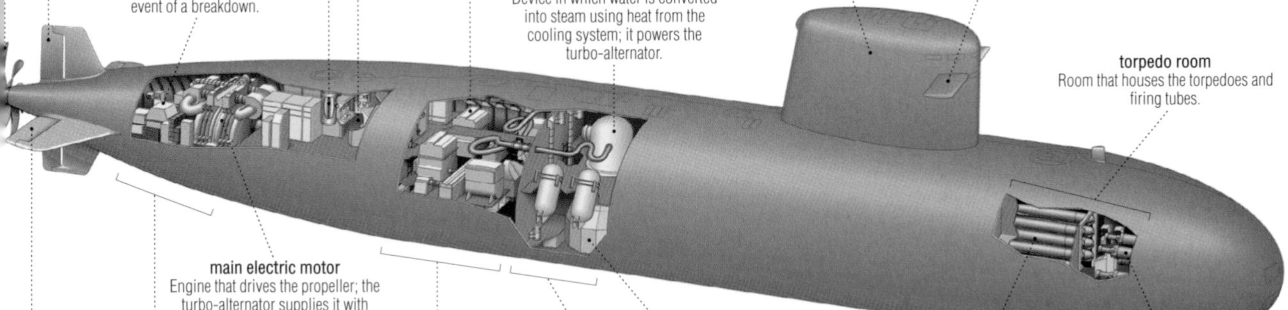
propeller
Device with blades that is connected to a propeller shaft; its movement generates the propulsion needed to drive the submarine.
airlock
Hatch that serves as a passage between the outside and the aft area of the submarine.
upper rudder
Movable part that allows the submarine to stay on course and turn right and left.
propulsion machinery control room
Command station for the engine room.
turbo-alternator
Device that uses steam to convert the mechanical force generated by the rotation of the turbine into electricity.
conning tower
The submarine's superstructure, from which the periscopes and antennas emerge.
sail plane
Adjustable fin at the front of the submarine; it is used for diving and surfacing.
emergency electric motor
Motor that replaces the main motor in the event of a breakdown.
steam generator
Device in which water is converted into steam using heat from the cooling system; it powers the turbo-alternator.
torpedo room
Room that houses the torpedoes and firing tubes.
main electric motor
Engine that drives the propeller; the turbo-alternator supplies it with electricity.
reactor
Device in which nuclear fission is produced; this releases the heat required to evaporate the water in the steam generator.
engine room
Room that houses the electric motors.
firing tube
Chamber that houses the torpedoes for firing.
electricity production room
Room where the instruments that produce electricity are housed.
nuclear boiler room
Room that houses the reactor.
torpedo
Self-propelled weapon containing an explosive charge that is designed to attack enemy ships and submarines.
diving plane
Adjustable rudder at the stern that allows the submarine to dive and surface.

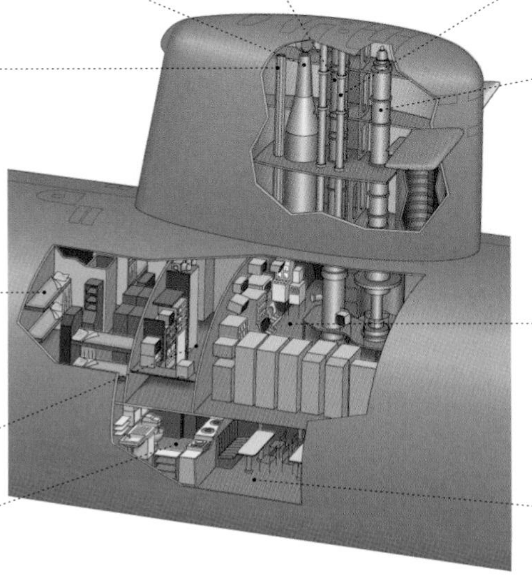
conning tower
The submarine's superstructure, from which the periscopes and antennas emerge.
attack periscope
Device used to examine the surface of the water; its discreet head allows the submarine to approach an enemy without being noticed.
radar antenna
Antenna designed to detect objects by emitting radio waves and capturing the echo they reflect.
radio antenna
Metal conductor transmitting and receiving radio waves for communications.
navigation periscope
Device used to examine the surface of the water; its wide head provides a broad field of vision.
multipurpose antenna
Device that transmits and receives radio waves on an extremely broad range of frequencies.
officers' quarters
Room where officers rest at night or between shifts.
operation control room
Room in which submarine combat operations and navigation maneuvers are coordinated.
computer room
Room in which radar, sonar and other data transmitted to the submarine are processed.
kitchen
Room where meals are prepared.
dining room
Hall for eating meals.

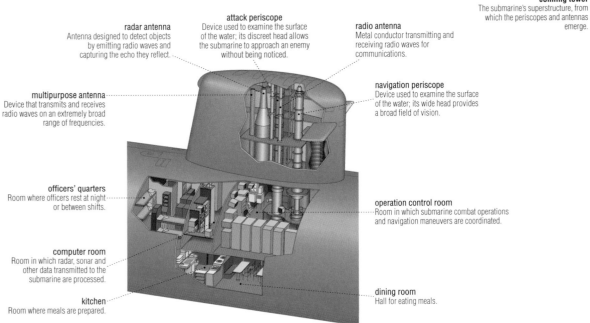

fire prevention

The means and instruments used to prevent and fight fires.

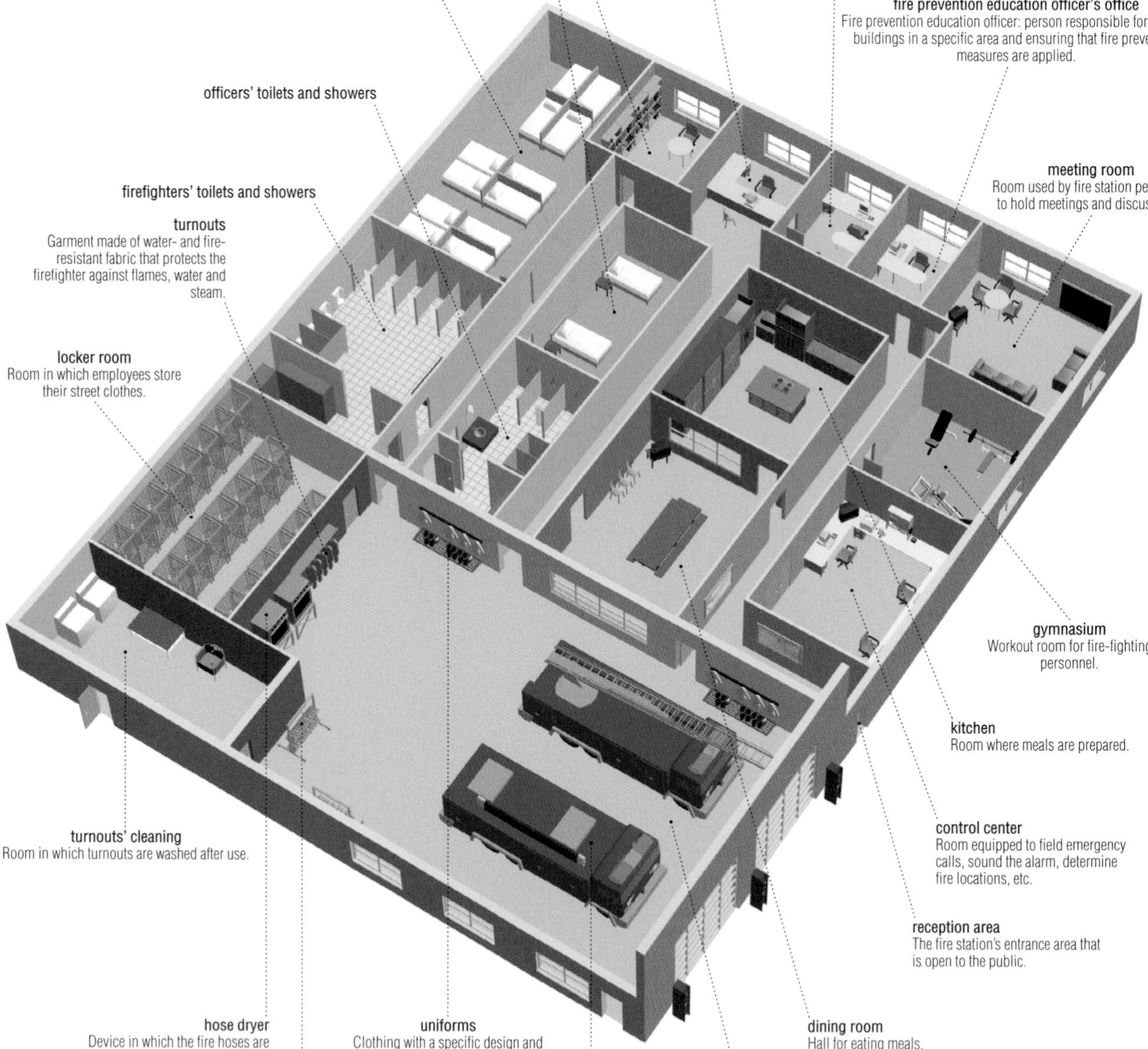
fire station
Building designed to house firefighters, fire trucks and fire-fighting materials.
officers' dormitory
Room where officers rest at night or between fire-fighting operations.
documentation center
Room used to store documentation such as security documents related to buildings in a specific area, maps and municipal emergency plans.
chief's office
Work area reserved for the fire chief.
firefighters' dormitory
Room furnished with several beds where firefighters rest at night or between fire-fighting operations.
administrative office
Workplace for administrative personnel.
fire prevention education officer's office
Fire prevention education officer: person responsible for visi buildings in a specific area and ensuring that fire preventio measures are applied.
officers' toilets and showers
meeting room
Room used by fire station persor to hold meetings and discussior
firefighters' toilets and showers
turnouts
Garment made of water- and fire-resistant fabric that protects the firefighter against flames, water and steam.
locker room
Room in which employees store their street clothes.
gymnasium
Workout room for fire-fighting personnel.
kitchen
Room where meals are prepared.
turnouts' cleaning
Room in which turnouts are washed after use.
control center
Room equipped to field emergency calls, sound the alarm, determine fire locations, etc.
reception area
The fire station's entrance area that is open to the public.
hose dryer
Device in which the fire hoses are placed to be dried after use.
uniforms
Clothing with a specific design and color that employees wear while on duty.
dining room
Hall for eating meals.
hose holder
Device used to hold fire hoses.
apparatus room
Part of the fire station where the fire trucks are parked.
fire truck
Motor vehicle designed to transport fire-fighting personnel and materials and to supply water to the fire hose nozzles.

hand lamp
Lighting device that is worn by the firefighter while on duty.

spotlight
Apparatus that projects concentrated high-intensity light beams.

strap
Band of leather or fabric secured to the spotlight; it can be held or worn as a shoulder strap.

battery
Device that converts chemical energy into electrical energy.

helmet
Headpiece designed to protect the head from impact, flames and water.

helmet
Headpiece designed to protect the head from impact, flames and water.

reflective stripe
Strip that reflects light so that it is easier to locate the firefighter when visibility is reduced.

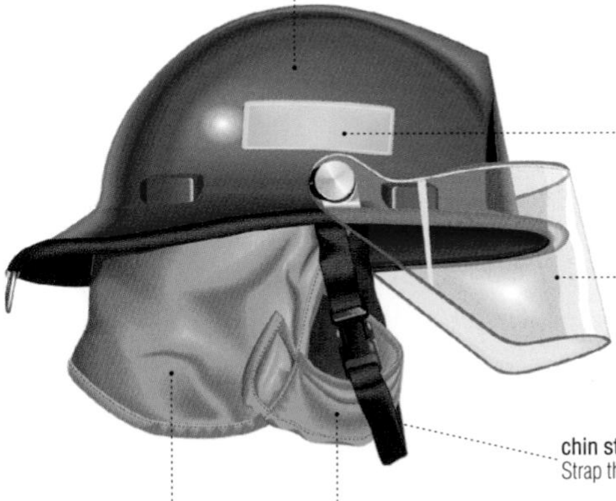

eye guard
Adjustable visor that protects the upper face area.

chin strap
Strap that fastens the helmet to the head.

neck guard
Fireproof fabric that protects the nape of the neck and the ears.

chin guard
Fireproof fabric that protects the lower face area.

firefighter
Person responsible for fighting fires, intervening in natural disasters and undertaking rescue operations.

helmet
Headpiece designed to protect the head from impact, flames and water.

compressed-air cylinder
Container filled with compressed air that allows the firefighter to breathe when the air is smoky or strongly contaminated.

full face mask
Mask that covers the entire face; it protects the respiratory tract and the eyes.

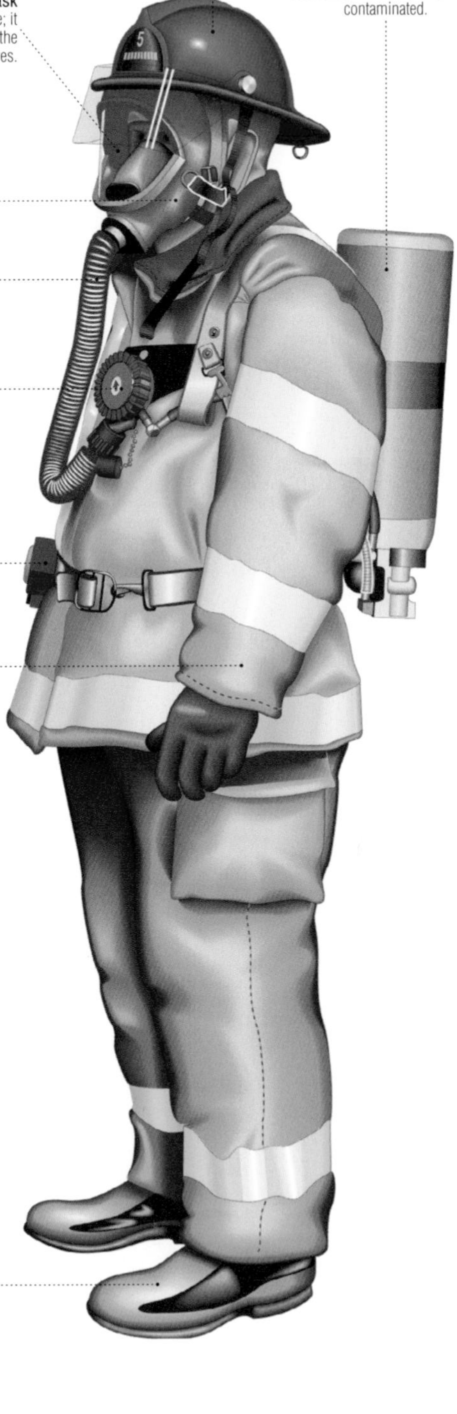

self-contained breathing apparatus
Device that protects against inhaling toxic gas, smoke, dust, etc.

air-supply tube
Conduit that funnels air from the cylinder to the mask.

pressure demand regulator
Device that reduces air pressure from the cylinder and regulates the flow of air to the mask.

mandown alarm
Device that emits a strong signal so that a firefighter can be located in a blaze; it is activated by the firefighter or after a 30-second period of immobility.

turnouts
Garment made of water- and fire-resistant fabric that protects the firefighter against flames, water and steam.

rubber boot
Water-resistant fireproof boot that protects the foot from burns and other injury.

fire prevention

fire trucks
Motor vehicles designed to transport fire-fighting personnel and materials and to supply water to the fire hose nozzles.

pumper
Motor vehicle with a water tank and a pump to funnel pressurized water to the fire hose nozzles.

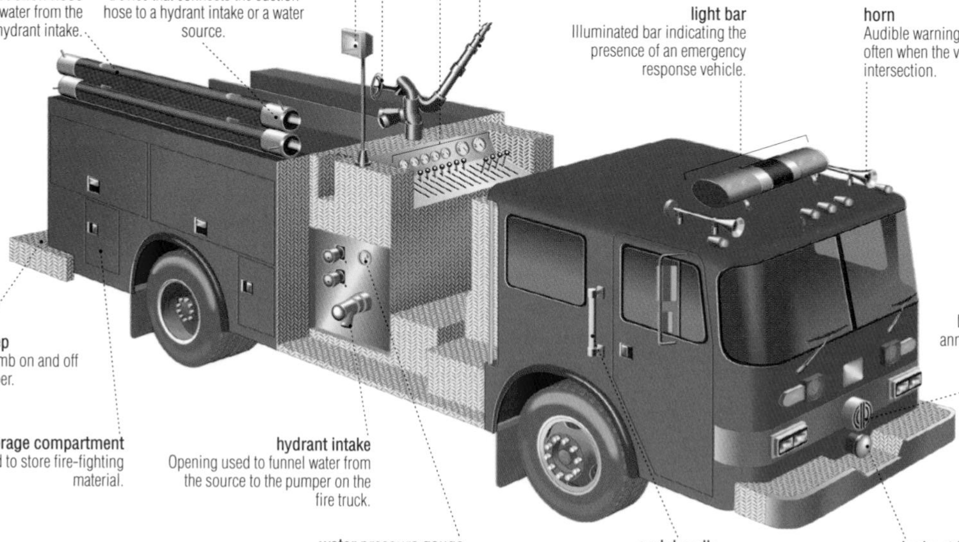
control wheel
Device used to operate the deluge gun.
control panel
Panel with a set of controls, which are used to operate the equipment.
spotlight
Device that emits a concentrated high-intensity light beam; it can be fully rotated.
deluge gun
Pump that delivers a strong jet of water.
fitting
Device that connects the suction hose to a hydrant intake or a water source.
suction hose
Tube that carries water from the source to a hydrant intake.
light bar
Illuminated bar indicating the presence of an emergency response vehicle.
horn
Audible warning device used most often when the vehicle crosses an intersection.
loudspeaker
Device used to issue public announcements or transmit radio communications.
rear step
Platform used to climb on and off the pumper.
storage compartment
Compartment used to store fire-fighting material.
hydrant intake
Opening used to funnel water from the source to the pumper on the fire truck.
water pressure gauge
Device that measures water pressure inside the tank.
grab handle
Vertical handle placed at shoulder level close to the door; it is used to climb into and out of the vehicle.
hydrant intake
Opening used to funnel water from the source to the pumper on the fire truck.

aerial ladder truck
Motor vehicle equipped with a tower ladder, which is used to fight a fire from above and access the upper reaches of a building from the outside.

telescopic boom
Extensible device that raises the sliding ladders of the tower ladder to the desired height.
Mars light
Revolving light on the roof of the moving vehicle; it is used when an operation is in progress.
ladder pipe nozzle
Device mounted on the end of the telescopic boom; it forms and directs a water jet onto a fire or onto the upper reaches of a building
elevating cylinder
Device that raises the tower ladder and keeps it stable.
turntable mounting
Pivoting device that supports and positions the tower ladder.
tower ladder
Set of extension ladders for changing the height of the tower ladder.
top ladder
Sliding ladder that makes up the highest part of the tower ladder.
spotlight
Device that emits a concentrated high-intensity light beam; it can be fully rotated.
storage compartment
Compartment used to store fire-fighting material.
outrigger
Device that stabilizes the vehicle when the ladders are deployed.

fire prevention

fire hydrant
A pipe connected to a water main; firefighters attach their hoses to it to supply their trucks.

cover
Part of the detector that shields the smoke detection mechanism.
test button
Device that is pressed to determine whether the sound signal is functioning.
base
Part of the detector that is attached to a surface; the cover screws into the base.
indicator light
Light indicating that the detector is in alarm mode.

smoke detector
Device that emits a powerful alarm signal when it detects smoke.

fire-fighting material

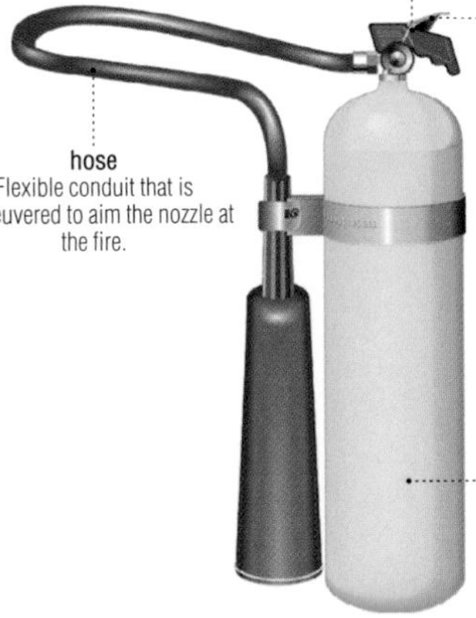
pin
Security device that is pulled to operate the trigger.
trigger
Device that is pressed to spray the fire area.
hose
Flexible conduit that is euvered to aim the nozzle at the fire.
tank
Metal container that is filled with pressurized liquid, powder or gas; it is replenished periodically.

portable fire extinguisher
Portable device used to extinguish a fire using liquid, powder or gas released under pressure.

nozzle
Device that is connected to the end of a fire hose; it forms and directs a jet of water.

ladder and hose strap
Band that connects two hoses or attaches a hose to a ladder or a fire escape, etc.

dividing breeching
Y-shaped device used to connect two hoses to a water outlet.

fire hose
Flexible hose that carries water from the pressurized water source to the nozzle.

fire hydrant wrench
Tool with a square opening nut used to manipulate the fire hydrant opening.

percussion bar
Tool with a deer foot that is used to force open locks, padlocks, etc.

hatchet
Tool with a sharp blade and a pick attached to the end of a handle; it is used to create openings by forcing open doors and windows.

pike pole
Tool with a hook and a pike attached to a long handle; it is used for operations such as piercing walls and ceilings and carrying out underwater searches.

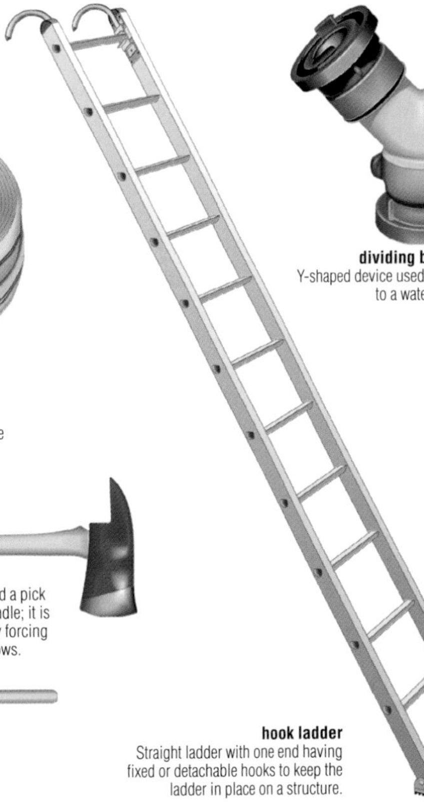

hook ladder
Straight ladder with one end having fixed or detachable hooks to keep the ladder in place on a structure.

crime prevention

The means used to prevent occurrences such as violence, delinquency and acts of aggression.

police station
Building that houses crime prevention personnel and offices.

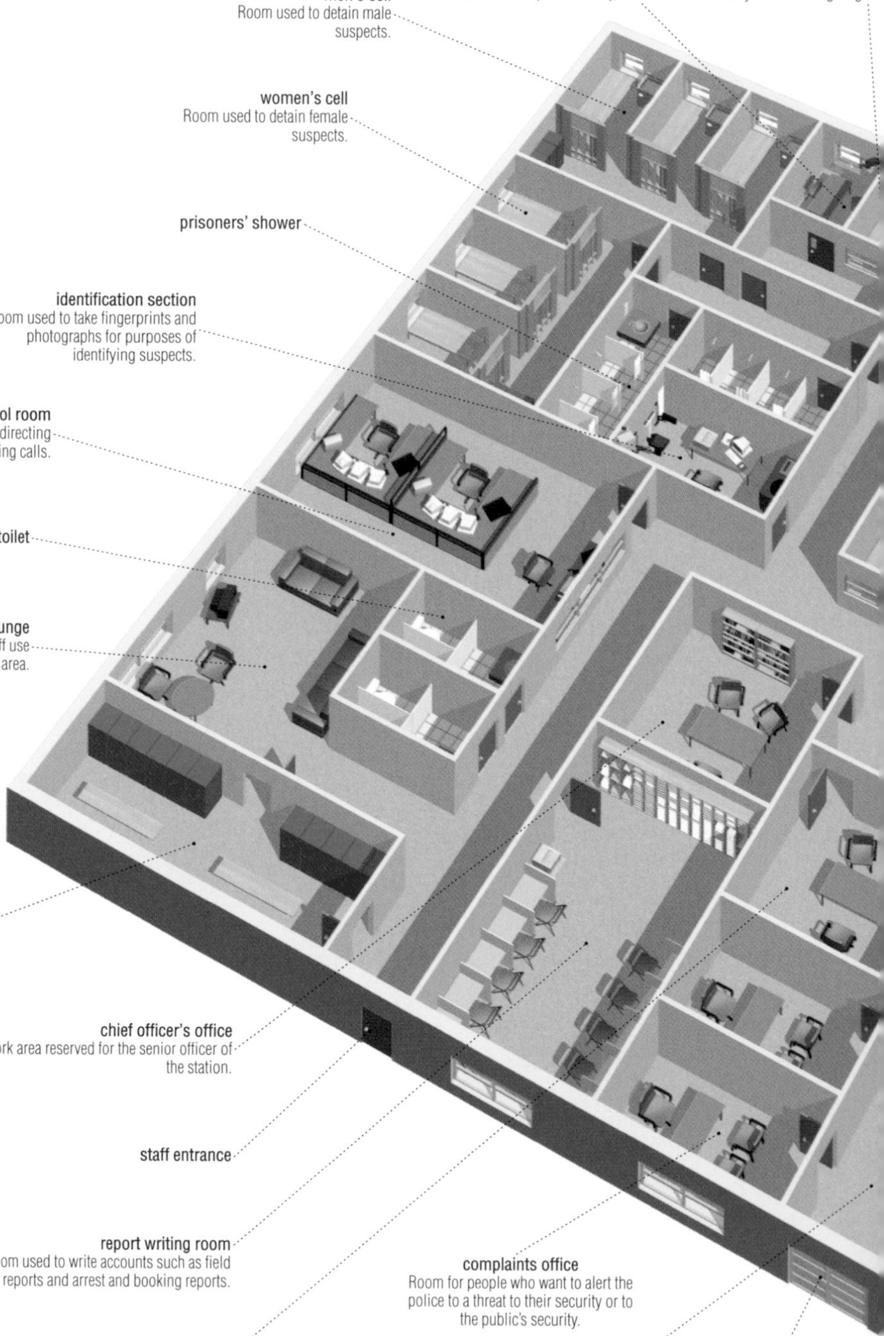

juvenile cell
Room used to detain suspects who have yet to reach legal age.
interrogation room
Room used to question suspects.
men's cell
Room used to detain male suspects.
women's cell
Room used to detain female suspects.
prisoners' shower
identification section
Room used to take fingerprints and photographs for purposes of identifying suspects.
control room
Room for receiving and directing incoming calls.
staff toilet
staff lounge
Room that police station staff use as a rest area.
locker room
chief officer's office
Work area reserved for the senior officer of the station.
staff entrance
report writing room
Room used to write accounts such as field reports and arrest and booking reports.
complaints office
Room for people who want to alert the police to a threat to their security or to the public's security.
junior officer's office
Work area reserved for the assistant to the chief officer.
waiting room
Area where citizens wait to see a police officer.
main entrance

garage
Part of the police station where vehicles are parked and maintained.
vehicle entrance
safe
Fireproof receptacle used to store important documents and pieces of evidence.
police car
Patrol vehicle equipped with a radio and a dashboard computer.
storage room
Room used to store a variety of objects.
archives
Room where documents are stored for possible use.
breath testing machine
Device used to determine a person's blood alcohol level by means of breath analysis.
equipment
Room used to store police equipment.
booking room
Room in which suspects are searched and informed of their rights before being led to a cell.
gun range
Room designed for firearms training using service pistols.
administrative office
Workplace for administrative personnel.
information desk
Area where information can be obtained on police services.

crime prevention

police officer
Uniformed person responsible for maintaining law and order.

cap
Brimless, somewhat soft headgear that has a peak and a flat crown.

badge
Symbol indicating the force an officer belongs to as well as the officer's identification number.

shoulder strap
Decorative tab attached to the shoulder and sometimes buttoned down; it is inspired by the military uniform.

rank insignia
Symbol indicating a police officer's rank.

identification badge
Symbol indicating a police officer's name.

uniform
Garment of a specific color and style that is worn by police officers on duty.

duty belt
Belt that the police officer wears to carry equipment.

microphone
Device that converts electric pulses into broadcast or recorded sounds.

latex glove case
Pouch for carrying gloves worn to pick up pieces of evidence or contaminated objects such as used syringes.

handcuff case
Pouch for storing handcuffs.

pistol
Short lightweight handgun that is loaded from the butt.

pepper spray
Container that emits an irritating gas to neutralize and control a person or a crowd.

ammunition pouch
Pouch for storing ammunition clips for the pistol.

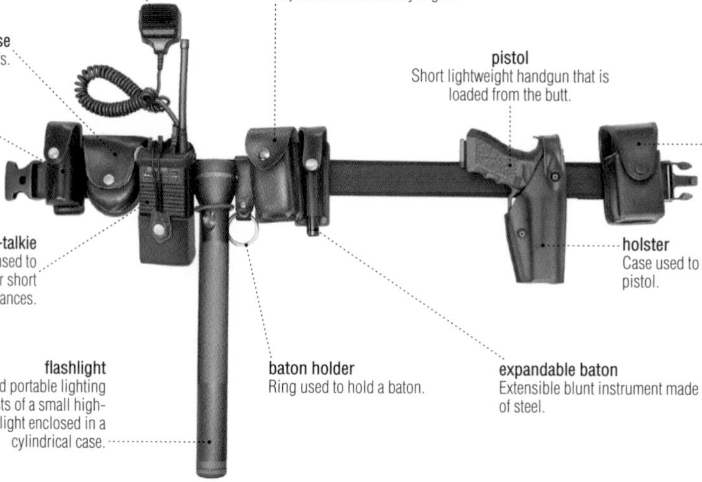

walkie-talkie
Portable two-way radio used to relay the human voice over short distances.

holster
Case used to carry and protect a pistol.

flashlight
Battery-operated portable lighting device; it consists of a small high-intensity light enclosed in a cylindrical case.

baton holder
Ring used to hold a baton.

expandable baton
Extensible blunt instrument made of steel.

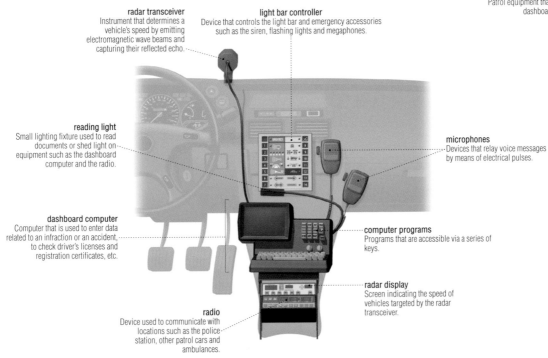

dashboard equipment
Patrol equipment that is installed on the dashboard's center console.

radar transceiver
Instrument that determines a vehicle's speed by emitting electromagnetic wave beams and capturing their reflected echo.

light bar controller
Device that controls the light bar and emergency accessories such as the siren, flashing lights and megaphones.

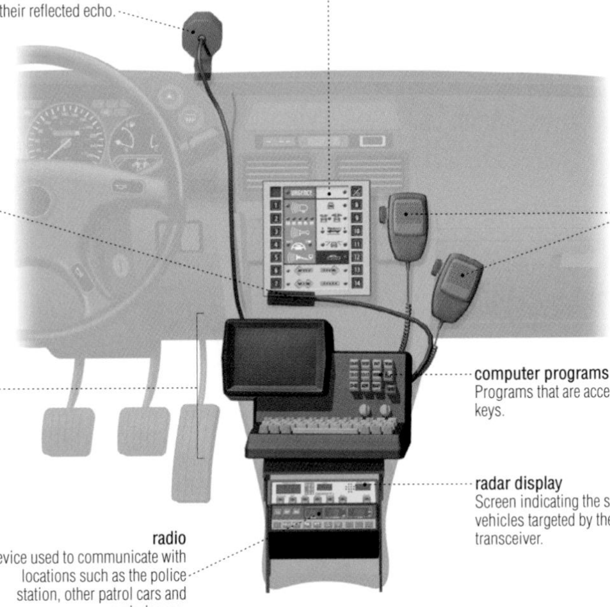

reading light
Small lighting fixture used to read documents or shed light on equipment such as the dashboard computer and the radio.

microphones
Devices that relay voice messages by means of electrical pulses.

dashboard computer
Computer that is used to enter data related to an infraction or an accident, to check driver's licenses and registration certificates, etc.

computer programs
Programs that are accessible via a series of keys.

radar display
Screen indicating the speed of vehicles targeted by the radar transceiver.

radio
Device used to communicate with locations such as the police station, other patrol cars and ambulances.

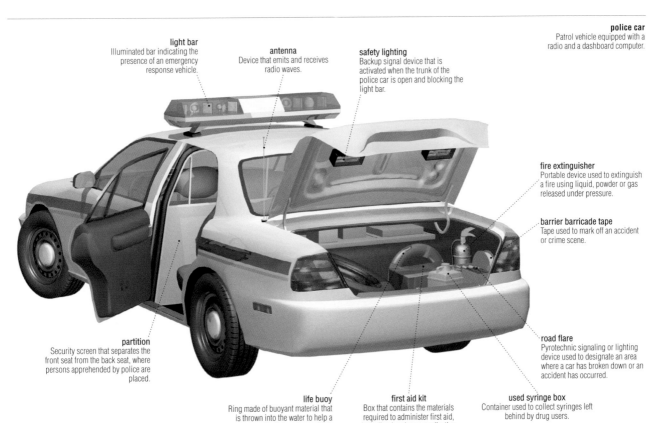

police car
Patrol vehicle equipped with a radio and a dashboard computer.

light bar
Illuminated bar indicating the presence of an emergency response vehicle.

antenna
Device that emits and receives radio waves.

safety lighting
Backup signal device that is activated when the trunk of the police car is open and blocking the light bar.

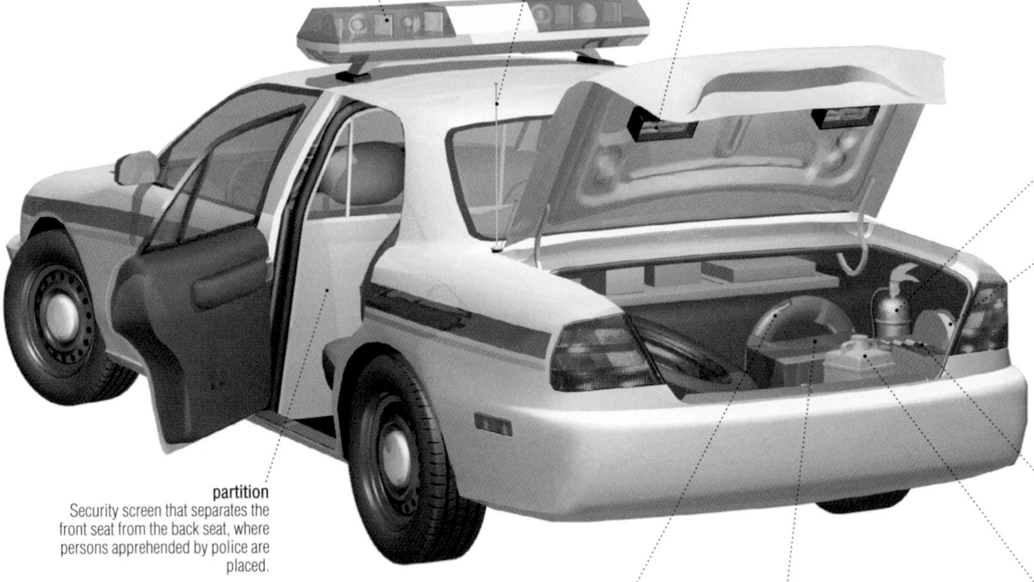

fire extinguisher
Portable device used to extinguish a fire using liquid, powder or gas released under pressure.

barrier barricade tape
Tape used to mark off an accident or crime scene.

road flare
Pyrotechnic signaling or lighting device used to designate an area where a car has broken down or an accident has occurred.

partition
Security screen that separates the front seat from the back seat, where persons apprehended by police are placed.

life buoy
Ring made of buoyant material that is thrown into the water to help a person in distress keep afloat.

first aid kit
Box that contains the materials required to administer first aid, including bandages, medication and instruments.

used syringe box
Container used to collect syringes left behind by drug users.

ear protection

Devices that reduce workplace noise and noise caused by power tools.

safety earmuffs
Pair of rigid shells that are connected by a headband and contain soft foam cushions.

headband
Flexible piece that keeps the earmuffs in place.

foam cushion
Soft material that fits around the ears to make the headband more comfortable.

earplugs
Device with plugs that are secured to the entrance of the auditory canal by a headband.

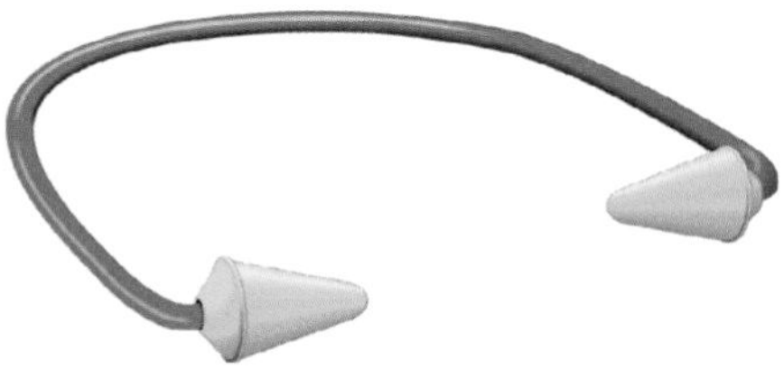

eye protection

Safety goggles that protect the eyes from impact, flying objects and heat.

safety glasses
Glasses that consist of plastic lenses attached to a frame with temples; they come with or without side protection.

safety goggles
Watertight glasses with a one-piece frame that provide front and side eye protection.

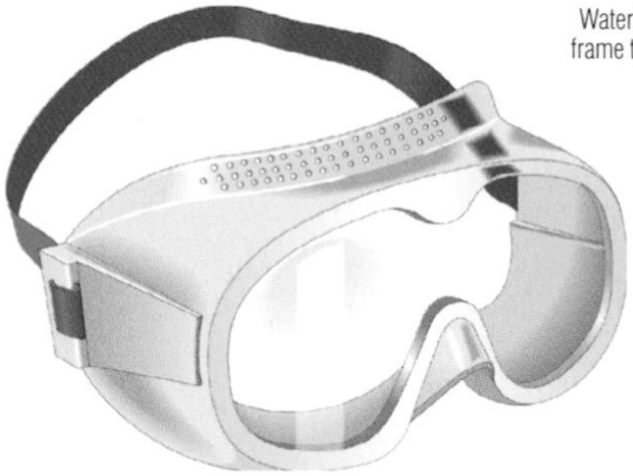

head protection

Safety helmet that protects against falling objects and impact.

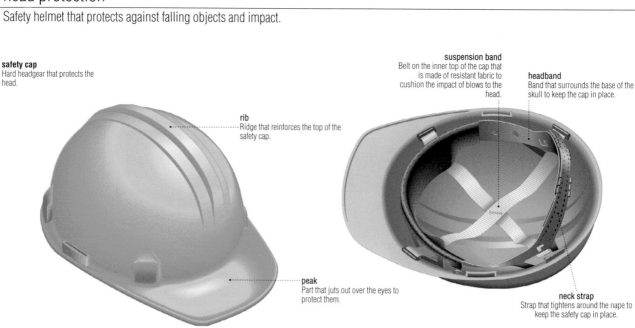

safety cap
Hard headgear that protects the head.

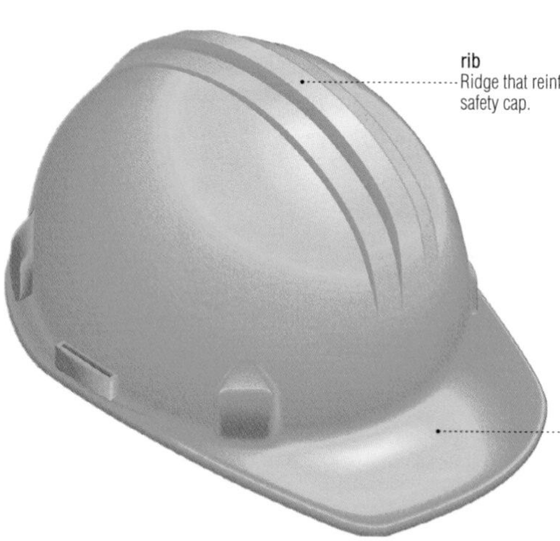

rib
Ridge that reinforces the top of the safety cap.

peak
Part that juts out over the eyes to protect them.

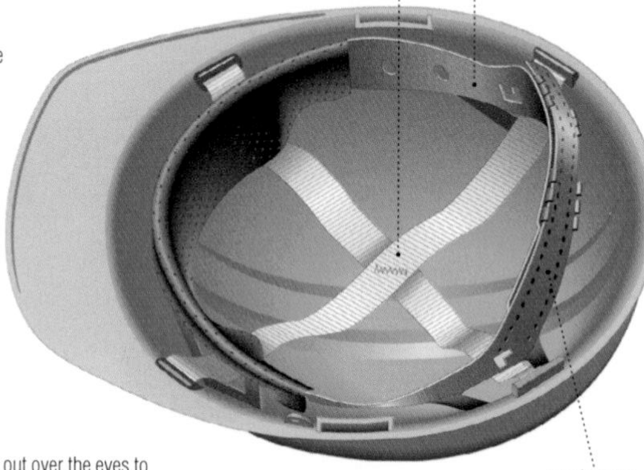

suspension band
Belt on the inner top of the cap that is made of resistant fabric to cushion the impact of blows to the head.

headband
Band that surrounds the base of the skull to keep the cap in place.

neck strap
Strap that tightens around the nape to keep the safety cap in place.

respiratory system protection

Mask used to protect the respiratory tract from elements such as polluted air, dust, smoke and volatile chemicals.

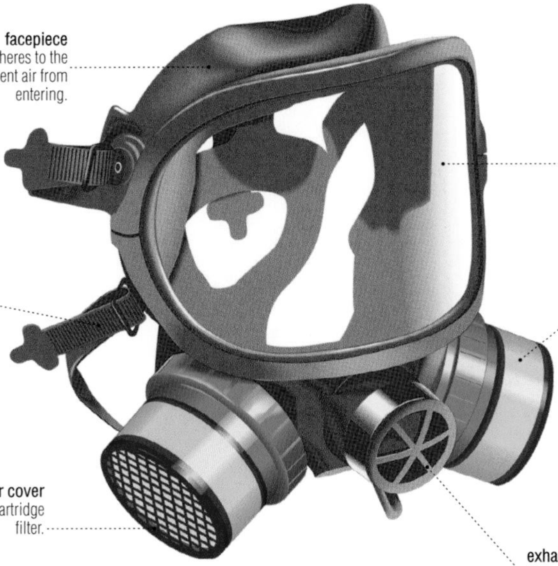

respirator
Mask that filters out contaminated air; it covers the entire facial area to protect the nose, mouth and eyes.
facepiece
Part of the mask that adheres to the face and prevents ambient air from entering.
visor
Transparent part of the mask that allows the user to see.
head harness
Straps that attach at the back of the head to secure the mask to the face.
cartridge
Device that filters out contaminated air by absorbing harmful substances.
inhalation valve
Device that allows air to enter the mask and prevents exhaled air from exiting through the air intake.
filter cover
Device that protects the cartridge filter.
exhalation valve
Device that allows air to be expelled from the mask.

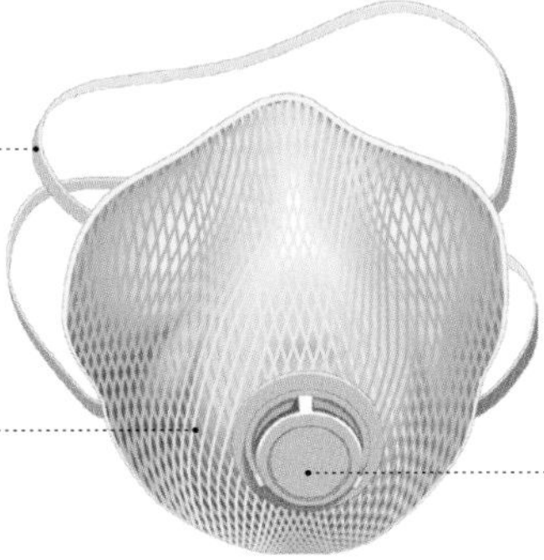

half-mask respirator
Mask that covers and protects the nose and mouth.
headband
Elastic band that secures the mask to the bottom of the face.
cup gasket
Part of the mask that adheres to the bottom of the face and prevents ambient air from entering.
exhalation valve
Device that allows air to be expelled from the mask.

foot protection

Shoes and accessories worn to protect the feet from dangers such as falling objects, intense heat and sharp tools.

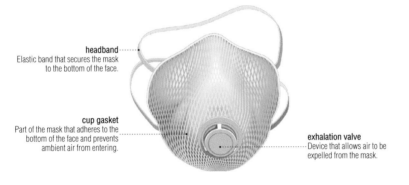

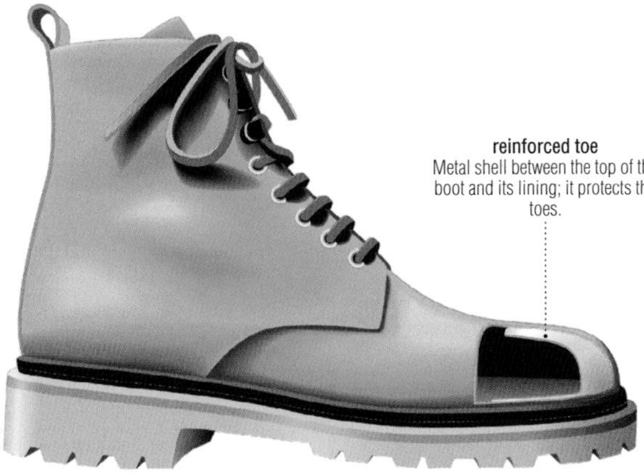

safety boot
Highly durable boot with an insulated nonslip sole and a reinforced toe; it comes up over the ankles.
reinforced toe
Metal shell between the top of the boot and its lining; it protects the toes.

toe guard
Accessory worn over a shoe to protect the end of the foot.

safety symbols

The pictograms used to warn of danger or indicate that safety equipment is mandatory.

dangerous materials
Pictogram warning of materials that pose a health or environmental risk owing to their properties or reactions.

corrosive
Pictogram warning of materials that can damage living tissue or other bodies such as metal.

electrical hazard
Pictogram warning of the danger of electrocution.

explosive
Pictogram warning of materials that explode by chemical reaction.

flammable
Pictogram warning of flammable materials.

radioactive
Pictogram warning of radioactive materials.

poison
Pictogram warning of materials harmful to an organism when inhaled, ingested or absorbed by the skin.

protection
Pictogram warning that protective equipment is mandatory on certain parts of the body.

eye protection
Pictogram warning that safety glasses are mandatory.

ear protection
Pictogram warning that equipment that reduces noise perception is mandatory.

head protection
Pictogram warning that safety caps are mandatory.

hand protection
Pictogram warning that protective gloves are mandatory.

foot protection
Pictogram warning that protective footwear or accessories are mandatory.

respiratory system protection
Pictogram warning that respirators are mandatory.

ambulance

Vehicle designed to transport the sick and injured to hospital and to administer first aid.

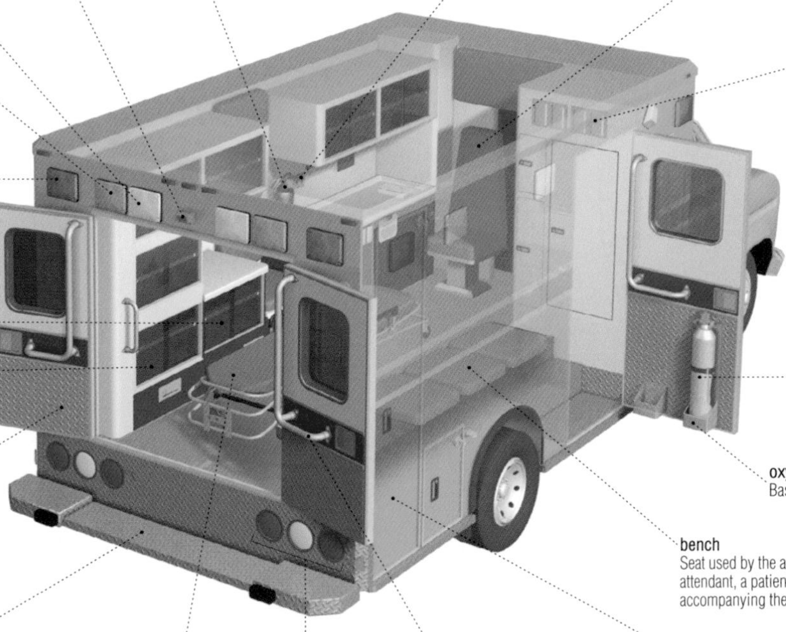

scene light
Spotlight that illuminates the rear of the vehicle during an operation.

camera
Device that allows the driver to see behind the vehicle.

aspirator
Device used to extract a liquid or a gas from one of the patient's orifices.

manometer
Instrument for measuring oxygen pressure inside the cylinder.

ambulance attendant's seat

air conditioning system
System that regulates the temperature and purifies the air inside the vehicle.

halogen light
High-intensity emergency light.

strobe light
Emergency light that emits a succession of brief flashes.

drug storage
Cabinet for storing the medications used most frequently (adrenaline, insulin).

first aid supplies
Cabinet for storing emergency response materials used by ambulance attendants (bandages, compresses, syringes).

rear door

portable oxygen cylinder
An easy-to-carry cylinder filled with compressed oxygen.

oxygen cylinder bracket
Base supporting the oxygen cylinder.

bench
Seat used by the ambulance attendant, a patient or a person accompanying the patient.

rear step
Platform at the back of the ambulance that is used to climb in and out.

stretcher
Folding bed on casters that is used to transport the sick and the injured.

taillights
Set of regulation lighting devices placed at the rear of a vehicle and used for signaling.

handle

backboard storage
Backboard: device used to immobilize a patient suspected of having a spinal injury.

first aid equipment

The instruments and equipment used to transport the sick and the injured and to administer first aid.

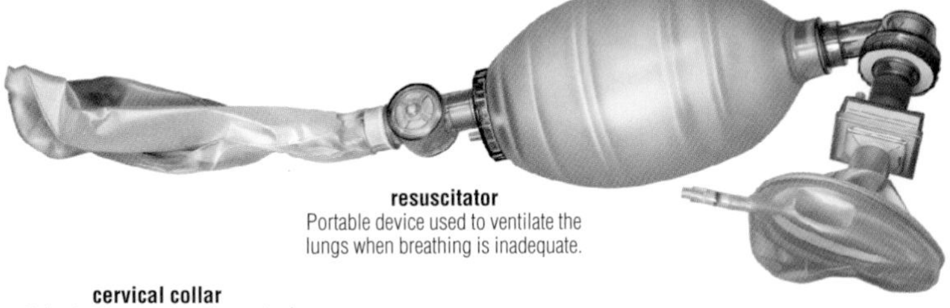

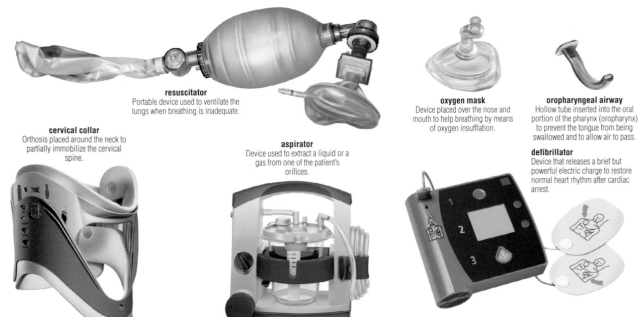

resuscitator
Portable device used to ventilate the lungs when breathing is inadequate.

oxygen mask
Device placed over the nose and mouth to help breathing by means of oxygen insufflation.

oropharyngeal airway
Hollow tube inserted into the oral portion of the pharynx (oropharynx) to prevent the tongue from being swallowed and to allow air to pass.

cervical collar
Orthosis placed around the neck to partially immobilize the cervical spine.

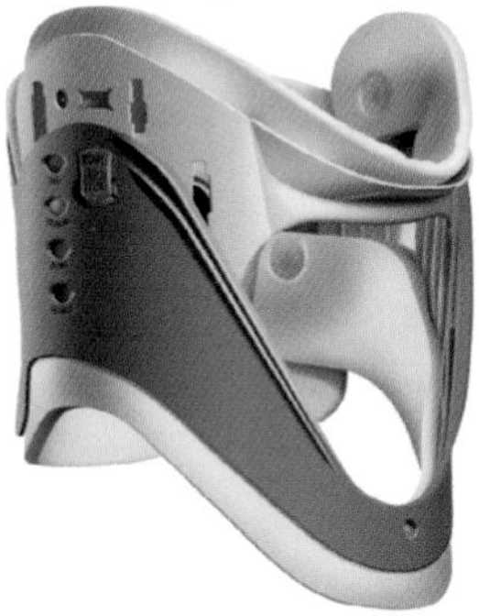

aspirator
Device used to extract a liquid or a gas from one of the patient's orifices.

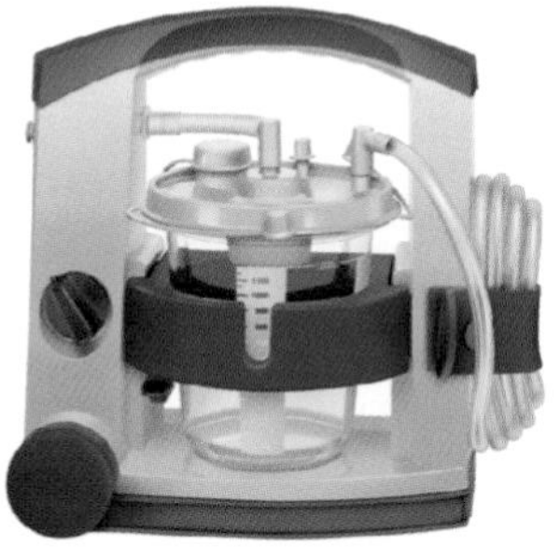

defibrillator
Device that releases a brief but powerful electric charge to restore normal heart rhythm after cardiac arrest.

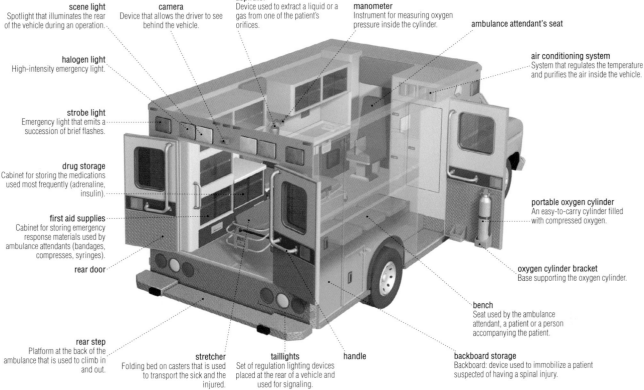

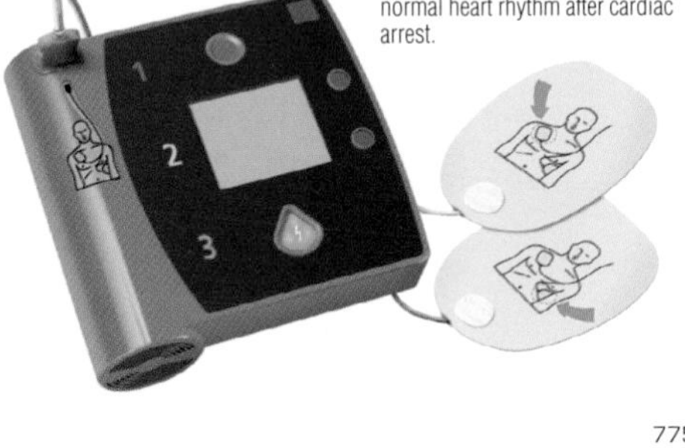

first aid equipment

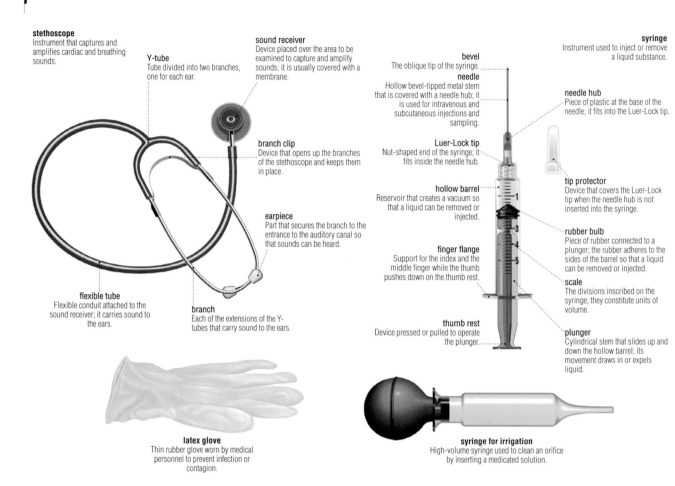

stethoscope
Instrument that captures and amplifies cardiac and breathing sounds.

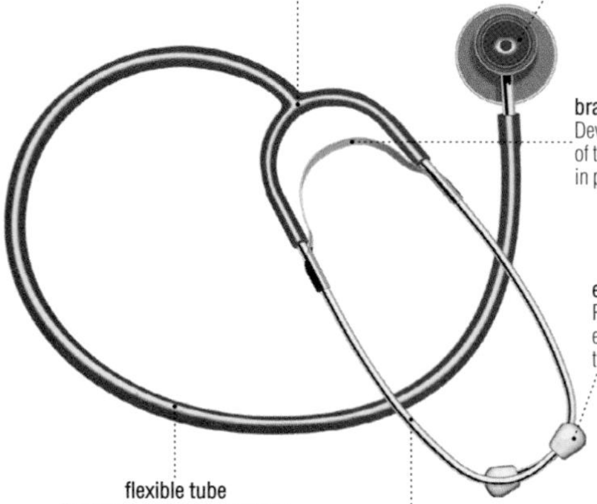

Y-tube
Tube divided into two branches, one for each ear.

sound receiver
Device placed over the area to be examined to capture and amplify sounds; it is usually covered with a membrane.

branch clip
Device that opens up the branches of the stethoscope and keeps them in place.

earpiece
Part that secures the branch to the entrance to the auditory canal so that sounds can be heard.

flexible tube
Flexible conduit attached to the sound receiver; it carries sound to the ears.

branch
Each of the extensions of the Y-tubes that carry sound to the ears.

syringe
Instrument used to inject or remove a liquid substance.

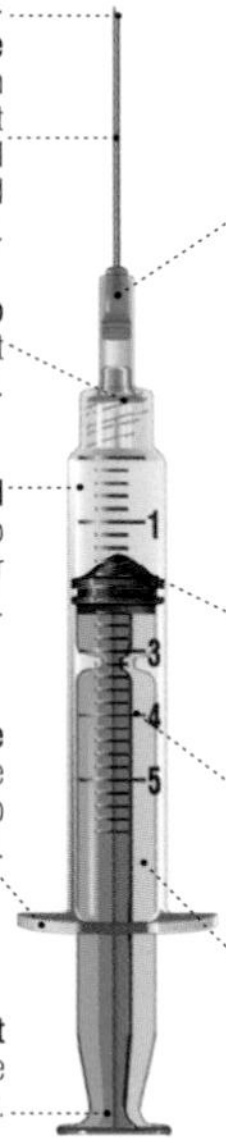

bevel
The oblique tip of the syringe.

needle
Hollow bevel-tipped metal stem that is covered with a needle hub; it is used for intravenous and subcutaneous injections and sampling.

Luer-Lock tip
Nut-shaped end of the syringe; it fits inside the needle hub.

hollow barrel
Reservoir that creates a vacuum so that a liquid can be removed or injected.

finger flange
Support for the index and the middle finger while the thumb pushes down on the thumb rest.

thumb rest
Device pressed or pulled to operate the plunger.

needle hub
Piece of plastic at the base of the needle; it fits into the Luer-Lock tip.

tip protector
Device that covers the Luer-Lock tip when the needle hub is not inserted into the syringe.

rubber bulb
Piece of rubber connected to a plunger; the rubber adheres to the sides of the barrel so that a liquid can be removed or injected.

scale
The divisions inscribed on the syringe; they constitute units of volume.

plunger
Cylindrical stem that slides up and down the hollow barrel; its movement draws in or expels liquid.

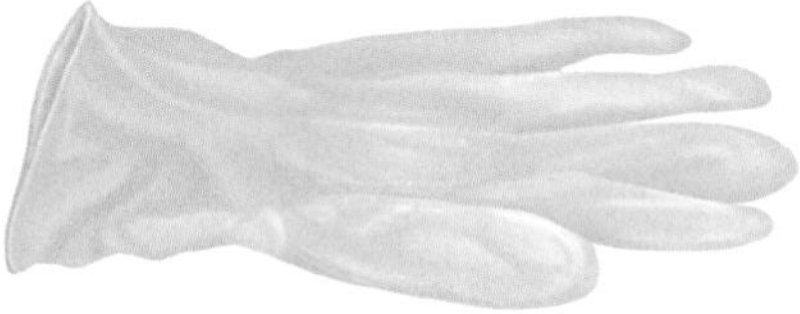

latex glove
Thin rubber glove worn by medical personnel to prevent infection or contagion.

syringe for irrigation
High-volume syringe used to clean an orifice by inserting a medicated solution.

cot
Folding bed on casters that is used to transport the sick and the injured.

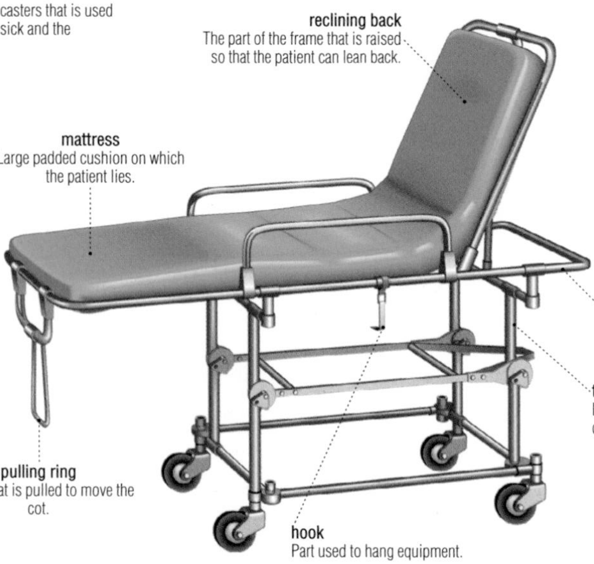

reclining back
The part of the frame that is raised so that the patient can lean back.

mattress
Large padded cushion on which the patient lies.

frame
Metal structure that supports the mattress above its feet.

telescopic leg
Extensible rods that stabilize the cot and regulate its height.

pulling ring
Device that is pulled to move the cot.

hook
Part used to hang equipment.

stretcher
Cloth-covered wooden or metal frame used to transport the sick and the injured.

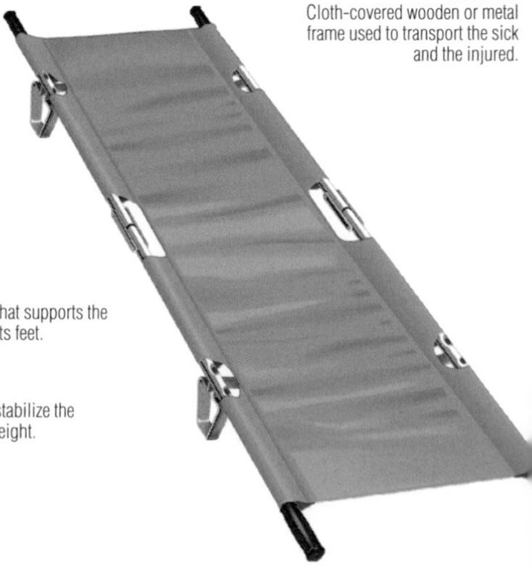

first aid kit

Box that contains the materials required to administer first aid, including bandages, medication and instruments.

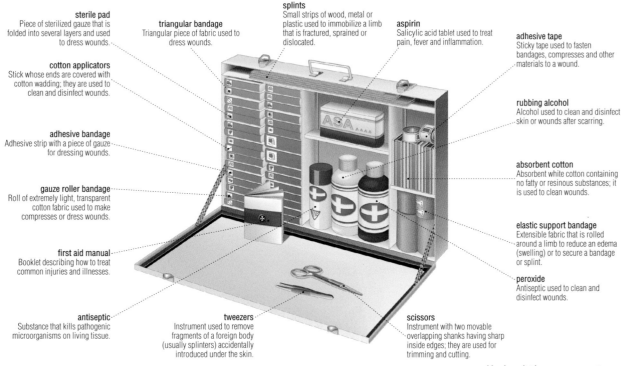

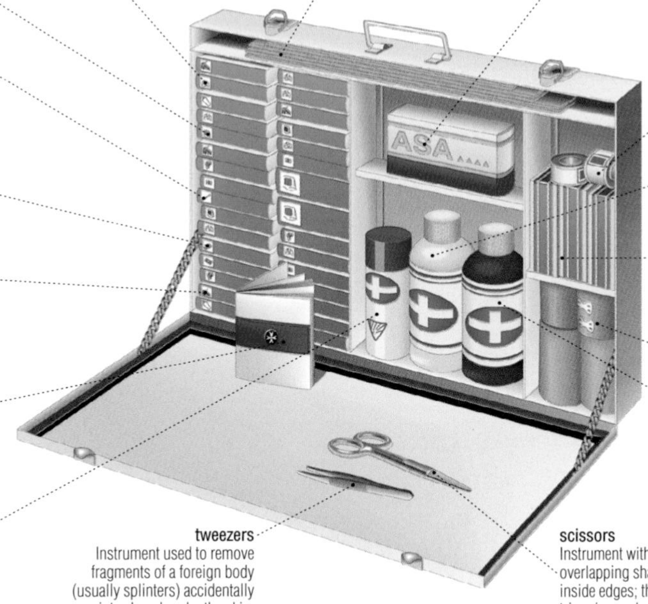
sterile pad
Piece of sterilized gauze that is folded into several layers and used to dress wounds.
triangular bandage
Triangular piece of fabric used to dress wounds.
splints
Small strips of wood, metal or plastic used to immobilize a limb that is fractured, sprained or dislocated.
aspirin
Salicylic acid tablet used to treat pain, fever and inflammation.
adhesive tape
Sticky tape used to fasten bandages, compresses and other materials to a wound.
cotton applicators
Stick whose ends are covered with cotton wadding; they are used to clean and disinfect wounds.
rubbing alcohol
Alcohol used to clean and disinfect skin or wounds after scarring.
ASA
adhesive bandage
Adhesive strip with a piece of gauze for dressing wounds.
absorbent cotton
Absorbent white cotton containing no fatty or resinous substances; it is used to clean wounds.
gauze roller bandage
Roll of extremely light, transparent cotton fabric used to make compresses or dress wounds.
elastic support bandage
Extensible fabric that is rolled around a limb to reduce an edema (swelling) or to secure a bandage or splint.
first aid manual
Booklet describing how to treat common injuries and illnesses.
peroxide
Antiseptic used to clean and disinfect wounds.
antiseptic
Substance that kills pathogenic microorganisms on living tissue.
tweezers
Instrument used to remove fragments of a foreign body (usually splinters) accidentally introduced under the skin.
scissors
Instrument with two movable overlapping shanks having sharp inside edges; they are used for trimming and cutting.

clinical thermometers

Instruments that measure body temperature; they can be auricular, oral, rectal, etc.

mercury thermometer
Thermometer graduated from 94°F to 108°F and containing mercury that expands as a function of body temperature; an arrow indicates normal body temperature (98.6°F).

digital thermometer
Thermometer that indicates the temperature in digits on a liquid crystal display screen.
38.0°C

blood pressure monitor

Device composed of an armlet and a pressure gauge; it is used to measure diastolic (heart dilatation) and systolic (heart contraction) pressure.

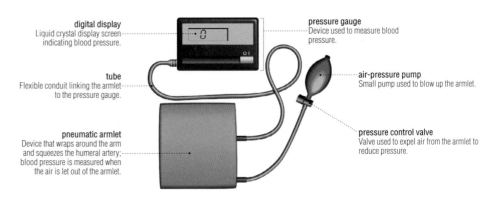

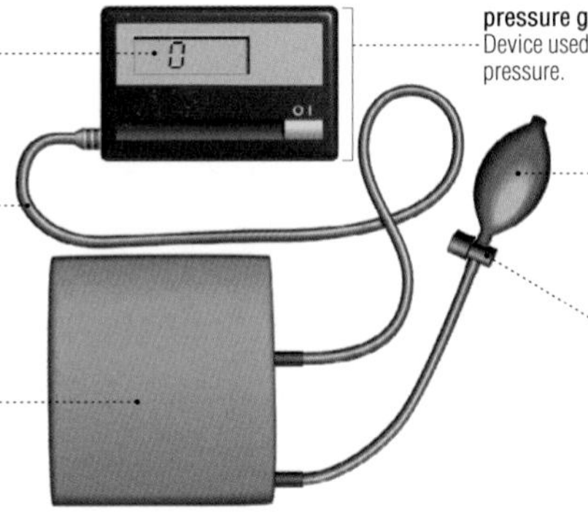
digital display
Liquid crystal display screen indicating blood pressure.
pressure gauge
Device used to measure blood pressure.
tube
Flexible conduit linking the armlet to the pressure gauge.
air-pressure pump
Small pump used to blow up the armlet.
pressure control valve
Valve used to expel air from the armlet to reduce pressure.
pneumatic armlet
Device that wraps around the arm and squeezes the humeral artery; blood pressure is measured when the air is let out of the armlet.

hospital

Establishment where the sick are given medical and surgical care and where babies are born.

emergency
Department that receives the sick and the injured who require immediate care.

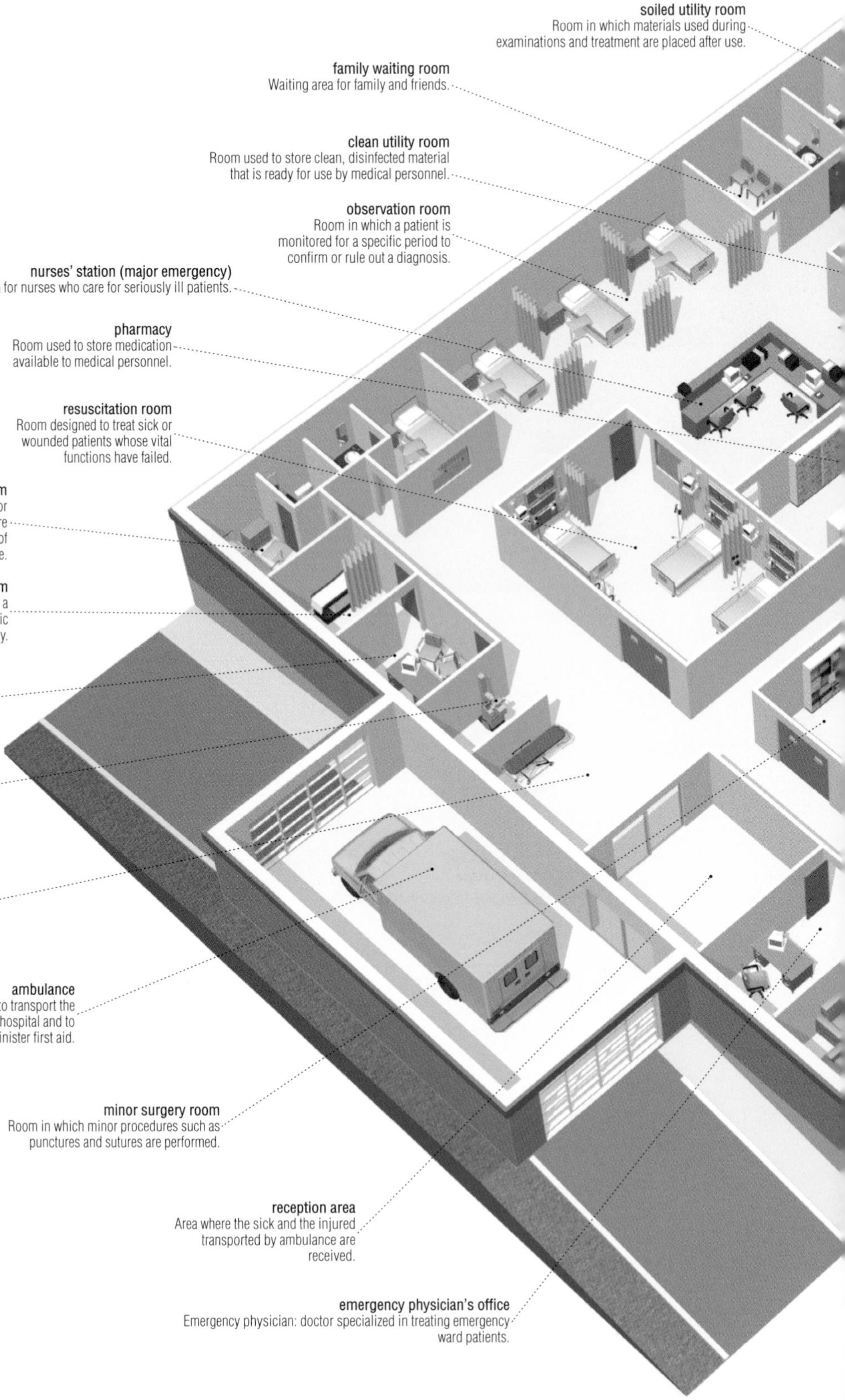

soiled utility room
Room in which materials used during examinations and treatment are placed after use.

family waiting room
Waiting area for family and friends.

clean utility room
Room used to store clean, disinfected material that is ready for use by medical personnel.

observation room
Room in which a patient is monitored for a specific period to confirm or rule out a diagnosis.

nurses' station (major emergency)
Work area for nurses who care for seriously ill patients.

pharmacy
Room used to store medication available to medical personnel.

resuscitation room
Room designed to treat sick or wounded patients whose vital functions have failed.

isolation room
Room in which contagious patients or patients vulnerable to infection are treated to avoid the transmission of disease.

psychiatric observation room
Room in which a patient is observed for a specific period to determine if a psychiatric referral is necessary.

psychiatric examination room
Room in which a patient meets with a psychiatrist for a mental health evaluation.

mobile X-ray unit
Instrument that captures an image of an internal body part by means of X-rays; this mobile unit moves around to various departments.

stretcher area
Area for patients on cots.

ambulance
Vehicle designed to transport the sick and injured to hospital and to administer first aid.

minor surgery room
Room in which minor procedures such as punctures and sutures are performed.

reception area
Area where the sick and the injured transported by ambulance are received.

emergency physician's office
Emergency physician: doctor specialized in treating emergency ward patients.

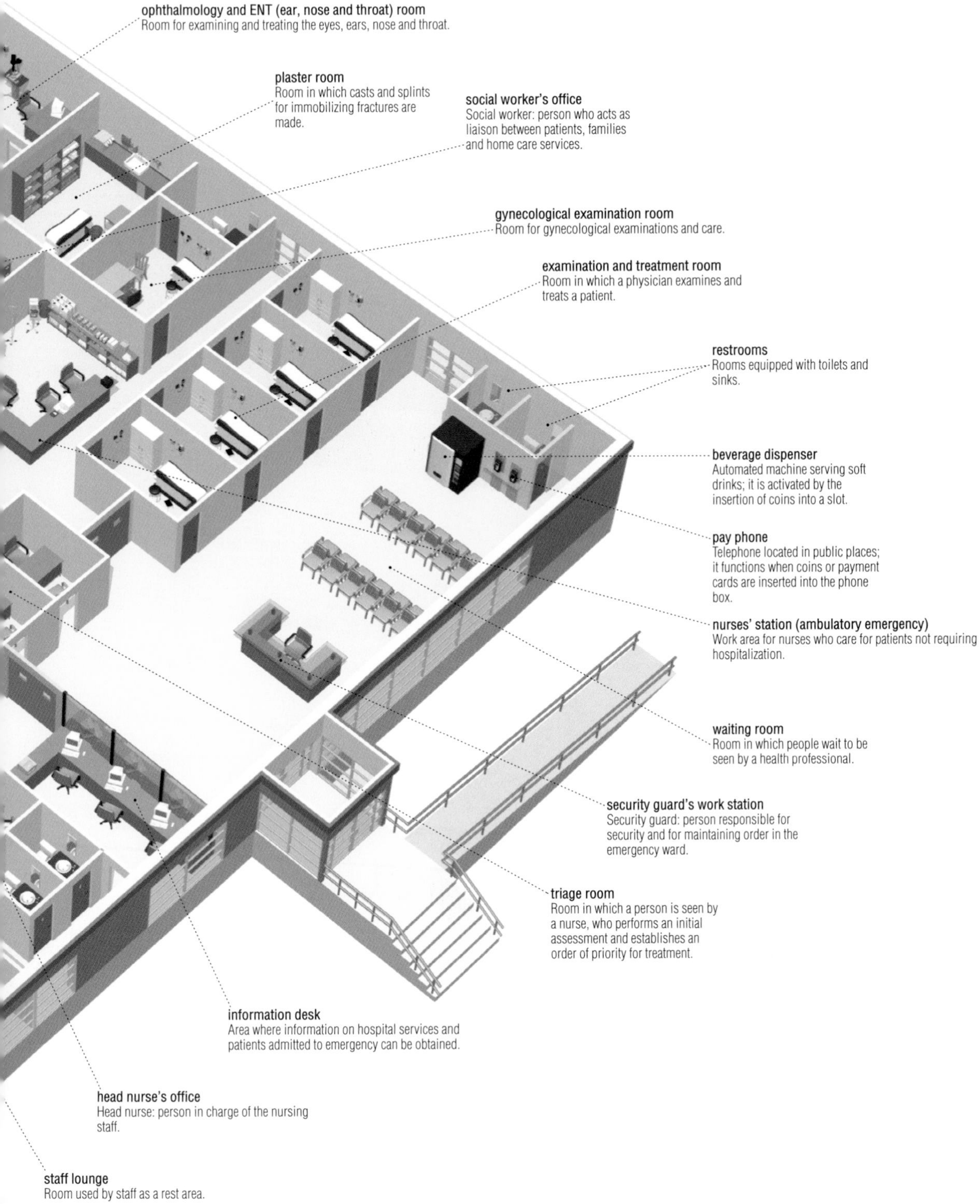

ophthalmology and ENT (ear, nose and throat) room
Room for examining and treating the eyes, ears, nose and throat.
plaster room
Room in which casts and splints for immobilizing fractures are made.
social worker's office
Social worker: person who acts as liaison between patients, families and home care services.
gynecological examination room
Room for gynecological examinations and care.
examination and treatment room
Room in which a physician examines and treats a patient.
restrooms
Rooms equipped with toilets and sinks.
beverage dispenser
Automated machine serving soft drinks; it is activated by the insertion of coins into a slot.
pay phone
Telephone located in public places; it functions when coins or payment cards are inserted into the phone box.
nurses' station (ambulatory emergency)
Work area for nurses who care for patients not requiring hospitalization.
waiting room
Room in which people wait to be seen by a health professional.
security guard's work station
Security guard: person responsible for security and for maintaining order in the emergency ward.
triage room
Room in which a person is seen by a nurse, who performs an initial assessment and establishes an order of priority for treatment.
information desk
Area where information on hospital services and patients admitted to emergency can be obtained.
head nurse's office
Head nurse: person in charge of the nursing staff.
staff lounge
Room used by staff as a rest area.

hospital

patient room
Room for hospitalized patients; it can be private (one bed), semiprivate (two beds) or common (more than two beds).

oxygen outlet
Device that supplies oxygen to a patient's room.

bedside lamp
Adjustable light fixture secured to the wall at the head of the bed.

resident
Graduate of medicine who does an apprenticeship of varying duration in a hospital as the final stage of medical training.

intravenous stand
Long metal rod with a hook that is supported by a base with casters; it is used to suspend a bag containing a solution that is slowly and continuously injected into the patient.

physician
Holder of a degree in medicine, the physician establishes the diagnosis and prescribes treatment and medication.

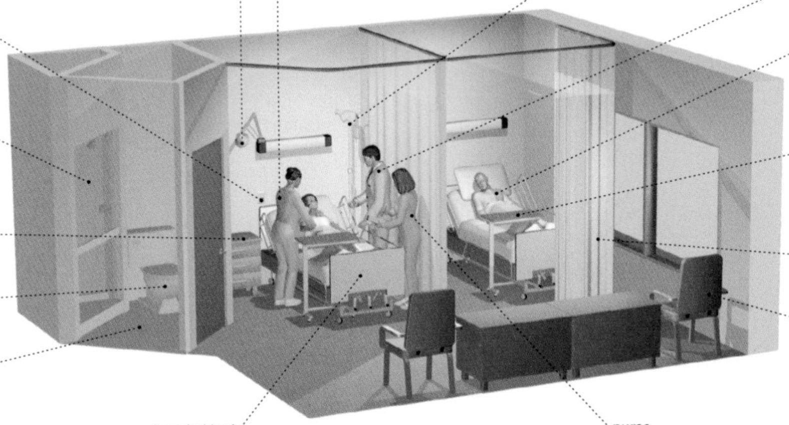

shower
Sanitary fixture for washing the body under a spray of water.

bedside table
Small table placed at the head of a bed; it might contain one or more drawers.

toilet
Plumbing fixture used to receive bodily waste; it has a bowl and a flusher.

bathroom
Room designed for personal hygiene; it is equipped with running water and sanitary fixtures.

hospital bed
Bed with an articulated base, casters and bars.

patient
Person who undergoes treatment, a medical examination or a surgical procedure.

overbed table
Table with casters and a tray that slides over the bed.

privacy curtain
Curtain used to separate one patient's area from another's or to provide privacy.

patient's chair
Chair for a patient or visitor.

nurse
Holder of a degree in nursing, the nurse treats patients under the direction of the physician.

operating suite
The rooms and equipment used for surgical procedures.

soiled utility room
Room in which surgical materials are placed after use.

operating room
Sterilized room used to perform surgical procedures.

medical gas cylinder
Device that supplies an anesthetic to the patient during a surgical procedure.

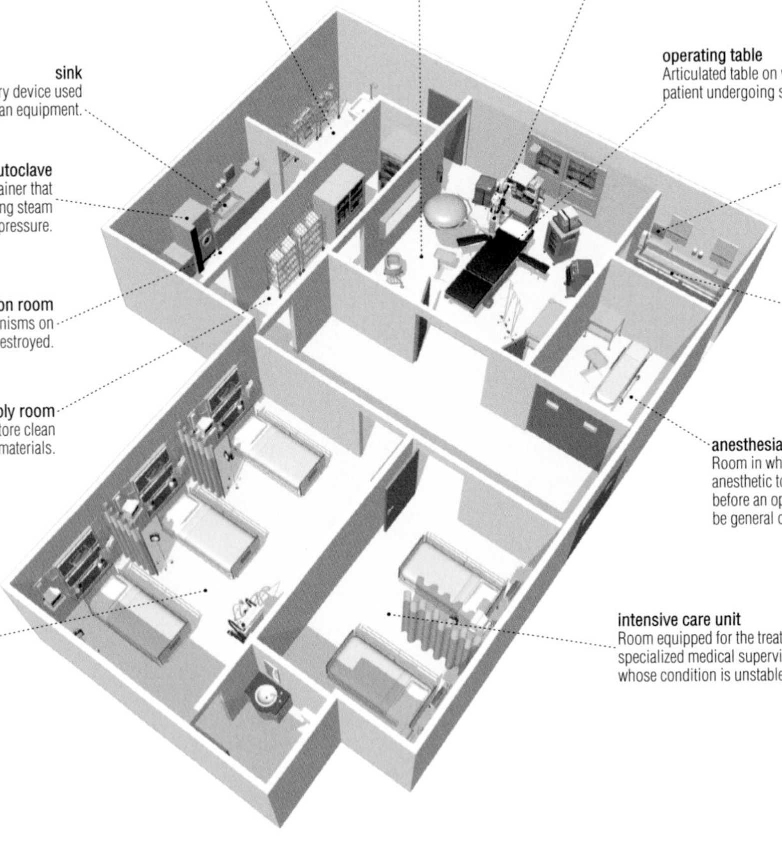

sink
Basin-shaped sanitary device used to clean equipment.

autoclave
Airtight metal container that sterilizes materials using steam under high pressure.

sterilization room
Room in which microorganisms on surgical instruments are destroyed.

supply room
Sterilized room used to store clean disinfected surgical materials.

recovery room
Room in which a patient awakens after receiving a general anesthetic as part of a surgical procedure.

operating table
Articulated table on which the patient undergoing surgery lies.

glove storage

scrub room
Room in which surgeons wash their hands before a surgical procedure.

anesthesia room
Room in which patients receive an anesthetic to dull sensitivity to pain before an operation; an anesthetic can be general or local.

intensive care unit
Room equipped for the treatment and specialized medical supervision of patients whose condition is unstable.

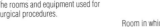

ambulatory care unit
Hospital unit that is divided into specialties and designed to deliver care and services to nonhospitalized patients who can move about on their own.

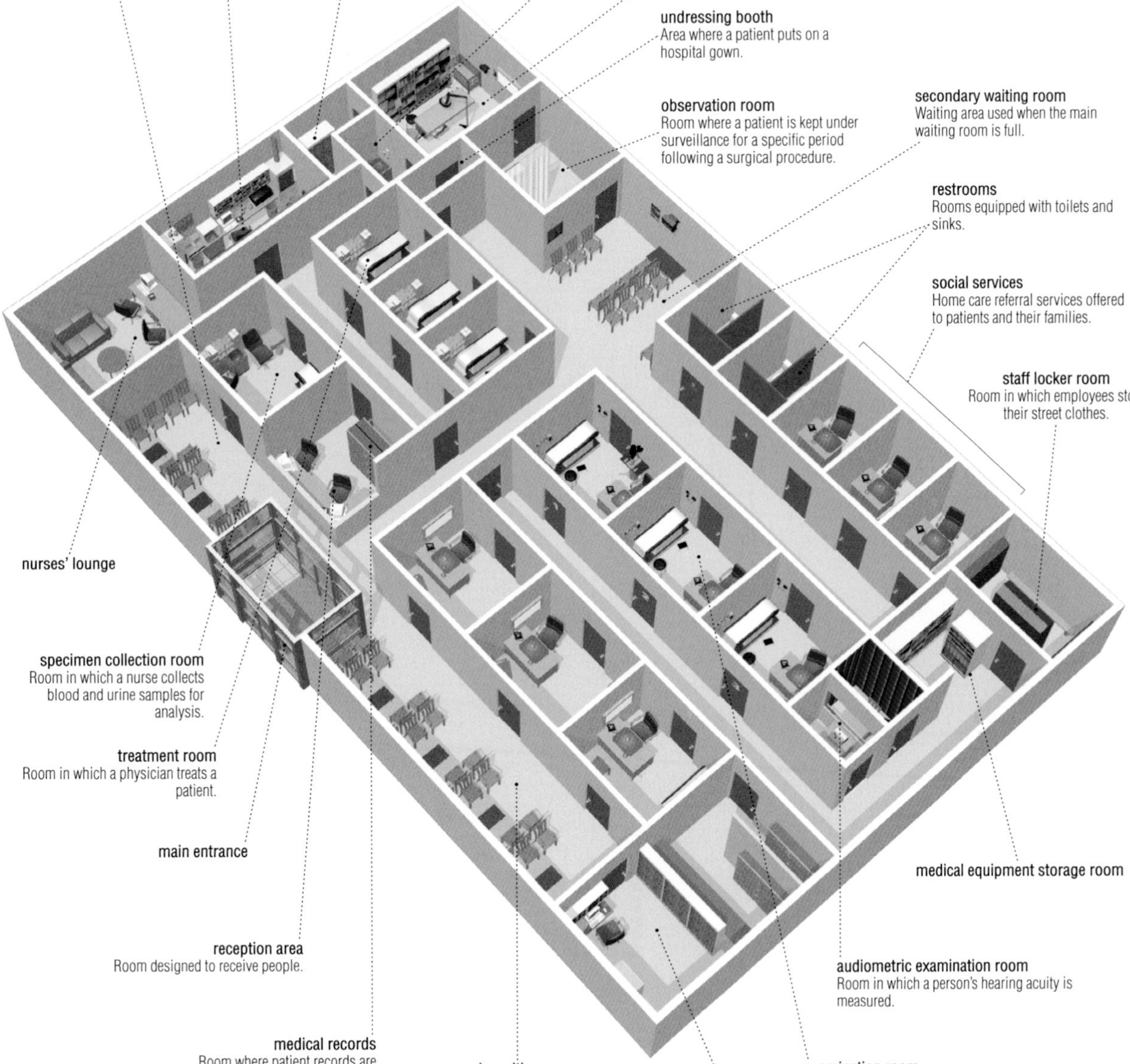
surgeon's sink
Plumbing fixture used by surgeons to disinfect their hands before minor surgery.
specimen collection center waiting room
Area where persons wait to have samples taken.
pathology laboratory
Room with the equipment required to analyze samples.
sterilization room
Room in which microorganisms on instruments used in treatment are destroyed.
operating room
Room used to perform minor surgical procedures.
undressing booth
Area where a patient puts on a hospital gown.
observation room
Room where a patient is kept under surveillance for a specific period following a surgical procedure.
secondary waiting room
Waiting area used when the main waiting room is full.
restrooms
Rooms equipped with toilets and sinks.
social services
Home care referral services offered to patients and their families.
staff locker room
Room in which employees store their street clothes.
nurses' lounge
specimen collection room
Room in which a nurse collects blood and urine samples for analysis.
treatment room
Room in which a physician treats a patient.
main entrance
medical equipment storage room
reception area
Room designed to receive people.
audiometric examination room
Room in which a person's hearing acuity is measured.
medical records
Room where patient records are stored for future consultation.
main waiting room
Area used by patients waiting for consultation.
examination room
Room in which a physician examines a patient.
pharmacy
Room used to store medication available to medical personnel.

SOCIETY

walking aids

Weight-bearing devices used to help a person move about.

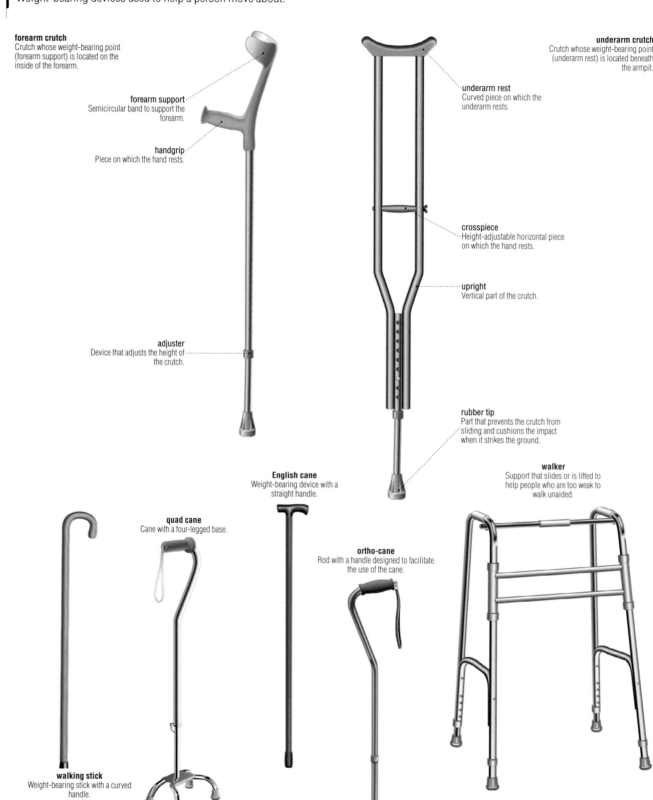

forearm crutch
Crutch whose weight-bearing point (forearm support) is located on the inside of the forearm.

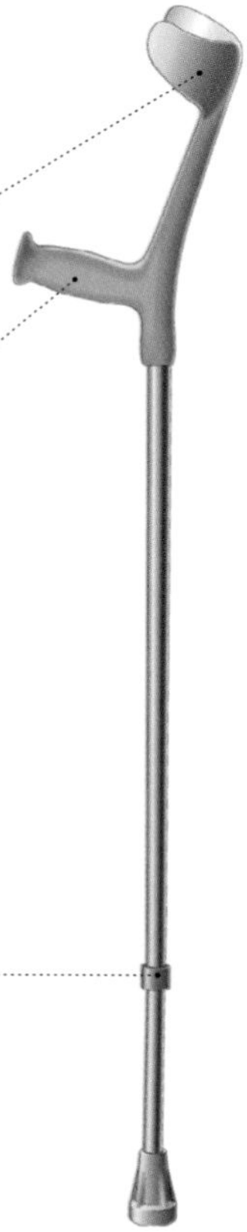

forearm support
Semicircular band to support the forearm.

handgrip
Piece on which the hand rests.

adjuster
Device that adjusts the height of the crutch.

underarm crutch
Crutch whose weight-bearing point (underarm rest) is located beneath the armpit.

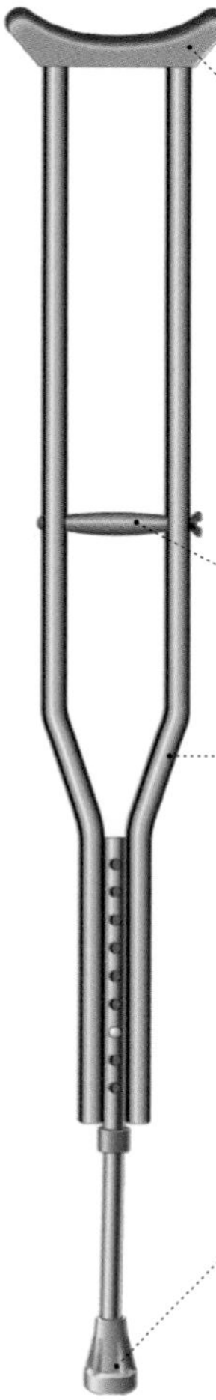

underarm rest
Curved piece on which the underarm rests.

crosspiece
Height-adjustable horizontal piece on which the hand rests.

upright
Vertical part of the crutch.

rubber tip
Part that prevents the crutch from sliding and cushions the impact when it strikes the ground.

walking stick
Weight-bearing stick with a curved handle.

quad cane
Cane with a four-legged base.

English cane
Weight-bearing device with a straight handle.

ortho-cane
Rod with a handle designed to facilitate the use of the cane.

walker
Support that slides or is lifted to help people who are too weak to walk unaided.

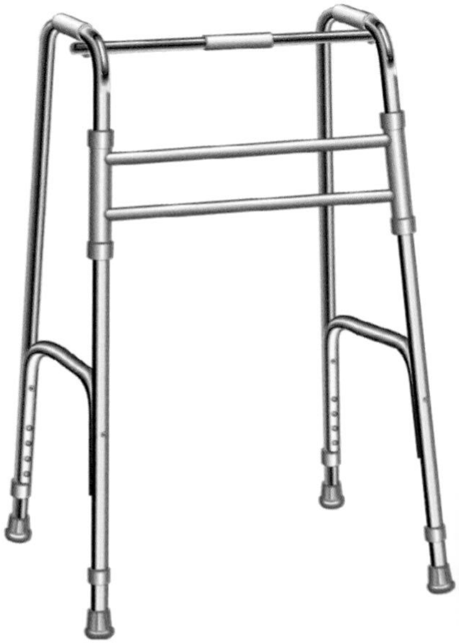

SOCIETY

wheelchair

Chair with arms and a back that is mounted on wheels; it enables a person who has difficulty walking to move about.

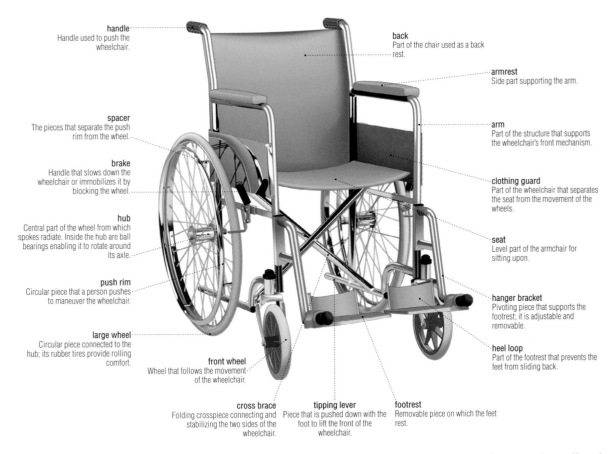

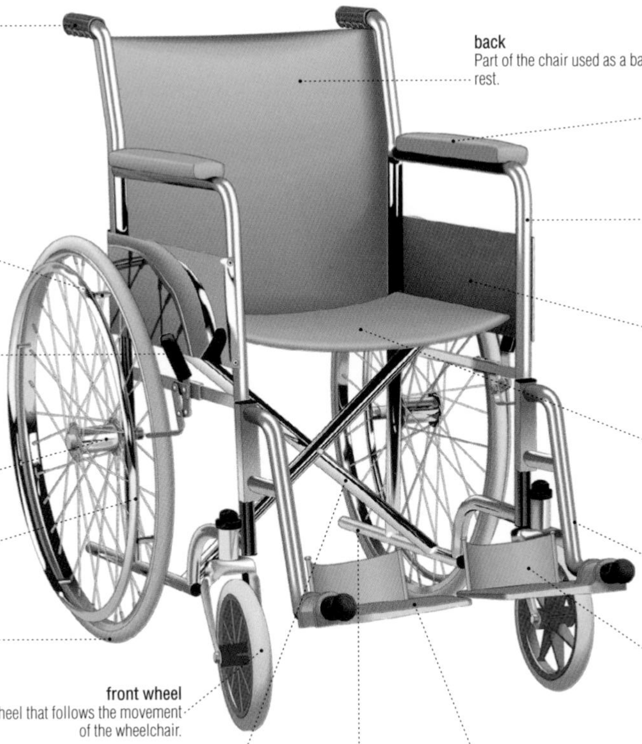

handle
Handle used to push the wheelchair.
spacer
The pieces that separate the push rim from the wheel.
brake
Handle that slows down the wheelchair or immobilizes it by blocking the wheel.
hub
Central part of the wheel from which spokes radiate. Inside the hub are ball bearings enabling it to rotate around its axle.
push rim
Circular piece that a person pushes to maneuver the wheelchair.
large wheel
Circular piece connected to the hub; its rubber tires provide rolling comfort.
front wheel
Wheel that follows the movement of the wheelchair.
cross brace
Folding crosspiece connecting and stabilizing the two sides of the wheelchair.
tipping lever
Piece that is pushed down with the foot to lift the front of the wheelchair.
footrest
Removable piece on which the feet rest.
back
Part of the chair used as a back rest.
armrest
Side part supporting the arm.
arm
Part of the structure that supports the wheelchair's front mechanism.
clothing guard
Part of the wheelchair that separates the seat from the movement of the wheels.
seat
Level part of the armchair for sitting upon.
hanger bracket
Pivoting piece that supports the footrest; it is adjustable and removable.
heel loop
Part of the footrest that prevents the feet from sliding back.

forms of medications

The various forms of medications that are commercially available.

cough syrup
Flavored solution containing a medication that suppresses the cough reflex.

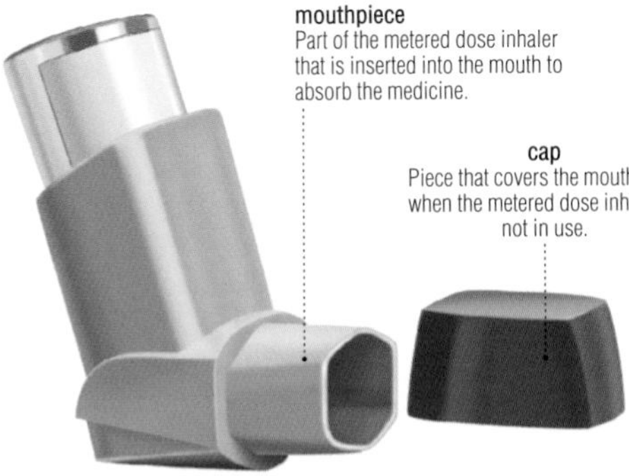

mouthpiece
Part of the metered dose inhaler that is inserted into the mouth to absorb the medicine.
cap
Piece that covers the mouthpiece when the metered dose inhaler is not in use.

metered dose inhaler
Aerosol device that releases a specific dose of medication into the respiratory tract; it is used mainly to treat asthma.

capsule
Small water-soluble pill with two sides that fit together; it is filled with a medication or a pharmaceutical product.

gelatin capsule
Receptacle filled with gelatin that contains a dose of medication or a pharmaceutical product.

tablet
Pill made of compressed powder that contains a dose of medication or a pharmaceutical product.

vial
Bulging glass tube sealed at its ends; it contains a specific dose of medication or a pharmaceutical product in liquid form.

family relationships

The relationships between the various generations of a family, including their spouses.

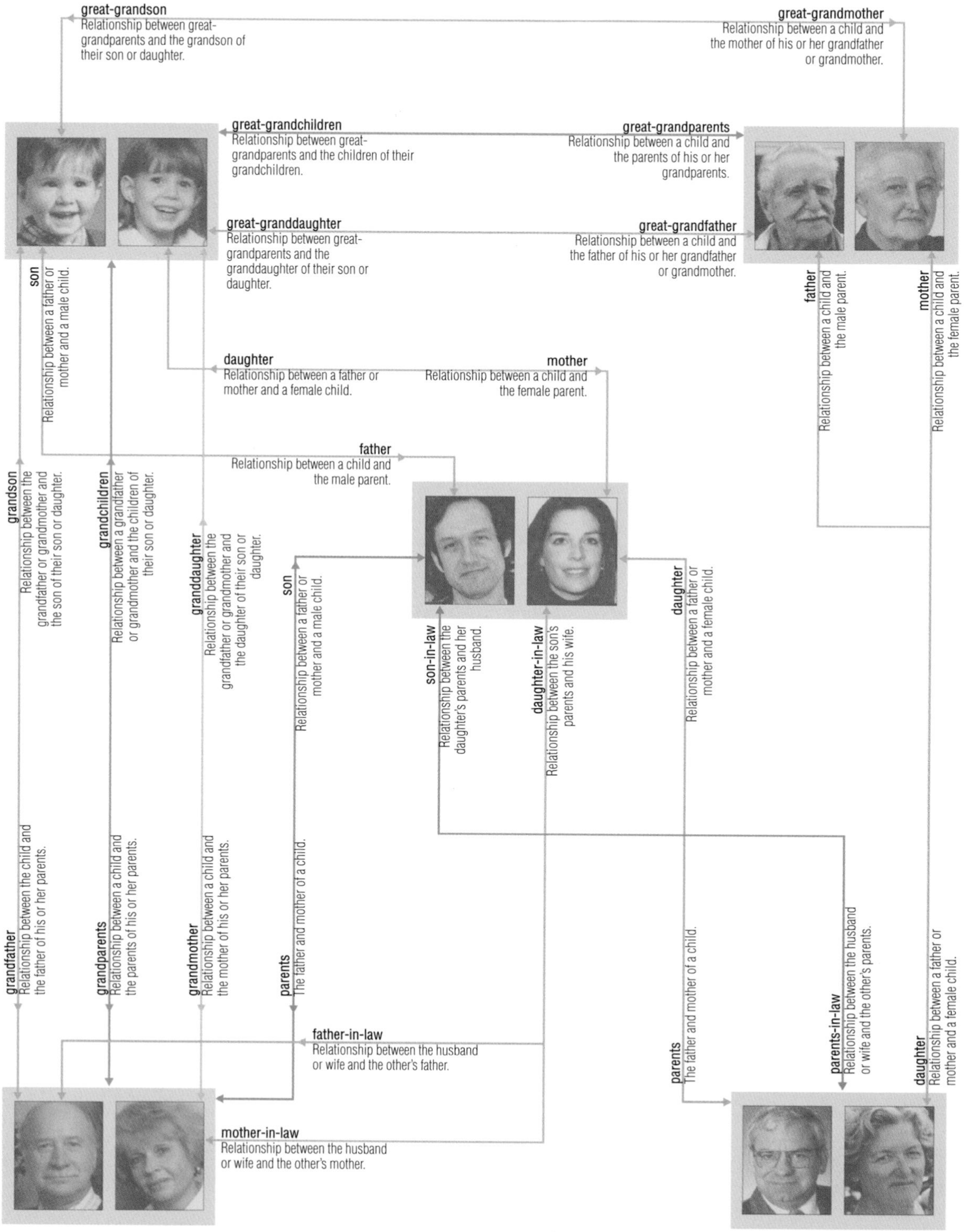
great-grandson
Relationship between great-grandparents and the grandson of their son or daughter.
great-grandmother
Relationship between a child and the mother of his or her grandfather or grandmother.
great-grandchildren
Relationship between great-grandparents and the children of their grandchildren.
great-grandparents
Relationship between a child and the parents of his or her grandparents.
great-granddaughter
Relationship between great-grandparents and the granddaughter of their son or daughter.
great-grandfather
Relationship between a child and the father of his or her grandfather or grandmother.
son
Relationship between a father or mother and a male child.
father
Relationship between a child and the male parent.
mother
Relationship between a child and the female parent.
daughter
Relationship between a father or mother and a female child.
mother
Relationship between a child and the female parent.
father
Relationship between a child and the male parent.
grandson
Relationship between the grandfather or grandmother and the son of their son or daughter.
grandchildren
Relationship between a grandfather or grandmother and the children of their son or daughter.
granddaughter
Relationship between the grandfather or grandmother and the daughter of their son or daughter.
son
Relationship between a father or mother and a male child.
son-in-law
Relationship between the daughter's parents and her husband.
daughter-in-law
Relationship between the son's parents and his wife.
daughter
Relationship between a father or mother and a female child.
grandfather
Relationship between the child and the father of his or her parents.
grandparents
Relationship between a child and the parents of his or her parents.
grandmother
Relationship between a child and the mother of his or her parents.
parents
The father and mother of a child.
parents
The father and mother of a child.
parents-in-law
Relationship between the husband or wife and the other's parents.
daughter
Relationship between a father or mother and a female child.
father-in-law
Relationship between the husband or wife and the other's father.
mother-in-law
Relationship between the husband or wife and the other's mother.

family relationships

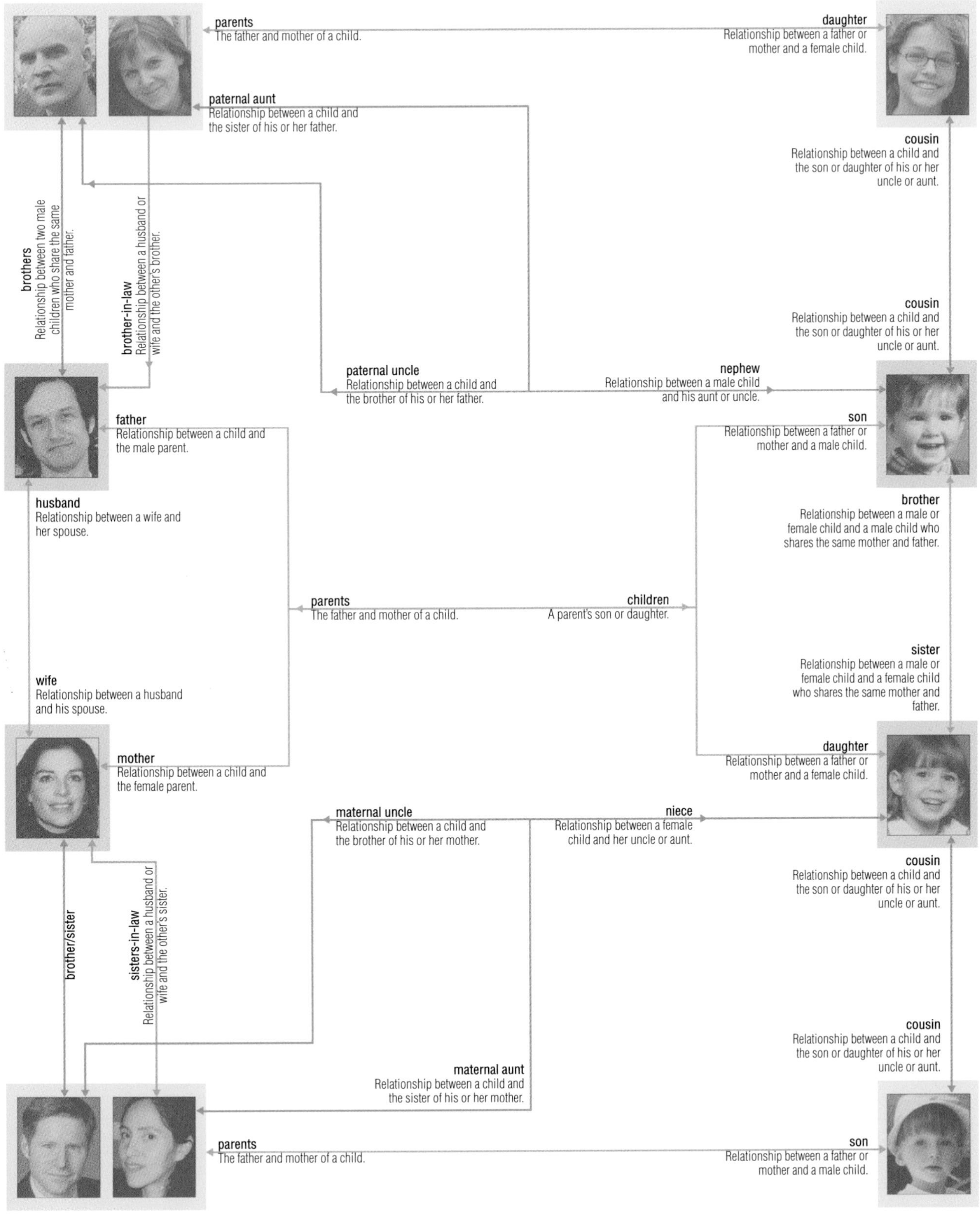
parents
The father and mother of a child.
daughter
Relationship between a father or mother and a female child.
paternal aunt
Relationship between a child and the sister of his or her father.
cousin
Relationship between a child and the son or daughter of his or her uncle or aunt.
brothers
Relationship between two male children who share the same mother and father.
brother-in-law
Relationship between a husband or wife and the other's brother.
cousin
Relationship between a child and the son or daughter of his or her uncle or aunt.
paternal uncle
Relationship between a child and the brother of his or her father.
nephew
Relationship between a male child and his aunt or uncle.
father
Relationship between a child and the male parent.
son
Relationship between a father or mother and a male child.
husband
Relationship between a wife and her spouse.
brother
Relationship between a male or female child and a male child who shares the same mother and father.
parents
The father and mother of a child.
children
A parent's son or daughter.
wife
Relationship between a husband and his spouse.
sister
Relationship between a male or female child and a female child who shares the same mother and father.
mother
Relationship between a child and the female parent.
daughter
Relationship between a father or mother and a female child.
maternal uncle
Relationship between a child and the brother of his or her mother.
niece
Relationship between a female child and her uncle or aunt.
cousin
Relationship between a child and the son or daughter of his or her uncle or aunt.
brother/sister
sisters-in-law
Relationship between a husband or wife and the other's sister.
cousin
Relationship between a child and the son or daughter of his or her uncle or aunt.
maternal aunt
Relationship between a child and the sister of his or her mother.
parents
The father and mother of a child.
son
Relationship between a father or mother and a male child.

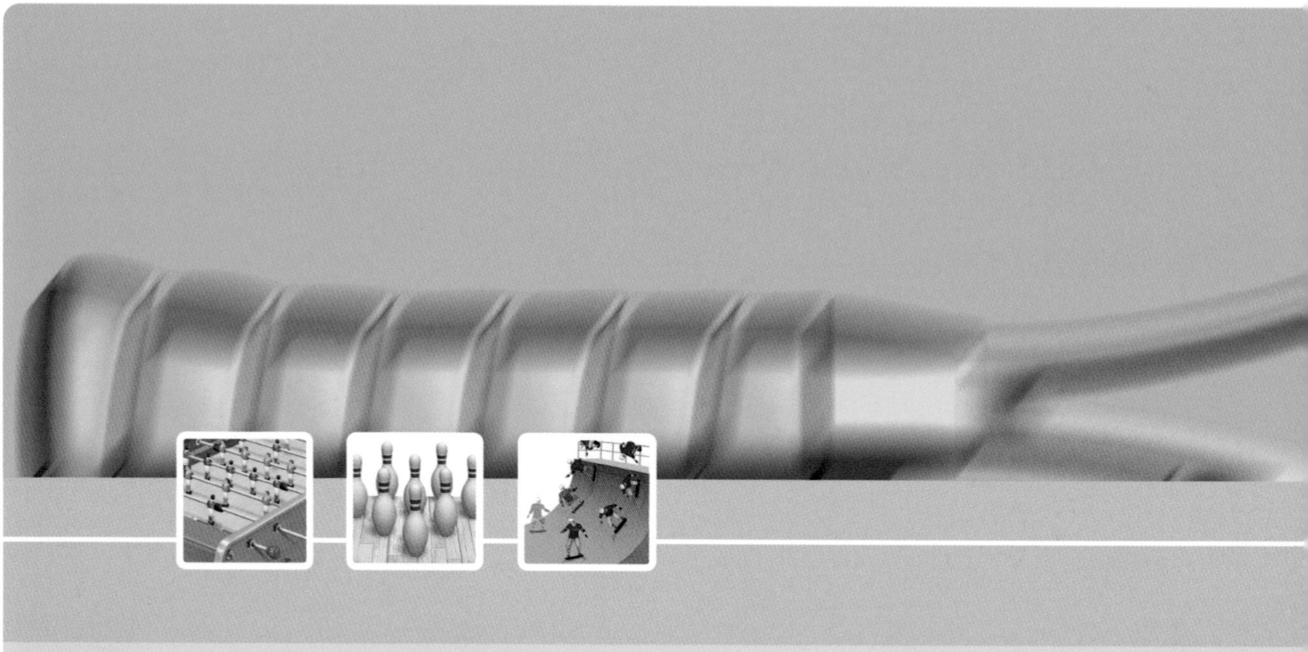

788 Sports facilities

Fields and installations designed for participating in sports and staging competitions.

790 Track and field

This sport brings together some 30 events: races, speed walking, marathon, jumps, shot put, combined events (heptathlon, decathlon).

794 Ball sports

Individual or team sports played by throwing o hitting a solid or inflated ball.

815 Racket sports

Popular all over the world, these sports have two to four opposing players with rackets; they rally a ball or shuttlecock on a defined playing surface.

823 Gymnastics

Gymnastic sports include rhythmic, artistic, acrobatic and aquatic gymnastics, as well as stretching. Gymnastics builds up the body and makes it supple.

827 Aquatic and nautical sports

Sports and recreational activities that take plac in or on water.

842 Combat sports

Sports in which two armed or unarmed opponents confront each other in combat.

850 Strength sports

Sports that develop muscular strength and size (weightlifting, power lifting and bodybuilding).

852 Equestrian sports

Sports practiced by a rider on a horse; they include competitions of skill, speed and endurance and team games.

SPORTS AND GAMES

Activities practiced for recreational purposes (fun, relaxation, health) and often taking the form of competitions sanctioned by official bodies.

59 Precision and accuracy sports

Sports whose objective is to hit a target of various shapes and sizes (such as a pocket, hole, jack or bowling pin) using various means (such as a bow, firearm, billiard cue, ball or club).

870 Cycling

Sport practiced on a bicycle.

872 Motor sports

Sports characterized by driving a motorized vehicle such as a race car, motorcycle, snowmobile or personal watercraft.

77 Winter sports

Sports practiced on snow or ice.

894 Sports on wheels

Sports that use a board or skates fitted with small wheels; they include team, acrobatic and speed activities.

896 Aerial sports

Sports or leisure activities done in the air using specialized apparatus and equipment.

00 Mountain sports

Sports or leisure activities connected with climbing and mountaineering.

902 Outdoor leisure

Leisure activities that take place outdoors.

914 Games

Leisure activities that are played according to established rules and require intelligence, skill and luck.

sports complex

Installations (buildings, playing fields, etc.) that are used for participating in sports.

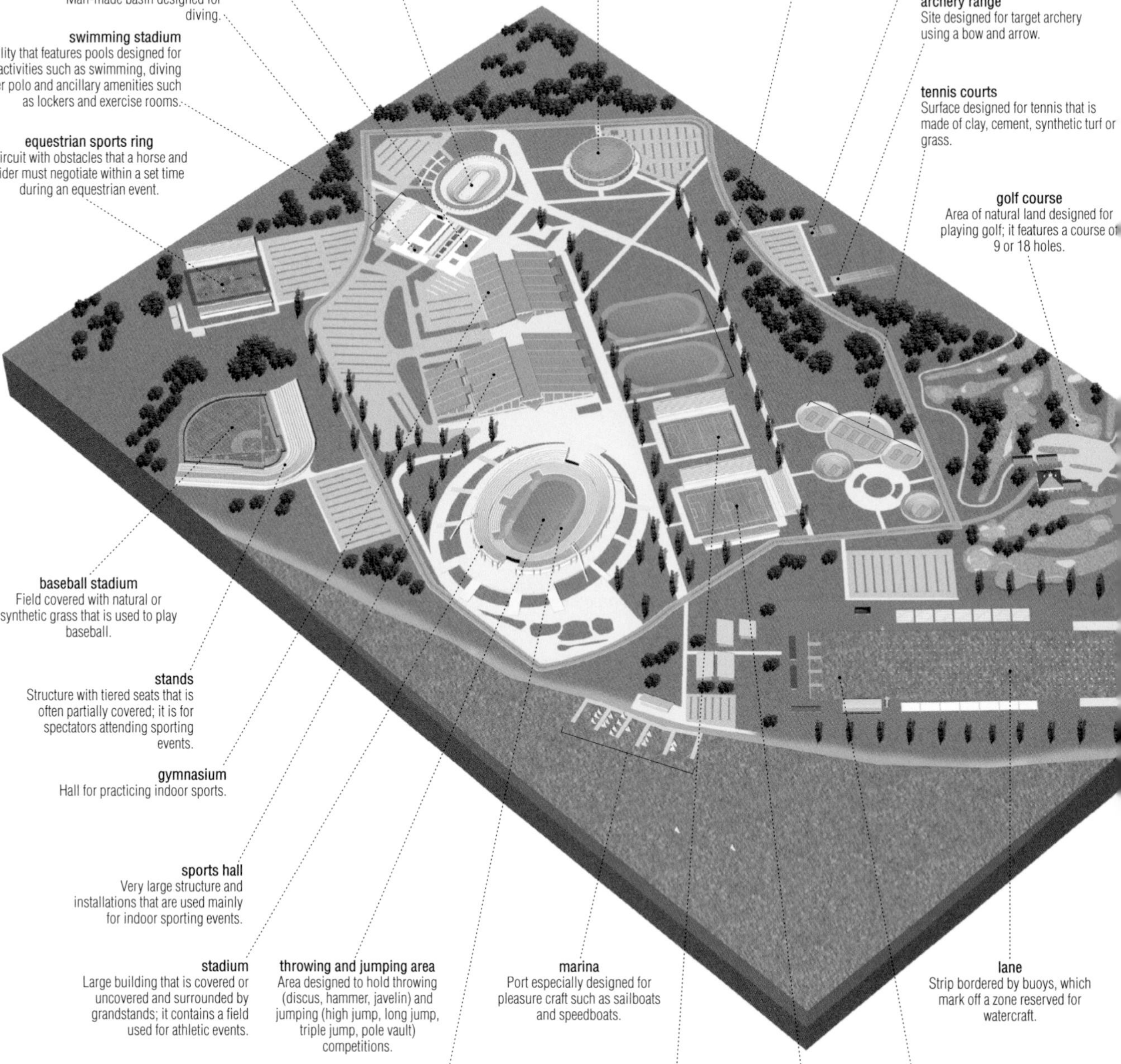

swimming pool
Man-made basin designed for swimming.

velodrome
Track designed for cycling competitions; its sharply banked turns allow competitors to reach high speeds.

arena
Building used mainly for ice sports; it houses a skating rink and ancillary amenities such as stands and locker rooms.

training area
Zone where athletes prepare for sports competitions by doing various exercises.

shooting range
Site designed for target shooting using firearms such as rifles and pistols.

diving well
Man-made basin designed for diving.

swimming stadium
Facility that features pools designed for aquatic activities such as swimming, diving and water polo and ancillary amenities such as lockers and exercise rooms.

archery range
Site designed for target archery using a bow and arrow.

tennis courts
Surface designed for tennis that is made of clay, cement, synthetic turf or grass.

equestrian sports ring
Circuit with obstacles that a horse and rider must negotiate within a set time during an equestrian event.

golf course
Area of natural land designed for playing golf; it features a course of 9 or 18 holes.

baseball stadium
Field covered with natural or synthetic grass that is used to play baseball.

stands
Structure with tiered seats that is often partially covered; it is for spectators attending sporting events.

gymnasium
Hall for practicing indoor sports.

sports hall
Very large structure and installations that are used mainly for indoor sporting events.

stadium
Large building that is covered or uncovered and surrounded by grandstands; it contains a field used for athletic events.

throwing and jumping area
Area designed to hold throwing (discus, hammer, javelin) and jumping (high jump, long jump, triple jump, pole vault) competitions.

marina
Port especially designed for pleasure craft such as sailboats and speedboats.

lane
Strip bordered by buoys, which mark off a zone reserved for watercraft.

athletic track
Oval circuit designed to hold races such as sprints, hurdles and relays.

field hockey field
Field covered with natural or synthetic grass that is used to play field hockey.

soccer field
Field covered with natural or synthetic grass that is used to play soccer.

competition course basin
Man-made basin of regulation size where aquatic competitions such as rowing and canoeing are held.

scoreboard

Display surface posting information related to a sporting event in progress (time, standings, results, etc.).

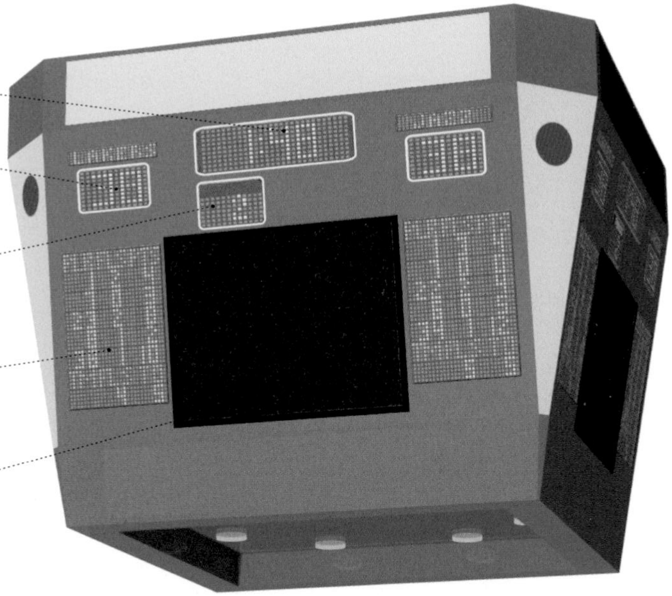

game clock
Instrument indicating the time left in a period.
score
Number of points scored by each team or player in a game.
period
Each of the segments of a match; its duration is fixed by the rules of the sport.
fouls/penalties
Sanctions imposed on a player who fails to follow the rules of the game; they take the form of penalty points or minutes.
video replay
Screen on which the highlights of a game are replayed for spectators.

competition

Sporting event in which several players or teams play against each other; it might be a championship, a cup, a tournament or a rally.

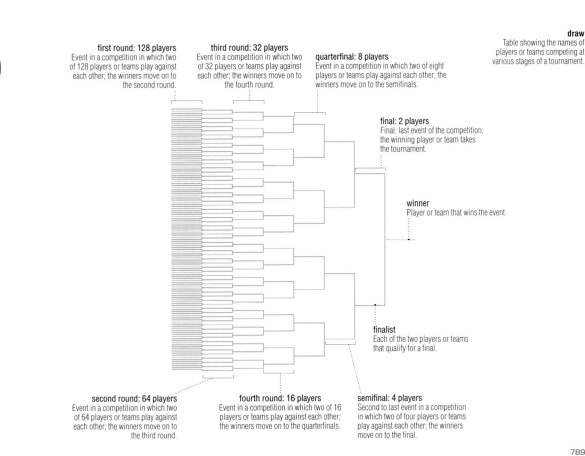

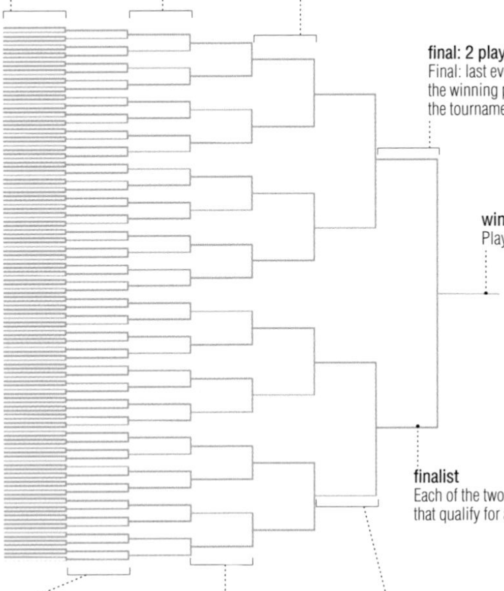

draw
Table showing the names of players or teams competing at various stages of a tournament.
first round: 128 players
Event in a competition in which two of 128 players or teams play against each other; the winners move on to the second round.
third round: 32 players
Event in a competition in which two of 32 players or teams play against each other; the winners move on to the fourth round.
quarterfinal: 8 players
Event in a competition in which two of eight players or teams play against each other; the winners move on to the semifinals.
final: 2 players
Final: last event of the competition; the winning player or team takes the tournament.
winner
Player or team that wins the event.
finalist
Each of the two players or teams that qualify for a final.
second round: 64 players
Event in a competition in which two of 64 players or teams play against each other; the winners move on to the third round.
fourth round: 16 players
Event in a competition in which two of 16 players or teams play against each other; the winners move on to the quarterfinals.
semifinal: 4 players
Second to last event in a competition in which two of four players or teams play against each other; the winners move on to the final.

arena

Field designed for participating in track and field and for staging competitions; it is often surrounded by grandstands for seating spectators.

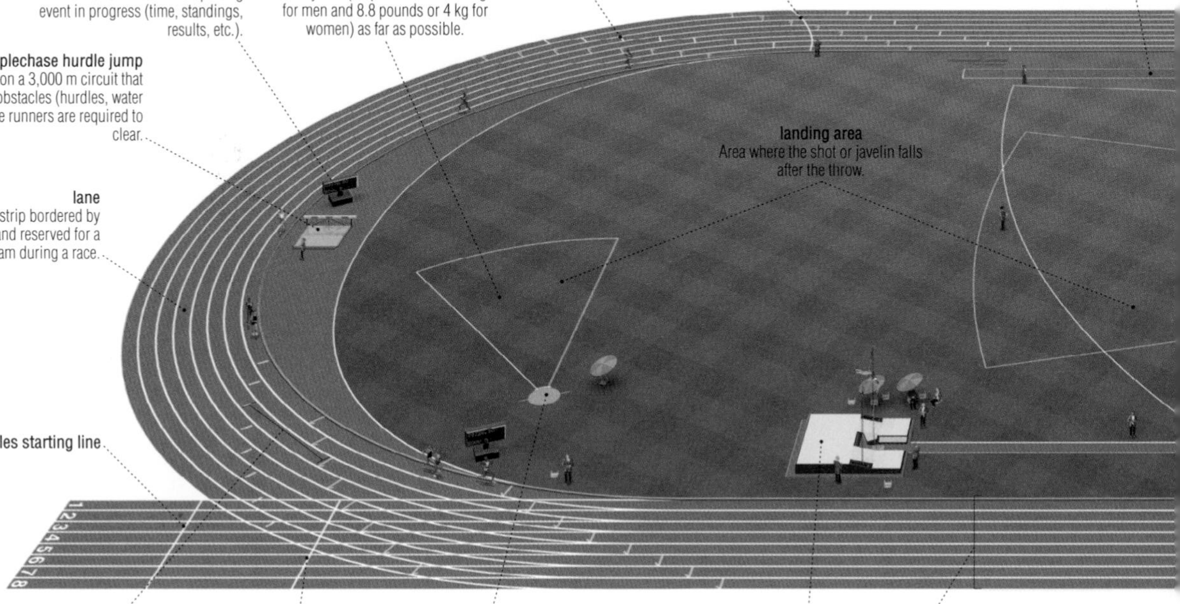
long jump and triple jump
Track and field event that requires jumping as far as possible from a given point (long jump) or taking several strides before jumping (triple jump).
200 m starting line
5,000 m starting line
scoreboard
Display surface posting information related to a sporting event in progress (time, standings, results, etc.).
shot put
Event in which athletes throw a heavy ball (12 pounds or 7.257 kg for men and 8.8 pounds or 4 kg for women) as far as possible.
steeplechase hurdle jump
Track event held on a 3,000 m circuit that includes artificial obstacles (hurdles, water jumps), which the runners are required to clear.
landing area
Area where the shot or javelin falls after the throw.
lane
Long narrow strip bordered by white lines and reserved for a runner or team during a race.
110 m hurdles starting line
takeover zone
Area in which the runners on a relay team pass the baton to the next runner.
100 m and 100 m hurdles starting line
throwing circle
Area where the athlete winds up to throw the shot; the thrower may not leave this area before the shot touches the ground.
pole vault
Athletic event in which a pole is used to vault over the highest possible crossbar.
track
Oval circuit designed to hold races such as sprints, hurdles and relays.

equipment

All the regulation equipment used for sporting events, including timekeeping systems, starting pistols, cameras and hurdles.

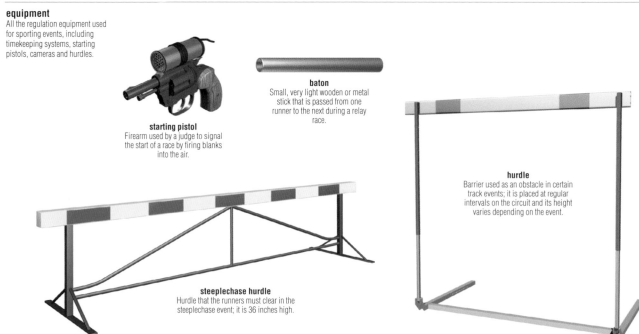

starting pistol
Firearm used by a judge to signal the start of a race by firing blanks into the air.

baton
Small, very light wooden or metal stick that is passed from one runner to the next during a relay race.

hurdle
Barrier used as an obstacle in certain track events; it is placed at regular intervals on the circuit and its height varies depending on the event.

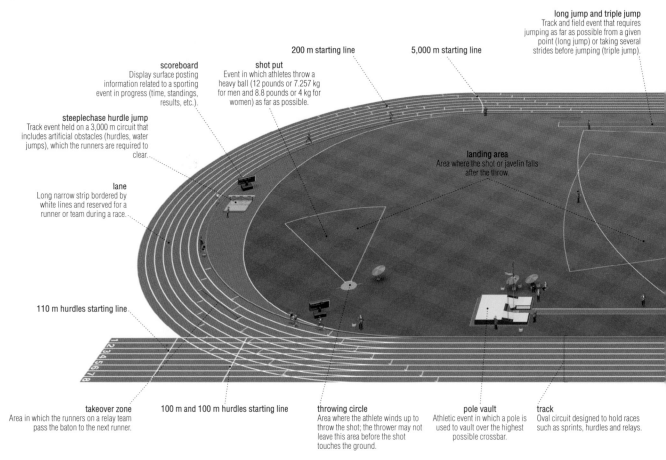

steeplechase hurdle
Hurdle that the runners must clear in the steeplechase event; it is 36 inches high.

arena

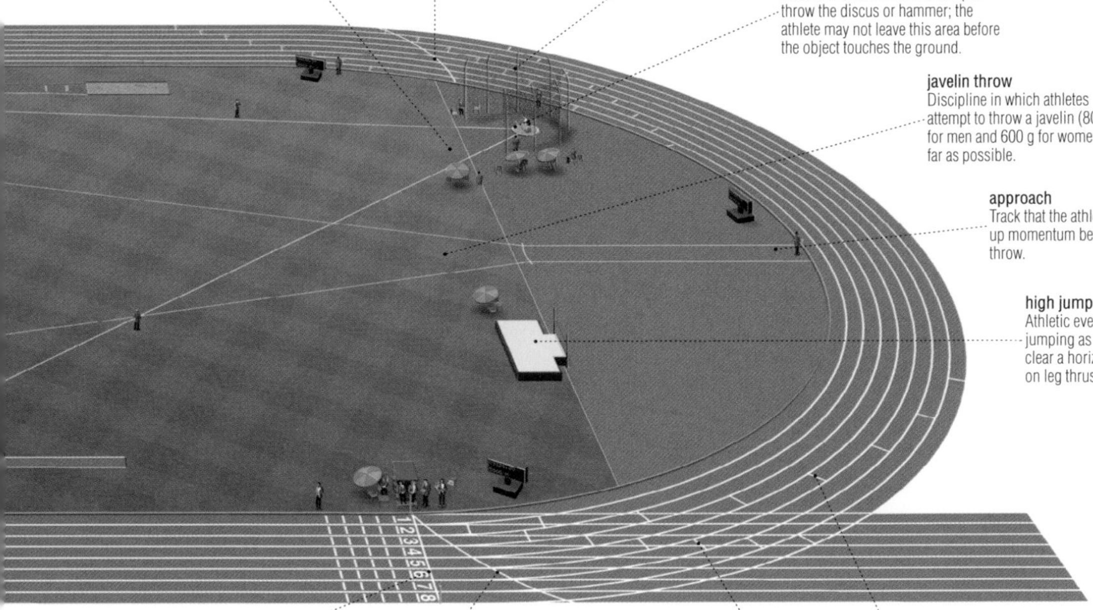
discus and hammer throw
Disciplines in which athletes attempt to throw a discus (2 kg for men and 1 kg for women) or hammer (16 lbs or 7.257 kg for men and 4 kg for women) as far as possible.
1,500 m starting line
safety cage
Wire fence bordering the throwing circle; it protects the spectators, competitors and officials in the event of a missed throw.
throwing circle
Area where the athlete winds up to throw the discus or hammer; the athlete may not leave this area before the object touches the ground.
javelin throw
Discipline in which athletes attempt to throw a javelin (800 g for men and 600 g for women) as far as possible.
approach
Track that the athlete uses to build up momentum before a javelin throw.
high jump
Athletic event that requires jumping as high as possible to clear a horizontal bar, relying solely on leg thrust.
12345678
finish line
Line marking the end of a race.
10,000 m and 4 x 400 m relay starting line
800 m starting line
400 m, 400 m hurdles, 4 x 100 m relay starting line

athlete: starting block

Starting block: device made up of two adjustable pedals that allow sprinters to give themselves momentum during a start.

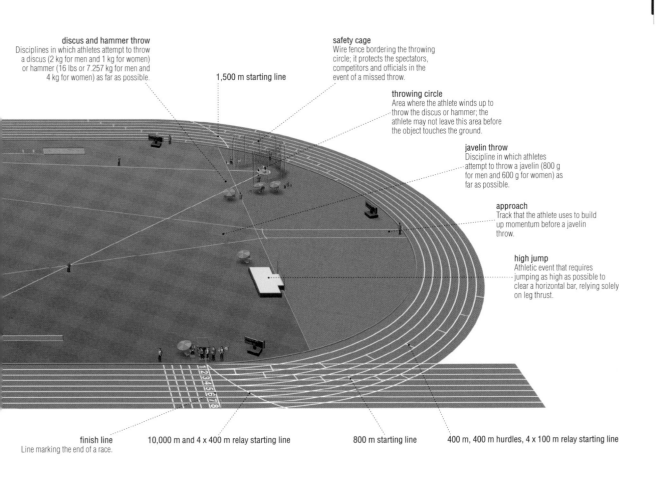

shirt
Supple, relatively tight-fitting garment covering the athlete's upper body.
number
Numbered piece of square fabric that athletes wear on their backs and chests for easy identification.
shorts
Very short pants covering only the top of the thighs.
pedal
Piece where the athlete places the feet; its angle can be adjusted.
track shoe
Shoe with a spiked sole that provides good traction during a race.
notch
Each of the grooves used to secure the pedals.
anchor
Piece that secures the starting block to the track.
starting line
Line marking the start of the race.
lane line
White band bordering the lanes on the track.
rack
Metal bar with notches that is used to adjust the position of the starting blocks.
spike
Metal piece attached to the front part of the sole to avoid slipping on the track and achieve better thrust.
block
Piece on which runners place their feet to give themselves momentum at the start of a race.
base
Piece that supports the pedal.

jumping

The four jumping events are the high jump, long jump, triple jump and pole vault.

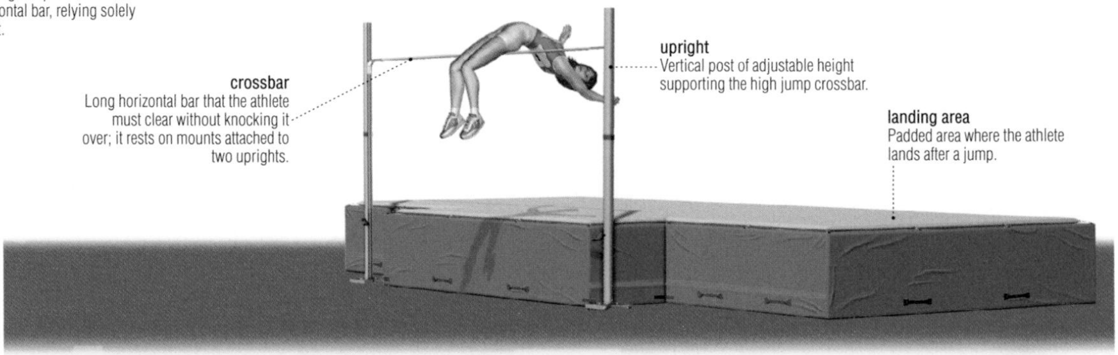
high jump
Athletic event that requires jumping as high as possible to clear a horizontal bar, relying solely on leg thrust.
crossbar
Long horizontal bar that the athlete must clear without knocking it over; it rests on mounts attached to two uprights.
upright
Vertical post of adjustable height supporting the high jump crossbar.
landing area
Padded area where the athlete lands after a jump.

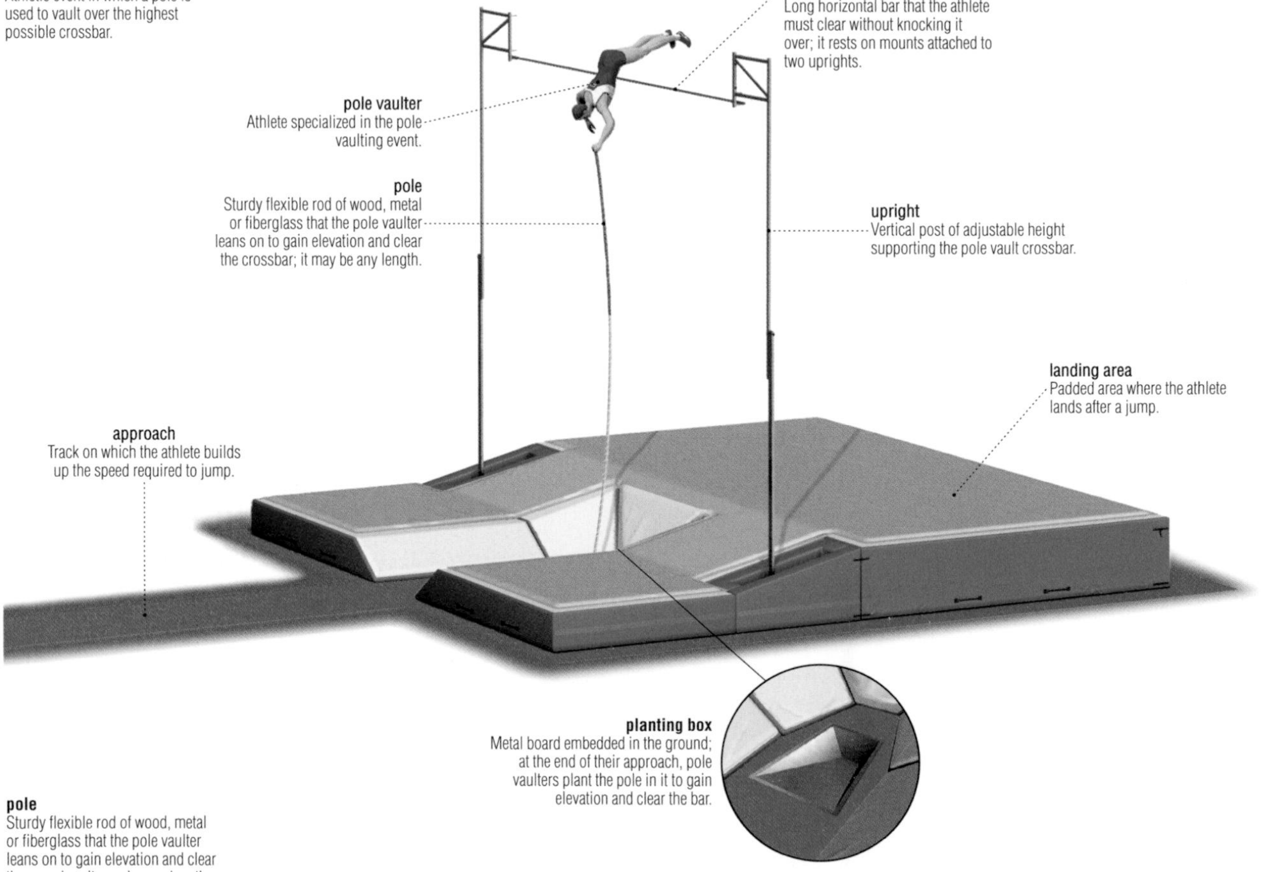
pole vault
Athletic event in which a pole is used to vault over the highest possible crossbar.
crossbar
Long horizontal bar that the athlete must clear without knocking it over; it rests on mounts attached to two uprights.
pole vaulter
Athlete specialized in the pole vaulting event.
pole
Sturdy flexible rod of wood, metal or fiberglass that the pole vaulter leans on to gain elevation and clear the crossbar; it may be any length.
upright
Vertical post of adjustable height supporting the pole vault crossbar.
landing area
Padded area where the athlete lands after a jump.
approach
Track on which the athlete builds up the speed required to jump.
planting box
Metal board embedded in the ground; at the end of their approach, pole vaulters plant the pole in it to gain elevation and clear the bar.

pole
Sturdy flexible rod of wood, metal or fiberglass that the pole vaulter leans on to gain elevation and clear the crossbar; it may be any length.
tip
Piece of rubber attached to the lower extremity of the pole to prevent it from slipping inside the planting box.

jumping

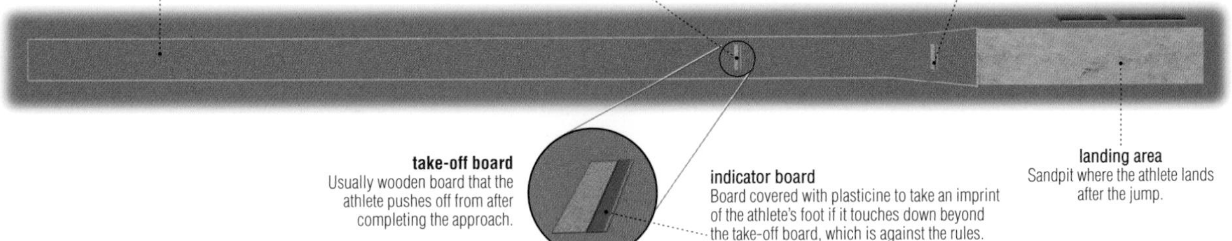
long jump and triple jump
Track and field events that require jumping as far as possible from a given point (long jump) or taking several strides before jumping (triple jump).
run-up track
Track on which the athlete builds up the speed required to jump.
triple jump take-off board
After clearing the take-off board, the athlete must perform a hop and a step before jumping into the landing area.
long jump take-off board
It is placed close to the landing area across which the athlete jumps as far as possible.
take-off board
Usually wooden board that the athlete pushes off from after completing the approach.
indicator board
Board covered with plasticine to take an imprint of the athlete's foot if it touches down beyond the take-off board, which is against the rules.
landing area
Sandpit where the athlete lands after the jump.

throwing

The throwing events are discus, shot put, hammer and javelin.

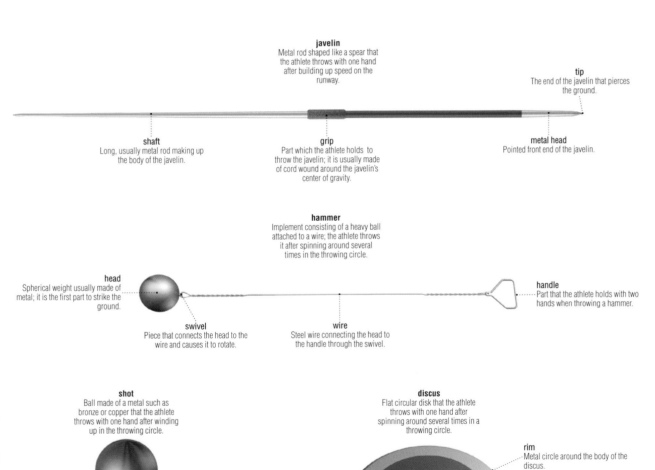

javelin
Metal rod shaped like a spear that the athlete throws with one hand after building up speed on the runway.
tip
The end of the javelin that pierces the ground.
shaft
Long, usually metal rod making up the body of the javelin.
grip
Part which the athlete holds to throw the javelin; it is usually made of cord wound around the javelin's center of gravity.
metal head
Pointed front end of the javelin.

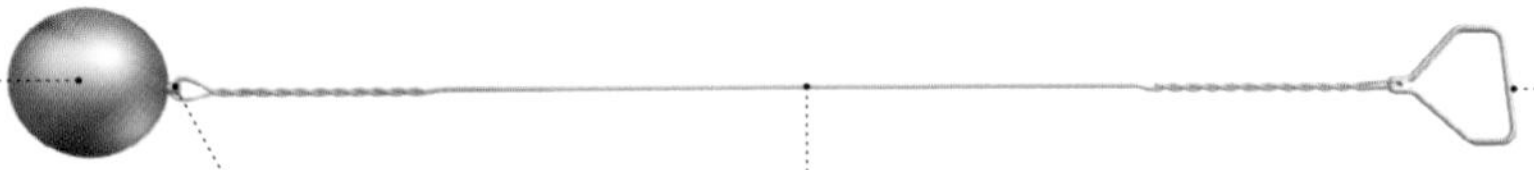
hammer
Implement consisting of a heavy ball attached to a wire; the athlete throws it after spinning around several times in the throwing circle.
head
Spherical weight usually made of metal; it is the first part to strike the ground.
handle
Part that the athlete holds with two hands when throwing a hammer.
swivel
Piece that connects the head to the wire and causes it to rotate.
wire
Steel wire connecting the head to the handle through the swivel.

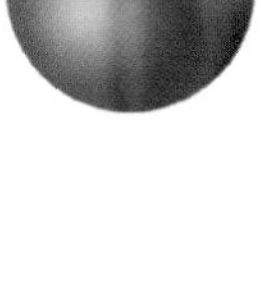
shot
Ball made of a metal such as bronze or copper that the athlete throws with one hand after winding up in the throwing circle.

discus
Flat circular disk that the athlete throws with one hand after spinning around several times in a throwing circle.
rim
Metal circle around the body of the discus.
weight
Heavy metal body at the center of the discus.
body
Part of the discus that is usually made of wood or plastic.

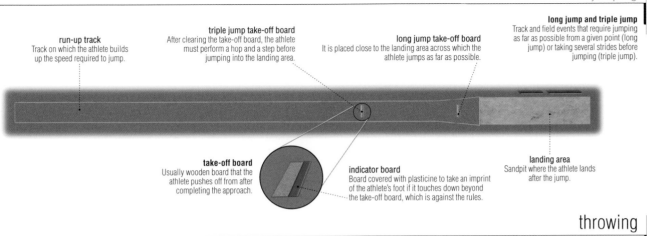

baseball

Sport with two opposing teams of nine players who attempt to score points by hitting a ball with a bat and running from one base to the next until they reach home plate; a game lasts nine innings, during which teams alternate from offense (at bat) to defense (in the field).

player positions
The team playing the field has nine players who try to prevent the opposing team from reaching bases and scoring points.

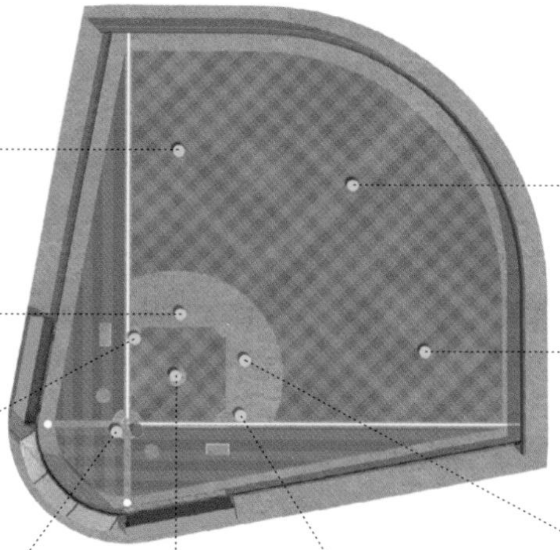

left fielder
Position that covers left field; if a fielder catches the ball before it touches the ground, the batter is retired.

shortstop
Position between second and third base; this player's role is to catch a ball hit in that direction and relay it to a teammate, depending on the game situation.

third baseman
Position near third base; this player needs a powerful arm to throw the ball directly to first base when the situation calls for it.

center fielder
Position in center field; covering the greatest area, this player anticipates where the ball will be hit and coordinates the positions of the outfielders.

right fielder
Position that covers right field; if a fielder catches the ball before it touches the ground, the batter is retired.

second baseman
Position near second base. This player, like all other infielders, retires an opponent by tagging the runner, ball in hand, before the runner reaches base.

catcher
Position behind home plate; this player catches the ball thrown by the pitcher and indicates the type of pitch to throw to retire the batter.

pitcher
Position opposite home plate; this player throws the ball to the opposing batter, using various pitches to try to prevent the batter from obtaining a hit.

first baseman
Position near first base that takes part in most defensive plays; the batter is retired if the first baseman, ball in hand, touches the base before the batter.

field
Surface on which a baseball game is played; it is in the shape of a quarter circle and is covered with dirt and natural or synthetic grass.

third base
Cushion attached to the ground that the player tries to reach after touching second base; if the player reaches home plate without being retired, one point is scored.

dugout
Partially closed area for the coaches, manager, substitute players and the team at bat.

coach's box
Each of two areas reserved for base coaches who use signals to communicate strategy to runners and batters.

foul line
Two straight lines bordering the playing field; they run from home plate to the outfield fence.

backstop
Chain-link barrier located behind home plate; it prevents the ball from reaching the spectators.

on-deck circle
Area reserved for the next batter; players on the team batting remain at bat until three outs have been recorded.

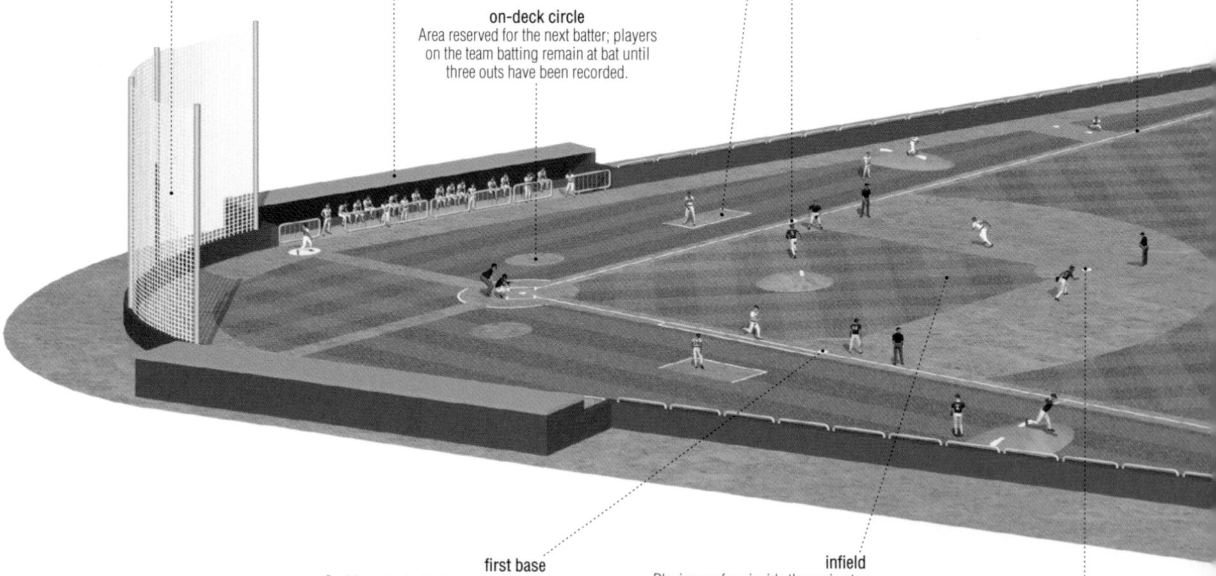

first base
Cushion attached to the ground that is the first base the batter reaches after hitting the ball; the player may stop there or move on to other bases.

infield
Playing surface inside the perimeter marked by the three bases and home plate; it includes a dirt area bordering the outfield.

second base
Cushion attached to the ground that the player tries to reach after touching first base, after the ball has been hit.

baseball

pitch
When the batter is in position, the pitcher throws the ball toward home plate; the batter judges the pitch and decides whether or not to try to hit it.

home-plate umpire
Official who calls balls and strikes, and signals when the batter has struck out (three strikes) or when a runner is retired at home plate.

batter
Player who takes position to hit the ball; to score a point, the batter must touch three successive bases and then home plate.

pitcher
Position opposite home plate; this player throws the ball to the opposing batter, using various pitches to try to prevent the batter from obtaining a hit.

catcher
Position behind home plate; this player catches the ball thrown by the pitcher and indicates the type of pitch to throw to retire the batter.

home plate
Rubber plate that the batter stands beside to face the pitcher; it marks the pitcher's strike zone and the umpire calls balls and strikes in relation to it.

pitcher's mound
Small mound of earth from which the pitcher throws the ball toward the batter; it is 10 inches higher than home plate.

pitcher's plate
Band of rubber attached to the ground; the pitcher stands on it to throw a pitch.

outfield fence
Barrier bordering the outfield, which is the playing surface between the two foul lines and beyond the infield.

left field
Section of the outfield behind third base, or to the left of the batter.

center field
Section of the outfield behind second base, directly facing the batter.

right field
Section of the outfield behind first base, or to the right of the batter.

foul line post
Each of the vertical posts indicating the end of the foul lines; a ball hit outside the foul lines is called a foul ball.

warning track
Area indicating to the outfielders that the fence is near; a home run is a ball hit over the fence and inside the foul lines.

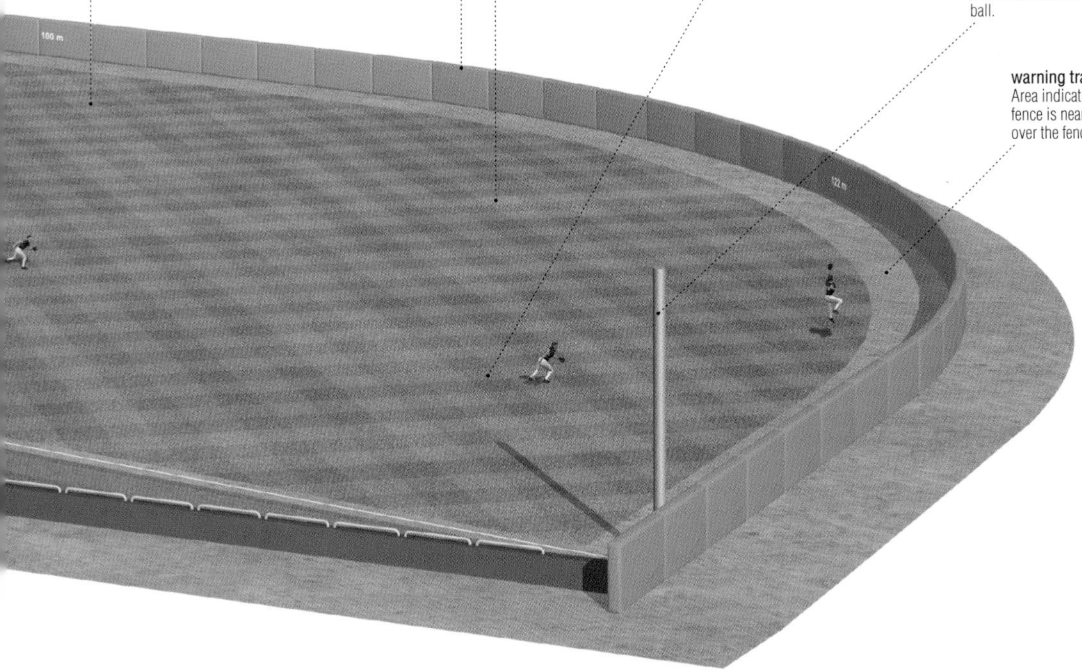

baseball

baseball
Hard ball with a circumference of 9 inches; its outer layer is made of two white pieces of leather sewn together.
bat
Piece of wood that the batter uses to hit the ball; its maximum length is 42 inches.
batter's helmet
Rigid piece of equipment for protecting the head from the ball's impact; it has side protection for the ears and temples.
batter
Player who takes position to hit the ball; the batter grasps the handle of the bat.
catcher
Position behind home plate; this player catches the ball thrown by the pitcher. The catcher wears equipment that protects against the ball, which can travel over 100 mph.
throat protector
Hard piece attached to the mask; it protects the catcher's neck and throat.
mask
Helmet with a wire cage that protects the catcher's head and face.
frame
Intersecting bars attached to the front of the mask; it protects the catcher's eyes and face while providing good visibility.
chest protector
Heavily padded vest that protects the catcher's chest.
catcher's glove
Glove with a heavily padded inside surface to cushion the impact of catching the ball.
team shirt
Flexible garment covering the upper body; it features the team emblem and the player's name and number.
undershirt
Relatively tight-fitting stretchy garment with short or long sleeves that players wear under the team shirt.
batting glove
Piece of leather covering the hand and wrist; it is designed to give the batter a good grip on the bat.
pants
Flexible stretchy garment covering the lower body from the waist to the shins or ankles.
stirrup sock
Colored sock whose lower extremity is an elastic that passes beneath the foot; it is usually worn over a white sock.
spiked shoe
Footwear whose sole contains small spikes to provide good traction.
toe guard
Piece of equipment made of hard molded plastic that protects the toes.
leg guard
Piece of equipment made of hard molded plastic that protects the leg.
knee pad
Piece of equipment made of hard molded plastic that protects the knee.
ankle guard
Piece of equipment made of hard molded plastic that protects the ankle and shin from impact when the ball ricochets off the bat.

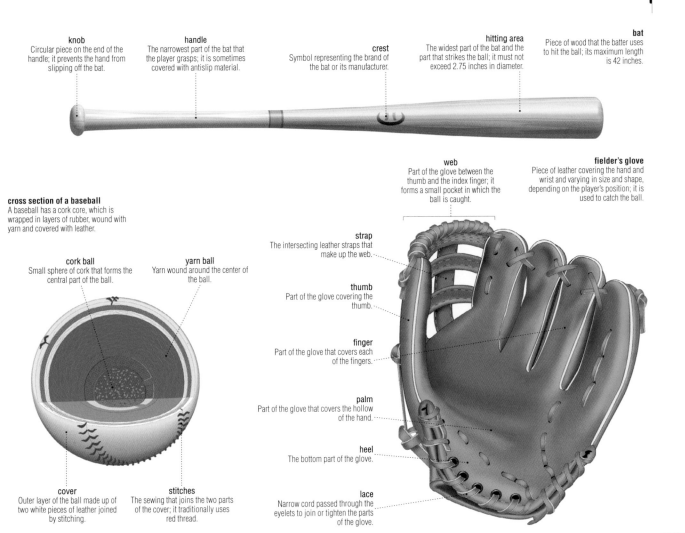

baseball

knob
Circular piece on the end of the handle; it prevents the hand from slipping off the bat.

handle
The narrowest part of the bat that the player grasps; it is sometimes covered with antislip material.

crest
Symbol representing the brand of the bat or its manufacturer.

hitting area
The widest part of the bat and the part that strikes the ball; it must not exceed 2.75 inches in diameter.

bat
Piece of wood that the batter uses to hit the ball; its maximum length is 42 inches.

cross section of a baseball
A baseball has a cork core, which is wrapped in layers of rubber, wound with yarn and covered with leather.

cork ball
Small sphere of cork that forms the central part of the ball.

yarn ball
Yarn wound around the center of the ball.

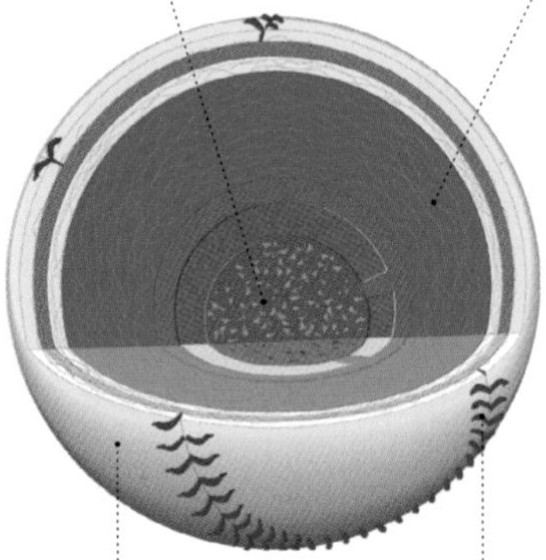

cover
Outer layer of the ball made up of two white pieces of leather joined by stitching.

stitches
The sewing that joins the two parts of the cover; it traditionally uses red thread.

web
Part of the glove between the thumb and the index finger; it forms a small pocket in which the ball is caught.

fielder's glove
Piece of leather covering the hand and wrist and varying in size and shape, depending on the player's position; it is used to catch the ball.

strap
The intersecting leather straps that make up the web.

thumb
Part of the glove covering the thumb.

finger
Part of the glove that covers each of the fingers.

palm
Part of the glove that covers the hollow of the hand.

heel
The bottom part of the glove.

lace
Narrow cord passed through the eyelets to join or tighten the parts of the glove.

softball

Sport akin to baseball but played on a smaller field; it differs from baseball in that the pitcher throws the ball underhand and not overhand.

softball glove
Piece of leather that the player uses to catch the ball; adapted to the dimensions of a softball, it is longer and wider than a baseball glove.

softball
Hard ball with a circumference of 12 inches; it is manufactured in the same way as a baseball.

softball bat
Piece of wood or aluminum that the batter uses to hit the ball; it is shorter and smaller in diameter than the baseball bat.

cricket

Sport with two opposing teams of 11 players who attempt to score points by hitting a ball with a bat and running between two wickets; teams alternate between offense (at the bat) and defense (in the field).

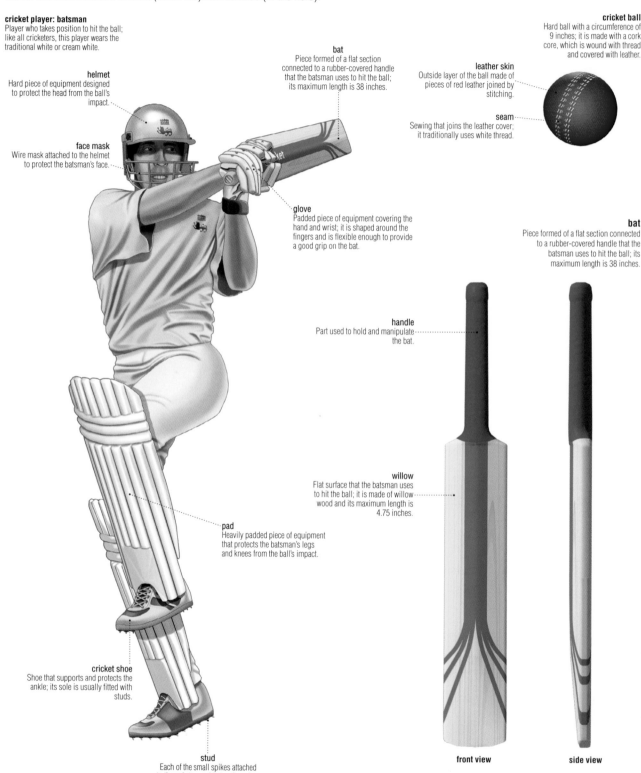

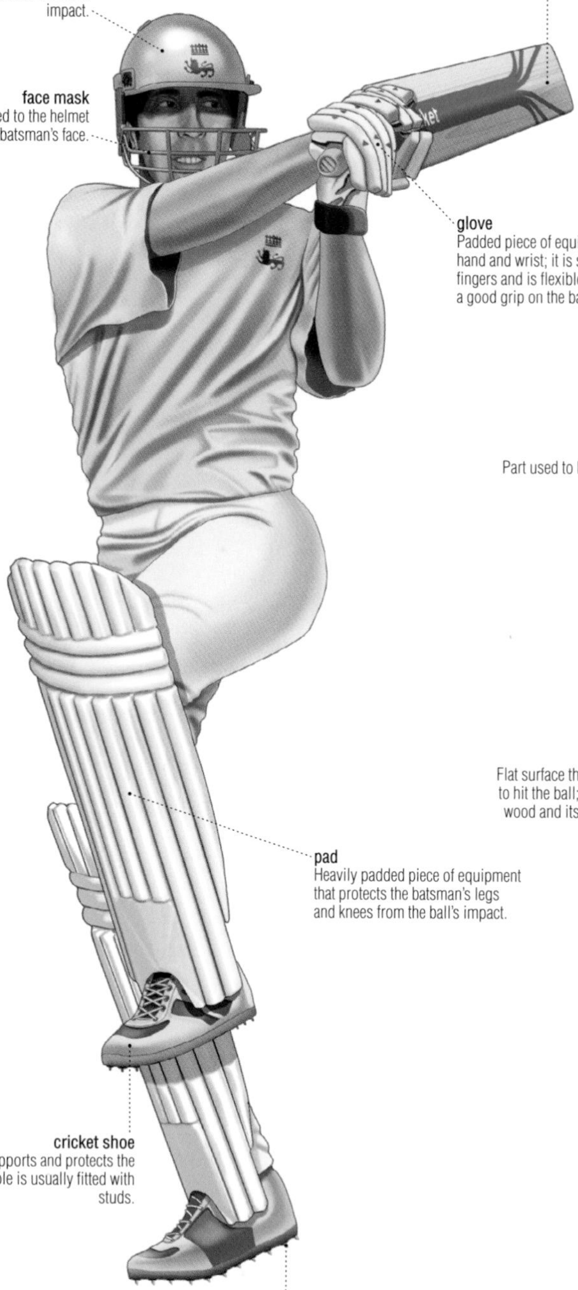
cricket player: batsman
Player who takes position to hit the ball; like all cricketers, this player wears the traditional white or cream white.
helmet
Hard piece of equipment designed to protect the head from the ball's impact.
face mask
Wire mask attached to the helmet to protect the batsman's face.
bat
Piece formed of a flat section connected to a rubber-covered handle that the batsman uses to hit the ball; its maximum length is 38 inches.
glove
Padded piece of equipment covering the hand and wrist; it is shaped around the fingers and is flexible enough to provide a good grip on the bat.
pad
Heavily padded piece of equipment that protects the batsman's legs and knees from the ball's impact.
cricket shoe
Shoe that supports and protects the ankle; its sole is usually fitted with studs.
stud
Each of the small spikes attached to the sole to provide traction when batting or running.

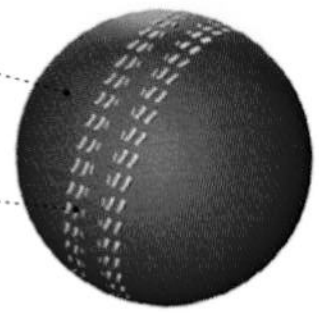
cricket ball
Hard ball with a circumference of 9 inches; it is made with a cork core, which is wound with thread and covered with leather.
leather skin
Outside layer of the ball made of pieces of red leather joined by stitching.
seam
Sewing that joins the leather cover; it traditionally uses white thread.

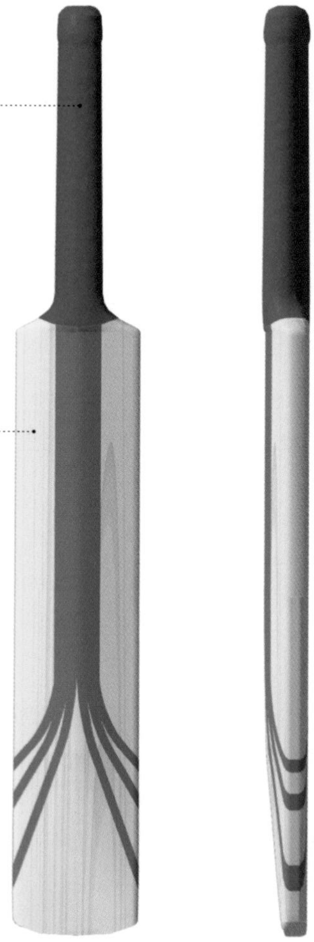
bat
Piece formed of a flat section connected to a rubber-covered handle that the batsman uses to hit the ball; its maximum length is 38 inches.
handle
Part used to hold and manipulate the bat.
willow
Flat surface that the batsman uses to hit the ball; it is made of willow wood and its maximum length is 4.75 inches.
front view
side view

cricket

field
Oval surface covered with natural or synthetic grass on which a cricket match is played; it is made up of a pitch and a field.

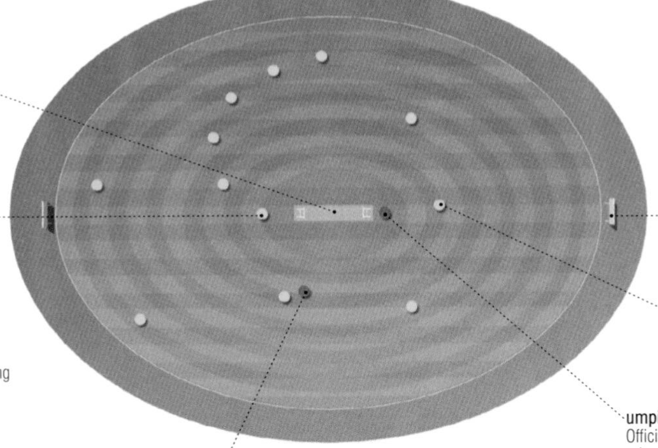

pitch
Rectangular surface in midfield where the bowler and the batsman face each other; it contains two wickets that are about 20 m apart.

wicketkeeper
Player positioned behind the batting wicket; the only defensive player who wears gloves, the wicketkeeper tries to catch balls missed by the batsman.

fielders
The team in the field, or the defending team, must catch the ball hit by the batsman and throw it toward one of the wickets to topple it.

screen
Rectangular surface behind each wicket; it minimizes distraction so that the batsman can follow the movement of the ball.

bowler
Player who throws the ball toward the batsman; the throw is made without bending the elbow and usually after running a few yards.

umpire
Official responsible for applying the rules of delivery; this umpire is positioned behind the bowler's wicket.

umpire
Official who enforces the rules; positioned to the side of the batsman's wicket, this umpire signals when a batsman is retired or when there is an infraction.

wicket
Piece made up of stumps with detachable bails; the wicket is considered toppled when at least one of the bails falls.

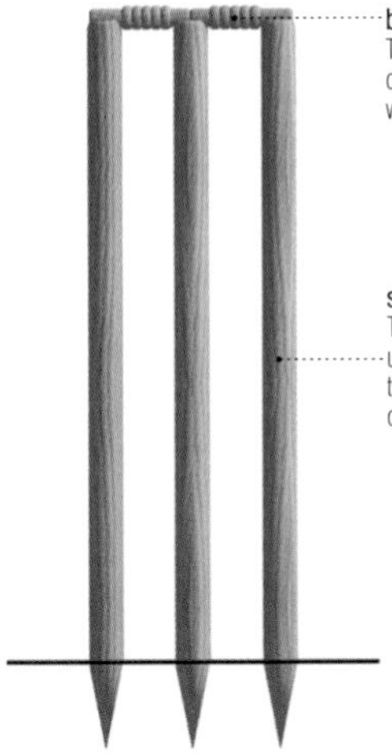

bail
The two horizontal pieces balanced on top of the stumps; they fall over when the ball strikes the wicket.

stump
The three vertical pieces that make up the wicket; the space between the stumps is smaller than the diameter of the ball.

pitch
Rectangular surface in midfield where the bowler and the batsman face each other; it contains two wickets that are 20 m apart.

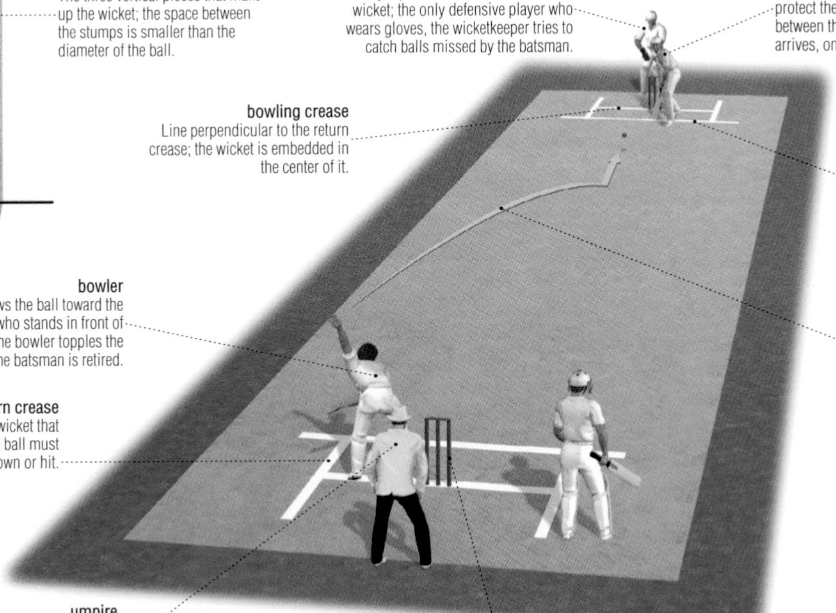

wicketkeeper
Player positioned behind the batting wicket; the only defensive player who wears gloves, the wicketkeeper tries to catch balls missed by the batsman.

batsman
Player who takes position to hit the ball and protect the wicket; each time the player runs between the two wickets before the ball arrives, one point is scored.

bowling crease
Line perpendicular to the return crease; the wicket is embedded in the center of it.

popping crease
Line drawn 4 feet from the wicket; at the end of a run, the batsman is safe after touching the ground behind this line with the bat or a part of the body.

bowler
Player who throws the ball toward the opposing batsman, who stands in front of the wicket; if the bowler topples the wicket, the batsman is retired.

delivery
Thrown at speeds reaching 100 mph, the ball usually bounces once before reaching the batsman.

return crease
The two lines on each side of wicket that demarcate the space in which the ball must be thrown or hit.

umpire
Official responsible for applying the rules of delivery; this umpire is positioned behind the bowler's wicket.

wicket
Piece made up of stumps with detachable bails; a defender can retire a batsman by toppling the wicket before the batsman completes the run between wickets.

field hockey

Sport with two opposing teams of 11 players who attempt to score in the opponent's goal by hitting a ball with a stick.

goalkeeper
Player whose role is to prevent the ball from entering the goal; the goalkeeper may touch the ball with any part of the body but cannot hold it with the hands.
helmet
Hard piece of equipment designed to protect the head.
face mask
Wire mask attached to the front of the helmet to protect the goalkeeper's face.
elbow pad
Piece of equipment worn under the shirt; its hard shell protects the elbow.
body pad
Heavily padded vest worn under the shirt to protect the goalkeeper's shoulders, chest and back.
glove
Padded piece of equipment covering the hand and wrist; its flexible design allows the goalkeeper to hold and manipulate the stick.
blocking glove
Rigid foam glove that is worn on the free hand; the goalkeeper uses its flat side to block the ball.
pad
Heavily padded piece of equipment that protects the goalkeeper's legs, knees and thighs from the ball's impact.
kicker
Piece made of rigid foam; it covers the goalkeeper's shoes and is used to kick the ball.

stick
Wooden or composite stick with a rounded side and a flat side, which is used to manipulate the ball.
handle
Part for holding and manipulating the stick.
tape
Rubber or plastic tape wound around the handle to prevent the hands from slipping.
toe
Curved end of the stick used to stop, manipulate and hit the ball.

hockey ball
Hard plastic ball with a circumference of 9 in; its traditionally white surface is usually grooved.

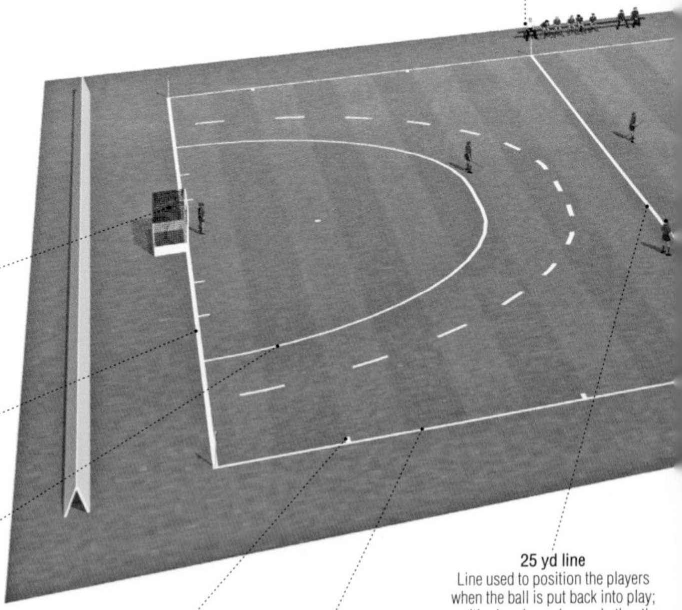
coach
The team's leader; the coach plots strategy and decides who plays in different situations.
goal
Cage made up of a net mounted on a frame; a goal is scored each time a team hits the ball into the opposing goal from inside the striking circle.
goal line
Line marking the ends of the playing field; the ball must cross this line for the goal to count as a point.
striking circle
Semicircle located in front of the goal; a goal can only be scored when the attacker hits the ball inside the opponent's striking circle.
5.5 yd line
Line where the attacker puts the ball back into play if the defenders push it behind their own goal line.
sideline
Line marking the sides of the playing field; when the ball crosses this line, the opposing team puts it back into play at the same place.
25 yd line
Line used to position the players when the ball is put back into play; positioning depends on whether the ball went out of play between the 25 yd lines or between one of them and the goal line.

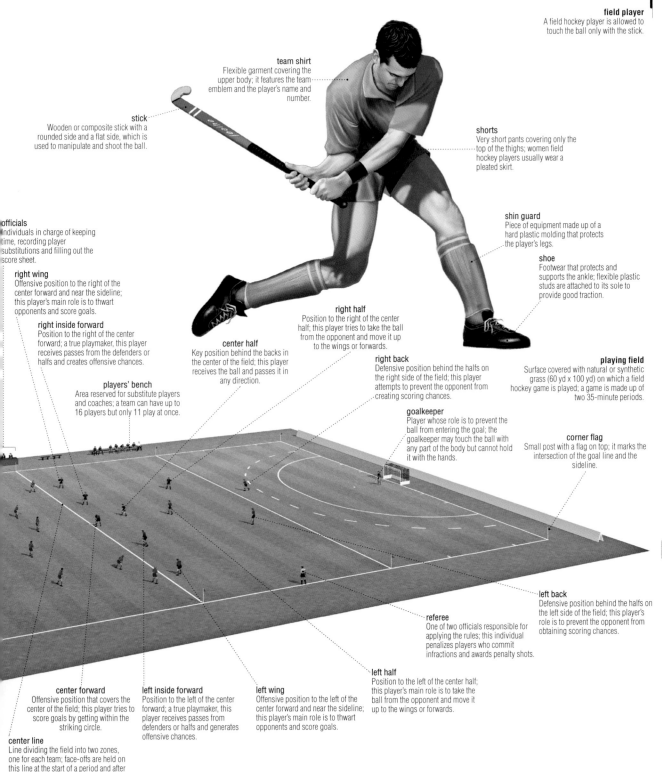

field hockey

field player
A field hockey player is allowed to touch the ball only with the stick.

team shirt
Flexible garment covering the upper body; it features the team emblem and the player's name and number.

stick
Wooden or composite stick with a rounded side and a flat side, which is used to manipulate and shoot the ball.

shorts
Very short pants covering only the top of the thighs; women field hockey players usually wear a pleated skirt.

shin guard
Piece of equipment made up of a hard plastic molding that protects the player's legs.

shoe
Footwear that protects and supports the ankle; flexible plastic studs are attached to its sole to provide good traction.

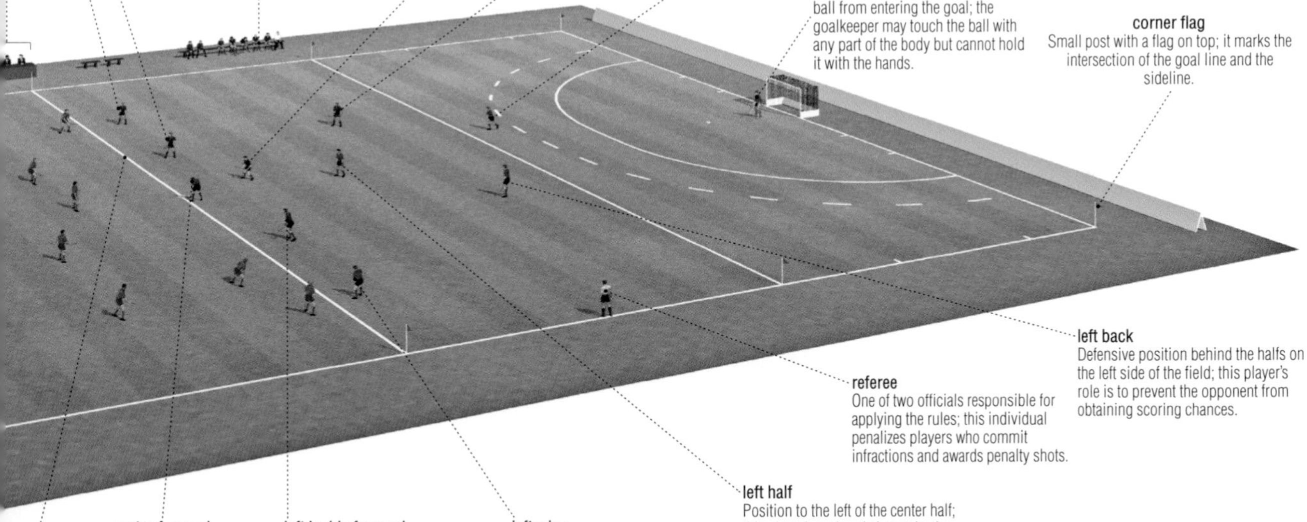

officials
Individuals in charge of keeping time, recording player substitutions and filling out the score sheet.

right wing
Offensive position to the right of the center forward and near the sideline; this player's main role is to thwart opponents and score goals.

right inside forward
Position to the right of the center forward; a true playmaker, this player receives passes from the defenders or halfs and creates offensive chances.

players' bench
Area reserved for substitute players and coaches; a team can have up to 16 players but only 11 play at once.

center half
Key position behind the backs in the center of the field; this player receives the ball and passes it in any direction.

right half
Position to the right of the center half; this player tries to take the ball from the opponent and move it up to the wings or forwards.

right back
Defensive position behind the halfs on the right side of the field; this player attempts to prevent the opponent from creating scoring chances.

playing field
Surface covered with natural or synthetic grass (60 yd x 100 yd) on which a field hockey game is played; a game is made up of two 35-minute periods.

goalkeeper
Player whose role is to prevent the ball from entering the goal; the goalkeeper may touch the ball with any part of the body but cannot hold it with the hands.

corner flag
Small post with a flag on top; it marks the intersection of the goal line and the sideline.

left back
Defensive position behind the halfs on the left side of the field; this player's role is to prevent the opponent from obtaining scoring chances.

referee
One of two officials responsible for applying the rules; this individual penalizes players who commit infractions and awards penalty shots.

left half
Position to the left of the center half; this player's main role is to take the ball from the opponent and move it up to the wings or forwards.

center forward
Offensive position that covers the center of the field; this player tries to score goals by getting within the striking circle.

left inside forward
Position to the left of the center forward; a true playmaker, this player receives passes from defenders or halfs and generates offensive chances.

left wing
Offensive position to the left of the center forward and near the sideline; this player's main role is to thwart opponents and score goals.

center line
Line dividing the field into two zones, one for each team; face-offs are held on this line at the start of a period and after a goal is scored.

soccer

Sport with two opposing teams of 11 players who attempt to score in the opponent's goal by kicking or knocking the ball in with any part of the body except the arms and hands.

soccer player
A soccer player is allowed to touch the ball with any part of the body except the arms and hands.

team shirt
Flexible garment covering the upper body; it features the team emblem and the player's name and number.

shorts
Very short pants covering only the top of the thighs.

shin guard
Piece of equipment made up of a hard plastic molding; it protects the soccer player's legs.

sock
Garment worn over the foot and up to the knee; it completely covers the shin guard.

soccer ball
Inflated ball made of leather or synthetic material; its circumference varies between 27 and 27.5 in.

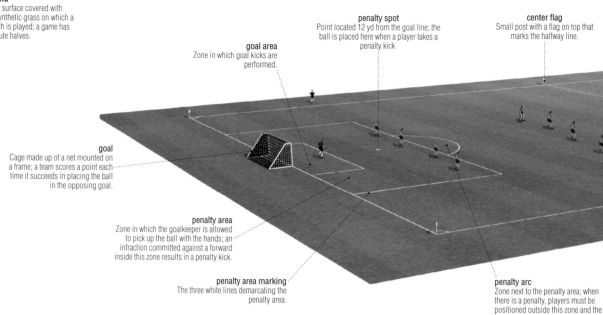

goalkeeper's gloves
Gloves that cover and protect the goalkeeper's hands and wrists and improve the grip on the ball.

interchangeable studs
Removable studs attached to the sole; they vary in size and can be changed to adapt to the state of the field.

soccer shoe
Shoe made of leather, soft rubber or plastic; studs are attached to its sole to provide good traction.

playing field
Rectangular surface covered with natural or synthetic grass on which a soccer match is played; a game has two 45-minute halves.

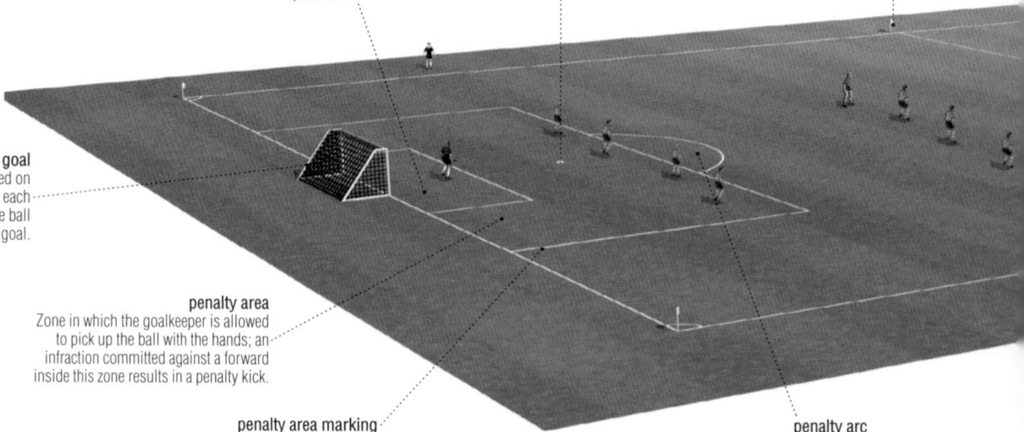

penalty spot
Point located 12 yd from the goal line; the ball is placed here when a player takes a penalty kick.

center flag
Small post with a flag on top that marks the halfway line.

goal area
Zone in which goal kicks are performed.

goal
Cage made up of a net mounted on a frame; a team scores a point each time it succeeds in placing the ball in the opposing goal.

penalty area
Zone in which the goalkeeper is allowed to pick up the ball with the hands; an infraction committed against a forward inside this zone results in a penalty kick.

penalty area marking
The three white lines demarcating the penalty area.

penalty arc
Zone next to the penalty area; when there is a penalty, players must be positioned outside this zone and the penalty area.

left back
Defensive position that covers the left side of the field; this player's main role is to slow or stop an opponent's progress toward the goal.

left midfielder
Center position that plays on the left side of the field; this player uses playmaking skills to pass the ball to the forwards.

defensive midfielder
Center position; this player tries to take the ball from the opponent before that player reaches the defenders and quickly mount a counterattack.

player positions
Various tactical schemes are used in soccer; among the best known is the 4-4-2, a formation with four defenders, four midfielders and two forwards.

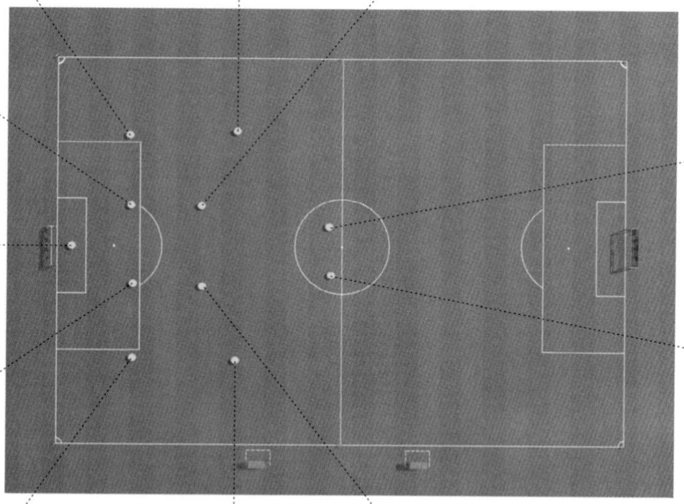

sweeper
Position that stays back, anticipates defensive mistakes by teammates and makes up for them; this player is not required to closely mark an opposing player.

forward
Offensive position usually placed behind the striker; this player uses speed to make crisp accurate passes.

goalkeeper
Position whose role is to prevent the ball from entering the goal; this is the only player allowed to touch the ball with the hands.

striker
Offensive position whose main role is to score goals; this player plays a forward position in the opposing team's zone.

stopper
Position that stays back, marks an opposing forward and prevents that player from being in a scoring position.

right back
Defensive position that covers the right side of the field; this player's role is to impede an opponent's progress toward the goal.

right midfielder
Center position that plays on the right side of the field; this player uses playmaking skills to pass the ball to the forwards.

defensive midfielder
Center position; this player tries to take the ball from the opponent before that player reaches the defenders and quickly mount a counterattack.

referee
Official responsible for applying the rules; this individual keeps time, signals penalties, issues warnings (yellow card) and ejects players (red card).

corner flag
Small post with a flag on top; it marks the intersection of the goal line and the touch line.

center spot
Point in the middle of the halfway line where the ball is placed before a kickoff at the start of a half or after a goal has been scored.

corner arc
Zone where the ball is placed when there is a corner kick, which is awarded when a defender puts the ball behind the goal line.

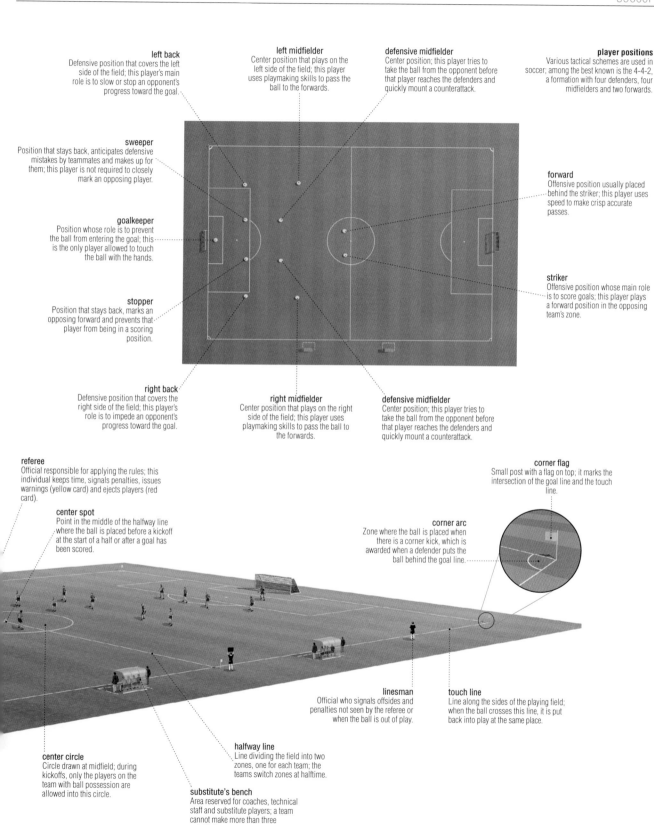

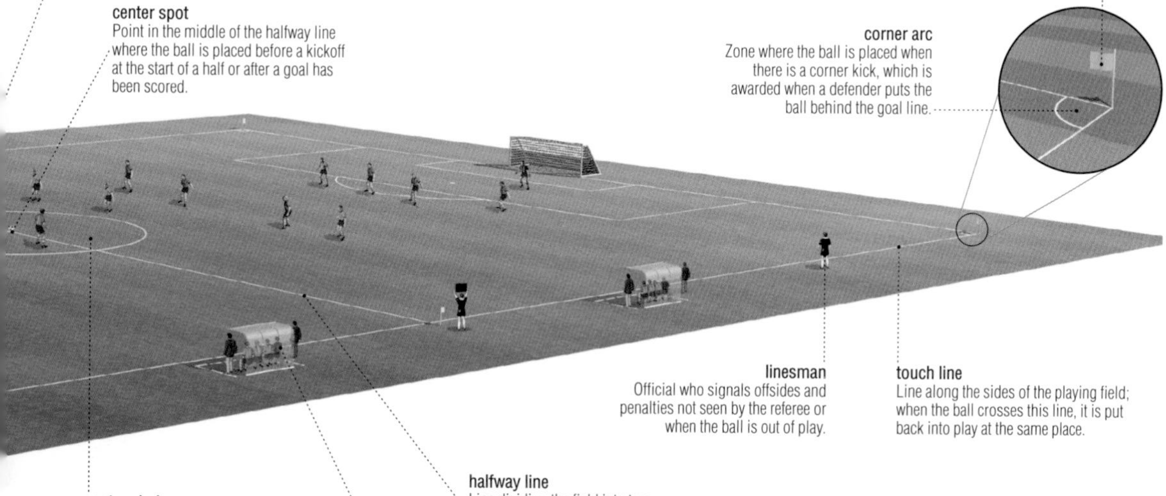

linesman
Official who signals offsides and penalties not seen by the referee or when the ball is out of play.

touch line
Line along the sides of the playing field; when the ball crosses this line, it is put back into play at the same place.

center circle
Circle drawn at midfield; during kickoffs, only the players on the team with ball possession are allowed into this circle.

halfway line
Line dividing the field into two zones, one for each team; the teams switch zones at halftime.

substitute's bench
Area reserved for coaches, technical staff and substitute players; a team cannot make more than three substitutions per game.

rugby

Sport with two opposing teams of 15 players that attempt to score points by carrying the ball into the in goal or kicking it between the uprights.

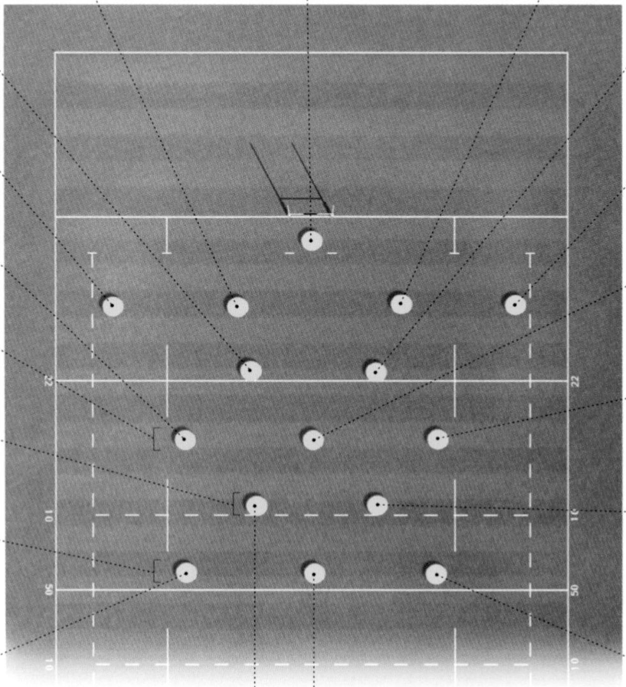
players' positions
A team is made up of seven backs and eight forwards; organized into three rows, the forwards take part in scrums and line-outs.
right center
Back positioned near the right wing; an excellent passer, this player challenges opposing centers and breaks down the defense.
fullback
Position in front of the goal; this player is the last line of defense for an opponent attempting to score a try.
left center
Back position near the left wing; an excellent passer, this player challenges opposing centers and breaks down the defense.
stand-off half
Position that acts as a link between the scrum half and the backs; an excellent strategist, this player directs the team's offense.
right wing
Back positioned on the right of the field; this player uses speed and agility to thwart opponents and score points.
flank forward
Third-row position to the right of the no. 8 forward; this player uses power and speed to play offensive and defensive roles.
third row
Group made up of the no. 8 forward and the two flank forwards; it is the last line of players in a scrum.
second row
Group made up of two forwards; one of its roles is to support the first row in a scrum.
first row
Group made up of the hooker and the two props; the first rows meet in the scrum and try to prevent the opponent from moving the ball forward.
tight head prop
Forward position to the right of the hooker; in a scrum, this player supports the hooker and pushes the opponent forward to gain field advantage.
scrum half
Position that acts as a link between the forwards and the backs; this player recovers the ball in a scrum and mounts the team's attack.
left wing
Back who covers the left side of the field; this player uses speed and agility to thwart opponents and score points.
no. 8 forward
Third-row position between the two flank forwards; when play is in progress, this player relays the ball from the forwards to the halfs.
flank forward
Third-row position to the left of the no. 8 forward; this player combines power with speed to play offensive and defensive roles.
lock forward
Second-row position on the left side of the field; this player's main role is to recover the ball during line-outs, rucks and mauls.
loose head prop
Forward positioned left of the hooker; in a scrum, this player supports the hooker and pushes the opponent to gain field advantage.
lock forward
Second-row position on the right of the field; one of this player's roles is to recover the ball during line-outs, rucks and mauls.
hooker
Position between the two props; this player attempts to gain possession of the ball in a scrum and to kick it back to teammates.

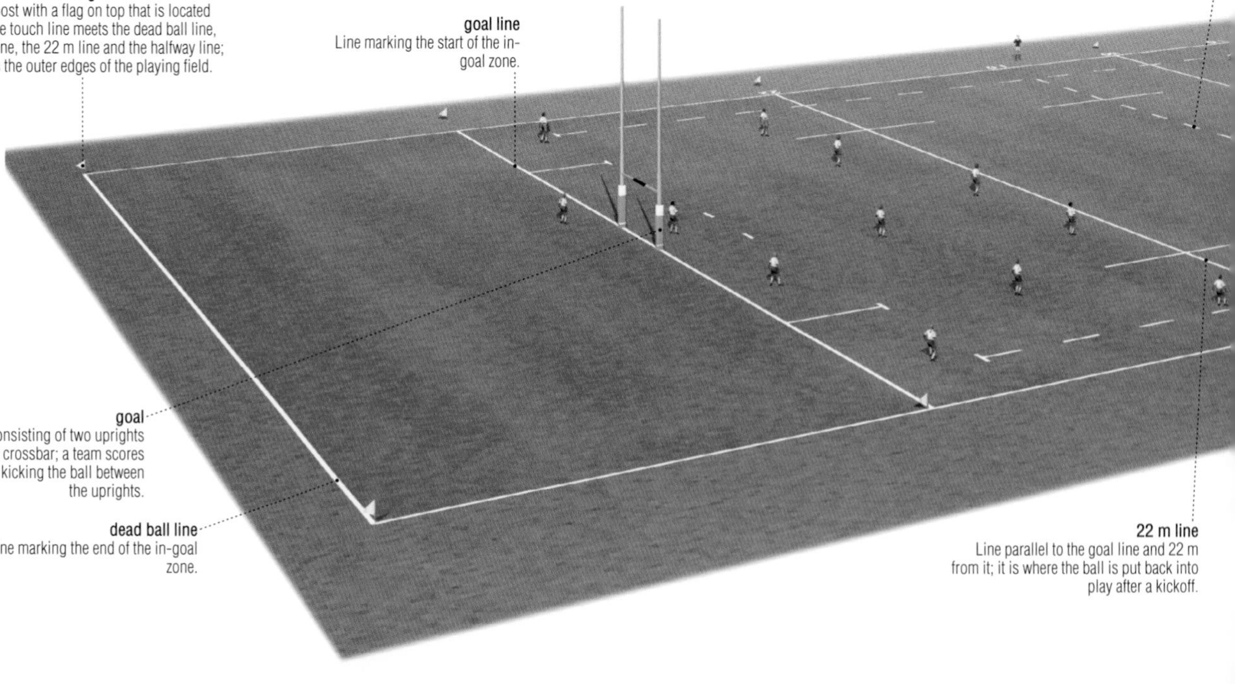
field
Rectangular surface covered with natural or synthetic grass on which a rugby game is played; a game consists of two 40-minute periods.
flag
Small post with a flag on top that is located where the touch line meets the dead ball line, the goal line, the 22 m line and the halfway line; it marks the outer edges of the playing field.
goal line
Line marking the start of the in-goal zone.
10 m line
Line parallel to the halfway line and 10 m from it; it marks the minimum distance the ball must travel during the kickoff.
goal
Frame consisting of two uprights and a crossbar; a team scores points by kicking the ball between the uprights.
dead ball line
Line marking the end of the in-goal zone.
22 m line
Line parallel to the goal line and 22 m from it; it is where the ball is put back into play after a kickoff.

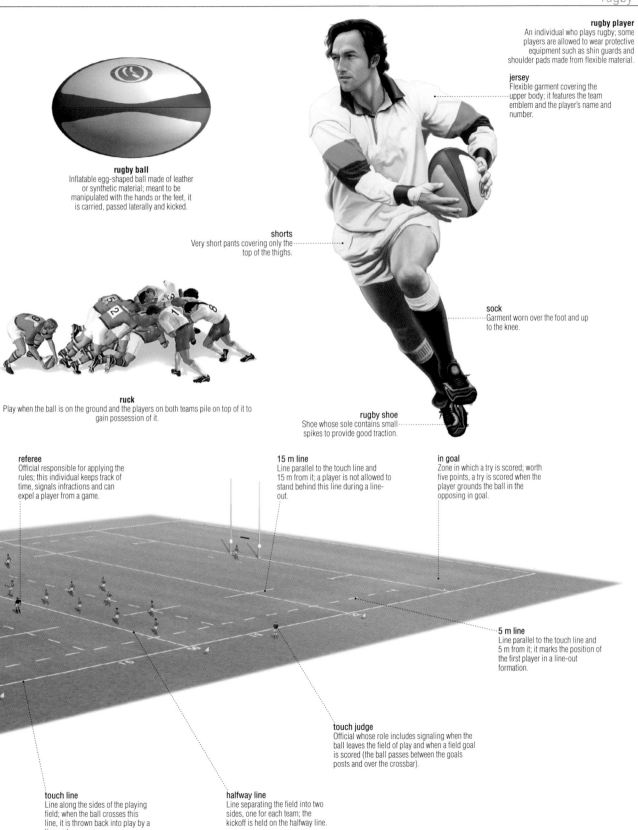

rugby ball
Inflatable egg-shaped ball made of leather or synthetic material; meant to be manipulated with the hands or the feet, it is carried, passed laterally and kicked.

rugby player
An individual who plays rugby; some players are allowed to wear protective equipment such as shin guards and shoulder pads made from flexible material.

jersey
Flexible garment covering the upper body; it features the team emblem and the player's name and number.

shorts
Very short pants covering only the top of the thighs.

sock
Garment worn over the foot and up to the knee.

rugby shoe
Shoe whose sole contains small spikes to provide good traction.

ruck
Play when the ball is on the ground and the players on both teams pile on top of it to gain possession of it.

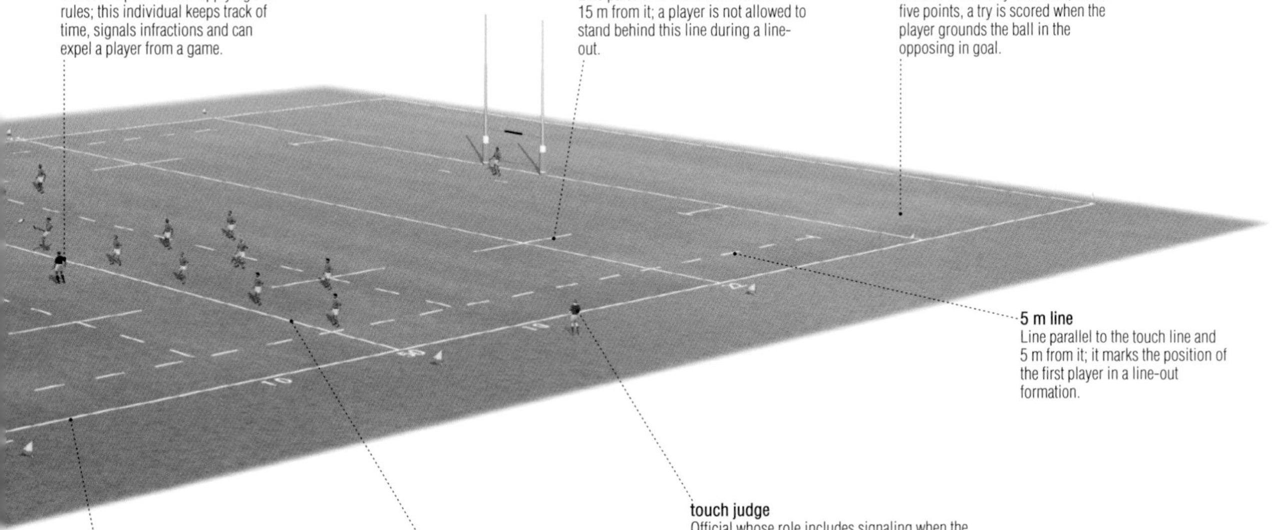

referee
Official responsible for applying the rules; this individual keeps track of time, signals infractions and can expel a player from a game.

15 m line
Line parallel to the touch line and 15 m from it; a player is not allowed to stand behind this line during a line-out.

in goal
Zone in which a try is scored; worth five points, a try is scored when the player grounds the ball in the opposing in goal.

5 m line
Line parallel to the touch line and 5 m from it; it marks the position of the first player in a line-out formation.

touch judge
Official whose role includes signaling when the ball leaves the field of play and when a field goal is scored (the ball passes between the goals posts and over the crossbar).

touch line
Line along the sides of the playing field; when the ball crosses this line, it is thrown back into play by a line-out.

halfway line
Line separating the field into two sides, one for each team; the kickoff is held on the halfway line.

football

Sport with two opposing teams of 11 players who attempt to score points by moving the ball into the end zone or kicking it between the goalposts.

scrimmage: defense
The defense tries to prevent the opponent's movement toward the end zone by stopping runs and passes.

right defensive end
Position to the right of the right defensive tackle; this player pressures the quarterback and tries to stop outside runs.

right cornerback
Position at the far right of the main defensive line; this player is very fast and covers the opposing team's wide receiver.

outside linebacker
Position near or behind the main defensive line on the right side of the field; agile and versatile, this player is effective against running and passing plays.

right defensive tackle
Position to the right of the middle linebacker; powerful and tough, this player is especially effective at stopping running plays.

right safety
Position behind the main defensive line on the right side of the field; this player is used mostly for the ability to cover passes.

left defensive tackle
Position to the left of the middle linebacker; powerful and tough, this player is especially effective at stopping running plays.

middle linebacker
Position behind the main defensiv line; this player combines speed and size especially to stop running plays in the center of the field.

inside linebacker
Position near or behind the main defensive line on the left side of the field; agile and versatile, this player is effective against passing and running plays.

left defensive end
Position on the outside of the left defensive tackle; this player pressures the quarterback and trie to stop the outside run.

neutral zone
Gap the equivalent of one ball length, it separates the offense and defense on the line of scrimmage and cannot be crossed before the snap.

left cornerback
Position at the far left of the main defensive line; this player is very fast and usually covers the opposing team's wide receiver.

left safety
Position behind the main defensive line on the left side of the field; an excellent tackler, this player is often relied on to stop running plays.

playing field
Rectangular surface (53.3 x 120 yards) covered with natural or synthetic grass on which a football game is played; a game consists of four 15-minute quarters.

inbounds line
The broken lines marking off yards; the lines and inbounds lines mark the line of scrimmage when play resumes.

goal line
Line marking the start of the end zone.

fifty-yard line
Line dividing the field into two zones, one for each team; it is 50 yards from the goal lines.

end zone
Zone in which a touchdown (six points) is scored when a player crosses it in possession of the ball.

end line
Line marking the far extremity of the end zone; the white area behind the goal is not part of the playing field.

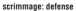

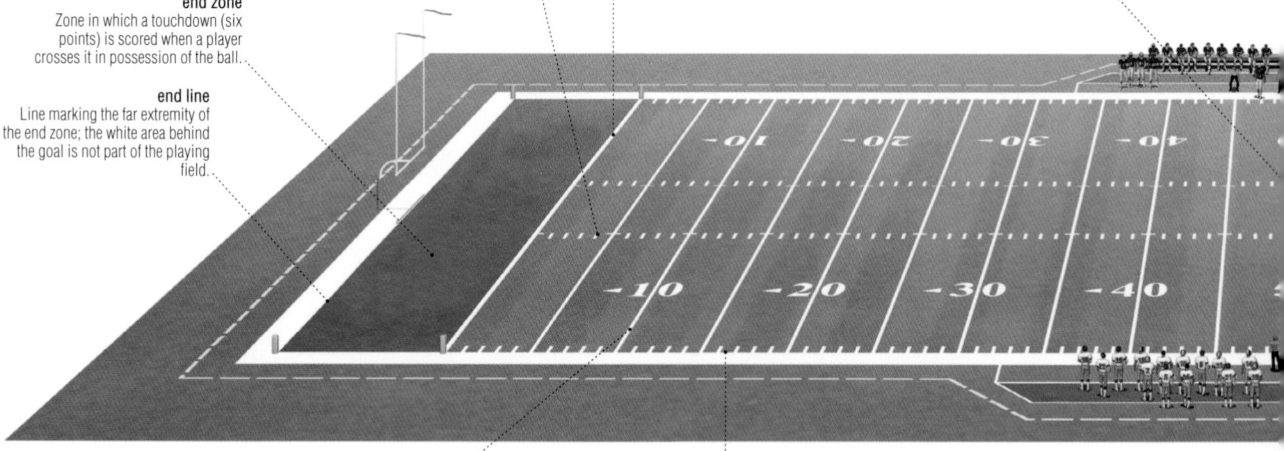

yard line
The solid lines at five-yard intervals that mark the distance from the goal line; at the start of a game, the ball is kicked off from the thirty-yard line.

sideline
Line demarcating the sides of the playing field; the play is whistled dead when the ball or a player in possession of the ball crosses it.

football

scrimmage: offense
The offense or team with ball possession has four downs to gain 10 yards. If it succeeds, it is given another four downs; if not, the ball is turned over to the other team by means of a punt.

quarterback
Position behind the center; the offensive leader, this player gathers teammates together between downs and communicates tactics.

left guard
Position to the left of the center; this player has a blocking role on passing and running plays.

left tackle
Position on the outside of the left guard; this player blocks the opposing defense and especially protects the quarterback in passing situations.

center
Position at the center of the offensive line; this player puts the ball in play by snapping it to the quarterback.

fullback
Position behind the quarterback; this player protects the quarterback in passing situations and blocks for the tailback.

tailback
Position behind the fullback; this fast player often carries the ball (running play).

right guard
Position to the right of the center; this player has a blocking role in passing and running situations.

right tackle
Position on the outside of the right guard; this player blocks the opposing defense and protects the quarterback in passing situations.

tight end
Position on the outside of the tackle; this versatile player blocks opposing players and catches passes.

wide receiver
Two positions at the far end of the offensive line; they use speed and agility to separate themselves from the defense and catch passes.

line of scrimmage
Imaginary line along which the offense and defense face one another before the ball is snapped.

back judge
Official who tracks the number of players on defense, follows the receivers and monitors the time elapsed between plays.

goal
Frame consisting of two goalposts and a crossbar; a team scores points by kicking the ball between the goalposts.

goalpost
One of the two vertical pieces making up the goal; they are 18.5 ft apart.

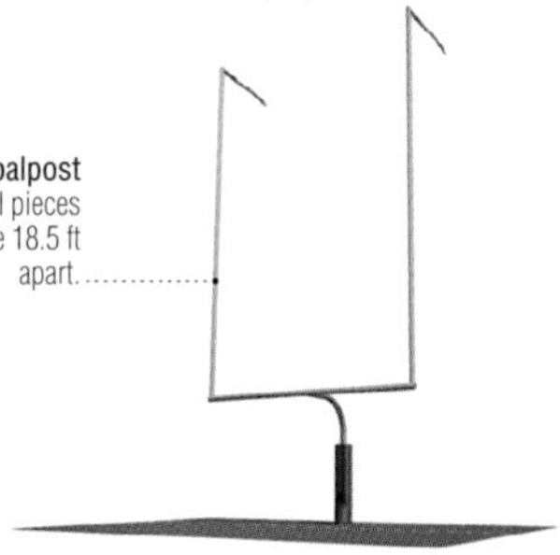

side judge
Official whose main role is to signal when a player crosses the sideline in possession of the ball.

line judge
Official whose role includes timekeeping, signaling stoppages in play and officiating during kickoffs and punts.

referee
Official responsible for applying the rules; this individual ensures that the game is properly played and supervises the work of the other officials.

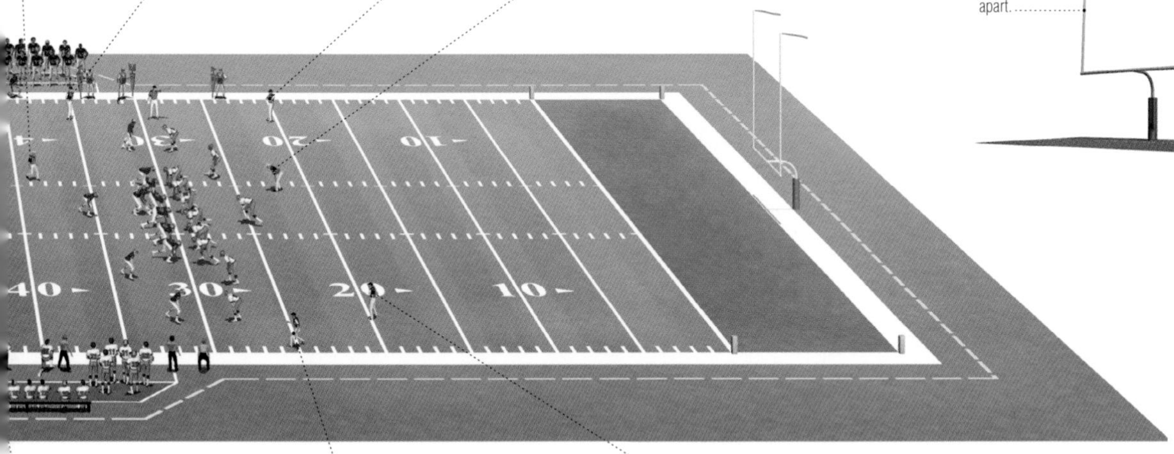

players' bench
Area for substitute players and coaches; a team's players are divided into three units: offense, defense and special teams.

umpire
Official in charge of checking player equipment and signaling infractions near the line of scrimmage.

head linesman
Official who signals stoppages in play and indicates exactly where to position the ball after it leaves the field of play.

football

football player
Football players' protective equipment varies depending on the player's role and position on the field.

helmet
Rigid piece of equipment designed to protect the head; it is lined with absorbent materials such as foam and air pockets.

chin strap
Strap that fastens the helmet to the head.

face mask
Metal cage attached to the helmet; it protects the football player's face.

player's number
Number identifying the player; special numbers are used to designate pass receivers.

team shirt
Flexible garment covering the upper body; it features the team emblem and the player's name and number.

wristband
Band of fabric that the quarterback wears around the wrist; it features a small window in which a note card is inserted.

pants
Light stretchy garment covering the lower body from the waist to the knees; it has pockets for holding protective pieces.

thigh pad
Padded piece of equipment that protects the thighs; it usually fits into a pocket inside the pants.

knee pad
Padded piece of equipment designed to protect the knee; it usually fits into a pocket inside the pants.

sock
Garment worn over the foot and up to the knee.

cleated shoe
Footwear whose sole contains small spikes to provide good traction.

protective equipment

Because of the violent contact and frequency of falls, football players wear heavy protective equipment.

tooth guard
Device that protects the football player's teeth; it fits between the cheeks and the teeth.

neck pad
Padded piece of equipment that protects the player's neck.

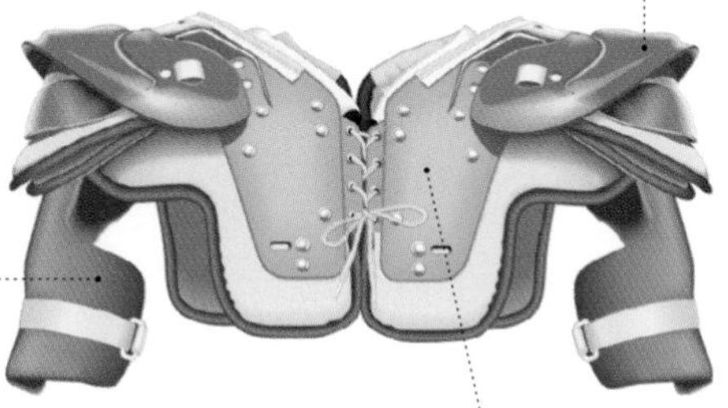

shoulder pad
Piece of equipment that consists of rigid molded plastic designed to protect the shoulder.

arm guard
Padded piece of equipment that protects the player's arms.

chest protector
Heavily padded vest that protects the football player's chest and back.

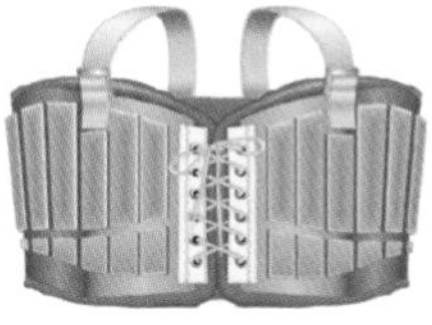

rib pad
Rigid jacket designed to protect the rib cage.

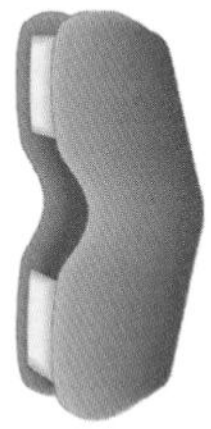

elbow pad
Padded piece of equipment designed to protect the elbow.

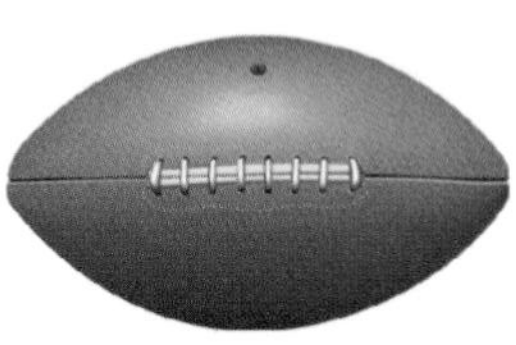

football
Inflatable oval leather ball that is smaller than a rugby ball; it has laces that provide a grip on the ball.

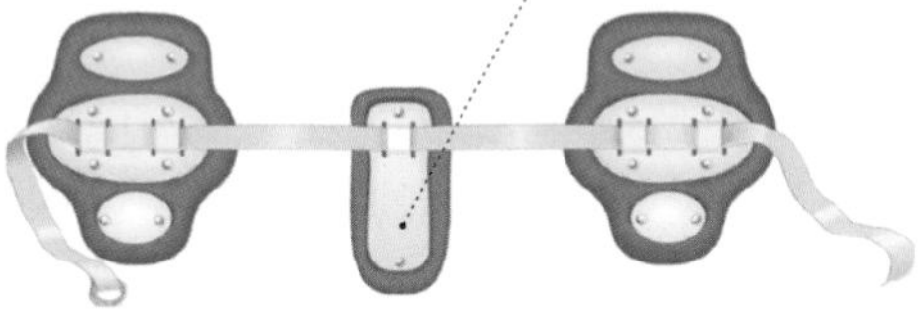

lumbar pad
Part of the hip pad that covers the coccyx.

hip pad
Piece of equipment consisting of three rigid molds designed to protect the hips and coccyx.

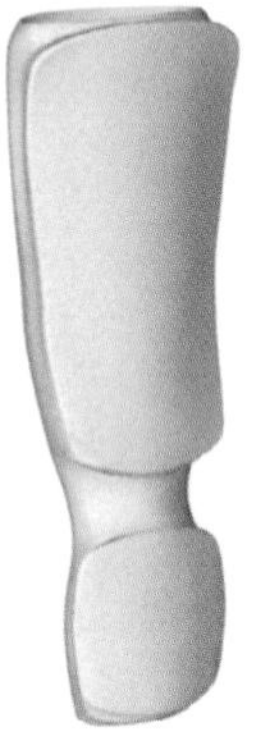

forearm pad
Padded piece of equipment designed to protect the forearm.

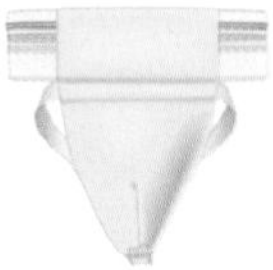

protective cup
Piece of equipment that consists of rigid molded plastic designed to cover a player's genital organs.

Canadian football

Similar to American football, it has two opposing teams of 12 players; the main difference is that there are only three downs to gain 10 yards.

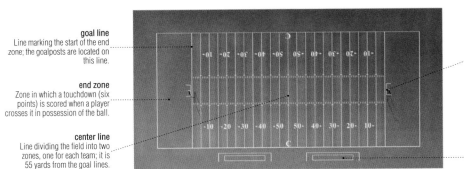

playing field for Canadian football
Rectangular surface covered with natural or synthetic grass; it is longer (150 yards) and wider (65 yards) than an American football field.

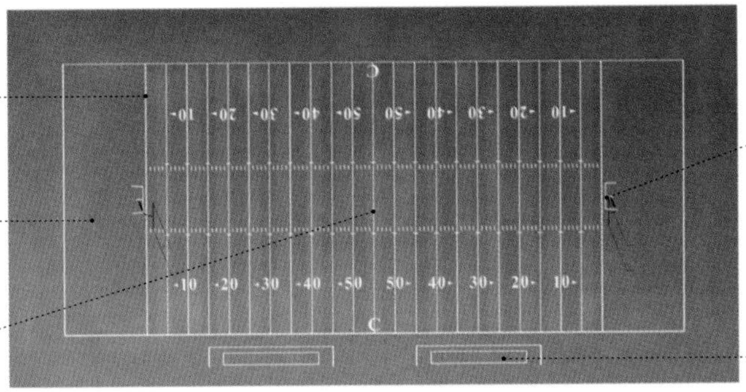

goal line
Line marking the start of the end zone; the goalposts are located on this line.

end zone
Zone in which a touchdown (six points) is scored when a player crosses it in possession of the ball.

center line
Line dividing the field into two zones, one for each team; it is 55 yards from the goal lines.

goal
Frame consisting of two goalposts and a crossbar; a team scores points by kicking the ball between the goalposts.

players' bench
Area for substitute players and coaches; a team's players are divided into three units: offense, defense and special teams.

netball

Sport played mainly by women with two opposing teams of seven players; teams score points by throwing a ball into the opponent's basket.

court
Hard rectangular surface (50 ft x 100 ft) on which a netball game is played; a game consists of four 15-minute periods.

goal
Structure made up of a basket and its supporting goalpost; a team scores each time it puts the ball into the opposing team's basket.

goal shooter
Position always in the goal third or goal circle; this player's role is to break away from the goalkeeper, catch passes and shoot on goal.

ring
Circular piece on which the netting is mounted; it is 15 in in diameter.

wing attack
Position that covers the center and goal thirds (except the goal circle); this player uses speed and agility to pass the ball to the shooter or the goal attack.

goalpost
Vertical post 10 ft high that supports the basket; it is attached to the floor in the middle of the back line.

goalkeeper
Position that defends the team's goal third; this player's role is to prevent the opposing shooter from gaining possession of the ball.

goal defense
Position that moves in the center and defense thirds (including the goal circle); one of this player's roles is to defend against the goal attack.

goal third
Area between the back line and the center third; defenders and the goalkeeper are not allowed to enter their team's goal third.

umpire
One of two officials responsible for applying the rules; this individual's role includes signaling infractions and when the ball leaves the court.

goal circle
Semicircular zone in front of the goal; shots can only be taken from this zone and only by a goal attack or goal shooter.

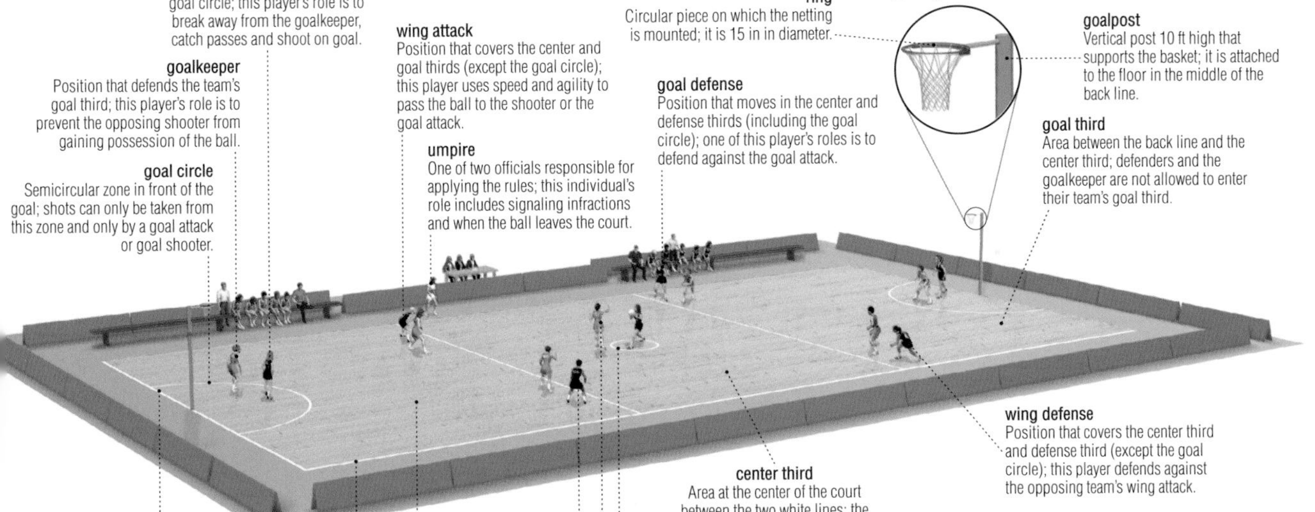

wing defense
Position that covers the center third and defense third (except the goal circle); this player defends against the opposing team's wing attack.

center third
Area at the center of the court between the two white lines; the goalkeepers and goal shooters are not allowed to enter this area.

back line
Line marking the ends of the court; when the ball crosses this line, one team puts it back into play at the same place.

central circle
Circular zone in the center of the court; at the start of a game and after a goal, the center on one of the teams puts the ball into play from this point.

sideline
Line along the sides of the playing field; when the ball crosses this line, it is put back into play at the same place.

center
Position that covers the entire court except the goal circles; this player is the link between the team's offense and defense thirds.

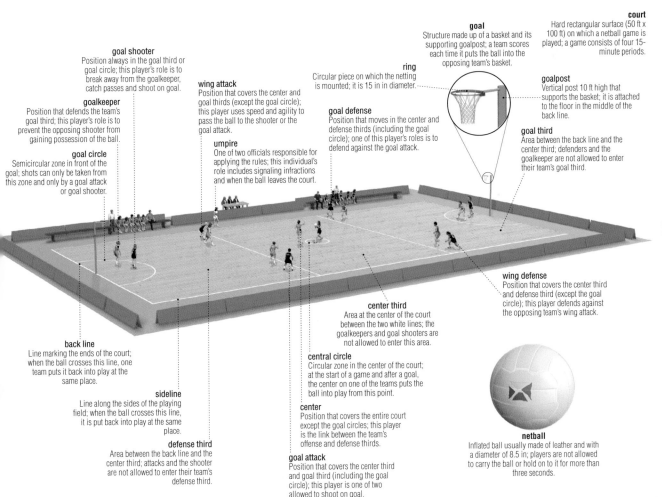

netball
Inflated ball usually made of leather and with a diameter of 8.5 in; players are not allowed to carry the ball or hold on to it for more than three seconds.

defense third
Area between the back line and the center third; attacks and the shooter are not allowed to enter their team's defense third.

goal attack
Position that covers the center third and goal third (including the goal circle); this player is one of two allowed to shoot on goal.

basketball

Sport with two opposing teams of five players who score points by throwing a ball into the opposing team's basket.

basketball player
Member of a basketball team; a player moves the ball forward by dribbling, which is bouncing the ball with one hand.
shirt
Flexible garment covering the upper body; it features the team emblem and the player's name and number.
basketball
Inflated orange ball made up of eight pieces of leather or synthetic material; it has a circumference of 30 in.
45
player's number
The number identifying a player; they are worn on the front and back of the shirt.
shorts
Short pants covering the top of the thighs.
shoe
Antiskid sneaker that protects the foot and provides ankle support.

scorer
Official who records points and fouls committed by the players.
timekeeper
Official who keeps time; this individual stops the clock when play stops and starts it again when play resumes.
court
Hard rectangular surface (50 ft x 94 ft) on which a basketball game is played.
clock operator
Official who keeps track of a team's possession time.
referee
Official who assists the first referee and also stays at the perimeter of the court so as not to interfere with the players.
referee
Official responsible for applying the rules; this individual does tip-offs and signals fouls.
sideline
Line along the sides of the court; when the ball crosses this line, it is put back into play at the same place.
semicircle
Semicircular zone where the player takes position to make a free throw, which is worth one point.
restricting circle
Circle around the center circle; players not taking part in the tip-off must be outside this circle.
center line
Line dividing the court into two halves, one for each team.
center circle
Circle at center court used for tip-offs at the start of a half and after a goal; a tip-off is when two players jump for the ball and try to push it toward their teammates.

player positions
Five players per team are on the court; they all play both offense and defense.

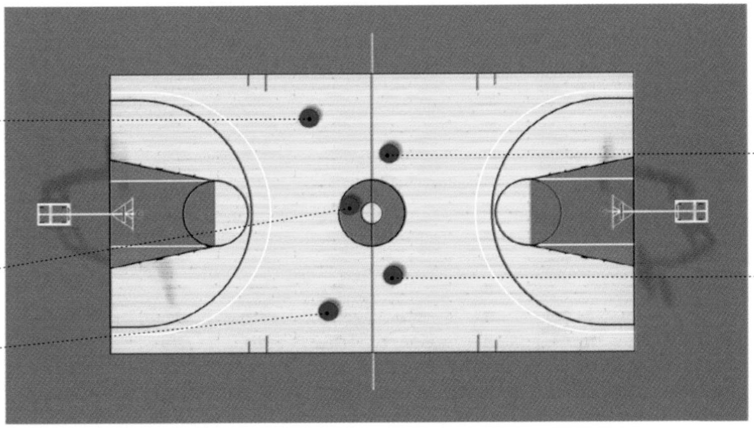

point guard
Position that directs the attack; this player is highly skilled at controlling and passing the ball.

left forward
Position that covers the left side of the court; this player has offensive (shooting, passing) and defensive abilities.

center
Position that defends the basket from close in and collects rebounds; this player is often the tallest on the team.

right forward
Position that covers the right side of the court; this player has offensive (shooting, passing) and defensive abilities.

guard
Position that assists the point guard; an excellent shooter, this player usually guards the opponent's most dangerous player.

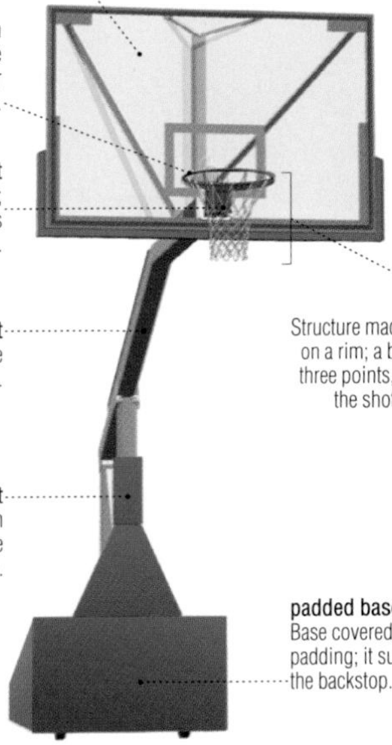

backboard
Rigid board attached to the back of the basket; it is usually made of transparent material so that spectators behind the basket can follow the action.

backstop
Structure made up of a basket and its support; a team scores each time it puts the ball into the opposing team's basket.

rim
Circular orange piece on which the net is mounted; it is 18 in in diameter and 10 ft above floor level.

net
Flexible netting attached to the rim; it slows the ball when it passes through the basket.

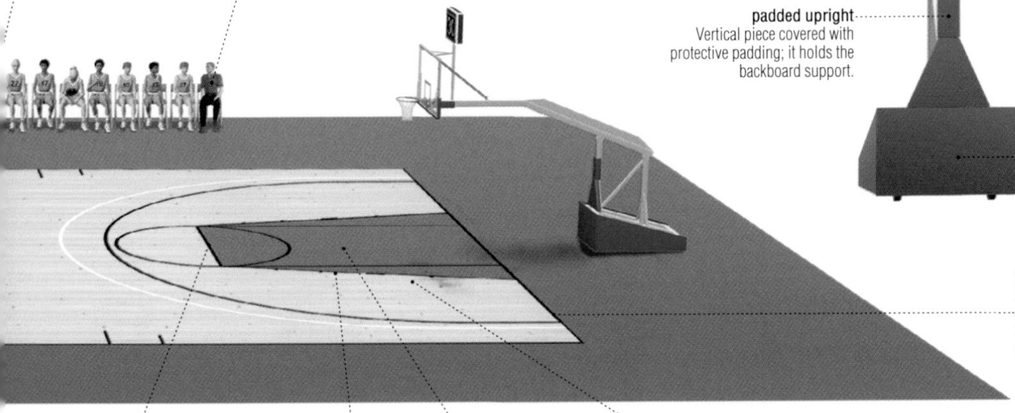

coach
The team's leader; the coach plots strategy and decides who plays in different situations.

basket
Structure made up of a net mounted on a rim; a basket is worth two or three points, depending on where the shot was taken from.

backboard support
Oblique piece that supports the backboard and the basket.

assistant coach
Person who assists the coach and can replace the coach if needed.

trainer
Individual who treats injured players.

padded upright
Vertical piece covered with protective padding; it holds the backboard support.

padded base
Base covered with protective padding; it supports and stabilizes the backstop.

end line
Line marking the ends of the court; when the ball crosses this line, one team puts it back into play at the same place.

free throw line
Line parallel to the end line; the shooter stands behind it for a free throw (throw awarded after a foul).

second space
Space along the restricted area near the free throw line; one of the shooter's teammates is in this space when there is a free throw.

restricted area
A trapezoidal area between the end line and the free throw line; an attacking player is not allowed to stay in it for more than three seconds.

first space
Space along the restricted area near the end line; one of the opposing players is in this space when there is a free throw.

SPORTS AND GAMES

volleyball

Sport with two opposing teams of six players who try to ground the ball in the opposing zone by hitting it over the net with their hands.

court
Hard rectangular surface (30 ft x 60 ft) on which a volleyball game is played; the first team to win three sets wins the game.

left attacker
Position to the left of the attack zone; this player's main role is making attack hits to score points.

end line
Line demarcating the ends of the court; the right back takes position behind this line to deliver a serve.

libero
Position specialized in receiving serves; this player only plays back while other teammates change positions during the course of a game.

umpire
Official who signals net faults or faults committed on the attack line and advises the referee when required.

white tape
Strip of tape with a cable passing through it; it is attached to posts to suspend the net.

free zone
Area at least 6.5 ft wide surrounding the court.

scorer
Official who fills in the score sheet, calls stoppages in play and supervises player rotations.

left back
Position on the left side of the back zone; this player's main role is making digs on short balls.

antenna
Flexible rods at each end of the net; they mark off the net area and the ball must stay inside them to remain in play.

linesman
One of four officials who use a red flag to signal a dead ball, service faults, contact with the antennas, etc.

players' bench
Area for substitute players and coaches; a team can have 12 players, six of whom are on the court during play.

back zone
Area between the attack line and the end line; it is usually occupied by the backs.

sideline
Line that demarcates the sides of the play area; a rally ends when the ball falls outside the sideline.

post
Upright used to stretch the net using white tape; the top of the net is just over 2 m above floor level.

referee
Official responsible for applying the rules; this individual follows the game from a raised platform set up at one end of the net.

center back
Position in the back zone; this player's main role is to recover long balls and blocked balls.

vertical side band
Vertical strip of white canvas at the ends of the net.

attack line
Line 10 ft from the net; the backs must make attack hits from behind this line.

net
Loosely stitched divider stretched across the middle of the court; players must hit the ball over it.

right back
Position on the right side of the back zone; this player's main role is making digs on short balls.

right attacker
Position to the right of the attack zone; this player's main role is making attack hits to score points.

center attacker
Position that covers the center of the attack zone; this player's main role is to counter the opponent's attacks.

attack zone
Area between the net and the attack line; it is usually occupied by the attackers.

volleyball
Inflated ball covered with soft leather and with a circumference of about 26 in; it must always be hit and cannot be held or thrown.

techniques

Players must master various techniques to dig up the ball, pass it and make attack hits.

dig
Technique used to play a long ball; the player lunges forward to hit the ball with one or two hands.

bump
Technique of extending the arms, joining the hands and striking the ball with the forearms; it is usually used to receive serves.

serve
Technique for putting the ball in play; a player usually serves the ball with one hand held above the head.

volleyball

beach volleyball
Sport with two opposing teams of two players who try to ground the ball in the opposing zone by hitting it over a net with their hands.

scorer
Official who holds the scorecard and signals stoppages in play.

second referee
Official who signals net faults or faults committed on the attack line and advises the first referee when required.

free zone
Area at least 10 ft wide surrounding the court.

court
Rectangular surface covered with sand on which a volleyball game is played; the first team to win two sets wins the match.

line judge
One of four officials who use a red flag to signal a dead ball, service faults, contact with the antennas, etc.

players' chairs
Rest area for players; a game is played barefoot and players wear a swimsuit or shorts and a shirt.

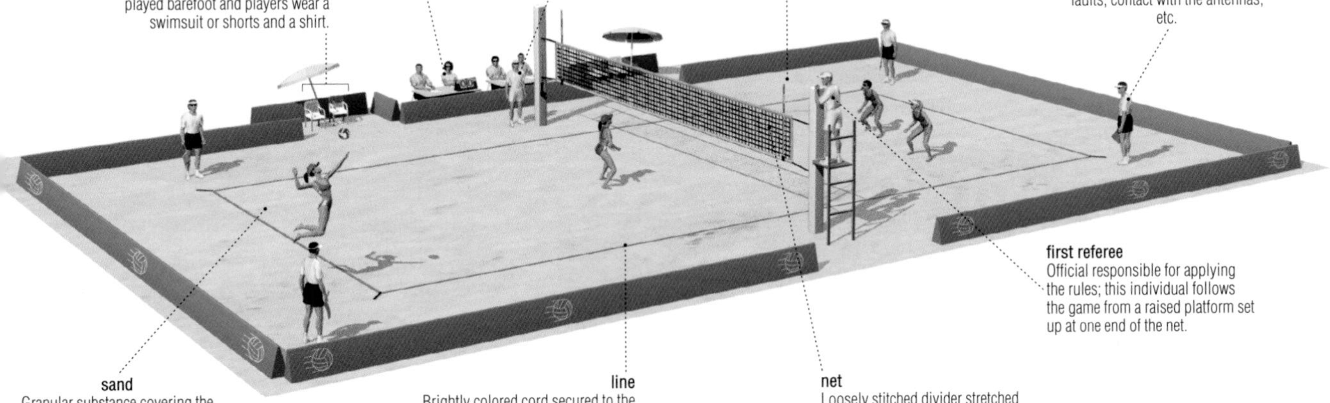

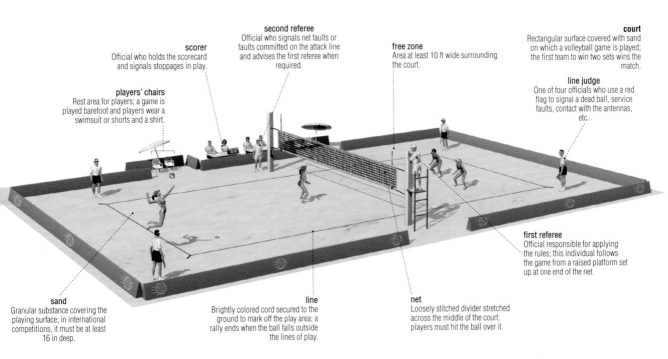

first referee
Official responsible for applying the rules; this individual follows the game from a raised platform set up at one end of the net.

sand
Granular substance covering the playing surface; in international competitions, it must be at least 16 in deep.

line
Brightly colored cord secured to the ground to mark off the play area; a rally ends when the ball falls outside the lines of play.

net
Loosely stitched divider stretched across the middle of the court; players must hit the ball over it.

beach volleyball
Ball with the same dimensions as a volleyball; it is heavier and contains less air mainly to counter the wind.

set
Pass executed with the fingertips, using a pushing motion with the arms; the set marks the transition between receiving and attacking.

spike
Offensive play that consists of striking the ball with the palm from above the level of the net.

block
Defensive play in which one or more front court players extend their arms and try to intercept the ball at the point where it crosses the net.

handball

Sport with two opposing teams of seven players who try to score points by throwing the ball into the opposing team's net.

player positions
Each team is allowed seven players on the court; players are not allowed to take more than three steps with the ball or to hold it for more than three seconds.

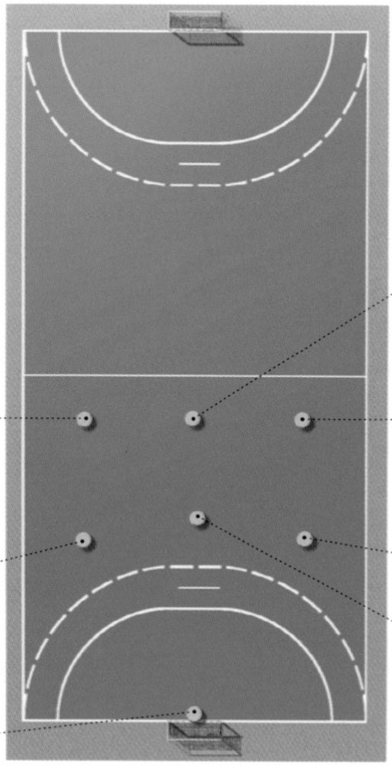

left winger
Position that covers the left side of the court; using speed and agility, this player is often at the sideline stretching the defense and creating scoring chances.

left back
Position behind the wingers on the left side of the court; an excellent shooter, this player also defends against the opponent's line player or back.

goalkeeper
Position whose role is to prevent the ball from entering the net; this player is the only one allowed to touch the ball with the feet.

center forward
Position in the center court area between the wingers; this player tries to slip through the defense and create holes in it.

right winger
Position that covers the right side of the court; using speed and agility, this player is often at the sideline stretching the defense and creating scoring chances.

right back
Position behind the wingers on the right side of the field; an excellent shooter, this player also defends against an opposing line player or back.

center back
Position in the center court area between the backs; this player is the team's offensive leader.

handball
Inflated ball usually covered with leather; it has a circumference of 21 in (women) to 24 in (men) and can be thrown, hit with the fist or dribbled.

court
Hard rectangular surface (20 m x 40 m) on which a handball game is played; a game is made up of two 30-minute periods with a 10-minute break between them.

goal line
Line at the ends of the court that demarcates the play area; a goal is scored when the ball crosses this line.

scorekeeper
Official in charge of timing the game and suspensions and substitute player changes.

timekeeper
Official in charge of timekeeping.

net
Loosely stitched netting attached to the back of the post; it keeps the ball inside the goal.

players' bench
Area for substitute players and coaches; a team can have up to 12 players, seven of whom are on the court at one time.

goal
Cage made up of a net mounted on a frame; a team scores a point each time it succeeds in placing the ball in the opposing goal.

goal line referee
Official responsible for applying the rules; positioned near the goal line, this individual signals infractions and decides if a goal counts.

secretary
Official who keeps the lineup card and marks the scorecard (goals allowed, expulsions, etc.).

goal area line
Arc drawn 6 m from the goal; it demarcates the goal area.

penalty mark
Line parallel to the goal line and 7 m from it; a 7 m free throw (a shot awarded after a penalty) is taken from behind this line.

court referee
Official responsible for applying the rules; positioned in the center of the court, this individual mainly signals player infractions.

sideline
Line along the sides of the court; when the ball crosses this line, it is put back into play at the same place.

goal area
Semicircular zone reserved for the goalkeeper; a player with ball possession may jump above this area when taking a shot.

free throw line
Arc drawn 9 m from the goal; during a 7 m free throw, all players except the shooter must be outside the zone demarcated by this line.

center line
Line dividing the court into two zones, one for each team; throw-offs are held on this line at the start of a period and after a goal.

table tennis

Sport with two or four opposing players with paddles; they hit a ball onto opposite sides of a net dividing a table in half.

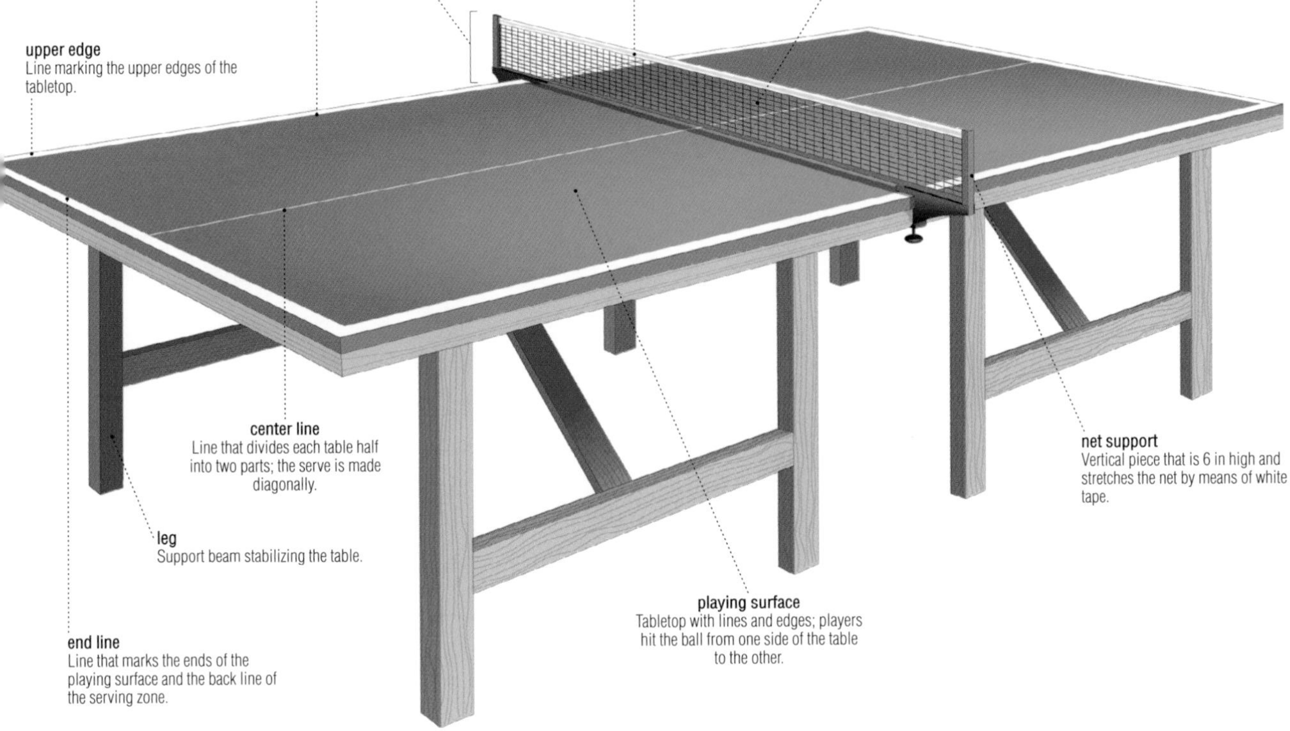

white tape
Strip of material with a cord passing through it; the cord is attached to the net supports to suspend the net.

mesh
The tiny squares make up the net; they are formed of interlaced threads.

table
Rectangular wooden table (9 ft x 5 ft) that is 2.5 ft above the ground; it is divided in half by a net.

net
Loosely stitched divider across the middle of the table; players must hit the ball over it.

sideline
Line marking the sides of the playing surface.

upper edge
Line marking the upper edges of the tabletop.

center line
Line that divides each table half into two parts; the serve is made diagonally.

net support
Vertical piece that is 6 in high and stretches the net by means of white tape.

leg
Support beam stabilizing the table.

playing surface
Tabletop with lines and edges; players hit the ball from one side of the table to the other.

end line
Line that marks the ends of the playing surface and the back line of the serving zone.

table tennis paddle
Paddle used to strike the ball; paddles come in a variety of shapes, sizes and weights.

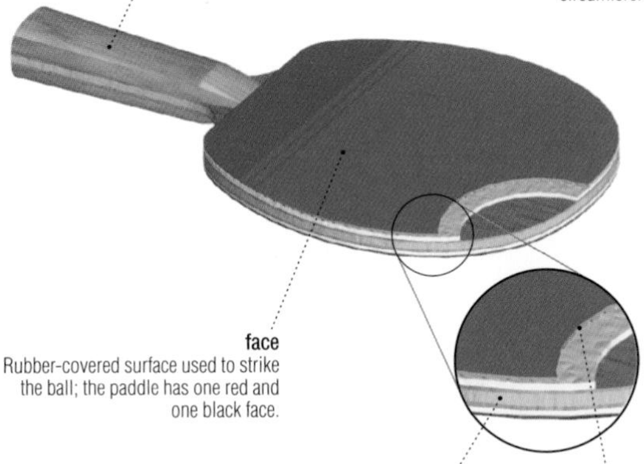

handle
Elongated part that the player grips to control the paddle.

face
Rubber-covered surface used to strike the ball; the paddle has one red and one black face.

blade
Hard flat portion containing at least 85% natural wood.

covering
Layer of rubber no more than .25 in thick that covers the faces of the blade.

table tennis ball
Ball made of celluloid or similar material; it is 1.6 in in circumference and weighs 0.09 oz.

types of grips
There are two principal paddle grips.

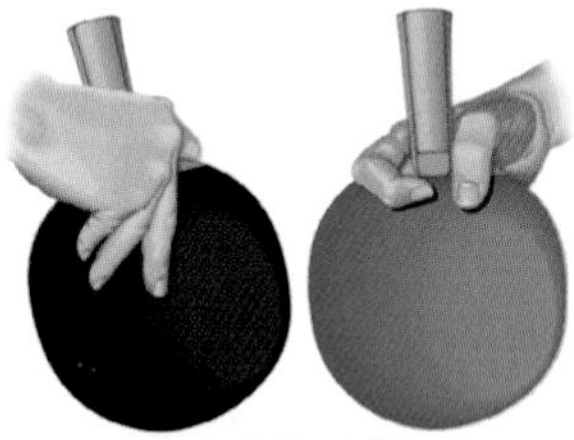

penholder grip
Grip that is suited to offensive play although it weakens the backhand: the table tennis player uses only one paddle face.

shake-hands grip
The most common grip; both paddle faces can be used and the player can hit forehand and backhand.

badminton

Sport with two or four opposing players that is similar to tennis; players use rackets to hit a shuttlecock onto opposite sides of a net that divides a court in half.

court
Synthetic or hardwood surface that is designed to provide good traction; badminton is usually played indoors.

service judge
Official who monitors the execution of the serve (player position, arrival of the shuttlecock in the appropriate zone, etc.).

center line
Line dividing each court half into two sides; the center line separates the left and right service zones.

linesman
One of 10 officials who ensure that the shuttlecock remains inside the lines of play and inform the umpire when a fault is committed.

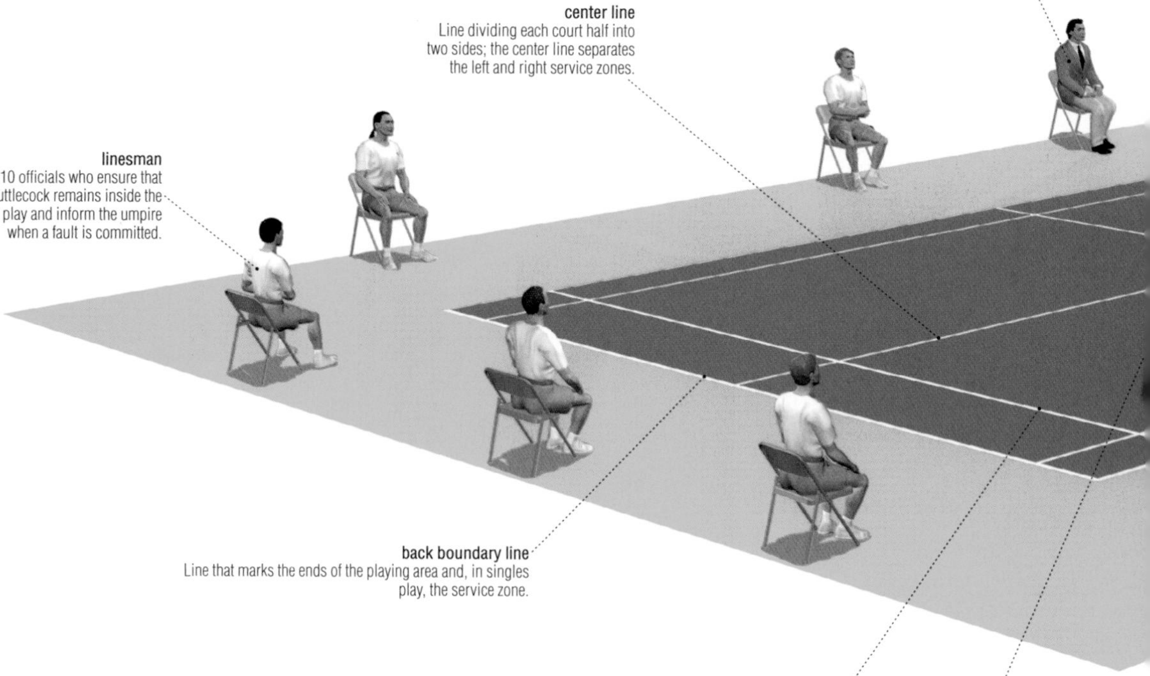

back boundary line
Line that marks the ends of the playing area and, in singles play, the service zone.

long service line
Line that marks the back of the service zone for doubles matches.

server
Player who puts the shuttlecock into play; the server and receiver stand diagonally opposite each other.

badminton racket
The racket used to strike the shuttlecock is lighter (about 3 oz) and narrower than a tennis racket; its head is about 9 in long and 11 in wide.

frame
Racket frame to which the stringing is attached.

handle
Part of the shaft that the player grips to control the racket.

stringing
Surface of interlaced strings of synthetic or natural fiber that is used to strike a shuttlecock.

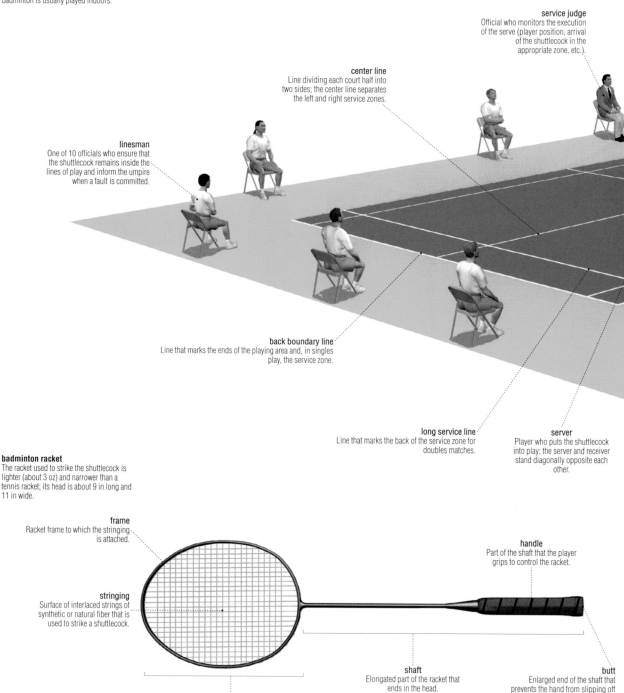

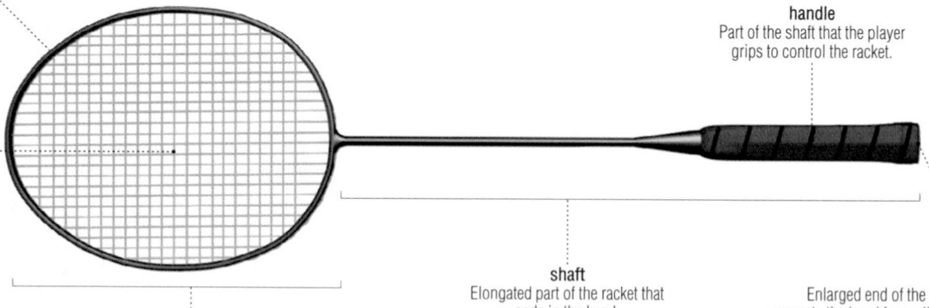

shaft
Elongated part of the racket that ends in the head.

butt
Enlarged end of the shaft that prevents the hand from slipping off the handle.

head
Oval part of the racket, including the frame and the stringing.

SPORTS AND GAMES

badminton

white tape
Strip of tape with a cord passing through it; it is attached to posts to suspend the net.

receiver
Player who receives the shuttlecock put into play by the server.

net
Loosely stitched divider stretched across the middle of the court at a height of 5 ft; players must hit the shuttlecock over it.

post
Vertical bar used to stretch the net by means of white tape.

umpire
Official responsible for applying the rules; the umpire ensures that the match runs smoothly and rules on contentious points.

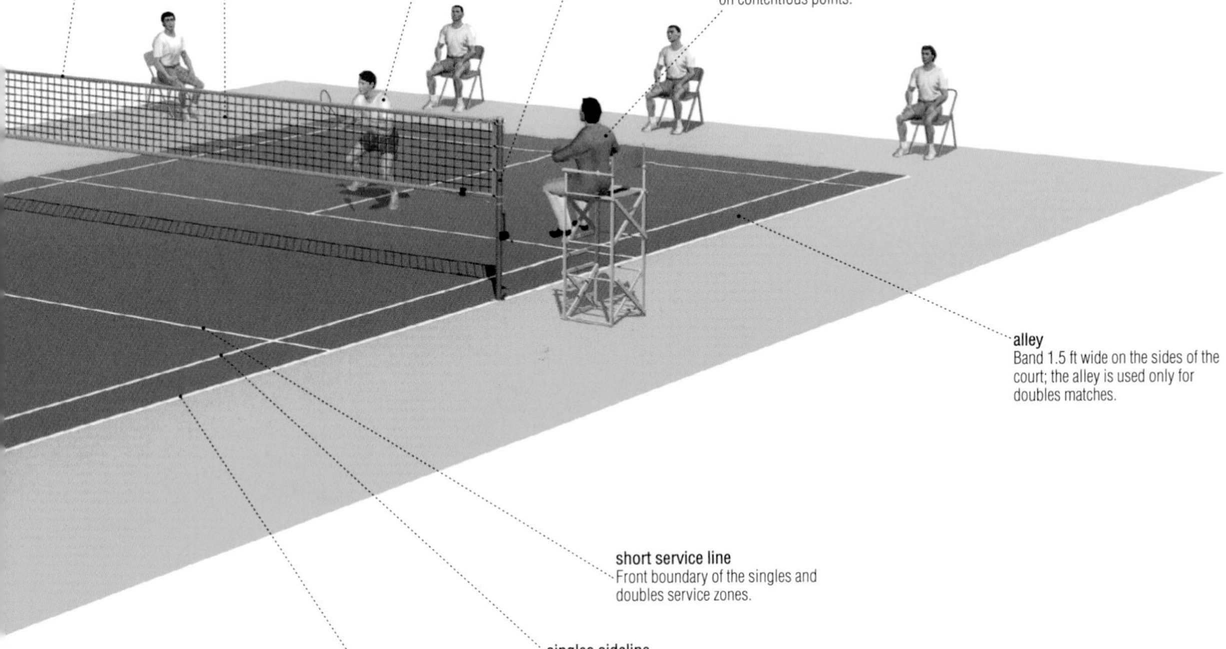

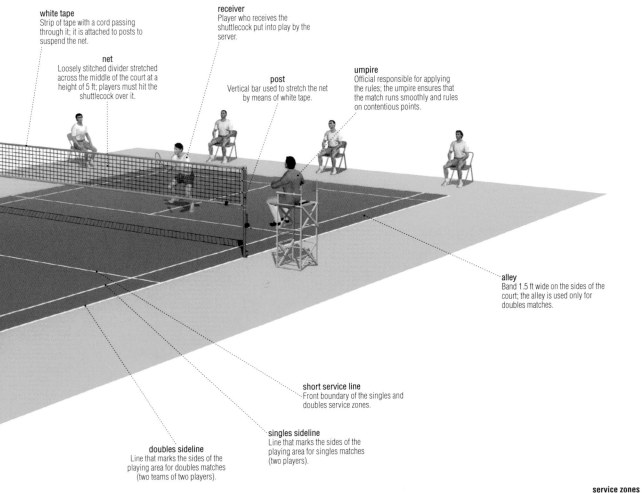

alley
Band 1.5 ft wide on the sides of the court; the alley is used only for doubles matches.

short service line
Front boundary of the singles and doubles service zones.

singles sideline
Line that marks the sides of the playing area for singles matches (two players).

doubles sideline
Line that marks the sides of the playing area for doubles matches (two teams of two players).

service zones
Zones where the server and receiver must remain for a serve; once the serve is delivered, players can move all over the court.

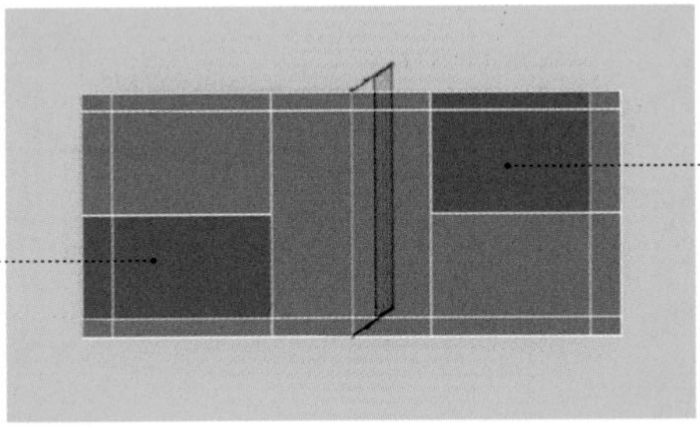

doubles service court
Service zone used by a player for doubles matches; the doubles playing area measures 44 ft x 20 ft.

singles service court
Service zone used by a player for singles matches; the singles playing area measures 44 ft x 17 ft.

synthetic shuttlecock
Small plastic cone that is sturdier than the feathered shuttlecock and is usually used for training; it weighs about 0.2 oz, the same as the feathered shuttlecock.

feathered shuttlecock
Small piece of cork with 14 to 16 feathers; it is used in competitions.

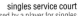

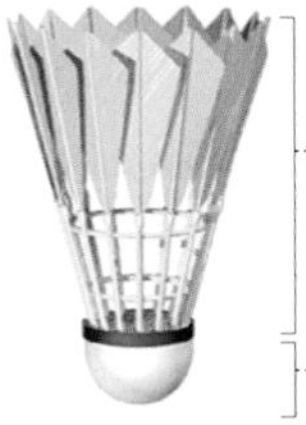

feather crown
Feathers or synthetic materials attached to the shuttlecock tip to stabilize it and make it aerodynamic.

cork tip
The rounded base of the shuttlecock; it can also be made of synthetic materials.

racquetball

Indoor sport with two or four opposing players with rackets; the players rally a bouncing ball using all surfaces of the court.

court
Enclosed space whose surfaces make up the playing area; it is 40 ft long, 20 ft wide and 20 ft high.

referee
Official responsible for applying the rules; the referee ensures that the match runs smoothly and rules on contentious points.

back wall
Wall marking the back of the court behind the players.

center court
Part of the court behind the short line and between the sidewalls; it is a strategic zone that players attempt to control.

sidewall
Wall marking the sides of the court.

ceiling
Horizontal surface making up the upper part of the court; the ceiling is part of the playing area.

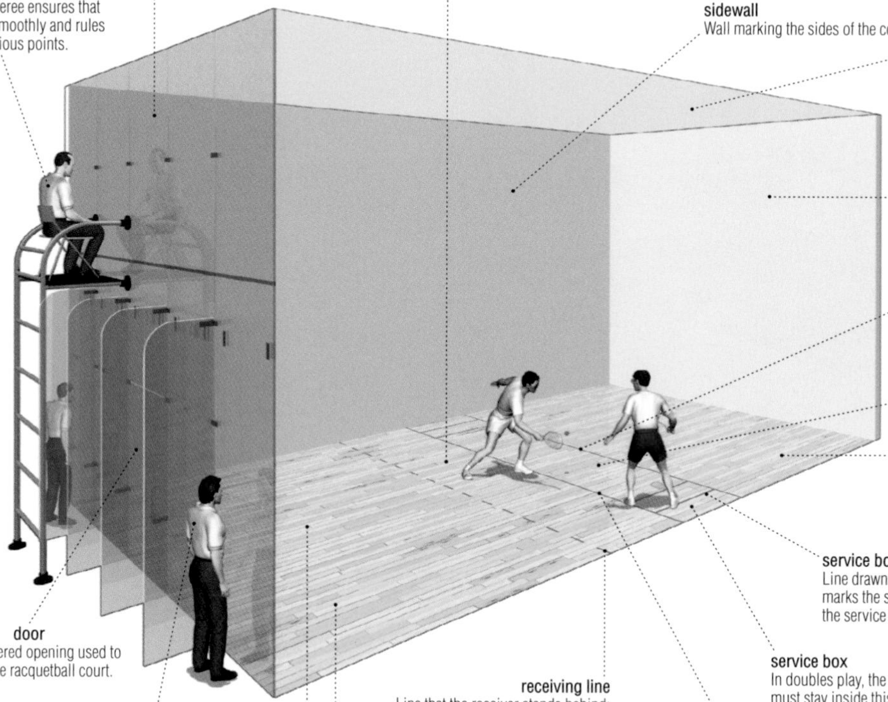

front wall
Wall facing the players; the service is made onto it.

service line
Line marking the front of the service zone.

service zone
Zone where a player stands to serve; the ball must bounce once in this zone before it is served.

frontcourt
Area between the front wall and the short line.

service box line
Line drawn 18 in from the sidewall that marks the service box at both ends of the service zone.

door
Glass-covered opening used to access the racquetball court.

receiving line
Line that the receiver stands behind; the receiver may not step over the receiving line until the serve crosses it.

service box
In doubles play, the server's partner must stay inside this area until the ball crosses the short line.

line judge
The two officials who, at the request of the referee or a player, confirm or reverse the referee's decision.

short line
Line dividing the court in half; the serve must cross the short line after bouncing off the front wall.

floor
Horizontal surface that is usually made of wooden slats; the ball may only bounce once on it.

backcourt
Zone between the short line and the back wall.

racquetball
Rubber ball that is filled with compressed air and weighs 1.4 oz; official balls bear the initials I.R.F. (International Racquetball Federation).

racquetball racket
Racket that is used to strike the ball; it has a short shaft, an elongated head and its maximum length is 22 in.

safety thong
Cord worn around the wrist to prevent accidental racket throws.

bumper guard
Strip of flexible material around the racket frame to protect it.

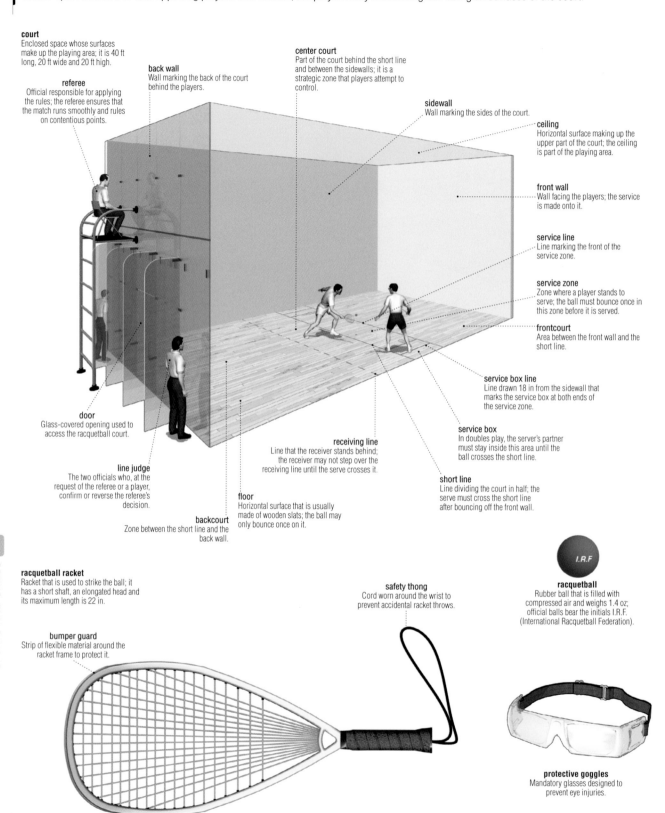

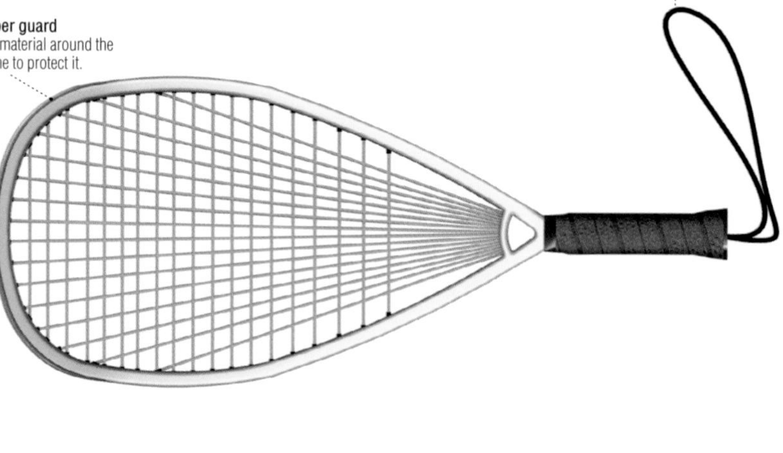

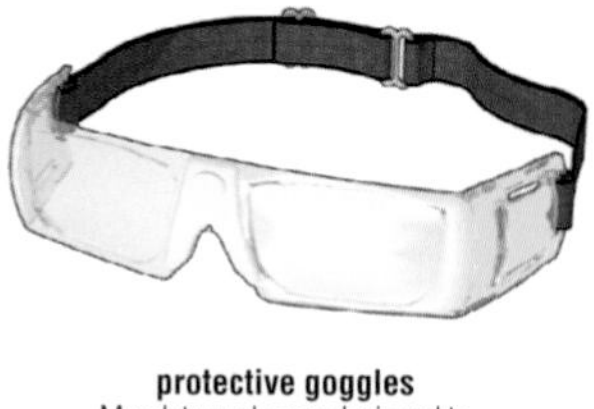

protective goggles
Mandatory glasses designed to prevent eye injuries.

squash

Sport similar to racquetball; its court size and equipment are different and the ceiling is excluded from the playing area.

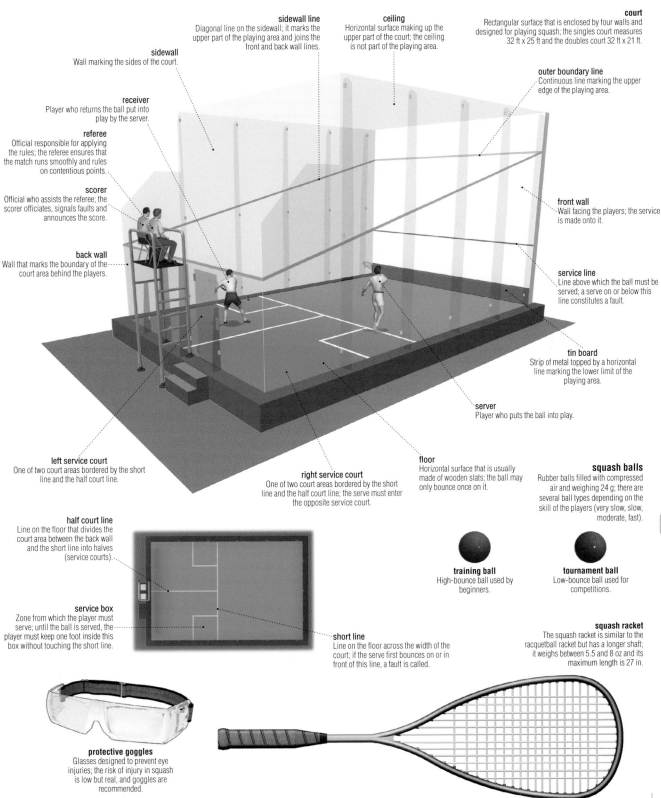

sidewall
Wall marking the sides of the court.

sidewall line
Diagonal line on the sidewall; it marks the upper part of the playing area and joins the front and back wall lines.

ceiling
Horizontal surface making up the upper part of the court; the ceiling is not part of the playing area.

court
Rectangular surface that is enclosed by four walls and designed for playing squash; the singles court measures 32 ft x 25 ft and the doubles court 32 ft x 21 ft.

outer boundary line
Continuous line marking the upper edge of the playing area.

receiver
Player who returns the ball put into play by the server.

referee
Official responsible for applying the rules; the referee ensures that the match runs smoothly and rules on contentious points.

scorer
Official who assists the referee; the scorer officiates, signals faults and announces the score.

back wall
Wall that marks the boundary of the court area behind the players.

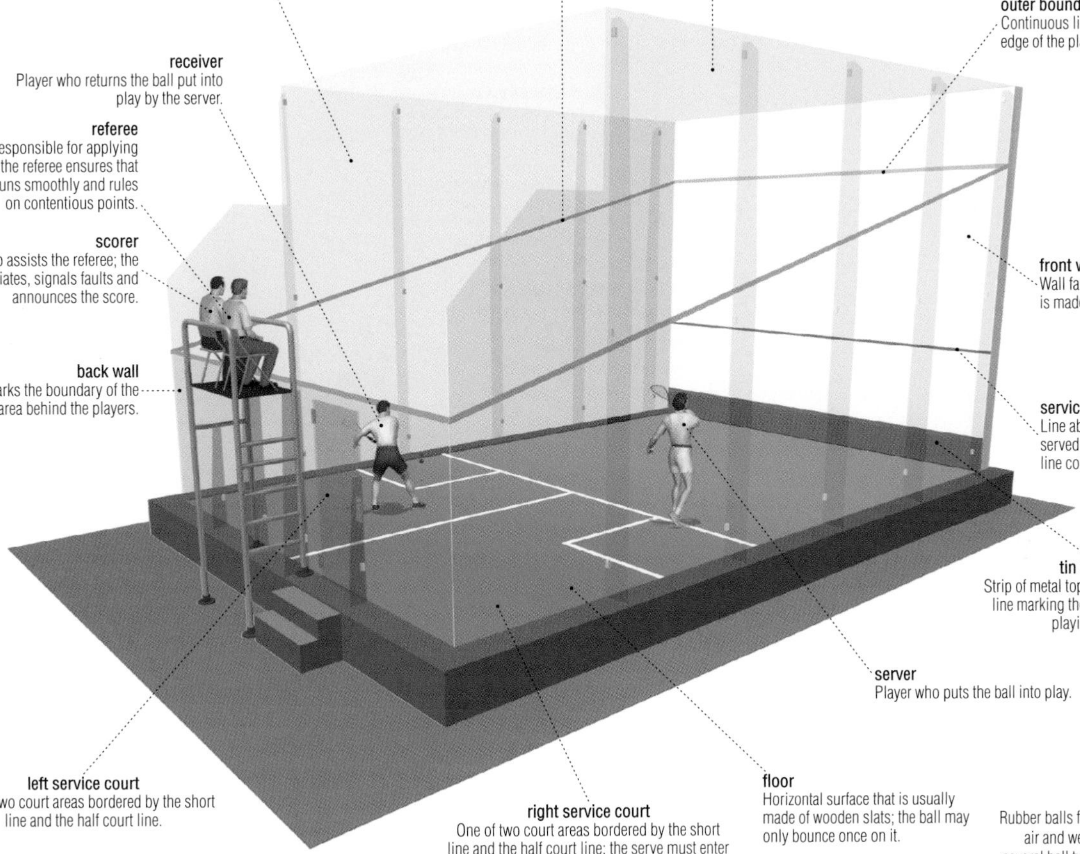

front wall
Wall facing the players; the service is made onto it.

service line
Line above which the ball must be served; a serve on or below this line constitutes a fault.

tin board
Strip of metal topped by a horizontal line marking the lower limit of the playing area.

server
Player who puts the ball into play.

left service court
One of two court areas bordered by the short line and the half court line.

right service court
One of two court areas bordered by the short line and the half court line; the serve must enter the opposite service court.

floor
Horizontal surface that is usually made of wooden slats; the ball may only bounce once on it.

half court line
Line on the floor that divides the court area between the back wall and the short line into halves (service courts).

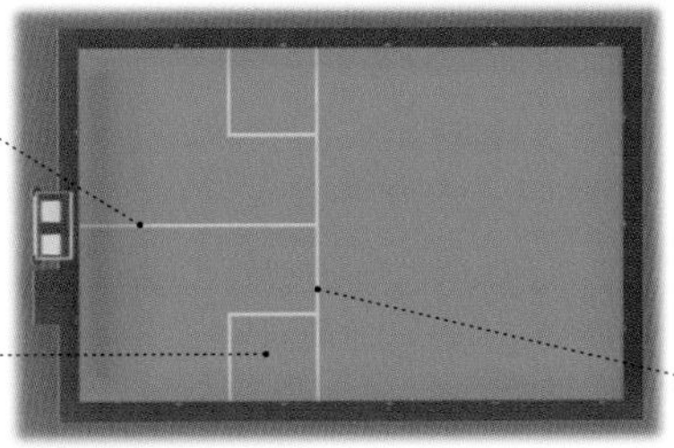

service box
Zone from which the player must serve; until the ball is served, the player must keep one foot inside this box without touching the short line.

short line
Line on the floor across the width of the court; if the serve first bounces on or in front of this line, a fault is called.

squash balls

Rubber balls filled with compressed air and weighing 24 g; there are several ball types depending on the skill of the players (very slow, slow, moderate, fast).

training ball
High-bounce ball used by beginners.

tournament ball
Low-bounce ball used for competitions.

squash racket
The squash racket is similar to the racquetball racket but has a longer shaft; it weighs between 5.5 and 8 oz and its maximum length is 27 in.

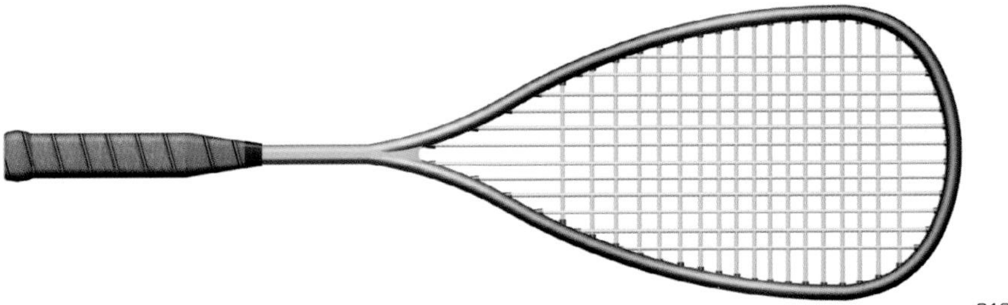

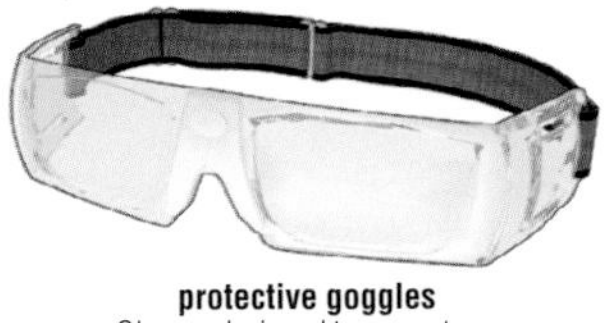

protective goggles
Glasses designed to prevent eye injuries; the risk of injury in squash is low but real, and goggles are recommended.

tennis

Sport with two or four opposing players with rackets who hit a ball onto opposite sides of a net dividing a court in half.

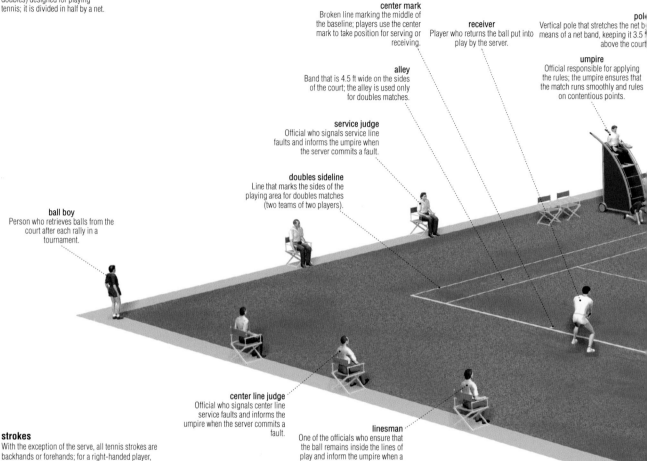

court
Rectangular surface (78 ft x 27 ft for singles, 78 ft x 36 ft for doubles) designed for playing tennis; it is divided in half by a net.

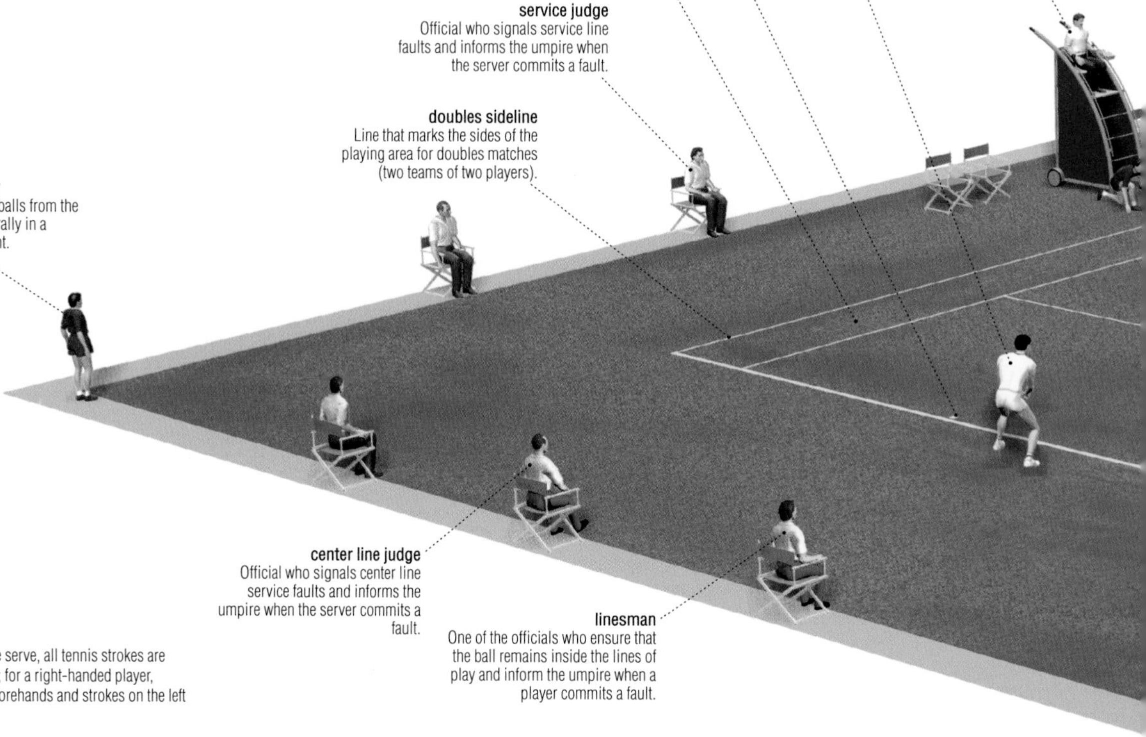
center mark
Broken line marking the middle of the baseline; players use the center mark to take position for serving or receiving.
receiver
Player who returns the ball put into play by the server.
pol
Vertical pole that stretches the net b means of a net band, keeping it 3.5 above the court
umpire
Official responsible for applying the rules; the umpire ensures that the match runs smoothly and rules on contentious points.
alley
Band that is 4.5 ft wide on the sides of the court; the alley is used only for doubles matches.
service judge
Official who signals service line faults and informs the umpire when the server commits a fault.
doubles sideline
Line that marks the sides of the playing area for doubles matches (two teams of two players).
ball boy
Person who retrieves balls from the court after each rally in a tournament.
center line judge
Official who signals center line service faults and informs the umpire when the server commits a fault.
linesman
One of the officials who ensure that the ball remains inside the lines of play and inform the umpire when a player commits a fault.

strokes
With the exception of the serve, all tennis strokes are backhands or forehands; for a right-handed player, strokes on the right are forehands and strokes on the left are backhands.

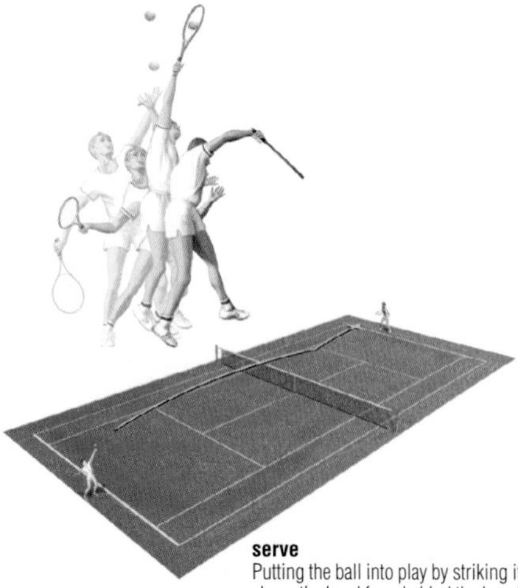

serve
Putting the ball into play by striking it above the head from behind the baseline; the server has two serves to put the ball diagonally into the service court.

half-volley
Stroke by which the ball is hit on the short hop below the knees; the half-volley is used mainly while approaching the net.

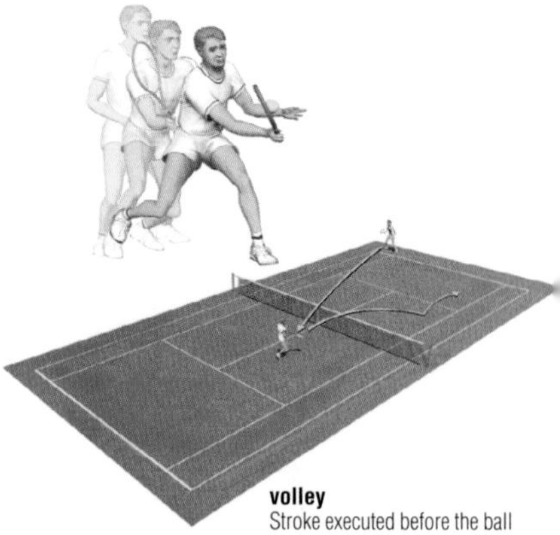

volley
Stroke executed before the ball bounces; it is usually played near the net.

tennis

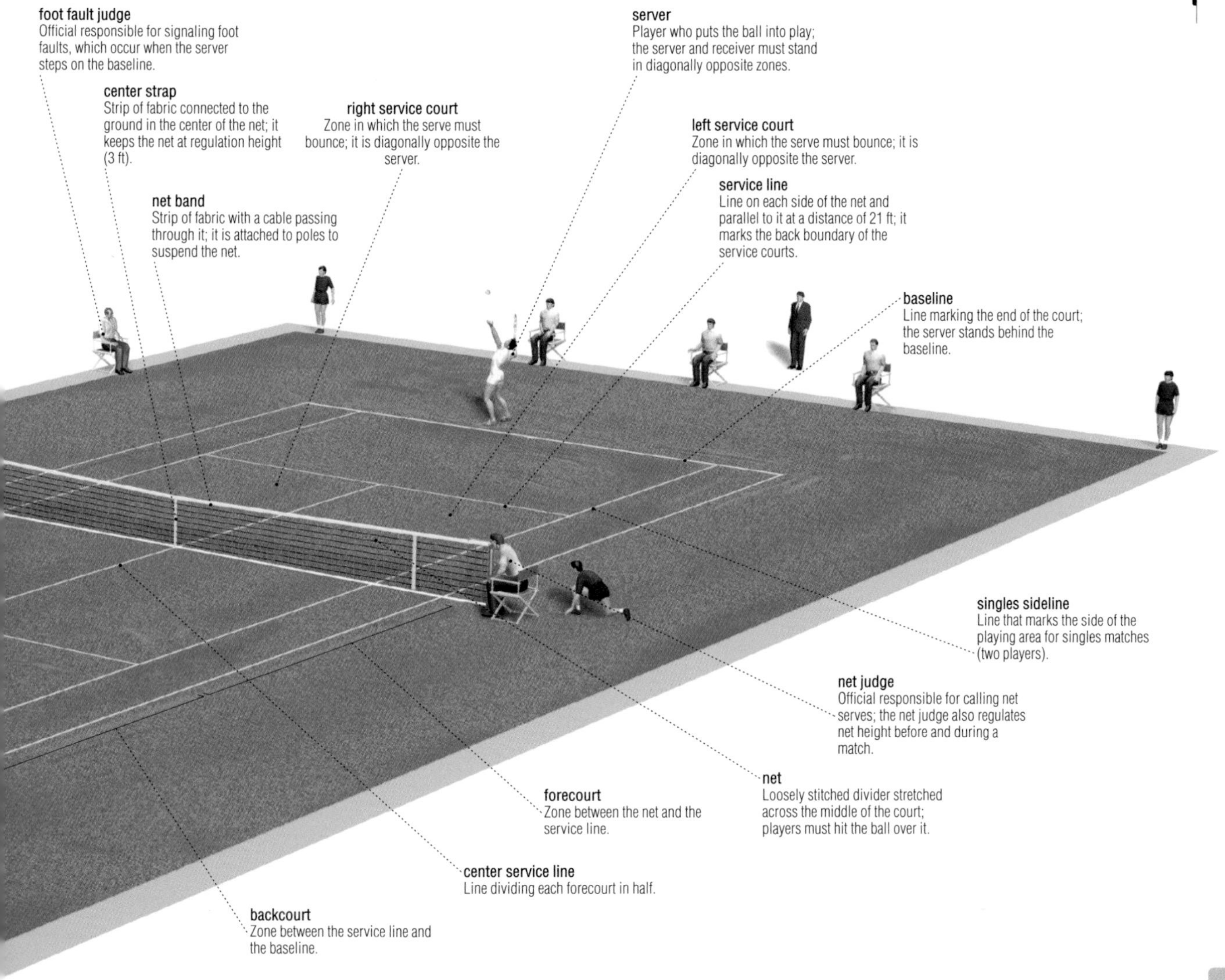
foot fault judge
Official responsible for signaling foot faults, which occur when the server steps on the baseline.
center strap
Strip of fabric connected to the ground in the center of the net; it keeps the net at regulation height (3 ft).
right service court
Zone in which the serve must bounce; it is diagonally opposite the server.
net band
Strip of fabric with a cable passing through it; it is attached to poles to suspend the net.
server
Player who puts the ball into play; the server and receiver must stand in diagonally opposite zones.
left service court
Zone in which the serve must bounce; it is diagonally opposite the server.
service line
Line on each side of the net and parallel to it at a distance of 21 ft; it marks the back boundary of the service courts.
baseline
Line marking the end of the court; the server stands behind the baseline.
singles sideline
Line that marks the side of the playing area for singles matches (two players).
net judge
Official responsible for calling net serves; the net judge also regulates net height before and during a match.
net
Loosely stitched divider stretched across the middle of the court; players must hit the ball over it.
forecourt
Zone between the net and the service line.
center service line
Line dividing each forecourt in half.
backcourt
Zone between the service line and the baseline.

lob
Stroke by which the ball is sent high into the air over the opponent's head when this player is in the forecourt.

drop shot
Short shot by which the ball falls just behind the net with almost no bounce.

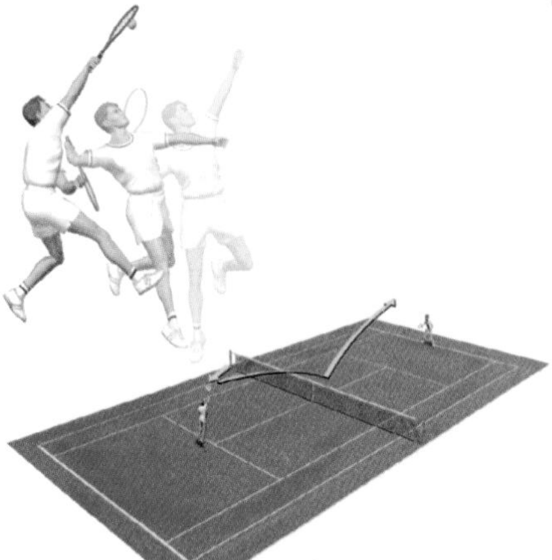

smash
Powerful stroke executed when the ball is over the head; usually played after a lob, the smash is meant to bounce out of the opponent's reach.

tennis

tennis racket
Racket with an oval head that is used to strike the ball; its maximum length is 29 in.

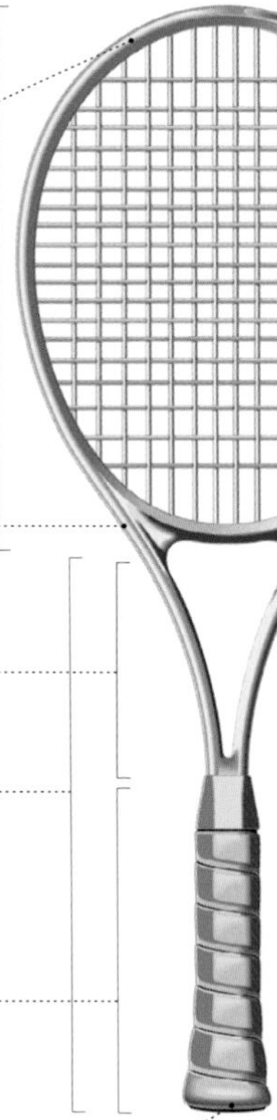

frame
Racket frame to which the stringing is attached.

head
Oval part of the racket, including the frame and the stringing.

shoulder
Base of the racket head joining it to the throat.

throat
Part joining the handle to the racket head.

shaft
Elongated part of the racket that ends in the head.

handle
Part that the player grips to control the racket.

butt
Enlarged end of the shaft that prevents the hand from slipping off the handle.

stringing
Synthetic or natural cords strung together to form a surface used to strike the ball.

tennis ball
Rubber ball that weighs about 2 oz and is filled with compressed air; it is covered with felt to make it more adherent.

polo shirt
Usually short-sleeved sweater that has a pointed turned-down collar; it is often fastened with a placket ending at mid-chest.

tennis player
Female competitors play in tournament matches of three sets; male competitors play in tournament matches of three or five sets.

wristband
Strip of fabric worn around the wrist; it absorbs sweat from the forehead and face.

skirt
Very short skirt covering only the upper thighs; women wear it to play tennis.

sock
Article of clothing that covers the foot and ankle.

tennis shoe
Light flexible shoe with a nonslip sole worn to play tennis.

scoreboard
Board that posts details on the match in progress; a match is divided into sets, games and points.

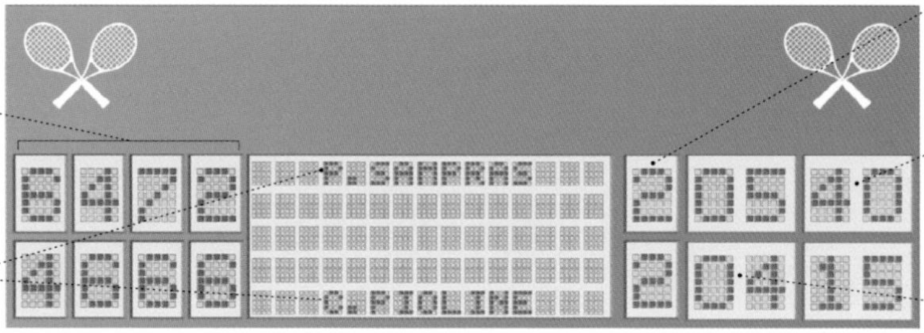

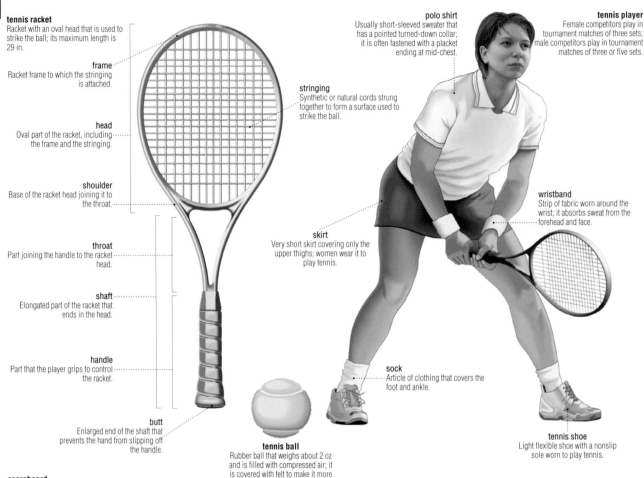

previous sets

players

set
Series of games; a tennis match consists of three or five sets (two or three winning sets).

points
Points that make up a game: 15 (1st point), 3 (2nd point), 40 (3rd point), game (4th point); the player who wins four points (or two consecutive points in the event of a deuce) wins the game.

game
Series of four points; the player who wins six games takes the set if this player holds a two-game lead.

playing surfaces

Tennis is played on various indoor and outdoor surfaces; playing strategies are adapted to the court surface.

grass
Extremely fast playing surface that favors a serve-and-volley game; grass surfaces are increasingly rare due to high maintenance costs.

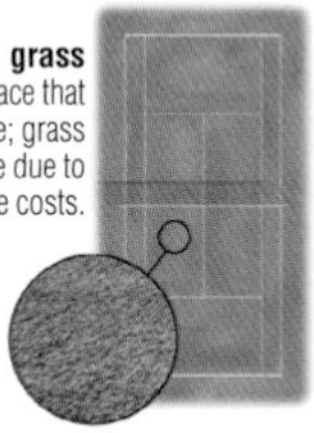

clay
Slow and comfortable surface given to long rallies; clay courts require regular but low-cost maintenance.

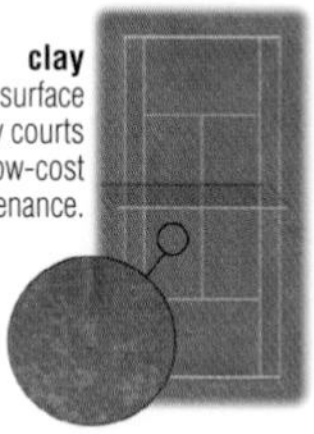

hard surface (cement)
Surface given to fast bounces; hard surfaces quickly wear out shoes and balls.

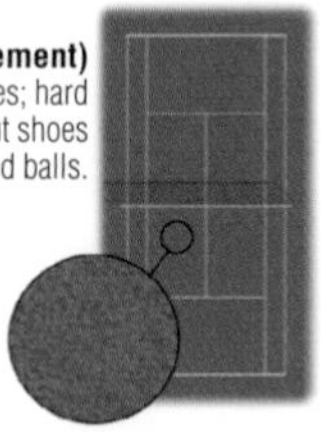

synthetic surface
Soft elastic surface that offers excellent bounce and reduces the risk of injury.

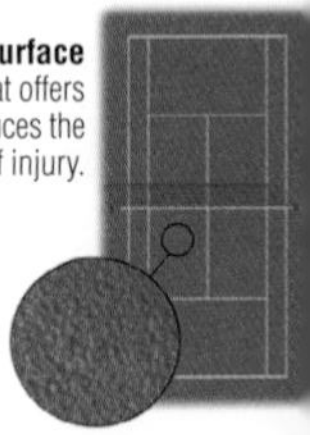

rhythmic gymnastics

Combining gymnastics with dance, this women's discipline requires suppleness, strength and dexterity for manipulating the apparatuses.

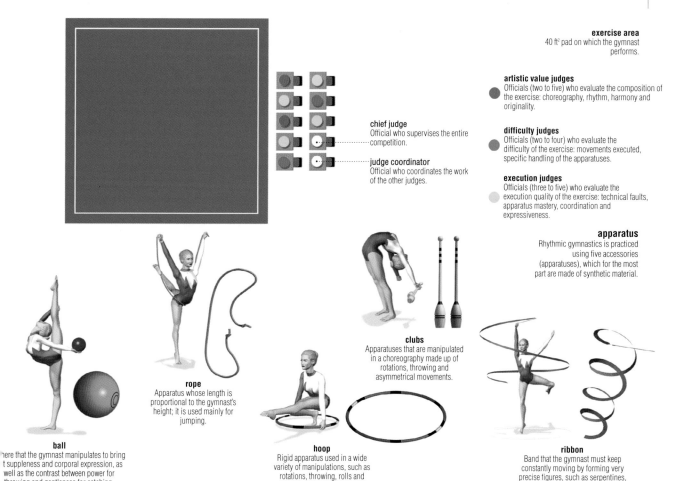

exercise area
40 ft² pad on which the gymnast performs.

chief judge
Official who supervises the entire competition.

judge coordinator
Official who coordinates the work of the other judges.

artistic value judges
Officials (two to five) who evaluate the composition of the exercise: choreography, rhythm, harmony and originality.

difficulty judges
Officials (two to four) who evaluate the difficulty of the exercise: movements executed, specific handling of the apparatuses.

execution judges
Officials (three to five) who evaluate the execution quality of the exercise: technical faults, apparatus mastery, coordination and expressiveness.

apparatus
Rhythmic gymnastics is practiced using five accessories (apparatuses), which for the most part are made of synthetic material.

ball
here that the gymnast manipulates to bring t suppleness and corporal expression, as well as the contrast between power for throwing and gentleness for catching.

rope
Apparatus whose length is proportional to the gymnast's height; it is used mainly for jumping.

clubs
Apparatuses that are manipulated in a choreography made up of rotations, throwing and asymmetrical movements.

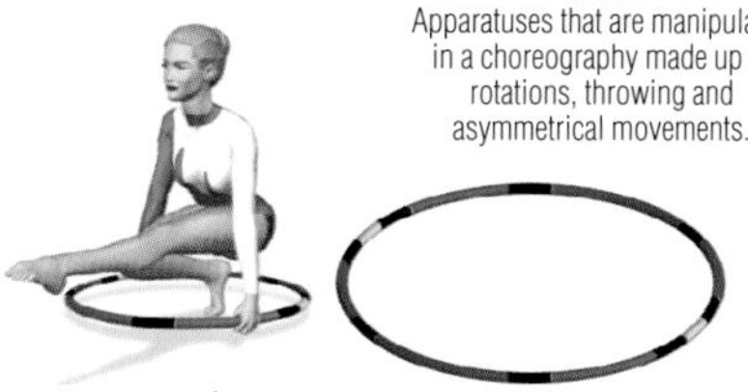

hoop
Rigid apparatus used in a wide variety of manipulations, such as rotations, throwing, rolls and passing through.

ribbon
Band that the gymnast must keep constantly moving by forming very precise figures, such as serpentines, spirals and circles.

trampoline

Apparatus made up of a bed stretched by springs; the gymnasts perform acrobatics by jumping and bouncing on it.

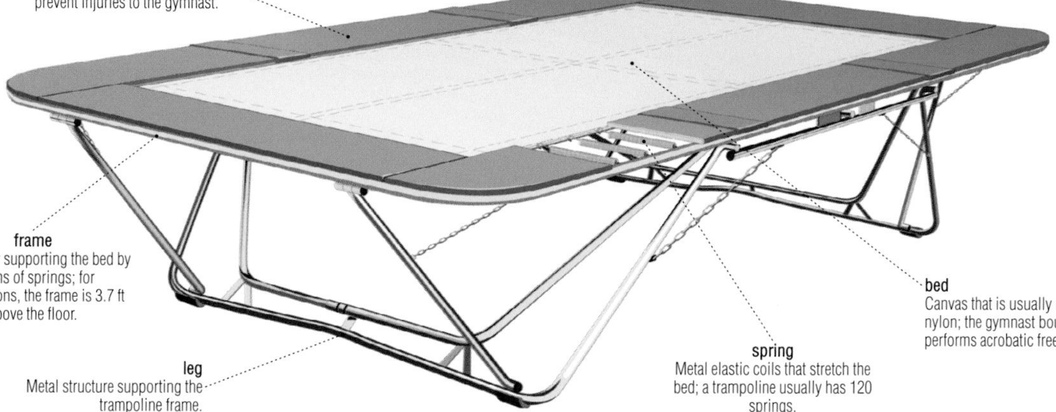

safety pad
Cushioned mat covering the frame to prevent injuries to the gymnast.

frame
Metal body supporting the bed by means of springs; for competitions, the frame is 3.7 ft above the floor.

leg
Metal structure supporting the trampoline frame.

spring
Metal elastic coils that stretch the bed; a trampoline usually has 120 springs.

bed
Canvas that is usually made of nylon; the gymnast bounces and performs acrobatic freestyle on it.

gymnastics

Sports discipline practiced on the ground with apparatuses such as rings, bars and beams.

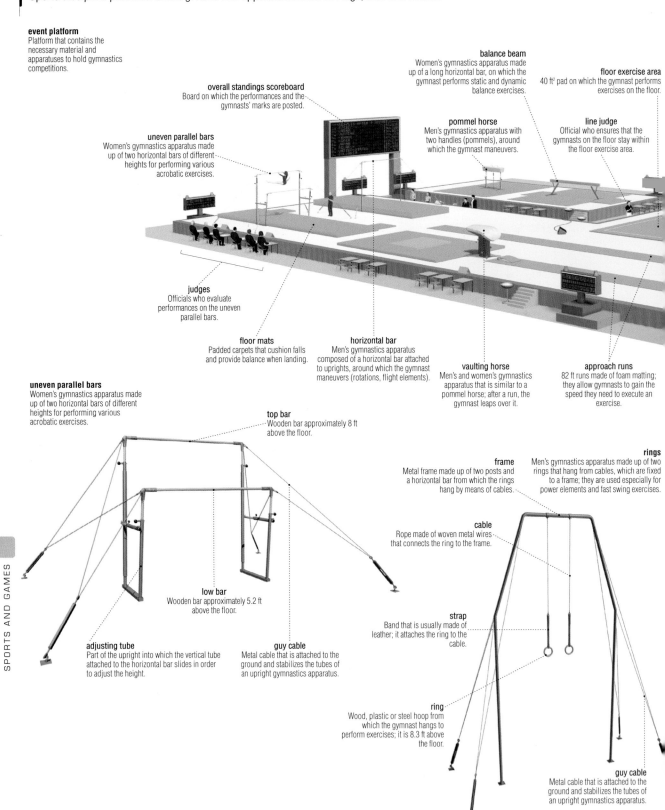

event platform
Platform that contains the necessary material and apparatuses to hold gymnastics competitions.

overall standings scoreboard
Board on which the performances and the gymnasts' marks are posted.

uneven parallel bars
Women's gymnastics apparatus made up of two horizontal bars of different heights for performing various acrobatic exercises.

balance beam
Women's gymnastics apparatus made up of a long horizontal bar, on which the gymnast performs static and dynamic balance exercises.

floor exercise area
40 ft² pad on which the gymnast performs exercises on the floor.

pommel horse
Men's gymnastics apparatus with two handles (pommels), around which the gymnast maneuvers.

line judge
Official who ensures that the gymnasts on the floor stay within the floor exercise area.

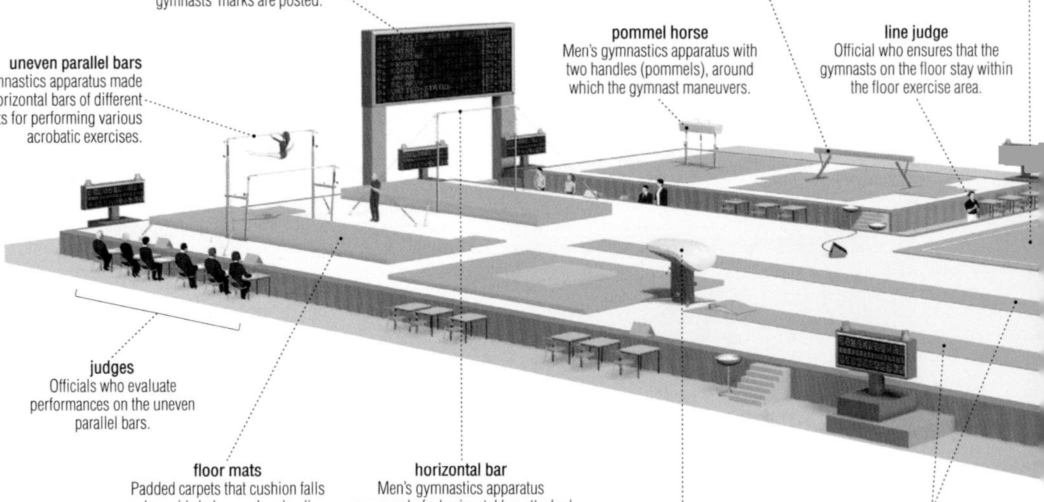

judges
Officials who evaluate performances on the uneven parallel bars.

floor mats
Padded carpets that cushion falls and provide balance when landing.

horizontal bar
Men's gymnastics apparatus composed of a horizontal bar attached to uprights, around which the gymnast maneuvers (rotations, flight elements).

vaulting horse
Men's and women's gymnastics apparatus that is similar to a pommel horse; after a run, the gymnast leaps over it.

approach runs
82 ft runs made of foam matting; they allow gymnasts to gain the speed they need to execute an exercise.

uneven parallel bars
Women's gymnastics apparatus made up of two horizontal bars of different heights for performing various acrobatic exercises.

top bar
Wooden bar approximately 8 ft above the floor.

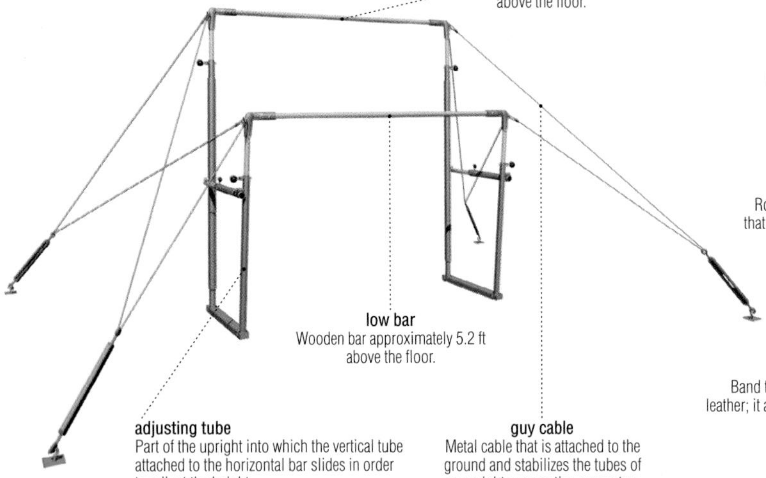

low bar
Wooden bar approximately 5.2 ft above the floor.

adjusting tube
Part of the upright into which the vertical tube attached to the horizontal bar slides in order to adjust the height.

guy cable
Metal cable that is attached to the ground and stabilizes the tubes of an upright gymnastics apparatus.

rings
Men's gymnastics apparatus made up of two rings that hang from cables, which are fixed to a frame; they are used especially for power elements and fast swing exercises.

frame
Metal frame made up of two posts and a horizontal bar from which the rings hang by means of cables.

cable
Rope made of woven metal wires that connects the ring to the frame.

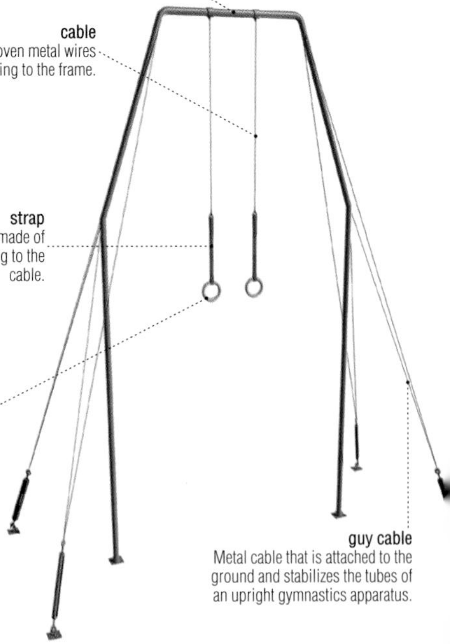

strap
Band that is usually made of leather; it attaches the ring to the cable.

ring
Wood, plastic or steel hoop from which the gymnast hangs to perform exercises; it is 8.3 ft above the floor.

guy cable
Metal cable that is attached to the ground and stabilizes the tubes of an upright gymnastics apparatus.

gymnastics

scoreboard
Board that displays information about a sports competition in progress such as gymnast's name, nationality and score.

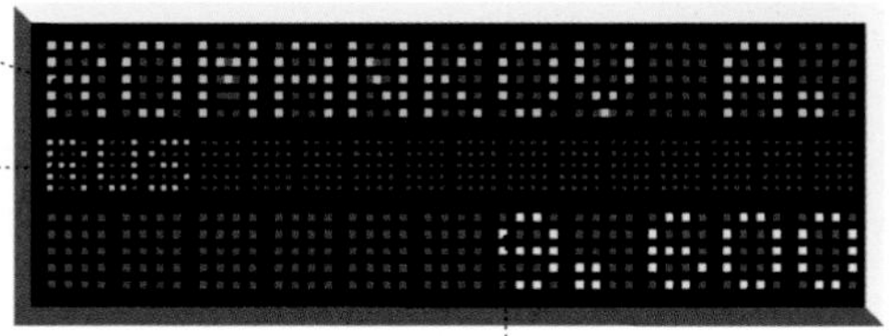

gymnast's name

nationality

score
Number of points awarded to a gymnast for a performance.

current event scoreboard
Judges grade exercises performed by the gymnasts based on execution, technique and artistic value.

judges
Officials who evaluate floor exercises.

vaulting horse
Men's and women's gymnastics apparatus that is similar to a pommel horse; after a run, the gymnast supports the body on it with both hands to make a jump.

rings
Men's gymnastics apparatus made up of two rings that hang from cables, which are fixed to a frame; they are used especially for power elements and fast swing exercises.

parallel bars
Men's gymnastics apparatus made up of two horizontal bars set at the same height; they are for performing various acrobatic exercises.

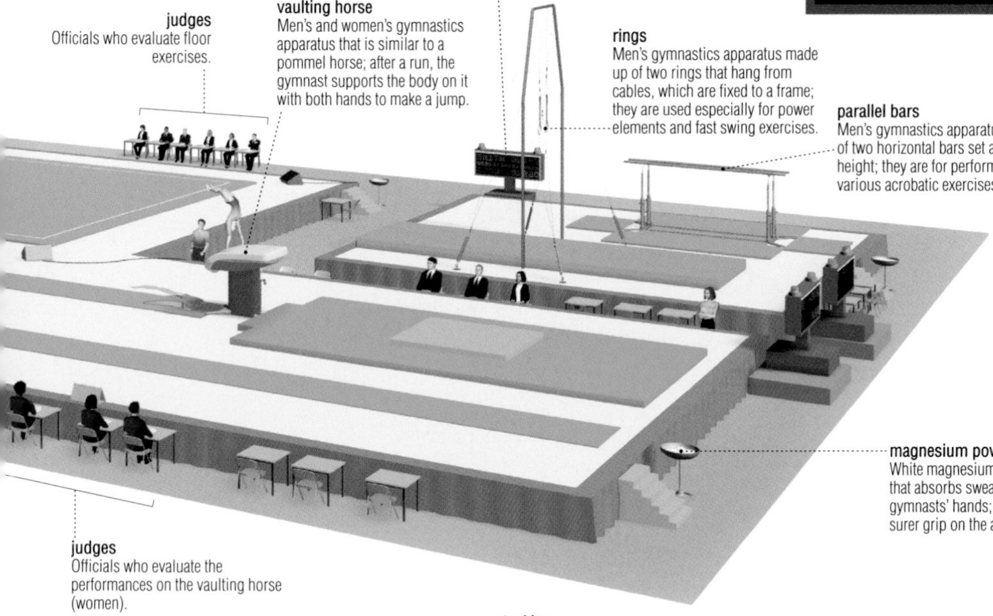

magnesium powder
White magnesium-based powder that absorbs sweat from the gymnasts' hands; this provides a surer grip on the apparatuses.

judges
Officials who evaluate the performances on the vaulting horse (women).

steel bar
Bar around which the gymnast maneuvers; it is 8.3 ft above the floor.

horizontal bar
Men's gymnastics apparatus composed of a horizontal bar attached to uprights, around which the gymnast maneuvers (rotations, flight elements).

guy cable
Metal cable that is attached to the ground and stabilizes the tubes of an upright gymnastics apparatus.

upright
Vertical post of adjustable height that supports the steel bar.

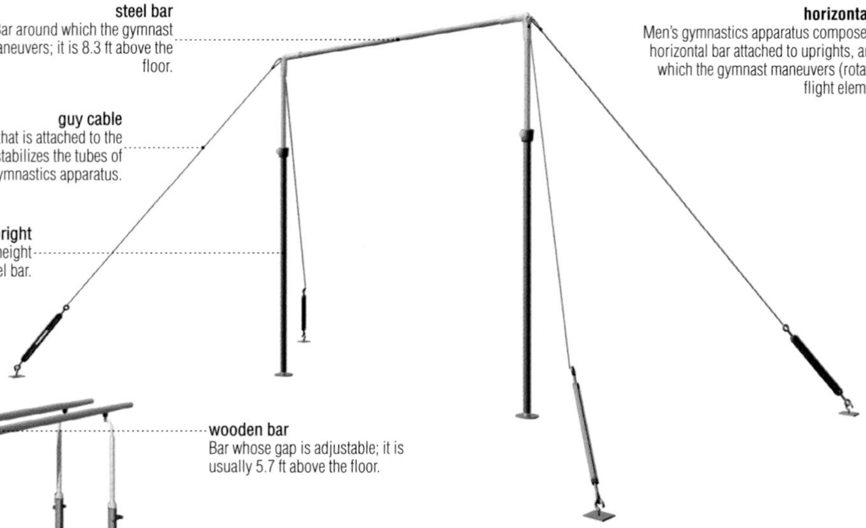

parallel bars
Men's gymnastics apparatus made up of two horizontal bars set at the same height; they are for performing various acrobatic exercises.

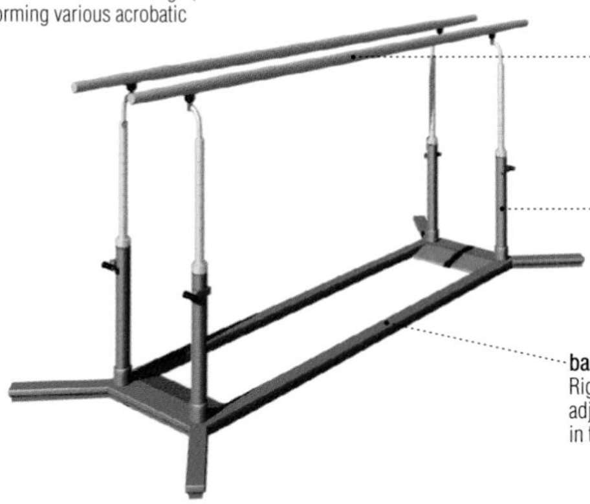

wooden bar
Bar whose gap is adjustable; it is usually 5.7 ft above the floor.

adjusting tube
Part of the upright into which the vertical tube attached to the horizontal bar slides in order to adjust the height.

base
Rigid support to which the adjusting tubes are attached, which in turn support the bars.

gymnastics

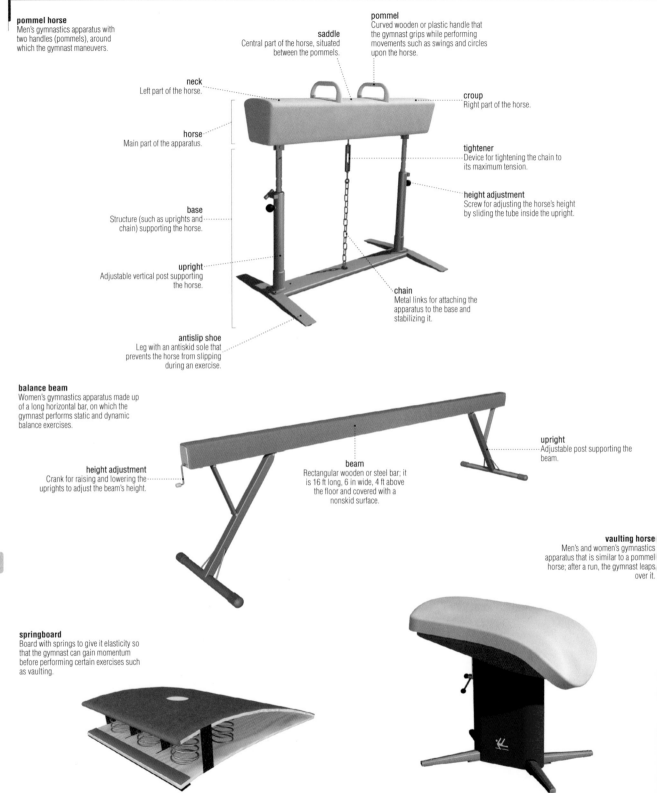

pommel horse
Men's gymnastics apparatus with two handles (pommels), around which the gymnast maneuvers.

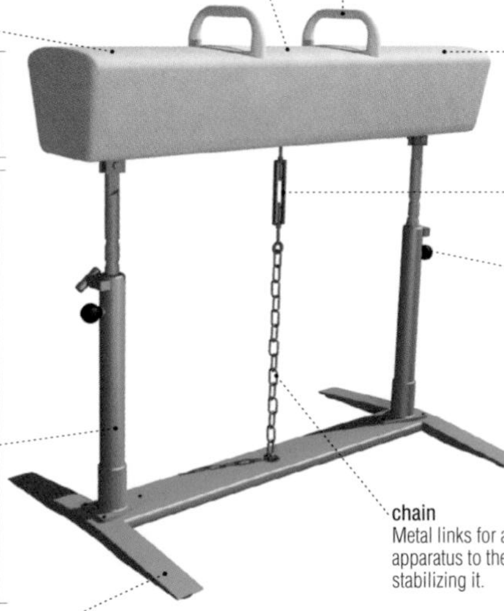
saddle
Central part of the horse, situated between the pommels.
pommel
Curved wooden or plastic handle that the gymnast grips while performing movements such as swings and circles upon the horse.
neck
Left part of the horse.
croup
Right part of the horse.
horse
Main part of the apparatus.
tightener
Device for tightening the chain to its maximum tension.
height adjustment
Screw for adjusting the horse's height by sliding the tube inside the upright.
base
Structure (such as uprights and chain) supporting the horse.
upright
Adjustable vertical post supporting the horse.
chain
Metal links for attaching the apparatus to the base and stabilizing it.
antislip shoe
Leg with an antiskid sole that prevents the horse from slipping during an exercise.

balance beam
Women's gymnastics apparatus made up of a long horizontal bar, on which the gymnast performs static and dynamic balance exercises.

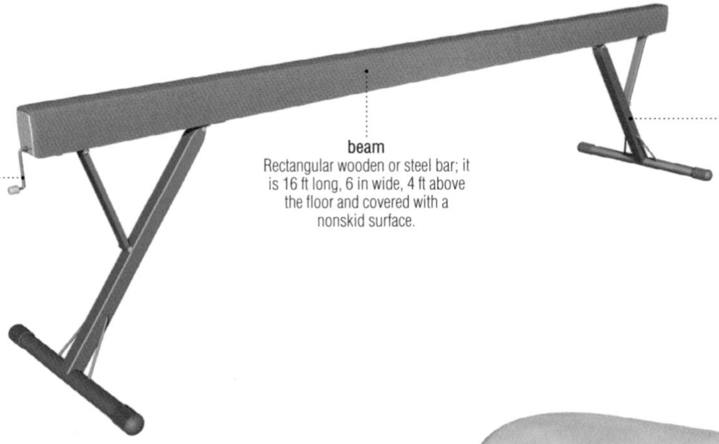
upright
Adjustable post supporting the beam.
beam
Rectangular wooden or steel bar; it is 16 ft long, 6 in wide, 4 ft above the floor and covered with a nonskid surface.
height adjustment
Crank for raising and lowering the uprights to adjust the beam's height.

vaulting horse
Men's and women's gymnastics apparatus that is similar to a pommel horse; after a run, the gymnast leaps over it.

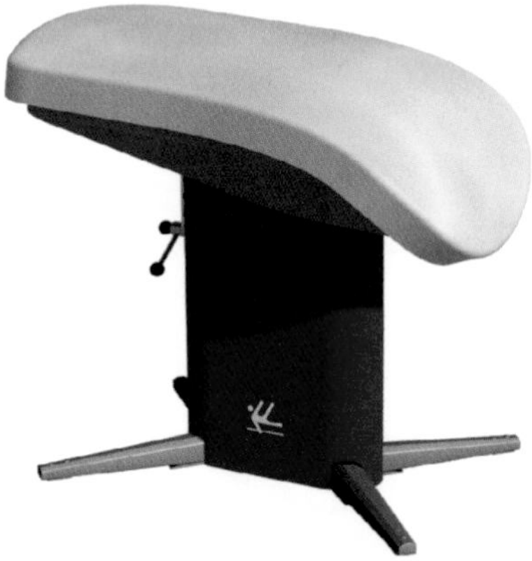

springboard
Board with springs to give it elasticity so that the gymnast can gain momentum before performing certain exercises such as vaulting.

water polo

Sport played in a pool with two teams of seven opposing players who attempt to score points at the opposite goal using a ball.

player
Member of a water polo team; during a game, the player must always stay in the water, never touch the bottom and not hold on to the sides of the pool.

water polo ball
Waterproof sphere that is filled with air and is usually yellow; the players (except for the goalkeeper) may not hold the ball with both hands.

cap
Flexible cap with ear protectors on which the player's number is written; each team wears a cap of a distinct color.

crossbar
Horizontal part connecting the two posts; the bar and the posts are made of plastic, metal or wood.

goal
Cage made up of a net mounted on a frame; a team scores a point each time it succeeds in placing the ball in the opposing goal.

post
Two vertical supports for the goal; they are located 10 ft from each other.

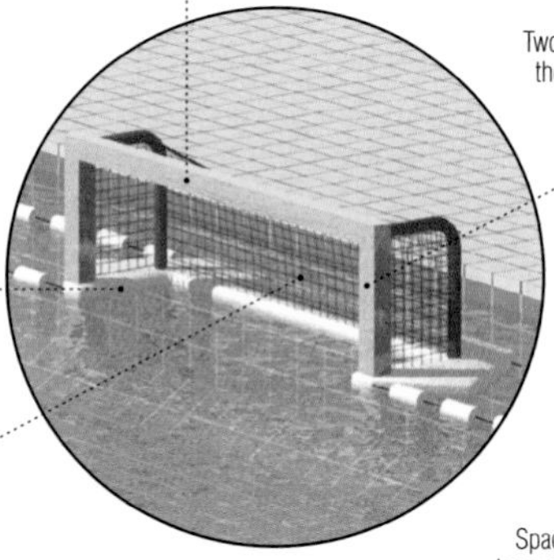

floater
Float that keeps the goal above the surface of the water; the goal is also held in place by cables attached to the sides of the pool.

net
Loosely stitched netting attached to the back of the post; it keeps the ball inside the goal.

swimming pool
Pool in which a water polo game takes place; a game has four periods of seven minutes each divided by breaks of two minutes each.

secretaries
Officials who write up the game's report (such as goals scored, fouls and exclusions) and signal the return of temporarily excluded players.

goal judge
Official whose main function is to decide on the validity of goals and to report balls gone behind the goal line (corners).

timekeepers
Officials in charge of the game's time, exclusions, continuous possession of the ball (maximum 35 seconds before taking a shot) and so on.

team bench
Space where substitute players and team officials sit; a team has 13 players but only seven are in the water at the same time.

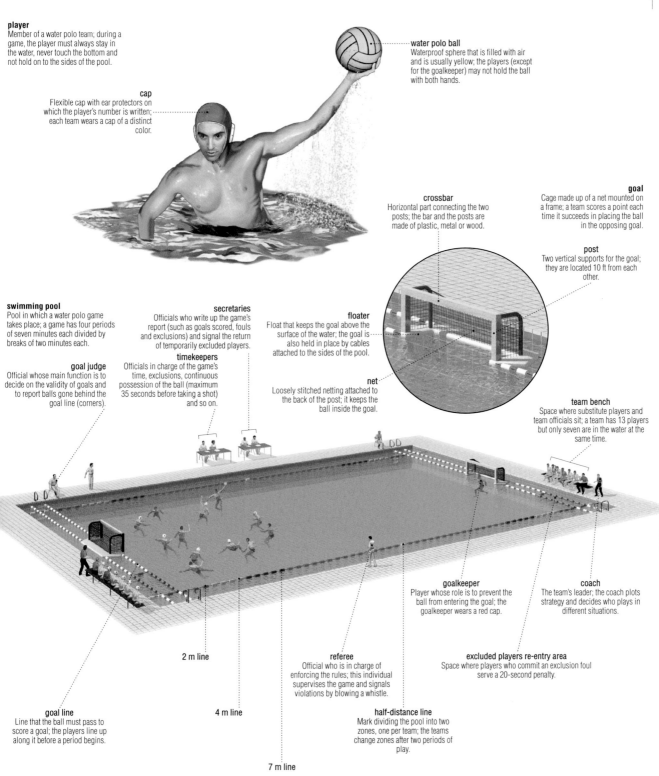

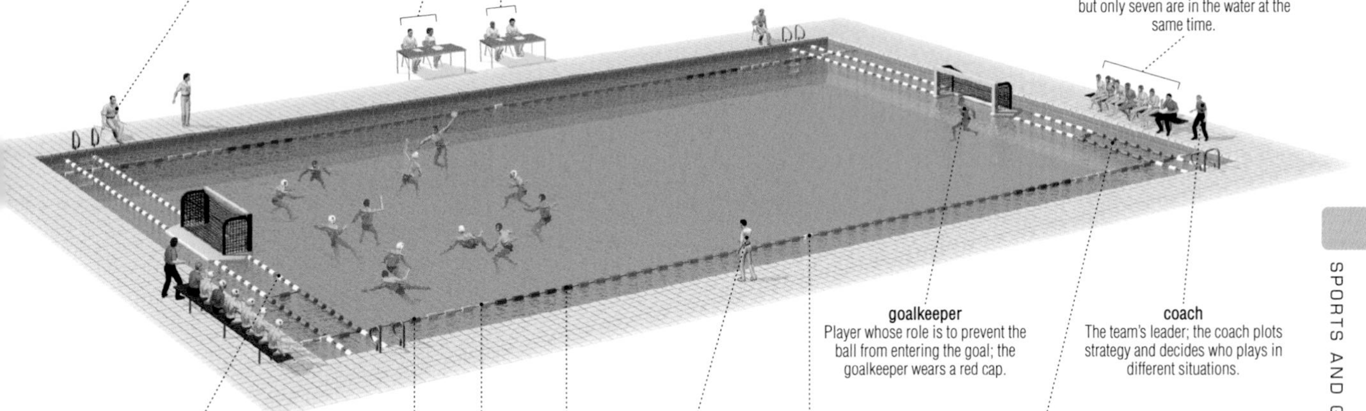

goalkeeper
Player whose role is to prevent the ball from entering the goal; the goalkeeper wears a red cap.

coach
The team's leader; the coach plots strategy and decides who plays in different situations.

2 m line

referee
Official who is in charge of enforcing the rules; this individual supervises the game and signals violations by blowing a whistle.

excluded players re-entry area
Space where players who commit an exclusion foul serve a 20-second penalty.

goal line
Line that the ball must pass to score a goal; the players line up along it before a period begins.

4 m line

half-distance line
Mark dividing the pool into two zones, one per team; the teams change zones after two periods of play.

7 m line

diving

Sport consisting of executing simple to complex dives into the water from a platform or a springboard.

starting positions

Dives are started with or without run-up walks and in one of the positions recognized by the International Amateur Swimming Federation (FINA).

reverse
Dive started facing the water; the athlete then performs one or more backward spins.

inward
Dive started with the back turned toward the water; the diver then performs one or more forward spins.

backward
Dive started with the back turned toward the water; the competitor then executes one or more backward spins.

forward
Dive started facing the water and followed by one or more forward spins.

armstand
Started on the hands for five seconds; this type of dive is done from a platform.

flights

Position of the body between the start and the entry; it must match one of the three positions authorized by FINA.

tuck position
Position in which the body is bent at the knees and hips with the knees and the feet together; the hands hold the legs.

straight position
Position in which the body remains perfectly straight and the arms are free (above the head or along the body).

pike position
Position in which the body is bent at the hips and the legs are outstretched; the arms are free.

diving installations

Equipment (such as springboards, platforms and tower) for diving; during a competition, the divers execute several dives and the points they earn are cumulative.

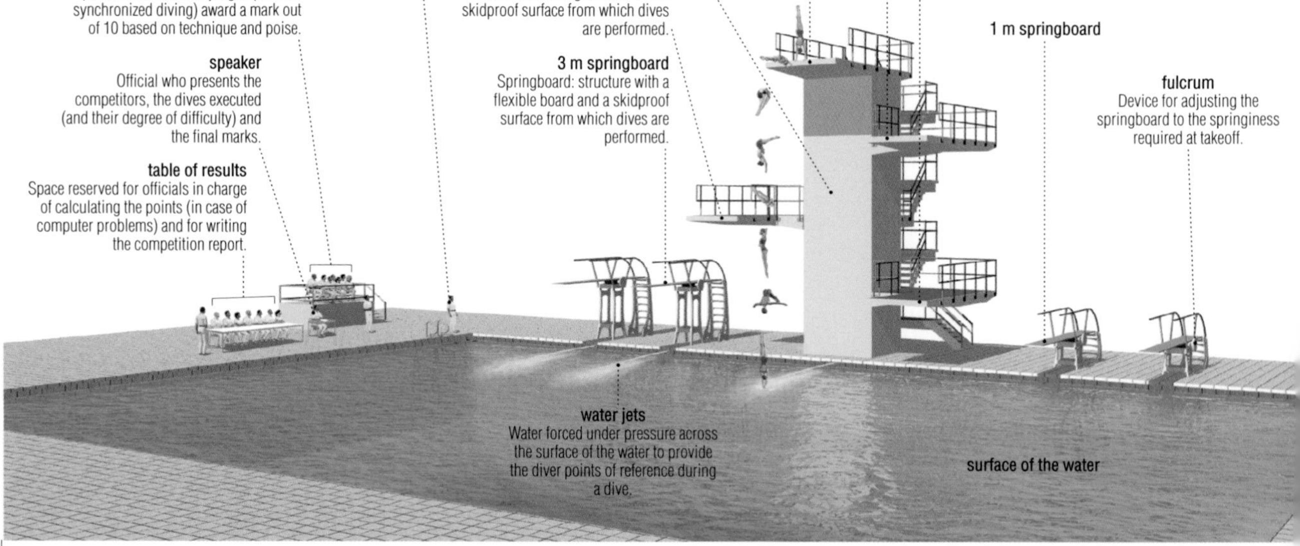

10 m platform

7.5 m platform

referee
Official in charge of enforcing the rules, giving the starting signal and marking the major errors committed during a dive.

diving tower
Fixed structure supporting several platforms of various heights; at the Olympic Games, only the 10 m platform is used.

3 m platform

judges
Individuals who evaluate the performances; seven judges (nine for synchronized diving) award a mark out of 10 based on technique and poise.

5 m platform
Platform: fixed rigid board with a skidproof surface from which dives are performed.

1 m springboard

speaker
Official who presents the competitors, the dives executed (and their degree of difficulty) and the final marks.

3 m springboard
Springboard: structure with a flexible board and a skidproof surface from which dives are performed.

fulcrum
Device for adjusting the springboard to the springiness required at takeoff.

table of results
Space reserved for officials in charge of calculating the points (in case of computer problems) and for writing the competition report.

water jets
Water forced under pressure across the surface of the water to provide the diver points of reference during a dive.

surface of the water

examples of dives

There are some 90 different dives that are distinguished by their start position, their form in flight and the figure presented (somersault, twist).

synchronized diving
Dive performed simultaneously by two athletes forming a team; the positions are the same as for individual events and must be executed simultaneously.

entries

The diver enters the water in the vertical position, head or feet first, while attempting to produce the least amount of splashing possible.

feet-first entry

head-first entry

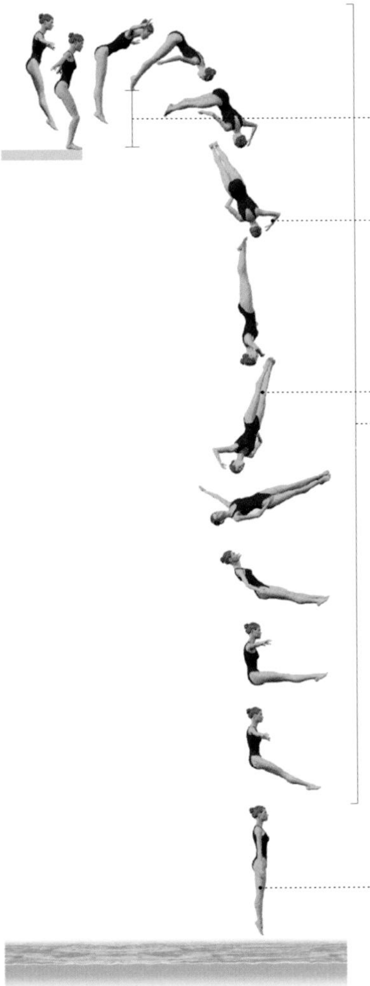

height of the dive
Elevation attained during takeoff; it must be sufficient enough for the diver to complete the series of planned movements.

arm position
Depending on the type of dive, the arms may be stretched along the body, toward the feet, over the head or by the sides.

leg position
While in flight, the feet must be together and the toes extended, regardless of the type of dive.

flight
Part of the dive between the start and the entry; whatever the type of dive chosen, the diver must demonstrate suppleness, elegance and fluidity.

entry
Final part of the dive, the moment when the diver enters the water.

forward somersault with a twist
Dive started with a run-up walk in the forward position; the diver then executes a forward body spin and enters the water feet first.

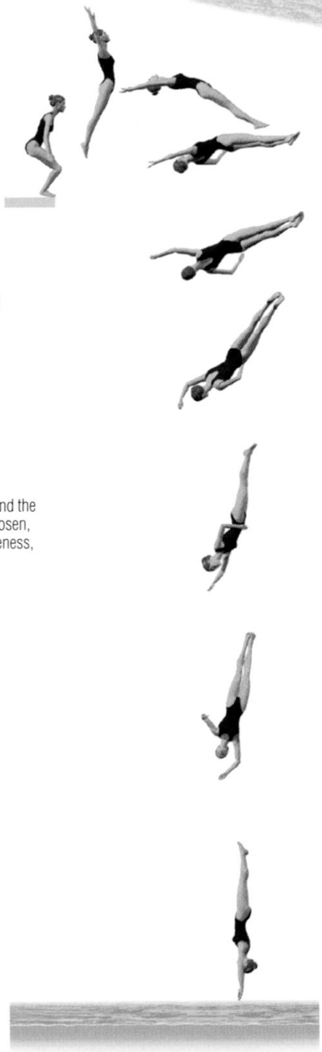

reverse dive with a twist
Dive started in reverse position; the athlete then executes a body spin and enters the water head first.

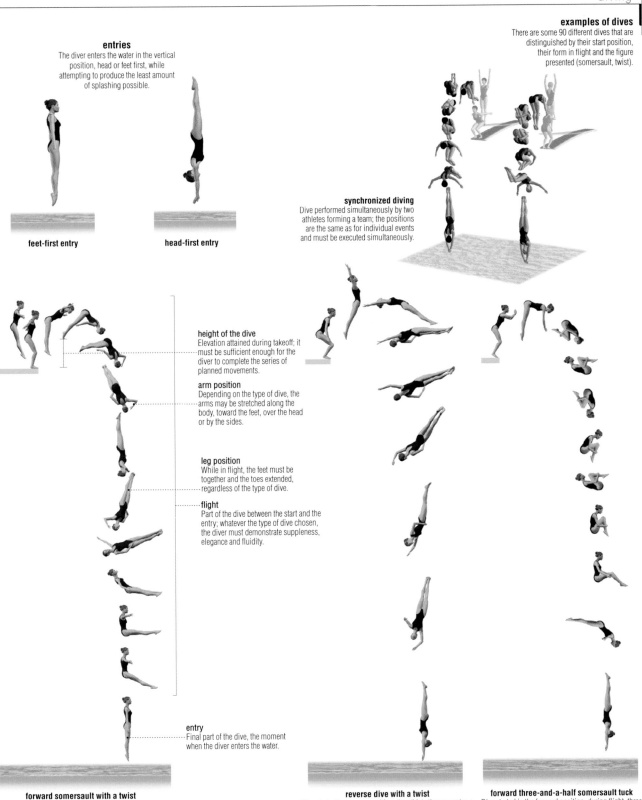

forward three-and-a-half somersault tuck
Dive started in the forward position; during flight, three and one-half rotations are executed in a tucked position and the water is entered head first.

swimming

Sport consisting of swimming a defined distance (which varies depending on the four recognized stroke categories) as quickly as possible.

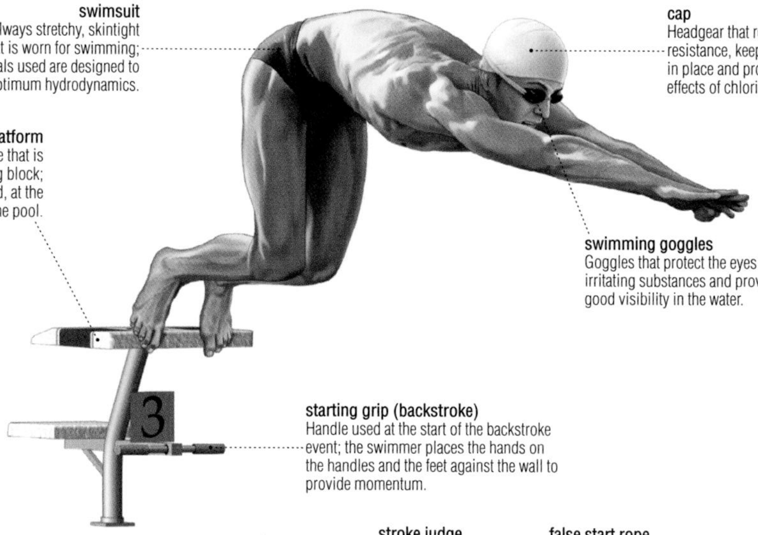

starting block
Metal elevated structure from which the swimmer dives into the pool to start a race.

swimsuit
Almost always stretchy, skintight clothing that is worn for swimming; the materials used are designed to provide optimum hydrodynamics.

cap
Headgear that reduces water resistance, keeps the swimmer's hair in place and protects it against the effects of chlorine.

platform
Rigid board with a nonskid surface that is attached to the top of the starting block; the swimmer takes position and, at the starter's signal, dives into the pool.

swimming goggles
Goggles that protect the eyes from irritating substances and provide good visibility in the water.

starting grip (backstroke)
Handle used at the start of the backstroke event; the swimmer places the hands on the handles and the feet against the wall to provide momentum.

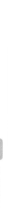

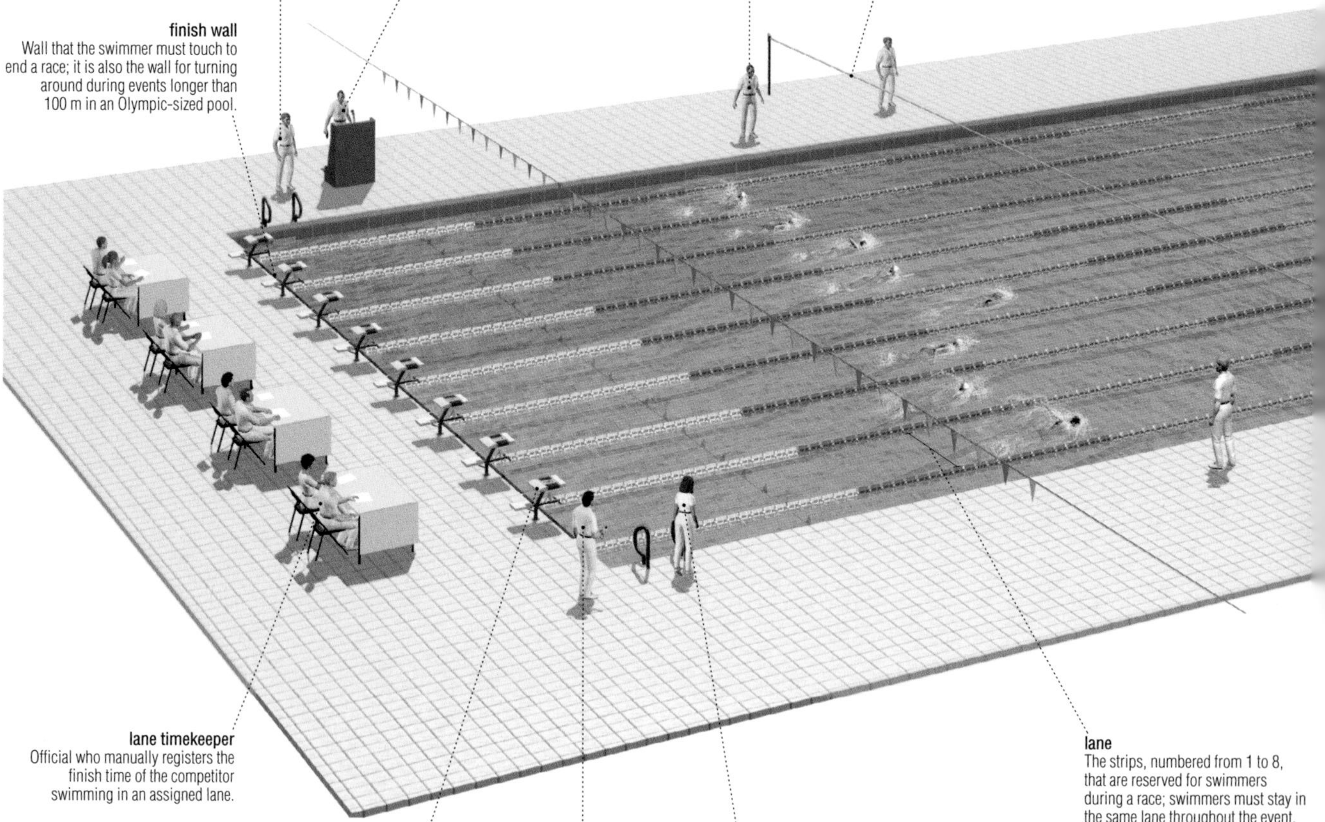

referee
Official who enforces the rules and oversees the progress of the competition; the referee ratifies the judges' decisions and resolves any disputes that may arise.

starter
Official who gives the start signal; false starts lead to the disqualification of the swimmer in error.

stroke judge
Each of the four officials checking the acceptability of the swimmers' movements, depending on the stroke category.

false start rope
Rope that is 50 ft from the wall; it is dropped into the water in the event of a false start to inform the swimmers that they must resume their starting positions.

finish wall
Wall that the swimmer must touch to end a race; it is also the wall for turning around during events longer than 100 m in an Olympic-sized pool.

lane timekeeper
Official who manually registers the finish time of the competitor swimming in an assigned lane.

lane
The strips, numbered from 1 to 8, that are reserved for swimmers during a race; swimmers must stay in the same lane throughout the event.

starting block
Metal elevated structure from which the swimmer dives into the pool to start a race.

chief timekeeper
Official who collects the times registered by the lane timekeepers; these data are used in the event the electronic timer fails.

placing judge
Official who confirms the times registered by the electronic timer after checking with the timekeepers.

swimming

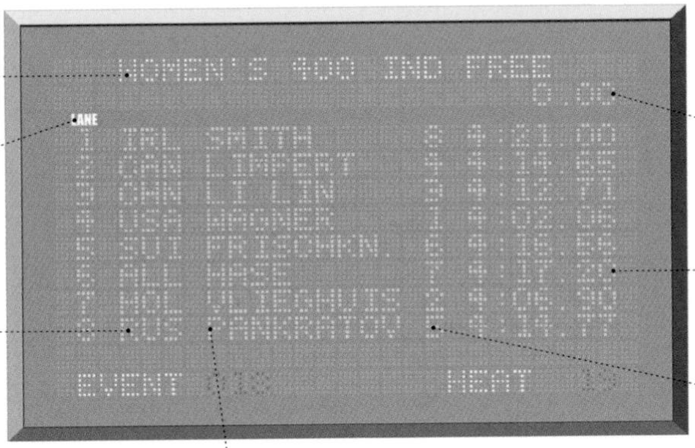

scoreboard
Posting surface displaying various data regarding the event in progress.

event
Type of competition in progress; it is based on the distance to swim and the category of stroke.

lane
Number of the lane assigned to each athlete.

swimmer's country

timer
Time elapsed since the beginning of the race.

swim times
Total duration of a contestant's race; it is measured in hundredths of a second.

order of finish
Classification of contestants at the end of the race in ascending order of finish times.

swimmer's name

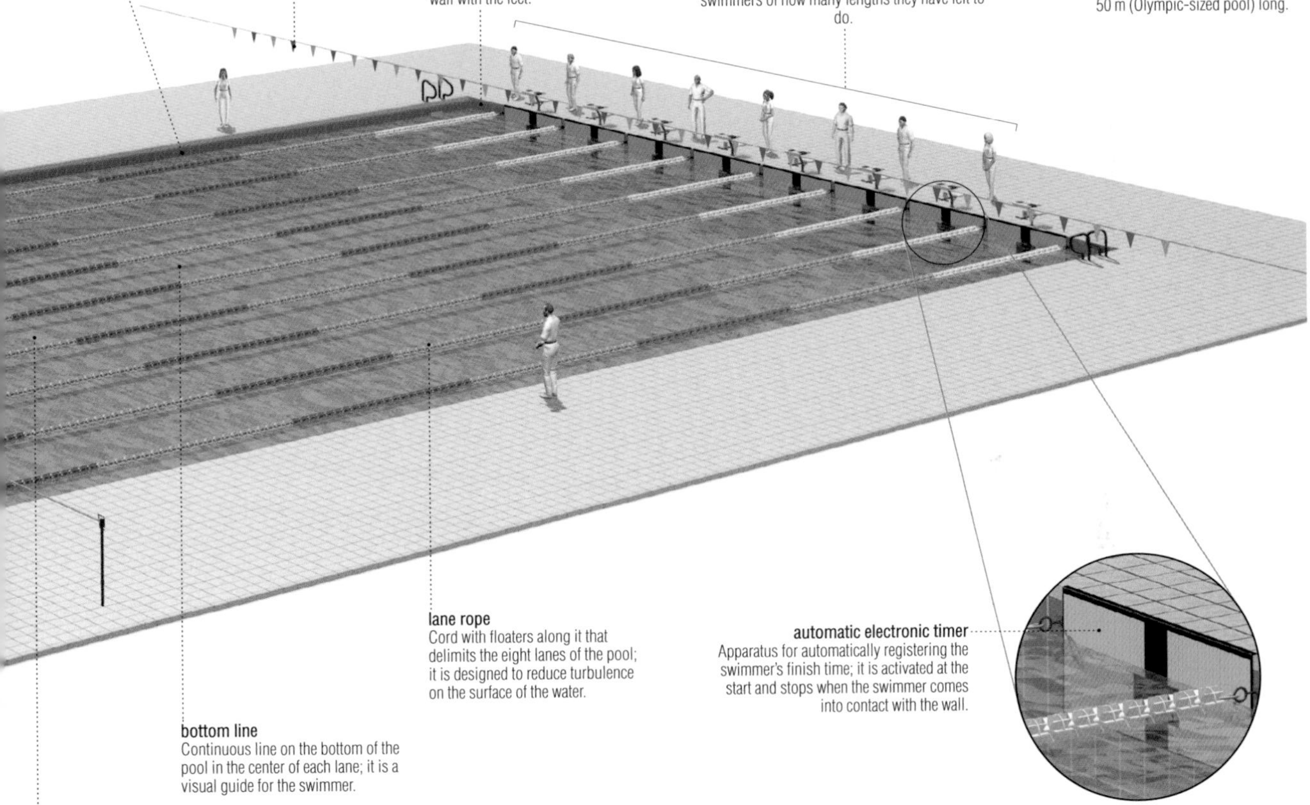

backstroke turn indicator
Rope with pennants that is strung 16 ft from the finish and turning walls; backstroke swimmers use it to judge distance.

sidewall
Wall forming the side of the pool; there is at least 20 in between the side wall and the outside lane ropes.

turning wall
Wall that the swimmer must touch before turning around; during the turn, the athlete pushes from the wall with the feet.

turning judges
Officials checking the validity of the turns; in the 800 m and 1500 m events, they inform the swimmers of how many lengths they have left to do.

competitive course
The events, for singles and teams, take place in a pool that is 25 m or 50 m (Olympic-sized pool) long.

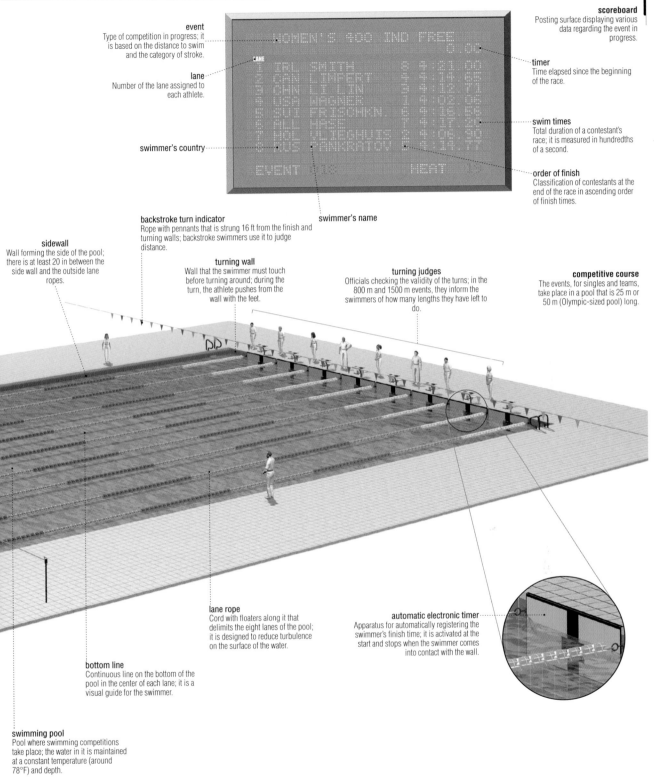

lane rope
Cord with floaters along it that delimits the eight lanes of the pool; it is designed to reduce turbulence on the surface of the water.

automatic electronic timer
Apparatus for automatically registering the swimmer's finish time; it is activated at the start and stops when the swimmer comes into contact with the wall.

bottom line
Continuous line on the bottom of the pool in the center of each lane; it is a visual guide for the swimmer.

swimming pool
Pool where swimming competitions take place; the water in it is maintained at a constant temperature (around 78°F) and depth.

swimming

types of strokes
Four basic categories are recognized by the International Amateur Swimming Federation (FINA): the breaststroke, the butterfly, the backstroke and freestyle (the crawl).

front crawl stroke
Stroke performed on the stomach in which the arms alternate in moving toward the front; it is very fast and is usually used in freestyle races.

breathing in
Action of drawing air into the lungs; to breathe in, the swimmer turns the head slightly, without lifting it.

starting dive
Dive enabling the swimmer to thrust the body into the water; the swimmer pushes off with the legs, extends the body and enters the water head first.

breathing out
Expulsion of air; the swimmer breathes out when the face is underwater.

turning wall
Wall that the swimmer must touch before turning around; during the turn, the athlete pushes from the wall with the feet.

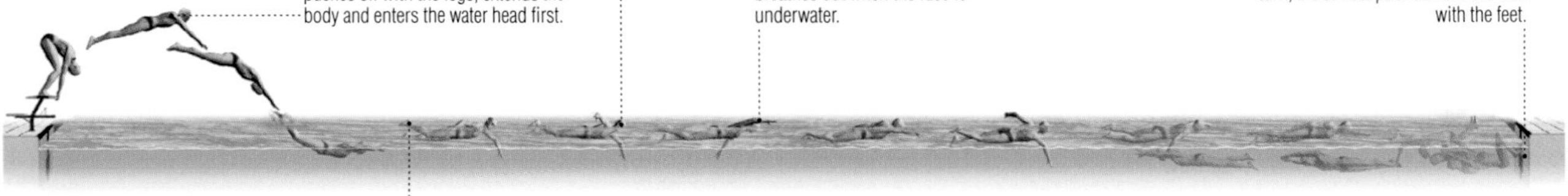

crawl kick
Movement in which the outstretched legs alternate in beating up and down.

flip turn
Movement for making a turn: the swimmer curls downward, pivots, then pushes from the wall with the feet.

breaststroke
Stroke characterized by a series of simultaneous arm movements (toward the front, toward the outside and toward the rear) that are synchronized with the beating of the legs.

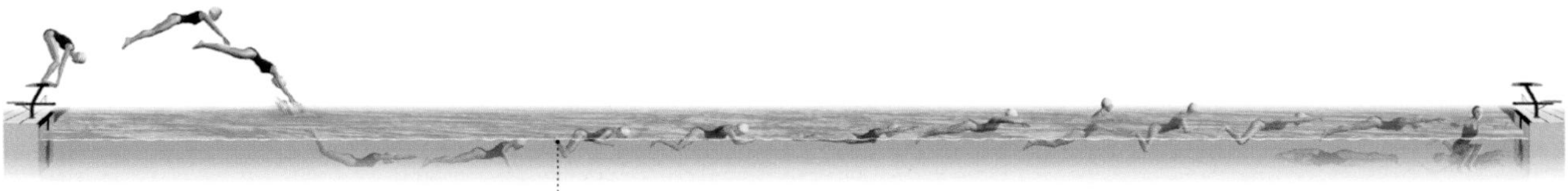

breaststroke kick
Movement in which the swimmer bends the legs and then stretches them simultaneously toward the outside; it is more powerful than other leg kicks.

breaststroke turn
Movement for making a half turn; the swimmer touches the wall with both hands, pivots, then pushes from the wall with the feet.

butterfly stroke
Stroke on the stomach in which the two arms are thrust simultaneously toward the front and then brought backward.

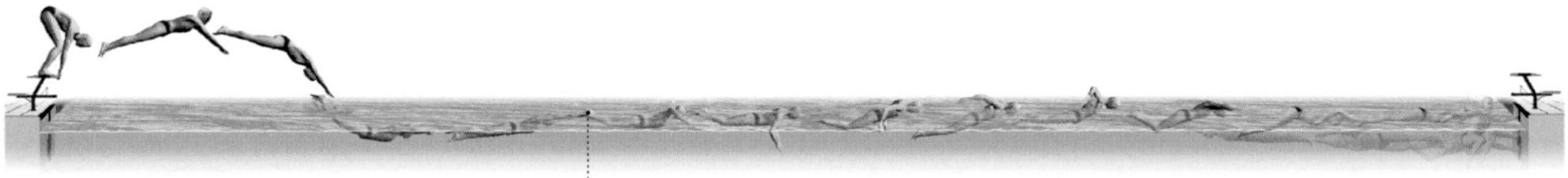

butterfly kick
Vertical simultaneous movement of the legs that completes an undulation started by the upper body; the legs always stay together.

butterfly turn
Movement for making a half turn; the swimmer touches the wall with both hands, pivots, then pushes from the wall with the feet.

backstroke
Stroke characterized by an alternating rotation of the arms toward the back; the outstretched legs make an alternating beating movement at the same time.

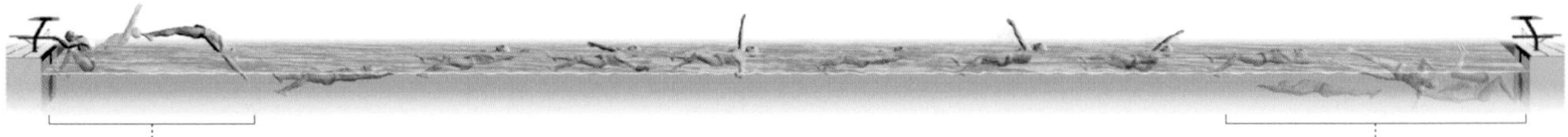

backstroke start
Movement by which the swimmer starts from within the pool; at the signal, the swimmer lets go of the starting grip and then pushes from the wall with the feet.

flip turn
Movement for making a turn; the swimmer arrives in the dorsal position, pivots, then pushes from the wall with the feet.

sailing

Sport navigation practiced on a sailboat. There are several classes of sailboats and various types of competitions such as regattas and transoceanic races.

wind
Displacement of air caused by variations in pressure between two regions of the atmosphere.

points of sailing
Courses of a sailboat relative to the direction of the wind; the sailboat navigates portside or starboardside, depending on which side the wind is coming from.

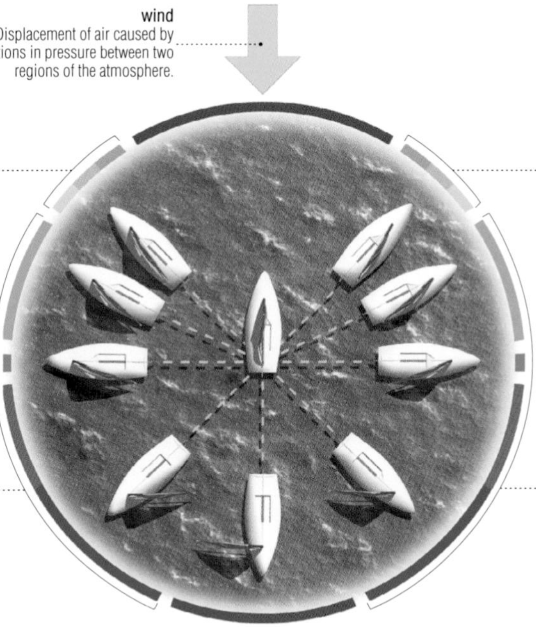

on the wind
Points of sailing in between a headwind and a close reach that are used especially when tacking; the sails are near the boat's center line.

on the wind
Points of sailing in between a headwind and a close reach that are used especially when tacking; the sails are near the boat's center line.

beam reach
Points of sailing in between a full and by and a down wind; the sails swing farther and farther from the boat's center line.

beam reach
Points of sailing in between a full and by and a down wind; the sails swing farther and farther from the boat's center line.

full and by
Point of sailing of a sailboat going against the wind, with its sail at an angle of about 60°.

beam reach
Point of sailing in between a wind abeam and a broad reach; the sailboat navigates by following the wind at an angle of about 135°.

on the wind
Point of sailing of a sailboat sailing against the wind, with its sail at an angle of about 45°.

headwind
Wind blowing against the sailboat's course; it is impossible to make headway.

close reach
Point of sailing in which the sailboat comes up against the wind, with its sail at an angle of about 70°.

broad reach
Fastest point of sailing, in between a beam reach and a down wind; the angle between the boat and the eye (axis) of the wind is wide.

close hauled
Point of sailing of a sailboat traveling near the wind's eye (axis), with its sail at an angle of about 45°; close hauled is the limit of sailing against the wind.

down wind
Point of sailing of a boat going in the same direction as the wind.

wind abeam
Point of sailing of a sailboat traveling at right angles to the wind.

course
Olympic events take place on a triangular course whose length varies depending on variables such as the characteristics of the water and the wind direction.

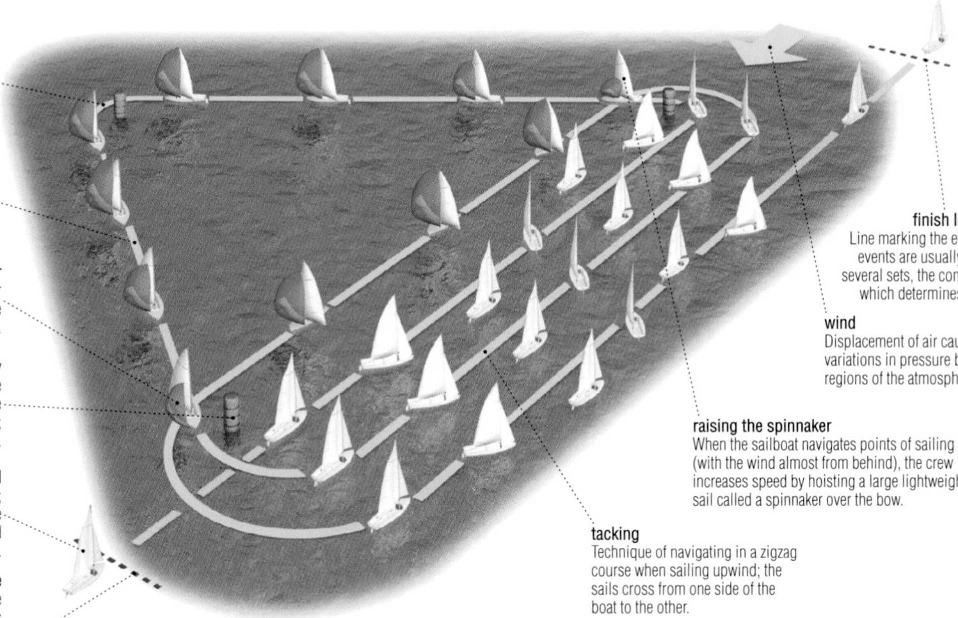

jibe
echnique for changing the sailboat's urse when the wind is coming from rear by letting the sails cross from one side of the boat to the other.

second leg at reach
he sailboat first navigates the beam each with the wind on the starboard side until the third buoy (first leg at reach), then sails a second straight ine to the beam reach with the wind on the port side.

lowering the spinnaker
The crew lowers the spinnaker when the sailboat turns into the wind, after the second leg at reach.

buoy
Floating object that marks out the race. An Olympic-type race has three buoys that are arranged in a triangle; they are rounded in a specific order.

start into a headwind
The race begins facing upwind; sailboats must then tack until the second buoy, which is located straight ahead.

starting line
Line marking the beginning of the race; when the starting signal is given, all the sailboats must be behind this line.

finish line
Line marking the end of the race; events are usually made up of several sets, the combined result of which determines the winner.

wind
Displacement of air caused by variations in pressure between two regions of the atmosphere.

raising the spinnaker
When the sailboat navigates points of sailing (with the wind almost from behind), the crew increases speed by hoisting a large lightweight sail called a spinnaker over the bow.

tacking
Technique of navigating in a zigzag course when sailing upwind; the sails cross from one side of the boat to the other.

sailing

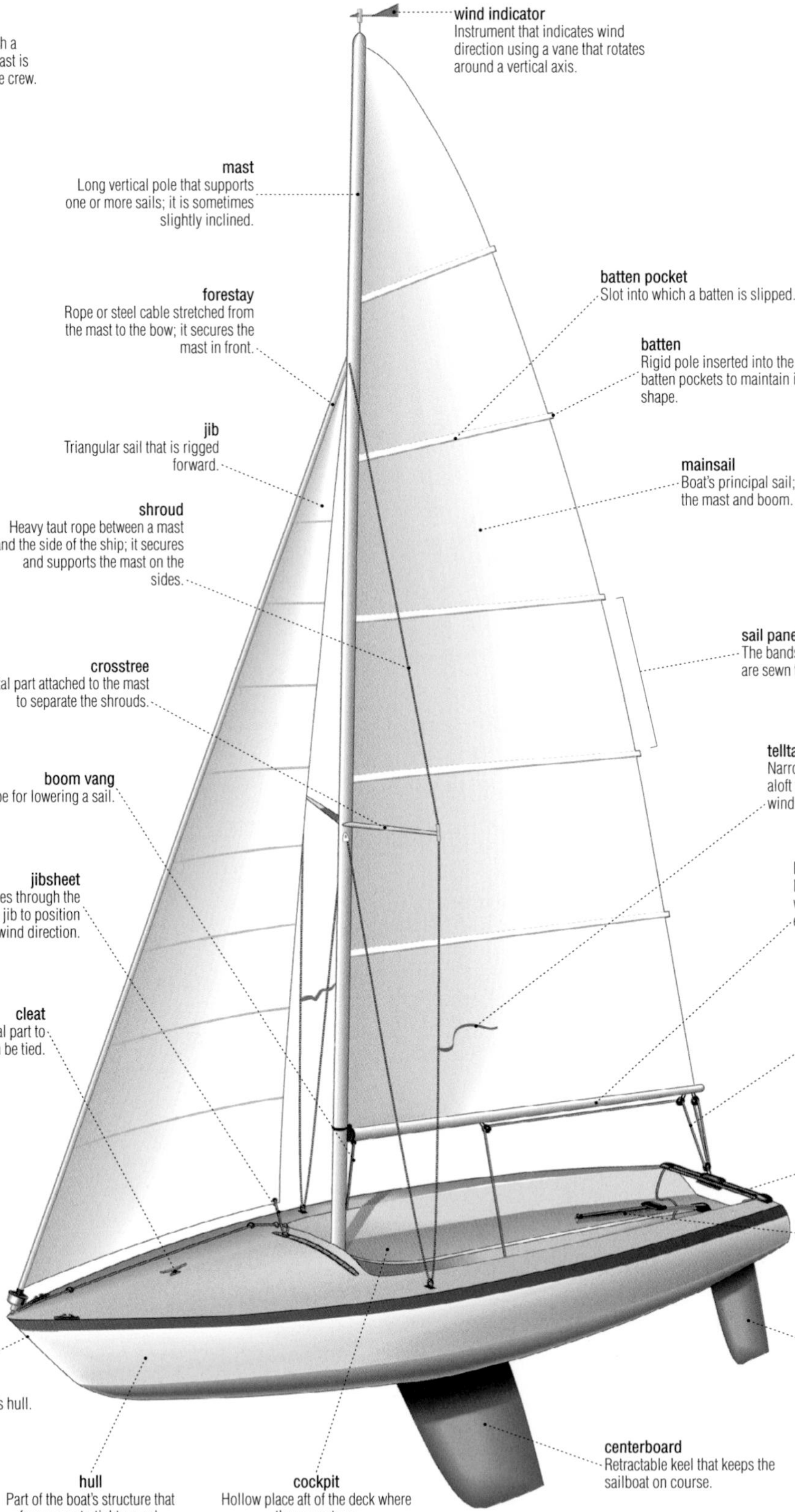
sailboat
Small monohull sailboat with a retractable centerboard; ballast is provided by the weight of the crew.
wind indicator
Instrument that indicates wind direction using a vane that rotates around a vertical axis.
mast
Long vertical pole that supports one or more sails; it is sometimes slightly inclined.
batten pocket
Slot into which a batten is slipped.
forestay
Rope or steel cable stretched from the mast to the bow; it secures the mast in front.
batten
Rigid pole inserted into the sail's batten pockets to maintain its shape.
jib
Triangular sail that is rigged forward.
mainsail
Boat's principal sail; it is rigged to the mast and boom.
shroud
Heavy taut rope between a mast and the side of the ship; it secures and supports the mast on the sides.
sail panel
The bands of canvas whose sides are sewn together to form a sail.
crosstree
Horizontal part attached to the mast to separate the shrouds.
telltale
Narrow light ribbon that is attached aloft to indicate the direction of the wind along the side of a sail.
boom vang
Short rope for lowering a sail.
boom
Long piece of metal that articulates with the mast; it supports the lower edge of the mainsail.
jibsheet
Cord that passes through the bottom corner of the jib to position it in relation to the wind direction.
mainsheet
Cord that passes through the bottom corner of the mainsail to position it in relation to the wind direction.
cleat
Anvil-shaped wood or metal part to which a rope can be tied.
traveler
Metal bar running across the deck; a car travels back and forth on it to move the mainsheet.
tiller
Unit for controlling the rudder; the coxswain is the person who holds a sailboat's tiller.
rudder
Submerged component that pivots on a vertical axle and is used to steer the boat.
bow
Forward part of the boat's hull.
centerboard
Retractable keel that keeps the sailboat on course.
hull
Part of the boat's structure that forms a watertight vessel.
cockpit
Hollow place aft of the deck where the crew stays.

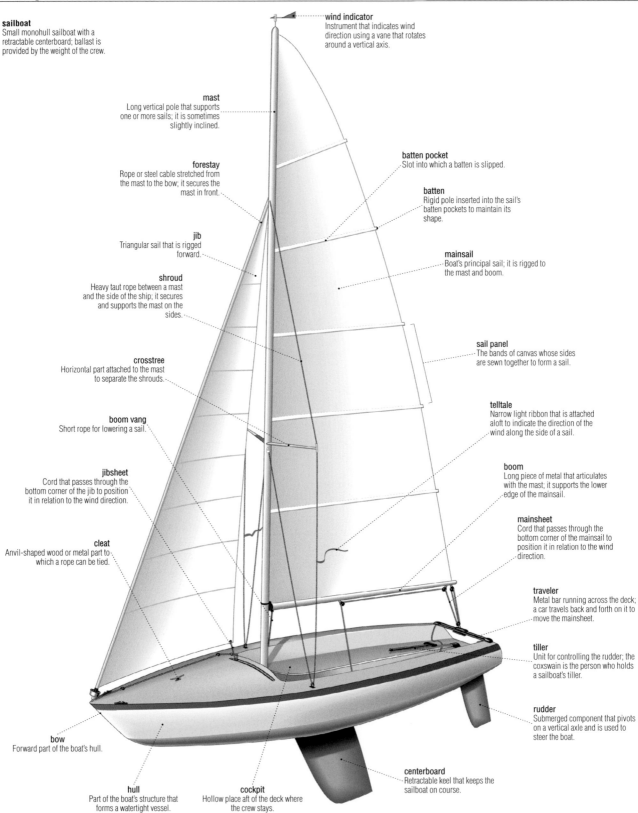

multihulls
Sailboats made out of two or three parallel hulls joined together; the hulls are long, narrow and lightweight so that high speeds can be attained.

trimaran
Sailboat consisting of a central hull stabilized by two smaller hulls on each side (floaters); the hulls are joined by two rigid link arms.

catamaran
Sailboat with two identical hulls that are connected by a rigid structure, which supports a cabin or a deck.

monohulls
Sailboats with a single hull; they are easier to handle but not as fast as multihulls.

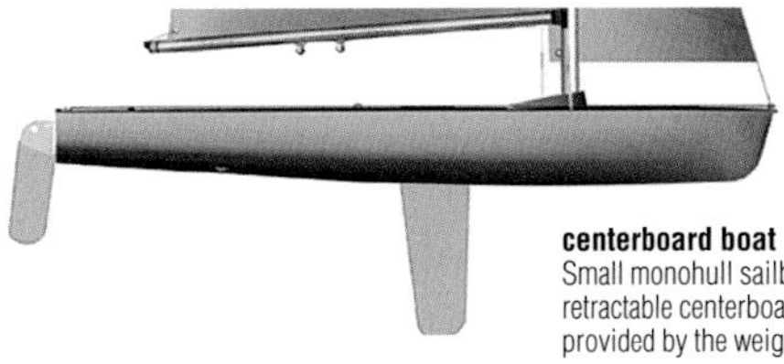

centerboard boat
Small monohull sailboat with a retractable centerboard; ballast is provided by the weight of the crew.

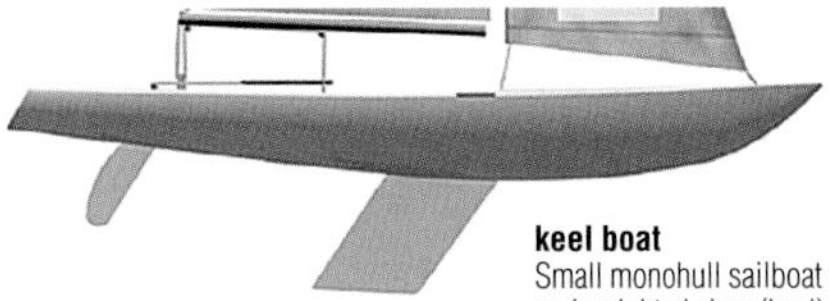

keel boat
Small monohull sailboat with a fixed and weighted skeg (keel) to keep the boat stable and prevent it from capsizing in the wind.

upperworks
Small equipment and accessories on a boat's deck especially for rigging, adjusting and handling the sails.

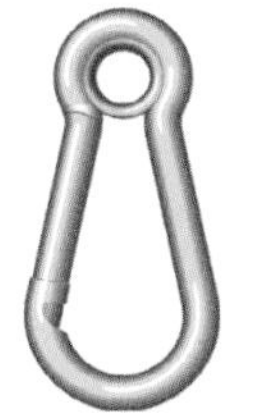

snap shackle
Metal ring that closes automatically with a spring; it is used to attach various elements such as sheets and sails.

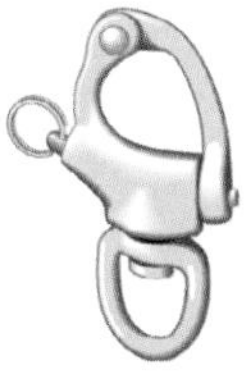

hank
Hook that is kept closed by a piston mechanism and set on a shank, which rotates on a ring; it prevents the ropes that are attached to it from twisting.

shackle
U-shaped part that closes with a threaded shank; it is used especially for joining two chains or for attaching ropes.

turnbuckle
Instrument for adjusting the tension of a rope; it is made up of a hollow cylindrical body with a threaded shank screwed onto each end.

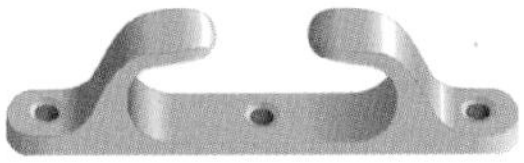

fairlead
Open part that is used to guide mooring ropes.

cleat
Anvil-shaped wood or metal part to which a rope can be tied.

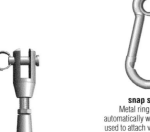

winch
Small crank for heaving a rope tight; it usually has a ratchet preventing it from rotating in the counter direction.

clam cleat
Device made up of two jaws with springs for locking a rope; after the rope is pulled, it stays in place.

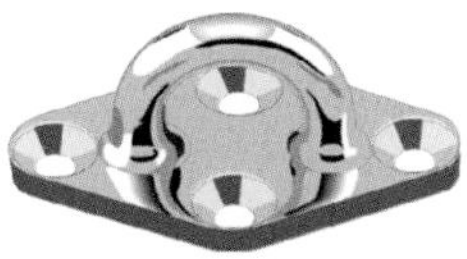

sheet lead
Ringed part through which a sheet passes to change its direction; it must be perfectly smooth to prevent wear on the rope.

traveler
Metal bar running across the deck; a car travels back and forth on it to move the mainsheet.

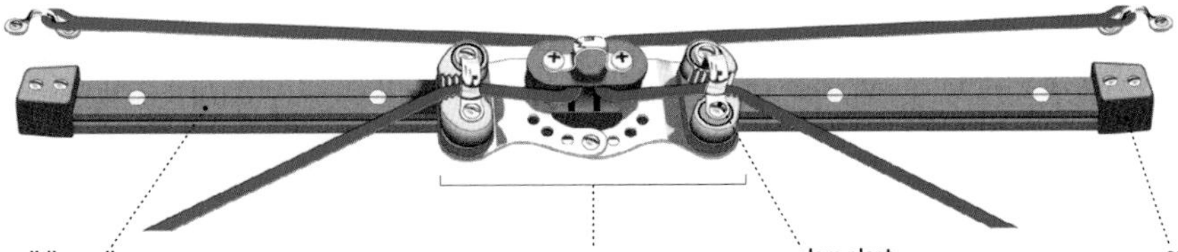

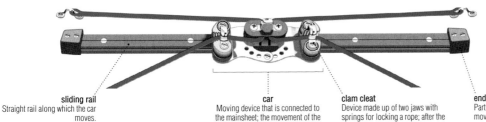

sliding rail
Straight rail along which the car moves.

car
Moving device that is connected to the mainsheet; the movement of the car quickly changes the sail position in relation to the wind.

clam cleat
Device made up of two jaws with springs for locking a rope; after the rope is pulled, it stays in place.

end stop
Part for locking the sideways movement of the car.

sailboard

Floating board with a sail; it is used in windsurfing, a sport consisting of gliding on water.

sail
Assembly of fabric or plastic sections that is rigged on a mast; it forms a surface that allows the board to sail with the wind.

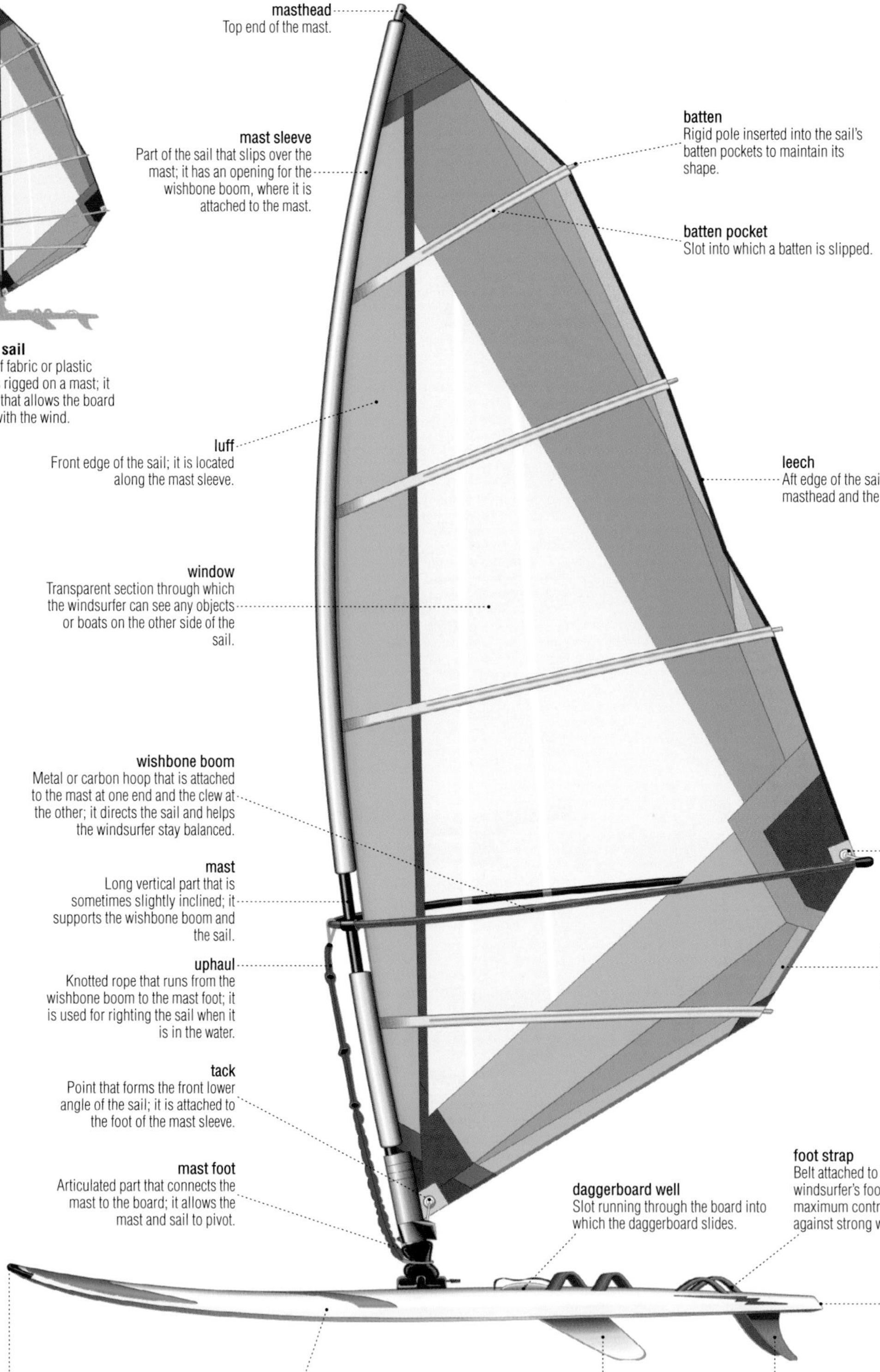
masthead
Top end of the mast.
batten
Rigid pole inserted into the sail's batten pockets to maintain its shape.
mast sleeve
Part of the sail that slips over the mast; it has an opening for the wishbone boom, where it is attached to the mast.
batten pocket
Slot into which a batten is slipped.
luff
Front edge of the sail; it is located along the mast sleeve.
leech
Aft edge of the sail between the masthead and the clew.
window
Transparent section through which the windsurfer can see any objects or boats on the other side of the sail.
wishbone boom
Metal or carbon hoop that is attached to the mast at one end and the clew at the other; it directs the sail and helps the windsurfer stay balanced.
clew
Point forming the small angle at the back of the sail; it is attached to the wishbone boom.
mast
Long vertical part that is sometimes slightly inclined; it supports the wishbone boom and the sail.
foot
Lower part of the sail between the clew and the tack.
uphaul
Knotted rope that runs from the wishbone boom to the mast foot; it is used for righting the sail when it is in the water.
tack
Point that forms the front lower angle of the sail; it is attached to the foot of the mast sleeve.
foot strap
Belt attached to the board to hold the windsurfer's foot in place; this provides maximum control of the board, especially against strong winds and waves.
mast foot
Articulated part that connects the mast to the board; it allows the mast and sail to pivot.
daggerboard well
Slot running through the board into which the daggerboard slides.
stern
Back part of the board.
bow
Forward part of the board; it curves slightly upward.
board
Floating device made of synthetic material on which the windsurfer rides; its shape varies depending on its use (racing, slalom, waves, jumping).
daggerboard
Usually retractable, vertical skeg that keeps the board on course.
skeg
One of the triangular parts aft and under the board that stabilize its course; the shorter the skegs, the easier the board is to handle.

canoe-kayak: whitewater

Sport of traveling in a canoe or kayak in water ranging from calm to turbulent in a river or man-made course.

canoe
Closed boat that is somewhat wider than a kayak and seats one or two people; it is propelled with a single-bladed paddle in a kneeling position.

single-bladed paddle
Instrument made up of a flat oar blade attached to a handle for propelling and steering a canoe.

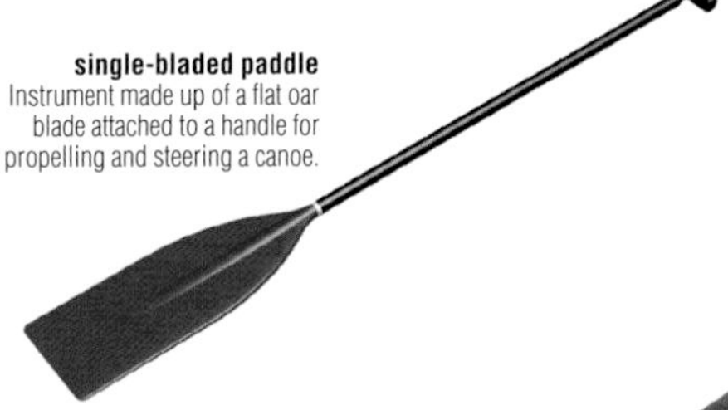

kayak
Long narrow closed boat with a round hull that provides stability and maneuverability; it is propelled with a double-bladed paddle in a seated position.

double-bladed paddle
Instrument with two curved oar blades that are attached to a handle; it propels and steers the kayak by paddling on alternating sides of the boat.

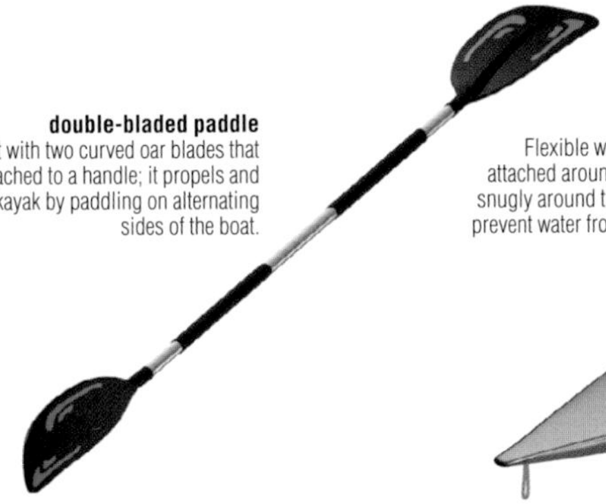

spray skirt
Flexible waterproof part that is attached around the opening; it fits snugly around the kayaker's waist to prevent water from entering the boat.

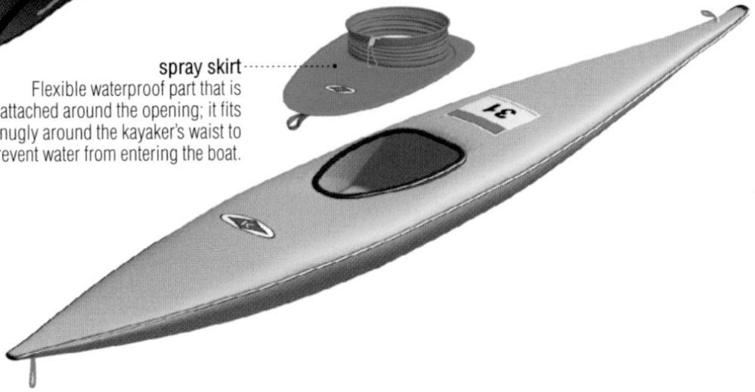

gate judge
Official who ensures that the paddler negotiates the gate as required without touching the poles; if the athlete makes a mistake, there is a time penalty.

whitewater
Race against time in turbulent water over a natural or man-made course; the route of the race is marked by 20 to 25 numbered gates.

upstream gate
Gate made with two red poles that must be negotiated against the current; races must have at least six upstream gates.

chief judge
Official who enforces the rules; this individual makes all the final decisions and ensures consistency among the various officials.

course gate
Space between two poles through which the competitor must pass; it hangs 6 in above the water from cables stretched from shore to shore.

downstream gate
Gate made of two green poles that is negotiated in the direction of the current.

safety officer
Official who manages the first aid staff, who are positioned along the course to be ready for emergencies.

rowing and sculling

Sport consisting of a speed race in a straight line over a maximum distance of 2000 m; races take place on calm water in boats designed for the purpose.

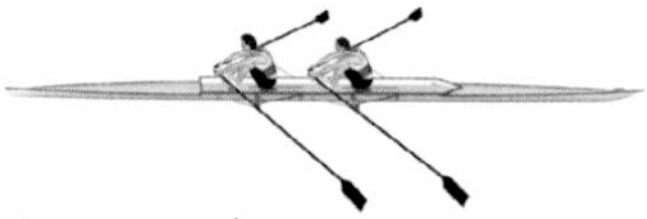

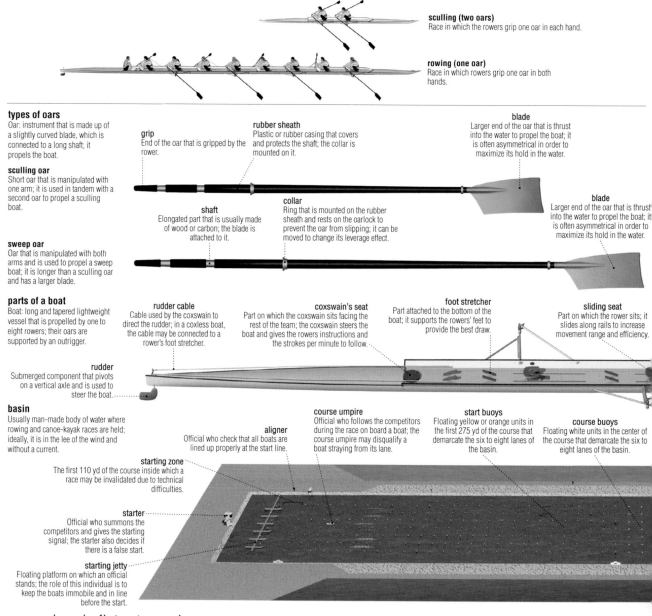

sculling (two oars)
Race in which the rowers grip one oar in each hand.

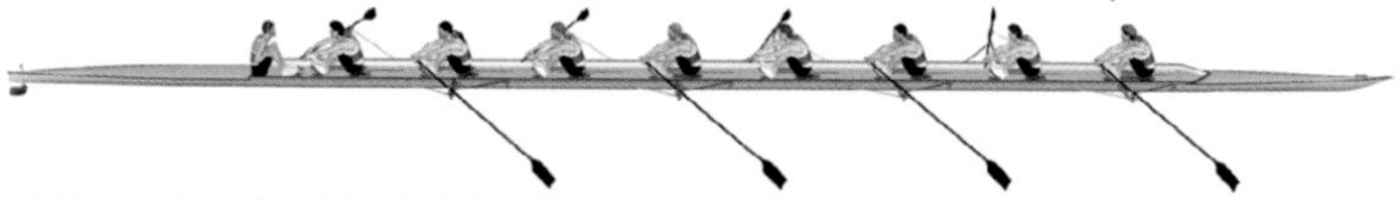

rowing (one oar)
Race in which rowers grip one oar in both hands.

types of oars

Oar: instrument that is made up of a slightly curved blade, which is connected to a long shaft; it propels the boat.

sculling oar
Short oar that is manipulated with one arm; it is used in tandem with a second oar to propel a sculling boat.

grip
End of the oar that is gripped by the rower.

rubber sheath
Plastic or rubber casing that covers and protects the shaft; the collar is mounted on it.

blade
Larger end of the oar that is thrust into the water to propel the boat; it is often asymmetrical in order to maximize its hold in the water.

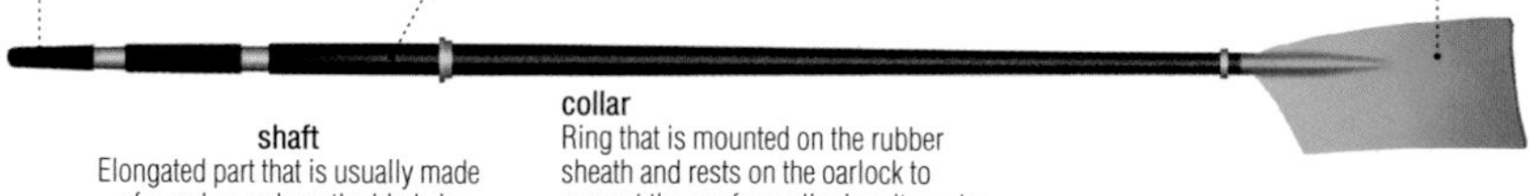

shaft
Elongated part that is usually made of wood or carbon; the blade is attached to it.

collar
Ring that is mounted on the rubber sheath and rests on the oarlock to prevent the oar from slipping; it can be moved to change its leverage effect.

blade
Larger end of the oar that is thrust into the water to propel the boat; it is often asymmetrical in order to maximize its hold in the water.

sweep oar
Oar that is manipulated with both arms and is used to propel a sweep boat; it is longer than a sculling oar and has a larger blade.

parts of a boat

Boat: long and tapered lightweight vessel that is propelled by one to eight rowers; their oars are supported by an outrigger.

rudder cable
Cable used by the coxswain to direct the rudder; in a coxless boat, the cable may be connected to a rower's foot stretcher.

coxswain's seat
Part on which the coxswain sits facing the rest of the team; the coxswain steers the boat and gives the rowers instructions and the strokes per minute to follow.

foot stretcher
Part attached to the bottom of the boat; it supports the rowers' feet to provide the best draw.

sliding seat
Part on which the rower sits; it slides along rails to increase movement range and efficiency.

rudder
Submerged component that pivots on a vertical axle and is used to steer the boat.

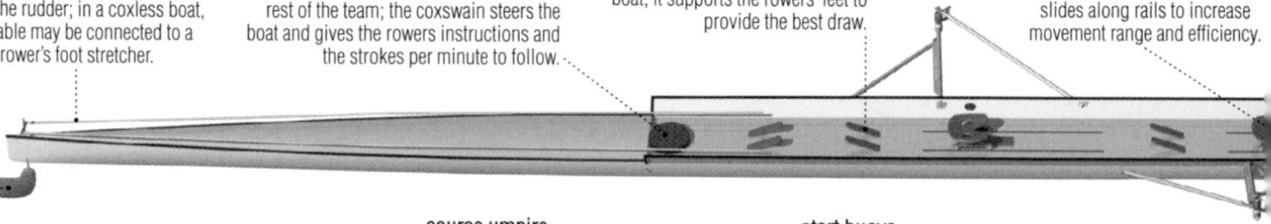

basin

Usually man-made body of water where rowing and canoe-kayak races are held; ideally, it is in the lee of the wind and without a current.

aligner
Official who check that all boats are lined up properly at the start line.

course umpire
Official who follows the competitors during the race on board a boat; the course umpire may disqualify a boat straying from its lane.

start buoys
Floating yellow or orange units in the first 275 yd of the course that demarcate the six to eight lanes of the basin.

course buoys
Floating white units in the center of the course that demarcate the six to eight lanes of the basin.

starting zone
The first 110 yd of the course inside which a race may be invalidated due to technical difficulties.

starter
Official who summons the competitors and gives the starting signal; the starter also decides if there is a false start.

starting jetty
Floating platform on which an official stands; the role of this individual is to keep the boats immobile and in line before the start.

canoe-kayak: flatwater racing

Sport consisting of a speed race in a straight line; races take place on calm water in canoes or kayaks with one or more places.

C1 canoe
Open pointed boat that is propelled with a single-bladed paddle in a kneeling position; the V-shaped hull is somewhat unstable but gives maximum glide.

deck
Enclosed area fore and aft; it reinforces the canoe's hull and prevents water from entering the cockpit.

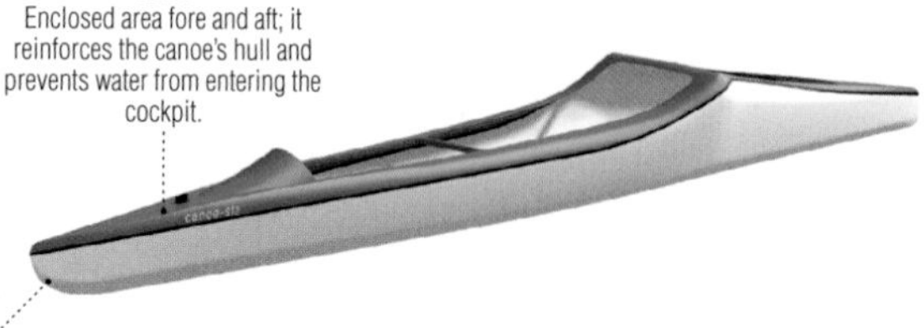

forestem
Somewhat pointed forward part of the canoe hull.

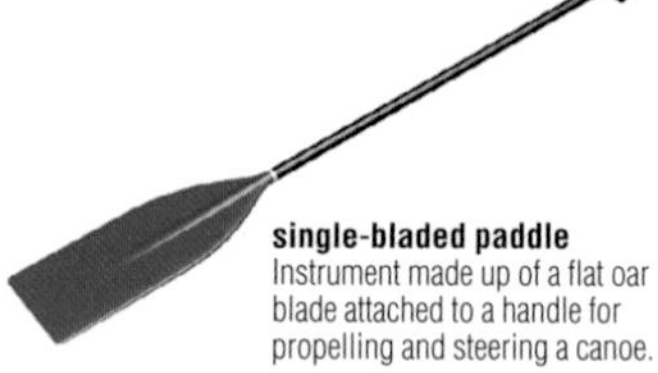

single-bladed paddle
Instrument made up of a flat oar blade attached to a handle for propelling and steering a canoe.

rowing and sculling

sculling boats

Boats in which the rowers have two oars and there are one, two, four and sometimes eight rowers; a sculling boat is rarely guided by a coxswain.

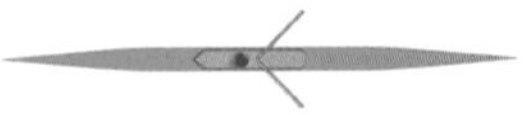

single scull
Sculling boat for one rower; it is the smallest and lightest of the rowboats.

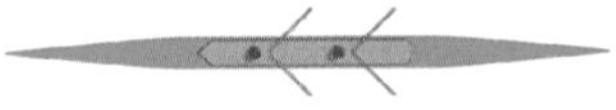

coxless double
Sculling boat for two rowers; like the single scull, it is rudderless and is steered by applying unequal force against the oars.

sweep boats

Boats in which the rowers have one oar and there are two, four or eight rowers; a sweep boat might be guided by a coxswain.

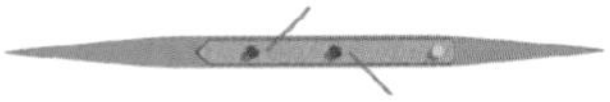

coxed pair

coxless pair

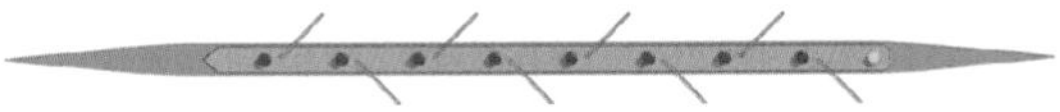

coxed eight

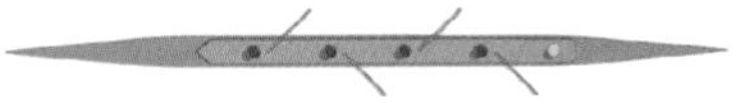

coxed four

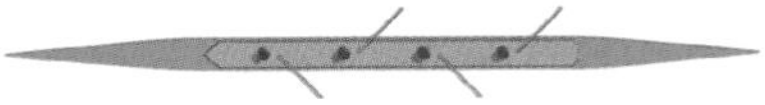

coxless four

oarlock
Piece of equipment on which the oar's collar rests; it keeps the oar in place while allowing it to move more easily.

outrigger
Metal adjustable structure that supports the oar within the rower's reach.

bow ball
Rubber or plastic globe forward on the hull; it is the deciding factor in a photo finish and serves as protection in the event of collision.

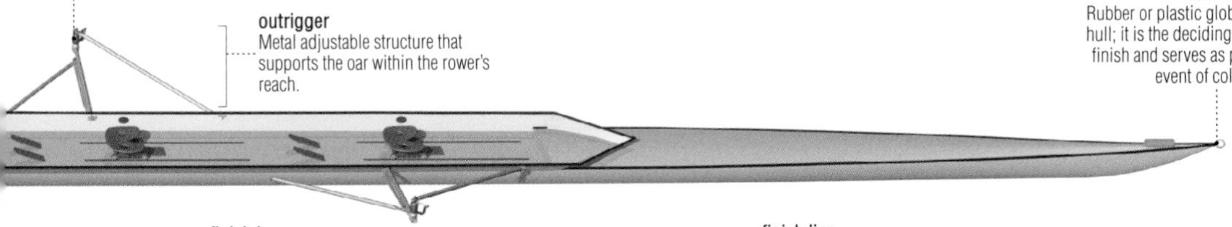

finish buoys
Floating yellow or orange units that demarcate the six to eight lanes of the basin for the last 275 yd of the course.

finish line judge
Official who validates the boats' placement and the race time.

finish line
Line marking the end of a race that is demarcated by two red flags atop buoys; a crew ends the race when the forward part of the boat crosses it.

floating dock
Floating platform used for launching boats into the water or for taking them out.

scoreboard
Display surface posting information related to a sporting event in progress (time, standings, results, etc.).

canoe-kayak: flatwater racing

K1 kayak

Closed tapered boat that is propelled with a double-bladed paddle in a seated position; it has a rudder to facilitate steering.

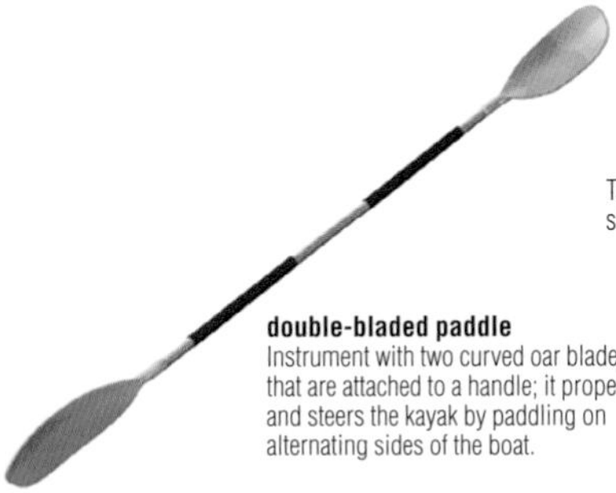

double-bladed paddle
Instrument with two curved oar blades that are attached to a handle; it propels and steers the kayak by paddling on alternating sides of the boat.

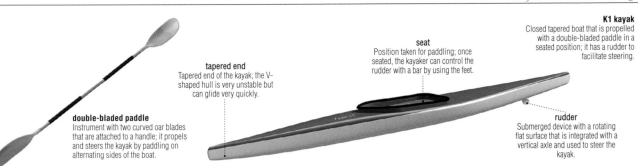

tapered end
Tapered end of the kayak; the V-shaped hull is very unstable but can glide very quickly.

seat
Position taken for paddling; once seated, the kayaker can control the rudder with a bar by using the feet.

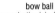

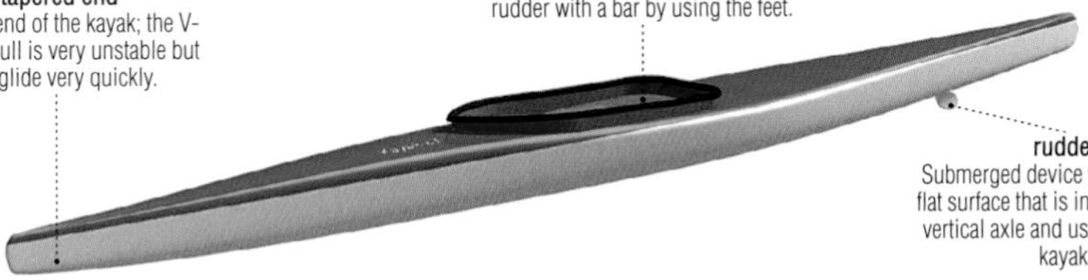

rudder
Submerged device with a rotating flat surface that is integrated with a vertical axle and used to steer the kayak.

water skiing

Sport in which the skier is towed by a motorboat and glides on the surface of the water on one or two skis; there are a number of disciplines, including jumping, slalom and figures.

examples of skis
Water skiing can be done on two skis (twin skis and jump skis) or on one ski (figures and slalom).

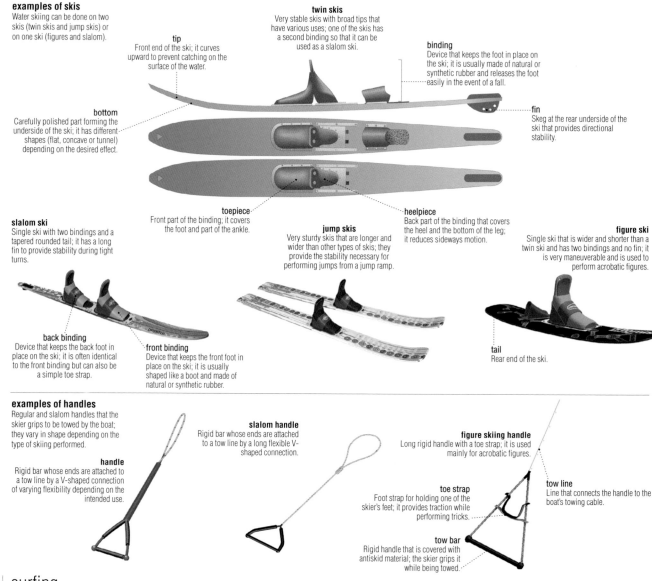

twin skis
Very stable skis with broad tips that have various uses; one of the skis has a second binding so that it can be used as a slalom ski.

tip
Front end of the ski; it curves upward to prevent catching on the surface of the water.

binding
Device that keeps the foot in place on the ski; it is usually made of natural or synthetic rubber and releases the foot easily in the event of a fall.

bottom
Carefully polished part forming the underside of the ski; it has different shapes (flat, concave or tunnel) depending on the desired effect.

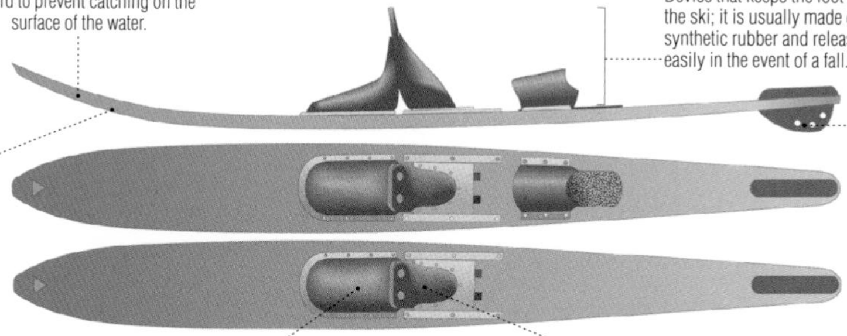

fin
Skeg at the rear underside of the ski that provides directional stability.

toepiece
Front part of the binding; it covers the foot and part of the ankle.

heelpiece
Back part of the binding that covers the heel and the bottom of the leg; it reduces sideways motion.

slalom ski
Single ski with two bindings and a tapered rounded tail; it has a long fin to provide stability during tight turns.

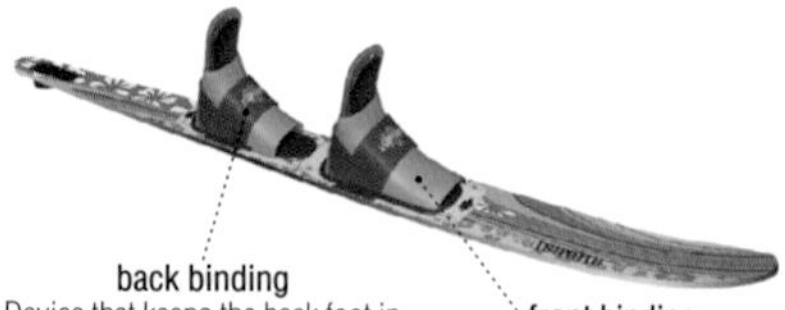

back binding
Device that keeps the back foot in place on the ski; it is often identical to the front binding but can also be a simple toe strap.

front binding
Device that keeps the front foot in place on the ski; it is usually shaped like a boot and made of natural or synthetic rubber.

jump skis
Very sturdy skis that are longer and wider than other types of skis; they provide the stability necessary for performing jumps from a jump ramp.

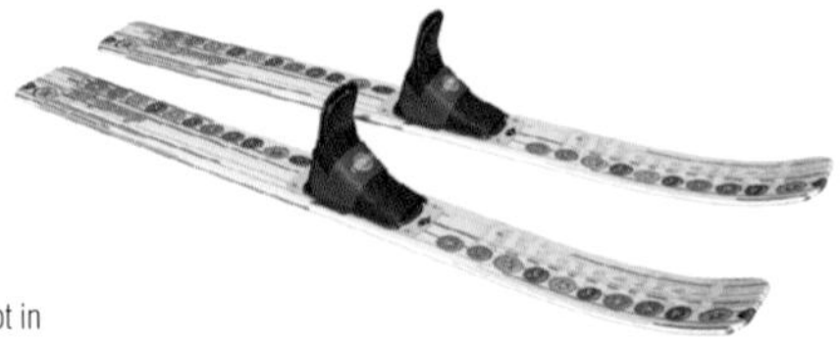

figure ski
Single ski that is wider and shorter than a twin ski and has two bindings and no fin; it is very maneuverable and is used to perform acrobatic figures.

tail
Rear end of the ski.

examples of handles
Regular and slalom handles that the skier grips to be towed by the boat; they vary in shape depending on the type of skiing performed.

handle
Rigid bar whose ends are attached to a tow line by a V-shaped connection of varying flexibility depending on the intended use.

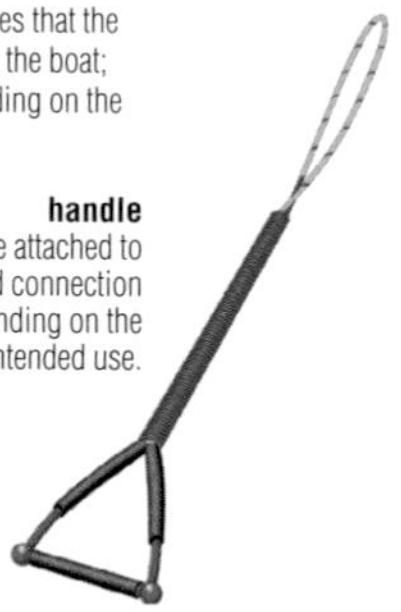

slalom handle
Rigid bar whose ends are attached to a tow line by a long flexible V-shaped connection.

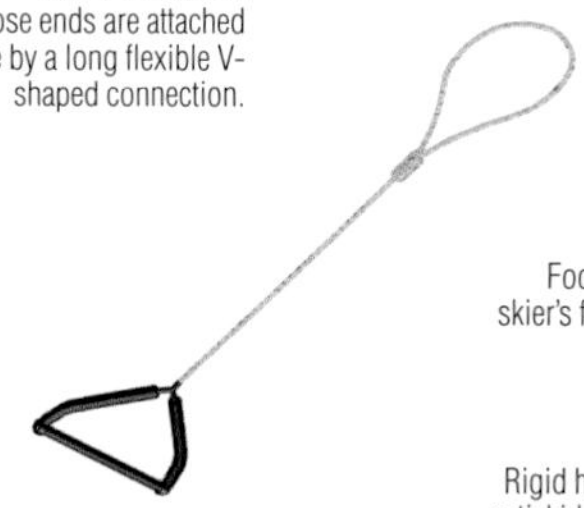

figure skiing handle
Long rigid handle with a toe strap; it is used mainly for acrobatic figures.

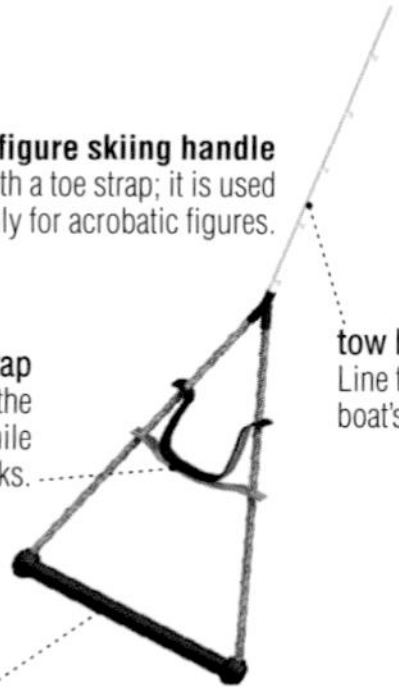

tow line
Line that connects the handle to the boat's towing cable.

toe strap
Foot strap for holding one of the skier's feet; it provides traction while performing tricks.

tow bar
Rigid handle that is covered with antiskid material; the skier grips it while being towed.

surfing

Sport consisting of riding the side of a breaking wave on a surfboard.

surfer
Athlete who practices surfing while standing, lying down or kneeling on a surfboard.

surfboard
Floating board made of synthetic material and covered with wax or antiskid strips; its length and shape vary depending on the intended use.

skeg
Triangular part at the rear underside of the board that provides directional stability.

boot
Synthetic rubber shoe that is used for surfing in cold water or for protecting the feet from coral and rocks.

SPORTS AND GAMES

scuba diving

Sport consisting of descending underwater and swimming around; it can be done holding one's breath or with scuba gear.

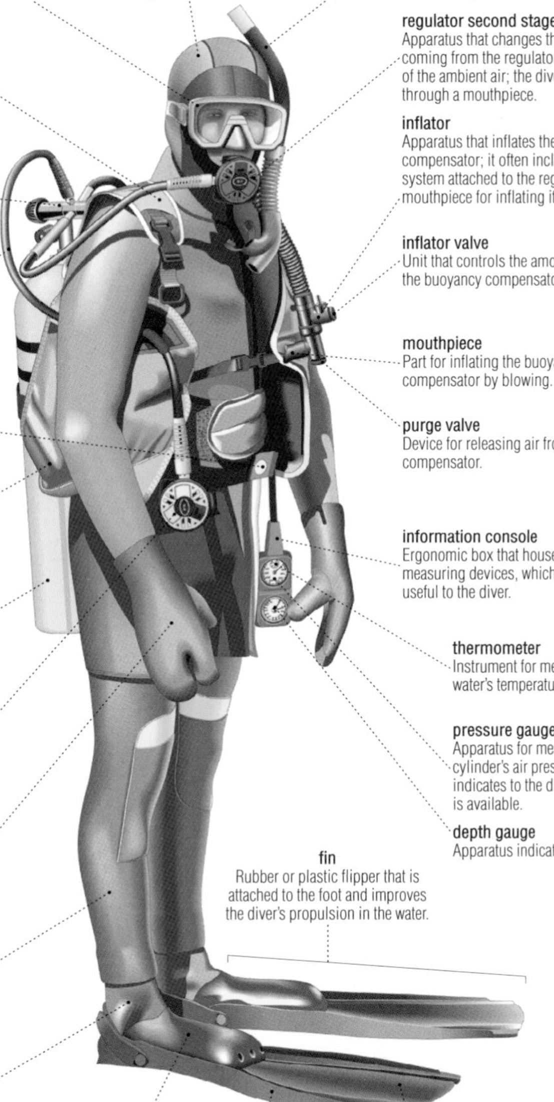

mask
Watertight part that is made up of glass surrounded by a rubber skirt; it covers the nose and eyes and provides good visibility underwater.

hood
Synthetic rubber cap that covers the head and neck to protect them against the cold.

snorkel
Rigid or flexible tube that enables the diver to breathe from just under the surface without lifting the head out of the water; it provides a comfortable and efficient position for swimming.

scuba diver
Person who practices scuba diving; the diver wears diving gear and carries equipment that makes it possible to stay underwater for as long as the air supply lasts.

harness
Piece of equipment with straps and suspenders; the diver uses it to carry one or more cylinders of compressed air on the back.

regulator second stage
Apparatus that changes the pressure of the air coming from the regulator first stage to the pressure of the ambient air; the diver breathes this air in through a mouthpiece.

inflator
Apparatus that inflates the buoyancy compensator; it often includes a mechanical system attached to the regulator as well as a mouthpiece for inflating it manually.

regulator first stage
Apparatus attached to the cylinder valve that lowers the air pressure coming from the cylinder to an intermediate value (medium pressure).

inflator valve
Unit that controls the amount of air entering the buoyancy compensator.

air hose
Flexible tube that connects the regulator first stage to the emergency regulator.

mouthpiece
Part for inflating the buoyancy compensator by blowing.

weight belt
Fabric sash worn around the waist; it contains a variable number of weights to compensate for the diver's natural flotation.

purge valve
Device for releasing air from the buoyancy compensator.

buoyancy compensator
Float device whose volume of air can be increased or decreased at will to stabilize the diver underwater; it can be used to return to the surface and to keep afloat without effort.

information console
Ergonomic box that houses various measuring devices, which are useful to the diver.

compressed-air cylinder
Device containing air of diminished volume due to pressure; it stores air that can be used by the diver to move underwater.

thermometer
Instrument for measuring the water's temperature.

emergency regulator
Regulator second stage that is connected by a hose to the regulator first stage; it is used to supply air to a diver in difficulty.

pressure gauge
Apparatus for measuring the cylinder's air pressure; this indicates to the diver how much air is available.

depth gauge
Apparatus indicating the diver's depth.

diving glove
Piece of synthetic rubber that covers the hand and wrist to protect them from the cold and from being hurt by underwater objects, plants and animals.

fin
Rubber or plastic flipper that is attached to the foot and improves the diver's propulsion in the water.

wet suit
Insulating outfit made out of synthetic rubber; a small amount of water is usually allowed to seep in and assume the diver's body temperature.

boot
Synthetic rubber boot that protects the foot and ankle from the cold and from being rubbed by the fin.

foot pocket
Part of the fin that covers the foot; it can be open at the heel and have an adjustable strap or be entirely closed.

rail
Side reinforcement of the fin; it makes the blade stiffer and improves the fin's efficiency.

blade
Thrusting part of the fin that is an extension of the foot pocket; its length and stiffness determine its thrusting power.

knife
Instrument made up of a handle and a cutting blade; it is often serrated for cutting rope, algae and other objects blocking the way.

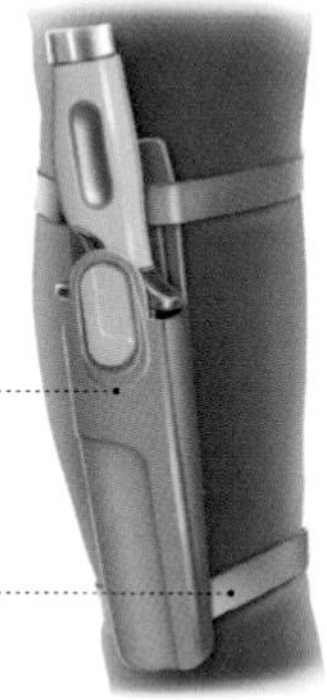

sheath
Usually hard casing that covers and protects the knife.

strap
Flexible strong belt that attaches the sheath to the diver (usually around the upper leg).

speargun
Weapon that uses pressurized air to launch an arrow at a fish or other marine animal underwater; the arrow is attached to the gun by a rope.

boxing

Sport in which two opponents wearing gloves fight each other with their fists (English boxing) or with their fists and feet (French boxing) following a code of rules.

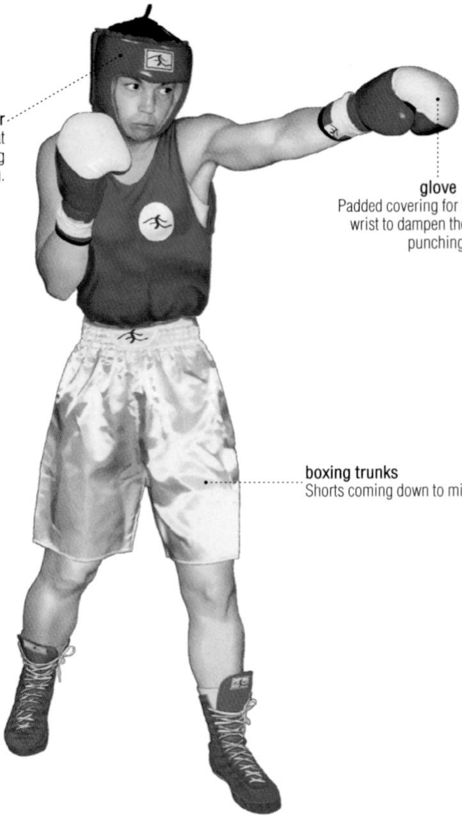

boxer
Athlete who practices boxing; boxers are classified into weight categories.

headgear
Rigid piece of equipment that protects the head especially during training and in Olympic boxing.

glove
Padded covering for the hand and wrist to dampen the impact of punching.

boxing trunks
Shorts coming down to mid-thigh.

punching bag
Leather or canvas bag that is filled with sand and weighs about 65 lb; the boxer trains by hitting it powerfully.

speed ball
Inflated leather bag that the boxer hits when training; it helps develop speed and punching coordination.

ring
Square podium that is surrounded by stretched ropes and measures from 18 to 22 ft on the inside of the ropes; the boxing bout takes place on it.

boxer
Athlete who practices boxing; boxers are classified into weight categories.

referee
Official who enforces the rules and directs the fight in the ring; after the bout, this individual collects and checks the judges' scores.

timekeeper
Official who controls the number of breaks and rounds and their duration by ringing a gong or bell, except in the case of a knockout.

rope
Grouping of threads forming a cable 1 to 2 in thick that stretches between posts to delimit the ring.

corner
Angle formed by the intersection of the ropes; the red and blue corners are reserved for the boxers, the other two are neutral.

turnbuckle
Metal part that is covered with padded matting and stretches the ropes around the ring.

ring step
Structural component for accessing the ring.

corner pad
Padded layer covering the posts to prevent injuries.

ring post
Pole located at the four corners of the ring that supports and stretches the ropes.

trainer
Person who supervises the boxer's training and is present during contests to coach the boxer on strategy.

second
Person who assists a boxer and ministers to him between rounds.

corner stool
Corner seat on which the boxer sits during breaks.

physician
Person who treats the boxers in the event of injury; a doctor's presence is mandatory and this individual may end a fight in the event of serious injury.

canvas
Covering for breaking falls that is made of flexible material and is about .5 in thick; a canvas is stretched on it.

ringside
Area surrounding the ring.

apron
Part of the ring that is outside the ropes; the floor of the ring is about 3 ft high and must extend beyond the ropes by at least 18 in.

judge
One of the three or five officials who evaluate the performances; they score the boxers and pick the winner.

boxing

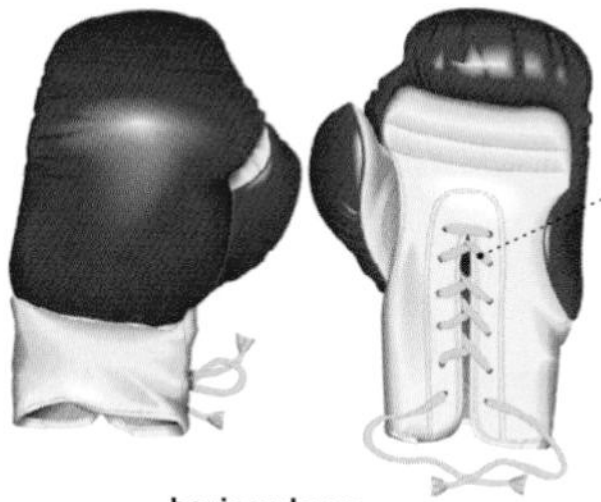

lace
Narrow cord that passes through the glove's eyelets to tighten it around the hand and wrist.

boxing gloves
The gloves are provided by the organizers before the bout.

bandage
Band of soft fabric (gauze) that is wrapped around the hand underneath the glove; it protects the hand against fractures and supports the wrist.

protective cup
Molded plastic equipment that protects an athlete's genitals.

mouthpiece
Protective device for the boxer's teeth that is placed between the cheeks and teeth during a fight.

wrestling

Sport in which two opponents fight bare-handed and seek to pin each other to the floor using various holds.

starting positions
The wrestlers start the bout standing on opposite sides of the white circle; this circle is in the middle of the central wrestling area and is 3.2 ft in diameter.

crouching position (freestyle wrestling)
Freestyle wrestling allows the wrestler to use the entire body; this provides for a larger variety of holds than in Greco-Roman wrestling.

standing position (Greco-Roman wrestling)
In Greco-Roman wrestling, it is forbidden to seize the opponent below the hips and to use one's legs for a hold or to defend oneself.

wrestler
Athlete who practices wrestling; wrestlers are classified into weight categories.

singlet
Tight-fitting one-piece outfit.

wrestling shoe
Flexible leather boot that covers the ankle; it has no heel and no metal parts.

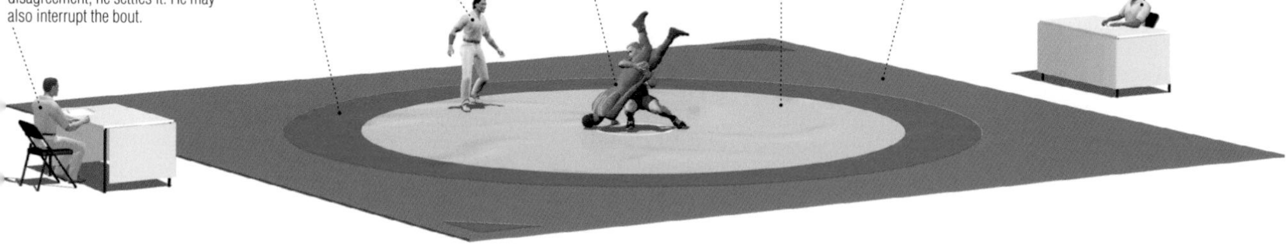

mat chairperson
Official who coordinates the work of the referee and the judge; in the event of disagreement, he settles it. He may also interrupt the bout.

passivity zone
Red band that is 3.2 ft wide; it delimits and is part of the wrestling surface (30 ft in diameter).

referee
Official in charge of enforcing the rules who directs the fight on the mat and wears red and blue sleeves to indicate points.

wrestler
Athlete who practices wrestling; wrestlers are classified into weight categories.

central wrestling area
Circle inside the passivity zone that is 23 ft in diameter; the bout takes place within it.

protection area
Area that is 5 ft wide and surrounds the passivity zone; it provides safety if the wrestler is thrown out of the wrestling area.

wrestling area
Mat with an area of 40 ft² for a wrestling match; a bout has two 3-minute periods with a break of 30 seconds.

judge
Official who assigns the points for the technical action as instructed by the referee or the mat chairperson and registers them on the scoreboard.

judo

Sport of Japanese origin that is practiced with bare hands and consists of unbalancing the opponent with holds; Judo means "the gentle way".

mat
Surface that measures 46 ft x 52 ft and is used for practicing judo; it is made up of smaller mat squares (tatamis).

contestant
One of two athletes (here, judokas) who confront each other in a bout; contestants are classified into weight categories.

scorers and timekeepers
The scorers show the results on the scoreboards and the timekeepers monitor the time during the bout.

scoreboard
Board that displays various data about the contest taking place (such as points and penalties); there are two scoreboards, one manual and one electronic, in each contest area.

medical team
Physicians tend to the judokas in the event of injury; their presence is mandatory and they may end a bout in the event of serious injury.

safety area
Surface that is 10 ft wide and surrounds the danger area; it provides safety if the contestant if thrown out of the contest area.

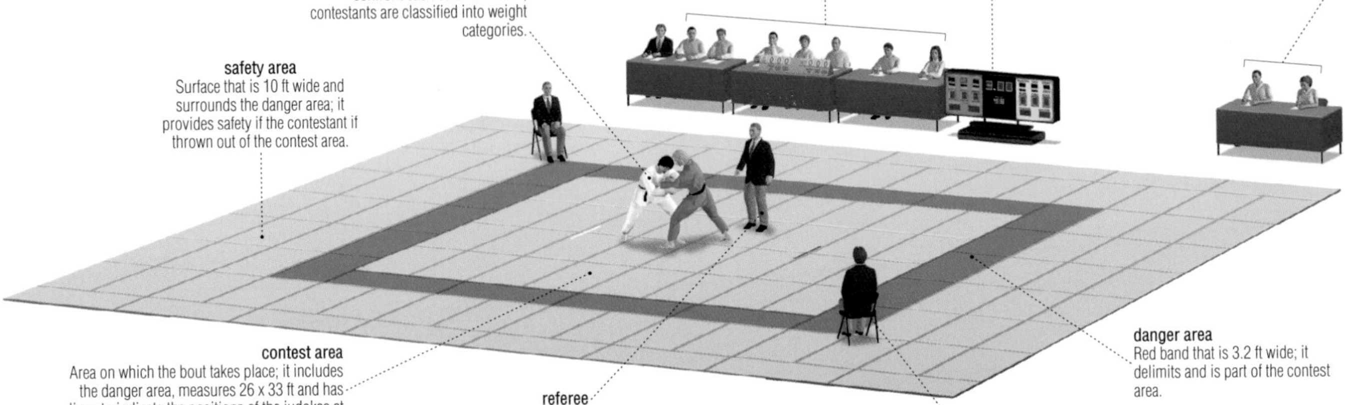

contest area
Area on which the bout takes place; it includes the danger area, measures 26 x 33 ft and has lines to indicate the positions of the judokas at the start and end of the bout.

referee
Official who enforces the rules and directs the bout on the mat; this individual is assisted by the two judges.

danger area
Red band that is 3.2 ft wide; it delimits and is part of the contest area.

judge
One of the two officials who assist the referee; they check especially that the holds are allowable and take place within the bounds of the contest area.

judogi
Clothing worn when practicing judo that is made of cotton or a similar fabric; one judoka wears a white judogi while the other wears a blue one.

jacket
Clothing with wide sleeves that covers the chest and part of the hips; women wear a white bodysuit or jerkin under the jacket.

trousers
Garment for the lower body; it extends from the waist or the hips to the ankles, covering each leg separately.

belt
Band of fabric about 10 ft long that is wrapped twice around the waist and whose color indicates the judoka's level.

examples of holds and throws

There are more than 40 holds in judo: floor grips (strangles, locks, holdings) and standing throws (shoulders, arms, hips, legs).

holding
The assailant uses pressure on the shoulders to pin the opponent to the floor.

stomach throw
The assailant pulls the opponent forward and puts a foot on the his stomach, causing the opponent to be thrown over the assailant's shoulder.

sweeping hip throw
The assailant pushes the opponent's leg, causing the opponent's torso to rotate and flip over the assailant's hip.

major outer reaping throw
Using the right leg, the assailant sweeps up the opponent's left leg from behind, causing the opponent to fall backward.

major inner reaping throw
Using the right leg, the assailant sweeps up the opponent's right leg from the front, causing the opponent to fall backward.

naked strangle
From behind, the assailant's arm puts pressure on the opponent's neck, constricting breathing or cutting off the flow of blood and oxygen to the brain.

arm lock
To force submission, the assailant exerts pressure on the opponent's elbow joint against its natural bending direction.

one-arm shoulder throw
Placing the forearms under the opponent's armpits, the assailant lifts the opponent over his back, propelling the opponent forward.

SPORTS AND GAMES

karate

Self-defense sport of Japanese origin that is practiced with bare hands; the blows, which are usually given with the hands and the feet, must stop before reaching the opponent's body.

karateka
Athlete who practices karate; some, but not all, organizations classify karatekas by weight.

karate-gi
Clothing worn when practicing karate; it includes a jacket and pants that are usually made of cotton.

obi
Long wide belt that is tied around the waist to close the jacket; its color indicates the contestant's level.

contest area
Mat with an area of 26 ft² on which the bout takes place; it is surrounded by a safety surface.

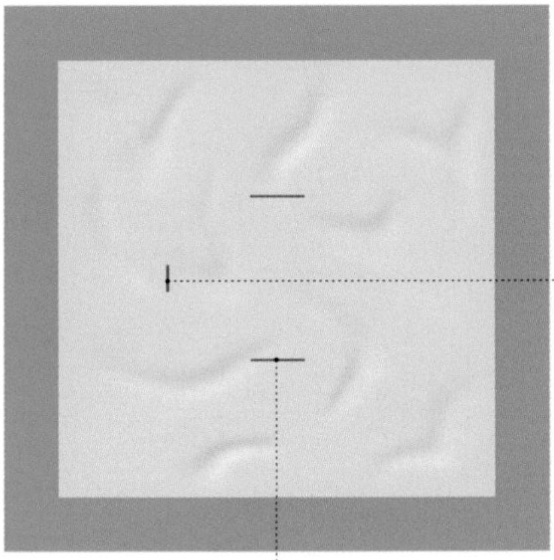

referee's line
Mark designating the regulation position of the referee during the bout.

competitors' line
Mark designating the karatekas' position at the start of the bout and after any interruption.

competition area
Surface for practicing karate; bouts last a maximum of three minutes.

arbitration committee
Group of upper-level officials who especially supervise the bout as it unfolds and check that the referee and the judges perform their duties correctly.

corner judge
One of the four officials who assist the referee, give their opinions especially about the referee's decisions and judge the actions of the karatekas.

scorekeeper
Official who tracks the karatekas' points and penalties.

timekeeper
Official who monitors the duration of the bout.

referee
Official who enforces the rules, directs the bout on the mat, awards the points and gives out warnings and penalties.

karateka
Athlete who practices karate; some, but not all, organizations classify karatekas by weight.

kung fu

One of several types of sport of Chinese origin practiced with or without weapons; it is similar to karate but requires more legwork.

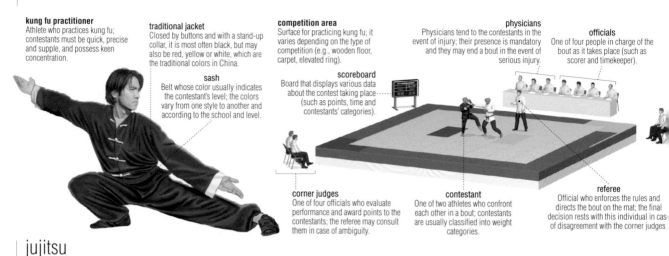

kung fu practitioner
Athlete who practices kung fu; contestants must be quick, precise and supple, and possess keen concentration.

traditional jacket
Closed by buttons and with a stand-up collar, it is most often black, but may also be red, yellow or white, which are the traditional colors in China.

sash
Belt whose color usually indicates the contestant's level; the colors vary from one style to another and according to the school and level.

competition area
Surface for practicing kung fu; it varies depending on the type of competition (e.g., wooden floor, carpet, elevated ring).

physicians
Physicians tend to the contestants in the event of injury; their presence is mandatory and they may end a bout in the event of serious injury.

officials
One of four people in charge of the bout as it takes place (such as scorer and timekeeper).

scoreboard
Board that displays various data about the contest taking place (such as points, time and contestants' categories).

corner judges
One of four officials who evaluate performance and award points to the contestants; the referee may consult them in case of ambiguity.

contestant
One of two athletes who confront each other in a bout; contestants are usually classified into weight categories.

referee
Official who enforces the rules and directs the bout on the mat; the final decision rests with this individual in case of disagreement with the corner judges.

jujitsu

Sport of Japanese origin based on throws, holds and blows to vital points of the body; it gave rise to judo.

competition area
Surface for practicing jujitsu.

scorekeepers
One of two officials who register the contestants' points and penalties, as given by the referee.

contestant
One of two athletes who confront each other in a bout; contestants are usually classified into weight categories.

obi
Long wide belt that is tied around the waist to close the jacket; its color indicates the contestant's level.

physicians
Physicians tend to the contestants in the event of injury; their presence is mandatory and they may end a bout in the event of serious injury.

timekeeper
Official who monitors the duration of the bout.

warning area
Red band that is 3.2 ft wide; it delimits the contest area.

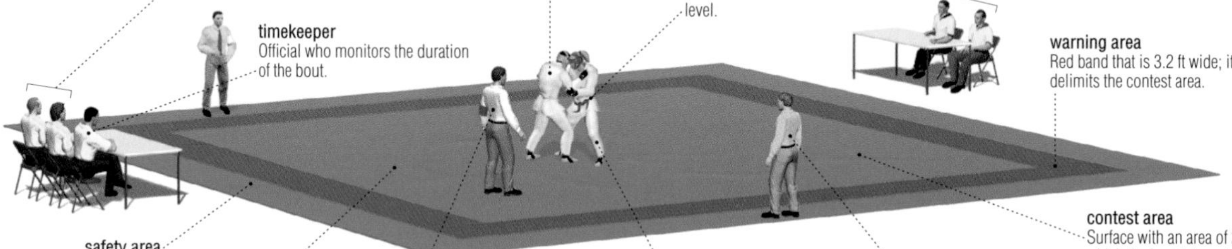

contest area
Surface with an area of 26 ft^2 on which the bout takes place.

safety area
Surface that is 3.2 ft wide and surrounds the warning area; it protects a contestant who is thrown out of the contest area.

tatami
Thick mat with an area of 40 ft^2 that is made up of smaller mat squares; jujitsu is practiced on it.

chief referee
Official who enforces the rules, directs the bout and awards the points and penalties to the contestants.

gi
Clothing worn when practicing jujitsu; it includes a cotton jacket and pants, which are usually white.

side referee
Two officials who stand outside the contest area and assist the chief referee; they are involved in the scoring of contestants.

aikido

Defensive sport of Japanese origin that consists of neutralizing an armed or unarmed opponent by means of dodging, throwing and holding, using bare hands.

aikidoka
Athlete who practices aikido; it requires good coordination, well-developed reflexes, suppleness and keen concentration.

aikidogi
Clothing worn for practicing aikido; for beginners, it consists of a white jacket made of sturdy cloth and white pants.

obi
Long wide belt that is tied around the waist to close the jacket; its color indicates the aikidoka's level.

hakama
Long skirt for hiding foot movement.

jo
Wooden stick about 4.2 ft long; it is used mainly for training.

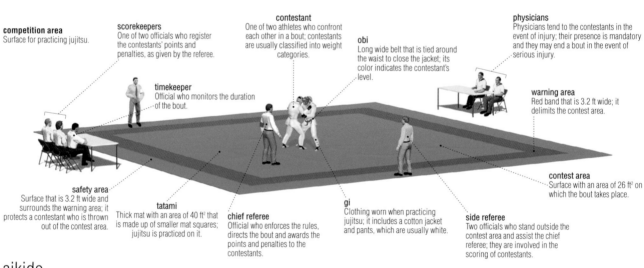

bokken
Wooden saber about 3.2 ft long that is used for training; the jo and the bokken help develop the concepts of distance and position.

kendo

Sport of Japanese origin that is a form of fencing; the opponents wear protection and fight with a bamboo saber.

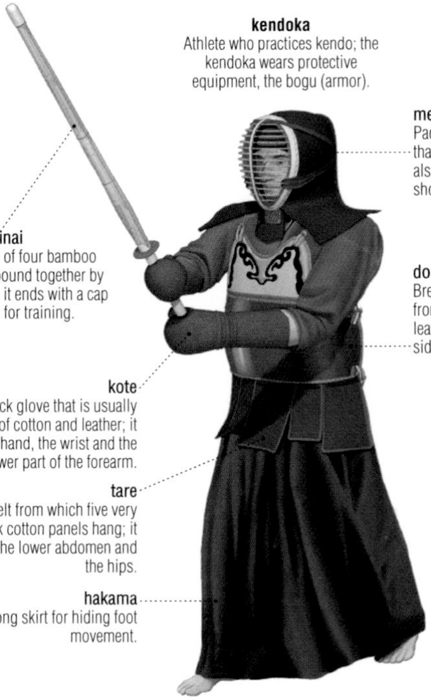

kendoka
Athlete who practices kendo; the kendoka wears protective equipment, the bogu (armor).

men
Padded helmet with a steel grate that protects the head and face; it also provides protection for the shoulders and throat.

shinai
Saber made up of four bamboo lades that are bound together by eces of leather; it ends with a cap and is used for training.

do
Breastplate that is usually made from bamboo blades covered with leather; it protects the front and sides of the torso.

kote
Very thick glove that is usually made of cotton and leather; it protects the hand, the wrist and the lower part of the forearm.

tare
Thick belt from which five very thick cotton panels hang; it protects the lower abdomen and the hips.

hakama
Long skirt for hiding foot movement.

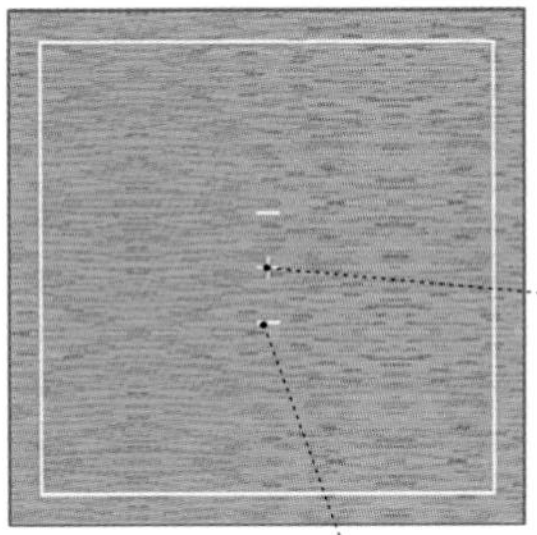

competition area
Smooth wooden floor on which the kendo bout takes place; a bout usually lasts five minutes.

center
Cross that indicates the center of the contest area.

danger zone
Band that is 5 ft wide and delimits the contest area.

competitors' line
Mark that designates the competitors' positions at the start of the bout.

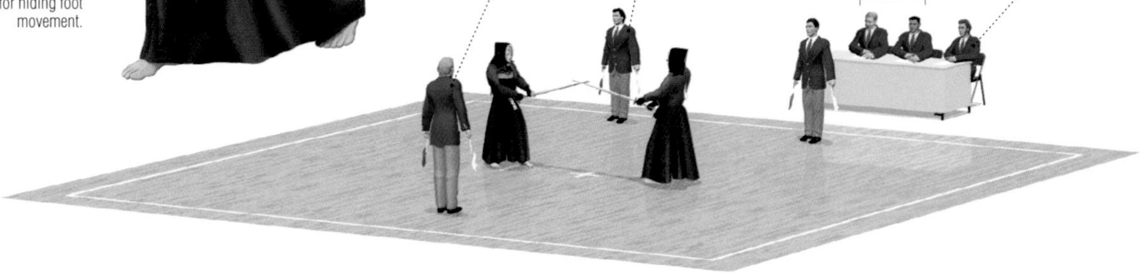

assistant referee
One of two officials who assist the chief referee and are involved in scoring the contestants, using flags.

chief referee
Official who enforces the rules, directs the bout and awards the points and penalties to the contestants.

scorekeepers
One of two officials who register the contestants' points and penalties, as given by the referee.

timekeeper
Official who monitors the duration of the bout.

sumo

Japanese wrestling that is linked to Shintoism; it is practiced by very large corpulent wrestlers who try to make the opponent touch the ground or throw him out of the contest area.

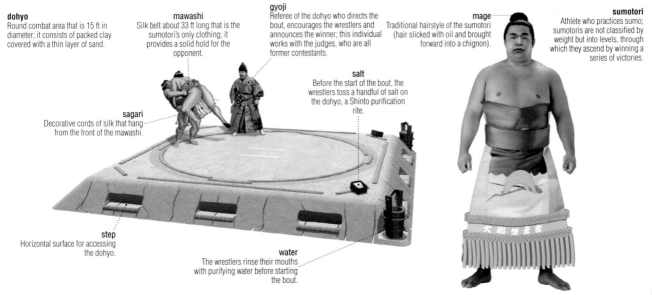

dohyo
Round combat area that is 15 ft in diameter; it consists of packed clay covered with a thin layer of sand.

mawashi
Silk belt about 33 ft long that is the sumotori's only clothing; it provides a solid hold for the opponent.

gyoji
Referee of the dohyo who directs the bout, encourages the wrestlers and announces the winner; this individual works with the judges, who are all former contestants.

salt
Before the start of the bout, the wrestlers toss a handful of salt on the dohyo, a Shinto purification rite.

sagari
Decorative cords of silk that hang from the front of the mawashi.

step
Horizontal surface for accessing the dohyo.

water
The wrestlers rinse their mouths with purifying water before starting the bout.

mage
Traditional hairstyle of the sumotori (hair slicked with oil and brought forward into a chignon).

sumotori
Athlete who practices sumo; sumotoris are not classified by weight but into levels, through which they ascend by winning a series of victories.

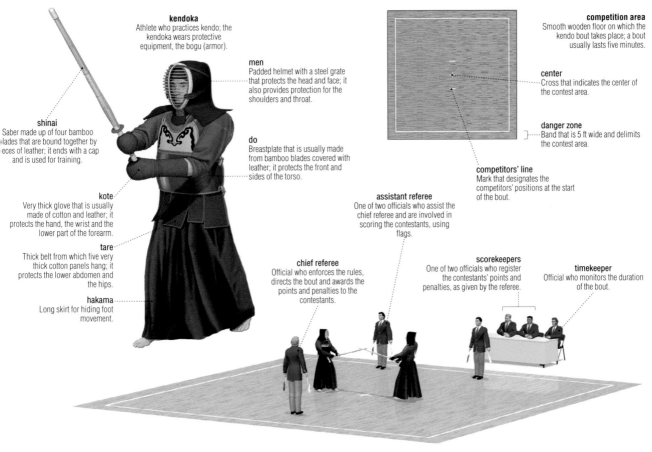

fencing

Sport with two opponents who attempt to touch each other with weapons (épée, foil or saber) on a specific part of the body.

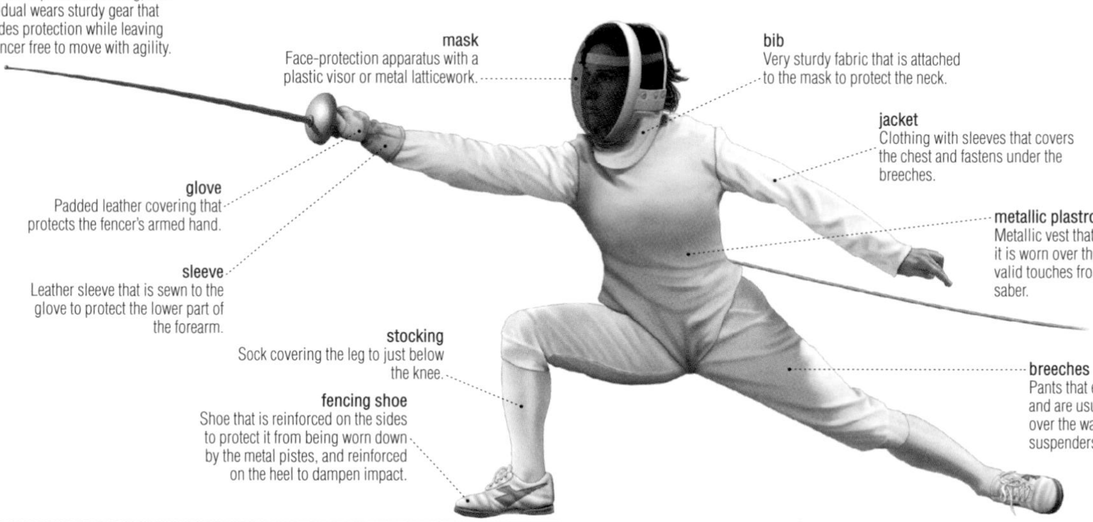

fencer
Athlete who practices fencing; this individual wears sturdy gear that provides protection while leaving the fencer free to move with agility.

mask
Face-protection apparatus with a plastic visor or metal latticework.

bib
Very sturdy fabric that is attached to the mask to protect the neck.

jacket
Clothing with sleeves that covers the chest and fastens under the breeches.

glove
Padded leather covering that protects the fencer's armed hand.

metallic plastron
Metallic vest that conducts electricity; it is worn over the jacket and detects valid touches from the electric foil or saber.

sleeve
Leather sleeve that is sewn to the glove to protect the lower part of the forearm.

stocking
Sock covering the leg to just below the knee.

breeches
Pants that extend below the knees and are usually pulled up very high over the waist and held up by suspenders.

fencing shoe
Shoe that is reinforced on the sides to protect it from being worn down by the metal pistes, and reinforced on the heel to dampen impact.

target areas

Depending on the weapon used, the fencer may touch different parts of an opponent's body to score points.

foilist
The valid touch surface is limited to the trunk and excludes the arms and head.

épéeist
Touches are valid everywhere on the body, including the mask and shoes.

sabreur
The valid touch surface includes the body from the waist up, mask and arms included.

piste
Area on which the match takes place; it is 46 ft long and between 5 and 6.5 ft wide.

timekeeper
Official who monitors the duration of the match; a single match is made up of three manches (sets) of three minutes, with a one-minute break between each manche.

electric foil
Its end contains an electric button that senses hits; a hit is registered only when the pressure on the tip of the blade is greater than 1.1 lb (maximum weight of the foil).

reel
Device that keeps the body wire under constant tension by following the forward and backward movements of the fencer.

foil warning line
Line 3.2 ft from the rear limit line warning the foilist that the end of the piste is near.

scoring light
Light that switches on to signal valid hits (red and green lights) and nonvalid hits (white lights).

electrical scoring apparatus
Electrical apparatus for registering the fencers' hits by means of a body wire.

judge
Each of the officials who assist the president; they stand beside the piste and especially check the validity of the hits.

on guard line
Line 6.5 ft from the center line; the fencer must stay behind it to start and when resuming combat after a valid hit.

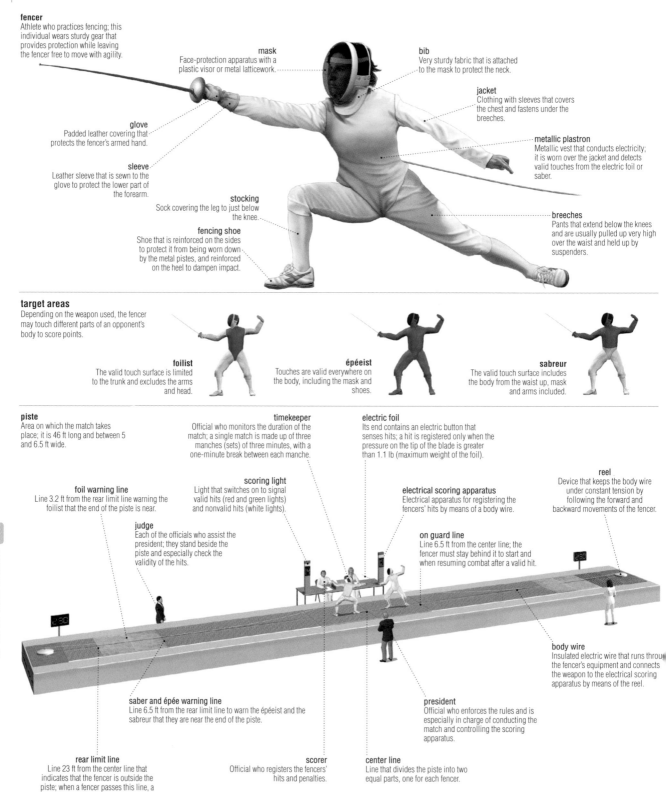

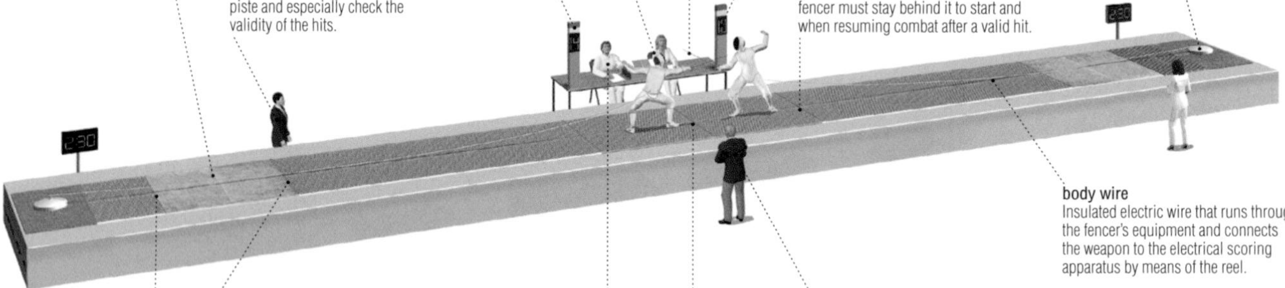

body wire
Insulated electric wire that runs throu the fencer's equipment and connects the weapon to the electrical scoring apparatus by means of the reel.

saber and épée warning line
Line 6.5 ft from the rear limit line to warn the épéeist and the sabreur that they are near the end of the piste.

president
Official who enforces the rules and is especially in charge of conducting the match and controlling the scoring apparatus.

rear limit line
Line 23 ft from the center line that indicates that the fencer is outside the piste; when a fencer passes this line, a hit is awarded to the opponent.

scorer
Official who registers the fencers' hits and penalties.

center line
Line that divides the piste into two equal parts, one for each fencer.

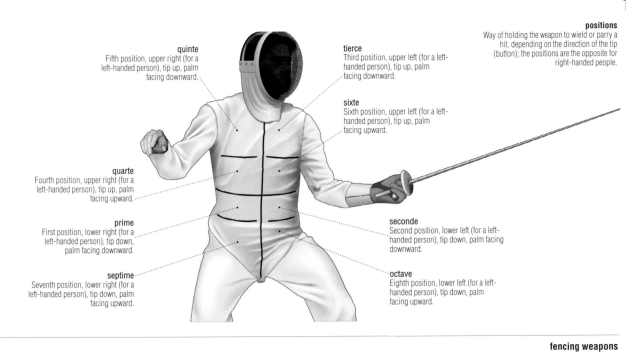

positions
Way of holding the weapon to wield or parry a hit, depending on the direction of the tip (button); the positions are the opposite for right-handed people.

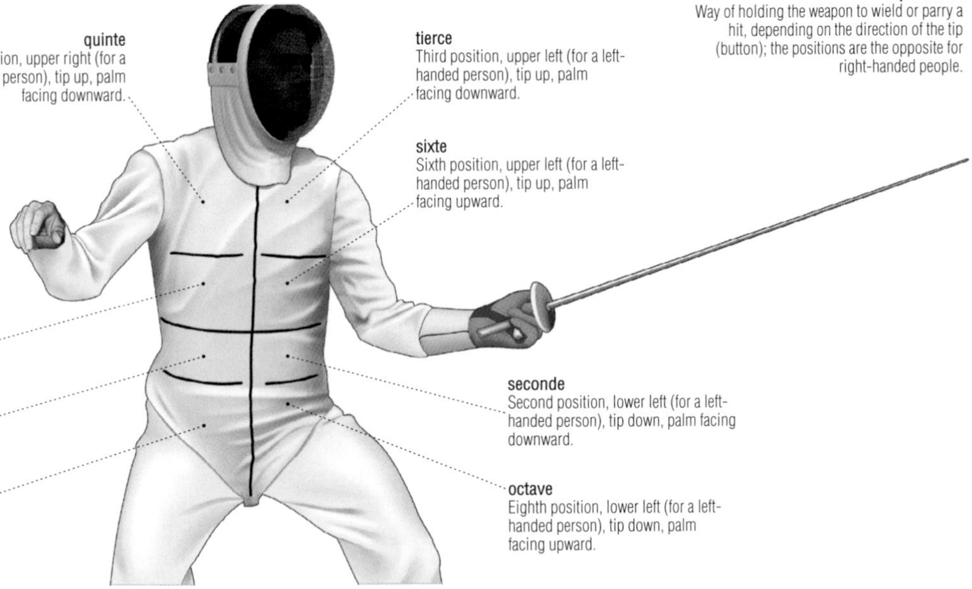

quinte
Fifth position, upper right (for a left-handed person), tip up, palm facing downward.

tierce
Third position, upper left (for a left-handed person), tip up, palm facing downward.

sixte
Sixth position, upper left (for a left-handed person), tip up, palm facing upward.

quarte
Fourth position, upper right (for a left-handed person), tip up, palm facing upward.

prime
First position, lower right (for a left-handed person), tip down, palm facing downward.

seconde
Second position, lower left (for a left-handed person), tip down, palm facing downward.

septime
Seventh position, lower right (for a left-handed person), tip down, palm facing upward.

octave
Eighth position, lower left (for a left-handed person), tip down, palm facing upward.

fencing weapons
In the Olympic Games, the foil, the épée and the saber are used by both men and women.

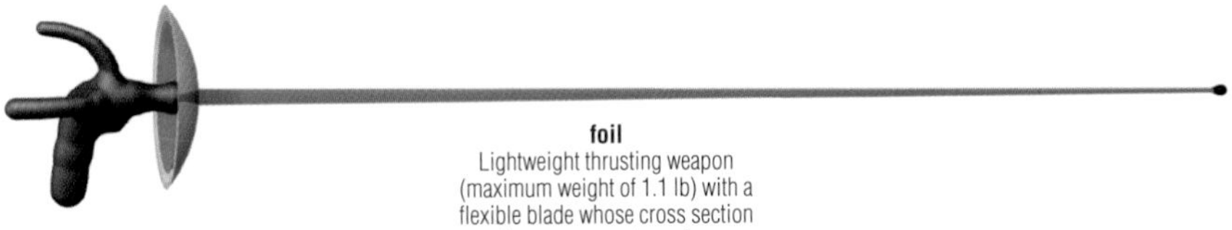

foil
Lightweight thrusting weapon (maximum weight of 1.1 lb) with a flexible blade whose cross section is square or rectangular.

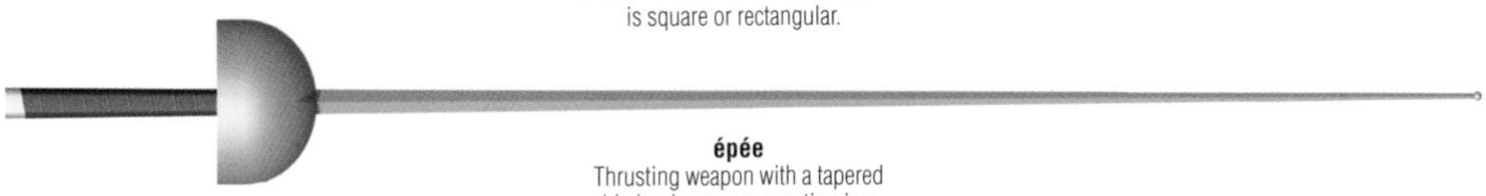

épée
Thrusting weapon with a tapered blade whose cross section is a triangle; it is more rigid and heavier than a foil, weighing up to 1.7 lb.

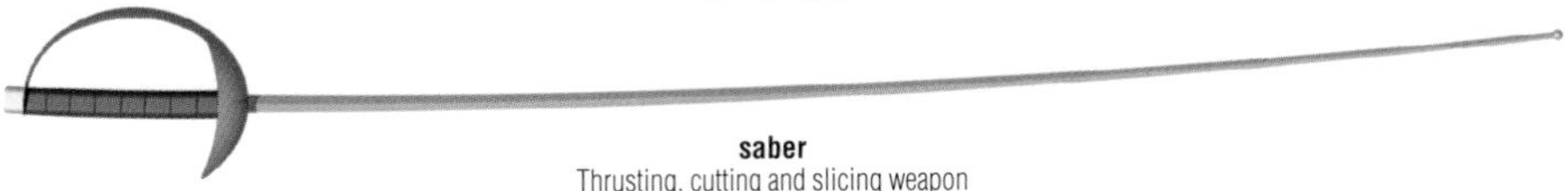

saber
Thrusting, cutting and slicing weapon whose blade is usually curved and sharp on one side only; its maximum weight is 1.1 lb, the same as that of the foil.

parts of the weapon
Weapons can be thrusting (touch made with the tip of the blade), cutting (with the blade) or slicing (with the back edge).

pommel
Metal knob at the end of the handle to balance the weapon.

mounting
Part of the weapon to which the blade is attached.

blade
Hitting part of the weapon; measuring about 3 feet, it is made of flexible metal and is thin and tapered.

button
Bulbous end of the blade; with electric weapons, the button triggers the switch of the electric apparatus when it makes a valid touch.

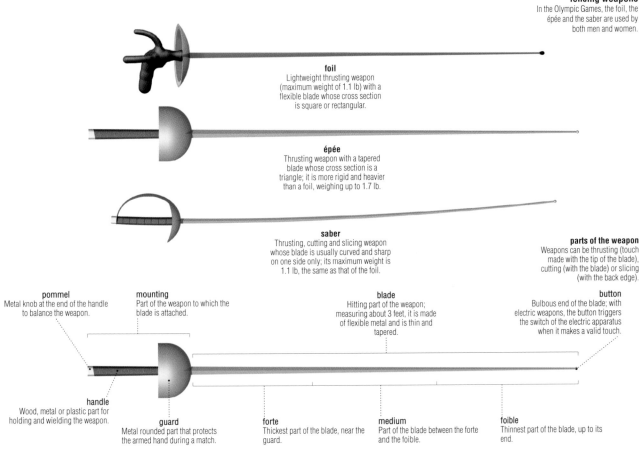

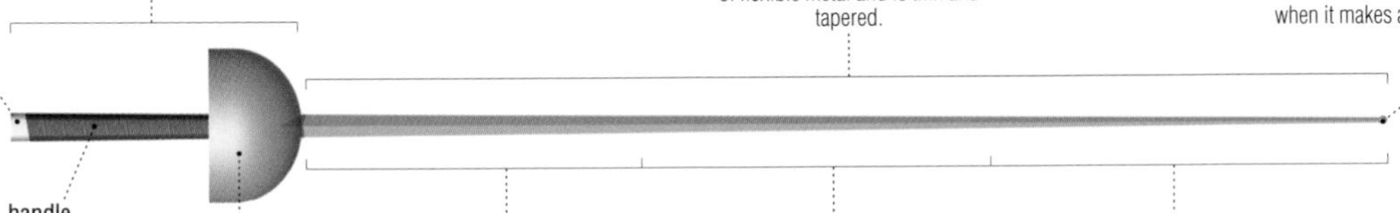

handle
Wood, metal or plastic part for holding and wielding the weapon.

guard
Metal rounded part that protects the armed hand during a match.

forte
Thickest part of the blade, near the guard.

medium
Part of the blade between the forte and the foible.

foible
Thinnest part of the blade, up to its end.

weightlifting

Sport that consists of lifting the heaviest load possible (barbell) over the head using two types of lifts (clean and jerk; snatch).

barbell
Gym equipment made up of cast-iron disks of various weights attached in equal weights to each end of a long bar, which is lifted with two hands.

wristband
Band of fabric that is 4 in wide or less and is worn around the wrist to support it when lifting.

weightlifting belt
Girdle that is 5 in wide or less and supports the dorsal and abdominal muscles during lifting.

sleeveless jersey
Tight top that covers the torso while leaving the shoulders free; a T-shirt may be worn under the jersey.

trunks
Tight shorts that end above the knees.

knee wrap
Band of fabric 1 ft wide or less that is worn around the knee to support it when lifting.

strap
Adjustable band for tightening the shoe around the foot.

weightlifting shoe
Shoe with an antiskid sole and raised heel that stabilizes the foot during lifting.

clean and jerk
Type of lift that is executed in two stages; the bar is first raised to shoulder level (clean) and then quickly raised over the head (jerk), using the leg muscles.

snatch
Type of lift that is more difficult than the clean and jerk; it consists of raising the load over the head as high as possible in a continuous quick movement.

fitness equipment

Material and apparatuses for carrying out exercises aimed at maintaining the physique and increasing muscular strength, flexibility and endurance.

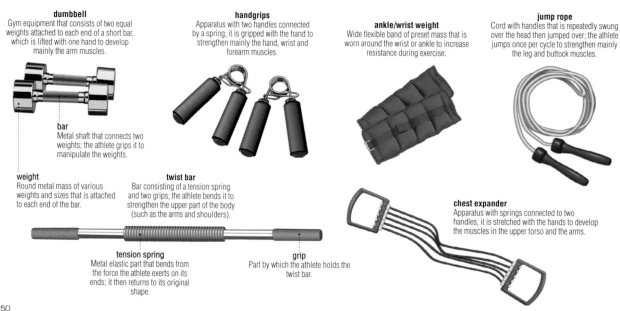

dumbbell
Gym equipment that consists of two equal weights attached to each end of a short bar, which is lifted with one hand to develop mainly the arm muscles.

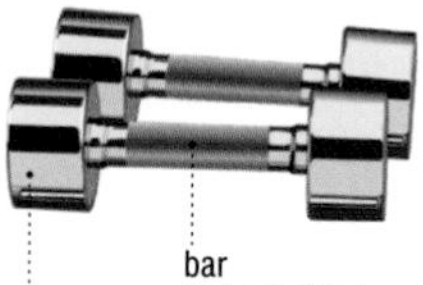

bar
Metal shaft that connects two weights; the athlete grips it to manipulate the weights.

weight
Round metal mass of various weights and sizes that is attached to each end of the bar.

handgrips
Apparatus with two handles connected by a spring; it is gripped with the hand to strengthen mainly the hand, wrist and forearm muscles.

ankle/wrist weight
Wide flexible band of preset mass that is worn around the wrist or ankle to increase resistance during exercise.

jump rope
Cord with handles that is repeatedly swung over the head then jumped over; the athlete jumps once per cycle to strengthen mainly the leg and buttock muscles.

twist bar
Bar consisting of a tension spring and two grips; the athlete bends it to strengthen the upper part of the body (such as the arms and shoulders).

tension spring
Metal elastic part that bends from the force the athlete exerts on its ends; it then returns to its original shape.

grip
Part by which the athlete holds the twist bar.

chest expander
Apparatus with springs connected to two handles; it is stretched with the hands to develop the muscles in the upper torso and the arms.

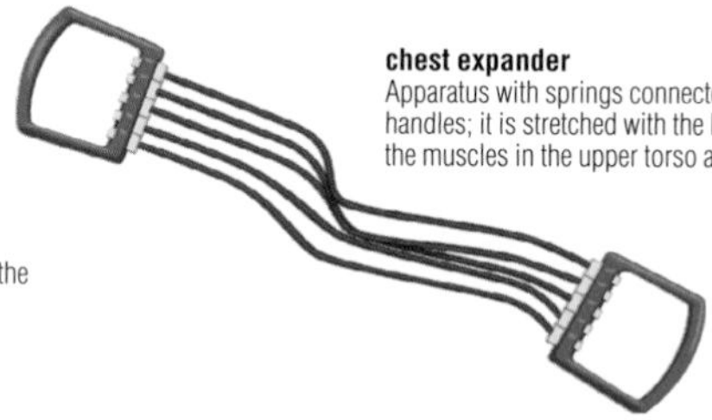

SPORTS AND GAMES

fitness equipment

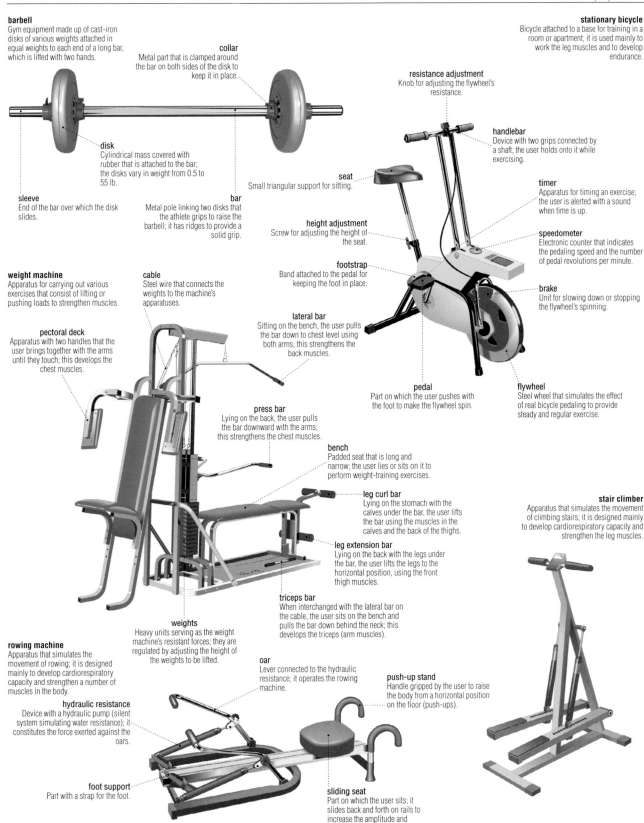

barbell
Gym equipment made up of cast-iron disks of various weights attached in equal weights to each end of a long bar, which is lifted with two hands.

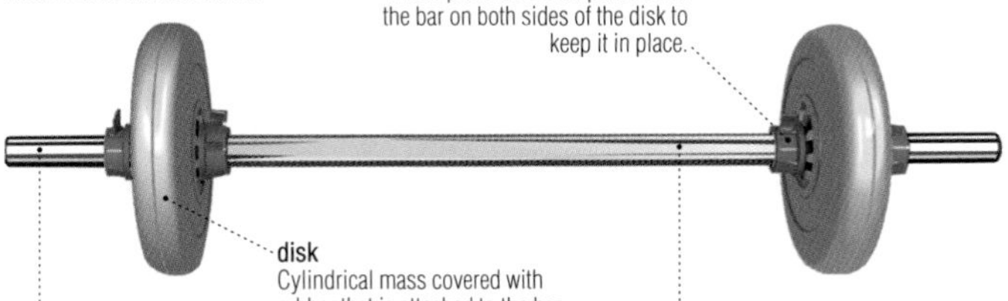

collar
Metal part that is clamped around the bar on both sides of the disk to keep it in place.

disk
Cylindrical mass covered with rubber that is attached to the bar; the disks vary in weight from 0.5 to 55 lb.

sleeve
End of the bar over which the disk slides.

bar
Metal pole linking two disks that the athlete grips to raise the barbell; it has ridges to provide a solid grip.

stationary bicycle
Bicycle attached to a base for training in a room or apartment; it is used mainly to work the leg muscles and to develop endurance.

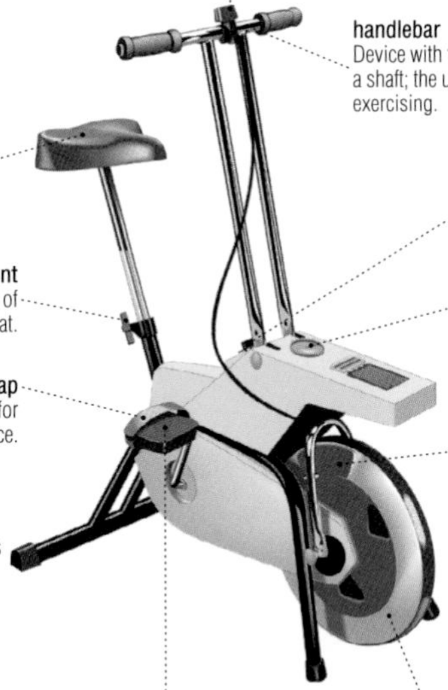

resistance adjustment
Knob for adjusting the flywheel's resistance.

handlebar
Device with two grips connected by a shaft; the user holds onto it while exercising.

seat
Small triangular support for sitting.

timer
Apparatus for timing an exercise; the user is alerted with a sound when time is up.

height adjustment
Screw for adjusting the height of the seat.

speedometer
Electronic counter that indicates the pedaling speed and the number of pedal revolutions per minute.

footstrap
Band attached to the pedal for keeping the foot in place.

brake
Unit for slowing down or stopping the flywheel's spinning.

pedal
Part on which the user pushes with the foot to make the flywheel spin.

flywheel
Steel wheel that simulates the effect of real bicycle pedaling to provide steady and regular exercise.

weight machine
Apparatus for carrying out various exercises that consist of lifting or pushing loads to strengthen muscles.

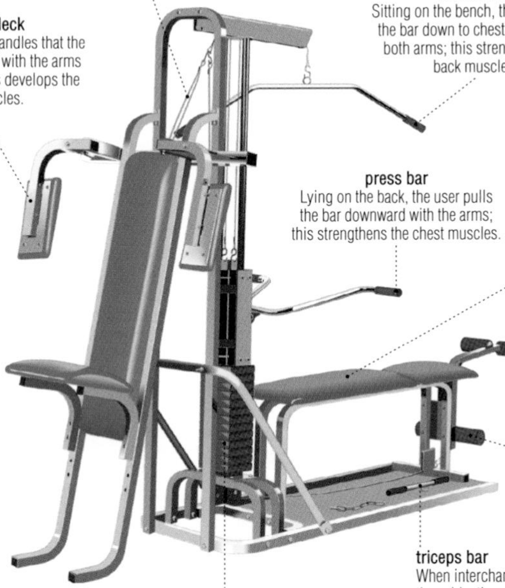

cable
Steel wire that connects the weights to the machine's apparatuses.

pectoral deck
Apparatus with two handles that the user brings together with the arms until they touch; this develops the chest muscles.

lateral bar
Sitting on the bench, the user pulls the bar down to chest level using both arms; this strengthens the back muscles.

press bar
Lying on the back, the user pulls the bar downward with the arms; this strengthens the chest muscles.

bench
Padded seat that is long and narrow; the user lies or sits on it to perform weight-training exercises.

leg curl bar
Lying on the stomach with the calves under the bar, the user lifts the bar using the muscles in the calves and the back of the thighs.

leg extension bar
Lying on the back with the legs under the bar, the user lifts the legs to the horizontal position, using the front thigh muscles.

triceps bar
When interchanged with the lateral bar on the cable, the user sits on the bench and pulls the bar down behind the neck; this develops the triceps (arm muscles).

weights
Heavy units serving as the weight machine's resistant forces; they are regulated by adjusting the height of the weights to be lifted.

stair climber
Apparatus that simulates the movement of climbing stairs; it is designed mainly to develop cardiorespiratory capacity and strengthen the leg muscles.

rowing machine
Apparatus that simulates the movement of rowing; it is designed mainly to develop cardiorespiratory capacity and strengthen a number of muscles in the body.

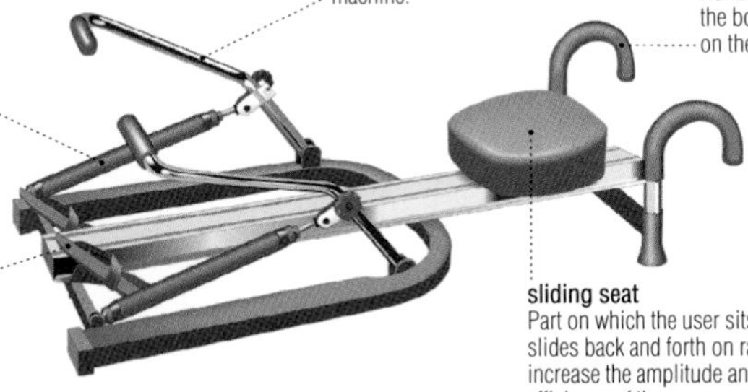

oar
Lever connected to the hydraulic resistance; it operates the rowing machine.

hydraulic resistance
Device with a hydraulic pump (silent system simulating water resistance); it constitutes the force exerted against the oars.

push-up stand
Handle gripped by the user to raise the body from a horizontal position on the floor (push-ups).

foot support
Part with a strap for the foot.

sliding seat
Part on which the user sits; it slides back and forth on rails to increase the amplitude and efficiency of the oars.

show-jumping

Competition during which a horse and its rider clear a series of different obstacles on a set course as quickly as possible.

obstacles
Elements that the horse and rider must clear during a competition; a penalty is given when the animal upsets one of the movable components of an obstacle.

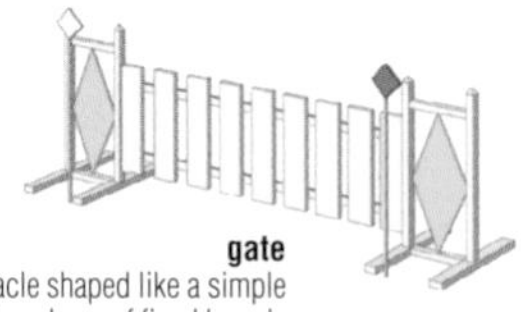

gate
Obstacle shaped like a simple fence and made up of fixed boards laid side by side.

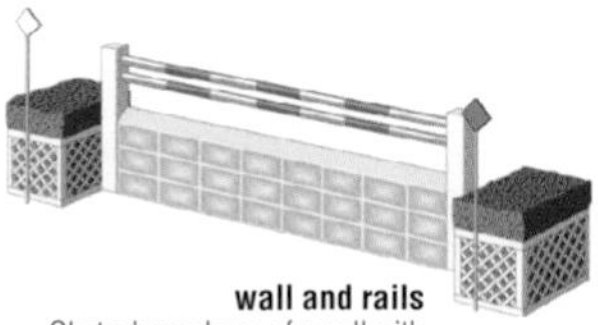

wall and rails
Obstacle made up of a wall with one or two movable bars on top.

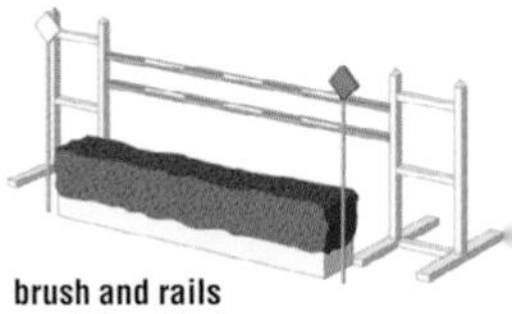

brush and rails
Obstacle composed of a vertical component with a hedge in front.

post and plank
Obstacle composed of wide movable boards (planks) that are laid one on top of another; planks are less stable than bars.

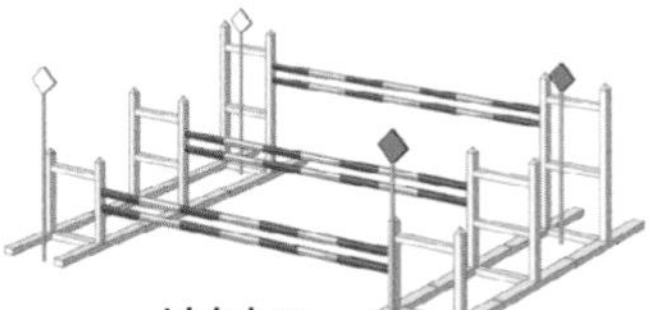

triple bars
Three-part obstacle composed of movable parallel bars; each successive obstacle increases in height.

post and rail
Obstacle composed of a set of movable bars that are laid one on top of another.

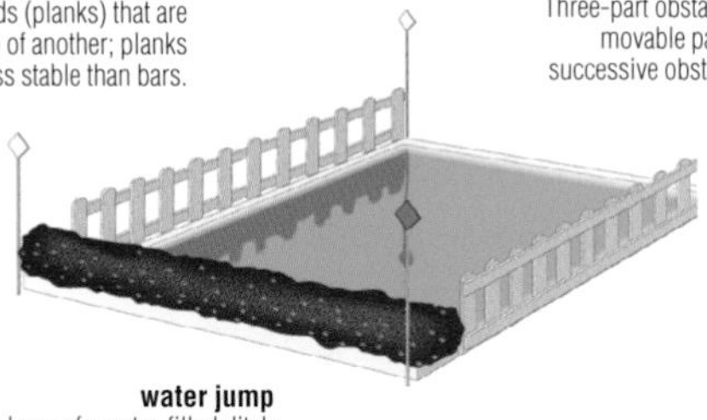

water jump
Obstacle made up of a water-filled ditch with a hedge in front; the horse commits a fault if it touches the water or the lath marking the end of the river.

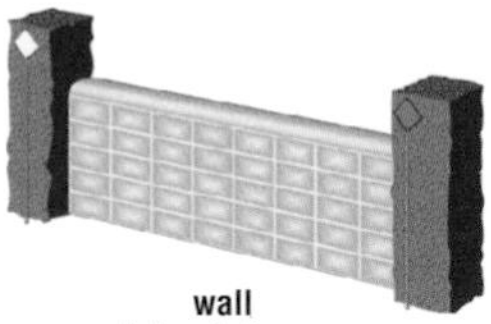

wall
Obstacle composed of a set of usually wooden, stacking blocks; the top of the wall is rounded to prevent the horses from being hurt.

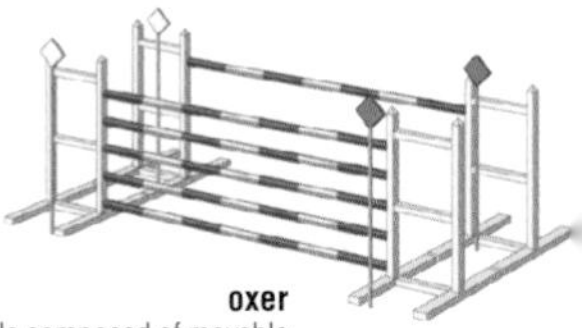

oxer
Two-part obstacle composed of movable parallel bars; there are two designs, one of identical heights (square oxer) and one of different heights (jumping oxer).

competition ring
Closed terrain marked with 12 to 15 obstacles that the horse and rider must clear in a set order while committing the fewest faults possible.

wall
Obstacle composed of a set of usually wooden, stacking blocks; the top of the wall is rounded to prevent the horses from being hurt.

post and plank
Obstacle composed of wide movable boards (planks) that are laid one on top of another; planks are less stable than bars.

combination
Set of two or more obstacles that are grouped together and count as a single obstacle; each of its obstacles must be cleared separately.

obstacle steward
Person in charge of righting the upset obstacles.

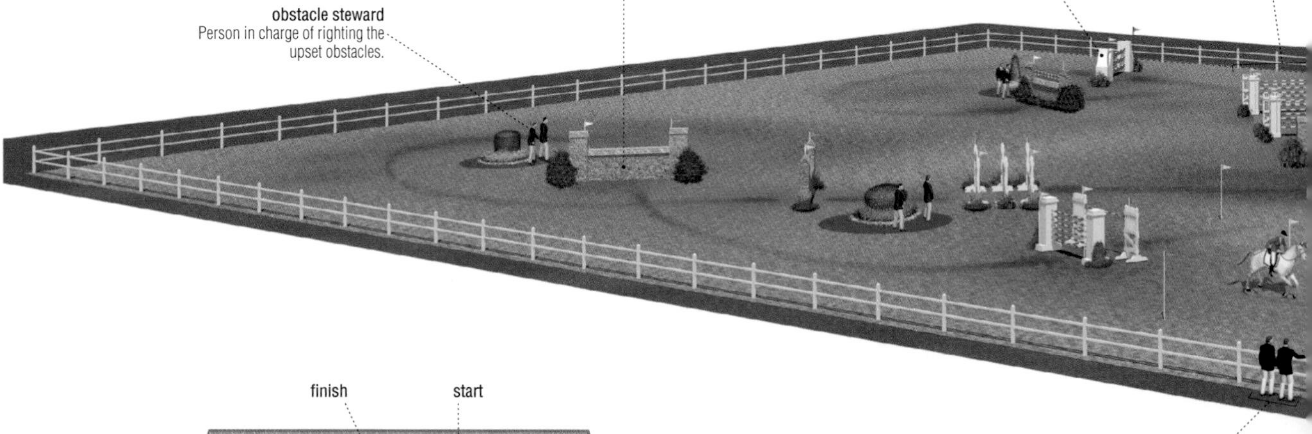

veterinarians
Doctors who treat animals; they examine the horses before the competition and may intervene in the event of injury.

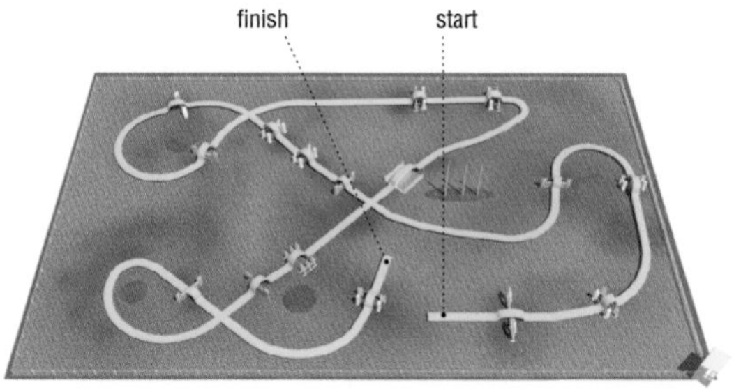

show-jumping

riding jacket
The rider's long dark-colored jacket; it is usually worn over a white shirt and a white tie.
riding cap
Reinforced hat that is traditionally covered with black velvet; it protects the rider's head against impact.
jodhpurs
Usually light-colored long pants that are very tight over the knees and legs and are kept stretched by foot straps.
saddle
Somewhat curved unit that is made mostly of leather; it is set on the horse's back for the rider to sit on.
rider
Person riding a horse; during a jump, the rider leans toward the horse's neck with the feet supported by the stirrups.
riding glove
Covering for the hand and wrist that takes the shape of the fingers; it provides a good grip on the reins and protects the hands from chafing.
saddlecloth
Padded part that is placed under the saddle to protect the horse's back from chafing; it also protects the saddle from the horse's sweat.
riding crop
Thin flexible stick that the rider uses to spur on the horse.
stirrup iron
Metal ring that hangs from each side of the saddle to support the rider's feet.
breastplate
Strap around the horse's chest that prevents the saddle from sliding back.
shin boot
Equipment placed around the cannon of the horse's leg to protect it from injury.
girth
Strap around the horse's belly that keeps the saddle on its back.
coronet boot
Usually rubber item of equipment that covers the horse's hoof to prevent injury.

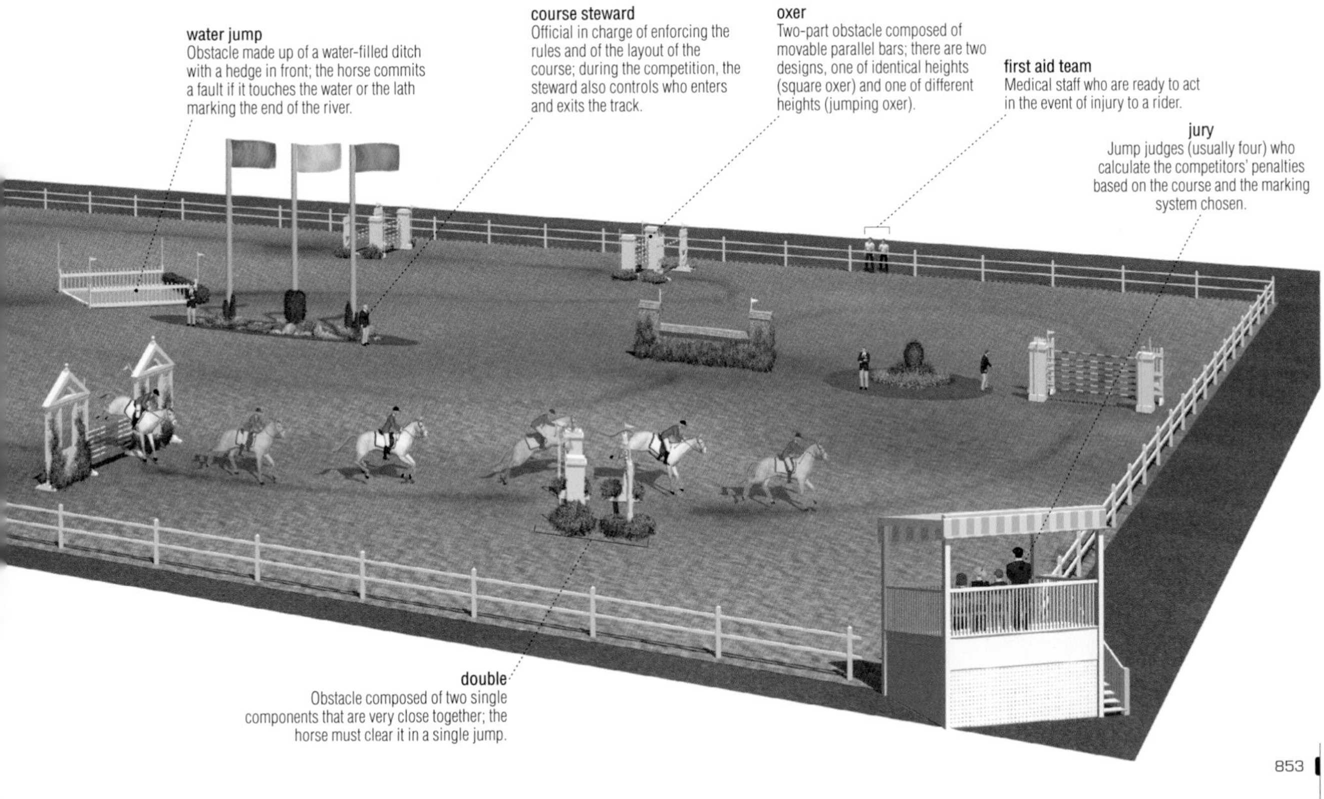
water jump
Obstacle made up of a water-filled ditch with a hedge in front; the horse commits a fault if it touches the water or the lath marking the end of the river.
course steward
Official in charge of enforcing the rules and of the layout of the course; during the competition, the steward also controls who enters and exits the track.
oxer
Two-part obstacle composed of movable parallel bars; there are two designs, one of identical heights (square oxer) and one of different heights (jumping oxer).
first aid team
Medical staff who are ready to act in the event of injury to a rider.
jury
Jump judges (usually four) who calculate the competitors' penalties based on the course and the marking system chosen.
double
Obstacle composed of two single components that are very close together; the horse must clear it in a single jump.

riding

Sport or recreation that consists of riding a horse; specialized equipment is necessary for steering and controlling the horse.

bridle
Head harness that enables the rider to steer a horse by using one or two bits in the horse's mouth, which are connected to the reins.

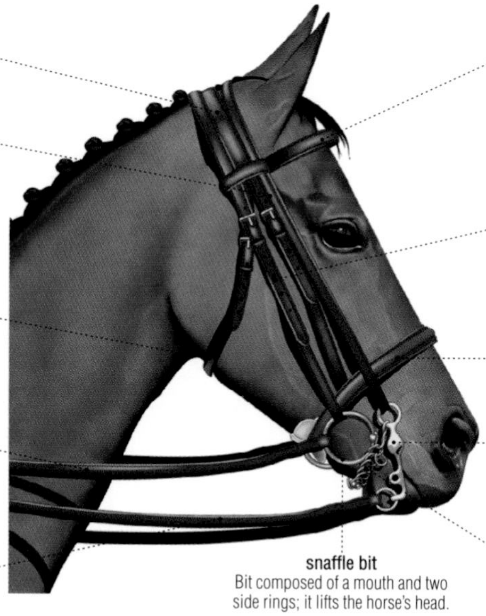

crownpiece
Strap that runs over the horse's head behind the ears; it keeps the snaffle and cheek straps in place.

cheek strap
Strap that runs along the horse's cheek and connects the crownpiece to the curb bit; it keeps the bit in the desired place in the horse's mouth.

throat latch
Strap that runs under the horse's throat to prevent the bridle from sliding forward; it must be loose enough to allow the horse to breathe freely.

snaffle rein
Strap that the rider holds to control the snaffle bit and thus steer the horse.

curb rein
Strap that the rider holds to control the curb bit and thus steer the horse.

snaffle bit
Bit composed of a mouth and two side rings; it lifts the horse's head.

browband
Strap that runs around the front of the horse's head; it prevents the bridle from sliding backward.

snaffle strap
Strap that runs along the horse's cheek and connects the crownpiece to the snaffle bit; it keeps the bit in the desired place in the horse's mouth.

noseband
Part of the bridle that runs around the head above the nostrils; it prevents the horse from opening its mouth and losing the bit.

curb bit
Bit composed of a mouth and two side bars; it lowers the horse's nose.

curb chain
Metal chain that hangs from the cheek rings and passes under the horse's jaw to secure the bit.

snaffle bit

Bit composed of a mouth and two side rings; it lifts the horse's head.

jointed mouth
Part composed of two articulated bars that is placed in the horse's mouth; it is controlled by the reins to steer the animal.

rein ring
Round part attached to the end of the mouth; the snaffle rein is attached to it.

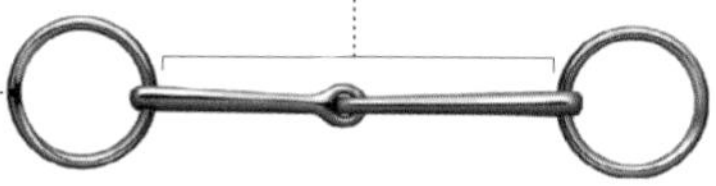

rubber snaffle bit
Bit made up of a straight mouth, which is covered with rubber; it is softer than steel and reduces the pressure of the bit on the horse's mouth.

egg butt snaffle bit
Bit composed of two fixed oval rings; it is designed to prevent injury to the corners of the horse's mouth.

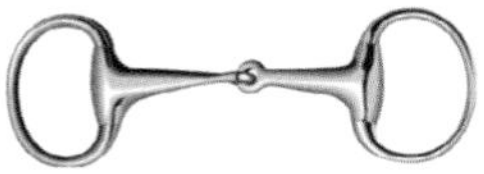

full cheek snaffle bit
Mouth with two side bars preventing the rings from entering the horse's mouth, while relaying clear signals through the reins.

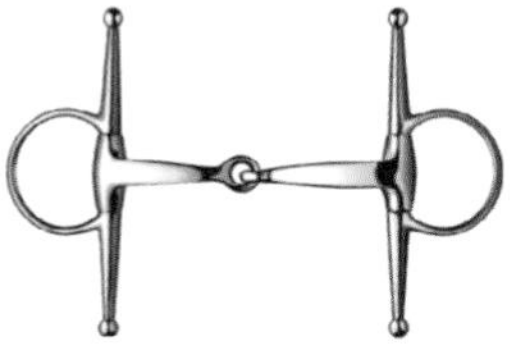

full cheek snaffle bit with toggles
Bit whose mouth has toggles, which make the horse relax its jaws.

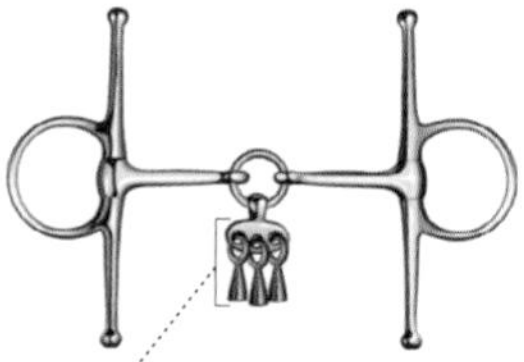

toggles
Metal chains that hang from the middle of the mouth; the horse tends to play with these parts, which makes it relax its jaws.

curb bit

Bit composed of a mouth and two side bars; it lowers the horse's nose.

port
Curvature of the mouth that is designed to reduce the pressure exerted by the bit on the horse's tongue.

upper cheek
Upper part of the bar that holds the mouth.

curb chain
Metal chain that hangs from the cheek rings and passes under the horse's jaw to secure the bit.

rein ring
Round part that is attached to the end of the lower cheek; the curb rein is attached to it.

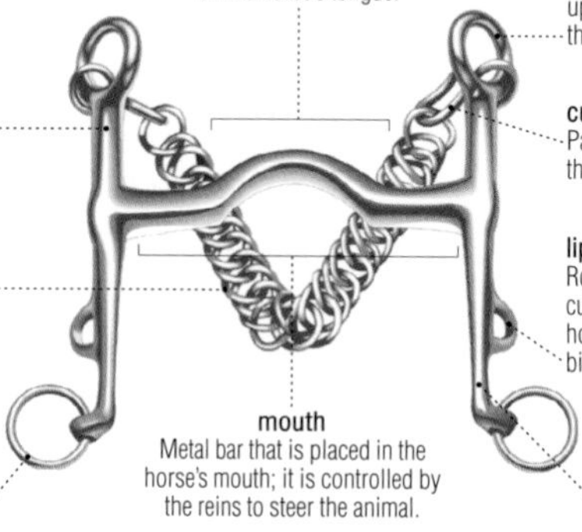

mouth
Metal bar that is placed in the horse's mouth; it is controlled by the reins to steer the animal.

cheek ring
Round part forming the end of the upper cheek; the curb chain and the cheek strap are attached to it.

curb hook
Part that connects the curb chain to the cheek ring.

lip strap ring
Round part for attaching a false curb chain (strap preventing the horse from seizing the arms of the bit's mouth with its mouth).

lower cheek
Lower part of the bar that holds the mouth; it is usually longer than the upper cheek.

sliding cheek bit
Bit whose mouth slides up and down the cheeks; this action is gentler to the horse but provides slightly less control.

jointed mouth bit
Curb bit whose mouth is composed of two articulated parts; it is gentler to the horse than a straight mouth bit.

Liverpool bit
Bit that can be used alone; it combines the characteristics of the snaffle and curb bits.

riding

saddle
Somewhat curved unit that is made mostly of leather; it is set on the horse's back for the rider to sit on.

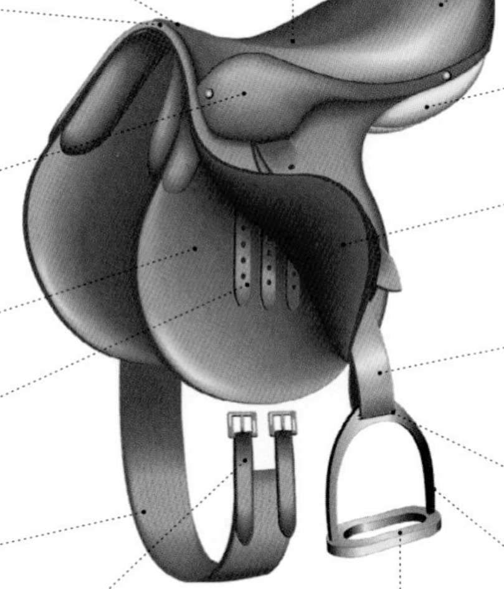

pommel
Front part of the saddle that is slightly rounded; the rider can hold onto it with the hand.
seat
Slightly concave part of the saddle on which the rider sits.
cantle
Back part of the saddle that is rounded slightly upward to support the lower back.
tree
Curved part under the pommel that is traditionally made of wood; it forms the front part of the saddle's framework.
panel
Padding for the saddle that is designed to dampen impact and protect the horse's back.
skirt
Piece of leather that is attached to the flap; it covers the stirrup leather buckles.
flap
Piece of leather that covers the knee roll and the tabs; the rider's thighs press against it.
knee roll
Piece of leather that forms the side of the saddle; it mainly protects the horse from the girth strap buckles.
stirrup leather
Adjustable strap that hangs from the saddle to support the stirrup iron.
tab
Belt with small holes that is attached to the knee roll; the girth strap is buckled to it.
eye
Slot in the top part of the stirrup iron through which the stirrup leather passes.
girth
Strap around the horse's belly that keeps the saddle on its back.
branch
One of two metal arms that connect the tread to the eye.
girth strap
Small belt that is attached to the end of the girth; it has a buckle for attaching it to the tab to tighten it.
tread
Lower part of the stirrup iron where the rider's foot is placed.

dressage

Discipline in which a rider takes a horse through a series of freestyle or school figures, called tests, on a ring especially designed for the purpose.

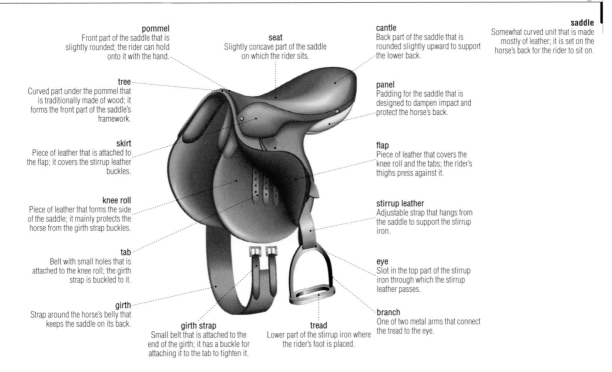

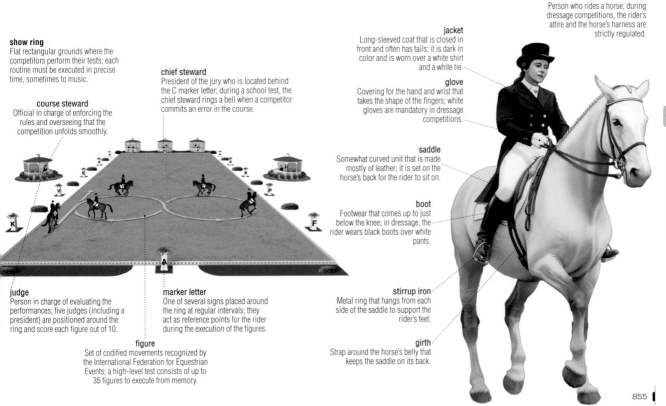

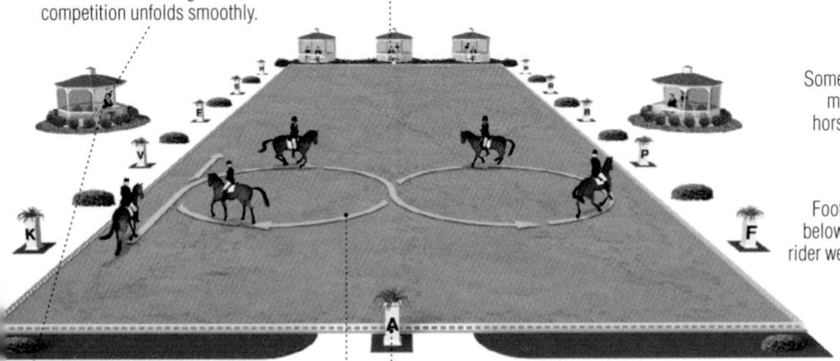

show ring
Flat rectangular grounds where the competitors perform their tests; each routine must be executed in precise time, sometimes to music.
chief steward
President of the jury who is located behind the C marker letter; during a school test, the chief steward rings a bell when a competitor commits an error in the course.
course steward
Official in charge of enforcing the rules and overseeing that the competition unfolds smoothly.
E
B
V
P
K
F
A
judge
Person in charge of evaluating the performances; five judges (including a president) are positioned around the ring and score each figure out of 10.
marker letter
One of several signs placed around the ring at regular intervals; they act as reference points for the rider during the execution of the figures.
figure
Set of codified movements recognized by the International Federation for Equestrian Events; a high-level test consists of up to 35 figures to execute from memory.

rider
Person who rides a horse; during dressage competitions, the rider's attire and the horse's harness are strictly regulated.
jacket
Long-sleeved coat that is closed in front and often has tails; it is dark in color and is worn over a white shirt and a white tie.
glove
Covering for the hand and wrist that takes the shape of the fingers; white gloves are mandatory in dressage competitions.
saddle
Somewhat curved unit that is made mostly of leather; it is set on the horse's back for the rider to sit on.
boot
Footwear that comes up to just below the knee; in dressage, the rider wears black boots over white pants.
stirrup iron
Metal ring that hangs from each side of the saddle to support the rider's feet.
girth
Strap around the horse's belly that keeps the saddle on its back.

horse racing: turf

Speed race on a track where jockeys ride horses, usually at a gallop.

jockey
Person who rides a racehorse; a jockey rides with very short stirrups and the body hunched over the horse's neck.

riding cap
Hard piece of equipment designed to protect the head.

shadow roll
Part that blocks the horse's view of the ground; this prevents the horse from mistaking shadows for obstacles to jump over.

saddle
Slightly curved part that is usually made of leather; it is laid on the horse's back for the jockey to sit on.

rein
Strap that the jockey holds to control the bit to steer the horse.

saddlecloth
Padded piece of cloth underneath the saddle that protects the horse's back from chafing and protects the saddle from the horse's sweat.

riding crop
Thin flexible stick that the rider uses to spur on the horse.

girth
Strap around the horse's belly that keeps the saddle on its back.

racetrack
Place that is designed for horse races; it is made up of an oval track (flat or with obstacles) and stands.

length post
Markers that are placed at regular intervals along the track so that jockeys can assess the distance still to cover.

judge's stand
Space reserved for the track judges who establish the horses' order of arrival at the finish line, using the videotape if necessary.

far turn
Last turn; the homestretch begins at the exit from it.

tote board
Display board that shows the various data on the race (such as class and betting information); it sometimes has a giant screen.

backstretch
Straight part on the side opposite the stands.

stable
Building where the horses are boarded and cared for.

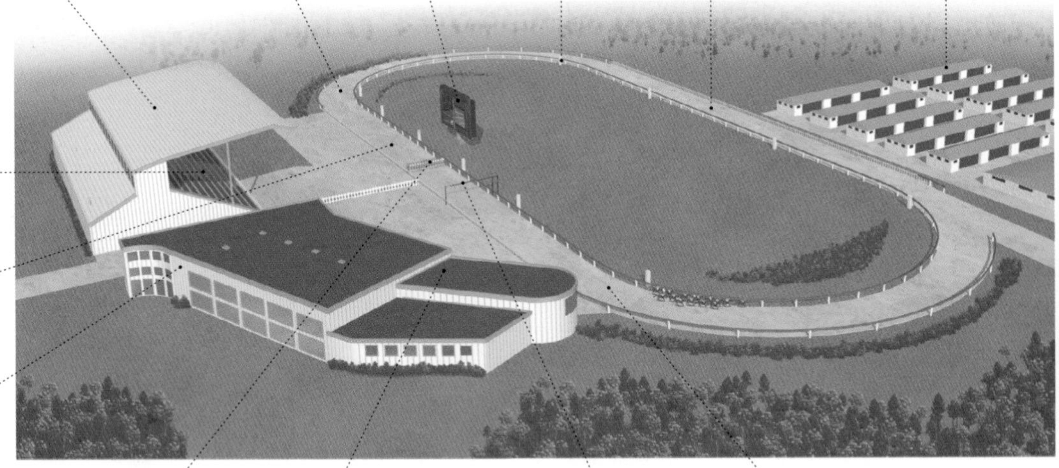

grandstand
Space reserved for spectators.

homestretch
Straight line between the far turn and the finish line; it constitutes the last sprint before the end of the race.

clubhouse
Building that houses various services such as bar, restaurant, glassed-in stands and betting booths.

starting gate
Mobile, compartmentalized barrier behind which the horses line up before the start; at a signal, all the compartment gates open at the same time.

paddock
Area where the horses and their jockeys are presented to the public before a race.

finish line
Line that marks the end of a race; a video camera helps identify the winner when the horses are bunched very close together.

clubhouse turn
First turn after the start and near the clubhouse; the jockeys try to position their horses on the inside track to reduce the distance to cover.

horse racing: harness racing

Speed race on a track for trotters or standardbred pacers harnessed to sulkies.

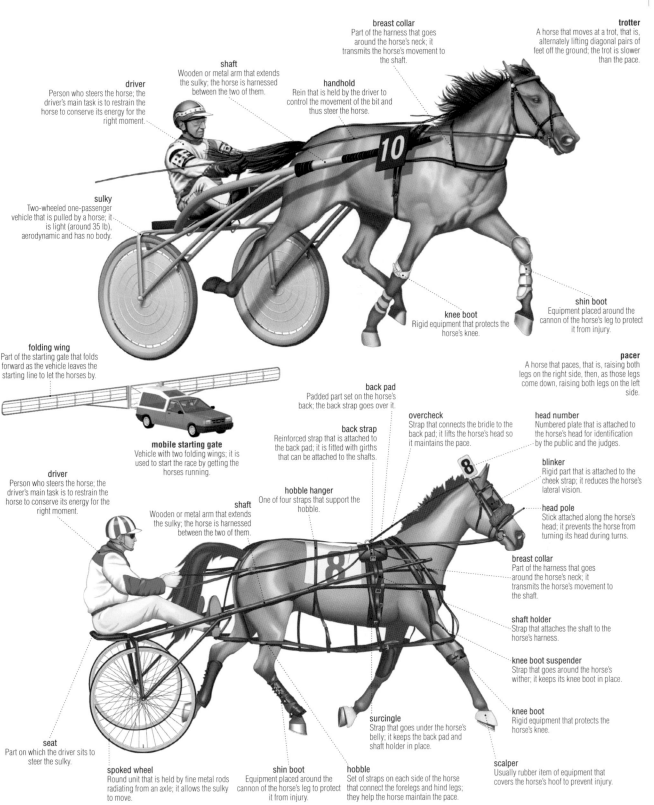

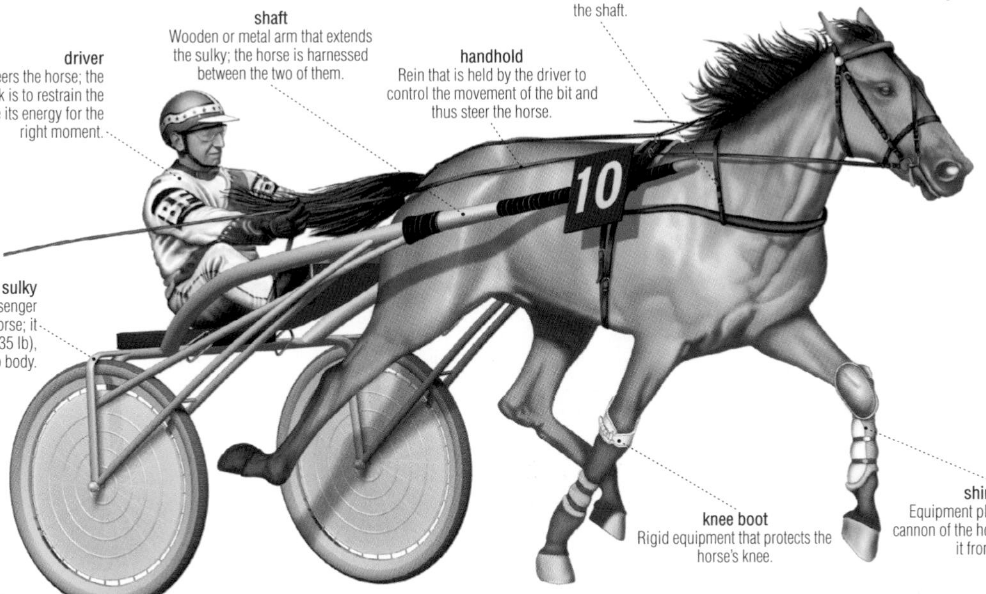
breast collar
Part of the harness that goes around the horse's neck; it transmits the horse's movement to the shaft.
trotter
A horse that moves at a trot, that is, alternately lifting diagonal pairs of feet off the ground; the trot is slower than the pace.
shaft
Wooden or metal arm that extends the sulky; the horse is harnessed between the two of them.
driver
Person who steers the horse; the driver's main task is to restrain the horse to conserve its energy for the right moment.
handhold
Rein that is held by the driver to control the movement of the bit and thus steer the horse.
10
sulky
Two-wheeled one-passenger vehicle that is pulled by a horse; it is light (around 35 lb), aerodynamic and has no body.
knee boot
Rigid equipment that protects the horse's knee.
shin boot
Equipment placed around the cannon of the horse's leg to protect it from injury.

folding wing
Part of the starting gate that folds forward as the vehicle leaves the starting line to let the horses by.
mobile starting gate
Vehicle with two folding wings; it is used to start the race by getting the horses running.

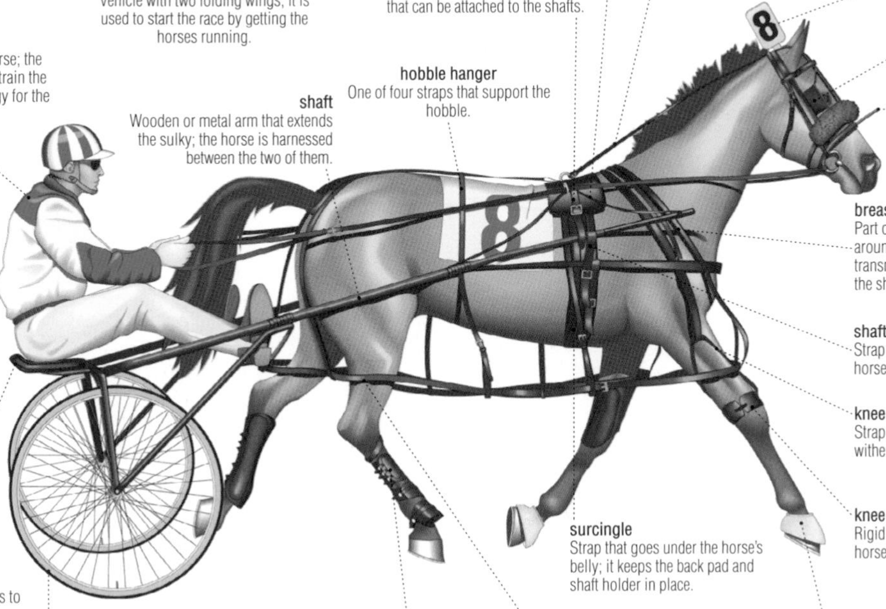
pacer
A horse that paces, that is, raising both legs on the right side, then, as those legs come down, raising both legs on the left side.
back pad
Padded part set on the horse's back; the back strap goes over it.
overcheck
Strap that connects the bridle to the back pad; it lifts the horse's head so it maintains the pace.
head number
Numbered plate that is attached to the horse's head for identification by the public and the judges.
back strap
Reinforced strap that is attached to the back pad; it is fitted with girths that can be attached to the shafts.
blinker
Rigid part that is attached to the cheek strap; it reduces the horse's lateral vision.
driver
Person who steers the horse; the driver's main task is to restrain the horse to conserve its energy for the right moment.
hobble hanger
One of four straps that support the hobble.
shaft
Wooden or metal arm that extends the sulky; the horse is harnessed between the two of them.
head pole
Stick attached along the horse's head; it prevents the horse from turning its head during turns.
8
breast collar
Part of the harness that goes around the horse's neck; it transmits the horse's movement to the shaft.
shaft holder
Strap that attaches the shaft to the horse's harness.
knee boot suspender
Strap that goes around the horse's wither; it keeps its knee boot in place.
knee boot
Rigid equipment that protects the horse's knee.
surcingle
Strap that goes under the horse's belly; it keeps the back pad and shaft holder in place.
seat
Part on which the driver sits to steer the sulky.
scalper
Usually rubber item of equipment that covers the horse's hoof to prevent injury.
spoked wheel
Round unit that is held by fine metal rods radiating from an axle; it allows the sulky to move.
shin boot
Equipment placed around the cannon of the horse's leg to protect it from injury.
hobble
Set of straps on each side of the horse that connect the forelegs and hind legs; they help the horse maintain the pace.

polo

Sport with two opposing teams of four riders who play on a level field; they try to score points through the opponents' goal by hitting a ball along the ground with a mallet.

rider and horse
The players ride horses whose manes are shaved and tails plaited to avoid catching; the players also change horses at every chukker (period).

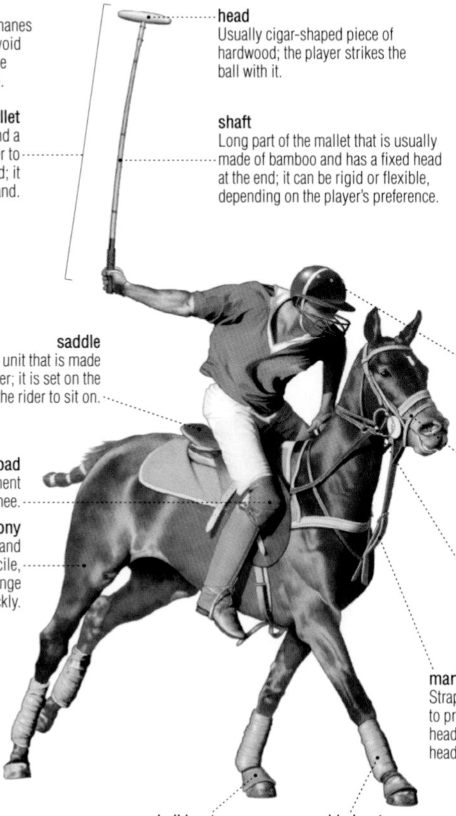

mallet
Part consisting of a shaft and a head that is used by the player to hit the ball along the ground; it must be held in the right hand.

head
Usually cigar-shaped piece of hardwood; the player strikes the ball with it.

shaft
Long part of the mallet that is usually made of bamboo and has a fixed head at the end; it can be rigid or flexible, depending on the player's preference.

saddle
Somewhat curved unit that is made mostly of leather; it is set on the horse's back for the rider to sit on.

knee pad
Hard leather piece of equipment that protects the rider's knee.

polo pony
Small horse that is bred and schooled for polo; calm and docile, it can start, stop and change directions very quickly.

helmet
Rigid piece of equipment that protects the rider's head; it usually has a protective grille.

noseband
Part of the bridle that runs around the head above the nostrils; it prevents the horse from opening its mouth and losing the bit.

bit
Device that is inserted in the horse's mouth; the rider steers the horse using the reins, which in turn move the bit in the horse's mouth.

martingale
Strap that is connected to the noseband to prevent the horse from throwing its head back; this prevents blows to its head during abrupt stops.

bell boot
Usually rubber item of equipment that covers the horse's hoof to prevent injury.

shin boot
Equipment placed around the cannon of the horse's leg to protect it from injury.

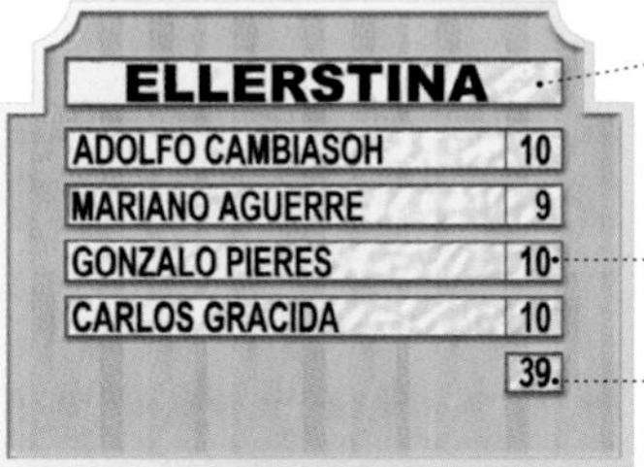

team name

player handicap
Index of skill assigned to each player on a scale from -2 to 10; a player with a handicap of 4 may play in international matches.

team handicap
Sum of the handicaps of all the players on the team; the team with the lowest handicap begins a match with a head start in goals.

handicaps board
Panel that displays the handicaps of the players and the teams.

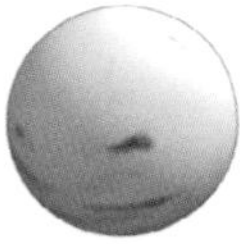

ball
White sphere of wood or plastic with a diameter of 3 to 3.5 in.

time clock
Apparatus that measures time, for managing a chukker's duration.

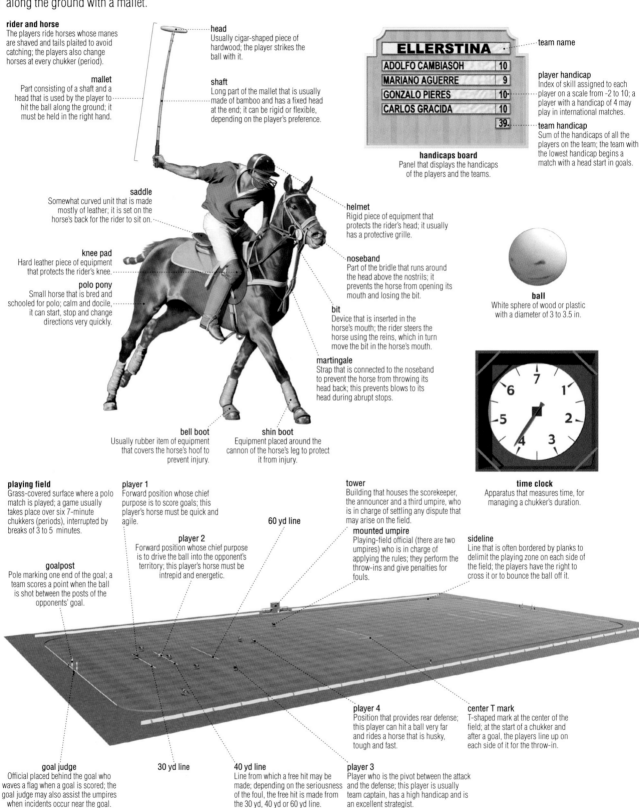

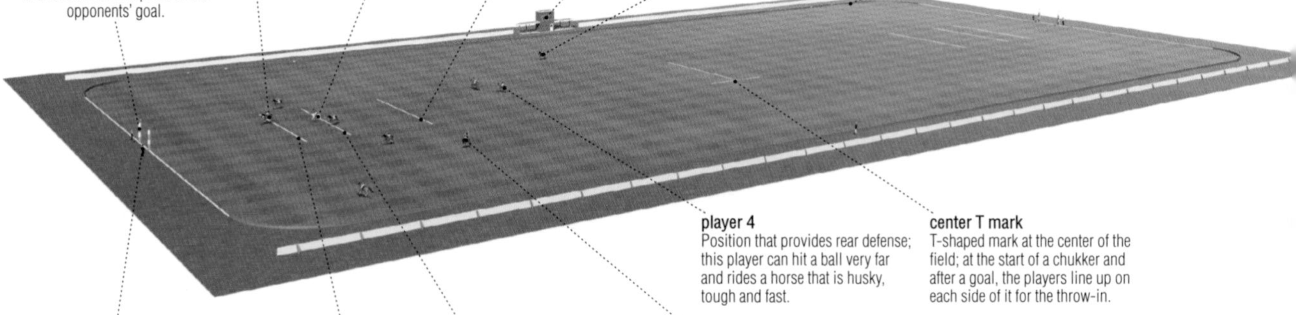

playing field
Grass-covered surface where a polo match is played; a game usually takes place over six 7-minute chukkers (periods), interrupted by breaks of 3 to 5 minutes.

player 1
Forward position whose chief purpose is to score goals; this player's horse must be quick and agile.

player 2
Forward position whose chief purpose is to drive the ball into the opponent's territory; this player's horse must be intrepid and energetic.

60 yd line

tower
Building that houses the scorekeeper, the announcer and a third umpire, who is in charge of settling any dispute that may arise on the field.

mounted umpire
Playing-field official (there are two umpires) who is in charge of applying the rules; they perform the throw-ins and give penalties for fouls.

sideline
Line that is often bordered by planks to delimit the playing zone on each side of the field; the players have the right to cross it or to bounce the ball off it.

goalpost
Pole marking one end of the goal; a team scores a point when the ball is shot between the posts of the opponents' goal.

player 4
Position that provides rear defense; this player can hit a ball very far and rides a horse that is husky, tough and fast.

center T mark
T-shaped mark at the center of the field; at the start of a chukker and after a goal, the players line up on each side of it for the throw-in.

goal judge
Official placed behind the goal who waves a flag when a goal is scored; the goal judge may also assist the umpires when incidents occur near the goal.

30 yd line

40 yd line
Line from which a free hit may be made; depending on the seriousness of the foul, the free hit is made from the 30 yd, 40 yd or 60 yd line.

player 3
Player who is the pivot between the attack and the defense; this player is usually team captain, has a high handicap and is an excellent strategist.

archery

Sport that consists of using a bow to shoot an arrow as close as possible to the middle of a target set a fixed distance away.

arrow
Projectile fired by a bow or a crossbow; it consists of a shaft, a point and a heel with a notch and fletching.

shaft
Long rod that makes up the body of the arrow; it is made of carbon fiber or an alloy of aluminum and carbon.

fletching
Feather or synthetic material attached to the base of the arrow to stabilize it during flight.

point
Pointed metal end of the arrow; depending on the power of the bow used, points of different weights are used.

nock
Slot into which the bowstring fits to keep the arrow in place while shooting it.

archer
Person who practices archery.

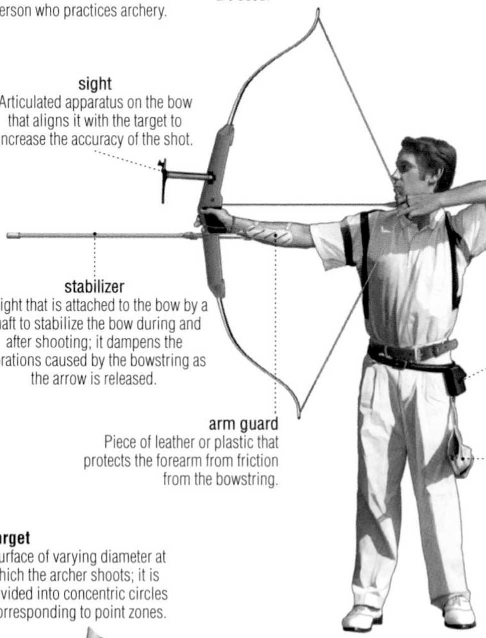

sight
Articulated apparatus on the bow that aligns it with the target to increase the accuracy of the shot.

stabilizer
Weight that is attached to the bow by a shaft to stabilize the bow during and after shooting; it dampens the vibrations caused by the bowstring as the arrow is released.

arm guard
Piece of leather or plastic that protects the forearm from friction from the bowstring.

accessory pouch

quiver
Case that is carried on the back or the hip; the arrows are stored in it during the shoot.

bare bow
Bow made up of a piece of wood and a string that are joined without screws; it is usually very powerful but is less accurate than a compound bow.

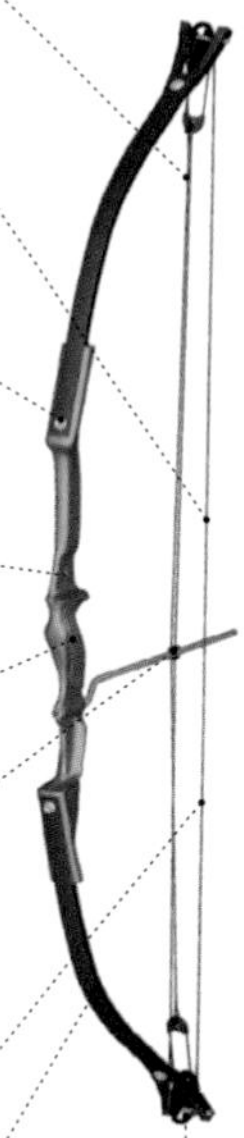

compound bow
Bow that uses a system of cables and wheels to increase its shooting power; it requires less effort on the part of the archer when aiming.

cable
Assembly of steel wires that runs around the wheels to increase the bow's power.

nocking point
Mark on the bowstring where the arrow's nock fits.

mounting bracket
Metal part with a threaded opening; a screw goes into it to attach the limb to the bow's grip.

arrow rest
Part against which the arrow shaft rests as the nock in fitted into the bowstring.

grip
Part between the two limbs that is gripped to manipulate the bow.

cable guard
Part that spreads the bowstring cables apart to prevent them from touching the arrow as the latter is nocked and shot.

bowstring
Fibers secured to a bow that were stretched to fire an arrow.

limb
Flexible part that stores the potential energy as the bow is stretched.

wheel
Small pulley attached to the ends of the limbs; it absorbs part of the force from the shot and it increases the shot's accuracy.

target
Surface of varying diameter at which the archer shoots; it is divided into concentric circles corresponding to point zones.

bull's-eye
Circle 4.8 in in diameter in the middle of the target; it is 4.3 ft from the ground and worth 10 points. The value of the other circles decreases toward the edge of the target.

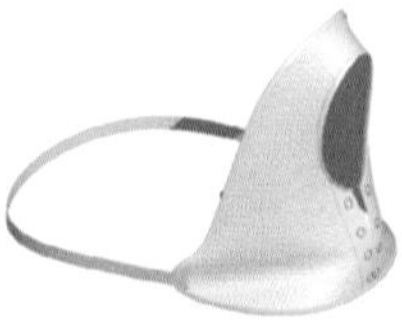

chest protector
Piece of leather or plastic that protects the chest from the friction of the bowstring and flattens the clothing to the body so it does not interfere with the shot.

finger tab
Piece of leather or plastic that protects the archer's fingers from the friction of the bowstring.

shooting range
Outdoor rectangular area that is 110 m long and set up for archery; it is surrounded by an exclusion zone for the protection of the spectators.

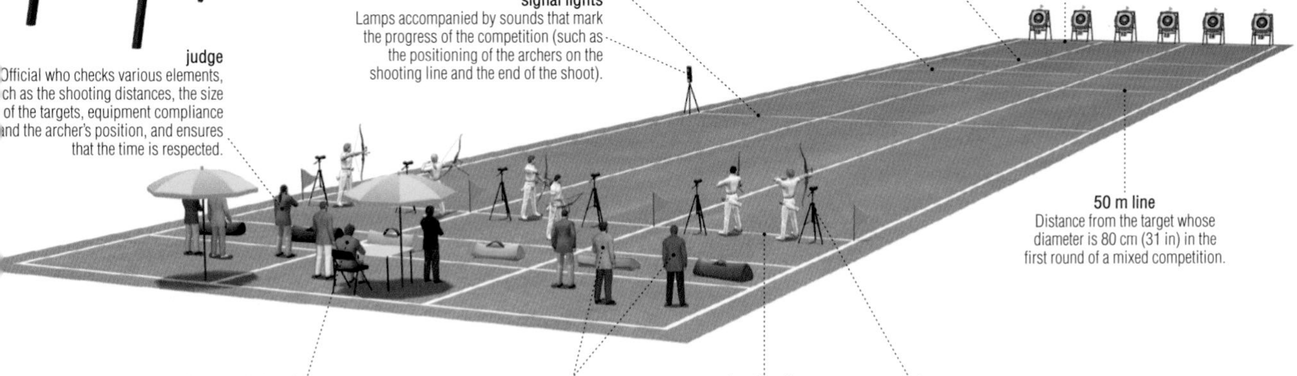

30 m line
Distance from the target whose diameter is 80 cm (31 in) in the first round of a mixed competition.

60 m line
Distance from the target whose diameter is 122 cm (48 in) in the first round of a women's competition.

70 m line
Distance from the target whose diameter is 122 cm (48 in) in the final round of a mixed competition.

90 m line
Distance from the target whose diameter is 122 cm (48 in) in the first round of a men's competition.

signal lights
Lamps accompanied by sounds that mark the progress of the competition (such as the positioning of the archers on the shooting line and the end of the shoot).

judge
Official who checks various elements, ch as the shooting distances, the size of the targets, equipment compliance nd the archer's position, and ensures that the time is respected.

50 m line
Distance from the target whose diameter is 80 cm (31 in) in the first round of a mixed competition.

director of shooting
Official whose responsibilities include monitoring the competition's progress, settling any disputes that may arise and monitoring the shooting time with sound signals.

scorers
Officials who are in charge of registering the points obtained by the archers.

shooting line
Line at which the archer stands to shoot with one foot placed on each side of it.

telescope
Optical instrument whose use is authorized for making out the precise spots where the arrows hit the target.

shotgun shooting

Sport that consists of shooting at a moving target using a shotgun; the gun is loaded with cartridges to destroy the target in flight.

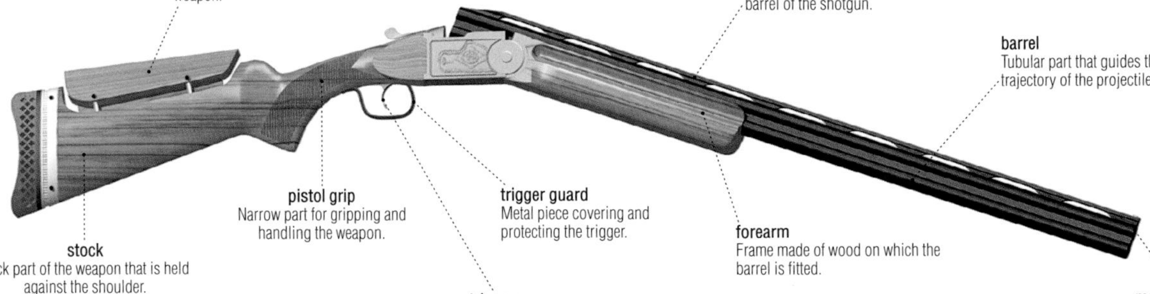

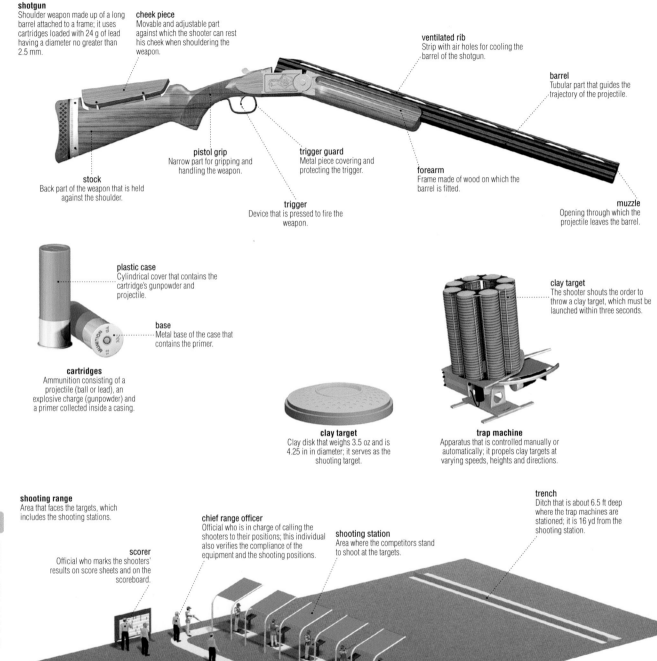

shotgun
Shoulder weapon made up of a long barrel attached to a frame; it uses cartridges loaded with 24 g of lead having a diameter no greater than 2.5 mm.

cheek piece
Movable and adjustable part against which the shooter can rest his cheek when shouldering the weapon.

ventilated rib
Strip with air holes for cooling the barrel of the shotgun.

barrel
Tubular part that guides the trajectory of the projectile.

stock
Back part of the weapon that is held against the shoulder.

pistol grip
Narrow part for gripping and handling the weapon.

trigger guard
Metal piece covering and protecting the trigger.

forearm
Frame made of wood on which the barrel is fitted.

trigger
Device that is pressed to fire the weapon.

muzzle
Opening through which the projectile leaves the barrel.

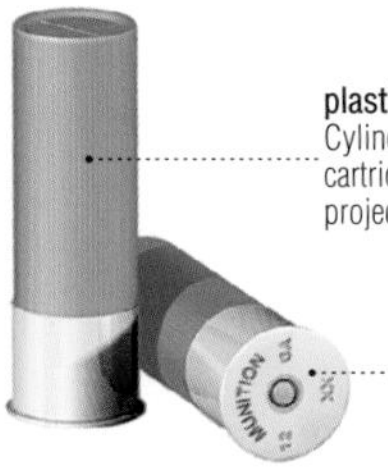

plastic case
Cylindrical cover that contains the cartridge's gunpowder and projectile.

base
Metal base of the case that contains the primer.

cartridges
Ammunition consisting of a projectile (ball or lead), an explosive charge (gunpowder) and a primer collected inside a casing.

clay target
Clay disk that weighs 3.5 oz and is 4.25 in in diameter; it serves as the shooting target.

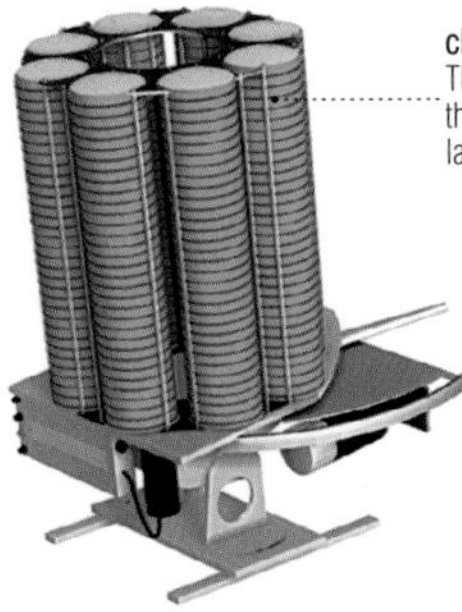

clay target
The shooter shouts the order to throw a clay target, which must be launched within three seconds.

trap machine
Apparatus that is controlled manually or automatically; it propels clay targets at varying speeds, heights and directions.

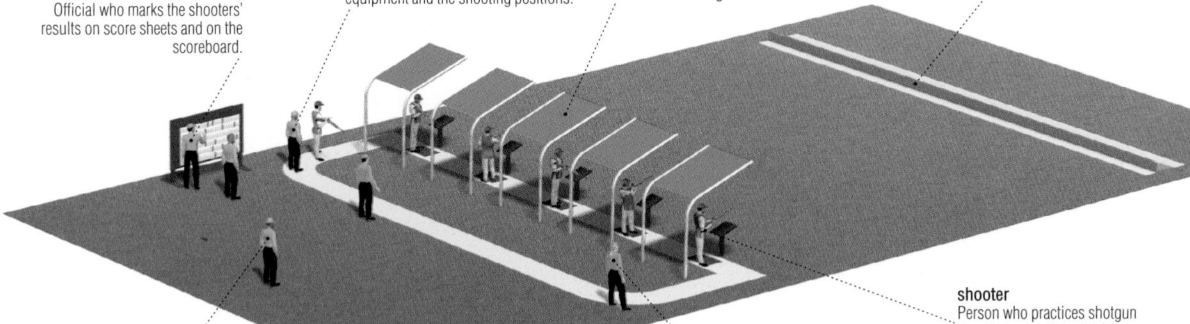

shooting range
Area that faces the targets, which includes the shooting stations.

chief range officer
Official who is in charge of calling the shooters to their positions; this individual also verifies the compliance of the equipment and the shooting positions.

trench
Ditch that is about 6.5 ft deep where the trap machines are stationed; it is 16 yd from the shooting station.

scorer
Official who marks the shooters' results on score sheets and on the scoreboard.

shooting station
Area where the competitors stand to shoot at the targets.

shooter
Person who practices shotgun shooting or participates in a competition.

chief referee
Official who is in charge of all technical and logistical aspects of the competition.

assistant referee
Official who checks whether or not the target has been hit; if it was not hit, the assistant referee reports this fact immediately.

rifle shooting

Sport that consists of using a rifle to shoot projectiles at a target a given distance away; the goal is to hit the target's center.

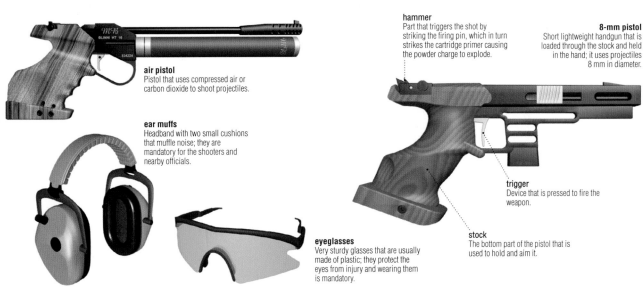

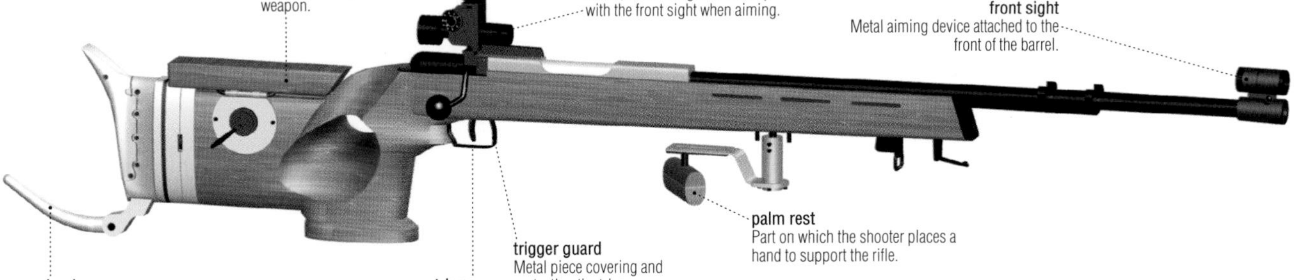

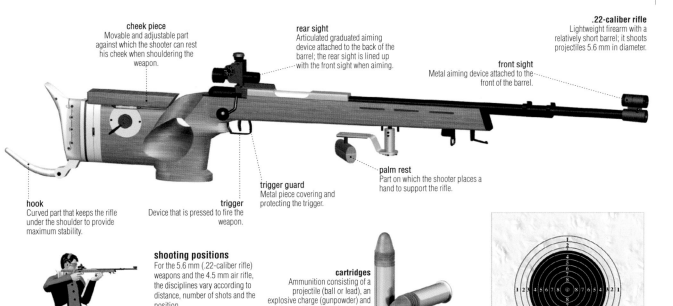

cheek piece
Movable and adjustable part against which the shooter can rest his cheek when shouldering the weapon.

rear sight
Articulated graduated aiming device attached to the back of the barrel; the rear sight is lined up with the front sight when aiming.

.22-caliber rifle
Lightweight firearm with a relatively short barrel; it shoots projectiles 5.6 mm in diameter.

front sight
Metal aiming device attached to the front of the barrel.

palm rest
Part on which the shooter places a hand to support the rifle.

trigger guard
Metal piece covering and protecting the trigger.

hook
Curved part that keeps the rifle under the shoulder to provide maximum stability.

trigger
Device that is pressed to fire the weapon.

shooting positions

For the 5.6 mm (.22-caliber rifle) weapons and the 4.5 mm air rifle, the disciplines vary according to distance, number of shots and the position.

cartridges
Ammunition consisting of a projectile (ball or lead), an explosive charge (gunpowder) and a primer collected inside a casing.

standing position
The shooter stands with two feet on the ground and no other support; the rifle is held in both hands, against the shoulder and along the aiming cheek.

kneeling position
Three points of contact with the ground are allowed: left foot, right knee and toe of the right foot (for a right-handed person); the rifle must be held in two hands, against the aiming shoulder.

prone position
Lying on the stomach, the shooter holds the weapon with two hands and one shoulder; the cheek can be held against the stock but the forearm cannot touch the ground.

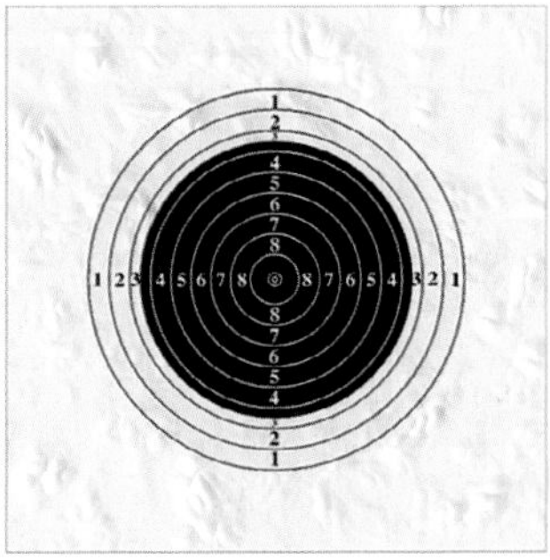

target
Surface 6.1 in in diameter that is marked by the bullets; it is divided into concentric circles corresponding to point zones.

pistol shooting

Sport that consists of using a pistol to shoot projectiles at a target a given distance away; the goal is to hit the target's center.

air pistol
Pistol that uses compressed air or carbon dioxide to shoot projectiles.

ear muffs
Headband with two small cushions that muffle noise; they are mandatory for the shooters and nearby officials.

eyeglasses
Very sturdy glasses that are usually made of plastic; they protect the eyes from injury and wearing them is mandatory.

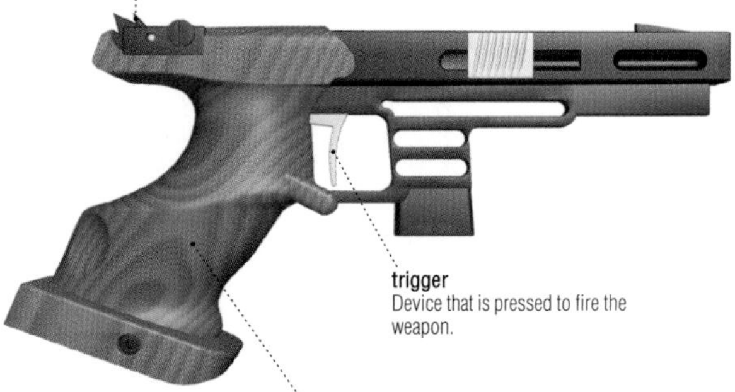

hammer
Part that triggers the shot by striking the firing pin, which in turn strikes the cartridge primer causing the powder charge to explode.

8-mm pistol
Short lightweight handgun that is loaded through the stock and held in the hand; it uses projectiles 8 mm in diameter.

trigger
Device that is pressed to fire the weapon.

stock
The bottom part of the pistol that is used to hold and aim it.

billiards

Games that are played on a special table; they use a cue to hit a cue ball either against two balls or to drive another into a pocket.

carom billiards
Game that is played on a pocketless table with three balls (one red and two white); players hit their own white balls to hit the other balls.

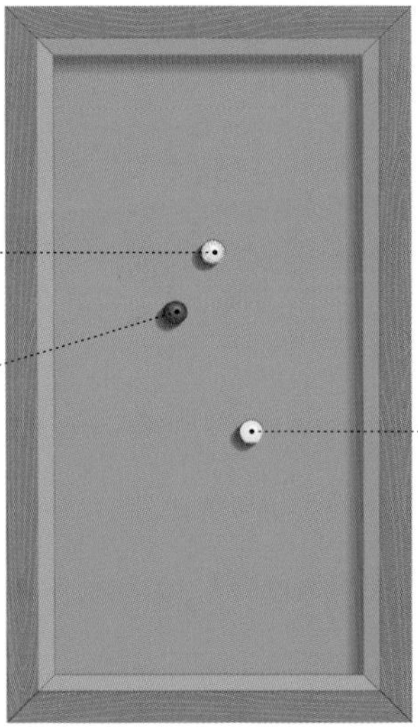

cue ball
White ball that the player hits with the cue to hit the red ball and the opponent's ball; it is the only ball that may be hit with the cue.

red ball
Ball the player must touch to score a carom.

white object ball
Ball the player must hit to score a carom (move in which the player's ball hits the two other balls); it is also the opponent's cue ball.

pool
Also known as American billiards, it is played on a table with six pockets using 15 object balls and a white ball; the goal is to drive the balls into the pockets in a set order.

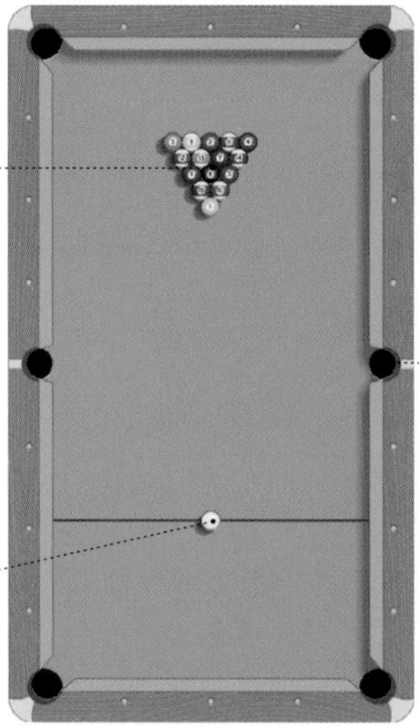

object balls
Balls that the player must drive into the pockets in a set order; at the start of the game, they are arranged in a triangle.

pocket
One of the six holes into which the player must drive the balls.

cue ball
White ball the player hits with the cue to hit the other balls and pocket them; it is the only ball that may be hit with the cue.

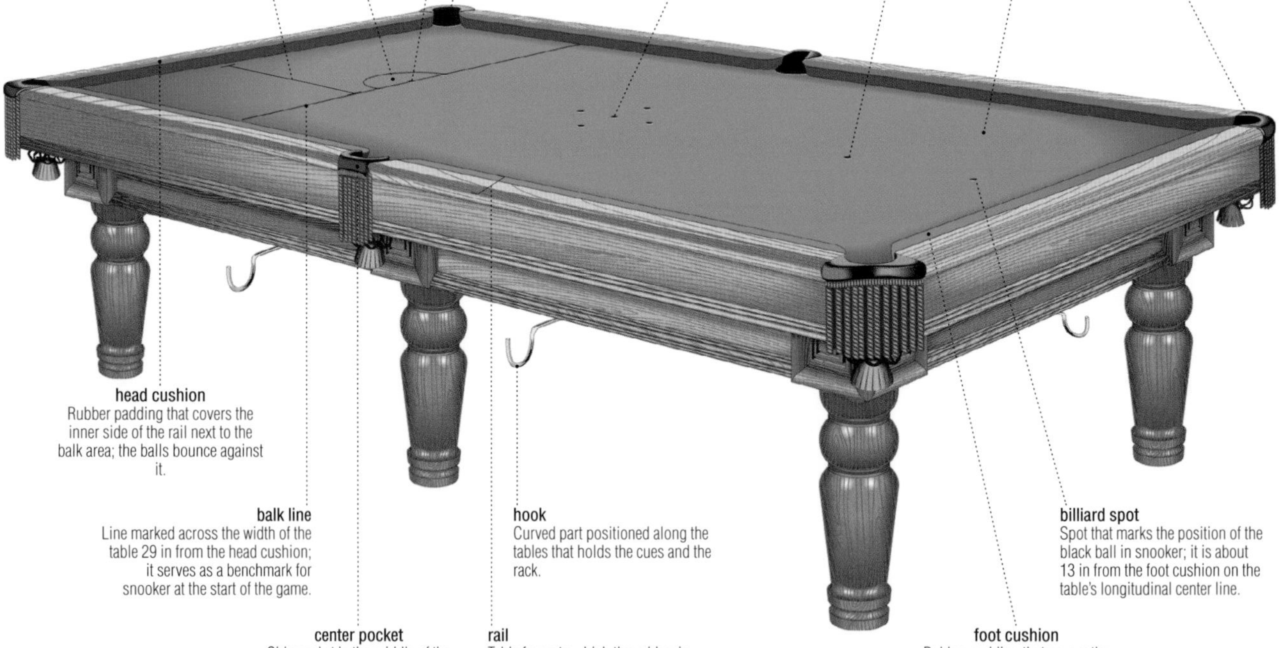

table
Surface on which the balls roll; it is supported by legs, has a rectangular top and is horizontal and level.

D
Semicircle whose center is on and in the middle of the balk line; the game starts from here.

balk line spot
Spot in the middle of the balk line that marks the position of the brown ball in snooker (there are two other spots at the intersections of the balk line and the "D").

pyramid spot
Spot that marks the position of the pink ball in snooker; it is halfway between the center spot and the foot cushion on the table's longitudinal center line.

baize
Felt fabric that covers the playing surface and the inner side of the rails.

balk area
Zone bordered by the balk line and the head cushion, including the "D"; this zone is used only in English billiards.

bottom pocket
Corner pocket located at the head cushion and next to the balk area.

center spot
Spot that marks the position of the blue ball in snooker; it is located halfway between the center pockets and the head and foot cushions.

top pocket
Corner pocket located at the foot cushion and opposite the balk area.

head cushion
Rubber padding that covers the inner side of the rail next to the balk area; the balls bounce against it.

balk line
Line marked across the width of the table 29 in from the head cushion; it serves as a benchmark for snooker at the start of the game.

hook
Curved part positioned along the tables that holds the cues and the rack.

billiard spot
Spot that marks the position of the black ball in snooker; it is about 13 in from the foot cushion on the table's longitudinal center line.

center pocket
Side pocket in the middle of the table's side rail.

rail
Table frame to which the rubber is attached and covered with felt; it delimits the playing surface.

foot cushion
Rubber padding that covers the inner side of the rail opposite the balk area; the balls bounce against it.

billiards

snooker
Billiards that is played on a table with six pockets and uses 22 balls (15 red, six of various colors and one white); the goal is to alternately pocket the red balls and the colored balls.

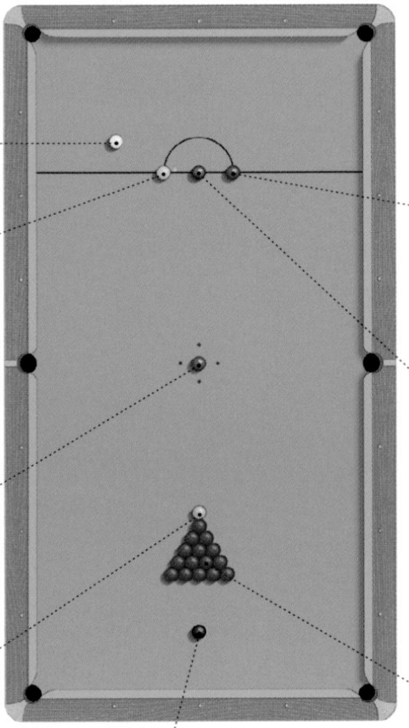

cue ball
White ball the player hits with the cue to hit the other balls and pocket them; it is the only ball that may be hit with the cue.

yellow ball
Ball that is worth two points; it is placed to the right of the "D", in relation to the head cushion.

blue ball
Ball that is worth five points; it is placed on the center spot.

pink ball
Ball that is worth six points; it is placed on the pyramid spot.

black ball
Ball that is worth seven points; it is placed on the billiard spot.

green ball
Ball that is worth three points; it is placed to the left of the "D", with respect to the head cushion.

brown ball
Ball that is worth four points; it is placed on the balk line spot.

red balls
Balls that are worth one point each. At the start of the game, they are arranged in a triangle behind the pink ball; as long as the player has not pocketed all the red balls, the colored balls are placed back on the table in their original spots.

English billiards
Billiards played in the United Kingdom on a table with six pockets using three balls (one red and two white); the goal is to pocket the balls or use one ball to hit the other two.

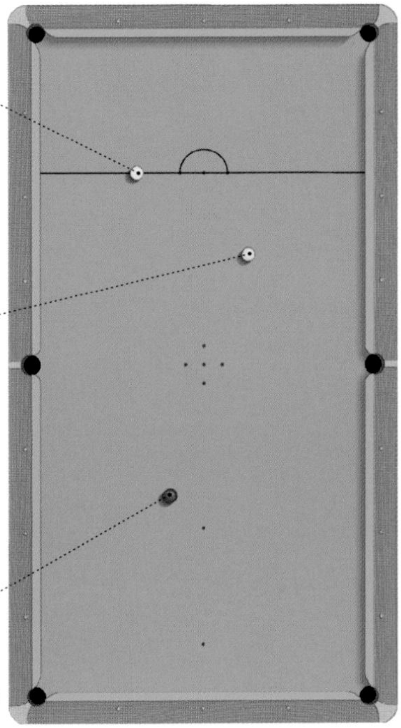

cue ball
White ball that belongs to one of the players; it is put into play from the "D".

white object ball
White ball that belongs to the other player; it is also the ball that the first player must hit or pocket.

red ball
Ball that the player must hit or pocket; at the start of the game, it is placed on the billiard spot.

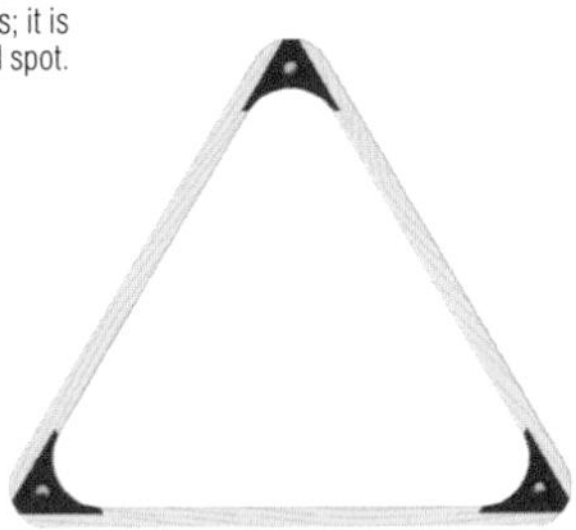

rack
Triangular piece of wood or plastic for lining up the balls on the table at the start of a game.

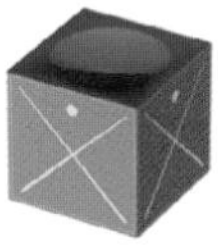

chalk
Small cube of chalky powder that is rubbed onto the tip of the cue to improve contact with the cue ball.

billiard cue
Long wooden stick that the player holds to hit the cue ball; the player chooses the cue's diameter, length and weight (no more than 25 oz).

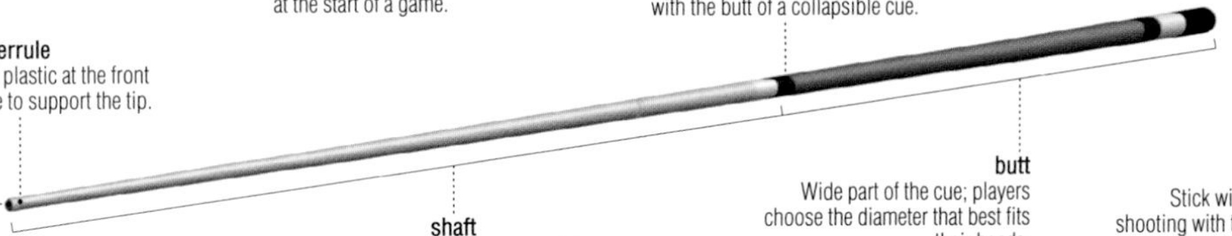

joint
Cylindrical part for joining the shaft with the butt of a collapsible cue.

ferrule
Piece of hard plastic at the front end of the cue to support the tip.

tip
Round piece of leather or felt on the end of the cue for hitting the cue ball; it is also the only component that can touch a ball.

shaft
Tapered part of the cue on which the player places the fingers to line up the shot.

butt
Wide part of the cue; players choose the diameter that best fits their hands.

bridge
Stick with a toothed head for shooting with the cue when the cue ball is out of the player's reach.

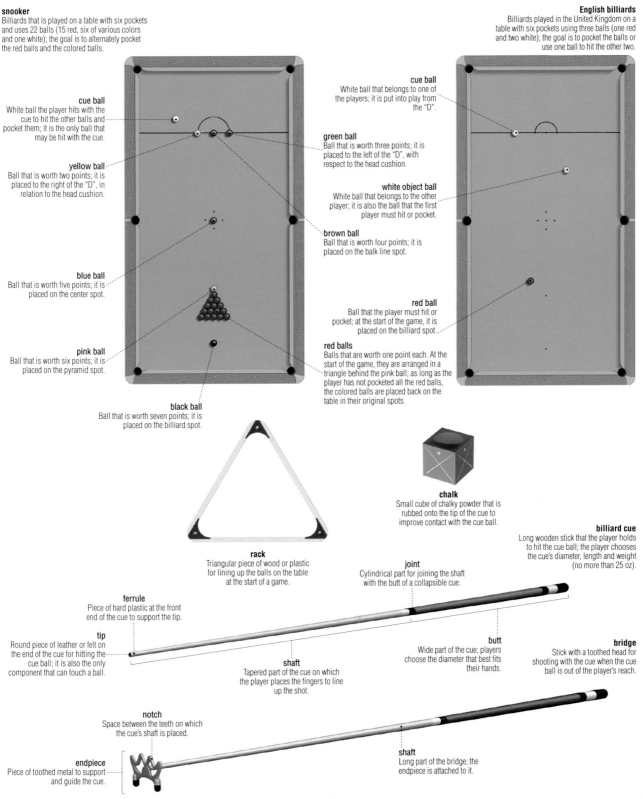

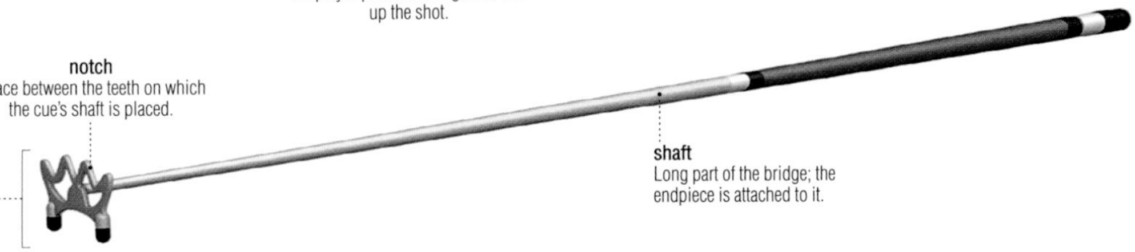

notch
Space between the teeth on which the cue's shaft is placed.

endpiece
Piece of toothed metal to support and guide the cue.

shaft
Long part of the bridge; the endpiece is attached to it.

lawn bowling

Ball sport of British origin in which two opposing players or teams play on a green; balls (bowls) are thrown as close as possible to a target (jack).

bowls
They are made of wood, rubber or other material and are not perfectly spherical (diameter of about 4.75 to 5.75 in, weight up to 3.5 lb).

jack
Small ball that is made of wood or lignite and is 2.5 in in diameter; it is the lawn bowling target and the point of reference for scoring.

bowling technique
The thrower takes three steps to wind up, unlike petanque where the thrower does not move.

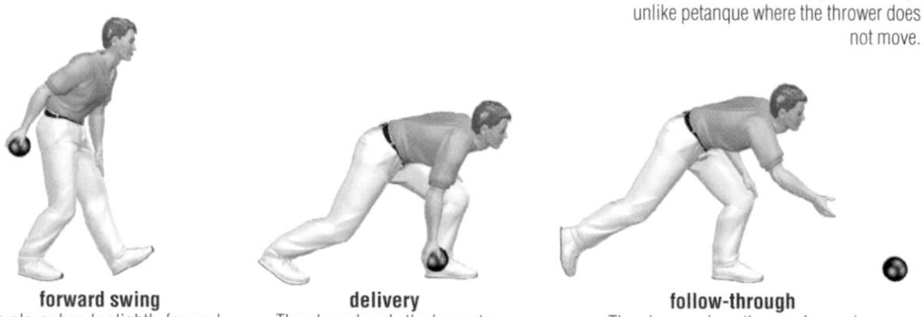

forward swing
The player bends slightly forward and places the arm behind the body to gain momentum for the throw.

delivery
The player bends the knees to accelerate the motion before releasing the bowl.

follow-through
The player swings the arm forward toward the jack after throwing the bowl.

green
Surface of natural or synthetic grass that is bordered by a ditch and a bank; the lawn bowling green is divided into several parallel playing surfaces.

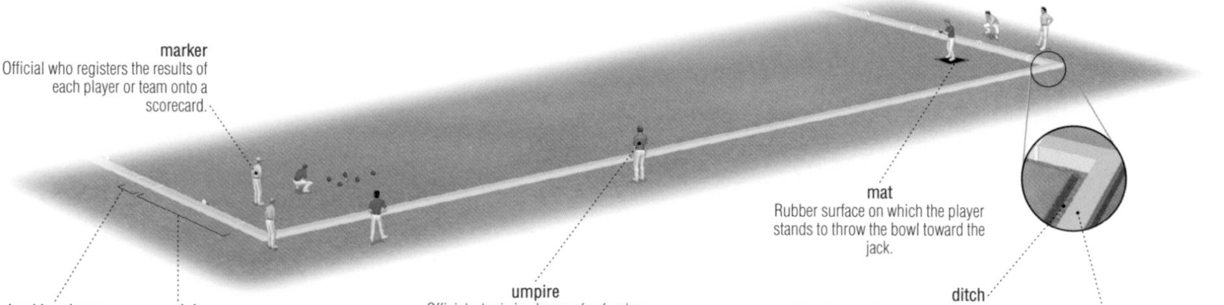

marker
Official who registers the results of each player or team onto a scorecard.

mat
Rubber surface on which the player stands to throw the bowl toward the jack.

dead bowl area
Zone outside the limits of the rink where bowls are considered out of bounds.

rink
Area 18 to 21 ft wide x 40 to 42 yd long that is laid out for playing lawn bowling.

umpire
Official who is in charge of enforcing the rules; the umpire can expel a player or team from the competition it they refuse to comply with a decision.

ditch
Small culvert that surrounds the green; a bowl falling into the ditch is considered out of bounds.

bank
Small wall that surrounds the ditch to delimit the playing field; it can be no higher than 9 in.

petanque

Ball sport that originated in the south of France in which two opposing players or teams throw balls (bowls) as close as possible to a target (jack).

playing field
Area laid out for playing petanque; matches can be played on a lawn, earth or sand. For international competitions, the field measures 13 ft x 49 ft.

referee
Official who is in charge of enforcing the rules; the referee ensures that the equipment and installation are in compliance.

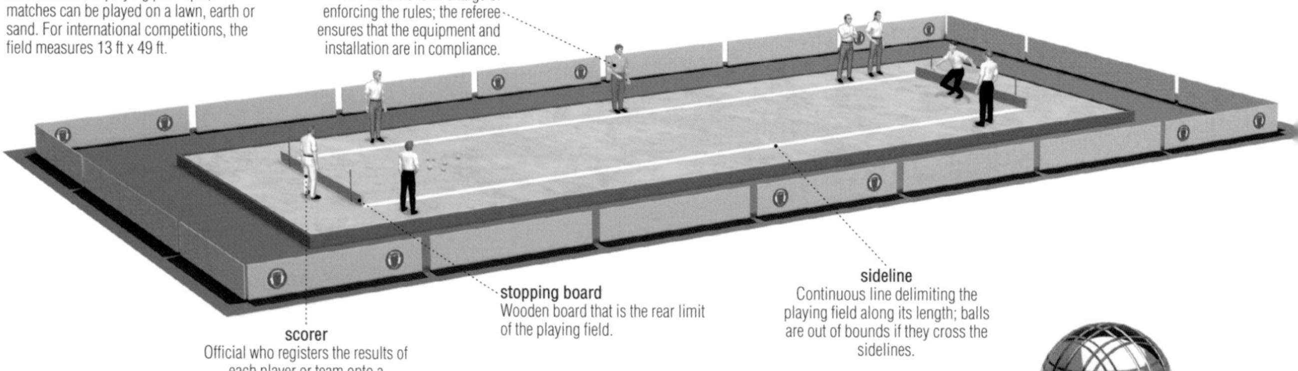

stopping board
Wooden board that is the rear limit of the playing field.

sideline
Continuous line delimiting the playing field along its length; balls are out of bounds if they cross the sidelines.

scorer
Official who registers the results of each player or team onto a scorecard.

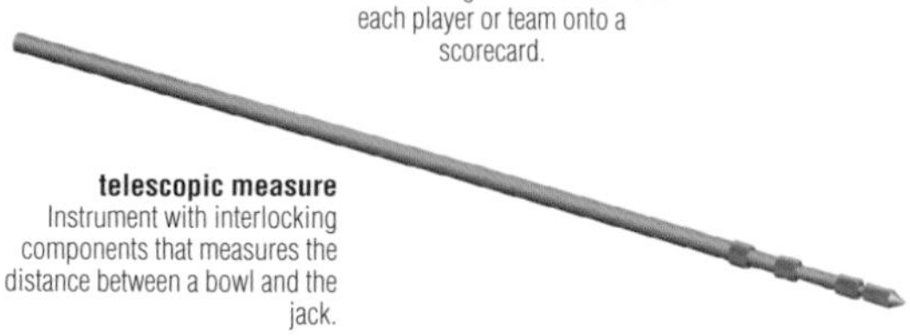

telescopic measure
Instrument with interlocking components that measures the distance between a bowl and the jack.

jack
Small ball whose diameter is between 1 and 1.35 in; it serves as the petanque target and the point of reference for scoring.

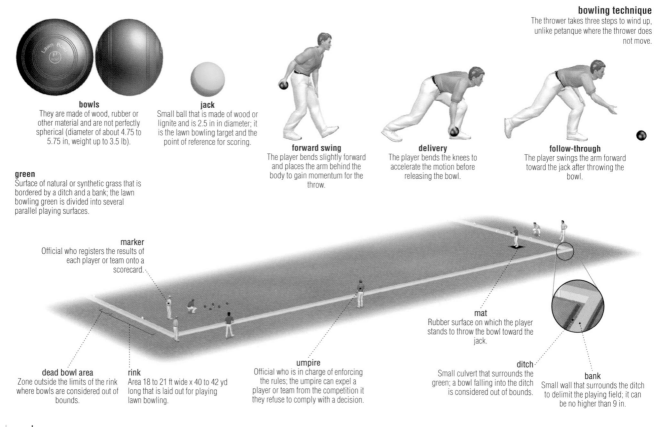

petanque bowl
Metal spherical ball that weighs between 1.4 and 1.7 lb and whose diameter is between 2.75 and 3.15 in.

bowling

Game of U.S. origin that consists of rolling a ball down a lane to knock down pins standing at the end.

examples of pins
Their shapes are specific to each variety of the game.

American duckpin
One of 10 pins that is lightweight and 9.4 in high; the game is played almost exclusively in the United States.

tenpin
Pin that weighs 3.5 to 3.7 lb and measures 15 in high; this is the most widespread type of bowling in the world.

candlepin
Cylindrical pin that is about 16 in high; this game with 10 pins is played in some provinces of Canada and states of the United States.

fivepin
Lightweight pin that is about 12 in high and has a rubber band around it; this five-pin game is very popular in Canada.

Canadian duckpin
Similar to American duckpin, it has a rubber band around it to make it heavier; this 10-pin game is very widespread in Canada.

shoe
For a right-handed person, the left sole is made of leather (for sliding) and the right sole of rubber (for stopping).

bowling ball
Large ball that the player rolls to hit the pins.

headpin
Also called the kingpin, it makes up the point of the triangle formed by the pins.

setup
Set of 10 pins arranged in an equilateral triangle at the end of each lane of the alley.

pin
Piece of wood that is covered with plastic; it is stood on end on the floor and the player knocks it over with a ball.

pocket
Tactical zone where the player rolls the ball to try to hit all the pins with one ball (strike).

ball return
Mechanical device (track) between the lanes that returns the balls the players threw toward the setup.

score console
Panel that displays the data of the game in progress (such as points for each frame for each player, total for previous games and the results for each team).

ball
Spherical object that is rolled using the hand to knock down the pins; there are two types: light and heavy. The heavy ball has three holes for gripping with the fingers.

bowler
Player who practices bowling; the first world championships for women took place in 1963.

keyboard
Set of keys for registering points scored (number of pins knocked over) for each frame and for the game total.

ball stand
Area where the bowls rack up after leaving the ball return.

setup
Set of 10 pins arranged in an equilateral triangle at the end of each lane of the alley.

bowling alley
Set of lanes that are made of wood or synthetic material and are laid out for bowling.

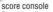

bowler
Player who practices bowling; the first world championships for men took place in 1954.

pit
Area at the end of the lane; the hit pins fall into it.

marker
Mark that helps the bowler define the ball's trajectory.

gutter
Ditch on both sides of the alley's lanes; a ball that falls into it is out of play.

approach
Lane on which the player makes the forward swing (usually three normal steps and one sliding) before rolling the ball.

foul line
Line behind which the player must stay when rolling the ball down the lane at delivery; crossing this line is a foul.

golf

Sport whose objective is to complete a set course by hitting a ball with a club; the player who uses the least number of strokes is the winner.

course
Area set up in a natural environment for playing golf, usually with 18 holes.

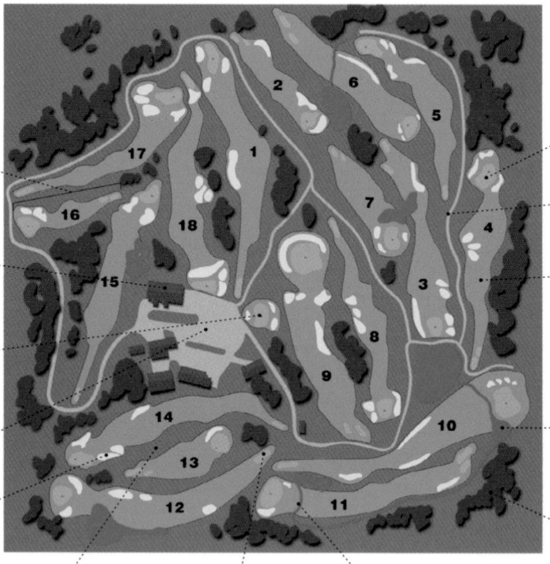

1
2
3
4
5
6
7
8
9
10
11
12
13
14
15
16
17
18
hole
Grass-covered fairway that is surrounded by plant growth; the golfer covers its distance by hitting a ball, despite the obstacles.
clubhouse
Structure located usually near the first and last holes that provides various services to golfers (such as a bar, restaurant and lockers).
practice green
Lawn similar to the green where golfers practice putting.
parking
Area for cars to park.
sand bunker
Section of the fairway of varying size that is filled with sand; if the ball becomes stuck here, the player uses a sand wedge to hit it out.
rough
Part of the course on the edge of the fairways where the grass grows freely.
teeing ground
Grassy surface mown very short from which the player tees off; teeing grounds are arranged at various distances from the hole as a function of the players' skill.
water hazard
Natural or man-made body of water (such as a lake, pond, river or reservoir) that constitutes an obstacle for the golfer.
green
Grass surface mown very short surrounding each of the course's holes; the golfer uses a putter to roll the ball into the hole.
cart path
Lane for golf carts to follow along the course.
fairway
Mown part of the course between the teeing ground for the hole and its green.
pond
Small shallow body of water that can be natural or man-made.
trees
Wooded part of the golf course.

holes
Grass-covered fairway surrounded by plant growth whose distance the golfer covers by hitting a ball, despite the obstacles; in principle, each hole is played in an estimated number of strokes, its par.

par 3 hole
The player tries to reach the green on the tee-off stroke and then make two putts; par 3s are often the most dreaded by golfers.

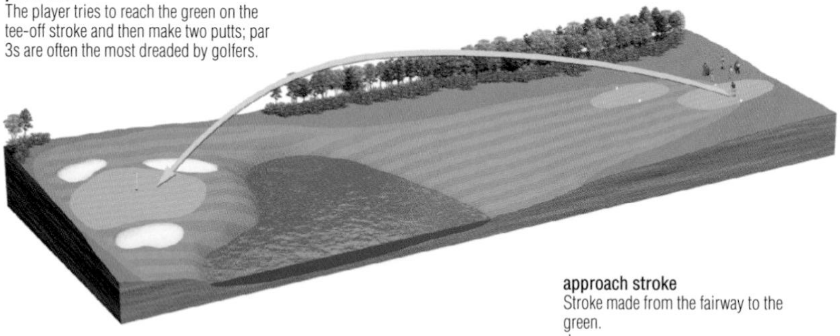

par 4 hole
The player tries to reach the green on the second stroke and then make two putts; it is called a birdie when a hole is sunk in one stroke under par.

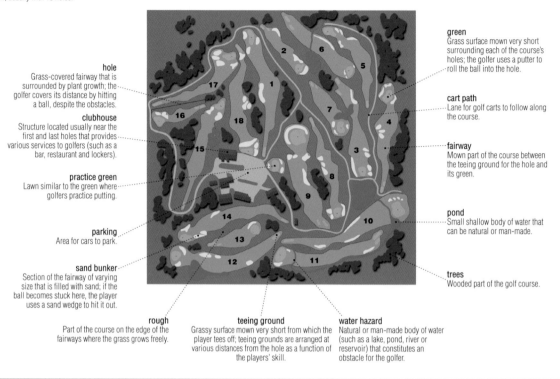

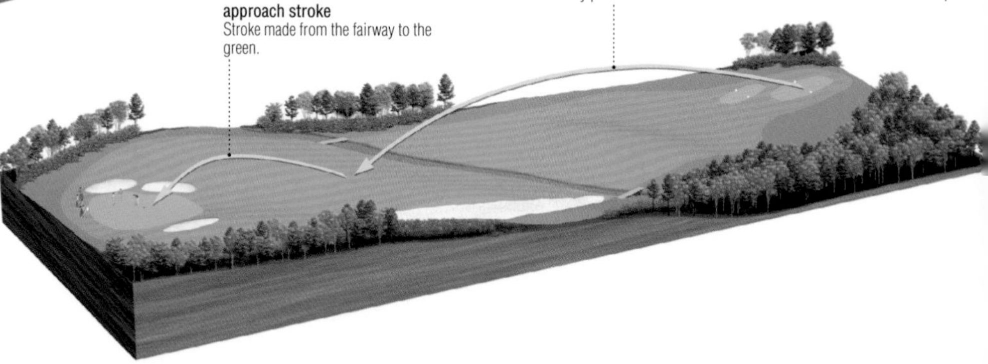

tee-off stroke
First stroke for a hole that is made from the teeing ground; the ball is usually placed on a tee.
approach stroke
Stroke made from the fairway to the green.

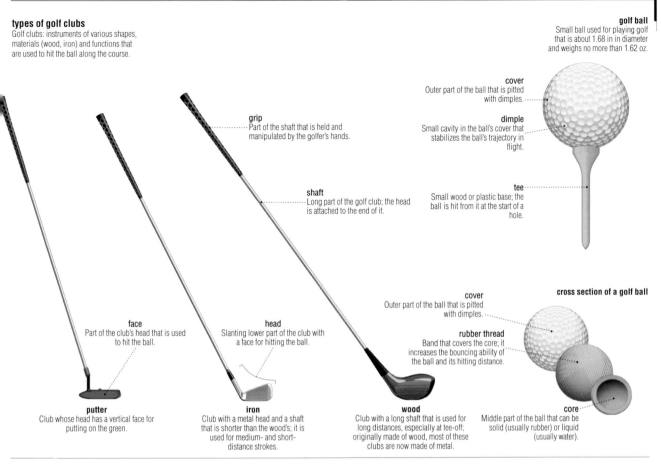

golf

types of golf clubs
Golf clubs: instruments of various shapes, materials (wood, iron) and functions that are used to hit the ball along the course.

golf ball
Small ball used for playing golf that is about 1.68 in in diameter and weighs no more than 1.62 oz.

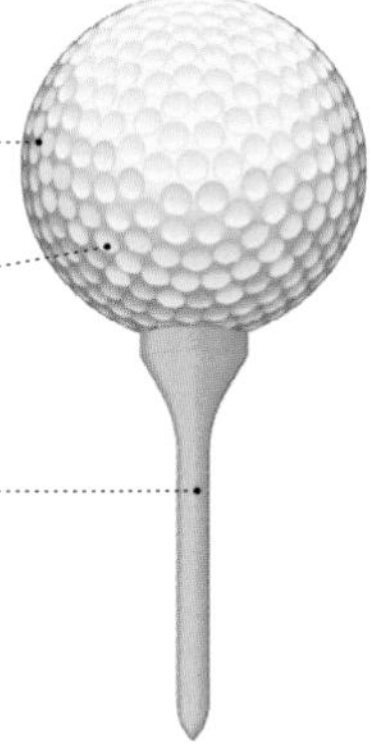

cover
Outer part of the ball that is pitted with dimples.

dimple
Small cavity in the ball's cover that stabilizes the ball's trajectory in flight.

tee
Small wood or plastic base; the ball is hit from it at the start of a hole.

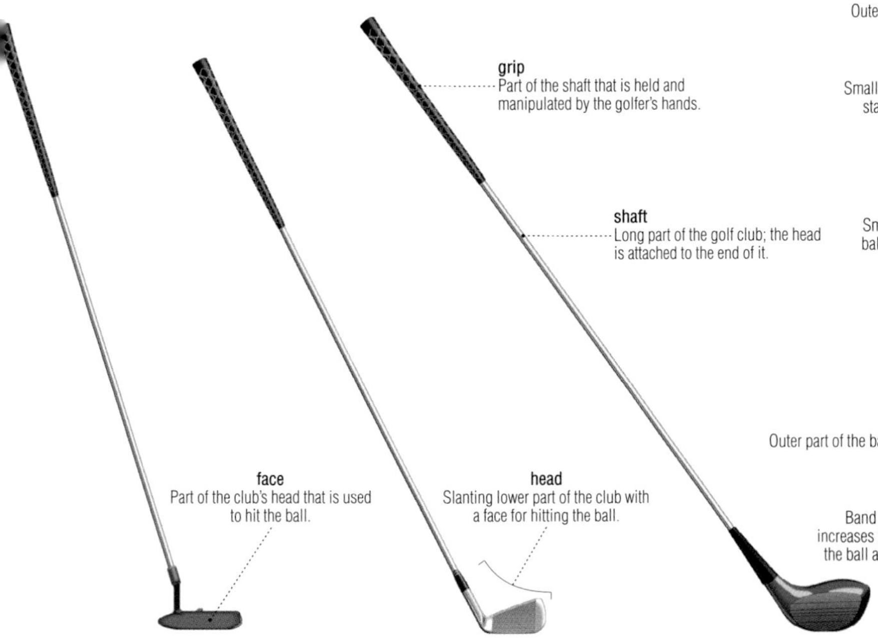

grip
Part of the shaft that is held and manipulated by the golfer's hands.

shaft
Long part of the golf club; the head is attached to the end of it.

face
Part of the club's head that is used to hit the ball.

head
Slanting lower part of the club with a face for hitting the ball.

putter
Club whose head has a vertical face for putting on the green.

iron
Club with a metal head and a shaft that is shorter than the wood's; it is used for medium- and short-distance strokes.

wood
Club with a long shaft that is used for long distances, especially at tee-off; originally made of wood, most of these clubs are now made of metal.

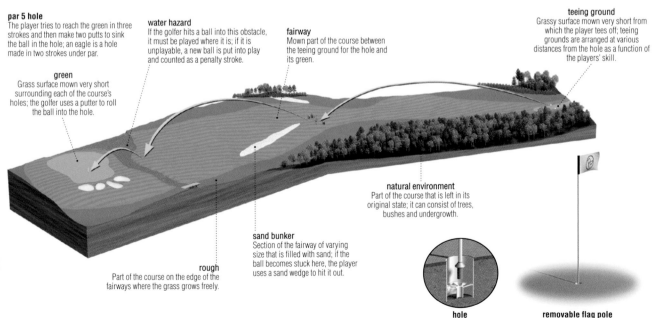

cross section of a golf ball

cover
Outer part of the ball that is pitted with dimples.

rubber thread
Band that covers the core; it increases the bouncing ability of the ball and its hitting distance.

core
Middle part of the ball that can be solid (usually rubber) or liquid (usually water).

par 5 hole
The player tries to reach the green in three strokes and then make two putts to sink the ball in the hole; an eagle is a hole made in two strokes under par.

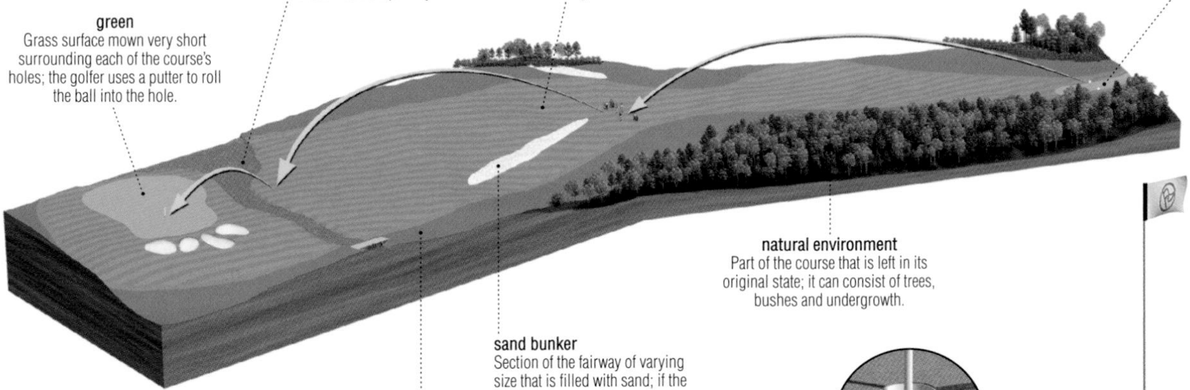

green
Grass surface mown very short surrounding each of the course's holes; the golfer uses a putter to roll the ball into the hole.

water hazard
If the golfer hits a ball into this obstacle, it must be played where it is; if it is unplayable, a new ball is put into play and counted as a penalty stroke.

fairway
Mown part of the course between the teeing ground for the hole and its green.

teeing ground
Grassy surface mown very short from which the player tees off; teeing grounds are arranged at various distances from the hole as a function of the players' skill.

natural environment
Part of the course that is left in its original state; it can consist of trees, bushes and undergrowth.

sand bunker
Section of the fairway of varying size that is filled with sand; if the ball becomes stuck here, the player uses a sand wedge to hit it out.

rough
Part of the course on the edge of the fairways where the grass grows freely.

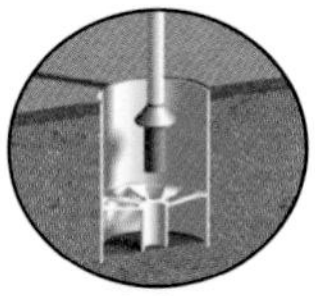

hole
Cavity dug out of the green; the player must roll the ball into it to complete a hole.

removable flag pole
Long rod with a flag that is planted in a hole to mark the hole's location so that it can be seen from far away.

golf

wood
The woods are usually numbered from 1 to 7, according to the inclination of their faces and the ranges of their strokes.

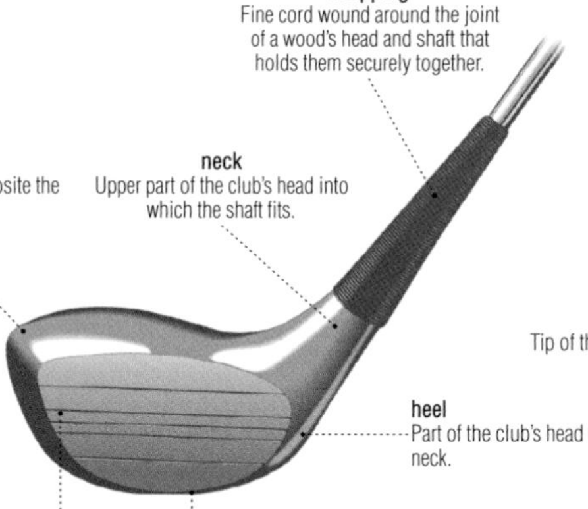
whipping
Fine cord wound around the joint of a wood's head and shaft that holds them securely together.
toe
Tip of the club's head, opposite the heel and the shaft.
neck
Upper part of the club's head into which the shaft fits.
heel
Part of the club's head under the neck.
groove
Fine indented lines on the face of the club that provide maximum control of the ball.
sole
Lower part of the club's head.

iron
Club used to hit the ball on the fairway or green. Irons are numbered from 1 to 9, according to the length of their shafts and their range; the angle of the sole increases in inclination to create curved trajectories of varying heights.

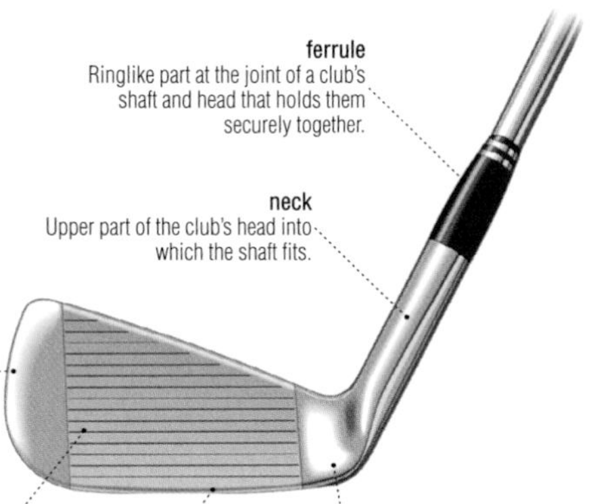
ferrule
Ringlike part at the joint of a club's shaft and head that holds them securely together.
neck
Upper part of the club's head into which the shaft fits.
toe
Tip of the club's head, opposite the heel and the shaft.
groove
Fine indented lines on the face of the club that provide maximum control of the ball.
sole
Lower part of the club's head.
heel
Part of the club's head under the neck.

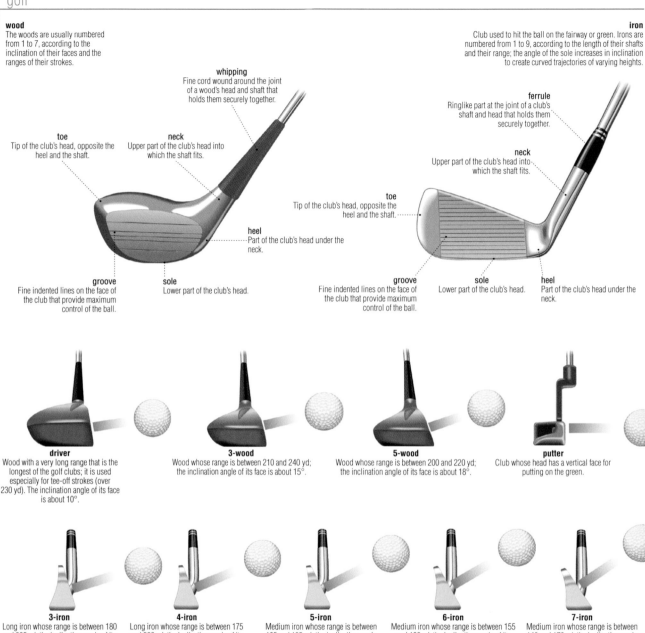

driver
Wood with a very long range that is the longest of the golf clubs; it is used especially for tee-off strokes (over 230 yd). The inclination angle of its face is about 10°.

3-wood
Wood whose range is between 210 and 240 yd; the inclination angle of its face is about 15°.

5-wood
Wood whose range is between 200 and 220 yd; the inclination angle of its face is about 18°.

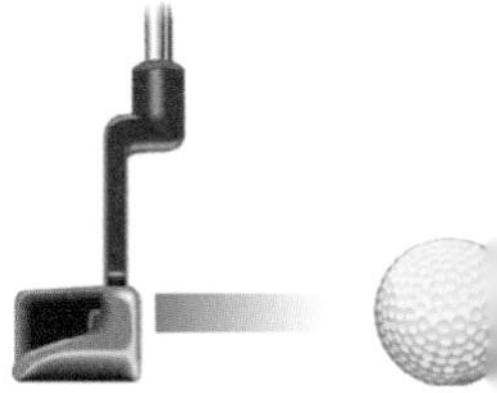

putter
Club whose head has a vertical face for putting on the green.

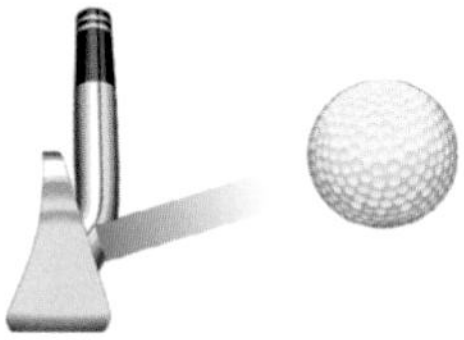

3-iron
Long iron whose range is between 180 and 205 yd; the inclination angle of its face varies from 20° to 22°.

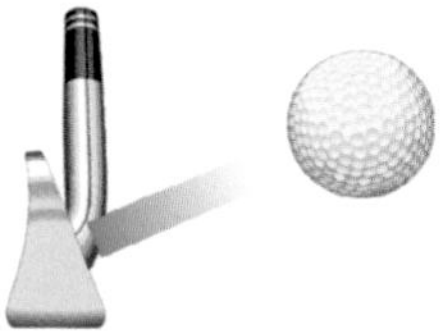

4-iron
Long iron whose range is between 175 and 200 yd; the inclination angle of its face varies from 22° to 24°.

5-iron
Medium iron whose range is between 165 and 195 yd; the inclination angle of its face varies from 26° to 28°.

6-iron
Medium iron whose range is between 155 and 180 yd; the inclination angle of its face varies from 30° to 32°.

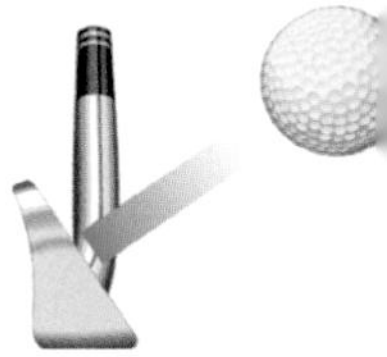

7-iron
Medium iron whose range is between 140 and 170 yd; the inclination angle of its face varies from 34° to 36°.

8-iron
Short iron whose range is between 135 and 155 yd; the inclination angle of its face varies from 38° to 40°.

9-iron
Short iron whose range is between 130 and 145 yd; the inclination angle of its face varies from 42° to 44°.

pitching wedge
Short iron used mainly for approach strokes on the fairway, at about 110 yd from the hole; the inclination angle of its face varies from 47° to 52°.

lob wedge
Short iron used for playing high and precise strokes near the green (less than 55 yd); the inclination angle of its face varies from 60° to 64°.

sand wedge
Short iron used mainly for hitting the ball out of sand bunkers; the inclination angle of its face varies from 54° to 58°.

golf cart
Two-wheeled rack that is pulled by a handle to transport the golf bag along the course.

shoulder strap
Large belt that distributes the weight of the golf bag on the shoulder.

pocket
Small exterior storage compartment that contains various accessories (such as balls, gloves and tees).

golf bag
Sack for transporting golf clubs and accessories; a player can use no more than 14 different clubs during a competition.

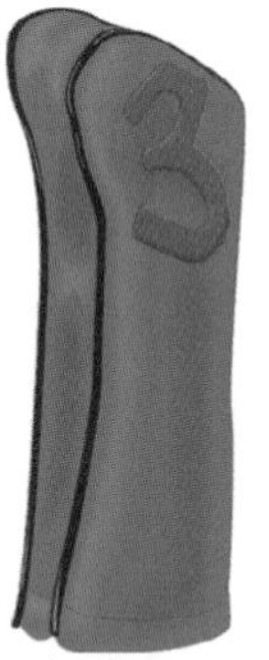

head cover
Part that covers and protects the head of a golf club while it is not being used.

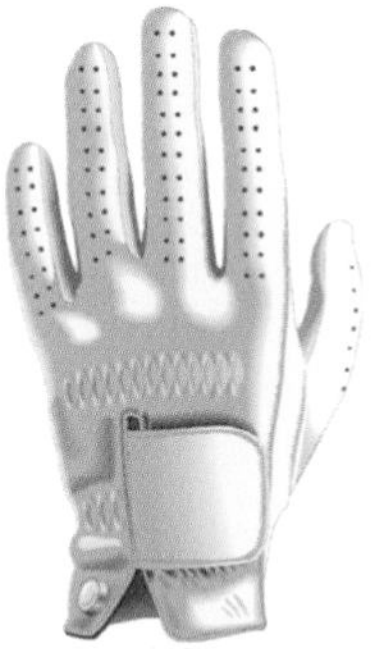

golf glove
Item that covers the hand to provide a better grip on the club; it is worn on one hand only (on the left hand for a right-handed person).

golf shoes
Leather shoes with cleats attached to the soles.

bag well
Rack at the back of the golf cart in which golfers carry their equipment over the golf course.

electric golf cart
Small motorized vehicle that is used by golfers to move from one hole to another along the golf course.

road racing

Sport that consists of racing a bicycle on a road for one day or in stages.

road-racing bicycle and cyclist
Road-racing bicycle: bicycle that is designed for speed; it has narrow tires, a lightweight frame and handlebars conducive to an aerodynamic position for the cyclist.

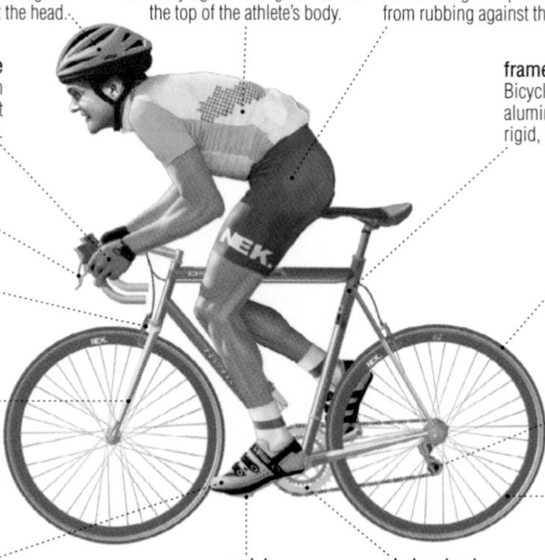

helmet
Hard piece of equipment designed to protect the head.

jersey
Stretchy tight clothing that covers the top of the athlete's body.

shorts
Tight clothing that covers the athlete's thighs to prevent them from rubbing against the seat.

glove
Leather item that reduces vibration and protects the hand against impact.

frame
Bicycle structure made of aluminum or carbon fiber; it is rigid, lightweight and very sturdy.

brake lever and shifter
The brake handle activates the brake caliper to which it is connected by a cable; the shifter is used to change the position of the chain.

tire
Structure made of cotton and steel fibers coated with rubber, mounted on the rim to form the casing for the inner tube.

brake
Mechanism composed of two brake pads that is activated by a brake cable; the pads are driven by a caliper and return springs to squeeze the wheel rim and slow down the wheel.

derailleur
Mechanism for changing the rear gears by lifting the chain from one gear wheel to another; it allows the cyclist to adapt to road conditions.

fork
Two tubes connected to the head tube and attached to each end of the front-wheel hub.

wheel
Disk that turns around an axle at its center and enables the bicycle to move; its weight and shape influence the bike's performance.

shoe
Shoe with notches in the sole that fit into a corresponding part on the pedal to keep the foot secure on the pedal.

pedal
Part attached to a crank that the cyclist rotates to provide the bicycle's power.

chain wheel
Wheel with teeth that, in combination with the rear sprockets, increases or decreases the distance traveled by a turn of the pedal crank.

road cycling competition
Event that consists of riding a bicycle a given distance on a road as quickly as possible.

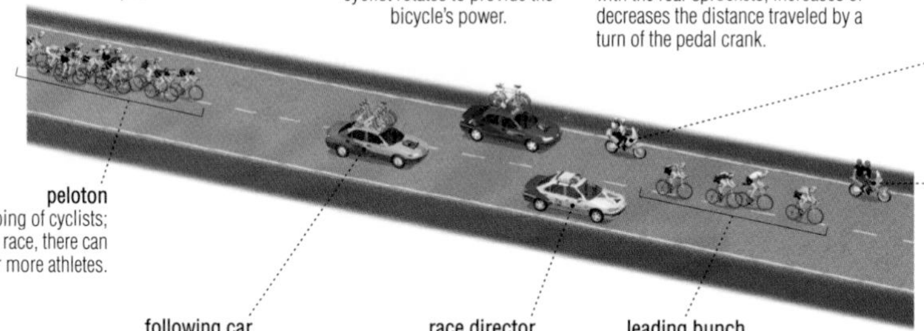

motorcycle-mounted camera
Motorcycle used by the cameraman who records the race for broadcast.

leading motorcycle
Motorcycle traveling in front of the first rider; its rider announces the cyclists coming up and checks that the way is clear.

peloton
Compact grouping of cyclists; depending on the race, there can be 150 or more athletes.

following car
Vehicle in which a team's coach, mechanics and trainers ride.

race director
Person who is in charge of organizing the race and monitors its progress from a car.

leading bunch
Compact grouping of cyclists at the front of the race.

mountain biking

Sport that consists of performing acrobatic exercises or racing offtrack (on a rough or steep course) on a bicycle.

cross-country bicycle and cyclist
Cross-country bicycle: relatively small, sturdy bicycle designed for performing acrobatics and competing in competitions on rough terrain.

goggles
Eyewear with plastic lenses fitted in a frame with arms; it protects the eyes from flying mud, stones and insects.

back suspension
Device that dampens vibrations from the wheels; this increases the bicycle's stability and its grip on the trail.

front fork
Fork whose air/oil or elastomer suspension provides a controlled ride over rough terrain.

clipless pedal
Pedal with a safety system so that the foot can be attached or detached quickly.

protective goggles
One-piece watertight eyewear that protects the eyes from flying mud, stones and insects.

downhill bicycle and cyclist
Downhill bicycle: small, very sturdy bicycle for racing on rough ground with steep hills and strewn with obstacles.

chin strap
Part of the helmet that protects the cyclist's chin.

raised handlebar
Grip whose elevated position makes the bicycle easier to steer when going downhill.

pedal with wide platform
Wide pedal providing good footing.

hydraulic disc brake
Brake with jaws that squeeze a disc to slow down the wheel; the braking power is produced by hydraulic pressure.

track cycling

Sport that consists of riding a bicycle on a closed track; the two types of track cycling events are speed and endurance.

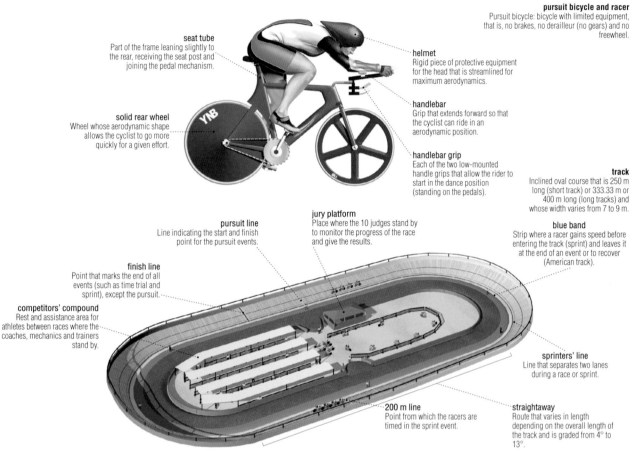

pursuit bicycle and racer
Pursuit bicycle: bicycle with limited equipment, that is, no brakes, no derailleur (no gears) and no freewheel.

seat tube
Part of the frame leaning slightly to the rear, receiving the seat post and joining the pedal mechanism.

helmet
Rigid piece of protective equipment for the head that is streamlined for maximum aerodynamics.

handlebar
Grip that extends forward so that the cyclist can ride in an aerodynamic position.

solid rear wheel
Wheel whose aerodynamic shape allows the cyclist to go more quickly for a given effort.

handlebar grip
Each of the two low-mounted handle grips that allow the rider to start in the dance position (standing on the pedals).

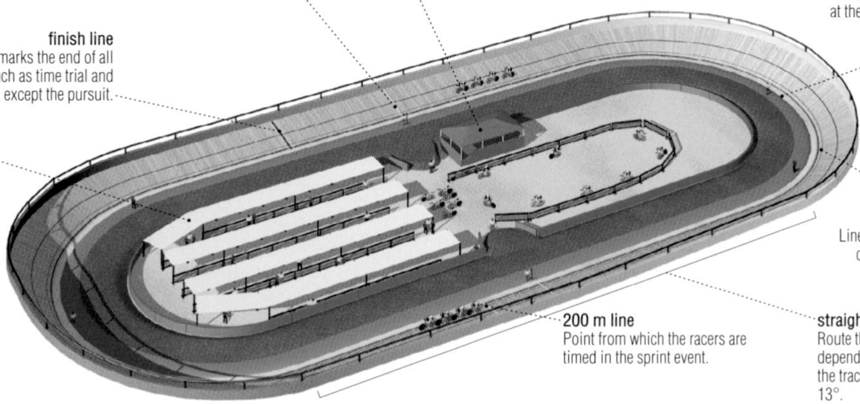

track
Inclined oval course that is 250 m long (short track) or 333.33 m or 400 m long (long tracks) and whose width varies from 7 to 9 m.

jury platform
Place where the 10 judges stand by to monitor the progress of the race and give the results.

pursuit line
Line indicating the start and finish point for the pursuit events.

blue band
Strip where a racer gains speed before entering the track (sprint) and leaves it at the end of an event or to recover (American track).

finish line
Point that marks the end of all events (such as time trial and sprint), except the pursuit.

competitors' compound
Rest and assistance area for athletes between races where the coaches, mechanics and trainers stand by.

sprinters' line
Line that separates two lanes during a race or sprint.

200 m line
Point from which the racers are timed in the sprint event.

straightaway
Route that varies in length depending on the overall length of the track and is graded from 4° to 13°.

BMX

Sport that consists of performing freestyle acrobatics using a small, one-speed bicycle.

half-pipe
Wooden U-shaped track that is set up for performing various acrobatic stunts (such as jumps and slides).

helmet
Hard piece of equipment designed to protect the head.

glove
Leather item that reduces vibration and protects the hand against impact.

handlebars
Grips with a system of rings that pivot around an axle; this enables the handlebars to turn 360°.

single chain wheel
Wheel with teeth that is connected to the sprocket by a chain enabling the wheel to turn; the wheel has only one chain wheel as there is only one gear.

single sprocket
Wheel with teeth that is connected to the chain wheel by a chain enabling the wheel to turn; the bicycle has only one sprocket as there is only one gear.

foot pegs
Supports attached to the hub; the athlete stands on them to perform certain freestyle acrobatics.

car racing

Speed event in which competitors driving race cars must make a predetermined number of laps around a track.

driver
Athlete who drives in a car race.

balaclava
Cap made of fireproof material that covers the head and neck and leaves the face uncovered.

undergarment
Clothing made of fireproof material that is worn under the suit; the undergarment and the driving suit must cover the neck, wrists and ankles.

flame-resistant driving suit
Molded one-piece outfit that is made of fireproof material; it protects the driver from serious burns for several seconds.

crash helmet
Hard piece of equipment designed to protect the head.

shoe
Fire-resistant shoe that covers the entire foot and ankle.

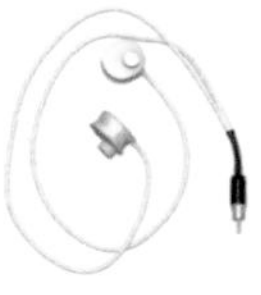

ear plugs/earbuds
Small plugs placed directly in the ears to dampen the noise from the engines and to allow radio communications between the driver and the team.

gloves
Item made of fireproof material that covers the hands and wrists; the gloves must fit tightly over the wrists and cover the sleeves of the suit.

wet-weather tire
Molded tire used on a wet track to evacuate a large quantity of water. At 185 mph, it evacuates more than 6.5 gallons of water per second.

dry-weather tire
Grooved tire providing a good grip on a dry track.

checkered flag
Black-and-white checkered flag that signals the end of a race or trial session.

starting grid
Position of the cars at the start of the race according to the time obtained during qualifications; the grid is made up of two cars per line in staggered formation.

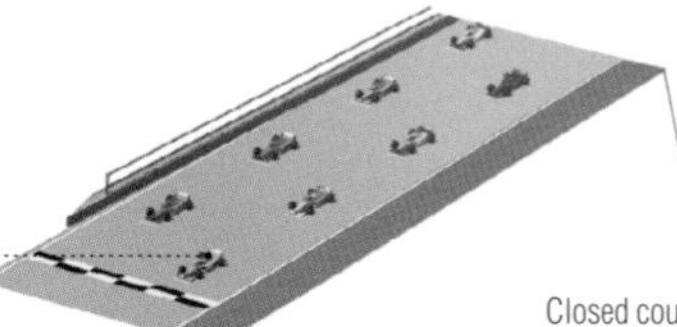

pole position
First position at the starting grid that is obtained by the driver who earned the best time during the qualification session.

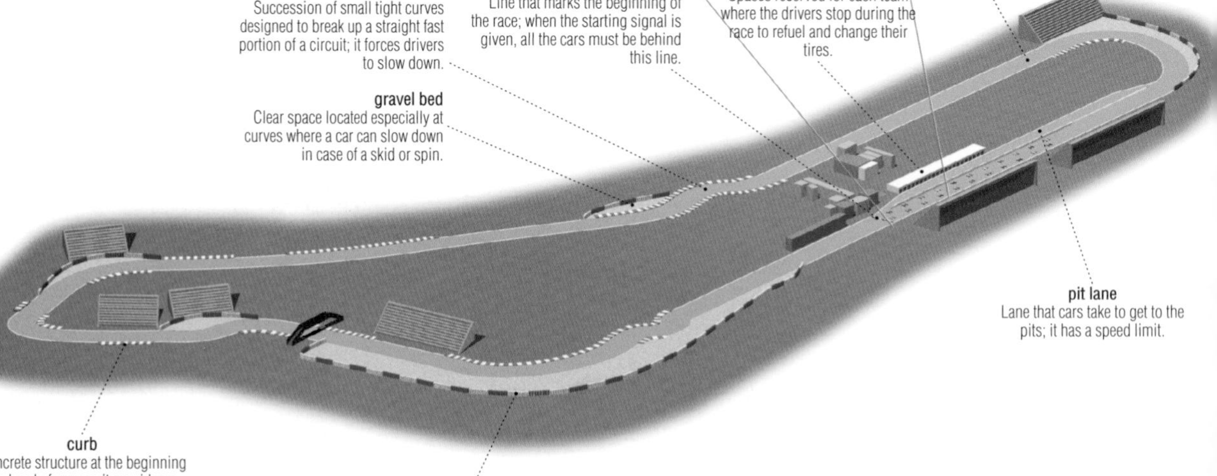

circuit
Driving surface of various lengths for race cars; the driver completes as many laps as necessary to accumulate 190 mi during a Grand Prix.

track
Closed course of a car race alternating between straight lines and more or less tight curves.

chicane
Succession of small tight curves designed to break up a straight fast portion of a circuit; it forces drivers to slow down.

starting line
Line that marks the beginning of the race; when the starting signal is given, all the cars must be behind this line.

pits
Spaces reserved for each team where the drivers stop during the race to refuel and change their tires.

gravel bed
Clear space located especially at curves where a car can slow down in case of a skid or spin.

pit lane
Lane that cars take to get to the pits; it has a speed limit.

curb
Concrete structure at the beginning and end of curves; it provides a visual landmark and delimits the track.

tire barrier
Security device for absorbing impact in case of collision or if cars leave the track.

car racing

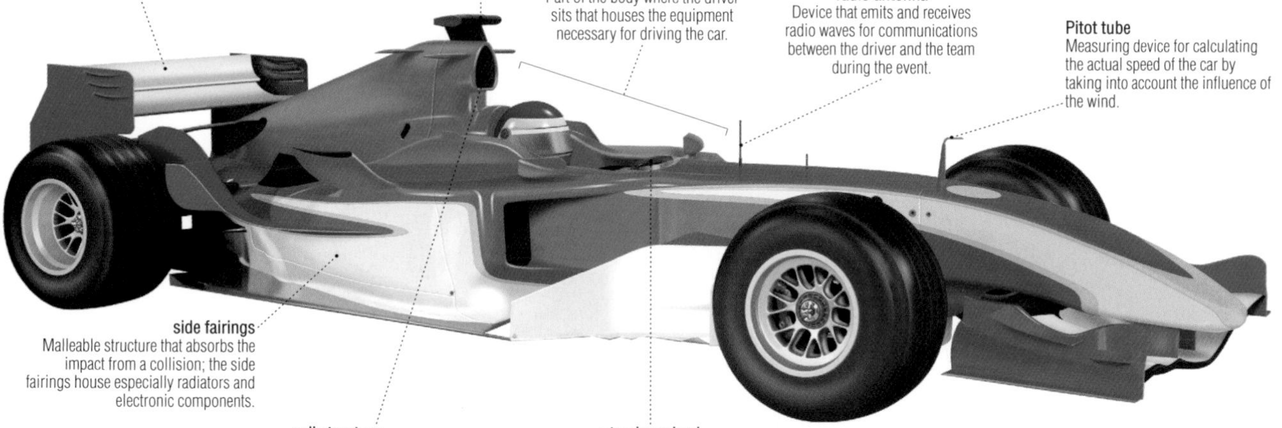
formula 1 car
Single-seater for racing on a closed circuit that can reach speeds of 225 mph; formula 1 is very popular in Europe.
wing
Part using air pressure to increase the load on the rear and front wheels to improve the tires' grip on the track.
camera
Exposure apparatus for following a driver's vehicle during an event; each car is equipped with at least one camera.
cockpit
Part of the body where the driver sits that houses the equipment necessary for driving the car.
radio antenna
Device that emits and receives radio waves for communications between the driver and the team during the event.
Pitot tube
Measuring device for calculating the actual speed of the car by taking into account the influence of the wind.
side fairings
Malleable structure that absorbs the impact from a collision; the side fairings house especially radiators and electronic components.
roll structure
Structure composed of metal loops to protect the driver if the car rolls over.
steering wheel
Unit enabling the driver to steer the turning wheels; a veritable dashboard, it is equipped with several controls such as the clutch and gear shifter.

rally car
Two-seater touring car for racing long distances on the road, in several stages and within a given time.

formula 3000 car
Single-seater that is less powerful than a formula 1 car but similar to it; formula 3000 is considered a school for formula 1.

formula Indy car
Sturdier and faster than a formula 1 in a straight line, it is designed to race on an oval or road circuit.

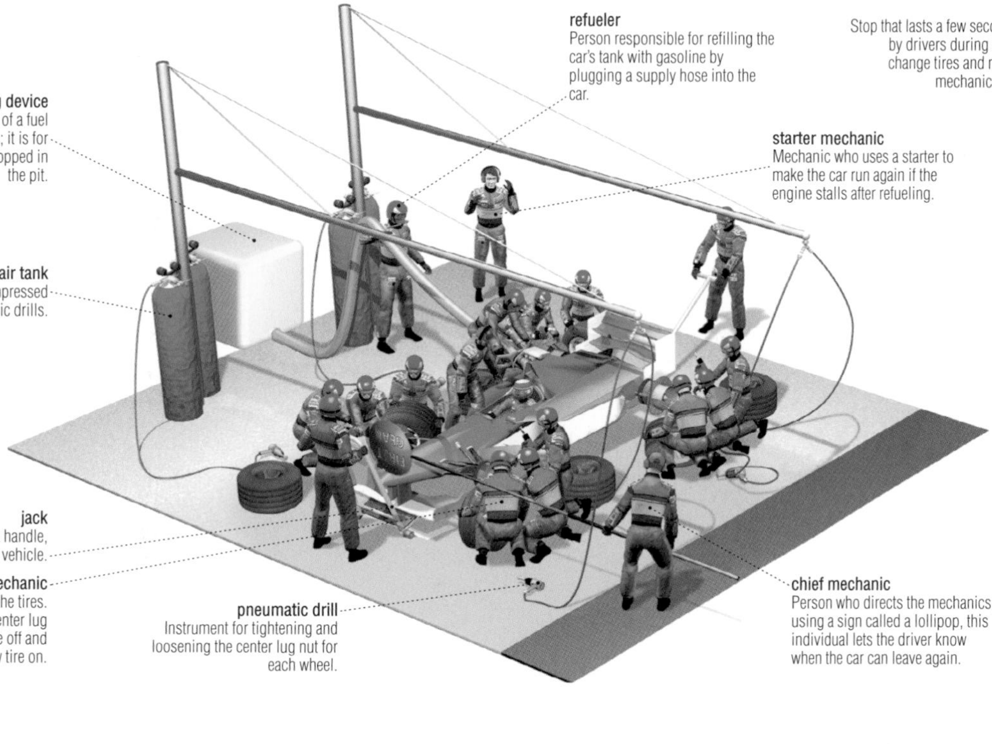
pit stop
Stop that lasts a few seconds; it is taken by drivers during a race to refuel, change tires and make necessary mechanical adjustments.
refueler
Person responsible for refilling the car's tank with gasoline by plugging a supply hose into the car.
refueling device
Assemblage consisting of a fuel tank connected to a hose; it is for refueling the car when stopped in the pit.
starter mechanic
Mechanic who uses a starter to make the car run again if the engine stalls after refueling.
compressed-air tank
Reservoir containing compressed air for the pneumatic drills.
jack
Mechanism activated by a handle, for raising the vehicle.
mechanic
Person in charge of changing the tires. One mechanic loosens the center lug nut, a second one takes the tire off and a third one puts the new tire on.
pneumatic drill
Instrument for tightening and loosening the center lug nut for each wheel.
chief mechanic
Person who directs the mechanics; using a sign called a lollipop, this individual lets the driver know when the car can leave again.

motorcycling

Competitions involving motorcycles whose engine cylinder size is larger than 125 cubic centimeters.

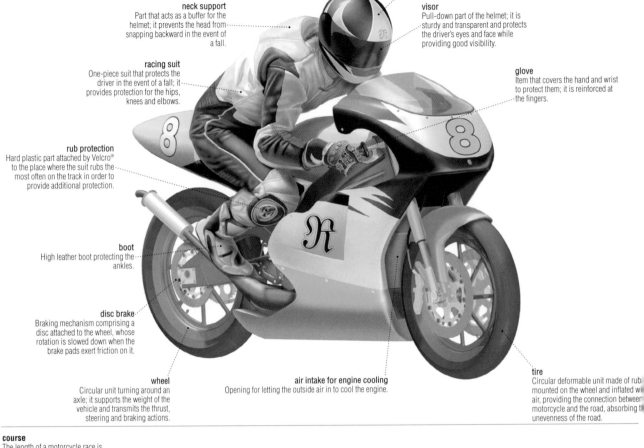

speed grand prix motorcycle and rider
Speed grand prix: streamlined motorcycle designed to race on a usually flat, closed road circuit; it can reach speeds of 200 mph.

full face helmet
Rigid piece of equipment that protects the head; it is equipped with a visor and a chin cup.

neck support
Part that acts as a buffer for the helmet; it prevents the head from snapping backward in the event of a fall.

visor
Pull-down part of the helmet; it is sturdy and transparent and protects the driver's eyes and face while providing good visibility.

racing suit
One-piece suit that protects the driver in the event of a fall; it provides protection for the hips, knees and elbows.

glove
Item that covers the hand and wrist to protect them; it is reinforced at the fingers.

rub protection
Hard plastic part attached by Velcro® to the place where the suit rubs the most often on the track in order to provide additional protection.

boot
High leather boot protecting the ankles.

disc brake
Braking mechanism comprising a disc attached to the wheel, whose rotation is slowed down when the brake pads exert friction on it.

wheel
Circular unit turning around an axle; it supports the weight of the vehicle and transmits the thrust, steering and braking actions.

air intake for engine cooling
Opening for letting the outside air in to cool the engine.

tire
Circular deformable unit made of rub mounted on the wheel and inflated wi air, providing the connection between motorcycle and the road, absorbing t unevenness of the road.

course
The length of a motorcycle race is between 2 and 6 mi.

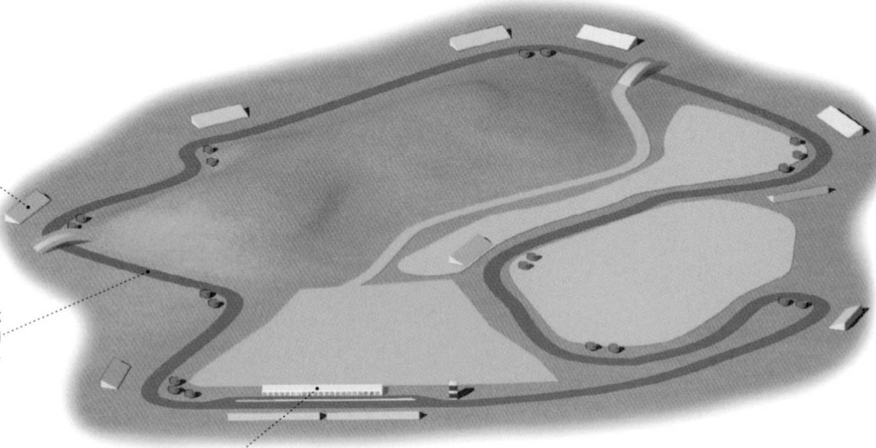

stands
Structure with tiered seats that is often partially covered; it is for spectators attending sporting events.

track
Driving surface of a motorcycling track; its minimum width is 32 ft.

pits
Spaces reserved for each team where the drivers stop during the race to refuel and change their tires.

motorcycling

trial motorcycle
Light motorcycle that is agile and easy to handle; it is designed for all-terrain obstacle races. The goal is to clear the obstacles while keeping both feet off the ground at all times.

rally motorcycle
All-terrain motorcycle designed to travel long distances on the road, in several stages and within a limited time.

motocross and supercross motorcycle
Slim lightweight motorcycle for racing on a closed rough circuit with uneven ground, bumps and hillocks.

protective suit
Clothing consisting of a top and pants that protect the driver in the event of a fall; protection (such as for the elbows, knees and back) is optional.

glove
Item that covers the hand and wrist in order to protect them; it is made of synthetic material and is padded inside and out.

pants
Garment for the lower body; it extends from the waist or the hips to the ankles, covering each leg separately.

helmet
Hard piece of equipment designed to protect the head.

protective goggles
Equipment that protects the eyes; it is covered with several layers of plastic, which the driver peels off when they become dirty.

hand protector
Rigid part in front of the handlebar to protect the hand in the event of impact.

number plate
Rectangular plate on the front and sides of the motorcycle; it carries a number to identify the driver.

fork
Sliding tube that encloses a spring; it forms the steering, suspension and shock-absorbing mechanisms of the front wheel.

nubby tire
Tire whose tread is fitted with blocks of rubber, providing better traction on rough terrain.

boot
High leather boot protecting the ankles.

protective plate
Metal part under the motorcycle that protects it from shocks and prevents it from striking obstacles.

multiple jumps
Series of several bumps that the racer clears in a single jump, as opposed to clearing each jump separately.

supercross circuit
Sometimes covered, man-made track that is composed of earth or a mixture of sand and clay; it is strewn with obstacles and bumps for jumps.

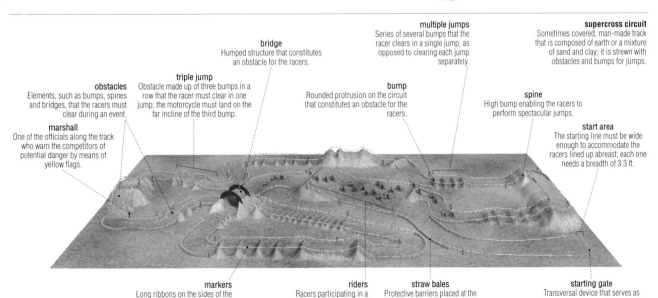

bridge
Humped structure that constitutes an obstacle for the racers.

triple jump
Obstacle made up of three bumps in a row that the racer must clear in one jump; the motorcycle must land on the far incline of the third bump.

obstacles
Elements, such as bumps, spines and bridges, that the racers must clear during an event.

marshall
One of the officials along the track who warn the competitors of potential danger by means of yellow flags.

bump
Rounded protrusion on the circuit that constitutes an obstacle for the racers.

spine
High bump enabling the racers to perform spectacular jumps.

start area
The starting line must be wide enough to accommodate the racers lined up abreast; each one needs a breadth of 3.3 ft.

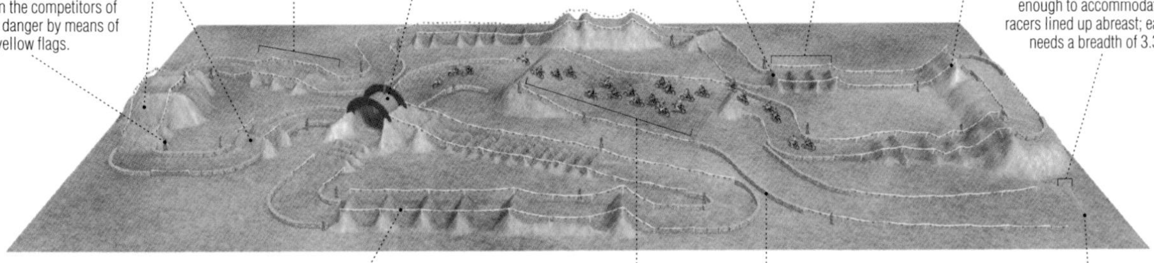

markers
Long ribbons on the sides of the track that delimit a safety zone for the racers and spectators.

riders
Racers participating in a motorcycling event.

straw bales
Protective barriers placed at the curves to absorb impact in the event a racer skids out.

starting gate
Transversal device that serves as the motorcycles' starting point; it folds up or down so that the racers can push off.

personal watercraft

Motorized boat that moves quickly on water (about 65 mph); it is propelled by a turbine that sucks in water in front of it and shoots it out behind.

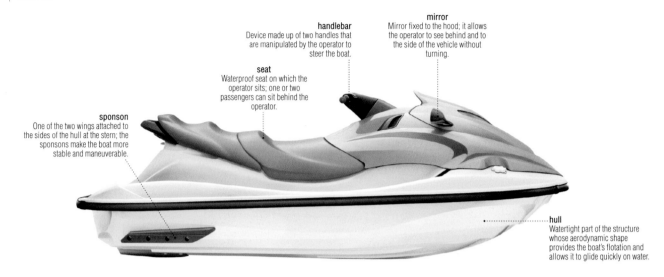

mirror
Mirror fixed to the hood; it allows the operator to see behind and to the side of the vehicle without turning.
handlebar
Device made up of two handles that are manipulated by the operator to steer the boat.
seat
Waterproof seat on which the operator sits; one or two passengers can sit behind the operator.
sponson
One of the two wings attached to the sides of the hull at the stern; the sponsons make the boat more stable and maneuverable.
hull
Watertight part of the structure whose aerodynamic shape provides the boat's flotation and allows it to glide quickly on water.

snowmobile

Motorized vehicle with a track and skis for moving rapidly on snow; some snowmobiles reach speeds of 125 mph.

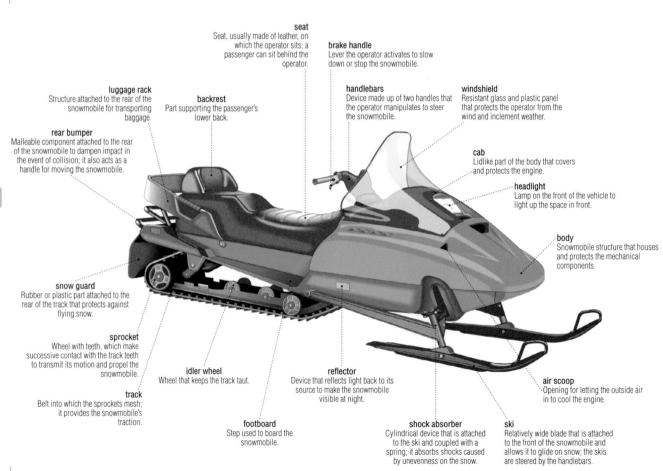

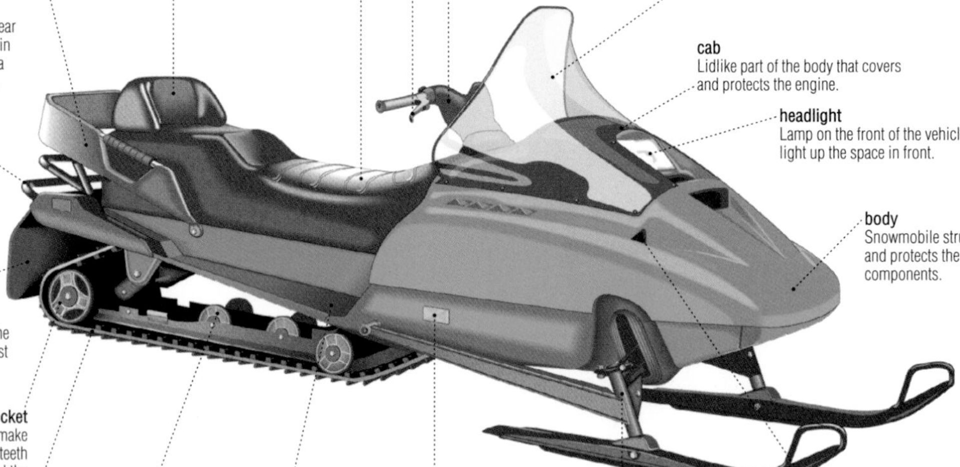
seat
Seat, usually made of leather, on which the operator sits; a passenger can sit behind the operator.
brake handle
Lever the operator activates to slow down or stop the snowmobile.
luggage rack
Structure attached to the rear of the snowmobile for transporting baggage.
backrest
Part supporting the passenger's lower back.
handlebars
Device made up of two handles that the operator manipulates to steer the snowmobile.
windshield
Resistant glass and plastic panel that protects the operator from the wind and inclement weather.
rear bumper
Malleable component attached to the rear of the snowmobile to dampen impact in the event of collision; it also acts as a handle for moving the snowmobile.
cab
Lidlike part of the body that covers and protects the engine.
headlight
Lamp on the front of the vehicle to light up the space in front.
body
Snowmobile structure that houses and protects the mechanical components.
snow guard
Rubber or plastic part attached to the rear of the track that protects against flying snow.
sprocket
Wheel with teeth, which make successive contact with the track teeth to transmit its motion and propel the snowmobile.
idler wheel
Wheel that keeps the track taut.
reflector
Device that reflects light back to its source to make the snowmobile visible at night.
air scoop
Opening for letting the outside air in to cool the engine.
track
Belt into which the sprockets mesh; it provides the snowmobile's traction.
footboard
Step used to board the snowmobile.
shock absorber
Cylindrical device that is attached to the ski and coupled with a spring; it absorbs shocks caused by unevenness on the snow.
ski
Relatively wide blade that is attached to the front of the snowmobile and allows it to glide on snow; the skis are steered by the handlebars.

curling

Sport with two opposing teams of four players who slide stones over an ice surface in the direction of a target.

curling brush
Brush that is rubbed over the ice in front of a moving stone to alter its trajectory or improve its sliding.

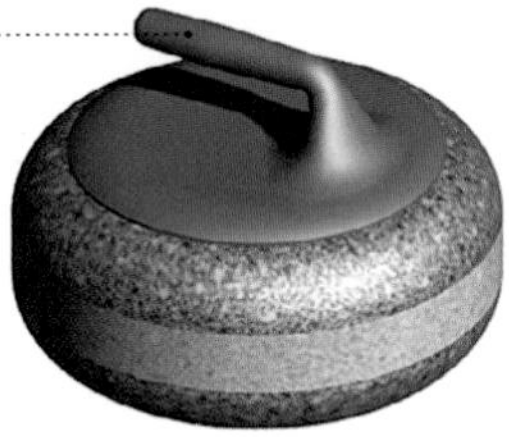

curling stone
Circular piece of polished granite; in the course of an end, each team takes turns to throw eight stones of the same color.

handle
Handle used to hold and maneuver the stone.

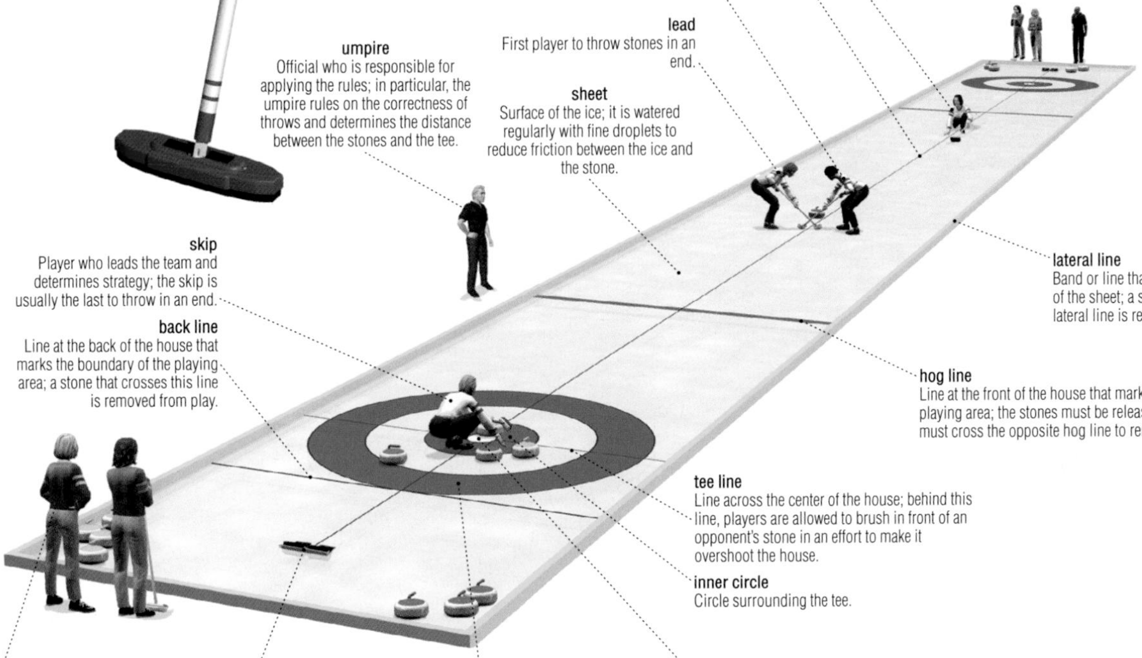

center line
Line that divides the sheet in half; the stone is thrown and released relatively close to this line.

sheet
Ice surface on which a match is played; when an end is complete, the next end starts from the opposite end of the sheet.

second
Second player to throw stones in an end.

vice-skip
Player who assists the skip in devising playing tactics; the vice-skip usually throws third in an end.

lead
First player to throw stones in an end.

umpire
Official who is responsible for applying the rules; in particular, the umpire rules on the correctness of throws and determines the distance between the stones and the tee.

sheet
Surface of the ice; it is watered regularly with fine droplets to reduce friction between the ice and the stone.

skip
Player who leads the team and determines strategy; the skip is usually the last to throw in an end.

back line
Line at the back of the house that marks the boundary of the playing area; a stone that crosses this line is removed from play.

lateral line
Band or line that delimits the sides of the sheet; a stone that strikes the lateral line is removed from play.

hog line
Line at the front of the house that marks the boundary of the playing area; the stones must be released before this line and must cross the opposite hog line to remain in play.

tee line
Line across the center of the house; behind this line, players are allowed to brush in front of an opponent's stone in an effort to make it overshoot the house.

inner circle
Circle surrounding the tee.

curler
Curling player who throws two stones in each of the 10 ends that make up a match.

hack
Rubber foothold at each end of the sheet that the thrower uses to push off.

outer circle
Circle forming the outer limit of the house.

tee
Circle forming the center of the house; once all the stones are thrown, the team with the stone closest to the tee wins the end.

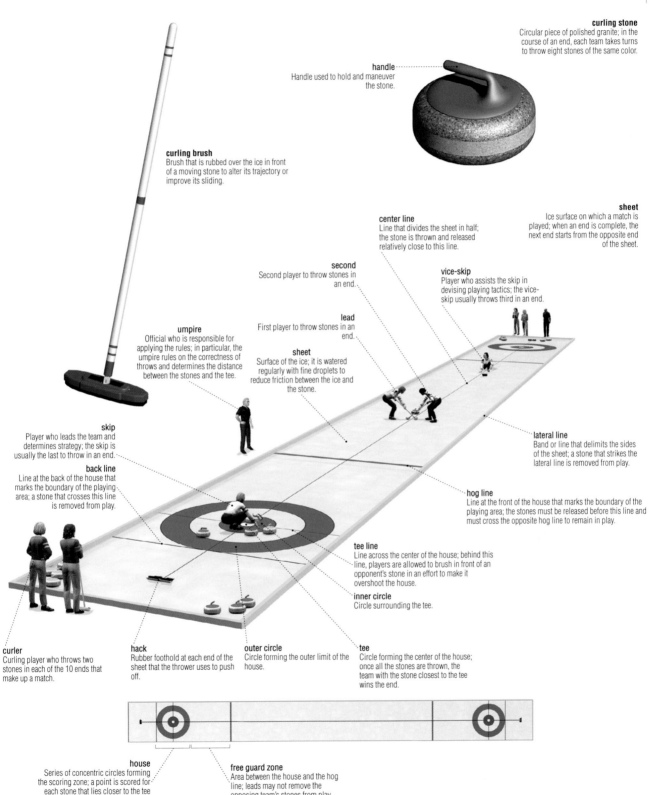

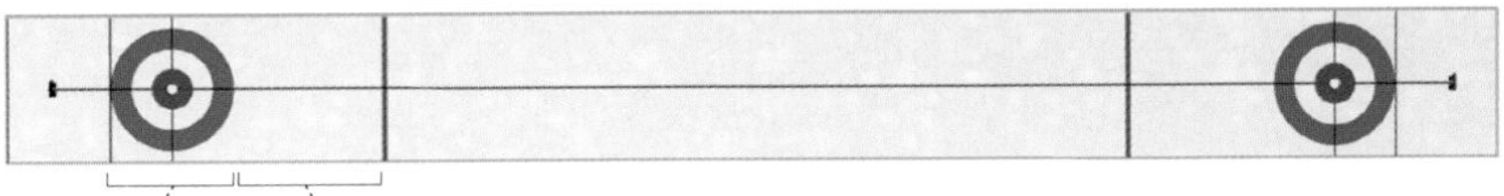

house
Series of concentric circles forming the scoring zone; a point is scored for each stone that lies closer to the tee than the opposing team's stones.

free guard zone
Area between the house and the hog line; leads may not remove the opposing team's stones from play.

ice hockey

Sport that is played on an ice rink with two opposing teams of six players; goals are scored by using a stick to put a puck in the opposing net.

ice hockey player
Member of an ice hockey team; players wear a variety of protective equipment to prevent injury caused by falls or body checks.

visor
Transparent piece of equipment secured to the front of the helmet to protect the eyes and upper face.

helmet
Hard piece of equipment designed to protect the head.

team's emblem
Logo representing the team that is printed on the front of the jersey.

player's number
Number that identifies the hockey player; numbers range from 1 to 99 and are sewn onto the back and the sleeves of the jersey.

glove
Padded covering for the hand and wrist that takes the shape of the fingers; it must be flexible enough to provide a good grip on the stick.

pants
Padded clothing attached around the waist by a belt or suspenders; they protect the pelvis, buttocks and thighs.

stocking
Stretchy piece of fabric that covers the leg and thigh; it is worn over the pads to keep the muscles warm.

skate
Reinforced boot equipped with a blade for gliding over ice.

blade
Narrow metal blade that is attached to the skate boot; its curved ends help the player to turn.

rink
Ice surface on which a hockey game is played; a game consists of three 20-minute periods with two 15-minute intermissions.

left defense
Position to the left of the center and behind the wing; this player tries to prevent the opponent from approaching the goal.

right defense
Position to the right of the center and behind the wing; this player tries to prevent the opponent from approaching the goal.

face-off spot
Each of the spots where a referee or linesman drops the puck to put it in play.

goal line
Red line that the puck must cross for a goal to be scored; the red line also marks the icing line.

glass protector
Reinforced glass panel that is mounted on top of the boards to protect spectators from high shots and players' sticks.

players' bench
Bench used by the coaches and by inactive players; each team has about 20 players but only six are on the ice at the same time.

rink corner
The four rounded corners of the rink where body checks are often thrown.

goal judge
Off-ice official who is positioned at the end of the rink behind the goal; the goal judge turns on a red light when the puck crosses the goal line.

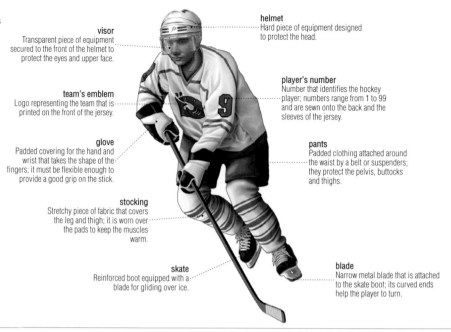

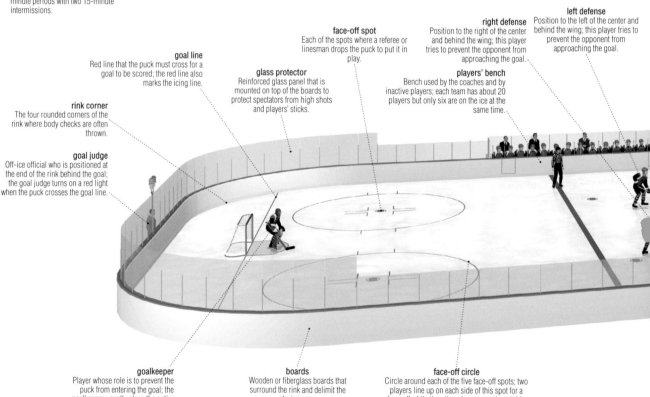

goalkeeper
Player whose role is to prevent the puck from entering the goal; the goalkeeper usually plays the entire game.

boards
Wooden or fiberglass boards that surround the rink and delimit the playing area.

face-off circle
Circle around each of the five face-off spots; two players line up on each side of this spot for a face-off while the other players remain outside the circle.

goalkeeper
Player whose role is to prevent the puck from entering the goal; the goalkeeper, who faces shots reaching speeds of 95 mph, wears heavy protective equipment.
face mask
Cage attached to the helmet to protect the goalkeeper's face and head; a flexible throat protector is attached to it.
blocking glove
Glove mounted with a hard flat rectangular piece that is used to block shots.
catching glove
Basket-shaped glove that is closed by pinching the hand; the goalkeeper uses it to catch and immobilize the puck.
goalkeeper's pad
Heavily padded piece of equipment that protects the goalkeeper's legs, knees and thighs from the impact of shots.
goalkeeper's stick
Stick featuring a large lower half and blade so that the goalkeeper can stop pucks more easily.

left wing
Offensive position to the left of the center; this player's role is to score goals and to check the opposing left wing.
coach
The team's leader; the coach plots strategy and decides who plays in different situations.
assistant coach
Person who assists the coach; there are usually two assistant coaches behind the bench, one in charge of the offense and the other in charge of the defense.
blue line
Two lines that divide the rink into three equal parts; an offside is called when a player crosses the opposing blue line before the puck.
goal crease
Semicircle reserved for the goalkeeper; the referee disallows a goal if a player interferes with the goalkeeper inside the goal crease.
referee
Official who is responsible for applying the rules; the referee, who wears a red armband, officiates and drops the puck for face-offs at the start of a period.
neutral zone
Area between the two blue lines where player changes are made and where various offensive and defensive strategies are initiated.
linesman
One of two officials who signal offsides and icings; they do most of the face-offs and also signal infractions to the referee.
goal
Cage formed of netting mounted on a metal frame; a team scores a goal each time it lodges the puck inside the opposing goal.
goal lights
The red light signals a goal while the green light, which is connected to the official time clock, signals a stoppage in play or the end of a period.
penalty bench official
Official who is responsible for maintaining order on the penalty bench.
penalty bench
Bench reserved for penalized players; penalties vary between two and 10 minutes, depending on the seriousness of the infraction.
center line
Line that divides the rink into two zones, one for each team; teams change zones after each period.
center face-off circle
Circle in the middle of the rink; face-offs are held in the center circle at the start of a period and after a goal.
center
Player who usually takes the face-offs; a key player on a team, the center plays an offensive and a defensive role.
right wing
Offensive position to the right of the center; this player's role is to score goals and to check the opposing right wing.
officials' bench
Bench reserved for some of the off-ice officials (timekeeper and penalty keeper, scorer, announcer).

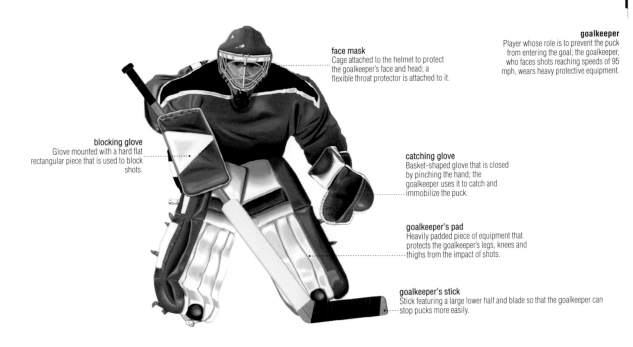

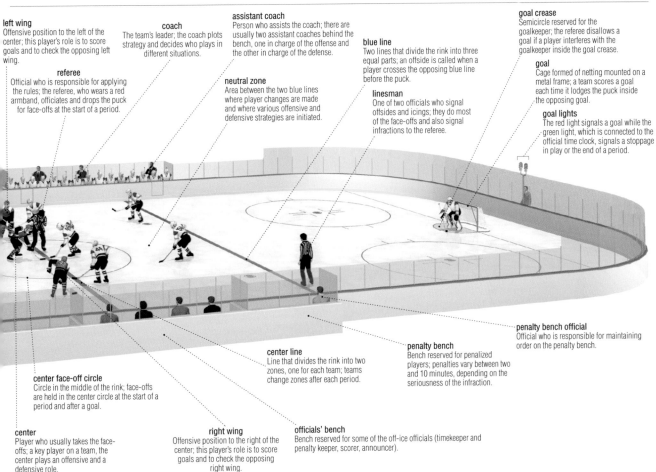

ice hockey

player's stick
Long, traditionally wooden stick that consists of a blade set at an angle to a shaft.

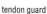

butt end
Upper end of the shaft; it is usually covered with rubber tape to prevent the hand from slipping off the stick.

shaft

heel
Back end of the blade.

blade
Lower part of the stick that is used to stop, pass and shoot the puck; it is curved to ease puck handling.

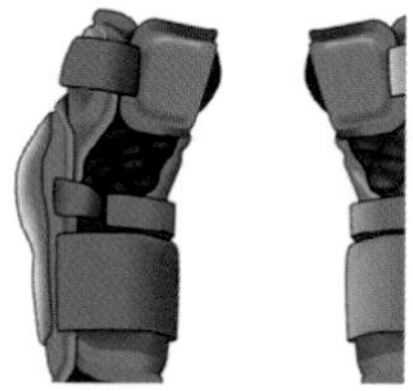

throat protector
Nylon neck guard that is worn under the shoulder pads to protect the hockey player's neck and throat.

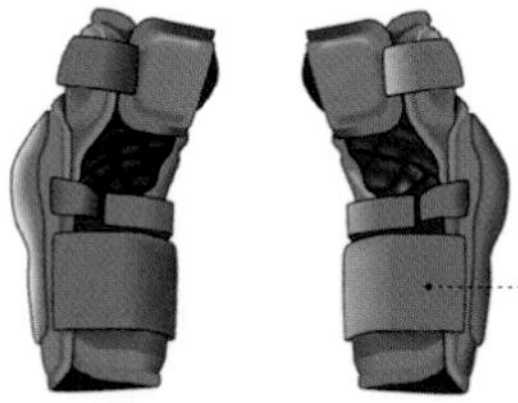

elbow pads
Piece of equipment that consists of a hard shell to protect the elbow; it also covers part of the arm and the forearm.

cuff
Elastic band that covers the upper part of the forearm; it fastens the elbow pad in place.

goalkeeper's stick
Stick featuring a large lower half and blade so that the goalkeeper can stop pucks more easily.

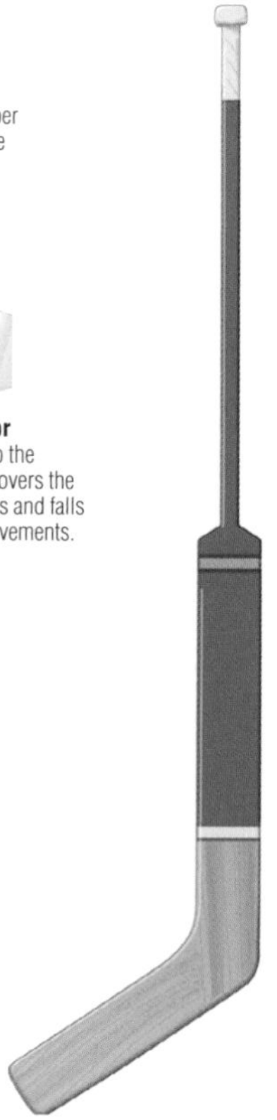

throat protector
Hard part secured to the goalkeeper's mask that covers the throat and the neck; it rises and falls with the goalkeeper's movements.

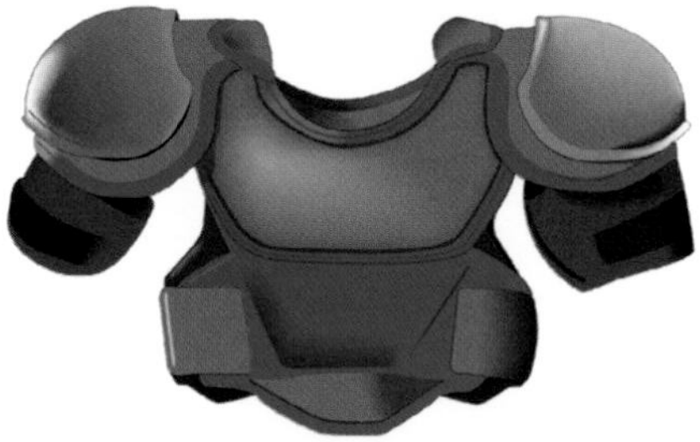

shoulder pads
Padded vest with two hard shells designed to protect the shoulders; they cover the chest and upper back but provide less coverage than the goalkeeper's chest pad.

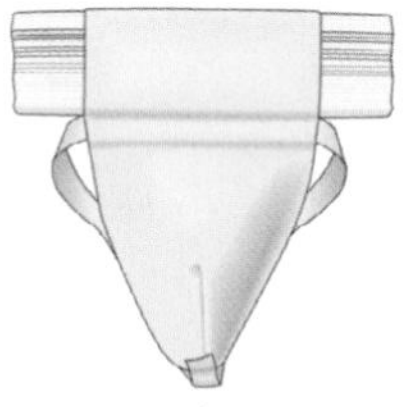

protective cup
Piece of equipment that consists of rigid molded plastic designed to cover a player's genital organs.

puck
Black disk that is made of hard rubber; the puck is refrigerated before a game to improve its sliding action and reduce bouncing.

arm pad
Part of the goalkeeper's chest pad that covers the arm.

goalkeeper's chest pad
Heavily padded vest that protects the goalkeeper's shoulders, chest, stomach, back and arms.

knee pad
Part of the pads that covers the knees.

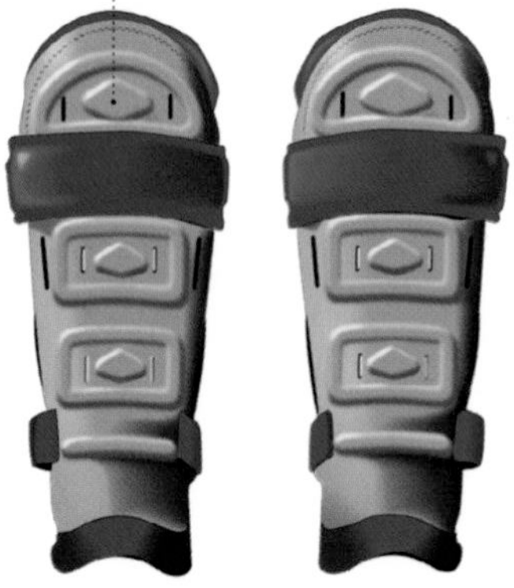

pads
Pieces of equipment that consist of hard molded plastic to protect the hockey player's legs and knees.

player's skate
Reinforced boot equipped with a blade for gliding over ice.

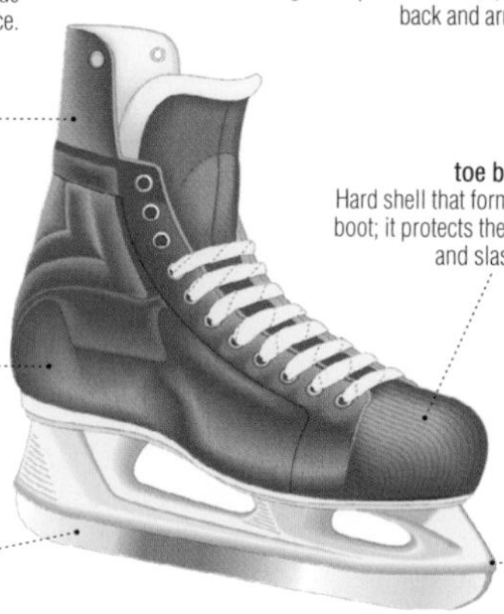

tendon guard
Rigid part that covers the lower leg.

toe box
Hard shell that forms the end of the boot; it protects the toes from shots and slashes.

boot
Sturdy flexible boot with a lace; it protects and supports the foot and ankle and is made of leather or synthetic materials.

blade
Narrow metal blade that is attached to the skate boot; its curved ends help the player to turn.

point
Front tip of the blade.

goalkeeper's skate
Skate that is reinforced on the sides and equipped with a long low straight blade; it is designed to improve the goalkeeper's balance.

SPORTS AND GAMES

figure skating

Sport that consists of executing jumps, spins and figures while skating to music; it includes singles skating, pairs skating and ice dancing.

figure skate
Reinforced boot with a blade that makes it possible to glide over the ice; figure skating is hard on the ankles so the skate provides maximum ankle support.

lining
Padded layer of fabric or leather that covers and protects the inside of the boot.

hook
Small piece of curved metal used to attach the lace.

backstay
Reinforcement at the back of the boot.

boot
Sturdy flexible boot with a lace; it protects and supports the foot and ankle and is made of leather or synthetic materials.

heel
Stiff part underneath the boot that supports the back of the foot.

stanchion
Vertical part that extends up from the blade to secure it to the sole.

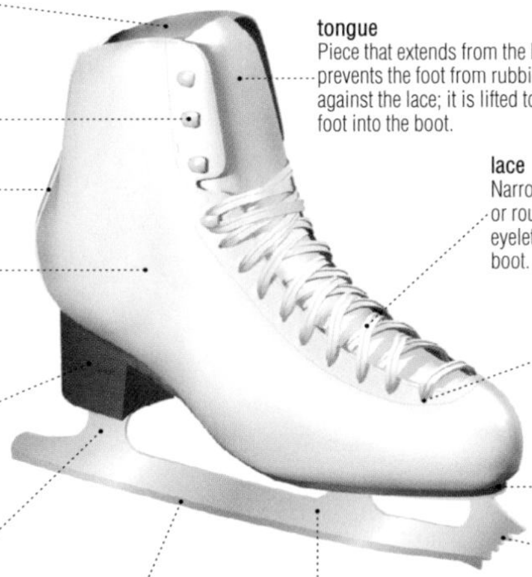

tongue
Piece that extends from the boot and prevents the foot from rubbing against the lace; it is lifted to slip the foot into the boot.

lace
Narrow cord of fabric or leather, flat or round, that is threaded through eyelets or hooks to tighten the boot.

eyelet
Small metal-rimmed hole through which the lace passes.

sole
Sturdy plastic or wooden sole that forms the bottom of the boot; the blade screws into the sole.

toe pick
Small teeth at the front end of the blade; they serve as the pivot point during spins and also make it possible to take off and land during jumps.

edge
Part of the blade that bites into the ice; the blade has two edges (inside and outside), which are separated by a groove.

blade
Narrow tapering strip of metal that is attached to the sole; the lower part is made of hardened steel to keep the edges sharp.

dance blade
Blade whose heel is shorter and whose toe picks are less pronounced to facilitate the execution of complex movements and to prevent the toe picks from catching.

free skating blade
Blade with toe picks that facilitate the execution of jumps and spins; its curvature is more pronounced than that of the dance blade.

examples of jumps

Jump: movement by which the skater leaves the ice and spins in the air before landing.

salchow
Single-rotation jump with takeoff from the back inside edge; the Swede Ulrich Salchow created it in 1909.

axel
Jump of one and a half rotations with takeoff from the forward edge; invented by the Norwegian Axel Paulsen in 1882, it is considered the most difficult jump.

toe loop
Single-rotation toe jump with takeoff and landing on the same foot; it is considered the easiest of the toe jumps.

flip
Single-rotation toe jump with takeoff from the back inside edge and landing on the opposite foot; the flip is in fact a toe salchow.

lutz
Single-rotation toe jump with takeoff from the back outside edge and landing on the opposite foot; the Austrian Alois Lutz invented it in 1913.

referee
Official who is responsible for the eligibility of officials, skaters and the judging panel and the allowability of controversial decisions.

assistant referee
Individual who assists the referee and is authorized to replace him or her if necessary.

technical delegates
Official who ensures that technical installations are in compliance with the standards of the International Skating Union (ISU).

judges
Officials who are responsible for evaluating performances; during international competitions, nine judges are chosen at random from the nations represented.

rink
Ice surface on which skaters execute their programs; program duration varies depending on the event (between 2 min. 40 sec. and 4 min. 30 sec.).

technical controller
Official who supervises the work of the technical specialist. He or she can immediately correct any error observed.

timekeeper
Person who monitors the length of performances to ensure that skaters respect the allotted time.

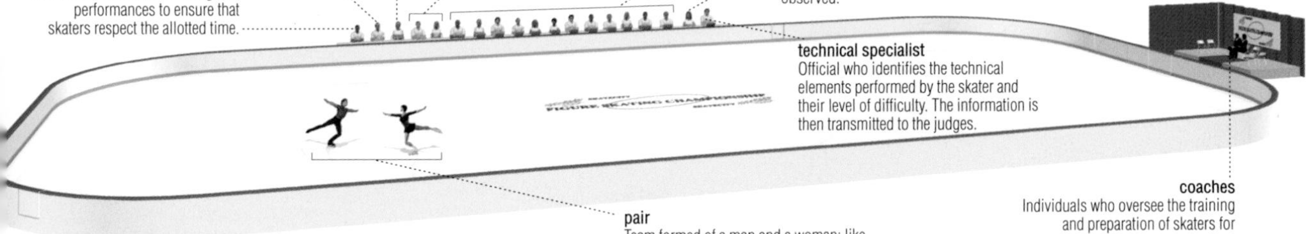

technical specialist
Official who identifies the technical elements performed by the skater and their level of difficulty. The information is then transmitted to the judges.

coaches
Individuals who oversee the training and preparation of skaters for competitions; coaches provide final advice prior to performances.

pair
Team formed of a man and a woman; like singles skaters, pairs take part in two events: the technical program and the free program.

speed skating

Race on ice between individuals or teams held on a long or short track.

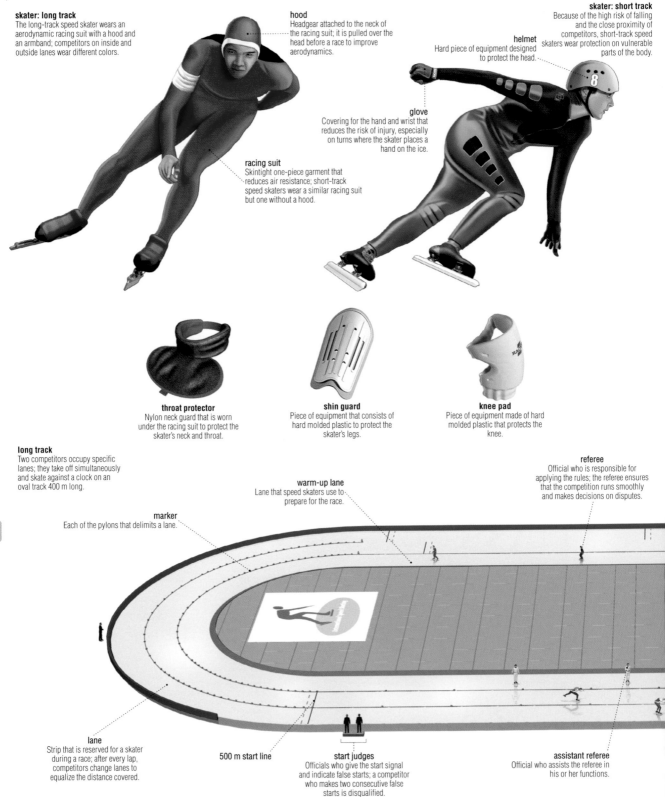

skater: long track
The long-track speed skater wears an aerodynamic racing suit with a hood and an armband; competitors on inside and outside lanes wear different colors.

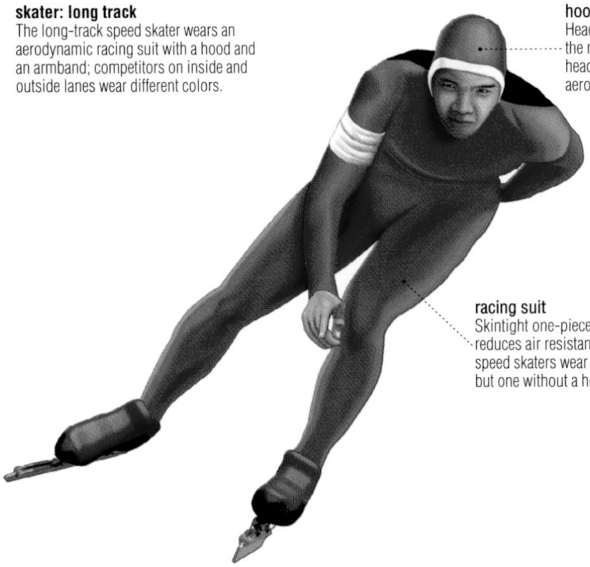

hood
Headgear attached to the neck of the racing suit; it is pulled over the head before a race to improve aerodynamics.

racing suit
Skintight one-piece garment that reduces air resistance; short-track speed skaters wear a similar racing suit but one without a hood.

skater: short track
Because of the high risk of falling and the close proximity of competitors, short-track speed skaters wear protection on vulnerable parts of the body.

helmet
Hard piece of equipment designed to protect the head.

glove
Covering for the hand and wrist that reduces the risk of injury, especially on turns where the skater places a hand on the ice.

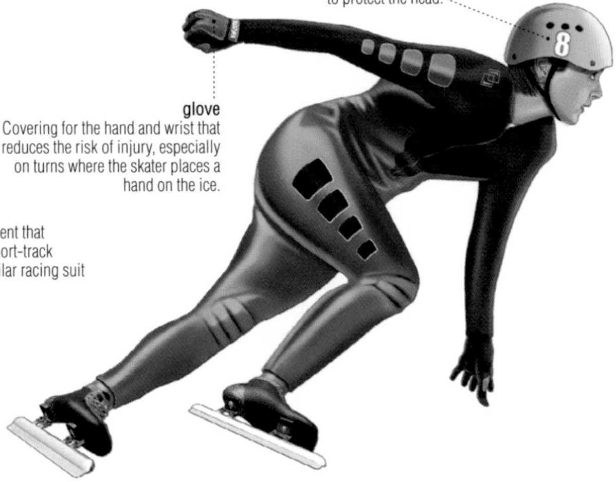

throat protector
Nylon neck guard that is worn under the racing suit to protect the skater's neck and throat.

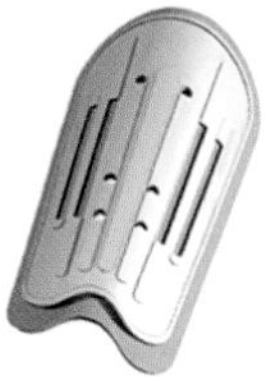

shin guard
Piece of equipment that consists of hard molded plastic to protect the skater's legs.

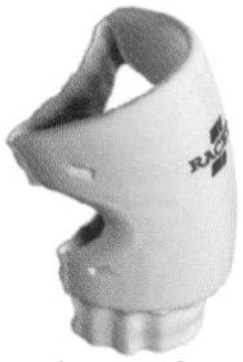

knee pad
Piece of equipment made of hard molded plastic that protects the knee.

long track
Two competitors occupy specific lanes; they take off simultaneously and skate against a clock on an oval track 400 m long.

warm-up lane
Lane that speed skaters use to prepare for the race.

referee
Official who is responsible for applying the rules; the referee ensures that the competition runs smoothly and makes decisions on disputes.

marker
Each of the pylons that delimits a lane.

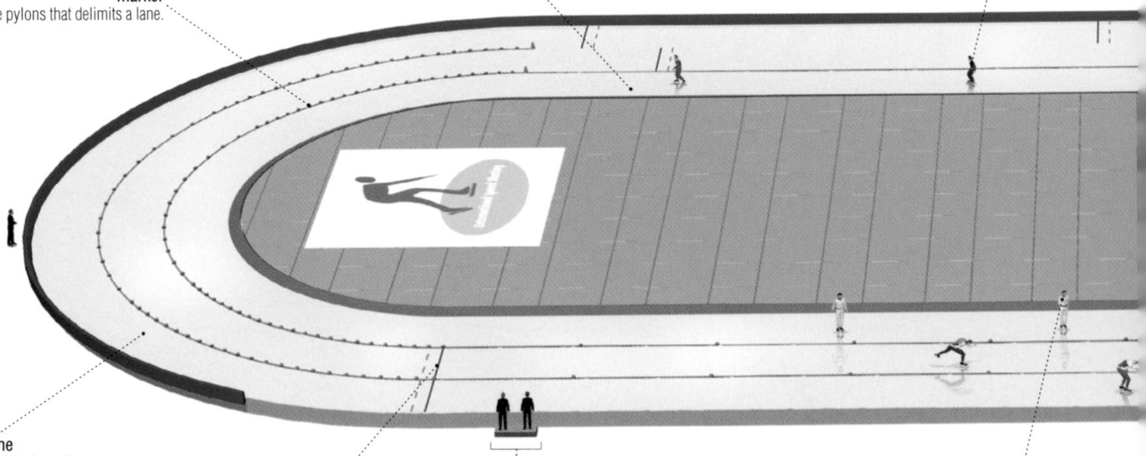

lane
Strip that is reserved for a skater during a race; after every lap, competitors change lanes to equalize the distance covered.

500 m start line

start judges
Officials who give the start signal and indicate false starts; a competitor who makes two consecutive false starts is disqualified.

assistant referee
Official who assists the referee in his or her functions.

speed skating

speed skates
Skates that consist of a lightweight boot, which takes the shape of the foot; they have long, very tapered blades to provide prolonged contact with the ice.

clapskate
Long-track skate with a blade that detaches from the heel; it provides longer contact with the ice to improve thrust.

short track skate
Skate with a blade that is curved in the direction of the turn and offset to the left for better cornering at high speed.

short track
Four to six skaters who race against one another; the skater who finishes with the fastest time wins the race.

start judge
Official who gives the start signal and indicates false starts; a competitor is disqualified for making two consecutive false starts.

finish judges
Officials who determine the order in which the skaters finish.

protective mat
Padding that covers the boards to cushion the impact when a skater falls.

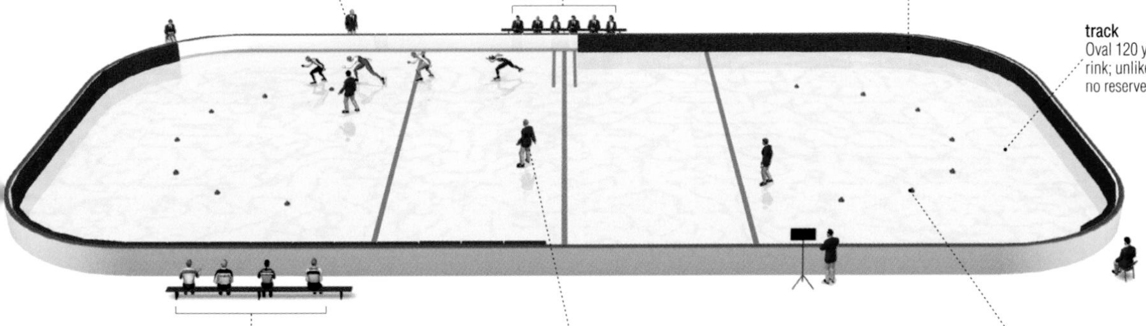

track
Oval 120 yd long on a standard rink; unlike the long track, there are no reserved lanes.

coaches
Individuals who train the skaters; they devise strategy and give instructions to the skaters throughout the race.

chief referee
Official who is responsible for applying the rules; in particular, the chief referee is authorized to disqualify a competitor who commits a fault.

marker
Each of the markers bordering the track; it is made of rubber or plastic and is not affixed to the ice to avoid damaging it.

assistant judges
Officials placed near the crossover area to ensure that lane changes are executed properly.

coaches
Individuals who train the skaters; they devise strategy and give instructions to the skaters throughout the race.

protective mat
Padding that covers the boards to cushion the impact when a skater falls.

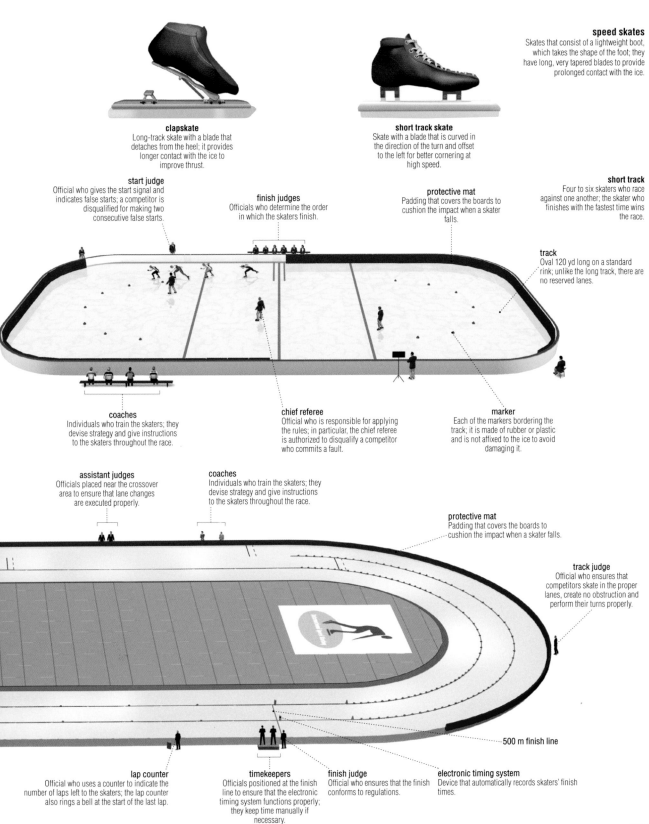

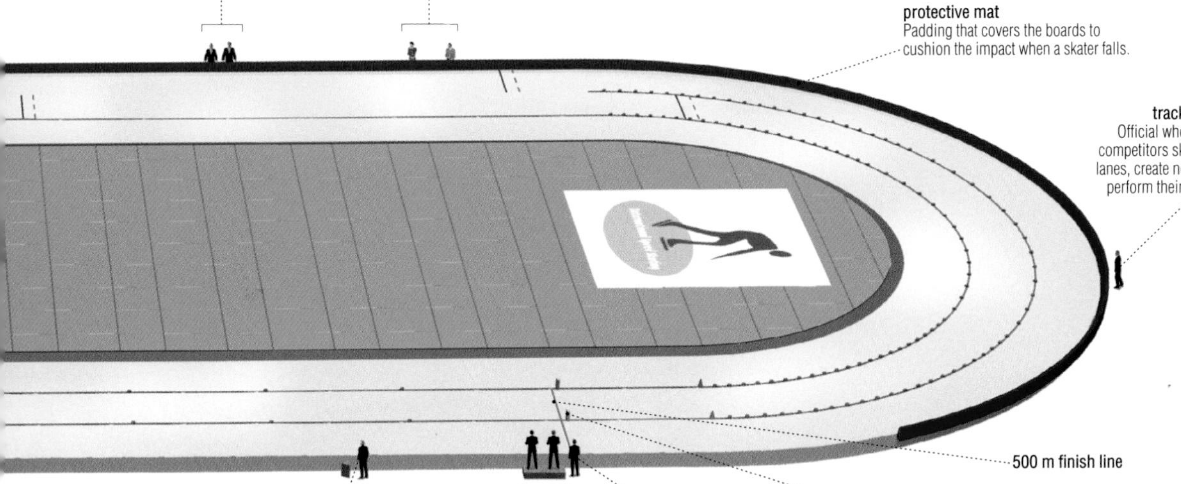

track judge
Official who ensures that competitors skate in the proper lanes, create no obstruction and perform their turns properly.

500 m finish line

lap counter
Official who uses a counter to indicate the number of laps left to the skaters; the lap counter also rings a bell at the start of the last lap.

timekeepers
Officials positioned at the finish line to ensure that the electronic timing system functions properly; they keep time manually if necessary.

finish judge
Official who ensures that the finish conforms to regulations.

electronic timing system
Device that automatically records skaters' finish times.

bobsled

Sport that consists of racing down an icy track on a two- or four-person bobsled; bobsleds reach speeds of over 85 mph.

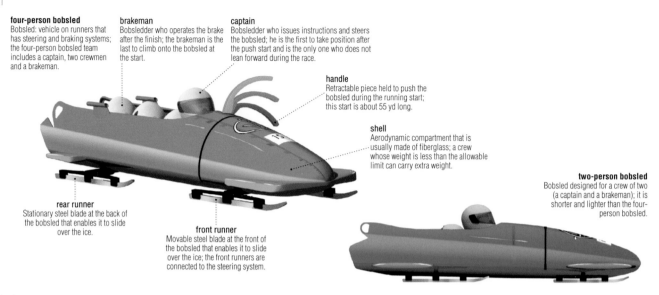

four-person bobsled
Bobsled: vehicle on runners that has steering and braking systems; the four-person bobsled team includes a captain, two crewmen and a brakeman.

brakeman
Bobsledder who operates the brake after the finish; the brakeman is the last to climb onto the bobsled at the start.

captain
Bobsledder who issues instructions and steers the bobsled; he is the first to take position after the push start and is the only one who does not lean forward during the race.

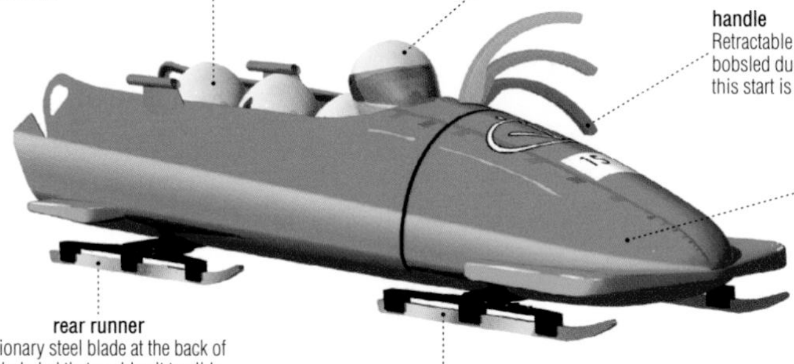

handle
Retractable piece held to push the bobsled during the running start; this start is about 55 yd long.

shell
Aerodynamic compartment that is usually made of fiberglass; a crew whose weight is less than the allowable limit can carry extra weight.

rear runner
Stationary steel blade at the back of the bobsled that enables it to slide over the ice.

front runner
Movable steel blade at the front of the bobsled that enables it to slide over the ice; the front runners are connected to the steering system.

two-person bobsled
Bobsled designed for a crew of two (a captain and a brakeman); it is shorter and lighter than the four-person bobsled.

luge

Speed sport that consists of racing down an icy track on a singles or doubles luge; luge racers lie on their backs with their feet forward and reach speeds of 90 mph.

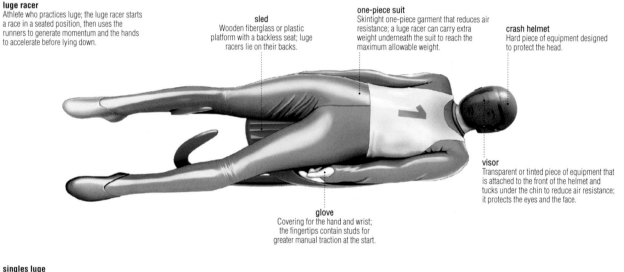

luge racer
Athlete who practices luge; the luge racer starts a race in a seated position, then uses the runners to generate momentum and the hands to accelerate before lying down.

sled
Wooden fiberglass or plastic platform with a backless seat; luge racers lie on their backs.

one-piece suit
Skintight one-piece garment that reduces air resistance; a luge racer can carry extra weight underneath the suit to reach the maximum allowable weight.

crash helmet
Hard piece of equipment designed to protect the head.

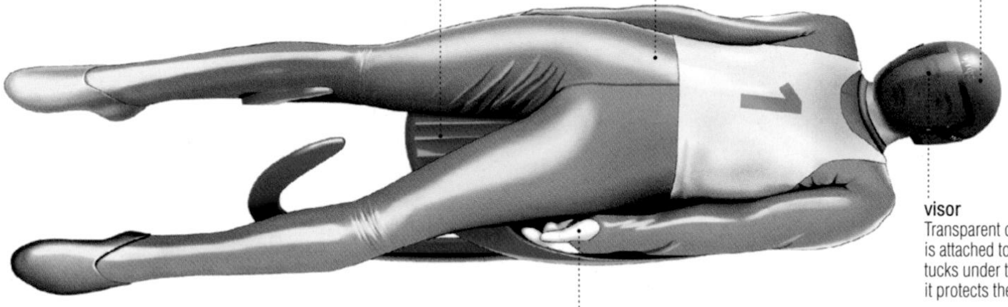

visor
Transparent or tinted piece of equipment that is attached to the front of the helmet and tucks under the chin to reduce air resistance; it protects the eyes and the face.

glove
Covering for the hand and wrist; the fingertips contain studs for greater manual traction at the start.

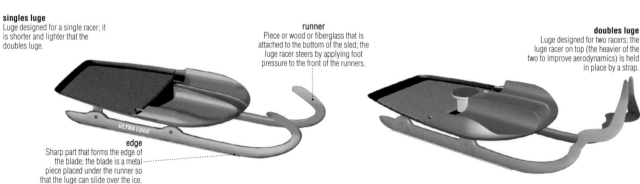

singles luge
Luge designed for a single racer; it is shorter and lighter that the doubles luge.

runner
Piece or wood or fiberglass that is attached to the bottom of the sled; the luge racer steers by applying foot pressure to the front of the runners.

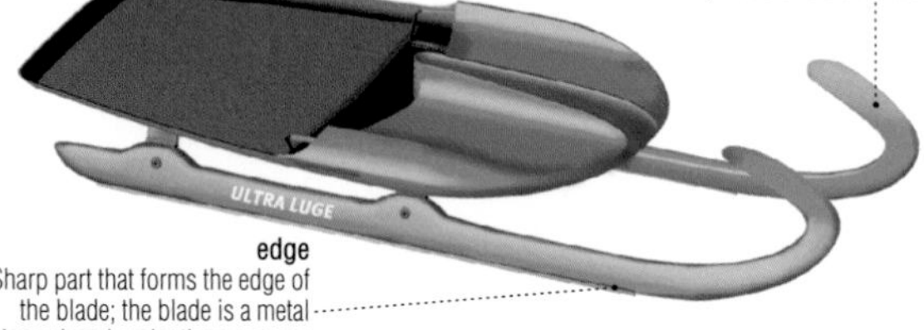

edge
Sharp part that forms the edge of the blade; the blade is a metal piece placed under the runner so that the luge can slide over the ice.

doubles luge
Luge designed for two racers; the luge racer on top (the heavier of the two to improve aerodynamics) is held in place by a strap.

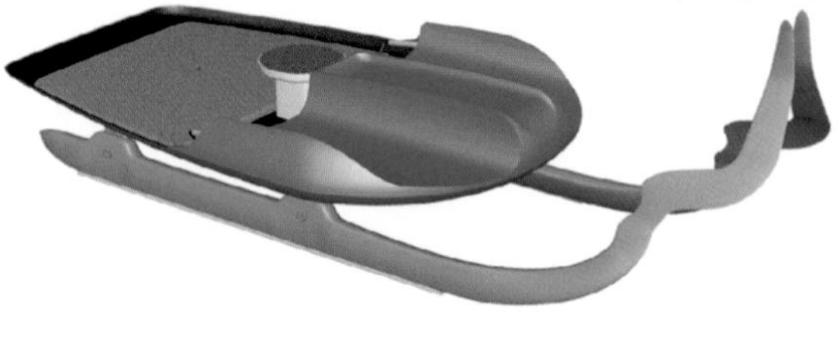

skeleton

Sport that consists of racing down an icy track on a skeleton, which can reach speeds of 85 mph; sledders lie head forward on their stomachs.

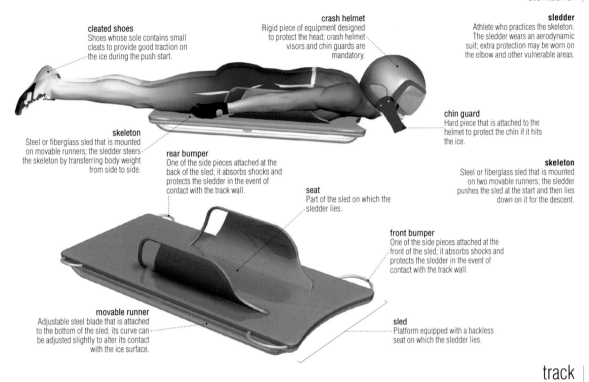

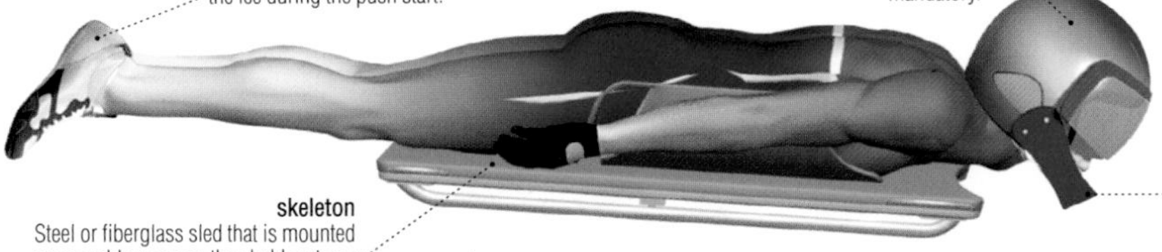
cleated shoes
Shoes whose sole contains small cleats to provide good traction on the ice during the push start.
crash helmet
Rigid piece of equipment designed to protect the head; crash helmet visors and chin guards are mandatory.
sledder
Athlete who practices the skeleton. The sledder wears an aerodynamic suit; extra protection may be worn on the elbow and other vulnerable areas.
chin guard
Hard piece that is attached to the helmet to protect the chin if it hits the ice.
skeleton
Steel or fiberglass sled that is mounted on movable runners; the sledder steers the skeleton by transferring body weight from side to side.

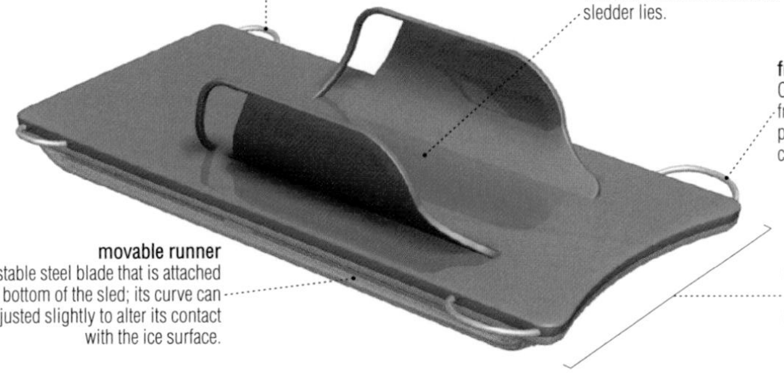
rear bumper
One of the side pieces attached at the back of the sled; it absorbs shocks and protects the sledder in the event of contact with the track wall.
seat
Part of the sled on which the sledder lies.
skeleton
Steel or fiberglass sled that is mounted on two movable runners; the sledder pushes the sled at the start and then lies down on it for the descent.
front bumper
One of the side pieces attached at the front of the sled; it absorbs shocks and protects the sledder in the event of contact with the track wall.
movable runner
Adjustable steel blade that is attached to the bottom of the sled; its curve can be adjusted slightly to alter its contact with the ice surface.
sled
Platform equipped with a backless seat on which the sledder lies.

track

Concrete structure that is covered with an artificial sheet of ice; bobsled, luge and skeleton races are held on it.

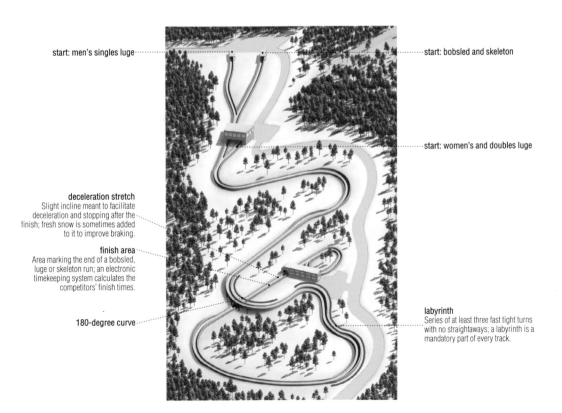

start: men's singles luge
start: bobsled and skeleton
start: women's and doubles luge
deceleration stretch
Slight incline meant to facilitate deceleration and stopping after the finish; fresh snow is sometimes added to it to improve braking.
finish area
Area marking the end of a bobsled, luge or skeleton run; an electronic timekeeping system calculates the competitors' finish times.
180-degree curve
labyrinth
Series of at least three fast tight turns with no straightaways; a labyrinth is a mandatory part of every track.

ski resort

Resort area with the facilities required for skiing and snowboarding; it also lodges skiers and snowboarders.

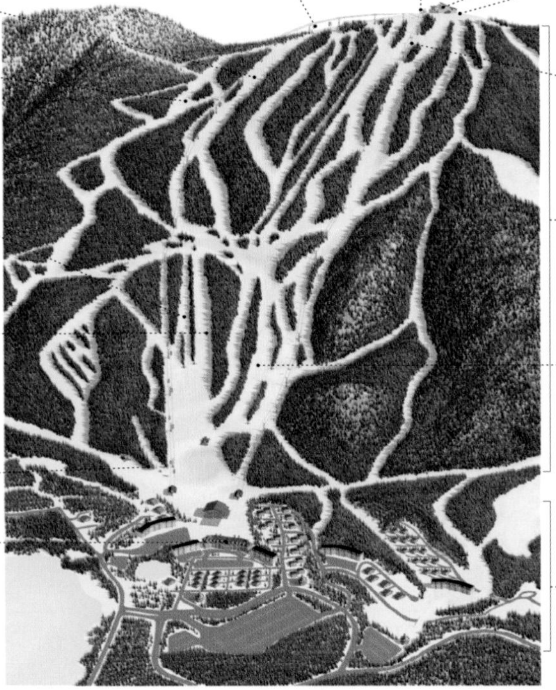

gondola
Mechanical lift made up of a series of closed cabins that are suspended from a single cable; skis and snowboards are hung outside the cabin.

intermediate slope
Relatively steep slope geared to intermediate skiers and snowboarders who know the basics of their sport.

easy slope
Wide gentle and well-cleared slope for skiing and snowboarding beginners.

expert slope
Extremely difficult slope geared to expert skiers and snowboarders; these slopes are usually very steep and include moguls and tight turns.

difficult slope
Steep slope geared to experienced skiers and snowboarders.

patrol and first aid station
Building reserved for the ski patrol; it houses equipment for administering first aid to injured or sick skiers.

main lodge
Building that brings together various services such as restaurants, bars, boutiques and day care.

snow-grooming machine
A tracked vehicle used to prepare trails; it packs fresh snow, evens out bumps and replaces snow on uncovered areas.

ski lift arrival area

summit lodge

summit
Highest point on the mountain; it marks the starting point of most alpine ski trails.

chair lift
Mechanical lift that is suspended from a single cable; it is made up of a series of seats for two to eight skiers or snowboarders who wear their equipment while going up and down.

ski area
Network of trails that makes up a ski resort; they can be built on one or more slopes, on one mountain or on adjacent mountains.

alpine ski trail
Slope groomed for alpine skiing or snowboarding; a sign indicates the level of difficulty by means of a pictogram.

lodging
The businesses, buildings and dwellings that make it possible to enjoy a relatively long-term stay at a ski resort.

ski school
Business that offers skiing or snowboarding lessons to individuals or groups of all levels.

T-bar
Mechanical lift that consists of a series of inverted T-shaped bars that hold two people; as the T-bar pulls them, their skis or snowboards slide along the ground.

cross-country ski trail
Trail groomed for cross-country skiing; a sign indicates the level of difficulty by means of a pictogram.

gondolas departure area

ice rink
Ice surface designed for skating.

hotel
Business establishment that lodges people for a fee.

information desk
Kiosk that provides information on a ski resort's facilities, events and services.

village
Place in which lodging and ski resort services are concentrated.

parking
Area for cars to park.

chair lift departure area

skiers' lodge
Multipurpose building providing a variety of services such as cafeteria, lockers, rental and repair shop and ski school.

condominium
Group of lodgings belonging to separate owners who share the building's maintenance costs.

mountain lodge
Small, usually wooden dwelling built on the side of a mountain; it sometimes provides direct access to the ski area.

snowboarding

Sport that consists of sliding over a snow-covered surface on a board fitted with foot bindings; the snowboard is steered by bending the knees.

hard boot
Boot used for alpine events; it provides firm support and makes it possible to immediately transfer body movement to the board.

helmet
Rigid piece of equipment that is designed to protect the head; helmets are mandatory for racing.

coveralls
Skintight one-piece garment that reduces air resistance.

glove
Covering for the hand and wrist that protects them against the cold and snow in the event of a fall.

snowboarder
Athlete who practices snowboarding; the snowboarder usually specializes in one particular discipline.

goggles
Equipment that protects the eyes against the sun and the elements; the filtered lenses optimize depth perception.

shin guard
Piece of equipment made of hard molded plastic that protects the snowboarder's legs.

snowboard
Board with foot bindings that is designed for sliding over snow-covered surfaces.

flexible boot
Flexible boot that is designed for freestyle and all-terrain snowboarding; it allows the snowboarder to perform a broad range of movements and figures.

freestyle snowboard
Wide flexible snowboard used for figures; the nose and tail are identical so that the snowboarder can take off and land in both directions.

soft binding
Binding used with flexible boots; the soft binding has straps to secure the foot and padded ankle supports.

plate binding
Binding used with hard boots; it has a metal toeplate that keeps the boot firmly in place to provide maximum stability.

alpine snowboard
Long narrow rigid snowboard that is designed to reach high speeds.

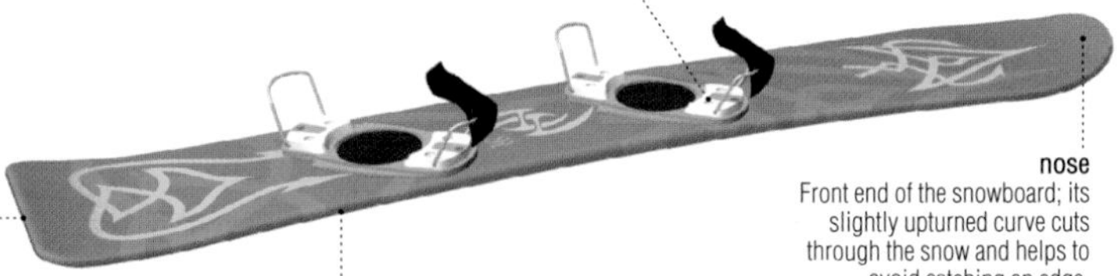

tail
Back end of the snowboard; unlike the tail of the freestyle snowboard, the alpine snowboard tail is not designed for going backward.

edge
Metal edge along the sole of the snowboard; the edge digs into the snow and makes turning possible.

nose
Front end of the snowboard; its slightly upturned curve cuts through the snow and helps to avoid catching an edge.

competition site: half-pipe
The half-pipe event is set to music and consists of executing acrobatic figures by sliding from one side of a track with banked edges (half-pipe) to the other.

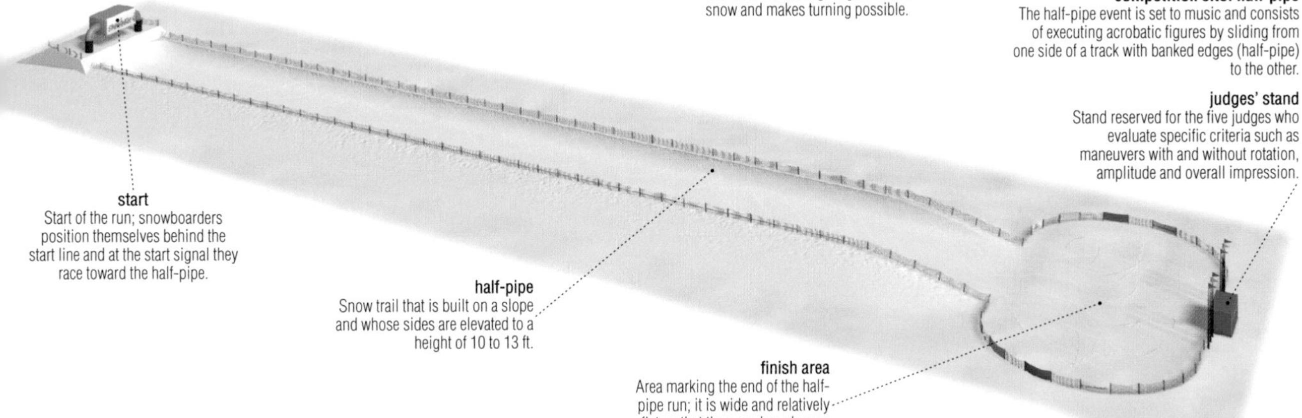

judges' stand
Stand reserved for the five judges who evaluate specific criteria such as maneuvers with and without rotation, amplitude and overall impression.

start
Start of the run; snowboarders position themselves behind the start line and at the start signal they race toward the half-pipe.

half-pipe
Snow trail that is built on a slope and whose sides are elevated to a height of 10 to 13 ft.

finish area
Area marking the end of the half-pipe run; it is wide and relatively flat so that the snowboarder can stop safely.

alpine skiing

Sport that consists of racing on alpine skis down a snow-covered slope with a medium or steep drop.

alpine skier
Athlete who practices alpine skiing; alpine skiers often specialize in one or more of four events.

ski goggles
Equipment that protects the eyes against the sun and the elements; the filtered lenses optimize depth perception.

ski suit
Skintight one-piece garment that reduces air resistance; various protective devices can be added, depending on the event.

helmet
Rigid piece of equipment that is designed to protect the head; helmets are mandatory for racing.

ski glove
Covering for the hand and wrist that protects them against the cold and bad weather; padded but flexible, it provides a solid grip on the handle.

basket
Circular piece attached to the bottom of the ski pole; it prevents the pole from sinking too deeply into the snow.

ski pole
Metal or composite fiber rod with a handle and a basket; the ski pole is used for maintaining balance and for turning.

ski boot
Rigid boot made of plastic or composite materials; the front and back of the ski boot attach to the ski.

wrist strap
Strap that is attached to the handle and worn around the wrist to prevent the skier from losing a pole when sticking it into the ground.

handle

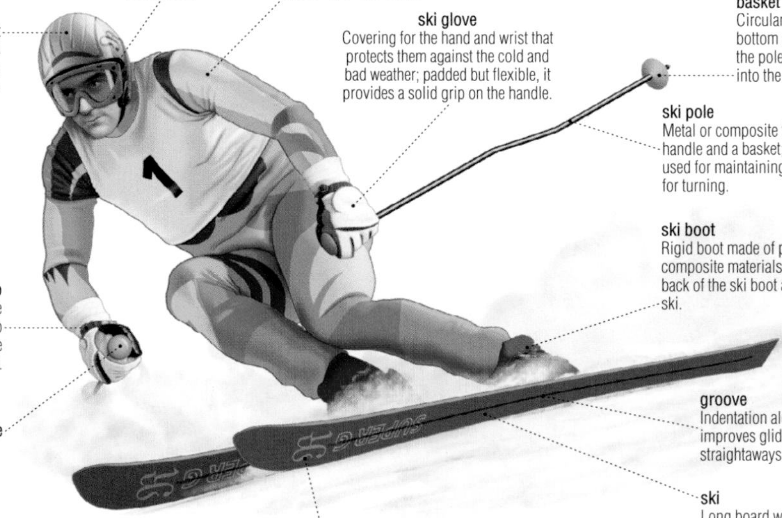

groove
Indentation along the bottom that improves glide and stability on straightaways.

ski
Long board with foot bindings that is designed for gliding over a snow-covered surface; it is usually made of wood or composite fibers.

bottom
Carefully polished piece that forms the bottom of the ski; a wax suited to snow conditions is applied to the bottom to obtain the best possible glide.

safety binding
Device that attaches the boot to the ski; it features an automatic release system that frees the boot when too much pressure is exerted on it.

tip
Rounded end of the shovel.

tail
Back end of the ski.

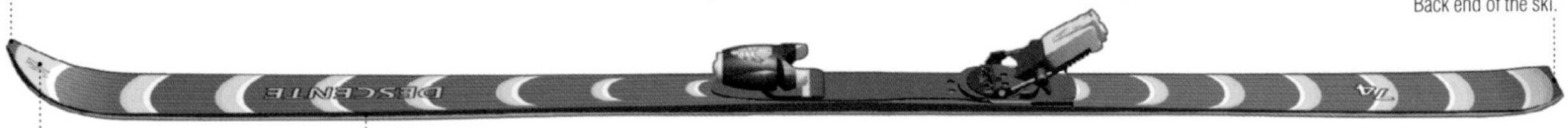

shovel
Front end of the ski; its upward curve cuts through snow and helps to avoid catching an edge.

edge
Metal edge that runs along the bottom of the ski; it bites into the snow and makes turning possible.

ski
Long board with foot bindings that is designed for gliding over a snow-covered surface; it is usually made of wood or composite fibers.

examples of skis

Skis are adapted to the requirements of each event; their performance on snow depends on their length, width and design.

slalom ski
Short narrow ski that makes it possible to quickly shift from one edge to the other; its dissymmetric shovel is designed to push back the gate poles in the event of contact.

giant slalom ski
Medium-length ski that provides greater flex than a downhill ski; it is suited to long turns and it remains stable at high speeds.

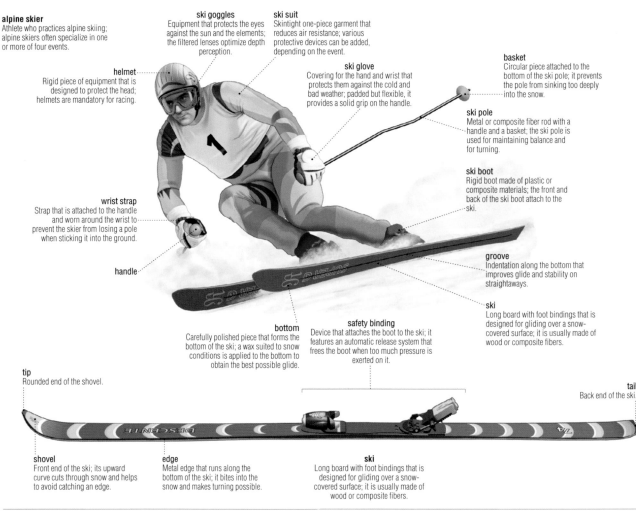

downhill and super-G ski
Long rigid ski that provides a high level of stability and excellent glide; it is designed for straightaways and for speed.

alpine skiing

technical events
During each event, skiers take turns attempting to complete the descent as fast as possible while following the established course.

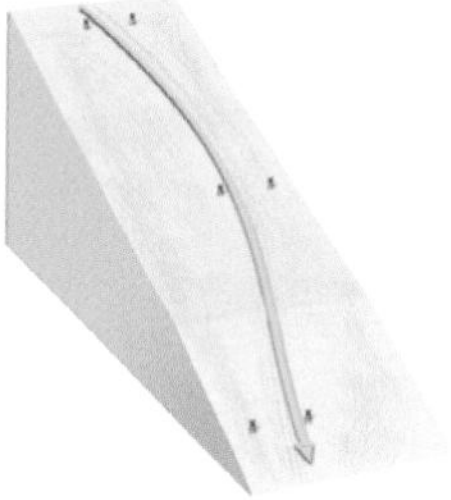

downhill
Speed event held on a steep course with long straightaways and wide fast turns; downhill skiers reach speeds of over 75 mph.

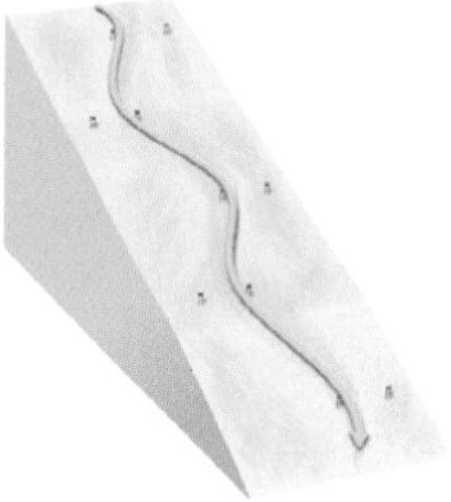

super giant (super-G) slalom
Event that combines the speed of downhill with the technique of giant slalom; the super-G course is shorter than the downhill course and has more gates.

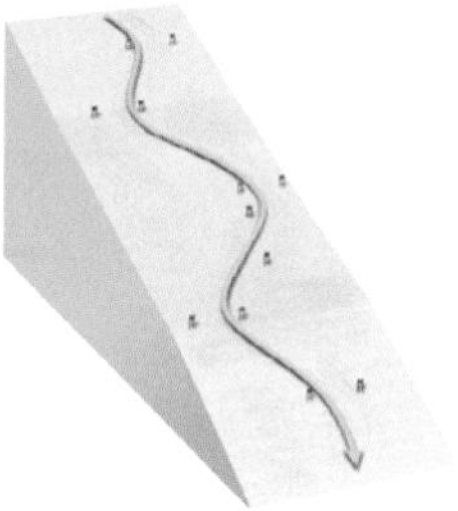

giant slalom
Technical event whose course has fewer gates and longer curves than the special slalom course.

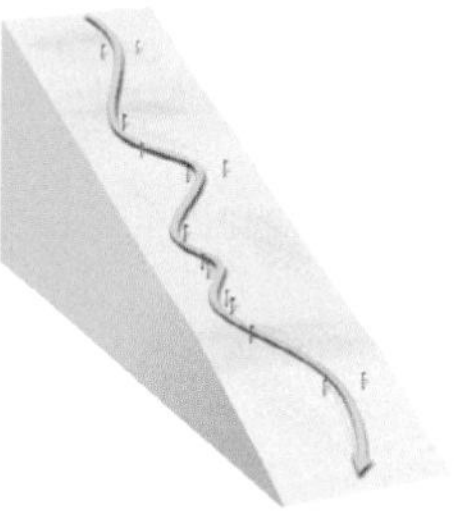

special slalom
Technical event whose course includes numerous sharp turns; the skier must graze the gate poles to keep the best trajectory.

ski boot
Rigid boot made of plastic or composite materials; the front and back of the ski boot attach to the ski.

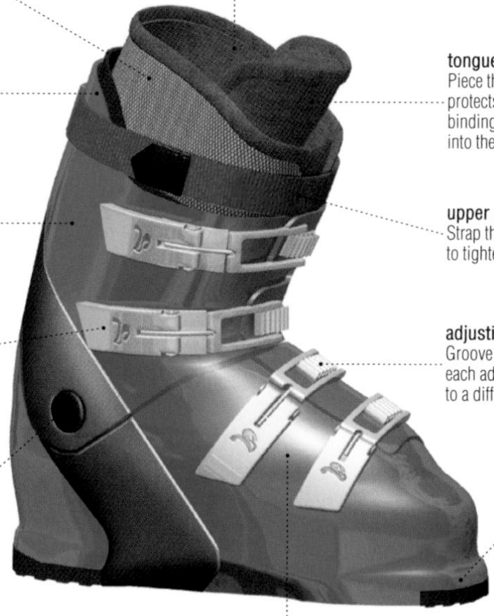

inner boot
Often removable padded lining designed to keep the feet warm and to provide comfort.

upper cuff
Relatively rigid piece that goes around the top of the inner boot.

upper
Reinforcement at the back of the boot.

upper shell
Part of the ski boot that covers the lower leg; its forward inclination is often adjustable, which makes it easier for the skier to lean forward.

buckle
Clip made up of a metal ring that fits into an adjusting catch to tighten the ski boot.

hinge
Piece connecting the upper and lower shells.

tongue
Piece that extends from the inner boot and protects the foot from rubbing against the binding system; it is raised to slip the foot into the inner boot.

upper strap
Strap that is attached to the upper to tighten the upper cuff.

adjusting catch
Groove in which the buckle latches; each adjusting catch corresponds to a different tightness.

sole
Sturdy piece that forms the bottom of the ski boot; it has molds at the heel and toe that fit into the binding.

lower shell
Part of the ski boot that covers the foot and the ankle.

safety binding
Device that attaches the boot to the ski; it features an automatic release system that frees the boot when too much pressure is exerted on it.

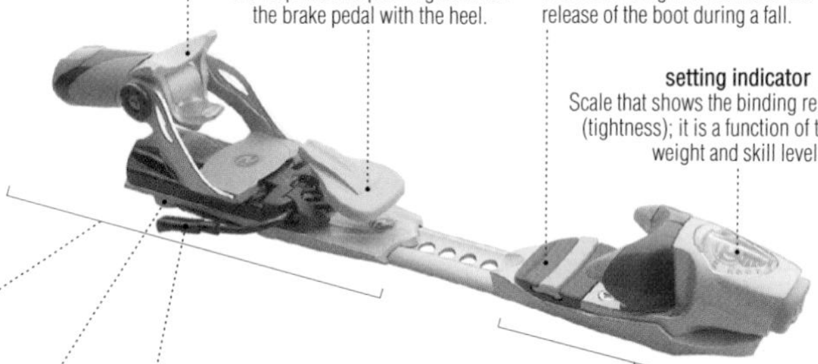

manual release
Manual device that releases the boot from the binding.

brake pedal
Device used to attach the binding by sliding the end of the sole into the toepiece and pushing down on the brake pedal with the heel.

antifriction pad
Part mounted on the toepiece that reduces friction between the sole and the binding and facilitates the release of the boot during a fall.

setting indicator
Scale that shows the binding release index (tightness); it is a function of the skier's weight and skill level.

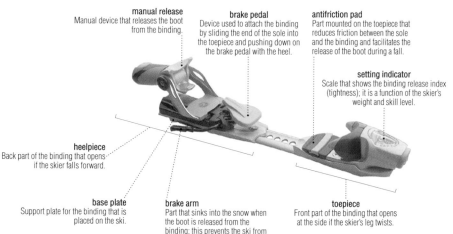

heelpiece
Back part of the binding that opens if the skier falls forward.

base plate
Support plate for the binding that is placed on the ski.

brake arm
Part that sinks into the snow when the boot is released from the binding; this prevents the ski from sliding down the slope.

toepiece
Front part of the binding that opens at the side if the skier's leg twists.

freestyle skiing

Sport that consists of performing various figures and tricks on skis; it includes three events: moguls, aerial skiing and acroski (ballet).

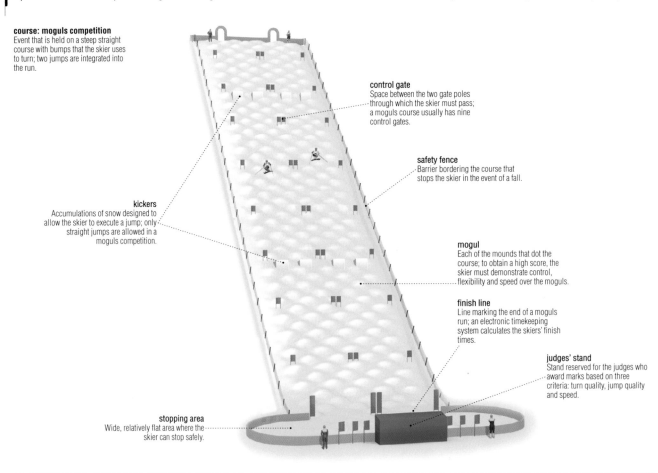

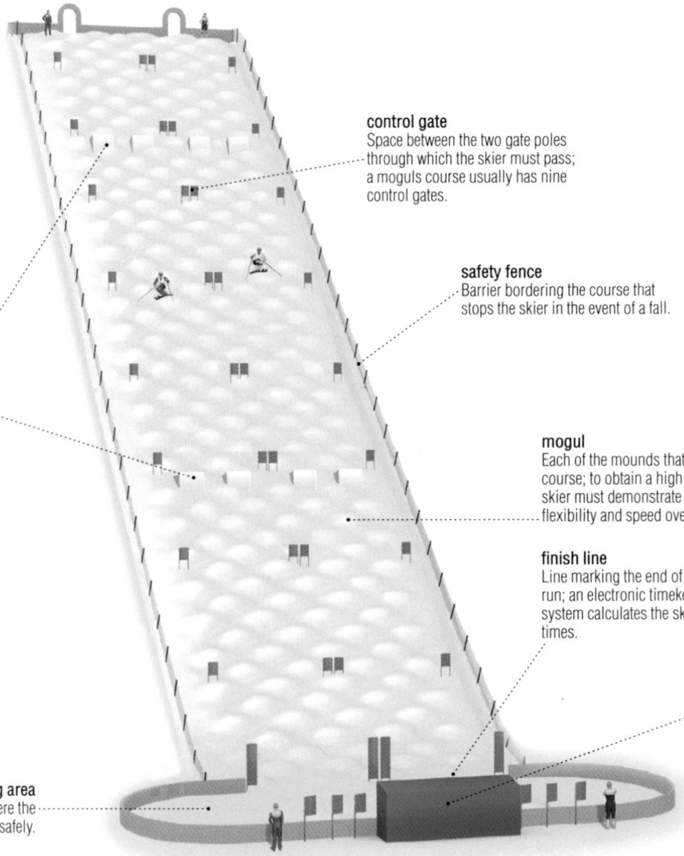
course: moguls competition
Event that is held on a steep straight course with bumps that the skier uses to turn; two jumps are integrated into the run.
control gate
Space between the two gate poles through which the skier must pass; a moguls course usually has nine control gates.
safety fence
Barrier bordering the course that stops the skier in the event of a fall.
kickers
Accumulations of snow designed to allow the skier to execute a jump; only straight jumps are allowed in a moguls competition.
mogul
Each of the mounds that dot the course; to obtain a high score, the skier must demonstrate control, flexibility and speed over the moguls.
finish line
Line marking the end of a moguls run; an electronic timekeeping system calculates the skiers' finish times.
judges' stand
Stand reserved for the judges who award marks based on three criteria: turn quality, jump quality and speed.
stopping area
Wide, relatively flat area where the skier can stop safely.

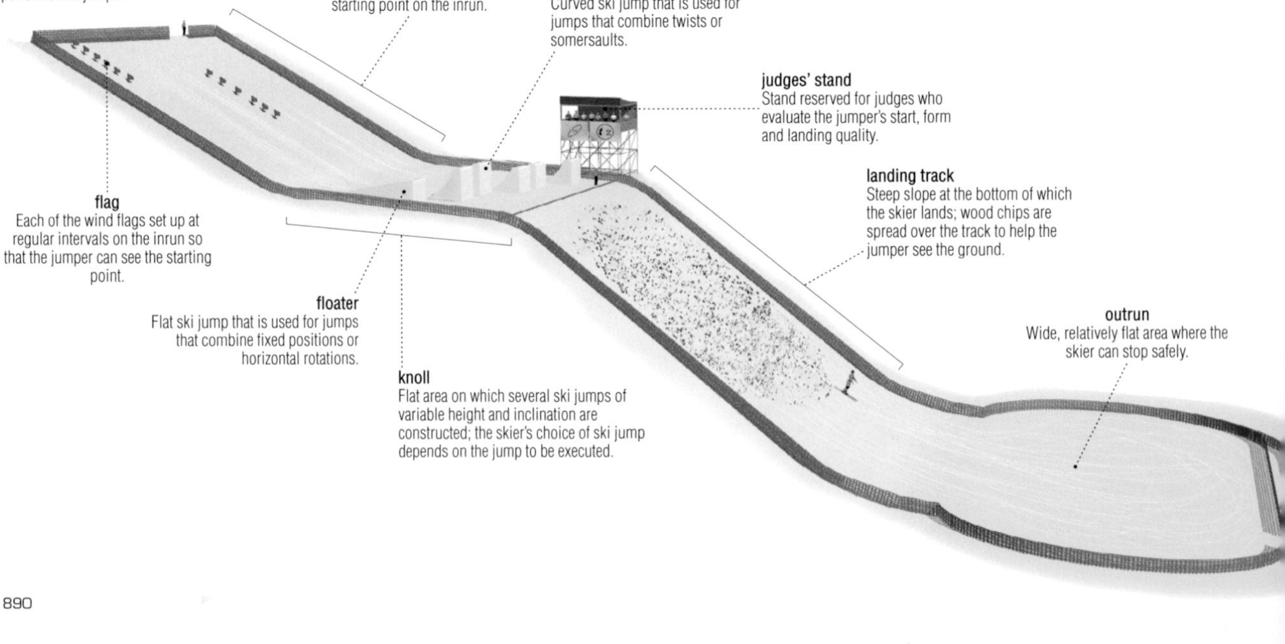
aerial site
During an aerial ski event, skiers take turns flying off a ski jump to perform aerial figures; each competitor performs two jumps.
inrun
Slope on which the jumper generates the speed needed for takeoff; the athlete can choose the starting point on the inrun.
kicker
Curved ski jump that is used for jumps that combine twists or somersaults.
judges' stand
Stand reserved for judges who evaluate the jumper's start, form and landing quality.
landing track
Steep slope at the bottom of which the skier lands; wood chips are spread over the track to help the jumper see the ground.
flag
Each of the wind flags set up at regular intervals on the inrun so that the jumper can see the starting point.
floater
Flat ski jump that is used for jumps that combine fixed positions or horizontal rotations.
knoll
Flat area on which several ski jumps of variable height and inclination are constructed; the skier's choice of ski jump depends on the jump to be executed.
outrun
Wide, relatively flat area where the skier can stop safely.

ski jumping

Sport that consists of covering the greatest possible distance in the air after jumping off a ski jump; the jumper's style is marked by judges.

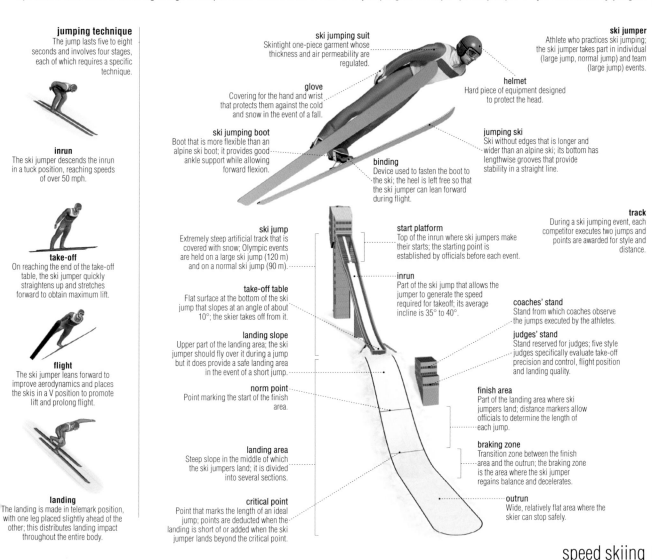

jumping technique
The jump lasts five to eight seconds and involves four stages, each of which requires a specific technique.

inrun
The ski jumper descends the inrun in a tuck position, reaching speeds of over 50 mph.

take-off
On reaching the end of the take-off table, the ski jumper quickly straightens up and stretches forward to obtain maximum lift.

flight
The ski jumper leans forward to improve aerodynamics and places the skis in a V position to promote lift and prolong flight.

landing
The landing is made in telemark position, with one leg placed slightly ahead of the other; this distributes landing impact throughout the entire body.

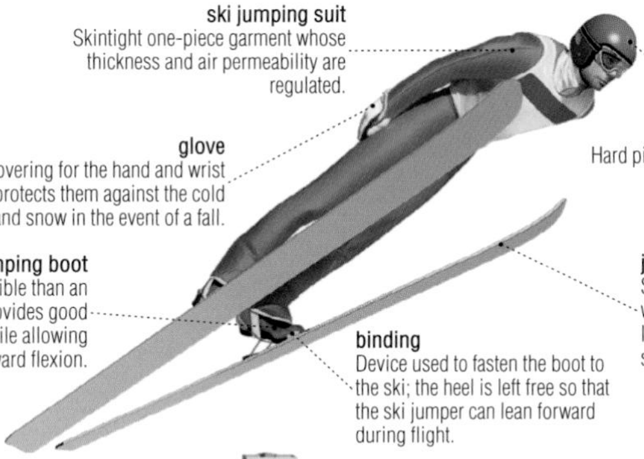

ski jumping suit
Skintight one-piece garment whose thickness and air permeability are regulated.

ski jumper
Athlete who practices ski jumping; the ski jumper takes part in individual (large jump, normal jump) and team (large jump) events.

glove
Covering for the hand and wrist that protects them against the cold and snow in the event of a fall.

helmet
Hard piece of equipment designed to protect the head.

ski jumping boot
Boot that is more flexible than an alpine ski boot; it provides good ankle support while allowing forward flexion.

jumping ski
Ski without edges that is longer and wider than an alpine ski; its bottom has lengthwise grooves that provide stability in a straight line.

binding
Device used to fasten the boot to the ski; the heel is left free so that the ski jumper can lean forward during flight.

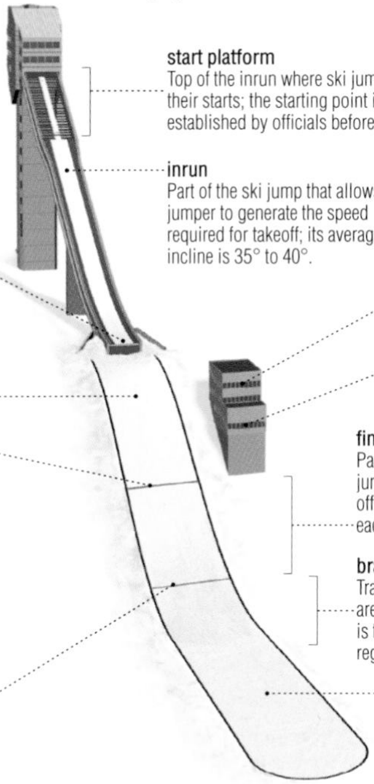

track
During a ski jumping event, each competitor executes two jumps and points are awarded for style and distance.

ski jump
Extremely steep artificial track that is covered with snow; Olympic events are held on a large ski jump (120 m) and on a normal ski jump (90 m).

start platform
Top of the inrun where ski jumpers make their starts; the starting point is established by officials before each event.

inrun
Part of the ski jump that allows the jumper to generate the speed required for takeoff; its average incline is 35° to 40°.

take-off table
Flat surface at the bottom of the ski jump that slopes at an angle of about 10°; the skier takes off from it.

coaches' stand
Stand from which coaches observe the jumps executed by the athletes.

judges' stand
Stand reserved for judges; five style judges specifically evaluate take-off precision and control, flight position and landing quality.

landing slope
Upper part of the landing area; the ski jumper should fly over it during a jump but it does provide a safe landing area in the event of a short jump.

norm point
Point marking the start of the finish area.

finish area
Part of the landing area where ski jumpers land; distance markers allow officials to determine the length of each jump.

landing area
Steep slope in the middle of which the ski jumpers land; it is divided into several sections.

braking zone
Transition zone between the finish area and the outrun; the braking zone is the area where the ski jumper regains balance and decelerates.

critical point
Point that marks the length of an ideal jump; points are deducted when the landing is short of or added when the ski jumper lands beyond the critical point.

outrun
Wide, relatively flat area where the skier can stop safely.

speed skiing

Sport that consists of skiing down an extremely steep straight slope to reach the highest possible speed.

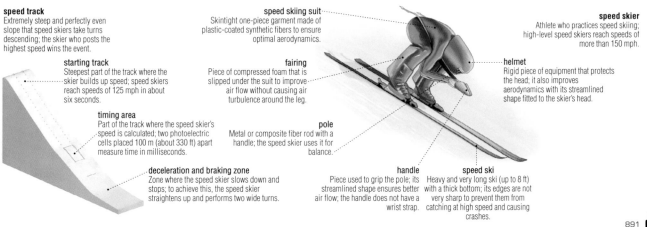

speed track
Extremely steep and perfectly even slope that speed skiers take turns descending; the skier who posts the highest speed wins the event.

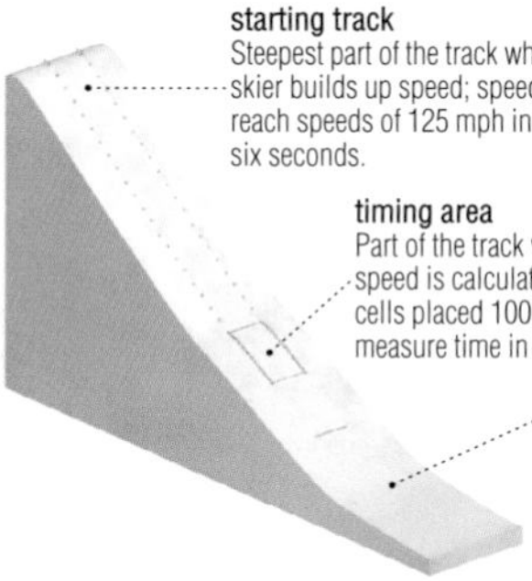

starting track
Steepest part of the track where the skier builds up speed; speed skiers reach speeds of 125 mph in about six seconds.

timing area
Part of the track where the speed skier's speed is calculated; two photoelectric cells placed 100 m (about 330 ft) apart measure time in milliseconds.

deceleration and braking zone
Zone where the speed skier slows down and stops; to achieve this, the speed skier straightens up and performs two wide turns.

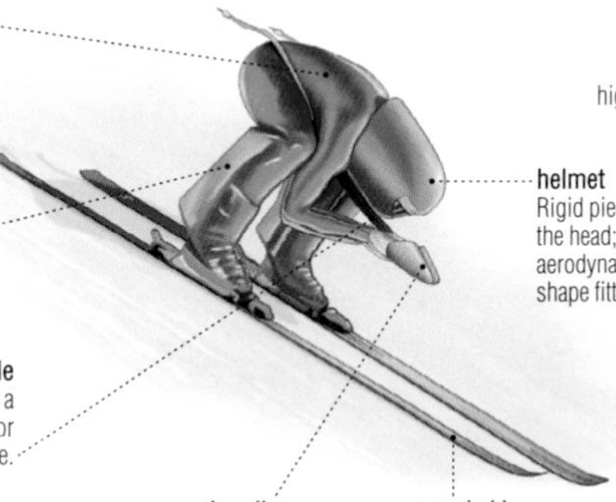

speed skiing suit
Skintight one-piece garment made of plastic-coated synthetic fibers to ensure optimal aerodynamics.

speed skier
Athlete who practices speed skiing; high-level speed skiers reach speeds of more than 150 mph.

fairing
Piece of compressed foam that is slipped under the suit to improve air flow without causing air turbulence around the leg.

helmet
Rigid piece of equipment that protects the head; it also improves aerodynamics with its streamlined shape fitted to the skier's head.

pole
Metal or composite fiber rod with a handle; the speed skier uses it for balance.

handle
Piece used to grip the pole; its streamlined shape ensures better air flow; the handle does not have a wrist strap.

speed ski
Heavy and very long ski (up to 8 ft) with a thick bottom; its edges are not very sharp to prevent them from catching at high speed and causing crashes.

cross-country skiing

Sport that consists of skiing over snow-covered surfaces on gently sloping terrain using a variety of techniques (skating step, diagonal step).

cross-country skier
Athlete who practices cross-country skiing; this athlete takes part in various individual (classic, freestyle, pursuit, sprint) and team (relay) events.

turtleneck
Knit fabric top with a high collar formed of ribbing that folds over around the neck; it has no closing mechanism.

ski hat
Headgear made of a tubular piece of fabric folded back to form a double layer; its top is sewn and sometimes features a pom-pom.

waxing kit
Kit that contains a number of waxes suited to a variety of snow conditions and the accessories used to apply or remove them.

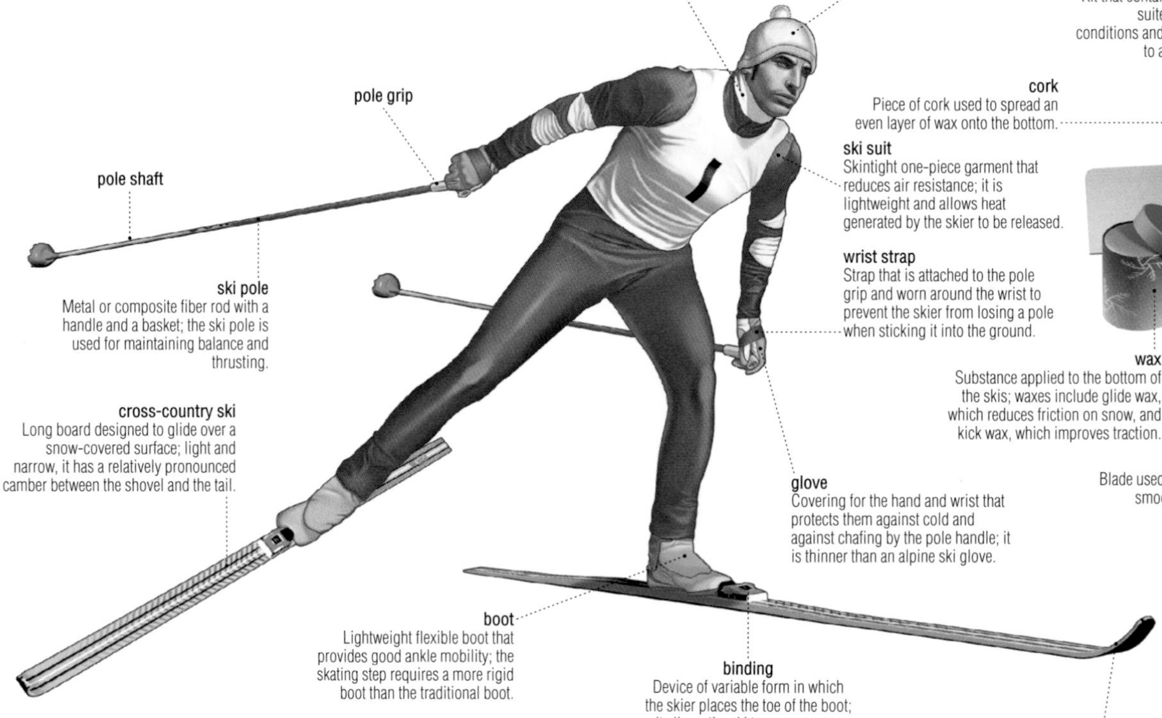

cork
Piece of cork used to spread an even layer of wax onto the bottom.

ski suit
Skintight one-piece garment that reduces air resistance; it is lightweight and allows heat generated by the skier to be released.

wrist strap
Strap that is attached to the pole grip and worn around the wrist to prevent the skier from losing a pole when sticking it into the ground.

ski pole
Metal or composite fiber rod with a handle and a basket; the ski pole is used for maintaining balance and thrusting.

wax
Substance applied to the bottom of the skis; waxes include glide wax, which reduces friction on snow, and kick wax, which improves traction.

cross-country ski
Long board designed to glide over a snow-covered surface; light and narrow, it has a relatively pronounced camber between the shovel and the tail.

scraper
Blade used to remove kick wax or smooth the ski bottom after applying glide wax.

glove
Covering for the hand and wrist that protects them against cold and against chafing by the pole handle; it is thinner than an alpine ski glove.

boot
Lightweight flexible boot that provides good ankle mobility; the skating step requires a more rigid boot than the traditional boot.

binding
Device of variable form in which the skier places the toe of the boot; it allows the ski to move as one with the skier.

shovel
Front end of the ski; its upward curve cuts through snow and helps to avoid catching an edge.

cross-country ski
Long board designed to glide over a snow-covered surface; light and narrow, it has a relatively pronounced camber between the shovel and the tail.

ski tip
Rounded end of the shovel.

toe binding
Binding with a mechanism that locks only the front of the boot.

shovel
Front end of the ski; its upward curve cuts through snow and helps to avoid catching an edge.

tail
Back end of the ski.

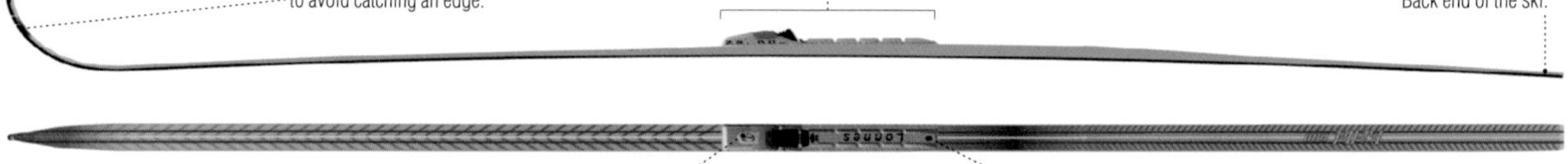

toepiece
Mechanism used to block the front end of the boot.

heelplate
Back part of the binding; it has notches that fit into the sole of the boot to prevent the foot from twisting to the side.

skating step
Technique that allows the cross-country skier to drive forward by pushing to the side like a skater; it is faster than the diagonal step.

diagonal step
Classic cross-country skiing technique; the skis remain parallel except in sharp turns or steep climbs.

skating kick
Side kick executed by leaning on the inside of one ski while keeping the body weight on the other ski.

gliding phase
Transition phase between two pushes; the skier returns the take-off leg to its initial position while moving the support ski forward.

pushing phase
Thrusting movement that begins by quickly pushing the take-off leg backwards; the skier alternates this movement from one leg to the other.

gliding phase
Transition phase between two pushes; the skier returns the take-off leg to its initial position while moving the support ski forward.

pushing phase
Rapid repetition of the pushing phase increases the skier's speed.

SPORTS AND GAMES

biathlon

Sport that combines cross-country ski racing with a precision shooting competition; the biathlon includes individual and team events (relays).

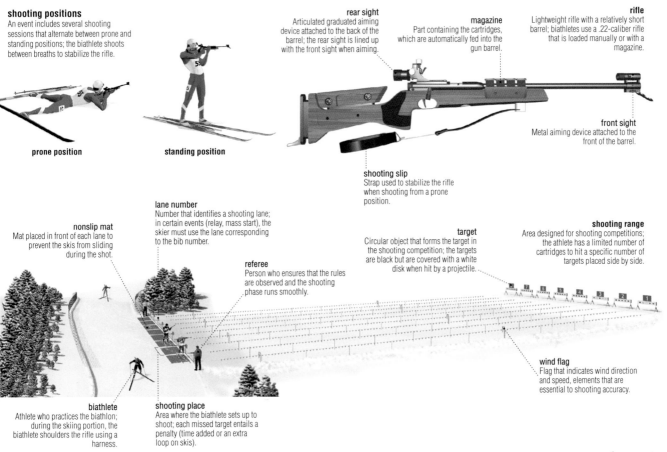

shooting positions
An event includes several shooting sessions that alternate between prone and standing positions; the biathlete shoots between breaths to stabilize the rifle.

prone position

standing position

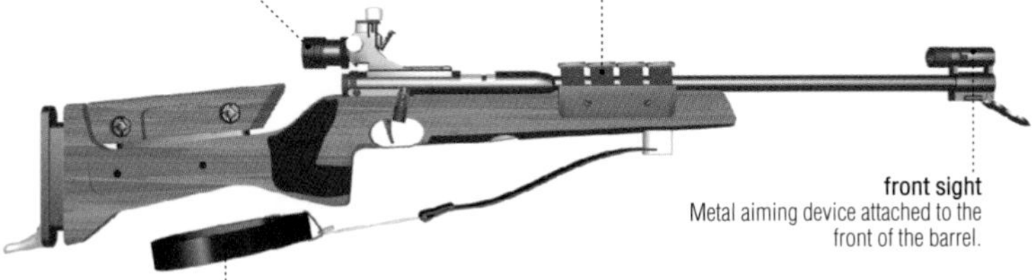

rear sight
Articulated graduated aiming device attached to the back of the barrel; the rear sight is lined up with the front sight when aiming.

magazine
Part containing the cartridges, which are automatically fed into the gun barrel.

rifle
Lightweight rifle with a relatively short barrel; biathletes use a .22-caliber rifle that is loaded manually or with a magazine.

front sight
Metal aiming device attached to the front of the barrel.

shooting slip
Strap used to stabilize the rifle when shooting from a prone position.

lane number
Number that identifies a shooting lane; in certain events (relay, mass start), the skier must use the lane corresponding to the bib number.

nonslip mat
Mat placed in front of each lane to prevent the skis from sliding during the shot.

referee
Person who ensures that the rules are observed and the shooting phase runs smoothly.

target
Circular object that forms the target in the shooting competition; the targets are black but are covered with a white disk when hit by a projectile.

shooting range
Area designed for shooting competitions; the athlete has a limited number of cartridges to hit a specific number of targets placed side by side.

wind flag
Flag that indicates wind direction and speed, elements that are essential to shooting accuracy.

biathlete
Athlete who practices the biathlon; during the skiing portion, the biathlete shoulders the rifle using a harness.

shooting place
Area where the biathlete sets up to shoot; each missed target entails a penalty (time added or an extra loop on skis).

snowshoes

Wide soles that come in a variety of shapes and are fitted to boots; snowshoes are used to walk on snow without sinking.

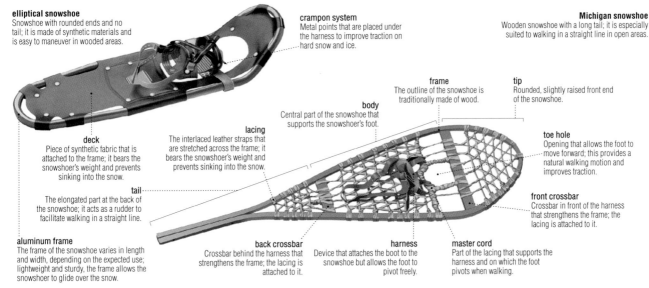

elliptical snowshoe
Snowshoe with rounded ends and no tail; it is made of synthetic materials and is easy to maneuver in wooded areas.

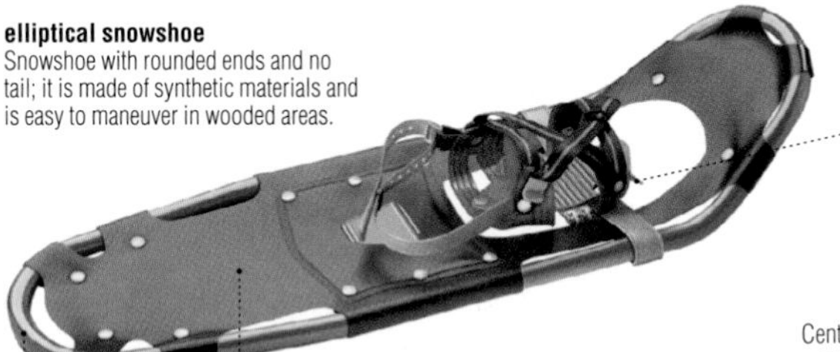

crampon system
Metal points that are placed under the harness to improve traction on hard snow and ice.

deck
Piece of synthetic fabric that is attached to the frame; it bears the snowshoer's weight and prevents sinking into the snow.

aluminum frame
The frame of the snowshoe varies in length and width, depending on the expected use; lightweight and sturdy, the frame allows the snowshoer to glide over the snow.

Michigan snowshoe
Wooden snowshoe with a long tail; it is especially suited to walking in a straight line in open areas.

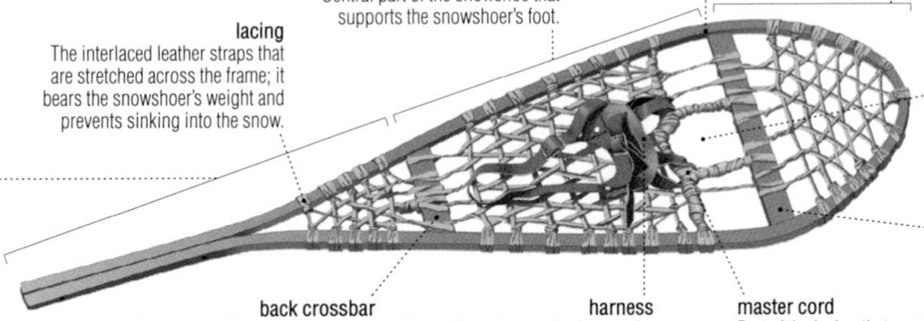

frame
The outline of the snowshoe is traditionally made of wood.

tip
Rounded, slightly raised front end of the snowshoe.

body
Central part of the snowshoe that supports the snowshoer's foot.

lacing
The interlaced leather straps that are stretched across the frame; it bears the snowshoer's weight and prevents sinking into the snow.

tail
The elongated part at the back of the snowshoe; it acts as a rudder to facilitate walking in a straight line.

toe hole
Opening that allows the foot to move forward; this provides a natural walking motion and improves traction.

front crossbar
Crossbar in front of the harness that strengthens the frame; the lacing is attached to it.

back crossbar
Crossbar behind the harness that strengthens the frame; the lacing is attached to it.

harness
Device that attaches the boot to the snowshoe but allows the foot to pivot freely.

master cord
Part of the lacing that supports the harness and on which the foot pivots when walking.

skateboarding

Sport that involves descents, turns and tricks on a specially designed or improvised surface; the skateboarder uses a board mounted on small wheels.

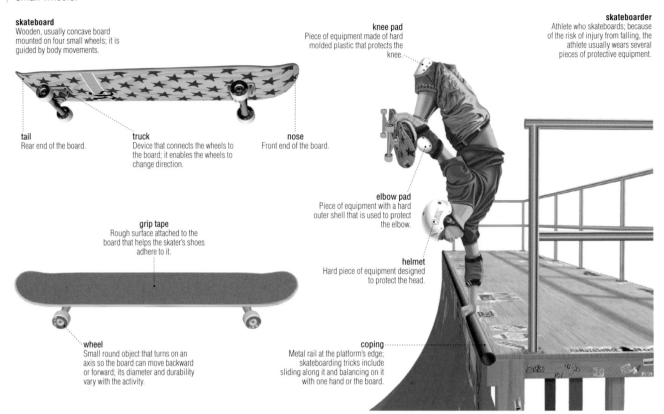

skateboard
Wooden, usually concave board mounted on four small wheels; it is guided by body movements.

tail
Rear end of the board.

truck
Device that connects the wheels to the board; it enables the wheels to change direction.

nose
Front end of the board.

grip tape
Rough surface attached to the board that helps the skater's shoes adhere to it.

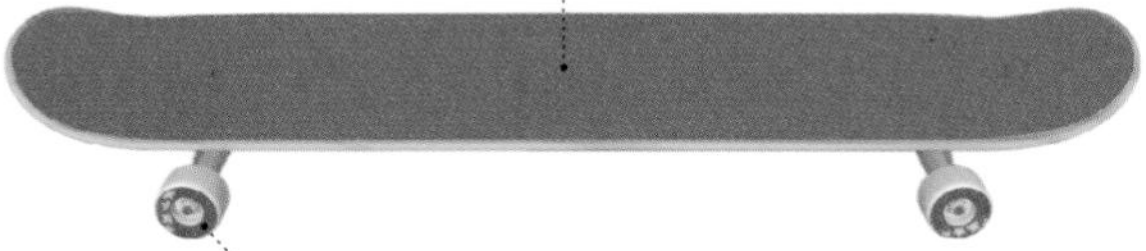

wheel
Small round object that turns on an axis so the board can move backward or forward; its diameter and durability vary with the activity.

knee pad
Piece of equipment made of hard molded plastic that protects the knee.

skateboarder
Athlete who skateboards; because of the risk of injury from falling, the athlete usually wears several pieces of protective equipment.

elbow pad
Piece of equipment with a hard outer shell that is used to protect the elbow.

helmet
Hard piece of equipment designed to protect the head.

coping
Metal rail at the platform's edge; skateboarding tricks include sliding along it and balancing on it with one hand or the board.

ramp
Wooden U-shaped track that is set up for performing various acrobatic stunts (such as jumps and slides).

guard rail
Metal handrail attached to the platform.

platform
Flat level surface at the top of the ramp; it can be more than 10 ft above the ground.

coping
Metal rail at the platform's edge; skateboarding tricks include sliding along it and balancing on it with one hand or the board.

vertical section
Level section at the end of the ramp; it is used by the skateboarder to gain sufficient height for doing tricks in the air.

flat
Flat level surface between the two curved sections of the ramp.

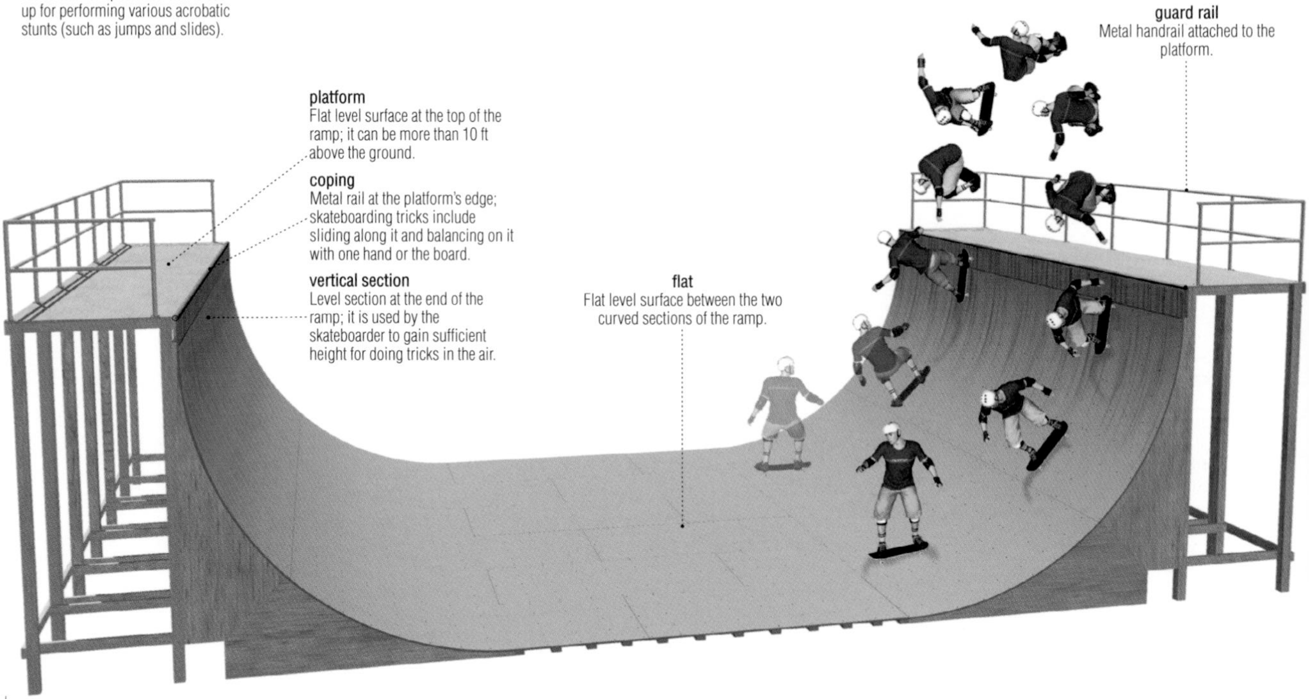

SPORTS AND GAMES

in-line skating

Range of activities that use skates fitted with small wheels: hockey, sprints, acrobatics on ramps or specially designed tracks, etc.

acrobatic skate
Skate with a plastic boot that is designed to provide maximum support and protect against impact when the skater is doing tricks.

inner boot
Cushioned, often removable lining that is designed for greater comfort inside the boot.

upper shell
Part of the boot that covers the lower part of the leg; it is usually hinged at the ankle.

frame
Device that is attached to the sole of the boot to support the wheels.

wheel
Round object that turns on an axis so the skate can move backward or forward.

in-line speed skate
Skate with a light low-cut soft boot that is often molded to the foot; it has five wheels to provide greater contact with the ground.

in-line hockey skate
Skate that is similar to an ice hockey skate; it is made up of a semisoft leather or nylon boot with reinforced side panels.

skater
Athlete who does in-line skating; because of the risk of injury from falling, the athlete usually wears several pieces of protective equipment.

helmet
Hard piece of equipment designed to protect the head.

elbow pad
Padded piece of equipment designed to protect the elbow.

knee pad
Piece of equipment made of hard molded plastic that protects the knee.

wrist guard
Piece of equipment with a hard plastic structure that protects the hand and the wrist.

in-line skate
Reinforced boot with four wheels placed in a straight line; it is used to move around on a hard, relatively smooth surface.

upper shell
Part of the boot that covers the lower part of the leg; it is usually hinged at the ankle.

inner boot
Cushioned, often removable lining that is designed for greater comfort inside the boot.

adjusting buckle
Clip made up of a metal ring that fits into an adjusting catch to tighten the boot.

boot
Ankle boot that protects the foot and ankle; depending on the intended use, it can be soft, semisoft or hard (shell).

axle
Wheel's rotational axis that connects it to the frame.

heel stop
Rubber pad at the back of the skate that enables the skater to slow down or stop.

wheel
Round object that turns on an axis so the skate can move backward or forward.

truck
Device that connects the wheels to the boot.

parachuting

Range of sporting activities that all include opening a parachute in the air after jumping from an airplane.

sky diving
Sport that consists of jumping out of an airplane, falling freely for a certain period while performing various maneuvers and then opening a parachute.

reserve parachute
Extra parachute used in the event the main one malfunctions; an automatic activation device deploys it when a predetermined safe altitude is reached.

main parachute
The parachute deployed by the sky diver when in the air; if a problem arises, the reserve parachute can be deployed.

helmet
Hard-shelled piece of equipment that protects the head against impact and the cold.

boot
Reinforced shoe used for sky diving that provides good ankle support for the landing.

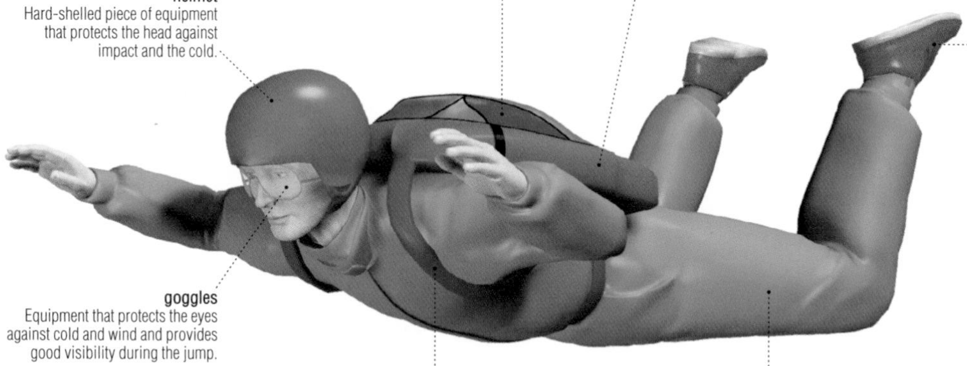

goggles
Equipment that protects the eyes against cold and wind and provides good visibility during the jump.

altimeter
Device that indicates the sky diver's altitude to help with the decision of when to open the parachute.

harness
Arrangement of straps that connects the sky diver to the suspension lines of the main and reserve canopies; it is stowed in a pack before departure.

one-piece coverall
Overalls designed to protect the sky diver against cold and reduce the danger of snagging on equipment.

canopy
Structure made of fabric cells that, when filled with air, forms a rectangular surface with the aerodynamic properties of an airplane wing.

parachute
Equipment consisting of a canopy that is connected to a harness by suspension lines; it is deployed at a given altitude to slow a sky diver's descent.

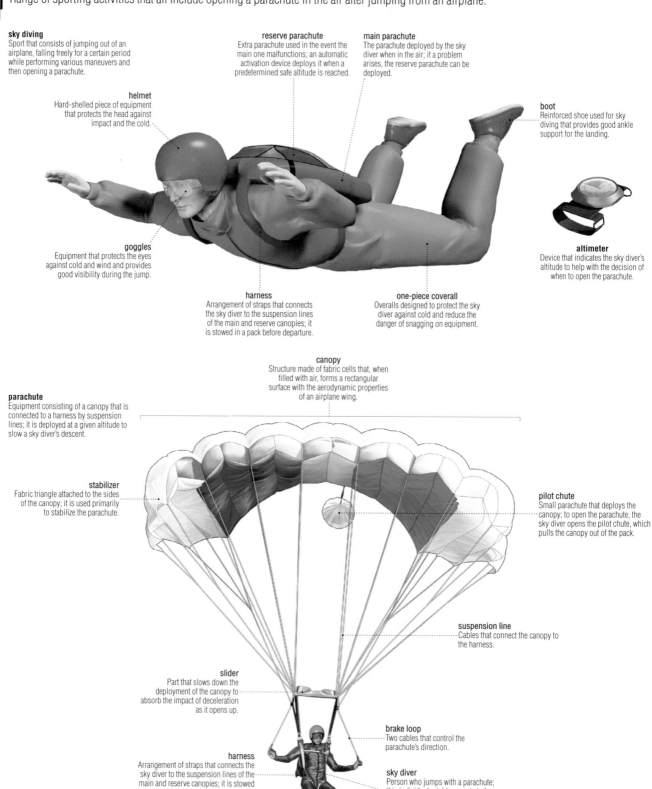

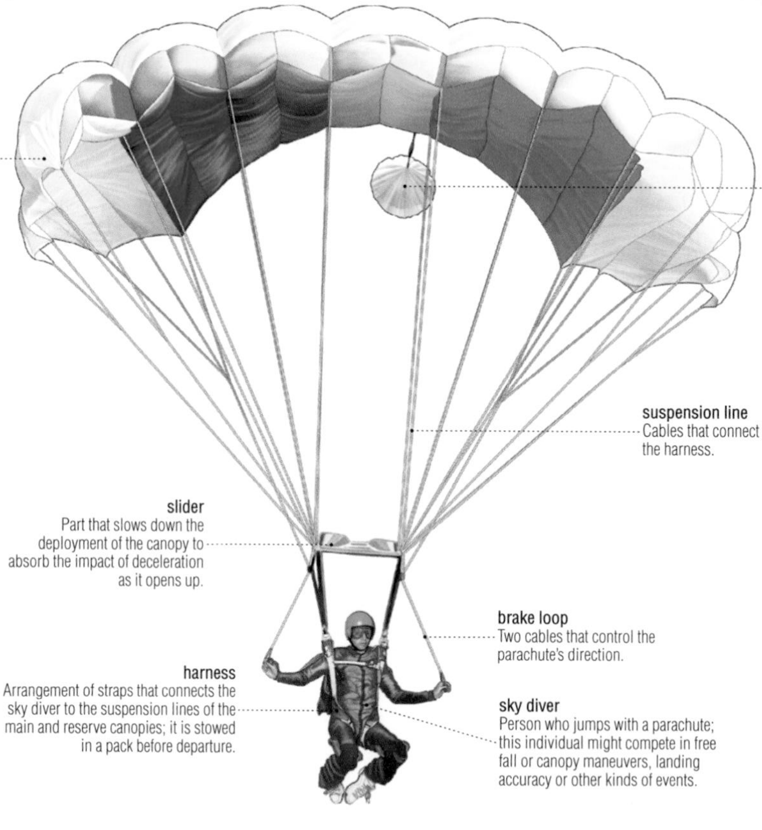

stabilizer
Fabric triangle attached to the sides of the canopy; it is used primarily to stabilize the parachute.

pilot chute
Small parachute that deploys the canopy; to open the parachute, the sky diver opens the pilot chute, which pulls the canopy out of the pack.

suspension line
Cables that connect the canopy to the harness.

slider
Part that slows down the deployment of the canopy to absorb the impact of deceleration as it opens up.

brake loop
Two cables that control the parachute's direction.

harness
Arrangement of straps that connects the sky diver to the suspension lines of the main and reserve canopies; it is stowed in a pack before departure.

sky diver
Person who jumps with a parachute; this individual might compete in free fall or canopy maneuvers, landing accuracy or other kinds of events.

hang gliding

Sport where a pilot strapped to a hang glider or a paraglider launches from a mountain slope, gains altitude and remains aloft for some distance.

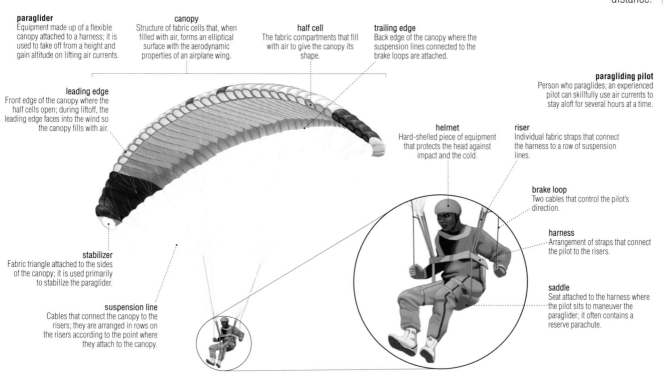

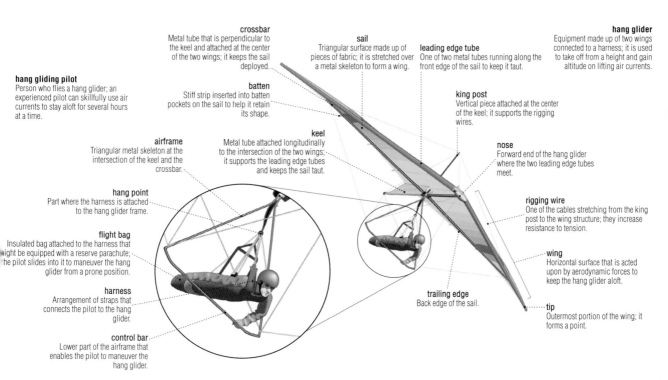

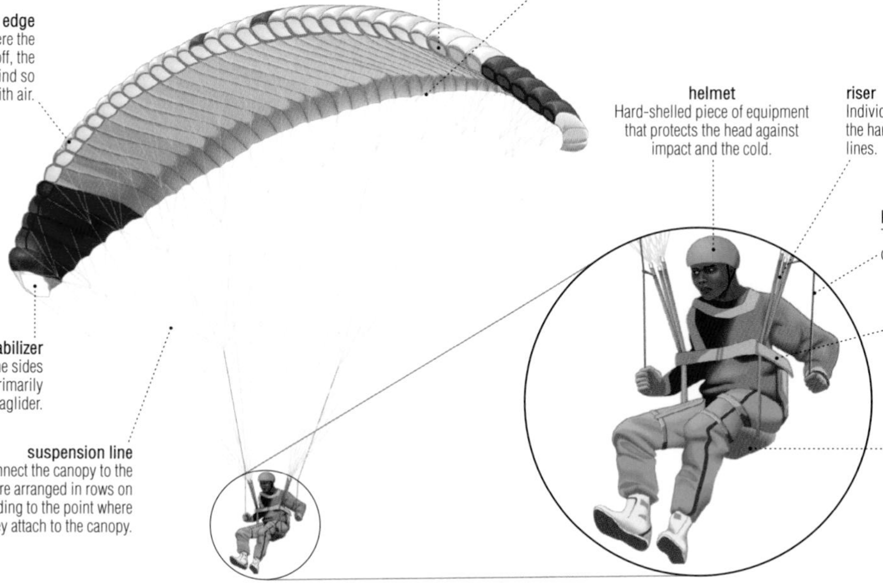
paraglider
Equipment made up of a flexible canopy attached to a harness; it is used to take off from a height and gain altitude on lifting air currents.
canopy
Structure of fabric cells that, when filled with air, forms an elliptical surface with the aerodynamic properties of an airplane wing.
half cell
The fabric compartments that fill with air to give the canopy its shape.
trailing edge
Back edge of the canopy where the suspension lines connected to the brake loops are attached.
paragliding pilot
Person who paraglides; an experienced pilot can skillfully use air currents to stay aloft for several hours at a time.
leading edge
Front edge of the canopy where the half cells open; during liftoff, the leading edge faces into the wind so the canopy fills with air.
helmet
Hard-shelled piece of equipment that protects the head against impact and the cold.
riser
Individual fabric straps that connect the harness to a row of suspension lines.
brake loop
Two cables that control the pilot's direction.
harness
Arrangement of straps that connect the pilot to the risers.
stabilizer
Fabric triangle attached to the sides of the canopy; it is used primarily to stabilize the paraglider.
saddle
Seat attached to the harness where the pilot sits to maneuver the paraglider; it often contains a reserve parachute.
suspension line
Cables that connect the canopy to the risers; they are arranged in rows on the risers according to the point where they attach to the canopy.

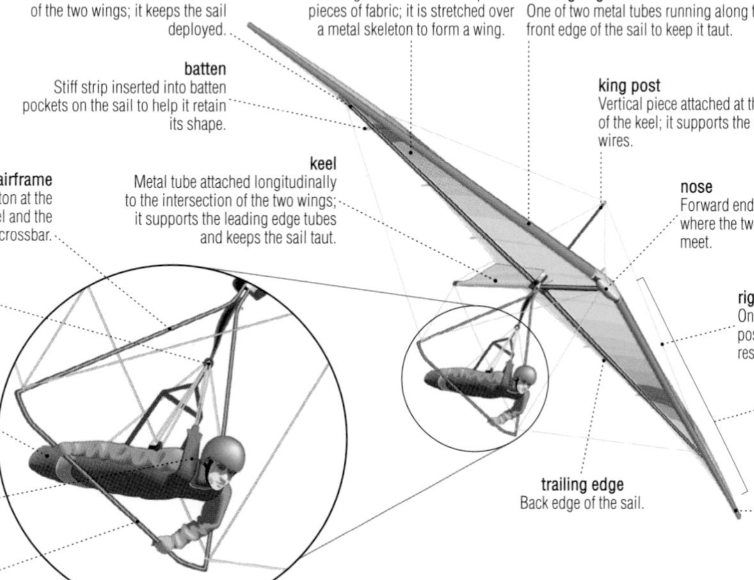
crossbar
Metal tube that is perpendicular to the keel and attached at the center of the two wings; it keeps the sail deployed.
sail
Triangular surface made up of pieces of fabric; it is stretched over a metal skeleton to form a wing.
leading edge tube
One of two metal tubes running along the front edge of the sail to keep it taut.
hang glider
Equipment made up of two wings connected to a harness; it is used to take off from a height and gain altitude on lifting air currents.
hang gliding pilot
Person who flies a hang glider; an experienced pilot can skillfully use air currents to stay aloft for several hours at a time.
batten
Stiff strip inserted into batten pockets on the sail to help it retain its shape.
king post
Vertical piece attached at the center of the keel; it supports the rigging wires.
keel
Metal tube attached longitudinally to the intersection of the two wings; it supports the leading edge tubes and keeps the sail taut.
airframe
Triangular metal skeleton at the intersection of the keel and the crossbar.
nose
Forward end of the hang glider where the two leading edge tubes meet.
hang point
Part where the harness is attached to the hang glider frame.
rigging wire
One of the cables stretching from the king post to the wing structure; they increase resistance to tension.
flight bag
Insulated bag attached to the harness that ight be equipped with a reserve parachute; he pilot slides into it to maneuver the hang glider from a prone position.
wing
Horizontal surface that is acted upon by aerodynamic forces to keep the hang glider aloft.
harness
Arrangement of straps that connects the pilot to the hang glider.
trailing edge
Back edge of the sail.
tip
Outermost portion of the wing; it forms a point.
control bar
Lower part of the airframe that enables the pilot to maneuver the hang glider.

glider

Small engineless aircraft that is launched by a tow plane and stays aloft on air currents.

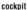

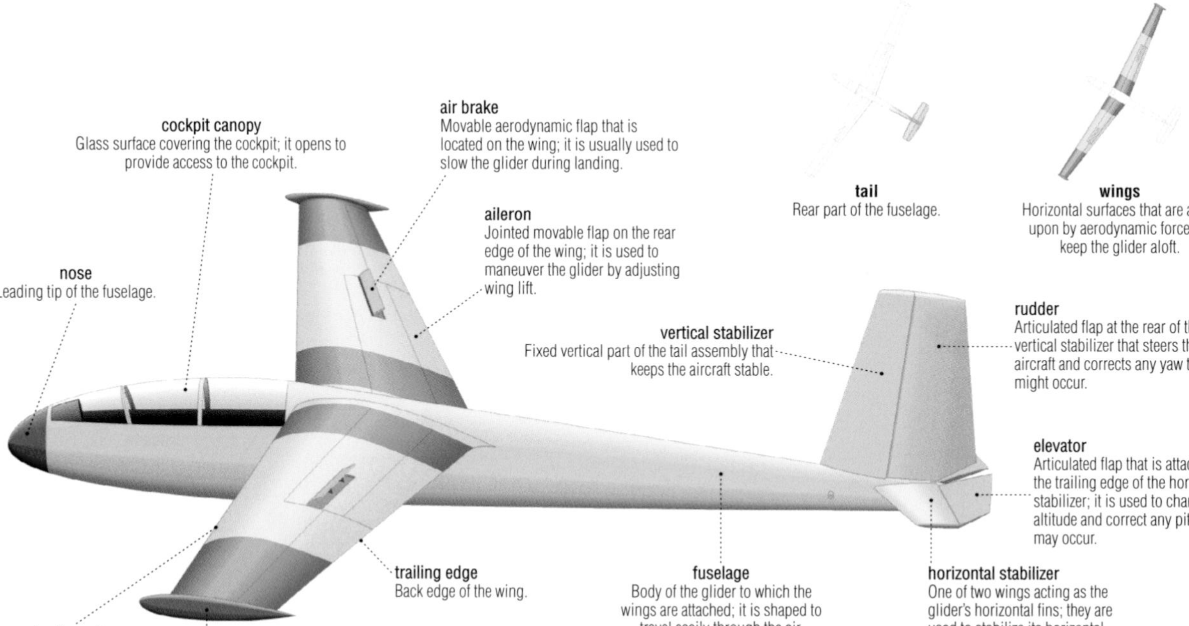
cockpit canopy
Glass surface covering the cockpit; it opens to provide access to the cockpit.
air brake
Movable aerodynamic flap that is located on the wing; it is usually used to slow the glider during landing.
tail
Rear part of the fuselage.
wings
Horizontal surfaces that are acted upon by aerodynamic forces to keep the glider aloft.
aileron
Jointed movable flap on the rear edge of the wing; it is used to maneuver the glider by adjusting wing lift.
nose
Leading tip of the fuselage.
rudder
Articulated flap at the rear of the vertical stabilizer that steers the aircraft and corrects any yaw that might occur.
vertical stabilizer
Fixed vertical part of the tail assembly that keeps the aircraft stable.
elevator
Articulated flap that is attached to the trailing edge of the horizontal stabilizer; it is used to change altitude and correct any pitch that may occur.
trailing edge
Back edge of the wing.
fuselage
Body of the glider to which the wings are attached; it is shaped to travel easily through the air.
horizontal stabilizer
One of two wings acting as the glider's horizontal fins; they are used to stabilize its horizontal movement.
leading edge
Front edge of the wing.
wing tip
Tapered piece that forms the lateral end of the wing.

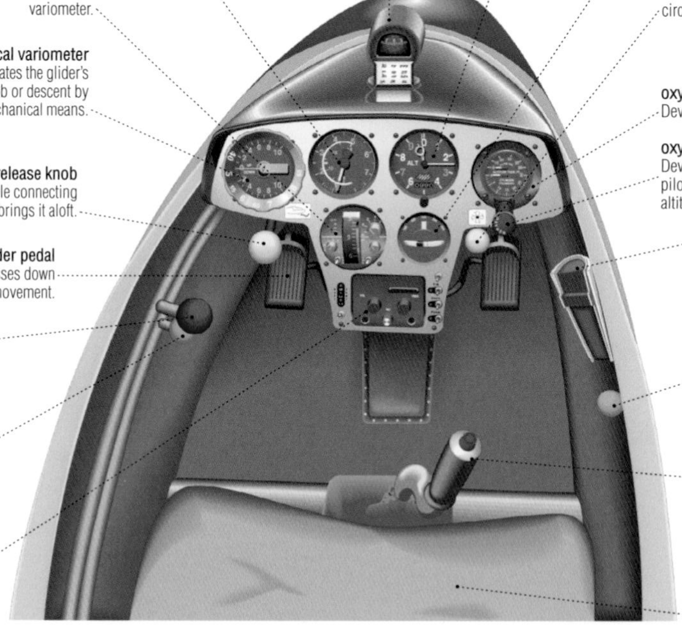
cockpit
Compartment where the glider pilot sits among all the instruments necessary to pilot the aircraft and control flight.
airspeed indicator
Device indicating the speed of the glider with respect to the air through which it is moving.
compass
Navigation instrument that indicates the glider's direction with respect to magnetic north.
altimeter
Device indicating the glider's altitude.
turn and slip indicator
Instrument with a gyroscope connected to a pointer that indicates the rate and direction of turning; it also has a ball that shows if the glider is rolling sideways.
electric variometer
Device that indicates the glider's vertical rate of climb or descent by means of an electric sensor; it is more accurate than a mechanical variometer.
cockpit ventilation
Device that controls the opening and closing of air vents to provide air circulation within the cockpit.
mechanical variometer
Device that indicates the glider's vertical rate of climb or descent by mechanical means.
oxygen feeding control
Device used to regulate the pilot's oxygen flow.
oxygen feeding knob
Device used to activate the system that provides the pilot with oxygen when the glider climbs to high altitudes.
tow release knob
Lever used to release the tow cable connecting the glider to the tow plane that brings it aloft.
microphone
Device that converts electric pulses into broadcast or recorded sounds.
rudder pedal
Foot lever that the pilot presses down to control rudder movement.
air brake handle
Lever used to raise and lower the air brakes.
canopy release knob
Lever that detaches the cockpit canopy from the fuselage so the pilot can eject in case of emergency.
turn and slip knob
Lever that maintains the position of the control stick to reduce pilot fatigue.
control stick
Lever used to control the ailerons and the elevator.
radio
Apparatus that sends and receives signals to communicate with another glider or with a ground station.
seat
Place where the pilot sits to maneuver the glider; the pilot is strapped into the seat and wears a mandatory reserve parachute.

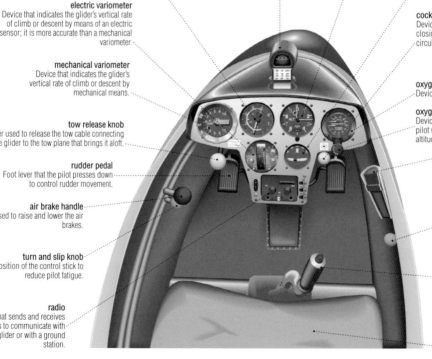

ballooning

Sport of traveling in a balloon carried along by the wind; flights take place at dawn and dusk, when winds are light and the air is stable.

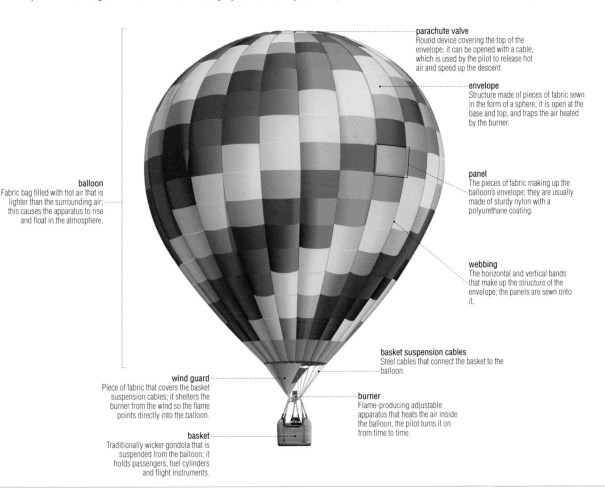

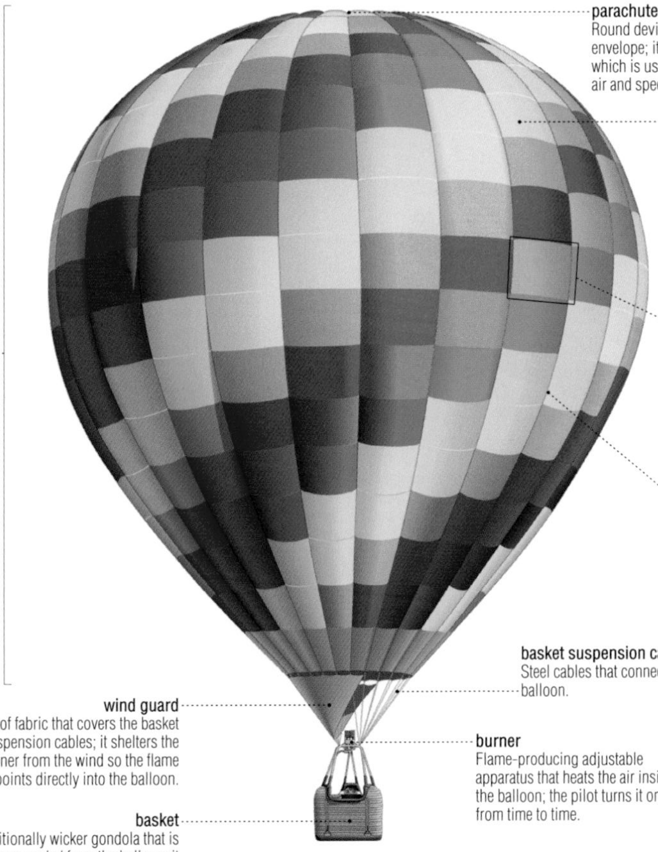
parachute valve
Round device covering the top of the envelope; it can be opened with a cable, which is used by the pilot to release hot air and speed up the descent.
envelope
Structure made of pieces of fabric sewn in the form of a sphere; it is open at the base and top, and traps the air heated by the burner.
balloon
Fabric bag filled with hot air that is lighter than the surrounding air; this causes the apparatus to rise and float in the atmosphere.
panel
The pieces of fabric making up the balloon's envelope; they are usually made of sturdy nylon with a polyurethane coating.
webbing
The horizontal and vertical bands that make up the structure of the envelope; the panels are sewn onto it.
basket suspension cables
Steel cables that connect the basket to the balloon.
wind guard
Piece of fabric that covers the basket suspension cables; it shelters the burner from the wind so the flame points directly into the balloon.
burner
Flame-producing adjustable apparatus that heats the air inside the balloon; the pilot turns it on from time to time.
basket
Traditionally wicker gondola that is suspended from the balloon; it holds passengers, fuel cylinders and flight instruments.

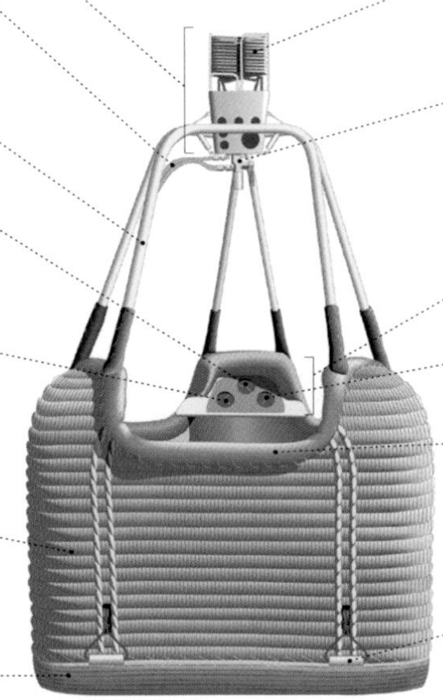
burner
Flame-producing adjustable apparatus that heats the air inside the balloon; the pilot turns it on from time to time.
heating coil
Tubing in which liquid fuel from the cylinders is heated; the fuel emerges as a gas and is then lit by a pilot flame.
basket
Traditionally wicker gondola that is suspended from the balloon; it holds passengers, fuel cylinders and flight instruments.
fuel lines
Flexible hoses that connect the fuel cylinders to the burner.
load support
Rigid framework that supports the burner; the basket suspension cables are attached to it.
blast valve
Part that opens so fuel can enter the burner.
flight instruments
Devices by which the pilot navigates and controls the flight; they include an altimeter, variometer, thermometer, compass and GPS.
variometer
Device that indicates the balloon's vertical rate of climb or descent.
altimeter
Device that indicates the balloon's altitude.
thermometer
Instrument that measures the temperature of the ambient air or of the hot air inside the envelope.
padding
Leather or foam trimming around the basket's upper rim that improves passenger comfort.
wicker basket
Very sturdy yet pliant gondola that can absorb the impact of landing.
hardwood base
Wooden floor that supports the passengers and any equipment carried in the basket.
basket handle
One of the parts used to hold and move the basket; they are also used as a means of anchoring the basket to the ground where necessary.

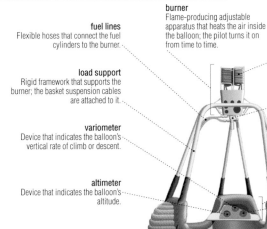

climbing

Leisure or competitive sport that consists of climbing up a natural rock face or an artificial climbing structure using bare hands and light equipment.

rock climber
Person who climbs natural rock faces or artificial climbing structures.

rock
Steep rock face ascended by rock climbers.

quickdraw
Piece of safety equipment that consists of a runner used to keep the rope away from the rock face so it can slide freely and is not worn away by rubbing.

belay rope
Rope that secures the climber in the event of a fall to ensure a safe climb up the rock face.

climbing shoe
Soft shoe with an adherent sole.

runner
Piece of equipment made up of two carabiners connected together by a nylon loop of variable length.

seat harness
Accessory connected to the rope that consists of a number of straps to support the climber's thighs and pelvis.

roped party
Group of climbers who are connected to one another by one or more ropes during an ascent.

leader
The most experienced climber who climbs at the head of the roped party and marks out the climbing route.

artificial climbing structure
Fixed or movable indoor or outdoor surface used by climbers as a rock face to practice their sport as a leisure or competitive activity.

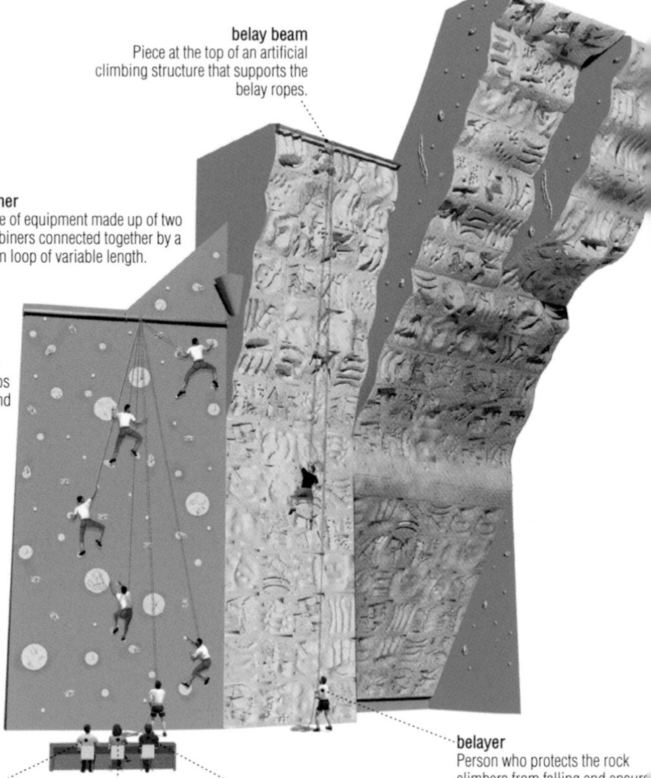

belay beam
Piece at the top of an artificial climbing structure that supports the belay ropes.

route judge
Person who ensures safety and observes the climbers' maneuvers.

president of the jury
Person who supervises all competition activities and presides over any disputes.

timekeeper
Person who ensures that the route is climbed within the set time frame.

belayer
Person who protects the rock climbers from falling and ensure they do not swap information during an event.

equipment
Complete range of accessories used in climbing.

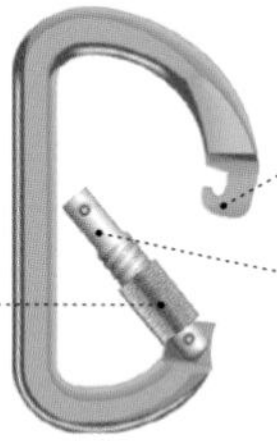

latch
Part over which the gate closes.

gate
Moving metal part that opens inward and has a spring-loaded closure.

screwsleeve
Device that locks the gate into a closed position.

locking carabiner
Metal ring with a gate that, once closed, can be locked with a screwsleeve; this makes it safer than the D carabiner.

D carabiner
Metal ring that opens and closes with a spring-loaded gate; it is used for attaching rope to a piton, a chock, etc.

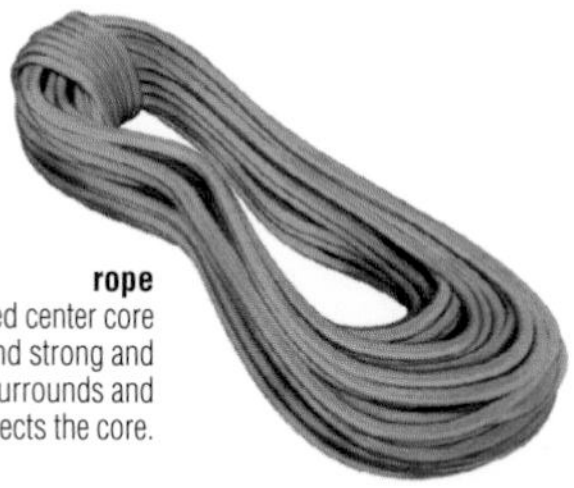

rope
Thin cable with a braided center core that makes it stretchy and strong and a woven sheath that surrounds and protects the core.

expansion piton
Piton that is driven into a hole previously made in the rock.

piton
Metal spike with a blade that is driven into a crack in the rock face; it ends in an eye to which a belay rope can be attached with a carabiner.

blade
Part that is driven into the crack in the rock face.

eye
Hole that is large enough for a carabiner to snap on so that a rope can be attached to the piton.

chock
Metal device that is inserted into a crack in the rock face and held in place by tension; it is extended by a steel cable to which a carabiner can snap on.

wire sling

descender
Metal accessory through which a rope slides that is used to protect the rope and the climber's hands; it acts as a brake during rappel descents.

seat harness
Accessory connected to the belay rope that consists of a number of straps to support the climber's thighs and pelvis.

climbing

handholds
Projection over which the hand is placed or hollow into which the fingers are inserted in order to advance.

pinch
Hold that is squeezed between the thumb and fingers.

crimp
Closed hold with the fingertips on the rock face and the thumb pushed against the index finger.

open hand
Open hold with the fingers outstretched and the palm gripping the rock.

foothold
Projection on which the foot is placed or hollow into which it is inserted in order to advance.

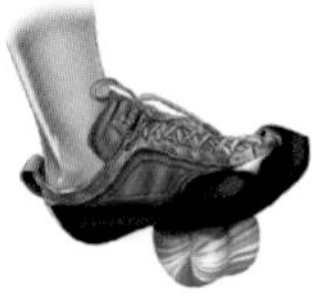

inside edge
Hold that consists of placing the foot's inside edge on a projection and turning the heel toward the rock face.

mountaineer
Person who climbs mountains.

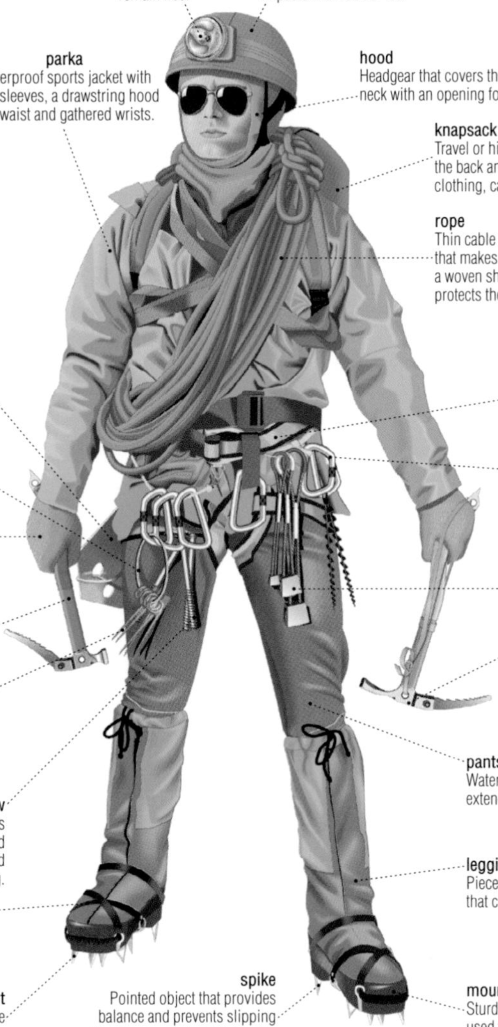

helmet lamp
Lamp that is attached to the helmet so that the mountaineer's hands remain free.

helmet
Solid piece of equipment to protect the head from falling rocks or impacts with rock or ice.

parka
Waterproof sports jacket with long sleeves, a drawstring hood and waist and gathered wrists.

hood
Headgear that covers the head and neck with an opening for the face.

knapsack
Travel or hiking bag that is worn on the back and is used to transport clothing, camping equipment, etc.

rope
Thin cable with a braided center core that makes it stretchy and strong and a woven sheath that surrounds and protects the core.

mountaineering shovel
Instrument used to dig and remove snow.

climbing harness
Accessory connected to the belay rope that consists of a number of straps; it supports the mountaineer's thighs and pelvis, back and sometimes shoulders.

piton-carrier
Metal ring on which pitons are hung.

carabiner
Metal ring that opens and closes with a spring-loaded gate and that might be equipped with a locking device; it is used to attach rope to a piton, a chock, etc.

mitten
Covering with a separation only for the thumb, providing better protection against the cold while allowing the wearer to grasp objects.

hammer ax
Hammer that doubles as an ice ax; it is used to drive in pitons, cut footholds, break ice on the rock face, etc.

chock
Metal device that is inserted into a crack in the rock face and held in place by tension; it is extended by a steel cable to which a carabiner can snap on.

ice ax
Small ax used by the mountaineer for cutting footholds, judging snow depth, gaining a firm grip in ice or hard-packed snow, etc.

ice piton
Metal spike with a blade that is driven into ice or hard-packed snow; it ends in an eye to which a belay rope can be attached using a carabiner.

pants
Waterproof pants that usually extend below the knee.

ice screw
Threaded metal tube that is screwed into ice or hard-packed snow to help with belaying and advancing.

legging
Piece of sturdy waterproof fabric that covers the leg.

crampon strap
Strap used to attach spikes to the sole of the shoe.

front point
Each of the front spikes; they are tilted at a 45° angle.

spike
Pointed object that provides balance and prevents slipping when the mountaineer is moving over snow or ice.

mountaineering boot
Sturdy shoe with spikes that is used to advance over snow or ice.

tubular ice screw
Threaded metal tube that is screwed into ice or hard-packed snow to help with belaying and advancing.

ring
Metal loop into which carabiners are inserted.

hammer ax
Hammer that doubles as an ice ax; it is used to drive in pitons, cut footholds, break ice on the rock face, etc.

hammer head
Flat surface used by the mountaineer to strike pitons.

pick
Part that is driven into ice or hard-packed snow in order to advance.

ice ax
Small ax used by the mountaineer for cutting footholds, judging snow depth, gaining a firm grip in ice or hard-packed snow, etc.

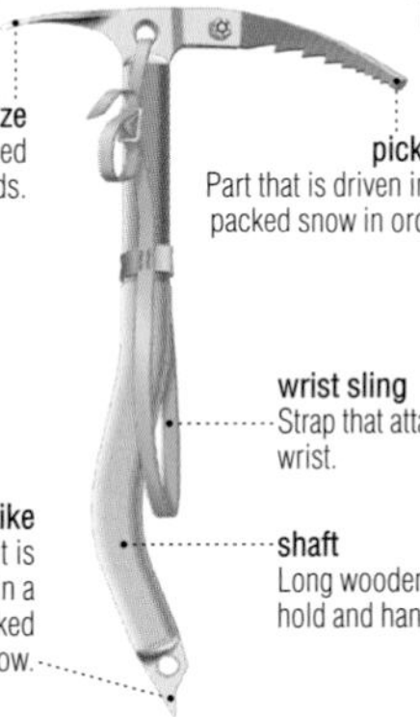

head
Semicircular part that contains the pick and the adze.

adze
Flat sharp-edged part that is used to cut footholds.

pick
Part that is driven into ice or hard-packed snow in order to advance.

wrist sling
Strap that attaches the ice ax to the wrist.

spike
Sharp-tipped end of the shaft; it is used to cut footholds and to gain a firm grip in ice or hard-packed snow.

shaft
Long wooden or metal part used to hold and handle the ice ax.

camping

Tourist activity that consists of sleeping in a portable shelter such as a tent or trailer and traveling with equipment designed for outdoor living.

examples of tents

Tents: portable waterproof soft-sided shelters that are stretched taut over a frame and temporarily pitched outdoors.

two-person tent
Tent that can accommodate two people.

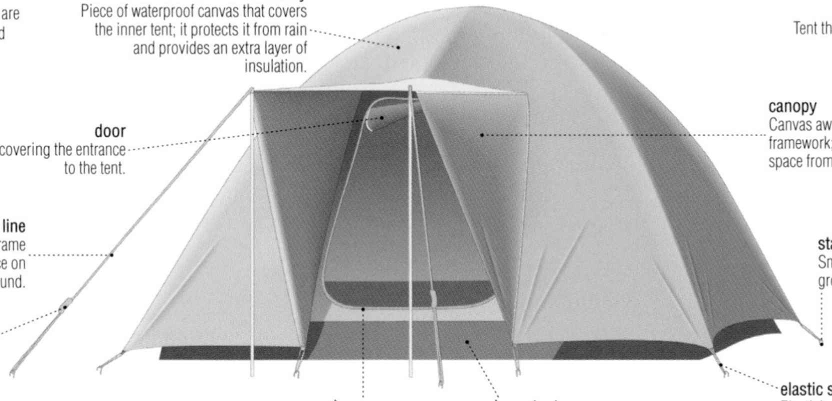

rainfly
Piece of waterproof canvas that covers the inner tent; it protects it from rain and provides an extra layer of insulation.

door
Piece of canvas covering the entrance to the tent.

guy line
Cable used to stretch the tent frame taut and hold it firmly in place on the ground.

strainer
Device used to stretch a guy line taut.

canopy
Canvas awning supported by a framework; it protects an outdoor space from the rain and sun.

stake
Small post that is driven into th ground to hold the tent in place

elastic strainer
Elasticized cable used to stretch the canvas taut and anchor it to the ground.

zipper
Closure made up of two lengths of tape edged with teeth that interlock by means of a slide.

inner tent
Part of the tent covered by the rainfly.

family tent
Spacious tent with several rooms that can accommodate about four people.

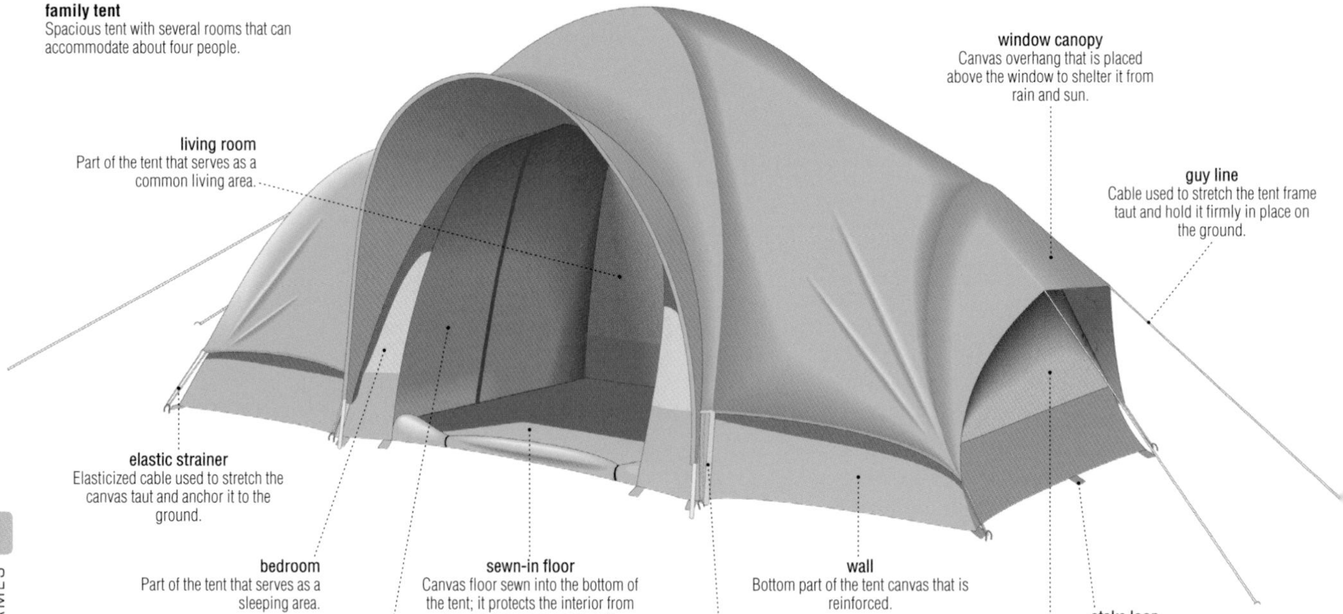

window canopy
Canvas overhang that is placed above the window to shelter it from rain and sun.

living room
Part of the tent that serves as a common living area.

guy line
Cable used to stretch the tent frame taut and hold it firmly in place on the ground.

elastic strainer
Elasticized cable used to stretch the canvas taut and anchor it to the ground.

bedroom
Part of the tent that serves as a sleeping area.

sewn-in floor
Canvas floor sewn into the bottom of the tent; it protects the interior from ground dampness and runoff.

wall
Bottom part of the tent canvas that is reinforced.

stake loop
One of the fabric circles attached to the tent's outer edge; stakes are driven through the loops to anchor the tent to the ground.

canvas divider
Partition that divides the tent's interior into separate rooms.

frame
Structure of stainless steel, plastic or carbon tubing that forms the framework of the tent and gives it shape.

screen window
Opening that lets air and light in and keeps mosquitoes out.

wagon tent
Spacious tent with sufficient interior capacity to accommodate a number of people or group activities.

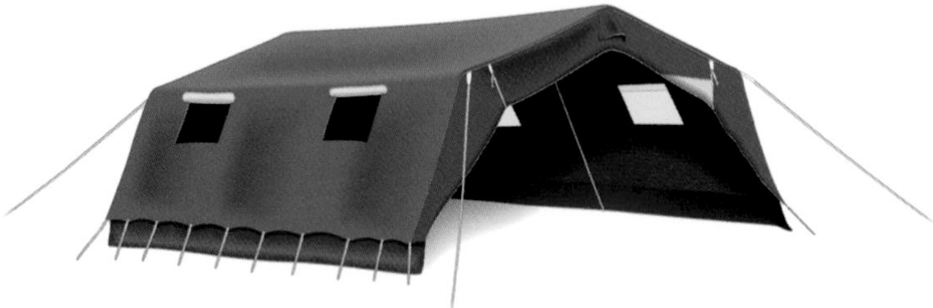

wall tent
Very spacious, rectangular tent that often has a number of interior dividers; it accommodates a number of people.

pup tent
Tent where the canvas is stretched taut on both sides of a summit rod, which is supported by two poles.

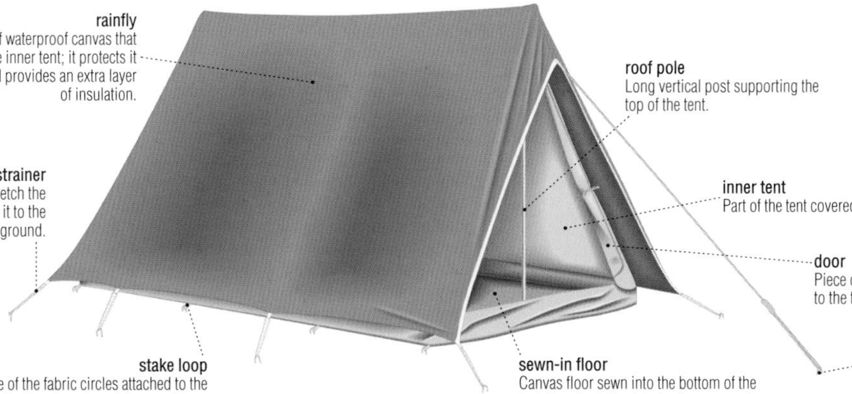

rainfly
Piece of waterproof canvas that covers the inner tent; it protects it from rain and provides an extra layer of insulation.

roof pole
Long vertical post supporting the top of the tent.

elastic strainer
Elasticized cable used to stretch the canvas taut and anchor it to the ground.

inner tent
Part of the tent covered by the rainfly.

door
Piece of canvas covering the entrance to the tent.

stake loop
One of the fabric circles attached to the tent's outer edge; stakes are driven through the loops to anchor the tent to the ground.

sewn-in floor
Canvas floor sewn into the bottom of the tent; it protects the interior from ground dampness and runoff.

stake
Small post that is driven into the ground to hold the tent in place.

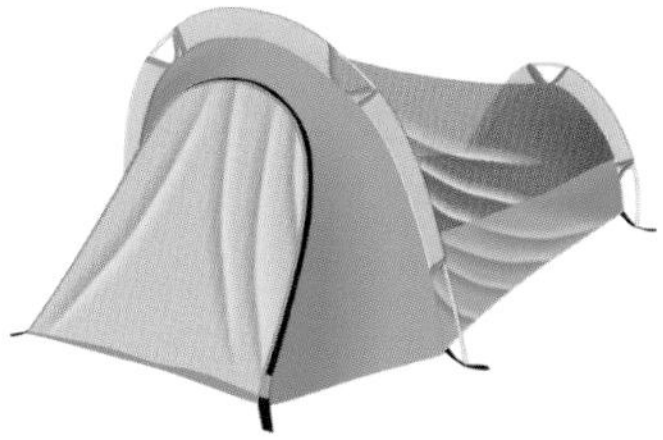

one-person tent
Small low-roofed tent with enough room to accommodate one person.

dome tent
Semicircular tent that, once pitched, can be moved without being taken down.

pop-up tent
Round tent with a framework that deploys automatically.

lantern
Safe portable light source that can be used both inside and outside a tent.

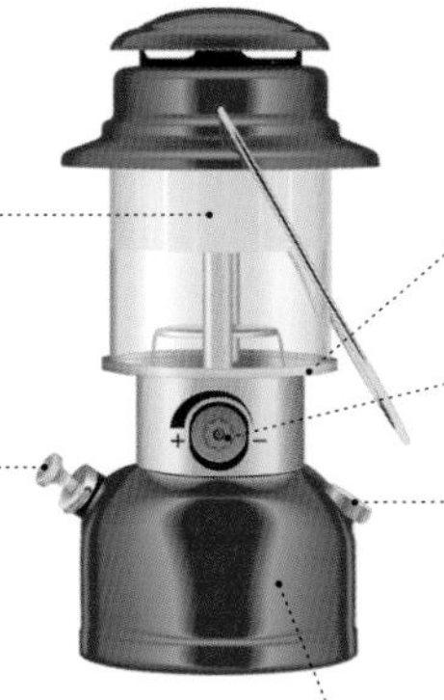

globe
Translucent or transparent heat-resistant covering that protects the light source and diffuses its light.

burner frame
Aluminum housing protecting the burner.

pressure regulator
Device that controls the pressure of the vaporized fuel and adjusts the light's brightness.

pump
Device that increases the air pressure inside the tank so the fuel vaporizes.

leakproof cap
Stopper for the fuel refill opening; it is threaded to prevent leakage.

tank
Canister containing the liquid fuel and air that supply the burner.

propane or butane accessories
Complete range of portable appliances that run on liquid or gas fuel and are used to light, cook or heat.

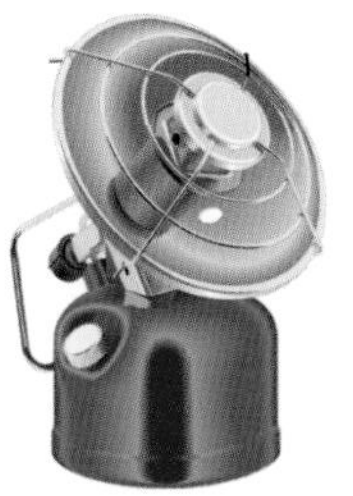

heater
Appliance with a heating element to generate heat and a reflector to radiate it.

double-burner camp stove
Two-burner appliance used to cook and reheat food.

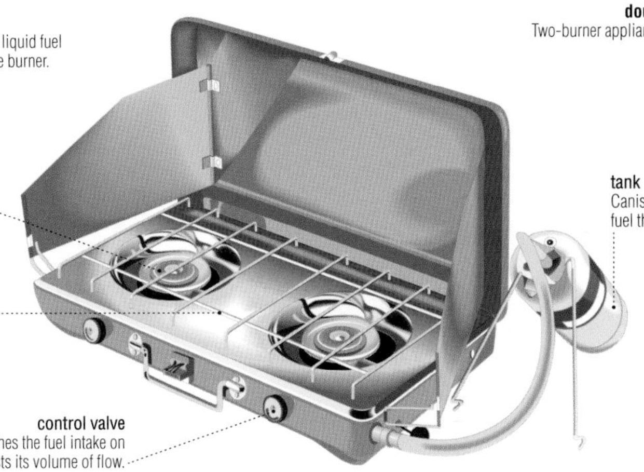

single-burner camp stove
Single-burner appliance used to cook and reheat food.

burner
Combustion device for an air-gas mixture.

wire support
Metal grill used as a base to support cooking utensils.

tank
Canister containing the pressurized fuel that supplies the burners.

control valve
Device that switches the fuel intake on and off and adjusts its volume of flow.

camping

examples of sleeping bags

Sleeping bags: insulated fabric coverings that close with a zipper and are used to stay warm when sleeping outdoors.

rectangular
Rectangular sleeping bag that is spacious enough to give the body room to move.

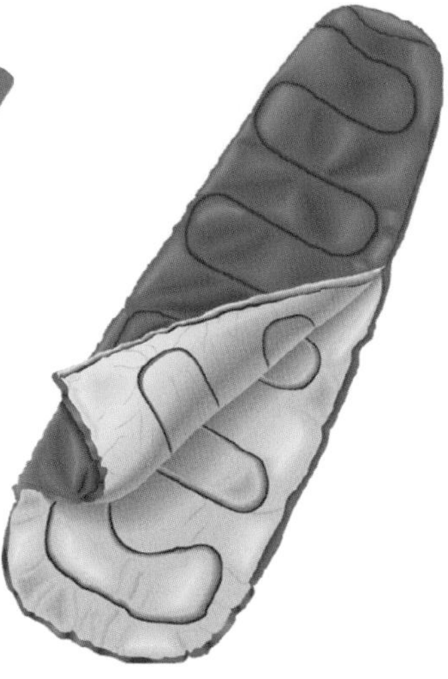

semi-mummy
Sleeping bag with a less spacious design to better retain body heat.

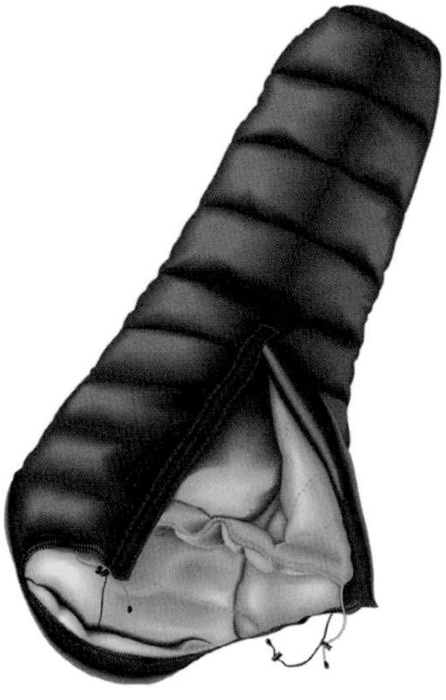

mummy
Sleeping bag shaped like the body; it has a part that covers the head and neck with an opening for the face.

bed and mattress

Accessories that a person lies down on to sleep or rest.

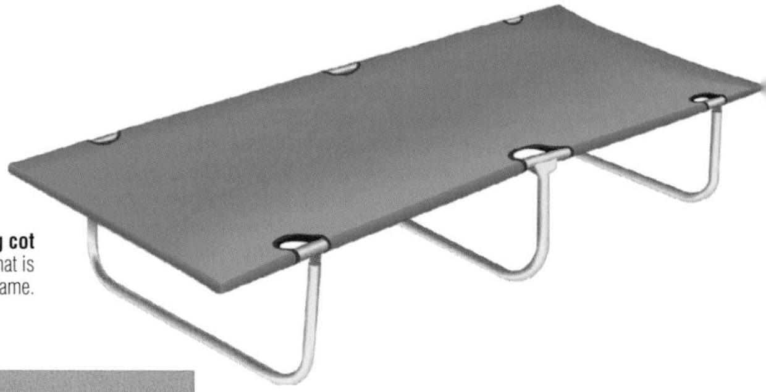

folding cot
Portable bed made of fabric that is stretched over a collapsible frame.

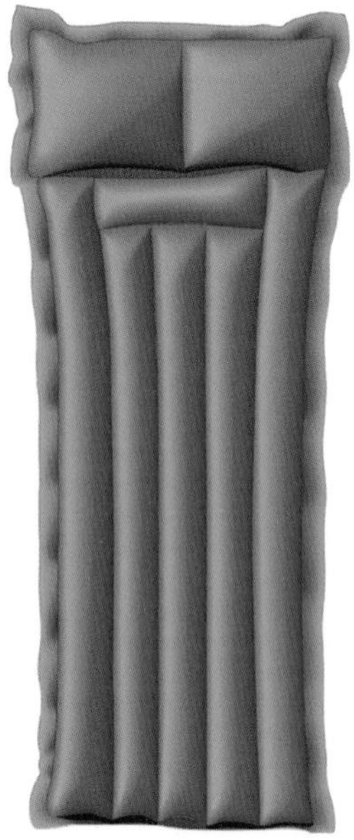

air mattress
Rubber or plastic bag that is filled with air; it usually has a pillow.

self-inflating mattress
Rubber, plastic or nylon bag that inflates with air by itself, without the need of an inflator.

foam pad
Long thin cushion made of soft material.

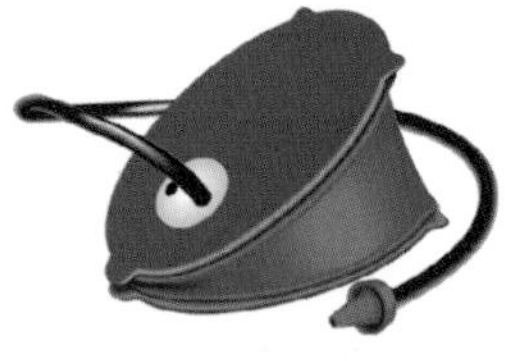

inflator-deflator
Device used to inflate and deflate air mattresses.

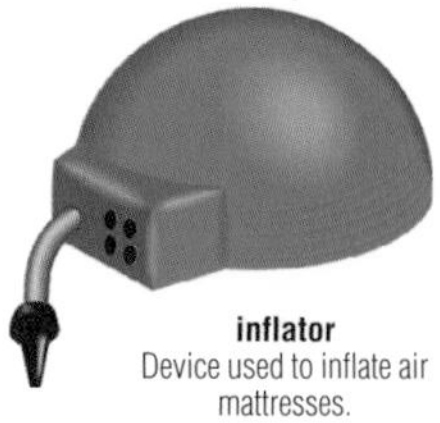

inflator
Device used to inflate air mattresses.

camping

cutlery set
Range of compact table utensils (knife, fork and spoon) used by the camper to eat.

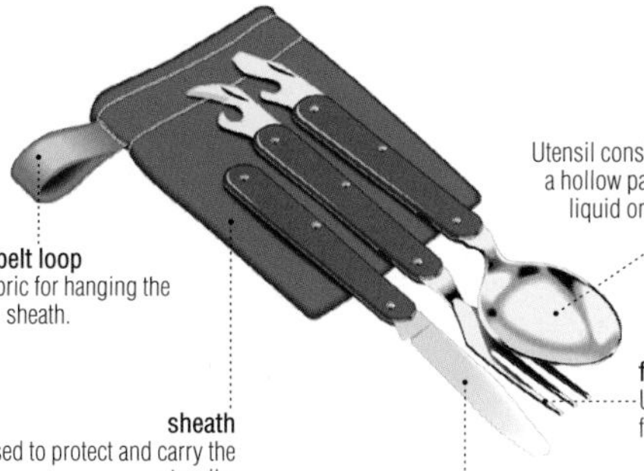

spoon
Utensil consisting of a handle and a hollow part that is used to eat liquid or semisolid foods.

belt loop
Strip of fabric for hanging the sheath.

fork
Utensil with tines used to spear food and carry it to the mouth.

sheath
Case used to protect and carry the utensils.

knife
Utensil consisting of a handle and a sharp blade used to cut food into bite-sized pieces.

cooking set
Stackable set of dishes, utensils and containers that are used to cook outdoors.

plate
Large piece of flat or shallow dinnerware, usually containing individual portions of solid food.

saucepan
Stockpot with somewhat high sides, used to cook food in a liquid.

handle
Part used to hold and move the frying pan.

frying pan
Utensil used to fry, sauté or brown food.

coffee pot
Container used to brew coffee.

cup
Container used to consume liquids or semisolid foods.

camping equipment
Range of accessories used when camping to store food, cut wood, etc.

Swiss Army knife
Multipurpose knife with a large assortment of blades and instruments.

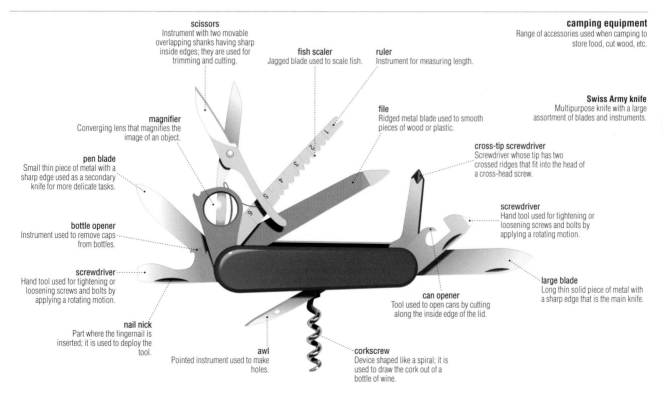

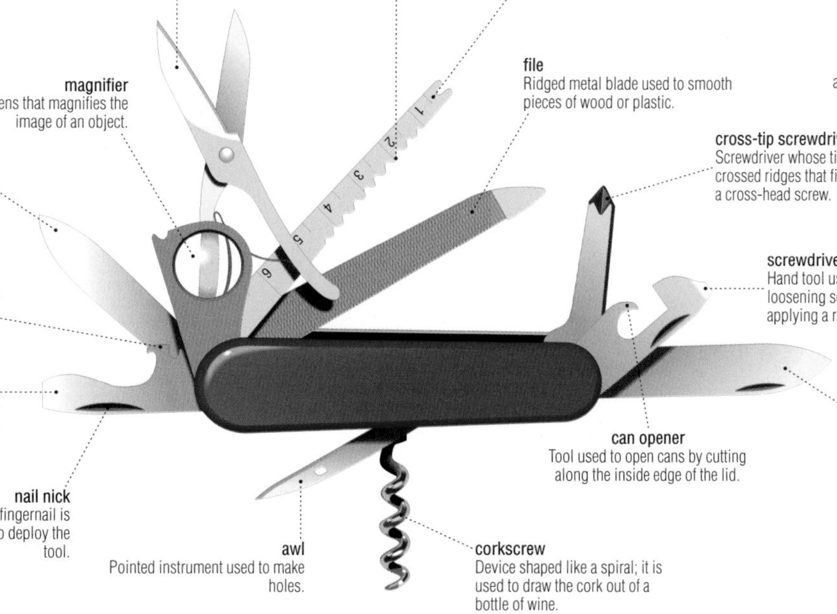

scissors
Instrument with two movable overlapping shanks having sharp inside edges; they are used for trimming and cutting.

fish scaler
Jagged blade used to scale fish.

ruler
Instrument for measuring length.

file
Ridged metal blade used to smooth pieces of wood or plastic.

magnifier
Converging lens that magnifies the image of an object.

pen blade
Small thin piece of metal with a sharp edge used as a secondary knife for more delicate tasks.

cross-tip screwdriver
Screwdriver whose tip has two crossed ridges that fit into the head of a cross-head screw.

screwdriver
Hand tool used for tightening or loosening screws and bolts by applying a rotating motion.

bottle opener
Instrument used to remove caps from bottles.

screwdriver
Hand tool used for tightening or loosening screws and bolts by applying a rotating motion.

large blade
Long thin solid piece of metal with a sharp edge that is the main knife.

can opener
Tool used to open cans by cutting along the inside edge of the lid.

nail nick
Part where the fingernail is inserted; it is used to deploy the tool.

awl
Pointed instrument used to make holes.

corkscrew
Device shaped like a spiral; it is used to draw the cork out of a bottle of wine.

SPORTS AND GAMES

camping

backpack
Travel or hiking bag that is worn on the back and is used to transport clothing, camping equipment, etc.

shoulder strap
Fabric band of variable length that goes over the shoulder so the bag can be carried on the back.

side compression strap
Fabric band that reduces the size of the bag and keeps the contents in place.

waist belt
Fabric strap that fits snugly around the hips and buckles there; it is designed to distribute the bag's weight.

top flap
Piece of fabric that folds over the opening of the backpack.

tightening buckle
Device used to adjust the length of the strap.

front compression strap
Fabric band connected to the top flap strap and used to fasten the backpack.

strap loop
Buckle through which the strap passes.

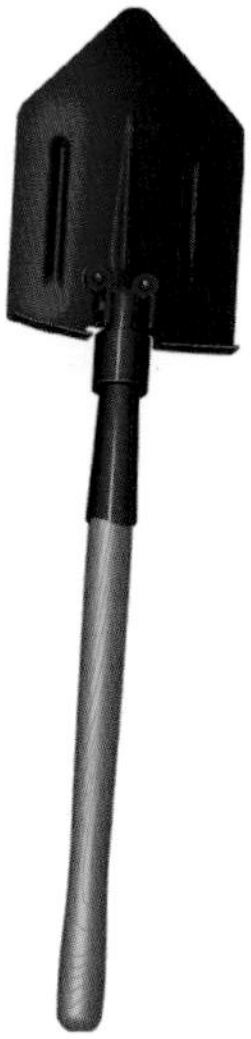

folding shovel
Tool with a collapsible handle; it is used as a shovel or a pickax.

hurricane lamp
Portable lantern with a glass globe and metal frame to protect the flame from wind and impact.

vacuum bottle
Container with a vacuum between the inner and insulated outer walls; it is designed to maintain its contents at a desired temperature.

bottle
Container used to hold liquids or semisolid foods.

stopper
Part used to close the neck of the bottle.

cup
Cap used as a container to consume liquid or semisolid foods.

canteen
Portable container used to store liquids.

cooler
Thermally insulated chest that is used to keep food cold with ice cubes or blocks of ice.

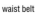

water carrier
Container with a spigot that is used to store drinking water when camping.

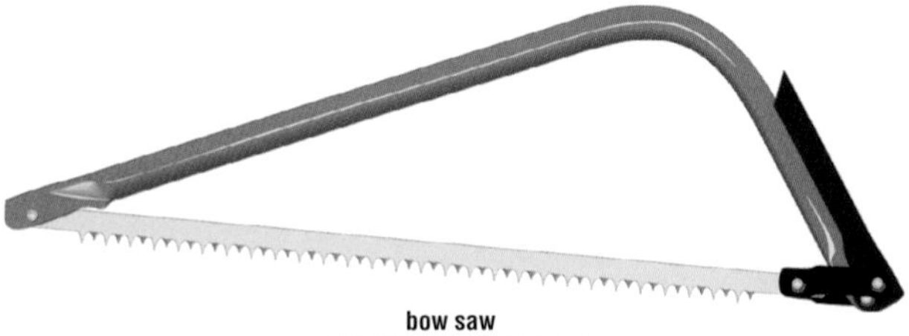

bow saw
Collapsible tool with a serrated blade; it is used to saw wood.

hatchet
Small ax used to cut wood.

leather sheath
Casing to cover the head of the hatchet when it is not in use.

knife
Tool consisting of a sharp blade and a handle; it is used to cut items such as rope and fishing line.

folding grill
Hinged metal utensil used to cook food over a campfire.

sheath
Casing to cover the knife blade when it is not in use.

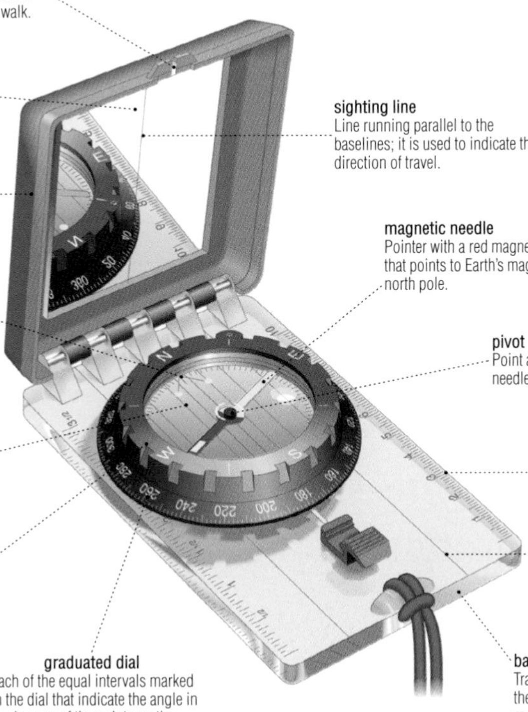

magnetic compass
Instrument for finding directions; it has a graduated compass card and a magnetic needle that points toward magnetic north.

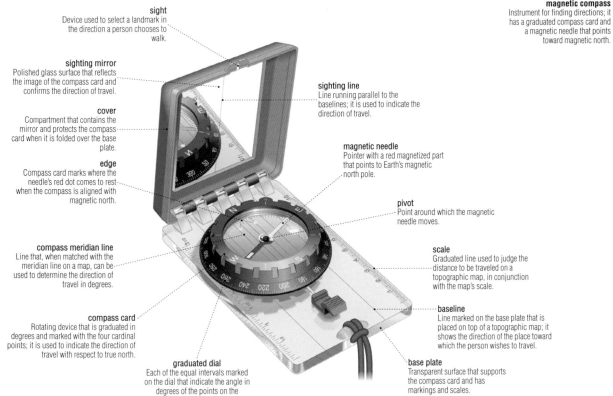

sight
Device used to select a landmark in the direction a person chooses to walk.

sighting mirror
Polished glass surface that reflects the image of the compass card and confirms the direction of travel.

cover
Compartment that contains the mirror and protects the compass card when it is folded over the base plate.

edge
Compass card marks where the needle's red dot comes to rest when the compass is aligned with magnetic north.

compass meridian line
Line that, when matched with the meridian line on a map, can be used to determine the direction of travel in degrees.

compass card
Rotating device that is graduated in degrees and marked with the four cardinal points; it is used to indicate the direction of travel with respect to true north.

graduated dial
Each of the equal intervals marked on the dial that indicate the angle in degrees of the points on the compass card.

sighting line
Line running parallel to the baselines; it is used to indicate the direction of travel.

magnetic needle
Pointer with a red magnetized part that points to Earth's magnetic north pole.

pivot
Point around which the magnetic needle moves.

scale
Graduated line used to judge the distance to be traveled on a topographic map, in conjunction with the map's scale.

baseline
Line marked on the base plate that is placed on top of a topographic map; it shows the direction of the place toward which the person wishes to travel.

base plate
Transparent surface that supports the compass card and has markings and scales.

knots

Intertwining of two ropes or of one rope back on itself; they are used to tie two ropes together or one rope to an object.

square knot
Knot used to join two ropes of equal diameter firmly together.

overhand knot
Basic all-purpose knot tied by simply looping the rope back on itself.

running bowline
Knot pulled tight around an object to hold it in place.

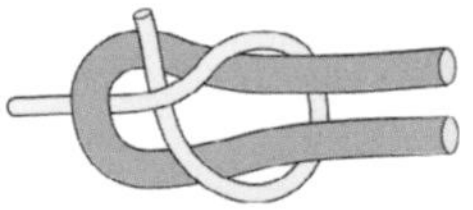

sheet bend
Knot used to join together two ropes of different diameters.

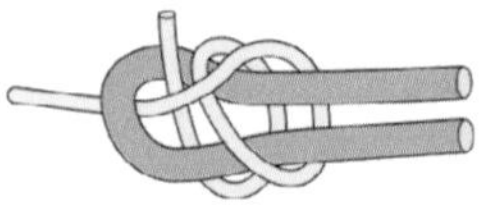

double sheet bend
Knot with the same function as the sheet bend but the second loop makes the knot stronger and more secure.

granny knot
Knot used to tie two ropes together; it is used only when they will need to be untied easily.

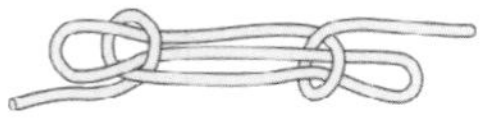

sheepshank
Knot used to temporarily shorten a rope.

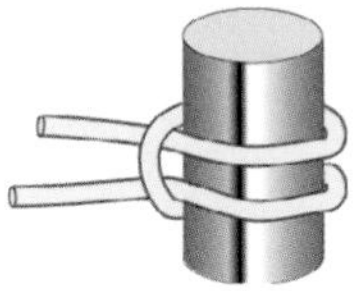

cow hitch
Knot used to join a rope to a ring, mast, yard, etc.

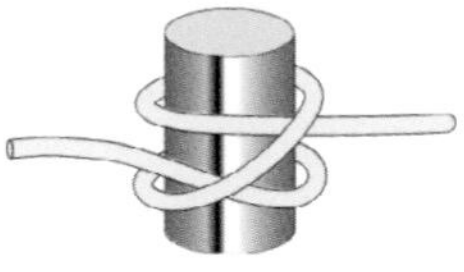

clove hitch
Knot used to join a rope to a stationary object or to another rope.

fisherman's knot
Knot used to tie together two ropes of equal diameter or two ends of fishing line.

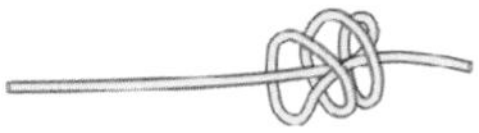

heaving line knot
Knot used to add weight to the end of a rope so it can be thrown.

figure-eight knot
Any knot used to increase the diameter of a rope end.

common whipping
Winding a cord around a rope end to prevent its strands from unraveling.

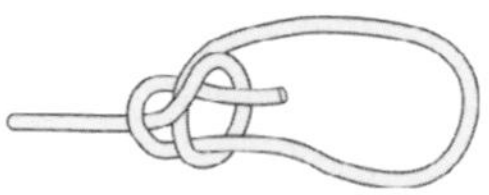

bowline
Knot used to create a loop at the end of a rope that cannot slip and in which a person can sit to be raised or lowered.

bowline on a bight
Knot with the same function as the bowline but with two ropes to make the loop; one forms the seat and the other goes around the waist.

short splice

Splice: joining two ropes by interweaving their strands.

forming
To create a splice, the strands of each rope are first unraveled and then interwoven.

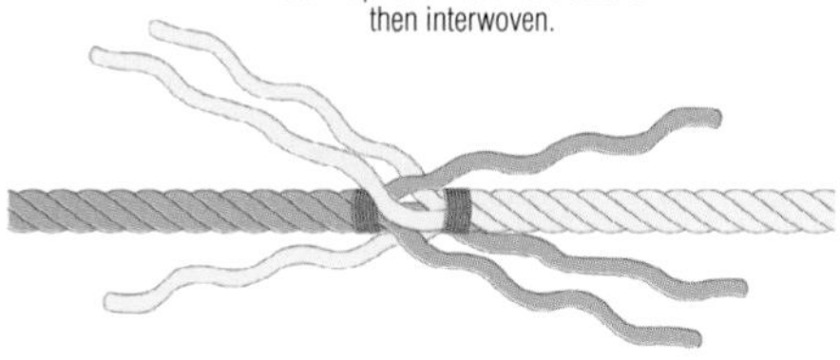

completion
To complete a splice, the strand ends of each rope are tucked into the other one.

cable

Flexible, very strong cord made of twisted or braided ropes.

twisted rope
Strand of rope that is twisted with others to make a cable.

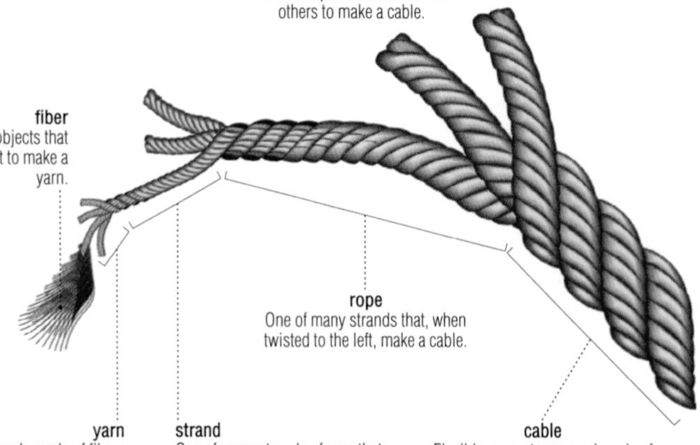

fiber
Each of the threadlike objects that are twisted to the right to make a yarn.

rope
One of many strands that, when twisted to the left, make a cable.

yarn
Each of the threads made of fibers that are twisted to the left to make a strand.

strand
One of many strands of yarn that, when twisted to the right, make a twisted rope.

cable
Flexible, very strong cord made of twisted ropes.

braided rope
Cable made by braiding strands together.

core
Mass of braided threads that give the rope its strength.

sheath
Casing made of interwoven threads that protects the core and makes it resistant to rubbing.

fishing

Outdoor leisure activity consisting of trying to catch fish with a fishing rod.

flyfishing
Fishing method that consists of delicately placing an artificial fly on or in the water; it simulates a real insect landing to attract fish.

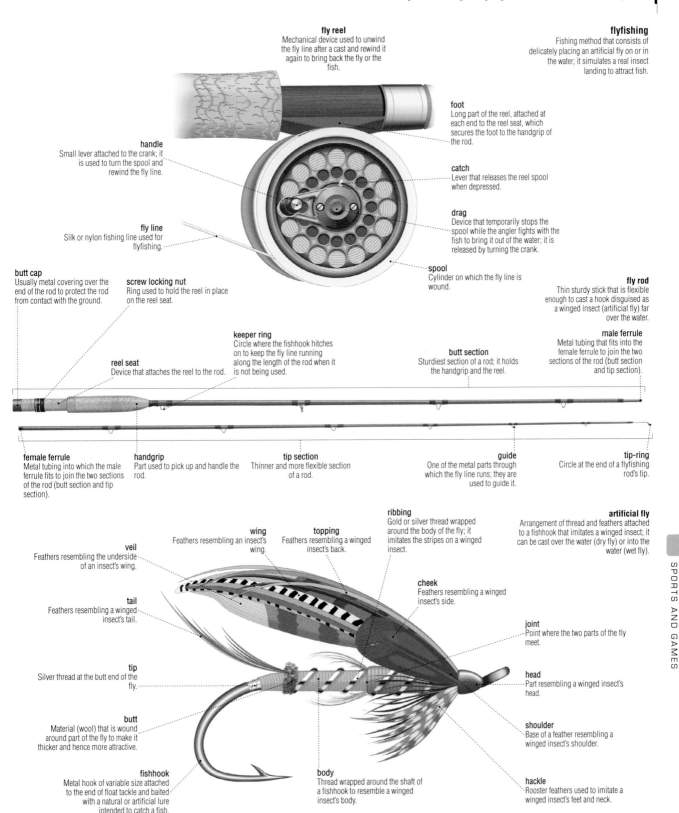

fly reel
Mechanical device used to unwind the fly line after a cast and rewind it again to bring back the fly or the fish.

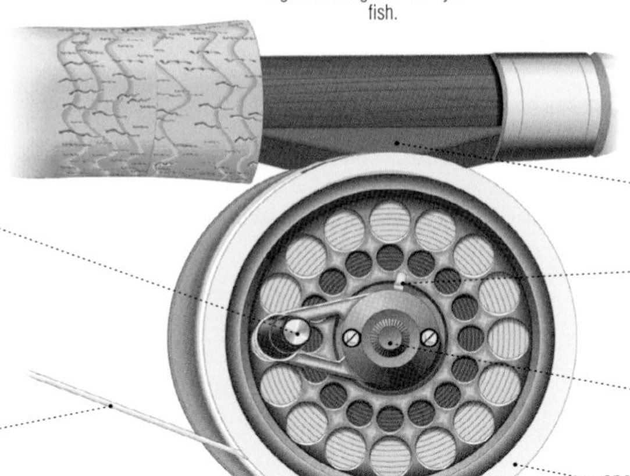

handle
Small lever attached to the crank; it is used to turn the spool and rewind the fly line.

fly line
Silk or nylon fishing line used for flyfishing.

foot
Long part of the reel, attached at each end to the reel seat, which secures the foot to the handgrip of the rod.

catch
Lever that releases the reel spool when depressed.

drag
Device that temporarily stops the spool while the angler fights with the fish to bring it out of the water; it is released by turning the crank.

spool
Cylinder on which the fly line is wound.

fly rod
Thin sturdy stick that is flexible enough to cast a hook disguised as a winged insect (artificial fly) far over the water.

butt cap
Usually metal covering over the end of the rod to protect the rod from contact with the ground.

screw locking nut
Ring used to hold the reel in place on the reel seat.

reel seat
Device that attaches the reel to the rod.

keeper ring
Circle where the fishhook hitches on to keep the fly line running along the length of the rod when it is not being used.

butt section
Sturdiest section of a rod; it holds the handgrip and the reel.

male ferrule
Metal tubing that fits into the female ferrule to join the two sections of the rod (butt section and tip section).

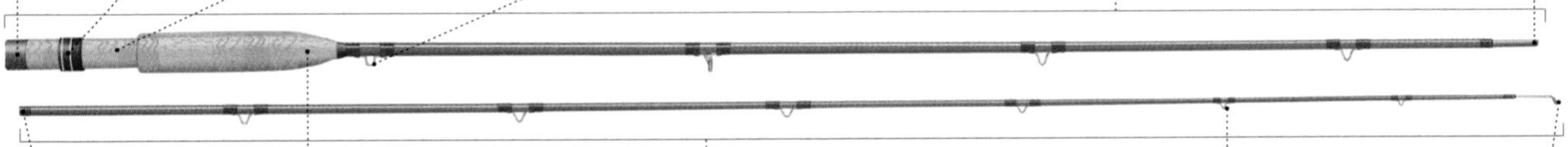

female ferrule
Metal tubing into which the male ferrule fits to join the two sections of the rod (butt section and tip section).

handgrip
Part used to pick up and handle the rod.

tip section
Thinner and more flexible section of a rod.

guide
One of the metal parts through which the fly line runs; they are used to guide it.

tip-ring
Circle at the end of a flyfishing rod's tip.

artificial fly
Arrangement of thread and feathers attached to a fishhook that imitates a winged insect; it can be cast over the water (dry fly) or into the water (wet fly).

veil
Feathers resembling the underside of an insect's wing.

wing
Feathers resembling an insect's wing.

topping
Feathers resembling a winged insect's back.

ribbing
Gold or silver thread wrapped around the body of the fly; it imitates the stripes on a winged insect.

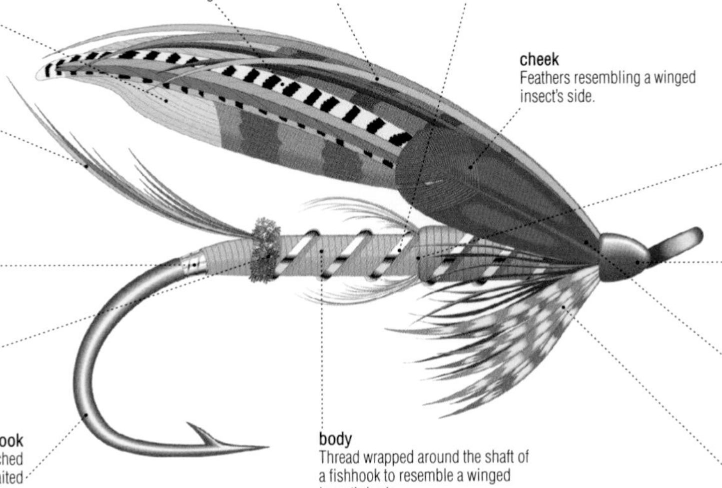

tail
Feathers resembling a winged insect's tail.

cheek
Feathers resembling a winged insect's side.

joint
Point where the two parts of the fly meet.

tip
Silver thread at the butt end of the fly.

head
Part resembling a winged insect's head.

butt
Material (wool) that is wound around part of the fly to make it thicker and hence more attractive.

shoulder
Base of a feather resembling a winged insect's shoulder.

fishhook
Metal hook of variable size attached to the end of float tackle and baited with a natural or artificial lure intended to catch a fish.

body
Thread wrapped around the shaft of a fishhook to resemble a winged insect's body.

hackle
Rooster feathers used to imitate a winged insect's feet and neck.

fishing

casting

Fishing that consists of letting a hook drop and sink into the water and reeling it back in to simulate the movement of a small fish.

spinning rod
Stick whose length and sturdiness varies with the kind of fishing being done; it is used to cast a hook carried along by a weight, sinker or spinner far over the water.

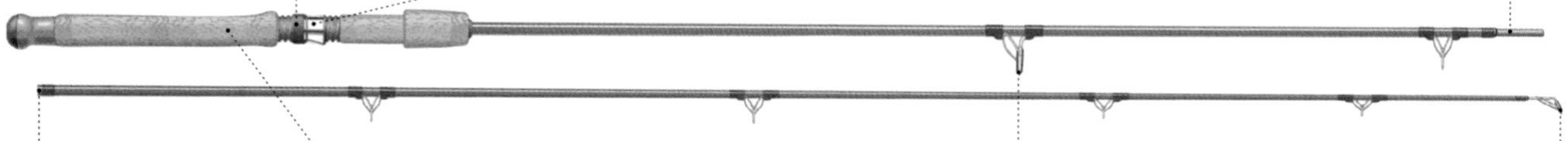
screw locking nut
Ring used to hold the reel in place on the reel seat.
reel seat
Device that attaches the reel to the rod.
male ferrule
Metal tubing that fits into the female ferrule to join the two sections of the rod (butt section and tip section).
female ferrule
Metal tubing into which the male ferrule fits to join the two sections of the rod (butt section and tip section).
butt grip
Part used to pick up and handle the rod.
butt guide
Large-diameter circle used to guide the slack line.
tip-ring
Circle at the end of a spinning rod's tip.

open-face spinning reel
Reel from which the line unwinds as it comes off the upper sides of the spool, which does not rotate but remains in place.

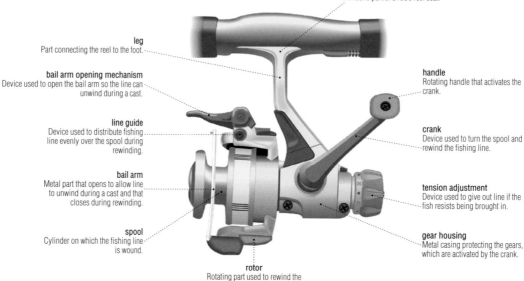

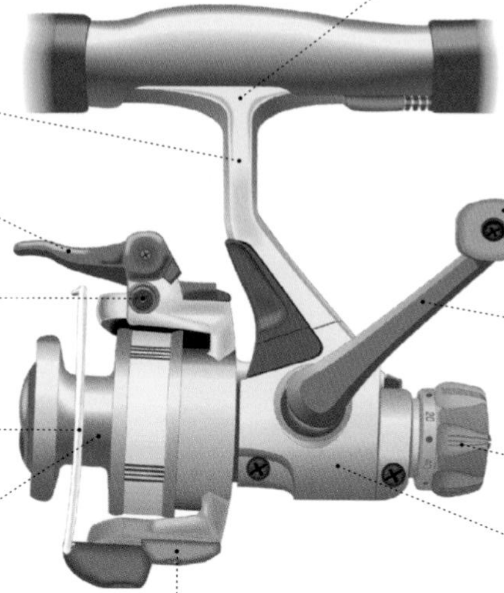
foot
Immobile part of a rod's reel seat.
leg
Part connecting the reel to the foot.
bail arm opening mechanism
Device used to open the bail arm so the line can unwind during a cast.
line guide
Device used to distribute fishing line evenly over the spool during rewinding.
bail arm
Metal part that opens to allow line to unwind during a cast and that closes during rewinding.
spool
Cylinder on which the fishing line is wound.
rotor
Rotating part used to rewind the fishing line.
handle
Rotating handle that activates the crank.
crank
Device used to turn the spool and rewind the fishing line.
tension adjustment
Device used to give out line if the fish resists being brought in.
gear housing
Metal casing protecting the gears, which are activated by the crank.

baitcasting reel
Reel from which the line unwinds due to the rotation of the spool on its axis.

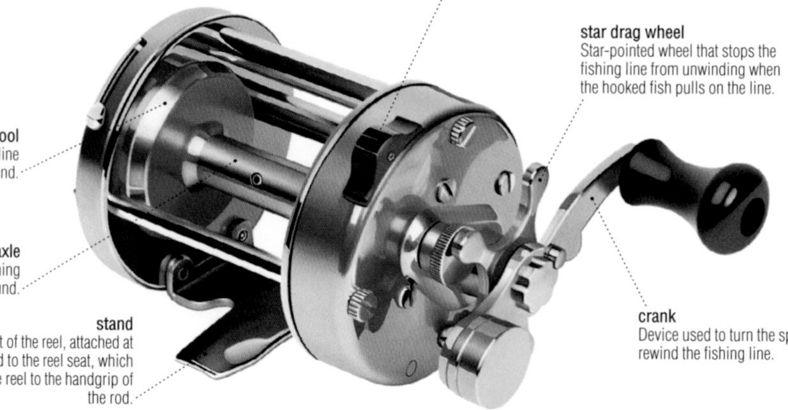
spool-release mechanism
Mechanism that releases the brake so the spool can once again turn freely.
star drag wheel
Star-pointed wheel that stops the fishing line from unwinding when the hooked fish pulls on the line.
spool
Cylinder on which the fishing line is wound.
spool axle
Metal rod around which the fishing line is wound.
stand
Long part of the reel, attached at each end to the reel seat, which secures the reel to the handgrip of the rod.
crank
Device used to turn the spool and rewind the fishing line.

fishhook
Metal hook of variable size attached to the end of float tackle and baited with a natural or artificial lure intended to catch a fish.

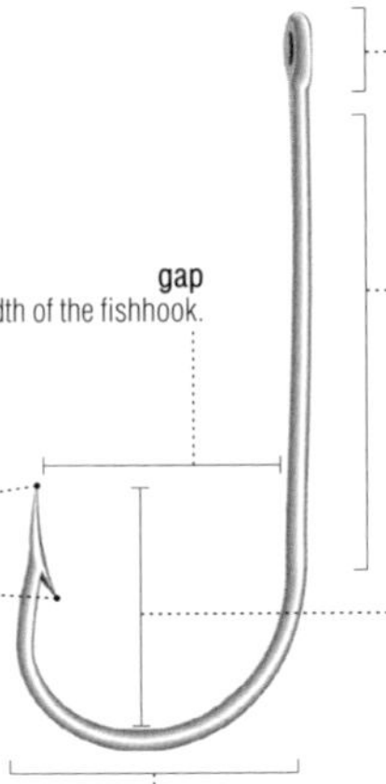

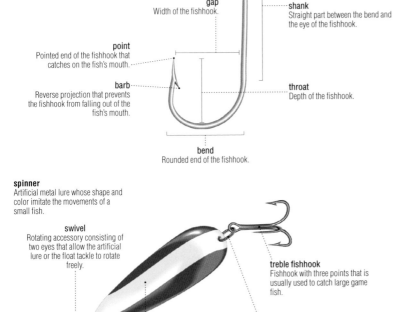

eye
Hole through which the fishing line passes so the fishhook can be attached to the line or to float tackle.

gap
Width of the fishhook.

shank
Straight part between the bend and the eye of the fishhook.

point
Pointed end of the fishhook that catches on the fish's mouth.

barb
Reverse projection that prevents the fishhook from falling out of the fish's mouth.

throat
Depth of the fishhook.

bend
Rounded end of the fishhook.

spinner
Artificial metal lure whose shape and color imitate the movements of a small fish.

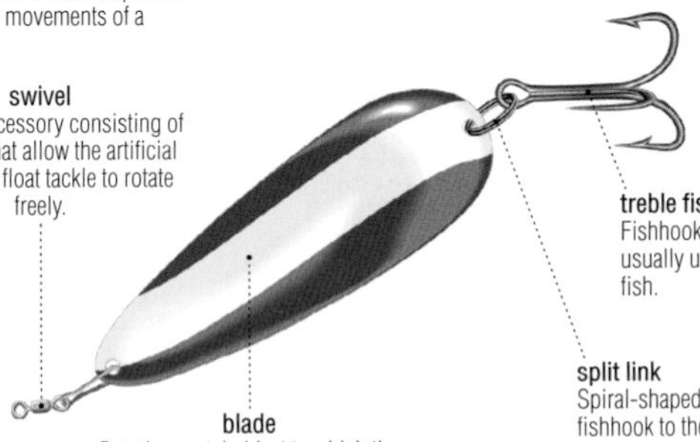

swivel
Rotating accessory consisting of two eyes that allow the artificial lure or the float tackle to rotate freely.

treble fishhook
Fishhook with three points that is usually used to catch large game fish.

split link
Spiral-shaped ring connecting the fishhook to the blade.

blade
Rotating metal object to which the swivel and the fishhook are attached.

float tackle
Range of accessories at the end of the fishing line and ending with the fishhook; the length of the leader depends on the kind of fish being caught.

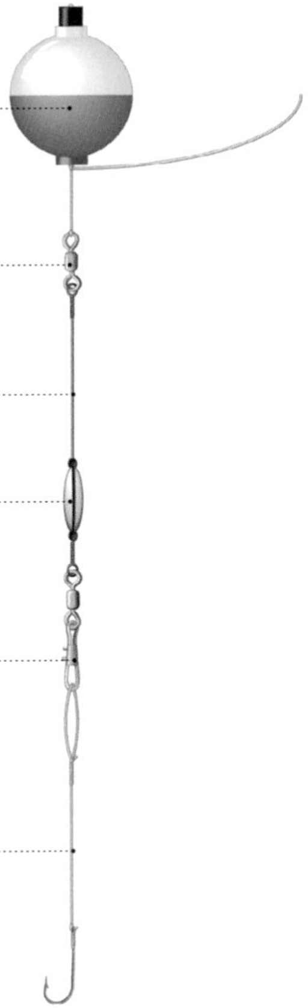

bobber
Light object filled with air that keeps the bait at a certain depth below water level and signals a bite by its movement.

swivel
Rotating accessory consisting of two eyes that allow the artificial lure or the float tackle to rotate freely.

leader
Length of steel wire between the fishing line and the fishhook that prevents the line from being cut by predatory fish such as pike.

sinker
Small lead object used to weight the line during the cast and to carry the fishhook underwater.

snap
Metal ring that opens and closes with a spring-loaded gate; it is used to connect the snelled fishhook to a swivel.

snelled fishhook
Ready-tied fishhook attached to float tackle at the end of the fishing line.

clothing and accessories

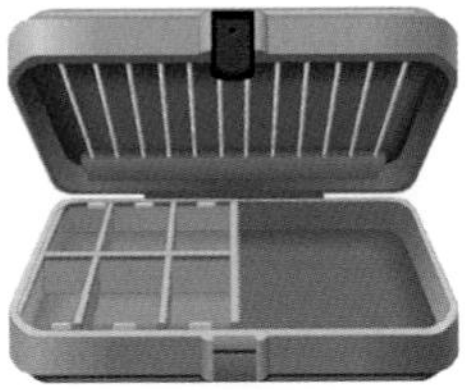

tackle box
Compartmentalized box used to store and carry bait and fishing equipment.

creel
Basket used to store and carry the catch.

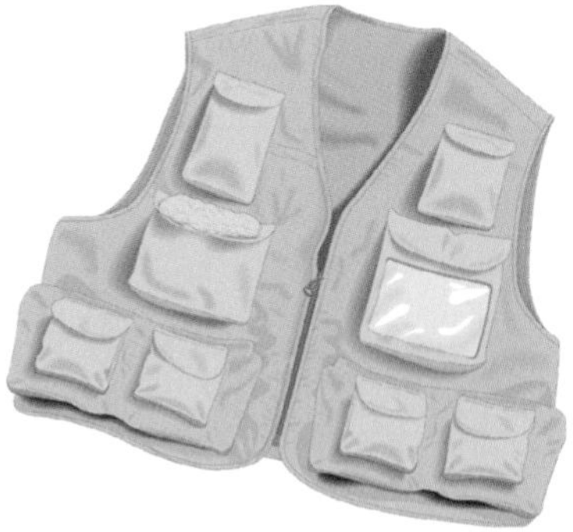

fishing vest
Sleeveless jacket with many pockets for carrying small objects (license, sinkers, etc.).

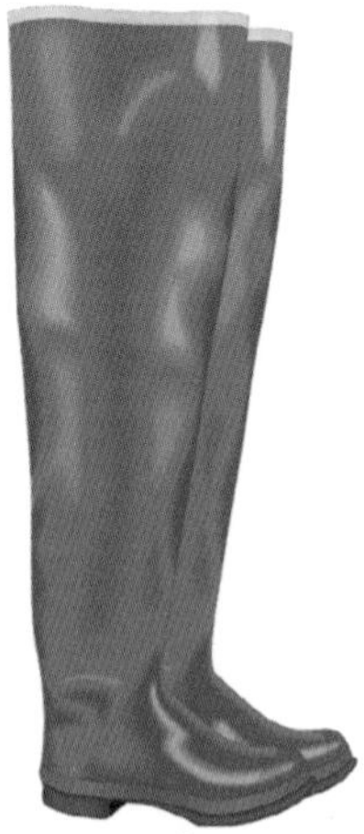

waders
Thigh-high rubber boots used to fish in shallow water.

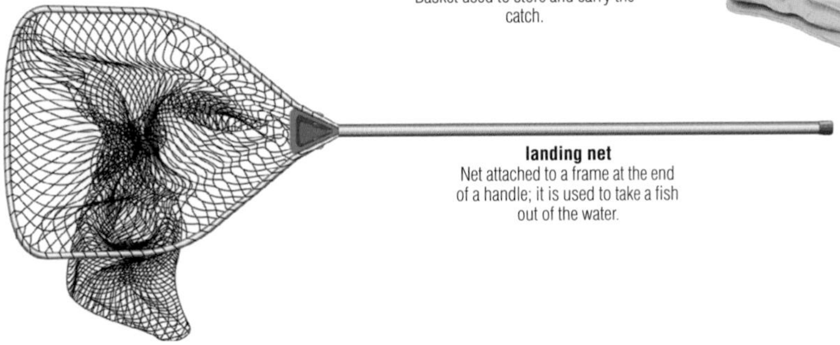

landing net
Net attached to a frame at the end of a handle; it is used to take a fish out of the water.

hunting

Outdoor activity that consists of lying in wait for or pursuing game in order to kill it.

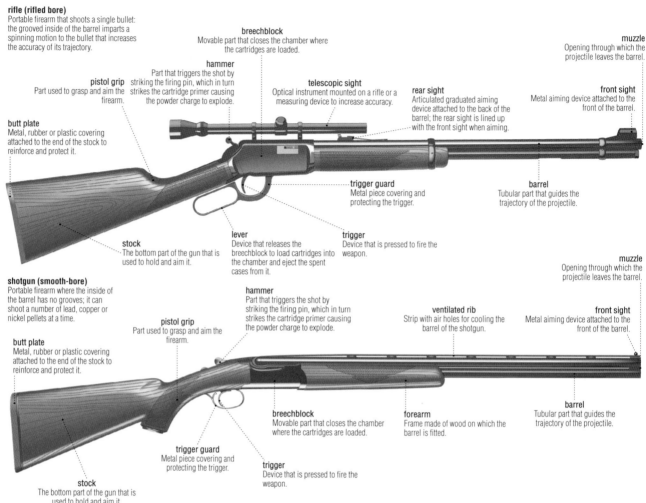

rifle (rifled bore)
Portable firearm that shoots a single bullet: the grooved inside of the barrel imparts a spinning motion to the bullet that increases the accuracy of its trajectory.

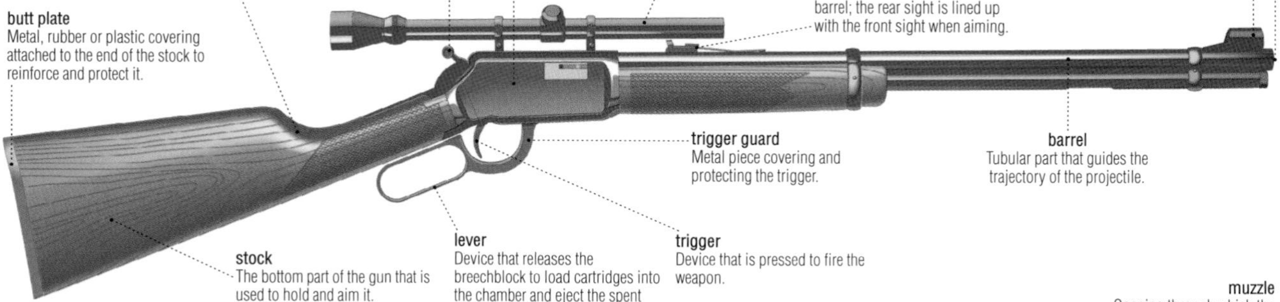

breechblock
Movable part that closes the chamber where the cartridges are loaded.
muzzle
Opening through which the projectile leaves the barrel.
hammer
Part that triggers the shot by striking the firing pin, which in turn strikes the cartridge primer causing the powder charge to explode.
pistol grip
Part used to grasp and aim the firearm.
telescopic sight
Optical instrument mounted on a rifle or a measuring device to increase accuracy.
rear sight
Articulated graduated aiming device attached to the back of the barrel; the rear sight is lined up with the front sight when aiming.
front sight
Metal aiming device attached to the front of the barrel.
butt plate
Metal, rubber or plastic covering attached to the end of the stock to reinforce and protect it.
trigger guard
Metal piece covering and protecting the trigger.
barrel
Tubular part that guides the trajectory of the projectile.
lever
Device that releases the breechblock to load cartridges into the chamber and eject the spent cases from it.
trigger
Device that is pressed to fire the weapon.
stock
The bottom part of the gun that is used to hold and aim it.

shotgun (smooth-bore)
Portable firearm where the inside of the barrel has no grooves; it can shoot a number of lead, copper or nickel pellets at a time.

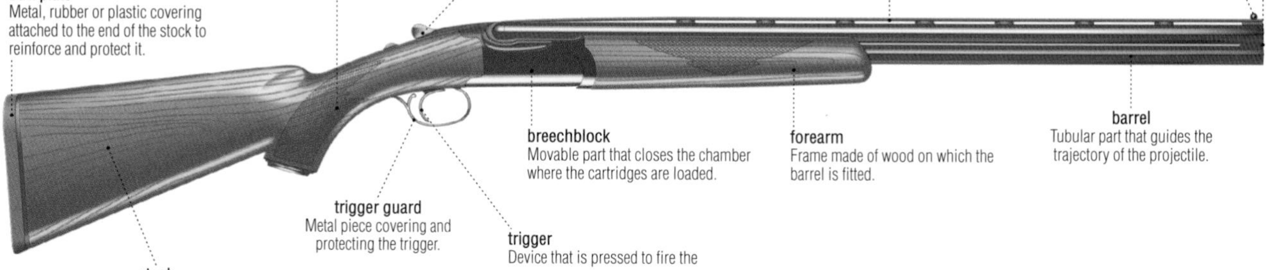

muzzle
Opening through which the projectile leaves the barrel.
hammer
Part that triggers the shot by striking the firing pin, which in turn strikes the cartridge primer causing the powder charge to explode.
ventilated rib
Strip with air holes for cooling the barrel of the shotgun.
front sight
Metal aiming device attached to the front of the barrel.
pistol grip
Part used to grasp and aim the firearm.
butt plate
Metal, rubber or plastic covering attached to the end of the stock to reinforce and protect it.
breechblock
Movable part that closes the chamber where the cartridges are loaded.
forearm
Frame made of wood on which the barrel is fitted.
barrel
Tubular part that guides the trajectory of the projectile.
trigger guard
Metal piece covering and protecting the trigger.
trigger
Device that is pressed to fire the weapon.
stock
The bottom part of the gun that is used to hold and aim it.

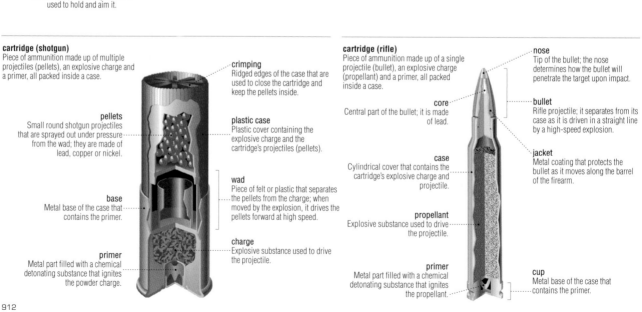

cartridge (shotgun)
Piece of ammunition made up of multiple projectiles (pellets), an explosive charge and a primer, all packed inside a case.

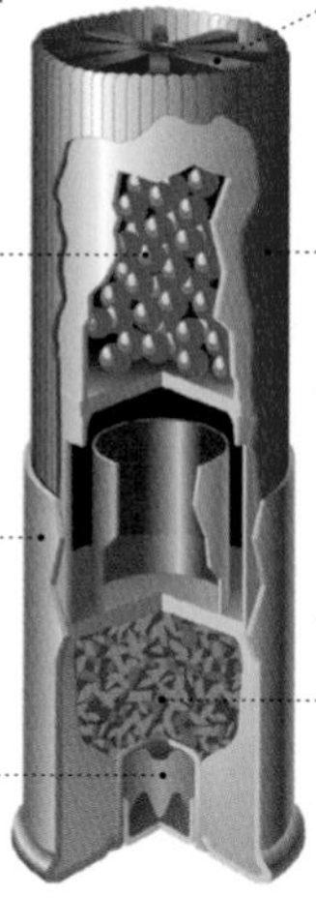

crimping
Ridged edges of the case that are used to close the cartridge and keep the pellets inside.
pellets
Small round shotgun projectiles that are sprayed out under pressure from the wad; they are made of lead, copper or nickel.
plastic case
Plastic cover containing the explosive charge and the cartridge's projectiles (pellets).
wad
Piece of felt or plastic that separates the pellets from the charge; when moved by the explosion, it drives the pellets forward at high speed.
base
Metal base of the case that contains the primer.
charge
Explosive substance used to drive the projectile.
primer
Metal part filled with a chemical detonating substance that ignites the powder charge.

cartridge (rifle)
Piece of ammunition made up of a single projectile (bullet), an explosive charge (propellant) and a primer, all packed inside a case.

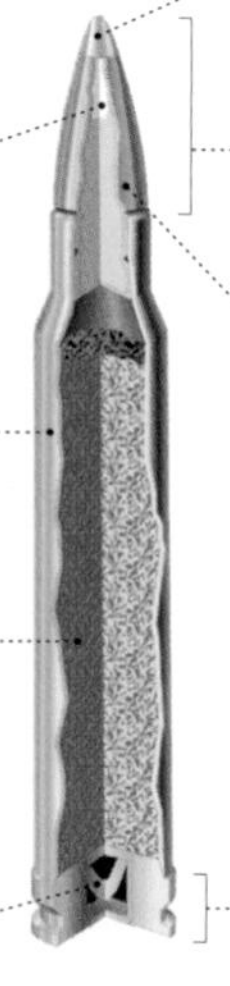

nose
Tip of the bullet; the nose determines how the bullet will penetrate the target upon impact.
core
Central part of the bullet; it is made of lead.
bullet
Rifle projectile; it separates from its case as it is driven in a straight line by a high-speed explosion.
jacket
Metal coating that protects the bullet as it moves along the barrel of the firearm.
case
Cylindrical cover that contains the cartridge's explosive charge and projectile.
propellant
Explosive substance used to drive the projectile.
primer
Metal part filled with a chemical detonating substance that ignites the propellant.
cup
Metal base of the case that contains the primer.

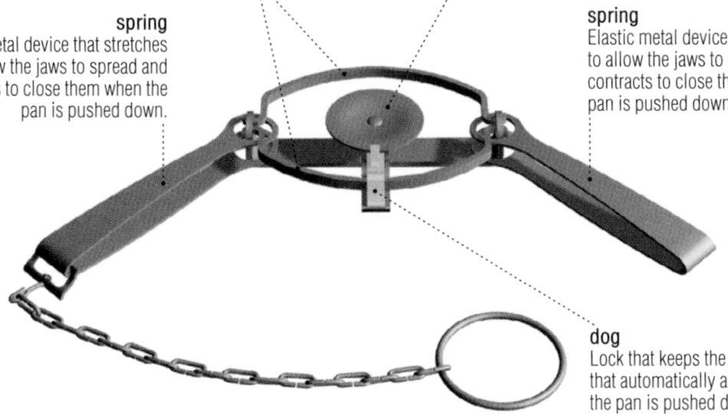
jaws
Metal parts that close over the animal's paw.
pan
Part that snaps the trap jaws shut when pushed down.
spring
Elastic metal device that stretches to allow the jaws to spread and contracts to close them when the pan is pushed down.
spring
Elastic metal device that stretches to allow the jaws to spread and contracts to close them when the pan is pushed down.
dog
Lock that keeps the trap open and that automatically activates it when the pan is pushed down.
leghold trap
Apparatus meant to capture an animal by the paw.

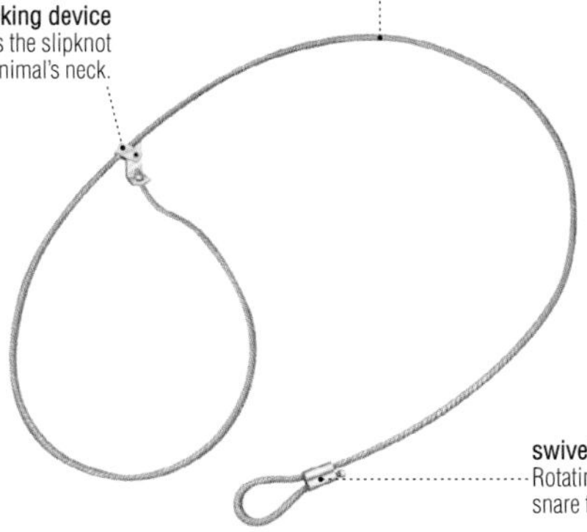
steel cable
Wire rope with a slipknot at one end.
locking device
Device that locks the slipknot around the animal's neck.
swivel
Rotating part that prevents the snare from twisting.
snare
Trap consisting of a steel cable ending in a slipknot; it is used to capture small game by the neck and strangle them.

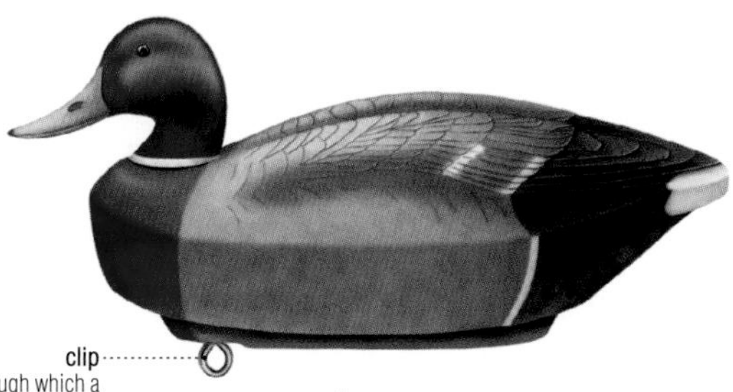
clip
Metal ring through which a weighted rope is passed to hold the decoy in place on the surface of the water.
decoy
Plastic or wooden lure used to attract wild ducks.

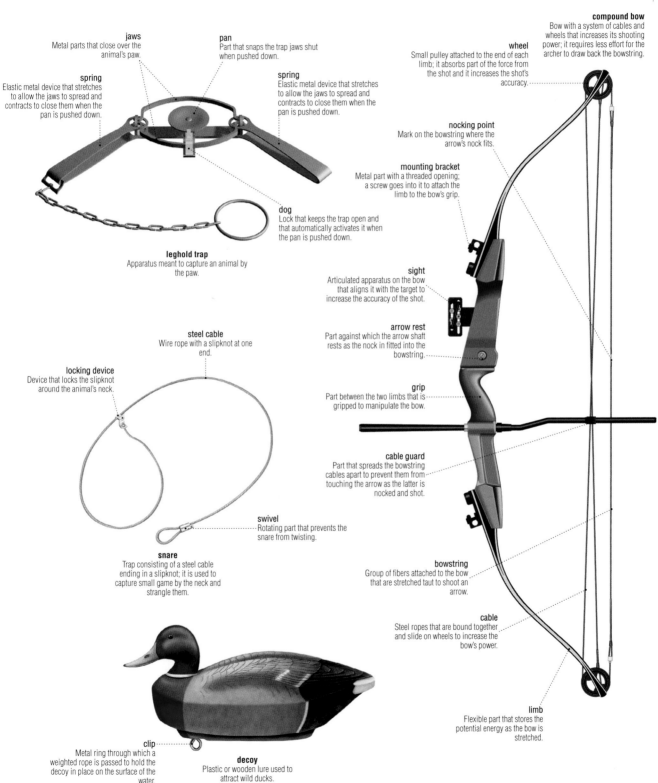

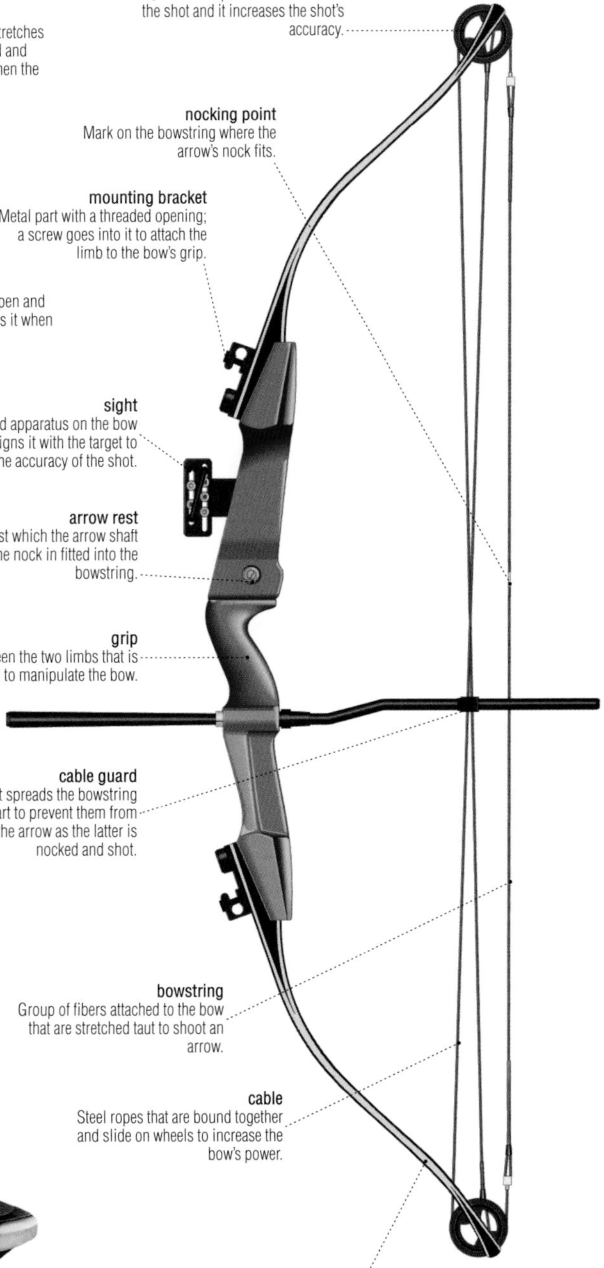
compound bow
Bow with a system of cables and wheels that increases its shooting power; it requires less effort for the archer to draw back the bowstring.
wheel
Small pulley attached to the end of each limb; it absorbs part of the force from the shot and it increases the shot's accuracy.
nocking point
Mark on the bowstring where the arrow's nock fits.
mounting bracket
Metal part with a threaded opening; a screw goes into it to attach the limb to the bow's grip.
sight
Articulated apparatus on the bow that aligns it with the target to increase the accuracy of the shot.
arrow rest
Part against which the arrow shaft rests as the nock in fitted into the bowstring.
grip
Part between the two limbs that is gripped to manipulate the bow.
cable guard
Part that spreads the bowstring cables apart to prevent them from touching the arrow as the latter is nocked and shot.
bowstring
Group of fibers attached to the bow that are stretched taut to shoot an arrow.
cable
Steel ropes that are bound together and slide on wheels to increase the bow's power.
limb
Flexible part that stores the potential energy as the bow is stretched.

dice and dominoes

Cubes (dice) or pieces divided into two ends (dominoes) with numbers indicated by pips or figures.

ordinary die
Small cube marked on each side with one to six pips; it is used in various games (backgammon, Monopoly®, Yahtzee®, etc.).

poker die
Small cube marked on each side with card symbols; it is used to play poker dice, a game similar to poker, which is played with five dice.

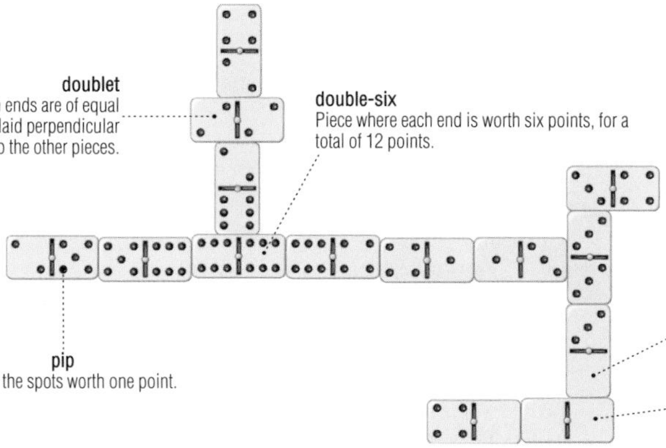

dominoes
Game that consists of setting up pieces in sequence according to their value, with adjoining pieces being identical.

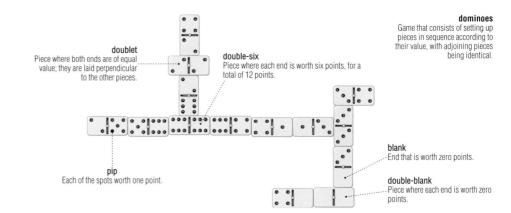

doublet
Piece where both ends are of equal value; they are laid perpendicular to the other pieces.

double-six
Piece where each end is worth six points, for a total of 12 points.

pip
Each of the spots worth one point.

blank
End that is worth zero points.

double-blank
Piece where each end is worth zero points.

cards

Rectangular pieces of cardboard used to play various games; they have figures, signs and numbers on one side and are divided into four suits.

symbols
The colors, figures and signs on a deck of cards.

heart
Red suit in a deck of cards that is shaped like a heart; this suit has the highest value.

diamond
Red suit in a deck of cards that is shaped like a lozenge; this suit has the second-highest value.

club
Black suit in a deck of cards that is shaped like a cloverleaf; this suit has the third-highest value.

spade
Black suit in a deck of cards that is shaped like a spearhead; this suit has the lowest value.

joker
Card depicting a court jester; in most games, its value is the cardholder's choice.

ace
Card with a single sign that usually has the highest value in the suit.

king
Figure depicting a king that usually has the second-highest value in the suit.

queen
Figure depicting a queen that usually has the third-highest value in the suit.

jack
Figure depicting an equerry that usually has the fourth-highest value in the suit.

standard poker hands
A poker hand consists of five cards whose combination confers a relative value on which the player bets; they have an ascending order of value.

high card
When none of the five cards in the hand can be combined with any other, the highest-ranked card is played.

one pair
Contains two cards of equal value.

two pairs
Contains two pairs.

three-of-a-kind
Contains three cards of equal value.

straight
Contains five consecutive cards of different suits.

flush
Contains five nonconsecutive cards of the same suit.

full house
Contains a three-of-a-kind and a pair.

four-of-a-kind
Contains four cards of equal value.

straight flush
Contains five consecutive cards of the same suit.

royal flush
Contains five consecutive cards of the same suit, from the 10 to the ace.

board games

Complete range of games that use a playing surface on which game pieces (tokens, dice, counters, etc.) are placed.

backgammon
Game of strategy in which two players move checkers around a board; players try to collect and bear them off while preventing the opponent's checkers from moving.

outer table
Area with 12 points that the checkers must move across to reach the inner table; opponents move in opposite directions.

inner table
Table that a player's checkers must enter before they can be borne off; the player who first bears off all his or her checkers wins the game.

dice cup
Container used to shake and throw the dice.

red
Red checkers that belong to one player.

die
One of the two small cubes marked on each side with one to six pips; the checker moves the same number of points as the number rolled.

doubling die
Die used to increase the game's stakes.

point
Each of the spaces on which the checkers are placed.

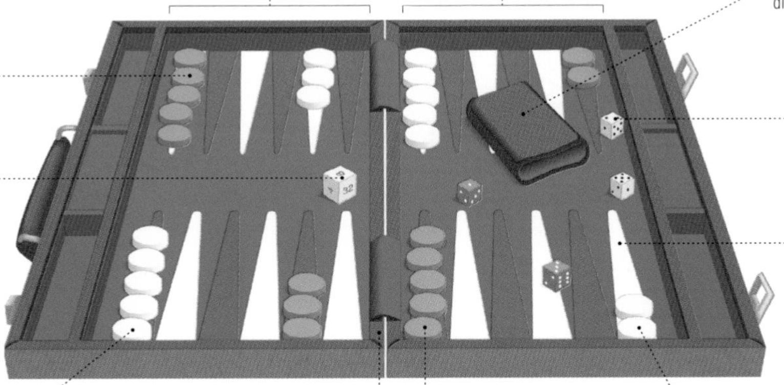

white
White checkers that belong to one player.

bar
Line that divides the board's inner and outer tables; the checkers hit by the opposing player are placed on it.

checkers
Each of the counters used to play; the checkers are moved from one point to the next based on the number of pips shown on the dice.

runner
One of two checkers belonging to a player placed at the start of the game on the opponent's inner table; it must leave that position before any other checkers of the same color can be moved.

snakes and ladders
Game of chance in which the goal is to reach the last space on the board by using the ladders and avoiding the snakes.

token
Small object representing a car, locomotive, hat, etc. that is used by players to move around the board.

die
One of the two small cubes marked on each side with one to six pips.

snake
When a token lands on the head of a snake, it must be moved down to the snake's tail.

ladder
When a token lands at the foot of a ladder, it is moved directly to the top of the ladder.

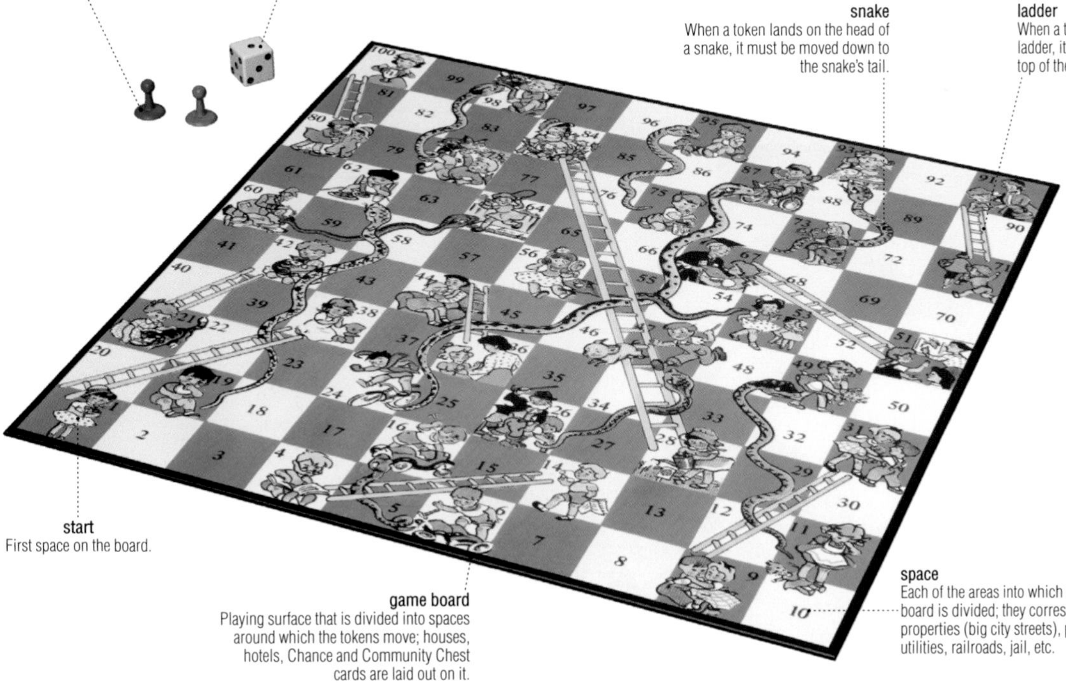

start
First space on the board.

game board
Playing surface that is divided into spaces around which the tokens move; houses, hotels, Chance and Community Chest cards are laid out on it.

space
Each of the areas into which the game board is divided; they correspond to properties (big city streets), public utilities, railroads, jail, etc.

board games

chess
Game where two players move pieces around a board in order to "checkmate" the opponent (i.e., attack the king in such a manner that no escape is possible).

chessboard
Board divided into 64 black and white squares; the corner square on each player's left must be black.

queen's side
Each of the pieces in columns *a* to *d* on the board.

king's side
Each of the pieces in columns *e* to *h* on the board.

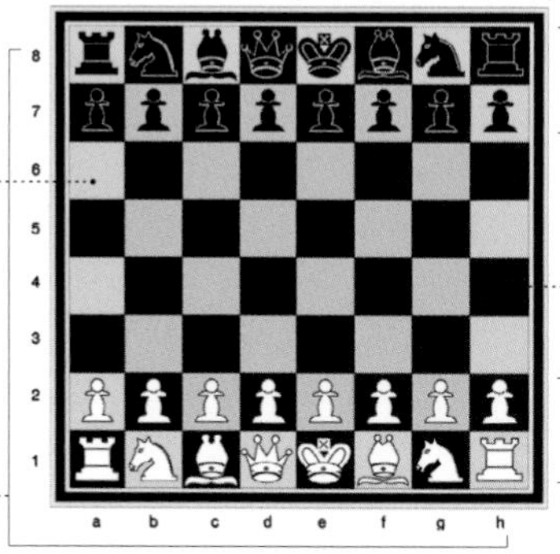

white square
Light-colored square; when the game begins, the white queen is on a square of her own color.

chess notation
Means of using letters and numbers to identify the chessboard squares; it is used to situate pieces, transcribe games, follow moves, etc.

Black
Pieces belonging to one of the two players.

black square
Dark-colored square; when the game begins, the black queen is on a square of her own color.

White
Pieces belonging to one of the two players; White starts the game.

chess pieces
At the beginning of the game, each player has 16 pieces with different moves and value: a king, a queen, two rooks, two bishops, two knights and eight pawns.

pawn
Piece that can advance one square at a time except at the beginning of the game, when it can advance one or two squares; it captures opposing pieces diagonally.

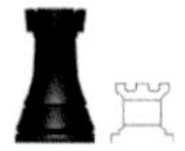

rook
Piece that can move backward or forward horizontally or vertically for as many squares as the player chooses.

bishop
Piece that can move backward or forward diagonally for as many squares as the player chooses.

knight
Piece that can move at right angles (square movement); the knight is the only piece that can jump over any other piece.

king
The most important piece in the game; it can move backward or forward in all directions one square at a time.

queen
The most powerful attack piece; it can move backward or forward in all directions for as many squares as the player chooses.

types of movements
Each piece moves in a specific way: diagonally, vertically, horizontally or in a square.

diagonal movement
Forward or backward movement along an oblique line.

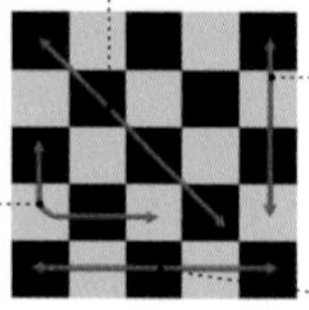

square movement
Moving one square forward or backward and then two squares laterally, or two squares forward or backward and then one square laterally.

vertical movement
Moving forward or backward along a column.

horizontal movement
Moving to the right or left along a row.

go
Japanese name for a strategic game that originated in China; players take turns placing stones on the intersections of a board to surround his or her opponent and control the most territory.

board
Grid made of 19 horizontal and vertical lines; the stones are placed where the lines intersect. The Japanese name for the board is "goban".

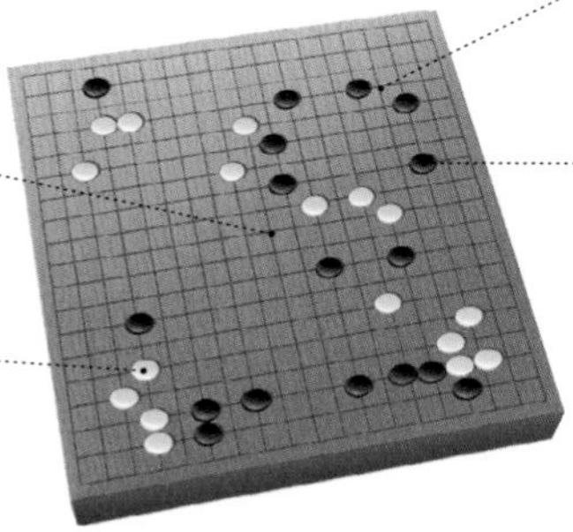

center
Central intersection on the board.

white stone
One player's token; in the game of go, there are 180 white stones.

handicap spot
Each of the nine points on the board where stones belonging to the weaker player are placed when the players are of unequal strength.

black stone
One player's token; in the game of go, there are 181 black stones and the player with these stones moves first.

major motions
The various movements are made by placing stones on a liberty, which is an empty, adjacent horizontal or vertical intersection.

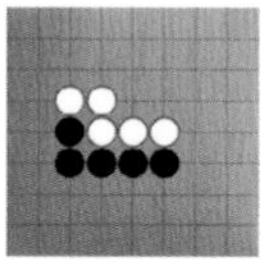

connection
When a stone occupies a liberty belonging to a stone of the same color, the two stones are connected; a chain is made up of two or more connected stones.

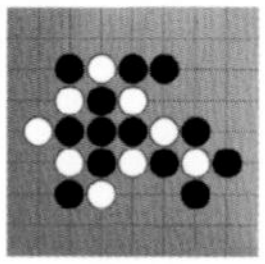

capture
When a stone or chain of stones is completely surrounded by the opponent's stones, it is captured and removed from the board.

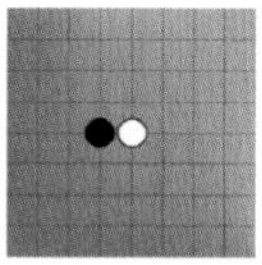

contact
Point where two stones occupying adjacent intersections meet.

checkers
Game that consists of capturing all the opposing counters by jumping over them, provided that the square behind each one is free.

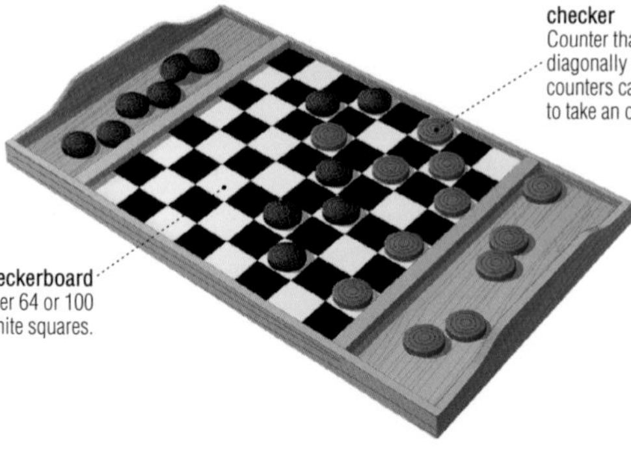

checker
Counter that can move forward diagonally one square at a time; counters can only move backward to take an opposing counter.

checkerboard
Board divided into either 64 or 100 black and white squares.

SPORTS AND GAMES

jigsaw puzzle

Puzzle that consists of a picture divided into irregularly shaped pieces that must be put back together.

piece
Each of the fragments that fit together to create a picture.

picture
Image put back together by assembling the pieces.

board
Flexible surface on which the puzzle pieces are laid out; it can be rolled up while the puzzle is still unfinished.

mah-jongg

Game for four players that originated in China; players score points by creating combinations of four sets of tiles (run, three-of-a-kind or square) and one pair.

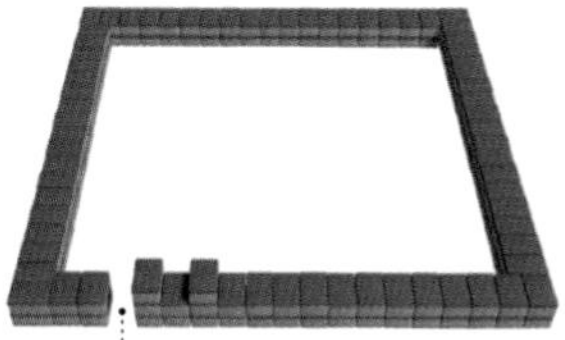

breaking the wall
Opening in the wall that determines the place from which the tiles will be drawn.

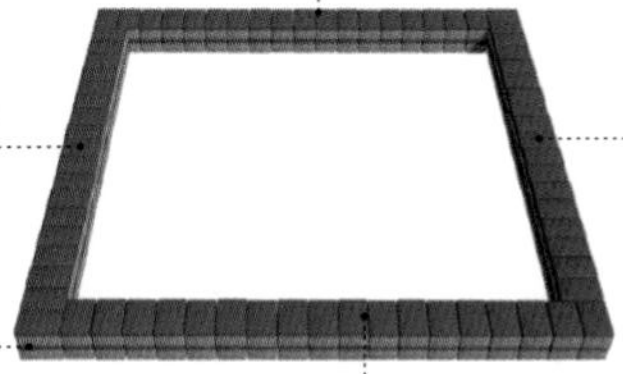

East
Player who is the East wind and who starts the game; this player's points are automatically doubled.

square
Four-sided structure of tiles divided into four cardinal points; each player is a wind from one of those points.

South
Player who is the South wind.

North
Player who is the North wind.

wall
Each player draws 36 tiles to build a wall that is 18 tiles long and two tiles high; the four walls are joined together to form a square.

West
Player who is the West wind.

suit tiles
Mah-jongg has 108 suit tiles: four matching sets of each of the nine circles, nine characters and nine bamboos.

circles
Each of the tiles depicting an ascending number of circles.

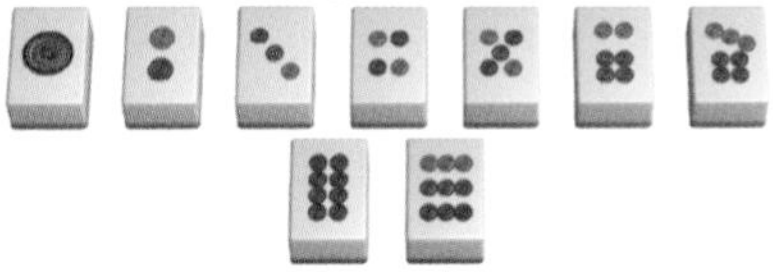

characters
Each of the tiles depicting an ideogram, which represents numbers one through nine.

bamboos
Each of the tiles depicting bamboo shoots, with the first tile showing a bird.

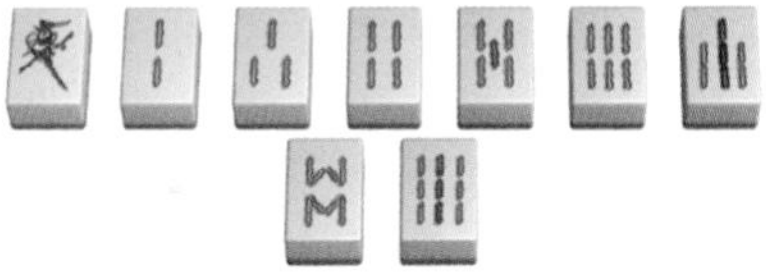

honor tiles
Mah-jongg has 28 honor tiles that are worth twice the points; there are four identical sets of four winds and four identical sets of three dragons.

winds
Each of the tiles representing the East, South, West and North winds.

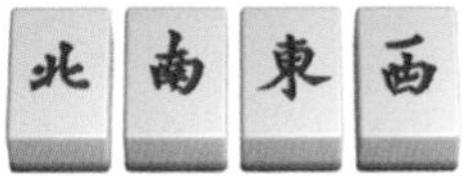

dragons
Each of the tiles depicting a red, green or white dragon.

bonus tiles
Mah-jongg has eight bonus tiles that are also known as Supreme Honor tiles; they are not used in making combinations but they add points.

flower tiles
Each of the four tiles depicting flowers.

season tiles
Each of the four tiles depicting the seasons.

video entertainment system

Group of units (game console and visual display) that allows a person to control the action in a game displayed on a screen by means of a controller.

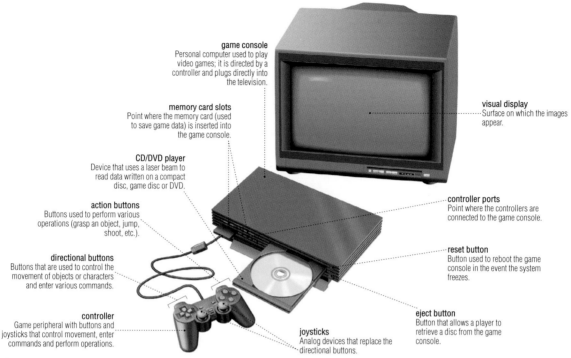

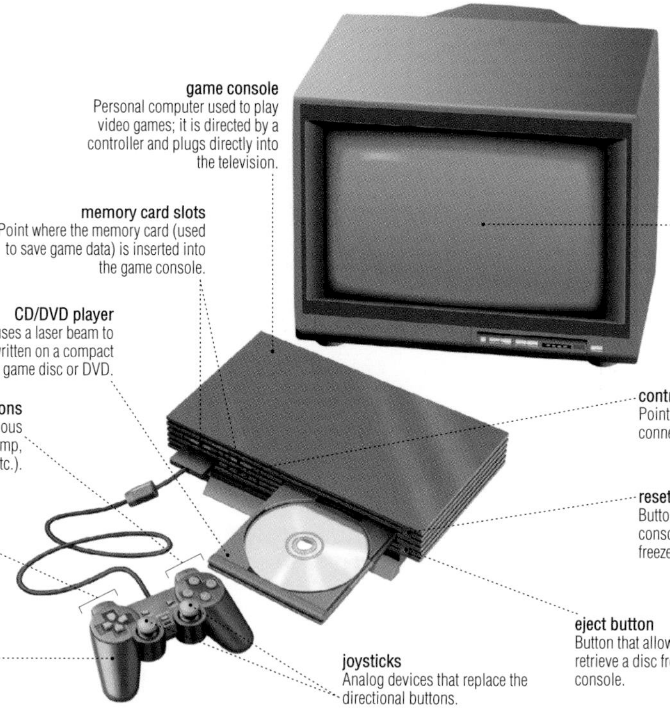
game console
Personal computer used to play video games; it is directed by a controller and plugs directly into the television.
memory card slots
Point where the memory card (used to save game data) is inserted into the game console.
CD/DVD player
Device that uses a laser beam to read data written on a compact disc, game disc or DVD.
action buttons
Buttons used to perform various operations (grasp an object, jump, shoot, etc.).
directional buttons
Buttons that are used to control the movement of objects or characters and enter various commands.
controller
Game peripheral with buttons and joysticks that control movement, enter commands and perform operations.
visual display
Surface on which the images appear.
controller ports
Point where the controllers are connected to the game console.
reset button
Button used to reboot the game console in the event the system freezes.
eject button
Button that allows a player to retrieve a disc from the game console.
joysticks
Analog devices that replace the directional buttons.

darts

Game of skill in which darts are thrown, three in succession, at a dartboard to accumulate a specific number of points (either 301 or 501).

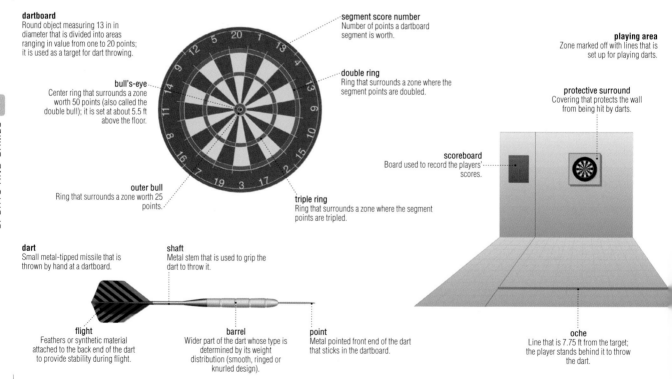

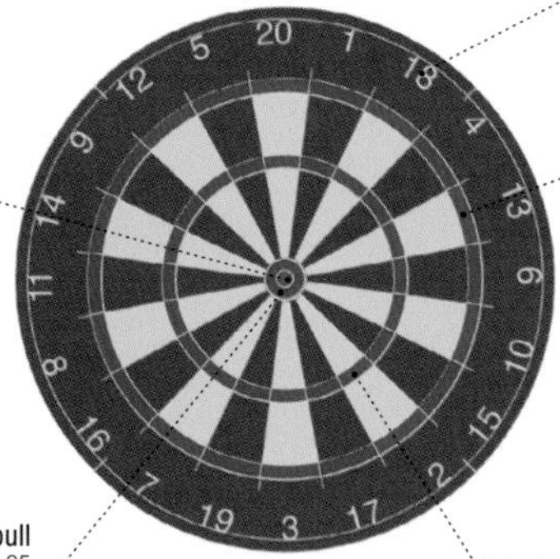
dartboard
Round object measuring 13 in in diameter that is divided into areas ranging in value from one to 20 points; it is used as a target for dart throwing.
bull's-eye
Center ring that surrounds a zone worth 50 points (also called the double bull); it is set at about 5.5 ft above the floor.
outer bull
Ring that surrounds a zone worth 25 points.
segment score number
Number of points a dartboard segment is worth.
double ring
Ring that surrounds a zone where the segment points are doubled.
triple ring
Ring that surrounds a zone where the segment points are tripled.
20 1 18 4 13 6 10 15 2 17 3 19 7 16 8 11 14 9 12 5

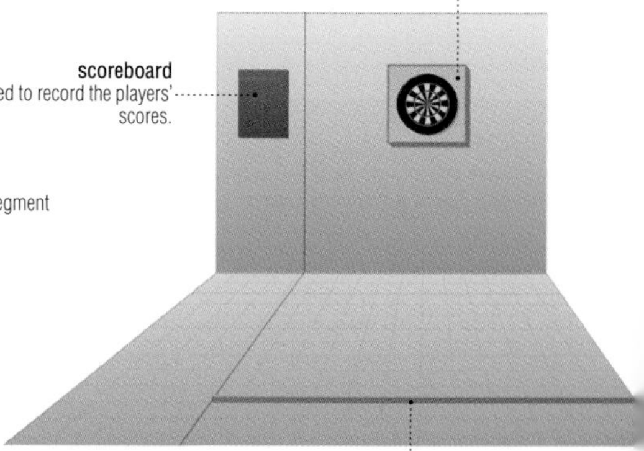
playing area
Zone marked off with lines that is set up for playing darts.
protective surround
Covering that protects the wall from being hit by darts.
scoreboard
Board used to record the players' scores.
oche
Line that is 7.75 ft from the target; the player stands behind it to throw the dart.

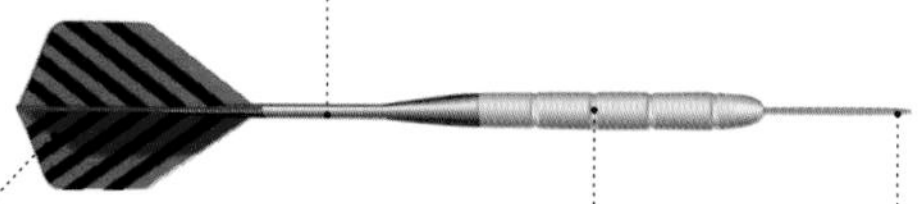
dart
Small metal-tipped missile that is thrown by hand at a dartboard.
shaft
Metal stem that is used to grip the dart to throw it.
flight
Feathers or synthetic material attached to the back end of the dart to provide stability during flight.
barrel
Wider part of the dart whose type is determined by its weight distribution (smooth, ringed or knurled design).
point
Metal pointed front end of the dart that sticks in the dartboard.

roulette table

Game made up of a roulette wheel and a betting layout; the aim is to bet on the winning number or color.

roulette wheel
Piece of equipment used to determine the winning number and color.

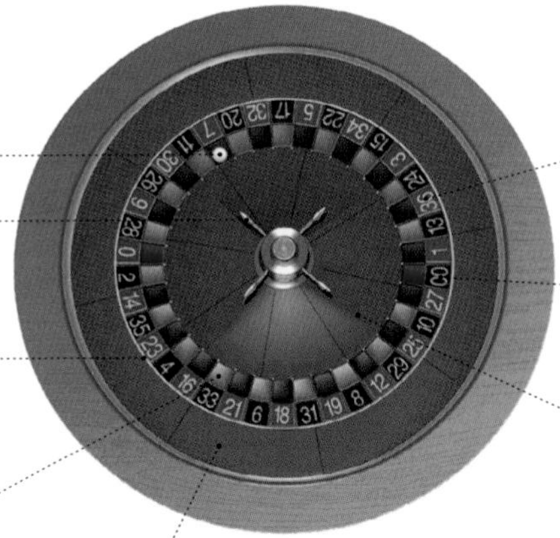

ivory ball
Small ball that the croupier drops into the stationary bowl; it rolls around the rotating wheel and stops in one of the compartments to determine the winning number and color.

cross handle
Grip shaped like a cross that is used by the croupier to rotate the wheel.

fret
Each of the metal edges separating the compartments.

compartment
Each of the hollow slots in front of a number where the ball can land to determine the winning number and color.

stationary bowl
Basin inside which the rotating wheel turns and into which the ivory ball is dropped.

number
Each of the red or black numbers 1 through 36, including a green zero and double zero.

double zero
Number added to the American roulette wheel.

rotating wheel
Wheel with 38 numbered compartments that turns inside a stationary bowl.

French roulette wheel
Piece of equipment used to determine the winning number and color; the French roulette wheel has no double zero compartment.

French betting layout
The French layout has all 36 numbers (even and odd, red and black, high and low) but only one zero.

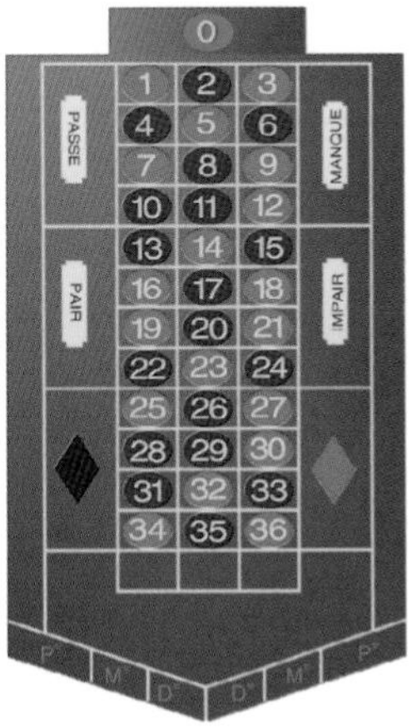

betting layout
Surface with designated betting spaces on which players place chips to represent their bets.

main section
Grid on which the numbered betting spaces are printed.

single zero
If the zero comes up, any chips that players bet on red, black, even, odd, high or low are imprisoned.

low (1 to 18)
The chip is placed on this square to bet on numbers 1 through 18; if one of those numbers comes up, the bet wins the original stake.

dozen (1 to 12)
The chip is placed on this square to bet on numbers 1 through 12; if one of those numbers comes up, the bet wins twice the original stake.

even
The chip is placed on this square to bet on the even numbers; if one of those numbers comes up, the bet wins the original stake.

red
The chip is placed on this square to bet on the red numbers; if one of those numbers comes up, the bet wins the original stake.

dozen (13 to 24)
The chip is placed on this square to bet on numbers 13 through 24; if one of those numbers comes up, the bet wins twice the original stake.

black
The chip is placed on this square to bet on the black numbers; if one of those numbers comes up, the bet wins the original stake.

en prison
Area where the chip is placed when the bet is imprisoned; it is either released or lost on the following turn.

odd
The chip is placed on this square to bet on the odd numbers; if one of those numbers comes up, the bet wins the original stake.

high (19 to 36)
The chip is placed on this square to bet on numbers 19 through 36; if one of those numbers comes up, the bet wins the original stake.

dozen (25 to 36)
The chip is placed on this square to bet on numbers 25 through 36; if one of those numbers comes up, the bet wins twice the original stake.

column
Each of the three vertical rows of 12 numbers.

double zero
Number added to the American betting layout; the chip is placed in the center of the square and if that number comes up, the bet wins back 35 times the original stake.

five-number bet
The chip is placed in the upper left hand corner of square 1; if 00, 0, 1, 2 or 3 comes up, the bet wins back six times the original stake.

square bet
The chip is placed at the intersection of four numbers; if one of those numbers comes up, the bet wins back eight times the original stake.

split bet
The chip is placed on a line dividing two numbers; if one of those two numbers comes up, the bet wins back 17 times the original stake.

line
The chip is placed on the line dividing the final two squares in two adjacent rows; if one of those six numbers comes up, the bet wins back five times the original stake.

straight bet
The chip is placed squarely in the center of any number; if that number comes up, the bet wins back 35 times the original stake.

street bet
The chip is placed on the outside edge of a row; if one of the three numbers in the row comes up, the bet wins 11 times the original stake.

two columns split bet
The chip is placed on one of the two lines between the three lower squares; if one of the numbers in those two columns comes up, the bet wins half the original stake.

slot machine

Electronic or mechanical gambling machine that is operated by inserting a coin into a slot in order to obtain a sequence of winning symbols.

cross section

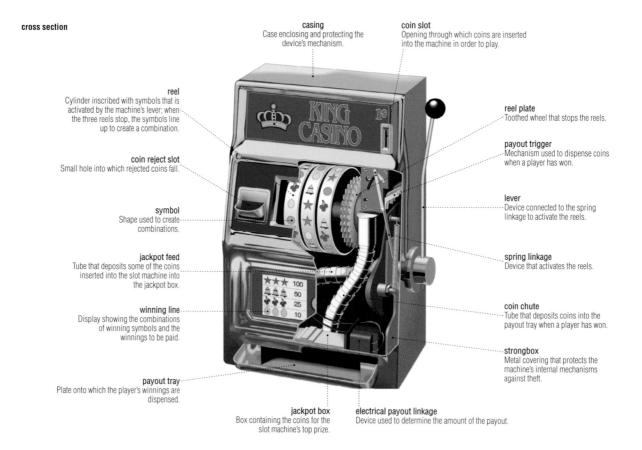

casing
Case enclosing and protecting the device's mechanism.
coin slot
Opening through which coins are inserted into the machine in order to play.
KING CASINO
1$
reel
Cylinder inscribed with symbols that is activated by the machine's lever; when the three reels stop, the symbols line up to create a combination.
reel plate
Toothed wheel that stops the reels.
payout trigger
Mechanism used to dispense coins when a player has won.
coin reject slot
Small hole into which rejected coins fall.
lever
Device connected to the spring linkage to activate the reels.
symbol
Shape used to create combinations.
spring linkage
Device that activates the reels.
jackpot feed
Tube that deposits some of the coins inserted into the slot machine into the jackpot box.
100
50
25
10
winning line
Display showing the combinations of winning symbols and the winnings to be paid.
coin chute
Tube that deposits coins into the payout tray when a player has won.
strongbox
Metal covering that protects the machine's internal mechanisms against theft.
payout tray
Plate onto which the player's winnings are dispensed.
jackpot box
Box containing the coins for the slot machine's top prize.
electrical payout linkage
Device used to determine the amount of the payout.

soccer table

Table soccer game with figures mounted on telescopic rods.

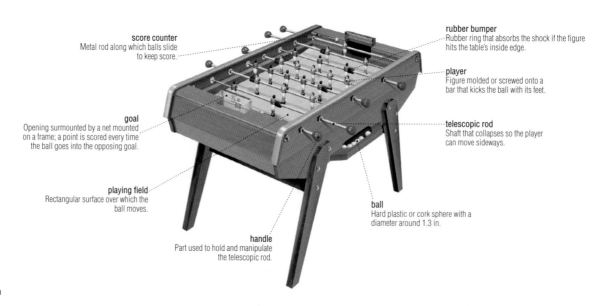

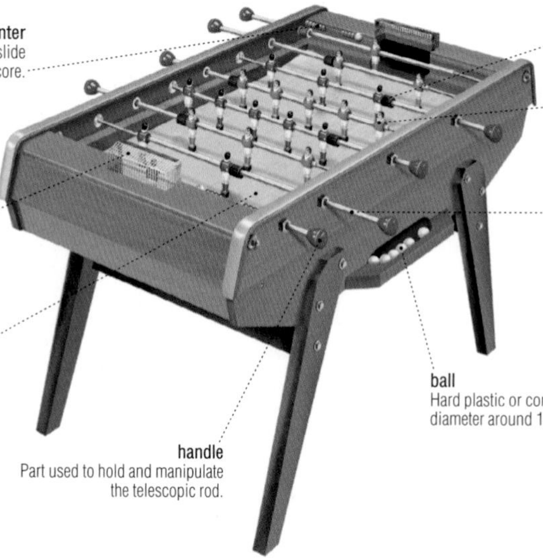
score counter
Metal rod along which balls slide to keep score.
rubber bumper
Rubber ring that absorbs the shock if the figure hits the table's inside edge.
player
Figure molded or screwed onto a bar that kicks the ball with its feet.
goal
Opening surmounted by a net mounted on a frame; a point is scored every time the ball goes into the opposing goal.
telescopic rod
Shaft that collapses so the player can move sideways.
playing field
Rectangular surface over which the ball moves.
ball
Hard plastic or cork sphere with a diameter around 1.3 in.
handle
Part used to hold and manipulate the telescopic rod.

Index

B

C

D

E

F

G

H

K

L

M

N

O

P

Q

R

S

T

U

X

Y

Z